KEY MAP®

HOUSTON HARRIS COUNTY ATLAS

DISCARD

53rd EDITION

CONTENTS

COPYRIGHT KEY MAPS 2017

S. HUBBS, CARTOGRAPHER   E. HUBBS, PRESIDENT

Information collected for the Houston-Harris County Atlas is gathered from multiple sources and compiled in a manner which insures maximum accuracy. Due to time lag between planning and construction we do show some roads and bridges as complete that do not exist as of publication. The Publishers cannot and do not guarantee the correctness of all information furnished to them, nor the complete absence of errors or omissions, hence no responsibility for same can be or is assumed.

We do request any inaccuracy found in the publication be brought to our attention so appropriate corrections can be made in future editions.

DISCARD

PUBLISHED BY HOUSTON MAP COMPANY
1212 DURHAM HOUSTON, TEXAS 77007
(713) 522-7949
www.keymap.com   sales@keymaps.com

How to Use Your KEY MAP®

For locating a street, follow the steps listed below:

Step #1	Step #3	Step #4	Step #2	
Street Name	**Block**	**Pg/Sq**	**Loc**	**Zip**
EASY ST	800	539Q	LP	77571

1. Locate the street name in the alphabetical listing. Note that numbered streets are in the front of the index.
2. Check the area location abbreviation and zip code to avoid incorrect street selection when a duplicate name is listed. The location abbreviation and zip code will also verify the street is in the area desired.
3. Many streets will have multiple listings indicating a continuation of the same street from page to page or indicating duplicate street names which are distinct and separate streets. To insure proper selection of the correct page and square check the block number and zip code.
4. Select the map page and square. Note that the square indicates where the name appears on the mapped page. Only names are indexed. Block numbers in the index indicate the lowest block number of the zip code listed or lowest block number for that page when the zip code continues between pages.
5. To key the location of the map page selected, check the Mini Map in the back of the book. Here you will find a layout of all the map pages. Each numbered rectangle refers to the corresponding book map pages. This is also an artery map, showing the most direct route from one area to another.
6. Remember, North is always at the top of the map. Map pages turn from East to West and are numbered consecutively. This means that if you add a number you are going East and if you subtract a number you are going West. North to South page numbers increase as you travel South and decrease as you travel North.

Scale of Individual Maps

All map pages are scaled 1/2 mile (2640') to the inch. Each small grid is exactly 3/4 mile square. A page covers 3 miles East-West by 4 1/2 miles North-South.

1" = one half mile (2,640')

Common Map Abbreviations

Alley . . . . ALY	Farm to Market Rd . . . . F.M.	Meadow . . . . MDW	Springs . . . . SPGS
Avenue . . . . AVE	Field . . . . FLD	Mount . . . . MT	Square . . . . SQ
Boulevard . . . . BLVD	Forest . . . . FRST	Mountain . . . . MTN	Street . . . . ST
Brook . . . . BRK	Forest Service . . . . F.S.	North . . . . N	Terrace . . . . TER
Circle . . . . CIR	Fort . . . . FT	Park . . . . PRK	Trail . . . . TRL
County Road . . . . C.R.	Freeway . . . . FRWY	Parkway . . . . PKWY	Valley . . . . VLLY
Court . . . . CT	Glen . . . . GLN	Place . . . . PL	View . . . . VW
Creek . . . . .CRK	Grove . . . . GRV	Point . . . . PT	Village . . . . VLLG
Drive . . . . .DR	Highway . . . . HWY	Proposed . . . . PROP	Water . . . . WTR
East . . . . E	Hollow . . . . HLLW	Ridge . . . . RDG	Way . . . . WY
Enchanted . . . . ECHTD	Interstate Highway . . . . I.H.	River . . . . RVR	West . . . . W
Estates . . . . ESTS	Lane . . . . LN	Saint . . . . ST	Willow . . . . WLLW
Extension . . . . EXT	Lake . . . . LK	South . . . . S	Wood . . . . WD

Location Abbreviations

Beach City . . . . BC	Hilshire . . . . HI	Piney Point . . . . PP	Northeast Brazoria County . . . . NEB
Bunker Hill . . . . BH	Hockley . . . . HK	Roman Forest . . . . RF	Northwest Brazoria County . . . . . . NWB
Brookside . . . . BK	Humble . . . . HM	Shoreacres . . . . SA	Chambers County . . . . CCO
Bellaire . . . . .BL	Huffman . . . . HU	Seabrook . . . . SB	Northeast Fort Bend County . . . . . NEF
Barret . . . . .BR	Jacinto City . . . . JC	Stage Coach . . . . SC	Northwest Fort Bend County . . . . . NWF
Baytown . . . . BT	Jersey Village . . . . JV	Shenandoah . . . . SD	Galveston County . . . . GCO
Crosby . . . . CB	Kemah . . . . KE	Stafford . . . . SF	Liberty County . . . . LCO
Clear Lake Shores . . . .CS	Katy . . . . KT	Sugar Land . . . . SG	Southeast Montgomery Co. . . . . . SEM
Channelview CV	League City LC	South Houston . . . . . . .SH	Southwest Montgomery Co. . . . . SWM
Cypress . . . . CY	La Porte . . . . LP	Spring . . . . SP	Waller County . . . . WCO
Dickinson . . . . DI	Mont Belvieu . . . . . . MB	Southside Place . . . . . .SS	Northeast Houston . . . . NEH
Deer Park . . . . DP	Missouri City . . . . MC	Spring Valley . . . . SV	Northwest Houston . . . . NWH
Downtown Houston . . . DT	Meadows Place . . . . . MD	Tomball . . . . TB	Southeast Houston . . . . SEH
El Lago . . . . .EL	McNair . . . . MN	Taylor Lake Village . . . .TL	Southwest Houston . . . . SWH
Friendswood . . . . FR	Morgans Point . . . . . . MP	Webster . . . . WB	Northeast Harris County . . . . NEC
Fresno . . . . FS	Nassau Bay . . . . NB	Woodlands. . . . . .WD	North-Central Harris County . . . . . NCC
Galena Park . . . . GP	Oak Ridge North . . . . OR	Waller . . . . WL	Northwest Harris County . . . . . . NWC
Hunters Creek . . . . . . .HC	Pasadena . . . . PA	West University . . . . . WU	Southeast Harris County . . . . SEC
Hedwig . . . . HE	Plum Grove . . . . PG	Woodbranch Village . . WV	Southwest Harris County . . . . SWC
Highlands . . . . HG	Pearland . . . . PL		

Como usar tu KEY MAP®

Para localizar una calle, siga los pasos en la lista de avajo:

	Paso #1		Paso #3	Paso #4	Paso #2	
	Street Name		**Block**	**Pg/Sq**	**Loc**	**Zip**
	EASY ST		800	539Q	LP	77571

1. Localice el nombre de la calle (Street Name) en la lista del alfabeto. Nota que calles con numeros para nombre de calle (Street Name) van antes en el alfabeto.
2. Cheque la abreviacion de la locacion (Loc) en esa area y codigo postal (Zip) para que no escoja la calle inexacto cuando hay nombres (Street Name) duplicado en la lista.
3. Varias calles estaran duplicado que indican la calle sige de pagina a pagina o que hay otra diferente por la diferencia en el codigo postal (Zip) o por el bloquee (Block).
4. Escoja la pagina y cuadro (Pg/Sq). Nota que la pagina y cuadro (Pg/Sq) indica donde esta el nombre (Street Name) de la calle nadamas. El bloquee (Block) en la lista del frente del libro indica que es el bloquee (Block) mas vajo de ese codigo postal (Zip) o en esa pagina.
5. Para hallar la locacion escogida, cheque el mapa chico en la ultima pagina del Key Map. Aqui hallas todos los numeros de las paginas incluido en azul. Esto es tambien una arteria que muestra la ruta mas directa de una area a otro.
6. Recuerde Norte siempre es arriba. Cuando gire la pagina es de Este y Oeste. Consecutive corren esas paginas. Eso quiere decir que si agregas una pagina vas al Este y si reduce un numero de pagina vas llendo Oeste. Norte y Sur las paginas aumentan cuando vas mas al Sur y las paginas reducen cuando vas mas al Norte.

La escala de Mapas Individuales

Todas las paginas de este libro se escalan 1/2 milla (2640') a la pulgada. Cada cuadro es exactamente 3/4 milla cuadrada. Cada pagina cubre 3 millas Este-Oeste por 4 1/2 millas Norte-Sur.

1"= una media milla (2,640')

Mapa Abreviaciones

Alley	ALY	Farm to Market Rd	F.M.	Meadow	MDW	Springs	SPGS
Avenue	AVE	Field	FLD	Mount	MT	Square	SQ
Boulevard	BLVD	Forest	FRST	Mountain	MTN	Street	ST
Brook	BRK	Forest Service	F.S.	North	N	Terrace	TER
Circle	CIR	Fort	FT	Park	PRK	Trail	TRL
County Road	C.R.	Freeway	FRWY	Parkway	PKWY	Valley	VLLY
Court	CT	Glen	GLN	Place	PL	View	VW
Creek	CRK	Grove	GRV	Point	PT	Village	VLLG
Drive	DR	Highway	HWY	Proposed	PROP	Water	WTR
East	E	Hollow	HLLW	Ridge	RDG	Way	WY
Enchanted	ECHTD	Interstate Highway	I.H.	River	RVR	West	W
Estates	ESTS	Lane	LN	Saint	ST	Willow	WLLW
Extension	EXT	Lake	LK	South	S	Wood	WD

Locacion Abreviaciones

Beach City	BC	Hilshire	HI	Piney Point	PP	Northeast Brazoria County	NEB
Bunker Hill	BH	Hockley	HK	Roman Forest	RF	Northwest Brazoria County	NWB
Brookside	BK	Humble	HM	Shoreacres	SA	Chambers County	CCO
Bellaire	BL	Huffman	HU	Seabrook	SB	Northeast Fort Bend County	NEF
Barret	BR	Jacinto City	JC	Stage Coach	SC	Northwest Fort Bend County	NWF
Baytown	BT	Jersey Village	JV	Shenandoah	SD	Galveston County	GCO
Crosby	CB	Kemah	KE	Stafford	SF	Liberty County	LCO
Clear Lake Shores	CS	Katy	KT	Sugar Land	SG	Southeast Montgomery Co.	SEM
Channelview	CV	League City	LC	South Houston	SH	Southwest Montgomery Co.	SWM
Cypress	CY	La Porte	LP	Southside Place	SS	Waller County	WCO
Dickinson	DI	Mont Belvieu	MB	Spring Valley	SV	Northeast Houston	NEH
Deer Park	DP	Missouri City	MC	Tomball	TB	Northwest Houston	NWH
Downtown Houston	DT	Meadows Place	MN	Taylor Lake Village	TL	Southeast Houston	SEH
El Lago	EL	McNair	MN	Webster	WB	Southwest Houston	SWH
Friendswood	FR	Morgans Point	MP	Woodlands	WD	Northeast Harris County	NEC
Fresno	FS	Nassau Bay	NB	Waller	WL	North-Central Harris County	NCC
Galena Park	GP	Oak Ridge North	OR	West University	WU	Northwest Harris County	NWC
Hunters Creek	HC	Pasadena	PA	Woodbranch Village	WV	Southeast Harris County	SEC
Hedwig	HE	Plum Grove	PG			Southwest Harris County	SWC
Highlands	HG	Pearland	PL				

HIGHWAYS

INTERSTATE NAME	LOCATION PAGE
10 East (East Freeway)	459, 460, 461, 462, 463, 494, 495, 496, 497, 498, 499
10 West (Katy Freeway, West Freeway)	444, 484, 485, 486, 487, 488, 489, 490, 491, 492, 493
45 North (North Freeway)	252, 292, 332, 372, 412, 413, 453
45 South (Gulf Freeway)	493, 494, 534, 535, 575, 576, 617, 618, 658
610 East (East Loop)	495, 535
610 North (North Loop)	452, 453, 454, 455, 495
610 South (South Loop)	531, 532, 533, 534, 535
610 West (West Loop)	451, 491, 531

U.S. HIGHWAY NAME	LOCATION PAGE
59 North (Eastex Freeway)	256, 257, 296, 335, 374, 375, 414, 454, 494
59 South (Southwest Freeway)	491, 492, 493, 529, 530, 531, 568, 569
90 (Beaumont Highway)	380, 381, 418, 420, 444, 445, 455, 456, 457, 458, 484, 485, 486, 487, 488, 489, 490, 491, 492, 493, 494, 495, 532, 533, 566, 567, 568, 569, 570, 571
290 (Northwest Freeway)	282, 283, 324, 325, 326, 366, 367, 368, 408, 409, 410, 450, 451

STATE HIGHWAY NAME	LOCATION PAGE
3 (Old Galveston Rd.)	535, 536, 576, 577, 617, 618, 658, 659
6	282, 323, 325, 326, 366, 367, 368, 408, 448, 488, 610
35	535, 575, 615
99 (Grand Parkway)	54, 55, 56, 87, 88, 89, 91, 92, 93, 253, 286, 290, 325, 365, 405, 445, 485, 525, 526, 566, 567
134	539, 499
146	462, 463, 501, 502, 540, 541, 580, 620, 660, 661
225 (LaPorte Frwy)	535, 536, 537, 538, 539, 540
249 (Tomball Parkway)	247, 248, 288, 328, 329, 369, 370, 371, 411, 412
288 (South Frwy., Nolan Ryan Expwy)	493, 533, 573, 613
330 SPUR (Decker Rd.)	499, 500, 501

TOLL ROAD NAME	LOCATION PAGE
Beltway 8 (Sam Houston Tollway)	369-376, 409, 416, 417, 449, 457, 489, 497, 498, 537, 570-577
Hardy Toll Road	292, 332, 333, 373, 413, 453
Tomball	288
Westpark Toll Road	491, 525, 526, 527, 528, 529, 530, 531
Fort Bend Toll Road	570, 571, 610

FARM MARKET ROADS

F.M. ROADS	LOCATION PAGE
FM 149	247
FM 270	659
FM 359	524, 566
FM 362	242, 282, 322
FM 517	660, 661
FM 518	613, 614, 615, 616, 620, 656, 657, 658, 659, 660
FM 521	532, 533, 572, 611, 612
FM 525	373, 374
FM 526	416, 417, 456, 496
FM 527	455
FM 528	656, 657, 658
FM 529	404, 405, 406, 407, 408
FM 565	463, 502, 503
FM 646	659, 660, 661
FM 686	340, 524
FM 723	524
FM 762	606
FM 865	613
FM 1092	569, 609
FM 1093	487, 488, 489, 490, 491, 524, 525, 526, 527
FM 1128	614
FM 1266	659, 660
FM 1314	254, 255, 295, 296
FM 1405	502, 503, 542
FM 1413	381
FM 1463	484

F.M. ROADS	LOCATION PAGE
FM 1464	527, 567
FM 1485	256, 257, 258
FM 1488	242, 243
FM 1774	247
FM 1876	528, 568
FM 1942	419, 420, 460, 461, 462, 463
FM 1959	577, 617
FM 1960	332, 333, 338, 339, 340
FM 1960 E	335, 336, 337, 338
FM 1960 W	331, 332, 333, 334, 335, 368, 369, 370, 408
1960 BYPASS E	335, 336
1960 BYPASS W	334, 335
FM 2094	619, 620, 659
FM 2100	259, 298, 299, 339, 379, 419, 459
FM 2234	570, 610, 611, 612, 613
FM 2351	616, 617, 656
FM 2354	503, 541, 542, 543
FM 2759	606, 607
FM 2920	249, 282, 283, 284, 285, 286, 287, 288, 289, 290, 291, 292
FM 2978	215, 249, 289
FM 3180	463, 503
FM 3345	610
FM 3360	463
FM 3436	660

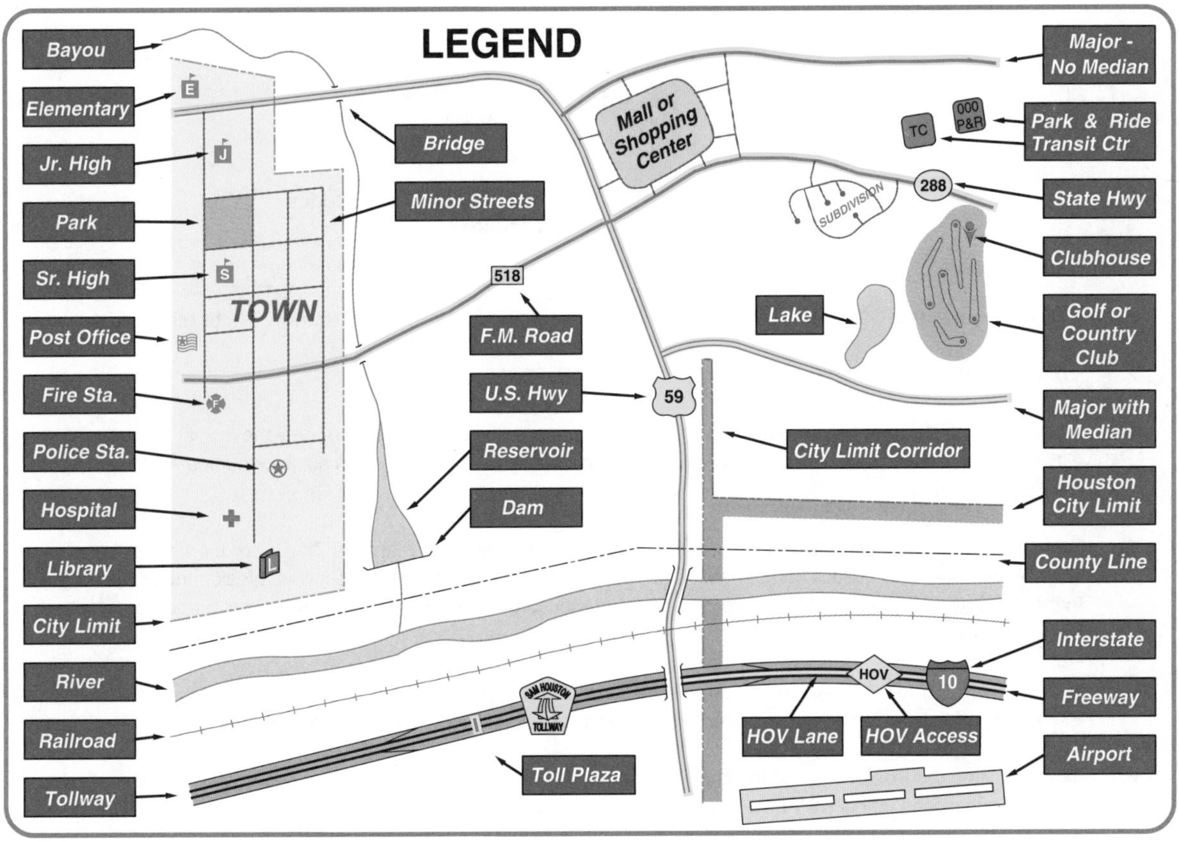

LEGEND

Bayou	Major - No Median
Elementary	Park & Ride Transit Ctr
Jr. High	State Hwy
Park	Clubhouse
Sr. High	Golf or Country Club
Post Office	Major with Median
Fire Sta.	Houston City Limit
Police Sta.	County Line
Hospital	Interstate
Library	Freeway
City Limit	Airport
River	
Railroad	
Tollway	

Bridge · Minor Streets · Mall or Shopping Center · TOWN · F.M. Road · U.S. Hwy · Reservoir · Dam · Lake · Subdivision · City Limit Corridor · 518 · 59 · 288 · TC · 000 P&R

Sam Houston Tollway · Toll Plaza · HOV · 10 · HOV Lane · HOV Access

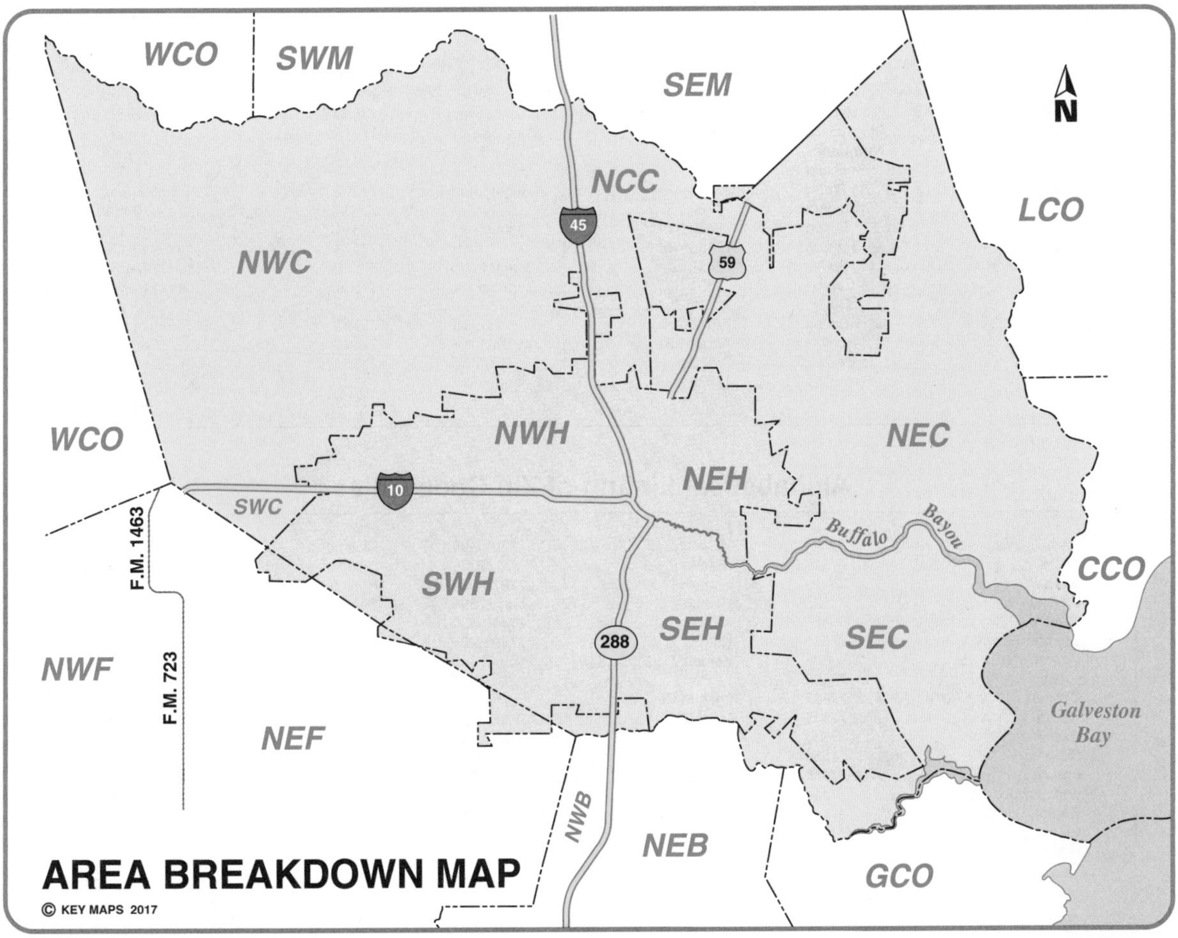

AREA BREAKDOWN MAP

WCO · SWM · SEM · NCC · LCO · NWC · NWH · NEC · WCO · NEH · SWC · 45 · 10 · 59 · SWH · SEH · SEC · CCO · Buffalo Bayou · F.M. 1463 · F.M. 723 · NWF · NEF · 288 · NWB · NEB · GCO · Galveston Bay

ZIP CODE ASSISTANCE

How to use your KEY MAP® in determining correct Zip Codes
A Step by Step Procedure

1. You will start with a Street Name and, in many cases, you will need a Block Number (Address).

2. Locate the Street Name in the alphabetical Street Index listings.

3. Use the Block Number to insure that the proper Zip Code is selected. Remember, only the lowest Block Number within the Zip Code is shown. If there is not an additional listing for that street then all block numbers appear within the Zip Code listed.

4. If an additional listing is shown it indicates the street appears in more than one Zip Code or on more than one **KEY MAP®** page. The block number shown for the additional listing denotes the lowest block number appearing in the Zip Code designated. If there are no additional listings then assume all remaining block numbers are within the final listing.

5. If "(even)" or "(odd)" appears within the street listing then there is a Zip Code line running down the center of that portion of the street. So Even addresses and Odd addresses will each be in different Zip Codes.

6. To determine the Postal City use the charts below. Keep in mind that Zip Codes do not usually follow city limits, so the location code in the **KEY MAP®** index should only be used to get a general idea of the Zip Code city.

Numerical Listing by Zip Code

Zip Code	City		Zip Code	City		Zip Code	City
77001-77099	Houston		77429	Cypress		77532	Crosby
77336	Huffman		77433	Cypress		77535	Dayton
77338-339	Humble		77447	Hockley		77536	Deer Park
77345-346	Humble		77449-450	Katy		77539	Dickinson
77355	Stagecoach		77459	Missouri City		77545	Fresno
77357	New Caney		77469	Richmond		77546	Friendswood
77362	Pinehurst		77477	Stafford		77547	Galena Park
77365	Porter		77478-479	Sugar Land		77562	Highlands
77372	Splendora		77484	Waller		77565	Kemah
77373	Spring		77489	Missouri City		77571	La Porte
77375	Tomball		77493-494	Katy		77573	League City
77379-382	Spring		77498	Sugar Land		77578	Manvel
77384-385	Conroe		77501-507	Pasadena		77580	Mont Belvieu
77386	Spring		77511	Alvin		77581	Pearland
77388-390	Spring		77518	Bacliff		77583	Rosharon
77396	Humble		77520-521	Baytown		77584	Pearland
77401	Bellaire		77523	Baytown		77586	Seabrook
77406-407	Richmond		77530	Channelview		77587	South Houston
						77598	Webster

Alphabetical Listing of Zip Code Cities

City	Zip		City	Zip		City	Zip
Alvin	77511		Houston	77001-99		Richmond	77406-407
Bacliff	77518		Huffman	77336		Richmond	77469
Baytown	77520-21		Humble	77338-339		Rosharon	77583
Baytown	77523		Humble	77345-346, 77396		Seabrook	77586
Bellaire	77401		Katy	77449-450		South Houston	77587
Channelview	77530		Katy	77493-494		Splendora	77372
Conroe	77384-385		Kemah	77565		Spring	77373, 77379-382
Crosby	77532		La Porte	77571		Spring	77386, 77388-390
Cypress	77429, 77433		League City	77573		Stafford	77477
Dayton	77535		Manvel	77578		Stagecoach	77355
Deer Park	77536		Missouri City	77459, 77489		Sugar Land	77478-79
Dickinson	77539		Mont Belvieu	77580		Sugar Land	77498
Fresno	77545		New Caney	77357		Tomball	77375
Friendswood	77546		Pasadena	77501-507		Waller	77484
Galena Park	77547		Pearland	77581, 77584		Webster	77598
Highlands	77562		Pinehurst	77362			
Hockley	77447		Porter	77365			

POST OAK AREA

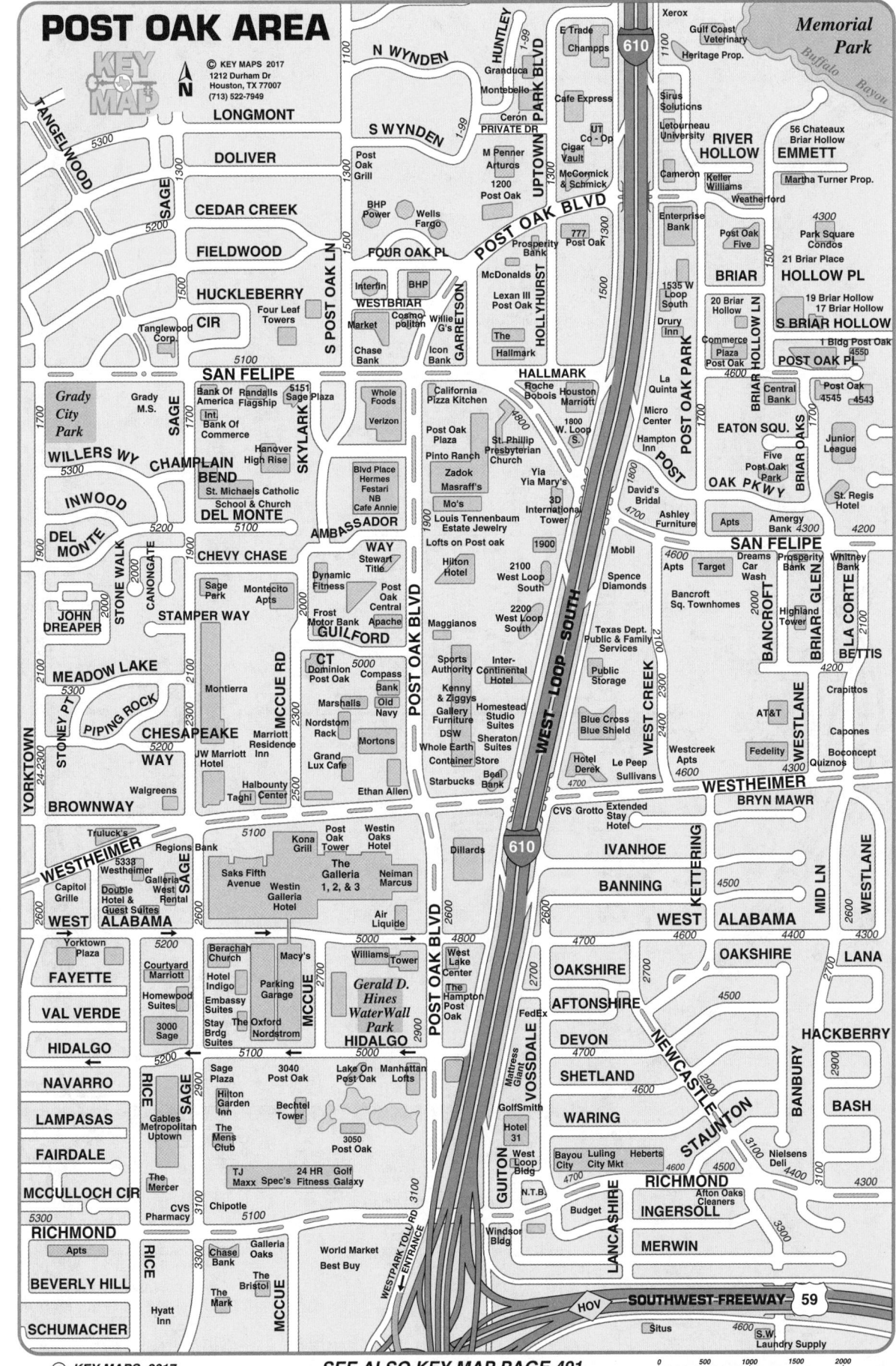

© KEY MAPS 2017
1212 Durham Dr
Houston, TX 77007
(713) 522-7949

Memorial Park

Scale in Feet
0   500   1000   1500   2000

DOWNTOWN

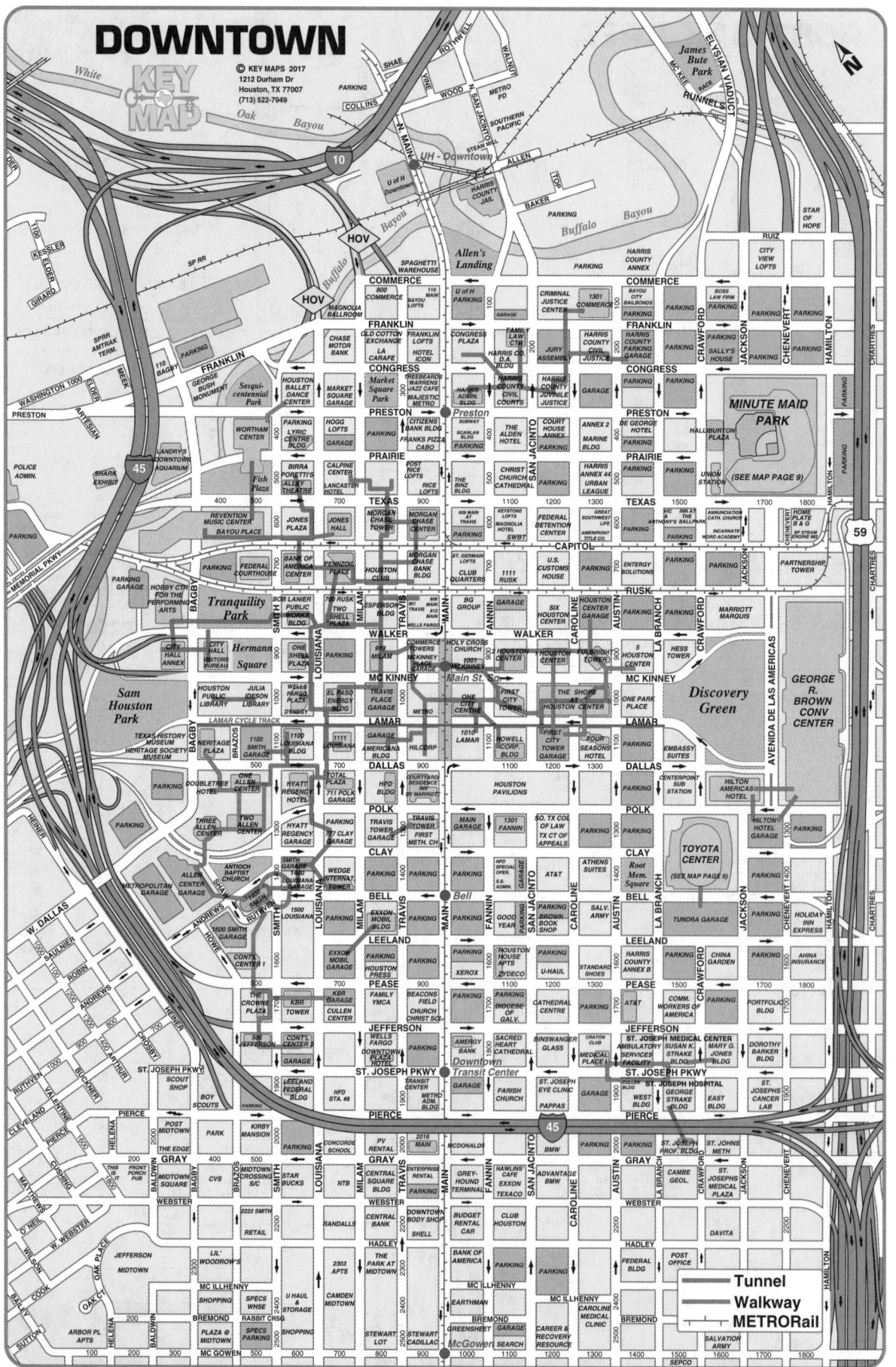

© KEY MAPS 2017
1212 Durham Dr
Houston, TX 77007
(713) 522-7949

8

© KEY MAPS 2017 (713) 522-7949

SEE ALSO KEY MAP PAGE 493

Tunnel
Walkway
METRORail

0   500   1000
Scale in Feet

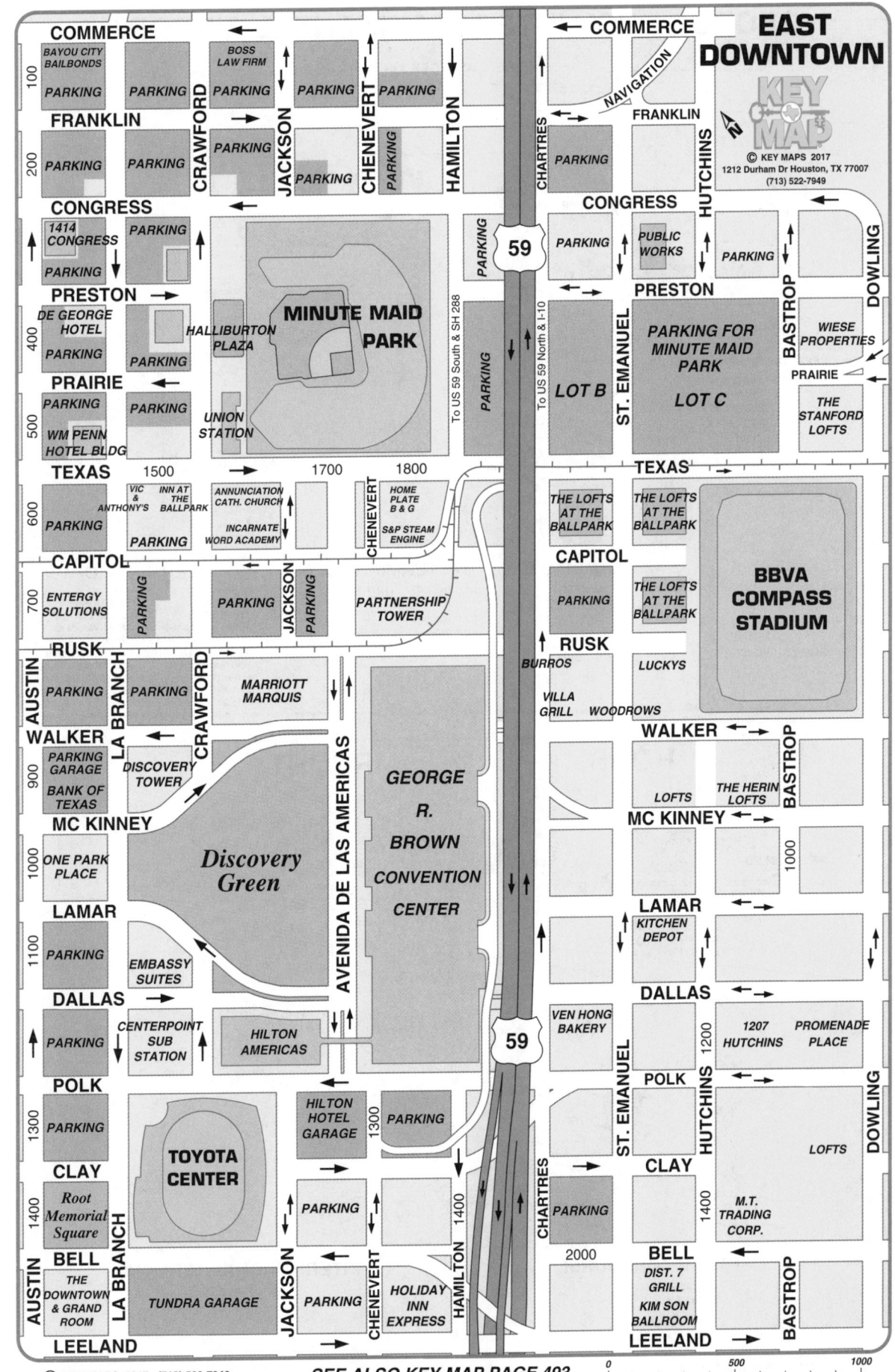

EAST DOWNTOWN

KEY MAPS

© KEY MAPS 2017
1212 Durham Dr Houston, TX 77007
(713) 522-7949

COMMERCE

BAYOU CITY BAILBONDS
PARKING
BOSS LAW FIRM
PARKING
PARKING
PARKING

FRANKLIN

PARKING
PARKING
CRAWFORD
PARKING
PARKING
CHENEVERT
PARKING
HAMILTON

CONGRESS

1414 CONGRESS
PARKING
PARKING

PRESTON

DE GEORGE HOTEL
PARKING
HALLIBURTON PLAZA
MINUTE MAID PARK

PRAIRIE

PARKING
PARKING
UNION STATION

WM PENN HOTEL BLDG

TEXAS 1500 1700 1800

PARKING
VIC & ANTHONY'S
INN AT THE BALLPARK
ANNUNCIATION CATH. CHURCH
INCARNATE WORD ACADEMY
CHENEVERT
HOME PLATE B & G
S&P STEAM ENGINE

CAPITOL

ENTERGY SOLUTIONS
PARKING
PARKING
JACKSON
PARKING
PARTNERSHIP TOWER

RUSK

AUSTIN
PARKING
LA BRANCH
PARKING
CRAWFORD
MARRIOTT MARQUIS

WALKER

PARKING GARAGE BANK OF TEXAS
DISCOVERY TOWER

MC KINNEY

ONE PARK PLACE
Discovery Green
AVENIDA DE LAS AMERICAS
GEORGE R. BROWN CONVENTION CENTER

LAMAR

PARKING
EMBASSY SUITES

DALLAS

PARKING
CENTERPOINT SUB STATION
HILTON AMERICAS

POLK

PARKING
HILTON HOTEL GARAGE
PARKING

CLAY

Root Memorial Square
TOYOTA CENTER

BELL

AUSTIN
THE DOWNTOWN & GRAND ROOM
LA BRANCH
TUNDRA GARAGE
JACKSON
PARKING
CHENEVERT
HOLIDAY INN EXPRESS
HAMILTON

LEELAND

COMMERCE
NAVIGATION
FRANKLIN
PARKING

CONGRESS
CHARTRES
PARKING
PUBLIC WORKS
HUTCHINS
PARKING
DOWLING

PRESTON
59
PARKING
ST. EMANUEL
PARKING FOR MINUTE MAID PARK
LOT C
WIESE PROPERTIES

PRAIRIE

To US 59 South & SH 288
To US 59 North & I-10
PARKING
LOT B
THE STANFORD LOFTS

TEXAS

THE LOFTS AT THE BALLPARK
THE LOFTS AT THE BALLPARK
BBVA COMPASS STADIUM

CAPITOL

PARKING
THE LOFTS AT THE BALLPARK

RUSK

BURROS
LUCKYS
VILLA GRILL
WOODROWS

WALKER

BASTROP
LOFTS
THE HERIN LOFTS

MC KINNEY

1000

LAMAR

KITCHEN DEPOT

DALLAS

VEN HONG BAKERY
ST. EMANUEL
1207 HUTCHINS
PROMENADE PLACE

POLK

CHARTRES
HUTCHINS
LOFTS
DOWLING

CLAY

PARKING
M.T. TRADING CORP.

BELL

2000
DIST. 7 GRILL
KIM SON BALLROOM
BASTROP

LEELAND

© KEY MAPS 2017 (713) 522-7949   **SEE ALSO KEY MAP PAGE 493**

0   500   1000
Scale in Feet

GEORGE BUSH INTERCONTINENTAL AIRPORT

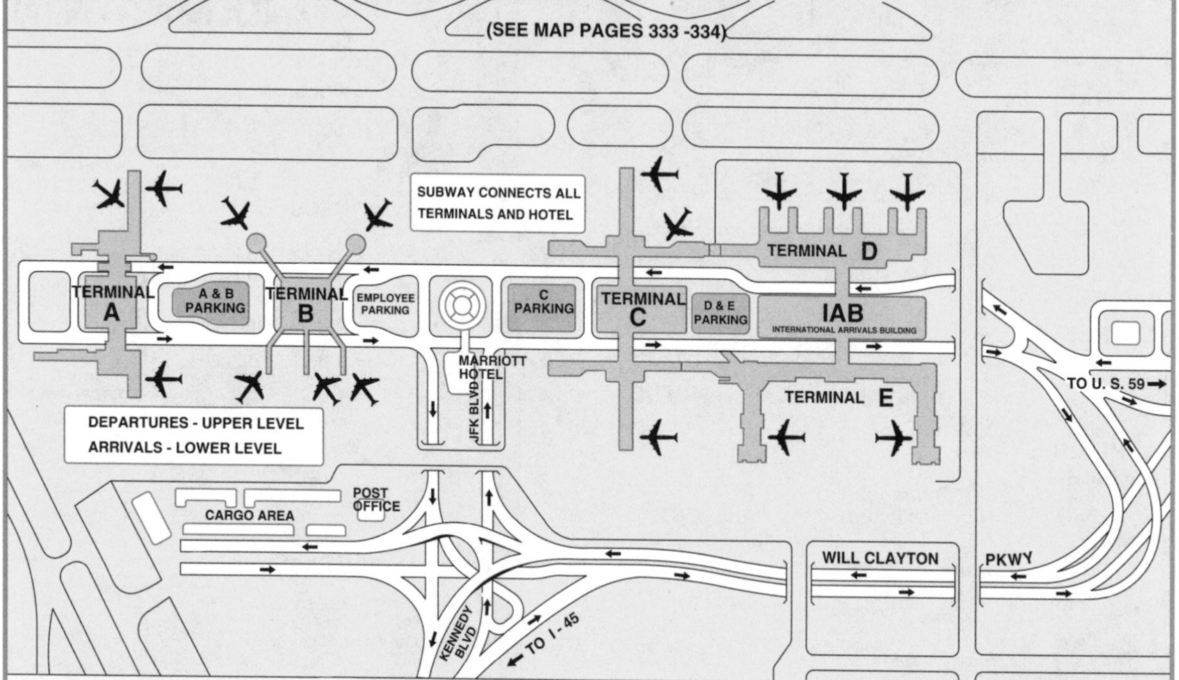

(SEE MAP PAGES 333 -334)

SUBWAY CONNECTS ALL TERMINALS AND HOTEL

TERMINAL A
A & B PARKING
TERMINAL B
EMPLOYEE PARKING
C PARKING
TERMINAL C
D & E PARKING
TERMINAL D
IAB — INTERNATIONAL ARRIVALS BUILDING
TERMINAL E

MARRIOTT HOTEL
JFK BLVD

DEPARTURES - UPPER LEVEL
ARRIVALS - LOWER LEVEL

POST OFFICE
CARGO AREA
WILL CLAYTON PKWY
TO U.S. 59
KENNEDY BLVD
TO I - 45

TERMINAL A

AIR CANADA	FRONTIER
ALASKA	SPIRIT
AMERICAN	TEXAS SKY
DELTA	UNITED
ELITE AIRWAYS	WESTJET

TERMINAL B
UNITED

TERMINAL C, E
UNITED

TERMINAL D

AEROMEXICO	KLM
AIR CHINA	KOREAN AIR
AIR FRANCE	LUFTHANSA
AIR NEW ZEALAND	QATAR AIRWAYS
ALL NIPPON AIRWAYS	SINGAPORE AIRLINES
AVIANCA	TURKISH AIRLINES
BRITISH AIRWAYS	VACATION EXPRESS
EMIRATES	VIVAAEROBUS
EVA AIR	VOLARIS
INTERJET	

HOBBY AIRPORT

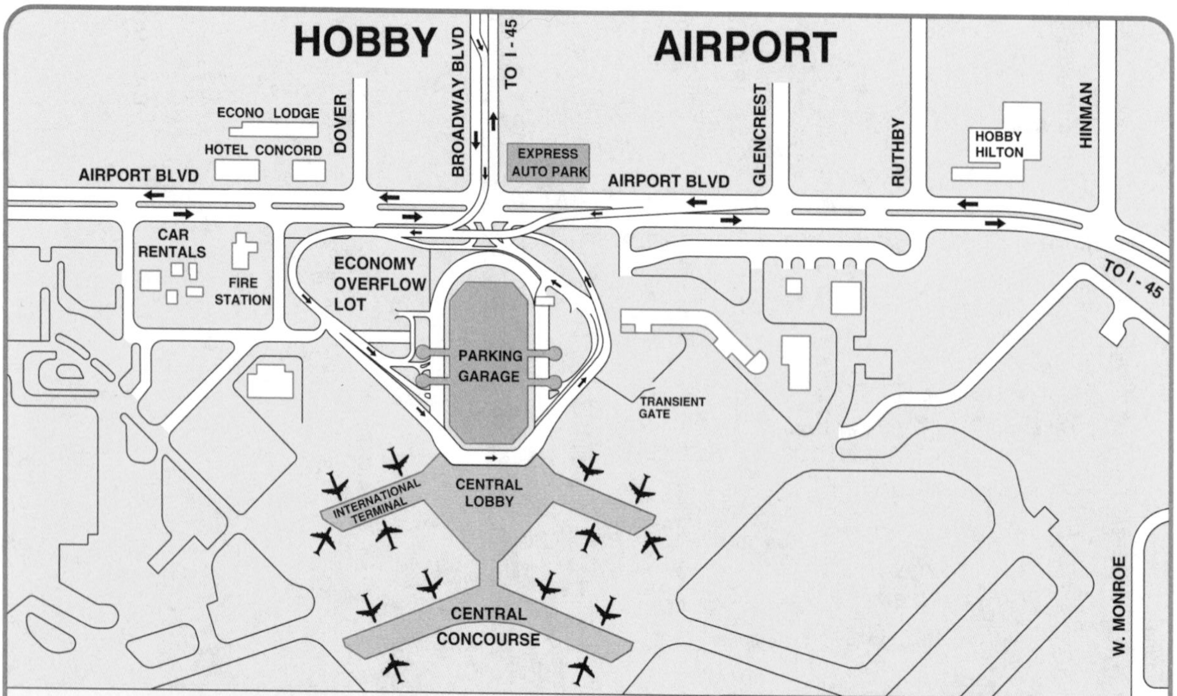

ECONO LODGE
HOTEL CONCORD
DOVER
BROADWAY BLVD
TO I - 45
EXPRESS AUTO PARK
AIRPORT BLVD
GLENCREST
RUTHBY
HOBBY HILTON
HINMAN
AIRPORT BLVD
CAR RENTALS
FIRE STATION
ECONOMY OVERFLOW LOT
PARKING GARAGE
TRANSIENT GATE
INTERNATIONAL TERMINAL
CENTRAL LOBBY
CENTRAL CONCOURSE
TO I - 45
W. MONROE

CENTRAL CONCOURSE
AMERICAN
DELTA
JET BLUE
SOUTHWEST

INTERNATIONAL TERMINAL
SOUTHWEST

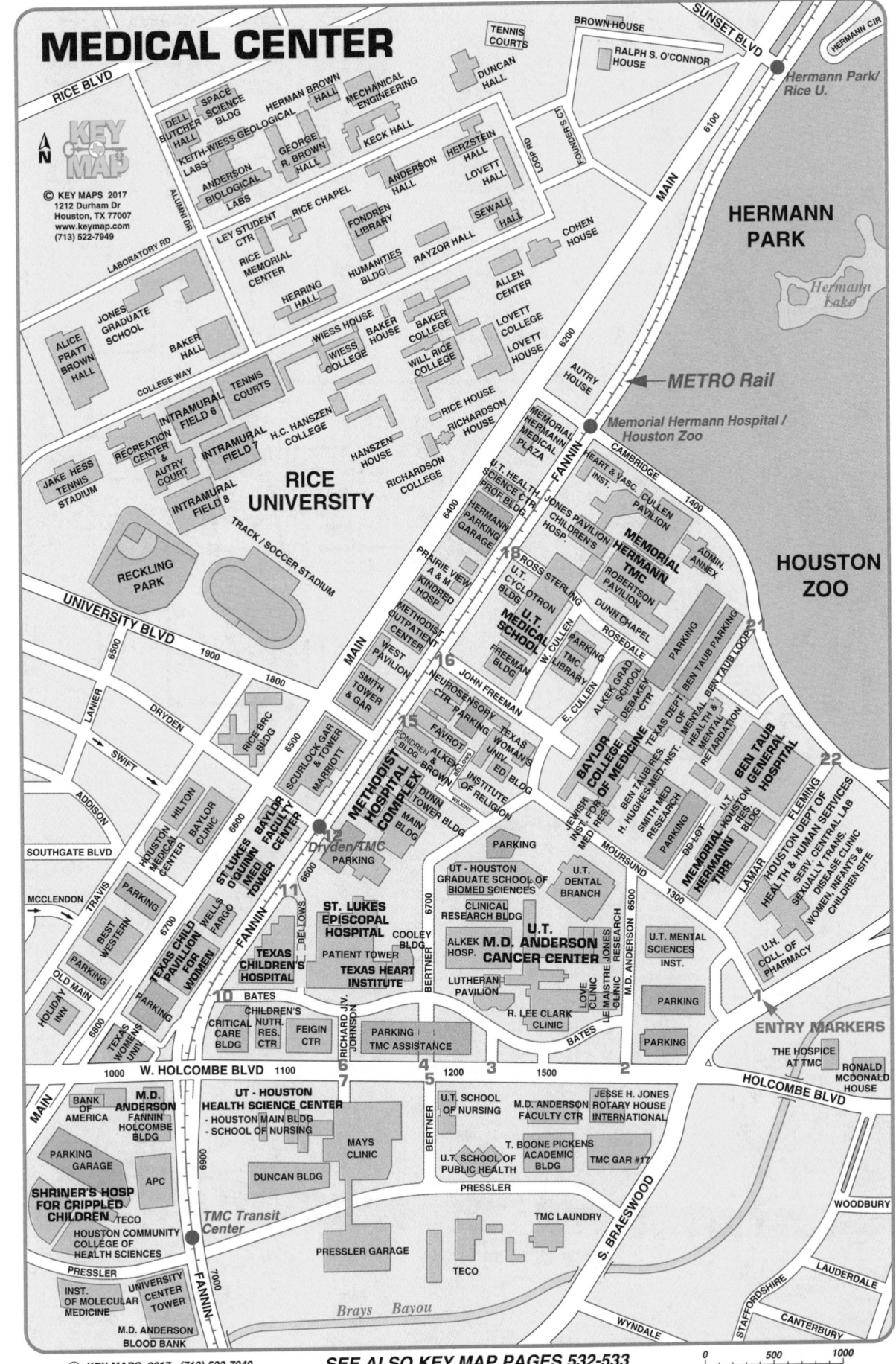

MEDICAL CENTER

© KEY MAPS 2017
1212 Durham Dr
Houston, TX 77007
www.keymap.com
(713) 522-7949

RICE UNIVERSITY

HERMANN PARK

HOUSTON ZOO

← METRO Rail

Memorial Hermann Hospital / Houston Zoo

MEMORIAL HERMANN TMC

U.T. MEDICAL SCHOOL

BAYLOR COLLEGE OF MEDICINE

BEN TAUB GENERAL HOSPITAL

METHODIST HOSPITAL COMPLEX

ST. LUKES EPISCOPAL HOSPITAL

TEXAS CHILDREN'S HOSPITAL

TEXAS HEART INSTITUTE

U.T. M.D. ANDERSON CANCER CENTER

SHRINER'S HOSP FOR CRIPPLED CHILDREN

UT - HOUSTON HEALTH SCIENCE CENTER
- HOUSTON MAIN BLDG
- SCHOOL OF NURSING

ENTRY MARKERS

Scale in Feet
0   500   1000

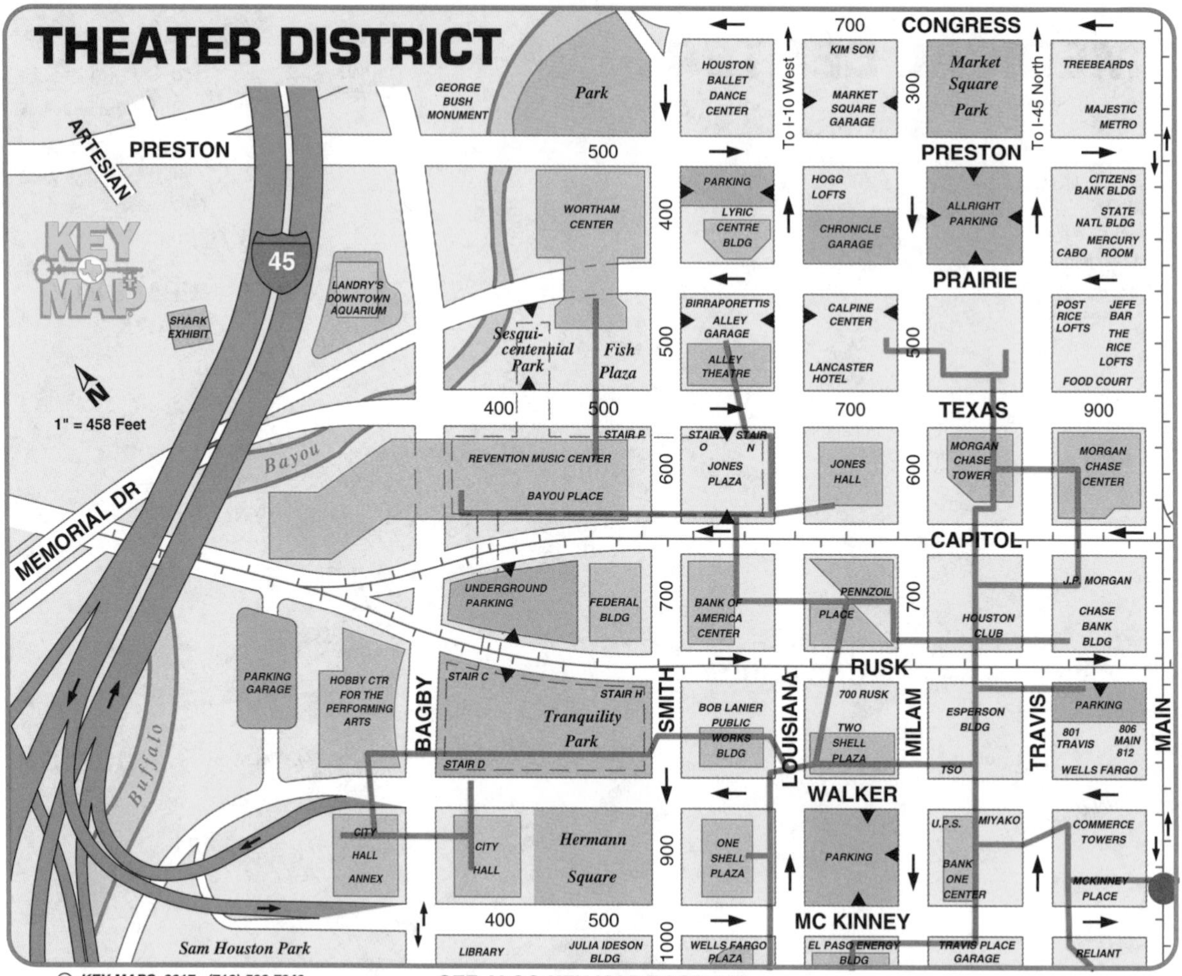

THEATER DISTRICT

CONGRESS

700

ARTESIAN

PRESTON

HOUSTON BALLET DANCE CENTER

KIM SON

MARKET SQUARE GARAGE

300

Market Square Park

TREEBEARDS

MAJESTIC METRO

To I-10 West

To I-45 North

Park

George Bush Monument

500

PRESTON

KEY MAP

45

LANDRY'S DOWNTOWN AQUARIUM

WORTHAM CENTER

400

PARKING

LYRIC CENTRE BLDG

HOGG LOFTS

CHRONICLE GARAGE

ALLRIGHT PARKING

CITIZENS BANK BLDG

STATE NATL BLDG

MERCURY ROOM

CABO

SHARK EXHIBIT

N

1" = 458 Feet

PRAIRIE

Sesqui-centennial Park

Fish Plaza

500

BIRRAPORETTIS ALLEY GARAGE

ALLEY THEATRE

CALPINE CENTER

LANCASTER HOTEL

500

POST RICE LOFTS

JEFE BAR

THE RICE LOFTS

FOOD COURT

400   500

Bayou

TEXAS   900

STAIR P

STAIR O   STAIR N

JONES PLAZA

JONES HALL

MORGAN CHASE TOWER

MORGAN CHASE CENTER

REVENTION MUSIC CENTER

BAYOU PLACE

600

600

MEMORIAL DR

CAPITOL

UNDERGROUND PARKING

FEDERAL BLDG

700

BANK OF AMERICA CENTER

PENNZOIL PLACE

HOUSTON CLUB

700

J.P. MORGAN

CHASE BANK BLDG

PARKING GARAGE

HOBBY CTR FOR THE PERFORMING ARTS

BAGBY

STAIR C

Tranquility Park

STAIR H

SMITH

RUSK

BOB LANIER PUBLIC WORKS BLDG

LOUISIANA

700 RUSK

TWO SHELL PLAZA

MILAM

ESPERSON BLDG

TSO

TRAVIS

PARKING

801 TRAVIS

806 MAIN

WELLS FARGO

812

MAIN

Buffalo

STAIR D

WALKER

CITY HALL ANNEX

CITY HALL

Hermann Square

900

ONE SHELL PLAZA

PARKING

U.P.S.

BANK ONE CENTER

MIYAKO

COMMERCE TOWERS

MCKINNEY PLACE

MC KINNEY

Sam Houston Park

400   500

LIBRARY

JULIA IDESON BLDG

1000

WELLS FARGO PLAZA

EL PASO ENERGY BLDG

TRAVIS PLACE GARAGE

RELIANT

© KEY MAPS 2017 (713) 522-7949

SEE ALSO KEY MAP PAGE 493

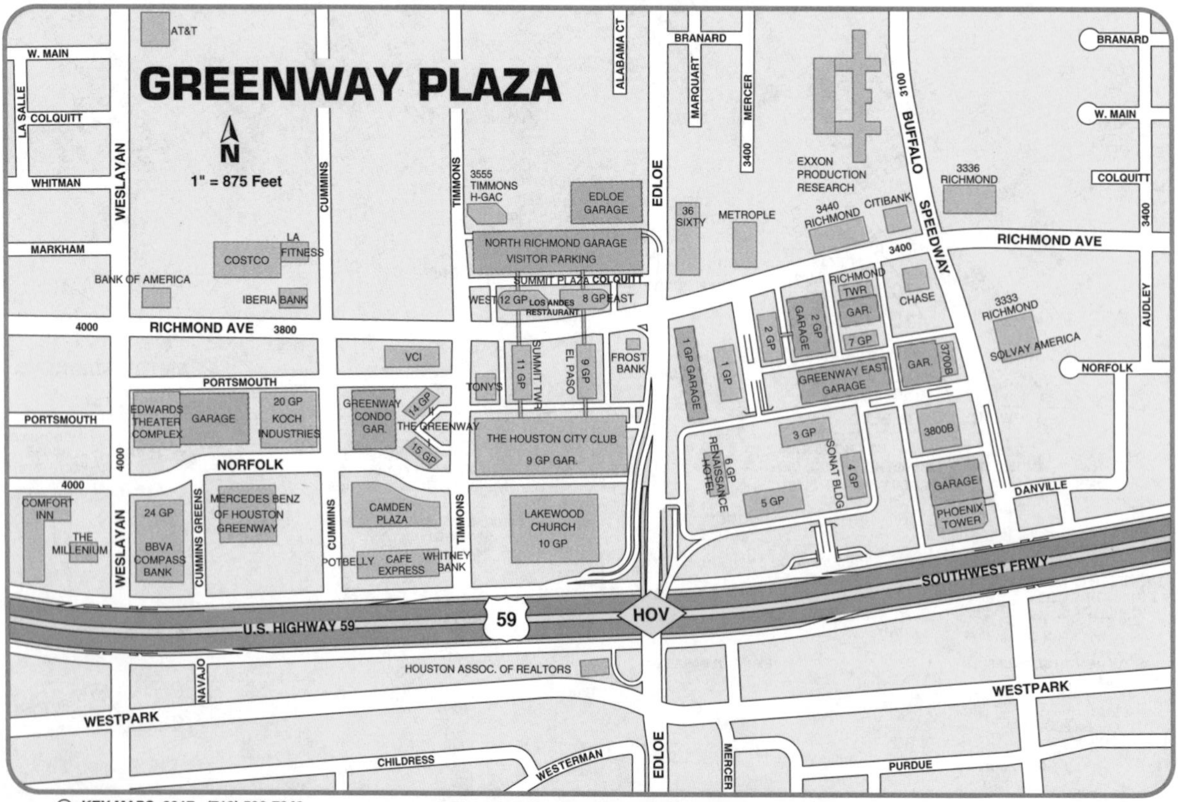

GREENWAY PLAZA

AT&T

BRANARD

BRANARD

W. MAIN

LA SALLE

COLQUITT

WESLAYAN

WHITMAN

N

1" = 875 Feet

CUMMINS

TIMMONS

3555 TIMMONS H-GAC

EDLOE GARAGE

ALABAMA CT

MARQUART

MERCER

3400

BUFFALO

3100

EXXON PRODUCTION RESEARCH

W. MAIN

3336 RICHMOND

COLQUITT

EDLOE

36 SIXTY

METROPLE

3440 RICHMOND

CITIBANK

SPEEDWAY

RICHMOND AVE

MARKHAM

LA FITNESS

COSTCO

NORTH RICHMOND GARAGE VISITOR PARKING

SUMMIT PLAZA COLQUITT

RICHMOND TWR

GAR.

CHASE

3333 RICHMOND

SOLVAY AMERICA

BANK OF AMERICA

IBERIA BANK

WEST 12 GP

LOS ANDES RESTAURANT

8 GP EAST

1 GP GARAGE

2 GP GARAGE

2 GP

7 GP

3708E

NORFOLK

4000

RICHMOND AVE

3800

VCI

11 GP

SUMMIT TWR

EL PASO

9 GP

FROST BANK

TONY'S

1 GP

GREENWAY EAST GARAGE

GAR.

PORTSMOUTH

EDWARDS THEATER COMPLEX

GARAGE

20 GP KOCH INDUSTRIES

GREENWAY CONDO GAR.

14 GP

THE GREENWAY

15 GP

THE HOUSTON CITY CLUB

9 GP GAR.

6 GP GARAGE

RENAISSANCE HOTEL

3 GP

SONAT BLDG

4 GP

3800B

GARAGE

PHOENIX TOWER

NORFOLK

PORTSMOUTH

4000

WESLAYAN

24 GP

BBVA COMPASS BANK

CUMMINS GREENS

MERCEDES BENZ OF HOUSTON GREENWAY

CAMDEN PLAZA

CUMMINS

TIMMONS

LAKEWOOD CHURCH 10 GP

5 GP

DANVILLE

COMFORT INN

THE MILLENIUM

POTBELLY

CAFE EXPRESS

WHITNEY BANK

AUDLEY

NORFOLK

SOUTHWEST FRWY

U.S. HIGHWAY 59

59

HOV

NAVAJO

HOUSTON ASSOC. OF REALTORS

EDLOE

MERCER

WESTPARK

WESTPARK

CHILDRESS

WESTERMAN

PURDUE

© KEY MAPS 2017 (713) 522-7949

SEE ALSO KEY MAP PAGE 492

TOLL ROADS

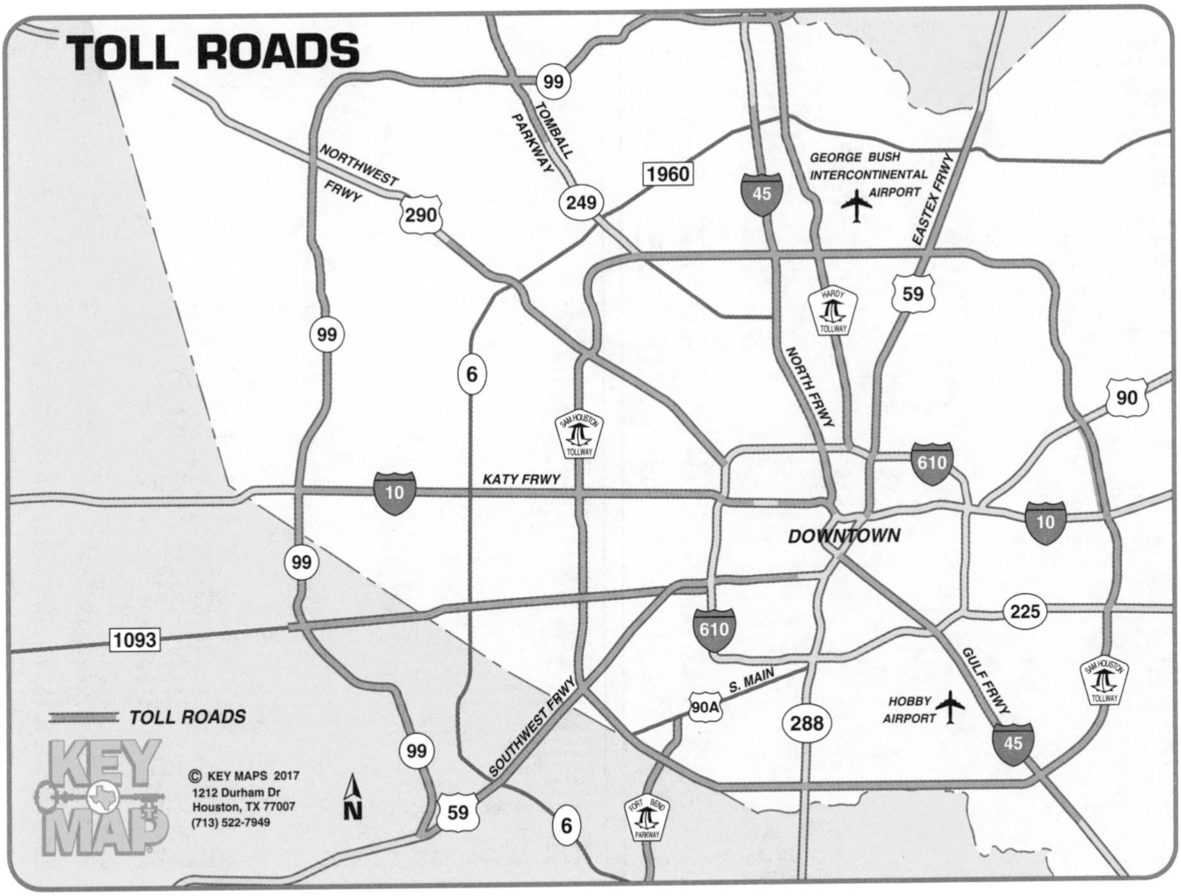

99

TOMBALL PARKWAY

NORTHWEST FRWY

1960

GEORGE BUSH INTERCONTINENTAL AIRPORT

EASTEX FRWY

249

290

45

99

HARDY TOLLWAY

59

6

NORTH FRWY

90

SAM HOUSTON TOLLWAY

610

10

10

DOWNTOWN

99

610

225

1093

S. MAIN

SAM HOUSTON TOLLWAY

90A

288

HOBBY AIRPORT

GULF FRWY

===== TOLL ROADS

99

SOUTHWEST FRWY

45

KEY MAP

© KEY MAPS 2017
1212 Durham Dr
Houston, TX 77007
(713) 522-7949

N

59

6

FORT BEND PARKWAY

KATY FRWY

HIGH OCCUPANCY VEHICLE LANES

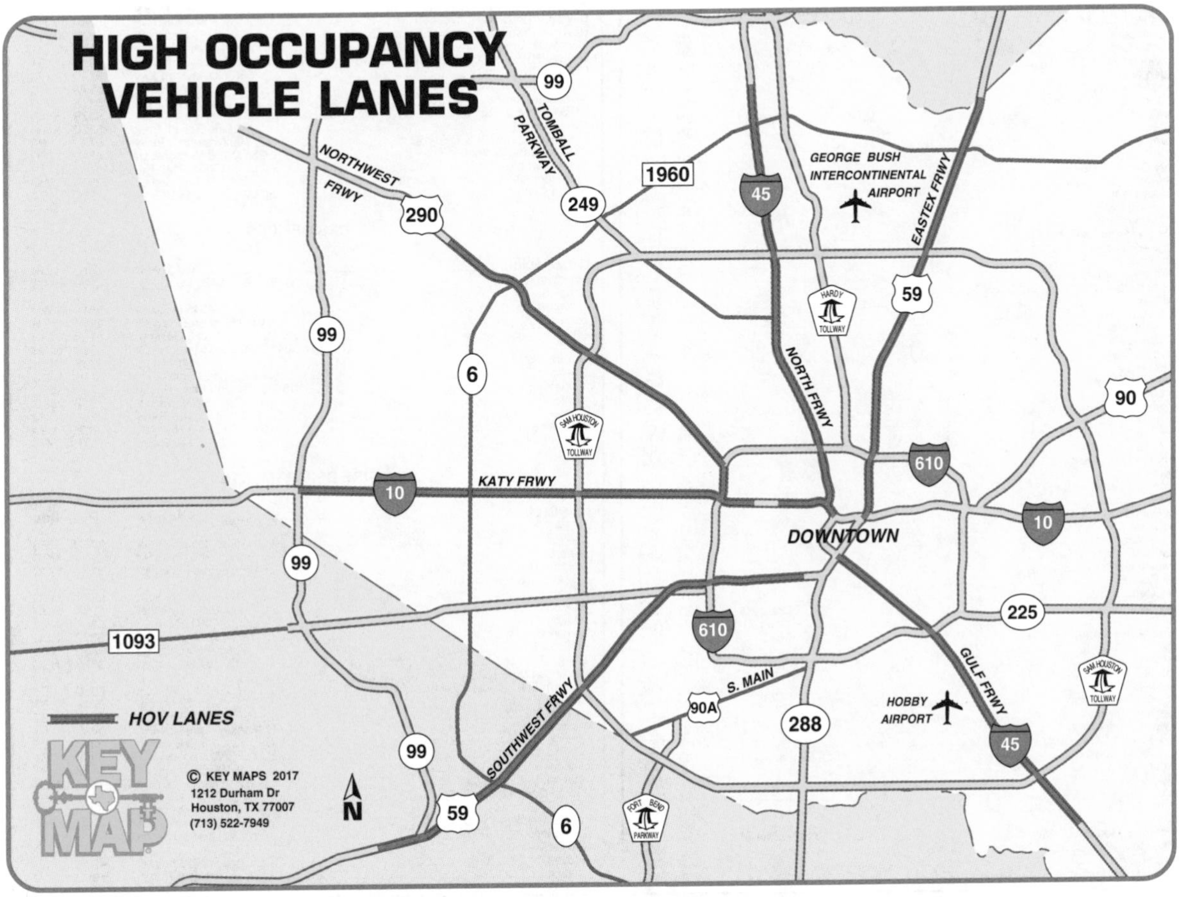

99

TOMBALL PARKWAY

NORTHWEST FRWY

1960

GEORGE BUSH INTERCONTINENTAL AIRPORT

EASTEX FRWY

249

290

45

99

HARDY TOLLWAY

59

6

NORTH FRWY

90

SAM HOUSTON TOLLWAY

610

10

10

DOWNTOWN

10

KATY FRWY

99

610

225

1093

S. MAIN

SAM HOUSTON TOLLWAY

90A

288

HOBBY AIRPORT

GULF FRWY

===== HOV LANES

99

SOUTHWEST FRWY

45

KEY MAP

© KEY MAPS 2017
1212 Durham Dr
Houston, TX 77007
(713) 522-7949

N

59

6

FORT BEND PARKWAY

For more information on HOV schedules & occupancy requirements please visit www.ridemetro.org

AIRPORTS

Airport Name	Address	Pg	Loc
Baytown Airport	5600 Barkaloo Rd	501D	NEC
Cardiff Brothers Airport	3139 Katy Hockley	484S	KT
Covey Trails Airport (pvt)	18 Kitty Hawk W	524J	NWF
Dan Jones International	16434 Kitzman	327C	NWC
Ellington Air Force Base	11900 Old Galveston Rd	577U	SEH
George Bush Intercontinental Airport	2800 N Terminal Rd	374G	NEH
George Bush Intercontinental Airport	2800 N Terminal Rd	334X	NEH
Hobby, William P. Airport	7800 Airport Blvd	575B	SEH
Hoffpauir Airport	2010 N. Mason	445V	NWC
Hooks, D.W. Mem. Airport	20803 Stuebner Airline Rd	290S	NWC
Ken-Ada Ranch Airfield (pvt)		242R	WCO
La Porte Municipal Airport	101 Airport Blvd	539Y	LP
Lyndon B. Johnson Space Center (NASA)	2101 Nasa Pkwy # 1	619N	SEH
Model Airplane Facility		487W	SWH
Polly Ranch Airstrip (pvt)	207 Oak Dr	657K	FR
R.W.J. Airpark	15111 Lakeview Dr	503R	CCO
Rogers Airport (pvt)	Holy Rd and Seaberg Rd	462C	CR
Skydive Houston Airport	15355 Penick Rd	322T	WCO
Skyway Manor Airport	2736 Piper Rd	614P	PL
Weiser Airpark	21904 Northwest Fwy	368T	NWC
West Houston Airport	18000 Groeschke Rd	447P	NWC
Westheimer Air Park	24215 FM 1093 Rd	524M	NEF
Williams Airfield	16990 Porter Ln	254Q	SEM

CEMETERIES

Cemetery Name	Address	Pg	Loc
Adath Israel Cem	4714 Airline Dr	453F	NEH
Aldine Cem	2202-2398 Aldine Meadows Rd	373V	NCC
Alief Cemetery	6900-6964 Dairy Ashford Rd	528H	SWH
Baker Cemetery	25546 Baker Cemetery Rd	247Y	SWM
Bammel Cem	Bammel Rd	332L	NWC
Baytown Memorial Cem	8624 Garth Rd	461K	NEC
Beeler Cemetery Park	1150 Enclave Pkwy	488F	SWH
Beth El Cem		491D	SWH
Beth Jacob Cemetery	2300 Almeda-Genoa Rd	573S	SWH
Bethany Cem	8501 Spencer Hwy	538Z	PA
Bonin Cem	23533 Gosling Rd	290D	NWC
Borgestedt Cem		368K	NWC
Brookside Memorial Park	13401 Eastex Fwy	414C	NEC
Budde Cem		292W	NWC
Burton Cem	County Road 25	322D	NWC
Busch Cem	Red Oak Dr	462Y	BT
Calvary Hill Cem	21723 Aldine Westfield Rd	333F	NCC
Cedar Crest	3010 Ferry Rd	502P	BT
Cemetery Beautiful	8401 Wheatley St	412T	NWH
Crosby Cem		419V	NEC
Crown Hill Cem		536C	SEC
De Zavala Cem		499N	SEC
Decker Prairie Cem	500-808 Virgie Community Rd	247Q	SWM
Dowdell Cem	12523 Twin Sisters Dr	368G	NWC
East River Cem	FM 1485	258P	SEM
Ehrhardt Cem		331T	NWC
Emanuel Memorial Park	8341 Bissonnet St	530T	SWH
Enloe Cem		295M	SEM
Evergreen Cem	13702 Sralla Rd	420S	NEC
Evergreen Plantation		541L	BT
Fairbanks Cem	14135 Packard St	410X	NWH
Fairview Cem	901 N Kansas St	658H	LC
Fieldstore Cem	FM 1488 Rd at Field Store Rd	242C	WCO
Forest Lawn Genoa Cem	8701 Almeda Genoa Rd	575Q	SEH
Forest Lawn North Cem	8700 Tavenor Ln	333K	NCC
Forest Park Cem	6900 Lawndale St	534D	SEH
Forest Park East Cem	21620 Gulf Fwy	658F	SEC
Forest Park West Cem	12800 Westheimer Rd	488V	SWH
Fritsche Cem		327M	NWC
Glendale Cem	8315 E Magnolia	535B	SEH
Glenwood Cem	2525 Washington Ave	493J	SWH
Golden Gate Cem	8400 Hirsch Rd	454F	NEH
Grand View Cem		538Y	DP
Hammer-Mc Faddin Cem		579Z	SEC
Harrington Cem	15525-15627 Garrett Rd	418N	NEC
Harris County Cem		456N	NEH
Harvey Cem		381S	NEC
Hegar Cem		284P	NWC
Henry Cem		579W	PA
Highlands Cem		459U	NEC
Hockley Cem		324J	NWC
Hollywood Cem		493C	SWH
Hollywood Cem	3506 N Main St	453S	NWH
Houston Memorial Gardens		613M	NEB
Houston National Cem	10410 Veterans Memorial Dr	372W	NWC
Huffman Cem		339A	NEC
Huffman Community Cem		339T	NEC
Hufsmith Cem		249T	NWC
Kidd Cem		256L	SEM
Klein Cem		330C	NWC
Klein Memorial Park Cem		247R	SWM
La Porte Cem		580F	LP
Lutheran Cem		326R	NWC
Lutheran Cem		287H	NWC
Lynch Cemetery		419G	NEC
Macedonia Cem		244Y	WCO
Magee Chapel		488N	SWH
Magnolia Cem		493J	SWH
Magnolia Cem		444S	KT
Magnolia Creek Cem		657V	LC
Memorial Oaks Cem	13001 Katy Fwy	488C	SWH
Morales Cem	14605 Luthe Rd	373Y	NCC
Morgan's Point Cem		541S	MP
Mueller Cem		367M	NWC
Oak Park Cem		454F	NEH
Oklahoma Cem		249J	SWM
Old Settlers Cem		615E	PL
Paradise Cemetery South		613M	NEB
Paradise North Cem		411M	NWH
Pate Cem		249J	SWM
Penn Cem		419T	NEC
Perry Cem	10477 Grant Rd	369G	NWC
Pillot Cem		288V	NWC
Prairie Grove Cem		528P	NEF
Ressurection Cem		615B	PL
Resthaven Cem		372L	NCC
Roberts Cem		285L	NWC
Roeder-Becker Cem		328X	NWC
Rose Hill-Siedel Cem		287N	NWC
Rosewood Cem		256X	SEM
Rosewood Park Cem		375L	HM
Sacred Heart Cem	500 FM 1942	419R	NEC
San Jacinto Cem	14659 Market St Rd	497G	NEC
Sanders Cem		495C	NEH
Sanders Cem		286F	NWC
Schloblom Cem		414B	NCC
Simms Cem		339W	NEC
Simms Cem		419K	NEC
South Park Memorial Cem	1310 N Main St	615A	PL
Spring Cem		292G	NCC
Springer Cem		244X	WCO
St. John's Urn Garden		492T	SWH
St. Joseph Cem		413P	NEH
St. Martin Cem		419V	NEC
St. Mary Cem		322A	WCO
Stewart-Prater Cem		335H	NEH
Tamina Cem		252B	SEM
Tettar Cem		334K	NCC
Waller Cem		282Z	NWC
Washington Cem		493J	SWH
Westfield Cem		333J	NCC
Whitcomb Cem		657F	FR
White Cem		459C	NEC
White Oak Cem		296B	SEM
Williams Cem		376E	NEC
Willow Creek Cem		289L	NWC
Woodlawn Cem	1101 Antoine Dr	491B	NWH
Zion Lutheran Cem		249Q	NWC

CITY HALLS

City Hall Name	Address	Pg	Loc
Baytown	2401 Market	541A	BT
Bellaire	7008 S. Rice	531G	BL
Brookside Village	6243 Brookside	614C	BK
Bunker Hill	11977 Memorial	490J	BH
Clear Lake Shores	1006 South Shore Dr	620X	CS
Deer Park	710 E. San Augustine	538Q	DP
El Lago	98 Lakeshore Dr	620J	EL
Friendswood	910 S. Friendswood Dr	657A	FR
Galena Park	2000 Clinton Dr	496W	GP
Hedwig Village	955 Piney Point	490C	HE
Hilshire Village	8301 Westview Dr	451W	HI
Houston	901 Bagby	493L	DT
Humble	114 West Higgins	335Y	HM
Hunters Creek Village	1 Hunters Creek Pl	490D	HC
Jacinto City	1301 Mercury Dr	496J	JC
Jersey Village	16327 Lakeview Dr	409Q	JV
Katy	901 Ave. C	444X	KT
Kemah	1401 Hwy 146	620Y	KE
La Porte	604 W. Fairmont Pkwy	580F	LP
League City	300 W. Walker	659J	LC
Meadows Place	1 Troyan Dr	569B	MD
Missouri City	1522 Texas Pkwy	570T	MC
Mont Belvieu	11607 Eagle Dr	463C	MB
Morgans Point	1415 E. Main	540Z	MP
Nassau Bay	1800 Space Park Dr #200	619S	NB
Oak Ridge North	27424 Robinson	252K	OR
Pasadena	1211 Southmore	536P	PA
Pearland	3519 Liberty	615U	PL
Piney Point Village	7676 Woodway Dr # 300	490R	PP
Roman Forest	2430 Roman Forest Blvd	257D	RF
Seabrook	1700 First Street	620P	SB
Shoreacres	601 Shore Acres Blvd	580U	SA
South Houston	1018 Dallas	536W	SH
Southside Place	6309 Edloe	532F	SS
Spring Valley	1025 Campbell Rd	490C	SV
Stafford	2610 S. Main	569R	SF
Sugar Land	2700 Town Center Blvd, N.	568X	SG
Taylor Lake Village	500 Kirby Blvd	619G	TL
Tomball	401 W. Market St	288H	TB
Waller	1118 Farr	282U	WL
Webster	217 Pennsylvania	618Y	WB
West University Place	3800 University Blvd	532B	WU

CONVENTION CENTERS

Facility Name	Address	Pg	Loc
Bay Area Houston Convention	604 Bradford Ave	620P	KE
Baytown Community Center	2407 Market St	540D	BT
George R. Brown Conv Ctr	1001 Ave de las Americas	493R	DT
Greater Houston Conv & Visitors Bureau	701 Avenida De Las Americas	493Q	DT
Humble Civic Center	8233 Will Clayton Pkwy	375D	HM
Johnnie Aroffo Civic Center	400 W. Walker St	659W	LC
NRG Astrodome	One Reliant Park	532R	SWH
NRG Center	One Reliant Park	532R	SWH
NRG Stadium	One Reliant Park	532Q	SWH
Pasadena Conv Ctr & Fairgrounds	7902 Fairmont Pkwy	578G	PA
Shenandoah Convention Center	19265 David Memorial Dr	251D	SD
Stafford Centre	10505 Cash Rd.	569L	SF
The Woodlands Convention Center	2301 N. Millbend Dr	252N	WD
Toyota Center	1510 Polk	493Q	DT

DPS OFFICES

Office Name	Address	Pg	Loc
Baytown	5420 Decker Dr	500F	BT
Houston			
Dacoma	4545 Dacoma	451V	NWH
East	11039 East Freeway, #B	496F	NEH
Gessner	12220 Gessner	570F	SWH
North	8418 Veterans Memorial Dr	412Q	NWH
South East	10810 Hwy 3	577S	SEH
Spring	4740 Spring Cypress Rd	291W	NWC
Vantatge Parkway E.	15403 Vantage Pkwy E. 300	373U	NCC
Winkler	9206 Winkler	535Z	SEH
Humble	7710 Will Clayton Pkwy	375C	HM
Pasadena	2783 Red Bluff Rd #100	537K	PA
Webster-Clear Lake DPS	111 Tristar	617F	SEH

FIRE DEPARTMENTS

Fire Station	Address	Pg	Loc
Aldine FD			
station 11	1009 Aldine Bender	373U	NEC
station 21	2301 Humble Westfield Rd	333J	NCC
station 31	20440 Imperial Valley Dr	332Z	NCC
Alief FD - Community VFD			
station 1	16003 Bellaire Blvd	527G	SWC
station 2	13802 Canyon Hill	528K	SWH
station 3	20304 FM 1093	526E	NEF
station 19	7642 Farmingham Rd	337Z	NEC
station 29	4000 Atascocita Rd	376D	NEC
station 39	19219 Oak Timber	337S	NEC
Atascocita VFD			
Baytown FD	201 E. Wye Dr	501Q	BT
station 1	4723 Garth	501F	BT
station 2	2323 Market	541A	BT
station 3	3311 Massey Tompkins Rd.	502K	BT
station 4	910 E. Fayle	501Z	BT
station 5	7722 Bayway Dr	500K	BT
station 6	10166 Pinehurst Dr	462Z	BT
station 7	7215 Eastpoint Blvd	461T	NEC
South Command	109 S Main	501Y	BT
Bellaire FD			
Brookside Village VFD	5101 Jessamine	531L	BL
Champions Area VFD	6241 Brookside Rd	614D	BK
Channelview VFD	12730 Champion Frst	370H	NWC
station 1	16229 Market	498G	CV
station 2	16010 Ridlon	498C	CV

Fire Station	Address	Pg	Loc
station 3	904 Dell Dale	498A	CV
Cloverleaf VFD			
station 1	911 Hollywood	497G	SEC
station 2	14422 Wallisville Rd	457S	NEC
Community VFD			
station 1	16003 Bellair Blvd	527G	SWC
station 2	13802 Canyon Hill Dr	528K	SWC
station 3	20304 FM 1093	526E	SWH
station 4	16005 Bellaire Blvd	527G	SWH
Crosby VFD			
station 81	2502 Highway 90	419G	CB
station 82	123 S. Diamondhead	419C	NEC
station 83	2409 Foley Rd	378Q	CB
station 84	18524 Crosby Eastgate	380Q	NEC
station 85	2819 FM 1942	420U	CB
Cy-Fair VFD			
station 1	9201 Rodney Ray Blvd	410K	NWC
station 2	11210 Tower Oaks	369T	NWC
station 3	11827 Telge Rd	368N	NWC
station 4	18006 Huffmeister	327S	NWC
station 5	16035 Aspenglenn North	448E	NWC
station 6	6404 N. Eldridge Rd	408V	NWC
station 7	20444 Cypresswood Dr	326X	NWC
station 8	18210 F.M. 529	407N	NWC
station 9	7922 Highway 6, N.	408J	NWC
station 10	11310 Steeplecrest	409A	NWC
station 11	18132 West Rd.	407A	NWC
station 12	19780 Keith Harrow	446C	NWC
Cypress Creek VFD			
station 21	14415 N. Eldridge Pkwy	328Z	NWC
station 22	11900 Cypress N. Houston	369J	NWC
station 23	9860 Cypresswood Dr	329Z	NWC
station 24	12073 Perry Rd.	369Q	NWC
Deer Park FD			
station 1	1302 Center	538K	DP
station 2	711 E. Pasadena Blvd	538U	DP
station 3	2211 E. X St	538M	DP
Eastex Freeway VFD			
station 1	14322 Old Humble Rd	375W	NEC
station 2	8523 E. North Belt	375V	NEC
Friendswood FD			
station 1	1000 S. Friendswood	657A	FR
station 2	2605 W. Parkwood Ave	656X	FR
station 3	4302 Laura Leigh	657B	FR
station 4	111 Woodlawn Dr	656C	FR
Galena Park FD			
Station 1	1713 2nd St	496W	GP
Station 2	12455 Industrial Rd	496Q	GP
Highlands VFD			
station 1	123 San Jacinto	459V	HG
station 2	2301 E. Wallisville Rd	460Q	NEC
Houston FD			
station 2	5880 Woodway at Bering	491K	SWH
station 3	3735 W. Alabama at Cummins	492S	SWH
station 4	6530 W. Little York near Bingle	411S	NWH
station 5	2020 Hollister at Hammerly	450V	NWH
station 6	3402 Washington at Lakin	493E	SWH
station 7	1402 Elgin at Austin	493T	SWH
station 8	1919 Louisiana	493Q	DT
station 9	702 Hogan at Freeman	493G	NEH
station 10	6600 Corporate Dr	529H	SWH
station 11	460 T.C. Jester @ Larkin	492C	SWH
station 12	1502 Alber at Terry	453Z	NEH
station 13	2215 W. 43rd near W. T. C. Jester	451M	NWH
station 15	5306 N. Main	453S	NWH
station 16	1700 Richmond at Dunlavy	492Z	SWH
station 17	2805 Navigation at Delano	494N	SEH
station 18	619 Telephone at Lockwood	494X	SEH
station 19	1801 Gregg at New Orleans	494F	NEH
station 20	6902 Navigation @ Marcario Garcia	494V	SEH
station 21	10515 S. Main near O'Meara	532T	SWH
station 22	7825 Harrisburg at 78th	495W	SEH
station 23	8005 Lawndale at Medina	535B	SEH
station 24	2625 Reed Rd	573A	SEH
station 25	3902 Scott at Rosewood	533D	SEH
station 26	7111 Dixie at Chaffin	534V	SEH
station 27	6515 Lyons	494H	NEH
station 28	3000 Chimney Rock at Dolores	491X	SWH
station 29	4831 Galveston Rd at Ahrens	535R	SEH
station 30	6702 Irvington at Frisco	453R	NEH
station 31	222 W. Crosstimbers at Old Yale	452M	NWH
station 32	8614 Tidwell near Mesa	455C	NEH
station 33	7117 Fannin	532M	SWH
station 34	3100 Laura Koppe @ Arkansas	454E	NEH
station 35	5535 Van Fleet near M.L.K.	534S	SEH
station 36	7720 Airport Blvd near Dover	575B	SEH
station 37	7026 Stella Link	532J	SWH
station 38	1120 Silber @ Hartland	491C	NWH
station 39	5810 Pickfair near Kelley	454U	NEH
station 40	5830 O.S.T. at Black	534G	SEH
station 41	805 Pearl at Amarillo	495F	NEH
station 42	8675 Clinton at Mississippi	495T	NEH
station 43	7330 N. Wayside at Dockal	455K	NEH
station 44	675 Maxey Rd at Church	496G	NEH
station 45	4910 N. McCarty near W. O. S. T.	455U	NEH
station 46	3902 Corder at Scott	533Q	SEH
station 47	2615 Tidewater at Kirkgard	572L	SWH
station 48	11616 Chimney Rock near Burdine	571B	SWH
station 49	1212 Gessner at Westview	450W	NWH
station 50	4420 Bingle at Malibou	451E	NWH
station 51	6902 Bellaire at Bintliff	530H	SWH
station 52	10343 Hartsook near Freewood	576K	SEH
station 53	13349 Vicksburg at Uvalde	497E	NEH
station 54	19006 Aldine Westfield	333Y	NEH
station 55	11212 Cullen near Selinski	573M	SEH
station 56	5820 E. Little York near Mapleleaf	414V	NEH
station 57	13602 Memorial Dr near Yorkchester	489F	SWH
station 58	10413 Fulton at Sunnyside	413X	NEH
station 59	13925 S. Post Oak at Prudence	571Q	SWH
station 60	2925 Jeannetta at Clarkcrest	490X	SWH
station 61	9726 Monroe at Swiss	575Q	SEH
station 62	1602 Seamist at Droxford	452W	NWH
station 63	5626 Will Clayton Pkwy at Lee	374D	NEH
station 64	3000 Greens Rd @ Morales	374N	NEH
station 65	11531 FM 1960 E	338R	NEH
station 66	5800 Teague at Hardison	450A	NWH
station 67	1616 W. Little York near Sealey	412X	NWH
station 68	8602 Bissonnet at S. Gessner	530T	SWH
station 69	1102 West Belt S. near Valley Forge	489R	SWH
station 70	11410 Beamer near Kirkvalley	576X	SEH
station 71	15200 Space Center Blvd	618F	SEH
station 72	17401 Saturn	618R	SEH
station 73	9640 Wilcrest near Bissonnet	529U	SWH
station 74	460 Aldine Bender at Lillja	373W	NEH
station 75	1995 S. Dairy Ashford	488R	SWH
station 76	7200 Cook Rd @ Sharpview	529J	SWH
station 77	10155 Kempwood @ Gessner	450J	SWH
station 78	15100 Memorial Dr @ Eldridge Pkwy	488C	SWH
station 80	16111 Chimney Rock @ Court Rd	611A	SWH
station 81	7990 Paul B. Koonce	575K	SEH
station 82	11250 Braesridge	570C	SWH
station 83	3350 Breezewood	489X	SWH
station 84	320 Grears Rd	372Q	NCC
station 86	14300 Briar Forest Dr	488J	SWH
station 90	16525 Park Row	447Y	NWH
station 92	3804 Will Clayton Pkwy (IAH)	374C	NEH
station 93	911 F.M. 1959	617B	SEH
station 94	235 El Dorado	617R	SEH
station 96	7409 Willowchase	370E	NWC
station 99	18580 Chanute	373H	NEH
station 101	1863 Kingwood Dr	336B	NEC
station 102	4102 Lake Houston Pkwy	297T	NEC
station 103	2907 High Valley Dr	297Z	NEC
station 104	910 Forest Cove Dr	336K	NEC
station 105	14014 W. Lake Houston Pkwy	377X	NEC
Huffman VFD	24141 F.M. 2100	339J	HU
Humble FD			
station 1	108 W. Main	335U	HM
station 2	501 Wilson Rd	336W	HM
Jacinto City VFD	1126 Mercury	495M	JC
Jersey Village VFD	16501 Jersey Dr	409Q	JV
Katy FD	1417 Ave D	444X	KT
Kemah VFD	905 Hwy. 146	620Y	KE
Klein Comm VFD			
station 1	18337 Stuebner-Airline	330B	NWC
station 2	14640 Gladebrook	331W	NWC
station 3	9755 Landry Blvd	329Q	NWC
station 4	16810 Squyres	330P	NWC
station 5	8230 Boudreaux Rd	290J	NWC
station 6	18822 N. Eldridge Pkwy	328H	NWC
station 7	19302 T.C. Jester Blvd	330D	NWC
station 8	9600 Crescent Clover Dr	289Y	NWC
LaPorte VFD			
station 1	124 S. 2nd	540Y	LP
station 2	9710 Spencer Hwy	539W	LP
station 3	2400 Sens Rd	540W	LP
station 4	2900 S. Broadway	580Q	LP
League City FD			
station 1	601 2nd	659E	LC
station 2	2120 Hobbs Rd	658U	LC
station 3	3575 F.M. 518 E.	659D	LC
station 4	175 W. Bay Area Blvd	657R	LC
station 5	2898 Bay Creek Dr	657G	LC
station 6	6060 South Shore Blvd	660E	LC
Little York VFD			
station 81	10410 Airline Dr	412H	NWH
station 82	2050 Aldine Western Rd	371V	NWC
station 83	14010 Walters	371L	NWC
station 84	1220 Rushworth Dr	372F	NWC
Magnolia VFD			
station 182	27114 FM 2978	249J	SWM
station 183	26555 Nichols Sawmill Rd	246N	SWM
station 184	27610 Decker Prairie	247V	SWM
McNair VFD	2610 Waco	460Y	MN
Missouri City FD			
station 2	12043 McClain	570L	MC
station 3	2496 Texas Pkwy	610B	MC
station 4	5955 Sienna Pkwy	610W	MC
Montgomery FD			
Nassau Bay VFD	120 Surf Ct	619S	NB
New Caney VFD			
station 151	19870 FM 1485 W.	256L	SEM
station 152	585 Roman Forest Blvd	257G	RM
station 153	27980 FM 1485	258P	SEM
North East FD	6930 Cypresswood Point Ave	334L	NCC
North Montgomery VFD			
Northwest VFD			
station 41	2950 Washington Dr	411H	NWC
station 42	5335 Green Pines	371N	NWC
station 43	7706 Fallbrook Dr	370Z	NWC
Pasadena VFD			
station 2	529 Pasadena Blvd	536M	PA
station 3	3004 Red Bluff Rd	537Q	PA
station 4	101 Queens	536R	PA
station 5	2710 Pansy	537Y	PA
station 6	1200 Kirby Rd	619H	PA
station 7	1600 Crenshaw Rd	577J	PA
station 8	4100 Space Center Blvd	578E	PA
station 9	4709 Donald	581W	PA
station 10	17200 Middlebrook	578Z	PA
Pearland FD			
station 1	2020 Old Alvin Rd	615K	PL
station 2	6050 Fite Road	614R	PL
station 3	3207 Yost Blvd	616S	PL
station 4	8333 Freedom Dr	613R	PL
station 5	3100 Kirby	612R	PL
Ponderosa VFD			
station 61	17061 Rolling Creek Dr	331R	NWC
station 62	4362 Louetta Rd	331B	NWC
station 63	21455 Imperial Valley	332V	NWC
Porter VFD			
station 121	23550 Loop 494	296B	SEM
station 122	17290 Porter Ln	254M	SEM
station 124	23317 Sorters Rd	295D	SEM
Rosehill VFD			
station 1	19000 FM 2920	286L	NWC
station 3	22531 FM 2920	285Q	NWC
station 4	24510 Running Iron Dr	324M	NWC
Seabrook VFD			
station 1	1850 Meyer	620L	SB
station 2	94 Lakeshore Dr	619M	SB
Sheldon VFD			
station 1	8407 C.E. King Pkwy	456G	NEC
station 2	9035 Johns Rd	418W	NEC
station 3	12911 South Lake Houston Pkwy	417J	NEC
Southeast VFD	12514 Astoria Blvd	616H	SEH
station 3	9830 Hughes Rd	616E	SEC
South Houston VFD	506 Georgia	536W	SH
station 1	502 Georgia	536W	SH
station 2	901 Ave D	536Y	SH
South Montgomery VFD			
station 11-1	335 Volunteer Ln.	252S	SWM
station 11-2	30710 Aldine Westfield	253S	SEM
station 11-3	27900 Robinson Rd	252K	SEM
station 11-4	2924 Birnham Woods Dr	253X	SEM
station 11-5	6425 Rayford Rd	294Q	SEM
station 11-6	3560 Discovery Creek Blvd	293F	SEM
Southside Place FD	6309 Edloe	532B	SS
Spring VFD			
station 70	22306 Springwoods Village Pkwy	292E	SP
station 71	646 E. Louetta Rd	292U	SP
station 72	23000 Northcrest	290H	NWC
station 73	4923 Treaschwig	333D	NCC
station 74	24030 Old Aldine Westfield Rd	293W	SP
station 75	3915 FM 2920	291T	NWC
station 76	8407 London Way	250W	NWC
station 77	2900 Cypresswood Dr	331D	NWC
station 78	1225 Booker Rd	292K	SP
Stafford FD			
station 1	2710 S. Main	569R	SF
station 2	10210 Mula Rd	569L	SF
station 3	11803 Kirkwood Rd	569B	SF
Sugar Land FD			
station 1	555 Matlage Way	568N	SG
station 2	1040 Industrial Rd	568H	SG
Timber Lakes VFD	3434 Royal Oaks	251N	SWM
Tomball FD			
central station	1200 Rudel	288G	TB
station 2	11725 Holderrieth	289S	TB

Fire Station	Address	Pg	Loc	Tri
County VFD				
station 1	29144 FM 1488	284C		WCO
Village FD	901 Corbindale	490C		HE
Waller VFD	612 Walnut St	282y		WL
Webster FD	18300 Highway 3	618Y		
Westfield VFD				
station 1	4102 Lauder	414B		NEC
station 3	2120 Aldine Mail Rd	413H		NEC
West I-10 VFD				
station 1	22125 Kingsland	485H		SWC
station 2	851 Dominion	486F		SWC
Westlake FD	19703 Saums Rd	446U		NWC
West Univ Pl FD	3800 University	532A		WU
Woodlands FD				
station 1	9951 Grogans Mill Rd	251G		WD
station 3	1522 Sawdust Rd	251U		WD
station 7	26722 Kuykendahl Rd	250Q		WD
station 8	11800 Gosling Rd	250M		WD

GOLF & COUNTRY CLUBS

Club Name	Address	Pg	Loc
Atascocita G.C.	20114 Pinehurst Dr	337R	NEC
Augusta Pines G.C.	18 Augusta Pines Dr	250T	NWC
Battleground G.C.	1600 Georgia Ave	538J	DP
Bay Forest C.C.	201 Bay Forest	580F	LP
Bay Oaks C.C. (pvt)	14545 Bay Oaks Blvd	618B	SEH
Beacon Lakes G.C.	801 F.M. 646	659T	LC
Bear Creek G.C.	16001 Clay Rd	448F	NWH
Blackhorse G.C.	12205 Fry Rd.	366M	NWC
Braeburn C.C.(pvt)	8101 Bissonnet	530U	SWH
Brock Park G.C.	8201 John Ralston Rd	456F	NEH
Carlton Woods CC, Creekside	1 Carlton Woods Creekside	250K	WD
Champions G.C. (pvt)	13722 Champions Dr.	370C	NWC
Clear Creek G.C.	3902 Fellows Rd	613D	SEH
Cypress Lakes G.C.	18700 Cypresswood Dr.	326Z	NWC
Cypresswood GC	21602 Cypresswood Dr.	334G	NCC
Gleannloch Pines G.C.	19393 Champion Forest Dr.	329C	NWC
Glenbrook Park G.C.	8205 North Bayou Dr.	535Q	SEH
Golfcrest C.C. (pvt)	2509 Country Club Dr.	616J	SEC
Gus Wortham Park G.C.	7000 Capitol Ave	494Z	SEH
Harrisburg C.C.	3618 Harrisburg Blvd	494N	SEC
Hearthstone C.C. (pvt)	7615 Ameswood	408K	NWC
Hermann Park G.C.	2155 N. Mac Gregor Way	533A	SWH
Heron Lakes G.C.	7910 N. Sam Houston Pkwy, W.	370S	NWC
High Meadow Ranch GC	37300 Golf Club Trl	246F	MG
Houston C.C. (pvt)	1 Potomac Dr	491J	SWH
Houston National G.C.	16500 Houston National Blvd	367U	NWC
Humble Oil Patch G.C.	2107 N. Houston Ave.	335M	NEC
Indian Shores G.C.	2141 Whitefeather Trail	378D	NEC
Jersey Meadow G.C.	8502 Rio Grande	409K	JV
Kingwood Cove G.C.	805 Hamblen Rd	336E	NEC
Lakeside C.C. (pvt)	100 Wilcrest Dr	489K	SWH
Lochinvar G.C.	2000 Farrell Rd	373B	NCC
Longwood G.C.	13300 Longwood Trace	328W	NWC
Magnolia Creek G.C.	1501 Bay Area Blvd	657Z	LC
Meadowbrook Farms G.C.	23230 Meadowbrook Farms Club Dr	525A	NEF
Melrose G.C.	401 Canino Rd	413T	NEH
Memorial Park G.C.	1001 E. Memorial Loop	492E	SWH
Northgate Frst C.C. (pvt)	17110 Northgate Frst Dr	331K	NWC
Oakhurst G.C.	20700 Mills Branch Dr	295M	SEM
Pasadena Municipal G.C.	1000 Duffer Ln	577P	SEH
Pearland Golf Club at Country Place	3123 Flower Field Ln	613B	NEB
Petroleum Club of Houston	1201 Louisiana Street, 35th floor	493Q	DT
Pine Crest C.C.	3080 Gessner	450J	NWH
Pine Forest C.C. (pvt)	18003 Clay Rd	447K	NWC
Raveneaux C.C. (pvt)	9415 Cypresswood Dr	330W	NWC
Red Wolf Golf Resort	27350 Afton Way	299P	NEC
Redstone C.C. (pvt)	5860 Wilson Rd	375Y	NEC
River Bend C.C. (pvt)	1214 Dulles Ave	569S	NEF
River Oaks C.C. (pvt)	1600 River Oaks Blvd	492P	SWH
River Terrace G.C.	16777 Wallisville	458P	NEH
Royal Oaks C.C.	2910 Royal Oaks Club Dr	489X	SWH
Sharpstown Park G.C.	6600 Harbor Town	530B	SWH
South Shore Harbour C.C.	4300 S. Shore Blvd	619Y	LC
Southwyck G.C.	2901 Club House Dr	613T	NEB
Spring Valley GC	25110 Gosling Rd	250Z	NWC
Stonebridge at Newport G.C.	16401 Country Club Dr	419A	NEC
Sugar Creek C.C.	420 Sugar Creek Blvd	568V	SG
Terra Verde G.C.	20 E Greenway Plaza	492X	SEC
Texaco C.C. (pvt)	12800 Texaco Rd	456Y	NEC
The Club at Cinco Ranch G.C.	23030 Cinco Ranch Blvd	485Q	NEF
The Club at Falcon Point G.C.	24503 Falcon Point Dr.	485E	NEF
The Clubs at Houston Oaks G.C.	22602 Hegar Rd	284B	WCO
The Clubs of Kingwood C.C.	1700 Lake Kingwood Trail	337E	NEC
The Clubs of Kingwood-Deerwood	1717 Forest Garden Dr.	337D	NEC
The Oaks & Panther Trail G.C.	2301 N. Millbend Dr	251Q	WD
The Woodlands C.C. East Course	1730 S. Millbend Dr	251M	WD
Timber Creek G.C.	4554 FM 2351	617N	FR
Tomball C.C. (pvt)	22303 Walden Wy	289P	NWC
Tour 18 G.C.	3102 F.M. 1960 E	376C	NEC
Walden on Lake Houston G.C.	18100 Wlden Frst Dr	337Z	NEC
Westwood C.C. (pvt)	8888 Country Creek Dr	530N	SWH
Wildcat G.C.	12000 Almeda Rd	572G	SWH
Willow Creek G.C. (pvt)	24525 Northcrest	250Y	NWC
Willow Fork C.C.	21055 Westheimer Pkwy	486S	SWC
Winchester C.C.	9607 Rio Grande Dr	409C	NWC
Wind Rose G.C.	6235 Pinelakes Blvd	290Z	NWC

HOSPITALS

Hospital Name	Address	Pg	Loc
Bay Area Regional Medical Center	200 Blossom St	618T	WB
Bayshore Medical Center	4000 Spencer Hwy	577A	PA
Bayside Medical Center	4001 Preston	577F	PA
Ben Taub General Hosp.**	1504 Taub Loop	533E	SWH
Clear Lake Reg. Med. Ctr	500 Medical Ctr Blvd	618X	WE
Cornerstone Hospital	709 Medical Ctr Blvd	618X	WB
Cy-Fair Medical Center Hosp.	10655 Steepletop	369W	NWC
Cypress Creek Hosp.	17750 Cali Dr	332J	NWC
DePelchin Children's - Main Campus	4950 Memorial Dr	492L	SWH
East Houston Regional Medical Ctr	13111 East Frwy	497E	NEH
Gulf Coast Hosp.	2800 Garth	501P	BT
HCA - W. Houston Medical Center	12141 Richmond Ave	489W	SWH
Houston NW Medical Ctr	710 Cypress Creek Pkwy	332J	NWC
Imperial Medical Center	1211 S.H. 6	568S	SG
Kingwood Medical Center	22999 US Hwy 59	335D	NCC
Lyndon B. Johnson Hosp.	5656 Kelley	454U	NEH
M.D. Anderson Cancer Center**	1515 Holcombe Blvd	533E	SWH
Memorial Hermann - Children's**	6411 Fannin	533E	SWH
Memorial Hermann - Cypress	27800 Northwest Freeway	326X	NWC
Memorial Hermann - Greater Heights	18955 Memorial N.	335X	HM
Memorial Hermann - Katy Hospital	23900 Katy Frwy	445X	KT
Memorial Hermann - Memorial City	921 Gessner	490A	SWH
Memorial Hermann - Northwest	1635 North Loop West	452T	NWH
Memorial Hermann - Pasadena	3620 Spencer Hwy	537W	PA
Memorial Hermann - Pearland	16100 South Freeway	613J	NEB
Memorial Hermann - Southeast	11800 Astoria Blvd	616H	SEC
Memorial Hermann - Southwest	7600 Beechnut	530L	SWH
Memorial Hermann - Texas Med Center**	6411 Fannin	532H	SWH
Memorial Hermann - The Woodlands	9250 Pinecroft	252A	WD
Memorial Hermann - Women's Memorial City	929 Gessner Road	490A	SWH
Memorial Hermann - Women's The Woodlands	9250 Pinecroft	252A	WD
Methodist - Med Center**	6565 Fannin	532H	SWH
Methodist - San Jacinto	4401 Garth Rd	501K	BT
Methodist - St. Catherine	701 S. Fry Rd	486C	SWC
Methodist - St. John	18300 St. John Dr	619S	NB
Methodist - West	18500 Katy Freeway (I-10)	447W	NWH
Methodist - Willowbrook	18220 Tomball Pkwy	370E	NWH
Michael DeBakey V.A. Med Center	2002 Holcombe	533J	SEH
Nexus Specialty Hospital	9182 Six Pines	251D	SD
OGA	7900 Fannin	532M	SWH
Park Plaza Hosp.	1313 Hermann Dr	533A	SWH
Patients Medical Center	10930 Resource Pkwy	616C	SEC
Quentin Mease Community Hosp.	3601 N. MacGregor Way	533H	SEH
Riverside General Hospital	3204 Ennis St	493Y	SEC
San Jacinto Methodist Hospital	1700 James Bowie Dr	502S	BT
Shriners Hospital for Children**	6977 S. Main	532H	SWH
Spring Branch Medical Center	8850 Long Point Rd	450V	NWH
St. Joseph Medical Center Hospital	1401 St. Joseph Pkwy	493Q	SEH
St. Lukes - Baylor Medical Center**	6720 Bertner	532H	SWH
St. Lukes - Patients Medical Center	4600 E. Sam Houston Pkwy S	577G	PA
St. Lukes - Sugar Land	1317 Lake Point Pkwy	568T	SG
St. Lukes - The Vintage	20171 Chasewood Park Dr	329Y	NWC
Sugar Land Medical Center	15300 Southwest Frwy	568U	SG
Sun Belt Regional - East Campus	15101 East Frwy	497H	NEH
Texas Children"s - West Campus	18200 Katy Fwy	447W	NWH
Texas Children's - Main Campus**	6621 Fannin	532H	SWH
Texas Heart Institute**	6720 Bertner St	532H	SWH
Texas Medical Center**	6550 Bertner	532H	SWH
Texas Orthopedic Hosp.	7401 S. Main	532L	SWH
Texas Specialty Hospital	6160 South Loop E	534L	SEC
Texas Sports Medical Center	28120 Tomball Pkwy	288L	TB
Tomball Regional Hosp.	605 Holderrieth Blvd	288L	TB
Triumph Hospital - North Houston	7407 North Fwy	412V	NEH
UT Mental Sciences Institute**	1300 Moursund	533E	SWH
Westbury Community Hospital	6060 Richmond Ave	491W	SWH
Women's Hospital of Texas	7600 Fannin	532M	SWH

LIBRARIES

Library Name	Address	Pg	Loc
Aldine Branch	11331 Airline	372Z	NEH
Atascocita Library	19520 Pinehurst Trail	337V	NEC
Baldwin Boettcher Branch	22248 Aldine Westfield Rd	333F	NCC
Barbara Bush Branch	6817 Cypresswood	330R	NWC
Bellaire	5111 Jessamine	531L	BL
Botts Memorial Library	2025 W. 11th St.	452Y	NWH
Bracewell	9002 Kingspoint Dr	576W	SEC
Cantor Rubin Kaplan Memorial Library	4525 Beechnut St	531R	SWH
Cardinal Beran Library	9845 Memorial Dr	491F	SWH
Carnegie Branch	1050 Quitman	493C	NEH
Central	500 McKinney	493L	DT
Cinco Ranch Branch	2620 Commercial Center Blvd.	485T	NEF
Clayton Genealogical	5300 Caroline	493W	SWH
Collier Savannah	6200 Pinemont	451F	NWC
Crosby Branch	135 Hare Rd	419C	CB
Deer Park Public Library	3009 Center	538T	DP
Dixon	8002 Hirsch	454K	NEH
Fairbanks	7122 N. Gessner	410S	NWC
Fairmont Branch	4330 Fairmont Pkwy	577F	PA
Fifth Ward	4014 Market	494F	NEH
Film Library	500 McKinney	493L	DT
Fine Arts and Recreation Library	500 McKinney	493L	DT
Flores Branch	110 N. Milby	494N	SEH
Freeman Memorial Branch	16616 Diana Ln	618P	SEH
Friendswood Public Library	416 S. Friendswood Dr	656D	FR
Galena Park	1500 Keene	496S	GP
Harris Administration	8080 El Rio	533N	SEH
Harris County	301 San Jacinto	493M	DT
Harris County - Tomball	701 James St	288L	TB
Harris County Law Library	1019 Congress	493L	DT
Heights Branch	1302 Heights Blvd	453W	NWH
Helen Hall Library	100 W. Walker	659J	LC
Henington-Alief Regional	7979 S. Kirkwood	529J	SWH
High Meadow	4500 Aldine Mail Route	414F	NEC
Hillendahl	2436 Gessner	450N	NWH
Houston Central	500 McKinney	493L	DT
Houston Public Library	3517 Reed Rd	573B	SEH
HPL Express Discorery Green	1500 McKinney	493Q	SWH
HPL Express Southwest	6400 High Star	531E	SWH
Jacinto City Branch	921 Akron	496E	JC
Johnson	3517 Reed Rd	573B	SEH
Jungman	5830 Westheimer	491T	SWH
Katherine Tyra Branch Library	16719 Clay Rd	447H	NWH
Katy Branch - Harris County	5414 Franz Rd	444U	KT
Kendall	609 N. Eldridge Pkwy	488G	SWH
Kingwood	4400 Bens View Ln	297X	NEC
La Porte (City)	600 S. Broadway	580C	LP
Lakewood	8815 Feland	455G	NEH
Looscan Branch	2510 Willowick	492S	SWH
LSC-CyFair Library	9191 Barker - Cypress Rd	407B	NWC
LSC-Tomball Library	30555 Tomball Pkwy	288A	TB
M.D. Anderson Branch	1515 Holcombe	533E	SWH
Mae Hilty Memorial Library	5912 Spencer Hwy	537Z	PA
Mamie George County Library	320 Dulles	569K	SF
Mancuso Branch	6767 Bellfort	534Y	SEH
Maud Smith Marks Branch	1815 Westgreen Blvd	486K	NWC
Mc Crane-Kashmere Gardens	5411 Pardee	454U	NEH
McGovern - Stella Link Regional	7405 Stella Link	532J	SWH
Meador, Evelyn Branch	2400 N. Meyer	620L	SEC
Melcher Library	7200 Keller	535E	SEH
Meyer Library	5005 W. Bellfort Ave	531Y	SWH
Missouri City Branch Library	1530 Texas Pkwy	570T	MC
Montrose	4100 Montrose	493S	SWH
Moody	9525 Irvington	453C	NWH
Morris Frank	10103 Fondren	530V	SWH
Neumann Library - UH Clear Lake	2700 Bay Area Blvd	618H	SEC
North Channel Library	15741 Wallisville Rd	457V	NEC
Northwest Branch	11355 Regency Green Dr	369J	NWC
Oak Forest Branch	1349 W. 43rd	452K	NWH
Octavia Fields	1503 S. Houston	375D	HM
Parent Resource Library	1500 Binz	533A	SWH
Park Place Branch	8145 Park Place	535P	SEH
Parker Williams Branch	10851 Scarsdale Blvd	616G	SEC
Pasaden Library	1201 Jeff Ginn Memorial Dr	537N	PA
Pasadena Fairmont Branch	4330 Fairmont	577F	PA
Pearland City	3523 Liberty Dr	615U	PL
Pleasantville	1520 Gellhorn	495K	NEH
R.B. Tullis Branch Library	21569 U.S. Highway 59	256U	SEM
Ring	8835 Longpoint	450V	NWH
Robert James Terry Library	3100 Cleburne	533C	SEH
Robert Pace & Ada Doherty Library - UST	1100 W Main St	493S	SWH
Robinson, J.W. Jr - Westchase	3223 Wilcrest	489Y	SWH
Scenic Woods	10677 Homestead	414Z	NEH
Shepard-Acres Homes	8501 W. Montgomery	412T	NWH
Smith	3624 Scott	533D	SEH
South Houston Branch	607 Avenue A	536X	SH
South Regional Library	2101 Lake Robbins Dr	251G	WD
Spring Branch Memorial	930 Corbindale	490C	HE
Stanaker	611 Macario Garcia Dr	494V	SEH
Sterling Municipal Library	Mary E. Wilbanks Ave	501X	BT

Stimley-Blue Ridge Branch	7007 W. Fuqua	571W	SWH
Stratford Branch	509 Stratford	459Q	NEC
Sugar Land Branch	550 Eldridge	568L	SG
Tax Library	910 Louisiana	493L	DT
Thurgood Marshall Law Library - TSU	3100 Cleburne St	533D	SEC
Trinity Gardens	7200 Hirsch	454K	NEH
Turner Memorial Branch	8301 W. Montgomery	412T	NWH
Tuttle	702 Kress	494H	NEH
U.S. Court Library	515 Rusk ste 6311	493L	DT
Vinson	3100 W. Fuqua Rd	572T	SWH
Walter Neighborhood	7660 Clarewood	530G	SWH
West University	6108 Auden	532A	WU
Wooster Branch	6014 Bayway	500N	BT
Youn Neighborhood Library	5260 Griggs (Palm Center)	534K	SEH

MUSEUMS

Museum Name	Address	Pg	Loc
1902 Perry House	109 W. Spreading Oaks	656D	FR
African American Heritage Museum	2101 Crawford	493U	SWH
Air Terminal Muesum	8325 Travelair	575E	SEH
American Cowboy Museum	11822 Almeda	572H	SWH
Art Car Museum	140 Hieghts Blvd	493E	SWH
Art League of Houston	1953 Montrose	493N	SWH
Barbers Hill Museum	11607 Eagle Dr	463C	MB
Bayou Bend Collection	1 Westcott	492L	SWH
Blaffer Art Museum	4173 Elgin	493N	SWH
Brown, Frank J. Heritage Museum	108 Skyview	656D	FR
Buffalo Soldiers National Museum	1834 Southmore	533B	SWH
Burke - Baker Planetarium	1 Hermann Cir	533A	SWH
Butler Longhorn Museum	1220 Coryell St	659E	CC
Byzantine Fresco Chapel	4011 Yupon	493W	SWH
Children's Museum	1500 Binz	533B	SWH
Contemporary Arts Museum	5216 Montrose	493W	SWH
Cy Twombly Gallery	1501 Branard St	493S	SWH
Czech Center Museum	4920 San Jacinto	493X	SWH
Diverse Works	3400 Main St	493M	DT
Durhan Bible Museum	7502 Fondren	530V	SWH
Health Museum	1515 Hermann Dr.	533A	SWH
Heritage Society Museum	1100 Bagby	493L	DT
Holocaust Museum	5401 Caroline	493W	SWH
Houston Center Contemporty Art	4848 Main St.	493X	SWH
Houston Center for Photography	1441 W. Alabama	493S	SWH
Houston Fire Museum	2403 Milam	493P	SWH
Houston Maritime Museum	2204 Dorrington	532G	SWH
Houston Museum of Natural Science	1 Herman Cir Dr	533A	SWH
Houston Police Museum	1200 Travis	493Q	DT
Humble Museum	219 E Main St	335Z	HM
Jung Center of Houston	5200 Montrose	493W	SWH
Katy Heritage Museum	6002 George Bush Dr	444X	KT
Katy Veterans Memorial Museum	6202 George Bush Dr	444X	KT
Lawndale Art Center	4912 Main	493W	SEH
McKay Clinic Medical Museum	110 N Avenue C	335Z	HM
Medical Museum	1515 Hermann Dr	533C	SWH
Menil Collection, The	1515 Sul Ross	492V	SWH
Military Museum of Texas	8611 Wallisville Rd	495B	NEH
Museum of Fine Arts	1001 Bissonnet	493W	SWH
Museum of Funeral History	415 Barren Spring Dr	332X	NCC
Museum of Health and Medical Science	1515 Hermann Dr	533A	SWH
Museum of Printing History	1324 W. Clay	493N	SWH
Museum of Southern History	14070 S.W. Freeway	568R	SG
Museum of Southern History at HBU	7502 Fondren	530L	SWH
Orange Show	2401 Munger	534B	SHE
Pearl Fincher Museum	6815 Cypresswood	330R	NWC
Pioneer Memorial Log House	1510 Cambridge St	533A	SWH
Projet Row Houses	2500 Holman	533D	SEH
Rice University Art Gallery	6100 Main, MS-21	532D	SWH
Rienzi	1406 Kirby	492Q	SWH
Rothko Chapel, The	1409 Sul Ross	493S	SWH
Russian Cultural Center	2337 Bissonnet	492Y	SWH
San Jacinto Museum of History	1 Monument Circle	539Q	SEC
Spring Historical Museum	403 Main	292Q	SP
Tomball Museum Complex	510 Pine St	288G	TB
West Bay Common School Children's Museum	210 N. Kansas Ave	659E	LC

PARK & RIDES

Park & Ride	Address	Pg	Loc
202 - Kuykendahl	12920 Kuykendahl	372G	NWC
203 - N. Shepherd	7821 N. Shepherd	412U	NWH
204 - Spring	17444 Carlsway	332L	NCC
205 - Kingwood	3210 Lake Houston Pkwy	297X	NEC
206 - Eastex	14400 Old Humble Rd	375W	NEC
212 - Seton Lake	7555 Seton Lake	371W	NWH
214 - Northwest Station	7373 Old Katy Rd	409E	NWC
216 - W. Little York	15010 Hempstead Hwy	409V	NWC
217 - Cypress	25210 N.W. Frwy @ Skinner	367F	NWC
221 - Kingsland	21669 Kingsland Blvd	486A	SWC
222 - Grand Parkway	1030 W. Grand Parkway North	445X	NWC
228 - Addicks	14230 Old Katy Rd	488B	NWC
236 - Maxey	515 Maxey Rd	496C	NEH
237 - Baytown	1496 San Jacinto Mall	461X	BT
244 - Monroe	88331/2 Gulf Frwy	535Z	SEH
246 - Bay Area	801 Bay Area Blvd	618T	SEH
247 - Fuqua	11755 Sabo Rd	576U	SEH
257 - Townsen	21003 Eastex Frwy	335V	HM
262 - Westwood	9990 Southwest Frwy	529V	SWH
265 - W. Bellfort	11415 Roark Rd	569C	SF
269 - Hillcroft	6220 Southwest Frwy	531A	SWH
270 - Missouri City	13849 Fondren Rd	570R	SWH
273 - Gessner	9925 Westpark @ Gessner	530A	SWH
274 - Westchase	11050 Harwin Dr.	529C	SWH
297 - South Point	12410 Kurland	576U	SEH

TRANSIT CENTERS

Transit Center Name	Address	Pg	Loc
Mission Bend Transit Center	13855 Alief-Clodine Rd	528F	SWC
Woodlands Development Corp.	Budde Rd & Pruitt	252W	WD
Acres Homes Transit Center	1220 W. Little York	412X	NWH
Bellaire Transit Center	5100 Bellaire Blvd @ Rice	531G	BL
Burnett Transit Center	Burnett St. & Everett St.	493H	NEH
Downtown Transit Center	1900 Main	493Q	DT
Eastwood Transit Center	4400 Gulf Fwy	412X	NWH
Fannin South Transit Center	1604 West Bellfort	532V	SWH
Fifth Ward/Denver Harbor Transit Center	1500 Lockwood	494G	NEH
Greenspoint Transit Center	12455 Greenspoint Dr	372R	NEH
Hiram Clark Transit Center	3600 W. Fuqua	572S	SWH
Hobby Transit Center	7800 Airport	575B	SEH
Kashmere Transit Center	5910 Hirsch Rd @ Kelley	454P	NEH
Magnolia Transit Center	6948 Harrisburg Blvd @ 70th	494Z	SEH
Mesa Transit Center	9419 Mesa @ Tidwell	455C	NEH
Mission Bend Transit Center	13855 Alief Clodine Rd	528F	SWC
Northline T.C.	Fulton @ Crosstimbers	453K	NEH
Northwest Transit Center	7373 Old Katy Rd	491D	NWC
Southeast Transit Center	6000 Scottcrest	533M	SEH
Tidwell Transit Center	9720 Epsom @ Hage	454A	NEH
TMC Transit Ceenter	6910 Fannin	532H	SWH
West Loop Transit Center	4675 S Braeswood @ South Loop	531V	SWH
Wheeler Station	4500 1/2 Main	493X	SWH

PARKS

Park Name	Address	Pg	Loc
Aaron Pasternak Memorial Park	2402 Parkview Dr.	657J	PL
Adair, Christia V. Park	15107 Cullen Blvd.	613D	SEH
Agnes Moffatt Park	W Sam Houston @ Hammerly	449Q	NWH
Alexander Duessen Park	12303 Sonnier	417H	NEH
Alief Amity Park	12509 Alief Clodine Rd.	528D	SWH
Alief Community Park	11903 Bellaire Blvd.	529E	SWH
Alkek Olympic Fest. Velodrome	19008 Saums Rd.	447S	NWH
Allenbrook Park	4111 Allenbrook	501L	BT
American Legion Park	3621 Golf Dr.	452P	NWH
Anderson Park	5701 Beverlyhill	491X	SWH
Andy Anderson Park	101 Atascocita Rd.	338U	NEH
Armand Bayou Nature Center	8500 Bay Area Blvd.	619B	PA
Armand Bayou Park	4300 Bay Area Blvd.	619C	PA
Arthur Bayer Park	24811 W. Hardy Rd.	292Y	NCC
Arthur Storey Park	7400 W. Sam Houston Pkwy S.	529L	SWH
Baldwin Park	1701 Elgin	493U	SEH
Bane Park	9600 W. Little York	410S	NWC
Barbara Jordan Park	6400 Winfield Rd.	415J	NEC
Barkuloo Park	1301 El Rancho Dr.	501M	BT
Barry Rose Park	1900 Barry Rose Rd	615G	PV
Bass Regional Park	7901 El Rio	613D	SEC
Bay Area Park	7500 Bay Area Blvd.	619A	PA
Baybrook Park	4221 Todville rd.	620H	SB
Bayer Park	1103 Spring Meadow Dr	292Y	NCC
Bayland Park	2641 State Hwy 146 Business	541E	BT
Bayland Park	6400 Bissonnet	530M	SWH
Bayou Bend Park	1 Westscott	538X	DP
Bayridge Park	2900 Mariner Dr	660J	LC
Bayside Park	1000 2nd St.	620Q	SB
Baytown Fairgrounds	7900 N. Main	461Q	NEC
Baytown Soccer Park	4700 Village Ln	500H	BT
Bear Creek Pioneers Park	3535 War Memorial Dr.	448L	NWH
Beeler Memorial Park	1150 Enclave Pkwy	488F	SWH
Bell Park	4790 Montrose Blvd.	493W	SWH
Bellaire Park	5113 Laurel	531G	BL
Ben Briar Park	1115 Bennett Dr.	537R	PA
Bendwood Park	12701 Barryknoll Ln.	489H	SWH
Beverly Hills Park	10201 Kingspoint Rd.	576S	SEH
Bicentennial Park	1001 Market St.	501X	BT
Big League Dreams Sports	1150 Big League Pkwy	658Z	LC
Bill Archer Dog Park	3201 State Hwy. 6 N.	448N	NWH
Bill Pickard Park	8201 Ross Rd.	530K	SWH
Bishop Joseph A. Fiorenza Park	4025 Eldridge Pkwy	528B	SWH
Bliss Meadows Park	5900 South Meadow Dr.	577D	PA
Blossom Heights Park	9000 Lipan Rd.	490X	SWH
Blueridge Park	5600 Court Rd.	573B	SEH
Boone Park	7700 Boone Rd.	529K	SWH
Bordersville Park (City)	19622 Carver Rd.	335W	NEH
Bowie Park	2200 Clayton Dr.	502S	BT
Bracher Park	1507 Bracher Rd.	450Z	NWH
Brentwood Park	13220 Landmark	572J	SWH
Brewster Park	1800 Des Chaumes	494E	
Briar Bend Park	7926 Woodway	490U	SWH
Briar Meadow Park	7703 Richmond Ave	490Z	SWH
Britton, W.C. Park	1305 Arizona	541E	BT
Brock Park	8201 John Ralston Rd.	456E	NEH
Brookline Park	3300 Real	534L	SEH
Brummershop	2622 Repsdorph Rd	620J	SB
Bud Hadfield Park	12405 Telge Rd.	367M	NWC
Buffalo Bayou Hiket Bike Trail	500 Allen Pkwy	488G	SWH
Buffalo Run Park	1122 Buffalo Run	570U	MC
Burke/Crenshaw Park	4950 Burke Rd.	577P	PA
Burnett Bayland Park	6000 Chimney Rock	531B	SWH
Burroughs Park	9738 Huffsmith Rd.	249X	NWC
Busby Park	6700 Hirsch	454P	
Cambridge Village Park	13099 Nitida	571H	SWH
Cameron Recreation Facility		409K	NEH
Campbell Woods Park	2315 Crestdale	450P	
Candlelight Park	1520 Candlelight	452E	NWH
Caney Creek Park	230 C.R. Rd 285	257P	SEM
Canterbury Park	12822 Northumb Rd.	572R	SWH
Carol Tree Park	11600 Memorial Dr.	490Q	PP
Carter Park	5150 FM 2351	574D	SEH
Caverdale Park	9920 Porto Rico Rd.	450A	NWH
Cedar Grove Park	7812 Crepe Myrtle Ln.	420S	NEC
Centennial Park	2200 S Friendswood Dr	657J	FR
Central Lttle League Park	1306 Garth Rd	501T	BT
Challenger Seven Memorial Park	2301 Nasa Pkwy	658E	SEC
Chandler Arboretum & Park	6434 Crosby Cedar Bayou Rd	461Z	NEC
Channelview Fairgrounds		458U	NEH
Channelview Sports Complex	16434 Wood Dr.	458V	CV
Charlton Park	8200 East Park Ct.	535P	SEH
Chimney Rock Park	11655 Chimney Rock	571B	SWH
Christy Park	900 Ave H	576B	SH
City Park	1900 Clinton Dr	496S	GP
City Park	City Park Dr. @ Garnier Dr	534X	SEH
Clark, Robert Park	9800 Clark Rd.	453B	NWH
Clear Creek Regional Park		613C	SEC
Clear Lake Park	5002 E. Nasa Pkwy	619L	SEC
Clear Lake Park Extension		619P	SEC
Cliff Tuttle Park	6201 Lyons Ave.	494H	NEH
Clinton Park	200 Mississippi	495U	NEH
Cloverland Park	3801 Hickory Ln.	573L	SEH
Cole Creek Park	7200 Drowsy Pine Dr.	411W	NWH
Collins Park	6727 Cypresswood Dr.	330R	NWC
Colonial Park	4130 Byron	532E	WU
Community Center Park	234 Matlage Way	568N	SG
Community Park	1700 Glen Lakes Ln	610K	MC
Corrigan Park	5409 Cunningham Dr.	614M	PL
Countryside Park	100 Alderwood	657Q	LC
County Pocket Park #1	1700 Campbell Rd. @ Spring Br. Dr	450U	NWH
County Pocket Park #2	6705 Housman	451Y	NWH
Covington West Park	13944 Oakwood Ln.	568F	SG
Crain Park	9051 Triola Ln.	530J	SWH
Creekwood Nature Area	3300 Maple Park Dr.	337A	NEC
Creekwood Park	3833 S. Panther Creek Dr.	251J	WD
Crestmont Park	5100 Selinsky Rd	576J	SEH
Crosby Park	419 Hare Rd.	419C	CB
Crowley Park	5700 Lauder Rd.	414C	NEC
Croyden Park		454H	NEH
Cullen Park	19008 Saums Rd.	447S	NWH
Cumberland Green Belt Park		255S	SEM
Cypress Creek Park		334F	NCC
Dads Club Community Park	5516 Daughtery Rd.	614T	PL
David Braun Park at Lake Nassau	18900 Upper Bay Rd	619W	NB
David Burnett Park	1704 Burnet ave	499D	CV
Deer Meadows	2500 Oklahoma Ave	538S	DP
Deer Ridge Park	2208 Deer Cove Trail	336G	NWC
Denver Harbor	6402 Market St.	494H	NEH
Deussen, Alexander Park	12303 Sonnier	417H	NEH
Discovery Green	1500 McKinney	493R	DT
Dodson Lake Park	8922 Dodson	454F	NEH
Doss Park	2500 Frick rd.	371Z	NWC
Dow Park	610 E San Augustine St	538Q	DP
Dow Park	7999 Wilmerdean	535X	SEH
Dow Park 1	15401 Greendale Dr.	373T	NCC
Driver Park	10918 Bentley	414T	NWC
Duke Hill Park	1377 Miriam	541B	BT
Dyess, A.E. Park	16822 Kitzman Rd.	327C	NWC
E. Southmore Park	3120 Red Bluff Rd.	573Q	PA
East Little League Park	1500 N Tenth St	501Z	BT

Park Name	Address	Pg	Loc
East Tidwell Park	9300 E. Tidwell	455D	NEH
Eastwood Park	5020 Harrisburg Blvd	494T	NEH
Edgewater Park	220 Hamblen Rd	335M	NEH
Eisenhower, Dwight D. Park	13201 Walton Rd.	418E	NEH
El Franco Lee Park	9400 Hall Road	575Z	SHE
El Jardin Park	7849 Harrisburg Blvd	581W	PA
Elbert Triangle	7000 Elbert	455J	NEH
Eldridge Park	2511 Eldridge Rd.	568B	SG
Eleanor Tinsley Park	500 Allen Pkwy	493K	SWH
Eliott, Mary Park	3000 Chevy Chase Dr.	492Q	SWH
Elizabeth Kaiser Meyer Park	7700 Cypresswood Dr.	330Q	NWC
Emancipation Park	3018 Dowling	493U	SEH
Enchanted Oaks Park	990 Highway 35 Bypass	332A	NWC
Equestrian Park		251Z	WD
Ervan Chew Park	4502 Dunlavy	492Z	SWH
Evergreen Park	4500 Evergreen	531M	BL
Fairmont Park	10216 Hillridge Rd	579B	LP
Falcon Park	12501 Market St	496L	NEH
Falconwing Park	5610 Rush Haven Dr	250C	WD
Feld Park	6406 Avenue B	531H	BL
FFA Center Park	1130 Cherry St	288M	TB
Finnigan Park	4900 Providence	494G	SEH
First Street Park	2501 First St	569V	SF
Flag Tree Park	8450 San Felipe St	490Q	PP
Fonde Park	5500 Carrolton	534F	SEH
Foote Park	2428 W Main St	541A	BT
Forest West Park	5915 Golden Forest Dr	451F	NWH
Forestgate Park	7505 S. Forestgate	250A	WD
Four Corners Recreation Center	15700 Old Richmond Rd	527U	NEF
Four Seasons Park	4702 Katy Hockley Cut Off Rd	444D	NWC
Freed Park	7020 Shadyvilla Ln	451Y	NWH
Freeway Manor Park	2241 Bronson	576F	SEH
Freshmeadow Park	4500 Campbell Rd	450F	NWH
Friendship Park	200 Park Dr	620G	SB
Friendswood Sportspark	2910 W Parkwood	656X	FR
Frontier Days (Amusement Park)		340D	LCO
Fry Road Park	19818 Franz Rd (On Franz off Fry)	446T	NWC
Garden Villas Park	6720 S Haywood Dr	534Z	SEH
Gardens Park	1300 Scott St	537J	PA
Gene Green Park	6500 E Sam Houston Pkwy N	457R	NEC
George Bush Park	16756 Westheimer Pkwy	487P	SWH
Gerber Park	4735 Gaston St	414Q	NEC
Gessner Park	1776 Gessner Dr	450S	NWH
Glen Meadows	801 Valley Brook	539X	LP
Godwin Park	5101 Rutherglenn Dr	531U	SWH
Golden Acres Park	5000 Oak Ave	581W	PA
Good Sam Park		488E	SWH
Gordon Fountain Lake Park	10511 Fountain Lake Dr	569E	SF
Grady Park	1700 Yorktown	491Q	SWH
Gragg Park	2999 S Wayside Dr	534G	SEH
Graham Park	540 West 34th	452R	NWH
Grand River Park	8400 Grand River	456E	
Green Acres	3501 Hooper Rd	618Z	WB
Greens Bayou Park	700 Westmont Dr	497E	NEH
Greenwood Park	622 Breseford Dr	497A	NEH
Grimes Park	5150 Reed Rd	574A	SEH
Grogans Point Park	180 Grogans Point Rd	251V	WD
Gulf Palms Park	11901 Palmsprings Dr	576Q	SEC
Gullo Park	1122 1/2 Pruitt Rd	292A	NCC
H & H Guest Ranch	4000 Greens Rd	374Q	NEH
Haden Park	1404 Witte Rd	450W	NWH
Halbert	200 E 23rd	453S	NWH
Harris County Katy Park	24927 Morton Rd	444R	KT
Hartman Park	9311 E Ave J	535C	SEH
Harwin Park	11305 Harwin	529C	SWH
Helen Gardens	701 E. Main	659E	LC
Hennessey Park	1900 Lyons Ave	493H	NEH
Herman Brown Park	400 Mercury Dr	456X	NEH
Hermann Park	6201 Hermann Park Dr	533A	SWH
Hester Garden Park	3029 Todville Rd	620T	SB
Highlands Park	1008 E Wallisville Rd	460N	HG
Highlands Park	2018 Colonists Park	568Z	SG
Hines Waterwall Park	5000 Hidalgo St	491U	SWH
Hobart Taylor Park (Liberty Park)	8100 Kenton St	455P	NEH
Hockley Park	28515 Old Washington Rd	323H	NWC
Hogg Park	2211 South St	493G	NEH
Hohl, Roy C, Nature Trail (Creek)	21014 Texas 249	329Y	NWC
Hollaway, J.C. Park	4219 Racoon Dr	502F	BT
Holly Spring Park	Cardinal Dr and Jay Way St	286E	NWC
Housman Pocket Park	6705 Housman	451Y	NWH
Houston Amateur Sports Park	12131 Kirby Dr	573J	SWH
Houston Arboretum	4501 Woodway Dr	491M	SWH
Houston Farm & Ranch Club	1 Abercrombie St	448J	NWH
Houston Gardens Park	6900 Camway St	454R	NEH
Huffsmith Park	9738 Huffsmith Rd	249W	NWC
Hunters Glen Park	1340 Independence Blvd	570X	MC
Huron Park	4700 Bush Rd	501E	BT
Hutcheson Park	5509 Minden St	454U	NEH
Hyde Park		658Q	LC
Imperial Oaks Park	31110 Imperial Oaks Blvd	252V	SEM
Independence City Park	3919 Liberty Dr	615U	PL
Independence Park	5515 Clara Rd	449D	NWC
Ingrando Park	7302 Keller St	535E	SEH
Irvington Park	4701 Robertson St	453V	NEH
James Driver Park	10918 Bentley St	414T	NEC
Jaycee Park	1300 Seamist	452W	NWH
Jenkins Memorial Park	4400 Crosby Cedar Bayou Rd	502E	BT
Jesse H. Jones County Park	20634 Kenswick Dr	335J	NCC
Johnson Park	9801 Tanner Rd	449D	NWC
Juergens Park	1331 Ulrich Rd	288C	TB
Katy City Park	5718 Second St	444T	KT
Katy Dog Park	5414 Franz Rd	444U	KT
Katy Park	24927 Morton Rd	444R	NWC
Keith Weiss Park	12300 Aldine Westfield Rd	414J	NCC
Kemah Park		620X	KE
King Estates Park	4791 E Orem	573R	SEH
Kipling Oaks Park		247K	SWM
Kirkwood South Park	10175 Sagetrail Dr	616A	SEC
Kitty Hollow Park	9555 State Hwy 6	610T	MC
Kleb Woods Park	20303 Draper Rd	286P	NWC
Klein Park	6530 N Major Dr	331B	NWC
Lafayette Park	4337 Lafayette St	531R	BL
Lake Forest Park	9200 Mesa Dr	455D	NEH
Lake Houston State Park	22031 Baptist Encampment Rd	257U	SEM
Lake Olympia Park		610P	MC
Lakewood		500J	BT
Lakewood Park	8827 Feland St	455G	NEH
Langwood Park	3975 Bolin Rd	451K	NWH
Law Park	8400 Mykawa Rd	574B	SEH
Lawndale Triangles		535C	SEH
League of Womens Voters Park	3111 Columbia St	501Q	BT
League Park		660H	GCO
Leavesly Park	901 Buckingham Dr	656M	FR
Lee, Jim W. Park	9025 Pitner	450L	NWH
Leon Z. Grayson Park		497B	CV
Levy Park	3801 Eastside St	492X	SWH
Lincoln Park	979 Grenshaw St	412Q	NWH
Lindsey - Lyons Park	2310 Atascocita Rd	376K	NEC
Lindsey Lyons Sports Complex	2310 Atascocita Rd	376K	NEC
Little Cedar Bayou Park	100 N Broadway St	580G	LP
Little Thicket Park	1831 W 23rd St	452T	NWH
Live Oak Park		492R	SWH
Lobit Park	FM 646 Rd E	659R	LC
Lomax Park	1508 Lomax Rd	539U	LP
Lonnie Green Park	130 First St	568P	SG
Lost Creek Park	3707 Lost Creek Blvd	569W	SG
Love Park	1000 W 12th St	452Z	NWH
Macco Park		568L	SG
MacGregor Park	5225 Calhoun Rd	534E	SEH
Mangum Manor Park	5235 Saxon Dr	451L	NWH
Mary Jo Peckham Park	5597 Gardenia Lane	444U	NWC
Mason Creek Hike and Bike Trail	2500 Porter Rd	445N	NWC
Mason Park	7601 Tipps St	535A	SEH
Matheson Park	1240 Ulrich	288C	TB
Maxey Road Park	601 Maxey Rd	496C	NEH
Maxie Beulah Park	2625 Monticello	572L	SWH
May, I.T. Park	2100 Wolf Rd	299Z	NEC
Mayfield Neighborhood Park	106 Avenue D	568N	SG
McHale Park	400 Todville Rd	620Q	SB
McLeod Park	10717 Langston Dr	463K	MB
McNair Memorial Park	418 Lakeshore Dr.	620J	EL
Meador, Rex Park	2200 N Meyer Ave	620L	SEC
Meadow Lake Park		568X	SG
Meadow Park		620L	SB
Meadowbrook Park	17410 River Rd	459X	NEC
Meadowcreek Park	5367 Berry Creek Dr	536S	SEH
Melrose Park	200 Carby Rd	413T	NEH
Memorial Park		492E	SWH
Memorial Park	500 W Jackson	536G	PA
Memorial Park-Friendswood		616Z	FR
Mercer Arboretum	22306 Aldine Westfield Rd	333F	NCC
Meyer, Elizabeth Kaiser Park	7700 Cypresswood Dr	330Q	NWC
Meyer, Rebecca Park	3200 Reba	492U	SWH
Meyerland Park	5151 Jason St	531Q	SWH
Milby, Chas H. Park		535G	SEH
Miller Park	1800 Eldridge Pkwy South	488Q	SWH
Millie Bush Bark Park	16101 Westheimer Pkwy	446T	NWC
Milroy Park	1205 Yale St	452Z	NWH
Miramar Park	1400 Delabrook Ct	620L	SB
Mission West Park	7536 C 1/3 Tetela	527K	NEF
MLK Park	403 Chestnut	288H	TB
Mohrhusen Park	110 2nd St	620Q	SB
Molly Pryor Memorial Orchard	15200 Memorial Dr	488C	SWH
Moncrief, Michael Park	16800 Bear Bayou	459S	CV
Montie Beach Park	300 N Post Oak Ln	453X	NEH
Moody Park	3725 Fulton St	453Y	NEH
Moritz Pech Family Park	1493 Moritz Dr	451W	NWH
Mulberry Park	700 Mulberry Ln	531H	BL
Nacol Park	4418 Bingle	451E	
New Kentucky Park	21710 FM 2920	285R	NWC
Newport Park	2398 Colonial Ct N	658P	LC
Nob Hill Park	10300 Timber Oak Dr	449V	NWH
North Little League Park	301 W. Cedar Bayou Lynchburg	501G	BT
North Park Recreation Area	2213 Northpark Dr	296Q	SEM
Northline Park	6902 Nording Rd	413W	NEH
Northshore Park	14440 Wallisville Rd	457S	NEC
Northwest Park	2002 N.P. St	539P	LP
Nottingham Park	14205 Kimberly Lane	489E	SWH
Oak Meadows Park	500 Ahrens St	536J	SEH
Oaks Park	3600 Locke Ln	492T	SWH
Oakwick Forest Park	39500 Ramblecreek Dr	610X	MC
Old City Park	300 Briarmeadow Ave	656E	FR
Park Meadows Park	610 E San Augustine	538U	DP
Parkview Park	2400 Burke Rd	537S	PA
Pasadena Blvd Park		536R	PA
Pasadena Fair Grounds	7902 Fairmont Pkwy	578G	SEC
Pasadena Parks Dept.	2910 Southmore Rd	573Q	PA
Pasadena Rodeo Grounds	7601 Red Bluff Rd	578G	PA
Paul D. Rushing Park	9114 Hockley Rd	404G	NWC
Peiser Park	8401 Lawndale St	535B	SEH
Pelham Park**	6701 Landor St	454M	NEH
Pelly Park	901 S Main St	541C	BT
Pep Mueller Park	14750 Henry Rd	413B	NCC
Pin Oak Stables		531D	BL
Pine Gully Park	535 Pine Gully Rd	620D	SB
Pitman, Russ Park	7112 Newcastle (Inside 610 Loop)	531M	BL
Pleasanton Manor Park	8501 Guinevere St	495K	NEH
Quail Green West Park	1802 Fresh Meadow Dr	570X	MC
Quebedeaux Park	1115 Congress St	493L	DT
Ramsey Community Center	16003 Lorenzo St	498G	CV
Randolph, Frankie Carter Park	5150 FM Rd 2351	616V	SEC
Ray Holbrook Park	2545 Owens Dr	660X	DI
Ray Miller Park	1800 Eldridge Pkwy	488P	SWH
Red Bluff Park	415 Delta St	537J	PA
Regency Park		369J	NWC
Renwick Sport Complex	205 Stadium Dr	656C	FR
Republic of Texas Plaza	5117 N. Main	501G	BT
Reveille Park	7700 Oak Vista St	535T	SEH
Ridgewood Park	4192 Woodrush Dr	251E	WD
Riley Chambers Park	808 Magnolia Ave	419X	BR
River Grove Park	953 Woodland Hills Dr	336M	NWC
River Terrace Park	16560 Market St	498H	SEC
Riverbend North Park		569S	SG
Riverbend South Park		569W	SG
Roane Park	1440 Turtle Creek Dr	610F	MC
Robert Stuart Park	7250 Belfort	534Z	SEH
Robinson Park	702 Red Bluff Rd	620G	SB
Roseland Park	100 Roseland Dr	542A	BT
Rosslyn Park	6500 Pinemont Dr	451A	NWH
Roy Campbell Burrough Park	9738 Huffsmith Rd	249Q	NWC
Rustic Oaks Park	5101 Orange Blossom	657V	LC
Ryan Park	11201 Harwin Dr	529C	SWH
Sage Meadow Park	11219 Sageyork Dr	616F	SEC
Sagemont Park	11507 Hughes	576Y	SEC
Sam Houston Park	1000 Bagby St	493L	DT
Sammuel Spaceway Park	12936 Samuel Ln	496M	NEH
Samuel Matthews Park	1728 E Huffsmith Rd	249W	NWC
San Jacinto State Park	1496 San Jacinto Mall	499P	SEH
Satsuma Park	1001 Satsuma St	537F	PA
Saums Park	200002 Beechview Ln	446T	NWC
Sawmill Park	2200 Millpark Dr	251V	WD
Schnur Park	12227 Cullen Blvd	573M	SEH
Schott's Park	8510 Will Clayton	376B	NEC
Schwartz Park	8203 Vogue	451N	
Schwartz Park	8303 Vogue Ln	451N	NWH
Scottcrest Park	10700 Rosehaven	573F	SEH
Seabrook Sport Complex	1805 N Meyer Ave	620L	SB
Seabrook Wildlife Refuge & Park	700 Red Bluff	620G	SB
Sesquicentennial Park	400 Texas St	493L	DT
Settegast Park	3001 Garrow St	494N	SEH
Shadow Bend Park	4192 Lake Woodlands Dr	251A	WD
Shadow Creek Ranch	Kingsley Dr	612G	PL
Shady Lane Park	10100 Sahdy Ln	414W	NEH
Shady Meadows Park		326X	NWC
Sheldon Park	8815 Pineland Rd	457B	NEH
Sheldon Sports Complex	8815 Pineland Rd	457B	NEH
Shepard Park	3402 N Shepard Dr	452G	NWH
Sims Bayou Park	3997 River Rd	574E	SEH
Slockett Memorial Park	12821 Nantucket Dr	568D	SG
Smokey Jasper Park	12900 River Trail Rd	415E	NEC
Songwood Park	548 Westshire Dr	496E	NEH
Sonny Tobias Park	5007 Camden	614R	PL
South Burke Park		577K	PA
South Park	801 S St	537K	PA
South Post Oak Park	5500 Hobby St	611B	SWH
Southdown Park	2150 Country Place Pkwy	613J	PL
Southwell Park	27419 Nelson St	292L	SP
Splash Town (Water Park)	21300 Interstate 45	292T	NCC
Sportsplex	1251 Link Rd	658V	LC

Park Name	Address	Pg	Loc
Spotts Park	401 S Heights Blvd	493J	SWH
Spring Branch Park	1700 Campbell	450U	NWH
Spring Creek Park	15012 Brown Rd	288A	NWC
Spring Klein Baseball Park	22430 Rothwood Rd	291J	NWC
Stafford Park	3108 5th St	569Q	SF
Sta-Mo Complex	1917 Moore Rd	610A	MC
Stanfield Park	8579 Ley Rd	455L	NEH
Stein Family Park	9601 Braes Bayou Dr	530U	SWH
Stevens & Pruett Ranch for Children	1210 Dallas Ln	612X	NWB
Stevenson Park	1000 S Friendswood Dr	657E	FR
Stratford Park	500 Stratford St	459Q	HG
Strawberry Park	1200 Parkside Dr	536Z	PA
Stude Park	1031 Stude St	493F	SWH
Sugar Lakes Park	120 Bayview Dr	568P	SG
Sugar Land City Park	321 7th St	568K	SG
Sugar Mill Park	13800 Hidden Lake Ln	568F	SG
Sunnyside Park	3502 Bellfort	533X	SEH
Sunset Park	914 W Hart Ave	536Q	PA
Sylvan Beach Park	400 N Bayshore Dr	580C	LP
Tamarac Park	1300 N Milbend Dr	251M	WD
Tanglewilde Park	9629 Windswept Ln	490W	SWH
Tanglewood Park	5801 Woodway Dr	491K	SWH
Tejas Park	505 Hafer St	501V	BT
Telge Road Park	12400 Pleasant Grove Rd	368J	NWC
Terry Hershey Park	15200 Memorial Dr	488L	SWH
Texas Park		618W	WB
The Woodlands Park		251Z	WD
Theis-Attaway Nature Center	13509 Theis Ln	288Q	SWM
Thomas Park	Fourth Street	444X	KT
Thomas, Cleveland Park	4100 Memorial Dr	492M	SWH
Tidwell Park	9720 Spaulding St	454D	NEH
Timber Lakes Park		251N	SWM
Tom & Vivian Edmonds		375W	NEC
Tom Bass Regional Park	15108 Cullen Blvd	613C	SEC
Tomball City Park	1001 Ulrich Rd	288H	TB
Townwood Park	3402 Simsbrook Dr	572P	SWH
Travis Park	7705 Bayway Dr	500F	BT
Trinity Gardens Park	4903 Bennington	454Q	NEH
Trotter Park	7809 E Little York	415T	NWH
Tuffly Park	3200 Russell St	454X	NEH
Turner Park	2800 West Little York	411Z	
Twin Creek Park		615B	FR
Unidad Park	2510 J B Lefevre Rd	501V	BT
Uvalde Park	1020 Uvalde Rd	497E	NEH
V.F.W. Park	6292 6th St Ave D	444X	KT
Verde Forest Park	8800 Brock Park Blvd	456B	NEB
Village Playfields		251Z	WD
W. 11TH Street Park	2400 W 11th St	452X	NWH
W. Little York Park	2800 Little York Rd	411V	NWH
Walnut Park	400 N Walnut St	618X	WB
Walter Hall Park	807 Hwy 3 N	659J	LC
Warren Park	3401 Topping St	454C	NEH
Washington, Edna Park	7613 Wade Rd	460U	MN
Watonga Parkway	4100 Watongo Blvd	451H	NWH
Wayne Gray Sports Complex	5200 East Rd	501G	BT
West Houston Methodist Park		445R	NWF
West Houston Sports Complex		446U	NWH
West Mount Houston Park	10300 N. Houston-Rosslyn	411J	
West Tidwell Trailhead	4700 W. Tidwell	451C	
Westbury Park	5635 Willowbend Blvd	531W	SWH
Westview Park		451W	NWH
Westwood Park	2407 Market St	500N	BT
White Oak Park		493B	NWH
Wildheather Park	14900 White Heather Dr	572S	SWH
Wildwood Park	2200 Oceanview Dr	620N	SB
Wilke Park	1022 Mercury Dr	495M	JC
Willow Park	4613 Waynesboro Dr	531Z	SWH
Wilson Memorial Park	100 Gilpin St	576F	SEH
Windsor Village Park	14441 Croquet Ln	571P	SWH
Winzer Park		412S	NWH
Woodcreek Park	2907 Crane	616S	PR
Woodland Park	212 Parkview	493C	NWH
Woodsland Park		484B	KT
Zube Park	17400 Roberts Rd	324H	NWC

PERFORMING ARTS

Venue Name	Address	Pg	Loc
A.D. Players Theater	5420 Westheimer Rd	491U	SWH
Alley Theatre	615 Texas Ave	493L	DT
Arena Theater	7326 Southwest Fwy	530G	SWH
Art Park Players	1302 Centers	538K	DP
Company Onstage	9647 Hillcroft	531S	SWH
Cynthia Woods Mitchell Pavillion	2005 Lake Robbins Dr	251H	WD
Encore Theatre	4112 Old Spanish Trail	533M	SEH
Hobby Center for Performing Arts	810 Bagby	493L	DT
Houston Ballet	601 Preston	493L	DT
Houston Grand Opera	510 Preston	493L	DT
Houston Symphony Orchestra	615 Louisiana	493L	DT
Jones Hall	615 Louisiana	493L	DT
Main Street Theater	2540 Times Blvd	532C	WU
Midtown Arts & Theater Center Houston	3400 Main St	493T	SWH
Miller Outdoor Theatre	6000 Hermann Park Dr	533A	SWH
Revention Music Center	520 Texas	493L	DT
Society for the Performing Arts	615 Louisiana	493L	DT
Stages Reportory Theater	3201 Allen Pkwy	492M	SWH
Super Happy Fun Land	3801 Polk St.	494S	SEH
The Ensemble Theater	3535 Main	493T	SWH
Theatre Under The Stars	800 Bagby	493L	DT
Toyota Center	1510 Polk	493Q	DT
White Oak Music Hall	2915 N Main St	493C	NEH
Wortham Theater Center	510 Preston	493L	DT

POINTS OF INTEREST

Name	Address	Pg	Loc
Battleship Texas	3527 Battleground Rd	499N	SEC
Baytown Nature Center	6813 Bayway Dr	500N	BT
Cynthia Woods Mitchell Pavillion	2005 Lake Robbins Dr	251H	WD
Discovery Green		493R	DT
Downtown Tunnel System	Downtown Houston	493L	DT
Galleria Mall	5001 Westheimer	491U	SWH
Helen's Garden		658M	LC
Houston Arboretum & Nature Center	4501 Woodway Dr	491M	SWH
Houston Pavilions		493Q	DT
Houston Zoo	1513 N. MacGregor	533E	SWH
IMAX Theatre		533E	SEH
Kemah Waterfront		620U	KE
Memorial Tennis Center		492E	SWH
Mercer Arboretum & Bontanic Garden	22306 Aldine Westfield	333F	NCC
Minute Maid Park	501 Crawford	493R	DT
NASA - L.B.J. Space Center	Nasa Rd 1 @ Space Ctr	619N	SEH
NRG Arena	One Reliant Park	532R	SWH
NRG Astrodome	One Reliant Park	532R	SWH
NRG Center	One Reliant Park	532R	SWH
NRG Stadium	One Reliant Park	532Q	SWH Old
Town Spring		292Q	SP
Pasadena Little Theater	4318 Allen Genoa	576H	PA
Pinebrook Farms	611 Virgie Community	248P	SWM
Saint Arnold Brewery	2522 Fairway Park Dr.	451Q	NWH
Saint Arnold Brewery	2000 Lyons Ave	493H	NEH
Sam Houston Race Park		370X	NWC
San Jacinto Monument	San Jacinto State Park	499T	SEC
Space Center Houston	1601 Nasa Pkwy	619N	SHE
Splashtown USA	21300 North Frwy	292T	NCC
Texas Medical Center	1155 Holcombe Blvd	533E	SWH
Tinseltown	1600 Lake Robbin Dr	251H	SWM
Toyota Center	1510 Polk	493Q	DT
Williams Tower/Fountain	Post Oak Blvd @ Hidalgo	491U	SWH
Yellow Rose Reception Hall	21130 Legion Rd	256U	SEM

POLICE STATIONS

Station	Address	Pg	Loc
Baytown McLemore Substation	3530 Market	500Z	BT
Baytown PD	3200 N. Main	501Q	BT
Bellaire PD	5110 Jessamine	531G	BL
Brookside PD	6243 Brookside	614C	BK
Bunker Hill PD	11981 Memorial	490J	BH
City of Houston - LP	22627 W. Shorewood Loop	338U	NEH
Clear Lake Shores PD	1006 S. Shore Dr.	620T	KE
Deer Park PD	2911 Center	538P	DP
El Lago PD	98 Lakeshore Dr	619M	EL
Friendswood PD	1600 Whitaker Dr	656M	FR
Galena Park	2207 Clinton Dr	496W	GP
Hedwig PD	9000 Gaylord	490D	HE
HPD - Acre Homes	6719 W. Montgomery	412Y	NWH
HPD - Airport HOU	7800 Airport	575B	SEH
HPD - Airport IAH	3100 N. Terminal Rd	374A	NEH
HPD - Aldine Community	10966 North Frwy	372Z	NEH
HPD - Ann Maria Lopez	1050 Quitman	493D	NEH
HPD - Braeburn	10101 Fondren, Suite 100	530U	SWH
HPD - Broadway Square	8751 Broadway	576K	SEH
HPD - Bush Airport	3100 Terminal Road North	334W	NEH
HPD - Central Command Station	61 Riesner	493L	DT
HPD - Clarkcrest	8940 Clarkcrest	490Y	SWH
HPD - Clear Lake	2855 Bay Area Blvd	618H	SEH
HPD - Denver Harbor	6402 Market St	495E	NEH
HPD - Downtown	1900 Rusk	493R	DT
HPD - East Freeway	12001 East Frwy	496G	NEH
HPD - East Side	7525 Sherman	495W	SWH
HPD - Ellington	7800 Airport Blvd	575B	SEH
HPD - Fifth Ward	4014 Market St	494F	NEH
HPD - Fondren	11168 Fondren	570C	SWH
HPD - Gessner	1331 Gessner	450W	NWH
HPD - Greenspoint	105 Greenspoint Dr	372R	NEH
HPD - Gulfton	5980 Renwick	531A	SWH
HPD - Heights	1127 N. Shepherd	492C	NWH
HPD - Hiram Clarke	14723 Hiram Clark	572S	SWH
HPD - Independence Heights	803 Crosstimbers	453J	NWH
HPD - Internal Affairs	1415 North Loop West	452P	NWH
HPD - Internal Affairs	1200 Travis	493Q	DT
HPD - Jensen	9211 Jensen	454A	NEH
HPD - Kingwood	3915 Rustic Woods	297X	NEH
HPD - Leija	4701 Galveston Rd	535R	SEH
HPD - Midwest	7277 Regency Square	530C	SWH
HPD - Navigation	4401 Navigation	494P	NEH
HPD - Near North	1335 West 43rd	452K	NWH
HPD - Near Town	802 Westheimer	493S	SWH
HPD - North	9455 W. Montgomery	412N	NWH
HPD - Northeast	8301 Ley Rd	455K	NEH
HPD - Northline	392 W. Little York	412V	NWH
HPD - Northwest	6000 Teague Rd	410W	NWH
HPD - Palm Center	5330 Griggs	534J	SEH
HPD - Ranchester	9146 Bellaire Blvd	530E	SWH
HPD - Richmond	6310 Richmond Ave	491W	SWH
HPD - South Central	2202 St Emanuel	493U	SEH
HPD - South Gessner	8605 Westplace Dr	570B	SWH
HPD - Southeast	8300 Mykawa	574C	SEH
HPD - Southmore	3711 Southmore	533H	SEH
HPD - Southwest	4503 Beechnut	531R	SWH
HPD - Special Operations DT Patrol	1415 Fannin St. 200	493Q	DT
HPD - Spring Branch	8400 Long Point # A	451S	NWH
HPD - Sunnyside	3511 Reed Rd	573B	SEH
HPD - Telephone	10201 Telephone Rd	575S	SEH
HPD - W. Side Command Sta	3203 S. Dairy Ashford	488Z	SWH
HPD - Westbury	5600 S. Willow Dr	571B	SWH
HPD - Westwood	9700 Bissonnet, Ste 1740W	529W	SWH
HPD - Willowbrook	17375 Tomball Pkwy	369M	NWC
Humble PD	310 Bender Ave	335U	HM
Jacinto City PD	10429 Market St Rd	496J	JC
Jersey Village PD	16401 Lakeview Dr	409Q	JV
Katy PD station 1	5456 Franz Rd	444U	KT
Katy PD station 2	Katy Mill Mall	484C	KT
Kemah PD	1401 State Hwy 146	620Y	KE
La Porte PD	3001 N. 23 St	540W	LP
Lakewood PD	12415 Louetta Rd	328V	NWC
League City PD	500 W. Walker	658M	LC
Meadows Place PD	1 Troyan	569B	MD
Memorial Villages PD	11981 Memorial Dr	490J	BH
Metro PD	810 N. San Jacinto	493M	DT
Mont Belvieu	11607 Eagle Dr	463C	MB
Montgomery County Annex	22354 Justice Dr	256U	SEM
Morgans Point PD	1415 E. Main	540Z	MP
Nassau Bay P.D.	18100 Upper Bay Rd	619S	SB
Oak Ridge PD	27424 Robinson Rd	252K	OR
Pasadena PD	1201 Davis	537N	PA
Pasadena Police Practice Range	6600 Genoa Red Bluff	578F	PA
Pearland PD	2703 Veterans Dr	615N	PL
Roman Forest	2403 Roman Forest Blvd	257D	RF
Seabrook PD	1400 Cook	620P	SB
Shoreacres PD	601 Shoreacres Blvd	580U	SA
South Houston PD	1023 Dallas	536W	SH
Southside Place PD	6309 Edloe	532A	SS
Spring Valley PD	1025 Campbell Rd	490C	SV
Stafford PD	2702 S. Main	569R	SF
Sugar Land PD	1200 S.H. 6	568S	SG
The Woodlands PD	9200 Grogans Mill Rd	251H	WD
Tomball PD	400 Fannin St.	288G	TB
Waller PD	1118 Farr St.	282U	WL
Webster PD	217 Pennsylvania	618Y	WB
West Univ. Place PD	3814 University	532A	WU
Precinct 3	2436 S. Grand Blvd	615N	PL
Precinct 2	303 Texas Parkway	570N	MC
Precinct 3	12803 Park One	568G	SG
Precinct 4	12919 Dairy Ashford	568M	SG

CONSTABLE OFFICES

Office	Address	Pg	Loc
Precinct 8	174 Calder Rd	658M	LC
Precinct 1	1302 Preston, 3rd Fl.	493M	DT
Precinct 1, Annex 31	7300 N. Sheperd	412U	NWH
Precinct 2	109 E. Shaw	536G	PA
Precinct 2, Annex 67	10851 Scarsdale	616G	SEC
Precinct 3	701 W. Baker	501L	BT
Precinct 3, Annex 2	14350 Wallisville Rd	457S	NEC
Precinct 3, Annex 3	903 Hollywood	497G	NEC
Precinct 4	6831 Cypresswood	330R	NWC
Precinct 4, Station 2	7900 Will Clayton Pkwy	375C	NWC
Precinct 5	17423 Katy Frwy	487B	SWC

Office	Address	Pg	Loc
Precinct 6 Place 1	333 Lockwood	494T	SEH
Precinct 6 Place 2	1001 M. Garcia Dr	494V	SEH
Precinct 7 Place 1	5737 Cullen Blvd	533H	SEH
Precinct 7 Place 2	5290 Griggs	534J	SEH
Precinct 8 Place 1	7330 Spencer Hwy Suite 107	538X	PA
Precinct 8 Place 2	16603 Buccaneer	618Q	SEH
Montgomery Co. Constables			
Precinct 3	1520 Lake Front Cir	251H	WD
Precinct 4	21130 US 59	256Q	SEM

WOODLANDS PATROL DIVISIONS

District 2 & 5	9200 Grogan's Mill Rd	251H	SWM
District 3	21130 U.S. Hwy 59	256Q	SEM

SHERIFF DEPARTMENTS

Harris Co. Central Sheriff Dept.	1200 Baker	493M	DT
Harris Co. District 1 (NW)	6831 Cypresswood	330R	NWC
Harris Co. District 2 (NE)	7900 Will Clayton Pkwy	375C	HM
Harris Co. District 3 (E & SE)	14350 Wallisville	457S	NEC
Harris Co. District 4 (W & SW)	16715 Clay Rd	447H	NWC
Harris Co. District 5	23828 FM 249	329E	NWC
District 2	7900 Will Clayton Pkwy	375C	HM

POST OFFICES

Post Office Name	Address	Pg	Loc
Addicks Barker Finance	16830 Barker Sprgs Rd	487B	NWC
Airport Mail Facility	19175 Lee Rd	335W	NEH
Albert Thomas Sta.	14917 El Camino Real	618E	NB
Almeda Sta.	3030 W. Fuqua	572T	SWH
Anson Jones Sta.	634 W. Cavalcade	453T	NWH
Ashford West	12655 Whittington	488R	SWH
Astrodome Sta	8205 Braesmain Dr	532L	SWH
Barker P.O.	211 Barker Rd	486D	SWH
Bay Area Postal	3118 F.M. 528	657C	FR
Baytown Main P.O.	601 W. Barker	501L	BT
Baytown Sta.	3508 Market	540D	BT
Bear Creek	16015 Cairnway	448A	NWC
Beechnut Sta.	11703 Beechnut	529N	SWH
Bellaire P.O.	5350 Bellaire Blvd	531F	BL
Bob Harris Sta.	102 Munger	536G	PA
Broadway Finance	4020 Broadway	535P	SEH
Channelview P.O.	531 Sheldon Rd	498F	CV
Civic Center Finance	700 Smith	493L	DT
Copperfield P.O.	8825 Hwy 6	408C	NWC
Cornerstone Station	14403 Walters Rd	331X	NWC
Crosby P.O.	133 Hare	419C	CB
Cypress P.O.	16635 Spring Cypress	367B	CY
Debora Sue Schatz Sta.	2909 Rodgerdale Rd	489Z	SWH
Deer Park P.O.	200 E. San Augustine	538Q	DP
Delbert L. Atkinson Sta.	6100 Spencer Hwy	537Z	PA
DeMoss Sta.	6500 DeMoss Dr	531E	SWH
Denver Harbor Sta.	5901 Market	494G	SEH
Eastwood Sta.	5415 Lawndale	494Y	SEH
Fairbanks Carrier Annex	7050 Brook Hollow	410S	NWC
Fleetwood	315 Addicks-Howell	488A	SWH
Foster Place Sta.	5210 Griggs Rd	534J	SEH
Foxbrook P.O.	7231 FM 1960 W.	334U	NCC
Fresno P.O.	2723 FM 521	611V	FS
Friendswood P.O.	310 Morningside	616Z	FR
Galena Park Main	1805 Clinton	496W	GP
Galleria Finance	5015 Westheimer	491U	SWH
Garden Oaks	3816 N. Shepherd Dr	452M	NWH
Genoa Sta.	10935 Almeda Genoa Rd	576P	GN
Granville W. Elder Sta.	550 Maxey Rd.	496C	NEH
Greenbriar Sta	3740 Greenbrair	492Y	SWH
Greens North Sta.	1530 Greensmark	372N	NWC
Greenway Plaza Finance	3 E. Greenway Plaza	492X	SWH
Harrisburg Sta.	8330 Manchester	535B	SEH
Heights Finance	1050 Yale	492D	NWH
Highlands P.O.	608 S. Main	459V	HG
Hockley P.O.	17210 Warren Ranch	324E	HK
Houston Mail Processing Center	4600 Aldine Bender Rd	374Y	NEH
Houston P.O.	401 Franklin	493L	DT
Huffman P.O.	24936 FM 2100	339K	HU
Humble P.O.	1202 1st St	335V	HM
Irvington Sta.	7825 Fulton	453B	NEH
James S. Griffith Sta.	9320 Emnora Ln	450Q	NWH
Jensen Drive Sta.	3520 Jensen Dr	454W	NEH
John Dunlop Sta	8728 Beverly Hill	490Y	SWH
John Foster Sta.	1520 S. Richey	536Q	PA
Julius Melcher Sta.	2802 Timmons Ln	492S	SWH
Katy Annex P.O.	1331 Pin Oak Rd	484G	KT
Katy P.O.	5701 4th	444X	KT
Katy Park Row Sta.	20180 Park Row	446X	NWC
Kemah P.O.	1129 Hwy 146	620Y	KE
Kingwood P.O.	4025 Feather Lakes Way	297X	NEH
Klein P.O.	9333 Spring Cypress	329M	NWC
Klein Station	7717 Louetta Rd.	330P	NWC
LaPorte P.O.	801 W. Fairmont Pkwy	580F	LP
League City P.O.	240 W. Galveston Rd	658M	LC
Long Point Sta.	8000 Long Point Rdvd	457S	NWH
Main P.O.	401 Franklin	493L	DT
Martin Luther King Sta.	9444 Cullen Blvd	573D	SEH
Medical Center Sta	7205 Almeda	533J	SEH
Memorial Park Sta.	10505 Town & Country Way	489D	SWH
Missouri City P.O.	1902 FM 2234	570X	MC
Mont Belvieu P.O.	10643 Eagle Dr	463H	MB
Nassau Bay Branch	18214 Upper Bay Rd	619S	NB
New Caney P.O.	20811 U.S. Hwy 59	256Q	SEM
North Shepherd Sta.	7511 N. Shepherd Dr	412U	NWH
Oak Forest Sta.	2499 Judiway	452N	NWH
Panther Creek P.O.	10800 Gosling Rd	250H	WD
Park Place Sta.	5302 Galveston Rd	535V	SEH
Pasadena Main P.O.	1199 Pasadena Blvd	536R	PA
Pearland P.O.	3519 E. Walnut	615P	PL
Pinehurst P.O.	34635 Wright Rd	247G	SWM
Porter P.O.	23550 Partners Way	296E	SEM
Rich Hill Sta.	2950 Unity	490Z	SWH
River Oaks Sta.	1900 W. Gray	492R	SWH
Roy Royall Sta.	4206 Little York Rd	414T	NEH
Sage Annex	3500 Sage Rd.	491Y	SWH
Sam Houston Finance P.O.	701 San Jacinto	493Q	SWH
Sam Houston Sta.	1500 Hadley	493U	DT
Seabrook P.O.	1600 2nd St	620P	SB
Silver Lake P.O.	2700 Cullen Blvd	613R	PL
South Houston P.O.	315 N. Allen Genoa	536Y	SH
South Post Oak Sta.	5505 Belrose Dr	571B	SWH
Southmore Sta.	4110 Almeda Rd.	493X	SWH
Spring P.O.	1411 Wunsche Loop	292P	SP
Spring Woodforest P.O.	155 Louetta Crossing	292T	NCC
Stafford P.O.	4110 Bluebonnett	569F	SF
Stafford P.O.	2810 S. Main	569Q	SF
Sugar Land P.O.	225 Matlage Way	568N	SG
T.W. House Sta.	1300 W. 19th	452U	NWH
Texas Southern P.O.	3100 Cleburne St	533D	SEH
Tomball P.O.	122 N. Holderrieth	288G	TB
University P.O.	1319 Richmond	493W	SWH
Waller P.O.	40090 Hempstead Hwy	282Y	WL
Webster P.O.	17077 Texas Ave.	618X	WB
Weslayan Finance	5340 Weslayan	492W	SWH
Westbrae Sta.	10910 S. Gessner	530X	SWH
Westbury Sta	11805 Chimney Rock	571B	SWH
Westchase Finance	3836 S. Gessner Dr	490W	SWH
Westfield Sta.	17119 Red Oak Dr	332J	NCC
William Rice Sta.	5201 Wakeforest	492Y	SWH
Willow Place Station	12955 Willow Place, W.	369M	NWC
Windmill Sta.	9898 Almeda Genoa	576N	SEH
Woodlands Sta	9450 Pinecroft	251D	WD

TOWNS & COMMUNITIES

Town Name	Address	Pg	Loc
Baytown		501N	BT
Bellaire		531G	BL
Brookside Village		614B	BK
Bunker Hill		490K	BH
Clear Lake Shores		620S	CS
Cypress		367A	CY
Deer Park		538Q	DP
Dickinson		659X	DI
El Lago		620E	EL
Fresno		611V	NEF
Friendswood		656R	FR
Galena Park		496T	GP
Hedwig		490B	HE
Hilshire		451W	HI
Hockley		323H	HK
Houston - Downtown		493L	DT
Hufsmith		249S	NWC
Humble		335Y	HM
Hunters Creek		490M	HC
Jacinto City		496J	JC
Jersey Village		409L	JV
Katy		444T	KT
Kemah		620X	KE
La Porte		540T	LP
League City		659K	LC
Meadows Place		569B	MD
Missouri City		610K	MC
Mont Belvieu		463J	MB
Morgans Point		540V	MP
Nassau Bay		619S	NB
Oak Ridge North		252F	OR
Pasadena		619A	PA
Pasadena		537U	PA
Pearland		615G	PL
Pinehurst		247C	PH
Piney Point		490G	PP
Plum Grove		259E	PG
Roman Forest		257D	RF
Seabrook		620F	SB
Shenendoah		252A	SD
Shoreacres		580P	SA
South Houston		536X	SH
Southside Place		532E	SS
Spring Valley		450Z	SV
Stafford		569K	SF
Stagecoach		246M	SC
Sugar Land		568L	SG
Taylor Lake Village		619M	TL
Texas City		660Z	TC
Tomball		288C	TB
Waller		282U	WL
Webster		618U	WB
West University Place		532A	WU
Woodbranch Village		257C	WV
Woodlands		251U	WD

UNIVERSITIES & COLLEGES

School or Facility Name	Address	Pg	Loc
Art Institute of Houston	1900 Yorktown #100	491Q	SWH
Baylor College of Medicine	One Baylor Plaza	532H	SWH
Bradford School of Business	4669 Southwest Frwy #300	491Z	SWH
Cinco Ranch Houston Comm. College		485Y	NEF
HCC Central-Hobby Airport Center	8880 Telephone Rd	575E	SEH
HCC Central-Palm Center	5400 Griggs Rd	534K	SEH
Houston Baptist University	7502 Fondren	530L	SWH
Houston Community College	1550 Fox Lake	446Y	NWC
Houston Community College	1265 Pinemont	452F	NWH
Houston Community College	1900 W. 34th	452P	NWH
Houston Community College	9400 Irvington	453C	NWH
Houston Community College	4638 Airline	453F	NEH
Houston Community College	401 Northline Mall	453K	NEH
Houston Community College	3821 Caroline	493T	SWH
Houston Community College	555 Community College	495H	NEH
Houston Community College	5407 Gulfton	531B	SWH
Houston Community College	5601 W. Loop South	531D	BL
Houston Community College	1900 Galen Dr	532H	SWH
Houston Community College	4242 Mason Rd	485Z	NEF
Houston Community College	4242 S. Mason Rd	485Z	NEF
Houston Community College	13803 Bissonnet	528P	SWC
Houston Community College	12401 S. Post Oak	571G	SWH
Houston Community College	1681 Cartwright	610B	MC
Houston Community College - Admin.	22 Waugh Dr	493T	SWH
Houston Community College - Alief-Elsik	12601 High Star Dr	528D	SWH
Houston Community College - Eastside	6815 Rustic	534H	SEH
Houston Community College - Greenbriar	13645 Murphy Rd	569L	SF
Houston Community College - Law Enf.	7907 Cowart	495J	NEH
Houston Community College - Stafford	9910 Cash Rd	569M	SF
Houston Community College - T & C	1010 W. Sam Hou. Pkwy N.	489D	NWH
Houston Community College	1300 Holman	493T	SWH
Houston Communtiy College-HealthScience	1900 Pressler	532H	SWH
Le Tourneau University	3 Riverway #130	491L	SWH
Lee College	511 S. Whiting	501X	BT
Lone Star College		333T	NCC
Lone Star College, Carver Center	2330 S. Victory	412S	NWH
Lone Star College, Cy-Fair College	9191 Barker Cypress	407A	NHC
Lone Star College, Fairbanks Center	14955 N W Freeway	410W	NHC
Lone Star College, Kingwood College	20000 Kingwood Dr.	295Z	SEM
Lone Star College, Parkway Center	16416 Northchase Dr	372R	NEH
Lone Star College, Tomball College	30555 Tomball Parkway	288A	TB
Lone Star College, Willow Chase Center	9494 Grant Rd	369H	NWC
Northwest Harris College	2700 W W Thorne	333T	NWH
Northwood University	6544 Post Oak Place	491R	SWH
Our Lady of Lake University	1900 Yorktown	491Q	SWH
Pearland College	2319 N. Grand Blvd	615J	PL
Rice University	6100 Main	532D	SWH
San Jacinto College - Central	8060 Spencer Hwy	578C	SEC
San Jacinto College - North	5800 Uvalde Rd	457T	NEC
San Jacinto College - South	13735 Beamer Rd	616H	SEH
School of Culinary Arts	1900 Yorktown	491Q	SWH
South Texas College of Law	1303 San Jacinto	493Q	DT
Texas Chiropractic College		537Z	PA
Texas College of Law		493Q	DT
Texas Southern University	3100 Cleburne	533C	SEH

Texas Womans University		532H	SWH
Texas Woman's University	6700 Fannin	532H	SWH
University of Houston - Clear Lake	2700 Bay Area Blvd	618H	PA
University of Houston - Downtown	One Main St	493L	DT
University of Houston - Fort Bend	1400 University Blvd	568S	SG
University of Houston - Katy	4242 S. Mason Rd	485Z	NEF
University of Houston - University Park	4800 Calhoun	534A	SEC
University of Phoenix	7900 N. Sam Houston Pkwy, W.	370W	NWC
University of Phoenix	11451 Katy Frwy. #200	489B	NWH
University of Phoenix	11511 Katy Freeway	489C	SWH
University of Phoenix Woodlands		252X	NWC
University of St. Thomas	3800 Montrose	493S	SWH
University of Texas - Medical	7000 Fannin	533A	SWH
Wharton County Jr. College (satellite)		568M	SG

HISD SPECIAL SERVICES

School or Facility Name	Address	Pg	Loc
Administration Bldg	4400 W. 18th	451V	NWH
Audio Visual Aid	3901 Telephone	534G	SEH
Barnett Stadium	6800 Fairway	534R	SEH
Butler, J.K. Stadium	13755 S. Main	571E	SWH
Career Oriented Education Ctr		494C	NEH
Central Warehouse	228 McCarty	495A	NEH
Contemporary Learning Center	1906 Cleburne	493X	SEH
Cooley Administration Bldg	300 W. 17th	452Z	NWH
Criminology Law Enforcement	4711 Dickson	492M	SWH
Delmar Stadium	2020 Mangum	451V	NWH
Grady Special School		491Q	SWH
H.S. for Engineering Prof.		453N	SWH
H.S. for Health Prof.	3100 Shenandoah	533F	SEH
H.S. for Perf. & Visual Arts	4001 Stanford	493S	SWH
Houston Technical Inst. (HTI)		493T	SWH
Jones-Vanguard High School		534S	SEH
Jordon, Barbara Technical		454T	NWH
M.O.T.E. Complex		495B	NEH
Oceanography Center		571B	SWH
Region, Central Office	812 W. 28th	452U	NWH
Region, East Office	1102 Telephone	494T	SEH
Region, North Office	5426 Cavalcade	454Y	NEH
Region, South Office	4040 W. Fuqua	572S	SWH
Region, West Office	5827 Chimney Rock	531B	SWH
Rogers T.H. Education Center	5840 San Felipe	491P	SWH
Special Service School		493T	SWH
Sterling Aerodynamics Academy		574K	SEH

HISD SCHOOL BUILDINGS

School or Facility Name	Address	Pg	Loc
Alcott Elem.	5859 Bellfort	534X	SEH
Allen Elem.	400 Victoria	453E	NWH
Almeda Elem.	14249 Bridgeport	572Y	SEH
Anderson Elem.	5727 Ludington	571A	SWH
Ashford Elem.	1815 Shannon Valley Dr	489N	CV
Askew, Jewel Elem.	11200 Wood Lodge	489P	SWH
Atherton Elem.	2011 Solo	494G	NEH
Attucks MS	4330 Bellfort	533Y	SEH
Austin, Stephen F. Sr.	1700 Dumble	494X	SEH
Barrick Elem.	12001 Winfrey	413U	NEH
Bastian Elem.	5051 Bellfort Ave	533Z	SEH
Baylor College of Medicine Aca	2610 Elgin	493Y	SEH
Bell, Kate Elem.	12323 Shaftsbury	569H	SWH
Bellaire Sr.	5100 Maple	531L	BL
Bellfort Acacemy	7647 Bellfort	535S	SEH
Benavidez Elem.	6262 Gulfton	531A	SWH
Benbrook Elem.	4026 Bolin Rd	451K	NWH
Berry Elem.	2310 Berry Rd	453H	NEH
Black, F.M. MS	1575 Chantilly	452J	NWH
Blackshear Elem.	2900 Holman	493Y	SEH
Bonham Elem.	8302 Braes River	530Q	SWH
Bonner Elem.	8100 Elrod	535U	SEH
Braeburn Elem.	7707 Rampart	531J	SWH
Briargrove Elem.	6145 San Felipe	491N	SWH
Briarmeadow Elem	3601 Dunvale	490Y	SWH
Briscoe Elem.	321 Forest Hill	494Z	SEH
Brookline Elem.	6301 South Loop East	534L	SEH
Browning Elem.	607 Northwood	453X	NWH
Burbank Elem.	216 Tidwell	453G	NEH
Burbank MS.	315 Berry Rd	453G	NEH
Burnet Elem.	5403 Canal	494U	SEH
Burrus Elem.	701 E. 33rd	453N	NEH
Bush Elem.	13800 Westerloch Dr	488K	SWC
Cage Elem.	4528 Leeland	494X	SEH
Carnegie, Vanguard HS	10401 Scott St	573G	SEH
Carrillo Elem.	960 S. Wayside	494Y	SEH
Carter Career Center HS	1700 Gregg	494F	NEH
Challenge Early College	5601 W. Loop S.	531D	SWH
Challenge Early College HS	5601 W. Loop S.	531D	SWH
Chavez Sr.	8501 Howard	535R	SEH
Clifton MS	6001 Golden Forest	451F	NWH
Codwell Elem.	4103 Brisbane	573G	SEH
Condit Elem.	7000 S. 3rd	531G	BL
Cook Elem.	7115 Lockwood	454L	NEH
Coop Elem.	10130 Aldine-Westfield	414W	NEH
Cornelius Elem.	7475 Westover	535S	SEH
Cowart Stadium		415U	NEH
Crawford Elem.	1510 Jenson Dr	494E	NEH
Crespo Elem.	7500 Office City	535J	SEH
Crockett Elem.	2112 Crockett	493F	SWH
Cullen MS.	6900 Scott	533Q	SEH
Cunningham, L.T. Elem	5100 Gulfton	531C	SWH
Daily Elem	12909 Briar Forest	488Q	SWH
Davila Elem.	7610 Dahlia	535E	SEH
De Chaumes Elem	155 Cooper	413X	NEH
De Zavala Elem.	7521 Avenue H	495S	SEH
Deady MS.	2500 Broadway	535F	SEH
DeAnda Elem	7980 Almeda Genoa	575P	SHE
DeBakey H.S. for Health Prof.	3100 Shenandoah St	533F	SWH
Dodson Elem.	1808 Sampson	493V	SEH
Dogan Elem.	4202 Liberty Rd	494B	NEH
Durham Elem.	4803 Brinkman	452G	NWH
Durkee Elem.	7301 Nording	413W	NEH
East Early College	220 N. Milby	494P	SEH
East Early College HS	220 N. Milby St	494P	SEH
Eastwood Academy	1315 dumble	494X	SEH
Edison MS	6901 Avenue I	494V	SEH
Eliot Elem.	6411 Laredo	494D	NEH
Elmore MS	8200 Tate	455T	NEH
Elrod H.W. Elem	6230 Dumfries	530V	SWH
Emerson Elem.	9533 Skyline	490X	SWH
Empowerment College Prep	5655 Selinsky	574F	SEH
Energized for STEM Academy	6201 Bissonnet	531J	SWH
Field Elem.	703 E. 17th	453W	NWH
Fleming, Lamar MS	4910 Collingsworth	454Y	NEH
Foerster Elem.	14200 Fonmeadow	570H	SWH
Fondren Elem.	12405 Carlsbad	570M	SWH
Fondren MS.	6333 S. Braeswood	530V	SWH
Fonville MS	725 E. Little York	413T	NEH
Fonwood Elem.	10719 Seneca	414V	NEH
Forest Brook MS	7525 Tidwell Rd	455A	NEH
Foster Elem	3919 Ward	533Q	SEH
Franklin Elem.	7101 Canal	494V	SEH
Frost Elem.	5650 Selinsky	574K	SEH
Furr Sr.	520 Mercury	495H	NEH
Gallegos Elem.	7415 Harrisburg	495W	SEH
Garcia Elem.	9550 Aldine-Westfield	454A	NEH
Garden Oaks Elem.	901 Sue Barnett	452L	NWH
Garden Villas Elem.	7185 Santa Fe	534Z	SEH
Golfcrest Elem.	7414 Fairway	535N	SEH
Gordon Elem.	6300 Avenue B	531H	BL
Gregg Elem.	6701 Roxbury	534U	SEH
Gregory/Lincoln Education Ctr.	1101 Taft	493P	SWH
Grimes Elem.	9220 Jutland	573D	SEH
Grissom Elem.	4900 Simsbrook	571R	SWH
Gross Elem.	12583 S. Gessner	570F	SEH
Halpin Childhood Center	10901 Sandpiper	530Z	SWH
Hamilton MS	139 E. 20th	453S	NWH
Harris, John Elem.	801 Broadway	535B	SEH
Harris, Roland Elem.	1262 Mae	496K	NEH
Hartman MS	7111 Westover	534V	SEH
Hartsfield Elem.	5001 Perry	534J	SEH
Harvard Elem.	810 Harvard	493A	NWH
Heights Sr.	413 E. 13th	453W	NWH
Helms Community Ctr.	503 W. 21st	452V	NWH
Henderson, J.P. Elem.	1800 Dismuke	534C	SEH
Henderson, Nat. Q. Elem.	701 Solo	494L	NEH
Henry, Patrick MS	10702 E. Hardy	413U	NEH
Herod Elem.	5627 Jason	531N	SWH
Herrera Elem.	525 Bennington Ave	453Q	NEH
Highland Heights Elem.	865 Paul Quinn	452C	NWH
Hillard Elem	8115 E. Houston Rd	455G	NEH
Hines - Caldwell	5515 W. Orem	571K	SWH
Hines - Caldwell	5515 West Orem	571K	SWH
Hines-Caldwell Elem	5515 W Orem	571Q	SWH
Hobby Elem.	4021 Woodmont Dr	572J	SWH
Hogg MS.	1100 Merrill	493B	NWH
Holland MS	1600 Gellhorn	495K	NEH
Horn Elem.	4535 Pine	531M	BL
Houston International Sudies	1810 Stuart	493U	SWH
Houston, Sam Sr	9400 Irvington	453D	NEH
Isaacs Elem.	3830 Pickfair	454Y	NEH
Janowski Elem.	7500 Bauman Rd	453L	NEH
Jefferson Elem.	5000 Sharman	453U	NEH
Jones, Jesse Sr	7414 St. Lo	534S	SEH
Jordon Tech. HS	5800 Eastex Frwy	454T	NEH
Judson Robinson Elem.	12425 Woodforest Dr	496C	NEH
Kaleidoscope MS.	6501 Bellaire	530H	SWH
Kashmere Gardens Elem.	4901 Lockwood	454U	NEH
Kashmere Sr.	6900 Wileyvale	454Q	NEH
Kelso Elem.	5800 Southmund	534N	SEH
Kennedy, J.F. Elem.	306 Crosstimbers	453J	NWH
Ketelsen Elem.	600 Quitman	493C	NEH
Key, Francis S. MS	4000 Kelley	454T	NEH
Kolter Elem.	9710 Runnymeade	531U	SWH
Lamar Sr.	3325 Westheimer	492T	SWH
Lanier MS	2600 Woodhead	492V	SWH
Lantrip Elem.	100 Telephone	494S	SEH
Las Americas Middle	6501 Bellaire	530H	SWH
Law & Criminal Justice H.S.	4701 Dickson	492M	NWH
Law Elem.	12401 South Coast Dr	573L	SEH
Lawson MS	14000 Stancliff	571R	SWH
Learning Academy	11433 Suburban Rd	415N	NEH
Lewis Elem.	7649 Rockhill	535X	SEH
Liberty HS	6400 SW Frwy Ste A	530D	SWH
Lockhart Elem.	3200 Rosedale	533C	SEH
Long MS	6501 Bellaire Blvd	530H	SWH
Longfellow Elem.	3617 Horris	532P	SWH
Looscan Elem.	3800 Robertson	453Z	NEH
Love Elem.	1120 W. 13th	452Z	NWH
Lovett Elem.	8814 S. Rice Ave	531Q	SWH
Lyons Elem.	800 Roxella	453C	NEH
MacGregor Elem.	4801 La Branch	493X	SEH
Mading Elem.	8511 Crestmont	574B	SEH
Madison Sr.	13719 White Heather	572J	SWH
Marshall MS.	1115 Noble	493D	NEH
Marshall, Thurgood Elem	6200 Winfield River	415J	NEH
Martinez, Clem Elem.	901 Hayes	493D	NEH
Martinez, R. Elem.	7211 Market	495E	NEH
McGowen Elem.	6820 Homestead	454R	NEH
McNamara Elem.	8714 McAvoy	530R	SWH
McReynolds MS	5910 Market	494G	SEH
Memorial Elem.	6401 Arnot	492F	SWH
Meyerland MS	10410 Manhattan	531X	SWH
Milby Sr.	1601 Broadway	535F	SEH
Milne Elem.	7800 Portal	530Y	SWH
Mitchell Elem.	10900 Gulfdale	575T	SEH
Montgomery Elem.	4000 Simsbrook	572N	SWH
Moreno, J.E. Elem.	620 E. Canino	413S	NEH
N. Houston Early College	99 Lyerly	453F	NEH
Navarro MS	5100 Polk	494X	SEH
Neff Elem.	8200 Carvel	530K	SWH
Ninth Grade College Prep	1303 Tidwell	453D	NEH
North Forest HS	10725 Mesa Dr	415U	NEH
North Houston Early College	99 Lyerly St	453F	NEH
Northline Elem.	821 Witcher Ln	453B	NWH
Northside Sr.	1101 Quitman	493D	NEH
Oak Forest Elem.	1401 W. 43rd	452K	NWH
Oates Elem.	10044 Wallisville	455Z	NEH
Ortiz MS.	6767 Telephone	535W	SEH
Osborne Elem.	800 Ringold	412U	NWH
Paige, Roderick Elem.	7501 Curry Rd	454J	NEH
Park Place Elem.	8235 Park Place Blvd	535P	SEH
Parker Elem.	10626 Atwell	531X	SWH
Patterson Elem.	5302 Allendale	536S	SEH
Peck Elem.	5909 England	533M	SEH
Performing & Visual Arts H.S.	4001 Stanford	493S	SWH
Pershing M.S.	3838 Bluebonnet	532J	WU
Petersen Elem.	14404 Waterloo	572P	SWH
Pilgram Academy K-8	6302 Skyline Dr	491W	SWH
Pin Oak Ms	4601 Glenmont	531D	BL
Piney Point Elem.	8921 Pagewood	490Y	SWH
Pleasantville Elem.	1431 Gellhorn	495L	NEH
Poe Elem.	5100 Hazard	492Z	SWH
Port Houston Elem.	1800 McCarty	495K	NEH
Project Chrysalis MS	4528 Leeland	494X	SEH
Pugh Elem.	1147 Kress	494M	SEH
Reach Charter	520 Mercury	496E	NEH
Red Elem.	4520 Tonawanda	531Z	SWH
Revere, Paul MS	10502 Briar Forest	489Q	SWH
Reynolds Elem.	9601 Rosehaven	573B	SEH
Rice K-8	7550 Seuss Dr	532L	SWH
River Oaks Elem.	2008 Kirby Dr	492Q	SWH
Roberts Elem.	6000 Greenbriar Dr	532G	SWH
Robinson Elem	12425 Woodforest	496C	NEC
Rodriguez Elem	5858 Chimney Rock	531B	SWH
Rogers, T.H., Elem	5840 San Felipe	491P	SWH
Roosevelt Elem	6700 Fulton	453Q	SEH
Ross Elem.	2819 Bay	454W	NEH
Rucker Elem.	5201 Vinett	536N	SEH
Rusk K-8	2805 Garrow	494N	SEH
Sam Houston Tech Cntr	9400 Irvington	453D	NEH
Sanchez, George I. Elem	2700 Berkley	535J	SEH
Scarborough Elem.	3021 Little York Rd	414T	NCC
Scarborough Sr	4141 Costa Rica	451L	NEH
Scott Elem.	3300 Russell	454X	NEH
Scroggins Elem	400 Boyles	494D	NEH
Seguin Elem.	5905 Waltrip	534V	SEH

School or Facility Name	Address	Pg	Loc
Shadowbriar Elem	2650 Shadowbriar	488V	SWH
Shadydale Elem	5905 Tidwell Rd	454C	NEH
Sharpstown MS	8330 Triola	530K	SWH
Sharpstown Sr	7504 Bissonnet	530Q	SWH
Shearn Elem	9802 Stella Link	532S	SWH
Sherman Elem	1909 McKee	493H	NEH
Sinclair Elem	6410 Grovewood	452X	SWH
Smith Education Ctr.	1701 Bringhurst	494F	NEH
Smith, K. Elem	4802 Crystell	451H	NEH
South Alternative	3555 Bellfort	533Y	SEH
Southmayd Elem	1800 Coral	535E	SEH
St. George Place Elem	5430 Hidalgo	491U	SWH
Sterling, Ross Sr	11625 Martindale	574K	SEH
Stevens Elem	1910 La Monte Dr	452J	NWH
Stevenson Elem	5410 Cornish	492G	SWH
Stevenson MS	9595 Winkler	536W	SEH
Sugar Grove Elem	8405 Bonhomme	530Q	SWH
Sutton Elem	7402 Albacore	530M	SWH
Tanglewood MS	5215 San Felipe	491Q	SWH
Thomas, Albert MS	5655 Selinsky	574F	SEH
Thompson Elem	6121Tierwester	533G	SEH
Tijerina Elem	6501 Sherman	494U	SEH
Tinsley Elem	11035 Bob White	570D	SWH
Travis Elem	3311 Beauchamp	493B	NWH
Twain, Mark Elem	7500 Braes	532J	SWH
Valley West Elem	10707 S. Gessner	530X	SWH
Wainwright Elem	5330 Milwee	451L	NWH
Walnut Bend Elem	10620 Briar Forest	489Q	SWH
Waltrip Sr	1900 W. 34th	452P	NWH
Washington, B.T. Sr	119 E. 39th	453N	NWH
Welch, Louie MS	11544 S. Gessner	570B	SWH
Wesley Elem	800 Dillard	412Y	NWH
West Briar MS	13733 Brimhurst	488K	SWH
West University Elem	3756 University Blvd	532A	WU
Westbury Sr	11911 Chimney Rock	571B	SWH
Westside HS	14201 Briar Forest	488J	SWH
Wharton Elem	900 W. Gray	493N	SWH
Wheatley Sr	4801 Providence	494G	NEH
Whidby Elem	7625 Springhill	533P	SEH
White Elem	9001 Triola	530J	SWH
Whittier Elem	10511 LaCrosse	496E	JC
Williams, M.C. MS	6100 Knox	452C	NWH
Wilson Elem	2100 Yupon	492R	SWH
Windsor Village Elem	14440 Polo	571P	SWH
Wisdom Sr	6529 Beverly Hill	490Z	SWH
Woodson Elem	10720 Southview	573G	SEH
Worthing Sr	9215 Scott	573C	SEH
Yates Sr	3703 Sampson	533D	SEH
Young, E.M. Elem	3555 Bellfort	533U	SEH

ALDINE ISD

School or Facility Name	Address	Pg	Loc
A.I.S.D Resource Center	14909 Aldine Westfield Rd	373V	NEH
A.W. Jones Elem	7903 Forest Point Dr	334R	NCC
Administration Bldg	14910 Aldine Westfield Rd	373V	NEH
Aldine 9th Grade School	10650 North Frwy	412D	NCC
Aldine Athletic Stadium		412D	NEH
Aldine MS	14908 Aldine Westfield Rd	373V	NEH
Aldine Sr	11101 Airline	412D	NEH
Aldine Teachers Credit Union		373U	NCC
Anderson Academy	7401 Wheatley	412T	NEH
Bethune Academy	2500 S. Victory Dr	412S	NEH
Black Elem	160 Mill Stream	372Z	NEH
Bussey Elem	11555 Airline Dr	372Z	NEH
Calvert Elem	1925 Marvell	373R	NCC
Campbell Educational Ctr	1865 Aldine Bender	373Z	NCC
Caraway IM	3031 Ellington	411R	NWH
Carmichael Elem	6902 Silver Star	371W	NWC
Carroll, Inez Academy	423 W. Gulfbank	412H	NCC
Carter Academy	3111 Fallbrook Dr	411C	NWC
Carver HS	2100 S. Victory Dr	412S	NEH
Compass	1617-A Lauder Rd	413D	NCC
Conley Elem	3345 W. Greens Rd	371Q	NWC
Cypresswood Elem	6901 Cypresswood Point Ave	334L	NCC
Davis 9th Grade School	12211 Ella Blvd	372K	NWH
Davis HS	12525 Ella Blvd	372K	NWH
De Santiago Pre-K	1420 Aldine Meadow	373U	NCC
Drew Academy	1910 W. Little York Rd	412W	NWH
Dunn Clifford Elem	2003 W. W. Thorne	333S	NEH
Eckert IM	1430 Aldine Meadows Rd	373U	NCC
Eisenhower 9th Grade School	3550 W. Gulfbank	411Q	NWH
Eisenhower Sr	7922 Antoine	411Q	NWH
Ermel Elem	7103 Woodsman Trail	411N	NWC
Escamilla, Vera IM	5241 E. Mt. Houston Rd	414L	NCC
Francis, Thomas Elem	14815 Lee Rd	374V	NEH
Garcia-Leza EC / Pre K	5311 E. Mount Houston Rd	414M	NEH
Goodman Elem	9325 Deer Trail	412L	NWH
Grantham Academy	13300 Chrisman Rd	413G	NCC
Gray, Thomas Elem	700 West Rd	412B	NWC
Greenspoint Elem	18028 Chisholm Trail	373J	NCC
Hall Education Center	15014 Aldine-Westfield	373V	NCC
Hambrick MS	4600 Aldine Mail Rd	414L	NCC
Harris Academy	3130 Holder Forest Dr	411V	NWH
Hill IM	2625 W. Mount Houston	411M	NWC
Hinojosa Ec/Pk	1620 Lauder Rd	413D	NCC
Hoffman MS	6101 W. Little York	411X	NWH
Houston Academy IM	8103 Carver	412S	NWH
Johnson Elem	5801 Hamil Rd	414H	NCC
Jones EC / Pre K	8003 Forest Point Dr	334R	NCC
Keeble Ec/Pk	203 W. Gulfbank Rd	413N	NCC
Kujawa EC / Pre K	7111 Fallbrook Dr	371W	NWC
Kujawa Elem	7007 Fallbrook Dr	370X	NWC
Lane School	2001 Aldine Bender	373Z	NEH
Lewis MS	21255 W Hardy Rd	332R	NCC
MacArthur 9th Grade School	12111 Gloger Rd	414F	NCC
MacArthur Sr	4400 Aldine Mail Rd	414F	NCC
Magrill Elem	21701 Rayford Rd	333M	NCC
Marcella IM	16250 Cotillion Dr	373S	NEC
Mendel Elem	3735 Topping	414X	NEH
Nimitz 9th Grade School	2425 W. W. Thorne Dr	333S	NCC
Nimitz Sr	2005 W.W. Thorne Blvd	333S	NCC
Odom Elem	14701 Henry Rd	413B	NCC
Oleson Elem	12345 Vickery	414G	NCC
Orange Grove Elem	4514 Mt. Houston Rd	414K	NCC
Parker, Otice L. IM	19850 E. Hardy Rd	333S	NCC
Plummer MS	11429 Spears Rd	372P	NWC
Project Recovery	1617-A Lauder Rd	413D	NCC
Rayford IM	21919 Rayford Rd	333L	NCC
Raymond Academy	1605 Connorvale Rd.	413D	NCC
Reece Pre-K - K	2223 Esther Dr	412S	NWH
Reed Academy	1616 Lauder Rd	413D	NCC
Sammons, Gloria B. Elem	2301 Frick Rd	372W	NWC
Shotwell MS	6515 Trail Valley Way	371X	NWC
Smith Academy	5815 W. Little York	411Y	NWH
Spence Elem	1300 Gears Rd.	372P	NWH
Stehlik IM	400 West Rd	412C	NWC
Stephens Elem	2402 Aldine Mail Rd	414E	NCC
Stovall Academy	3025 Ellington	411R	NWH
Stovall, Thomas J. MS	11201 Aldine Dr	412D	NEH
Teague MS	21700 Rayford Rd	333M	NCC
Thompson Elem	220 Casa Grande	372Z	NEH
Victory Early College HS	2330 S. Victory	412S	NCC
Vines Ec/Pk	7220 Inwood Park	411V	NWH
W.W. Thorne Stadium	1865 Aldine Bender	373V	NCC
Wilson IM	3131 Fallbrook	411C	NWC
Worsham, Bill Elem	3007 Hartwick	414N	NCC

ALIEF ISD

School or Facility Name	Address	Pg	Loc
Administration Bldg	4250 Cook Rd	529E	SWH
Albright MS	6315 Winkleman	527H	SWC
Alexander Elem	8500 Brookwulf	528R	SWC
Alief ALC	4427 Belle Park Dr	529F	SWH
Alief Athletic Stadium Complex		529A	SWH
Alief MS	4415 Cook Rd	529E	SWH
Best Elem	10000 Centre Pkwy	529V	SWH
Boone Elem	11400 Bissonnet	529T	SWH
Budewig IM	12570 Richmond Ave	488Z	SWH
Bush Elem	9730 Stroud	529H	SWH
Chambers Elem	10700 Carvel Ln	529L	SWH
Chancellor Elem	4350 Boone Rd	529F	SWH
Collins Elem	9829 Town Park Dr	529H	SWH
Cummings Elem	10455 S. Kirkwood	529W	SWH
Elsik 9th Grade Center	6767 Dairy Ashford	528H	SWH
Elsik Sr	12601 High Star	528H	SWH
Hastings 9th Grade Center	6750 Cook	528H	SWH
Hastings Sr	4410 Cook Rd	528H	SWH
Hearne Elem	13939 Rio Bonito	528F	SWC
Heflin Elem	3303 Synott	488Y	SWC
Hicks Elem	8520 Hemlock Hill Dr	528P	SWC
Holmquist Elem	15040 Westpark Dr	527D	SWC
Holub MS	9515 S. Dairy Ashford	528V	SWH
Horn Elem	10734 Bissonnet	529U	SWH
Kennedy Elem	10200 Huntington Place	528V	SWH
Kerr HS	8150 Howell Sugarland Rd	528J	SWC
Killough MS	7600 Synott Rd	528L	SWH
Klentzman IM	11100 Stancliff	529X	SWH
Landis Elem	10255 Spice Ln	529Q	SWH
Liestman Elem	7610 Synott Rd	528L	SWH
Mahanay Elem	13215 High Star	528G	SWH
Martin Elem	11718 Hendon Ln	529J	SWH
Mata IM	9225 S. Dairy Ashford	528V	SWH
Miller IM	15025 Westpark	527D	SWC
O'Donnell MS	14041 Alief-Clodine	528F	SWC
Olle MS	9200 Boone Rd	529T	SWH
Outley Elem	12355 Richmond	488Z	SWH
Owens IM	6900 Turtlewood Dr	529L	SWH
Petrosky Elem	6703 Winkleman	527H	SWC
Rees Elem	16305 Kensley Dr	527B	SWC
Smith Elem	11300 Stancliff	529X	SWH
Sneed Elem	9855 Pagewood Ln	490W	SWH
Taylor HS	7555 Howell Sugar Land	528K	SWC
Youens Elem	12141 High Star	529E	SWH
Youngblood IM	8410 Dairyview Ln	528R	SWH

ALVIN ISD

School or Facility Name	Address	Pg	Loc
Glenn York Elem	2720 Kingsley Dr	612P	PL
Laura Ingalls Wilder Elem	2225 Kingsley Dr	612L	PL
Marek, Mary Elem	1947 Kirby	612M	PL
Nolan Ryan Jr	11500 Shadow Creek Pkwy	612H	PL
Red Duke Elem	2900 County Rd. 59	613S	MV
Wilder Elem	2225 Kingsley	612L	PL

BARBERS HILL ISD

School or Facility Name	Address	Pg	Loc
Barbers Hill Elem South	9600 Eagle Dr	463M	MB
Barbers Hill IM	9616 Eagle Dr	463M	MB
Barbers Hill Kinder Center	9600 Eagle Dr.	463M	MB
Barbers Hill MS North	9600 Eagle Dr	463M	MB
Barbers Hill Sr	9696 Eagle Dr	463M	MB
DAEP	9600 Eagle Dr.	463M	MB
Primary School	9600 Eagle Dr.	463M	MB

CHANNELVIEW ISD

School or Facility Name	Address	Pg	Loc
Aruirre Jr	15726 Wallisville Road	457V	CV
Administration Bldg	1403 Sheldon Rd	458T	CV
Apollo School	828 Sheldon Rd	498C	CV
Channelview HS	1100 Sheldon	458Y	CV
Cobb Elem	915 Dell Dale	498A	CV
Crenshaw Primary	16204 Wood Dr	458U	CV
De Zavala Elem	16150 2nd	498G	CV
Endeavor Learning Ctr	828 Sheldon Rd	498C	CV
Hamblen Elem	1019 Dell Dale	458W	CV
Harvey Brown Primary	16550 Wallisville Rd	458P	NEC
Johnson, Alice Jr	15500 Proctor	458X	CV
Kolarik Center, L.W.	1120 Sheldon Rd	458Y	CV
McMullan, F., Primary	1290 Dell Dale	458W	CV
Pre K & Day Care Center	828 Sheldon Rd	498C	CV
Schochler, Carroll Primary	910 Deer pass	498A	CV
Transportation Ctr	1407 Sheldon Rd	458X	CV

CLEAR CREEK ISD

School or Facility Name	Address	Pg	Loc
Administration Bldg	2425 E. Main	659B	LC
Armand Bayou Elem	16000 Hickory Knoll	618C	SEH
Bauerschlag Elem	2051 League City Pkwy	658U	LC
Bay, James Elem	1502 Bayport	620K	SB
Bayside IM	4430 Village Way	660K	LC
Brookside IM	3535 E. Parkwood	657C	FR
Brookwood Elem	16850 Middlebrook Dr	578Z	PA
Clear Brook HS	4607 F.M. 2351	617S	FR
Clear Creek IM	2451 E. Main St	659B	LC
Clear Creek Sr	2305 E. Main	659B	LC
Clear Falls HS	4380 Village Way	660K	LC
Clear Lake City Elem	1707 Fairwind	618K	SEH
Clear Lake IM	15545 El Camino Real	618K	SEH
Clear Lake Sr	2929 Bay Area Blvd	618H	SEH
Clear Path Alternative HS	400 S. Kansas	659J	LC
Clear Springs HS	501 Palomino Dr	658J	LC
Clear View HS	400 S. Walnut	618X	WB
Creekside IM	4320 W. Main	658N	LC
Falcon Pass Elem	2465 Falcon Pass Dr	618G	SEH
Ferguson, Lloyd R. Elem	1910 Compass Rose Blvd	619Z	LC
Gilmore Elem	3552 League City Pkwy	658S	LC
Goforth Elem	2610 Webster Rd	659L	LC
Greene, P.H., Elem	2903 Friendswood Link Rd	657C	SEH

School or Facility Name	Address	Pg	Loc
Hall, W.G. Elem	5931 Meadowside	657V	LC
Hyde Elem	3700 F.M. 518 East	660A	LC
La Vace Stewart Elem	330 F.M. 2094	620X	GCO
Landolt Elem	2104 Pilgrims Point	617Y	SEC
League City Elem	709 E. Wilkins	659J	GCO
League City IM	2588 Webster	659L	GCO
Margaret S. McWhirter Elem	300 Pennsylvania	618Y	WB
Mossman Elem	4050 Village Way	660K	LC
Ninth Grade Ctr - Clear Ck HS	2451 E. Main	659B	LC
Ninth Grade Ctr - Clear Lk HS	2903 Falcon Pass	618G	SEH
North Pointe Elem	3200 Almond Creek Dr	578W	SEH
Parr Elem	1315 hwy 3 South	659N	LC
Robinson Elem	451 Kirby Dr	619L	PA
Ross, J.H., Elem	2401 W. Main	658K	LC
Seabrook IM	2401 E. Meyer	620K	SB
Space Center IM	17400 Saturn Ln	618Q	SEH
Victory Lakes IM	2880 W. Walker	659W	LC
Ward, John F. Elem	1440 Bouldercrest Dr	618E	SEH
Weber Elem	11955 Blackhawk Blvd	616K	SEH
Wedgewood Elem	4000 Friendswood Link	657C	LC
Westbrook IM	302 W. El Dorado Blvd	617U	SHE
Whitcomb, G.H. Elem	900 Reseda Dr	618P	SEH
White, E.H. Elem	1708 Les Talley Dr	620E	EL

CONROE ISD

School or Facility Name	Address	Pg	Loc
Academy of Science & Technolog	27330 Oak Ridge School Rd	252A	SEM
Birnham Woods Elem	3110 Birnham Woods Dr	253T	SEM
Bradley Elem	4200 Falls Lake Drive	253T	SEM
Broadway Elem	2855 Spring Trls Bnd	293K	SEM
Buckalew Elem	4909 W. Alden Bridge Dr	216N	WD
Bush Elem	7420 Crownridge Dr	216R	WD
Collins IM	6020 Shadowbend Place	217X	WD
Coulson Tough K-6	11660 Crane Brook	215Y	SWM
Cox IM, Tom	3333 Waterbend Cove	293C	SEM
David Elem	5301 Shadowbend Place	251A	WD
Deretchin Elem	11000 Merit Okas Dr	215U	WD
Dolly Vogel IM	27100 Geffert Wright	252P	SEM
Ford Elem	25460 Richard Rd	252T	SEM
Galatas Elem	9001 Cochrans Crossing Dr	216U	WD
Glen Loch Elem	27505 Glen Loch Dr	251J	WD
Hailey Elem	12051 Sawmill Rd	251V	WD
Houser Elem	27370 Oak Ridge School Rd	252F	OR
Irons Jr	16780 Needham Rd	218Q	SEM
Kaufman Elem	31202 Aldine Westfield	253N	SEM
Knox Jr	12104 Sawmill Rd	251V	WD
Lamar Elem	1300 Many Pines	251M	WD
McCullough Jr	3800 S. Panther Creek Dr	251J	WD
Mitchell, George IM	6800 Alden Bridge	216L	WD
Oak Ridge Elem	19675 I-45 South	252A	SEM
Oak Ridge HS	27330 Oak Ridge School Rd	252A	OR
Patterson Elem	640 Beach Airport Rd	158V	NEM
Powell Elem	7332 Cochrans Crossing Dr	216V	WD
Ride Elem	4920 W. Panther Creek	251E	WD
Snyder Elem	28601 Birnham Woods Dr	293B	SEM
Sue Park Broadway Elem	2855 Spring Trails Bend	293F	SEM
The Woodlands College Park HS	3701 College Park Dr	217Q	SWM
Wilkerson IM	12312 Sawmill Rd	251V	WD
Woodlands 9th Grade	10010 Branch Crossing Dr	216J	WD
Woodlands HS	6101 Research Forest Dr	217S	WD
York Jr	27310 Oakridge School Rd	252A	SEM

CROSBY ISD

School or Facility Name	Address	Pg	Loc
Administration Bldg	706 Runneburg Rd	419H	CB
Barrett Primary	815 F.M. 1942	420S	CB
Cougar Stadium		419L	CB
Crosby Kindergarten	805 Runneburg Rd	419H	CB
Crosby MS	14703 F.M. 2100	419L	CB
Crosby Sr	333 Red Summit Dr	419L	CB
Drew Elem	223 Red Oak	419Y	CB
Instructional Annex	5910 Pecan	419D	CB
Newport Elem	430 N. Diamondhead Blvd	379T	NEC

CY-FAIR ISD

School or Facility Name	Address	Pg	Loc
Adam Elem	11303 Honeygrove Ln	368U	NWC
Adaptive Behavior Center	12508 Windfern Rd.	369U	NWC
Administration Bldg	12630 Windfern	369U	NWC
Alternative Learning Center, E.	12508 Windfern Rd.	369U	NWC
Alternative Learning Center, W.	19350 Rebel Yell	406V	NWC
Andre' Elem	8111 Fry Rd	407G	NWC
Anthony MS	10215 Greenhouse Rd	366Z	NWC
Aragon MS	16823 West Rd	407G	NWC
Arnold MS	11111 Telge Rd	368S	NWC
Ault Elem	21010 Maple Village Dr	326S	NWC
Bane Elem	5805 Kaiser	450B	NWH
Bang Elem	8900 Rio Grande	409G	NWC
Berry Center	8877 Barker Cypress	407A	NWC
Birkes Elem	8500 Queenston Blvd	407G	NWC
Black Elem	14155 Grant Rd	328T	NWC
Bleyl MS	10800 Mills Rd	369F	NWC
Bridgeland HS	10707 Mason Rd	365V	NWC
Campbell MS	11415 Bobcat Rd	369U	NWC
Carlton Pre-Vocational Center	16825 Spring Cypress Rd	367B	NWC
Cook MS	9111 Wheatland	409G	NWC
Copeland Elem	18018 Forest Heights	407K	NWC
Cypress Creek HS	9815 Grant Rd	369G	NWC
Cypress Fairbanks HS	22602 Hempstead Hwy	367R	NWC
Cypress Falls HS	9811 Huffmeister	368X	NWC
Cypress Lakes HS	5750 Greenhouse	406Z	NWC
Cypress Park HS	7425 Westgreen Blvd	406J	NWC
Cypress Ranch HS	10700 Fry Rd	366Q	NWC
Cypress Ridge HS	7900 N. Eldridge Pkwy	408M	NWC
Cypress Springs HS	7909 Fry Rd	406L	NWC
Cypress Woods HS	16825 Spring Cypress Rd	367F	CY
Danish Elem	11850 Fallbrook Dr	369S	NWC
Dean MS	14104 Reo	410X	NWH
Duryea, Dr. Peggy Bell Elem	20150 Arbor Creek	406Q	NWC
Emery Elem	19636 Plantation Myrtles	406Y	NWC
Emmott Elem	11750 Steepleway Blvd	409A	NWC
Farney Elem	14425 Barker-Cypress	327X	NWC
Fiest Elem	8425 Pine Falls	408E	NWC
Francone Elem	11250 Perry Rd	369U	NWC
Frazier Elem	8300 Little River Rd	410G	NWH
Gleason Elem	9203 Willowbridge Park Blvd	409H	NWC
Goodson MS	17333 Huffmeister	327T	NWC
Hairgrove Elem	7120 N. Eldridge Pkwy	408R	NWC
Hamilton Elem	12050 Kluge Rd	328Y	NWC
Hamilton MS	12330 Kluge Rd	328Y	NWC
Hancock Elem	13801 Schroeder Rd	369D	NWC
Hemmenway Elem	20400 West Little York Rd	406X	NWC
Holbrook Elem	6402 Langfield Rd	411W	NWH
Holmsley Elem	7315 Hudson Oak Dr	407K	NWC
Hoover Elem	6425 Greenhouse Rd	406V	NWC
Hopper MS	7811 Fry Rd	406L	NWC
Horne Elem	14950 W. Little York Rd	408T	NWC
Jersey Village Sr	7600 Solomon	409R	NWC
Jowell Elem	6355 Greenhouse Rd	406V	NWC
Kahla Ms	16212 W. Little York	407V	NWC
Keith, Gwen Wyman Elem	20550 Fairfield Green	326N	NWC
Kirk Elem	12421 Tanner Rd	449A	NWC
Labay MS	15435 Willow River Dr	408E	NWC
Lamkin Elem	11521 Telge Rd	368N	NWC
Langham Creek HS	17610 F.M. 529	407P	NWC
Lee Elem	12900 W Little York Rd	407V	NWC
Lieder Elem	17003 Keith Harrow Blvd	447D	NWH
Lowery Elem	15950 Ridge Park	408J	NWC
Maintenance Ctr		369U	NWC
Matzke Elem	10002 Mills Road	369L	NWC
McFee Elem	19315 Plantation Cove	406Z	NWC
Metcalf Elem	6100 Queenston	407U	NWC
Millsap Elem	12424 Huffmeister	368K	NWC
Moore Elem	13734 Lakewood Forest Dr	369A	NWC
Owens Elem	7939 Jackrabbit	408L	NWC
Pope Elem	19019 N. Bridgeland Lake Pkwy	366E	NWC
Post Elem	7600 Equador	409R	NWC
Postma Elem	18425 West Rd	407A	NWC
Pridgeon Stadium	11355 Falcon Rd	369U	NWH
Reed Elem	8700 Tami Renee Ln	410K	NWC
Rennell Elem	19500 Tuckerton Blvd	366Z	NWC
Reo Administrative Annex	14103 Reo	410X	NWH
Robinson, M. Elem	4321 Westfield Village	446F	NWC
Robison Elem	13600 Skinner Rd	367F	NWC
Rodeo Arena	Telge Rd	368N	NWC
Salyards MS	21757 Fairfield Place Dr	325R	NWC
Salyards MS	21757 Fairfield Place Dr	325R	NWC
Sampson Elem	16002 Coles Crossing	367G	NWC
Sheridan Elem	19790 Keith Harrow Blvd	446C	NWC
Smith MS	19325 Cypress N. Houston	366A	NWC
Spillane MS	17500 Jarvis	367F	CY
Swenke Elem	22400 Fairfield Place Dr	325M	NWC
Thornton MS	19802 Keith Harrow Blvd	446C	NWC
Tipps Elem	5611 Queenston Blvd	407Y	NWC
Transportation Ctr	11430 Falcon	369S	NWC
Truitt MS	6600 Addicks-Satsuma	408T	NWC
Walker Elem	6424 Settlers Village	406T	NWC
Warner Elem	19545 Cypress N. Houston	366Z	NWC
Watkins MS	4800 Cairnvillage	447D	NWH
Wells Elem	10607 Mason Road	365V	NWC
Willbern Elem	10811 Goodspring Dr	369Z	NWC
Wilson Elem	18015 Keith Harrow	447B	NWH
Windfern HS	12630 Windfern Rd	369U	NWC
Woodard Elem	17501 Cypress N. Houston	367P	NWC
Yeager Elem	13615 Champions Frst Dr	330Y	NWC

DEER PARK ISD

School or Facility Name	Address	Pg	Loc
Abshire Stadium		538P	DP
Administration Bldg	203 Ivy	538G	DP
Bonnette Jr	5010 Pasadena Blvd	538T	DP
Carpenter, W.A. Elem	5002 Pasadena Blvd	538S	DP
Dabbs Elem	302 E. Lambuth	538Y	DP
Deepwater Elem	309 Glenmore	537G	PA
Deepwater Jr	501 Glenmore	537L	PA
Deer Park Elem	2920 Luella	538Q	DP
Deer Park Jr	410 E. 9th	538L	DP
Deer Park Sr, N. Campus	402 Ivy	538L	DP
Deer Park Sr, S. Campus	710 W. San Augustine	538P	DP
Early Childhood Center	401 Glenmore	537G	PA
Fairmont Elem	4315 Heathfield	578E	PA
Fairmont Jr	4911 Holly Bay Ct	578F	PA
Parkwood Elem	404 Parkwood	537M	PA
San Jacinto Elem	1302 E. 13TH	538L	DP
Wolters Accelerated HS	400 Ivy	538G	DP

DICKINSON ISD

School or Facility Name	Address	Pg	Loc
Barber MS	5651 FM 517 East	660X	DI
Dickinson HS	3800 Baker Dr	660X	DI
Dunbar MS	2901 23rd St	659Y	DI
Silbernagel Elem	4201 25th St	659Z	GCO

FORT BEND ISD

School or Facility Name	Address	Pg	Loc
Armstrong Elem	3440 Independence	569Y	MC
Barbara Jordan Elem	17800 West Oak Village	527E	NEF
Barrington Place Elem	2100 Squire Dobbins	568D	SG
Blue Ridge Elem	6241 McHard Rd	611F	SWH
Briargate Elem	15817 Blue Ridge Rd	571W	SWH
Crocket MS, David	19001 Beechnut	526P	NEF
Drabek Elem	11325 Lake Woodbridge	568A	NEF
Dulles Elem	630 Dulles Ave	569N	SF
Dulles HS	550 Dulles Ave	569N	SF
Dulles MS	500 Dulles Ave	569N	SF
Fleming Elem	14850 Bissonnet	527V	NEF
Fort Bend Athletic Complex	16403 Lexington Blvd	568Y	NEF
George Bush HS	6707 FM 1464	527E	NEF
Glover Elem	1510 Columbia Blue Dr	610A	MC
Highlands Elem	2022 Colonist Park	568Z	SG
Hightower HS	3333 Hurricane Ln	610Z	MC
Hodges Bend MS	16510 Bissonnet	527P	NEF
Holley, Mary Austin Elem	16655 Bissonnet	527T	NEF
Hunters Glen Elem	8295 Independence Blvd	570Y	MC
Jones, E.A. Elem	302 Martin Ln	570N	MC
Kempner Stadium	223 Fifth	568K	SG
Lakeview Elem	314 Lakeview Dr	568K	SG
Lantern Lane Elem	3323 Mission Valley	610F	MC
M.R. Wood High School	139 Avenue E	568J	SG
Marshall HS	1227 Texas Pkwy	570T	SF
McAuliffe, Christa MS	16650 S. Post Oak	611B	SWH
Meadows Elem	12037 Pender Ln	569A	MD
Mission Bend Elem	16200 Beechnut	527K	NEF
Mission Glen Elem	16053 Mission Glen	527Q	NEF
Mission West Elem	7325 Clodine-Reddick Rd	527J	NEF
Missouri City MS	202 Martin Ln	570N	MC
Oakland Elem	4455 Waterside Estates Dr	526W	NEF
Parks, Rosa Elem	19101 Chimney Rock	611S	SWH
Progressive HS	1555 Independence Rd	570X	MC
Ridgegate Elem	6015 W. Ridge Creek Dr	571X	SWH
Ridgemont Elem	4910 Raven Ridge Dr	611C	SWH
Sequin Elem	7817 Grand Mission Blvd	526L	NEF
Sugar Land MS	321 7th	568K	SG
Sugar Mill Elem	13707 Jess Pirtle	568K	SG
Technical Education	540 Dulles Avenue	569N	MC
Townewest Elem	13927 Old Richmond Rd	528T	NEF
Travis HS	11111 Harlem Rd	526Y	NEF
Willowridge HS	16301 Chimney Rock	611B	SWH

FRIENDSWOOD ISD

School or Facility Name	Address	Pg	Loc
Administration Bldg	302 Laurel Dr	656D	FR
Bales IM	211 Stadium	656C	FR
Cline Elem	505 Briarmeadow	656H	FR
Football Stadium		656G	FR

School or Facility Name	Address	Pg	Loc
Friendswood Jr	1000 Manison Parkway	657N	FR
Friendswood Sr	702 Greenbriar	656G	FR
Friendswood Transportation Ctr	400 Woodlawn	656D	FR
Westwood Elem	506 W. Edgewood Ave	656C	FR
Windsong IM	2100 W. Parkwood	656U	FR

GALENA PARK ISD

School or Facility Name	Address	Pg	Loc
Accelerated Ctr for Educ.	13601 Woodforest Blvd	497B	NEC
Becker Early Childhood Cntr	1908 2nd St	496W	GP
Center for Success	13838 Woodforest	497B	NEC
Cimarron Elem	816 Cimarron	497E	NEC
Cloverleaf Elem	1035 Frankie	497F	NEC
Cobb 6th Grade Campus	6722 Uvalde	457P	NEC
Cunningham MS	14110 Wallisville Rd	456Z	NEC
Galena Park Area Voc.	1001 Parkside	496S	GP
Galena Park Elem	401 N. Main	496W	GP
Galena Park High School	1000 Keene	496S	GP
Galena Park MS	400 Keene	496W	GP
Galena Park Transportation		496H	NEC
Green Valley Elem	13350 Woodforest	497A	NEC
Havard Elem	15150 Wallisville Rd	457U	NEC
Jacinto City Elem	10910 Wiggins	496J	JC
MacArthur Elem	1801 N. Main	496S	GP
Normandy Crossing Elem	12500 Normandy Crossing	496H	NEH
North Shore Elem	14310 Duncannon	497C	NEC
North Shore High School	13501 Holly Park	497B	NEC
North Shore MS	120 Castlegory	457U	NEC
North Shore Sr	353 N. Castlegory	457T	NEC
Purple Sage Elem	6500 Purple Sage	457N	NEC
Pyburn Elem	12302 Coulson	496L	NEC
Sam Houston Elem	4101 E. Sam Houston Pkwy N	497D	NEC
Tice, Kenneth Elem	14120 Wallisville	456V	NEC
Williamson Elem	6720 New Forest Pkwy	457P	NEC
Woodland Acres Elem	12936 Sarah's Ln	496M	NEC
Woodland Acres MS	12947 Myrtle Ln	496M	NEC
Zotz Education Center	13801 Holly Park	497B	NEC

GOOSE CREEK ISD

School or Facility Name	Address	Pg	Loc
Alamo Elem	302 YMCA Dr	501Q	BT
Alternative Learning Program	4026 Decker Dr	500M	BT
Ashbel Smith Elem	403 E. James	501X	BT
Austin Elem	3022 E. Massey Tompkins	502K	BT
Banuelos Elem	7770 Eastpoint Blvd	461S	NEC
Baytown Jr	7707 Bayway Dr	500F	BT
Bowie Elem	2200 Clayton	502S	BT
Cedar Bayou Jr	2610 Elvinta	502P	BT
Clark Elem	6033 N. Hwy 146	502G	BT
Community Guidance Center	401 Jones Rd	459V	HG
Community Guidance Center	4026 1/2 Decker Dr	500L	BT
Crockett Elem	4500 Barkaloo	501H	BT
De Zavala Elem	305 Tri-City Beach Rd	541D	BT
Early College HS	200 Lee Rd	501X	BT
Gentry Jr	1919 E. Archer Rd	502A	BT
George Washington Carver Elem	600 S. Pruett	541B	BT
Goose Creek Memorial HS	6001 E. Wallisville	461Q	NEC
Harlem Elem	3333 I-10	460Y	MN
Highlands Elem	200 E. Wallisville Rd	459R	NEC
Highlands Jr	1212 E. Wallisville Rd	460N	MN
Hopper Primary	405 E. Houston	459R	NEC
Horace Mann Jr	310 S. Hwy 146	541D	BT
Hyland, Peter E. Center	1906 Decker Dr	501T	BT
Lamar Elem	816 N. Pruett	501Y	BT
Lee, Robert E. Sr	1809 Market	501W	BT
Memorial Stadium		501X	BT
Pumphrey Elem	4901 Fairway Dr	500M	BT
San Jacinto Elem	2615 Virginia	540D	BT
Special Assignment Clinic	607 W. Baker	501K	BT
Stallworth Stadium		502A	BT
Sterling, Ross Sr	300 W. Baker Rd	501L	BT
Stuart Career Ctr	300 YMCA Dr	501Q	BT
Travis Elem	100 Robin Rd	500F	BT
Walker Elem, Victoria	4711 Seabird	461T	NEC

HUFFMAN ISD

School or Facility Name	Address	Pg	Loc
Administration Bldg	24302 F.M. 2100	339K	NEC
Ben Bowen Early Childhood	24403 E. Lake Houston Pkwy	338M	NEH
Copeland Elem	24405 E. Lake Houston Pkwy	338M	NEH
Hargrave Hs	25400 Willy Ln	339H	NEC
Huffman Intermediate	24403 E. Lake Houston Pkwy	338M	NEH
Huffman MS	3407 Huffman-Eastgate	339H	NEC
Jack Spence Stadium	24403 E. Lake Houston Pkwy	338M	NEH
Transportation	3403 Huffman-Eastgate	339H	NEC

HUMBLE ISD

School or Facility Name	Address	Pg	Loc
Administration Bldg	20200 Eastway Village Dr	335V	HM
Atascocita HS	13300 Will Clayton Parkway	377B	NEC
Atascocita MS	18810 W. Lake Houston Pkwy	337Z	NEC
Atascocita Springs Elem	13515 Valley Lodge Pkwy	377K	NEC
Bear Branch Elem	3500 Garden Lake Dr	296Z	NEC
Career & Technology Center	9155 Will Clayton Pkwy	376A	HM
Charles Street Stadium	Charles	335V	HM
Community Learning Center	18901 Timber Forest	337W	NEC
Creekwood MS	3603 Lake Houston Pkwy	297X	NEC
Deerwood Elem	2920 Forest Garden Dr	297Y	NEC
Eagle Springs Elem	12500 Will Clayton Pkwy	377A	NEC
Elm Grove Elem	2815 Clear Ridge	297S	NEC
Fall Creek Elem	14435 Mesa Rd	375Y	NEC
Fields, Jack M. Elem	2505 S. Houston Ave	375H	HM
Foster Elem	1800 Trailwood Village Dr	336C	NEC
Greentree Elem	3502 Brook Shadow	297X	NEC
Hidden Hollow Elem	4104 Appalachian Trail	297T	NEC
Humble Elem	20252 Fieldtree	335Q	HM
Humble ISD Football Stadium		376A	HM
Humble MS	11207 Will Clayton Pkwy	376D	NEC
Humble Sr	1700 Wilson Rd	376A	HM
Kingwood MS	2407 Pine Terrace	296Z	NEH
Kingwood Park HS	4015 Woodland Hills Dr	296V	NEC
Kingwood Sr	2701 Kingwood Dr	337A	NEC
Lakeland Elem	1500 Montgomery Ln	335Z	HM
Lakeshore Elem	13333 Breakwater Path	377L	NEC
Maplebrook Elem	7935 Farmingham Rd	337Z	NEC
North Belt Elem	8105 North Belt Dr	375U	NEC
Oak Forest Elem	6400 Kingwood Glen	337X	NEH
Oaks Elem	5858 Upper Lake Dr	337T	NEC
Park Lakes Elem	4400 Wilson Rd	376N	NEC
Pine Forest Elem	19702 W. Lake Houston Pkwy	337V	NEC
Quest HS	18901 Timber Forest	337W	NEC
Ridge Creek Elem	15201 Woodland Hills Dr	376V	NEC
River Pines Elem	2400 Cold River Dr	376A	HM
Riverwood MS	2910 High Valley	297Z	NEC
Shadow Forest Elem	2300 Mills Branch Dr	297V	NEC
Sterling MS, Ross	1131 Wilson Rd	376A	HM
Summer Creek HS	14000 Weckford Blvd	376Z	NEC
Summerwood Elem	14000 Summerwood lakes	377X	NEC
Timbers Elem	6910 Lonesome Woods Trail	337Y	NEC
Timberwood MS	18450 Timber Forest	337W	NEC
Transportation & Maint Ctr	1703 Wilson Rd	376A	HM
Whispering Pines Elem	17321 Woodland Hills Dr	376H	HM
Willow Creek Elem	2002 Willow Terrace	338A	NEC
Woodcreek MS	14600 Woodson Park Dr	376Z	NEC
Woodland Hills Elem	2222 Tree Ln	296Z	NEC

KATY ISD

School or Facility Name	Address	Pg	Loc
Alexander-Roosevelt Elem	6161 S. Fry Rd	525C	NEF
Bear Creek Elem	4815 Hickory Downs	448A	NWH
Beckendorff JR	8200 South Fry Rd	485W	NEF
Beck-Rodger & Ellen Jr	5200 S. Fry Rd	525D	NEF
Bethke Elem	4535 E. Ventana Pkwy	445B	NWC
Cardiff Jr	3900 Dayflower	446M	NWC
Cimarron Elem	1100 S. Peek Rd	485G	SWC
Cinco Ranch HS	23440 Cinco Ranch Blvd	485P	NEF
Cinco Ranch Jr	23420 Cinco Ranch Blvd	485P	NEF
Creech, Betty Sue Elem	5905 S. Mason	526A	NEF
Davidson Elem	26906 Pine Mill Ranch Dr	484W	NEF
Exley Elem	21800 Westheimer Parkway	485V	NEF
Fielder Elem	2100 Greenway Village Dr	485Q	NEF
Franz Elem	2751 Westgreen Blvd	446S	NWC
Garland McMeans Jr	21000 Westheimer Pkwy	486S	NEF
George Bush Soccer Complex		486T	SWH
Golbow Elem	3535 Lakes of Bridgewater	446J	NWC
Griffin Elem	7800 S. Fry Rd	485W	NEF
Hayes Elem	21203 Park Timbers	486J	SWH
Holland Elem	23720 Seven Meadows	525E	NEF
Hutsell, Zelma Elem	5360 Franz Rd	444U	KT
Jenks Elem	27602 Westridge Creek Ln	484N	NEF
Katy Elem	5726 George Bush Avenue	444Y	KT
Katy HS	6331 Highway Blvd	484A	KT
Katy Jr	5350 Franz Rd	444U	KT
Kilpatrick Elem	626 Danover	484C	KT
King Elem	1901 Charlton House Ln	445S	NWC
Mayde Creek Elem	2698 Greenhouse Rd	446V	KT
Mayde Creek HS	19202 Groeschke	447S	NWH
Mayde Creek Jr	2700 Greenhouse Rd	446R	KT
McDonald Jr	3635 Lakes of Bridgewater	446J	NWC
McRoberts Elem	3535 N. Fry Rd	446L	NWC
Memorial Parkway Elem	21603 Park Tree Ln	486E	SWC
Memorial Parkway Jr	21203 Highland Knoll	486J	SWC
Miller Vocational School	1734 Katyland Dr	444V	KT
Morton Ranch Elem	2502 Mason Rd	446N	NWC
Morton Ranch JR	2498 N Mason Rd	446N	NWC
Morton Ranch SR	2100 Franz Rd	445V	NWC
Nottingham Country Elem	20500 Kingsland Blvd	486B	SWC
O.A.C. Center	1732 Katyland Dr	444V	KT
Pattison Elem	19910 Stonelodge	486L	SWC
Rhodes, Jack F. Mem. Stadium	1733 Katy-Fort Bend	444V	KT
Rylander Elem	24831 Westheimer Parkway	485S	NEF
Schmalz Elem	18605 Green Land Way	447J	NWC
Seven Lakes HS	9251 South Fry Rd	524D	NEF
Seven Lakes Jr	6026 Katy-Gaston Rd	524D	NEF
Shafer Elem	5150 Ranch Point Dr	524A	NEF
Stanley Elem	26633 Cinco Terrace Dr	524B	NEF
Stephens Elem	2715 Fry Rd	446U	NWC
Stockdick Jr	4777 Peek Rd	445B	NWC
Sundown Elem	20100 Saums Rd	446T	KT
Taylor, James E., HS	20700 Kingsland Blvd	486B	SWC
Tays Jr	26721 Hawks Prairie Blvd	484T	NEF
Tompkins HS	4400 Falcon Landing Blvd	484U	NEF
Transportation & Maint Ctr		444U	KT
West Memorial Elem	22605 Provincial Blvd	485C	SWC
West Memorial Jr	22311 Provincial Blvd	485C	SWC
Williams, James E. Elem	3900 S. Peek Rd	485U	NEF
Wilson Elem	5200 Falcon Landing	484X	NEF
Winborn Elem	22555 Prince George	445U	NWC
Wolfe Elem	502 Addicks-Howell Rd	488A	SWH
Woodcreek Elem	1155 Woodcreek Bend Ln	484F	KT
Woodcreek Jr	1801 Woodcreek Bend Ln	484E	KT

KLEIN ISD

School or Facility Name	Address	Pg	Loc
Administration Bldg	7200 Spring Cypress Rd	330B	NWC
Benfer Elem	18027-B Kuykendahl	331F	NWC
Benignus Elem	7225 Alvin A. Klein	290U	NWC
Blackshear Elem	11211 Lacey Rd	329F	NWC
Brill Elem	9102 Herts Rd	330S	NWC
Doerre IM	18218 Theiss Mail Rd	330E	NWC
Ehrhardt Elem	6603 Rosebrook Ln	330C	NWC
Eiland Elem	6700 N. Klein Circle Dr	411J	NWC
Epps Island Elem	7403 Smiling Wood Ln	411A	NWC
Frank Elem	9225 Crescent Clover	289Y	NWC
French Elem	5802 W. Rayford	250V	NWC
Greenwood Forest Elem	12100 Misty Valley	370H	NWC
Hassler Elem	9325 Lochlea Ridge Dr	329H	NWC
Haude Elem	3111 Louetta Rd	291Z	NWC
Hildebrandt IM	22800 Hildebrandt Rd	290G	NWC
Kaiser Elem	13430 Bammel-N. Houston	371E	NWC
Kleb IM	7425 Louetta Rd	330L	NWC
Klein ALC	16503 Stuebner-Airline	330Q	NWC
Klein Cain HS	10201 Spring Cypress	329L	NWC
Klein Collins HS	20811 Ella Blvd	291X	NWC
Klein Forest Sr	11400 Misty Valley	371E	NWC
Klein IM	4710 W. Mt Houston Rd	411L	NWC
Klein Oak Sr	22603 Northcrest Dr	290G	NWC
Klein Sr	16715 Stuebner Airline	330L	NWC
Klenk Elem	6111 Bourgeois Rd	370M	NWC
Kohrville Elem	11600 Woodland Shore	329A	NWC
Krahn Elem	9502 Eday	329R	NWC
Kreinhop Elem	20820 Ella Blvd	291U	NWC
Krimmel IM	7070 FM 2920	290P	NWC
Kuehnle Elem	5510 Winding Ridge Dr	330H	NWC
Lemm Elem	19034 Joan Leigh Dr	332F	NCC
Mahaffey Elem	10255 Mahaffey Rd	289G	NWC
McDougle El	10410 Kansack Ln	370Z	NWC
Metzler Elem	8500 West Rayford	290A	NWC
Mittelstadt Elem	7525 Kleingreen	330Q	NWC
Mueller Elem	7074 FM 2920	290P	NWC
Nitsch Elem	4702 W. Mt Houston Rd	411L	NWC
Northampton Elem	6404 Root Rd	290G	NWC
Roth Elem	21623 Castlemont	291S	NWC
Schindewolf IM	20903 Ella Blvd	291U	NEC
Schultz Elem	7920 Willow Forest	290E	NWC
Strack IM	18027-S Kuykendahl Rd	331F	NWC
Theiss Elem	17510 Theiss Mail Rd	330K	NWC
Ulrich IM	10103 Spring Cypress Rd	329L	NWC
Vistas HS	12550 Bammel N. Houston	371J	NWC
Wunderlich IM	11800 Misty Valley	370H	NWC
Zwink Elem	22200 Frassati Way	291K	NWC

LAMAR CONS. ISD

School or Facility Name	Address	Pg	Loc
Adolphus Elem	7910 Winston Ranch Pkwy	525Z	NEF
Bentley Elem	9910 FM 359	524S	NWF
Hubenak Elem	11344 Rancho Bella Pkwy	524M	NEF
McNeill Elem	7300 S. Mason Rd	526J	NEF

LA PORTE ISD

School or Facility Name	Address	Pg	Loc
Administration Bldg	1002 San Jacinto	580C	LP
Baker, James H. 6th Grade	9800 Spencer Hwy	579A	LP
Bayshore Elem	800 McCabe Rd	580K	LP
College Park Elem	4315 Luella	539Y	LP
DeWalt Campus	401 N. 2nd	540Y	LP
Heritage Elem	4301 E. Blvd	538Z	DP
LaPorte Elem	725 S. Broadway	580C	LP
LaPorte Jr	401 S. Broadway	580C	LP
LaPorte Sr	301 E. Fairmont Pkwy	580C	LP
Lomax Elem	10615 N. Avenue L	539U	LP
Lomax Jr	9801 N. Avenue L	539S	LP
Reid, Jennie Elem	10001 W. Fairmont Pkwy	579B	LP
Rizzuto Elem	3201 Farrington	579C	LP

MAGNOLIA ISD

School or Facility Name	Address	Pg	Loc
Branch Elem	8909 FM 1488	215J	SWM
Bear Branch Jr	31310 F.M. 2978	215Q	SWM
Bear Branch Jr 6th Grade	8040 Kenlake	215Q	SWM
Ellisor, Tom R. Elem	33040 Egypt Ln	215M	WD
Lyon, J.L. Elem	27035 Nichols Sawmill Rd	246N	MG
Nichols Sawmill Elem	28750 Nichols Sawmill	246E	SWM
Smith, Cedric Elem	28747 Hardin Store Rd	248D	SWM
9th Grade Campus	22500 Eagle Dr	256V	SEM

NEW CANEY ISD

School or Facility Name	Address	Pg	Loc
Administration Bldg	21584 Loop 494	256U	SEM
Aikin Elem	600 Dogwood Ln	257D	SEM
Bens Branch Elem	24160 Briar Berry Ln	295H	SEM
Crippen Elem	18690 Cumberland	255T	SEM
Keefer Crossing MS	20350 F.M. 1485	256L	SEM
Kings Manor Elem	21111 Royal Crossing	296W	SEM
Learning Center, The	20419 F.M. 1485, W.	256L	SEM
Maint Trans Bldg	668 Loop 494	256R	SEM
New Caney 6th Grade Campus	22784 Hwy 59 S	296B	SEM
New Caney Elem	20501 F.M. 1485	256L	SEM
New Caney HS	21650 Loop 494	256U	SEM
Porter Elem	22256 Ford Rd	296K	SEM
Porter HS	22625 Sandy Ln	255Y	SEM
Six Grade Campus	Opening Fall 2007	256U	SEM
Sorters Mill Elem	23300 Sorters Rd	295C	SEM
Valley Ranch Elem	21700 Valley Ranch Crossing Dr	256X	SEM
White Oak MS	24161 Briar Berry Ln	295M	SEM

PASADENA ISD

School or Facility Name	Address	Pg	Loc
Administration Annex		536G	PA
Administration Bldg	1515 Cherrybrook	537S	PA
Atkinson Elem	9602 Kingspoint	576S	PA
Auxilary Stadium		537X	PA
Bailey Elem	2707 Lafferty	536Z	PA
Beverly Hills IM	11111 Beamer	576T	SEH
Bondy IM	5101 Keith Rd	577G	PA
Burnett Elem	11825 Teaneck	616D	SEH
Bush, Laura Elem	9100 Blackhawk	575V	SEH
Career & Technical HS	1846 E. Sam Houston Pkwy	537V	PA
Challenger IM	11111 Beamer	576X	SEH
Community Evening School	4949 Burke	577K	PA
De Zavala 5th Grade	101 E. Jackson	536G	PA
Dobie, J. Frank Hs	10220 Blackhawk	615D	SEH
Fisher Elem	2920 Watters	537X	PA
Football Stadium		537W	PA
Frazier Elem	10503 Hughes Rd	616B	SEH
Freeman Elem	2323 Theta	576F	SEH
Gardens Elem	1105 E. Harris	536M	PA
Garfield Elem	10301 Hartsook	576K	SEH
Genoa Elem	12900 Almeda-Genoa	576R	SEH
Golden Acres Elem	5232 Sycamore	537Y	PA
Guidance Center	3010 Bayshore	537W	PA
Jackson IM	1020 E. Thomas	536M	PA
Jensen Elem	3514 Tulip	577B	PA
Jessup Elem	9301 Almeda-Genoa	575R	SEH
Keller MS	3102 San Augustine	537Q	PA
Kruse Elem	400 Park Ln	536G	PA
Lomax MS	1519 Genoa Red-Bluff	577K	PA
Matthys Elem	1500 Main	576A	SH
McMasters Elem	1011 Bennett Dr	537M	PA
Meador Elem	10701 Seaford	576T	SEH
Melillo MS	9220 Hughes Rd	615H	SEC
Miller, Vincent W. IM	1002 Farimont Pkwy	576H	SEH
Milstead MS	338 Gilpin	576L	SEH
Moore Elem	8880 Southbluff	615D	SEC
Morales Elem	305 W. Harris	536L	PA
Morris 5th Grade Cntr	10415 Fuqua	576T	SEH
Park View IM	3003 Dabney	537X	PA
Parks Elem	3302 San Augustine	537Q	PA
Pasadena Memorial High	4410 Crenshaw Rd	577K	PA
Pasadena Sr	206 S. Shaver	536G	PA
Pearl Hall Elem	1504 9th St	576C	SEH
Pomeroy Elem	920 Burke Rd	537K	PA
Queens IM	1112 Queens Rd	536T	PA
Red Bluff Elem	416 Bearle	537J	PA
Richey Elem	610 S. Richey	536K	PA
Roberts MS	13402 Conklin Ln	577S	SHE
Sam Rayburn Hs	2121 Cherrybrook Ln	537T	PA
San Jacinto IM	3600 Red Bluff	537Q	PA
Schneider, Rick MS	8920 Easthaven	575H	SEH
Shaw MS	1201 Houston Ave	537N	PA
Skill Center	4320 Crenshaw	577F	PA
Smith, L. F. Elem	1401 Avenue A	536Y	PA
Smythe, Mae Elem	2202 Pasadena Blvd	537T	PA
South Belt Elem	1801 Riverstone Ranch	616E	SEH
South Houston Elem	900 Main	536W	PA
South Houston IM	900 College	576A	SEH
South Houston Sr	3820 S. Shaver	576C	SEH
South Shaver Elem	2020 S. Shaver	536U	PA
Southmore IM	2000 Patricia Ln	537S	PA
Sparks, Genevieve Elem	2503 E. Southmore	537P	PA
Stuchbery Elem	11210 Hughes Rd	616C	SEH
Teague, Carol Elem	4200 Crenshaw Rd	577K	SEH
Tegeler Career Center	4949 Burke	577K	PA
Thompson IM	11309 Sagedowne	616C	SEH
Turner Elem	4333 Lily	577G	PA
Williams Elem	1522 Scarborough	536P	PA
Young, Adella Elem	4221 Fox Meadow	576H	PA

PEARLAND ISD

School or Facility Name	Address	Pg	Loc
Administration Bldg	2337 N. Galveston Ave	615K	PL
Alexander MS	3001 Old Alvin Rd	615T	PL
Carleston Elem	3010 Harkey	614Q	PL
Challenger Elem	9434 Hughes Ranch Rd	613L	PL
Cockrell, Barbara Elem	3500 McHard rd	615F	PL
Glenda Dawson HS	2050 Cullen Blvd	613H	PL
Harris Elem	2314 Schleider Dr	615L	PL
Jamison MS	2506 Woody Rd	614R	PL
Lawhon Elem	5810 Brookside	614B	BK
Magnolia Elem	5350 Magnolia	614V	PL
Massey Ranch Elem	3900 Manvel Rd	614W	PL
Miller Jr High, Berry	3301 Manvel Rd	614T	PL
Pace Alternate	2314 Old Alvin Rd	615K	PL
Pearland Jr High East	2315 Old Alvin Rd	615K	PL
Pearland Jr High South	4719 Bailey Rd	615W	PL
Pearland Jr High West	2337 N. Galveston Ave	615K	PL
Pearland Sr (North & South)	3775 S. Main	615X	PL
Presner Stadium		615K	PL
Robert Turner HS	4717 Bailey Rd	615W	PL
Rogers Ms	3121 Manvel Rd	614P	PL
Rustic Oak Elem	1302 Rustic Ln	616W	NEB
Sablatura MS	2201 N. Galveston Rd	615K	PL
Searcy Ninth Grade, Sheryl	3775 South Main	615X	PL
Shadycrest Elem	2405 Shadybend	615V	PL
Silvercrest Elem	3003 Southwyek Pkwy	613T	PL
Silverlake Elem	2550 C.R. 90	613W	NEB

SHELDON ISD

School or Facility Name	Address	Pg	Loc
Administration Bldg	1411 C.E. King Pkwy	456G	NEC
Carroll Elem	10210 C.E. King Pkwy	416Z	NEC
Crenshaw Stadium		456D	NEC
King, C.E. MS	8530 C.E. King Pkwy	456D	NEC
King, C.E. Sr	8540 C.E. King Pkwy	456D	NEC
Monahan Elem	8901 Deep Valley	456D	NEC
Null, Michael R. Elem	12117 Garrett Rd	416Q	NEC
Royalwood Elem	7715 Royalwood	457J	NEC
Sheldon Early Childhood	17010 Beaumont Hwy	418X	NEC
Sheldon Elem	17203 Hall-Sheppard	418X	NEC
Stephanie Cravens Academy Elem	13210 Tidwell	457A	NEC

SPRING ISD

School or Facility Name	Address	Pg	Loc
Administration Bldg	16717 Ella Blvd	332N	NWC
Anderson Elem	6218 Lynngate Dr	334F	NCC
Bailey MS	3377 James Leo Dr.	293U	NCC
Bammel Elem	17309 Red Oak Dr	332J	NWC
Bammel MS	16711 Ella	332S	NWC
Beneke Elem	3840 Briarchase Dr	371B	NWC
Booker, Carolee Elem	22352 Imperial Valley Rd	332L	NCC
Burchett Elem	26000 Cypresswood	293T	NCC
Clark Elem	12625 River Laurel	372E	NWC
Clark IM	1825 Rushworth	372E	NWC
Claughton MS	3000 Spears Rd	371G	NWC
Cooper Elem	18665 Imperial Valley Dr	372D	NCC
DeKaney HS	22351 Imperial Valley Dr.	332L	NCC
Dueitt MS	1 Eagle Crossing	333D	NCC
Eickenroht Elem	15252 Grand Point Dr	332X	NWC
Heritage Elem	12255 T.C. Jester Blvd	371H	NWC
Hirsch Elem	2633 Trailing Vine Rd	333A	NCC
Hoyland Elem	2200 Wittershaw Dr	372B	NWC
Jenkins Elem	4615 Reynaldo	333D	NCC
Lewis Elem	3230 Spears Rd	371G	NWC
Link Elem	2815 Ridge Hollow	371M	NWC
Major Elem	900 Wunsche Loop	292Q	SP
McNabb Elem	743 E. Cypresswood Dr	292Y	NCC
Meyer Elem	16330 Forest Way	332T	NWC
Northgate Crossing Elem	23437 Northgate Crossing Blvd	292F	NCC
Ponderosa Elem	17202 Butte Creek Rd	331R	NWC
Reynolds Elem	3975 Gladeridge Dr	331S	NWC
Richey Road MS	100 E Richey Rd	333U	NCC
Roberson MS	15252 Grand Point Dr	332X	NWC
Salyers Elem	922 Wunsche Loop	292U	NWC
Smith Elem	26000 Cypresswood	293T	NCC
Spring Sr	19428 North Frwy	292X	NCC
Thompson Elem	12470 Walters Rd	371G	NWC
Twin Creeks MS	27100 Cypresswood	293W	NCC
Wells MS	4033 Gladeridge	331S	NWC
Westfield Athletic Complex	South Ridge	332S	NWC
Westfield HS 9th Grade	1500 Southridge	332S	NWC
Westfield Sr	16713 Ella Blvd	332N	NWC
Winship, John A. Elem	2175 Spring Creek Dr	292V	NCC
Wunsche School	900 Wunsche Loop	292Q	SP

SPRING BRANCH ISD

School or Facility Name	Address	Pg	Loc
Administration Bldg	955 Campbell Rd	490C	HE
Bear Blvd. School, The Elem	8860 Westview Dr	450Z	NWH
Bendwood Elem	12750 Kimberly	489H	SWH
Buffalo Creek Elem	2801 Blalock	450K	NWH
Bunker Hill Elem	11950 Taylorcrest	490E	SWH
Cedar Brook Elem	2121 Ojeman	450R	NWH
Cornerston Academy MS	9016 Westview	450Y	SWH
Darrell Tully Stadium	1050 Dairy Ashford	488D	SWH
Edgewood Elem	8655 Emnora	450R	NWH
Frostwood Elem	12214 Memorial Dr	490J	BH
Grob Stadium		450Z	SV
Guthrie Center, The HS	10660 Hammerly	449Q	NWH
High School of Choice	9016 Westview	450Z	SV
Hollibrook Elem	3602 Hollister	450M	NWH
Housman Elem	6705 Housman	451U	NWH
Hunters Creek Elem	10650 Beinhorn	491A	SV
Landrum Jr	220 Ridgecrest	451N	NWH
Lion Lane School, The Elem	2210 Ridgecrest	451S	NWH
Meadow Wood Elem	14230 Memorial Dr	489E	SWH
Memorial Drive Elem	11202 Smithdale	490G	PP
Memorial MS	12550 Vindon	489D	SWH
Memorial Sr	935 Echo Ln	490B	SWH
Natatorium	10404 Tiger Trail	449R	NWH
Northbrook MS	3030 Rosefield	450K	NWH
Northbrook Sr	1 Raider Cir	450P	NWH
Nottingham Elem	570 Nottingham Oaks	488G	SWH
Panda Path, The Elem	8575 Pitner	450M	NWH
Pine Shadows Elem	9900 Neuens	450S	NWH
Ridgecrest Elem	2015 Ridgecrest	451S	NWH
Rummel Creek Elem	625 Brittmore	489G	SWH
Shadow Oaks Elem	1335 Shadowdale	449Z	NWH
Sherwood Elem	1700 Sherwood Forest	449X	NWH

School or Facility Name	Address	Pg	Loc
Spring Branch Elem	1700 Campbell Rd	450U	NWH
Spring Branch MS	1000 Piney Point Rd	490C	SWH
Spring Branch School of Choice	9016 Westview	450Y	NWH
Spring Forest MS	14240 Memorial Dr	489E	SWH
Spring Oaks MS	2150 Shadowdale	449R	NWH
Spring Shadows Elem	9725 Kempwood	450K	NWH
Spring Woods MS	9810 Neuens	450T	NWH
Spring Woods Sr	2045 Gessner	450N	NWH
Stratford Sr	14555 Fern	488H	SWH
Terrace Elem	10400 Rothbury	449R	NWH
Thornwood Elem	14400 Fern	488H	SWH
Tiger Trail School, The Elem	10406 Tiger Trail	449V	NWH
Transportation Ctr	1066 Gessner	490A	SWH
Treasure Forest Elem	7635 Amelia	451T	NWH
Valley Oaks Elem	8390 Westview	451W	NWH
Westchester Ed Ctr	901 Yorkchester	489B	SWH
Westwood Elem	2100 Shadowdale	449R	NWH
Wilchester Elem	13618 St. Mary's	489B	SWH
Wildcat Way School, The Elem	12754 Kimberley Ln	489C	NWH
Woodview Elem	9749 Cedardale	450X	NWH

STAFFORD ISD

School or Facility Name	Address	Pg	Loc
Administration Annex	1625 Staffordshire	570W	SF
Stafford Alt Campus	13645 Murphy Rd Ste. 225	569L	SF
Stafford Elem	1625 Staffordshire	570W	SF
Stafford HS	1625 Staffordshire	570W	SF
Stafford IM	1625 Staffordshire	570W	SF
Stafford MS	1625 Staffordshire	570W	SF
Stafford Primary School	1625 Staffordshire	570W	SF

TOMBALL ISD

School or Facility Name	Address	Pg	Loc
Administration Bldg	221 W. Main	288H	TB
Ancillary Services	310 Cherry	288H	TB
Canyon Pointe Elem	13002 Northpointe Blvd	328F	NWC
Creekside Forest Elem	5949 Creekside Forest	250R	NWC
Creekview Elem	8877 West New Harmony Trail	249R	NWC
Decker Prairie Elem	27427 Decker Prairie-Rosehl	247V	SWM
Lakewood Elem	15614 Gettysburg	329S	NWC
Northpointe IM	11855 Northpointe Blvd	328H	NWC
Oakcrest IM	18202 Shaw Rd	328F	NWC
Rosehill Elem	17950 Waller Tomball Rd	287N	NWC
Special Services	1302 Keefer St	288F	TB
Student Service & Trans	1055 Baker Dr	288C	TB
Timber Creek Elem	8455 Creekside Green Dr	250N	NWC
Tomball Alternative Center	1302 Keefer St	288F	TB
Tomball Elem	1110 Inwood	288G	TB
Tomball HS	30330 Quinn	288C	TB
Tomball IM	723 W. Main	288G	TB
Tomball Jr	30403 Quinn	288B	TB
Tomball Memorial HS	19031 Northpointe Ridge	328F	NWC
Wildwood Elem	13802 Northpointe Blvd	328E	NWC
Willow Creek Elem	18302 N. Eldridge Pkwy	328H	TB
Willow Wood Jr	11770 Gregson Rd	328M	NWC

WALLER ISD

School or Facility Name	Address	Pg	Loc
Administration Bldg	1918 Key	282Q	WL
Fields Store Elem	31670 Giboney	242B	WCO
Holleman Elem	2200 Brazeal	282Q	WL
Jones Elem	19115 Owens Rd	281L	PV
Roberts Road Elem	24920 Zube Rd	324H	NWC
Schultz MS	19010 Stokes Rd	282Z	WL
Turlington Elem	23400 Hegar Rd	244X	WCO
Waller HS	20950 Fieldstore Rd	282L	NWC
Waller Jr	2402 Waller	282U	WL

PRIVATE HIGH SCHOOLS

School or Facility Name	Address	Pg	Loc
Academy Hall HS	3911 Campbell Rd	450K	NWH
Alexander-Smith Academy HS	10255 Richmond Ave	489Z	SWH
Awty International School	7455 Awty School Ln	491D	NWH
Banff School, The	13726 Cutten Rd	370A	NWC
Beren Academy	11333 Cliffwood Dr	571D	SWH
Briarwood School	12207 Whittington	489N	CV
Duchesne Academy	10202 Memorial Dr	491B	SWH
Episcopal HS	4650 Bissonnet	531D	SWH
Faith Christian Academy	3519 Burke Rd	577A	PA
Fort Bend Babtist Academy	1520 Seventh St	568L	SG
HLA - Fort Bend H.S.	3964 Bluebonnet	569F	SF
HLA - Fort Bend HS	3964 Bluebonnet	569G	SWH
Houston Christian HS	2700 W. Sam Houston Pkwy	449M	NWH
Incarnate Word Academy	609 Crawford	493R	DT
Kinkaid School, The	201 Kinkaid School Dr	490Q	PP
Lutheran HS South	12555 Ryewater Dr	617A	SHE
Lutheran North HS	1130 W. 34th	452Q	NWH
Memorial Hall School	2501 Central Parkway	451U	NWH
Mt. Carmel HS	6700 Mt. Carmel Dr	534Y	SEH
Northland Christian School	4363 Sylvanfield Dr	331W	NWC
Pope John XXIII HS	1800 N. Grand Pkwy	485K	SWC
Rosehill Christian School	19830 F.M. 2920	286K	NWC
School of the Woods HS	1321 Wirt Rd	451W	HI
Second Baptist School	6410 Woodway Dr	490R	SWH
St. Agnes Academy	9000 Bellaire Blvd	530E	SWH
St. John's School	2401 Claremont Ln	492T	SWH
St. Pius X HS	811 W. Donovan	452G	NWH
St. Stephen's Episcopal	1800 Sul Ross	492V	SWH
St. Thomas Episcopal School	4900 Jackwood	531Q	SWH
St. Thomas HS	4500 Memorial Dr	492M	SWH
Strake Jesuit HS	8900 Bellaire Blvd	530E	SWH
Texas Christian HS	17800 Keith Harrow Blvd	447C	NWC
The Emery / Weiner School	9825 Stella Link	532S	SWH
The John Cooper School	1 John Cooper Dr	250C	WD
Westbury Christian HS	10420 Hillcroft	531W	SWH
Woodlands Christian Academy	5800 Alden Woods Dr	217P	WD

INTERSTATE HIGHWAYS

Street Name	Block	Pg/Sq	Loc	Zips
EAST (I.H. 10 E) FRWY	0	459Y	CV	77530
EAST (I.H. 10 E) FRWY	0	460Z	NEC	77521
EAST (I.H. 10 E) FRWY	0	461V	NEC	77521
EAST (I.H. 10 E) FRWY	0	462S	NEC	77521
EAST (I.H. 10 E) FRWY	0	463N	CCO	77520
EAST (I.H. 10 E) FRWY	1000	493L	DT	77002
EAST (I.H. 10 E) FRWY	1500	494H	NEH	77020
EAST (I.H. 10 E) FRWY	1500	494H	NEH	77020
EAST (I.H. 10 E) FRWY	1700	460Z	NEC	77521
EAST (I.H. 10 E) FRWY	4300	461V	NEC	77521
EAST (I.H. 10 E) FRWY	7100	462S	NEC	77521
EAST (I.H. 10 E) FRWY	7800	495F	NEH	77029
EAST (I.H. 10 E) FRWY	7800	495F	NEH	77029
EAST (I.H. 10 E) FRWY	10000	463N	CCO	77520
EAST (I.H. 10 E) FRWY	10300	496F	NEH	77029
EAST (I.H. 10 E) FRWY	10300	496F	NEH	77029
EAST (I.H. 10 E) FRWY	12200	496F	NEH	77015
EAST (I.H. 10 E) FRWY	12200	496F	NEH	77015
EAST (I.H. 10 E) FRWY	13100	497K	NEC	77015
EAST (I.H. 10 E) FRWY	13100	497K	NEC	77015
EAST (I.H. 10 E) FRWY	15000	498E	CV	77530
EAST (I.H. 10 E) FRWY	15000	498E	CV	77530
EAST (I.H. 10 E) FRWY	17000	499B	NEC	77530
EAST (I.H. 10 E) FRWY	17000	499B	NEC	77530
EAST (I.H. 10 E) FRWY	17500	459Y	CV	77530
GULF (I.H. 45 S) FRWY	100	658B	LC	77573
GULF (I.H. 45 S) FRWY	100	658B	LC	77573
GULF (I.H. 45 S) FRWY	2400	493Q	SEH	77003
GULF (I.H. 45 S) FRWY	2400	493Q	SEH	77003
GULF (I.H. 45 S) FRWY	2600	493V	SEH	77004
GULF (I.H. 45 S) FRWY	2600	493V	SEH	77004
GULF (I.H. 45 S) FRWY	2601	493V	SEH	77003
GULF (I.H. 45 S) FRWY	2601	493V	SEH	77003
GULF (I.H. 45 S) FRWY	3400	494W	SEH	77004
GULF (I.H. 45 S) FRWY	3400	494W	SEH	77004
GULF (I.H. 45 S) FRWY	4100	494W	SEH	77004
GULF (I.H. 45 S) FRWY	4100	494W	SEH	77004
GULF (I.H. 45 S) FRWY	4101	494W	SEH	77023
GULF (I.H. 45 S) FRWY	4101	494W	SEH	77023
GULF (I.H. 45 S) FRWY	4300	534H	SEH	77023
GULF (I.H. 45 S) FRWY	4300	534H	SEH	77023
GULF (I.H. 45 S) FRWY	6600	534H	SEH	77087
GULF (I.H. 45 S) FRWY	6600	534H	SEH	77087
GULF (I.H. 45 S) FRWY	7200	535Y	SEH	77017
GULF (I.H. 45 S) FRWY	7200	535Y	SEH	77017
GULF (I.H. 45 S) FRWY	9000	575D	SEH	77017
GULF (I.H. 45 S) FRWY	9000	575D	SEH	77017
GULF (I.H. 45 S) FRWY	9800	576U	SEH	77034
GULF (I.H. 45 S) FRWY	9800	576U	SEH	77034
GULF (I.H. 45 S) FRWY	15600	617F	SEH	77546
GULF (I.H. 45 S) FRWY	15600	617F	SEH	77546
GULF (I.H. 45 S) FRWY	15601	617F	SEH	77598
GULF (I.H. 45 S) FRWY	15601	617F	SEH	77598
GULF (I.H. 45 S) FRWY	19700	618W	WB	77598
GULF (I.H. 45 S) FRWY	19700	618W	WB	77598
GULF (I.H. 45 S) FRWY	20000	658B	WB	77598
GULF (I.H. 45 S) FRWY	20000	658B	WB	77598
KATY (I.H. 10 W) FRWY	1200	493E	SWH	77007
KATY (I.H. 10 W) FRWY	4000	492A	SWH	77007
KATY (I.H. 10 W) FRWY	4000	492A	SWH	77007
KATY (I.H. 10 W) FRWY	7200	491B	SWH	77024
KATY (I.H. 10 W) FRWY	7200	491B	SWH	77024
KATY (I.H. 10 W) FRWY	8600	490A	SWH	77024
KATY (I.H. 10 W) FRWY	8600	490A	SWH	77024
KATY (I.H. 10 W) FRWY	10700	489B	SWH	77079
KATY (I.H. 10 W) FRWY	10700	489B	SWH	77079
KATY (I.H. 10 W) FRWY	12200	488C	SWH	77079
KATY (I.H. 10 W) FRWY	12200	488C	SWH	77079
KATY (I.H. 10 W) FRWY	14800	487C	SWH	77094
KATY (I.H. 10 W) FRWY	14800	487C	SWH	77094
KATY (I.H. 10 W) FRWY	19000	486D	SWC	77094
KATY (I.H. 10 W) FRWY	19000	486D	SWC	77094
KATY (I.H. 10 W) FRWY	20000	485B	NWC	77449
KATY (I.H. 10 W) FRWY	20000	485B	NWC	77449
KATY (I.H. 10 W) FRWY	20001	485B	SWC	77450
KATY (I.H. 10 W) FRWY	20001	485B	SWC	77450
KATY (I.H. 10 W) FRWY	24000	484A	KT	77494
KATY (I.H. 10 W) FRWY	24000	484A	KT	77494
KATY (I.H. 10 W) FRWY	24900	444Z	KT	77493
KATY (I.H. 10 W) FRWY	24900	444Z	KT	77493
EAST LOOP (I.H. 610) N.	0	495Q	NEH	77029
EAST LOOP (I.H. 610) S.	0	535C	SEH	77012
NORTH LOOP (I.H. 610)	100	453N	NWH	77008
NORTH LOOP (I.H. 610) E.	100	454U	NEH	77009
NORTH LOOP (I.H. 610) W.	100	452Q	NWH	77018
NORTH LOOP (I.H. 610)	101	453N	NWH	77018
NORTH LOOP (I.H. 610) E.	101	454U	NEH	77022
NORTH LOOP (I.H. 610) W.	101	452Q	NWH	77008
NORTH LOOP (I.H. 610)	600	453N	NWH	77009
NORTH LOOP (I.H. 610)	601	453N	NWH	77022
NORTH LOOP (I.H. 610) E.	2000	454U	NEH	77026
NORTH LOOP (I.H. 610) W.	2400	452Q	NWH	77092
NORTH LOOP (I.H. 610) W.	2401	452Q	NWH	77008
NORTH LOOP (I.H. 610) E.	6600	455X	NEH	77028
NORTH LOOP (I.H. 610) E.	8100	455X	NEH	77029
NORTH LOOP (I.H. 610) E.	9400	495C	NEH	77029
SOUTH LOOP (I.H. 610) W.	400	533S	SWH	77054
SOUTH LOOP (I.H. 610) W.	1400	532U	SWH	77054
SOUTH LOOP (I.H. 610) E.	2200	533T	SEH	77021
SOUTH LOOP (I.H. 610) W.	3200	532U	SWH	77025
SOUTH LOOP (I.H. 610) E.	3900	533T	SEH	77051
SOUTH LOOP (I.H. 610) W.	4300	531V	SWH	77096
SOUTH LOOP (I.H. 610) E.	4400	534N	SEH	77033
SOUTH LOOP (I.H. 610) E.	6051	534N	SEH	77087
SOUTH LOOP (I.H. 610) E.	6052	534N	SEH	77087
SOUTH LOOP (I.H. 610) E.	6100	534N	SEH	77087
SOUTH LOOP (I.H. 610) E.	7700	535F	SEH	77017
SOUTH LOOP (I.H. 610) E.	7701	535F	SEH	77012
SOUTH LOOP (I.H. 610) E.	8500	535F	SEH	77017
WEST LOOP (I.H. 610) N.	1	491M	SWH	77024
WEST LOOP (I.H. 610) S.	1	491V	SWH	77027
WEST LOOP (I.H. 610) N.	1100	451Z	NWH	77055
WEST LOOP (I.H. 610) N.	1500	451Z	NWH	77008
WEST LOOP (I.H. 610) S.	5200	531M	SWH	77401
WEST LOOP (I.H. 610) S.	5201	531M	SWH	77081
WEST LOOP (I.H. 610) S.	5500	531M	SWH	77401
WEST LOOP (I.H. 610) S.	8500	531M	SWH	77096
NORTH (I. H. 45 N) FRWY	1000	493C	NWH	77009
NORTH (I. H. 45 N) FRWY	1000	493C	NWH	77009
NORTH (I. H. 45 N) FRWY	2400	453A	NWH	77009
NORTH (I. H. 45 N) FRWY	2400	453A	NWH	77009
NORTH (I. H. 45 N) FRWY	3800	453A	NWH	77022
NORTH (I. H. 45 N) FRWY	3800	453A	NWH	77022
NORTH (I. H. 45 N) FRWY	5400	453A	NWH	77076
NORTH (I. H. 45 N) FRWY	5400	453A	NWH	77076
NORTH (I. H. 45 N) FRWY	6200	412C	NWH	77076
NORTH (I. H. 45 N) FRWY	6200	412C	NWH	77076
NORTH (I. H. 45 N) FRWY	7500	412M	NEH	77037
NORTH (I. H. 45 N) FRWY	7500	412M	NEH	77037
NORTH (I. H. 45 N) FRWY	10700	372Q	NWH	77037
NORTH (I. H. 45 N) FRWY	10700	372Q	NWH	77037
NORTH (I. H. 45 N) FRWY	11400	372Q	NWC	77060
NORTH (I. H. 45 N) FRWY	11400	372Q	NWC	77060
NORTH (I. H. 45 N) FRWY	13700	372Q	NWC	77090
NORTH (I. H. 45 N) FRWY	13700	372Q	NWC	77090
NORTH (I. H. 45 N) FRWY	15200	332K	NWC	77090
NORTH (I. H. 45 N) FRWY	15200	332K	NWC	77090
NORTH (I. H. 45 N) FRWY	18700	332K	NCC	77373
NORTH (I. H. 45 N) FRWY	18700	332K	NCC	77373
NORTH (I. H. 45 N) FRWY	18701	332K	NWC	77388
NORTH (I. H. 45 N) FRWY	18701	332K	NWC	77388
NORTH (I. H. 45 N) FRWY	19500	292K	NCC	77373
NORTH (I. H. 45 N) FRWY	19500	292K	NCC	77373
NORTH (I. H. 45 N) FRWY	19501	292K	NWC	77388
NORTH (I. H. 45 N) FRWY	19501	292K	NWC	77388
NORTH (I. H. 45 N) FRWY	22100	292K	NCC	77373
NORTH (I. H. 45 N) FRWY	22100	292K	NCC	77373
NORTH (I. H. 45 N) FRWY	22101	292K	NWC	77389
NORTH (I. H. 45 N) FRWY	22101	292K	NWC	77389
NORTH (I. H. 45 N) FRWY	24000	252J	SEM	77386
NORTH (I. H. 45 N) FRWY	24000	252J	SEM	77386
NORTH (I. H. 45 N) FRWY	24001	252J	SWM	77380
NORTH (I. H. 45 N) FRWY	24001	252J	SWM	77380
NORTH (I. H. 45 N) FRWY	27000	252J	SEM	77385
NORTH (I. H. 45 N) FRWY	27000	252J	SEM	77385
NORTH (I. H. 45 N) FRWY	27001	252J	SWM	77380
NORTH (I. H. 45 N) FRWY	27001	252J	SWM	77380
NORTH (I. H. 45 N) FRWY	28601	252J	SWM	77381
NORTH (I. H. 45 N) FRWY	28601	252J	SWM	77381

U.S. HIGHWAYS

Street Name	Block	Pg/Sq	Loc	Zips
EASTEX (U.S. 59 N) FRWY	0	256Q	SEM	77357
EASTEX (U.S. 59 N) FRWY	0	256Q	SEM	77357
EASTEX (U.S. 59 N) FRWY	0	257A	SEM	77357
EASTEX (U.S. 59 N) FRWY	0	257A	SEM	77357
EASTEX (U.S. 59 N) FRWY	100	494A	NEH	77020
EASTEX (U.S. 59 N) FRWY	100	494A	NEH	77020
EASTEX (U.S. 59 N) FRWY	1800	494A	NEH	77026
EASTEX (U.S. 59 N) FRWY	1800	494A	NEH	77026
EASTEX (U.S. 59 N) FRWY	3100	454P	NEH	77026
EASTEX (U.S. 59 N) FRWY	3100	454P	NEH	77026
EASTEX (U.S. 59 N) FRWY	6600	454P	NEH	77093
EASTEX (U.S. 59 N) FRWY	6600	454P	NEH	77093
EASTEX (U.S. 59 N) FRWY	10100	414L	NCC	77093
EASTEX (U.S. 59 N) FRWY	10100	414L	NCC	77093
EASTEX (U.S. 59 N) FRWY	11700	414L	NCC	77039
EASTEX (U.S. 59 N) FRWY	11700	414L	NCC	77039
EASTEX (U.S. 59 N) FRWY	14000	375F	NEC	77396
EASTEX (U.S. 59 N) FRWY	14000	375F	NEC	77396
EASTEX (U.S. 59 N) FRWY	14001	375F	NEC	77032
EASTEX (U.S. 59 N) FRWY	14001	375F	NCC	77032
EASTEX (U.S. 59 N) FRWY	14400	375F	NEH	77396
EASTEX (U.S. 59 N) FRWY	14400	375F	NEH	77396
EASTEX (U.S. 59 N) FRWY	18100	335U	HM	77338
EASTEX (U.S. 59 N) FRWY	18100	335U	HM	77338
EASTEX (U.S. 59 N) FRWY	21000	335H	NEH	77339
EASTEX (U.S. 59 N) FRWY	21000	335H	NEH	77339
EASTEX (U.S. 59 N) FRWY	23000	296K	SEM	77365
EASTEX (U.S. 59 N) FRWY	23000	296K	SEM	77365
NORTHWST (U.S. 290) FRWY	9800	451E	NWH	77092
NORTHWST (U.S. 290) FRWY	9800	451E	NWH	77092
NORTHWST (U.S. 290) FRWY	12800	450D	NWH	77040
NORTHWST (U.S. 290) FRWY	12800	450D	NWH	77040
NORTHWST (U.S. 290) FRWY	13600	410X	NWH	77040
NORTHWST (U.S. 290) FRWY	13600	410X	NWH	77040
NORTHWST (U.S. 290) FRWY	15100	409K	JV	77040
NORTHWST (U.S. 290) FRWY	15100	409K	JV	77040
NORTHWST (U.S. 290) FRWY	17500	409K	NWC	77065
NORTHWST (U.S. 290) FRWY	17500	409K	NWC	77065
NORTHWST (U.S. 290) FRWY	20000	368X	NWC	77065
NORTHWST (U.S. 290) FRWY	20000	368X	NWC	77065
SOUTHWEST (U.S. 59 S) FRWY	100	493X	SWH	77004
SOUTHWEST (U.S. 59 S) FRWY	100	493X	SWH	77004
SOUTHWEST (U.S. 59 S) FRWY	400	493X	SWH	77002
SOUTHWEST (U.S. 59 S) FRWY	400	493X	SWH	77002
SOUTHWEST (U.S. 59 S) FRWY	600	493X	SWH	77006
SOUTHWEST (U.S. 59 S) FRWY	600	493X	SWH	77006
SOUTHWST (U.S. 59 S) FRWY	1900	492X	SWH	77098
SOUTHWST (U.S. 59 S) FRWY	1900	492X	SWH	77098
SOUTHWST (U.S. 59 S) FRWY	3200	492X	SWH	77027
SOUTHWST (U.S. 59 S) FRWY	3200	492X	SWH	77027
SOUTHWST (U.S. 59 S) FRWY	5000	491X	SWH	77056
SOUTHWST (U.S. 59 S) FRWY	5000	491X	SWH	77056
SOUTHWST (U.S. 59 S) FRWY	5600	491X	SWH	77057
SOUTHWST (U.S. 59 S) FRWY	5600	491X	SWH	77057
SOUTHWST (U.S. 59 S) FRWY	6200	531A	SWH	77074
SOUTHWST (U.S. 59 S) FRWY	6200	531A	SWH	77074
SOUTHWST (U.S. 59 S) FRWY	6500	530H	SWH	77074
SOUTHWST (U.S. 59 S) FRWY	6500	530H	SWH	77074
SOUTHWST (U.S. 59 S) FRWY	9900	529Z	SWH	77074
SOUTHWST (U.S. 59 S) FRWY	9900	529Z	SWH	77074
SOUTHWT (U.S. 59 S) FRWY	11000	569E	SWH	77031
SOUTHWT (U.S. 59 S) FRWY	11000	569E	SWH	77031
SOUTHWT (U.S. 59 S) FRWY	11900	569E	SF	77477
SOUTHWT (U.S. 59 S) FRWY	11900	569E	SF	77477
SOUTHWT (U.S. 59 S) FRWY	13100	568X	SG	77478
S. U.S. HWY 59	0	531A	SWH	77081
S. U.S. HWY 59	0	531A	SWH	77081
S. U.S. HWY 59	0	568R	SG	77478
S. U.S. HWY 59	0	568R	SG	77478
U.S. HWY 90	0	380M	NEC	77532
U.S. HWY 90	0	380M	NEC	77532
U.S. HWY 90	0	381F	LCO	77535
U.S. HWY 90	0	381F	LCO	77535
U.S. HWY 90	0	418X	NEC	77049
U.S. HWY 90	0	418X	NEC	77049
U.S. HWY 90	0	420A	NEC	77532
U.S. HWY 90	0	420A	NEC	77532
U.S. HWY 90	0	444Z	KT	77493
U.S. HWY 90	0	444Z	KT	77493
U.S. HWY 90	0	445W	NWC	77493
U.S. HWY 90	0	445W	NWC	77493
U.S. HWY 90	0	455X	NEH	77029
U.S. HWY 90	0	455X	NEH	77029
U.S. HWY 90	0	456N	NEH	77013
U.S. HWY 90	0	456N	NEH	77013
U.S. HWY 90	0	457K	NEC	77049
U.S. HWY 90	0	457K	NEC	77049
U.S. HWY 90	0	458B	NEC	77049
U.S. HWY 90	0	458B	NEC	77049
U.S. HWY 90	0	486D	SWC	77094
U.S. HWY 90	0	486D	SWC	77094
U.S. HWY 90	0	487D	SWH	77094
U.S. HWY 90	0	487D	SWH	77094
U.S. HWY 90	0	492A	SWH	77007
U.S. HWY 90	0	492A	SWH	77007
U.S. HWY 90	0	533L	SEH	77021
U.S. HWY 90	0	533L	SEH	77021
U.S. HWY 90 E.	1500	494G	NEH	77020
U.S. HWY 90 E.	1500	494G	NEH	77020
U.S. HWY 90	5200	444Y	KT	77493
U.S. HWY 90	5200	444Y	KT	77493
U.S. HWY 90 E.	7800	495B	NEH	77029
U.S. HWY 90 E.	7800	495B	NEH	77029
U.S. HWY 90 E.	8100	455T	NEH	77028
U.S. HWY 90 E.	8100	455T	NEH	77028
U.S. HWY 90A	0	532T	SWH	77025
U.S. HWY 90A	0	532T	SWH	77025
U.S. HWY 90A	0	570P	MC	77489
U.S. HWY 90A	0	570P	MC	77489
U.S. HWY 90A	0	571F	SWH	77035
U.S. HWY 90A	0	571F	SWH	77035
U.S. HWY 90A S.	2000	569R	SF	77477
U.S. HWY 90A S.	2000	569R	SF	77477
U.S. HWY 90A S.	5000	568L	SG	77478
U.S. HWY 90A S.	5000	568L	SG	77478
U.S. HWY 90A NORTH	100	495E	NEH	77020
U.S. HWY 90A NORTH	100	495E	NEH	77020
U.S. HWY 90A NORTH	3900	455V	NEH	77013
U.S. HWY 90A NORTH	3900	455V	NEH	77013
W. U.S. HWY 290	22600	367K	CY	77429
W. U.S. HWY 290	22600	367K	CY	77429
W. U.S. HWY 290	26100	366D	NWC	77429
W. U.S. HWY 290	26100	366D	NWC	77429
W. U.S. HWY 290	28000	326X	NWC	77433
W. U.S. HWY 290	28000	326X	NWC	77433
W. U.S. HWY 290	30000	325U	NWC	77429
W. U.S. HWY 290	30000	325U	NWC	77429
W. U.S. HWY 290	32100	324L	NWC	77447
W. U.S. HWY 290	32100	324L	NWC	77447
W. U.S. HWY 290	35700	323D	NWC	77447
W. U.S. HWY 290	35700	323D	NWC	77447
W. U.S. HWY 290	37500	283S	NWC	77484
W. U.S. HWY 290	37500	283S	NWC	77484

TOLLWAYS

Street Name	Block	Pg/Sq	Loc	Zips
HARDY TOLL RD	0	453H	NEH	77093
HARDY TOLL RD	0	453H	NEH	77093
HARDY TOLL RD	0	413G	NCC	77039
HARDY TOLL RD	0	413G	NCC	77039
HARDY TOLL RD	0	373K	NCC	77032
HARDY TOLL RD	0	373K	NCC	77032
HARDY TOLL RD	0	333W	NCC	77073
HARDY TOLL RD	0	333W	NCC	77073
HARDY TOLL RD	0	332R	NCC	77073
HARDY TOLL RD	0	332R	NCC	77073
HARDY TOLL RD	0	292M	NCC	77373
HARDY TOLL RD	0	292M	NCC	77373
EAST SAM HOUSTON PKWY S.	0	577P	SEH	77034
EAST SAM HOUSTON PKWY	100	498W	NEC	77015
EAST SAM HOUSTON PKWY S.	100	537V	PA	77503
EAST SAM HOUSTN PKWY S.	3100	577P	PA	77505
EAST SAM HOUSTN PKWY N.	4800	457A	NEC	77015
EAST SAM HOUSTN PKWY N.	5600	457A	NEC	77049
EAST SAM HOUSTN PKWY N.	8200	457A	NEC	77044
EAST SAM HOUSTN PKWY N.	9200	416H	NEC	77044
NORTH SAM HOUSTN PKWY W.	0	370S	NWC	77064
NORTH SAM HOUSTN PKWY E.	100	372V	NEH	77060
NORTH SAM HOUSTN PKWY W.	100	372S	NWH	77038
NORTH SAM HOUSTN PKWY E.	300	373S	NEH	77060
NORTH SAM HOUSTN PKWY E.	800	373S	NCC	77032
NORTH SAM HOSTN PKWY E.	2400	374U	NEH	77032
NORTH SAM HOSTN PKWY W.	3200	371U	NWC	77086
NORTH SAM HOSTN PKWY E.	5700	375U	NEC	77396
NORTH SAM HOSTN PKWY E.	9700	376S	NEC	77396
SOUTH SAM HOUSTN PKWY E.	1	572Z	SWC	77047
SOUTH SAM HOUSN PKWY E.	1800	573Y	SEH	77047
SOUTH SAM HOUSN PKWY W.	3000	571S	SWH	77053
SOUTH SAM HOUSN PKWY E.	4100	574X	SEH	77048
SOUTH SAM HOUSN PKWY W.	6200	571Y	SWH	77085
SOUTH SAM HOUSN PKWY E.	7200	575Y	SEH	77075
SOUTH SAM HOUSN PKWY E.	9400	576Y	SEH	77089
SOUTH SAM HOUSN PKWY W.	9500	570K	MC	77071
SOUTH SAM HOUS PKWY W.	10700	569D	SWH	77031
SOUTH SAM HOUS PKWY W.	11300	569D	SWH	77031
WEST SAM HOUSTN PKWY N.	100	489M	SWH	77024
WEST SAM HOUSTN PKWY S.	100	489Z	SWH	77042
WEST SAM HOUSTN PKWY N.	1000	449U	NWH	77043
WEST SAM HOUSTN PKWY N.	4300	449G	NWH	77041
WEST SAM HOUSTN PKWY S.	5800	529M	SWH	77072
WEST SAM HOUSTN PKWY N.	6000	409Y	NWC	77041
WEST SAM HOUSTN PKWY N.	7000	410N	NWC	77040
WEST SAM HOUSTN PKWY N.	8500	409D	NWC	77064
WEST SAM HOUSTN PKWY S.	8800	529M	SWH	77099
WEST SAM HOUS PKWY N.	10000	369Z	NWC	77064
WESTPARK TOLLROAD	5600	491X	SWH	77057
WESTPARK TOLLROAD	5600	491X	SWH	77057
WESTPARK TOLLROAD	6100	531A	SWH	77057
WESTPARK TOLLROAD	6100	531A	SWH	77057
WESTPARK TOLLROAD	9800	530A	SWH	77057
WESTPARK TOLLROAD	9800	530A	SWH	77057
WESTPARK TOLLROAD	10800	529C	SWH	77057
WESTPARK TOLLROAD	10800	529C	SWH	77057
WESTPARK TOLLROAD	12800	528C	SWH	77057
WESTPARK TOLLROAD	12800	528C	SWH	77057

STATE HIGHWAYS

Street Name	Block	Pg/Sq	Loc	Zips
LA PORTE (S.H. 225) FRWY	1200	537E	LP	77506
LA PORTE (S.H. 225) FRWY	1200	537E	LP	77506
LA PORTE (S.H. 225) FRWY	4600	538H	DP	77536
LA PORTE (S.H. 225) FRWY	4600	538H	DP	77536
LA PORTE (S.H. 225) FRWY	7100	539K	LP	77571
LA PORTE (S.H. 225) FRWY	7100	539K	LP	77571
LA PORTE (S.H. 225) FRWY	7900	535H	SEH	77012
LA PORTE (S.H. 225) FRWY	7900	535H	SEH	77012
LA PORTE (S.H. 225) FRWY	8500	535H	SEH	77017
LA PORTE (S.H. 225) FRWY	8500	535H	SEH	77017
LA PORTE (S.H. 225) FRWY	10000	536E	SEH	77017
LA PORTE (S.H. 225) FRWY	10000	536E	SEH	77017
LA PORTE (S.H. 225) FRWY	12000	540N	LP	77571
LA PORTE (S.H. 225) FRWY	12000	540N	LP	77571
LA PORTE RD	8100	535F	SEH	77012
NOLAN RYAN EXPRESSWAY	0	613J	PL	77584
NOLAN RYAN EXPRESSWAY	0	613J	PL	77584
SOUTH (S.H. 288) FRWY	4300	533W	SWH	77004
SOUTH (S.H. 288) FRWY	4300	533W	SWH	77004
SOUTH (S.H. 288) FRWY	7500	533W	SWH	77021
SOUTH (S.H. 288) FRWY	7500	533W	SWH	77021
SOUTH (S.H. 288) FRWY	8100	533W	SWH	77051
SOUTH FRWY	8100	533W	SWH	77051
SOUTH (S.H. 288) FRWY	11900	573J	SWH	77047
SOUTH (S.H. 288) FRWY	11900	573J	SWH	77047
S.H. 3	100	659J	LC	77573
S.H. 3	100	659J	LC	77573
S.H. 3	500	536W	SH	77587
S.H. 3	500	536W	SH	77587
S.H. 3	1300	659T	DI	77539
S.H. 3	1300	659T	DI	77539
S.H. 3	1500	576G	SH	77587
S.H. 3	1500	576G	SH	77587
S.H. 3	7200	576M	SEH	77034
S.H. 3	7200	576M	SEH	77034
S.H. 3	9000	535Z	SEH	77017
S.H. 3	9000	535Z	SEH	77017
S.H. 3	10500	577S	SEH	77034
S.H. 3	10500	577S	SEH	77034
S.H. 3	12000	617G	SEH	77598
S.H. 3	12000	617G	SEH	77598
S.H. 3	15000	618T	WB	77598
S.H. 3	15000	618T	WB	77598
S.H. 3	18200	658C	WB	77598
S.H. 3	18200	658C	WB	77598
S.H. 6	0	282T	WL	77484
S.H. 6	0	282T	WL	77484
S.H. 6	0	323B	NWC	77484
S.H. 6	0	323B	NWC	77484
S.H. 6	0	325U	NWC	77447
S.H. 6	0	325U	NWC	77447
S.H. 6	0	326X	NWC	77433
S.H. 6	0	326X	NWC	77433
S.H. 6	0	366D	NWC	77429
S.H. 6	0	366D	NWC	77429
S.H. 6	0	367K	CY	77433
S.H. 6	0	367K	CY	77433
S.H. 6	0	368X	NWC	77065
S.H. 6	0	368X	NWC	77065
S.H. 6	0	408B	NWC	77095
S.H. 6	0	408B	NWC	77095
S.H. 6	0	610X	MC	77459
S.H. 6	0	610X	MC	77459
S. S.H. 6	100	488E	SWH	77079
S. S.H. 6	100	488E	SWH	77079
S.H. 6	100	568X	SG	77479
S.H. 6	100	568X	SG	77479
S. S.H. 6	1000	488N	SWH	77077
S. S.H. 6	1000	488N	SWH	77077
N. S.H. 6	1000	448W	NWH	77079
N. S.H. 6	1000	448W	NWH	77079
N. S.H. 6	1200	448J	NWH	77084
N. S.H. 6	1200	448J	NWH	77084
S. S.H. 6	2500	488N	SWH	77082
S. S.H. 6	2500	488N	SWH	77082
S. S.H. 6	3500	528A	SWC	77082
S. S.H. 6	3500	528A	SWC	77082
S.H. 6	3900	609G	MC	77479
S.H. 6	3900	609G	MC	77479
N. S.H. 6	5000	408W	NWC	77084
N. S.H. 6	5000	408W	NWC	77084
S. S.H. 6	6200	528A	SWC	77083
S. S.H. 6	6200	528A	SWC	77083
N. S.H. 6	7000	408B	NWC	77095
N. S.H. 6	7000	408B	NWC	77095
S. S.H. 6	9500	528W	NEF	77498
S. S.H. 6	9500	528W	NEF	77498
S.H. 35	1000	615Y	PL	77581
S.H. 35	1000	615Y	PL	77581
S.H. 35	3000	535J	SEH	77087
S.H. 35	3000	535J	SEH	77087
S.H. 35	6400	575W	SEH	77061
S.H. 35	6400	575W	SEH	77061
S.H. 35	9200	575W	SEH	77075
S.H. 35	9200	575W	SEH	77075
S.H. 96	0	659Q	LC	77573
S.H. 96	0	659Q	LC	77573
S.H. 96	0	660F	LC	77573
S.H. 96	0	660F	LC	77573
S.H. 99	0	445T	NWC	77449
S.H. 99	0	445T	NWC	77449
S.H. 99	0	485B	SWC	77450
S.H. 99	0	485B	SWC	77450
S.H. 99	0	525K	NEF	77407
S.H. 99	0	525K	NEF	77407
S.H. 99	0	526X	NEF	77406
S.H. 99	0	526X	NEF	77407
S.H. 134	100	539E	DP	77571
S.H. 134	100	539E	DP	77571
S.H. 134	1900	499N	SEC	77571
S.H. 134	1900	499N	SEC	77571
S.H. 146	0	541A	BT	77520
S.H. 146	0	541A	BT	77520
S.H. 146	0	540H	BT	77520
S.H. 146	0	540H	BT	77520
S.H. 146	0	580F	LP	77571
S.H. 146	0	580F	LP	77571
N. S.H. 146	0	463J	MB	77521
N. S.H. 146	0	463J	MB	77521
S.H. 146	100	501U	BT	77520
S.H. 146	100	501U	BT	77520
S.H. 146	400	620B	SB	77586
S.H. 146	400	620B	SB	77586
S.H. 146	600	620Y	KE	77565
S.H. 146	600	620Y	KE	77565
S.H. 146	2400	502P	BT	77520
S.H. 146	2400	502P	BT	77520
S.H. 146	3000	660C	GCO	77518
S.H. 146	3000	660C	GCO	77518
N. S.H. 146	7000	462V	BT	77520
N. S.H. 146	7000	462V	BT	77520
S.H. 225	100	536E	PA	77506
S.H. 225	100	536E	PA	77506
S.H. 225	1400	537E	PA	77506
S.H. 225	1400	537E	PA	77506
S.H. 225	2900	537E	PA	77503
S.H. 225	2900	537E	PA	77503
S.H. 225	5000	538G	DP	77536
S.H. 225	5000	538G	DP	77536
S.H. 225	7000	535H	SEH	77017
S.H. 225	7000	535H	SEH	77017
S.H. 225	7100	539K	LP	77571
S.H. 225	7100	539K	LP	77571
S.H. 225	10000	536E	SEH	77017
S.H. 225	10000	536E	SEH	77017
S.H. 225	11800	540N	SEC	77571

Street Name	Block	Pg/Sq	Loc	Zips
S.H. 225	11800	540N	SEC	77571
S.H. 249	700	412J	NWC	77038
S.H. 249	700	412J	NWC	77038
S.H. 249	11500	411B	NWC	77086
S.H. 249	11500	411B	NWC	77086
S.H. 249	14000	371W	NWC	77086
S.H. 249	14000	371W	NWC	77086
S.H. 249	14500	370Z	NWC	77086
S.H. 249	14500	370Z	NWC	77086
S.H. 249	16300	370Z	NWC	77064
S.H. 249	16300	370Z	NWC	77064
S.H. 249	17900	369H	NWC	77070
S.H. 249	17900	369H	NWC	77070
S.H. 249	20400	329T	NWC	77070
S.H. 249	20400	329T	NWC	77070
S.H. 249	22600	329T	NWC	77375
S.H. 249	22600	329T	NWC	77375
S.H. 249	24200	328H	NWC	77377
S.H. 249	24200	328H	NWC	77377
S.H. 249	26700	288Z	NWC	77375
S.H. 249	26700	288Z	NWC	77375
S.H. 249	31200	248W	SWM	77362
S.H. 249	31200	248W	SWM	77362
S.H. 249	32000	247M	SWM	77362
S.H. 249	32000	247M	SWM	77362
S.H. 288	0	613W	NEB	77584
S.H. 288	0	613W	NEB	77584
S.H. 288	4000	493T	SWH	77004
S.H. 288	4000	493T	SWH	77004
S.H. 288	7500	533K	SEH	77021
S.H. 288	7500	533K	SEH	77021
S.H. 288	8700	533W	SEH	77051
S.H. 288	8700	533W	SEH	77051
S.H. 288	9100	573J	SEH	77051
S.H. 288	9100	573J	SEH	77051
S.H. 288	11900	573W	SEH	77047
S.H. 288	11900	573W	SEH	77047
S.H. 290	0	410X	NWH	77040
S.H. 290	0	410X	NWH	77040
S.H. 330	0	499D	NEC	77520
S.H. 330	0	499D	NEC	77520
S.H. 330	0	500A	BT	77520
S.H. 330	0	500A	BT	77520
S.H. 330	0	501N	BT	77520
S.H. 330	0	501N	BT	77520

LOOPS (State Highways)

Street Name	Block	Pg/Sq	Loc	Zips
LOOP 207	0	463E	MB	77580
LOOP 207	0	463E	MB	77580
LOOP 410	0	540X	LP	77571
LOOP 410	0	540X	LP	77571
LOOP 410	0	580L	LP	77571
LOOP 410	0	580L	LP	77571
LOOP 494	19300	256U	SEM	77357
LOOP 494	19300	256U	SEM	77357
LOOP 494	22000	335H	NEH	77339
LOOP 494	22000	335H	NEH	77339
LOOP 494	22400	335H	SEM	77339
LOOP 494	22400	335H	SEM	77339
LOOP 494	22600	296S	SEM	77365
LOOP 494	22600	296S	SEM	77365

FARM to MARKET ROADS

Street Name	Block	Pg/Sq	Loc	Zips
F.M. 149	0	247B	SWM	77362
F.M. 270	100	659A	LC	77573
F.M. 359	0	524W	NWF	77406
F.M. 362	0	282B	WCO	77484
F.M. 362	0	282T	WCO	77484
F.M. 362	0	242N	WCO	77484
F.M. 362	0	242C	WCO	77484
F.M. 362	15000	322E	WCO	77484
F.M. 517	0	660Z	GCO	77539
F.M. 518	0	613R	PL	77581
F.M. 518	0	614Q	PL	77581
F.M. 518	0	615Q	PL	77581
F.M. 518	0	616T	PL	77581
F.M. 518	0	656D	FR	77546
F.M. 518	0	657J	FR	77546
F.M. 518	0	658L	LC	77573
F.M. 518	0	659E	LC	77573
F.M. 518	0	660A	LC	77573
F.M. 518	900	620X	KE	77565
F.M. 521	100	612J	NEF	77545
F.M. 521	2500	611Z	FS	77545
F.M. 521	8600	533S	SWH	77054
F.M. 521	10500	532Z	SWH	77045
F.M. 521	10900	572H	SWH	77045
F.M. 521	13400	572Q	SWC	77053
F.M. 525	1	373W	NEH	77060
F.M. 525	200	373U	NCC	77060
F.M. 525	800	373U	NCC	77032
F.M. 525	2400	374X	NCC	77032
F.M. 526	1	496C	NEH	77013
F.M. 526	5800	456R	NEC	77049
F.M. 526	7400	456R	NEC	77044
F.M. 526	9000	416Z	NEC	77044
F.M. 526	12000	417J	NEC	77044
F.M. 527	5400	455L	NEH	77028
F.M. 528	0	658A	FR	77546
F.M. 528	0	657D	SEC	77598
F.M. 528	0	656Q	FR	77546
F.M. 529	11000	409N	NWC	77041
F.M. 529	12700	408N	NWC	77041
F.M. 529	14400	408N	NWC	77095
F.M. 529	16200	407Q	NWC	77095
F.M. 529	18000	406Q	NWC	77433
F.M. 529	21600	405Q	NWC	77449
F.M. 529	25000	404Q	NWC	77493
F.M. 565	0	502H	CCO	77520
F.M. 565	0	503E	CCO	77520
F.M. 565	1700	463E	MB	77580
F.M. 646	100	659R	LC	77573
F.M. 646	100	659X	LC	77539
F.M. 646	4800	660P	LC	77539
F.M. 686	0	340D	LCO	77535
F.M. 723	6200	524Q	NEF	77406
F.M. 865	0	613H	NEB	77584
F.M. 1092	200	569Y	SF	77477
F.M. 1092	1000	569Y	MC	77459
F.M. 1092	2200	609C	MC	77459
F.M. 1093	0	490V	SWH	77057
F.M. 1093	0	491S	SWH	77057
F.M. 1093	11300	489S	SWH	77077
F.M. 1093	12400	488U	SWH	77077
F.M. 1093	15100	487V	SWH	77082
F.M. 1093	16200	527B	SWH	77082
F.M. 1093	17400	526E	NEF	77450
F.M. 1093	21000	525G	NEF	77450
F.M. 1093	23500	524J	NEF	77406
F.M. 1128	2100	614T	NEB	77584
F.M. 1266	0	659R	LC	77573
F.M. 1266	2500	660J	LC	77573
F.M. 1314	0	254H	SEM	77365
F.M. 1314	0	255N	SEM	77365
F.M. 1314	0	295D	SEM	77365
F.M. 1314	0	296F	SEM	77365
F.M. 1405	0	503N	CCO	77520
F.M. 1405	0	502V	CCO	77520
F.M. 1405	4000	542C	CCO	77520
F.M. 1413	0	381H	LCO	77535
F.M. 1463	0	484B	KT	77494
F.M. 1464	0	527J	NEF	77407
F.M. 1464	6500	527T	NEF	77498
F.M. 1485	0	256R	SEM	77357
F.M. 1485	0	256F	SEM	77357
F.M. 1485	0	257P	SEM	77357
F.M. 1485	0	258P	SEM	77357
F.M. 1488	0	243F	WCO	77447
F.M. 1488	33500	242C	WCO	77484
F.M. 1774	0	247B	SWM	77362
F.M. 1876	100	568C	SG	77478
F.M. 1876	2500	528U	NEF	77478
F.M. 1942	0	463A	MB	77580
F.M. 1942	100	419V	BR	77532
F.M. 1942	900	420S	NEC	77532
F.M. 1942	3900	460D	NEC	77532
F.M. 1942	4000	461F	NEC	77532
F.M. 1942	7600	462A	CCO	77521
F.M. 1959	100	577X	SEH	77034
F.M. 1959	400	617B	SEH	77034
F.M. 1960	0	340D	LCO	77535
W. F.M. 1960	100	332N	NWC	77090
F.M. 1960	100	332M	NCC	77073
F.M. 1960	100	338P	NEH	77336
W. F.M. 1960	1200	331R	NWC	77090
F.M. 1960	1600	333K	NCC	77073
E. F.M. 1960	2100	335V	NEC	77338
W. F.M. 1960	2300	331W	NWC	77068
W. F.M. 1960	3100	333L	NCC	77338
E. F.M. 1960	4100	336U	NEC	77346
W. F.M. 1960	4500	370F	NWC	77069
E. F.M. 1960	4700	337W	NEC	77346
F.M. 1960	5000	334N	NCC	77338
W. F.M. 1960	5100	334N	NCC	77338
W. F.M. 1960	7300	370F	NWH	77070
F.M. 1960	8400	335S	NCC	77338
W. F.M. 1960	8400	335S	NCC	77338
E. F.M. 1960	8400	338Q	NEC	77346
W. F.M. 1960	8600	369M	NWC	77070
F.M. 1960	10600	339K	NEC	77336
W. F.M. 1960	11000	369W	NWC	77065
W. F.M. 1960	12700	368Z	NWC	77065
W. F.M. 1960	13100	408C	NWC	77065
E. F.M. 1960 BYPASS	100	335V	HM	77338
E. F.M. 1960 BYPASS	1500	336S	HM	77338
W. F.M. 1960 BYPASS	7700	334V	NCC	77338
F.M. 1960 BYPASS	8400	335T	HM	77338
F.M. 2094	0	619Z	LC	77573
F.M. 2094	0	659B	LC	77573
F.M. 2094	200	620W	LC	77565
F.M. 2100	0	298M	NEC	77336
F.M. 2100	1100	459R	HG	77562
F.M. 2100	5900	419L	NEC	77532
F.M. 2100	16900	379U	NEC	77532
F.M. 2100	21400	339S	NEC	77336
F.M. 2100	29000	299X	NEC	77336
F.M. 2100	0	258Z	NEC	77357
F.M. 2234	1200	570X	MC	77489
F.M. 2234	2500	610G	MC	77489
F.M. 2234	8500	611G	NEF	77053
F.M. 2234	8700	612E	NEF	77053
F.M. 2234 (Prop)	0	613F	NEB	77584
F.M. 2351	0	617K	SEH	77546
F.M. 2351	100	616Z	FR	77546
F.M. 2351	500	656F	NEB	77511
F.M. 2354	0	503G	CCO	77520
F.M. 2354	0	543X	CCO	77520
F.M. 2354	0	542Y	BT	77520
F.M. 2354	0	541H	BT	77520
F.M. 2920	1500	292S	NWC	77388
F.M. 2920	2500	291T	NWC	77388
F.M. 2920	6000	290P	NWC	77379
F.M. 2920	9000	289E	TB	77375
F.M. 2920	14000	288J	NWC	77377
F.M. 2920	15500	287P	NWC	77377
F.M. 2920	18100	286R	NWC	77377
F.M. 2920	20000	285S	NWC	77447
F.M. 2920	24100	284R	NWC	77447
F.M. 2920	27900	283U	NWC	77484
F.M. 2920	30700	282V	NWC	77484
F.M. 2978	19500	289E	NWC	77375
F.M. 2978	24600	249N	SWM	77354
F.M. 3180	0	463H	MB	77520
F.M. 3180	0	503D	CCO	77520
F.M. 3345	0	610B	MC	77489
F.M. 3360	0	463C	MB	77520
F.M. 3436	0	660Z	TC	77539

NUMBERED STREETS

Street Name	Block	Pg/Sq	Loc	Zips
1ST	0	491Y	BL	77401
1ST	0	531C	BL	77401
1ST	0	611V	FS	77545
FIRST EXT	0	335U	HM	77338
N. 1ST	1	501Y	BT	77520
W. 1ST	100	538G	DP	77536
N. 1ST	100	540Y	LP	77571
E. 1ST	100	538G	DP	77536
S. 1ST	100	501Y	BT	77520
E. 1ST	100	335V	HM	77338
1ST	100	296C	SEM	77365
1ST	100	459Z	HG	77562
1ST	100	568P	SG	77498
1ST	100	580C	LP	77571
1ST	300	536X	SH	77587
1ST	300	620T	KE	77565
S. 1ST	400	541B	BT	77520
1ST	600	620Q	SB	77586
1ST	1000	496W	GP	77547
1ST	1300	463A	MB	77580
1ST	1400	339K	HU	77336
1ST	1500	570N	MC	77489
1ST	2200	569V	SF	77477
FIRST	2800	659Y	GCO	77539
1ST	3800	615N	PL	77581
1ST	4800	576M	SEH	77504
FIRST	5200	419C	NEC	77532
1ST	5200	444Y	KT	77493
1ST	6300	531G	BL	77401
1ST	11600	418Q	NEC	77044
1ST	13700	497P	NEC	77015
1ST	14000	331X	NWC	77014
FIRST	15800	498G	CV	77530
1ST	23400	256R	SEM	77357
1ST	26100	292R	SP	77373
2ND	0	527Z	NEF	77498
2ND	0	576R	SEH	77034
2ND	0	612S	FS	77545
SECOND	0	659Y	DI	77539
2ND	0	658M	LC	77573
2ND	0	659E	LC	77573
W. 2ND	100	538G	DP	77536
N. 2ND	100	501Y	BT	77520
N. 2ND	100	540Y	LP	77571
E. 2ND	100	493E	SWH	77007
E. 2ND	100	538G	DP	77536
S. 2ND	100	501Y	BT	77520
2ND	100	296C	SEM	77365
2ND	100	459Z	HG	77562
2ND	100	568K	SG	77498
2ND	100	580C	LP	77571
2ND	100	619N	SEH	77058
2ND	200	570N	MC	77489
2ND	300	335V	HM	77338
2ND	300	536X	SH	77587
2ND	400	620U	KE	77565
2ND	500	531G	BL	77401
2ND	600	620K	SB	77586
N. 2ND	800	531C	BL	77401
2ND	800	491Y	BL	77401
S. 2ND	900	541C	BT	77520
2ND	1000	496W	GP	77547
2ND	1100	620Q	SB	77586
2ND	1300	463A	MB	77580
2ND	2200	495Z	GP	77547
2ND	3400	615N	PL	77581
2ND	4800	576M	SEH	77504
SECOND	5300	419G	NEC	77532
2ND	5500	444Y	KT	77493
2ND	11600	418Q	NEC	77044
2ND	14000	331X	NWC	77014
SECOND	15800	498G	CV	77530
2ND	23400	256R	SEM	77357
2ND ST	0	339K	HU	77336
3-J RANCH RD	0	247A	SWM	77355
3RD	0	612S	FS	77545
3RD	0	658M	LC	77573
3RD	0	659E	LC	77573
THIRD	0	659Y	DI	77539
N. 3RD	1	501Y	BT	77520
S. 3RD	1	501Y	BT	77520
W. 3RD	100	538F	DP	77536
N. 3RD	100	540X	LP	77571
E. 3RD	100	538G	DP	77536
N. 3RD	100	459R	HG	77562
3RD	100	531L	BL	77401
S. 3RD	100	459V	HG	77562
3RD	100	536X	SH	77587
3RD	100	568K	SG	77498
3RD	100	580B	LP	77571
3RD	100	619S	SEH	77058
3RD	400	335V	HM	77338
3RD	400	620U	KE	77565
3RD	600	620P	SB	77586
N. 3RD	800	531C	BL	77401
S. 3RD	900	541C	BT	77520
3RD	1000	463A	MB	77580
3RD	1000	496W	GP	77547
3RD	1400	339K	HU	77336
N. 3RD	1500	491Y	BL	77401
3RD	1600	570N	MC	77489
3RD	2200	495Z	GP	77547
3RD	3900	615N	PL	77581
E. 3RD	5000	444Y	KT	77493
3RD	5000	444Y	KT	77493
3RD	10800	574E	SEH	77048
3RD	11600	418Q	NEC	77044
3RD	13800	497P	NEH	77015
3RD	14000	331X	NWC	77014
3RD	23400	256R	SEM	77357
4TH	0	333X	NCC	77073
4TH	0	576R	SEH	77034
4TH	0	619N	SEH	77058
4TH	0	658H	LC	77573
4TH	0	611V	FS	77545
W. 4TH	1	620T	KE	77565
4TH	1	331X	NWC	77014
W. 4TH	100	538F	DP	77536
S. 4TH	100	459U	HG	77562
S. 4TH	100	580B	LP	77571
N. 4TH	100	501Y	BT	77520
N. 4TH	100	540X	LP	77571
E. 4TH	100	493E	NWH	77007
E. 4TH	100	538G	DP	77536
S. 4TH	100	501Y	BT	77520
4TH	100	459Q	HG	77562
4TH	100	459Z	HG	77562
4TH	100	492H	NWH	77007
4TH	100	568K	SG	77498
4TH	100	620U	KE	77565
4TH	100	536X	SH	77587
4TH	300	335V	HM	77338
E. 4TH 1/2	600	493E	NWH	77007
4TH	600	576B	SH	77587
4TH	600	620P	SB	77586
4TH	600	659E	LC	77573
4TH	800	491Y	BL	77401
S. 4TH	900	541C	BT	77520
4TH	1000	496W	GP	77547
4TH	2200	495Z	GP	77547
E. 4TH	5400	444Y	KT	77493
4TH	5400	444Y	KT	77493
4TH	10000	574E	SEH	77048
4TH AVE	100	419G	CB	77532
4TH AVE	600	659S	LC	77573
4TH ST	0	339K	HU	77336
S. 5TH	0	531G	BL	77401
5TH	0	333W	NCC	77073
5TH	0	611V	FS	77545
5TH	0	619N	SEH	77058
5TH	0	659E	LC	77573
W. 5TH	1	620T	KE	77565
5TH	1	331Y	NWC	77014
W. 5TH	100	492D	NWH	77007
W. 5TH	100	538F	DP	77536
S. 5TH	100	459U	HG	77562
S. 5TH	100	541C	BT	77520
S. 5TH	100	580B	LP	77571
N. 5TH	100	501Y	BT	77520
N. 5TH	100	540X	LP	77571
E. 5TH	100	493A	NWH	77007
E. 5TH	100	538G	DP	77536
5TH	100	459Q	HG	77562
5TH	100	459Z	HG	77562
5TH	100	568K	SG	77498
5TH	100	536X	SH	77587
N. 5TH	200	531G	BL	77401
5TH	400	620U	KE	77565
5TH	500	335V	HM	77338
E. 5TH 1/2	600	493A	NWH	77007
5TH	600	576B	SH	77587
5TH	600	620P	SB	77586
5TH	1000	496W	GP	77547
5TH	1500	570S	MC	77489
5TH	2100	569Y	NEF	77477
5TH	2200	495Z	GP	77547
5TH	3600	609C	MC	77459
E. 5TH	5000	444Y	KT	77493
5TH	5000	444Y	KT	77493
5TH	10800	574E	SEH	77048
5TH	11500	418Q	NEC	77044
5TH	11900	529A	SWH	77072
6TH	0	333W	NCC	77073
6TH	0	418Q	NEC	77004
6TH	0	611V	FS	77545
6TH	0	619P	SEH	77058
W. 6TH	1	620X	KE	77565
6TH	1	331Y	NWC	77014
W. 6TH	100	492D	NWH	77007
W. 6TH	100	538F	DP	77536
S. 6TH	100	459U	HG	77562
S. 6TH	100	541C	BT	77520
S. 6TH	100	580B	LP	77571
N. 6TH	100	501Y	BT	77520
N. 6TH	100	540X	LP	77571
E. 6TH	100	538G	DP	77536
6TH	100	459Q	HG	77562
6TH	100	459Z	HG	77562
6TH	100	568K	SG	77498
6TH	100	536X	SH	77587
6TH	400	620U	KE	77565
6TH	500	335V	HM	77338
E. 6TH 1/2	600	493A	NWH	77007
6TH	600	576B	SH	77587
6TH	600	620Q	SB	77586
SIXTH	700	612S	FS	77545
E. 6TH 1/2	1000	493A	NWH	77009
6TH	1000	496W	GP	77547
6TH	2100	570S	SF	77477
6TH	2200	495Z	GP	77547
6TH	5200	419H	CB	77532
6TH	10000	370Y	NWC	77064
6TH	11900	529A	SWH	77072
W. 7TH	1	620X	KE	77565
7TH	1	331Y	NWC	77014
W. 7TH	100	492D	NWH	77007
W. 7TH	100	538K	DP	77536
S. 7TH	100	541C	BT	77520
S. 7TH	100	580B	LP	77571
N. 7TH	100	501Y	BT	77520
N. 7TH	100	540X	LP	77571
E. 7TH	100	493A	NWH	77007
7TH	100	459Q	HG	77562
7TH	100	459Z	HG	77562
7TH	100	568K	SG	77498
7TH	100	658H	LC	77573
7TH	100	536X	SH	77587
7TH	300	335V	HM	77338
7TH	400	620Y	KE	77565
7TH	500	620P	SB	77586
E. 7TH 1/2	600	493A	NWH	77007
7TH	600	576B	SH	77587
7TH	600	373X	NCC	77060
SEVENTH	700	612S	FS	77545
W. 7TH 1/2	900	492D	NWH	77007
E. 7TH	1000	493A	NWH	77009
E. 7TH 1/2	1000	493A	NWH	77009
7TH	1000	659A	LC	77573
7TH	1000	496S	GP	77547
7TH	2200	495V	GP	77547
7TH	11500	418Q	NEC	77044
7TH 1/2	11900	418R	NEC	77044
7TH	11900	529A	SWH	77072
N. 8TH	0	540T	LP	77571
W. 8TH	1	620X	KE	77565
8TH	1	331Y	NWC	77014
W. 8TH	100	492D	NWH	77007
W. 8TH	100	538K	DP	77536
S. 8TH	100	501Z	BT	77520
S. 8TH	100	580F	LP	77571
N. 8TH	100	501Z	BT	77520
N. 8TH	100	540X	LP	77571
E. 8TH	100	493A	NWH	77007
E. 8TH	100	538L	DP	77536
8TH	100	459Q	HG	77562
8TH	100	459Z	HG	77562
8TH	100	536X	SH	77587
8TH	400	620Y	KE	77565
E. 8TH 1/2	600	493A	NWH	77007
8TH	600	576B	SH	77587
8TH	700	620T	SB	77586
8TH	1000	496S	GP	77547
8TH	2200	495V	GP	77547
8TH	10800	574E	SEH	77048
8TH	11600	418R	NEC	77044
9TH	0	620T	SB	77586
9TH	1	331Y	NWC	77014
W. 9TH	100	492D	NWH	77007
W. 9TH	100	538L	DP	77536
E. 9TH	100	493A	NWH	77007
E. 9TH	100	538L	DP	77536
E. 9TH	100	659P	LC	77573
9TH	100	459Q	HG	77562
9TH	100	459Z	HG	77562
9TH	100	536Y	SH	77587
9TH	500	620Y	KE	77565
9TH	600	576C	SH	77587
9TH	700	620Y	SB	77586
9TH	1000	496S	GP	77547
9TH	2200	495V	GP	77547
9TH	9500	410C	NWC	77064
9TH	9600	370Y	NWC	77064
9TH	10600	574F	SEH	77048
9TH	11600	418R	NEC	77044
10TH	0	373Z	NCC	77039
10TH	0	418R	NEC	77044
10TH	0	620T	SB	77586
10TH	1	331Y	NWC	77014
W. 10TH	100	492D	NWH	77008
W. 10TH 1/2	100	492D	NWH	77008
E. 10TH	100	493A	NWH	77008
E. 10TH	100	538L	DP	77536
10TH	100	459Q	HG	77562
10TH	100	459Z	HG	77562
10TH	100	536Y	SH	77587

Street Name	Block	Pg/Sq	Loc	Zips
N. 10TH	100	540T	LP	77571
10TH	500	620Y	KE	77565
E. 10TH 1/2	600	493A	NWH	77008
10TH	600	576C	SH	77587
10TH	600	620Y	SB	77586
N. 10TH	700	501Z	BT	77520
10TH	1000	496S	GP	77547
10TH	2200	495V	GP	77547
10TH	5400	444Y	KT	77493
11TH	1	331Y	NWC	77014
W. 11TH	100	452Z	NWH	77008
E. 11TH	100	538L	DP	77536
E. 11TH	100	659Q	LC	77573
11TH	100	459Q	HG	77562
11TH	100	459Z	HG	77562
11TH	100	620U	SB	77586
S. 11TH	100	540X	LP	77571
N. 11TH	100	540X	LP	77571
E. 11TH	100	453W	NWH	77008
11TH	100	536Y	SH	77587
S. 11TH	300	580B	LP	77571
E. 11TH 1/2	600	453W	NWH	77008
11TH	600	576C	SH	77587
E. 11TH	1000	453W	NWH	77009
11TH	1100	659T	LC	77573
11TH	1100	496S	GP	77547
11TH	2200	495V	GP	77547
W. 11TH	2300	492B	NWH	77008
W. 11TH	3800	492B	NWH	77055
W. 11TH PLACE	5300	493W	SWH	77005
11TH	6300	444U	KT	77493
12TH	0	444U	KT	77493
12TH	0	620T	SB	77586
12TH	0	660N	LC	77539
12TH	1	331Y	NWC	77014
W. 12TH	100	538L	DP	77536
S. 12TH	100	540X	LP	77571
N. 12TH	100	540T	LP	77571
E. 12TH	100	453W	NWH	77008
E. 12TH	100	538L	DP	77536
E. 12TH	100	659Q	LC	77573
W. 12TH	100	452W	NWH	77008
12TH	100	459Q	HG	77562
12TH	100	459Z	HG	77562
12TH	100	536Y	SH	77587
12TH	300	620U	SB	77586
E. 12TH 1/2	600	453W	NWH	77008
12TH	600	576C	SH	77587
12TH	1000	496S	GP	77547
12TH	2200	495V	GP	77547
W. 12TH	3700	451Z	NWH	77055
13TH	1	331Y	NWC	77014
W. 13TH	100	452Z	NWH	77008
W. 13TH	100	538K	DP	77536
S. 13TH	100	540X	LP	77571
E. 13TH	100	453W	NWH	77008
E. 13TH	100	659U	LC	77573
13TH	100	459Z	HG	77562
E. 13TH	100	538M	DP	77536
N. 13TH	300	540T	LP	77571
13TH	400	576C	SH	77587
E. 13TH 1/2	600	453W	NWH	77008
13TH	1000	496S	GP	77547
13TH	2200	495V	GP	77547
E. 13TH	2600	539J	DP	77536
13TH	5500	444U	KT	77493
14TH	1	331Y	NWC	77014
W. 14TH	100	452Y	NWH	77008
E. 14TH	100	453W	NWH	77008
S. 14TH	300	580B	LP	77571
S. 14TH	300	580B	LP	77571
N. 14TH	500	540X	LP	77571
14TH	600	576C	SH	77587
E. 14TH	800	453W	NWH	77009
14TH	1000	496S	GP	77547
W. 14TH 1/2	1800	452Y	NWH	77008
N. 14TH	5400	530D	SWH	77036
14TH	16200	367L	CY	77429
W. 15TH	100	452Y	NWH	77008
E. 15TH	100	453W	NWH	77008
15TH	100	576C	SH	77587
S. 15TH	300	580A	LP	77571
W. 15TH 1/2	900	452Y	NWH	77008
15TH	1000	496S	GP	77547
15TH	2200	495V	GP	77547
W. 16TH	100	452Y	NWH	77008
E. 16TH	100	453W	NWH	77008
N. 16TH	100	540W	LP	77571
16TH	100	580E	LP	77571
E. 16TH	1000	453W	NWH	77009
16TH	1000	496S	GP	77547
16TH	1000	576C	SH	77587
16TH	1700	659U	LC	77573
17TH	0	576D	PA	77504
W. 17TH	100	452U	NWH	77008
S. 17TH	100	580A	LP	77571
N. 17TH	100	540W	LP	77571
E. 17TH	700	453S	NWH	77008
17TH	1000	496S	GP	77547
17TH	1600	659T	LC	77573
17TH GREEN	7300	337U	NEC	77346
W. 18TH	100	452U	NWH	77008
S. 18TH	100	580A	LP	77571
N. 18TH	100	540W	LP	77571
E. 18TH	100	453S	NWH	77008
18TH	1200	495V	GP	77547
18TH	2200	496S	GP	77547
18TH	2600	659U	GCO	77539
W. 18TH	4400	451V	NWH	77092
18TH ST	0	576Q	SEH	77034
W. 19TH	100	452U	NWH	77008
E. 19TH	600	453S	NWH	77008
19TH	2800	659Y	GCO	77539
19TH ST	0	576Q	SEH	77034
E. 20TH	0	660T	GCO	77539
W. 20TH	100	452U	NWH	77008
E. 20TH	100	453S	NWH	77008
20TH	2000	659Y	DI	77539
20TH	4300	660M	BC	77518
20TH ST	0	576Q	SEH	77034
E. 21ST	0	659V	GCO	77539
E. 21ST	0	660S	GCO	77539
W. 21ST	200	452U	NWH	77008
E. 21ST	600	453S	NWH	77008
21ST	2200	659Y	DI	77539
21ST ST	0	576Q	SEH	77034
E. 22ND	100	453S	NWH	77008
W. 22ND	200	452U	NWH	77008
22ND	2200	659Y	DI	77539
E. 22ND	4800	660S	GCO	77539
22ND ST	0	576Q	SEH	77034
22ND ST	400	249A	WCO	77445

Street Name	Block	Pg/Sq	Loc	Zips
E. 23RD	100	453S	NWH	77008
W. 23RD	200	452T	NWH	77008
E. 23RD	800	453S	NWH	77009
23RD	2200	659Y	DI	77539
N. 23RD	2900	540W	LP	77571
23RD	4600	660S	GCO	77539
E. 24TH	100	453S	NWH	77008
W. 24TH	200	452T	NWH	77008
E. 24TH	800	453S	NWH	77009
24TH	2200	659Y	DI	77539
24TH	4400	660S	GCO	77539
24TH CT	0	659V	GCO	77539
24TH CT	0	659V	GCO	77539 S.
25TH	100	540W	LP	77571
N. 25TH	100	540W	LP	77571
E. 25TH	100	453S	NWH	77008
W. 25TH	200	452T	NWH	77008
E. 25TH	800	453S	NWH	77009
25TH	2700	659Y	DI	77539
25TH	4200	659V	GCO	77539
25TH	4400	660S	GCO	77539
E. 26TH	100	453S	NWH	77008
W. 26TH	200	452U	NWH	77008
E. 26TH	700	453S	NWH	77009
26TH	1200	540S	LP	77571
26TH	2300	659Y	DI	77539
26TH	4600	660W	GCO	77539
E. 27TH	0	659V	GCO	77539
E. 27TH	100	453S	NWH	77008
W. 27TH	200	452T	NWH	77008
E. 27TH	700	453S	NWH	77009
27TH	2300	659Y	DI	77539
27TH	4100	660W	GCO	77539
E. 28TH	100	453N	NWH	77008
W. 28TH	200	452Q	NWH	77018
E. 28TH	700	453N	NWH	77009
28TH	2200	659Y	DI	77539
28TH	4200	659Z	GCO	77539
28TH	4400	660W	GCO	77539
E. 29TH	400	453N	NWH	77008
E. 29TH	700	453N	NWH	77009
29TH	2400	659Y	DI	77539
29TH	4200	659Z	GCO	77539
29TH	4400	660W	GCO	77539
W. 30TH	200	452Q	NWH	77018
E. 30TH	200	453N	NWH	77018
E. 30TH	1300	453N	NWH	77022
30TH	2300	659Y	DI	77539
30TH	4200	659Z	GCO	77539
30TH	4400	660W	GCO	77539
E. 31ST 1/2	100	453N	NWH	77018
W. 31ST	200	452Q	NWH	77018
E. 31ST	200	453N	NWH	77018
E. 31ST	600	453N	NWH	77022
31ST	4300	659Z	GCO	77539
31ST	4400	660W	GCO	77539
N. 32ND	0	531C	BL	77401
E. 32ND	0	660W	GCO	77539
E. 32ND	100	453N	NWH	77018
W. 32ND	200	452Q	NWH	77018
E. 32ND	600	453N	NWH	77022
E. 32ND 1/2	600	453P	NWH	77022
32ND	4200	659Z	GCO	77539
32ND	4400	660W	GCO	77539
E. 33RD	100	453N	NWH	77018
W. 33RD	200	452R	NWH	77018
E. 33RD	600	453N	NWH	77022
33RD	4200	659Z	GCO	77539
33RD	4400	660W	GCO	77539
E. 34TH	100	453N	NWH	77018
W. 34TH	200	452P	NWH	77018
E. 34TH	600	453N	NWH	77022
W. 34TH 1/2	1400	452P	NWH	77018
W. 34TH	3400	451P	NWH	77092
34TH	4200	659Z	GCO	77539
34TH	4400	660W	GCO	77539
E. 35TH	200	453N	NWH	77018
E. 35TH	500	453N	NWH	77022
W. 35TH	900	452Q	NWH	77018
35TH	4200	659Z	GCO	77539
35TH	4400	660W	GCO	77539
E. 36TH	200	453N	NWH	77018
E. 36TH	500	453N	NWH	77022
36TH	4200	660W	GCO	77539
E. 37TH	100	453P	NWH	77018
E. 37TH	500	453P	NWH	77022
E. 38TH	100	453P	NWH	77018
E. 38TH	500	453P	NWH	77022
W. 38TH	600	452R	NWH	77018
E. 39TH	100	453P	NWH	77018
E. 39TH	500	453P	NWH	77022
W. 39TH	700	452Q	NWH	77018
E. 40TH 1/2	100	453J	NWH	77018
E. 40TH	200	453N	NWH	77018
E. 40TH	400	453N	NWH	77022
E. 40TH 1/2	500	453J	NWH	77022
E. 41ST	100	453J	NWH	77018
E. 41ST	300	453J	NWH	77022
W. 41ST	700	452L	NWH	77018
E. 42ND	100	453J	NWH	77018
42ND 1/2	100	453J	NWH	77018
E. 42ND	300	453J	NWH	77022
W. 42ND	700	452K	NWH	77018
E. 43RD	100	453J	NWH	77018
E. 43RD	300	453J	NWH	77022
W. 43RD	600	452K	NWH	77018
W. 43RD	4300	451F	NWH	77092
W. 43RD	7200	450H	NWH	77040
E. 44TH	100	453J	NWH	77018
W. 44TH	200	452M	NWH	77018
E. 45TH	100	453J	NWH	77018
S. 65TH	100	494U	SEH	77011
65TH	100	494U	SEH	77011
S. 66TH	100	494Y	SEH	77011
66TH	100	494V	SEH	77011
S. 69TH	100	494Z	SEH	77011
69TH	100	494R	SEH	77011
69TH	2500	494R	SEH	77020
S. 70TH	100	494Z	SEH	77011
N. 70TH	100	495N	SEH	77011
70TH	100	494V	SEH	77011
S. 71ST	100	494Z	SEH	77011
71ST	100	494Z	SEH	77011
71ST	700	495S	SEH	77011
S. 72ND	100	494Z	SEH	77011
72ND	100	495S	SEH	77011
73RD	100	495W	SEH	77011
S. 74TH	100	495W	SEH	77011
74TH	100	495S	SEH	77011
S. 74TH 1/2	200	495W	SEH	77011
S. 75TH	100	495W	SEH	77011
75TH	100	495W	SEH	77011

Street Name	Block	Pg/Sq	Loc	Zips
S. 75TH	500	535A	SEH	77023
76TH	100	495W	SEH	77012
S. 76TH	800	535A	SEH	77023
S. 77TH	100	495W	SEH	77012
77TH	100	495W	SEH	77012
S. 77TH	900	535A	SEH	77023
S. 78TH	100	495W	SEH	77012
78TH	100	495X	SEH	77012
S. 79TH	100	535A	SEH	77012
79TH	100	495X	SEH	77012
S. 80TH	100	495X	SEH	77012
80TH	100	495X	SEH	77012
S. 80TH	600	535B	SEH	77012
81ST	100	495X	SEH	77012
92ND	300	535C	SEH	77012
93RD	300	535C	SEH	77012
95TH	200	535D	SEH	77012
96TH	300	535D	SEH	77012
97TH	500	535D	SEH	77012
102ND	300	497P	NEC	77015

ALPHABETICAL STREETS

A

Street Name	Block	Pg/Sq	Loc	Zips
A AVE	16700	499A	CV	77530
A DR	0	290L	NWC	77389
A F SAND RD	13400	408V	NWC	77041
A I S D	19300	335T	NEH	77338
A J FOYT RD	23800	285N	NWC	77447
A J FOYT RD	23900	284R	NWC	77447
A K J	500	570S	SF	77477
A STREET	600	282T	WL	77484
A STREET	800	444T	KT	77493
A STREET	1800	536A	NEH	77029
A, AVENUE	400	656A	NEB	77581
A, AVENUE	0	659Y	GCO	77539
A, AVENUE	1	568N	SG	77478
S. A, AVENUE	100	335Y	HM	77338
N. A, AVENUE	100	335Y	HM	77338
A, AVENUE	100	569Q	SF	77477
A, AVENUE	300	536Y	SH	77587
A, AVENUE	800	444Y	KT	77493
A, AVENUE	1000	660M	BC	77518
A, AVENUE	1100	463A	MB	77580
A, AVENUE	1200	611X	FS	77545
A, AVENUE	12500	419V	BR	77532
A, AVENUE	16700	498D	CV	77530
AARON	2900	539S	DP	77536
AARON ST	0	538V	DP	77536
AARONDALE CIR	1	381Q	LCO	77535
AARONDALE CT	1	381Q	LCO	77535
AARONDALE DR	1	381U	LCO	77535
W. AARONDALE LN	1	381U	LCO	77535
AARONDALE TRAIL	0	381P	LCO	77535
AARONGLEN CIR	1	381U	LCO	77535
AARONGLEN CT	1	381V	LCO	77535
AARONGLEN DR	1	381U	LCO	77535
AARONGLEN PASS	0	381T	LCO	77535
AARROYO HILL CT	6400	526E	NEF	77450
ABAFT CT	17700	379T	NEC	77532
ABALAR	17800	375R	NEC	77396
ABALONE COVE	3800	609Q	MC	77459
ABALONE WAY	12800	456D	NEC	77044
ABALONE WAY	13000	457A	NEC	77044
ABANA LN	1000	332J	NWC	77090
ABARGO	0	617E	SEH	77089
ABASCAL HILLS LN	0	446G	NWC	77449
ABBAWOOD	0	410V	NWH	77040
ABBERTON HILL DR	15900	330T	NWC	77379
ABBEY CT	24900	250W	NWC	77389
ABBEY LN	0	657U	LC	77573
ABBEY LN	0	252T	SEM	77386
ABBEY LN	13800	568B	SG	77498
ABBEY BROOK PLACE	1	250D	WD	77381
ABBEY CHASE CT	15400	408B	NWC	77095
ABBEY CHASE LN	9200	408A	NWC	77095
ABBEYDALE DR	8800	570A	SWH	77031
ABBEY FIELD DR	2700	613V	NEB	77584
ABBEY FIELD DR	3200	297J	SEM	77365
ABBEY MANOR LN	0	444C	NWC	77493
ABBEY OAK CIR	21200	333E	NCC	77073
ABBEY OAK DR	1600	333E	NCC	77073
ABBEY POINT LN	0	457K	NEC	77049
ABBEY SPRINGS LN	26700	484Y	NEF	77494
ABBEYWOOD DR	3600	613U	NEB	77584
ABBEYWOOD DR	16600	618M	SEH	77058
ABBIE LN	5000	660W	DI	77539
ABBOTGLEN LN	25600	485W	NEF	77494
ABBOTSHALL	9300	456D	NEC	77044
ABBOTSWOOD CT	600	486A	SWC	77450
ABBOTT	300	500P	BT	77520
ABBOTT	500	493J	SWH	77007
ABBOTT CIR	400	568K	SG	77498
ABBOTT DR	1000	613G	NEB	77584
ABBUTSFORD LN	22700	485U	NEF	77450
ABBY CT	1100	444W	KT	77493
ABBY LN	3000	538U	DP	77536
ABBY LN	17200	330J	NWC	77379
ABBY ALDRICH LN	1500	445V	NWC	77449
ABBY GLEN WAY	18200	407X	NWC	77084
ABBY LANE CIR	8100	330J	NWC	77379
ABBY RIDGE WAY	0	416M	NEC	77044
ABEL LN	0	286A	SWM	77355
ABELLFIELD LN	1700	568Y	SG	77478
ABER	16200	458Y	CV	77530
ABERCREEK AVE	5000	617X	FR	77546
ABERCROMBIE DR	1	448N	NWH	77084
ABERDEEN	200	569J	SF	77477
ABERDEEN CT	8800	407D	NWC	77095
ABERDEEN DR	2000	658P	LC	77573
ABERDEEN RD	1100	536V	PA	77502
ABERDEEN RD	1300	537S	PA	77502
ABERDEEN FIELDS CT	16100	407D	NWC	77095
ABERDEEN FIELDS DR	8900	407D	NWC	77095
ABERDEEN FOREST DR	16000	407D	NWC	77095
ABERDEEN GLEN DR	8900	407D	NWC	77095
ABERDEEN GREEN DR	16000	408A	NWC	77095
ABERDEEN HOLLOW LN	18700	328G	NWC	77377
ABERDEEN LAKE DR	9200	407D	NWC	77095
ABERDEEN OAKS DR	8800	407D	NWC	77095
ABERDEEN PALMS DR	8700	408A	NWC	77095
ABERDEEN PARK DR	8800	407D	NWC	77095
ABERDEENSHIRE DR	17400	527W	NEF	77407
ABERDEEN TRAILS DR	15700	408A	NWC	77095
ABERDEEN WAY	500	459Q	HG	77562
ABERDEEN WAY	3100	532J	SWH	77025
ABERDOVEY LN	15000	497D	NEC	77530
ABERGREEN TRAIL	16100	408A	NWC	77095
ABERGREEN TRAIL	16200	407D	NWC	77095
ABERHAM DR	3600	371K	NWC	77066
ABERMORE LN	0	527W	NEF	77478

Street Name	Block	Pg/Sq	Loc	Zips
ABERNATHY	2200	494B	NEH	77026
ABERSHAM CT	400	485C	SWC	77450
ABERTON CT	19700	291W	NWC	77379
ABERTON LN	5100	290Z	NWC	77379
ABERTON LN	5200	291W	NWC	77379
ABERTON FOREST DR	6100	407X	NWC	77084
ABER TRAIL CT	8900	407D	NWC	77095
ABIDE DR	13200	571K	SWH	77085
ABIDIE GARDENS DR	0	376S	NEC	77396
ABIDING CT	0	373E	NCC	77073
ABIGAIL DR	0	527T	NEF	77498
ABIGAIL LN	0	657M	FR	77546
ABIGAIL GRACE CT	9800	532S	SWH	77025
ABIGAIL GRACE LN	21500	255U	SEM	77365
ABIGAL WAY	4100	609Y	NEF	77459
ABILENE	1900	659F	LC	77573
ABILENE	6900	494H	NEH	77020
ABILENE	7100	495E	NEH	77020
ABILENE CREEK LN	0	660K	LC	77573
ABINGER LN	3400	411R	NWH	77088
ABINGTON COVE DR	20700	295M	SEM	77365
ABINGTON WAY	6100	492B	NWH	77008
ABLESIDE DR	4300	658N	LC	77573
ABLOOM LN	11600	371N	NWC	77066
ABNEY DR	100	372Q	NCC	77060
ABOTTING RD	0	617T	SEC	77546
ABRIGO	0	616H	SEH	77089
ABRIOLA CT	0	525J	NEF	77406
ABRUZZO DR	0	571L	SWH	77085
ABRUZZO DR	12900	571L	SWH	77085
ABSHIER	0	578C	LP	77505
ABSINTHE	0	408S	NWC	77084
ACACIA	1900	658K	LC	77573
ACACIA	4400	531H	BL	77401
ACACIA DR	1300	536P	PA	77502
ACACIA DR	3500	609J	SG	77479
ACACIA DR	22600	245U	SWM	77355
ACACIA LN	0	460W	BT	77521
N. ACACIA LN	1900	658K	LC	77573
ACACIA ARBOR LN	12400	409W	NWC	77041
ACACIA FAIR LN	0	611S	FS	77545
ACACIA FALLS CT	7900	526R	NEF	77407
ACACIA FOREST TRAIL	10300	616G	SEC	77089
ACACIA GLEN LN	0	524B	NEF	77494
ACACIA GLEN LN	0	524B	NEF	77494
ACACIA PLACE	700	609V	MC	77459
ACACIA ROSE CT	0	526T	NEF	77469
ACACIAWOOD WAY	0	572H	SEH	77051
ACACIA WOOD WAY	3700	446L	NWC	77449
ACADEMY	1	619M	TL	77586
ACADEMY	5000	532A	WU	77005
ACADEMY	6800	532J	SWH	77025
ACADEMY LN	700	538Y	DP	77536
ACADEMY TRACE DR	0	253T	SEM	77386
ACADIAN DR	11700	529W	SWH	77099
ACADIANA DR	2500	620K	SB	77586
ACAMPO PLACE	1200	569Y	MC	77477
ACANTHUS LN	11000	367U	NWC	77095
ACAPULCO DR	15700	409Q	JV	77040
ACAPULCO COVE CT	8300	338N	NEC	77346
ACAPULCO COVE DR	20300	338N	NEC	77346
ACAPULCO VILLAGE DR	600	336W	HM	77338
ACCORD DR	0	293G	SEM	77386
ACE	3600	530B	SWH	77063
ACE LN	22000	332R	NCC	77073
ACHGILL	8300	409L	JV	77040
ACKLEY DR	6400	415A	NEC	77396
ACKLEY MANOR	0	367D	NWB	77429
ACME CT	300	453E	NWH	77022
ACOMA DR	10500	413X	NEH	77076
ACORN	300	659N	LC	77573
ACORN	4900	451E	NWH	77092
ACORN CIR	3200	659Z	GCO	77539
ACORN CT	1000	616R	FR	77546
ACORN CT	1400	610B	MC	77489
ACORN CT	5300	657V	LC	77573
ACORN CT	6400	614P	PL	77584
ACORN DR	0	612Y	NWB	77583
ACORN LN	3700	297U	NEH	77345
ACORN BROOK	0	447N	NWC	77084
ACORN CHASE DR	22200	291L	NWC	77389
ACORN CLEARING PATH	0	418T	NEC	77044
ACORN CLUSTER CT	1	251B	WD	77381
ACORN FALLS DR	0	449X	NWH	77043
ACORN FIELD TRAIL	0	377E	NEC	77346
ACORN FOREST DR	6300	411S	NWH	77088
ACORN GLEN TRAIL DR	2000	611S	FS	77545
ACORN GREEN CT	15300	458W	NEC	77530
ACORN GROVE DR	22300	291L	NWC	77389
ACORN MEADOW DR	1500	372N	NWC	77067
ACORN OAK	100	298C	NEC	77336
ACORN OAK	12000	251U	WD	77380
ACORN OAKS DR	0	445N	NWC	77493
ACORN RIDGE WAY	0	326Y	NWC	77433
ACORN RUN LN	3500	291L	NWC	77389
ACORN SPRINGS LN	3400	291L	NWC	77389
ACORN SQUARE CT	2200	445S	NWC	77493
ACORN TREE	200	332F	NWC	77388
ACORN TREE CT	200	332F	NWC	77388
ACORN VALLEY DR	22200	291L	NWC	77389
ACORN VALLEY DR	22700	291G	NWC	77389
ACORN WAY LN	3400	291L	NWC	77389
ACORN WOOD WAY	2800	618B	SEH	77059
ACORN WOOD WAY	3500	578X	SEH	77059
ACROPOLIS WAY	4200	610Q	MC	77459
ACUNA LN	14400	572P	SWH	77045
ADA	100	484A	KT	77494
ADA	2800	493C	NWH	77009
ADA LN	20000	257R	SEM	77357
ADAGIO AVE	7700	410P	NWC	77040
ADAGIO LN	9300	410N	NWC	77040
ADAIR	3100	493Z	SEH	77004
ADAIR	3500	533D	SEH	77004
ADAM CT	200	288M	TB	77375
ADAM LN	100	493R	DT	77003
ADAM'S RUN	12000	368J	NWC	77429
ADAMBURY CT	23300	292G	NCC	77373
ADAMO LN	300	613H	PL	77581
ADAM PRAIRIE DR		325S	NWC	77447
ADAMS	0	614V	PL	77581
ADAMS	1	494T	SEH	77011
W. ADAMS	100	540X	LP	77571
N. ADAMS	100	494T	SEH	77011
ADAMS	1200	501Z	BT	77520
ADAMS	1600	502W	BT	77520
ADAMS	1800	570S	SF	77477
ADAMS	6700	444X	KT	77494
ADAMS	21900	296P	SEM	77365
ADAMS AVE	800	570S	MC	77489
ADAMS DR	1500	538V	DP	77536
ADAMS DR	1700	538U	PL	77581
ADAMS LN	13700	247B	SWM	77362

Street Name	Block	Pg/Sq	Loc	Zips
ADAMS ACRES	100	296P	SEM	77365
ADAMSBOROUGH DR	10500	529U	SWH	77099
ADAMS MILL LN	10100	528W	NEF	77498
ADAMS RIDGE LN	0	377E	NEC	77346
ADAMS WALK CT	1500	488K	SWH	77077
ADAMS WAY	22200	285D	SWM	77355
ADAMWOOD CT	3600	331B	NWC	77338
ADANA	0	616H	SEH	77089
ADDENMOOR CT	13300	371C	NWC	77014
ADDICKS-CLODINE RD	3500	527G	SWC	77083
ADDICKS CLODINE RD	3300	487Y	SWC	77082
ADDICKS CLODINE RD	3500	527U	NEF	77083
ADDICKS FAIRBANKS	0	408V	NWC	77041
ADDICKS HOWELL RD	200	488A	SWH	77079
ADDICKS HOWELL RD	2500	488J	SWH	77082
ADDICKS HOWELL RD	7500	528J	SWC	77083
ADDICKS HOWELL RD	9500	528W	NEF	77498
ADDICKS LEVEE DR	0	447W	NWH	77084
ADDICKS OAKS PLACE	0	449U	NWH	77043
ADDICKS SATSUMA RD	1000	448S	NWH	77079
ADDICKS SATSUMA RD	1300	448S	NWH	77084
ADDICKS SATSUMA RD	5000	408X	NWC	77084
ADDICKS SATSUMA CUTOFF	5300	408W	NWC	77084
ADD IN LN	0	330W	NWC	77069
ADDINGTON CT	3600	299S	NEC	77336
ADDINGTON CT	3600	299S	NEC	77336
ADDISON DR	3800	613G	NEB	77584
ADDISON RD	1900	532G	SWH	77030
ADDISON FOREST TRAIL		484W	NEF	77494
ADDISON FOREST TRAIL		484W	NEF	77494
ADDISON FOREST TRAIL		484W	NEF	77494
ADDISON HILLS LN	5200	485X	NEF	77494
ADDISON PARK LN	1000	292B	NCC	77373
ADDLESTON DR	0	295V	SEM	77365
ADDLESTONE RIDGE LN	0	524H	NEF	77494
ADE	3700	530B	SWH	77063
ADEL RD	11300	372J	NWC	77067
ADELAIDE DR	0	527X	NEF	77469
ADELAIDE MEADOWS CT	19600	406U	NWC	77449
ADELAIDE MEADOWS DR	19700	406U	NWC	77449
ADELA POINT		289P	NWC	77375
ADELBERT	7300	454J	NEH	77093
ADELE	400	500N	BT	77520
ADELE	800	453T	NWH	77009
ADELFINA	15000	527Z	NEF	77498
ADELIA	3000	494A	NEH	77026
ADELIA CT	12600	496L	NEH	77015
ADELINE LN	9900	532T	SWH	77054
ADELLA CT	6800	614T	PL	77584
ADELLE	7200	454J	NEH	77093
ADELL ROSE LN	0	449X	NWH	77043
ADELPHI	2200	492Y	SWH	77098
ADEN DR	0	493V	SEH	77004
ADEN MIST DR	0	493V	SEH	77004
ADINA SPRINGS LN	17400	367X	NWC	77095
ADIRONDACK DR	12500	617A	SEH	77089
ADKINS RD	1000	490C	SV	77055
ADKINS RD	1200	450Y	NWH	77055
ADKINS FOREST DR	19400	329D	NWC	77379
ADLER DR	10700	463S	CCO	77520
ADLER DR	13200	572V	SWH	77047
ADLER LAKE DR	8300	527Q	NEF	77083
ADLONG JOHNSON RD	17500	380P	NEC	77532
ADLONG SCHOOL RD	16400	420C	NEC	77532
ADLONG SCHOOL RD	16600	380U	NEC	77532
ADMIRAL CT	4100	609C	MC	77459
ADMIRAL DR	2600	619Z	LC	77573
ADMIRAL RD	2600	659C	LC	77573
ADMIRAL BAY LN	600	484D	NEF	77494
ADMIRAL OAK CT	0	376H	NEC	77346
ADMIRALTY DR	3600	299S	NEC	77336
ADMIRALTY DR	3700	299S	NEC	77336
ADMIRALTY BEND LN	0	251G	WD	77380
ADMIRALTY WAY	300	620W	LC	77565
ADOBE CIR	16500	367Y	NWC	77095
ADOBE DR	9900	367Y	NWC	77095
ADOBE LN	4500	501M	BT	77521
ADOBE CANYON LN	19200	328D	NWC	77377
ADOBE FALLS DR	0	253W	SEM	77386
ADOBE FALLS DR	1800	292N	NWC	77388
ADOBEPINE LN	0	447G	NWC	77084
ADOBE RIDGE LN	0	445N	NWC	77493
ADOBE RIDGE LN	0	615H	PL	77089
ADOBE ROSE DR	0	376E	HM	77396
ADOBE SKY CT	9200	527N	NEF	77407
ADOBE STONE DR	1700	376E	HM	77396
ADOBE TRACE LN	17900	447F	NWC	77084
ADOBE VISTA LN	6500	609J	NEF	77479
ADOLPH DR	1000	452B	NWH	77091
ADOLPH BAETHE RD	33000	322N	WCO	77484
ADONIS AVE	8000	461T	NEC	77521
ADONIS RD	3900	333C	NCC	77373
W. ADOUE	100	501Y	BT	77520
E. ADOUE	100	501Y	BT	77520
ADOWA SPRINGS LOOP	0	292U	NCC	77373
ADRIA HILLS CIR	0	251W	SWM	77389
ADRIAN	7700	535F	SEH	77012
ADRIAN HILLS LN	0	293K	SEM	77386
ADRIFT CT	1000	419B	NEC	77532
ADRIFT ROW LN	0	296Q	SEM	77365
ADVANCE DR	11500	369N	NWC	77065
ADVANCE DR	12100	368R	NWC	77065
ADVENTURE GREEN DR	0	325M	NWC	77429
ADWICK CT	23000	485C	SWC	77450
AEGEAN	1	491L	SWH	77056
AEGEAN DR	0	610V	MC	77459
AERIAL BROOK TRAIL	3800	611W	FS	77545
AERIE DR	11800	328C	NWC	77377
AEROBIC AVE	7500	377D	NEC	77346
AEROPARK DR	5200	374U	NEH	77032
AEROSPACE AVE	12000	577X	SEH	77034
AESTIVAL	23400	295B	SEM	77365
AFFIRMED DR	4200	538N	PA	77503
AFFIRMED WAY	16100	617T	SEC	77546
AFLOAT WAY	1200	419B	NEC	77532
AFORE DR	15800	419F	NEC	77532
AFSAR AVE	0	371G	NWC	77014
AFTON	1000	491C	NWH	77055
AFTON	1200	451U	NWH	77055
AFTON CT	1000	289A	TB	77375
AFTON CT	2500	658P	LC	77573
AFTON FOREST LN	0	446J	NWC	77449
AFTON HOLLOW LN	18100	526M	NEF	77407
AFTON MEADOW	13000	528Q	SWH	77072
AFTON MEADOW LN	0	528Q	SWC	77072
AFTON OAK LN	2700	253N	SEM	77386
AFTON PLACE	0	500C	NEC	77521
AFTON PORT LN	0	416Z	NEC	77044
AFTON POST LN	0	416Z	NEC	77044
AFTON RIDGE LN	5600	407Z	NWC	77084
AFTONSHIRE DR	4700	491V	SWH	77027
AFTON WAY	27000	299W	NEC	77336

Street Name	Block	Pg/Sq	Loc	Zips
AFTON WOODS DR	6900	451Y	NWH	77055
AFT WAY	300	379T	NEC	77532
AGAR LN	2400	449Q	NWH	77043
AGARITA LN	13200	528G	SWH	77083
AGARITA RD	0	244K	WCO	77447
AGASSI ACE CT	6200	331J	NWC	77379
AGATE	23400	291A	NWC	77389
AGATE CANYON WAY	11500	367Q	NWC	77095
AGATE PRAIRE DR	16500	367U	NWC	77095
AGATE STREAM PLACE	1	250C	WD	77381
AGAVE DR	0	525B	NEF	77494
AGAVE DR	0	659G	LC	77573
AGAVE RIDGE	11200	616E	SEC	77089
AGDON DR	0	296R	NEH	77339
AGEAN DR	0	377A	NEC	77346
AGEE	0	576T	SEH	77089
AGG RD	200	288M	TB	77375
AGG RD	600	289J	TB	77375
AGGIE LN	1900	658K	LC	77573
AGGIE LN	11900	413T	NEH	77076
AGILE PINES DR	18600	377D	NEC	77346
AGNES	3600	534L	SEH	77087
AGUA VISTA DR	18700	447E	NWC	77084
AGUILA	9600	455Z	NEH	77013
AGUSTA CT	16400	330S	NWC	77379
AGUSWOOD LN	20700	333P	NCC	77073
AHOY CT	400	379X	NEC	77532
AHRENS	300	536N	SEH	77017
AIKEN LN	15500	373R	NCC	77032
AIKENS-OWENS	22000	286M	NWC	77377
AIKEN WOODS DR	0	257E	SEM	77357
AIMUA CT	7600	527J	NEF	77083
AINSDALE DR	1500	488Q	SWH	77077
AINSWORTH DR	11500	569B	SWH	77099
AINSWORTH DR	11800	569B	MD	77477
W. AIR CARGO	0	575B	SEH	77061
E. AIR CARGO	0	575B	SEH	77061
AIR CARGO	0	575B	SEH	77061
AIR CENTER BLVD	16100	373L	NCC	77032
AIRE	7700	495B	NEH	77029
AIRFIELD LN	20100	254L	SEM	77365
AIRFOIL RD	18000	374A	NEH	77032
AIRFREIGHT RD	2800	374A	NEH	77032
S. AIRHART DR	100	501S	BT	77520
N. AIRHART DR	100	501S	BT	77520
S. AIRHART DR	1100	500Z	BT	77520
S. AIRHART DR	1400	540D	BT	77520
AIRLINE DR	1000	444U	KT	77493
AIRLINE DR	1400	453X	NWH	77009
AIRLINE DR	2000	657K	FR	77546
AIRLINE DR	3000	453P	NWH	77022
AIRLINE DR	5400	413X	NEH	77076
AIRLINE DR	7500	413N	NCC	77037
AIRLINE DR	10000	412H	NCC	77037
AIRLINE DR	15300	372Z	NEH	77037
N. AIRLINE RD	1800	612Y	NWB	77578
AIRLINE-FT BEND RD	300	612V	NWB	77583
AIRLINE-FT BEND RD	2000	613T	NEB	77584
AIRLINE-FT BEND RD #2	900	612U	NWB	77583
AIRMAIL RD	18300	374A	NEH	77032
AIRPORT BLVD	100	539Z	LP	77571
AIRPORT BLVD	2900	573F	SEH	77051
W. AIRPORT BLVD	3400	572E	SWH	77045
AIRPORT BLVD	3400	572H	SWH	77045
AIRPORT BLVD	4100	573F	SEH	77047
AIRPORT BLVD	4700	574E	SEH	77048
W. AIRPORT BLVD	5500	571E	SWH	77035
AIRPORT BLVD	6600	575A	SEH	77061
W. AIRPORT BLVD	7500	570F	SWH	77071
AIRPORT BLVD	9000	575D	SEH	77061
W. AIRPORT BLVD	9400	569G	SWH	77031
W. AIRPORT BLVD	10500	569B	MD	77477
W. AIRPORT BLVD	12000	568D	SG	77478
AIRPORT LOOP	9000	575B	SEH	77061
AIRSTREAM LOOP	13700	417W	NEC	77044
E. AIRTEX DR	1	372D	NCC	77073
AIRTEX DR	100	372B	NWC	77090
E. AIRTEX DR	1300	373C	NCC	77073
AIRWAY DR	1	413J	NCC	77037
AIRYBROOK LN	400	486D	SWC	77094
AJAX	3500	453N	NWH	77022
AJUGA CT	17100	328Q	NWC	77377
AKARD	3000	573F	SEH	77051
AKARD	4100	573G	SEH	77047
AKIN DR	19100	379P	NEC	77532
AKRON	900	496J	JC	77029
AKRON OAK ST	13201	369G	NWC	77070
AKUMAL LN	2800	333P	NCC	77073
AKUMAL CALLE	5000	660S	GCO	77539
W. ALABAMA	100	493S	SWH	77002
W. ALABAMA	200	493S	SWH	77006
ALABAMA	700	444W	KT	77494
ALABAMA	900	493X	SWH	77002
ALABAMA	1000	493T	SWH	77004
S. ALABAMA	1200	537V	PA	77503
ALABAMA	1200	575D	SH	77587
ALABAMA	1500	541A	BT	77520
ALABAMA	1600	537V	PA	77503
W. ALABAMA	1700	492T	SWH	77098
ALABAMA	1900	540D	BT	77520
W. ALABAMA	3400	492T	SWH	77027
ALABAMA	3500	533D	SEH	77004
W. ALABAMA	4900	491U	SWH	77056
ALABAMA	700	484A	KT	77494
ALABAMA AVE	200	659A	LC	77573
ALABAMA CT	1	492T	SWH	77027
ALABASTER CT	16800	527P	NEF	77083
ALABASTER DR	8200	527P	NEF	77083
ALABASTER OAKS LN	0	376N	NEC	77396
ALABONSON RD	4300	451F	NWH	77092
ALABONSON RD	6800	411P	NWC	77088
ALADDIN CT	700	656B	FR	77546
ALAMAN DR	14200	332W	NWC	77090
ALAMANCE	4300	501J	BT	77521
ALAMANNI DR	0	616P	PL	77581
ALAMAR DR	0	408K	NWC	77095
ALAMBRA	2300	495P	NEH	77029
ALAMEDA POINT LN	0	409W	NWC	77041
ALAMETOS DR	16100	527K	NEF	77083
ALAMO	0	500Z	BT	77520
ALAMO	800	461X	BT	77521
ALAMO	1400	493F	SWH	77007
ALAMO AVE	4400	609E	SG	77479
ALAMO DR	11700	539R	LP	77571
ALAMO LN	24000	243P	WCO	77484
ALAMO RD	0	410Z	NWH	77040
ALAMO LAKE CT	15500	328N	NWC	77429
ALAMOSA CT	14200	568E	SG	77498
ALAMOSA LN	5200	331E	NWC	77379
ALAN	1100	538L	DP	77536
ALANA LN	300	252K	SEM	77386
ALANA SPRINGS DR	1900	486Q	SWC	77450

Street Name	Block	Pg/Sq	Loc	Zips
ALANNAH LAGOON CT	14600	527R	NEF	77083
ALANNAH LAGOON DR	8200	527R	NEF	77083
ALANNEIL DR	5500	531J	SWH	77081
ALAN THAI LN	0	376G	NEC	77396
ALANTIC BREEZE LN	0	526J	NEF	77407
ALANWOOD	7700	535X	SEH	77061
ALASKA	4000	535Q	SEH	77017
ALASKA AVE	1800	659P	LC	77573
ALASSIO ISLE CT	0	610P	MC	77459
ALASTAIR DR	100	537K	PA	77506
ALBA	7300	412U	NWH	77088
ALBA RD	2800	452Q	NWH	77018
ALBA RD	5300	452C	NWH	77091
ALBACORE DR	7000	530M	SWH	77074
ALBANS RD	1700	532D	SWH	77005
ALBANY	1300	538P	DP	77536
ALBANY	2600	493P	SWH	77006
ALBANY CREST LN	0	578T	SEH	77059
ALBANY PARK CT	21000	290T	NWC	77379
ALBANY PARK LN	21000	290T	NWC	77379
ALBANY SPRINGS LN	0	417D	NEH	77044
ALBA ROSE DR	0	292D	SEM	77386
ALBATROSS DR	4300	620G	SB	77586
ALBATROSS LN	31500	246X	SWM	77355
ALBEE DR	22300	445R	NWC	77449
ALBELIA MEADOWS DR	13200	528L	SWH	77083
ALBEMARLE DR	3000	537L	PA	77503
ALBEMARLE LN	5100	534F	SEH	77021
ALBER	500	453Z	NEH	77009
ALBERENE DR	9200	530S	SWH	77074
ALBERT DR	5800	374V	NEH	77396
ALBERT DR	5900	375S	NEH	77396
ALBERT DR	23100	296M	SEM	77365
ALBERTA	3600	533L	SEH	77021
ALBERTINE DR	0	286Q	NWC	77377
ALBERTI SONATA DR	0	444M	NWC	77493
ALBERT MANOR	0	376R	NEC	77346
ALBERTON LN	2200	613Q	NEB	77584
ALBIN LN	7800	570C	SWH	77071
ALBION CRESCENT DR	6600	406R	NWC	77449
ALBION FALLS TRAIL	0	330C	NWC	77379
ALBRECHT DR	0	524A	NEF	77494
ALBRIGHT	0	543U	BC	77520
ALBRIGHT DR	2400	536T	SEH	77017
ALBRITTON CT	0	289D	NWC	77375
ALBRITTON TERRACE DR	0	295M	SEM	77365
ALBURY	8900	530Z	SWH	77096
ALBURY DR	8900	530R	SWH	77074
ALBURY DR	9400	530V	SWH	77096
ALBURY PARK LN	10000	289T	NWC	77375
ALCALA CT	9400	455D	NEH	77078
ALCANTERRA DR	9700	455D	NEH	77078
ALCAZAR	0	616H	SEH	77089
ALCEA CT	20000	289Z	NWC	77379
ALCHESTER LN	13300	489F	SWH	77079
ALCOMITA DR	7400	527M	SWC	77083
ALCONBURY LN	4300	533H	SEH	77021
ALCORN	500	568P	SG	77478
ALCORN	9000	453H	NEH	77093
ALCOTT DR	8500	450R	NWH	77080
ALCOTT DR	10400	449Q	NWH	77043
ALCOTT MANOR LN	0	526F	NEF	77450
ALCOVE LN	17000	331R	NWC	77090
ALCOVE FOSTER CT	0	611N	FS	77545
ALCOVE GLEN LN	0	329F	NWC	77375
ALDATES DR	1800	457V	NEC	77015
ALDEBURGH CT	8600	330T	NWC	77379
ALDEN	6100	408T	NWC	77084
ALDEN CIR	0	573R	SEH	77048
ALDEN CIR	0	573R	SEH	77048
ALDENBROOK DR	0	408F	NWC	77095
ALDENHAM PLACE	16600	330M	NWC	77379
ALDEN MANOR LN	3300	485T	NEF	77494
ALDEN OAKS DR	0	327D	NWC	77429
ALDEN RIDGE DR	16000	611B	SWH	77053
ALDENSHIRE CT	25100	485W	NEF	77494
ALDENSTONE LN	0	408W	NWC	77084
ALDENWALE LN	0	572U	SWH	77047
ALDENWICK LN	600	332Q	NCC	77073
ALDENWILDS LN	0	527W	NEF	77469
ALDER	0	375M	NEC	77396
ALDER CIR	0	657L	LC	77598
ALDER DR	5400	531F	SWH	77081
ALDER BEND LN	22200	291J	NWC	77389
ALDER BRANCH LN	0	257E	SEM	77357
ALDERBROOK DR	1500	568F	SG	77498
ALDERCY	21500	333F	NCC	77338
ALDERDALE LN	0	289R	NWC	77375
ALDERETE DR	15500	331S	NWC	77068
ALDERFER	3500	573U	SEH	77047
ALDERFIELD	5800	407Z	NWC	77084
ALDERFIELD MANOR LN	5300	484W	NEF	77494
ALDERFORD CT	10600	369K	NWC	77070
ALDERGROVE DR	3400	331C	NWC	77388
ALDERLEAF PLACE	2700	291Z	NWC	77388
ALDERLY DR	7400	250T	NWC	77389
ALDERMOOR DR	18300	331H	NWC	77388
ALDERNEY DR	6900	491B	NWH	77055
ALDER PASS CT	3800	446L	NWC	77449
ALDER PLACE	1	251V	WD	77380
ALDERSBY LN	0	657U	LC	77573
ALDERSGATE CT	600	486C	SWC	77450
ALDERSON	5900	494D	NEH	77020
ALDERSON	7300	495A	NEH	77020
ALDERSON	13700	497B	NEC	77015
ALDER SPRINGS CT	7200	525B	NEF	77494
ALDER SPRINGS LN	7300	525B	NEF	77494
ALDERWICK DR	14700	528S	NEF	77498
ALDERWOOD DR	0	657Q	LC	77573
ALDERWOOD DR	3600	331G	NWC	77388
ALDERWOOD DR	12600	570J	MC	77489
ALDINE BENDER RD	0	375X	NEC	77396
ALDINE BENDER RD	1	372V	NEH	77060
ALDINE BENDER RD	200	373T	NEH	77060
ALDINE BENDER RD	800	373T	NCC	77032
ALDINE BENDER RD	2300	374W	NCC	77032
ALDINE BENDER RD	5800	375W	NEC	77396
ALDINE MAIL RD	100	413E	NCC	77037
ALDINE MAIL RD	1100	413G	NCC	77039
ALDINE MAIL RD	2400	414F	NCC	77039
ALDINE MEADOWS RD	1100	373V	NCC	77032
ALDINE PARK LN	1700	413R	NCC	77093
ALDINE WESTERN RD	1000	372S	NWC	77038
ALDINE WESTERN RD	2400	371V	NWC	77038
ALDINE WESTFIELD RD	0	253S	SEM	77386
ALDINE WESTFIELD RD	2300	454E	NEH	77093
ALDINE WESTFIELD RD	9500	453D	NEH	77093
ALDINE WESTFIELD RD	10000	413V	NEH	77093
ALDINE WESTFIELD RD	12400	413V	NEH	77039
ALDINE WESTFIELD RD	14800	373G	NCC	77032
ALDINE WESTFIELD RD	17000	373G	NCC	77073
ALDINE WESTFIELD RD	19700	333F	NCC	77338

Street Name	Block	Pg/Sq	Loc	Zips
ALDINE WESTFIELD RD	22500	293W	NCC	77373
ALDINE WESTFIELD RD	24200	292V	NCC	77373
ALDINE WESTFIELD RD	29800	293S	SEM	77386
ALDINE WESTFIELD RD	31700	253J	SEM	77385
ALDIS	10400	576S	SEH	77075
ALDON	2400	454A	NEH	77093
ALDRICH	1300	451Y	NWH	77055
ALDRIDGE DR	3200	610U	MC	77459
ALDSWORTH DR	1900	412K	NWC	77088
ALDWELL CT	9900	409G	NWC	77064
ALEAH CT	2500	291V	NWC	77388
ALECIA DR	4000	537R	PA	77503
ALECIA DR	4200	538N	PA	77503
ALEDO	3900	533Y	SEH	77051
ALEE CT	17900	379T	NEC	77532
ALEEN	500	495F	NEH	77029
ALEGRIA DR	7400	527K	NEF	77083
ALEJO DR	8900	411S	NWH	77088
ALEMARBLE OAK	0	326V	NWC	77429
ALEMARBLE OAK	0	327S	NWC	77429
ALENTINA CT	2800	659M	LC	77573
ALENZO DR	15300	373Q	NCC	77032
ALEPIN	19500	245R	SWM	77355
ALEPO GROVE DR	0	293G	SEM	77386
E. ALESSANO LN	0	445E	NWC	77493
ALETA DR	7800	330E	NWC	77379
ALETHA LN	6100	531J	SWH	77081
ALEUTIAN BAY CT	17400	376H	NEC	77346
ALEUTIAN BAY LN	17300	377E	NEC	77346
ALEX LN	11800	570B	SWH	77071
ALEXA FOREST DR	0	296A	SEM	77365
ALEXANDER	800	492D	NWH	77007
ALEXANDER	900	452Z	NWH	77008
ALEXANDER BLVD		289P	NWC	77375
S. ALEXANDER DR	100	501Z	BT	77520
N. ALEXANDER DR	100	501Z	BT	77520
S. ALEXANDER DR	200	541C	BT	77520
ALEXANDER DR	3200	502P	BT	77520
ALEXANDER LN	2100	615L	PL	77581
ALEXANDER LN	20100	254L	SEM	77365
ALEXANDER CROSSING LN	24500	485T	NEF	77494
ALEXANDER PARC DR	3100	615K	PL	77581
ALEXANDRA	0	569P	SF	77477
ALEXANDRA LN	0	539W	DP	77571
ALEXANDRA PARK DR	1300	329H	NWC	77379
ALEXANDRA SPRINGS LN	0	293K	SEM	77386
ALEXANDRIA CT	7900	330A	NWC	77379
ALEXANDROS CT	3100	613R	PL	77584
ALEXIS CIR	4000	371B	NWC	77014
ALEXIS TATE CIR	4000	609Q	MC	77459
ALEX LANDING DR	0	375X	NEC	77396
ALEX LANDING DR	0	415C	NEC	77396
ALFANO	5400	453A	NEH	77076
ALFANO	6300	413W	NEH	77076
ALFANO	7700	413S	NEH	77037
ALFENA AVE	15800	419D	CB	77532
ALFONS	100	293S	NCC	77373
ALFORD	300	501Z	BT	77520
ALFORD RD	1000	245B	SWM	77355
ALFRED LN	10000	410W	NWH	77041
ALGEN	10300	576P	SEH	77075
ALGER DR	15800	570Z	SWH	77489
ALGERIAN WAY	2500	492Y	SWH	77098
ALGERNON DR	3800	333C	NCC	77373
ALGIERS RD	9900	450A	NWH	77041
ALGONQUIN DR	11500	616D	SEH	77089
ALGRAVE DR	16000	330S	NWC	77379
ALGREGG	600	453W	NWH	77008
ALGREGG	900	453W	NWH	77009
ALHAMBRA CT	800	569N	SG	77478
ALHAVEN DR	17300	331G	NWC	77388
ALIANA CREEK WAY	0	527W	NEF	77469
ALIANA LAKES CT	0	527X	NEF	77407
ALIANA LAKES CT	0	527X	NEF	77407
W. ALIANA TRACE DR	0	526Y	NEF	77469
E. ALIANA TRACE DR	0	527X	NEF	77469
ALICE	2800	533K	SWH	77054
ALICE	3200	533R	SEH	77021
ALICE	3900	615E	PL	77581
ALICE	3700	611X	FS	77545
ALICE	31000	288B	TB	77375
ALICE AVE	1100	536H	PA	77506
ALICE DR	3500	569W	SG	77478
ALICE LN	300	538L	DP	77536
ALICE LN	12600	496M	NEH	77015
ALICE LN	20100	256L	SEM	77357
ALICE LN	31000	248X	TB	77375
ALICE RD	13700	288P	NWC	77377
ALICE CROSSING LN	0	660J	LC	77573
ALICE FOSTER	16600	527T	NEF	77498
ALICIA WAY DR	6300	444P	KT	77493
ALI CREEK CT	24500	250X	NWC	77389
ALIEF CLODINE RD	11600	529A	SWH	77082
ALIEF CLODINE RD	12300	528C	SWH	77082
ALIEF CLODINE RD	13600	527F	SWC	77082
ALIEF PLACE DR	11900	529A	SWH	77072
ALIEF VILLAGE DR	4100	529A	SWH	77072
ALINA LN	0	252T	SEM	77386
ALINAWOOD CT	19300	337S	NEC	77346
ALINAWOOD DR	19500	337S	NEC	77346
ALINE	4400	534Q	SEH	77087
ALISA LN	6400	408S	NWC	77084
ALISA BEND CT	0	376G	NEC	77396
ALISIMPSON	3000	533F	SWH	77021
ALISO BEND LN	12400	409W	NWC	77041
ALISO CANYON LN	8200	527P	NEF	77083
ALISO RIDGE CT	0	609S	NEF	77479
ALISO SHADOW CT	0	615H	PL	77089
ALIVIA CT	0	293W	NCC	77373
ALJEAN LN	7400	538X	DP	77536
ALKAY	14400	572P	SWH	77045
ALKAY	15100	572T	SWH	77053
ALKIRE	0	568Q	SG	77478
ALKIRE LAKE DR	200	568Q	SG	77478
W. ALKIRE LAKE DR	300	568Q	SG	77478
ALLADDIN LN	1	251P	WD	77380
ALLAN	400	656D	FR	77546
ALLBRITTON DR	2900	414W	NEH	77093
ALLDAY DR	5800	530B	SWH	77036
ALLEGHENY	6300	533K	SEH	77021
E. ALLEGRO	1900	450U	NWH	77080
S. ALLEGRO	9100	450U	NWH	77080
N. ALLEGRO	9100	450U	NWH	77080
ALLEGRO CT	7600	410P	NWC	77040
ALLEGRO DR	4300	620G	SB	77586
ALLEGRO DR	7500	410P	NWC	77040
ALLEGRO BEND BLVD	0	293G	SEM	77386
ALLEGRO ESTATES BLVD	0	293G	SEM	77386
ALLEGRO SHORES LN	20300	338N	NEC	77346
ALLEMAND LN	16800	367C	NWC	77429
ALLEN	100	536W	SH	77587
ALLEN	1200	493M	NEH	77002

Street Name	Block	Pg/Sq	Loc	Zips
ALLEN	3000	537G	PA	77503
ALLEN	3100	493E	SWH	77007
ALLEN	4100	492G	SWH	77007
ALLEN	17900	459N	NEC	77530
ALLEN CIR	0	542C	CCO	77520
ALLEN CT	1000	492G	SWH	77007
ALLEN LN	2000	460X	MN	77521
ALLEN LN	8300	530X	SWH	77071
ALLEN RD	3600	614W	NEB	77584
ALLEN RD	15100	527Z	NEF	77498
ALLENBROOK DR	3700	501L	BT	77521
ALLENBY LN	0	573T	SEC	77047
W. ALLENDALE	100	536U	PA	77502
ALLENDALE	100	531L	BL	77401
ALLENDALE RD	4500	535V	SEH	77017
ALLENDALE RD	5200	536N	SEH	77017
ALLENDALE RIDGE TRAIL	0	526N	NEF	77407
ALLENDE DR	7600	527K	NEF	77083
ALLENE DR	30600	286C	SWM	77355
ALLENFORD CT	0	484Z	NEF	77494
S. ALLEN GENOA RD	100	536Y	SH	77587
N. ALLEN GENOA RD	100	536Y	SH	77587
ALLEN GENOA RD	100	536J	SEH	77017
ALLEN GENOA RD	1300	536T	PA	77502
ALLEN GENOA RD	3700	576H	PA	77504
ALLEN GENOA RD	5300	577N	PA	77034
ALLENHAM CT	21200	334M	NCC	77338
ALLENHAM LN	21100	334M	NCC	77338
ALLEN PINES LN	7400	406K	NWC	77433
ALLEN PKWY	500	493J	SWH	77002
ALLEN PKWY	1500	493J	SWH	77019
ALLEN PKWY	3900	492M	SWH	77019
ALLENSBY	7000	453P	NEH	77022
ALLEN SHORE CIR	0	366K	NWC	77433
W. ALLEN SHORE DR	12100	366K	NWC	77433
E. ALLEN SHORE DR	18100	366L	NWC	77433
ALLENS LANDING DR	10700	368U	NWC	77065
ALLENTOWN DR	6000	290G	NWC	77389
ALLENWICK LN	0	407Z	NWC	77084
ALLENWICK HILLS CT	0	326U	NWC	77429
ALLERTON	6200	408S	NWC	77084
ALLERTON DR	1800	570X	MC	77489
ALLEY	0	540X	LP	77571
ALLEY	0	537Q	PA	77503
ALLEY CT	500	292W	NWC	77388
S. ALLEY CT	15700	527C	SWC	77082
ALLIANCE	100	282T	WL	77484
ALLIANT DR	100	374Y	NEH	77032
ALLIE CT	0	293K	SEM	77386
ALLIGATOR LN	1200	335C	SEM	77339
ALLIGATOR GAR CT	0	366S	NWC	77433
ALLINGHAM LN	23700	485T	NEF	77494
ALLINGTON COVE LN	0	376R	NEC	77346
ALLIS	200	332B	NCC	77373
ALLISA	0	569T	SF	77477
ALLISON CT	2200	609D	MC	77459
ALLISON CT	25000	250X	NWC	77389
ALLISON DR	2800	376G	NEC	77396
ALLISON LN	9900	532T	SWH	77054
ALLISON RD	4100	573R	SEH	77048
ALLISON RD	4600	574N	SEH	77048
ALLISON BEND CT	10900	370V	NWC	77086
ALLISON MEADOWS CT	0	293K	SEM	77386
ALLISTER CT	23300	485T	NEF	77494
ALLMAN	1700	541C	BT	77520
ALLPOINT CT	7200	525L	NEF	77407
ALLSTON	500	492D	NWH	77007
ALLSTON	900	452Z	NWH	77008
ALLSTON	4100	452M	NWH	77018
ALLSUP	7400	574G	SEH	77061
ALLUM RD	4600	571G	SWH	77045
ALLVIEW LN	19000	486D	SWC	77094
ALLWOOD	7900	454D	NEH	77016
ALLWOOD	11200	414Q	NEC	77093
ALLYSON CT	2600	293T	NCC	77373
ALLYSON LN	2800	293T	NCC	77373
ALLYSUM CT	13200	328Y	NWC	77429
ALLYSUM LN	13100	328Y	NWC	77429
ALMA	100	493C	NWH	77009
ALMA	800	288K	TB	77375
ALMA	6700	574Z	BK	77581
ALMA	12400	419U	BR	77532
ALMAHURST CIR	13800	328T	NWC	77429
ALMAHURST LN	13800	328T	NWC	77429
ALMARIE DR	25600	257Q	SEM	77357
E. ALMEDA	8800	533S	SWH	77054
E. ALMEDA	10500	532Z	SWH	77051
ALMEDA RD	3500	493X	SWH	77004
ALMEDA RD	5100	533N	SWH	77004
ALMEDA RD	6100	533N	SWH	77021
ALMEDA RD	6900	533N	SWH	77030
ALMEDA RD	6901	533N	SWH	77021
ALMEDA RD	7000	533N	SWH	77054
ALMEDA RD	10500	532Z	SWH	77045
ALMEDA RD	10900	572Q	SWH	77045
ALMEDA RD	13400	572Q	SWH	77053
ALMEDA RD	14600	612B	SWC	77053
ALMEDA BEND CT	9500	575R	SEH	77075
ALMEDA FOREST CT	0	532S	SWH	77045
ALMEDA GENOA RD	100	572U	SWH	77047
ALMEDA GENOA RD	1900	573T	SEH	77047
ALMEDA GENOA RD	4100	574Q	SEH	77048
ALMEDA GENOA RD	6700	575N	SEH	77075
ALMEDA GENOA RD	9700	576N	SEH	77075
ALMEDA GENOA RD	10500	576Q	SEH	77034
ALMEDA MEADOWS DR	0	573R	SEH	77048
ALMEDA MEADOWS DR	0	573R	SEH	77048
ALMEDA OAKS DR	9800	576N	SEH	77075
ALMEDA PARK	0	532S	SWH	77045
ALMEDA PINES DR	9500	575R	SEH	77075
ALMEDA PLAZA DR	2600	572L	SWH	77045
ALMEDA SCHOOL RD	13400	572Y	SWH	77047
ALMEDA SCHOOL RD	14600	612C	SWC	77047
ALMEDA TRACE DR	0	572Q	SWH	77045
ALMEECE	14400	572P	SWH	77045
ALMEECE	15100	572T	SWH	77053
ALMENAR CIR	2500	412E	NWC	77038
ALMENDARES AVE	2600	537P	PA	77506
ALMERA FALLS DR	0	407E	NWC	77433
ALMINGTON LN	3400	411V	NWH	77088
ALMONASTER	12100	370L	NWC	77066
ALMOND CT	3900	293M	SEM	77386
ALMOND DR	0	500E	BT	77520
ALMOND ST	900	501M	BT	77521
ALMOND BAY LN	14100	528N	SWC	77083
ALMOND BLOSSOM DR	0	657H	FR	77546
ALMOND BROOK LN	1400	617H	SEH	77062
ALMOND COVE CT	0	612U	PL	77584
ALMOND CREEK DR	2900	578W	SEH	77059
S. ALMONDELL CIR	0	249A	SWM	77354
N. ALMONDELL CIR	0	249A	SWM	77354
ALMONDELL CT	0	249B	SWM	77354
ALMONDELL DR	0	249B	SWM	77354
S. ALMONDELL WAY	0	249B	SWM	77354
N. ALMONDELL WAY	0	249B	SWM	77354
ALMOND GLEN CT	0	417W	NEC	77044
ALMOND GROVE	10900	376U	NEC	77396
ALMOND GROVE CT	12100	489J	SWH	77077
ALMOND GROVE DR	1200	489J	SWH	77077
ALMOND LAKE CT	14700	613D	SEC	77047
ALMOND LAKE DR	4000	613D	SEC	77047
ALMOND ORCHARD LN	25000	485W	NEF	77494
ALMOND PARK CT	19800	486L	SWC	77450
ALMOND PARK LN	19800	486L	SWC	77450
ALMOND PARK LN	19800	486L	SWC	77450
ALMOND PLACE LN	18000	526R	NEF	77407
ALMOND POINTE	900	658R	LC	77573
ALMOND SPRINGS DR	7500	407L	NWC	77095
ALMONDWOOD LN	3400	291L	NWC	77389
ALMONT DR	7100	415T	NEH	77016
ALMONTE LN	18100	328H	NWC	77377
ALOE	1	492L	SWH	77007
ALOE AVE	5200	461T	NEC	77521
ALOFT CT	2000	418D	NEC	77532
ALOHA TRAIL DR	11900	456C	NEC	77044
ALON CT	13700	371C	NWC	77014
ALON LN	13600	371C	NWC	77014
ALORA LANDING TRAIL	0	617E	SEH	77089
ALORA SPRINGS TRACE	0	367P	NWC	77433
ALORIA HILLS TRAIL	0	484N	NEF	77494
ALPENA LN	11500	367R	NWC	77095
ALPERTON DR	7600	411R	NWH	77088
ALPHA	3600	492R	SWH	77019
ALPHA	12100	529N	SWH	77072
ALPHA	12900	614B	BK	77581
S. ALPHA DR	0	614N	PL	77584
N. ALPHA DR	0	614N	PL	77584
ALPHA DR	1100	537N	PA	77506
ALPHA LN	1300	419D	NEC	77532
ALPHA LN	1400	420A	NEC	77532
ALPILLES MOUNTAIN DR	0	450K	NWH	77080
ALPINE CIR	0	609P	MC	77459
ALPINE CT	1	531H	BL	77401
ALPINE DR	100	569J	SF	77477
W. ALPINE DR	6700	574C	SEH	77061
E. ALPINE DR	6700	574C	SEH	77061
ALPINE BROOK CT	2100	611W	FS	77545
ALPINE BROOK LN	0	376K	NEC	77346
ALPINE CREST LN		484S	NEF	77494
ALPINE HEIGHTS DR	5300	297E	NEC	77365
ALPINE MOUNTAIN LN	0	328F	NWC	77429
ALPINE PARK LN	7500	407K	NWC	77433
ALPINE RIDGE WAY	12500	617E	SEH	77089
ALPINE ROSE LN	0	484U	NEF	77494
ALPINE TRAIL LN	0	524H	NEF	77494
ALPINE TRAIL LN	0	524H	NEF	77494
ALPINE VALE CT	11600	411H	NWC	77088
ALP SPRINGS LN	25600	292U	NCC	77373
ALPSTRINE	24500	257P	SEM	77357
ALROVER	14400	572P	SWH	77045
ALROVER	15000	572T	SWH	77053
ALSACE	3600	533M	SEH	77021
ALSAY	0	370L	NWC	77066
ALSEA BAY CT	0	377F	NEC	77346
ALSETH CIR	10900	370V	NWC	77086
ALSEY ROSE DR	0	376R	NEC	77346
ALSHIRE DR	4000	333G	NCC	77373
ALSTEAD CT	15900	570Z	SWH	77489
ALSTEAD DR	6100	408Y	NWC	77041
ALSTON	12400	568D	SG	77478
ALSTON DR	12000	569A	MD	77477
ALSTON RD	12400	568C	SG	77478
ALSTON PLACE	0	615W	PL	77584
ALSTON HILLS DR	0	406H	NWC	77433
ALSUMA	8500	455X	NEH	77029
ALSWORTH	3200	660H	BC	77518
ALTA LN	0	539W	DP	77571
ALTAIR DR	13400	571Q	SWH	77085
ALTAIR DR	14100	248X	TB	77375
ALTAIR DR	14200	248X	TB	77375
ALTAIR WAY	0	571L	SWH	77085
ALTAI TERRACE DR		289Y	NWC	77389
ALTA LOMA WAY	9900	576S	SEH	77075
ALTA MAR DR	15800	527L	NEF	77083
ALTA MESA DR	15300	527G	SWC	77083
ALTAMIRE DR	0	658S	LC	77573
ALTAMONT DR	8900	530T	SWH	77074
ALTA OAK DR	0	484Z	NEF	77494
ALTA PEAK WAY	0	445D	NWC	77449
ALTA PEAK WAY CT	0	445D	NWC	77449
ALTAVILLA LN	0	659H	LC	77573
ALTA VISTA	0	494Z	SEH	77011
ALTA VISTA	1600	534D	SEH	77023
ALTA VISTA DR	300	536V	PA	77502
ALTHEA DR	900	452J	NWH	77018
ALTHEA DR	2100	451M	NWH	77018
ALTIC	1	494U	SEH	77011
ALTIC	600	494U	SEH	77023
ALTIC LANE CT	11500	370M	NWC	77066
ALTMAN TRAIL	0	371D	NWC	77014
ALTMOR LN	10200	575U	SEH	77075
ALTO	700	413B	NCC	77060
ALTO LAKE DR	11700	372J	NWC	77067
ALTON	100	495W	SEH	77012
ALTONBURY LN	10000	569G	SWC	77031
ALTON SPRINGS DR	0	406H	NWC	77433
ALTON WRIGHT RD	32100	247S	SWM	77355
ALTON WRIGHT RD	33000	246R	SWM	77355
ALTOONA	2300	494B	NEH	77026
ALTO PEAK LN	0	406T	NWC	77433
ALTURA DR	0	328K	NWC	77377
ALTUS DR	3000	573K	SEH	77051
S. ALTWOOD CIR	1	250A	WD	77382
ALUM ROCK LN	0	574Z	SEH	77048
ALVA	1	501V	BT	77520
ALVA CT	0	258E	SEM	77357
ALVAR DR	0	371G	NWC	77014
ALVARADO DR	5700	571E	SWH	77035
ALVERSTON DR	0	484V	NEF	77494
ALVIN	500	537J	PA	77506
ALVIN	3600	533Y	SEH	77051
ALVIN	4700	533Z	SEH	77033
ALVIN-SUGARLAND RD	3600	609F	MC	77479
ALVIN-SUGARLAND RD	6900	610S	MC	77459
ALVIN A-KLEIN DR	0	290V	NWC	77379
ALVIN A KLEIN DR	0	290T	NWC	77379
ALVIN A KLEIN DR	0	290P	NWC	77379
ALVY DR	1700	539U	LP	77571
ALYDAR DR	2000	538S	PA	77503
ALYSE	600	538L	DP	77536
ALYSHEBA LN	4200	617T	SEC	77546
ALYSSA AVE	12700	570J	MC	77489
ALYSSA CT	9700	376S	NEC	77396
ALYSSA LN	21700	255V	SEM	77365
ALYSSA GARDEN LN	8400	375Y	NEC	77396
ALY TRACE CT	10800	370W	NWC	77064
ALZAADA LN	9300	369M	NWC	77070
AMADO DR	12300	368R	NWC	77065
AMADO LN	0	658Y	LC	77573
AMADWE	8500	533Z	SEH	77051
AMALFI DR	0	619V	LC	77565
AMALFI COAST DR	0	407E	NWC	77433
AMALFI SHORES CT	0	610T	MC	77459
AMALFI SHORES CT	0	610T	MC	77459
AMALIE	4000	414X	NEH	77093
AMALIE	4500	454B	NEH	77093
AMANDA CT	3600	578A	PA	77505
AMANDA CT	4800	609A	SG	77478
AMANDA LN	3000	490X	SWH	77063
AMANDA'S CROSSING BLVD	0	616L	SEC	77089
AMANDA GRACE LN	0	328S	NWC	77429
AMANDA LEE DR	0	615U	PL	77581
AMANDA MEADOWS	0	616L	SEC	77089
AMANDA PARK LN	0	616L	SEC	77089
AMANDA PINES	12200	616L	SEC	77089
AMANDAS WAY	28500	293C	SEM	77386
AMANI LN	10300	367X	NWC	77095
AMAPOLA DR	15600	527G	SWC	77083
AMARA CT	1	251J	WD	77381
AMARANTH DR	2600	446U	NWC	77084
AMARANTH MEADOW LN	0	571G	SWH	77085
AMARANTO LN	0	525J	NEF	77406
AMARGOS DR	16400	527K	NEF	77083
AMARILLO	800	536X	SH	77587
AMARILLO	6900	495E	NEH	77020
AMARILLO	7100	495F	NEH	77029
AMARYLLIS AVE	0	461N	NEC	77521
AMARYLLIS RD	0	460W	BT	77521
AMARYLLIS RED TRAIL	0	326J	NWC	77433
AMASA	6500	453P	NEH	77022
AMAZON DR	22800	254Z	SEM	77365
AMBASSADOR CT	1800	610K	MC	77459
AMBASSADOR WAY	5000	491Q	SWH	77056
AMBER	6700	453Q	NEH	77022
AMBER CT	6900	370A	NWC	77069
AMBER LN	200	658K	LC	77573
AMBER ALCOVE CT	4600	297P	NEH	77345
AMBER ASH CT	6800	337Q	NEC	77346
AMBER BAY DR	12900	328L	NWC	77377
W. AMBER BLUFF LN	0	524G	NEF	77494
E. AMBER BLUFF LN	0	524G	NEF	77494
AMBER BOUGH CT	800	617H	SEH	77062
AMBER CANYON DR	11500	367R	NWC	77095
AMBER CHASE DR	1700	486Q	SWH	77450
AMBER CLIFF DR	2900	446T	NWC	77449
AMBER COVE DR	8200	338N	NEC	77346
AMBER CREEK CT	0	612L	PL	77584
AMBERCREEK CT	17300	407L	NWC	77095
AMBER CREEK DR	0	612G	PL	77584
AMBERCREST CT	6500	290G	NWC	77389
AMBERCREST DR	6600	290G	NWC	77389
AMBER CROSSING	0	525V	NEF	77406
AMBER DAISY LN	0	326N	NWC	77433
AMBER DALE CT	2800	578W	SEH	77059
AMBER DAWN LN	25500	485W	NEF	77494
AMBER ELM TRAIL	21900	325R	NWC	77433
AMBERFIELD LN	6500	407N	NWC	77449
AMBER FOREST DR	0	253P	SEM	77386
AMBER FOREST DR	0	253P	SEM	77386
AMBER FOREST DR	3200	331P	NWC	77068
AMBERGATE DR	1300	489J	SWH	77077
AMBERGATE DR	10700	376U	NEC	77396
AMBER GLADE CT	1100	485G	SWC	77494
AMBER GLEN DR	2000	485Q	NEF	77494
AMBER GRAIN LN	0	325R	NWC	77429
AMBERGRIS CT	21200	334M	NCC	77338
AMBER GROVE CT	14100	528N	SWC	77083
AMBER HILL	0	526T	NEF	77407
AMBER HILL TRAIL	2900	615Y	PL	77581
AMBER HOLLOW CT	0	609P	NEF	77479
AMBER HOLLOW CT	14100	327Z	NWC	77429
AMBER HOLLOW LN	15500	327Z	NWC	77429
AMBER HOLLY CT	3200	297K	NEH	77345
AMBER KNOLL CT	1400	617H	SEH	77062
AMBER LAKE DR	4200	447F	NWC	77084
AMBER LEAF CT	1	251A	WD	77381
AMBERLEAF CT	24600	484D	NEF	77494
AMBERLEE CT	4000	293H	SEM	77386
AMBERLIGHT LN	20100	486L	SWC	77450
AMBER LODGE LN	13400	528Q	SWC	77083
AMBERLY CT	2100	490V	SWH	77063
AMBERLY CT	2400	613Q	NEB	77584
AMBER MANOR LN	0	377P	NEC	77346
AMBER MEADOW DR	3100	446Q	NWC	77449
AMBER MIST	17600	407F	NWC	77095
AMBERMIST LN	17200	407B	NWC	77095
AMBERN DR	5500	611B	SWH	77053
AMBER PINE CT	6700	337Q	NEC	77346
AMBER QUEEN CT	5700	448D	NWC	77041
AMBER QUEEN LN	13400	448D	NWC	77041
AMBER ROSE LN	3600	414B	NCC	77039
AMBERSHADOW DR	100	457Y	NEC	77015
AMBER SHORE	0	659D	LC	77573
AMBER SKY PLACE	1	250C	WD	77381
AMBER SPRINGS DR	2200	486P	SWC	77450
AMBERTON LN	1	490K	BH	77024
AMBER VALLEY CT	11400	370M	NWC	77066
AMBERVIEW DR	0	457V	NEC	77530
AMBER VILLAGE CIR	0	526K	NEF	77407
AMBER VILLAGE LN	0	526K	NEF	77407
AMBERVINE CIR	20000	486G	SWC	77450
AMBER WHEAT CT	2300	611W	MC	77545
AMBERWICK DR	9600	569H	SWH	77031
E. AMBER WILLOW TRAIL	0	325R	NWC	77433
S. AMBER WILLOW TRAIL	20800	326F	NWC	77433
AMBERWOOD DR	0	334M	NCC	77338
AMBLE LN	13900	571Q	SWH	77085
AMBLE OAK CT	4500	618B	SEH	77059
AMBLE OAK TRAIL	2700	618B	SEH	77059
AMBLER DR	6600	330L	NWC	77379
AMBLER SPRINGS DR	13500	328F	NWC	77377
AMBLEWOOD DR	8300	529P	SWH	77072
AMBLEWOOD DR	8600	529X	SWH	77099
AMBLEWOOD DR	11800	569A	MD	77477
AMBOY	1100	494F	NEH	77020
AMBROSA DR	0	457A	NEC	77044
AMBROSIA SPRINGS LN	0	484Z	NEF	77494
AMBROSDEN LN	1000	458W	NEC	77530
AMBROSE	12400	572P	SWH	77045
AMBROSIA FALLS DR	19400	329A	NWC	77375
AMBROSIA PLACE	1	250B	WD	77381
AMBRY	0	408W	NWC	77084
AMBURSEN	10400	576K	SEH	77034
AMC DR	1200	484H	KT	77494
AMCREEK RD	16200	331Q	NWC	77068
AMELIA	1700	541F	BT	77520
AMELIA DR	12200	572M	SWH	77045
AMELIA RD	7400	451S	NWH	77055
AMELIA ST	0	568T	SG	77478
AMELIA ISLAND DR	0	366Q	NWC	77433
AMELIA LAKE LN	0	377H	NEH	77346
AMELIA PINE LN	17200	377K	NEC	77346
AMENO DR	2400	616K	PL	77581
AMERICAN	300	501X	BT	77520
AMERICAN DR	5500	494L	NEH	77020
AMERICANA DR	1200	569Y	MC	77477
AMERICAN BEAUTY CT	5400	448C	NWC	77041
AMERICAN BEECH TRAIL		249P	NWC	77375
AMERICAN ELM LN	6800	250U	NWC	77389
AMERICAN FORK CT	0	332W	NWC	77090
AMERICAN HOLLY CT	7500	406M	NWC	77433
AMERICAN PETROLEUM RD	12800	496V	NEH	77015
AMERICAN YELLOW WOOD PL	0	296A	SEM	77365
AMERSHAM CT	25800	250T	NWC	77389
AMERSON CT	3900	613Y	NEB	77584
AMERSON DR	3100	613Y	NEB	77584
AMES	2300	613K	PL	77584
AMES CIR	1	490M	PP	77024
AMES CT	500	332C	NCC	77373
AMESBURY CIR	3500	613Q	NEB	77584
AMESBURY CT	3100	569N	SF	77478
AMESBURY DR	15800	408W	NWC	77084
AMESBURY LN	15300	568Y	SG	77478
AMESBURY MANOR LN	18000	486D	SWC	77094
AMESBURY MEADOW LN	21300	290Q	NWC	77379
AMESWOOD RD	7600	408K	NWC	77095
AMETHYST DR	0	367Q	NWC	77095
AMETHYST ARBOR LN	0	524H	NEF	77494
AMHERST	2400	532A	WU	77005
AMHERST LN	700	538Y	DP	77536
AMHERST POINT	0	487A	SWC	77094
AMICI ST	15200	286D	SWM	77355
AMIDON DR	16800	330L	NWC	77379
AMIGO	8100	410U	NWC	77040
AMIGO LN	100	659Z	DI	77539
AMIR	4100	529A	SWH	77072
AMIRA DR	11200	369S	NWC	77065
AMISTAD CT	12000	289W	NWC	77375
AMISTAD DR	19300	328D	NWC	77375
AMISTAD DR	19400	288Z	NWC	77375
AMISTAD LAKE CIR	0	406D	NWC	77433
AMITY DR	0	293G	SEM	77386
AMMANN CT	0	377D	NEH	77346
AMMAR ST	0	530Z	SWH	77096
AMMICK CT	22900	290H	NWC	77389
AMMI TRAIL	18100	373J	NCC	77060
AMMONS	700	536Y	SH	77587
AMMONS	2700	501Q	BT	77521
AMOCO, B P	13500	488B	SWH	77079
AMOOR	3600	455X	NEH	77029
AMORGAS ISLE DR	4900	291N	NWC	77388
AMORTABROOK DR	8200	407G	NWC	77095
AMOS	3500	533Q	SEH	77021
AMPTON DR	6600	330R	NWC	77379
AMSBURY LN	13600	368A	NWC	77429
AMSDEN LN	0	286Q	NWC	77377
AMSLER	600	413E	NCC	77037
AMSTERDAM DR	12300	616D	SEH	77089
AMUDARYA DR	0	295B	SEM	77365
AMUNDSEN	100	453Y	NEH	77009
AMUR DR	22900	294D	SEM	77365
AMURWOOD LN	8100	290E	NWC	77375
AMWELL RD	6000	250Z	NWC	77389
AMY	0	409L	JV	77040
AMY	5100	455N	NEH	77028
N. AMY DR	900	538Q	DP	77536
S. AMY DR	1100	538Q	DP	77536
AMY DR	1600	502S	BT	77520
AMY LN	0	255V	SEM	77357
AMY LN	0	375D	HM	77338
AMY ANN	0	299N	NEC	77336
AMY BROOK CT	8600	375Z	NEC	77396
AMYFORD CT	14300	328X	NWC	77429
AMYFORD BEND	11700	328X	NWC	77429
AMY MICHELLE LN	1700	458V	CV	77530
AMY POINT LN	0	527N	NEF	77407
AMY RIDGE RD	16300	611C	SWH	77053
AMY SHORES CT	2900	485N	NEF	77494
AMYS WAY	0	609S	NEF	77479
AMY WILLOW LN	0	293K	SEM	77386
ANABEL LN	100	453A	NWH	77076
ANACACHO	4400	577F	PA	77504
ANACACHO DR	500	252T	SEM	77386
ANACACHO LN	400	613B	NEB	77584
ANACORTES	8100	535Y	SEH	77061
ANADA BAY CT	14400	327Y	NWC	77429
ANADARKO LN	17400	367X	NWC	77095
ANADELL	8000	451W	HI	77055
ANAGNOST RD	13500	572V	SWH	77047
ANAGNOST RD	14000	612D	SWH	77047
ANA LEE	700	463E	MB	77521
ANALISA CIR	17000	407Q	NWC	77084
ANAQUA DR	5800	451A	NWH	77092
ANAQUITAS CREEK CT	0	525H	NEF	77407
ANARK CT	0	290P	NWC	77379
ANASTASIA TRAIL	0	616L	SEC	77089
ANCHICK	11900	413T	NEH	77076
ANCHOR	0	412W	NWH	77091
ANCHOR	2500	411Z	NWH	77088
ANCHOR DR	6200	407U	NWC	77084
ANCHORAGE LN	500	488A	SWH	77079
ANCHOR BAY CT	2000	613E	PL	77584
ANCHOR BAY LN	0	338W	NEC	77346
ANCHOR LAKE LN	1900	484K	NEF	77494
ANCHOR PARK	16800	617X	SEC	77546
ANCHOR POINT CIR	0	569X	MC	77459
ANCHOR POINT CT	4500	569X	MC	77459
ANCHOR POINTE CT	2100	658V	LC	77573
ANCHOR POINT PLACE	1	251F	WD	77381
ANCHOR RANCH DR	24000	325J	NWC	77447
ANCHOR WAY	0	379X	NEC	77532
ANCHOR WAY	200	660K	LC	77573
ANCIENT ELM LN	0	289C	NWC	77375
ANCIENT FOREST DR	16400	376H	NEH	77346
ANCIENT LORE DR	0	289P	NWC	77375
ANCIENT OAKS DR	5700	337T	NEC	77346
ANCIENT WILLOW DR	8800	290J	NWC	77375
ANCLA LN	22000	338Z	NEC	77532
ANCONA CT	0	445A	NWC	77493
ANDALUSIAN DR	18500	407N	NWC	77433
ANDANTE DR	8700	410K	NWC	77040
ANDERS AVE	1100	620K	SB	77586
ANDERS LN	2000	660B	KE	77565
ANDERSON	0	571S	SWH	77489
ANDERSON	100	453P	NEH	77022
ANDERSON	100	536G	PA	77506
ANDERSON	800	531C	BL	77401
ANDERSON	1200	531C	BL	77081

Street Name	Block	Pg/Sq	Loc	Zips
ANDERSON	24000	339K	HU	77336
ANDERSON CIR	0	295R	SEM	77365
E. ANDERSON RD	100	572V	SWH	77047
ANDERSON RD	700	296S	SEM	77339
ANDERSON RD	3100	572S	SWC	77053
ANDERSON RD	3400	502N	BT	77521
ANDERSON RD	6200	571U	SWH	77085
ANDERSON RD	26000	248K	SWH	77354
ANDERSON, M D	1100	532H	SWH	77030
ANDERSON OAKS	5500	571U	SWH	77053
ANDERSON OAKS CT	5600	571U	SWH	77053
ANDERSON POINT LN	2400	332A	NWC	77388
ANDERSON RANCH LN	0	657P	FR	77546
ANDERSON WOODS DR	13300	369B	NWC	77070
ANDERS RUN RD	0	377K	NEC	77346
ANDERWOOD KNOLL TRACE	0	526L	NEF	77407
ANDERWOOD RIDGE LN	0	249V	NWC	77375
ANDERWOODS CT	13400	369F	NWC	77070
ANDIRON CT	7300	408L	NWC	77041
ANDORRA CT	14000	457Y	NEC	77015
ANDORRA LN	100	457Y	NEC	77015
ANDORRA BAY CROSSING	0	484N	NEF	77494
ANDORRA BEND LN	0	297J	SEM	77365
ANDORRA COVE DR	0	405T	NWC	77493
ANDORRA FALLS TRACE	0	405P	NWC	77493
ANDORR HILLS LN	0	406X	NWC	77449
ANDORRA POINTE TRACE	0	526N	NEF	77407
ANDOVE HILLS CT	0	657Y	LC	77573
ANDOVER	600	332C	NCC	77373
ANDOVER DR	1000	613E	NEB	77584
ANDOVER HARVEST LN	0	328P	NWC	77429
ANDOVER MANOR DR	12900	367H	NWC	77429
ANDOVER TRACE LN	0	609U	MC	77459
ANDOWER WOODS CT	8300	407G	NWC	77095
ANDRAU LN	12000	489W	SWH	77082
ANDREA	4900	534N	SEH	77021
ANDREA LN	1800	537P	PA	77502
ANDREA SOPHIA LN	3600	578A	PA	77505
ANDREA WAY LN	14200	528N	NEF	77083
ANDREE FOREST CT	0	253P	SEM	77386
ANDREW LN	20500	446K	NWC	77449
ANDREW LN	22900	295D	SEM	77365
ANDREW LN	23200	296A	SEM	77365
ANDREW ARBOR CT	0	366R	NWC	77433
ANDREW CHASE LN	1500	293K	SEM	77386
ANDREWS	200	493P	SWH	77019
ANDREWS CT	0	580L	LP	77571
ANDREW SPRINGS LN	0	293K	SEM	77386
ANDREW SPRINGS LN	27500	293G	SEM	77386
ANDREWS RIDGE LN	0	375X	NEC	77396
ANDREW WAY CT	13500	488X	SWC	77082
ANDRICKS RD	3100	579A	LP	77571
E. ANDRICKS RD	9600	579A	LP	77571
ANDRIS LN	0	252T	SEM	77386
ANDRUS CT	0	524U	NEF	77084
ANDWOOD	6100	534V	SEH	77021
ANDY DR	7300	412U	NWH	77091
ANDY LN	26000	248K	SWH	77354
ANGARA CT	19200	294H	SEM	77365
ANGEL LN	3300	572F	SWH	77045
ANGELA	1100	538Q	DP	77536
ANGELA CT	9800	289U	NWC	77379
ANGELA DR	1	245F	SWM	77355
ANGELA LN	0	569P	SF	77477
ANGELAS MEADOWS	9100	408B	NWC	77375
ANGELA WAY DR	0	253S	SEM	77386
ANGEL FALLS LN	5900	408Y	NWC	77041
ANGEL FIRE LN	13800	369A	NWC	77070
ANGEL GATE CT	23300	485T	NEF	77494
ANGELINA AVE	1000	536H	PA	77506
ANGELINE	1800	453T	NWH	77009
ANGELINE SPRINGS LN	0	366V	NWC	77433
ANGELIQUE DR	11200	368U	NWC	77065
ANGEL ISLAND LN	16300	611B	SWH	77053
ANGEL LAKE DR	0	524Q	NWF	77040
ANGEL LEAF RD	100	291D	WD	77380
ANGEL MEADOW CT	14300	568E	SG	77498
ANGELO	5300	453U	NEH	77009
ANGEL OAKS CT	7000	526H	NEF	77407
ANGEL PARK DR	0	253Q	SEM	77386
ANGEL RUN LN	0	297K	NEH	77377
ANGEL SHORES LN	12300	449A	NWC	77041
ANGELS REST CT	0	293U	NCC	77373
ANGELWOOD SPRINGS LN	0	249V	NWC	77375
ANGENI TRAIL	0	297J	SEM	77365
ANGIE LN	9600	412F	NWC	77038
ANGLEFISH COVE	3100	542P	BT	77520
ANGLER DR	7600	377D	NEC	77346
ANGLER BEND DR	15900	377Q	NWC	77044
ANGLERBEND LANDING	7300	407L	NWC	77095
ANGLER COVE DR	0	366J	NWC	77433
ANGLER LEAF CT	16000	377Q	NEC	77044
ANGLER PARK	32400	252R	SEM	77385
ANGLESIDE LN	9700	528T	NEF	77498
ANGLETON	4700	533Z	NEH	77033
ANGLIN	1200	453M	NEH	77022
ANGLING CT	0	293R	SEM	77386
ANGORA	26200	247T	SWM	77355
ANGUS	6000	614U	PL	77584
ANGUS	7800	455P	NWH	77088
ANGUS DR	19800	380H	NEC	77532
ANICE	1500	413G	NCC	77039
ANICE	2400	414E	NCC	77039
ANICE	3500	414M	NCC	77039
ANIMAL CRACKER	0	296T	SEM	77339
ANITA	300	493P	SWH	77004
ANITA	1000	493Z	SEH	77004
ANITA	3900	494W	SEH	77004
ANKELE LN	0	448K	NWH	77084
ANLU DR	0	524J	NWF	77084
ANN	1000	536M	PA	77506
ANN	2200	494J	SEH	77004
ANN	20100	256K	SWH	77357
ANN CIR	21800	285H	SWM	77447
ANN CT	3600	533D	SEH	77004
ANN CT	27200	252E	OR	77385
ANN LN	3900	614W	NEB	77064
ANN LN	12100	369R	NWH	77064
ANNA	900	656B	NEB	77546
ANNADEL GARDENS DR	16800	407U	NWC	77084
ANNA GREEN	16800	407U	NWC	77084
ANNA HELD	10500	534R	SEH	77048
ANNANDALE TERRACE DR	13900	367D	NWH	77429
ANNAPOLIS	0	532G	WU	77005
ANNAPOLIS	1	619W	TL	77586
ANNAPOLIS	5800	532C	WU	77005
ANN ARBOR CT	3100	569N	SG	77478
ANN ARBOR DR	2800	490Y	SWH	77047
ANNATTO DR	0	461Q	NEC	77521
ANNATTO LN	0	419C	NEC	77532
ANNA WAY	0	656R	FR	77546
ANNAWOOD CIR	4200	331F	NWC	77388
ANNE	1000	450Y	NWH	77055
ANNE	1100	490C	SV	77055
ANNE AVE	1200	335Z	HM	77338
ANNE DR	18100	618Z	WB	77058
ANNE LN	32000	248N	SWM	77355
ANNE'S CT	1	252J	WD	77380
ANNE'S WAY	200	569P	SF	77477
ANNE BLUSH DR	0	286Q	NWC	77377
ANNENDALE CIR	20900	295R	SEM	77365
ANNETTE LN	1	453B	NEH	77076
ANNETTE LN	100	616Y	FR	77546
ANNFRAN CIR	11900	328X	NWC	77429
ANNICE LN	32000	248S	SWM	77355
ANNIE LEE LN	0	656B	NEB	77581
ANNISTON DR	2500	450N	NWH	77080
ANN LOUISE RD	12000	411C	NWC	77086
ANN LOUISE RD	13000	371Y	NWC	77086
ANNOLA LN	7900	330P	NWC	77379
ANNUNCIATION	5500	414R	NEH	77016
ANNUNCIATION	6100	415N	NEH	77016
ANOKA CT	14700	497D	NEC	77015
ANOKA DR	14800	497D	NEC	77530
ANSBURY DR	1200	452P	NWH	77018
ANSDELL CT	5400	408W	NWC	77084
ANSELM ST	4400	572E	SWH	77045
ANSLEY RD	33500	247P	SWM	77355
ANSLEY WAY	0	616T	PL	77581
ANSON CIR	800	537L	PA	77503
ANSON FALLS CT	20100	486G	SWC	77450
ANSON GROVE LN	14100	568A	SG	77498
ANSON POINT LN	6800	411S	NWH	77047
ANTAGNOST RD	13700	572V	SWH	77047
ANTAGNOST RD	14100	572Z	SWH	77047
ANTEAN WAY CT	12500	408D	NWC	77065
ANTELOPE LN	100	379A	NEC	77532
ANTELOPE DR	600	378D	NEC	77532
ANTELOPE DR	8600	490Y	NWC	77063
ANTELOPE LN	16000	246T	SWM	77355
ANTELOPE CREEK LN	0	484S	NEF	77494
ANTELOPE HILLS DR	2800	610U	MC	77459
ANTELOPE SHORE DR	0	537V	PA	77503
ANTHA	4400	454C	NEH	77093
ANTHA	4600	454D	NEH	77016
ANTHEM COVE	1500	484K	NEF	77494
ANTHONETTE LN	1300	497L	NEC	77015
ANTHONIA LN	6000	524Y	NEF	77445
ANTHONY CT	900	536H	PA	77506
ANTHONY LN	2300	614H	PL	77581
ANTHONY LN	4600	577M	PA	77505
ANTHONY HAY CT	22700	445U	NWC	77449
ANTHONY HAY LN	2000	445U	NWC	77449
ANTHONY PINE LN	2500	412J	NWH	77088
ANTHONY TRAILS LN	0	293F	SEM	77386
ANTHONY TRAILS LN	0	293F	SEM	77386
ANTHURIUM CT	19200	406R	NWC	77449
ANTIBES LN	0	529B	SWH	77082
ANTIETAM LN	8400	527P	NEF	77375
ANTIGUA LN	1300	618Z	NB	77058
ANTIGUA LN	1500	619S	NB	77058
ANTILLES LN	1	619W	SB	77058
ANTIOCH DR	15700	571Z	SWH	77053
ANTIQUA ESTATES CT	22900	252L	SEM	77385
ANTIQUE LN	22700	256Q	SEM	77357
ANTIQUE CEDAR LN	6800	250U	NWC	77389
ANTIQUE MEADOWS DR	4600	617S	SEC	77546
ANTLER DR	0	376N	NEC	77396
ANTLER LN	4900	333H	NCC	77338
ANTLERS CIR	24400	296M	SEM	77365
ANTLER TRAILS CT	0	378Q	NEC	77532
ANTLER TRAILS LN	0	378Q	NEC	77532
ANTOINE DR	700	491B	SWH	77024
ANTOINE DR	1000	451Q	NWH	77055
ANTOINE DR	2800	451G	NWH	77091
ANTOINE DR	5300	451G	NWH	77091
ANTOINE DR	6100	411Y	NWH	77091
ANTOINE DR	7000	411B	NWH	77088
ANTOINE DR	10000	371T	NWC	77086
ANTOINE DR	11000	371P	NWC	77067
ANTOINE DR	12300	371P	NWC	77067
ANTOINETTE	4000	534L	SEH	77004
ANTOINETTE LN	100	419R	BR	77532
ANTON DR	28000	248N	NWC	77449
E. ANTONE CIR	15300	570G	MC	77071
W. ANTONE CIR	15400	570G	MC	77071
ANTONIA	12700	570J	SF	77477
ANTONIA LN	31100	288B	TB	77375
ANTONIA LN	31200	248X	TB	77375
ANTONIA MANOR CT	0	525V	NEF	77445
ANTONIO ST	4400	572E	SWH	77045
ANTRIM	2600	616J	PL	77581
ANTRIM LN	9900	579C	LP	77571
ANTRIM LN	10300	539X	LP	77571
ANTRIM PLACE	14400	368A	NWC	77429
ANTWERP COVE	9300	329U	NWC	77070
ANVIL CIR	17400	331M	NWC	77090
ANVIL DR	17400	331M	NWC	77090
ANVIL LN	0	255T	SEM	77365
ANVIL COVE DR	0	250Q	NWC	77373
ANVIL IRON LN		524L	NWF	77406
ANWAR DR	13700	528F	SWC	77083
ANY WAY	0	297N	NWH	77339
ANZA CIR	7900	535F	SEH	77012
ANZAC	7100	494H	NEH	77020
ANZAC	7200	495E	NEH	77020
ANZAC DR	0	615W	PL	77584
ANZAC MEADOW CT	0	325Q	NWC	77433
ANZALONE DR	2500	333A	NCC	77373
ANZIO RD	5200	534S	SEH	77033
APACHE	500	453L	NEH	77022
APACHE	6900	454R	NEH	77028
APACHE	7300	455N	NEH	77028
APACHE CT	4200	461S	NEC	77520
APACHE DR	1100	503F	CCO	77520
APACHE DR	6300	538W	PA	77532
APACHE DR	4600	461A	NEC	77532
APACHE ST	0	658Y	LC	77573
APACHE CROSSING	0	658U	LC	77573
APACHE FALLS DR	1000	485G	SWC	77450
APACHE GARDENS LN	20100	446M	NWC	77449
APACHE HILLS DR	17300	328M	NWC	77377
APACHE LAKE DR	20300	448P	NWC	77449
APACHE LEAF DR	0	656K	FR	77546
APACHE MEADOWS DR	4300	446N	NWC	77449
APACHE PLUME DR	7500	570C	SWH	77071
APACHE POINT DR	4500	375V	NWC	77429
APACHE TRAIL	1100	501M	BT	77521
APACHE TRAIL	4500	613V	NEB	77584
APACHE TRAIL	18300	295F	SEM	77365
APACHE TRAIL	20200	378H	NEC	77532
APACHE TRAIL	26600	248M	SWM	77354
APACHE WAY DR	10400	367X	NWC	77095
APACHE WELLS DR	0	485J	NEF	77494
APAR DR	5000	374Y	NCC	77032
APEN LEAF LN	0	376S	NEC	77396
APGAR	5500	374R	NEH	77032
APOLLO	800	618U	SEH	77058
APOLLO	4100	452K	NWH	77018
APOLLO	6500	412X	NWH	77091
APOLLO CT	17900	257D	RF	77357
APOTHECARY LN	8300	410G	NWC	77064
APPAIN OAK ST	0	326Y	NWC	77429
APPALACHIAN TRAIL	3200	297T	NEH	77345
APPALOOSA AVE	0	408X	NWC	77084
APPALOOSA FALLS CT	0	368B	NWC	77429
APPALOOSA RIDGE DR	20000	334R	NCC	77338
APPALOOSA TRAIL	20500	378G	NEC	77532
APPELT DR	2200	498J	NEC	77015
APPIA DR	0	619V	LC	77565
APPIAN RIDGE	24400	296M	SEM	77365
APPIAN WAY	1600	497E	NEH	77015
APPIAN WAY	26000	258F	RF	77357
APPIAN WAY	2200	613K	PL	77584
APPIN CT	9200	407D	NWC	77095
APPIN FALLS	0	329V	NWC	77070
APPIN FALLS DR	9100	330S	NWC	77379
APPLE	0	293M	SEM	77386
APPLE DR	3100	610F	MC	77459
APPLE LN	700	657V	LC	77573
APPLE ARBOR DR	23000	333A	NCC	77373
APPLE BEND CIR	0	377W	NEC	77044
APPLEBERRY DR	0	406L	NWC	77433
APPLEBERRY DR	0	524F	NEF	77494
APPLE BLOOM WAY	15400	498A	NEC	77530
APPLE BLOSSOM CIR	20600	257P	SEM	77357
APPLE BLOSSOM DR	700	613E	NEB	77584
APPLEBLOSSOM LN	5000	617W	FR	77546
APPLEBLOSSOM LN	5300	657A	FR	77546
APPLE BLUFF CT	0	377G	NWC	77433
APPLE BLUFF LN	6100	609X	NEF	77479
APPLE BOUGH CIR	11700	372J	NWC	77067
APPLE BROOK LN	0	445K	NWC	77493
APPLE BUD CT	0	373E	NCC	77073
APPLE DR	12200	570E	SWH	77031
APPLE CREEK RD	0	571F	SWH	77085
APPLE CREEK RD	5400	536W	SEH	77017
APPLECREEK BEND DR	0	569T	NEF	77477
APPLECREST WAY	19100	291X	NWC	77388
APPLECROSS LN	16800	407Z	NWC	77084
APPLECROSS LN	17000	407Z	NWC	77084
APPLE DALE DR	0	447K	NWC	77494
APPLE DALE DR	0	447K	NWC	77494
APPLE FORD DR	1100	619G	TL	77586
APPLE FOREST CT	2900	297Q	NEH	77345
APPLE FOREST TRAIL	12800	368Y	NWC	77065
APPLEGATE DR	22400	334N	NWC	77373
APPLE GLEN DR	13000	528L	SWH	77072
APPLE GREEN	700	413B	NWC	77060
APPLE GROVE DR	3500	613X	NEB	77578
APPLE HARVEST LN	0	367P	NWC	77433
APPLE HEDGE TRAIL	0	524D	NEF	77494
APPLE HILL	18800	447N	NWC	77084
APPLE HOLLOW CT	16400	376L	NEC	77396
APPLE HOLLOW LN	0	376L	NEC	77396
APPLE KNOLL CT	13600	577Z	SEH	77059
APPLE KNOLL CT	13700	618A	SEH	77059
APPLE MILL DR	8800	408A	NWC	77095
APPLEMINT CIR	20600	326J	NWC	77433
APPLE OAK CT	7000	526H	NEF	77407
APPLE PARK CT	1400	485M	SWC	77450
APPLE PARK DR	1400	486J	SWC	77450
APPLERIDGE CT	7500	570Z	SWH	77489
APPLERIDGE DR	9700	369L	NWC	77070
APPLERIDGE LN	15300	570Z	SWH	77489
APPLE RIVER DR	0	366Q	NWC	77433
APPLEROCK DR	4000	501K	BT	77521
APPLEROCK TRAIL	15800	326S	NWC	77433
APPLE SEED CT	2900	487Z	SWC	77082
APPLE SPRING	0	538R	DP	77536
APPLE SPRINGS DR	4800	614R	PL	77584
APPLETON	6800	453L	NEH	77022
APPLETON DR	1900	610B	MC	77489
APPLETON DR	3300	613Y	NEB	77584
APPLETON HILLS TRAIL	0	406D	NWC	77433
APPLETON MEADOW TRACE	0	406W	NWC	77449
APPLE TREE W. CIR	3700	579B	LP	77571
APPLE TREE N. CIR	10300	579B	LP	77571
APPLE TREE S. CIR	10300	579B	LP	77571
APPLE TREE RD	13000	489F	SWH	77079
APPLETREE HILL LN	18700	447J	NWC	77084
APPLETREE HILL LN	18900	446M	NWC	77084
APPLETREE RIDGE RD	18900	447A	NWC	77084
APPLETREE RIDGE RD	19000	446J	NWC	77084
APPLEVALE CT	5200	297P	NEH	77345
APPLE VALLEY LN	3000	609H	MC	77459
APPLE VALLEY LN	3000	610F	MC	77459
APPLE VALLEY LN	6100	370C	NWC	77069
APPLE VALLEY LN	6100	370B	NWC	77069
APPLEWHITE DR	100	485D	SWC	77450
APPLEWOOD	11600	490P	BH	77024
APPLEWOOD DR	300	656L	FR	77546
APPLEWOOD DR	1100	579C	LP	77571
APPLEWOOD FOREST DR	6300	524F	NEF	77494
APPLEYARD LN	16100	324S	NWC	77433
APPOMATTOX	8900	538Z	LP	77571
APPOMATTOX DR	800	251V	SWM	77380
W. APRICOT BLUSH CT	0	325Q	NWC	77433
E. APRICOT BLUSH CT	0	325Q	NWC	77433
APRICOT BLUSH W. CT	14600	325Q	NWC	77433
APRICOT BLUSH E. CT	14700	325Q	NWC	77433
APRIL	12300	614D	BK	77581
APRIL LN	3000	451L	NWH	77092
APRIL LN	3800	451G	NWH	77092
APRIL ARBOR CT	8700	530X	NWH	77433
APRIL COVE CT	2700	613X	NEB	77578
APRIL CREEK LN	7200	407Q	NWC	77095
APRIL FALLS TRAIL	16300	527P	NEF	77083
APRIL GLEN CT	14100	326Z	NWC	77429
APRIL GLEN CT	17200	407Q	NWC	77084
APRIL HILL	16600	407L	NWC	77095
APRIL KNOLL CT	10900	369S	NWC	77429
APRIL MEADOW DR	0	290N	NWC	77379
APRIL MIST CT	13200	328F	SWC	77082
E. APRIL RAIN CT	1300	610B	MC	77489
W. APRIL RAIN CT	1400	610B	MC	77489
APRIL RIDGE DR	16100	527P	NEF	77083
APRIL RUN CT	2600	298W	NEH	77073
APRIL SHOWERS LN	10700	449G	NWC	77041
APRIL SPRINGS LN	22600	525F	NEF	77494
APRIL WAY CT	11000	490M	HC	77024
APRIL WIND DR	3000	371G	NWC	77014
APSLEY MANOR TRAIL	0	451Y	NWH	77055
AQUA BAY CT	7300	529E	SWH	77072
AQUA CT	0	326J	NWC	77433
AQUA DR	5000	293Y	NCC	77373
AQUARIAN CT	16400	419B	NEC	77532
AQUATIC DR	18700	378B	NEC	77346
AQUA VISTA DR	0	620L	SB	77586
AQUA VISTA DR	900	336J	NEH	77339
AQUEDUCT RD	11700	417R	NEC	77044
AQUILLA CT	5000	609K	MC	77459
AQUILLALAKE CIR	0	366Z	NWC	77433
AQUILLA CT	0	293M	SEM	77386
ARABELLA	6500	412X	NWH	77091
ARABELLA	8700	412P	NEH	77088
ARABELLE	2000	492B	NWH	77007
ARABELLE	14800	408X	NWC	77084
ARABIAN TRAIL	0	612Z	NEB	77578
ARAGON DR	7100	527L	NEF	77083
ARAGON GREEN DR	15100	325R	NWC	77433
ARAGON MEADOW LN	0	457K	NEC	77049
ARAMIS DR	16000	332V	NCC	77073
ARANAS CT	0	447A	NWC	77449
ARANAS LN	0	447A	NWC	77449
ARANSAS DR	9100	412K	NWH	77088
ARAPAHO BEND LN	0	327U	NWC	77429
ARAPAHOE	5200	494G	NEH	77020
ARAPAHOE PASS LN	0	526Q	NEF	77407
ARAPAHO HILL LN	0	377E	NEC	77346
ARAPAHO SHADOW CT	13800	328P	NWC	77429
ARAPAHO TRAIL	24100	296M	SEM	77365
ARAPAJO	4100	461S	NEC	77521
ARAPAJO	4200	577F	PA	77504
ARBERRY	7700	535F	SEH	77012
ARBOLADA GREEN CT	20200	337U	NEC	77346
ARBOLDS DR	5200	571A	SWH	77035
ARBOR	100	500P	BT	77520
ARBOR	1000	533B	SWH	77004
ARBOR	2200	533C	SEH	77004
ARBOR	0	659N	LC	77573
E. ARBOR CIR	3300	620F	SB	77586
ARBOR CT	500	613G	NEB	77584
ARBOR DR	0	538U	DP	77536
ARBOR DR	3800	613G	NEB	77584
ARBOR LN	0	245R	SWM	77355
ARBOR LN	3300	620E	SB	77586
ARBOR LN	4400	578G	PA	77505
ARBOR LN	6000	525H	NEF	77450
ARBOR BEND CT	19300	331A	NWC	77379
ARBOR BEND CT	27000	337Q	NWC	77346
ARBOR BEND DR	1	369H	NWC	77070
ARBOR BLUE LN	0	366J	NWC	77433
N. ARBOR BOUGH CIR	1200	611X	NEF	77545
W. ARBOR BOUGH CIR	3800	611X	NEF	77545
E. ARBOR BOUGH CIR	3800	611X	NEF	77545
ARBOR BREEZE CT	0	525D	NEF	77450
ARBOR BRIDGE CT	5300	297P	NEH	77345
ARBOR BROOK CT	4400	578E	PA	77505
ARBOR BROOK LN	0	612P	PL	77545
W. ARBOR CAMP CIR	0	250Q	NWC	77389
E. ARBOR CAMP CIR	0	250R	NWC	77389
ARBOR CANYON LN	0	488N	SWH	77077
ARBOR COVE	0	484K	NEF	77494
ARBOR COVE CT	23400	525L	NEF	77407
ARBOR COVE LN	22200	525L	NEF	77407
ARBOR CREEK DR	19700	406Q	NWC	77449
ARBORCREST	14200	618A	SEH	77062
ARBORDALE LN	11900	490J	BH	77024
ARBORETUM DR	4200	578F	PA	77505
ARBOR FALLS LN	4900	447A	NWC	77084
ARBOR FIELD LN	12700	456D	NEC	77044
ARBOR FIELD LN	12700	456D	NEC	77044
ARBOR FOREST LN	0	253Q	SEM	77386
ARBOR FOREST TRAIL	1700	338A	NEH	77345
ARBORG DR	30400	252V	SEM	77386
ARBOR GARDEN LN	0	371E	NWC	77066
ARBOR GATE DR	0	612N	PL	77545
ARBORGATE DR	22500	334B	NCC	77373
ARBOR GLEN RD	7900	570G	MC	77071
ARBORGROVE LN	5000	333M	NCC	77338
ARBOR GROVE LN	20800	290U	NWC	77373
ARBOR HAVEN CIR	0	366J	NWC	77433
ARBOR HILL LN	0	613T	NEB	77584
ARBOR HOLLOW LN	12600	328G	NWC	77377
ARBOR IVY LN	0	377Y	NWC	77044
ARBOR KNOLL CT	0	376H	NWC	77346
ARBOR KNOLL LN	0	376H	NWC	77346
ARBOR LAKE DR	15800	329S	NWC	77377
ARBOR LEA LN	16000	617X	SEC	77546
ARBOR LODGE DR	0	366J	NWC	77433
ARBOR MEADOW	7900	570G	MC	77071
ARBOR MIST	3200	578S	SWC	77059
ARBOR MIST	300	487A	SWC	77094
ARBORMONT DR	18100	366D	CY	77429
ARBOR OAK DR	7000	411Y	NWC	77088
ARBOR OAK LEAF CT	0	326L	NWC	77429
ARBOR PARADISE DR	4400	414B	NWC	77039
ARBOR PARK CT	7200	407Q	NWC	77095
ARBOR PINE	800	288B	TB	77375
ARBOR PINES LN	19300	338W	NWC	77346
ARBOR PLACE	1000	493X	SWH	77004
ARBOR PLACE	3500	609E	SG	77479
ARBOR POINT CT	3600	486W	NEF	77450
ARBOR POINT LN	3700	617X	SEC	77546
ARBOR RANCH CT	0	698G	LC	77573
ARBOR RIDGE DR	12700	570G	MC	77071
W. ARBOR ROSE LN	6300	290P	NWC	77379
E. ARBOR ROSE LN	6300	290P	NWC	77379
ARBOR ROSE LN	6300	290U	NWC	77379
ARBORS EDGE LN	0	326Q	NWC	77433
ARBOR SPRING CT	17400	330D	NWC	77379
ARBOR SPRINGS LN	0	253Q	SEM	77386
ARBOR STREAM LN	22600	485Y	NEC	77450
ARBOR TERRACE CT	3500	331H	NWC	77388
ARBOR TERRACE DR	18300	331H	NWC	77388
ARBOR TRACE CT	14700	327W	NWC	77429
ARBOR TRACE LN	14700	325Q	NWC	77396
ARBOR TRAILS DR	0	333G	NCC	77338
ARBOR TRELLIS DR	0	371E	NWC	77066
ARBOR VALLEY WAY	0	368Z	NWC	77065
ARBOR VILLA LN	0	377U	NWC	77044
ARBOR VILLAS LN	0	326L	NWC	77429
ARBOR VISTA BLVD	0	326Q	NWC	77433
ARBOR VITAE DR	5300	451F	NWH	77092
ARBOR WALK DR	8600	335N	NCC	77338
ARBOR WIND LN	0	407J	NWC	77057
ARBORWAY	200	491F	SWH	77057
ARBOR WIND DR	0	407J	NWC	77057
ARBORWOOD DR	1000	657V	LC	77573
ARBOR WOOD DR	8800	411S	NWH	77040
ARBRE LN	0	657E	FR	77546
ARBROATH CT	24900	250W	NWC	77433
ARBUCKLE	2600	532G	WU	77005

Street Name	Block	Pg/Sq	Loc	Zips
ARBURY LN	0	376A	NEC	77338
ARBURY LN	0	376A	NEC	77338
ARBURY GLEN LN	8000	334M	NCC	77338
ARBURY HILL LN	0	375Z	NEC	77396
ARC	3700	530B	SWH	77063
ARCADE DR	9500	330S	NWC	77379
ARCADIA	700	498G	CV	77530
ARCADIA	2400	494B	NEH	77026
ARCADIA DR	1800	568A	SG	77498
ARCADIA DR	7300	578F	PA	77505
ARCADIA BAY DR	0	612J	PL	77545
ARCADIA BEND CT	0	409W	NWC	77041
ARCADIA BEND LN	0	409W	NWC	77041
ARCADIA COVE CT	0	326U	NWC	77429
ARCADIA GLEN CT	25600	485W	NEF	77494
ARCADIA GLEN LN	5200	485W	NEF	77494
ARCADIA HEIGHTS BLVD	0	487A	SWC	77494
ARCADIAN DR	100	419U	BR	77532
ARCADIAN SHORES DR	6100	408T	NWC	77084
ARCADIAN SHORES LN	0	612N	PL	77545
ARCADIAN SPRING LN	0	329F	NWC	77375
ARCADIA PARK LN	21100	335J	NCC	77338
ARCADIA POINT LN	17600	377E	NEC	77346
ARCADIA RIDGE LN	2500	445R	NWC	77449
ARCANE CT	25100	250Y	NWC	77389
ARCARO GLEN CT	18700	337Z	NEC	77346
ARCHCREST CT	0	406G	NWC	77433
ARCHDALE CT	25400	524G	NEF	77494
ARCHDUKE DR	15800	373P	NCC	77032
ARCHED OAKS DR	0	368X	NWC	77095
ARCHED OAKS DR	0	408B	NWC	77095
ARCHER	200	453X	NWH	77009
E. ARCHER	2700	462X	NEC	77521
E. ARCHER RD	1	501C	NEC	77521
W. ARCHER RD	100	501C	NEC	77521
E. ARCHER RD	2000	502A	NEC	77521
ARCHER FALLS DR	0	326K	NWC	77433
ARCHER GLEN DR	19300	372D	NCC	77073
ARCHER OAK PALCE	0	249C	SWM	77382
ARCHER PARK	32100	252M	SEM	77385
ARCHGATE DR	6400	334F	NCC	77373
ARCHIBALD BLAIR LN	22500	445U	NWC	77449
ARCHLEY DR	1200	451W	HI	77055
ARCHMONT DR	10500	369F	NWC	77070
ARCH ROCK DR	0	406H	NWC	77433
ARCHWAY CT	5100	539X	LP	77571
ARCHWAY DR	4900	539X	LP	77571
ARCHWAY DR	16100	527C	SWC	77082
ARCHWOOD	13900	457F	NEC	77049
ARCHWOOD LN	12600	368R	NWC	77429
ARCHWOOD TRAIL	500	493J	SWH	77007
W. ARCHWYCK CIR	0	249C	SWM	77382
S. ARCHWYCK CIR	0	249C	SWM	77382
N. ARCHWYCK CIR	0	249C	SWM	77382
ARCHWYCK CIR	0	249C	SWM	77382
ARCIDIAN FOREST DR	6200	411K	NWC	77088
ARCOLA CT	0	250X	NWC	77389
ARCOLA MANOR CT	0	445F	NWC	77493
ARCOLA RIDGE CT	13700	528P	SWC	77083
ARCOLA RIDGE DR	8600	528P	SWC	77083
ARCOTT LN	0	570T	MC	77489
ARCOTT BEND DR	0	328F	NWC	77429
ARCRIDGE CIR	4700	611D	SWH	77053
ARCTIC TERN CT	400	568P	SG	77478
ARDASIA DR	0	290D	NWC	77389
ARDEN CT	9400	573D	SEH	77033
ARDENDALE LN	0	485W	NEF	77494
ARDEN FOREST CT	1100	329G	NWC	77379
ARDEN GLEN LN	0	377W	NEC	77044
ARDENNES	7300	533V	SEH	77033
ARDEN PARK DR	21000	525R	NEF	77407
ARDEN RIDGE LN	0	371D	NWC	77014
ARDENT OAK CIR	3400	578X	SEH	77059
ARDEN TRAIL DR	0	293G	SEM	77386
ARDENWOOD PARKWAY	0	444L	KT	77493
ARDFIELD DR	13600	370E	NWH	77070
ARDKINGLAS DR	17000	527W	NEF	77407
ARDLEY CIR	8600	412Q	NWH	77088
ARDMORE	5500	533G	SEH	77021
ARDMORE	6800	533K	SWH	77054
ARDWELL DR	14300	528S	NEF	77498
ARDWICK CT	24100	289D	NWC	77375
AREBA	2400	412W	NWH	77091
AREBA	3000	411Z	NWH	77091
ARENA DR	5400	531D	SWH	77081
ARENA DR	6900	530G	SWH	77036
ARENAS TIMBERS DR	5600	337T	NEC	77346
ARENDALE	10900	575T	SEH	77075
ARENDALE LN	2100	292D	SEM	77386
AREZZO CIR	0	657L	FR	77546
ARGENT CT	0	299X	NEC	77336
ARGENT DR	0	299X	NEC	77336
ARGENTINA CIR	4200	577B	PA	77504
ARGENTINA DR	7900	409M	JV	77040
ARGONNE	0	659Z	GCO	77539
ARGONNE	2000	492U	SWH	77019
ARGONNE	2900	492U	SWH	77098
ARGONNE WOODS	0	296Q	SEM	77365
ARGOS CT	3400	610Q	MC	77459
ARGOS DR	2700	610Q	MC	77459
ARGOSY BEND PLACE	100	249R	NWH	77375
ARGOSY BEND PLACE	100	249R	NWH	77375
ARGYLE RD	16900	418X	NEC	77049
ARIA CT	2600	660W	DI	77539
ARICA LN	0	293W	NCC	77373
ARIEL	5200	531N	SWH	77096
ARIEL	5900	530P	SWH	77074
ARIEL CT	12100	569E	SF	77477
ARIETTA WAY	0	293F	SEM	77386
ARION LN	600	536U	PA	77502
ARISTA DR	7200	527K	NEF	77083
ARISTATA DR	0	524E	NEF	77494
ARIZONA	400	580C	LP	77571
ARIZONA	500	576B	SH	77587
ARIZONA	1300	541A	BT	77520
ARIZONA	4500	535U	SEH	77017
ARIZONA AVE	1600	659P	LC	77573
ARIZONA SKY CT	15000	376U	NEC	77396
ARKANSAS	500	576B	SH	77587
ARKANSAS	2400	494A	NEH	77026
ARKANSAS	3200	540D	BT	77520
N. ARKANSAS	7900	454J	NEH	77093
ARKANSAS AVE	2600	659U	LC	77573
ARKANSAS AVE	2800	659Z	GCO	77539
ARKANSAS POST LN	12200	377J	NEC	77346
ARKDALE CT	15900	330S	NWC	77379
ARKO	14800	413A	NCC	77060
ARLAN LAKE DR	18700	332A	NWC	77388
ARLEDGE	8800	575H	SEH	77075
ARLEN	8700	455H	NEH	77078
ARLENE DR	21600	285D	SWM	77355
ARLENE DR	21800	245Z	SWM	77355

Street Name	Block	Pg/Sq	Loc	Zips
ARLETTA	8000	535T	SEH	77061
ARLICIOUS	3300	455W	NEH	77020
ARLINGTON	200	493E	NWH	77007
ARLINGTON	900	453W	NWH	77008
ARLINGTON	3000	453E	NWH	77018
ARLINGTON	4200	453J	NWH	77022
ARLINGTON	5500	453A	NWH	77076
ARLINGTON FOREST DR	8900	411K	NWC	77088
ARLINGTON MEADOWS LN	0	328L	NWC	77377
ARLINGTON PLACE	14300	327Z	NWC	77429
ARLINGTON POINTE DR	0	658R	LC	77573
ARLINGTON SQUARE DR	3900	576G	SEH	77034
ARLON TRAIL	13300	488X	SWC	77082
ARMADA DR	900	452B	NWH	77091
ARMADA DR	3100	451D	NWH	77091
ARMADILLO	14900	327X	CY	77429
ARMAND	6800	532F	SS	77025
ARMAND VIEW DR	4200	578F	PA	77505
ARMANT PLACE DR	14000	367D	NWC	77429
ARMATTA CT	10000	576N	SEH	77075
ARMBULL CT	18900	337X	NEC	77346
ARMENTO DR	0	329Y	NWC	77070
ARMER	0	543Q	BC	77520
ARMILLARY DR	0	406Y	NWC	77449
ARMILLARY DR	0	406Y	NWC	77449
ARMITAGE AVE	14800	527V	NEF	77498
ARMOR AVE	700	536V	PA	77502
ARMOR AVE	1300	537S	PA	77502
ARMOR OAKS DR	0	296X	SEM	77339
ARMOR SMITH DR	26900	296W	NEC	77339
ARMORY	0	373U	NCC	77032
ARMOUR DR	5400	494Q	NEH	77020
ARMOURDALE	0	501S	BT	77520
ARMOUR TRAIL	800	373J	NCC	77060
ARMSTEAD	1200	453X	NWH	77009
ARMSTRONG	100	495Z	NEH	77029
ARMSTRONG	3900	530B	SWH	77063
ARMSTRONG LN	5900	484B	KT	77494
ARMSTRONG LN	11100	612V	PL	77584
ARMSTRONG LN	11500	613S	PL	77584
ARNAGE LN	0	571L	SWH	77085
ARNAGE LN	12900	571L	SWH	77085
ARNCLIFFE DR	5400	411Q	NWH	77088
ARNDT LN	21300	285H	SWM	77447
ARNDT RD	14300	417X	NEC	77044
ARNDT WAY	0	285H	SWM	77355
ARNELL DR	4400	451H	NWH	77018
ARNETT LN	100	413S	NEH	77037
ARNETTE PARK LN	0	377F	NEC	77346
ARNEWAY DR	9000	289D	NWC	77375
ARNICA CT	1	250M	WD	77381
ARNIM	7300	535J	SEH	77087
ARNO	400	536Z	PA	77502
ARNOLD	100	492L	SWH	77007
ARNOLD	800	288G	TB	77375
ARNOLD	3700	532A	WU	77005
ARNOLD DR	4500	613Z	NEB	77584
ARNOLD DR	4700	614W	NEB	77584
ARNOLD CREEK LN	0	257F	SEM	77357
ARNOT	6200	492F	SWH	77007
ARNOUX-RUE	15800	246V	SWM	77355
ARON	400	501Z	BT	77520
ARP	12500	570R	SWH	77085
ARRAMORE LN	8600	407D	NWC	77095
ARRIETA DR	0	257F	SEM	77357
ARRINGTON FOREST LN	8000	334M	NCC	77338
ARRIOLA	0	363C	NWC	77447
ARROMANCHES LN	3400	291U	NWC	77388
ARRONDI CIR	12400	408D	NWC	77065
ARRONS WAY DR	0	371E	NWC	77066
ARROW	0	576E	SEH	77034
E. ARROW DR	0	257C	WV	77357
N. ARROWANA LN	6000	530D	SWC	77036
S. ARROWANA LN	6100	530D	SWC	77036
S. ARROWANA POINTE	0	530D	SWH	77036
N. ARROWANA POINTE	0	530D	SWH	77036
ARROWBROOK CT	7300	525B	NEF	77494
S. ARROW CANYON CIR	0	250Q	NWC	77389
N. ARROW CANYON CIR	0	250Q	NWC	77389
ARROWCHASE CT	6800	406P	NWC	77449
ARROW COVE CT	8200	338N	NEC	77346
ARROW COVE DR	20300	338N	NEC	77346
ARROW CREEK LN	0	290T	NWC	77379
W. ARROWDALE DR	100	413N	NCC	77037
ARROWDALE DR	200	413N	NCC	77037
ARROWFEATHER PLACE	0	250N	NWC	77389
ARROW FIELD LN	20400	486T	NEF	77450
ARROW FLINT COVE	18400	447J	NWC	77084
ARROW GLEN DR	0	524S	NWF	77406
ARROW GRAND CT	0	526Q	NEF	77407
ARROWGRASS DR	9500	409C	NWC	77064
ARROW HEAD	0	656F	FR	77546
ARROWHEAD CT	1	568V	SG	77478
ARROWHEAD CT	1800	610K	MC	77459
ARROWHEAD DR	5000	500M	BT	77521
ARROWHEAD LN	7700	575T	SEH	77075
ARROWHEAD CREEK LN	2600	615R	PL	77581
ARROWHEAD GLEN DR	12000	570F	SWH	77071
ARROWHEAD RIDGE DR	0	376Q	NEC	77396
ARROWHEAD RUN LN		366U	NWC	77433
ARROWHEAD TERRACE LN	9500	375V	NEC	77396
ARROWHEAD TRAIL	28100	246B	SWM	77355
ARROW HILL RD	1000	488F	SWH	77077
ARROW LAKE DR	900	485G	SWC	77450
ARROWMILL LN	0	328F	NWC	77377
ARROWOOD GLEN DR	0	488Q	SWH	77077
ARROW POINT DR	4600	453E	NWH	77022
ARROW RIDGE CT	1500	372J	NWC	77067
ARROW RIDGE DR	11600	372J	NWC	77067
ARROW ROCK TRAIL	8000	415L	NEC	77050
ARROWSMITH CT	2400	613Q	NEB	77584
ARROWSMITH DR	19800	334V	NCC	77338
ARROWS PEAK LN	17000	367Y	NWC	77095
ARROW STAR CT	0	445S	NWC	77493
ARROW STAR DR	0	445S	NWC	77493
ARROWWOOD	12300	248J	SWM	77362
N. ARROWWOOD CIR	2000	490P	PP	77063
ARROWWOOD N. CIR	2000	490P	PP	77063
ARROWWOOD CIR	11600	490P	PP	77063
ARROWWOOD DR	18400	257C	WV	77357
ARROYO CIR	1	502F	BT	77521
ARROYO CIR	22200	338Z	NEH	77532
ARROYO COLORADO CT	0	366Z	NWC	77433
ARROYO CREEK LN	11500	328D	NWC	77377
ARROYO VERDE LN	12000	409W	NWC	77041
ARROYO VERDE LN	12000	449B	NWH	77041
ARROYO VISTA CT	2000	371M	NWC	77067
ARROYO VISTA LN	11900	371M	NWC	77067
ARROYO WILLOW TRAIL	0	326Q	NWC	77429
ARSENAL	4200	451K	NWH	77092
ART	11500	413U	NEH	77076
ARTDALE	3700	530B	SWH	77063

Street Name	Block	Pg/Sq	Loc	Zips
ARTEM CT	0	572M	SEH	77051
ARTESIA	400	332C	NCC	77373
ARTESIA DR	0	539R	DP	77536
ARTESIAN PLACE	1	493L	SWH	77002
ARTESIAN PLAZA DR	400	335V	HM	77338
ARTESIAN SPRINGS	0	612N	PL	77545
ARTESIAN WAY	18700	336Z	NEC	77346
ARTESIAN WAY	26100	257D	RF	77357
ARTHINGTON AVE	5400	571X	SWH	77053
ARTHUR	900	493P	SWH	77019
ARTHUR CT	4100	502K	BT	77521
ARTHUR RD	26000	292M	SP	77373
ARTHURIAN DREAM CT	0	289T	NWC	77375
ARTIC DR	4600	336Z	NEC	77346
ARTIC DR	4800	337W	NEC	77346
ARTISAN SPRINGS LN	0	485X	NEF	77494
ARTO	6600	453R	NEH	77093
ARTOYS DR	15500	329T	NWC	77377
ARTWOOD LN	17000	610F	SWH	77489
ARUBA DR	3800	450L	NWH	77080
ARUBA LN	0	333R	NCC	77338
ARUBA CALLE	0	660S	GCO	77539
ARUM RD	0	570T	MC	77489
ARUNDEL DR	14900	497H	NEC	77530
ARVADA BAY CT	0	526Q	NEF	77407
ARVANA	300	576F	SEH	77034
ARVILLA LN	4700	534E	SEH	77021
ARVIN	9100	455C	NEH	77028
ARVIN	9600	455C	NEH	77078
ARVONSHIRE CT	0	457P	NEC	77049
ARWADY VIEW LN	0	613R	PL	77584
ASBURY	100	492L	SWH	77007
ASBURY CT	0	615K	PL	77581
ASBURY LN	1300	538M	DP	77536
ASBURY BROOK CT	0	444T	KT	77493
ASBURY GARDEN	0	538M	DP	77536
ASBURY GLEN CT	3300	253N	SEM	77386
ASBURY PARK CT	1	609J	SG	77479
ASBURY PARK DR	1	609J	SG	77479
ASBURY PLACE	1	492L	SWH	77007
ASCALON CIR	5600	330Y	NWC	77069
ASCOT LN	3600	452N	NWH	77092
ASCOT LN	3900	451R	NWH	77092
ASCOT GARDEN	0	609Z	MC	77459
ASCOT GLEN LN	13200	528B	SWH	77082
ASH	0	282Y	WCO	77484
ASH	0	540T	LP	77571
ASH	200	568J	SG	77498
ASH	400	288H	TB	77375
ASH	1200	541B	BT	77520
ASH	33000	247R	SWM	77362
ASH LN	3400	538U	DP	77536
ASH LN	6800	444W	KT	77493
ASH RD	2500	614S	NEB	77584
ASH ST	0	282Y	WCO	77484
ASH ARBOR WAY	1400	618Q	SEH	77058
N. ASHBEL	1	501Y	BT	77520
S. ASHBEL	100	501Y	BT	77520
ASHBERRY CT	400	658N	LC	77573
ASHBERRY PINE LN	0	446E	NWC	77449
ASHBLOOM LN	0	450V	NWH	77080
ASHBLUFF LN	0	371G	NWC	77014
ASHBOURNE SPRINGS LN	15600	408A	NWC	77095
ASHBRIDGE CT	0	291L	NWC	77389
ASHBRIDGE CT	16800	329R	NWC	77379
ASHBROOK DR	5100	531B	SWH	77081
ASHBROOK LN	28700	245D	SWM	77355
ASHBROOK DOVE LN	0	328A	NWC	77429
ASHBROOK DOVE LN	0	328A	NWC	77377
ASHBRROK LN	0	612Q	PL	77584
ASHBURN	5600	574A	SEH	77033
ASHBURN	6900	534Z	SEH	77061
ASHBURN	7400	535W	SEH	77061
ASHBURN	6700	574D	SEH	77061
ASHBURNHAM DR	3700	528C	SWH	77082
ASHBURN SPUR	6700	534Z	SEH	77061
ASHBURTON DR	15300	409M	JV	77040
ASHBURY LN	1300	538M	DP	77536
ASHBURY PARK CT	13900	488J	SWH	77077
ASHBURY PARK LN	0	253N	SEM	77385
ASHBURY PARK LN	1500	488P	SWH	77077
ASH BUTTE DR	17200	331R	NWC	77090
ASHBY	100	500P	BT	77520
ASHBY	4500	492Z	SWH	77005
ASHBY	4600	532D	SWH	77005
ASHCLIFT DR	12600	488Z	SWH	77082
ASHCOTT DR	11000	529F	SWH	77072
ASH CREEK DR	3400	610U	MC	77459
ASH CREEK DR	11200	489B	NWH	77043
ASHCROFT DR	6300	531J	SWH	77081
ASHCROFT DR	8300	531W	SWH	77096
ASHCROFT DR	11300	571E	SWH	77035
ASHDALE DR	1100	568F	SG	77498
ASHDALE LN	13900	528P	SWC	77083
ASHDOWN FOREST DR	9500	329G	NWC	77379
ASHEBORO DR	100	485D	SWC	77450
ASHE CREEK	0	658K	LC	77573
ASHE LAKE RD	24300	252X	SEM	77386
ASHENTREE WAY	13800	528T	NEF	77083
ASHE PARK CT	0	377F	NEC	77346
ASHER HOLLOW LN	0	445E	NWC	77493
ASHER MEADOWS DR	19500	366V	NWC	77433
ASHER OAKS LN	0	295M	SEM	77365
ASHFIELD DR	3100	488Z	SWH	77082
ASHFORD	2300	282U	WL	77484
ASHFORD LN	0	568D	SG	77478
ASHFORD ARBOR DR	3100	488Y	SWH	77082
ASHFORD BEND DR	3000	488Y	SWH	77082
ASHFORD BROOK DR	12700	488U	SWH	77082
ASHFORD CHASE DR	12600	488Y	SWH	77082
ASHFORD COVE DR	0	613Y	NEB	77584
ASHFORD CREEK DR	12700	488U	SWH	77082
ASHFORD FOREST DR	400	488M	SWH	77079
ASHFORD GLEN CT	12300	568D	SG	77478
ASHFORD GREEN CT	12300	568D	SG	77478
ASHFORD GREEN LN	0	528Q	SWC	77072
ASHFORD GREEN LN	8000	528Q	SWH	77072
ASHFORD GROVE	21600	486J	SWC	77450
ASHFORD HAVEN	11400	568D	SG	77478
ASHFORD HILLS DR	11200	568D	SG	77478
ASHFORD HILLS DR	12600	488Q	SWH	77077
ASHFORD HOLLOW	12300	568D	SG	77478
ASHFORD HOLLOW LN	1500	488R	SWH	77077
ASHFORD KNOLL DR	12700	488U	SWH	77082
ASHFORD LAKES DR	11100	568D	SG	77478
ASHFORD MEADOW DR	12500	488U	SWH	77082
ASHFORD MEADOWS DR	12200	568D	SG	77478
ASHFORD OAK DR	2600	488Y	SWH	77082
ASHFORD PARK DR	2600	488V	SWH	77082
ASHFORD PARK DR	12200	528Z	SG	77478
ASHFORD PINE	11400	568D	SG	77478
ASHFORD PINE DR	12600	488Y	SWH	77082

Street Name	Block	Pg/Sq	Loc	Zips
ASHFORD PKWY	900	488R	SWH	77077
ASHFORD PLACE DR	12300	568D	SG	77478
ASHFORD POINT	11100	528Z	SG	77478
ASHFORD POINT DR	12600	528C	SWH	77082
ASHFORD POINT LN	0	615J	PL	77089
ASHFORD POND DR	11300	568D	SG	77478
ASHFORD RIDGE LN	0	525C	NEF	77450
ASHFORD RIVER	0	528M	SWH	77072
ASHFORD SHADOW DR	0	528M	SWH	77072
ASHFORD SHORE DR	0	528M	SWH	77072
ASHFORD SKY LN		484J	NEF	77494
ASHFORD SPRINGS LN	0	375Z	NEC	77396
ASHFORD SQUARE ST	0	329B	NWC	77375
ASHFORD TERRACE DR	0	528M	SWH	77072
ASHFORD TRACE DR	0	528R	SWH	77072
ASHFORD TRAIL DR	2700	488Y	SWH	77082
ASHFORD VALLEY DR	12200	528Z	SG	77478
W. ASHFORD VILLA LN	3700	528D	SWH	77082
E. ASHFORD VILLA LN	3700	528D	SWH	77082
ASHFORD VILLA LN	3700	528D	SWH	77082
S. ASHFORD VILLA LN	12500	528D	SWH	77082
N. ASHFORD VILLA LN	12500	528D	SWH	77082
ASHFORD WAY	1200	336H	NEH	77339
ASHFORD WAY	12200	528Z	SG	77478
ASHFORD WILLOW	11400	568D	SG	77478
ASHFORD WIND DR	11400	568D	SG	77478
ASH FOREST DR	1800	485L	SWC	77450
ASH FORK DR	10000	409C	NWC	77064
ASHFORK DR	21100	446C	NWC	77449
ASH GARDEN CT	8200	527P	NEF	77083
ASHGATE DR	5500	334E	NCC	77373
ASH GLADE CT	3800	297U	NEH	77345
ASH GLEN CT	20200	291Y	NWC	77388
ASH GLEN DR	3500	291Y	NWC	77388
ASH GREEN DR	0	325L	NWC	77433
ASHGROVE DR	2000	489S	SWH	77077
ASH HAVEN LN	2600	446N	NWC	77449
ASH HOLLOW DR	3900	527D	SWC	77082
ASHINGTON DR	2600	371R	NWC	77067
ASHKIRK DR	8700	528R	SWH	77099
ASHLAND	600	492D	NWH	77007
ASHLAND	800	458X	CV	77530
ASHLAND	900	452V	NWH	77008
ASHLAND	3000	452M	NWH	77018
ASHLAND BLVD	800	498B	CV	77530
ASHLAND BRIDGE LN	10800	527Z	NEF	77498
ASHLAND BROOK CT	19800	446Q	NWH	77084
ASHLAND CREEK LN	4100	658W	LC	77573
ASHLAND FOREST DR	6600	411J	NWC	77088
ASHLAND HOLLOW LN	0	484U	NEF	77494
ASHLAND LANDING DR	14100	367D	NWC	77429
ASHLAND PARK LN	3100	253N	SEM	77386
ASHLAND PINES LN	14700	375Z	NEC	77396
ASHLAND POINT LN		328k	NWC	77429
ASHLAND SPRINGS LN	0	406M	NWC	77433
ASHLAND WAY	0	450Z	NWH	77055
ASHLAND WOODS DR	0	293D	SEM	77386
ASHLAWN DR	8200	527Q	NEF	77083
ASHLEE LN	3800	371B	NWC	77014
ASHLEN DR	600	372H	NCC	77073
ASHLEY	2700	535K	SEH	77017
ASHLEY	4000	460M	NEC	77562
ASHLEY	10000	370Y	NWC	77064
ASHLEY	20300	446P	NWC	77449
ASHLEY CT	1400	288M	TB	77375
ASHLEY CT	3600	610U	MC	77459
ASHLEY CT	5000	449B	NWC	77041
ASHLEY DR	25200	244C	WCO	77447
ASHLEY LN	0	539W	DP	77571
ASHLEY LN	0	462Z	BT	77521
ASHLEY LN	0	462Z	BT	77521
ASHLEY LN	9900	616K	SEC	77089
ASHLEY RD	18800	447N	NWC	77084
ASHLEY RD	18900	446R	NWC	77084
ASHLEY BAY LN	0	370E	NWH	77070
W. ASHLEY CIRCLE DR	12200	570G	SWH	77071
S. ASHLEY CIRCLE DR	12200	570G	SWH	77071
N. ASHLEY CIRCLE DR	12200	570G	SWH	77071
E. ASHLEY CIRCLE DR	12200	570G	SWH	77071
ASHLEY COVE CT	600	487A	SWC	77094
ASHLEY CREEK CT	0	376W	NEC	77396
ASHLEY FALLS	13800	488F	SWH	77077
ASHLEY GLEN CIR	0	332Z	NCC	77073
ASHLEY GROVE	6000	407U	NWC	77084
ASHLEY GROVE CT	12100	569E	SF	77477
ASHLEY HALL CT	6300	408T	NWC	77084
ASHLEY HOPE DR	0	524B	NEF	77494
ASHLEY MANOR BLVD	3700	253P	SEM	77386
ASHLEY OAK DR	0	325S	HK	77447
ASHLEY OAK DR		325S	NWC	77447
ASHLEY PINES DR	22700	292K	SP	77373
ASHLEY RIDGE LN	2400	568A	SG	77498
ASHLEY RUN	13600	488K	SWH	77077
ASHLEY SPRING CT	5700	525C	NEF	77494
ASHLEY TERRACE LN	0	406M	NWC	77433
ASHLEYVILLE RD	1	501Q	BT	77521
ASHLEY WOODS CT	0	330K	NWC	77379
ASHLING DR	12200	529W	SWH	77477
ASHLOCK DR	3100	488Z	SWH	77082
ASHLY MANOR DR	6300	250U	NWC	77389
ASHLYN RIDGE LN	0	293E	SEM	77386
ASHLYN TIMBER CT	16300	246Y	SWM	77355
ASHLYN TIMBER LN	31400	246Y	SWM	77355
ASHMEAD DR	11900	489J	SWH	77077
ASH MEADOW DR	1400	331R	NWC	77090
ASHMERE LN	5200	331E	NWC	77379
ASHMOLE LN	7400	411V	NWH	77088
ASHMOND LN	0	289Q	NWC	77375
ASHMONT CT	2200	610A	MC	77489
ASHMONT DR	2300	610A	MC	77489
ASHMONT DR	2426	609D	MC	77459
ASHMOOR CT	16700	618R	SEH	77058
ASHMOOR WAY	16800	618R	SEH	77058
ASHMORE CT	1700	570T	MC	77489
ASHMORE DR	1500	570T	MC	77489
ASHMORE DR	6700	370B	NWC	77069
ASHMORE ESTATES CT	22900	252M	SEM	77385
ASHMORE PARK DR	5200	525C	NEF	77494
ASH OAK DR	1400	570T	MC	77489
ASH OAK DR	5700	451C	NWH	77091
ASH OAK DR	6200	411Y	NWH	77091
ASHOGLEN LN	13500	488F	SWH	77077
ASHPARK DR	0	371S	NWC	77066
ASH PARK DR	3600	337E	NEH	77339
ASH PLACE	1	259N	NEC	77357
ASH PLACE	1000	493K	SWH	77007
ASH POINTE	900	658R	LC	77573
ASHRIDGE PARK DR	8600	330S	NWC	77379
ASH RUN CT	1500	616P	PL	77581
ASHTEX DR	13700	415B	NEC	77396
ASHTEX DR	14900	375T	NEH	77396
ASHTON	6400	411Z	NWH	77091

Street Name	Block	Pg/Sq	Loc	Zips
ASHTON DR	7500	407H	NWC	77095
ASHTON LN	3100	578D	LP	77571
ASHTON LN	32000	248S	SWM	77355
ASHTON GROVE CT	0	376W	NEC	77396
ASHTON HILLS CT	13500	367H	NWC	77429
ASHTON HILLS DR	15800	367H	NWC	77429
ASHTON OAKS DR	0	612U	PL	77584
ASHTON PARK DR	3000	614V	PL	77584
ASHTON PARK DR	3100	488Z	SWH	77082
ASHTON PINES LN	0	290T	NWC	77379
ASHTON TRAIL DR	4600	414C	NCC	77039
ASHTON VILLAGE CT	31300	252Q	SEM	77386
ASHTON VILLAGE DR	1500	252Q	SEM	77386
ASH TREE LN	21800	332M	NCC	77073
ASHURST DR	12000	489S	SWH	77077
ASHVALE DR	16100	329N	NWC	77377
ASH VALLEY DR	8000	330E	NWC	77379
ASH VALLEY DR	8300	329M	NWC	77379
ASH VIEW LN	0	611W	FS	77545
ASHVILLE DR	9200	573F	SEH	77051
ASHWAY	1300	252G	SEM	77385
ASHWELL CT	7800	250W	NWC	77389
ASHWOOD	2800	532L	SWH	77025
ASHWOOD	11200	336S	NEC	77338
ASHWOOD CIR	3800	579D	LP	77571
ASHWOOD DR	1200	568G	SG	77498
ASHWOOD DR	3900	615W	PL	77584
ASHWOOD DR	5000	500M	BT	77521
ASHWOOD CREEK LN	0	484X	NEF	77494
ASHWOOD CROSSING DR	0	524Q	NWF	77406
ASHWOOD VALLEY DR	9600	407B	NWC	77095
ASHWORTH	11500	414M	NEH	77016
ASHWORTH	11700	414M	NEH	77050
ASHWYNE CT	3300	578D	LP	77571
ASHWYNE LN	8400	578D	LP	77571
ASIA LN	0	660S	GCO	77539
ASINO DR	0	445E	NWC	77493
ASKEW	2700	534L	SEH	77087
ASKINS LN	4800	414U	NEH	77093
ASKINS LN	5300	414V	NEH	77016
ASPEN	5100	531K	BL	77401
ASPEN	5400	531K	SWH	77081
ASPEN CIR	6800	290C	NWC	77389
ASPEN CT	4300	609F	MC	77459
ASPEN CT	8000	463S	CCO	77520
ASPEN DR	3800	579C	LP	77571
ASPEN DR	4800	577L	PA	77505
ASPEN DR	12000	368D	NWC	77429
ASPEN DR	12700	247R	SWM	77362
ASPEN LN	0	539S	DP	77571
ASPEN LN	0	568D	SG	77478
ASPEN LN	1700	620K	SB	77586
ASPEN LN	2700	614Q	PL	77584
ASPEN LN	12100	569E	SF	77477
ASPEN RD	1000	620W	CS	77565
ASPEN ARBOR CT	16200	617X	SEC	77546
ASPEN BEND DR	3200	331N	NWC	77068
ASPEN BOUGH CIR	13200	368U	NWC	77065
ASPENBRANCH LN	17900	447B	NWC	77084
ASPENBROOK CT	3300	615F	PL	77581
ASPEN BROOK LN	4300	291T	NWC	77388
ASPEN CANYON DR	20500	526A	NEF	77450
ASPEN CHASE LN	0	375Z	NEC	77396
ASPEN COVE CT	13900	488K	SWH	77077
ASPEN COVE DR	13700	488K	SWH	77077
ASPEN CREEK CT	2900	297Q	NEH	77345
ASPEN DALE DR	0	292D	SEM	77386
ASPEN FAIR TRAIL	0	291M	NWC	77389
ASPEN FALLS LN	0	376W	NEC	77396
ASPEN FALLS LN	0	376X	NEC	77396
ASPEN FARMS LN	5900	609X	NEF	77479
ASPENFIELD LN	2300	486N	SWC	77450
ASPEN GLADE DR	1900	296U	NEH	77339
ASPENGLEN DR	4300	448E	NWC	77084
ASPEN GLEN LN	3500	291Y	NWC	77388
ASPENGLENN DR	16000	448E	NWC	77084
ASPEN GROVE DR	1600	489N	SWH	77077
ASPEN HAZE LN	0	375Y	NEC	77396
ASPEN HEIGHTS TRAIL	0	326V	NWC	77429
ASPEN HILLS DR	14900	618E	SEH	77062
ASPEN HOLLOW CT	0	484F	KT	77494
ASPEN HOLLOW LN	13800	488X	SWH	77082
ASPEN KNOLL CT	13800	618A	SEH	77059
ASPEN LAKE CT	3100	613T	NEB	77578
ASPEN LAKE CT	5300	297P	NEH	77345
ASPEN LAKE DR	3300	613W	NEB	77578
ASPENLODGE LN	25200	485W	NEF	77494
ASPEN MANOR LN	0	406C	NWC	77433
ASPEN MEADOW DR	8800	570A	SWH	77071
ASPEN MIST LN	21800	445H	NWC	77449
ASPEN MOUNTAIN TRAIL	3900	337B	NEH	77345
ASPEN OAK CT	17400	330D	NWC	77379
ASPEN PARK LN	2900	447N	NWC	77084
ASPEN PASS DR	0	297R	NEH	77345
ASPEN PINE TRAIL	0	326N	NWC	77433
ASPEN PINE WAY	0	326N	NWC	77433
ASPEN PLACE DR	8800	570A	SWH	77071
ASPEN POINT DR	5200	446B	NWC	77449
ASPEN RANCH CT	0	484S	NEF	77494
ASPEN RESERVE WAY	0	449X	NWH	77043
ASPEN RIDGE CT	17400	527J	NEF	77407
ASPEN RIVER LN	1900	618F	SEH	77062
ASPEN SHADOW LN	0	338A	NEH	77345
ASPEN SHORES CT	0	406R	NWC	77449
ASPEN SPRING DR	0	538R	DP	77536
ASPEN STAR CT	0	572W	SWC	77053
ASPEN TERRACE CT	12800	367E	NWC	77433
ASPEN TRACE LN	0	335P	NCC	77338
ASPEN TRAILS DR	19300	406R	NWC	77449
ASPEN TREE CT	0	371D	NWC	77014
ASPENVIEW CT	8600	412P	NWH	77088
ASPEN VILLA LN	0	484Y	NEF	77494
ASPENWAY DR	11500	369A	NWC	77070
ASPENWILDE DR	20300	326T	NWC	77433
ASPENWOOD DR	10200	410M	NWC	77040
ASPHODEL CT	5700	331J	NWC	77379
ASPHODEL LN	17700	331J	NWC	77379
ASPLEY CT	1700	486L	SWC	77094
ASPLEY DR	0	615Z	PL	77581
ASPREY CT	8600	330T	NWC	77379
ASTE LN	12300	368R	NWC	77065
ASTER	13000	571G	SWH	77045
ASTER DR	800	444X	KT	77493
ASTER RD	0	570T	MC	77489
ASTERBEND	13800	528P	SWC	77083
ASTER CREST CT	10500	329B	NWC	77379
ASTER ESTATES LN	14100	366D	NWC	77429
ASTERGLEN CT	19500	446L	NWC	77449
ASTER MANOR CT	15900	367D	NWC	77429
ASTER MANOR CT	15900	367D	NWC	77429
S. ASTERN DR	800	419F	NEC	77532
W. ASTERN DR	15700	419F	NEC	77532

Street Name	Block	Pg/Sq	Loc	Zips
E. ASTERN DR	15700	419F	NEC	77532
ASTER PETAL CT	0	325R	NWC	77433
ASTILBE CT	19900	289Y	NWC	77379
ASTIN MANSION LN	0	366J	NWC	77433
ASTIPALIA DR	21500	291N	NWC	77388
ASTLEY LN	7900	330K	NWC	77379
ASTLEY ACRES LN		328P	NWC	77429
ASTON	13700	450C	NWH	77040
ASTON	14200	410X	NWH	77040
ASTON LAKE LN	12800	408V	NWC	77041
ASTON MAIN DR	0	366N	NWC	77433
ASTON PARK DR	0	451X	NWH	77055
ASTONSHIRE LN	0	332W	NWC	77014
ASTORIA BLVD	9900	616K	SEC	77089
ASTORIA BLVD	11200	616G	SEC	77089
ASTORIA BLVD	11900	617A	SEH	77089
ASTORIA LN	0	659M	LC	77573
ASTORIA LN	0	659M	LC	77573
ASTORIA BROOK LN	0	253K	SEM	77386
ASTRACHAN RD	0	527W	NEF	77469
ASTRAPIA BAY CROSSING	0	330C	NWC	77379
ASTRAPIA VALLEY LN	0	406D	NWC	77433
ASTRODOME	0	532R	SWH	77054
ASTROWORLD	0	532V	SWH	77054
ASTWOOD CT	4200	330V	NWC	77068
ASTWOOD CT	8300	330P	NWC	77379
ATAHOUSE	0	329N	NWC	77377
S. ATASCA DR	0	377C	NEC	77346
ATASCA CREEK DR	6600	377C	NEC	77346
ATASCA OAKS BLVD	0	377F	NEC	77346
ATASCA OAKS DR	18600	337T	NEC	77346
ATASCA SOUTH CT	6700	337X	NEC	77346
ATASCA SOUTH DR	18600	337Y	NEC	77346
ATASCA VILLAS DR	20000	337R	NEC	77346
ATASCA WOODS TRACE	18400	377C	NEC	77346
ATASCA WOODS WAY	18400	377C	NEC	77346
ATASCOCITA RD	100	375M	NEC	77396
ATASCOCITA RD	1200	376F	NEC	77396
ATASCOCITA RD	4000	377A	NEC	77346
ATASCOCITA RD	5500	337X	NEC	77346
ATASCOCITA BEND DR	0	376K	NEC	77396
ATASCOCITA FOREST DR	18600	337X	NEC	77346
ATASCOCITA GREENS LN	0	338S	NEC	77346
ATASCOCITA LAKE DR	20100	338N	NEC	77346
ATASCOCITA LAKE WAY	8300	338N	NEC	77346
ATASCOCITA MEADOWS LN	18300	376D	NEC	77346
ATASCOCITA PARK DR	18600	337W	NEC	77346
ATASCOCITA PINES DR	19500	337V	NEC	77346
ATASCOCITA PLACE DR	2100	337M	NEC	77346
ATASCOCITA POINT DR	20900	337M	NEC	77346
ATASCOCITA SHORES DR	19500	338S	NEC	77346
ATASCOCITA SHORES DR	20400	337M	NEC	77346
ATASCOCITA TIMBERS NORTH	5400	337W	NEC	77346
ATASCOCITA TOWN CTR	0	337Y	NEC	77346
ATASCOCITA TRACE DR	18900	337Y	NEC	77346
ATASCOCITA TRAIL	4400	376D	NEC	77346
ATASCOCITA VILLAGE	0	375M	NEC	77396
ATASCOCITA WAY	3900	376F	NEC	77396
ATASCOCITA WEST TRLS	5300	337S	NEC	77346
ATCHISON	0	290D	NWC	77389
ATHEA GLEN CIR	20800	525D	NEF	77450
ATHENA CT	3300	610Q	MC	77459
ATHENS	4000	494W	SEH	77023
ATHENS DR	3700	578A	PA	77505
ATHENS DR	25200	257G	RF	77357
ATHENS WAY		610Q	MC	77459
ATHERINGTON PLACE	17200	330K	NWC	77379
ATHERSTONE	28700	293A	SEM	77386
ATHERSTONE	29500	253W	SEM	77386
ATHERTON LN	19200	486H	SWC	77094
ATHERTON BEND LN	0	326Y	NWC	77433
ATHERTON CANYON LN	3100	331Y	NWC	77014
ATHLONE CT	3900	411U	NWH	77088
ATHLONE DR	7200	411U	NWH	77088
ATHOS	1900	535F	SEH	77012
ATLANTA	1300	538N	DP	77536
ATLANTA	17000	375F	HM	77396
ATLANTIC	1	501W	BT	77520
ATLANTIC	2600	493C	NEH	77009
ATLANTIC DR	0	337W	NEC	77346
ATLAS DR	2500	610Q	MC	77459
ATLAS CEDAR DR	32600	322B	WCO	77484
ATLASRIDGE DR	0	574Y	SEH	77048
ATLASTA LN	13200	413J	NCC	77037
ATLAW DR	12400	570F	SWH	77071
ATMORE FOREST DR	0	330N	NWC	77379
ATMORE PLACE DR	14900	487Z	SWC	77082
ATRIUM	0	373S	NEH	77060
ATRIUM PLACE	0	257A	WV	77357
ATRIUM PLACE DR	19400	446Y	NWC	77084
ATRIUM WOODS CT	1	251B	WD	77381
ATTAR	1700	492F	SWH	77007
ATTAWAY	10200	575T	SEH	77075
ATTAYAC	0	503M	CCO	77520
ATTERBURY DR	14700	528S	NEF	77498
ATTERBURY DR	14800	527V	NEF	77498
ATTINGHAM DR	600	489H	SWH	77024
ATTLEE DR	12100	489N	SWH	77077
ATTLEE DR	12300	488R	SWH	77077
ATTRIDGE RD	2900	452Q	NWH	77018
ATTUCKS	3500	533D	SEH	77004
ATTWATER	7700	455P	NEH	77028
ATTWATER WAY	2500	658T	LC	77573
ATWATER CANYON LN	22100	525G	NEF	77494
ATWDOOD BEND TRAIL	0	526Q	NEF	77407
S. ATWELL DR	600	531K	BL	77401
ATWELL DR	6300	531K	SWH	77081
ATWELL DR	8000	531P	SWH	77096
ATWELL DR	11100	571B	SWH	77035
ATWOOD LN	10300	413Y	NEH	77076
ATWOOD LN	15200	420G	NEC	77532
ATWOOD BAY TRAIL	0	326T	NWC	77433
ATWOOD FALLS LN	0	658Y	LC	77573
ATWOOD FALLS LN	0	377K	NEC	77346
ATWOOD GLEN CT	12900	371D	NWC	77014
ATWOOD GLEN LN	2400	371D	NWC	77014
ATWOOD GROVE LN	0	411A	NWC	77086
ATWOOD HILLS LN	0	334R	NCC	77338
ATWOOD HILLS TRAIL	0	405S	NWC	77493
ATWOOD LANDING LN	0	405P	NWC	77493
ATWOOD MANOR CT	7700	527J	NEF	77407
ATWOOD PRESERVE LN	0	294J	NWC	77386
AUBERT	900	536N	SEH	77017
AUBRELL RD	3500	614Y	PL	77584
AUBREY FALLS CT	2400	486P	SWC	77450
AUBREY HILLS LN	9700	524F	NEF	77494
AUBREY OAKS CT	0	609U	MC	77459
AUBREY ROSE LN	0	366Z	NWC	77433
AUBREYWOOD LN	12500	369M	NWC	77070
AUBURN	3200	535K	SEH	77017
AUBURN DR	0	250U	NWC	77389
AUBURN DR	2000	444R	KT	77493

Street Name	Block	Pg/Sq	Loc	Zips
AUBURN DR	2900	613V	NEB	77584
AUBURN DR	18100	290J	NWC	77375
AUBURN ASH CIR	6500	337Q	NEC	77346
AUBURN BAY BLVD	0	326V	NWC	77429
AUBURN BEND DR	0	250U	NWC	77389
AUBURN BLUFF DR	0	407C	NWC	77095
AUBURN BROOK LN	4600	609S	NEF	77479
AUBURN CLIFF TRAIL	0	484N	NEF	77494
AUBURN COLONY CT	0	253T	SEM	77386
AUBURN CREEK DR	0	612G	PL	77584
AUBURN CREEK LN	0	659H	LC	77573
AUBURN CREST DR	21300	296J	SEM	77365
AUBURNDALE	2300	534C	SEH	77023
AUBURN FALLS DR	2900	612G	PL	77584
AUBURN FALLS LN	2900	447N	NWC	77084
AUBURN FALLS LN	24100	296J	SEM	77365
AUBURN FIELDS DR	21200	296J	SEM	77365
AUBURN FOREST DR	7500	330E	NWC	77379
AUBURN GLEN LN	8700	407B	NWC	77095
AUBURN GREEN DR	0	296E	SEM	77365
AUBURN GROVE CIR	3700	609G	MC	77459
AUBURN GROVE LN	12800	408V	NWC	77041
AUBURN HEIGHTS TRAIL	0	527S	NEF	77407
AUBURN HILLS DR	12000	328V	NWC	77377
AUBURN HILLS DR	12100	329S	NWC	77377
AUBURN HOLLOW LN	3200	486S	NEF	77450
AUBURN KEY CT	0	609S	NEF	77479
AUBURN KNOLL AVE	0	457L	NEC	77049
AUBURN LAKES DR	6100	250Z	NWC	77389
AUBURN LYNN DR	0	250U	NWC	77389
AUBURN MANE DR	0	249V	NWC	77375
AUBURN MEADOWS DR	19600	486G	SWC	77094
AUBURN OAK TRAIL	6700	337Q	NEC	77346
AUBURN PARK LN	19700	291W	NWC	77379
AUBURN PINE CT	20600	337Q	NEC	77346
AUBURN PLACE	0	492X	SWH	77005
AUBURN PLACE	1	492X	SWH	77005
AUBURN REACH DR	0	296E	SEM	77365
AUBURN RIDGE LN	20900	290U	NWC	77379
AUBURN RUN LN	0	290V	NWC	77379
AUBURN SHORES	12300	449A	NWC	77041
AUBURN SHORES CT	0	612G	PL	77584
AUBURN SHORES DR	0	612G	PL	77584
AUBURN SKY CT	2000	660L	LC	77573
AUBURN SPRINGS LN	12700	366H	NWC	77433
AUBURN TERRACE CT	6300	250U	NWC	77389
AUBURN TERRACE DR	0	250U	NWC	77389
AUBURN THICKET TRAIL	0	405T	NWC	77493
AUBURN TRACE CT	0	525D	NEF	77450
AUBURN TRACE CT	20900	525D	NEF	77450
AUBURN TRAILS DR	24200	296J	SEM	77365
AUBURN TRAILS LN	11900	612R	PL	77584
AUBURN TREE DR	0	326U	NWC	77429
AUBURN VALE	2100	445S	NWC	77493
AUBURN WOODS CT	24100	296J	SEM	77365
AUBURN WOODS DR	2900	615Y	PL	77581
AUBURN WOODS DR	6100	407X	NWC	77084
AUBURN WOODS DR	18200	367A	CY	77429
AUBURN WOODS DR	18500	326Z	CY	77429
AUCKLAND POINT	12000	368C	NWC	77429
AUCUBA LN	11500	367Q	NWC	77095
AUDEN	5100	492W	SWH	77005
AUDEN	5400	532E	SS	77005
AUDEN DR	1400	620Q	SB	77586
AUDLEY	3000	492X	SWH	77098
AUDRA LN	0	252T	SEM	77386
AUDRA LN	13700	528F	SWC	77083
AUDREY CT	12000	248N	SWM	77362
AUDREY LN	300	457X	NEC	77015
AUDREY ARBOR WAY	17000	527T	NEF	77407
AUDREY MANOR LN	0	446G	NWC	77449
AUDREY SPRINGS CT	0	484N	NEF	77494
AUDRIE RAE LN	0	407E	NWC	77433
AUDUBON	0	614V	PL	77584
AUDUBON	400	658K	LC	77573
AUDUBON CIR	0	366J	NWC	77433
AUDUBON CT	3100	569N	SG	77478
AUDUBON CT	12100	568H	SF	77477
AUDUBON FOREST DR	7600	375U	NEC	77396
AUDUBON GROVE LN	0	328N	NWC	77429
AUDUBON HILL CT	0	411D	NWC	77038
AUDUBON PARK DR	9600	329G	NWC	77379
AUDUBON PLACE	3400	493S	SWH	77006
AUDUBON PLACE	3300	614V	PL	77584
AUDUBON SPRINGS DR	0	410T	NWC	77040
AUDUBON WOOD TRAIL	2200	611S	FS	77545
AUGER PLACE	10900	251P	WD	77380
AUGHTON CT	24900	250W	NWC	77389
AUGHTON DR	25000	250W	NWC	77389
AUGRAE PARK CT	0	525M	NEF	77407
AUGUST RD	11900	367M	CY	77429
AUGUSTA	4900	492L	SWH	77007
AUGUSTA	9000	503Z	BC	77520
AUGUSTA BLVD	0	501K	BT	77521
AUGUSTA CT	1	409K	JV	77064
AUGUSTA CT	5800	491P	SWH	77057
AUGUSTA DR	0	539S	DP	77536
AUGUSTA DR	600	491P	SWH	77057
AUGUSTA DR	2100	659D	LC	77573
AUGUSTA DR	2300	616J	PL	77581
AUGUSTA DR	4500	578K	PA	77505
AUGUSTA BREEZE LN		524C	NEF	77494
AUGUSTA CREEK CT	7500	250X	NWC	77389
AUGUSTA MIST LN	0	406R	NWC	77449
AUGUSTA OAKS CT	0	419A	NEC	77532
AUGUSTA PINES DR	1	250N	NWC	77389
AUGUSTA PINES COVE	6900	250T	NWC	77389
W. AUGUSTA PINES PARKWAY	7700	250T	NWC	77389
AUGUSTA PINES PKWY E	6500	250U	NWC	77389
AUGUSTA PINES WAY	8000	250S	NWC	77389
AUGUSTA POINTE CT		524C	NEF	77494
AUGUSTA SPRING DR	0	290R	NWC	77379
AUGUST CROW DR	0	285Q	NWC	77447
AUGUST HILL DR	0	338B	NEH	77345
AUGUSTINE DR	7000	530J	SWH	77036
AUGUSTIN LANDING DR	15800	367H	NWC	77429
AUGUST LEAF DR	22500	290E	NWC	77375
AUGUST LIGHT LN	0	407C	NWC	77095
AUGUST MEADOWS LN	17700	330J	NWC	77379
AUGUST SUNSET DR	0	376U	NEC	77396
AUGUSTUS VENTURE CT	12200	366K	NWC	77433
AUGUSWOOD LN	20800	333P	NCC	77073
AULIA LN	0	252T	SEM	77386
AULINE LN	1500	451X	NWH	77055
AURA CT	2300	610Q	MC	77459
AURA DR	0	325R	NWC	77433
AURELIA LN	0	659G	LC	77573
AURELIA MIST LN	7400	375X	NEC	77396
AURONIA DR	12200	371H	NWC	77067
AURORA	100	453S	NWH	77008
AURORA	700	453S	NWH	77009
AURORA	15100	527Z	NEF	77498

Street Name	Block	Pg/Sq	Loc	Zips
AURORA FALLS LN	7100	528K	SWC	77083
AUROR AMIST LN	0	572W	SWC	77053
AURORA PARK LN	0	335P	NCC	77338
S. AUSTIN	100	618Y	WB	77598
N. AUSTIN	100	618X	WB	77598
AUSTIN	100	493Q	DT	77002
AUSTIN	600	535Z	SH	77587
AUSTIN	800	493Q	DT	77010
AUSTIN	1200	493Q	DT	77002
AUSTIN	1200	576A	SH	77587
AUSTIN	1300	501V	BT	77520
AUSTIN	1900	659K	LC	77573
AUSTIN	2300	493T	SWH	77004
AUSTIN	5400	533A	SWH	77004
AUSTIN	27000	324E	HK	77447
AUSTIN	1500	659H	LC	77573
AUSTIN	1600	500U	BT	77520
W. AUSTIN AVE	100	536Q	PA	77502
AUSTIN AVE	400	536R	PA	77502
N. AUSTIN AVE	2100	615J	PL	77581
S. AUSTIN AVE	2400	615N	PL	77581
AUSTIN DR	6100	609Z	MC	77459
AUSTIN'S PLACE	2600	568Y	SG	77478
W. AUSTIN BAYOU CT	0	367W	NWC	77433
E. AUSTIN BAYOU CT	0	367W	NWC	77433
AUSTIN BLUFF LN	0	328F	NWC	77377
AUSTIN BREEZE LN	0	660J	LC	77573
AUSTIN COVE LN	0	415C	NEH	77396
AUSTIN CREEK	0	656R	FR	77546
AUSTIN EAST	2500	537P	PA	77502
AUSTIN HOLLOW CT	0	417C	NEH	77044
AUSTIN LAKE DR	3800	615Y	PL	77581
AUSTIN MANOR CT	1200	329B	NWC	77375
AUSTIN OAK LN	0	526M	NEF	77407
AUSTIN PKWY	3800	609E	NEF	77479
AUSTIN SHORE CIR	0	366K	NWC	77433
N. AUSTIN SHORE CT	0	366K	NWC	77433
N. AUSTIN SHORE DR	12300	366L	NWC	77433
S. AUSTIN SHORE DR	18100	366K	NWC	77433
AUSTIN SPRINGS	0	292U	NCC	77373
AUSTIN THOMAS DR	0	407E	NWC	77433
AUSTINVILLE DR	6300	407S	NWC	77449
AUSTRALIA	15600	409R	JV	77040
AUSTRALIA REEF DR	0	445R	NWC	77449
AUSTRIAN PINE PLACE	8500	289R	NWC	77375
AUTAUGA	8900	450K	NWH	77080
AUTOPARK WAY	14100	528N	SWC	77083
AUTOPARK WAY	14600	527R	NEF	77083
AUTREY	1000	493W	SWH	77006
AUTREY DR	1700	538S	DP	77536
AUTUMN	0	616G	SEC	77089
AUTUMN	0	660T	GCO	77539
AUTUMN CT	0	614U	PL	77584
AUTUMN CT	1000	657V	LC	77573
AUTUMN LN	3500	502F	BT	77521
AUTUMN LN	8100	454G	NEH	77016
AUTUMN LN	19200	256F	SEM	77357
AUTUMN LN	28100	248S	SWM	77362
AUTUMN ALCOVE CT	4700	297P	NEH	77345
AUTUMN ARBOR DR	6000	451B	NWH	77092
AUTUMN ASPEN LN	7300	526J	NEF	77407
AUTUMN BEND DR	0	327D	NWC	77429
AUTUMN BLOSSOM CT	17200	407Q	NWC	77095
AUTUMN BLUFF LN	17600	526M	NEF	77407
AUTUMN BRANCH CT	0	484U	NEF	77494
AUTUMN BREEZE CT	5400	331E	NWC	77379
AUTUMN BREEZE DR	18600	330D	NWC	77379
AUTUMN BRIDGE LN	3200	447N	NWC	77084
AUTUMN BROOK	0	407F	NWC	77095
AUTUMNBROOK DR	15500	331N	NWC	77068
AUTUMNBROOK LN	0	612Q	PL	77584
AUTUMN BROOK LN	2900	660E	LC	77573
AUTUMN BROOK ST	900	620G	SB	77586
AUTUMN CANYON LN	30000	253N	SEM	77386
AUTUMN CANYON TRACE	14300	617H	SEH	77062
AUTUMN CHASE DR	11400	409A	NWC	77065
AUTUMN COVE CT	2900	657G	FR	77546
AUTUMN COVE DR	2100	620W	LC	77573
AUTUMN CREEK CT	0	657G	FR	77546
AUTUMN CREEK DR	2900	657G	FR	77546
AUTUMN CREEK DR	2900	657H	FR	77546
AUTUMN CREEK DR	12000	369Q	NWC	77070
AUTUMN CREEK LN	19500	338S	NEC	77346
AUTUMNCREST CT	24400	245V	SWM	77355
AUTUMN CREST DR	2900	657H	FR	77546
AUTUMN CREST LN	0	525M	NEF	77407
AUTUMN CYPRESS LN	0	366R	NWC	77433
AUTUMN DAWN CT	1400	610B	MC	77489
AUTUMN DAWN WAY	4600	447A	NWC	77084
AUTUMN DOGWOOD WAY	5800	338A	NEH	77345
AUTUMN FALL	7800	463S	CCO	77520
AUTUMN FALLS DR	0	612P	PL	77545
AUTUMN FALLS LN	16000	407H	NWC	77095
AUTUMN FERN DR	2000	486P	SWC	77450
AUTUMN FIELD CT	17300	407Q	NWC	77095
AUTUMN FLOWERS DR	6600	407N	NWC	77449
AUTUMN FOREST DR	3200	614T	PL	77584
AUTUMN FOREST DR	5000	451C	NWH	77091
AUTUMN FOREST DR	5800	451B	NWH	77092
AUTUMN GARDEN CT	2500	298W	NEH	77345
AUTUMN GLADE PLACE	19600	446M	NWC	77449
AUTUMN GLEN	0	528M	SWH	77072
AUTUMN GLEN CT	14700	327W	NWC	77429
AUTUMNGLOW CT	2900	485N	NEF	77494
AUTUMN GOLD CT	0	366R	NWC	77433
AUTUMN GREEN DR	1100	569T	MC	77459
AUTUMN GROVE DR	7100	528M	SWH	77072
AUTUMN HARVEST DR	2900	657H	FR	77546
AUTUMN HARVEST DR	9000	369U	NWC	77064
AUTUMN HARVEST DR	9600	369V	NWC	77064
AUTUMN HAZE LN	13200	328Q	NWC	77429
AUTUMN HILLS CT	3000	657D	FR	77546
AUTUMN HILLS DR	17500	407P	NWC	77084
AUTUMN HILLS DR	18000	407N	NWC	77449
AUTUMN HOLLOW LN	7800	408L	NWC	77041
AUTUMNJOY DR	3100	613X	NEB	77584
AUTUMN JOY DR	9400	289Y	NWC	77375
AUTUMN KNOLL CIR	3700	446K	NWC	77449
AUTUMN LAKE DR	2000	619Z	LC	77573
AUTUMN LAKE DR	2600	485Q	NEF	77450
AUTUMN LAKES	4700	609E	NEF	77459
AUTUMN LAKE TRAIL	9900	613K	PL	77584
AUTUMN LAUREL DR	0	407L	NWC	77095
AUTUMN LAUREL TRAIL	7800	407L	NWC	77095
AUTUMN LEAF N. CIR	10200	248L	SWM	77354
AUTUMN LEAF S. CIR	10200	248L	SWM	77354
AUTUMN LEAF DR	3100	657G	FR	77546
AUTUMN LEAF LN	12500	528M	SWH	77072
AUTUMN LEIGH DR	16300	527U	NEF	77083
AUTUMNLIGHT LN	0	366M	NWC	77433
AUTUMN LONG TRAIL	0	376W	NEC	77396
AUTUMN MANOR DR	19300	525Z	NEF	77406

Street Name	Block	Pg/Sq	Loc	Zips
AUTUMN MANOR LN	0	407J	NWC	77433
AUTUMN MEADOW LN	10200	369X	NWC	77064
AUTUMN MEADOWS DR	4200	446H	NWC	77449
AUTUMN MILL DR	12300	369L	NWC	77070
AUTUMN MIST	14100	328T	NWC	77429
AUTUMN MIST CT	2300	619Y	LC	77573
AUTUMN MIST CT	4300	485Z	NEF	77450
AUTUMN MIST LN	2300	619Y	LC	77573
AUTUMN OAK	0	502F	NEC	77521
AUTUMN OAK CT	17300	330D	NWC	77379
AUTUMN OAKS	18600	257D	RF	77357
AUTUMN OAKS DR	900	489C	SWH	77079
AUTUMN OAK WAY	0	330D	NWC	77379
AUTUMN ORCHARD CT	26500	484Y	NEF	77494
AUTUMN ORCHARD LN	0	253J	SEM	77385
AUTUMN ORCHARD LN	4700	484Y	NEF	77494
AUTUMN PARK CIR	0	447P	NWC	77084
AUTUMN PARK CT	2800	657D	FR	77546
AUTUMN PARK DR	18300	447P	NWC	77084
AUTUMN PINE LN	4600	447F	NWC	77084
AUTUMN PINES TRAIL	3900	447G	NWC	77084
AUTUMN POINT LN	800	292G	NCC	77373
AUTUMN PRAIRIE DR	21100	525R	NEF	77407
AUTUMN RAIN LN	6800	290T	NWC	77379
AUTUMN REDWOOD WAY	20800	326S	NWC	77433
AUTUMN RIDGE LN	0	407N	NWC	77449
AUTUMN RIDGE TRAIL DR	13900	573Z	SEH	77048
AUTUMN RIVER LN	0	524T	NWF	77406
AUTUMN ROSE LN	0	609Q	MC	77459
AUTUMN RUN DR	0	290S	NWC	77379
AUTUMN SAGE LN	0	297V	NEH	77345
AUTUMN SHORE CIR	2500	486P	SWC	77450
AUTUMN SHORE DR	20400	486P	SWC	77450
AUTUMN SKY LN	15400	408B	NWC	77095
AUTUMNSONG DR	9000	369Z	NWC	77064
AUTUMN SPRINGS DR	1600	610K	MC	77459
AUTUMN SPRINGS LN	2200	293T	NCC	77373
AUTUMNSTONE DR	0	526X	NEF	77469
AUTUMN STREAM	22400	289J	NWC	77375
AUTUMN SUN DR	0	528J	SWC	77083
AUTUMN SUNSET LN	6500	290Q	NWC	77379
AUTUMN TERRACE LN	20400	486K	SWC	77450
AUTUMN THISTLE DR	6400	407S	NWC	77449
AUTUMN TIMBERS LN	0	366V	NWC	77433
AUTUMN TRACE CT	8100	528L	SWC	77083
AUTUMN TRAILS LN	17400	407P	NWC	77084
AUTUMN TRAILS LN	18000	407P	NWC	77449
AUTUMNVALE LN	14900	368A	NWC	77429
AUTUMN VALLEY DR	13200	328U	NWC	77429
AUTUMN VIEW DR	4100	573V	SEH	77048
AUTUMN VILLAGE DR	1100	569T	MC	77459
AUTUMN WATER ST	0	296T	SEM	77365
AUTUMNWAY CT	10100	409D	NWC	77064
AUTUMNWAY DR	9700	409C	NWC	77064
AUTUMN WILLOW DR	8100	290E	NWC	77375
AUTUMNWIND CT	25500	485W	NEF	77494
AUTUMN WIND DR	8300	410J	NWC	77040
AUTUMN WIND DR	16200	332T	NWC	77090
AUTUMNWOOD CT	1	251L	WD	77380
AUTUMNWOOD DR	0	248F	SWM	77354
AUTUMNWOOD DR	600	496F	NEH	77013
AUTUMN WOOD LN	0	616Z	FR	77546
AUTUMN WOODS DR	22200	296C	SEM	77365
AUTUMN WOODS DR	22300	256Y	SEM	77365
N. AUTUMNWOOD WAY	1	251L	WD	77380
AUTUMNWOOD WAY	10700	251Q	WD	77380
AUTUMTWOOD DR	0	248G	SWM	77354
AVALANGE CT	13100	367H	CY	77429
AVALON CT	7400	578F	PA	77505
AVALON CT	13700	417X	NEC	77044
AVALON LN	4100	502K	BT	77521
AVALON AQUA WAY	0	290P	NWC	77379
AVALON BAY LN	0	525A	NEF	77494
AVALON BEND CIR	0	290P	NWC	77379
AVALON BEND CT	0	253P	SEM	77386
AVALON BROOK LN	0	406C	NWC	77433
AVALON CANYON CT	22200	485Y	NEF	77450
AVALON CASTLE DR	3500	253X	SEM	77386
AVALON CASTLE DR	3500	253X	SEM	77386
AVALON COVE LN	0	614J	PL	77581
AVALON CREST DR	0	290K	NWC	77379
AVALON FOREST CT	0	253N	SEM	77386
AVALON GARDEN LN	3800	525B	NEF	77494
AVALON LAKE LN	0	614N	PL	77581
AVALON LORDS CIR	0	290K	NWC	77379
AVALON MANOR LN	0	614J	NEB	77581
AVALON PARK CT	24500	296J	SEM	77365
AVALON PARK DR	24000	296J	SEM	77365
AVALON PLACE	2100	492P	SWH	77019
AVALON POINT CT	17800	327W	NWC	77429
AVALON QUEEN DR	0	290P	NWC	77379
AVALON RIDGE DR	0	293G	SEM	77386
AVALON SPRING CT	0	253K	SEM	77386
AVALON SPRINGS DR	19000	329A	NWC	77375
AVALON TERRACE	3000	491X	SWH	77057
AVALON TRACE	0	526K	NEF	77407
AVALON TRACE LN	0	614J	NEB	77581
AVALON WAY	5600	491T	SWH	77057
AVALON WOODS DR	0	253P	SEM	77386
AVANA FALLS LN	0	524R	NEF	77406
AVANA GLEN LN	2000	568A	SG	77498
AVANAK	5500	290M	NWC	77389
AVANTA COVE DR	0	407E	NWC	77433
AVANTI CT	3000	613V	NEB	77584
AVANTI DR	2900	613V	NEB	77584
AVAST WAY	0	419B	NEC	77532
AVEBURY CT	2100	486Q	SWC	77450
AVE G	0	662N	GCO	77539
AVE H	0	661R	GCO	77539
AVE H	0	662S	GCO	77539
AVE H	0	571V	SWH	77053
AVELEIGH LN	0	376C	NEC	77396
AVELLINO CT	24500	524M	NEF	77406
AVE M	0	571V	SWH	77053
AVENEL DR	6300	578J	PA	77505
AVENEL IRON DR	10800	370S	NWC	77064
AVENELL RD	2200	576F	SEH	77034
AVENFIELD RD	16400	328R	NWC	77377
AVENIDA DE LAS AMERICAS	1000	493R	DT	77010
AVENIDA LA QUINTA	2100	488U	SWH	77077
AVENIDA MONTEREY PLACE	0	525X	NEF	77406
AVENIDA VAQUERO	12700	488U	SWH	77077
AVENPLACE RD	16200	328R	NWC	77377
AVENS	4300	452M	NWH	77018
AVENSTONE	0	328R	NWC	77377
AVENTINE PLANTATION DR	0	406Y	NWC	77449
AVENTINO WAY	0	450V	NWH	77080
AVENTS RIDGE DR	0	524K	NWF	77406
AVENUE OF MAPLES	0	257N	SEM	77357
AVENUE OF OAKS	100	453U	NEH	77009
AVENU MALKENU AVE	0	449T	NWH	77043
AVERA CREEK DR	30400	253T	SEM	77386

Street Name	Block	Pg/Sq	Loc	Zips
AVERILL	3700	453U	NEH	77009
AVERNUS	2600	453P	NWH	77022
AVERS DR	0	252Q	SEM	77386
AVERSA DR	0	445E	NWC	77493
AVERT CT	8200	412Q	NWH	77088
AVERY	0	534U	SEH	77087
AVERY CT	2600	620K	SB	77586
AVERY LN	0	656R	FR	77546
AVERY ARBOR LN		367S	NWC	77433
AVERY BROOK LN	14400	368N	NWC	77429
AVERY COVE LN	0	525D	NEF	77450
AVERY GROVE CT	0	406G	NWC	77433
AVERY HILL LN	25300	293P	NCC	77373
AVERY HOLLOW CT	4500	658S	LC	77573
AVERY JANE CIR	19200	255U	SEM	77365
AVERY OAKS LN		524K	NWF	77406
AVERY PARK DR	2300	568A	SG	77498
AVERY POINT DR	20400	446K	NWC	77449
AVERY RIDGE LN	13000	328K	NWC	77377
AVERY TRACE CT	11000	368V	NWC	77065
AVERY VALE CT	12400	371H	NWC	77014
AVERY VALE LN	12500	371H	NWC	77014
AVES	9900	576K	SEH	77034
AVETEX	19800	286U	NWC	77377
AVETT DR	21300	296J	SEM	77365
AVETT MEADOW LN	21300	296J	SEM	77365
AVEY CT	3600	613Y	NEB	77584
AVIATOR WAY	0	251C	WD	77380
AVIGNON CT	3501	529B	SWH	77082
AVILA DR	2500	412E	NWC	77038
AVILA BEND DR	14800	408P	NWC	77095
AVILION CT	1500	613L	PL	77584
AVINGTON RD	8400	578D	LP	77571
AVION	13700	417X	NEC	77044
AVION VILLAGE DR	0	366P	NWC	77433
AVIVA LN	13700	528K	SWC	77083
AVOCA DR	0	572M	SEH	77051
AVOCET CT	0	610F	MC	77489
AVOCET LN	0	411S	NWH	77040
AVOGADRO DR	0	445J	NWC	77493
AVON	300	538K	DP	77536
AVON	1900	541A	BT	77520
AVONBROOK LN	0	577W	SEH	77034
AVONBURY LN	24500	485S	NEF	77494
AVONCREST LN	21000	525H	NEF	77407
AVONDALE	100	493S	SWH	77006
AVONDALE	400	658H	LC	77573
AVONDALE LN	300	616Y	FR	77546
AVONDALE MEADOW LN	0	450K	NWH	77080
AVONELLE LN	12900	571M	SWH	77045
AVON GATE CT	0	484J	NEF	77494
AVONGATE LN	14100	488W	SWH	77082
AVONGLEN LN	22000	291L	NWC	77389
AVONLAKE LN	0	375Z	NEC	77396
AVON LANDING LN	0	290Z	NWC	77379
AVONMOOR DR	6600	457Q	NEC	77049
AVON OAK LN	0	486N	SWH	77450
AVON PLACE	11300	370M	NWC	77066
AVONSHIRE DR	13200	528G	SWH	77083
AVON WAY	1300	336H	NEH	77339
AWEIGH DR	500	419B	NEC	77532
AWESOME LN	0	539W	DP	77571
AWNING CT	1000	419B	NEC	77532
AWTY SCHOOL LN	6000	491D	NWH	77055
AXIAL	0	257Q	SEM	77357
AXILDA	100	536J	SEH	77017
AXILDA	800	535M	SEH	77017
AXIS RIDGE	0	458S	NEC	77049
AXTON FALLS	16300	367C	NWC	77429
AYCLIFF DR	2400	374W	NCC	77039
AYERS LN	0	296S	SEM	77365
AYERS PARK DR	1600	327Y	NWC	77429
AYERS PARK LN	16000	327Y	NWC	77429
AYERS ROCK LN	0	292G	NCC	77373
AYLESBURY LN	7900	330E	NWC	77379
AYLESWORTH CT	3000	485S	NEF	77494
AYRSHIRE PARK LN	0	449X	NWH	77043
AYRSHIRE PLACE	0	616K	SEC	77089
AYSCOUGH LN	23700	445N	NWC	77493
AYSHA PARK DR	0	529S	SWM	77099
AYSTON DR	18900	329F	NWC	77375
AZAHAR CT	2200	660G	LC	77573
AZALEA	100	568S	SG	77478
AZALEA	700	452L	NWH	77018
AZALEA	7100	535A	SEH	77023
AZALEA BLVD	0	296B	SEM	77365
AZALEA CT	0	657Q	LC	77573
AZALEA CT	1200	536K	PA	77506
AZALEA CT	8200	535V	SEH	77017
AZALEA CT	27000	248F	SWM	77354
AZALEA DR	400	500E	BT	77520
AZALEA ARBOR	0	406W	NWC	77449
AZALEA BROOK TRAIL	0	615Y	PL	77581
AZALEA BROOK WAY	19600	446Q	NWC	77084
AZALEA CREEK TRAIL	12700	368Z	NWC	77065
AZALEADELL DR	300	452L	NWH	77018
AZALEA GARDEN DR	2300	411D	NWC	77038
AZALEA GLEN CT	19000	446R	NWC	77084
AZALEA HILL TRAIL	0	293U	NCC	77373
AZALEA HILL TRAIL	0	293U	NCC	77373
AZALEA LEAF CT	0	406R	NWC	77449
AZALEA MEADOW LN	0	484Q	NEF	77494
AZALEA PARK DR	25400	250T	NWC	77389
AZALEA POINTE	900	658R	LC	77573
AZALEA RANCH DR	0	484R	NEF	77494
AZALEA RANCH DR	0	484R	NEF	77494
AZALEA SANDS DR	3400	253T	SEM	77386
AZALEA SHORES CT	15800	377Q	NEC	77044
AZALEA SHORES DR	15600	329U	NWC	77070
AZALEA TRACE DR	5000	371J	NWC	77066
AZALEA TRAIL	1500	657F	FR	77546
AZALEA TRAIL LN	1	531G	BL	77401
AZALEA VALLEY CT	6900	406Q	NWC	77449
AZALEA VALLEY DR	19400	406Q	NWC	77449
AZALEA VILLAGE	0	411J	NWC	77088
AZALEA WAY	18900	330A	NWC	77379
AZEEM AVE	9600	529S	SWH	77099
AZELA SHORE	0	296Q	SEM	77365
AZIMUTH DR	16000	419A	NEC	77532
AZROCK	18600	250N	NWC	77375
AZTEC	4200	577F	PA	77504
AZTEC	29000	323G	NWC	77484
AZTEC CT	2600	659W	LC	77573
AZTEC DR	1900	538R	DP	77536
AZTEC DR	18200	295F	SEM	77365
AZTEC LN	7000	459K	NEC	77049
AZTEC CANYON DR	0	253S	SEM	77386
AZTEC THRUSH DR	0	484P	NEF	77494
AZTEC WOOD DR	3400	447K	NWC	77084
AZUCAR CT	800	568G	SG	77498
AZUL SKY CT	0	366Z	NWC	77433
AZURE LN	18800	295F	SEM	77365

Street Name	Block	Pg/Sq	Loc	Zips
AZURE BROOK DR	8100	615H	SEC	77089
AZURE CRYSTAL CT	2000	293W	NCC	77373
AZURE LAKE CT	0	485J	NEF	77494
S. AZURE MIST CT	0	325M	NWC	77433
N. AZURE MIST CT	0	325M	NWC	77433
AZURE PASS DR	0	485J	NEF	77494
AZURE SKY DR	24100	293W	NCC	77373
AZUSA CANYON RD	600	490G	PP	77024

B

Street Name	Block	Pg/Sq	Loc	Zips
B	100	580Q	LP	77571
B	3800	529A	SWH	77072
B AVE	0	410P	NWC	77040
B AVE	100	660R	GCO	77518
B AVE	16700	499A	CV	77530
B DR	0	290L	NWC	77389
B F E DR	0	338Z	NEC	77336
B J LEWIS DR	0	412T	NWH	77088
B P AMOCO	13500	488B	SWH	77079
B STREET	700	282T	WL	77484
B STREET	1800	536A	NEH	77547
B, AVENUE	0	568N	SG	77498
B, AVENUE	0	656A	NEB	77581
B, AVENUE	0	659Y	GCO	77539
S. B, AVENUE	100	335Y	HM	77338
N. B, AVENUE	100	335V	HM	77338
B, AVENUE	200	569Q	SF	77477
B, AVENUE	300	536Y	SH	77587
B, AVENUE	700	444Y	KT	77494
B, AVENUE	800	444Y	KT	77493
B, AVENUE	900	463E	MB	77521
B, AVENUE	1100	660R	GCO	77518
B, AVENUE	1200	611X	FS	77545
B, AVENUE	6300	531H	BL	77401
B, AVENUE	7400	495W	SEH	77012
B, AVENUE	12400	419V	BR	77532
B, AVENUE	16700	498D	CV	77530
BABBITT CT	0	577S	SEH	77034
BABBITT ST	0	576V	SEH	77034
BABBITT ST	0	577S	SEH	77034
BABBLING CREEK DR	3500	297T	NEH	77345
BABBLING SPRING CT	9600	329L	NWC	77375
BABER CT	15300	408B	NWC	77095
BABER DR	9100	408B	NWC	77095
BABER RUN CIR	9200	408B	NWC	77095
BABY BLUE LN	0	524D	NEF	77494
BACA	1	456W	NEH	77013
BACA	500	496A	NEH	77013
BACA	1000	496J	JC	77029
BACARD LN	13000	528Q	SWC	77099
BACCHUS	3300	453N	NWH	77022
BACE CT	1	492H	SWH	77007
BACE DR	8900	490C	SV	77055
BACH ELM ST	13001	369G	NWC	77070
BACHER	5200	455P	NEH	77028
BACH ORCHARD TRAIL	0	411D	NWC	77038
BACH SPRINGS CT	14400	327Z	NWC	77429
BACHWOOD DR	9500	410F	NWC	77040
BACK BAY CT	1900	619W	NB	77058
BACK BAY BROOK TRAIL	0	572P	SWH	77045
BACK BAY RIDGE WAY	12000	616G	SEC	77089
BACKCOVE CT	8600	409H	NWC	77064
BACKEN LN	18300	407S	NWC	77084
BACKENBERRY CT	15900	617T	SEC	77546
BACKENBERRY DR	4500	617T	SEC	77546
BACKLAND CT	1000	292B	NCC	77373
BACKSTAY CT	800	419B	NEC	77532
BACON	3400	533P	SEH	77021
BACONS CASTLE LN	14900	408T	NWC	77084
S. BACOPA DR	0	250Q	NWC	77389
N. BACOPA DR	0	250Q	NWC	77389
BADE	1000	490C	SV	77055
BADEN	3800	453Y	NEH	77009
BADEN HOLLOW LN	20500	406K	NWC	77433
BADEN OAKS CT	3300	485U	NEF	77494
S. BADEN OAKS DR	1700	615Z	PL	77581
BADEN OAKS DR	4100	615Z	PL	77581
BADGER CT	0	446R	NWC	77084
BADGER CANYON DR	10500	367Y	NWC	77095
BADGER FOREST DR	3700	411V	NWH	77088
BADGER HOLLOW DR	21700	245R	SWM	77355
S. BADGER LODGE CIR	0	250K	NWC	77389
N. BADGER LODGE CIR	0	250K	NWC	77389
BADGER LODGE DR	0	250K	NWC	77389
BADGERWOOD DR	11600	496B	NEH	77013
BADLANDS BEND LN	0	376M	NEC	77346
BADTKE RD	17100	324F	HK	77447
BAER	2600	493J	NEH	77020
BAETHE LN	32100	322P	WCO	77484
BAFFIN LN	1000	331H	NWC	77090
BAFING DR	13100	528Q	SWC	77099
BAFING DR	13200	528Q	SWC	77083
BAGBY	100	493L	DT	77002
BAGBY	2300	493P	SWH	77006
BAGEFIELD CT	3600	486S	NEF	77450
BAGGETT LN	1500	451X	NWH	77055
BAGLEY GARDEN CT	0	446G	NWC	77449
BAGNOLI ROSE LN	3200	613V	PL	77584
BAGPIPE LN	4400	447H	NWC	77084
BAHAMA DR	1500	620K	SB	77586
BAHAMA BLUE DR		526S	NEF	77407
BAHAMA COVE CT	0	609T	NEF	77479
BAHAMAS LN	18200	618Z	NB	77058
BAHIA LN	7100	571W	SWH	77489
BAHIA LN	7300	570Z	SWH	77489
BAHME SPRINGS LN	0	295M	SEM	77365
BAIAMONTE	14300	570M	SWH	77085
BAIKAL CT	0	377H	NEH	77346
BAILEY	900	493P	SWH	77019
BAILEY	1900	493P	SWH	77006
BAILEY RD	3500	613Z	NEB	77578
BAILEY RD	4500	614X	NEB	77584
BAILEY RD	7300	615W	PL	77584
BAILEY RD	23400	289D	NWC	77375
BAILEY, D S LN	6500	412X	NWH	77091
BAILEY, D S LN	6500	412X	NWH	77091
BAILEY'S RUN	0	528C	SWH	77082
BAILEY BEND DR	0	657S	FR	77546
BAILEY BROOK LN	0	658Z	LC	77573
BAILEY HILLS LN	0	377F	NEC	77346
BAILEYS CROSSING DR	0	368A	NWC	77429
BAILEY SPRINGS CT	5800	525B	NEF	77450
BAILEYS RUN LN	0	524E	NEF	77494
BAILEYS RUN LN	0	524E	NEF	77494
BAILEYS TOWN CT	0	377T	NEC	77044
BAILEYWOOD DR	21100	525R	NEF	77407
BAIN	3000	454X	NEH	77026
BAIN DR	0	609Z	MC	77459
BAINBRIDGE	10300	414Z	NEH	77016
W. BAINBRIDGE CIR	2600	613U	NEB	77584
E. BAINBRIDGE CIR	2700	613U	NEB	77584

Street Name	Block	Pg/Sq	Loc	Zips
BAINBRIDGE CT	3000	569S	SG	77478
BAINBRIDGE LN	19700	290Z	NWC	77379
BAINBRIDGE ESTATES DR	3600	331C	NWC	77388
BAINBRIDGE TRAIL	13000	368Y	NWC	77065
BAINBROOK LN	14700	375U	NEC	77396
BAINFORD CT	23500	485X	NEF	77494
BAIRD	1200	494X	SEH	77023
BAIRD AVE	1400	444Y	KT	77493
BAIRD CT	5600	449C	NWC	77041
BAIRD MOUNT CT	0	376M	NEC	77346
BAIRNSDALE LN	7400	370A	NWC	77070
BAIRNSDALE LN	8100	369D	NWC	77070
BAITLAND DR	0	609U	MC	77459
BAKER	0	296T	SEM	77365
BAKER	300	288G	TB	77375
BAKER	1200	493M	NEH	77002
BAKER	3500	660W	DI	77539
BAKER	8200	578C	LP	77571
BAKER AVE	100	660M	BC	77518
BAKER DR	100	288G	TB	77375
BAKER DR	8200	535Q	SEH	77017
BAKER RD	100	486H	SWC	77094
BAKER RD	100	501K	BT	77521
BAKER RD	800	656F	FR	77546
E. BAKER RD	900	501M	BT	77521
E. BAKER RD	1300	502J	BT	77521
BAKER RD	2000	336S	NEH	77338
BAKER RD	5500	500K	BT	77520
BAKER CEMETERY RD	25200	247Y	SWM	77355
BAKER COVE	1	490G	PP	77024
BAKER ESTATES DR	0	486L	SWC	77450
BAKER LAKE DR	31100	252Q	SEM	77385
BAKER SPRINGS CT	0	657P	FR	77546
BAKERS VILLAGE DR	0	407B	NWC	77095
BAKERSWOOD DR	0	253T	SEM	77386
BAKER TRAIL	1900	486L	SWC	77094
BAKERWOOD DR	0	409F	NWC	77064
BALA LAKE CT	1200	329G	NWC	77379
BALARAMA DR	12900	528Q	SWC	77099
BALBO	5100	451D	NWH	77091
BALBOA DR	4400	609J	SG	77479
BALCH SPRINGS	700	292Q	NCC	77373
BALCH SPRINGS LN	0	445L	NWC	77449
BALCONES DR	3900	576G	SEH	77034
BALCONES HILL CT	0	366Z	NWC	77433
BALCONES PINE ST	19000	326U	NWC	77429
BALCONES RIDGE LN	0	578T	SEH	77059
BALCREST DR	13300	369F	NWC	77070
BALD CYPRESS BLVD	0	487Z	SWC	77082
BALD CYPRESS CT		332Q	NCC	77073
BALD EAGLE CT	14100	377W	NEC	77044
BALDINGER	200	494Z	SEH	77011
BALD MOUNTAIN CIR	11900	371L	NWC	77067
BALDOVIN WAY		289P	NWC	77375
BALDRIDGE LN	1500	484K	NEF	77494
BALD RIDGE LN	10000	367X	NWC	77095
BALD SPRINGS TRAIL	1700	338A	NEH	77345
BALDSWELLE DR	15500	329S	NWC	77377
BALDWIN	0	531H	BL	77401
BALDWIN	1900	493P	SWH	77002
BALDWIN	2300	493T	SWH	77006
BALDWIN RD	20600	295D	SEM	77365
BALDWIN RD	20900	296A	SEM	77365
BALDWIN ELM	0	526T	NEF	77407
BALDWIN HILL CT	0	377L	NEC	77346
BALDWIN HILL LN	0	377K	NEC	77346
BALDWIN OAKS	20100	446L	NWC	77449
BALDWIN SPRUCE TRAIL	0	329B	NWC	77375
BALEARIC ISLAND CT	4500	660F	LC	77573
BALFOUR	5300	455Q	NEH	77028
BAL HARBOR	100	419U	BR	77532
BAL HARBOUR DR	18000	619P	NB	77058
BALIE LN	8700	335N	NCC	77338
BALKIN	4000	533M	SEH	77021
BALKIN	4900	534N	SEH	77021
BALL	3100	494P	SEH	77003
BALLANTINE	9700	575P	SEH	77075
BALLANTRAE CT	13600	457T	NEC	77015
BALLANTRAE LN	100	457T	NEC	77015
BALLANTRAE LN	300	457X	NEC	77015
BALLANTYNE	26000	247V	SWM	77355
BALLARD CT	2400	291V	NWC	77388
BALLARD DR	0	444D	NWC	77493
BALLARDVALE LN	12000	371L	NWC	77067
BALLARDWOOD CT	900	292B	NCC	77373
BALLAST RD	13500	377Q	NEC	77044
BALLENTINE LN	0	620Q	SB	77586
BALLFOUR PARK LN	14000	573Z	SEC	77047
BALLINA CANYON CT	12300	409W	NWC	77041
BALLINA CANYON LN	5600	409W	NWC	77041
BALLINA MEADOWS CT	6300	406U	NWC	77449
BALLINA MEADOWS DR	19600	406U	NWC	77449
BALLINA RIDGE CT	8300	527N	NEF	77083
BALLIN DAVID DR	9500	329L	NWC	77379
BALLINGER CIR	10100	409G	NWC	77064
BALLINGER DR	8600	409G	NWC	77064
BALLINGER CREEK LN	0	660P	LC	77573
BALLINGER RIDGE CT	20000	526E	NEF	77407
BALLISTER	0	541S	SEH	77571
BALLSTONEFIELD LN	0	484V	NEF	77494
BALLY CASTLE DR	16900	329Q	NWC	77070
BALMANO PLACE	10100	527S	NEF	77407
BALMANO PLACE	10100	527S	NEF	77407
BALMFORTH LN	9900	531U	SWH	77096
BALMORAL CT	700	656M	FR	77546
BALMORAL CT	0	657Q	LC	77573
BALMORAL LN	3800	613Y	NEB	77584
BALMORAL LN	11800	490K	BH	77024
BALMORAL GLEN LN	0	446W	NWC	77449
BALMORA LHILLS DR	0	376V	NEC	77346
BALMORE CIR	13300	370D	NWC	77069
BALMORE CIR	13500	330Y	NWC	77069
BALMORHEA AVE	1100	413C	NCC	77039
BALMORHEA AVE	2400	414A	NCC	77039
BALMORHEA DR	5300	614Z	PL	77584
BALSAM LN	9300	455D	NEH	77078
BALSAM BREEZE LN	0	612F	PL	77545
BALSAM BROOK LN	21600	525G	NEF	77450
BALSAM CROSSING LN	0	407K	NWC	77433
W. BALSAM FIR CIR	0	294P	SEM	77386
E. BALSAM FIR CIR	0	294Q	SEM	77386
BALSAM FIR CT	4000	294P	SEM	77386
BALSAM FIR LN	0	293M	SEM	77386
BALSAM LAKE CT	0	612F	PL	77545
BALSAM LAKE LN	0	612F	PL	77545
BALSAM LAKE LN	2100	658U	LC	77573
BALSAM PARK CT	4300	609X	NEF	77479
BALSAM RIDGE WAY	2500	611S	FS	77545
BALSA ROCK CT		484W	NEF	77494
BALSAS DR	0	255X	SEM	77365
BALTHAMWOOD LN	0	329N	NWC	77377
BALTHASAR	23300	333D	NCC	77373

Street Name	Block	Pg/Sq	Loc	Zips
BALTIC	0	376D	NEC	77346
BALTIC DR	0	336Z	NEC	77346
BALTIC LN	700	332E	NWC	77090
BALTIC LN	1200	331M	NWC	77090
BALTIC RAIN DR	0	285L	NWC	77447
BALTIMORE	7600	495X	SEH	77012
BALTIMORE OHIO	0	247Z	SWM	77355
BALTRUSOL DR	14000	408K	NWC	77095
BALTZELL DR	300	247G	SWM	77362
BALTZELL DR	7800	250W	NWC	77389
BALUCHI DR		289X	NWC	77379
BALVANO DR	0	525J	NEF	77406
BALVENIE CT	9300	407D	NWC	77095
BALZANO CT	0	445F	NWC	77493
BALZAR	3100	659Z	GCO	77539
BALZY RD	3500	452P	NWH	77018
BAMBI CIR	1	338L	NEH	77336
BAMBIWOODS CT	19700	337T	NEC	77346
BAMBIWOODS DR	19900	337P	NEC	77346
BAMBOO RD	9300	450A	NWH	77041
BAMBOO FOREST	0	457A	NEC	77044
BAMBOO FOREST TRAIL	12800	456D	NEC	77044
BAMBRIAR DR	18000	331H	NWC	77090
BAMBRIDGE DR	18000	331H	NWC	77090
BAMBROOK LN	18000	331G	NWC	77090
BAMCREST DR	2000	331H	NWC	77090
BAMMEL LN	2600	492T	SWH	77098
BAMMEL RD	100	332L	NCC	77073
BAMMEL FIELDS CT	0	331V	NWC	77014
BAMMEL NORTH HOUSTON	10000	371S	NWC	77086
BAMMEL NORTH HOUSTON	11000	371E	NWC	77066
BAMMEL NORTH HOUSTON	14000	331X	NWC	77014
BAMMEL OAKS CT	0	331V	NWC	77014
BAMMEL TIMBERS LN	2400	331Q	NWC	77068
BAMMEL VILLAGE DR	15700	331U	NWC	77014
BAMMEL WESTFIELD RD	100	332K	NWC	77090
BAMMELWOOD DR	2300	331V	NWC	77014
BAMPTON DR	9300	329M	NWC	77379
BAMWICK DR	1500	331H	NWC	77090
BAMWOOD DR	17000	332N	NWC	77090
BAMWOOD DR	17200	331M	NWC	77090
BANANA BEND DR	100	458H	NEC	77562
BANBURY	0	615X	PL	77584
BANBURY GREEN LN	0	328E	NWC	77377
BANBURY PLACE	3100	491Z	SWH	77027
BANCHESTER CT	12600	369K	NWC	77070
BANCHORY AVE	17000	329R	NWC	77379
BANCOCK CT	25300	245Q	SWM	77355
BANCROFT	2000	491V	SWH	77027
BANCROFT MIST LN		325N	NWC	77447
BANDELIER DR	2500	450N	NWH	77080
BANDELL DR	3000	572F	SWH	77045
BANDERA	13400	497F	NEC	77015
BANDERA BROOK LN	21000	525H	NEF	77450
BANDERA CREEK LN	0	376M	NEC	77346
BANDERA CREEK LN	0	657P	FR	77546
BANDERA FALLS BEND	15200	328N	NWC	77429
BANDERA GLEN LN	0	484S	NEF	77494
BANDERA HILLS LN	0	526J	NEF	77407
BANDERA HOLLOW LN	4200	527B	SWC	77082
BANDERA PARK CT	0	578T	SEH	77059
BANDERA RANCH LN	0	446N	NWH	77449
BANDERA RESERVE LN	0	578T	SEH	77059
BANDERA RIDGE LN	0	367S	NWC	77433
BANDERA RUN CT	4500	577G	PA	77505
BANDERA VALLEY CT	11400	616E	SEC	77089
BANDIT TRAIL DR	11100	367P	NWC	77095
BANDLON DR	10700	529F	SWH	77072
BANDON LN	700	372H	NCC	77073
BANDRIDGE RD	8400	578D	LP	77571
BANDROCK TERRACE		526S	NEF	77407
BANEBERRY DR	23000	333A	NCC	77373
BANEBERRY RD	1	245T	SWM	77355
BANESTONE BLVD	0	289Q	NWC	77375
BANEWAY DR	4300	529K	SWH	77072
BANEWOOD DR	0	289Q	NWC	77375
BANFF	15400	618K	SEH	77062
BANFF BROOK WAY		289G	NWC	77375
BANFF MOUNTAIN TRAIL	2900	411H	NWC	77088
BANFF SPRINGS CT	0	376H	NEC	77346
BANFIELD CT	10300	575V	SEH	77075
BANGLE	8100	535F	SEH	77012
BANGS RD	1	413X	NEH	77076
BANISTER COVE	2100	484K	NEF	77494
BANJO	7400	412U	NWH	77088
BANK	11900	418R	NEC	77044
BANK DR	200	495Z	GP	77547
BANKERS HOUSE DR	19300	406Z	NWC	77449
BANKERS HOUSE DR	19300	406Z	NWC	77449
BANKS	1000	493W	SWH	77006
BANKS	1700	492Z	SWH	77098
BANKS	19400	335S	NEH	77338
BANKSFIELD CT	3200	485S	NEF	77494
BANKSFIELD CT	21700	445M	NWC	77449
BANK SHADE CT	22900	290F	NWC	77375
BANKSIA DR	0	257E	SEM	77357
BANKSIDE DR	5500	531W	SWH	77096
BANKSIDE DR	7500	530Y	SWH	77071
BANKSIDE DR	9100	530W	SWH	77031
BANKS MILL DR	0	257E	SEM	77357
BANKS RIDGE LN	3800	445H	NWC	77449
BANKS RUN CT	21300	446J	NWC	77449
BANKS RUN DR	0	612H	PL	77584
BANKS RUN LN	3500	446J	NWC	77449
BANKS VIEW CT	0	578X	SEH	77059
BANKWAY CT	0	411R	NWH	77088
BANNER DR	4000	455Y	NEH	77013
BANNERMANS WAY	10800	527X	NEF	77407
BANNER MEADOW LN	0	406P	NWC	77433
BANNER RIDGE LN	14700	375Y	NEC	77396
BANNING DR	4500	491V	SWH	77027
BANNING PARK CT	4700	484Z	NEF	77494
BANNING PARK LN	26300	484Z	NEF	77494
BANNING POINT CT	23600	485T	NEF	77494
BANNISTER LN	11200	413X	NEH	77076
BANNOCK	7100	462Z	BT	77521
BANNON FIELD LN	0	526J	NEF	77407
BANNOWSKY LN	0	457V	NEC	77049
BANPO CT	0	377D	NEC	77346
BANQUO DR	22800	333D	NCC	77373
BANTA DR	6500	571X	SWH	77489
BANTAM BROOK LN	4900	371J	NWC	77066
BANTAM RIDGE CT	0	611C	SWH	77053
BANTER POINT LN	0	445L	NWC	77449
BANTER TRAIL LN	0	609T	NEF	77479
BANTER TRAILS CT	15400	457U	NEC	77049
BANTER TRAILS DR	300	457U	NEC	77049
BANTING	8400	456E	NEH	77078
BANTON	700	498B	CV	77530
BANTRY MEADOW DR	1200	373J	NCC	77060
BANTRY MEADOW DR	1200	373J	NCC	77060
BANTUM	10400	414W	NEH	77093
BANTY FALLS CT	15500	331P	NWC	77068
BANYAN	6900	454M	NEH	77028
BANYAN	7300	455J	NEH	77028
BANYAN CREST LN	0	446J	NWC	77449
BANYAN WOOD WAY	0	614Y	PL	77584
BANYON GULCH LN	0	444S	KT	77493
BANYON OAK CT		526T	NEF	77407
BANZER	8700	450Z	NWH	77055
BAPTIST	200	569V	SF	77477
BAPTIST ENCAMPMENT RD	20400	257P	SEM	77357
BAPTIST UNIVERSITY	0	530L	SWH	77074
BAR-A (PVT)	0	287P	NWC	77377
BARABIN	0	571R	SWH	77045
BARADA	10300	576K	SEH	77034
BARAJAS LN	900	373U	NCC	77039
BARANY CT	6000	406Z	NWC	77449
BARAZI OAKS CT	11600	490F	BH	77024
BARBADOS DR	6600	411J	NWH	77088
BARBADOS CALLE	5100	660S	GCO	77539
BARBARA	700	288L	TB	77375
BARBARA	15000	246U	SWM	77355
BARBARA	1300	460N	HG	77562
E. BARBARA CIR	15300	570G	MC	77071
W. BARBARA CIR	15400	570G	MC	77071
BARBARA CT	0	539V	LP	77571
BARBARA CT	1800	538M	DP	77536
BARBARA LN	1700	537N	PA	77502
BARBARA LN	2600	532G	WU	77005
BARBARA MAE	200	457Y	NEC	77015
BARBARA MAE	300	497C	NEC	77015
BARBARELLA CT	6600	411N	NWH	77088
BARBAROSSA DR	15100	527P	NEF	77083
BARBEE	1200	493X	SWH	77004
BARBER	0	463A	MB	77580
BARBER	400	492M	SWH	77007
BARBER RD	0	462D	MB	77521
BARBER GROVE LN	15600	408A	NWC	77095
BARBER RUN CIR	9200	408B	NWC	77095
BARBERRY CT	0	615F	PL	77581
BARBERRY DR	3000	573B	SEH	77051
BARBERRY LN	400	500A	BT	77520
BARBERRY BRANCH ST	0	451S	NWH	77055
BARBERRY PINE LN	0	377F	NEC	77346
BARBERS CT	12800	570K	MC	77489
BARBERS HILL RD	100	459H	NEC	77562
BARBERS HILL RD	700	460E	NEC	77562
BARBERS HILL RD	4500	461E	NEC	77562
BARBERTON DR	7400	530K	SWH	77036
BARBETTA CT	100	659D	LC	77573
BARBIL LN	100	299W	NEH	77336
BARBIZON DR	12300	617E	SEH	77089
BARBIZON DR	12300	616H	SEH	77089
BARBONS HEATH CT	0	446W	NWC	77449
E. BARBOURS CUT BLVD.	1	540X	LP	77571
W. BARBOURS CUT BLVD.	100	540W	LP	77571
E. BARBOURS CUT BLVD.	3000	541S	MP	77571
BARBOURS CUT TERM	0	541S	MP	77571
BARBSTONE DR	13300	377X	NEC	77044
BARBUDA DR	0	333M	NCC	77338
BARBUDA LN	18100	618U	NB	77058
BARBUDA LN	18700	619W	NB	77058
BARCAN CIR	21700	485R	SWC	77450
BARCAROLE DR	21300	291Q	NWC	77388
BARCA ROSA CIR	0	445A	NWC	77493
BARCELONA CIR	700	501V	BT	77520
BARCELONA CT	1	609C	MC	77459
BARCELONA DR	16000	617W	FR	77546
BARCELONA DR	16500	657B	FR	77546
BARCELONA WAY	0	659S	LC	77573
BARCELONA WAY	1500	501V	BT	77520
BARCHAN POINT		526S	NEF	77407
BARCHETTA TRAIL	0	445E	NWC	77493
BARCLAY LAKE LN	2400	332A	NWC	77388
BARCO CT	4000	293M	SEM	77386
BARCUS LN	12900	496M	NEH	77015
BARDET	5900	614Q	PL	77584
BARDWELL	1100	493D	NEH	77009
BARDWELL LAKE CT	0	377L	NEH	77346
BARDWELL LAKE CT	1500	526X	NEF	77407
BARE BRANCH LN	18100	407E	NWC	77433
BARELEY LN	10800	369P	NWC	77070
BARELY ROSE CT	0	325M	NWC	77429
BAREMEADOW LN	0	407S	NWC	77449
BAREN BROOK WAY	0	326V	NWC	77429
BARENTS	0	376D	NEC	77346
BARENTS DR	0	336Z	NEC	77346
BARE OAK	3000	487Z	SWC	77082
BARE SKY DR	0	612M	PL	77584
BARE SKY DR	8600	407D	NWC	77095
BARGER	1900	659B	LC	77573
BARGER RD	9600	530S	SWH	77074
BARGEWAY	16100	419B	NEC	77532
BAR HARBOUR CT	16100	419B	NEC	77532
BARINWOOD CT	0	289Q	NWC	77375
BARK LN	13000	497A	NEC	77015
BARKALOO RD	3700	501H	NEC	77521
BAR KAY LN	24100	325J	NWC	77447
BAR KAY LN	24200	324M	NWC	77447
BARK CABIN DR	0	377K	NEC	77346
BARKDULL	800	493W	SWH	77006
BARKENTINE LN	16700	617U	SEC	77546
BARKER	1000	569Y	MC	77477
N. BARKER	17300	407Q	NWC	77084
BARKER DR	8700	456C	NEC	77044
BARKER-CYPRESS	0	527A	SWC	77082
S. BARKER-CYPRESS	300	487W	SWH	77094
BARKER BAYOU CT	14200	367B	NWC	77429
BARKER BEND CT	20500	406P	NWC	77449
BARKER BEND LN	6600	406P	NWC	77449
BARKER BLUFF LN	0	367P	NWC	77433
BARKER CANYON LN	21000	525H	NEF	77450
BARKER CLODINE RD	200	487E	SWC	77094
BARKER CORNER DR	0	327X	CY	77429
BARKER CYPRESS RD	300	487A	SWC	77094
BARKER CYPRESS RD	1000	447N	NWC	77094
BARKER CYPRESS RD	5000	407X	NWC	77084
BARKER CYPRESS RD	7000	407F	NWC	77433
BARKER CYPRESS RD	9500	367T	NWC	77433
BARKER CYPRESS RD	13000	367H	CY	77429
BARKER CYPRESS RD	14400	327X	CY	77429
BARKER GATE CT	0	367S	NWC	77433
BARKER GROVE DR	0	367S	NWC	77433
BARKER HOLLOW DR	0	524B	NEF	77494
BARKER LAKE CT	0	367T	NWC	77433
BARKER MARSH DR	16500	327X	NWC	77429
BARKERMIST LN	6100	525H	NEF	77450
BARKER OAKS DR	2200	488S	SWH	77077
BARKER PARK CT	0	367P	NWC	77433
BARKER PELICAN CT	14400	327X	NWC	77429
BARKER RANCH CT	16500	327X	CY	77429
BARKER RIDGE CT	0	249B	SWM	77354
BARKERS BRANCH DR	0	447K	NWC	77084
BARKERS COVE	500	488A	SWH	77079
BARKERS CREST DR	18200	447K	NWC	77084
BARKERS FOREST LN	3200	447N	NWC	77084
BARKERS GREEN WAY	18200	447P	NWC	77084
BARKERS LANDING CT	400	488B	SWH	77079
BARKERS LANDING RD	15600	488B	SWH	77079
S. BARKERS LANDING RD	15800	488B	SWH	77079
N. BARKERS LANDING RD	15800	488A	SWH	77079
BARKERS POINT LN	16000	488A	SWH	77079
BARKER SPRINGS RD	16600	487B	NWH	77084
BARKERS WOOD LN	3001	447P	NWC	77084
BARKER TRACE DR	0	367P	NWC	77433
BARKER TRACE DR	0	367P	NWC	77433
BARKERVIEW CT	14100	408Y	NWC	77084
BARKER VIEW DR	0	367S	NWC	77433
BARKER VILLAGE CT	0	407S	NWC	77449
BARKER VILLAGE LN	0	407S	NWC	77449
BARKER WEST DR	0	367P	NWC	77433
BARKLEA RD	16100	327Y	CY	77429
BARKLEY	400	453J	NWH	77022
BARKLEY DR	4900	535R	SEH	77017
BARKLEY BEND LN	0	377K	NEC	77346
BARKLY CT	1100	615B	PL	77581
BARK RIDGE LN	0	407C	NWC	77095
BARKSDALE AVE	0	568W	SG	77479
BARKSDALE DR	2900	414S	NEH	77093
BARKSHIRE DR	13700	372E	NWC	77014
BARKSTON CT	20600	486F	SWC	77450
BARKSTON DR	1000	486F	SWC	77450
BARKWITH LN	0	457Z	NEC	77530
BARKWOOD	100	452H	NWH	77022
BARLETON WAY	1700	618R	SEH	77058
BARLETTA DR	0	257F	SEM	77357
BARLEY	5800	444X	KT	77494
BARLEY LN	0	484B	KT	77494
BARLEYCORN LN	5300	524D	NEF	77494
BARLEY MILL CT	16600	407G	NWC	77095
BARLEY SPRINGS LN	0	253P	SEM	77386
BARLOW	8100	455T	NEH	77028
BARLOW BEND LN	5000	525C	NEF	77450
BARLOW SPRINGS LN	0	376N	NEC	77396
BARMBY CT	8400	250W	NWC	77389
BARMBY DR	24900	250W	NWC	77389
BARMBY DR	25000	249Z	NWC	77375
BARMONT DR	9700	579A	LP	77571
BARNACLE DR	300	379Y	NEC	77532
BARNES	300	500P	BT	77520
BARNES	3500	492H	SWH	77007
BARNES LN	0	612Z	NEB	77578
BARNESDALE CT	0	372M	NCC	77073
BARNES RIDGE LN	7900	528L	SWH	77072
BARNESVILLE DR	700	498A	CV	77530
BARNESWORTH DR	13200	456Q	NEH	77049
BARNETT	3800	535P	SEH	77017
S. BARNETT LN	26500	246N	SWM	77355
BARNETT LN	26600	246N	SWM	77355
BARNEY RD	6600	451J	NWH	77092
BARNGATE CT	16100	327Y	NWC	77429
BARNGATE MEADOW LN	0	406F	NWC	77433
BARNHAM	10300	414Y	NEH	77016
BARNHART BLVD	13900	488P	SWH	77077
BARNHART LN	9200	409A	NWC	77065
BARNHART HILL DR		366R	NWC	77433
BARNHILL DR	7800	334V	NCC	77338
BARNHOUSE LN	0	325F	NWC	77447
BARN RED CT	0	326Y	NWC	77433
BARN RUN LN		325S	NWC	77447
BARNSFORD LN	800	289R	NWC	77375
BARNSFORD LN	9200	289R	NWC	77375
BARNSFORD LN	9200	289R	NWC	77375
BARNSFORD LN	9200	289R	NWC	77375
BARNSLEY LN	1900	412K	NWC	77088
BARNSTABLE CT	10500	329B	NWC	77379
BARNSTABLE PLACE	1	250D	WD	77381
BARNSTON	6100	454N	NEH	77026
BARN SWALLOW LN	0	328K	NWC	77429
BARNWELL DR	4100	527D	SWC	77082
BAROMETER DR	0	379Y	NEC	77532
BAROMETER BEND DR	0	377Q	NEC	77044
BARON	2600	494J	NEH	77020
W. BARON LN	1	609C	MC	77459
BARON LN	1	609C	MC	77459
BARON LN	4200	538Y	DP	77536
BARON RD	4500	501F	BT	77521
BARON BEND LN	20400	406P	NWC	77449
BARON BROOK DR	0	406Q	NWC	77433
BARONBROOK LN	13900	417B	NEC	77044
BARON COVE LN	22200	525C	NEF	77450
BARONEAL DR	0	336U	NEH	77338
BARONESS LN	0	405W	NWC	77493
BARONET DR	0	404Z	NWC	77493
BARON GATE CT	6800	290Q	NWC	77379
BARON GROVE DR	0	338B	NEH	77345
BARON HOLLOW CT	13100	371D	NWC	77014
BARON OAKS CT	5500	330Y	NWC	77069
BARON OAKS DR	14200	330Y	NWC	77069
BARONRIDGE DR	600	619G	TL	77586
BARON RIDGE DR	7000	502C	BT	77521
BARON RIDGE LN	0	407E	NWC	77433
BARON RIDGE LN	0	525A	NEF	77469
BARONS BRIDGE DR	13700	330Y	NWC	77069
BARONS COVE	5200	448D	NWC	77041
BARONS COVE CT	0	612K	PL	77545
BARONS GLEN	1900	568Y	SG	77478
BARONSHIRE DR	17200	329L	NWC	77070
BARONSHIRE ROUND	9900	329L	NWC	77070
BARONS LAKE LN	13600	328P	NWC	77429
BARONSLEDGE LN	0	446J	NWC	77449
BARONSMEDE DR	9200	528U	SWC	77083
BARONS POINT CT	5700	609T	NEF	77479
BARON TRACE LN	5200	485X	NEF	77494
BAROSSA VALLEY LN	0	446E	NWC	77449
BARR	2000	450Q	NWH	77080
BARR CIR	9200	450Q	NWH	77080
BARRACUDA CT	1	490B	SWH	77024
BARRACUDA LN	3800	580V	LP	77571
BARRANCA DR	13200	528Q	SWC	77083
BARRAUD CT	1500	445Z	NWC	77449
BARRED OWL DR	0	333G	NCC	77338
BARRELL SPRINGS LN	22400	289J	NWC	77375
BARREL OAK DR	0	450U	NWH	77080
BARREL RUN DR	0	285P	NWC	77447
BARREL RUN DR	0	285P	NWC	77447
BARREMORE	5400	534C	SEH	77023
BARREN SPRINGS DR	400	332X	NWC	77090
BARREN WAY	8700	410F	NWC	77064
BARRETT	5200	453E	NEH	77022
BARRETT	5400	453E	NEH	77076
BARRETT BRAE DR	11300	529P	SWH	77072
BARRETT CREEK LN	0	525M	NEF	77407
BARRETT KNOLLS DR	0	525U	NEF	77469
BARRETT KNOLLS DR	0	525U	NEF	77469
BARRETT POST LN	0	367Y	NWC	77095
BARRETT RIDGE LN	13800	377Y	NEH	77044
BARRETTS CROSSING DR	0	330K	NWC	77379
BARRETTS GLEN CT	9400	408D	NWC	77065
BARRETTS GLEN DR	1800	615Z	PL	77581
BARRETT STATION	0	419U	BR	77532
BARRETT WOODS CT	6000	525R	NEF	77407
BARRETT WOODS DR	21000	525R	NEF	77407
BARR FOREST DR	0	377A	NEC	77346
BARRIER CT	0	502K	BT	77521
BARRINGER LN	500	617M	SEH	77598
BARRINGTON CT	0	615W	PL	77584
BARRINGTON CT	2600	528Y	SG	77478
BARRINGTON RD	3300	491X	SWH	77056
BARRINGTON BRANCH DR	2700	293T	NCC	77373
BARRINGTON CREEK TRACE	0	405T	NWC	77493
BARRINGTON FAIRWAY	13900	370B	NWC	77069
BARRINGTON GARDEN	6600	370B	NWC	77069
BARRINGTON GREEN	6600	370B	NWC	77069
BARRINGTON GROVE TRACE	0	526Q	NEF	77407
BARRINGTON HILLS LN	1600	485L	SWC	77450
BARRINGTON LODGE LN	0	484S	NEF	77494
BARRINGTON MEADOW TRACE	0	526N	NEF	77407
BARRINGTON PLACE DR	2100	568C	SG	77478
BARRINGTON PLACE DR	2500	528Y	SG	77478
BARRINGTON POINTE CT	100	659D	LC	77573
BARRINGTON POINTE DR	2000	659D	LC	77573
BARRINGTON POINTE DR	2100	660A	LC	77573
BARRINGTON SPRINGS	0	405T	NWC	77493
BARRINGTON SPRINGS LN	0	658Z	LC	77573
BARRINGTON WAY	0	615W	PL	77584
BARRISTER DR	0	570E	SWH	77071
BARRISTER CREEK DR	0	287G	NWC	77377
BARR LAKE DR	9900	368X	NWC	77095
BARRON LN	1	498G	CV	77530
BARRON LN	3000	610D	SWH	77489
BARRONE DR	14100	368P	NWC	77429
BARRONETT BEND	1900	568C	SG	77478
BARRONTON DR	6600	290G	NWC	77389
W. BARRON WOOD CIR	8500	528N	SWC	77083
E. BARRON WOOD CIR	8500	528P	SWC	77083
BARROW	1200	463E	MB	77521
BARROW LN	11100	368R	NWC	77065
BARROW LN	11100	368V	NWC	77065
BARROW COVE DR	15800	367D	NWC	77429
BARROW CREEK	0	615H	PL	77089
BARROW DOWNS WAY	500	577W	SEH	77034
BARROW DOWNS WAY	500	617A	SEH	77034
BARROW EDGE LN	0	366Y	NWC	77433
BARROWFIELD LN	0	527W	NEF	77478
BARROWGATE DR	1100	568F	SG	77498
BARROW GLEN CT	0	291N	NWC	77388
BARROW GLEN DR	0	524E	NEF	77494
BARROWHOLLOW DR	9200	528U	SWC	77083
BARROW POINT LN	13200	371D	NWC	77014
BARROW RIDGE LN	4200	527B	SWC	77082
BARR SPRING DR	0	376E	HM	77396
BARRY CT	0	573L	SEH	77470
BARRY LN	18700	337X	NEC	77346
BARRY LN	28500	283Q	NWC	77484
BARRYBROOK LN	8500	578C	LP	77571
BARRYCLIFF CT	12000	369Q	NWC	77070
BARRY ESTATE CT	1500	444Z	KT	77493
BARRY ESTATE DR	1500	445W	NWC	77493
BARRYGATE CIR	22200	334F	NCC	77373
BARRYGATE CT	22200	334F	NCC	77373
BARRYGATE DR	6400	334F	NCC	77373
BARRYKNOLL CT	800	489B	SWH	77079
BARRYKNOLL LN	11800	490A	SWH	77024
BARRYKNOLL LN	13100	489A	SWH	77079
BARRYKNOLL LN	14400	488D	SWH	77079
BARRY MOORE DR	0	615T	PL	77581
BARRYMORE BLVD	600	541A	BT	77520
BARRY OAKS LN	8600	578D	LP	77571
BARRY ROSE RD	0	615H	PL	77089
BARRY ROSE RD	1900	615L	PL	77581
BARRYS CT	11100	409P	NWC	77041
BARRYS WAY	600	338M	NEH	77336
BARRYTREE CT	12000	369Q	NWC	77070
BARRYTREE DR	11900	369Q	NWC	77070
BARSTONE LN	0	525H	NEF	77450
BARSTOW	23600	290D	NWC	77389
BARSTOW BEND LN	4900	446D	NWC	77449
BART LN	8600	410P	NWC	77040
S. BARTELL DR	2800	532U	SWH	77054
W. BARTELL DR	8400	532U	SWH	77054
BARTLETT	900	493W	SWH	77006
BARTLETT	2100	492Y	SWH	77098
BARTLETT RD	7100	444X	KT	77493
BARTLETT BEND DR	100	459M	HG	77562
BARTLETT COVE DR	1200	372J	NWC	77067
BARTLETT LANDING DR	0	326U	NWC	77429
BARTLETT PEAR CT	0	457L	NEC	77049
BARTLETTS HARBOR CT	8500	411S	NWH	77040
BARTLETT WAY DR	0	615F	PL	77581
BARTON	5600	455S	NEH	77028
BARTON	8800	575H	SEH	77075
BARTON CT	2500	658P	LC	77573
BARTON CT	2900	613T	NEB	77584
BARTON CT	9200	579A	LP	77571
BARTON DR	3000	613T	NEB	77584
BARTON BEND LN	0	406D	NWC	77433
BARTON CREEK CT	20000	486L	SWC	77450
BARTON CREEK DR	0	485J	NEF	77494
BARTON CREEK DR	2100	612H	PL	77584
BARTON CREEK DR	2100	612M	PL	77584
BARTON CREEK DR	5100	578J	PA	77505
BARTON CREEK TRAIL	1600	486L	SWC	77450
BARTON CROSSING LN	9400	527S	NEF	77407
BARTON FALLS	5600	449A	NWC	77041
BARTON FALLS CT	2100	658S	LC	77573
BARTON GATE LN	0	488T	SWH	77077
BARTON GROVE LN	14700	376W	NEC	77396
BARTON HILLS CT	0	371D	NWC	77014
BARTON HOLLOW CT	6300	407T	NWC	77449
BARTON HOLLOW LN		525R	NEF	77469
BARTON LAKE CT	7400	525L	NEF	77469
BARTON MEADOW LN	2800	485N	NEF	77494
BARTON OAKS CT	17000	407Q	NWC	77095
BARTON OAKS DR	7200	407L	NWC	77095
BARTON ORCHARD LN	0	377P	NEC	77044
BARTON PARK LN	21800	486W	NEF	77450
BARTON POINT LN	0	527N	NEF	77083
BARTON RIDGE LN	0	527J	NEF	77407
BARTON RIVER LN	0	417B	NEC	77044
BARTONS CT	3900	609E	SG	77479
BARTONS LN	3600	609E	SG	77479
BARTON SHORES DR	0	612J	PL	77545
BARTON SPRINGS LN	0	377E	NEC	77346
BARTON SPRINGS ST	0	659L	LC	77573
BARTON VALE LN	0	526F	NEF	77407
BARUNA	12300	528M	SWH	77072

Street Name	Block	Pg/Sq	Loc	Zips
BARWICK DR	19500	292Y	NCC	77373
BARWOOD	3200	251X	SWM	77380
BARWOOD DR	10200	449V	NWH	77043
BARWOOD BEND DR	11300	368Q	NWC	77065
BARZIZA	400	494U	SEH	77011
BASAL BRIAR CT	1	251J	WD	77381
BASALT DR	0	461T	NEC	77521
BASALT LN	14400	488J	SWH	77077
BASCOM	8400	451J	NWH	77080
BASE LIGHT DR	0	285L	NWC	77447
BASHAW DR	30000	252Y	SEM	77386
BASH PLACE	1	491Z	SWH	77027
BASIL	4100	494P	SEH	77003
BASIL CT	0	614Y	PL	77584
BASIL DR	0	461Q	NEC	77521
BASIL LN	7500	529M	SWH	77036
BASILAN LN	1300	618V	NB	77058
BASIL BRANCH DR	0	451S	NWH	77055
BASILBROOK CT	0	484R	NEF	77494
BASIL CREST LN	0	615K	PL	77581
N. BASILDON CT	21100	332U	NCC	77073
BASIL FIELD CT	0	524F	NEF	77494
BASILICA	11700	529W	SWH	77099
BASIL TRACE DR	0	253T	SEM	77386
BASIL VIEW LN	0	524F	NEF	77494
BASIN	1600	495S	SEH	77011
BASIN BEND	100	297L	NEH	77365
BASKET	2000	536V	PA	77502
BASKET FLOWER DR	20100	289Y	NWC	77379
BASKET OAK DR	24100	339J	NEH	77336
BASKING	1400	450W	NWH	77080
BASKOVE DR	8800	411J	NWC	77088
BASLOW DR	5400	446C	NWC	77449
BASS	1500	492H	SWH	77007
BASS CT	1500	492H	SWH	77007
BASSBROOK DR	21300	291Q	NWC	77388
BASS COVE CT	0	445N	NWC	77493
BASSDALE DR	11300	329X	NWC	77070
BASSELFORD DR	9600	528U	SWC	77083
BASSETDALE LN	6000	407V	NWC	77084
BASSETT	8100	533X	SEH	77051
BASSETT HALL LN	24100	445T	NWC	77493
BASSFIELD LN	0	484V	NEF	77494
BASSFIELD LN	0	484V	NWF	77494
BASSFORD DR	13000	528U	SWC	77099
BASSFORD DR	13200	528U	SWC	77083
BASSINGHAM DR	2700	296V	NEH	77339
BASSINGHAM DR	3100	297N	NEH	77339
BASSOON DR	9000	532N	SWH	77025
BASS POINT WAY	9400	375R	NEC	77396
BASS PRO DR	0	484C	KT	77494
BASSWOOD	100	453L	NEH	77022
BASSWOOD DR	0	657Q	LC	77573
BASSWOOD DR	200	252N	SEM	77386
BASSWOOD LN	4400	531D	BL	77401
BASSWOOD DALE DR	5500	407W	NWC	77084
BASSWOOD FOREST DR	0	407L	NWC	77095
BASSWOOD SPRINGS CT	1400	617D	SEH	77062
BASTIAN	7300	533V	SEH	77033
BASTION SETTLE DR	0	285L	NWC	77447
BASTOGNE RD	7300	533V	SEH	77033
BASTON CREEK DR	0	326K	NWC	77433
BASTONE	25800	247V	SWM	77355
N. BASTROP	1	494J	SEH	77003
BASTROP	300	493R	SEH	77003
BASTROP	1300	536P	PA	77506
BASTROP	2300	493Y	SEH	77004
BASTROP BAYOU CT	0	367W	NWC	77433
BASTROP GLEN LN	0	660J	LC	77573
BATAAN DR	2100	658R	LC	77573
BATAAN RD	4900	534N	SEH	77033
BATEAU	11300	368T	NWC	77429
BATEAU CT	11300	368T	NWC	77429
BATEAU DR	14100	368T	NWC	77429
BATEMAN LN	7700	411P	NWH	77088
BATES AVE	1100	532H	SWH	77030
BATES LN	12600	569H	SF	77477
BATESBROOKE CT	1	250C	WD	77381
BATESWOOD DR	700	489E	SWH	77079
BATH	100	620Q	SB	77586
BATHGATE LN	0	408W	NWC	77084
BATHURST	31000	248U	TB	77375
BATHURST DR	14200	572N	SWH	77045
BATHURST DR	14800	572S	SWH	77053
BATING HOLLOW	12000	490J	SWH	77024
BATON CT	0	373E	NEC	77073
BATON PASS	19100	338W	NEC	77346
BATON ROUGE	4600	454Q	NEH	77028
BATSON	0	418U	NEC	77049
BATTEN WAY	500	379T	NEC	77532
BATTER SEA GARDEN DR	15300	458S	NEC	77530
BATTERSON	6000	454N	NEH	77026
BATTERY ST	1100	568T	SG	77478
BATTLE	0	459C	NEC	77562
N. BATTLEBELL RD	100	459V	HG	77562
N. BATTLEBELL RD	700	460S	HG	77562
BATTLEBELL RD	3000	460V	NEC	77521
BATTLEBELL RD	4000	461S	NEC	77521
BATTLE CREEK	0	407H	NWC	77095
BATTLE CREEK	3400	609K	MC	77459
BATTLECREEK DR	7600	410R	NWC	77040
BATTLECREEK DR	16300	407G	NWC	77095
BATTLEFORD DR	0	289V	NWC	77375
BATTLE HILLS DR	7200	410Q	NWC	77040
BATTLEOAK DR	7600	410R	NWC	77040
BATTLEPINE CT	7500	410R	NWC	77040
BATTLEPINE DR	7600	410R	NWC	77040
BATTLE PLAINS DR	8400	410Q	NWC	77040
BATTLE SPRING DR	0	293T	NCC	77373
BATTLEVIEW RD	300	539Z	LP	77571
BATTLEWOOD DR	7300	410R	NWH	77040
BAUER AVE	800	659K	LC	77573
BAUER DR	1900	450Q	NWH	77080
BAUER RD	16500	325P	NWC	77429
BAUER RD	18100	285T	NWC	77447
BAUER CANYON DR	0	285Q	NWC	77447
BAUER CREEK DR	0	285L	NWC	77447
BAUER ELM ST	0	418T	NEC	77044
BAUER HOCKLEY RD	18900	326B	NWC	77377
BAUER HOCKLEY RD	20000	325A	NWC	77447
BAUER HOCKLEY RD	24200	324D	NWC	77447
BAUERLE CT	1	490K	BH	77024
BAUERLEIN DR	9400	411A	NWC	77086
BAUER OAKS DR	0	407D	NWC	77095
S. BAUER POINT CIR	0	250Q	NWC	77389
BAUER POINT CIR	0	250Q	NWC	77389
BAUER POINT CT	0	250Q	NWC	77389
BAUER RIDGE DR	16000	367H	NWC	77429
BAUERS	0	285P	NWC	77447
BAUER SKY DR	0	285K	NWC	77447
BAUGHMAN RIDGE DR		484W	NEF	77494
BAUMAN RD	6900	453G	NEH	77022
BAUMAN RD	9400	413Y	NEH	77076
BAUMAN RD	12400	413Q	NEH	77037
BAUMEADOW LN	1900	568A	SG	77498
BAUMGARTNER DR	21800	333L	NCC	77338
BAUXHALL CT	300	486C	SWC	77450
BAVARIA DR	9600	329U	NWC	77070
BAXTER AVE	15300	408S	NWC	77084
BAXTER GROVE	0	367H	NWC	77429
BAXTER HILLS LN	0	369G	NWC	77077
BAXTERS CT	0	484V	NEF	77494
BAY	200	580L	LP	77571
BAY	2400	454W	NEH	77026
BAY AVE	100	660D	KE	77565
BAY AVE	200	620U	KE	77565
BAY LN	20700	254P	SEM	77365
W. BAY RD	0	542C	CCO	77520
W. BAY RD	0	502U	CCO	77520
BAY RD	6300	578A	PA	77505
BAYARD LN	4800	493W	SWH	77006
BAYARD LN	5300	493W	SWH	77005
W. BAY AREA BLVD	100	618S	WB	77598
W. BAY AREA BLVD	100	657R	LC	77573
BAY AREA BLVD	400	618Q	SEH	77058
W. BAY AREA BLVD	1200	617Z	SEC	77546
W. BAY AREA BLVD	1201	617Z	SEC	77598
W. BAY AREA BLVD	2600	657C	SEC	77598
BAY AREA BLVD	7700	580N	SEC	77507
BAY AREA BLVD	7700	579Y	SEC	77507
BAYBERRY AVE	0	659P	LC	77573
BAYBERRY CT	11700	328R	NWC	77377
BAYBERRY DR	3900	572N	SWH	77045
BAY BERRY LN	1400	619D	PA	77586
BAYBERRY LN	1400	619D	PA	77586
W. BAYBERRY BEND DR	0	528H	SWH	77072
S. BAYBERRY BEND DR	0	528H	SWH	77072
E. BAYBERRY BEND DR	0	528H	SWH	77072
BAYBERRY PARK LN	9800	289U	NWC	77375
BAY BLUE WAY	0	326N	NWC	77433
BAYBORO PARK CT	15500	617S	SEC	77546
BAYBORO PARK DR	4800	617S	SEC	77546
BAY BOWER LN	19400	446H	NWC	77449
BAYBREEZE	0	620Y	KE	77565
BAY BREEZE DR	3400	620E	SB	77586
BAYBRIAR DR	15700	570Z	SWH	77489
BAY BRIDGE	8400	613V	PL	77584
BAYBRIDGE DR	200	568P	SG	77478
BAY BRIDGE DR	10800	370S	NWC	77064
BAYBROOK DR	15300	618K	SEH	77062
BAYBROOK MALL	1	617V	SEH	77546
BAYBROOK SQUARE DR	0	617Z	SEC	77598
BAYBROOK VILLAGE	0	617Z	SEC	77598
BAY CEDAR CT	5000	573M	SEH	77048
BAY CEDAR DR	10900	573M	SEH	77048
BAYCHESTER LN	1400	332V	NCC	77073
BAY CLIFF CT	0	250E	WD	77381
BAYCLIFF CT	500	659H	LC	77573
BAYCLIFF CT	2000	612H	PL	77584
BAY CLUB DR	600	620H	SB	77586
BAY COAST LN	0	539Z	LP	77571
BAY COLONY	100	580V	LP	77571
BAY COLONY CIR	200	580V	LP	77571
BAY COVE CT	15400	618B	SEH	77059
BAY CREEK DR	3000	657G	FR	77546
BAY CREST	0	612M	PL	77584
S. BAY CREST CIR	0	377C	NEC	77346
N. BAY CREST CIR	0	377C	NEC	77346
E. BAY CREST CIR	0	377C	NEC	77346
BAYCREST DR	300	660K	LC	77573
BAYCREST DR	2300	619T	NB	77058
BAY CROSSING DR	11500	612M	PL	77584
BAYER	3200	579A	LP	77571
BAYER	18500	246X	SWM	77355
BAYER RD	200	292R	SP	77373
BAYEUX LN	20900	291U	NWC	77388
BAYFAIR	4700	578J	PA	77505
BAYFIELD DR	5600	574A	SEH	77033
BAYFIELD GLEN LN	13900	573U	SEC	77047
BAY FOREST DR	15500	618G	SEH	77062
BAY FRONT CT	0	612H	PL	77584
BAYFRONT CT	0	612L	PL	77584
BAYFRONT DR	0	612L	PL	77584
BAY FRONT DR	13600	488P	SWH	77077
BAY GARDENS DR	13800	528X	NEF	77498
BAYGLEN CT	4200	330V	NWC	77068
BAY GREEN CT	15400	618C	SEH	77059
BAY GROVE LN	0	539Z	LP	77571
BAY HARBOR DR	1	580L	LP	77571
BAY HAVEN WAY	1900	619Z	LC	77573
BAY HILL	0	501K	BT	77521
BAY HILL BLVD	24100	485E	NEF	77494
BAY HILL BLVD	24500	484H	NEF	77494
BAY HILL DR	2100	659C	LC	77573
BAYHILL DR	2300	541H	BT	77520
BAY HILL LN	5100	577C	PA	77505
BAY HOLLOW CT	2900	485U	NEF	77450
BAY HOLLOW DR	0	612M	PL	77584
BAY HOLLOW DR	22500	485U	NEF	77450
BAYHURST DR	11700	490K	BH	77024
BAY ISLAND BLVD	100	542P	BT	77520
BAY ISLE CT	2900	578S	SEH	77059
BAYLAND AVE	100	493B	NWH	77009
BAYLAND PARK DR	0	531J	SWH	77074
BAY LEAF CT	1300	610B	MC	77489
BAY LEAF DR	0	461P	NEC	77521
BAYLEAF DR	22700	333A	NCC	77373
BAYLEAF LN	1	251M	WD	77380
BAY LEDGE	3500	617X	SEC	77546
BAY LEDGE CT	16800	617X	SEC	77546
BAY LEDGE DR	11500	612M	PL	77584
BAYLESS DR	1100	541B	BT	77520
BAYLESS DR	7800	535K	SEH	77017
BAYLEYS CT	0	406Z	NWC	77494
BAYLISS MANOR LN	0	326T	NWC	77433
BAYLISS RETREAT LN	0	294J	NWC	77386
BAY LODGE LN	15400	370U	NWC	77086
BAYLOR	2100	501U	BT	77520
BAYLOR	2200	453T	NWH	77009
BAYLOR DR	2000	444U	KT	77493
BAYLOR CREEK LN	0	660P	LC	77573
BAYLOR PLAZA	1	532D	SWH	77030
BAY MANOR	2400	612M	PL	77584
BAYMEADOW CT	0	612L	PL	77584
BAYMEADOW DR	0	612L	PL	77584
BAY MEADOW DR	1000	618J	SEH	77062
BAY MILLS DR	0	250Q	NWC	77389
BAY MILLS PLACE	0	250Q	NWC	77389
BAYMIST CT	22100	525C	NEF	77450
BAY MIST RIDGE LN		524C	NEF	77494
BAYNARD DR	4100	529B	SWH	77072
BAY OAKS BLVD	14000	618A	SEH	77059
BAY OAKS DR	100	580Q	LP	77571
BAY OAKS DR	600	660B	KE	77565
BAY OAKS DR	5300	577L	PA	77505
BAY OAKS RD	800	492C	NWH	77008
BAY OAKS HARBOR DR	2300	542J	BT	77520
BAYONET LN	0	246M	SWM	77355
BAYONNE CIR	13300	288Y	NWC	77377
BAYONNE DR	5800	290G	NWC	77389
W. BAYOU	0	580T	SA	77571
E. BAYOU	0	580U	SA	77571
BAYOU	1	494J	NEH	77020
BAYOU	3000	538U	DP	77536
BAYOU AVE	2500	502T	BT	77520
BAYOU BLVD	0	536L	PA	77506
E. BAYOU BLVD	3600	502B	BT	77521
BAYOU BLVD	3800	502G	NEC	77521
BAYOU BLVD	6000	462X	NEC	77521
BAYOU DR	100	542A	BT	77520
BAYOU DR	100	498D	CV	77530
BAYOU DR	800	458Z	CV	77530
BAYOU DR	2200	659B	LC	77573
BAYOU DR	3000	580Q	SA	77571
BAYOU DR	3300	453P	NWH	77022
N. BAYOU DR	8200	535Q	SEH	77017
BAYOU LN	1	620T	CS	77565
BAYOU RD	0	618H	PA	77059
BAYOU RD	0	619E	PA	77059
BAYOU ARBOR LN	25700	484Z	NEF	77494
BAYOU BEND	600	538T	DP	77536
BAYOU BEND CT	5800	533G	SEH	77004
S. BAYOU BEND DR	100	502C	BT	77521
N. BAYOU BEND DR	100	502C	BT	77521
BAYOU BEND DR	100	620W	LC	77573
BAYOU BEND LN	0	444S	KT	77493
BAYOU BLUFF CT	17100	329R	NWC	77379
BAYOU BLUFF DR	9000	329R	NWC	77379
BAYOU BRANCH	18200	447K	NWC	77084
BAYOU BRIDGE DR	6100	530V	SWH	77096
BAYOU BROOK	1	490N	SWH	77063
S. BAYOU CLUB CT	0	250K	NWC	77389
BAYOU COVE CT	400	489L	SWH	77042
BAYOU COVE LN	2100	658S	LC	77573
BAYOU CREST DR	6300	411J	NWC	77088
BAYOU ELM DR	22700	333E	NCC	77373
BAYOU FOREST DR	3400	580P	LP	77571
S. BAYOU FOREST DR	3500	580T	SA	77571
BAYOU FOREST DR	7100	411P	NWC	77088
BAYOU GLEN DR	1200	539P	LP	77571
BAYOU GLEN LN	0	491J	SWH	77057
BAYOU GLEN RD	5200	491L	SWH	77056
BAYOU GLEN RD	5700	491K	SWH	77057
BAYOU GLEN RD	6500	491J	SWH	77057
BAYOU GLEN RD	10000	489L	SWH	77042
BAYOU GROVE DR	4000	619L	TL	77586
BAYOU ISLAND DR	1000	490N	SWH	77063
BAYOU JUNCTION CT	18500	366K	NWC	77433
BAYOU JUNCTION RD	12000	366K	NWC	77433
BAYOU KNOLL DR	400	488G	SWH	77079
S. BAYOU KNOLL DR	6100	528G	SWH	77072
BAYOU LAKE LN	9400	410N	NWC	77040
BAYOU MANOR LN	10100	409B	NWC	77064
BAYOU MEAD CT	12600	377B	NEC	77346
BAYOU MEADOW LN	3400	493J	SEH	77007
BAYOU MEAD TRAIL	18100	377B	NEC	77346
BAYOU MEAD WAY	0	377B	NEC	77346
BAYOU MIST CT	0	488T	SWH	77077
BAYOU OAKS	1200	656L	FR	77546
BAYOU OAKS DR	7200	411T	NWH	77088
BAYOU OAKS VISTA DR	1200	493K	SWH	77019
BAYOU PARKWAY CT	13700	488F	SWH	77077
BAYOU PINE CT	8400	410K	NWC	77040
BAYOU PKWY	900	488F	SWH	77077
BAYOU PLACE CT	10700	529X	SWH	77099
BAYOU PLACE DR	11100	529X	SWH	77099
BAYOU PLACE LN	11200	529X	SWH	77099
BAYOU POINTE DR	1	490N	SWH	77063
BAYOU RIDGE DR	8900	335T	NEH	77338
BAYOU RIDGE ST	0	444D	NWC	77493
BAYOU RIVER CT	15900	488E	SWH	77079
BAYOU RIVER DR	800	488E	SWH	77079
BAYOU SHADOWS	1	490J	SWH	77024
BAYOU TERRACE LN	0	485W	NEF	77494
BAYOU TESCH DR	26400	248J	SWM	77354
BAYOU TIMBER LN	5000	491L	SWH	77056
BAYOU TRAIL CT	10100	409B	NWC	77064
BAYOU TRAIL LN	10200	369X	NWC	77064
BAYOU VIEW	0	502G	BT	77521
BAYOU VIEW CIR	0	619R	EL	77586
BAYOU VIEW DR	100	619R	EL	77586
BAYOU VIEW DR	200	620J	EL	77586
BAYOU VIEW DR	6400	411Y	NWH	77091
BAYOU VISTA	600	538T	DP	77536
BAYOU VISTA	7200	462Y	BT	77521
BAYOU VISTA CIR	0	484F	KT	77494
BAYOU VISTA CT	0	484F	KT	77494
BAYOU VISTA DR	1200	493K	SWH	77019
BAYOU VISTA DR	4200	451C	NWH	77091
BAYOU VISTA LN	0	484F	KT	77494
BAYOU WOODS DR	7200	411T	NWH	77088
BAYOU WOODS LN	9000	462Y	BT	77521
BAY PALMS DR	21600	446B	NWC	77449
BAY PARK DR	2903	657D	FR	77546
BAYPARK RD	12900	579G	SEC	77507
BAY PINES DR	5200	446B	NWC	77449
BAY PLACE DR	13100	543D	BC	77520
BAY POINTE CT	14100	617H	SEH	77062
BAYPORT	100	620F	SB	77586
BAYPORT BLVD	9500	579U	SEC	77507
BAYPORT CT	3800	293H	SEM	77386
BAYPORT DR	0	612L	PL	77584
BAYPORT LN	0	660J	LC	77573
BAYRAM DR	1500	451W	NWH	77055
BAY RIDGE	100	540Z	LP	77571
BAYRIDGE	200	660K	LC	77573
BAYRIDGE	1	541W	MP	77571
BAYRIDGE BLVD	0	543X	BC	77520
BAY RIDGE CT	3100	657G	FR	77546
BAYRIDGE RD	59	541S	MP	77571
BAYSHELL CT	0	620A	SB	77586
BAYSHORE BLVD	3000	537W	PA	77502
BAYSHORE BLVD	3100	537W	PA	77504
BAY SHORE DR	0	620E	SB	77586
E. BAYSHORE DR	0	500N	BT	77520
BAYSHORE DR	1	580G	LP	77571
W. BAYSHORE DR	100	499R	BT	77520
BAYSHORE DR	100	499R	BT	77520
BAYSHORE DR	100	580Q	LP	77571
BAYSHORE DR	1400	620Y	KE	77565
BAYSHORE DR	2600	660D	GCO	77518
BAY SHORE DR	4000	609K	MC	77459
BAYSIDE	0	543W	BC	77520
BAYSIDE CT	0	526J	NEF	77407
BAYSIDE DR	100	580Q	LP	77571
BAYSIDE CROSSING DR	0	539Z	LP	77571
BAY SKY WAY	0	620H	SB	77586
BAY SPRING DR	300	660A	LC	77573
BAY SPRING DR	22100	485V	NEF	77450
BAY STAR BLVD	800	617C	SEH	77598
BAYSWATER DR	1200	572V	SWH	77047
BAYTHORNE DR	9200	450B	NWH	77041
BAYTOWN	0	500Z	BT	77520
BAYTOWN CENTRAL BLVD	4500	501F	BT	77521
BAYTOWN LOOP 201	0	501W	BT	77520
BAYTOWN LOOP 201	0	502P	BT	77520
BAYTOWN TUNNEL	0	540L	SEH	77520
BAY TREE DR	13800	568F	SG	77498
BAYTREE DR	15700	329U	NWC	77070
BAY TREE LANDING	15400	367H	CY	77429
BAYVIEW	7800	543W	BC	77520
BAYVIEW CT	4600	610P	MC	77459
BAY VIEW DR	100	568P	SG	77478
BAYVIEW DR	500	620J	EL	77586
BAYVIEW DR	1900	620F	SB	77586
BAYVIEW RD	0	660D	KE	77518
BAYVIEW COVE DR	0	532U	SWH	77054
BAY VILLA	1	500T	BT	77520
BAY VISTA	0	539V	LP	77571
BAY VISTA	600	620L	SB	77586
BAYWATER DR	0	612L	PL	77584
BAYWATER CANYON DR	0	612L	PL	77584
BAYWATER CREEK LN	0	615M	PL	77089
BAYWATER PARK LN	0	609J	NEF	77479
BAYWAY DR	5000	500F	BT	77520
BAYWICK DR	24800	250S	NWC	77389
BAY WIND CT		484V	NEF	77494
BAY WIND CT		484V	NEF	77494
BAY WINDS CT	2500	618C	SEH	77059
BAYWOOD	100	580U	SA	77571
BAYWOOD	200	494Q	SEH	77011
BAYWOOD	400	620D	SB	77586
BAYWOOD CT	200	252N	SEM	77386
BAYWOOD DR	400	621A	SB	77586
BAYWOOD DR	4700	578J	PA	77505
BAY WOOD LN	0	657U	LC	77573
BAYWOOD PARK DR	3000	331P	NWC	77068
BAZELBRIAR DR	15800	570Z	SWH	77489
BAZEL BROOK DR	6400	571W	SWH	77489
BAZIN	10800	576T	SEH	77089
BAZZEL LN	0	339G	NEC	77336
BEACAVE BEND CT	10900	370V	NWC	77086
BEACH	11900	418R	NEC	77044
BEACHAM DR	15100	329T	NWC	77070
BEACH BAY CT	9400	416Y	NEC	77044
BEACHCOMBER LN	700	618K	SEH	77062
BEACHGROVE LN	22000	525C	NEF	77494
BEACH HAVEN RD	0	503V	CCO	77339
BEACHSIDE	3300	378T	NEC	77532
BEACHTON	1300	493G	SWH	77007
BEACHWALK DR	1700	419A	NEC	77532
BEACHWATER DR	3200	485U	NEF	77450
BEACHWOOD	6800	533Q	SEH	77021
BEACHY CT	19600	406Y	NWC	77449
BEACON	500	497F	NEC	77015
BEACON CIR	0	619T	LC	77573
BEACON CT	3600	613X	NEB	77578
BEACON RD	0	618U	WB	77058
BEACON BAY CIR	2700	657C	SEC	77546
BEACON BEND CT	3400	613V	PL	77584
BEACON BEND LN	8500	613V	PL	77584
BEACON BROOK LN	0	446S	NWC	77449
BEACON BROOK LN	0	446S	NWC	77449
BEACON PARK CT	0	333A	NCC	77373
BEACON COVE CT	1700	486K	SWC	77450
BEACON CREEK CT	0	253K	SEM	77386
BEACON CROSSING LN	0	366Y	NWC	77433
BEACON FALLS DR	5800	297Z	NEH	77345
BEACON GREEN LN	0	253P	SEM	77386
BEACON GREEN LN	0	615G	PL	77581
BEACON GROVE ST	0	291M	NWC	77389
BEACON HILL DR	3400	613U	NEB	77584
BEACON HILL DR	4400	619M	TL	77586
BEACON HOLLOW CT	12300	368Q	NWC	77429
BEACON LIGHT LN	2100	611W	FS	77545
BEACON MANOR LN	6700	408V	NWC	77041
BEACONRIDGE DR	5900	611B	SWH	77053
BEACONSFIELD DR	1	245D	SWM	77355
BEACONSFIELD DR	14800	457Z	NEC	77015
BEACONSHIRE RD	1500	488Q	SWH	77077
BEACONS HOLLOW LN	500	657Y	LC	77573
BEACONS LIGHT PLACE	100	249R	NWH	77375
BEACONS LIGHT PLACE	100	249R	NWH	77375
BEACON SPRINGS LN	0	446N	NWH	77449
BEACON SPRINGS LN	0	609U	NEF	77479
BEACONS TRACE DR	0	330U	NWC	77069
BEACONS VIEW	3500	617X	SEC	77546
BEACON TRACE CT	14300	330T	NWC	77069
BEACON TREE CT	12200	377A	NEC	77346
BEACON VIEW CT	3300	613V	PL	77584
BEALEY LN	4000	573Z	SEC	77047
BEALL	1300	452U	NWH	77008
BEALL	5500	452C	NWH	77091
BEALL WOODS LN	0	377F	NEC	77346
BEAMER RD	10600	576T	SEH	77089
BEAMER RD	10800	616C	SEH	77089
BEAMER RD	15500	617N	SEH	77546
BEAN	0	500V	BT	77520
BEAN	9200	455C	NEH	77028
BEAN	9600	455C	NEH	77078
BEANCREST LN	0	457P	NEC	77049
BEAR-RAM RD	0	528H	SWH	77072
BEAR BAYOU DR	15700	458Z	CV	77530
BEARBOROUGH DR	25700	252P	SEM	77386
BEAR BROOK DR	3200	337C	NEH	77345
BEAR CANYON CT	6300	526F	NEF	77450
BEAR CAVE LN	5500	446C	NWC	77449
BEARCLAW CT	27100	246Q	SWM	77355
BEARCOVE CIR	9100	409H	NWC	77064
BEAR CREEK DR	3001	448K	NWH	77084
S. BEAR CREEK DR	17000	447H	NWC	77084
N. BEAR CREEK DR	17000	447H	NWC	77084
BEAR CREEK MEADOWS LN	3800	449G	NWH	77043
BEAR CREEK TRACE	4100	501K	BT	77521
BEAR CUB LN	21400	378C	NEH	77532
BEARD CT	3400	493J	SWH	77007
BEARD RD	14000	457B	NEC	77044
BEARD RD	14000	417Y	NEC	77044
BEARDEN RD	100	259T	NEC	77336
BEARDEN CREEK LN	9300	376W	NEC	77396
BEARDEN FALLS LN	7100	375X	NEC	77396
BEARDEN LAKE DR	16200	328R	NWC	77377
BEARDEN PLACE LN	4200	527B	SWC	77082
BEAR HILL DR	16000	448E	NWC	77084
BEAR HUNTERS DR	5400	406Y	NWC	77449
BEAR HUNTERS DR	5400	446B	NWC	77449
BEARHURST DR	0	250Q	NWC	77389
BEARING STAR LN	31300	248X	TB	77375

Street Name	Block	Pg/Sq	Loc	Zips
BEARKAT CIR	0	330L	NWC	77379
BEAR LAKE DR	3600	297T	NEH	77345
BEARLE	100	537E	PA	77506
BEAR LODGE DR	4200	447F	NWC	77084
BEAR MEADOW CT	19300	406V	NWC	77449
BEAR MEADOW LN	5600	406X	NWC	77449
BEAR MEADOW LN	19400	406V	NWC	77449
BEAR MEADOWS LN	0	377K	NEC	77346
BEAR MIST DR	17300	407B	NWC	77095
BEAR OAKS DR	6900	527F	NEF	77083
BEAR PASS CT	5200	446B	NWC	77449
BEAR PATH LN	21100	446C	NWC	77449
BEAR PAW CIR	5500	446C	NWC	77449
BEAR RIVER LN	0	377F	NEC	77346
BEAR RUN LN	21100	446C	NWC	77449
BEAR SPRINGS DR	19300	406V	NWC	77449
BEAR TRACK LN	6000	577D	PA	77505
BEAR TRAIL LN	5500	446C	NWC	77449
BEAR TREE TRAIL	21100	446C	NWC	77449
BEAR VALLEY DR	12400	528H	SWH	77072
BEARWOOD RD	13800	371U	NWC	77038
BEASLEY HILLS LN	0	452Y	NWH	77008
BEATRICE	5500	453A	NEH	77076
BEATRICE	6400	413W	NEH	77076
BEATTY	2400	534G	SEH	77023
BEATTY DR	14800	375S	NEH	77396
BEAU LN	3500	414F	NCC	77039
BEAU LN	4800	414G	NCC	77039
BEAUCHAMP	2600	493B	NWH	77009
BEAUDRY DR	5900	571A	SWH	77035
BEAUDRY DR	6000	570D	SWH	77035
BEAUFORD DR		484J	NEF	77494
BEAU FOREST LN	23200	285T	NWC	77447
BEAUFORT DR	7800	330J	NWC	77379
BEAUFORT SEA DR	1200	372J	NWC	77067
BEAU GESTE DR	6300	411S	NWH	77088
BEAU HARP CT	6000	457S	NEC	77049
BEAU HARP DR	14300	457S	NEC	77049
BEAUJOLAIS LN	1300	489J	SWH	77077
BEAULINE ABBEY	12500	328R	NWC	77377
BEAU MONDE DR	8700	528Q	SWC	77099
BEAUMONT	200	535Z	SH	77587
BEAUMONT	600	536W	SH	77587
BEAUMONT	1300	576A	SH	77587
BEAUMONT	1300	501V	BT	77520
BEAUMONT	7400	495S	SEH	77011
BEAUMONT	600	659J	LC	77573
BEAUMONT HWY	0	381F	LCO	77535
BEAUMONT HWY	100	419T	BR	77532
BEAUMONT HWY	4000	420A	NEC	77532
BEAUMONT HWY	8400	380R	NEC	77532
BEAUMONT HWY	9800	455V	NEH	77078
BEAUMONT HWY	11600	456P	NEH	77049
BEAUMONT HWY	13100	457D	NEC	77049
BEAUMONT HWY	16300	418W	NEC	77049
BEAUMONT PLACE	7200	456M	NEC	77049
BEAUPRE POINT DR	600	496C	NEC	77015
BEAUREGARD CT	3400	610U	MC	77459
BEAUREGARD DR	12100	490J	SWH	77024
BEAUVOIR DR	11200	368Q	NWC	77065
BEAVER	7900	462V	BT	77520
BEAVER	31900	246T	SWM	77355
BEAVER CT	0	246X	SWM	77355
BEAVER DR	3600	455X	NEH	77029
BEAVER LN	15900	246T	SWM	77355
BEAVER BEND CT	7600	461S	NEC	77521
BEAVER BEND CT	9200	412M	NCC	77037
BEAVER BEND RD	200	412M	NCC	77037
BEAVER BEND RD	800	412K	NWH	77088
BEAVERBROOK DR	5200	408W	NWC	77084
BEAVER CREEK DR	5400	539X	LP	77571
BEAVER CREEK DR	17900	331L	NWC	77090
BEAVER DAM	0	378C	NEH	77532
BEAVER DAM	23000	291E	NWC	77389
BEAVERDELL DR	18000	328H	NWC	77377
BEAVER FALLS DR	5800	338A	NEH	77345
BEAVER GLEN DR	3000	297N	NEH	77339
BEAVERHEAD CIR	3200	251T	SWM	77380
BEAVERHEAD CT	3200	251T	SWM	77380
BEAVERHILL DR	5100	448A	NWC	77084
BEAVERHILL DR	5200	408W	NWC	77084
BEAVERHOLLOW DR	5100	448A	NWC	77084
BEAVER LAKE CT	7800	337R	NEC	77346
BEAVER LODGE DR	5300	337D	NEH	77345
BEAVER PASS LN	5600	406Y	NWC	77449
BEAVER POND CIR	4800	447A	NWC	77084
BEAVER RUN DR	25600	338H	NEC	77336
BEAVER SPRINGS CIR	1600	331R	NWC	77090
BEAVER SPRINGS CT	1600	331R	NWC	77090
BEAVER SPRINGS DR	17000	331R	NWC	77090
BEAVER TAIL POINT	1	490N	SWH	77024
BEAVER TRAIL DR	11000	371S	NWC	77086
BEAVER VALLEY	0	618F	SEH	77062
BEAVERWOOD DR	23800	293T	NCC	77373
BEAVERWOOD DR	25300	293N	NCC	77373
BEAWOOD DR	8800	528P	SWC	77083
BEBINGTON CT	0	611T	FS	77545
E. BECCA CIR	3700	452N	NWH	77092
N. BECCA LN	2900	452N	NWH	77092
BECCA CROSSING WAY	0	372J	NWC	77076
BECK	800	453T	NWH	77009
BECK-MASTEN	0	369S	NWC	77065
BECKENDORF BEND LN	0	328M	NWC	77377
BECKENDORFF RD	22000	405P	NWC	77449
BECKENDORFF RD	23000	404T	NWC	77493
BECKENHAM DR	9200	528Q	SWC	77099
N. BECKER	0	458Y	CV	77530
BECKER	0	324V	NWC	77447
BECKER	800	498C	CV	77530
BECKER	1000	458Y	CV	77530
BECKER	9100	535C	SEH	77012
BECKER RD	16000	325S	NWC	77447
BECKER RD	18500	285S	NWC	77447
BECKER CEMETERY RD	13400	328T	NWC	77429
BECKERDELL LN	0	328M	NWC	77377
BECKER GLEN	3300	611W	FS	77545
BECKER LINE DR	6200	330M	NWC	77379
BECKER PINES LN	0	484X	NEF	77494
BECKER PINES LN	0	484X	NEF	77494
BECKET	2900	613K	NEB	77584
BECKETS CROSSING LN	700	292G	NCC	77373
BECKETT LN	0	450Z	NWH	77055
BECKETT CREEK LN	0	375Y	NEC	77396
BECKETT RIDGE DR	3600	376G	NEC	77396
BECKETTS KNOLL CT	0	484E	NEF	77494
BECKETTS OAKS CT	16900	527J	NEF	77083
BECKET WOODS LN	14100	568A	SG	77498
BECKFIELD CT	12200	528Z	SWH	77099
BECKFIELD DR	10600	528Z	SWH	77099
BECKFORD DR	8700	528Q	SWC	77099
BECKHAM SPRINGS CT	0	292U	NCC	77373
BECKINS CLIFF DR	9200	329G	NWC	77379

Street Name	Block	Pg/Sq	Loc	Zips
BECKLAND LN	16500	407V	NWC	77084
BECKLEDGE LN	0	573T	SEC	77047
BECKLEY	7700	412N	NWH	77088
BECKLIN LN	12900	528Q	SWC	77099
BECKMAN	700	413Y	NEH	77076
BECKMAN DR	1600	339P	HU	77336
BECK RIDGE DR	16000	611B	SWH	77053
BECKTON LN	1000	613F	NEB	77584
BECKWITH DR	13800	372F	NWC	77014
BECKWOOD CIR	1200	372F	NWC	77014
BECKWOOD DR	0	293D	SEM	77386
BECKWOOD POST DR	9600	407B	NWC	77095
BECKY	0	614D	BK	77581
BECKY	5600	614U	PL	77584
BECURTESY CT	0	328N	NWC	77429
BEDELL BRIDGE LN	0	377K	NEC	77346
BEDFORD	0	257H	SEM	77357
BEDFORD	100	495W	SEH	77012
BEDFORD	11000	529Z	SWH	77031
BEDFORD	11300	569D	SWH	77031
BEDFORD AVE	0	613K	NEB	77584
BEDFORD CHASE	13500	367C	NWC	77429
BEDFORD FALLS DR	12800	367H	NWC	77429
BEDFORD FORREST CT	3300	610U	MC	77459
BEDFORD FORREST DR	2900	610U	MC	77459
BEDFORD GLEN DR	15200	458W	NEC	77530
BEDFORD OAK	0	611S	FS	77545
BEDFORD PASS DR	17200	367X	NWC	77095
BEDFORD PEAK CT	17100	377K	NEC	77346
BEDFORD SPRINGS LN	0	657Y	LC	77573
BEDIAS CREEK CT	0	525H	NEF	77407
BEDIAS CREEK DR	0	525H	NEF	77407
BEDIAS GREEN CIR	0	366N	NWC	77433
BEDWORTH LN	8700	412K	NWC	77088
BEE LN	11800	371M	NWC	77067
BEE BAYOU LN	3600	609E	SG	77479
BEEBE LN	1	490E	BH	77024
BEEBRUSH PLACE	0	250K	NWC	77389
BEEBRUSH PLACE	0	250K	NWC	77389
BEECAVE CT	3000	609D	MC	77459
W. BEE CAVE SPRINGS CIR		367W	NWC	77095
S. BEE CAVE SPRINGS CIR		367W	NWC	77095
N. BEE CAVE SPRINGS CIR		367W	NWC	77095
E. BEE CAVE SPRINGS CIR		367W	NWC	77095
BEECH	1100	500Z	BT	77520
BEECH	4500	531G	BL	77401
BEECH DR	1300	252G	SEM	77385
BEECHAM CT	3000	331P	NWC	77068
BEECHAM DR	15100	331P	NWC	77068
BEECHAM LAKE CT	7400	526K	NEF	77407
BEECHAM LAKE LN	19700	526K	NEF	77407
BEECHAVEN	8400	578D	LP	77571
BEECHAVEN DR	4700	611D	SWH	77053
BEECHBEND DR	500	570Y	MC	77489
BEECH BEND DR	1700	489N	SWH	77077
BEECH CANYON DR	23100	485F	SWC	77494
BEECH COVE	1400	580F	LP	77571
BEECH COVE LN	7600	529J	SWH	77072
BEECHCRAFT	3400	615P	PL	77581
BEECHCRAFT	4500	620G	SB	77586
BEECH CREEK CT	0	366Z	NWC	77433
BEECH CREEK SPRINGS CIR	0	366P	NWC	77433
BEECHCREST	8600	528P	SWC	77083
BEECH CROSSING DR	8000	528N	SWC	77083
BEECHDALE CT	13100	371D	NWC	77014
BEECHER	600	541A	BT	77520
BEECHER DR	3600	538T	DP	77536
BEECH FERN DR	4900	526X	NEF	77406
BEECH FORK LN	15100	527Z	NEF	77498
BEECHGATE LN	13401	528L	SWC	77083
BEECH GLEN DR	14100	528J	SWC	77083
BEECHGLEN LN	13400	528L	SWC	77083
BEECHGROVE DR	900	618U	SEC	77058
BEECH HILL DR	3400	331G	NWC	77388
BEECH HOLLOW LN	13800	488X	SWH	77082
BEECHKNOLL LN	4900	446D	NWC	77449
BEECH LANDING LN	21000	525H	NEF	77450
BEECH MEADOW DR	14100	528J	SWC	77083
BEECH MEADOW LN	7900	528L	SWC	77083
BEECHMONT RD	100	490P	SWH	77024
BEECHMOOR DR	14800	408K	NWC	77095
BEECHNUT	4200	531P	SWH	77096
BEECHNUT	5700	530L	SWH	77074
BEECHNUT	8000	530J	SWH	77036
BEECHNUT	10100	529N	SWH	77072
BEECHNUT	13100	528J	SWC	77083
BEECHNUT	14800	527L	NEF	77083
BEECHNUT	17500	526Q	NEF	77407
BEECHNUT	20000	525R	NEF	77469
BEECHNUT LANDING DR	0	528L	SWH	77083
BEECH PARK DR	8300	528N	SWC	77083
BEECH PARK LN	7900	528L	SWC	77083
BEECH POINT DR	3300	297X	NEH	77345
BEECH RIDGE LN	13500	528K	SWC	77083
S. BEECH SPRINGS CIR	0	250L	NWC	77389
S. BEECH SPRINGS CIR	0	250L	NWC	77389
N. BEECH SPRINGS CIR	0	250L	NWC	77389
N. BEECH SPRINGS CIR	0	250L	NWC	77389
BEECH TREE CT	3100	446P	NWC	77449
BEECH TREE DR	20700	446P	NWC	77449
BEECHURST CT	1500	618F	SEH	77062
BEECHURST DR	14900	618E	SEH	77062
BEECHVIEW LN	20000	446T	NWC	77449
S. BEECHWOOD CT	3900	578X	SEH	77059
N. BEECHWOOD CT	4000	578X	SEH	77059
BEECHWOOD DR	1200	656L	FR	77546
BEECHWOOD DR	3900	615W	PL	77584
BEECHWOOD LN	0	245D	SWM	77355
BEECROFT DR	1100	568G	SG	77498
BEEF CANYON DR	24000	325J	NWC	77447
BEEF CANYON DR	24200	324M	NWC	77447
BEE HIVE	6000	577D	PA	77505
BEEKMAN RD	4900	534F	SEH	77021
BEEKMAN PLACE DR	10100	450W	NWH	77043
BEELA RD	6700	574R	SEH	77048
BEE LINE CT	0	372M	NCC	77073
BEEMAN WAY	9200	410X	NWH	77040
BEE MEADOW LN	8300	610G	SWH	77489
BEESTON HALL CT	0	290R	NWC	77388
BEESTON HILL DR	0	406U	NWC	77449
BEETLE RD	28500	298Z	NEH	77336
BEEVILLE DR	11800	369R	NWC	77064
BEFAYE RD	600	453A	NEH	77076
BEGGS	3700	453Y	NEH	77009
BEGONIA	500	531L	BL	77401
BEGONIA BLVD	8100	460U	NEC	77562
BEGONIA LN	100	459M	HG	77562
BEGONIA CREEK CT	21100	326N	NWC	77433
BEGONIA ESTATES CT	14200	366D	NWC	77429
BEGONIA MEADOWS DR	25000	249Z	NWC	77375
BEHAN	0	411X	NWH	77092
BEHLER RD	3400	613Y	NEB	77584

Street Name	Block	Pg/Sq	Loc	Zips
BEHRENS PASS LN		366T	NWC	77433
BEIGEWOOD LN	20300	335N	NCC	77338
BEINHORN DR	11800	369N	NWC	77065
BEINHORN RD	10400	491E	HC	77024
BEINHORN RD	10700	490D	HC	77024
BEISERT CIR	0	286D	SWM	77355
BEKONSCOT DR	1100	329G	NWC	77379
BEL RD	500	620Y	KE	77565
BELARBOR	5600	534W	SEH	77033
BELARBOR	6200	534Y	SEH	77087
BELASCO LN	9400	528U	SWC	77099
BELAYA LN	1000	331H	NWC	77090
BELBAY	7600	534X	SEH	77033
BELCAMP CT	10200	575V	SEH	77075
BELCARA VIEW	0	660F	LC	77573
BELCOURT	10400	368Y	NWC	77065
BELCREST	5600	534W	SEH	77033
BELCREST	6200	534Y	SEH	77087
BELDART	5600	534W	SEH	77033
BELDART	6200	534Y	SEH	77087
BELDART CT	5400	534W	SEH	77033
BELDEN	0	575D	SEH	77034
BELFAST RD	9100	579A	LP	77571
BELFAST GLEN TRACE	0	297F	SEM	77365
BELFIELD	1200	495U	NEH	77029
BELFORD PARK LN	0	526K	NEF	77407
BELFRY CT	4100	485Z	NEF	77450
BELGARD	7600	534X	SEH	77033
BELGIAN BEAUTY CT	0	377S	NEC	77044
BELGIUM DR	6200	578E	PA	77505
BELGIUM WAY	0	371G	NWC	77014
BELGOLD	7000	370K	NWC	77066
BELGRADE DR	3800	572E	SWH	77045
BELGRAVE DR	12900	328V	NWC	77429
W. BELGRAVIA DR	1000	613F	NEB	77584
E. BELGRAVIA DR	1000	613F	NEB	77584
S. BELGRAVIA DR	2600	613J	NEB	77584
N. BELGRAVIA DR	2600	613F	NEB	77584
BELGRAVIA WAY	1200	336H	NEH	77339
BELHAM RIDGE CT	1300	329H	NWC	77379
BELHAVEN DR	13400	330Z	NWC	77069
BELIN DR	1300	496K	JC	77029
BELINDA CT	13600	370B	NWC	77069
BELIN MANOR DR	300	490K	BH	77024
BELISSIMA AURORA LN	0	406R	NEF	77433
BELK	3600	534Q	SEH	77087
BELKNAP	200	568N	SG	77478
S. BELKNAP	300	568N	SG	77478
BELKNAP CT	100	568N	SG	77478
BELKNAP RD	9900	528X	NEF	77498
BELKNAP PLACE	0	528Z	NEF	77099
BELL	0	292P	NWC	77388
W. BELL	300	493N	SWH	77019
BELL	600	493Q	DT	77002
W. BELL	1400	492R	SWH	77019
BELL	1600	493V	SEH	77003
BELL	4100	494S	SEH	77023
BELL	8400	370Y	NWC	77064
BELL	17000	323H	HK	77447
BELL AVE	24100	297J	SEM	77365
BELL DR	0	612L	PL	77584
BELLA DR	13800	368P	NWC	77429
BELLA ARBOR LN	0	366J	NWC	77433
BELLA DULCE CT	21300	290Q	NWC	77379
BELLA FLORA CT	21300	290Q	NWC	77379
BELLA FLORENCE DR	24200	524M	NEF	77406
BELLAFORTE CT	10900	524R	NEF	77406
BELLAGIO	0	408S	NWC	77084
BELLAGIO DR	0	525J	NEF	77406
BELLAGO LN	0	527X	NEF	77469
BELLAIRE	900	580D	LP	77571
BELLAIRE BLVD	0	526G	NEF	77407
BELLAIRE BLVD	2600	532F	WU	77025
BELLAIRE BLVD	4300	531E	SWH	77401
BELLAIRE BLVD	5500	531E	SWH	77081
BELLAIRE BLVD	6300	530H	SWH	77074
BELLAIRE BLVD	7300	530F	SWH	77036
BELLAIRE BLVD	10000	529F	SWH	77072
BELLAIRE BLVD	13200	528E	SWH	77083
BELLAIRE BLVD	14800	527H	SWC	77083
BELLAIRE BLVD	20000	525K	NEF	77406
BELLAIRE CT	100	531H	BL	77401
BELLAIRE ESTATES DR	13100	528G	SWC	77083
BELLAIRE GARDENS DR	0	528G	SWH	77083
BELLAIRE GARDENS TRAIL	0	528G	SWH	77083
BELLA JESS DR	21300	290Q	NWC	77379
BELLA LAKES LN	4800	447C	NWC	77084
BELLA LUNA CT	21300	290Q	NWC	77379
BELLA MEDA LN	0	524J	NEF	77406
BELLA MOUNTAIN DR	21300	290Q	NWC	77379
BELLAMY LN	8400	528Q	SWC	77083
BELLA NOCHE DR	0	290Q	NWC	77379
BELLA PINE CT	9300	455D	NEH	77078
BELLARIA LANDING LN	0	484T	NEF	77494
BELLA SERA DR	6400	290Q	NWC	77379
BELLA STAR DR	0	290Q	NWC	77379
BELLA TERRA BLVD	0	525N	NEF	77469
BELLA TERRA PKWY	0	525K	NEF	77469
BELLA TERRA PKWY	0	525K	NEF	77469
BELLA VENEZA DR	24200	524M	NEF	77406
BELLA VIDA LN	0	528C	SWH	77082
BELLAVISTA	3300	453P	NWH	77022
BELLAVISTA CT	12000	409W	NWC	77041
BELLAVISTA CT	12000	409W	NWC	77041
BELLA VISTA POINT	13300	368H	NWC	77429
BELLAVISTA POINT	13300	368H	NWC	77429
BELLAVITA DR	0	616K	PL	77581
BELLAW WOODS DR	19300	335S	NCC	77338
BELLBIRD CT	1	251R	WD	77380
BELLBROOK DR	11000	530Z	SWH	77096
BELL CANYON LN	24400	485S	NEF	77494
BELLCHASE	2000	292V	NCC	77373
BELLCHASE	2300	293N	NCC	77373
BELLCHASE CIR	25300	292V	NCC	77373
BELL CHASE DR	0	371C	NWC	77014
BELL CLIFF CT	0	578T	SEH	77059
BELL CREEK CT	0	612L	PL	77584
BELL CREEK DR	0	612L	PL	77584
BELL CREEK LN	0	406P	NWC	77449
BELLE CT	11900	248N	SWM	77355
BELLE CT	25100	249S	NWC	77375
BELLEAU WOOD DR	19000	336U	NEH	77338
BELLECLAIRE	9300	416Z	NEC	77044
BELLE COTE DR	18500	378T	NEC	77532
BELLEFIELD CT	2800	485N	NEF	77494
BELLEFONTAINE	2200	532G	SWH	77030
BELLEFONTAINE	2600	532E	SWH	77025
W. BELLEFONTAINE WAY	0	328V	NWC	77377
BELLEFROST LN	0	525D	NEF	77450
BELLE GLADE DR	4400	452E	NWH	77018
BELLE GLEN DR	6800	529J	SWH	77072
BELLE GLEN DR	8700	529N	SWH	77099

Street Name	Block	Pg/Sq	Loc	Zips
BELLE GLOS CT	0	286Q	NWC	77377
BELLE HEAVEN	11700	369S	NWC	77065
BELLE HELENE CIR	13400	367G	NWC	77429
BELLE HOLLOW DR	4400	448E	NWC	77084
BELLE ISLE DR	0	336U	NEH	77338
BELLE MANOR LN	0	609S	NEF	77479
BELLE PARK DR	3900	529F	SWH	77072
BELLE PARK DR	8600	529P	SWH	77099
BELLERIVE DR	7000	530C	SWH	77036
BELLERIVE DR	11000	529B	SWH	77072
BELLE RIVER LN	14300	488N	SWH	77077
BELLEROSE LN	10400	369G	NWC	77070
BELLESHIRE GLEN LN	16001	407V	NWB	77084
BELLE TERRE DR	1600	339A	NEC	77336
BELLE VERNON DR	23500	290C	NWC	77389
BELLEVUE	2800	535K	SEH	77017
BELLEVUE FALLS LN		609S	NEF	77479
BELLE WAY	0	615S	PL	77584
BELLE WAY DR	19800	336U	NEH	77338
BELLEWOOD DR	7600	451X	NWH	77055
BELLFAIR DR	10700	529G	SWH	77072
BELLFALL CT	14900	527D	SWC	77082
BELLFIELD MANOR LN	6500	408S	NWC	77084
BELLFLORA CT	14800	527M	SWC	77083
BELL FLOWER	8900	490X	SWH	77063
BELLFLOWER GLEN DR	0	526T	NEF	77469
BELLFLOWER PASS LN	0	660N	LC	77573
BELLFOREST CT	0	417B	NEC	77044
W. BELLFORT	4300	531X	SWH	77035
W. BELLFORT	5400	571A	SWH	77035
BELLFORT	6200	534W	SEH	77087
W. BELLFORT	7500	570B	SWH	77071
BELLFORT	7500	535T	SEH	77061
W. BELLFORT	8600	570B	SWH	77031
W. BELLFORT	9300	569D	SWH	77031
W. BELLFORT	10600	529W	SWH	77099
W. BELLFORT	11700	529W	SWH	77477
W. BELLFORT	13600	528Y	SWH	77478
W. BELLFORT AVE	0	527W	NEF	77469
W. BELLFORT AVE	2300	532T	SWH	77054
BELLFORT AVE	3000	533W	SEH	77051
W. BELLFORT AVE	4000	532S	SWH	77025
BELLFORT AVE	4800	534W	SEH	77033
BELLFORT AVE	4900	533Z	SEH	77033
BELLFORT CT	5300	534W	SEH	77033
BELLFORT CHASE DR	10200	569C	SWH	77031
BELLFORT VILLAGE DR	11900	569C	SWH	77031
BELL GARDENS DR	10300	449M	NWC	77041
BELLGATE CT	22400	334E	NCC	77373
BELLGREEN DR	6800	532G	SWH	77030
BELLGREEN LN	1000	618E	SEH	77062
BELLGROVE DR	1300	620E	EL	77586
BELLHAVEN LN	0	658N	LC	77573
BELLHAVEN SPRINGS DR	0	296J	SEM	77365
BELL HOLLOW LN	3800	525B	NEF	77494
BELLINA DR	0	525N	NEF	77469
BELLINA DR	0	525N	NEF	77469
BELLINGHAM DR	7600	455E	NEH	77028
BELLINGTON CT	4400	337F	NEH	77345
BELLIS LN	15800	571X	SWH	77489
BELLKNAP RD	8200	410Y	NWH	77040
BELL MANOR CT	13000	572R	SWH	77047
BELLMAR DR	200	413N	NCC	77037
BELLMAR DR	300	616Y	FR	77546
BELLMART DR	13200	528G	SWC	77083
BELLMEAD DR	4900	609K	MC	77459
BELLMEADE	1900	492P	SWH	77019
BELL MEADE BLVD	0	406Z	NWC	77449
BELLMONTE	0	491P	SWH	77057
BELLMOOR LN	16800	407Z	NWC	77084
BELL MOUNTAIN DR	0	484X	NEF	77494
BELL MOUNTAIN DR	0	484X	NEF	77494
BELLNOLE DR	4800	535R	SEH	77017
BELLOWGLEN DR	0	445R	NWC	77449
BELLOWS LN	6500	532H	SWH	77030
BELLOWS BEND	22300	485U	NEF	77450
BELLOWS BEND CT	3900	485V	NEF	77450
BELLOWS FALLS LN	0	375Z	NEC	77396
BELLOWS GATE CT	13900	366D	NWC	77429
BELLOWS VIEW DR	0	484Z	NEF	77494
BELLPORT DR	15300	408S	NWC	77084
BELL SHADOW LN	1400	412F	NWC	77038
BELLSPRING LN	11000	529B	SWH	77072
BELL TELEPHONE RD	0	458C	NEC	77049
BELL TIMBERS	5400	337W	NEC	77346
BELL TOWNE DR	10000	528S	NEF	77498
BELL VALLEY CT	0	578T	SEH	77059
BELLVIEW	100	501L	BT	77521
BELLVIEW DR	4700	531L	BL	77401
BELLVILLE DR	1300	412F	NWC	77038
BELLWEATHER CT	1	251K	WD	77381
BELLWICK LN	0	406L	NWC	77433
BELLWICK CREST PLACE	0	405T	NWC	77493
BELLWOOD LN	9200	529H	SWH	77036
BELLWOOD LAKE DR	1400	526X	NEF	77406
BELLWOOD PINES DR	0	524E	NEF	77494
BELLWOOD SPRINGS LN	4600	609S	NEF	77479
BEL MAR	800	568P	SG	77478
BELMARHEIGHTS DR	0	327D	NWC	77429
BELMARK	5600	534W	SEH	77033
BELMARK	6200	534Y	SEH	77087
BELMAS	0	572L	SWH	77045
BELMONT	200	288M	TB	77375
BELMONT	500	536D	PA	77506
W. BELMONT	1100	536F	PA	77506
BELMONT	5100	492X	SWH	77005
BELMONT	5400	532F	WU	77005
BELMONT CIR	13000	368Y	NWC	77065
S. BELMONT CT	10500	368Y	NWC	77065
N. BELMONT CT	10700	368Y	NWC	77065
BELMONT DR	500	656P	FR	77546
BELMONT BEND	6500	526E	NEF	77450
BELMONTE POINTE DR	15800	367D	NWC	77429
BELMONT FARMS DR	21200	289P	NWC	77375
BELMONT LEGEND CT	0	572Q	SWH	77047
BELMONT PARK DR	0	406C	NWC	77433
BELMONT PINE CT	0	326Z	NWC	77429
BELMONT SHORE CT	3600	609L	MC	77459
BELMONT SHORE LN	3800	609L	MC	77459
BELMORE LN	0	615W	PL	77584
BELNEATH	5400	534W	SEH	77033
BELNEATH CT	5400	534W	SEH	77033
BELRIDGE	10400	414Y	NEH	77016
BEL RIPOSO LN	0	659R	LC	77573
BELROIT	7800	455P	NEH	77028
BELROSE DR	5500	571A	SWH	77035
BELROSE FALLS LN	0	251W	NWC	77389
BELSHILL ST	10600	527W	NEF	77407
BELSHIRE RD	1100	536V	PA	77502
BELSHIRE RD	1300	537S	PA	77502
BELT LN	1201	570S	MC	77489
BELTED KINGFISHER TRAIL	0	291H	NWC	77389

Street Name	Block	Pg/Sq	Loc	Zips
BELTERRAZA CT	7900	527M	SWC	77083
BELTERRAZA DR	14700	527M	SWC	77083
BELTON BEND CT	0	406D	NWC	77433
BELTONE DR	500	485D	SWC	77450
BELTON LAKE DR	0	293G	SEM	77386
BELTON SHORE DR	0	406H	NWC	77433
BELTWAY 8 TOLL BRDG	0	538A	NEC	77015
BELTWAY 8 TOLL BRDG	0	538A	SEC	77503
BELTWOOD DR	2700	371V	NWC	77038
BELVAMERA RD	0	527X	NEF	77469
BELVAN CT	14500	328X	NWC	77429
BELVEDERE	4800	534J	SEH	77021
BELVEDERE DR	1600	502S	BT	77520
BELVEDERE PARK LN	0	572U	SWH	77047
BELVEDERE POINT	0	292F	NWC	77389
BELVOIR DR	14900	497H	NEC	77530
BELVOIR PARK DR	3900	486S	NEF	77450
BELVON VALLEY DR	0	296J	SEM	77365
BELVON VALLEY LN	24600	296J	SEM	77365
BELWIN DR	500	485D	SWC	77450
BELWOOD PARK LN	0	367P	NWC	77433
BEMANDO	0	452A	NWC	77091
BEMBRIDGE DR	1600	252V	SEM	77386
BEN DR	100	453F	NEH	77022
BENARD CT	4200	538N	PA	77503
BEN BLUM RD	13000	457E	NEC	77049
BENBOW WAY	1700	450U	NWH	77080
BENBROOK DR	100	413T	NEH	77076
BENBROOK MANOR LN	0	406H	NWC	77433
BENBROOK SPRINGS LN	0	445M	NWC	77449
BENBURY DR	22900	485B	SWC	77450
BENCHFIELD DR	900	452B	NWH	77091
BENCHLEY DR	9200	528Q	SWC	77099
BENCHMARK DR	16700	611B	SWH	77053
BENCREST DR	0	371T	NWC	77066
BEND CT	4900	569W	SG	77478
W. BEND DR	0	657U	LC	77573
E. BEND LN	1	492K	SWH	77007
BEND LN	13700	415C	NEC	77396
BEND COVE CT	0	660E	LC	77573
BEND CREEK LN	0	612L	PL	77584
BENDELL DR	8000	535U	SEH	77017
BENDER	0	374R	NEH	77396
BENDER AVE	100	335U	HM	77338
BENDER CT	15800	375Q	NEC	77396
BENDER RD	5800	375N	NEH	77396
BENDERS LN	3800	293C	SEM	77386
BENDERS CROSSING CT	3700	293C	SEM	77386
BENDERS CROSSING DR	28600	293C	SEM	77386
BENDERS DOCK CT	28500	293C	SEM	77386
BENDERS LANDING BLVD	0	253Y	SEM	77386
W. BENDERS LANDING BLVD	3100	293C	SEM	77386
E. BENDERS LANDING BLVD	27000	293M	SEM	77386
E. BENDERS LANDING BLVD	27300	293D	SEM	77386
E. BENDERS LANDING BLVD	28500	253Y	SEM	77386
BENDERWOOD CT	28600	293C	SEM	77386
BENDING BIRCH CT	20300	326P	NWC	77433
BENDING BIRCH DR	15600	326P	NWC	77433
BENDING BOUGH LN	1900	332A	NWC	77388
BENDING BOUGH LN	1900	292W	NWC	77388
BENDING BRANCH LN	8400	407E	NWC	77433
BENDING BRANCH PLACE	1	250C	WD	77381
BENDING BROOK LN	0	369T	NWC	77064
BENDING CREEK LN	16800	617X	SEC	77546
BENDING CYPRESS RD	17300	327J	NWC	77429
BENDING GREEN WAY	0	486N	SWC	77450
BENDING KEY CT	0	609U	MC	77479
BENDING MAPLE DR	0	330Z	NWC	77069
BENDING OAK CT	17200	327W	NWC	77429
S. BENDING OAK LN	0	614T	PL	77584
E. BENDING OAK LN	0	614T	PL	77584
BENDING OAK LN	1	490L	PP	77024
BENDING OAKS	6100	415E	NEH	77050
BENDING PECAN CT	8400	410E	NWC	77040
BENDING PINES CT	4900	484Z	NEF	77494
BENDING PINES LN	0	290T	NWC	77379
BENDING PINES LN	26300	484Z	NEF	77494
BENDING POINT	0	376V	NEC	77346
BENDING POST DR	17300	367X	NWC	77095
BENDING SHORE CT	100	660A	LC	77573
BENDING SPRING DR	0	612L	PL	77584
BENDING STREAM DR	0	656R	FR	77546
BENDING STREAM DR	1800	660L	LC	77573
BENDING WILLOW LN	9500	409D	NWC	77064
BEND ROCK WAY	0	377M	NEH	77346
BENDSTONE CIR	2000	486Q	SWC	77450
BENDWICK DR	1500	459E	NEC	77562
BEND WILLOW CT	21900	485V	NEF	77450
BEND WILLOW LN	3200	485V	NEF	77450
BENDWOOD DR	1	569N	SG	77478
BENDWOOD DR	400	489H	SWH	77024
BENDWOOD LN	0	660E	LC	77573
BENDWOOD LN	1	569N	SG	77478
BENELLI CT	0	376F	NEC	77396
BENELVA	0	498T	NEC	77015
BENET	0	497M	NEC	77015
BENEVENTO CT	0	445E	NWC	77493
BENE VISTA DR	0	447E	NWC	77084
BENEVOLENT WAY	0	289T	NWC	77375
BENFER RD	14400	330Z	NWC	77069
BENFIELD DR	3400	488Y	SWH	77082
BENFIELD MEADOWS	0	485Z	NEF	77450
BENFORD DR	13000	528U	SWC	77099
BENFORD DR	13200	528U	SWC	77083
BENFORD RIDGE LN	20500	406K	NWC	77433
BEN HUR DR	1000	490D	SV	77055
BEN HUR DR	1200	450Z	SV	77055
BENICIA DR	0	366Q	NWC	77433
BENIGNUS RD	400	489H	SWH	77024
BENITA	14200	570M	SWH	77085
BENJAMIN	7100	494Z	SEH	77011
BENJAMIN CIR	0	656X	FR	77546
BENJAMIN LN	6800	578A	PA	77505
BENJAMIN FRANKLIN LN	3500	569U	MC	77459
BENJIS PLACE	0	252N	SEM	77380
BEN LEIDI DR	16600	447D	NWC	77084
BENMAR DR	100	372R	NEH	77060
BENMAR DR	800	373P	NCC	77032
BENMORE DR	12100	528Z	SWH	77099
BENNE CT	2900	371G	NWC	77014
BENNET CHASE DR	15800	367D	NWC	77429
BENNET RIDGE DR	0	406K	NWC	77433
BENNETT	8100	495P	NEH	77029
BENNETT DR	400	537M	PA	77503
BENNETT DR	1000	537R	PA	77503
BENNETT PASS DR	0	294E	SEM	77386
BENNETT RIDGE DR	0	253X	SEM	77386
BENNETTS RIDGE LN	0	296J	SEM	77365
BENNETT TRAILS DR	0	253X	SEM	77386
BENNETT VIEW DR	0	328K	NWC	77377
BEN NEVIS	10200	460F	NEC	77532
BEN NEVIS DR	16600	447D	NWC	77084
BENNIE	100	453K	NEH	77022
BENNIE RD	0	249W	NWC	77375
BENNIGAN	2000	658T	LC	77573
BENNING	0	530Z	SWH	77096
BENNING DR	4300	571D	SWH	77035
BENNING DR	5200	571B	SWH	77035
BENNING DR	5500	531W	SWH	77096
BENNING DR	8800	530W	SWH	77031
BENNING CREST LN	0	573X	SEC	77047
BENNINGCREST LN	0	573X	SEC	77047
BENNINGFIELD LN	8500	370N	NWC	77064
BENNING POINT LN	0	373E	NCC	77073
BENNINGTON	100	453P	NEH	77022
BENNINGTON	1700	453Q	NEH	77093
BENNINGTON	3700	454P	NEH	77016
BENNINGTON	4900	454Q	NEH	77028
BENNINGTON CT	2500	658V	LC	77573
BENNINGTON DR	3100	537L	PA	77503
BENNINGTON SPRINGS DR	0	524E	NEF	77494
BENRUS CT	3200	613Y	NEB	77584
BENS LN	800	338M	NEH	77336
BENS BRANCH DR	2600	337B	NEH	77339
BENSON	1200	494F	NEH	77020
BENSON DR	2200	496S	GP	77547
BENSON FALLS DR	0	526W	NEF	77406
BENSON LANDING DR	0	326U	NWC	77429
BENSON SPRINGS LN	29600	253W	SEM	77386
BENS TOWN DR	0	337B	NEH	77339
BENS VIEW LN	0	337F	NEH	77345
BENS VIEW LN	0	337F	NEH	77345
BENS VIEW TRAIL	2200	337F	NEH	77339
BENTANA CT	17000	407L	NWC	77095
BENT ARBOR CT	21800	525C	NEF	77450
BENT ARBOR LN	5800	525C	NEF	77450
BENT ASPEN CT	20300	326T	NWC	77433
BEN TAUB LOOP	1500	533E	SWH	77030
BENT BOUGH LN	5200	411T	NWH	77088
BENT BRANCH DR	6900	411T	NWH	77088
BENTBROOK DR	0	617V	SEH	77546
BENT BROOK WAY	3200	445M	NWC	77449
BENT CREEK	0	612R	PL	77584
BENT CREEK LN	1800	658U	LC	77573
BENTCREST CT	0	528Q	SWC	77072
BENTCREST CT	13100	528Q	SWH	77072
BENT CYPRESS DR	17300	331L	NWC	77388
BENT CYPRESS DR	17600	331G	NWC	77388
BENT ELM DR	18400	331B	NWC	77388
BENTFIELD CT	16800	618R	SEH	77058
BENTFIELD WAY	16700	618R	SEH	77058
BENTFORD DR	0	335D	NEH	77339
BENTFORD PARK ST	8000	525Z	NEF	77406
BENTGATE DR	0	293Y	NCC	77373
BENTGRASS CT	21400	486S	NEF	77450
BENTGRASS DR	3000	486S	NEF	77450
BENTGRASS RUN LN	0	293G	SEM	77386
BENT GREEN LN	7800	250S	NWC	77389
BENTGREEN CHASE CT		484T	NEF	77494
BENTGROVE LN	0	366R	NWC	77433
BENT GULCH LN		328P	NWC	77429
BENT HOLLOW LN	24700	485N	NEF	77494
BENT HORN LN	27800	246J	SWM	77355
BENTHOS DR	9100	528Q	SWC	77083
BENT LAKE DR	21000	446J	NWC	77449
BENTLAKE LN	1400	615G	PL	77581
BENT LAKE LN	13400	328Q	NWC	77429
BENTLEY	10300	414P	NCC	77093
BENTLEY CT	2900	613V	NEB	77584
BENTLEY DR	4000	613V	NEB	77584
BENTLEY DR	10000	245T	SWM	77447
BENTLEY LN	0	528K	SWC	77083
BENTLEY PARK CT	1	369D	NWC	77070
BENTLY GLEN LN	0	485S	NEF	77494
BENTLY GREEN LN	0	452Y	NWH	77008
BENT MEADOW CT	0	484Z	NEF	77494
BENT OAK	0	244B	WCO	77447
BENT OAK DR	1600	570U	MC	77489
BENT OAK DR	9600	410S	NWC	77040
BENT OAK DR	10000	409R	NWC	77040
BENT OAK LN	8000	330P	NWC	77379
BENT OAK LN	27500	249G	SWM	77354
BENTON DR	0	577J	PA	77504
BENTON CREEK DR	0	328J	NWC	77429
BENTON CREEK DR	0	328J	NWC	77377
BENTONDALE LN	0	575U	SEH	77075
BENTONGROVE LN	0	457A	NEC	77044
BENTONITE BLVD	4700	461N	BT	77521
BENTON PARK	0	328C	NWC	77377
BENTON SPRINGS LN	20000	526K	NEF	77407
BENTPATH CT	3700	371B	NWC	77014
BENTPATH DR	13900	371B	NWC	77014
BENT PINE DR	12300	369J	NWC	77429
BENT PINE DR	19800	337U	NEC	77346
BENTRIDGE DR	15100	377X	NEC	77044
BENTRIDGE VALLEY LN		249V	NWC	77375
BENT SAGE CT	24700	485X	NEF	77494
BENT SAIL CT	0	660J	LC	77573
BENT SAIL LN	800	660E	LC	77573
BENTSEN LN	9800	369H	NWC	77070
BENTSHIRE WAY	16600	618R	SEH	77058
BENT SPRING CT	3300	445M	NWC	77449
BENT SPRINGS LN	3600	445M	NWC	77449
BENT SPUR CT	10600	409F	NWC	77064
BENT SPUR LN	8700	409F	NWC	77064
BENT SPUR LN	9500	409B	NWC	77064
BENT TRAIL CT	11500	370Q	NWC	77066
BENT TREE CIR	5900	337P	NEC	77346
BENT TREE TRAIL	2700	659C	LC	77573
BENT TWIG WAY	15300	325R	NWC	77433
BENTVINE CIR	19300	446V	NWC	77084
BENTVINE DR	0	612N	PL	77545
BENTVINE DR	1900	446Z	NWC	77084
BENT WAY DR	11400	369J	NWC	77433
BENTWOOD CT	900	616V	FR	77546
BENTWOOD DR	1400	570T	MC	77489
BENTWOOD DR	24300	244C	WCO	77447
BENTWOOD RD	5000	617S	FR	77546
BENTWOOD ELM	5500	291W	NWC	77379
BENTWOOD OAKS CIR	20400	295R	SEM	77365
BENTWOOD OAKS DR	19900	295R	SEM	77365
BENTWOOD OAKS DR	21000	296N	SEM	77365
BENTWOOD PKWY	25000	295R	SEM	77365
BENTWORTH DR	2000	489S	SWH	77077
BEN VENUE	10200	460G	NEC	77532
BENWEST CT	0	291X	NWC	77388
BENWICH CIR	7100	408P	NWC	77095
BENWICK	9100	329M	NWC	77379
BERAN DR	3100	572K	SWH	77045
BERCLAIR DR	10500	372W	NWC	77038
BERDEEN DR	0	326K	NWC	77433
BERENDO	6000	451K	NWH	77092
BERESFORD	400	497A	NEH	77015
BERETTA CT	16300	610C	SWH	77489
BERETTA BEND DR	17000	376K	NEC	77396
BERGAMO DR	11001	524M	NEF	77406
BERGAMO LAKE DR	0	445B	NWC	77493
BERGEN BAY LN	0	611S	FS	77545
BERGENFIELD CT	5600	526A	NEF	77450
BERGENIA DR	14400	368A	NWC	77429
BERGIN	3000	454W	NEH	77026
BERGMAN LN	22600	286A	SWM	77355
BERGSTROM	5400	452C	NWH	77091
BERING	2700	494J	SEH	77003
BERING CIR	5700	491K	SWH	77057
BERING CT	0	491T	SWH	77057
BERING DR	400	491P	SWH	77057
BERING BRIDGE LN	0	377E	NEC	77346
BERING LANDING DR	0	406L	NWC	77433
BERINGWOOD DR	9200	528P	SWC	77083
BERKELEY LAKE LN	1200	618E	SEH	77062
BERKELY CT	8100	461P	NEC	77521
BERKLEY	1200	535K	SEH	77012
BERKLEY	2900	535P	SEH	77017
BERKLEY	3600	535P	SEH	77087
BERKLEY HALL CT	0	250E	WD	77381
BERKLEY PARK CT	3800	618D	PA	77058
BERKRIDGE DR	5800	571X	SWH	77053
W. BERKSHIRE	0	488L	SWH	77077
E. BERKSHIRE	0	488L	SWH	77077
BERKSHIRE	100	531L	BL	77401
BERKSHIRE	9500	454A	NEH	77093
BERKSHIRE DOWNS DR	0	248Z	TB	77375
BERKSHIRE ELM	2100	445S	NWC	77493
BERKSHIRE FOREST DR	0	407C	NWC	77098
BERKSHIRE GREEN DR	15000	527R	NEF	77083
BERKSHIRE HILLS DR	5800	297Z	NEH	77345
BERKSHIRE MANOR LN	0	408W	NWC	77084
BERKSHIRE OAK	0	326Y	NWC	77429
BERKSHIRE PARK DR	6100	407X	NWC	77084
BERKSHIRE TRACE	9700	613K	PL	77584
BERKWAY TRAIL	11600	369S	NWC	77065
BERKWOOD CT	13100	371Z	NWC	77038
BERLANDIER ASH LN	0	289C	NWC	77375
BERLIN CT	9600	329U	NWC	77070
BERLINETTA DR	2900	613V	NEB	77584
BERLINO DR	1600	616P	PL	77581
BERMAR	31200	246Y	SWM	77355
BERMONDSEY DR	0	329J	NWC	77377
BERMUDA	0	538N	PA	77503
BERMUDA	4100	537R	PA	77503
BERMUDA	4400	609J	SG	77479
BERMUDA AVE	0	461N	NEC	77521
BERMUDA DUNES CT	13600	370B	NWC	77069
BERMUDA DUNES DR	2400	609G	MC	77459
BERMUDA DUNES DR	5600	330Y	NWC	77069
BERMUDA DUNES DR	5900	370B	NWC	77069
BERN	2300	659F	LC	77573
BERNADETTE LN	2700	449M	NWH	77043
BERNALDA CIR	0	524R	NEF	77406
BERNARD	1200	536H	PA	77506
BERNARD	1300	537E	PA	77506
BERNARD	3200	579A	LP	77571
BERNARD CT	19000	295B	SEM	77365
BERNARD WAY	1600	618R	SEH	77058
BERNDALE	8500	495L	NEH	77029
BERNICE	5900	534V	SEH	77087
BERNICE DR	34500	247F	SWM	77362
BERNINA LN	14700	417V	NEC	77044
BERNINA LN	15900	418T	NEC	77044
BERNLEY	16200	367L	CY	77429
BERNSHIRE LN	6100	407V	NWC	77084
BERRIDGE HOUSE CT	9600	411B	NWC	77086
BERRINGTON DR	14100	528N	SWC	77083
BERRY	700	493T	SWH	77002
BERRY	1000	493Y	SEH	77004
BERRY CT	3000	493Y	SEH	77004
BERRY LN	23700	290B	NEC	77389
BERRY RD	1	453G	NEH	77022
BERRY RD	1500	454E	NEH	77093
BERRY BLOSSOM CT	1	251R	WD	77380
BERRY BLOSSOM DR	1	251R	WD	77380
BERRY BRANCH DR	18000	407X	NWC	77084
BERRYBRIAR LN	10000	289U	NWC	77375
BERRY BROOK DR	5500	535V	SEH	77017
BERRY CREEK DR	5100	536S	SEH	77017
BERRY CRESENT DR	22300	291L	NWC	77389
BERRYDALE	4500	535R	SEH	77017
BERRYFIELD DR	1800	489N	SWH	77077
BERRYFIELD LN	3100	615T	PL	77581
BERRYFROST LN	1	251V	WD	77380
BERRY GARDEN LN	0	330C	NWC	77379
BERRY GROVE DR	3400	291Q	NWC	77388
BERRY HEDGE LN	0	325K	NWC	77447
BERRY HILL	10200	289U	NWC	77375
BERRY HILL	18600	328C	NWC	77377
BERRY HILL CT	5400	535V	SEH	77017
BERRYHILL LN	3100	291R	NWC	77388
BERRY KNOLL CT	4900	297Q	NEH	77345
BERRY LAUREL LN	12200	372E	NWC	77014
BERRY LEAF CT	18500	447S	NWC	77084
BERRY LIMB DR	9900	529W	SWH	77099
BERRYLINE	0	251F	WD	77381
S. BERRYLINE CIR	1	251F	WD	77381
N. BERRYLINE CIR	1	251B	WD	77381
BERRY MEADOW DR	11700	570A	SWH	77071
BERRY OAKS LN	17800	330J	NWC	77379
BERRY ORCHARD LN	9800	289U	NWC	77375
BERRYPATCH LN	9800	289U	NWC	77375
BERRYPICK LN	1	251P	WD	77380
BERRY PINE DR	23000	333A	NCC	77373
BERRY PLACE DR	11800	570A	SWH	77071
BERRY POINT DR	17700	327A	NWC	77429
BERRY RIDGE LN	21300	289T	NWC	77375
BERRY SHOALS LN	0	328L	NWC	77377
BERRY SPRINGS DR	0	370E	NWC	77069
BERRYSTONE LN	9800	289U	NWC	77375
BERRYSTONE TRAIL	1200	569X	MC	77459
BERRY THICKET LN	20500	379E	NEC	77532
BERRY TREE DR	10800	369X	NWC	77064
BERRY VIEW CT	1	251R	WD	77380
BERRY VINE	21200	289U	NWC	77375
BERRY VINE DR	8600	610G	SWH	77489
BERRYWICK DR	0	289D	NWC	77375
BERRYWOOD LN	1200	488M	SWH	77077
BERRYWOOD BEND DR	20900	289U	NWC	77375
BERSEY LN	5600	452B	NWH	77091
BERTANI LN	14000	368P	NWC	77429
BERTASZ DR	0	457V	NEC	77049
BERTELL LN	11600	328T	NWC	77429
BERTELLI'S LN	5500	451D	NWH	77091
BERTHA	4000	454X	NEH	77026
BERTHA'S LN	1400	496M	NEH	77015
BERTHEA	900	493W	SWH	77006
BERTLOMA	200	536Z	PA	77502
BERTNER	6500	532H	SWH	77030
BERTNER AVE	7000	532M	SWH	77030
W. BERTRAND	400	412R	NCC	77037
BERTRAND	2000	413R	NCC	77093
BERTRAND	2400	414N	NCC	77093
BERTRAND CT	0	620K	SB	77586
BERTWOOD	7900	454D	NEH	77016
BERWICK	13100	497E	NEH	77015
N. BERWICK DR	22000	368W	NWC	77095
BERWICK LN	6100	657U	LC	77573
BERWICK MANOR CT	1200	329B	NWC	77379
BERWYN DR	7900	412M	NCC	77037
BERYL	6600	530M	SWH	77074
BERZIN CT	3200	444M	NWC	77493
BESS	4300	531R	BL	77401
BESS RD	1100	659X	GCO	77539
BESSEMER	9900	576J	SEH	77034
BESSEMER CT	0	251C	WD	77381
BESSIE SWINDLE WAY	0	573L	SEH	77089
BESTIN LN	9700	368Z	NWC	77065
BESTIN OAKS DR	0	615Z	PL	77581
BESTOWAL LN	0	404Z	NWC	77493
BETA CIR	700	537L	PA	77503
BETANNA DR	7400	408K	NWC	77095
BETH LN	100	498F	CV	77530
BETH LN	12000	248E	SWM	77354
BETHAL GREEN DR	400	485B	SWC	77450
BETHAN GLEN LN	16700	407Z	NWC	77084
BETHANY	2900	447S	NWC	77084
BETHANY LN	3500	414J	NCC	77039
BETHANY LN	4800	414G	NCC	77039
BETHANY BAY DR	0	612L	PL	77584
BETHANY BAY DR	7200	609Q	MC	77459
BETHANY MANOR CT	0	407X	NWC	77449
BETHANY PARK DR	0	252R	SEM	77385
BETHEL BLVD	3800	451K	NWH	77092
BETHEL BAPTIST RD	19900	256M	SEM	77357
BETHEL BEND LN	0	487A	SWC	77494
BETHEL CREEK CT	0	326U	NWC	77433
BETHEL MILLS CT	0	484N	NEF	77494
BETHEL VALLEY TRACE	0	484P	NEF	77494
BETHJE	100	492L	SWH	77007
BETHLEHEM	900	452E	NWH	77018
BETHLEHEM	2000	451H	NWH	77018
BETH MARIE	28200	246G	SWM	77355
BETHNAL GREEN DR	11300	371P	NWC	77066
BETHPAGE LN	7400	250X	NWC	77389
BETHUNE DR	6500	412W	NWH	77091
BETHUNE WAY	13400	571K	SWH	77085
BETHY DR	0	413T	NEH	77037
BETKA RD	26800	324J	HK	77447
BETKA RD	30000	323J	NWC	77484
BETKA RD	30900	322F	WCO	77484
BETONICA LN	6500	407S	NWC	77449
BETRAL	100	452H	NWH	77022
BETSY LN	4000	492S	SWH	77027
BETSY ROSS CT	1200	569Y	MC	77477
BETTENCOURT LN	0	373A	NCC	77073
BETTINA CT	800	490E	SWH	77024
BETTIS DR	4200	491V	SWH	77027
BETTY	1500	379R	NEC	77532
BETTY	4300	531M	BL	77401
BETTY	4800	614W	NEB	77584
BETTY LN	1300	537N	PA	77502
BETTY LN	13000	570J	SF	77477
BETTY LN	17400	447G	NWC	77084
BETTY LN	22101	256K	SEM	77357
BETTY RD	400	536Y	SH	77587
BETTYANN LN	700	336J	NEH	77336
BETTY BOOP	7900	455P	NEH	77028
BETTY JANE LN	7600	491B	NWH	77055
BETTY JOYCE	0	335T	NEH	77338
BETTY SUE LN	500	572Y	SWH	77047
BETTYWOOD CT	8000	290E	NWC	77375
BETTYWOOD LN	23300	290E	NWC	77375
BEUFORT WAY	6000	250Z	NWC	77389
BEULAH	3000	493Z	SEH	77004
BEUSCH DR	1400	537N	PA	77502
BEUTEL DR	1300	450Y	SV	77055
BEVERLY	700	493A	NWH	77007
BEVERLY	900	453W	NWH	77008
BEVERLY	2400	537Z	PA	77503
BEVERLY AVE	900	536M	PA	77506
BEVERLY CIR	600	570S	SF	77477
S. BEVERLY CIR	2300	570S	SF	77477
BEVERLY DR	11800	369N	NWC	77065
BEVERLY LN	100	531M	BL	77401
BEVERLY RD	0	484E	KT	77494
BEVERLY CHASE DR	21300	525Z	NEF	77406
BEVERLY GARDENS CT	0	491X	SWH	77057
BEVERLY HILL	5300	491X	SWH	77056
BEVERLY HILL	5600	491W	SWH	77057
BEVERLY HILL	7900	490W	SWH	77063
BEVERLY HILLS	0	490Y	SWH	77063
BEVERLY HILLS WALK	5700	491X	SWH	77057
BEVERSBROOK DR	9700	569H	SWH	77031
BEVIAMO ST	0	530X	SWH	77031
BEVINGTON OAKS CIR	2000	485M	SWC	77450
BEVINGTON OAKS CT	21700	485M	SWC	77450
BEVIS	1500	452U	NWH	77008
BEVKEN CT	13600	328T	NWC	77429
BEVLYN DR	8500	532P	SWH	77025
BEXAR	11700	539R	LP	77571
BEXAR DR	8700	409H	NWC	77064
BEXHILL DR	11500	369N	NWC	77065
BEXHILL DR	12100	368R	NWC	77065
BEXHILL DR	13000	368Q	NWC	77065
BEXLEY DR	10600	529N	SWH	77099
BEXLEY DR	12300	528R	SWH	77099
BHANDARA CT	3200	444M	KT	77493
BIANCA CT	9400	455D	NEH	77078
BIANCA SPRING LN	0	484X	NEF	77494
BIANCO LN	0	659M	LC	77573
BIARRITZ CT	3500	529A	SWH	77082
BIBB DR	13300	330Z	NWC	77069
BICENTENNIAL CT	4700	371A	NWC	77066
BICHESTER LN	12300	414E	NCC	77039
BICKETT LN	200	332C	NCC	77373
BICKFORD CT	24500	485S	NEF	77494
BICKFORD PLACE	0	330Z	NWC	77069
BICKHAM DR	0	366N	NWC	77433
BICKWOOD CT	11300	616C	SEC	77089
BICKWOOD DR	11500	616C	SEC	77089
BIDDIE WILBER RD	0	614G	PL	77581
BIDDLE DR	0	296E	SEM	77365
BIDEFORD LN	7500	330W	NWC	77070
BIDEFORD LN	8100	329Z	NWC	77070
BIDIAS	4500	577F	PA	77504
BIENVILLE AVE	6700	502C	BT	77521
BIENVILLE LN	500	496D	NEC	77015
BIG BASIN LN	0	377F	NEC	77346
BIG BEND DR	1500	450Y	NWH	77055
BIG BEND LN	1600	538R	DP	77536

Street Name	Block	Pg/Sq	Loc	Zips
BIG BRANCH DR	0	409D	NWC	77064
BIG CANYON DR	19800	526F	NEF	77450
BIG CEDAR CIR	4800	609K	MC	77459
BIG CEDAR DR	2500	337C	NEH	77345
BIG CREEK DR	8300	410H	NWC	77064
BIG CREEK FALLS CT	16600	330P	NWC	77379
BIG CYPRESS DR	18300	331H	NWC	77388
BIG CYPRESS DR	18600	331C	NWC	77388
BIG DEER DR	100	379A	NEC	77532
BIG DEER DR	600	378D	NEC	77532
BIG ELM CIR	4800	609K	MC	77459
BIG ELM DR	0	366P	NWC	77433
BIGELOW	700	453Z	NEH	77009
W. BIGELOW OAK CT	1	251E	WD	77381
E. BIGELOW OAK CT	1	251E	WD	77381
BIG FALLS DR	4800	337C	NEH	77345
BIG FIR DR	3200	297Z	NEH	77345
BIGGS CT	6700	535W	SEH	77061
BIG HICKORY DR	3400	297Y	NEH	77345
BIG HOLLOW LN	100	489K	SWH	77042
BIG HOLLY LN	11400	252D	SEM	77385
BIG HOLLY LN	11600	253A	SEM	77385
BIGHORN	7500	461S	NEC	77521
BIG HORN CT	3100	568Z	SG	77478
BIG HORN DR	1400	331M	NWC	77090
BIGHORN RIVER LN	0	377E	NEC	77346
BIGHORN VALLEY LN	0	526N	NEF	77407
BIG JOHN	0	460N	HG	77562
BIG JOHN	11600	411H	NWC	77038
BIG LAKE DR	1600	489P	SWH	77077
BIG LAKE LN	0	609Y	NEF	77459
BIG LEAF DR	0	369J	NWC	77429
BIG LEAF PASTURE LN	0	407A	NWC	77433
BIG LEAGUE DREAMS PKWY	1100	658Z	LC	77573
BIG MEADOW LN	0	484Z	NEF	77494
BIG MEADOWS DR	2900	296Y	NEH	77339
BIG OAK CIR	16200	286C	SWM	77355
BIG OAK LN	26300	248J	SWM	77354
BIG OAKS	700	490F	SWH	77024
BIG OAKS DR	12400	415E	NEH	77050
BIG OAKS GROVE	17400	527E	NEF	77407
BIG OAK TRAIL DR	8000	410L	NWC	77040
BIG PINES	1300	288B	TB	77375
BIG PINE TRAIL	0	366S	NWC	77433
BIG PINEY DR	3600	297U	NEH	77345
BIG REED DR	0	377K	NEC	77346
BIGRIVER CT	0	245R	SWM	77355
BIG RIVER DR	2300	337C	NEH	77345
BIGRIVER DR	2300	245R	SWM	77355
BIG ROCK LN	19300	328C	NWC	77377
BIG SANDY	8100	533S	SEH	77051
BIG SKY DR	22600	485G	SWC	77450
BIG SPRING	4900	609K	MC	77459
BIG SPRING DR	0	614Z	PL	77541
BIG SPRINGS DR	2300	336C	NEH	77339
BIG SPRINGS DR	2800	296Y	NEH	77339
BIG SPRING TRAIL	12700	377B	NEC	77346
BIG SPRUCE DR	3200	297S	NEH	77339
BIG STONE DR	12600	370D	NWC	77066
BIG SUR DR	14400	408K	NWC	77095
BIG TIMBER CT	19600	337P	NEC	77346
BIG TIMBER DR	19800	337T	NEC	77346
BIG TREE DR	20600	381A	NEC	77532
BIG TREE DR	21100	380D	NEC	77532
BIG VALLEY DR	7300	408N	NWC	77095
BIG WELLS DR	20500	446P	NWC	77449
BIG WILLOW LN	9700	409D	NWC	77064
BIG WILLOW CREEK CIR	0	366N	NWC	77433
BIGWOOD	7300	455A	NEH	77016
BIGWOOD	7900	455B	NEH	77078
BIG WOOD SPRINGS DR	21500	486J	SWC	77450
BIHIA FOREST DR	5800	411K	NWC	77088
BILAL RD	0	372J	NWC	77067
BILLABONG CRESCENT CT	18100	327W	NWC	77429
BILL CROWLEY PK, W E RD	0	414C	NCC	77039
BILLFISH BLVD	0	377G	NEC	77345
BILLIE LEE DR	25000	257T	SEM	77357
BILLIE LOU	0	299W	NEH	77336
BILLIKIN DR	6500	371T	NWC	77086
BILLINEYS PARK	19400	406U	NWC	77449
BILLINGFORD DR	200	485C	SWC	77450
BILLINGHAM CT	6800	330Q	NWC	77379
BILLINGS DR	1400	450Y	NWH	77055
BILLINGSLEY	3500	453Y	NEH	77009
BILLINGTON	6200	408S	NWC	77084
BILLINSGATE DR	6200	407S	NWC	77449
BILLIT WAY DR	1300	486H	SWC	77094
BILLY	4300	494K	NEH	77020
BILOXI	8500	535L	SEH	77017
BILTMORE	7800	375G	HM	77396
BIMINI ST	0	377G	NEC	77345
BIMINI COVE WAY	0	296Q	SEM	77365
S. BIMINI TWIST CIR	0	249R	NWC	77375
N. BIMINI TWIST CIR	0	249R	NWC	77375
BIMINI WAY	1700	620K	SB	77586
BIMMS DR	9600	252B	SEM	77385
BINALONG DR	6400	406U	NWC	77449
BINBROOK DR	0	445M	NWC	77449
BINEFIELD	28700	293A	SEM	77386
BINEFIELD	29200	253W	SEM	77386
BINFORD CIR	21300	283J	NWC	77484
BINFORD RD	21100	283N	NWC	77484
BINFORD PLACE	30000	283J	NWC	77484
BINGHAM	1000	493F	SWH	77007
BINGHAM MANOR LN	0	491Y	SWH	77401
BINGHAMPTON RD	11900	616H	SEH	77089
BINGLE RD	900	490D	SV	77055
BINGLE RD	1100	450V	NWH	77055
BINGLE RD	4000	451J	NWH	77092
BINGLE RD	6100	411W	NWH	77092
BINION FOREST LN	5100	291J	NWC	77389
BINK CT	13800	371B	NWC	77014
BINLEY CT	13000	488U	SWH	77077
BINLEY DR	2300	488U	SWH	77077
BINNACLE WAY	300	419C	NEC	77532
BINON CIR	0	527W	NEF	77469
E. BINON LN	0	527S	NEF	77469
BINON LN	0	527S	NEF	77469
BINTLIFF CT	0	530C	SWH	77036
BINTLIFF DR	5600	530C	SWH	77036
BINTLIFF DR	6500	530R	SWH	77074
BINZ	1000	493W	SWH	77004
BINZ	1200	533B	SWH	77004
BIRCH	0	375M	NEC	77396
BIRCH	0	444X	KT	77493
BIRCH	800	620X	CS	77565
BIRCH	1300	616T	PL	77581
BIRCH	4500	531M	BL	77401
BIRCH	16600	418Q	NEC	77044
BIRCH	22800	296Q	SEM	77365
BIRCH CT	0	657L	LC	77598
BIRCH DR	800	537M	PA	77503

Street Name	Block	Pg/Sq	Loc	Zips
BIRCH DR	10800	579C	LP	77571
N. BIRCH LN	0	407J	NWC	77433
BIRCH LN	3400	538U	DP	77536
BIRCH ARBOR CT	0	375Z	NEC	77396
BIRCHAVEN LN	0	528Q	SWC	77072
BIRCHBANK LN	21100	446J	NWC	77449
BIRCHBARK DR	7800	334V	NCC	77338
BIRCH BAY CT	21400	446B	NWC	77449
BIRCH BEND CIR	1500	372N	NWC	77067
BIRCH BOUGH	300	615Y	PL	77581
BIRCH BOUGH CT	4900	297Q	NEH	77345
BIRCHBROOK CT	1	251T	WD	77380
N. BIRCHCANE CT	1	251J	WD	77381
N. BIRCHCANE DR	1	251J	WD	77381
BIRCH CANOE CT	100	249R	NWH	77375
BIRCH CANOE CT	100	249R	NWH	77375
BIRCH CANOE DR	100	249R	NWH	77375
BIRCH CANOE DR	100	249R	NWH	77375
BIRCH CANYON CT	2300	611W	MC	77545
BIRCH CANYON CT	13600	408L	NWC	77041
BIRCH CANYON DR	8000	408L	NWC	77041
BIRCH COLONY CT	0	297E	SEM	77365
BIRCH COVE	4600	448E	NWC	77084
BIRCH CREEK DR	2900	297S	NEH	77339
BIRCHCROFT DR	4300	411U	NWH	77088
W. BIRCHDALE DR	2700	610E	MC	77489
E. BIRCHDALE DR	2700	610E	MC	77489
BIRCH FALLS RD	12700	368Z	NWC	77065
BIRCHFIELD OAK CT		484W	NEF	77494
BIRCH FOREST LN	17800	330J	NWC	77379
BIRCHGATE DR	5500	334A	NCC	77373
BIRCH GLEN DR	12900	328U	NWC	77429
BIRCHGLEN LN	8100	369D	NWC	77070
BIRCH GREEN WAY	0	292D	SEM	77386
BIRCH GROVE DR	13000	528U	SWC	77099
BIRCH GROVE DR	13300	528U	SWC	77083
BIRCH HAVEN DR	4000	297S	NEH	77339
BIRCH HEIGHTS	0	406X	NWC	77449
BIRCH HOLLOW LN	13800	488X	SWH	77082
BIRCH KNOLL LN	14300	573X	SEC	77047
BIRCHLAND CT	3300	297Y	NEH	77345
BIRCH LANDING CT	0	612Q	PL	77584
BIRCHLEAF DR	3100	446P	NWC	77449
BIRCHLINE DR	10200	329C	NWC	77379
BIRCH MANOR LN	0	524D	NEF	77494
BIRCH MAPLE DR	0	444Z	KT	77493
BIRCH MAPLE DR	0	444Z	KT	77493
BIRCH MEADOW DR	11700	570A	SWH	77071
BIRCHMERE CT	2600	486P	SWC	77450
BIRCH MILL CT	0	336B	NEH	77339
BIRCHMONT DR	4900	451C	NWH	77091
BIRCHMONT DR	5800	451B	NWH	77092
BIRCHMOOR CT	2100	297V	NEH	77345
BIRCH PARK LN	2900	333P	NCC	77073
BIRCH PLACE	1	259P	NEC	77357
BIRCH POINT DR	22500	485L	SWC	77450
BIRCH RAIN CT	20600	446K	NWC	77449
BIRCHRIDGE	0	299S	NEC	77336
BIRCH RIDGE DR	10200	335Q	HM	77338
BIRCH RIDGE DR	22500	291J	NWC	77389
BIRCH RIVER DR	15700	487Y	SWC	77082
BIRCH ROW RD	12400	411D	NWC	77038
BIRCH RUN CT	1500	372J	NWC	77067
BIRCH RUN LN	11600	372J	NWC	77067
BIRCHSAY MANOR DR	0	329C	NWC	77379
BIRCH SPRINGS DR	0	407C	NWC	77095
BIRCHSTONE DR	1000	569T	MC	77459
BIRCHTON	4100	450G	NWH	77080
BIRCHTREE FOREST DR	7200	411V	NWH	77088
BIRCH VALE LN	0	609Y	NEF	77479
BIRCH VALE RD	16000	448E	NWC	77084
BIRCH VALLEY CT	1200	485M	SWC	77450
BIRCH VALLEY DR	22000	485M	SWC	77450
BIRCH VIEW	900	498A	NEC	77530
BIRCHVIEW CT	800	613F	NEB	77584
BIRCHVIEW DR	5800	328R	NWC	77377
BIRCHVIEW DR	15600	329S	NWC	77377
BIRCH VILLA DR	3600	297X	NEH	77345
BIRCHWOOD	1400	413Q	NEC	77093
BIRCHWOOD	11200	336S	NEC	77338
BIRCHWOOD DR	1	298B	NEC	77336
BIRCHWOOD DR	200	252N	SEM	77386
BIRCHWOOD DR	1300	536P	PA	77502
BIRCHWOOD BEND CT	0	405T	NWC	77493
BIRCHWOOD CREEK CT	0	291A	NWC	77389
BIRCHWOOD GROVE BLVD	0	367P	NWC	77433
BIRCHWOOD KNOLL CT	0	524R	NEF	77406
BIRCHWOOD LAKE LN	0	405S	NWC	77493
BIRCHWOOD MEADOW CT	0	484P	NEF	77494
BIRCHWOOD SPRINGS	0	296Q	SEM	77365
BIRCHWOOD TRAIL	0	328R	NWC	77377
BIRCHWOOD WAY LN	0	658Y	LC	77573
W. BIRD RD	100	536Q	PA	77502
E. BIRD RD	100	536Q	PA	77502
BIRDCALL LN	13300	368L	NWC	77429
BIRD CREEK DR	16900	407U	NWC	77084
BIRD DOG DR	16300	610B	SWH	77489
BIRD FOREST DR	8600	411L	NWC	77088
BIRDHAVEN LN	16900	610G	SWH	77489
BIRDHILL CIR	10900	369X	NWC	77064
BIRDIE CIR	0	580K	LP	77571
BIRDIE CT	2100	616K	PL	77581
BIRDIE LN	12400	496Q	GP	77015
BIRD MEADOW LN	8300	610G	SWH	77489
BIRD RUN DR	8300	610G	SWH	77489
BIRDSALL	1	492L	SWH	77007
BIRDSALL MARKET PLACE	0	492L	SWH	77007
BIRDSEYE MAPLE LN	6800	250U	NWC	77389
BIRDS EYE MAPLE LN	9600	410A	NWC	77064
BIRDSNEST TRAIL	9600	527U	NEF	77498
BIRDSONG DR	500	659E	LC	77573
BIRDSONG DR	800	501K	BT	77521
BIRDSONG DR	3800	537M	PA	77503
BIRDWING LN	11300	371R	NWC	77067
BIRDWOOD CT	8900	531N	SWH	77096
BIRDWOOD RD	5100	531P	SWH	77096
BIRDWOOD RD	5800	530P	SWH	77074
BIRDY	0	404F	NWC	77447
BIRKDALE CT	1200	485E	NEF	77494
BIRKENHEAD CIR	4600	569T	MC	77459
BIRKLAND PINE	0	449X	NWH	77043
BIRMINGHAM	7800	455K	NEH	77028
BIRNAM GARDEN LN	0	411A	NWC	77086
BIRNAM WOOD BLVD	20000	333R	NEH	77338
BIRNAM WOOD BLVD	22800	333C	NCC	77373
BIRNAM WOOD BLVD	23500	293T	NCC	77373
BIRNEY POINT LN	13700	417D	NEC	77044
BIRNHAM CT	0	299T	NEC	77336
BIRNHAM BEND CIR	3700	293C	SEM	77386
BIRNHAM OAKS BLVD	0	253T	SEM	77386
BIRNHAM WOODS BLVD	800	537M	PA	77503
BIRNHAM WOODS CT	0	253K	SEM	77386

Street Name	Block	Pg/Sq	Loc	Zips
BIRNHAM WOODS DR	0	253X	SEM	77386
BIRNHAM WOODS DR	28300	293G	SEM	77386
BIRSAY	9600	329R	NWC	77379
BIRTHSTONE DR	0	404Z	NWC	77493
BISBANE DR	2500	371H	NWC	77014
BISBEE	1200	535G	SEH	77012
BISBEE	2500	535L	SEH	77017
BISBEE RD	0	658Y	LC	77573
BISCAYNE BLVD	200	620J	EL	77586
BISCAYNE BLVD	300	619M	EL	77586
BISCAYNE CT	2200	568C	SG	77478
BISCAYNE BAY DR	0	612F	PL	77584
BISCAYNE BEND LN	600	658S	LC	77573
BISCAYNE HILL CT	20100	290Z	NWC	77379
BISCAYNE LAKE CT	0	612F	PL	77545
BISCAYNE LAKE DR	0	612F	PL	77545
BISCAYNE PASS LN	11800	376H	NEC	77346
BISCAYNE POND CT	0	485J	NEF	77494
BISCAYNE RIDGE LN	17000	367Y	NWC	77095
BISCAYNE SHOALS DR	16000	617T	SEC	77546
BISCAYNE SPRINGS LN	0	612P	PL	77545
BISCAYNE VALLEY LN	0	446A	NWC	77449
BISCAYNE WAY	11200	413X	NEH	77076
BISHOP	100	459V	HG	77562
BISHOP	300	493G	NEH	77009
BISHOP BEND LN	14100	573Z	SEC	77047
BISHOP BOBUIS DR	0	486C	SWC	77450
BISHOP KNOLL LN	16700	407Z	NWC	77084
BISHOP PLACE DR	1300	329G	NWC	77379
BISHOPS RD	23500	245Y	SWM	77447
BISHOPS BRIDGE	0	660K	LC	77573
BISHOPS GATE LN	19700	335N	NCC	77338
BISHOPS GLEN CT	5700	408W	NWC	77084
BISHOPS GLEN LN	15800	408W	NWC	77084
BISHOPS MANOR LN	1	369H	NWC	77070
BISHOPS MILL CT	21300	296X	SEM	77339
BISHOPS TERRACE	0	299S	NEC	77336
BISHOPS TERRACE DR	3600	299S	NEC	77336
BISHOPTON	3100	615C	PL	77581
BISHOPTON CIR	3300	615C	PL	77581
BISHOPVALE DR	800	413K	NCC	77037
BISHOP WAY DR	13400	528T	SWC	77083
BISLEY LN	8700	412K	NWC	77088
BISMARK	1600	493K	SWH	77007
BISON DR	700	488G	SWH	77079
BISON BACK DR	18400	377C	NEC	77346
BISONTINE	2100	617X	SEC	77546
BISSONNET	900	493W	SWH	77005
BISSONNET	1000	492Y	SWH	77005
BISSONNET	3700	532A	WU	77005
BISSONNET	4300	531H	BL	77401
BISSONNET	5400	531H	SWH	77081
BISSONNET	6300	530M	SWH	77074
BISSONNET	9500	529V	SWH	77036
BISSONNET	10300	529S	SWH	77099
BISSONNET	13200	528Q	SWC	77083
BISSONNET	14700	527T	NEF	77083
BISTRO LN	11500	529B	SWH	77082
BITON DR	7000	528F	SWC	77083
BITRIDGE CIR	15800	611D	SWH	77053
BITTERCREEK DR	1900	489P	SWH	77042
BITTERIDGE	0	408T	NWC	77084
BITTERNUT DR	5800	451A	NWH	77092
BITTERNUT HICKORY LN		289G	NWC	77375
BITTER ROOT CT	0	295L	SEM	77365
BITTER ROOT DR	20000	295M	SEM	77365
BITTERROOT RANCH DR	0	406U	NWC	77449
BITTERWOOD CIR	1	251J	WD	77381
BITTERWOOD CT	1	251J	WD	77381
BITTS CT	17300	379W	NEC	77532
BIVENS BEND	18400	330E	NWC	77379
BIVENS BROOK DR	2100	371V	NWC	77067
BIZERTE	100	453E	NWH	77022
BIZZELL LN		289D	NWC	77375
BJORN DR	0	571F	SWH	77085
BLACK	2800	534G	SEH	77023
BLACK LN	0	614S	PL	77584
BLACK ALDER LN	0	329L	NWC	77379
BLACKAMORE CIR	9600	409A	NWC	77065
BLACK BEAR	2100	252D	SEM	77385
BLACK BEAR	2200	253A	SEM	77385
BLACKBEAR DR	1400	378C	NEH	77532
BLACKBERRY CIR	3600	610X	MC	77459
BLACKBERRY DR	1100	537N	PA	77506
BLACKBERRY LN	26300	257R	SEM	77357
BLACKBERRY HOLLOW DR	1200	332R	NCC	77073
BLACKBERRY TRAIL LN	0	326Q	NWC	77429
BLACK BIRCH LN		289G	NWC	77375
BLACKBIRD DR	13300	368Q	NWC	77429
BLACKBIRD LN	7800	463S	CCO	77520
BLACKBLUFF CT	21100	446E	NWC	77449
BLACKBRISTLE LN	20900	290U	NWC	77379
BLACKBROOK LN	12800	408V	NWC	77041
BLACKBROOK LN	26700	484Y	NEF	77494
BLACKBURN	8300	535F	SEH	77012
BLACKBURN CT	6100	657U	LC	77573
BLACKBURN DR	1400	537W	PA	77502
BLACKBURN COVE CT	15100	327V	NWC	77429
BLACK CANYON DR	19800	526A	NEF	77450
BLACK CANYON LN	0	612L	PL	77545
BLACKCAP VIREO DR	0	366N	NWC	77433
BLACKCASTLE DR	3100	331P	NWC	77068
BLACK CHERRY	30000	249D	SWM	77354
BLACK CHERRY CT	1	251J	WD	77381
BLACKCHERRY LN	8000	463S	CCO	77520
BLACK CHERRY BEND CT	19800	326X	NWC	77433
BLACK CHERRY CROSSING	0	524D	NEF	77494
BLACKCLIFF LN	0	575U	SEH	77075
BLACK COVE DR	0	366K	NWC	77433
BLACK CRICKET CT	3600	376G	NEC	77396
BLACK DUCK DR	0	658T	LC	77573
BLACK EAGLE DR		484P	NEF	77494
BLACK FALCON CT	33100	322J	WCO	77484
BLACK FALCON RD	16000	322N	WCO	77484
BLACK FALLS CT	11000	527Z	NEF	77498
BLACK FALLS LN	15200	527Z	NEF	77498
BLACK FIN LN	7800	528M	SWH	77072
BLACKFOOT TRAIL RUN	13900	328P	NWC	77429
BLACK FOREST	0	250S	NWC	77389
BLACK FOREST CT	10200	252G	SEM	77385
BLACK FOREST DR	200	332B	NWC	77388
BLACK GAP DR	0	407J	NWC	77433
BLACKGATE DR	0	576L	SEH	77034
BLACK GOLD CT	2400	333S	NCC	77073
BLACK GUM DR	5800	411W	NWH	77092
BLACKGUM DR	22600	245Q	SWM	77447
BLACK HAW	1000	488C	NWH	77079
BLACK HAW	1100	448Y	NWH	77079
BLACKHAWK BLVD	9500	575V	SEH	77075
BLACKHAWK BLVD	9900	616E	SEC	77089
BLACKHAWK BLVD	15300	617W	FR	77546
BLACKHAWK BLVD	16400	657C	FR	77546

Street Name	Block	Pg/Sq	Loc	Zips
BLACKHAWK CIR	9300	575Z	SEH	77075
BLACKHAWK RIDGE LN	0	575Y	SEH	77075
BLACKHAWK TRAIL CT	3100	293U	NCC	77373
BLACK HEARTH TRAIL	0	325R	NWC	77433
BLACKHEATH CT	1300	485K	SWC	77494
BLACK HICKORY CT	20200	446T	NWC	77449
BLACK HORSE COVE	7900	609Z	MC	77459
BLACKHORSE TRAIL	26300	366H	NWC	77433
BLACKJACK CT	7800	411Q	NWH	77088
BLACKJACK LN	5500	411Q	NWH	77088
BLACK JACK LN	28000	249D	SWM	77354
N. BLACKJACK OAK CIR	11900	251U	WD	77380
S. BLACKJACK OAK CIR	12000	251U	WD	77380
BLACKJACK OAK PLACE	2500	251U	WD	77380
BLACK LAB LN	0	444F	NWC	77493
BLACKLAND PRAIRIE DR	0	366P	NWC	77433
BLACK LOCUST DR	3400	411U	NWH	77088
BLACKMAN	0	456M	NEC	77044
BLACK MAPLE LN	4300	411X	NWH	77088
BLACK MESA CT	4200	446E	NWC	77449
BLACK MESA RANCH LN	0	366V	NWC	77433
BLACK MOUNTAIN ASH CT		289G	NWC	77375
BLACK MOUNTAIN WAY	21700	445H	NWC	77449
BLACKMYRTLE DR	0	376S	NEC	77396
BLACK OAK CT	6200	578J	PA	77505
BLACK OAK DR	5800	451A	NWH	77092
BLACK OAK DR	7700	249C	SWM	77354
BLACK OPAL LN	0	296X	SEM	77339
BLACK OWL DR	0	333G	NCC	77338
BLACK PEARL CT	0	372D	NCC	77073
BLACK PINE CIR	0	328A	NWC	77377
BLACK POOL	8300	461P	NEC	77521
BLACKPOOL PLACE	12900	371F	NWC	77066
BLACKRAVEN	0	334N	NCC	77338
BLACKRIDGE RD	2400	371M	NWC	77067
BLACK ROCK	4700	461N	NEC	77521
BLACK ROCK LN	0	615L	PL	77581
BLACK ROCK RD	1	497C	NEC	77015
BLACK ROCK RD	300	457U	NEC	77015
BLACK ROSE TRAIL	17600	327N	NWC	77429
BLACK SANDS DR	10400	367Y	NWC	77095
BLACKSBURG CT	22100	485Y	NEF	77450
BLACKSHEAR	200	289E	TB	77375
BLACKSHEAR	3900	453J	NWH	77018
BLACKSHIRE LN	0	492A	NWH	77055
BLACK SKIMMER CT	2500	658T	LC	77573
BLACKSMITH CT	7500	410H	NWC	77064
BLACKSMITH DR	8300	410H	NWC	77064
BLACKSMITH'S LN	4000	609A	SG	77479
BLACK SPUR CT	0	526W	NEF	77469
BLACKSTOCK LN	13400	528Q	SWC	77083
BLACK STONE	4700	461N	NEC	77521
BLACKSTONE CT	12500	488M	SWH	77077
BLACKSTONE LN	0	253Q	SEM	77386
BLACKSTONE CREEK LN	6000	338E	NEH	77345
BLACKSTONE GATE LN	0	297K	NEH	77365
BLACKSTONE RIVER DR	0	377E	NEC	77346
BLACKSTONE TRAILS DR	0	376G	NEC	77396
BLACKSTONE TRAILS DR	0	376G	NEC	77396
BLACKSTONE VILLA LN	0	446E	NWC	77449
BLACKSTREAM CT	11400	366Q	NWC	77433
BLACK SWAN CT	0	249B	SWM	77354
BLACKTAIL CT	26800	324S	NWC	77447
BLACK TERN LN	0	411S	NWH	77040
BLACKTHORNE DR	1300	486G	SWC	77094
BLACKTIP DR	0	445R	NWC	77449
BLACK TOOTH WAY	9200	375R	NEC	77396
BLACK WALNUT DR	100	457Y	NEC	77015
BLACK WATER DR	21100	446C	NWC	77449
BLACKWATER LN	200	457Y	NEC	77015
S. BLACKWELL	100	536F	PA	77506
N. BLACKWELL	100	536F	PA	77506
BLACKWELL	100	540Z	LP	77571
BLACK WILLOW DR	22600	290E	NWC	77375
BLACKWOOD AVE	1100	373U	NCC	77032
BLACKWOOD BRIDGE LN	0	484Y	NEF	77494
BLADE BOROUGH CT	12000	616G	SEC	77089
BLADENBORO DR	14400	366D	CY	77429
BLADENBORO DR	14600	326Z	NWC	77429
BLADES	10300	415W	NEH	77016
BLADES	11200	415N	NEH	77016
BLADESDALE CT	1200	485K	SWC	77494
BLADESTONE LN	0	485U	NEF	77494
BLADON DR	0	376N	NEC	77396
BLADWIN SQUARE DR	0	488K	SWH	77077
BLAESSER DR	3200	613Z	NEB	77584
BLAFFER	0	500Z	BT	77520
BLAFFER	3900	454Z	NEH	77026
BLAHA	0	285T	NWC	77447
BLAINE LAKE DR	9800	411A	NWC	77086
BLAINE OAKS LN	0	253K	SEM	77386
BLAIR	1300	452Z	NWH	77008
BLAIR LN	100	336J	NEH	77339
BLAIR RD	300	252K	SEM	77385
BLAIR CROSSING	10000	252K	SEM	77385
BLAIRE CT	15900	408A	NWC	77095
BLAIR HILL LN	13500	417A	NEC	77044
BLAIR MANOR CT	2500	445Q	NWC	77449
BLAIR MANOR LN	22500	445Q	NWC	77449
BLAIR MEADOW DR	11600	529W	MD	77477
BLAIR MEADOW DR	12000	569A	MD	77477
BLAIRMONT LN	1300	618K	SEH	77062
BLAIRMORE CT	5400	486W	NEF	77450
BLAIR RIDGE DR	14100	367D	NWC	77429
BLAIRSTONE	0	407R	NWC	77084
BLAIRSTONE	16700	407Q	NWC	77084
BLAIRS WAY	100	249R	NWH	77375
BLAIRS WAY	100	249R	NWH	77375
BLAIRWOOD DR	16800	458B	NEC	77049
BLAISEFIELD CT	4900	484Z	NEF	77494
BLAKE	9900	527T	NEF	77498
BLAKE AVE	1400	537N	PA	77502
BLAKE CT	6800	614T	PL	77584
BLAKE RD	1900	568D	SG	77478
BLAKE BEND CIR	9100	408B	NWC	77095
BLAKELEY TRAILS CT	0	293F	SEM	77386
BLAKELEY TRAILS CT	0	293F	SEM	77386
BLAKELY GROVE LN	0	615R	PL	77581
BLAKE POINT LN	0	328F	NWC	77377
BLAKE VALLEY LN	18100	326V	NWC	77429
BLAKE WAY	15400	373R	NCC	77032
BLAKEWOOD CT	3400	331N	NWC	77068
BLANCH PINES CT	0	490G	HE	77024
N. BLALOCK	0	490F	HE	77024
BLALOCK CIR	1	490L	PP	77024
BLALOCK LN	11600	490P	BH	77024
BLALOCK RD	100	490P	PP	77024
BLALOCK RD	1100	450Y	NWH	77055
BLALOCK RD	1500	450Y	NWH	77080
BLALOCK RD	4300	450B	NWH	77041
BLALOCK FOREST	11600	490K	BH	77024
BLALOCK WOODS	1	490G	BH	77024

Street Name	Block	Pg/Sq	Loc	Zips
BLANCA SPRINGS	2800	337X	NEC	77346
BLANCA SPRINGS CT	8500	337X	NEC	77346
BLANCA TERRACE DR	0	376S	NEC	77396
BLANCHARD	13200	419V	BR	77532
BLANCHARD GROVE DR	26500	524E	NEF	77494
BLANCHARD HILL LN	800	572Q	SWH	77047
BLANCHARD PARK LN	0	366Y	NWC	77433
BLANCHARD SPRINGS DR	0	407D	NWC	77095
BLANCHE	200	494P	SEH	77011
BLANCHMONT LN	18200	619S	NB	77058
BLANCKE BLVD	0	579Q	SEC	77507
BLANCO	3200	490X	SWH	77063
BLANCO DR	5000	614Z	PL	77584
BLANCO ARBOR DR	0	526K	NEF	77407
W. BLANCO BEND DR		367W	NWC	77095
N. BLANCO BEND DR		367W	NWC	77095
BLANCO CREEK DR		289H	NWC	77375
BLANCO FALLS LN	13900	328S	NWC	77429
BLANCO HILLS LN	10400	367X	NWC	77095
BLANCO LAKE CT	19200	331B	NWC	77388
BLANCO PINES DR	6900	377C	NEC	77346
BLANCO RIDGE LN	0	526J	NEF	77407
BLANCO RIVER CT	0	253Y	SEM	77386
BLANCO TERRACE LN	0	409W	NWC	77041
BLANCO TRAILS LN	15700	328S	NWC	77429
BLANCROFT CT	100	568V	SG	77478
BLAND	1100	412W	NWH	77091
BLAND	4700	581W	PA	77586
BLAND	4700	621A	PA	77586
BLANDFORD LN	6900	451X	NWH	77055
BLANDING DR	600	497D	NEC	77015
BLAND MILLS LN	0	527W	NEF	77469
BLANE	24400	445W	NWC	77493
BLANEFIELD LN	0	289R	NWC	77375
BLANK	1400	496M	NEH	77015
BLANKENSHIP DR	7700	451N	NWH	77055
BLANKENSHIP DR	8400	450K	NWH	77080
BLANKET FLOWER CT	1	251B	WD	77381
BLANTON BLVD	4700	451H	NWH	77092
BLANTON LN	12700	528Y	SG	77478
BLANTON BROOK DR	0	406P	NWC	77433
BLANTON FOREST DR	0	377L	NEC	77346
BLANTYRE WAY	1300	336H	NEH	77339
BLARNEY DR	3700	573Q	SEH	77047
BLASS CT	0	457A	NEC	77044
BLAZEY CIR	7600	408L	NWC	77095
BLAZEY DR	13300	408L	NWC	77041
BLAZEY DR	14000	408L	NWC	77095
BLAZING GAP	7800	609Z	MC	77459
BLAZING STAR CT	1	251L	WD	77380
BLAZING STAR DR	0	539S	DP	77536
BLEKER	2000	494B	NEH	77026
BLEKER	6700	454K	NEH	77016
BLEND STONE	16800	407U	NWC	77084
BLENFIELD	22700	485U	NEF	77450
BLENHEIM DR	6900	330L	NWC	77379
BLENHEIM PALACE CT	14300	408Q	NWC	77095
BLENHEIM PALACE LN	7100	408Q	NWC	77095
BLENHEIM TERRACE LN	0	293H	SEM	77386
BLEVINS DR	17100	367X	NWC	77095
BLIGH	14200	572N	SWH	77045
BLINDLAKE DR	1700	446Z	NWC	77084
BLIND RIVER DR	4200	577E	PA	77504
BLINKIN AVE	100	419U	BR	77532
BLINKWOOD PARK	0	484J	KT	77494
BLINNWOOD LN	12500	369M	NWC	77070
BLISS	4500	535U	SEH	77017
BLISS CANYON CT	24900	485W	NEF	77494
BLISSFIELD LN	21300	486N	SWC	77450
BLISSFULL BRANCH BLVD	0	366V	NWC	77433
BLISSFULL HAVEN CT	0	366J	NWC	77433
BLISSFULL VALLEY LN	0	329F	NWC	77375
BLISS MEADOWS DR	3200	537Z	PA	77505
BLISS MEADOWS DR	3400	577D	PA	77505
BLISS STATION DR	0	373G	NCC	77073
BLISS TRAIL	6600	407Q	NWC	77084
BLISSWOOD DR	14000	377X	NEC	77044
BLISSWOOD DR	14000	377X	NEC	77044
BLITHE OAK CT	0	329B	NWC	77375
BLOCKER LN	1100	570X	MC	77489
BLODGETT	800	493X	SWH	77004
BLODGETT	2400	533C	SEH	77004
BLOECHERCREST LN	0	328M	NWC	77377
BLOOM DR	6800	413X	NEH	77076
BLOOMBURY LN	8600	370N	NWC	77064
BLOOMFIELD	3000	573B	SEH	77051
BLOOMFIELD DR	0	612P	PL	77545
BLOOMHILL PLACE	0	249B	SWM	77382
BLOOMINGDALE MANOR DR	14100	367D	NWC	77429
BLOOMING GARDEN CT	4400	658N	LC	77573
BLOOMING GROVE LN	1	488F	SWH	77077
BLOOMING IVY LN	9900	616K	SEC	77089
BLOOMING MEADOW LN	0	415X	NWH	77078
BLOOMING ORCHARD LN	0	485V	NEF	77450
BLOOMING PARK LN	1900	486J	SWC	77450
BLOOMING PEAR CT	20900	326N	NWC	77433
BLOOMING PLUM DR	0	366P	NWC	77433
BLOOMING ROCK LN	21400	290Q	NWC	77379
E. BLOOMING ROSE CT	17300	327P	NWC	77429
W. BLOOMING ROSE CT	17400	327P	NWC	77429
BLOOMING SAGE CT	6000	406Y	NWC	77449
BLOOMINGTON LN	11800	569B	MD	77477
BLOOM MEADOW TRAIL	16200	326N	NWC	77433
BLOOM MIST CT	0	528Q	SWC	77072
BLOOMRIDGE CIR	22700	485Y	NEF	77450
BLOOMS RISE DR	0	286Q	NWC	77377
BLOSSOM	0	659T	LC	77573
BLOSSOM	100	618X	WB	77598
BLOSSOM	3800	492L	SWH	77007
BLOSSOM	11900	418R	NEC	77044
BLOSSOM CT	3800	613Y	NEB	77584
BLOSSOM LN	0	460X	BT	77521
BLOSSOM BAY CT	2500	618C	SEH	77059
BLOSSOM BAY DR	15000	618C	SEH	77059
BLOSSOM BELL LN	8300	610G	SWH	77489
BLOSSOM BROOK LN	21800	525C	NEF	77450
BLOSSOMBURY CT	0	446A	NWC	77449
BLOSSOM CREEK CT	1600	336B	NEH	77339
BLOSSOM CREEK DR	2000	336B	NEH	77339
BLOSSOM CREEK TRAIL	2100	336B	NEH	77339
BLOSSOM CREST LN	0	293Z	NCC	77373
BLOSSOM FALLS	16200	406R	NWC	77449
BLOSSOM FIELD CT	0	457A	NEC	77044
BLOSSOM FIELD CT	16200	326N	NWC	77433
BLOSSOM GREEN LN	0	326N	NWC	77433
BLOSSOM GROVE LN	21700	290L	NWC	77379
BLOSSOMHEATH RD	12800	368E	NWC	77429
BLOSSOM LAKE CT	0	366R	NWC	77433
BLOSSOM LAKE CT	0	253P	SEM	77386
BLOSSOM MEADOW CT	22100	525G	NEF	77494
BLOSSOMMIST LN	7400	527J	NEF	77407
BLOSSOM WALK CT	0	612Q	PL	77584

Street Name	Block	Pg/Sq	Loc	Zips
BLOSSOM WALK LN	12600	409S	NWC	77041
BLOSSOMWOOD DR	300	658N	LC	77573
BLOUNT	1600	453W	NWH	77008
BLUE	7900	455P	NEH	77028
BLUE AARON CT	0	325M	NWC	77429
BLUE AGAVE WAY	0	329C	NWC	77379
BLUE ASH DR	14100	372C	NWC	77090
BLUE ASH DR	15200	332X	NWC	77090
BLUEBANK LN	0	485X	NEF	77494
BLUE BEECH DR	20300	446S	NWC	77449
BLUE BELL	100	459M	HG	77562
BLUE BELL RD	100	412H	NCC	77037
BLUE BELL RD	700	412G	NWC	77038
BLUEBERRY	100	452M	NWH	77018
BLUEBERRY LN	1200	656L	FR	77546
BLUEBERRY LN	2100	537S	PA	77502
BLUEBERRY LN	8800	458A	NEC	77049
BLUEBERRY CEDAR DR	0	366N	NWC	77433
BLUEBERRY HILL CT	15800	448A	NWC	77084
BLUEBERRY HILL DR	4700	448B	NWC	77084
BLUEBERRY HILL DR	5300	408W	NWC	77084
BLUEBERRY HILL DR	19900	252K	SEM	77385
S. BLUEBILL BAY	100	542P	BT	77520
N. BLUEBILL BAY	100	542P	BT	77520
BLUE BIRD	9800	539T	LP	77571
BLUEBIRD	20900	286N	NWC	77447
BLUEBIRD	31600	248S	SWM	77362
BLUEBIRD LN	100	536U	PA	77502
BLUE BIRD LN	14000	489E	SWH	77079
W. BLUEBIRD LN	18000	286M	NWC	77377
BLUEBIRD RD	0	455G	NEH	77028
BLUEBIRD BEND	7300	375K	HM	77396
BLUEBIRD PARK LN	0	333F	NCC	77338
BLUEBIRD PARK LN	0	333F	NCC	77338
BLUEBIRD PLACE	10000	252L	SEM	77385
BLUEBIRD WAY	3200	614X	PL	77584
BLUE BONNET	0	619H	TL	77586
BLUEBONNET	100	568S	SG	77478
BLUE BONNET	800	444X	KT	77493
BLUEBONNET	2700	619U	LC	77565
BLUEBONNET	3100	537Y	PA	77505
BLUEBONNET	3300	577C	PA	77505
BLUEBONNET	8500	460P	NEC	77562
BLUEBONNET BLVD	2200	532L	SWH	77030
BLUEBONNET BLVD	3000	532J	SWH	77025
BLUEBONNET DR	3500	612A	SWC	77053
BLUEBONNET DR	3900	569F	SF	77477
BLUE BONNET DR	4500	611D	SWH	77053
BLUEBONNET LN	23900	243T	WCO	77484
BLUEBONNET BEND	14100	328N	NWC	77429
BLUEBONNET DALE DR	15500	326S	NWC	77433
BLUEBONNET MEADOW LN	21400	291Q	NWC	77388
BLUEBONNET MEADOWS LN	3200	447J	NWC	77084
BLUEBONNET PLACE CIR	8000	493K	SWH	77019
BLUEBONNET POND LN	6100	338B	NEH	77345
BLUE BONNET RUN CT	7500	407M	NWC	77095
BLUEBONNET TRACE DR	0	293C	SEM	77386
BLUEBONNET TRAIL	3900	539S	DP	77536
BLUE BOTTLE LN	6700	407T	NWC	77449
BLUE BUNGALOW DR	0	250R	NWC	77389
BLUE CANDLE DR	3400	331C	NWC	77388
BLUE CANOE CT	0	620K	SB	77586
BLUE CANYON DR	22500	485Q	NEF	77450
BLUE CASTLE CT	100	457X	NEC	77015
BLUE CASTLE LN	200	457X	NEC	77015
BLUE CEDAR	0	294J	SEM	77386
BLUE CEDAR CT	4400	294N	SEM	77386
BLUE CEDAR LN	0	294N	SEM	77386
BLUE CEDAR LN	0	335P	NCC	77338
BLUE COVE CT	0	406D	NWC	77433
BLUE COVE LN	0	366K	NWC	77433
BLUE CREEK DR	0	612L	PL	77584
BLUE CREEK DR	2600	613W	NEB	77578
BLUE CREEK DR	5100	297Y	NEH	77345
BLUE CREEK RANCH DR	15000	370Z	NWC	77086
BLUECREEK RIDGE LN	0	406Y	NWC	77449
BLUE CREST DR	0	296E	SEM	77365
BLUECREST LN	5000	485W	NEF	77494
BLUE CROMIS LN	0	572E	SWH	77045
BLUE CRULS WAY	9700	329C	NWC	77379
BLUE CYPRESS CT	0	657Z	LC	77573
BLUE CYPRESS DR	3400	331G	NWC	77388
BLUE CYPRESS LN	0	657Z	LC	77573
BLUE DAWN DR	2900	446T	NWC	77449
BLUE DIAMOND DR	1100	570X	MC	77489
BLUE DOLPHIN	0	620P	SB	77586
BLUE DUSK DR	0	326N	NWC	77433
BLUE EGRET DR	0	325Q	NWC	77433
BLUE FALLS DR	13900	528W	NEF	77498
BLUE FEATHER DR	11000	370S	NWC	77064
BLUEFIELD DR	3300	537Q	PA	77503
BLUEFIELD LN	0	406X	NWC	77449
BLUEFIELD LN	18100	526H	NEF	77407
BLUEFIN	16500	419B	NEC	77532
BLUE FOREST DR	4100	376H	NEC	77396
BLUE FOVANT CT	0	291Z	NWC	77388
BLUE FOX CT	1	251V	WD	77380
BLUE FOX RD	1	251V	WD	77380
BLUE GAMA DR	11400	367R	NWC	77095
BLUE GAP	0	609Z	NEF	77459
BLUEGATE	8400	532P	SWH	77025
BLUEGATE CT	8400	532Q	SWH	77025
BLUE GILL DR	0	366S	NWC	77433
BLUE GLADE DR	0	525U	NEF	77469
BLUE GLADE DR	0	525U	NEF	77469
BLUE GLEN DR	2700	333T	NCC	77073
BLUEGRASS	4100	452M	NWH	77018
BLUEGRASS CT	2900	609F	MC	77459
BLUEGRASS LN	13700	417T	NEC	77044
BLUEGRASS ST	0	452R	NWH	77018
BLUE HAVEN	12700	414G	NCC	77039
BLUEHAW MEADOW LN	8700	524D	NEF	77494
BLUE HEATHER CT	0	445R	NWC	77449
BLUE HERON	100	657K	FR	77546
BLUE HERON	10400	574G	SEH	77048
BLUE HERON DR	0	656B	PL	77581
BLUE HERON RUN DR	0	291H	NWC	77389
BLUE HILL LN	0	328F	NWC	77429
BLUE HILLS DR	3100	610F	MC	77459
BLUE HILLS RD	6500	370B	NWC	77069
BLUE HOLLOW HEIGHTS DR	18400	366P	NWC	77433
W. BLUE HYACINTH DR	0	326J	NWC	77433
S. BLUE HYACINTH DR	0	326J	NWC	77433
N. BLUE HYACINTH DR	11900	326J	NWC	77433
BLUE IRIS TRAIL	0	488G	SWH	77079
BLUE ISLAND DR	11900	456C	NEC	77044
BLUE JACK LN	28000	249C	SWM	77354
BLUE JASMINE	0	578U	SEH	77059
BLUE JASMINE CT	4000	578Y	SEH	77059
BLUE JAY	6300	574R	SEH	77048
BLUE JAY	7400	575N	SEH	77075
BLUE JAY CIR	2700	375L	HM	77396

Street Name	Block	Pg/Sq	Loc	Zips
BLUE JAY LN	8000	463S	CCO	77520
BLUE JAY LN	25100	295Q	SEM	77365
BLUE JAY LN	31600	248S	SWM	77362
BLUE JAY LN		484P	NEF	77494
BLUEJAY TRAILS CT	0	324M	NWC	77447
BLUEJAY TRAILS CT	0	324M	NWC	77447
BLUEJAY TWIN CIR	7700	375Q	NEC	77396
BLUE JUNIPER DR	20200	446T	NWC	77449
BLUE LAGOON CT	0	610T	MC	77459
BLUE LAGOON DR	0	456C	NEC	77044
BLUE LAKE	3500	331C	NWC	77388
BLUE LAKE CT	0	298B	NEC	77336
BLUE LAKE DR	1	298G	NEC	77336
BLUE LAKE DR	3100	336Q	NEH	77338
BLUE LAKE CREEK TRAIL	0	524A	NEF	77494
BLUE LAKES LN	2900	609H	MC	77459
BLUE LAKE VIEW LN	0	335P	NCC	77338
BLUE LILY LN	0	367W	NWC	77095
BLUE MARLIN LN	13500	528K	SWC	77083
BLUE MEADOW LN	3500	414J	NCC	77039
BLUE MESA RIDGE DR	15000	617T	SEC	77546
BLUEMIST	0	496G	NEH	77013
BLUE MIST CT	0	446N	NWC	77449
BLUE MIST CT	19900	335N	NCC	77338
BLUE MORNING DR	15200	370Y	NWC	77086
BLUE MOUND TERRACE	17200	367U	NWC	77095
BLUE MOUNTAIN DR	12000	371L	NWC	77067
BLUE NILE DR	0	326K	NWC	77433
BLUE NORTHER DR	0	249Q	NWC	77375
BLUE OAK DR	10300	368Y	NWC	77065
BLUE OPAL LN	0	524G	NEF	77494
BLUE ORCHID CT	13700	417A	NEC	77044
BLUE PEARL DR		526S	NEF	77407
BLUE PINE CIR	0	326Q	NWC	77429
BLUE POINT RD	200	620T	CS	77565
BLUE POINT JUNIPER DR	0	575R	SEH	77075
BLUE PRATO CT	0	445F	NWC	77493
BLUE QUAIL DR	1800	657N	FR	77546
BLUE QUAIL DR	8300	610C	SWH	77489
BLUE REEF DR	0	445R	NWC	77449
BLUERIDGE	1500	536P	PA	77502
BLUE RIDGE DR	200	252A	SD	77381
BLUE RIDGE DR	400	251D	SD	77381
BLUE RIDGE DR	1300	252G	SEM	77385
BLUE RIDGE DR	7200	534V	SEH	77087
BLUERIDGE RD	2300	611N	FS	77545
BLUE RIDGE RD	3000	610G	NEF	77489
BLUE RIDGE RD	12700	571N	SWH	77085
BLUE RIDGE RD	15000	571W	SWH	77489
BLUE RIDGE RD	16100	611A	SWH	77489
BLUE RIDGE GRACE WAY	0	616L	SEC	77089
BLUE RIDGE PARK LN	30900	253N	SEM	77386
BLUE RIDGE SUNSET CT	0	616L	SEC	77089
BLUE RIVER DR	12200	415J	NEH	77050
BLUE RIVER BIRCH LN	0	289C	NWC	77375
BLUEROCK	2400	414A	NCC	77039
BLUE ROCK CT	700	413B	NCC	77060
BLUE ROCK SPRINGS DR	16300	332R	NCC	77073
BLUE ROSE CIR	4600	609B	MC	77459
BLUE ROSE DR	2200	569X	MC	77459
BLUE ROSE DR	2400	609B	MC	77459
BLUE SAGE DR	1800	484L	NEF	77494
BLUE SAGE DR	4900	614S	NEB	77584
BLUE SAGE TERRACE	4200	331B	NWC	77388
BLUE SHADOW DR	2400	291R	NWC	77388
BLUE SKY	2800	411R	NWH	77088
BLUES POINT DR	0	327W	NWC	77429
BLUE SPRING DR	3800	331S	NWC	77068
BLUE SPRING WAY	0	330H	NWC	77379
BLUE SPRING WAY	0	330H	NWC	77379
BLUE SPRUCE	11900	370R	NWC	77066
BLUE SPRUCE LN	0	339P	HU	77336
BLUE SPRUCE HILL ST	0	376D	NEC	77346
BLUE SPRUCE HILL ST	0	377A	NEC	77346
BLUE SPRUCE TRAIL	0	615Y	PL	77581
BLUE SPRUCE VALE WAY	12400	617E	SEH	77089
BLUESTEM	0	572E	SWH	77045
BLUESTEM DR	0	411R	NWH	77088
BLUESTEM RIDGE CT	0	445E	NWC	77493
BLUESTONE CT	4100	569Y	MC	77459
BLUESTONE DR	1100	569Y	MC	77459
BLUESTONE DR	6300	415S	NEH	77016
BLUESTONE CANYON DR	0	524K	NWF	77406
BLUESTONE HOLLOW LN	18900	328F	NWC	77377
BLUESTONE SPRINGS LN	0	290U	NWC	77379
BLUE SWALLOW DR	13300	370Z	NWC	77086
BLUE SWALLOW DR	13500	370V	NWC	77086
BLUESWIFT DR	0	406Q	NWC	77433
BLUE TAIL DR	300	338L	NEH	77336
BLUE THISTLE DR	15100	325R	NWC	77433
BLUE TIMBER CT	0	416Z	NEC	77044
BLUE TOPAZ DR	0	525V	NEF	77406
BLUE VANGA LN	0	328Q	NWC	77433
BLUE VANGA LN	0	328B	NWC	77377
BLUE VERVAIN DR	0	293G	SEM	77386
BLUE VIOLET CT	100	249R	NWH	77375
BLUE VIOLET CT	100	249R	NWH	77375
BLUE VISTA CT	2200	568A	NEF	77498
BLUE VISTA DR	13700	568A	NEF	77498
BLUE VISTA DR	16600	367Q	NWC	77095
BLUE WAHOO LN	0	407K	NWC	77433
BLUE WATER CT	4200	578F	PA	77505
BLUEWATER DR	4100	569U	MC	77459
BLUE WATER LN	2300	451H	NWH	77018
BLUEWATER BAY DR	0	484H	NEF	77494
BLUE WATER BAY DR	1800	485J	NEF	77494
BLUEWATER COVE DR	18200	377D	NEC	77346
BLUEWATER WAY	0	337L	NEC	77346
BLUE WATER WAY	100	619V	LC	77565
BLUE WILDFLOWER PLACE	0	249A	SWM	77354
BLUE WILLOW DR	100	489U	SWH	77042
BLUE WIND CT	2700	447P	NWC	77084
BLUFF CT	26800	295Y	SEM	77365
BLUFF CANYON WAY	19700	526B	NEF	77450
BLUFF CREEK DR	2100	337C	NEH	77345
BLUFFDALE DR	15900	448A	NWC	77084
BLUFF HAVEN LN	0	366J	NWC	77433
BLUFF MEADOW	0	293G	SEM	77386
BLUFF OAK DR	0	450U	NWH	77080
BLUFF PARK CT	0	327U	NWC	77429
BLUFF POINT DR	7600	371S	NWC	77086
BLUFF POINT DR	7700	370V	NWC	77086
BLUFFRIDGE CIR	14800	408P	NWC	77095
BLUFF SPRINGS DR	16400	367Z	NWC	77095
BLUFFSTONE CT	0	609Q	MC	77459
BLUFFTON LN	2100	486J	SWC	77450
BLUFF TRAIL DR	7800	334R	NCC	77338
BLUFFVIEW DR	18400	378S	NEC	77532
BLUFF VIEW COVE LN	0	293G	SEM	77386
BLUMA RANCH DR	25100	485N	NEF	77494
BLUME AVE	10200	577Y	SEH	77034
BLUNDELL DR	18000	331F	NWC	77388

Street Name	Block	Pg/Sq	Loc	Zips
BLUSHDAWN SIERRA CT	0	406R	NEF	77433
BLUSHING MEADOWS DR	0	366J	NWC	77433
BLUSHING PEAR CT	0	407U	NWC	77084
BLYTHE	13000	497E	NEH	77015
BLYTHEWOOD	5300	534E	SEH	77021
BOARDWALK LN	10700	489Q	SWH	77042
BOARDWALK PKWY	100	569P	SF	77477
BOATBILL LN	0	328A	NWC	77429
BOATER'S CROSSING DR	0	444J	KT	77493
BOAT HOOK	17500	379T	NEC	77532
BOATSWAIN CT	15900	419F	NEC	77532
BOB	300	494T	SEH	77011
BOB	400	536V	PA	77502
BOB LN	0	256K	SEM	77357
BOBBIE	3200	411C	NWC	77086
BOBBITT LN	7500	451X	NWH	77055
BOBBITT HEIGHTS LN	0	451X	NWH	77055
BOBBITT MANOR	0	451X	NWH	77055
BOBBY	0	257A	SEM	77357
BOBBY	1100	615B	PL	77581
BOBBY	11301	249W	NWC	77375
BOBBY LN	20100	254M	SEM	77365
BOBBY BURNS	5400	455P	NEH	77028
BOBBY JACK LN	0	410K	NWC	77040
BOBBY JONES RD		484N	NEF	77494
BOBBY LEE LN	1800	534H	SEH	77087
BOBCAT DR	11400	369U	NWC	77064
BOBCAT LN	31900	246T	SWM	77355
BOBCAT PATH CT	0	372M	NCC	77073
BOBCAT TRAIL	16500	327F	NWC	77429
BOB LINK	1	245P	SWM	77355
BOBOLINK	5400	536N	SEH	77017
BOBOLINK CIR	4300	609F	MC	77459
BOBOLINK CIR	22600	286M	NWC	77377
BOB SMITH RD	100	501R	BT	77521
BOB SMITH RD	1500	502N	BT	77521
BOB WHITE	2200	253E	SEM	77385
BOB WHITE DR	1100	657N	FR	77546
BOB WHITE DR	8100	530M	SWH	77074
BOB WHITE DR	9400	530V	SWH	77096
BOB WHITE DR	11400	570H	SWH	77035
BOB WHITE LN	1200	444Z	KT	77493
BOCA CT	3600	610J	MC	77459
BOCA CT	10300	528V	SWH	77099
BOCA CHICA LN	0	447J	NWC	77084
BOCA GRANDE LN	0	377M	NEC	77346
BOCA RATON	0	619V	LC	77565
BOCA RATON DR	3300	610J	MC	77459
BOCA RATON DR	13100	370B	NWC	77069
BOCEPHUS	11100	529B	SWH	77082
BODART CIR	1600	331R	NWC	77090
BODART CT	1600	331R	NWC	77090
BODART DR	1400	331R	NWC	77090
BODEGA BAY DR	16300	611B	SWH	77053
BODEN	2100	659G	LC	77573
BODEN LN	3900	293H	SEM	77386
BODINE DR	3200	613Z	NEB	77584
BOENEMAN DR	700	412U	NWH	77091
BOERNE CANYON LN	13600	328S	NWC	77429
BOERNE COUNTRY DR	0	328N	NWC	77429
BOERNE CREEK DR	7300	525M	NEF	77407
BOGAN FLATS CT	16400	367R	NWC	77095
BOGAN FLATS DR	11400	367R	NWC	77095
BOGARD CT	0	568W	SG	77479
BOGART	0	322P	WCO	77484
BOGDEN LN	8600	410E	NWC	77040
BOGDEN VILLAGE CIR	3900	446L	NWC	77449
BOGEY CIR	0	580K	LP	77571
BOGEY WAY	11700	616K	SEC	77089
BOGGESS RD	7200	415W	NEH	77016
BOGIE LN	0	322P	WCO	77484
BOGIE WAY	0	577H	PA	77505
BOGOTA DR	3800	578A	PA	77505
BOGS CT	11700	249S	NWC	77375
BOGS RD	11300	249S	NWC	77375
BOHEME DR	12100	490E	SWH	77024
BOHEME DR	13000	489L	SWH	77079
BOHEMIAN HALL RD	13000	420B	NEC	77532
BOHEMIAN HALL RD	16400	380X	NEC	77532
BOHLSSEN RD	31500	258U	NEC	77357
BOHNHOF STRASSE	16300	329Q	NWC	77070
BOICEWOOD	4500	454G	NEH	77016
BOIS D'ARC	2300	282U	WL	77484
BOIS D'ARC	5900	534V	SEH	77087
BOIS D'ARC	10600	539Q	LP	77571
BOIS D'ARC LN	7300	462Y	BT	77521
BOISE	0	500N	BT	77520
BOISE	13400	497F	NEH	77015
BOIX MANOR LN	21500	296J	SEM	77365
BO JACK DR	8100	410K	NWC	77040
BOLDEN	100	495V	NEH	77029
BOLDERE LN	14700	457P	NEC	77049
BOLD FOREST DR	8600	411K	NWC	77088
BOLD RIVER RD	0	329B	NWC	77375
BOLD RULER DR	600	570S	SF	77477
BOLERO CT	11700	528Z	MD	77477
BOLERO DR	7000	459K	NEC	77049
BOLERO POINT CIR	5800	449A	NWC	77041
BOLERO POINT CT	5700	449A	NWC	77041
BOLERO POINT LN	5700	409W	NWC	77041
BOLERO POINT LN	12000	449A	NWC	77041
BOLES	300	495W	SEH	77011
BOLIN RD	3500	451P	NWH	77092
BOLINAS CT	23800	293C	SEM	77386
BOLINGTON DR	8600	528P	SWC	77083
BOLIN POINT LN	0	446K	NWC	77449
BOLIVAR	500	531G	BL	77401
BOLIVAR POINT LN	0	657N	FR	77546
BOLIVIA	3900	577B	PA	77504
BOLIVIA BLVD	3700	451L	NWH	77092
BOLIVIA BLVD	5100	451C	NWH	77091
BOLLARD DR	16000	419A	NEC	77532
BOLLA RIDGE	0	286D	SWM	77355
BOLLING LN	700	453B	NEH	77076
BOLLINGBROOK DR	9200	528U	SWC	77083
BOLLINGER CT	24200	485T	NEF	77494
BOLSA CHICA LN	6300	408U	NWC	77041
BOLSOVER	1700	532D	SWH	77005
BOLSOVER SKY CT	0	446E	NWC	77449
BOLSTER	100	541B	BT	77520
BOLT	3000	573B	SEH	77051
BOLTE TIMBERS LN	0	328M	NWC	77377
BOLTON CT	900	288D	TB	77375
BOLTON DR	0	657T	LC	77573
BOLTON DR	900	570P	MC	77489
BOLTON BRIDGE LN	19700	335S	NCC	77338
BOLTON GARDENS CT	11500	371Q	NWC	77066
BOLTON GARDENS DR	3200	371Q	NWC	77066
BOLTON PLACE	500	491H	SWH	77024
BOLTON TRAILS LN	0	484Y	NEF	77494
BOMAR	300	493N	SWH	77006
BOMBAY	3500	453N	NWH	77022

Street Name	Block	Pg/Sq	Loc	Zips
BOMBAY	16900	373K	NCC	77032
BOMFORD AVE	14800	497M	NEC	77015
BOMOSEEN LAKE RD	0	377G	NEH	77346
BONAIRE	7700	455T	NEH	77028
BONAIRE CALLE	0	660S	GCO	77539
BONANN DR	10100	329P	NWC	77070
BONANZA RD	700	618Q	SEH	77062
BONAPARTE DR	11200	368N	NWC	77429
BONAVENTURE DR	13700	368P	NWC	77065
BONAVENTURE WAY	0	568S	SG	77479
BONAZZI BLVD	9800	411R	NWH	77088
BOND	3000	537G	PA	77503
BOND	4300	494B	NEH	77026
BOND	8200	410U	NWC	77040
BONDALE	8400	410U	NWC	77040
BONDI CT	600	486D	SWC	77094
BONDS CREEK LN	0	291X	NWC	77388
BONERWOOD	0	610D	SWH	77489
BONESS RD	5800	374M	NEH	77396
BONESS RD	6000	375J	NEH	77396
BONGODERO DR	0	487Z	SWC	77082
BONHAM	0	500V	BT	77520
BONHAM	6900	494H	NEH	77020
BONHAM	7100	495E	NEH	77020
BONHAM	13700	497F	NEC	77015
BONHAMFORD CT	0	375Z	NEC	77396
BONHAM LAKES LN	0	376S	NEC	77396
BONHAM OAKS CT	18200	526M	NEF	77407
BONHAM OAKS LN	0	573Y	SEC	77047
BONHAM PARK LN	0	335J	NCC	77338
BONHAM PINES LN	0	660J	LC	77573
BONHAM SPRINGS TRAIL	0	366Z	NWC	77433
BONHILL CT	8300	330T	NWC	77379
BONHOMME RD	5600	530C	SWH	77036
BONHOMME RD	8100	530Q	SWH	77074
BONILLA LN	13500	528K	SWC	77083
BONITA	6700	454K	NEH	77016
BONITA LN	3800	580V	LP	77571
BONITA CREEK	0	609Z	NEF	77459
BONITA SPRINGS DR	15300	527H	SWC	77083
BONITA WAY	0	660F	LC	77573
BONITA WAY	2200	542A	BT	77520
BONITO LN	0	659Z	DI	77539
BONNABELL LN	0	369G	NWC	77077
BONNAMERE LN	23900	485T	NEF	77494
BONNARD CIR	17200	330K	NWC	77379
BONNEBRIDGE WAY BLVD	3000	489X	SWH	77082
BONNEBRIDGE WAY BLVD	3400	529A	SWH	77042
BONN ECHO LN	6000	535Z	SEH	77017
E. BONNER	1000	492H	SWH	77007
BONNER	3000	580Q	LP	77571
BONNER	10800	449Y	NWH	77043
BONNER DR	1000	492H	SWH	77007
BONNER DR	8000	535Q	SEH	77017
BONNERCREST DR	13900	528T	NEF	77083
BONNERS PARK CIR	0	407W	NWC	77449
BONNERS PARK CT	0	407W	NWC	77449
BONNER VIEW LN	0	492H	SWH	77007
BONNETBRIAR LN	0	528T	NEF	77083
BONNET CREEK DR	0	407C	NWC	77095
BONNETTE	500	288N	NWC	77377
BONNEY BRIAR DR	3000	609H	MC	77459
BONNEY BRIER DR	14100	330X	NWC	77069
BONNEYBROOK CT	0	292B	NCC	77373
W. BONNEYMEAD CIR	1	250C	WD	77381
S. BONNEYMEAD CIR	1	250C	WD	77381
E. BONNEYMEAD CIR	1	250C	WD	77381
BONNEYWOOD LN	12700	368J	NWC	77429
BONNIE	400	536X	SH	77587
BONNIE LN	12800	570J	SF	77477
BONNIE BAY CT	400	657Y	LC	77573
BONNIE BRAE	1200	493W	SWH	77006
BONNIE BRAE	1500	492Z	SWH	77006
BONNIE CHASE	6300	407S	NWC	77449
BONNIEDOON	0	657A	FR	77546
BONNIE DOON	800	656D	FR	77546
BONNIEFIELD LN	1100	488K	SWH	77077
BONNIE GLEN	900	336K	NEH	77339
BONNIE PARK CT	15500	331N	NWC	77068
BONNIE SEAN DR	16700	329R	NWC	77379
BONNIEVILLE DR	1300	460N	HG	77562
BONNINGTON DR	13900	617B	SEH	77034
BONNO PLACE	1700	494E	NEH	77020
BONNY DALE	5100	531C	SWH	77081
BONNY LOCH LN	4800	447C	NWC	77084
BONNY RIDGE CT	16600	611H	SWH	77053
BONNYTON LN	1600	332W	NWC	77014
BONNYVIEW DR	8800	408A	NWC	77095
BONOVER	1800	492H	NWH	77007
BONSRELL	5500	534C	SEH	77023
BONTURA	16200	367G	CY	77429
BONWAY DR	13500	572K	SWH	77045
BOOKER	100	292L	SP	77373
BOOKER	100	502G	BT	77520
BOOKER	7700	455T	NEH	77028
BOOKER T	1000	494F	NEH	77020
BOOKERTEE	1100	541B	BT	77520
BOOKREN CT	4500	613V	NEB	77584
BOOM DR	15900	419F	NEC	77532
BOONE	0	577X	SEH	77034
BOONE	2500	494A	NEH	77026
BOONE CT	400	538Y	DP	77536
BOONE RD	4000	529B	SWH	77072
BOONE RD	8500	529P	SWH	77099
BOONE LOOP RD	9500	529T	SWH	77099
BOONE MEADOWS	0	408B	NWC	77095
BOONES COVE CT	0	377F	NEC	77346
BOONRIDGE RD	15700	571Z	SWH	77053
BOONWAY DR	13400	572K	SWH	77045
BOOTH	700	493C	NEH	77009
BOOTH	15000	611D	SEF	77053
BOOTH	15000	612A	NEF	77053
BOOTH BAY CT	800	660E	LC	77573
BOOTH BAY LN	1600	619W	NB	77058
BOOT HILL RD	15900	246M	SC	77355
BOOT RIDGE RD	16100	611D	SWH	77053
BOOTS RD	5400	452C	NWH	77091
BOQUILLAS CANYON DR	19200	328C	NWC	77377
BORAGE ST	0	419C	NEC	77532
BORAH PEAK WAY	21500	445H	NWC	77449
BORAX BEND CT		526S	NEF	77469
BORDACE CT	0	290P	NWC	77379
BORDEN	600	568T	SG	77478
BORDEN	8900	495U	NEH	77029
BORDEN BLUFF LN	0	407B	NWC	77095
BORDEN MANOR DR	0	331R	NWC	77090
BORDEN MILL RD	0	366K	NWC	77433
BORDEN SHORE CIR	0	366K	NWC	77433
BORDER	13900	573V	SEH	77048
BORDER	26500	292L	SP	77373
BORDER LAKE LN	0	377H	NEH	77346
BORDERS DR	19300	335T	NEH	77338

Street Name	Block	Pg/Sq	Loc	Zips
BORDERWOOD DR	11600	496B	NEH	77013
BORDLEY DR	5300	491P	SWH	77056
BORDLEY DR	6100	491N	SWH	77057
BORDLEY DR	9900	489Q	SWH	77042
BOREAS DR	12300	414G	NCC	77039
BORG DR	2300	535L	SEH	77017
BORG BREAKPOINT DR	6200	331N	NWC	77379
BORGESTEDT CEM RD	14000	368K	NWC	77429
BORIDGE CIR	15800	611D	SWH	77053
BORIS COVE TRAIL	0	572R	SWH	77047
BORNISH HILL CT	0	377K	NEC	77346
BOROS DR	900	491A	HC	77024
BOROUGH LN	17400	330K	NWC	77379
BOROUGH PARK DR	24500	252S	SWM	77380
BOSC DR	0	615F	PL	77581
BOSLEY LN	6400	408S	NWC	77084
BOSPHORUS ST	0	377D	NEC	77346
BOSQUE	5500	491T	SWH	77056
BOSQUE RIVER CT	0	253Y	SEM	77386
BOSQUE RIVER DR	0	367S	NWC	77433
BOSS GASTON RD	15500	527U	NEF	77498
BOSSINGHAM LN	0	457V	NEC	77049
BOSSUT DR	0	525L	NEF	77407
BOSTIC	1700	453H	NEH	77093
BOSTIC	4700	454F	NEH	77016
BOSTON	800	538K	DP	77536
BOSTON	2600	493P	SWH	77006
BOSTON GREEN WAY	0	537V	PA	77503
BOSTON POST RD	16500	367B	CY	77429
BOSWELL	1100	453Z	NEH	77009
BOSWORTH	5100	535R	SEH	77017
BOTANICAL VISTA DR	0	249V	NWC	77375
BOTANY LN	3700	573L	SEH	77047
BOTANY LN	5300	574J	SEH	77048
BOTANY LN	8000	575K	SEH	77075
BOTANY BAY LN	19700	486Q	SWC	77450
BOTHWELL	11300	490G	PP	77024
BOTKINS RD	23000	285W	NWC	77447
BOTKINS RD	24100	284Z	NWC	77447
BOTTIGLIA WAY	0	659R	LC	77573
BOTTLEBRUSH CT	11200	367U	NWC	77095
BOTTLEBRUSH LN	11400	367U	NWC	77095
BOTWOOD	0	457V	NEC	77530
BOUDREAUX CIR	25800	288Y	NWC	77377
BOUDREAUX RD	6800	290K	NWC	77375
BOUDREAUX RD	8900	289V	NWC	77375
BOUDREAUX RD	12000	288Z	NWC	77375
BOUDREAUX RD	13900	328A	NWC	77377
BOUDREAUX RD	15900	327D	NWC	77429
BOUDREAUX ESTATES DR	13200	288X	NWC	77377
BOUGAINVILLA LN	15700	617W	FR	77546
BOUGAINVILLA LN	16900	657B	FR	77546
BOUGAINVILLA BLOSSOM LN	20500	326N	NWC	77433
BOUGANVILLEA	0	255Y	SEM	77365
BOUGH CT	5600	451B	NWH	77092
BOUGH GLEN	0	618A	SEH	77062
BOUGH KNOLL CT	0	328N	NWC	77429
BOUGHTON LN	0	376N	NEC	77396
BOULDER	1200	535G	SEH	77012
BOULDER DR	4100	614Z	PL	77584
BOULDER BAY LN	0	338W	NEC	77346
BOULDER BEND LN	0	485W	NEF	77494
BOULDER BEND LN	0	658Z	LC	77573
BOULDER BLUFF DR	700	332V	NCC	77073
W. BOULDER CLIFF LN	0	375X	NEC	77396
S. BOULDER CLIFF LN	0	375X	NEC	77396
E. BOULDER CLIFF LN	0	375X	NEC	77396
BOULDER CLIFF LN	0	253N	SEM	77386
BOULDER COVE CT	26500	484T	NEF	77494
BOULDER CREEK CT	0	612L	PL	77584
BOULDER CREEK DR	0	612L	PL	77584
BOULDER CREEK DR	2900	296Y	NEH	77339
BOULDERCREST DR	1400	618E	SEH	77062
BOULDER FALLS CT	14000	617D	SEH	77062
BOULDER FIELD LN	0	417A	NEC	77044
BOULDER HILL LN	0	484S	NEF	77494
BOULDER HOLLOW LN	0	327U	NWC	77429
BOULDER LAKE CT	6000	297Z	NEH	77345
BOULDER LAKE CT	24800	484M	NEF	77494
BOULDER MEADOW LN	4900	446D	NWC	77449
BOULDER OAKS DR	15500	448B	NWC	77084
BOULDER OAKS DR	15800	408X	NWC	77084
BOULDER PARK CT	32500	253N	SEM	77385
BOULDER POINT CT	3100	578X	SEH	77059
BOULDER POND	0	250R	NWC	77389
BOULDER RIDGE	0	615A	PL	77581
BOULDER RIDGE CT	17200	407L	NWC	77095
BOULDER SPRINGS DR	8800	528N	SWC	77083
BOULDER SPRINGS LN	20000	488N	SWH	77077
BOULDER SPRINGS LN	22200	289J	NWC	77375
BOULDER TRACE LN	0	446C	NWC	77449
BOULDER VALLEY DR	6200	406T	NWC	77449
BOULDERWOODS DR	1200	618E	SEH	77062
BOULDGREEN	16600	407U	NWC	77084
BOULEVARD GREEN	1	531H	BL	77401
BOUNDARY	400	493C	NEH	77009
BOUNDARY CT	900	616Y	FR	77546
E. BOUNDARY PEAK WAY	4000	445H	NWC	77449
N. BOUNDARY PEAK WAY	21500	445H	NWC	77449
BOUNDS LN	1	258Y	NEC	77336
BOUNTIFUL LN	6200	454V	NEH	77016
BOUNTY DR	100	619Z	LC	77573
BOUNTY LN	12600	328Q	NWC	77377
BOUNTY MAIN	0	616X	GCO	77546
BOURELLE DR	0	245Z	SWM	77355
BOURGAIN DR	25900	288X	NWC	77377
BOURGEOIS RD	4500	371J	NWC	77066
BOURGEOIS RD	5500	370Q	NWC	77066
BOURGEOIS FOREST DR	11600	370M	NWC	77066
BOURLAND BLVD	0	328N	NWC	77429
BOURNEMOUTH DR	1200	577J	PA	77504
BOURNEWOOD DR	700	568F	SG	77498
E. BOURNEWOOD DR	12800	568G	SG	77478
BOURRELET WAY	16200	419B	NEC	77532
BOVA RD	7900	410G	NWC	77064
BOVEDA DR	14700	528J	SWC	77083
BOVINGTON DR	23900	250W	NWC	77389
BOW LN	15400	571Y	SWH	77053
BOWCREEK LN	21500	445H	NWC	77449
BOWDEN	1200	493W	SWH	77005
BOWDEN CT	2800	610U	MC	77459
BOWDEN DR	22000	256K	SEM	77357
BOWDEN CHASE CT	1400	289X	NWC	77379
BOWDEN CHASE DR	10600	289X	NWC	77379
BOWDEN CREEK DR	13700	367H	NWC	77429
BOWDIN CREST DR	0	325M	NWC	77433
BOWEN	1100	569Y	NEF	77477
BOWEN	7700	533U	SEH	77051
BOWEN DR	1400	537R	PA	77503
BOWEN DR	6300	406U	NWC	77449
BOWER	300	336W	HM	77338
BOWERBANK CT	0	249B	SWM	77382

Street Name	Block	Pg/Sq	Loc	Zips
BOWERS	8700	495U	NEH	77029
BOWERS PINE CT	0	292E	NWC	77389
BOWFIN RD	10100	329U	NWC	77070
BOWHEAD DR	11600	496B	NEH	77013
BOWIE	100	499K	NEC	77520
BOWIE	100	541B	BT	77520
BOWIE	7200	535A	SEH	77012
BOWIE	800	500V	BT	77520
BOWIE DR	11700	539R	LP	77571
BOWIE LN	24000	296F	SEM	77365
BOWIE ST	0	658Y	LC	77573
BOWIE BEND LN	0	484X	NEF	77494
BOWIE RIDGE LN	16100	611C	SWH	77053
BOWING OAKS DR	12800	328V	NWC	77429
BOWLAN LN	11500	570D	SWH	77035
BOWLER RD	0	243A	WCO	77484
BOWLES CT	0	290R	NWC	77388
BOWLIN CT	0	571Y	SWH	77053
BOWLINE RD	1600	618K	SEH	77062
BOWLING GREEN	5600	533F	SEH	77021
BOWMAN	4900	453E	NWH	77022
BOWMAN CT	5000	291N	NWC	77388
BOWMORE CT	9300	408A	NWC	77095
BOWRIDGE LN	16100	571X	SWH	77053
BOWRIDGE LN	16200	611B	SWH	77053
BOWSMAN DR	12400	328G	NWC	77377
BOWSPIRIT WAY	0	296U	SEM	77365
BOWSPRIT LN	15000	618K	SEH	77062
BOW STRING COVE	700	488B	SWH	77079
BOWTRAIL	6300	407V	NWC	77084
BOW WILLOW DR	0	369M	NWC	77070
BOW WOOD CT	25000	250Y	NWC	77389
BOXBERRY CT	1	252J	WD	77380
BOX CANYON DR	17200	325J	NWC	77447
BOX ELDER	11900	370R	NWC	77066
BOXELDER DR	3200	487Y	SWC	77082
BOXELDER POINTE	900	658R	LC	77573
BOXELDER POINTE CT	600	658K	LC	77573
BOXFIELD LN	0	484Y	NEF	77494
BOXFORD CT	1100	292B	NCC	77373
BOX FORT LN	0	366N	NWC	77433
BOXHILL DR	11600	371K	NWC	77066
BOX OAK PLACE	2400	251U	WD	77380
BOXRIDGE LN	20000	446W	NWC	77449
BOXSTER CT	800	375M	NEC	77396
BOXTHORN CT	24600	485S	NEF	77494
BOX TURTLE LN	1	251M	WD	77380
BOXWOOD	100	500A	BT	77520
BOXWOOD	6100	614C	BK	77581
BOXWOOD CIR	0	614C	BK	77581
BOXWOOD CT	1800	568B	SG	77498
BOXWOOD BRIDGE LN	6600	409S	NWC	77041
BOXWOOD RIDGE LN	0	526K	NEF	77407
BOXWOOD TERRACE DR	13200	528L	SWH	77083
BOXWOOD WAY LN	12500	409S	NWC	77041
BOY	7800	455P	NEH	77028
BOYCE	6900	494M	NEH	77020
BOYCE	7100	495J	NEH	77020
BOYCE SPRINGS DR	5100	370D	NWC	77066
BOYD	0	611C	SWH	77053
BOYD	8200	453F	NEH	77022
BOYD CT	900	536H	PA	77506
BOYDEN KNOLL DR	0	524E	NEF	77494
BOYER LN	13100	457X	NEC	77015
BOYETT	3200	539Z	LP	77571
BOYKIN	2100	576A	SEH	77034
BOYLAN	0	659N	LC	77573
BOYLES	100	494D	NEH	77020
BOYLSTON DR	14700	497D	NEC	77015
BOYNTON DR	3100	572J	SWH	77045
BOYNTON DR	5100	571L	SWH	77045
BOYS COUNTRY	0	284Z	NWC	77447
BOY SCOUT DR	4400	617T	SEC	77546
BOYSEN CT	0	377F	NEC	77346
BOYSENBERRY LN	7300	407L	NWC	77095
BOYTON LN	17000	329M	NWC	77379
BRA-MOR	2000	502N	BT	77521
BRABANT CT	6900	411N	NWH	77088
BRACE	6600	574D	SEH	77061
BRACE	7300	535W	SEH	77061
BRACE RD	23200	325B	NWC	77447
W. BRACEBRIDGE CIR	1	250A	WD	77382
E. BRACEBRIDGE CIR	1	250A	WD	77382
BRACEBRIDGE CT	14100	568A	SG	77498
BRACEBRIDGE DR	1	250A	WD	77382
BRACENHURST LN	0	457P	NEC	77049
BRACE RIDGE LN	0	444T	KT	77493
BRACHER	1400	450Z	SV	77055
BRACK BAMBOO LN	0	524E	NEF	77494
BRACKEN FALLS BLVD	0	578X	SEH	77059
BRACKEN FERN CT	1	251M	WD	77380
BRACKENFERN RD	3300	446L	NWC	77449
BRACKENFIELD DR	18400	331G	NWC	77388
BRACKEN HURST DR	0	484X	NEF	77494
BRACKEN HURST DR	0	484X	NEF	77494
BRACKENRIDGE	1700	494A	NEH	77026
BRACKENRIDGE	5600	454S	NEH	77026
BRACKENTON CREST CT	20000	289Z	NWC	77379
BRACKENTON CREST DR	9400	289Z	NWC	77379
BRACKET CT	1700	615Z	PL	77581
BRACKET CT	9700	408D	NWC	77065
BRACKET DR	3900	615Z	PL	77581
BRACKLEY LN	8700	412K	NWH	77088
BRACKNELL	6100	535Z	SEH	77017
BRACKSTONE CT	0	525M	NEF	77407
BRAD CT	500	618X	WB	77598
BRADBRIDGE LN	13100	528B	SWH	77082
BRADBURN HILL LN	2501	371D	NWC	77014
BRADBURY	0	245A	SWM	77355
BRADBURY DR	2200	244B	WCO	77447
BRADBURY LN	100	244A	WCO	77447
BRADBURY FOREST DR	2100	293S	NCC	77373
BRADBURY PATH CT	2100	293S	NCC	77373
BRADDOCK RD	16500	367B	CY	77429
BRADDOCK HILLS LN	0	290J	NWC	77375
BRADEHALL LN	0	290P	NWC	77379
N. BRADEN DR	3934	573Y	SEC	77047
E. BRADEN DR	14500	573Y	SEC	77047
BRADENWAY LN	12100	616L	SEC	77089
BRADFIELD CT	1	490F	BH	77024
BRADFIELD RD	700	373P	NEH	77060
BRADFORD	200	620U	KE	77565
BRADFORD	3400	532F	SWH	77025
BRADFORD	7400	535N	SEH	77087
BRADFORD DR	2300	610A	MC	77489
BRADFORD LN	0	657U	LC	77573
BRADFORD COLONY DR	14500	408T	NWC	77084
BRADFORD CREEK CT	20700	326N	NWC	77433
BRADFORD FOREST DR	0	406F	NWC	77433
BRADFORD LAKE TRAIL	0	326N	NWC	77433
BRADFORD PINES CT	0	366R	NWC	77433
BRADFORD SHORES DR	16100	326N	NWC	77433

Street Name	Block	Pg/Sq	Loc	Zips
BRADFORD VILLAGE DR	31300	252R	SEM	77386
BRADFORD VILLAGE RD	1900	610B	MC	77489
BRADFORD WAY	10900	575Z	SEH	77075
BRADFORD WAY DR	10800	575Z	SEH	77075
BRADGATE CT	23200	485K	SWC	77494
BRAD HURST CT	0	484Q	NEF	77494
BRADIE CT	6100	657U	LC	77573
BRADLEY	600	620L	SB	77586
BRADLEY	3700	453X	NWH	77009
BRADLY LN	5200	444M	KT	77493
BRADMAR	7500	412S	NWH	77088
BRADMORE DR	1800	489P	SWH	77077
BRADNEY DR	1500	488R	SWH	77077
BRADSHAW	1900	453S	NWH	77008
BRADSHAW NURSERY	1400	659N	LC	77573
BRADSHIRE	4200	619G	TL	77586
BRADSHIRE CT	200	538U	DP	77536
BRADSTONE CT	4900	447B	NWC	77084
BRADSTONE DR	4700	447B	NWC	77084
BRADWELL DR	800	618J	SEH	77062
BRADWORTHY DR	5900	407W	NWC	77449
BRADY	4400	494U	SEH	77011
BRADY LN	10000	289K	NWC	77375
BRADY BEND DR	0	292K	SP	77373
BRADY BRANCH LN	0	406D	NWC	77433
BRAE LN	2200	659B	LC	77573
BRAE ACRES CT	7600	530Q	SWH	77074
BRAE ACRES RD	8000	530P	SWH	77074
BRAEBERRY CT	7500	526M	NEF	77407
BRAEBERRY LN	0	407S	NWC	77449
BRAEBURN DR	4500	531K	BL	77401
BRAEBURN ST	0	530M	SWH	77074
BRAEBURN BEND DR	10800	530W	SWH	77031
BRAEBURN GLEN BLVD	9200	530P	SWH	77074
BRAEBURN VALLEY DR	7700	530Q	SWH	77074
BRAECOVE CIR	0	526F	NEF	77450
BRAECREST	12600	456H	NEC	77044
BRAELOCH DR	0	528W	SG	77498
BRAEMAR RD	10100	460G	NEC	77562
BRAEMAR CRESCENT	7800	407H	NWC	77095
BRAEMAR FOREST	1	251A	WD	77381
BRAE POINT CT	21100	446J	NWC	77449
BRAER RIDGE	2200	484M	NEF	77494
BRAES BLVD	6800	532J	SWH	77025
BRAES ANCHOR	11900	570B	SWH	77071
BRAES BAYOU DR	9100	530U	SWH	77074
BRAES BAYOU DR	10700	530Y	SWH	77071
BRAES BEND DR	10600	530X	SWH	77071
BRAES BOUGH DR	11900	570B	SWH	77071
BRAES CREEK	10000	530X	SWH	77071
BRAES CROSSING	11900	570B	SWH	77071
BRAESDALE LN	7600	530U	SWH	77071
BRAES FERRY	11900	570B	SWH	77071
BRAES FOREST DR	9900	530U	SWH	77071
BRAES FOREST DR	11200	570C	SWH	77071
BRAESGLEN DR	7600	530U	SWH	77071
BRAESHEATHER CIR	9400	530V	SWH	77096
BRAESHEATHER CT	9400	531U	SWH	77096
BRAESHEATHER DR	4900	531S	SWH	77096
BRAESHEATHER DR	6100	530V	SWH	77096
BRAES LANDING	11900	570B	SWH	77071
BRAES LAUNCH	11900	570B	SWH	77071
BRAESMAIN DR	8000	532L	SWH	77025
BRAES MEADOW DR	7600	530Y	SWH	77071
BRAESMONT DR	8800	531T	SWH	77096
BRAES PARK DR	11300	570B	SWH	77071
BRAES PARK DR	11900	570B	SWH	77071
BRAESRIDGE CT	7700	530Y	SWH	77071
BRAESRIDGE DR	9800	530U	SWH	77071
BRAESRIDGE DR	11200	570G	SWH	77071
BRAES RIVER DR	8100	530Q	SWH	77074
BRAES VALLEY DR	4700	531Q	SWH	77096
BRAESVIEW DR	3200	613Y	NEB	77584
BRAESVIEW LN	7600	530U	SWH	77071
BRAESWEST DR	13500	488T	SWH	77082
BRAESWOOD BLVD	1000	532M	SWH	77030
S. BRAESWOOD BLVD	1700	532M	SWH	77030
N. BRAESWOOD BLVD	1900	532J	SWH	77030
S. BRAESWOOD BLVD	2500	532M	SWH	77025
N. BRAESWOOD BLVD	2900	532J	SWH	77025
S. BRAESWOOD BLVD	4200	531T	SWH	77096
N. BRAESWOOD BLVD	4200	531T	SWH	77096
N. BRAESWOOD BLVD	5900	531T	SWH	77074
S. BRAESWOOD BLVD	7500	530U	SWH	77071
S. BRAESWOOD BLVD	8600	530U	SWH	77071
S. BRAESWOOD BLVD	8900	530U	SWH	77074
BRAESWOOD CT	1400	532L	SWH	77030
BRAESWOOD PARK DR	2200	532L	SWH	77030
BRAESWOOD SQUARE	1	531T	SWH	77096
BRAEWICK DR	7100	530M	SWH	77074
BRAEWICK DR	9400	530Z	SWH	77096
BRAEWICK DR	11400	570D	SWH	77035
BRAEWIN CT	3500	331S	NWC	77068
BRAEWOOD GLEN LN	12700	528M	SWH	77072
BRAFFERTON LN	22500	445Q	NWC	77449
BRAGG	1100	453R	NEH	77009
BRAHMAN DR	0	613W	NEB	77578
BRAHMAN DR	2900	612Z	NEB	77578
BRAHMS CT	7800	410J	NWC	77040
BRAHMS LN	9100	410K	NWC	77040
S. BRAIDED BRANCH DR	0	249R	NWC	77375
N. BRAIDED BRANCH DR	0	249R	NWC	77375
BRAIDWOOD DR	20200	486C	SWC	77450
BRAILSFORT	2300	493Z	SEH	77004
BRAKEN CARTER LN	22500	445U	NWC	77449
BRAKEN MANOR LN	22500	445Q	NWC	77449
BRAKERS CROSSING AVE	0	447P	NWC	77084
BRALEY CT	25100	406Q	NWC	77433
BRALEYBROOK CT	25100	485W	NEF	77494
BRALEY PARK LN	2500	252R	SEM	77385
BRAMBLE	1800	493M	SWH	77003
BRAMBLE LN	5300	660X	DI	77539
BRAMBLEBURY DR	1100	568G	SG	77478
BRAMBLE CREEK DR	3400	501N	BT	77521
BRAMBLE CREST CT	15400	408N	NWH	77095
BRAMBLE FERN PLACE	3500	446L	NWC	77449
BRAMBLE HILL CT	3100	578T	SEH	77059
BRAMBLEVINE DR	22600	245U	SWM	77355
BRAMBLE WAY	16500	618R	SEH	77058
BRAMBLEWOOD DR	14400	488M	SWH	77079
BRAMBLING DR	16400	618D	SEH	77059
BRAMFORD CT	10600	369K	NWC	77070
BRAMFORD POINT LN	12900	369G	NWC	77070
BRAMLEY DR	6200	538W	PA	77503
BRAMPTON CT	15900	330S	NWC	77379
BRAMPTON MILL CT	0	406D	NWC	77433
BRAMSHAW GLEN	0	457Q	NEC	77049
BRAMWELL DR	22100	445M	NWC	77449
BRANARD	300	493S	SWH	77006
BRANARD	1700	492U	SWH	77098
BRANARD	3400	492S	SWH	77027
BRANARD CT	300	492V	SWH	77098

Street Name	Block	Pg/Sq	Loc	Zips
BRANBURY CT	0	332R	NCC	77073
BRANCH	4500	533R	SEH	77021
BRANCH	11800	418R	NEC	77044
BRANCH AVE	1500	524U	NEF	77406
BRANCH LN	1300	332D	NCC	77373
BRANCH RD	27200	292L	SP	77373
BRANCH BEND DR	0	490P	BH	77024
BRANCHBERRY LN	4700	291S	NWC	77388
BRANCH CANYON CT	17200	367U	NWC	77095
BRANCH CREEK DR	0	367P	NWC	77433
W. BRANCH CROSSING	0	249B	SWM	77382
BRANCHDALE LN	18400	330F	NWC	77379
BRANCH ELM	0	258N	SEM	77357
BRANCH FOREST DR	14800	488W	SWH	77082
BRANCHGROVE LN	0	526J	NEF	77407
BRANCH HILL DR	1800	615Z	PL	77581
BRANCHING CT	18100	526H	NEF	77407
BRANCH LAKE DR	5900	370R	NWC	77066
BRANCHMEAD CT	4400	485Z	NEF	77450
BRANCH PARK DR	9800	409D	NWC	77064
BRANCH POINT DR	7400	408J	NWC	77095
BRANCHPORT DR	0	408A	NWC	77095
BRANCH VIEW LN	2500	609C	MC	77459
BRANCHWATER LN	14200	528W	NEF	77498
BRANCHWEST DR	0	488W	SWH	77082
BRANCHWOOD	34900	247F	SWM	77362
BRANCHWOOD CT	10100	410M	NWH	77040
BRANCOTT WAY	0	531W	SWH	77096
BRAND LN	100	569P	SF	77477
BRANDEMERE WAY	4000	371E	NWC	77066
BRANDING IRON	5600	660T	DI	77539
BRANDING IRON CIR	5600	660T	DI	77539
BRANDING IRON LN	200	413A	NCC	77060
BRANDING IRON LN	27800	246J	SWM	77355
BRANDMERE DR	3500	613Y	NEB	77584
BRANDON	7800	533Y	SEH	77051
BRANDON CT	3600	578A	PA	77505
BRANDON DR	20600	256R	SEM	77357
BRANDON BEND DR	12600	570J	MC	77489
BRANDON CHASE LN	9200	526Q	NEF	77407
BRANDON GATE	11100	367V	NWC	77095
BRANDON OAKS WAY	19800	446L	NWC	77449
BRANDONWAY	11700	490F	BH	77024
BRANDONWOOD CT	15400	330U	NWC	77069
BRANDONWOOD PLACE	15300	330U	NWC	77069
BRANDT	500	292Q	SP	77373
BRANDT	3800	493T	SWH	77006
BRANDT LN	0	448L	NWH	77084
BRANDY	0	569T	NEF	77459
BRANDY LN	11300	418P	NEC	77044
BRANDY LN	11900	328V	NWC	77377
BRANDY BRANCH CT	0	660J	LC	77573
BRANDY CREEK CT	8100	334R	NCC	77338
BRANDY CREEK LN	19800	334V	NCC	77338
BRANDYGATE CT	23100	292G	NCC	77373
BRANDY MILL RD	2400	371M	NWC	77067
BRANDYWINE LN	11800	490F	BH	77024
BRANDYWOOD CIR	9900	329K	NWC	77375
BRANDYWYNE CT	13300	488P	SWH	77077
BRANDYWYNE DR	100	616Y	FR	77546
BRANDYWYNE DR	12300	488R	SWH	77077
BRANFORD	6500	412X	NWH	77091
BRANFORD GREENS DR	13700	528P	SWC	77083
BRANFORD GROVE DR	0	290N	NWC	77379
BRANFORD HILLS LN	21200	486J	SWC	77450
BRANFORD MANOR DR	13700	528P	SWC	77083
BRANFORD OAK LN	0	615H	PL	77089
BRANFORD PARK LN	0	615M	PL	77089
BRANFORD PARK LN	7200	527J	NEF	77407
BRANHAM DR	0	528N	SWC	77083
BRANIFF	7600	575K	SEH	77061
BRANNAN DR	0	446L	NWC	77449
BRANNOCK AVE	0	527W	NEF	77478
BRANNOK LN	0	289L	NWC	77375
BRANNON	8600	453H	NEH	77093
BRANNON FIELD LN	13700	408L	NWC	77041
BRANNON HILL LN	20900	335N	NCC	77338
BRANNON PARK LN	1000	292F	NCC	77373
BRANNON POINT LN	0	376S	NEC	77396
BRANNON RIDGE LN	0	485S	NEF	77494
BRANSON LN	13600	328T	NWC	77429
S. BRANSON CREEK WAY	0	250K	NWC	77389
S. BRANSON CREEK WAY	0	250K	NWC	77389
BRANSON PARK LN	0	334R	NCC	77338
BRANT DR	3000	444K	KT	77493
BRANT ARBOR LN	0	253P	SEM	77386
BRANT ARBOR LN	0	609U	NEF	77479
BRANT CROSSING DR	0	484V	NEF	77494
BRANTDALE RD	0	251E	WD	77381
BRANTFIELD CT	9400	408B	NWC	77095
BRANTFIELD PARK LN	13100	328F	NWC	77377
BRANT GROVE LN	0	377L	NEC	77346
BRANTLEY	0	577Y	SEH	77034
BRANTLEY	0	617C	SEH	77034
BRANTLEY	5300	291J	NWC	77389
BRANTLEY HAVEN DR	11800	329A	NWC	77375
BRANT ROCK DR	12600	528D	SWH	77082
BRANTS WAY CT	12500	408D	NWC	77065
BRANUM	9700	535M	SEH	77017
BRASHEAR	400	335V	HM	77338
BRASHEAR	1000	493F	SWH	77007
BRASIL LN	16600	367U	NWC	77095
BRASS HAMMER CT	11300	409A	NWC	77065
BRASS LANTER DR	0	290W	NWC	77379
BRASS TOP LN	0	299U	NEC	77336
BRASS TOWN LN	0	527J	NEF	77083
BRASSTOWN MOUNTAIN WAY	21400	446E	NWC	77449
BRASSWOOD CT	22200	245R	SWM	77355
BRATEN LN	15200	617R	SEH	77598
BRATTLE DR	24700	484G	NEF	77494
BRAUNSTON LN	8700	412N	NWC	77088
BRAUTIGAM RD	24400	247X	SWM	77355
BRAVE LEGION WAY	0	289P	NWC	77375
BRAVERY DR	21800	285M	NWC	77447
BRAVO	2500	537P	PA	77502
BRAVOS MANOR LN	1900	611T	NEF	77545
BRAWLEY CREEK LN	0	376W	NEC	77396
BRAXTON DR	3900	490Y	SWH	77063
BRAXTON DR	5600	530C	SWH	77036
BRAXTON GROVE LN	0	330H	NWC	77379
BRAXTONS BEND	0	370M	NWC	77066
BRAXTONSHIRE CT	5400	330Y	NWC	77069
BRAYBEND LN	0	486N	SWC	77450
BRAYDEN CT	27700	293H	SEM	77386
BRAYDEN HILL TRAIL	0	484N	NEF	77494
BRAYDEN ROCK LN	17200	377K	NEC	77346
BRAYDON BEND DR	13600	408L	NWC	77041
BRAYFORD PLACE CT	13900	372A	NWC	77014
BRAYFORD PLACE DR	14000	332W	NWC	77014
BRAYMARK DR	0	372A	NWC	77014
BRAYMOORE DR	10700	449L	NWH	77065
BRAYPARK LN	0	486N	SWC	77450
BRAYS	7900	535A	SEH	77012
BRAYSON OAKS PLACE	0	449U	NWH	77043
BRAYSWORTH DR	4300	529F	SWH	77072
BRAYTON CT	13000	368Y	NWC	77065
BRAZEAL	2200	282Q	WL	77484
BRAZIL	4200	577B	PA	77504
BRAZIL	7000	454J	NEH	77093
BRAZORIA	0	612S	FS	77545
BRAZORIA	2400	492Q	SWH	77019
BRAZORIA PLACE	6100	614L	PL	77581
BRAZOS	0	255X	SEM	77365
BRAZOS	900	493L	DT	77002
BRAZOS	2300	493P	SWH	77006
BRAZOS DR	15900	568X	SG	77479
BRAZOS DR	20000	255R	SEM	77357
BRAZOS DR	20600	256N	SEM	77357
BRAZOS DR	22800	295C	SEM	77365
BRAZOS BEND	0	615N	PL	77584
BRAZOS BEND DR	4600	609K	MC	77459
BRAZOS BEND TRAIL	12500	377B	NEC	77346
BRAZOS RIVER BLVD	0	253U	SEM	77386
BRAZOS SAGE DR	0	366U	NWC	77433
BRAZZEL LN	3200	339G	NEC	77336
BRAZZO CT	0	659L	LC	77573
BREA CT	3800	293C	SEM	77386
BREA CREST	200	413N	NCC	77037
BREA CREST	1100	413Q	NEH	77037
BREA CREST	2000	414N	NCC	77093
BREAKER CT	3800	609Q	MC	77459
BREAKER POINT DR	0	617B	SEC	77546
BREAKERS POINT DR	3000	657C	SEC	77546
BREAKLINE PLACE	0	250P	NWC	77389
BREAKWATER	800	419B	NEC	77532
BREAKWATER PATH DR	0	377L	NEC	77044
BREAKWATER PATH DR	0	377L	NEC	77346
BREAKWATER PATH DR	0	377M	NEC	77346
BREAKWATER PATH LOOP	0	377M	NEC	77346
BREAKWOOD DR	4000	532N	SWH	77025
BREAKWOOD DR	4300	531R	SWH	77096
BREANNA LN	15900	457V	NEC	77049
BREAUX TRACE	2500	620J	SB	77586
BRECCIA DR	7300	408Q	NWC	77041
BRECHIN CT	9200	407D	NWC	77095
BRECHIN LN	16200	407D	NWC	77095
BRECK	13800	330Z	NWH	77066
BRECK	13800	371A	NWC	77066
BRECKAN CT	11600	328X	NWC	77429
BRECKENRIDGE DR	3300	371N	NWC	77066
BRECKENRIDGE DR	4200	371Q	NWC	77066
BRECKENRIDGE COVE LN	1100	658L	LC	77573
BRECKENRIDGE DALE LN	0	293U	NCC	77373
BRECKENRIDGE DALE LN	0	293U	NCC	77373
BRECKENRIDGE FOREST CT	0	293U	NCC	77373
BRECKENRIDGE FOREST DR	23800	293U	NCC	77373
BRECKENWOOD MILLS	0	376R	NEC	77346
BRECKINRIDGE CT	3200	610V	MC	77459
BRECKINRIDGE LN	3300	610V	MC	77459
BRECKONRIDGE CIR	1100	615B	PL	77581
BRECON HALL DR	1100	489J	SWH	77077
BREDA DR	7300	461W	NEC	77521
BREECH DR	900	419B	NEC	77532
BREEDS HILL CT	200	490J	BH	77024
BREELAND PARK CT	14200	568A	SG	77498
BREEN DR	4800	411F	NWC	77086
BREEN DR	7500	410G	NWC	77064
BREEN VISTA DR	0	293F	SEM	77386
S. BREEZE DR	2600	613W	NEB	77578
BREEZE FOREST CT	0	376V	NEC	77396
BREEZELOCH DR	0	407A	NWC	77433
BREEZE PARK DR	300	457W	NEC	77015
BREEZEPORT CT	0	612J	PL	77545
BREEZEPORT DR	0	612J	PL	77545
BREEZEWAY	7200	410R	NWH	77040
BREEZE WAY	12900	413P	NCC	77037
BREEZEWAY CT	3900	620E	SB	77586
BREEZEWAY DR	0	569X	MC	77459
BREEZEWAY DR	3800	620E	SB	77586
BREEZEWAY LN	0	612G	PL	77545
BREEZEWAY BEND DR	2200	612M	PL	77584
BREEZEWAY BEND LN	0	485X	NEF	77494
BREEZEWAY BEND LN	300	658U	LC	77573
BREEZEWAY COVE CIR	0	366J	NWC	77433
BREEZEWOOD	3300	489X	SWH	77082
BREEZEWOOD CT	3900	620E	SB	77586
BREEZEWOOD DR	3800	620E	SB	77586
BREEZEWOOD DR	3800	620E	SB	77586
BREEZIN CT	1800	251R	WD	77380
BREEZY CT	18600	295E	SEM	77365
BREEZY CT	28300	246L	SWM	77355
BREEZY BEND DR	1200	484G	NEF	77494
BREEZY BIRCH CT	0	484S	NEF	77494
BREEZY COVE CT	0	289X	NWC	77375
BREEZY CYPRESS CREEK TRL	0	368P	NWC	77429
BREEZY FOREST LN	0	331A	NWC	77388
BREEZY GLEN LN	0	407J	NWC	77433
BREEZY HILL DR	21900	445R	NWC	77449
BREEZY HOLLOW LN	6100	525G	NEF	77450
BREEZY KNOLL DR	11500	369U	NWC	77064
BREEZY LANDING LN	0	577W	SEH	77034
BREEZY MEADOW CT	13700	417A	NEC	77044
BREEZY MEADOW DR	12000	569E	SF	77477
BREEZY MEADOW LN	12900	417A	NEC	77044
BREEZY OAK CT	0	406L	NWC	77433
BREEZY PINES CT	3100	337E	NEH	77339
BREEZY PINES LN	2700	613F	NEB	77584
BREEZY POINT DR	4600	337C	NEH	77345
BREEZY POINT PLACE	1	250H	WD	77381
BREEZY RETREAT CT	0	253K	SEM	77386
BREEZY SHORE LN	21100	525M	NEF	77407
BREEZY WATERS CT	0	377L	NEH	77044
W. BREEZY WAY	0	251K	WD	77380
E. BREEZY WAY	0	251K	WD	77380
BREEZY WAY	0	251K	WD	77380
BRELAND	5700	454C	NEH	77016
BREMAN CREST LN	9500	410F	NWC	77040
BREMEN DR	11500	371N	NWC	77066
BREMERTON LN	19300	331C	NWC	77388
BREMERTON FALLS DR	0	610Q	MC	77459
BREMOND	200	493P	SWH	77006
BREMOND	1000	493T	SWH	77002
BREMOND	1400	493T	SWH	77004
BREMOND	3400	494W	SEH	77004
W. BREMONDS BEND CT	0	366L	NWC	77433
E. BREMONDS BEND CT	0	366L	NWC	77433
BREMONDS BEND DR	0	366L	NWC	77433
W. BRENDA	100	413W	NEH	77076
BRENDA	500	413W	NEH	77076
BRENDA	1100	538Q	DP	77536
BRENDA LN	300	252E	OR	77385
BRENDA LN	900	375D	HM	77338
BRENDA LN	1600	537N	PA	77502
BRENDAM LN	7100	528L	SWH	77072
BRENDON CT	16600	330M	NWC	77379
BRENDON PARK LN	500	616Y	FR	77546
BRENDON TRACE LN	0	293F	SEM	77386
BRENDON TRAIL CT	28000	293J	SEM	77386
BRENDON TRAIL DR	0	293J	SEM	77386
BRENDON TRAILS CT	10800	289X	NWC	77379
BRENDON TRAILS DR	1300	289X	NWC	77379
BRENFORD DR	1100	572R	SWH	77047
BRENHAM CT	9400	409H	NWC	77064
BRENHAVEN DR	12600	412A	NWC	77038
BRENLY DR	14700	328X	NWC	77429
BRENNAN	23600	245X	SWM	77447
BRENNAN RIDGE LN	5600	525D	NEF	77450
BRENNER	4900	453E	NWH	77022
BRENNER CT	4000	569S	SG	77478
BRENNER CREEK CT	10800	489C	SWH	77079
BRENNER RIDGE LN	0	573Y	SEC	77047
BRENT DR	6300	571T	SWH	77085
BRENTA CT	0	444S	KT	77493
BRENTA MOUNTAIN LN	0	445F	NWC	77493
BRENTA VALLEY DR	0	257F	SEM	77357
W. BRENTCHASE CIR	0	371B	NWC	77014
S. BRENTCHASE CIR	0	371B	NWC	77014
BRENTCROSS DR	0	329N	NWC	77377
BRENTFORD CT	16500	527P	NEF	77083
BRENTFORD DR	8100	527P	NEF	77083
BRENTHAVEN SPRINGS LN	9600	329F	NWC	77375
BRENTLAWN CT	0	572E	SWH	77045
BRENTLAWN CT	0	572E	SWH	77045
BRENTLEYWOOD CT	9300	369M	NWC	77070
BRENTLEYWOOD LN	12300	369M	NWC	77070
BRENTMOOR DR	0	295V	SEM	77365
BRENTON	4500	414P	NCC	77093
S. BRENTON KNOLL DR	12000	329A	NWC	77375
N. BRENTON KNOLL DR	12000	329A	NWC	77375
BRENTON OAKS DR	16600	330M	NWC	77379
BRENTONRIDGE LN	19600	291W	NWC	77379
BRENTONWOOD LN	13300	488P	SWH	77077
BRENTRIDGE MANOR LN	0	328A	NWC	77429
BRENTRIDGE MANOR LN	0	328A	NWC	77377
BRENTSHIRE LN	14200	330U	NWC	77069
BRENTWAY DR	10500	369F	NWC	77070
W. BRENTWOOD	400	498E	CV	77530
N. BRENTWOOD	15000	498A	NEC	77530
N. BRENTWOOD	15100	498A	CV	77530
S. BRENTWOOD	15200	498E	CV	77530
E. BRENTWOOD	15500	498B	CV	77530
BRENTWOOD DR	0	656F	FR	77546
BRENTWOOD DR	700	501T	BT	77520
BRENTWOOD DR	2000	492Q	SWH	77019
BRENTWOOD LN	0	615K	PL	77581
BRENTWOOD LAKES CIR	9300	329L	NWC	77379
BRENTWOOD LAKES DR	17500	329L	NWC	77379
BRENTWOOD OAKS CT	1	251A	WD	77381
BRENTWOOD PARK	0	572E	SWH	77045
BRENTWOOD PARK	0	572E	SWH	77045
BRENWICK CT	600	486B	SWC	77450
BRENWOOD CIR	0	407T	NWC	77449
S. BRENWOOD DR	0	407W	NWC	77449
BRENWOOD DR	18000	407X	NWC	77449
BRENWOOD GLEN TRAIL	5800	407W	NWC	77449
BRENWOOD MANOR DR	18300	407W	NWC	77449
BRENWOOD PARK DR	6400	407W	NWC	77449
BRENWOOD PEAK DR	0	406Z	NWC	77449
BRENWOOD TRAILS LN	5800	406Z	NWC	77449
BRESCIA CT	0	447A	NWC	77449
BRESSINGHAM DR	18900	329F	NWC	77375
BRESSLYN CT	9500	416Z	NEC	77044
BRESSLYN LN	16200	326V	NWC	77429
BRESSLYN LN	16200	326V	NWC	77429
BRETAGNE DR	13300	497B	NEC	77015
BRETFORD CT	13000	368Y	NWC	77065
BRETON BAY PASS	0	609Y	MC	77459
BRETON FALLS LN	0	526L	NEF	77407
BRETON GLEN LN	0	370E	NWH	77070
BRETON POINT DR	22900	292G	NCC	77373
BRETON RIDGE	13100	370E	NWH	77070
BRETON SHORE LN	0	485X	NEF	77494
BRETONWOOD LN	25100	485N	NEF	77494
BRETSHIRE DR	5000	414Z	NEH	77016
BRETSHIRE DR	6400	454D	NEH	77016
BRETSHIRE DR	7300	455A	NEH	77016
BRETT	13100	328Q	NWC	77429
BRETT CT	0	610Q	MC	77459
BRETT DR	5100	614R	PL	77584
BRETTON DR	10100	414Z	NEH	77016
BRETTON MILL DR	21000	337P	NEC	77346
BRETTWOOD CIR	11700	616D	SEC	77089
BRETTWOOD CT	11700	616D	SEC	77089
BRETTWOOD DR	11200	616D	SEC	77089
BREWER LN	19500	335T	NEH	77338
BREWSTER	1600	494A	NEH	77020
BREWSTER	1900	454W	NEH	77026
BREWSTER	6800	454N	NEH	77093
BREWSTER LN	0	609Y	MC	77459
BREYANA PARK LN	0	376W	NEC	77396
BRIA LN	0	542J	BT	77520
BRIAN	7800	375G	HM	77396
BRIAN HAVEN DR	4700	452F	NWH	77018
BRIAN HAVEN DR	5400	452B	NWH	77091
BRIANWOOD CT	18400	331B	NWC	77388
BRIAR	3000	537L	PA	77503
BRIAR CIR	2100	615K	PL	77581
BRIAR CIR	23900	296E	SEM	77365
BRIAR CT	1400	616T	PL	77581
BRIAR CT	3100	569N	SG	77478
BRIAR CT	3200	500R	BT	77521
BRIAR DR	5200	491F	SWH	77056
BRIAR DR	10000	489M	SWH	77042
BRIAR LN	20100	257M	SEM	77357
BRIAR ARBOR	17700	487A	SWC	77094
BRIARBANK DR	1500	568F	SG	77498
BRIAR BARK LN	23800	296E	SEM	77365
BRIAR BAYOU DR	1100	488L	SWH	77077
S. BRIAR BAYOU DR	6000	528G	SWH	77072
BRIARBEND DR	4300	531Z	SWH	77035
BRIARBEND DR	5300	531X	SWH	77096
BRIAR BERRY LN	0	296J	SEM	77365
BRIAR BERRY LN	23800	295M	SEM	77365
BRIAR BLUFF LN	0	488W	SWH	77082
BRIAR BRANCH DR	2200	489V	SWH	77042
BRIAR BRANCH LN	10800	490D	HC	77024
BRIAR BRIDGE	0	491N	SWH	77057
BRIARBROOK DR	800	489R	SWH	77042
BRIAR BROOK DR	14000	414A	NCC	77039
BRIARBROOK LN	0	488P	SWH	77077
BRIAR CANYON CT	6300	526E	NEF	77450
BRIAR CANYON CT	11600	329N	NWC	77377
BRIAR CHASE CIR	0	295H	SEM	77365
BRIARCHASE CT	14100	371B	NWC	77014
BRIARCHASE DR	3800	371B	NWC	77014
BRIAR CHASE DR	20800	295H	SEM	77365
BRIAR CHASE DR	20900	296E	SEM	77365
BRIARCHASE MANOR	0	371B	NWC	77014
BRIARCHESTER DR	1700	485M	SWC	77450
BRIAR CLIFF	1300	252G	SEM	77385
BRIARCLIFF DR	300	453C	NEH	77076
BRIARCLIFT LN	600	501L	BT	77521
BRIAR COVE CIR	20800	295H	SEM	77365
BRIAR COVE CIR	20900	296E	SEM	77365
BRIARCRAFT CT	15100	570V	SWH	77489
BRIARCRAFT DR	15100	570V	SWH	77459
BRIAR CREEK	1000	656M	FR	77546
BRIARCREEK BLVD	1700	333J	NCC	77073
BRIARCREEK BLVD	22600	333A	NCC	77373
BRIARCREEK BLVD	23600	293W	NCC	77373
BRIAR CREEK CIR	23600	296E	SEM	77365
BRIAR CREEK DR	600	539X	LP	77571
BRIARCREEK DR	800	501M	BT	77521
BRIAR CREST CT	0	616T	PL	77581
BRIARCREST DR	100	252S	SEM	77386
BRIARCREST DR	2000	488S	SWH	77077
BRIARCROSS CT	0	609J	NEF	77459
BRIAR CROSS CT	6300	408T	NWC	77084
BRIARDALE CT	1	491R	SWH	77027
BRIAR FALLS CT	13500	578W	SEH	77059
BRIARFIELD DR	6700	330G	NWC	77379
BRIAR FOREST DR	8900	490P	SWH	77024
BRIAR FOREST DR	9300	490P	SWH	77063
BRIAR FOREST DR	9700	489R	SWH	77042
BRIAR FOREST DR	11300	489N	SWH	77077
BRIAR FOREST DR	12200	488J	SWH	77077
BRIARGATE CIR	6600	571W	SWH	77489
BRIARGATE CT	15600	570Z	SWH	77489
BRIARGATE CT	15600	571X	SWH	77489
BRIARGATE DR	6600	571W	SWH	77489
BRIARGATE TRAILS	6500	571X	SWH	77489
BRIAR GLADE DR	6000	529G	SWH	77072
BRIAR GLEN CT	400	616V	FR	77546
BRIARGLEN DR	100	659E	LC	77573
BRIAR GLEN DR	2000	491V	SWH	77027
BRIARGLEN DR	2500	616T	PL	77581
BRIAR GLEN LN	200	539P	LP	77571
BRIARGREEN	800	537L	PA	77503
BRIARGREEN DR	2000	488S	SWH	77077
BRIARGREEN DR	2500	488W	SWH	77082
BRIAR GROVE DR	300	372B	NWC	77090
BRIARGROVE DR	2600	491N	SWH	77057
BRIAR HARBOR	12700	328Q	NWC	77377
BRIAR HAVEN CIR	20800	295H	SEM	77365
BRIAR HAVEN CIR	20900	296J	SEM	77365
BRIAR HEATH DR	14000	488K	SWH	77077
BRIAR HILL DR	1	489R	SWH	77042
BRIARHILLS PKWY	13900	488E	SWH	77077
BRIAR HOLLOW	1	491R	SWH	77027
BRIAR HOLLOW DR	3800	660X	DI	77539
S. BRIAR HOLLOW LN	1	491R	SWH	77027
E. BRIAR HOLLOW LN	1	491R	SWH	77027
BRIAR HOLLOW PLACE	4500	491R	SWH	77027
BRIAR HOME DR	1600	488J	SWH	77077
BRIARHORN DR	22900	290G	NWC	77389
BRIARHURST DR	2300	491S	SWH	77057
BRIARHURST PARK	2800	491S	SWH	77057
BRIARHURST PARK	6200	491S	SWH	77057
BRIAR IVY LN	0	488S	SWH	77082
BRIAR KNOLL DR	500	488G	SWH	77079
S. BRIAR KNOLL DR	3200	488Y	SWH	77082
S. BRIAR KNOLL DR	6200	528G	SWH	77072
BRIAR LAKE	0	292R	NCC	77373
BRIARLAKE LN	0	658U	LC	77573
BRIARLAND LN	25500	485W	NEF	77494
BRIAR LANDING LN	21500	525D	NEF	77450
BRIARLEAF CT	1700	527J	NEF	77083
BRIARLEE DR	1900	488S	SWH	77077
BRIAR LODGE DR	21200	296J	SEM	77365
BRIAR MAPLE	0	295M	SEM	77365
BRIAR MAPLE CIR	20800	295M	SEM	77365
BRIAR MAPLE CIR	20900	296J	SEM	77365
BRIARMEAD DR	1000	491N	SWH	77057
BRIAR MEADOW	0	568D	SG	77478
BRIAR MEADOW	0	657E	FR	77546
BRIAR MEADOW	27700	288P	NWC	77377
BRIARMEADOW AVE	300	656H	FR	77546
BRIARMOOR CT	1700	618F	SEH	77062
N. BRIAR MOSS LN	0	407S	NWC	77449
BRIAR OAK	21300	334M	NCC	77338
BRIAR OAKS LN	1800	491R	SWH	77027
BRIAR OAKS COVE	200	491L	SWH	77056
BRIARPARK DR	1	489R	SWH	77042
BRIARPARK DR	2700	489Z	SWH	77042
BRIARPARK TRAIL LN	10000	369Y	NWC	77064
BRIAR PATCH	10400	463S	CCO	77520
BRIAR PATCH RD	12600	488L	SWH	77077
BRIARPATH DR	500	488H	SWH	77079
BRIARPINE CT	12900	408V	NWC	77041
BRIAR PLACE DR	13900	488N	SWH	77077
BRIARPORT DR	2200	488S	SWH	77077
BRIAR RIDGE	2400	491S	SWH	77057
BRIAR RIDGE DR	800	491J	SWH	77057
BRIAR RIVER DR	10300	489V	SWH	77042
BRIAR ROCK RD	100	252S	SEM	77380
BRIAR ROSE CT	0	612K	PL	77545
BRIAR ROSE DR	0	612K	PL	77545
BRIAR ROSE DR	6100	491N	SWH	77057
BRIAR ROSE DR	7500	490R	SWH	77063
BRIAR ROSE DR	10000	489R	SWH	77042
BRIAR ROSE DR	11300	489P	SWH	77077
BRIAR RUN CT	7500	570Z	SWH	77489
BRIARSAGE CT	0	488N	SWH	77077
BRIARSAGE DR	14000	488N	SWH	77077
BRIAR SAGE LN	0	615C	PL	77581
BRIAR SEASONS DR	6200	571X	SWH	77489
BRIARSEDGE CT	19500	446L	NWC	77449
BRIARSIDE DR	13500	569Q	SF	77477
BRIAR SPRING CIR	20800	295M	SEM	77365
BRIAR SPRING CT	15500	571X	SWH	77489
BRIAR SQUARE	0	408T	NWC	77084
BRIARSTEAD DR	15700	571W	SWH	77489
BRIARSTEM DR	2000	488S	SWH	77077
BRIARSTONE CT	20000	290Y	NWC	77379
BRIARSTONE LN	6400	290Y	NWC	77379
BRIARSTONE BAY	0	406W	NWC	77449
BRIARSTONE BEND LN	0	367P	NWC	77433
BRIARSTONE GLEN CT	0	368F	NWC	77429
BRIARSTONE HARBOR TRAIL	0	445F	NWC	77493
BRIARSTONE HOLLOW DR	0	526P	NEF	77407
BRIARSTONE POINT LN	0	484N	NEF	77494
BRIARSTONE RIDGE LN	0	291A	NWC	77389
BRIAR SUMMIT LN	0	485X	NEF	77494
BRIAR SUMMIT LN	0	485X	NEF	77494
BRIAR TERRACE DR	6100	529G	SWH	77072
BRIAR THICKET DR	23900	296E	SEM	77365
BRIAR THISTLE LN	23700	296E	SEM	77365

Street Name	Block	Pg/Sq	Loc	Zips
BRIAR TIMBER CIR	0	296E	SEM	77365
BRIAR TIMBER DR	20900	296E	SEM	77365
BRIARTOWN LN	6100	491S	SWH	77057
BRIARTRACE CT	9690	416Z	NEC	77044
BRIAR TRAIL	1	491G	SWH	77056
BRIAR TREE CIR	0	296E	SEM	77365
BRIAR TREE DR	23600	296E	SEM	77365
BRIARTURN DR	1900	488S	SWH	77077
BRIARVIEW DR	2000	488S	SWH	77077
BRIAR VIEW DR	2600	616T	PL	77581
BRIAR VILLA DR	12700	328Q	NWC	77377
BRIAR VISTA WAY	0	526N	NEF	77407
BRIAR WALK DR	20900	296E	SEM	77365
BRIARWAY	1	491R	SWH	77027
BRIARWAY	800	537L	PA	77503
BRIARWEST BLVD	2200	488U	SWH	77077
BRIARWEST CIR	12800	488U	SWH	77077
BRIARWICK DR	19300	255T	SEM	77365
BRIARWICK LN	2900	414S	NEH	77093
BRIARWICK LN	5200	414V	NEH	77016
BRIARWICK LN	19600	257L	SEM	77357
BRIARWICK PARK LN	7300	407J	NWC	77433
BRIARWILD LN	9800	450S	NWH	77080
BRIAR WILLOW DR	20100	296E	SEM	77365
BRIARWOOD	0	529W	MD	77477
BRIARWOOD	1300	536P	PA	77502
BRIARWOOD CT	1	492T	SWH	77019
BRIARWOOD CT	100	659F	LC	77573
BRIARWOOD CT	900	538P	DP	77536
N. BRIARWOOD DR	0	247F	SWM	77362
BRIARWOOD DR	200	541C	BT	77520
BRIARWOOD COVE CIR	0	366J	NWC	77433
BRIARWOOD FOREST DR	5400	411L	NWC	77088
BRIARWOOD PASS	0	293D	SEM	77386
BRIARWOOD TRAIL	0	245D	SWM	77355
BRIARWORTH DR	13900	488N	SWH	77077
BRICELAND SPRINGS DR	14700	487Z	SWC	77082
BRICK LN	6600	456K	NEC	77049
BRICKARBOR DR	1400	446W	NWC	77449
BRICKELL BUSH CIR	0	366N	NWC	77433
BRICKEN LN	0	572Q	SWH	77047
BRICKER	4500	533V	SEH	77051
BRICKER	4700	533V	SEH	77033
BRICKHAVEN LN	8400	528Q	SWC	77083
BRICKHILL LN	25800	250T	NWC	77389
BRICKMAN CT	15800	407Z	NWC	77084
BRICKSTONE CT	800	252T	SEM	77386
BRICK VILLAGE DR	9800	367X	NWC	77095
BRICKYARD CT	10300	450E	NWH	77041
BRIDAL OAK CT	0	291C	WD	77380
BRIDAL PASS DR		524L	NWF	77406
BRIDEN OAK CT	18100	330E	NWC	77379
BRIDENWOOD CT	7600	330E	NWC	77379
BRIDEWELL LN	0	527J	NEF	77407
BRIDGE CT	2000	418D	NEC	77532
BRIDGE DR	16000	418D	NEC	77532
BRIDGEBAY LN	3800	446J	NWC	77449
BRIDGEBERRY LN	3200	489X	SWH	77082
BRIDGEBLUFF LN	3500	446E	NWC	77449
BRIDGEBROOK DR	22100	334E	NCC	77373
BRIDGE COVE DR	0	366F	NWC	77433
BRIDGE CREEK LN	4900	485Y	NEF	77494
BRIDGE CREEK LN	5000	525C	NEF	77494
BRIDGE CREEK FALLS CT	16600	330P	NWC	77379
BRIDGE CREST BLVD	100	527E	SWC	77082
BRIDGE CREST CT	1	527A	SWC	77082
BRIDGE CROSS LN	2000	371M	NWC	77067
BRIDGEDALE DR	3600	414A	NCC	77039
BRIDGEDALE LN	19800	335N	NCC	77338
BRIDGEDOWN DR	11100	369X	NWC	77065
BRIDGE END LN	21800	291T	NWC	77388
BRIDGE FALLS CT	21100	446J	NWC	77449
BRIDGE FALLS WAY	18500	447N	NWC	77084
BRIDGEFIELD LN	0	290X	NWC	77379
BRIDGEFOOT LN	8300	410G	NWC	77064
BRIDGE FOREST DR	5400	411L	NWC	77088
BRIDGEGATE DR	5500	334F	NCC	77373
BRIDGEHAVEN CT	5500	525C	NEF	77494
BRIDGEHAVEN DR	22300	525C	NEF	77494
BRIDGE HOLLOW CT	900	618E	SEH	77062
BRIDGELAKE BLVD	0	445R	NWC	77449
BRIDGELAND LN	4100	291T	NWC	77388
BRIDGELAND LN	10200	450E	NWH	77041
BRIDGELAND RD	0	366P	NWC	77433
BRIDGELAND CREEK PARKWAY	0	366P	NWC	77433
BRIDGELAND HEIGHTS DR	0	366Q	NWC	77433
N. BRIDGELAND LAKE PKWY	0	366F	NWC	77433
BRIDGELAND LANDING DR	0	366Q	NWC	77433
BRIDGE LIGHT LN	0	445R	NWC	77449
BRIDGE MANOR LN	0	526E	NEF	77450
BRIDGEMEADOWS LN	21100	446J	NWC	77449
BRIDGEMONT LN	4700	291S	NWC	77388
BRIDGE PARK DR	8600	409H	NWC	77064
BRIDGEPARK LN	0	406M	NWC	77433
BRIDGEPATH CT	13300	408Y	NWC	77041
BRIDGEPATH LN	13400	408Y	NWC	77041
BRIDGEPATH COVE	13500	408Y	NWC	77041
BRIDGEPOINT LN	21300	291S	NWC	77388
BRIDGEPORT RD	13500	572U	SWH	77047
W. BRIDGEPORT PASS CIR	0	406D	NWC	77433
S. BRIDGEPORT PASS CIR	0	406D	NWC	77433
N. BRIDGEPORT PASS CIR	0	406D	NWC	77433
E. BRIDGEPORT PASS CIR	0	406D	NWC	77433
BRIDGER BEND LN	0	377F	NEC	77346
BRIDGES FAIRWAY CT	0	331U	NWC	77068
BRIDGES FAIRWAY LN	0	331U	NWC	77068
BRIDGESIDE LN	0	609Y	MC	77459
BRIDGE SPRINGS LN	21100	446J	NWC	77449
BRIDGESTONE LN	21500	291T	NWC	77388
BRIDGESTONE BEND DR	4600	291P	NWC	77388
BRIDGESTONE CANYON DR	22300	291P	NWC	77388
BRIDGESTONE CEDAR DR	4400	291P	NWC	77388
BRIDGESTONE CLIFF DR	4500	291P	NWC	77388
BRIDGESTONE CROSSING DR	22000	291P	NWC	77388
BRIDGESTONE EAGLE CT	0	291T	NWC	77388
BRIDGESTONE GLENRIDGE	22300	291P	NWC	77388
BRIDGESTONE HAWK CT	0	291T	NWC	77388
BRIDGESTONE LAKES DR	4400	291P	NWC	77388
BRIDGESTONE MAPLE DR	4300	291P	NWC	77388
BRIDGESTONE OAK DR	22100	291P	NWC	77388
BRIDGESTONE PALM CT	22300	291P	NWC	77388
BRIDGESTONE PARK LN	0	253N	SEM	77386
BRIDGESTONE PATH DR	0	291P	NWC	77388
BRIDGESTONE PINE CT	22100	291P	NWC	77388
BRIDGESTONE POINT DR	4500	291P	NWC	77388
BRIDGESTONE SHADOW CT	0	291P	NWC	77388
BRIDGESTONE TRAILS DR	4500	291P	NWC	77388
BRIDGESTONE VALLEY DR	4500	291P	NWC	77388
BRIDGESTONE WAY CT	22000	291P	NWC	77388
BRIDGETON LN	0	573X	SEC	77047
BRIDGETON HOLLOW DR	0	484V	NEF	77494
BRIDGETON PLACE LN	0	609S	NEF	77479

Street Name	Block	Pg/Sq	Loc	Zips
BRIDGETT LN	3300	463H	MB	77520
BRIDGEVIEW CIR	4600	291W	NWC	77388
BRIDGE VIEW LN	0	484E	KT	77494
BRIDGEVIEW LN	4600	291W	NWC	77388
BRIDGEVILLAGE DR	4400	293Y	NCC	77373
BRIDGEVILLE LN	4800	291S	NWC	77388
BRIDGEWALK LN	13300	408Y	NWC	77041
BRIDGEWALK COVE	13500	408Z	NWC	77041
BRIDGEWATER CIR	22800	333E	NCC	77373
BRIDGEWATER DR	22000	245R	SWM	77355
BRIDGEWATER DR	22600	333E	NCC	77373
BRIDGEWATER DR	24400	246N	SWM	77355
BRIDGEWATER MANOR LN	3000	445R	NWC	77449
BRIDGEWATER MEADOW	0	446E	NWC	77449
BRIDGEWATER POINTE	21400	446E	NWC	77449
BRIDGEWATER VILLAGE DR	21700	445M	NWC	77449
BRIDGE WAY	24100	290C	NWC	77389
BRIDGEWOOD	10900	490H	HC	77024
BRIDGEWOOD DR	18600	378Q	NEC	77532
BRIDLE CT	14500	377T	NEC	77044
BRIDLE BEND DR	14800	408X	NWC	77084
BRIDAL BLUFF CT		484S	NEF	77494
BRIDLE CANYON	23700	287A	SWM	77355
BRIDLECHASE LN	14000	371A	NWC	77014
BRIDLE CREEK DR	25600	287A	SWM	77355
BRIDLECREEK GLEN DR	0	368B	NWC	77429
BRIDLEDON LN	4100	371B	NWC	77014
BRIDLE FALLS	25700	287A	SWM	77355
BRIDLE GROVE CT	18600	328G	NWC	77377
BRIDLE MEADOW LN	18200	328K	NWC	77377
BRIDLE OAK DR	16000	326K	NWC	77433
BRIDLEPARK CIR	10900	414V	NEH	77016
BRIDLE PATH DR	7200	456L	NEC	77044
BRIDLE PATH LN	0	656X	FR	77546
BRIDLE PATH LN	2800	656X	FR	77546
BRIDLE RIDGE LOOP	700	332V	NCC	77073
BRIDLE RUN LN	0	327Y	NWC	77429
BRIDLE SPRINGS LN	0	377W	NEC	77044
BRIDLE SPUR LN	1300	451W	HI	77055
BRIDLE TRAIL DR	21000	332V	NCC	77073
BRIDLEWAY CIR	10900	414V	NEH	77016
BRIDLEWAY CIR	26900	246Q	SWM	77355
BRIDLEWOOD	10700	490H	HC	77024
BRIDLINGTON	5700	571P	SWH	77085
BRIDOON DR	18500	407N	NWC	77433
BRIEFWAY	7300	534R	SEH	77087
BRIEFWAY	7400	535N	SEH	77087
BRIER GARDENS DR	3600	527D	SWC	77082
BRIERLEY LN	0	407Y	NWC	77084
BRIERVINE CT	1	250M	WD	77381
BRIG-O-DOON CIR	9400	530V	SWH	77096
BRIGADE	10200	450N	NWH	77043
BRIGADE CT	2500	609B	MC	77478
BRIGADE TRAILS DR	6400	406V	NWC	77449
BRIGADOON	100	656C	FR	77546
BRIGHT CT	0	419A	NEC	77532
N. BRIGHT DR	800	332V	NCC	77073
BRIGHT ANGEL LN	0	406C	NWC	77433
BRIGHT BLOOM LN	6300	290U	NWC	77379
BRIGHT BLUFF LN	0	573Y	SEC	77047
BRIGHTBROOK DR	14900	408F	NWC	77095
BRIGHT CANYON LN	0	366R	NWC	77433
BRIGHT DAWN CT	0	484U	NEF	77494
BRIGHT EMBER CT	800	617M	SEH	77062
BRIGHTEN GLEN LN	0	377K	NEC	77346
BRIGHT FALLS LN	6300	407S	NWC	77449
BRIGHT FEATHER LN	0	526K	NEF	77407
BRIGHTFIELD DR	13700	568F	SG	77498
BRIGHT GLEN DR	0	612J	PL	77545
BRIGHT GLEN LN	0	572W	SWC	77053
BRIGHTGLEN LN	0	332H	NCC	77373
BRIGHT GROVE CT	8500	407G	NWC	77095
BRIGHT HARBOR DR	0	406D	NWC	77433
BRIGHT HOLLOW LN	0	485J	NEF	77494
BRIGHTLAKEBEND CT	0	526J	NEF	77407
BRIGHT LAKE BEND LN	7400	525M	NEF	77407
BRIGHTLAKE WAY	1700	569X	MC	77459
BRIGHTLAKE WAY LN	0	612K	PL	77545
BRIGHT LANDING CT	12000	612U	PL	77584
BRIGHT LANDING LN	0	612U	PL	77584
BRIGHTLING LN	16500	332P	NWC	77090
BRIGHT MEADOW LN	20500	379E	NEC	77532
BRIGHT MEADOWS DR	2000	610A	MC	77489
BRIGHT NIGHT DR	0	527P	NEF	77407
BRIGHT OAK CT	0	293Z	NCC	77373
BRIGHTON	0	568D	SG	77478
BRIGHTON CT	1	609C	MC	77459
BRIGHTON LN	0	258G	SEM	77357
BRIGHTON LN	3700	613G	NEB	77584
BRIGHTON LN	10100	569C	SWC	77031
BRIGHTON LN	10600	569A	MD	77477
BRIGHTON BROOK LN	0	253P	SEM	77386
BRIGHTON BROOK LN	0	328M	NWC	77377
BRIGHTON BROOK LN	0	526P	NEF	77407
BRIGHTON BROOK LN	0	615G	PL	77581
BRIGHTONFERN LN	0	457Q	NEC	77049
BRIGHTON FORT DR	0	332R	NCC	77073
BRIGHTON GARDENS DR	0	524P	NWF	77406
BRIGHTON GLEN LN	7300	527J	NEF	77407
BRIGHTON HILL LN	6800	525H	NEF	77450
BRIGHTON HOLLOW LN	21400	406X	NWC	77449
BRIGHTON KNOLLS LN	7500	527J	NEF	77407
BRIGHTON LAKE LN	8300	407F	NWC	77095
BRIGHTON PARK DR	13800	377Y	NEC	77044
BRIGHTON PLACE CT	8100	408F	NWC	77095
BRIGHTON SKY LN		484S	NEF	77494
BRIGHTON SPRINGS LN	3700	446J	NWC	77449
BRIGHTON TRACE LN	0	526M	NEF	77407
BRIGHTON TRACE LN	14400	377Y	NEH	77044
BRIGHTON TRAIL CT	12700	328G	NWC	77377
BRIGHTON TRAIL LN	18800	328G	NWC	77377
BRIGHTONWOOD CT	6600	290U	NWC	77379
BRIGHTONWOOD LN	20300	290U	NWC	77379
BRIGHT PENNY LN	600	497H	NEC	77015
BRIGHT POINT CT	0	289W	NWC	77375
BRIGHTRIDGE LN	6900	290T	NWC	77379
BRIGHT SAIL CIR	2000	619Z	LC	77573
BRIGHTS BEND	4300	609R	MC	77459
BRIGHT SKY CT	2900	253N	SEM	77386
BRIGHT SKY CT	26400	484Y	NEF	77494
BRIGHTSPRING CT	0	446N	NWC	77449
BRIGHT SPRING LN	0	290Q	NWC	77379
BRIGHT STAR RD	23100	334A	NCC	77373
BRIGHTSTONE DR	19800	334R	NCC	77338
BRIGHT SUMMER LN	0	526F	NEF	77407
BRIGHT SUNRISE TRAIL	0	611N	FS	77545
BRIGHT TIMBER LANDING DR	0	294E	SEM	77386
BRIGHT VIEW LN	13500	577W	SEH	77034
BRIGHTWATER DR	2000	569X	MC	77459
BRIGHTWATER DR	2400	609B	MC	77459
BRIGHTWATER CENTER BLVD	0	609C	MC	77459
BRIGHTWELL DR	0	335H	NEH	77339

Street Name	Block	Pg/Sq	Loc	Zips
BRIGHT WILLOW LN	0	417C	NEH	77044
BRIGHTWOOD	4000	609C	MC	77459
BRIGHTWOOD DR	3900	331S	NWC	77068
BRIGHTWOOD DR	4500	330V	NWC	77068
BRIGHTWOOD LN	25100	339E	HU	77336
BRIGHTWOOD HEIGHTS CT	0	366R	NWC	77433
BRIGHTWOOD PARK LN	18100	526M	NEF	77407
BRIGHTWORK WAY	0	251G	WD	77380
BRIGID PLACE DR	12900	369J	NWC	77429
BRIGSTONE PARK DR	5600	525D	NEF	77450
BRILEY	2000	493Z	SEH	77004
BRILEY DR	0	620D	SB	77586
BRILL	3000	454X	NEH	77026
BRILL DR	1600	656M	FR	77546
BRILL LN	24600	249X	NWC	77375
BRILLIANT CIR	0	444D	NWC	77493
BRILLIANT LAKE DR	9800	376S	NEC	77396
BRILLOCK AVE	900	373U	NCC	77032
BRIM	7000	454M	NEH	77028
BRIMBERRY	1900	452E	NWH	77018
BRIMBERRY	2100	451H	NWH	77018
BRIMFIELD DR	16000	527C	SWC	77082
BRIMHILL RD	0	369P	NWC	77070
BRIMHURST DR	13500	488K	SWH	77077
BRIMMAGE DR	2200	371H	NWC	77067
BRIMRIDGE LN	0	574Y	SEH	77048
BRIMSTONE CT	1	251T	WD	77380
BRIMWOOD DR	3400	331S	NWC	77068
BRINDISI CT	0	610T	MC	77459
BRINDLE TRAIL	0	377S	NEC	77044
BRINGATE CT	12200	371J	NWC	77066
BRINGATE LN	5300	370M	NWC	77066
BRINGEWOOD CHASE DR	1000	329H	NWC	77379
BRINGHURST	1	494K	NEH	77020
BRINGHURST	2000	494B	NEH	77026
BRINKLEY	4100	533Y	SEH	77051
BRINKLEY	4700	533Y	SEH	77033
BRINKLOW CROSSING DR	0	295M	SEM	77365
BRINKLOW POINT DR	0	406H	NWC	77433
BRINKMAN	2500	452U	NWH	77008
BRINKMAN	3400	452G	NWH	77018
BRINKMAN	5200	452G	NWH	77091
BRINKMAN CT	0	452G	NWH	77091
BRINKWOOD DR	16200	332T	NWC	77090
BRINKWORTH LN	7500	370A	NWC	77070
BRINKWORTH LN	8100	369D	NWC	77070
BRINMONT PLACE	3200	485T	NEF	77494
BRINMONT PLACE CT	23500	485X	NEF	77494
BRINSON CT	1200	329B	NWC	77375
BRINTON CT	16200	407D	NWC	77095
BRINTON FOREST CT	0	446E	NWC	77449
BRINTON OAKS CT	2100	486N	SWC	77450
BRINTON SADDLE LN	0	446E	NWC	77449
BRINTON SPRING LN	0	615F	PL	77581
BRINTON TRAILS LN	3200	485U	NEF	77494
BRINWOOD DR	10100	450W	NWH	77043
BRINWOOD DR	10200	449Z	NWH	77043
BRISBANE DR	0	406U	NWC	77449
BRISBANE DR	0	574H	SEH	77061
BRISBANE DR	100	575E	SEH	77061
BRISBANE DR	3000	573L	SEH	77051
BRISBANE DR	4100	573L	SEH	77047
BRISBANE DR	4900	573M	SEH	77048
BRISBANE MEADOWS DR	0	406U	NWC	77449
BRISCOE	4500	533V	SEH	77051
BRISCOE	4700	533V	SEH	77033
BRISCOE CT	0	613S	PL	77584
BRISCOE LN	0	612V	PL	77584
BRISCOE LN	0	613S	PL	77584
BRISCOE BEND LN	0	406C	NWC	77433
BRISK SPRING CT	25500	292V	NCC	77373
BRISTLEBROOK DR	9200	528T	NEF	77083
BRISTLECONE DR	2700	446N	NWC	77449
BRISTLE CONE PINE LN	0	250V	NWC	77389
BRISTLECONE PLACE	2000	251R	WD	77380
BRISTLECONE TRAIL	3300	251S	SWM	77380
BRISTLE CREEK DR	0	407D	NWC	77095
BRISTLE HAVEN DR	0	528H	SWH	77072
BRISTLELEAF DR	3600	446M	NWC	77449
N. BRISTLE PINE DR	8400	330N	NWC	77379
S. BRISTLE PINE DR	17200	330N	NWC	77379
BRISTLESTAR DR	19200	446M	NWC	77449
BRISTOL	4600	453U	NEH	77009
BRISTOL CT	0	258F	SEM	77357
W. BRISTOL CT	400	658Q	LC	77573
S. BRISTOL CT	1100	658Q	LC	77573
N. BRISTOL CT	1100	658Q	LC	77573
BRISTOL CT	2700	569N	SG	77478
BRISTOL LN	1000	569T	MC	77459
BRISTOL BAND LN	2300	486N	SWC	77450
BRISTOL BANKS CT	5200	449A	NWC	77041
BRISTOL BAY CT	18400	377C	NEC	77346
BRISTOL BERRY DR	12900	328Y	NWC	77429
BRISTOL BREEZE DR	0	612G	PL	77545
BRISTOL BREEZE LN	2100	658T	LC	77573
BRISTOL CLIFF BLVD		328k	NWC	77429
BRISTOL COVE	5100	491Y	SWH	77056
S. BRISTOL GATE PLACE	1	251R	WD	77380
N. BRISTOL GATE PLACE	1	251R	WD	77380
E. BRISTOL HARBOR CIR	6200	408T	NWC	77084
S. BRISTOL HARBOR CIR	14700	408T	NWC	77084
BRISTOL HILLS LN	0	332R	NCC	77073
BRISTOL KNOLL DR	0	525R	NEF	77407
BRISTOL LANE CT	11500	370L	NWC	77066
BRISTOL MANOR BLVD	0	366L	NWC	77433
BRISTOL MEADOW LN	0	657S	FR	77546
BRISTOL MEADOW LN	0	406F	NWC	77433
BRISTOL MEMORIAL DR	0	330B	NWC	77379
BRISTOL PARK	6500	409S	NWC	77041
BRISTOL PATH LN	0	609X	NEF	77479
BRISTOL POINT LN	0	328K	NWC	77377
BRISTOL POINT LN	18500	328K	NWC	77377
BRISTOL RIDGE DR	7200	408N	NWH	77095
BRISTOL WATER DR	0	612L	PL	77584
BRISTOL WATERS	0	449A	NWC	77041
BRISTOL WAY	1000	613F	NEB	77584
BRISTOLWOOD CT	22400	525G	NEF	77494
BRISTOL WOODS LN	0	368A	NWC	77429
BRITANNIA DR	20000	486C	SWC	77450
BRITE GLEN CT	0	290K	NWC	77379
BRITFORD	16700	407Q	NWC	77084
BRITISH KNOLL CT	12600	371H	NWC	77014
BRITISH WOODS LN	700	616Y	FR	77546
BRITOAK LN	10800	489A	SWH	77079
BRITON CENTER CT	7000	370A	NWC	77069
BRITON COVE DR	14500	408T	NWC	77084
BRITT RD	12400	614C	BK	77581
BRITTAN LEAF LN	11000	577S	SEH	77034
BRITTANY CT	17000	407Q	NWC	77084
BRITTANY DR	13400	568C	SG	77478
BRITTANY LN	13700	415B	NEC	77396
BRITTANY COLONY DR	2100	658R	LC	77573

Street Name	Block	Pg/Sq	Loc	Zips
BRITTANY CREEK DR	19300	331D	NWC	77388
BRITTANY FERRY LN	6600	457P	NEC	77049
BRITTANY KNOLL DR	16000	407R	NWC	77095
BRITTANY LAKES DR	2500	658U	LC	77573
BRITTANY PARK LN	6300	370R	NWC	77066
BRITTANY ROSE PLACE	100	249R	NWH	77375
BRITTANY ROSE PLACE	100	249R	NWH	77375
BRITTERIDGE	15000	408T	NWC	77084
BRITTMOORE RD	600	489C	SWH	77079
BRITTMOORE RD	1000	449U	NWH	77043
BRITTMOORE RD	4300	449G	NWC	77041
BRITTMOORE RD	5900	409U	NWC	77041
BRITTMOORE OAKS PLACE	0	449U	NWH	77043
BRITTMOORE PARK DR	10900	449B	NWC	77041
BRITTMORE NORTH	4300	449C	NWC	77041
BRITT OAKS DR	6400	656W	NEB	77511
BRITTON	1800	541A	BT	77520
BRITTON HILL WAY	21600	445H	NWC	77449
BRITTON KEY LN	0	293F	SEM	77386
BRITTON KEY LN	0	293F	SEM	77386
BRITTON RIDGE	2600	484M	NEF	77494
BRITTWAY	10900	449U	NWH	77043
BRITTYN LAKE DR	0	293D	SEM	77386
BROAD	2400	534Q	SEH	77087
BROAD RD	2300	460Y	MN	77521
BROAD ST	0	568T	SG	77478
BROAD BAY LN	0	612F	PL	77545
BROAD BAY LN	0	659M	LC	77573
BROAD BEND DR	0	366L	NWC	77433
BROADBLUFF LN	18000	407K	NWC	77433
BROAD BRANCH CT	24700	293N	NCC	77373
BROADCREST CT	25500	485W	NEF	77494
BROAD CYPRESS CT	0	331W	NWC	77068
BROADELM DR	7200	407Q	NWC	77095
BROADFIELD BLVD	1200	487D	NWH	77084
BROADFIELD BLVD	1400	447Z	NWH	77084
BROADFORD	27000	247Z	SWM	77355
BROAD GLEN	0	446F	NWC	77449
BROADGLEN CT	16200	527B	SWC	77082
BROADGREEN DR	2200	610A	MC	77489
BROADGREEN DR	14200	489E	SWH	77079
BROADGREEN DR	14400	488H	SWH	77079
BROAD HARBOR LN	0	406C	NWC	77433
BROAD HAVEN DR	2500	371R	NWC	77067
BROADHEAD MANOR CT	9300	289Z	NWC	77379
BROADHEAD MANOR DR	19700	289Z	NWC	77379
BROADHILL DR	0	296S	NEH	77365
BROAD HOLLOW CT	20900	290U	NWC	77379
BROADHURST DR	1	572Y	SWH	77047
BROADKNOLL LN	17300	527J	NEF	77407
BROADLAWN DR	2100	618M	SEH	77058
BROADLEAF	4200	297T	NEH	77345
BROADLEAF AVE	0	461N	NEC	77521
BROADLEY DR	9700	528S	NEF	77498
BROADMARK LN	4500	333M	NCC	77338
BROADMEAD DR	2500	532P	SWH	77025
BROADMEADOW LN	13500	488F	SWH	77077
BROADMOOR	1600	494X	SEH	77023
BROADMOOR CIR	2700	609H	MC	77459
BROADMOOR CT	2100	659D	LC	77573
BROADMOOR DR	0	577C	PA	77505
BROADMOOR DR	400	656P	FR	77546
BROADMOOR DR	3000	569S	SG	77478
BROADMOOR DR	4700	659D	LC	77573
BROAD OAK CT	15900	329N	NWC	77377
BROAD OAKS CIR	100	491F	SWH	77056
W. BROAD OAKS DR	1	491K	SWH	77056
E. BROAD OAKS DR	1	491K	SWH	77056
BROAD OAKS DR	6500	524Y	NEF	77406
BROAD OAKS LN	1	491L	SWH	77056
BROAD OAKS PARK	5400	491L	SWM	77056
BROAD OAKS TRAIL	100	491F	SWH	77056
BROAD PINE DR	24800	338M	NEH	77336
BROAD RIDGE RD	16000	611D	SWH	77053
BROADRIPPLE DR	200	338M	NEH	77336
BROAD RUN LN	0	526K	NEF	77407
BROADSIDE CT	15900	419E	NEC	77532
BROADSKY DR	20300	446X	NWC	77449
BROAD SPRINGS CT	23100	525K	NEF	77407
BROADSTAIRS	10300	496A	NEH	77013
BROADSTONE DR	21500	446J	NWC	77449
BROADSWEEP DR	11200	369U	NWC	77064
BROADSWORD DR		289P	NWC	77375
BROAD TIMBERS DR	2400	293S	NCC	77373
BROAD VALE CIR	18200	377A	NEC	77346
BROAD VALLEY CT	5800	334E	NCC	77373
BROADVIEW DR	7600	535W	SEH	77061
BROADWATER DR	16000	418D	NEC	77532
BROADWAY	0	536H	PA	77506
BROADWAY	0	616S	PL	77581
N. BROADWAY	100	540U	LP	77571
BROADWAY	100	535B	SEH	77012
S. BROADWAY	700	580C	LP	77571
E. BROADWAY	1000	615P	PL	77581
BROADWAY	2700	535T	SEH	77017
BROADWAY	3900	535T	SEH	77087
W. BROADWAY	4000	614R	PL	77581
BROADWAY	8100	535T	SEH	77061
N. BROADWAY	8800	576K	SEH	77034
BROADWAY	8800	575B	SEH	77061
BROADWAY	16000	418D	NEC	77532
S. BROADWAY	100	540Y	LP	77571
W. BROADWAY AVE	100	536G	PA	77506
BROADWAY	1000	612R	PL	77584
BROADWAY	2300	613R	PL	77584
BROADWAY	4200	614N	PL	77581
BROADWAY BEND DR	0	612R	PL	77584
BROADWIND LN	19100	446D	NWC	77449
BROCK	3500	534F	SEH	77023
BROCKET PLACE	200	569J	SF	77477
BROCKHAMPTON	500	496E	NEH	77013
BROCKINGTON DR	6800	525F	NEF	77494
BROCKLAND LN	0	406H	NWC	77433
BROCK LAND LN	0	326V	NWC	77429
BROCK LAND LN	0	326V	NWC	77429
BROCKLEY LN	7300	534V	SEH	77087
BROCKLEY LN	7400	535S	SEH	77087
BROCKMAN	200	536G	PA	77506
BROCK MEADOW DR	0	250U	NWC	77389
BROCK MEADOW DR	0	250U	NWC	77389
BROCK PARK BLVD	8500	456A	NEH	77078
BROCKTON	8000	535L	SEH	77017
BROCKWELL	0	334J	NCC	77338
BROCKWOOD DR	14600	573Z	SEC	77047
BROCKWOOD DR	14700	613D	SEC	77047
BROC SPRINGS LN	0	293F	SEM	77386
BROC SPRINGS LN	0	293F	SEM	77386
BRODIE LN	0	446S	NWC	77449
BRODIE LN	0	446S	NWC	77449
BRODT RD	700	420C	NEC	77532
BRODY FALLS CT	0	377W	NEC	77044
BROGAN CT	8600	249Z	NWC	77375

Street Name	Block	Pg/Sq	Loc	Zips
BROGDEN RD	700	490D	HE	77024
BROKEN ARROW	1500	502J	BT	77521
BROKEN ARROW	7400	461S	NEC	77521
BROKEN ARROW DR	12100	490E	SWH	77024
BROKEN BACK DR	17100	379W	NEC	77532
BROKEN BOUGH CIR	11700	490F	BH	77024
BROKEN BOUGH DR	3300	609H	MC	77459
BROKEN BOUGH DR	11900	490E	SWH	77024
BROKEN BOUGH DR	12500	489H	SWH	77024
BROKEN BOUGH DR	25000	251T	SWM	77380
BROKEN BOUGH LN	19500	258J	SEM	77357
BROKEN BOW LN	12100	247R	SWM	77362
BROKEN BOW LN	24000	325J	NWC	77447
BROKEN BOW LN	24200	324M	NWC	77447
BROKEN BRANCH CT	2000	484K	NEF	77494
BROKEN BRIDGE DR	13600	571J	SWH	77085
BROKEN BRIDGE LN	3000	615L	PL	77581
BROKEN BROOK CIR	1	250C	WD	77381
BROKEN BROOK CT	13000	368E	NWC	77429
BROKEN CACTUS DR	0	406D	NWC	77433
BROKEN CREEK CT	0	612L	PL	77584
BROKEN CREEK CT	2600	612L	PL	77584
BROKEN CREEK LN	0	612L	PL	77584
BROKEN CREEK LN	12300	612L	PL	77584
BROKEN CYPRESS CIR	15500	457Q	NEC	77049
BROKEN ELM DR	3500	331F	NWC	77388
S. BROKEN FERN DR	1	251R	WD	77380
N. BROKEN FERN DR	1	251M	WD	77380
BROKEN HILLS LN	0	377U	NEC	77044
BROKEN LANCE LN	0	407J	NWC	77433
BROKEN LIMB TRAIL	21800	325R	NWC	77433
W. BROKEN OAK CT	1	251J	WD	77381
E. BROKEN OAK CT	1	251J	WD	77381
BROKEN PASS LN	0	367P	NWC	77433
BROKEN PEBBLE CT	22100	485Z	NEF	77450
BROKEN PINE CT	0	609Q	MC	77459
BROKEN PINE LN	26400	366M	NWC	77433
BROKEN RIDGE DR	7400	408J	NWC	77095
BROKEN SKY CT	9800	369U	NWC	77064
BROKEN SKY DR	10800	369U	NWC	77064
BROKEN SPEAR LN	0	256W	SEM	77365
BROKEN SPOKE	15900	246M	SC	77355
BROKEN STONE	6500	407U	NWC	77084
BROKEN TIMBER CIR	16200	407H	NWC	77095
BROKEN TIMBER WAY	8200	407H	NWC	77095
BROKEN TRACE CT	0	376B	NEC	77369
BROKENVIEW DR	3000	613P	NEB	77584
BROLETTO CT	0	525J	NEF	77406
BROLIE LN	0	454V	NEH	77026
BROLLIER	2300	533S	SWH	77054
BROM BONES BLVD	2600	616N	PL	77581
BROMEL STATION	9900	329L	NWC	77070
BROMLEY	8000	451W	HI	77055
BROMPTON	6300	532F	WU	77005
BROMPTON	6800	532K	SWH	77025
BROMPTON CT	1	490L	PP	77024
BROMPTON CT	300	459Q	HG	77562
W. BROMPTON DR	1000	613E	NEB	77584
E. BROMPTON DR	1000	613K	NEB	77584
S. BROMPTON DR	2600	613J	NEB	77584
N. BROMPTON DR	2600	613F	NEB	77584
BROMPTON LN	500	459Q	HG	77562
BROMPTON PLACE DR	8300	527P	NEF	77083
BROMPTON SQUARE DR	0	532F	SEH	77005
BRONCO DR	9100	450Y	NWH	77055
BRONCO BLUFF CT	3100	486T	SWC	77450
BRONCROFT CT	12900	377X	NEC	77044
BRONDESBURY DR	20100	486K	SWC	77450
BRON HOLLY DR	2000	452N	NWH	77018
BRONSON	2100	576F	SEH	77034
BRONTIE SPRINGS CT	0	526P	NEF	77407
BRONTON	3000	452N	NWH	77092
BRONWYNN LN	2700	573T	SEC	77047
BRONZE BAY CT	15100	618C	SEH	77059
BRONZE BLUFF DR	20200	446P	NWC	77449
BRONZE FINCH DR	14700	325L	NWC	77433
BRONZEHILL LN	0	484Y	NEF	77494
BRONZE LEAF CT	21900	325R	NWC	77433
BRONZE LEAF DR	21900	325R	NWC	77433
BRONZE LOQUATE CT	2700	446N	NWC	77449
BRONZE SUNSET CT	1700	338A	NEH	77345
BRONZE TRAIL DR	7600	377D	NEC	77346
BROODING OAK CIR	9400	530V	SWH	77096
BROOK LN	600	536U	PA	77502
BROOK AMBER CIR	1700	538M	DP	77536
BROOK ARBOR CT	15300	618F	SEH	77062
BROOK ARBOR LN	0	612K	PL	77545
BROOK ARBOR LN	0	660E	LC	77573
BROOKBANK DR	3700	331S	NWC	77068
BROOKBEND DR	10600	531Y	SWH	77035
S. BROOKBERRY CT	1	251E	WD	77381
E. BROOKBERRY CT	1	251E	WD	77381
BROOKBLUFF LN	13500	488P	SWH	77077
BROOKCHASE DR	29300	293A	SEM	77386
BROOKCHASE DR	29600	253W	SEM	77386
BROOKCHASE LOOP	21500	326S	NWC	77433
BROOKCHASE WAY	15600	326S	NWC	77433
BROOKCHESTER	1700	485M	SWC	77450
BROOK COVE DR	0	366K	NWC	77433
BROOKCREST CIR	8600	528R	SWH	77072
BROOKDALE DR	100	657Q	LC	77573
BROOKDALE DR	2300	297S	NEH	77339
BROOKDALE LN	3100	538T	DP	77536
BROOKDALE BAY LN	0	405U	NWC	77493
BROOKDALE HEIGHTS PLACE	0	291A	NWC	77389
BROOKDALE MEADOW TRACE	0	405R	NWC	77493
BROOKDALE PARK LN	0	526Q	NEF	77407
BROOKEFIELD CIR	1	245D	SWM	77355
BROOKELAND MEADOWS CT	0	570Z	SWH	77489
BROOKES BEND	18000	487A	SWC	77094
BROOKE VISTA LN	0	576V	SEH	77034
BROOKFALLS DR	11600	329S	NWC	77070
BROOKFIELD	7800	462V	CCO	77520
BROOKFIELD DR	0	571Z	SWH	77053
BROOKFIELD DR	2900	572S	SWH	77045
BROOKFIELD DR	4700	571P	SWH	77085
BROOKFIELD PARK	12600	409S	NWC	77041
BROOKFIELD RUN LN	4000	609J	NEF	77479
BROOKFIR LN	7000	411S	NWH	77040
BROOKFLOWER RD	1	252J	WD	77380
BROOKFORD CT	16200	578Y	SEH	77059
BROOKFORD DR	500	570Y	MC	77489
BROOKFORD DR	15700	618C	SEH	77059
BROOKFORD DR	15900	578Y	SEH	77059
BROOK FOREST CT	0	618H	SEH	77059
BROOK FOREST DR	15700	618H	SEH	77059
BROOK FOREST RD	22000	257A	SEM	77357
BROOK FOREST RD	23500	256D	SEM	77357
BROOK FOREST TRAIL	200	568N	SG	77478
BROOK GARDEN LN	3900	446J	NWC	77449
BROOKGATE DR	6100	334B	NCC	77373
BROOKGLADE CIR	12300	528R	SWH	77099
BROOKGLEN DR	5100	535V	SEH	77017
BROOKGREEN	0	578Y	SEH	77059
BROOKGREEN	0	618C	SEH	77059
BROOKGREEN DR	3200	297W	NEH	77339
BROOKGREEN FALLS DR	21500	486J	SWC	77450
BROOK GROVE DR	1200	485L	SWC	77450
BROOK GROVE DR	3100	297Y	NEH	77345
BROOK HAVEN	0	537X	PA	77502
BROOKHAVEN	3100	538T	DP	77536
BROOKHAVEN	3900	537X	PA	77504
BROOKHAVEN	4300	533Q	SEH	77051
BROOKHAVEN CT	1100	615B	PL	77581
BROOK HAVEN DR	2100	659C	LC	77573
BROOKHAVEN DR	25100	252S	SEM	77386
BROOKHAVEN PARK CIR	12500	408D	NWC	77065
BROOKHAVEN PARK DR	9500	408D	NWC	77065
BROOKHEAD TRAIL	4000	371E	NWC	77066
BROOKHILL DR	6100	534L	SEH	77087
BROOKHOLLOW	3000	528Q	NWF	77045
BROOK HOLLOW CT	0	244G	WCO	77447
BROOK HOLLOW DR	0	614G	PL	77581
BROOKHOLLOW DR	1000	538S	DP	77536
BROOK HOLLOW DR	13500	568F	SG	77498
BROOKHOLLOW DR	24200	244G	WCO	77447
BROOKHOLLOW COURT DR	0	407Y	NWC	77084
BROOKHOLLOW COURT DR	0	407Y	NWC	77084
BROOKHOLLOW CROSSING	0	407Y	NWC	77084
BROOKHOLLOW GROVE CT	17200	407Y	NWC	77084
BROOKHOLLOW MIST CT	17200	407Y	NWC	77084
BROOKHOLLOW OAKS TRAIL	5500	407Y	NWC	77084
BROOKHOLLOW PINES CT	5500	407Y	NWC	77084
BROOKHOLLOW PINE TRAIL	0	407Y	NWC	77084
BROOKHOLLOW TRACE CT	17200	407Y	NWC	77084
BROOKHOLLOW WEST DR	6900	410S	NWC	77040
BROOKHURST	0	296S	NEH	77365
BROOKHURST DR	0	295V	NEH	77365
BROOKHURST LN	3100	538T	DP	77536
BROOKINGS DR	18000	447F	NWC	77084
W. BROOKLAKE CT	1400	489K	SWH	77077
W. BROOKLAKE DR	1300	489K	SWH	77077
E. BROOKLAKE DR	1300	489K	SWH	77077
BROOKLAWN DR	4700	371J	NWC	77066
BROOKLAWN DR	6200	571T	SWH	77085
BROOKLEA	6000	534Q	SEH	77087
BROOKLEAF DR	7400	408M	NWC	77041
BROOKLEDGE DR	11400	529X	SWH	77099
BROOKLET DR	9600	529Y	SWH	77099
BROOKLET VIEW CT	13800	618A	SEH	77059
BROOKLINE CT	1	251B	WD	77381
BROOKLINE DR	2800	609H	MC	77459
BROOKLYN	11400	413M	NCC	77093
BROOKMALL DR	0	524H	NEF	77494
BROOKMALL DR	0	524H	NEF	77494
BROOKMEADE DR	1300	538S	DP	77536
BROOKMEADE DR	3700	572J	SWH	77045
BROOKMEADE DR	5000	571L	SWH	77045
BROOK MEADOW	0	568D	SG	77478
BROOK MEADOW	1500	539P	LP	77571
BROOK MEADOW CIR	11300	616D	SEC	77089
BROOK MEADOW CT	11200	616D	SEC	77089
BROOK MEADOW DR	11400	616D	SEC	77089
BROOK MEADOW LN	9900	616K	SEC	77089
BROOK MEADOWS CT	12100	569A	MD	77477
BROOK MEADOWS LN	11200	569A	MD	77477
BROOKMERE DR	2300	452S	NWH	77008
BROOK MILL CT	11100	368U	NWC	77065
BROOKMONT LN	12000	456H	NEC	77044
BROOK MOSS LN	0	415C	NEC	77396
BROOKNEY RD	0	613L	NEB	77584
BROOKNOLL DR	18000	407X	NWC	77084
BROOKNOLL DR	18100	447B	NWC	77084
BROOK PARK WAY	14700	618E	SEH	77062
S. BROOK PEBBLE CT	1	251Z	WD	77380
N. BROOK PEBBLE CT	1	251Z	WD	77380
BROOK PINE LN	15700	487Y	SWC	77082
BROOKPOINT DR	14900	618E	SEH	77062
BROOKREN CIR	8600	528R	SWH	77072
BROOKREN CT	4500	613V	NEB	77584
BROOKRIDGE LN	16600	611H	SWH	77053
BROOK RISE LN	20700	326S	NWC	77433
BROOKRIVER DR	9800	410N	NWC	77040
BROOKROCK CIR	21100	446J	NWC	77449
BROOK RUN LN	7000	411S	NWH	77040
BROOKS	500	493H	NEH	77009
BROOKS	1700	494E	NEH	77026
BROOKS	2700	494E	NEH	77020
BROOKS CT	0	494E	NEH	77020
BROOKS CT	0	610Q	MC	77459
BROOKS CT	3000	613Y	NEB	77584
BROOKS ARBOR LN	0	405T	NWC	77493
BROOKSBURG LN	0	328P	NWC	77429
BROOKS CROSSING DR	0	462V	BT	77521
BROOKS CROSSING DR	0	462V	BT	77521
BROOK SHADOW DR	3400	297X	NEH	77345
BROOKSHIRE	0	258T	SEM	77358
BROOKSHIRE	300	459X	CV	77530
BROOKSHIRE	9600	450F	NWH	77041
BROOKSHIRE LN	10600	449H	NWH	77041
BROOKSHIRE CHASE LN	0	449X	NWH	77043
BROOK SHORE CT	400	568P	SG	77478
BROOK SHORE CT	3000	297Q	NEH	77345
BROOKSHORE LN	10000	613K	PL	77584
BROOKSIDE	9800	539T	LP	77571
BROOKSIDE CT	4700	569X	MC	77459
BROOKSIDE DR	1800	657J	FR	77546
BROOKSIDE DR	3500	580V	SA	77571
BROOKSIDE DR	6300	494Y	SEH	77023
BROOKSIDE DR	13100	528Y	SG	77478
BROOKSIDE LN	0	258Q	LCO	77357
BROOKSIDE LN	20500	258U	NEC	77357
BROOKSIDE RD	4300	613H	PL	77581
BROOKSIDE RD	4800	614E	NEB	77581
BROOKSIDE RD	4900	614A	BK	77581
BROOKSIDE CEMETERY RD	4100	615A	PL	77581
BROOKSIDE FOREST DR	14700	410E	NWC	77040
BROOKSIDE PINE LN	1700	337H	NEH	77345
BROOKSIDE WILLOW LN	0	407V	NWC	77084
BROOKS PLACE	2600	494E	NEH	77026
BROOKSPRING DR	11600	489P	SWH	77077
BROOK SPRINGS DR	7700	408J	NWC	77095
BROOKS SPUR 58	100	568S	SG	77478
BROOKSTON	3000	572F	SWH	77045
BROOKSTON	4600	571M	SWH	77045
BROOKSTONE CT	3500	613Y	NEB	77584
BROOKSTONE DR	7100	411S	NWH	77040
BROOKSTONE LN	4500	658N	LC	77573
BROOKSURE CIR	8600	528R	SWH	77072
BROOKTONDALE CT	16800	407Z	NWC	77084
BROOK TRAIL CIR	7900	410L	NWC	77040
BROOKTRAIL DR	1300	336E	NEH	77339
BROOKTREE	10200	449Z	NWH	77043
BROOKTREE DR	2000	452S	NWH	77008
BROOKTREE LN	3200	251P	SWM	77380
BROOKVALE CT	3700	297U	NEH	77345
BROOKVALE DR	12600	412A	NWC	77038
BROOKVALLEY DR	11900	570C	SWH	77071
BROOKVALLEY DR	12200	570G	SWH	77071
BROOKVIEW	9800	539T	LP	77571
BROOKVIEW DR	200	497D	NEC	77530
BROOKVIEW DR	2900	613P	NEB	77584
BROOKVILLA DR	15700	618C	SEH	77059
BROOK VILLAGE	19000	446Q	NWC	77084
BROOKWATER DR	300	338D	NEC	77336
BROOK WAY	17700	325F	NWC	77447
BROOKWAY DR	0	407Y	NWC	77084
BROOKWAY DR	0	407Y	NWC	77084
BROOKWAY WILLOW DR	5200	290Z	NWC	77379
BROOKWIND DR	3800	578D	LP	77571
BROOKWOOD CT	1400	620Q	SB	77586
BROOKWOOD DR	3400	578H	LP	77571
BROOKWOOD LN	0	245D	SWM	77355
BROOKWOOD LN	0	614S	NEB	77584
BROOKWOOD LN	3100	538S	DP	77536
BROOKWOOD BRIDGE LN	15000	527Z	NEF	77498
BROOKWOOD FOREST DR	0	295U	SEM	77365
BROOKWOOD HOLLOW	0	526N	NEF	77407
BROOKWOOD PARK BLVD	0	405T	NWC	77493
BROOKWOOD PARK LN	0	658Z	LC	77573
BROOKWOODS DR	3600	452N	NWH	77092
BROOKWOODS DR	4000	451R	NWH	77092
BROOKWULF DR	8500	528R	SWH	77072
BROOKWULF DR	8600	528R	SWH	77099
BROOM	4500	451G	NWH	77091
BROOMSEDGE DR	2600	446U	NWC	77084
BROOT RD	0	420C	NEC	77532
BRORA CT	16800	447D	NWC	77084
BROTHERS PURCHASE CIR	12200	366L	NWC	77433
BROU LN	7300	530M	SWH	77074
BROUGHTON	25100	293P	NCC	77373
BROUGHWOOD CIR	20500	446W	NWC	77449
BROUSSARD	0	577X	SEH	77034
W. BROUSSARD	100	419R	BR	77532
E. BROUSSARD	100	419R	BR	77532
BROUSSARD CT	2600	620K	SB	77586
BROWAY LN	16300	326R	NWC	77429
BROWER	8500	535L	SEH	77017
BROWER CREST DR	5000	577K	PA	77504
BROWN	0	569R	SF	77477
BROWN	2000	570N	MC	77489
BROWN	23400	289H	NWC	77375
BROWN DR	200	537F	PA	77506
BROWN LN	0	657A	FR	77586
BROWN LN	700	538Y	DP	77536
BROWN RD	14100	288E	NWC	77377
BROWN RD	14900	287H	NWC	77377
BROWN RD	34600	247J	SWM	77362
BROWN BARK DR	6100	451F	NWH	77092
BROWN BEND CT	0	406D	NWC	77433
BROWN BRIDGE CT	10600	528W	NEF	77498
BROWNCROFT	5100	534J	SEH	77021
BROWNDALE CT	23800	485T	NEF	77494
BROWNE	0	493J	SWH	77007
S. BROWNELL	100	540Y	LP	77571
N. BROWNELL	100	540Y	LP	77571
S. BROWNELL	500	580D	LP	77571
BROWN EYED SUSAN CT	15100	325R	NWC	77433
BROWNFIELDS CT	4900	371N	NWC	77066
BROWNFIELDS DR	4700	371N	NWC	77066
BROWN HILL DR	2600	293T	NCC	77373
BROWN HUFFSMITH RD	0	288B	TB	77375
BROWNIE CAMPBELL RD	2700	371T	NWC	77038
BROWNIE CAMPBELL RD	3200	371T	NWC	77086
BROWNING	1200	539P	LP	77571
BROWNING	3800	532A	WU	77005
BROWNING FERRIS LANDFILL		611R	FS	77545
BROWNING TRACE LN	0	527W	NEF	77469
BROWN LEAF CIR	9400	530V	SWH	77096
BROWNLEE LN	5200	331J	NWC	77379
BROWN MAPLE DR	2400	611T	NEF	77545
BROWN MEADOW CT	4100	446H	NWC	77449
BROWNOOR LN	3700	446J	NWC	77449
BROWN PELICAN LN	2600	658T	LC	77573
BROWN REDBUD CT	0	407J	NWC	77433
BROWN SADDLE	300	491K	SWH	77057
BROWNSTONE LN	3900	572S	SWH	77053
BROWNSTONE LN	4600	571V	SWH	77053
BROWNSTONE MILLS DR	0	406R	NWC	77433
BROWNSTONE PLACE	0	614N	NEB	77584
BROWNSVILLE	6500	494D	NEH	77020
BROWNSVILLE	7100	495A	NEH	77020
BROWNSVILLE	13700	497C	NEC	77015
BROWN TRAIL	0	329N	NWC	77377
BROWNWAY	5200	491U	SWH	77056
BROWNWIND TRAIL	3800	539S	DP	77536
BROWNWOOD	6200	500N	BT	77520
BROWNWOOD	6900	494H	NEH	77020
BROWNWOOD	7100	495E	NEH	77020
BROWNWOOD	13700	497F	NEC	77015
BROWNWOOD LN	23200	287F	NWC	77377
BROYLES	3400	454X	NEH	77026
BROZE RD	20800	334N	NCC	77338
BROZZI LN	0	659R	LC	77573
BRUCE	0	659J	LC	77573
BRUCE	0	660Y	DI	77539
BRUCE	3700	453X	NWH	77009
BRUCE DR	2000	502W	BT	77520
BRUCE SUMMERS PLACE	0	616H	SEC	77089
BRUCE TREE RIDGE DR	0	376T	NWC	77396
BRUMBLEY	7700	535F	SEH	77012
BRUMLOW	1000	458Z	CV	77530
BRUMMEL DR	8700	528Q	SWC	77099
BRUMMERHOP	600	620Q	SB	77586
BRUN	1700	492R	SWH	77019
BRUNDAGE DR	2100	372B	NWH	77090
BRUNELLO ST	0	659P	LC	77573
BRUNER RD	31400	242C	WCO	77484
BRUNO WAY	3100	613V	PL	77584
BRUNS GLEN LN	0	328M	NWC	77377
BRUNSON FALLS DR	21000	525R	NEF	77407
BRUNSON GROVE LN	6000	524E	NEF	77494
BRUNSWICK	5100	414M	NEC	77039
BRUNSWICK DR	0	658H	LC	77573
BRUNSWICK DR	800	569S	SG	77478
BRUNSWICK ST		289P	NWC	77375
BRUNSWICK CROSSING LN	0	573U	SEC	77047
BRUNSWICK LAKES BLVD	0	573Z	SEC	77047
BRUNSWICK MEADOWS DR	0	573X	SEC	77047
BRUNSWICK PLACE	0	573Y	SEC	77047
BRUNSWICK POINT LN	14200	573X	SEC	77047
BRUSHBIRD LN	0	446W	NWC	77449
BRUSH CANYON DR	11800	329N	NWC	77377
BRUSHFIELD RD	8100	410G	NWC	77064
BRUSHFORD DR	0	446J	NWC	77449
BRUSH HILL	6000	290U	NWC	77379
BRUSH HOLLOW RD	2400	371M	NWC	77067
BRUSHILL CT	100	658N	LC	77573
BRUSHTON DR	20100	291S	NWC	77379
BRUSHWOOD CT	1	252N	WD	77380
BRUSHWOOD DR	0	411Y	NWH	77088
BRUSHWOOD DR	7200	411U	NWH	77088
BRUSHY CT	7500	411T	NWH	77088
BRUSHY ARBOR LN	0	375X	NEC	77396
BRUSHY CANYON DR	20900	332Y	NCC	77073
BRUSHY CREEK CIR	1900	446Y	NWC	77084
BRUSHY CREEK DR	1800	568Z	SG	77478
BRUSHY CREEK DR	25000	244E	WCO	77447
BRUSHY FOREST	0	285B	SWM	77447
BRUSHY GLEN DR	300	332V	NCC	77073
BRUSHY MEADOW CT	26700	484Y	NEF	77494
BRUSHY OAKS	23600	285B	SWM	77447
BRUSHY PINES	23300	285B	SWM	77447
BRUSHY RANCH TRAIL	0	458T	NEC	77049
BRUSHY RIDGE DR	20900	332Z	NCC	77073
BRUSHY RIVER CT	10600	367T	NWC	77095
BRUSHY RIVER CT	17500	367T	NWC	77095
BRUSHY TRAILS	23600	285B	SWM	77447
BRUSHY WOODS	23600	285B	SWM	77447
BRUTON PARK LN	0	445V	NWC	77449
BRUTUS	7900	535F	SEH	77012
BRUTUS DR	25900	257D	RF	77357
BRUTUS HILL LN	13000	528M	SWH	77072
BRYAM	8700	535Y	SEH	77061
BRYAN	1	494T	SEH	77011
N. BRYAN	100	494P	SEH	77011
BRYAN	900	536H	PA	77506
BRYAN	1400	541A	BT	77520
BRYAN	2600	494J	NEH	77020
BRYAN AVE	800	620P	SB	77586
BRYAN CT	0	613L	PL	77584
BRYANHURST LN	5200	331E	NWC	77379
BRYAN POND CT	0	445L	NWC	77449
BRYANT	9200	575H	SEH	77075
BRYANT LN	2700	657M	LC	77598
BRYANT CROSSING LN	0	293F	SEM	77386
BRYANT PARK CT	6500	411B	NWC	77086
BRYANT POND DR	5800	408Y	NWC	77041
BRYANT RIDGE RD	4600	571Z	SWH	77053
BRYBERRY CT	1	251A	WD	77381
BRYCE	1100	452Y	NWH	77008
BRYCE CANYON CT	8800	330n	NWC	77379
BRYCE CANYON DR	6300	526E	NEF	77450
BRYCE MANOR CT	0	376H	NEC	77346
BRYCE MANOR LN	0	376H	NEC	77346
BRYCE MEADOW LN	14300	573X	SEC	77047
BRYCE MILL CT	0	376H	NEC	77346
BRYCE PECAN WAY DR	0	325S	HK	77447
BRYCE SUMMIT LN		484S	NEF	77494
BRYDAN DR	11700	328X	NWC	77429
BRYKERWOODS DR	7500	451X	NWH	77055
BRYMOOR CT	3500	613Q	NEB	77584
BRYNGROVE LN	0	408W	NWC	77084
BRYN MAWR CIR	200	490M	HC	77024
BRYN MAWR LN	4500	491V	SWH	77027
BRYNN BRANCH LN		484X	NEF	77494
BRYONSTON DR	11600	371K	NWC	77066
BRYONWOOD DR	7600	491B	NWH	77055
BRYSTONE DR	5000	449B	NWC	77041
BRYTON PARK DR	7000	528F	SWC	77083
BUBBLING BROOKS LN	7200	407Q	NWC	77095
BUBBLING SPRING LN	7500	410D	NWC	77086
BUBBLING WELL CT	15500	617S	SEC	77546
BUCAN	1	413X	NEH	77076
BUCCANEER DR	0	502K	BT	77521
BUCCANEER LN	15700	618K	SEH	77062
BUCCANEER LN	16800	618K	SEH	77058
BUCHANAN	0	247R	SWM	77355
BUCHANAN	1500	537N	PA	77502
BUCHANAN	7900	495P	NEH	77029
BUCHANAN DR	2100	502W	BT	77520
BUCHANAN BEND CT	0	407A	NWC	77433
BUCHANAN HILL LN	0	484U	NEF	77494
BUCHANAN OAKS LN	0	377K	NEC	77346
BUCHANNAN	2300	539U	LP	77571
BUCHANS DR	1300	252U	SEM	77386
BUCK	2900	494F	NEH	77020
BUCK	33200	246T	SWM	77355
BUCK CT	0	246T	SWM	77355
BUCK RD	33300	247S	SWM	77355
BUCKBOARD DR	100	372Z	NEH	77060
BUCKEYE CT	0	614N	NEB	77584
BUCKEYE DR	0	463S	CCO	77520
BUCKEYE DR	100	485C	SWC	77450
BUCKEYE LN	0	614S	NEB	77584
BUCKEYE BROOK WAY	15300	458W	NEC	77530
BUCKEYE CREEK RD	4000	297T	NEH	77339
BUCKEYE FURNACE LN	10700	528W	NEF	77498
BUCKEYE GLEN LN	8200	335N	NCC	77338
BUCKEYE HILL ST	0	328N	NWC	77429
BUCKEYE PASS	0	526P	NEF	77407
BUCKEYE PLACE	800	610S	MC	77459
BUCKEYE RIDGE	0	446R	NWC	77084
BUCKHAVEN DR	0	616K	SEC	77089
BUCKHEAD CT	16100	329N	NWC	77377
BUCK HOLLOW DR	1000	378D	NEC	77532
BUCKHOLT	2200	616W	PL	77581
BUCKHORN RANCH	0	418N	NEC	77044
BUCKHURST DR	3800	371P	NWC	77066
BUCKINGHAM CT	1000	656M	FR	77546
BUCKINGHAM DR	300	491G	SWH	77024
BUCKINGHAM DR	800	656M	FR	77546
BUCKINGHAM DR	1700	577E	PA	77504
BUCKINGHAM LN	14000	288B	TB	77375
BUCKINGHAM COURT CIR	0	490G	HE	77024
BUCKINGHAM PLACE	200	569J	SF	77477
BUCKINGHAM WAY	1300	336H	NEH	77339
BUCK ISLAND CT	17500	377E	NEC	77354
BUCK KNIFE	6400	531E	SWH	77081
BUCKLAND LN	12300	414E	NCC	77039
BUCKLAND PARK DR	19400	406U	NWC	77449
BUCKLE LN	15100	372Z	NEH	77060
BUCKLE BERRY WAY	0	486D	SWC	77094
BUCKLERIDGE RD	4500	611D	SWH	77053
BUCKMANN CT	1500	450W	NWH	77043
BUCKMINSTER	2500	293A	SEM	77386
BUCKNELL CT	3000	569N	SG	77478
BUCKNELL RD	10300	414Z	NEH	77016
BUCKNER	1000	493P	SWH	77019
BUCKNER CT	0	372M	NCC	77073
BUCKNER CT	3100	610U	MC	77459
BUCKOW DR	5600	374M	NEH	77396
BUCK RIDGE	0	376P	NEC	77396
S. BUCK RIDGE	1	251B	WD	77381
N. BUCK RIDGE	1	251B	WD	77381
BUCKSKIN	2400	444P	KT	77493
BUCKSKIN DR	0	328C	NWC	77377
BUCKSKIN E. DR	21600	255U	SEM	77365

Street Name	Block	Pg/Sq	Loc	Zips
BUCKSKIN W. DR.	21600	255T	SEM	77365
BUCKSKIN BRIDGE CT	14800	568A	NEF	77498
BUCKSKIN TRAIL CT	20500	486T	SWC	77450
BUCK SPRINGS TRAIL	11600	329N	NWC	77377
BUCKS RUN	15500	287H	NWC	77377
BUCKTAIL DR	0	250P	NWC	77389
BUCKTHORNE PLACE	2100	251Q	WD	77380
BUCK TRAIL PLACE	0	250Q	NWC	77389
BUCKTROUT LN	22000	445Z	NWC	77449
BUCROFT	8400	495P	NEH	77029
BUD LN	300	501G	BT	77521
BUDD	2900	536Z	PA	77502
BUDDE RD	24600	252W	SWM	77380
BUDDE CEMETERY RD	20300	292W	NWC	77388
BUDDY COX LN	0	292J	NWC	77389
BUELL CT	1	493N	SWH	77006
BUELOW	5800	534G	SEH	77023
BUENA PARK CT	9900	576S	SEH	77089
BUENA PARK DR	9700	576S	SEH	77089
BUENA VISTA	4200	569K	SF	77477
BUENA VISTA	7400	535N	SEH	77087
BUENA WAY	27400	293C	SEM	77386
BUESCHER	22000	287L	NWC	77377
BUESCHER CT	4600	615N	PL	77581
BUESCHER DR	1300	449X	NWH	77043
BUFFALO BEND DR	0	444S	KT	77493
BUFFALO BEND DR	10300	369X	NWC	77064
BUFFALO BEND LN	9200	615H	SEC	77089
BUFFALO CANYON DR	0	253T	SEM	77386
BUFFALO CLOVER CIR	0	526W	NEF	77406
BUFFALO COVE LN	0	445N	NWC	77493
BUFFALO CREEK DR	0	525Z	NEF	77406
BUFFALO GAP	5700	609Z	MC	77459
BUFFALO GAP DR	9800	367Z	NWC	77095
BUFFALO LAKE CIR	0	367S	NWC	77433
BUFFALO LAKE CT	4400	526W	NEF	77406
BUFFALO PASS DR	17200	367P	NWC	77095
BUFFALO PEAK CT	17000	377J	NEC	77346
BUFFALO RIDGE CIR	1	491F	SWH	77056
BUFFALO RIVER WAY	18700	446R	NWC	77084
BUFFALO RUN	0	570T	MC	77489
BUFFALO RUN CIR	1500	372N	NWC	77067
BUFFALO SPEEDWAY	0	612B	SWC	77047
BUFFALO SPEEDWAY	2600	492T	SWH	77098
BUFFALO SPEEDWAY	5100	532F	WU	77005
BUFFALO SPEEDWAY	6800	532F	SWH	77025
BUFFALO SPEEDWAY	9900	532T	SWH	77054
BUFFALO SPEEDWAY	13800	572P	SWH	77045
BUFFALO SPRINGS	0	292U	NCC	77373
BUFFALO SPRINGS CT	25500	292U	NCC	77373
BUFFALO SPRINGS LN	0	660J	LC	77573
BUFFALO SPRINGS WAY	900	292U	NCC	77373
BUFFALO TERRACE	2000	493J	SWH	77019
BUFFALO TRAIL	4500	501H	BT	77521
BUFFALO TRAIL	20200	378H	NEC	77532
BUFFALO TRAIL	27300	244A	WCO	77447
BUFFALO VIEW LN	7900	407J	NWC	77433
BUFFINGTON	600	373X	NCC	77060
BUFFKIN LN	6900	330W	NWC	77069
BUFFLEHEAD CT	13200	377Y	NEC	77044
BUFFUM	9200	573B	SEH	77051
BUFFWOOD DR	700	488B	SWH	77079
BUFORD	6300	534G	SEH	77023
BUGLE RD	4100	529F	SWH	77072
BUGLE RUN DR	1400	446W	NWC	77449
BUHLER CT	15800	367D	NWC	77429
BUI DR	6100	614G	PL	77581
BULEN AVE	5300	657A	FR	77546
BULIAN DR	0	461R	NEC	77521
BULKHEAD WAY	17000	379X	NEC	77532
BULL LN	400	570P	MC	77489
BULLARD CREEK DR	0	366N	NWC	77433
BULL CREEK RD	7400	408K	NWC	77095
BULLFINCH	6300	534Z	SEH	77087
BULLHEAD DR	0	658Y	LC	77573
BULLINGER DR	6800	330L	NWC	77379
BULLIS GAP DR	17100	324M	NWC	77447
BULLOCK LN	1300	450W	NWH	77055
BULL PINE DR	18400	331E	NWC	77379
BULL RIDGE CIR	20900	295R	SEM	77365
BULL RIDGE DR	22700	295R	SEM	77365
BULL RUN	8900	578D	LP	77571
BULL RUN CT	2900	610U	MC	77459
BULL RUN DR	300	658P	LC	77573
BULRUSH CANYON TRAIL	7800	525A	NEF	77494
BULWARK DR	900	419A	NEC	77532
BUMBLEBEE CT	0	658X	LC	77573
BUMBLEBEE CT	0	245V	SWM	77355
BUNCHE DR	6500	412W	NWH	77091
BUNDICK DR	6200	412X	NWH	77091
BUNDY LN	9500	450P	NWH	77080
BUNGALOW LN	4300	573L	SEH	77047
BUNGALOW LN	5100	574J	SEH	77048
BUNKER LN	32000	322P	WCO	77484
BUNKER BEND CT	20000	338S	NEC	77346
BUNKER BEND DR	8300	337R	NEC	77346
BUNKER BEND DR	8500	338S	NEC	77346
BUNKER BLUFF CT	0	484W	NEF	77494
BUNKER COVE DR	0	366K	NWC	77433
BUNKER HILL CIR	11800	490F	BH	77024
BUNKER HILL CT	2200	615J	PL	77581
BUNKER HILL LN	0	656X	FR	77546
BUNKER HILL RD	200	490B	SWH	77024
BUNKER HILL RD	1000	450X	NWH	77055
BUNKER OAK LN	0	299U	NEC	77336
BUNKER RIDGE RD	15900	611D	SWC	77053
BUNKER WOOD LN	7700	410D	NWC	77086
BUNKER WOOD LN	7900	370Z	NWC	77086
BUNNINGHAM LN	8700	490D	SV	77055
BUNNY LN	12000	248S	SWM	77355
BUNNY RUN DR	8800	412L	NWH	77088
BUNTE	5400	454U	NEH	77026
BUNTING CT	8000	375Q	NEC	77396
BUNTING RD	30600	242G	WCO	77484
BUNTING MEADOW CT	4200	446H	NWC	77449
BUNTING MEADOW DR	4200	446H	NWC	77449
BUNTON	900	453Z	NEH	77009
BUNZEL	1900	412K	NWC	77088
BUNZEL	2400	412J	NWC	77088
BUOY RD	300	618N	SEH	77598
BUOY RD	700	618P	SEH	77062
BURBANK	1	453B	NEH	77076
BURBANK	1300	541A	BT	77520
BURBERRY CIR	0	377L	NEC	77346
BURCAN CT	23000	292G	NCC	77373
BURCH	3800	494P	SEH	77003
BURDEN	8600	453D	NEH	77093
BURDEN	10200	413Z	NEH	77093
BURDINE	9100	531T	SWH	77096
BURDINE	11500	571B	SWH	77035
BURDINE	12600	571F	SWH	77085
BURDINE CT	6400	571K	SWH	77085

Street Name	Block	Pg/Sq	Loc	Zips
BURDOM	0	335Y	HM	77338
BURFORD LN	8700	412K	NWC	77088
BURFORD PLACE	0	488L	SWH	77077
BURG LN	8300	412N	NWH	77088
BURGANDY OAKS	100	249R	NWH	77375
BURGANDY OAKS	100	249R	NWH	77375
BURGE	0	616F	SEC	77089
BURGER LN	9100	410P	NWC	77040
BURGESS	6900	533K	SWH	77021
BURGESS CT	2800	614S	NEB	77584
BURGESS BEND WAY	0	250N	NWC	77389
BURGESS HEIGHTS LN	0	524H	NEF	77494
BURGH CASTLE DR	25000	250W	NWC	77389
BURGHEA DHARBOUR DR	0	610P	NEF	77459
BURGOYNE DR	5800	491S	SWH	77057
BURGOYNE DR	7500	490V	SWH	77063
BURGOYNE DR	10000	489U	SWH	77042
BURGOYNE DR	11300	489T	SWH	77077
BURGOYNE DR	13700	488T	SWH	77077
BURGOYNE DR	14200	488S	SWH	77077
BURGUNDY LN	100	658L	LC	77573
BURGUNDY LN	3500	534G	SEH	77023
BURGUNDY SKY WAY	0	326V	NWC	77429
BURHAM LN	500	657Y	LC	77573
BURHAM PARK DR	16300	367C	NWC	77429
BURK	10800	574R	SEH	77075
BURKDALE DR	2300	568C	SG	77478
BURKE RD	100	537F	PA	77506
BURKE RD	1300	537P	PA	77502
BURKE RD	3100	577K	PA	77504
BURKE FOREST DR	14000	370A	NWC	77070
BURKEGATE DR	4200	333C	NCC	77373
BURKEHALL LN	0	407V	NWC	77084
BURKE LAKE LN	0	377H	NEH	77346
BURKE RIDGE DR	4300	577K	PA	77504
BURKES GARDEN DR	10800	369S	NWC	77065
BURKESHIRE LN	0	577F	PA	77504
BURKETT	2300	493Z	SEH	77004
BURKETT	6600	533G	SEH	77021
BURKETT DR	3400	579A	LP	77571
BURKETTE RD	23100	296D	SEM	77357
BURKHARDT RD	18000	286R	NWC	77377
BURKHART	0	287N	NWC	77377
BURKHART CIR	8300	451W	SV	77055
BURKHART CT	8300	451W	SV	77055
BURKHART RD	8000	451W	SV	77055
BURKHART RD	8600	450Z	SV	77055
BURKHART RIDGE DR	0	407B	NWC	77095
BURKLIN LN	16500	246U	SWM	77355
BURKRIDGE DR	7300	408R	NWC	77041
BURKS CT	0	574R	SEH	77075
BURKS TRAIL DR	24100	296J	SEM	77365
BURK WAY	1	258R	NEC	77357
BURL	8800	455G	NEH	77028
BURLCREEK	16600	407V	NWC	77084
BURLE OAK CT	19700	337S	NEC	77346
BURLE OAK DR	19800	337N	NEC	77346
BURLESON	900	412X	NWH	77091
BURLESON CT	8800	409H	NWC	77064
BURLINGAME DR	11600	569B	SWH	77099
BURLINGHALL DR	5500	571A	SWH	77035
BURLINGTON	3400	493T	SWH	77006
N. BURLINGTON	6400	411X	NWH	77092
BURLINGTON	25600	247Y	SWM	77355
BURLMONT LN	15100	458W	NEC	77530
BURLWOOD DR	11500	616D	SEC	77089
BURMA RD	4800	533R	SEH	77033
BURMA RD	4900	534S	SEH	77033
BURMAN	7900	495J	NEH	77029
BURMAN	10300	496J	JC	77029
BURMESE LN	11200	568D	SG	77478
BURNABY	3800	451K	NWH	77092
BURNABY	25100	293P	NCC	77373
W. BURNABY CIR	24700	293S	NCC	77373
N. BURNABY CIR	24700	293S	NCC	77373
E. BURNABY CIR	24700	293S	NCC	77373
BURNABY TRAIL CT	21800	332Q	NCC	77073
BURNELL OAKS LN	16500	332N	NWC	77090
BURNET	0	500U	BT	77520
BURNET BROOK LN	0	367S	NWC	77433
N. BURNETT	100	500E	BT	77520
BURNETT	400	493H	NEH	77009
BURNETT	1700	493H	NEH	77026
BURNETT	2700	494E	NEH	77020
BURNETT AVE	1700	499H	NEC	77520
BURNETT DR	100	500E	BT	77520
S. BURNETT DR	300	500J	BT	77520
BURNETT CT (1600 Jensen)	0	494E	NEH	77020
BURNETT HILLS LN	0	578T	SEH	77059
BURNETT PLACE	700	501K	BT	77521
BURNEY RD	700	568A	NEF	77498
BURNEY RD	11000	568E	SG	77498
BURNEY BEND LN	0	576V	SEH	77034
BURNHAM	14100	572X	SWC	77053
BURNHAM CIR	1	568V	SG	77478
BURNINGBUSH LN	11000	415T	NEH	77016
BURNING HILLS DR	7600	530U	SWH	77071
BURNING OAK LN	7900	527J	NEF	77407
BURNING PALMS CT	3600	489Y	SWH	77042
BURNING TREE	4600	501J	BT	77521
BURNING TREE LN	2800	609M	MC	77459
BURNING TREE LN	26500	258J	SEM	77357
BURNING TREE RD	700	336E	NEH	77339
BURNING TREE RD	5900	530A	SWH	77036
BURNISHED OAKS CT	100	249R	NWH	77375
BURNISHED OAKS CT	100	249R	NWH	77375
BURNLEY	1100	413P	NEH	77037
BURNS HOLLOW DR	0	325S	HK	77447
BURNSIDE LN	10000	450A	NWH	77041
BURNT AMBER LN	20700	333P	NCC	77073
BURNT ASH DR	8200	335J	NCC	77338
BURNT CANDLE DR	18600	331H	NWC	77388
BURNTFORK	9900	369Y	NWC	77064
BURNTFORK	10000	409C	NWC	77064
BURNT LEAF LN	17800	331J	NWC	77379
BURNT WOOD CT	0	253J	SEM	77385
BURNWOOD LN	900	332G	NCC	77073
BUR OAK	6000	330D	NWC	77379
BUR OAK CT	17100	330D	NWC	77379
BUR OAK DR	5200	578J	PA	77505
BURR	1	494T	SEH	77011
N. BURR	100	494P	SEH	77011
BURRARD	25100	293N	NCC	77373
BUR REED RD	0	526T	NEF	77407
BURRESS	1	453G	NEH	77022
E. BURRESS	200	453E	NWH	77022
BURRIS PARK DR	200	332C	NCC	77373
BURR OAK DR	2800	657H	FR	77546
BURR OAK DR	5400	451A	NWH	77092
BURR OAK TRACE	7000	249D	SWM	77354
BURRO MESA DR	2600	293F	SEM	77386
BURRO SPRINGS DR	29100	293F	SEM	77386

Street Name	Block	Pg/Sq	Loc	Zips
BURROWDALE CT	17001	407U	NWC	77084
BURT	3100	452F	NWH	77018
BURT	5800	452B	NWH	77091
BURT	7500	412T	NWH	77088
BURT	5800	412X	NWH	77091
BURTCLIFF	14000	413E	NCC	77060
BURTCLIFF	14800	413A	NCC	77060
BURTON	16000	418W	NEC	77049
BURTON CEMETERY RD	29000	323A	NWC	77484
BURTON CEMETERY RD	30700	322D	NWC	77484
BURTON RIDGE DR	3100	253S	SEM	77386
BURWELL	5600	534C	SEH	77023
BURWELL RD	100	459M	HG	77562
BURWOOD CIR	20500	446W	NWC	77449
BURWOOD CT	16600	618R	SEH	77058
BURWOOD DR	0	615W	PL	77584
BURWOOD PARK DR	8300	330P	NWC	77379
BURWOOD WAY	16700	618M	SEH	77058
BUS BARN RD	0	463H	MB	77521
BUSCH	0	542C	CCO	77520
BUSCH	100	413E	NCC	77060
BUSCH RD	2100	501V	BT	77520
BUSCHONG	500	373X	NCC	77060
BUSCHONG	800	373Y	NCC	77039
BUSH RD	5100	501E	NEC	77521
BUSHMEADE LN	0	406P	NWC	77449
BUSH OAK LN	1	252J	WD	77380
BUSH SAGE DR	14300	368A	NWC	77429
BUSHWOOD DR	19100	291X	NWC	77388
BUSHY CREEK DR	10300	369L	NWC	77070
BUSHY OAKS TRAIL	16100	286C	SWM	77355
BUSIEK	4300	453J	NWH	77022
BUSINESS CENTER	0	613N	PL	77584
BUSINESS CENTER DR	0	613E	PL	77584
BUSINESS CENTER DR	1100	449Y	NWH	77043
BUSINESS PARK DR	6700	409U	NWH	77041
BUSSE CIR	800	537L	PA	77503
BUSTER CIR	900	288D	TB	77375
BUSY BEE DR	0	366N	NWC	77433
BUTANO SPRINGS LN	0	377F	NEC	77346
BUTE	3800	493T	SWH	77006
BUTE	4200	493T	SWH	77002
BUTERA RD	15900	246T	SWM	77355
BUTLER	2000	657K	FR	77546
BUTLER	3000	493J	SWH	77007
BUTLER AVE	0	659J	LC	77573
BUTLER AVE	2600	658Q	LC	77573
BUTLER BLVD	1900	533J	SWH	77030
BUTLER DR	1400	537N	PA	77502
BUTLER DR	5800	614L	PL	77581
BUTLERCREST	1400	450W	NWH	77080
BUTLER HILL CT	25000	249S	NWC	77375
BUTLER OAKS CT	6600	250Y	NWC	77389
BUTLER SPRINGS CT	0	484Z	NEF	77494
BUTLER SPRINGS LN	0	484Z	NEF	77494
W. BUTTE CANYON RD	12800	411D	NWC	77038
E. BUTTE CANYON RD	12800	411D	NWC	77038
BUTTE CREEK RD	17000	331L	NWC	77090
BUTTE MEADOWS LN	3700	573U	SEC	77047
BUTTER BROOKS LN	0	326U	NWC	77429
BUTTERCUP	3200	490Y	SWH	77063
BUTTERCUP	5600	657V	LC	77573
BUTTER CUP LN	1200	336F	NEH	77339
BUTTERCUP LN	27000	248F	SWM	77354
BUTTERCUP COVE LN	0	293F	SEM	77386
BUTTERCUP HILL CT	0	366Z	NWC	77433
BUTTERCUP SPRINGS LN	0	410E	NWC	77064
BUTTERFIELD RD	500	332P	NWC	77090
BUTTERFLY CIR	5800	577D	PA	77505
BUTTERFLY CT	400	489F	SWH	77079
BUTTERFLY CT	18500	295J	SEM	77365
BUTTERFLY LN	12800	489G	SWH	77024
BUTTERFLY LN	13300	489F	SWH	77079
BUTTERFLY LN	24000	295E	SEM	77365
BUTTERFLY BUSH LN	0	328F	NWC	77429
BUTTERFLY COVE LN	0	332N	NWC	77090
BUTTERFLY IRIS LN	0	406D	NWC	77433
BUTTERFLY PATH DR	4700	376S	NEC	77396
BUTTERGROVE DR	5700	408Y	NWC	77041
BUTTER MILL LN	1500	372N	NWC	77067
BUTTERNUT CT	4200	411U	NWH	77088
BUTTER NUT LN	7700	249G	SWM	77354
BUTTERNUT GROVE PLACE	0	250E	NWC	77375
BUTTEROAK DR	16800	330H	NWC	77379
BUTTEROAK LN	16800	330H	NWC	77379
BUTTERSTONE	0	529D	SWH	77042
BUTTERSTONE RIDGE LN	0	526R	NEF	77469
BUTTERSTONE RIDGE LN	0	526R	NEF	77469
BUTTERSTONE RIDGE LN	8801	527N	NEF	77407
BUTTERWICK DR	23800	250W	NWC	77389
BUTTONBUSH CT	1	251L	WD	77380
BUTTONHILL DR	2300	570Y	MC	77489
BUTTONWOOD DR	1200	656L	FR	77546
BUTTONWOOD CREEK TRAIL		249T	NWC	77375
BUVINGHAUSEN	17000	329N	NWC	77377
BUXLEY	13000	571M	SWH	77045
BUXLEY	14700	571V	SWH	77053
BUXTON	9700	536J	SEH	77017
BUXTON WOOD DR	0	295U	SEM	77365
BY DR	0	419F	NEC	77532
BYCREEK DR	2500	331K	NWC	77068
BYLAKE CT	13600	488P	SWH	77077
BYLANE DR	200	490P	BH	77024
BYRD	2100	620N	SB	77586
BYRD	6300	534U	SEH	77087
BYRNE	100	493B	NWH	77009
BYRON	100	658H	LC	77573
BYRON	1300	538L	DP	77536
BYRON	3800	532E	WU	77005
BYRON AVE	2400	615P	PL	77581
BYRON CT	7800	330A	NWC	77379
BYRON MEADOWS DR	0	406U	NWC	77449
BYRONSTONE DR	11500	371P	NWC	77066
BYSTREET RD	800	576H	SEH	77504
BY THE LAKE WAY CT	0	326Z	NWC	77429
BYTRAIL	0	376H	NEC	77346
BYWATER CT	2000	619Z	LC	77573
BYWATER DR	1900	488P	SWH	77077
BYWAY	3300	580Q	SA	77571
BYWAY	6200	492F	SWH	77007
BYWOOD	7000	454H	NEH	77028
BYWOOD	7300	455E	NEH	77028

C

Street Name	Block	Pg/Sq	Loc	Zips
C	2800	580Q	LP	77571
C	3800	529A	SWH	77072
C AVE	0	410P	NWC	77040
C DR	0	290L	NWC	77389
C STREET	0	282T	WL	77484
C STREET	1800	536A	NEH	77547
N. C STREET	12200	540W	LP	77571

Street Name	Block	Pg/Sq	Loc	Zips
C, AVENUE	0	419V	BR	77532
C, AVENUE	0	568N	SG	77478
C, AVENUE	0	569Q	SF	77477
C, AVENUE	0	619N	SEH	77058
C, AVENUE	0	656A	NEB	77581
S. C, AVENUE	100	335Z	HM	77338
N. C, AVENUE	100	335Z	HM	77338
C, AVENUE	100	459U	HG	77562
C, AVENUE	100	536W	SH	77587
C, AVENUE	800	444X	KT	77493
C, AVENUE	1100	611X	FS	77545
C, AVENUE	1500	659Z	GCO	77539
C, AVENUE	5300	419G	CB	77532
C, AVENUE	6400	494V	SEH	77011
C, AVENUE	7500	495W	SEH	77012
C, AVENUE	15400	498F	CV	77530
C, H M	5500	533F	SEH	77021
C.R. 48 (AIRLINE RD N)	0	612Y	NWB	77578
C.R. 59 (AIRLINE-FT BD)	900	612T	NWB	77584
C.R. 59 (AIRLINE-FT BD)	2000	613T	NEB	77584
C.R. 71 (DUESENBERG DR)	4400	613V	NEB	77584
C.R. 71A (LEYLAND DR)	4400	613V	NEB	77584
C.R. 71B (BURLINETTA DR)	2900	613V	NEB	77584
C.R. 71C (MORRIS CT)	4300	613V	NEB	77584
C.R. 72 (PLANTATION DR)	2500	613R	NEB	77584
C.R. 72A (PLANTATION CT)	0	613R	NEB	77584
C.R. 72B (PECAN GROVE)	4600	613R	NEB	77584
C.R. 72C (PECAN GRV CT)	2500	613R	NEB	77584
C.R. 72D (CHESTNUT CIR)	2500	614S	NEB	77584
C.R. 72E (WALNUT GRV CT)	2500	614N	NEB	77584
C.R. 72F (MEADOWHURST)	2500	614N	NEB	77584
C.R. 72G (HUNTINGTON WY)	2800	614S	NEB	77584
C.R. 72H (CLOVER LN)	4800	614S	NEB	77584
C.R. 72J (MEADOWGLEN DR)	4800	614N	NEB	77584
C.R. 72K (CLOVERFLD DR)	4800	614S	NEB	77584
C.R. 72L (CLOVERFLD CT)	2600	614S	NEB	77584
C.R. 72M (FOXDEN)	2500	614S	NEB	77584
C.R. 72N (LINDEN PLACE)	4500	613V	NEB	77584
C.R. 72P (KIMBALL DR)	4500	613V	NEB	77584
C.R. 72Q (KIMBALL PLACE)	2700	613V	NEB	77584
C.R. 72R (ABBEY FIELD)	2700	613V	NEB	77584
C.R. 72S (RUSSET PLACE)	4500	613V	NEB	77584
C.R. 72T (RUSSET PL, W)	2800	613V	NEB	77584
C.R. 72U (BOOKREN CT)	4500	613V	NEB	77584
C.R. 72V (RUSSET PL, S)	4500	613V	NEB	77584
C.R. 72W (THALERFIELD)	0	613V	NEB	77584
C.R. 72X (DUESENBERG CT)	4300	613V	NEB	77584
C.R. 72Y (GLENCULLEN LN)	2700	614S	NEB	77584
C.R. 72Z (SENTRY WOODS)	4800	614S	NEB	77584
C.R. 73 (BURGESS HILL)	2800	614S	NEB	77584
C.R. 74A (HUGGINWAY)	3500	613U	NEB	77584
C.R. 74B (GARRETSVILLE)	0	613U	NEB	77584
C.R. 74C (HANSFORD PL)	3500	613U	NEB	77584
C.R. 74D (PRINCETON DR)	2500	613U	NEB	77584
C.R. 76 (ABBEYWOOD DR)	3800	613U	NEB	77584
C.R. 76A (ROTHBURY DR)	2900	613U	NEB	77584
C.R. 76B (HANBERRY LN)	3800	613U	NEB	77584
C.R. 76C (PEEKSKILL CT)	3000	613U	NEB	77584
C.R. 76D (ELSBURY LN)	2900	613U	NEB	77584
C.R. 89 (OLD CHOC BYU)	2400	613Z	NEB	77584
C.R. 90 (BEHLER RD)	0	613U	NEB	77584
C.R. 91 (DAUGHERTY RD)	3500	613R	NEB	77584
C.R. 91 (DAUGHERTY RD)	4800	614N	NEB	77584
C.R. 93 (MILLER RANCH)	1200	613P	PL	77584
C.R. 93A (CAMELOT'S CT)	3200	613K	PL	77584
C.R. 93B (EXCALIBER'S)	3200	613K	PL	77584
C.R. 93C (KING ARTHUR'S)	3200	613K	PL	77584
C.R. 93D (AVILION CT)	0	613L	PL	77584
C.R. 94 (SMITH RANCH)	2400	613P	NEB	77584
C.R. 101 (BAILEY RD)	3700	613Z	NEB	77578
C.R. 101 (BAILEY RD)	4600	614X	NEB	77584
C.R. 101 (BAILEY RD)	7400	615W	PL	77584
C.R. 101A (HOLLINGSWORTH)	0	614X	NEB	77584
C.R. 101B (RESTHOME)	0	614W	NEB	77584
C.R. 102C (ANN LN)	0	614W	NEB	77584
C.R. 103 (HARKEY RD)	14700	614Q	PL	77584
C.R. 104 (MCLEAN RD)	2600	614Z	PL	77584
C.R. 105 (ROY RD)	0	614K	PL	77581
C.R. 105A (ROBIN SOUND)	0	614F	PL	77581
C.R. 105B (ROBIN SPUR)	0	614F	PL	77581
C.R. 106 (BROOKSIDE RD)	4300	613H	PL	77581
C.R. 106 (BROOKSIDE RD)	4800	614E	NEB	77581
C.R. 106 (BROOKSIDE RD)	4900	614B	BK	77581
C.R. 106A (MCHARD RD)	2600	613E	PL	77584
C.R. 106AA (TEAKWOOD LN)	3500	613G	NEB	77584
C.R. 106B (COUNTRY PL E)	0	613F	NEB	77584
C.R. 106BB (WOODFERN GLN)	800	613G	NEB	77584
C.R. 106C (COUNTRY PL W)	0	613F	NEB	77584
C.R. 106CC (REDWOOD BEND)	600	613G	NEB	77584
C.R. 106D (COUNTRY PLACE)	800	613F	NEB	77584
C.R. 106E (FLOWERFIELD)	3000	613F	NEB	77584
C.R. 106F (FLOWER FLD CT)	0	613F	NEB	77584
C.R. 106G (PEACH HLLW, W)	0	613F	NEB	77584
C.R. 106H (BIRCHVIEW CT)	800	613F	NEB	77584
C.R. 106J (PEACH HLLW, S)	2700	613F	NEB	77584
C.R. 106K (PRIMRS MDWS S)	3300	613F	NEB	77584
C.R. 106L (PRIMRS MDWS W)	900	613F	NEB	77584
C.R. 106M (PRIMRS MDWS E)	900	613F	NEB	77584
C.R. 106N (THORNWOOD CT)	800	613F	NEB	77584
C.R. 106P (POPLAR CRK LN)	2800	613F	NEB	77584
C.R. 106Q (MAPLE BRCH LN)	700	613F	NEB	77584
C.R. 106R (POSTWOOD LN)	900	613F	NEB	77584
C.R. 106S (ROSEFIELD CT)	700	613F	NEB	77584
C.R. 106T (LAUREL GRV LN)	700	613F	NEB	77584
C.R. 106U (BREEZY PINES)	2700	613F	NEB	77584
C.R. 106V (FOREST OAKS)	800	613F	NEB	77584
C.R. 106W (PEACH HLLW, S)	2700	613F	NEB	77584
C.R. 106X (PEACH HLLW, S)	900	613F	NEB	77584
C.R. 106Y (LARKSPUR CIR)	0	613F	NEB	77584
C.R. 107	0	614H	PL	77581
C.R. 107 (MONA)	4500	614W	NEB	77581
C.R. 107C (ARNOLD DR)	4500	613Z	NEB	77584
C.R. 107E (ETHEL)	0	614W	NEB	77584
C.R. 108	0	614P	PL	77581
C.R. 108 (MAX RD)	12300	574W	BK	77581
C.R. 108 (MAX RD)	12500	614E	BK	77581
C.R. 109 (GARDEN RD)	12400	574X	BK	77581
C.R. 109 (GARDEN RD)	12600	614K	PL	77581
C.R. 124	2100	656A	NEB	77581
C.R. 125	0	656B	NEB	77581
C.R. 126 (DIXIE FARM RD)	0	615Z	PL	77581
C.R. 127 (HASTINGS-FRWD)	0	656A	NEB	77581
C.R. 129 (DONALSON RD)	1500	656J	NEB	77511
C.R. 129A (CHOATE DR)	0	656N	NEB	77511
C.R. 129B (POWELL)	0	656N	NEB	77511
C.R. 129C (FLORES)	0	656N	NEB	77511
C.R. 130 (PENNYWAYNE LN)	1000	656B	NEB	77546
C.R. 131 (RUSTIC LN)	0	656B	NEB	77546
C.R. 131 (RUSTIC LN)	0	616X	NEB	77546
C.R. 132 (FRIENDSWOOD W)	0	656F	NEB	77546
C.R. 133 (MOORE RD)	0	656W	NEB	77546
C.R. 134	0	656W	FR	77511

Street Name	Block	Pg/Sq	Loc	Zips
C.R. 218 (NORTON RD)	0	613Y	NEB	77578
C.R. 222 (SOUTHWESTERN)	0	613Y	NEB	77578
C.R. 250 (BARDET ST)	0	614Q	PL	77584
C.R. 252 (QUINN RD)	1900	656F	NEB	77581
C.R. 253 (WEST FRDWD RD)	0	656B	NEB	77546
C.R. 285	900	656J	NEB	77511
C.R. 286 (KIMBALL LN)	0	656E	NEB	77511
C.R. 297 (ASH RD)	2500	614S	NEB	77584
C.R. 298 (OAK RD)	2500	614S	NEB	77584
C.R. 303 (ANNA LEE LN)	900	656B	NEB	77546
C.R. 354	0	259E	PG	77327
C.R.354	0	258H	SEM	77327
C.R.354	0	259E	SEM	77327
C.R. 389 (COVEY LN)	0	614S	NEB	77584
C.R. 391	0	656A	NEB	77581
C.R. 391 (STEVENSON RD)	0	656A	NEB	77581
C.R. 391 (STEVENSON RD)	0	616W	NEB	77581
C.R. 403 (HUGHES RANCH)	1900	612M	PL	77584
C.R. 403 (HUGHES RANCH)	2600	613M	PL	77584
C.R. 403 (HUGHES RANCH)	4700	614J	PL	77581
C.R. 403A (BRYAN CT)	0	613L	PL	77584
C.R. 406 (SHARONDALE)	6000	614Y	PL	77584
C.R. 408 (NELSON RD)	0	614Q	PL	77584
C.R. 430 (DACE RD)	0	656E	NEB	77584
C.R. 460 (STERLING, W)	3400	613L	PL	77584
C.R. 474 (TREASURE LN)	4500	613Z	NEB	77584
C.R. 474A (APACHE TRL)	4500	613V	NEB	77584
C.R. 512	0	614L	PL	77581
C.R. 542 (HILLHOUSE RD)	600	613M	PL	77584
C.R. 548 (HAST-FRNWD)	0	656F	FR	77546
C.R. 551	0	656J	NEB	77511
C.R. 553 (WILLOW)	6100	614Y	PL	77584
C.R. 553A (COTTONWOOD)	6100	614Y	PL	77584
C.R. 554 (TERRELL DR)	5900	614Y	PL	77584
C.R. 555 (WAGONTRAIL RD)	14700	614U	PL	77584
C.R. 556 (GARDENS RD)	14000	614J	PL	77581
C.R. 560 (CLIFF STONE)	5000	614F	PL	77581
C.R. 561 (STONE RD, N)	12600	614A	PL	77581
C.R. 561A (LONGLEAF)	4900	614E	PL	77581
C.R. 562 (SMITH RNCH #1)	0	613J	PL	77584
C.R. 563 (SMITH RNCH #2)	2600	613J	PL	77584
C.R. 564 (WOODFIN RD)	3200	612W	NWB	77583
C.R. 564A (PALM)	100	612W	FS	77545
C.R. 565 (SEDDON RD)	4400	614E	PL	77581
C.R. 589 (BLUE SAGE DR)	4900	614S	NEB	77584
C.R. 603 (LINDA LN)	1100	613L	NEB	77584
C.R. 648 (NORTHFORK DR)	3400	613V	NEB	77584
C.R. 648 (NORTHFORK DR)	4800	614S	NEB	77584
C.R. 648A (ARROWSMITH CT)	2400	614S	NEB	77584
C.R. 648B (FALCON RIDGE)	2500	613U	NEB	77584
C.R. 648B (HANOVER CIR)	3600	613U	NEB	77584
C.R. 648C (AMBERLY CT)	2400	613Q	NEB	77584
C.R. 648D (WOODBURY CT)	2400	613U	NEB	77584
C.R. 648E (COVINGTON WAY)	2400	613Q	NEB	77584
C.R. 648E (WOODBINE PL)	3400	613Q	NEB	77584
C.R. 648F (LANDSDOWN CT)	3500	613Q	NEB	77584
C.R. 648G (AMESBURY CIR)	3500	613Q	NEB	77584
C.R. 648H (BRYMOOR CT)	3500	613Q	NEB	77584
C.R. 648J (CHARTER OAKS)	2400	613Q	NEB	77584
C.R. 648K (LAKECREST DR)	2600	613U	NEB	77584
C.R. 648L (HEATHERBEND)	2600	613U	NEB	77584
C.R. 648M (WILLOWICK CT)	2600	613U	NEB	77584
C.R. 648P (MORGAN RD)	0	613U	NEB	77584
C.R. 648Q (BENTLEY DR)	4000	613V	NEB	77584
C.R. 648R (SOUTHFORK DR)	0	613Y	NEB	77584
C.R. 648S (AVANTI DR)	2900	613V	NEB	77584
C.R. 648T (LOTUS DR)	4000	613V	NEB	77584
C.R. 648V (AVANTI CT)	3000	613V	NEB	77584
C.R. 648W (AUBURN DR)	2900	613V	NEB	77584
C.R. 648Y (VERSAILLE DR)	0	613V	NEB	77584
C.R. 648Z (BODINE DR)	3200	613Z	NEB	77584
C.R. 649 (NORTHAMPTN DR)	0	613L	NEB	77584
C.R. 649A (SHELDON DR)	3400	613L	NEB	77584
C.R. 649B (ST. JOHN DR)	1000	613G	NEB	77584
C.R. 649C (WELLINGTON DR)	3400	613L	NEB	77584
C.R. 649D (WENTWORTH DR)	1000	613G	NEB	77584
C.R. 649E (CANTERBURY DR)	1000	613G	NEB	77584
C.R. 649F (CHATWOOD DR)	3500	613G	NEB	77584
C.R. 649G (ABBOTT DR)	1000	613G	NEB	77584
C.R. 649H (WALDEN DR)	3500	613G	NEB	77584
C.R. 649I (NORTHAMPTN CT)	0	613G	NEB	77584
C.R. 649J (COVINGTON CT)	0	613G	NEB	77584
C.R. 649K (HAMPTON DR, E)	800	613G	NEB	77584
C.R. 649L (WELLSFORD, S)	800	613G	NEB	77584
C.R. 649M (WELLSFORD, N)	0	613G	NEB	77584
C.R. 649N (BRIGHTON LN)	3700	613G	NEB	77584
C.R. 649P (SOHO DR)	3700	613G	NEB	77584
C.R. 650 (SOUTHDOWN DR)	2600	613F	NEB	77584
C.R. 650A (BROMPTON DR S)	2600	613J	NEB	77584
C.R. 650B (BELGRAVIA, S)	2600	613J	NEB	77584
C.R. 650C (BELGRAVIA, W)	1000	613F	NEB	77584
C.R. 650D (BROMPTON DR N)	2600	613F	NEB	77584
C.R. 650E (BROMPTON DR E)	1000	613K	NEB	77584
C.R. 650F (BELGRAVIA, N)	2600	613F	NEB	77584
C.R. 650G (KENSINGTON DR)	2900	613F	NEB	77584
C.R. 650H (LAMBETH DR)	2700	613K	NEB	77584
C.R. 650J (BROMPTON DR W)	1000	613E	NEB	77584
C.R. 650K (BELGRAVIA, E)	1000	613F	NEB	77584
C.R. 650L (PIMLICO DR)	1000	613F	NEB	77584
C.R. 650M (WOODBRIDGE AV)	1000	613F	NEB	77584
C.R. 650N (HELMSLEY DR)	2900	613F	NEB	77584
C.R. 650P (HUNTINGTON DR)	1000	613K	NEB	77584
C.R. 650Q (SHERBORNE)	3000	613F	NEB	77584
C.R. 650R (WINDEMERE DR)	2900	613F	NEB	77584
C.R. 650S (MELFORD AVE)	1000	613F	NEB	77584
C.R. 650T (BECKET)	2900	613K	NEB	77584
C.R. 650U (NORWICH)	2900	613K	NEB	77584
C.R. 650V (BEDFORD AVE)	0	613K	NEB	77584
C.R. 650W (MARGATE CT)	1000	613K	NEB	77584
C.R. 650X (OXFORD DR)	1000	613K	NEB	77584
C.R. 653L (COUNTRY GRV E)	600	613G	NEB	77584
C.R. 658 (WESTGATE DR)	1900	614N	PL	77581
C.R. 664 (SHELDON RD)	900	613H	PL	77581
C.R. 666 (SMITH RD)	0	613Q	PL	77584
C.R. 667 (HAWK RD)	3800	613H	PL	77584
C.R. 742 (BECKY LN)	6100	614U	PL	77584
C.R. 742A (JERRY CREST)	6100	614Y	PL	77584
C.R. 742B (LARRY CREST)	6100	614Y	PL	77584
C.R. 742C (PATRIDGE DR)	6100	614Y	PL	77584
C.R. 742D (WAGON TRAIL)	14700	614U	PL	77584
C.R. 751 (LORRIE LN)	5800	614L	PL	77581
C.R. 782 (GARDENIA)	5600	614L	PL	77581
C.R. 782A (LAZY BEND DR)	14600	614Q	PL	77581
C.R. 782B (THELMA)	14600	614Q	PL	77581
C.R. 801 (PIPER RD)	14600	614P	PL	77584
C.R. 817 (SHARON DR)	5600	614F	PL	77581
C.R. 826 (RODRIQUEZ RD)	0	614N	PL	77584
C.R. 831 (HOLLAND RD)	16600	614X	NEB	77584
C.R. 834 (CONFEDERATE)	0	614Z	PL	77584
C.R. 834A (COLONIAL DR)	6600	614V	PL	77584
C.R. 834B (LEE RD)	16100	614Z	PL	77584
C.R. 844 (WEST LEA LN)	5400	614X	PL	77584

Street Name	Block	Pg/Sq	Loc	Zips
C.R. 844A (MEADOW LN)	5300	614X	PL	77584
C.R. 844B (MOCKINGBIRD)	5300	614X	PL	77584
C.R. 844C (HERON LN)	5300	614X	PL	77584
C.R. 844D (MOCKINGBIRD W)	0	614X	PL	77584
C.R. 844E (SKYLARK WAY)	3200	614X	PL	77584
C.R. 844F (WINGTAIL WAY)	3200	614X	PL	77584
C.R. 844G (MEADWLARK WY)	3200	614X	PL	77584
C.R. 844H (BLUEBIRD WAY)	3200	614X	PL	77584
C.R. 862	6100	614U	PL	77584
C.R. 880 (MCKNIGHT RD)	5100	614W	NEB	77584
C.R. 883 (BUTLER RD)	5800	614L	PL	77581
C.R. 883A (MARSHA LN)	5800	614K	PL	77581
C.R. 883B (KELLY DR)	5800	614L	PL	77581
C.R. 883D (MICHAEL LN)	13900	614L	PL	77581
C.R. 883E (MELANIE LN)	13900	614L	PL	77581
C.R. 883F (OLIN DR)	6000	614L	PL	77581
C.R. 883G (CARROLL DR)	13500	614G	PL	77581
C.R. 883H (STEVEN DR)	0	614L	PL	77581
C.R. 884 (CURTIS DR)	0	613Z	NEB	77584
C.R. 895 (MUSTANG)	1900	612X	NWB	77583
C.R. 896 (GLOSSON RD)	0	612R	PL	77584
C.R. 899 (CANTU RD)	6300	614Q	PL	77584
C.R. 899A (OCHOA RD)	0	614Q	PL	77584
C.R. 905 (RIVERS RD)	3400	613Z	NEB	77578
C.R. 914 (AUBRELL RD)	15900	614Y	PL	77584
C.R. 922 (JESKE RD)	0	613X	NEB	77584
C.R. 926 (JOSEPHINE)	0	614Q	PL	77584
C.R. 954 (RAZA RD)	6100	614Y	PL	77584
C.R. 963	0	616W	PL	77584
C.R. 967 (HONEYSUCKLE)	0	612T	NWB	77584
C.R. 990 (SORENSON DR)	0	613Z	NEB	77584
C.R. 990A (FORRESTER DR)	3100	613Z	NEB	77584
C.R. 990B (WEBBER DR, E)	0	613Z	NEB	77584
C.R. 990C (WEBBER DR, N)	4100	613V	NEB	77584
C.R. 990D (WEBBER DR, S)	4100	613Z	NEB	77584
C.R. 990E (WEBBER CT, S)	3100	613Z	NEB	77584
CABALLERO DR	9700	455D	NEH	77078
CABALLITO LN	0	461P	NEC	77521
CABALLO ST	0	461P	NEC	77521
CABANA CANYON CT	5800	609T	NEF	77479
N. CABANGO CT	0	295A	SEM	77365
S. CABANGO DR	0	295E	SEM	77365
N. CABANGO DR	0	295A	SEM	77365
CABANISS AVE	1	499R	BT	77520
CABANISS AVE	100	500N	BT	77520
CABANISS CIR	18500	331E	NWC	77379
CABANNA RD	22800	291E	NWC	77389
CABBAGE	5000	331A	NWC	77379
CABBAGE PATCH CT	18500	255A	SEM	77302
CABBOT COVE	11300	289X	NWC	77375
CABELA RIDGE CT	0	372C	NCC	77073
CABELL	1200	453P	NWH	77022
CABERNET LN	0	451S	NWH	77055
CABEZA DR	2500	528Z	SG	77478
CABILDO DR	15400	527G	SWC	77083
CABIN CREEK DR	9200	409G	NWC	77064
CABIN CREEK DR	9500	409C	NWC	77064
CABIN GATE PLACE	100	249R	NWH	77375
CABIN GATE PLACE	100	249R	NWH	77375
CABIN GREEN CT	18000	377B	NEC	77346
CABIN LINE LN	24600	485A	NEF	77494
CABIN PLACE	3500	609E	SG	77479
CABIN RUN LN	14900	528W	NEF	77498
CABLE BROOK LN	20100	446L	NWC	77449
CABLE CAR CT	2200	611W	FS	77545
CABLE TERRACE DR	22900	485L	SWC	77494
CABLE WAY	1100	379T	NEC	77532
CABO BLANCO CT	12200	449A	NWC	77041
CABO ISLE LN	0	409W	NWC	77041
CABOOSE CT	17500	379S	NEC	77532
CABOT	7400	455A	NEH	77016
CABOT	7900	455B	NEH	77078
CABOT COVE	0	614V	PL	77584
CABOT CREEK CIR	15600	329T	NWC	77070
CABOT HILL ST	0	416L	NEC	77044
CABOT LAKES DR	1400	659W	LC	77573
CABOT LODGE LN	0	326Y	NWC	77433
CABOT POINT DR	0	486Q	SWC	77450
CABOT RIDGE LN	0	326U	NWC	77429
CABOTS LANDING DR	15000	408S	NWC	77084
CABOTWAY	29500	249W	NWC	77375
CABRA CT	19500	406U	NWC	77449
CABRERA CT	13600	528K	SWC	77083
CABRERA CT	13600	528K	SWC	77083
CABRERA LN	13500	528K	SWC	77083
CABRERA RD	3200	609N	NEF	77479
CABRILLO LANDING CT	0	525A	NEF	77494
CABRINA LN	7200	528L	SWH	77083
CABRINA TRACE CT	0	373E	NCC	77073
CACTUS	1300	536K	PA	77506
CACTUS	3000	454X	NEH	77026
CACTUS	22900	296C	SEM	77357
CACTUS DR	300	252F	SEM	77385
CACTUS DR	1100	501M	BT	77521
CACTUS LN	0	406M	NWC	77433
CACTUS BLOOM LN	2100	485P	NEF	77494
CACTUS BLOSSOM TRAIL	0	326J	NWC	77433
CACTUS BRANCH CT	0	578T	SEH	77059
CACTUS CREEK DR	3400	253X	SEM	77386
CACTUS FLOWER DR	10400	371S	NWC	77086
CACTUS FOREST DR	5400	411L	NWC	77088
CACTUS GARDEN CIR	0	525X	NEF	77406
CACTUS HEIGHTS LN	0	615K	PL	77581
CACTUS POINT CT	11100	367T	NWC	77095
CACTUS ROSE DR	19200	446M	NWC	77449
CACTUS SAGE TRAIL	24900	485J	NEF	77494
CACTUS THORN DR	19200	406M	NWC	77433
CACTUS VALLEY CT	11200	616E	SEC	77089
CACTUS WREN LN	14700	288A	NWC	77377
CADAWAC RD	8100	530Q	SWH	77074
CADBURY CIR	4100	502K	BT	77521
CADBURY DR	18100	447F	NWC	77084
CADBURY CASTLE LN	0	611S	FS	77545
CADDO	7100	462Y	BT	77520
CADDO CT	7600	461S	NEC	77521
CADDO CT	9200	579A	LP	77571
CADDO RD	7300	455A	NEH	77016
CADDO RD	7900	415X	NEH	77078
CADDO RD	8400	455D	NEH	77078
CADDO CREEK LN	11200	616E	SEC	77089
CADDO HEIGHTS ST	21000	525R	NEF	77407
CADDO LAKE LN	6800	528G	SWH	77083
CADDO PARK CT	21300	525Z	NEF	77406
CADDO PASSWAY	25700	525A	NEF	77494
CADDO POINT CT	0	409W	NWC	77041
CADDO RIDGE LN	0	367W	NWC	77433
CADDO RIDGE LN	0	407A	NWC	77433
CADDO SPRINGS CT	0	406D	NWC	77433
CADDO TERRACE LN	5900	409W	NWC	77041
CADDO TRAIL	9900	248L	SWM	77354
CADDY CIR	19000	337Z	NEC	77346
CADE CT	15800	408A	NWC	77095

Street Name	Block	Pg/Sq	Loc	Zips
CADE DR	8800	408A	NWC	77095
CADEAUX CIR	0	332G	NCC	77073
CADE HILLS LN	0	293F	SEM	77386
CADENA CT	10300	329B	NWC	77375
CADENA RD	3500	577A	PA	77504
CADEN CREEK	0	256X	SEM	77365
CADENCREST CT	4900	484Z	NEF	77494
CADENHEAD RD	23800	257N	SEM	77357
CADENHORN LN	15800	408W	NWC	77084
CADEN ROCK LN	0	328K	NWC	77429
CADENZA CT	7700	410P	NWC	77040
CADES COVE DR	2300	333A	NCC	77373
CADES CREEK CT	10200	616G	SEC	77089
CADILLAC	6600	533L	SEH	77021
CADIZ CIR	2500	412E	NWC	77038
CADIZ CT	4400	660G	LC	77573
CADMAN CT	9400	531U	SWH	77096
CADMUS	4300	453J	NWH	77022
CADOGAN CT	20200	486K	SWC	77450
CADOGAN LN	1600	486K	SWC	77450
CADY CT	13800	488K	SWH	77077
CAELWOOD DR	5900	337X	NEC	77346
CAESAR DR	11400	528Z	SWH	77477
CAESARS CIR	18300	257C	RF	77357
CAFFERTY TRACE	0	620K	SB	77586
CAFFREY	9600	576S	SEH	77075
CAGE	100	494F	NEH	77020
CAGLE	0	247Q	SWM	77355
CAGNEY LN	0	610H	NEF	77489
CAHILL CT	13700	328T	NWC	77429
CAHILL LN	13300	328T	NWC	77429
CAICOS CALLE	0	660W	GCO	77539
CAIN CIR	1	496Q	GP	77015
CAINE HILL CT	1400	659W	LC	77573
CAIRNGALE	16900	447D	NWC	77084
CAIRNGORM AVE	16100	407H	NWC	77095
CAIRNGORM DR	16500	447H	NWC	77084
CAIRNGROVE LN	16500	407V	NWC	77084
CAIRNLADDIE	17000	447C	NWC	77084
CAIRNLASSIE	17000	447C	NWC	77084
CAIRNLEIGH CT	16700	447D	NWC	77084
CAIRNLEIGH DR	4600	447D	NWC	77084
CAIRNLEIGH DR	5000	407Z	NWC	77084
CAIRNLOCH	16900	447D	NWC	77084
CAIRNLOMOND	4600	447H	NWC	77084
CAIRN MEADOWS	10000	329B	NWC	77375
CAIRN OAKS PLACE	1	251C	WD	77381
CAIRNS DR	19500	406U	NWC	77449
CAIRNSEAN	4600	447C	NWC	77084
CAIRNTOSH	16900	447C	NWC	77084
CAIRNVILLAGE	4600	447C	NWC	77084
CAIRNWAY DR	16000	448A	NWC	77084
CAIRNWAY DR	16300	447H	NWC	77084
CAITLYN CT	600	486D	SWC	77094
CAITLYN BLOSSOM LN	0	366Y	NWC	77433
CAITLYN FALLS LN	0	375Y	NEC	77396
CAJON CIR	22000	338Z	NEC	77532
CAJON CANYON CT	20400	526E	NEF	77450
CAKEBREAD ST		484J	NEF	77494
CAL DR	13400	368Q	NWC	77065
CALABRIA BAY CT	0	610T	MC	77459
CALABRIAN PINE CT	9200	527N	NEF	77407
CALADERO DR	7000	527G	SWC	77083
CALAIS RD	7200	533V	SEH	77033
CALAMUS CIR	0	461P	NEC	77521
CALANDRA LARK LN	0	328A	NWC	77377
CALAVATRA CT	0	377D	NEH	77346
CALAVATRA LN	0	378A	NEC	77346
CALAVERAS BLUE LN	0	445L	NWC	77449
CALAVERAS CREEK CT	28400	298X	NEH	77336
CALAVERAS LAKE DR	0	293C	SEM	77386
CALAWAY COVE CT	12200	449A	NWC	77041
CALAWAY FALLS LN		484S	NEF	77494
CALAWAY OAKS LN	0	484W	NEF	77494
CALCATERRA CT	18100	327W	NWC	77429
CALCUTTA SPRING DR	0	528K	SWC	77083
CALDBECK LN	0	611S	FS	77545
CALDER	400	658V	LC	77573
CALDER	6300	492F	SWH	77007
N. CALDER DR	0	658M	LC	77573
CALDERA CT	5100	371N	NWC	77066
CALDERA LN	0	406G	NWC	77433
CALDERA CANYON CT	17100	367X	NWC	77095
CALDERA CANYON DR	10000	367X	NWC	77095
CALDERBROOK DR	21900	445M	NWC	77449
CALDERMONT CT	15800	407Z	NWC	77084
CALDERSTONE CT	0	485S	NEF	77494
CALDERWOOD DR	900	332G	NCC	77073
CALDICOTE DR	5600	337X	NEC	77346
CALDRA WAY	0	611W	FS	77545
CALDWALDER LN	6900	375F	NEH	77396
CALDWELL	100	500E	BT	77520
CALDWELL	3900	534L	SEH	77087
CALDWELL CANYON LN	0	371D	NWC	77014
CALDWELL POINTE CT	0	377J	NEC	77346
CALEBS COVE	3300	502B	NEC	77521
CALEDONIA DR	19300	406R	NWC	77449
CALENDAR	3800	453Y	NEH	77009
CALENDAR LAKE DR	2800	609F	MC	77459
CALGARY CIR	0	569U	MC	77459
CALGARY CIR	3800	569U	MC	77459
CALGARY LN	5000	414Y	NEH	77016
CALGARY POINTE DR	26800	296X	SEM	77339
CALGARY WOODS LN	0	524H	NEF	77494
CALGARY WOODS LN	0	524H	NEF	77494
CALHOUN	3000	660H	BC	77518
CALHOUN RD	4300	534A	SEH	77004
CALHOUN RD	5100	534A	SEH	77021
CALHOUN RD	5900	533V	SEH	77033
CALHOUN CT (1700 Ennis)	3000	493V	SEH	77003
CALI DR	17000	332J	NWC	77090
CALI DR	18200	331H	NWC	77090
CALICHE CREEK DR	0	571R	SWH	77045
CALICO LN	11400	490G	PP	77024
CALICO CANYON DR	8200	290N	NWC	77375
CALICO CANYON LN	1600	615F	PL	77581
CALICO CORNERS LN	23100	334A	NCC	77373
CALICO CREEK LN	0	612P	PL	77545
CALICO CROSSING LN	0	525D	NEF	77450
CALICO FALLS LN	12200	409W	NWC	77041
CALICO FIELD CT	14400	327Y	NWC	77429
CALICO FIELD DR	14400	327Y	NWC	77429
CALICO GLEN LN	17900	447B	NWC	77084
CALICO HEIGHTS LN	0	326T	NWC	77433
CALICO HILL LN	2000	568D	SG	77478
CALICO HILLS CIR	400	486D	SWC	77094
CALICO PEAK WAY	0	326E	NWC	77433
CALICO PLACE LN	0	326U	NWC	77429
CALICO POINT CT	7400	526K	NWF	77407
CALICO RIDGE LN	22900	292L	NCC	77373
N. CALICO ROCK LN	1100	332R	NCC	77073
W. CALICO ROCK LN	16400	332R	NCC	77073

Street Name	Block	Pg/Sq	Loc	Zips
CALICO WOODS LN	0	485J	NEF	77494
CALICO WOODS LN	6600	408V	NWC	77041
CALIFORNIA	1000	493S	SWH	77006
CALIFORNIA	1000	540D	BT	77520
CALIFORNIA	1800	660W	GCO	77539
CALIFORNIA RD	2700	611T	FS	77545
CALISTOGA CT	16300	611B	SWH	77053
CALISTOGA DR		484J	NEF	77494
CALIX LN	7100	528J	SWC	77083
CALJON DR	0	334V	NCC	77338
CALLAHAN DR	14000	456V	NEC	77049
CALLAN LN	0	458S	NEC	77049
CALLE CACERES PLACE	0	492L	SWH	77007
CALLE CADIZ PLACE	0	492L	SWH	77007
CALLE CATALINA PLACE	0	492L	SWH	77007
CALLE CORDOBA PLACE	0	492L	SWH	77007
CALLE IRIS	200	494P	SEH	77003
CALLE LOZANO DR	6400	408U	NWC	77041
CALLE MONTILLA PLACE	0	492L	SWH	77007
CALLEPINE LN	18900	328F	NWC	77377
CALLE RONDA PLACE	0	492L	SWH	77007
CALLE ROSA	0	494P	SEH	77003
CALLERY CREEK DR	4600	571Z	SWH	77053
CALLES	1100	494G	NEH	77020
CALLE SEVILLA PLACE	0	492L	SWH	77007
CALLE VIOLETA	200	494P	SEH	77003
CALLEY PATH	0	568W	SG	77479
CALLIE	0	255C	SEM	77357
CALLIE	2300	494W	SEH	77004
CALLIE CT	1	491E	HC	77024
CALLOWAY	100	495V	NEH	77029
CALLOWAY CIR	2300	616K	PL	77581
CALLY CT	0	612Z	NEB	77578
CALM CT	0	407X	NWC	77084
CALMAR DR	1600	252Z	SEM	77386
CALM BROOK CT	17900	407K	NWC	77095
CALM CREEK CT	900	498A	NEC	77530
CALM LAGOON CT	17000	407G	NWC	77095
CALMONT DR	13900	369A	NWC	77070
CALMONT DR	14000	329W	NWC	77070
CALM STREAM WALK LN		289G	NWC	77375
CALMWATER LN	0	417B	NEC	77044
CALM WIND WAY	0	572P	SWH	77045
CALORA	4400	251E	WD	77381
CALORO	5400	444Q	KT	77493
CALTHORTE CT	700	486G	SWC	77450
CALTON COVE CIR	6300	411B	NWC	77086
S. CALUMET	1000	533B	SEH	77004
N. CALUMET	1000	533B	SEH	77004
CALUMET	1000	493W	SWH	77004
CALUMET	1300	533B	SWH	77004
CALUMET	6800	290C	NWC	77389
CALUMET DR	2300	528Z	SG	77478
CALVANO DR	0	326V	NWC	77429
CALVARY LN	2500	445Q	NWC	77449
CALVARYMAN LN	1500	445U	NWC	77449
CALVERT RD	27500	288J	NWC	77377
CALVERT COVE CT	4100	293H	SEM	77386
CALVERT COVE CT	4100	294E	SEM	77386
CALVERT CROSSING CT	0	446P	NWC	77449
CALVERTON DR	9700	528S	NEF	77498
CALVERTON PINES LN	8500	407F	NWC	77095
CALVI CT	100	531M	BL	77401
CALVIN	100	536L	PA	77506
CALVIN AVE	900	412X	NWH	77088
CALVIN AVE	2400	412W	NWH	77088
CALVIN RD	15700	332X	NEC	77090
CALVINS RD	28000	298X	NEH	77336
CALVIT KNOLLS DR	0	526W	NEF	77406
CALWOOD CIR	9400	329R	NWC	77379
CALYPSO LN	100	619X	LC	77573
CALYPSO BAY CT	0	612G	PL	77584
CALYPSO BAY DR	0	612G	PL	77584
CALYPSO COVE CT	1800	619D	PA	77586
CAM CT	1	451W	SV	77055
CAMARA LN	13700	489F	SWH	77079
CAMARGO CT	9400	530T	SWH	77074
CAMARILLO CT	0	411M	NWC	77088
CAMAROSA DR	0	577J	OY	77504
CAMAY DR	8500	454D	NEH	77016
CAMBER CT	16700	419B	NEC	77532
CAMBER CT	16800	379X	NEC	77532
CAMBER BROOK CT	8800	615D	SEC	77089
CAMBER BROOK DR	8600	615D	SEC	77089
CAMBERLEIGH LN	4900	291S	NWC	77388
CAMBERWELL CT	1	251Z	WD	77380
CAMBERWELL GREEN CT	10000	329Q	NWC	77070
CAMBERWELL GREEN LN	16900	329Q	NWC	77070
CAMBORNE LN	8200	369D	NWC	77070
CAMBRIA CT	0	659S	LC	77573
CAMBRIA CT	0	659S	LC	77573
CAMBRIDGE	6800	533J	SWH	77030
CAMBRIDGE	7400	533N	SWH	77054
CAMBRIDGE BLVD	0	257H	SEM	77357
CAMBRIDGE BLVD	0	258F	SEM	77357
CAMBRIDGE CT	1200	620G	SB	77586
CAMBRIDGE CT	2100	612Y	NWB	77578
S. CAMBRIDGE CT	2200	658P	LC	77573
N. CAMBRIDGE CT	2200	658P	LC	77573
CAMBRIDGE CT	3500	577B	PA	77504
CAMBRIDGE DR	800	459Q	HG	77562
CAMBRIDGE DR	1200	656L	FR	77546
CAMBRIDGE LN	2800	609D	MC	77459
CAMBRIDGE BAY LN	0	612F	PL	77545
CAMBRIDGE CIRCUS	2900	615L	PL	77581
CAMBRIDGE COVE CIR	7200	609Q	MC	77459
CAMBRIDGE COVE DR	0	613T	NEB	77584
CAMBRIDGE DALE CT	2200	445S	NWC	77493
CAMBRIDGE EAGLE DR	12800	377T	NEC	77044
CAMBRIDGE FALLS DR	3400	611T	FS	77545
CAMBRIDGE GLEN DR	6300	570D	SWH	77035
CAMBRIDGE OAKS CIR	1600	486H	SWC	77094
CAMBRIDGE SHORES CT	0	612K	PL	77545
CAMBRIDGE SQUARE LN	0	611S	FS	77545
CAMBRIDGE VALE CT	0	326Y	NWC	77429
CAMBRIDGE VIEW DR	15800	617X	FR	77546
CAMBRIDGE VILLAGE DR	500	336W	HM	77338
CAMBRY CROSSING CT	2900	485U	NEF	77494
CAMBRY LANDING LN	6000	609X	NEF	77479
CAMBRY PARK	4100	486S	NEF	77450
CAMBURY DR	13700	372F	NWH	77014
CAMBY PARK DR	11800	572R	SWH	77047
CAMDEN DR	2300	533F	SWH	77021
CAMDEN LN	5000	614R	PL	77584
CAMDEN RD	1000	536V	PA	77502
CAMDEN RD	1300	537S	PA	77502
CAMDEN BAY CT	0	366Q	NWC	77433
CAMDEN BEND CT	4100	485Z	NEF	77450
CAMDEN BEND LN	21900	485Z	NEF	77450
CAMDEN BROOK LN	4700	484Y	NEF	77494
CAMDEN COVE LN	0	417A	NEC	77044
CAMDEN CREEK LN	0	488T	SWH	77077

Street Name	Block	Pg/Sq	Loc	Zips
CAMDEN CROSS LN	0	289Y	NWC	77379
CAMDEN FALLS LN	0	488T	SWH	77077
CAMDEN FOREST DR	0	376C	NEC	77396
CAMDEN GARDEN LN		524C	NEF	77494
CAMDEN GLEN LN	27100	366Q	NWC	77433
CAMDEN HILLS LN	0	615H	PL	77089
CAMDEN HOLLOW LN	7800	375Y	NEC	77396
CAMDEN LANDING TRAIL	1700	611W	FS	77545
CAMDEN MEADOW DR	12200	328D	NWC	77375
CAMDEN OAK	0	526H	NEF	77407
CAMDEN OAKS LN	17700	527E	NEF	77407
CAMDEN PARK DR	2500	252R	SEM	77385
CAMDEN PARK LN	0	660P	LC	77573
N. CAMDEN PKWY	2400	371L	NWC	77067
S. CAMDEN PKWY	2500	371L	NWC	77067
CAMDEN RIDGE LN	24300	250Z	NWC	77389
CAMDEN ROW CT	0	407G	NWC	77095
CAMDEN VALLEY CT	0	407R	NWC	77084
CAMDEN VILLAGE DR	31400	252R	SEM	77386
CAMDON DR	0	538R	DP	77536
CAMELBACK CT	15100	488G	SWH	77079
CAMELIA CIR	2200	502W	BT	77520
CAMELIA CT	26300	248F	SWM	77354
CAMELIA CHASE CT	0	293U	NCC	77373
CAMELIA CHASE CT	0	293U	NCC	77373
CAMELIA CREST	0	615K	PL	77581
CAMELIA CREST LN	0	410A	NWC	77064
CAMELIA GLEN LN	3900	611W	FS	77545
CAMELLA EVERGREEN LN	0	526T	NEF	77469
CAMELLIA	100	568S	SG	77478
CAMELLIA	3200	577C	PA	77505
CAMELLIA	6000	492G	SWH	77007
CAMELLIA	18000	327C	NWC	77429
CAMELLIA CT	0	657F	FR	77546
CAMELLIA BEND CIR	19400	291W	NWC	77379
CAMELLIA BEND CIR	19500	330D	NWC	77379
CAMELLIA CREEK	0	406W	NWC	77449
CAMELLIA DALE TRAIL	18700	447N	NWC	77084
CAMELLIA ESTATES LN	18200	366D	NWC	77429
CAMELLIA GARDENS DR	9800	527S	NEF	77407
CAMELLIA KNOLL TRAIL	19300	446Q	NWC	77084
S. CAMELLIA PARK CIR	0	250J	NWC	77389
CAMELLIA WAY ST	0	659G	LC	77573
CAMELOT	700	616X	FR	77546
CAMELOT	3500	502K	BT	77521
CAMELOT LN	700	491E	HC	77024
CAMELOT LN	1100	616X	PL	77581
CAMELOT LN	2800	609D	MC	77459
CAMELOT LN	25200	244M	WCO	77447
CAMELOT CENTRE CT	13700	370A	NWC	77069
CAMELOT GROVE DR	22100	296X	SEM	77339
CAMELOT LEGEND DR		289P	NWC	77375
CAMELOT PLACE	1300	569S	SG	77478
CAMELOTS CT	3200	613K	PL	77584
CAMEL WALK DR	0	449T	NWH	77043
CAMEO CT	1900	659F	LC	77573
CAMEO DR	3100	450M	NWH	77080
CAMEO FALLS LN	0	524F	NEF	77494
CAMEO ROSE DR	0	326J	NWC	77433
CAMERON	2300	492U	SWH	77098
CAMERON CT	6100	657U	LC	77573
CAMERON LN	29100	243Q	WCO	77447
CAMERON RD	33000	282A	WCO	77484
CAMERON BLUFF LN	0	484T	NEF	77494
CAMERON COVE LN	6000	525H	NEF	77450
CAMERON PARK LN	0	293K	SEM	77386
CAMERON REACH CT		328k	NWC	77377
CAMERON REACH DR	13200	328K	NWC	77377
W. CAMERON RIDGE DR	0	325M	NWC	77429
E. CAMERON RIDGE DR	0	326J	NWC	77433
CAMERONS CAMP DR	19200	526P	NEF	77407
CAMILLE	1600	537F	PA	77506
CAMILLE	1700	247J	SWM	77362
CAMILLE DR	28100	248X	TB	77375
CAMILLIA CT	0	444X	KT	77493
CAMILLIA DR	2400	460Q	NEC	77562
CAMILLIA RIDGE WAY	24200	445S	NWC	77493
CAMILLIA TRAIL	15900	328R	NWC	77377
CAMILLO CT	0	487E	SWC	77094
CAMINITO TRAIL	6400	337U	NEC	77346
CAMINO CT	1	250A	WD	77382
CAMINO DEL SOL DR	15100	527L	NEF	77083
CAMINO OAKS DR	11100	370T	NWC	77064
CAMINO RANCHO DR	14700	528E	SWC	77083
CAMINO RANCHO DR	14900	527M	SWC	77083
CAMINO REAL	7300	460Y	MN	77521
CAMINO VERDE DR	7300	527L	SWC	77083
CAMINO VILLAGE DR	1000	618V	SEC	77058
CAMIRILLO CREEK LN		524C	NEF	77494
CAMMY LN	2100	539S	LP	77571
CAMP RD	300	460N	HG	77562
CAMPAIGN CIR	0	526W	NEF	77406
CAMPANA	0	369J	NWC	77429
CAMPANILE DR	0	446S	NWC	77449
CAMPBELL	100	536Q	PA	77502
CAMPBELL	1200	493D	NEH	77009
CAMPBELL	1700	494A	NEH	77026
CAMPBELL	4500	494C	NEH	77020
CAMPBELL CT	0	450Y	NWC	77055
CAMPBELL DR	4800	614R	PL	77584
CAMPBELL RD	900	490C	HE	77024
CAMPBELL RD	1000	450Y	NWH	77055
CAMPBELL RD	1700	450U	NWH	77080
CAMPBELL RD	4300	450B	NWH	77041
CAMPBELL RD	9200	450U	NWH	77080
CAMPBELLFORD DR	18100	328H	NWC	77377
CAMPBELL PIT RD	21600	257X	SEM	77357
CAMP COVE DR	0	327S	NWC	77429
CAMPDEN CT	16000	330R	NWC	77379
CAMPDEN DR	6600	330R	NWC	77379
CAMPDEN HILL RD	14400	571V	SWH	77045
CAMPDEN HILL RD	15200	571Z	SWH	77053
CAMPEACHY CIR	13200	528L	SWH	77083
CAMPEACHY LN	7100	528L	SWH	77083
CAMPECHE DR	4600	571R	SWH	77045
CAMPERS CREST DR	18500	377D	NEC	77346
CAMPFIELD CT	3500	446L	NWC	77449
CAMPFIELD DR	19700	446L	NWC	77449
CAMP FIRE RD	15800	617T	SEC	77546
CAMPHOR DR	3700	527C	SWC	77082
CAMPHOR TREE DR	20700	446N	NWC	77449
CAMPHORWOOD DR	11200	616C	SEC	77089
CAMPIONE CT	24200	524M	NEF	77406
CAMP LILLIE RD	100	338S	NEH	77346
CAMP MANISON RD	1600	657J	FR	77546
CAMPOREE LN	7400	528L	SWH	77083
CAMPOS DR	11500	369N	NWC	77065
CAMPOS DR	12100	368R	NWC	77065
CAMPSITE TRAIL	12500	368L	NWC	77429
CAMPTON CT	1200	451Y	NWH	77055
CAMPTOWN CIR	6600	330W	NWC	77069
CAMPWELL	0	500N	BT	77520
CAMPWOOD DR	1900	568Y	SG	77478
CAMPWOOD LN	13800	328S	NWC	77429
CAMRANH ST	0	529P	SWH	77072
CAMRON POINT CIR	0	407W	NWC	77449
CAMROSE CIR	0	571S	SWH	77085
CAMROSE CIR	1	571S	SWH	77085
CAMROSE CT	0	292F	NCC	77373
CAMROSE CT	9600	371W	NWC	77086
CAMWAY	6700	454R	NEH	77028
CAMWOOD	1	245T	SWM	77355
CAMWOOD	7600	535N	SEH	77087
CANAAN BRIDGE DR	13300	408Y	NWC	77041
CANABURY DR	28500	299S	NEC	77336
CANADA DR	6000	577H	PA	77505
CANADA DR	6100	578E	PA	77505
CANADA RD	3100	538Z	LP	77571
CANADA RD	3200	578D	LP	77571
CANADA DRY	2100	534B	SEH	77023
CANADIAN	200	453V	NEH	77009
CANADIAN	3200	444K	KT	77493
CANADIAN RIVER CT	4600	253U	SEM	77386
CANADIAN RIVER DR	4300	569W	SG	77478
CANADY PARK LN	0	575V	SEH	77075
CANAL	1900	494N	SEH	77003
CANAL	4400	494N	SEH	77011
CANAL	7500	495W	SEH	77012
CANAL CT	1	494P	SEH	77011
CANAL DR	0	656X	FR	77511
W. CANAL RD	100	459M	HG	77562
E. CANAL RD	100	459M	HG	77562
E. CANAL RD	800	460J	HG	77562
S. CANAL RD	1800	460T	HG	77562
CANAL RD	22500	525K	NEF	77406
CANARAS CT	19100	406Z	NWC	77449
CANARIDGE DR	16100	571X	SWH	77053
CANARIO DR	16200	527K	NEF	77083
CANARY	300	257H	RF	77357
CANARY	700	536U	PA	77502
CANARY CIR	1600	658Q	LC	77573
CANARY CIR	20400	295R	SEM	77365
CANARY LN	2800	375K	HM	77396
CANARY LN	25100	295R	SEM	77365
CANARY GRASS LN	3700	578Y	SEH	77059
CANARY ISLE CT	4200	485Y	NEF	77450
CANARY POINT DR	25200	524L	NWF	77406
CANARY POINT LN	0	407E	NWC	77433
CANARYWOOD DR	10900	616C	SEC	77089
S. CANARY YELLOW CIR	14800	325Q	NWC	77433
W. CANARY YELLOW CIR	22000	325Q	NWC	77433
E. CANARY YELLOW CIR	22000	325R	NWC	77433
CANASTA LN	7400	528L	SWH	77083
CANAVERAL CREEK LN	0	609T	NEF	77479
CANBERRA	8600	575E	SEH	77061
CANBY	17200	324E	HK	77447
CANBY POINT LN	0	326T	NWC	77429
S. CANCUN DR	0	571M	SWH	77045
N. CANCUN DR	0	571M	SWH	77045
E. CANCUN DR	0	571M	SWH	77045
CANDA LN	7200	528L	SWH	77083
CANDACE	8700	450V	NWH	77055
CANDACE CT	12800	570E	MC	77489
CANDACE POINT CT		366U	NWC	77433
CANDELA CT	7700	527J	NEF	77083
CANDELA DR	17000	527J	NEF	77083
CANDEL RAY DR	0	299X	NEC	77336
CANDIZ LANDING CIR	1300	298Z	NEH	77336
CANDLE LN	7800	530Y	SWH	77071
CANDLE BEND DR	3000	332A	NWC	77388
CANDLEBERRY DR	13700	415C	NEC	77396
CANDLEBROOK CIR	19200	331D	NWC	77388
CANDLEBROOK DR	3400	331D	NWC	77388
CANDLE CABIN LN	3100	331D	NWC	77388
CANDLE CANYON CT	0	366Y	NWC	77433
CANDLE CANYON CT	0	366Y	NWC	77433
CANDLECHASE DR	18600	331H	NWC	77388
CANDLE COVE CT	0	609T	NEF	77479
CANDLE CREEK	0	291Z	NWC	77388
CANDLECREEK DR	18900	331D	NWC	77388
CANDLECREST DR	4900	452F	NWH	77018
CANDLECREST DR	5400	452C	NWH	77091
CANDLE GATE LN	0	484X	NEF	77494
CANDLE GATE LN	0	484X	NEF	77494
CANDLEGLOW DR	4900	452G	NWH	77018
CANDLEGREEN LN	7600	570G	SWH	77071
CANDLE GROVE DR	3000	331D	NWC	77388
CANDLE HILL DR	3000	332A	NWC	77388
CANDLE HOLLOW DR	3000	331D	NWC	77388
CANDLEKNOLL DR	3200	331D	NWC	77388
CANDLELEAF DR	4900	452G	NWH	77018
CANDLELIGHT	19600	257M	SEM	77357
CANDLE LIGHT CT	0	568E	SG	77498
CANDLELIGHT CT	1900	657K	FR	77546
CANDLELIGHT LN	1000	452F	NWH	77018
CANDLELIGHT CRESCENT RD	18900	331D	NWC	77388
CANDLELIGHT PARK LN	0	290S	NWC	77379
CANDLELIGHT PLACE DR	1900	452E	NWH	77018
CANDLELIGHT TRAIL	1900	657K	FR	77546
CANDLELON DR	3300	331D	NWC	77388
CANDLEMIST DR	4900	452G	NWH	77018
CANDLEMIST DR	5400	452C	NWH	77091
CANDLEOAK DR	3300	331D	NWC	77388
CANDLE PARK DR	18700	331D	NWC	77388
CANDLEPINE DR	3200	331D	NWC	77388
CANDLE PINE WAY	3100	331D	NWC	77388
CANDLE PLACE DR	3000	331D	NWC	77388
CANDLE POINT DR	19900	526F	NEF	77407
CANDLE POND LN	3100	331D	NWC	77388
W. CANDLER DR	100	413N	NCC	77037
CANDLER DR	200	413N	NCC	77037
CANDLERIDGE DR	3300	331D	NWC	77388
CANDLE RIDGE PARK DR	3300	333N	NCC	77073
CANDLE RIVER LN	19000	331D	NWC	77388
CANDLEROCK CT	16300	407H	NWC	77095
CANDLESHADE	5500	452B	NWH	77091
CANDLESHADE LN	13300	571M	SWH	77045
CANDLESHINE CIR	8700	407D	NWC	77095
CANDLE STICK LN		484T	NEF	77494
CANDLESTON LN	1600	486L	SWC	77450
CANDLETRAIL DR	19100	331D	NWC	77388
CANDLETREE DR	4900	452F	NWH	77018
CANDLETREE DR	5400	452B	NWH	77091
CANDLEVIEW DR	18600	331D	NWC	77388
CANDLEWAY DR	3200	331D	NWC	77388
CANDLEWICK	13100	497E	NEH	77015
CANDLEWISP CIR	3300	331D	NWC	77388
CANDLEWISP DR	3400	331D	NWC	77388
CANDLEWOOD	0	658S	LC	77573
CANDLEWOOD	700	657V	LC	77573
CANDLEWOOD DR	5400	491K	SWH	77056
CANDLEWOOD DR	10000	489Q	SWH	77042
CANDLEWOOD LN	5800	491K	SWH	77057
CANDLEWOOD GLEN LN	0	371D	NWC	77014
CANDLEWOOD OAKS LN	19600	329C	NWC	77379
CANDLEWOOD PARK LN	4300	485Y	NEF	77494
CANDOVER CT	400	486B	SWC	77450
CANDY	0	247Y	SWM	77355
CANDY	2000	247N	SWM	77362
CANDY	8600	495L	NEH	77029
CANDY CT	9800	289V	NWC	77379
CANDY LN	1400	463A	MB	77521
CANDYRIDGE CT	16500	611C	SWH	77053
CANDY TUFT	1500	412F	NWC	77038
CANEBRAKE LN	7400	528L	SWH	77083
CANEBREAK CROSSING	2200	568Y	SG	77478
CANE CREEK	9700	329U	NWC	77070
CANE CREEK CT	16100	329U	NWC	77070
CANEFIELD OAKS CIR	22600	485Y	NEF	77450
CANE FIELDS RD	0	445N	NWC	77493
CANEGROVE LN	0	575U	SEH	77075
CANE ISLAND PKWY	0	444S	KT	77493
CANEMONT	11300	570H	SWH	77035
CANERIDGE DR	6200	571X	SWH	77053
CANE RIVER LN	0	377E	NEC	77346
CANESHAW DR	0	614Z	PL	77584
CANE VALLEY CT	0	417D	NEH	77044
CANEY	0	297L	NEH	77365
CANEY DR	21000	257T	SEM	77357
CANEY DR	21900	256F	SEM	77357
CANEYBROOK CT	21800	445M	NWC	77449
CANEY MOUNTAIN DR	0	377K	NEC	77346
CANEY SPRINGS LN	0	417C	NEH	77044
CANFIELD	2100	493Z	SEH	77004
CANFIELD	3400	533D	SEH	77004
CANFIELD	9200	490X	SWH	77063
CANFIELD OAKS LN	4100	485Y	NEF	77450
CANFORD CT	4600	337B	NEH	77345
CANGELOSI RD	1200	570Q	MC	77489
CANIFF	0	579A	LP	77571
W. CANINO RD	1	412V	NCC	77037
E. CANINO RD	100	413S	NCC	77037
CANINO RD	100	413T	NEH	77076
CANMERE CT	10700	369K	NWC	77070
CANMORE SPRINGS DR	0	253S	SEM	77386
CANN DR	3800	537M	PA	77503
CANNA	700	498A	NEC	77530
CANNA CT	10600	463S	CCO	77520
CANNABERRY WAY	20200	292W	NWC	77388
CANNABERRY WAY	20400	291Z	NWC	77388
CANNADY CT	13600	370B	NWC	77069
CANNA LILY CT	3200	297Q	NEH	77345
CANNATA DR	14400	572Q	SWH	77045
CANNIFF	200	575D	SH	77587
CANNIFF	8600	575D	SEH	77017
CANNION FALLS DR	15600	328V	NWC	77377
CANNOCK CT	0	258F	SEM	77357
CANNOCK RD	7300	530G	SWH	77074
CANNOCK CHASE CT	9400	409A	NWC	77065
CANNOCK CHASE DR	9400	409A	NWC	77065
CANNON	7700	533T	SEH	77021
CANNON	7900	533T	SEH	77051
CANNON CT	0	610X	MC	77459
CANNON LN	0	252L	SEM	77385
CANNONADE DR	2000	538S	PA	77503
CANNON ANELLO CT	0	445J	NWC	77493
CANNON BALL DR	400	252S	SWM	77380
CANNON BALL DR	600	251V	SWM	77380
CANNONBALL RUN	0	656X	FR	77546
CANNON CREEK TRAIL	23300	287H	NWC	77377
CANNONDALE LN	4100	485Z	NEF	77450
CANNON FALLS LN	0	417A	NEC	77044
CANNON FIRE DR	19600	406Y	NWC	77449
CANNONGATE DR	4400	293Y	NCC	77373
CANNON HILLS LN	0	526Q	NEF	77407
CANNON KNOLLS	6300	408T	NWC	77084
CANNON PASS CT	3300	568Z	SG	77478
CANNONS POINT CT	2300	609A	SG	77478
CANNONS POINT DR	2300	609A	SG	77478
CANNONWAY DR	5500	374Z	NCC	77032
CANNONWOOD LN	12500	369M	NWC	77070
CANNOWAY LAKE DR	14200	568E	SG	77498
CANOE CREST CT	18900	338W	NEC	77346
CANOGA LN	9800	450S	NWH	77080
CANONERO	900	570S	SF	77477
CANONGATE DR	2000	491U	SWH	77056
CANONSBURG LN	4400	658S	LC	77573
CANOPY LN	18400	295E	SEM	77365
CANOPY GREEN DR	100	249R	NWH	77375
CANOPY GREEN DR	100	249R	NWH	77375
CANOSA DR	17000	366P	NWC	77433
CANOVA HILL LN	0	377L	NEC	77346
CANSFIELD CT	6800	525E	NEF	77494
CANSFIELD WAY	23400	525F	NEF	77494
CANSTON CT	24900	250Y	NWC	77389
CANTABRIA LN	2200	660K	LC	77573
CANTAONWOOD CT	0	416Z	NEC	77044
CANTATA CT	9300	410J	NWC	77040
CANTERBOROUGH PLACE	0	250E	NWC	77375
CANTERBURY	1900	533J	SWH	77030
CANTERBURY	3500	502L	BT	77521
CANTERBURY CIR	24600	244M	WCO	77447
CANTERBURY CT	2100	538Q	DP	77536
CANTERBURY DR	1000	613G	NEB	77584
CANTERBURY DR	9800	335T	HM	77338
CANTERBURY DR	12700	371H	NWC	77014
CANTERBURY LN	20000	295D	SEM	77365
CANTERBURY FOREST DR	15300	329S	NWC	77377
CANTERBURY PARK LN	0	615W	PL	77584
CANTERBURY WAY	4800	330V	NWC	77069
CANTERDALE	1100	572R	SWH	77047
CANTERHURST CIR	9800	409A	NWC	77065
CANTERHURST WAY	12000	409A	NWC	77065
CANTERLANE DR	1200	572R	SWH	77047
W. CANTERRA CIR	10500	367Y	NWC	77095
E. CANTERRA CIR	10500	367Z	NWC	77095
CANTERRA CT	10500	367Z	NWC	77095
CANTERRA WAY	11600	367Q	NWC	77095
CANTERTROT DR	9700	335Q	HM	77338
CANTERVIEW DR	1200	572V	SWH	77047
CANTERVILLE RD	1100	572R	SWH	77047
CANTERWAY DR	5200	574E	SEH	77048
CANTERWELL RD	13400	572U	SWH	77047
CANTERWOOD DR	4200	330V	NWC	77068
CANTHO ST	0	529P	SWH	77072
CANTIANO CT	0	525J	NEF	77406
CANTIGNY CT	22800	485L	SWC	77450
CANTIGNY LN	1600	485L	SWC	77450
CANTON	100	495W	SEH	77012
CANTON DR	3800	613G	NEB	77584
CANTON ACRES CT	0	294J	NWC	77386
CANTON BLUFF LN	400	332Q	NCC	77073
CANTON CLIFF CT	0	377K	NEC	77346
CANTON COMMON LN	0	406F	NWC	77433
CANTON CREST DR	0	484V	NWF	77494
CANTON CREST DR	0	484V	NWF	77494
CANTONE GROTTO CT	0	445E	NWC	77493
CANTON FOREST	17300	527E	NEF	77407
CANTON HILLS CT	0	377J	NEC	77346
CANTON HILLS LN	0	609U	MC	77459
CANTON OAKS CT	3500	331S	NWC	77068
CANTON PARK LN	8900	408E	NWC	77095
CANTON PASS LN	21800	525G	NEF	77494
CANTON PASS LN	26700	366R	NWC	77433
CANTON SPRING LN	0	377W	NEC	77044
CANTOR CIR	14800	408X	NWC	77084
CANTOR TRAILS LN	4000	609T	NEF	77479
CANTRELL	8100	530R	SWH	77074
CANTRELLE MANOR	13900	367D	NWC	77429
CANTU RD	5700	614Q	PL	77584
CANTURBERRY DR	0	659D	LC	77573
CANTWELL DR	4200	578E	PA	77505
CANTWELL DR	13800	372F	NWC	77014
CANTWELL BEND	14700	328X	NWC	77429
CANVAS CT	600	419B	NEC	77532
CANVASBACK	3200	444K	KT	77493
CANVASBACK LN	0	573Y	SEC	77047
S. CANVASBACK CAY	0	542N	BT	77520
N. CANVASBACK CAY	0	542J	BT	77520
CANVASBACK GLEN CT	0	291N	NWC	77388
CANYON	7800	533T	SEH	77051
CANYON CT	3000	609D	MC	77459
CANYON CT	11600	252M	SEM	77385
CANYON DR	2800	613U	NEB	77584
N. CANYON LN	0	328G	NWC	77377
CANYON LN	0	336Z	NEC	77346
CANYON ARBOR WAY	12100	367Q	NWC	77095
CANYONBACK LN	0	292L	SP	77373
CANYON BAY DR	19200	328C	NWC	77377
CANYON BEND DR	11500	328D	NWC	77377
CANYON BLANCO DR	0	571G	SWH	77045
CANYON BLOOM LN	17700	527N	NEF	77407
CANYON BLUFF CT	3800	578X	SEH	77059
CANYON BLUFF DR	2600	613S	NEB	77578
CANYON BRANCH LN	30100	253W	SEM	77386
CANYON BREEZE DR	11600	328D	NWC	77377
CANYON BROOK CT	4000	578Z	PA	77059
CANYON BROOK CT	11100	368V	NWC	77065
CANYON CHASE DR	6300	526A	NEF	77450
CANYON CHASE DR	16100	367Q	NWC	77095
CANYON CLIFF CT	0	409S	NWC	77041
CANYON COVE DR	18400	378S	NEC	77532
CANYON CREEK	0	248N	SWM	77362
CANYON CREEK CT	1900	616S	PL	77581
CANYON CREEK DR	0	485K	NEF	77494
CANYON CREEK RD	17900	331M	NWC	77090
CANYON CREEK SQUARE	6900	408P	NWC	77084
CANYON CREST DR	600	658N	LC	77573
CANYON CREST LN	10400	371W	NWC	77086
CANYON CROSS	11400	252D	SEM	77385
CANYON CROSS	11500	253A	SEM	77385
CANYON CROSSING CT	25500	524L	NWF	77406
CANYON CROSSING DR	25500	524L	NWF	77406
CANYON CYPRESS CT	6400	407T	NWC	77084
CANYON CYPRESS LN	18100	407S	NWC	77084
CANYON DEW LN	0	484W	NEF	77494
CANYON DROP DR	11700	328H	NWC	77377
CANYON ECHO DR	12500	368V	NWC	77065
CANYON FALLS CT	2200	658X	LC	77573
CANYON FALLS DR	2600	613W	NEB	77578
CANYON FALLS DR	11800	289W	NWC	77375
CANYON FERRY LN	19101	526L	NEF	77407
CANYON FIELDS DR	0	524K	NWF	77406
CANYON FOREST CT	21600	525D	NEF	77450
CANYON FOREST DR	5400	411L	NWC	77088
CANYON FORK CT	3600	485V	NEF	77450
CANYON FROST DR	19000	328G	NWC	77377
CANYON GALE LN	0	612N	PL	77545
CANYON GARDEN DR	700	485G	SWC	77450
CANYON GATE BLVD	20100	526A	NEF	77450
CANYON GATE DR	4900	578J	PA	77505
CANYON GATE DR	11500	328D	NWC	77377
CANYON GLEN DR	12100	367Q	NWC	77095
CANYON GREEN DR	11500	367Q	NWC	77095
CANYON HEIGHTS CT	1100	485G	SWC	77494
CANYON HILL DR	13800	528K	SWC	77083
CANYON HOLLOW DR	0	407Y	NWC	77084
CANYON HOLLOW DR	0	407Y	NWC	77084
CANYON HOLLOW LOOP	0	528K	SWC	77083
CANYON KNOLL DR	17400	407Q	NWC	77095
CANYON LAKE CT	0	538R	DP	77536
CANYON LAKE DR	0	286T	NWC	77377
CANYON LAKE DR	0	538R	DP	77536
CANYON LAKE DR	3800	615Y	PL	77581
CANYON LAKE DR	22700	333A	NCC	77373
CANYON LAKE DR	23700	293W	NCC	77373
CANYON LAKES MANOR DR	0	406H	NWC	77433
CANYON LAKES PARK	4900	375V	NEC	77396
W. CANYON LAKE SPRINGS DR	0	406D	NWC	77433
S. CANYON LAKE SPRINGS DR	0	407A	NWC	77433
N. CANYON LAKE SPRINGS DR	0	407A	NWC	77433
E. CANYON LAKE SPRINGS DR	0	407A	NWC	77433
CANYONLANDS LN	0	377E	NEC	77346
CANYON LAUREL CT	16900	330N	NWC	77379
CANYON LINKS CT	21600	485V	NEF	77450
CANYON LINKS DR	3100	485V	NEF	77450
CANYON MAPLES LN	13900	328S	NWC	77429
CANYON MEADOWS DR	2300	610A	MC	77489
CANYON MILL LN	11900	328C	NWC	77377
CANYON MILLS CT	16300	367Q	NWC	77095
CANYON MILLS DR	11600	367Q	NWC	77095
CANYON MIST LN	11700	328D	NWC	77377
CANYON OAK CT	3100	331T	NWC	77068
CANYON OAK DR	16600	367U	NWC	77095
CANYON OAK PLACE	1	251U	WD	77380
CANYON PARK DR	6200	526A	NEF	77450
CANYON PASS DR	0	484S	NEF	77494
CANYON PEAK LN	21700	485V	NEF	77450
CANYON PINE DR	8400	330N	NWC	77379
CANYON POST	0	367Q	NWC	77095
CANYON RANCH DR	0	253W	SEM	77386
CANYON RANCH DR	0	612N	PL	77545
CANYON REACH DR	0	484W	NEF	77494
CANYON RIDGE CT	16800	330N	NWC	77379
CANYON RIDGE CT	20200	526E	NEF	77450
CANYON RIDGE DR	8500	330N	NWC	77379
CANYON RIVER LN	19000	446R	NWC	77084
CANYON ROCK LN	11900	328H	NWC	77377
CANYON ROCK WAY	6200	526B	NEF	77450
CANYON ROSE	10200	369G	NWC	77070
CANYON ROSE DR	0	328H	NWC	77377
CANYON ROYAL DR	18900	328G	NWC	77377
CANYON RUN CT	6200	526A	NEF	77450
CANYON SAGE LN	4800	484V	NEF	77494
CANYON SANDS LN	25600	524K	NWF	77406
CANYON SHADOW DR	20400	526E	NEF	77450
CANYON SHORE DR	0	376U	NEC	77396
CANYON SHORE DR	4700	376S	NEC	77396

Street Name	Block	Pg/Sq	Loc	Zips
CANYON SIDE CT	30000	253W	SEM	77386
CANYON SIDE LN	30100	253W	SEM	77386
CANYON SPRINGS	17200	331R	NWC	77090
CANYON SPRINGS DR	0	612L	PL	77545
CANYON SPRINGS DR	500	539X	LP	77571
CANYON SPRINGS LN	16900	617X	SEC	77546
CANYON SQUARE	0	253S	SEM	77386
CANYON SQUARE	0	253S	SEM	77386
CANYON SQUARE	2900	253S	SEM	77386
CANYON SQUARE	2900	253S	SEM	77386
CANYON SQUARE DR	2900	253W	SEM	77386
CANYON STAR CT	19000	328H	NWC	77377
CANYON STAR LN	11900	328H	NWC	77377
CANYON STREAM CT	17100	407L	NWC	77095
CANYON SUMMER LN	30100	253W	SEM	77386
CANYON SUN LN	11700	328D	NWC	77377
CANYON TERRACE LN	21500	485M	SWC	77450
CANYON TERRACE LN	21800	486J	SWC	77450
CANYON TIMBERS DR	11900	328G	NWC	77377
CANYON TOP CT	6200	526A	NEF	77450
CANYON TRACE	0	334R	NCC	77338
CANYON TRACE CT	6200	526A	NEF	77450
W. CANYON TRACE DR	12000	367Q	NWC	77095
E. CANYON TRACE DR	12100	367Q	NWC	77095
N. CANYON TRACE DR	16500	367Q	NWC	77095
CANYON TRAIL DR	11100	370L	NWC	77066
CANYON TRAILS DR	11100	370R	NWC	77066
CANYON TREE CT	11100	524L	NWF	77406
CANYON VALLEY CT	19000	328G	NWC	77377
CANYON VALLEY DR	11900	328G	NWC	77377
CANYON VIEW	37800	246F	SWM	77355
CANYONVIEW CT	2900	486T	SWC	77450
CANYON VIEW CT	38700	246F	SWM	77355
CANYON VILLA RD	0	526P	NEF	77407
CANYON VILLAGE TRACE DR	0	375V	NEC	77396
CANYON VISTA LN	11700	328H	NWC	77377
CANYON VISTA LN	19100	328G	NWC	77377
CANYON WALK DR	0	366U	NWC	77433
CANYON WAY DR	6600	371T	NWC	77086
CANYON WHISPER DR	16700	327X	CY	77429
CANYON WOODS DR	11500	328D	NWC	77377
W. CANYON WREN CIR	0	250P	NWC	77389
W. CANYON WREN CIR	0	250P	NWC	77389
E. CANYON WREN CIR	0	250P	NWC	77389
E. CANYON WREN CIR	0	250P	NWC	77389
CANYON WREN DR	0	250P	NWC	77389
CANYON WREN DR	0	250P	NWC	77389
CAPALONA CT	0	257F	SEM	77357
CAPARRA CREEK LN	0	405T	NWC	77493
CAPE LN	0	609Y	MC	77459
CAPE BAHAMAS LN	18200	618Z	NB	77058
CAPE BREEZE DR	0	329U	NWC	77070
CAPE BREEZE DR	9700	367X	NWC	77095
CAPE CHARLES LN	18600	619W	NB	77058
CAPE CHESTNUT DR	1	251J	WD	77381
CAPE CLOVER TRAIL	19900	526T	NEF	77407
CAPE COD LN	1	490H	HC	77024
CAPE CORAL CT	800	660J	LC	77573
CAPE CORAL CT	17200	407F	NWC	77095
CAPE COTTAGE	20500	526J	NEF	77407
CAPE COTTAGE CT	23300	292G	NCC	77373
CAPE COTTAGE LN	700	292G	NCC	77373
CAPECREST DR	2800	613T	NEB	77584
CAPE FOREST DR	2800	297X	NEH	77345
CAPE FOREST DR	3600	297X	NEH	77345
CAPE FORWARD DR	6300	528F	SWC	77083
CAPE HARBOUR PLACE	0	251G	SWM	77380
N. CAPE HARBOUR WAY	0	251L	SWM	77380
CAPE HATTERAS DR	5900	408Y	NWC	77041
CAPE HENRY	8401	659M	LC	77459
CAPE HENRY LN	6100	408X	NWC	77084
CAPEHILL DR	300	618S	SEH	77598
CAPE HOPE	15900	419F	NEC	77532
CAPE HYANNIS DR	11700	573M	SEH	77048
CAPE HYANNIS DR	12700	573R	SEH	77048
CAPE LANDING DR	0	612L	PL	77584
CAPE LAUREL	12700	371H	NWC	77014
CAPELLA CIR	31200	248X	TB	77375
CAPELLA PARK DR	5600	291W	NWC	77379
CAPELLA RIVIERA DR	0	445A	NWC	77493
CAPELLO DR	5700	571A	SWH	77035
CAPE LOOKOUT WAY	18300	377A	NEC	77346
CAPE MAY CT	0	253K	SEM	77386
CAPE MEADOW CT	0	485X	NEF	77494
CAPE PROVINCE DR	13200	528L	SWH	77083
CAPER GROVE LN	0	524F	NEF	77494
CAPERIDGE CT	27200	299S	NEC	77336
CAPE RISE TRAIL	0	418T	NEC	77044
CAPER MEADOW LN	0	524F	NEF	77494
CAPERNAUM CROSSING CT	7100	290T	NWC	77379
CAPE ROYAL DR	0	406G	NWC	77433
CAPERTON	600	453M	NEH	77022
CAPE SABLE CT	12500	377A	NEC	77346
CAPESBROOK CT	4900	484Z	NEF	77494
CAPETOWN DR	18500	619W	NB	77058
CAPEVIEW CROSSING	7200	290T	NWC	77379
CAPE VISTA CT	0	253P	SEM	77386
CAPEWALK DR	0	532T	SWH	77036
CAPEWOOD CT	1	251E	WD	77381
CAPEWOOD DR	300	659N	LC	77573
CAPEWOOD DR	16600	376L	NEC	77396
CAPILANO CT	24600	484H	NEF	77494
CAPISTRANO	12300	496L	NEH	77015
CAPISTRANO FALLS DR	16000	617T	SEC	77546
CAPITAL	2300	537T	PA	77502
CAPITAL CT	3100	613R	PL	77584
CAPITAL PARK DR	11000	449H	NWH	77041
CAPITOL	0	444Y	KT	77493
CAPITOL	400	493R	DT	77002
W. CAPITOL	1400	493K	SWH	77007
CAPITOL	1600	493R	SEH	77003
CAPITOL	3900	494N	SEH	77023
CAPITOL	4700	494T	SEH	77011
S. CAPITOL	5000	494U	SEH	77011
N. CAPITOL	5000	494U	SEH	77011
CAPITOL	7500	495W	SEH	77012
CAPITOL HEIGHTS DR	11700	369S	NWC	77065
CAPITOL LANDING LN	22500	445Q	NWC	77449
CAPLAN	800	580C	LP	77571
CAPLIN	100	453Q	NEH	77022
CAPLIN	1800	454P	NEH	77026
CAPONI FALLS LN		524C	NEF	77494
CAPPAMORE	500	496E	NEH	77013
CAPRI	100	568P	SG	77478
CAPRI	11000	490D	HE	77024
CAPRI CIR	7800	408K	NWC	77095
CAPRI CT	0	659M	LC	77573
CAPRI CT	2200	616K	PL	77581
E. CAPRI DR	2200	616K	PL	77581
S. CAPRI DR	2300	616K	PL	77581
CAPRI DR	15900	409L	JV	77040
CAPRI LN	1700	620K	SB	77586
CAPRICCIO DR	0	293K	SEM	77386
CAPRICE LN	18200	618V	NB	77058
CAPRICE BEND PLACE	100	249R	NWH	77375
CAPRICE BEND PLACE	100	249R	NWH	77375
CAPRICORN DR	12700	569L	SF	77477
CAPRIDGE DR	0	574Y	SEH	77048
CAPRI ISLE CT	0	488P	SWH	77077
CAPRI PLACE	1400	616K	PL	77581
CAPROCK DR	5000	614Z	PL	77584
CAPROCK DR	15700	618N	SEH	77598
CAPROCK BLUFF LN	0	406D	NWC	77433
CAPROCK COVE LN	14200	375Y	NEC	77396
CAPROCK FALLS CT	0	406D	NWC	77433
CAPROCK SPRINGS DR	0	366Q	NWC	77433
S. CAPROCK WAY	12400	377B	NEC	77346
N. CAPROCK WAY	12400	377B	NEC	77346
CAPRON	1100	494F	NEH	77020
CAPSHAW CT	9400	408D	NWC	77065
CAPSTAN RD	1600	618K	SEH	77062
CAPSTONE DR	0	411M	NWC	77088
CAPTAIN DR	7000	530E	SWH	77036
CAPTAIN'S CT	4400	609R	MC	77459
CAPTAINS WALK	300	488A	SWH	77079
S. CAPTIAN BLVD	0	290Y	NWC	77379
N. CAPTIAN BLVD	0	290Y	NWC	77379
CARA CIR	5000	577C	PA	77505
CARACARA DR	0	411S	NWH	77040
CARACAS DR	7200	527F	NEF	77083
CARADINE	14000	571T	SWH	77085
CARADOC SPRINGS CT	27500	293K	SEM	77386
W. CARAMEL APPLE TRAIL	0	325M	NWC	77433
N. CARAMEL APPLE TRAIL	0	326J	NWC	77433
E. CARAMEL APPLE TRAIL	0	326J	NWC	77433
CARA PLACE	4100	532W	SWH	77025
CARAQUET CT	30800	252U	SEM	77386
CARAQUET DR	25700	252Q	SEM	77386
N. CARAQUET DR	26200	252Q	SEM	77386
CARAVAN DR	10500	530W	SWH	77031
CARAVEL CIR	4000	609Q	MC	77459
CARAVEL CT	0	620W	LC	77573
CARAVEL CT	4100	609Q	MC	77459
CARAVEL DR	2000	620W	LC	77573
CARAVEL LN	6700	609Q	MC	77459
CARAVELLE CT	1300	485E	NEF	77494
CARAWAY	0	658Z	LC	77573
CARAWAY CIR	0	461Q	NEC	77521
CARAWAY CIR	8300	461P	NEC	77521
CARAWAY LN	9500	529M	SWH	77036
CARAWAY LAKE DR	5200	461P	NEC	77521
CARAWAY RIDGE DR	0	406H	NWC	77433
CARAWAY VILLAGE DR	0	451W	NWH	77055
CARBERRY HILLS CT	0	377P	NEC	77044
CARBIDE LN	7400	410P	NWC	77040
CARBON CANYON LN	11700	328D	NWC	77377
CARBONEAR DR	1500	457V	NEC	77530
CARBRIDGE DR	16600	407Z	NWC	77084
CARBRIDGE DR	18000	407X	NWC	77084
CARBROOK CT	4500	331B	NWC	77388
W. CARBY RD	100	413N	NCC	77037
E. CARBY RD	100	413N	NCC	77037
CARBY RD	100	413P	NCC	77037
W. CARBY RD	200	412R	NCC	77037
CARDAMON LN	8300	461P	BT	77521
CARDIFF RD	11700	413U	NEH	77076
CARDIFF RD	12400	413Q	NEH	77037
CARDIFF BEND DR	0	484S	NEF	77494
CARDIFF HILLS DR	0	332R	NCC	77073
CARDIFF MIST DR	0	484S	NEF	77494
CARDIFF PARK LN	19500	486G	SWC	77094
CARDIFF RANCH DR	0	484W	NEF	77494
CARDIFF ROCKS LN	0	484S	NEF	77494
CARDIGAN BAY CIR	1200	329G	NWC	77379
CARDINAL	1800	658Q	LC	77573
CARDINAL	9800	539T	LP	77571
CARDINAL	19900	286J	NWC	77447
CARDINAL AVE	1000	568U	SG	77478
CARDINAL CIR	700	536U	PA	77502
CARDINAL LN	2600	375L	HM	77396
CARDINAL LN	14000	489E	SWH	77079
CARDINAL LN	22600	286H	NWC	77377
CARDINAL LN	26700	444K	NWC	77493
CARDINAL BAY	5500	448D	NWC	77041
CARDINAL BAY CT	0	612L	PL	77584
CARDINAL BEND LN	1	369H	NWC	77070
CARDINAL BROOK WAY	4500	297Q	NEH	77345
CARDINAL COVE CT	13600	328T	NWC	77429
CARDINAL CREEK CT	14500	617H	SEH	77062
CARDINAL CREEK WAY	5900	298W	NEH	77345
CARDINAL CREST LN	0	450K	NWH	77080
CARDINAL ELM	2300	611W	MC	77545
CARDINAL FLOWERS DR	13500	368A	NWC	77429
CARDINAL GROVE CT	19100	326U	NWC	77429
CARDINAL HILLS CT	0	367P	NWC	77433
CARDINAL LAKE RD	0	446H	NWC	77449
CARDINAL LANDING LN	0	406L	NWC	77433
CARDINAL MEADOWS DR	0	568H	SG	77478
CARDINAL OAKS LN	0	619V	LC	77565
CARDINAL POINT DR	0	335H	NEH	77339
CARDINAL RIDGE CIR	2000	657J	FR	77546
CARDONO LN	15700	571W	SWH	77489
CARDSTON CIR	0	328H	NWC	77377
CARDSTON CT	12200	328H	NWC	77377
CARDUCCI DR	0	525J	NEF	77406
CARDWELL CT	1	490C	SV	77055
CARDWELL DR	8800	490C	SV	77055
CAREFREE CIR	5300	657V	LC	77573
CAREFREE DR	1200	657V	LC	77573
CARELIA LN	17700	330F	NWC	77379
CAREN CT	12400	570E	SWH	77031
CAREW	5000	531Q	SWH	77096
CAREW	5700	530Q	SWH	77074
CAREY	100	498F	CV	77530
CAREY	5300	454L	NEH	77028
CAREY LN	200	656D	FR	77546
CAREYBROOK LN	0	446G	NWC	77449
CAREY CHASE DR	7500	570V	SWH	77489
CAREY RIDGE CT	200	486D	SWC	77094
CAREYWOOD DR	12800	410T	NWC	77040
CAREYWOOD DR	12800	568C	SG	77478
CARGILL	7900	495P	NEH	77029
CARIBBEAN LN	11000	576S	SEH	77089
CARIBE LN	1400	572Z	SWH	77047
CARIBOU	5100	291A	NWC	77389
CARIBOU CT	8000	462V	CCO	77520
CARIBOU RIDGE DR	19100	329A	NWC	77375
CARIDAS DR	12300	570L	SWH	77085
CARILLO DR	5500	451D	NWH	77091
CARINA CT	2300	619T	LC	77573
CARINA FOREST CT	0	376W	NEC	77396
CARINO DR	5500	451D	NWH	77091
CARINO STRADA DR	24200	524R	NEF	77406
CARIO	700	498B	CV	77530
CARIS	4800	451C	NWH	77091
CARISBROOK LN	21200	333M	NCC	77338
CARISLE CT	4200	502K	BT	77521
CARISLE PARK CIR	0	657U	LC	77573
CARISO CT	0	524M	NEF	77406
CARITAS CIR	9600	408D	NWC	77065
CARL	1700	493C	NEH	77009
CARL	100	536G	PA	77506
CARL CT	2200	569V	SF	77477
CARL LN	11800	490K	BH	77024
CARL RD	6800	294X	NCC	77373
CARLA	11500	413U	NEH	77076
CARLA LN	23500	256Z	SEM	77357
CARLAND ARBOR LN	0	446B	NWC	77449
CARLANG	100	498F	CV	77530
CARLA OAKS DR	0	446K	NWC	77449
CARLARIS CT	12900	408V	NWC	77041
CARLA WAY	12900	369E	NWC	77429
CARLEEN RD	2300	451H	NWH	77018
CARLEEN RD	4600	451H	NWH	77092
CARLEEN CREEK TRAIL	21300	290N	NWC	77379
CARLENE LN	25900	247X	SWM	77355
CARLFORD CIR	3000	452P	NWH	77018
CARLIE WAY	100	569P	SF	77477
CARLIN BEND LN	9200	407D	NWC	77095
CARLINGFORD LN	700	489A	SWH	77079
CARLINGTON DR	10300	414W	NEH	77093
CARLINGWOOD DR	13700	368D	NWC	77070
CARLISLE	3000	580Q	LP	77571
CARLISLE	8500	535L	SEH	77017
CARLISLE CT	4200	502K	BT	77521
CARLISLE LN	6100	657U	LC	77573
CARLISLE BEND CT	0	484N	NEF	77494
CARLISLE CREEK TRACE	0	526N	NEF	77407
CARLISLE FALL CT	0	616H	SEC	77089
CARLISLE GLEN DR	0	526P	NEF	77407
CARLISLE GROVE TRACE	0	406W	NWC	77449
CARLISLE HILLS TRACE	0	405R	NWC	77493
CARLISLE MEADOW CT	0	253T	SEM	77386
CARLISLE PARK LN	16000	407Z	NWC	77084
CARLISLE VALLEY TRACE	0	405P	NWC	77493
CARLON	3700	532E	SS	77005
CARLOS	8500	455X	NEH	77029
CARLOS CREEK DR	0	524K	NWF	77406
CARLOTA CT	1	531N	SWH	77074
CARLOTA CT	9000	531N	SWH	77074
CARLOTA CT	10600	531W	SWH	77096
CARLOW LN	9000	579A	LP	77571
CARL RD EXT	0	334C	NCC	77373
CARLSBAD	4100	409Q	JV	77040
CARLSBAD	12000	570R	SWH	77085
CARLSBAD	1	570M	SWH	77085
S. CARLSBAD LN	1800	538R	DP	77536
N. CARLSBAD LN	1800	538R	DP	77536
CARLSON LN	3700	573L	SEH	77047
CARLSON MANOR CT	0	484J	KT	77494
CARLSON MANOR DR	0	484J	KT	77494
CARLSWAY RD	0	332L	NCC	77073
CARLTON	1200	541B	BT	77520
CARLTON DR	10800	573G	SEH	77047
CARLTON RD	24100	296M	SEM	77365
CARLTON HEIGHTS	2000	455L	NEH	77028
CARLTON OAKS	12400	328V	NWC	77377
CARLTON OAKS ST	0	524Y	NEF	77406
CARLTON PARK CT	1	490Q	PP	77024
CARLTON SPRINGS LN	0	524H	NEF	77494
CARLTON SPRINGS LN	0	524H	NEF	77494
CARLTON VALE CT	16400	328U	NWC	77377
CARLTON WOODS CREEKSIDE DR	0	250F	WD	77381
CARLWOODS DR	0	503F	CCO	77520
CARLY COVE CT	1800	293E	SEM	77386
CARLY COVE LN	28500	293E	SEM	77386
CARLY PARK WAY	6700	407U	NWC	77084
CARMALEE	9200	575Z	SEH	77075
CARMALEE	9600	576S	SEH	77075
CARMEL	2400	412W	NWH	77091
CARMEL	3000	411Z	NWH	77091
CARMEL CIR	4600	578E	PA	77505
CARMEL CIR	8000	408K	NWC	77095
CARMEL COVE CT	6000	409W	NWC	77041
CARMEL DALE LN	12300	617E	SEH	77089
CARMEL FALLS LN		484Y	NEF	77494
CARMEL GROVE	0	373A	NCC	77073
CARMEL GROVE LN	0	526R	NEF	77494
CARMEL HILL LN	0	612U	PL	77584
CARMELITE CT	20100	486C	SWC	77450
CARMELLA DR	600	536G	PA	77506
CARMEL LAKE DR	0	526K	NEF	77494
CARMEL POINT CT	3900	611W	FS	77545
CARMEL RIDGE WAY	0	537V	PA	77503
CARME LRIVER LN	0	331B	NWC	77388
CARMEL VALLEY CT	20900	406P	NWC	77449
CARMEL VALLEY DR	3100	609G	MC	77459
CARMELWOOD CT	8200	335N	NCC	77338
CARMELWOOD LN	8200	335N	NCC	77338
CARMEL WOODS DR	2500	620E	SB	77586
CARMEN	4600	573D	SEH	77051
CARMEN LN	23600	296G	SEM	77365
CARMENCITA WAY	0	575Q	SEH	77075
CARMICHAEL CIR	5300	656W	AV	77511
CARMICHAEL CT	200	659D	LC	77573
CARMILINDA	13500	413K	NCC	77037
CARMINE GLEN LN	0	457P	NEC	77049
CARMINE OAK CT	20600	337Q	NEC	77346
CARMITA	19400	252B	SEM	77385
CARMONA LN	5000	614R	PL	77584
CARMOYLE WAY	10400	527W	NEF	77407
CARMS	23500	296E	SEM	77365
CARNAGIE PARK CT	0	618D	PA	77058
CARNARVON DR	100	491G	SWH	77024
CARNATION	800	444W	KT	77493
CARNATION	3400	453P	NWH	77022
CARNATION CT	0	460W	BT	77521
CARNEGIE	400	501X	BT	77520
CARNEGIE	700	541B	BT	77520
CARNEGIE	2800	532F	WU	77005
CARNELIAN CT	4400	529F	SWH	77072
CARNELIAN DR	4000	529F	SWH	77072
CARNESWOOD LN	14100	288B	TB	77375
CARNEYS POINT LN	6200	290R	NWC	77379
CARNOUSTIE CT	1200	485E	NEF	77494
CARNOUSTIE DR	2800	609M	MC	77459
CAROL	800	531K	BL	77401
CAROL CT	9500	410J	NWC	77040
CAROL LN	0	247R	SWM	77362
CAROL LN	4900	534J	SEH	77021
CAROL RD	21600	257X	SEM	77357
CAROL RD	26700	299W	NEC	77336
CAROLA FOREST DR	12100	416L	NEC	77044
CAROLANE TRAIL	1	490F	BH	77024
CAROL CHASE CIR	15000	570V	SWH	77489
CAROL COLLIER CT		484N	NEF	77494
CAROL CREST	0	542K	BT	77520
CAROLCREST CIR	14100	489J	SWH	77079
CAROLCREST DR	14200	489E	SWH	77079
CAROLCREST DR	14400	488H	SWH	77079
CAROLDEAN	0	484T	NEF	77494
CAROLE LN	10000	502D	BT	77521
CAROLINA	1700	540D	BT	77520
CAROLINA	6800	444W	KT	77493
CAROLINA	700	484A	KT	77494
CAROLINA AVE	1900	659P	LC	77573
CAROLINA CT	1500	657E	FR	77546
CAROLINA CHERRY CT	0	250Q	NWC	77389
CAROLINA CHERRY LN	0	250U	NWC	77389
CAROLINA FALLS LN	14600	326X	NWC	77433
N. CAROLINA GREEN DR	0	325Q	NWC	77433
E. CAROLINA GREEN DR	21700	325Q	NWC	77433
CAROLINA GROVE LN	0	373A	NCC	77073
CAROLINA HILLS DR	14900	326X	NWC	77433
CAROLINA HOLLOW LN	14400	377Y	NEH	77044
CAROLINA LAKE LN	0	406F	NWC	77433
CAROLINA LAKE LN	0	406F	NWC	77433
CAROLINA MILL LN	0	406G	NWC	77433
CAROLINA OAKS DR	15100	326X	NWC	77433
CAROLINA SHORES LN	4000	658S	LC	77573
CAROLINA WAY	0	255C	SEM	77357
CAROLINA WAY	2600	532G	WU	77005
CAROLINA WREN CIR	0	373E	NCC	77073
CAROLINE	100	292Q	SP	77373
CAROLINE	200	493Q	DT	77002
CAROLINE	800	493Q	DT	77002
CAROLINE	801	493Q	DT	77010
CAROLINE	900	493Q	DT	77010
CAROLINE	1100	493Q	DT	77002
CAROLINE	1101	493Q	DT	77010
CAROLINE	1200	493Q	DT	77010
CAROLINE	2300	493T	SWH	77004
CAROLINE	4700	581W	SEC	77586
CAROLINE	5800	533A	SWH	77030
CAROLINE	1600	660T	DI	77539
CAROLINE DR	0	415C	NEH	77396
CAROLINE CHASE CT	22400	525C	NEF	77494
CAROLINE COVE LN	22300	485Z	NEF	77450
CAROLINE CREEK CT	24500	293T	NCC	77373
CAROLINE GREEN CT	6000	334F	NCC	77373
CAROLINE PARK LN	2200	293E	SEM	77386
CAROLINE RIDGE DR	0	375Y	NEC	77396
CAROLINE SHORE WAY	11900	616F	SEC	77089
CAROLINE WAY CT	20300	372D	NCC	77073
CAROLING OAKS CT	19700	337T	NEC	77346
CAROL LYNN DR	600	570S	MC	77489
CAROLS WAY CIR	12200	328Z	NWC	77070
CAROLS WAY DR	14600	328Z	NWC	77070
CAROLTON CT	1	245D	SWM	77355
CAROLTON WAY	17800	373C	NCC	77073
CAROLWOOD DR	7800	455F	NEH	77028
CAROLYN	500	620X	KE	77565
CAROLYN	1000	335Z	HM	77338
CAROLYN	1100	538L	DP	77536
CAROLYN	3000	660H	BC	77518
CAROLYN CT	9800	289V	NWC	77379
CAROLYN CT	19100	330A	NWC	77379
CAROLYNDALE DR	0	527X	NEF	77478
CAROTHERS	3200	534R	SEH	77087
CAROTHERS	6800	454M	NEH	77028
CAROTHERS	7300	455J	NEH	77028
CAROUSEL CIR	5400	500H	BT	77521
CAROUSEL CT	13300	448C	NWC	77041
CAROUSEL LN	8800	450P	NWH	77080
CAROUSEL CREEK CT	0	326V	NWC	77429
CARPENTER	7500	375F	HM	77396
CARPENTER AVE	1300	536X	PA	77502
CARPENTER RD	1000	376E	HM	77396
CARPENTER BEE DR	0	256Z	SEM	77357
CARPENTER BEE DR	0	296D	SEM	77357
CARPENTERS HOLLOW CT	0	457V	NEC	77049
CARPENTERS LANDING WAY	0	457R	NEC	77049
CARPET BAGGER DR	19200	406V	NWC	77449
CARR	900	494A	NEH	77020
CARR	1600	494A	NEH	77026
CARR	3200	454W	NEH	77026
CARRACK TURN DR	16700	617Y	SEC	77546
CARRAU	5500	449C	NWC	77041
CARRAWAY CT	15000	328J	NWC	77429
CARRAWAY LN	8700	249J	SWM	77354
CARR CREEK LN	0	377F	NEC	77346
CARRELL RD	24100	288H	TB	77375
CARRERA CT	2800	659M	LC	77573
CARRIAGE	2500	569V	SF	77477
CARRIAGE CT	1100	620G	SB	77586
CARRIAGE CT	13500	417X	NEC	77044
CARRIAGE CT	18600	619W	NB	77058
CARRIAGE DR	800	375D	HM	77338
CARRIAGE LN	3400	500M	BT	77521
CARRIAGE LN	18200	618V	NB	77058
CARRIAGE BEND DR	5000	485Z	NEF	77450
CARRIAGE BROOK WAY	1900	618G	SEH	77062
CARRIAGE CREEK DR	8300	410H	NWC	77064
CARRIAGE CREEK LN	300	657F	FR	77546
CARRIAGE CREST DR	0	290S	NWC	77379
CARRIAGE CROSSING LN	17800	327W	NWC	77429
CARRIAGE DALE CT	17100	330J	NWC	77379
CARRIAGE GLEN DR	12700	328L	NWC	77377
CARRIAGE HILL DR	11800	489J	SWH	77077
CARRIAGE HILL DR	12300	488M	SWH	77077
CARRIAGE LAKE DR	11100	368Z	NWC	77065
CARRIAGE LAMP DR	0	299T	NEC	77336
CARRIAGE MANOR LN	0	296X	SEM	77339
CARRIAGE OAK CIR	12100	377A	NEC	77346
CARRIAGE PARK DR	14700	376U	NEC	77396
CARRIAGE PINES CT	1	251B	WD	77381
CARRIAGE POINT DR	20600	333N	NCC	77073
CARRIAGE RUN CT	1700	611X	FS	77545
CARRIAGE RUN PLACE	0	611W	FS	77545
CARRIAGE VALE LN	0	329B	NWC	77375
CARRIAGE VIEW LN	0	298X	NEH	77336
CARRIAGE WALK LN	13700	488K	SWH	77077
CARRIAGE WAY	1700	568Z	SG	77478
CARRICK	9200	453F	NEH	77022
CARRICK BEND DR	0	250U	NWC	77389
CARRIE	100	572U	SWH	77047
CARRIE LN	7300	538X	DP	77536
CARRIE LN	22300	245U	WCO	77355
CARRIE CASSIA LN	0	527T	NEF	77407
CARRIE COVE CT	3000	293H	SEM	77386
CARRIGAN PLACE	14000	528P	SWC	77083
CARRIGE RIDGE CT	12000	369Q	NWC	77070
CARRIGE RIDGE DR	11900	369Q	NWC	77070
CARRILL BEND LN	0	328F	NWC	77377
CARRINGTON CT	4900	614S	NEB	77584
CARRINGTON LN	13800	368A	NWC	77429
CARRINGTON RIDGE LN	0	377C	NEC	77346
CARRINGTON WOODS LN	0	527W	NEF	77469

Street Name	Block	Pg/Sq	Loc	Zips
CARRIZO	12800	571F	SWH	77085
CARRIZO FALL CT	0	409W	NWC	77041
CARRIZO SPRINGS CT	2900	446P	NWC	77449
S. CARROL LN	26500	246N	SWM	77355
CARROL LN	26600	246N	SWM	77355
CARROLL	0	543U	BC	77520
N. CARROLL	100	540Y	LP	77571
S. CARROLL	600	580D	LP	77571
CARROLL	1200	537N	PA	77506
CARROLL	1900	533J	SWH	77030
CARROLL	13500	614G	PL	77581
CARROLL LAKE DR	17100	330N	NWC	77379
CARROLL PLACE LN	0	527N	NEF	77407
CARROLLTON LN	0	243A	WCO	77484
CARROLLTON CREEK CT	5700	407Z	NWC	77084
CARROLLTON CREEK LN	16800	407Z	NWC	77084
CARROLTON	2500	534F	SEH	77023
CARROT	18400	331A	NWC	77379
CARRSWOLD DR	12100	570F	SWH	77071
CARRUTH LN	13400	528F	SWC	77083
CARSA LN	13600	371C	NWC	77014
CARSEN BEND	14700	328X	NWC	77429
CARSEN BEND	15000	457Q	NEC	77049
CARSEN SPRING CT	20800	406P	NWC	77449
CARSEN SPRING CT	20800	406P	NWC	77449
CARSEY LN	11300	490L	PP	77024
CARSHALTON CT	17100	407U	NWC	77084
CARSON	0	257E	SEM	77357
CARSON AVE	0	613S	PL	77584
CARSON AVE	11100	612V	PL	77584
CARSON CIR	16200	570J	MC	77489
CARSON CT	0	612V	PL	77584
CARSON CT	100	533B	SEH	77004
CARSON DR	2600	444Q	KT	77493
CARSON RD	6100	574L	SEH	77048
CARSONDALE	8600	535Z	SEH	77017
CARSON FIELD LN	0	366R	NWC	77433
CARSON HILL LN	5100	541F	NWH	77092
CARSONMONT LN	9400	369M	NWC	77070
CARSON PEAK LN	0	446E	NWC	77449
CARSON RIDGE DR	400	252T	SEM	77386
CARSTAIRS DR	11200	329X	NWC	77070
CARSTONE CT	1500	485L	SWC	77450
CARTAGE KNOLLS DR	13900	367C	NWC	77429
CARTAGENA DR	4000	616X	PL	77581
CARTAGENA DR	5500	571A	SWH	77035
CARTAGENA DR	6000	570D	SWH	77035
CARTER	0	248F	SWM	77354
CARTER	2100	453S	NWH	77008
CARTER	3000	537G	PA	77503
CARTER	5300	574X	SEH	77048
CARTER	27000	244S	WCO	77447
CARTER RD	10100	329P	NWC	77070
CARTER GATE DR	22700	334A	NCC	77373
CARTER MOIR LN	22500	445U	NWC	77449
CARTERS GROVE LN	1500	445Z	NWC	77449
CARTERSVILLE	300	495V	NEH	77029
CART GATE CT	14100	408Q	NWC	77095
CART GATE DR	7100	408Q	NWC	77095
CARTHAGE DR	10000	576S	SEH	77089
CARTWRIGHT RD	0	610B	MC	77489
CARTWRIGHT RD	1400	610A	MC	77489
CARTWRIGHT RD	2500	609C	MC	77459
CARTWRIGHT RIDGE	25900	251N	SWM	77380
CARUSO FOREST DR	5800	411K	NWC	77088
CARUTHERS LN	200	490M	HC	77024
CARVED ROCK DR	6600	571J	SWH	77085
CARVED STONE LN	6600	526Q	NEF	77407
CARVEL CIR	7300	528M	SWH	77072
CARVEL LN	6600	530M	SWH	77074
CARVEL LN	7900	530J	SWH	77036
CARVEL LN	10700	529K	SWH	77072
CARVEL LN	13200	528M	SWH	77083
CARVER	100	502H	BT	77520
CARVER	800	541B	BT	77520
CARVER RD	6200	412W	NWH	77091
CARVER RD	7000	412S	NWH	77088
CARVER RD	19500	335S	NCC	77338
CARVER PINES DR	0	524E	NEF	77494
CARY	0	502E	NEC	77521
CARY	2800	494N	SEH	77003
CARYA CIR	3700	609E	SG	77479
CARY DOUGLAS DR	0	325S	HK	77447
CARY FARM	0	370M	NWC	77066
CARY FARM RD	0	371J	NWC	77066
CASA LN	100	659Z	DI	77539
CASABA CT	13700	328X	NWC	77429
CASA BATILLO DR	0	406Y	NWC	77449
CASA BATILLO DR	0	406Y	NWC	77449
CASA BLANCA CIR	0	406D	NWC	77433
CASABLANCA DR	6600	411J	NWH	77088
CASA CALVET DR	0	406Z	NWC	77449
CASA CALVET DR	0	406Z	NWC	77449
CASA DEL LAGO DR	4100	610K	MC	77459
CASA DEL MONTE DR	6600	527G	SWC	77083
CASA DEL SOL	0	290A	NWC	77389
CASA GRANDE CT	0	658Y	LC	77573
CASA GRANDE DR	0	658Y	LC	77573
CASA GRANDE DR	1	372Z	NEH	77060
CASA GRANDE DR	300	373W	NEH	77060
CASA LINDA DR		325N	NWC	77447
CASA LINDA DR		325S	NWC	77447
CASA LOMA DR	9700	450F	NWH	77041
CASA MARE	0	620D	SB	77586
CASA MILA DR	0	406Y	NWC	77449
CASA MILA DR	0	406Y	NWC	77449
CASA TEJAS LN	300	339W	NEC	77532
CASCADA	6600	338Y	NEH	77532
CASCADE	1200	536P	PA	77502
CASCADE CIR	17300	367T	NWC	77095
CASCADE DR	500	531L	BL	77401
CASCADE BASIN FALLS		289D	NWC	77375
CASCADE BEND LN	14800	326Z	NWC	77429
CASCADE CAVERNS CT	0	328N	NWC	77429
CASCADE CAVERNS CT	0	417A	NEC	77044
CASCADE CAVERNS LN	0	417A	NEC	77044
CASCADE CREEK DR	700	485G	SWC	77450
CASCADE CREEK DR	3100	297S	NEH	77339
CASCADE FALLS DR	0	656R	FR	77546
CASCADE FALLS DR	14100	618A	SEH	77062
CASCADE GLEN DR	2500	485P	NEF	77494
CASCADE GREEN CT	0	372C	NCC	77073
CASCADE HILL DR	0	370U	NWC	77086
CASCADE HILL LN	0	370U	NWC	77086
CASCADE HOLLOW LN	0	407E	NWC	77433
CASCADE HOLLOW LN	21700	290L	NWC	77379
CASCADE HOUSE CT	0	376E	HM	77396
CASCADE HOUSE DR	0	376B	HM	77396
CASCADE MIST DR	0	328E	NWC	77429
CASCADE OAKS CT	4100	447E	NWC	77084
CASCADE PINES DR	200	457U	NEC	77049
CASCADE POINT DR	15600	448B	NWC	77084

Street Name	Block	Pg/Sq	Loc	Zips
CASCADERA DR	6000	411B	NWC	77086
CASCADE RIDGE	0	485F	SWC	77494
CASCADE SPRINGS CT	2800	613X	NEB	77578
CASCADE SPRINGS DR	3400	613X	NEB	77578
CASCADE SPRINGS DR	22100	525F	NEF	77494
CASCADE TIMBERS LN	18400	328G	NWC	77377
CASCADE VIEW CT	0	659H	LC	77573
CASCADE WOODS LN	0	366V	NWC	77433
CASCADIA DR	3400	527C	SWC	77082
CASCADIA DR	15900	527C	SWC	77082
CASCADIA KNOLL CT	12900	337X	NEC	77346
CASCADING BROOK CT	20600	326S	NWC	77433
CASCADING BROOK WAY	15500	326S	NWC	77433
CASCADING FALLS BLVD	0	326K	NWC	77433
CASCADING OAKS DR	0	256T	SEM	77357
CASCADING SPRINGS LN	0	377F	NEC	77346
CASCET CT	700	486B	SWC	77450
CASCIANO CT	0	659M	LC	77573
CASE	3800	532A	WU	77005
CASEMONT DR	4500	331F	NWC	77388
CASERTA DR	13800	369C	NWC	77070
CASETA DR	14800	487Z	SWH	77082
CASEY	400	501V	BT	77520
CASEY CT	6800	614T	PL	77584
CASEY DR	700	498B	CV	77530
CASEY LN	27700	258K	SEM	77357
CASEY RD	0	258U	NEC	77357
CASEY RD	400	541B	BT	77520
CASEY CREEK CT	19300	526F	NEF	77407
CASH DR	5200	444Z	KT	77493
CASH RD	0	569K	SF	77477
CASH RD	9800	569L	SF	77477
S. CASHEL CIR	4600	330Z	NWC	77069
N. CASHEL CIR	4600	330Z	NWC	77069
CASHEL CASTLE DR	4600	330Z	NWC	77069
CASHEL FOREST DR	14000	330Z	NWC	77069
CASHEL GLEN DR	4500	330Z	NWC	77069
S. CASHEL OAK DR	4700	330Z	NWC	77069
N. CASHEL OAK DR	14200	330Z	NWC	77069
CASHEL PARK LN	0	407Z	NWC	77084
CASHEL SPRING DR	4600	330Z	NWC	77069
CASHEL WOOD DR	14200	330Z	NWC	77069
CASHEW	3000	446U	NWC	77084
CASHIER CT	0	293U	NCC	77373
CASHMERE WAY	0	614Y	PL	77584
CASH OAKS DR	6200	331N	NWC	77379
CASON	2600	532E	WU	77005
CASPER CT	600	332C	NCC	77373
CASPER DR	18700	332C	NCC	77373
CASPER CLIFF CT		484Y	NEF	77494
CASPERSON DR	1600	496K	JC	77029
CASPIAN DR	0	337W	NEC	77346
CASPIAN LN	1000	332J	NWC	77090
CASRORDELL DR	0	618S	SEH	77598
CASS CT	0	293R	SEM	77386
CASSANDRA LN	11800	369R	NWC	77064
CASSANDRA PARK	16000	330R	NWC	77379
CASSELBERRY DR	24600	296J	SEM	77365
CASSENA GROVE PLACE	0	249U	NWC	77375
CASSIA CIR	11800	369N	NWC	77065
CASSIA SPRINGS DR	0	451W	NWH	77055
CASSIDY CREEK CT	0	408G	NWC	77095
CASSIDY PARK LN	4100	485Z	NEF	77450
CASSIDY PLACE	4800	371A	NWC	77066
CASSINA LN	17400	331G	NWC	77388
CASSINI CT	0	525L	NEF	77407
CASSINI CT	0	251C	WD	77381
CASSINI DR	0	457A	NEC	77044
CASSIUS CT	18100	257D	RF	77357
CASSOWARY	1	252N	WD	77380
CASSOWARY CT	3100	293X	NCC	77373
CAST CT	800	419B	NEC	77532
CASTAWAY CT	15900	419F	NEC	77532
CASTELLINA LN	0	451Y	NWH	77055
CASTELLINA LN	0	491C	NWH	77055
CASTERLY CT	0	611S	FS	77545
CASTILIAN DR	13400	457X	NEC	77015
CASTILLE LN	11200	529B	SWH	77082
CASTING SPRINGS WAY	0	292U	NCC	77373
CASTLE	2500	282T	WL	77484
CASTLE	25000	244R	WCO	77447
CASTLE CT	1300	493W	SWH	77006
CASTLE CT	1400	492Z	SWH	77006
CASTLE CT	2900	615Q	PL	77581
CASTLE DR	2000	658T	LC	77573
CASTLE LN	3100	569N	SG	77478
CASTLE RD	29000	283B	NWC	77484
CASTLE RD	34000	282D	NWC	77484
CASTLE ARCH CT	27100	296X	SEM	77339
CASTLEBAR CT	400	497C	NEC	77015
CASTLEBAR LN	0	569X	MC	77459
CASTLEBAY CT	3300	613V	PL	77584
CASTLE BAY DR	2200	619Z	LC	77573
CASTLEBAY DR	6500	451A	NWH	77092
CASTLE BEACH CT	2100	619Z	LC	77573
CASTLE BEND DR	20600	486K	SWC	77450
CASTLE BLUFF LN	0	417D	NEC	77044
CASTLEBRIDGE DR	12100	409E	JV	77065
CASTLEBRIDGE LN	100	409E	JV	77065
CASTLEBROOK CT	1	569S	SG	77478
CASTLEBROOK RD	5000	291E	NWC	77389
CASTLEBURY LN	0	526E	NEF	77450
CASTLECLIFF LN	26800	296X	SEM	77339
CASTLECOMBE DR	13200	377X	NEC	77044
CASTLE COMBE WAY	1300	336H	NEH	77339
CASTLE COURT PLACE	4400	492Z	SWH	77006
CASTLE COVE LN	600	660E	LC	77573
CASTLE COVE LN	14400	377Y	NEH	77044
CASTLE CREEK CT	0	658J	LC	77573
CASTLE CREEK DR	1600	570T	MC	77489
CASTLECREEK LN	5000	571Y	SWH	77053
CASTLECREEK LN	5300	611C	SWH	77053
CASTLE CREST CT	0	527R	NEF	77083
CASTLE CREST DR	9801	528U	SWH	77083
CASTLEDALE DR	900	413Q	NEH	77037
CASTLEDALE DR	2600	414P	NCC	77093
CASTLE DISCORDIA ST	0	444C	NWC	77493
CASTLE FALLS CT	6400	407T	NWC	77449
CASTLE FALLS DR	3600	613W	NEB	77578
CASTLEFORD	8100	450C	NWH	77040
CASTLE FOREST DR	0	253T	SEM	77386
CASTLE FRASER DR	16500	447D	NWC	77084
CASTLEGAP CT	19700	289Z	NWC	77379
CASTLEGAP DR	9300	289Z	NWC	77379
CASTLE GARDENS CT	0	446S	NWC	77449
CASTLE GARDENS LN	0	446S	NWC	77449
CASTLE GATE DR	15100	527R	NEF	77083
CASTLEGATE LN	100	409E	JV	77065
CASTLE GLEN DR	1200	457Y	NEC	77015
CASTLEGORY	100	457X	NEC	77015
N. CASTLEGORY	300	457U	NEC	77049
CASTLEGORY CT	13600	457X	NEC	77015

Street Name	Block	Pg/Sq	Loc	Zips
CASTLEGREEN DR	19900	291Z	NWC	77388
CASTLEGROVE CT	16100	328R	NWC	77377
CASTLE GUARD	0	444H	NWC	77493
W. CASTLE HARBOR	200	656T	FR	77546
E. CASTLE HARBOR	200	656Q	FR	77546
CASTLE HAVEN LN	18300	330B	NWC	77379
CASTLE HAWK TRAIL	0	525Q	NEF	77407
CASTLEHEAD DR	0	289Q	NWC	77375
CASTLEHEATH CT	2100	486Q	SWC	77450
CASTLE HEATH LN	17900	447F	NWC	77084
CASTLE HILLS BLVD	22100	286K	NWC	77377
CASTLE HILLS CT	10700	369K	NWC	77070
CASTLE HILL TRAIL	800	336A	NEH	77339
CASTLE HOLLOW DR	0	250U	NWC	77389
CASTLE KNOLL DR	12900	371A	NWC	77066
CASTLELAKE DR	200	616Y	FR	77546
CASTLE LANE DR	6300	370R	NWC	77066
CASTLE MANOR DR	0	253T	SEM	77386
CASTLEMILLS CT	20600	486K	SWC	77450
CASTLEMIST DR	1300	252Q	SEM	77386
CASTLEMONT DR	0	528N	NEF	77083
CASTLEMONT LN	21100	291T	NWC	77388
CASTLEMOOR CT	26000	367N	NWC	77433
CASTLE OAKS DR	1800	615Z	PL	77581
CASTLE PEAK CT	0	485S	NEF	77494
CASTLE PEAK DR	10800	367U	NWC	77095
CASTLE PEAK LN	6100	657Y	LC	77573
CASTLE PINE LN	6500	330G	NWC	77379
CASTLE PINES DR	4100	501K	BT	77521
CASTLE PLACE	2500	569V	SF	77477
CASTLE POINT LN	20500	379E	NEC	77532
CASTLE POND CT	3400	613V	PL	77584
CASTLE POND CT	8300	407G	NWC	77095
CASTLE RAIN DR	0	377G	NEC	77346
CASTLEREAGH DR	14300	572N	SWH	77045
CASTLEREAGH LAKE LN	0	405S	NWC	77493
CASTLE RIDGE DR	11800	489J	SWH	77077
CASTLEROCK CT	2900	613T	NEB	77584
CASTLEROCK DR	3100	613T	NEB	77584
CASTLE ROCK RD	1400	331M	NWC	77090
CASTLEROCK SPRINGS LN	9600	329F	NWC	77375
CASTLE SPRINGS DR	22000	485M	SWC	77450
CASTLESTONE DR	12500	408D	NWC	77065
CASTLE TERRACE CT	0	290Q	NWC	77379
CASTLETON	10300	414Z	NEH	77016
CASTLETON BAY LN	0	612P	PL	77545
CASTLETON CREEK CT	22700	485L	SWC	77450
CASTLETON FARMS RD	16900	330K	NWC	77379
CASTLETOWN PARK CT	16000	330R	NWC	77379
CASTLEVIEW CIR	4600	501F	BT	77521
CASTLEVIEW DR	4600	501F	BT	77521
CASTLEVIEW LN	6600	571W	SWH	77489
CASTLEVIEW LN	7300	570Z	SWH	77489
CASTLE WAY LN	200	456Z	NEC	77015
CASTLEWIND CIR	22000	485V	NEF	77450
CASTLEWIND CT	2000	619Z	LC	77573
CASTLEWIND CT	22000	485V	NEF	77450
CASTLEWIND DR	3100	485V	NEF	77450
CASTLEWIND LN	0	612F	PL	77545
CASTLEWOOD	3000	532P	SWH	77025
W. CASTLEWOOD AVE	100	656L	FR	77546
CASTLEWOOD AVE	100	656L	FR	77546
E. CASTLEWOOD AVE	200	657A	FR	77546
CASTLEWOOD DR	200	252J	OR	77386
CASTOFF CT	16800	379X	NEC	77532
CASTOLAN DR	1000	372W	NWC	77038
CASTOR	3300	453J	NWH	77022
CASTOR	14100	248X	NWC	77375
CASTOR CT	31400	248X	TB	77375
CASTORDEL	0	618S	SEH	77598
CASTOR GLEN	0	618N	SEH	77598
CASTORGLEN DR	15700	617R	SEH	77598
CASTRIES CT	0	377G	NEC	77345
CASUAL LN	600	659N	LC	77573
CASUAL SHORE CT	100	619Z	LC	77573
CASWELL CT	900	486F	SWC	77450
CATALANO CT	13500	368A	NWC	77429
CATALDO CT	0	410T	NWC	77040
CATALINA CT	0	485V	NEF	77450
CATALINA DR	2100	538S	PA	77503
CATALINA DR	3300	609J	SG	77479
CATALINA DR	3700	538S	DP	77536
CATALINA LN	7400	575S	SEH	77075
CATALINA HARBOR CT	0	525A	NEF	77494
CATALINA ISLAND DR	0	525A	NEF	77494
CATALINA LEAF LN	9600	329C	NWC	77379
CATALINA SHORES DR	0	612L	PL	77584
CATALINA SHORES DR	12100	409W	NWC	77041
CATALINA VILLAGE DR	13500	528F	SWC	77083
CATALONIA COVE	0	660F	LC	77573
CATALPA CIR	11800	369N	NWC	77065
CATALPA PLACE	800	610S	MC	77459
CATAMARAN DR	2000	619Z	LC	77573
CATAMARAN DR	18500	378A	NEC	77346
CATAMARAN COVE DR	0	612F	PL	77584
CATAMARAN PASS DR	0	407G	NWC	77095
CATAMORE	11000	413Y	NEH	77076
CATANIA LN	0	659L	LC	77573
CATANIA BAY CT	0	610P	NEF	77459
CATARINA CIR	6700	407Q	NWC	77084
CATAWISSA DR	8800	407D	NWC	77095
CATBIRD CT	16100	375Q	NEC	77396
CATCH SPRINGS DR	0	406D	NWC	77433
CATCLAW DR	0	293F	SEM	77386
CATES	31800	248S	SWM	77362
CAT FEET CT	1	250D	WD	77381
CATFORD	11000	575X	SEH	77075
CATHCART DR	6600	412W	NWH	77091
CATHEDRAL DR	9300	573B	SEH	77051
CATHEDRAL FALLS DR	0	328Y	NWC	77429
CATHEDRAL GROVE LN	7900	410L	NWC	77040
CATHEDRAL PINES DR	0	377G	NEC	77346
CATHER	400	453A	NEH	77076
CATHERINE	200	453Y	NEH	77009
CATHERINE ANNE CT	0	325M	NWC	77433
CATHERINE BAY LN	0	377T	NEC	77044
CATHERWOOD LN	5800	407Z	NWC	77084
CATHERWOOD PLACE	800	497A	NEH	77015
CATHEY	16000	458U	CV	77530
CAT HOLLOW CT	0	367W	NWC	77095
CATHY	0	244L	WL	77447
CATHY	9100	450U	NWH	77080
CATHY DR	11800	369N	NWC	77065
CATHYS WAY	20000	254L	SEM	77365
CATINA LN	13200	571L	SWH	77045
CATINA LN	13900	571Q	SWH	77045
CATLETT LN	9300	579A	LP	77571
CATLINA MANOR LN	0	526P	NEF	77407
CATOOSA DR	21800	290R	NWC	77388
CATRON CROSSING	6300	405S	NWC	77493
CATROSE LN	11700	328X	NWC	77429
CATSK DEER DR	0	378Q	NEC	77532

Street Name	Block	Pg/Sq	Loc	Zips
CATSKILL DR	1200	569X	MC	77459
CATSKILL BLUFF LN	17000	367Y	NWC	77095
CATSKILL CREST DR	12100	328D	NWC	77375
CAT SPRING DR	0	327U	NWC	77429
CAT SPRINGS CT	20500	446P	NWC	77449
CATTAIL CROSSING	19800	526T	NEF	77407
CATTAIL GATE CT	9200	375V	NEC	77396
CATTAIL PARK CT	0	253J	SEM	77385
CATTAIL PLACE	1	250H	WD	77381
CATTAILS LN	6300	570H	SWH	77035
CAT TAIL SPRING CT	9500	408B	NWC	77095
CATTERPILLAR CT	18800	295F	SEM	77365
CATTLE RD	0	380G	NEC	77532
CATTLE CALL WAY	0	525A	NEF	77494
CAUDLE DR	1200	450Z	SV	77055
CAUFIELD CT	0	249B	SWM	77382
CAUSEWAY	14800	497M	NEC	77015
CAUSEWAY DR	8600	528Q	SWC	77083
CAUSEWAY RD	0	541F	BT	77520
W. CAVALCADE	100	453T	NWH	77009
CAVALCADE	100	453V	NEH	77009
CAVALCADE	2600	454Y	NEH	77026
CAVALCADE	6900	454Y	NEH	77028
CAVALIER	300	536U	PA	77502
CAVALIER	6000	534Q	SEH	77087
CAVALIER	20000	379H	NEC	77532
CAVALLO	0	255T	SEM	77365
CAVALLO PASS LN	0	659P	LC	77573
CAVALRY CIR	100	658K	LC	77573
CAVALRY RD	11500	539Z	LP	77571
CAVAN	0	616J	PL	77581
CAVANAUGH	5600	534J	SEH	77021
CAVATINA WAY	0	293F	SEM	77386
CAVE CREEK CT	0	376V	NEC	77346
CAVE CREEK DR	0	376V	NEC	77346
CAVEHILL CT	800	572Q	SWH	77047
CAVELL LN	8700	490D	SV	77055
CAVEN	13800	375W	NEC	77396
CAVENDALE CT	4000	485U	NEF	77494
CAVENDISH DR	15700	578Y	SEH	77059
CAVERLY LN		289G	NWC	77375
CAVERN DR	4700	617X	SEC	77546
CAVERN SPRINGS DR	19400	329A	NWC	77375
CAVERSHAM DR	5200	531P	SWH	77096
CAVE RUN DR	4900	609F	MC	77459
CAVE SPRINGS DR	3300	296Y	NEH	77339
CAVESSON DR	7400	407J	NWC	77433
CAWDER WOODS LN	0	328G	NWC	77377
CAWDOR WAY	11700	490F	HE	77024
CAWOOD PLACE	0	330K	NWC	77379
CAXTON	10200	414Y	NEH	77016
CAXTON BEND DR	0	328F	NWC	77377
CAYAHOGA CT	0	250P	NWC	77389
CAYEY	11200	415P	NEC	77016
CAYLEBAITE	1000	538X	DP	77536
CAYLIN DR	14200	377Y	NEH	77044
CAYLOR	1	494U	SEH	77011
CAYMAN BEND LN	0	612F	PL	77545
CAYMAN BEND LN	1000	659M	LC	77573
CAYMAN ESTATES	22900	252M	SEM	77385
CAYMAN MIST DR	9700	575Z	SEH	77075
CAYMAN POINT DR	21700	485V	NEF	77450
CAYMAN WAY	0	333M	NCC	77338
CAYMUS DR	0	293Z	NCC	77373
CAYO HUESO LN	0	447J	NWC	77084
CAY SOL CT	9400	416Y	NEC	77044
CAYTON	6600	574D	SEH	77061
CAYTON	7400	535X	SEH	77061
CAYUGA	7300	533P	SWH	77054
CAYWOOD LN	1300	451X	NWH	77055
CEAL RD	19600	295L	SEM	77365
CEBRA	5600	452A	NWH	77091
CEBRA	6300	412W	NWH	77091
CEBRUN	5700	452B	NWH	77091
CECE GLEN CT	28500	293E	SEM	77386
CECIL ST	7200	532M	SWH	77030
CECILE LN	6500	458N	NEC	77049
CECILIA CIR	16200	286C	SWM	77355
CECIL SUMMERS CT	0	616J	SEC	77089
CECIL SUMMERS WAY	11400	616E	SEC	77089
CECINA ST	0	659Q	LC	77573
CEDAR	0	337B	NEH	77339
CEDAR	100	459R	HG	77562
CEDAR	100	580G	LP	77571
CEDAR	800	538K	DP	77536
CEDAR	2100	614M	PL	77581
CEDAR	2500	502T	BT	77520
CEDAR	3200	572T	SWC	77053
CEDAR	4600	531G	BL	77401
CEDAR	4700	581W	PA	77586
CEDAR	16400	498H	CV	77530
CEDAR	16600	418P	NEC	77044
CEDAR	3100	543M	BC	77520
CEDAR AVE	500	659A	LC	77573
CEDAR BLVD	4100	542B	CCO	77520
CEDAR CIR	200	257B	WV	77357
CEDAR CIR	7000	375X	NEC	77396
CEDAR LN	100	498D	CV	77530
CEDAR LN	100	619M	EL	77586
CEDAR LN	6500	444W	KT	77493
CEDAR LN	14100	375X	NEC	77396
CEDAR LN	17400	246T	SWM	77355
CEDAR LN	19100	287P	NWC	77377
CEDAR RD	800	620T	CS	77565
CEDAR RD	2100	484L	NEF	77494
CEDAR RD	8300	340U	LCO	77535
CEDAR BAY DR	5500	337D	NEH	77345
CEDAR BAYOU RD	100	501V	BT	77520
CEDAR BAYOU RD	2000	502T	BT	77520
CEDAR BAYOU BAYSHORE	0	502Y	CCO	77520
CEDAR BAYOU BAYSHORE	0	542G	CCO	77520
CEDAR BAYOU LAKE DR	0	542P	BT	77520
W. CEDAR BAYOU LYNCHBURG	1	501E	NEC	77521
E. CEDA BAYOU LYNCHBURG	100	501H	NEC	77521
E. CEDA BAYOU LYNCHBURG	1300	502F	NEC	77521
W. CEDA BAYOU LYNCHBURG	2000	500B	NEC	77521
CEDAR BEND DR	4100	610P	MC	77459
CEDAR BEND CREEK	5200	448D	NWC	77041
CEDARBERRY LN	9900	289U	NWC	77375
CEDAR BLUFF DR	0	657G	FR	77546
CEDAR BLUFF DR	3100	657G	FR	77546
CEDAR BLUFF DR	5700	502G	BT	77521
CEDAR BLUFF DR	9600	369U	NWC	77064
CEDARBRAKE	2100	502S	BT	77520
CEDARBRAKE DR	8300	451W	SV	77055
CEDARBRAKE DR	8600	450Z	SV	77055
CEDAR BRAKE RD	0	250H	WD	77381
CEDAR BRANCH	9800	502G	BT	77521
CEDAR BRANCH DR	100	658P	LC	77573
CEDAR BREAK CT	12400	377A	NEC	77346
CEDAR BRIDGE	10900	576S	SEH	77075
CEDAR BROOK CIR	2600	569V	NEF	77477

Street Name	Block	Pg/Sq	Loc	Zips
CEDARBROOK CT	1400	620L	SB	77586
CEDARBROOK DR	1400	450Z	SV	77055
CEDAR BROOK LN	0	657Z	LC	77573
CEDAR BRUSH CIR	8000	330K	NWC	77379
CEDARBURG DR	5500	574J	SEH	77048
CEDAR BUSH DR	4500	414C	NCC	77039
CEDAR CANYON DR	21000	326S	NWC	77433
CEDAR CHASE PLACE	1	250D	WD	77381
CEDARCLIFF CT	12000	369Q	NWC	77070
CEDARCLIFF DR	10800	369Q	NWC	77070
CEDAR CLIFF LN	12800	368Q	NWC	77429
CEDAR COVE	1500	580F	LP	77571
CEDAR COVE CT	1700	486J	SWC	77450
CEDAR COVE DR	4900	501F	BT	77521
CEDAR COVE DR	21500	486J	SWC	77450
CEDAR COVE LN	0	253U	SEM	77386
CEDAR CREEK CT	200	247G	SWM	77362
CEDAR CREEK CT	1700	489P	SWH	77077
CEDAR CREEK DR	0	612M	PL	77584
CEDAR CREEK DR	100	658K	LC	77573
CEDAR CREEK DR	2100	502S	BT	77520
CEDAR CREEK DR	5000	491Q	SWH	77056
CEDAR CREEK DR	5800	491P	SWH	77057
CEDAR CREEK DR	6100	491N	SWH	77057
CEDAR CREEK DR	10000	489Q	SWH	77042
CEDAR CREEK DR	11300	489P	SWH	77077
CEDAR CREEK POINT	13300	528Y	SG	77478
CEDARCREST	5100	534P	SEH	77087
CEDARCREST DR	3000	537L	PA	77503
CEDAR CREST CEMETERY	0	502P	BT	77520
CEDAR CROSSING WAY	0	528Q	SWC	77083
CEDARDALE DR	8600	450Z	SV	77055
CEDARDALE DR	10000	450W	NWH	77055
CEDARDALE FALLS DR	0	524F	NEF	77494
CEDARDALE PINES DR	0	524A	NEF	77494
CEDAREDGE DR	9800	409C	NWC	77064
CEDAREDGE DR	10100	369Y	NWC	77064
CEDAR EDGE DR	18500	330A	NWC	77379
CEDAR FALLS DR	2200	336G	NEH	77339
CEDAR FERN CT	2100	293E	SEM	77386
CEDARFIELD RD	0	484Y	NEF	77494
CEDARFIELD RD	0	484Y	NEF	77494
CEDAR FIELD WAY	0	407Y	NWC	77084
CEDAR FOREST DR	3900	297T	NEH	77339
CEDAR FORK DR	500	658P	LC	77573
CEDAR FORM LN	11700	568D	MD	77477
CEDAR GAP LN	12100	529N	SWH	77072
CEDAR GARDENS DR	3600	527D	SWC	77082
CEDAR GLEN LN	3600	291Y	NWC	77388
CEDAR GROVE CT	12700	337X	NEC	77346
CEDAR GROVE DR	13200	420S	BR	77532
CEDAR GULLY	0	543H	BC	77520
CEDAR GULLY DR	16000	617X	SEC	77546
CEDAR GULLY RD	0	657R	LC	77573
CEDAR HAWK CT	0	444S	KT	77493
CEDAR HILL	9900	462R	BT	77521
CEDAR HILL CT	0	615N	PL	77581
CEDAR HILL DR	0	615N	PL	77581
CEDAR HILL DR	25200	244C	WCO	77447
CEDAR HILL LN	2800	414S	NCC	77093
CEDAR HILL LN	5400	414V	NEH	77016
CEDAR HOLLOW	3300	502B	NEC	77521
CEDAR HOLLOW CT	300	613B	NEB	77584
S. CEDAR HOLLOW DR	2700	613B	NEB	77584
E. CEDAR HOLLOW DR	3000	613B	NEB	77584
CEDARHURST DR	9600	531U	SWH	77096
CEDAR ISLE DR	14700	408X	NWC	77084
CEDAR JUMP RD	0	377D	NEC	77346
CEDAR KEY TRAIL	0	377B	NEC	77346
CEDAR KNOLLS DR	2300	296Z	NEH	77339
CEDAR KNOLLS DR	3100	297W	NEH	77339
CEDAR KNOLLS DR	3400	337A	NEH	77339
CEDAR LAKE DR	100	658P	LC	77573
CEDAR LAKE RD	100	338V	NEH	77336
CEDAR LANDING DR	0	658K	LC	77573
CEDAR LANDING DR	9800	502G	BT	77521
CEDAR LANE CIR	100	619M	TL	77586
CEDAR LANE DR	200	619M	TL	77586
CEDAR LAWN CIR	6800	578K	PA	77505
CEDAR LODGE CT	5300	297P	NEH	77345
CEDAR MANOR CT	16600	367F	CY	77429
W. CEDAR MEADOW CIR	6000	525C	NEF	77494
E. CEDAR MEADOW CIR	6000	525C	NEF	77494
S. CEDAR MEADOW CIR	22400	525C	NEF	77494
N. CEDAR MEADOW CIR	22400	525C	NEF	77494
CEDAR MESA DR	11800	576L	SEH	77034
CEDAR MILL CT	3400	297Z	NEH	77345
CEDAR MILLS DR	3500	297Z	NEH	77345
CEDARMONT DR	3200	579A	LP	77571
CEDARMOOR CT	2600	488U	SWH	77082
CEDAR MOSS CT	0	257F	SEM	77357
CEDAR MOUND LN	0	528Q	SWC	77083
CEDAR OAK	200	656D	FR	77546
CEDAR OAKS DR	18600	330A	NWC	77379
CEDAR OAKS LN	4600	531M	BL	77401
CEDAR PARK LN	10400	371W	NWC	77086
CEDAR PARK FOREST	0	329Q	NWC	77070
CEDAR PASS CT	1400	489N	SWH	77077
CEDAR PASS DR	11800	489N	SWH	77077
CEDAR PATH	6700	527E	NEF	77407
CEDAR PATH CT	0	657T	FR	77546
CEDAR PATH LN	0	252M	SEM	77385
CEDAR PLACE	1	259P	LCO	77357
CEDAR PLACID CIR	2900	331P	NWC	77068
CEDAR PLACID LN	17200	331P	NWC	77068
CEDAR POINT CIR	9300	329Q	NWC	77070
CEDAR POINT CT	11700	329W	NWC	77070
CEDAR POINT CT	11700	329W	NWC	77070
CEDAR POINT DR	100	658N	LC	77573
CEDAR POINT DR	6800	578J	PA	77505
CEDAR POINT DR	13500	368D	NWC	77429
CEDAR POINT DR	13600	369A	NWC	77070
CEDAR POINT DR	14000	329W	NWC	77070
CEDAR POINT RD	5500	542Z	CCO	77520
CEDAR POINT PLACE	6200	407S	NWC	77449
CEDAR POND DR	100	375G	HM	77396
CEDAR POST CT	1000	289A	TB	77375
CEDAR POST LN	1000	490B	NWH	77055
CEDAR POST LN	1100	450X	NWH	77055
CEDARPOST SQUARE ST	0	450X	NWH	77055
CEDARPOST TREE SPRINGS PL	0	450X	NWH	77055
CEDAR PRAIRIE DR	0	658N	LC	77573
CEDAR RAIN DR	20500	446P	NWC	77449
CEDAR RIDGE CT	3200	657G	FR	77546
CEDAR RIDGE CT	4000	527D	SWC	77082
CEDAR RIDGE DR	15000	527D	SWC	77082
CEDAR RIDGE LN	0	615H	PL	77089
CEDAR RIDGE TRAIL	4200	578Y	SEH	77059
CEDAR RIDGE TRAIL	2800	657H	FR	77546
CEDAR ROCK DR	0	324M	NWC	77447
CEDAR RUN CIR	0	330C	NWC	77379
CEDAR RUN FALLS	9000	249Z	NWC	77375

Street Name	Block	Pg/Sq	Loc	Zips
CEDAR SAGE DR	16400	367Q	NWC	77095
CEDAR SANDS LN		328k	NWC	77377
CEDAR SCURRY CIR	0	332X	NWC	77090
CEDAR SHADE LN	1	251M	WD	77380
CEDAR SHADE RD	0	524B	NEF	77494
CEDARSHAM LN	0	446M	NWC	77449
CEDAR SHOALS RD	1100	618E	SEH	77062
CEDAR SHORES LN	15900	377L	NEC	77044
CEDAR SPRING DR	4900	609F	MC	77459
CEDAR SPRINGS PLACE	25500	292U	NCC	77373
CEDAR SPRING TRAIL	0	337Q	NEC	77346
CEDARSPUR DR	8300	451W	SV	77055
CEDARSPUR DR	8600	450Z	SV	77055
CEDAR SUMMER CROSSING	0	526L	NEF	77407
W. CEDAR SUN TRAIL	3000	446Q	NWC	77449
E. CEDAR SUN TRAIL	3000	446Q	NWC	77449
N. CEDAR SUN TRAIL	20000	446Q	NWC	77449
CEDAR SUN TRAIL CT	0	446Q	NWC	77449
CEDAR TOP DR	8900	411R	NWH	77088
CEDARTOWNE LN	10400	528X	NEF	77498
CEDAR TRACE DR	8400	330N	NWC	77379
CEDAR TRAIL	0	527E	NEF	77407
CEDAR TRAIL	0	527J	NEF	77407
E. CEDAR TRAIL CT	4000	615S	PL	77584
CEDAR TREE	6000	530C	SWH	77036
CEDARVALE LN	11600	329N	NWC	77377
CEDAR VALLEY DR	3700	609M	MC	77459
CEDAR VALLEY DR	4200	337C	NEH	77345
CEDAR VIEW	7900	463S	CCO	77520
CEDARVIEW	25000	248N	SWM	77354
CEDAR VIEW DR	5700	502G	BT	77521
CEDARVIEW LN	11000	409Y	NWC	77041
CEDAR VILLAGE CT	22700	485L	SWC	77450
CEDAR VILLAGE DR	3000	297Y	NEH	77345
CEDARVILLE DR	2700	297Z	NEH	77345
CEDAR VINE LN	0	328M	NWC	77377
CEDAR VISTA LN	0	452Q	NWH	77018
CEDAR WALK DR	8600	249Z	NWC	77375
CEDAR WING CT	3000	610B	MC	77489
CEDARWING LN	1	251M	WD	77380
CEDARWOOD	11200	336S	NEC	77338
CEDARWOOD CT	1800	568B	SG	77498
CEDARWOOD DR	0	656D	FR	77546
CEDARWOOD DR	500	656D	FR	77546
CEDARWOOD DR	1300	536P	PA	77502
CEDARWOOD DR	3900	615W	PL	77584
CEDAR WOODS PLACE	2800	331P	NWC	77068
CEDARWOOD TRACE DR	0	253X	SEM	77386
CEDAR YARD LN	0	366N	NWC	77433
CEDEL DR	7600	451P	NWH	77055
CEDEL DR	8500	450R	NWH	77055
CEILA	0	255D	SEM	77357
CELANO DR	11100	524M	NEF	77406
CELEBRATION WAY	0	609Y	NEF	77459
CELESTE CT	0	250J	NWC	77389
CELESTE RIVER CT	17300	367T	NWC	77095
CELESTIAL LN	5100	414G	NCC	77039
CELESTITE DR	4300	529E	SWH	77072
CELIA DR	12600	496M	NEH	77015
CELINA LN	8200	450C	NWH	77040
CELLAR DOOR	10000	530X	SWH	77031
CELLINI DR	14100	368P	NWC	77429
CELTIC OAK DR	0	578J	PA	77505
CELTIC TERRACE DR	0	484V	NEF	77494
CELTIS	11500	496K	JC	77029
CEMBRA WALK	20300	290V	NWC	77379
CEMETERY RD	0	249U	NWC	77375
CEMETERY RD	18500	247Q	SWM	77355
CENIZO PARK LN	0	484X	NEF	77494
CENIZO PARK LN	0	484X	NEF	77494
CENTENARY	2600	532G	WU	77005
CENTENNIAL DR	1300	450W	NWH	77055
CENTENNIAL LN	5000	617X	FR	77546
CENTENNIAL BRIDGE CT	10400	528W	NEF	77498
CENTENNIAL BRIDGE LN	15100	528W	NEF	77498
CENTENNIAL GLEN DR	5800	525D	NEF	77450
CENTENNIAL GLEN DR	5900	526A	NEF	77450
CENTENNIAL VILLAGE DR	3000	614V	PL	77584
CENTER	0	498X	DP	77536
CENTER	100	502N	BT	77520
CENTER	100	499D	NEC	77520
CENTER	100	538B	DP	77536
CENTER	200	536H	PA	77506
CENTER	300	460S	HG	77562
CENTER	300	570S	SF	77477
CENTER	1500	493F	SWH	77007
CENTER	2500	282U	WL	77484
CENTER	3900	492H	SWH	77007
CENTER	5100	578B	PA	77505
CENTER	499	569V	SF	77477
CENTER CT	0	493E	SWH	77007
CENTER CT	100	538P	DP	77536
CENTER CT	100	538T	DP	77536
CENTER DR	100	496W	GP	77547
CENTERBROOK CT	0	612K	PL	77545
CENTERBROOK LN	2200	486P	SWC	77450
CENTER COURT CIR	17300	330D	NWC	77379
CENTER COURT DR	5800	330D	NWC	77379
CENTERFIELD DR	0	616U	FR	77546
CENTERFIELD DR	13500	370E	NWH	77070
CENTER HILL DR	700	488A	SWH	77079
CENTERLAKE LN	19700	291W	NWC	77379
CENTER MEADOW	0	288C	TB	77375
CENTER PARK DR	0	327U	NWC	77429
CENTERPARK DR	7600	370E	NWH	77070
CENTER PARK DR	19100	332C	NCC	77373
CENTER POINT DR	9200	532Y	SWH	77054
CENTERPOINTE DR	0	658R	LC	77573
CENTERRASPRINGS DR	0	328A	NWC	77429
CENTER RIDGE DR	0	366N	NWC	77433
CENTER SPRING CT	25800	292U	NCC	77373
CENTERTON DR	0	485U	NEF	77494
CENTER VILLAGE DR	5300	525C	NEF	77494
CENTERWOOD DR	600	496F	NEH	77013
CENTIFOLIA LN	0	286L	NWC	77377
CENTOLANI ST	0	659P	LC	77573
CENTRAL	200	535C	SEH	77012
CENTRAL	700	536V	PA	77502
CENTRAL	1700	535G	SEH	77017
CENTRAL	11400	414L	NCC	77093
CENTRAL DR	100	568V	SG	77478
CENTRAL DR	11900	367K	CY	77433
CENTRALCREST	5600	451P	NWH	77092
CENTRAL FALLS DR	5900	408Y	NWC	77041
CENTRAL GREEN BLVD	16500	373K	NCC	77032
CENTRAL LAKES	0	376U	NEC	77396
CENTRAL PARK CIR	2300	578X	SEH	77059
CENTRAL PARK DR	0	373L	NCC	77032
CENTRAL PKWY	2200	451U	NWH	77092
CENTRAL TRAIL DR	0	285L	NWC	77447
CENTRE AVE	0	580P	SA	77571
CENTRE CT	12400	528M	SWH	77072

Street Name	Block	Pg/Sq	Loc	Zips
CENTRE COURT PLACE	16300	330M	NWC	77379
CENTRE GROVE CT	7100	370E	NWC	77069
CENTRE GROVE DR	7000	370A	NWC	77069
CENTRE OAKS DR	7000	370E	NWC	77069
CENTREPARK DR	10200	450J	NWH	77043
CENTRE PKWY	9600	529V	SWH	77036
CENTRE PLACE CIR	6500	330M	NWC	77379
CENTURIAN CIR	25600	257D	RF	77357
N. CENTURY CIR	2100	657K	FR	77546
S. CENTURY CT	2200	657K	FR	77546
CENTURY DR	100	657K	FR	77546
CENTURY DR	12700	569K	SF	77477
CENTURY LN	12900	496M	NEH	77015
CENTURY PLANT DR	0	525B	NEF	77494
CENTURY PLAZA DR	300	332Y	NCC	77073
CENTURY PLAZA DR	1400	373A	NCC	77073
CENTURY SQUARE BLVD	100	568M	SG	77478
CEOLE CIR	1000	658R	LC	77573
CEOLE LN	400	658R	LC	77573
CERCA CT	7000	371W	NWC	77086
CERCA BLANCA DR	15800	527L	NEF	77083
CEREMONIAL LN	0	404Z	NWC	77493
CEREMONIAL LN	0	444D	NWC	77493
CEREZA DR	16100	527L	NEF	77083
CERMAK	0	529S	SWH	77099
CERRITOS DR	5600	571A	SWH	77035
CERRITOS DR	6000	570D	SWH	77035
CERRO PUENTE WAY	0	527X	NEF	77469
CERTOSA DR	23700	525N	NEF	77469
S. CESAR CHAVEZ BLVD	100	494Z	SEH	77011
N. CESAR CHAVEZ BLVD	100	494V	SEH	77011
N. CESAR CHAVEZ BLVD	300	494V	SEH	77011
CESSNA	3500	615P	PL	77581
CETIND CT	0	373F	NCC	77073
CETIND CT	0	373F	NCC	77073
CETTI	2800	493D	NEH	77009
CETTI	3400	453Z	NEH	77009
CETTIPARK ST	0	453Z	NEH	77009
CHABLIS RIDGE CT	0	446E	NWC	77449
CHACO	2600	493V	SEH	77004
CHACO HILL LN	0	526R	NEF	77469
CHAD CT	16200	246Y	SWM	77355
CHAD LN	900	501M	BT	77521
CHAD LN	20100	256K	SEM	77357
CHAD ARBOR TRAIL	20100	326P	NWC	77433
CHADBOURNE CT	600	488H	SWH	77079
CHADBOURNE DR	14000	489E	SWH	77079
CHADBOURNE DR	14400	488H	SWH	77079
CHADBOURNE TRACE LN	0	525M	NEF	77407
CHADBROOK LN	11700	569B	SWH	77099
CHADBURY LN	800	619L	TL	77586
CHADBURY PARK DR	20400	486P	SWC	77450
CHADDINGTON CT	0	289L	NWC	77375
CHADELL POINT LN	3000	445R	NWC	77449
CHADINGTON LN	3300	291Y	NWC	77388
CHADWAY CROSSING	6100	525G	NEF	77494
CHADWELL DR	11900	570A	SWH	77031
CHADWELL GLEN LN	3400	528C	SWH	77082
CHADWICK	7900	495J	NEH	77029
CHADWICK	10300	496J	JC	77029
CHADWICK DR	3600	613X	NEB	77578
CHAFFIN	3100	534R	SEH	77087
CHAFFINCH DR	0	405R	NWC	77493
CHAGALL LN	17200	330K	NWC	77379
CHAIN	7600	533V	SEH	77033
CHALCOS DR	8500	535Q	SEH	77017
CHALCOTT CT	0	289R	NWC	77375
CHALET	0	411D	NWC	77038
CHALET	16500	286C	SWM	77355
CHALETFORD DR	0	457A	NEC	77044
CHALETFORD DR	0	457A	NEC	77044
CHALFIELD CIR	12900	377X	NEC	77044
CHALFIELD CT	14600	377X	NEC	77044
CHALFONT	11500	369W	NWC	77065
CHALFONT CT	3300	371Q	NWC	77066
CHALFONT DR	3200	371Q	NWC	77066
CHALFORD DR	9500	528S	NEF	77083
CHALFORD DR	9700	528S	NEF	77498
CHALICE KNOLL ST	0	444D	NWC	77493
CHALICE TRAIL	0	568J	NEF	77498
CHALK HILL	0	609Z	MC	77459
CHALK MAPLE CT	11400	367U	NWC	77095
CHALK MAPLE LN	16500	367U	NWC	77095
CHALK ROCK DR	1200	372N	NWC	77067
CHALKSTONE LN	13700	415B	NEC	77396
W. CHALLE CIR	19000	332B	NCC	77373
E. CHALLE CIR	19000	332B	NCC	77373
CHALLENGER CT	2000	418H	NEC	77532
CHALLENGER DR	15100	418H	NEC	77532
CHALLENGER RD	0	487W	SWH	77094
N. CHALLENGER 7 PKWY	0	577X	SEH	77034
CHALLENGER PARK	0	658E	WB	77598
CHALLENGER SEVEN DR	10100	495M	JC	77029
CHALLIE LN	7700	411P	NWH	77088
CHALLIS PARK CT	0	410T	NWC	77040
CHALMETTE	500	658K	LC	77573
CHALMETTE	12400	496D	NEC	77015
CHALMETTE PARK	16500	367G	NWC	77429
CHALTON CT	8300	330P	NWC	77379
CHAMBERING CT	5700	525R	NEF	77407
CHAMBERLAIN	1300	413V	NCC	77093
CHAMBERLAIN	2400	414S	NCC	77093
CHAMBERLAIN DR	12800	488Q	SWH	77077
CHAMBERLAIN DR	17400	407K	NWC	77095
CHAMBERLAIN COVE	2100	484K	NEF	77494
CHAMBERS	100	419Y	BR	77532
CHAMBERS	10400	576K	SEH	77034
CHAMBLER CT	5200	330U	NWC	77069
CHAMBLY DR	500	497A	NEC	77015
CHAMBOARD LN	900	452K	NWH	77018
CHAMELEON CT	2600	572L	SWH	77045
N. CHAMFER CT	15800	419F	NEC	77532
S. CHAMFER WAY	700	419F	NEC	77532
N. CHAMFER WAY	800	419F	NEC	77532
W. CHAMFER WAY	15700	419F	NEC	77532
E. CHAMFER WAY	15700	419F	NEC	77532
CHAMISAL CT	0	376E	HM	77396
CHAMOMILE CT	16100	527Q	NEF	77083
CHAMOMILE GREEN CT	10400	369G	NWC	77070
CHAMOMILE MEADOW TRAIL	0	524D	NEF	77494
S. CHAMPAGNE CIR	15600	287R	NWC	77377
W. CHAMPAGNE CIR	21500	287R	NWC	77377
E. CHAMPAGNE CIR	21500	287R	NWC	77377
E. CHAMPAGNE CT	0	287R	NWC	77377
W. CHAMPAGNE CT	15500	287R	NWC	77377
CHAMPAGNE CT	15500	287M	NWC	77377
CHAMPAGNE DR	15600	287R	NWC	77377
CHAMPAGNE FALLS CT	16600	330P	NWC	77379
CHAMPAGNE FALLS DR	16600	330P	NWC	77379
CHAMPAIGN	13400	413H	NCC	77039
CHAMPION DR	2300	616J	PL	77581
CHAMPION LN	6700	412X	NWH	77091

Street Name	Block	Pg/Sq	Loc	Zips
CHAMPION COVE CIR	0	329V	NWC	77070
CHAMPION FOREST	0	329H	NWC	77379
CHAMPION FOREST	0	330J	NWC	77379
CHAMPION FOREST CIR	8300	330N	NWC	77379
CHAMPION FOREST DR	0	289T	NWC	77375
CHAMPION FOREST DR	10000	371W	NWC	77086
CHAMPION FOREST DR	11300	370D	NWC	77066
CHAMPION FOREST DR	13000	330T	NWC	77069
CHAMPION FOREST DR	15800	330T	NWC	77379
CHAMPION LAKE CT	25600	252S	SWM	77380
CHAMPION LAKE DR	400	252S	SWM	77380
CHAMPION LAKES ESTS	17100	329K	NWC	77375
CHAMPION LAKES TRAIL	16000	329K	NWC	77375
CHAMPION OAKS RD	28400	248D	SWM	77354
CHAMPION PINES DR	7300	330K	NWC	77379
CHAMPION PLACE DR	0	370B	NWC	77069
CHAMPIONS CT	4400	619Z	LC	77573
CHAMPIONS DR	2200	610E	MC	77459
CHAMPIONS DR	13000	370B	NWC	77069
CHAMPIONS DR	15800	330S	NWC	77379
CHAMPIONS DR	28600	246B	SWM	77355
CHAMPIONS ARBOR DR	0	369D	NWC	77070
CHAMPIONS BEND CIR	1	330Y	NWC	77069
CHAMPIONS BEND DR	0	330Y	NWC	77069
CHAMPIONS CENTRE CT	7000	370A	NWC	77069
CHAMPIONS CENTRE DR	12800	370F	NWH	77066
CHAMPIONS CENTRE DR	13500	370E	NWC	77069
CHAMPIONS CEN ESTS DR	7000	370E	NWC	77069
W. CHAMPIONS COLONY	1	370B	NWC	77069
E. CHAMPIONS COLONY	1	370C	NWC	77069
CHAMPIONS COURT TRAIL	1	330X	NWC	77069
CHAMPIONS COURT WAY	1	330X	NWC	77069
CHAMPIONS COVE CIR	16500	329V	NWC	77379
CHAMPIONS COVE CT	16500	329V	NWC	77379
CHAMPIONS COVE DR	9500	329V	NWC	77379
CHAMPIONS GLEN DR	5600	330X	NWC	77069
CHAMPIONS GREEN DR	0	371N	NWC	77066
CHAMPIONS GREEN DR	0	371S	NWC	77066
CHAMPIONS GROVE CT	11700	370H	NWC	77066
CHAMPIONS GROVE LN	11700	370M	NWC	77066
CHAMPIONS HAMLET LN	0	330Y	NWC	77069
CHAMPIONSHIP DR	0	656X	FR	77546
CHAMPIONSHIP LN	14200	330W	NWC	77069
CHAMPIONS LAKEWAY	17000	329K	NWC	77375
CHAMPIONS PARK DR	13000	370F	NWC	77069
CHAMPIONS PLACE	1	370B	NWC	77069
CHAMPIONS PLAZA DR	6800	370F	NWC	77069
CHAMPIONS POINT	0	370M	NWC	77066
CHAMPIONS POINT LN	0	370M	NWC	77066
CHAMPION SPRINGS BLVD	16800	330N	NWC	77379
CHAMPION SPRINGS CIR	8800	330N	NWC	77379
CHAMPION SPRINGS CT	8800	330N	NWC	77379
CHAMPIONS RIDGE RD	28400	248D	SWM	77354
CHAMPIONS TRACE LN	0	370M	NWC	77066
CHAMPIONS WALK LN	11600	370M	NWC	77066
CHAMPIONS WAY LN	5300	370M	NWC	77066
CHAMPION TRAIL	0	444S	KT	77493
CHAMPION VILLA DR	1	330X	NWC	77069
CHAMPION VILLAGE CT	6800	370B	NWC	77069
CHAMPION VILLAGE DR	14100	370B	NWC	77069
CHAMPION WOODS DR	11200	329K	NWC	77375
CHAMPLAIN BEND	5200	491Q	SWH	77056
CHAMPOUX	33300	242F	WCO	77484
CHAMPS	700	498B	CV	77530
CHANAS CT	0	290R	NWC	77388
CHANAY LN	2200	296V	NEH	77339
CHANCE CT	3000	613U	NEB	77584
CHANCE LN	700	501M	BT	77521
CHANCEL DR	7900	570G	MC	77071
CHANCEL ARCH CT	0	258E	SEM	77357
CHANCELLOR DR	6600	330Q	NWC	77379
CHANCELLORSVILLE CT	2500	658P	LC	77573
CHANCERY RD	13700	577W	SEH	77034
CHANCEWOOD LN	8100	334R	NCC	77338
CHANDELEUR COVE	0	609Y	MC	77459
CHANDLER	5200	492L	SWH	77007
CHANDLER DR	100	501R	BT	77521
CHANDLER LN	3300	538S	DP	77536
CHANDLER CHASE CT	13000	377X	NEC	77044
CHANDLER COVE LN	0	577J	PA	77504
N. CHANDLER CREEK CIR	0	250B	WD	77381
S. CHANDLER CREEK CIR	1	250B	WD	77381
CHANDLER CREEK CT	1	250B	WD	77381
CHANDLER HOLLOW	0	328X	NWC	77429
CHANDLER HOLLOW LN	0	609U	MC	77459
CHANDLER HOLLOW LN	15100	457U	NEC	77049
CHANDLER POINT DR	0	325S	HK	77447
CHANDLER RIDGE LN	16300	326R	NWC	77429
CHANDLERS WAY	0	246V	SWM	77355
CHANDLERS WAY	0	448D	NWC	77041
CHANDON MIST DR	0	406Y	NWC	77449
CHANDON MIST DR	0	406Y	NWC	77449
CHANEL DR	0	457A	NEC	77044
CHANEY ALLEN	7900	412N	NWH	77088
CHANG-AN DR	100	570P	MC	77489
CHANGING OAK RIDGE CT	15000	487Z	SWC	77082
CHANNCELORSVILLE LN	0	527P	NEF	77083
CHANNEL BEND DR	0	366L	NWC	77433
CHANNELBROOK LN	6200	290U	NWC	77379
CHANNEL CITY RD	0	497Z	SEH	77015
CHANNEL CITY RD	100	537D	PA	77503
CHANNELS CT	1100	419B	NEC	77532
CHANNELSIDE	7700	535C	SEH	77012
CHANNELVIEW DR	15900	498G	CV	77530
CHANNEL WOOD DR	0	366L	NWC	77433
CHANNELWOOD LN	2300	486N	SWC	77450
CHANNING SPRINGS DR	0	293K	SEM	77386
CHANNING SPRINGS DR	0	293G	SEM	77386
CHANNING WAY	16200	367L	CY	77429
CHANTALLE DR	6600	406V	NWC	77449
CHANTELOUP	0	573N	SEH	77047
CHANTEL WAY	0	525A	NEF	77469
CHANTILLY CIR	4600	452L	NWH	77018
CHANTILLY LN	900	452K	NWH	77018
CHANTILLY LN	4800	451L	NWH	77092
CHANTRY DR	5000	447B	NWC	77084
CHANUTE RD	17200	373H	NEH	77032
CHAPADA HIGHLANDS DR	0	406H	NWC	77433
CHAPAL GATE LN	14800	377Y	NEH	77044
CHAPARRAL CIR	22800	296C	SEM	77365
CHAPARRAL CT	22800	296G	SEM	77365
CHAPARRAL DR	0	659W	LC	77573
CHAPARRAL DR	1900	449V	NWH	77043
CHAPARRAL DR	3700	501M	BT	77521
CHAPARRAL DR	22800	296C	SEM	77365
CHAPARRAL RD	29200	323W	NWC	77447
CHAPARRAL BERRY DR	0	406H	NWC	77433
CHAPARRAL CROSSING	0	659W	LC	77573
CHAPARRAL WAY	3200	251X	SWM	77380
CHAPEL BELLE LN	300	490K	BH	77024
CHAPEL BEND DR	3200	331T	NWC	77068
CHAPEL BROOK DR	5400	330U	NWC	77069

Street Name	Block	Pg/Sq	Loc	Zips
CHAPELBROOK LN	14700	408G	NWC	77095
CHAPEL CANYOU LN	0	527S	NEF	77407
CHAPEL CONE LN	0	484F	NEF	77494
CHAPEL COVE CT	14700	327W	NWC	77429
CHAPEL CREEK CT	2500	371L	NWC	77067
CHAPEL CREST DR	0	296X	SEM	77339
CHAPELFIELD LN	0	457P	NEC	77049
CHAPEL GLEN CT	20400	486P	SWC	77450
CHAPEL HILL DR	10500	528Z	SWH	77099
CHAPEL HOLLOW LN	14200	327Z	NWC	77429
CHAPEL LAKE DR	15500	367C	NWC	77429
CHAPELLE CT	11700	489J	SWH	77077
CHAPEL MEADOW LN	0	526F	NEF	77450
CHAPEL OAKS DR	12100	371H	NWC	77067
CHAPEL PARK CT	17000	578Y	SEH	77059
CHAPEL PARK WAY	16900	578Y	SEH	77059
CHAPEL PINE CT	9400	329M	NWC	77379
CHAPEL PINE DR	17200	329M	NWC	77379
CHAPEL PINES DR	16800	330K	NWC	77379
CHAPEL RIDGE LN	25300	293N	NCC	77373
CHAPEL ROCK LN	0	253K	SEM	77386
CHAPEL SQUARE DR	3400	331F	NWC	77388
CHAPELSTONE CT	0	416Z	NEC	77044
CHAPEL VALLEY CT	0	366Z	NWC	77433
CHAPELWOOD CT	400	490L	PP	77024
CHAPELWOOD LN	11800	490K	BH	77024
CHAPEREL DR	4700	614Z	PL	77584
CHAPIN	0	373Q	NCC	77032
CHAPIS	2400	414W	NEH	77093
CHAPLIN	15100	373Q	NCC	77032
CHAPLIN PLACE DR	2800	376K	NEC	77396
CHAPMAN	0	577X	SEH	77034
CHAPMAN	800	493H	NEH	77002
CHAPMAN	1500	493H	NEH	77009
CHAPMAN	3500	453V	NEH	77009
CHAPMAN	6100	453V	NEH	77022
CHAPMAN	17800	418R	NEC	77044
CHAPMAN BLUFF DR	0	293L	SEM	77386
CHAPMAN FALLS DR	0	524K	NWF	77406
CHAPMAN LAKE CT	0	377G	NEH	77346
CHAPMANS	0	420A	NEC	77532
CHAPMANS COUNT RD	18300	366K	NWC	77433
CHAPPARAL CT	0	609C	MC	77459
CHAPPARAL LN	23100	296C	SEM	77365
CHAPPARAL WAY	3200	251X	SWM	77380
CHAPPEL HILL DR	300	656H	FR	77546
CHAPPEL HILL DR	4900	609K	MC	77459
CHAPPELL LN	2100	610P	MC	77459
CHAPPELL KNOLL DR	20600	326S	NWC	77433
CHAPPLEWOOD DR	3100	613X	NEB	77584
CHAPPLEWOOD DR	3100	613X	NEB	77584
CHAPWOOD CT	900	292B	NCC	77373
CHARA CT	19800	366V	NWC	77433
CHARADE DR	4700	371A	NWC	77066
CHARBONNEAU	0	579Q	SEC	77507
CHARDONNAY DR	1300	489P	SWH	77077
CHARIDGES CT	13700	617A	SEH	77034
CHARIDGES DR	400	617A	SEH	77034
CHARING CROSS DR	12200	569D	SWH	77031
CHARING CROSS WAY	1200	336H	NEH	77339
CHARING WAY	0	572E	SWH	77045
CHARING WAY	0	572E	SWH	77045
CHARIOT DR	11400	529W	SWH	77477
CHARIOT RD	18600	257G	RF	77357
CHARIS PLACE	1	331D	NWC	77388
CHARISS GLEN DR	100	659D	LC	77573
CHARLBROOK DR	9800	528S	NEF	77498
CHARLENES WAY DR	0	484S	NEF	77494
CHARLES	0	413Y	NEH	77076
CHARLES	100	536G	PA	77506
CHARLES	4700	581W	PA	77586
CHARLES	3000	660H	BC	77518
CHARLES AVE	1	541D	BT	77520
CHARLES AVE	3300	614W	NEB	77584
CHARLES CIR	0	285M	SWM	77355
CHARLES LN	2600	528X	NEF	77498
CHARLES RD	100	413X	NEH	77076
CHARLES RD	200	335V	HM	77338
CHARLES RD	1100	412T	NWH	77088
CHARLES RD	1500	414W	NEH	77093
CHARLES RD	11200	409P	NWC	77041
CHARLES E SELECMAN DR	12200	569G	SF	77477
CHARLESMONT	7600	415W	NEH	77016
CHARLESMONT	8000	415X	NEH	77078
CHARLES OATES	0	496K	JC	77029
CHARLES PLACE	700	501M	BT	77521
S. CHARLESTON	1	569N	SG	77478
N. CHARLESTON	1	569N	SG	77478
CHARLESTON	100	657E	FR	77546
CHARLESTON	2400	533G	SEH	77021
CHARLESTON PARK DR	1	532S	SWH	77025
CHARLESTON SQUARE	500	336W	HM	77338
CHARLESTOWN COLONY CT	6000	408X	NWC	77084
CHARLESTOWN COLONY DR	5500	408X	NWC	77084
CHARLETON MILL LN	14800	528W	NEF	77498
CHARLIE	7400	412S	NWH	77088
CHARLIE LN	0	377S	NEC	77044
CHARLIE VOIX AVE	500	497A	NEC	77015
CHARLINE	3000	533K	SWH	77054
CHARLISA SPRINGS DR	20400	446G	NWC	77449
CHARLMONT DR	14700	528N	NEF	77083
CHARLMONT DR	14800	527R	NEF	77083
CHARLOTTE	0	414T	NCC	77093
CHARLOTTE	5800	532C	WU	77005
CHARLOTTE DR	0	245V	SWM	77355
CHARLOTTE DR	2000	502P	BT	77520
CHARLOTTES BEQUEST DR	12000	366K	NWC	77433
CHARLSON PLACE	100	501L	BT	77521
CHARLTON	100	496W	GP	77547
CHARLTON CT	9800	335Q	HM	77338
CHARLTON GREEN LN	24500	250Z	NWC	77389
CHARLTON HOUSE LN	1700	445S	NWC	77493
CHARLTON OAKS CT	1700	485K	NEF	77494
CHARLTON PARK DR	1200	488F	SWH	77077
CHARLTON WAY DR	13900	488F	SWH	77077
CHARLYNN OAKS DR	13900	329Z	NWC	77070
CHARLYNN OAKS DR	14000	370A	NWC	77070
CHARMING CREEK CT	6000	338E	NEH	77345
CHARMING RIVER DR	2700	293W	NCC	77373
CHARMONT RD	9700	579B	LP	77571
CHARNCROSS LN	0	289R	NWC	77375
CHARNEY LN	8700	412K	NWC	77088
CHARNWICK CT	5200	330U	NWC	77069
CHARNWOOD	1100	453H	NEH	77022
CHAROLAIS DR	15600	327Z	CY	77429
CHARPIOT	0	377T	NEC	77044
CHARPIOT LN	7000	375P	NEH	77396
CHARPIOT LN	12500	456M	NEC	77049
S. CHARPIOT LN	15800	375P	NEH	77396
N. CHARPIOT LN	15900	375P	NEH	77396
CHARRIN DR	5300	374Z	NCC	77032
CHARRINGTON DR	6000	250Z	NWC	77389

Street Name	Block	Pg/Sq	Loc	Zips
CHARRITON DR	600	413E	NCC	77060
CHARRITON DR	1500	413H	NCC	77039
CHARRITON DR	2300	414G	NCC	77039
CHARRO	1800	656U	FR	77546
CHART DR	1400	419A	NEC	77532
CHART DR	1800	418D	NEC	77532
CHARTER LN	31500	322C	WCO	77484
CHARTER BAY DR	0	532U	SWH	77054
CHARTER GROVE DR	11200	370R	NWC	77066
CHARTERHOUSE WAY	0	568B	SG	77498
CHARTER LAKE CIR	0	524B	NEF	77494
CHARTER LAKE LN	0	524B	NEF	77494
CHARTERLAWN CIR	9300	329Q	NWC	77070
CHARTERMILL LN	0	366E	NWC	77433
CHARTERMOSS CIR	9400	329Q	NWC	77070
CHARTER OAKS	2900	414S	NEH	77093
CHARTER OAKS CT	2400	613Q	NEB	77584
CHARTER PARK LN	0	524H	NEF	77494
CHARTER PINE	9300	329U	NWC	77070
CHARTER POINTE CT	2000	619Z	LC	77573
CHARTER RIDGE DR	9400	329Q	NWC	77070
CHARTER ROCK DR	16100	329U	NWC	77070
CHARTERSTONE DR	16000	329Q	NWC	77070
CHARTERWOOD DR	10000	329T	NWC	77070
CHART HOUSE CT	15900	377Q	NEC	77044
CHARTLEY FALLS DR	14100	377X	NEC	77044
CHARTRES	1	493R	SEH	77002
CHARTRES	600	493R	SEH	77003
CHARTRES	4000	493X	SWH	77004
CHARTRES	5400	533B	SWH	77004
CHARTRESE AVE	6700	502C	BT	77521
CHARTREUSE CT	11400	529B	SWH	77082
CHARTREUSE WAY	3300	489X	SWH	77082
CHARTREUSE WAY CT	11400	529B	SWH	77082
CHARTWELL CT	11600	490F	BH	77024
CHARTWELL DR	12200	569D	SWH	77031
CHARWELL CROSSING	13500	330Y	NWC	77069
CHARWON	4400	414Q	NEC	77093
CHARWOOD CT	3600	331T	NWC	77068
CHAS LN	800	452C	NWH	77091
CHASE	1400	494A	NEH	77026
CHASE	7400	454J	NEH	77093
CHASE BRODERICK LN	0	366U	NWC	77433
CHASEBROOK TRAIL	2300	297V	NEH	77345
CHASECREEK DR	7600	570V	SWH	77489
CHASEFIELD DR	7800	570V	SWH	77489
CHASEGROVE LN	0	526J	NEF	77407
CHASE HARBOR	5500	449A	NWC	77041
CHASE HARBOR LN	0	612K	PL	77545
CHASEHILL DR	15100	570V	SWH	77489
CHASE HOLLOW LN	0	406C	NWC	77433
CHASE LAKE DR	11800	489N	SWH	77077
CHASELAND LN	12800	488Q	SWH	77077
CHASELOCH	17200	329M	NWC	77379
CHASEMONT DR	14500	570V	SWH	77489
CHASEMORE DR	16100	329V	NWC	77379
CHASEPOINT DR	7700	570V	SWH	77489
CHASERIDGE DR	14900	570V	SWH	77489
CHASESTONE CT	20000	486G	SWC	77450
CHASEVIEW DR	7700	570V	SWH	77489
CHASEVILLAGE DR	14500	570V	SWH	77489
CHASEWAY DR	7700	570V	SWH	77489
CHASEWICK CIR	4100	371B	NWC	77014
CHASEWIND DR	7700	570V	SWH	77489
CHASEWOOD DR	6800	571S	SWH	77489
CHASEWOOD DR	7100	570V	SWH	77489
CHASEWOOD MEADOWS LOOP	0	570V	SWH	77489
CHASEWOOD PARK DR	20400	329Y	NWC	77070
CHASON CT	17000	407Q	NWC	77084
CHASTE TREE LN	19900	335N	NCC	77338
CHASTON DR	13000	408M	NWC	77041
CHASWORTH DR	13200	408R	NWC	77041
CHATAM LN	12000	490J	BH	77024
CHATAM GLEN LN	0	526K	NEF	77407
CHATANOOGA	0	247Z	SWM	77355
CHATBURN DR	1800	489P	SWH	77077
CHATDALE LN	0	326R	NWC	77429
CHATEAU	1300	420A	NEC	77532
CHATEAU	7900	455P	NEH	77028
CHATEAU	13500	288X	NWC	77377
CHATEAU LN	10400	252F	SEM	77385
CHATEAU BEND CT	1700	486K	SWC	77450
CHATEAU BEND DR	20100	486K	SWC	77450
CHATEAU COVE	3700	293G	SEM	77386
CHATEAU CREEK WAY	4400	294N	SEM	77386
CHATEAUCREST CT	0	573Y	SEC	77047
CHATEAU FOREST DR	8900	411T	NWH	77088
CHATEAU GATE CT	0	375Y	NEC	77396
CHATEAU LAKE DR	26900	296X	NEC	77339
CHATEAU LAKE DR	26900	296X	NEC	77339
CHATEAU PARK LN	0	253N	SEM	77385
CHATEAU POINT LN	7700	408L	NWC	77041
CHATEAU RIDGE CT	19300	286G	NWC	77377
CHATEAU SPRINGS CT	28500	293E	SEM	77386
CHATEAU TRAIL	11800	328V	NWC	77377
CHATEAU WOODS LN	23100	285X	NWC	77447
CHATEAU WOODS PKWY DR	200	252G	SEM	77385
CHATFIELD	9600	532T	SWH	77025
CHATFIELD MANOR LN	13000	328F	NWC	77377
CHATFIELD RUN CT	0	366Y	NWC	77433
CHATFORD HOLLOW LN	2500	371D	NWC	77014
CHATHAM AVE	0	568S	SG	77479
CHATHAM LN	4000	492S	SWH	77027
CHATHAM COVE	0	609Y	MC	77459
CHATHAM HILL DR	5200	408W	NWC	77084
CHATHAM ISLAND LN	6400	570D	SWH	77035
CHATHAM LAKE LN	0	526E	NEF	77450
CHATHAM SPRINGS LN	0	406M	NWC	77433
CHATHAM WAY DR	17500	407Y	NWC	77084
CHATHAM WOODS DR	6000	407X	NWC	77084
CHATSWORTH	0	407V	NWC	77084
CHATSWORTH	0	491G	SWH	77024
CHATSWORTH DR	8500	491C	SWH	77024
CHATSWORTH SKY CT	0	377F	NEC	77346
CHATTANOOGA	8900	578D	LP	77571
CHATTAROY PLACE	1900	568C	SG	77478
CHATTEN WAY	11400	490C	HE	77024
CHATTERBIRD LN	1	251R	WD	77380
CHATTERLY LN	0	373J	NCC	77060
CHATTERTON DR	10100	449V	NWH	77043
CHATTERTON DR	11000	449T	NWH	77043
CHATWOOD DR	3500	613G	NEB	77584
CHATWOOD DR	8800	455H	NEH	77078
CHAU'S CT	22800	485Y	NEF	77494
CHAUCER DR	5400	532C	SWH	77005
CHAUCER LN	0	502L	BT	77521
CHAUCER OAKS CT	11400	489X	SWH	77082
CHAUMONT DR	12700	617E	SEH	77089
CHAVILE	12900	368M	NWC	77429
CHAVILE	13000	369E	NWC	77429
CHAZEN DR	1600	496K	JC	77029
CHAZENWOOD DR	0	409F	NWC	77064

Street Name	Block	Pg/Sq	Loc	Zips
CHEAM CIR	700	496D	NEH	77015
CHEANEY CT	11500	371P	NWC	77066
CHEANEY DR	3300	371P	NWC	77066
CHEATHAM	400	298X	NEH	77336
CHEATHAM LN	1400	496M	NEH	77015
CHECKERBERRY	2000	615V	PL	77581
CHECKERBERRY PARK LN	10000	289U	NWC	77375
CHECKERBOARD	9700	531X	SWH	77096
CHEDDAR CT	24100	289D	NWC	77375
CHEDDAR RIDGE DR	1000	329H	NWC	77379
CHEDDINGTON DR	200	485C	SWC	77450
CHEDWORTH DR	400	618J	SEH	77062
CHEECA LODGE LN	7400	377C	NEC	77346
CHEENA DR	4000	532S	SWH	77025
CHEENA DR	4300	531X	SWH	77096
CHEENA DR	6000	530Z	SWH	77096
CHEER	8900	490X	SWH	77063
CHEETHAM	0	366P	NWC	77433
CHEETHAM DR	0	366N	NWC	77433
CHEEVES DR	9700	415W	NEH	77016
CHEEVES DR	10000	415N	NEH	77016
CHELMSFORD LN	8700	330T	NWC	77379
CHELSEA	500	531L	BL	77401
CHELSEA BLVD	1	493W	SWH	77006
CHELSEA BLVD	800	493W	SWH	77002
CHELSEA LN	200	616X	FR	77546
CHELSEA LN	1100	616X	PL	77581
CHELSEA BEND CT	8200	527P	NEF	77083
CHELSEABROOK CT	8800	616A	SEC	77089
CHELSEABROOK LN	10300	616A	SEC	77089
CHELSEA CANYON CT	20200	526A	NEF	77450
CHELSEA CREEK LN	0	293E	SEM	77386
CHELSEA ELM CT	12000	411D	NWC	77038
CHELSEA FAIR LN	5400	291W	NWC	77379
CHELSEAHURST LN	14000	573T	SEC	77047
CHELSEA KNOLL LN	10900	371R	NWC	77067
CHELSEA OAK	11500	369S	NWC	77065
CHELSEA OAK ST	11100	369T	NWC	77065
CHELSEA PARK CT	20400	486K	SWC	77450
CHELSEA PARK DR	0	486K	SWC	77450
W. CHELSEA PLACE	400	620E	EL	77586
CHELSEA RIDGE CT	2200	486P	SWC	77450
CHELSEA VALE DR	0	611W	FS	77545
CHELSEA WALK DR	11300	371P	NWC	77066
CHELSEA WAY	1300	336H	NEH	77339
CHELSEN BRIDGE LN	23000	485B	SWC	77450
CHELSEY CIR	0	525Z	NEF	77406
CHELSHAM LN	15300	458W	NEC	77530
CHELSHURST WAY	1200	329B	NWC	77375
CHELSHURST WAY CT	1200	329B	NWC	77375
CHELSTON CT	2300	568C	SG	77478
CHELSWORTH DR	8700	527R	NEF	77083
CHELTENHAM DR	700	486B	SWC	77450
CHELTENHAM DR	5500	531S	SWH	77096
CHELTON	13100	497E	NEH	77015
CHELWOOD PLACE	13700	330Y	NWC	77069
CHEMICAL RD	9700	579V	SEC	77507
CHENEVERT	1	493Q	DT	77002
CHENEVERT	600	493Q	DT	77003
CHENEVERT	800	493Q	DT	77010
CHENEVERT	1200	493Q	DT	77003
CHENEVERT	2300	493U	SWH	77004
CHENEVERT	5200	533A	SWH	77004
CHENNAULT RD	4900	534N	SEH	77033
CHER CT	8900	410K	NWC	77040
CHERANNA DR	0	332X	NWC	77090
CHERBOURG RD	4500	534N	SEH	77033
CHERIDAN CIR	6100	524Y	NEF	77406
CHERIE COVE DR	0	411L	NWC	77088
CHERIE CREST CT	5300	411L	NWC	77088
CHERIE GROVE CIR	0	411L	NWC	77088
CHERILYNN CT	14100	374X	NCC	77032
CHERISH TRAIL	5500	525A	NEF	77494
CHERISTA	0	295L	SEM	77365
CHEROKEE	0	461S	NEC	77521
CHEROKEE	600	536Q	PA	77506
CHEROKEE	1300	538R	DP	77536
CHEROKEE	4500	492Z	SWH	77005
CHEROKEE	5300	532D	SWH	77005
CHEROKEE	9600	462Y	BT	77521
CHEROKEE	29000	323G	NWC	77484
CHEROKEE DR	23600	295F	SEM	77365
CHEROKEE RD	26700	248M	SWM	77354
CHEROKEE BLUFF DR	19400	328D	NWC	77375
CHEROKEE HOLLOW DR	1200	485G	SWC	77450
CHEROKEE LAKE LN	0	377G	NEH	77346
CHEROKEE TRACE	100	297J	SEM	77365
CHERRINGTON CT	23000	485Q	NEF	77450
CHERRINGTON DR	2000	485Q	NEF	77450
CHERRY	0	459Q	HG	77562
S. CHERRY	100	288R	TB	77375
N. CHERRY	100	288G	TB	77375
CHERRY	1100	500Z	BT	77520
CHERRY	1600	282U	WL	77484
CHERRY	4500	614M	PL	77581
CHERRY	21000	256J	SEM	77357
CHERRY CT	300	579C	LP	77571
CHERRY LN	1200	419T	NEC	77532
CHERRY LN	1200	454W	NEH	77026
CHERRY LN	2100	537S	PA	77502
CHERRYBARK LN	0	489G	SWH	77079
CHERRYBARK OAK DR	3200	487Z	SWC	77082
CHERRY BEND DR	1700	489S	SWH	77077
CHERRY BLOOM TRAIL	0	488G	SWH	77079
CHERRY BLOSSOM DR	0	613E	NEB	77584
CHERRY BLOSSOM DR	5100	657V	LC	77573
CHERRY BLOSSUM DR	8200	460Q	NEC	77562
CHERRY BRANCH DR	0	293G	SEM	77386
CHERRYBROOK LN	1400	537S	PA	77502
CHERRY CANYON LN	21200	289U	NWC	77375
CHERRY COVE LN	0	366J	NWC	77433
CHERRY CREEK CT	1400	610F	MC	77459
CHERRY CREEK DR	0	612R	PL	77584
CHERRY CREEK DR	3100	610F	MC	77459
CHERRY CREEK DR	5400	536S	SEH	77017
CHERRY CREEK BEND	12500	449A	NWC	77041
CHERRY CREEK BEND CT	5500	449A	NWC	77041
CHERRYDALE DR	6500	534U	SEH	77087
CHERRYDOWN DR	13600	568F	SG	77498
CHERRY FOREST DR	3200	411V	NWH	77088
CHERRY FORK DR	0	369P	NWC	77065
CHERRYGLADE CT	0	417W	NEC	77044
CHERRY GLEN CT	2500	298W	NEH	77345
CHERRY GREEN WAY	0	445P	NWC	77493
CHERRY GROVE CT	3000	578S	SEH	77059
CHERRY HAVEN CIR	20400	446S	NWC	77449
CHERRYHILL	6000	534P	SEH	77087
CHERRY HILL DR	24200	284G	WCO	77447
CHERRY HILLS DR	0	409F	JV	77064
CHERRY HILLS DR	2100	659D	LC	77573
CHERRY HILLS DR	2900	610F	MC	77459
CHERRY HILLS LN	3700	577C	PA	77505

Street Name	Block	Pg/Sq	Loc	Zips
CHERRY HILLS RD	6300	330X	NWC	77069
CHERRY HILLS RD	6900	370A	NWC	77069
CHERRY HOLLOW LN	13700	488X	SWH	77082
CHERRYHURST	1600	492V	SWH	77006
CHERRYKNOLL DR	11600	489P	SWH	77077
CHERRY LAKE CIR	0	288S	NWC	77377
CHERRY LAUREL	1	298E	NEC	77336
CHERRY LAUREL	3500	296Y	NEH	77339
CHERRY LAUREL CIR	24200	297E	SEM	77365
CHERRY LAUREL DR	300	288M	TB	77375
CHERRY LAUREL DR	1800	252Z	SEM	77386
CHERRY LIMB DR	10200	529W	SWH	77099
CHERRY MEADOW DR	3700	414K	NCC	77039
CHERRY MILL CT	2900	578X	SEH	77059
CHERRY MOUND DR	13700	488E	SWH	77077
CHERRY OAK CIR	4100	411U	NWH	77088
CHERRYOAK LN	4400	411U	NWH	77088
CHERRY OAKS LN	19700	337U	NEC	77346
CHERRY OAK WAY	0	578U	SEH	77059
CHERRY ORCHARD CT	2800	446T	NWC	77449
CHERRY ORCHARD LN	20300	446T	NWC	77449
CHERRY PARK DR	7100	408J	NWC	77095
CHERRY PLACE CT	7800	337V	NEC	77346
CHERRY QUARTZ CT	0	524G	NEF	77494
CHERRY RANCH DR	0	484R	NEF	77494
CHERRY RIDGE	0	288M	TB	77375
CHERRY RIDGE DR	1600	489P	SWH	77077
CHERRY RUN	6300	408T	NWC	77084
CHERRYSHIRE CT	8200	527Q	NEF	77083
CHERRYSHIRE DR	16100	527P	NEF	77083
CHERRY SPRINGS CT	1400	610F	MC	77459
CHERRY SPRINGS DR	900	412A	NWC	77038
CHERRY SPRINGS DR	2900	610F	MC	77459
CHERRY SPRINGS LN	400	292U	NCC	77373
CHERRYSTONE DR	0	334R	NCC	77338
CHERRY TREE	5500	451E	NWH	77092
CHERRY TREE LN	100	616Z	FR	77546
CHERRYTREE GROVE DR	18500	447N	NWC	77084
CHERRYTREE PARK CIR	1900	618B	SEH	77062
CHERRYTREE RIDGE LN	2100	618F	SEH	77062
CHERRY VALLEY DR	100	338M	NEH	77336
CHERRYVILLE DR	2100	411D	NWC	77038
CHERRYWOOD	100	531L	BL	77401
CHERRYWOOD CIR	5100	657V	LC	77573
CHERRYWOOD BEND DR	0	366V	NWC	77433
CHERTON CT	0	572E	SWH	77045
CHERTON CT	0	572E	SWH	77045
CHERTSEY CIR	1400	457Z	NEC	77530
CHERYL	14300	570M	SWH	77085
CHERYL	31000	247Z	SWM	77362
CHERYL CT	2700	609B	MC	77459
CHERYL DR	2000	615K	PL	77581
CHERYL LYNNE LN	3800	572E	SWH	77045
CHESAPEAKE	1800	501W	BT	77520
CHESAPEAKE CT	3500	613Y	NEB	77584
CHESAPEAKE BAY CT	1700	447W	NWH	77084
CHESAPEAKE WAY	5200	491U	SWH	77056
CHESAPEKE BEND LN	3000	446N	NWC	77449
CHESHAM CT	12100	569D	SWH	77031
CHESHIRE LN	1000	452G	NWH	77018
CHESHIRE LN	5500	451L	NWH	77092
CHESHIRE BEND LN	15701	408W	NWC	77084
CHESHIRE EDGE LN	0	484J	NEF	77494
CHESHIRE GROVE LN	16500	332N	NWC	77090
CHESHIRE OAKS DR	0	532X	SWH	77054
CHESHIRE PARK RD	6800	411J	NWC	77088
CHESHIRE PLACE DR	16700	527N	NEF	77083
CHESHIREVALE	8300	491A	HC	77024
CHESHUNT LN	15300	458W	NEC	77530
S. CHESKA LN	1	490L	PP	77024
N. CHESKA LN	1	490L	PP	77024
CHESLYN CT	9400	289R	NWC	77375
CHESNEY DOWNS DR	9000	528N	NEF	77083
CHESNEY DOWNS DR	9100	527R	NEF	77083
CHESSGATE CT	1800	485M	SWC	77450
CHESSGATE FALLS BLVD	0	294J	SEM	77386
CHESSINGTON DR	11600	569D	SWH	77031
CHESSINGTON DR	12400	570E	SWH	77031
CHESSIRE	1	488L	SWH	77077
CHESSNUT GLEN DR	3500	291Y	NWC	77388
CHESSWOOD CIR	2100	568C	SG	77478
CHESSWOOD DR	11500	529B	SWH	77072
CHESTER	4100	492H	SWH	77007
CHESTER	17800	418R	NEC	77044
CHESTER DR	0	420J	NEC	77532
CHESTER DR	100	656C	FR	77546
CHESTER DR	2800	614R	PL	77584
CHESTER BEND LN	0	484P	NEF	77494
CHESTERBROOK DR	12300	569H	SWH	77031
CHESTERFIELD DR	9300	573F	SEH	77051
CHESTERFIELD LN	3100	569J	SF	77477
CHESTER FORT DR	2100	293S	NCC	77373
CHESTER GABLES CT	13700	528Q	SWC	77083
CHESTER GABLES DR	13600	528Q	SWC	77083
CHESTERGATE DR	4200	333D	NCC	77373
CHESTER GLEN CROSSING	0	291A	NWC	77389
CHESTER KNOLL CT	0	484N	NEF	77494
CHESTER MEADOW LN	0	487A	SWC	77494
CHESTER MILLS CROSSING	0	526N	NEF	77407
CHESTER OAK DR	0	527F	NEF	77083
CHESTER PARK DR	9100	409C	NWC	77064
CHESTERPOINT DR	1300	252Q	SEM	77386
CHESTERSHIRE DR	3100	537L	PA	77503
CHESTER SPRINGS LN	0	406X	NWC	77449
CHESTERTON CT	24200	485T	NEF	77494
CHESTERWICK DR	21900	485M	SWC	77450
CHESTERWOOD DR	900	616X	PL	77581
S. CHESTNUT	100	288H	TB	77375
N. CHESTNUT	100	288H	TB	77375
CHESTNUT	200	459Q	HG	77562
CHESTNUT	200	500A	BT	77520
CHESTNUT	1500	493H	NEH	77009
CHESTNUT	4800	531G	BL	77401
CHESTNUT CIR	0	657L	LC	77598
CHESTNUT CIR	2500	614S	NEB	77584
CHESTNUT LN	2100	537S	PA	77502
CHESTNUT BEND ST	0	292D	SEM	77386
CHESTNUT BLUFF DR	17300	367X	NWC	77095
CHESTNUT BOUGH	1100	458W	NEC	77530
CHESTNUT BRANCH TRAIL	0	327R	NWC	77429
CHESTNUT BROOK CT	19600	446Q	NWC	77084
CHESTER BUSINESS PARK DR	400	288H	TB	77375
CHESTNUT COVE CIR	0	366J	NWC	77433
CHESTNUT CREEK CT	17100	330J	NWC	77379
CHESTNUT CREEK WAY	10000	613K	PL	77584
CHESTNUT CREST DR	18700	377D	NEC	77346
CHESTNUT FALLS DR	14400	326T	NWC	77433
CHESTNUTFIELD CT	19400	486D	SWC	77094
CHESTNUT FOREST DR	8200	411K	NWC	77088
CHESTNUT GLEN	15000	327Z	NWC	77429
CHESTNUT GROVE	4400	658N	LC	77573
CHESTNUT GROVE LN	1400	337D	NEH	77345

Street Name	Block	Pg/Sq	Loc	Zips
CHESTNUT GROVE LN	1700	338A	NEH	77345
CHESTNUT HILL CT	1	251X	WD	77380
CHESTNUT HILLS CT	700	486B	SWC	77450
CHESTNUT HILLS DR	20600	486A	SWC	77450
CHESTNUT HOLLOW CT	12400	377A	NEC	77346
CHESTNUT ISLE CT	5400	297P	NEH	77345
CHESTNUT MILLS RD	2400	371H	NWC	77067
CHESTNUT OAK DR	1700	610P	MC	77459
CHESTNUT OAK LN	0	578Y	SEH	77059
CHESTNUT OAK PLACE	2300	251U	WD	77380
CHESTNUT PARK DR	0	612X	NWB	77545
CHESTNUT PASS WAY	0	294A	SEM	77386
CHESTNUT PEAK CT	6200	298W	NEH	77345
CHESTNUT PINES DR		484W	NEF	77494
CHESTNUT PLACE	19500	486D	SWC	77094
CHESTNUT RIDGE CT	4400	610P	MC	77459
CHESTNUT RIDGE RD	1100	336E	NEH	77339
CHESTNUT RIDGE RD	18300	257B	WV	77357
CHESTNUT RIVER LN	0	366R	NWC	77433
CHESTNUT ROSE RD	0	286Q	NWC	77377
CHESTNUT SHADOW DR	0	369L	NWC	77070
CHESTNUT SPRINGS LN	1300	618E	SEH	77062
CHESTNUT SQUARE DR	0	366P	NWC	77433
CHESTNUT TRAIL	16200	329N	NWC	77377
CHESTNUT TRAIL	17400	527E	NEF	77407
CHESTNUT TREE LN	1500	372N	NWC	77067
CHESTNUT WOODS TRAIL	11200	368V	NWC	77065
CHESTON DR	1300	496K	JC	77029
S. CHESTWOOD DR	11400	490G	HE	77024
N. CHESTWOOD DR	11400	490G	HE	77024
CHESWICK DR	8100	412R	NCC	77037
CHESWOOD	5600	534Q	SEH	77087
CHETCO LN	4500	461S	NEC	77521
CHETLAND PLACE DR	14800	408K	NWC	77095
CHETMAN DR	11400	368R	NWC	77065
CHETMAN DR	11700	368Q	NWC	77065
CHETWOOD CIR	900	658M	LC	77573
CHETWOOD DR	6600	531F	SWH	77081
CHEVAL DR	14100	368P	NWC	77429
CHEVALIER ST	0	444D	NWC	77493
CHEVERY DR	0	572W	SWC	77053
CHEVIOT CIR	11400	529P	SWH	77099
CHEVIOT HILLS LN	3400	611X	FS	77545
CHEVY ST	0	657L	FR	77546
CHEVY CHASE CIR	600	568R	SG	77478
CHEVY CHASE CIR	700	569N	SG	77478
CHEVY CHASE DR	2900	492N	SWH	77019
CHEVY CHASE DR	5000	491S	SWH	77056
CHEVY CHASE DR	6100	491S	SWH	77057
CHEVY CHASE DR	7500	490V	SWH	77063
CHEVY CHASE DR	10000	489Q	SWH	77042
CHEVY CHASE DR	11300	489P	SWH	77077
CHEVY CHASE DR	14100	488S	SWH	77077
CHEVY CHASE DR	21900	255Y	SEM	77365
CHEVY OAKS LN	0	526Q	NEF	77407
CHEW	1600	494C	NEH	77020
CHEWTON CT	12500	328Q	NWC	77377
CHEWTON GLEN	16600	328Q	NWC	77377
CHEYENNE AVE	4700	537Y	PA	77505
CHEYENNE CT	7900	461S	NEC	77521
CHEYENNE DR	17100	503F	CCO	77520
CHEYENNE BEND DR	0	328P	NWC	77429
CHEYENNE MEADOWS DR	900	485G	SWC	77450
CHEYENNE RIVER CIR	1800	569W	SG	77478
CHEYNE CIR	7600	330Q	NWC	77379
CHIA	1500	536P	SEH	77017
CHIANTI RIDGE DR	0	407E	NWC	77433
CHIAPAS DR	0	293G	SEM	77386
CHIARA CT	1200	659M	LC	77573
CHIA VALLEY CT	9200	615H	SEC	77089
CHICADEE	1800	658Q	LC	77573
CHICAGO	2800	535K	SEH	77017
CHICAGO BRIDGE-IRON	8400	410C	NWC	77064
CHICHESTER LN	15300	409M	JV	77040
CHICKADEE LN	10400	574G	SEH	77048
CHICKADEE LN	18800	286G	NWC	77377
CHICKAMAUGA LN	8400	527P	NEF	77083
CHICKASAW	7100	462Y	BT	77521
CHICKASAW LN	10000	450A	NWH	77041
CHICKASAW PLUM WAY	0	524D	NEF	77494
CHICKASAW TRAIL	24100	297J	SEM	77365
CHICKERING	3000	454X	NEH	77026
CHICKFIELD CT	10200	575U	SEH	77075
CHICKORY FIELD LN	500	613G	NEB	77584
CHICKORY TRAIL LN	0	616E	SEC	77089
CHICKORY TRAILS	21300	525D	NEF	77450
CHICKORY WOOD CT	400	613C	NEB	77584
CHICKORY WOODS LN	7000	527E	NEF	77083
CHICKORY WOODS LN	7100	527J	NEF	77083
CHICKWOOD DR	11500	616C	SEC	77089
CHICO LN	100	659Z	DI	77539
CHICOMA ST	0	290Y	NWC	77379
CHICORY DR	0	461P	NEC	77521
CHICORY DR	17400	447X	NWH	77084
CHICORY CHASE CT	0	524F	NEF	77494
CHICORY STAR LN	9000	524C	NEF	77494
CHIEF DR	5200	614V	PL	77584
CHILDERS CT	0	332D	NCC	77373
CHILDERS CT	800	569T	NEF	77477
CHILDERS LN	1300	332D	NCC	77373
CHILDERSBURG CT	7600	526M	NEF	77407
CHILDRES POND CT	0	250Q	NWC	77389
CHILDRESS	3500	492W	SWH	77005
CHILE DR	3800	577A	PA	77504
CHILTON DR	1700	502W	BT	77520
CHILTON LN	1400	444Y	KT	77493
CHILTON RD	1700	492Q	SWH	77019
CHILTON BLUFF BLVD	0	406F	NWC	77433
CHILTREN CIR	15900	330S	NWC	77379
CHIMERALN DR	0	610U	MC	77459
CHIMES DR	12800	488Q	SWH	77077
CHIMIRA LN	3000	573F	SEH	77051
CHIMNEY BROOK LN	3200	331P	NWC	77068
CHIMNEY HILL CT	15200	408J	NWC	77095
CHIMNEY RIDGE RD	4600	611D	SWH	77053
CHIMNEY ROCK DR	200	491B	SWH	77024
CHIMNEY ROCK DR	700	491K	SWH	77056
CHIMNEY ROCK DR	5300	531F	SWH	77081
CHIMNEY ROCK DR	6700	531K	BL	77401
CHIMNEY ROCK DR	8600	531K	SWH	77096
CHIMNEY ROCK DR	11300	571B	SWH	77035
CHIMNEY ROCK DR	13500	571K	SWH	77085
CHIMNEY ROCK DR	15700	571X	SWH	77489
CHIMNEY ROCK DR	16100	611B	SWH	77053
CHIMNEY ROCK RD	0	611S	FS	77545
CHIMNEY ROCK CENT BLVD	0	531B	SWH	77081
CHIMNEY ROSE CT	0	573T	SEC	77047
CHIMNEYSTONE CIR	2400	609A	SG	77479
CHIMNEYSTONE DR	16300	407H	NWC	77095
CHIMNEY SWEEP DR	13100	408L	NWC	77041
CHIMNEY TRAIL LN	0	616E	SEC	77089
CHIMNEY VINE LN	1700	336F	NEH	77339
CHINABERRY DR	5800	451A	NWH	77092
CHINABERRY HILL LN	0	526J	NEF	77407
CHINA BERRY PARK LN	0	658S	LC	77573
CHINABERRY PARK LN	9900	289U	NWC	77375
CHINA BLUE LN	0	325M	NWC	77429
CHINA DOLL CT	5400	448D	NWC	77041
CHINA FIR	20300	446S	NWC	77449
CHINA GREEN DR	0	325M	NWC	77429
CHINA ROSE CT	1	251B	WD	77381
CHINA SPRINGS	25500	292Y	NCC	77373
CHINA YELLOW TRAIL	0	325M	NWC	77429
CHINESE FIR LN	0	296A	SEM	77365
CHINKAPIN OAK DR	500	252T	SEM	77386
CHINNI CIR	19400	486D	SWC	77094
CHINNI CT	900	486D	SWC	77094
CHINNOK	7100	462Y	BT	77521
CHINN RIDGE LN	16600	527P	NEF	77083
CHINO ST	0	658Y	LC	77573
CHINON CIR	7800	570G	MC	77071
CHINO VALLEY CT	3200	610U	MC	77459
CHINQUAPIN LN	20500	258U	NEC	77357
CHINQUAPIN PLACE	900	486H	SWC	77094
CHINQUAPIN SCHOOL	0	460Q	NEC	77562
CHIPLEY DR	4200	578F	PA	77505
CHIPMAN LN	14800	413A	NEH	77060
CHIPMAN LN	15000	412D	NEH	77060
CHIPMAN LN	15400	372Z	NEH	77060
CHIPMAN GLEN DR	13100	528B	SWH	77082
CHIPPAWA LN	1200	577E	PA	77504
CHIPPED SPARROW PLACE	0	250P	NWC	77389
CHIPPED SPARROW PLACE	0	250P	NWC	77389
CHIPPENDALE	0	451R	NWH	77092
CHIPPENDALE CT	3100	569T	SG	77478
CHIPPENDALE RD	1200	452J	NWH	77018
CHIPPENHAM DR	900	486F	SWC	77450
CHIPPENHAM LN	0	569X	MC	77459
CHIPPERFIELD DR	15000	457Z	NEC	77530
CHIPPEWA	7500	461S	NEC	77521
CHIPPEWA BLVD	5400	411F	NWC	77086
CHIPPEWA LN	1	295F	SEM	77365
CHIPPEWA RIDGE CT	11400	616E	SEC	77089
CHIPPEWA TRAIL	0	250Q	NWC	77389
CHIPPING LN	8700	412J	NWC	77088
W. CHIPPINGHAM	0	488L	SWH	77077
E. CHIPPINGHAM	0	488L	SWH	77077
CHIPPLEGATE DR	19800	334R	NCC	77338
CHIPSHOT	0	337Z	NEC	77346
CHIPSTEAD CIR	9700	329V	NWC	77070
CHIPSTEAD CT	9700	329V	NWC	77070
CHIPSTEAD DR	16200	329V	NWC	77379
CHIPSTEAD DR	16400	329V	NWC	77070
CHIPSTONE CT	26800	366M	NWC	77433
CHIPWOOD DR	24400	245V	SWM	77355
CHIRPING SPARROW CT	500	247G	SWM	77362
CHIRPING SQUIRREL CT	200	247L	SWM	77362
CHISELHURST	0	409B	NWC	77064
CHISELHURST DR	9700	408D	NWC	77065
CHISELHURST WAY	10000	369W	NWC	77065
CHISELHURST WAY CT	11300	369X	NWC	77065
CHISEL POINT DR	800	486H	SWC	77094
CHISEL STONE CT	0	657P	FR	77546
CHISHOLM	0	539S	DP	77536
CHISHOLM TRAIL	5500	660X	DI	77539
CHISHOLM TRAIL	18000	373J	NCC	77060
CHISHOLM WOOD LN	8900	575V	SEH	77075
CHISLE STONE LN	19300	446D	NWC	77449
CHISOLM CREEK CT	0	446N	NWC	77449
CHISOS TRAIL	600	332E	NWC	77388
CHISUM	4500	494F	NEH	77020
CHISWELL	2800	532Q	SWH	77025
CHISWICK RD	12600	572V	SWH	77047
CHITWOOD CT	500	486D	SWC	77094
CHIVALRY CT	26100	296X	SEM	77339
CHOATE	0	580S	SEC	77571
CHOATE	10800	580S	SEC	77507
CHOATE CIR	1000	536N	SEH	77017
CHOATE DR	0	656N	NEB	77511
CHOCTAW	0	579A	LP	77571
S. CHOCTAW	7300	461S	NEC	77521
CHOCTAW	18400	295G	SEM	77365
CHOCTAW DR	17100	503F	CCO	77520
CHOCTAW TRAIL	1500	296M	SEM	77365
CHOCTAW TRAIL	1600	297J	SEM	77365
CHOKE CANYON LN	0	660N	LC	77573
CHOKECHERRY AVE	0	296A	SEM	77365
CHOLLA VIEW CT	0	410E	NWC	77064
CHOLLA CANYON LN	8000	406H	NWC	77433
CHOLLA VIEW LN	19400	406M	NWC	77433
CHOLLA WALK LN	0	410E	NWC	77064
CHOPIN CT	11900	368N	NWC	77429
CHORALE CT	8000	410J	NWC	77040
CHORIN	400	540J	SEC	77571
CHOWNING RD	800	490C	HE	77024
CHRIS CT	37000	246G	SWM	77355
CHRIS DR	3200	490Z	SWH	77063
CHRIS LN	22200	256Z	SEM	77357
CHRIS LN	28100	248W	TB	77375
CHRIS RD	15000	612D	PL	77047
CHRISMAN RD	12300	413G	NCC	77039
CHRISMAN RD	14200	373Y	NCC	77039
CHRIS RIDGE CT	27500	293K	SEM	77386
CHRISSIE DR	4800	614R	PL	77584
CHRISTA LN	1500	536Y	SH	77587
CHRISTAL LAKE LN	0	525F	NEF	77494
CHRISTEN CANYON LN	0	524J	NWF	77406
CHRISTENSEN	100	494P	SEH	77003
CHRISTIAN DR	11000	417R	NEC	77044
CHRISTIANA DR	27600	247V	SWM	77355
CHRISTIE	2900	454X	NEH	77026
CHRISTILYNN LN	14300	374W	NCC	77032
CHRISTINA CT	12800	570E	MC	77489
CHRISTINA LN	300	616Y	FR	77546
CHRISTINA LOOP	0	542J	BT	77520
CHRISTINE	300	536J	SEH	77017
CHRISTINE	1000	535R	SEH	77017
CHRISTINE CROSSING DR	19200	526Q	NEF	77407
CHRISTI PLACE	100	536W	SH	77587
CHRISTMAS RD	0	610H	NEF	77489
CHRISTMAS FERN	11000	370S	NWC	77064
CHRISTMAS TREE LN	0	371G	NWC	77014
CHRISTOPHER	1300	569Z	NEF	77477
CHRISTOPHER CT	7200	408Q	NWC	77041
CHRISTOPHER DR	0	542K	BT	77520
CHRISTOPHER DR	0	610Q	MC	77459
CHRISTOPHER LN	0	501M	BT	77521
CHRISTOPHER LN	20500	446K	NWC	77449
CHRISTOPHER GLEN PLACE	0	332Z	NCC	77073
CHRISTOPHER LAKE CT	0	325M	NWC	77429
CHRISTOPHER PARK ST	0	325N	HK	77447
CHRISTOPHER PLACE	4500	371A	NWC	77066
CHRISTOPHER WALK CT	12000	616G	SEC	77089
CHRISTOPHER WREN	0	445Z	NWC	77449
CHRISTPHER WALK'S TRAIL	11900	616G	SEC	77089
CHRISTY	3600	538U	DP	77536
CHRISTY'S CT	0	244C	WCO	77447
CHRISTY GLEN CT	11800	616G	SEC	77089
CHRISTY MILL CT	12200	328Z	NWC	77070
CHRISTY PARK CIR	18600	447E	NWC	77084
CHRISWOOD DR	12600	328V	NWC	77429
CHRITIEN POINT CT	4900	569W	SG	77478
CHRYSANTHEMUM DR	0	571G	SWH	77085
CHRYSTELL LN	4600	451F	NWH	77092
CHUCK DR	0	657L	FR	77546
CHUCKANUT LN	1	490Q	PP	77024
CHUCKBERRY ST	0	450Q	NWH	77080
CHUCKSON DR	11500	368Q	NWC	77065
CHUCKWAGON TRAIL	28000	246J	SWM	77355
CHUCKWOOD RD	13800	371V	NWC	77038
CHUKAR CIR	0	449L	NWH	77084
CHUN LN	6200	411X	NWH	77092
CHURCH	400	500P	BT	77520
CHURCH	500	419H	CB	77532
W. CHURCH	600	568J	SG	77498
E. CHURCH	600	568K	SG	77498
CHURCH	23600	296F	SEM	77365
CHURCH LN	10800	449Y	NWH	77043
CHURCH RD	12400	496G	NEH	77013
CHURCH COLONY	0	525D	NEF	77450
CHURCH COLONY	5000	525D	NEF	77450
CHURCHHILL FALLS CT	16600	330P	NWC	77379
CHURCHILL	2300	493C	NEH	77009
CHURCHILL	2700	615P	PL	77581
CHURCHILL CT	11900	490F	BH	77024
CHURCHILL COVE LN	0	615M	PL	77089
CHURCHILL GARDENS LN	3500	371K	NWC	77066
CHURCHILL GRAND CT	0	326Z	NWC	77429
CHURCHILL WAY CIR	11300	369W	NWC	77065
CHURCHILL WAY DR	9800	409A	NWC	77065
CHURCHILL WAY DR	10000	369W	NWC	77065
CHURCH LIGHT LN	8300	410H	NWC	77064
CHURCHVILLE DR	8400	451J	NWH	77080
CHUTE CT	3400	612Z	NWB	77578
CIANO LN	0	491C	NWH	77055
CIAS TRAIL LN	2000	293E	SEM	77386
CIBOLA RD	2200	659C	LC	77573
CIBOLA PARK LN	0	409W	NWC	77041
CIBOLD CREEK CT	0	366Z	NWC	77433
CIBOLO	9600	455Z	NEH	77013
CIBOLO PINE LN	0	366Z	NWC	77433
W. CICADA CIR	23800	296D	SEM	77357
E. CICADA CIR	23800	296D	SEM	77357
CICADA DR	7600	610N	MC	77459
CICADA LN	3500	414G	NCC	77039
CICELY CT	0	578Y	SEH	77059
CICERO RD	14000	408C	NWC	77095
CICETER RD	12900	414G	NCC	77039
CICLO CT		524M	NEF	77406
CIDERCREEK LN	21100	289U	NWC	77375
CIDERWOOD DR	2500	333A	NCC	77373
CIDERWOOD DR	2900	333B	NCC	77373
CIELIO BAY CT	5700	449A	NWC	77041
CIELIO BAY LN	12100	449A	NWC	77041
CIELITO LN	0	461P	NEC	77521
CIEN RD	400	620Y	KE	77565
CIEN RD	600	660C	KE	77565
CIENNA DR	8200	410L	NWC	77040
CILANTRO LN	5200	461T	NEC	77521
CILE	3000	538X	DP	77536
CIMARRON	800	497A	NEH	77015
CIMARRON FALLS	0	289D	NWC	77375
CIMARRON PASS	0	293U	NCC	77373
CIMARRON PKWY	21000	486E	SWC	77450
CIMARRON PKWY	21600	485H	SWC	77450
CIMARRON PLACE DR	0	485G	SWC	77494
CIMARRON VALLEY LN	0	612U	PL	77584
CIMBER LN	23100	333C	NCC	77373
CIMMARON DR	16200	246M	SC	77355
CIMMARON CREEK CT	5800	330H	NWC	77379
CIMMARON OAK LN	0	526R	NEF	77407
CINCO BLVD	21500	485V	NEF	77450
CINCO CROSSING LN	5000	485W	NEF	77494
CINCO ESTATES DR	0	485W	NEF	77494
CINCO FALLS DR	0	524A	NEF	77494
CINCO FOREST TRAIL DR	0	524A	NEF	77494
CINCO LAKES CT	22200	485R	NEF	77450
CINCO LAKES DR	2500	485U	NEF	77450
CINCO MANOR LN	24900	485W	NEF	77494
CINCO PARK RD	15000	526A	NEF	77450
CINCO PARK RD	21100	526A	NEF	77450
CINCO PARK PLACE	2300	485Q	NEF	77494
CINCO PARK PLACE CT	23200	485Q	NEF	77494
CINCO RANCH BLVD	21500	485Q	NEF	77450
CINCO RANCH BLVD	23100	485Q	NEF	77494
CINCO RANCH BLVD	23100	524C	NEF	77494
CINCO RANCH COMPLEX		485P	NEF	77494
CINCO RANCH H.S. BLVD		485P	NEF	77494
CINCO RIDGE DR	0	524G	NEF	77494
CINCO ROSE DR	0	524F	NEF	77494
CINCO TERRACE DR	0	524G	NEF	77494
CINCO TRACE DR		484S	NWF	77494
CINCO VILLAGE CENTER BLVD	0	485T	NEF	77494
CINDER CONE TRAIL	12700	456D	NEC	77044
CINDER CREEK CT	0	290E	NWC	77375
CINDERELLA	7800	455T	NEH	77028
CINDERWOOD CT	14600	457Y	NEC	77015
CINDERWOOD DR	18200	326Z	NWC	77429
CINDY LN	6200	452X	NWH	77008
CINDY ANN WAY	0	372D	NCC	77073
CINDY LYNN LN	22300	245U	SWM	77355
CINDYRELLA DR	400	460N	HG	77562
CINDYWOOD CIR	14100	489E	SWH	77079
CINDYWOOD DR	14100	489E	SWH	77079
CINDYWOOD DR	14400	488H	SWH	77079
CINNABAR CT	15400	408N	NWC	77095
CINNABAR DR	4300	529E	SWH	77072
CINNABAR BAY CT	200	660A	LC	77573
CINNABAR BAY DR	200	660A	LC	77573
CINNABERRY LN	10200	289U	NWC	77375
CINNAMON	5100	500H	BT	77521
CINNAMON DR	100	485C	SWC	77450
CINNAMON LN	8200	529Q	SWH	77072
CINNAMON ST	4200	501M	BT	77521
CINNAMON ASH CT	0	407J	NWC	77433
CINNAMON COVE DR	3900	659Z	GCO	77539
CINNAMON CREEK CIR	5800	408U	NWC	77084
CINNAMON FERN	8900	369V	NWC	77064
CINNAMON FERN CT	3900	578X	SEH	77059
CINNAMON FERN LN	11000	369V	NWC	77064
CINNAMON GLEN DR	3100	333P	NCC	77073
CINNAMON LAKE DR	5300	461P	NEC	77521
CINNAMON OAK LN	100	489L	SWH	77079
CINNAMON OAK LN	300	489G	SWH	77079
CINNAMON OAK LN	700	489C	SWH	77079
CINNAMON RUN	8200	250J	NWC	77389
CINTOLA LN	0	659R	LC	77573
CIPRO ST	0	530X	SWH	77031
W. CIRCLE	100	462V	BT	77521
S. CIRCLE	100	462V	BT	77521
E. CIRCLE	100	462V	BT	77521
CIRCLE	500	580C	LP	77571
W. CIRCLE DR	0	570C	SWH	77071
CIRCLE DR	1	455U	NEH	77013
S. CIRCLE DR	400	541C	BT	77520
N. CIRCLE DR	400	541C	BT	77520
CIRCLE DR	500	580G	LP	77571
E. CIRCLE DR	700	570C	SWH	77071
CIRCLE DR	800	531C	BL	77401
W. CIRCLE DR	3400	615V	PL	77581
E. CIRCLE DR	3400	615V	PL	77581
N. CIRCLE DR	8000	570C	SWH	77071
S. CIRCLE DR	12000	570C	SWH	77071
CIRCLE BEND DR	900	570P	MC	77489
CIRCLECHASE DR	14500	570V	SWH	77489
CIRCLE COVE CT	9000	412L	NWH	77088
CIRCLE DEMATEL	0	486C	SWC	77450
CIRCLEGATE DR	5500	334E	NCC	77373
CIRCLE LAKE DR	0	247C	SWM	77354
CIRCLE LAKE DR	1100	484E	NWF	77494
S. CIRCLE PARK	1400	577J	PA	77504
N. CIRCLE PARK	1400	577J	PA	77504
W. CIRCLE PARK	5000	577J	PA	77504
S. CIRCLEWOOD GLEN	1	251E	WD	77381
N. CIRCLEWOOD GLEN	1	251E	WD	77381
CIRCLEWOOD WAY	14400	618A	SEH	77062
CIRCLING HAWK CT	15200	408N	NWC	77095
CIRCULAR QUAY LN	0	327S	NWC	77429
CIRRUS CT	1	251Y	WD	77380
CISCO CT	0	406D	NWC	77433
CISCO HILL CT	20400	486X	NEF	77450
CITADEL LN	3700	451J	NWH	77092
CITADEL PLAZA DR	2600	452T	NWH	77008
CITATION	4100	537R	PA	77503
CITATION CT	8600	412P	NWH	77088
CITATION DR	700	570S	SF	77477
CITRINE DR	0	367U	NWC	77095
CITRUS	12000	409X	NWC	77041
CITRUS CT	8000	463S	CCO	77520
CITRUS FIELD LN	0	406V	NWC	77449
W. CITRUS ROSE CT	0	325M	NWC	77429
E. CITRUSROSE CT	0	325M	NWC	77429
CITRUSWOOD LN	10000	616K	SEC	77089
CITY CT	3300	371C	NWC	77014
CITY CLUB DR	1	492W	SWH	77046
CITY PARK CENTRAL DR	11800	573N	SWH	77047
CITYPARK LOOP	8500	455U	NEH	77013
CITY PLACE DR	10500	489U	SWH	77042
CITY PLAZA DR	0	292E	NCC	77373
CITY SHORES LN	0	524E	NEF	77494
CITY VIEW PLACE	16800	373N	NEH	77060
CITY WALK DR	15000	568X	SG	77479
CITYWAY DR	0	489U	SWH	77042
CITYWEST BLVD	1500	489U	SWH	77042
CIVIC CIR	0	541A	BT	77520
CIVIC DR	0	541A	BT	77520
CIVIL DR	100	658P	LC	77573
CLABURY CT	12600	369K	NWC	77070
E. CLADY CT	800	252P	SEM	77386
W. CLADY DR	700	252P	SEM	77386
CLAIBORNE	1700	658L	LC	77573
CLAIBORNE	7400	455A	NEH	77016
CLAIBORNE	7900	455B	NEH	77078
CLAINERT	2000	296T	SEM	77365
CLAIRCREST LN	5000	485S	NEF	77494
CLAIRE CT	2000	569W	SG	77478
CLAIRE LN	400	497A	NEC	77015
CLAIRE BROOK DR	0	525L	NEF	77407
CLAIRFIELD LN	4500	333M	NCC	77338
CLAIRFIELD LN	4800	334J	NCC	77338
CLAIRHILL DR	100	249M	NWH	77375
CLAIRHILL DR	100	249M	NWH	77375
CLAIRMONT DR	9700	579B	LP	77571
CLAIRSON LN	7300	407J	NWC	77433
CLAIRY CT	100	413T	NEH	77076
CLAN MACGREGOR DR	16800	407Y	NWC	77084
CLAN MACINTOSH DR	16800	407Y	NWC	77084
CLANTON	9200	450K	NWH	77080
CLANTON PINES DR	0	376N	NEC	77396
CLAPTON PATH	0	293L	SEM	77386
CLARA LN	0	248S	SWM	77354
CLARA RD	400	536Y	SH	77587
CLARA RD	800	379Z	NEC	77532
CLARA RD	5300	449D	NWC	77041
CLARA RD	6000	409Z	NWH	77041
CLARA RD	10800	456S	NEH	77013
CLARADEEN CT	0	572R	SWH	77047
CLARADON POINT LN	22100	485Z	NEF	77450
CLARA HILLS LN	12400	416Z	NEC	77044
CLARA VISTA DR	0	376S	NEC	77396
CLARBLAK LN	4000	450K	NWH	77080
CLARBOROUGH DR	1200	449Y	NWH	77043
CLARCEL	5900	415A	NEC	77039
W. CLARE	2200	538P	DP	77536
E. CLARE	2200	538P	DP	77536
CLAREHOUSE LN	0	573T	SEC	77047
CLAREMONT	1500	537N	PA	77502
CLAREMONT	1900	492T	SWH	77019
CLAREMONT	5000	494X	SEH	77023
CLAREMONT DR	0	658N	LC	77573
CLAREMONT CROSSING	0	658P	LC	77573
CLAREMONT GARDEN CIR	0	572R	SWH	77047
CLAREMORE CT	21000	406T	NWC	77449
CLARENCE	500	288G	TB	77375
CLARENCE	3300	454J	NEH	77093
CLARENDON LN	11900	490J	BH	77024
CLARENDON BEND LN	7600	526M	NEF	77407
CLARE POINT DR	0	249A	SWM	77354
CLARESHOLM	12200	328G	NWC	77377
CLARESTONE DR	3700	613Q	NEB	77584
CLARET CUP LN	0	410L	NWC	77040
CLARETFIELD CT	21300	335J	NCC	77338
CLARETON CT	14700	368A	NWC	77429
CLARETON LN	13500	368A	NWC	77429
CLAREWOOD	0	529H	SWH	77036
CLAREWOOD DR	5300	531F	SWH	77081
CLAREWOOD DR	7000	530G	SWH	77036
CLAREWOOD DR	12000	529E	SWH	77072
CLAREWOOD DR	13400	528F	SWC	77083
CLARIDGE DR	5600	531W	SWH	77096
CLARIDGE DR	7600	530Y	SWH	77071
CLARIDGE DR	9200	530W	SWH	77031
CLARIDGE PARK CT	25500	484V	NEF	77494
CLARIDGE PARK LN	4800	484V	NEF	77494
CLARINGTON	8600	454G	NEH	77016
CLARION WAY	7900	410J	NWC	77040
CLARK	0	577X	SEH	77034
CLARK	300	494E	NEH	77020

Street Name	Block	Pg/Sq	Loc	Zips
CLARK CT	400	494J	NEH	77020
CLARK DR	0	620H	SB	77586
CLARK DR	18700	254C	SEM	77302
CLARK RD	4200	450H	NWH	77040
CLARK RD	9400	453B	NEH	77076
CLARK RD	10000	413X	NEH	77076
CLARKCREST	8900	490X	SWH	77063
CLARKDALE CT	1200	486H	SWC	77094
CLARKDON CT	5300	370M	NWC	77066
CLARKE SPRINGS DR	15700	571Z	SWH	77053
CLARKE SPRINGS DR	15800	611D	SWH	77053
CLARKGATE DR	4200	333C	NCC	77373
CLARK GROVE LN	10400	575V	SEH	77075
CLARKMAN RIDGE LN	0	406F	NWC	77433
CLARKS FORK CT	15600	370U	NWC	77086
CLARKS FORK DR	13600	370U	NWC	77086
CLARKSON LN	5900	451Z	NWH	77055
CLARKSTON LN	5200	291W	NWC	77379
CLARKSTON LN	5300	290Z	NWC	77379
CLARKSVILLE	2900	579A	LP	77571
CLARK TOWNE LN	13800	528T	NEF	77498
CLAUDIA	0	456X	NEH	77013
CLAUDIA DR	12400	496Q	GP	77015
CLAVERTON DR	3500	371P	NWC	77066
CLAWSON	6500	451Y	NWH	77055
CLAWSON RD	0	420L	NEC	77532
CLAXTON	1000	535E	SEH	77087
CLAY	100	493Q	DT	77002
W. CLAY	300	493N	SWH	77019
W. CLAY	1400	492R	SWH	77019
CLAY	1600	493V	SEH	77003
CLAY	3900	494S	SEH	77023
CLAY CT	0	539J	DP	77536
CLAY RD	1200	569Z	NEF	77477
CLAY RD	8600	450H	NWH	77080
CLAY RD	10300	449H	NWH	77041
CLAY RD	11000	448H	NWH	77084
CLAY RD	16300	447H	NWC	77084
CLAY RD	19100	446F	NWC	77449
CLAY RD	22000	445F	NWC	77449
CLAY RD	23000	444F	NWC	77493
CLAYBECK LN	0	485S	NEF	77494
CLAYBERRY ST	0	450Q	NWH	77080
CLAYBROOK	0	616A	SEC	77089
CLAYBROOK DR	10300	615D	SEC	77089
CLAY CANYON DR	4300	485Y	NEF	77450
CLAYCLIFF CT	12800	576V	SEH	77034
CLAY CREEK CT	2600	615R	PL	77581
CLAY CREEK DR	16100	448E	NWC	77084
CLAYCREST	15100	327Z	NWC	77429
CLAYCRESTE CT	15100	327Z	NWC	77429
CLAYCROFT CT	14500	368A	NWC	77429
CLAYGATE DR	12400	573Q	SEH	77047
CLAY HILL DR	4200	448E	NWC	77084
CLAYHORN CT	0	526F	NEF	77450
CLAY LANDING LN	0	446F	NWC	77449
CLAYMILL CT	4800	446C	NWC	77449
CLAYMILL LN	0	615F	PL	77581
CLAYMONT HILL DR	13800	367C	NWC	77429
CLAYMORE CT	1	490G	PP	77024
CLAYMORE RD	11100	490L	PP	77024
CLAYMORE MEADOW LN	5300	250Z	NWC	77389
CLAYMORE PARK DR	3000	449L	NWH	77043
CLAY PIGEON CT	16300	610C	SWH	77489
CLAY POINT CT	400	490L	PP	77024
CLAYPOOL	15100	373U	NCC	77032
CLAYRIDGE DR	6200	571X	SWH	77053
CLAYSPRINGS LN	22200	525L	NEF	77407
CLAYSTONE LN	0	527S	NEF	77407
CLAYTHORNE CT	0	527W	NEF	77407
CLAYTON	100	453P	NEH	77022
CLAYTON	500	288L	TB	77375
CLAYTON DR	1600	502S	BT	77520
CLAYTON LN	0	612Z	NEB	77578
CLAYTON BEND CT	4000	527G	SWC	77082
CLAYTON BEND DR	15700	527G	SWC	77082
CLAYTON BLUFF LN	0	407K	NWC	77433
CLAYTON CANYON LN	0	524J	NWF	77406
CLAYTON GATE DR	4000	527G	SWC	77082
CLAYTON GREENS CT	4000	527C	SWC	77082
CLAYTON GREENS DR	16000	527C	SWC	77082
CLAYTON HILL DR	13300	408Y	NWC	77041
CLAYTON LAKE LN	0	377L	NEH	77044
CLAYTON OAKS DR	0	487Z	SWC	77082
CLAYTON RIDGE CT	2900	487Z	SWC	77082
CLAYTONS BEND CT	0	293J	SEM	77396
CLAYTONS PARK LN	0	377A	NEC	77346
CLAYTON TERRACE DR	0	610V	MC	77459
CLAYTON TRACE TRAIL	0	527C	SWC	77082
CLAYTON WOODS BLVD	0	527D	SWC	77082
CLAYTON WOODS DR	3200	527D	SWC	77082
CLAYWOOD	11700	490K	BK	77024
CLAYWOOD CT	11700	490K	BH	77024
CLEAR ARBOR LN	0	576Z	SEH	77034
CLEAR BEND LN	6400	525H	NEF	77450
CLEARBOURNE LN	8900	575U	SEH	77075
CLEARBROOK DR	2200	610E	MC	77489
CLEARBROOK LN	800	491J	SWH	77057
CLEARBROOK LN	19000	245D	SWM	77355
CLEAR BROOK OAK	11900	616G	SEC	77089
CLEAR CANYON DR	6200	526F	NEF	77450
CLEAR CAPE LN	13000	571K	SWH	77085
CLEAR CIBOLO CREEK CIR	0	366N	NWC	77433
CLEAR COVE LN	10400	449H	NWH	77041
CLEAR CREEK	0	620K	SB	77586
CLEAR CREEK	5100	614A	BK	77581
S. CLEAR CREEK	24800	244V	WCO	77447
CLEAR CREEK AVE	200	659J	LC	77573
CLEAR CREEK CIR	0	244V	WCO	77447
CLEAR CREEK CIR	0	461T	NEC	77521
CLEAR CREEK CIR	0	657A	FR	77546
S. CLEAR CREEK DR	300	657F	FR	77546
N. CLEAR CREEK DR	300	657E	FR	77546
CLEAR CREEK LN	0	657A	FR	77546
CLEAR CREEK RD	0	244Z	WCO	77447
N. CLEAR CREEK RD	24500	244V	WCO	77447
CLEAR CREEK MEADOWS DR	100	658N	LC	77573
CLEAR CREEK WAY	0	297Q	NEH	77345
CLEARCREST DR	15700	618D	SEH	77059
CLEAR DALE DR	19700	337U	NEC	77346
CLEAR FALLS DR	3600	297W	NEH	77339
CLEARFIELD DR	11000	417R	NEC	77044
CLEARFIELD CANYON DR	0	524K	NWF	77406
CLEARFIELD SPRINGS CT	0	615K	PL	77581
CLEAR FOREST DR	13900	528W	NEF	77498
CLEAR FORK DR	10800	376U	NEC	77396
CLEARFORK DR	12200	489J	SWH	77077
CLEAR GLEN DR	19700	337U	NEC	77346
CLEARGROVE LN	0	575Q	SEH	77075
CLEARHAVEN CT	15300	327V	NWC	77429
CLEAR HOLLOW LN	12100	616G	SEC	77089
CLEAR LAKE	100	620T	CS	77565
CLEAR LAKE CT	4400	609K	MC	77459
CLEAR LAKE RD	1	459P	HG	77562
CLEAR LAKE CITY BLVD	1600	617L	SEH	77062
CLEAR LAKE CITY BLVD	2000	618A	SEH	77062
CLEAR LAKE CITY BLVD	2600	578X	SEH	77059
S. CLEAR LAKE LOOP	0	612Q	PL	77584
N. CLEAR LAKE LOOP	0	612M	PL	77584
E. CLEAR LAKE LOOP	0	612M	PL	77584
W. CLEAR LAKE LOOP	0	612L	PL	77584
CLEARLIGHT LN	17800	330F	NWC	77379
CLEAR MEADOW DR	16000	458Y	CV	77530
CLEAR MEADOW LN	9900	616K	SEC	77089
CLEAR MILL LN	26400	484T	NEF	77494
CLEARMONT DR	16300	611C	SWH	77053
CLEAR OAKS LN	0	253J	SEM	77385
CLEAR OAK WAY	16600	618M	SEH	77058
CLEAR POINTE DR	15600	327Z	NWC	77429
CLEAR RIDGE DR	2200	296V	NEH	77339
CLEAR RIDGE DR	2800	297S	NEH	77339
CLEAR RIVER DR	12200	415E	NEH	77050
CLEARSABLE LN	11000	577W	SEH	77034
CLEAR SAGE CT	0	250A	WD	77382
CLEARSKY CT	0	660E	LC	77573
CLEAR SKY DR	19200	337R	NEC	77346
CLEARSMOKE CIR	8700	407D	NWC	77095
CLEAR SPRINGS DR	400	489E	SWH	77079
CLEAR SPRINGS COVE CT		366R	NWC	77433
CLEAR SPRINGS WAY	25700	292U	NCC	77373
CLEARSTONE CIR	0	524T	NWF	77406
CLEAR TRAIL LN	13700	577S	SEH	77034
CLEAR VALLEY DR	1000	372E	NWC	77014
CLEAR VALLEY DR	15400	408N	NWC	77095
CLEARVIEW	7800	533V	SEH	77033
CLEARVIEW AVE	0	571Z	SWH	77053
CLEARVIEW AVE	100	656D	FR	77546
CLEARVIEW AVE	400	617W	FR	77546
CLEARVIEW CIR	0	532X	SWH	77025
CLEARVIEW ST	0	532X	SWH	77025
CLEARVIEW VILLAGE BLVD	0	577W	SEH	77034
CLEARVIEW VILLA WAY	3300	532X	SWH	77054
CLEAR VILLA LN	10900	577W	SEH	77034
CLEARWATER	0	568Z	SG	77478
CLEARWATER	300	495V	GP	77029
CLEARWATER CT	3400	569W	SG	77478
CLEARWATER CT	4200	609B	MC	77459
CLEARWATER CREEK DR	1600	569W	SG	77478
CLEARWATER CROSSING	8100	375U	NEC	77396
CLEAR WATER PARK DR	3000	485V	NEF	77450
CLEARWAY DR	9200	574E	SEH	77033
CLEAR WING CT	3100	333B	NCC	77373
CLEARWOOD	8900	575M	SEH	77075
CLEARWOOD CT	0	657U	LC	77573
CLEARWOOD DR	0	657U	LC	77573
CLEARWOOD CRSSING BLVD	10400	575V	SEH	77075
CLEAR WOODS CT	0	293D	SEM	77386
CLEAR WOODS DR	0	293D	SEM	77386
CLEBURNE	1000	493X	SWH	77004
CLEBURNE	3000	533D	SEH	77004
CLEBURNE DR	4100	614Z	PL	77584
CLEE LN	6800	330L	NWC	77379
CLEEVE CLOSE	18700	337X	NEC	77346
CLEEVES DR	0	527W	NEF	77478
CLEFT STONE DR	6700	408P	NWC	77084
CLEGHORN LN	0	491F	SWH	77024
CLEMATIS LN	10600	531Y	SWH	77035
CLEMATIS LN	11100	571C	SWH	77035
CLEMENS DR	0	406B	NWC	77433
CLEMENT	5600	454S	NEH	77026
CLEMENTINE	2100	494C	NEH	77020
CLEMENTINE	2800	494C	NEH	77026
CLEMENTSHIRE	5600	534U	SEH	77087
CLEMENTS SQUARE PLACE	0	250N	NWC	77389
CLEMSON	6300	451J	NWH	77092
CLEMSON DR	2000	444U	KT	77493
CLEMWOOD LN	0	297U	NEH	77345
CLENNIE NEEDAM RD	23900	296K	SEM	77365
CLEO	600	611Y	FS	77545
CLEO	6700	614D	BK	77581
CLEO BROOK	0	329Z	NWC	77070
CLEOBROOK DR	14000	369D	NWC	77070
CLEPPER	0	248P	SWM	77354
CLEPPER	13200	248U	NWC	77375
CLEPPERWOOD LN	300	247G	SWM	77362
CLERKENWELL DR	5700	407Y	NWC	77084
CLERMONT CT	0	246T	SWM	77355
CLERMONT HARBOR CT	0	572E	SWH	77045
CLERMONT HARBOR CT	0	572E	SWH	77045
CLEVEDON LN	15300	409M	JV	77040
W. CLEVELAND	100	541C	BT	77520
E. CLEVELAND	100	541C	BT	77520
CLEVELAND	700	493P	SWH	77019
CLEVELAND	1500	538V	DP	77536
CLEVELAND	1800	536V	PA	77502
CLEVELAND	3200	611Z	FS	77545
CLEVELAND DR	1	568K	SG	77498
CLEVELAND BAY CT	9600	409A	NWC	77065
CLEVERA WALK LN	0	447R	NWC	77084
CLEVERA WALK LN	0	447R	NWC	77084
CLIFF CT	1	412Z	NWH	77076
CLIFF DR	13200	419R	BR	77532
CLIFFBROOK CT	15700	407R	NWC	77095
CLIFF CREEK CT	0	293G	SEM	77386
CLIFFDALE	2400	412W	NWH	77091
CLIFFDALE	3000	411Z	NWH	77091
CLIFFDALE DR	1800	570X	MC	77489
CLIFFGATE DR	11400	529N	SWH	77072
CLIFF HAVEN CT	16300	367Z	NWC	77095
CLIFF HAVEN DR	16200	367Z	NWC	77095
CLIFFHILL CT	25600	485W	NEF	77494
CLIFF MANOR LN	0	406F	NWC	77433
CLIFF MARSHALL	3200	411R	NWH	77088
CLIFFMONT LN		658W	LC	77573
CLIFFORD	900	490D	HE	77024
CLIFF PARK DR	1200	485G	SWC	77450
CLIFF PARK DR	10200	368Y	NWC	77065
CLIFFPOINT CT	4800	446D	NWC	77449
CLIFF POINTE LN		484W	NEF	77494
CLIFFROSE CT	11100	616E	SEC	77089
CLIFFROSE LN	16500	618Q	SEH	77062
CLIFFSAGE CT	0	406M	NWC	77433
CLIFFSHIRE CT	8200	527P	NEF	77083
CLIFFSIDE DR	400	413U	NEH	77076
CLIFFSTONE LN	0	446C	NWC	77449
W. CLIFF STONE RD	5100	614E	NEB	77581
CLIFF SWALLOW CT	3100	333B	NCC	77373
CLIFFWOOD	23100	256R	SEM	77357
CLIFFWOOD CT	0	531R	SWH	77096
CLIFFWOOD DR	9000	531R	SWH	77096
CLIFFWOOD DR	10000	531R	SWH	77035
CLIFFWOOD DR	11300	571D	SWH	77035
CLIFT HAVEN	4700	452L	NWH	77018
CLIFT HAVEN	5400	452C	NWH	77091
CLIFTON	1	494U	SEH	77011
CLIFTON	3900	660M	BC	77518
CLIFTON FORGE DR	10800	369S	NWC	77065
CLIFTON OAKS DR	0	529S	SWM	77099
CLIMBER CT	5300	448C	NWC	77041
CLIMBING BRANCH DR	15100	331P	NWC	77068
CLIMBING IVY CIR	0	447A	NWC	77084
CLIMBING OAKS DR	19400	337T	NEC	77346
CLINE	2500	494K	NEH	77020
CLINE	3300	501R	BT	77521
CLINE	3500	502N	BT	77521
CLINE LN	27900	258K	SEM	77357
CLINE RD	9500	416E	NEC	77050
CLINT NEIDGK RD	28100	248L	SWM	77354
CLINTON DR	1	496Y	GP	77547
CLINTON DR	2200	495Z	GP	77547
CLINTON DR	2500	494K	NEH	77020
CLINTON DR	7800	495T	NEH	77029
CLINTON DR	12500	496Y	NEH	77015
CLINTON PARK	200	495V	NEH	77029
CLINTRIDGE DR	5500	407X	NWC	77084
CLINTWAY DR	13800	372E	NWC	77014
CLIO	700	453X	NWH	77009
CLIPPER	0	419B	NEC	77532
CLIPPER AVE	0	620L	SB	77586
CLIPPER HILL CT	0	293Z	NCC	77373
CLIPPER HILL LN	0	293Z	NCC	77373
CLIPPER POINTE DR	15900	367D	NWC	77429
CLIPPERS BAY	0	619S	NB	77058
CLIPPERS COVE DR	2400	619S	NB	77058
CLIPPER WINDS WAY	3100	447P	NWC	77084
CLIPPERWOOD PLACE	9200	528P	SWC	77083
CLIVEDEN DR	11600	371P	NWC	77066
CLOAKSDALE LN	0	407N	NWC	77433
CLOBOURNE CROSSING LN	3800	617X	SEC	77546
CLOCHESTER LN	0	657Z	LC	77573
CLOCKWISE	400	372F	NWH	77014
CLODINE	0	527J	NEF	77083
CLODINE REDDICK RD	7300	527K	NEF	77083
CLOISTER DR	1600	419A	NEC	77532
CLOIS VISTA DR		366V	NWC	77433
CLORINDA	6000	455N	NEH	77028
CLOSEWOOD TERRACE DR	16000	367D	NWC	77429
CLOSE WOOD WAY	0	446F	NWC	77449
CLOTELL CIR	0	574J	SEH	77048
CLOTHIER	0	577X	SEH	77034
CLOUDBERRY LN	9900	289T	NWC	77375
CLOUDBERRY LN		289Q	NWC	77375
CLOUDBRIDGE CT	100	660A	LC	77573
CLOUDBRIDGE DR	0	485V	NEF	77450
CLOUDBRIDGE DR	100	660A	LC	77573
CLOUDBROOK LN	21300	446E	NWC	77449
CLOUDBURST LN	0	612J	PL	77545
CLOUDCAP CT	13900	417B	NEC	77044
CLOUDCLIFF LN	4900	484Z	NEF	77494
CLOUD CLIFF LN	14200	488N	SWH	77077
CLOUDCRAFT CT	5200	485W	NEF	77494
CLOUDCROFT DR	0	539N	DP	77536
CLOUD CROFT DR	1800	657N	FR	77546
CLOUDHAVEN CT	4900	446D	NWC	77449
CLOUD LAKE CT	0	525D	NEF	77450
CLOUDMOUNT DR	4500	448E	NWC	77084
CLOUD PEAK DR	19300	328C	NWC	77377
CLOUDS HILL CT	1300	329G	NWC	77379
CLOUDS REST	23900	287A	SWM	77355
CLOUD SWEPT LN	6600	371W	NWC	77086
CLOUDY BAY DR	0	611N	FS	77545
CLOVE CIR	10100	415X	NEH	77078
CLOVER	4100	533Y	SEH	77051
CLOVER	4700	534W	SEH	77033
CLOVER LN	2700	572G	SWH	77045
CLOVER LN	3600	539S	DP	77536
CLOVER LN	4800	614S	NEB	77584
W. CLOVER LN	18000	656E	NEB	77511
CLOVERBANK LN	0	524S	NWF	77406
CLOVERBROOK DR	3700	572N	SWH	77045
CLOVER CANYON CIR	7600	407M	NWC	77095
CLOVERCREEK BLVD	0	246A	SWM	77355
CLOVER CREEK BLVD	19000	246A	SWM	77355
CLOVER CREEK DR	3500	297U	NEH	77345
CLOVER CREEK LN	0	612Q	PL	77584
CLOVER CREEK POINT LN	13000	377K	NEC	77346
CLOVER CREST DR	0	368W	NWC	77095
CLOVERDALE	3200	532P	SWH	77025
CLOVERDALE DR	3000	659H	LC	77573
CLOVER FALLS LN	0	485X	NEF	77494
CLOVER FIELD	0	656E	NEB	77511
CLOVERFIELD CT	2600	614S	NEB	77584
CLOVERFIELD DR	1900	484H	NEF	77494
CLOVERFIELD DR	4800	614S	NEB	77584
CLOVER GARDENS DR	8100	408E	NWC	77095
CLOVER GLEN LN	18700	447J	NWC	77084
CLOVER GREEN LN	11300	372J	NWC	77067
CLOVER GREEN LN	11300	372N	NWC	77067
CLOVER GROVE CT	18400	447N	NWC	77084
CLOVERHILL	17900	487A	SWC	77094
CLOVER HILLS CIR	25500	251V	SWM	77380
CLOVER HOLLOW LN	0	449X	NWH	77043
CLOVER KNOLL CT	7800	407G	NWC	77095
CLOVER LAKE CT	0	410M	NWC	77040
CLOVER LAND CT	8500	335N	NCC	77338
CLOVERLAND PARK LN	26200	367E	NWC	77433
CLOVER LANE CT	11500	370L	NWC	77066
CLOVERLEAF	500	497G	NEC	77015
CLOVERLEAF CT	3200	613X	NEB	77578
CLOVERLEAF DR	19100	245D	SWM	77355
CLOVERMEADOW	20900	290U	NWC	77379
CLOVER MEADOWS	3700	577D	PA	77505
CLOVERMILL DR	11500	371N	NWC	77066
CLOVERMIST DR	0	409F	NWC	77064
CLOVER MIST LN	0	656A	NEB	77584
CLOVER NOOK LN	4100	619G	TL	77586
CLOVER NUT CT	0	407J	NWC	77433
CLOVER PARK DR	18000	376D	NEC	77346
CLOVER PATH	18600	295B	SEM	77365
CLOVER POINT DR	14100	528W	NEF	77498
CLOVER RANCH CIR	3100	484R	NEF	77494
CLOVER RANCH DR	25100	484R	NEF	77494
CLOVER RIDGE	0	659G	LC	77573
CLOVER RIDGE	200	656B	FR	77546
CLOVER RIDGE	6000	534Q	SEH	77087
CLOVER RIDGE LN	4100	609U	NEF	77479
CLOVER SHORE DR	0	253Y	SEM	77386
CLOVER SPRINGS DR	1800	296Y	NEH	77339
CLOVERSTONE CT	19500	486G	SWC	77094
CLOVER TRACE DR	0	253P	SEM	77386
CLOVER TRAIL LN	1500	372N	NWC	77067
CLOVER TRAILS	23800	525E	NEF	77494
CLOVERVALE DR	14000	372E	NWC	77014
CLOVER VALLEY DR	3300	297U	NEH	77345
CLOVERVIEW DR	0	328L	NWC	77377
CLOVER WALK LN	12500	409S	NWC	77041
CLOVERWALK LN	12900	528Q	SWC	77072
CLOVERWICK LN	16300	330R	NWC	77379
CLOVERWOOD DR	12600	328V	NWC	77429
CLOVERWOOD DR	19100	245D	SWM	77355
CLOVESTONE PATH	10800	527W	NEF	77407
CLOVIS RD	1100	452X	NWH	77008
CLOW RD	4200	330V	NWC	77068
CLOYANNA RD	18900	337X	NEC	77346
CLUB CT	700	620X	CS	77565
CLUB DR	0	322T	WCO	77484
CLUB LN	12700	528Y	SWH	77099
CLUB CREEK DR	9300	530S	SWH	77036
CLUB CREEK DR	9700	529R	SWH	77036
CLUB GREEN CT	0	576Z	SEH	77034
CLUBHOLLOW	4100	486S	NEF	77450
CLUBHOUSE DR	1500	656T	FR	77546
CLUBHOUSE LN	37300	246F	SWM	77355
CLUB LAKE DR	7400	407M	NWC	77095
CLUB LAKE DR	7500	408J	NWC	77095
CLUB OAK CT	1	337F	NEH	77339
W. CLUB POINT DR	8000	337R	NEC	77346
E. CLUB POINT DR	8000	337R	NEC	77346
CLUB VALLEY DR	3900	527D	SWC	77082
CLUETT	6900	455K	NEH	77028
CLUSTER CT	17800	331F	NWC	77379
CLUSTERING OAK CT	7000	526H	NEF	77407
CLUSTER OAKS DR	19400	337T	NEC	77346
CLUSTER PINE DR	12900	328U	NWC	77429
CLUSTER PINES CT	14200	371Q	NWC	77066
CLYBURN CT	3100	610U	MC	77459
CLYDE	6000	492F	SWH	77007
CLYDE DR	300	501W	BT	77520
CLYDE DR	20200	256Q	SEM	77357
CLYDEHURST GROVE CT	0	484Y	NEF	77494
CLYDEHURST GROVE CT	0	484Y	NEF	77494
CLYDESDALE	4600	447D	NWC	77084
CLYDESDALE RIDGE DR	0	334R	NCC	77338
CLYMER MEADOW	0	609Y	MC	77459
COACH RD	100	372Z	NEH	77060
COACH RD	300	373W	NEH	77060
COACHCREEK DR	7000	571J	SWH	77085
COACHFIELD LN	11500	570D	SWH	77035
COACHGATE DR	6000	334F	NCC	77373
COACH HOUSE DR	0	299T	NEC	77336
COACH LAMP LN	100	372Z	NEH	77060
COACH LAMP LN	300	373W	NEH	77060
COACHLIGHT DR	900	488F	SWH	77077
COACH LIGHT LN	3400	500H	BT	77521
COACH LIGHT LN	26500	258J	SEM	77357
COACHMAKER DR	17000	617Y	SEC	77546
COACHMAN	400	490K	BH	77024
COACHMAN DR	3400	500M	BT	77521
COACHMAN LN	12200	247R	SWM	77362
COACHPOINT	0	530A	SWH	77042
COACHWOOD DR	0	299T	NEC	77336
COACHWOOD DR	6300	570D	SWH	77035
COACHWOOD DR	7500	570C	SWH	77071
COAHUILA	9600	455Z	NEH	77013
COAL	2400	454W	NEH	77026
COAL CREEK LN	0	367P	NWC	77433
COALDALE	0	410T	NWC	77040
COALFIELD LN	0	366R	NWC	77433
COALPORT CT	800	332Q	NCC	77073
COAMING CT	17000	379X	NEC	77532
COAN	9500	454A	NEH	77093
COAPITES	4000	577F	PA	77504
COASTAL CT	0	619X	LC	77573
COASTAL GREENS DR	0	532T	SWH	77054
COASTAL GROVE LN	0	524E	NEF	77494
COASTAL MEADOW	23700	525E	NEF	77494
COASTAL OAK DR	2700	618C	SEH	77059
COASTAL PRAIRIE LN	0	445N	NWC	77493
COASTAL SPRINGS DR	0	290T	NWC	77379
COASTAL WAY	5500	571L	SWH	77085
COAST BRIDGE SE	9400	575Z	SEH	77075
COAST LINE	5400	461T	NEC	77521
COASTWAY LN	8100	575X	SEH	77075
COASTWOOD LN	400	613B	NEB	77584
COATS CREEK LN	0	406P	NWC	77449
COATSWORTH DR	0	527U	NEF	77083
COBA CT	21300	333K	NCC	77073
COBA CALLE	5100	660S	GCO	77539
COBALT	5500	414R	NEH	77016
COBALT	6100	415N	NEH	77016
COBALT CREEK LN	9600	407D	NWC	77095
COBALT GLEN DR	14000	568A	NEF	77498
COBALT GREEN DR	0	325R	NWC	77433
COBB	0	457T	NEC	77049
COBB	0	498A	CV	77530
COBB	3500	533D	SEH	77004
COBBDALE LN	0	371D	NWC	77014
COBBLE LN	5200	331E	NWC	77379
COBBLE COVE CIR	0	366J	NWC	77433
COBBLE CREEK DR	1700	333J	NCC	77073
COBBLE FALLS CT	0	407B	NWC	77095
COBBLEFIELD LN	7900	570C	SWH	77071
COBBLE GATE CT	0	251C	WD	77381
COBBLE GROVE LN	0	447A	NWC	77084
COBBLE HILL CIR	1	250D	WD	77381
COBBLE HILL DR	8000	415L	NEC	77050
COBBLE HILL PLACE	1	250D	WD	77381
COBBLE MANOR LN	3600	290U	NWC	77379
COBBLE MEADOW CT	0	366R	NWC	77433
COBBLER LN	10100	289U	NWC	77375
COBBLERS WAY	2500	617Y	SEC	77546
COBBLESHIRE CT	9300	412M	NCC	77037
COBBLESHIRE CT	23400	256D	SEM	77357
COBBLESHIRE DR	9000	412M	NCC	77037
COBBLE SHORES DR	17100	328Q	NWC	77377
COBBLESKILL LN	3500	609L	MC	77459
COBBLE SPRINGS DR	0	486K	SWC	77450
COBBLE SPRINGS DR	0	612L	PL	77584
COBBLE SPRINGS LN	0	612L	PL	77584
COBBLESTONE	18200	326Z	NWC	77429
COBBLESTONE DR	11700	490E	SWH	77024
COBBLESTONE DR	12500	489H	SWH	77024
COBBLESTONE LN	3400	500H	BT	77521
COBBLESTONE CREEK WAY	3200	447N	NWC	77084
COBBLESTONE HILL	6500	297V	NEH	77345
COBBLESTONE PATH	6900	408P	NWC	77084
COBBLETON DR	300	577W	SEH	77034
COBBLE TREE CT	9000	527N	NEF	77407
COBBS COVE LN	9900	416Z	NEC	77044
COBBS CREEK CT	12000	371M	NWC	77067
COBBS CREEK RD	12100	371M	NWC	77067
COBDEN CT	12800	576V	SEH	77034
COBIA DR	0	485B	SWC	77450
COBIA DR	0	485F	SWC	77494
COBLES	5100	330Z	NWC	77069
COBLESKILL LN	10500	528Z	SWH	77099
COBOLT CREEK LN	0	407D	NWC	77095
COBOLT FALLS DR	10400	367Z	NWC	77095

Street Name	Block	Pg/Sq	Loc	Zips
COBRE VALLEY CIR	15400	618F	SEH	77062
COBRE VALLEY DR	14500	618E	SEH	77062
COBURN	300	500P	BT	77520
COBURN AVE	300	659E	LC	77573
COCHET SPRING DR	16100	330M	NWC	77379
COCHISE TRAIL	0	658U	LC	77573
COCHITI TRAIL	0	377L	NEH	77346
COCHRAN	0	493H	NEH	77009
COCHRAN	1900	493D	NEH	77009
COCHRAN	6100	453M	NEH	77022
COCHRAN DR	24400	296L	SEM	77365
COCHRAN LN	100	463F	MB	77520
COCHRAN PARK TRAIL	0	293G	SEM	77386
COCHRANS CROSSING DR	3300	250C	WD	77381
COCKBURN	8600	415Y	NEH	77078
COCKEREL	200	452R	NWH	77018
COCKRUM BLVD	7000	370F	NWH	77066
COCO	31000	248W	SWM	77362
COCO RD	30100	325Q	NWC	77429
COCOA LN	2500	537P	PA	77502
COCOBOLA LN	0	407J	NWC	77433
COCONA LN	2800	333P	NCC	77073
COCONINO LN	11700	328C	NWC	77377
COCOPLUM DR	20500	446S	NWC	77449
COCO SHORES CT	0	377K	NEC	77044
CODWELL, DR JOHN DR	0	495D	NEH	77013
CODY	200	453Y	NEH	77009
CODY'S RUN	14900	328W	NWC	77429
COE CT	10000	411N	NWH	77088
COE RD	100	247K	SWM	77362
COE COUNTRY	0	247Y	SWM	77355
COE LOOP	15000	287A	SWM	77355
COE LOOP	15500	286D	SWM	77355
COFFE DR	3600	578A	PA	77505
COFFEE	7400	533V	SEH	77033
COFFEE	8600	573D	SEH	77033
COFFEEBEND	0	484R	NEF	77494
COFFEE MILL LAKE CT	17900	367S	NWC	77433
COFFMAN CT	2800	454W	NEH	77026
COGBURN PARK DR	0	572R	SWH	77047
COG HILL DR	6300	578J	PA	77505
COGLIN	1200	494G	NEH	77020
COHASSET PLACE	100	249M	NWH	77375
COHASSET PLACE	100	249M	NWH	77375
COHEN GREEN LN	0	486H	SWC	77094
COHN	700	492G	NWH	77007
COHN	6500	412Y	NWH	77091
COHO LN	12600	572K	SWH	77045
COHUTTA LN	11000	414T	NCC	77093
COKE	4200	494L	NEH	77020
COKEBERRY	1	251R	WD	77380
COLA	1000	412T	NWH	77088
COLBERT	8500	249Z	NWC	77375
COLBROOK	0	612X	NWB	77583
COLBURY CT	2000	486Q	SWC	77450
COLBY	1	493R	SEH	77003
COLBY DR	1500	502W	BT	77520
COLBY LN	10000	289F	NWC	77375
COLBY BEND LN	2400	485Q	NEF	77450
COLBY LODGE DR	2300	486P	SWC	77450
COLBY RUN CT	7300	527J	NEF	77407
COLCHESTER	4400	452E	NWH	77018
COLCHESTER WAY	4600	569X	MC	77459
COLCHESTER WAY	4300	577E	PA	77504
COLDALE GLEN LN	17900	527J	NEF	77407
COLDDE MEADOW LN	0	290P	NWC	77379
COLDFIELD	0	406Y	NWC	77449
COLD HARBOR LN	16600	527T	NEF	77083
COLD LAKE DR	8500	411R	NWH	77088
COLD RAIN DR	0	525R	NEF	77407
COLD RIVER CT	9300	376A	HM	77396
COLD RIVER DR	0	376E	HM	77396
COLD RIVER DR	2000	376A	HM	77396
COLD SPRINGS	13700	415A	NEC	77396
COLDSPRINGS CT	1	291B	WD	77380
COLD SPRINGS DR	11200	449X	NWH	77043
COLD SPRINGS WAY	9800	329L	NWC	77375
COLDSTONE CREEK CT	0	525M	NEF	77407
COLDSTREAM DR	6300	578E	PA	77505
COLDSTREAM RD	1000	491C	NWH	77055
COLDWATER LN	600	336K	NEH	77339
COLDWATER BRIDGE CT	10900	528W	NEF	77498
COLDWATER BRIDGE LN	2100	658U	LC	77573
COLD WATER CANYON	0	446J	NWC	77449
COLDWATER CANYON LN	3200	445M	NWC	77449
COLDWATER COVE LN	0	366J	NWC	77433
COLDWATER MEADOW LN	0	335N	NCC	77338
COLDWATER MEADOW LN	20200	335N	NCC	77338
COLDWATER MEADOW LN	20200	335N	NCC	77338
COLE AVE	100	618X	WB	77598
COLE BRIDGE CT	18200	326R	NWC	77429
COLE BRIDGE LN	16100	326V	NWC	77429
COLEBROOK CT	3400	613V	PL	77584
COLEBROOK DR	11000	529F	SWH	77072
COLEBURN DR	16000	407D	NWC	77095
COLECHESTER CT	900	292B	NCC	77373
COLE CREEK DR	6700	451A	NWH	77092
COLE CREEK DR	9200	410S	NWC	77040
COLECREST CT	0	328S	NWC	77429
COLECREST LN	0	488T	SWH	77077
COLECREST LN	0	488T	SWH	77077
COLE CROSSING	0	367D	NWC	77429
COLEFIELD LN	7300	407K	NWC	77433
COLEMAN	900	537J	PA	77506
COLEMAN CT	6700	609Y	NEF	77459
COLEMAN BOYLIN	1200	659N	LC	77573
COLEMAN OAKS DR	0	326U	NWC	77429
COLEMANS WAY CT	0	616L	SEC	77089
COLENDALE DR	9100	412M	NCC	77037
COLE PARK CIR	22200	485R	NEF	77450
COLE POINT DR	0	375Y	NEC	77396
COLE POINT DR	0	415C	NEH	77396
COLERIDGE	3800	532A	WU	77005
COLERIDGE LN	20600	526J	NEF	77407
COLERIDGE ST	0	568W	SG	77479
COLESBERRY CT	5300	486W	NEF	77450
COLES CROSSING	16200	367C	NWC	77429
COLES CROSSING DR	12900	367H	NWC	77429
COLES CROSSING NORTH DR	13600	367H	NWC	77429
COLES FARM DR	1700	568Z	SG	77478
COLES WAY CT	0	616L	SEC	77089
COLETO	8100	535K	SEH	77017
COLETO CREEK CT	4500	526X	NEF	77406
COLETO CREEK LN	0	660P	LC	77573
COLE TRACE LN	26400	484Y	NEF	77494
COLETTE	33000	246V	SWM	77355
COLETTE LN	24900	296Q	SEM	77365
COLEUS LN	0	461P	NEC	77521
COLEWICK CT	900	292B	NCC	77373
COLFAX	5600	494D	NEH	77020
COLGATE	3700	535T	SEH	77087
COLGATE	8000	535T	SEH	77061

Street Name	Block	Pg/Sq	Loc	Zips
COLIMA DR	7200	527K	NEF	77083
COLINDALE RIDGE LN	0	326U	NWC	77429
COLIN SPRINGS LN	27500	293F	SEM	77386
COLLEEN DR	2300	615U	PL	77581
COLLEEN RD	8900	450L	NWH	77080
COLLEEN MEADOWS CIR	3500	450M	NWH	77080
COLLEEN WOODS CIR	3500	450M	NWH	77080
COLLEGE	100	459R	HG	77562
COLLEGE	500	531L	BL	77401
COLLEGE	500	536W	SH	77587
COLLEGE	700	576A	SH	77587
COLLEGE	1400	575D	SH	77587
COLLEGE	1700	575D	SEH	77017
COLLEGE	5600	532E	WU	77005
W. COLLEGE	6700	532E	WU	77005
E. COLLEGE	6700	532E	WU	77005
COLLEGE	18400	322A	WCO	77484
COLLEGE GREEN DR	1700	618R	SEH	77058
COLLEGE PARK DR	4300	538Y	DP	77536
COLLETON DR	0	257E	SEM	77357
COLLEVILLE SUR MER LN	0	291U	NWC	77388
COLLEY	2300	454A	NEH	77093
COLLEY	2400	454B	NEH	77093
COLLIER	1200	494X	SEH	77023
COLLIER	2000	534F	SEH	77023
COLLIFORD CREEK CT	0	484J	NEF	77494
COLLIFORD CREEK CT		484J	NEF	77494
COLLINA SPRINGS CT	6300	409W	NWC	77041
COLLINA SPRINGS CT	6300	409W	NWC	77041
COLLINFORD CT	23700	485T	NEF	77494
COLLINGATE LN	0	407J	NWC	77433
COLLINGDALE	8400	538Y	LP	77571
COLLINGSFIELD DR	2100	568C	SG	77478
COLLINGSWOOD DR	10200	579C	LP	77571
COLLINGSWORTH	300	453Z	NEH	77009
COLLINGSWORTH	2400	454Z	NEH	77026
COLLINGTON CT	4500	609P	MC	77459
COLLINGTREE DR	25100	250S	NWC	77389
COLLINGWOOD DR	16800	527X	NEF	77407
COLLINGWOOD RD	10300	579B	LP	77571
COLLINGWOOD MESQUITE	0	579D	LP	77571
COLLIN JOHN TRAIL	19200	255R	SEM	77365
COLLIN PARK	10300	575V	SEH	77075
COLLINS	100	298X	NEH	77336
COLLINS RD	1300	413L	NCC	77093
COLLINS RD	4500	414L	NCC	77093
COLLINS RD	5500	414M	NEH	77016
COLLINS PLACE	1	493M	NEH	77002
COLLINS VIEW DR	0	257E	SEM	77357
COLLINSVILLE DR	0	328V	NWC	77377
N. COLLOSSEUM CIR	0	257D	RF	77357
N. COLLOSSEUM CIR	0	258A	SEM	77357
S. COLLOSSEUM CIR	0	257D	RF	77357
S. COLLOSSEUM CIR	0	258A	SEM	77357
COLMAR WAY	3500	447J	NWC	77084
COLMESNEIL	5000	614Q	PL	77584
COLOGNE DR	13300	368Q	NWC	77065
COLOMA LN	11300	490L	PP	77024
COLOMBA ST	0	572E	SWH	77045
COLOMBIA DR	4200	577B	PA	77504
COLOMBIA DR	4800	577C	PA	77505
COLONA	0	288S	NWC	77377
COLONEL FISCHER BLVD	18800	334Y	NEH	77032
COLONEL FORBINS ST	0	449T	NWH	77043
COLONES	0	578J	PA	77505
COLONIAL	0	659D	LC	77573
COLONIAL	1100	531C	BL	77401
S. COLONIAL CT	2200	658P	LC	77573
N. COLONIAL CT	2200	658P	LC	77573
COLONIAL CT	2300	610J	MC	77459
COLONIAL CT	5100	577C	PA	77505
COLONIAL DR	300	616Z	FR	77546
COLONIAL DR	2000	502N	BT	77520
COLONIAL DR	6600	614V	PL	77584
COLONIAL LN	7700	533U	SEH	77051
COLONIAL BEND LN	21700	485V	NEF	77450
COLONIAL BIRCH LN	0	445W	NWC	77493
COLONIAL BIRCH LN	0	445W	NWC	77493
COLONIAL BRIDGE LN	15700	333S	NCC	77073
COLONIAL CREST DR	1500	444Z	KT	77493
COLONIAL ELM DR	24600	445W	NWC	77493
COLONIAL FALLS LN	8500	375Z	NEC	77396
COLONIAL FOREST CIR	18100	330E	NWC	77379
COLONIAL FOREST LN	8200	330E	NWC	77379
COLONIAL FOREST LN	8300	329M	NWC	77379
COLONIALGATE DR	22500	334B	NCC	77373
COLONIAL GLEN CT	0	612U	PL	77584
COLONIAL HILL DR	0	366P	NWC	77433
COLONIAL HILLS	700	413B	NCC	77060
COLONIAL LAKES DR	2600	609F	MC	77459
COLONIAL MANOR DR	1200	445W	NWC	77493
COLONIAL MAPLE DR	24500	445W	NWC	77493
COLONIAL OAKS LN	8200	330J	NWC	77379
COLONIAL PARK LN	5200	485X	NEF	77494
COLONIAL PINES CT	25600	250T	NWC	77389
COLONIAL PKWY	23600	445W	NWC	77449
COLONIAL PKWY	24900	444Z	KT	77493
COLONIAL RIDGE DR	2300	617Y	SEC	77546
COLONIAL ROW DR	0	251L	SWM	77380
COLONIAL SPRINGS LN	2300	293F	SEM	77386
COLONIAL TRAIL DR	11300	370R	NWC	77066
COLONIST PARK DR	2000	568Z	SG	77478
COLONNADE DR	1700	532M	SWH	77030
COLONY	0	614M	PL	77581
COLONY	7700	529M	SWH	77036
COLONY CT	0	577C	PA	77505
COLONY CT	10200	450E	NWH	77041
COLONY LN	600	453A	NEH	77076
COLONY LN	2400	614R	PL	77581
COLONY LN	6500	375W	NEC	77396
COLONY LN	19300	256F	SEM	77357
COLONY BAY DR	0	609L	MC	77459
COLONY BEND DR	16700	617U	SEC	77546
COLONY BEND LN	7200	609R	MC	77459
COLONY COVE DR	9100	329R	NWC	77379
COLONY CREEK	0	656J	NEB	77511
COLONY CREEK DR	16800	330N	NWC	77379
COLONY CREEK DR	17100	329R	NWC	77379
COLONY CREST CT	3200	489X	SWH	77082
COLONY GLEN CT	800	617H	SEH	77062
COLONY GREEN DR	23100	485K	SWC	77494
COLONY GROVE LN	19100	446D	NWC	77449
COLONY HAVEN CIR	2600	293T	NCC	77373
COLONY HEATH LN	0	571K	SWH	77085
COLONY HILL LN	0	371D	NWC	77014
COLONY HILL LN	0	371D	NWC	77014
COLONY HURST TRAIL	0	293Y	NCC	77373
COLONY KNOLL CT	2600	609G	MC	77459
COLONY LAKE CT	0	366U	NWC	77433
COLONY LAKE ESTATES	0	569T	NEF	77459
COLONY LAKES DR	1200	568W	SG	77479
COLONY OAKS CT	8400	330J	NWC	77379

Street Name	Block	Pg/Sq	Loc	Zips
COLONY POINT CT	7700	407L	NWC	77095
COLONY POINT LN	0	609P	MC	77459
COLONYPOND DR	9200	329R	NWC	77379
COLONY SHORE CIR	0	366K	NWC	77433
E. COLONY SHORE DR	12100	366K	NWC	77433
COLONY SHORE DR	12100	366K	NWC	77433
W. COLONY SHORE DR	12200	366K	NWC	77433
N. COLONY SHORE DR	18600	366K	NWC	77433
S. COLONY SHORE DR	18700	366K	NWC	77433
COLONY SPRING LN	0	446D	NWC	77449
COLONY STREAM DR	17400	329R	NWC	77379
COLONY TRAIL LN	19300	446D	NWC	77449
COLONY VIEW LN	7300	609R	MC	77459
COLONYWAY CT	9200	329R	NWC	77379
COLONYWOOD PLACE	10800	251Q	WD	77380
COLORADO	0	375H	HM	77396
COLORADO	0	659E	LC	77573
COLORADO	700	493F	SWH	77007
COLORADO	1300	540D	BT	77520
COLORADO AVE	2300	660W	GCO	77539
COLORADO DR	22700	255Y	SEM	77365
COLORADO DR	22800	295C	SEM	77365
COLORADO RIVER DR	0	253Z	SEM	77386
COLORADO SPRINGS CT	0	292U	NCC	77373
COLORADO SPRINGS LN	0	406F	NWC	77433
COLOSSEUM CT	26300	258A	SEM	77357
COLQUITT	100	493W	SWH	77002
COLQUITT	400	493W	SWH	77006
COLQUITT	1700	492Y	SWH	77098
COLQUITT	3700	492X	SWH	77027
COLSON LN	5200	502B	NEC	77521
COLSON SPRINGS DR	0	326T	NWC	77429
COLSON WAY	0	568W	SG	77479
COLT	0	656D	FR	77546
COLT	10300	574E	SEH	77033
COLT CANYON	9300	616E	SEC	77089
COLT CREEK CT	0	377K	NEC	77346
COLTER STONE DR	21700	290Q	NWC	77388
COLTON	5900	414Z	NEH	77016
COLTON	7300	415W	NEH	77016
COLTON COVE DR	0	368W	NWC	77095
COLTON COVE DR	0	408A	NWC	77095
COLTON HOLLOW DR	2400	371M	NWC	77067
COLTON WAY	0	659S	LC	77573
W. COLT SHADOW LN	0	294J	SEM	77386
S. COLT SHADOW LN	0	294J	SEM	77386
N. COLT SHADOW LN	0	294J	SEM	77386
E. COLT SHADOW LN	0	294J	SEM	77386
COLT SPRINGS CT	0	327U	NWC	77429
COLT SPRINGS LN	0	327U	NWC	77429
COLTWOOD DR	3300	331C	NWC	77388
COLT WOOD DR	3500	331F	NWC	77388
COLUMBA CT	31200	248X	TB	77375
COLUMBIA	0	577B	PA	77504
COLUMBIA	200	493A	NWH	77007
COLUMBIA	900	453W	NWH	77008
COLUMBIA	2100	501Q	BT	77521
COLUMBIA	3000	453W	NWH	77018
COLUMBIA LN	700	538Y	DP	77536
COLUMBIA LN	2100	612Y	NWB	77578
COLUMBIA BLUE DR	1000	570W	MC	77489
COLUMBIA BLUE DR	1400	610B	MC	77489
COLUMBIA CIRCLE	2300	619Y	LC	77573
COLUMBIA FALLS CT	21800	525G	NEF	77494
COLUMBIA FALLS LN	6100	525G	NEF	77494
COLUMBIA FOREST DR	0	408F	NWC	77095
COLUMBIA GLEN CT	0	250U	NWC	77389
COLUMBIA KEY DR	0	328K	NWC	77429
COLUMBIA KEY DR		328k	NWC	77377
COLUMBIA PINES LN	11400	366Q	NWC	77433
COLUMBIA SPRINGS CT	0	366U	NWC	77433
COLUMBINE DR	0	293B	SEM	77386
COLUMBINE LN	7400	456M	NEC	77049
COLUMBINE LN	13100	457J	NEC	77049
COLUMBUS	1000	493N	SWH	77019
COLUMBUS CT	8400	613V	PL	77584
COLUMBUS MILL DR	0	257F	SEM	77357
COLVILLE	15200	498E	CV	77530
COLVILLE DR	14900	497H	NEC	77530
COLVIN	3700	456X	NEH	77013
COLWELL RD	2300	331Q	NWC	77068
COLWYN LN	15300	409M	JV	77040
COMA	8300	533Y	SEH	77051
COMAL	1300	536K	PA	77506
COMAL	4700	614D	PL	77581
COMAL	7800	533U	SEH	77051
COMAL	0	253Y	SEM	77386
COMAL DR	0	539N	DP	77536
COMAL BEND LN	16000	328S	NWC	77429
COMAL KARST DR	0	293F	SEM	77386
COMAL PARK CT	0	578T	SEH	77059
N. COMAL RIVER	0	366Z	NWC	77433
E. COMAL RIVER	0	406D	NWC	77433
COMAL RIVER CT	0	253U	SEM	77386
S. COMAL RIVER DR	0	406D	NWC	77433
COMAL RIVER LOOP	0	253U	SEM	77386
COMAL SPRINGS DR	0	538R	DP	77536
COMANCHE	1200	538R	DP	77536
COMANCHE	4200	577F	PA	77504
COMANCHE	7400	461S	NEC	77521
COMANCHE DR	18400	295G	SEM	77365
COMANCHE LN	10000	410W	NWH	77041
COMANCHE SPRINGS CT	10400	367U	NWC	77095
COMANCHE TRAIL	33500	247Q	SWM	77355
COMBINE LN	0	458S	NEC	77049
COMEAUX LN	0	527W	NEF	77469
COMELY LN	13600	489F	SWH	77079
COMET DR	11900	411E	NWC	77086
COMET VIEW CT	4600	376S	NEC	77396
COMFORT CT	15500	328N	NWC	77429
COMFORT GLEN CT	12000	573L	SEH	77047
COMILE	500	453Q	NEH	77022
COMINSKY DR	0	457V	NEC	77049
COMMANDER	2100	536V	PA	77502
COMMERCE	0	459D	NEC	77562
S. COMMERCE	100	501Y	BT	77520
N. COMMERCE	100	501U	BT	77520
COMMERCE	100	288G	TB	77375
COMMERCE	800	493M	DT	77002
COMMERCE	2400	494N	SEH	77003
E. COMMERCE	200	618Y	WB	77598
COMMERCE AVE	0	296F	SEM	77365
COMMERCE BUSINESS DR	0	569U	NEF	77477
COMMERCE CREEK DR	0	410T	NWC	77040
COMMERCE GREEN BLVD	100	568Q	SG	77478
COMMERCE OAKS DR	27600	252K	OR	77385
COMMERCE PARK DR	8100	530N	SWH	77036
COMMERCIAL	13700	572X	SWH	77047
COMMERCIAL LN	22700	289L	NWC	77375
COMMERCIAL CENTER BLVD	2600	485T	NEF	77494
COMMERCIAL PARK DR	0	335S	NEH	77338
COMMERCIAL PARK LN	27700	288Q	TB	77375

Street Name	Block	Pg/Sq	Loc	Zips
COMMERICAL PARK DR	0	288R	TB	77375
COMMODORE WAY	300	488A	SWH	77079
COMMON	1500	493H	NEH	77009
COMMON CREST DR	15000	408F	NWC	77095
COMMON OAK DR	0	450U	NWH	77080
COMMON PARK DR	1200	493D	NEH	77009
COMMONS CT	8100	408F	NWC	77095
COMMONS BREEZE DR	800	298G	NEC	77336
COMMONS COVE CT	0	375X	NEC	77396
COMMONS ENCLAVE	0	298K	NEC	77336
COMMONS FOREST CT	30000	298L	NEC	77336
COMMONS FOREST DR	29100	298Q	NEC	77336
COMMONS GLEN DR	0	450V	NWH	77080
COMMONS HILL LN	0	450V	NWH	77080
COMMONS LAKE DR	100	298N	NEC	77336
COMMONS LAKE EDGE DR	800	298G	NEC	77336
COMMONS LAKEVIEW DR	600	298L	NEC	77336
COMMONS MEADOW LN	0	450V	NWH	77080
COMMONS OAK LN	30500	298L	NEC	77336
COMMONS OAKS DR	0	298U	NEC	77336
COMMONS PARK DR	30100	298L	NEC	77336
COMMONS PINE LN	900	298L	NEC	77336
COMMONS ROYAL VIEW DR	30200	298L	NEC	77336
COMMONS SCENIC VIEW DR	30200	298L	NEC	77336
COMMONS SPRING CREEK DR	800	298L	NEC	77336
COMMONS SUPERIOR DR	29400	298L	NEC	77336
COMMONS TRAIL LN	300	298L	NEC	77336
COMMONS VIEW DR	500	298T	NEH	77336
S. COMMONS VIEW DR	900	298Y	NEH	77336
N. COMMONS VIEW DR	900	298Y	NEH	77336
COMMONS VISTA DR	300	298Q	NEC	77336
COMMONS WALK LN	0	375X	NEC	77396
COMMONS WATERWAY	0	298U	NEC	77336
COMMONS WAY CT	800	298L	NEC	77336
COMMONS WOODS CT	30000	298L	NEC	77336
COMMONWEALTH	1600	493N	SWH	77006
COMMONWEALTH BLVD	3300	609J	SG	77479
COMMUNITY	0	491Z	SWH	77027
COMMUNITY CT	12900	568C	SG	77478
E. COMMUNITY DR	100	256Z	SEM	77357
COMMUNITY DR	1600	537J	PA	77506
COMMUNITY DR	5300	492W	SWH	77005
COMMUNITY DR	5500	532E	WU	77005
COMMUNITY DR	22400	256Y	SEM	77357
COMMUNITY CENTER DR	24600	250W	NWC	77389
COMMUNITY COLLEGE DR	500	495H	NEH	77013
COMORO LN	17500	330K	NWC	77379
COMPANION DR	600	419F	NEC	77532
COMPAQ CENTER DR	0	329T	NWC	77377
W. COMPAQ CENTER DR	11100	329X	NWC	77070
COMPASS CT	17600	379T	NEC	77532
COMPASS COVE CIR	1000	329H	NWC	77379
S. COMPASS ROSE BLVD	1900	619Z	LC	77573
N. COMPASS ROSE CIR	400	379T	NEC	77532
S. COMPASS ROSE CIR	17500	379T	NEC	77532
COMPASS ROSE DR	7300	525M	NEF	77407
COMPASS ROSE PKWY	0	620W	LC	77573
COMPTON	8400	454D	NEH	77016
COMPTON CIR	4300	531D	BL	77401
COMPTON MANOR DR	19400	329D	NWC	77379
COMPTON POINT	0	660A	LC	77573
COMPTON POINTE	0	660A	LC	77573
COMSTOCK CIR	17400	331Q	NWC	77090
COMSTOCK MEADOWS DR	0	407B	NWC	77095
COMSTOCK SPRINGS DR	800	485G	SWC	77450
COMVEST PARK DR	14600	528A	SWC	77082
CONANT CT	24600	484G	NEF	77494
CONCERT DR	100	533A	SWH	77030
CONCERTO CIR	8600	410K	NWC	77040
CONCHA LN	0	531W	SWH	77096
CONCHO	6800	530M	SWH	77074
CONCHO	8000	530K	SWH	77036
CONCHO	10700	529L	SWH	77072
CONCHO BAY CT	12000	409W	NWC	77041
CONCHO BAY DR	6300	409W	NWC	77041
CONCHO BAY DR	12000	409W	NWC	77041
CONCHO CREEK LN	0	367W	NWC	77095
CONCHO MOUNTAIN	7100	370A	NWC	77069
CONCHO RIVER CT	0	253Y	SEM	77386
CONCHO RIVER CT	1800	569W	SG	77478
CONCHO SPRINGS DR	19400	406V	NWC	77449
CONCHO SPRINGS DR	19500	406U	NWC	77449
CONCHO VALLEY DR	0	249V	NWC	77375
CONCORD	1500	538N	DP	77536
CONCORD	8100	535K	SEH	77017
CONCORD CIR	1	490K	BH	77024
CONCORD CIR	2600	659C	LC	77573
CONCORD DR	2600	659C	LC	77573
CONCORD LN	9200	410A	NWC	77064
CONCORD RD	1900	537N	PA	77502
CONCORDANCE DR	0	293G	SEM	77386
CONCORD BRIDGE CT	0	408Z	NWC	77041
CONCORD BRIDGE DR	5700	408Z	NWC	77041
CONCORD GLEN LN	0	484Z	NEF	77494
CONCORD GREEN DR	0	447A	NWC	77084
CONCORD GROVE	14400	408T	NWC	77084
CONCORD HILL DR	20200	326X	NWC	77433
CONCORDIA CT	2800	659M	LC	77573
CONCORDIA DR	100	485C	SWC	77450
CONCORDIA PARK LN	21100	525H	NEF	77407
CONCORD KNOLL DR	0	615U	PL	77581
CONCORD MEADOW LN	14000	573T	SEC	77047
CONCORD PARK DR	6600	410S	NWH	77040
CONCORD PLACE	1200	569Y	MC	77477
CONCORD TRACE	0	450V	NWH	77055
CONCOURSE DR	9300	529R	SWH	77036
CONCRETE ST	100	535C	SEH	77012
CONDESSA DR	16200	527F	NEF	77083
CONDON LN	5500	571X	SWH	77053
CONDOR DR	800	657N	FR	77546
CONDORS NEST	0	485E	SWC	77494
CONDOR WAY	7000	571S	SWH	77489
CONDREY CT	18700	328F	NWC	77377
CONE CREEK DR	2000	331L	NWC	77090
CONECREST CT	5600	411U	NWH	77088
CONEFALL CT	23900	293X	NCC	77373
CONEFLOWER RD	0	659G	LC	77573
CONERY GROVE DR	0	295L	SEM	77365
CONESTOGA CIR	700	485H	SWC	77450
CONESTOGA LANE CT	11500	370L	NWC	77066
CONFEDERATE	6800	614Z	PL	77584
CONFEDERATE CT	3300	610V	MC	77459
CONFEDERATE DR	3200	610V	MC	77459
CONFEDERATE RD	1100	450X	NWH	77055
CONFEDERATE SOUTH DR	3100	610V	MC	77459
CONFEDERATE WAY	200	619M	EL	77586
CONGER	8800	575H	SEH	77075
CONGO LN	8600	410P	NWC	77040
CONGO LN	15300	409R	JV	77040
CONGRESS	600	493M	DT	77002
CONGRESS	2200	493M	SEH	77003
CONGRESSIONAL CIR	0	250K	NWC	77389

Street Name	Block	Pg/Sq	Loc	Zips
CONICA CT	5600	291S	NWC	77379
CONIFER DR	2900	580L	LP	77571
CONIFER RD	13000	489F	SWH	77079
CONIFER BAY CT	15400	618B	SEH	77059
CONIFER CHASE	0	486D	SWC	77094
CONIFER CREEK TRAIL	1900	338B	NEH	77345
CONIFER FARM DR	0	325F	NWC	77447
CONIFER POINT LN	17500	447C	NWC	77084
CONIFER RIDGE WAY	0	376H	NEC	77346
CONIFER SPRINGS CT	11900	371L	NWC	77067
CONIFER SPRINGS LN	11900	371L	NWC	77067
CONIPER CIR	0	580F	LP	77571
CONKLIN	700	412Q	NWH	77088
CONKLIN	1900	412N	NWH	77088
CONKLIN LN	12400	576V	SEH	77034
CONKLIN LN	13400	577S	SEH	77034
CONLAN BAY DR	6100	408Y	NWC	77041
CONLEY	5800	533M	SEH	77021
CONLON	6600	535X	SEH	77061
CONNAUGHT GARDEN DR	8500	528Q	SWC	77083
CONNAUGHT WAY	300	457X	NEC	77015
CONNECTICUT	300	495Z	NEH	77029
CONNELLY RD	1500	501E	NEC	77521
CONNEMARA DR	7400	407J	NWC	77433
CONNER CT	5000	577K	PA	77504
CONNER COVE	0	525R	NEF	77407
CONNER CREEK CT	0	377L	NEC	77346
CONNER GROVE CT	0	445S	NWC	77493
CONNER LAKE LN	0	377H	NEH	77346
CONNER PARK DR	13900	367D	NWC	77429
CONNER REINHARDT RD	0	256H	SEM	77357
CONNERS RD	1	259S	NEC	77336
CONNERS ACE DR	15600	330R	NWC	77379
CONNIE	200	413X	NEH	77076
CONNIES COURT LN	4500	609B	MC	77459
CONNOR	11700	414K	NCC	77039
CONNORDALE LN	28500	293E	SEM	77386
CONNOR LANDING LN	0	366Z	NWC	77433
CONNOR REINHARDT RD	0	257J	SEM	77357
CONNOR RUN CT		366T	NWC	77433
CONNORS PATH CT	0	333E	NCC	77073
CONNORVALE CT	700	413F	NCC	77060
CONNORVALE LN	500	413E	NCC	77060
CONNORVALE RD	900	413H	NCC	77039
CONNORVALE RD	2300	414F	NCC	77039
CONOLY	100	453X	NWH	77009
CONOVER CT	14700	497D	NEC	77015
CONQUISTADOR DR	22000	339W	NEC	77532
CONRAD	100	536H	PA	77506
CONRAD LN	3100	446K	NWC	77449
CONRAD SAUER DR	1000	489D	NWH	77043
CONRAD SAUER DR	1100	449Z	NWH	77043
CONROE HUFSMITH RD	26000	249N	SWM	77354
CONROE LAKE CT	3800	615Y	PL	77581
CONROY	4100	454X	NEH	77026
CONROY POINTE LN	6000	524E	NEF	77494
CONSER	0	576Q	SEH	77034
CONSORT DR	10800	372U	NWC	77038
CONSTANCE DR	900	490B	HE	77024
CONSTANCE KNOLLS DR	0	338M	NEH	77336
CONSTANTINE	26200	258A	RF	77357
CONSTANTINE DR	3100	258A	SEM	77357
CONSTELLATION BLVD	400	619X	LC	77573
CONSTELLATION LN	8000	575P	SEH	77075
CONSTELLATION POINT DR	0	251C	WD	77380
CONSTITUTION AVE	1300	570S	SF	77477
CONSTITUTION LN	15500	617S	SEC	77546
CONSUELA DR	9600	530S	SWH	77074
CONSUELA DR	10200	530W	SWH	77031
CONSUL CT	0	258F	SEM	77357
CONSULAR CT	3200	613V	PL	77584
CONSULATE PLAZA DR	5300	374Q	NEH	77032
CONTADO CT	13500	368A	NWC	77429
CONTEMPORARY GARDEN OAKS	0	452M	NWH	77018
CONTENDER LN	15500	617T	SEC	77546
CONTI	1300	493H	NEH	77002
CONTI	2500	494E	NEH	77020
CONTINENTAL DR	3200	609D	MC	77459
CONTINENTAL DR	4300	529E	SWH	77072
CONTINENTAL PKWY	18400	377A	NEC	77346
CONTINENTAL PKWY	18600	337W	NEC	77346
CONTOUR PLACE	5000	531T	SWH	77096
CONVERSE	1000	493N	SWH	77006
CONVOY CT	16000	419A	NEC	77532
CONWARD DR	4100	371N	NWC	77066
CONWAY	2800	532K	SWH	77025
CONWAY LANDING	14000	367D	NWC	77429
CONWAY MEADOWS CT	0	484V	NWF	77494
CONWAY PLACE	13500	368B	NWC	77429
COOK	1000	620P	SB	77586
COOK	1400	493P	SWH	77006
COOK	20000	286S	NWC	77377
COOK	21000	285V	NWC	77377
S. COOK CIR	4300	658N	LC	77573
N. COOK CIR	4300	658N	LC	77573
COOK DR	1	541D	BT	77520
COOK RD	3800	529E	SWH	77072
COOK RD	8600	528Z	SWH	77099
COOK, A B RD	0	244Z	WCO	77447
COOK FOREST DR	0	377G	NEC	77346
COOKGLASS DR	8400	529N	SWH	77072
COOK LANDING DR	0	527T	NEF	77469
COOK POINT CT	0	484X	NEF	77494
COOK POINT LN	0	484X	NEF	77494
COOK RIDGE DR	0	406B	NWC	77433
COOKRIDGE LN	14001	372A	NWC	77014
COOKSTEEL DR	8400	529N	SWH	77072
COOKWIND DR	8400	529N	SWH	77072
COOKWOOD DR	8400	529N	SWH	77072
COOLAIRE	0	419V	BR	77532
COOL CREEK CT	6000	338E	NEH	77345
COOLGREEN AVE	12400	456Z	NEH	77013
COOLGROVE DR	7900	457F	NEC	77049
COOLIDGE	600	498G	CV	77530
COOLIDGE	8300	535F	SEH	77012
COOLIDGE DR	1400	538R	DP	77536
COOL MIST DR	500	496B	NEH	77013
COOLRIDGE CT	14600	618E	SEH	77062
COOLRIDGE CREEK DR	0	328K	NWC	77429
COOLRIDGE CREEK DR		328k	NWC	77377
COOL RIVER DR	1900	371M	NWC	77067
COOL SHADOWS	11700	418P	NEC	77044
COOLSHIRE LN	8100	369D	NWC	77070
COOL SPRING DR	300	412M	NCC	77037
COOL SPRING DR	1400	412K	NWH	77088
COOL SPRINGS LN	2300	568A	SG	77498
COOLWOOD DR	500	496F	NEH	77013
COONS RD	23500	329E	NWC	77375
COON TREE CT	5500	337S	NEC	77346
COOPER RD	1	413X	NEH	77076
COOPER BREAKS DR	0	377F	NEC	77346
COOPER CANYON DR	12000	328C	NWC	77377

Street Name	Block	Pg/Sq	Loc	Zips
COOPER COVE LN	0	660J	LC	77573
COOPER CREEK FALLS		249Z	NWC	77375
COOPER MOUNTAIN LN	0	526P	NEF	77407
COOPER RIDGE LN	16000	611C	SWH	77053
COOPERS DRAW LN	17100	617Y	SEC	77546
COOPERS GULCH TRAIL	0	406X	NWC	77449
COOPERS HAWK CT	14000	377W	NEC	77044
COOPERS HAWK DR	12900	377W	NEC	77044
COOPERS POST LN	2500	568Y	SG	77478
COOPERSTOWN DR	12500	617E	SEH	77089
S. COOTER	31900	246T	SWM	77355
N. COOTER	31900	246T	SWM	77355
N. COOTER CT	15900	246T	SWM	77355
COPELAND	1400	494F	NEH	77020
COPELAND LN	17200	254M	SEM	77365
COPELAND RD	12900	369F	NWC	77070
COPELAND MILL LN	2700	573X	SEC	77047
COPELAND OAKS BLVD	13400	328T	NWC	77429
COPINSAY DR	0	407W	NWC	77449
COPLEY LN	11000	414T	NCC	77093
COPPAGE	6200	492F	SWH	77007
COPPER	18200	285X	NWC	77447
COPPERAS BEND CT	8200	407F	NWC	77095
COPPERAS COVE	1600	488K	SWH	77077
COPPER BEAN DR	19100	328D	NWC	77375
COPPER BLUFF LN	0	407F	NWC	77095
COPPERBLUFF LN	0	407F	NWC	77095
COPPER BOTTOM DR	0	287V	NWC	77377
COPPER BOTTOM DR	0	288S	NWC	77377
COPPER BRANCH	0	408A	NWC	77095
COPPERBROOK DR	8500	408G	NWC	77095
COPPER CANYON DR	16000	617X	SEC	77546
COPPER CAVE LN	20500	526S	NEF	77407
COPPER CLIFF DR	2900	446T	NWC	77449
COPPER COVE DR	0	407D	NWC	77095
COPPER CREEK	4100	501K	BT	77521
COPPER CREEK DR	1000	485G	SWC	77450
COPPER CREEK LN	1000	485G	SWC	77450
COPPER CREEK LN	8300	609V	NEF	77459
COPPER CREST	0	371N	NWC	77066
COPPERCREST DR	1300	252Q	SEM	77386
COPPER CROSSING CT	0	407Y	NWC	77084
COPPERDALE LN	10200	409G	NWC	77064
COPPER DOCKS TRAIL	0	332X	NWC	77090
COPPERFIELD DR	12400	569H	SWH	77031
COPPER GABLES LN	16100	327Y	NWC	77429
COPPER GROVE BLVD	0	408B	NWC	77095
COPPER GROVE BLVD	15300	408B	NWC	77095
COPPER HARBOR CT	0	407C	NWC	77095
COPPER HAVEN LN	0	407G	NWC	77095
COPPER HEATH LN	8500	407F	NWC	77095
COPPER HOLLOW LN	10000	416Z	NEC	77044
COPPER ISLES LN	0	407F	NWC	77095
COPPER JUNCTION DR	0	367W	NWC	77095
S. COPPERKNOLL CIR	100	250D	WD	77381
COPPER KNOLL LN	0	616J	PL	77089
W. COPPER LAKE DR	17300	407F	NWC	77095
W. COPPER LAKES CT	8000	407F	NWC	77095
COPPER LAKES CT	8000	407G	NWC	77095
COPPER LANTERN DR	0	366N	NWC	77433
COPPERLEAF DR	26000	252Q	SEM	77386
COPPER LILLY LN	0	290D	NWC	77389
COPPER MANOR CT	0	485W	NEF	77494
COPPERMEADE CT	11500	372P	NWC	77067
COPPERMEADE DR	1200	372N	NWC	77067
COPPER MILL DR	12600	369L	NWC	77070
COPPER MIST LN	9700	407B	NWC	77095
COPPER MOUNTAIN LN		526Q	NEF	77406
COPPER OAK LN	0	408N	NWC	77084
COPPER PINE DR	0	328E	NWC	77377
COPPER POINT LN	0	527J	NEF	77407
COPPER RIDGE LN	0	615B	PL	77581
W. COPPER SAGE CIR	1	250C	WD	77381
S. COPPER SAGE CIR	1	250C	WD	77381
E. COPPER SAGE CIR	1	250C	WD	77381
COPPER SHORE CIR	8100	407G	NWC	77095
COPPER SHORE DR	17000	407G	NWC	77095
COPPER SHORES LN	0	524M	NEF	77406
COPPER SKY CT	0	484U	NEF	77494
COPPER SKY CT	0	612K	PL	77545
COPPER SKY DR	0	612K	PL	77545
COPPER SKY LN	0	484U	NEF	77494
COPPERSMITH DR	100	485C	SWC	77450
COPPER SPRINGS LN	0	408S	NWC	77084
COPPER STAR	3300	447L	NWC	77084
COPPERSTONE RD	0	407H	NWC	77095
COPPER TRACE LN	14300	367C	CY	77429
COPPERTREE LN	12100	570H	SWH	77035
COPPER VALLEY CT	2500	371L	NWC	77067
COPPER VERDE LN	0	407V	NWC	77084
COPPER VILLA LN	0	408S	NWC	77084
W. COPPER VILLAGE DR	8200	407H	NWC	77095
E. COPPER VILLAGE DR	8200	407H	NWC	77095
COPPERVINE LN	19300	446Z	NWC	77084
COPPERWILLOW CT	14000	417B	NEC	77044
COPPERWOOD DR	8200	410L	NWC	77040
COPPERWOOD DR	10100	410M	NWH	77040
COPPERWOOD PARK LN	2000	252R	SEM	77386
COPPERWOOD RUN WAY	0	407R	NWC	77084
COPRA LN	2800	333P	NCC	77073
COQUINA DR	0	524H	NEF	77494
CORA	7400	412S	NWH	77088
CORA	10700	412J	NWC	77088
CORAL	500	535A	SEH	77023
CORAL	1000	535E	SEH	77012
CORAL	6700	494M	NEH	77020
CORAL CIR	3500	620E	SB	77586
CORAL DR	0	613W	NEB	77578
CORAL DR	500	580K	LP	77571
CORAL BAY	16100	419C	NEC	77532
CORAL BAY DR	100	619Z	LC	77573
CORAL BAY DR	200	659D	LC	77573
CORAL BEAN DR	14000	568A	NEF	77498
CORAL BELL LN	6000	457S	NEC	77049
CORALBEND DR	16800	367U	NWC	77095
CORALBERRY CT	1	251J	WD	77381
CORALBERRY RD	1	251J	WD	77381
CORAL BRIDGE LN	20900	291U	NWC	77388
CORAL CANE DR	0	285Q	NWC	77447
CORAL CANYON	15400	287D	NWC	77377
CORAL CHASE CT	22400	525G	NEF	77494
CORAL COVE CT	0	612G	PL	77584
CORAL COVE CT	2000	619Z	LC	77573
CORAL COVE CT	17100	407F	NWC	77095
CORAL COVE DR	0	612L	PL	77584
CORAL COVE LN	0	658T	LC	77573
CORAL CREEK DR	5100	535R	SEH	77017
CORALCREST CT	12900	448D	NWC	77041
CORAL GABLE DR	5000	330Z	NWC	77069
CORAL GABLES DR	5000	370C	NWC	77069
CORAL GARDEN LN	0	377M	NEC	77346
CORAL GARDEN LN	10800	575U	SEH	77075

Street Name	Block	Pg/Sq	Loc	Zips
CORAL GLEN CT	14800	618F	SEH	77062
CORAL HAVEN CT	0	297U	NEH	77345
CORAL LEAF TRAIL	15400	325R	NWC	77433
CORAL LILLY DR	400	660E	LC	77573
CORAL MEADOW CT	4100	446H	NWC	77449
CORALMONT	1400	412F	NWC	77038
CORAL OAK CT	15100	618G	SEH	77059
CORAL OAK WAY	0	297L	NEH	77345
CORAL PARK DR	30900	252U	SEM	77386
CORAL POINTE DR	5500	448H	NWC	77041
CORAL REEF DR	3700	620E	SB	77586
CORAL REEF DR	11900	456C	NEC	77044
CORAL RIDGE CT	3200	660A	LC	77573
CORAL RIDGE CT	13100	370C	NWC	77069
CORAL RIDGE DR	3200	660A	LC	77573
CORAL RIDGE RD	5400	370C	NWC	77069
CORAL ROCKS CT	0	610T	MC	77459
CORAL ROSE CT	4500	375V	NEC	77396
CORAL SANDS DR	15000	618F	SEH	77062
CORAL SHADOWS DR	3900	446M	NWC	77449
CORAL SPRINGS CT	5800	525C	NEF	77494
CORAL SPRINGS DR	3400	613X	NEB	77578
CORAL STONE RD	10000	371T	NWC	77086
CORAL TREE PLACE	800	610S	MC	77459
CORALVILLE CT	12800	448D	NWC	77041
CORALVINE CT	1	251R	WD	77380
CORAL WAY DR	1300	619H	TL	77586
CORAL WOOD LN	0	528T	NEF	77498
CORBEL LN	8500	528Q	SWC	77083
CORBEN CREEK LN	9800	527S	NEF	77407
CORBETT CT	3500	610U	MC	77459
CORBIN	6500	451Y	NWH	77055
CORBIN CREEK DR	0	326K	NWC	77433
CORBINDALE RD	600	490C	HE	77024
CORBINGATE DR	24800	250Y	NWC	77389
CORBIT GROVE CT	0	526K	NEF	77407
CORBITT RD	27400	484S	NEF	77494
CORBRIDGE CREEK CT	0	251W	SWM	77389
CORBRIDGE GLEN CT	0	406X	NWC	77449
CORBUT BEND CT	8300	337Z	NEC	77346
CORCORAN	0	577Y	SEH	77034
CORCORAN DR	3600	446K	NWC	77449
CORDELL	200	453X	NWH	77009
CORDELLA PLACE	0	249B	SWM	77382
CORDELL BRICK LN	0	456N	NEH	77078
CORDELL FALLS CT	0	377F	NEC	77346
CORDELL LANDING DR	0	525R	NEF	77407
CORDER	2800	533P	SWH	77054
CORDER	3400	533P	SEH	77021
CORDERO DR	0	571H	SWH	77045
CORDES DR	100	338C	NEH	77336
CORDES DR	2500	568Y	SG	77479
CORDIER CT	1	494N	SEH	77003
CORDOBA CT	7700	337M	NEC	77346
CORDOBA DR	8600	412J	NWC	77088
CORDOBA DR	11500	412J	NWC	77038
CORDOBA COVE	0	660K	LC	77573
CORDOBA PINES DR	10600	412J	NWH	77088
CORDON	2900	454W	NEH	77026
CORDONA DR	6400	406V	NWC	77449
CORELAND LN	18200	326R	NWC	77429
COREOPSIS CT	0	698G	LC	77539
COREY BEND CT	0	526F	NEF	77407
COREY COVE LN	25600	485W	NEF	77494
COREY WOODS CT	8300	407G	NWC	77095
CORIANDER DR	22000	485D	SWC	77450
CORIANDER DR	22600	245Q	SWM	77355
CORIANNE CT	0	444X	KT	77493
CORIANNE ST	0	444X	KT	77493
CORINALDO CT	0	445E	NWC	77493
CORINE	900	569V	NEF	77477
CORINNA DR	0	528E	SWC	77083
CORINNE CT	3500	446L	NWC	77449
CORINTH	7800	533T	SEH	77051
CORINTH DR	6600	578A	PA	77505
CORINTHIAN PARK DR	5800	290Z	NWC	77379
CORINTHIAN PARK LN	5800	290Z	NWC	77379
CORINTHIAN POINTE	0	571L	SWH	77085
CORINTH MEADOW CT	0	445L	NWC	77449
CORK	2000	659X	DI	77539
CORK CIR	2400	616J	PL	77581
CORK DR	3500	573Q	SEH	77047
CORK LN	4200	538Y	DP	77536
CORKSIE	3000	573F	SEH	77051
CORKTREE KNOLLS	14300	327Z	NWC	77429
CORKWOOD CT	11800	576Z	SEC	77089
CORKWOOD DR	11500	576Z	SEC	77089
CORL	5600	534Q	SEH	77087
CORLANDER LN	0	461P	BT	77521
CORLEY	0	460N	HG	77562
CORMORANT	0	610F	MC	77489
CORMORANT CT	17300	376F	NEC	77396
CORNELIA DR	14100	368P	NWC	77429
CORNELL	0	453J	NWH	77022
CORNELL	2100	501U	BT	77520
CORNELL	2500	453S	NWH	77009
CORNELL	3100	453N	NWH	77022
CORNELL LN	6100	657U	LC	77573
CORNELL PARK CT	3900	619A	PA	77058
CORNELL PARK LN	24200	484D	NEF	77494
CORNERBROOK LN	0	525C	NEF	77494
CORNER CHASE	0	527C	SWC	77082
CORNER CREEK	6400	407V	NWC	77084
CORNER OAKS LN	9300	529R	SWH	77036
CORNER SQUARE	0	620L	SB	77586
CORNERSTONE	4500	615S	PL	77584
CORNERSTONE ARBOR DR	19400	366V	NWC	77433
CORNERSTONE PARK DR	0	331X	NWC	77014
CORNERSTONE PLACE DR	1700	485M	SWC	77450
CORNERSTONE VILLAGE DR	14100	331X	NWC	77014
CORNETT DR	9200	410E	NWC	77064
CORNFLOWER LN	0	525B	NEF	77494
CORNICHE	1600	619U	LC	77573
CORNINA DR	0	335N	NCC	77338
CORNING DR	12400	616D	SEH	77089
CORNISH	4300	492G	NWH	77007
CORNOUSTIE	4700	578J	PA	77505
CORNWALL	0	258F	SEM	77357
CORNWALL	16400	409L	JV	77040
CORNWALL BRIDGE LN	7300	408Q	NWC	77041
CORNWALL WAY	1200	336H	NEH	77339
CORNWELL	10000	370Z	NWC	77086
CORNWELL WAY	0	336G	NEH	77339
COROLA FOREST	12300	416L	NEC	77044
COROLA TRAIL DR	11300	370R	NWC	77066
CORONA LN	10700	529L	SWH	77072
CORONA LN	12300	528M	SWH	77072
CORONA DEL MAR DR	1700	610K	MC	77459
CORONA DEL MAR DR	15100	527M	SWC	77083
CORONADO	100	453X	NWH	77009
CORONADO	1800	656U	FR	77546
CORONADO	4500	620H	SB	77586

Street Name	Block	Pg/Sq	Loc	Zips
CORONADO CT	0	367W	NWC	77095
CORONADO LAKES DR	1500	659W	LC	77573
CORONADO PARK LN	17300	377E	NEC	77346
CORONADO SPRINGS DR	0	330H	NWC	77379
CORONADO WAY	2200	659C	LC	77573
CORONAL WAY	0	568E	NEF	77498
CORONATION DR	1	576G	SEH	77034
CORONDO CT	3500	532F	WU	77005
CORONET RIDGE CT	100	249R	NWH	77375
CORONET RIDGE CT	100	249R	NWH	77375
CORPORATE DR	5700	529D	SWH	77036
CORPORATE DR	9800	568M	SG	77478
CORPORATE DR	10500	569J	SF	77477
CORPORATE CENTRE DR	11000	449D	NWH	77041
CORPUS CHRISTI	6300	494D	NEH	77020
CORPUS CHRISTI	7100	495A	NEH	77020
CORPUS CHRISTI	12800	496D	NEH	77015
CORPUS CHRISTI	12900	497A	NEH	77015
CORRAL	17100	326M	NWC	77429
CORRAL DR	1400	331M	NWC	77090
CORRAL CORNER CT	9100	409G	NWC	77064
CORRAL CORNER LN	9800	409G	NWC	77064
CORRALES DR	7900	527L	NEF	77083
CORRAL GATE CT	0	372M	NCC	77073
CORRAL GATE CT	3500	486S	NEF	77450
CORRAL PATH CT	9800	409G	NWC	77064
CORRAL TRAIL	2500	617Y	SEC	77546
CORRAN PARK CIR	0	410L	NWC	77040
CORRIDOR PLACE	300	569P	SF	77477
CORRIDOR WAY	400	569T	NEF	77477
CORRIGAN	0	614R	PL	77584
CORRIGAN CT	3300	371C	NWC	77014
CORRIGAN DR	13600	371C	NWC	77014
CORRIGAN SPRINGS DR	0	368E	NWC	77429
CORSAIR RD	15300	571X	SWH	77053
CORSAIR RD	16200	611B	SWH	77053
CORSICA	700	496D	NEC	77015
CORSICANA	6900	494M	NEH	77020
CORSICANA	7100	495J	NEH	77020
CORSICANA LAKE LN	0	409W	NWC	77041
CORTA CALLE DR	7100	527G	SWC	77083
CORTELYOU LN	5100	534K	SEH	77021
CORTENRIDGE	0	574Z	SEH	77048
CORTES DR	7400	527K	NEF	77083
CORTINA DR	7600	528K	SWC	77083
CORTINA VALLEY DR	0	406G	NWC	77433
CORTIS	1200	532H	SWH	77030
CORTLAND RIDGE LN	10600	366V	NWC	77433
CORTLANDT	200	493E	NWH	77007
CORTLANDT	900	453W	NWH	77008
CORTLANDT	3000	453W	NWH	77018
CORTLANDT	5500	453A	NWH	77076
CORTO	3800	454K	NEH	77016
CORTONA CT	0	659P	LC	77573
CORTONA LN	0	657L	FR	77546
CORUM	11300	576W	SEH	77089
CORVALLIS DR	0	368W	NWC	77095
CORVETTE CT	700	413F	NCC	77060
CORVETTE LN	500	413F	NCC	77060
CORWIN	300	413S	NEH	77076
CORWIN PLACE	1	490H	HC	77024
CORY LN	4400	609B	MC	77459
CORY CROSSING LN	2000	293E	SEM	77386
CORYDON DR	100	338R	NEH	77336
CORYDON DR	900	339J	NEH	77336
CORYELL	400	659E	LC	77573
W. CORYELL	400	658H	LC	77573
CORY TERRACE CT	28500	293E	SEM	77386
CORZA CT	0	571H	SWH	77045
CORZATT DR	13300	368U	NWC	77065
COSBURN LN	0	289R	NWC	77375
COSBY	3600	533M	SEH	77021
COSBY	4900	534N	SEH	77021
COSMOS	100	493C	NEH	77009
COSSEY RD	9400	329P	NWC	77070
COSTA	0	494J	NEH	77020
COSTA BRAVA DR	0	407E	NWC	77433
COSTA BRAVA PARK	0	660K	LC	77573
COSTA DEL REY CT	12000	409W	NWC	77041
COSTA MESA CIR	2500	659S	LC	77573
COSTA MESA DR	6300	611B	SWH	77053
COSTA RICA RD	3700	451G	NWH	77092
COSTA SIENNA LN	0	409S	NWC	77041
COSTERO DR	17000	527K	NEF	77083
COSTMARY LN	0	450V	NWH	77055
COTILLION DR	15500	373S	NEH	77060
COTORRA COVE CT	0	409S	NWC	77041
COTSWALD TRAIL	3000	613G	NEB	77584
COTSWOLD CT	3900	453Y	NEH	77009
COTSWOLD BLVD	1400	336H	NEH	77339
S. COTSWOLD MANOR DR	2700	336G	NEH	77339
N. COTSWOLD MANOR DR	2700	336H	NEH	77339
S. COTSWOLD MANOR LOOP	1100	337E	NEH	77339
N. COTSWOLD MANOR LOOP	1400	336G	NEH	77339
COTTAGE	100	453X	NWH	77009
W. COTTAGE	300	453X	NWH	77009
E. COTTAGE	300	453X	NWH	77009
COTTAGE	9700	613K	PL	77584
COTTAGE	22300	340Y	LCO	77532
COTTAGE BAY CT	1800	658Y	LC	77573
COTTAGE BROOK LN	0	615G	PL	77581
COTTAGE COVE CT	1400	620G	SB	77586
COTTAGE COVE LN	0	525H	NEF	77450
COTTAGE CREEK DR	0	407G	NWC	77095
COTTAGE CREEK DR	0	612Q	PL	77584
COTTAGE CYPRESS LN	26400	366M	NWC	77433
COTTAGE ELM CT	0	616G	SEC	77089
COTTAGE FIELD RD	10200	450J	NWC	77041
COTTAGE GATE	23500	285B	SWM	77447
COTTAGE GATE DR	23500	245X	SWM	77447
COTTAGE GATE LN	8500	412P	NWH	77088
COTTAGE GLEN CT	5000	297Q	NEH	77345
COTTAGE GROVE CT	500	658S	LC	77573
COTTAGE GROVE PLACE	1	250C	WD	77381
COTTAGE HEATH LN	20500	526J	NEF	77407
COTTAGE HILL LN	25200	293N	NCC	77373
COTTAGE IVY CIR	0	328V	NWC	77377
COTTAGE LANDING LN	1600	488N	SWH	77077
COTTAGE MANOR LN	0	484U	NEF	77494
COTTAGE OAK LN	0	484F	KT	77494
COTTAGE OAK LN	0	484F	KT	77494
COTTAGE OAK LN	1000	452F	NWH	77091
COTTAGE PARK CIR	19600	486G	SWC	77094
COTTAGE PINES DR	0	407W	NWC	77449
COTTAGE PINES LN	0	253P	SEM	77386
COTTAGE POINT DR	1600	485K	NEF	77494
COTTAGE RIDGE LN	0	484F	KT	77494
COTTAGE ROSE TRAIL	16600	327N	NWC	77429
COTTAGE SPRING CT	0	484Y	NEF	77494
COTTAGE SPRINGS DR	0	612L	PL	77584
COTTAGE STEP TRAIL	2600	611S	NEF	77545
COTTAGE STONE LN	4800	446C	NWC	77449

Street Name	Block	Pg/Sq	Loc	Zips
COTTAGE STREAM CT	0	290U	NWC	77379
COTTAGE STREAM LN	6200	290U	NWC	77379
COTTAGE TIMBERS CT	0	417B	NEC	77044
COTTAGE TIMBERS LN	14400	377Y	NEH	77044
COTTAGE WEST LN	0	446A	NWC	77449
COTTAGE WIND LN	0	484U	NEF	77494
COTTER DR	600	292Y	NCC	77373
COTTER LAKE CIR	3000	609F	MC	77459
COTTER LAKE DR	4900	609F	MC	77459
COTTINGHAM	13000	574S	SEH	77048
COTTON CIR	2600	610A	MC	77489
COTTON DR	6700	451E	NWH	77092
COTTON BLUFF LN	0	328J	NWC	77429
COTTON BROOK CT	11700	329A	NWC	77375
COTTON CREEK DR	19500	288Z	NWC	77375
COTTONDALE CT	2500	485Q	NEF	77450
COTTONDALE CT	20700	486S	SWC	77450
COTTON FIELD LN	6100	406V	NWC	77449
COTTON FIELD LN	19100	406V	NWC	77449
COTTONFIELD WAY	2900	609E	SG	77479
COTTON FOREST CT	0	253K	SEM	77386
COTTON GIN DR	19100	406V	NWC	77449
COTTONGLADE LN	20000	334R	NCC	77338
COTTONGLEN CT	5000	449H	NWH	77041
COTTON GROVE LN	0	377L	NEC	77346
COTTON LAKE CT	4900	526X	NEF	77407
COTTON MEADOWS LN	13900	573U	SEC	77047
COTTON RANCH DR	0	485N	NEF	77494
COTTON RANCH DR	0	485N	NEF	77494
COTTON RIDGE TRAIL	4800	611C	SWH	77053
COTTON RUN CT	8600	411S	NWH	77040
COTTONSHIRE DR	3000	333B	NCC	77373
COTTONTAIL DR	100	419Z	BR	77532
COTTONTAIL DR	700	420W	BR	77532
COTTONTOP CT	11000	371S	NWC	77086
COTTON VALLEY LN	0	256W	SEM	77365
COTTONWOOD SHORES CT		367S	NWC	77433
COTTONWOOD	1300	536P	PA	77502
COTTONWOOD	5900	534V	SEH	77087
COTTONWOOD	6100	614Y	PL	77584
COTTONWOOD	33000	247R	SWM	77355
COTTONWOOD CIR	6800	375X	NEC	77396
COTTONWOOD CT	1800	568B	SG	77498
COTTONWOOD CT	2200	609D	MC	77459
COTTONWOOD CT	4400	658S	LC	77573
COTTONWOOD DR	400	616U	FR	77546
COTTONWOOD DR	2800	444P	KT	77493
COTTONWOOD DR	3800	579C	LP	77571
COTTONWOOD DR	7200	462Y	BT	77521
COTTONWOOD LN	11900	368D	NWC	77429
COTTONWOOD BEND CT	10300	409D	NWC	77064
COTTONWOOD CANYON DR	10100	367X	NWC	77095
COTTONWOOD COVE LN	24400	251W	SWM	77380
COTTONWOOD CREEK	0	657V	LC	77573
COTTONWOOD HEIGHTS DR	14300	332W	NWC	77090
COTTONWOOD HOLLOWS TRAIL		367W	NWC	77095
COTTONWOOD PARK LN	6400	409S	NWC	77041
COTTONWOOD TRAIL CT	8100	407G	NWC	77095
COTTONWOOD TRAIL LN	17600	407K	NWC	77095
COTTONWOOD WALK	2700	332A	NWC	77388
COTTONWOOD WALK CT	2800	332A	NWC	77388
COTTONWOOD WAY	16900	578Z	SEH	77059
COTTRELL CT	13700	488F	SWH	77077
COUCH	2100	452T	NWH	77008
COUCH	3400	452P	NWH	77018
COUCH	6500	412X	NWH	77091
COUGAR	0	369U	NWC	77064
COUGAR	24000	287A	SWM	77355
COUGAR DR	24000	247W	SWM	77355
COUGAR BEND LN	0	484S	NEF	77494
COUGAR CREEK	1400	253E	SEM	77385
COUGAR FALLS CT	16600	330P	NWC	77379
COUGAR PEAK DR	19200	328D	NWC	77377
COUGAR PLACE	1	533D	SEH	77004
COUGOT	5000	452H	NWH	77022
COULCREST DR	1900	450V	NWH	77055
COULSON	12200	496L	NEH	77015
COULSON CIR	12000	496L	NEH	77015
COULTER DR	0	293G	SEM	77386
COULTER PINE CT		289G	NWC	77375
COUNCIL GROVE CT	5600	411Q	NWH	77088
COUNCIL GROVE LN	5200	411Q	NWH	77088
COUNSELOR	11500	368P	NWC	77065
COUNT	7900	455B	NEH	77028
COUNT ERIC DR	2600	446V	NWC	77084
COUNTER POINT DR	1900	451T	NWH	77055
COUNTRY CIR	13500	248Y	TB	77375
COUNTRY CT	1	490M	PP	77024
COUNTRY LN	100	248G	SWM	77354
COUNTRY LN	100	657V	LC	77573
COUNTRY LN	700	491E	HC	77024
COUNTRY LN	13500	248Y	TB	77375
COUNTRY LN	23300	244C	WCO	77447
COUNTRY RD	0	613Y	NEB	77578
COUNTRY RD	3600	577D	PA	77505
COUNTRY RD	5900	484B	KT	77494
COUNTRYAIRE	5600	657V	LC	77573
COUNTRY ARBOR LN	12500	409S	NWC	77041
COUNTRY BEND	17700	246S	SWM	77355
COUNTRY BEND RD	16000	407H	NWC	77095
COUNTRY BOY CT	0	293U	NCC	77373
COUNTRYBREEZE CT	0	331B	NWC	77338
COUNTRY BRIDGE RD	16800	407L	NWC	77095
COUNTRY BROOK CT	8600	407G	NWC	77095
COUNTRY BROOK LN	17100	407G	NWC	77095
COUNTRYCANYON DR	0	331B	NWC	77338
COUNTRYCLOUD DR	0	331B	NWC	77388
S. COUNTRY CLUB	800	580T	SA	77571
N. COUNTRY CLUB	800	580T	SA	77571
W. COUNTRY CLUB	3300	580T	SA	77571
E. COUNTRY CLUB	3300	580Q	SA	77571
COUNTRY CLUB BLVD	1500	568V	SG	77478
COUNTRY CLUB BLVD	3200	569J	SF	77477
COUNTRY CLUB CT	16000	409L	JV	77040
COUNTRY CLUB DR	1	656T	FR	77546
COUNTRY CLUB DR	500	258B	RF	77357
COUNTRY CLUB DR	500	258B	SEM	77357
COUNTRY CLUB DR	1400	419A	NEC	77532
COUNTRY CLUB DR	2000	616J	PL	77581
COUNTRY CLUB DR	2600	615R	PL	77581
COUNTRY CLUB DR	4800	501J	BT	77521
COUNTRY CLUB DR	6400	494Y	SEH	77023
COUNTRY CLUB COVE	1600	501F	BT	77521
COUNTRY CLUB COVE DR	1700	501E	BT	77521
COUNTRY CLUB CROSSING	0	615R	PL	77581
COUNTRY CLUB GREEN	0	289N	NWC	77375
S. COUNTRY CLUB GREEN	10900	289P	NWC	77375
N. COUNTRY CLUB GREEN	10900	289P	NWC	77375
COUNTRY CLUB GREEN CIR	21500	289P	NWC	77375
COUNTRY CLUB GREEN WAY	21600	289P	NWC	77375
COUNTRY CLUB VIEW DR	4400	501J	BT	77521
COUNTRY CORNER CT	1900	484F	NEF	77494

Street Name	Block	Pg/Sq	Loc	Zips
COUNTRY COVE CT	0	325H	NWC	77377
COUNTRY COVE DR	0	325H	NWC	77377
COUNTRY COVE LN	22500	525C	NEF	77494
COUNTRY CREEK DR	8800	529R	SWH	77036
COUNTRY CREST	17700	246S	SWM	77355
COUNTRYCROSSING DR	4300	331B	NWC	77388
COUNTRY DELL DR	4000	291X	NWC	77388
COUNTRY ESTATES DR	24600	257K	SEM	77357
COUNTRY ESTATES LN	1	257K	SEM	77357
COUNTRY FAIR DR	23700	285B	SWM	77447
COUNTRY FAIR LN	15600	326N	NWC	77433
COUNTRY FALLS LN	5900	338A	NEH	77345
COUNTRY FIELDS	17800	246S	SWM	77355
COUNTRY FOREST CT	1	251Z	WD	77380
COUNTRY GATE DR	0	249V	NWC	77375
COUNTRY GLEN	5600	657R	LC	77573
COUNTRY GREEN	5600	657V	LC	77573
COUNTRY GREEN CT	13500	578W	SEH	77059
COUNTRYGREEN DR	4000	291X	NWC	77388
COUNTRY GROVE	17600	246S	SWM	77355
W. COUNTRY GROVE CIR	600	613G	NEB	77584
E. COUNTRY GROVE CIR	600	613G	NEB	77584
COUNTRY HAVEN CT	14400	377Y	NEH	77044
COUNTRY HEIGHTS	26200	246S	SWM	77355
COUNTRY HEIGHTS CT	4200	331B	NWC	77388
COUNTRY HILL CT	13600	248Y	TB	77375
COUNTRY HILLS	17800	287E	NWC	77377
COUNTRYHILLS CT	19200	331B	NWC	77388
COUNTRY HOLLOW	26100	246S	SWM	77355
COUNTRY KNOLL DR	10100	411B	NWC	77086
COUNTRY LAKE DR	19000	246E	SWM	77355
COUNTRY LAKE DR	19200	245H	SWM	77355
COUNTRY LAKE ESTATES DR	19200	331B	NWC	77388
COUNTRYLAND CT	0	331B	NWC	77338
COUNTRY MANOR DR	13900	528W	NEF	77498
COUNTRY MEADOW	17400	246S	SWM	77355
COUNTRY MEADOW LN	10700	329E	NWC	77375
COUNTRYMEADOW LN	19300	331B	NWC	77388
COUNTRY MEADOWS	6100	614L	PL	77581
COUNTRY MEADOWS CT	3300	613F	NEB	77584
COUNTRYMEADOWS DR	0	331B	NWC	77338
COUNTRY MEADOWS DR	30500	248Y	TB	77375
W. COUNTRY MEADOWS LN	800	613F	NEB	77584
S. COUNTRY MEADOWS LN	3300	613F	NEB	77584
COUNTRY MILL WAY	4100	331B	NWC	77388
COUNTRYMOUNTAIN CT	0	331B	NWC	77338
COUNTRY OAKS CT	4300	331B	NWC	77388
N. COUNTRY OAKS RD	1500	378R	NEC	77532
COUNTRY ORCHARD LN	12100	616K	SEC	77089
COUNTRY PARK CT	21700	486J	SWC	77450
COUNTRY PARK DR	1400	486J	SWC	77450
COUNTRY PARK DR	1500	485M	SWC	77450
COUNTRYPARK DR	4100	331B	NWC	77388
COUNTRY PARK WAY	15700	326S	NWC	77433
COUNTRY PATH WAY	0	371Z	NWC	77038
COUNTRY PATH WAY	13400	371Z	NWC	77038
COUNTRY PINE CT	13600	248Y	TB	77375
COUNTRY PINES CT	1	245B	SWM	77355
COUNTRYPINES DR	0	331B	NWC	77338
COUNTRY PINES RD	1	245F	SWM	77355
COUNTRY PLACE	0	488D	SWH	77079
COUNTRY PLACE	5800	657V	LC	77573
W. COUNTRYPLC BLVD	0	613F	NEB	77584
E. COUNTRYPLC BLVD	0	613F	NEB	77584
COUNTRYPLC BLVD	800	613F	NEB	77584
COUNTRY PLACE CIR	1200	489A	SWH	77079
COUNTRY PLACE DR	700	489A	SWH	77079
COUNTRY PLACE DR	3700	569U	NEF	77477
COUNTRY PLACE DR	17800	255A	SEM	77302
COUNTRY PLACE PKWY	1800	613E	NEB	77584
COUNTRY PLACE RD	0	246A	SWM	77355
COUNTRY PLACE RD	29400	245D	SWM	77355
COUNTRYRANCH CT	0	331B	NWC	77338
COUNTRY RIDGE	0	246S	SWM	77355
COUNTRYRIDGE DR	0	331B	NWC	77388
COUNTRY RIDGE DR	2000	618F	SEH	77062
COUNTRYRIVER CT	0	331B	NWC	77388
COUNTRY ROSE LN	14700	327W	NWC	77429
COUNTRY RUN CT	0	610Y	MC	77459
COUNTRYSHIRE LN	2000	524V	NEF	77406
COUNTRYSIDE DR	300	657Q	LC	77573
COUNTRYSIDE LN	21400	334J	NCC	77338
COUNTRYSIDE LN	21600	333H	NCC	77338
COUNTRYSIDE VIEW CT	0	331B	NWC	77388
COUNTRY SPRINGS RD	0	447E	NWC	77084
COUNTRY SQUARE DR	19000	446R	NWC	77084
S. COUNTRY SQUIRE	11000	490M	PP	77024
N. COUNTRY SQUIRE	11000	490M	PP	77024
COUNTRY SQUIRE BLVD	10200	462V	CCO	77520
COUNTRY TIMBERS	26000	246S	SWM	77355
COUNTRY TIME CIR	13600	248Y	TB	77375
COUNTRY TIMES	300	296G	SEM	77365
COUNTRY TRAIL	0	257K	SEM	77357
COUNTRY TRAIL	15800	329S	NWC	77377
COUNTRY TRAILS CT	4300	331B	NWC	77388
COUNTRY VIEW DR	8200	410L	NWC	77040
COUNTRY VILLAGE BLVD	1800	336W	HM	77338
COUNTRY VILLAGE DR	19200	291X	NWC	77388
COUNTRY WALK DR	17900	330E	NWC	77379
COUNTRY WAY	0	246S	SWM	77355
COUNTRY WAY DR	11700	490K	BH	77024
COUNTRY WIND CT	8100	410J	NWC	77040
COUNTRY WIND LN	8300	410J	NWC	77040
COUNTRY WOOD LN	12300	414H	NCC	77039
COUNTRY WOODS TRAIL	26100	246S	SWM	77355
COUNTY CRESS DR	14500	573Z	SEC	77047
COUNTY CRESS DR	14700	613D	SEC	77047
COUNTY DOWN CT	24700	484H	NEF	77494
COUNTY FAIR DR	100	372Z	NEH	77060
COUNTY FAIR DR	300	373W	NCC	77060
COUNTY LINE		244H	WCO	77447
W. COUPLAND DR	1900	539T	LP	77571
COURAGEOUS DR	100	619Y	LC	77573
COURAGEOUS DR	20300	285M	NWC	77447
COURBEN CIR	9300	455D	NEH	77078
COURBEN LN	9700	455D	NEH	77078
COURREGE LN	13400	413J	NCC	77037
COURS	6500	454N	NEH	77093
S. COURSE DR	8300	529Q	SWH	77072
S. COURSE DR	8500	529Q	SWH	77099
COURSEVIEW CT	24700	250Y	NWC	77389
COURSE VIEW LN	6500	250Y	NWC	77389
COURT	0	615N	PL	77581
COURT	1000	493E	SWH	77007
COURT RD	1700	610A	MC	77489
COURT RD	4700	611C	SWH	77053
COURT RD	7300	610C	SWH	77489
COURT ST	0	568T	SG	77478
COURT AMBER TRAIL	15300	325R	NWC	77433
COURTCLIFF DR	11300	370R	NWC	77066
COURTESY LN	700	620Y	KE	77565
COURTESY RD	800	373T	NCC	77032

Street Name	Block	Pg/Sq	Loc	Zips
COURT GLEN DR	9700	529T	SWH	77099
COURT GREEN TRAIL	15300	325R	NWC	77433
COURTLAND	800	659K	LC	77573
COURTLAND CIR	16500	330P	NWC	77379
COURTLAND CT	100	459M	HG	77562
COURTLAND MANOR LN	3300	297X	NEH	77339
COURTLAN DOAKS ST	0	485A	NEF	77494
COURTLAND PLACE	300	656H	FR	77546
COURTLANDT PLACE	1	493T	SWH	77006
COURTLANDT PLACE	1	493S	SWH	77006
COURTLAND VIEW	800	659K	LC	77573
COURTLEA	4500	336Z	NEC	77346
COURTLEY	10400	368Y	NWC	77065
COURTLY ESTATES LN	18100	366D	NWC	77429
COURTLY MANNER CT		289P	NWC	77375
COURTLY MEADOW LN	7000	408Q	NWC	77041
COURTNEY	3200	460M	NEC	77562
COURTNEY	3600	494B	NEH	77026
COURTNEY	14500	247N	SWM	77362
COURTNEY CT	2200	609D	MC	77459
COURTNEY LN	5200	657R	LC	77573
COURTNEY BEND CIR	10900	370V	NWC	77086
COURTNEY GREEN RD	0	616L	SEC	77089
COURTNEY LANE DR	1900	489Q	SWH	77042
COURTNEY MANOR LN	0	485W	NEF	77494
COURTNEY PINE CIR	17400	329M	NWC	77379
COURT OF LION	5600	330Y	NWC	77069
COURT OF LORDS	13800	330Y	NWC	77069
COURT OF REGENTS	14000	330Y	NWC	77069
COURT OF YORK	5200	330Y	NWC	77069
COURTSHIRE DR	11000	413Y	NEH	77076
COURTSHIRE LN	2000	569W	SG	77478
W. COURTSIDE DR	800	659K	LC	77573
E. COURTSIDE DR	800	659K	LC	77573
COURTSIDE DR	1100	659K	LC	77573
COURTSIDE PLACE DR	1800	570X	MC	77489
COURTYARD	0	613K	PL	77584
COURTYARD BLVD	100	500K	BT	77520
COUSHATTA CT	13800	328P	NWC	77429
COVE	9100	533S	SWH	77054
E. COVE RD	100	502H	CCO	77520
COVE RD	1200	463B	MB	77580
COVE BEND LN	0	366K	NWC	77433
COVE BLUFF CT	0	366K	NWC	77433
COVEBRIDGE DR	0	485U	NEF	77450
COVEBROOK CT	2200	613T	NEB	77584
COVEBROOK DR	2900	613T	NEB	77584
COVE CREEK LN	100	489L	SWH	77042
COVECREST DR	100	338R	NEH	77336
COVE EDGE LN	0	366K	NWC	77433
COVE FOREST DR	0	366J	NWC	77433
COVE HARBOR LN	0	366J	NWC	77433
COVE HILL LN	0	366J	NWC	77433
COVE HOLLOW DR	22300	485L	SWC	77450
COVE LAKE DR	6600	406P	NWC	77449
COVE LANDING DR	0	366E	NWC	77433
COVELIGHT LN	0	526J	NEF	77407
COVE MANOR DR	0	366J	NWC	77433
COVE MILL LN	0	366K	NWC	77433
COVENANT CREST DR	0	570U	MC	77489
COVENANT SPRINGS CT	14100	377W	NEC	77044
COVENEY DR	14000	332W	NWC	77090
COVENS FOREST DR	11900	416K	NEC	77044
COVENT GARDEN DR	8700	570A	SWH	77031
COVENTINA CIR	0	410L	NWC	77040
COVENTRY BLVD	25600	250T	NWC	77389
COVENTRY CT	0	258E	SEM	77357
COVENTRY CT	300	536U	PA	77502
COVENTRY CT	5100	617S	FR	77546
COVENTRY CT	9800	335Q	HM	77338
COVENTRY LN	0	245R	SWM	77355
COVENTRY BAY DR	0	615M	PL	77089
COVENTRY CREEK LN	0	484Y	NEF	77494
COVENTRY FALLS	6000	407Y	NWC	77084
COVENTRY FIELD LN	6200	407U	NWC	77084
COVENTRY MEADOWS LN	0	407T	NWC	77084
COVENTRY OAKS DR	17400	407X	NWC	77084
COVENTRY PARK DR	17000	407Y	NWC	77084
COVENTRY SQUARE DR	9300	529N	SWH	77099
COVENTRY SQUIRE DR	17500	407X	NWC	77084
COVE PARK DR	1800	619V	LC	77565
COVE POINTE DR	0	366K	NWC	77433
COVERED BRIDGE	10900	575V	SEH	77075
COVEREDGATE CT	22200	334F	NCC	77373
COVERED WAGON LN	18600	246J	SWM	77355
COVE RIDGE LN	0	366J	NWC	77433
COVERLEA CT	0	292W	NWC	77388
COVERN	100	535W	SEH	77061
COVE ROYALE LN	0	526L	NEF	77407
COVESIDE	2100	619V	LC	77565
COVE SPRINGS CT	0	366J	NWC	77433
COVE SPRINGS DR	0	366E	NWC	77433
COVESVILLE LN	14800	408T	NWC	77084
COVE TIMBERS LN	8100	290E	NWC	77375
COVEVIEW DR	100	338V	NEH	77336
COVE VIEW DR	3400	620E	SB	77586
W. COVE VIEW TRAIL	0	250Q	NWC	77389
E. COVE VIEW TRAIL	0	250Q	NWC	77389
COVE VIEW TRAIL CT	0	250Q	NWC	77389
COVE VISTA DR	0	366J	NWC	77433
COVE VISTA LN	0	366J	NWC	77433
COVEWOOD DR	2100	296Z	NEH	77339
COVEY CIR	2900	610E	MC	77459
COVEY CT	10300	528U	SWH	77099
COVEY LN	2500	614S	NEB	77584
COVEY LN	12700	528U	SWH	77099
COVEY RUN DR	16300	610C	SWH	77489
COVEY TRAIL	3400	609G	MC	77459
COVEY TRAILS	0	366N	NWC	77433
COVEY WOOD CT	18600	447E	NWC	77084
COVINGTON CT	1000	613G	NEB	77584
COVINGTON DR	5100	452E	NWH	77018
COVINGTON DR	6600	412W	NWH	77091
COVINGTON DR	7700	407H	NWC	77095
COVINGTON BRIDGE DR	21100	291U	NWC	77388
COVINGTON GLEN DR	0	369G	NWC	77077
COVINGTON LAKE CT	0	405S	NWC	77493
COVINGTON WAY	2400	613Q	NEB	77584
COWAN	500	537J	PA	77506
W. COWAN DR	100	492K	SWH	77007
E. COWAN DR	200	492K	SWH	77007
COWARDS CREEK CT	1000	656G	FR	77546
COWARDS CREEK DR	700	656G	FR	77546
COWART	7200	495J	NEH	77020
COWART	7900	495K	NEH	77029
COWBOY WAY	1	524X	NWF	77406
COWDEN CT	1100	570X	MC	77489
COWLING	400	494U	SEH	77011
COW OAK DR	23800	290B	NWC	77389
COX	22500	296C	SEM	77357
COX RD	11100	252K	SEM	77385
COX MANOR DR		325S	NWC	77447

Street Name	Block	Pg/Sq	Loc	Zips
COXSWAIN CT	16700	379Y	NEC	77532
COXWOLD LN	19100	329B	NWC	77375
COY DR	100	419U	BR	77532
COY DR	2700	538T	DP	77536
COYETO	0	570E	SWC	77477
COYLE	0	340U	LCO	77535
COYLE	3400	494W	SEH	77003
COYLE	4300	494W	SEH	77023
COYOTE LN	1100	501M	BT	77521
COYOTE BRIDGE LN	0	526L	NEF	77407
COYOTE CALL CT	0	406Y	NWC	77449
COYOTE CREEK DR	0	407C	NWC	77095
COYOTE ECHO DR	0	406X	NWC	77449
COYOTE RIDGE LN	20000	446Q	NWC	77449
COYOTE SPRINGS CT	25800	292U	NCC	77373
COYOTE TRAIL CT	2900	610U	MC	77459
COYOTE TRAIL CT	2900	610V	MC	77459
COYOTE TRAIL DR	2700	610U	MC	77459
COYOTE TRAIL DR	3200	610V	MC	77459
COYOTILLO LN	16700	367U	NWC	77095
COYRIDGE LN	16100	571X	SWH	77053
COYRIDGE LN	16200	611B	SWH	77053
COZ CT	0	457V	NEC	77049
COZAC LN	0	609P	NEF	77479
COZY CABIN DR	0	406Y	NWC	77449
COZY HOLLOW LN	15000	377Y	NEC	77044
COZY TERRACE LN	5600	407Z	NWC	77084
CRAB APPLE CT	11900	369J	NWC	77429
CRABAPPLE DR	100	500A	BT	77520
CRABAPPLE COVE	6700	408N	NWC	77084
CRAB ORCHARD RD	5900	491J	SWH	77057
CRABTREE CT	0	249B	SWM	77354
CRADDOCK DR	10700	528Z	SWH	77099
CRADLE	15300	571Y	SWH	77053
CRADLE COVE CT	17100	407G	NWC	77095
CRAFT CT	17700	379T	NEC	77532
CRAFTMADE LN	14000	417X	NEC	77044
CRAGGY BARK DR	1900	292X	NWC	77388
CRAGMORE DR	1000	619G	TL	77586
CRAIG	100	501L	BT	77521
CRAIG	2900	492T	SWH	77098
CRAIG	4800	576M	SEH	77504
CRAIG	5300	534C	SEH	77023
CRAIG DR	1000	496S	GP	77547
CRAIGCHESTER LN	19100	332A	NWC	77388
CRAIGHEAD DR	10600	532W	SWH	77025
CRAIGHILL PLACE	8000	334R	NCC	77338
CRAIGHURST CT	3500	618D	SEH	77059
CRAIGHURST DR	15700	618D	SEH	77059
CRAIGMONT	2300	534G	SEH	77023
CRAIGMONT BLVD	4300	500L	BT	77521
CRAIGMONT BRIDGE DR	7300	406K	NWC	77433
CRAIGSHIRE CT	16100	330T	NWC	77379
CRAIGWAY RD	6000	290G	NWC	77389
CRAIGWOOD LN	12600	368L	NWC	77429
CRAIL DR	9600	329R	NWC	77379
CRAINFELD DR		525M	NEF	77407
CRAKSTON	6100	408T	NWC	77084
CRAMER CT	700	486B	SWC	77450
CRAMMOND	10000	370Y	NWC	77064
CRAMPTON LN	17000	330H	NWC	77379
CRAMPTON LN	17200	330C	NWC	77379
CRANBERRY CIR	2300	333A	NCC	77373
CRANBERRY BEND	1	250B	WD	77381
CRANBERRY CROSSING LN	21300	289U	NWC	77375
CRANBERRY GATE DR	17200	328R	NWC	77377
CRANBERRY HILL CT	900	488E	SWH	77079
CRANBERRY HILL DR	900	488E	SWH	77079
CRANBERRY TRAIL	22700	333A	NCC	77373
CRANBOURNE DR	15100	618J	SEH	77062
CRANBROOK LN	400	657Y	LC	77573
CRANBROOK RD	5500	491K	SWH	77056
CRANBROOK RD	10600	489L	SWH	77042
CRANBROOK CANYON CT	5900	609X	NEF	77479
CRANBROOK CREEK LN	0	377W	NEC	77044
CRANBROOK FALLS LN	0	526J	NEF	77407
CRANBROOK HOLLOW LN	8100	407F	NWC	77095
CRANBROOK SQUARE CT	6800	527E	NEF	77407
CRANBROOK TERRACE LN	0	484N	NEF	77494
CRANBROOK WAY	1400	536P	PA	77502
CRANDALL RD	3200	579A	LP	77571
CRANDON	2900	454X	NEH	77026
CRANE	2600	454Y	NEH	77026
CRANE DR	2500	616P	PL	77581
CRANE HARBOR CT	0	526N	NEF	77407
CRANE HAWK LN	0	658X	LC	77573
CRANE HOLLOW LN	0	333F	NCC	77338
CRANES CREEK CT	0	524G	NEF	77494
CRANESPARK	12500	328Q	NWC	77377
CRANFIELD CT	600	486B	SWC	77450
CRANFIELD DR	20600	486B	SWC	77450
CRANHURST LN	15400	572W	SWH	77053
CRANLEIGH CT	9400	531U	SWH	77096
CRANSLEY DR	18200	447F	NWC	77084
CRANSTON CT	2000	492C	NWH	77008
CRANSWICK RD	4800	450B	NWH	77041
CRANWATER BRIDGE LN	0	525L	NEF	77407
CRANWAY DR	1600	450Z	NWH	77055
CRANWOOD DR	16100	330M	NWC	77379
CRAPE MYRTLE BEND LN	0	698L	LC	77539
CRATE FALLS DR	0	285P	NWC	77447
CRATER LAKE CT	12100	377B	NEC	77346
CRATER RANCH RD	13900	371C	NWC	77014
CRAVEN RD	1800	570K	SF	77477
CRAVENRIDGE DR	13900	528T	NEF	77083
CRAVENS	0	457T	NEC	77049
CRAVENS	600	453C	NEH	77076
S. CRAVENS RD	200	570P	MC	77489
CRAWFORD	0	247V	SWM	77355
CRAWFORD	1	493Q	DT	77002
CRAWFORD	800	493Q	DT	77010
CRAWFORD	1200	493Q	DT	77002
CRAWFORD	1200	616U	FR	77546
CRAWFORD	2300	493U	SWH	77004
CRAWFORD	5300	533B	SWH	77004
CRAWFORD	5500	449D	NWC	77041
CRAWFORD	5900	409Z	NWH	77041
CRAWFORD	16000	409L	JV	77040
CRAWFORD DR	3700	537R	PA	77503
CRAWFORD HILL LN	0	330D	NWC	77379
CRAWFORD RIDGE CT	0	298Y	NEH	77336
CRAWFORD RIDGE CT	0	298Y	NEC	77336
CRAWLEY CT	1400	457Z	NEC	77530
CRAYFORD CT	11200	369W	NWC	77065
CRAYFORD DR	11400	369W	NWC	77065
CRAYTON RD	1	322V	WCO	77484
CRAZY HORSE TRAIL	8700	409G	NWC	77064
CRAZY HORSE VALLEY DR	20000	446X	NWC	77449
C RD, T K	25100	249T	NWC	77375
CREAGER	800	576A	SEH	77034
CREEDE	9500	410F	NWC	77040
CREEGAN PARK CT	1800	572R	SWH	77047

Street Name	Block	Pg/Sq	Loc	Zips
CREEK	2200	541A	BT	77520
E. CREEK CIR	13500	370V	NWC	77086
W. CREEK DR	0	657U	LC	77573
CREEK DR	1700	450V	NWH	77055
CREEK DR	1800	450V	NWH	77080
W. CREEK DR	6200	614D	BK	77581
E. CREEK DR	13900	528T	NEF	77498
CREEK DR	19300	256G	SEM	77357
S. CREEK DR	26100	248R	SWM	77354
N. CREEK DR	27300	248M	SWM	77354
CREEK LN	0	568Z	SG	77478
CREEK ARBOR CIR	2700	446R	NWC	77084
CREEK BANK LN	3100	615L	PL	77581
CREEK BEND	0	246V	SWM	77355
CREEKBEND	0	568T	SG	77478
CREEK BEND	300	657V	LC	77573
CREEK BEND DR	0	249S	NWC	77375
CREEK BEND DR	2800	657D	FR	77546
CREEKBEND DR	3400	501Q	BT	77521
CREEKBEND DR	4300	531Z	SWH	77035
CREEKBEND DR	5200	531X	SWH	77096
CREEKBEND DR	7500	530Y	SWH	77071
CREEK BEND DR	19300	331D	NWC	77388
CREEK BEND RD	24400	244U	WCO	77447
CREEK BEND TRAIL	19700	446Q	NWC	77084
CREEK BLUFF LN	2500	609B	MC	77459
CREEK BLUFF LN	17600	367T	NWC	77433
CREEK BRANCH	0	290E	NWC	77375
CREEKBRIAR CT	15600	331N	NWC	77068
CREEKBRIAR DR	3400	331N	NWC	77068
CREEK BRIDGE LN	0	446H	NWC	77449
W. CREEK CLUB DR	3100	609L	MC	77459
E. CREEK CLUB DR	3500	609M	MC	77459
CREEK CREST DR	7200	408P	NWC	77095
CREEK CROSSING	0	609Z	MC	77459
CREEK CROSSING LN	18000	295F	SEM	77365
CREEKDALE DR	2300	331Q	NWC	77068
CREEKDALE BEND DR	0	406C	NWC	77433
CREEK EDGE CT	21000	446J	NWC	77449
CREEK FALLS CT	0	615L	PL	77581
CREEKFIELD CT	18500	330F	NWC	77379
CREEKFIELD DR	7400	330E	NWC	77379
CREEKFORD CIR	1200	568V	SG	77478
CREEKFORD CT	1300	568V	SG	77478
CREEK FOREST CIR	600	251V	SWM	77380
CREEK FOREST LN	600	251V	SWM	77380
CREEK GATE DR	0	658J	LC	77573
CREEK GATE RD	10600	252D	SEM	77385
CREEK GATE RD	10800	253A	SEM	77385
CREEK GLEN DR	7500	408J	NWC	77095
CREEK GLEN DR	8200	568P	SG	77478
CREEK GROVE CT	14000	371U	NWC	77066
CREEK GROVE DR	3300	371U	NWC	77066
CREEKHAVEN CT	4800	448B	NWC	77084
CREEKHAVEN CT	5400	657Z	LC	77573
CREEKHAVEN DR	15500	448B	NWC	77084
CREEK HICKORY RD	2300	331L	NWC	77068
CREEK HILL LN	15800	327S	NWC	77429
CREEK HOLLOW DR	1300	620J	EL	77586
CREEK HOLLOW LN	4000	609B	MC	77459
CREEK HURST	0	528V	SWH	77099
CREEKHURST DR	11400	529X	SWH	77099
CREEK KNOLL BLVD	0	292G	NCC	77373
CREEKLAND CIR	5200	291E	NWC	77389
CREEK LANDING CT	0	407S	NWC	77449
CREEKLEA RD	16700	331Q	NWC	77068
CREEKLEAF RD	2300	331L	NWC	77068
CREEK LINE DR	16900	657F	FR	77546
CREEKLINE GLEN CT	11100	369K	NWC	77429
CREEKLINE GREEN CT	11100	369K	NWC	77429
CREEKLINE MEADOW CT	11100	369K	NWC	77429
CREEK MANOR CT	5500	296R	NEH	77339
CREEK MANOR DR	2800	296R	NEH	77339
CREEK MANOR DR	3000	297N	NEH	77339
CREEK MEADOW DR	2400	446U	NWC	77084
CREEK MEADOWS DR	2300	610A	MC	77459
CREEKMILL CT	0	327W	NWC	77429
CREEK MIST CIR	0	407U	NWC	77084
CREEKMIST CT	0	484F	NEF	77494
CREEK MIST DR	0	367P	NWC	77433
CREEKMONT DR	1000	451H	NWH	77091
CREEKMONT TRACE LN	0	452F	NWH	77091
CREEKMORE CIR	5200	291E	NWC	77389
CREEK MOUNTAIN DR	16900	407Z	NWC	77084
CREEK PARK DR	9500	568T	SG	77478
CREEK PARK DR	23000	291E	NWC	77389
CREEKPINE LN	0	328K	NWC	77377
CREEKPINE LN	11700	289W	NWC	77375
CREEK PINE LN	11700	289W	NWC	77375
CREEK POINT DR	19900	406U	NWC	77449
CREEKRIDGE DR	2400	616P	PL	77581
CREEK RIDGE DR	23800	293T	NCC	77373
CREEK RIDGE LN	4000	609B	MC	77459
CREEK RUN DR	0	612F	PL	77545
CREEK RUN DR	19300	331D	NWC	77388
CREEK SAGE LN	0	658S	LC	77573
CREEKS EDGE DR	2400	615R	PL	77581
CREEKS END BLVD	0	525H	NEF	77407
CREEKS END CT	0	525H	NEF	77407
CREEKS GATE CT	8900	527N	NEF	77407
CREEK SHADE DR	3300	331C	NWC	77388
CREEK SHADOWS DR	3200	297N	NEH	77339
CREEK SHADOWS DR	4900	296R	NEH	77339
CREEK SHADOWS DR	5100	297N	NEH	77339
CREEKSHIRE DR	1800	569W	SG	77478
CREEK SHOAL TRACE	0	446Q	NWC	77084
CREEKSHORE DR	19700	406Q	NWC	77449
CREEK SHORE LN	0	615L	PL	77581
CREEKSIDE	12100	247R	SWM	77362
CREEKSIDE	18800	257G	RF	77357
CREEKSIDE CIR	1	491E	HC	77024
N. CREEKSIDE CT	0	491A	SV	77024
CREEKSIDE CT	0	246A	SWM	77355
S. CREEKSIDE CT	2	491A	SV	77024
CREEKSIDE CT	400	657M	LC	77573
CREEKSIDE DR	0	444S	KT	77493
CREEKSIDE DR	100	657M	LC	77573
W. CREEKSIDE DR	700	491E	HC	77024
E. CREEKSIDE DR	700	491E	HC	77024
CREEKSIDE DR	1600	568U	SG	77478
CREEKSIDE DR	1800	657J	FR	77546
CREEKSIDE DR	4100	525Y	NEF	77406
CREEKSIDE LN	700	491A	SV	77024
CREEKSIDE LN	700	491E	HC	77024
CREEKSIDE LN	6100	657Q	LC	77573
CREEKSIDE LN	7500	578G	PA	77505
CREEKSIDE BEND BLVD	0	366S	NWC	77433
CREEKSIDE CROSSING DR	0	366P	NWC	77433
CREEKSIDE FARMS LN	0	330D	NWC	77379
CREEKSIDE FOREST DR		249Q	NWC	77375
CREEKSIDE GATE CT	22900	290F	NWC	77375
CREEKSIDE GREEN DR	0	250Q	NWC	77389
CREEKSIDE GREEN DR	8600	249R	NWH	77375
CREEKSIDE GREEN DR	8600	249R	NWH	77375
CREEKSIDE GROVE LN	14300	331W	NWC	77068
CREEKSIDE HAVEN TRAIL	0	291A	NWC	77389
CREEKSIDE LANDING BLVD		249V	NWC	77375
CREEKSIDE PARK BLVD	0	250R	NWC	77389
CREEKSIDE PARK DR	13100	488Y	SWH	77082
CREEKSIDE RANCH DR	0	615M	PL	77089
CREEKSIDE RANCH DR	0	524S	NWF	77406
CREEKSIDE TERRACE CT		329k	NWC	77375
CREEKSIDE TIMBERS DR	22900	290F	NWC	77389
CREEKSIDE WILLOW DR	22900	290E	NWC	77375
CREEKSOUTH RD	16200	331P	NWC	77068
CREEK SPRINGS DR	13400	528B	SWC	77083
CREEKSTONE CIR	8300	451W	HI	77055
CREEKSTONE DR	3500	613U	NEB	77584
CREEKSTONE CROSSING DR	0	609U	MC	77459
CREEKSTONE LAKE DR	0	532U	SWH	77054
CREEKSTONE VILLAGE DR	0	609Q	MC	77459
CREEKSTONE VILLAGE DR	0	609U	MC	77459
CREEKSTONE VILLAGE DR	12500	369K	NWC	77429
CREEK TERRACE DR	2600	609G	MC	77459
CREEK TERRACE LN	0	376W	NEC	77396
CREEK TERRACE LN	0	609F	MC	77459
CREEK TRACE LN	0	407S	NWC	77449
CREEKTRACE LN	0	406Y	NWC	77449
CREEK TRAIL	16600	407V	NWC	77084
CREEK TREE DR	10500	369F	NWC	77070
CREEK VALLEY LN	1900	569W	SG	77478
CREEKVIEW	0	657A	FR	77546
CREEKVIEW	4900	539X	LP	77571
CREEK VIEW	6100	609W	NEF	77479
CREEK VIEW CIR	0	447A	NWC	77084
CREEK VIEW CT	1000	568T	SG	77478
CREEKVIEW CT	1800	609D	MC	77459
CREEKVIEW DR	0	657R	LC	77573
CREEKVIEW DR	23500	290D	NWC	77389
CREEKVIEW DR	24200	250Z	NWC	77389
CREEK VIEW LN	11600	252H	SEM	77385
CREEK VIEW LN	11700	253E	SEM	77385
CREEK VIEW LN	16700	327X	NWC	77429
CREEKVIEW PARK DR	13100	488Y	SWH	77082
CREEK VILLAGE DR	6700	406R	NWC	77449
CREEK VINE DR	9400	410E	NWC	77040
CREEK WATER DR	0	447A	NWC	77084
CREEK WATER DR	8800	329M	NWC	77379
CREEKWAY CIR	2500	609D	MC	77459
CREEK WAY DR	0	568T	SG	77478
CREEKWAY DR	12600	368H	NWC	77429
CREEKWAY BEND DR	0	376U	NEC	77396
CREEK WILLOW DR	8400	290E	NWC	77375
CREEKWIND CIR	0	407U	NWC	77084
CREEKWOOD DR	6500	490R	SWH	77063
CREEK WOOD DR	23500	290A	NWC	77389
N. CREEKWOOD HILLS LN	0	369A	NWC	77070
CREEKWOOD HILLS LN	0	369A	NWC	77070
CREEK WOOD WAY	800	490D	HC	77024
CREEL CIR	3200	579A	LP	77571
CREEPING VINE LN	8800	412K	NWH	77088
CREIGHTON CT	11300	409A	NWC	77065
CREIGHTON DR	1800	570X	MC	77489
CREMONA CT	11000	525N	NEF	77469
CRENCHRUS CT	11000	371T	NWC	77086
CRENSHAW	0	578J	PA	77505
CRENSHAW	4200	535Q	SEH	77017
CRENSHAW RD	100	576M	SEH	77504
CRENSHAW RD	1200	577F	PA	77504
CRENSHAW RD	6300	578J	PA	77505
CRENSHAW RD	12400	456D	NEC	77044
CREPE MYRTLE	8200	535V	SEH	77017
CREPE MYRTLE LN	4700	577C	PA	77505
CRESCENDA CT	0	293U	NCC	77373
CRESCENDO CT	7600	410P	NWC	77040
CRESCENT	0	580L	LP	77571
CRESCENT	1900	580L	LP	77571
CRESCENT	14000	248X	TB	77375
CRESCENT DR	0	656X	FR	77546
CRESCENT DR	100	536L	PA	77506
CRESCENT DR	3500	613Y	NEB	77584
CRESCENT ARBOR LN	0	290T	NWC	77379
CRESCENT BAY DR	100	660A	LC	77573
CRESCENT BAY DR	19000	486H	SWC	77094
CRESCENT BEND RD	2900	331D	NWC	77388
CRESCENT BLUFF DR	0	612M	PL	77584
CRESCENT BLUFF LN	10100	369C	NWC	77070
CRESCENT BREEZE LN	0	528Q	SWC	77072
CRESCENT BRIDGE CT	0	375X	NEC	77396
CRESCENT CANYON CT	8000	407F	NWC	77095
CRESCENT CANYON DR	17100	407F	NWC	77095
CRESCENT COMMON DR	1900	485L	NEF	77494
CRESCENT CORAL DR	2100	619Z	LC	77573
CRESCENT COVE	0	612M	PL	77584
CRESCENT COVE CT	22400	525C	NEF	77494
CRESCENT FALLS CT	1	251F	WD	77381
CRESCENT FOREST CT	15300	618F	SEH	77062
CRESCENT FOUNTAIN RD	18900	331D	NWC	77388
CRESCENT GATE CT	300	491H	SWH	77024
CRESCENT GATE LN	8600	491H	SWH	77024
CRESCENT GREEN CT	1400	486H	SWC	77094
CRESCENT GREEN DR	0	486C	SWC	77094
CRESCENT GREEN DR	1400	486H	SWC	77094
CRESCENT HEIGHTS	21600	291S	NWC	77388
CRESCENT HOLLOW CT	2300	291R	NWC	77388
CRESCENT HOLLOW DR	21500	291R	NWC	77388
CRESCENT KNOLLS DR	8000	525Z	NEF	77406
CRESCENT LAKE CIR	0	461N	NEC	77521
CRESCENT LANDING DR	14200	617H	SEH	77062
CRESCENT LILLY DR	15100	325V	NWC	77433
CRESCENT MANOR LN	0	528Q	SWC	77072
CRESCENT MANOR LN	13000	528Q	SWH	77072
CRESCENT MEADOW DR	0	366J	NWC	77433
CRESCENT MOON DR	9000	369V	NWC	77064
CRESCENT MOUNTAIN LN	0	377E	NEC	77346
CRESCENT OAK DR	1400	610P	MC	77459
CRESCENT OAKS PARK LN	2900	253N	SEM	77386
CRESCENT PALM CT	2000	488P	SWH	77077
CRESCENT PARK DR	2300	489S	SWH	77077
N. CRESCENT PARK DR	12000	372J	NWC	77067
S. CRESCENT PARK DR		372J	NWC	77067
CRESCENT PARK VILLAGE	0	528Q	SWC	77072
CRESCENT PARK VILLAGE DR		528Q	SWH	77072
CRESCENT PARKWAY CT	1300	486G	SWC	77094
CRESCENT PASS DR	19100	329A	NWC	77375
CRESCENT PINE DR	0	407F	NWC	77095
CRESCENT PLAZA DR	0	488P	SWH	77077
CRESCENT POINT CIR	23400	485K	NEF	77494
CRESCENT POINT DR	1600	485K	NEF	77494
CRESCENT POINTE DR	2100	619V	LC	77573
N. CRESCENTRIDGE DR	1	251C	WD	77381
CRESCENT ROYALE WAY	0	377A	NEC	77346
CRESCENT SHORE	100	580L	LP	77571
CRESCENT SHORE DR	1900	619Z	LC	77573
CRESCENT SHORES LN	1500	619D	PA	77586
CRESCENT SPRINGS DR	19000	336A	NEH	77339
CRESCENT STAR CT	0	525D	NEF	77450
CRESCENT STAR RD	2800	331D	NWC	77388
CRESCENT TIDE LN	0	658Z	LC	77573
CRESCENT TIMBER LN	0	253Q	SEM	77386
CRESCENT VALLEY	0	338W	NEC	77346
CRESCENT VIEW	100	580L	LP	77571
CRESCENT VIEW CT	1	251B	WD	77381
CRESCENT VIEW LN	0	609T	NEF	77479
CRESCENT VILLAGE LN	0	527J	NEF	77407
CRESCENT WOOD LN	8400	330J	NWC	77379
CRESENT DR	0	656X	FR	77546
CRESENT COVE CT	0	484E	KT	77494
CRESENT COVE LN	0	484E	KT	77494
CRESENT CREEK	0	406U	NWC	77449
CRESENT OAKS CT	15400	331P	NWC	77068
CRESENT PALM CT	2000	488P	SWH	77077
CRESENT PALM LN	0	488T	SWH	77077
CRESENT PALM LN	2100	488P	SWH	77077
CRESENT POINT DR	21600	486J	SWC	77450
CRESLINE	300	413Y	NEH	77076
CRESLINE	1500	414W	NEH	77093
CRESSIDA GLEN LN	13000	528L	SWH	77072
CRESSWELL	0	296S	NEH	77365
CRESSWELL CT	3500	610U	MC	77459
CRESSWELL DR	0	295Z	NEH	77365
S. CREST	3900	660M	BC	77518
CREST	6300	534P	SEH	77033
CREST CT	100	569V	SF	77477
CREST CT	5900	534P	SEH	77033
CRESTA PLACE DR	6300	578A	PA	77505
CRESTBEND CT	300	490N	SWH	77042
CRESTBEND DR	300	490N	SWH	77042
CRESTBOURNE CT	0	372A	NWC	77014
CRESTBRIAR CT	1	501M	BT	77521
CRESTBRIDGE LN	3200	291U	NWC	77388
CRESTBROOK DR	900	412A	NWC	77038
CRESTBROOK DR	15700	618C	SEH	77059
CRESTBROOK BEND LN	2800	446N	NWC	77449
CRESTBROOK COVE	21700	445M	NWC	77449
CRESTBROOK MANOR LN	0	407K	NWC	77433
CRESTBROOK PARK LN	11200	289J	NWC	77375
CRESTBURY CT	7100	407N	NWC	77433
CRESTBURY LN	7200	407N	NWC	77433
CREST COVE DR	0	366J	NWC	77433
CRESTDALE CIR	9700	450P	NWH	77080
CRESTDALE DR	1400	450T	NWH	77080
CRESTDALE DR	2400	450P	NWH	77080
CRESTED BUTTE CT	2700	371M	NWC	77067
CRESTED CLOUD CT	1	251Y	WD	77380
CRESTED GREEN DR	4000	527C	SWC	77082
CRESTED HILL LN	0	406L	NWC	77433
CRESTED IRIS DR	13700	368A	NWC	77429
CRESTED JAY LN	1	252N	WD	77380
CRESTED LARK CT	22800	485L	SWC	77450
CRESTED MOSS AVE	0	286Q	NWC	77377
CRESTED PEAK LN	0	366Z	NWC	77433
CRESTED PINES CT	1	251C	WD	77381
CRESTED SONG CIR	0	525R	NEF	77407
CRESTED TERN CT	1	251R	WD	77380
CRESTED DUCK LN	0	324S	NWC	77447
CRESTED VALLEY DR	21000	525R	NEF	77407
CRESTED WOOD CT	0	525R	NEF	77407
CRESTERRACE DR	6300	578A	PA	77505
CRESTFIELD CT	10700	369F	NWC	77070
CRESTFORD LN	6300	538W	PA	77505
CRESTFORD LN	6500	578A	PA	77505
CRESTFORD PARK LN	6000	407Z	NWC	77084
CRESTFORD PARK LN	25800	524D	NEF	77494
CREST GATE	1	527F	SWC	77082
CRESTGLEN CT	18100	526M	NEF	77407
CRESTGLEN LN	0	369D	NWC	77070
CRESTGROVE DR	3300	578A	PA	77505
CRESTHAVEN CIR	5000	573M	SEH	77048
CREST HAVEN LN	0	366J	NWC	77433
CRESTHAVEN PARK	0	538W	PA	77505
CRESTHILL	6600	534P	SEH	77033
CREST HILL LN	3400	493J	SWH	77007
CRESTHOLLOW LN	0	488W	SWH	77082
CRESTING KNOLLS CIR	6100	525R	NEF	77407
CREST LAKE DR	12300	529J	SWH	77072
CRESTLAWN	0	658N	LC	77573
CRESTLEA CT	3400	578A	PA	77505
CRESTLINE RD	17200	376G	NEC	77396
CRESTLINE BAY LN	11100	524L	NWF	77406
CRESTMEADOW DR	3300	578A	PA	77505
CRESTMONT	5200	500G	BT	77521
CRESTMONT	6300	534T	SEH	77033
CRESTMONT	8600	574B	SEH	77033
CRESTMONT CIR	2000	610E	MC	77459
CRESTMONT DR	0	538R	DP	77536
CRESTMONT DR	1600	570S	SF	77477
CRESTMONT PLACE LOOP	0	570P	MC	77489
CRESTMONT SPRINGS LN	0	253P	SEM	77386
CRESTMONT TRAIL DR	0	570P	MC	77489
CRESTMOON CT	0	616E	SEC	77089
CRESTMOOR WAY	16200	527B	SWH	77082
CRESTMORE	11000	531W	SWH	77096
CRESTON DR	1700	454N	NEH	77026
CRESTON DR	1900	252V	SEM	77386
CRESTON CLIFF CT		484T	NEF	77494
CRESTON COVE CT	0	406M	NWC	77433
CRESTON HILLS	0	615B	PL	77581
CRESTON MEADOW DR	25500	524L	NWF	77406
CRESTON SPRINGS CT	0	330M	NWC	77379
CRESTON WOODS DR	26300	524E	NEF	77494
CREST PARK DR	2800	488Y	SWH	77082
CREST PEAK WAY	0	445H	NWC	77449
CREST PEAK WAY CT	0	445H	NWC	77449
CRESTRIDGE	6300	534S	SEH	77033
CRESTSHIRE LN	22900	292G	NCC	77373
CRESTSIDE DR	6300	578A	PA	77505
CRESTVALE DR	12600	412A	NWC	77038
CRESTVIEW	0	246A	SWM	77355
CRESTVIEW	0	580L	LP	77571
CRESTVIEW CT	0	245N	SWM	77355
CRESTVIEW CT	1800	610K	MC	77459
CRESTVIEW DR	0	245D	SWM	77355
CRESTVIEW DR	7800	455F	NEH	77028
CRESTVIEW DR	8800	455H	NEH	77078
CRESTVIEW TRAIL	1	527B	SWC	77082
CRESTVILLE	6200	534P	SEH	77033
CRESTWATER BLVD	0	527B	SWC	77082
CRESTWATER CT	500	527B	SWC	77082
CRESTWATER TRAIL	100	527B	SWC	77082
CRESTWAY	4900	539X	LP	77571
CRESTWAY DR	100	500E	BT	77520
CRESTWICK DR	8000	527M	SWC	77083
CREST WIND	0	369P	NWC	77065
CRESTWIND CT	100	612G	PL	77584
CRESTWIND CT	12100	369P	NWC	77070
CRESTWIND DR	12800	612F	PL	77584
CRESTWOOD CIR	1	568V	SG	77478
CRESTWOOD DR	0	538R	DP	77536
CRESTWOOD DR	1	492K	SWH	77007
CRESTWOOD DR	300	620E	EL	77586
CRESTWOOD DR	2900	613T	NEB	77584
CRESTWOOD LN	700	570S	MC	77489
CRESTWOOD LN	1600	537P	PA	77502
CRESTWOOD COVE CT	0	367S	NWC	77433
CRESTWOOD COVE CT	0	367S	NWC	77433
CRESTWOOD ESTATES DR	1	490G	PP	77024
CRESTWOOD PARK	31500	252R	SEM	77385
CRESTWORTH LN	21900	446A	NWC	77449
CRESWELL CT	18200	407X	NWC	77084
CRETE	800	494F	NEH	77020
CRETE DR	300	538L	DP	77536
CRETIAN POINT CT	16300	367C	NWC	77429
CRIBBAGE CT	0	527V	NEF	77083
CRICHTON CT	0	297U	NEH	77345
CRICKET AVE	1500	296M	SEM	77365
CRICKET AVE	1600	297J	SEM	77365
S. CRICKET CIR	4300	291P	NWC	77388
N. CRICKET CIR	4300	291P	NWC	77388
E. CRICKET CIR	21800	291P	NWC	77388
CRICKET DR	21800	291P	NWC	77388
CRICKET LN	2900	414S	NEH	77093
CRICKETBRIAR CT	17200	407Q	NWC	77084
CRICKET HOLLOW PLACE	1	250D	WD	77381
CRICKET HOLLOW PLACE	100	251A	WD	77381
CRICKET MILL DR	0	376H	NEC	77346
CRICKETT HOLLOW DR	13700	330Y	NWC	77069
CRICKETT HOLLOW LN	12600	368J	NWC	77429
CRICKET WOOD CIR	13400	528B	SWH	77082
CRICKLEWOOD LN	1200	329G	NWC	77379
CRICKLEWOOD CREEK LN	13400	528Q	SWC	77083
CRIEFFE RD	13000	414G	NCC	77039
CRIM CT	6400	456Q	NEH	77049
CRIM RD	13100	456Q	NEH	77049
CRIM LILLY CT	7100	406P	NWC	77433
CRIMSON BAY DR	100	660A	LC	77573
CRIMSON BEECH DR	0	253Y	SEM	77386
CRIMSON BERRY TRAIL	1900	338A	NEH	77345
CRIMSON BLUFF LN	0	484E	KT	77494
CRIMSON CANYON DR	10300	367Y	NWC	77095
S. CRIMSON CLOVER CT	200	251B	WD	77381
CRIMSON CLOVER CROSSING	8700	524D	NEF	77494
CRIMSON COAST CT	400	660E	LC	77573
CRIMSON COAST DR	400	660E	LC	77573
CRIMSON COVE CT	2200	619Z	LC	77573
CRIMSON ELM DR	0	325R	NWC	77433
CRIMSON FLOWER LN	16400	326J	NWC	77433
CRIMSON FLOWER LN	16400	326F	NWC	77433
CRIMSON LAKE LN	2100	658T	LC	77573
CRIMSON LEAF CT	20700	326N	NWC	77433
CRIMSON LEAF LN	0	326N	NWC	77433
CRIMSON MAPLE CT	3300	297P	NEH	77345
CRIMSON MEADOWS DR	4100	573Z	SEH	77048
CRIMSON OAK CIR	20400	337Q	NEC	77346
CRIMSON OAK CT	4100	578Y	SEH	77059
CRIMSON OAK TRAIL	20600	337Q	NEC	77346
S. CRIMSON RIDGE CIR	0	250B	WD	77382
N. CRIMSON RIDGE CIR	0	250B	WD	77382
CRIMSON RIDGE CT	1	250G	WD	77381
CRIMSON SKY DR	0	528J	SWC	77083
CRIMSON STAR TERRACE	0	525F	NEF	77494
CRIMSON TRAIL	14800	408P	NWC	77084
CRIMSON VALLEY CT	2300	297U	NEH	77345
CRIMSON WOOD DR	0	524L	NWF	77406
CRINKLEAWN DR	11000	371T	NWC	77086
CRINKLEROOT CT	1	251R	WD	77380
CRINUM LILY DR	0	328M	NWC	77377
CRIPPLE BROOK CT	5500	535V	SEH	77017
CRIPPLE CREEK CT	4700	535R	SEH	77017
CRIPPLE CREEK DR	4700	535V	SEH	77017
CRIPPLE CREEK DR	33300	247M	SWM	77362
CRIPPLE CREEK LN	1800	616N	PL	77581
CRISFIELD CT	22400	485U	NEF	77450
CRISP APPLE WAY	0	611N	FS	77545
CRISPIN LN	9400	450T	NWH	77080
CRISP SPRING LN	25600	292U	NCC	77373
CRISP WOOD LN	7300	411A	NWC	77086
CRISP WOOD LN	7500	410D	NWC	77086
CRISTIWOOD CT	19700	289Y	NWC	77379
CRITES	4100	494P	SEH	77003
CRITES	4600	494P	SEH	77011
CRITTENDEN	2400	454S	NEH	77026
CROCALE PATCH DR	700	338M	NEH	77336
CROCKER	1000	493N	SWH	77019
CROCKER	1800	493S	SWH	77006
CROCKETT	0	499K	NEC	77520
CROCKETT	0	500V	BT	77520
S. CROCKETT	400	538Y	DP	77536
N. CROCKETT	400	538Y	DP	77536
CROCKETT	400	498G	CV	77530
CROCKETT	1100	493G	SWH	77007
CROCKETT	11700	539R	LP	77571
CROCKETT	21200	256N	SEM	77357
CROCKETT CT	0	528Y	SG	77478
CROCKETT BEND CT	0	377J	NEC	77346
CROCKETT BEND LN	0	377J	NEC	77346
CROCKETT CANYON CT	17000	377K	NEC	77346
CROCKETT CREEK CT	0	578T	SEH	77059
CROCKETT RIDGE DR	6900	525V	NEF	77406
CROES DR	8800	450Z	SV	77055
CROFT CT	11700	369W	NWC	77065
CROFTER GLEN DR	4400	657B	FR	77546
CROFTON	7300	455E	NEH	77028
CROFTON	9400	455A	NEH	77016
CROFTSMILL DR	0	257E	SEM	77357
CROFTWOOD DR	14900	331S	NWC	77068
CROKER RIDGE RD	4600	571Z	SWH	77053
CROMART	0	534A	SEH	77004
CROMARTY CT	16600	447D	NWC	77084
CROMDALE MANOR CT	10400	329C	NWC	77379
CROMWELL	1000	413U	NEH	77037
CROMWELL	1400	413V	NCC	77093
CROMWELL	2400	414N	NCC	77093
CROMWELL CT	0	568B	SG	77498
CRONDELL CIR	14900	457Z	NEC	77530
CROOKED LN	2300	446V	NWC	77084
CROOKED ARROW DR	15700	527U	NEF	77498
CROOKED CREEK CT	23600	245Y	SWM	77447
S. CROOKED CREEK DR	5400	536S	SEH	77017
N. CROOKED CREEK DR	5400	536S	SEH	77017
CROOKED CREEK LN	1800	616N	PL	77581
CROOKED CREEK RD	23500	285C	SWM	77447
CROOKED CREEK RD	23600	245Y	SWM	77447
CROOKED GATE LN	20500	379E	NEC	77532
S. CROOKED LAKE WAY	15900	326N	NWC	77433
N. CROOKED LAKE WAY	15900	326N	NWC	77433
CROOKED OAK DR	17000	327T	CY	77429
CROOKED OAK WAY	18400	330H	NWC	77379

Street Name	Block	Pg/Sq	Loc	Zips
CROOKED PINE DR	11200	369J	NWC	77429
CROOKED POST RD	5800	334A	NWC	77373
CROOKED WOOD	9400	370Z	NWC	77086
CROOKS WAY CT	10200	369W	NWC	77065
CROOMS	5400	492L	SWH	77007
CROQUET LN	13400	571K	SWH	77085
CROQUET LN	13800	571P	SWH	77085
CROQUET LN	15400	571X	SWH	77053
CROSBY	0	339K	HU	77336
CROSBY	0	500V	BT	77520
CROSBY	700	493K	SWH	77019
CROSBY	1000	493P	SWH	77019
CROSBY	12100	339J	HU	77336
W. CROSBY CIR	16400	420A	NEC	77532
E. CROSBY CIR	16400	420A	NEC	77532
CROSBY RD	0	463A	MB	77521
CROSBY BARBERS HILL	900	420Y	NEC	77532
CROSBY BARBERS HILL	4000	460D	NEC	77532
CROSBY BARBERS HILL	4200	461A	NEC	77521
CROSBY BARBERS HILL	7600	462B	CCO	77521
CROSBY CEDAR BAYOU RD	100	502J	NEC	77521
CROSBY CEDAR BAYOU RD	4600	501D	NEC	77521
CROSBY CEDAR BAYOU RD	6500	461L	NEC	77521
CROSBY CEDAR BAYOU RD	7100	461Z	NEC	77521
CROSBY DAYTON RD	500	419D	CB	77532
CROSBY DAYTON RD	1300	380W	NEC	77532
CROSBY EASTGATE RD	18000	380G	NEC	77532
CROSBY EASTGATE RD	21400	340Q	LCO	77535
CROSBY FIELD LN	0	577W	SEH	77034
CROSBY FRWY	0	458A	NEC	77049
CROSBY FRWY	0	418Z	NEC	77049
CROSBY FRWY	0	419T	NEC	77532
CROSBY LYNCHBURG RD	100	459D	NEC	77562
CROSBY LYNCHBURG RD	10500	419L	NEC	77532
CROSBY VILLAGE DR	0	419C	NEC	77532
CROSLIN	0	455R	NEH	77078
CROSS	0	499L	NEC	77520
CROSS	21300	256V	SEM	77357
S. CROSS LN	0	290T	NWC	77379
CROSSBAY CT	0	658U	LC	77573
CROSSBEND DR	23100	485Q	NEF	77494
CROSSBILL	0	251V	WD	77380
CROSSBOW DR	300	252T	SEM	77386
CROSSBOW ARROW CT		289T	NWC	77375
CROSSBRANCH CT	3400	615F	PL	77581
CROSSBRANCH DR	19600	486G	SWC	77094
CROSSBRIDGE DR	800	292F	NCC	77373
CROSSBROOK CT	2200	619Z	LC	77573
CROSSBROOK CT	3000	485V	NEF	77450
CROSSBROOK DR	22000	485V	NEF	77450
CROSS CANYON LN	18100	526M	NEF	77407
CROSSCOACH LN	1700	446T	NWC	77449
CROSS CONTINENTS DR	0	374U	NEH	77032
CROSS COUNTRY DR	8100	338W	NEC	77346
CROSSCOVE CT	17400	407F	NWC	77095
CROSSCREEK CT	3500	610J	MC	77459
CROSS CREEK CT	5200	657V	LC	77573
CROSS CREEK DR	0	612N	PL	77545
CROSS CREEK LN	4900	658W	LC	77573
CROSSCUT	0	407T	NWC	77084
CROSSCUT PASS DR	23300	293Y	NCC	77373
CROSS DRAW DR	1200	372J	NWC	77067
CROSSFAIR DR	0	486P	SWC	77450
CROSSFALLS LN	0	406M	NWC	77433
CROSSFELL RD	2900	291Q	NWC	77388
CROSSFELL FIELDS LN	0	328W	NWC	77429
CROSSFENCE DR	0	249V	NWC	77375
CROSSFENCE DR		249V	NWC	77375
CROSSFIELD DR	900	486F	SWC	77450
CROSSFIELD DR	16300	407H	NWC	77095
CROSS FOX LN	1	251P	WD	77380
CROSSGATE BLVD	0	292F	NCC	77373
CROSSGLADE CT	0	417C	NEH	77044
CROSSGLEN CT	21800	334F	NCC	77373
CROSS GREEN LN	3600	293P	NCC	77373
CROSS GROVE LN	0	485N	NEF	77494
CROSSHAVEN CT	13700	457X	NEC	77015
CROSSHAVEN DR	13800	457Y	NEC	77015
CROSSHILL CT	0	372C	NCC	77073
CROSS HOLLOW LN	0	484F	NEF	77494
CROSS HOLLOW LN	26200	367J	NWC	77433
CROSSING DR	13000	408Q	NWC	77041
CROSSING NEXUS LN	2000	486N	SWC	77450
CROSSINGTON WAY	0	292F	NCC	77389
CROSS JUNCTION	14500	408T	NWC	77084
CROSSLAKES LN	0	609E	SG	77479
CROSSLAND CT	18200	407N	NWC	77433
CROSSLAND PARK LN	26100	367E	NWC	77433
CROSSLYN LN	13400	328W	NWC	77429
CROSSMAN DR	3200	297J	SEM	77365
CROSSMEADOW LN	0	527N	NEF	77407
CROSSMILL LN	0	486N	SWC	77450
CROSS OAK	0	250M	WD	77381
CROSSON LN	0	250T	NWC	77389
CROSSOUT CT	0	293U	NCC	77373
CROSSOVER RD	27000	484N	NEF	77494
CROSSPARK PLACE	3300	493J	SWH	77007
CROSS PLAINS CT	9400	408A	NWC	77095
CROSSPOINT AVE	1600	532U	SWH	77054
CROSSRIDGE DR	0	408H	NWC	77065
CROSSRIVER LN	8600	407F	NWC	77095
CROSSROADS DR	700	488E	SWH	77079
CROSSROADS PARK DR	12400	408D	NWC	77065
CROSSROADS PLAZA DR	10600	613S	PL	77584
CROSSROADS TRAIL	26700	299T	NEC	77346
CROSS SADDLE CT	1000	292F	NCC	77373
CROSS SPRING CT	11500	612R	PL	77584
CROSS SPRING DR	11600	612R	PL	77584
CROSS SPRING LN	0	658U	LC	77573
CROSS SPRING PARK LN	32300	253N	SEM	77385
CROSS SPRINGS CT	8200	407G	NWC	77095
CROSS SPRINGS DR	17100	407G	NWC	77095
CROSS STONE CT	14800	327W	NWC	77429
CROSS TIDE LN	2600	617X	SEC	77546
E. CROSSTIMBERS	1	453L	NEH	77022
W. CROSSTIMBERS	100	452M	NWH	77018
CROSSTIMBERS	100	453L	NWH	77018
CROSSTIMBERS	300	453K	NWH	77022
E. CROSSTIMBERS	1700	454J	NEH	77093
E. CROSSTIMBERS	4000	454J	NEH	77016
CROSS TIMBERS LN	0	616U	FR	77546
CROSSTON	4500	452M	NWH	77018
CROSSTREES LN	13700	415B	NEC	77396
CROSSVALE LN	0	573Y	SEC	77047
CROSS VALLEY DR	5400	371N	NWC	77066
CROSSVIEW DR	2700	490Y	SWH	77063
CROSSVIEW LAKE DR		366V	NWC	77433
CROSSVIEW TIMBERS		367S	NWC	77433
CROSSVINE CIR	2600	251P	WD	77380
CROSSVINE TRAIL CT	21200	326S	NWC	77433
CROSSVINE TRAIL LN	20000	326X	NWC	77433
CROSSWAY DR	6300	407U	NWC	77084
CROSSWAY OAKS	28000	246A	SWM	77355
CROSSWELL	6400	534Y	SEH	77087
CROSSWELL	6800	574C	SEH	77087
CROSSWICK LN	0	292F	NCC	77373
CROSSWIND DR	0	612R	PL	77584
CROSSWINDS	0	289R	NWC	77379
CROSSWINDS DR	14600	374V	NEH	77032
CROSSWINDS WAY	18300	378S	NEC	77532
CROSSWOOD RD	13900	371U	NWC	77038
CROSSWOOD TRAILS LN	26100	367E	NWC	77433
CROSSWORTH DR	0	257F	SEM	77357
CROTEAU DR	8700	456D	NEC	77044
CROTON RD	7400	530K	SWH	77036
CROW RD	1	500N	BT	77520
CROW RD	100	499R	BT	77520
CROW COURT DR	12000	368Q	NWC	77429
CROWELL LN	2600	502B	NEC	77521
E. CROWN	100	536D	PA	77506
CROWN	100	495E	NEH	77020
CROWN	100	496T	GP	77547
CROWN LN	4500	501F	BT	77521
CROWN ARBOR	0	568J	NEF	77498
CROWN BEND	0	568E	NEF	77498
CROWNBERRY CT	1	251K	WD	77381
CROWN BROOK CT	8800	528N	SWC	77083
CROWN CHASE DR	27000	296W	SEM	77339
CROWN COLONY	5400	370D	NWC	77069
CROWN COVE LN	0	296X	SEM	77339
CROWN DALE	0	371J	NWC	77066
CROWNED CT	0	404Z	NWC	77493
CROWNFIELD LN	22500	485U	NEF	77450
CROWN FOREST DR	3000	297Z	NEH	77345
CROWN GLEN CT	14000	617D	SEH	77062
CROWN GROVE	0	568J	NEF	77498
CROWN HAVEN CT	26900	296W	SEM	77339
CROWN HAVEN DR	26900	296W	SEM	77339
CROWNHILL LN	0	407V	NWC	77084
CROWN LAKE CIR	0	330B	NWC	77379
CROWN MEADOW CT	17100	407L	NWC	77095
CROWNOVER RD	1700	450U	NWH	77080
CROWN PARK DR	11200	372N	NWC	77067
CROWN PLACE	0	568J	NEF	77498
CROWN POINT DR	10500	529X	SWH	77099
CROWN PROMENADE	0	568J	NEF	77498
CROWN RIDGE CT	3900	578X	SEH	77059
CROWN ROCK DR	27000	296W	NEC	77339
CROWNSEDGE DR	10600	329B	NWC	77379
CROWN TRAIL	0	568J	NEF	77498
CROWNWEST DR	7100	528M	SWH	77072
CROWNWOOD DR	4100	619G	TL	77586
CROW RIDGE CT	13900	328P	NWC	77429
CROWS NEST DR	2100	619X	LC	77573
CROWS NEST WAY	17300	379X	NEC	77532
CROW VALLEY DR	3400	610J	MC	77459
CROW VALLEY DR	4100	609R	MC	77459
CROW VALLEY LN	12700	528Y	SWH	77099
CROXTON DR	14800	457Z	NEC	77015
CROY CREEK CT		289H	NWC	77375
CROYDON CT	2000	492C	NWH	77008
CRUSADER WAY	6500	530E	SWH	77036
CRUSE DR	500	536M	PA	77506
CRUSE RD	4700	454H	NEH	77016
CRUTCHFIELD LN	1500	445Y	NWC	77449
CRY BABY LN	1	339A	NEC	77336
CRYER CREEK CIR	0	366P	NWC	77433
CRYSTAL	300	658H	LC	77573
CRYSTAL BLVD	9900	502C	BT	77521
CRYSTAL CT	0	328F	NWC	77429
CRYSTAL CT	1800	452S	NWH	77008
CRYSTAL BAY CT	0	408W	NWC	77084
CRYSTAL BAY DR	5100	408W	NWC	77084
CRYSTAL BAY DR	22300	485V	NEF	77450
CRYSTAL BAY LN	800	660E	LC	77573
CRYSTAL BLUE LN	7400	526K	NEF	77407
CRYSTAL BLUFF CT		526S	NEF	77407
CRYSTAL BRIDGE LN	0	525H	NEF	77450
CRYSTAL BROOK DR	15800	331N	NWC	77068
W. CRYSTAL CANYON CIR	0	250R	NWC	77389
E. CRYSTAL CANYON CIR	0	250R	NWC	77389
E. CRYSTAL CANYON CT	0	250R	NWC	77389
CRYSTAL CASCADE CIR	0	330B	NWC	77379
CRYSTAL CASCADE LN	0	660E	LC	77573
CRYSTAL COVE CIR	8600	457A	NEC	77044
CRYSTAL COVE CIR	9300	329Q	NWC	77070
CRYSTAL COVE CT	8600	457A	NEC	77044
CRYSTAL COVE DR	12800	456D	NEC	77044
CRYSTAL COVE LN	0	524J	NWF	77406
CRYSTAL CREEK CT	16200	330T	NWC	77379
CRYSTAL CREEK DR	1	568Z	SG	77478
CRYSTAL DOVE DR	3400	291Q	NWC	77388
CRYSTAL DOWELS DR	6900	578K	PA	77505
CRYSTAL DOWNS CT	23000	485Q	NEF	77450
CRYSTAL DOWNS DR	2000	485Q	NEF	77450
CRYSTAL DOWNS LN	0	409K	JV	77064
CRYSTAL FALLS DR	2700	297X	NEH	77345
CRYSTAL FALLS DR	3700	609M	MC	77459
CRYSTAL FOREST CT	0	444P	KT	77493
CRYSTAL FOREST TRAIL	0	444P	KT	77493
CRYSTAL GLEN LN	7300	407R	NWC	77095
CRYSTAL GREENS DR	20100	486W	NEF	77450
CRYSTAL GROVE DR	15700	487Y	SWC	77082
CRYSTAL HILLS	2100	488V	SWH	77077
CRYSTAL HILLS DR	1300	489N	SWH	77077
CRYSTAL ISLE LN	7600	375Y	NEC	77396
CRYSTAL IVY LN	0	291X	NWC	77388
W. CRYSTAL LAKE CIR	1300	613L	NEB	77584
E. CRYSTAL LAKE CIR	1300	613M	NEB	77584
S. CRYSTAL LAKE CIR	1300	613M	NEB	77584
N. CRYSTAL LAKE CIR	3900	613L	NEB	77584
CRYSTAL LAKE DR	4100	613M	NEB	77584
CRYSTAL LAKE LN	1	251V	WD	77380
CRYSTAL LEAF LN	0	524G	NEF	77494
CRYSTAL MEADOW PLACE	0	484L	NEF	77494
CRYSTAL MOON DR	0	410L	NWC	77040
CRYSTAL PARK DR	0	376Y	NEC	77396
CRYSTAL PASS CT	3900	446J	NWC	77449
CRYSTAL PINES DR	0	253W	SEM	77386
CRYSTAL POINT	6400	609K	MC	77459
CRYSTAL POINT DR	6800	406V	NWC	77449
CRYSTAL REEF DR	100	660A	LC	77573
CRYSTAL REEF LN	0	612L	PL	77545
CRYSTAL REEF PLACE	0	612F	PL	77545
CRYSTAL RIVER DR	2000	337C	NEH	77345
CRYSTAL ROCK CT	12601	528M	SWH	77072
CRYSTAL SKY	0	525E	NEF	77494
CRYSTAL SPRINGS DR	1900	336G	NEH	77339
CRYSTAL STONE LN	0	524G	NEF	77494
CRYSTAL STREAM TRAIL	0	338B	NEH	77345
CRYSTAL VIEW CIR	1600	407H	NWC	77095
CRYSTAL VIEW CT	16500	407H	NWC	77095
CRYSTAL WAY	7100	530D	SWC	77036
CRYSTAL WIND LN	0	484Q	NEF	77494
CRYSTALWOOD DR	11600	496C	NEH	77013
CRYSTALYNN LN	0	326Y	NWC	77433
CRYSTOLA PARK	19100	332C	NCC	77373
CUADRO LN	0	451Y	NWH	77055
CUB LN	9300	575L	SEH	77075
CUBALIBRE DR	22000	339W	NEC	77532
CUCCERRE RD	8000	412V	NEH	77037
CUCKLEBUR CIR	10000	367Y	NWC	77095
CUDHAM	0	255P	SEM	77365
CUFFLEY	21900	256K	SEM	77357
CUFFMAN DR	0	450S	NWH	77080
CUJANES	4000	577F	PA	77504
CUKERBAUM	0	524S	NWF	77406
CULBERSON	6200	533L	SEH	77021
CULEBRA	9700	455Z	NEH	77013
CULICO FALLS CT	0	253K	SEM	77386
CULLEN BLVD	100	613R	PL	77584
CULLEN BLVD	700	494S	SEH	77023
CULLEN BLVD	2100	534A	SEH	77004
CULLEN BLVD	3700	533D	SEH	77004
CULLEN BLVD	5700	533R	SEH	77021
CULLEN BLVD	7300	533R	SEH	77051
CULLEN BLVD	8600	573D	SEH	77051
CULLEN BLVD	10200	573Z	SEH	77047
CULLEN BLVD	14800	613D	SEC	77047
CULLEN CIR	6400	533E	SWH	77030
CULLEN CT	300	539Z	LP	77571
CULLEN ESTATES DR	0	613Z	NEB	77584
CULLEN MEADOW CT	12000	573L	SEH	77047
CULLEN RIDGE DR	0	295L	SEM	77365
CULLEN TERRACE	0	293J	SEM	77386
CULLUM ROADWAY	0	257R	SEM	77357
CULMORE DR	4800	534J	SEH	77021
CULMORE DR	6300	534L	SEH	77087
CULROSS CT	18900	337X	NEC	77346
CULROSS CLOSE	5800	337X	NEC	77346
CULVER	1300	536T	PA	77502
CULVER	9200	573C	SEH	77051
CUMBERLAND	2300	534C	SEH	77023
CUMBERLAND BLVD	18600	255S	SEM	77365
CUMBERLAND CT	3200	610U	MC	77459
CUMBERLAND DR	2800	610U	MC	77459
CUMBERLAND DR	5200	657R	LC	77573
CUMBERLAND BRIDGE LN	14800	568A	NEF	77498
CUMBERLAND BROOK LN		484S	NEF	77494
CUMBERLAND FALLS DR	0	330C	NWC	77379
CUMBERLAND OAK CT	1599	326N	NWC	77433
CUMBERLAND OAK CT	2300	297V	NEH	77345
CUMBERLAND OAK WAY	15300	325V	NWC	77433
CUMBERLAND PARK LN	0	377E	NEC	77346
CUMBERLAND RIDGE	0	325R	NWC	77433
CUMBERLAND RIDGE LN	0	657Y	LC	77573
CUMBERLAND TRAIL	16100	326P	NWC	77433
CUMBERLAND WAY	21300	325V	NWC	77433
CUMBRE DR	22800	295B	SEM	77365
CUMBRIA DR	15900	330S	NWC	77379
CUMI	8900	460R	NEC	77562
CUMMINGS LN	20200	256K	SEM	77357
CUMMINS	3000	492S	SWH	77027
CUMMINS GREEN	4200	492W	SWH	77027
CUNEY DR	3800	533C	SEH	77004
CUNNINGHAM DR	0	578C	SEC	77505
CUNNINGHAM DR	2300	614R	PL	77581
CUNNINGHAM DR	24300	296K	SEM	77365
CUNNINGHAM RD	5700	449B	NWC	77041
CUNNINGHAM RD	5900	409X	NWC	77041
CUNNINGHAM FIR TRAIL		249P	NWC	77375
CUPIDS BOWER CT	5000	291N	NWC	77388
CUPSHIRE DR	0	406B	NWC	77433
CURACAO DR	7000	459K	NEC	77049
CURIO GRAY TRAIL	0	325L	NWC	77433
CURLEE CIR	0	576K	SEH	77034
CURLEE RD	8800	576K	SEH	77034
CURLEE SPRING LN	0	292E	NWC	77389
CURLEW CT	0	610E	MC	77489
CURLEW DR	7100	406Q	NWC	77433
CURLING	1700	450V	NWH	77055
CURLY OAKS DR	3900	572S	SWH	77053
CURLY OAKS DR	4600	571V	SWH	77053
S. CURLY WILLOW CIR	100	249R	NWH	77375
S. CURLY WILLOW CIR	100	249R	NWH	77375
N. CURLY WILLOW CIR	100	249R	NWH	77375
N. CURLY WILLOW CIR	100	249R	NWH	77375
S. CURLY WILLOW CIR		249R	NWC	77375
N. CURLY WILLOW CIR		249Q	NWC	77375
CURRAWONG CT	0	367P	NWC	77433
CURRENCY	9200	495G	NEH	77013
CURRIE	10400	577X	SEH	77034
CURRIN FOREST DR	12200	416L	NEC	77044
CURRY	0	457T	NEC	77049
CURRY	600	620Q	SB	77586
CURRY LN	3617	659Z	DI	77539
CURRY RD	0	613X	NEB	77584
CURRY RD	6900	454J	NEH	77093
CURRY RD	20500	252K	SEM	77385
CURRY ST	900	501M	BT	77521
CURRY CREEK LN	14100	332W	NWC	77090
CURRYDALE WAY	100	250J	NWC	77375
CURRY LANDING DR	0	407C	NWC	77095
CURRY RIDGE LN	11600	328D	NWC	77377
CURT LN	12900	408R	NWC	77041
CURTIAN RIDGE	1	297R	NEH	77345
CURTIN	700	452K	NWH	77018
CURTIN	4900	494T	SEH	77023
CURTIS	0	379Q	NEC	77532
CURTIS	3500	613Z	NEB	77578
CURTIS	3900	494F	NEH	77020
W. CURTIS AVE	100	536Q	PA	77502
CURTIS AVE	100	536R	PA	77502
CURTIS CROSSING	0	570S	MC	77489
CURWOOD DR	0	251Y	WD	77380
CURZON	800	257Y	SEM	77357
CUSHING	1100	493P	SWH	77019
CUSHING	2800	494C	NEH	77026
CUSHMAN DR	0	257E	SEM	77357
CUSTARD APPLE TRAIL	5500	524D	NEF	77494
CUSTER	4300	453Y	NEH	77009
CUSTER DR	2800	658S	LC	77573
CUSTER LN	5600	614B	BK	77581
CUSTER CREEK DR	4100	569U	MC	77459
CUSTOMS	0	289V	NWC	77375
CUSTUS	1000	493E	SWH	77007
CUTA CT	13100	414F	NCC	77039
CUTLASS DR	3500	375M	NEC	77396
CUTLER RIDGE LN	13100	457A	NEC	77044
CUTTEN RD	10100	370L	NWC	77066
CUTTEN RD	13100	370L	NWC	77069
CUTTEN RD	14000	370A	NWC	77069
CUTTEN RD	15800	329U	NWC	77070
CUTTEN PKWY	6700	370A	NWC	77069
CUTTER CT	0	620K	SB	77586
CUTTER DR	0	659D	LC	77573
CUTTER DR	2000	660A	LC	77573
CUTTER MILL DR	22500	291J	NWC	77389
CUTTER RAYS	700	612S	FS	77545
CUTTER WAY	17100	379X	NEC	77532
CUTTING HORSE LN	10200	409G	NWC	77064
CUTTLER RD	22200	256U	SEM	77357
CY-CREEK Y	0	369C	NWC	77070
CY-FAIR FIRE	0	326R	NWC	77429
CYAN SKY DR	16400	325R	NWC	77433
CYBERONICS BLVD	100	618M	SEH	77058
CYBERONICS BLVD	300	618M	SEH	77058
CYMBAL CT	9200	410P	NWC	77040
CYMBAL DR	9700	569H	SF	77477
CYNDA BROOKE DR	4300	501J	BT	77521
CYNTHIA	4300	531M	BL	77401
CYNTHIA ANN CT	9800	532S	SWH	77025
W. CYPRESS	0	368G	NWC	77429
E. CYPRESS	0	368G	NWC	77429
CYPRESS	0	330D	NWC	77379
CYPRESS	0	375M	NEC	77396
CYPRESS	100	298E	NEC	77336
CYPRESS	100	459Q	HG	77562
CYPRESS	100	580G	LP	77571
CYPRESS	1100	500Z	BT	77520
CYPRESS	2600	537T	PA	77502
CYPRESS	5200	537U	PA	77503
CYPRESS	5700	531N	SWH	77074
CYPRESS	7700	535B	SEH	77012
CYPRESS CIR	0	368Q	NWC	77065
CYPRESS CIR	12500	368K	NWC	77429
CYPRESS CIR	14200	375X	NEC	77396
CYPRESS CIR	17000	254D	SEM	77302
CYPRESS CIR	31800	282V	WL	77484
CYPRESS CT	2600	620J	SB	77586
CYPRESS CT	11200	369J	NWC	77065
CYPRESS DR	100	419Y	BR	77532
CYPRESS DR	7500	375C	HM	77396
CYPRESS DR	12200	367K	CY	77433
CYPRESS LN	1	609A	SG	77478
CYPRESS LN	300	539P	LP	77571
CYPRESS LN	1200	336F	NEH	77339
CYPRESS LN	1200	459E	NEC	77562
CYPRESS LN	6300	444P	KT	77493
CYPRESS LN	13500	369E	NWC	77429
CYPRESS RD	0	446H	NWC	77449
CYPRESS RD	26700	295Y	SEM	77365
CYPRESS ARBOR CT	19300	446H	NWC	77449
CYPRESS ARBOR DR	19200	446G	NWC	77449
CYPRESS BANK DR	18900	331C	NWC	77388
CYPRESS BAY BLVD	0	619V	LC	77565
CYPRESS BAY CT	19400	446H	NWC	77449
CYPRESS BAY DR	0	446H	NWC	77449
CYPRESS BAY DR	19200	446H	NWC	77449
CYPRESS BEND	100	257J	SEM	77357
CYPRESS BEND CT	4600	615N	PL	77581
CYPRESS BEND DR	16200	367G	CY	77429
CYPRESS BEND LN	2000	569W	SG	77478
CYPRESS BLOOM LN	0	406M	NWC	77433
CYPRESS BLUFF DR	7400	406K	NWC	77433
CYPRESSBLUFF LN	0	446H	NWC	77449
CYPRESS BOUGH DR	19600	446G	NWC	77449
CYPRESS BRANCH DR	14400	328S	NWC	77429
CYPRESS BREEZE CT	7200	290T	NWC	77379
CYPRESS BREEZE CT	14000	328Q	NWC	77429
CYPRESS BREEZE DR	20600	406K	NWC	77433
CYPRESS BRIDGE DR	16500	327X	CY	77429
CYPRESS BROOK CT	16500	327X	CY	77429
CYPRESSBROOK DR	8700	408F	NWC	77095
CYPRESS BROOK WILLOW DR	0	368P	NWC	77429
CYPRESS CANYON DR	19100	446H	NWC	77449
CYPRESS CASCADE LN	14300	331W	NWC	77068
CYPRESS CHASE	0	487A	SWC	77094
CYPRESS CHASE BLVD	0	366D	NWC	77429
CYPRESS CHATEAU DR	18800	331D	NWC	77388
CYPRESS CHURCH RD	18200	326Q	NWC	77429
CYPRESS CLIFF DR	19200	446G	NWC	77449
CYPRESS COLONY LN	4201	446H	NWC	77449
CYPRESS CORNER	0	368P	NWC	77065
CYPRESS CORNER DR	0	368P	NWC	77065
N. CYPRESS CORNER PLACE	0	368P	NWC	77065
CYPRESS CORNER WAY	0	368P	NWC	77065
CYPRESS COTTAGE CT	14600	367A	NWC	77429
CYPRESS COVE	1400	580F	LP	77571
CYPRESS COVE DR	1500	331H	NWC	77090
CYPRESS COVE PARK DR	0	366E	NWC	77433
CYPRESS CREEK BLVD	14100	368K	NWC	77429
CYPRESS CREEK PKWY	0	331T	NWC	77068
CYPRESS CREEK BANK DR	0	368P	NWC	77429
CYPRESS CREEK BEND LN	0	366Y	NWC	77433
CYPRESS CREEK FOREST DR	0	368P	NWC	77429
CYPRESS CREEK LAKES DR	11600	366R	NWC	77433
CYPRESS CRESCENT DR	0	406K	NWC	77433
CYPRESS CREST DR	14200	328S	NWC	77429
CYPRESSCROFT	12800	366H	NWC	77433
CYPRESS CROSSING DR	12300	368M	NWC	77429
CYPRESSDALE DR	3400	331C	NWC	77388
CYPRESS DAWN LN	4700	446H	NWC	77449
CYPRESS DOWNS DR	16500	327X	CY	77429
CYPRESS ECHO DR	0	406K	NWC	77433
CYPRESSEDGE CT	0	327Z	NWC	77429
CYPRESS EDGE DR	0	406K	NWC	77433
CYPRESS ENCLAVE LN	0	253U	SEM	77386
S. CYPRESS ESTATES CIR	300	332B	NWC	77388
N. CYPRESS ESTATES CIR	300	332B	NWC	77388
CYPRESS ESTATES CT	19100	332B	NWC	77388
CYPRESS ESTATES DR	18900	332F	NWC	77388
CYPRESS FALLS DR	14000	328T	NWC	77429
CYPRESS FARMS RANCH	16000	327Y	CY	77429
CYPRESS FIELD	0	369P	NWC	77065
CYPRESS FIELDS AVE	17100	327P	NWC	77429
CYPRESS FIELDS RD	14800	327T	CY	77429
CYPRESS FLOWER DR	19100	446G	NWC	77449
E. CYPRESS FOREST DR	13200	369C	NWC	77070
W. CYPRESS FOREST DR	13300	369B	NWC	77070
CYPRESS GARDEN DR	8600	408A	NWC	77095
CYPRESS GARDEN DR	14200	328T	NWC	77429
CYPRESS GARDEN DR	15500	287V	NWC	77377
CYPRESS GARDENS	0	408A	NWC	77095
CYPRESS GARDENS	15300	330U	NWC	77069
CYPRESSGATE DR	5500	334E	NCC	77373
CYPRESSGATE DR	22500	334E	NCC	77373
CYPRESS GLADE DR	17000	327P	CY	77429
CYPRESS GLADES CIR	19300	406R	NWC	77449
CYPRESS GLADES CT	19300	406R	NWC	77449
CYPRESS GLADES DR	6500	406R	NWC	77449
CYPRESS GLEN	17500	327K	NWC	77429
CYPRESS GREEN DR	14900	328W	NWC	77429
CYPRESS GREEN LN	20600	406K	NWC	77433
CYPRESS GROVE LN	3700	411U	NWH	77088
CYPRESS GROVE MDWS DR	0	331U	NWC	77014
CYPRESS GULLY DR	0	406P	NWC	77449
CYPRESS GUN CLUB	0	368A	NWC	77429

Street Name	Block	Pg/Sq	Loc	Zips
CYPRESS HALL DR	15800	367D	NWC	77429
CYPRESS HARBOR DR	19200	446G	NWC	77449
CYPRESS HARROW DR	0	446D	NWC	77449
CYPRESS HAVEN LN	0	331P	NWC	77068
CYPRESS HEATH CT	13500	328P	NWC	77429
CYPRESS HILL	2400	568Y	SG	77479
W. CYPRESS HILL CIR	17700	326H	NWC	77429
E. CYPRESS HILL CIR	17900	326H	NWC	77429
CYPRESS HILL CT	17300	331L	NWC	77388
CYPRESS HILL DR	3700	331G	NWC	77388
CYPRESS HILLTOP WAY	0	325F	NWC	77447
CYPRESS HOLLOW	0	258Q	NEC	77357
CYPRESS HOLLOW	1600	616T	PL	77581
CYPRESS HOLLOW	17500	327K	NWC	77429
CYPRESS HURST	0	293Y	NCC	77373
CYPRESS ISLAND DR	0	333F	NCC	77073
CYPRESS KEY DR	3700	291Y	NWC	77388
CYPRESS KNEE DR	17000	327T	CY	77429
CYPRESS KNEE LN	3900	414B	NCC	77039
CYPRESS KNOLL	14400	328T	NWC	77429
CYPRESS KNOLL DR	0	326T	NWC	77429
CYPRESS LAKE RD	3900	331G	NWC	77388
CYPRESS LAKE VILLAGE DR	18300	326V	NWC	77429
CYPRESS LAKE VILLAGE DR	18300	326V	NWC	77429
CYPRESS LANDING DR	2100	331V	NWH	77090
CYPRESS LAUREL	17600	407F	NWC	77095
CYPRESS LEAF DR	14400	328S	NWC	77429
CYPRESS LEDGE BLVD	15000	326V	NWC	77429
CYPRESS LILLY DR	0	406P	NWC	77449
CYPRESS LINKS TRAIL	14400	326Z	NWC	77429
CYPRESS LOCH DR	18700	329D	NWC	77379
CYPRESS LODGE CT	0	366V	NWC	77433
CYPRESS MANOR	6800	330R	NWC	77379
CYPRESS MANOR DR	1600	339N	HU	77336
CYPRESS MARSH CT	16600	327X	NWC	77429
CYPRESS MEADE CT	14900	326Z	NWC	77429
CYPRESS MEADE LN	18200	327W	NWC	77429
CYPRESS MEADE LN	18400	326Z	NWC	77429
CYPRESS MEADOW CT	3700	291Y	NWC	77388
CYPRESS MEADOW DR	0	573Y	SEC	77047
CYPRESS MEADOW DR	14200	328S	NWC	77429
CYPRESS MEADOWS	0	287V	NWC	77377
CYPRESS MEADOWS DR	15600	367M	CY	77429
CYPRESS MILL PARK DR	17900	327W	NWC	77429
CYPRESS MIST CT	0	367P	NWC	77433
CYPRESS MOSS DR	19500	446G	NWC	77449
CYPRESS MOUND CT	0	330H	NWC	77379
CYPRESS MOUNTAIN DR	18800	331C	NWC	77388
CYPRESS NEEDLE DR	0	327W	NWC	77429
CYPRESS N HOUSTON BLVD	0	367P	NWC	77095
CYPRESS N HOUSTON RD	11000	369K	NWC	77065
CYPRESS N HOUSTON RD	11300	368Q	NWC	77429
CYPRESS N HOUSTON RD	15100	367R	CY	77429
CYPRESS OAK DR	0	446H	NWC	77449
CYPRESS OAKS DR	0	332F	NWC	77388
CYPRESS OAKS DR	14400	368E	NWC	77429
CYPRESS ORCHARD LN	0	327X	NWC	77429
CYPRESS OVERLOOK TRAIL	0	334L	NCC	77338
CYPRESS PALMS CT		328P	NWC	77429
CYPRESS PARK DR	11800	368Q	NWC	77065
CYPRESSPARK GLEN LN	0	324M	NWC	77447
CYPRESSPARK GLEN LN	0	324M	NWC	77447
CYPRESS PARK SPUR	13300	368Q	NWC	77065
W. CYPRESS PASS LOOP	12700	367H	CY	77429
E. CYPRESS PASS LOOP	12700	367H	CY	77429
CYPRESS PASTURE TRAIL	0	325F	NWC	77447
CYPRESS PATH CT	16500	327X	CY	77429
CYPRESS PEAK LN	19200	446D	NWC	77449
CYPRESS PELICAN DR	16500	327X	NWC	77429
S. CYPRESS PINE DR	1	250M	WD	77381
N. CYPRESS PINE DR	1	250M	WD	77381
CYPRESS PINES	0	369P	NWC	77065
CYPRESS PLACE DR	11700	369N	NWC	77065
CYPRESS PLANTATION DR	17400	327F	NWC	77429
CYPRESS PLAZA PKWY	0	366U	NWC	77433
CYPRESS POINT DR	0	656U	FR	77546
CYPRESS POINT DR	2700	610E	MC	77459
CYPRESS POINT DR	6500	370B	NWC	77069
CYPRESS POINT DR	16100	367C	CY	77429
CYPRESS POINTE DR	0	658R	LC	77573
CYPRESS POND CIR	13700	328T	NWC	77429
CYPRESS POND CT	4400	578U	SEH	77059
CYPRESS POND RD	13600	328T	NWC	77429
CYPRESS POST DR	0	406K	NWC	77433
CYPRESS POST LN	15100	327V	CY	77429
CYPRESS POST LN	15100	327V	CY	77429
CYPRESS PRAIRIE DR	7100	406Q	NWC	77433
CYPRESS RAIN LN	19100	446H	NWC	77449
CYPRESS RANCH DR	0	327X	CY	77429
CYPRESS RIDGE DR	14200	328S	NWC	77429
CYPRESS RIDGE GROVE LN	14900	327W	NWC	77429
CYPRESS RILL DR	14300	331W	NWC	77068
CYPRESS RIVER DR	0	609A	SG	77478
CYPRESS RIVER DR	19200	446H	NWC	77449
CYPRESS ROSE CT	0	446D	NWC	77449
CYPRESS ROSEHILL RD	14000	367A	CY	77429
CYPRESS ROSEHILL RD	16100	327E	NWC	77429
CYPRESS ROSEHILL RD	19100	287W	NWC	77377
CYPRESS ROSEHILL-DECKER	0	287E	NWC	77377
CYPRESS ROYAL DR	0	446H	NWC	77449
CYPRESS RUN	300	487A	SWC	77094
CYPRESS RUN CT	4800	569W	SG	77478
CYPRESS RUN DR	1900	569W	SG	77478
CYPRESS SAGE DR	0	368P	NWC	77429
CYPRESS SHADOWS	11200	369N	NWC	77065
CYPRESS SHORES DR	12200	328D	NWC	77375
CYPRESS SIDE DR	0	367P	NWC	77433
CYPRESS SPRING	0	331G	NWC	77388
CYPRESS SPRING DR	4900	609P	MC	77459
CYPRESS SPRING DR	17300	331L	NWC	77388
CYPRESS SPRINGS	0	366U	NWC	77433
CYPRESS SPRINGS DR	0	612L	PL	77584
CYPRESS SPRINGS LN	0	612L	PL	77584
CYPRESS SQUARE CT	8700	330N	NWC	77379
CYPRESS SQUARE DR	9100	330N	NWC	77379
CYPRESS STAR LN	0	368P	NWC	77429
CYPRESS STATION DR	100	332F	NWC	77090
CYPRESS STEPPE LN	0	407A	NWC	77433
CYPRESS STONE LN	18200	326Z	NWC	77429
CYPRESS TERRACE DR	17400	327F	NWC	77429
CYPRESS THICKET DR	16500	327X	CY	77429
CYPRESSTHORN LN	19400	446D	NWC	77449
CYPRESS TIMBER DR	14800	327X	CY	77429
CYPRESS TIMBER LN		366R	NWC	77433
CYPRESS TRACE DR	16000	367C	CY	77429
CYPRESS TRACE RD	18000	332E	NWC	77090
CYPRESS TRAIL	0	373Z	NCC	77039
CYPRESS TRAIL	0	413D	NCC	77039
CYPRESS TRAIL	11800	369N	NWC	77065
CYPRESSTREE DR	2000	333A	NCC	77373
CYPRESS TREE LN	20600	291Y	NWC	77388
CYPRESS VALE DR	0	406P	NWC	77449
CYPRESS VALLEY DR	14200	328S	NWC	77429
CYPRESS VALLEY DR	16200	367C	CY	77429
CYPRESS VALLEY LN	18000	327W	NWC	77429
CYPRESS VALLEY RD	12700	367H	CY	77429
CYPRESS VIEW DR	14200	328S	NWC	77429
CYPRESS VIEW COVE	0	524A	NEF	77494
CYPRESS VILLA LN	0	366U	NWC	77433
CYPRESS VILLAGE CT	6100	614U	PL	77584
CYPRESS VILLAGE DR	0	406P	NWC	77449
CYPRESS VILLAGE DR	6100	614Y	PL	77584
W. CYPRESS VILLAS DR	4400	331F	NWC	77379
S. CYPRESS VILLAS DR	17700	331F	NWC	77379
CYPRESSVINE DR	2300	446U	NWC	77084
CYPRESS VISTA	300	487A	SWC	77094
CYPRESS WALK LN	0	367A	NWC	77429
CYPRESS WATERS CT	16500	327X	CY	77429
CYPRESS WATERS DR	14900	327T	CY	77429
CYPRESS WAY DR	11200	369N	NWC	77065
CYPRESSWELL CT	0	330H	NWC	77379
CYPRESSWICK CIR	0	330H	NWC	77379
CYPRESSWICK LN	0	330M	NWC	77379
CYPRESS WILLOW DR	0	446D	NWC	77449
CYPRESS WIND	0	487A	SWC	77094
CYPRESSWOOD	0	326X	NWC	77433
CYPRESSWOOD CT	4300	331F	NWC	77388
CYPRESSWOOD CT	19600	292X	NWH	77388
CYPRESSWOOD DR	0	325V	NWC	77433
E. CYPRESSWOOD DR	100	292Y	NCC	77373
CYPRESSWOOD DR	100	332A	NWC	77388
CYPRESSWOOD DR	2900	331K	NWC	77388
CYPRESSWOOD DR	4400	330R	NWC	77379
CYPRESSWOOD DR	9500	329Z	NWC	77070
CYPRESSWOOD DR	10000	369C	NWC	77070
CYPRESSWOOD DR	12100	368D	NWC	77070
CYPRESSWOOD DR	18000	327W	CY	77429
CYPRESSWOOD DR	18200	326Z	CY	77429
CYPRESSWOOD DR	20200	334P	NCC	77338
CYPRESSWOOD DR	22000	334A	NCC	77373
CYPRESSWOOD DR	23400	293T	NCC	77373
CYPRESSWOOD DR	23900	293W	NCC	77373
CYPRESSWOOD DR	24200	324R	NWC	77447
CYPRESSWOOD BEND	800	292Y	NCC	77373
CYPRESSWOOD BOUGH	800	292Y	NCC	77373
CYPRESSWOOD BROOK LN	0	292X	NCC	77373
CYPRESSWOOD CHASE RD	20300	292T	NEH	77373
CYPRESSWOOD COVE	700	292Y	NCC	77373
CYPRESSWOOD CREEK	19900	292Y	NCC	77373
CYPRESSWD CROSSING BL	13900	369A	NWC	77070
CYPRESSWOOD DALE	19800	292X	NCC	77373
CYPRESSWOOD ESTATES LN	600	292X	NCC	77373
CYPRESSWD ESTATES RUN	19800	292Y	NCC	77373
CYPRESSWOOD FALLS	19800	292X	NCC	77373
CYPRESSWOOD FOREST CT	18900	331D	NWC	77388
CYPRESSWD FOREST VW LN	3100	331D	NWC	77388
CYPRESSWOOD GLEN	19900	292X	NEH	77373
CYPRESSWOOD GLEN DR	19900	291Y	NWC	77388
CYPRESSWD GLEN TRAILS LN	0	324R	NWC	77447
CYPRESSWD GLEN TRAILS LN	0	324R	NWC	77447
CYPRESSWOOD GREEN CT	21900	334E	NCC	77373
CYPRESSWOOD GREEN DR	6000	334E	NCC	77373
CYPRESSWOOD GROVE RD	0	297P	NEH	77345
CYPRESSWOOD HARBOR CIR	600	292X	NCC	77373
CYPRESSWOOD HAVEN	0	292X	NCC	77373
CYPRESSWOOD HILL	500	292T	NEH	77373
CYPRESSWOOD KNOLL	500	292T	NEH	77373
CYPRESSWOOD LAKE CT	700	292Y	NCC	77373
CYPRESSWOOD LAKE DR	19600	292Y	NCC	77373
CYPRESSWD MEDWS DR	20500	291Y	NWC	77388
CYPRESSWD MEDICAL DR	15600	331U	NWC	77014
CYPRESSWOOD MILL	700	292Y	NCC	77373
CYPRESSWOOD NORTH LP	0	292U	NCC	77373
CYPRESSWOOD PLACE DR	11500	369A	NWC	77070
CYPRESSWOOD POINT AVE	0	334L	NCC	77338
CYPRESSWOOD RIDGE	600	292T	NCC	77373
CYPRESSWOOD SHORE	19800	292Y	NCC	77373
CYPRESSWOOD SPRINGS	19800	292Y	NCC	77373
CYPRESSWOOD SPRINGS LN		328k	NWC	77429
CYPRESSWOOD SQUARE	0	292U	NCC	77373
CYPRESSWOOD SUMMIT DR	0	334K	NCC	77338
CYPRESSWOOD TRACE	500	292Y	NCC	77373
CYPRESSWOOD TRACE	19700	292Y	NCC	77373
CYPRESSWOOD TRAIL CT	0	369A	NWC	77070
CYPRESSWOOD TRAIL DR	0	369A	NWC	77070
CYPRESSWOOD VIEW LN	0	253K	SEM	77386
CYPRIATE TRAIL	0	326Y	NWC	77433
CYPRUS CEDAR CT	17900	322B	WCO	77484
CYPRUS CEDAR LN	17800	322B	WCO	77484
CYPRUS FIELD	12000	369P	NWC	77070
CYR	7400	451T	NWH	77055
CYRIL DR	3600	376L	NEC	77396
CYRL LN	7900	456F	NEC	77044
W. CYRUS DR	11100	370S	NWC	77064
E. CYRUS DR	11100	370S	NWC	77064
CYRUS LN	0	282P	WCO	77484
CYRUS HILL DR	0	446N	NWH	77449

D

Street Name	Block	Pg/Sq	Loc	Zips
D	100	580Q	LP	77571
E. D	800	540Z	LP	77571
D	3800	529A	SWH	77072
D AVE	0	410P	NWC	77040
D DR	0	290L	NWC	77389
N. D AVENUE	11100	539Z	LP	77571
D PLUS	0	457G	NEC	77049
D S BAILEY LN	6500	412X	NWH	77091
D STREET	0	282T	WL	77484
D STREET	0	611X	FS	77545
D STREET	1300	536A	NEH	77015
D, AVENUE	0	569Q	SF	77477
D, AVENUE	0	619N	SEH	77058
D, AVENUE	0	656A	NEB	77581
D, AVENUE	1	536X	SH	77587
S. D, AVENUE	100	335Z	HM	77338
N. D, AVENUE	100	335V	HM	77338
D, AVENUE	100	459U	HG	77562
D, AVENUE	100	568J	SG	77498
D, AVENUE	800	444X	KT	77493
D, AVENUE	5400	419G	CB	77532
D, AVENUE	15900	498C	CV	77530
D, SOUTH	1000	541W	MP	77571
D'AMICO	3000	492M	SWH	77019
DABNEY	3400	454Z	NEH	77026
DABNEY DR	1400	537W	PA	77502
DABNEY MANOR CT	2400	445Q	NWC	77449
DABNEY MANOR LN	22500	445Q	NWC	77449
DACCA DR	3000	573F	SEH	77051
DACCA DR	4100	573G	SEH	77047
DACOMA	3700	452S	NWH	77092
DACOMA	3900	451U	NWH	77092
DACUS DR	900	496J	JC	77029
DADE	1400	536Q	PA	77502
DADEBROOK CT	12800	408V	NWC	77041
DADEBURY LN	16600	407Z	NWC	77084
DADEMOUNT CT	20600	526J	NEF	77407
DADE PEAK WAY	0	445D	NWC	77449
DAEHNE DR	13700	371B	NWC	77014
DAFFODIL	8600	490Y	SWH	77063
DAFFODIL CT	18600	295A	SEM	77365
DAFFODIL LN	23500	295A	SEM	77365
DAFFODIL RD	1400	570T	MC	77489
DAFFODILL DR	2400	460Q	NEC	77562
DAFFODIL MEADOW PLACE	100	249R	NWH	77375
DAFFODIL MEADOW PLACE	100	249R	NWH	77375
DAGG RD	4300	613D	SEH	77048
DAGG RD	4700	614A	SEH	77048
DAHLIA	7200	535E	SEH	77012
DAHLIA LN	4200	538U	DP	77536
DAHLIA LN	5600	444T	KT	77493
DAHLIA RD	0	460W	BT	77521
DAHLIA BROOK WAY	0	526T	NEF	77407
DAHLIA FIELD WAY	0	527D	SWC	77082
DAHLIA GLEN LN	0	326V	NWC	77429
DAHLIA GREEN WAY	0	371Z	NWC	77038
DAHLIA GREEN WAY	13400	371Z	NWC	77038
DAHLIA HILL	3500	611W	MC	77545
DAHLIA VALE WALK	0	418T	NEC	77044
DAILEY	500	541B	BT	77520
DAIN PLACE DR	3500	336U	NEH	77338
DAINTREE PLACE	0	405P	NWC	77493
N. DAIRY ASHFORD RD	100	488C	SWH	77079
S. DAIRY ASHFORD RD	1200	488V	SWH	77077
S. DAIRY ASHFORD RD	2800	488V	SWH	77082
S. DAIRY ASHFORD RD	6100	528H	SWH	77072
S. DAIRY ASHFORD RD	8600	528H	SWH	77099
DAIRY ASHFORD RD	11500	568H	SG	77478
DAIRY BROOK DR	12700	528R	SWH	77099
DAIRY GATE DR	22700	334A	NCC	77373
DAIRY OAKS DR	4200	380H	NEC	77532
DAIRY VIEW LN	8400	528R	SWH	77072
DAIRY VIEW LN	9300	528R	SWH	77099
DAISEY BELLE LN	1500	372N	NWC	77067
DAISY	1000	535A	SEH	77012
DAISY	2700	659Z	GCO	77539
DAISY	3100	537Y	PA	77505
DAISY	3400	577C	PA	77505
DAISY	6600	614D	BK	77581
DAISY LN	18400	295E	SEM	77365
DAISY BLOOM CT	20500	326N	NWC	77433
DAISY CHAIN	0	287Y	NWC	77377
DAISY CLOVER CT	0	616L	SEC	77089
DAISY COVE LN	0	410E	NWC	77064
DAISY CREEK TRAIL	16300	326F	NWC	77433
DAISYETTA	14200	570R	SWH	77085
DAISY MEADOW CT	12500	409S	NWC	77041
DAISY MEADOW DR	4200	446G	NWC	77449
DAISY MIST LN	9700	412F	NWC	77038
DAISY WOOD LN	0	616L	SEC	77089
DAKAR DR	11500	369N	NWC	77065
DAKAR DR	12100	368U	NWC	77065
DAKOTA	600	535Z	SH	77587
DAKOTA	1600	659P	LC	77573
DAKOTA BEND DR	14400	328P	NWC	77429
DAKOTA HILL CT	0	406F	NWC	77433
DAKOTA RIDGE CT	10000	367X	NWC	77095
DAKOTA RIDGE DR	17200	367X	NWC	77095
DAKOTA RIDGE PLACE	1	250B	WD	77381
DAKOTA RUN LN	1900	445S	NWC	77493
DAKOTA SPRINGS DR	19500	328C	NWC	77377
DAKTON DR	13100	414F	NCC	77039
DALAT ST	0	529P	SWH	77072
DALBY	300	576F	SEH	77034
DALE	100	413E	NCC	77060
DALE	900	502W	BT	77520
DALE DR	12500	368B	NWC	77429
DALEBROOK DR	11000	415N	NEH	77016
DALEBURG DR	14300	374Z	NCC	77032
DALEBURY CT	12200	371J	NWC	77066
DALEBURY DR	0	337U	NEC	77346
DALECREST DR	9500	450X	NWH	77080
DALEFORD LN	12900	456M	NEC	77049
DALE FOREST CT	18400	377A	NEC	77346
DALE GREEN LN	0	611S	FS	77545
DALEGROVE CT	7200	337U	NEC	77346
DALE HOLLOW LN	14600	368J	NWC	77429
DALEHURST CT	10300	575V	SEH	77075
DALE OAK WAY	16600	618R	SEH	77058
DALE RIVER RD		289G	NWC	77375
DALEROSE CT	1300	618E	SEH	77062
DALESIDE DR	12100	528Z	SWH	77099
DALE SPRINGS CT	0	572L	SWH	77045
DALEWOOD DR	500	413E	NCC	77060
DALEWOOD DR	500	570U	MC	77489
DALKEY DR	0	572H	SEH	77051
DALLAM CT	8700	409G	NWC	77064
DALLAM LN	10100	409G	NWC	77064
W. DALLAS	100	493J	SWH	77002
DALLAS	100	612S	FS	77545
DALLAS	100	493V	DT	77002
DALLAS	200	658M	LC	77573
DALLAS	300	536W	SH	77587
W. DALLAS	600	611U	FS	77545
W. DALLAS	700	493J	SWH	77019
DALLAS	1300	493V	DT	77002
DALLAS	1301	493V	DT	77010
DALLAS	1400	576B	SH	77587
DALLAS	1400	537S	PA	77502
DALLAS	1500	501V	BT	77520
DALLAS	1600	493V	DT	77003
DALLAS	1601	493V	DT	77010
DALLAS	2000	493V	SEH	77003
W. DALLAS	3000	492M	SWH	77019
DALLAS	3900	494S	SEH	77023
DALLAS	7100	494Z	SEH	77011
DALLAS	7100	460Y	MN	77521
DALLAS	21200	256N	SEM	77357
DALLAS LN	3100	613W	NWB	77578
DALLAS RD	18800	378R	NEC	77532
DALLAS ACORN AVE	0	455C	NEH	77078
DALLAS STREET RD	0	611V	FS	77545
DALLUM DR	0	447C	NWC	77084
DALMALLY	9500	329L	NWC	77379
DALMATIAN DR	3100	572N	SWH	77045
DALMATIAN DR	4600	571R	SWH	77045
DALMATION LN	3400	538U	DP	77536
DALMORE CT	9300	407D	NWC	77095
DALRYMPLE RD	3700	528A	SWC	77082
DALSTON DR	0	613D	SEC	77047
DALSTROM	3500	573U	SEC	77047
DALTON	2700	535K	SEH	77017
DALTON CREST DR	0	406F	NWC	77433
DALTON OAKS DR	14500	457U	NEC	77015
DALTONRIDGE DR	4100	293L	SEM	77386
DALTON SHADOW LN	17900	527N	NEF	77407
DALTON SPRING LN	21500	446J	NWC	77449
DALTON PARK CT	0	333A	NCC	77373
DALVIEW	2400	412W	NWH	77091
DALVIEW	3000	411Z	NWH	77091
DALY DR	14400	488E	SWH	77077
DALY PLACE	1	493G	NEH	77009
DAMACSO COVE	0	660F	LC	77573
DAMASCON CT	12500	371H	NWC	77014
DAMASCUS DR	8500	412Q	NWH	77088
DAMON CT	800	493N	SWH	77006
DAN	1400	494B	NEH	77020
DAN CIR	0	285D	SWM	77355
DANA DR	100	460S	HG	77562
DANA DR	22600	288P	NWC	77377
W. DANA LN	500	490G	PP	77024
DANA LEIGH DR	5100	370D	NWC	77066
DANALYN CT	18800	337X	NEC	77346
DANA LYNN LN	4500	613Z	NEB	77584
DANANG ST	0	529P	SWH	77072
DANA WAY	2000	537N	PA	77502
DANBRIDGE CT	18900	328G	NWC	77377
DANBRIDGE GULCH LN		484W	NEF	77494
DANBRIDGE HILLS LN		484T	NEF	77494
DANBURY CIR	0	656Y	FR	77546
DANBURY CT	1101	615B	PL	77581
DANBURY RD	900	451X	NWH	77055
DANBURY BRIDGE DR	17300	407B	NWC	77095
DANBURY CHASE TRAIL	3400	611W	FS	77545
DANBURY HOLLOW LN	0	575U	SEH	77075
DANBURY PARK LN	500	332Q	NCC	77073
DANBURY RUN DR	13600	408Y	NWC	77041
DANBURY SPRINGS LN	0	657T	FR	77546
DANBY HEATH LN	1400	332R	NCC	77073
DANCING GREEN DR	0	325L	NWC	77433
DAN COX AVE	1400	444Z	KT	77493
DANCY RD	0	409Y	NWC	77041
DANCY RD	5400	449C	NWC	77041
DANDALK	0	329R	NWC	77379
DANDELION LN	9500	570C	SWH	77071
DANDELION FIELD	7000	528J	NEF	77083
DANDELION MEADOW LN	5300	485W	NEF	77494
DANDRIDGE AVE	1300	536X	PA	77502
DANDY	7800	454C	NEH	77016
DANDYLINE WAY	10200	289U	NWC	77375
DANDY PARK CT	11700	572R	SWH	77047
DANE	7200	454J	NEH	77093
DANE LN	0	539W	DP	77571
DANEBRIDGE DR	5100	447B	NWC	77084
DANE HILL DR	7400	250T	NWC	77389
DANEK RD	3200	460G	NEC	77532
DANEK RD	4500	461A	NEC	77532
DANESWOOD CT	2300	291R	NWC	77388
DANETTE CT	8000	330E	NWC	77379
DANFIELD DR	100	572Y	SWH	77047
DANFIELD DR	4800	571Y	SWH	77053
DANFORD DR	15700	571X	SWH	77053
DANFORD LN	11400	415J	NEH	77016
DANFORTH DR	1000	617H	SEH	77062
DANFORTH CROSSING LN	8200	375Y	NEC	77396
DANFORTH WAY	9200	528P	SWC	77083
DANGLER	600	620Q	SB	77586
DANI LN	200	660X	DI	77539
DANIEL	900	541B	BT	77520
DANIEL CIR	0	656K	FR	77546
DANIEL RD	23100	256Z	SEM	77357
DANIELLA DR	10600	576K	SEH	77034
DANIELLE CT	9100	529T	SWH	77099
DANIELLE CT	19100	255U	SEM	77365
DANIELLE DR	5200	578C	PA	77505
DANIELLE LN	1300	616U	PL	77581
S. DANIEL OAK CIR	3400	291L	NWC	77389
N. DANIEL OAK CIR	3400	291L	NWC	77389
E. DANIEL OAK CIR	22300	291L	NWC	77389
DAN JOHN	1700	258K	SEM	77357
DANNA	800	659A	LC	77573
DANNA LN	100	453U	NEH	77009
DANO CT	0	332W	NWC	77090
DANO CT	0	332W	NWC	77090
DANOVER	400	484B	KT	77494
DANPHE LANDING CT	19200	329B	NWC	77375
DANPREE	3900	577E	PA	77504
DAN RIVER DR	24200	445S	NWC	77493
DANSEE	800	453X	NEH	77009
DANSHIRE CT	6300	456R	NEH	77049
DANSHIRE DR	13300	456R	NEH	77049
DANTE DR	15900	571Y	SWH	77053
DANTON FALLS DR	13900	408Y	NWC	77041
DANUBE	1000	533U	SEH	77051
DANUBINA	1	541D	BT	77520
DANUBINA	300	501Z	BT	77520
DANVERS DR	11800	456K	NEC	77044
DANVERS DR	12600	456M	NEC	77049
DANVILLE	0	492X	SWH	77098
DAPHNE	3300	533L	SEH	77021
DAPPER	600	412Q	NWH	77088
DAPPLE LN	9600	408D	NWC	77065
DAPPLED CT	0	328E	NWC	77377
DAPPLED GROVE TRAIL	0	376H	NEC	77346
DAPPLED GROVE TRAIL	0	377E	NEC	77346
DAPPLED RIDGE WAY	0	615Y	PL	77581
DAPPLED SUN PLACE	1	251G	WD	77381
DAPPLED TRAIL	4100	376H	NEC	77396
DAPPLED VALE TRAIL	0	293Y	NCC	77373
DAPPLED VALE TRAIL	0	293Y	NCC	77373
DAPPLED WALK WAY	0	328E	NWC	77377
DAPPLE FILLY DR	0	249V	NWC	77375
DAPPLEWOOD LN	5500	406X	NWC	77449
DARA SPRINGS LN	0	293K	SEM	77386
DARBY CIR	100	252L	SEM	77385
DARBY CT	3500	613Y	NEB	77584
DARBY BROOK DR	0	611S	FS	77545
DARBY COVE	13900	488N	SWH	77077
DARBYDALE DR	14800	332X	NWC	77090
DARBYDALE CROSSING LN	0	332X	NWC	77090
DARBY HOUSE	16400	367G	NWC	77429
DARBY HOUSE CT	13500	367G	NWC	77429
DARBY LOOP	10400	252L	SEM	77385
DARBY MILL LN	0	367X	NWC	77095
DARBY RETREAT LN	14900	326T	NWC	77433
DARBY RIDGE CT	19200	291W	NWC	77379
DARBY ROSE LN	13600	417A	NEC	77044
DARBY SPRINGS WAY	14100	326Y	NWC	77429
DARBY SQUARE TRAIL	0	407X	NWC	77084
DARBY WAY	6000	290C	NWC	77389
DARCUS	3700	532E	SS	77005
DARDEN	3400	454F	NEH	77093
DARDEN LN	500	339E	HU	77336
DARDEN LN	1300	620G	SB	77586
DARFIELD CT	1500	332W	NWC	77014
DARGAIL	11000	528Z	NEF	77478
DARIA CT	700	488E	SWH	77079
DARIA DR	800	488A	SWH	77079

Street Name	Block	Pg/Sq	Loc	Zips
DARIEN	4300	455W	NEH	77028
DARIEN	4800	455J	NEH	77028
DARJEAN	13400	415A	NEC	77039
DARK CANYON CT	4800	446D	NWC	77449
DARK CAVERN CT	17200	367P	NWC	77095
DARK ELM DR	2400	611T	NEF	77545
DARK HOLLOW LN		289Y	NWC	77379
DARKHORSE	0	334N	NCC	77338
DARK SIDE RD	0	377G	NEC	77338
DARKWOOD DR	5900	411T	NWH	77088
DARLA CT	0	539V	LP	77571
DARLA LN	9600	412G	NWC	77038
DARLENE	0	611X	FS	77545
DARLENE	3900	576G	SEH	77034
DARLENE LN	19700	255Y	SEM	77365
DARLING	3000	537G	PA	77503
DARLING	4800	492C	NWH	77007
DARLING CREEK LN	0	405T	NWC	77493
DARLINGHURST DR	3500	572N	SWH	77045
DARLINGHURST DR	5700	571P	SWH	77085
DARLING POINT CT	18000	327W	NWC	77429
DARLINGTON CT	6100	657U	LC	77573
DARLINGTON DR	7800	455K	NEH	77028
DARLINGTON MEADOW CT	0	332R	NCC	77073
DARLINGTON OAK ST	0	414V	NEH	77016
DARLINGTON RIDGE LN	0	377T	NEC	77044
DARMERA DR	0	368A	NWC	77429
DARNAY DR	7600	533V	SEH	77033
DARNELL	5000	531Q	SWH	77096
DARNELL	5800	530Q	SWH	77074
DARNELL CIR	7400	530Q	SWH	77074
DARNELL CT	3600	610U	MC	77459
DARNLEY LN	1500	488K	SWH	77077
DAROCA DR	2200	660F	LC	77573
DARONE CT	700	252P	SEM	77386
DARRAH DR	14100	332W	NWC	77090
DARREL	2900	536Z	PA	77502
DARRELL SPRINGS LN	10000	329F	NWC	77375
DARRIAN LN	0	458S	NEC	77530
DARRINGTON LN	13700	370B	NWC	77069
DARSCHELLE	14300	330T	NCC	77379
DARSCHELLE CT	14300	330U	NWC	77069
DARSCHELLE DR	5400	330T	NWC	77069
DARSEY	4300	531M	BL	77401
DART	900	493G	SWH	77007
DARTER ST	0	453Z	NEH	77009
DARTFORD CT	6900	330L	NWC	77379
DARTFORD SPRINGS LN	0	524H	NEF	77494
DARTHOUTH CHASE DR	0	376S	NEC	77396
DARTMAKER CT	25600	295V	NEH	77365
DARTMOOR RIDGE TRAIL	0	371S	NWC	77066
DARTMOOR TERRACE DR	0	488P	SWH	77077
DARTMOUTH	0	619M	TL	77586
DARTMOUTH	2200	444U	KT	77493
DARTMOUTH	4100	532A	WU	77005
DARTMOUTH DR	3000	537L	PA	77503
DARTMOUTH LN	700	538Y	DP	77536
DARTMOUTH FIELD LN	3300	611W	FS	77545
DARTMOUTH HILL CT	2300	445N	NWC	77493
DARTON DR	15800	571Y	SWH	77053
DARTWOOD DR	14100	456V	NEC	77049
DARTWOOD DR	14400	457N	NEC	77049
DARWIN	3900	414U	NEC	77093
DARWOOD CT	16100	527Q	NEF	77083
DARYNS LANDING DR	0	411D	NWC	77038
DASHWOOD DR	5300	531F	SWH	77081
DASHWOOD DR	5301	531F	BL	77401
DASHWOOD DR	5500	531F	SWH	77081
DASHWOOD DR	7600	530E	SWH	77036
DASHWOOD DR	11800	529E	SWH	77072
DASHWOOD FOREST	1	251A	WD	77381
DATE	3500	454W	NEH	77026
DATE	17400	418R	NEC	77044
DATE MEADOW LN	10000	289U	NWC	77375
DATEWOOD LN	9900	289U	NWC	77375
DATONIA	100	531L	BL	77401
DATTNER RD	1	456Y	NEH	77013
DAUBERN CT	14700	328X	NWC	77429
DAUGHERTY	1300	495N	NEH	77029
DAUGHERTY	1900	282U	WL	77484
DAUGHERTY RD	3600	613R	PL	77584
DAUGHERTY RD	4900	614N	NEB	77584
DAUGHTIE LN	0	249K	SWM	77354
DAUN	5500	414M	NEC	77039
DAUNTLESS CT	5100	371N	NWC	77066
DAUPHIN CT	2500	619T	NB	77058
DAVENMOOR CT	3100	485S	NEF	77494
DAVENPORT	3600	533Z	SEH	77051
DAVENPORT HILLS LN	13000	377K	NEC	77346
DAVENPORT MANOR DR	13900	367D	NWC	77429
DAVEN RIDGE LN	0	573X	SEC	77047
DAVEN RIDGE LN	0	573X	SEC	77047
DAVENTRY LN	12300	414E	NCC	77039
DAVENWAY DR	17300	407U	NWC	77084
DAVENWOOD CIR	11700	616D	SEC	77089
DAVENWOOD CT	11700	616D	SEC	77089
DAVENWOOD DR	11400	616D	SEC	77089
DAVEY CROCKETT	0	458Y	CV	77530
DAVEY OAKS	3000	614S	NEB	77584
DAVEY WOODS DR	0	377K	NEC	77346
DAVID	400	656D	FR	77546
DAVID	500	659F	LC	77573
S. DAVID	8400	532V	SWH	77054
DAVID	22600	256Y	SEM	77357
DAVID LN	10700	460D	NEC	77532
DAVID LN	20151	256K	SEM	77357
DAVID GLEN DR	16100	617W	FR	77546
DAVID GLEN DR	16500	657B	FR	77546
DAVID HILL LN	0	325S	HK	77447
DAVID MEMORIAL	0	252A	SD	77380
DAVID PINES CT	0	253T	SEM	77386
DAVIDS CREST CT	22300	485Y	NEF	77450
DAVIDSON	700	452C	NWH	77091
DAVIDSON LN	1	258Y	NEC	77336
DAVID VETTER BLVD	100	252A	SEM	77385
DA VINA LN	0	368D	NWC	77429
DA VINCI DR	0	616K	PL	77089
DA VINCI LN	0	368D	NWC	77429
DAVIS	100	335Z	HM	77338
DAVIS	100	619X	LC	77573
DAVIS	800	537N	PA	77506
DAVIS	900	659B	LC	77573
DAVIS	1600	494A	NEH	77026
DAVIS	3000	580Q	LP	77571
DAVIS	3400	454W	NEH	77026
DAVIS OAK DR	0	294E	SEM	77386
DAVISON	0	497W	PA	77506
DAVISON	0	537A	PA	77506
DAVISON CT	0	658U	LC	77573
DAVIS PRAIRIE LN	0	657S	FR	77546
DAVIS RUN DR	0	368E	NWC	77429
DAVON LN	1300	619W	NB	77058

Street Name	Block	Pg/Sq	Loc	Zips
DAVY CROCKETT CT	0	366S	NWC	77433
DAVY JONES CT	16300	419B	NEC	77532
DAWKINS	1700	460T	HG	77562
DAWKINS LN	2500	371D	NWC	77014
DAWN	0	615L	PL	77581
DAWN	4100	532W	SWH	77025
DAWN	12000	372P	NWC	77067
DAWN AVE	200	656D	FR	77546
DAWN CT	5600	657V	LC	77573
DAWN DR	500	657V	LC	77573
DAWN-DUSK RD	17000	367P	NWC	77433
DAWNBLUSH LN	8700	407D	NWC	77095
DAWN BREAK TRAIL	0	446F	NWC	77449
DAWNBRIAR CT	7500	570Z	SWH	77489
DAWN BROOK CT	2200	613K	PL	77584
DAWN BROOK DR	10000	613K	PL	77584
DAWNBROOK DR	15000	331T	NWC	77068
DAWNBURST DR	5200	337S	NEC	77346
DAWN CANYON RD	19300	446R	NWC	77084
DAWNCHASE CT	5500	330T	NWC	77069
DAWNCHASE DR	0	330Y	NWC	77069
DAWN CLOUD LN	0	484V	NEF	77494
DAWN CREEK LN	4200	291T	NWC	77388
DAWN CREST CT	2000	659D	LC	77573
S. DAWN CYPRESS CT	3900	578Y	SEH	77059
N. DAWN CYPRESS CT	4000	578Y	SEH	77059
DAWN FALLS LN	0	330B	NWC	77379
DAWNFIELDS DR	9200	369Y	NWC	77064
DAWNGATE DR	5000	293Z	NCC	77373
DAWNGLEN CT	0	290U	NWC	77379
DAWN HARVEST CT	9600	369U	NWC	77064
DAWN HARVEST DR	11100	369Y	NWC	77064
DAWN HARVEST LN	11100	369Y	NWC	77064
DAWN HAVEN CT	17300	407F	NWC	77095
DAWNHEATH DR	0	367N	NWC	77095
DAWNHEATH DR		367N	NWC	77433
DAWN HILL DR	300	656T	FR	77546
DAWNHOLLOW LN	1900	485L	NEF	77494
DAWN HOLLOW LN	13000	528Q	SWC	77072
DAWN HOLLOW LN	13000	528Q	SWH	77072
DAWN LIGHT CIR	0	574N	SEH	77048
DAWN LILY DR	5000	291S	NWC	77388
DAWN MARIE LN	16100	527U	NEF	77498
DAWN MEADOWS DR	15100	331T	NWC	77068
DAWN MILL LN	0	367P	NWC	77433
DAWNMIST CT	0	612U	PL	77584
DAWN MIST CT	0	337R	NEC	77346
DAWN MIST CT	19700	337S	NEC	77346
DAWN MIST DR	19800	337N	NEC	77346
DAWN MISTY LN	0	574P	SEH	77048
DAWN PINE FOREST TRAIL	0	329B	NWC	77375
DAWN POINT CT	12500	368Z	NWC	77065
DAWN QUAIL CT	8200	610C	SWH	77489
DAWNRIDGE DR	2800	613U	NEB	77584
DAWNRIDGE DR	5500	571A	SWH	77035
DAWNRIDGE DR	7600	570C	SWH	77071
DAWNRIDGE DR	8900	570B	SWH	77071
DAWNRIDGE LN	9000	529P	SWH	77099
DAWN RIDGE WAY	0	620L	SB	77586
DAWN RISE CT	3900	611W	FS	77545
DAWN RIVER LN	0	614N	PL	77581
DAWN ROSE CT	0	290T	NWC	77379
DAWNS EDGE DR	0	574J	SEH	77048
DAWN SHADOWS DR	0	376H	NEC	77346
DAWN SHADOW WAY	2200	611W	FS	77545
DAWNS HEIGHTS CT	0	574K	SEH	77048
DAWN SKY LN	800	660E	LC	77573
DAWN SQUARE	20300	446K	NWC	77449
DAWN STAR DR	2600	610B	MC	77489
DAWN STAR DR	6700	337X	NEC	77346
DAWN TERRACE CT	0	574N	SEH	77048
DAWN TERRACE LN	0	574P	SEH	77048
DAWN TIMBERS CT	21600	334M	NCC	77338
DAWNTREADER DR	0	326Y	NWC	77433
DAWN VALE DR	14600	618E	SEH	77062
DAWNVIEW	6000	534V	SEH	77087
DAWN VIEW LN	0	574P	SEH	77048
DAWN WIND LN	2200	293F	SEM	77386
DAWNWOOD DR	3200	251N	SWM	77380
DAWNWOOD DR	11800	496F	NEH	77013
DAWSON LN	3000	573B	SEH	77051
DAWSON RD	0	613S	PL	77584
DAWSON RD	11100	612V	PL	77584
DAWSON CREEK DR	6300	538W	PA	77503
DAWSON MILL CT	0	407G	NWC	77095
DAWSON SPRINGS DR	11100	524L	NWF	77406
DAY	3800	493T	SWH	77006
DAY DR	2300	613L	PL	77584
DAY RD	10900	449Y	NWH	77043
DAYBREAK LN	11100	368T	NWC	77429
DAYCO	4000	451E	NWH	77092
DAYCOACH LN	8300	410H	NWC	77064
DAYFLOWER DR	4100	446H	NWC	77449
DAYHILL DR	0	330K	NWC	77379
DAY HOLLOW LN	12600	369L	NWC	77070
DAYLIGHT LN	7200	407R	NWC	77095
DAYLIGHT WOOD WAY	0	377E	NEC	77346
DAYLILLY CREEK DR	7900	528L	SWH	77083
DAYLILY HILLS DR	21400	292N	NWC	77388
DAY LILY WAY	1800	371V	NWC	77067
DAYPORT	5500	451D	NWH	77091
DAYRIDGE CT	0	574Z	SEH	77048
DAYRIDGE LN	0	574Y	SEH	77048
DAYS DAWN DR	17500	328L	NWC	77377
DAYSPRING DR	0	366V	NWC	77433
DAYSTAR DR	16900	503F	CCO	77520
DAYTON	0	500Z	BT	77520
DAYTON	7700	495X	SEH	77012
DAYTONA CT	2400	656U	FR	77546
DAYTON RIDGE LN	0	406H	NWC	77433
DAYTON SPRINGS DR	0	326U	NWC	77429
DAY TRAIL LN	10500	329B	NWC	77379
DAY TRIP TRAIL	0	326V	NWC	77429
DAYWOOD DR	13100	371Z	NWC	77038
DEAD HORSE	8000	375G	HM	77396
DEADWOOD DR	7400	410R	NWH	77040
DEAFSMITH	0	459A	NEC	77562
DEAFSMITH	10600	539Q	LP	77571
DEAFSMITH RD	18800	458D	NEC	77049
DE AKINS	0	285N	NWC	77447
DEAL	1700	532P	SWH	77025
DEAMS	1700	453M	NEH	77093
DEAMS	2300	454J	NEH	77093
DEAN	0	249J	SWM	77354
DEAN	5500	414D	NEC	77039
DEAN	22500	292P	SP	77373
DEAN DALE CT	0	446B	NWC	77449
DEANMONT DR	6300	611C	SWH	77053
DEANNA	9900	455A	NEH	77016
DEANNA	10000	415W	NEH	77016
DEANNE	100	501Z	BT	77520
DEANWOOD	9300	410R	NWH	77040

Street Name	Block	Pg/Sq	Loc	Zips
DEARBORN	7100	451T	NWH	77055
DEASA DR	2300	333A	NCC	77373
DEATON DR	7900	337R	NEC	77346
DEATON MILL DR	0	407C	NWC	77095
DEATS RD	100	659Z	GCO	77539
DEAUVILLE DR	20700	291U	NWC	77388
DEAUVILLE PLAZA DR	5400	451Q	NWH	77092
DEBBI LN	31000	246Z	SWM	77355
DEBBIE	12500	372Q	NCC	77060
DEBBIE	16000	458U	CV	77530
DEBBIE LN	0	661M	GCO	77539
DEBBIE LN	0	248N	SWM	77362
DEBBIE LN	1100	490B	NWH	77055
DEBBIE LN	9700	412F	NWC	77038
DEBBIE'S CT	20100	257J	SEM	77357
DEBBIE GAY DR	8100	410K	NWC	77040
DEBBIE TERRACE DR	0	407E	NWC	77433
DEBENEY DR	1500	413H	NCC	77039
DEBENEY DR	3300	414G	NCC	77039
DE BOLL	1	453G	NEH	77022
DEBORAH	2600	570W	NEF	77477
DEBORAH	2700	569Z	NEF	77477
DEBORAH	3500	451P	NWH	77092
DEBORAH	7100	535J	SEH	77087
DEBORAH	8400	370Y	NWC	77064
DEBORAH LN	5100	500H	BT	77521
DEBORAH ANN WAY	0	332Z	NCC	77073
DEBORAH COLONY LN	0	376W	NEC	77396
DEBRA	23600	296G	SEM	77365
DEBRA RD	10800	456S	NEH	77013
DEBRAH LN	9600	412G	NWC	77038
DEBRAS TRACE LN	4600	485Z	NEF	77450
DEBRA TERRACE CT	1000	488E	SWH	77077
DEBRAY DR	0	290R	NWC	77388
DECATHALON CT	18800	338W	NEC	77346
DECATUR	1500	493K	SWH	77007
DECATUR AVE	6700	502C	BT	77521
DECEMBER PINE LN	17600	330J	NWC	77379
DECHIRICO CIR	17200	330K	NWC	77379
DECISION DR	21800	285M	NWC	77447
DECK CT	16800	379X	NEC	77532
DECK LN	0	299J	NEC	77336
DECKARD	6600	535X	SEH	77061
S. DECKER	13100	247L	SWM	77355
N. DECKER	13100	247L	SWM	77355
W. DECKER	33600	247L	SWM	77355
DECKER DR	0	484V	NEF	77494
DECKER DR	100	501N	BT	77520
DECKER DR	3500	500A	BT	77520
DECKER DR	14100	247N	SWM	77355
DECKER CREST DR	0	484W	NEF	77494
DECKER FIELD LN	0	612Q	PL	77584
DECKER FORREST BLVD	800	248F	SWM	77354
DECKER HILLS DR	29500	248B	SWM	77354
DECKER HOLLOW	0	247S	SWM	77355
DECKER INDUSTRIAL CIR	31700	248S	SWM	77362
DECKER OAKS DR	12000	248N	SWM	77355
DECKER OAKS DR	32000	248N	SWM	77355
DECKER PINES	32100	247V	SWM	77355
DECKER PLACE	0	247Q	SWM	77355
DECKER PRAIRIE-ROSEHILL	22000	287A	NWC	77377
DECKER PRAIRIE-ROSEHILL	23100	287E	SWM	77355
DECKER PRAIRIE-ROSEHILL	23900	247W	SWM	77355
DECKER RIDGE CT	6000	406T	NWC	77449
DECKER RIDGE DR	20200	406T	NWC	77449
DECKER WOODS DR	26800	248F	SWM	77354
DECOSTER BLVD	0	656W	AV	77511
DEDMAN	2400	537Z	PA	77503
DEDMAN RD	4000	577H	PA	77505
DEE DR	5900	577D	PA	77505
DEE RD	6100	614G	PL	77581
DEEDA DR	4500	535U	SEH	77017
DEEDS RD	2800	447N	NWC	77084
DEEN DR	200	338D	NEH	77336
DEE OAKS DR	19400	337T	NEC	77346
DEEP ANCHOR WAY	2700	378N	NEC	77532
DEEPBROOK DR	2000	615V	PL	77581
DEEP BROOK DR	17600	331E	NWC	77379
DEEP CANYON DR	6300	526F	NEF	77450
DEEP CLIFF DR	23500	485K	NEF	77494
DEEP CORAL CT	24800	484D	NEF	77494
DEEP COVE DR	0	612L	PL	77584
DEEP COVE LN	14200	568A	SG	77498
DEEP CREEK LN	5600	451C	NWH	77091
DEEP DALE DR	19800	334V	NCC	77338
DEEP FALLS DR	0	326K	NWC	77433
DEEP FOREST CIR	5700	451B	NWH	77092
DEEP FOREST DR	7000	411T	NWH	77088
DEEP GLEN LN	4800	446D	NWC	77449
W. DEEPGROVE DR	100	413N	NCC	77037
DEEPGROVE DR	100	413N	NCC	77037
DEEP LAKE DR	2400	297Z	NEH	77345
DEEP MEADOW DR	11500	369U	NWC	77064
DEEP MEADOW DR	23300	289B	NWC	77375
DEEP MEADOW DR	24400	249X	NWC	77375
DEEP OAK CT	2500	618C	SEH	77059
DEEP PINES	16800	330K	NWC	77379
DEEP PINES CT	21700	255S	SEM	77365
DEEP PRAIRIE DR	17300	407B	NWC	77095
DEEP RIVER CT	3200	336H	NEH	77339
DEEPSHADE CT	0	377E	NEC	77346
DEEPSOUTH CT	0	406Z	NWC	77449
DEEP SOUTH DR	6000	406Z	NWC	77449
DEEP SPRING LN	12400	488M	SWH	77077
DEEP VALLEY DR	8600	456D	NEC	77044
DEEP VALLEY DR	9500	416Z	NEC	77044
DEEPWATER AVE	100	537G	PA	77503
DEEPWELL LN	900	490B	HE	77024
DEEPWOOD DR	1200	657A	FR	77546
DEEPWOOD DR	6000	534K	SEH	77023
DEEPWOODS DR	11800	368D	NWC	77429
DEER AVE	1300	538L	DP	77536
DEER CT	3400	615T	PL	77581
DEER LN	31600	248T	SWM	77362
DEERBEND CT	3700	293C	SEM	77386
DEERBERRY CT	1	251M	WD	77380
DEERBROOK CT	3500	613Y	NEB	77584
DEERBROOK DR	3400	297W	NEH	77339
DEER BROOK DR	24200	244G	WCO	77447
DEERBROOK PARK BLVD	20100	335P	NCC	77338
DEERBROOK PARK CT	0	335P	NCC	77338
DEER CHASE DR	3900	527D	SWC	77082
DEER COVE LN	12800	408Z	NWC	77041
DEER COVE TRAIL	2200	336G	NEH	77339
DEER CREEK	29000	246D	SWM	77355
DEERCREEK CIR	0	444P	KT	77493
DEER CREEK CT	7100	330L	NWC	77379
DEER CREEK DR	2900	568V	SG	77478
DEER CREEK DR	16800	330F	NWC	77379
DEER CREEK DR	19900	380H	NEC	77532
DEER CREEK WAY	33500	247N	SC	77355
DEERCREST DR	700	498A	NEC	77530

Street Name	Block	Pg/Sq	Loc	Zips
DEER CROSSING DR	18400	378A	NEC	77346
DEER FALLS CT	3800	297X	NEH	77345
DEER FERN DR	400	659H	LC	77573
DEERFIELD	100	453L	NEH	77022
DEERFIELD	2400	444P	KT	77493
DEERFIELD CT	0	444T	KT	77493
DEERFIELD DR	3000	613T	NEB	77584
DEERFIELD VILLAGE DR	4000	447F	NWC	77084
N. DEERFOOT CIR	1	252J	WD	77380
S. DEERFOOT CIR	100	252J	WD	77380
DEERFOOT CT	1	252J	WD	77380
DEER FOREST DR	0	293S	NCC	77373
DEER GLEN	2900	331K	NWC	77068
DEER GRASS CT	3800	578Y	SEH	77059
DEER GRASS LN	9500	417X	NEC	77044
DEERGROVE DR	12300	414E	NCC	77039
DEERHAVEN DR	21300	291Q	NWC	77388
DEER HOLLOW DR	2800	297Y	NEH	77345
DEERHURST LN	1900	412N	NWC	77088
DEERING DR	9500	529V	SWH	77036
DEER KEY CIR	18800	446V	NWH	77084
DEER KNOLL CT	1400	611X	NEF	77545
DEER LAKE CT	0	293P	NCC	77373
DEER LAKE CT	1	251B	WD	77381
N. DEER LAKE RD	100	338L	NEH	77336
DEER LAKE RD	100	338L	NEH	77336
DEER LAKE PLACE	0	293P	NCC	77373
DEERLAND CT	3400	297Y	NEH	77345
DEER LEAP DR	4100	447E	NWC	77084
DEER LICK DR	16100	332T	NWC	77090
DEER LODGE DR	4400	452E	NWH	77018
DEER MEADOW DR	2300	610A	MC	77489
DEER MEADOW DR	7900	570G	SWH	77071
N. DEER MEADOW DR	8900	570E	SWH	77071
DEER MEADOW DR	8900	570E	SWH	77071
DEER MEADOW LN	0	444T	KT	77493
DEERMEADOW FALLS LN	0	524B	NEF	77494
DEERMOSS DR	3200	446R	NWC	77449
DEER MOUNTAIN CT	2500	298W	NEH	77345
DEERPASS	700	498A	NEC	77530
DEER PASS DR	1100	458W	NEC	77530
DEERPATH CT	15800	329N	NWC	77377
DEERPATH WAY	18600	378Q	NEC	77532
DEER POINT DR	4600	291E	NWC	77389
DEER RIDGE DR	1200	659J	LC	77573
DEER RIDGE LN	6600	371X	NWC	77086
DEER RIDGE ESTATES BLVD	1	336G	NEH	77339
W. DEER RIVER CIR	0	250N	NWC	77389
E. DEER RIVER CIR	0	250N	NWC	77389
DEER RUN	14000	247T	SWM	77355
DEER RUN CT	2200	444T	KT	77493
DEER RUN DR	3100	336P	NEH	77338
DEER RUN LN	19500	258J	SEM	77357
DEER RUN CROSSING	0	444T	KT	77493
DEER SAGE CT	12900	408Z	NWC	77041
DEER SHADOW CT	5700	408Z	NWC	77041
DEERSLAYER TRAIL	20400	378M	NEC	77532
DEER SPRINGS DR	2000	336G	NEH	77339
DEER TIMBERS LN	5400	337S	NEC	77346
DEER TIMBERS TRAIL	5200	337S	NEC	77346
DEER TRACE CT	0	378Q	NEC	77532
DEER TRACE DR	0	378Q	NEC	77532
DEER TRACK CT	0	370Y	NWC	77086
DEER TRAIL	1	381Q	LCO	77535
DEERTRAIL	1800	538R	DP	77536
DEER TRAIL	6000	577D	PA	77505
DEER TRAIL	25300	244F	WCO	77447
DEER TRAIL CIR	3500	376P	NEC	77396
DEER TRAIL CT	0	381P	LCO	77535
DEER TRAIL DR	8000	250S	NWC	77389
DEER TRAIL DR	8900	412L	NWH	77088
DEER TRAIL DR	9500	412G	NWC	77038
DEER TRAILS CIR	3400	376P	NEC	77396
DEER TRAILS DR	1000	376N	NEC	77396
DEERVALLEY	1800	538R	DP	77536
DEER VALLEY	36700	246D	SWM	77355
DEER VALLEY DR	2000	293N	NCC	77373
DEERWICK CT	9000	289D	NWC	77375
DEERWOOD	0	538V	DP	77536
DEERWOOD CIR	4800	501E	BT	77521
DEERWOOD CT	0	444P	KT	77493
DEERWOOD CT	0	615K	PL	77581
W. DEERWOOD DR	1900	524U	NEF	77406
E. DEERWOOD DR	2000	524U	NEF	77406
DEERWOOD DR	7000	524U	NEF	77406
DEERWOOD LN	3300	610J	MC	77459
DEERWOOD RD	5800	491J	SWH	77057
DEERWOOD RD	10300	489L	SWH	77042
DEERWOOD GLEN DR	0	538J	DP	77536
DEERWOOD LAKE DR	7800	377D	NEC	77346
DEERWOOD PARK LN	31000	252R	SEM	77386
DEERWOOD TRAIL	12200	247R	SWM	77362
DEE WOODS DR	18900	337Y	NEC	77346
W. DE FEE	100	501Y	BT	77520
E. DE FEE	100	501Y	BT	77520
DEFEE	600	335Z	HM	77338
DEFENDER	700	495U	NEH	77029
DEFIANCE	8900	578D	LP	77571
DEFOE DR	2700	445R	NWC	77449
DEFOREST RIDGE	22800	485Y	NEF	77494
DE FORREST	12000	371A	NWC	77066
DE FOUR TRACE	2500	620J	SB	77586
DEGAS LN	9800	454D	NEH	77016
DE GEORGE	4100	453X	NWH	77009
DE GRASSI	200	259T	LCO	77336
DE HAVEN	100	495V	NEH	77029
DEIHL RD	6300	411X	NWH	77092
DEIHL RD	6400	451B	NWH	77092
DEIRDRE ANNE DR	6300	411S	NWH	77088
DEKADINE CT	0	290P	NWC	77379
DEKE SLAYTON	0	656C	FR	77546
DEKE SLAYTON HWY	0	660A	LC	77573
DEKE SLAYTON HWY	0	615Q	PL	77581
DEKE SLAYTON HWY	0	616S	PL	77581
DEKE SLAYTON HWY	0	657K	FR	77546
DEKE SLAYTON HWY	0	658N	LC	77573
DEKE SLAYTON HWY	0	659B	LC	77573
DE KOVEN	200	495W	SEH	77011
DELABROOK CT	1400	620L	SB	77586
DELACEY LN	13600	328T	NWC	77429
DELACHASE CIR	8500	330N	NWC	77379
DELAFIELD	2300	534F	SEH	77023
DE LAGOS CIR	4800	291E	NWC	77389
DE LA LUNA CT	1	502G	BT	77521
DELAMERE DR	0	528S	NEF	77498
DELANEY	100	453Q	NEH	77009
DELANEY KNOLL	0	250U	NWC	77389
DE LANGE LN	4500	451F	NWH	77092
N. DELANO	1	494N	SEH	77003
DELANO	2400	493V	SEH	77004
DELAVAN DR	7500	455J	NEH	77028
DELAWARE	300	495V	NEH	77029

Street Name	Block	Pg/Sq	Loc	Zips
DELAWARE AVE	1600	659P	LC	77573
DE LAY DR	0	617M	SEH	77598
DELBARTON DR	14700	527R	NEF	77083
DELBURY	5800	571P	SWH	77085
DEL CIRO CT	0	502F	BT	77521
DEL CLAIR CIR	2800	610E	MC	77489
DE LEON	3600	535T	SEH	77087
DE LEON	8000	535T	SEH	77061
DELEON FIELDS DR	0	253T	SEM	77386
DELERY DR	2000	451T	NWH	77055
DELESANDRI	900	660A	LC	77565
DELETTE	1200	538N	PA	77503
DELEWARE AVE	0	659T	LC	77573
DELEWARE AVE	0	659T	LC	77573
DELFAN CIR	6100	375J	NEH	77396
DELFORD WAY	0	568W	SG	77479
DELFREN LN	5600	444T	KT	77493
DELGADO DR	16200	527F	NEF	77083
DEL GLEN LN	7500	528L	SWH	77072
DELHI	3300	453J	NWH	77022
DELIA	2800	494A	NEH	77026
DELICADO DR	0	376E	HM	77396
DELILAH	8700	533Z	SEH	77033
DELL	6200	492F	SWH	77007
DELL CT	200	453Y	NEH	77009
DELLA	6700	454N	NEH	77093
DELLA CREEK WAY DR	4400	609K	MC	77459
DEL LAGO CT	29000	298J	NEC	77336
DELLAPINES DR	0	327D	NWC	77429
DELLBRIDGE LN	16900	332Q	NCC	77073
DELLBROOK DR	900	372X	NWC	77038
DELL DALE	100	498E	CV	77530
DELL DALE	1000	458W	CV	77530
DELLFERN CT	11800	570D	SWH	77035
DELLFERN DR	5900	571A	SWH	77035
DELLFERN DR	6000	570D	SWH	77035
DELLFOREST CT	1	251E	WD	77381
DELLHAVEN LN	0	330E	NWC	77379
DELL HOLLOW DR	11500	371N	NWC	77066
DELLORE LN	1900	659F	LC	77573
DELLROSE CROSSING DR	0	524K	NWF	77406
DELLWILD CT	15200	457Q	NEC	77049
DELL WOOD LN	5900	290Z	NWC	77379
DELLWOOD SPRINGS DR	0	407C	NWC	77095
DELMACK	5600	374V	NCC	77032
DELMAN	11300	414P	NEC	77093
DELMAR	1	494U	SEH	77011
N. DELMAR	100	494U	SEH	77011
DEL MAR	100	619V	LC	77565
DELMAR	600	494T	SEH	77023
DELMAR PARK LN	0	334R	NCC	77338
DELMAR TERRACE DR	0	293F	SEM	77386
DELMAS	1000	535E	SEH	77087
DEL MONTE	100	459M	HG	77562
DEL MONTE	2900	609H	MC	77459
DEL MONTE DR	100	656F	FR	77546
DEL MONTE DR	200	537H	PA	77503
DEL MONTE DR	2100	492N	SWH	77019
DEL MONTE DR	5100	491P	SWH	77056
DEL MONTE DR	6100	491N	SWH	77057
DEL MONTE DR	7500	490R	SWH	77063
DEL MONTE DR	10000	489R	SWH	77042
DEL MONTE DR	11300	489P	SWH	77077
DEL NORTE	400	452F	NWH	77018
DEL NORTE	2200	451H	NWH	77018
DEL NORTE DR	3300	502F	BT	77521
DEL NORTE CANYON DR	18900	328H	NWC	77377
DELOACHE AVE	7400	334R	NCC	77338
DE LOREAN CT	800	375M	NEC	77396
DELORES	1100	660B	KE	77565
DELORES LN	5200	334E	NCC	77373
DEL ORO DR	3700	502F	BT	77521
DE LOZIER	16100	409L	JV	77040
DEL PAPA	13400	572U	SWH	77047
DEL PAPA	14600	612C	SWC	77047
DEL PASO CIR	4600	578E	PA	77505
DELPHI CT	4300	610Q	MC	77459
DELPHI LN	1900	371M	NWC	77067
DELPHINIUM PLACE	0	249C	SWM	77382
DEL PRADO DR	0	527G	SWC	77083
DEL REY LN	7600	530U	SWH	77071
DELRIDGE DR	21400	291R	NWC	77388
DEL RIO	5600	533L	SEH	77021
DELSANTOS ST	12700	572E	SWH	77045
DEL SOL CT	1	502G	BT	77521
DEL SUR	5100	452H	NWH	77018
DEL SUR DR	3500	502F	BT	77521
DELTA	100	537F	PA	77506
DELTA DR	0	295A	SEM	77365
DELTA BRIDGE CT	0	612M	PL	77584
DELTA BRIDGE CT	11500	568A	NEF	77498
DELTA BRIDGE DR	0	612M	PL	77584
DELTA ESTATES CT	18100	366D	NWC	77429
DELTA QUEEN DR	19200	406Z	NWC	77449
DELTA SPRING LN	21400	525D	NEF	77450
DELTA SPRINGS LN	17700	447C	NWC	77084
DELTAWOOD	0	578Y	SEH	77059
DELTA WOOD CT	4100	578Y	SEH	77059
DELTA WOOD TRAIL	6700	337Q	NEC	77346
DE LUCA LN	14700	288X	NWC	77377
DELUXE	13500	573V	SEH	77047
DELWIN	2400	576F	SEH	77034
DELWOOD	8000	535T	SEH	77087
DELWOOD SPRINGS LN	0	377L	NEC	77346
DELWOODS TERRACE	0	376R	NEC	77346
DE LYN LN	0	614U	PL	77584
DELYNN	7800	462X	NEC	77521
DELZ	300	452H	NWH	77018
E. DELZ DR	300	453E	NWH	77022
DEMARCO CT	0	571G	SWH	77045
DEMARCO DR	0	571G	SWH	77045
DEMAREE LN	1400	495K	NEH	77029
DEMARET LN	1200	450W	NWH	77055
DEMENT RD	11000	289B	NWC	77375
DEMETER DR	0	610Q	MC	77459
DEMI LN	2900	463L	MB	77520
DEMIA CT	11800	569A	MD	77477
DE MILO DR	1700	452E	NWH	77018
DE MILO DR	4300	451F	NWH	77092
DEMINC	14900	497H	NEC	77530
DEMOCRACY CT	8000	330E	NWC	77379
DEMONT PARK	0	575V	SEH	77075
DEMONTROND	100	372G	NWH	77090
DE MOSS DR	5900	530H	SWH	77081
DE MOSS DR	6500	530H	SWH	77074
DE MOSS DR	7600	530E	SWH	77036
DEMPLEY DR	13600	408Y	NWC	77041
DEMPSEY FIELD DR	0	296E	SEM	77365
DEMSEY MILL DR	9400	527U	NEF	77498
DEMSEY OAKS DR	18700	337Z	NEC	77346
W. DENALI DR	0	538V	DP	77536
DENALI LN	0	377E	NEC	77346
DENALI RANGE CT	21700	445H	NWC	77449
DENARD LN	500	570N	MC	77489
DENBRIDGE CT	14100	528S	NEF	77083
DENBRIDGE DR	9200	528N	NEF	77083
DENBROOK DR	0	330V	NWC	77068
DENBURY WAY	9400	532S	SWH	77025
DENBY	400	541B	BT	77520
DENBY	8400	535F	SEH	77012
DENFIELD CT	0	369L	NWC	77070
DENFORD CT	20600	486K	SWC	77450
DENHAM	100	536Q	PA	77506
S. DENHAM RIDGE LN	5600	250Z	NWC	77389
N. DENHAM RIDGE LN	24500	250Z	NWC	77389
DENIO DR	3500	488Y	SWH	77082
DENISE	1100	538U	DP	77536
DENISE	9200	249Z	NWC	77375
DENISE	31000	248W	SWM	77362
DENISE DR	11500	490B	HE	77024
DENISE DALE LN	18400	447J	NWC	77084
DENISE TERRACE DR	0	325S	HK	77447
DENISE TERRACE DR		325S	NWC	77447
DENISON	6900	494H	NEH	77020
DENISON	7100	495E	NEH	77020
DENISON OAKS DR	0	524E	NEF	77494
DENKMAN	2900	538W	PA	77503
DENLAN BLVD	0	447F	NWC	77084
DENMAN	900	492Q	SWH	77019
DENMARK	0	578E	PA	77505
DENMARK	3200	454J	NEH	77093
DENMARK	4000	454L	NEH	77016
DENMARK	5400	454L	NEH	77028
DENMARK DR	6000	577H	PA	77505
DENMERE CT	4400	337B	NEH	77345
DENNING DR	9800	455D	NEH	77078
DENNINGTON DR	18500	407S	NWC	77449
DENNIS	1	493P	SWH	77006
DENNIS	100	335Z	HM	77338
DENNIS	1000	493T	SWH	77002
DENNIS	1100	493U	SEH	77004
DENNIS	3800	494W	SEH	77004
DENNIS WAY LN	0	457A	NEC	77044
DENNY	100	459R	HG	77562
DENNY	6800	410Z	NWC	77040
DENNY	10200	370W	NWC	77064
DENNY LN	5500	291E	NWC	77389
DEN OAK DR	0	524W	NWF	77406
DEN OAK DR	10300	368Y	NWC	77065
DENORAN DR	4700	573H	SEH	77048
DENORAN DR	5600	574F	SEH	77048
DENRIDGE DR	2200	411D	NWC	77038
DENSLOW CIR	9600	453C	NEH	77076
DENSMORE DR	5900	571E	SWH	77035
DENSMORE DR	6000	570H	SWH	77035
DENT DR	1	501L	BT	77521
DENTON	0	248C	SWM	77354
DENTON	100	619L	PA	77586
DENTON	7600	455K	NEH	77028
W. DENTON DR	0	335U	HM	77338
E. DENTON DR	0	335U	HM	77338
DENTON MEADOWS CT	0	446K	NWC	77449
DENTON TRACE DR	0	295L	SEM	77365
DENTWOOD DR	13800	372F	NWC	77014
DENVER	3200	493V	SEH	77003
DENVER	3300	494S	SEH	77003
DENVER ARBOR CT	0	572W	SWC	77053
DENVER OAKS DR	13300	368U	NWC	77065
DEPARTURE	17300	379W	NEC	77532
DEPELCHIN	1500	493F	SWH	77007
DE PETRIS DR	0	444M	NWC	77493
DEPOT NORTH	0	372N	NWC	77067
DE PRIEST	6200	412U	NWH	77091
DE PRIEST	7300	412U	NWH	77088
DERBY CT	0	657Y	LC	77573
DERBY DR	1900	371M	NWC	77067
DERBY LN	600	570Y	MC	77489
DERBYBROOK CT	25100	485W	NEF	77494
DERBY GATE CT	0	407U	NWC	77084
DERBYHALL DR	3500	371K	NWC	77066
DERBYSHIRE DR	400	617B	SEH	77034
DERBYSHIRE DR	5300	444U	KT	77493
DERBYSHIRE MEADOWS LN	0	334R	NCC	77338
DERBYWOOD GLEN LN	0	484X	NEF	77494
DERBYWOOD GLEN LN	0	484X	NEF	77494
DEREK DR	3700	502J	BT	77521
DERHAM PARC	1	490G	PP	77024
DERING CT	20100	486C	SWC	77450
DERMOTT DR	11500	369S	NWC	77065
DERMOTT DR	12100	368U	NWC	77065
DERMOTT RIDGE DR	0	524L	NWF	77406
DERRICK DR	300	336W	NEC	77338
DERRICK FIELD LN	0	613W	NEB	77578
DERRIK DR	9200	450K	NWH	77080
DERRIL LN	0	527D	SWC	77082
DERRINGTON RD	9300	370W	NWC	77064
DERWENT LN	11800	369R	NWC	77065
DESCARTES DR	0	525L	NEF	77407
DES CHAUMES	1600	494A	NEH	77020
DES CHAUMES	1800	454W	NEH	77026
DES CHAUMES CT	0	494A	NEH	77026
DESCO DR	7600	334R	NCC	77338
DESERET DR	500	656H	FR	77546
E. DESERT DR	3600	579A	LP	77571
DESERT AIRE DR	500	656P	FR	77546
DESERT BLUFF LN	0	526G	NEF	77407
DESERT BROOK LN	0	526J	NEF	77407
DESERT CALICO LN	0	526P	NEF	77407
DESERT CANYON CT	7800	408L	NWC	77041
DESERT CANYON DR	13800	408L	NWC	77041
DESERT CLIFF CT	4400	484Y	NEF	77494
DESERT CLOUD CT	9400	410E	NWC	77040
DESERT CLOUD LN	8700	410E	NWC	77040
DESERT EAGLE DR	0	328F	NWC	77429
DESERT FLOWER LN	9300	410D	NWH	77086
DESERT FLOWER LN	9600	370Z	NWC	77086
DESERT GOLD	23600	525E	NEF	77494
DESERT IVY DR	19400	486G	SWC	77094
DESERT MAIZE LN	17200	367X	NWC	77095
DESERT MARIGOLD DR	18500	372H	NCC	77073
DESERT MOON DR	19200	406M	NWC	77433
DESERT OAKS CT	7200	525L	NEF	77407
DESERT OAK WAY	5700	330D	NWC	77379
DESERT OASIS LN	2900	446U	NWC	77449
DESERT PALMS DR	8600	330N	NWC	77379
DESERT PARK LN	0	252R	SEM	77385
DESERT ROCK LN	0	615L	PL	77089
DESERT ROSE LN	6400	371W	NWC	77086
DESERT ROSE PLACE	800	610S	MC	77459
DESERT RUN DR	3600	579A	LP	77571
DESERT SAGE DR	2500	446S	NWC	77449
DESERT SHADOWS LN	0	406K	NWC	77433
DESERT SPRINGS CIR	10500	367U	NWC	77095
DESERT SPRINGS CIR	11300	367Q	NWC	77095
DESERT SPRINGS CT	2000	658T	LC	77573
DESERT STAR	0	525E	NEF	77494
DESERT STAR CT	0	328S	NWC	77429
DESERT TRACE CT	13900	377Y	NEH	77044
DESERT VINE CT	2200	568B	SG	77498
DESERT WILLOW CT	300	659H	LC	77573
DESERT WILLOW DR	400	659H	LC	77573
DESERT WILLOW DR	2400	446P	NWC	77449
DESERT WILLOW DR	22200	245Q	SWM	77355
DESIRABLE DR	9200	579A	LP	77571
DESIREABLE	500	339E	HU	77336
DES JARDINES	1200	494Y	SEH	77023
DES JARDINES	1600	534B	SEH	77023
DES MOINES	4700	537Y	PA	77505
DESNA CT	19300	295E	SEM	77365
DESNA DR	19300	295A	SEM	77365
DESOTA	1800	656U	FR	77546
DESOTA DR	0	656Q	FR	77546
DE SOTO	1100	452A	NWH	77091
DE SOTO	2700	451D	NWH	77091
DESOTO	3600	451D	NWH	77091
DESOTO DR	25700	244K	WCO	77447
DESOTO GLEN CT	0	457L	NEC	77049
DESTIN LN	1700	656U	FR	77546
DESTIN SHORE DR	2900	447N	NWC	77084
DESTINY LN	12900	419V	NEC	77532
DESTINY COVE	1	251G	WD	77381
DESTINY PARK CT	5900	407W	NWC	77449
DESTREHAN DR	16300	367C	NWC	77429
DETERING	1500	492C	NWH	77007
DETERMINED DR	12300	414F	NCC	77039
DETRIC LN	16200	611C	SWH	77053
DETROIT	7800	535K	SEH	77017
DEUSSEN PKWY	12700	417D	NEH	77044
DEUSSEN PKWY	13400	377X	NEC	77044
DEUSTER LN	20100	254L	SEM	77365
DEUTSER	2300	414W	NEH	77093
DE VAL	10500	368T	NWC	77429
DEVENCREST DR	11300	370R	NWC	77066
DEVEREAUX CT	20100	486C	SWC	77450
DEVERELL DR	9700	528S	NEF	77498
W. DEVEREUX DR	1100	658M	LC	77573
DEVERON LN	700	332N	NWC	77090
DE VILLE DR	22100	485D	SWC	77450
DEVILLE DR	22100	485D	SWC	77450
DEVIN LN	15200	420G	NEC	77532
DEVINSTONE DR	0	449X	NWH	77043
DEVINWOOD DR	0	502H	BT	77520
DEVIVO CT		525M	NEF	77407
DEVLIN DR	7700	337Z	NEC	77346
DEVON	4500	491V	SWH	77027
DEVON LN	0	258F	SEM	77357
DEVONBERRY LN	4600	485Y	NEF	77450
DEVONCROFT DR	9100	570A	SWH	77031
DEVON DALE DR	100	249R	NWH	77375
DEVON DALE DR	100	249R	NWH	77375
DEVON GLEN DR	1300	489K	SWH	77077
DEVON GREEN DR	5100	446B	NWC	77449
DEVON OAKS	0	368A	NWC	77429
DEVOENPORT DR	6700	406U	NWC	77449
DEVONPORT LN	800	619G	TL	77586
DEVONSHIRE	2200	492Q	SWH	77019
DEVONSHIRE DR	2400	613P	PL	77584
DEVONSHIRE CASTLE ST	0	444D	NWC	77493
DEVONSHIRE CRESCENT CIR	1800	533E	SWH	77030
DEVONSHIRE KNOLL ST	0	444C	NWC	77493
DEVONSHIRE MANOR LN	0	451Y	NWH	77055
DEVONWOOD LN	8100	369D	NWC	77070
DEVYN FOREST LN	0	293G	SEM	77386
DEW CIR	23300	339P	HU	77336
DEWALT	800	412P	NWH	77088
DEW ARBOR	11400	372N	NWC	77067
DEWBERRY	4500	533M	SEH	77021
DEWBERRY	4700	534P	SEH	77021
DEWBERRY LN	2100	537S	PA	77502
DEWBERRY BLOSSOM LN	0	410E	NWC	77064
DEWBERRY BROOK CT	1700	338A	NEH	77345
DEWBERRY CREEK LN	0	406P	NWC	77449
DEWBERRY CREEK LN	20700	406P	NWC	77449
DEWBERRY CREEK LN	20700	406P	NWC	77449
DEWBERRY CRESCENT DR	0	367W	NWC	77095
DEWBERRY SHORES LN	0	375X	NEC	77396
DEW CREST DR	6700	407N	NWC	77449
DEW DROP CT	25200	245Q	SWM	77355
DEW DROP LN	16200	407R	NWC	77095
DE WEESE	0	572D	SWH	77045
DEWEY	1200	496L	NEH	77015
DEWEY	2100	282U	WL	77484
DEWEY LN	100	493K	SWH	77007
DEWEY EVE CT	10400	369G	NWC	77070
DEWEY MEADOW RUN CT	27800	294J	SEM	77386
DEW FALL CT	1	251Z	WD	77380
DEWFLOWER DR	0	525B	NEF	77494
DEWGRASS DR	17000	373N	NEH	77060
DEWITT RD	7800	455K	NEH	77028
DEWLIGHT PLACE	0	249A	SWM	77354
DEW MEADOWS CT		367S	NWC	77433
DEW MIST LN	7200	407R	NWC	77095
DEWMONT LN	9300	369M	NWC	77070
DEWSTONE	0	296T	SEM	77365
DEWTHREAD CT	1	251L	WD	77380
DEWVILLE LN	6600	413W	NEH	77076
DEWVILLE LN	7600	413S	NEH	77037
DEW WOOD LN	23100	333D	NCC	77373
DEXTER	8700	575M	SEH	77075
DEXTER BLUFF CT	0	609X	NEF	77479
DEXTER POINT DR	16300	367C	NWC	77429
DE ZAVALLA RD	15900	498L	CV	77530
DIABLO DR	1200	338Y	NEH	77532
DIABLO CANYON LN	19200	328D	NWC	77377
DIAKOVIC DR	12400	496D	NEC	77015
DIAMANTE DR	0	577J	PA	77504
DIAMANTE DR	4400	660F	LC	77573
DIAMANTINA CT	0	405T	NWC	77493
DIAMOND	0	452E	NWH	77018
DIAMOND	100	616Z	FR	77546
DIAMOND CT	19700	245D	SWM	77355
DIAMOND DR	0	298N	NEC	77336
DIAMONDALE CT	3900	485U	NEF	77450
DIAMOND BACK	9500	530B	SWH	77036
DIAMOND BAY CT	6000	409W	NWC	77041
DIAMOND BROOK DR	1400	617D	SEH	77062
DIAMONDCLIFF CT	0	446A	NWC	77449
DIAMOND COVE LN	0	526J	NEF	77407
DIAMOND CREEK DR	28400	245C	SWM	77355
DIAMOND CREST	0	570Y	MC	77489
DIAMOND FALLS LN	7100	250T	NWC	77389
DIAMOND FIELD DR	0	407L	NWC	77095
DIAMOND GROVE CT	3900	578X	SEH	77059
S. DIAMONDHEAD BLVD	100	419E	NEC	77532
N. DIAMONDHEAD BLVD	900	379S	NEC	77532
S. DIAMONDHEAD BLVD	1700	418H	NEC	77532
DIAMOND H FARMS	0	284Z	NWC	77447
DIAMOND HILLS LN	0	446C	NWC	77449
DIAMOND HOLLOW CT	3100	486T	SWH	77450
DIAMOND KNOLL CT	23200	485F	SWC	77494
DIAMOND LAKE CT	8700	528N	SWC	77083
DIAMONDLEAF CT	0	609Y	NEF	77459
DIAMOND LEAF LN	600	489G	SWH	77079
DIAMOND M	0	336V	NEC	77346
DIAMOND OAK CT	1	250M	WD	77381
DIAMOND PARK CIR	19300	332C	NCC	77373
DIAMOND PEAK CT	17900	377B	NEC	77346
DIAMOND RANCH DR	0	485N	NEF	77494
DIAMOND RIDGE DR	16000	571X	SWH	77053
DIAMOND ROCK CT	21100	406T	NWC	77449
DIAMOND ROCK DR	6200	406T	NWC	77449
DIAMOND ROCK DR	16000	327Y	NWC	77429
DIAMOND RUN CT	0	524G	NEF	77494
DIAMOND SHORE CT	22500	485U	NEF	77450
DIAMOND SPRINGS DR	2000	488P	SWH	77077
DIAMONDS SPGS DR	0	612L	PL	77584
DIAMOND STAR DR	0	487Y	SWC	77082
DIAMOND WAY	100	298X	NEH	77336
DIAMOND WAY CT	8300	613V	PL	77584
DIAN	1300	452Y	NWH	77008
DIANA	11700	368R	NWC	77065
DIANA CT	1400	618F	SEH	77062
DIANA LN	15000	618F	SEH	77062
DIANA LN	16800	618Q	SEH	77058
DIANE	1900	247P	SWM	77362
DIANE CT	5400	334E	NCC	77373
DIANE DR	22100	334E	NCC	77373
DIANE LN	12000	371M	NWC	77067
DIANE MANOR LN	0	376W	NEC	77396
DIANE OAKS DR	5700	334A	NCC	77373
DIANESHIRE CT	400	332B	NWC	77388
DIANESHIRE DR	19100	332A	NWC	77388
DICK	4500	494L	NEH	77020
DICKENS RD	4900	534F	SEH	77021
DICKEY PLACE	2100	492U	SWH	77019
DICKINSON	11000	576Y	SEH	77089
DICKINSON AVE	300	659P	LC	77573
DICKINSON AVE	2000	659V	GCO	77539
DICKINSON MANOR DR	0	406K	NWC	77433
DICK SCOBEE DR	0	487W	SWH	77094
DICKSON	3800	492L	SWH	77007
DICKSON PARK DR	19200	332C	NCC	77373
DICKSON WAY	6500	571S	SWH	77085
DICKSON WAY	7000	571S	SWH	77489
DIEGO SPRINGS DR	9900	329F	NWC	77375
DIEHLWOOD PLACE	4800	291S	NWC	77388
DIEPPE	5000	534S	SEH	77033
DIERKER DR	5800	450B	NWH	77041
DIERKER DR	5900	410X	NWH	77041
DIESEL	1200	493E	SWH	77007
DIETZ	0	494W	SEH	77023
DIEZ	1000	494X	SEH	77023
DIJON CT	12500	496D	NEC	77015
DIJON DR	600	496D	NEC	77015
DI JON DR	25900	288X	NWC	77377
DIKE	0	500V	BT	77520
DILLARD	600	412Y	NWH	77091
DILLARD DR	0	409Q	JV	77040
DILL CANYON LN	0	524F	NEF	77494
DILLON	6600	574D	SEH	77061
DILLON	7300	575A	SEH	77061
DILLON	7500	535W	SEH	77061
DILLON CREEK LN	5700	524D	NEF	77494
DILLON HILL CIR	15400	370U	NWC	77086
DILLONWOOD CT	0	619V	LC	77565
DILLON WOOD CT	3000	445R	NWC	77449
DILLSBURY CT	19200	406R	NWC	77449
DI MAMBRO LN	21200	285V	NWC	77377
DIMMETT WAY	0	291N	NWC	77388
DIMROD	3000	660H	BC	77518
DIMSDALE DR	5800	250Z	NWC	77389
DINASTIA VIEW CT	0	660F	LC	77573
DINCANS	4900	492Y	SWH	77005
DINERO DR	19200	337Z	NEC	77346
DINERSTEIN DR	400	617R	SEH	77598
DING-AN-SICH DR	0	381V	LCO	77535
DINGHY CT	17500	379X	NEC	77532
DINIA CT	0	372J	NWC	77067
DINNER CREEK CT	6600	407T	NWC	77449
DINNER CREEK DR	18000	407N	NWC	77449
DINORAH CT	600	486D	SWC	77094
DINWIDDIE DR	0	656S	NEB	77546
DIONNE DR	6800	413X	NEH	77076
DIPLOMACY DR	0	410N	NWC	77040
DIPLOMAT CT	8600	412Q	NWH	77088
DIPLOMATIC PLAZA DR	15300	374U	NEH	77032
DIPLOMAT WAY	1300	412Q	NWH	77088
DIPPING LN	1	453B	NEH	77076
DIPPING LN	20500	258P	SEM	77357
DIRBY	8800	575H	SEH	77075
DIRECTORS DR	12400	569J	SF	77477
DIRECTORS ROW	4000	451V	NWH	77092
DISCIPLINE AVE	0	371G	NWC	77014
DISCOVERY LN	0	609Z	MC	77459
DISCOVERY LN	0	609Z	MC	77459
DISCOVERY LN	14900	408T	NWC	77084
DISCOVERY BAY DR	0	613J	PL	77584
DISCOVERY CREEK BLVD	0	293F	SEM	77386
DISCUS CIR	500	258A	SEM	77357
DISCUS DR	8500	338W	NEC	77346
DISHER CIR	1	258Y	NEC	77336
DISMUKE	1100	494Y	SEH	77023
DISNEY DR	0	371G	NWC	77014
DISTANT ROCK LN	16300	407H	NWC	77095
DISTANT WOODS CT	8800	407C	NWC	77095
DISTANT WOODS DR	8700	407C	NWC	77095
DISTRIBUTION BLVD	3800	452R	NWH	77018
DITE	13900	377Y	NEH	77044
DITMAS LN	5100	534K	SEH	77021
DITTMANS CT	3100	494E	NEH	77020
DIVELLEC LN	20800	291U	NWC	77388
DIVEN CIR	14600	328X	NWC	77429
DIVERSION DR	19300	328D	NWC	77375
DIVERS WAY	1500	459W	CV	77530
DIVIDEND DR	400	495D	NEH	77013
DIVINE	10200	573H	SEH	77033
DIVING DUCK CT	0	376K	NEC	77396
DIVISION	2400	493Y	SEH	77004
DIVOT DR	32000	322P	WCO	77484
DIX	15000	571T	SWH	77085
DIXIE CT	4800	609A	SG	77478
DIXIE DR	100	538Q	DP	77536
DIXIE DR	300	658P	LC	77573
DIXIE DR	2300	533G	SEH	77021
DIXIE DR	6100	534U	SEH	77087
DIXIE DR	7400	535S	SEH	77087
DIXIE FARM RD	1000	617E	SEH	77089
DIXIE FARM RD	2300	616S	PL	77581

Street Name	Block	Pg/Sq	Loc	Zips
DIXIE FARM RD	3000	616L	SEC	77089
DIXIE FARM RD	3700	615Z	PL	77581
DIXIE FRIENDSWOOD	16700	615Z	PL	77581
DIXIE HILL CT	1600	615Z	PL	77581
DIXIE HOLLOW	1600	616P	PL	77581
DIXIELAND DR	0	415A	NWC	77039
DIXIE WOODS DR	2300	616T	PL	77581
DIXON CT	2900	613T	NEB	77584
DIXON DR	2800	613T	NEB	77584
DOAK LN	8800	575U	SEH	77075
DOBBIN	13000	574R	SEH	77048
DOBBIN HUFSMITH RD	26000	249N	SWM	77354
DOBBIN HUFSMITH RD	27000	248D	SWM	77354
DOBBINS DR	0	613Y	NEB	77584
DOBBIN SPRINGS LN	4900	297T	NEH	77345
DOBBIN STREAM LN	3200	447J	NWC	77084
DOBBS VIEW LN	0	292J	NWC	77389
DOBIE	10100	573D	SEH	77033
DOBSON DR	15500	373Q	NCC	77032
DOCHFOUR LN	0	289V	NWC	77375
DOCK CT	300	379Y	NEC	77532
DOCK CT	4000	569Y	MC	77459
DOCKAL RD	7900	455K	NEH	77028
DOCK BAR CT	16100	617T	SEC	77546
DOCKENS FOREST LN	6700	457Q	NEC	77049
DOCKSIDE	16000	419B	NEC	77532
DOCKSIDE CT	400	568P	SG	77478
DOCKSIDE CT	4300	609B	MC	77459
DOCKSIDEHILL LN	0	338W	NEC	77346
DOCKSIDE LANDING DR	0	367S	NWC	77433
DOCKSIDE LANDING DR	0	367S	NWC	77433
DOCKSIDE LANDING DR	0	367S	NWC	77433
DOCKSIDE TERRACE	0	484D	NEF	77494
DOCKSIDE TERRACE CT	24700	484D	NEF	77494
DOCK VIEW LN	3800	569Y	MC	77459
DODAR CEDAR LN	32800	322B	WCO	77484
DODD LN	1500	488R	SWH	77077
DODD RIDGE LN	0	332P	NWC	77090
DODGE	1400	536F	PA	77506
DODIEWOOD LN	8000	370Y	NWC	77086
DODSON	8200	454F	NEH	77093
DODSON	10200	414X	NEH	77093
DODSON TRACE DR	0	253S	SEM	77386
DOE CIR	1	338L	NEH	77336
DOE CIR	24400	296M	SEM	77365
DOE CT	14000	247S	SWM	77355
DOE DR	32300	247S	SWM	77355
DOE MEADOW DR	12200	568H	SF	77477
DOE PATH	0	376N	NEC	77396
DOE PATH CIR	0	376P	NEC	77396
DOERNER LN	0	492S	SWH	77027
DOERRE RD	19000	290X	NWC	77379
S. DOE RUN DR	1	251L	WD	77380
N. DOE RUN DR	1	251L	WD	77380
DOE RUN RD	3000	610B	MC	77489
DOE TRAIL	24500	246X	SWM	77355
DOG RUN LN	22500	296C	SEM	77357
DOGWOOD	0	246V	SWM	77355
DOGWOOD	0	290E	NWC	77375
DOGWOOD	0	375M	NEC	77396
DOGWOOD	1	297P	NEH	77365
DOGWOOD	100	568S	SG	77478
DOGWOOD	500	453Q	NEH	77022
DOGWOOD	11200	336S	NEC	77338
DOGWOOD	33100	247R	SWM	77362
DOGWOOD CIR	400	616U	FR	77546
DOGWOOD CT	0	615W	PL	77584
DOGWOOD DR	1100	537N	PA	77506
DOGWOOD DR	2000	570W	MC	77489
DOGWOOD DR	8700	289H	NWC	77375
W. DOGWOOD DR	10800	579C	LP	77571
DOGWOOD DR	10900	579C	LP	77571
DOGWOOD LN	1	256P	SEM	77357
DOGWOOD LN	1	257L	SEM	77357
DOGWOOD LN	100	254P	SEM	77365
DOGWOOD LN	800	444W	KT	77493
DOGWOOD LN	7300	462Y	BT	77521
DOGWOOD LN	12000	368D	NWC	77429
DOGWOOD LN	17700	257D	SEM	77357
DOGWOOD LN	18000	258E	SEM	77357
S. DOGWOOD LN	26500	246P	SWM	77355
N. DOGWOOD LN	26600	246P	SWM	77355
DOGWOOD RD	800	620T	CS	77565
DOGWOOD ST	2200	659G	LC	77573
DOGWOOD ACRES	0	297P	NEH	77365
DOGWOOD BLOOM CT	19200	331A	NWC	77379
DOGWOOD BLOSSOM CT	0	615Y	PL	77581
DOGWOOD BLOSSOM TRAIL	13000	368U	NWC	77065
DOGWOOD BLOSSOM TRAIL	0	615Y	PL	77581
DOGWOOD BOUGH LN	3900	611W	FS	77545
DOGWOOD BRANCH LN	2301	252R	SEM	77386
DOGWOOD BROOK TRAIL	1600	618E	SEH	77062
DOGWOOD CANYON LN	3900	609J	NEF	77479
DOGWOOD CREEK CT	2800	326J	NWC	77433
DOGWOOD CREEK CT	20800	326F	NWC	77433
DOGWOOD CREST LN	0	375X	NEC	77396
DOGWOOD FALLS RD	7300	407L	NWC	77095
DOGWOOD GLEN CT	13000	328T	NWC	77429
DOGWOOD HILL	0	410E	NWC	77064
DOGWOOD HILL	0	537V	PA	77503
DOGWOOD KNOLL LN	0	524M	NEF	77406
DOGWOOD MOUNTAIN RD	12000	371N	NWC	77066
DOGWOOD PARK CT	0	406R	NWC	77449
DOGWOOD PARK LN	0	406R	NWC	77449
DOGWOOD PLACE	1	259P	LCO	77357
DOGWOOD RIDGE LN	4500	297T	NEH	77345
DOGWOOD SPRINGS DR	3100	333P	NCC	77073
DOGWOOD TERRACE LN	0	253P	SEM	77386
DOGWOOD TRAIL	0	245S	SWM	77447
DOGWOOD TRAIL	18400	286V	NWC	77377
DOGWOOD TRAIL	24400	257B	WV	77357
DOGWOOD TRAIL	32600	246V	SWM	77355
DOGWOOD TRAIL DR	7200	337Y	NEC	77346
DOGWOOD TRAIL LN	0	657U	LC	77573
DOGWOOD TREE	14300	413A	NCC	77060
DOGWOOD TREE	15000	373W	NEH	77060
DOGWOOD VIEW LN	0	328A	NWC	77429
DOGWOOD VIEW LN	0	328A	NWC	77377
DOGWOOD WALK CT	19600	332A	NWC	77388
DOHERTY CIR	20000	446L	NWC	77449
DOHERTY PLACE	3300	446L	NWC	77449
DOLA DR	0	283Q	NWC	77484
DOLAN BROOK LN	0	377U	NEC	77044
DOLAN FALL LN	21400	525D	NEF	77450
DOLAN FALLS LN	0	615M	PL	77089
DOLAN HEIGHTS CT	0	406F	NWC	77433
DOLAN HILLS CT	2100	485P	NEF	77494
DOLAN LAKE DR	2300	568A	NEF	77498
DOLAN SPRINGS DR	19300	328C	NWC	77377
DOLBEAU DR	500	497A	NEC	77015
DOLBEN CT	9900	411N	NWH	77088
DOLBEN MEADOWS LN	0	326T	NWC	77429
DOLGO DR	12500	369J	NWC	77429
DOLIVER CIR	1900	610B	MC	77489
DOLIVER DR	0	491P	SWH	77057
DOLIVER DR	5000	491Q	SWH	77056
DOLIVER DR	5700	491N	SWH	77057
DOLIVER DR	9400	490P	SWH	77063
DOLIVER DR	10000	489R	SWH	77042
DOLIVER POINT	9400	490P	SWH	77063
DOLLAN PARK LN	0	371D	NWC	77014
DOLLINS	800	444X	KT	77493
DOLLY WRIGHT	800	412S	NWH	77088
DOLLY WRIGHT	2500	411V	NWH	77088
DOLORES	5500	491X	SWH	77056
DOLORES	5600	491X	SWH	77057
DOLPHIN	1	542A	BT	77520
DOLPHIN CT	1	490B	SWH	77024
DOLPHIN CT	3000	620N	SB	77586
DOLPHIN DR	1700	620K	SB	77586
DOLPHIN LN	3800	580V	LP	77571
DOLPHIN ARC DR	7600	377D	NEC	77346
S. DOLPHIN HARBOR	0	542J	BT	77520
N. DOLPHIN HARBOR	0	542J	BT	77520
DOMENICO LN	2700	659M	LC	77573
DOMER DR	8300	330P	NWC	77379
DOMINA ST	0	525J	NEF	77406
DOMINECO LN	2400	486P	SWC	77450
DOMINGO DR	7000	459K	NEC	77049
DOMINIC CT	0	458S	NEC	77530
DOMINIC LN	0	458S	NEC	77530
DOMINICA DR	0	377G	NEC	77345
DOMINION DR	1	486B	SWC	77450
DOMINION ESTATES DR	0	452F	NWH	77091
W. DOMINION FALLS LN	0	415C	NEH	77396
S. DOMINION FALLS LN	0	415C	NEH	77396
N. DOMINION FALLS LN	0	415C	NEH	77396
DOMINION PARK DR	100	372B	NWC	77090
DOMINION POINT DR	0	452F	NWH	77091
DOMINIQUE DR	13900	368T	NWC	77429
DOMINO LN	7300	412V	NEH	77076
DOMINO RD	0	293W	NCC	77373
DOMINO RD	0	293Q	NCC	77373
DOMINQUEZ SPRING DR	2500	293F	SEM	77386
DON	600	537K	PA	77506
DONALBAIN DR	4000	333H	NCC	77373
DONALD	4700	581W	PA	77586
DONALD	26600	292R	SP	77373
DONALD DR	10100	453C	NEH	77076
DONALDSON	300	540Z	MP	77571
DON ALEJANDRO	0	452A	NWC	77091
DONATA CIR	21500	333F	NCC	77338
DONCASTER RD	11900	490J	BH	77024
DONCREST DR	700	497D	NEC	77530
DONDELL DR	700	497D	NEC	77530
DONEGAL	2300	615R	PL	77581
DONEGAL CT	2200	538P	DP	77536
DONEGAL WAY	10600	573G	SEH	77047
DONELLAN DR	2700	411M	NWC	77088
DONELSON LN	14600	328X	NWC	77429
DONERAIL DR	4100	537R	PA	77503
DONEY	2700	534G	SEH	77023
DONFIELD DR	700	497D	NEC	77530
DONFORTH DR	15700	571X	SWH	77053
DON GIL	10000	576N	SEH	77075
DON HENLEY CT	1600	494E	NEH	77020
DONLEN	6700	453Q	NEH	77022
DONLEY DR	8600	412K	NWH	77088
DONNA DR	10800	410M	NWC	77041
DONNA DR	12400	372P	NWC	77067
DONNA LN	14700	420M	NEC	77532
DONNA BELL LN	3700	452J	NWH	77018
DONNACOREY DR	500	496F	NEH	77013
DONNA LYNN CT	5100	451L	NWH	77092
DONNA LYNN DR	4100	451L	NWH	77092
DONNELL LAKE DR	0	366Q	NWC	77433
DONNET LN	15500	373R	NCC	77032
DONNITA LN	0	656E	NEB	77511
DONNY BROOK	0	569A	SWH	77477
DONNYBROOK	0	569A	SWH	77477
DONNYVILLE	0	539N	LP	77571
DONOHO	5900	534T	SEH	77033
W. DONOVAN	300	452H	NWH	77091
DONOVAN	1500	501V	BT	77520
DONREL WAY	0	371H	NWC	77067
DONWELL LN	0	328T	NWC	77429
DON WHITE	5900	411P	NWH	77088
DONYS CT	1	410K	NWC	77040
DONYS DR	8700	410K	NWC	77040
DOOLITTLE BLVD	4700	534S	SEH	77033
DOONSIDE DR	19800	406U	NWC	77449
DOPEY HOLLOW	0	528C	SWH	77082
DOPSLAUF DR	0	448K	NWH	77084
DORA	0	493W	SWH	77006
DORA	5300	533A	SWH	77005
DORA LN	15200	527Z	NEF	77498
DORADO CIR	31200	248X	TB	77375
DORADO DR	0	377G	NEC	77345
DORADO DR	1	656T	FR	77546
DORAL	4300	578E	PA	77505
DORAL CT	700	656Q	FR	77546
DORAL CT	1400	541H	BT	77520
DORAL CT	2900	659D	LC	77573
DORAL DR	2400	541H	BT	77520
S. DORAL DR	2700	609H	MC	77459
N. DORAL DR	2700	609H	MC	77459
DORAL LN	900	332L	NCC	77073
DORALDALE CT	8500	410F	NWC	77040
DORAL ROCK CT	0	407J	NWC	77433
DORAL ROSE LN	0	446N	NWC	77449
DORA MEADOWS DR	9300	527Q	NEF	77083
DORAN LN	15500	373Q	NCC	77032
DORANTES LN	0	338M	NEH	77336
DORBRANDT	5500	534C	SEH	77023
DORCHESTER	100	453Q	NEH	77022
DORCHESTER	3700	454P	NEH	77016
DORCHESTER CT	3400	569S	SG	77478
DORCHESTER FOREST DR	13200	369H	NWC	77070
DORENE	1300	536T	PA	77502
DORIC CT	11200	368T	NWC	77429
DORINGTON DR	0	410L	NWC	77040
DORIS	400	536V	PA	77502
DORIS	900	620W	GCO	77565
DORIS	1000	538L	DP	77536
DORIS	4500	500H	BT	77521
DORIS CT	1900	570S	SF	77477
DORIS OAKS CIR	0	455G	NEH	77028
DORITA LN	9600	412G	NWC	77038
DORKING CT	14900	457Z	NEC	77530
DORMAN CT	2200	484K	NEF	77494
DORMAN DRAW LN	0	377D	NEC	77346
DORMSTOM LN	1900	412K	NWC	77088
DORNOCH DR	2100	659C	LC	77573
DORNOCH DR	9400	329Q	NWC	77379
DORNOCH DR	9900	329R	NWC	77070
DOROTHY	700	492D	NWH	77007
DOROTHY	900	452Z	NWH	77008
DOROTHY	2000	536T	PA	77502
DOROTHY	4300	531M	BL	77401
DOROTHY LN	3600	615U	PL	77581
DOROTHY LN	20200	257L	SEM	77357
DOROTHY ANN DR	5600	453A	NEH	77076
DORRANCE	0	568D	SG	77478
DORRANCE LN	9900	569D	SWC	77031
DORRANCE LN	11300	569A	MD	77477
DORRAY LN	14800	487Z	SWC	77082
DORRCREST LN	8100	369D	NWC	77070
DORRINGTON	2200	532G	SWH	77030
DORRINGTON ESTATES LN	23900	252R	SEM	77385
DORRIS	1800	501S	BT	77520
DORSAL WAY	400	379X	NEC	77532
W. DORSET	0	488L	SWH	77077
E. DORSET	0	488L	SWH	77077
DORSET	0	257H	SEM	77357
DORSET CT	0	258F	SEM	77357
DORSETSHIRE DR	1200	577E	PA	77504
DORSETSHIRE DR	7100	411N	NWH	77040
DORSET SQUARE	1	251F	SWM	77381
DORSETT	700	495E	NEH	77029
DORSETTE CT	0	568B	SG	77498
DORSEY CT	100	494K	NEH	77020
DORSEY LN	0	614U	PL	77584
DORSEY FALLS DR	0	524Q	NWF	77406
DORSTON DR	20200	257Q	SEM	77357
DORTMUND DR	0	293F	SEM	77386
DORWAYNE CT	12200	496L	NEH	77015
DORYLEE DR	6300	415A	NEC	77396
DORYWOOD RD	13800	371V	NWC	77038
DOSIA	8500	533Z	SEH	77051
DOSKOCIL DR	0	457A	NEC	77044
DOSSEY	2000	539V	LP	77571
DOTSON RD	13200	369H	NWC	77070
DOUBLE	8100	412T	NWH	77088
DOUBLE BAY	0	327W	NWC	77429
DOUBLE BAYOU CT	0	366Z	NWC	77433
DOUBLEDAY DR	12000	616D	SEH	77089
DOUBLE EAGLE DR	4900	578K	PA	77505
DOUBLE JACK CT	0	293U	NCC	77373
DOUBLE LAKE DR	2600	609K	MC	77459
DOUBLE LILLY DR	17200	407B	NWC	77095
DOUBLE MEADOW CT	0	407L	NWC	77095
DOUBLE MEADOWS DR	20600	406L	NWC	77433
DOUBLE OAK CIR	0	366P	NWC	77433
DOUBLE PINE DR	13800	457Y	NEC	77015
DOUBLE SHOALS CIR	14300	332W	NWC	77090
DOUBLE TRAIL CT	3900	609G	MC	77459
DOUBLE TREE DR	11800	369Q	NWC	77070
DOUBLETREE GLEN DR	0	332Q	NCC	77073
DOUBLETREE PARK DR	0	332Q	NCC	77073
DOUBLETREE PLAZA	0	374P	NEH	77032
DOUBLETREE RANCH DR	0	366P	NWC	77433
DOUD	10600	531U	SWH	77035
DOUGLAS	2400	615P	PL	77581
DOUGLAS	4000	453N	NWH	77018
DOUGLAS DR	300	500P	BT	77520
DOUGLAS LN	300	570N	MC	77489
DOUGLAS RD	0	658X	LC	77573
DOUGLAS CREEK LN	0	253S	SEM	77386
DOUGLAS FIR	11900	370R	NWC	77066
DOUGLAS LAKE RD	0	377G	NEH	77346
DOUGLAS PARK DR	0	526A	NEF	77450
DOUGLAS PASS	0	660E	LC	77573
DOUGLAS SPUR CT	0	525U	NEF	77469
DOUGLAS SPUR CT	0	525U	NEF	77469
DOUGLAS SPUR DR	0	525U	NEF	77469
DOUGLAS SPUR DR	0	525U	NEF	77469
DOULTON DR	5000	534S	SEH	77033
DOUNREAY DR	16300	447H	NWC	77084
DOVE	1200	496L	NEH	77015
DOVE CT	1900	657N	FR	77546
DOVE CT	3400	615T	PL	77581
DOVE BROOK CT	12800	408Z	NWC	77041
DOVE CALL CT	0	249B	SWM	77382
DOVE CANYON LN	22000	256W	SEM	77365
DOVECOTT LN	8400	528Q	SWC	77083
DOVE COUNTRY DR	2700	569U	NEF	77477
DOVE COVE RD	3100	375L	HM	77396
DOVE CREEK CIR	10900	371S	NWC	77086
DOVE CREEK SPRINGS TRAIL	0	367W	NWC	77433
DOVEDALE CT	11300	371R	NWC	77067
DOVE FERN CT	6100	408Z	NWC	77041
DOVEFIELD LN	18100	407K	NWC	77433
DOVE FOREST LN	5300	337N	NEC	77346
DOVE HAVEN CT	21400	256W	SEM	77365
DOVE HAVEN LN	0	659G	LC	77573
DOVE HOLLOW DR	4600	414C	NCC	77039
DOVE LAKE TRAIL	0	366V	NWC	77433
DOVE MANOR CT	8600	329D	NWC	77379
DOVE OAKS CT	12900	408Z	NWC	77041
DOVE PARK CT	10900	575Z	SEH	77075
DOVE PARK DR	0	569U	NEF	77477
DOVE PASS CT	0	527J	NEF	77407
DOVE POINT LN	12800	408Z	NWC	77041
DOVE PRAIRIE CT	6200	408Z	NWC	77041
DOVER	2800	535K	SEH	77017
DOVER	3700	535T	SEH	77087
DOVER	3900	538U	DP	77536
DOVER	8100	535X	SEH	77061
DOVER	8800	575B	SEH	77061
DOVER	11100	569D	SWH	77031
DOVER LN	0	657U	LC	77573
DOVER LN	200	616Y	FR	77546
DOVER LN	400	332C	NCC	77373
DOVER BLUFF LN	0	609U	NEF	77479
DOVERBROOK DR	27200	299S	NEC	77336
DOVER CLIFF CT	16500	419B	NEC	77532
DOVER CREEK LN	6000	524E	NEF	77494
DOVER FALLS CT	0	376B	NEC	77369
W. DOVERFIELD DR	100	413N	NCC	77037
DOVERFIELD DR	200	413N	NCC	77037
DOVERGLEN DR	2300	570Y	MC	77489
DOVERGREEN LN	19900	291Z	NWC	77388
DOVER HEIGHTS LN	1800	611T	NEF	77545
DOVER HILL RD	9700	579B	LP	77571
DOVER HOUSE WAY	6000	250V	NWC	77389
DOVE RIDGE DR	0	444S	KT	77493
DOVE RIDGE LN	5700	408Z	NWC	77041
DOVER MEADON	12000	369P	NWC	77070
DOVER MIST LN	0	446S	NWC	77449
DOVER MIST LN	0	446S	NWC	77449
DOVER MIST LN	0	615G	PL	77581
DOVER OAKS LN	0	253K	SEM	77386
DOVER PARK LN	0	525D	NEF	77450
DOVERSHIRE	24000	250Z	NWC	77389
DOVERSHIRE BLUFF WAY	5900	250Z	NWC	77389
DOVERSHIRE KNOLL CT	5900	250Z	NWC	77389
DOVERSIDE	600	453G	NEH	77022
DOVER SPRINGS CT	9700	524G	NEF	77494
DOVERTON LN	16300	328U	NWC	77377
DOVE RUN CT	7700	406M	NWC	77433
DOVER VALLEY DR	0	578T	SEH	77059
DOVER WAY	6600	290C	NWC	77389
DOVERWICK DR	24000	289D	NWC	77375
DOVERWOOD WAY	16600	618R	SEH	77058
DOVES GATE CT	0	524G	NEF	77494
DOVESHIRE CT	3300	446L	NWC	77449
DOVES LANDING	19200	329B	NWC	77375
DOVES NEST CT	0	332N	NWC	77090
DOVE SPRINGS DR	4600	371J	NWC	77066
DOVE STONE DR	0	408N	NWC	77084
DOVETAIL LN	0	527J	NEF	77407
DOVETAIL ARBOR TRACE	0	406W	NWC	77449
DOVETAIL BLUFF LN	0	253T	SEM	77386
DOVETAIL COLONY CT	0	445F	NWC	77493
DOVETAIL COVE CT	0	249U	NWC	77375
DOVETAIL CREEK CT	0	367P	NWC	77433
DOVETAIL MEADOW LN	0	405T	NWC	77493
DOVETAIL RIDGE CT		328P	NWC	77429
DOVETON LN	19100	291X	NWC	77388
S. DOVE TRACE CIR	1	250B	WD	77382
DOVE TRACE CIR	1	250B	WD	77382
DOVE TRAIL CT	16000	327S	NWC	77429
DOVE TRAILS	1300	288B	TB	77375
DOVE TREE	17600	330J	NWC	77379
DOVEVALLEY	0	256X	SEM	77365
DOVE WAY	9100	575V	SEH	77075
DOVEWOOD LN	2700	333A	NCC	77373
DOVIE DR	3300	251S	SWM	77380
DOVINGTON CT	21700	291S	NWC	77388
DOW CIR	2700	538U	DP	77536
DOW RD	5200	450H	NWH	77040
DOWBER RD	6000	452D	NWH	77076
DOWCREST DR	6600	290C	NWC	77389
DOWDELL RD	7600	290F	NWC	77389
DOWDELL RD	8000	289M	NWC	77375
DOWLWOOD DR	15600	373P	NCC	77032
DOWNDALE CIR	22500	485Y	NEF	77450
DOWNDALE LN	22600	485Y	NEF	77450
DOWNEY	11000	413T	NEH	77076
DOWNEY VIOLET LN	0	416Q	NEC	77044
DOWNFORD DR	15300	329S	NWC	77377
DOWNGATE DR	4100	447F	NWC	77084
DOWNHEATH LN	15700	333S	NCC	77073
DOWNING	2900	615L	PL	77581
DOWNING	5600	494D	NEH	77020
DOWNING CIR	1100	658M	LC	77573
DOWNING CIR	3600	538U	DP	77536
DOWNING DR	0	573N	SWH	77045
DOWNING PARK BLVD	0	524C	NEF	77494
DOWNING PARK BLVD	0	524C	NEF	77494
DOWNINGTON CT	8000	330E	NWC	77379
DOWNS LN	4300	414X	NEH	77093
DOWNS LN	10000	454B	NEH	77093
DOWNTOWN HOUSTON	0	493L	DT	77002
DOWNWOOD FOREST DR	6000	411K	NWC	77088
DOYLE	1700	538N	PA	77503
DOYLE	3200	454E	NEH	77093
DOZENT LN	100	502B	NEC	77521
DRACAENA CT	14400	328Z	NWC	77070
DRACO	0	411R	NWH	77088
DRAGON CT	25000	244R	WCO	77447
DRAGONFLY	30000	288A	NWC	77377
DRAGONFLY DR	0	326H	NWC	77429
DRAGONFLY MEADOW CT	9900	376T	NEC	77396
DRAGONFLY MEADOW CT	9900	376T	NEC	77396
DRAGONWICK DR	2600	572L	SWH	77045
DRAGONWOOD TRAIL	9000	527R	NEF	77083
DRAKE	3700	492W	SWH	77005
DRAKE CT	6000	444K	KT	77493
DRAKE LN	0	657U	LC	77573
DRAKE BROOK LN	0	326U	NWC	77429
DRAKE FALLS CT	4600	485Z	NEF	77450
DRAKE FALLS DR	0	612G	PL	77584
DRAKEFIELD CT	24200	485S	NEF	77494
DRAKE FIELD LN	0	334R	NCC	77338
DRAKEFORD CT	0	573T	SEC	77047
DRAKELAND DR	10800	376U	NEC	77396
DRAKEMILL DR	12200	489J	SWH	77077
DRAKE PRAIRIE LN	12300	368L	NWC	77429
DRAKESBURY LN	0	485T	NEF	77494
DRAKE SHADOWS LN	0	446G	NWC	77449
DRAKE SPRINGS LN	0	612Q	PL	77584
DRAKESTONE BLVD	4800	571Z	SWH	77053
DRAKESTONE BLVD	5500	571Y	SWH	77053
DRAKEWOOD DR	13700	568F	SG	77498
DRAKEWOOD DR	20400	446K	NWC	77449
DRANE CT	900	492C	NWH	77008
DRAPER RD	0	286P	NWC	77377
DRAPER RD	15000	331U	NWC	77014
DRAVA LN	1000	332J	NWC	77090
DRAVA LN	1100	331M	NWC	77090
DRAWBRIDGE DR	3600	376G	NEC	77396
DRAWBRIDGE LN	1400	252U	SEM	77386
DRAYCOTT LN	14400	571V	SWH	77045
DRAYCUTT DR	0	484E	NEF	77494
DRAYCUTT DR		484J	NEF	77494
DRAYTON LN	2100	412J	NWC	77088
DRAYTON HALL	0	609Z	MC	77459
DREAM CT	5900	571K	SWH	77085
DREAMER	16800	325P	NWC	77429
DREAMLAND BLVD	100	419U	BR	77532
DREAMSCAPE CIR	0	573Y	SEH	77047
DREAMWEAVER CIR	1	251Z	WD	77380
DRENNAN	1	494N	SEH	77003
N. DRENNAN	100	494P	SEH	77003
DRENNANBURG CT	3100	446Q	NWC	77449
DRENNER PARK LN	5900	411B	NWC	77086
DRESDEN	100	495W	SEH	77012
DRESDEN RIDGE LN	12900	369G	NWC	77070
DRESHER DR	600	292Y	NCC	77373
DREW	1	493P	SWH	77006
W. DREW	100	493N	SWH	77006
DREW	1000	493T	SWH	77002
DREW	1100	493U	SWH	77004
DREW	3800	494W	SEH	77004
DREW	3800	530B	SWH	77063
DREWBERRY ST	0	450Q	NWH	77080
DREWFALLS CT	22100	525Q	NEF	77407
DREWFALLS DR	6500	525Q	NEF	77407
DREW FOREST LN	4800	376D	NEC	77346
DREW FOREST LN	5000	377A	NEC	77346
DREW HAVEN LN	8300	330E	NWC	77379
DREWLAINE FIELDS LN	6700	407P	NWC	77449
DREW MEADOWS DR	0	253X	SEM	77386
DREWSER	1300	491P	SWH	77057
DREWS MANOR CT	2900	485S	NEF	77494
DREXEL CIR	2300	492S	SWH	77027
DREXEL DR	1000	444U	KT	77493

Street Name	Block	Pg/Sq	Loc	Zips
DREXEL DR	2000	492S	SWH	77027
DREXELBROOK DR	11800	489N	SWH	77077
DREXEL HILL DR	11900	489J	SWH	77077
DREXELRIDGE LN	0	327D	NWC	77429
DREYFUS	1000	532M	SWH	77030
DREYFUS	3400	533Q	SEH	77021
DRIBECK CT	3800	331X	NWC	77014
DRIFT ANCHOR PLACE	0	250N	NWC	77389
DRIFTDALE PLACE	0	250R	NWC	77389
DRIFTER CT	2400	613T	NEB	77584
DRIFTERS BEND	0	293G	SEM	77386
S. DRIFTING LEAF CT	1	251Z	WD	77380
N. DRIFTING LEAF CT	1	251Z	WD	77380
DRIFTING OAKS CT	0	408A	NWC	77095
DRIFTING OAKS DR	0	408A	NWC	77095
DRIFTING PINE CT	12200	371J	NWC	77066
DRIFTING ROSE DR	15800	327S	NWC	77429
DRIFTING WILLOW CT	7500	406M	NWC	77433
DRIFTING WINDS DR	11900	456C	NEC	77044
DRIFTSTONE DR	8800	330N	NWC	77379
DRIFTSTONE DR	9100	329R	NWC	77379
DRIFTWOOD	0	539Y	LP	77571
DRIFTWOOD	0	579C	LP	77571
DRIFTWOOD	200	658M	LC	77573
DRIFTWOOD	4600	501E	BT	77521
DRIFTWOOD	6700	533Q	SEH	77021
DRIFTWOOD CT	3400	569S	SG	77478
DRIFTWOOD DR	100	619H	TL	77586
DRIFTWOOD DR	2700	613X	NEB	77578
DRIFTWOOD LN	2600	620E	SB	77586
DRIFTWOOD BEND CT	0	610Z	MC	77545
DRIFTWOOD BEND DR	0	610Z	MC	77545
DRIFTWOOD HARBOR		249V	NWC	77375
DRIFTWOOD OAK CT	15400	618B	SEH	77059
DRIFTWOOD PARK DR	9900	368W	NWC	77095
DRIFTWOOD PRAIRIE LN	0	367W	NWC	77095
DRIFTWOOD SHORES CT	0	367W	NWC	77095
DRIFTWOOD SPRINGS DR	0	407W	NWC	77449
DRIPPING POINT LN	3500	484T	NEF	77494
DRIPPING SPRINGS DR	13400	528C	SWC	77083
DRISCOLL	1500	492R	SWH	77019
DRISCOLL	3800	492V	SWH	77098
DRISCOLL PARK DR	6000	525R	NEF	77407
DRISTONE DR	2200	296Z	NEH	77339
DRIVER FOREST DR	0	295L	SEM	77365
DRIVER GREEN DR	1800	445S	NWC	77493
DRODDY	4800	451C	NWH	77091
DROITWICH DR	18500	337W	NEC	77346
DROUET	7500	535W	SEH	77061
DROWSY PINE DR	6900	411W	NWH	77092
DROWSY PINE DR	25900	257M	SEM	77357
DROXFORD LN	1500	452X	NWH	77008
DROXSHIRE DR	10100	335Q	HM	77338
DRUCKER DR	0	371Q	NWC	77066
DRUID	2300	412W	NWH	77091
DRUID	3000	411Z	NWH	77091
DRUID'S GLEN PLACE	0	249D	SWM	77382
DRUMCLIFFE CT	300	457X	NEC	77015
DRUM HELLER LN	18000	328G	NWC	77377
DRUMLIN FIELD WAY		526S	NEF	77407
DRUMMER DR	2500	658P	LC	77573
DRUMMET BLVD	14600	374X	NEH	77032
DRUMMOND	3200	532J	SWH	77025
DRUMMOND CLIFF LN	0	410E	NWC	77064
DRUMMOND PARK DR	11900	416K	NEC	77044
DRUM ROLL DR	8300	410G	NWC	77064
DRUMWOOD LN	12600	368L	NWC	77429
DRURY LN	1200	451X	NWH	77055
DRYAD DR	5300	571A	SWH	77035
DRYAD DR	6000	570H	SWH	77035
DRY ARBOR CT	0	326L	NWC	77429
DRYBANK DR	3100	445M	NWC	77449
DRY BANK LN	0	612K	PL	77545
DRYBANK CREEK LN		484S	NEF	77494
DRYBERRY CT	16200	527U	NEF	77083
DRYBROOK RD	24900	250S	NWC	77389
DRYBROOK CROSSING LN	0	526L	NEF	77407
DRYBURGH CT	3400	299N	NEC	77336
DRY CANYON CT	0	406Z	NWC	77449
DRY CREEK DR	3700	578A	PA	77505
DRY CREEK DR	14200	367B	CY	77429
DRY CREEK LN	16700	327X	CY	77429
DRY CREEK RD	27500	249F	SWM	77354
DRY CREEK FALLS BLVD	0	326K	NWC	77433
DRY CREEK RANCH RD	13800	367B	NWC	77429
DRYDEN LN	5200	578J	PA	77505
DRYDEN RD	1700	532G	SWH	77030
DRYDEN MILLS LN	13600	369G	NWC	77070
DRY DESERT WAY	9500	579A	LP	77571
DRYER PARK DR	0	293U	NCC	77373
DRYFALLS CT	21000	446J	NWC	77449
DRY RIDGE CT	0	376V	NEC	77346
DRY SAND DR	9500	579A	LP	77571
DRYSDALE LN	9800	450B	NWH	77041
DRY SPRING DR	24000	293T	NCC	77373
DRY SPRINGS DR	9500	579A	LP	77571
DRY STONE CT	0	657S	FR	77546
DRYSTONE LN	16300	407H	NWC	77095
DRY WILLOW LN	0	616J	PL	77089
DRYWOOD CREEK	0	659W	LC	77573
DRYWOOD CROSSING CT	23000	292G	NCC	77373
DUAL CIRCLE CT	12200	367M	CY	77429
DUAN	7000	453K	NEH	77022
DUANE	2300	539Y	LP	77571
DUANE	8600	533Y	SEH	77051
DUANE	9000	573H	SEH	77047
DUART DR	11700	490F	HE	77024
DU BARRY LN	1100	452N	NWH	77018
DUBINWOOD DR	0	524E	NEF	77494
DUBLIN	13900	571J	SWH	77085
DUBLIN CIR	2300	616K	PL	77581
DUBLIN CT	0	569K	SF	77477
DUBLIN DR	1800	658U	LC	77573
DUBLIN DR	1900	538P	DP	77536
DUBLIN LN	5900	614L	PL	77581
DUBLIN BAY BLVD	0	286Q	NWC	77377
DU BOIS	3600	533U	SEH	77051
DU BOISE RD	6800	411Z	NWH	77091
DUCCIO RIVER WAY	0	445E	NWC	77493
DUCHAMP DR	10100	529R	SWH	77036
DUCHESS CT	1	490E	BH	77024
DUCHESS LN	12600	369K	NWC	77070
DUCHESS PARK CT	3400	657G	FR	77546
DUCHESS PARK LN	3100	657G	FR	77546
DUCHESS TRAIL	0	490E	BH	77024
DUCHESS WAY	2400	569V	SF	77477
DUCK CREEK LN	0	450J	NWH	77080
DUCKETT PARK DR	6400	411B	NWC	77086
DUCKLAKE LN	2100	446Y	NWC	77084
DUCK TAIL LN	0	324S	NWC	77447
DUCKWALK	7200	530L	SWH	77074
DUCKWATER COVE	16800	367U	NWC	77095

Street Name	Block	Pg/Sq	Loc	Zips
DUCLAIR LN	16200	324S	NWC	77447
DUDE RD	10200	409G	NWC	77064
DUDE WILLABY RD	0	258K	SEM	77357
DUDLEY	3000	533F	SWH	77021
DUESENBERG CT	4300	613V	PL	77584
DUESENBERG DR	4400	613V	PL	77584
DUFF LN	600	453G	NEH	77022
DUFFER LN	800	577P	SEH	77034
DUFFIELD LN	7800	570C	SWH	77071
DUFFTON	16200	367Q	CY	77429
DUFFY LN	0	612Z	NEB	77578
DUHON PLACE	2400	620K	SB	77586
DUKE	1100	541B	BT	77520
DUKE	2800	532F	WU	77005
DUKE LN	3300	657L	FR	77546
DUKE'S ALEXANDER DR	0	296X	SEM	77339
DUKE LAKE DR	0	332A	NWC	77388
DUKE OF YORK CT	13300	369F	NWC	77070
DUKE OF YORK LN	10500	369F	NWC	77070
DUKES BEND	300	569V	SF	77477
DUKES RUN	0	293Y	NCC	77373
DUKE TRAIL LN	0	609X	NEF	77479
DUKE TRAIL LN	0	609X	NEF	77479
DULA LN	11800	368R	NWC	77429
DU LAC TRACE	2500	620J	SB	77586
DULANEY	0	247Y	SWM	77355
DULANEY RD	2900	447N	NWC	77084
DULCIMER	9200	573B	SEH	77051
DULCINA DR	0	286Q	NWC	77377
DULCREST	3000	573F	SEH	77051
DULLER LN	8000	535K	SEH	77017
DULLES AVE	100	569N	SF	77477
DULLES AVE	1200	609B	MC	77478
DULLES AVE	1700	609B	MC	77459
DU LOCK LN	1300	450W	NWH	77055
DULUTH	13300	497F	NEH	77015
DUMAS	11200	576R	SEH	77034
DUMBARTON	3500	532J	SWH	77025
DUMBARTON RD	3700	537H	PA	77503
DUMBLE	400	494T	SEH	77011
DUMBLE	600	494X	SEH	77023
DUMBLE	6300	533R	SEH	77021
DUMFRIES DR	4900	531S	SWH	77096
DUMFRIES DR	6000	530V	SWH	77096
DUMONT	600	536W	SH	77587
DUMORE DR	4900	573H	SEH	77048
DUMORE DR	5200	574J	SEH	77048
DUNAIN PARK CT	9200	407D	NWC	77095
DUNAWAY	1600	496Q	GP	77015
DUNBAR	800	453T	NWH	77009
DUNBAR	19500	335S	NCC	77338
DUNBAR CT	6100	657U	LC	77573
DUNBAR CAVE CT	12900	377F	NEC	77346
DUNBAR ESTATES DR	100	616Y	FR	77546
DUNBAR POINT CT	10400	329C	NWC	77379
DUNBARRIDGE DR	0	327D	NWC	77429
DUNBARTON	0	460H	NEC	77532
DUNBEATH DR	11400	490C	HE	77024
DUNBLAINE	0	490J	SWH	77024
DUNBROOK DR	10500	369B	NWC	77070
DUNBROOK PARK LN	5500	406X	NWC	77449
DUNCAN	1100	458Y	CV	77530
DUNCAN	7700	454J	NEH	77093
DUNCAN GROVE DR	15300	367H	CY	77429
DUNCANNON DR	13900	457X	NEC	77015
DUNCAN RUN LN		366U	NWC	77433
DUNCANSBY VALE RD	7900	407H	NWC	77095
DUNCASTER	300	489F	SWH	77079
DUNCASTER CT	3400	609G	MC	77459
DUNCASTER DR	3400	609G	MC	77459
DUNCUM	10300	496E	NEH	77013
DUNCUM	13700	497F	NEC	77015
DUNDALK	9400	329R	NWC	77379
DUNDAS DR	0	328E	NWC	77377
DUNDEE CT	0	367L	CY	77429
DUNDEE RD	16200	367L	CY	77429
DUNEBERRY TRAIL	0	376H	NEC	77346
DUNE BROOK DR	8100	615H	SEC	77089
DUNE GATE CT	9200	375V	NEC	77396
DUNES DR	2600	659D	LC	77573
DUNES DR	15900	418H	NEC	77532
DUNES RIDGE WAY	400	660E	LC	77573
DUNFIELD LN	11500	569B	SWH	77099
DUNFORD CT	300	459Q	HG	77562
DUNHAM DR	600	453A	NEH	77076
DUNHAM CREEK LN	0	325S	HK	77447
DUNHAM LAKE DR	0	325S	HK	77447
DUNHAVEN CT	1100	618E	SEH	77062
DUNHILL CT	23300	485T	NEF	77494
DUNHILL LN	1300	537N	PA	77506
DUNHURST LN	0	573T	SEC	77047
DUNKIRK RD	7300	533V	SEH	77033
DUNKLEY DR	400	413W	NEH	77076
DUNLAP	6500	531E	SWH	77074
DUNLAP	8000	531J	SWH	77074
DUNLAP	10600	531S	SWH	77096
DUNLAP	11400	571A	SWH	77035
DUNLAP	12000	570M	SWH	77035
DUNLAP FIELD LN	0	526J	NEF	77407
DUNLAP MEADOWS LN	25200	485S	NEF	77494
DUNLAVY	600	492V	SWH	77019
DUNLAVY	1500	492V	SWH	77006
DUNLAVY CT	1100	616X	PL	77581
DUNLAVY DR	3800	616X	PL	77581
DUNLAVY LN	0	657Y	LC	77573
DUNLAY SPRINGS DR	0	406H	NWC	77433
DUNLEIGH MEADOWS LN	0	492A	NWH	77055
DUNLEITH CIR	16500	367G	NWC	77429
DUNLEITH LN	5200	331E	NWC	77379
DUNLIN MEADOW CT	1	251E	WD	77381
DUNLIN MEADOW DR	1	251E	WD	77381
DUNLOGGIN LN	1	251P	WD	77381
DUNLOP	5100	453U	NEH	77009
DUNMAN LN	15900	418T	NEC	77044
DUNMAN RD	7800	375L	NEC	77396
DUNMOOR DR	15700	578Y	SEH	77059
DUNMORE CT	13300	370D	NWC	77069
DUNN	4400	494L	NEH	77020
DUNN	20700	256S	SEM	77357
DUNN	20700	256T	SEM	77357
DUNN CIR	2600	538Q	DP	77536
DUNN DR	0	419K	NEC	77532
DUNN LN	23300	296E	SEM	77365
DUNNAM LN	1	490K	BH	77024
DUNNAM PLACE	1	297U	NEH	77345
DUNNEL RIDGE LN	16200	326V	NWC	77429
DUNNETHEAD DR	5000	407Z	NWC	77084
DUNNON BAY POINT CT	18000	327W	NWC	77429
DUNOON BAY POINT CT	0	327W	NWC	77429
DUNRAVEN LN	2200	492U	SWH	77019
DUNRICH CT	2900	660L	LC	77573
DUNSFORD CT	16800	527E	NEF	77083

Street Name	Block	Pg/Sq	Loc	Zips
DUNSINANE	11500	490G	PP	77024
DUNSLEY DR	5800	407W	NWC	77449
DUNSMERE	2800	452Q	NWH	77018
DUNSMERE	5400	452G	NWH	77091
DUNSMERE CT	2700	613T	NEB	77584
DUNSMORE CLIFF TRACE	0	326T	NWC	77433
DUNSMORE GLEN CROSSING	0	616H	SEC	77089
DUNSMORE HARBOR	0	406W	NWC	77449
DUNSMORE LANDING DR	0	578U	SEH	77059
DUNSMORE MANOR CT	0	253T	SEM	77386
DUNSMORE PLACE	14400	368A	NWC	77429
DUNSMORE RIVER TRAIL	0	405P	NWC	77493
DUNSMORE SPRINGS LN	0	291A	NWC	77389
DUNSON GLEN DR	500	332X	NWC	77090
DUNSTABLE LN	15100	458W	NEC	77530
DUNSTAN	1700	532D	SWH	77005
DUNSTAN RD	1100	536V	PA	77502
DUNSTAN RD	1300	537S	PA	77502
DUNSTER LN	14900	457Z	NEC	77530
DUNSTON FALLS DR	1200	329B	NWC	77379
DUNVALE RD	2700	490U	SWH	77063
DUNVEGAN WAY	10000	495H	NEH	77013
DUNVEGAN WAY	10300	496F	NEH	77013
DUNWELL CT	800	252P	SEM	77386
DUNWICK	5900	574U	SEH	77048
DUNWICK LN	300	536Y	PA	77502
DUNWOOD DR	1100	247K	SWM	77362
DUNWOODY DR	700	413Y	NEH	77076
DUOTO	5300	452A	NWH	77091
DUPONT	2400	537Z	PA	77503
DUPONT	4100	533M	SEH	77021
DUPREE	2800	533K	SWH	77054
DUQUESNE LN	3700	577C	PA	77505
DURAL DR	18400	486D	SWC	77094
DURAN DR	2700	613S	NEB	77584
DURAN CANYON CT	11900	371L	NWC	77067
DURAN CANYON LN	11900	371L	NWC	77067
DURAND OAK CT	20800	326S	NWC	77433
DURAND OAK DR	20700	326S	NWC	77433
DURAN FALLS CT	13800	377Y	NEC	77044
DURANGO DR	0	615T	PL	77581
DURANGO DR	1400	450Y	NWH	77055
DURANGO BAY LN	6100	409W	NWC	77041
DURANGO BEND LN	0	657K	FR	77546
DURANGO CANYON LN	0	253P	SEM	77386
DURANGO CANYON LN	0	484X	NEF	77494
DURANGO CANYON LN	0	484X	NEF	77494
DURANGO CREEK LN	6900	406P	NWC	77449
DURANGO FALLS LN	25600	524F	NEF	77494
DURANGO LODGE LN	0	526P	NEF	77407
DURANGO LODGE LN		526Q	NEF	77406
DURANGO MIST LN	0	406Z	NWC	77449
DURANGO PASS DR	0	612J	PL	77545
DURANGO PATH LN	0	366Y	NWC	77433
DURANGO POINT CT	0	328M	NWC	77377
DURANGO POINT LN	0	329V	NWC	77070
DURANGO RIDGE WAY	9500	410F	NWC	77040
DURANGO VALLEY LN	0	406B	NWC	77433
DURANT	4300	538X	DP	77536
DURANZO CT	2200	660F	LC	77573
DURBAN DR	2600	449M	NWH	77043
DURBAN DR	4400	449H	NWH	77041
DURBAN OAKS DR	0	484V	NEF	77494
DURBRIDGE CT	10600	368Y	NWC	77065
DURBRIDGE TRAIL DR	13000	368Y	NWC	77065
DURFEY LN	1500	445V	NWC	77449
DURFORD DR	6200	492F	SWH	77007
DURHAM CT	0	258G	SEM	77357
N. DURHAM DR	700	492C	NWH	77008
N. DURHAM DR	1000	452U	NWH	77008
N. DURHAM DR	3000	452U	NWH	77018
DURHAM CANYON LN	0	406G	NWB	77433
DURHAM CHASE LN	0	408G	NWC	77095
DURHAM CHASE LN	2700	446N	NWC	77449
DURHAM COVE LN	0	327U	NWC	77429
DURHAM HILL LN		328P	NWC	77449
DURHAM KNOLL LN	5100	291J	NWC	77389
DURHAMMANOR LN	0	575U	SEH	77075
DURHAM RIDGE LN	0	376H	NEC	77346
DURHAM RUN LN	0	526L	NEF	77407
DURHAM TRACE DR	24500	293S	NCC	77373
DURHILL	3200	532P	SWH	77025
DURKLYN LN	8000	329Z	NWC	77070
DURLEY DR	600	489F	SWH	77079
DURNESS WAY	3300	532J	SWH	77025
DURR	100	620Y	KE	77565
DURR	200	660C	KE	77565
DURRAIN FERRY RD	1800	541A	BT	77520
DURRETT DR	0	286E	SWM	77447
DURRETTE DR	11700	490K	SWH	77024
S. DURRETTE DR	11900	490J	SWH	77024
N. DURRETTE DR	11900	490J	SWH	77024
DURWOOD	2900	414S	NEH	77093
DURWOOD PINES LN	0	366V	NWC	77433
DUSK ST	0	373J	NCC	77060
DUSK HAVEN LN	17000	367Y	NWC	77095
DUSK VALLEY CT	8210	329D	NWC	77379
DUSKY LILAC TRAIL	0	325R	NWC	77433
DUSKY MEADOW PLACE	1	250D	WD	77381
DUSKY ROSE LN	900	536U	PA	77502
DUSTIN	0	420M	NEC	77532
DUSTIN	4401	420M	NEC	77532
DUSTIN	4401	420M	NEC	77532
DUSTIN LN	26900	248E	SWM	77354
DUSTIN PLACE CT	2500	375K	NEC	77396
DUSTY CT	0	612Z	NEB	77578
DUSTY CANYON LN	0	526L	NEF	77407
DUSTY CREEK DR	19700	406U	NWC	77449
DUSTY DAWN DR	6600	371X	NWC	77086
DUSTY GLEN LN	21100	290T	NWC	77379
DUSTY HEATH LN	0	525D	NEF	77450
DUSTY HOLLOW LN	10200	616G	SEC	77089
DUSTY MANOR LN	9700	524F	NEF	77494
DUSTY MEADOW LN	0	609P	NEF	77479
DUSTY PATH LN	16100	327Y	NWC	77429
DUSTY PATTY CT	17700	527N	NEF	77407
DUSTY RIDGE CT	0	610K	MC	77459
DUSTY RIDGE LN	9700	416Z	NEC	77044
DUSTY ROSE CIR	7000	609P	MC	77459
DUSTY ROSE CT	0	253J	SEM	77385
DUSTY ROSE CT	0	657S	FR	77546
DUSTY ROSE LN	18800	328G	NWC	77377
DUSTY TERRACE LN	18100	407S	NWC	77449
DUSTY TRACE CT	0	615B	PL	77581
DUSTY TRACE CT	0	615B	PL	77581
DUSTY TRAIL DR	10700	371S	NWC	77086
DUSTY YAUPON LN	19500	406M	NWC	77433
DUTCH AVE	800	538K	DP	77536
DUTCH HARBOR LN	0	377E	NEC	77346
DUTCH OAK CIR	8000	330J	NWC	77379
DUTTON HILL CT	22100	332Q	NCC	77073
DUTTON POINT CT	0	445S	NWC	77493

Street Name	Block	Pg/Sq	Loc	Zips
DUTTON POINT DR	0	445S	NWC	77493
DUTTON TRACE LN	16300	527B	SWC	77082
DUVAL	4000	534M	SEH	77087
DUVAL	4000	534L	SEH	77087
DUXBURY	5500	571A	SWH	77035
DUXBURY	6000	570D	SWH	77035
DWARF HONEYSUCKLE CT	0	446D	NWC	77084
DWIGHT	900	496M	NEH	77015
DWINELL	1000	537M	PA	77503
DWINELL	5700	534C	SEH	77023
DWINNELL	500	502W	BT	77520
DWIRE DR	1	580Q	LP	77571
DWYER DR	5800	374V	NEH	77396
DYCHE CT	2800	454S	NEH	77026
DYER	1	501U	BT	77520
DYER	7400	412S	NWH	77088
DYER BROOK DR	6000	408Z	NWC	77041
DYER GLEN	10300	369K	NWC	77070
DYER LAKE LN	0	452Y	NWH	77008
DYERSVILLE CT	0	293U	NCC	77373
DYLAN DR	5800	502G	BT	77521
DYLAN LN	0	538V	DP	77536
DYLAN HILLS LN	0	328G	NWC	77377
DYLAN LANDING CIR		366U	NWC	77433
DYLANS CROSSING DR	0	411D	NWC	77038
DYLANS POINT CT	17600	447G	NWC	77084
DYLAN SPRINGS LN	6400	525H	NEF	77450
W. DYNA DR	100	372Z	NEH	77037
DYNA DR	100	373W	NEH	77060
DYNASTY DR	0	405W	NWC	77493
DYSON LN	11000	409U	NWC	77041

E

Street Name	Block	Pg/Sq	Loc	Zips
E	0	659E	LC	77573
E. A	100	540Y	LP	77571
E. B	100	540Z	LP	77571
E. C	200	540Y	LP	77571
E. D	100	580C	LP	77571
E. E	100	580C	LP	77571
E. E	1100	540Z	MP	77571
E. E	2800	580Q	LP	77571
E AVE	0	410P	NWC	77040
E RD	0	532M	SWH	77030
E STREET	0	282T	WL	77484
E, AVENUE	0	568J	SG	77498
E, AVENUE	0	619S	SEH	77058
S. E, AVENUE	100	335Z	HM	77338
N. E, AVENUE	100	335V	HM	77338
E, AVENUE	100	459U	HG	77562
E, AVENUE	100	536X	SH	77587
E, AVENUE	100	569Q	SF	77477
E, AVENUE	1800	496W	NEH	77547
E, AVENUE	5700	419G	CB	77532
E, AVENUE	6500	494V	SEH	77011
E, AVENUE	7500	495W	SEH	77012
E, AVENUE RD	100	569T	NEF	77478
E, B F DR	0	338Z	NEC	77336
EAGAN MILL DR	13600	488P	SWH	77077
EAGAR DR	0	658X	LC	77573
EAGLE	100	536H	PA	77506
EAGLE	1000	493X	SWH	77002
EAGLE	1100	493Y	SEH	77004
EAGLE	1800	658Q	LC	77573
EAGLE	3600	533D	SEH	77004
EAGLE CT	1	251R	WD	77380
EAGLE CT	3000	610B	MC	77489
EAGLE CT	10600	503H	CCO	77520
EAGLE CT	10600	463S	CCO	77520
EAGLE DR	6800	463C	MB	77580
EAGLE LN	0	580K	LP	77571
EAGLE LN	7500	290S	NWC	77379
EAGLE BEND	0	291S	NWC	77379
EAGLE BEND	20900	486S	NEF	77450
EAGLE BEND DR	20000	290V	NWC	77379
EAGLEBEND LN	4900	485Y	NEF	77494
EAGLE BLUFF CT	4000	527C	SWC	77082
EAGLE BROOK LN	6500	290Y	NWC	77379
EAGLE CANYON WAY	19700	526B	NEF	77450
EAGLE CHASE LN	25600	250T	NWC	77389
EAGLECLIFF CT	18100	526M	NEF	77407
EAGLE COVE	28000	246F	SWM	77355
EAGLE COVE DR	0	612K	PL	77545
EAGLECOVE DR	8900	409H	NWC	77064
EAGLE CREEK DR	0	656R	FR	77546
EAGLE CREEK DR	2800	297Y	NEH	77345
EAGLE CREEK LN	9300	529R	SWH	77036
EAGLE CREST DR	0	485K	NEF	77494
EAGLECREST DR	1600	333N	NCC	77073
EAGLE CREST LN	0	613L	PL	77584
EAGLE CROSSING	0	333D	NCC	77373
EAGLE EYE LN	9600	527T	NEF	77498
EAGLE FALLS	0	656R	FR	77546
EAGLE FALLS CT	1800	489N	SWH	77077
EAGLE FALLS DR	1800	489N	SWH	77077
EAGLE FIELDS DR	5400	326U	NWC	77429
EAGLE FORK CT	0	539Y	LP	77571
EAGLE FORK DR	4300	448E	NWC	77084
EAGLE GLEN DR	10400	449H	NWH	77041
EAGLE GROVE LN	20100	291W	NWC	77379
EAGLE HAVEN DR	0	485E	SWC	77494
EAGLE HOLLOW DR	0	376B	NEC	77369
EAGLE HOLLOW LN	0	657Y	LC	77573
EAGLE ISLAND LN	11800	576L	SEH	77034
EAGLE LAKE DR	100	657J	FR	77546
EAGLE LAKE DR	2900	615Y	PL	77581
EAGLE LAKES DR	100	656R	FR	77546
EAGLE LANDING	0	571L	SWH	77085
EAGLE LEDGE DR	17200	328Q	NWC	77377
EAGLE LEDGE LN	12700	328Q	NWC	77377
EAGLE MEADOW DR	22000	485M	SWC	77450
EAGLE MILLER DR	0	369H	NWC	77070
EAGLE MILLS CT	20200	335N	NCC	77338
EAGLE MOUNTAIN CT	4400	526W	NEF	77406
EAGLE NEST CT	10500	579C	LP	77571
EAGLE NEST CT	20300	446P	NWC	77449
EAGLE NEST DR	3100	579C	LP	77571
EAGLE NEST DR	3150	539Y	LP	77571
EAGLE NEST LN	0	253J	SEM	77385
EAGLE NEST LN	0	657S	FR	77546
EAGLENEST LN	2600	375L	HM	77396
EAGLE PASS	0	494D	NEH	77020
EAGLE PASS	7100	495A	NEH	77020
EAGLE PASS	13700	497B	NEC	77015
EAGLE PASS FALLS CT	0	377B	NEC	77346
EAGLE PEAK CT	9700	524G	NEF	77494
EAGLE PINES LN	25900	250T	NWC	77389
EAGLE POINT RD	1700	378C	NEC	77532
EAGLE POINT TRAIL DR	2900	446U	NWC	77449
EAGLE RIDGE DR	6800	406R	NWC	77449
EAGLE RIDGE DR	28400	246B	SWM	77355
EAGLE RIDGE WAY	3100	446R	NWC	77084

Street Name	Block	Pg/Sq	Loc	Zips
EAGLE RISE PLACE	1	250A	WD	77382
EAGLE ROCK CIR	1	250D	WD	77381
EAGLEROCK CIR	2800	610E	MC	77489
EAGLE ROCK CT	100	250D	WD	77381
EAGLE ROCK CT	10500	579C	LP	77571
EAGLE ROCK DR	2000	450N	NWH	77080
EAGLE ROCK PLACE	1	250D	WD	77381
EAGLE RUN	8900	578D	LP	77571
EAGLES DR	0	411Q	NWH	77088
EAGLE SAGE LN	0	445N	NWC	77493
EAGLES BRANCH DR	0	376U	NEC	77396
EAGLES BROOK CT	0	406C	NWC	77433
EAGLES COVE	100	657J	FR	77546
EAGLES GLEN DR	0	330Z	NWC	77069
EAGLES GLIDE DR	700	372B	NWC	77090
EAGLE SHORE TRAIL	0	376W	NEC	77396
EAGLES KNOLL CT	3200	485U	NEF	77494
EAGLE SKY BLVD	0	406X	NWC	77449
EAGLES LANDING	26700	299T	NEC	77336
EAGLES LEDGE CT	0	333K	NCC	77338
EAGLE SPRINGS PARKWAY	18100	377B	NEC	77346
EAGLE SPRINGS PARKWAY	18500	337X	NEC	77346
EAGLES REST	20600	290S	NWC	77379
EAGLES RUN DR	0	256T	SEM	77357
EAGLESTONE CT	3200	291U	NWC	77388
EAGLES WALK	3800	485U	NEF	77450
EAGLES WAY	2300	616K	PL	77581
EAGLES WING	1	248F	SWM	77354
EAGLE TALON CT	24500	484M	NEF	77494
EAGLETON LN	10000	460A	NEC	77532
EAGLETON LN	11900	420S	BR	77532
EAGLE TRAIL DR	0	406G	NWC	77433
EAGLE TRAIL DR	4700	448A	NWC	77084
EAGLET TRAIL	0	614Y	PL	77584
EAGLE VALLEY DR	0	326U	NWC	77429
EAGLE VIEW DR	11300	371R	NWC	77067
EAGLE VISTA DR	14700	488J	SWH	77077
EAGLE WATCH CT	22800	485Q	NEF	77450
EAGLEWOOD CT	3400	613Y	NEB	77584
EAGLEWOOD DR	3200	613Y	NEB	77584
EAGLEWOOD DR	11500	616C	SEC	77089
EAGLEWOOD FOREST DR	0	295M	SEM	77365
EAGLEWOOD GLEN TRAIL	9200	527P	NEF	77083
EAGLEWOOD GREEN LN	6400	290Y	NWC	77379
EAGLEWOOD SHADOWS CT	9300	527Q	NEF	77083
EAGLEWOOD SHADOWS DR	16300	527Q	NEF	77083
EAGLEWOOD SPRING CT	16100	527Q	NEF	77083
EAGLEWOOD SPRING DR	9200	527Q	NEF	77083
EAGLEWOOD TRACE	0	295M	SEM	77365
EARHART	7900	455P	NEH	77028
EARL	3000	492T	SWH	77098
EARL	3000	537G	PA	77503
EARLE	1000	532M	SWH	77030
EARLHAM DR	1	657A	FR	77546
EARLINE	4500	454G	NEH	77016
EARLINGTON MANOR CT	1400	329C	NWC	77379
EARLINGTON MANOR DR	10100	329C	NWC	77379
EARLMIST DR	22700	333E	NCC	77373
EARLMIST DR	23000	333A	NCC	77373
EARL OF DUNMORE LN	1500	445V	NWC	77449
EARL PORTER DR	0	463B	MB	77520
EARLS COURT DR	500	485C	SWC	77450
EARLSFERRY DR	900	497D	NEC	77530
EARLSFERRY DR	1000	457Z	NEC	77530
EARLSWOOD DR	14700	527R	NEF	77083
EARLWOOD CT	0	615W	PL	77584
EARLY LN	1500	451X	NWH	77055
EARLY AUTUMN CT	4500	375V	NEC	77396
EARLY BREEZE PLACE	0	446Q	NWC	77084
EARLY DAWN CT	1	251J	WD	77381
EARLY DEW CT	0	572Q	SWH	77045
EARLY EDGE LN		484W	NEF	77494
EARLY ELM CT	0	457L	NEC	77049
EARLY FALL DR	6500	334P	NCC	77338
EARLY FOREST LN	11500	489A	NWH	77043
EARLY HARVEST CIR	11000	369Z	NWC	77064
EARLY HOLLOW LN	14700	368E	NWC	77429
EARLY HORIZON CT	0	574K	SEH	77048
EARLY LIGHT CT	0	293Y	NCC	77373
EARLY LIGHT CT	0	293Y	NCC	77373
EARLY MAPLE CT	0	445N	NWC	77493
EARLY MIST CT	11500	369V	NWC	77064
EARLY MORNING DR	0	574P	SEH	77048
EARLY SPRING CIR	11200	369U	NWC	77064
EARLY SPRING DR	9800	369U	NWC	77064
EARLY SQUARE CT	10400	369G	NWC	77070
EARLY TURN CT	2800	657C	SEC	77598
EARLY TURN DR	2800	657C	SEC	77598
EARLY WALK WAY	0	537V	PA	77503
EARLY WINTER DR	0	334K	NCC	77338
EARLYWOOD LN	12800	368J	NWC	77429
EARNESTWOOD DR	8800	528P	SWC	77083
EARTHSTONE DR	24000	525A	NEF	77494
EASINGWOLD DR	14800	457Z	NEC	77015
EASINGWOLD DR	15000	457V	NEC	77530
EASLEY	19100	252A	SD	77385
EAST	0	494J	SEH	77003
EAST	0	501S	BT	77520
EAST	0	580C	LP	77571
EAST	200	502N	BT	77520
EAST	1200	493E	SWH	77007
EAST	7000	460Y	MN	77521
EAST	21300	256S	SEM	77357
EAST AVE	800	444Y	KT	77493
EAST BLVD	0	538R	DP	77536
EAST CT	3900	538U	DP	77536
EAST DR	0	658Z	LC	77573
EAST DR	200	619V	LC	77565
EAST DR	300	493M	SEH	77003
EAST DR	14900	254A	SEM	77302
EAST (I.H. 10 E) FRWY	0	459Y	CV	77530
EAST (I.H. 10 E) FRWY	0	460Z	NEC	77521
EAST (I.H. 10 E) FRWY	0	461V	NEC	77521
EAST (I.H. 10 E) FRWY	0	462S	NEC	77521
EAST (I.H. 10 E) FRWY	0	463N	CCO	77520
EAST (I.H. 10 E) FRWY	1000	493L	DT	77002
EAST (I.H. 10 E) FRWY	1500	494H	NEH	77020
EAST (I.H. 10 E) FRWY	1500	494H	NEH	77020
EAST (I.H. 10 E) FRWY	1700	460Z	NEC	77521
EAST (I.H. 10 E) FRWY	4300	461V	NEC	77521
EAST (I.H. 10 E) FRWY	7100	462S	NEC	77521
EAST (I.H. 10 E) FRWY	7800	495F	NEH	77029
EAST (I.H. 10 E) FRWY	7800	495F	NEH	77029
EAST (I.H. 10 E) FRWY	10000	463N	CCO	77520
EAST (I.H. 10 E) FRWY	10300	496F	NEH	77029
EAST (I.H. 10 E) FRWY	10300	496F	NEH	77029
EAST (I.H. 10 E) FRWY	12200	496F	NEH	77015
EAST (I.H. 10 E) FRWY	12200	496F	NEH	77015
EAST (I.H. 10 E) FRWY	13100	497K	NEC	77015
EAST (I.H. 10 E) FRWY	13100	497K	NEC	77015
EAST (I.H. 10 E) FRWY	15000	498E	CV	77530
EAST (I.H. 10 E) FRWY	15000	498E	CV	77530
EAST (I.H. 10 E) FRWY	17000	499B	NEC	77530
EAST (I.H. 10 E) FRWY	17000	499B	NEC	77530
EAST (I.H. 10 E) FRWY	17500	459Y	CV	77530
EAST LN	3900	454X	NEH	77026
EAST RD	1400	610A	MC	77489
EAST RD	1800	533J	SWH	77054
EAST RD	5000	501G	BT	77521
EAST BAY BLVD	0	251G	SWM	77380
EAST BELT	0	417N	NEC	77044
EAST BELT	0	497H	NEC	77015
EAST BELTWAY	0	537M	PA	77503
EASTBOURNE DR	13700	577W	SEH	77034
EASTBOURNE LN	1100	613L	NEB	77584
EASTBROOK DR	12400	496C	NEH	77013
EASTCAPE CT	400	618N	SEH	77598
EASTCAPE DR	15500	618N	SEH	77598
EAST CHASE	0	461T	NEC	77521
EAST COPPER LAKES CT	17000	407G	NWC	77095
EAST COPPER LAKES DR	8000	407G	NWC	77095
EASTCOVE CIR	8900	409H	NWC	77064
EASTCREST PARK DR	13900	367D	NWC	77429
EASTEN	12600	371H	NWC	77014
EASTER	5900	452A	NWH	77091
EASTER	6200	412S	NWH	77088
EASTERLING DR	11500	368P	NWC	77065
EASTERLY LN		366U	NWC	77433
EASTERN BLUEBIRD DR	7800	375Q	NEC	77396
EASTERN FORK CT	0	366L	NWC	77433
EASTERN REDBUD LN	14300	377X	NEC	77044
EASTERN RUN TRAIL	2700	371Z	NWC	77038
EASTERWOOD TRAIL LN		289G	NWC	77375
EASTEX (U.S. 59 N) FRWY	0	256Q	SEM	77357
EASTEX (U.S. 59 N) FRWY	0	256Q	SEM	77357
EASTEX (U.S. 59 N) FRWY	0	257A	SEM	77357
EASTEX (U.S. 59 N) FRWY	0	257A	SEM	77357
EASTEX (U.S. 59 N) FRWY	100	494A	NEH	77020
EASTEX (U.S. 59 N) FRWY	100	494A	NEH	77020
EASTEX (U.S. 59 N) FRWY	1800	494A	NEH	77026
EASTEX (U.S. 59 N) FRWY	1800	494A	NEH	77026
EASTEX (U.S. 59 N) FRWY	3100	454P	NEH	77026
EASTEX (U.S. 59 N) FRWY	3100	454P	NEH	77026
EASTEX (U.S. 59 N) FRWY	6600	454P	NEH	77093
EASTEX (U.S. 59 N) FRWY	6600	454P	NEH	77093
EASTEX (U.S. 59 N) FRWY	10100	414L	NCC	77093
EASTEX (U.S. 59 N) FRWY	10100	414L	NCC	77093
EASTEX (U.S. 59 N) FRWY	11700	414L	NCC	77039
EASTEX (U.S. 59 N) FRWY	11700	414L	NCC	77039
EASTEX (U.S. 59 N) FRWY	14000	375F	NEC	77396
EASTEX (U.S. 59 N) FRWY	14000	375F	NEC	77396
EASTEX (U.S. 59 N) FRWY	14001	375F	NCC	77032
EASTEX (U.S. 59 N) FRWY	14001	375F	NCC	77032
EASTEX (U.S. 59 N) FRWY	14400	375F	NEH	77396
EASTEX (U.S. 59 N) FRWY	14400	375F	NEH	77396
EASTEX (U.S. 59 N) FRWY	18100	335U	HM	77338
EASTEX (U.S. 59 N) FRWY	18100	335U	HM	77338
EASTEX (U.S. 59 N) FRWY	21000	335H	NEH	77339
EASTEX (U.S. 59 N) FRWY	21000	335H	NEH	77339
EASTEX (U.S. 59 N) FRWY	23000	296K	SEM	77365
EASTEX (U.S. 59 N) FRWY	23000	296K	SEM	77365
EASTFIELD CIR	2000	610F	MC	77459
EAST FIELD DR	0	617V	SEH	77598
EASTGATE	100	495W	SEH	77012
EASTGATE VILLAGE DR	22900	292L	NCC	77373
EASTGROVE LN	2600	492S	SWH	77027
EASTHAMPTON DR	5300	414H	NEC	77039
EAST HARDY	0	292L	SP	77373
EASTHAVEN BLVD	6600	535Z	SEH	77017
EASTHAVEN BLVD	8000	575D	SEH	77034
EASTHAVEN BLVD	8400	575H	SEH	77075
EASTHAVEN BLVD	10000	575R	SEH	77075
EASTHAVEN DR	1500	537N	PA	77506
EASTHEIMER	8800	370S	NWC	77064
EASTLAKE	300	576F	SEH	77034
EASTLAND	2100	658U	LC	77573
EASTLAND	5000	455P	NEH	77028
EASTLAND CT	2100	658T	LC	77573
EASTLEIGH LN	6600	457P	NEC	77049
EASTLOCH DR	0	329H	NWC	77379
EAST LOOP (I.H. 610) N.	0	495Q	NEH	77029
EAST LOOP (I.H. 610) S.	0	535C	SEH	77012
EASTMAN	1100	536Q	PA	77506
EASTMAN	2400	453T	NWH	77009
EASTMAN	3000	453P	NWH	77022
EASTMAN PLACE	19900	446L	NWC	77449
EASTMONT LN	1900	570S	MC	77489
EASTMOORE CT	13900	372A	NWC	77014
EASTON	7800	535K	SEH	77017
EASTON BEND LN	26200	367J	NWC	77433
EASTON COMMONS DR	8400	408F	NWC	77095
EASTON GATE LN	0	377U	NEC	77044
EASTON GROVE LN	0	615H	PL	77089
EASTON MEADOWS DR	18300	328K	NWC	77377
EASTON PARK DR	15100	408J	NWC	77095
EASTON POINT DR	0	524S	NWF	77406
EASTON SKY LN	0	366Y	NWC	77433
EASTON SPRINGS	0	612M	PL	77584
EASTOVER	8200	455K	NEH	77028
EASTPARK DR	4300	454V	NEH	77028
EASTPOINT BLVD	8100	461S	NEC	77521
EAST RIDGE	8200	410L	NWC	77040
EASTRIDGE DR	0	253S	SEM	77386
EAST SAM HOUSTON PKWY S.	0	577P	SEH	77034
EAST SAM HOUSTON PKWY	100	498W	NEC	77015
EAST SAM HOUSTON PKWY S.	100	537V	PA	77503
EAST SAM HOUSTN PKWY S.	3100	577P	PA	77505
EAST SAM HOUSTN PKWY N.	4800	457A	NEC	77015
EAST SAM HOUSTN PKWY N.	5600	457A	NEC	77049
EAST SAM HOUSTN PKWY N.	8200	457A	NEC	77044
EAST SAM HOUSTN PKWY N.	9200	416H	NEC	77044
EASTSHORE	4000	609C	MC	77459
EAST SHORE DR	0	251F	SWM	77380
EASTSIDE	2500	492T	SWH	77019
EASTSIDE	3000	492T	SWH	77098
EAST TIMBERLOCH TRAIL	31100	246Y	SWM	77355
EASTTOWN LN	0	297F	SEM	77365
EASTVALE DR	1600	252V	SEM	77386
EASTWAY	100	496W	GP	77547
EASTWAY VILLAGE DR	100	335U	HM	77338
EASTWICK LN	3100	578D	LP	77571
EASTWIND DR	1900	538K	DP	77536
EASTWOOD	1	494T	SEH	77011
N. EASTWOOD	100	494P	SEH	77011
EASTWOOD	600	494S	SEH	77023
EASTWOOD	5800	533M	SEH	77021
EASTWOOD CIR	17400	407K	NWC	77095
EASTWOOD CT	900	569S	SG	77478
EASTWOOD DR	400	257C	WV	77357
EASTWOOD DR	26700	252J	OR	77386
EASTWOOD HILLS DR	26100	252K	SEM	77385
EASTWOOD LAKE CT	1900	336B	HM	77339
EASTWOOD LAKE LN	7500	525G	NEF	77407
EASY	800	539Q	LP	77571
EASY	2500	537P	PA	77502
EASY	3400	494C	NEH	77026
EASY	3600	454Y	NEH	77026
EASY	3900	659Z	GCO	77539
EASYBROOK LN	7500	330F	NWC	77379
EASY JET DR	600	570S	SF	77477
EASY STREET	36100	246L	SWM	77355
EASY WIND LN	0	449T	NWH	77043
EATON	1300	532M	SWH	77030
EATON CT	1	490K	BH	77024
EATON CREEK TRAIL	0	406X	NWC	77449
EATON CREEK TRAIL CT	0	406X	NWC	77449
EATON GLEN LN	0	407V	NWC	77084
EATON SQUARE	1	491R	SWH	77027
EAVES DR	2100	502S	BT	77520
EBB	9700	576W	SEH	77089
EBBETS FIELD DR	22300	291K	NWC	77389
EBBTIDE DR	2800	572L	SWH	77045
EBERHARD	900	493N	SWH	77019
EBERHART STAR CT	1600	484L	NEF	77494
EBERSBERG WAY	0	328N	NWC	77429
EBEYS LANDING LN	17400	376H	NEC	77346
EBLE	0	368F	NWC	77429
EBLEN DR	9300	410R	NWH	77040
EBONY LN	1300	452N	NWH	77018
EBONY OAKS PLACE	0	249C	SWM	77382
EBURY DR	3800	371P	NWC	77066
ECHELON	0	446S	NWC	77449
ECHINACEA DR	0	461T	NEC	77521
ECHO AVE	100	656D	FR	77546
ECHO LN	100	298Z	NEH	77336
ECHO LN	700	490C	HE	77024
ECHO LN	2700	251U	WD	77380
ECHO LN	19800	257L	SEM	77357
ECHO BEND DR	0	250D	WD	77381
ECHOBEND LN	17800	330F	NWC	77379
S. ECHO BRANCH	0	609Z	MC	77459
N. ECHO BRANCH	0	609Z	MC	77459
ECHO BROOK DR	6600	413W	NEH	77076
ECHO BROOK DR	7600	413S	NEH	77037
ECHO BROOK LN	0	658Z	LC	77573
ECHO CANYON CT	0	253K	SEM	77386
ECHO CANYON DR	12000	328G	NWC	77377
ECHO CANYON DR	15600	448B	NWC	77084
ECHOCHASE DR	14600	570V	SWH	77489
ECHO CLEARING CT	0	376H	NEC	77346
ECHO CREEK LN	900	570P	MC	77489
ECHO FALLS DR	4300	297T	NEH	77345
ECHO FALLS DR	20100	486G	SWC	77450
ECHO FALLS LN	10400	367X	NWC	77095
ECHOGLADE CT	9500	409D	NWC	77064
W. ECHO GLEN DR	100	412Z	NEH	77076
E. ECHO GLEN DR	100	413W	NEH	77076
ECHO GROVE LN	3500	449L	NWH	77043
ECHO HARBOR	16900	617X	SEC	77546
ECHO HARBOR DR	0	612L	PL	77584
ECHO HEIGHTS DR	16800	366P	NWC	77433
ECHO HILL DR	15700	618C	SEH	77059
ECHO HOLLOW	11500	490G	HE	77024
ECHO HOLLOW	32700	246V	SWM	77355
ECHO LAKE CT	0	330X	NWC	77069
ECHO LAKE LN	5900	330X	NWC	77069
ECHO LAKES CIR	4000	609L	MC	77459
ECHO LAKES LN	6200	609L	MC	77459
ECHO LANDING DR	0	369M	NWC	77070
ECHO LEDGE	11400	372N	NWC	77067
ECHO LODGE DR	15700	408J	NWC	77095
ECHO LODGE DR	15900	407M	NWC	77095
ECHOLS RD	1500	502W	BT	77520
ECHO MANOR DR	0	285Q	NWC	77447
ECHO MAR LN	0	407X	NWC	77084
ECHO MOUNTAIN DR	3200	297T	NEH	77345
ECHO PEAKS LN	9400	375V	NEC	77396
ECHO PINES DR	7100	337Y	NEC	77346
ECHO POINT LN	7600	407M	NWC	77095
ECHO RIDGE	2000	568Z	SG	77478
ECHO RIDGE CT	2000	296Y	NEH	77339
ECHO SPRING LN	11600	369P	NWC	77065
ECHO STABLE LN	0	327U	NWC	77429
ECHO STREAM PLACE	2900	447N	NWC	77084
ECHOTA DR	0	291N	NWC	77388
ECHO VALLEY DR	8800	490D	SV	77055
ECHOWAY CT	9400	409D	NWC	77064
ECHOWAY DR	9400	409D	NWC	77064
ECHO WOODS	11500	490G	HE	77024
ECLIPSE	0	452E	NWH	77018
ECLIPSE	2200	451H	NWH	77018
ECRU HILLS DR	0	406P	NWC	77433
ECTOR	0	411E	NWH	77086
ECTOR	3100	491X	SWH	77056
ECUADOR DR	3900	577A	PA	77504
ED DR	21600	285D	SWM	77355
EDAY LN	9600	329R	NWC	77379
EDDIE	3600	494B	NEH	77026
EDDIE DR	6000	375S	NEH	77396
EDDIE DR	14800	375S	NEH	77396
EDDINGTON	700	494T	SEH	77023
EDDLEMONT DR	16400	458S	NEC	77049
EDDLEWOOD CT	1900	458S	NEC	77049
EDDY	100	336W	HM	77338
EDDY'S EDGE CT	9500	616E	SEC	77089
EDDYROCK DR	10800	576T	SEH	77089
EDDYSTONE DR	10100	449V	NWH	77043
EDELL	9300	454A	NEH	77093
EDELWEISS DR	0	659H	LC	77573
EDEN	7200	535E	SEH	77012
EDEN CT	17300	329M	NWC	77379
EDENA DR	1700	458S	NEC	77049
EDENBRIDGE CT	17300	329M	NWC	77379
EDENBRIDGE DR	9000	329M	NWC	77379
EDEN COVE CT	7000	609P	MC	77459
EDEN COVE LN	0	612U	PL	77584
EDEN CREEK DR	0	612M	PL	77584
EDEN CREST CT	5700	525R	NEF	77407
EDEN CROSSING LN	7300	526M	NEF	77407
EDENDALE CIR	1	245D	SWM	77355
EDENDALE CIR	2000	485R	SWC	77450
EDENDERRY CT	4500	569X	MC	77459
EDENDERRY LN	1300	569X	MC	77459
EDEN ELM PLACE	1	250D	WD	77381
EDEN FALLS CIR	17300	407Q	NWC	77095
EDEN FALLS CT	17200	407Q	NWC	77095
EDENGLEN CT	6300	457N	NEC	77049
EDENGLEN DR	13900	456R	NEC	77049
EDENGLEN DR	14400	457N	NEC	77049
EDEN GLENN LN	0	615F	PL	77581
EDENGROVE DR	0	328L	NWC	77377
EDENHOLLOW CT	6300	457N	NEC	77049
EDEN KNOLL LN	0	377U	NEC	77044
EDEN MANOR LN	13800	417D	NEC	77044
EDEN MEADOWS DR	0	293K	SEM	77386
EDEN PARK CT	8000	525Z	NEF	77406
EDEN PARK LN	0	452G	NWH	77018
EDEN PINES	20200	291S	NWC	77379
EDEN POINT CT	0	484Y	NEF	77494
EDEN POINT LN	0	484Y	NEF	77494
EDENPORT CT	6300	457N	NEC	77049
EDEN PRAIRIE DR	6100	525R	NEF	77407
EDEN RIDGE LN	0	613K	PL	77584
EDEN RUN CT	0	367P	NWC	77433
EDENS AVE	100	659F	LC	77573
EDENSBOROUGH DR	19700	446Q	NWC	77449
EDENS DAWN DR	19100	329A	NWC	77375
EDEN SPRINGS LN	12100	449A	NWC	77041
EDENSTONE DR	0	368N	NWC	77429
EDEN TRAILS LN	18200	487A	SWC	77094
EDENVALE	15500	617W	FR	77546
EDENVALE CT	5100	617W	FR	77546
EDEN VALLEY DR	9900	329C	NWC	77379
EDENWAY CT	6300	457N	NEC	77049
EDENWAY DR	17400	329M	NWC	77379
EDENWOOD DR	8100	250S	NWC	77389
EDFIELD	4500	533V	SEH	77051
EDFIELD	4600	533V	SEH	77033
EDGAR	8400	533Y	SEH	77051
EDGAR	10600	573L	SEH	77047
EDGAR RD	14200	373X	NCC	77039
EDGEBASTON CT	20900	332Y	NCC	77073
EDGEBORO	13200	457E	NEC	77049
EDGE BRANCH LN	0	377H	NEH	77346
EDGEBROOK	800	501L	BT	77521
E. EDGEBROOK DR	1	576C	SEH	77034
EDGEBROOK DR	300	576E	SEH	77034
EDGEBROOK DR	8800	575H	SEH	77075
EDGEBROOK FOREST CT	8100	411Q	NWC	77088
EDGEBROOK FOREST DR	5500	411Q	NWC	77088
EDGECLIFF FALLS CT	0	445L	NWC	77449
EDGECRAFT DR	7400	570V	SWH	77459
EDGECREEK DR	3200	371Q	NWC	77066
EDGECREST DR	0	299W	NEC	77336
EDGECROFT CT	19000	328G	NWC	77377
EDGEDALE DR	2300	610C	MC	77489
EDGEFIELD DR	3300	537M	PA	77503
EDGEFIELD LAKES DR	0	532X	SWH	77054
EDGEGATE DR	4900	293Z	NCC	77373
EDGEGLEN DR	0	332Y	NCC	77073
EDGEGROVE CT	13900	372E	NWC	77014
EDGEHAVEN DR	17300	610G	SWH	77489
EDGEHILL DR	12800	456M	NEC	77049
EDGEHILL DR	13100	457J	NEC	77049
EDGEHILL RD	1700	537N	PA	77502
EDGE LAKE BLVD	0	377L	NEH	77346
EDGELOCH DR	9100	289Z	NWC	77379
EDGE MANOR LN	19100	526K	NEF	77407
EDGEMERE DR	0	295V	NEH	77365
EDGEMONT DR	16300	611C	SWH	77053
EDGEMOOR DR	5500	531E	SWH	77081
EDGEMOOR DR	6300	530H	SWH	77074
EDGEMOOR DR	7800	530F	SWH	77036
EDGE PARK CIR	0	372C	NCC	77073
EDGE ROSE CT	0	526W	NEF	77406
EDGESTONE DR		609T	NEF	77479
EDGETON CT	300	457W	NEC	77015
EDGEVALE CT	7500	407M	NWC	77095
EDGEVIEW RD	4500	447E	NWC	77084
EDGEWATER DR	0	573Y	SEC	77047
EDGEWATER DR	0	568Z	SG	77478
EDGEWATER DR	1300	656R	FR	77546
EDGEWATER DR	4800	414Y	NEH	77093
EDGEWATER BEND CT	3300	613V	PL	77584
EDGEWATER BEND LN	8400	613V	PL	77584
EDGEWATER COVE CIR	0	366J	NWC	77433
EDGEWAY DR	7600	491B	NWH	77055
EDGEWICK CT	800	569N	SG	77478
EDGEWICK CT	5600	330Y	NWC	77069
EDGEWICK ELM	0	611S	FS	77545
EDGEWOOD	1	494T	SEH	77011
N. EDGEWOOD	100	494Q	SEH	77011
EDGEWOOD	100	541D	BT	77520
EDGEWOOD	100	580L	LP	77571
EDGEWOOD	300	658H	LC	77573
EDGEWOOD	600	494T	SEH	77023
EDGEWOOD	12000	490E	BH	77024
W. EDGEWOOD AVE	100	616Y	FR	77546
E. EDGEWOOD AVE	100	616Z	FR	77546
W. EDGEWOOD AVE	400	656C	FR	77546
EDGEWOOD DR	2300	609B	MC	77459
EDGEWOOD DR	3100	613Y	NEB	77584
EDGEWOOD DR	3100	659Z	GCO	77539
EDGEWOOD DR	16000	618D	PA	77059
EDGEWOOD FOREST CIR	1	251A	WD	77381
EDGEWOOD HAVEN DR	0	366J	NWC	77433
EDGEWOOD HILL CT	3800	611W	FS	77545
EDGEWOOD MANOR CT	9800	329L	NWC	77375
EDGEWOOD PARK DR	12700	411D	NWC	77038
EDGEWOOD PLACE DR	5500	331A	NWC	77379
EDGEWOOD VILLAGE TRAIL	0	457G	NEC	77049
EDGEWORTH	9500	454A	NEH	77093
EDGON DR	0	328U	NWC	77429
EDGWARE DR	17000	407Y	NWC	77084
EDIE	3600	611X	FS	77545
EDIFICATION AVE	300	419V	NEC	77532
EDINBURG	6100	535S	SEH	77087
EDINBURG AVE	1800	658T	LC	77573
EDINBURGH CT	14100	488J	SWH	77077
EDINBURGH DR	1200	656M	FR	77546
EDINBURGH LN	4600	569X	MC	77459
EDINSTON PLACE	4900	291S	NWC	77388
EDISON	1300	541A	BT	77520
EDISON	3500	453Y	NEH	77009
EDISON BROOK LN	0	610Q	MC	77459
EDISON LIGHT TRAIL	0	326V	NWC	77429
EDISON PARK	0	531C	SWH	77081
EDISON PARK LN	0	531C	SWH	77081
EDISON TRACE LN	13200	328K	NWC	77377
EDISTO CT	14500	408X	NWC	77084
EDITH	200	460S	HG	77562
EDITH	4300	531M	BL	77401
EDITH	5300	531P	SWH	77096
EDITH	5500	531P	SWH	77081
EDITH	23300	325B	NWC	77447
EDLOE	2600	492X	SWH	77027
EDLOE	3600	492X	SWH	77046
EDLOE	5100	532F	WU	77005
EDLOE	7200	532K	SWH	77025
ED LOU LN	0	328J	NWC	77429
EDMOND AVE	1400	537J	PA	77506
EDMONSON DR	0	257M	SEM	77357
EDMONT LN	7100	412X	NWH	77088
EDMONTON DR	3100	537L	PA	77503
EDMUND	4400	494L	NEH	77020
EDMUNDSON	1300	494S	SEH	77003
EDMUNDSON	2200	494S	SEH	77004
EDMUND WAY	0	659X	LC	77539

Street Name	Block	Pg/Sq	Loc	Zips
EDNA	1000	541B	BT	77520
EDNA	3600	611X	FS	77545
EDNA	5800	419G	NEC	77532
EDNA	7100	534R	SEH	77087
EDNA	7400	535N	SEH	77087
EDO CIR	0	527Q	NEF	77083
EDSALL DR	17300	331L	NWC	77388
EDSEE	4300	453X	NWH	77009
EDWARD DR	1100	536Y	SH	77587
EDWARD DR	5500	374V	NEH	77032
EDWARD DR	5800	375S	NEH	77396
EDWARD LN	22300	286L	NWC	77377
EDWARDS	1000	493F	SWH	77007
EDWARDS	10000	370Z	NWC	77086
EDWARDS AVE	0	613S	PL	77584
EDWARDS LN	0	613S	PL	77584
EDWARDS LN	0	613S	PL	77584
EDWAY	4300	573V	SEH	77048
EDWINA BLVD	12200	572M	SWH	77045
EDWINSTOWE TRAIL	0	449X	NWH	77043
EDWORTHY RD	20000	326T	NWC	77433
EEBING WIND WAY	0	251G	SWM	77380
E. F	100	580C	LP	77571
EFFIE	900	659K	LC	77573
EFFIE	4300	531M	BL	77401
EFFIE LN	1300	537P	PA	77502
EFFINGHAM DR	5500	571E	SWH	77035
EFFINGHAM DR	6000	570H	SWH	77035
EGAN	500	494K	NEH	77020
EGANVILLE CIR	18100	328G	NWC	77377
EGANVILLE DR	12100	328H	NWC	77377
EGBERT	5100	492C	NWH	77007
EGGLESTON	0	572L	SWH	77051
EGGLING LN	0	448F	NWH	77041
EGRET	0	375U	NEC	77396
EGRET CT	3900	293C	SEM	77390
EGRET DR	4300	620G	SB	77586
EGRET BAY BLVD	0	659A	LC	77573
EGRET BAY BLVD	18100	618Z	WB	77058
S. EGRET CANAL	100	542J	BT	77520
N. EGRET CANAL	100	542J	BT	77520
EGRET CHASE CT	2500	611S	FS	77545
EGRET FIELD LN	0	457V	NEC	77049
EGRET GLEN CT	19100	326Y	NWC	77429
EGRET HAVEN LN	0	366J	NWC	77433
EGRET HILL CT	12600	617E	SEH	77089
EGRET LAKE WAY	0	376H	NEC	77346
EGRET MEADOW LN	3200	446R	NWC	77084
EGRET NEST LN	0	332N	NWC	77090
EGRET OAKS	0	618Z	WB	77058
EGRET WOOD WAY	0	326Y	NWC	77433
EGYPT	0	578E	PA	77505
EGYPT	1000	453Z	NEH	77009
EGYPT DR	6000	577H	PA	77505
EGYPTIAN	600	489K	SWH	77042
EHRHARDT LN	0	568S	SG	77479
EICHLER DR	7000	529H	SWH	77036
EICHWURZEL LN	100	453U	NEH	77009
EIFFEL WAY	0	377D	NEH	77396
EIGEL	4100	492H	SWH	77007
EIGHTEENTH FAIRWAY DR	19900	337V	NEC	77346
EIGHT WILLOWS RD	7500	570R	SWH	77489
EIKER RD	12300	614C	BK	77581
EILEEN	3000	538U	DP	77536
EILEEN	17000	247T	SWM	77355
EINRA LN	1100	420N	BR	77532
EISENHOWER RD	7300	533V	SEH	77033
S. EISENHOWER PARK DR	0	418E	NEH	77044
N. EISENHOWER PARK DR	0	418A	NEH	77044
ELAINE RD	13000	572R	SWH	77047
ELAINE WAY	0	615S	PL	77584
ELAM	1900	620N	SB	77586
EL AMBAR DR	0	574L	SEH	77048
ELAN BLVD	0	253T	SEM	77386
ELANA LN	0	569P	SF	77477
ELANDER BLOSSOM DR	0	249V	NWC	77375
ELBE DR	19200	294D	SEM	77365
ELBECK DR	11100	571D	SWH	77035
ELBERRY RD	6000	250V	NWC	77389
ELBERT	3000	492T	SWH	77098
ELBERT	6400	455J	NEH	77028
ELBERTA	1000	533U	SEH	77051
ELBERTA	5700	414M	NEC	77050
ELBRIDGE LN	7400	538X	DP	77536
EL BUEY RD	900	577J	SEH	77034
EL BUEY WAY	2300	535M	SEH	77017
EL BUEY WAY	5100	536J	SEH	77017
EL CAMINO	2600	533N	SWH	77054
EL CAMINO DEL REY	5000	531B	SWH	77081
EL CAMINO REAL	14000	617D	SEH	77062
EL CAMINO REAL	14700	618J	SEH	77062
EL CAMINO REAL	16800	618U	SEH	77058
EL CAMINO VILLAGE DR	1300	618U	SEC	77058
EL CAPITAN DR	7900	527M	NEF	77083
EL CENTRO	5100	452H	NWH	77018
EL CHACO LN	9600	462Y	BT	77521
EL CID TRAIL	7000	459K	NEC	77049
ELCOTT LN	0	572W	SWH	77053
EL CRESTA DR	7300	527L	NEF	77083
ELDARICA PINE CT	0	289G	NWC	77375
ELDARICA WAY	0	524E	NEF	77494
ELDEN HILLS CT	23900	485J	NEF	77494
ELDEN HILLS WAY	1400	485J	NEF	77494
ELDER	800	493G	SWH	77002
ELDER	1100	493G	SWH	77007
ELDER LN	20100	252L	SEM	77385
ELDER RD	2600	444Q	KT	77493
ELDERBERRY AVE	0	659P	LC	77573
ELDERBERRY LN	500	613C	NEB	77584
ELDERBERRY LN	13000	457E	NEC	77049
W. ELDERBERRY ST	0	659T	LC	77573
ELDERBERRY ARBOR	5500	526T	NEF	77407
ELDERBERRY PARK LN	10000	289U	NWC	77375
ELDER BRIDGE DR	13400	528X	NEF	77498
ELDER GLEN DR	300	618S	SEH	77598
ELDER GROVE CT	400	613F	NEB	77584
N. ELDER GROVE DR	300	613B	NEB	77584
ELDERGROVE LN	7700	527J	NEF	77407
ELDERHEDGE RD	5700	525R	NEF	77407
ELDER MILL LN	10100	527Z	NEF	77498
ELDER PARK CT	2600	446N	NWC	77449
ELDERVISTA CIR	400	618S	SEH	77598
ELDERVISTA DR	300	618S	SEH	77598
ELDERWOOD DR	4000	619L	TL	77586
ELDERWOOD TERRACE DR	0	526W	NEF	77406
ELDON	200	373W	NEH	77060
ELDON BROOK DR	0	295R	SEM	77365
ELDON PARK CT	13700	367C	CY	77429
ELDORA DR	8800	450L	NWH	77080
EL DORADO	1	656Y	FR	77546
EL DORADO BLVD	100	617R	SEH	77598
EL DORADO BLVD	600	618K	SEH	77062

Street Name	Block	Pg/Sq	Loc	Zips
W. EL DORADO BLVD	2100	617U	SEC	77546
ELDORADO BLVD	3000	609G	MC	77459
EL DORADO BLVD	3000	578T	SEH	77059
EL DORADO BLVD	3000	609H	MC	77459
EL DORADO DR	6800	375X	NEC	77396
ELDORADO CENTRE LN	7100	370A	NWC	77069
ELDORADO GLEN DR	0	335P	NCC	77338
EL DORADO OAKS CT	3600	578Y	SEH	77059
EL DORADO OAKS DR	15700	578Y	SEH	77059
ELDORA SPRINGS CT	0	329V	NWC	77070
ELDORO CANYON LN	17000	367Y	NWC	77095
ELDRIDGE RD	100	568G	SG	77478
ELDRIDGE CHASE	13100	408R	NWC	77041
ELDRIDGE CHASE CT	7200	408R	NWC	77041
ELDRIDGE GARDEN CIR	13800	528E	SWC	77083
ELDRIDGE GLEN	0	409W	NWC	77041
ELDRIDGE GLEN DR	5700	408Z	NWC	77041
ELDRIDGE MEADOW CT	7100	408R	NWC	77041
ELDRIDGE MEADOW DR	13100	408R	NWC	77041
ELDRIDGE PARK DR	13000	368D	NWC	77429
N. ELDRIDGE PARKWAY	0	368R	NWC	77429
ELDRIDGE PARK WAY	2600	528Y	NEF	77498
N. ELDRIDGE PKWY	100	488C	SWH	77079
S. ELDRIDGE PKWY	900	488T	SWH	77077
N. ELDRIDGE PKWY	1200	448U	NWH	77084
S. ELDRIDGE PKWY	2500	488T	SWH	77082
N. ELDRIDGE PKWY	5700	408V	NWC	77041
S. ELDRIDGE PKWY	6200	528K	SWC	77083
N. ELDRIDGE PKWY	8700	368H	NWC	77065
N. ELDRIDGE PKWY	12300	368H	NWC	77429
N. ELDRIDGE PKWY	13800	328Z	NWC	77070
N. ELDRIDGE PKWY	15000	328Z	NWC	77429
N. ELDRIDGE PKWY	16000	328R	NWC	77377
ELDRIDGE PLACE DR	12800	408Z	NWC	77041
ELDRIDGE SPRINGS WAY	13600	528F	SWC	77083
ELDRIDGE TRACE CT	13500	528K	SWC	77083
ELDRIDGE VIEW DR	6300	528F	SWC	77083
ELDRIDGE VILLA	13400	528X	NEF	77498
ELDRIDGE VILLA WAY	0	568B	SG	77498
ELDRIDGE WAY	0	448D	NWC	77041
ELDRIGE VALLEY DR	13600	528F	SWC	77083
ELEANOR	100	453Q	NEH	77009
ELEANOR LN	0	245F	SWM	77355
ELEANOR MEADOW LN	0	326U	NWC	77429
ELEANOR TINSLEY WAY	2200	534B	SEH	77023
ELECTRA DR	100	489L	SWH	77079
ELECTRA DR	300	489G	SWH	77024
ELECTRA DR	600	489G	SWH	77079
ELEGANT WAY LN	0	371S	NWC	77066
ELEGIA DR	3200	450M	NWH	77080
ELENA	400	459R	HG	77562
ELENAS BEND CT	0	524A	NEF	77494
ELEPHANT WALK	23000	291F	NWC	77389
ELEVATOR	0	495T	NEH	77029
ELF CIR	23400	339P	HU	77336
EL FLETA LN	15500	527U	NEF	77498
ELFWOOD CT	100	457Y	NEC	77015
ELGARD LN	0	329B	NWC	77375
ELGIN	100	493T	SWH	77006
ELGIN	1000	493Y	SEH	77004
ELGIN	3900	494W	SEH	77004
ELGIN	15400	498B	CV	77530
ELGIN	15600	458X	CV	77530
ELGIN CT	3300	493Z	SEH	77004
EL GRANDE DR	14700	528E	SWC	77083
EL GRANDE DR	14900	527H	SWC	77083
EL GRECO DR	0	527G	SWC	77083
ELI	4100	492H	SWH	77007
ELIAS PEAK CT	1400	332R	NCC	77073
ELI COVE LN	0	328K	NWC	77377
ELIJAH CT	22000	249S	NWC	77375
ELIJAH HILLS LN	28001	293F	SEM	77386
ELINOR CT	14300	327Z	NWC	77429
ELISE DR	13700	572U	SWH	77047
ELI WAY	0	659S	LC	77573
ELIZABETH	1300	463A	MB	77580
ELIZABETH	3600	538U	DP	77536
ELIZABETH CT	3700	532S	SWH	77025
ELIZABETH CT	7200	408R	NWC	77041
ELIZABETH CT	11800	248N	SWM	77355
ELIZABETH DR	0	658M	LC	77573
ELIZABETH LN	10700	539U	LP	77571
ELIZABETH RD	9000	450Y	NWH	77055
ELIZABETH BAY	0	327W	NWC	77429
ELIZABETH BROOK DR	0	524J	NWF	77406
ELIZABETH MEADOW CT	7000	408R	NWC	77041
ELIZABETH PLACE CT	22400	525C	NEF	77494
ELIZABETH ROSE CT	10300	616F	SEC	77089
ELIZABETH ROSE DR	10200	616F	SEC	77089
ELIZABETHS GLEN LN	9600	329F	NWC	77375
W. ELIZABETH SHORE LOOP	12300	366K	NWC	77433
E. ELIZABETH SHORE LOOP	12300	366K	NWC	77433
S. ELIZABETH SHORE LOOP	18200	366K	NWC	77433
N. ELIZABETH SHORE LOOP	18300	366K	NWC	77433
EL JAMES DR	3400	331G	NWC	77388
EL JARDIN DR	4800	621A	PA	77586
EL JARDIN DR	4800	581W	PA	77586
ELK	0	527Q	NEF	77083
ELK DR	100	379A	NEC	77532
ELK DR	600	378D	NEC	77532
ELKANA DEANE LN	22500	445Q	NWC	77449
ELK BEND DR	9100	329R	NWC	77379
ELK BLUFF LN	0	484X	NEF	77494
ELK CANYON CT	6000	298W	NEH	77345
ELK CREEK DR	2300	337C	NEH	77345
ELKCREEK DR		325N	NWC	77447
ELK CROSSING DR	1	250D	WD	77381
ELKDALE DR	3100	487Z	SWC	77082
ELKFIELD LN	5000	333H	NCC	77338
ELK FORES TTRAIL	0	416R	NEC	77044
ELKGROVE LN	5000	333H	NCC	77338
ELKHART	800	452B	NWH	77091
ELKHAVEN	0	256X	SEM	77365
ELK HILL CT	14800	618F	SEH	77062
ELKHORN LN	4900	333H	NCC	77338
ELKHORN RANCH DR	0	409B	NWC	77064
ELKINGTON CT	11800	570B	SWH	77071
ELKINS RD	14800	413A	NEH	77060
ELKINS HOLLOW LN	0	660J	LC	77573
ELK LAKE CT	0	377B	NEC	77346
ELK MEADOW DR	12200	568H	SF	77477
ELKMONT CT	4800	614S	NEB	77584
ELK PARK LN	15700	618G	SEH	77062
ELK PASS DR	0	378Q	NEC	77532
ELK POINT LN	10200	369Y	NWC	77064
ELK RIDGE LN	0	484T	NEF	77494
ELK RIVER CIR	17900	331M	NWC	77090
ELK RIVER RD	1400	331L	NWC	77090
ELK RUN CIR	800	488F	SWH	77079
ELKS DR	2900	484R	NEF	77494
ELKS DR	3000	485N	NEF	77494
ELK SPRINGS CIR	11900	371L	NWC	77067

Street Name	Block	Pg/Sq	Loc	Zips
ELK SPRINGS LN	0	253K	SEM	77386
ELKTON CT	0	486N	SWC	77450
ELKTON CT	2400	613U	NEB	77584
ELK VALLEY CIR	17900	331L	NWC	77090
ELK VISTA CT	0	484S	NEF	77494
ELKWAY LN	5000	333H	NCC	77338
ELKWOOD DR	1400	570T	MC	77489
ELKWOOD DR	13800	371U	NWC	77038
ELKWOOD FOREST DR	6000	411K	NWC	77088
ELKWOOD GLEN CT	0	329F	NWC	77375
ELKWOOD GLEN LN	0	329F	NWC	77375
ELL RD	10800	414U	NEC	77093
ELLA	100	288L	TB	77375
ELLA	400	616Y	FR	77546
ELLA	6700	614D	BK	77581
ELLA BLVD	0	291U	NWC	77388
ELLA BLVD	1100	452X	NWH	77008
ELLA BLVD	3000	452F	NWH	77018
ELLA BLVD	9200	412K	NWC	77088
ELLA BLVD	9700	412B	NWC	77038
ELLA BLVD	10700	372P	NWH	77067
ELLA BLVD	13800	372K	NWC	77014
ELLA BLVD	15300	332N	NWC	77090
ELLA BLVD	17000	331M	NWC	77090
ELLA BLVD	18300	331C	NWC	77388
ELLA CIR	1400	331M	NWC	77090
ELLA BLVD CT	0	412F	NWC	77038
S. ELLA CREEK DR	0	372K	NWH	77067
N. ELLA CREEK DR	0	372K	NWH	77067
ELLA CROSSING DR	0	332N	NWC	77090
ELLA GATE CT	0	376W	NEC	77396
W. ELLAINE AVE	100	536K	PA	77506
ELLAINE AVE	400	536M	PA	77506
ELLA LEE	0	488V	SWH	77077
ELLA LEE	0	490S	SWH	77063
ELLA LEE LN	2300	492U	SWH	77019
ELLA LEE LN	3400	492S	SWH	77027
ELLA LEE LN	5600	491T	SWH	77056
ELLA LEE LN	6100	491S	SWH	77057
ELLA LEE LN	7800	490V	SWH	77063
ELLA LEE LN	10000	489U	SWH	77042
ELLA LEE LN	11300	489T	SWH	77077
ELLA LEE LN	12400	488T	SWH	77077
ELLA PARK DR	0	372K	NWH	77067
ELLA RIDGE LN	0	372K	NWH	77067
ELLA VIEW LN	0	372K	NWH	77067
ELLEA LN	0	568H	SG	77478
ELLEDGE RD	24700	252X	SEM	77386
ELLEN	6100	614C	BK	77581
ELLEN	9600	502C	BT	77521
ELLEN AVE	300	659F	LC	77573
ELLEN DR	300	538L	DP	77536
ELLEN LN	12800	497N	NEH	77015
ELLENA RD	300	413W	NEH	77076
ELLENA RD	600	453B	NEH	77076
ELLENBERGER AVE	6500	375W	NEC	77396
ELLENDALE CT	15800	327Y	NWC	77429
ELLENVILLE DR	12300	616D	SEH	77089
ELLERBE SPRINGS LN	0	524B	NEF	77494
ELLERSLIE LN	13400	367G	NWC	77429
ELLERTON LN	800	332N	NWC	77090
ELLERY DR	0	484G	NEF	77494
ELLESBOROUGH LN	3300	291Y	NWC	77388
ELLESMERE DR	13000	457W	NEC	77015
ELLICOTT ROCK DR	0	377J	NEC	77346
ELLIES GATE LN	3500	613W	NWB	77578
ELLINGER LN	7900	450C	NWH	77040
ELLINGHAM DR	400	486B	SWC	77450
ELLINGTON	800	412N	NWH	77088
ELLINGTON	2700	411R	NWH	77088
ELLINGTON FIELD	1	577U	SEH	77034
ELLINGTON PARK DR	0	617B	SEH	77598
ELLIOTT	1200	494X	SEH	77023
ELLIOTT, T K	0	525V	NEF	77406
ELLIS	100	620T	SB	77586
ELLIS	14000	569R	SF	77477
ELLIS CT	3200	494E	NEH	77020
ELLIS CT	3900	530C	SWH	77063
ELLIS DR	7700	570Z	SWH	77489
ELLIS DR	12500	614C	BK	77581
ELLIS RD	1	657R	LC	77573
ELLIS BEND DR	0	366K	NWC	77433
ELLIS LANDING	0	658K	LC	77573
ELLISON RIDGE DR	11000	524L	NWF	77406
ELLIS SANDS LN	0	377K	NEC	77044
ELLIS SCHOOL RD	100	459Z	HG	77562
ELLIS SCHOOL RD	1900	460X	BT	77521
ELLIS SPRINGS LN	0	375X	NEC	77396
ELLISTON	900	494X	SEH	77023
ELLSCOTT CT	3300	253S	SEM	77386
ELLSWORTH DR	1100	536R	PA	77506
ELLWOOD	11000	251P	WD	77380
ELM	0	337B	NEH	77339
ELM	0	375M	NEC	77396
ELM	0	540T	LP	77571
ELM	1	298E	NEC	77336
S. ELM	100	288M	TB	77375
N. ELM	100	288H	TB	77375
ELM	100	419Y	BR	77532
ELM	100	459R	HG	77562
ELM	100	536M	PA	77506
ELM	100	619H	TL	77586
ELM	300	282Y	WL	77484
ELM	1100	494X	SEH	77023
ELM	1200	541B	BT	77520
ELM	4500	531H	BL	77401
ELM	4700	581W	PA	77586
ELM	4800	614M	PL	77581
ELM	5100	531C	SWH	77081
ELM	5101	531C	BL	77401
ELM	5300	531A	SWH	77081
E. ELM	7300	535B	SEH	77012
ELM	7400	535A	SEH	77023
ELM	17000	418R	NEC	77044
ELM	17800	257A	WV	77357
ELM	20000	257Q	SEM	77357
ELM	25400	257Y	SEM	77357
ELM	26700	292Q	SP	77373
ELM AVE	100	538K	DP	77536
W. ELM CIR	2800	444P	KT	77493
E. ELM CIR	2800	444P	KT	77493
ELM CIR	14000	375X	NEC	77396
ELM CT	6200	531C	BL	77401
ELM CT	13600	568B	SG	77498
ELM CT	26800	295Y	SEM	77365
ELM DR	12000	368D	NWC	77429
ELM LN	0	531J	SWH	77081
ELM LN	100	257M	SEM	77357
ELM LN	3900	660M	BC	77518
ELM LN	4200	291K	NWC	77389
ELM LN	26600	246P	SWM	77355
ELM RD	800	620T	CS	77565

Street Name	Block	Pg/Sq	Loc	Zips
EL MAR LN	1700	620K	SB	77586
EL MATADOR LN	22100	338Z	NEC	77532
ELMBANK DR	16000	407H	NWC	77095
ELM BARK	22700	290E	NWC	77375
ELM BAYOU CT	10800	369X	NWC	77064
ELM BEND CT	10200	335Q	HM	77338
ELM BLUFF CT	10200	369Y	NWC	77064
ELM BOUGH CT	12500	368Z	NWC	77065
ELM BRANCH CT	1	251Y	WD	77380
S. ELM BRANCH PLACE	1	251Y	WD	77380
N. ELM BRANCH PLACE	1	251Y	WD	77380
ELM BRIDGE CT	11000	368U	NWC	77065
ELMBROOK DR	4500	331F	NWC	77388
ELM CANYON CT	3000	297Q	NEH	77345
ELM CREEK DR	25300	251V	SWM	77380
ELM CREEK FALLS DR		367S	NWC	77433
ELMCREST DR	3200	411V	NWH	77088
ELM CREST TRAIL	4000	578U	SEH	77059
ELMCROFT DR	11200	529T	SWH	77099
ELM CROSSING TRAIL	0	292D	SEM	77386
ELMDALE DR	10500	369B	NWC	77070
ELMDON DR	18300	447F	NWC	77084
ELM DRAKE LN	8700	335N	NCC	77338
ELM EDGE WAY	0	447K	NWC	77084
ELM EDGE WAY	0	447K	NWC	77084
ELMEN	600	620H	SB	77586
ELMEN	1500	492R	SWH	77019
ELMER BAILEY PARKWAY	0	404G	NWC	77493
ELM ESTATES DR	11600	489P	SWH	77077
ELMFIELD	14000	572X	SWH	77047
ELMFIELD DR	25800	250S	NWC	77389
ELM FOREST DR	0	331F	NWC	77388
ELM FOREST DR	2300	613K	PL	77584
ELM FORK DR	19800	337U	NEC	77346
ELMGATE DR	2000	450P	NWH	77080
ELM GLEN DR	3600	297W	NEH	77339
ELM GLEN DR	3900	609M	MC	77459
ELM GREEN	25400	293P	NCC	77373
ELM GROVE CT	2800	297S	NEH	77339
ELMGROVE RD	5900	290C	NWC	77389
ELMGROVE PARK LN	1100	619C	PA	77586
ELMHAVEN RD	8400	578D	LP	77571
ELM HILL CT	19000	446R	NWC	77084
ELM HOLLOW	2500	616T	PL	77581
ELMHURST	10000	576N	SEH	77075
ELM HURST LN	21500	486N	SWC	77450
ELMHURST TRAILS LN	1100	619H	PA	77586
ELMINGTON CT	12900	328U	NWC	77429
ELMINGTON DR	12900	328U	NWC	77429
ELMIRA	24800	249W	NWC	77375
EL MIRANDA DR	14800	408P	NWC	77095
ELM KNOLL CT	10300	369X	NWC	77064
ELM KNOLL TRAIL	10000	369X	NWC	77064
ELMLAKE	400	338V	NEH	77336
ELM LAKE DR	8400	527Q	NEF	77083
ELMLAWN DR	5500	574A	SEH	77033
ELM LEAF PLACE	15300	326V	NWC	77429
ELMLEY PLACE	25800	250T	NWC	77389
ELM MEADOW TRAIL	9900	369Y	NWC	77064
ELMONT DR	14600	408K	NWC	77095
ELMORA	3700	532E	SS	77005
ELM ORCHARD TRAIL	0	377E	NEC	77346
ELMORE	600	659E	LC	77573
ELMORE DR	19000	252A	SEM	77385
ELMPARK CT	13900	371B	NWC	77014
ELM PARK WAY	16600	618M	SEH	77058
ELM PLACE	1	259Q	LCO	77357
ELM POINT CT	16100	407M	NWC	77095
ELM POINTE	900	658R	LC	77573
ELMRIDGE	3200	532P	SWH	77025
ELMRIDGE CT	0	610X	MC	77459
ELM RIDGE DR	500	252T	SEM	77386
ELMS CT	3600	609L	MC	77459
ELMSBURY CT	20000	446L	NWC	77449
ELMSCOTT DR	1500	568F	SG	77498
ELMSCOTT DR	6500	578E	PA	77505
ELMSFORD CT	8200	527Q	NEF	77083
ELMSGROVE LN	11100	369E	NWC	77070
ELM SHADOW DR	1800	570W	MC	77489
ELM SHORES DR	13600	377Q	NEC	77044
ELMSIDE DR	2700	490W	SWH	77042
ELM SPRINGS DR	5500	574E	SEH	77048
ELM SQUARE CT	0	326V	NWC	77429
ELM SQUARE ST	0	326V	NWC	77429
ELMSTONE CT	4500	337B	NEH	77345
ELM STREAM CT	3900	611W	FS	77545
ELMSWORTH DR	10500	529Q	SWH	77099
ELMTEX DR	14800	375T	NEH	77396
ELM TRACE DR	28500	246E	SWM	77355
ELM TRAIL LN	13900	371B	NWC	77014
ELM TREE DR	5500	574E	SEH	77048
ELM TREE DALE DR	0	446F	NWC	77449
ELMTREE ESTATES DR	19400	406R	NWC	77449
EL MUNDO	8000	533N	SWH	77054
ELM VALLEY CT	19800	337U	NEC	77346
ELM VIEW CIR	4800	446D	NWC	77084
ELM VIEW CT	600	569V	SF	77477
ELMVIEW DR	1600	450T	NWH	77080
ELMVIEW TRACE LN	9500	450T	NWH	77080
ELM WING LN	22800	485G	SWC	77450
ELMWOOD	0	369E	NWC	77429
ELMWOOD	200	252N	OR	77386
ELMWOOD	1700	539V	LP	77571
ELMWOOD	3900	533Y	SEH	77051
ELMWOOD	19800	336S	NEC	77338
ELMWOOD CIR	300	616U	FR	77546
ELMWOOD CT	1800	568B	SG	77498
ELMWOOD CT	4900	501F	BT	77521
ELMWOOD CT	23500	290D	NWC	77389
ELMWOOD CT	24200	297E	SEM	77365
ELMWOOD DR	700	501T	BT	77520
ELMWOOD DR	3900	615W	PL	77584
ELMWOOD DR	23600	296H	SEM	77365
ELMWOOD DR	23900	297E	SEM	77365
ELMWOOD LN	1200	536P	PA	77502
ELMWOOD BEND LN	0	257E	SEM	77357
ELMWOOD BROOK CT	20300	326T	NWC	77433
ELMWOOD DALE DR	0	611W	FS	77545
ELMWOOD GLEN CT	16800	407L	NWC	77095
ELMWOOD HILL LN	5900	338E	NEH	77345
ELMWOOD MANOR DR	16000	367D	NWC	77429
ELMWOOD PARK CT	16200	618D	PA	77059
ELMWOOD RIDGE DR	0	366V	NWC	77433
EL ORO DR	0	574L	SEH	77048
EL PADRE DR	15200	527H	SWC	77083
EL PASEO	1800	532R	SWH	77054
EL PASEO	2000	533N	SWH	77054
EL PASO	700	536W	SH	77587
EL PASO	6900	494H	NEH	77020
EL PASO	7100	495E	NEH	77020
EL PASO	29600	248C	SWM	77354
EL PICO DR	7900	527L	NEF	77083

Street Name	Block	Pg/Sq	Loc	Zips
ELPYCO	3000	573F	SEH	77051
EL RANCHO	1300	501M	BT	77521
EL RANCHO	7500	535S	SEH	77087
ELRINGTON CREEK CT	0	526Q	NEF	77407
ELRINGTON HEIGHTS LN	0	405T	NWC	77493
ELRINGTON POINTE LN	0	484P	NEF	77494
ELRINGTON WOOD PLACE	0	406C	NWC	77433
EL RIO	7900	533N	SWH	77054
ELROD	0	445M	NWC	77449
ELROD	8000	535U	SEH	77017
ELROD RD	2000	445R	NWC	77449
ELROY	3800	453Z	NEH	77009
EL RUBI DR	0	574L	SEH	77048
ELSA	600	536V	PA	77502
EL SABIO DR	0	527Q	NEF	77083
EL SALVADOR DR	4500	371A	NWC	77066
ELSBETH RD	300	498M	CV	77520
ELSBURY	4300	493W	SWH	77006
ELSBURY LN	2900	613U	NEB	77584
ELSER	2800	493D	NEH	77009
ELSER	3400	453Z	NEH	77009
EL SERENO DR	7100	527M	SWC	77083
ELSIE LN	0	377U	NEC	77044
ELSIE LN	8800	410B	NWC	77064
ELSIE LN	12900	496M	NEH	77015
ELSIE WOOD DR	0	293Y	NCC	77373
ELSINORE DR	22000	485D	SWC	77450
ELSTREE DR	14800	457Z	NEC	77015
ELSTREE DR	14900	457Z	NEC	77530
EL SUENO ST	0	447J	NWC	77084
EL TESORO DR	14700	527H	SWC	77083
EL TIGRE LN	0	461P	NEC	77521
ELTON	500	575H	SEH	77034
ELTON	1400	576E	SEH	77034
ELTON	2200	502T	BT	77520
ELTON DR	15600	420E	CB	77532
ELTON KNOLLS	6000	406U	NWC	77449
EL TOPACIO DR	0	574L	SEH	77048
EL TORO	200	659F	LC	77573
EL TORO CT	16000	618S	SEH	77598
EL TORO LN	300	618S	SEH	77598
EL TORO LN	700	618P	SEH	77062
EL TURQUESA DR	0	574L	SEH	77048
ELVERA	7700	535F	SEH	77012
ELVERSON OAKS DR	0	329N	NWC	77377
W. ELVINTA	2400	502S	BT	77520
E. ELVINTA	2400	502N	BT	77520
ELWOOD	7700	495W	SEH	77012
ELWOOD DR	15600	409M	JV	77040
ELWOOD HILLS CT	1	251F	WD	77381
ELYSIAN	800	493D	NEH	77020
ELYSIAN	1400	493D	NEH	77026
ELYSIAN	2400	453V	NEH	77009
ELYSIAN ST VIADUCT	0	493D	NEH	77020
ELYSON BLVD	0	405P	NWC	77493
ELYSON FALLS DR	0	405T	NWC	77493
ELYSON GROVE WAY	0	405P	NWC	77493
ELYSON HOLLOW DR	0	405S	NWC	77493
ELYSON WOODS CROSSING	0	405R	NWC	77493
EMANCIPATION	300	493R	SEH	77003
EMANCIPATION	2300	493R	SEH	77004
EMANCIPATION	4700	533B	SEH	77004
EMBARCADERO DR	3600	527C	SWC	77082
EMBASSY LN	800	491C	SWH	77024
EMBASSY PLAZA DR	5300	374Q	NEH	77032
EMBE	2100	537S	PA	77502
EMBER LN	4200	538U	DP	77536
EMBER CANYON LN	2501	446N	NWC	77449
EMBER GLEN CT	15200	408J	NWC	77095
EMBERGLO FIELD TRAIL	0	325Q	NWC	77433
EMBER ISLES LN	12100	449A	NWC	77041
EMBER LAKE RD	12100	371J	NWC	77066
EMBER SKY CT	19600	486C	SWC	77094
EMBER SKY DR	0	612L	PL	77584
EMBER SPRING DR	3700	297S	NEH	77339
EMBER TRAIL LN	31500	253N	SEM	77386
EMBER TRAILS CT	300	487A	SWC	77094
EMBER TRAILS DR	18600	486D	SWC	77094
EMBER VILLAGE LN	0	328C	NWC	77377
EMBERWOOD DR	16200	329U	NWC	77070
EMBERWOOD FALLS DR	0	524F	NEF	77494
EMBERWOOD VIEW LN	0	575Q	SEH	77075
EMBLA DR	8000	457F	NEC	77049
EMBRY	300	493C	NEH	77009
EMBRY HILLS DR	16300	332R	NCC	77073
EMERALD CIR	0	369Q	NWC	77070
EMERALD CIR	1	656D	FR	77546
EMERALD CIR	18200	255D	SEM	77357
EMERALD CT	100	453Y	NEH	77009
EMERALD CT	1900	486L	SWC	77094
EMERALD CT	18200	255D	SEM	77357
EMERALD DR	6600	578A	PA	77505
EMERALD DR	10200	529Y	SWH	77074
EMERALD LN	19700	255C	SEM	77357
EMERALD ARBOR	0	251C	WD	77381
EMERALD ASH CT	6600	337Q	NEC	77346
EMERALD BAY CIR	3500	446J	NWC	77449
EMERALD BAY DR	0	612M	PL	77584
EMERALD BAY POINT LN	0	297K	NEH	77365
EMERALD BLUFF CT	7900	407K	NWC	77095
EMERALD BRANCH LN	3700	485V	NEF	77450
EMERALD BREEZE CT	0	615H	PL	77089
EMERALD BRIAR LN	0	407Z	NWC	77084
EMERALD BROOK	5300	449A	NWC	77041
EMERALD BROOK LN	0	612Q	PL	77584
EMERALD BROOK LN	0	657Z	LC	77573
EMERALD CANYON RD	6500	526E	NEF	77450
EMERALD CLIFF LN	20100	526K	NEF	77407
EMERALD CLOUD LN	100	619Y	LC	77573
EMERALD COVE CT	0	488P	SWH	77077
EMERALD COVE DR	2100	658V	LC	77573
EMERALD CREEK DR	10000	369Q	NWC	77070
EMERALD CYPRESS LN	14600	327W	NWC	77429
EMERALD FALLS CT	3500	578X	SEH	77059
EMERALD FALLS DR	3600	578X	SEH	77059
EMERALD FALLS LN	0	615B	PL	77581
EMERALD FIELD DR	0	537H	PA	77530
EMERALD FOREST CT	13900	568F	SG	77498
EMERALD FOREST DR	0	369Q	NWC	77070
EMERALD FOREST DR	1	255C	SEM	77357
EMERALD GARDEN LN	17600	447G	NWC	77084
EMERALD GLADE LN	0	375X	NEC	77338
EMERALD GLENN DR	0	369Q	NWC	77070
EMERALD GREEN DR	1700	486L	SWC	77094
EMERALD GREEN LN	1200	486L	SWC	77094
EMERALD GROVE DR	3000	297Y	NEH	77345
EMERALD HEIGHTS CT	8700	528N	SWC	77083
EMERALD HILL DR	11700	369Q	NWC	77070
EMERALD ISLE DR	17300	407K	NWC	77095
EMERALD ISLE LN	0	660E	LC	77573
EMERALD ISLE LN	2800	660E	LC	77573
EMERALD LAKE CT	1600	617D	SEH	77062

Street Name	Block	Pg/Sq	Loc	Zips
EMERALD LEAF DR	0	569E	SF	77477
EMERALD LEAF DR	19600	486G	SWC	77094
EMERALD LOFT CIR	2000	485R	SWC	77450
EMERALD MANOR LN	0	250U	NWC	77389
EMERALD MEADOW	7500	525B	NEF	77494
EMERALD MEADOW LN	8200	375Y	NEC	77396
EMERALD MIST PKWY	0	290S	NWC	77379
EMERALD MIST PKWY	0	290S	NWC	77379
EMERALD MOSS CT	14900	327W	NWC	77429
EMERALD MOUNTAIN DR		526S	NEF	77407
EMERALD OAKS CT	28000	246F	SWM	77355
EMERALD OAKS DR	10000	369Q	NWC	77070
EMERALD PARK DR	10100	369Q	NWC	77070
EMERALD PARK POINTE DR	4400	414B	NCC	77039
EMERALD PATHWAY DR	1800	292N	NWC	77388
EMERALD PINE DR	10300	369Q	NWC	77070
EMERALD POINT LN	1901	660P	LC	77573
EMERALD POINT LN	22300	289K	NWC	77375
EMERALD POOL LN	0	330B	NWC	77379
EMERALD POOL FALLS DR		249Z	NWC	77375
EMERALD RIDGE CIR	21600	485V	NEF	77450
EMERALD RIDGE LN	19600	486C	SWC	77094
EMERALD RIVER DR	1600	485K	NEF	77494
EMERALD RUN LN	7200	290T	NWC	77379
EMERALDS COVE CT	0	488P	SWH	77077
EMERALD SHIRE LN	6700	408V	NWC	77041
EMERALD SHORE CT	8800	407F	NWC	77095
EMERALD SPRINGS CT	0	612L	PL	77584
EMERALD SPRINGS CT	1500	486G	SWC	77094
EMERALD SPRINGS DR	0	612L	PL	77584
EMERALD SPRINGS DR	19700	486G	SWC	77094
EMERALD SPRUCE CT	20600	337Q	NEC	77346
EMERALD STONE CIR	0	614L	PL	77581
EMERALD STONE LN	18200	487A	SWC	77094
EMERALD TERRACE	25600	250U	NWC	77389
EMERALD TRACE CT	0	609J	NEF	77459
EMERALD TRAIL DR	10300	369Q	NWC	77070
EMERALD TREE CIR	0	447A	NWC	77084
EMERALD VALLEY CT	8400	408E	NWC	77095
EMERALD VISTA DR	0	293G	SEM	77386
EMERALD WAY	19700	245H	SWM	77355
EMERALD WOODS DR	11700	369Q	NWC	77070
EMERSON	200	493T	SWH	77006
EMERSON CREEK DR	0	253T	SEM	77386
EMERSON CREEK LN	24200	296J	SEM	77365
EMERSON RIDGE DR	0	292N	NWC	77388
EMERY DR	10600	529W	SWH	77099
EMERY CLIFF PLACE	1	250D	WD	77381
EMERY HEIGHTS LN	0	484U	NEF	77494
EMERY HILL CT	14800	527V	NEF	77498
EMERY HILL DR	9400	527V	NEF	77498
EMERY MANOR LN	0	295M	SEM	77365
EMERY MEADOWS LN	18800	328G	NWC	77377
EMERY MILLS LN	21000	334R	NCC	77338
EMERY OAKS LN	0	328M	NWC	77377
EMERY SPUR LN	0	366Y	NWC	77433
EMHOUSE LN	0	366P	NWC	77433
EMILE	100	494K	NEH	77020
N. EMILE	500	494K	NEH	77020
EMILEE POINT LN	0	293E	SEM	77386
EMILIA CT	16400	329V	NWC	77379
EMIL MARKS LN	0	444R	NWC	77493
EMILY CT	12500	568M	SG	77478
EMILY LN	20500	446K	NWC	77449
EMILY ANN CT	20100	326P	NWC	77433
EMILY FORSET TRAIL		484W	NEF	77494
EMILY PARK LN	0	525C	NEF	77450
EMILY TRACE LN	22900	485U	NEF	77494
EMILY VISTA LN	3000	611S	NEF	77545
EMILY WAY	24500	244V	WCO	77447
EMIR	1800	453T	NWH	77009
EMITE CT	1	494U	SEH	77011
EMMA	1700	453P	NWH	77009
EMMA DR	2400	614L	PL	77581
EMMA BAY BLVD	0	328K	NWC	77429
EMMA GARDENS LN	28000	293K	SEM	77386
EMMA LOU	7000	412S	NWH	77088
EMMA SPRINGS CT	0	376W	NEC	77396
EMMAUS LN	0	366N	NWC	77433
EMMEL CREEK LN	0	332N	NWC	77090
EMMET	3900	454X	NEH	77026
EMMET HUTTO BLVD	4000	501K	BT	77521
EMMETT RD	12500	408V	NWC	77041
EMMIT CREEK LN	5900	609T	NEF	77479
EMMOTT RD	8500	410T	NWC	77040
EMNORA LN	8500	450N	NWH	77080
EMNORA LN	10200	449R	NWC	77043
EMORY	4100	532A	WU	77005
EMORY BROOK CT	12100	377A	NEC	77346
EMORY COVE DR	0	293G	SEM	77386
EMORY GREEN	24200	445S	NWC	77493
EMORY HILL	14400	326Y	NWC	77429
EMORY KNOLL DR	2300	611W	FS	77545
EMORY MILL RD	0	526T	NEF	77407
EMORY OAK CT	1	250M	WD	77381
EMORY OAK LN	3100	613B	NEB	77584
EMORY TRAIL	19100	332F	NWC	77388
EMPANADA DR	14300	528J	SWC	77083
EMPANADA DR	14900	527L	NEF	77083
EMPEROR LN	7900	528R	SWH	77072
EMPERORS PASS	0	610W	MC	77459
W. EMPIRE	400	412R	NCC	77037
EMPIRE CIR	18700	258E	SEM	77357
EMPIRE CENTRAL DR	6900	410N	NWC	77040
EMPIRE GOLD DR	0	325L	NWC	77433
EMPIRE HEIGHTS CT	14300	328T	NWC	77429
EMPIRE LANDING VIEW	0	525A	NEF	77494
EMPIRE OAKS LN	0	485N	NEF	77494
EMPOLI LN	0	659Q	LC	77573
EMPORIA	12800	496D	NEH	77015
EMPORIA	13000	497E	NEH	77015
EMPORIA CHASE CT	0	484L	NEF	77494
EMPORIA LAKE LN	0	377H	NEH	77346
EMPORIA POINT CT	0	484L	NEF	77494
EMPRESS	300	658L	LC	77573
EMPRESS DR	200	576G	SEH	77034
EMPRESS LN	4100	525Y	NEF	77406
EMPRESS COVE LN	0	328L	NWC	77377
EMPRESS CROSSING DR	0	289Y	NWC	77379
EMPRESS OAKS CT	11700	489W	SWH	77082
EMPSON DR	15500	373Q	NCC	77032
EMPTY NESS DR	0	327U	NWC	77429
EMPTY SADDLE CT	20400	486T	NEF	77450
EMROSE LN	17900	327N	CY	77429
EMSCO	6700	574G	SEH	77061
EMSWORTH CIR	12700	488M	SWH	77077
ENBROOK MEADOW LN	0	446N	NWH	77449
ENCENADA GREEN CT	0	337U	NEC	77346
ENCENADA GREEN TRAIL	6300	337T	NEC	77346
ENCHANTED DR	12900	368F	NWC	77429
ENCHANTED DR	28700	251D	SD	77381
ENCHANTED LN	500	332A	NWC	77388

Street Name	Block	Pg/Sq	Loc	Zips
ENCHANTED CACTUS DR	0	525B	NEF	77494
ENCHANTED CREEK DR	7100	406Q	NWC	77433
ENCHANTED CROSSING	0	525E	NEF	77494
ENCHANTED FOREST DR	8000	411L	NWC	77088
ENCHANTED FOREST DR	32800	246V	SWM	77355
ENCHANTED GATE	4200	333C	NCC	77373
ENCHANTED GROVE DR	19500	332B	NWC	77388
ENCHANTED HOLLOW DR	500	332A	NWC	77388
ENCHANTED HOLLOW LN	3100	291U	NWC	77388
ENCHANTED ISLE DR	2200	618A	SEH	77062
ENCHANTED LAKE CT	9200	289M	NWC	77375
ENCHANTED LAKE DR	0	612P	PL	77545
ENCHANTED LAKE DR	0	485Q	NEF	77450
ENCHANTED LAKE DR	2100	619Z	LC	77573
ENCHANTED LANDING CT	2800	485U	NEF	77494
ENCHANTED LANDING LN	23000	485T	NEF	77494
ENCHANTED MEADOW DR	0	484Z	NEF	77494
ENCHANTED MEADOW LN	4600	484Y	NEF	77494
ENCHANTED MIST DR	5200	337S	NEC	77346
ENCHANTED OAKS CT	100	332B	NWC	77388
ENCHANTED OAKS DR	18900	332F	NWC	77388
ENCHANTED PARK DR	1900	252R	SEM	77386
ENCHANTED PARK LN	2000	486N	SWC	77450
ENCHANTED PATH DR	11900	456C	NEC	77044
ENCHANTED RIVER DR	200	332A	NWC	77388
ENCHANTED ROCK DR	500	332U	NCC	77073
ENCHANTED ROCK LN	0	609Y	MC	77459
ENCHANTED ROCK LN	4600	291W	NWC	77388
ENCHANTED ROCK TRAIL	18100	377B	NEC	77346
ENCHANTED ROSE	0	406L	NWC	77433
ENCHANTED SPRING DR	19400	332A	NWC	77388
ENCHANTED SPRINGS CT	0	609X	NEF	77479
ENCHANTED STONE CT	10200	369L	NWC	77070
ENCHANTED STONE DR	9900	369L	NWC	77070
ENCHANTED STREAM DR	19100	332E	NWC	77388
ENCHANTED TIMBERS DR	5100	337S	NEC	77346
ENCHANTED TIMBERS LN	0	253Q	SEM	77386
ENCHANTED TRAIL DR	200	332A	NWC	77388
ENCHANTED VALLEY DR	14400	368E	NWC	77429
ENCHANTED WOODS DR	1	336L	NEH	77339
ENCHANTFORD CT	19400	332B	NWC	77388
ENCHANTINGTON CIR	19400	332B	NWC	77388
ENCHANTMENT DR	23300	339P	HU	77336
ENCINITA DR	7800	527L	NEF	77083
ENCINITAS COVE CT	22700	289M	NWC	77375
ENCINITAS COVE DR	8200	289M	NWC	77375
ENCINO	0	568R	SG	77478
ENCINO AVE	0	659S	LC	77573
ENCINO DR	5000	617W	FR	77546
ENCINO LN	2500	569N	SG	77478
ENCINO COVE CT	10000	369Y	NWC	77064
ENCINO PASS TRAIL	10300	369X	NWC	77064
ENCLAVE CT	0	568G	SG	77478
ENCLAVE CT	1700	569X	MC	77459
ENCLAVE CT	12200	569E	SF	77477
ENCLAVE LN	0	488Q	SWH	77077
ENCLAVE CREEK LN	0	445M	NWC	77449
ENCLAVE FOUNTAIN LN	5500	452A	NWH	77091
ENCLAVE GREENS DR	0	486H	SWC	77094
ENCLAVE LAKE DR	900	488F	SWH	77077
ENCLAVE LAKE LN	0	613J	PL	77584
ENCLAVE LAKE LN	11300	612H	PL	77584
ENCLAVE MANOR DR	0	609P	NEF	77479
ENCLAVE MIST LN	0	445H	NWC	77449
ENCLAVE OAKS LN	0	331T	NWC	77068
ENCLAVE PKWY	100	488Q	SWH	77077
ENCLAVE ROUND	0	488L	SWH	77077
N. ENCLAVE SQUARE	0	488F	SWH	77077
S. ENCLAVE SQUARE	1000	488F	SWH	77077
W. ENCLAVE SQUARE	1100	488F	SWH	77077
E. ENCLAVE SQUARE	1100	488F	SWH	77077
ENCLAVE TERRACE	0	568T	SG	77478
ENCLAVE TRAIL	3200	488P	SWH	77077
ENCLAVE VISTA LN	0	409W	NWC	77041
ENCLAVE VISTA LN	0	409W	NWC	77041
ENCLAVE WATERS LN	5500	452A	NWH	77091
ENCREEK RD	2300	331L	NWC	77068
ENDEAVOR CT	1900	620K	SB	77586
ENDEAVOR DR	7600	528M	SWH	77072
ENDELL CT	700	486B	SWC	77450
ENDEL WAY	0	527W	NEF	77407
ENDICOTT LN	2100	568C	SG	77478
ENDICOTT LN	3300	613Y	NEB	77584
ENDICOTT LN	8500	531Q	SWH	77096
ENDICOTT LN	10600	531X	SWH	77035
ENDICOTT LN	10600	571B	SWH	77035
ENDICOTT ROCK LN	0	377K	NEC	77346
ENDOR	7700	535B	SEH	77012
ENELO DR	0	450D	NWH	77092
ENERGY DR	0	292F	NWC	77389
ENERO DR	14900	527M	SWC	77083
ENFIELD DR	300	459Q	HG	77562
ENFORD CT	700	486B	SWC	77450
ENGEL	100	494Q	SEH	77011
ENGELKE	2500	494N	SEH	77003
ENGELMOHR	1900	532R	SWH	77054
ENGELMOHR	2300	533N	SWH	77054
ENGLAND	5800	533H	SEH	77021
W. ENGLAND CT	0	533H	SEH	77021
E. ENGLAND CT	0	533H	SEH	77021
ENGLEBROOK DR	14600	408G	NWC	77095
ENGLEFIELD CT	3900	446L	NWC	77449
ENGLEFORD	4100	454X	NEH	77026
ENGLE FOREST CIR	4900	377A	NEC	77346
ENGLEWOOD	100	531L	BL	77401
ENGLEWOOD	3500	454Z	NEH	77026
ENGLEWOOD DR	1	568Y	SG	77478
ENGLEWOOD DR	100	658M	LC	77573
ENGLEWOOD DR	3600	613Y	NEB	77584
ENGLEWOOD PARK LN	14100	328P	NWC	77429
ENGLEWOOD PLACE	0	568Y	SG	77478
ENGLEWOOD POINT CT	5200	485W	NEF	77494
ENGLISH	200	453U	NEH	77009
ENGLISH BROOK CIR	12100	377A	NEC	77346
ENGLISH CHASE CT	0	368A	NWC	77429
ENGLISH COLONY DR	2800	657C	SEC	77598
ENGLISH ELM	1900	371V	NWC	77067
ENGLISH GLADE CT	1	251F	WD	77381
ENGLISH GREEN WAY	2100	611W	FS	77545
ENGLISH HOLLY CT		249T	NWC	77375
ENGLISH IVY LN	17800	331J	NWC	77379
ENGLISH LAKE DR	0	615Y	PL	77581
ENGLISH MANOR DR	0	406C	NWC	77433
ENGLISH OAKS BLVD	3000	614U	PL	77584
ENGLISH OAKS DR	23800	293T	NCC	77373
ENGLISH ROSE LN	11200	489X	SWH	77082
ENGLISH TURN DR		484W	NEF	77494
ENID	200	453T	NWH	77009
ENID	6500	453P	NEH	77022
ENLIGHTENMENT AVE	300	419V	NEC	77532
ENLOE RD	23800	295H	SEM	77365
ENMORE CT	9300	407D	NWC	77095

Street Name	Block	Pg/Sq	Loc	Zips
N. ENNIS	1	494N	SEH	77003
ENNIS	300	494N	SEH	77003
ENNIS	800	493V	SEH	77003
ENNIS	3000	533C	SEH	77004
ENNIS RD	15300	527U	NEF	77498
ENNIS RD	16300	527U	NEF	77498
ENNIS LN	6800	330L	NWC	77379
ENNSBURY DR	18100	447F	NWC	77084
ENOCH	2200	533S	SWH	77054
ENOLA DR	14500	366D	CY	77429
ENO LOOP	0	331U	NWC	77014
ENOS ST	10000	370Z	NWC	77086
ENRIDGE LN	0	574Y	SEH	77048
ENSBROOK DR	10800	569B	SWH	77099
ENSEMBLE CT	9000	410K	NWC	77040
ENSEMBLE DR	7800	410K	NWC	77040
ENSENADA DR	15200	527M	NEF	77083
ENSENADA CANYON LN	0	409W	NWC	77041
ENSLEY WOOD DR	13100	528C	SWH	77082
ENSTONE CIR	9500	330S	NWC	77379
ENSWORTH DR	7100	415T	NEH	77016
ENTERPRISE	700	412U	NWH	77088
ENTERPRISE AVE	100	619U	LC	77573
ENTERPRISE CIR	1600	619U	LC	77573
ENTRADA CT	20200	337U	NEC	77346
ENTRANCE	0	492F	SWH	77007
ENVOY	10100	414Z	NEH	77016
ENYART	4900	534N	SEH	77021
EOLA CREEK LN	0	458S	NEC	77049
EPERNAY	0	409L	JV	77040
EPHRAM DR	2200	484K	NEF	77494
EPIC DR	3900	293L	SEM	77386
EPONA CT	0	410L	NWC	77040
EPORIUM DR	0	447P	NWC	77084
EPPES	4700	534J	SEH	77021
EPPES	6300	534R	SEH	77087
EPPINGDALE DR	3600	371K	NWC	77066
EPPING FOREST WAY	1	609J	SG	77479
EPPOLITO	300	569V	SF	77477
EPPS	100	288G	TB	77375
EPRIGHT DR	0	326U	NWC	77429
EPSILON	1200	577J	PA	77504
EPSOM RD	9800	454A	NEH	77093
EPSOM RD	10900	414T	NEC	77093
EPSOM DOWNS DR	7400	407J	NWC	77433
EPSTEIN CT	1	493J	SWH	77007
EQUADOR	7600	409R	JV	77040
EQUINOX	500	419B	NEC	77532
EQUITY DR	10800	449H	NWH	77041
ERA LN	22300	296C	SEM	77365
ERASMUS LANDING CT	0	378A	NEC	77346
ERASTUS	1900	494C	NEH	77020
ERASTUS	2800	494C	NEH	77026
ERATH	7400	535A	SEH	77023
E. ERATH	7600	535B	SEH	77012
ERATH ALLEY	7600	535B	SEH	77012
ERBY	3600	534G	SEH	77023
ERBY	3900	534M	SEH	77087
ERIC	29700	246D	SWM	77355
ERICA LN	0	287R	NWC	77377
ERICA LN	0	460N	HG	77562
ERICA LN	3000	573B	SEH	77051
ERICK CIR	0	290K	NWC	77379
ERICSON CT	5900	330D	NWC	77379
ERICSTON DR	11300	329S	NWC	77070
ERIC TRAIL DR	0	325S	HK	77447
ERIE	3700	535P	SEH	77017
ERIE	3900	535T	SEH	77087
ERIE	7800	461S	NEC	77521
ERIE	8000	535T	SEH	77061
ERIE	18200	295F	SEM	77365
ERIE COVE CT	27700	294E	SEM	77386
ERIKA CT	21600	255V	SEM	77365
ERIKA WAY DR	19900	486L	SWC	77450
ERIN	300	453Z	NEH	77009
ERIN CT	100	539Z	LP	77571
ERIN CT	8100	570G	SWH	77071
ERIN CT	14000	568E	SG	77498
ERIN DR	0	570F	SWH	77071
ERIN DR	2300	616K	PL	77581
ERIN ASHLEY LN	0	524B	NEF	77494
ERIN COVE CT	7900	407L	NWC	77095
ERIN CREEK CT	15900	618G	SEH	77062
ERINCREST CT	21900	485V	NEF	77450
ERIN DALE CT	14200	528N	SWC	77083
ERIN GLEN CT	2200	538N	DP	77536
ERIN GLEN WAY	10000	613K	PL	77584
ERIN HOLLOW CT	19900	526K	NEF	77407
ERIN KNOLL CT	3400	578X	SEH	77059
ERIN VIEW DR	0	612P	PL	77545
ERIN WAY CT	17400	407P	NWC	77095
ERINWOOD CT	100	330F	NWC	77379
ERINWOOD DR	7400	330F	NWC	77379
ERLINGTON BEND TRACE	0	297J	SEM	77365
ERNEST	0	374V	NEH	77396
ERNEST CIR	21800	245Z	SWM	77355
ERNESTINE	1300	494W	SEH	77023
ERNIE RD	5000	454L	NEH	77016
ERNST CT	500	332B	NWC	77388
ERNSTES RD	400	485A	SWC	77494
EROC AVE	0	572H	SEH	77051
EROS LN	2700	610Q	MC	77459
ERRINGTON DR	7900	457F	NEC	77049
ERSKINE CT	10300	369K	NWC	77070
ERTEL LN	7000	410T	NWC	77040
ERVA DR	400	413J	NCC	77037
ERVIN	1200	658Z	LC	77573
ERVIN HILL LN	0	295M	SEM	77365
ERWIN RD	1300	413L	NCC	77039
ESCALA DR	21100	334R	NCC	77338
ESCALANTE DR	0	367P	NWC	77433
ESCHER RD	15800	326P	NWC	77433
ESCON	0	444G	NWC	77493
ESCONDIDO CIR	6600	527G	SWC	77083
ESCONDIDO DR	6500	527G	SWC	77083
ESELLE CREEK DR	0	289H	NWC	77375
ESKRIDGE	5500	534C	SEH	77023
ESPADA ST	0	447J	NWC	77084
ESPERANZA	1700	534D	SEH	77023
ESPERIA ST	0	525J	NEF	77406
ESPERSON	6000	494U	SEH	77011
ESPINOSA DR	16100	527K	NEF	77083
ESPINOSA LN	19500	256K	SEM	77357
ESPLANADE BLVD	0	372V	NEH	77060
N. ESPLANADE LN	200	569Q	SF	77477
S. ESPLANADE LN	300	569Q	SF	77477
ESPLANADE PLACE	100	569Q	SF	77477
ESPLANADE WAY	0	569Q	SF	77477
S. ESPLANADE WAY	100	569Q	SF	77477
ESPUELA LN	0	461P	NEC	77521
ESSENBRUK DR	12000	371J	NWC	77066
ESSENDINE LN	14400	571R	SWH	77045

Street Name	Block	Pg/Sq	Loc	Zips
ESSEX	0	257M	SEM	77357
ESSEX	0	258J	SEM	77357
ESSEX CT	1100	620G	SB	77586
ESSEX CT	2500	658V	LC	77573
ESSEX DR	700	656M	FR	77546
ESSEX LN	3900	492S	SWH	77027
ESSEX GREEN	3800	492S	SWH	77027
ESSEX PLACE	200	569J	SF	77477
ESSEX TERRACE	2700	492S	SWH	77027
ESSIE RD	3200	411C	NWC	77086
ESSLEMONT CT	10000	527S	NEF	77407
ESSLEMONT CT	10000	527S	NEF	77407
ESSMAN LN	20500	333N	NCC	77073
ESTANCIA PLACE	0	250K	NWC	77389
ESTARIL CIR	2500	412E	NWC	77038
ESTATE	2500	538S	PA	77503
ESTATE	3100	569Q	SF	77477
ESTATE DR	1900	538T	DP	77536
ESTATE DR	4500	501E	BT	77521
ESTATES AT CULLEN PARK	0	447T	NWC	77084
ESTATES CREEK BLVD	2900	331D	NWC	77388
ESTEBAN POINT LN	0	293K	SEM	77386
ESTELLA	400	576H	PA	77504
ESTELLA CT	0	660G	LC	77573
ESTELLA LN	15700	332T	NWC	77090
ESTELLE	1	494P	SEH	77003
ESTELLE LN	0	248S	SWM	77354
ESTELLE LN	5300	334E	NCC	77373
ESTERBROOK DR	3400	487Y	SWC	77082
ESTES	3900	534G	SEH	77023
ESTES BROOK LN	0	572W	SWC	77053
ESTES GLEN LN	9500	410F	NWC	77040
ESTES LAKE LN	0	485S	NEF	77494
ESTES PARK LN	11900	371L	NWC	77067
ESTHER	1200	620W	GCO	77565
ESTHER	4200	569P	SF	77477
ESTHER AVE	2500	537P	PA	77502
ESTHER DR	0	411V	NWH	77088
ESTHER DR	1100	412S	NWH	77088
ESTHERWOOD PLACE	0	249A	SWM	77354
ESTONIA CT	5900	330D	NWC	77379
ESTRADA DR	6200	528E	SWC	77083
ESTRELLA CT	0	571H	SWH	77045
ESTRELLITA DR	14800	413A	NEH	77060
ESTURAY CIR	0	250P	NWC	77389
ETCHSTONE DR	6600	290C	NWC	77389
ETHAN CREEK DR		289H	NWC	77375
ETHAN TRAILS LN	0	293K	SEM	77386
ETHEL	4800	614S	NEB	77584
ETHEL	7700	455P	NEH	77028
ETHEL LN	4300	569P	NEF	77477
ETHELINE DR	5000	414H	NEC	77039
ETHERIDGE	5600	534Q	SEH	77087
ETHYL RD	100	537G	PA	77503
ETHYL RD	1100	497Y	SEC	77503
ETON	3700	535N	SEH	77087
ETON DR	2100	615L	PL	77581
ETON BROOK LN	16400	332R	NCC	77073
ETON RIDGE CT	0	526M	NEF	77407
ETTA	8900	454E	NEH	77093
ETTRICK DR	5500	571E	SWH	77035
ETTRICK DR	6000	570H	SWH	77035
ETZEL CIR	0	572S	SWH	77053
EUBANKS	300	453L	NEH	77022
EUBANKS	1700	453M	NEH	77093
EUCLAIRE DR	11700	411F	NWC	77086
EUCLID	300	493B	NWH	77009
EUCLID	400	498G	CV	77530
EUEL	1100	453V	NEH	77009
EUELL RD	2500	420C	NEC	77532
EUGENE	6900	454N	NEH	77093
EUGENIO SANTANA DR	22900	500Z	BT	77520
EULA AVE	5000	577C	PA	77505
EULA MORGAN RD	3000	444K	NWC	77493
EULE DR	5000	444Z	KT	77493
EUNICE	3100	493C	NWH	77009
EUNICE	17800	418R	NEC	77044
EUNICE JOHNSON LN	0	322A	WCO	77484
EUPHRATES	5200	578Q	PA	77059
EUREKA	6100	492B	NWH	77008
EUROPA	3300	453J	NEH	77022
EUSTON STATION	0	532Z	SWH	77045
EVA	1000	536V	PA	77502
EVA	2600	454J	NEH	77093
EVA DR	800	444W	KT	77493
EVANFEILD CT	27000	366U	NWC	77433
EVANGELINE	11900	419Z	BR	77532
EVANGELINE DR	0	620K	SB	77586
EVANGELINE DR	10800	456S	NEH	77013
EVANGELINE SPRINGS LN	0	524H	NEF	77494
EVANHALEBEND DR	0	327D	NWC	77429
EVANMILL LN	0	524H	NEF	77494
EVAN RIDGE CT	1	251C	WD	77381
EVANS	6600	574D	SEH	77061
EVANS	7300	575A	SEH	77061
EVANS RD	1400	610A	MC	77489
EVANS GATE	0	656R	FR	77546
EVANS GROVE LN	0	484T	NEF	77494
EVANS MILL LN	0	484T	NEF	77494
EVANSTON	1	457X	NEC	77015
EVANSTON	500	497B	NEH	77015
EVE	1	456X	NEH	77013
EVELLA	2600	454W	NEH	77026
EVELLA	4500	494C	NEH	77026
EVELO	8400	533Z	SEH	77051
EVELYN	200	453U	NEH	77009
S. EVELYN CIR	11700	570L	MC	77071
N. EVELYN CIR	11700	570L	MC	77071
EVENDALE CT	19200	486H	SWC	77094
EVENING LN	24200	295K	SEM	77365
EVENING ST	0	373J	NCC	77060
EVENING BAY DR	0	612Q	PL	77584
EVENING CLOUD CT	1400	485L	SWC	77450
EVENING GLEN CT	12200	328D	NWC	77375
EVENING GLEN DR	19300	328D	NWC	77375
EVENING MEADOW DR	0	367S	NWC	77433
EVENING MOON LN	0	446B	NWC	77449
EVENING OAKS CT	18200	330C	NWC	77379
EVENING PRIMROSE LN	20200	289W	NWC	77375
EVENING ROSE LN	0	289Y	NWC	77379
EVENING ROSE LN	0	407S	NWC	77449
EVENING RUN LN	0	527N	NEF	77083
EVENING SHADE CT	2700	610B	MC	77489
EVENING SHADES CT	19500	337V	NEC	77346
EVENING SHADOWS LN	5700	334B	NCC	77373
EVENING SHORE CT	12500	449A	NWC	77041
EVENING SHORE DR	5500	449A	NWC	77041
EVENING SHORE LN	0	612Q	PL	77584
EVENING SONG CT	1	251Z	WD	77380
EVENING STAR CT	0	612K	PL	77545
EVENING STAR CT	16000	419A	NEC	77532
EVENING TRAIL DR	3800	331F	NWC	77388
EVENING WIND CT	0	612J	PL	77545
EVENING WIND DR	0	612J	PL	77545
EVENSONG LN	11100	368T	NWC	77429
EVENTIDE DR	14100	368P	NWC	77429
EVERBEAR	1300	577J	PA	77504
EVERBLOOM MEADOW	0	525B	NEF	77494
EVEREST DR	1500	336B	NEH	77339
EVEREST LN	2700	333P	NCC	77073
EVERETT	1500	493H	NEH	77009
EVERETT DR	2800	656X	FR	77546
EVERETT GLEN LN	0	524E	NEF	77494
EVERETT OAKS LN	0	407C	NWC	77095
EVERFROST LN	0	290X	NWC	77379
EVERGLADE	0	416W	NEC	77078
S. EVERGLADE DR	0	538R	DP	77536
N. EVERGLADE DR	0	538R	DP	77536
EVERGLADE DR	1200	537W	PA	77502
EVERGLADE DR	8800	415Z	NEH	77078
EVERGREEN	0	297P	NEH	77365
EVERGREEN	700	656H	FR	77546
EVERGREEN	4500	531M	BL	77401
EVERGREEN	5400	531K	SWH	77081
EVERGREEN	5401	531K	BL	77401
EVERGREEN	5500	531K	SWH	77081
EVERGREEN	5600	531K	BL	77401
EVERGREEN	6100	531J	SWH	77081
EVERGREEN CIR	1000	251H	WD	77380
EVERGREEN DR	400	535A	SEH	77023
EVERGREEN DR	500	459Q	HG	77562
EVERGREEN DR	1000	535E	SEH	77087
EVERGREEN DR	2300	616T	PL	77581
EVERGREEN DR	13300	248Y	TB	77375
EVERGREEN DR	23300	296M	SEM	77365
EVERGREEN LN	1600	619D	PA	77586
EVERGREEN RD	100	541L	BT	77520
EVERGREEN RD	100	611U	FS	77545
EVERGREEN ST	0	463S	CCO	77520
EVERGREEN BAY CT	2500	618C	SEH	77059
EVERGREEN BEND DR	0	250V	NWC	77389
EVERGREEN BROOK WAY	7600	407M	NWC	77095
EVERGREEN CANYON RD	5400	371N	NWC	77066
EVERGREEN CLIFF TRAIL	2700	297Z	NEH	77345
EVERGREEN ELM CT	4300	578Y	SEH	77059
EVERGREEN ELM WAY	17000	578Y	SEH	77059
EVERGREEN FALLS DR	18600	447N	NWC	77084
EVERGREEN GLADE CT	3000	296Y	NEH	77339
EVERGREEN GLADE DR	2900	296Y	NEH	77339
EVERGREEN GLEN	0	578Y	SEH	77059
EVERGREEN GROVE DR	15400	527R	NEF	77083
EVERGREEN HAVEN CT	0	447A	NWC	77084
EVERGREEN HILLS DR	29401	253X	SEM	77386
EVERGREEN KNOLL LN	15200	326T	NWC	77433
EVERGREEN LAKE LN	16200	367C	NWC	77429
EVERGREEN MEADOW CT	4500	446H	NWC	77449
EVERGREEN OAK DR	3100	331T	NWC	77068
EVERGREEN PARK	31300	252R	SEM	77385
EVERGREEN PLACE DR	15300	527Q	NEF	77083
EVERGREEN RIDGE WAY	14700	618F	SEH	77062
EVERGREEN SPRINGS CT	6600	290Y	NWC	77379
EVERGREEN SPRINGS LN	20200	290Y	NWC	77379
EVERGREEN SQUARE TRAIL	3500	611W	MC	77545
EVERGREEN TERRACE DR	7900	410L	NWC	77040
EVERGREEN TIMBERS	16200	246Y	SWM	77355
EVERGREEN TRAILS	6400	409W	NWC	77041
EVERGREEN VALLEY DR	5200	297U	NEH	77345
EVERGREEN VILLAGE DR	4000	297T	NEH	77345
EVERHART LN	6900	410E	NWC	77040
EVERHART BROOK LN	0	377G	NEC	77346
EVERHART KEY LN	0	334R	NCC	77338
EVERHART MANOR LN	5400	524D	NEF	77494
EVERHART POINTE DR	12600	328Q	NWC	77377
EVERHART SPRINGS LN	0	366Y	NWC	77433
EVERHILL CIR	6500	526E	NEF	77450
EVERINGTON CIR	22900	485C	SWC	77450
S. EVERINGTON DR	400	485C	SWC	77450
EVERINGTON DR	400	485C	SWC	77450
EVERLEAF DR	8300	330N	NWC	77379
EVERLY BEND DR	0	293G	SEM	77386
EVERMORE MANOR LN	0	373E	NCC	77073
EVERSEEN LN	8400	410K	NWC	77040
EVERSHAM WAY	1200	336H	NEH	77339
S. EVERS PARK DR	10600	491E	HC	77024
N. EVERS PARK DR	10600	491E	HC	77024
EVERTON	100	494N	SEH	77003
EVERTS AVE	5200	656W	AV	77511
EVERWOOD LN	10800	490H	HC	77024
EVERWOOD GREEN LN	0	326K	NWC	77433
EVESBOROUGH DR	10500	529T	SWH	77099
EVESHAM DR	1600	457U	NEC	77015
EVIE LN	7400	538X	DP	77536
EVONNE	400	536N	SEH	77017
EWELL DR	2500	658P	LC	77573
EWING	1100	533B	SWH	77004
EWING CT	3100	613W	NWB	77578
EWING DR	3300	613W	NWB	77578
EWOOD	1000	615A	PL	77581
EXBURY CT	12300	328R	NWC	77377
EXBURY WAY	1	491L	SWH	77056
EXCALIBER'S CT	3200	613K	PL	77584
EXCALIBUR CT	700	656B	FR	77546
EXCALIBUR CT	19800	486L	SWC	77094
EXCALIBUR DR	0	486L	SWC	77094
EXCHANGE	300	495A	NEH	77020
EXCHANGE DR	12500	569J	SF	77477
EXECUTIVE DR	12600	569J	SF	77477
EXECUTIVE DR	12900	569J	SG	77478
EXETER	9000	453D	NEH	77093
EXETER	10000	413Z	NEH	77093
EXETER	11700	413R	NCC	77093
EXETER CIR	2200	444Q	KT	77493
EXETER LN	0	657U	LC	77573
EXETER TRAIL	3300	613F	NEB	77584
EXMOOR TERRACE DR	0	488T	SWH	77077
EXMOUTH CT	3600	299S	NEC	77336
EXMOUTH CT	3600	299S	NEC	77336
EXPLORER DR	13400	377L	NEC	77044
EXPLORER COVE	3200	609E	SG	77479
EXPORT PLAZA DR	15500	374Q	NEH	77032
EXPRESS LN	7000	456J	NEH	77078
EXTOL WAY	0	445K	NWC	77493
EXTON LN	13400	369F	NWC	77070
EZEKIEL RD	11500	329A	NWC	77375
EZZARD CHARLES LN	6300	412W	NWH	77091

F

Street Name	Block	Pg/Sq	Loc	Zips
F	2900	580Q	LP	77571
F	3800	529A	SWH	77072
F AVE	0	536X	SH	77587
F CIR	0	290L	NWC	77389
S. F, AVENUE	100	335Z	HM	77338
N. F, AVENUE	100	335V	HM	77338
F, AVENUE	100	536X	SH	77587
F, AVENUE	100	568J	SG	77498
F, AVENUE	100	569Q	SF	77477
F, AVENUE	1800	496W	GP	77547
F, AVENUE	2000	659Y	DI	77539
F, AVENUE	6500	494V	SEH	77011
F, AVENUE	7500	495W	SEH	77012
FABER RD	13800	413F	NCC	77037
FABIOLA DR	0	575R	SEH	77075
FABLE CT	14300	327Z	NWC	77429
FABLE SPRINGS LN	0	367P	NWC	77433
FACULTY LN	4300	534E	SEH	77004
FADEWAY LN	13000	571G	SWH	77045
FADING ROSE LN	0	326N	NWC	77433
FAGAN WAY	0	568S	SG	77479
FAILSAFE	600	453Q	NEH	77022
FAIR	700	412U	NWH	77088
N. FAIR CT	21100	332V	NCC	77073
FAIR DR	0	579F	SEC	77507
FAIR LN	1100	540T	LP	77571
FAIR ACRES	7800	528M	SWH	77072
FAIR ACRES DR	1100	568F	SG	77498
FAIRBANKS	200	453U	NEH	77009
FAIRBANKS	2400	454T	NEH	77026
FAIRBANKS-N HOUSTON	5600	450C	NWH	77040
FAIRBANKS-N HOUSTON	6000	410T	NWC	77040
FAIRBANKS-N HOUSTON	8000	410T	NWC	77064
FAIRBANKS-N HOUSTON	9800	370T	NWC	77064
FAIRBANKS-N HOUSTON	10700	370T	NWC	77086
FAIRBANKS-WHITE OAK	7400	410U	NWC	77040
FAIRBAY CIR	2100	620W	LC	77573
FAIRBAY DR	22300	485U	NEF	77450
FAIR BEAUTY CT	0	612P	PL	77545
FAIRBEND	8700	450Z	NWH	77055
FAIRBLOOM LN	8800	410F	NWC	77040
FAIRBOURNE DR	6300	578E	PA	77505
FAIRBRANCH CT	2000	485K	NEF	77494
FAIRBRANCH DR	23300	485K	NEF	77494
FAIR BREEZE LN	0	612F	PL	77545
FAIRBRIDGE LN	12700	368L	NWC	77429
FAIRBROOK LN	8400	578C	LP	77571
FAIRBROOK LN	25300	293N	NCC	77373
FAIRBROOK LN	25700	292R	NCC	77373
FAIRBROOK PARK CT	21300	290U	NWC	77379
FAIRBROOK PARK CT	21300	290U	NWC	77379
FAIRBROOK PARK CT	21300	290U	NWC	77379
FAIRBROOK PARK LN	6500	290U	NWC	77379
FAIRBROOK PARK LN	6500	290U	NWC	77379
FAIRBROOK PARK LN	6500	290U	NWC	77379
FAIR BROOK WAY	9600	613L	PL	77584
FAIRBUFF LN	14300	331Y	NWC	77014
FAIRBURY DR	11800	616D	SEH	77089
FAIRBURY DR	12200	617A	SEH	77089
FAIR CASTLE DR	0	406L	NWC	77433
FAIRCHILD	0	577Y	SEH	77034
FAIRCHILD	5100	455P	NEH	77028
FAIRCLIFF LN	0	406P	NWC	77449
FAIR COUNTRY LN	0	446F	NWC	77449
FAIRCOURT DR	26800	296X	SEM	77339
FAIRCREEK LN	5400	525D	NEF	77450
FAIRCREST	700	413U	NEH	77076
FAIRCREST	4800	577G	PA	77505
FAIRCROFT DR	9200	574E	SEH	77033
FAIRCROFT DR	10600	574E	SEH	77048
FAIRDALE	4800	577G	PA	77505
FAIRDALE LN	5300	491Y	SWH	77056
FAIRDALE LN	5600	491W	SWH	77057
FAIRDALE LN	7600	490W	SWH	77063
FAIRDALE RD	500	656H	FR	77546
FAIRDALE ESTATES CT	0	491W	SWH	77057
E. FAIRDALE OAKS	0	491W	SWH	77057
FAIR DAWN CT	3000	485V	NEF	77450
FAIRDAWN LN	0	658W	LC	77573
FAIRDAY LN	700	413U	NEH	77076
FAIR ELM CT	0	527D	SWC	77082
FAIR FALLS DR	3200	297Q	NEH	77345
FAIR FALLS LOOP	21200	326N	NWC	77433
FAIR FALLS WAY	16100	326N	NWC	77433
FAIRFAX	800	538K	DP	77536
FAIRFAX	9900	495M	JC	77029
FAIRFAX	10300	496J	JC	77029
FAIRFAX LN	0	536H	PA	77506
FAIRFAX GREEN DR	4700	333D	NCC	77373
S. FAIRFAX VILLAGE CIR	4800	333D	NCC	77373
N. FAIRFAX VILLAGE CIR	4800	333D	NCC	77373
W. FAIRFAX VILLAGE CIR	22800	333D	NCC	77373
E. FAIRFAX VILLAGE CIR	22800	333D	NCC	77373
FAIRFIELD	100	580Q	SA	77571
FAIRFIELD	6600	534C	SEH	77023
S. FAIRFIELD CT	1900	658Q	LC	77573
N. FAIRFIELD CT	1900	658Q	LC	77573
FAIRFIELD ARBOR DR	0	578T	SEH	77059
FAIRFIELD BEND PLACE	0	484N	NEF	77494
FAIRFIELD CHASE CROSSING	0	297K	SEM	77365
FAIRFIELD CREEK DR	0	326X	NWC	77433
FAIRFIELD FALLS DR	0	326N	NWC	77433
FAIRFIELD FALLS WAY	0	325V	NWC	77433
FAIRFIELD FALLS WAY	15200	326S	NWC	77433
FAIRFIELD GREEN	21200	325R	NWC	77433
FAIRFIELD GREEN BLVD	20500	326N	NWC	77433
FAIRFIELD GREEN CIR	16000	326N	NWC	77433
FAIRFIELD LAKES CT	20300	326P	NWC	77433
FAIRFIELD MANOR WAY	0	526L	NEF	77407
FAIRFIELD PARK DR	0	326N	NWC	77433
FAIRFIELD PARK DR	21800	325R	NWC	77433
FAIRFIELD PARK WAY	20300	326N	NWC	77433
FAIRFIELD PLACE	22000	325R	NWC	77433
FAIRFIELD TRACE DR	20100	326N	NWC	77433
FAIRFIELD VILLAGE	0	326X	NWC	77433
FAIRFORD DR	4800	609S	NEF	77479
FAIR FOREST DR	5400	411K	NWC	77088
FAIRGATE DR	900	486G	SWC	77094
FAIRGATE LN	7700	575S	SEH	77075
FAIR GLADE CT	13900	328T	NWC	77429
FAIR GLADE LN	14000	328T	NWC	77429
FAIRGLEN	4200	577G	PA	77505
FAIR GRANGE LN	0	407J	NWC	77433
FAIRGRANGE KEY LN	0	373E	NCC	77073
FAIRGRANGE PLACE LN	0	446G	NWC	77449
FAIRGREEN DR	0	610A	MC	77489
FAIRGREEN DR	2200	610E	MC	77489
FAIRGREEN LN	4100	573L	SEH	77047
FAIRGREEN LN	4700	574J	SEH	77048
FAIRGREEN GLEN DR	13200	414B	NCC	77039
FAIRGROVE CT	2700	613T	NEB	77584
FAIR GROVE DR	0	296R	NEH	77339
FAIRGROVE PARK CT	8200	407F	NWC	77095
FAIRGROVE PARK DR	17500	407F	NWC	77095
FAIRGROVE RIDGE	0	572Q	SWH	77045
W. FAIR HARBOR LN	300	488B	SWH	77079
E. FAIR HARBOR LN	300	488B	SWH	77079
FAIRHAVEN	4800	577G	PA	77505
FAIRHAVEN	6400	532E	WU	77005
FAIRHAVEN CT	0	325H	NWC	77377
FAIRHAVEN CREEK DR	0	325H	NWC	77377
FAIRHAVEN FALLS DR	0	325H	NWC	77377
FAIRHAVEN GATEWAY DR	0	326E	NWC	77377
FAIRHAVEN HILLS DR	0	325H	NWC	77377
FAIRHAVEN ISLAND CT	0	325H	NWC	77377
FAIRHAVEN LAKE DR	0	326E	NWC	77377
FAIRHAVEN MANOR CIR	0	325H	NWC	77377
FAIRHAVEN MEADOW DR	0	325H	NWC	77377
FAIRHAVEN PARK CT	0	326E	NWC	77377
FAIRHAVEN SUNRISE CT	0	326E	NWC	77377
FAIRHAVEN SUNSET CT	0	326E	NWC	77377
FAIRHILL	4300	577G	PA	77505
FAIRHILL DR	3700	490Z	SWH	77063
S. FAIRHOLLOW LN	11800	449L	NWH	77043
N. FAIRHOLLOW LN	11800	449L	NWH	77043
FAIRHOPE	2800	532P	SWH	77025
FAIRHOPE LN	1	245D	SWM	77355
FAIRHOPE GROVE CIR	3700	446L	NWC	77449
FAIRHOPE MEADOW LN	0	296W	SEM	77339
FAIRHOPE OAK	0	537V	PP	77503
FAIRHOPE OAK CT	18200	447P	NWC	77084
FAIRHOPE PLACE	8200	532P	SWH	77025
FAIRIDGE CT	6000	250V	NWC	77389
FAIR KNOLL WAY	14200	618A	SEH	77062
FAIRLAKE DR	22600	338R	NEH	77336
FAIRLAND DR	9300	573F	SEH	77051
FAIRLAND DR	10800	573K	SEH	77051
FAIRLANE	0	614C	BK	77581
FAIRLANE DR	10600	491E	HC	77024
FAIRLANE MEADOWS DR	0	369G	NWC	77077
FAIRLANE OAKS DR	0	369G	NWC	77077
FAIRLANE SQUARE	1100	458W	NEC	77530
FAIRLAWN	6500	534U	SEH	77087
FAIRLEAF CIR	22900	485L	NEF	77494
FAIRLEE CT	0	249B	SWM	77382
FAIRMEADE	0	334N	NCC	77338
FAIRMEADE CT	1	251A	WD	77381
FAIRMEADE BEND DR	1	251A	WD	77381
FAIRMEADOW DR	11800	570C	SWH	77071
FAIR MEADOW LN	0	525A	NEF	77494
FAIRMONT	200	459X	CV	77530
FAIRMONT	5000	492W	SWH	77005
FAIRMONT	11300	570H	SWH	77035
FAIRMONT CT	3100	569N	SG	77478
FAIRMONT GREENS PKWY	0	580K	LP	77571
W. FAIRMONT PKWY	100	580E	LP	77571
E. FAIRMONT PKWY	100	580C	LP	77571
FAIRMONT PKWY	100	576D	PA	77504
FAIRMONT PKWY	1400	577G	PA	77504
FAIRMONT PKWY	4700	577G	PA	77505
FAIRMONT PKWY	6300	578G	PA	77505
FAIRMONT PKWY	7500	578G	PA	77507
FAIRMONT PKWY	8900	579H	LP	77571
FAIRMONT SPRINGS CT	0	326Z	NWC	77429
FAIRMOOR	4800	577G	PA	77505
FAIR OAK	2500	613K	PL	77584
FAIR OAK CT	300	569V	SF	77477
FAIR OAK DR	300	569V	SF	77477
FAIR OAK DALE LN	0	376H	NEC	77346
FAIROAKS	1600	620E	EL	77586
FAIROAKS RD	900	494Y	SEH	77023
FAIR PARK CT	19800	337U	NEC	77346
FAIR PARK DR	13800	372E	NWC	77014
FAIRPINES DR	0	291W	NWC	77379
FAIRPLUM DR	10000	529S	SWH	77099
FAIRPOINT DR	11000	529X	SWH	77099
FAIRPOINT DR	12400	528V	SWH	77099
FAIR POINTE DR	2200	619Z	LC	77573
FAIRPORT LN	500	488A	SWH	77079
FAIRPORT HARBOR LN	23600	525F	NEF	77407
FAIR REIGN DR	0	296X	NEC	77339
FAIRSHIRE	4800	577G	PA	77505
FAIRSTONE DR	10800	369Y	NWC	77064
FAIR TIDE	1700	419A	NEC	77532
FAIRTIDE CT	1	251F	WD	77381
FAIRTIDE CT	2400	619Y	LC	77573
FAIRTIDE DR	5200	461T	NEC	77521
FAIRVALLEY DR	3600	331S	NWC	77068
FAIRVENT	4900	577G	PA	77505
FAIRVIEW	0	537W	PA	77502
FAIRVIEW	100	493N	SWH	77006
FAIRVIEW	1900	492V	SWH	77019
FAIRVIEW	3300	577A	PA	77504
FAIRVIEW	7000	409N	NWC	77041
FAIRVIEW	10100	460H	NEC	77532
FAIRVIEW DR	10200	252G	SEM	77385
FAIRVIEW FOREST DR	5400	411K	NWC	77088
FAIRVIEW PARK DR	0	372D	NCC	77073
FAIRVIEW VALLEY CT	18200	447P	NWC	77084
FAIRVINE PARK DR	23100	485Q	NEF	77494
FAIR WALNUT WAY	0	446F	NWC	77449
FAIRWATER DR	20700	486N	SWC	77450
FAIRWATER PARK DR	2100	620W	LC	77573
FAIRWATER PARK DR	2200	619Z	LC	77573
FAIRWAY	0	568R	SG	77478
FAIRWAY	4200	577G	PA	77505
FAIRWAY CIR	2200	616J	PL	77581
FAIRWAY CT	7200	411T	NWH	77088
FAIRWAY CT	7800	250S	NWC	77389
FAIRWAY DR	0	580K	LP	77571
FAIRWAY DR	2500	569N	SG	77478
FAIRWAY DR	2800	656T	FR	77546
FAIRWAY DR	4800	500M	BT	77521
FAIRWAY DR	6300	534M	SEH	77087
FAIRWAY DR	11100	370S	NWC	77064
FAIRWAY DR	28200	246F	SWM	77355
FAIRWAY BEND	20900	486S	NEF	77450
FAIRWAY BEND CT	5800	290V	NWC	77379
FAIRWAY BEND DR	20000	290V	NWC	77379
FAIRWAY CROSSING	0	299X	NEC	77339
FAIRWAY ESTATES DR	2800	331P	NWC	77068
FAIRWAY FARMS LN	800	336A	NEH	77339
FAIRWAY GREEN DR	2000	337F	NEH	77339
FAIRWAY ISLAND DR	19600	337V	NEC	77346
FAIRWAY MANOR LN	5900	334E	NCC	77373
FAIRWAY MEADOW LN	20500	290V	NWC	77379
FAIRWAY OAKS CT	6200	330C	NWC	77379
FAIRWAY OAKS CT	26700	299T	NEC	77336
E. FAIRWAY OAKS DR	0	299U	NEC	77336
FAIRWAY OAKS DR	0	299T	NEC	77336
FAIRWAY OAKS DR	17400	330C	NWC	77379
FAIRWAY PARK DR	2200	451U	NWH	77092
FAIRWAY PINES DR	0	570U	MC	77489
FAIRWAY PLAZA DR	0	577D	PA	77505
FAIRWAY POINTE DR	2200	619Y	LC	77573
FAIRWAY SHORES LN	0	297K	NEH	77365
FAIRWAY SQUARE DR	0	408P	NWC	77084
FAIRWAY TRACE LN	2000	299X	NEC	77336
FAIRWAY TRAILS LN	20300	290U	NWC	77379
FAIRWAY VALLEY LN	0	525A	NEF	77494

Street Name	Block	Pg/Sq	Loc	Zips
FAIRWEATHER CIR	0	525D	NEF	77450
FAIRWEATHER CT	5200	525D	NEF	77450
FAIRWICK CT	5300	526A	NEF	77450
FAIRWIND DR	1600	618L	SEH	77062
FAIRWIND LN	0	609U	MC	77459
FAIRWOOD	2000	616S	PL	77581
FAIRWOOD	4200	577G	PA	77505
FAIRWOOD DR	6300	411P	NWH	77088
FAIRWOOD DR	10900	539Y	LP	77571
FAIRWOOD BREEZE	14000	328T	NWC	77429
FAIRWOOD CREEK CT	0	376Q	NEC	77396
FAIRWOOD CREEK LN	0	657X	LC	77573
FAIRWOOD CREEK LN	6500	609Y	NEF	77459
FAIRWOOD KNOLL LN	0	611W	FS	77545
FAIRWOOD MEADOW CT	18200	447P	NWC	77084
FAIRWOOD SPRINGS CT	14000	328T	NWC	77429
FAIRWOOD SPRINGS DR	13900	328T	NWC	77429
FAIRWORTH PLACE LN	20500	406L	NWC	77433
FAIRWYCK CT	0	289T	NWC	77375
FAITH	0	284Z	NWC	77447
FAITH	100	459Z	HG	77562
FAITH LN	7400	538X	DP	77536
FAITH MILLSTREAM DR	0	335P	NCC	77338
FAITH PLACE	13500	571K	SWH	77085
FAITH VALLEY DR	0	368E	NWC	77429
FAKE	0	656P	FR	77546
FALA	10600	415W	NEH	77016
FALBA RD	12800	370A	NWC	77070
FALCO	2200	659Y	DI	77539
FALCON	1200	496G	NEH	77015
FALCON	10900	369U	NWC	77064
FALCON'S NEST	1	490Q	PP	77024
FALCON CHASE CT	20100	290Z	NWC	77379
FALCON CREEK CT	0	525Z	NEF	77406
FALCON CREST DR	18500	377D	NEC	77346
FALCON FLIGHT LN	0	289Q	NWC	77375
FALCON FOREST CT	18000	377A	NEC	77346
FALCON FOREST DR	4700	376D	NEC	77346
FALCON FOREST DR	5000	377A	NEC	77346
FALCON GATE CT	0	333F	NCC	77338
FALCON GATE CT	0	333F	NCC	77338
FALCON GATE DR	24900	485K	NEF	77494
FALCONGROVE LN	0	485J	NEF	77494
FALCON HEIGHTS DR	13900	367C	NWC	77429
FALCONHILL CT	19800	406M	NWC	77433
FALCON HILL LN	0	485N	NEF	77494
FALCON HILL ST	0	334P	NCC	77388
FALCON HOLLOW LN	25000	485N	NEF	77494
FALCON KNOLL LN	2500	485N	NEF	77494
FALCON LAIR LN	0	485N	NEF	77494
FALCON LAKE CIR	200	657J	FR	77546
FALCON LAKE DR	200	657J	FR	77546
FALCON LANDING BLVD	0	484V	NEF	77494
FALCON LANDING BLVD	0	484X	NEF	77494
FALCON LANDING BLVD	0	484X	NEF	77494
FALCON LANDING BLVD	0	485N	NEF	77494
FALCON LANDING BLVD	0	524B	NEF	77494
FALCON LANDING BLVD	0	524B	NEF	77494
FALCON MEADOW DR	4200	446H	NWC	77449
FALCON PASS	0	578D	LP	77571
FALCON PASS DR	2900	618L	SEH	77062
FALCON POINT DR	24100	485E	NEF	77494
FALCON REACH DR	0	450S	NWH	77080
FALCON RIDGE	2500	613U	NEB	77584
FALCON RIDGE BLVD	1600	656M	FR	77546
FALCON RIDGE BLVD	2000	657N	FR	77546
FALCON RIDGE DR	15200	375U	NEC	77396
FALCONS COVE DR	16500	367Y	NWC	77095
FALCONS NEST LANDING DR	0	324M	NWC	77447
FALCONS NEST LANDING DR	0	324M	NWC	77447
FALCON SPRING	33900	324Q	NWC	77447
FALCON TALON CT	24500	485J	NEF	77494
FALCON TRAIL DR	3400	293U	NCC	77373
FALCONWING DR	10800	250C	WD	77381
FALCONWOOD LN	22100	334E	NCC	77373
FALDO DR	0	250X	NWC	77389
FALES LN	0	657Y	LC	77573
FALHER DR	30100	252Z	SEM	77386
FALK AVE	200	580Q	LP	77571
FALK CT	3000	580Q	LP	77571
FALKIRK CT	6100	657U	LC	77573
FALKIRK LN	4000	532J	SWH	77025
FALKLAND WAY	0	527Q	NEF	77083
FALL	3100	533K	SWH	77054
FALL	19200	256G	SEM	77357
FALL LN	31800	248S	SWM	77362
FALL ASTER DR	0	293W	NCC	77373
FALL BRANCH DR	3600	485V	NEF	77450
FALL BRANCH LN	0	612U	PL	77584
FALL BREEZE DR	11100	369V	NWC	77064
FALL BRIAR DR	15500	571X	SWH	77489
FALLBROOK	0	451H	NWH	77018
FALLBROOK CT	0	613X	NEB	77584
FALLBROOK DR	0	610Q	MC	77459
FALLBROOK DR	0	613X	NEB	77584
FALLBROOK DR	1300	372W	NWC	77038
FALL BROOK DR	4400	451H	NWH	77018
FALLBROOK DR	6400	411C	NWC	77086
FALLBROOK DR	7500	370Z	NWC	77086
FALLBROOK DR	9100	369X	NWC	77064
FALLBROOK DR	11000	368V	NWC	77065
FALLBROOK DR	11100	369X	NWC	77065
FALLBROOK DR	12100	368V	NWC	77065
FALLBROOK LN	0	612U	PL	77584
FALL CHASE CT	14000	377W	NEC	77044
FALL CREEK DR	300	338M	NEH	77336
FALL CREEK BEND	14600	375Y	NEC	77396
FALL CREEK BEND CT	14600	375U	NEC	77396
FALL CREEK CROSSING	14600	375U	NEC	77396
FALL CREEK RESERVE DR	0	376W	NEC	77396
FALL CREEK VIEW DR	14600	376W	NEC	77396
FALLCREST	11000	368V	NWC	77065
W. FALLENBOUGH	0	449D	NWH	77041
N. FALLENBOUGH	0	449D	NWH	77041
E. FALLENBOUGH DR	4900	449H	NWH	77041
N. FALLENBOUGH DR	10400	449D	NWH	77041
FALLEN BRANCH DR	2400	485Q	NEF	77494
FALLENGATE CT	22200	334F	NCC	77373
FALLENGATE DR	5500	334E	NCC	77373
FALLEN LEAF	0	609Z	NEF	77459
FALLEN LEAF PLACE	0	248G	SWM	77354
FALLEN LEAF PLACE	0	248K	SWM	77354
FALLEN LEAF WAY	16600	618R	SEH	77058
FALLEN OAK CT	1300	616P	PL	77581
FALLEN OAKS DR	4200	451C	NWH	77091
FALLEN PALMS CT	3600	489Y	SWH	77042
FALLEN PINE LN	2500	412J	NWH	77088
FALLENSTONE DR	1	250D	WD	77381
FALLEN TIMBER CT	20100	291W	NWC	77379
FALLEN TIMBERS	0	490K	BH	77024
FALLEN WOODS DR	0	450S	NWH	77080
FALL FAIR CT	0	326Y	NWC	77433
FALL FAIR LN	0	326Y	NWC	77433
FALL FOLIAGE DR	20400	334Q	NCC	77338
FALL GLEN DR	7900	410M	NWC	77040
FALL GROVE	18000	328M	NWC	77377
FALL GROVE CT	3700	578X	SEH	77059
FALL HOLLOW DR	7900	408L	NWC	77041
FALLING BRIAR LN	0	609X	NEF	77479
FALLING BROOK DR	3000	297X	NEH	77345
FALLING CEDAR CT	0	253P	SEM	77386
FALLING CEDAR CT	0	326Y	NWC	77433
FALLING CHERRY PLACE	7000	457L	NEC	77049
FALLING CREEK DR	14500	331X	NWC	77014
FALLING CREEK DR	14600	331S	NWC	77068
FALLING ELM LN	14000	457Y	NEC	77015
FALLING FOREST LN	0	619V	LC	77565
FALLING HARBOR		289Y	NWC	77379
FALLING LEAF	0	656K	FR	77546
FALLING LEAF	1300	619H	TL	77586
FALLING LEAF DR	400	656D	FR	77546
FALLING LEAF DR	700	656G	FR	77546
FALLING LEAF LN	1	490C	HE	77024
FALLING LEAF LN	3200	251S	SWM	77380
FALLING LEAVES	0	296R	SEM	77365
FALLING LIMB CT	15500	457Q	NEC	77049
FALLING OAK CT	5000	577M	PA	77505
FALLING OAK DR	7200	290B	NWC	77389
FALLING OAKS	2100	411D	NWC	77038
FALLING OAK WAY	18400	330H	NWC	77379
FALLING RAIN CT	0	328P	NWC	77429
FALLING RAPIDS CT	10400	369G	NWC	77070
FALLING RIVER DR	10400	367X	NWC	77095
FALLING ROCK LN	37000	484X	NEF	77494
FALLING SPRING	0	292Q	NCC	77373
FALLING SPRINGS LN	800	660E	LC	77573
FALLING STAR CT	1	251F	WD	77381
FALLING STAR RD	1	251F	WD	77381
FALLING STREAM DR	19700	329A	NWC	77375
FALLING TIMBER LN	0	526G	NEF	77407
FALLING TREE	0	457X	NEC	77015
FALLING TREE CT	13800	457Y	NEC	77015
FALLING WATER CT	8200	568P	SG	77478
FALLING WATER DR	0	484E	KT	77494
FALLINGWATER ESTATES	0	485S	NEF	77494
FALLING WATERS DR	6600	330G	NWC	77379
FALL LAKE DR	10900	372S	NWH	77067
FALL MEADOW DR	1800	610E	MC	77459
FALL MEADOW LN	11700	414J	NCC	77039
FALLMIST CT	23200	485L	NEF	77494
FALLMONT CIR	10100	411B	NWC	77086
FALLMONT CT	10100	411B	NWC	77086
FALLMONT DR	0	411B	NWC	77086
FALLOON LN	500	496F	NEH	77013
FALL ORCHARD CT	2500	298W	NEH	77345
FALLOW LN	0	458S	NEC	77049
FALLOW LN	400	616Z	FR	77546
FALL POINT DR	0	368U	NWC	77065
FALL RIDGE CIR	1700	485L	NEF	77494
FALL RIVER CIR	17900	331M	NWC	77090
FALL RIVER CT	300	491F	SWH	77024
FALL RIVER RD	400	491F	SWH	77024
FALL RIVER PASS CT	17600	377E	NEC	77346
FALL RIVER PASS LN	12000	377E	NEC	77346
FALLS	3900	454T	NEH	77026
FALLS CIR	0	609P	MC	77459
FALLS AT FAIRDALE	0	491W	SWH	77057
FALLSBRIDGE DR	10600	368Y	NWC	77065
FALLS BROOK CT	0	609Q	MC	77459
FALLS CANYON CT	4900	484Z	NEF	77494
FALLS CHURCH DR	2400	371M	NWC	77067
FALLS COPPICE LN	12100	616L	SEC	77089
FALLSCREEK CT	2900	613P	NEB	77584
FALLS DOCK CT	0	372C	NCC	77073
FALLS FROST DR	0	525R	NEF	77407
FALLS GULCH CT	0	406C	NWC	77433
FALL SHADOWS CT	3900	578Z	PA	77059
FALLSHIRE DR	1	251A	WD	77381
FALLS LAKE DR	0	253T	SEM	77386
FALL SPRING LN	7200	375X	NEC	77396
FALLSTONE RD	10500	529Y	SWH	77099
FALLSVIEW DR	0	612N	PL	77545
FALLSVIEW LN	13100	488Q	SWH	77077
FALL VALLEY DR	1600	489P	SWH	77077
FALL WIND CT	23200	485P	NEF	77494
FALLWOOD DR	11500	368Q	NWC	77065
FALMOUTH AVE	15300	408N	NWC	77084
FALMOUTH DR	15700	618C	SEH	77059
FALSE CYPRESS LN	4200	331W	NWC	77068
FALUN CT	3700	293G	SEM	77386
FALVEL RD	20500	291U	NWC	77388
FALVEL RD	22000	291L	NWC	77389
FALVEL COVE DR	3900	291P	NWC	77388
FALVEL LAKE DR	21500	291P	NWC	77388
FALVEL MEADOWS LN	0	291Q	NWC	77388
FALVEL MISTY DR	21500	291Q	NWC	77388
FALVEL SHADOW CREEK DR	3900	291P	NWC	77388
FALVEL SUNRISE CT	21500	291P	NWC	77388
FALVEL SUNSET CT	21600	291P	NWC	77388
FALVEY	4700	536J	SEH	77017
FALWORTH DR	300	372M	NCC	77060
FAMILY CIR	13400	571K	SWH	77085
FAMWORTH CIR	0	657U	LC	77573
FAMWORTH LN	0	657U	LC	77573
FANA CT	14400	374Y	NCC	77032
FANESTIEL	2300	502N	BT	77520
FANNETTE	8600	495L	NEH	77029
FANNIN	0	499K	NEC	77520
FANNIN	0	500V	BT	77520
FANNIN	100	288H	TB	77375
FANNIN	100	493Q	DT	77002
FANNIN	900	493Q	DT	77002
FANNIN	901	493Q	DT	77010
FANNIN	1000	493Q	DT	77002
FANNIN	3000	493Q	SWH	77004
FANNIN	5500	533A	SWH	77030
FANNIN	6500	532H	SWH	77030
FANNIN	7400	532H	SWH	77054
W. FANNIN STATION	0	532Z	SWH	77045
S. FANNIN STATION	0	532Z	SWH	77045
N. FANNIN STATION	0	532Z	SWH	77045
E. FANNIN STATION	0	532Z	SWH	77045
FANNIN STATION	0	532Z	SWH	77045
FAN PALM PLACE	0	250P	NWC	77389
FANTAIL CT	1	245Y	SWM	77355
FANTAIL CT	18000	419A	NEC	77532
FANTAIL DR	16000	419A	NEC	77532
FANTASIA DR	23300	339P	HU	77336
FANTASY DR	12300	414G	NCC	77039
FANTASY WOODS DR	1700	486L	SWC	77094
FANWICK	22600	289R	NWC	77375
FANWICK CT	9300	289R	NWC	77375
FARADAY CT	0	251C	WD	77381
FARADAY DR	13100	572V	SWH	77047
FARAWAY LN	25100	339E	HU	77336
FARB DR	5100	414Y	NEH	77016
FARBER	3700	532E	SS	77005
FAR FETCH LN	4600	421S	NEC	77532
FARGO	100	493N	SWH	77006
FARGO	5600	660X	DI	77539
FARGO WOODS CIR	14500	457Y	NEC	77015
FARGO WOODS DR	100	457Y	NEC	77015
FARHILLS CT	1300	332W	NWC	77090
FARING RD	16800	418X	NEC	77049
FARISH CIR	1	491G	SWH	77024
FARISS	200	532W	SWH	77054
FARLAN LN	3700	371B	NWC	77014
FARLEY	6000	577Q	SEH	77034
FARLEY DR	5400	374V	NCC	77032
FARLEY PASS DR	0	407C	NWC	77095
FARLINGTON CIR	12700	488M	SWH	77077
FARLOW LN	2700	612Z	NWB	77578
F.M. 149	0	247B	SWM	77362
F.M. 270	100	659A	LC	77573
F.M. 359	0	524W	NWF	77406
F.M. 362	0	282B	WCO	77484
F.M. 362	0	282T	WCO	77484
F.M. 362	0	242N	WCO	77484
F.M. 362	0	242C	WCO	77484
F.M. 362	15000	322E	WCO	77484
F.M. 517	0	660Z	GCO	77539
F.M. 518	0	613R	PL	77581
F.M. 518	0	614Q	PL	77581
F.M. 518	0	615Q	PL	77581
F.M. 518	0	616T	PL	77581
F.M. 518	0	656D	FR	77546
F.M. 518	0	657J	FR	77546
F.M. 518	0	658L	LC	77573
F.M. 518	0	659E	LC	77573
F.M. 518	0	660A	LC	77573
F.M. 518	900	620X	KE	77565
F.M. 521	100	612J	NEF	77545
F.M. 521	2500	611Z	FS	77545
F.M. 521	8600	533S	SWH	77054
F.M. 521	10500	532Z	SWH	77045
F.M. 521	10900	572H	SWH	77045
F.M. 521	13400	572Q	SWC	77053
F.M. 525	1	373W	NEH	77060
F.M. 525	200	373U	NCC	77060
F.M. 525	800	373U	NCC	77032
F.M. 525	2400	374X	NCC	77032
F.M. 526	1	496C	NEH	77013
F.M. 526	5800	456R	NEC	77049
F.M. 526	7400	456R	NEC	77044
F.M. 526	9000	416Z	NEC	77044
F.M. 526	12000	417J	NEC	77044
F.M. 527	5400	455L	NEH	77028
F.M. 528	0	658A	FR	77546
F.M. 528	0	657D	SEC	77598
F.M. 528	0	656Q	FR	77546
F.M. 529	11000	409N	NWC	77041
F.M. 529	12700	408N	NWC	77041
F.M. 529	14400	408N	NWC	77095
F.M. 529	16200	407Q	NWC	77095
F.M. 529	18000	406Q	NWC	77433
F.M. 529	21600	405Q	NWC	77449
F.M. 529	25000	404Q	NWC	77493
F.M. 565	0	502H	CCO	77520
F.M. 565	0	503E	CCO	77520
F.M. 565	1700	463E	MB	77580
F.M. 646	100	659R	LC	77573
F.M. 646	100	659X	LC	77539
F.M. 646	4800	660P	LC	77539
F.M. 686	0	340D	LCO	77535
F.M. 723	6200	524Q	NEF	77406
F.M. 865	0	613H	NEB	77584
F.M. 1092	200	569Y	SF	77477
F.M. 1092	1000	569Y	MC	77459
F.M. 1092	2200	609C	MC	77459
F.M. 1093	0	490V	SWH	77057
F.M. 1093	0	491S	SWH	77057
F.M. 1093	11300	489S	SWH	77077
F.M. 1093	12400	488U	SWH	77077
F.M. 1093	15100	487V	SWH	77082
F.M. 1093	16200	527B	SWH	77082
F.M. 1093	17400	526E	NEF	77450
F.M. 1093	21000	525G	NEF	77450
F.M. 1093	23500	524J	NEF	77406
F.M. 1128	2100	614T	NEB	77584
F.M. 1266	0	659R	LC	77573
F.M. 1266	2500	660J	LC	77573
F.M. 1314	0	254H	SEM	77365
F.M. 1314	0	255N	SEM	77365
F.M. 1314	0	295D	SEM	77365
F.M. 1314	0	296F	SEM	77365
F.M. 1405	0	503N	CCO	77520
F.M. 1405	0	502V	CCO	77520
F.M. 1405	4000	542C	CCO	77520
F.M. 1413	0	381H	LCO	77535
F.M. 1463	0	484B	KT	77494
F.M. 1464	0	527J	NEF	77407
F.M. 1464	6500	527T	NEF	77498
F.M. 1485	0	256R	SEM	77357
F.M. 1485	0	256F	SEM	77357
F.M. 1485	0	257P	SEM	77357
F.M. 1485	0	258P	SEM	77357
F.M. 1488	0	243F	WCO	77447
F.M. 1488	33500	242C	WCO	77484
F.M. 1774	0	247B	SWM	77362
F.M. 1876	100	568C	SG	77478
F.M. 1876	2500	528U	NEF	77478
F.M. 1942	0	463A	MB	77580
F.M. 1942	100	419V	BR	77532
F.M. 1942	900	420S	NEC	77532
F.M. 1942	3900	460D	NEC	77532
F.M. 1942	4000	461F	NEC	77532
F.M. 1942	7600	462A	CCO	77521
F.M. 1959	100	577X	SEH	77034
F.M. 1959	400	617B	SEH	77034
F.M. 1960	0	340D	LCO	77535
W. F.M. 1960	100	332N	NWC	77090
F.M. 1960	100	332M	NCC	77073
F.M. 1960	100	338P	NEH	77336
W. F.M. 1960	1200	331R	NWC	77090
F.M. 1960	1600	333K	NCC	77073
E. F.M. 1960	2100	335V	NEC	77338
W. F.M. 1960	2300	331W	NWC	77068
F.M. 1960	3100	333L	NCC	77338
E. F.M. 1960	4100	336U	NEC	77346
W. F.M. 1960	4500	370F	NWC	77069
E. F.M. 1960	4700	337W	NEC	77346
F.M. 1960	5000	334N	NCC	77338
W. F.M. 1960	5100	334N	NCC	77338
W. F.M. 1960	7300	370F	NWH	77070
F.M. 1960	8400	335S	NCC	77338
W. F.M. 1960	8400	335S	NCC	77338
E. F.M. 1960	8400	338Q	NEC	77346
W. F.M. 1960	8600	369M	NWC	77070
F.M. 1960	10600	339K	NEC	77336
W. F.M. 1960	11000	369W	NWC	77065
W. F.M. 1960	12700	368Z	NWC	77065
W. F.M. 1960	13100	408C	NWC	77065
E. F.M. 1960 BYPASS	100	335V	HM	77338
E. F.M. 1960 BYPASS	1500	336S	HM	77338
W. F.M. 1960 BYPASS	7700	334V	NCC	77338
F.M. 1960 BYPASS	8400	335T	HM	77338
F.M. 2094	0	619Z	LC	77573
F.M. 2094	0	659B	LC	77573
F.M. 2094	200	620W	LC	77565
F.M. 2100	0	298M	NEC	77336
F.M. 2100	1100	459R	HG	77562
F.M. 2100	5900	419L	NEC	77532
F.M. 2100	16900	379U	NEC	77532
F.M. 2100	21400	339S	NEC	77336
F.M. 2100	29000	299X	NEC	77336
F.M. 2100	0	258Z	NEC	77357
F.M. 2234	1200	570X	MC	77489
F.M. 2234	2500	610G	MC	77489
F.M. 2234	8500	611G	NEF	77053
F.M. 2234	8700	612E	NEF	77053
F.M. 2234 (Prop)	0	613F	NEB	77584
F.M. 2351	0	617K	SEH	77546
F.M. 2351	100	616Z	FR	77546
F.M. 2351	500	656F	NEB	77511
F.M. 2354	0	503G	CCO	77520
F.M. 2354	0	543X	CCO	77520
F.M. 2354	0	542Y	BT	77520
F.M. 2354	0	541H	BT	77520
F.M. 2920	1500	292S	NWC	77388
F.M. 2920	2500	291T	NWC	77388
F.M. 2920	6000	290P	NWC	77379
F.M. 2920	9000	289E	TB	77375
F.M. 2920	14000	288J	NWC	77377
F.M. 2920	15500	287P	NWC	77377
F.M. 2920	18100	286R	NWC	77377
F.M. 2920	20000	285S	NWC	77447
F.M. 2920	24100	284R	NWC	77447
F.M. 2920	27900	283U	NWC	77484
F.M. 2920	30700	282V	NWC	77484
F.M. 2978	19500	289E	NWC	77375
F.M. 2978	24600	249N	SWM	77354
F.M. 3180	0	463H	MB	77520
F.M. 3180	0	503D	CCO	77520
F.M. 3345	0	610B	MC	77489
F.M. 3360	0	463C	MB	77520
F.M. 3436	0	660Z	TC	77539
FARM & RANCH DR	0	448N	NWH	77084
FARM COUNTRY LN	0	325J	NWC	77447
FARMCREEK DR	27200	299S	NEC	77336
FARMER	3100	494F	NEH	77020
FARMER RD	0	526W	NEF	77406
FARMERS FIELD	3100	615L	PL	77581
FARM GARDEN LN	0	325K	NWC	77447
FARM HILL DR	23700	293X	NCC	77373
FARMINGHAM DR	10500	528Z	SWH	77099
FARMINGHAM RD	7500	337Z	NEC	77346
FARMINGHAM RD	8000	338W	NEC	77346
FARMINGTON	3000	450M	NWH	77080
FARMLAND AVE	0	445N	NWC	77493
FARM PASTURE TRAIL	0	325K	NWC	77447
FARM RD 270	18100	618Z	WB	77598
FARM RIDGE LN	0	335P	NCC	77338
FARM RIDGE LN	8200	335N	NCC	77338
FARM WEST TRAIL		484W	NEF	77494
FARNABY CT	6800	330Q	NWC	77379
FARNDALE DR	15100	618J	SEH	77062
FARNELL CT	16400	330P	NWC	77379
FARNHAM	3700	492Y	SWH	77098
FARNHAM CIR	0	490R	PP	77024
FARNHAM CIR	3400	613Q	NEB	77584
FARNHAM CT	0	490R	PP	77024
FARNHAM PARK DR	1	490R	PP	77024
FARNINGTON DR	4600	447B	NWC	77084
FARNSFIELD DR	18200	447B	NWC	77084
FARNSWORTH	7100	453L	NEH	77022
FARNWORTH CIR	200	657U	LC	77573
FAR PINES DR	700	292L	SP	77373
FAR POINT CT	9500	408B	NWC	77095
FAR POINT MANOR DR	13200	367G	CY	77429
FARQUESON	8500	455X	NEH	77029
FARR	1600	282U	WL	77484
FARR AVE	15900	374N	NEH	77032
FARRAGUT	9700	455B	NEH	77078
FARRAH	1000	569T	NEF	77477
FARRAWOOD DR	14500	328X	NWC	77429
FARRAWOOD PARK LN	22900	292L	NCC	77373
FARREL HILL	3300	611W	FS	77545
FARRELL	1	453F	NEH	77022
FARRELL CIR	32000	246S	SWM	77355
FARRELL DR	9500	369L	NWC	77070
FARRELL LN	100	569Z	NEF	77477
FARRELL RD	1400	373B	NCC	77073
FARRELL RD	1900	333R	NCC	77073
FARRELL RD	3300	333U	NEH	77338
FARRELLEY LN	0	573X	SEC	77047
FARRIER DR		524L	NWF	77406
FARRIERS BEND DR	2300	617Y	SEC	77546
N. FARRINGTON BLVD	0	579B	LP	77571
N. FARRINGTON BLVD	200	539Y	LP	77571
FARRINGTON DR	0	539X	LP	77571
FARRIS GREEN RD	22100	296F	SEM	77365
FARRISWOOD CT	18300	407J	NWC	77433
FARTEX	22800	287G	NWC	77377
FARTHER POINT	1	491F	SWH	77024
FARWELL DR	5700	571E	SWH	77035
FARWOOD	1200	493C	NEH	77009
W. FARWOOD TERRACE	0	326E	NWC	77433
E. FARWOOD TERRACE	0	326E	NWC	77433
FASCO	10000	573C	SEH	77051
FASHION	800	494T	SEH	77023
FASHION HILL DR	1400	412Q	NWH	77088
FASIG TIPTON LN	0	526Z	NEF	77469
FASTGREEN CIR	0	616E	SEC	77581
FASTWATER BEND LN	0	328A	NWC	77429
FASTWATER CREEK CT	0	612K	PL	77545
FATHEREE DR	21900	255Z	SEM	77365
FATHEREE DR	22800	295C	SEM	77365
FATHOM LN	15700	618K	SEH	77062
FATIMA LN	5400	452H	NWH	77091
FATIMA LAKE DR	0	529S	SWM	77099
FAUBURG DR	0	257E	SEM	77357
FAUCETTE	5600	534B	SEH	77023
FAULKEY GULLEY CIR	11400	329W	NWC	77070
FAULKEY GULLEY CT	11400	329W	NWC	77070
FAULKEY GULLY	14100	329W	NWC	77070
FAULKEY GULLY CIR	11400	329W	NWC	77070
FAULKEY GULLY CT	11400	329W	NWC	77070
FAULKNER	3700	533Q	SEH	77021

Street Name	Block	Pg/Sq	Loc	Zips
FAULKNER RIDGE DR	6200	526E	NEF	77450
FAUNA	6600	574D	SEH	77061
FAUNA	7300	575A	SEH	77061
FAUNA	11400	417N	NEC	77044
FAUNAWOODS CT	14400	417X	NEC	77044
FAUST LN	100	489H	SWH	77024
FAVIAN CT	7100	528F	SWC	77083
FAVISCA PLACE	0	252N	SEM	77380
FAVOR BEND CT	17500	376G	NEC	77396
FAVOR BEND DR	17500	376G	NEC	77396
FAWCETT DR	13200	370F	NWC	77069
FAWLEY LN	0	457P	NEC	77049
FAWN	21500	378C	NEH	77532
FAWN CIR	24400	296M	SEM	77365
FAWN CT	600	496D	NEH	77015
FAWN CT	1200	658S	LC	77573
FAWN CT	2900	610B	MC	77489
FAWN DR	600	496D	NEH	77015
FAWN LN	25100	295R	SEM	77365
FAWN LN	31600	248S	SWM	77362
FAWNBRAKE DR	13900	568F	SG	77498
FAWN BRIDGE LN	0	378Q	NEC	77532
FAWNBROOK CT	20500	486K	SWC	77450
FAWNBROOK HOLLOW LN	4500	297T	NEH	77345
FAWN CANYON CT	20400	326T	NWC	77433
FAWNCHASE CT	1	251J	WD	77381
FAWNCLIFF DR	6700	370F	NWC	77069
FAWN CREEK DR	3000	296Z	NEH	77339
FAWN CREEK DR	4000	297S	NEH	77339
FAWNCREST DR	12600	412A	NWC	77038
FAWNDALE	0	501E	BT	77521
FAWNDALE LN	8000	450C	NWH	77040
FAWNDALE WAY	3100	500H	BT	77521
FAWN GLEN DR	3800	297X	NEH	77345
FAWNGROVE DR	11300	574J	SEH	77048
FAWN GULLY CT	0	447L	NWC	77084
FAWN HAVEN DR	0	486Q	SWC	77450
FAWN HILL CT	0	609T	NEF	77479
FAWN HILL DR	0	406B	NWC	77433
FAWN HILL LN	0	366Y	NWC	77433
FAWN HOLLOW CT	20000	337V	NEC	77346
FAWNHOPE DR	1300	452W	NWH	77008
FAWNLAKE	6000	444P	KT	77493
N. FAWN LAKE	6100	444P	KT	77493
S. FAWN LAKE	6200	444P	KT	77493
FAWNLAKE CIR	0	444P	KT	77493
FAWNLAKE DR	100	489L	SWH	77079
FAWNLILY	10900	251P	WD	77380
FAWN LILY DR	13599	368A	NWC	77429
FAWN MEADOW DR	1600	376P	NEC	77396
FAWN MEADOW DR	1600	376P	NEC	77396
FAWN MEADOW LN	2100	524Z	NEF	77406
FAWNMIST COVE	0	329F	NWC	77375
FAWN MOUNTAIN DR	2600	611S	NEF	77545
FAWN PARK CT	9400	375V	NEC	77396
FAWNPOINTE CT	0	250S	NWC	77389
FAWN REST PLACE	20400	290T	NWC	77379
FAWNRIDGE DR	7300	455E	NEH	77028
FAWN RIDGE FOREST DR	24700	293T	NCC	77373
FAWN RIVER CIR	7100	330F	NWC	77379
N. FAWN RIVER CIR	7200	330F	NWC	77379
W. FAWN RIVER CIR	17600	330F	NWC	77379
FAWN RIVER DR	6800	330G	NWC	77379
FAWN RUN LN	18500	447N	NWC	77084
FAWNS CROSSING DR	19700	289W	NWC	77375
FAWNSHADOW CT	9000	409F	NWC	77064
FAWN SPRINGS CT	0	366Q	NWC	77433
FAWN TERRACE DR	7600	570G	SWH	77071
FAWN TIMBER TRAIL	0	337P	NEC	77346
FAWN TRACE DR	900	336L	NEH	77339
FAWN TRAIL LN	5400	337N	NEC	77346
FAWN VALLEY DR	1200	659N	LC	77573
FAWNVIEW DR	10500	369B	NWC	77070
FAWNVIEW DR	12000	368D	NWC	77070
FAWN VIEW LN	31200	253P	SEM	77386
FAWN VILLA DR	15400	331S	NWC	77068
FAWN VISTA	16000	331N	NWC	77068
FAWNWAY DR	11400	574J	SEH	77048
FAWN WIND CT	8400	410J	NWC	77040
FAWNWOOD DR	500	570U	MC	77489
FAWNWOOD DR	6200	290C	NWC	77389
FAWNWOOD LN	2300	252Z	SEM	77386
FAWNWOOD LN	25000	247W	SWM	77355
FAY	1100	620Y	KE	77565
FAY	2800	534F	SEH	77023
FAY CT	2300	538Q	DP	77536
FAYDUR CT	0	612T	NWB	77583
FAYE RD	0	286T	NWC	77377
FAYE OAKS CT	19700	337S	NEC	77346
FAYE OAKS DR	19800	337N	NEC	77346
FAYETTE	5300	491U	SWH	77056
FAYE WAY	0	286S	NWC	77377
W. FAYLE	100	501Y	BT	77520
E. FAYLE	100	501Y	BT	77520
E. FAYLE	1600	502W	BT	77520
FAYLE	2300	460T	MN	77521
FAYRIDGE DR	0	574Y	SEH	77048
FAYWOOD DR	15500	373W	NCC	77060
S. FAZIO WAY	0	250K	NWC	77389
FEAGAN	3700	492M	SWH	77007
FEAGAN	4000	492L	SWH	77007
FEAMSTER DR	600	453E	NWH	77022
FEARLESS DR	21600	285M	NWC	77447
FEATHER BRANCH CT	1	251A	WD	77381
FEATHER COVE CT	4600	609J	NEF	77479
FEATHER CRAFT LN	16800	618T	SEH	77058
FEATHER CRAFT LN	17100	618T	WB	77598
FEATHER CREEK DR	6600	371T	NWC	77086
FEATHER FALL LN	17000	367Y	NWC	77095
FEATHERFIELD LN	17900	526M	NEF	77407
FEATHER GLEN CT	2800	485N	NEF	77494
FEATHER GLEN LN	0	657T	FR	77546
FEATHER GREEN TRAIL	0	611S	FS	77545
FEATHER LAKES WAY	4000	297X	NEH	77339
FEATHER LANCE DR	19000	407J	NWC	77433
FEATHER MILL LN	0	526Q	NEF	77407
FEATHER RIDGE DR	1900	570X	MC	77489
FEATHER RUN	12500	409S	NWC	77041
FEATHERS LANDING DR	0	328L	NWC	77377
FEATHER SPRINGS DR	7800	407K	NWC	77095
FEATHERSTAR LN	11300	371R	NWC	77067
FEATHERSTONE	0	615X	PL	77584
FEATHERSTONE	1400	494F	NEH	77020
FEATHER TAIL LN	0	324N	NWC	77447
FEATHERTON CT	2300	568C	SG	77478
FEATHER VALLEY LN	0	485P	NEF	77493
FEATHERWIND DR	3600	446L	NWC	77449
FEATHERWOOD DR	11500	576U	SEH	77034
N. FEATHERWOOD DR	12600	576U	SEH	77034
FEBRUARY	12800	614D	BK	77581
FECHSER LN	0	527W	NEF	77469
FEDERAL	3100	537W	PA	77504

Street Name	Block	Pg/Sq	Loc	Zips
FEDERAL	3300	577A	PA	77504
FEDERAL RD	700	496U	GP	77015
FEDERAL PLAZA DR	0	451F	NWH	77092
FELAND	8800	455G	NEH	77028
FELD DR	14800	612B	SWC	77053
FELDMAN	2800	572D	SWH	77045
FELDSPAR	6300	451J	NWH	77092
FELECIA	5800	452A	NWH	77091
FELGATE CREEK CT	6600	408T	NWC	77084
FELGATE CREEK DR	15000	408T	NWC	77084
FELICE DR	5500	531J	SWH	77081
FELICIA DR	3900	609J	SG	77479
FELICIANA LN	7600	330Q	NWC	77379
FELICIA OAKS TRAIL	6500	370Y	NWC	77064
FELICITY AIME	13700	367C	NWC	77429
FELIX	0	494J	SEH	77020
FELIX	0	494T	SEH	77011
FELIZA LN	8200	527N	NEF	77083
FELLOWS RD	1	572Y	SWC	77047
FELLOWS RD	1900	573W	SWC	77047
FELLOWS RD	3500	613C	SEC	77047
FELLOWSHIP LN	5400	331E	NWC	77379
FELLOWSHIP PINE CIR	5300	331E	NWC	77379
FELSCHER LN	4300	380C	NEC	77532
FELTON	100	501X	BT	77520
FELTON MILLS CT	0	524L	NWF	77494
FENCE POST RD	400	656G	FR	77546
FENCHURCH DR	9300	330S	NWC	77379
FENELON DR	0	500F	BT	77520
FENHAM LN	4500	333M	NCC	77338
FENIAN CT	14500	528S	NEF	77498
FENIMORE CT	12000	528Z	NEF	77478
FENLAND FIELD LN	12900	572Q	SWH	77047
FENN	300	452M	NWH	77018
FENNEL DR	0	461P	NEC	77521
FENNELL	100	535B	SEH	77012
FENNEMORE	11900	411E	NWC	77086
FENNIGAN CT	2200	658T	LC	77573
FENNIGAN LN	2100	658T	LC	77573
FENNY BRIDGE LN	17000	329M	NWC	77379
FENSKE RD	18000	327N	NWC	77429
FENSKE RD	18400	326R	NWC	77429
FENTON LN	14200	568A	SG	77498
FENTON PLACE	0	332Z	NCC	77073
FENTON ROCK LN	0	484P	NEF	77494
FENWAY PARK WAY	4400	291K	NWC	77389
FENWICK	1400	453X	NWH	77009
FENWICK DR	0	285B	SWM	77447
FENWOOD	2600	532C	WU	77005
FENWOOD	2700	619V	LC	77565
FENWOOD DR	2200	536U	PA	77502
FERDINAND	8600	533Y	SEH	77051
FERDINAND	9700	573C	SEH	77051
FERGIS DR	5900	406Z	NWC	77449
FERGUSON	1	501Y	BT	77520
FERGUSON	500	335Z	HM	77338
FERGUSON WAY	900	412N	NWH	77088
FERGUSON WAY	2700	411R	NWH	77088
FERGUS PARK CT	1800	572R	SWH	77047
FERMI DR	0	445J	NWC	77493
FERN	1000	459M	HG	77562
FERN	3000	537M	PA	77503
FERN	3000	537G	PA	77503
FERN	4800	531L	BL	77401
FERN	12400	488H	SWH	77079
FERN	16100	327D	NWC	77429
FERN CIR	8500	460P	NEC	77562
FERN CT	6300	614Q	PL	77584
FERN DR	14200	488H	SWH	77079
FERN LN	900	444W	KT	77493
FERNANDEZ FALLS CT	0	616M	SEC	77089
FERNBANK DR	7900	457F	NEC	77049
FERNBANK FOREST DR	0	377K	NEC	77346
FERN BASIN DR	15600	448B	NWC	77084
FERN BASIN DR	15800	408X	NWC	77084
FERN BEND LN	0	484P	NEF	77494
FERNBLUFF CT	100	330F	NWC	77379
FERNBLUFF DR	17900	330F	NWC	77379
FERNBROOK LN	7500	370A	NWC	77070
FERNBROOK LN	8100	369D	NWC	77070
FERNBUSH DR	20600	333W	NCC	77073
FERNCHASE CIR	17300	407Q	NWC	77095
FERNCHASE CT	17200	407Q	NWC	77095
FERNCLIFF LN	15900	408E	NWC	77095
FERN COVE DR	4900	501F	BT	77521
FERN CREEK LN	0	536T	SEH	77017
FERN CREEK LN	2700	616N	PL	77581
FERN CREEK TRAIL	12500	377B	NEC	77346
FERN CREEK TRAIL	2100	297V	NEH	77345
FERNCREST CT	12200	369L	NWC	77070
FERNCROFT	0	619V	LC	77565
FERNDALE	0	531L	BL	77401
FERNDALE	1200	620J	EL	77586
FERNDALE	2600	492U	SWH	77098
FERNDALE	8700	535Z	SEH	77017
FERNDALE CT	700	656C	FR	77546
FERNDALE DR	3000	659H	LC	77573
FERNDALE MEADOWS DR	0	484V	NEF	77494
W. FERNDALE PLACE DR	0	369V	NWC	77064
S. FERNDALE PLACE DR	9000	369V	NWC	77064
N. FERNDALE PLACE DR	9000	369V	NWC	77064
FERNDALE VIEW DR	0	369V	NWC	77064
FERNDELL	11800	415R	NEC	77016
FERNE DR	18300	255P	SEM	77365
FERNE LEAF DR	21000	255P	SEM	77365
FERNESS LN	14900	497D	NEC	77530
FERNESS LN	15100	498A	NEC	77530
FERNEY LN	18800	295F	SEM	77365
FERN FOREST DR	11900	456C	NEC	77044
FERN GARDEN CT	500	297Q	NEH	77345
FERNGATE DR	22400	334F	NCC	77373
FERN GLADE	0	331W	NWC	77014
FERNGLADE DR	3600	331T	NWC	77068
FERNGLEN DR	1	251R	WD	77380
FERNGLEN DR	24700	484G	NEF	77494
FERN GROVE LN	2300	618A	SEH	77059
FERNHAVEN DR	19700	446L	NWC	77449
FERN HILL DR	2500	293X	NCC	77373
FERN HILL DR	2900	293T	NCC	77373
FERNHILL DR	13500	568F	SG	77498
FERN HOLLOW CT	5900	407W	NWC	77449
FERNHOLLOW LN	20900	291W	NWC	77388
W. FERNHURST	23500	485B	SWC	77450
E. FERNHURST DR	500	485B	SWC	77450
FERN LACY CT	0	291R	NWC	77388
FERN LACY DR	2200	291R	NWC	77388
FERNLAKE DR	13700	456R	NEH	77049
FERNLEA	11800	415R	NEC	77016
FERN MANOR	0	297T	NEH	77345
FERN MEADOW DR	400	609V	MC	77459
FERN MEADOW DR	12300	569E	SF	77477
FERN MEADOW LN	12000	414F	NCC	77039

Street Name	Block	Pg/Sq	Loc	Zips
FERN MILL CT	12900	408Z	NWC	77041
FERN MIST CT	0	484P	NEF	77494
FERN MIST LN	0	484P	NEF	77494
FERNOAKS DR	3200	291Q	NWC	77388
FERN PARK DR	5200	297N	NEH	77339
FERN PINE CT	20300	446N	NWC	77449
FERN RIDGE DR	15600	408X	NWC	77084
FERNRIDGE RD	0	251M	WD	77380
FERN RIVER DR	3500	297T	NEH	77345
FERN ROCK DR	3100	538Z	LP	77571
FERN ROCK DR	3200	578D	LP	77571
FERN ROCK FALLS CT	16600	330P	NWC	77379
FERNROSE CT	0	245U	SWM	77355
FERN SHADOWS CT	19000	446R	NWC	77084
FERNSIDE DR	4200	578E	PA	77505
FERNSPRAY LN	1900	447W	NWH	77084
FERN SPRINGS CT	800	617H	SEH	77062
FERNSTONE LN	9800	369L	NWC	77070
FERN TERRACE DR	10800	575Z	SEH	77075
FERN TRACE CT	500	252T	SEM	77386
FERN TRAIL CT	18300	447P	NWC	77084
FERN VALE CT	12500	368Z	NWC	77065
FERN VALLEY DR	8800	456D	NEC	77044
FERN VIEW DR	3700	297T	NEH	77345
FERN WALK CT	12600	617E	SEH	77089
FERNWAY LN	12800	456M	NEC	77049
FERNWILLOW DR	9100	289Z	NWC	77379
FERN WING CT	1	250C	WD	77381
FERNWOOD	0	412D	NEH	77060
FERNWOOD CT	4300	534E	SEH	77021
FERNWOOD CT	20000	336S	NEC	77338
FERNWOOD DR	600	656G	FR	77546
FERNWOOD DR	3900	533H	SEH	77021
FERNWOOD DR	3900	615W	PL	77584
FERNWOOD BEND DR	0	328L	NWC	77377
FERN WOOD FOREST	9400	410N	NWC	77040
FERNWOOD WAY	16600	618M	SEH	77058
FEROL LN	100	460S	HG	77562
FEROL RD	7600	415S	NEH	77016
FERON LN	0	406F	NWC	77433
FERRARA DR	7300	527F	NEF	77083
FERRARI DR	800	375M	NEC	77396
FERRARO RD	8500	413N	NCC	77037
FERRIS DR	6400	531F	SWH	77081
FERRIS DR	6600	531F	BL	77401
FERRIS DR	8500	531P	SWH	77096
S. FERRISBURG CT	2200	568C	SG	77478
N. FERRISBURG CT	2300	528Y	SG	77478
FERRO ST	4100	569P	SF	77477
FERRY RD	2500	502P	BT	77520
FERRY RD	4500	502L	BT	77520
FERRY BOAT DR	19100	406V	NWC	77449
FERRY COVE LN	0	612P	PL	77545
FERRY HILL LN	13000	457W	NEC	77015
FERRY LANDING	2500	568Z	SG	77478
FERTILE VALLEY LN	0	526N	NEF	77407
FESCUE DR	0	293F	SEM	77386
FESTIVAL DR	900	618K	SEH	77062
FESTIVAL HILL CT	0	366S	NWC	77433
FESTUS	13300	572S	SWH	77047
FETLOCK DR	12200	409A	NWC	77065
FETLOCK DR	12300	408D	NWC	77065
FEUHS LN	100	453G	NEH	77022
FICHTER	1	453G	NEH	77022
FICUS CT	17400	331L	NWC	77388
FID CT	17000	379W	NEC	77532
FIDDLELEAF CT	1	251J	WD	77381
FIDDLERS COVE PLACE	1	250D	WD	77381
FIDDLERS GREEN DR	0	609U	NEF	77459
FIDDLERS GREEN DR	3600	527C	SWC	77082
FIDELIA	11800	490P	BH	77024
FIDELIA CT	11700	490P	SWH	77024
FIDELITY	100	495M	NEH	77029
FIELD CT	0	614G	PL	77581
FIELDBLOOM LN	0	528T	NEF	77083
FIELDBLUFF LN	18300	407S	NWC	77449
FIELD BRIAR DR	1700	485M	SWC	77450
FIELD BRIAR LN	0	609Q	MC	77459
FIELDBROOK DR	11600	489P	SWH	77077
FIELDCLIFF CT	12800	408V	NWC	77041
FIELD COTTAGE LN	0	526G	NEF	77407
FIELD COTTAGE LN	7600	334M	NCC	77338
FIELDCREEK DR	300	657F	FR	77546
E. FIELDCREST	11700	539V	LP	77571
FIELDCREST DR	11100	539V	LP	77571
FIELDCROSS LN	0	573T	SEC	77047
FIELD CYPRESS LN	0	366V	NWC	77433
FIELDER DR	22000	485M	SWC	77450
FIELDER BROOK LN	0	484X	NEF	77494
FIELD FLOWER CT	1	251Z	WD	77380
FIELDGLEN CT	0	658N	LC	77573
FIELDGLEN DR	17500	407P	NWC	77084
FIELD GREEN DR	0	325V	NWC	77433
FIELDHAVEN CT	26300	366H	NWC	77433
FIELD HAZE TRAIL	16200	326F	NWC	77433
FIELD HOLLOW DR	0	612N	PL	77545
FIELD HOUSE CT	21100	334R	NCC	77338
FIELDING LN	12600	456M	NEC	77049
FIELDLARK LN	1600	610B	MC	77489
FIELD MANOR LN	0	525H	NEF	77450
FIELD MANOR LN	0	573Y	SEC	77047
FIELD MEADOW CT	4600	446G	NWC	77449
FIELD MEADOW DR	4200	446G	NWC	77449
FIELDMONT LN	0	373A	NCC	77073
FIELD RIDGE DR	7400	408J	NWC	77095
FIELDRIDGE LN	0	486J	SWC	77450
FIELDROSE CT	23300	525F	NEF	77407
FIELD ROW TRAIL	0	325F	NWC	77447
FIELD RUN CT	600	457Q	NEC	77049
FIELDS	7700	455T	NEH	77028
FIELDS LN	22100	291J	NWC	77389
FIELDSBORO DR	12200	570E	SWH	77031
FIELDSHIRE	6900	525E	NEF	77494
FIELDSHIRE CIR	0	446M	NWC	77449
FIELD SPRINGS LN	13500	578W	SEH	77059
FIELDSPUR TRAIL		526S	NEF	77406
FIELDS STORE RD	0	242Y	NWC	77484
FIELDS STORE RD	0	242H	WCO	77484
FIELDS STORE RD	1400	282L	NWC	77484
FIELDSTONE	0	407H	NWC	77095
FIELDSTONE	2700	568V	SG	77478
FIELDSTONE CT	7600	407H	NWC	77095
FIELDSTONE DR	0	613X	NEB	77584
FIELDSTONE DR	1300	610B	MC	77489
FIELD STONE DR	10200	450J	NWC	77041
FIELDSTONE DR	13700	408Q	NWC	77041
FIELDSTONE TERRACE CT		526S	NEF	77407
FIELDTHORN CT	3600	486S	NEF	77450
FIELDTREE DR	19800	335Q	HM	77338
FIELD VIEW CT	9200	575Z	SEH	77075
FIELDVINE CT	21900	486W	NEF	77450
FIELDWICK LN	4600	333M	NCC	77338

Street Name	Block	Pg/Sq	Loc	Zips
FIELDWOOD DR	5000	491Q	SWH	77056
FIELDWORTH DR	12500	413P	NEH	77037
FIELD YUCCA LN	0	327U	NWC	77429
FIERY BROWN TRAIL	0	326J	NWC	77433
FIESTA DR	800	453F	NEH	77022
FIESTA LN	100	659Z	DI	77539
FIESTA LN	4300	534A	SEH	77004
FIESTA FLOWER	7200	525E	NEF	77494
FIESTA ROSE CT	0	326J	NWC	77433
FIFE CT	1400	658P	LC	77573
FIFE LN	17200	657C	SEC	77598
FIFI	6700	614D	BK	77581
FIGARO DR	12800	489G	SWH	77024
FIGG LN	0	377D	NEH	77346
FIGG LN	0	377D	NEC	77346
FIGHTING COLT	8300	530X	SWH	77071
FIGLAND	5800	614U	PL	77584
FIG ORCHARD RD	100	459M	HG	77562
FIG ORCHARD RD	700	460J	HG	77562
FIG ORCHARD RD	3000	460M	NEC	77562
FIG TREE	1100	459M	HG	77562
FIGURINE CT	20800	525D	NEF	77450
FIJI CT	600	419B	NEC	77532
FILAREE RIDGE LN	9200	616E	SEC	77089
FILAREE TRAIL	0	416Q	NEC	77044
FILEY CT	10300	496E	NEH	77013
FILEY LN	10700	496E	NEH	77013
FILLMONT	0	456D	NEC	77044
FILLMONT LN	9500	416Z	NEC	77044
FILLMORE	7900	495P	NEH	77029
FILLTOP	8000	455P	NEH	77028
FILLY PASS CT	0	327U	NWC	77429
FILMONT CT	0	326Z	NWC	77429
FILMORE LN	3600	538Z	DP	77536
FINBOROUGH DR	16400	328U	NWC	77377
FINBURY LN	23600	485T	NEF	77494
FINBURY OAKS LN	0	446N	NWC	77449
FINCASTLE DR	22100	485D	SWC	77450
FINCH	1000	453Z	NEH	77009
FINCH	5500	454M	NEH	77028
FINCH	7300	455J	NEH	77028
S. FINCH CIR	7500	455J	NEH	77028
N. FINCH CIR	7500	455J	NEH	77028
FINCH BROOK DR	12900	328Y	NWC	77429
FINCHER DR	15700	617W	SEC	77546
FINCH FALLS LN	0	450K	NWH	77080
FINCHGROVE LN	0	485W	NEF	77494
FINCH GROVE LN	0	332N	NWC	77090
FINCH LANDING LN	0	333F	NCC	77338
FINCH LANDING LN	0	333F	NCC	77338
FINCHLEY DR	3700	528C	SWH	77082
FINCH SPRINGS LN	0	484S	NEF	77494
FINCHWOOD LN	10100	529R	SWH	77036
FIND HORN LN	9300	407D	NWC	77095
FINDLAY	5200	577D	PA	77505
FINDLAY	7900	535K	SEH	77017
FINDLAY CT	0	535Q	SEH	77017
FINESSE DR	800	373T	NCC	77032
FINESSE DR	1000	373U	NCC	77032
FINEWOOD WAY	16600	618R	SEH	77058
FINFEATHER DR	0	249Z	NWC	77375
FINFROCK	300	536K	PA	77506
FINGERLING PLACE	0	250P	NWC	77389
FINN	7000	453K	NEH	77022
FINN CORNER WAY	0	250N	NWC	77389
FINNEGAN DR	0	494G	NEH	77020
FINN GROVE LN	0	486H	SWC	77094
FINNIGANS CIR	0	377L	NEC	77346
FINN WAY DR	0	415C	NEC	77396
FINSBURY	0	374T	NEH	77032
FINSBURY FIELD DR	5300	444U	KT	77493
FINTONA WAY	400	497C	NEC	77015
FINTRY HILLS ST	0	377Q	NEC	77044
FINWOOD LN	15800	377Q	NEC	77044
FIONA PINES TRAIL	0	524F	NEF	77494
FIONA SKY LN	0	524F	NEF	77494
FIORELLA WAY	3300	333F	NCC	77338
FIR	0	375M	NEC	77396
FIR	7100	535E	SEH	77087
FIR	7300	535E	SEH	77012
FIR LN	12200	247M	SWM	77362
FIR CANYON TRAIL	19000	326Y	NWC	77429
FIR COVE	1800	296Y	NEH	77339
FIR CREEK LN	21500	291T	NWC	77388
FIR CREST CT	2700	569U	NEF	77477
FIRDALE CIR	15200	498A	NEC	77530
FIREBIRD DR	11900	529W	SWH	77099
FIREBRICK DR	13200	408M	NWC	77041
FIRE BROOK CT	0	250U	NWC	77389
FIRE CREEK DR	10900	449T	NWH	77043
FIRECREEK RIDGE DR	17200	367Q	NWC	77095
FIREDEL	11800	415R	NEC	77016
FIREFALL CT	1	251X	WD	77380
FIREFALL LN	1	251X	WD	77380
FIRE FLICKER PLACE	1	250H	WD	77381
FIREFLY	5300	536N	SEH	77017
FIREFLY CT	100	295F	SEM	77365
FIREFLY DR	18600	295E	SEM	77365
FIREFLY RD	0	615T	PL	77581
FIREGATE DR	23800	293Y	NCC	77373
FIREHILLS	0	411D	NWC	77038
W. FIREMIST CT	0	325L	NWC	77429
E. FIREMIST CT	0	325M	NWC	77429
FIREMIST WAY	0	325M	NWC	77429
FIRENZA DR	5700	571E	SWH	77035
FIRENZE DR	0	657L	FR	77546
FIREROCK DR	13700	571J	SWH	77085
FIRE SAGE CT	10300	376C	NEC	77396
FIRE SAGE DR	10300	376C	NEC	77396
FIRESIDE DR	17600	331E	NWC	77379
FIRESIDE LN	24100	339J	HU	77336
FIRESIGN DR	19600	337U	NEC	77346
FIRE STATION RD	0	326R	NWC	77429
FIRESTONE CT	2100	659C	LC	77573
FIRESTONE DR	2100	659C	LC	77573
FIRESTONE DR	4300	531V	SWH	77035
FIRE THORN LN	7900	406M	NWC	77433
FIRETHORNE CREEK CT	7700	250T	NWC	77389
FIRE TIGER CT	0	250N	NWC	77389
FIRE TOWER HILL PLACE	0	366S	NWC	77433
FIREWATER LN	0	612F	PL	77584
FIREWEED TRAIL	0	325L	NWC	77433
FIRE WHEEL DR	0	293C	SEM	77386
FIREWILLOW PLACE	1	250C	WD	77381
FIRE WIND CT	21200	290U	NWC	77379
FIREWOOD LN	25100	293P	NCC	77373
FIR FOREST	0	331C	NWC	77388
FIR FOREST DR	4000	331F	NWC	77388
FIR GLEN LN	13000	328U	NWC	77429
FIR GROVE DR	2300	296Z	NEH	77339
FIRHILL DR	1800	489N	SWH	77077
FIR HOLLOW CIR	18400	377A	NEC	77346

Street Name	Block	Pg/Sq	Loc	Zips
FIR HOLLOW WAY	0	615Y	PL	77581
FIR KNOLL WAY	0	326Y	NWC	77433
FIR MEADOW LN	0	698M	LC	77539
FIRNAT	600	453H	NEH	77022
FIRNAT	2000	454E	NEH	77093
FIRNAT	4500	455A	NEH	77016
FIR PLACE	1	259Q	LCO	77357
FIR RIDGE CT	24500	338L	NEH	77336
FIR RIDGE DR	200	338M	NEH	77336
FIR SPRINGS DR	2000	296U	NEH	77339
FIRST	0	373U	NCC	77032
FIRST	0	620L	SB	77586
FIRST BEND CT	0	366L	NWC	77433
FIRST BEND DR	0	366L	NWC	77433
FIRST BEND CROSSING DR	0	366K	NWC	77433
FIRST COLONY BLVD	1400	568W	SG	77479
FIRST CROSSING BLVD	2000	568Z	SG	77478
FIRST LANDING DR	0	366P	NWC	77433
FIRST VOYAGE CT	18400	366K	NWC	77433
FIRTH DR	3200	613F	NEB	77584
FIRTH LN	16700	447D	NWC	77084
FIRTHRIDGE CT	15700	618N	SEH	77598
FIR TREE DR	1900	658T	LC	77573
FIRTREE WAY	2000	618G	SEH	77062
FIR VALLEY DR	4300	297X	NEH	77345
FIRWOOD DR	1600	536P	PA	77502
FIRWOOD LN	0	575U	SEH	77075
FIR WOODS LN	15300	327S	NWC	77429
FISH RD	24400	247X	SWM	77355
FISH CREEK DR	0	486A	SWC	77450
FISHEL	11900	414N	NCC	77093
FISHER	800	452L	NWH	77018
FISHER	1200	463E	MB	77520
FISHER	6300	409Z	NWH	77041
S. FISHER CT	1900	537T	PA	77502
N. FISHER CT	1900	537T	PA	77502
FISHER DR	19200	326D	NWC	77377
FISHER DR	19300	286Z	NWC	77377
FISHER LN	0	502P	BT	77520
FISHER RD	200	335Y	HM	77338
FISHER RD	17600	322A	WCO	77484
FISHER, COLONEL DR	18800	334Y	NEH	77032
FISHER COLONY DR	0	524L	NWF	77406
FISHER GLEN LN	8000	528L	SWH	77072
FISHER GROVE LN	0	377F	NEC	77346
FISHERMAN CT	9000	293L	SEM	77386
FISHERMANS COVE	4400	609R	MC	77459
FISHER PARK DR	0	408B	NWC	77095
FISHER RIDGE LN	0	328C	NWC	77377
FISHER RIVER LN	0	377J	NEC	77346
FISHER TRACE CT	0	332D	NCC	77373
FISHHAWK WAY	400	379X	NEC	77532
FISH HOOK CT	4000	293H	SEM	77386
FISIOLA ST	0	530X	SWH	77031
FISK	4600	453U	NEH	77009
FITCH	4400	454G	NEH	77016
FITE RD	0	613R	NEB	77584
FITE RD	5100	614R	PL	77584
FITZ	0	285D	SWM	77355
FITZ	21300	286A	SWM	77355
FITZGERALD	6100	412Y	NWH	77091
FITZGERALD RD	10900	463A	MB	77580
FITZHUGH	6000	455Q	NEH	77028
FITZLEE	2300	282U	WL	77484
FITZROY CT	14200	528S	NEF	77083
FITZWATER DR	3900	333D	NCC	77373
FIVE ASHES DR	15900	330T	NWC	77379
FIVE FORKS DR	6800	330F	NWC	77379
FIVE IRON DR	2100	616K	SEC	77089
FIVE KNOLLS DR	4600	617X	SEC	77546
FIVE OAKS DR	5000	291A	NWC	77389
FIVE OAKS DR	5400	290D	NWC	77389
FIVE SPOT CT	9600	289Y	NWC	77379
FJORD CT	5000	371S	NWC	77066
FLACK DR	5600	531J	SWH	77081
FLAGHOIST LN	500	488G	SWH	77079
FLAGHORNE CT	18800	328G	NWC	77377
FLAGLER	7100	578B	PA	77505
FLAGLER	11700	570L	MC	77071
FLAGMORE CT	20700	486F	SWC	77450
FLAGMORE DR	1000	486F	SWC	77450
FLAGSHIP CT	2300	619Y	LC	77573
FLAGSHIP DR	8700	495Q	NEH	77029
FLAGSTAFF LN	0	658U	LC	77573
FLAGSTAFF LN	12600	456M	NEC	77049
FLAGSTAFF LN	13100	457J	NEC	77049
FLAGSTONE DR	13700	408L	NWC	77041
FLAGSTONE CREEK RD	18800	447N	NWC	77084
FLAGSTONE DALE	0	616G	SEC	77089
FLAGSTONE HILL LN	0	526J	NEF	77407
FLAGSTONE HILLS	0	526K	NEF	77407
FLAGSTONE PASS CT	0	609T	NEF	77479
FLAGSTONE PASS LN	9300	616E	SEC	77089
FLAGSTONE TERRACE	1000	536S	SEH	77017
FLAGSTONE TRACE WAY	0	328E	NWC	77429
FLAGSTONE TRACE WAY	0	328E	NWC	77377
FLAGSTONE TRAIL CT	20600	326J	NWC	77433
FLAGSTONE WALK WAY	0	457R	NEC	77049
FLAIR CIR	6300	457N	NEC	77049
FLAIR DR	14100	456R	NEC	77049
FLAIR DR	14400	457N	NEC	77049
FLAIR OAKS DR	7500	410Q	NWC	77040
FLAMBOROUGH DR	3000	537L	PA	77503
FLAME	0	375P	NEH	77396
FLAMELEAF GARDENS CT	15200	326S	NWC	77433
FLAMENCO DR	7000	459K	NEC	77562
FLAMENCO GARDENS	0	660F	LC	77573
FLAMING AMBER WAY	0	325M	NWC	77429
FLAMING ARROW TRAIL	20900	378C	NEC	77532
FLAMING CANDLE DR	3100	331D	NWC	77388
S. FLAMINGO	0	610N	MC	77459
N. FLAMINGO	0	610N	MC	77459
N. FLAMINGO	600	620H	SB	77586
W. FLAMINGO	1000	620H	SB	77586
FLAMINGO	1300	252G	SEM	77385
FLAMINGO	1800	658Q	LC	77573
S. FLAMINGO	4500	620H	SB	77586
FLAMINGO CT	700	656C	FR	77546
FLAMINGO CT	4100	613M	NEB	77584
FLAMINGO CT	25800	257G	RF	77357
FLAMINGO DR	5400	534W	SEH	77033
FLAMINGO DR	6200	534Y	SEH	77087
FLAMINGO'S BEAK	0	381U	LCO	77535
FLAMINGO BAY DR	3900	610N	MC	77459
N. FLAMINGO BIGHT	0	542J	BT	77520
S. FLAMINGO BIGHT	100	542J	BT	77520
FLAMINGO ISLAND CT	2300	610N	MC	77459
FLAMINGO ISLAND DR	1	610N	MC	77459
FLAMINGO LAKES CT	12000	369W	NWC	77065
FLAMINGO LANDING	1	610N	MC	77459
FLAMINGO PARK	15200	375U	NEC	77396
FLANAGAN RD	12000	368L	NWC	77429

Street Name	Block	Pg/Sq	Loc	Zips
FLANDERS DR	3200	297J	SEM	77365
FLANDERS FIELD LN	1400	568E	SG	77498
FLANNER'S CT	800	292G	NCC	77373
FLANNERY CT	22000	485Z	NEF	77450
FLANNERY BRIDGE LN	20900	291V	NWC	77388
FLANNERY PARK LN	400	487A	SWC	77094
FLANNERY RIDGE LN	0	573U	SEC	77047
FLANNIGAN WAY	0	292J	NWC	77389
FLATBROOK DR	0	293Z	NCC	77373
FLAT CREEK DR	0	612L	PL	77545
FLAT CREEK LN	21200	446J	NWC	77449
FLAT IRON DR	0	335P	NCC	77338
FLATRIDGE CT	16100	527Q	NEF	77083
FLAT ROCK	1800	656R	FR	77546
FLAT ROCK LN	0	573U	SEC	77047
FLATROCK CREEK	0	372J	NWC	77067
FLATROCK CREEK DR	0	257E	SEM	77357
FLATROCK PARK LN	0	373A	NCC	77073
FLATROCK TRAIL	8000	415L	NEC	77050
FLAT SPRINGS LN	0	407J	NWC	77433
FLAT STONE	1	251B	WD	77381
FLATTOP LN	11900	328C	NWC	77377
FLATWOOD CT	3100	614S	NEB	77584
FLATWOOD DR	3800	446L	NWC	77449
FLATWOODS PLUM DR	0	249R	NWC	77375
FLAX CT	24100	289A	TB	77375
FLAX DR	7700	570C	SWH	77071
FLAX BOURTON	5200	337W	NEC	77346
FLAX BOURTON CLOSE	18700	337W	NEC	77346
FLAXEN DR	12000	409A	NWC	77065
FLAXEN DR	12300	408D	NWC	77065
FLAXEN MANOR CT	10500	329B	NWC	77379
FLAX FLOWER DR	0	526T	NEF	77407
FLAXMAN LN	7100	495K	NEH	77029
FLAXMAN LN	10300	496J	JC	77029
FLAXSEED WAY	12500	569M	SF	77477
FLAXWOOD DR	19300	337S	NEC	77346
FLECHERWOOD CT	0	290R	NWC	77388
FLEDGLING TRAIL	0	526T	NEF	77407
FLEET LN	4200	538U	DP	77536
FLEETHAVEN CT	5700	407Z	NWC	77084
FLEETHAVEN LN	16000	407Z	NWC	77084
FLEETWAY DR	200	490M	HC	77024
FLEETWELL DR	13800	572P	SWH	77045
FLEETWOOD	200	658M	LC	77573
FLEETWOOD	2900	414S	NEH	77093
FLEETWOOD	4700	531C	BL	77401
FLEETWOOD DR	0	579C	LP	77571
FLEETWOOD DR	0	539Y	LP	77571
FLEETWOOD DR	700	501X	BT	77520
FLEETWOOD FALLS LN	0	293G	SEM	77386
FLEETWOOD GROVE CROSSING	0	328E	NWC	77377
FLEETWOOD OAKS DR	15700	488A	SWH	77079
FLEET WOOD PARK	0	295M	SEM	77365
FLEET WOOD PARK	0	295M	SEM	77365
FLEETWOOD PLACE CIR	0	488E	SWH	77079
FLEETWOOD PLACE DR	800	488E	SWH	77079
FLEMING	0	502B	BT	77521
FLEMING	3300	462X	NEC	77521
FLEMING CT	700	496E	NEH	77013
FLEMING DR	2900	537K	PA	77506
FLEMING DR	10100	495H	NEH	77013
FLEMING DR	10300	496E	NEH	77013
FLEMING DOWNE LN	4700	291S	NWC	77388
FLEMING SPRINGS DR	0	376F	NEC	77338
FLEMING SPRINGS DR	0	376F	NEC	77338
FLEMINGTON AVE	15300	408S	NWC	77084
FLETA DR	6200	455P	NEH	77028
FLETCHER	1800	493C	NEH	77009
FLETCHER BRIDGE CT	14800	568A	NEF	77498
FLETCHER BRIDGE LN	10700	568A	NEF	77498
FLETCHER WAY DR	19400	372D	NCC	77073
FLEUR DR	11200	368U	NWC	77065
FLEUR DE LIS BLVD	13800	368T	NWC	77429
FLEWELLENS FALLS LN	7000	330B	NWC	77379
FLICKER DR	1600	610B	MC	77489
FLICKERING CANDLE DR	3200	331H	NWC	77388
FLICKERING LEAF LN	2400	611N	NEF	77545
FLINT	1100	496J	JC	77029
FLINT BRIDGE CT	14800	568A	NEF	77498
FLINT BROOK CT	2300	611W	FS	77545
FLINT COVE CT	17200	407L	NWC	77095
FLINT CREEK DR	4000	297S	NEH	77339
FLINTCREST DR	0	457V	NEC	77015
FLINTDALE RD	400	490F	BH	77024
FLINT FOREST LN	11600	490F	BH	77024
FLINTGATE CT	2600	371D	NWC	77014
FLINT HILL DR	18300	407W	NWC	77449
FLINTLOCK	11500	539Z	LP	77571
FLINTLOCK DR	22100	405Y	NWC	77449
FLINTLOCK RD	5900	410Y	NWH	77040
FLINTLOCK RD	6300	410U	NWC	77040
FLINT OAK CT	0	372C	NCC	77073
FLINTON DR	0	524P	NWF	77406
FLINT POINT DR	400	490L	PP	77024
FLINTRIDGE	0	250H	WD	77381
FLINTRIDGE DR	0	250A	WD	77382
FLINTRIDGE DR	0	250G	WD	77381
FLINTRIDGE DR	7800	455F	NEH	77028
FLINT RIDGE RD	200	618T	WB	77598
FLINTRIDGE LAKE LN	15100	326U	NWC	77429
FLINT RIVER DR	800	491A	HC	77024
FLINTROCK CIR	2700	371L	NWC	77067
FLINTROCK CT	3900	609E	SG	77479
FLINTROCK DR	2900	613Y	NEB	77584
FLINTROCK LN	3700	609E	SG	77479
FLINTROCK RD	0	539Z	LP	77571
FLINTSIDE DR	19500	406R	NWC	77449
FLINTSTONE DR	11800	368D	NWC	77070
FLINT TRAIL	21400	255U	SEM	77365
FLINT VALLEY LN		484V	FL	77441
FLINTWICK DR	7100	459J	NEC	77049
FLINTWOOD CT	11600	490F	BH	77024
FLINTWOOD DR	11700	490F	BH	77024
FLISER DR	7300	408R	NWC	77041
FLORA	3400	493T	SWH	77006
FLORA DR	4200	578F	PA	77505
FLORA RD	0	657T	FR	77546
FLORABUNDA LN	100	379K	NEC	77532
FLORADORA LN	100	452D	NWH	77076
FLORA FAUNA DR	0	335K	NCC	77338
FLORAFIELD LN	10500	368S	NWC	77429
FLORAGATE DR	23800	293Z	NCC	77373
FLORAL	1400	535E	SEH	77087
FLORAL BLOOM WAY	2500	611S	FS	77545
FLORAL CREST DR	9200	527P	NEF	77083
FLORAL GARDEN LN	0	297K	NEH	77365
FLORALGATE LN	17200	407F	NWC	77095
FLORAL GLEN LN	0	406R	NWC	77449
FLORAL PARK CT	9400	408A	NWC	77095
FLORAL PARK LN	0	457U	NEC	77049
FLORAL RIDGE DR	2200	291R	NWC	77388

Street Name	Block	Pg/Sq	Loc	Zips
FLORAL WAY CT	3900	611X	FS	77545
FLORA MEADOW DR	24500	293T	NCC	77373
FLORAMORGAN LN	12100	616L	SEC	77089
FLORA ROCK LN	0	366Y	NWC	77433
FLORA ROCK LN	4100	609T	NEF	77479
FLORA ROCK LN		609T	NEF	77479
FLORA VIEW CT	20700	290V	NWC	77379
FLORA VISTA DR	300	618S	SEH	77598
FLORENCE	100	288H	TB	77375
FLORENCE	2300	537P	PA	77502
FLORENCE	2700	493B	NWH	77009
FLORENCE	4800	531L	BL	77401
FLORENCE	17800	257A	SEM	77357
FLORENCE DR	0	658X	LC	77573
FLORENCE RD	13400	528X	NEF	77498
FLORENCE BEND DR	0	328J	NWC	77429
FLORENCE BEND DR	0	328J	NWC	77377
FLORENCE CREST DR	0	526P	NEF	77407
FLORENCE KNOLL DR	0	328J	NWC	77429
FLORENCE KNOLL DR	0	328J	NWC	77377
FLORENCE RUN LN	0	328K	NWC	77377
FLORENCE RUN LN		328K	NWC	77377
FLORES	0	656N	NEB	77511
FLORET ESTATES CT	14300	367A	NWC	77429
FLORET HILL LN	12500	568D	SG	77478
FLORETTE LN	20900	291U	NWC	77388
FLORHAM PARK DR	19100	329H	NWC	77379
FLORIA ST	0	256V	SEM	77357
FLORIDA	900	659P	LC	77573
FLORIDA	1500	541A	BT	77520
FLORIDA	1900	540D	BT	77520
FLORIDA	2800	494A	NEH	77026
FLORIDA DR	1700	620K	SB	77586
FLORIDA LN	0	620K	SB	77586
FLORIDA VIEW LN	0	377L	NEC	77346
FLORINA RANCH DR	0	484R	NEF	77494
FLORINDA	3600	533M	SEH	77021
FLORINE	3600	534L	SEH	77087
FLOSSIE MAE	8600	495L	NEH	77029
FLOSSMOOR	13700	417T	NEC	77044
FLOWER DR	0	248E	SWM	77354
FLOWER BRIDGE CT	4500	375V	NEC	77396
FLOWER BUD	23800	525E	NEF	77494
FLOWER CREEK LN	0	658Z	LC	77573
FLOWER CREEK LN	14200	488N	SWH	77077
FLOWER CREST	0	570Z	MC	77489
FLOWERCROFT CT	15900	367C	CY	77429
FLOWER CROFT CT	20900	526J	NEF	77407
FLOWERDALE	7400	451X	NWH	77055
FLOWERFIELD CT	0	613F	NEB	77584
FLOWERFIELD LN	3000	613F	NEB	77584
FLOWERFIELD LN	17000	373N	NEH	77060
FLOWER GARDEN LN	1900	488N	SWH	77077
FLOWER GATE DR	5800	334A	NCC	77373
FLOWER GROVE CT	18100	526M	NEF	77407
FLOWER HILL CT	20700	290V	NWC	77379
FLOWERINGMAPLEMEADOW CT	0	616L	SEC	77089
FLOWERING ASH CROSSING	8800	524C	NEF	77494
FLOWERING AZALEA CT	0	296A	SEM	77365
FLOWERING CRAB APPLE DR	0	296A	SEM	77365
FLOWERING CRAPE MYRTLE DR	0	296A	SEM	77365
FLOWERING DOGWOOD CIR	0	296A	SEM	77365
FLOWERING OAK CT	18100	526H	NEF	77407
FLOWERINGVALLEY CIR	0	290Q	NWC	77379
FLOWER MIST CT	17100	328Q	NWC	77377
FLOWER MIST LN	16800	367Q	NWC	77095
FLOWER MOUND	0	248F	SWM	77354
FLOWER MOUND LN	26400	248F	SWM	77354
FLOWER PATH	8600	457A	NEC	77044
FLOWER REEF CIR	3200	660A	LC	77573
FLOWER RIDGE	23300	296M	SEM	77365
FLOWER RIDGE CT	5000	485W	NEF	77494
FLOWERS	1700	534H	SEH	77087
FLOWERS	2700	537Y	PA	77503
FLOWER STALK PLACE	0	250P	NWC	77389
FLOWERTUFT CT	1	252J	WD	77380
FLOWER VIEW CT	0	411R	NWH	77088
FLOWERWOOD CT	1100	618E	SEH	77062
FLOWERWOOD DR	14700	618E	SEH	77062
FLOWING OAK LN	0	406L	NWC	77433
FLOWING PALM LN	2500	611T	NEF	77545
FLOYD	100	658M	LC	77573
FLOYD	3800	492F	SWH	77007
FLOYD LN	15300	458X	CV	77530
FLOYD RD	1600	658S	LC	77573
FLUKINGER RD	23000	242W	WCO	77484
FLUOR DANIEL DR	1	568T	SG	77478
FLUOR DANIEL DR	200	568T	SG	77479
FLUSHING MEADOWS DR	11700	616D	SEH	77089
FLUSHING MEADOWS DR	11900	617A	SEH	77089
FLUTTERBY RD	0	327E	NWC	77429
FLYCASTER DR	1800	292N	NWC	77388
FLYCATCHER CT	0	461N	NEC	77521
FLYCATCHER COVE DR	0	658X	LC	77573
W. FLYING BRIDGE CIR	0	250P	NWC	77389
N. FLYING BRIDGE CIR	0	250P	NWC	77389
E. FLYING BRIDGE CIR	0	250P	NWC	77389
FLYING BRIDGE CIR	0	250P	NWC	77389
S. FLYING BRIDGE WAY	0	379X	NEC	77532
FLYING BRIDGE WAY	700	379X	NEC	77532
FLYING CLOUD TRAIL	20900	378C	NEC	77532
FLYING DOVE TRAIL	2000	378M	NEC	77532
FLYING DUTCHMAN	400	419B	NEC	77532
FLYING EAGLE CT	9500	527U	NEF	77083
FLYING GEESE LN	11200	329B	NWC	77375
FLYNN	1	494J	SEH	77003
FLYNN DR	1900	537T	PA	77502
FLYWAY LN	8700	462J	NEC	77521
FOGLE	4000	454X	NEH	77026
FOLCON CT	0	461N	NEC	77521
FOLEY	1500	450Y	NWH	77055
FOLEY	3500	494K	SEH	77003
FOLEY RD	100	379N	NEC	77532
FOLEY RD	1100	378Q	NEC	77532
FOLEY PARK CT	0	407J	NWC	77433
FOLEY POINT DR	0	327S	NWC	77429
FOLGER	2700	414W	NEH	77093
FOLGER	3400	454B	NEH	77093
FOLIAGE GREEN LN	2500	296V	NEH	77339
FOLIAGE GREEN LN	2700	297S	NEH	77339
FOLKCREST WAY	12500	569H	SF	77477
FOLK FESTIVAL PLACE	0	366S	NWC	77433
FOLKGLEN CT	12800	576V	SEH	77034
FOLKLORE CT	0	250Q	NWC	77389
FOLKLORE WAY	12500	569H	SF	77477
FOLKNOLL DR	9700	569M	SF	77477
FOLKSTONE CIR	0	524H	NEF	77494
FOLKSTONE LN	7700	575S	SEH	77075
FOLKWAY DR	100	372M	NCC	77060
FOLLOWFIELD LN	13000	571K	SWH	77085
FOLLY FIELD DR	0	326U	NWC	77429
FOLSOM DR	16900	458B	NEC	77049

Street Name	Block	Pg/Sq	Loc	Zips
FOLWELL LN	300	490K	BH	77024
FONDA	11100	531X	SWH	77035
FONDREN	3000	580Q	LP	77571
W. FONDREN CIR	15300	570G	MC	77071
E. FONDREN CIR	15300	570G	MC	77071
FONDREN RD	2000	490U	SWH	77063
FONDREN RD	5600	530G	SWH	77036
FONDREN RD	7400	530G	SWH	77074
FONDREN RD	9600	530U	SWH	77096
FONDREN RD	11300	570G	SWH	77035
FONDREN RD	13100	570M	SWH	77085
FONDREN RD	13900	570U	MC	77489
FONDREN BEND DR	12000	570E	SWH	77071
FONDREN GROVE CIR	12700	570J	MC	77489
FONDREN GROVE DR	16300	570J	MC	77489
FONDREN LAKE DR	8100	570B	SWH	77071
FONDREN MEADOW DR	11900	570B	SWH	77071
FONDREN PLACE DR	12000	570E	SWH	77071
FONDREN VILLAGE DR	8700	570E	SWH	77071
FONES RD	21200	287N	NWC	77377
FONES RD	21700	286R	NWC	77377
FONMEADOW	0	571E	SWH	77035
FONMEADOW DR	14200	570H	SWH	77035
FONTAIN LN	300	419R	BR	77532
FONTAINBLEU	8600	491D	SWH	77024
FONTAINE DR	3200	613Y	NEB	77584
FONTANA DR	2600	449M	NWH	77043
FONTANA RD	21200	286R	NWC	77377
FONTANA WAY	0	659S	LC	77573
FONTENELLE DR	5500	571E	SWH	77035
FONTENELLE DR	6000	570H	SWH	77035
FONTHILL DR	8000	330P	NWC	77379
FONTINOT	2100	494C	NEH	77020
FONTINOT	2800	494C	NEH	77026
FONVILLA	7000	530R	SWH	77074
FONVILLE DR	9600	576S	SEH	77075
FOOTBRIDGE WAY	0	250N	NWC	77389
FOOTE	2700	494J	NEH	77020
FOOTHILL	3000	451R	NWH	77092
FOOTSTEP PATH	0	446F	NWC	77449
FORBES RD	11000	575N	SEH	77075
FORBESBURY DR	3900	447K	NWC	77084
FORBES FIELD TRAIL	22500	291K	NWC	77389
FORCE	6200	494D	NEH	77020
FORCE	7100	495A	NEH	77020
FORCE	13100	497A	NEH	77015
FORCE MAIN	0	616L	SEC	77089
FORD	1400	536F	PA	77506
FORD	7800	495W	SEH	77012
FORD RD	1200	569Z	NEF	77477
W. FORD RD	22000	296F	SEM	77365
FORD RD	22200	296M	SEM	77365
FORD RD	23900	297J	SEM	77365
FORDHAM	5800	532C	WU	77005
FORDHAM CIR	2200	444Q	KT	77493
FORDHAM PARK CT	3800	618D	PA	77058
FORDINBRIDGE CT	9300	329R	NWC	77379
FORDINBRIDGE DR	17000	329R	NWC	77379
FORDSHIRE DR	9100	532N	SWH	77025
FORECASTLE	16000	419B	NEC	77532
FORECASTLE CT	500	419B	NEC	77532
FOREDALE	9600	576S	SEH	77075
FORELAND CT	13300	488Q	SWH	77077
FORELAND DR	1900	488P	SWH	77077
FORELAND DR	2200	488U	SWH	77077
FORELLE DR	0	615F	PL	77581
FORELOCK WAY	16600	379W	NEC	77532
FOREMAN	9700	535M	SEH	77017
FOREMAN	9900	536J	SEH	77017
FORESET THICKET LN	0	372K	NWH	77067
FOREST	100	580G	LP	77571
FOREST	400	494T	SEH	77011
FOREST	800	620T	CS	77565
FOREST	1600	616S	PL	77581
FOREST AVE	100	580Q	SA	77571
FOREST CIR	24800	244Q	WCO	77447
W. FOREST CIR	25700	339A	NEC	77336
FOREST CT	4800	500M	BT	77521
FOREST CT	12300	368C	NWC	77429
FOREST CT	23700	285B	SWM	77447
W. FOREST DR	1000	489A	NWH	77043
W. FOREST DR	1200	449W	NWH	77043
W. FOREST DR	19500	257M	SEM	77357
E. FOREST DR	19500	257M	SEM	77357
FOREST DR	19900	291Y	NWC	77388
E. FOREST LN	100	457Y	NEC	77015
FOREST LN	23400	338R	NEH	77336
FOREST ACRES DR	13000	416J	NEC	77050
FOREST ACRES DR	13500	416E	NEC	77050
FOREST ARBOR CT	8500	407F	NWC	77095
FORESTAY CT	1800	419A	NEC	77532
FORESTAY LN	7400	461T	NEC	77521
FOREST BANK LN	2100	615L	PL	77581
FOREST BARK LN	0	372K	NWH	77067
FOREST BAY CT	800	617H	SEH	77062
FOREST BEND AVE	16100	617W	FR	77546
FOREST BEND AVE	16300	657B	FR	77546
FOREST BEND LN	601	616V	FR	77546
FOREST BEND CREEK WAY	18600	331A	NWC	77379
FOREST BIRCH CT	3900	578Z	PA	77059
FOREST BLOOM LN	12800	416Z	NEC	77044
FOREST BLUFF DR	3900	296V	NEH	77339
FOREST BRANCH BLVD	14500	331W	NWC	77014
FOREST BREEZE LN	8000	330J	NWC	77379
FOREST BRIAR DR	15100	527R	NEF	77083
FOREST BRIDGE WAY	5300	371J	NWC	77066
FORESTBROOK DR	2600	333A	NCC	77373
FORESTBROOK DR	3000	333B	NCC	77373
FOREST BROOK LN	0	253P	SEM	77386
FORESTBURG CT	25600	252U	SEM	77386
FORESTBURG DR	0	252U	SEM	77386
FORESTBURG DR	900	412A	NWC	77038
FORESTBURG DR	1700	252R	SEM	77386
FOREST CANYON CT	20600	290V	NWC	77379
FOREST CANYON LN	24700	485N	NEF	77494
FOREST CEDARS DR	17900	407X	NWC	77084
FOREST CENTER DR	0	295Z	NEH	77365
FOREST CENTER DR	0	296W	NEH	77365
FOREST CIRCLE LN	1200	339A	NEC	77336
FOREST CITY DR	3500	297W	NEH	77339
FOREST COLONY DR	0	296A	SEM	77365
FOREST COMMONS	8100	408F	NWC	77095
FOREST COURSE CIR	1	337F	NEH	77339
FOREST COURSE WAY	1	337K	NEH	77339
FOREST COVE CT	0	252M	SEM	77385
FOREST COVE DR	1	336K	NEH	77339
FOREST COVE DR	13300	368H	NWC	77429
FOREST CREEK DR	4400	609B	MC	77459
FOREST CREEK DR	8900	289D	NWC	77375
FOREST CREEK LN	0	612P	PL	77545
FOREST CREEK FARMS DR	15300	327R	NWC	77429
FOREST CREST	0	244B	WCO	77447

Street Name	Block	Pg/Sq	Loc	Zips
FORESTCREST DR	23900	290C	NWC	77389
FOREST CROSS LN	7700	527J	NEF	77407
FOREST DALE LN	9300	455D	NEH	77078
FOREST DAWN WAY	7400	407L	NWC	77095
FOREST DEER RD	18700	447E	NWC	77084
FOREST DEW DR	18300	407S	NWC	77449
FOREST EDGE DR	0	372L	NWH	77067
FOREST ELMS DR	18300	331H	NWC	77388
FOREST ELMS DR	18800	331C	NWC	77388
FOREST ENCLAVE LN	14800	331T	NWC	77068
FORESTER	0	493F	NWH	77009
FORESTER PARK LN	0	253N	SEM	77385
FOREST ESTATES DR	12000	370H	NWC	77066
FOREST FALLS CT	0	368U	NWC	77065
FOREST FALLS DR	2000	337D	NEH	77345
FOREST FERN CT	19300	337S	NEC	77346
FOREST FERN DR	19500	337S	NEC	77346
FOREST FIR	800	372F	NWH	77067
FOREST FLOOR LN	0	292D	SEM	77386
FOREST FORGE DR	18500	407J	NWC	77433
FOREST GARDEN DR	1700	337C	NEH	77345
FOREST GARDEN DR	2800	297Y	NEH	77345
S. FORESTGATE DR	0	250A	WD	77382
FOREST GATE DR	2900	502F	NEC	77521
FORESTGATE DR	6200	334F	NCC	77373
FOREST GATE LN	0	253U	SEM	77386
FOREST GLADE CT	10200	252G	SEM	77385
FOREST GLADE DR	21200	333M	NCC	77338
FOREST GLEN	3200	251P	SWM	77380
FOREST GLEN	11700	490K	BH	77024
FOREST GLEN DR	0	334R	NCC	77338
FOREST GLEN LN	0	619V	LC	77565
FOREST GLEN OAKS DR	0	406D	NWC	77433
FOREST GREEN DR	1700	339P	HU	77336
FOREST GREEN DR	28200	246B	SWM	77355
FOREST GREEN LN	23200	296D	SEM	77357
FOREST GREEN TRAIL	1900	337F	NEH	77339
FOREST GROVE DR	8500	450M	NWH	77080
FOREST GULLY	13500	372F	NWH	77067
FORESTHAVEN DR	5100	370D	NWC	77066
FOREST HAVEN TRAIL	17600	329L	NWC	77375
FOREST HEIGHTS BLVD	0	407L	NWC	77095
FOREST HEIGHTS DR	18000	407K	NWC	77095
FOREST HILL BLVD	100	494Z	SEH	77011
FOREST HILL BLVD	1500	534D	SEH	77023
FORESTHILL DR	0	245D	SWM	77355
FOREST HILLS DR	14100	288B	TB	77375
FOREST HILLSIDE LN	0	372K	NWH	77067
FOREST HOLLOW DR	1300	569X	MC	77459
FOREST HOLLOW DR	8800	415Z	NEH	77078
FOREST HOLLOW DR	9600	462Y	BT	77521
FOREST HOLLY DR	3500	297X	NEH	77345
FOREST HOME DR	1000	488J	SWH	77077
FOREST HOME DR	4500	569X	MC	77459
FOREST HURST DR	4900	293Z	NCC	77373
FOREST HURST GLEN	0	293Y	NCC	77373
FOREST IVY LN	0	372K	NWH	77067
FOREST KNOLL DR	13200	457F	NEC	77049
FOREST LAKE CIR	0	296Q	SEM	77365
FOREST LAKE DR	100	619L	TL	77586
FORESTLAKE TRAIL	0	444P	KT	77493
FOREST LAND DR	5800	407X	NWC	77084
FOREST LANE CIR	18600	256F	SEM	77357
FOREST LAUREL DR	2800	296Z	NEH	77339
FOREST LEAF CIR	4100	569Y	MC	77459
FOREST LEAF DR	10600	528W	NEF	77498
FOREST LEDGE DR	0	296U	SEM	77365
FORESTLIGHT CT	0	335J	NCC	77338
FOREST LOCH DR	0	293Z	NCC	77373
FOREST LODGE CIR	14800	328Z	NWC	77070
FOREST LODGE CT	14900	329W	NWC	77070
FOREST LODGE DR	14500	329W	NWC	77070
FOREST LODGE DR	15000	328Z	NWC	77070
FOREST MAGIC LN	21400	333M	NCC	77338
FOREST MANOR DR	1900	336C	NEH	77339
FOREST MEADOW DR	12800	328V	NWC	77429
FOREST MEW CT	6700	457Q	NEC	77049
FOREST MILL LN	6600	527E	NEF	77407
FOREST MIST DR	17500	330G	NWC	77379
FOREST MIST WAY	0	293D	SEM	77386
FOREST MOON DR	0	365M	NWC	77433
FOREST MOSS CT	0	446D	NWC	77084
FOREST MOUNTAIN CT	2000	338A	NEH	77345
FOREST MUSE DR	0	249D	SWM	77382
FOREST NOOK CT	5000	452E	NWH	77018
FOREST NORTH DR	23200	296W	NEH	77339
FOREST OAK LN	0	253J	SEM	77385
FOREST OAK PARK CT	3100	253N	SEM	77385
FOREST OAKS BLVD	2400	536N	SEH	77017
FOREST OAKS LN	800	613F	NEB	77584
W. FOREST PARK	0	615G	PL	77581
E. FOREST PARK	0	615G	PL	77581
FOREST PARK CT	0	252M	SEM	77385
FOREST PARK CT	12300	368C	NWC	77429
FOREST PARK DR	3800	527C	SWC	77082
FOREST PARK DR	12200	368C	NWC	77429
FOREST PARK LN	0	615L	PL	77581
FOREST PARK LN	17600	330J	NWC	77379
FOREST PARK CEMETERY	0	534D	SEH	77023
FOREST PARK TRAIL	0	252M	SEM	77385
FOREST PASS LN	0	328S	NWC	77429
FOREST PATH CT	2400	293S	NCC	77373
FOREST PINE CT	0	253J	SEM	77385
FOREST PINE LN	26400	484T	NEF	77494
FOREST PINES CT	400	657F	FR	77546
FOREST PINES VILLAGE LN	13500	372K	NWH	77067
FORESTPLACE CT	25300	250S	NWC	77389
FOREST PLAZA CT	6000	370R	NWC	77066
FOREST POINT DR	0	334R	NCC	77338
FOREST POINT DR	0	334R	NCC	77338
FOREST POINT DR	2700	659G	LC	77573
FOREST POINT DR	7800	335N	NCC	77338
FOREST RAIN LN	4100	376H	NEC	77346
FOREST RANCH DR	210	458S	NEC	77049
FOREST RIDGE DR	2500	610A	MC	77459
FOREST RIDGE DR	8200	330E	NWC	77379
FOREST RIDGE DR	8300	329H	NWC	77379
FOREST RIDGE DR	19000	246A	SWM	77355
FOREST RIDGE POINT	0	447G	NWC	77084
FOREST RIDGE POINT	0	447G	NWC	77084
FOREST RIVER DR	900	459W	CV	77530
FOREST ROW DR	3400	297Z	NEH	77345
FOREST RUN DR	15500	326T	NWC	77433
FORESTRY DR	30700	252U	SEM	77386
FOREST SAGE LN	0	524C	NEF	77494
FOREST SAGE LN	12000	612U	PL	77584
FOREST SHADOWS DR	4600	333M	NCC	77338
FOREST SHORES DR	1	336D	NEH	77339
FORESTSIDE LN	8400	408E	NWC	77095
FOREST SOUNDS LN	0	296T	SEM	77365
FOREST SPRING LN	10000	613K	PL	77584
FOREST SPRINGS DR	5400	297N	NEH	77339
FOREST SPRINGS LAKE	25500	292V	NCC	77373
FOREST STAR	800	372K	NWH	77067
FOREST STONE	7900	463S	CCO	77520
FOREST STREAM DR	20500	337R	NEC	77346
FOREST TERRACE DR	4800	293Z	NCC	77373
FOREST THICKET LN	0	372K	NWH	77067
FOREST TIMBERS CIR	19400	337T	NEC	77346
FOREST TIMBERS CT	0	293S	NCC	77373
FOREST TIMBERS CT	19400	337T	NEC	77346
FOREST TIMBERS DR	5200	337T	NEC	77346
FOREST TOWN DR	18200	447F	NWC	77084
FOREST TRACE DR	18900	337Y	NEC	77346
FOREST TRAIL	5000	502B	NEC	77521
FOREST TRAIL	16600	458Z	CV	77530
FOREST TRAIL	16800	459W	CV	77530
FOREST TRAIL	23600	285B	SWM	77447
FOREST TRAIL	23800	245X	SWM	77447
FOREST TRAIL	24100	296L	SEM	77365
FOREST TRAILS DR	5400	407X	NWC	77084
FOREST TRAILS DR	14700	408K	NWC	77095
FOREST VALE CT	2800	297S	NEH	77339
FOREST VALLEY	11100	369N	NWC	77065
FOREST VIEW	800	656D	FR	77546
FORESTVIEW	800	258A	SEM	77357
FOREST VIEW	9000	455H	NEH	77078
FORESTVIEW DR	1	245B	SWM	77355
FOREST VIEW TRAIL	11900	253E	SEM	77385
FOREST VILLAGE DR	3300	296Z	NEH	77339
FOREST VINE CT	17500	328M	NWC	77377
FOREST VISTA DR	21400	333M	NCC	77338
FOREST WAY DR	16100	332T	NWC	77090
FOREST WILLOW LN	3200	331T	NWC	77068
FOREST WIND LN	11600	370L	NWC	77066
FORESTWOOD DR	200	457W	NEC	77015
FORGE CREEK RD	2500	371M	NWC	77067
FORGE CREEK RD	12000	371M	NWC	77067
FORGE HILL PLACE	1	250H	WD	77381
FORGE RIVER RD	400	618U	WB	77598
FORGE STONE DR	2500	617Y	SEC	77546
S. FORK BLVD	11100	616L	SEC	77089
S. FORK CIR	12100	616G	SEC	77089
S. FORK CT	12100	616G	SEC	77089
W. FORK DR	0	657U	LC	77573
FORK CREEK DR	11900	368V	NWC	77065
FORKED BOUGH DR	11200	489P	SWH	77042
FORKLAND DR	13100	488L	SWH	77077
FORMAT	15800	458T	NEC	77530
FORMENTERA PLACE	0	660F	LC	77573
FORNEY DR	5600	530D	SWH	77036
FORNEY RIDGE LN	3900	573Y	SEC	77047
FORREST	1	501U	BT	77520
W. FORREST LN	100	538P	DP	77536
E. FORREST LN	100	538Q	DP	77536
FORRESTAL	7300	533V	SEH	77033
FORRESTER DR	3100	613Z	NEB	77584
FORRESTER TRAIL	0	524A	NEF	77494
FORREST HILLS DR	300	659H	LC	77573
FORSTALL DR	0	371H	NWC	77014
FORSYTHE LN	900	332H	NCC	77073
FORT AUGUSTA CT	0	250X	NWC	77389
FORT AUGUSTA DR	0	250X	NWC	77389
FORT BEND TOLL RD	0	570Z	SWH	77489
FORT BEND TOLL RD	0	570Z	NEF	77459
FORT BEND TOLL RD	0	610L	NEF	77459
FORT BEND TOLL RD	0	610R	NEF	77459
FORT BEND TOWN CENTER	3800	610Y	MC	77459
FORT BOWIE CT	20000	446T	NWC	77449
FORTBRIDGE CT	16700	447D	NWC	77084
FORT BRIDGER RD	2000	446T	NWC	77449
FORT CUSTER CT	20000	446T	NWC	77449
FORT DAVIS CT	19900	446U	NWC	77449
FORT DENISON BLVD	0	327S	NWC	77429
FORT DODGE DR	20000	446U	NWC	77449
FORT DUPONT	12400	377E	NEC	77346
FORTHBRIDGE DR	4600	447D	NWC	77084
FORTHLIN CIR	4200	485Y	NEF	77494
FORTHLOCH CT	16800	447D	NWC	77084
FORTINBERRY	100	501S	BT	77520
FORT ISABELLA DR	0	248Z	NWC	77375
FORT LARAMIE DR	2100	446X	NWC	77449
FORT LEATON LN	0	366N	NWC	77433
FORTNER	100	500P	BT	77520
FORTON DR	0	372M	NCC	77073
FORT PATH DR	24500	293S	NCC	77373
FORTROSE CT	7900	369D	NWC	77070
FORTROSE GARDEN	18800	328G	NWC	77377
FORT ROYAL DR	2600	411H	NWC	77038
FORT SETTLEMENT DR	1	568Z	SG	77478
FORT SETTLEMENT DR	24500	293T	NCC	77373
FORT SETTLEMENT TRAIL	2600	293T	NCC	77373
FORT SMITH	14200	488A	SWH	77079
FORT STANTON DR	19800	446X	NWC	77449
FORT STOCKTON DR	2900	446P	NWC	77449
FORT SUMTER CT	5500	408X	NWC	77084
FORT SUMTER LN	5600	408X	NWC	77084
FORT TIMBERS CT	0	293S	NCC	77373
FORTUNA DR	0	616K	PL	77581
FORTUNA DR	2600	444Q	KT	77493
FORTUNA BELLA DR	2100	616K	PL	77581
FORTUNATA WAY	0	445E	NWC	77493
FORTUNE	700	412U	NWH	77088
FORTUNE DR	800	501V	BT	77520
FORTUNE PARK DR	0	572R	SWH	77047
FORT WORTH	1700	501V	BT	77520
FORTY FOUR LN	24000	324H	NWC	77447
FORUM CT	17900	257D	RF	77357
FORUM DR	8500	450V	NWH	77055
FORUM PARK DR	9600	529V	SWH	77036
FORUM PLACE DR	10500	529Z	SWH	77036
FORUM WEST DR	10000	529Z	SWH	77036
FOSBAK	800	453F	NEH	77022
FOSSIL CANYON DR	9400	375V	NEC	77396
FOSSIL CREEK CIR	22700	485Q	NEF	77450
FOSSIL PARK DR	1600	485K	NEF	77494
FOSSIL POINT CT	0	377E	NEC	77346
FOSSIL POINT LN	0	377E	NEC	77346
FOSSIL RIDGE LN	0	377F	NEC	77346
FOSSIL ROCK LN	11700	576L	SEH	77034
FOSSIL STONE LN	0	526T	NEF	77407
FOSSIL TRAILS DR	21400	292N	NWC	77388
FOSSIL VALLEY LN	0	406C	NWC	77433
FOSSIL WOOD LN	0	327H	NWC	77429
FOSSILWOOD LN	0	328E	NWC	77377
FOSTER	100	288D	TB	77375
FOSTER	100	500N	BT	77520
FOSTER	900	537J	PA	77506
FOSTER	1600	495S	SEH	77011
FOSTER	5800	533M	SEH	77021
FOSTER LN	30100	252Y	SEM	77386
FOSTER RD	21100	291V	NWC	77388
FOSTER BROOK LN	7800	526L	NEF	77407
FOSTER GARDENS LN	0	446E	NWC	77449
FOSTER HILL CT	0	297Q	NEH	77345
FOSTER HILL DR	2800	297Q	NEH	77345
FOSTER POINT LN	0	367Y	NWC	77095
FOSTERS BEND LN	7400	526K	NEF	77407
FOSTERS CANYON LN	0	373A	NCC	77073
FOSTERS CREEK DR	14000	367D	NWC	77429
FOSTER KNOLL LN	24100	296J	SEM	77365
FOSTERS PARK CT	0	256W	SEM	77365
FOSTER SPRING LN	15200	408B	NWC	77095
FOSTERS RUN LN	0	375X	NEC	77396
FOSTORIA LN	600	453A	NEH	77076
FOUNDARY DR	2000	445S	NWC	77493
FOUNDERS BLVD	0	444S	KT	77493
FOUNDERS CT	3000	609C	MC	77459
FOUNDERS CIRCLE BLVD	0	250X	NWC	77389
FOUNDERS GREEN CIR	3100	615L	PL	77581
FOUNDERS SHORE CIR	0	366K	NWC	77433
FOUNDERS SHORE S. DR	12000	366K	NWC	77433
FOUNDERS SHORE N. DR	12100	366K	NWC	77433
FOUNDERS WAY CT	0	452F	NWH	77091
FOUNDING DR	6100	406T	NWC	77449
FOUNTAIN	500	580K	LP	77571
FOUNTAIN	7900	533X	SEH	77051
FOUNTAIN DR	2100	568C	SG	77478
FOUNTAIN ARBOR LN	0	406X	NWC	77449
FOUNTAIN BEND DR	19700	289W	NWC	77375
FOUNTAINBLEAU	25900	288X	NWC	77377
FOUNTAIN BRIDGE LN	5200	330U	NWC	77069
FOUNTAIN BROOK CT	0	612R	PL	77584
FOUNTAINBROOK CT	2900	612R	PL	77584
FOUNTAIN BROOK DR	0	612R	PL	77584
FOUNTAINBROOK DR	0	612R	PL	77584
FOUNTAINBROOK LN	0	609N	MC	77459
FOUNTAINBROOK PARK CT	0	253N	SEM	77386
FOUNTAINBROOK PARK LN	0	253N	SEM	77386
FOUNTAIN CREEK DR	4400	578E	PA	77505
FOUNTAIN CREST CT	13200	408M	NWC	77041
FOUNTAIN CREST DR	7400	408M	NWC	77041
FOUNTAINE	6700	454M	NEH	77028
FOUNTAINGATE DR	10100	569H	SF	77477
FOUNTAINGLEN LN	0	485S	NEF	77494
FOUNTAINGROVE LN	7600	330P	NWC	77379
FOUNTAINHEAD DR	1	569P	SF	77477
FOUNTAINHEAD DR	4400	371A	NWC	77066
FOUNTAIN HILLS CT	13400	370U	NWC	77086
FOUNTAIN HILLS DR	3200	610V	MC	77459
FOUNTAIN LAKE CIR	12500	569E	SF	77477
FOUNTAIN LAKE DR	10400	569E	SF	77477
FOUNTAIN LAKE WAY	20300	326P	NWC	77433
FOUNTAIN LILLY DR	7000	377C	NEC	77346
FOUNTAIN MEADOW	7200	525E	NEF	77494
FOUNTAIN MESA LN	0	408S	NWC	77084
FOUNTAIN MIST DR	0	612J	PL	77545
FOUNTAIN ROCK DR	0	612K	PL	77545
FOUNTAIN SHORES DR	10300	369W	NWC	77065
FOUNTAINS PLAZA	0	251H	WD	77380
FOUNTAIN SPRAY	7300	525E	NEF	77494
FOUNTAIN SPRING DR	3400	371U	NWC	77066
FOUNTAIN SQUARE	1900	491T	SWH	77057
FOUNTAIN STONE LN	0	376W	NEC	77396
S. FOUNTAIN VALLEY DR	2100	610J	MC	77459
N. FOUNTAIN VALLEY DR	2100	610J	MC	77459
FOUNTAIN VIEW	26000	257D	RF	77357
FOUNTAIN VIEW	1000	491T	SWH	77057
FOUNTAIN VIEW CT	1900	484K	NEF	77494
FOUNTAIN VIEW LN	600	659S	LC	77573
FOUNTAINWOOD	0	408N	NWC	77084
FOUNTAINWOOD GROVE LN	0	407R	NWC	77084
FOURCADE	1600	494X	SEH	77023
FOUR CORNERS LN	0	406D	NWC	77433
FOUR HILL	4900	578J	PA	77505
FOUR LEAF DR	15500	448B	NWC	77084
FOUR LEAF CLOVER	3000	374N	NEH	77032
FOURNACE PLACE	4500	531C	BL	77401
FOUR OAKS DR	21300	333J	NCC	77073
FOUR OAKS PLACE	0	491Q	SWH	77056
FOUR PINES DR	2800	297Y	NEH	77345
FOUR RIVERS	0	408S	NWC	77084
FOUR RIVERS CT	5200	452F	NWH	77091
FOUR SEASONS DR	5100	448B	NWC	77084
FOUR SIXES LN	24000	325J	NWC	77447
FOUR SIXES LN	24200	324M	NWC	77447
FOUR WINDS DR	2800	609R	MC	77459
FOUR WINDS DR	14900	571S	SWH	77489
FOWLER	300	492M	SWH	77007
FOWLER PARK	2500	252M	SEM	77385
FOWLER PINES DR	0	377K	NEC	77346
FOWLIE	7800	455P	NEH	77028
FOX	2700	494J	SEH	77003
FOX	8000	463S	CCO	77520
FOX CT	3400	615T	PL	77581
FOX DR	3100	502B	NEC	77521
FOX LN	0	448K	NWH	77084
FOX RD	9800	410A	NWC	77064
FOX AMIS DR	0	366N	NWC	77433
FOX ARBOR LN	0	484T	NEF	77494
FOX ARROW LN	12800	408Z	NWC	77041
FOXBEND DR	22100	405Y	NWC	77449
FOXBEND LN	7200	334Q	NCC	77338
FOXBEND LN	24100	339J	HU	77336
FOXBERRY GLEN LN	0	524H	NEF	77494
FOXBERRY GLEN LN	0	524H	NEF	77494
FOX BLUFF DR	12000	289W	NWC	77375
FOXBOROUGH LN	600	570Y	MC	77489
FOX BRANCH TRAIL	21200	334M	NCC	77338
FOX BRIAR LN	300	569N	SG	77478
FOX BRIAR LN	25200	292V	NCC	77373
FOXBRICK LN	7100	334U	NCC	77338
FOXBROOK DR	6900	334Q	NCC	77338
FOX BRUSH LN	12800	408Z	NWC	77041
FOXBURO DR	11500	369S	NWC	77065
FOXBURO DR	12100	368U	NWC	77065
FOX CANYON	28700	293B	SEM	77386
FOX CANYON DR	2800	293A	SEM	77386
FOX CHAPEL PLACE	0	249C	SWM	77382
FOX CHASE CT	6200	408Z	NWC	77041
FOXCHESTER LN	19900	334Q	NCC	77338
FOX CLEARING TRAIL	7300	334L	NCC	77338
FOX CLIFF LN	20700	334L	NCC	77388
FOX COVE TRAIL	7300	334M	NCC	77338
FOX CREEK CT	0	444T	KT	77493
FOXCREST CT	7300	334L	NCC	77388
FOXCREST LN	7200	334L	NCC	77388
FOXCROFT LN	6900	334L	NCC	77338
FOX CROSSING CIR	7900	330P	NWC	77379
FOX CROSSING LN	16200	330P	NWC	77379
FOX CUB LN	0	334L	NCC	77388
FOXDALE CT	5000	447B	NWC	77084
FOXDEN DR	2500	614S	NEB	77584
FOXFERN	6600	456R	NEH	77049
FOXFERN CIR	6400	456R	NEH	77049
FOXFIELD DR	17200	610G	SWH	77489
FOXFIELD LN	6900	334Q	NCC	77338
FOX FIRE	2400	460Q	NEC	77562
FOXFIRE CIR	2800	609H	MC	77459
FOXFORD WAY	13800	457X	NEC	77015
FOX FOREST TRAIL	7200	334L	NCC	77388
FOX FOUNTAIN LN	0	293A	SEM	77386
FOXGATE RD	15700	488B	SWH	77079
FOX GLEN LN	20100	334Q	NCC	77338
FOXGLEN LN	20600	334M	NCC	77388
FOXGLOVE DR	0	539S	DP	77536
FOXGLOVE DR	500	570Y	MC	77489
FOXGLOVE DR	2400	460Q	NEC	77562
FOXGLOVE DR	2400	613P	NEB	77584
FOXGLOVE LN	400	453A	NEH	77076
FOXGLOVE ST	0	659G	LC	77573
FOXGLOVE OAKS CT	0	615L	PL	77581
FOX GRASS TRAIL	4800	297P	NEH	77345
FOX GROVE LN	20000	334R	NCC	77338
FOX HALL LN	7200	334L	NCC	77388
FOX HAVEN LN	20000	334R	NCC	77338
FOXHILL	4000	414P	NCC	77093
FOXHILL DR	2000	570W	MC	77489
FOX HILLSIDE WAY	0	334L	NCC	77388
FOX HOLLOW	600	576H	PA	77504
FOX HOLLOW BLVD	4600	291E	NWC	77389
FOX HOLLOW CT	22900	291E	NWC	77389
FOX HOLLOW DR	100	502B	NEC	77521
FOX HOLLOW DR	24200	244G	WCO	77447
FOX HOUND LN	20700	334M	NCC	77388
FOX HUNT DR	23000	291F	NWC	77389
FOXHUNTER RD	6200	456R	NEH	77049
FOXHURST LN	6900	334Q	NCC	77338
FOXINGHAM CIR	0	293A	SEM	77386
FOXKESTREL TRAIL	0	328B	NWC	77377
FOX KNOLL LN	6900	334Q	NCC	77338
FOXLAKE DR	1500	446Y	NWC	77084
FOXLAND CT	6000	290Z	NWC	77379
FOX LEAF TRAIL	0	334L	NCC	77338
FOXLEIGH CT	13200	456Q	NEH	77049
FOXLEIGH RD	6100	456Q	NEH	77049
FOXLINE DR	6900	334Q	NCC	77338
FOXLODGE LN	20600	334L	NCC	77388
FOX LYNN DR	28700	293B	SEM	77386
FOXMAR LN	0	334R	NCC	77338
FOXMAR LN	6900	334Q	NCC	77338
FOX MEADOW DR	12300	568H	SF	77477
FOXMEADOW LN	3900	576H	PA	77504
FOX MESA LN	6800	334L	NCC	77338
FOX MILL LN	0	291E	NWC	77389
FOXMONT LN	6900	334Q	NCC	77338
FOXMOOR	13500	330Y	NWC	77069
FOX MOUNTAIN DR	2800	293A	SEM	77386
FOX ORCHARD CT	0	334L	NCC	77338
FOX PATH	0	484P	NEF	77494
FOX PITT RD	2700	293B	SEM	77386
FOX POINT DR	0	366P	NWC	77433
FOXPORT LN	6900	334Q	NCC	77338
FOX PRAIRIE LN	18700	447J	NWC	77084
FOX PUP LN	21400	378C	NEH	77532
FOXRIDGE DR	12300	413Q	NEH	77037
FOX RIDGE LN		484T	NEF	77494
FOX RIVER DR	29300	293A	SEM	77386
FOX RIVER LN	2400	293A	SEM	77386
FOXROW LN	10200	369X	NWC	77064
FOX RUN	3500	615S	PL	77584
FOX RUN	23300	290C	NWC	77389
FOX RUN BLVD	28700	293A	SEM	77386
FOXRUN CT	9800	450P	NWH	77080
FOX RUN LN	400	657M	LC	77573
FOXRUN VISTA DR	0	484V	NWF	77494
FOXSHADOWS LN	7200	334L	NCC	77388
FOXSHIRE LN	1	572Y	SWH	77047
W. FOXSHIRE LN	100	572X	SWC	77053
FOXSIDE LN	6900	334Q	NCC	77338
FOX SPARROW	0	251R	WD	77380
FOX SPRINGS DR	15600	408X	NWC	77084
FOX SQUARE TRAIL	0	334L	NCC	77338
FOX SQUIRREL CT	200	247L	SWM	77362
FOX STAR LN	0	334L	NCC	77388
FOX STONE LN	2400	339J	HU	77336
FOX STONE LN	20200	334Q	NCC	77338
FOX SWIFT CT	0	334M	NCC	77338
FOXTAIL CT	300	659H	LC	77573
FOXTAIL LILLY CIR	0	447A	NWC	77084
FOXTAIL PINE DR	0	486A	SWC	77450
FOXTAIL PLACE	1900	251R	WD	77380
FOXTON RD	12200	574Q	SEH	77048
FOXTON PLACE CT	7400	407M	NWC	77095
FOX TRACE LN	12400	371J	NWC	77066
FOX TRAIL	900	576D	PA	77504
FOX TRAIL LN	6900	334Q	NCC	77338
FOXTREE LN	19100	486M	SWC	77094
FOX TROT CT	0	334L	NCC	77338
FOXVALLEY LN	6900	334L	NCC	77338
FOX VIEW CIR	2700	293B	SEM	77386
FOXVIEW DR	2600	293A	SEM	77386
FOXVILLE DR	2500	371M	NWC	77067
FOXVISTA LN	0	334L	NCC	77388
FOXWAITHE LN	0	334R	NCC	77338
FOXWAITHE LN	6900	334R	NCC	77338
FOXWALK LN	0	334L	NCC	77388
FOX WALK TRAIL	0	334M	NCC	77338
FOX WATER DR	2400	293A	SEM	77386
FOXWAY LN	7100	334Q	NCC	77338
FOXWICK LN	6900	334Q	NCC	77338
FOX WIND CT	6100	408Z	NWC	77041
FOXWOOD	28300	248S	SWM	77362
FOXWOOD CT	1700	570U	MC	77489
FOXWOOD LN	24100	339J	HU	77336
FOXWOOD RD	1300	452T	NWH	77008
FOXWOOD ARBOR LN	0	328A	NWC	77429
FOXWOOD CREEK LN	0	377P	NEC	77044
FOXWOOD FAIR LN	0	334L	NCC	77388
FOXWOOD FOREST BLVD	19900	334Q	NCC	77338
FOXWOOD FOREST CT	7100	334Q	NCC	77338
FOXWOOD GARDEN DR	20700	334L	NCC	77388
FOXWOOD GLEN LN	20700	334L	NCC	77388
FOXWOOD MIST TRAIL	0	334L	NCC	77338
FOY LN	10300	414N	NCC	77093
FOYCE	100	453K	NEH	77022
FOYER CIR	7300	609R	MC	77459
FOYT, A J RD	23800	285N	NWC	77447
FOYT, A J RD	23900	284R	NWC	77447
FRAGRANT CLOUD CT	5500	448D	NWC	77041
FRAGRANT PINE LN	15200	457Q	NEC	77049
FRAGRANT ROSE CT	17600	327N	NWC	77429
FRAIL LN	600	413S	NEH	77076
FRAISER FIR PLACE	0	250U	NWC	77389
FRA MAURO CT	2600	659D	LC	77573
FRA MAURO DR	0	659D	LC	77573
FRAMPTON CT	16700	330H	NWC	77379
FRANCE LN	6000	577H	PA	77505

Street Name	Block	Pg/Sq	Loc	Zips
FRANCE LN	6100	578E	PA	77505
FRANCEL LN	12200	328X	NWC	77429
FRANCES	1000	538L	DP	77536
FRANCES DR	2000	614M	PL	77581
FRANCES LN	16200	246U	SWM	77355
FRANCES PARK DR	0	525R	NEF	77407
FRANCHETTI DR	0	444M	NWC	77493
FRANCINE LN	5000	414Y	NEH	77016
W. FRANCIS	100	501U	BT	77520
E. FRANCIS	100	501U	BT	77520
FRANCIS	600	493T	SWH	77002
FRANCIS	1000	493Y	SEH	77004
FRANCIS	12800	570J	SF	77477
FRANCIS CT	600	659A	LC	77573
FRANCIS CT	3300	493Z	SEH	77004
FRANCIS DR	900	537J	PA	77506
FRANCIS LN	12700	570J	MC	77489
FRANCISCO CT	4100	293H	SEM	77386
FRANCIS MARION DR	6200	411Y	NWH	77091
FRANCITAS DR	900	412A	NWC	77038
FRANCOISE BLVD	10900	489P	SWH	77042
FRANDORA LN	700	490F	HE	77024
FRANK	1500	379R	NEC	77532
FRANK	7400	495S	SEH	77011
FRANK	15100	527Z	NEF	77498
FRANK LN	13000	570J	SF	77477
FRANK RD	2400	374S	NCC	77032
FRANKFORD CT	0	573M	SEH	77048
FRANKIE	500	497F	NEC	77015
FRANKLIN	0	500Y	BT	77520
FRANKLIN	100	493M	DT	77002
FRANKLIN	9800	369G	NWC	77070
FRANKLIN HILLS CT	0	376Q	NEC	77396
FRANKLIN PARK CT	18300	331E	NWC	77379
FRANKLIN PARK DR	0	524D	NEF	77494
FRANKS ST	24600	293S	NCC	77373
FRANK SHORE DR	0	612F	PL	77545
FRANK SHORES DR	0	612F	PL	77545
FRANKTON WAY	17800	373C	NCC	77073
FRANKWAY DR	8800	531R	SWH	77096
FRANTA	600	419C	CB	77532
FRANZ RD	5100	444T	KT	77493
FRANZ RD	19100	446U	NWC	77084
FRANZ RD	19900	446T	NWC	77449
FRANZ RD	21000	445T	NWC	77449
FRANZ RD	24900	444V	KT	77493
FRASER DR	0	295A	SEM	77365
FRASER POINT CT	6500	330R	NWC	77379
FRASIER	0	658Z	LC	77573
FRASIER	500	493A	NWH	77007
FRAWLEY	100	453U	NEH	77009
FRAZER LN	400	412H	NEH	77037
FRAZER LN	800	412G	NWH	77038
FRAZIER RIVER DR	12100	415E	NEH	77050
FREAMAN	800	501X	BT	77520
FRED	100	412T	NWH	77088
FRED	100	484A	KT	77494
FREDA DR	400	536Y	SH	77587
FRED E MITCHELL DR	0	495G	NEH	77029
FREDERICK RD	18900	328B	NWC	77377
FREDERICKSBURG DR	2500	658P	LC	77573
FREDERICKSBURG LN	8400	527P	NEF	77083
FREDONIA DR	1700	373C	NCC	77073
FREDRICK LN	0	660Q	LC	77573
FREE LN	35100	247F	SWM	77362
FREECREST	9800	576R	SEH	77034
FREECROFT	9800	576R	SEH	77034
FREEDALE	9800	576R	SEH	77034
FREEDMAN	18100	325B	NWC	77447
FREEDOM	0	573H	SEH	77033
FREEDOM CT	2000	609C	MC	77459
FREEDOM DR	0	613R	PL	77581
FREEDOM RIVER DR	0	335P	NCC	77338
FREEDOM TREE CT	1800	610P	MC	77459
FREEDOM TREE DR	4200	610P	MC	77459
FREEDONIA DR	1400	450Y	NWH	77055
FREEHILL	9800	576R	SEH	77034
FREELAND	8500	575G	SEH	77061
FREELAND	8550	575H	SEH	77075
FREEMAN	1500	493G	NEH	77009
FREEMAN AVE	1400	444Z	KT	77493
FREEMAN RD	18000	407N	NWC	77040
FREEMAN RD	18800	406P	NWC	77040
FREEMAN RD	23100	405P	NWC	77493
FREEMAN RD	24500	404P	NWC	77493
FREEMONT	4200	453Y	NEH	77009
FREEMONT FAIR CT	9400	576J	SEH	77075
FREEMONT PEAK LN	0	377F	NEC	77346
FREEPORT BLVD	100	457X	NEC	77015
FREEPORT BLVD	300	497F	NEC	77015
FREER CT	13600	328T	NWC	77429
FREERIDGE CT	0	445M	NWC	77449
FREESIA CT	0	460W	BT	77521
FREESIA CT	100	249M	NWH	77375
FREESIA CT	100	249M	NWH	77375
FREESTONE	9800	576Q	SEH	77034
FREESTONE AVE	0	612V	PL	77584
FREESTONE AVE	0	613S	PL	77584
FREESTONE PEACH LN	15200	326S	NWC	77433
FREESTONE PLUM CT	0	457G	NEC	77049
FREESTONE STREAM CT	0	250P	NWC	77389
FREESTONE STREAM PLACE	0	250P	NWC	77389
FREETON	3900	576L	SEH	77034
FREEWOOD	8500	576K	SEH	77034
FREIDA LN	17800	330F	NWC	77379
FRELS LN	1	413T	NEH	77076
FREMONT MANOR LN	0	524H	NEF	77494
S. FREMONT RIDGE	0	250Q	NWC	77389
N. FREMONT RIDGE	0	250Q	NWC	77389
S. FREMONT RIDGE LOOP	0	250Q	NWC	77389
N. FREMONT RIDGE LOOP	0	250Q	NWC	77389
FREMONT TRAILS DR	0	293T	NCC	77373
FRENCH RD	0	447C	NWC	77084
FRENCH RD	17000	447C	NWC	77084
FRENCH CHATEAU DR	6300	411S	NWH	77088
FRENCH COLONY	0	659B	LC	77573
FRENCH CREEK DR	5100	536S	SEH	77017
FRENCHMANS CROSSING DR	0	292G	NCC	77373
FRENCH OAK LN	11200	489X	SWH	77082
S. FRENCH OAKS CIR	0	249B	SWM	77382
FRENCH PLACE	1600	502S	BT	77520
FRENCH VILLAGE DR	1700	451S	NWH	77055
FRENSHAM CIR	5300	448C	NWC	77041
FRESA RD	100	536V	PA	77502
FRESA RD	1300	537S	PA	77502
FRESCO DR	2900	446P	NWC	77449
FRESCO WELLS DR	3000	446P	NWC	77449
FRESCURA DR	14200	528E	SWC	77083
FRESH CANYON CT	0	484S	NEF	77494
FRESH DAWN DR	2600	611N	NEF	77545
FRESH MEADOW	5600	657V	LC	77573
FRESH MEADOW	9500	450F	NWH	77041

Street Name	Block	Pg/Sq	Loc	Zips
FRESHMEADOW DR	1800	570X	MC	77489
FRESHMEADOWS DR	2900	490Z	SWH	77063
FRESHWATER BAY CT	1300	329G	NWC	77379
FRESH WIND LN	0	659M	LC	77573
FRESNO DR	7900	527L	NEF	77083
FREY RD	2100	576K	SEH	77034
FRIAR CIR	16200	330P	NWC	77379
FRIAR LN	1800	449T	NWH	77043
FRIARCREEK LN	1300	451W	HI	77055
FRIARCREEK LN	1300	451W	HI	77055
FRIARDALE CT	12200	328D	NWC	77375
FRIAR GLEN LN	0	332V	NCC	77073
FRIAR GROVE	0	296R	NEH	77339
FRIAR LAKE LN	25300	292R	NCC	77373
FRIAR POINT RD	3000	573F	SEH	77051
FRIAR POINT RD	4100	573G	SEH	77047
FRIARS LN	800	501L	BT	77521
FRIARS COURT LN	7600	330Q	NWC	77379
FRIARS HILL	10500	369P	NWC	77070
FRIARS LEGEND DR	2200	253S	SEM	77386
FRIAR TUCK	24700	244R	WCO	77447
FRIAR TUCK DR	5300	444U	KT	77493
W. FRIAR TUCK LN	300	491G	SWH	77024
E. FRIAR TUCK LN	300	491G	SWH	77024
FRIAR VILLAGE DR	12700	328L	NWC	77377
FRIARWOOD TRAIL	2200	296R	NEH	77339
FRICK RD	2200	372W	NWC	77038
FRICK RD	3200	371Y	NWC	77086
FRIENDLY RD	8900	454B	NEH	77093
FRIENDLY RD	10100	414X	NEH	77093
FRIENDSHIP RD	8500	450R	NWH	77080
FRIENDS KNOLL LN	200	616Y	FR	77546
S. FRIENDSWOOD DR	100	616Z	FR	77546
N. FRIENDSWOOD DR	100	616T	FR	77546
S. FRIENDSWOOD DR	300	656D	FR	77546
S. FRIENDSWOOD DR	1000	657E	FR	77546
FRIENDSWOOD LAKE BLVD	0	656R	FR	77546
FRIENDSWOOD LINK RD	1300	657B	SEC	77546
FRIENDSWOOD LINK RD	2900	657B	SEC	77598
FRIENDSWOOD LINK RD	3700	657A	FR	77546
FRIENDSWOOD WEBSTER RD	0	657B	FR	77546
FRIES CT	1	490D	SV	77055
FRIES RD	1000	490D	SV	77055
FRIES RD	1200	450Z	SV	77055
FRIESIAN ESTATES DR		289X	NWC	77379
FRIESIAN MEADOW LN	0	334R	NCC	77338
FRIESIAN TRAIL	0	334R	NCC	77338
FRIGATE DR	16600	617X	SEC	77546
FRINGETREE BARK CT	0	249U	NWC	77375
FRINGEWOOD DR	8600	455C	NEH	77028
FRIO	300	535B	SEH	77012
FRIO	0	538R	DP	77536
FRIOBEND LN	8600	410L	NWC	77040
S. FRIO RIVER CIR	0	367W	NWC	77433
N. FRIO RIVER CIR	0	367W	NWC	77095
E. FRIO RIVER CIR	0	367W	NWC	77095
FRIO RIVER LOOP	0	253U	NWC	77389
FRIO SPRINGS CT	0	328S	NWC	77429
FRIO SPRINGS LN	0	328S	NWC	77429
FRISCO	1	453Q	NEH	77022
FRISCO	6300	453Q	NEH	77022
FRITSCHE CEMETERY RD	16100	327L	NWC	77429
FRITZ	0	246W	SWM	77355
FRITZ LN	0	331U	NWC	77068
FRITZ LN	22700	291F	NWC	77389
FROENZA CT	0	524R	NEF	77406
FRONT	600	535B	SEH	77012
FRONT		611U	FS	77545
FRONTENAC DR	8200	570F	SWH	77071
FRONTIER	1200	656L	FR	77546
FRONTIER DR	3900	609A	SG	77479
FRONTIER DR	4400	450G	NWH	77041
FRONTIER RD	15800	246R	SC	77355
FRONTIER CREEK CT	0	328L	NWC	77377
FRONTIERSMAN CT	21600	285M	NWC	77447
FROSA LN	0	659P	LC	77573
FROST	5800	374Z	NEH	77396
FROST BAY CT	0	617H	SEH	77062
FROST CREEK DR	0	612J	PL	77545
FROST CREEK LN	0	657S	FR	77546
FROSTDALE LN	0	573Y	SEC	77047
FROSTED LILAC CT	0	249V	NWC	77375
S. FROSTED POND DR	1	250B	WD	77381
N. FROSTED POND DR	1	250B	WD	77381
FROSTED POND PLACE	1	250C	WD	77381
FROSTFIELD LN	0	524C	NEF	77494
FROSTGATE CT	0	445R	NWC	77449
FROST LAKE CT	4100	609B	MC	77459
FROSTMEADOW CT	3600	486S	NEF	77450
FROST PASS	0	609A	SG	77479
FROSTPORT BLVD	0	495H	JC	77029
FROST RANCH	0	609F	MC	77479
FROST RIVER CT	11300	329N	NWC	77377
FROST SPRINGS	0	293E	SEM	77386
FROSTVIEW LN	7200	570Z	SWH	77489
FROSTWOOD DR	100	252N	SEM	77386
FROSTWOOD DR	400	490A	SWH	77024
FROSTWOOD DR	3300	613T	NEB	77584
FROSTWOOD VALLEY CT	7600	407M	NWC	77095
FROSTY BROOK DR	6300	571K	SWH	77085
FROSTY PASS DR	0	293X	NCC	77373
FRUEND	3500	494P	SEH	77003
FRUGE RD	1100	612D	SWC	77047
FRUITA	0	282T	WCO	77484
FRUITVALE DR	900	412A	NWC	77038
FRUITWOOD DR	11400	616D	SEC	77089
FRY CT	21500	485Z	NEF	77450
FRY RD	0	524D	NEF	77494
S. FRY RD	0	485Z	NEF	77450
S. FRY RD	0	525D	NEF	77450
S. FRY RD	100	486P	SWC	77450
FRY RD	1000	446Y	NWC	77084
FRY RD	1001	446Y	NWH	77449
FRY RD	3000	446G	NWC	77449
FRY RD	5100	406Y	NWC	77449
FRY RD	7000	406L	NWC	77433
FRY RD	11500	366H	NWC	77433
FUCHSIA LN	6900	337Y	NEC	77346
FUDGE	100	458Y	CV	77530
FUEL STORAGE RD	2000	333Z	NEH	77032
FUERTE DR	14700	528J	SWC	77083
E. FUGATE	0	453X	NEH	77009
FUGATE	400	453W	NWH	77009
W. FUGATE	700	453W	NWH	77009
FULFORD CT	4000	486S	NEF	77450
FULFORD POINT LN	2900	485P	NEF	77494
FULHAM CT	2000	490V	SWH	77063
FULLER	0	408X	NWC	77084
FULLER BLUFF DR	3500	253X	SEM	77386
FULLERS GRANT CT	12000	366K	NWC	77433
FULLERTON DR	10900	449Q	NWH	77043
FULLGARDEN CT	5700	406Y	NWC	77449

Street Name	Block	Pg/Sq	Loc	Zips
FULMER	300	453U	NEH	77009
FULSHEAR-GASTON RD	25100	524N	NWF	77406
FULTON	1400	493D	NEH	77009
FULTON	3400	453Y	NEH	77009
FULTON	6100	453B	NEH	77022
FULTON	9400	453B	NEH	77076
FULTONDALE LN	0	575Q	SEH	77075
FULTONMANOR LN	0	327D	NWC	77429
FULTON MEADOWS LN	6000	541F	NWH	77092
FULTON POINT DR	0	330M	NWC	77379
FULTON SPRINGS CT	11100	524L	NWF	77406
FULVETTA CROSSING	0	405P	NWC	77493
FULVETTA PARK TRAIL	0	297K	SEM	77365
FUN DR	0	531J	SWH	77074
FUNSTON	100	495W	SEH	77012
W. FUQUA	2900	572S	SWH	77045
FUQUA	2900	573V	SEH	77047
W. FUQUA	4600	571U	SWH	77045
W. FUQUA	6300	571W	SWH	77489
FUQUA	6500	574V	SEH	77048
W. FUQUA	7300	570Z	MC	77489
FUQUA	7700	575U	SEH	77075
FUQUA	10000	576S	SEH	77089
FUQUA	11500	576R	SEH	77034
FUQUA BREEZE DR	0	575V	SEH	77075
FUQUA GARDENS DR	8300	575T	SEH	77075
FUQUA GARDENS VIEW RD		571U	SWH	77053
FUQUA GLEN LN	0	575V	SEH	77075
FUQUA OAKS LN	0	575U	SEH	77075
FUQUA RIDGE LN	0	575U	SEH	77075
FUQUA VILLAS LN	0	575V	SEH	77075
FURAY RD	6900	415Q	NEC	77016
FURLONG LN	8100	570F	SWH	77071
FURMAN RD	12000	573P	SEH	77047
FUR MARKET DR	7500	410H	NWC	77064
FURRAY RD	8000	455K	NEH	77028
FURROW CT	24100	295F	SEM	77365
FUSSELL RD	10500	252L	SEM	77385

G

Street Name	Block	Pg/Sq	Loc	Zips
G	4000	529A	SWH	77072
G AVE	0	410P	NWC	77040
G, AVENUE	0	569R	SF	77477
G, AVENUE	0	659Y	DI	77539
S. G, AVENUE	100	335Z	HM	77338
N. G, AVENUE	100	335V	HM	77338
G, AVENUE	100	568J	SG	77498
G, AVENUE	200	576B	SH	77587
G, AVENUE	1800	496W	GP	77547
G, AVENUE	7000	533J	SWH	77030
G, AVENUE	7200	532M	SWH	77030
G.H. CIR	18700	282S	WL	77484
GABARDINE CREEK	0	327Z	NWC	77429
GABLE LN	5000	371N	NWC	77066
GABLE BRIDGE LN	0	526K	NEF	77407
GABLE COVE LN	0	366J	NWC	77433
GABLE CROSSING DR	0	526T	NEF	77469
GABLE CROSSING DR	0	526T	NEF	77469
GABLE GLEN LN	0	407B	NWC	77095
GABLE GROVE LN	0	485X	NEF	77494
GABLE HILL LN	10800	371V	NWC	77067
GABLE HOLLOW LN	1900	486N	SWC	77450
GABLE LANDING LN	0	253K	SEM	77386
GABLE LODGE CT	300	491H	SWH	77024
GABLE LODGE DR	23300	485P	NEF	77494
GABLE MEADOWS LN	21300	290P	NWC	77379
GABLEMILLS DR	0	366J	NWC	77433
GABLE MOUNTAINS CIR	14500	332W	NCC	77090
GABLEOAK LN	0	407E	NWC	77433
GABLE PARK CT	0	615F	PL	77581
GABLEPARK LN	3200	615F	PL	77581
GABLE POINT DR	0	612N	PL	77545
GABLE POINT DR	7700	407L	NWC	77095
GABLE POINT DR	20000	486G	SWC	77450
GABLE RIDGE DR	20400	486P	SWC	77450
GABLE RUN CT	0	526J	NEF	77407
GABLE STONE LN	0	615G	PL	77581
GABLESTONE LN	6000	525H	NEF	77450
GABLE WIND CT	17300	407E	NWC	77095
GABLE WIND MILL LN	12700	416Z	NEC	77044
GABLE WING LN	0	609N	NEF	77459
GABLEWINN CT	9300	369M	NWC	77070
GABLE WOODS DR	19700	289W	NWC	77375
GABRIEL	9000	490X	SWH	77063
GABRIEL	20500	256L	SEM	77357
GABRIELLA BLUFF LN	0	412N	NWH	77088
GABRIELLA BLUFF LN	0	573L	SEH	77089
GABRIELLE CANYON CT	6300	526B	NEF	77450
N. GABRIEL RIVER CIR	1300	569S	SG	77478
S. GABRIEL RIVER CIR	1500	569S	SG	77478
GABY VIRBO DR	13200	528G	SWH	77083
GADDIS OAKS DR	0	250U	NWC	77389
GADDIS OAKS DR	0	250U	NWC	77389
GADSDEN	17000	375F	HM	77396
GADSHILL CIR	14400	377X	NEC	77044
GADWALL CT	14400	377Y	NEH	77044
GADWALL BAYOU LN	26900	324S	NWC	77447
GADWIN PARK DR	0	250Y	NWC	77389
GAELDOM DR	16300	448E	NWC	77084
GAELDOM DR	16500	447H	NWC	77084
GAELIC CT	4600	447D	NWC	77084
GAELIC DR	16600	447D	NWC	77084
GAELICGLEN LN	17000	407Y	NWC	77084
GAELIC GREEN ST	0	572Q	SWH	77045
GAFF CT	16900	379X	NEC	77532
GAFF LN	30700	286D	SWM	77355
GAFFNEY LN	0	576R	SEH	77034
GAFFNEY LN	5600	407Z	NWC	77084
GAFNA CIR	0	410L	NWC	77040
GAGE	7300	411E	NWH	77086
GAGE CT	1	490F	SWH	77024
GAGE DAVID LN	0	366Z	NWC	77433
GAGELAKE LN	19300	446V	NWC	77084
GAGER	3400	414X	NEH	77093
GAGE SPRING CT	0	293Z	NCC	77373
GAGNE	2200	494C	NEH	77020
GAIL	22300	256Z	SEM	77357
GAIL DR	1200	247K	SWM	77362
GAIL LN	0	577C	PA	77505
GAIL RD	3400	502N	BT	77521
GAILEY LN	7300	410P	NWC	77040
GAILLARD	1	501Y	BT	77520
N. GAILLARD	100	501Y	BT	77520
GAILLARDIA CT	200	247G	SWM	77362
GAIL MEADOW CT	0	484U	NEF	77494
GAIL SHORE DR	18600	366K	NWC	77433
GAINES	1100	453V	NEH	77009
GAINES RD	8100	527V	NEF	77498
GAINES MEADOW DR	8200	527M	NEF	77083
GAINESVILLE	6200	494D	NEH	77020
GAINESVILLE	7100	495A	NEH	77020

Street Name	Block	Pg/Sq	Loc	Zips
GAINESVILLE	13700	497C	NEC	77015
GAINESWAY DR	13400	328T	NWC	77429
GAINS LN	23200	296L	SEM	77365
GAINSBOROUGH CT	9700	569H	SWH	77031
GAINSBOROUGH DR	12200	569H	SWH	77031
GAIRLOCH DR	2000	658T	LC	77573
GAIRLOCH LN	4100	532J	SWH	77025
GALA CT	0	569T	NEF	77477
GALAPAGOS CT	0	445R	NWC	77449
GALAXY	9600	455B	NEH	77078
GALAXY BLVD	18000	258E	SEM	77357
GALAYDA	11600	411E	NWH	77086
GALBREATH DR	11300	370M	NWC	77066
GALE	200	453U	NEH	77009
GALE	600	620Q	SB	77586
GALEFIELD DR	6300	578E	PA	77505
GALENA	100	496T	GP	77547
GALENA CREEK	13400	370U	NWC	77086
GALENA MANOR	100	495Z	GP	77547
GALENA STONE LN	0	524F	NEF	77494
GALENTINE POINT	11900	368H	NWC	77429
GALESBURG	3900	533Z	SEH	77051
GALEWOOD LN	21800	332M	NCC	77073
GALEWOOD WAY	16600	618M	SEH	77058
GALIANI DR	0	445J	NWC	77493
GALICIA LN	0	660L	LC	77573
GALIUM MEADOWS	0	249Z	NWC	77375
GALLAGHER DR	4300	572N	SWH	77045
GALLAGHER DR	5000	571Q	SWH	77045
GALLAGHER LN	1400	538N	DP	77536
GALLAHAD	7800	455B	NEH	77078
GALLANT CT	0	527C	SWC	77082
GALLANT FLAG DR	0	289T	NWC	77375
GALLANT FOREST DR	6000	411K	NWC	77088
GALLANT FOX	4100	537R	PA	77503
GALLANT FOX DR	2400	570S	SF	77477
GALLANT GLEN LN	7100	407Q	NWC	77095
GALLANT KNIGHT LN	26100	296X	SEM	77339
GALLANT RIDGE LN	11200	529B	SWH	77082
GALLANT RIDGE LN	11400	489W	SWH	77082
GALLATIN LN	19300	328C	NWC	77377
GALLENA STONE LN	0	615F	PL	77581
GALLEON DR	2100	620W	LC	77573
GALLEON DR	7100	530L	SWH	77036
GALLEON OAKS DR	1600	486K	SWC	77450
GALLEON POINT CT	0	612L	PL	77584
GALLEON POINT DR	0	612M	PL	77584
GALLERY CT	16700	611B	SWH	77053
GALLETA CT	0	250L	NWC	77389
GALLETA CT	0	250L	NWC	77389
S. GALLEY	700	419F	NEC	77532
E. GALLEY	15700	419F	NEC	77532
S. GALLEY CT	15600	419F	NEC	77532
GALLEY MIST DR	3500	331C	NWC	77388
GALLINAS WAY	0	290Y	NWC	77379
GALLING DR	15800	571W	SWH	77489
GALLINULE LN	10500	574G	SEH	77048
GALLO	0	570D	SWH	77035
GALLOWAY DR	4000	613Z	NEB	77584
GALLOWAY LN	6100	657U	LC	77573
GALLOWAY GATES CT	0	287Z	NWC	77377
GALLOWAY REACH DR	0	366P	NWC	77433
GALLOWGATE LN	0	527W	NEF	77478
GALLUP DR	0	539N	DP	77536
GALLUP DR	0	539N	DP	77536
GALMICHE RD	0	458F	NEC	77049
GALSTON LN	9600	329R	NWC	77379
GALVANI DR	14100	368P	NWC	77429
S. GALVESTON	0	615J	PL	77581
GALVESTON	0	658M	LC	77573
GALVESTON	0	659J	LC	77573
GALVESTON	0	659N	LC	77573
W. GALVESTON	100	658M	LC	77573
GALVESTON	100	611Z	FS	77545
GALVESTON	200	612W	FS	77545
GALVESTON	800	576A	SH	77587
GALVESTON S. AVE	0	615P	PL	77581
GALVESTON AVE	1900	615K	PL	77581
GALVESTON DR	11900	367K	CY	77433
GALVESTON RD	0	536W	SH	77587
GALVESTON RD	1900	535L	SEH	77012
GALVESTON RD	2400	535L	SEH	77017
GALVESTON RD	7200	576B	SEH	77034
GALVESTON RD	10500	577X	SEH	77034
GALVESTON RD	12000	617H	SEH	77598
GALVESTON RD	15600	618T	SEH	77598
GALVESTON-LEAGUE CITY	0	658D	SEC	77598
S. GALWAN CIR	9800	369Q	NWC	77070
W. GALWAN CIR	11800	369Q	NWC	77070
E. GALWAN CIR	11800	369Q	NWC	77070
GALWAY DR	500	538P	DP	77536
GALWAY LN	3600	450L	NWH	77080
GAMBEL DR	0	293G	SEM	77386
GAMBIER LN	6500	531H	BL	77401
GAMBIT DR	12300	529W	SWH	77477
GAMBLE OAK DR	19500	338S	NEC	77346
GAMBREL OAK PLACE	1	251U	WD	77380
GAMEBIRD LN	9300	576P	SEH	77034
GAME COVE LN	13600	417P	NEC	77044
GAMEWOOD CT	25700	252T	SEM	77386
GAMEWOOD DR	300	252T	SEM	77386
GAMLIN BEND DR	3700	527C	SWC	77082
GAMMA	1200	577J	PA	77504
GAMMA	1300	419H	CB	77532
GAMMAGE	4900	534J	SEH	77021
GAMMAGE	6300	534R	SEH	77087
GAMMILL	5700	452D	NWH	77091
GAMMON DR	400	453E	NWH	77022
GAMMON OAKS DR	0	407C	NWC	77095
GANADO CREEK CT	0	445L	NWC	77449
GANADO CREEK CT	0	445L	NWC	77449
GANDER LAKE LN	0	461N	NEC	77521
GANDERWOOD DR	11500	616C	SEC	77089
GANGES CT	22800	294D	SEM	77365
W. GANGWAY CT	1000	419F	NEC	77532
S. GANGWAY DR	800	419F	NEC	77532
W. GANGWAY DR	15600	419F	NEC	77532
GANNET HOLLOW PLACE	1	250D	WD	77381
GANNET PEAK WAY	21500	445H	NWC	77449
GANNETT	3100	532P	SWH	77025
GANNOWAY LAKE CT	1600	568E	SG	77498
GANO	1500	493D	NEH	77009
GANO	3400	453V	NEH	77009
GANS	100	495Z	NEH	77029
GANT RD	6600	370L	NWC	77066
GANTON DR	21500	486W	NEF	77450
GANYARD DR	1800	449V	NWH	77043
GARAPAN	900	412X	NWH	77091
GARAPAN	2700	411Z	NWH	77091
GARBER LN	10500	496E	JC	77029
GARBER LN	13700	497G	NEC	77015
GARCIA, STAFF SGT M DR	100	494V	SEH	77011

Street Name	Block	Pg/Sq	Loc	Zips
GARCROFT	9700	495R	NEH	77029
GARDEN	7000	535E	SEH	77087
GARDEN	7200	535E	SEH	77012
S. GARDEN	11500	570F	MC	77071
N. GARDEN	11500	570F	MC	77071
GARDEN CIR	1500	538M	DP	77536
GARDEN CT	1300	538M	DP	77536
GARDEN DR	100	656C	FR	77546
GARDEN LN	2900	609E	SG	77479
GARDEN RD	0	614K	PL	77581
GARDEN RD	12400	574X	BK	77581
GARDEN RD	12600	614K	PL	77581
GARDEN ARBOR LN	20800	525H	NEF	77407
GARDEN BEND CIR	15600	326T	NWC	77433
GARDEN BLOOM LN	0	407J	NWC	77433
GARDEN BLOOM LN	0	407J	NWC	77433
GARDEN BRANCH CT	4000	485Z	NEF	77450
GARDEN BREEZE DR	9000	575Z	SEH	77075
GARDEN BRIDGE	9400	575V	SEH	77075
GARDEN BROOK LN	7100	290T	NWC	77379
GARDEN CANYON CT	1000	485G	SWC	77450
GARDEN CANYON DR	6400	406T	NWC	77449
GARDEN CANYON DR	22700	485G	SWC	77450
GARDEN CHASE CT	2100	485Q	NEF	77494
GARDEN CHASE DR	23200	485P	NEF	77494
GARDEN CITY DR	2600	411R	NWC	77088
GARDEN COVE CT	4100	485U	NEF	77494
GARDEN CREEK DR	17200	329M	NWC	77379
GARDEN CREEK WAY	13800	578W	SEH	77059
GARDEN CREST LN	0	452Q	NWH	77018
GARDENCREST LN	1100	488F	SWH	77077
GARDENDALE DR	1000	452Q	NWH	77018
GARDENDALE DR	3700	451R	NWH	77092
GARDENDALE DR	5600	451P	NWH	77092
GARDEN EDGE LN	0	326L	NWC	77429
GARDENEST	0	528M	SWH	77072
GARDEN ESTATE	12400	528M	SWH	77072
GARDEN FALLS CT	20400	326T	NWC	77433
GARDEN FALLS DR	2700	613X	NEB	77578
GARDEN FERN CT	1900	618G	SEH	77062
GARDEN FIELD LN	0	612U	PL	77584
GARDEN FIELD LN	3200	485V	NEF	77450
GARDEN FIELD LN	7200	527J	NEF	77407
GARDEN FLOWER CT	5800	406Y	NWC	77449
GARDEN FORD DR	4900	337C	NEH	77345
GARDEN FOREST DR	0	328Q	NWC	77377
GARDEN GALE LN	12300	416Z	NEC	77044
GARDEN GATE CT	0	372C	NCC	77073
GARDEN GATE WAY	3400	578X	SEH	77059
GARDEN GLADE CT	17100	407L	NWC	77095
GARDEN GLEN DR	11700	369A	NWC	77070
GARDEN GLEN DR	12000	368D	NWC	77070
GARDEN GLEN LN	1300	615G	PL	77581
GARDEN GREEN WAY	3700	446L	NWC	77449
GARDEN GROVE CT	13400	488X	SWC	77082
GARDEN GROVE DR	3300	371U	NWC	77066
GARDENGROVE LN	0	571Z	SWH	77053
GARDEN HEATH LN	0	445R	NWC	77449
GARDEN HEATH LN	0	446N	NWC	77449
GARDEN HEATH LN	0	526E	NEF	77407
GARDEN HILL LN	16000	407M	NWC	77095
GARDEN HILLS LN	4300	297U	NEH	77345
GARDEN HOLLOW CT	5000	297Z	NEH	77345
GARDENIA	5800	614L	PL	77581
GARDENIA CT	26300	248B	SWM	77354
GARDENIA DR	0	460T	NEC	77562
GARDENIA DR	900	452K	NWH	77018
GARDENIA DR	2100	451M	NWH	77018
GARDENIA LN	5500	444T	KT	77493
GARDENIA BEND DR	14700	572S	SEH	77053
GARDENIA BREEZE LN		289Z	NWC	77379
GARDENIA ESTATES LN	0	366D	NWC	77429
GARDENIA GARDENS	1	258V	NEC	77336
GARDENIA MEADOW LN		289Z	NWC	77379
GARDENIA MEADOW LN		329D	NWC	77379
GARDENIA RANCH DR	0	484V	NEF	77494
GARDENIA TRACE DR	0	253T	SEM	77386
GARDENIA TRAIL	4800	537Y	PA	77505
GARDEN IVY LN	0	615G	PL	77581
GARDEN KNOLL LN	7500	375X	NEC	77396
GARDEN LAKE DR	3400	296Z	NEH	77339
GARDEN LAKE DR	3700	297W	NEH	77339
GARDEN LAKES DR	1400	656R	FR	77546
GARDEN LAND CT	900	332V	NCC	77073
GARDEN LANDING DR	0	406L	NWC	77433
GARDEN LAUREL LN	12300	371H	NWC	77014
GARDEN LEAF LN	6500	408V	NWC	77041
GARDENLILY CT	4600	484Y	NEF	77494
GARDEN MANOR DR	17900	407X	NWC	77084
GARDEN MEADOW DR	4500	446H	NWC	77449
GARDEN MESA DR	0	337D	NEH	77345
GARDEN MIST LN	7000	377B	NEC	77346
GARDEN MIST LN	21400	406X	NWC	77449
GARDEN OAK CT	20600	337Q	NEC	77346
GARDEN OAKS BLVD	300	452M	NWH	77018
GARDEN PARK LN	1100	538M	DP	77536
GARDEN PARKS DR	7300	575S	SEH	77075
GARDEN PATH CT	16400	578Z	PA	77059
GARDEN PATH PLACE	100	249R	NWH	77375
GARDEN PATH PLACE	100	249R	NWH	77375
GARDEN PLACE DR	10600	528W	NEF	77498
GARDEN PLANTATION DR	0	609J	NEF	77479
GARDEN POINT DR	2100	337D	NEH	77345
GARDEN POOL LN	19400	329A	NWC	77375
GARDEN RIDGE CANYON	0	526W	NEF	77406
GARDEN ROSE LN	0	452Q	NWH	77018
GARDEN ROW DR	9600	527V	NEF	77498
GARDEN ROW DR	9600	528V	NEF	77478
GARDEN RUN CT	2900	446Q	NWC	77084
GARDENSAGE LN	26300	484Z	NEF	77494
GARDEN SHADOW LN	0	452Q	NWH	77018
GARDEN SHADOWS LN	11400	367N	NWC	77433
GARDENSPRINGS	0	290Q	NWC	77379
GARDEN SPRINGS	13600	528F	SWC	77083
GARDEN SPRINGS DR	4100	297S	NEH	77339
GARDEN STONE LN	0	290Y	NWC	77379
GARDENS TRAIL CT	6300	528G	SWH	77083
GARDEN STREAM CT	2200	618F	SEH	77062
GARDEN TERRACE DR	1500	485L	NEF	77494
GARDEN TRACE LN	0	452Q	NWH	77018
GARDEN TRAIL CT	0	528G	SWH	77072
GARDEN TREE	0	458B	NEC	77049
GARDEN TREE DR	8900	418X	NEC	77049
GARDEN TREE DR	11200	418T	NEC	77044
GARDEN VALLEY LN	15300	408B	NWC	77095
GARDENVIEW DR	1400	372E	NWC	77014
GARDEN VIEW DR	11600	372K	NWC	77067
GARDENVIEW POINT CT	0	484J	NEF	77494
GARDEN VILLA	700	444Q	KT	77493
GARDEN VILLAGE DR	4200	297N	NEH	77339
GARDENVILLE ST	0	576V	SEH	77034
GARDENVILLE ST	0	577S	SEH	77034
GARDEN VISTA DR	15100	326S	NWC	77433
GARDEN WALK	700	580F	LP	77571
GARDEN WALK	1500	538M	DP	77536
GARDEN WAY DR	500	537M	PA	77503
GARDEN WIND CT	20400	290V	NWC	77379
GARDENWOOD DR	3500	297N	NEH	77339
GARDNER	500	453X	NWH	77009
W. GARDNER	900	453W	NWH	77009
GARDNERBROOK	0	456Q	NEH	77049
GARETT GREEN CIR	15200	408B	NWC	77095
GARFIELD	1	580G	LP	77571
GARFIELD	200	536G	PA	77506
GARFIELD	2400	412S	NWH	77088
GARFIELD	2700	411V	NWH	77088
GARFIELD	7900	495N	NEH	77029
GARFIELD PARK LN	9200	575V	SEH	77075
GARGAN	300	493G	NEH	77009
GARLAND	1500	535E	SEH	77087
GARLAND	8000	535U	SEH	77017
GARLAND FALLS	0	329A	NWC	77375
GARLAND GROVE PLACE	1	250G	WD	77381
GARLAND LEAVES ST	0	447P	NWC	77084
GARLAND MIST LN	0	526K	NEF	77407
GARLAND PATH BEND		525R	NEF	77469
GARLANG	15700	498F	CV	77530
GARLENDA LN	0	576R	SEH	77034
GARLINGTON DR	0	366P	NWC	77433
GARNER CT	2700	613N	NEB	77584
GARNER RD	400	536R	PA	77502
GARNERCREST DR	17500	407K	NWC	77095
GARNER GROVE LN	0	446J	NWC	77449
GARNER LAKE LN	6100	609Y	NEF	77459
GARNER MILL LN	12100	616K	SEC	77089
GARNER PARK DR	0	615N	PL	77581
GARNET	3700	532E	SS	77005
GARNET CT	2600	613S	NEB	77584
GARNET FALLS LN	0	376W	NEC	77396
GARNETFIELD LN	0	485S	NEF	77494
GARNETFIELD LN	0	657P	FR	77546
GARNETFIELD LN	5200	485S	NEF	77494
GARNET GROVE CT	0	524D	NEF	77494
GARNET HILL LN	7000	377C	NEC	77346
GARNET RED RD	0	328E	NWC	77429
GARNET SHADOW LN	0	524G	NEF	77494
GARNET SPRINGS LN	0	406X	NWC	77449
GARNET STONE LN	0	524G	NEF	77494
GARNIER DR	0	573N	SWH	77045
GARRET KNOLLS LN	0	526L	NEF	77407
GARRETSON LN	1500	491R	SWH	77056
S. GARRETT	500	537J	PA	77506
GARRETT BLVD	2500	539S	DP	77536
GARRETT RD	9000	415R	NEC	77078
GARRETT RD	9500	416Q	NEC	77044
GARRETT RD	12800	417Q	NEC	77044
GARRETT RD	15000	418N	NEC	77044
GARRETT GREEN LN	0	527N	NEF	77407
GARRETTS DR	3600	613U	NEB	77584
GARRETTS COVE CT	7200	375X	NEC	77396
GARRETTS GALE LN	2900	485T	NEF	77494
GARRICK CT	10500	496E	NEH	77013
GARRICK LN	10600	496E	NEH	77013
GARRISON CT	3300	371C	NWC	77014
GARRISON POINT CT	0	410L	NWC	77040
GARRISON POINT DR	0	410L	NWC	77040
GARRISON RUN DR	3500	253X	SEM	77386
GARRISON TRAIL LN	0	293F	SEM	77386
GARROTSVILLE	100	453K	NEH	77022
GARROTT	3400	493S	SWH	77006
GARROTT	4300	493S	SWH	77002
GARROW	2500	494N	SEH	77003
GARROW	4400	494T	SEH	77011
GARSEE DR	7600	410R	NWH	77040
GARTH RD	1200	501K	BT	77520
GARTH RD	2800	501B	BT	77521
GARTH RD	6700	461P	NEC	77521
GARTH RD	10200	461P	NEC	77532
GARVEY DR	2100	537F	PA	77506
GARVINS CT	100	493F	SWH	77007
GARWOOD	0	411Z	NEH	77091
GARWOOD DR	2400	412W	NWH	77091
GARWOOD TRACE DR	0	366P	NWC	77433
GARY	6900	451X	NWH	77055
GARY AVE	900	536V	PA	77502
GARY CT	12200	367M	CY	77429
GARY LN	3200	251N	SWM	77380
GARZA	19000	379R	NEC	77532
GASLAMP DR	16400	407D	NWC	77095
GASLAMP POINT CT	19100	326Y	NWC	77429
GASLIGHT CT	0	620G	SB	77586
GAS LIGHT LN	19500	258J	SEM	77357
GASLIGHT KNOLL DR	0	376S	NEC	77396
GASLIGHT VILLAGE DR	8800	407D	NWC	77095
GASMER DR	4600	571B	SWH	77035
GASSER LN	0	571F	SWH	77085
GASSER LN	5700	571F	SWH	77085
GASTON	4400	414R	NEC	77093
GASTON	5600	415N	NEH	77016
GASTON RD	0	484Z	NEF	77494
GASTON RD	0	524D	NEF	77494
GASTON RD	0	525E	NEF	77494
GASTON RD	2300	484P	NEF	77494
GASTONBURY CT	400	658N	LC	77573
GASTONBURY LN	20900	334R	NCC	77338
GATEBRIAR CT	7400	570Z	SWH	77489
GATEBRIAR DR	15700	570Z	SWH	77489
GATEBROOK DR	0	617V	SEH	77546
GATE CANYON CT	5400	334E	NCC	77373
GATECRAFT DR	7400	570V	SWH	77459
GATE CREEK	0	615Z	PL	77581
GATE CREEK CT	23200	485Q	NEF	77494
GATECREST DR	700	373P	NCC	77032
GATE HILL DR	1	250H	WD	77381
GATEHOUSE DR	7800	410L	NWC	77040
GATEMERE CT	300	485C	SWC	77450
GATEMONT CT	12200	370M	NWC	77066
GATEMOUND CT	20600	526J	NEF	77407
GATEPOINT DR	21100	332V	NCC	77073
GATE RIDGE CT	7600	407J	NWC	77433
GATERIDGE DR	7300	408R	NWC	77041
GATE RIDGE LN	18400	407J	NWC	77433
GATES	7900	455T	NEH	77028
GATESBURY CT	3200	487Y	SWC	77082
GATESBURY DR	15200	487Z	SWC	77082
GATESBURY NORTH DR	3000	487Z	SWC	77082
GATESDEN DR	11000	329S	NWC	77377
GATES FARM LN	14900	568A	NEF	77498
GATESHIP DR	600	332V	NCC	77073
GATESIDE DR	800	373P	NCC	77032
GATES RANDAL CT		366U	NWC	77433
GATESTONE	0	485L	SWC	77450
S. GATE STONE	300	493J	SWH	77007
N. GATE STONE	400	493J	SWH	77007
GATEVIEW DR	20900	332Z	NCC	77073
GATEVIEW LN	15400	570Z	SWH	77489
GATEWAY DR	10300	414W	NEH	77093
E. GATEWICK	0	332L	NCC	77073
GATEWOOD	3800	380Q	NEC	77532
GATEWOOD	4800	571U	SWH	77053
GATEWOOD MANOR DR	0	524F	NEF	77494
GATLIN LN	0	293K	SEM	77386
GATLINBURG DR	10900	530W	SWH	77031
GATLINBURG DR	11800	570A	SWH	77031
GATLING CT	19900	446U	NWC	77449
GATMERE CT	9400	527V	NEF	77498
GATOR	0	457T	NEC	77049
GATOR HAWK DR	0	333W	NCC	77073
GATTON PARK DR	13000	371E	NWC	77066
GATWICK DR	0	330S	NWC	77379
GATWICK LN	0	445U	NWC	77449
GAUCHO CIR	1700	539T	LP	77571
GAUCHO DR	17300	527N	NEF	77083
GAUGE HOLLOW CT	8900	527N	NEF	77407
GAUGUIN DR	8900	411S	NWH	77088
GAULT RD	1500	413D	NCC	77039
GAULT RD	2400	414A	NCC	77039
GAUTHIER RD	15600	323X	NWC	77447
GAUTIER CT	13200	368U	NWC	77065
GAUTIER DR	11200	368U	NWC	77065
GAVIN CT	1690	329C	NWC	77379
GAVIN LN	0	458S	NEC	77530
GAVINGALE DR	0	327D	NWC	77429
GAVIN MANOR CT	0	407X	NWC	77449
GAVIN PLACE DR	11200	411M	NWC	77088
GAWAIN LN	10500	491E	HC	77024
GAY	6100	453Q	NEH	77022
GAYHART	15800	373Q	NCC	77032
GAYLA LN	5100	500H	BT	77521
GAYLAWOOD DR	12200	371A	NWC	77066
GAYLIN HILLS CT	2100	293F	SEM	77386
GAYLORD DR	8700	490D	HE	77024
GAYLYN CIR	1000	332Z	NCC	77073
GAYMOOR DR	11300	571B	SWH	77035
GAYNOR	0	611Z	FS	77545
E. GAYWOOD DR	300	489G	SWH	77079
GAYWOOD DR	300	489F	SWH	77079
GAYWOOD ST	0	449Q	NEH	77043
GAZANIA	11800	369J	NWC	77065
GAZELLE LN	0	614Y	PL	77584
GAZIN	500	494H	NEH	77020
GEAREN CT	0	328N	NWC	77429
GEARS RD	100	372Q	NWH	77067
GEARS RD	2100	371Q	NWC	77067
W. GEARS LOOP	1000	372P	NWC	77067
GEAT OAK CT	0	252G	SEM	77385
GEFFERT WRIGHT RD	27100	252P	SEM	77386
GEHAN WOODS DR	0	329F	NWC	77375
GEHRING	6200	533F	SWH	77021
GELLHORN DR	0	495D	NEH	77013
GELLHORN DR	200	495G	NEH	77013
GELLHORN DR	500	495K	NEH	77029
GEMBROOK LN	12000	616G	SEC	77089
GEMCO	0	528Z	SWH	77099
GEM DALE CT	5000	526S	NEF	77407
GEMINI	15000	571V	SWH	77053
GEMINI AVE	800	618U	SEC	77058
GEMSTONE COVE CT	0	524G	NEF	77494
GEMSTONE HILL LN	0	524G	NEF	77494
GEMSTONE PARK RD	5300	526S	NEF	77407
GENA CT	10300	370U	NWC	77064
GENADENA	100	576R	SEH	77034
S. GENA LEE DR	6500	370U	NWC	77064
N. GENA LEE DR	6500	370U	NWC	77064
GENARD RD	9800	450A	NWH	77041
GENDLEY DR	13200	408R	NWC	77041
GENE CAMPBELL BLVD	0	254H	SEM	77357
GENE CAMPBELL BLVD	0	255G	SEM	77357
GENE CAMPBELL BLVD	0	256E	SEM	77357
GENEMAURY	9800	411R	NWH	77088
GENERAL COLONY DR	2300	617X	SEC	77546
GENERAL GRESHAM LN	13400	367G	NWC	77429
GENERAL LEE	0	578D	LP	77571
GENERAL LEE	8900	578D	LP	77571
GENERIC DR	0	420X	NEC	77532
GENESEE	1000	493P	SWH	77019
GENESEE	1900	493P	SWH	77006
GENESIS COVE CT	7000	330B	NWC	77379
GENESIS PLANTATION LN	0	377U	NEC	77044
GENESSE CREEK LN	3000	657B	SEC	77546
GENESSE VALLEY DR	0	250U	NWC	77389
GENET DR	0	524E	NEF	77494
GENEVA	4400	531D	BL	77401
GENEVA DR	4500	371A	NWC	77066
GENEVA DR	5100	617W	FR	77546
GENEVA DR	28900	292C	SEM	77386
GENEVA DR	29500	252Y	SEM	77386
W. GENEVA DR	30100	252Y	SEM	77386
E. GENEVA DR	30100	252U	SEM	77386
GENEVA FIELDS DR	0	326U	NWC	77429
GENEVA GREEN DR	0	372D	NCC	77073
GENEVA HILLS LN	27700	293K	SEM	77386
GENEVA SPRINGS LN	28101	293F	SEM	77386
GENIE	14800	457P	NEC	77049
GENIE LN	7300	455M	NEH	77078
GENIE COVE LN	0	415S	NEH	77016
GENOA	700	576A	SH	77587
GENOA	3000	258A	SEM	77357
GENOA RED BLUFF RD	100	576R	SEH	77034
GENOA RED BLUFF RD	400	577K	SEH	77034
GENOA RED BLUFF RD	1100	577K	SEH	77034
GENOA RED BLUFF RD	1101	577K	PA	77504
GENOA RED BLUFF RD	1701	577K	PA	77505
GENOA RED BLUFF RD	3800	578K	PA	77505
GENOA RED BLUFF RD	5600	578M	SEH	77507
GENOVA	900	568Q	SG	77478
GENOVA	1000	493D	NEH	77009
GENS CT	1	451W	SV	77055
GENTILLY DR	200	485D	SWC	77450
GENTILLY PLACE	300	490K	BH	77024
GENTLE BEND DR	1100	570X	MC	77489
GENTLE BEND DR	6600	370B	NWC	77069
GENTLE BREEZE CT	15200	328N	NWC	77429
GENTLE BROOK CT	2400	618A	SEH	77062
GENTLEBROOK DR	0	612Q	PL	77584
GENTLE COVE CT	0	446D	NWC	77084
GENTLE CREEK WAY	0	326Y	NWC	77433
GENTLE GLEN LN	0	334K	NCC	77388
GENTLE MIST CT	20300	326N	NWC	77433
GENTLE MIST LN	20400	326N	NWC	77433
GENTLE MOSS LN	7300	525E	NEF	77494
GENTLE MOSS LN	23800	525E	NEF	77494
GENTLE RIDGE CT	20500	326S	NWC	77433
GENTLE SHADOW DR	0	285Q	NWC	77447
GENTLE SLOPE LN	0	377L	NEC	77346
GENTLE STONE CT	8700	407C	NWC	77095
GENTLE STONE DR	16600	407C	NWC	77095
GENTLE WATER DR	13000	377L	NEC	77044
GENTLE WILLOW LN	7300	525E	NEF	77494
GENTLE WIND	0	660E	LC	77573
GENTLE WINDS LN	0	377L	NEC	77346
GENTLEWOOD CT	8300	407H	NWC	77095
GENTLEWOOD DR	5900	609Y	NEF	77479
GENTRY	200	292Q	SP	77373
GENTRY	600	541B	BT	77520
GENTRY	1500	493H	NEH	77009
GENTRY DR	800	375D	HM	77338
GENTRY RD	21400	368S	NWC	77429
GENTRY OAK CT	1	251C	WD	77381
GENTRY SHADOWS LN	0	376S	NEC	77396
GENTRYSIDE CT	1800	488Q	SWH	77077
GENTRYSIDE DR	2000	488Q	SWH	77077
GENTRYSIDE LN	1800	488Q	SWH	77077
GEOFFREY CT	0	335R	HM	77338
GEORGE	300	659F	LC	77573
GEORGE	1400	537N	PA	77502
GEORGE	2900	660H	BC	77518
GEORGE	3300	454T	NEH	77026
N. GEORGE	3400	454T	NEH	77026
GEORGE	7600	463W	CCO	77520
GEORGE	7700	501X	BT	77520
GEORGE	2600	616T	PL	77581
GEORGE ALTVATER BLVD	0	540Y	MP	77571
GEORGE ALTVATER BLVD	0	541S	SEH	77571
GEORGE BUSH	0	444X	KT	77493
GEORGES WAY	24401	338M	NEH	77336
GEORGETOWN	2100	444Q	KT	77493
GEORGETOWN	2800	532B	WU	77005
GEORGETOWN DR	13100	528Y	SG	77478
GEORGETOWN COLONY DR	5600	408X	NWC	77084
GEORGETOWN GLEN CIR	0	406D	NWC	77433
GEORGETOWN PARK CT	12300	618D	PA	77058
GEORGE WASHINGTON LN	3500	569U	MC	77459
GEORGI LN	5000	451L	NWH	77092
GEORGIA	100	495V	NEH	77029
GEORGIA	100	536W	SH	77587
GEORGIA	1100	575D	SH	77587
GEORGIA	1700	540D	BT	77520
GEORGIA AVE	100	538N	DP	77536
GEORGIA AVE	500	659J	LC	77573
GEORGIANNA DR	6300	538W	PA	77503
GEORGIAN ROW	0	251K	SWM	77380
GEORGIA PINE DR	3100	333B	NCC	77373
GEORGIBELLE DR	10200	489D	NWH	77043
GERAL LN	15300	408S	NWC	77084
GERALD	0	500N	BT	77520
GERALD	2700	538W	PA	77503
GERALD BROOK LN	0	366V	NWC	77433
GERALDINE	2800	581W	PA	77586
GERBER LN	9200	375R	NEC	77396
GERDA	6700	614D	BK	77581
GERENT LN	0	405W	NWC	77493
GERHART DR	4300	572E	SWH	77045
GERLACH ST	10300	576V	SEH	77034
GERMAN BAUER DR	0	285P	NWC	77447
GERMAN BEND DR	0	376S	NEC	77396
GERMAN OAK LN	0	295M	SEM	77365
GERNGROSS LN	0	457A	NEC	77044
GERONA ST	0	660L	LC	77573
GERONIMO	3900	577G	PA	77505
GERONIMO	33400	247Q	SWM	77355
GERONIMO CT	700	485H	SWC	77450
GERONIMO LAKE CT	14600	573Z	SEC	77047
GERONIMO LAKE DR	4000	573Z	SEC	77047
GERRARDS CROSS DR	13200	528B	SWH	77082
GERSHWIN DR	100	489L	SWH	77079
GERSHWIN OAK ST	12300	617E	SEH	77089
GERTIN	3800	533H	SEH	77004
GERTIN CIR	3900	533H	SEH	77004
GERVAISE DR	0	328N	NWC	77429
S. GESSNER DR	0	570J	MC	77489
GESSNER DR	1	490A	SWH	77024
GESSNER DR	1000	450W	NWH	77055
S. GESSNER DR	1000	490W	SWH	77063
GESSNER DR	1400	450J	NWH	77080
GESSNER DR	4300	450J	NWH	77041
S. GESSNER DR	5700	530E	SWH	77036
GESSNER DR	5900	410W	NWH	77041
N. GESSNER DR	6600	410W	NWH	77040
S. GESSNER DR	8400	530X	SWH	77074
S. GESSNER DR	9600	530X	SWH	77071
S. GESSNER DR	11200	570B	SWH	77071
GESSNER RD	0	370N	NWC	77064
GESSPORT BLVD	0	570F	SWH	77071
GETITON DR	0	487X	SWH	77094
GETTIE	3500	611X	FS	77545
GETTY RD	7300	411E	NWH	77086
GETTYSBURG CT	12000	329S	NWC	77377
GETTYSBURG DR	0	615S	PL	77584
GETTYSBURG DR	2500	658P	LC	77573
GETTYSBURG DR	15300	329S	NWC	77377
GETTYSBURG VALLEY CT	6300	406V	NWC	77449
GETTYSBURG VALLEY DR	19100	406V	NWC	77449
GAREY PLACE	0	332Z	NCC	77073
GHANA LN	5900	577H	PA	77505
GHODSI RD	0	333Y	NCC	77073
GIANNA CT	0	528N	NEF	77083
GIANNA BELLA CT	0	615M	PL	77089
GIANNA SPRINGS CT	0	376G	NEC	77396
GIANNA WAY	0	333K	NCC	77338
GIANT HICKORY DR	0	245R	SWM	77355
GIANT PINE LN	0	326U	NWC	77429
GIARDINI DR	0	445E	NWC	77493
GIBBONS	8300	535F	SEH	77012
GIBBONS CREEK LN	0	445L	NWC	77449
GIBBONS CREEK WAY	0	406D	NWC	77433
GIBBONS HILL LN	0	660J	LC	77573
GIBBS	900	453T	NWH	77009
GIBBS BEND CT	0	333K	NCC	77073
GIBONEY RD	31600	242B	WCO	77484
GIBRALTAR CIR	2500	412E	NWC	77038
GIBRALTER PLACE	0	526S	NEF	77407
GIBSON	3900	492L	SWH	77007
GIBSON CROSSING WAY	0	372J	NWC	77076
GIBSON GRASS CT	0	330R	NWC	77379
GIDDINGS LN	8600	409L	NWC	77064
GIFFORD HILL	0	409T	NWC	77041
GIG CT	400	379X	NEC	77532
GILA CT	0	658U	LC	77573
GILA DR	22800	254Z	SEM	77365
GILA BEND LN	11600	328D	NWC	77377
GILA CLIFF LN	17600	377E	NEC	77346
GILBERT	300	536H	PA	77506
GILBERT	3400	615B	PL	77581
GILBERT AVE	0	571R	SWH	77045
GILBERT DR	24500	296K	SEM	77365
GILBERTYN DR	15600	329S	NWC	77377
GILBOUGH DR	24500	249Z	NWC	77375

Street Name	Block	Pg/Sq	Loc	Zips
GILCREST DR	0	331U	NWC	77014
GILCREST FOREST CT	1	251A	WD	77381
GILDED CREST CT	0	249C	SWM	77382
GILDER RD	8900	369M	NWC	77064
GILDUS DR	0	290K	NWC	77379
GILDWOOD PLACE	100	249M	NWH	77375
GILDWOOD PLACE	100	249M	NWH	77375
GILES RD	0	500C	NEC	77521
GILFORD LN	3000	485T	NEF	77494
GILFORD CREST DR	10600	289X	NWC	77379
GIL JR LN	10000	576N	SEH	77075
GILL	17400	418R	NEC	77044
GILL DR	1600	659X	DI	77539
GILLEN	7000	534R	SEH	77087
GILLESPI	1	372Y	NEH	77038
GILLESPIE	2800	494K	NEH	77020
GILLETTE	600	493P	SWH	77019
GILLETTE	1900	493P	SWH	77006
GILLETTE DR	1600	502S	BT	77520
GILLIAN PARK DR	6300	407W	NWC	77449
GILLINGHAM LN	100	568L	SG	77478
GILLINGHAM WAY	1700	577E	PA	77504
GILLIOM DR	2600	446V	NWC	77084
GILLMAN DR	9800	455D	NEH	77078
GILLMAN PARK	13700	372H	NCC	77073
GILLSIDE MANOR DR	0	524H	NEF	77494
GILMAN TRACE LN	6000	541F	NWH	77092
GILMAR CT	3000	609D	MC	77459
GILPIN	100	576F	SEH	77034
GILRODRIGUEZ LOOP E	0	575X	SEH	77075
GILRODRIGUEZ LOOP W	0	575X	SEH	77075
GILSON LN	10000	370Z	NWC	77086
GILTSPUR WAY	24700	250V	NWC	77389
GIMBALS WAY	17700	379U	NEC	77532
GINA	13100	570J	SF	77477
GINA LN	13100	413P	NCC	77037
GINERIDGE DR	5500	571X	SWH	77053
GINERWOOD CREST CT	4600	609X	NEF	77479
GINGER	6200	451C	NWH	77091
GINGER DR	8100	250J	NWC	77389
GINGER LN	0	659Z	DI	77539
GINGER LN	3600	615U	PL	77581
GINGER LN	15600	409M	JV	77040
GINGER BELL DR	5500	407X	NWC	77084
GINGER BLUFF TRAIL		484W	NEF	77494
GINGER BROOK	6500	409S	NWC	77041
GINGER COVE LN	0	698D	LC	77573
GINGER COVE LN	0	411A	NWC	77086
GINGER COVE LN	0	612N	PL	77545
GINGER CREEK LN	3700	253P	SEM	77386
GINGER CREEK TRAIL	20000	486L	SWC	77450
GINGER FIELD CT	0	615E	PL	77581
GINGER FIELDS LN	17100	328M	NWC	77377
GINGER GABLES LN	0	524F	NEF	77494
GINGER HILL LN	0	406X	NWC	77449
GINGERLEAF LN	1600	451S	NWH	77055
GINGER LEI LN	11900	456C	NEC	77044
GINGER LILY LN	0	524J	NEF	77406
GINGER OAK ST	0	451S	NWH	77055
GINGER PARK DR	8100	461P	NEC	77521
W. GINGER PEAR CT	0	325Q	NWC	77433
E. GINGER PEAR CT	0	325Q	NWC	77433
GINGER PONDS DR	0	449A	NWC	77041
GINGER RANCH DR	0	484R	NEF	77494
GINGER RIDGE LN	0	328L	NWC	77377
E. GINGER SPICE CT	0	325Q	NWC	77433
GINGERSTICK	0	457U	NEC	77049
GINGER TRACE DR	0	253T	SEM	77386
GINGERWOOD DR	3200	613T	NEB	77584
GINGERWOOD HILLS LN	0	326U	NWC	77429
GINGHAM DR	400	490L	PP	77024
GINGHAM CHECK CT	0	446F	NWC	77449
GINGHAM CHECK CT	0	446F	NWC	77449
GINKO	0	375M	NEC	77396
GINNY COVE CT	0	293K	SEM	77386
GINNYDALE DR	0	406K	NWC	77433
GINSENG DR	5200	461T	NEC	77521
GINTER LN	3000	484V	NEF	77494
GIRARD	600	493L	SWH	77007
GIRL SCOUT LN	4400	617T	SEC	77546
GIRL SCOUT RD	2100	257U	SEM	77357
GIRNIGOE DR	5100	407Z	NWC	77084
GIRONDE DR	7900	570G	MC	77071
GIRVAN LN	10700	527X	NEF	77407
GISBORNE LN	0	373A	NCC	77073
GIVENCHY DR	0	457A	NEC	77044
GIVENS	1200	493E	SWH	77007
GIVERNY CT	1100	329G	NWC	77379
GLACIER DR	2600	371L	NWC	77067
GLACIER LN	4200	538U	DP	77536
GLACIER BAY CT	18300	377B	NEC	77346
GLACIER BROOK CT	16300	618D	PA	77059
GLACIER CREEK DR	0	524E	NEF	77494
GLACIER FALLS DR	20100	289W	NWC	77375
GLACIER HILL DR	1000	488E	SWH	77077
GLACIER POINT CT	17300	377E	NEC	77346
GLADDEN DR	12500	456M	NEC	77049
GLADDEN DR	13100	457J	NEC	77049
GLADE	2300	613L	PL	77584
GLADE CT	1400	611X	NEF	77545
GLADEBECK LN	13300	328F	NWC	77377
GLADEBRIAR DR	0	297P	NEH	77345
GLADE BRIDGE CT	0	328P	NWC	77429
GLADEBROOK CT	3900	331S	NWC	77068
GLADEBROOK DR	14600	331W	NWC	77068
GLADEBROOK GLEN LN	16000	407R	NWC	77095
GLADE CANYON	21800	290R	NWC	77388
GLADE CREEK DR	3600	297W	NEH	77339
GLADE ESTATES DR	4200	297N	NEH	77339
GLADEFIELD DR	11200	529T	SWH	77099
GLADE FOREST DR	3700	297W	NEH	77339
GLADE HILL	0	297Y	NEH	77345
GLADEHILL DR	5100	297V	NEH	77345
GLADE HOLLOW DR	13800	372E	NWC	77014
GLADE LANDING LN	17600	527N	NEF	77407
GLADEMILL CT	20500	406F	NWC	77433
GLADEPARK CT	5600	407X	NWC	77084
GLADE POINT DR	14300	327X	NWC	77429
GLADERIDGE DR	3800	331S	NWC	77068
GLADE RIVER LN	11700	328M	NWC	77377
GLADESDALE PARK LN	4500	485Z	NEF	77450
GLADESIDE DR	5100	446B	NWC	77449
GLADE SPRINGS DR	0	612Q	PL	77584
GLADE SPRINGS DR	3100	297S	NEH	77339
GLADESTONE LN	0	485Y	NEF	77450
GLADE VALLEY DR	3900	296U	NEH	77339
GLADEWATER CT	0	406D	NWC	77433
GLADEWATER CT	19300	328D	NWC	77375
GLADEWATER DR	0	612H	PL	77584
GLADEWATER DR	19400	328D	NWC	77375
GLADEWATER DR	19600	288Z	NWC	77375
GLADEWATER LN	0	660E	LC	77573
GLADEWELL DR	6100	529G	SWH	77072
GLADEWICK DR	12100	489N	SWH	77077
GLADEWICK DR	14700	376Y	NEC	77396
GLADEWOOD	0	449M	NWH	77041
GLADEWOOD DR	10300	449H	NWC	77041
GLADEWOOD LN	11800	570C	SWH	77071
GLADIOLA	2400	460U	NEC	77562
GLADIOLA AVE	0	461N	NEC	77521
GLADSTONE	7800	533U	SEH	77051
GLADSTONE DR	0	658M	LC	77573
GLADSTONE DR	1000	658R	LC	77573
GLADWAY MANOR DR	0	484J	KT	77494
GLADWYNE	3100	578D	LP	77571
GLADWYNE CT	8800	578D	LP	77571
GLADYS	600	493B	NWH	77009
GLADYS YOAKUM DR	0	525U	NEF	77406
GLAMIS LN	16600	447D	NWC	77084
GLAMORGAN DR	15300	409M	JV	77040
GLASCOCK LN	8600	409H	NWC	77064
GLASER DR	1700	493G	NEH	77009
GLASER DR	11200	413X	NEH	77076
GLASGOW	100	536F	PA	77506
GLASGOW	2400	454S	NEH	77026
GLASGOW DR	4600	569X	MC	77459
GLASGOW PLACE	14100	488J	SWH	77077
GLASHOLM DR	0	373A	NCC	77073
GLASS	6700	454K	NEH	77016
GLASS	27700	243R	WCO	77447
GLASS CIR	7800	454K	NEH	77016
GLASS CT	4400	454Q	NEH	77016
GLASSBLOWER LN	7500	410H	NWC	77064
GLASSBOTTOM	4400	531R	SWH	77096
GLASSCOW GREEN	0	616K	SEC	77089
GLASSFORD DR	0	616K	SEC	77089
GLASTONBURY DR	3100	615B	PL	77581
GLAZEBROOK DR	100	412D	NEH	77060
GLAZEBROOK DR	300	373W	NEH	77060
GLAZED BRANCH DR	0	376V	NEC	77396
GLEAMING ROSE DR	0	368A	NWC	77429
GLEANN ARBOR BLVD	0	329C	NWC	77379
GLEANNBURY POINTE DR	0	289Y	NWC	77379
GLEANNLOCH ESTATES DR	8700	329D	NWC	77379
GLEANNLOCH FOREST DR	0	289X	NWC	77379
GLEANNLOCH FOREST DR	9300	329G	NWC	77379
GLEANNLOCH LAKES	0	329G	NWC	77379
GLEASON RD	7200	415W	NEH	77016
GLEBE RD	4200	451M	NWH	77018
GLEE LN	800	373U	NCC	77032
GLEN	0	257E	SEM	77357
GLEN AVE	900	412T	NWH	77088
GLEN AVE	2400	412S	NWH	77088
GLEN CT	0	615W	PL	77584
S. GLEN LN	4900	658W	LC	77573
GLEN ABBEY DR	0	485E	SWC	77494
GLENAIRE	8500	535X	SEH	77061
GLENALBYN	1000	497E	NEH	77015
GLEN ALLEN LN	5600	330X	NWC	77069
GLENALTA	7700	535X	SEH	77061
GLEN ARBOR DR	3500	532K	SWH	77025
GLEN ARDEN LN	8500	528Q	SWC	77083
GLEN ARDEN LN	22000	485M	SWC	77450
GLENARM	5600	494D	NEH	77020
GLEN AVON DR	4200	578E	PA	77505
GLENBANK CT	0	407Q	NWC	77095
GLENBANK WAY	7200	407Q	NWC	77095
GLENBAY CT	1100	539X	LP	77571
GLEN BAY CT	11800	616G	SEC	77089
GLENBORO DR	2000	252V	SEM	77386
GLENBOROUGH DR	100	372Q	NWH	77067
GLENBRAE	7500	535X	SEH	77061
GLENBRANCH DR	21300	291R	NWC	77388
GLEN BREEZE CT	20100	337U	NEC	77346
GLEN BRIAR LN	18500	447J	NWC	77084
GLENBRIAR PLACE	7500	570Z	SWH	77489
GLENBRIAR SPRINGS LN	26200	367E	NWC	77433
GLENBROOK	8100	535P	SEH	77017
GLENBROOK CT	4100	535T	SEH	77087
GLENBROOK KNOLL LN	16000	407R	NWC	77095
GLEN BURN CT	20100	337U	NEC	77346
GLENBURN DR	2300	337C	NEH	77345
GLENBURNIE DR	300	453E	NWH	77022
GLENBURN MANOR LN	22000	445M	NWC	77449
GLEN BURROW CT	0	484K	NEF	77494
GLENBURY DR	9100	412M	NCC	77037
GLEN CAIRN CT	200	338Q	NEH	77336
GLEN CANON LN	14100	330Y	NWC	77069
GLEN CANYON CT	6500	526E	NEF	77450
GLENCASTLE CT	0	297Q	NEH	77345
GLEN CHASE CT	7100	408N	NWC	77095
GLEN CHASE DR	15400	408N	NWC	77095
GLENCHASE LN	4200	371A	NWC	77014
GLENCHESTER	300	489B	SWH	77079
GLENCLAN LN	17000	447C	NWC	77084
GLENCLIFFE LN	8100	369D	NWC	77070
GLENCOE	6000	534Q	SEH	77087
GLENCOVE	6000	492K	SWH	77007
GLEN COVE BLVD	400	619Z	LC	77565
GLEN COVE CIR	3800	610K	MC	77459
GLEN COVE CT	4100	533H	SEH	77021
GLEN COVE DR	0	620N	SB	77586
GLEN COVE DR	4000	533H	SEH	77021
GLENCREEK	0	335Q	HM	77338
GLENCREEK DR	27100	299T	NEC	77336
GLENCREST	8100	535T	SEH	77061
GLENCREST	8800	575B	SEH	77061
GLENCREST DR	1100	539X	LP	77571
GLENCREST DR	1200	537W	PA	77502
GLENCROFT	9300	455D	NEH	77078
GLENCROFT CT	200	338Q	NEH	77336
GLENCROSS	8400	535X	SEH	77061
GLEN CROSSING CIR	12100	377A	NEC	77346
GLEN CROSSING LN	0	377A	NEC	77346
GLEN CULLEN LN	2700	614S	NEB	77584
GLENCULLEN LN	2700	614S	NEB	77584
GLENDA	1100	615B	PL	77581
GLENDA	12900	413P	NCC	77037
GLENDA KAY DR	10700	368U	NWC	77065
GLENDALE	100	495W	SEH	77012
GLENDALE	22400	296G	SEM	77365
GLENDALE DR	2700	614R	PL	77584
GLENDALE HILL DR	0	524F	NEF	77494
GLENDALE RIDGE CT	0	376R	NEC	77396
GLENDAVEN WAY	15400	487Y	SWC	77082
GLENDAVON LN	2200	486N	SWC	77450
GLENDELL CT	7900	535T	SEH	77061
GLENDENING	1	490M	HC	77024
GLENDO CT	0	377F	NEC	77346
GLENDORA	100	495W	SEH	77012
GLENDOWER DR	4700	333D	NCC	77373
GLENDOWN LN	9500	369L	NWC	77070
GLENEAGLE DR	0	659D	LC	77573
GLENEAGLES CT	5000	447D	NWC	77084
GLENEAGLES DR	300	656P	FR	77546
GLENEAGLES DR	4800	447D	NWC	77084
GLENEAGLES DR	6300	578F	PA	77505
GLEN ECHO	0	609M	MC	77459
GLEN ECHO DR	1100	412L	NWH	77088
GLEN ECHO LN	700	490G	HE	77024
GLEN ECHO LN	2700	610J	MC	77459
GLEN EDEN CT	1900	568A	SG	77498
GLEN ERICA DR	13100	370D	NWC	77069
GLEN ERICA DR	13500	330Z	NWC	77069
GLENEVISS DR	17000	447C	NWC	77084
GLENFAIR CT	9100	289Z	NWC	77379
GLEN FALLS	7100	456M	NEC	77049
GLEN FALLS LN	0	615G	PL	77581
GLEN FERRY LN	0	332V	NCC	77073
GLENFIELD	0	530Z	SWH	77096
GLENFIELD	9400	531S	SWH	77096
GLENFIELD CT	1	531N	SWH	77074
GLENFIELD HOLLOW LN	0	366R	NWC	77433
GLENFIELD MANOR LN	0	371C	NWC	77014
GLENFIELD PARK LN	10200	369G	NWC	77070
GLENFIELD SPRING LN	5300	250Z	NWC	77389
GLENFINCH LN	19600	291W	NWC	77379
GLENFORD DR	700	570Y	MC	77489
GLEN FOREST CT	8000	535T	SEH	77061
GLENGARRY RD	3800	573Q	SEH	77047
GLENGARRY RD	4500	574N	SEH	77048
GLENGATE DR	23900	293Y	NCC	77373
GLENGATE LN	10000	529R	SWH	77036
GLENGREEN DR	1600	570T	MC	77489
GLEN GREEN LN	14100	330X	NWC	77069
GLENGROVE	5800	374M	NEH	77396
GLENGYLE CT	24000	338Q	NEH	77336
GLENHAGEN CT	17700	407T	NWC	77084
GLENHAGEN DR	6300	407T	NWC	77084
GLEN HAVEN BLVD	2100	532L	SWH	77030
W. GLEN HAVEN BLVD	2600	532L	SWH	77025
S. GLEN HAVEN BLVD	2600	532L	SWH	77025
E. GLEN HAVEN BLVD	2600	532L	SWH	77025
GLEN HAVEN BLVD	2600	532J	SWH	77025
GLEN HAVEN CIR	0	330E	NWC	77379
GLEN HAVEN CT	200	659G	LC	77573
GLEN HAVEN DR	200	659G	LC	77573
GLENHAVEN DR	5000	500M	BT	77521
GLEN HAVEN ESTATES DR	0	330E	NWC	77379
GLENHEATH	7500	535X	SEH	77061
GLENHEATHER DR	3800	331S	NWC	77068
GLENHEW RD	17300	376G	NEC	77396
GLENHILL DR	3700	613Y	NEB	77584
GLENHILL DR	6100	290C	NWC	77389
GLENHILLSHIRE DR	0	451W	HI	77055
GLEN HOLLOW DR	900	375D	HM	77338
GLEN HOLLOW DR	8100	534W	SEH	77033
GLEN HOLLOW DR	10800	573M	SEH	77048
GLENHOLLY LN	0	485W	NEF	77494
GLENHOLLY PARK DR	0	568B	SG	77498
GLENHOPE DR	6700	406R	NWC	77449
GLENHOUSE CT	8700	412P	NWH	77088
GLENHOUSE DR	8800	412P	NWH	77088
GLENHURST DR	5700	534T	SEH	77033
GLEN IRIS DR	3000	660E	LC	77573
GLENIRISH DR	0	484Y	NEF	77494
GLENIRISH DR	0	484Y	NEF	77494
GLEN IVY DR	3800	297T	NEH	77345
GLENKIRK DR	9900	575Z	SEC	77089
GLENKIRK DR	10100	616A	SEC	77089
GLEN KNOLL CT	11600	489P	SWH	77077
GLEN KNOLL DR	2100	489P	SWH	77077
GLEN LAKE CT	2900	291Z	NWC	77388
GLEN LAKE DR	19900	291Z	NWC	77388
GLEN LANDING DR	19400	446M	NWC	77449
GLEN LANE CT	11500	370M	NWC	77066
GLEN LAUREL LN	0	615G	PL	77581
GLENLEA	400	616Z	FR	77546
GLENLEA	7700	535X	SEH	77061
GLENLEA CT	900	616U	FR	77546
GLENLEDI DR	17000	407Y	NWC	77084
GLENLEDI DR	17900	407X	NWC	77084
GLENLEE DR	5800	374M	NEH	77396
GLENLEE DR	5900	375J	NEH	77396
GLENLEIGH DR	12300	371H	NWC	77014
GLENLEIGH PLACE	1	250G	WD	77381
GLENLEVAN LN	0	484V	NEF	77494
GLEN LIEF CT	0	290Z	NWC	77379
GLENLOCH DR	8000	535X	SEH	77061
GLENLOCH DR	8800	575B	SEH	77061
GLEN LOCH DR	23800	291B	SEM	77380
GLEN LOCH DR	26500	251P	WD	77381
GLEN MANOR DR	7300	455E	NEH	77028
GLEN MAR DR	0	366N	NWC	77433
GLEN MAR DR	16000	527C	SWC	77082
GLENMARK DR	17500	407T	NWC	77084
GLENMAWR DR	10100	576S	SEH	77075
GLEN MAY PARK CT	10300	329C	NWC	77379
GLEN MAY PARK DR	1600	329C	NWC	77379
GLENMEADE DR	3700	618C	SEH	77059
GLENMEADOW DR	4900	531U	SWH	77096
GLENMEADOW DR	12300	569E	SF	77477
GLENMEADOWS DR	100	539X	LP	77571
GLENMERE LN	5200	331J	NWC	77379
GLEN MILLS REACH DR		325N	NWC	77447
GLEN MIST CT	1600	412F	NWC	77038
GLEN MIST LN	5600	330X	NWC	77069
GLENMONT BLVD	21900	285H	SWM	77447
GLENMONT DR	4400	531B	SWH	77081
GLENMONT DR	4700	531D	BL	77401
GLENMONT DR	6500	530C	SWH	77036
GLENMONT ESTATES BLVD	22000	285D	SWM	77355
GLENMONT ESTATES BLVD	22500	245Z	SWM	77355
GLENMONT PARK DR	17100	618T	WB	77598
GLENMONT RIDGE CT	0	611S	FS	77545
GLENMORE	3400	534L	SEH	77023
GLENMORE DR	200	537G	PA	77503
GLENMORE FOREST	1400	451W	NWH	77055
GLENMORE MEADOWS DR	0	253X	SEM	77386
GLENMORIN CT	5600	456V	NEC	77049
GLENMORRIS CT	6500	407T	NWC	77084
GLENMORRIS DR	17300	407T	NWC	77084
GLENN	0	411V	NWH	77088
GLENN	0	537E	PA	77506
GLENN	1100	536M	PA	77506
GLENN	1200	541C	BT	77520
GLENNALE CT	4100	447H	NWC	77084
GLENNALE DR	4000	447H	NWC	77084
GLENN CLIFF DR	7800	370S	NWC	77064
GLENN ELM DR	8200	330E	NWC	77379
GLENN NEVIS	4800	447C	NWC	77084
GLENNEYRE LN	5900	407V	NWC	77084
GLENN HAVEN ESTATES DR	18500	330E	NWC	77379
GLENN HILLS LN	0	657X	LC	77573
GLENN LAKES DR	6500	370B	NWC	77069
GLENN LAKES LN	1800	610J	MC	77459
GLENN LAKES LN	2800	609L	MC	77459
GLENNLAST LN	13200	413K	NCC	77037
GLENN LEIGH DR	0	330E	NWC	77379
GLEN NOOK DR	5200	414Y	NEH	77016
GLENN RICKI DR	3800	572E	SWH	77045
GLENN RIVER DR	12300	415E	NEH	77050
GLENNVILLE CT	200	490M	HC	77024
GLENOAK DR	0	615Z	PL	77581
GLEN OAKS	0	247T	SWM	77355
GLEN OAKS DR	1300	252G	SEM	77385
GLEN OAKS RD	1500	492C	NWH	77008
GLENORA DR	10700	369S	NWC	77065
GLENOVER DR	22900	485G	SWC	77450
GLEN PARK	100	493C	NEH	77009
GLEN PARK DR	300	570S	SF	77477
GLEN PARK DR	1900	570S	SF	77477
GLENPARK DR	4800	539X	LP	77571
GLENPATTI DR	17300	407P	NWC	77084
GLENPINE DR	3600	331S	NWC	77068
GLEN PINES DR	5600	330X	NWC	77069
GLEN POLARA DR	6800	407P	NWC	77084
GLEN PRAIRIE DR	7600	535T	SEH	77061
GLEN RAY DR	6500	407P	NWC	77084
GLENRIDGE CT	5500	571Y	SWH	77053
GLENRIDGE LN	4600	571Z	SWH	77053
GLENRIDGE FOREST	200	487A	SWC	77094
GLEN RILEY DR	8200	527Q	NEF	77083
GLEN RIO	5300	571L	SWH	77045
GLENROCK DR	6500	534Z	SEH	77087
GLENROCK HILLS	26600	524F	NEF	77494
S. GLENROCK HILLS CT	0	524E	NEF	77494
N. GLENROCK HILLS CT	0	524E	NEF	77494
GLENROCK HILLS DR	0	524E	NEF	77494
GLENROCK HILLS DR	26600	524F	NEF	77494
GLEN ROSA DR	6900	525F	NEF	77494
GLENROSE	3500	533T	SEH	77051
GLEN ROYAL CT	18000	296W	NEH	77365
GLENROYAL CT	21700	336A	SEM	77339
GLEN RYDER CT	0	372M	NCC	77073
GLENSCOTT	7900	535Y	SEH	77061
GLEN SHADOW DR	8700	412L	NWH	77088
GLENSHADOW WAY	9700	412F	NWC	77038
GLENSHANNON	16400	618D	SEH	77059
GLENSHANNON AVE	1000	656M	FR	77546
GLENSHIRE DR	4000	533N	SWH	77025
GLENSIDE	8600	574A	SEH	77033
GLEN SPRING DR	3000	297S	NEH	77339
GLENSTEIN DR	6800	407Q	NWC	77084
GLENSTONE	200	456Y	NEH	77013
GLENTHORPE CT	24400	485S	NEF	77494
GLENTHORPE LN	3000	485S	NEF	77494
GLENTIDE CIR	12800	572F	SWH	77045
GLEN TURRET CT	9300	408A	NWC	77095
GLENTWORTH CT	5100	447B	NWC	77084
GLENVALE DR	400	413A	NCC	77060
GLEN VALLEY	4900	539X	LP	77571
GLEN VALLEY DR	1000	375D	HM	77338
GLEN VALLEY DR	8000	535X	SEH	77061
GLENVIEW CT	5100	539X	LP	77571
GLENVIEW DR	900	656B	PL	77581
GLENVIEW DR	1000	616X	PL	77581
GLENVIEW DR	4900	539X	LP	77571
GLENVIEW DR	5400	337D	NEH	77345
GLENVIEW DR	7600	535S	SEH	77061
GLENVIEW DR	8000	535Q	SEH	77017
GLENVILLAGE	4600	447C	NWC	77084
GLENVINE DR	16400	375J	NEH	77396
GLENVISTA	7500	535X	SEH	77061
GLENWATER CT	15000	377Y	NEC	77044
GLENWAY DR	10500	369B	NWC	77070
GLENWAY DR	12000	368D	NWC	77070
GLENWAY FALLS DR	19400	406R	NWC	77449
GLENWELL CT	4500	337B	NEH	77345
GLENWEST DR	19100	617V	SEH	77546
GLENWICK CT	7200	407P	NWC	77433
GLENWILD N. CIR	0	250J	NWC	77389
GLENWILD S. CIR	0	250J	NWC	77389
GLENWILD DR	1800	570W	MC	77489
GLENWILLOW	21100	289Q	NWC	77375
S. GLEN WILLOW LN	7500	570V	SWH	77489
E. GLEN WILLOW RD	14400	570V	SWH	77489
GLENWOLDE DR	10500	529Q	SWH	77099
GLENWOLDE DR	11600	529S	SWH	77099
GLENWOLDE DR	12800	528Q	SWH	77099
GLENWOLF DR	17500	407T	NWC	77084
GLENWOOD	100	492L	SWH	77007
GLENWOOD	10100	461E	NEC	77532
GLENWOOD AVE	4500	538X	DP	77536
GLENWOOD BLVD	23700	245X	SWM	77447
GLENWOOD DR	0	326K	NWC	77433
GLENWOOD DR	1100	444Z	KT	77493
GLENWOOD DR	1500	656L	FR	77546
GLENWOOD DR	3000	613S	NEB	77584
GLENWOOD DR	28000	258T	SEM	77357
GLENWOOD RD	4300	538X	DP	77536
GLENWOOD CANYON LN	0	406H	NWC	77433
GLENWOOD CANYON LN	1100	488J	SWH	77077
GLENWOOD FOREST DR	9600	455C	NEH	77078
GLENWOOD PARK DR	15300	408E	NWC	77095
GLENWOOD RIDGE DR	400	252T	SEM	77386
GLENWOODS DR	0	381P	LCO	77535
GLENWOODS LN	0	381P	LCO	77535
GLENWOOD SPRINGS DR	3500	297T	NEH	77345
GLENWORTH LN	24100	485T	NEF	77494
GLENWYCK	12800	572J	SWH	77045
GLENYORK CT	12900	328U	NWC	77429
GLESBY	9000	495C	NEH	77029
GLIDDEN STREAM LN	0	366N	NWC	77433
GLOBE	500	576E	SEH	77034
GLOBE	1400	575D	SEH	77034
GLOGER	11700	414K	NCC	77039
GLORIA CT	1100	568T	SG	77478
GLORIA DR	10800	456S	NEH	77013
GLORIA LN	10000	462V	CCO	77521
GLORIETA DR	8100	527R	NEF	77083
GLORIETTA TURN	16500	331T	NWC	77068
GLORY AVE	24100	296K	SEM	77365
GLORYBOWER CT	1	251L	WD	77380
GLORY GARDEN WAY	0	250P	NWC	77389
GLORY HILL TRAIL	0	450U	NWH	77080
GLORYLAND	0	533V	SEH	77033
GLORY ROSE CT	17600	327N	NWC	77429
GLORY VISTA LN	0	366V	NWC	77433
GLORYWHITE CT	12800	576V	SEH	77034
GLOSRIDGE DR	1900	451S	NWH	77055
GLOSSON RD	2200	612R	PL	77584
GLOSTER DR	14900	497D	NEC	77530
GLOUCESTER	0	257M	SEM	77357
GLOUCESTER	0	258J	SEM	77357
GLOUCHESTER LN	900	332G	NCC	77073
GLOURIE CIR	1000	491A	HI	77055
GLOURIE DR	1000	451W	HI	77055

Street Name	Block	Pg/Sq	Loc	Zips
GLOVER	7700	535K	SEH	77012
GLOVER MEADOWS LN	3700	573U	SEC	77047
GLOYNA	9900	411R	NWH	77088
GLUDECCA ST	0	530X	SWH	77031
GLYNN WAY DR	100	491G	SWH	77056
GNARLED CHESNUT CT	9400	576J	SEH	77075
GNARLED OAKS CT	5900	337T	NEC	77346
GNARLWOOD DR	11400	616C	SEC	77089
GNEISS HOLLOW RD	5101	526S	NEF	77407
GN PLACE, I &	0	493M	SEH	77002
GOAR RD	12600	488R	SWH	77077
GOBER	100	536J	SEH	77017
GOBER	800	535M	SEH	77017
GODFREY	2000	460T	MN	77521
GODFREY COVE CT	26600	484X	NEF	77494
GODSEY CT	400	490K	BH	77024
GODSTONE	0	329V	NWC	77070
GODSTONE LN	9100	330S	NWC	77379
GODWIN	1400	494X	SEH	77023
GOEDECKE RD	100	292M	SP	77373
GOETTEE CIR	5600	451C	NWH	77091
GOFORTH	5800	533M	SEH	77021
GOLBOW DR	0	448K	NWH	77084
GOLD	5100	454S	NEH	77026
GOLD BRIDGE CT	16700	611B	SWH	77053
GOLD BROOK LN	10100	527Z	NEF	77498
W. GOLD BUTTERCUP CT	0	325M	NWC	77429
E. GOLD BUTTERCUP CT	0	325M	NWC	77429
GOLD CANDLE DR	3400	331C	NWC	77388
GOLD CANDLESTICK DR	0	285K	NWC	77447
GOLD CANYON RD	0	418P	NEC	77044
GOLD CREEK DR	8400	451J	NWH	77080
GOLDCREST	9100	453G	NEH	77022
GOLDCREST	9600	453C	NEH	77076
GOLDCREST CT	25500	250T	NWC	77389
GOLD CUP WAY	9800	409A	NWC	77065
GOLD DUST LN	7500	410H	NWC	77064
GOLDEN DR	5200	500G	NEC	77521
GOLDEN LN	900	339E	NEH	77336
GOLDEN LN	1300	539P	LP	77571
GOLDEN RD	2200	251U	SWM	77380
GOLDEN APPALOOSA CIR	14500	377T	NEC	77044
GOLDEN AURORA DR	0	527N	NEF	77083
GOLDEN BAY LN	2000	619Z	LC	77573
GOLDEN BEAR LN	600	336A	NEH	77339
GOLDEN BELL DR	25600	250T	NWC	77389
GOLDEN BEND DR	400	459M	HG	77562
GOLDEN BLUFF LN	0	417B	NEC	77044
GOLDEN BLUFF LN	0	417B	NEC	77044
GOLDEN BOUGH LN	8300	375Z	NEC	77396
GOLDEN BROOK DR	12600	571F	SWH	77085
GOLDEN BROOK LN	5000	485Y	NEF	77450
GOLDEN BUD LN	0	325R	NWC	77433
GOLDEN CANYON LN	17900	527J	NEF	77407
GOLDEN CAPE DR	2900	660E	LC	77573
GOLDEN CEDAR DR	21900	325R	NWC	77433
GOLDEN CHORD CIR	8600	410K	NWC	77040
GOLDEN CIRCLE WAY	13600	528F	SWC	77083
GOLDEN COVE LN	22100	296X	NEC	77339
GOLDEN COVE LN	22100	296X	NEC	77339
GOLDEN CREEK DR	0	446J	NWC	77449
GOLDEN CREEK LN	0	612P	PL	77545
GOLDEN CYPRESS LN	14200	367B	CY	77429
GOLDEN CYPRESS LN	14400	327Y	CY	77429
GOLDENDALE CT	7100	406L	NWC	77433
GOLDENDALE DR	1200	619G	TL	77586
GOLDEN DOVE DR	21300	291U	NWC	77388
GOLDEN EAGLE	0	370H	NWC	77066
GOLDEN EAGLE AVE	0	371E	NWC	77066
GOLDEN EAGLE DR	15100	375Q	NEC	77396
GOLDEN EAGLE LN	0	245N	SWM	77355
GOLDEN ELM CIR	0	325R	NWC	77433
GOLDEN EYE	3200	444K	KT	77493
GOLDENEYE DR	0	461N	NEC	77521
GOLDENEYE LN	2500	658X	LC	77573
GOLDEN FALLS LN	0	330C	NWC	77379
GOLDEN FERN CT	11000	575Z	SEH	77075
GOLDEN FIELD DR	13200	578S	SEH	77059
GOLDEN FLAME CT	19600	486G	SWC	77094
GOLDEN FLORAL CT	0	249A	SWM	77354
GOLDEN FOLIAGE TRAIL	0	335P	NCC	77338
GOLDEN FOREST DR	4800	451G	NWH	77091
GOLDEN FOREST DR	5700	451B	NWH	77092
GOLDEN FORK DR	0	485P	NEF	77493
GOLDEN GARDENS	4500	415A	NEC	77039
GOLDEN GATE	0	409Q	NWH	77041
GOLDENGLADE CIR	9500	409D	NWC	77064
GOLDENGLADE DR	9500	409D	NWC	77064
GOLDEN GLADE LN	17500	367T	NWC	77095
GOLDEN GLEN DR	9900	529S	SWH	77099
GOLDEN GRAIN DR	10800	369Y	NWC	77064
GOLDEN GROVE DR	0	407H	NWC	77095
GOLDENGROVE DR	7600	330E	NWC	77379
GOLDEN GROVE LN	5600	334A	NCC	77373
GOLDEN HARBOUR	0	610W	NEF	77459
GOLDEN HAWK TRAIL	14700	325Q	NWC	77433
GOLDEN HAWTHORNE CT	20600	337Q	NEC	77346
GOLDEN HEARTH LN	0	366U	NWC	77433
GOLDEN HEATH LN	0	526G	NEF	77407
GOLDEN HILLS LN	3000	609H	MC	77459
GOLDEN HOLLOW CT	5500	334E	NCC	77373
GOLDEN KINGS CT	20800	337Q	NEC	77346
GOLDEN LAKE DR	3700	297T	NEH	77345
GOLDENLEAF DR	0	616U	FR	77546
GOLDEN LEAF DR	2700	297S	NEH	77345
GOLDEN LEGION LN	0	366Q	NWC	77433
GOLDEN LODGE LN	11800	370L	NWC	77066
GOLDEN LODGE LN	11801	370L	NWC	77066
GOLDEN MANE RD	0	249Z	NWC	77375
GOLDEN MANOR LN	16100	367D	NWC	77429
GOLDEN MEADOW DR	9100	369Y	NWC	77064
GOLDEN MESA DR	20000	446P	NWC	77449
GOLDEN MEWS LN	2300	485J	NEF	77494
GOLDEN MILLS		295V	NEH	77365
GOLDEN MORNING CIR	0	447A	NWC	77084
GOLDEN NUGGET DR	1000	485M	SWC	77450
GOLDEN OAK LN	0	339P	HU	77336
GOLDEN OAK CHASE CT	27800	294J	SEM	77386
GOLDEN OAK PARK LN	0	252M	SEM	77385
GOLDEN OASIS LN	0	376V	NEC	77396
GOLDEN ORCHARD PLACE	0	249A	SWM	77354
GOLDEN PARK LN	9600	411N	NWH	77088
GOLDEN PASS	2400	371L	NWC	77067
GOLDEN PINE DR	11800	329S	NWC	77070
GOLDEN PLACE	1	250H	WD	77381
GOLDEN POND DR	1800	337C	NEH	77345
GOLDEN POND DR	14400	408U	NWC	77084
GOLDEN PRAIRIE LN	9800	411C	NWC	77086
GOLDEN RAINBOW DR	12900	328Y	NWC	77429
GOLDEN RAINTREE DR	20800	446N	NWC	77449
GOLDEN RAY DR	11200	369J	NWC	77429
GOLDEN REED DR	0	486P	SWC	77450
GOLDEN RIDGE DR	18000	407X	NWC	77084
GOLDEN RIVER LN	6600	528F	SWC	77083
GOLDENROD	100	493C	NEH	77009
GOLDENROD	2200	460P	NEC	77562
GOLDENROD	2600	537U	PA	77503
GOLDENROD LN	4300	609F	MC	77459
GOLDEN ROSE DR	6700	406Q	NWC	77449
GOLDEN SAGE LN	16100	367C	CY	77429
GOLDEN SAILS DR	2100	620W	LC	77573
GOLDEN SAILS DR	2200	619Z	LC	77573
GOLDEN SANDS DR	16100	407D	NWC	77095
GOLDEN SHORES DR	0	610U	MC	77459
GOLDEN SHORES LN	2300	619Y	LC	77573
GOLDEN SKY LN	0	526J	NEF	77407
GOLDENSONG CT	23200	292G	NCC	77373
GOLDEN SPIKE LN	8500	410D	NWH	77086
GOLDEN SPUR TRAIL	20200	378G	NEC	77532
GOLDEN STAR DR	0	528J	SWC	77083
GOLDEN STATE	0	570B	SWH	77071
GOLDEN STREAM DR	5300	371N	NWC	77066
GOLDEN SUMMER CT	0	376V	NEC	77396
GOLDEN SUN CT	1300	619H	PA	77586
GOLDEN SUNSHINE DR	9100	369V	NWC	77064
GOLDEN SUNSHINE DR	10700	369X	NWC	77064
GOLDEN SYCAMORE TRAIL	16200	326F	NWC	77433
GOLDEN TAYLOR DR	0	615F	PL	77581
GOLDEN TEE CT	3300	609G	MC	77459
GOLDEN TEE CT	10500	528U	SWH	77099
GOLDEN TEE LN	3500	609M	MC	77459
GOLDEN TEE LN	12700	528U	SWH	77099
GOLDEN TERRACE CT	0	485X	NEF	77494
GOLDEN THISTLE	12400	619A	PA	77058
GOLDEN THISTLE LN	7500	407J	NWC	77433
GOLDEN TRACE CT	8100	528L	SWC	77083
GOLDEN TRAILS DR	2100	254K	SEM	77365
GOLDEN TRAILS DR	3300	297X	NEH	77345
GOLDEN VALLEY DR	13200	328T	NWC	77429
GOLDEN VIEW	13000	528F	SWC	77083
GOLDEN VIEW CT	0	528F	SWC	77083
GOLDENVIEW PARK LN	0	528W	NEF	77498
GOLDEN VILLAS	2500	538S	PA	77503
GOLDEN VINES LN	0	253X	SEM	77386
GOLDEN WATER CT	13000	377P	NEC	77044
GOLDENWAVE CT	0	525E	NEF	77494
GOLDEN WAVE DR	0	446D	NWC	77449
GOLDEN WEST DR	900	485H	SWC	77450
GOLDEN WILLOW CT	3800	446M	NWC	77449
GOLDEN WILLOW DR	3200	297N	NEH	77339
GOLDEN WILLOW DR	3500	446M	NWC	77449
GOLDEN WINGS CT	5300	448D	NWC	77041
GOLDEN WOOD LN	9300	410D	NWC	77086
GOLDERS GREEN DR	3400	528C	SWH	77082
GOLDFARB	13000	572T	SWH	77045
GOLDFIELD LN	10500	409B	NWC	77064
GOLDFINCH	4300	571D	SWH	77035
GOLDFINCH AVE	900	568Q	SG	77478
GOLDFINCH DR	7300	375K	HM	77396
GOLDFINCH LN	0	658T	LC	77573
GOLDFINCH LN	18700	286H	NWC	77377
GOLDFINCH RD	10600	463S	CCO	77520
GOLD FIRE DR	6500	571J	SWH	77085
GOLD HAVEN DR		526S	NEF	77407
GOLDHURST LN	0	289Q	NWC	77375
GOLDKING RD	0	338V	NEC	77336
GOLDKING CROSS CT	23400	293Y	NCC	77373
GOLDLAKE DR	19800	406Q	NWC	77449
GOLD LANTANA TRAIL	5000	291E	NWC	77389
GOLDLEAF CT	0	609Y	NEF	77459
GOLDLEAF CT	0	609Y	NEF	77459
GOLD LEAF TRAIL	21900	325R	NWC	77433
GOLDMAR CT	0	372M	NCC	77073
GOLD MEDAL CIR	5300	448C	NWC	77041
GOLD MESA CT	900	618J	SEH	77062
GOLD MESA TRAIL	14800	618E	SEH	77062
GOLD MOSS DR	6500	571J	SWH	77085
GOLD NUGGET	0	339F	NEC	77336
GOLD PANNING CT	17200	246K	SWM	77355
GOLD POINT DR	10300	409G	NWC	77064
GOLD RIDGE LN	16400	611C	SWH	77053
N. GOLD RIVER CIR	6800	609Q	MC	77459
S. GOLD RIVER CIR	6900	609Q	MC	77459
GOLD RUSH SPRINGS DR	9600	329G	NWC	77375
GOLDSMITH	2000	532G	SWH	77030
GOLDSPIER	5400	451D	NWH	77091
GOLDSPIER	7000	411Z	NWH	77088
GOLDSPRING LN	2000	293T	NCC	77373
GOLDSTONE DR	22100	485D	SWC	77450
GOLDSTREAM CT	11700	328M	NWC	77377
GOLD TEE CT	6500	530F	SWH	77036
GOLD TEE DR	8200	530F	SWH	77036
GOLDTHREAD CT	1	250M	WD	77381
GOLDWATER CT	13600	377Y	NEC	77044
GOLF CT	800	570S	SF	77477
GOLF DR	3400	452K	NWH	77018
GOLF DR	5400	452F	NWH	77091
GOLF CLUB DR	15900	379W	NEC	77532
GOLF CLUB DR	16700	419E	NEC	77532
GOLF COURSE DR	0	448E	NWH	77084
GOLFCREST BLVD	2900	534M	SEH	77087
GOLFCREST DR	2300	616K	PL	77581
GOLF GREEN CIR	8000	530F	SWH	77036
GOLF GREEN CT	5300	657Z	LC	77573
GOLF LINKS CT	1	337F	NEH	77339
GOLF RIDGE CIR	0	616J	SEC	77581
GOLF VIEW LN	27500	299T	NEC	77336
GOLF VIEW TRAIL	14200	578X	SEH	77059
GOLFWAY	6800	534M	SEH	77087
GOLIAD	1000	493G	SWH	77002
GOLIAD	1200	493G	SWH	77007
GOLIAD RUN	6600	461Y	BT	77521
GOLOBY DR	0	525M	NEF	77407
GOLONDRINA DR	7800	527L	NEF	77083
GO MAN GO DR	600	570S	SF	77477
GOMEL DR	0	406Z	NWC	77449
GOMEZ	6400	500D	SEC	77521
GONDOLA	900	568Q	SG	77478
GONDOLA DR	11400	529W	SWH	77477
GONZALES	6900	494H	NEH	77020
GONZALES	7100	495E	NEH	77020
GONZALES LN	21700	256K	SEM	77357
GOOD DALE LN	23000	334A	NCC	77373
GOOD DAY DR	0	569Y	MC	77459
GOODE	7800	535B	SEH	77012
GOODFELLOW DR	23100	333D	NCC	77373
GOODFELLOW DR	23400	293Z	NCC	77373
GOODFIELD CT	16800	329R	NWC	77379
GOODHOPE	3400	533P	SEH	77021
GOODING HILL LN	0	371D	NWC	77014
GOOD INTENTION RD	0	380D	NEC	77532
GOODLAE DR	10100	411J	NWH	77088
GOODLEY CT	11600	328T	NWC	77429
GOODLOE	2300	414W	NEH	77093
GOODLOE PLACE	0	660E	LC	77573
GOODMAN	15100	408S	NWC	77084
GOODMAN RIDGE DR	0	610V	MC	77459
GOODMANVILLE CT	0	527W	NEF	77469
GOODMEADOW DR	9000	369V	NWC	77064
GOODNIGHT	0	539S	DP	77536
GOODNIGHT TRAIL	800	373J	NCC	77060
GOODRICH	2300	614M	PL	77581
GOODRIDGE DR	0	574V	SEH	77048
GOODRUM RD	10000	450E	NWH	77041
GOODRUM RD	10200	449D	NWH	77041
GOOD SAM	1000	488E	SWH	77079
GOODSON DR	1	372Z	NEH	77060
GOODSON DR	300	373W	NEH	77060
GOODSON LOOP RD	100	247A	SWM	77362
GOODSPRING DR	10800	369Z	NWC	77064
GOOD SPRING DR	11800	371M	NWC	77067
GOODTIMES	0	445P	NWC	77449
GOODWIN DR	2000	445S	NWC	77493
GOODWIN DR	24300	445S	NWC	77493
GOODWIN RD	20000	252L	SEM	77385
GOODYEAR DR	1900	535H	SEH	77017
GOOSEBERRY LN	18700	295F	SEM	77365
GOOSECREEK DR	4900	500M	BT	77521
GOOSE CREEK LANDING	0	461N	NEC	77521
GOOSELAKE LN	19400	446U	NWC	77084
GORDONSCASTLE	10400	489L	SWH	77042
GORDY	0	620Y	KE	77565
GORDY	0	660C	KE	77565
GORDY RD	100	660M	BC	77518
GORE	900	537J	PA	77506
GORE DR	7200	415W	NEH	77016
GORE GRASS CT	16000	330R	NWC	77379
GORHAM DR	15300	408S	NWC	77084
GORHAM PARK CIR	11500	372N	NWC	77067
GORKIPARK DR	0	445R	NWC	77449
GORMAN DR	5700	457S	NEC	77049
GORMAN BROOK DR	0	407C	NWC	77095
GOROM CT	2900	613U	NEB	77584
GORTON DR	0	406U	NWC	77449
GOSFORTH DR	5400	446C	NWC	77449
GOSLING RD	0	250H	WD	77381
GOSLING RD	9300	251A	WD	77381
GOSLING RD	20000	290M	NWC	77389
GOSLING RD	24500	250Z	NWC	77389
GOSLING CEDAR PLACE	0	290R	NWC	77388
GOSLING MALLARD DR	0	290R	NWC	77388
GOSLING OAKS LN	0	290R	NWC	77388
GOSPEL WAY	13400	571K	SWH	77085
GOSS RD	5700	500C	NEC	77521
GOSSETT	100	459R	HG	77562
GOSS HOLLOW LN	0	406X	NWC	77449
GOSS SPRING CT	22500	292K	NCC	77373
GOSTICK	2000	453S	NWH	77008
GOSWELL LN	1300	458W	NEC	77530
GOTHAM DR	12400	616D	SEH	77089
GOTHIC LN	22800	285C	SWM	77447
GOUDIN DR	7600	570Z	SWH	77489
GOULBURN DR	3700	572N	SWH	77045
GOULD	2400	534G	SEH	77023
GOULD'S CT	2600	494A	NEH	77026
GOULD CHAMBERS RD	19000	255P	SEM	77365
GOVERNMENT, U S RD	0	448W	NWH	77084
GOVERNMENT, U S RD	0	447Y	NWH	77084
W. GOVERNORS CIR	2000	451V	NWH	77092
E. GOVERNORS CIR	2000	452S	NWH	77092
GOVERNORSHIRE DR	22900	485B	SWC	77450
GOVERNORS PLACE DR	400	485C	SWC	77450
GOWLAND	14200	572N	SWH	77045
GOYA	0	576S	SEH	77075
GRAB RD	2000	373R	NCC	77032
GRABLE COVE LN	1600	289Y	NWC	77379
GRACE	0	284Z	NWC	77447
GRACE	0	458H	HG	77562
GRACE	200	494S	SEH	77003
GRACE	1000	538L	DP	77536
GRACE LN	1	459F	NEC	77562
GRACE LN	800	375D	HM	77338
GRACE LN	5500	534J	SEH	77021
GRACE LN	22300	256L	SEM	77357
GRACECHURCH DR	11300	371P	NWC	77066
GRACE FALLS DR	0	525R	NEF	77407
GRACEFIELD CT	4000	573Z	SEC	77047
GRACEFIELD HAVEN LN	0	524M	NEF	77406
GRACEFIELD MANOR CT	5500	525D	NEF	77450
GRACEFUL BEND LN	8500	375Z	NEC	77396
GRACEFUL ELM CT	1	251C	WD	77381
GRACEFUL OAK CROSSING	8500	524D	NEF	77494
GRACEFUL PATH WAY	0	292D	SEM	77386
GRACE HALL DR	0	369P	NWC	77065
GRACE HILLS LN	0	484T	NEF	77494
GRACE HOLLOW DR	10400	366V	NWC	77433
GRACELAND	200	453U	NEH	77009
GRACELY PARK LN	0	526F	NEF	77407
GRACE MEADOW LN	0	568A	SG	77498
GRACENOTE PLACE	0	250J	NWC	77389
GRACE POINT DR	100	568J	SG	77498
GRACEPOINT LN	5200	574J	SEH	77048
GRACETON LN	0	291V	NWC	77388
GRACIA	7100	413S	NEH	77076
GRACIA	7500	413S	NEH	77037
GRACKLE DR	7000	407J	NWC	77433
GRACKLE RUN LN	0	335P	NCC	77338
GRACYS LANDING LN	0	524E	NEF	77494
GRACYS LANDING LN	0	524E	NEF	77494
GRADUATE CIR	4300	534E	SEH	77004
GRADY	8800	454C	NEH	77016
GRAFF NET CT	6200	330M	NWC	77379
GRAF NET DR	0	330M	NWC	77379
GRAFTON	7900	535P	SEH	77017
GRAFTON DR	0	256T	SEM	77357
GRAFTON BRIDGE LN	13900	573V	SEC	77047
GRAFTONDALE CT	0	407Z	NWC	77084
GRAHAM	1	541B	BT	77520
GRAHAM	2400	534G	SEH	77023
GRAHAM DR	100	495Z	GP	77547
GRAHAM DR	900	288K	TB	77375
GRAHAMCREST DR	7600	535W	SEH	77061
GRAHAM PARK LN	0	445L	NWC	77449
GRAHAM SPRINGS CT	13400	377L	NEH	77044
GRAHAM TRACE	0	660J	LC	77573
GRAHAMWOOD LN	2700	573X	SEC	77047
GRAINGER SPRINGS	0	370E	NWH	77070
GRAMERCY	2300	532G	SWH	77030
GRAMERCY	2700	532E	SWH	77025
GRAMERCY CT	3100	613Y	NEB	77584
GRAMMAR RD	100	572Y	SWC	77047
GRAMOND HALL DR	0	289Z	NWC	77379
GRAMPIN DR	16600	407Z	NWC	77084
S. GRANADA	0	569Y	MC	77477
N. GRANADA	0	569Y	MC	77477
GRANADA	13200	497A	NEH	77015
GRANBERRY	100	335Z	HM	77338
GRANBERRY	500	493A	NWH	77007
GRANBERRY GATE DR	17200	328R	NWC	77377
GRANBOROUGH DR	0	295Z	NEH	77365
GRANBY TERRACE	2000	333A	NCC	77373
GRAN CANARY DR	0	660L	LC	77573
GRAND	100	498E	CV	77530
GRAND	500	537K	PA	77506
GRAND	7600	455W	NEH	77020
GRAND AVE	100	660R	GCO	77518
GRAND AVE	8400	370Y	NWC	77064
GRAND BLVD	0	660Y	DI	77539
N. GRAND BLVD	2100	615J	PL	77581
S. GRAND BLVD	2400	615N	PL	77581
GRAND BLVD	6100	533F	SWH	77021
GRAND BLVD	6900	533K	SWH	77054
N. GRAND PKWY	0	445X	NWC	77449
GRAND ARBOR LN	0	253P	SEM	77386
GRAND ARBOR LN	0	407J	NWC	77433
GRAND ARCHES LN	0	377J	NEC	77346
GRAND ASHFORD DR	18900	329B	NWC	77375
GRAND BAY LN	21600	445M	NWC	77449
GRANDBLUFF CT	14900	326Z	NWC	77429
GRAND BLUFF LN	0	657X	LC	77573
GRAND BLUFF GROVE	19900	526J	NWF	77407
GRANDBROOK	0	616A	SEC	77089
GRAND BROOK CT	8600	615D	SEC	77089
GRAND BROOK DR	10300	615D	SEC	77089
W. GRAND BROOKS	5900	525D	NEF	77450
E. GRAND BROOKS	5900	525D	NEF	77450
S. GRAND BROOKS	21700	525D	NEF	77450
N. GRAND BROOKS	21700	525D	NEF	77450
GRAND BROOKS LN	21700	525D	NEF	77450
GRANDBURY CT	0	406D	NWC	77433
GRAND BUTTE CT	0	525G	NEF	77494
GRAND CANYON	0	377B	NEC	77346
GRAND CANYON DR	2400	371G	NWC	77067
GRAND CANYON GATE DR	6300	526A	NEF	77450
GRAND CAYMAN CT	3200	609E	SG	77479
GRAND CAYMAN DR	4300	609E	SG	77479
GRAND CHATEAU LN	4800	447B	NWC	77084
GRAND CIRCLE BLVD	0	445X	NWC	77449
GRAND COLONY CT	19300	406Y	NWC	77449
GRAND COLONY DR	5900	406Z	NWC	77449
GRAND COLONY DR	5900	406Z	NWC	77449
GRAND CORNER DR	0	525F	NEF	77497
GRAND CORRAL LN	14800	327Y	NWC	77429
GRAND COVE CT	22100	525C	NEF	77450
GRAND CREEK CT	0	658J	LC	77573
GRAND CREEK CT	21900	525C	NEF	77450
GRAND CREEK DR	0	658J	LC	77573
GRAND CREEK LN	5700	525C	NEF	77450
GRAND CREEK LN	11200	289K	NWC	77375
GRAND CROSS LN	12700	528M	SWH	77072
GRAND CYPRESS LN	6400	407T	NWC	77084
GRAND DRIFT CT	0	525G	NEF	77494
GRAND ELM CIR	3000	331P	NWC	77068
GRANDE MONDE DR	0	572L	SWH	77045
GRAND ESTATES DR	10700	368Z	NWC	77065
GRAND FALLS DR	1300	569Y	MC	77459
GRAND FALLS DR	2700	297X	NEH	77345
GRAND FIELD CT	21200	334M	NCC	77338
GRAND FIR TRAIL	0	326R	NWC	77433
GRAND FLORA CT	0	409S	NWC	77041
GRAND FLORAL BLVD	5600	448C	NWC	77041
GRAND FLORAL CT	5700	448C	NWC	77041
GRAND FOREST DR	5300	447B	NWC	77084
GRAND FORKS DR	22000	485H	SWC	77450
GRAND FOUNTAINS DR	0	532X	SWH	77054
GRAND GLEN CT	6100	525G	NEF	77494
GRAND HARBOR DR	0	484D	NEF	77494
GRAND HARBOUR DR	0	485U	NEF	77450
GRAND HAVEN DR	6400	411K	NWC	77088
GRAND HEIGHTS CT	14000	617D	SEH	77062
GRAND HILLS LN	3700	617S	SEC	77546
GRAND HOLLOW LN	21300	525H	NEF	77450
GRANDIN WOOD CT	21100	334R	NCC	77338
GRAND ISLE CT	9400	416Y	NEC	77044
GRAND JOUST DR	0	296X	NEH	77339
GRAND JUNCTION DR	900	485H	SWC	77450
GRAND KNOLLS DR	8400	527Q	NEF	77083
GRAND LAKE	5100	531K	SWH	77401
GRAND LAKE	5400	531K	SWH	77081
GRAND LAKE	5401	531K	BL	77401
GRAND LAKE	5522	531K	BL	77401
GRAND LAKEVIEW DR	3000	291Z	NWC	77388
GRAND LANCELOT DR	21800	296X	SEM	77339
GRAND LINDEN CT	21200	334M	NCC	77338
GRAND MANOR LN	14200	375Y	NEC	77396
GRAND MASTERPIECE CT	5600	448C	NWC	77041
GRAND MASTERPIECE LN	13400	448C	NWC	77041
GRAND MEADOW DR	7100	525E	NEF	77494
GRAND MEADOWS CT	1600	485K	NEF	77494
GRAND MEADOWS DR	23200	485K	NEF	77494
GRAND MESA DR	2100	337D	NEH	77345
GRANDMILL LN	2100	485P	NEF	77494
GRAND MISSION BLVD	0	526G	NEF	77407
GRAND MIST DR	0	525G	NEF	77494
GRAND MOUNTAIN CT	7900	407G	NWC	77095
GRAND NOBLE CIR	3000	331P	NWC	77068
GRAND NUGGET CT	14800	618E	SEH	77062
GRAND NUGGET LN	900	618E	SEH	77062
GRAND OAK CT	3800	609G	MC	77459
GRANDOAK DR	0	615Z	PL	77581
GRAND OAK PARK	0	447E	NWC	77084
GRAND OAKS BLVD	300	457W	NEC	77015
GRAND OAKS DR	500	497A	NEC	77015
GRAND OAKS DR	700	496H	NEH	77015
GRAND OAKS WIND	0	294E	SEM	77386
GRAND PARK DR	1100	570W	MC	77489
GRAND PASS LN	0	485X	NEF	77494
GRAND PEAK LN	0	409W	NWC	77041
GRAND PEBBLE LN	0	484U	NEF	77494
GRAND PHILLIPS LN	5000	485Y	NEF	77450
GRAND PINES DR	10600	528W	NEF	77498
GRAND PKWY	0	485K	NEF	77494
GRAND PKWY	0	525V	NEF	77407
GRAND PKWY	0	526W	NEF	77407
GRAND PLAINS DR	700	332X	NWC	77090
GRAND PLANTATION	0	609G	MC	77459
GRAND PLANTATION CT	2600	609G	MC	77459
GRAND PLAZA DR	800	372T	NWH	77067
GRAND POINT RD	15100	372B	NWC	77090
GRAND POINT RD	15200	332X	NWC	77090
GRAND PORTAGE LN	0	377J	NEC	77346
GRAND PRAIRIE DR	13700	415B	NEC	77396
GRAND PRAIRIE DR	14600	375T	NEH	77396
GRAND PRIX DR	3500	375R	NEC	77396
GRAND PROMENADE LN	0	569Q	SF	77477
GRAND PROMINENCE CT	0	525G	NEF	77494
GRAND RANCH LN	0	657K	FR	77546
GRAND RANCH LN	0	657K	FR	77546

Street Name	Block	Pg/Sq	Loc	Zips
GRAND RAPIDS LN	22900	333B	NCC	77373
GRAND RESERVE DR	0	485F	SWC	77494
GRANDRIDGE DR	7900	457F	NEC	77049
GRANDRIVER DR	8800	456E	NEH	77078
GRAND PRINCE LN	1400	332V	NCC	77073
GRAND SAGE DR	0	326U	NWC	77429
GRAND SAGE DR	0	326U	NWC	77429
GRAND SHORE LN	0	612K	PL	77545
GRAND SHORES CT	6100	525G	NEF	77494
GRAND SPRINGS DR	23300	485P	NEF	77494
W. GRAND STAR	0	525H	NEF	77450
S. GRAND STAR	0	525H	NEF	77450
N. GRAND STAR	0	525H	NEF	77450
E. GRAND STAR	0	525H	NEF	77450
GRAND SUMMIT CT	0	525G	NEF	77494
GRAND TERRACE CT	7400	407K	NWC	77095
GRAND TERRANE LN	0	445L	NWC	77449
GRAND TETON DR	2400	371L	NWC	77067
GRAND TETON TRAIL	12500	377B	NEC	77346
GRAND TRACE LN	0	485X	NEF	77494
GRAND TRAVERSE DR	0	328F	NWC	77377
GRANDVALE DR	6100	529G	SWH	77072
GRAND VALLEY CIR	17900	331M	NWC	77090
GRAND VALLEY DR	1400	331M	NWC	77090
GRANDVIEW	7900	533X	SEH	77051
GRANDVIEW PARK DR	9200	330N	NWC	77379
GRAND VIEW TERRACE	300	493J	SEH	77007
GRAND VILLA LN	8800	526Q	NEF	77407
GRANDVILLE	5400	455T	NEH	77028
GRAND VISTA LN	5100	525C	NEF	77494
GRAND VISTA LAKES DR	0	526L	NEF	77407
GRAND WEST BLVD	0	445Y	NWC	77449
GRAND WIMBLEDON DR	0	331N	NWC	77379
GRAND WINDS LN	2700	446R	NWC	77084
GRAND WINDS LN	2701	446R	NWC	77084
GRANDWOOD LN	0	525D	NEF	77450
GRANDY	14200	375W	NEC	77396
GRANGER	1300	494F	NEH	77020
GRANGER	8600	335S	NCC	77338
GRANGER BLUFF	0	406F	NWC	77433
GRANGER LAKE CT	1700	526W	NEF	77406
GRANGER OAKS CT	25500	485S	NEF	77494
GRANGER OAKS LN	0	485S	NEF	77494
GRANGER RIDGE LN	0	526F	NEF	77450
GRANIER MOUNTAIN DR	0	450K	NWH	77080
GRANITE	6300	451J	NWH	77092
GRANITE CT	2600	613S	NEB	77584
GRANITE BIRCH LN	0	366Y	NWC	77433
GRANITE BLUFF LN		524C	NEF	77494
GRANITE CREEK CT	21000	406T	NWC	77449
GRANITE FALLS CT	0	375Y	NEC	77396
GRANITE FALLS LN	0	609U	MC	77459
GRANITE GORGE DR	8600	330N	NWC	77379
GRANITE HAVEN LN	0	446N	NWH	77449
GRANITE ISLE CT	0	616H	SEC	77089
GRANITE KNOLL LN	26500	366R	NWC	77433
GRANITE LAKE CT	4900	609F	MC	77459
GRANITE LAKE DR	3000	609F	MC	77459
GRANITE MANOR LN	0	367P	NWC	77433
GRANITE MEADOW DR	0	524D	NEF	77494
GRANITE MOUNTAIN	0	457R	NEC	77049
GRANITE PARK CT	16300	367C	NWC	77429
GRANITE PARK WAY	0	375R	NEC	77396
GRANITE PATH PLACE	0	250Q	NWC	77389
GRANITE PEAK LN	0	526Q	NEF	77407
GRANITE RIDGE LN	7500	407L	NWC	77095
GRANITE RIVER LN	0	253J	SEM	77385
GRANITE ROCK LN	0	329B	NWC	77375
GRANITE SHADOW LN	0	297K	NEH	77365
GRANITE SHOALS CT	0	612M	PL	77584
GRANITE SHOALS CT	15000	328W	NWC	77429
GRANITE SHOALS DR	0	612L	PL	77584
GRANITE SPRINGS LN	3600	445H	NWC	77449
GRANITE TRAIL LN	0	525M	NEF	77407
GRANITE VALE RD	2900	447N	NWC	77084
GRANITE VALLEY LN	26800	366H	NWC	77433
GRANITEVILLE DR	0	455D	NEH	77078
GRANITE WOODS CT	12200	377A	NEC	77346
GRANNIS	9000	575M	SEH	77075
GRANT	200	538Y	DP	77536
GRANT	1800	493S	SWH	77006
GRANT	3000	537G	PA	77503
W. GRANT	4300	538Y	DP	77536
GRANT RD	9000	369F	NWC	77070
GRANT RD	11000	369F	NWC	77429
GRANT RD	11900	368D	NWC	77429
GRANT RD	12400	328J	NWC	77429
GRANT RD	15900	327L	NWC	77429
GRANT'S HARBOUR LN	0	658Z	LC	77573
GRANTCHESTER MEADOWS	0	413N	NCC	77037
GRANTHAM RD	100	501P	BT	77521
GRANTLEY DR	12100	528Z	SWH	77099
GRANT MEADOWS TRAIL	0	328J	NWC	77429
GRANT MILLS LN	10400	527Z	NEF	77498
GRANTMOOR LN	13200	571M	SWH	77045
GRANTON	6100	454Z	NEH	77026
GRANTS CREEK CT	0	338W	NEC	77346
GRANTS HARBOR LN	0	484T	NEF	77494
GRANTS HOLLOW LN	0	526F	NEF	77407
GRANTS LAKE BLVD	2500	568Y	SG	77479
GRANTS LAKE CIR	1	568Y	SG	77479
GRANTS MANOR CT	0	327U	NWC	77429
GRANTS RIDGE LN	0	328K	NWC	77377
GRANTS TRACE TRAIL	0	369G	NWC	77070
GRANTWOOD	5100	533H	SEH	77004
GRANUM DR	30100	252Z	SEM	77386
GRANVIA DR	7200	527M	SWC	77083
GRAN VILLA DR	0	407E	NWC	77433
GRANVILLE	100	501S	BT	77520
GRANVILLE DR	600	412Y	NWH	77091
GRAN VISTA DR	15100	527M	SWC	77083
GRAPE	5000	531P	SWH	77096
GRAPE	5800	530R	SWH	77074
GRAPE	8800	530N	SWH	77036
GRAPE	17000	418R	NEC	77044
GRAPE LN	2300	537X	PA	77502
GRAPE CREEK CIR	0	406D	NWC	77433
GRAPE CREEK GROVE LN	0	367W	NWC	77095
GRAPE ORCHARD CT	0	325R	NWC	77433
GRAPEVINE	3700	572N	SWH	77045
GRAPEVINE	5500	571Q	SWH	77085
GRAPEVINE CT	12000	569A	SF	77477
GRAPEVINE GALLEY DR	10200	366Z	NWC	77433
GRAPEVINE HILL LN	0	615G	PL	77581
GRAPEVINE LAKE CT	0	526W	NEF	77407
GRAPEVINE SHORE LN	0	367S	NWC	77433
GRAPEVINE SHORE LN	0	367S	NWC	77433
GRAPEVINE TRAIL	6800	527E	NEF	77407
GRAPEVINE WOOD LN	0	445L	NWC	77449
GRAPEWOOD CIR	11500	576Z	SEC	77089
GRAPEWOOD CT	11500	576Z	SEC	77089
GRAPEWOOD DR	11400	616D	SEC	77089
GRAPEWOOD DR	11700	576Z	SEC	77089
GRAPEWOOD TRAIL	2200	538V	DP	77536
GRAPHITE CANYON CT		526S	NEF	77407
GRAPPA DR	0	445F	NWC	77493
GRASILLA DR	0	571H	SWH	77045
GRASMERE DR	16100	367L	CY	77429
GRASS CREEK LN	0	615K	PL	77581
GRASSHOPPER CT	23500	295F	SEM	77365
GRASSHOPPER LN	100	488A	SWH	77079
GRASSINGTON DR	14900	497D	NEC	77530
GRASSINGTON DR	15100	498A	NEC	77530
GRASS LAKE LN	11301	524K	NWF	77406
GRASSLAND CIR	10400	369P	NWC	77070
GRASSLAND CT	1800	568Y	SG	77478
GRASSMERE	2900	573B	SEH	77051
GRASSMONT DR	700	498A	NEC	77530
GRASSNOOK DR	22400	289R	NWC	77375
GRASS PALM CT	0	618B	SEH	77059
GRASS SKIPPER LN	700	338M	NEH	77336
GRASS VALLEY	4400	451H	NWH	77018
GRASSY BRIAR LN	0	571K	SWH	77085
GRASSY COVE DR	10100	329T	NWC	77070
GRASSY CREEK DR	16100	527C	SWC	77082
GRASSY FIELDS CT	17900	373J	NWC	77060
GRASSY GLEN DR	11000	369Z	NWC	77064
GRASSY GROVE LN	0	526G	NEF	77407
GRASSY HAVEN LN	0	524E	NEF	77494
GRASSY HILL LN	21800	291P	NWC	77388
GRASSY KNOLL CT	2800	609A	SG	77478
GRASSY MEADOW DR	10800	369Y	NWC	77064
GRASSY SHORES LN	0	377L	NEC	77044
GRASSY VIEW DR	900	372D	NCC	77073
GRAUSTARK	3300	493S	SWH	77006
GRAUSTARK LN	22400	285F	SWM	77447
GRAVEN HILL DR	16300	330P	NWC	77379
GRAVENHURST LN	18100	328G	NWC	77377
GRAVESTONE LN	10000	616K	SEC	77089
W. GRAY	100	493N	SWH	77019
GRAY	100	493P	SWH	77002
GRAY	1200	460S	HG	77562
W. GRAY	1500	492R	SWH	77019
GRAY	1600	493U	SEH	77003
GRAY	2700	493V	SEH	77004
GRAY CT	1	493V	SEH	77004
GRAY BEAR CIR	14000	328T	NWC	77429
GRAYBILL CT	26900	324S	NWC	77447
GRAY BIRCH DR	1800	568X	SG	77479
GRAYCLIFF DR	5700	457S	NEC	77049
GRAYDEN DR	0	406B	NWC	77433
GRAY FALLS DR	2000	489S	SWH	77077
GRAYFEATHER CT	2500	291R	NWC	77388
GRAYFORD CT	0	373A	NCC	77073
GRAY FOREST TRAIL	11700	329N	NWC	77377
GRAY FOREST TRAIL CT	16000	329N	NWC	77377
GRAY FOX DR	24000	339N	NEH	77336
GRAY HAWK DR	2100	446T	NWC	77449
S. GRAY HERON CT	14800	325Q	NWC	77433
N. GRAY HERON CT	14900	325R	NWC	77433
GRAY JAY CT	0	410L	NWC	77040
GRAY JAY DR	0	410L	NWC	77040
GRAYLING LN	11300	371R	NWC	77067
GRAYMONT HILLS	0	330H	NWC	77379
GRAY MOSS CT	2700	609A	SG	77478
GRAY MOSS LN	1100	491B	NWH	77055
GRAY OAK CT	0	407J	NWC	77433
GRAY OAK PLACE	12100	251U	WD	77380
GRAY PEARL CT	0	325L	NWC	77433
GRAY RIDGE CT	0	527D	SWC	77082
GRAY RIDGE DR	15000	527D	SWC	77082
GRAY SLATE DR	1900	610B	MC	77489
GRAYSON	800	577P	SEH	77034
GRAYSON	2500	494J	NEH	77020
GRAYSON BEND DR	0	524E	NEF	77494
GRAYSON FALLS LN	24500	251W	NWC	77389
GRAYSON FIELD LN	0	657P	FR	77546
GRAYSON FIELD LN	0	657P	FR	77546
GRAYSON GARDENS DR	9800	527T	NEF	77407
GRAYSON LAKES	0	484P	NEF	77494
GRAYSON LAKES BLVD	1200	484K	NEF	77494
GRAYSON OAKS LN	0	297J	NEH	77365
GRAYSON OAKS PLACE	0	449U	NWH	77043
GRAYSON POINT LN	0	446N	NWC	77449
GRAYSON VALLEY LN	0	615M	PL	77089
GRAY SPORTS COMPLEX	0	501G	BT	77521
GRAYSTONE LN	5100	330Z	NWC	77069
GRAYSTONE BLUFF CT	6000	338E	NEH	77345
GRAYSTONE CREEK CT	1400	338E	NEH	77345
GRAYTON LN	13600	408U	NWC	77041
GRAYTON EDGE CT	0	377F	NEC	77346
GRAY WOLF	21000	378C	NEC	77532
GRAYWOOD CT	10900	579C	LP	77571
GRAYWOOD CT	11600	616C	SEC	77089
GRAYWOOD DR	11400	616D	SEC	77089
GRAYWOOD GROVE LN	14600	618E	SEH	77062
GREAT BASIN CT	11900	377E	NEC	77346
GREAT BLUFF LN	0	406P	NWC	77449
GREAT BRIDGE DR	10800	369S	NWC	77065
GREATBROOK LN	0	525H	NEF	77450
GREAT CREEK DR	0	612K	PL	77545
GREAT CREEK LN	21900	525C	NEF	77450
GREAT DOVER CIR	1300	458W	NEC	77530
GREAT EASTON LN	1400	332R	NCC	77073
GREAT ELMS CT	7000	406Q	NWC	77433
GREAT ELMS DR	19900	406Q	NWC	77433
GREAT FOREST	16300	376H	NEC	77346
GREAT FOREST CT	4000	376H	NEC	77346
GREAT GLEN DR	16000	407Z	NWC	77084
GREAT GLEN DR	17900	447C	NWC	77084
GREAT HAWK LN	10900	575Y	SEH	77075
GREAT HERON DR	0	250R	NWC	77389
GREAT HERON PLACE	0	250Q	NWC	77389
GREAT HERON PLACE	0	250Q	NWC	77389
GREAT HILL CT	6900	527F	NEF	77083
GREAT HORSE LN	0	610W	MC	77459
GREAT LAKE	20100	283Q	NWC	77484
GREAT LAKES AVE	2700	609E	SG	77479
GREAT LAUREL CT	1	251C	WD	77381
GREAT LAUREL CT	20700	337Q	NEC	77346
GREAT MEADOWS DR	0	445S	NWC	77493
GREAT OAK BLVD	11600	252H	SEM	77385
GREAT OAK LN	1300	568X	SG	77479
GREAT OAKS DR	2400	609B	MC	77459
GREAT OAKS DR	6100	415E	NEH	77050
GREAT OAKS BAY DR	0	527F	NEF	77083
GREAT OAKS GLEN DR	16500	527F	NEF	77083
GREAT OAKS HOLLOW DR	16700	527F	NEF	77083
GREAT OAKS SHADOW DR	0	527F	NEF	77083
GREAT PINES DR	0	406B	NWC	77433
GREAT PLAINS LN	10200	409C	NWC	77064
GREAT PRAIRIE LN	0	485K	NEF	77494
GREAT RIDGE CT	0	527F	NEF	77083
GREAT RIVER CT	10500	615D	SEC	77089
GREAT SALT DR	0	377M	NEH	77346
GREAT SANDS CT	0	377F	NEC	77346
GREAT SANDS DR	0	377F	NEC	77346
GREAT SPRINGS CT	0	485X	NEF	77494
GREAT TIMBERS LN	0	253P	SEM	77386
GREATWOOD DR	900	496F	NEH	77013
GRECIAN WAY	600	490G	PP	77024
GREELEY	3800	493S	SWH	77006
GREEN	0	288H	TB	77375
GREEN	0	448A	NWC	77084
GREEN	100	569R	MC	77489
GREEN	400	501U	BT	77520
GREEN	900	282U	WL	77484
GREEN	3000	494E	NEH	77020
GREEN	100	258Q	NEC	77357
GREEN	400	500V	BT	77520
GREEN LN	5300	371N	NWC	77066
GREEN RD	0	329K	NWC	77375
GREEN ACRES DR	14000	420K	NEC	77532
GREEN APPLE DR	3100	615K	PL	77581
GREEN ARBOR DR	10800	576P	SEH	77089
GREEN ASH DR	5700	531B	SWH	77081
GREEN ASH DR	6500	530C	SWH	77036
GREEN ASPEN LN	0	573Y	SEC	77047
GREENBANK LN	8200	408E	NWC	77095
GREEN BARK	22900	290E	NWC	77375
GREENBAY	11000	490K	BH	77024
GREENBAY CIR	1	490L	PP	77024
GREENBELT DR	300	488L	SWH	77079
GREEN BELT DR	500	568K	SG	77498
W. GREEN BELT DR	700	568K	SG	77498
E. GREEN BELT DR	800	568K	SG	77498
GREENBELT DR	800	488C	SWH	77079
GREENBEND	0	372T	NWH	77038
GREENBERRY DR	2500	336B	NEH	77339
GREENBERRY DR	2700	296X	NEH	77339
GREENBLADE DR	0	612J	PL	77545
GREEN BLADE DR	11400	367R	CY	77429
GREEN BLADE LN	1	251R	WD	77380
GREEN BLOSSOM TRAIL	0	326J	NWC	77433
GREEN BLUFF DR	12000	416L	NEC	77044
GREEN BLUFFS CT	0	337U	NEC	77346
GREEN BOUGH CT	1	251Z	WD	77380
GREENBOUGH DR	10400	569Q	SF	77477
GREENBOW LN	200	459H	NEC	77562
GREEN BOWER LN	1	251R	WD	77380
GREENBRAE LN	5200	485W	NEF	77494
GREENBRANCH DR	0	487Z	SWC	77082
GREEN BRANCH DR	3300	336Q	NEH	77338
GREENBRIAR	0	659F	LC	77573
GREENBRIAR	100	656G	FR	77546
GREENBRIAR	1400	537N	PA	77502
GREENBRIAR	2600	492Y	SWH	77098
GREENBRIAR	4500	532C	SWH	77005
GREENBRIAR	5700	532C	SWH	77030
GREENBRIAR	8000	532R	SWH	77054
GREENBRIAR DR	100	500J	BT	77520
GREENBRIAR DR	1700	568B	SG	77498
GREENBRIAR DR	3700	569K	SF	77477
GREENBRIAR DR	4000	610K	MC	77459
GREENBRIAR DR	13400	568B	SG	77498
GREENBRIAR COLONY DR	1600	373R	NCC	77032
GREENBRIAR PARK DR	17900	373J	NCC	77060
GREENBRIAR PLAZA DR	16600	373S	NEH	77060
GREENBRIAR POINT LN	16600	407C	NWC	77095
GREENBRIAR SPRINGS DR	3000	333P	NCC	77073
GREEN BRIDGE	0	485L	SWC	77494
GREENBROOK DR	21600	332M	NCC	77073
S. GREENBUD CT	1	251Z	WD	77380
N. GREENBUD CT	1	251Z	WD	77380
GREENBUSCH RD	1000	484M	NEF	77494
GREENBUSCH FARM RD	0	484M	NEF	77494
GREENBUSH	7900	532K	SWH	77025
GREEN BUSH PARK	0	484R	NEF	77494
GREEN BUTTE CT	12000	416M	NEC	77044
GREEN CANARY CIR	14900	325Q	NWC	77433
GREEN CANDLE DR	3400	331D	NWC	77388
GREENCANYON DR	11700	416K	NEC	77044
GREENCANYON DR	12200	416L	NEC	77044
GREENCAP LN	16300	324N	NWC	77447
GREENCAPE CT	9400	376W	NEC	77396
GREEN CASTLE CT	0	408A	NWC	77095
GREEN CASTLE WAY	8800	407D	NWC	77095
GREEN CEDAR DR	100	658P	LC	77573
GREEN CEDAR DR	8300	527Q	NEF	77083
GREENCHASE DR	12500	372R	NEH	77060
GREEN CHASE LN	19400	372D	NCC	77073
GREENCLIFF LN	0	526J	NEF	77407
GREEN COLLING PARK DR	0	572R	SWH	77047
GREEN CORAL DR	12000	416L	NEC	77044
GREEN COTTAGE LN	4600	569X	MC	77459
GREENCOURT DR	2000	570W	MC	77489
GREEN COURT DR	15700	618G	SEH	77062
GREEN COVE	400	490L	PP	77024
GREEN COVE DR	14000	420P	NEC	77532
GREEN COVE BEND LN	5300	449A	NWC	77041
GREENCRAIG DR	5600	571E	SWH	77035
GREEN CREEK CIR	11900	369Q	NWC	77070
GREEN CREEK DR	2800	610B	MC	77489
GREEN CREEK DR	9900	369P	NWC	77070
GREEN CREEK ISLE	11900	416M	NEC	77044
GREENCREEK MEADOWS LN	0	290T	NWC	77379
GREENCREST DR	2000	570W	MC	77489
GREEN CREST DR	2800	487Z	SWH	77082
GREEN CREST DR	3600	527D	SWC	77082
GREENCROFT	1100	458Y	CV	77530
GREENCROSS LN	25000	485J	NEF	77494
GREEN CYPRESS CT	18400	326Z	NWC	77429
GREEN CYPRESS LN	6300	407T	NWC	77449
GREENDALE DR	1300	610B	MC	77489
GREENDALE DR	15100	373T	NCC	77032
GREENDALE PARK LN	0	252R	SEM	77385
GREENDELL	100	459M	HG	77562
GREEN DEVON DR	7800	408E	NWC	77095
GREEN DOLPHIN	12800	456Z	NEH	77013
GREENDOWNS	7500	535N	SEH	77087
GREENE	0	659L	LC	77573
W. GREENE AVE	400	618Y	WB	77598
GREEN EDGE CT	4100	337F	NEH	77339
GREENEDGE DR	7800	410L	NWC	77040
GREEN ELM LN	17700	330M	NWC	77379
GREEN EMERALD CT	0	524G	NEF	77494
GREEN ESTATES CT	23700	293T	NCC	77373
GREEN FALLS DR	0	612R	PL	77584
GREEN FALLS DR	5800	411P	NWH	77088
GREEN FALLS DR	12000	612Q	PL	77584
GREEN FEATHER DR	16400	458S	NEC	77049
GREEN FERN CT	0	291R	NWC	77388
GREENFIELD	0	330R	NWC	77379
GREENFIELD	8700	410F	NWC	77064
GREENFIELD	26300	292Q	SP	77373
N. GREENFIELD DR	15700	330M	NWC	77379
GREEN FIELD PLACE	1	252N	WD	77380
GREEN FIELDS DR	3700	609E	SG	77479
GREENFIELD TRAIL	20700	337P	NEC	77346
GREEN FIR TRAIL	15300	325R	NWC	77433
GREENFORD GLEN DR	0	328E	NWC	77377
GREEN FOREST	6200	451B	NWH	77092
GREEN FOREST	23200	285B	SWM	77447
GREEN FOREST	23400	245X	SWM	77447
GREEN FOREST DR	200	332B	NWC	77388
GREEN FOREST LN	0	615U	PL	77581
GREEN FOREST LN	0	294U	SEM	77386
GREEN FOREST LN	0	294U	SEM	77386
GREEN FOREST BLUFF TRAIL	0	524A	NEF	77494
GREEN FOREST PASS	0	447G	NWC	77084
GREEN FOREST PASS	0	447G	NWC	77084
GREENFORK DR	10000	529R	SWH	77036
GREEN GABLE MANOR	6600	250Y	NWC	77389
GREEN GARDEN LN	2200	446U	NWC	77084
GREENGATE DR	21200	291R	NWC	77388
GREENGLADE CT	1	251J	WD	77381
GREEN GLADE DR	11400	529X	SWH	77099
GREEN GLADE DR	12200	528V	SWH	77099
GREENGLADE LN	2300	252Z	SEM	77386
GREEN GLEN	16000	373P	NCC	77032
GREENGLEN DR	11700	416K	NEC	77044
GREENGLEN DR	12500	416L	NEC	77044
GREENGRASS CT	1800	452S	NWH	77008
GREENGRASS DR	1300	452S	NWH	77008
GREEN GROVE RD	7000	459K	NEC	77049
GREENHAM CT	3200	291R	NWC	77388
GREENHAM DR	21300	291Q	NWC	77388
GREEN HAVEN DR	1	251J	WD	77381
GREENHAVEN DR	25800	251N	SWM	77380
GREENHAVEN LN	3000	451R	NWH	77092
GREENHAVEN LAKE LN	0	328S	NWC	77429
GREEN HAZEL CT	5300	447B	NWC	77084
GREEN HAZEL DR	18000	447B	NWC	77084
GREENHEAD	3200	444K	KT	77493
GREENHEATH CT	7200	250T	NWC	77389
GREENHEATH LN	5500	525D	NEF	77450
GREEN HEATHER LN	0	571K	SWH	77085
GREEN HERON DR		484P	NEF	77494
GREEN HILL DR	2100	373M	NEH	77032
GREENHILL RD	5400	614B	BK	77581
GREENHILL FOREST DR	5400	411L	NWC	77088
GREEN HILLS DR	0	488T	SWH	77077
GREEN HOLLOW CT	2700	610B	MC	77489
GREEN HOLLOW LN	8600	329M	NWC	77379
GREEN HOOD	6500	412W	NWH	77091
GREENHOUSE	0	486D	SWC	77094
GREENHOUSE RD	0	406Z	NWC	77449
GREENHOUSE RD	0	367A	CY	77429
GREENHOUSE RD	300	656N	NEB	77511
GREENHOUSE RD	2600	446M	NWC	77084
GREENHOUSE RD	5000	406V	NWC	77449
GREENHURST	6500	412W	NWH	77091
GREEN IMPERIAL LN	0	326Q	NWC	77429
GREENINGDON	1	251A	WD	77381
GREEN ISLAND DR	2500	373M	NEH	77032
GREEN ISLE AVE	0	660X	DI	77539
GREEN IVY CT	0	537H	PA	77530
GREEN IVY CT	13900	578X	SEH	77059
GREEN IVY TRAIL	0	298W	NEH	77345
GREEN JADE	3900	293M	SEM	77386
GREEN JEWEL DR	0	326J	NWC	77433
GREEN JUTE LEDGE DR	0	294E	SEM	77386
GREEN KNOLL DR	2100	371M	NWC	77067
GREEN KOLBE LN	0	450R	NEH	77080
GREENLAKE DR	2700	291Q	NWC	77388
GREENLAND CT	10300	569Q	SF	77477
GREENLAND DR	13500	569Q	SF	77477
GREENLAND OAK CT	23700	293U	NCC	77373
GREEN LAND WAY	18600	447J	NWC	77084
GREEN LAWN DR	7500	411P	NWH	77088
GREENLEAF	2600	493B	NWH	77009
GREENLEAF	8200	463S	CCO	77520
GREEN LEAF DR	0	295M	SEM	77365
GREENLEAF DR	4000	291K	NWC	77389
E. GREEN LEAF LN	3100	580Q	SA	77571
GREENLEAF LN	15100	618F	SEH	77062
GREENLEAF LAKE DR	8300	408E	NWC	77095
GREENLEAF LODGE LN	0	611W	FS	77545
GREEN LEAF MEADOWS	0	528Q	SWC	77083
GREENLEAF RIDGE CT	19000	326Y	NWC	77429
GREEN LEAF SPRING LN	24101	485A	NEF	77494
GREENLEE DR	14900	497D	NEC	77530
GREENLET CT	3000	293X	NCC	77373
GREENLOCH LN	11800	416K	NEC	77044
GREEN LODGE CIR	2800	293T	NCC	77373
GREENLODGE LN	0	328P	NWC	77429
GREENLOW DR	13500	372K	NWH	77067
GREENMANOR DR	16000	375N	NEH	77396
GREEN MANSIONS CT	1400	610B	MC	77489
GREEN MAPLE CT	0	527S	NEF	77407
GREEN MEADOW	9800	539T	LP	77571
GREEN MEADOW CT	0	657Z	LC	77573
GREEN MEADOW CT	2700	610B	MC	77489
GREEN MEADOW LN	700	412Y	NWH	77091
GREEN MEADOW RD	27700	288P	NWC	77377
GREEN MEADOWS	3600	577D	PA	77505
GREEN MEADOWS LN	0	444T	KT	77493
GREEN MEADOW WAY	0	293D	SEM	77386
GREENMESA DR	11700	416K	NEC	77044
GREENMESA DR	12300	416L	NEC	77044
GREEN MESA DR	18800	253A	SEM	77385
GREEN MILL CT	28400	293E	SEM	77386
GREEN MILLS DR	0	369H	NWC	77070
GREENMIST LN	0	485X	NEF	77494
GREENMONT DR	5900	451B	NWH	77092
GREENMOOR DR	0	249A	SWM	77354
GREEN MOSS CT	1400	610B	MC	77489
GREEN MOSS DR	24600	338L	NEH	77336
GREEN MOUNTAIN DR	0	612J	PL	77545
GREEN MOUNTAIN DR	16000	373M	NEH	77032
GREEN OAK DR	1200	373P	NCC	77032
GREEN OAK DR	1900	336B	NEH	77339
GREEN OAK DR	2700	296X	NEC	77339
GREEN OAK FALLS LN	13300	414B	NCC	77039
GREEN OAK MEADOW LN	17900	373J	NWC	77060
GREEN OAK PLACE	1500	336B	NEH	77339
GREEN OAKS	11500	490K	BH	77024
GREEN OAKS	22900	256V	SEM	77357
GREEN OAKS DR	300	657R	LC	77573
GREEN OAKS DR	16100	373R	NEH	77032
GREEN OAKS LN	0	447E	NWC	77084
GREEN OAK TERRACE CT	1400	336B	NEH	77339
GREEN OASIS CT	19600	406Y	NWC	77449
GREEN ORCHARD DR	0	371K	NWC	77066
GREENOUGH DR	24800	484G	NEF	77494
GREEN PALMETTO LN	0	613R	PL	77584
GREEN PARK DR	200	488C	SWH	77079
S. GREENPARK DR	3200	488Y	SWH	77082

Street Name	Block	Pg/Sq	Loc	Zips
S. GREENPARK DR	6100	528C	SWH	77072
GREENPARK MANOR LN	6200	571K	SWH	77085
GREEN PEAK LN	0	407A	NWC	77433
GREEN PEAR LN	6500	457Q	NEC	77049
GREEN PINE	1600	296X	NEC	77339
GREEN PINE	2800	296X	NEC	77339
GREEN PINES CIR	11900	371N	NWC	77066
GREEN PINES DR	5300	371N	NWC	77066
GREEN PINES DR	5600	370R	NWC	77066
GREEN PINES DR	21800	256Z	SEM	77357
GREEN PINES FOREST	800	372K	NWH	77067
GREEN PLAZA DR	11400	372U	NWH	77038
GREEN PLUM LN	16101	324S	NWC	77447
GREEN POINT CT	400	490L	PP	77024
GREENPORT LN	0	407V	NWC	77084
S. GREENPRINT CIR	0	249M	NWC	77375
S. GREENPRINT CIR	0	250J	NWC	77375
N. GREENPRINT CIR	0	250J	NWC	77375
GREEN QUAIL DR	16800	610F	SWH	77489
GREEN RANCH DR	13600	414A	NCC	77039
GREEN RAY DR	8900	407D	NWC	77095
GREENRICH DR	0	373J	NCC	77060
GREENRIDGE CIR	100	658J	LC	77573
GREENRIDGE DR	2700	491S	SWH	77057
GREENRIDGE DR	3100	609D	MC	77459
W. GREENRIDGE DR	3300	491W	SWH	77057
E. GREENRIDGE DR	3300	491W	SWH	77057
GREENRIDGE DR	13600	568B	SG	77498
GREENRIDGE FOREST CT	1	251F	WD	77381
GREENRIDGE FOREST DR	1	251F	WD	77381
S. GREEN RIDGE TRAIL	0	325R	NWC	77433
N. GREEN RIDGE TRAIL	0	325R	NWC	77433
GREEN RIPPLE	0	325L	NWC	77433
E. GREEN RIPPLE CIR	0	326J	NWC	77433
GREEN RIVER DR	7800	455K	NEH	77028
N. GREEN RIVER DR	8500	455G	NEH	77028
N. GREEN RIVER DR	8800	456E	NEH	77078
GREEN RIVER DR	11700	456G	NEC	77044
GREENRIVER VALLEY DR	4900	297P	NEH	77345
GREENROCK LN	11900	416L	NEC	77044
GREEN ROCK RD	2200	373M	NEH	77032
GREENRUSH DR	22900	485L	NEF	77494
W. GREENS	0	370Q	NWC	77066
GREENS CT	11400	371R	NWC	77067
W. GREENS RD	0	372P	NWH	77067
W. GREENS RD	100	372N	NWC	77067
GREENS RD	100	372R	NEH	77060
GREENS RD	1200	373P	NCC	77032
GREENS RD	2400	374Q	NEH	77032
W. GREENS RD	3100	371N	NWC	77066
GREENS RD	5800	375N	NEH	77396
W. GREENS RD	7200	370K	NWH	77064
GREENS RD	9600	376N	NEC	77396
GREEN SAGE DR	0	370U	NWC	77086
GREENS BAYOU	12400	496G	NEH	77015
GREENSBORO DR	2500	533F	SWH	77021
GREENSBROOK FOREST DR.	11700	416K	NEC	77044
GREENSBROOK GARDEN DR	11800	416Q	NEC	77044
GREENS COURT WAY	4400	337F	NEH	77339
GREENS COVE WAY	15400	618B	SEH	77059
GREENS CROSSING BLVD	10400	412C	NWC	77038
GREENS CROSSING BLVD	10900	372U	NWH	77067
GREENS EDGE DR	1	337G	NEH	77339
GREENSFORD CT	2000	458S	NEC	77049
GREEN SHADE DR	16200	332T	NWC	77090
GREEN SHADOW DR	1400	373P	NCC	77032
GREEN SHADOW DR	3700	537M	PA	77503
GREENSHIRE	0	573R	SEH	77048
GREENSHIRE DR	0	573M	SEH	77048
GREENSHIRE DR	100	659H	LC	77573
GREENSHIRE DR	11500	573M	SEH	77048
GREEN SHOALS LN	6300	370L	NWC	77066
GREEN SHORE DR	0	377P	NEC	77044
GREENSHORES LN	0	526J	NEF	77407
GREENSIDE DR	13800	528P	SWC	77083
GREENSIDE CIR E	0	337U	NEC	77346
GREENSIDE CIR N	0	337U	NEC	77346
GREENSIDE CIR W	0	337T	NEC	77346
GREENSIDE HILL LN	19700	406Y	NWC	77449
GREENS LANDING DR	100	372Y	NWH	77038
GREEN SLOPE PLACE	1	250D	WD	77381
GREENS MANOR LN	12900	456D	NEC	77044
GREENSMARK DR	1400	372N	NWC	77067
GREEN SMOKE DR	16200	407D	NWC	77095
GREENSPARK LN	11800	416L	NEC	77044
GREENS PKWY	500	372P	NWH	77067
GREENSPOINT DR	12000	372R	NEH	77060
GREENSPOINT PARK DR	16700	372R	NEH	77060
GREEN SPRING CT	1000	569T	MC	77459
GREEN SPRINGS DR	5100	371A	NWC	77066
GREEN SPRINGS DR	5700	370H	NWC	77066
GREEN SPRINGS LN	0	447E	NWC	77084
GREEN SPUR	16100	373M	NEH	77032
GREEN SQUARE CT	22700	292L	SP	77373
GREEN STAR CT	1800	570W	MC	77489
GREEN STAR DR	1800	570W	MC	77489
GREEN STAR LN	0	327U	NWC	77429
GREEN STEM PATH	0	484Z	NEF	77494
GREENSTILL DR	4400	336Z	NEC	77346
GREENSTILL DR	4700	337W	NEC	77346
GREENSTOCK	1	259S	NEC	77336
GREENSTONE	7400	535N	SEH	77087
GREEN STONE CT	400	486D	SWC	77094
GREEN STONE CT	6700	408P	NWC	77084
GREEN STONE DR	15000	408P	NWC	77084
GREENSTONE PARK LN	11000	616A	SEC	77089
GREEN SUMMER LN	0	334P	NCC	77373
GREEN SUMMER LN	0	334Q	NCC	77373
GREENSWARD	17800	418R	NEC	77044
GREENSWARD RD	9300	450U	NWH	77080
GREENSWARTH LN	7400	575S	SEH	77075
GREEN TAVERN CT	15100	328W	NWC	77429
GREEN TEAL LN	13500	414B	NCC	77039
GREEN TEE DR	2000	615R	PL	77581
GREEN TEE DR	2900	616J	PL	77581
GREEN TEE DR	4400	501J	BT	77521
GREEN TEE LN	3800	258B	SEM	77357
GREEN TERRACE LN	5800	411T	NWH	77088
GREEN THICKET CT	21500	292N	NWC	77375
GREEN THICKET DR	0	612N	PL	77545
GREENTHREAD DR	0	659G	LC	77573
GREEN TIMBERS DR	5100	337S	NEC	77346
GREEN TOP CT	5800	407X	NWC	77084
GREEN TRAIL CT	0	537H	PA	77530
GREEN TRAIL DR	1100	372W	NWC	77038
GREEN TRAIL DR	4600	448A	NWC	77084
GREEN TRAIL CROSSING DR	0	612P	PL	77584
GREEN TRAILS DR	1900	569E	SF	77477
GREEN TREE	25800	248J	SWM	77354
GREEN TREE CT	3000	609H	MC	77459
GREEN TREE CT	4300	578F	PA	77505
GREEN TREE DR	5500	609S	NEF	77479
GREEN TREE DR	16100	373M	NEH	77032
GREEN TREE LN	0	288C	TB	77375
GREEN TREE RD	5000	491L	SWH	77056
GREEN TREE RD	5900	491K	SWH	77057
GREEN TREE RD	10000	489M	SWH	77042
GREEN TREE PARK LN	0	493J	SEH	77007
GREEN TURTLE DR	0	578A	PA	77505
GREENVALE	11300	490L	PP	77024
GREENVALE LN	6300	370Q	NWC	77066
GREEN VALLEY DR	1100	490D	SV	77055
GREEN VALLEY DR	2200	373R	NEH	77032
GREEN VALLEY DR	2200	538V	DP	77536
GREEN VALLEY DR	2600	539S	DP	77536
GREEN VALLEY DR	8600	490D	SV	77055
GREEN VALLEY LN	9800	409C	NWC	77064
GREENVALLEY TRAIL DR	2900	446T	NWC	77449
GREEN VELVET TRAIL	0	326J	NWC	77433
GREENVIEW DR	0	325R	NWC	77433
GREENVIEW DR	16000	373M	NEH	77032
GREENVIEW GLEN DR		367N	NWC	77433
GREEN VILLA	0	660Z	TC	77539
GREEN VILLAGE DR	3300	296Z	NEH	77339
GREENVILLE	6900	494H	NEH	77020
GREENVILLE	7200	495E	NEH	77020
GREENVILLE	13700	497F	NEC	77015
GREENVILLE DR	2600	659C	LC	77573
GREENVINE CIR	0	484E	NEF	77494
GREEN VISTA	2900	331P	NWC	77068
GREENWADE CIR	20300	446X	NWC	77449
GREENWATER DR	10400	368Z	NWC	77065
GREENWAY CT	3600	535P	SEH	77087
GREENWAY DR	1700	458U	CV	77530
GREENWAY DR	3600	501L	BT	77521
GREENWAY DR	13400	568B	SG	77498
GREENWAY CHASE	6800	528L	SWH	77072
GREENWAY CHASE CT	12900	528L	SWH	77072
GREENWAY FOREST LN	6100	411P	NWC	77088
GREENWAY MANOR LN	5900	334E	NCC	77373
GREENWAY PARK CIR	0	485L	NEF	77450
GREENWAY PLAZA DR	1	492X	SWH	77046
GREENWAY PLAZA EAST	0	492X	SWH	77046
GREENWAY VIEW TRAIL	1	337F	NEH	77339
GREENWAY VILLAGE CIR	23200	485L	NEF	77494
GREENWAY VILLAGE CT	23200	485Q	NEF	77494
GREENWAY VILLAGE DR	1400	485Q	NEF	77494
GREENWELL DR	0	372B	NWC	77014
GREENWELL SPRINGS LN	0	524B	NEF	77494
GREENWEST DR	1800	570X	MC	77489
GREEN WHISPER DR	0	325V	NWC	77433
GREENWICH	9500	455B	NEH	77078
GREENWICH PLACE	0	492R	SWH	77019
GREENWICH TERRACE DR	1900	492R	SWH	77019
GREENWICHWOOD LN	1400	332V	NCC	77073
N. GREENWICH CT	12800	571K	SWH	77085
GREENWICK LN	6200	571K	SWH	77085
N. GREENWICK LOOP	6200	571K	SWH	77085
S. GREENWICK LOOP	6300	571K	SWH	77085
W. GREENWICK LOOP	12800	571K	SWH	77085
E. GREENWICK LOOP	12800	571K	SWH	77085
GREENWILLOW CT	0	531R	SWH	77096
GREENWILLOW DR	9000	531V	SWH	77096
GREENWILLOW DR	10000	571D	SWH	77035
GREEN WILLOW FALLS DR	0	289W	NWC	77375
GREENWIND CHASE DR	19300	486L	SWC	77094
GREENWOOD	1	494U	SEH	77011
GREENWOOD	1300	502W	BT	77520
W. GREENWOOD	4200	542G	CCO	77520
GREENWOOD DR	0	614Z	PL	77584
N. GREENWOOD DR	300	494Q	SEH	77011
GREENWOOD DR	3400	569W	SG	77478
GREENWOOD LN	0	571V	SWH	77053
GREENWOOD S. LN	13701	417B	NEC	77044
GREENWOOD COLONY CT	0	578U	SEH	77059
GREENWOOD ESTATES DR	12000	370H	NWC	77066
GREENWOOD FOREST DR	12000	370D	NWC	77066
GREENWOOD FOREST DR	12700	371E	NWC	77066
GREENWOOD GLEN DR	3000	297Y	NEH	77345
GREENWOOD LAKES LN	13200	417B	NEC	77044
GREENWOOD MANOR DR	13400	367G	NWC	77429
GREENWOOD OAKS DR	1900	618B	SEH	77062
GREENWOOD PINES DR	16000	618G	SEH	77062
GREENWOOD PLACE	3300	538S	DP	77536
GREENWOOD POINT DR	7000	406R	NWC	77433
GREENWOOD SPRINGS PLACE	0	405T	NWC	77493
GREENWOOD TRACE LN	4400	484Y	NEF	77494
GREENWOOD VALLEY PLACE	0	405R	NWC	77493
GREENYARD DR	6600	371T	NWC	77086
GREGDALE RD	6900	456L	NEC	77049
GREGG	100	494J	NEH	77020
GREGG	1937	494A	NEH	77026
GREGORY	4300	454X	NEH	77026
GREGORY BLVD	14800	570L	MC	77071
GREGORY CT	800	569T	NEF	77477
GREGORY CROSSING WAY	0	372J	NWC	77076
GREGSON RD	11400	329J	NWC	77377
GREGSON RD	11700	328M	NWC	77377
GREGS WAY	700	338M	NEH	77336
GREGWAY LN	2700	609B	MC	77459
GREGWOOD CT	4300	485Y	NEF	77450
GREIG AVE	10200	577T	SEH	77034
GREINER DR	8600	450L	NWH	77080
GREN	4900	534N	SEH	77021
GRENADA LN	0	333R	NCC	77338
GRENADA LN	18800	619W	NB	77058
GRENADA FALLS DR	0	407D	NWC	77095
GRENADIER DR	9700	576W	SEH	77089
W. GRENFELL LN	100	412Z	NEH	77076
W. GRENFELL LN	200	413W	NEH	77076
GRENFELL LN	600	413Y	NEH	77076
GRENNOCH LN	3300	532J	SWH	77025
GRENOBLE LN	20700	526A	NEF	77450
GRENSHAW	800	412Q	NWH	77088
GRESAK	3200	251X	SWM	77380
GRESHAM	1	501T	BT	77520
GRESS	10000	370Z	NWC	77086
GRESSET LN	0	296T	SEM	77365
GRETEL DR	400	489G	SWH	77024
GRETNA GREEN DR	4800	447D	NWC	77084
GRETNA GREEN DR	5100	407Z	NWC	77084
GREY BLOOM AVE	0	286Q	NWC	77377
GREY BOULDER DR	0	408N	NWC	77084
GREYBURN LN	2200	450P	NWH	77080
GREYFIELD LN	0	573T	SEC	77047
GREY FINCH CT	1	251B	WD	77381
GREY FOX DR	24100	339N	NEH	77336
GREYFRIAR DR	100	413N	NCC	77037
GREYHAWK CT	21000	525R	NEF	77407
GREY HOLLOW LN	13000	328W	NWC	77429
GREY KIRBY DR	0	658X	LC	77573
GREYLAKE PLACE	0	249B	SWM	77382
GREYLOG DR	5200	574E	SEH	77048
GREY MILLS DR	9400	369H	NWC	77070
GREY MIST CT	3000	657C	SEC	77546
GREY MIST DR	17100	617Y	SEC	77546
GREY MIST DR	17300	657C	SEC	77546
GREYMOSS LN	20600	333P	NCC	77073
GREY OAKS DR	6100	415E	NEH	77050
GREY PEBBLE LN	0	406D	NWC	77433
GREY PEREGINE DR	0	484P	NWF	77494
GREYROCK DR	0	328A	NWC	77429
GREYS LN	0	408G	NWC	77095
GREY SPARROW DR		484P	NEF	77494
GREY SPRINGS CT	0	326V	NWC	77429
GREYSTONE DR	700	498A	CV	77530
GREYSTONE LN	21700	255U	SEM	77365
GREY SWAN DR		484P	NEF	77494
GREYTIP CT	0	445R	NWC	77449
GREY WILLOW TRAIL	0	488T	SWH	77077
GREYWOOD DR	13400	568F	SG	77498
GRGICH HILL DR	0	484J	NEF	77494
GRIFFIN	900	536M	PA	77506
GRIFFIN	1100	453V	NEH	77009
GRIFFIN	1100	541B	BT	77520
GRIFFIN LN	2800	444Q	KT	77493
GRIFFIN HOUSE LN	23800	445T	NWC	77493
GRIFFIN WILLOW RD	14500	570V	SWH	77489
GRIGGS CT	2500	613Q	NEB	77584
GRIGGS RD	3500	533G	SEH	77021
GRIGGS RD	4600	534J	SEH	77021
GRIGGS RD	5900	534H	SEH	77023
GRIGGS RD	6800	535A	SEH	77023
GRIGGS POINT LN	15300	527U	NEF	77498
GRIGIO PINES DR	0	445B	NWC	77493
GRIGSBY	2600	494A	NEH	77026
GRIMALDI ST	0	524M	NEF	77406
GRIMES	0	323D	NWC	77484
GRIMES	4000	534L	SEH	77087
GRIMES	27000	324E	HK	77447
GRIMES AVE	0	612V	PL	77584
GRIMES AVE	0	613S	PL	77584
GRINNELL	0	453T	NWH	77009
GRISBEE RD	14000	408Q	NWC	77095
GRISBY RD	0	487B	SWC	77094
GRISBY RD	13800	488B	SWH	77079
GRISBY RD	14800	487D	SWH	77094
GRISSOM RD	2700	658E	LC	77598
GRISSOM RD	2800	657M	LC	77598
GRISSOM RD	4400	657L	LC	77598
GRIST MILL LN	0	617Y	SEC	77546
GRISWOLD	0	247V	SWM	77355
GROGANS MILL RD	9000	251Q	WD	77380
GROGANS PARK DR	1	251V	WD	77380
GROGANS POINT CT	1	251T	WD	77380
GROGANS POINT RD	1	251Y	WD	77380
GROLLWOOD	800	498B	CV	77530
GROMMET CT	16500	419A	NEC	77532
GROMWELL DR	22000	245V	SWM	77355
GROSBEAK DR	6200	574F	SEH	77048
GROSBEAK LN	18900	286G	NWC	77377
GROSCHKE RD	16100	448N	NWH	77084
GROSCHKE RD	17100	447Q	NWH	77084
GROSCHKE RD	18000	447P	NWH	77084
GROSS	1000	492R	SWH	77019
GROSSMOUNT DR	12300	371E	NWC	77066
GROSVENOR	13700	617A	SEH	77034
GROSVENOR SQUARE	5500	330Y	NWC	77069
GROS VENTRE LN	0	408G	NWC	77095
GROTA	100	493C	NEH	77009
GROTHE LN	100	453G	NEH	77009
GROTON DR	3000	573F	SEH	77051
GROTON DR	3800	573G	SEH	77047
GROTTO POINT DR	0	327S	NWC	77429
GROUND BRIER CT	1	251J	WD	77381
GROUSE CT	5000	447D	NWC	77084
GROUSE MOOR DR	16700	447D	NWC	77084
GROVE	1	494J	NEH	77020
GROVE	100	580G	LP	77571
GROVE	100	620T	CS	77565
GROVE	800	538L	DP	77536
GROVE CT	0	454Y	NEH	77026
GROVE ARBOR LN	0	370A	NWH	77070
GROVE BRIAR LN	21100	525M	NEF	77407
GROVE BROOK LN	18200	326V	NWC	77429
GROVE BROOK LN	0	326V	NWC	77429
GROVE CANYON CT	0	457G	NEC	77049
GROVE COURT DR	1800	570X	MC	77489
GROVE CREEK DR	17600	329M	NWC	77379
GROVECREST	6600	451A	NWH	77092
GROVEDALE DR	20900	332V	NCC	77073
GROVE ESTATES LN	14200	366D	NWC	77429
GROVE FIELD LN	6600	408T	NWC	77084
GROVE GARDENS DR	15000	527D	SWC	77082
GROVE GLEN DR	10100	529S	SWH	77099
GROVE HAVEN DR	9200	527Q	NEF	77083
GROVEHILL	6500	451A	NWH	77092
GROVE HOLLOW CT	12500	368Z	NWC	77065
GROVE KNOLL DR	0	327X	NWC	77429
GROVE LAKE DR	1900	336G	NEH	77339
GROVELAND LN	3200	492Q	SWH	77019
GROVELAND HILLS DR	0	406H	NWC	77433
GROVELEIGH LN	0	368N	NWC	77429
GROVELEIGH PARK CT	0	253N	SEM	77386
GROVE MANOR DR	2700	297Z	NEH	77345
GROVE MEADOW DR	12300	569E	SF	77477
GROVEMILL DR	12900	572F	SWH	77045
GROVEMIST LN	14100	488W	SWH	77082
GROVEN	3000	451R	NWH	77092
GROVE OAKS DR	3500	297N	NEH	77339
GROVE PARK	32100	322F	WCO	77484
GROVE PARK CT	31900	253J	SEM	77385
GROVE PARK DR	0	658N	LC	77573
GROVE PARK DR	8500	408E	NWC	77095
GROVE PARK DR	12600	570J	MC	77489
GROVE POINT	12200	370M	NWC	77066
GROVER	10000	410W	NWH	77041
GROVE RIDGE DR	7800	535S	SEH	77061
GROVESHIRE CT	3100	569N	SG	77478
GROVESHIRE DR	700	497D	NEC	77530
GROVESIDE DR	13900	414A	NCC	77039
GROVESNOR	0	614Y	PL	77584
GROVESNOR CT	0	614Y	PL	77584
GROVESPRING DR	15500	331S	NWC	77068
GROVE SQUARE CT	0	446B	NWC	77449
GROVE STONE CT	12000	568H	SF	77498
GROVE TERRACE DR	3000	297X	NEH	77345
GROVETON	4900	573H	SEH	77033
GROVETON	5100	574E	SEH	77033
GROVETON CT	0	484T	NEF	77494
GROVETON LN	5000	614Q	PL	77584
GROVETON PARK DR	0	251D	SD	77380
GROVETON PARK DR	0	251D	SD	77381
GROVETON RIDGE LN	400	486D	SWC	77094
GROVE VALLEY TRAIL	19000	446R	NWC	77084
GROVE VIEW TRAIL	0	611S	FS	77545
GROVEWAY DR	4500	534L	SEH	77087
GROVEWAY DR	19100	255U	SEM	77365
GROVE WEST BLVD	4900	568H	SF	77477
GROVEWOOD CT	7700	614E	NEB	77581
GROVEWOOD LN	1000	452X	NWH	77008
GROVEWOOD PARK	2100	252R	SEM	77385
GROVEY	3000	494B	NEH	77026
GROW LN	7800	450C	NWH	77040
GRUENWALD AVE	400	620P	SB	77586
GRUMBACH	5600	494C	NEH	77020
GRUMMAN CASTLE LN	0	244M	WCO	77447
GRUNEWALD DR	2000	537X	PA	77502
GRUSS DR	100	372Q	NCC	77060
GTE	0	461Q	NEC	77521
GUADALAJARA	0	569Z	NEF	77477
GUADALCANNAL RD	7300	533V	SEH	77033
GUADALUPE	0	415N	NEH	77016
GUADALUPE	1200	569Z	NEF	77477
GUADALUPE	5500	414R	NEH	77016
GUADALUPE	5700	660X	DI	77539
GUADALUPE RIVER BLVD	0	253U	SEM	77386
GUADALUPE RIVER DR	11800	371L	NWC	77067
GUADALUPE SPRINGS LN	15400	328S	NWC	77429
GUADALUPE TRAIL CT	17400	376H	NEC	77346
GUADALUPE TRAIL LN	12000	376H	NEC	77346
GUANG MING WAY	0	248H	SWM	77354
GUARDSMAN LN	22500	445Q	NWC	77449
GUBBIO LN	0	659Q	LC	77573
GUENTHER	100	568N	SG	77478
GUERNSEY DR	11700	328R	NWC	77377
GUESE RD	1300	452X	NWH	77008
GUESE RD	3000	452P	NWH	77018
GUESSENA	4200	456W	NEH	77013
GUEST	9400	455C	NEH	77028
GUEST	9600	455C	NEH	77078
GUHN RD	5400	450C	NWH	77040
GUHN RD	6200	410Y	NWH	77040
GUILBEAU LN	2400	620J	SB	77586
GUILDED MEADOW LN	0	377F	NEC	77346
GUILDWICK CIR	20400	335Q	HM	77338
GUILFORD CT	5000	491U	SWH	77056
GUILFORD RD	7300	530L	SWH	77074
GUILFORD GLEN LN	0	524H	NEF	77494
GUILLEN LN	800	569P	SF	77477
GUINEA DR	1100	491A	HI	77055
GUINESS CT	9000	408A	NWC	77095
GUINEVERE	8400	495L	NEH	77029
GUINN	16600	418Q	NEC	77044
GUINN HILL RD	19400	295G	SEM	77365
GUINSTEAD DR	15800	330S	NWC	77379
GUITON	4800	491Z	SWH	77027
GULDAN DR		525M	NEF	77407
GULF	0	501W	BT	77520
W. GULF	1	501Y	BT	77520
E. GULF	1	501Y	BT	77520
E. GULF	500	541D	BT	77520
GULF	1100	536T	PA	77502
GULF	3600	535P	SEH	77017
GULF	4000	535T	SEH	77087
GULF (I.H. 45 S) FRWY	100	658B	LC	77573
GULF (I.H. 45 S) FRWY	100	658B	LC	77573
GULF (I.H. 45 S) FRWY	2400	493Q	SEH	77003
GULF (I.H. 45 S) FRWY	2400	493Q	SEH	77003
GULF (I.H. 45 S) FRWY	2600	493V	SEH	77004
GULF (I.H. 45 S) FRWY	2600	493V	SEH	77004
GULF (I.H. 45 S) FRWY	2601	493V	SEH	77003
GULF (I.H. 45 S) FRWY	2601	493V	SEH	77003
GULF (I.H. 45 S) FRWY	3400	494W	SEH	77004
GULF (I.H. 45 S) FRWY	3400	494W	SEH	77004
GULF (I.H. 45 S) FRWY	4100	494W	SEH	77004
GULF (I.H. 45 S) FRWY	4100	494W	SEH	77004
GULF (I.H. 45 S) FRWY	4101	494W	SEH	77023
GULF (I.H. 45 S) FRWY	4101	494W	SEH	77023
GULF (I.H. 45 S) FRWY	4300	534H	SEH	77023
GULF (I.H. 45 S) FRWY	4300	534H	SEH	77023
GULF (I.H. 45 S) FRWY	6600	534H	SEH	77087
GULF (I.H. 45 S) FRWY	6600	534H	SEH	77087
GULF (I.H. 45 S) FRWY	7200	535Y	SEH	77017
GULF (I.H. 45 S) FRWY	7200	535Y	SEH	77017
GULF (I.H. 45 S) FRWY	9000	575D	SEH	77017
GULF (I.H. 45 S) FRWY	9000	575D	SEH	77017
GULF (I.H. 45 S) FRWY	9800	576U	SEH	77034
GULF (I.H. 45 S) FRWY	9800	576U	SEH	77034
GULF (I.H. 45 S) FRWY	15600	617F	SEH	77546
GULF (I.H. 45 S) FRWY	15600	617F	SEH	77546
GULF (I.H. 45 S) FRWY	15601	617F	SEH	77598
GULF (I.H. 45 S) FRWY	15601	617F	SEH	77598
GULF (I.H. 45 S) FRWY	19700	618W	WB	77598
GULF (I.H. 45 S) FRWY	19700	618W	WB	77598
GULF (I.H. 45 S) FRWY	20000	658B	WB	77598
GULF (I.H. 45 S) FRWY	20000	658B	WB	77598
GULF PINES DR	100	332K	NWC	77090
GULF BANK	0	411N	NWH	77088
W. GULF BANK RD	100	412L	NCC	77037
W. GULF BANK RD	100	413K	NCC	77037
W. GULF BANK RD	700	411Q	NWH	77088
W. GULF BANK RD	7000	410Q	NWC	77040
W. GULF BANK RD	10000	409R	NWC	77040
GULF BREEZE DR	15400	617B	SEH	77598
GULFBRIAR PLACE	7500	570Z	SWH	77489
GULF BRIDGE	9400	575V	SEH	77075
GULF BRIDGE CIR	10900	575V	SEH	77075
GULF BRIDGE CT	10900	575V	SEH	77075
GULFBROOK DR	0	617V	SEH	77546
GULF CENTRAL DR	2100	534B	SEH	77023
GULF COMPRESS RD	0	496W	GP	77547
GULF CREEK DR	2700	535J	SEH	77012
GULFCREST	4600	534A	SEH	77023
GULF CYPRESS LN	0	325K	NWC	77447
GULFDALE DR	10900	575T	SEH	77075
GULFGATE MALL	1	535J	SEH	77087
GULF HILL LN	2000	541E	BT	77520
GULF ISLE CT	7900	407F	NWC	77095
GULFLOW	2600	534H	SEH	77087
GULF MEADOWS DR	10200	575T	SEH	77075
GULF MOUNTAIN DR	0	450C	NWH	77091
GULFPALMS ST	9900	576Q	SEH	77034
GULF POINTE DR	11800	576U	SEH	77089
GULF PUMP RD	100	419S	NEC	77532
GULFSHADOW DR	0	328A	NWC	77429
GULF SHORE LN	0	525M	NEF	77407
GULF SPRING LN	8200	575T	SEH	77075
GULFSTREAM CT	13900	528W	NEF	77498
GULFSTREAM LN	10200	528W	NEF	77498
GULFSTREAM PARK	12100	617B	SEH	77598
GULF TERMINAL DR	2100	534B	SEH	77023
GULFTON	5100	531B	SWH	77081
GULFTON	7600	530B	SWH	77036
GULFTON DR	1100	616X	PL	77581
GULF TREE LN	8200	575X	SEH	77075
GULF VALLEY	10900	575T	SEH	77075
GULFWAY DR	4600	502G	BT	77521

Street Name	Block	Pg/Sq	Loc	Zips
GULFWIND CT	19800	486G	SWC	77094
GULFWIND DR	19700	486G	SWC	77094
GULF WOOD LN	8200	575T	SEH	77075
GULICK LN	8000	575P	SEH	77075
GULL CT	16600	419C	NEC	77532
GULL ROCK PLACE	0	250Q	NWC	77389
N. GULLS CUT	0	542J	BT	77520
S. GULLS CUT	100	542J	BT	77520
GULLWOOD DR	11400	616C	SEC	77089
GUM	0	660Y	DI	77539
GUM	5200	419H	CB	77532
GUM DR	4100	660Y	DI	77539
GUMAS	3100	572T	SWH	77053
GUM GROVE LN	4300	411X	NWH	77088
N. GUM GULLY DR	300	379J	NEC	77532
GUM GULLY RD	100	379J	NEC	77532
GUM GULLY RD	1000	378M	NEC	77532
GUM ISLAND RD	0	381V	LCO	77535
GUMMERT RD	18600	407W	NWC	77449
GUMMERT RD	19200	406Z	NWC	77449
GUM SPRING LN	2300	293X	NCC	77373
GUM TREE LN	1300	339E	NEC	77336
GUM VALLEY DR	11500	411G	NWC	77088
GUNCOTTON AVE	0	285Q	NWC	77447
GUNDA HEIGHTS DR	18500	366P	NWC	77433
GUNDLE RD	19100	333X	NCC	77073
GUNNERHYDE	4300	493W	SWH	77006
GUNNISON	5100	571Z	SWH	77053
GUN OAK PLACE	12200	251V	WD	77380
GUN POWDER LN	2600	616N	PL	77581
GUNRANGE RD	0	659R	LC	77573
GUNRANGE RD	0	660N	LC	77573
GUNSTON CT	2300	528Y	SG	77478
GUNTER	4200	494K	NEH	77020
GUNTERS RIDGE DR	20000	289Z	NWC	77379
GUNTHER SPRINGS CT	0	372C	NCC	77073
GUNWALE	1600	618L	SEH	77062
GURNEY LN	900	413S	NEH	77037
GUS RD	100	292Q	SP	77373
GUSE	6700	413W	NEH	77076
GUSTAV	0	333J	NCC	77073
GUSTAV	1200	494X	SEH	77023
GUSTER DR		484W	NEF	77494
GUSTINE CT	10300	530S	SWH	77031
GUSTINE LN	8700	530S	SWH	77031
GUSTON HALL LN	0	445R	NWC	77449
GUSTON HALL LN	22500	445Q	NWC	77449
GUSTY TRAIL LN	6300	408V	NWC	77041
GUSTY WINDS CT	10800	369Y	NWC	77064
GUSTY WINDS DR	9400	369Y	NWC	77064
GUTHRIE DR	3500	537R	PA	77503
GUTHRIE RIDGE LN	0	524C	NEF	77494
GUTHRIE RIDGE LN	0	524C	NEF	77494
GUY CT	600	379T	NEC	77532
GUYER	300	568J	SG	77498
GUY ODELL LN	20100	256L	SEM	77357
GUYS	0	339J	HU	77336
GUYWOOD	9200	410R	NWH	77040
G WAY	0	290L	NWC	77389
GWEN	10400	413Z	NEH	77093
GWENFAIR DR	0	293W	NCC	77373
GWENN RIDDELL	0	500H	BT	77521
GWINN	0	534H	SEH	77023
GYPSUM CT	6300	408U	NWC	77041
GYPSY	0	538N	PA	77503
GYPSY FOREST DR	4700	376D	NEC	77346
GYPSY POPS DR	4200	538N	PA	77503
GYPSY RED DR	0	326J	NWC	77433
GYRFALCON FORK	0	328B	NWC	77377
H				
H	3800	529A	SWH	77072
H AVE	0	410P	NWC	77040
H AVE	0	569R	SF	77477
H CT	0	290L	NWC	77389
H AND R RD	20600	333N	NCC	77073
H M C	5500	533F	SEH	77021
N. H STREET	9700	539T	LP	77571
H, AVENUE	0	569R	SF	77477
H, AVENUE	0	577X	SEH	77034
H, AVENUE	0	659T	LC	77573
H, AVENUE	0	659Y	DI	77539
S. H, AVENUE	100	335Z	HM	77338
N. H, AVENUE	100	335Z	HM	77338
H, AVENUE	100	568J	SG	77498
H, AVENUE	300	576C	SH	77587
H, AVENUE	1800	496W	GP	77547
H, AVENUE	4700	494P	SEH	77011
H, AVENUE	7500	495S	SEH	77012
E. H, AVENUE	9400	535H	SEH	77012
S. HABERMACHER	0	486T	SWH	77450
N. HABERMACHER	0	486T	SWH	77450
HABERSHAM CT	4500	609K	MC	77459
HABERSHAM LN	11500	490K	PP	77024
HABLO DR	7500	527K	NEF	77083
W. HACHITA CIR	0	290Y	NWC	77379
E. HACHITA CIR	0	290Y	NWC	77379
HACIENDA LN	1	490G	PP	77024
HACKAMORE CT	0	255T	SEM	77365
HACKAMORE LN	11800	490F	BH	77024
HACKAMORE BROOK CT	0	446B	NWC	77449
HACKAMORE HOLLOW LN	2700	331U	NWC	77014
HACKBERRY	100	500K	BT	77520
HACKBERRY	200	459Q	HG	77562
HACKBERRY	800	570S	SF	77477
HACKBERRY	800	580Q	LP	77571
HACKBERRY	12900	247R	SWM	77362
HACKBERRY CT	3400	291Y	NWC	77388
HACKBERRY DR	23700	485K	NEF	77494
HACKBERRY LN	0	616U	FR	77546
HACKBERRY LN	1	491V	SWH	77027
HACKBERRY LN	2800	444P	KT	77493
HACKBERRY CREEK DR	23900	485E	NEF	77494
HACKER	600	412R	NEH	77037
HACKETT DR	2400	452T	NWH	77008
HACKINSON DR	0	253S	SEM	77365
HACKLEY DR	0	568L	SG	77478
HACKMATACK WAY	0	371S	NWC	77066
HACKNEY	0	656K	FR	77546
HACKNEY	900	459Y	SEH	77023
HACKNEY	1500	534B	SEH	77023
HADDEN RD	8500	461M	NEC	77521
HADDEN HOLLOW DR	2100	371V	NWC	77067
HADDEN PARK CT	32500	253N	SEM	77386
HADDICK	9200	455C	NEH	77028
HADDICK	9600	415Y	NEH	77078
HADDINGTON DR	10000	450S	NWH	77080
HADDINGTON DR	10100	449V	NWH	77043
HADDOCK CT	6300	408U	NWC	77041
HADDON	1400	492R	SWH	77006
HADDON	1900	492R	SWH	77019
HADDONFIELD LN	7900	369D	NWC	77070
HADE FALLS LN	0	373A	NCC	77073
HADE MEADOW LN	0	373A	NCC	77073
HADEN RD	1500	497K	NEC	77015
HADEN CREST CT	16200	367C	NWC	77429
HADEN PARK DR	22100	485V	NEF	77450
HADEN RUN DR	0	367W	NWC	77095
HADERIA CT	9300	289Z	NWC	77379
HADLEY	300	493Q	SWH	77002
HADLEY	1600	493V	SEH	77003
HADLEY	2700	493V	SEH	77004
HADLEY CIR	2500	528Y	SG	77478
HADLEY FALLS DR	11900	371M	NWC	77067
HADLEY ROCK DR	0	524E	NEF	77494
HADLEY SPRINGS LN	0	293F	SEM	77386
HADLOCK PLACE	0	250Q	NWC	77389
HADRIAN DR	21300	446B	NWC	77449
HAFER	1	501V	BT	77520
HAFER RD	16300	332P	NWC	77090
HAFFA	0	375U	NEC	77396
HAFNER DR	1700	451U	NWH	77055
HAGAN CT	16000	419A	NEC	77532
HAGE	3100	454B	NEH	77093
N. HAGERMAN	100	494P	SEH	77011
HAGERMAN	100	494T	SEH	77011
HAGERSON RD	100	609X	NEF	77479
HAGGARD NEST DR		484V	NEF	77494
HAGGARD NEST DR		484V	NEF	77494
HAGILBERT CT	21600	334M	NCC	77338
HAHL RD	6900	410S	NWC	77040
HAHLO	100	494H	NEH	77020
HAHNECK VALLEY CT	22000	526A	NEF	77450
HAHNECK VALLEY LN	5200	526A	NEF	77450
HAHNS PEAK DR	10500	367Y	NWC	77095
HAIDER AVE	6700	502C	BT	77521
HAIGHT	5300	455P	NEH	77028
HAIGSHIRE DR	24500	249Z	NWC	77375
HAILE	4900	414Q	NEC	77093
HAILEY	1600	494A	NEH	77020
HAILEY	1900	494A	NEH	77026
HAILEY'S COMET	0	539N	DP	77536
HAILEY BEND	0	656R	FR	77546
HAILEY GROVE LN	0	445M	NWC	77449
HAILEY PAIGE DR	0	407E	NWC	77433
HAILEY SPRINGS LN	0	375X	NEC	77396
HAILWOOD DR	0	249B	SWM	77389
HAIN	3800	453U	NEH	77009
HAINES CREEK DR	0	253W	SEM	77386
HAITI LN	4200	578E	PA	77505
HAITI LN	7000	459K	NEC	77530
HALAMAR LN	14300	368A	NWC	77429
HALBERT	1000	535E	SEH	77087
HALBERT DR	2200	614M	PL	77581
HALBROOK COVE LN	0	328A	NWC	77429
HALBROOK GLEN LN	0	484U	NEF	77494
HALCYON LN	1	501P	BT	77521
HALCYON DAYS DR	0	334P	NCC	77373
HALCYON TIME TRAIL	0	572Q	SWH	77045
HALDANE DR	2300	451P	NWH	77055
HALES HUNT CT	0	290R	NWC	77388
HALESWORTH LN	0	290Z	NWC	77379
HALEWOOD DR	800	618J	SEH	77062
HALEY CT	6800	614T	PL	77584
HALEY LN	0	294U	SEM	77386
HALEY LN	0	294U	SEM	77386
HALEY RD	33100	322E	WCO	77484
HALEY FALLS LN	17200	407L	NWC	77095
HALEYS COMET CIR	9700	329L	NWC	77375
HALEYS LANDING LN	15600	408A	NWC	77095
HALEY WOODS CT	7300	407Q	NWC	77095
HALF BRANCH BEND LN	0	289C	NWC	77375
HALF DOLLAR BAR RD	22300	256Y	SEM	77357
HALFF BEND DR	0	366P	NWC	77433
HALFMOON CT	1	251X	WD	77380
HALF MOON CT	19400	337S	NEC	77346
HALFMOON BAY	0	612Q	PL	77584
HALFMOON BAY DR	0	612Q	PL	77584
HALF MOON TRAIL	18400	337X	NEC	77346
HALFPENNY RD	7000	408P	NWC	77095
HALF VOLLEY CIR	18700	337Z	NEC	77346
HALIFAX	8700	410T	NWC	77040
HALIFAX	12700	497A	NEH	77015
HALIFAX LN	0	657U	LC	77573
HALIFAX BROOK	12600	616G	SEC	77089
HALIK	3700	615E	PL	77581
HALKEIS	300	536Y	SH	77587
HALKEIS RD	2400	536Y	PA	77502
HALKIN CT	16700	330L	NWC	77379
HALKIRK	9200	329R	NWC	77379
HALL	200	620P	SB	77586
HALL	31800	282U	WL	77484
HALL CT	0	539J	DP	77536
S. HALL DR	100	568S	SG	77478
N. HALL DR	100	568S	SG	77478
HALL RD	7700	575X	SEH	77075
HALL RD	9400	575Z	SEC	77089
HALL RD	10700	576X	SEC	77089
HALL RD	10800	616B	SEH	77089
HALLBROOK LN	0	527J	NEF	77407
HALLBROOK WAY	0	250F	WD	77381
HALL COLONY CT	20900	406T	NWC	77449
HALLCROFT LN	0	373A	NCC	77073
HALL CROFT CHASE LN	0	446G	NWC	77449
HALLDALE DR	8000	527M	SWC	77083
HALLEN	4100	660M	BC	77518
HALLEN DALE LN	0	487A	SWC	77094
HALLETT DR	24800	295K	SEM	77365
HALLFIELD DR	13800	372E	NWC	77014
HALL FOREST DR	0	575X	SEH	77075
HALL GREENS CT	0	575X	SEH	77075
HALLIE DR	500	489H	SWH	77024
HALLIE LN	19200	255V	SEM	77357
HALLIFORD DR	9800	569D	SWH	77031
HALLIMORE DR	0	293F	SEM	77386
HALL LAKE DR	0	575X	SEH	77075
HALLMARK DR	4700	491R	SWH	77056
HALLMARK LN	9800	613K	PL	77584
HALLMARK FAIR CT	3900	618D	PA	77059
HALLMARK OAK ST	0	292D	SEM	77386
HALLMARK OAK ST	800	620H	SB	77586
HALL MEADOW LN	25300	524G	NEF	77494
HALL MEADOWS CT	0	575X	SEH	77075
HALL OAKS DR	0	575X	SEH	77075
HALLOW CANE DR	0	285Q	NWC	77447
HALLOWED STREAM LN	11800	366M	NWC	77433
HALLOWICK CT	0	572E	SWH	77045
HALLOWICK CT	0	572E	SWH	77045
HALLOWING POINT RD	11800	371M	NWC	77067
HALL PARK SUBDIVISION DR	0	575X	SEH	77075
HALL PINES CT	0	575X	SEH	77075
HALL PLACE	1400	453W	NWH	77008
HALL POND CT	0	406U	NWC	77449
HALL RANCH CT	0	575X	SEH	77075
HALL RIDGE CT	0	575X	SEH	77075
HALL RIDGE TRACE LN	1800	371V	NWC	77067
HALLS BRIDGE	0	659E	LC	77573
HALLS CREEK CT	0	657K	FR	77546
HALL SHEPHERD RD	16900	418W	NEC	77049
HALLSHIRE DR	7100	454D	NEH	77016
HALLSHIRE DR	7200	455A	NEH	77016
HALLSLEIGH LN	700	332P	NWC	77090
HALLSTONE KNOLLS DR	0	338M	NEH	77336
HALL TERRACE CT	0	575X	SEH	77075
HALL THOMPSON RD	0	444J	KT	77493
HALL VIEW DR	0	575X	SEH	77075
HALLWELL CT	14700	368A	NWC	77429
HALLWORTHY DR	0	371S	NWC	77066
HALMART	5700	534U	SEH	77087
HALPERN	700	493D	NEH	77009
HALPERN CT	0	493D	NEH	77009
HALPREN FALLS CIR	13700	367D	NWC	77429
HALPREN FALLS LN	16000	367D	NWC	77429
HALPRIN CREEK DR	14000	367C	NWC	77429
HALSEY	900	496H	NEH	77015
HALSHEAD LN	0	657U	LC	77573
HALSLO	23000	333H	NCC	77373
HALSTEAD	1800	570X	MC	77489
HALSTEAD DR	2500	293A	SEM	77386
HALSTEAD MEADOWS CIR	6400	411B	NWC	77086
HALSTON DR	10000	528S	NEF	77498
HALSTON RIDGE CT	19300	328D	NWC	77375
HALTON CT	2800	337B	NEH	77345
HALYARD DR	1800	418D	NEC	77532
HAMBLEDON VILLAGE DR	4100	371B	NWC	77014
HAMBLEN	0	374V	NCC	77032
HAMBLEN	1100	453V	NEH	77009
HAMBLEN	5800	375S	NEH	77396
HAMBLEN CT	4600	620H	SB	77586
HAMBLEN RD	100	335H	NEH	77339
HAMBLEN RD	300	336L	NEH	77339
HAMBLETON CIR	13700	330Y	NWC	77069
HAMBLETON DR	13800	330Y	NWC	77069
HAMBLETON WAY CIR	9800	409A	NWC	77065
HAMBLETON WAY CIR	10000	369W	NWC	77065
HAMBLETON WAY DR	11200	369W	NWC	77065
HAMBLIN	0	457T	NEC	77049
HAMBLIN RD	11800	367L	CY	77429
HAMBRICK CT	700	413F	NCC	77060
W. HAMBRICK RD	100	412D	NCC	77037
HAMBRICK RD	100	413E	NCC	77060
HAMDEN CT	400	486B	SWC	77450
HAMDEN VALLEY DR	25200	524L	NWF	77406
HAMID BLVD	3800	611Z	FS	77545
HAMILL RD	5400	414H	NEC	77039
HAMILLCREST DR	12400	371H	NWC	77014
HAMILL RANCH LN	0	370M	NWC	77066
N. HAMILTON	1	493M	SEH	77002
W. HAMILTON	100	452D	NWH	77076
E. HAMILTON	100	453A	NWH	77076
HAMILTON	100	493U	SWH	77002
W. HAMILTON	300	452D	NWH	77091
HAMILTON	600	493U	SWH	77003
HAMILTON	800	493U	SWH	77010
HAMILTON	900	282U	WL	77484
HAMILTON	1200	493Q	SWH	77003
HAMILTON	3100	580Q	LP	77571
HAMILTON	2300	493U	SWH	77004
HAMILTON CIR	7800	409R	JV	77040
HAMILTON DR	9600	613P	PL	77584
HAMILTON LN	0	657U	LC	77573
HAMILTON LN	500	536L	PA	77506
HAMILTON BEND LN	0	253K	SEM	77386
HAMILTON FALLS LN	0	330B	NWC	77379
HAMILTON GROVE LN	0	573X	SEC	77047
HAMILTON GROVE LN	0	573X	SEC	77047
HAMILTON HILLS DR	0	407A	NWC	77433
E. HAMILTON HILLS DR		367W	NWC	77095
HAMILTON MILL CT	24500	485P	NEF	77494
HAMILTON PARK DR	16600	367C	NWC	77429
HAMILTON POOL DR	0	326K	NWC	77433
HAMILWOOD DR	17100	407K	NWC	77095
HAMISH RD	18900	328B	NWC	77377
HAMLET	7800	455B	NEH	77078
HAMLET CT	14000	330Y	NWC	77069
HAMLET LN	0	609U	NEF	77459
HAMLET PARK CT	22500	292K	NCC	77373
HAMLET RIDGE LN	0	446S	NWC	77449
HAMLET SHADOW LN	0	366Z	NWC	77433
HAMLET VALE CT	10400	369G	NWC	77070
HAMLET WAY	1200	336H	NEH	77339
HAMLIN LAKE DR	0	250N	NWC	77375
HAMLIN VALLEY DR	1400	331R	NWC	77090
HAMM RD	2900	616S	PL	77581
HAMMAN	6000	492F	SWH	77007
HAMMER	600	620L	SB	77586
HAMMER LN	0	255T	SEM	77365
HAMMERLY BLVD	7200	451N	NWH	77055
HAMMERLY BLVD	8600	450R	NWH	77080
HAMMERLY BLVD	10200	449R	NWH	77043
HAMMERMILL LN	12900	456D	NEC	77044
HAMMERSMITH DR	12300	328V	NWC	77377
HAMMERSMITH LN	0	657Y	LC	77573
HAMMERWOOD CIR	3100	614S	NEB	77584
HAMMERWOOD CT	16300	328U	NWC	77377
HAMMERWOOD DR	1900	570Y	MC	77489
HAMMOCK	1100	493D	NEH	77009
HAMMOCK DUNES PLACE	0	250K	NWC	77389
HAMMOND DR	11500	369W	NWC	77065
W. HAMMOND DR	20900	296J	SEM	77365
E. HAMMOND DR	21700	296K	SEM	77365
HAMMONDSPROT LN	0	326V	NWC	77429
HAMMON WAY	0	295K	SEM	77365
HAMON DR	700	536M	PA	77506
HAMPDEN CT	0	568W	SG	77479
HAMPDEN POINT CT	0	411S	NWH	77040
HAMPDEN POINT CT	0	411S	NWH	77040
HAMPSHIRE	3300	615P	PL	77581
HAMPSHIRE LN	2500	609D	MC	77459
S. HAMPSHIRE LN	12000	616G	SEC	77089
HAMPSHIRE ROCKS DR	20200	486F	SWC	77450
HAMPSTEAD CT	3600	299S	NEC	77336
W. HAMPTON	0	609L	MC	77459
HAMPTON	1000	412N	NWH	77088
W. HAMPTON CIR	14800	570L	MC	77071
E. HAMPTON CIR	14800	570L	MC	77071
HAMPTON CT	1	490H	HC	77024
S. HAMPTON CT	300	459Q	HG	77562
N. HAMPTON CT	300	459Q	HG	77562
HAMPTON CT	1400	656M	FR	77546
HAMPTON CT	4500	577B	PA	77504
HAMPTON CT	6100	250B	NWC	77389
HAMPTON CT	7000	290B	NWC	77389
HAMPTON CT	13600	568F	SG	77498
W. HAMPTON DR	0	613K	PL	77584
S. HAMPTON DR	0	613K	PL	77584
E. HAMPTON DR	800	613G	NEB	77584
HAMPTON DR	2300	658P	LC	77573
HAMPTON DR	2800	609H	MC	77459
HAMPTON, WADE DR	800	491A	HC	77024
HAMPTON BAY DR	0	612K	PL	77545
HAMPTON BAY LN	0	485X	NEF	77494
HAMPTON BEND LN	13300	369G	NWC	77070
HAMPTON CREEK LN	0	377W	NEC	77044
HAMPTON DALE	16000	330R	NWC	77379
HAMPTON FALLS CT	6100	408Z	NWC	77041
HAMPTON FALLS DR	13200	408Z	NWC	77041
HAMPTON FOREST LN	23000	290H	NWC	77389
HAMPTON GLEN CT	0	527E	NEF	77083
HAMPTON GREEN LN	14600	377Y	NEH	77044
HAMPTON HILLS DR	0	376B	NEC	77369
HAMPTON LAKES CT	1900	445S	NWC	77493
HAMPTON LAKES DR	24400	445V	NWC	77493
HAMPTON LODGE	0	250G	WD	77381
HAMPTONMERE LN	12900	328K	NWC	77377
HAMPTON OAK CT	6200	407S	NWC	77449
HAMPTON OAK CT	18200	330E	NWC	77379
HAMPTON OAK DR	17900	330E	NWC	77379
HAMPTON OAKS CIR	1600	486H	SWC	77094
HAMPTON OAKS DR	23900	290C	NWC	77389
HAMPTON PARK	18100	330F	NWC	77379
HAMPTON PINES LN	0	250Q	NWC	77389
HAMPTON PLACE	1	251F	SWM	77381
HAMPTON POINTE BLVD	5600	250Z	NWC	77389
HAMPTON RIDGE CT	5600	330Y	NWC	77069
HAMPTONSHIRE LN	23800	485S	NEF	77494
HAMPTON SPRINGS DR	2600	620A	SB	77586
HAMPTON TERRACE LN	24300	250Z	NWC	77389
HAMPTON VILLA LN	1000	572R	SWH	77047
HAMPTON VILLAGE LN	0	328P	NWC	77377
HAMPTON WAY CT	6100	250Z	NWC	77389
HAMPTON WOOD DR	19800	287T	NWC	77377
HAMSFIELD CT	12300	328R	NWC	77377
HAMSTEAD PARK DR	14500	408U	NWC	77084
HANBERRY LN	3800	613U	NEB	77584
HANBERRY LN	17800	326G	NWC	77429
HANBURY CT	1800	568A	SG	77498
HANBY CREEK CT	19400	486H	SWC	77094
HANCOCK	1300	536X	PA	77502
HANCOCK	5200	533G	SEH	77004
HANCOCK ELM	0	326Y	NWC	77429
HANCOCK OAK ST	0	326Y	NWC	77433
HANCOCK RUN	0	578D	LP	77571
HANCOCK RUN	8900	578D	LP	77571
HANDBRIDGE PLACE	0	250J	NWC	77389
HANDBROOK DR	5300	330U	NWC	77069
HANDELL LN	300	536Y	PA	77502
HANDSPIKE WAY	800	379X	NEC	77532
HANES	7100	412X	NWH	77088
HANEY RD	8400	461N	NEC	77562
HANEY RD	8700	460M	NEC	77562
HANFORD	9600	455B	NEH	77078
HANFRO LN	7700	412T	NWH	77088
HANGING MOSS TRAIL	9500	409D	NWC	77064
HANGING OAK CIR	0	408P	NWC	77095
HANKA DR	10000	450W	NWH	77080
HANKA DR	10100	450W	NWH	77043
HANKAMER	1400	537J	PA	77506
HANKAR WAY	0	527W	NEF	77407
HANKAR WAY	17400	527W	NEF	77407
HANKLA	1	453B	NEH	77076
HANLEY	8300	409L	JV	77040
HANLEY LN	4200	414Q	NEC	77093
HANLEY LN	6300	415N	NEH	77016
HANLEY WATER DR	0	326U	NWC	77429
HANLON CT	6700	527F	NEF	77083
HANNA	7800	455P	NEH	77028
HANNA RD	1400	252F	SEM	77385
HANNA RD	26100	252K	SEM	77386
HANNA RD	26600	252F	SEM	77385
HANNAH LN	300	656W	AV	77511
HANNAH'S WAY	0	660Q	LC	77573
HANNAH COVE LN	0	293F	SEM	77386
HANNAH CREEK	0	615M	PL	77089
HANNAH GLEN LN	14400	368N	NWC	77429
HANNAH MEADOW LN	0	484N	NEF	77494
HANNAH OAKS LN	0	376G	NEC	77396
HANNAHS CROSSING LN		528L	SWH	77072
HANNA NASH RD	19900	378M	NEC	77532
HANNECK CT	22000	526A	NEF	77450
HANNECK VALLEY LN	5200	526A	NEF	77450
HANNING LN	11000	409Y	NWC	77041
HANNINGTON DR	1200	486F	SWC	77450
HANNINGTON LN	20600	486F	SWC	77450
HANNOCK GLEN LN	800	292L	NCC	77373
HANNON DR	9400	410R	NWH	77040
HANNOVER GROVE LN	0	446N	NWC	77449
HANNOVER VALLEY CT	0	291R	NWC	77388
HANNOVER VILLAGE CT	0	291R	NWC	77388
HANNOVER VILLAGE TRAIL	0	291R	NWC	77388
HANOI BLVD	0	529Q	SWH	77072
HANOVER	100	495W	SEH	77012
HANOVER CIR	3600	613U	NEB	77584
HANOVER LN	0	657U	LC	77573
HANOVER BREEZE LN	0	377P	NEC	77044
HANOVER ESTATES DR	21300	291V	NWC	77388
HANOVER FOREST D	21300	291V	NWC	77388
HANOVER GLEN LN	18100	527J	NEF	77407
HANOVER HOLLOW LN	29900	253X	SEM	77386
HANOVERIAN DR	0	527W	NEF	77469
HANOVER LAKE DR	0	408F	NWC	77095
HANOVER MILL LN	9500	410F	NWC	77040
HANOVER PINES DR	21300	292N	NWC	77388
HANOVER RIDGE DR	21700	291R	NWC	77388
HANOVER SQUARE DR	0	371F	NWC	77066
HANOVER VILLAGE DR	21600	291R	NWC	77388
HANOVER WAY	2100	291R	NWC	77388
HANOVER WAY CT	21500	292N	NWC	77388
HANOVER WOODS DR	0	292S	NWC	77388
HANS	0	614Y	PL	77584
HANS CT	8700	330S	NWC	77379
HANSEL LN	12800	489G	SWH	77024
HANSEN RD	7600	575D	SEH	77061
HANSFORD	5600	534B	SEH	77023
HANSFORD CT	3400	613U	NEB	77584
HANSFORD PLACE	3400	613U	NEB	77584
HANSOM DR	21600	255T	SEM	77365
HANSOM RD	3000	411C	NWC	77038
HANSON	100	620X	GCO	77565
HANSON	24300	245Y	SWM	77355
HANSONS CT	0	294K	SEM	77386
HANSONS CREEK CT	14200	377X	NEC	77044
HANSONS SPRING DR	0	295M	SEM	77365
HANSTON CT	2400	613U	NEB	77584
HANSTON CT	19200	486H	SWC	77094
HANUS CIR	9500	410R	NWH	77040
S. HANWORTH DR	9600	569D	SWH	77031

Street Name	Block	Pg/Sq	Loc	Zips
N. HANWORTH DR	11700	569D	SWH	77031
HAPPY LN	12900	328U	NWC	77429
HAPPY HOLLOW	5000	452E	NWH	77018
HAPPY VALLEY DR	1700	502S	BT	77520
HARALDSON FOREST DR	12000	416L	NEC	77044
HARBIN DR	11100	369N	NWC	77065
HARBINGER CT	0	249B	SWM	77354
HARBOR	100	495A	NEH	77020
HARBOR	1100	500Z	BT	77520
HARBOR	2100	495N	NEH	77029
S. HARBOR	6900	495S	SEH	77011
HARBOR BLVD	100	495A	NEH	77020
HARBOR LN	1	620X	GCO	77565
HARBOR BEND LN	0	658Z	LC	77573
HARBOR BEND LN	0	698D	LC	77573
HARBOR BREEZE LN	0	444T	KT	77493
HARBOR BREEZE LN	0	658U	LC	77573
HARBOR CANYON DR	0	376T	NWC	77396
HARBOR CHASE CT	0	612K	PL	77545
HARBOR CHASE DR	0	612K	PL	77545
HARBOR COVE DR	1	251K	WD	77381
HARBORCREST DR	100	619M	TL	77586
HARBORCREST DR	1800	620K	SB	77586
HARBOR CROSSING LN	0	485A	NEF	77494
HARBOR FALLS DR	0	326K	NWC	77433
HARBOR GLEN LN	4800	447C	NWC	77084
HARBOR HILLS DR	0	532X	SWH	77054
HARBOR KEY CIR	18800	446Z	NWH	77084
HARBOR LAKES DR	0	325H	NWC	77377
HARBOR LAKES LN	700	485A	NEF	77494
HARBOR LANDING DR	0	612K	PL	77545
HARBOR MIST	5200	461T	NEC	77521
HARBOR MIST	6400	609K	MC	77459
HARBOR MIST CT	16800	379X	NEC	77532
HARBOR MIST DR	300	379Y	NEC	77532
HARBOR OAKS DR	0	489L	SWH	77042
HARBOR PASS DR	0	612K	PL	77545
HARBOR PASS LN	3500	617X	SEC	77546
HARBOR POINT DR	4000	609C	MC	77459
HARBOR POINT DR	8000	570B	SWH	77071
HARBOR RANCH LN	5900	250Z	NWC	77389
HARBOR RIDGE	0	615G	PL	77089
HARBOR RIDGE	0	449A	NWC	77041
HARBORSIDE CIR	300	620W	LC	77565
HARBORSIDE LN	0	612F	PL	77545
HARBORSIDE WAY	400	619V	LC	77565
HARBOR SPRINGS LN		289Y	NWC	77379
HARBOR TERRACE LN	0	524R	NEF	77406
HARBORTOWN DR	1200	568F	SG	77498
HARBOR TOWN DR	6500	530F	SWH	77036
HARBOR VIEW BLVD	100	542J	BT	77520
HARBORVIEW DR	300	619Z	LC	77565
HARBOR WATER DR	0	325H	NWC	77377
HARBOUR	0	543L	BC	77520
HARBOUR	1	619X	NB	77058
HARBOUR CIR	1900	659D	LC	77573
HARBOUR CIR	4100	569X	MC	77459
HARBOUR DR	1900	620N	SB	77586
HARBOUR BEND S. LN	13300	377L	NEC	77044
HARBOUR BEND E. LN	16000	377L	NEC	77044
HARBOUR BREEZE LN	3300	613V	PL	77584
HARBOUR BRIDGE POINT DR	17800	327W	NWC	77429
HARBOUR CHASE DR	3400	485U	NEF	77450
HARBOUR COVE CIR	4100	609P	MC	77459
HARBOUR COVE DR	1900	620K	SB	77586
HARBOUR ESTATES CIR	0	619D	TL	77586
HARBOUR GATEWAY LN	6200	609L	MC	77459
HARBOUR LAKE CT	0	376U	NEC	77396
HARBOUR LIGHT DR	16000	377L	NEC	77044
HARBOUR PLACE	500	568P	SG	77478
HARBOUR PLACE	4300	609R	MC	77459
HARBOUR POINTE DR	0	619Y	LC	77573
HARBOUR SANDS DR	1000	486H	SWC	77094
HARBOURSIDE LN	6400	609P	MC	77459
HARBOURVIEW CT	4200	609B	MC	77459
HARBOUR VILLAGE DR	0	619D	TL	77586
HARBROOK DR	3300	613Y	NEB	77584
HARBROOK DR	5600	534V	SEH	77087
HARBURLY CT	1	329G	NWC	77379
HARBY	4300	494W	SEH	77023
HARCOURT DR	6300	415S	NEH	77016
HARCOURT BRIDGE CT	14600	408T	NWC	77084
HARCOURT BRIDGE DR	6400	408T	NWC	77084
HARCROFT	3500	495M	GP	77029
HARD RD	27000	243D	WCO	77447
HARDAGE CT	24100	297E	SEM	77365
HARDEMAN CT	8700	409G	NWC	77064
HARDESTY AVE	800	620P	SB	77586
HARDIE	3300	454T	NEH	77026
HARDIMAN ROW	0	292E	NWC	77389
HARDIN RD	2500	502J	BT	77521
HARDING	500	541B	BT	77520
HARDING	1500	537N	PA	77502
HARDING RD	600	498H	CV	77530
HARDING RD	7700	535F	SEH	77012
HARDIN HOLLY RD	1	297L	NEH	77365
HARDIN STORE RD	24000	248N	SWM	77354
HARDIN STORE RD	28900	249A	SWM	77354
HARDISON LN	10000	450A	NWH	77041
HARDLEE	0	249K	SWM	77354
HARD ROCK DR	15000	408P	NWC	77084
HARDSCRABBLE	0	485K	NEF	77494
HARDSVILLE DR	19900	291Y	NWC	77388
HARDWAY	4800	451G	NWH	77092
HARDWICKE RD	100	412D	NEH	77060
HARDWICKE RD	300	373W	NEH	77060
HARDWICK HILLS LN		484W	NEF	77494
HARDWICK OAKS DR	20700	332Z	NCC	77073
HARDWIDGE CT	20100	486F	SWC	77450
HARDWOOD CIR	3100	614S	NEB	77584
HARD WOOD DR	24200	338M	NEH	77336
HARDWOOD LN	2300	414S	NEH	77093
HARDWOOD DALE WAY	0	334P	NCC	77388
HARDWOOD FOREST DR	5400	411Q	NWC	77088
HARDWOOD RIDGE TRAIL	0	326Y	NWC	77433
HARDWOOD TRAIL	21900	256C	SEM	77357
W. HARDY RD	0	373A	NCC	77073
W. HARDY RD	0	373E	NCC	77073
HARDY RD	800	493D	NEH	77020
HARDY RD	1300	493D	NEH	77026
HARDY RD	2400	453V	NEH	77009
W. HARDY RD	6000	453D	NEH	77022
E. HARDY RD	7600	453D	NEH	77093
E. HARDY RD	10000	413U	NEH	77093
W. HARDY RD	10100	413U	NEH	77076
W. HARDY RD	12100	413B	NEH	77037
W. HARDY RD	13100	413B	NCC	77060
W. HARDY RD	14100	373P	NEH	77060
E. HARDY RD	14100	373A	NCC	77032
HARDY RD	14200	373X	NCC	77032
HARDY RD	17800	333N	NCC	77073
W. HARDY RD	20000	333W	NCC	77073
HARDY RD	20400	257P	SEM	77357
HARDY RD	20700	332D	NCC	77373
E. HARDY RD	21300	332M	NCC	77073
HARDY RD	23600	292V	NCC	77373
W. HARDY RD	26300	292L	SP	77373
E. HARDY RD	26300	292Q	SP	77373
HARDY ELM ST	8100	290N	NWC	77379
E. HARDY EXTENSION	0	252H	SEM	77385
HARDY STONE DR	0	373F	NCC	77073
HARDY STONE DR	0	373F	NCC	77073
HARDY TOLL RD	0	453H	NEH	77093
HARDY TOLL RD	0	453H	NEH	77093
HARDY TOLL RD	0	413G	NCC	77039
HARDY TOLL RD	0	413G	NCC	77039
HARDY TOLL RD	0	373K	NCC	77032
HARDY TOLL RD	0	373K	NCC	77032
HARDY TOLL RD	0	333W	NCC	77073
HARDY TOLL RD	0	333W	NCC	77073
HARDY TOLL RD	0	332R	NCC	77073
HARDY TOLL RD	0	332R	NCC	77073
HARDY TOLL RD	0	292M	NCC	77373
HARDY TOLL RD	0	292M	NCC	77373
HARDY TRACE DR	18700	328F	NWC	77377
HARE	3000	494F	NEH	77020
HARE RD	100	419C	CB	77532
HARE COOK RD	100	379U	NEC	77532
HARE COOK RD	1600	380S	NEC	77532
HAREFIELD LN	0	407Z	NWC	77084
HAREWOOD CT	0	615W	PL	77584
HARFORD MILLS DR	0	528P	SWC	77083
HARGRAVE	100	536G	PA	77506
HARGRAVE RD	0	298F	NEC	77336
HARGRAVE RD	0	244H	WCO	77447
HARGRAVE RD	12900	369H	NWC	77070
HARGRAVE RD	14500	370A	NWC	77069
HARGRAVE RD	23200	245E	WCO	77447
W. HARGRAVES	100	298G	NEC	77336
HARGRAVES RD	100	298G	NEC	77336
HARGROVE RD	0	325S	HK	77447
HARKEY RD	14800	614Q	PL	77584
HARKNESS	1	453B	NEH	77076
HARLAN LN	27000	252E	OR	77385
HARLAND DR	1800	451T	NWH	77055
HARLAND DR	3800	451K	NWH	77092
HARLAND LAKE LN	0	377G	NEH	77346
HARLEM	1800	494C	NEH	77020
HARLEM RD	6500	526U	NEF	77407
HARLEM RD	7100	460Y	MN	77521
HARLEQUIN CT	0	658T	LC	77573
HARLEQUIN LN	26900	324N	NWC	77447
HARLEY	2800	613P	PL	77584
HARLEY CT	2500	454A	NEH	77093
HARLOW DR	18500	328K	NWC	77377
HARMAN	0	568J	SG	77498
HARMAN DR	0	340U	LCO	77535
HARMASTON RD	0	415X	NEH	77078
HARMEIR	18900	286M	NWC	77377
HARMILL HOUSE DR	0	376B	NEC	77338
HARMILL HOUSE DR	0	376B	NEC	77338
HARMON	4900	414Q	NEC	77093
HARMON	6300	415N	NEH	77016
HARMON PARK CT	0	333A	NCC	77373
HARMONT RIVER CT	0	406W	NWC	77449
HARMONY CIR	22800	296D	SEM	77357
HARMONY LN	8300	457H	NEC	77049
HARMONY BLUFF LN	0	487A	SWC	77494
HARMONY BRANCH DR	0	293G	SEM	77386
HARMONY BRIDGE	0	250B	SWM	77381
HARMONY COVE	7100	530D	SWC	77036
HARMONY CREEK LN	0	293F	SEM	77386
HARMONY DALE LN	0	293F	SEM	77386
HARMONY ESTATES LN	18100	366D	NWC	77429
HARMONY FOREST LN	0	293F	SEM	77386
HARMONY GLADE LN	0	293F	SEM	77386
HARMONY GLEN LN	8300	410G	NWC	77064
HARMONY HALL CT	0	612U	PL	77584
HARMONY HALL LN	0	377E	NEC	77346
HARMONY HILL CT	9100	329R	NWC	77379
HARMONY HILL DR	17000	330N	NWC	77379
HARMONY HILL DR	17200	329R	NWC	77379
HARMONY LAKE LN	0	405T	NWC	77493
HARMONY LIGHT CT	7600	290S	NWC	77379
HARMONY MEADOWS LN	0	293F	SEM	77386
HARMONY MILL CT	0	484X	NWF	77494
HARMONY OAKS BLVD	0	293G	SEM	77386
HARMONY PINES BLVD	0	293G	SEM	77386
HARMONY POINT LN	0	293F	SEM	77386
HARMONY SHORES DR	0	524E	NEF	77494
HARMONY SHORES DR	0	524E	NEF	77494
HARMONY SPRINGS DR	0	407C	NWC	77095
HARMONY VALLEY LN	0	293F	SEM	77386
HARMONY VIEW LN	0	293F	SEM	77386
HARMONY WOODS BLVD	0	293G	SEM	77386
HARMS RD	0	409N	NWC	77041
HARMS RD	7600	409J	NWC	77041
HARNELL	0	454W	NEH	77026
HARNESS LN	15100	617M	SEH	77598
HARNESS CREEK LN	8800	491G	SWH	77024
HARNESS OAKS CT	1500	488K	SWH	77077
HARNESS PATH CT	24500	293S	NCC	77373
HARNESS TRAIL CT	0	299X	NEC	77336
HARNESS TRAIL DR	0	299X	NEC	77336
HARNETT DR	18300	366D	CY	77429
HARNWELL CROSSING DR	10400	329C	NWC	77379
HAROLD	600	493S	SWH	77006
HAROLD	1700	492V	SWH	77098
HAROLD LN	1	501P	BT	77521
HAROLDS RD	800	338M	NEH	77336
HARPER	3700	532E	SS	77005
HARPER DR	2100	536U	PA	77502
HARPER LN	25100	251U	SWM	77380
HARPER CREEK LN	0	524B	NEF	77494
HARPER FOREST DR	5400	411L	NWC	77088
HARPERGATE DR	23100	333C	NCC	77373
HARPER RIVER CT	0	524A	NEF	77494
HARPERS BRIDGE DR	13200	408Y	NWC	77041
HARPERS FERRY DR	2500	658P	LC	77573
HARPERS GLEN LN	7500	528L	SWH	77072
HARPERS LANDING LN	0	526Q	NEF	77407
HARPERS RIDGE LN	0	446B	NWC	77449
HARPERWOOD LN	0	371D	NWC	77014
HARPETH OAK LN	0	609X	NEF	77479
HARPINGS WAY	1100	379X	NEC	77532
HARPOON CT	16100	419B	NEC	77532
HARPOST MANOR	0	331E	NWC	77379
HARPSWELL LN	600	332Q	NCC	77073
HARREL DWYER RD	0	332S	NWC	77090
HARRELL	8600	454E	NEH	77093
HARRIER CT	0	484P	NWF	77494
HARRIETT	5400	534C	SEH	77023
HARRIETTE	2600	537T	PA	77502
HARRIMAN	3700	494B	NEH	77026
HARRINGTON	300	493H	NEH	77009
HARRINGTON	1700	494E	NEH	77026
HARRINGTON DR	0	620G	SB	77586
HARRINGTON DR	10100	613K	PL	77584
HARRIS	0	580V	PA	77586
HARRIS	100	495A	NEH	77020
HARRIS	400	620U	KE	77565
HARRIS	1200	453X	NWH	77009
HARRIS	27000	324E	HK	77447
HARRIS AVE	0	612V	PL	77584
HARRIS AVE	0	613S	PL	77584
HARRIS AVE	100	536L	PA	77506
HARRIS AVE	100	536M	PA	77506
HARRIS AVE	1200	537K	PA	77506
HARRIS CT	100	453X	NWH	77009
HARRIS RD	100	459V	HG	77562
HARRIS RD	2300	460X	MN	77521
HARRISBURG BLVD	2500	494N	SEH	77003
HARRISBURG BLVD	4400	494N	SEH	77011
HARRISBURG BLVD	7500	495X	SEH	77012
HARRIS CANYON LN	0	327U	NWC	77429
HARRIS COUNTY DR	0	322D	NWC	77484
HARRIS MEADOW BLVD	0	446B	NWC	77449
HARRIS MILL DR	0	446M	NWC	77449
HARRIS MILL LN	0	659H	LC	77573
HARRISON	1500	538V	DP	77536
HARRISON	7100	460T	MN	77521
HARRISON AVE	500	501V	BT	77520
HARRISON CT	1700	538N	PA	77503
HARRISON CT	6200	526A	NEF	77450
HARRISON HILL CT	0	488T	SWH	77077
HARRISON LAKES CIR	17500	329L	NWC	77379
HARRIS SETTLEMENT CT	12000	366K	NWC	77433
HARRISTOWN DR	0	572R	SWH	77047
HARROP AVE	1400	537J	PA	77506
HARROW	3000	533X	SEH	77051
HARROW	11300	414P	NCC	77093
W. HARROW DR	5000	447C	NWC	77084
W. HARROW DR	5600	407Y	NWC	77084
HARROW LN	8300	330P	NWC	77379
HARROWBY DR	23000	333A	NCC	77373
HARROWGATE DR	9700	569H	SWH	77031
HARROW HILL CT	4200	447F	NWC	77084
HARROW HILL DR	18200	447F	NWC	77084
HARSTON DR	10800	329B	NWC	77375
HART	100	536P	PA	77506
HART	1300	496J	JC	77029
HARTAWAY LN	14700	368A	NWC	77429
HARTCLIFF CIR	3100	446Q	NWC	77449
HARTCREST DR	13900	367D	NWC	77429
HARTE CT	2700	445R	NWC	77449
HARTFIELD LN	3200	291Q	NWC	77388
HARTFIELD BLUFF LN	0	366V	NWC	77433
HARTFORD	7900	535P	SEH	77017
HARTFORD CT	0	568B	SG	77498
HARTFORD BAY TRAIL	0	368F	NWC	77429
HARTFORD BEND CROSSING	0	405P	NWC	77493
HARTFORD BLUFF CT	0	617E	SEC	77089
HARTFORD CLIFF CT	0	405P	NWC	77493
HARTFORD FALLS LN	0	526Q	NEF	77407
HARTFORD GROVE LN	0	484P	NEF	77494
HARTFORD LANDING LN	0	609T	NEF	77479
HARTFORD SPRINGS TRAIL	0	405R	NWC	77493
HARTGLEN CIR	1900	485L	SWC	77450
HART HOLLOW LN	12700	328G	NWC	77377
HARTINGTON DR	3400	371P	NWC	77066
HARTLAND	6800	491C	NWH	77055
HARTLEPOOL LN	12700	371E	NWC	77066
HARTLEY RD	11300	414P	NCC	77093
HARTLINE GREEN DR	0	366N	NWC	77433
HARTMAN	600	492M	SWH	77007
HARTMAN DR	700	501M	BT	77521
HARTMAN DR	2300	528Y	SG	77478
HARTMAN RD	7100	456M	NEC	77049
HARTMAN RD	15900	246R	SWM	77355
HARTMAN RIDGE CT	16600	611H	SWH	77053
HARTRIDGE DR	0	331R	NWC	77090
HARTS	0	244Y	WCO	77447
HARTSDALE DR	3900	490Z	SWH	77063
HARTSDALE DR	5600	530D	SWH	77036
HARTSHILL CT	12900	377X	NEC	77044
HARTSHILL DR	14200	377X	NEC	77044
HARTSHORN CT	0	299X	NEC	77336
HARTSHORN DR	0	299X	NEC	77336
HARTSOOK	10100	576K	SEH	77034
HARTSVILLE RD	3000	573F	SEH	77051
HARTSVILLE RD	4100	573G	SEH	77047
HARTT	1600	502S	BT	77520
HARTT	4100	532W	SWH	77025
HARTWELL DR	5000	447B	NWC	77084
HARTWICK	0	413Q	NCC	77093
W. HARTWICK LN	100	413N	NCC	77037
HARTWICK RD	200	413N	NCC	77037
HARTWICK RD	1300	414N	NCC	77093
HARTWICK RD	5500	415N	NEH	77016
HARTWICK FALLS DR	24500	296J	SEM	77365
HARTWICK PINES DR	0	377K	NEC	77346
HARTWILL DR	0	524F	NEF	77494
HARTWOOD	16600	618R	SEH	77058
HARVARD	1	493A	NWH	77007
HARVARD	800	538L	DP	77536
HARVARD	900	453S	NWH	77008
HARVARD	1100	501U	BT	77520
HARVARD	2700	537T	PA	77502
HARVARD	3600	453N	NWH	77018
HARVARD	5600	452D	NWH	77076
HARVARD CRESCENT	2100	612U	NWB	77578
HARVARD ESTATES BLVD	2100	612Y	NWB	77578
HARVARD HOLLOW	2100	612Y	NWB	77578
HARVARD POINTE DR	0	658R	LC	77573
HARVARD TRAIL	3600	612Y	NWB	77578
HARVARD WAY	2100	612Y	NWB	77578
HARVEST LN	0	444S	KT	77493
HARVEST LN	0	461R	NEC	77521
HARVEST LN	4300	534A	SEH	77004
HARVEST BEND BLVD	11200	369U	NWC	77064
HARVEST BROOK CT	13600	617D	SEH	77059
HARVEST CHASE CT	14700	327W	NWC	77429
HARVEST CHASE LN	5000	609S	NEF	77479
HARVEST COVE	2500	617Y	SEC	77546
HARVEST CREEK CT	2200	338A	NEH	77345
HARVEST DALE AVE	11100	368V	NWC	77065
HARVEST DAWN CT	7400	408N	NWC	77095
HARVESTER	7800	407H	NWC	77095
HARVESTER LN	0	609R	MC	77459
HARVEST FALL LN	15300	458W	NEC	77530
HARVEST FIELD LN	0	290T	NWC	77379
HARVEST GABLES DR	0	290D	NWC	77389
HARVEST GLEN CT	14300	618B	SEH	77062
HARVEST GLEN DR	6800	337U	NEC	77346
HARVEST GROVE CT	21300	291R	NWC	77388
HARVEST HILL CT	2800	657H	FR	77546
HARVEST HILL DR	2800	657G	FR	77546
HARVEST HILL LN	20600	333P	NCC	77073
HARVEST HOLLOW CT	17300	527J	NEF	77407
HARVEST KNOLL DR	5000	291J	NWC	77389
HARVEST LANDING LN	0	406L	NWC	77433
HARVEST MEADOWS DR	10800	369T	NWC	77065
HARVEST MILL CT	7600	407G	NWC	77095
HARVEST MILL LN	7600	527J	NEF	77407
HARVEST MOON DR	2500	610B	MC	77489
HARVEST MOON LN	0	612U	PL	77584
HARVEST MOON LN	700	488M	SWH	77077
HARVEST OAK LANDING DR	0	294E	SEM	77386
HARVEST POINTE LN	0	484W	NEF	77494
HARVEST RIDGE RD	14300	618E	SEH	77062
HARVEST RIVER DR	0	406G	NWC	77433
HARVEST RUN LN	129	456D	NEC	77044
HARVEST SPRING DR	5200	297P	NEH	77345
HARVEST STREAM WAY	0	446R	NWC	77084
HARVEST SUMMER CT	16200	618D	PA	77059
HARVEST SUN DR	10800	369Z	NWC	77064
HARVEST TERRACE CT	6100	290V	NWC	77379
HARVEST TERRACE CT	6100	290V	NWC	77379
HARVEST TERRACE LN	20800	290Q	NWC	77379
HARVEST TIME LN	600	373J	NEH	77060
HARVEST TRAIL LN	0	407S	NWC	77449
HARVEST VALLEY LN	0	615B	PL	77581
HARVEST WIND CT	9100	369V	NWC	77064
HARVEY	0	528Z	SWH	77099
HARVEY	0	570T	MC	77489
HARVEY AVE	100	501U	BT	77520
HARVEY BLVD	100	500N	BT	77520
HARVEY DR	700	247F	SWM	77362
HARVEY RD	3300	380U	NEC	77532
HARVEY RD	5200	381S	NEC	77532
HARVEY RD	12900	456Y	NEH	77013
HARVEYS WAY	21600	334M	NCC	77338
HARVEY WILSON DR	5500	494L	NEH	77020
HARVIN	0	532M	SWH	77030
HARVRENEE DR	14900	368J	NWC	77429
HARWELL DR	2200	534H	SEH	77023
HARWICH LN	0	609Y	MC	77459
HARWICK DR	15900	330T	NWC	77379
HARWIN DR	6500	530C	SWH	77036
HARWIN DR	11200	529C	SWH	77072
HARWIN DR	12800	528D	SWH	77072
HARWOOD DR	100	659D	LC	77573
HARWOOD DR	2300	451P	NWH	77055
HARWOOD HEIGHTS DR	0	524E	NEF	77494
HARWOOD MILLS RD	0	377G	NEH	77346
HARWOOD SPRINGS DR	0	450S	NWH	77080
HASBROOK	100	534M	SEH	77087
HASIE DR	5000	374Z	NCC	77032
HASINA KNOLL	16700	327X	CY	77429
HASKELL	6200	492F	SWH	77007
HASSELL DR	0	484G	KT	77494
HASSELT DR	0	329U	NWC	77070
HASSLER RD	200	290H	NWC	77389
HASTING OAK CT	1	251J	WD	77381
HASTINGS	3100	535K	SEH	77017
HASTINGS	22400	256Y	SEM	77357
HASTINGS CIR	19800	656N	NEB	77511
HASTINGS LN	4200	538U	DP	77536
HASTINGS RD	19600	656N	NEB	77511
HASTINGS ST	0	609S	NEF	77479
HASTINGS GREEN DR	11900	368Z	NWC	77065
HASTINGWOOD DR	5000	447B	NWC	77084
HASTY LN	8200	460Q	NEC	77562
HAT	10600	528Z	SWH	77099
HATCH CT	16900	379X	NEC	77532
HATCHER LN	1	657E	FR	77546
HATCHER SPRING LN	0	452Y	NWH	77008
HATCHERVILLE RD	12300	462C	MB	77521
HATCHMERE PLACE	1400	329G	NWC	77379
HATCHMERE PLACE CT	1500	329G	NWC	77379
N. HATFIELD	12400	614L	PL	77581
HATFIELD RD	1700	614V	PL	77581
HATFIELD RD	2900	614V	PL	77584
HATFIELD GLEN DR	5800	407W	NWC	77449
HATFIELD HOLLOW DR	15500	329T	NWC	77377
HATHORN WAY DR	1000	486H	SWC	77094
HATTERAS POINT DR	4400	617T	SEC	77546
HATTIE	1500	412T	NWH	77088
HATTON	8400	532P	SWH	77025
HATTON FALLS DR	0	366P	NWC	77433
HATWELL	1800	534C	SEH	77023
HAUDE RD	19300	332A	NWC	77388
HAUDE RD	19300	331D	NWC	77388
HAUDE RD	20000	291Z	NWC	77388
HAUGHLAND DR	18500	407N	NWC	77433
HAUGHTON DR	6500	290C	NWC	77389
HAUNA LN	0	660S	GCO	77539
HAUSER	1400	494X	SEH	77023
HAUSWORTH CT	22900	292G	NCC	77373
HAVANA	3600	538S	DP	77536
HAVANT CIR	12700	488L	SWH	77077
HAVARD RD	100	338H	NEC	77336
HAVARD RD	800	339E	NEC	77336
HAVARD OAKS DR	11500	367Q	NWC	77095
HAVASU DR	0	326K	NWC	77433
HAVEL	3000	451R	NWH	77092
HAVELOCK DR	1300	252Q	SEM	77386
E. HAVEN CT	700	656C	FR	77546
HAVEN DR	19200	255R	SEM	77365
HAVEN ARBOR DR	0	366J	NWC	77433
HAVEN BEND LN	0	526L	NEF	77407
HAVEN BROOK	2700	297X	NEH	77339
HAVEN BROOK LN	0	615G	PL	77581
HAVEN CLIFF LN	0	331B	NWC	77388
HAVEN COVE LN	21800	445H	NWC	77449
HAVEN CREEK DR	6700	406Q	NWC	77449
HAVEN CREEK DR	7000	406Q	NWC	77433
HAVENCREST CT	2400	613P	PL	77584
HAVENCREST DR	1600	412A	NWC	77038
HAVENCREST DR	2400	411D	NWC	77038
HAVENCREST DR	2700	613P	NEB	77584
HAVENCREST DR	9000	527R	NEF	77083
HAVEN CROSSING CT	9600	408D	NWC	77065
HAVENDALE DR	6100	529C	SWH	77072
HAVENDALE LN	0	457P	NEC	77049
HAVEN FALLS LN	13100	528Y	SG	77478
HAVENFIELD CT	22900	485X	NEF	77494
HAVENFIELD RIDGE LN		249V	NWC	77375
HAVEN FOREST CT	0	326E	NWC	77377
HAVENGATE CIR	13400	457W	NEC	77015
HAVEN GLEN DR	3800	296V	NEH	77339
HAVEN GREEN CIR	3300	446L	NWC	77449
HAVEN HILLS DR	15900	448A	NWC	77084
HAVEN HOLLOW CT		328P	NWC	77429
HAVENHOUSE DR	1900	252V	SEM	77386
HAVENHURST DR	15700	618C	SEH	77059
HAVENHURST DR	16200	578Y	SEH	77059
HAVEN LAKE DR	3600	296Z	NEH	77339

Street Name	Block	Pg/Sq	Loc	Zips
HAVEN LAKE DR	25500	249V	NWC	77375
HAVEN LAKE DR	25800	250S	NWC	77375
HAVEN LAKE PLACE	8600	249V	NWC	77375
HAVEN LAKE POINT	0	249V	NWC	77375
HAVENLARK DR	0	371N	NWC	77066
HAVEN LOCK DR	1500	489P	SWH	77077
HAVENMEADOW LN	0	290T	NWC	77379
HAVEN MEADOWS LN	14700	375X	NEC	77396
HAVENMIST DR	12100	329A	CY	77429
HAVENMOOR PLACE	3600	446K	NWC	77449
HAVEN OAKS DR	3400	331P	NWC	77068
HAVEN OAKS DR	4200	297N	NEH	77339
HAVENPARK DR	16300	618C	SEH	77059
HAVEN PINES DR	3500	297T	NEH	77345
HAVEN POINT DR	5600	407X	NWC	77084
S. HAVENRIDGE DR	1	251E	WD	77381
N. HAVENRIDGE DR	1	251E	WD	77381
HAVENRIDGE DR	14900	527R	NEF	77083
HAVENROCK DR	12600	412A	NWC	77038
HAVENS	9400	453C	NEH	77076
HAVENS LN	0	569P	SF	77477
HAVENS EDGE CT	20400	335Q	HM	77338
HAVENSGLADE CT	0	526W	NEF	77469
HAVEN SHORE LN	5300	609T	NEF	77479
HAVENSTONE LN	0	525C	NEF	77450
HAVEN TRAIL	8500	249V	NWC	77375
HAVEN VALLEY DR	5300	446C	NWC	77449
HAVENVIEW DR	5100	449D	NWC	77041
HAVEN WAY	8500	249V	NWC	77375
HAVENWAY LN	9200	410F	NWC	77064
HAVENWOOD CT	0	367P	NWC	77433
HAVENWOOD RIDGE LN	0	524H	NEF	77494
HAVENWOODS DR	4700	371A	NWC	77066
HAVENWOODS DR	5700	370H	NWC	77066
HAVEN WOODS WAY	8600	249V	NWC	77375
HAVER	1600	492V	SWH	77006
HAVERBAY CT	21700	445M	NWC	77449
HAVERDOWN DR	9800	409A	NWC	77065
HAVERFIELD CT	15100	328W	NWC	77429
HAVERFORD LN	1	657A	FR	77546
HAVERFORD RD	24700	250Z	NWC	77389
HAVERGATE DR	0	250L	WD	77389
HAVERHILL DR	1600	452X	NWH	77008
HAVERHILL DR	9800	335T	HM	77338
HAVERING LN	15900	330T	NWC	77379
HAVERLING DR	2900	613S	NEB	77584
HAVERS LN	0	569P	SF	77477
HAVERSHAM DR	100	490J	SWH	77024
HAVERSHIRE DR	3400	609G	MC	77459
HAVERSHIRE LN	13300	489B	SWH	77079
HAVERSTOCK DR	8700	570A	SWH	77031
HAVERSTROM LN	21700	291S	NWC	77388
HAVERTON DR	7000	415P	NEH	77016
HAVERTY DR	14300	374Z	NCC	77032
HAVEY DR	0	532L	SWH	77025
HAVILAND	11500	570H	SWH	77035
HAVILAND FALLS DR	0	376N	NEC	77396
HAVIS LN	0	448W	NWH	77084
HAVNER CT	8500	412R	NCC	77037
W. HAVNER LN	100	413N	NCC	77037
HAVNER LN	200	413Q	NEH	77037
HAVNER LN	1700	413R	NCC	77093
HAVNER LN	2800	414N	NCC	77093
HAWAII	8200	409M	JV	77040
HAWAII AVE	1600	659N	LC	77573
HAWES RD	6200	375J	NEH	77396
HAWICK DR	4000	447F	NWC	77084
HAWK RD	3800	613H	PL	77584
HAWK CREEK	0	609Z	MC	77459
HAWKE BAY LN	0	657P	FR	77546
HAWKES BAY CT	5900	525C	NEF	77494
HAWKEYE	6500	456R	NEH	77049
HAWKEYE CT	6500	456R	NEH	77049
HAWK HAVEN LN	17800	330F	NWC	77379
HAWKHILL DR	1100	657N	FR	77546
HAWKHURST CT	0	249B	SWM	77354
HAWKHURST DR	0	249A	SWM	77354
HAWKIN LN	17500	287J	NWC	77377
HAWKING	0	656N	NEB	77511
HAWKINS	100	413E	NCC	77037
HAWKINS	2500	494N	SEH	77003
HAWKINS CREEK CT	23600	485F	NEF	77494
HAWKINS MANOR LN	0	406X	NWC	77449
HAWKINS RIDGE LN	19800	526K	NEF	77407
HAWKLEY DR	0	525Z	NEF	77406
HAWK MEADOW DR	4200	446G	NWC	77449
HAWK MEADOWS	0	614J	PL	77581
HAWK PARK	7900	375Q	NEC	77396
HAWK RIDGE	0	609Z	MC	77459
HAWKS RD	1500	610E	MC	77489
HAWKS HARBOR CT	0	524G	NEF	77494
HAWKS LANDING DR	0	324M	NWC	77447
HAWKS LANDING DR	0	324M	NWC	77447
HAWKSMOOR CT	0	328N	NWC	77429
HAWKS NEST DR	0	372J	NWC	77067
HAWKS NEST DR	1200	372J	NWC	77067
HAWKS PRAIRIE BLVD	0	484P	NWF	77494
HAWKSPUR CIR	21000	525R	NEF	77407
HAWKSTONE CT	26700	484Y	NEF	77494
HAWKWOOD DR	22600	334B	NCC	77373
HAWLEY LN	5600	450C	NWH	77040
HAWLEY CREEK DR	0	253X	SEM	77386
HAWN RD	25700	250S	NWC	77389
HAWTHORNE	100	493S	SWH	77006
HAWTHORNE	300	536R	PA	77506
HAWTHORNE	800	620T	CS	77565
HAWTHORNE	1300	541A	BT	77520
HAWTHORNE	1700	492V	SWH	77098
HAWTHORNE	4700	581W	PA	77586
W. HAWTHORNE	29400	252Z	SEM	77386
E. HAWTHORNE	29600	252Z	SEM	77386
HAWTHORNE CT	900	288M	TB	77375
HAWTHORNE BEND DR	0	524A	NEF	77494
HAWTHORNE BLOSSOM DR	0	250V	NWC	77389
HAWTHORNE BROOK LN	2100	611S	FS	77545
HAWTHORNE CREEK DR	0	330H	NWC	77379
HAWTHORNE DALE CT	0	445P	NWC	77493
HAWTHORNE FALLS LN	0	457Q	NEC	77049
HAWTHORNE GARDEN WAY	0	524D	NEF	77494
HAWTHORNE HILL CIR	12100	377A	NEC	77346
HAWTHORNE RIDGE RD	0	326Y	NWC	77429
HAWTHORNE SHORES DR	0	377K	NEC	77044
HAWTHORN GLEN CT	0	611Y	FS	77545
HAWTHORN PLACE	500	610S	MC	77459
HAWTHORN VALLEY LN	0	408F	NWC	77095
HAYBROOK DR	8100	615H	SEC	77089
HAYDEE RD	3100	291R	NWC	77388
HAYDEN CT	3700	293C	SEM	77386
HAYDEN COVE DR	8200	289M	NWC	77375
HAYDEN FALLS DR	0	524K	NWF	77406
HAYDEN GROVE DR	0	406H	NWC	77433
HAYDEN LAKES DR	0	328A	NWC	77377

Street Name	Block	Pg/Sq	Loc	Zips
HAYDENLAKES DR	0	328A	NWC	77429
HAYDEN SPRINGS CT	0	376G	NEC	77396
HAYDEN SPRINGS CT	0	376G	NEC	77396
HAYDEN WOOD DR	19100	328D	NWC	77375
HAYES	0	502P	BT	77520
HAYES	1400	489P	SWH	77077
HAYES	2800	489X	SWH	77082
HAYESFORD LN	16300	326R	NWC	77429
HAYES RANCH RD	18800	253A	SEM	77385
HAYFORD DR	0	335D	NEH	77339
HAYGOOD	4300	453J	NWH	77022
HAYLEE WAY	21500	333G	NCC	77338
HAYLIE HOLLOW CT	1600	293J	SEM	77396
HAYMAN CT	0	406U	NWC	77449
HAYMAN DR	6300	406U	NWC	77449
HAYMARKET LN	100	497C	NEC	77015
HAYMARKET LN	300	457Y	NEC	77015
HAY MEADOW CT	20700	283P	NWC	77484
HAY MEADOW LN	11800	414K	NCC	77039
HAYNES	7400	411R	NWH	77088
HAYNES DR	13800	370B	NWC	77069
HAYNES RD	12000	370F	NWC	77066
HAYNESWORTH LN	5700	577N	SEH	77034
HAYS	700	493D	NEH	77009
HAYS	3000	537Q	PA	77503
HAYSDEN LN	0	657V	LC	77573
HAYS HIGHLANDS LN	0	578X	SEH	77059
HAYSLIP LN	11000	409Y	NWC	77041
HAYSTREAM DR	19200	446M	NWC	77449
HAYWARD CT	7700	407L	NWC	77095
HAYWARD CROSSING LN	0	524H	NEF	77494
HAYWOOD	4100	414Y	NEH	77093
HAYWOOD	5000	414Y	NEH	77016
HAYWOOD CT	3400	569S	SG	77478
N. HAYWOOD DR	6300	535W	SEH	77061
S. HAYWOOD DR	6700	535W	SEH	77061
HAYWOOD DR	7400	535W	SEH	77061
HAYWOOD OAKS DR	0	367W	NWC	77095
HAZARD	1500	492R	SWH	77019
HAZARD	2600	492V	SWH	77098
HAZARD	5300	532D	SWH	77005
HAZEL	100	580G	LP	77571
HAZEL	1200	493N	SWH	77019
HAZEL	1600	493N	SWH	77006
HAZEL	2700	616T	PL	77581
HAZEL	5300	500G	BT	77521
HAZEL ALDER WAY	5700	524D	NEF	77494
HAZEL ARBOR WAY	0	526T	NEF	77407
HAZEL BERRY WAY	5500	524D	NEF	77494
HAZEL BROOK CT	4800	297Q	NEH	77345
HAZEL COVE DR	7100	407Q	NWC	77095
HAZEL CREEK CIR	7200	407Q	NWC	77095
N. HAZELCREST CIR	100	250A	WD	77382
HAZELCREST DR	200	250A	WD	77382
HAZELDALE DR	0	368E	NWC	77429
HAZEL FIELD CT	23100	485F	SWC	77494
HAZEL GLADE CT	3900	578X	SEH	77059
HAZEL GREEN LN	4100	611W	FS	77545
HAZEL GROVE DR	0	329E	NWC	77375
HAZELGROVE DR	5300	447B	NWC	77084
HAZELHURST DR	10000	450W	NWH	77080
HAZELHURST DR	10100	449X	NWH	77043
HAZELL HILLS DR	0	367S	NWC	77433
HAZELL HILLS DR	0	367S	NWC	77433
HAZELNUT LN	0	460W	BT	77521
HAZEL OAK LN	0	578U	SEH	77059
HAZEL PARK DR	3000	488X	SWH	77082
HAZEL POINTE TRAIL	0	253T	SEM	77386
HAZEL RANCH DR	0	484R	NEF	77494
HAZEL RIDGE LN	14000	618A	SEH	77062
HAZEL ROSE SKY DR	0	335N	NCC	77338
HAZEL THICKET TRAIL	15300	326V	NWC	77429
HAZELTINE DR	4900	578J	PA	77505
HAZELTON DR	4300	531Z	SWH	77035
HAZELWAY LN	12800	328U	NWC	77429
HAZELWOOD DR	3900	614Z	PL	77584
HAZELWOOD LN	12500	488M	SWH	77077
HAZELWOOD HOLLOW DR		328k	NWC	77377
HAZEL WOODS CT	0	527S	NEF	77469
HAZEN	5600	531J	SWH	77081
HAZEN	6800	530M	SWH	77074
HAZEN	8000	530J	SWH	77036
HAZEN	10600	529L	SWH	77072
HAZEN POINT DR	0	326T	NWC	77429
HAZEPOINT DR	0	484X	NEF	77494
HAZEPOINT DR	0	484X	NEF	77494
HAZLITT DR	2100	373R	NCC	77032
HAZY LN	20100	446T	NWC	77449
HAZY BLUFF CT	0	446J	NWC	77449
HAZY BROOK LN	7900	375U	NEC	77396
HAZY CREEK DR	2300	446U	NWC	77084
HAZYCREST DR	18400	330E	NWC	77379
HAZY FOREST LN	31200	252R	SEM	77386
HAZYGLEN DR	12400	488Z	SWH	77082
HAZY HILL DR	11900	456C	NEC	77044
HAZY HILLSIDE CT	2800	297Z	NEH	77345
HAZYKNOLL LN	1700	371R	NWC	77067
HAZY LANDING CT	27400	294T	SEM	77386
HAZYL SHADOW DR	0	289Q	NWC	77375
HAZY MEADOW LN	8500	410E	NWC	77040
HAZY MILLS LN	0	253T	SEM	77386
HAZY MIST CT	0	524M	NEF	77406
HAZY PARK DR	3000	488X	SWH	77082
HAZY PINES CT	16200	618D	PA	77059
HAZY RIDGE LN	14600	367A	NWC	77429
HAZYSTONE CT	31100	292L	SP	77373
HAZYSTONE LN	0	615F	PL	77581
HAZY VALLEY LN	10700	371S	NWC	77086
HEADLAND DR	18500	407J	NWC	77433
HEADSTALL DR	0	249V	NWC	77375
HEADWATER DR	0	250K	NWC	77389
HEADWATERS FOREST DR	0	377K	NEC	77346
HEAGANS CT	14500	528S	NEF	77498
HEALTH RIVER LN	0	609U	NEF	77479
HEANEY DR	200	453C	NEH	77076
HEANEY DR	1600	453D	NEH	77093
HEARNE DR	2300	537T	PA	77502
HEARTBROOK FIELD LN	0	406G	NWC	77433
HEART GROVE DR	4100	376H	NEH	77346
HEARTH DR	8400	532Q	SWH	77054
HEARTHGLEN LN	0	609N	MC	77459
HEARTHGLEN LN	0	290U	NWC	77379
S. HEARTHSHIRE CIR	0	249A	SWM	77354
N. HEARTHSHIRE CIR	0	249A	SWM	77354
E. HEARTHSHIRE CIR	0	249B	SWM	77354
HEARTHSHIRE CT	0	249A	SWM	77354
HEARTHSHIRE DR	0	249A	SWM	77354
HEARTHSIDE CIR	200	657Q	LC	77573
HEARTHSTONE CT	500	252T	SEM	77386
N. HEARTHSTONE GREEN CT	7200	408Q	NWC	77095
W. HEARTHSTONE GREEN DR	7100	408P	NWC	77095
N. HEARTHSTONE GREEN DR	7200	408P	NWC	77095

Street Name	Block	Pg/Sq	Loc	Zips
S. HEARTHSTONE GREEN DR	14600	408P	NWC	77095
HEARTHSTONE HILL LN	22700	292L	SP	77373
HEARTHSTONE MEADOWS DR	14500	408P	NWC	77095
HEARTHSTONE PLACE DR	0	408P	NWC	77084
HEARTHWICK RD	0	250J	NWC	77375
HEARTHWICK PLACE	0	249M	NWC	77375
HEARTHWOOD DR	9600	411N	NWH	77040
HEARTLAND LN	0	336Z	NEC	77346
HEARTLAND GROVE DR	18400	524L	NWF	77406
HEARTLAND KEY LN	0	484T	NEF	77494
HEARTLEAF CT	1	251K	WD	77381
HEART PINE WAY	5500	524D	NEF	77494
HEARTSONG DR	0	328E	NWC	77377
HEARTWIND CT	17400	367T	NWC	77095
HEARTWOOD CREEK DR	0	289C	NWC	77375
HEARTWOOD OAK TRAIL	20900	326N	NWC	77433
HEARTWOOD OAK WAY	3200	297P	NEH	77345
HEARTWOOD WAY	15800	326P	NWC	77433
HEARTY ORANGE CT	0	325L	NWC	77433
HEARTY ORANGE DR	0	325L	NWC	77433
HEATH	6300	415N	NEH	77016
HEATH CT	11100	415T	NEH	77016
HEATHBROOK LN	200	486D	SWC	77094
HEATHCLIFF CT	800	490C	HE	77024
HEATHCLIFF DR	800	570Y	MC	77489
HEATHCOTE CT	1	251T	WD	77380
HEATHCOTE LN	1400	332V	NCC	77073
HEATHER	2200	460Q	NEC	77562
HEATHER	5800	657V	LC	77573
HEATHER CIR	8800	490D	SV	77055
HEATHER CT	800	490C	HE	77024
HEATHER CT	27800	252E	OR	77385
HEATHER LN	100	252E	OR	77385
S. HEATHER LN	500	656H	FR	77546
N. HEATHER LN	500	656H	FR	77546
HEATHER LN	600	501L	BT	77521
HEATHER LN	3100	446P	NWC	77449
HEATHER LN	3700	615V	PL	77581
HEATHER LN	19500	258J	SEM	77357
HEATHERBANK DR	8500	408A	NWC	77095
HEATHER BEND CT	16300	618D	PA	77059
HEATHERBEND DR	2600	613U	NEB	77584
HEATHER BERRY LN	0	367S	NWC	77433
HEATHERBLOOM DR	3100	572N	SWH	77045
HEATHERBLOOM DR	5700	571P	SWH	77085
HEATHER BLOSSOM LN	5900	338E	NEH	77345
HEATHER BLUFF CT	8600	575Y	SEF	77075
HEATHER BLUFF CT	8600	575Y	SEH	77075
HEATHER BLUFF LN	10000	575Y	SEH	77075
HEATHER BLUFF LN	10000	575Y	SEH	77075
HEATHERBRIAR LN	0	524D	NEF	77494
HEATHERBROOK DR	3100	572N	SWH	77045
HEATHERBROOK DR	5600	571P	SWH	77085
HEATHERCLIFF LN	10800	575U	SEH	77075
HEATHER COVE CT	1800	618A	SEH	77062
HEATHERCREST	4900	571Q	SWH	77045
HEATHERCROFT DR	22900	485B	SWC	77450
HEATHERDALE DR	15700	618C	SEH	77059
HEATHERDAWN CT	0	484Z	NEF	77494
HEATHERED OAKS	0	328T	NWC	77429
HEATHER FALLS DR	0	368U	NWC	77065
HEATHER FALLS WAY	14200	618A	SEH	77062
HEATHERFIELD DR	14100	489J	SWH	77079
HEATHERFIELD DR	14400	488M	SWH	77079
HEATHERFORD CT	10300	450E	NWH	77041
HEATHERFORD DR	10600	449H	NWH	77041
HEATHER GATE LN	200	379E	NEC	77532
HEATHERGLEN	4900	531U	SWH	77096
HEATHERGOLD DR	2300	446V	NWC	77084
HEATHER GREEN DR	2100	618G	SEH	77062
HEATHER GROVE CT	20800	337Q	NEC	77346
HEATHER HEIGHTS WAY	7800	407M	NWC	77095
HEATHER HILL DR	10100	371S	NWC	77086
HEATHERHILL PLACE	14100	488J	SWH	77077
HEATHER HOLLOW DR	6800	407N	NWC	77449
HEATHERKNOLL DR	2600	333A	NCC	77373
HEATHER LAKE CT	2900	297Q	NEH	77345
HEATHERLAND DR	8300	330E	NWC	77379
HEATHER LANDING LN	0	528H	SWH	77072
HEATHERLY DR	8700	527R	NEF	77083
HEATHER MEADOW CT	16500	618D	PA	77059
HEATHERMILL DR	11300	371P	NWC	77066
HEATHER MIST CT	15200	325R	NWC	77433
W. HEATHEROCK CIR	3100	609E	SG	77479
E. HEATHEROCK CIR	3100	609E	SG	77479
HEATHEROSE DR	29700	252Z	SEM	77386
HEATHERPARK DR	3000	297Y	NEH	77345
HEATHER PARK DR	4200	578E	PA	77505
HEATHER POINTE	0	658R	LC	77573
HEATHER RIDGE CT	2400	617Y	SEC	77598
HEATHER ROW LN	7200	456L	NEC	77044
HEATHER RUN	5500	448D	NWC	77041
HEATHERSAGE DR	3900	447F	NWC	77084
HEATHERSIDE	8800	454C	NEH	77016
HEATHER SPRINGS DR	0	329R	NWC	77379
HEATHER SPRINGS DR	500	539X	LP	77571
HEATHER SPRINGS LN	1600	658W	LC	77573
HEATHER SPRINGS LN	19000	526G	NEF	77407
HEATHERTON HILL LN	0	572U	SWH	77047
HEATHERTON MILL LN	0	328P	NWC	77377
HEATHER TRAIL DR	11000	575Z	SEH	77075
HEATHERVALE CT	5200	297P	NEH	77345
HEATHER VALLEY WAY	14800	618F	SEH	77062
HEATHERVIEW DR	8600	529Q	SWH	77099
HEATHER WAY CT	22500	445Q	NWC	77449
HEATHERWICK DR	12100	328V	NWC	77429
HEATHERWIND LN	0	573X	SEC	77047
HEATHERWOOD CT	0	484E	KT	77494
HEATHERWOOD CT	400	659H	LC	77573
HEATHERWOOD DR	100	252N	SEM	77386
HEATHERWOOD DR	2100	570Y	MC	77489
HEATHERWOOD DR	2700	501E	BT	77521
HEATHERWOOD DR	11000	413Y	NEH	77076
HEATHERWOOD DR	21900	255Y	SEM	77365
HEATHERWOOD PARK CIR	19700	486L	SWC	77094
HEATH FALLS LN		328P	NWC	77429
HEATHFIELD CT	5100	447B	NWC	77084
HEATHFIELD DR	0	497D	NEC	77530
HEATHFIELD DR	1000	457Z	NEC	77530
HEATHFIELD DR	4100	578E	PA	77505
HEATHGATE CT	15000	618J	SEH	77062
HEATHGATE DR	100	618J	SEH	77062
HEATHGLEN LN	0	575U	SEH	77075
HEATHGLEN LN	0	575U	SEH	77075
HEATH GREEN CIR	0	325R	NWC	77433
HEATH GROVE LN	17300	527E	NEF	77407
HEATH HOLLOW DR	1200	329B	NWC	77379
HEATH HOLLOW LN	0	573T	SEC	77047
HEATH HOLLOW WAY	16600	618R	SEH	77058
HEATH HOUSE DR	0	295Q	SEM	77365
HEATHLAND DR	0	299X	NEC	77336
HEATH MEADOW CT	21900	334F	NCC	77373

Street Name	Block	Pg/Sq	Loc	Zips
HEATHMOOR LN	6000	407V	NWC	77084
HEATH PARK TRAIL	0	616L	SEC	77089
HEATHRIDGE LN	18300	407J	NWC	77433
HEATH RIVER LN	0	406C	NWC	77433
HEATH RIVER LN	0	609U	MC	77459
HEATHROW LN	7900	330Q	NWC	77379
HEATHROW FOREST PKWY	14300	374X	NEH	77032
HEATH SPRING CT	13600	377Y	NEC	77044
HEATHSTONE PLACE	1	250C	WD	77381
HEATHTON DR	8800	529Q	SWH	77099
HEATH VILLA LN	0	526L	NEF	77407
HEATHWICK LN	1200	449W	NWH	77043
HEATHWOOD CT	1100	489N	SWH	77077
HEATHWOOD DR	1200	489J	SWH	77077
HEATHWOOD BROOK LN	21200	290Q	NWC	77379
HEATON CT	17500	246N	SWM	77355
HEATON DR	18000	447B	NWC	77084
S. HEATON LN	26000	246T	SWM	77355
HEATON LN	26600	246P	SWM	77355
HEATON RD	0	615T	PL	77581
HEATON HALL	8200	335S	NCC	77338
HEAVEN LEIGH TRAIL	10100	370U	NWC	77064
HEAVY ANCHOR	9700	376S	NEC	77396
HEBBURN CT	0	250J	NWC	77389
HEBERT	1200	535G	SEH	77012
HEBERT TRAIL DR	2900	487Z	SWC	77082
HEBRON LN	0	524K	NWF	77406
HECHT LN	16800	254Q	SEM	77365
HECTOR	1700	453H	NEH	77093
HECTOR	2400	454E	NEH	77093
HECTOR AVE	700	536V	PA	77502
HECTOR AVE	1300	537S	PA	77502
HEDDON OAKS CT	9800	329G	NWC	77379
HEDEN RD	16200	330N	NWC	77379
HEDGE LN	23300	296M	SEM	77365
HEDGEBELL CT	1	251L	WD	77380
HEDGECROFT	16500	373S	NEH	77060
W. HEDGECROFT DR	1600	620E	EL	77586
E. HEDGECROFT DR	1600	620E	EL	77586
HEDGEDALE WAY	0	250P	NWC	77389
HEDGEDOWN DR	12000	408D	NWC	77065
HEDGEGATE DR	11900	409A	NWC	77065
HEDGE MAPLE CT	6300	337P	NEC	77346
HEDGEPARK DR	6000	525R	NEF	77407
HEDGEROW DR	6900	330Q	NWC	77379
HEDGE SPARROW LN	0	405T	NWC	77493
HEDGESTONE CT	8700	578D	LP	77571
HEDGETON CT	6500	290G	NWC	77389
HEDGE WAY DR	10100	369W	NWC	77065
HEDGEWICK CT	21700	291S	NWC	77388
HEDGEWICK DR	6800	408T	NWC	77084
HEDGEWICK LN	0	291S	NWC	77388
HEDGEWOOD LN	7000	415P	NEH	77016
HEDGLEY PLACE	13400	330Y	NWC	77069
W. HEDRICK	800	495S	SEH	77011
E. HEDRICK	800	495S	SEH	77011
HEDWIG	200	490M	PP	77024
HEDWIG CIR	1	490D	HE	77024
HEDWIG CT	1	490H	PP	77024
HEDWIG LN	11100	490H	PP	77024
HEDWIG GREENS	11000	490H	HC	77024
HEDWIG SHADOWS DR	1	490H	HC	77024
HEDWIG WAY	800	490H	HE	77024
HEFFERNAN	5600	534Q	SEH	77087
HEFLIN LN	14900	408P	NWC	77095
HEFLIN COLONY DR	9400	527V	NEF	77498
HEGAR RD	17300	324A	HK	77447
HEGAR RD	18400	284N	NWC	77447
HEGAR RD	23000	244S	WCO	77447
HEGAR RD	27300	243V	WCO	77447
HEGAR JOSEPH RD	0	243K	WCO	77484
HEGAR MAGNOLIA	22800	282Y	WCO	77447
HEIDELBERG CT	9600	329U	NWC	77070
HEIDEN CIR	16400	330P	NWC	77379
HEIDI LN	0	256V	SEM	77357
HEIDI LN	28100	288B	TB	77375
HEIDI OAKS LN	0	375Y	NEC	77396
HEIDRICH	300	452M	NWH	77018
HEIGHTMONT ESTATES	27500	249F	SWM	77354
HEIGHTS	1200	537P	PA	77503
HEIGHTS BLVD	1	493A	NWH	77007
HEIGHTS BLVD	900	453W	NWH	77008
HEIGHTS BLVD	20000	257R	SEM	77357
HEIGHTS DR	1300	444U	KT	77493
HEIGHTS CROSSING LN	0	375X	NEC	77396
HEIGHTS HARVEST LN	0	327U	NWC	77429
W. HEIGHTS HOLLOW LN	700	493J	SWH	77007
E. HEIGHTS HOLLOW LN	700	493J	SWH	77007
S. HEIGHTS HOLLOW LN	3000	493J	SWH	77007
N. HEIGHTS HOLLOW LN	3000	493J	SWH	77007
HEILIG RD	7400	531J	SWH	77074
HEINER	1000	493P	SWH	77002
HEIRLOOM LN	0	444D	NWC	77493
HEIRLOOM LN	0	445A	NWC	77493
HEISER	5600	534Q	SEH	77087
HEITE	4300	453J	NWH	77022
HELBERG RD	2600	451R	NWH	77092
HELEN	2000	536T	PA	77502
HELEN	2800	493B	NWH	77009
HELEN DR	200	538L	DP	77536
HELEN DR	1400	252Y	SEM	77386
HELEN LN	0	614W	NEB	77584
HELEN LN	3600	615U	PL	77581
HELEN LN	31200	248Y	TB	77375
HELENA	2000	493P	SWH	77002
HELENA	2300	493P	SWH	77006
HELENA HILLS LN	0	657P	FR	77546
HELENE	6400	455P	NEH	77028
HELENE	6700	614D	BK	77581
HELENE CT	11900	248N	SWM	77362
HELENIUM LN	0	293F	SEM	77386
W. HELGRA	100	538K	DP	77536
HELINBACK	300	656J	NEB	77511
HELIOS DR	1400	610Q	MC	77459
S. HELM CT	16200	419B	NEC	77532
N. HELM CT	16200	419B	NEC	77532
HELMERS	4900	453L	NEH	77009
HELMERS	6100	453G	NEH	77022
HELMS	0	616A	SEC	77089
HELMS DR	23600	296E	SEM	77365
HELMS DR	25300	339E	NEH	77336
W. HELMS RD	100	412M	NCC	77037
E. HELMS RD	100	413J	NCC	77037
HELMS RD	100	412L	NWH	77088
HELMSBROOK DR	8700	616A	SEC	77089
HELMSDALE	10200	450N	NWH	77043
HELMSDALE	10400	449R	NWH	77043
HELMSLEY DR	2900	613F	NEB	77584
HELMSMAN	500	419B	NEC	77532
HELVICK BLVD	0	572M	SEH	77051
HELVICK CRESCENT AVE	0	572M	SEH	77051
HEMINGSTONE LN	20000	291Z	NWC	77388

Street Name	Block	Pg/Sq	Loc	Zips
HEMINGTON CIR	19100	329B	NWC	77375
HEMINGTON DR	19100	329B	NWC	77375
HEMINGWAY DR	6400	534Z	SEH	77087
HEMINGWAY PASS LN	0	293D	SEM	77386
HEMLOCK	0	500H	BT	77521
HEMLOCK	6700	534H	SEH	77087
HEMLOCK	7200	535E	SEH	77012
HEMLOCK	12100	248J	SWM	77362
HEMLOCK CIR	3200	659Z	GCO	77539
HEMLOCK DR	1300	536P	PA	77502
HEMLOCK DR	4500	500M	BT	77521
HEMLOCK BRIDGE CT	14800	568A	NEF	77498
HEMLOCK GROVE DR	0	377K	NEC	77346
HEMLOCK HILL DR	8400	528P	SWC	77083
HEMLOCK LAKES DR	2000	337D	NEH	77345
HEMLOCK PARK DR	0	333F	NCC	77073
HEMLOCK RED CT		484W	NEF	77494
HEMPHILL	0	501X	BT	77520
HEMPHILL	500	493F	SWH	77007
HEMPSTEAD AVE	1300	536P	PA	77506
HEMPSTEAD RD	8000	492A	NWH	77008
HEMPSTEAD RD	8800	452W	NWH	77008
HEMPSTEAD RD	9400	451P	NWH	77092
HEMPSTEAD RD	12900	450G	NWH	77040
HEMPSTEAD RD	14200	410W	NWH	77040
HEMPSTEAD RD	15000	409V	NWC	77040
HEMPSTEAD RD	17500	409K	NWC	77065
HEMPSTEAD RD	18500	408C	NWC	77065
HEMPSTEAD RD	20700	368X	NWC	77429
HEMPSTEAD RD	22400	367E	CY	77429
HEMPSTEAD RD	26200	367E	NWC	77429
HEMPSTEAD RD	27000	325V	NWC	77433
HEMPSTEAD RD	28000	325N	NWC	77429
HEMPSTEAD RD	30100	324E	HK	77447
HEMPSTEAD RD	36100	324E	NWC	77484
HEMPSTEAD RD	38700	283W	NWC	77484
HEMPSTEAD RD	39000	282T	WCO	77484
HEMWICK DR	10400	368T	NWC	77429
HEMWICK COVE DR	13600	528P	SWC	77083
HEMWOOD CT	4100	414B	NCC	77039
HENDERSON	500	493F	SWH	77007
HENDERSON	900	618Z	WB	77058
HENDERSON	27200	292L	SP	77373
HENDERSON LN	0	657U	LC	77573
HENDERSON LN	2400	538P	DP	77536
HENDERSON POINT DR	15200	367H	NWC	77429
HENDON LN	6700	530M	SWH	77074
HENDON LN	8700	530J	SWH	77036
HENDON LN	11200	529K	SWH	77072
HENDRICK'S PASS DR	6000	406X	NWC	77449
HENDRICKS	1500	453H	NEH	77093
HENDRICKSEN	13000	574N	SEH	77048
HENDRICKS LAKES DR	0	332A	NWC	77388
HENDRIX PARK DR	0	293G	SEM	77386
HENKE	500	494H	NEH	77020
HENLEY DR	11500	369U	NWC	77064
HENNESSEE LN	400	617M	SEH	77598
HENNESSY LN	7900	290A	NWC	77389
HENNIKER CT	5800	408Z	NWC	77041
HENNIKER DR	5700	408Z	NWC	77041
HENNINGER	1200	494X	SEH	77023
HENNINGTON DR	4900	291S	NWC	77388
HENO	9400	573C	SEH	77051
HENRIETTA	100	618X	WB	77598
HENRIETTA	9000	412P	NWH	77088
HENRY	200	493C	NEH	77009
HENRY	300	656W	AV	77511
HENRY RD	14000	413F	NCC	77060
HENRY RD	15200	373X	NCC	77060
HENRY SHREVE RD	0	367C	NWC	77429
HENSEN CREEK DR	15300	370U	NWC	77086
HENSON	7900	455P	NEH	77028
HENSON FALLS DR	0	524E	NEF	77494
HEPBURN	2100	533N	SWH	77054
HERA DR	3500	610Q	MC	77459
HERALD	3700	455X	NEH	77029
HERALD OAK CT	1	251F	WD	77381
HERALD SQUARE DR	10500	529P	SWH	77099
HERBEN	9200	454A	NEH	77093
HERBERT	900	536M	PA	77506
HERBERT	7000	534D	SEH	77023
HERBRAND DR	13600	617A	SEH	77034
HERCULES AVE	1000	618U	WB	77058
HERD	0	492H	SWH	77007
HERDSMAN DR	800	488F	SWH	77079
HEREFORD	4800	380M	NEC	77532
HEREFORD	7500	535S	SEH	77087
HEREFORD	16500	328R	NWC	77377
HEREFORD CIR	3100	613W	NEB	77578
HEREFORD LN	18100	619S	NB	77058
HERITAGE	0	614V	PL	77584
HERITAGE	18100	619S	NB	77058
HERITAGE	19700	285V	NWC	77377
HERITAGE CT	17700	657D	SEC	77598
W. HERITAGE DR	100	656C	FR	77546
E. HERITAGE DR	100	616Z	FR	77546
HERITAGE LN	5400	484G	KT	77494
HERITAGE LN	11900	490F	BH	77024
HERITAGE BAY DR	17200	657C	SEC	77598
HERITAGE BEND CT	2300	657C	SEC	77598
HERITAGE BEND DR	17500	657C	SEC	77598
HERITAGE CANYON DR	0	406G	NWC	77433
HERITAGE COLONY CT	17800	617Y	SEC	77598
HERITAGE COLONY DR	2100	617Y	SEC	77546
HERITAGE COLONY DR	2400	657D	SEC	77598
HERITAGE COLONY DR	3600	609K	MC	77459
HERITAGE COUNTRY CT	15500	617S	SEC	77546
HERITAGE COUNTRY LN	4600	617S	SEC	77546
HERITAGE COVE CT	17700	657D	SEC	77598
HERITAGE COVE DR	17500	657C	SEC	77598
HERITAGE CREEK CT	17500	657C	SEC	77598
HERITAGE CREEK DR	17600	657C	SEC	77598
HERITAGE CREEK LANDING	0	452X	NWH	77008
HERITAGE CREEK OAKS	0	452X	NWH	77008
HERITAGE CREEK PARK	1200	452X	NWH	77008
HERITAGE CREEK TERRACE	3000	452X	NWH	77008
HERITAGE CREEK VILLAGE	1100	452X	NWH	77008
HERITAGE CROWN CT	12000	573L	SEH	77047
HERITAGE ELM CT	19600	446Q	NWC	77084
HERITAGE FALLS DR	15600	617T	SEC	77546
HERITAGE FARMSTEAD LN	0	366P	NWC	77433
HERITAGE FOREST LN	21300	256W	SEM	77365
W. HERITAGE GRAND CIR	0	485W	NEF	77494
S. HERITAGE GRAND CIR	0	485W	NEF	77494
N. HERITAGE GRAND CIR	0	485W	NEF	77494
E. HERITAGE GRAND CIR	0	485W	NEF	77494
HERITAGE GREEN DR	3100	615L	PL	77581
HERITAGE GROVE DR	12200	371K	NWC	77066
N. HERITAGE HILL CIR	1	250C	WD	77381
HERITAGE HILL CIR	1	250C	WD	77381
HERITAGE HOUSE CIR	17300	657C	SEC	77598
HERITAGE HOUSE DR	2900	657C	SEC	77598
HERITAGE LANDING	2300	615L	PL	77581
HERITAGE MAPLE DR	25800	250U	NWC	77389
W. HERITAGE MILL CIR	0	249H	NWC	77375
N. HERITAGE MILL CIR	0	250E	NWC	77375
E. HERITAGE MILL CIR	0	250J	NWC	77375
W. HERITAGE OAKS DR	23100	296G	SEM	77365
E. HERITAGE OAKS DR	23400	296G	SEM	77365
HERITAGE OAKS LN	200	490Q	PP	77024
HERITAGE PARK W	0	444L	KT	77493
HERITAGE PARK CIR	0	444S	KT	77493
HERITAGE PARK DR	0	444S	KT	77493
HERITAGE PARK DR	5000	444M	KT	77493
HERITAGE PINES DR	7500	337V	NEC	77346
HERITAGE PLAINS DR	4800	617S	SEC	77546
HERITAGE POINT BLVD	18900	246A	SWM	77355
HERITAGE RIDGE DR	0	290S	NWC	77379
HERITAGE ROW CT	0	444S	KT	77493
HERITAGE STAR CROSSING	8200	485W	NEF	77494
HERITAGESTONE DR	4100	371E	NWC	77066
HERITAGE STREAM DR	0	484X	NEF	77494
HERITAGE STREAM DR	0	484X	NEF	77494
HERITAGE TRAIL DR	0	573L	SEH	77047
HERITAGE WATERS CT	9900	376S	NEC	77396
HERITAGE WOOD DR	14800	527D	SWC	77082
HERKIMER	700	492D	NWH	77007
HERKIMER	900	452Z	NWH	77008
HERMAN	100	335Z	HM	77338
HERMANN DR	1000	533A	SWH	77004
HERMANN RD	5900	414M	NEC	77050
HERMANN RD	6100	415J	NEC	77050
HERMANN LAKE DR	6300	533F	SWH	77021
HERMANN MUSEUM CIR	5700	533B	SEH	77004
HERMANN PARK CT	1	533F	SWH	77021
HERMAN PARK DR	5900	533A	SWH	77030
HERMITAGE LN	12900	489L	SWH	77079
HERMITAGE HOLLOW LN	2600	296R	NEH	77339
HERMITAGE OAKS CT	12100	328V	NWC	77377
HERMITAGE OAKS DR	15200	328V	NWC	77377
HERMITAGE OAKS DR	15700	329S	NWC	77377
HERMITAGE TRACE	0	412E	NWC	77038
HERMIT THRUSH LN	14700	288A	NWC	77377
HERMOSA CT	11200	490L	PP	77024
HERMOSA ARROYO DR	0	660G	LC	77573
HERNANDEZ RD	1000	577J	PA	77504
HERNDON	0	494C	NEH	77020
HERNDON PLACE	0	568W	SG	77479
HERNGRIF	16000	373R	NEH	77032
HERON CT	0	245X	SWM	77355
HERON CT	1100	568U	SG	77478
N. HERON DR	1000	620H	SB	77586
S. HERON DR	1300	620G	SB	77586
HERON DR	5400	574A	SEH	77033
HERON DR	6200	534Y	SEH	77087
HERON LN	600	536U	PA	77502
HERON LN	5300	614X	PL	77584
HERON LN	18800	286H	NWC	77377
HERON COVE CT	18600	447E	NWC	77084
HERON CREST DR	0	366P	NWC	77433
HERON FALLS LN	0	659H	LC	77573
HERON FIELD CT	13500	578W	SEH	77059
HERON FLIGHT	8700	370S	NWC	77064
HERON FOREST LN	18000	376D	NEC	77346
HERONGATE DR	15800	448A	NWC	77084
S. HERON INLET	0	542J	BT	77520
N. HERON INLET	0	542J	BT	77520
HERON LAKES CT	0	370S	NWC	77064
HERON LAKES DR	0	370S	NWC	77064
HERON MARSH DR	14300	327X	NWC	77429
HERON MEADOW LN	0	327V	NWC	77429
HERON MEADOWS DR	0	367Y	NWC	77095
HERON NEST	8900	369V	NWC	77064
HERON NEST	11000	370S	NWC	77064
HERON NEST DR	8700	370S	NWC	77064
HERON PARK CT	7600	375U	NEC	77396
HERON PARK DR	15200	375U	NEC	77396
HERON POINT DR	16400	327X	NWC	77429
HERONS CREST	0	333F	NCC	77338
HERONS FLIGHT PLACE	100	250L	NWC	77389
HERONS GROVE LN	0	524G	NEF	77494
HERON SHADOW CT	0	526K	NEF	77407
HERONS TERRACE	0	525Z	NEF	77406
HERON TRAIL	15900	328R	NWC	77377
HERON VIEW	8700	370S	NWC	77064
HERON VILLAGE DR	11000	370S	NWC	77064
HERON WALK	8700	370S	NWC	77064
HERON WAY	1000	568Q	SG	77478
HERON WAY	11000	370S	NWC	77064
HERONWOOD DR	5400	337N	NEC	77346
HERRICK CT	700	486B	SWC	77450
HERRIDGE	4300	453J	NWH	77022
HERRING BONE DR	0	570Y	MC	77489
HERRIN LANDING BLVD	0	609X	NEF	77479
HERRIN LANDING LN	0	366Y	NWC	77433
HERRITAGE SHORE	300	487A	SWC	77094
HERRNHUT DR	17300	657C	SEC	77598
HERSCHELL	4600	455X	NEH	77028
HERSCHELL ST	0	455K	NEH	77028
HERSCHELWOOD	8000	534W	SEH	77033
HERSHE	4200	494F	NEH	77020
HERSHE	7900	495E	NEH	77029
HERSHE	13700	497F	NEC	77015
HERSHEY	0	574R	SEH	77048
HERTFORD	6000	574U	SEH	77048
HERTFORD PARK DR	6700	408P	NWC	77084
HERTFORDSHIRE CIR	8000	330K	NWC	77379
HERTFORDSHIRE DR	7600	330K	NWC	77379
HERTS RD	8200	330P	NWC	77379
HERVEY LN	0	658Q	LC	77573
HERVIE	0	576V	SEH	77034
HESLEP	600	453X	NWH	77009
HESPERIAN	5300	452E	NWH	77091
HESS LN	0	531W	SWH	77096
HESSE CT	22200	445R	NWC	77449
HESSETT CREEK DR	0	295R	SEM	77365
HESSON	0	576U	SEH	77034
HESS VALLEY	0	287A	SWM	77355
HESTA LN	6100	454D	NEH	77016
HESTER	600	620Q	SB	77586
HEWES POINT LN	0	609Y	NEF	77459
HEWING DR	17100	617Y	SEC	77546
HEWITT	1600	659L	LC	77573
HEWITT CIR	0	410P	NWC	77040
HEWITT DR	1300	452J	NWH	77018
HEWITT DR	5500	451K	NWH	77092
HEWITT DR	9300	251C	WD	77381
HEWN ROCK	0	613P	PL	77584
HEWRICK	3300	455W	NEH	77020
HEXHAM CT	9500	330S	NWC	77379
HEXHAM DR	16100	330S	NWC	77379
HEYSHAM	500	496E	NEH	77013
HEZEKIAH LN	7200	412S	NWH	77088
HH RANCH	0	374Q	NEH	77032
HIACINTAS WAY	0	333K	NCC	77338
HIALEAH DR	1700	620K	SB	77586
HIALEAH DR	2200	451M	NWH	77018
HIALEAH DR	4900	451L	NWH	77092
HIALEAH LN	4300	538N	PA	77503
HIAWATHA	7800	461S	NEC	77521
HIAWATHA DR	7700	530E	SWH	77036
HIAWATHA LN	3900	577G	PA	77505
HIBERNIA DR	9900	411J	NWH	77088
HIBISCUS LN	16400	657A	FR	77546
HIBISCUS LN	16600	657B	FR	77546
HIBISCUS POINT DR	16700	367Y	NWC	77095
HIBURY CT	0	490N	SWH	77024
HIBURY DR	1	490J	SWH	77024
HICKMAN	5600	454U	NEH	77016
HICKMAN MANOR LN	21500	406X	NWC	77449
HICKOK	8000	575K	SEH	77075
HICKOK LN	3000	573L	SEH	77047
HICKORY	600	288G	TB	77375
HICKORY	1000	493G	SWH	77007
HICKORY	3400	538U	DP	77536
HICKORY CT	0	295Y	SEM	77365
HICKORY CT	1	297E	SEM	77365
HICKORY CT	1500	616P	PL	77581
HICKORY CT	28000	245K	SWM	77355
HICKORY DR	0	615B	PL	77581
HICKORY DR	23500	297E	SEM	77365
HICKORY LN	0	257M	SEM	77357
HICKORY LN	1200	336K	NEH	77339
HICKORY LN	1200	419T	NEC	77532
HICKORY LN	2100	537S	PA	77502
HICKORY LN	7300	462Y	BT	77521
HICKORY LN	19400	286A	SWM	77355
HICKORY ASHE DR	18700	337Z	NEC	77346
HICKORYBARK DR	1	250M	WD	77381
HICKORY BAY CT	2000	486K	SWC	77450
HICKORY BEND	0	615G	PL	77581
HICKORY BEND CT	0	615G	PL	77581
HICKORY BEND CT	3100	447N	NWC	77084
HICKORY BEND DR	12600	369L	NWC	77070
HICKORY BLUFF DR	0	290S	NWC	77379
HICKORY BOUGH CT	6300	297V	NEH	77345
HICKORY BRANCH LN	8600	335N	NEC	77338
HICKORY BROOK LN	3200	297X	NEH	77345
HICKORY BURL CT	0	446B	NWC	77449
HICKORY CANYON CT	7300	375X	NEC	77396
HICKORY CHASE CT	20300	486K	SWC	77450
HICKORY CHASE DR	1700	486K	SWC	77450
HICKORY COVE DR	15900	407M	NWC	77095
HICKORY CREEK CIR	0	366N	NWC	77433
HICKORY CREEK DR	1900	336C	NEH	77339
HICKORY CREEK DR	3400	615B	PL	77581
HICKORYCREST DR	6100	290C	NWC	77389
HICKORY DALE	15300	327S	NWC	77429
HICKORY DOWNS DR	4300	448E	NWC	77084
HICKORY FALLS DR	3000	297Y	NEH	77345
HICKORY FARM DR	20800	446N	NWC	77449
HICKORY FIELD CT	26300	366H	NWC	77433
HICKORY FOREST DR	5400	411Q	NWC	77088
HICKORY GARDENS LN	0	447N	NWC	77084
HICKORYGATE DR	4300	293Y	NCC	77373
HICKORY GLEN CT	0	296V	NEH	77339
HICKORY GLEN DR	1900	570W	MC	77489
HICKORY GREEN CT	4900	297Q	NEH	77345
HICKORY GROVE DR	4300	448E	NWC	77084
HICKORY GROVE LN	0	253P	SEM	77386
HICKORY GROVE LN	3200	613B	NEB	77584
HICKORY HARVEST DR	5400	526T	NEF	77407
HICKORY HILL CT	1800	569W	SG	77478
HICKORY HILL LN	11800	368D	NWC	77429
HICKORY HILL RD	24700	251T	SWM	77380
HICKORY HILLS DR	0	366R	NWC	77433
HICKORY HOLLOW	900	491A	HC	77024
HICKORY HOLLOW LN	2300	252Z	SEM	77386
HICKORY HOLLOW LN	12000	247R	SWM	77362
HICKORY HOLLOW RD	3200	251N	SWM	77380
HICKORY HOLLOW PLACE	1	250H	WD	77381
HICKORY KNOB CT	3700	297W	NEH	77339
HICKORY KNOLL DR	15700	618C	SEH	77059
HICKORY KNOLLS DR	0	615B	PL	77581
HICKORY LAKE DR	1400	611X	NEF	77545
HICKORY LAKES LN	0	257F	SEM	77357
HICKORY LAWN DR	1900	489S	SWH	77077
HICKORY LIMB CT	2800	659H	LC	77573
HICKORY MANOR DR	1800	339P	HU	77336
HICKORY MEADOW LN	0	446R	NWC	77084
HICKORY MEADOWS CT	13900	417B	NEC	77044
HICKORY MILL CT	7800	407K	NWC	77095
HICKORY OAK DR	1	251A	WD	77381
HICKORY OAK DR	4200	291K	NWC	77389
HICKORY PARK DR	2000	337D	NEH	77345
HICKORY POINT CT	7500	407M	NWC	77095
HICKORY POINT RD	16100	407M	NWC	77095
HICKORY POST CT	1000	289A	TB	77375
HICKORY POST LN	300	489J	SWH	77079
HICKORY RANCH DR	17500	324H	NWC	77447
HICKORY RIDGE	0	490N	SWH	77063
HICKORY RIDGE DR	1	490J	SWH	77024
HICKORY RIDGE DR	1	298H	NEC	77336
HICKORY RIDGE DR	100	251D	SD	77381
HICKORY RIDGE DR	200	299E	NEC	77336
HICKORY RIDGE DR	300	620J	EL	77586
HICKORY SHADOWS DR	1	491A	HI	77055
HICKORY SPRINGS DR	5600	297Z	NEH	77345
HICKORY SPRINGS LN	0	612P	PL	77545
HICKORY STREAM CT	14300	331S	NWC	77068
HICKORY TERRACE DR	29300	253X	SEM	77386
HICKORYTEX DR	14800	375T	NEH	77396
HICKORY TRACE CT	9900	329L	NWC	77375
HICKORY TRAIL	10000	369Y	NWC	77064
HICKORY TRAIL PLACE	2100	486P	SWC	77450
HICKORY TREE CT	10900	368Z	NWC	77065
HICKORY TUNNEL LN	0	447J	NWC	77084
HICKORY TWIG LN	0	292W	NWC	77388
HICKORY TWIG WAY	19600	292W	NWC	77388
HICKORY VALLEY LN	25300	292V	NCC	77373
HICKORY VIEW CT	3800	617X	SEC	77546
HICKORY VILLAGE DR	5300	297Y	NEH	77345
HICKORY WIND DR	19900	337Q	NEC	77346
HICKORY WIND DR	19900	337V	NEC	77346
HICKORY WOOD	11900	248N	SWM	77362
HICKORYWOOD LN	800	490C	HE	77024
HICKORY WOOD LN	3200	613B	NEB	77584
HICKS	500	288G	TB	77375
HICKS	2800	493E	SWH	77007
HICKSFIELD	0	494X	SEH	77023
HICKS FIELD LN	0	660K	LC	77573
HIDALGO	5000	491U	SWH	77056
HIDALGO	6500	500C	NEC	77521
HIDALGO FALLS BLVD	0	326K	NWC	77433
HIDALGO VALLEY LN	0	332X	NWC	77090
HIDDEN CIR	0	250C	WD	77381
HIDDEN CT	0	248D	SWM	77354
HIDDEN CT	9200	248D	SWM	77354
HIDDEN ACRES DR	16000	448A	NWC	77084
HIDDEN ALLEY DR	0	524H	NEF	77494
HIDDEN ALLEY DR	0	524H	NEF	77494
HIDDEN ARBOR LN	6300	411S	NWH	77088
HIDDEN ARBOR LN	7000	411S	NWH	77040
HIDDEN BAY CT	2700	612R	PL	77584
HIDDENBAY CT	8000	330A	NWC	77379
HIDDEN BAY DR	11300	612R	PL	77584
HIDDENBAY WAY	18500	330E	NWC	77379
HIDDEN BEND DR	11000	369Y	NWC	77064
HIDDEN BLUFF LN	28500	293E	SEM	77386
HIDDEN BOUGH LN	0	609U	MC	77459
HIDDEN BRANCH DR	15900	458S	NEC	77049
HIDDEN BREEZE DR	0	458S	NEC	77049
HIDDEN BRIDLE CT	21000	332V	NCC	77073
HIDDEN BROOK LN	1700	658W	LC	77573
HIDDEN BROOK LN	3700	445M	NWC	77449
HIDDEN CANYON RD	800	485H	SWC	77450
HIDDEN CASTLE DR	12700	457W	NEC	77015
HIDDEN CHASE DR	0	458S	NEC	77049
HIDDEN CHESTNUT LN	4800	446D	NWC	77084
HIDDEN CLIFF DR	0	450J	NWH	77080
HIDDEN CLOVER CIR	15000	325U	NWC	77433
HIDDEN COVE	0	246G	SWM	77355
HIDDEN COVE	1	610N	MC	77459
HIDDEN COVE	15800	488A	SWH	77079
HIDDEN COVE CT	1900	619Z	LC	77573
HIDDEN COVE CT	28600	248D	SWM	77354
HIDDEN CREEK DR	1900	336C	NEH	77339
HIDDEN CREEK DR	2500	615Q	PL	77581
HIDDEN CREEK LN	700	616V	FR	77546
HIDDEN CREST DR	0	458S	NEC	77049
HIDDEN CYPRESS LN	0	611N	FS	77545
HIDDEN DALE POINT DR	0	328Y	NWC	77429
HIDDEN DEER CORNER CT	1	250L	WD	77381
HIDDEN DELL CT	13500	578W	SEH	77059
HIDDEN FALLS CT	21800	525C	NEF	77450
HIDDEN FALLS DR	10000	613K	PL	77584
HIDDEN FOREST DR	17500	330J	NWC	77379
HIDDEN FORT LN	4000	609F	MC	77459
HIDDEN FOX LN	0	447E	NWC	77084
HIDDEN GARDEN DR	2600	297S	NEH	77339
HIDDEN GLEN DR	3900	297S	NEH	77339
HIDDEN GLEN LN	0	615G	PL	77581
HIDDEN GROVE CT	11500	329N	NWC	77377
HIDDEN GROVE LANDING DR	0	294J	SEM	77386
HIDDEN GROVE LANDING DR	27000	294T	SEM	77386
HIDDEN GROVE TRAIL	16200	329N	NWC	77377
HIDDEN HARBOR	400	488A	SWH	77079
HIDDEN HAVEN	15700	408A	NWC	77095
HIDDEN HILL CIR	1500	336K	NEH	77339
HIDDEN HOLLOW LN	0	252M	SEM	77385
HIDDEN KEY CT	0	332W	NWC	77090
HIDDEN KEY CT	0	332W	NWC	77090
HIDDEN KNOLL CT	2700	609A	SG	77478
E. HIDDEN LAKE	9100	249A	SWM	77354
W. HIDDEN LAKE	10100	524P	NWF	77406
W. HIDDEN LAKE	28600	248D	SWM	77354
HIDDEN LAKE DR	0	249A	SWM	77354
HIDDEN LAKE DR	100	620W	LC	77573
HIDDEN LAKE LN	10100	524P	NWF	77406
HIDDEN LAKE LN	13800	568F	SG	77498
HIDDEN LAKE RD	24500	251W	SWM	77380
HIDDEN LAKES DR	0	298W	NEH	77345
HIDDEN LAKES DR	5700	337D	NEH	77345
HIDDEN LANDING DR	2700	612R	PL	77584
HIDDEN LEAF DR	0	457V	NEC	77530
HIDDEN LINKS CT	4200	337F	NEH	77339
HIDDEN LODGE CT	24900	485N	NEF	77494
HIDDEN MANOR DR	0	458S	NEC	77049
HIDDEN MAPLE DR	23500	293W	NCC	77373
HIDDEN MEADOW DR	14200	568A	SG	77498
HIDDEN MEADOW LN	0	615M	PL	77089
HIDDEN MILL DR	5000	291J	NWC	77389
HIDDEN MIST CT	3000	613P	NEB	77584
HIDDEN MOON DR	10400	369Y	NWC	77064
HIDDEN NEST CT	0	447A	NWC	77084
HIDDEN OAK CT	0	330E	NWC	77379
HIDDEN OAK LN	700	616R	FR	77546
HIDDEN OAKS	1100	658L	LC	77573
HIDDEN OAKS LN	7700	407M	NWC	77095
HIDDEN PARK DR	1700	458S	NEC	77049
HIDDEN PARK DR	1800	457V	NEC	77049
HIDDEN PARK LN	2500	252R	SEM	77385
HIDDEN PINE LN	600	616V	FR	77546
HIDDEN PINES CT	200	658N	LC	77573
HIDDEN PINES DR	3400	296Y	NEH	77339
HIDDEN POINT LN	20400	526J	NEF	77407
HIDDEN POINTE SHORES LN	13300	414B	NCC	77039
HIDDEN PORT LN	10000	616L	SEC	77089
HIDDEN RANCH DR	0	406X	NWC	77449
W. HIDDEN RIDGE	700	332V	NCC	77073
E. HIDDEN RIDGE	800	332V	NCC	77073
HIDDEN RIDGE CT	6500	609J	NEF	77479
HIDDEN RIVER DR	14500	528S	NEF	77083
HIDDEN RIVER LN	0	612Q	PL	77584
HIDDEN ROSE LN	0	416Z	NEC	77044
HIDDEN SHADOW LN	19700	406M	NWC	77433
HIDDEN SHIRE LN	0	328K	NWC	77377
HIDDEN SHORE CIR	20600	486P	SWC	77450
HIDDEN SHORE DR	2400	486P	SWC	77450
HIDDEN SPRING FALLS DR	2700	293B	SEM	77386
HIDDEN SPRINGS CIR	2800	613X	NEB	77578
HIDDEN SPRINGS DR	4500	448B	NWC	77084
HIDDEN SPRING VALE DR	2700	293A	SEM	77386
HIDDEN TERRACE DR	0	458S	NEC	77049
HIDDEN TIMBERS LN	0	484E	KT	77494
HIDDEN TRACE CT	4400	371F	NWC	77066
HIDDEN TRAIL CT	17700	330J	NWC	77379
HIDDEN TRAIL DR	8400	330J	NWC	77379
HIDDEN TRAIL DR	28700	248D	SWM	77354
HIDDEN TRAIL LN	8000	330J	NWC	77379
HIDDEN TREASURE CIR	16900	657C	SEC	77546
HIDDEN VALLEY DR	500	412M	NCC	77037
HIDDEN VALLEY DR	700	412L	NWH	77088
HIDDEN VALLEY WATERS DR	0	328Z	NWC	77429
S. HIDDEN VIEW CIR	1	250C	WD	77381
N. HIDDEN VIEW CIR	1	250C	WD	77381
HIDDEN VIEW PLACE	1	250C	WD	77381
HIDDEN VILLAS DR	1700	336G	NEH	77339
HIDDEN VISTA LN	0	326L	NWC	77429
HIDDEN WINDS DR	4000	294J	SEM	77386
HIDDEN WINDS DR	4000	293M	SEM	77386
HIDDENWOOD DR	15000	329S	NWC	77070
HIDDEN WOODS LN	0	253K	SEM	77386
HIDDEN WOODS LN	700	616V	FR	77546
N. HIDE CT	21100	332V	NCC	77073
HIDEAWAY	3500	331H	NWC	77388
HIDEAWAY CIR	1	530U	SWH	77074
E. HIDEAWAY CT	8100	250S	NWC	77389

Street Name	Block	Pg/Sq	Loc	Zips
W. HIDEAWAY CT	8200	250S	NWC	77389
HIDEAWAY BEND LN	9900	416Z	NEC	77044
HIDEAWAY GREEN DR	0	524S	NWF	77406
HIDEAWAY LAKE CIR	8100	250S	NWC	77389
HIDEAWAY PARK DR	12400	369J	NWC	77429
HIDEAWAY PASS LN	0	609T	NEF	77479
HIDEAWAY RUN CT	8200	250S	NWC	77389
HIDEAWAY RUN DR	25200	250S	NWC	77389
HIENSLEY	300	493G	NEH	77009
HIFORD DR	3700	573Q	SEH	77047
HIGBIE DR		325S	NWC	77447
W. HIGGINS	100	335U	HM	77338
HIGGINS	100	335U	HM	77338
HIGGINS	900	463E	MB	77580
HIGGINS	4800	573D	SEH	77033
HIGGINS	5100	574A	SEH	77033
HIGGINS ST	0	335Z	HM	77338
HIGH	1	541C	BT	77520
HIGH	200	288G	TB	77375
HIGH	3500	493E	SWH	77007
HIGH BANKS LN	13500	577W	SEH	77034
HIGHBRIDGE CT	11400	369W	NWC	77065
HIGH BRIDGE CT	24700	485X	NEF	77494
HIGHBRIDGE FOREST LN	24500	296J	SEM	77365
HIGHBROOK DR	0	408F	NWC	77095
HIGHBURY CT	5700	407Y	NWC	77084
HIGHBURY VIEW CT	13100	572Q	SWH	77047
HIGH CANYON CT	2900	486S	SWC	77450
HIGH CANYON CT	4500	658N	LC	77573
HIGH CANYON LN	19100	328D	NWC	77377
HIGH CASTLE CT	3000	578S	SEH	77059
HIGH CHAPARRAL	36300	246G	SWM	77355
HIGHCLERE MANOR LN	0	451Y	NWH	77055
HIGHCLERE PARK DR	1	329D	NWC	77379
HIGHCLIFF CT	15001	457Q	NEC	77049
HIGHCLIFF LN	0	526L	NEF	77407
HIGH COTTON LN	0	528H	SWH	77072
HIGH CREEK DR	17800	329M	NWC	77379
HIGHCREST DR	0	451T	NWH	77055
HIGHCREST DR	1900	570X	MC	77489
HIGHCREST DR	7500	451S	NWH	77055
HIGHCREST DR	8600	450U	NWH	77080
HIGHCROFT DR	14100	488J	SWH	77077
HIGHDALE CT	19700	337U	NEC	77346
HIGH DESERT LN	0	485P	NEF	77494
HIGHET PLACE	20800	289T	NWC	77375
HIGH FALLS DR	3500	331S	NWC	77068
HIGH FALLS LN	0	615G	PL	77581
HIGH FERRY LN	13800	327Z	NWC	77429
HIGHFIELD DR	15600	408E	NWC	77095
HIGHFIELD PARK DR	0	406C	NWC	77433
HIGHFIELD RIDGE LN	0	332H	NCC	77373
HIGH FOREST DR	0	376H	NEH	77346
HIGH GARDEN LN	0	611S	FS	77545
HIGH GATE CT	1800	569W	SG	77478
HIGHGATE LN	0	450V	NWH	77080
HIGHGLEN CT	5200	297P	NEH	77345
HIGHGREEN DR	3500	297W	NEH	77339
HIGHGROVE DR	11300	489P	SWH	77077
HIGHGROVE PARK	700	491B	SWH	77024
HIGH HAVEN DR	8800	527R	NEF	77083
HIGH HILL	0	244E	WCO	77447
HIGH HOLLOW LN	7900	369D	NWC	77070
HIGH ISLAND WAY	0	333K	NCC	77073
HIGH KNOB DR	10900	368V	NWC	77065
HIGHKNOLL LN	4000	619L	TL	77586
HIGH KNOLL LN	7900	407K	NWC	77095
HIGHLAND	100	493B	NWH	77009
HIGHLAND CIR	1	251B	WD	77381
S. HIGHLAND CT	1	251B	WD	77381
N. HIGHLAND CT	1	251B	WD	77381
HIGHLAND CT	2700	569N	SG	77478
HIGHLAND DR	0	257K	SEM	77357
HIGHLAND GAP LN	0	615B	PL	77581
HIGHLAND ARBOR DR	7800	370A	NWC	77070
HIGHLAND BAY CT	2000	486K	SWC	77450
HIGHLAND BLUFF LN	0	332D	NCC	77373
HIGHLAND BRANCH DR	6200	337T	NEC	77346
HIGHLAND BROOK DR	12900	527Q	NEF	77083
HIGHLAND CANYON DR	17000	407G	NWC	77095
HIGHLAND CASTLE LN	13400	457W	NEC	77015
HIGHLAND CLIFF LN	0	445E	NWC	77493
HIGHLAND COUNTRY DR	0	366N	NWC	77433
HIGHLAND COVE DR	0	369D	NWC	77070
HIGHLAND COVE DR	0	370E	NWC	77069
HIGHLAND CREEK RANCH DR	20200	406Q	NWC	77449
HIGHLAND CROSS DR	100	332L	NCC	77073
HIGHLAND ELM	15200	326S	NWC	77433
HIGHLANDER DR	16000	487Y	SWC	77082
HIGHLANDER DR	16100	527C	SWC	77082
HIGHLAND ESTATES CT	22900	252L	SEM	77385
HIGHLAND FALLS LN	5200	525D	NEF	77450
HIGHLAND FARMS RD	7500	407M	NWC	77095
HIGHLAND FERN CT	2700	337B	NEH	77345
HIGHLAND FIELD LN	4500	609J	NEF	77479
HIGHLANDGATE DR	22200	334F	NCC	77373
HIGHLAND GLADE CT	21800	296X	SEM	77339
HIGHLAND GLEN DR	7801	370E	NWC	77070
HIGHLAND GLEN LN	1600	615F	PL	77581
HIGHLAND GREEN CT	0	370E	NWC	77069
HIGHLAND HAVEN DR		366R	NWC	77433
HIGHLAND HILLS	12800	328V	NWC	77429
HIGHLAND HILLS DR	2000	568Y	SG	77478
HIGHLAND HOLLOW LN	20700	333P	NCC	77073
HIGH LANDING	0	485P	NEF	77493
HIGH LANDING LN	0	485P	NEF	77493
HIGHLAND KNOLLS DR	19900	486J	SWC	77450
HIGHLAND KNOLLS DR	21600	485M	SWC	77450
HIGHLAND LAKE LN	0	612P	PL	77545
HIGHLAND LAKES DR	2800	609M	MC	77459
HIGHLAND LAKES DR	3500	297W	NEH	77339
HIGHLAND LAUREL DR	2900	297X	NEH	77345
HIGHLAND LODGE LN	0	457A	NEC	77044
HIGHLAND MAPLE CT	0	332D	NCC	77373
HIGHLAND MEADOW DR	11500	616C	SEC	77089
HIGHLAND MEADOWS DR	0	615M	PL	77089
HIGHLAND MEADOW VLLG DR	10900	616C	SEC	77089
HIGHLAND MIST CIR	400	457W	NEC	77015
HIGHLAND OAK CT	7200	527J	NEF	77407
HIGHLAND OAK LN	0	486K	SWC	77450
HIGHLAND OAK LN	17300	527J	NEF	77407
HIGHLAND PARK CT	13400	370E	NWC	77070
HIGHLAND PARK DR	13501	370E	NWC	77070
HIGHLAND PARK LN	0	615F	PL	77581
HIGHLAND PLACE DR	0	446E	NWC	77449
HIGHLAND POINT CT	0	332H	NCC	77373
HIGHLAND POINT CT	0	615F	PL	77581
HIGHLAND POINT LN	0	332H	NCC	77373
HIGHLAND POINT LN	0	615F	PL	77581
HIGHLANDS, THE DR	2500	568Z	SG	77478
HIGHLAND SAGE LN	0	332H	NCC	77373
E. HIGHLANDS BAYOU DR	0	367W	NWC	77095

Street Name	Block	Pg/Sq	Loc	Zips
HIGHLAND SHORES DR	100	459E	NEC	77562
HIGHLAND SPRING DR	0	489P	SWH	77077
HIGHLAND STONE CT	2100	486P	SWC	77450
HIGHLAND STONE DR	0	486P	SWC	77450
HIGHLANDS VIEW CT	15700	448B	NWC	77084
HIGHLAND TERRACE	100	658L	LC	77573
HIGHLAND TIMBERS DR	0	370E	NWC	77070
HIGHLAND TRACE DR	0	370E	NWC	77070
HIGHLAND TRAIL	18700	447J	NWC	77084
HIGHLAND VALE CT	3900	611W	FS	77545
HIGHLAND VIEW	0	446J	NWC	77449
HIGHLAND VILLA LN	16700	376K	NEC	77396
HIGHLAND WAY LN	14800	527V	NEF	77498
HIGHLAND WOODS DR	400	459Q	HG	77562
HIGHLAND WOODS DR	10600	528W	NEF	77498
HIGHLAWN	9200	453F	NEH	77022
HIGH LEVEL RD	8500	495T	NEH	77029
HIGH LIFE DR	6900	370Q	NWC	77066
W. HIGHLINE DR	100	538P	DP	77536
E. HIGHLINE DR	100	538Q	DP	77536
HIGHMANOR DR	12700	412A	NWC	77038
HIGH MEADOW	5800	657V	LC	77573
HIGH MEADOW	7500	490T	SWH	77063
HIGH MEADOW	27700	288P	NWC	77377
S. HIGH MEADOW CIR	30500	245N	SWM	77355
N. HIGH MEADOW CIR	30500	245N	SWM	77355
HIGHMEADOW DR	7500	490S	SWH	77063
HIGHMEADOW LN	19200	326C	NWC	77377
HIGHMEADOW LN	19400	286Y	NWC	77377
HIGHMEADOW BEND LN	0	406Q	NWC	77449
HIGH MEADOW RANCH	300	247A	SWM	77355
HIGH MESA CT	13400	578X	SEH	77059
HIGHMORE DR	16800	375E	NCC	77396
HIGH MOUNTAIN DR	8500	411R	NWH	77088
HIGH NOON	3000	336T	NEC	77338
HIGH NOON CT	0	366Q	NWC	77433
HIGH OAK LN	34800	247F	SWM	77362
S. HIGH OAKS CIR	1	251Z	WD	77380
N. HIGH OAKS CIR	1	251Z	WD	77380
HIGH PARK CIR	0	332H	NCC	77373
HIGH PINE DR	3300	609G	MC	77459
HIGHPINES DR	3800	331W	NWC	77068
HIGH PLAINS DR	2900	446P	NWC	77449
HIGH POINT LN	3900	572S	SWH	77053
HIGH POINT LN	4600	571V	SWH	77053
HIGHPOINT CROSSING	0	298P	NEC	77336
HIGHPOINTE GREEN	1500	329C	NWC	77379
HIGHPOINTE RUN LN		328k	NWC	77377
HIGH POINT PINES DR	22500	292K	NCC	77373
HIGHRIDGE	200	456Z	NEH	77013
HIGH RIDGE CIR	900	657J	FR	77546
HIGH RIDGE DR	500	657J	FR	77546
HIGHROCK RD	6600	451A	NWH	77092
HIGH SEA DR	12600	328Q	NWC	77377
HIGH SIERRA LN	3500	447J	NWC	77084
HIGHSPRINGS DR	15200	331S	NWC	77068
HIGH STAR DR	5800	531E	SWH	77081
HIGH STAR DR	6400	531E	SWH	77074
HIGH STAR DR	7700	530A	SWH	77036
HIGH STAR DR	10600	529E	SWH	77072
HIGH STAR DR	12500	528H	SWH	77072
HIGH STAR DR	13200	528H	SWH	77083
HIGH STAR LANDING DR	0	528H	SWH	77072
HIGHSTONE CT	2200	658S	LC	77573
HIGH STONE LN	6600	406P	NWC	77449
HIGH SUMMIT LN	0	407A	NWC	77433
HIGH THICKET CT	0	332H	NCC	77373
HIGH TIDE LN	0	612K	PL	77545
HIGH TIMBERS DR	0	251M	WD	77380
HIGH TIMBERS DR	2400	251G	WD	77380
HIGHTOWER LN	19300	335T	NEH	77338
HIGH TREE TRAIL	0	616H	SEC	77089
HIGH VALLEY DR	0	338A	NEH	77345
HIGH VALLEY DR	1700	298W	NEH	77345
HIGH VALLEY DR	2900	297Z	NEH	77345
HIGHVIEW DR	2500	414A	NCC	77039
HIGH VILLAGE DR	7700	407M	NWC	77095
HIGHWAY BLVD	5000	444Y	KT	77494
HIGHWIND BEND LN	6600	406U	NWC	77449
HIGHWOOD RD	13100	489G	SWH	77079
HIGHWORTH DR	17000	329M	NWC	77379
HIKER'S PATH DR	0	377D	NEC	77346
HIKERS TRAIL DR	18900	338W	NEC	77346
HIKS BAY LN	0	525L	NEF	77407
HILARY	5600	454U	NEH	77026
HILBERT	2200	412J	NWC	77088
HIL CRIS RD	1500	569Z	NEF	77477
W. HILCROFT AVE	0	610C	SWH	77489
HILDA	9000	533Z	SEH	77033
HILDA OAKS DR	0	455G	NEH	77028
HILDEBRANDT RD	22000	290L	NWC	77389
HILL	200	298X	NEH	77336
HILL	1200	494E	NEH	77020
HILL	1600	659Y	GCO	77539
HILL	1800	541A	BT	77520
HILL AVE	1600	659Z	GCO	77539
S. HILL DR	2500	616M	SEC	77089
HILL RD	100	413K	NCC	77037
HILL RD	1300	413L	NCC	77039
HILLARD	0	577X	SEH	77034
HILLARD	8100	412S	NWH	77088
HILLARD GREEN LN	14300	573X	SEC	77047
W. HILLARY CIR	400	568K	SG	77498
E. HILLARY CIR	400	568K	SG	77498
HILLARY CIR	500	568K	SG	77498
HILLBARN DR	7700	410L	NWC	77040
HILL BRANCH DR	12700	488Y	SWH	77082
HILLBROOK CT	15200	329S	NWC	77070
HILLBROOK DR	3800	613Y	NEB	77584
HILLBROOK DR	11600	329S	NWC	77070
HILL CANYON LN	0	528Q	SWC	77072
HILL CANYON LN	13000	528Q	SWH	77072
HILL COUNTRY DR	15200	328N	NWC	77429
HILL CREEK RD	23100	334A	NCC	77373
HILL CREEK BEND	0	612N	PL	77545
HILL CREEK FALLS CT		249Z	NWC	77375
HILLCREST	1700	499H	NEC	77520
HILLCREST	12000	248J	SWM	77362
HILLCREST	12100	247M	SWM	77362
S. HILLCREST DR	20000	295D	SEM	77365
N. HILLCREST DR	20000	255V	SEM	77365
HILLCREST RD	7200	409R	JV	77040
HILLCREST ST	0	532T	SWH	77025
HILLCROFT	2700	490Z	SWH	77057
HILLCROFT	5600	530D	SWH	77036
HILLCROFT	6000	531A	SWH	77081
HILLCROFT	8300	531W	SWH	77096
HILLCROFT	11300	571E	SWH	77035
HILLCROFT	12700	571N	SWH	77085
HILLCROFT	14500	570V	SWH	77489
HILLDALE	9100	490C	SV	77055
HILLDALE PARK CT	31300	253N	SEM	77386

Street Name	Block	Pg/Sq	Loc	Zips
HILLDALE PARK LN	0	253N	SEM	77386
HILLENBERG LN	0	576R	SEH	77034
HILLENBERG LN	0	576R	SEH	77034
HILLENDAHL BLVD	1400	451W	NWH	77055
HILLER	1300	496L	NEH	77015
HILL FOREST DR	4200	297Y	NEH	77345
HILLGLEN CT	15200	618J	SEH	77062
HILLGREEN DR	1800	484G	NEF	77494
HILL GROVE CT	0	295L	SEM	77365
HILL GROVE DR	0	295L	SEM	77365
HILLHAVEN CT	6500	290Y	NWC	77379
HILLHOUSE RD	500	613H	PL	77584
HILLHURST DR	500	501P	BT	77521
HILLINGDALE LN	13700	369D	NWC	77070
HILLINGDON LN	0	328H	NWC	77377
HILLINGTON CT	0	289R	NWC	77375
HILLINGWORTH CT	0	407Z	NWC	77084
HILLIS	9200	455C	NEH	77028
HILLIS	9600	455C	NEH	77078
HILLIS	9900	455C	NEH	77078
HILL JUNCTION CT	0	406C	NWC	77433
HILL LAKES CT	17300	327T	NWC	77429
HILLMAN	5100	494Y	SEH	77023
HILLMEADOW DR	3400	291Q	NWC	77388
HILLMERE LN	10200	369G	NWC	77070
HILLMIST CT	0	328K	NWC	77377
HILLMONT	7200	450D	NWH	77040
HILLMONT	8300	450C	NWH	77040
HILLMONT SPRINGS DR	0	295R	SEM	77365
HILL OAK DR	4100	451K	NWH	77092
HILLOCK LN	0	614T	PL	77584
HILLOCK BLUFF CIR	600	332V	NCC	77073
HILLOCK GLEN LN	18000	327H	NWC	77429
HILLOCK WOODS	1	251T	WD	77380
HILL PARK DR	22200	485L	SWC	77450
HILL PLACE	0	494E	NEH	77020
HILLRIDGE DR	9900	252K	SEM	77385
HILLRIDGE RD	10000	579B	LP	77571
HILLSBORO	5500	494H	NEH	77020
HILLSBORO	7900	495E	NEH	77029
HILLSBORO	13700	497G	NEC	77015
HILLS BRIDGE CT	14800	568A	NEF	77498
HILLS BRIDGE LN	11500	568A	NEF	77498
HILLSDALE	3100	579A	LP	77571
HILLSDALE BRIDGE LN	10600	528W	NEF	77498
HILLSDALE FOREST DR	20700	296J	SEM	77365
HILLSGATE CT	11700	328M	NWC	77377
HILLSGROVE CT	8800	412K	NWH	77088
HILLSHIRE DR	1800	538S	DP	77536
W. HILLSHIRE PARK	0	451W	NWH	77092
E. HILLSHIRE PARK	0	451W	NWH	77055
HILLSIDE CT	0	252J	OR	77386
HILLSIDE CT	0	500K	BT	77520
HILLSIDE CT	200	252N	OR	77386
W. HILLSIDE DR	5500	414D	NEC	77039
E. HILLSIDE DR	5500	414D	NEC	77039
HILLSIDE DR	11500	414L	NEC	77039
HILLSIDE DR	13000	414H	NEC	77039
HILLSIDE DR	26300	252N	OR	77386
HILLSIDE DR	32200	248J	SWM	77362
HILLSIDE BAYOU DR	0	450S	NWH	77080
HILLSIDE CLEARING TRAIL	0	446F	NWC	77449
HILLSIDE CREEK DR	0	376U	NEC	77396
HILLSIDE ELM	1500	618E	SEH	77062
HILLSIDE FALLS TRAIL	15700	618G	SEH	77062
HILLSIDE GLEN TRAIL	11100	368Z	NWC	77065
HILLSIDE HICKORY CT	14300	617H	SEH	77062
HILLSIDE MILL	0	376Q	NEC	77396
HILLSIDE OAK LN	1900	618F	SEH	77062
HILLSIDE PARK WAY	15100	326T	NWC	77433
HILLSIDE SPRINGS CIR	19500	446R	NWC	77084
HILLSIDE TERRACE LN	15400	328S	NWC	77429
HILLSIDE WOODS CT	0	457G	NEC	77049
HILLSMAN LN	100	527Y	NEF	77498
HILL SPRINGS DR	3500	297X	NEH	77345
HILLSTAR ST	0	453Z	NEH	77009
HILLSTONE DR	3300	609E	SG	77479
HILLSTONE DR	13200	457J	NEC	77049
HILLSTROM PARK DR	0	484J	KT	77494
HILLSVIEW LN	0	257E	SEM	77357
HILLSWIND CIR	17000	330K	NWC	77379
HILL TIMBERS DR	5200	337W	NEC	77346
HILLTOP DR	29400	252Y	SEM	77386
HILL TOP LN	0	257L	SEM	77357
HILLTOP LN	1600	336K	NEH	77339
HILLTOP LN	18800	286M	NWC	77377
HILLTOP HARBOR WAY	0	367S	NWC	77433
HILLTOP PARK LN	0	366U	NWC	77433
HILL TOP RANCH RD	0	285T	NWC	77447
HILLTOPVALLEY DR	0	327D	NWC	77429
HILLTOP VIEW DR	15200	328N	NWC	77429
HILLVALE DR	14000	488J	SWH	77077
HILLVIEW	17000	330J	NWC	77379
HILLVIEW DR	10000	252K	SEM	77385
HILLWAY DR	5100	333H	NCC	77373
HILLWOOD LN	18400	407S	NWC	77449
HILSHIRE GLEN CT	0	450R	NWH	77080
HILSHIRE GREEN DR	7900	491A	HI	77055
HILSHIRE GROVE LN	1	451W	HI	77055
HILSHIRE LAKE DR	0	450Q	NWH	77080
HILSHIRE OAKS CT	1	491A	HI	77055
HILSHIRE PARK DR	0	450Q	NWH	77080
HILSHIRE TERRACE CT	0	450R	NWH	77080
HILSHIRE TRAIL DR	0	450R	NWH	77080
HILTON	8500	454F	NEH	77093
HILTONCREST	8200	370Y	NWC	77064
HILTON HEAD CT	3300	610F	MC	77459
HILTON HEAD DR	1500	610F	MC	77459
HILTON HEAD LN	16000	327Y	CY	77429
HILTON HOLLOW CT	6400	407U	NWC	77084
HILTON HOLLOW DR	17000	407U	NWC	77084
HILTONVIEW RD	4900	371S	NWC	77086
HILTONVIEW RD	5400	370V	NWC	77086
HIMLEY DR	0	366N	NWC	77433
HINDS	9900	576E	SEH	77034
HINES	1	501U	BT	77520
HINESBURG CT	10300	575V	SEH	77075
HINESDALE PARK LN	0	484X	NEF	77494
HINESDALE PARK LN	0	484X	NEF	77494
HINKLEY DR	0	293G	SEM	77386
HINKLEY GLEN CT	17000	527W	NEF	77407
HINMAN	8300	535Y	SEH	77061
HINMAN	8800	575C	SEH	77061
HINSDALE SPRINGS LN	0	572S	SWC	77053
HINTERWOOD WAY	0	250E	NWC	77375
HINTON BLVD	3100	453P	NWH	77022
HINTON DR	0	530L	SWH	77074
HIRA LAKE DR	0	529S	SWM	77099
HIRAM CLARKE RD	12000	571R	SWH	77045
HIRAM CLARKE RD	14700	571R	SWH	77053
HIRAM CLARKE RD	15900	611D	SWH	77053
HIRIDGE	8500	450V	NWH	77055

Street Name	Block	Pg/Sq	Loc	Zips
HIRONDEL	5400	574A	SEH	77033
HIRONDEL	6200	574C	SEH	77087
HIRSCH	100	335V	HM	77338
HIRSCH AVE	100	335V	HM	77338
HIRSCH DR	29800	288B	TB	77375
HIRSCH RD	1	494K	NEH	77020
HIRSCH RD	4000	454T	NEH	77026
HIRSCH RD	6700	454T	NEH	77016
HIRSCH RD	10200	414M	NEH	77016
HIRSCH RD	11700	414M	NEC	77050
HIRSCHFIELD RD	2700	333C	NCC	77373
HIRSCHFIELD RD	13700	288K	NWC	77377
HISPANIA VIEW DR	0	660G	LC	77573
HISTORY ROW	0	251L	WD	77380
HITCH CT	1100	379X	NEC	77532
HITCHCOCK	2300	414W	NEH	77093
HITCHCOCK	2600	454B	NEH	77093
HITCHIN LN	1300	458W	NEC	77530
HITCHING POST CIR	27200	246N	SWM	77355
HITCHING POST CT	16100	327U	NWC	77429
HITCHING RACK LN	28000	246J	SWM	77355
HITHER	0	340M	LCO	77535
HITHERFIELD DR	1200	568F	SG	77498
HIXON CREEK DR	20800	295R	SEM	77365
HOAD DEUCE CT	6500	330R	NWC	77379
HOATZIN CT	4300	609F	MC	77459
HOBART	5200	291A	NWC	77389
HOBART DR	9800	527V	NEF	77498
HOBBS RD	0	658Y	LC	77573
HOBBS RD	100	658L	LC	77573
HOBBS REACH LN	0	452Y	NWH	77008
HOBBS TERRACE DR	12600	328L	NWC	77377
HOBBY	4500	610D	SWH	77489
HOBBY	5500	611A	SWH	77053
HOBBY RD	5500	611B	SWH	77053
HOBBY, WILLIAM, AIRPORT	0	575B	SEH	77061
HOBBY FOREST LN	18000	377A	NEC	77346
HOBSONS CORNER	0	296U	SEM	77365
HOCKADAY DR	22100	485D	SWC	77450
HOCKLEY	0	500Z	BT	77520
HOCKLEY	0	501W	BT	77520
HOCKLEY	0	501W	BT	77520
HOCKLEY	7800	535B	SEH	77012
HOCKLEY DR	14200	408G	NWC	77095
HOCKLEY GARDEN LN	0	457K	NEC	77049
HODA DR	0	372J	NWC	77067
HODGEFIELD LN	16600	332N	NWC	77090
HODGE HILL LN	9800	366Y	NWC	77433
HODGE LAKE LN	1700	568V	SG	77478
HODGES	2300	460X	MN	77521
HODGES	12100	570M	SWH	77085
HODGES BEND CIR	2400	568Y	SG	77479
HODGES BEND DR	9200	527P	NEF	77083
HODGES GROVE LN	0	328M	NWC	77377
HODGES RUN LN	0	376S	NEC	77396
HODGKINS	800	373T	NCC	77032
HOEKE LN	0	452R	NWH	77018
HOFFER	10800	576S	SEH	77075
HOFFER	11000	576S	SEH	77089
HOFFMAN	100	494G	NEH	77020
HOFFMAN	3800	454Y	NEH	77026
HOFFMAN	6000	454Q	NEH	77028
HOFFMAN	7700	454L	NEH	77016
HOFFMAN ESTATES BLVD	19100	328B	NWC	77377
HOFFMAN ESTATES BLVD	19300	288X	NWC	77377
HOGAN	100	493H	NEH	77009
HOGAN BRIDGE CT	0	250W	NWC	77389
HOGAN BRIDGE DR	0	250W	NWC	77389
HOGANS ALLEY	700	336E	NEH	77339
HOGG	2000	494E	NEH	77026
HOGGARD DR	12200	568D	MD	77477
HOGUE	5600	534Q	SEH	77087
HOHEN CIR	5500	451D	NWH	77091
HOHL	700	453G	NEH	77022
HOHL	2800	454E	NEH	77093
HOHLDALE	100	452H	NWH	77022
HOHLDALE	300	452H	NWH	77091
HOHLFORD ST	1	452D	NWH	77076
HOHN RD	0	340R	LCO	77535
HOLBECH LN	900	497D	NEC	77530
HOLBECH LN	1000	457Z	NEC	77530
HOLBORNE DR	700	617B	SEH	77034
HOLBROOK	11000	414T	NCC	77093
HOLBROOK SPRINGS CT	0	445L	NWC	77449
HOLBROOK SPRINGS CT	0	445L	NWC	77449
HOLCOMB	0	339H	NEC	77336
HOLCOMBE BLVD	1000	533E	SWH	77030
W. HOLCOMBE BLVD	2100	532G	SWH	77030
HOLCOMBE BLVD	2400	533E	SEH	77021
W. HOLCOMBE BLVD	2600	532G	SWH	77025
HOLDEN MILLS DR	6300	250Z	NWC	77389
HOLDEN PARK PLACE	0	528K	NWC	77083
HOLDER	0	373X	NCC	77060
HOLDER FOREST CIR	7200	411V	NWH	77088
HOLDER FOREST CT	7200	411V	NWH	77088
HOLDER FOREST DR	3100	411V	NWH	77088
HOLDER RAMBO DR	2000	298K	NEC	77336
HOLDERRIETH BLVD	100	288L	TB	77375
HOLDERRIETH RD	11300	289S	NWC	77375
HOLDERRIETH RD	11900	288U	NWC	77375
HOLDERRIETH SOUTH	0	288L	TB	77375
HOLFORD CT	14200	329W	NWC	77070
HOLIDAN WAY	11300	490G	PP	77024
HOLIDAY	300	288H	TB	77375
HOLIDAY CT	23700	297E	SEM	77365
HOLIDAY LN	8000	575P	SEH	77075
HOLIDAY BAY CT	0	484U	NEF	77494
HOLLAND	100	496P	GP	77547
HOLLAND	900	496K	JC	77029
HOLLAND	3800	456X	NEH	77013
HOLLAND	10500	569B	MD	77477
HOLLAND CT	300	535B	SEH	77012
HOLLAND RD	0	614X	NEB	77584
HOLLANDALE DR	12700	488Y	SWH	77082
HOLLANDBRIDGE LN	600	332Q	NCC	77073
HOLLANDER CT	200	659D	LC	77573
HOLLAND FIELDS CIR	15200	408B	NWC	77095
HOLLAND GROVE CT	0	326T	NWC	77433
HOLLES DR	14500	528S	NEF	77498
HOLLEY CT	11200	416R	NEC	77044
HOLLEYGATE CT	24000	293Y	NCC	77373
HOLLEY RIDGE DR	1	336G	NEH	77339
HOLLIER DR	0	656W	FR	77511
HOLLINGERS ISLAND	1	485R	NEF	77450
HOLLINGSWORTH DR	3700	614W	NEB	77584
HOLLINGSWORTH PINE LN		484N	NEF	77494
HOLLINGTON DR	0	289X	NWC	77375
HOLLINS	200	252B	SEM	77385
HOLLINS WAY	16600	618R	SEH	77058
HOLLINWELL DR	2800	485V	NEF	77450
HOLLIS	2300	414W	NEH	77093
HOLLISBROOK LN	8300	457E	NEC	77044

Street Name	Block	Pg/Sq	Loc	Zips
HOLLIS GARDEN DR	19000	328D	NWC	77375
HOLLISTER DR	1500	450V	NWH	77055
HOLLISTER DR	1800	450M	NWH	77080
HOLLISTER DR	5200	450D	NWH	77040
HOLLISTER DR	5900	410V	NWH	77040
HOLLISTER DR	8300	410H	NWC	77064
HOLLISTER DR	9400	370Z	NWC	77086
HOLLISTER DR	9500	410R	NWH	77040
HOLLISTER DR	12900	370V	NWC	77086
HOLLISTER ST	0	370M	NWC	77066
HOLLISTER ST	12000	370G	NWC	77066
HOLLISTER COLE	0	410Z	NWC	77040
HOLLISTER COMMONS LN	0	450V	NWH	77080
HOLLISTER RIDGE	0	410Z	NWC	77040
HOLLISTER SPRING	0	410Z	NWC	77040
HOLLISTER SQUARE CT	0	450V	NWH	77080
HOLLISTER TREE CROSSING	0	450V	NWH	77080
HOLLISTER WOODS	0	410Z	NWC	77040
HOLLOCK	8800	575M	SEH	77075
HOLLOCK	9700	576J	SEH	77075
HOLLOW CIR	3100	610E	MC	77459
HOLLOW DR	400	489H	SWH	77024
S. HOLLOW LN	0	526J	NEF	77407
HOLLOW LN	0	658W	LC	77573
HOLLOW ASH CT	14600	457U	NEC	77015
HOLLOW ASH LN	1200	485L	SWC	77450
HOLLOWAY CT	1	573H	SEH	77048
HOLLOWAY DR	4100	573G	SEH	77047
HOLLOWAY CLIFF LN	0	406C	NWC	77433
HOLLOWAY HILLS TRL	0	328E	NWC	77377
HOLLOWAY SQUARE LN	6600	527E	NEF	77407
HOLLOWBACK DR	0	524B	NEF	77494
HOLLOW BANKS LN	8700	407F	NWC	77095
HOLLOW BAY CT	0	444S	KT	77493
HOLLOW BAY LN	0	407B	NWC	77095
HOLLOW BEND CT	5000	452F	NWH	77018
HOLLOW BLOOM LN	0	485P	NEF	77493
HOLLOW BLUFF LN	0	527J	NEF	77407
HOLLOW BRANCH CT	5100	486W	NEF	77450
HOLLOW BRANCH CT	18300	327W	NWC	77429
HOLLOW BRANCH LN	1400	619H	PA	77586
HOLLOW BROOK DR	13000	488Y	SWH	77082
HOLLOW CANYON CT	10300	528W	NEF	77498
HOLLOW CANYON DR	10100	528W	NEF	77498
HOLLOW CEDAR DR	7100	457L	NEC	77049
HOLLOW CHASE LN	4600	609J	NEF	77479
HOLLOW COVE CT	7400	407J	NWC	77433
HOLLOW CREEK CT	3100	488Y	SWH	77082
HOLLOW CREEK DR	2800	488Y	SWH	77082
HOLLOWCREEK PARK DR	13100	488Y	SWH	77082
HOLLOWCREEK POINT LN	0	406C	NWC	77433
HOLLOWCREST DR	11100	616E	SEC	77089
HOLLOW FIELD CT	7400	407J	NWC	77433
HOLLOW FIELD LN	7100	407P	NWC	77433
HOLLOW FIELD LN	21800	486W	NEF	77450
HOLLOW GATE MEADOW CT	0	251W	SWM	77389
HOLLOWGATE PARK LN		249V	NWC	77375
HOLLOW GLEN LN	1	329F	NWC	77375
HOLLOW GLEN LN	7600	528L	SWH	77072
HOLLOWGREEN CT	13500	488X	SWC	77082
HOLLOWGREEN DR	13500	488X	SWH	77082
HOLLOW HARVEST LN	0	407S	NWC	77449
HOLLOW HARVEST LN	0	407S	NWC	77449
HOLLOWHAVEN CT	8100	407F	NWC	77095
HOLLOW HEARTH DR	6800	408T	NWC	77084
HOLLOW HILL LN	0	527N	NEF	77407
HOLLOW HOOK RD	1600	450N	NWH	77080
HOLLOW HOOK RD	4300	450E	NWH	77041
HOLLOW LODGE CT	22700	485L	SWC	77450
HOLLOWLOG DR	19200	446Q	NWC	77449
HOLLOWMILL LN	14100	488W	SWH	77082
HOLLOW MIST LN	0	615L	PL	77581
HOLLOW OAKS CIR	18300	255W	SEM	77365
HOLLOW OAKS DR	6400	415E	NEH	77050
HOLLOWOOD LN	1200	570X	MC	77489
HOLLOW PASS LN	0	484S	NEF	77494
HOLLOW PINE CT	14000	456R	NEC	77049
HOLLOW PINE DR	5000	456V	NEC	77049
HOLLOW QUILL DR	8000	411J	NWC	77088
HOLLOW REEF CIR	2100	620W	LC	77573
HOLLOW RIDGE DR	7400	408J	NWC	77095
HOLLOW RIDGE RD	16500	611C	SWH	77053
HOLLOW ROCK DR	15800	329U	NWC	77070
HOLLOW SAGE LN	31200	252R	SEM	77386
HOLLOW SANDS CT	0	407Y	NWC	77084
HOLLOW SHORE	2200	612M	PL	77584
HOLLOW SPRINGS LN	28300	293E	SEM	77386
HOLLOW STONE LN	26400	366M	NWC	77433
HOLLOW TRACE LN	0	485X	NEF	77494
HOLLOW TREE	900	580P	LP	77571
HOLLOW TREE LN	1	332K	NWC	77090
HOLLOWVINE LN	4800	485S	NEF	77494
HOLLOW VISTA DR	0	369H	NWC	77070
HOLLOW WIND DR	1800	486Q	SWC	77450
HOLLOW WOOD	0	449H	NWH	77041
HOLLOW WOOD DR	16200	332T	NWC	77090
HOLLSBROOK CT	3400	569S	SG	77478
HOLLVALE	0	412D	NEH	77060
HOLLY	0	254P	SEM	77365
HOLLY	0	256V	SEM	77357
HOLLY	0	258K	SEM	77357
HOLLY	0	420P	NEC	77532
N. HOLLY	100	500E	BT	77520
HOLLY	100	297P	NEH	77365
HOLLY	100	298E	NEC	77336
HOLLY	1100	493G	SWH	77007
HOLLY	2400	282Y	WL	77484
HOLLY	4500	531M	BL	77401
HOLLY	5500	531J	SWH	77081
HOLLY	5700	531J	SWH	77074
HOLLY	11700	411G	NWC	77086
HOLLY	11700	419Y	BR	77532
HOLLY	14600	373X	NCC	77060
HOLLY	24000	297J	SEM	77365
W. HOLLY AVE	2400	537X	PA	77502
HOLLY AVE	4700	537Y	PA	77503
HOLLY CT	3100	609L	MC	77459
HOLLY CT	5500	614G	PL	77581
HOLLY CT	19400	245D	SWM	77355
HOLLY DR	0	659N	LC	77573
HOLLY DR	100	500E	BT	77520
HOLLY DR	600	460N	HG	77562
HOLLY DR	24700	257T	SEM	77357
HOLLY DR	25500	249S	NWC	77375
HOLLY LN	0	538Z	DP	77536
HOLLY LN	0	245S	SWM	77447
HOLLY LN	0	247U	SWM	77355
HOLLY LN	1200	658Z	LC	77573
HOLLY LN	12100	248J	SWM	77362
HOLLY LN	13500	369E	NWC	77429
HOLLY LN	24400	257B	WV	77357
HOLLY BARR LN	20500	406K	NWC	77433

Street Name	Block	Pg/Sq	Loc	Zips
HOLLY BAY CT	4900	578F	PA	77505
HOLLY BEND CT	5300	447B	NWC	77084
HOLLY BEND DR	18100	447B	NWC	77084
HOLLYBERRY	0	247Q	SWM	77355
HOLLY BERRY CT	7800	406M	NWC	77433
HOLLYBERRY CT	18200	255S	SEM	77365
HOLLYBERRY DR	1500	333J	NCC	77073
HOLLYBOUGH DR	0	299S	NEC	77336
HOLLYBRANCH CT	18500	255T	SEM	77365
HOLLYBRANCH DR	21900	290J	NWC	77375
HOLLY BRANCH LN	0	619V	LC	77565
HOLLYBROOK DR	0	247Q	SWM	77355
HOLLY BROOK DR	2500	620L	SB	77586
HOLLYBROOK LN	3500	414G	NCC	77039
HOLLYBUSH DR	1500	568F	SG	77498
HOLLYBUSH LN	25300	293N	NCC	77373
HOLLY CANYON CT	6300	526E	NEF	77450
HOLLY CHASE	10000	489Z	SWH	77042
HOLLY COURT ESTATES DR	7300	408K	NWC	77095
HOLLY COVE LN	0	406R	NWC	77449
HOLLY CREEK CT	300	251E	WD	77381
HOLLY CREEK TRAIL	22000	287K	NWC	77377
HOLLY CREST DR	500	252T	SEM	77386
HOLLYCREST DR	700	498A	NEC	77530
HOLLY CROSSING	3200	489Z	SWH	77042
HOLLYDALE DR	14800	618F	SEH	77062
HOLLYDALE RIDGE LN	0	524H	NEF	77494
HOLLY FALLS CT	17100	407G	NWC	77095
HOLLYFARE DR	0	484X	NEF	77494
HOLLYFARE DR	0	484X	NEF	77494
HOLLY FERN CT	300	659H	LC	77573
HOLLY FERN DR	400	659H	LC	77573
HOLLYFIELD LN	2100	445T	NWC	77493
HOLLYFLOWER PLACE		249Q	NWC	77375
HOLLY FOREST DR	17900	407Y	NWC	77084
HOLLYGATE LN	0	326R	NWC	77429
HOLLY GLADE LN	2000	568A	SG	77498
HOLLY GLEN	0	257L	SEM	77357
HOLLYGLEN DR	10100	414Z	NEH	77016
HOLLYGLENN	300	257A	WV	77357
HOLLY GREEN CT	3900	297S	NEH	77339
HOLLY GREEN DR	2900	297S	NEH	77339
HOLLY GREEN DR	18100	407X	NWC	77084
HOLLY GROVE DR	6700	535W	SEH	77061
HOLLY HALL	1900	532R	SWH	77054
HOLLY HALL	3300	533N	SWH	77021
HOLLY HILL DR	0	290E	NWC	77375
HOLLY HILL DR	900	568J	SG	77498
HOLLY HILL DR	28700	251D	SD	77381
HOLLY HILL LN	10900	409Y	NWC	77041
HOLLY HILLS DR	8600	289H	NWC	77375
HOLLYHOCK DR	0	569T	NEF	77477
HOLLY HOLLOW	22900	287E	NWC	77377
HOLLYHURST LN	1300	491R	SWH	77056
HOLLY KNOLL DR	2200	489S	SWH	77077
HOLLY LAKE	1	332C	NCC	77373
HOLLY LAKE DR	22500	485L	SWC	77450
HOLLY LAKES DR	22000	287J	NWC	77377
HOLLYLEAF	0	247Q	SWM	77355
HOLLY LEAF CT	21600	255S	SEM	77365
HOLLYLEAF DR	8200	330J	NWC	77379
HOLLY LOOP	0	375M	NEC	77396
HOLLY LORD	26900	247Z	SWM	77355
HOLLY LYNN	0	488K	SWH	77077
HOLLY MANOR LN	0	526M	NEF	77407
HOLLY MEADOW	3200	489Z	SWH	77042
HOLLYMIST DR	2600	446V	NWC	77084
HOLLY OAK CT	3100	331T	NWC	77068
HOLLYOAK DR	1800	447X	NWH	77084
S. HOLLY OAKS CIR	30200	245P	SWM	77355
N. HOLLY OAKS CIR	30300	245P	SWM	77355
HOLLY OAKS CT	25100	245P	SWM	77355
HOLLY PARK DR	4800	537Y	PA	77505
HOLLY PARK DR	13200	497C	NEC	77015
HOLLY PATH	3200	489Z	SWH	77042
HOLLY PINES WAY	0	447K	NWC	77084
HOLLY RANCH DR	3100	484R	NEF	77494
HOLLY RIDGE	0	295F	SEM	77365
HOLLYRIDGE DR	800	490E	SWH	77024
HOLLYRIDGE DR	1700	570Y	MC	77489
HOLLY RIDGE RD	23400	295G	SEM	77365
HOLLY RIVER DR	1500	489P	SWH	77077
HOLLY SHADE CT	19200	291W	NWC	77379
HOLLY SHORES	3200	489Z	SWH	77042
HOLLY SPRINGS	200	656F	FR	77546
HOLLY SPRINGS DR	2700	615N	PL	77584
HOLLY SPRINGS DR	5200	491K	SWH	77056
HOLLY SPRINGS DR	6100	491J	SWH	77057
HOLLY SPRINGS DR	10000	489Q	SWH	77042
HOLLY SPRINGS PLACE	25500	292U	NCC	77373
HOLLY STONE DR	11900	369Q	NWC	77070
HOLLY TERRACE	5100	491L	SWH	77056
HOLLY TERRACE CT	4300	578E	PA	77505
HOLLY THICKET	3200	489Z	SWH	77042
HOLLY THORN	0	329F	NWC	77375
HOLLY TRAIL DR	16500	618Q	SEH	77058
HOLLY TREE	0	247Q	SWM	77355
HOLLY TREE	1	332C	NCC	77373
HOLLYTREE DR	15800	331N	NWC	77068
HOLLYVALE DR	100	412D	NCC	77060
HOLLYVALE DR	300	413A	NCC	77060
HOLLY VALLEY DR	0	489M	SWH	77042
HOLLY VIEW CIR	6200	411Y	NWH	77091
HOLLY VIEW DR	5200	411Y	NWH	77091
HOLLYVINE LN	10100	616L	SEC	77089
HOLLY WALK	19700	332A	NWC	77388
HOLLY WALK LN	2500	332A	NWC	77388
HOLLY WALK LANE CT	19800	332A	NWC	77388
HOLLY WAY	18700	447J	NWC	77084
HOLLYWELL DR	18000	447B	NWC	77084
HOLLYWICK DR	24200	289D	NWC	77375
HOLLYWIND CIR	19700	486L	SWC	77094
HOLLYWOOD	400	497G	NEC	77015
HOLMAN	600	493T	SWH	77002
HOLMAN	1000	533D	SEH	77004
S. HOLMES	100	540Z	LP	77571
N. HOLMES	100	540Y	LP	77571
S. HOLMES	500	580D	LP	77571
HOLMES BLVD	0	536H	PA	77506
HOLMES RD	1	572A	SWH	77045
HOLMES RD	600	532Y	SWH	77045
HOLMES RD	2300	533S	SWH	77051
HOLMES RD	4200	525W	NEF	77406
HOLMES RD	4500	533S	SEH	77033
HOLMSLEY LN	7100	410T	NWC	77040
HOLMWOOD DR	8200	410L	NWC	77040
HOLSBERRY CT	17300	328Q	NWC	77377
HOLSTEIN	19800	380H	NEC	77532
HOLSTON HILLS CT	5600	370C	NWC	77069
HOLSTON HILLS DR	13100	370C	NWC	77069
HOLT	0	282U	WL	77484
HOLT	4300	531M	BL	77401

Street Name	Block	Pg/Sq	Loc	Zips
HOLT	8300	533N	SWH	77054
HOLT ALLEY	3000	454S	NEH	77026
HOLTCAMP	7300	495W	SEH	77011
HOLTMAN	100	413E	NCC	77060
HOLTON	800	531C	BL	77401
HOLTON AVE	1000	538X	DP	77536
HOLTON GRIPP DR	0	524E	NEF	77494
HOLTON RIDGE DR	0	484V	NEF	77494
HOLTS LANDING DR	0	366Q	NWC	77433
HOLTWOO DOAK DR	0	377K	NEC	77346
HOLUB	25800	244K	WCO	77447
HOLWORTH DR	11000	529F	SWH	77072
HOLY RD	3000	420V	NEC	77532
HOLY RD	4100	421S	NEC	77532
HOLYHEAD DR	200	457Y	NEC	77015
HOLYOKE LN	25100	293P	NCC	77373
HOLY ROOD LN	700	491G	SWH	77024
HOLY SEE	17800	324H	NWC	77447
HOLZWARTH RD	0	292E	NWC	77389
HOLZWARTH RD	1500	292X	NWC	77388
E. HOMAN	1	501U	BT	77520
W. HOMAN	200	501U	BT	77520
HOMAR	0	372Q	NWC	77067
HOMBLY CT	11300	371Q	NWC	77066
HOMBLY DR	3200	371Q	NWC	77066
HOMCO	6600	494Z	SWH	77023
HOME	3400	493E	SWH	77007
HOME CT	0	371Z	NWC	77038
HOMEBRIAR CT	15700	570Z	SWH	77489
HOMEBROOK DR	1600	372W	NWC	77038
HOMED LARK PLACE CT	0	250P	NWC	77389
HOMED LARK PLACE CT	0	250P	NWC	77389
HOMELAND DR	9200	528T	SWC	77083
HOMEMONT LN	24100	339J	HU	77336
S. HOME PLACE	3500	609E	SG	77479
N. HOME PLACE	3500	609E	SG	77479
HOME POINT DR	0	452F	NWH	77091
HOMER	700	412Y	NWH	77091
HOMER	2600	412W	NWH	77091
HOMERDALE	0	288K	NWC	77377
HOMESTEAD CT	6600	454R	NEH	77028
HOMESTEAD RD	3600	414Z	NEH	77028
HOMESTEAD RD	8700	454H	NEH	77016
HOMESTEAD RD	10100	414R	NEH	77016
HOMESTEAD RD	11700	414D	NEC	77050
HOMESTEAD RD	12800	414D	NEC	77039
HOMESTEAD RD	13900	414D	NEC	77396
HOMESTEAD PASS DR	24000	293U	NCC	77373
HOMETTE	13700	417T	NEC	77044
HOMEVIEW DR	6100	457N	NEC	77049
HOMEWOOD LN	5000	500M	BT	77521
HOMEWOOD LN	7800	455F	NEH	77028
HOMEWOOD LN	8800	455H	NEH	77078
HOMEWOOD LN	11900	490E	BH	77024
HOMEWOOD ROW LN	1	491L	SWH	77056
HON CT	19700	406U	NWC	77449
HONDO	3200	533T	SEH	77051
HONDO HILL RD	10200	409G	NWC	77064
HONDURAS DR	4000	577A	PA	77504
HONEY	14700	571S	SWH	77085
HONEY CIR	5000	533H	SEH	77004
HONEY LN	6000	577D	PA	77505
HONEYBEAR LN	5400	334A	NCC	77373
HONEYBEE	23200	296D	SEM	77357
HONEY BEE CT	13900	414B	NCC	77039
HONEY BEE LN	0	297A	SEM	77357
HONEYBIRD MEADOW CIR	0	405P	NWC	77493
HONEY BROOK CT	0	609T	NEF	77479
HONEY BROOK DR	3800	297T	NEH	77345
HONEYCOMB	0	251R	WD	77380
HONEYCOMB LN	14600	368J	NWC	77429
HONEY CREEK CT	4600	615N	PL	77581
HONEY CREEK DR	3200	487Y	SWC	77082
HONEY CREEK DR	3400	569W	SG	77478
HONEY CREEK LN	7500	407M	NWC	77095
HONEY CREEK TRAIL	12500	377B	NEC	77346
HONEY CREEK WAY	18200	377B	NEC	77346
HONEYCREST LN	0	250U	NWC	77389
HONEYCREST LN	0	250U	NWC	77389
HONEY DAFFODIL PLACE	0	251R	WD	77380
HONEY DAISY CT	17800	367T	NWC	77433
HONEY DALE LN	20500	379E	NEC	77532
HONEYFIELD LN	8000	330A	NWC	77379
HONEY GOLD TRAIL	0	325V	NWC	77433
HONEY GROVE LN	11200	368V	NWC	77065
HONEYGUIDE CT	0	297K	NEH	77365
HONEY HARVEST LN	0	407R	NWC	77084
HONEY HILL DR	1000	488F	SWH	77077
HONEY LOCUST DR	2400	446S	NWC	77449
HONEY LOCUST HILL DR	20200	292W	NWC	77388
HONEY MEADOW CT	0	616J	PL	77089
HONEY MEADOW LN	0	616J	PL	77089
HONEY MESQUITE WAY	0	524D	NEF	77494
HONEYMOON BRIDGE LN	14900	528W	NEF	77498
HONEY OAKS DR	4000	619G	TL	77586
HONEY PINE LN	0	406L	NWC	77433
HONEY RIDGE DR	0	253X	SEM	77386
HONEYSICKLE	0	331D	NWC	77388
HONEYSICKLE	1500	612T	NWB	77584
HONEYSUCKLE	0	295F	SEM	77365
HONEYSUCKLE	5900	534V	SEH	77087
HONEYSUCKLE	8500	460P	NEC	77562
HONEYSUCKLE DR	100	500F	BT	77520
HONEYSUCKLE DR	1900	570W	MC	77489
HONEYSUCKLE DR	23900	295E	SEM	77365
HONEYSUCKLE LN	4800	537Y	PA	77505
HONEYSUCKLE LN	5700	374H	NEH	77396
HONEYSUCKLE LN	5900	375E	NEH	77396
HONEY SUCKLE HAVEN DR		367N	NWC	77433
HONEYSUCKLE SPRINGS RD	0	377F	NEC	77346
HONEYSUCKLE WALK	2500	292W	NWC	77388
HONEYSUCKLE WALK	2700	331D	NWC	77388
HONEY TREE DR	2100	252H	SEM	77385
HONEYVINE DR	5200	573V	SEH	77048
HONEYVINE DR	5300	574N	SEH	77048
HONEYVINE DR	5300	660X	DI	77539
HONEYWELL	9600	530S	SWH	77074
HONEY WHEAT WAY	0	325K	NWC	77447
HONEYWOOD CT	4500	578Y	SEH	77059
HONEYWOOD TRAIL	12300	488M	SWH	77077
HONOLULU	15600	409M	JV	77040
HONOR CT	5700	448D	NWC	77041
HONOR DR	5500	448D	NWC	77041
HONOR PARK DR	12500	408D	NWC	77065
HONSINGER	3200	493E	SWH	77007
HOOD	5700	534G	SEH	77023
HOOK	10000	370Y	NWC	77064
HOOKER	500	373X	NCC	77060
HOOK LEFT DR	0	616E	SEC	77581
HOOKS RD	0	613P	PL	77584
HOOKS CREEK CT	8600	407H	NWC	77095
HOOKS M H	0	413M	NCC	77093

Street Name	Block	Pg/Sq	Loc	Zips
HOOPER RD	13400	572Z	SWH	77047
HOOPER RD	14000	288K	NWC	77377
HOOPER RD	14600	612D	SWC	77047
HOOPS	0	287L	NWC	77377
HOOTEN LN	26100	248K	SWM	77354
HOOTON	6000	531A	SWH	77081
HOOT OWL RD	10400	409F	NWC	77064
HOOT OWL RD	10400	409F	JV	77064
HOOVER	4900	451F	NWH	77092
HOOVER DR	0	289V	NWC	77379
HOOVER DR	1400	538R	DP	77536
HOOVER RD	600	498G	CV	77530
HOOVER GARDENS DR	17400	367X	NWC	77095
HOPE	0	284Y	NWC	77447
HOPE RD	300	340U	LCO	77535
HOPE FARM LN	16600	367G	NWC	77429
HOPE HILLS LN	0	326U	NWC	77429
HOPE RANCH LN	5300	609T	NEF	77479
HOPE SHADOW CT	15300	326U	NWC	77429
HOPE SPRINGS DR	19500	366V	NWC	77433
HOPETON DR	0	253S	SEM	77386
HOPETOWN DR	5700	457S	NEC	77049
HOPE VALLEY PLACE	1	250A	WD	77382
HOPEVIEW	19200	406R	NWC	77449
HOPE VILLAGE RD	15400	617S	SEC	77546
HOPEWELL DR	23700	445P	NWC	77493
HOPEWELL LN	7500	570C	SWH	77071
HOPE WOOD MILLS DR	6300	524E	NEF	77494
HOPFE RD	17600	325C	NWC	77447
HOPFE RD	18500	285U	NWC	77447
HOPI	7100	462Z	BT	77521
HOPI CT	0	658Y	LC	77573
HOPI DR	0	658Y	LC	77573
HOPI LN	23500	295F	SEM	77365
HOPKINS	1900	493S	SWH	77006
HOPKINS CEDAR	0	376R	NEC	77346
HOPKINS PARK DR	1300	486H	SWC	77094
HOPPER CIR	1100	413Q	NEH	77037
HOPPER RD	1200	413Q	NEH	77037
HOPPER RD	1300	414N	NCC	77093
HOPPER RD	5400	415N	NEH	77016
HOPPERS CREEK DR	19800	446L	NWC	77449
HOPSON	1400	493K	SWH	77019
HOPSON MEADOW DR	0	524K	NWF	77406
HOPSON MEADOW LN	0	524L	NWF	77406
HOPVINE CT	1	251J	WD	77381
HOPWOOD	0	490F	BH	77024
HORACE	4100	454X	NEH	77026
HORACE RD	2700	569V	NEF	77477
HORATIO	1300	496K	JC	77029
HORDEN CREEK DR	19400	288Z	NWC	77375
HORDS CREEK DR	29100	293F	SEM	77386
HORIZON DR	16000	419A	NEC	77532
HORIZON BAY LN	0	484N	NEF	77494
HORIZON FALLS LN	0	375Y	NEC	77396
HORIZON GROVE LN	25600	524F	NEF	77494
S. HORIZON RIDGE CT	1	250B	WD	77381
N. HORIZON RIDGE CT	1	250B	WD	77381
W. HORIZON RIDGE PLACE	1	250B	WD	77381
E. HORIZON RIDGE PLACE	1	250B	WD	77381
HORIZON SIDE WAY	0	445J	NWC	77493
HORIZON VIEW CIR	0	609P	NEF	77479
HORNBEAM DR	3400	527D	SWC	77082
S. HORNBEAM PLACE	1	251V	WD	77380
N. HORNBEAM PLACE	1	251V	WD	77380
HORNBERGER RD	0	417N	NEC	77044
HORNBILL CT	1	252N	WD	77380
HORNBROOK DR	11400	529X	SWH	77099
HORNCASTLE CT	3400	613Q	NEB	77584
HORNCASTLE DR	700	498B	CV	77530
HORNE	1000	412P	NWH	77088
HORNED OWL DR	0	484P	NWF	77494
HORNET DR	18400	295E	SEM	77365
HORNPIPE LN	9900	450N	NWH	77080
HORNWOOD DR	5800	531E	SWH	77081
HORNWOOD DR	6500	530H	SWH	77074
HORNWOOD DR	7500	530E	SWH	77036
HORSE LN	16900	611E	NEF	77053
HORSE CAVE CIR	9200	329H	NWC	77379
HORSEPEN BAYOU DR	6300	408T	NWC	77084
HORSE PRAIRIE DR	0	406Y	NWC	77449
HORSESHOE CIR	0	255T	SEM	77365
HORSESHOE DR	0	255T	SEM	77365
HORSESHOE DR	0	656K	FR	77546
HORSESHOE DR	1000	568Q	SG	77478
N. HORSESHOE DR	1200	568Q	SG	77478
HORSESHOE BEND	0	614M	PL	77581
HORSESHOE BEND	10000	409C	NWC	77064
HORSESHOE BEND	0	538R	DP	77536
HORSESHOE CANYON DR	0	406C	NWC	77433
HORSESHOE FALLS	0	610W	MC	77433
HORSESHOE FALLS LN	0	366Q	NWC	77433
HORSESHOE HILL CT	16100	327Y	NWC	77429
HORSESHOE LAKE LN	19500	446U	NWC	77084
HORSESHOE RUN DR	23400	293Y	NCC	77373
HORSESHOE SPRINGS LN	0	332X	NWC	77090
HORSESHOE TRAIL	0	374H	NEH	77396
HORSESHOE TRAIL	18600	246J	SWM	77355
HORSETAIL FALLS DR	20400	289W	NWC	77375
HORSETOOTH CANYON DR	17200	367X	NWC	77095
HORTON	5700	454S	NEH	77026
HORTON LANDING LN	0	376S	NEC	77396
HOSANNA WAY	0	370M	NWC	77066
HOSFORD MEADOWS DR	24600	296J	SEM	77365
HOSKINS DR	1900	450Q	NWH	77080
HOSPITAL	18100	619S	NB	77058
HOSPITAL RD	600	288D	TB	77375
HOSTLER DR	0	249V	NWC	77375
HOTCHKISS	1200	535F	SEH	77012
HOT CREEK CT	18400	377C	NEC	77346
HOT CREEK TRACE	7000	377C	NEC	77346
HOT SPRINGS DR	2700	614R	PL	77584
HOT SPRINGS DR	8300	408E	NWC	77095
HOUGHTON RD	200	486C	SWC	77450
HOUND DOG	0	372T	NWC	77038
HOUNDS LAKE DR	0	257E	SEM	77357
HOUSE	0	364D	NWC	77433
HOUSE	2100	537T	PA	77502
HOUSE RD	0	365N	NWC	77433
HOUSE RD	15000	325W	NWC	77447
HOUSE RD	15700	365A	NWC	77447
HOUSE HAHL RD	15700	366J	NWC	77433
HOUSE HAHL RD	20000	365M	NWC	77433
HOUSE HAHL RD	24500	364V	NWC	77433
HOUSE MARTIN LN	0	328K	NWC	77429
HOUSMAN	6600	451Y	NWH	77055
W. HOUSTON	0	611Z	FS	77545
N. HOUSTON	0	658H	LC	77573
HOUSTON	0	500V	BT	77520
W. HOUSTON	100	459Q	HG	77562
S. HOUSTON	100	618Y	WB	77598
N. HOUSTON	100	618X	WB	77598

Street Name	Block	Pg/Sq	Loc	Zips
HOUSTON	100	288G	TB	77375
HOUSTON	100	536Q	PA	77502
E. HOUSTON	100	459R	HG	77562
HOUSTON	100	611Z	FS	77545
HOUSTON	200	612W	FS	77545
HOUSTON	200	620U	SB	77586
E. HOUSTON	800	460N	HG	77562
HOUSTON	1200	501U	BT	77520
HOUSTON	10700	539Q	LP	77571
S. HOUSTON AVE	100	335Z	HM	77338
N. HOUSTON AVE	100	335R	HM	77338
HOUSTON AVE	500	493G	SWH	77007
S. HOUSTON AVE	1600	375H	HM	77396
N. HOUSTON AVE	2100	615J	PL	77581
HOUSTON AVE	2200	660W	GCO	77539
S. HOUSTON AVE	2400	615N	PL	77581
HOUSTON AVE	2500	493G	NWH	77009
HOUSTON BLVD	400	576B	SH	77587
HOUSTON DR	16900	367K	CY	77433
E. HOUSTON RD	5200	455Q	NEH	77028
HOUSTON-ROSSLYN	0	411X	NWH	77091
HOUSTON ACORN AVE	0	455C	NEH	77078
W. HOUSTON CENTER BLVD	12100	489W	SWH	77082
W. HOUSTON CENTER BLVD	13000	529A	SWH	77082
HOUSTON CHRONICLE BLVD	1000	487B	NWH	77084
HOUSTON CHRONICLE BLVD	1200	447X	NWH	77084
HOUSTONIAN DR	4700	491H	SWH	77024
HOUSTON LAKE CT	0	615Y	PL	77581
HOUSTON LAKE DR	3700	615Y	PL	77581
HOUSTON NATIONAL BLVD	16500	367U	NWC	77095
HOUSTON OAKS DR	10100	409D	NWC	77064
HOUSTON POLICE ACADEMY	0	373H	NEH	77032
HOUSTON SHIP CHANNEL	0	495T	SEH	77029
HOUSTON SHIP CHANNEL	0	536B	SEH	77017
HOUSTON SHIP CHANNEL	0	497S	SEH	77015
HOUSTON SHIP CHANNEL	0	499P	SEH	77571
HOVEDEN CT	20600	486K	SWC	77450
HOVEDEN DR	1400	486K	SWC	77450
HOVENKAMP	0	535Z	SEH	77017
HOWALD	100	580L	LP	77571
N. HOWARD	100	288H	TB	77375
HOWARD	200	536G	PA	77506
HOWARD	900	335Z	HM	77338
HOWARD	7900	535R	SEH	77017
HOWARD AVE	600	538F	DP	77536
HOWARD CT	0	258E	SEM	77357
HOWARD LN	1000	531D	BL	77401
HOWARD ALLEY	2900	454S	NEH	77026
HOWCHER	4100	573L	SEH	77047
HOWCHER	5100	573M	SEH	77048
HOWE	1000	493P	SWH	77002
HOWE RD	13000	574Q	SEH	77048
HOWELL	5600	374R	NEH	77032
HOWELL GROVE LN	15600	408A	NWC	77095
HOWELL SUGAR LAND RD	6200	528J	SWC	77083
HOWES DR	0	253S	SEM	77386
HOWLAND	15000	408T	NWC	77084
HOWLAND CT	6100	408T	NWC	77084
HOWSER DR	24900	257T	SEM	77357
HOWTH AVE	0	572H	SEH	77051
HOWTON	7100	454R	NEH	77028
S. HOWTON	7700	455N	NEH	77028
N. HOWTON	7700	455N	NEH	77028
HOWTON	8000	455Q	NEH	77028
HOXTON DR	0	327D	NWC	77429
HOYA CT	14700	328Z	NWC	77070
HOYT DR	100	484E	NWF	77494
HOYT LN	1300	445V	NEC	77449
HOYTE DR	10600	530W	SWH	77031
HOYTE PARK LN	19700	291W	NWC	77379
HRONAS DR	0	446F	NWC	77449
HUB	1100	494Y	SEH	77023
HUBBARDCREEK CT	0	366Z	NWC	77433
HUBBARD RUN DR	0	296E	SEM	77365
HUBBELL DR	6100	614U	PL	77584
S. HUBBS	0	373L	NCC	77032
E. HUBBS	0	373L	NCC	77032
HUBERCAMP RD	9300	462U	NEC	77521
HUBERS CT	12800	570K	MC	77489
HUBERT	100	618X	WB	77598
HUBSTONE WAY	0	615K	PL	77581
HUCKELTON LN	4200	291X	NWC	77388
HUCKINSTON CT	9100	289Z	NWC	77379
HUCKLEBERRY	2900	609F	MC	77459
HUCKLEBERRY CIR	5100	491Q	SWH	77056
HUCKLEBERRY CT	26800	246N	SWM	77355
HUCKLEBERRY LN	2100	537W	PA	77502
HUCKLEBERRY LN	5100	491Q	SWH	77056
HUCKLEBERRY LN	18500	295B	SEM	77365
HUCKLEBERRY BRANCH CT	19600	332A	NWC	77388
HUCKLEBERRY HARVEST TRAIL	0	328A	NWC	77429
HUDDERSFIELD DR	0	330E	NWC	77379
HUDDLER	7400	531J	SWH	77074
HUDDLESTON DR	0	326U	NWC	77429
HUDGENS AVE	1300	444Z	KT	77493
HUDSON	7800	535A	SEH	77012
HUDSON CIR	0	490P	SWH	77024
HUDSON CT	0	568B	SG	77498
HUDSON LN	22600	256Y	SEM	77357
HUDSON BEND CIR	9300	408A	NWC	77095
HUDSON FALLS LN	0	484F	KT	77494
HUDSON KNOLL DR	0	295L	SEM	77365
HUDSON OAKS DR	6900	407P	NWC	77095
HUDSON PLACE	0	490P	SWH	77024
HUDSON RIVER TRAIL	9600	576J	SEH	77075
HUE ST	0	529Q	SWH	77072
HUENI RD	1	297K	NEH	77365
HUEY	4000	534M	SEH	77087
HUFF DR	10500	530X	SWH	77031
HUFFMAN LN	3000	336T	NEC	77338
HUFFMAN-CLEVELAND RD	0	258V	NEC	77336
HUFFMAN-CLEVELAND RD	27300	298R	NEC	77336
HUFFMAN-NEW CANEY RD	31700	258V	SEM	77357
HUFFMAN EASTGATE RD	1700	339G	NEC	77336
HUFFMAN OAKS LN	12200	339J	HU	77336
HUFFMEISTER RD	6000	408P	NWC	77084
HUFFMEISTER RD	7000	408K	NWC	77095
HUFFMEISTER RD	10000	368T	NWC	77065
HUFFMEISTER RD	11100	368A	NWC	77429
HUFFMEISTER RD	15000	367D	NWC	77429
HUFFMEISTER RD	15100	327T	CY	77429
HUFFMEISTER RD	18400	326V	NWC	77429
W. HUFSMITH	100	288G	TB	77375
HUFSMITH RD	300	288D	TB	77375
HUFSMITH RD	900	289A	TB	77375
HUFSMITH RD	1000	249X	NWC	77375
HUFSMITH-KOHRVILLE RD	16100	329K	NWC	77070
HUFSMITH-KOHRVILLE RD	16400	329K	NWC	77375
HUFSMITH-KOHRVILLE RD	19500	289P	NWC	77375
HUFSMITH-KOHRVILLE RD	24600	249W	NWC	77375
HUFSMITH CEMETERY RD	25000	249T	NWC	77375
HUFSMITH KUYKENDAHL RD	6000	290A	NWC	77375

Street Name	Block	Pg/Sq	Loc	Zips
HUFSMITH KUYKENDAHL RD	8500	289C	NWC	77375
HUFSMITH KUYKENDAHL RD	10800	249X	NWC	77375
HUGE OAKS	1400	451W	NWH	77055
HUGGINS	1300	540D	BT	77520
HUGGINS DR	11100	571D	SWH	77035
HUGGINSWAY	3500	613U	NEB	77584
HUGH RD	1200	372J	NWC	77067
HUGH ECHOLS BLVD	3800	501L	BT	77521
HUGHES	100	494Y	SEH	77011
HUGHES	300	494Y	SEH	77023
HUGHES CT	0	296A	SEM	77365
HUGHES LN	100	248N	SWM	77354
HUGHES RD	0	615H	SEC	77089
HUGHES RD	9800	616B	SEC	77089
HUGHES RD	11400	576Y	SEH	77089
HUGHES CROSSING DR	0	368E	NWC	77429
HUGHES LANDING BLVD	0	251C	WD	77380
HUGHES RANCH RD	2300	613M	NEB	77584
HUGHES RANCH RD	4300	614J	PL	77581
HUGHES RANCH RD	9800	616E	SEC	77089
HUGHEY AVE	0	257A	SEM	77357
HUGHLETT DR	0	366P	NWC	77433
HUISACHE	4600	531M	BL	77401
HUISACHE	5400	531K	SWH	77081
HUISACHE BLVD	3400	615T	PL	77581
HUISACHE CT	3300	615T	PL	77581
HUISACHE BRANCH CT	19600	332A	NWC	77388
HULDY	1700	492V	SWH	77019
HULDY	2600	492V	SWH	77098
HULL	4000	533M	SEH	77021
HULL	4900	534N	SEH	77021
HULLSMITH DR	2700	490V	SWH	77063
W. HULLWOOD CIR	0	250R	NWC	77389
E. HULLWOOD CIR	0	250R	NWC	77389
E. HULLWOOD CT	0	250Q	NWC	77389
HUMAYA DR	0	255X	SEM	77365
HUMBLE	0	500Z	BT	77520
HUMBLE	0	501W	BT	77520
W. HUMBLE	100	501Y	BT	77520
E. HUMBLE	100	541C	BT	77520
HUMBLE DR	2100	620F	SB	77586
HUMBLE DR	3000	613X	NEB	77578
HUMBLE PKWY	18200	375B	NEH	77338
HUMBLE RD	0	288P	NWC	77377
HUMBLE BROOK DR	0	335P	NCC	77338
HUMBLE BY-PASS	0	334V	NCC	77338
HUMBLE BY-PASS	0	335T	HM	77338
HUMBLE BY-PASS	0	336S	NEC	77338
W. HUMBLE BYPASS	7700	334V	NCC	77338
W. HUMBLE BYPASS	8400	335T	HM	77338
HUMBLE CROSBY RD	16800	379A	NEC	77532
HUMBLE CROSBY RD	22300	339N	HU	77336
HUMBLE CROSBY RD	27000	299W	NEC	77336
HUMBLE CROSBY RD	29000	298V	NEC	77336
HUMBLE GULLY RUN	0	376Q	NEC	77396
HUMBLE HUFFMAN RD	0	337Y	NEC	77346
HUMBLE LAKE RD	14400	288N	NWC	77377
HUMBLE PLACE DR	1700	336W	HM	77338
HUMBLE WESTFIELD RD	1600	333L	NCC	77073
HUMBLE WESTFIELD RD	4800	334P	NCC	77338
HUMBLE WESTFIELD RD	5700	335T	HM	77338
HUMBLE WESTFIELD LOOP	1600	333J	NCC	77073
HUMBOLDT PARK LN	0	524C	NEF	77494
HUMBOLDT PARK LN	0	524C	NEF	77494
HUMMING BIRD	9800	539T	LP	77571
HUMMINGBIRD	25800	257H	RF	77357
HUMMINGBIRD CT	200	536U	PA	77502
HUMMINGBIRD DR	4300	531Z	SWH	77035
HUMMINGBIRD DR	5400	531X	SWH	77096
HUMMINGBIRD DR	7800	530Y	SWH	77071
HUMMINGBIRD DR	400	413A	NCC	77060
HUMMINGBIRD LN	2600	375L	HM	77396
HUMMINGBIRD LN	18600	286H	NWC	77377
HUMMINGBIRD GLEN CT	0	289R	NWC	77375
HUMMINGBIRD PLACE	10800	252M	SEM	77385
HUMMINGBIRD POINT LN	0	332S	NWC	77090
HUMPHREVILLE	3000	580Q	LP	77571
HUMPHREYS DR	8600	528Q	SWC	77083
HUNDRED BRIDGE LN	11100	568A	NEF	77498
HUNGARY LN	6200	578E	PA	77505
HUNKLER DR	10600	573H	SEH	77047
W. HUNNICUT	100	501Y	BT	77520
E. HUNNICUT	100	501Y	BT	77520
HUNSTANTON CT	3500	486S	NEF	77450
HUNT	0	499L	NEC	77520
HUNT	1	494T	SEH	77003
HUNT	1800	657J	FR	77546
HUNT RD	600	461X	BT	77521
HUNTBROOK DR	0	570T	MC	77489
HUNTBROOK DR	6800	330G	NWC	77379
HUNTCREST LN	0	376U	NEC	77396
HUNTER	1500	495V	GP	77547
HUNTER	2200	501S	BT	77520
W. HUNTER	3800	460M	NEC	77562
E. HUNTER	3800	460M	NEC	77562
HUNTER	9000	495U	NEH	77029
HUNTER LN	25700	484Q	NEF	77494
HUNTER HART DR	21400	296J	SEM	77365
HUNTERCLIFF LN	20300	406Q	NWC	77449
HUNTER CREEK CT	0	294U	SEM	77386
HUNTER CREEK CT	0	294U	SEM	77386
HUNTER CREEK DR	0	294U	SEM	77386
HUNTER CREEK DR	0	294U	SEM	77386
HUNTERCREST	600	620E	EL	77586
HUNTERFIELD DR	12800	328V	NWC	77429
HUNTERMOOR CIR	8200	335S	NCC	77338
HUNTER PARK	32300	252R	SEM	77385
HUNTER PARK CT	2300	252R	SEM	77385
HUNTER RANCH WAY	24500	324M	NWC	77447
HUNTERS CT	1800	570Y	MC	77489
HUNTERS LN	0	657J	FR	77546
HUNTERS RD	29600	246D	SWM	77355
HUNTERS BEND	0	657J	FR	77546
HUNTERS BEND DR	15300	287H	NWC	77377
HUNTERS BRANCH DR	1	490D	HE	77024
HUNTERS CANYON	0	502K	BT	77520
HUNTERS CANYON LN	0	328Y	NWC	77429
HUNTERS CHASE LN	13800	327Z	NWC	77429
W. HUNTERS COURT DR	1300	451X	NWH	77055
E. HUNTERS COURT DR	1300	451X	NWH	77055
S. HUNTERS COURT DR	7700	451X	NWH	77055
N. HUNTERS COURT DR	7700	451X	NWH	77055
HUNTERS COVE	0	657J	FR	77546
HUNTERS COVE CT	13900	414B	NCC	77039
HUNTERS CREEK DR	8300	491A	HC	77024
HUNTERS CREEK LN	0	462T	NEC	77521
HUNTERS CREEK PLACE	1	490D	HC	77024
HUNTERS CREEK WAY	100	285P	NWC	77447
W. HUNTERS CREEK WAY DR	1200	451X	NWH	77055
E. HUNTERS CREEK WAY DR	1200	451X	NWH	77055
S. HUNTERS CREEK WAY DR	7700	451X	NWH	77055
N. HUNTERS CREEK WAY DR	7700	451X	NWH	77055

Street Name	Block	Pg/Sq	Loc	Zips
S. HUNTERS CROSSING CIR	1	250G	WD	77381
N. HUNTERS CROSSING CIR	1	250G	WD	77381
HUNTERS CROSSING CT	1	250G	WD	77381
HUNTERS CROSSING DR	0	250G	WD	77381
HUNTERS CROSSING LN	0	461T	NEC	77521
HUNTERS DEN DR	500	488H	SWH	77079
HUNTERS FIELD LN	0	456D	NEC	77044
HUNTERS FIELD LN	0	457A	NEC	77044
HUNTERS FIELD LN	8700	578D	LP	77571
HUNTERS FOREST	0	657J	FR	77546
HUNTERS FOREST DR	10800	490H	HC	77024
HUNTERS GATE CT	0	609U	MC	77479
HUNTERSGLEN CIR	17300	376G	NEC	77396
HUNTERS GLEN DR	2900	610E	MC	77459
HUNTERS GROVE	15500	246V	SWM	77355
HUNTERS GROVE LN	600	491E	HC	77024
HUNTERS HOLLOW DR	24700	251S	SWM	77380
HUNTERS HOLLOW DR	26300	251J	SWM	77380
HUNTERS LAKE WAY	0	417A	NEC	77044
HUNTERS LAKE WAY	14000	377X	NEC	77044
HUNTERS LOCKE	2500	568Y	SG	77479
HUNTERS LODGE LN	0	461T	NEC	77521
HUNTERS PARK DR	1400	570T	MC	77489
HUNTERS PARK DR	11000	490H	HC	77024
HUNTERS PARK LN	400	490H	HC	77024
HUNTERS PARK WAY	1200	451X	NWH	77055
HUNTERS PEAK LN	7700	462V	CCO	77520
HUNTERS PRAIRIE LN	0	444X	KT	77493
HUNTER SPRING CIR	23800	293X	NCC	77373
HUNTERS RIDGE CT	1	490M	HC	77024
HUNTERS RIDGE DR	0	502K	BT	77520
HUNTERS RIVER LN	0	569Q	SF	77477
HUNTERS SHORE DR		524A	NEF	77494
HUNTERS SIDE TRAIL	0	611N	FS	77545
HUNTERS TERRACE DR	0	376C	NEC	77369
HUNTERSTONE CT	6400	407U	NWC	77084
HUNTERS TRACE DR	1900	489P	SWH	77042
HUNTERS TRACE LN	0	462T	NEC	77521
HUNTERS TRAIL	0	257L	SEM	77357
HUNTERS TRAIL	300	491J	HC	77024
HUNTERS TRAIL	0	657J	FR	77546
HUNTERS TREE DR	22600	291J	NWC	77389
HUNTERS VIEW LN		328K	NWC	77429
HUNTERS VILLAGE DR	8300	378A	NEC	77346
HUNTERS WAY	0	462T	NEC	77521
HUNTERS WAY CT	600	491E	HC	77024
HUNTERWOOD DR	400	491E	HC	77024
HUNTER WOOD DR	1200	659N	LC	77573
HUNTERWOOD DR	3200	609H	MC	77459
HUNTERWYCK LN	0	462T	NEC	77521
HUNTFORD LN	12000	416Z	NEC	77044
W. HUNTING	4500	454T	NEH	77026
HUNTING BRIAR DR	12500	528U	SWH	77099
HUNTING BROOK DR	12500	528U	SWH	77099
HUNTINGDALE DR	1900	485L	SWC	77450
HUNTING DOG LN	16300	610C	SWH	77489
HUNTINGDON PLACE	3200	492P	SWH	77019
HUNTING MEADOW DR	4500	446H	NWC	77449
HUNTING PATH CT	11000	368V	NWC	77065
HUNTING PATH PLACE	1	250C	WD	77381
HUNTINGSHIRE	0	257G	SEM	77357
HUNTINGTON	600	616Y	FR	77546
HUNTINGTON	21900	255Y	SEM	77365
HUNTINGTON CT	3000	444K	KT	77493
HUNTINGTON DR	0	570Y	MC	77489
HUNTINGTON DR	1000	613K	NEB	77584
HUNTINGTON DR	2100	537F	PA	77506
HUNTINGTON LN	0	462T	NEC	77521
HUNTINGTON LN	1800	524Y	NEF	77406
HUNTINGTON COVE	900	490M	HC	77063
HUNTINGTON CREST DR	10400	528V	SWH	77099
HUNTINGTON DALE DR	10200	528V	SWH	77099
HUNTINGTON ESTATES DR	10400	528Y	SWH	77099
HUNTINGTON FIELD DR	12300	528U	SWH	77099
HUNTINGTON GLEN	11900	529S	SWH	77099
HUNTINGTON HILL DR	9500	529S	SWH	77099
HUNTINGTON PARK	0	411U	NWH	77088
HUNTINGTON PARK CIR	1	490E	BH	77024
HUNTINGTON PARK CT	1	490E	BH	77024
HUNTINGTON PARK DR	12000	529W	SWH	77099
HUNTINGTON PLACE DR	9500	528V	SWH	77099
HUNTINGTON POINT DR	10400	528V	SWH	77099
HUNTINGTON VALLEY DR	10400	528Z	SWH	77099
HUNTINGTON VENTURE DR	12100	528Y	SWH	77099
HUNTINGTON VIEW DR	10200	528V	SWH	77099
HUNTINGTON WAY	2700	614S	NEB	77584
HUNTINGTON WAY DR	9500	529S	SWH	77099
HUNTINGTON WAY DR	10400	528Z	SWH	77099
HUNTINGTON WICK DR	9500	529S	SWH	77099
HUNTINGTON WILLOW LN	0	332X	NWC	77090
HUNTINGTON WOOD DR	10200	528Z	SWH	77099
HUNTINGTON WDS ESTATES DR	1	287L	NWC	77377
HUNTING VALLEY CT	24700	485N	NEF	77494
HUNTING VALLEY LN	2600	485N	NEF	77494
HUNTINGWICK DR	12300	490E	SWH	77024
HUNTINGWICK DR	12500	489H	SWH	77024
HUNTINGWOOD DR	23400	285B	SWM	77447
HUNTINGWOOD DR	23500	245X	SWM	77447
HUNT LAKE LN	19500	446Y	NWC	77084
HUNTLAND CT	3700	485V	NEF	77450
HUNTLEIGH WAY	13000	568C	SG	77478
HUNTLEY MANOR DR	0	293F	SEM	77386
HUNTMONT DR	14500	366D	CY	77429
HUNTMONT DR	14700	326Z	NWC	77429
HUNTON DR	4000	529D	SWH	77042
HUNTRESS LN	1900	618L	SEH	77062
HUNTSMAN DR	0	371L	NWC	77067
HUNTSMANS HORN CIR	1	251M	WD	77380
HUNTSWELL CT	5200	485W	NEF	77494
HUNTWICK LN	24100	339J	HU	77336
HUNTWICK PARC CT	5000	330Z	NWC	77069
HUNTWOOD CT	3700	485V	NEF	77450
HUNTWOOD HILLS LN	0	484Y	NEF	77494
HUNTWYCK	0	248N	SWM	77354
HUNTWYCK CT	11000	490H	HC	77024
HURFUS DR	2100	451V	NWH	77092
HURLEY	600	453C	NEH	77022
HURLEY	2800	454A	NEH	77093
HURLINGHAM	2800	414N	NCC	77093
HURLOCK	700	332C	NCC	77373
HURLPLAN	3100	454A	NEH	77093
HURON	23700	291A	NWC	77389
HURON CT	7800	461S	NEC	77521
HURON BEND DR	0	296E	SEM	77365
HURON PARK TRAIL	18400	337X	NEC	77346
HURRICANE LN	0	333T	NCC	77073
HURRICANE LN	3300	610Z	MC	77545
HURST	100	543U	BC	77520
HURST	6100	492B	NWH	77008
HURST CT	12200	367M	CY	77429
S. HURST DR	0	616G	SEC	77089
HURSTFIELD POINTE CT	13900	367D	NWC	77429

Street Name	Block	Pg/Sq	Loc	Zips
HURSTFIELD POINTE DR	15800	367D	NWC	77429
HURST FOREST DR	7600	337V	NEC	77346
HURST GREEN LN	0	611T	FS	77545
HURST HILL LN	0	575U	SEH	77075
HURST MANOR DR	1400	329G	NWC	77379
HURSTON GLEN LN	0	524C	NEF	77494
HURSTON GLEN LN	0	524C	NEF	77494
HURST PARK DR	1200	329G	NWC	77379
HURST POINT LN	0	457P	NEC	77049
HURSTSHIRE BEND	0	485A	NEF	77494
HURSTWOOD	0	337V	NEC	77346
HURTA RD	100	419Q	BR	77532
HURTGEN FOREST RD	7300	534S	SEH	77033
HUSE	5500	414M	NEC	77039
HUSSION	1300	494S	SEH	77003
N. HUTCHESON	1	494N	SEH	77003
HUTCHESON	100	494N	SEH	77003
HUTCHINS	1	493R	SEH	77002
HUTCHINS	300	493R	SEH	77003
HUTCHINS	2300	493U	SEH	77004
HUTCHINS DR	0	613Y	NEB	77584
HUTCHINSON	0	577X	SEH	77034
HUTCHINSON	15200	570K	MC	77071
W. HUTCHINSON CIR	15200	570L	MC	77071
E. HUTCHINSON CIR	15200	570L	MC	77071
HUTTO	0	457P	NEC	77049
HUTTON	2100	494B	NEH	77026
HUTTON COURT LN	0	527W	NEF	77469
HUTTON PARK DR	0	524A	NEF	77494
HUXLEY, T LN	2	609C	MC	77459
HYACINTH	3000	493C	NEH	77009
HYACINTH PATH WAY	0	457V	NEC	77049
HYACINTH PLACE	800	610S	MC	77459
S. HYANNIS PORT	500	419B	NEC	77532
N. HYANNIS PORT	500	419B	NEC	77532
HYCLIFF CT	6600	609K	MC	77459
HYCOHEN RD	13600	573S	SEH	77047
HYDE COVE CT	0	526R	NEF	77407
HYDE PARK BLVD	1	493N	SWH	77006
HYDE PARK DR	0	327U	NWC	77429
HYDE PARK PLACE	14900	330V	NWC	77069
HYDETHORPE DR	8800	527R	SWC	77083
HYDRO-55	0	373C	NCC	77073
HYDROVILLE CT	0	455D	NEH	77078
HYLAND LN	0	658M	LC	77573
HYLANDER DR	11200	329T	NWC	77070
HYLAND GREENS LN	24300	292B	NCC	77373
HYLAND PARK	2300	371H	NWC	77014
HYTA	200	452M	NWH	77018

I

Street Name	Block	Pg/Sq	Loc	Zips
W. I	100	580B	LP	77571
I AVE	0	410P	NWC	77040
I AVE	0	501S	BT	77520
I AVE	0	569R	SF	77477
I CT	0	290L	NWC	77389
I & GN PLACE	0	493M	SEH	77002
I, AVENUE	0	569R	SF	77477
I, AVENUE	0	659T	LC	77573
I, AVENUE	0	659Y	DI	77539
I, AVENUE	400	576C	SH	77587
I, AVENUE	6500	494P	SEH	77011
I, AVENUE	7500	495X	SEH	77012
E. I, AVENUE	9400	535D	SEH	77012
IAGO CT	0	659P	LC	77573
IBARRA LN	0	660G	GCO	77539
IBERIA DR	11100	368R	NWC	77065
IBERIAN CT		289Y	NWC	77379
IBERIS MEADOWS DR	25000	249Z	NWC	77375
IBERVILLE GLEN DR	0	484X	NEF	77494
IBERVILLE GLEN DR	0	484X	NEF	77494
IBEX LN	0	457P	NEC	77049
IBIS	0	333M	NCC	77338
IBIS RD	19600	284V	NWC	77447
IBISCO CT	0	525J	NEF	77406
IBIS LAKE CT	0	446B	NWC	77449
IBIS POND LN	0	334P	NCC	77388
IBIS WAY	0	610F	MC	77489
IBIZA LN	0	660G	GCO	77539
IBRIS RANCH DR	25100	485N	NEF	77494
ICE PALACE DR	0	532S	SWH	77025
IDA	0	494K	NEH	77020
IDA BELL	100	492L	SWH	77007
IDAHO	100	540Y	LP	77571
IDAHO	300	580C	LP	77571
IDAHO	500	576B	SH	77587
IDAHO	1300	541E	BT	77520
IDAHO	1600	659N	LC	77573
IDAHO	3300	533Q	SEH	77021
IDAHO	4900	534N	SEH	77021
IDA ROSE CT	6000	406T	NWC	77449
IDA WELLS FOREST DR	7400	415S	NEC	77016
IDA WELLS FOREST DR	7400	415S	NEC	77016
IDEAL	2500	493C	NEH	77009
IDLEBROOK DR	10500	369B	NWC	77070
IDLEBROOK DR	11600	369A	NWC	77070
IDLE GLEN ROADWAY	20400	258T	SEM	77357
IDLELOCH DR	28200	299S	NEC	77336
IDLE WATER LN	13000	377L	NEC	77044
IDLE WILDE ROADWAY	20400	258P	SEM	77357
IDLE WIND DR	0	525Z	NEF	77406
IDLEWOOD	3900	530A	SWH	77042
IDLEWOOD CIR	0	250H	WD	77381
IDLEWOOD CT	500	616V	FR	77546
IDLEWOOD CT	10900	579C	LP	77571
IDLEWOOD DR	0	250H	WD	77381
IDLEWOOD DR	0	616V	FR	77546
IDLEWOOD DR	700	501T	BT	77520
E. IDLEWOOD DR	10800	579C	LP	77571
IDLEWOOD CROSSING DR	0	524L	NWF	77406
IDLE WOOD ROADWAY	20800	258T	NEC	77357
IDYLWILD	1200	453T	NWH	77009
IDYLWILD WOOD WAY	0	326Y	NWC	77433
IDYLWOOD DR	1300	534D	SEH	77023
IGLOO RD	2900	374A	NEH	77032
IKES LN	0	338M	NEH	77336
IKES RD	1200	539P	LP	77571
IKES POND DR	0	250W	NWC	77389
IKES TREE DR	0	250X	NWC	77389
ILEX	6700	534H	SEH	77087
ILEX	7200	535E	SEH	77012
ILFREY	100	499D	NEC	77520
ILFREY LN	5100	491U	SWH	77056
ILFREY LN	5100	491U	SWH	77057
ILLENE DR	11500	414C	NWC	77093
ILLIAD CT	11500	529W	SWH	77477
ILLINOIS	0	376E	HM	77396
ILLINOIS	0	659K	LC	77573
ILLINOIS	500	576A	SH	77587
ILLINOIS	3100	540D	BT	77520
ILLINOIS	6300	533L	SEH	77021

Street Name	Block	Pg/Sq	Loc	Zips
N. ILLINOIS AVE	100	659E	LC	77573
S. ILLINOIS AVE	200	659J	LC	77573
ILLINOIS RD	3000	611T	FS	77545
ILONA LN	8500	532N	SWH	77025
IMANI LN	13500	571L	SWH	77085
IMBER	700	536K	PA	77506
IMBER FOREST DR	18000	376D	NEC	77346
IMHOF	27000	284N	NWC	77447
IMHOF	27600	283Q	NWC	77484
IMOGENE	4700	531Q	SWH	77096
IMOGENE	5800	530R	SWH	77074
IMOGENE	8900	530N	SWH	77036
IMPERIAL	100	616Z	FR	77546
IMPERIAL	900	338C	NEH	77336
IMPERIAL	4900	531C	BL	77401
IMPERIAL	11200	413Q	NCC	77093
IMPERIAL CT	13800	568F	SG	77498
IMPERIAL RD	300	568N	SG	77498
IMPERIAL ARBOR LN	0	332Q	NCC	77073
IMPERIAL ARBOR LN	0	332Q	NCC	77073
IMPERIAL BEND DR	0	372D	NCC	77073
IMPERIAL BLUFF CT	31400	253P	SEM	77386
IMPERIAL BROOK DR	0	372D	NCC	77073
IMPERIAL CANYON CT	14100	568A	SG	77498
IMPERIAL CANYON LN	2100	568A	SG	77498
IMPERIAL COLONY LN	0	446C	NWC	77449
IMPERIAL COVE CT	0	253T	SEM	77386
IMPERIAL CREEK DR	29400	288E	NWC	77377
IMPERIAL CROSSING DR	2600	252M	SEM	77385
IMPERIAL CROSSING DR	12600	328L	NWC	77377
IMPERIAL CROWN DR	1500	450S	NWH	77043
IMPERIAL FALLS CT	15800	408E	NWC	77095
IMPERIAL FOREST LN	15900	332R	NCC	77073
IMPERIAL GREEN DR	0	372D	NCC	77073
IMPERIAL GROVE DR	5300	371N	NWC	77066
IMPERIAL GROVE DR	5500	370V	NWC	77066
IMPERIAL GROVE LN	0	253J	SEM	77386
IMPERIAL HILLS DR	19300	328D	NWC	77375
IMPERIAL IVY CT	22700	292L	SP	77373
IMPERIAL LAKE DR	0	372D	NCC	77073
IMPERIAL LANDING LN	0	446J	NWC	77449
IMPERIAL LEAF LN	6700	290U	NWC	77379
IMPERIAL LEGENDS DR	30500	253S	SEM	77386
IMPERIAL MANOR LN	1500	332R	NCC	77073
IMPERIAL NORTH LN	0	253P	SEM	77386
IMPERIAL OAK DR	20400	245F	SWM	77355
IMPERIAL OAKS BLVD	30000	252V	SEM	77386
IMPERIAL PARK LN	0	252R	SEM	77385
IMPERIAL PARK LN	0	332Q	NCC	77073
S. IMPERIAL PATH LN	0	252R	SEM	77386
N. IMPERIAL PATH LN	0	252V	SEM	77386
IMPERIAL PLAZA DR	400	373S	NEH	77060
IMPERIAL POINT	7200	529L	SWH	77072
IMPERIAL PROMENADE DR	0	253P	SEM	77386
IMPERIAL RIDGE LN	20900	290T	NWC	77379
IMPERIAL SHORES DR	0	612K	PL	77545
IMPERIAL SPRINGS CT	14200	367D	NWC	77429
IMPERIAL STONE DR	0	372D	NCC	77073
IMPERIAL VALLEY CT	14800	413A	NEH	77060
IMPERIAL VALLEY DR	14800	413A	NEH	77060
IMPERIAL VALLEY DR	15700	373W	NEH	77060
IMPERIAL VALLEY DR	16100	373S	NEH	77060
IMPERIAL VALLEY DR	17200	373N	NEH	77060
IMPERIAL VALLEY DR	18100	372D	NCC	77073
IMPERIAL VALLEY DR	20400	332Z	NCC	77073
IMPERIAL VIEW DR	0	252R	SEM	77385
IMPERIAL WALK CT	0	253N	SEM	77386
IMPERIAL WALK LN	0	253N	SEM	77386
IMPERIAL WOODS LN	11700	328X	NWC	77429
IMPERIUM LN	3000	258A	SEM	77357
INA	5100	455S	NEH	77028
INA	10700	415S	NEH	77016
INCA	23500	295F	SEM	77365
INCA DR	6300	538W	PA	77503
INCA DOVE PLACE	0	366S	NWC	77433
INCE LN	0	410M	NWC	77040
INCE LN	9100	410V	NWC	77040
INCH RD	7600	451T	NWH	77055
INCLINE DR	5100	371N	NWC	77066
INDEPENDENCE	7700	533U	SEH	77051
INDEPENDENCE AVE	0	659P	LC	77573
E. INDEPENDENCE AVE	100	659P	LC	77573
INDEPENDENCE BLVD	0	461X	BT	77521
INDEPENDENCE BLVD	0	570X	MC	77489
INDEPENDENCE BLVD	0	609D	MC	77459
INDEPENDENCE DR	300	617W	FR	77546
INDEPENDENCE RD	1500	570Y	MC	77489
INDEPENDENCE PARK	0	615U	PL	77581
INDEPENDENCE RUN	0	578D	LP	77571
INDEPENDENCE RUN	8900	578D	LP	77571
INDIA	13800	572U	SWH	77047
INDIAN	0	376E	HM	77396
INDIAN CIR	5600	491F	SWH	77056
INDIAN CIR	5700	491F	SWH	77057
INDIANA	0	375H	HM	77396
INDIANA	100	536W	SH	77587
INDIANA	1100	376E	HM	77396
INDIANA	1200	575D	SH	77587
INDIANA	1400	492R	SWH	77006
INDIANA	1800	492R	SWH	77019
INDIANA	3100	540D	BT	77520
INDIANA RD	3000	611T	FS	77545
INDIANAPOLIS	12800	497A	NEH	77015
INDIANAPOLIS	2100	658V	LC	77573
INDIAN AUTUMN	0	618A	SEH	77062
INDIAN AUTUMN TRACE	1100	618A	SEH	77062
INDIAN BAYOU	300	491F	SWH	77057
INDIAN BLANKET DR	400	659G	LC	77573
INDIAN BLANKET LN	13200	528G	SWH	77083
INDIAN BLUFF	5700	491F	SWH	77057
INDIAN BROOK CT	5500	334E	NCC	77373
INDIAN CEDAR LN	1	251R	WD	77380
INDIAN CHERRY FOREST LN	19700	326X	NWC	77433
INDIAN CLEARING TRAIL	0	292D	SEM	77386
INDIAN CLOVER DR	1	251E	WD	77381
INDIAN COVE CT	7700	337M	NEC	77346
INDIAN CREEK	0	609Z	NEF	77459
INDIAN CREEK RD	13000	489F	SWH	77079
INDIAN CREEK FALLS	9200	289D	NWC	77375
INDIAN CREST CT	23900	485E	NEF	77494
INDIAN CYPRESS DR	16000	327Y	CY	77429
INDIAN DESERT DR	0	406M	NWC	77433
INDIAN FALLS DR	6600	571W	SWH	77489
INDIAN FIELD CT	6300	408T	NWC	77084
INDIAN FOREST DR	3500	293P	NCC	77373
INDIAN GARDENS WAY	4300	375R	NEC	77396
INDIANGRASS CT	0	524H	NEF	77494
INDIAN GRASS DR	19100	446M	NWC	77449
INDIANGRASS LN	0	524H	NEF	77494
INDIAN GROVE LN	20300	486T	SWC	77450
INDIAN HARBOR LN	14100	367D	NWC	77429
INDIAN HAWTHORN CT	1300	486H	SWC	77094
INDIAN HAWTHORN DR	19300	486H	SWC	77094
INDIAN HILL RD	7000	250K	NWC	77389
INDIAN HILLS CIR	23600	287D	NWC	77377
INDIAN HILLS WAY	23700	485K	NEF	77494
INDIAN HILL TRAIL	800	336K	NEH	77339
INDIAN KNOLL DR	22600	485G	SWC	77450
INDIAN LAKE DR	6600	571W	SWH	77489
INDIAN LEDGE DR	10800	369X	NWC	77064
INDIAN LODGE LN	0	375Z	NEC	77396
INDIAN MAPLE DR	8700	335N	NCC	77338
INDIAN MEADOW DR	300	659H	LC	77573
INDIAN MILL DR	16100	527C	SWC	77082
INDIAN MOUND CT	2700	378N	NEC	77532
INDIAN MOUND TRAIL	2700	378N	NEC	77532
INDIAN MOUNTAIN LN	0	377F	NEC	77346
INDIAN OAKS	11600	418P	NEC	77044
INDIAN OCEAN	0	376D	NEC	77346
INDIAN OCEAN DR	0	336Z	NEC	77346
INDIANOLA DR	5400	374V	NCC	77032
INDIAN PAINTBRUSH LN	10400	367U	NWC	77095
INDIAN QUAIL CIR	14900	408P	NWC	77095
INDIAN RIDGE CT	1000	485G	SWC	77450
INDIAN RIDGE DR	22300	485G	SWC	77450
INDIAN RILL CT		289G	NWC	77375
INDIAN RIVER DR	8900	412L	NWH	77088
INDIAN RUN DR	2500	375K	NEC	77396
W. INDIAN SAGE CIR	1	250B	WD	77381
S. INDIAN SAGE CIR	1	250B	WD	77381
INDIAN SAGE DR	0	485Z	NEF	77450
INDIAN SHORES LN	5300	449A	NWC	77041
INDIAN SHORES RD	100	379E	NEC	77532
INDIAN SHORES RD	1200	378H	NEC	77532
INDIAN SPRING DR	900	656L	FR	77546
INDIAN SPRINGS TRAIL	15900	246M	SC	77355
INDIAN SPRINGS WAY	0	292U	NCC	77373
INDIAN SPRING TRAIL	8000	415L	NEC	77050
INDIAN STONE LN	19100	446D	NWC	77449
INDIAN SUMMER CT	3300	657G	FR	77546
INDIAN SUMMER DR	0	299N	NEC	77336
INDIAN SUMMER TRAIL	3100	657G	FR	77546
INDIAN SUNRISE CT	4200	618D	PA	77059
INDIAN TRACE LN	16300	527B	SWC	77082
INDIAN TRAIL	2500	539S	DP	77536
INDIAN TRAIL	3200	500R	BT	77521
INDIAN TRAIL	5700	491F	SWH	77057
INDIAN TRAIL	10700	329K	NWC	77375
INDIAN TRAIL	17300	254M	SEM	77365
INDIAN TRAIL	19500	257L	SEM	77357
INDIAN TRAIL CT	1500	610B	MC	77489
INDIAN TRAIL DR	2600	610B	MC	77489
INDIAN VISTA DR	10800	369X	NWC	77064
INDIAN WELLS CT	3100	610F	MC	77459
INDIAN WELLS DR	1700	610F	MC	77459
INDIAN WELLS DR	11900	370H	NWC	77066
INDIAN WELLS DR	14100	330X	NWC	77069
INDIAN WOODS DR	15400	571W	SWH	77489
INDIDO KEY CT	0	366Z	NWC	77433
INDIGO	4600	531R	SWH	77096
INDIGO	5800	530R	SWH	77074
S. INDIGO CIR	0	250C	WD	77381
N. INDIGO CIR	0	250C	WD	77381
INDIGO CT	0	295J	SEM	77365
INDIGO CT	0	419A	NEC	77532
INDIGO CT	1	245T	SWM	77355
INDIGO DR	0	612R	PL	77584
INDIGO DR	0	612R	PL	77584
INDIGO LN	0	295J	SEM	77365
INDIGO LN	3100	609F	MC	77459
INDIGO BAY CT	0	612K	PL	77545
INDIGO BAY CT	9700	524G	NEF	77494
INDIGO BAY DR	0	612K	PL	77545
INDIGO BAY CREEK LN	0	612K	PL	77545
INDIGO BROOK CT	10300	615D	SEC	77089
INDIGO BUNTING PLACE	0	250K	NWC	77389
INDIGO BUNTING PLACE	0	250K	NWC	77389
INDIGO BUSH DR	0	406D	NWC	77433
INDIGO COVE CT	0	658X	LC	77573
INDIGO COVE LN	0	409W	NWC	77041
INDIGO CREEK LN	11400	289J	NWC	77375
INDIGO FALLS LN	5300	449A	NWC	77041
INDIGO FIELD LN	2100	525H	NEF	77407
INDIGO HARBOUR LN	2300	619Y	LC	77573
INDIGO HILL LN	21500	526A	NEF	77450
INDIGO HILLS DR	16800	246P	SWM	77355
INDIGO ILLUSION CIR	0	288S	NWC	77377
INDIGO ISLES LN	5600	449A	NWC	77041
INDIGO LAKE CT	13500	488P	SWH	77077
INDIGO LAKE CT	28100	245H	SWM	77355
INDIGO LAKE DR	19000	246J	SWM	77355
INDIGO LAKE DR	19200	245G	SWM	77355
INDIGO LOCH LN	17600	447G	NWC	77084
INDIGO MIST CT	0	407U	NWC	77084
INDIGO PARK DR	1700	252V	SEM	77386
INDIGO PASS CT	4700	577G	PA	77505
INDIGO PASS LN	0	525D	NEF	77450
INDIGO PINES LN	22200	525C	NEF	77450
INDIGO RIVER LN	20700	406P	NWC	77449
INDIGO RUTH DR	0	290P	NWC	77379
INDIGO RUTH DR	21500	290J	NWC	77379
INDIGO SANDS DR	13400	612K	PL	77545
INDIGO SHORE WAY	0	253X	SEM	77386
INDIGO SKY CIR	0	250C	WD	77381
INDIGO SPIRES DR	13600	368A	NWC	77429
INDIGO STONE LN	2700	446N	NWC	77449
INDIGO TRACE CT	13400	369G	NWC	77070
INDIGO VILLA LN	8300	527N	NEF	77083
INDIGO WAY	18400	295K	SEM	77365
INDUS	11000	576S	SEH	77089
INDUSTRIAL	12300	496Q	GP	77015
INDUSTRIAL BLVD	100	568M	SG	77478
INDUSTRIAL DR	1500	570N	MC	77489
E. INDUSTRIAL PKWY	0	255C	SEM	77357
W. INDUSTRIAL PKWY	18900	255C	SEM	77357
INDUSTRIAL RD	8700	495Q	NEH	77029
INDUSTRIAL RD	12300	496M	NEH	77015
INDUSTRIAL RD	13000	497N	NEC	77015
INDUSTRIAL PARK DR	31600	247V	SWM	77362
INDUSTRIAL PARK RD	0	495Z	NEH	77029
INDUSTRIAL WAY	400	494R	SEH	77011
INDUSTRIAL WAY	20400	252K	SEM	77385
INDUSTRY	14100	572X	SWC	77053
INDUSTRY LN	22800	289L	NWC	77375
INEZ	2800	534G	SEH	77023
INEZ	3600	611X	FS	77545
INGA LN	11500	369R	NWC	77064
INGALTON	0	619P	PA	77058
INGEBORG	1600	494W	SEH	77023
INGERSOL AVE	2300	537F	PA	77506
INGERSOLL	4400	491Z	SWH	77027
INGEWOOD	16900	458B	NEC	77049
INGHAM DR	19500	406U	NWC	77449
INGHRAM LN	0	366P	NWC	77433
INGLEBROOK LN	0	528Q	SWC	77083
INGLE OAK CT	13600	408L	NWC	77041
INGLE OAK DR	7900	408L	NWC	77041
INGLESIDE CT	4800	291S	NWC	77388
INGLESIDE PARK	16700	367C	CY	77429
INGLEWOOD DR	5100	578J	PA	77505
INGOLD	3700	532E	SS	77005
INGOMAR WAY	4800	571Y	SWH	77053
INGRAM PLACE	13800	369A	NWC	77070
INIESTA LN	0	660H	GCO	77539
INKAHOOTS	29000	323G	NWC	77484
INKBERRY DR	6900	451A	NWH	77092
INKBERRY VALLEY LN	0	572E	SWH	77045
INKER	4500	492H	SWH	77007
INLAND DR	0	614Y	PL	77584
INLAND RD	100	298M	NEC	77336
INLAND GROVE CT	19100	326Y	NWC	77429
INLAND HILL ST	0	572Q	SWH	77045
INLAND OAKS DR	17800	527E	NEF	77407
INLAND PRAIRIE DR	0	250N	NWC	77375
INLAND SPRING CT	13800	578W	SEH	77059
INLANE	100	535A	SEH	77012
INLET CT	0	611W	FS	77545
INMAN	4500	494K	NEH	77020
INNISBROOK DR	16500	407G	NWC	77095
INNISFALL CIR	12200	328G	NWC	77377
INNISFREE	11300	490G	PP	77024
INNSBRUCK	5600	531D	BL	77401
INNSBRUK CT	12200	371J	NWC	77066
INNSBRUK DR	4600	371J	NWC	77066
INNSBURY DR	11600	414N	NCC	77093
INNSDALE DR	300	453C	NEH	77076
INNSHIRE LN	13300	571M	SWH	77045
INSCHO LN	2000	485M	SWC	77450
INSCHO POINT CIR	2000	619Z	LC	77573
INSIGHT AVE	300	419V	NEC	77532
INSLEY	14400	572P	SWH	77045
INSLEY	15000	572T	SWH	77053
INSPIRE CREST LN	0	294E	SEM	77386
INSTITUTE LN	5300	533A	SWH	77005
INTERCHANGE DR	8800	532U	SWH	77054
INTERCONTINENTAL BLVD	0	336W	HM	77338
INTERCONTINENTAL AIRPORT	0	374F	NEH	77032
INTERCONTINENT GATEWY DR	0	375B	NEH	77396
INTERCONTINENTAL PK BLVD	0	373V	NCC	77032
W. INTERDRIVE	14100	374W	NCC	77032
E. INTERDRIVE	14100	374W	NCC	77032
INTERLACHEN DR	5000	500M	BT	77521
INTERNATIONAL BLVD	700	491B	SWH	77024
INTERNATIONAL PLAZA DR	15300	374P	NEH	77032
INTERNATIONAL VLLG	500	336W	HM	77338
INTERPID OAK LN	0	332V	NCC	77073
INTERPORT	0	373L	NCC	77032
INTERURBAN	100	658M	LC	77573
INTERVALE	8800	575M	SEH	77075
INTERWOOD N PKWY	3700	374T	NEH	77032
INTERWOOD S PKWY	3700	374X	NEH	77032
INTREPID	7700	528M	SWH	77072
INTREPID ELM	2900	447N	NWC	77084
INTREPID WAY	2400	619X	LC	77573
INVERGARRY WAY	0	289V	NWC	77375
INVERGYEL LN	0	289Q	NWC	77375
INVERLOCH WAY	9800	335Q	HM	77338
INVERMERE DR	1900	252V	SEM	77386
INVERNESS	1300	656F	FR	77546
INVERNESS CT	3600	616W	PL	77581
INVERNESS DR	3600	492N	SWH	77019
INVERNESS DR	5000	500M	BT	77521
INVERNESS LN	1500	616W	PL	77581
INVERNESS CROSSING BLVD	22500	289R	NWC	77375
INVERNESS FOREST BLVD	21700	332M	NCC	77073
INVERNESS LAKE DR	21000	337K	NEC	77346
INVERNESS PARK CIR	1	450Z	SV	77055
INVERNESS PARK WAY	1	450Z	SV	77055
INVERNESS WAY	6400	578J	PA	77505
INVERRARY CT	7900	408K	NWC	77095
INVERRARY DR	14800	408K	NWC	77095
INVIERNO	10800	496J	JC	77029
INVINCIBLE CIR	3000	619Y	LC	77573
INVINCIBLE DR	3300	619Y	LC	77573
INWAY CIR	23900	290C	NWC	77389
INWAY DR	6100	290C	NWC	77389
INWAY OAKS DR	0	290D	NWC	77389
INWAY TRAIL DR	0	290D	NWC	77389
INWAY TRAIL DR	23800	290D	NWC	77389
INWOOD	500	288G	TB	77375
INWOOD CT	3100	569N	SG	77478
INWOOD DR	200	501P	BT	77521
INWOOD DR	200	616U	FR	77546
INWOOD DR	2100	492N	SWH	77019
INWOOD DR	5300	491P	SWH	77056
INWOOD DR	5300	444Y	KT	77493
INWOOD DR	5800	491N	SWH	77057
INWOOD DR	7500	490R	SWH	77063
INWOOD DR	10000	489Q	SWH	77042
INWOOD DR	11300	489P	SWH	77077
INWOOD LN	100	459M	HG	77562
INWOOD LN	1000	536P	PA	77502
INWOOD LN	15900	571W	SWH	77489
INWOOD BROOK LN	0	446N	NWC	77449
INWOOD FOREST DR	3700	411Q	NWH	77088
INWOOD GLEN LN	0	253N	SEM	77386
INWOOD GREEN	0	411R	NWH	77088
INWOOD HOLLOW LN	10100	411J	NWH	77088
INWOOD NORTH DR	8900	411J	NWH	77088
INWOOD OAKS DR	1	490H	HC	77024
INWOOD PARK CT	5800	491P	SWH	77057
INWOOD PARK DR	7000	411Z	NWH	77088
INWOOD SHADOWS	9900	411K	NWH	77088
INWOOD TRAIL DR	0	411R	NWH	77088
INWOOD VILLAGE LN	0	446B	NWC	77449
INWOOD VISTA CT	0	411R	NWH	77088
INWOOD WEST DR	6500	411N	NWH	77088
INYO NATIONAL DR	0	377K	NEC	77346
IOLA	2800	535K	SEH	77017
IONE	4300	531H	BL	77401
IOWA	100	540Y	LP	77571
IOWA	400	580C	LP	77571
IOWA	400	576A	SH	77587
IOWA	3100	540D	BT	77520
S. IOWA AVE	100	659E	LC	77573
N. IOWA AVE	100	659E	LC	77573
IPSWICH RD	100	575E	SEH	77061
IRA	4500	494P	SEH	77011
IRBY	6100	412X	NWH	77091
IRBY	9300	412P	NWH	77088
IRELAND	4300	454C	NEH	77093
IRELAND	4500	454C	NEH	77016
IRELAND LN	4400	577H	PA	77505
IRENE	100	538F	DP	77536
IRENE	14800	570L	SWH	77085
IRENE	15100	527V	NEF	77498
IRENE DR	400	460N	HG	77562
IRENE RD	100	453Y	NEH	77009
IRENE RD	6000	456L	NEC	77049
IRENELL DR	19500	295C	SEM	77365
IRIE	0	330X	NWC	77069
IRIS	0	495A	NEH	77020
IRIS	3200	460R	NEC	77562
IRIS CT	0	460W	BT	77521
IRIS CT	2600	613U	NEB	77584
IRIS LN	4200	538U	DP	77536
IRIS LN	5500	444P	KT	77493
IRIS LN	18800	295F	SEM	77365
IRIS ARBOR LN	8600	407C	NWC	77095
IRIS BLOOM CT	0	292D	SEM	77386
IRIS BLUFF LN	0	326V	NWC	77429
IRIS BROOK WAY	0	368Z	NWC	77065
IRIS CANYON DR	12000	328H	NWC	77377
IRIS CHASE TRAIL	0	526L	NEF	77407
IRIS CREST	0	406X	NWC	77449
IRIS CROSSING LN	0	612U	PL	77584
IRIS CROSSING LN	0	612U	PL	77584
IRIS CROSSING LN	15300	457U	NEC	77049
IRIS EDGE WAY	0	327H	NWC	77429
IRIS FIELD CT	0	445P	NWC	77493
IRIS GABLE CT	0	484P	NEF	77494
IRIS GARDEN LN	0	417A	NEC	77044
IRIS GLEN LN	7800	526L	NEF	77407
IRISH BEND LN	2900	613V	NEB	77584
IRISH ELM CT	15000	326U	NWC	77429
IRISH HILL DR	5500	571X	SWH	77053
IRISH IVY CT	4100	293M	SEM	77386
IRISH MAPLE ST	800	620L	SB	77586
IRISH MIST CT	1200	485L	SWC	77450
IRISH OAKS CT	1700	527J	NEF	77083
IRIS HOLLOW WAY	0	616H	SEC	77089
IRISH RIDGE WAY	0	611W	FS	77545
IRISH SHORES LN	3300	613V	PL	77584
IRISH SPRING DR	2100	371V	NWC	77067
IRIS LAKE CT	77070	369G	NWC	77070
IRIS LEE LN	11300	490Q	PP	77024
IRIS MANOR CT	0	446C	NWC	77449
IRIS MILLS LN	0	326V	NWC	77429
IRIS PARK CT	0	487A	SWC	77094
IRIS VALLEY WAY	0	371Y	NWC	77038
IRISWOOD DR	11600	616C	SEC	77089
IRONBARK CT	400	618N	SEH	77598
IRONBARK CT	300	618S	SEH	77598
IRONBARK DR	400	618N	SEH	77598
IRON BRIDGE DR	3500	371F	NWC	77066
IRON CASTLE CT	4300	486W	NEF	77450
IRONCLAD DR	2500	658P	LC	77573
IRONCREST LN	20900	291W	NWC	77388
IRON CROWN CIR	3100	331P	NWC	77068
IRONFORK DR	15800	571X	SWH	77053
IRONGATE DR	0	495T	NEH	77029
IRON HILL LN	0	366U	NWC	77433
IRON HORSE	5700	609Z	NEF	77459
IRON HORSESHOE LN	14500	377T	NEC	77044
IRON KNOLL DR	22000	296X	NEC	77339
IRON KNOLL DR	22000	296X	NEC	77339
IRON LAKE DR	18500	447N	NWC	77084
IRON LIEGE CT	8600	412Q	NWH	77088
IRONLOFT CT	3500	486S	NEF	77450
IRON MANOR LN	26800	296X	SEM	77339
IRON MILL DR	0	285L	NWC	77447
IRON ORE	0	247E	SWM	77362
IRON ORE RD	0	377A	NEC	77346
IRON ORE RD	1700	339F	NEC	77336
IRON RIDGE	1900	568Z	SG	77478
IRON RIDGE LN	0	657S	FR	77546
IRON RIVER DR	0	370Y	NWC	77086
IRON ROCK	6000	534Q	SEH	77087
IRON SEAT DR	0	285Q	NWC	77447
IRON SEAT DR	0	285Q	NWC	77447
IRONSIDE RD	23800	293X	NCC	77373
IRONSIDE CREEK DR	15700	571X	SWH	77053
IRONSIDE HILL DR	15700	571X	SWH	77053
IRONSIDE TURN DR	6000	571X	SWH	77053
IRON SPRINGS	8800	576L	SEH	77034
IRON SPRINGS DR	9000	576L	SEH	77034
IRONSPUR LN	0	327Y	NWC	77429
IRON SQUIRE DR	26800	296X	SEM	77339
IRONSTONE CT	11700	371L	NWC	77067
IRONTON PL	100	249R	NWH	77375
IRONTON PLACE		249Q	NWC	77375
IRON TREE LN	8400	524D	NEF	77494
IRON WEED DR	11500	367Q	NWC	77095
IRONWIND LN	0	250P	NWC	77389
IRONWOOD	4600	501J	BT	77521
IRONWOOD	22700	296C	SEM	77365
IRONWOOD	31700	282U	WL	77484
IRONWOOD BLVD	900	497F	NEH	77015
IRONWOOD DR	0	294A	SEM	77386
IRONWOOD LN	7300	462Y	BT	77521
IRONWOOD ESTATES DR	10700	573E	SEH	77051
IRONWOOD MEADOW LN	0	328A	NWC	77429
IRONWOOD RETREAT BLVD		484S	NEF	77494
IROQUOIS	0	295G	SEM	77365
IROQUOIS	12700	413Q	NEH	77037
IROQUOIS DR	4200	577F	PA	77504
IROQUOIS LN	0	247Q	SWM	77355
W. IRVIN	0	299N	NEC	77336
E. IRVIN	29000	299N	NEC	77336
IRVINE	0	493J	SWH	77007
IRVINE PARK LN	0	657U	LC	77573
IRVING LN	2700	537K	PA	77506
IRVINGTON BLVD	3300	453U	NEH	77009
IRVINGTON BLVD	6100	453U	NEH	77022
IRVINGTON BLVD	9400	453U	NEH	77076
IRVINGTON DR	2800	613T	NEB	77584
IRVINGTON COURTS	100	493C	NEH	77009
IRVINGWAY	4900	535N	SEH	77087
ISAAC	1600	538N	PA	77503
ISAACKS RD	100	335Z	HM	77338
ISAACKS DR EXT	0	336W	HM	77338
ISABEL BAY LN	0	406C	NWC	77433
ISABELL	2300	460T	MN	77521
ISABELLA	800	493X	SWH	77002
ISABELLA	1000	493X	SWH	77004
ISABELLA LILAC LN	0	406X	NWC	77449
ISABELLA MEADOW WAY	0	484N	NEF	77494
ISABELLA WAY	0	616L	SEC	77089
ISADORE CT	3300	494A	NEH	77026
ISAIAH DR	0	614N	PL	77584
ISBELL DR	13200	248U	NWC	77375
ISETTA LN	800	413F	NCC	77060
ISFALL PARK PLACE	4500	611D	SWC	77053
ISHMEAL	100	452D	NWH	77076
ISHMEAL	300	452D	NWH	77091
ISIDORA MEZA DR	0	495H	NEH	77013
ISLA	6700	614D	BK	77581
ISLA DR	2000	615K	PL	77581

Street Name	Block	Pg/Sq	Loc	Zips
ISLA CANELA LN	0	660G	GCO	77539
ISLAMORADA CT	9400	416Y	NEC	77044
ISLAMORADA DR	11900	416Y	NEC	77044
ISLAND BLVD	1	610N	MC	77459
S. ISLAND DR	3000	620E	SB	77586
N. ISLAND DR	3000	620E	SB	77586
ISLAND DR	12400	328Q	NWC	77377
ISLAND BREEZE	11500	612M	PL	77584
ISLAND BREEZE CIR	100	660A	LC	77573
ISLAND BREEZE DR	5500	448D	NWC	77041
ISLANDBREEZE DR	18500	330A	NWC	77379
ISLAND CROSSING	0	612M	PL	77584
ISLAND CROSSING LN	0	659M	LC	77573
ISLANDER WAY	1700	620L	SB	77586
ISLAND FALLS CT	1800	658U	LC	77573
ISLAND FALLS CT	12900	448D	NWC	77041
ISLAND FERN CT	5600	338E	NEH	77345
ISLAND GREEN CT	1	337K	NEH	77339
ISLAND GROVE CT	15700	488B	SWH	77079
ISLAND HEATHER CT	5900	297Z	NEH	77345
ISLAND HILLS DR	4100	618D	PA	77059
E. ISLAND LAKE LOOP	7400	334M	NCC	77338
W. ISLAND LAKE LOOP	21600	334M	NCC	77338
ISLAND MANOR	11500	612M	PL	77584
ISLAND MANOR DR	0	407G	NWC	77095
ISLAND MANOR LN	0	658U	LC	77573
ISLAND MEADOW CT	800	617H	SEH	77062
ISLAND OAK	2000	618B	SEH	77062
ISLAND PALM CT	13500	578W	SEH	77059
ISLAND SHORE BLVD	0	367Q	NWC	77095
ISLAND SHORE CIR	12100	367Q	NWC	77095
ISLAND SHORE CT	16600	367Q	NWC	77095
ISLAND SONG DR	11900	456C	NEC	77044
ISLAND SPRING CT	500	292U	NCC	77373
ISLAND SPRING LN	17800	328M	NWC	77377
ISLAND VIEW	1000	619V	LC	77565
ISLAND VILLAS DR	2100	619Z	LC	77573
ISLANDWOODS DR	14200	408Q	NWC	77095
ISLA VISA DR	0	660C	GCO	77565
ISLA VISTA CIR	0	660G	LC	77573
ISLA VISTA CT	6000	409W	NWC	77041
ISLE OF PINES CT	0	457G	NEC	77049
ISLE ROYALE CT	18000	377B	NEC	77346
ISLE ROYALE WAY	12600	377B	NEC	77346
ISLE VISTA DR	12000	409W	NWC	77041
ISLEWOOD BLVD	0	251L	WD	77380
ISLINGTON DR	28400	299S	NEC	77336
ISOLDE DR	300	489G	SWH	77024
ISOM	1600	413M	NCC	77039
ISSACKS WAY	3900	609A	SG	77479
ITALY LN	4400	578E	PA	77505
ITASCA CT	2000	658T	LC	77573
ITASCAP INE DR	0	377K	NEC	77346
ITHACA	7900	535P	SEH	77017
ITHACA DR	3300	610U	MC	77459
IVANHOE	4500	491V	SWH	77027
IVANHOE SPRINGS DR	8500	528P	SWC	77083
IVAN REID DR	8000	410K	NWC	77040
IVE DR	2900	580K	LP	77571
IVER IRONWOOD TRAIL	16900	527S	NEF	77407
IVIE LEE	1500	502S	BT	77520
IVORY	23400	291A	NWC	77389
IVORY ASH CT	6500	337Q	NEC	77346
IVORY BROOK DR	19700	486G	SWC	77094
IVORY CREEK DR	11500	612M	PL	77584
IVORY CREEK LN	20400	486P	SWC	77450
IVORY CREST DR	0	528H	SWH	77072
IVORY CROSSING CT	1400	619H	PA	77586
IVORY CROSSING LN	18000	407K	NWC	77433
IVORY FALLS CT	17100	407L	NWC	77095
IVOR YFIELD LN	0	377P	NEC	77044
IVORY FOREST LN	0	253N	SEM	77386
IVORY GATE LN	21500	446N	NWC	77449
IVORY GLASS DR	0	404Z	NWC	77493
IVORY LAKE CT	0	524C	NEF	77494
IVORY MEADOWS LN	4900	447C	NWC	77084
IVORY MILLS LN	19500	486M	SWC	77094
IVORY MILLS LN	19900	486L	SWC	77094
IVORY MIST LN	5600	449A	NWC	77041
IVORY MOON PLACE	1	250C	WD	77381
IVORY PEARL CT	0	444D	NWC	77493
IVORY POINTE DR	3200	660E	LC	77573
IVORY PRESS DR	0	405W	NWC	77493
IVORY RIDGE LN	800	486G	SWC	77094
IVORY ROSE LN	0	485W	NEF	77494
IVORY STONE LN	500	659H	LC	77573
IVORY STONE WAY	0	410E	NWC	77064
IVORY SUNSET LN	0	405W	NWC	77493
IVORY VALLEY LN	0	406C	NWC	77433
IVY	100	538L	DP	77536
IVY	800	620T	CS	77565
IVY	2500	454S	NEH	77026
IVY	4800	577C	PA	77505
S. IVY CIR	17000	447H	NWC	77084
N. IVY CIR	17000	447H	NWC	77084
IVY CT	27400	248B	SWM	77354
IVY ARBOR LN	0	615K	PL	77581
IVY ARBOR LN	0	615F	PL	77581
IVY ARBOR LN	1	369H	NWC	77070
IVY BEND DR	3100	613Z	NEB	77584
IVY BEND LN	0	609T	NEF	77479
IVY BLOSSOM LN	21500	526A	NEF	77450
IVY BLUFF CT	14000	618A	SEH	77062
IVY BRANCH WAY	0	528N	NEF	77083
IVY BRIDGE LN	15900	408E	NWC	77095
IVY BROOK CT	17400	407P	NWC	77095
IVY BUSH BEND LN	0	525R	NEF	77407
IVY CLIFF CT	0	376C	NEC	77338
IVY COVE	2100	484K	NEF	77494
IVY COVE DR	4900	501E	BT	77521
IVYCREEK CT	0	657Z	LC	77573
IVY CREEK LN	17000	373N	NEH	77060
IVY CREST CT	2000	488N	SWH	77077
IVYCROFT LN	900	292C	NCC	77373
IVYDALE DR	12800	456M	NEC	77049
IVYDALE DR	13000	457J	NEC	77049
IVY DELL CT	2700	578W	SEH	77059
IVY FAIR WAY	0	446B	NWC	77449
IVY FALLS	6400	609K	MC	77459
IVY FALLS CT	8500	409G	JV	77040
IVY FALLS DR	3100	331N	NWC	77068
IVY FIELD CT	10200	369C	NWC	77070
IVYFORD CT	14500	328X	NWC	77429
IVY FOREST DR	12600	328V	NWC	77429
IVYGATE DR	22400	334E	NCC	77373
IVY GLEN CT	300	659H	LC	77573
IVY GLEN DR	2300	488V	SWH	77077
IVY GREEN DR	3900	527D	SWC	77082
IVY GROVE DR	16500	618R	SEH	77058
IVY HARBOR CT	0	615F	PL	77581
IVY HEATH LN	6500	408V	NWC	77041
IVY HILL DR	3100	296Y	NEH	77339
IVY HOLLOW DR	700	498A	NEC	77530
IVY HOLLOW LN	10300	367T	NWC	77433
IVYHURST LN	13100	488U	SWH	77082
IVYKNOLL DR	6300	570D	SWH	77035
IVY LEAF	1	298H	NEC	77336
IVY LEAF	11100	414R	NEH	77016
IVY LEAF CT	0	659N	LC	77573
IVY MANOR CT	0	326J	NWC	77433
IVY MEADOW LN	4700	446H	NWC	77449
IVYMIST CT	0	417D	NEH	77044
IVYMOUNT DR	13800	568F	SG	77498
IVY OAKS LN	10300	450E	NWH	77041
IVY OAKS LN	10400	449H	NWH	77041
IVY PARK	0	575Y	SEH	77075
IVY PARKWAY DR	900	488F	SWH	77077
IVY PATH CT	7600	407L	NWC	77095
IVYPATH LN	0	407B	NWC	77095
IVY POINT CIR	20200	337R	NEC	77346
IVY POINT CT	8200	527Q	NEF	77083
IVY RIDGE	23300	296M	SEM	77365
IVYRIDGE RD	10200	449Z	NWH	77043
IVY RUN CT	2400	486P	SWC	77450
IVYSIDE DR	13100	488U	SWH	77077
IVY SPRINGS LN	8800	412L	NWH	77088
IVY STONE CT	4900	446D	NWC	77449
IVY STONE CT	22300	485V	NEF	77450
IVY STONE LN	0	657P	FR	77546
IVY STREAM DR	17400	367X	NWC	77095
W. IVY TERRACE CIR	0	525C	NEF	77450
S. IVY TERRACE CIR	0	525C	NEF	77450
N. IVY TERRACE CIR	0	525C	NEF	77450
E. IVY TERRACE CIR	0	525C	NEF	77450
IVY TERRACE CT	21500	486N	SWC	77450
IVY TRACE LN	25000	485N	NEF	77494
IVY TRAIL CT	7900	407L	NWC	77095
IVY WALL CT	700	488B	SWH	77079
IVY WALL DR	800	488E	SWH	77079
IVY WICK CT	11500	289W	NWC	77375
IVY WILD LN	16800	367U	NWC	77095
IVY WOOD CT	14500	375X	NEC	77396
IVYWOOD DR	3900	614Z	PL	77584
IVYWOOD DR	26900	299X	NEC	77336
IVY WOOD LN	0	252M	SEM	77385
IWO JIMA RD	7300	534S	SEH	77033

J

Street Name	Block	Pg/Sq	Loc	Zips
W. J	100	580B	LP	77571
J	4100	529A	SWH	77072
J CIR	0	290L	NWC	77389
J M HESTER	9700	335U	HM	77338
J B LE FEVRE RD	0	501W	BT	77520
J F K BLVD	12200	414B	NCC	77039
J F K BLVD	16000	374F	NEH	77032
J H K BLVD	0	619C	PA	77586
J L REAUX	11500	415W	NEH	77016
J W PEAVY DR	6900	495S	SEH	77011
J-STAR CT	1	490F	BH	77024
J, A K	500	570S	SF	77477
J, AVENUE	0	659Y	DI	77539
J, AVENUE	100	501S	BT	77520
J, AVENUE	400	576C	SH	77587
J, AVENUE	1700	496W	GP	77547
J, AVENUE	4700	494Q	SEH	77011
J, AVENUE	7500	495S	SEH	77012
E. J, AVENUE	9300	535D	SEH	77012
J, R W	0	503M	BC	77520
J.C. OAKS CIR	0	455G	NEH	77028
J.R. DR	0	612Z	NEB	77578
J.R. TOWLES DR	18900	379Q	NEC	77532
JABERWALKY	11500	371P	NWC	77066
JABOT AVE	0	611W	FS	77545
JACANA CT	22200	245V	SWM	77355
JACANA DR	24700	245V	SWM	77355
JACARANDA	0	255T	SEM	77365
JACARANDA PLACE	11900	369J	NWC	77429
JACEY LANDING LN	0	368X	NWC	77095
JACINTH CT	11500	371N	NWC	77066
S. JACINTO	0	417V	NEC	77044
W. JACINTO DR	11200	417R	NEC	77044
E. JACINTO DR	11200	417R	NEC	77044
JACINTO PORT BLVD	14800	497M	NEC	77015
JACINTO PORT BLVD	15100	498N	NEC	77015
W. JACK	100	501Y	BT	77520
E. JACK	100	501Y	BT	77520
JACK	300	536V	PA	77502
JACK	1300	616T	PL	77581
JACK	3800	493S	SWH	77006
JACK LN	11800	490K	BH	77024
JACK RD	25000	364G	NWC	77447
JACK BLOCK CT	1100	379X	NEC	77532
JACKIE LANDING LN	0	528H	SWH	77072
JACK LONDON CT	16100	419B	NEC	77532
JACK PINE CIR	22700	289R	NWC	77375
JACKPINE DR	27400	299S	NEC	77336
JACK PINE PLACE	8500	289R	NWC	77375
JACKRABBIT RD	7000	408C	NWC	77095
JACKSON	0	660M	BC	77518
JACKSON	0	576A	SH	77587
JACKSON	1	493Q	DT	77002
W. JACKSON	100	536G	PA	77506
JACKSON	100	536H	PA	77506
JACKSON	300	497P	NEC	77506
JACKSON	600	493Q	DT	77003
JACKSON	800	493Q	DT	77010
JACKSON	900	575D	SH	77587
JACKSON	1200	493Q	DT	77003
JACKSON	1500	538V	DP	77536
JACKSON	2300	493U	SWH	77004
JACKSON	5300	533B	SWH	77004
JACKSON AVE	0	613S	PL	77584
JACKSON BLVD	1000	493N	SWH	77006
JACKSON LN	2300	658K	LC	77573
JACKSON RD	0	537A	PA	77506
JACKSON RD	0	497W	SEH	77506
JACKSON BAYOU	100	419G	CB	77532
JACKSON BLUFF DR	3800	446M	NWC	77449
JACKSON BROOK WAY	0	326Y	NWC	77433
JACKSON CREEK BEND LN	8400	375Z	NEC	77396
JACKSON FIELD RD	0	244Q	WCO	77447
JACKSON HILL	300	492M	SWH	77007
JACKSON MANOR LN	0	412N	NWH	77088
JACKSON MANOR LN	0	573L	SEH	77089
JACKSON PARK LN	0	524C	NEF	77494
JACKSON PARK LN	0	524C	NEF	77494
JACKSON PINES DR	17300	331Q	NWC	77090
JACKSON SAWMILL LN	14900	528W	NEF	77498
JACKSONS CROSSING	0	527J	NEF	77083
JACKSON SPRINGS LN	0	293J	SEM	77386
JACKSTAFF	0	616T	PL	77581
JACKSTONE DR	7900	457F	NEC	77049
JACK TAR DR	17100	379X	NEC	77532
JACKTREE LN	0	460W	BT	77521
JACKWOOD	4600	531R	SWH	77096
JACKWOOD	5800	530R	SWH	77074
JACKWOOD	8800	530N	SWH	77036
JACKWOOD ST	7500	530Q	SWH	77074
JACOB CT	2600	660W	DI	77539
JACOB LN	4700	614J	PL	77581
JACOB BEND DR		484W	NEF	77494
JACOB CANYON DR	6200	526B	NEF	77450
JACOB CROSSING DR		524J	NWF	77406
JACOB FIELD LN	0	412N	NWH	77088
JACOB FIELD LN	0	573L	SEH	77089
JACOBSCREEK DR	0	327D	NWC	77429
JACOBS LANDING LN	0	524B	NEF	77494
JACOBS TRACE CT	12400	371J	NWC	77066
JACOBS WELL CT	21800	525L	NEF	77407
JACOBS WELL DR	7300	525L	NEF	77407
JACQUELYN DR	1500	451T	NWH	77055
JACQUELYN DR	2400	615K	PL	77581
JACQUELYNE CIR	700	537L	PA	77503
JACY CREEK DR		289H	NWC	77375
JADE	22800	296Q	SEM	77365
JADE CT	1	412Z	NWH	77076
JADE BLOOM CT	0	524G	NEF	77494
JADE BLUFF LN	0	525D	NEF	77450
JADE BROOK CT	22600	525B	NEF	77494
JADE CANYON LN	19100	328H	NWC	77377
JADE CLOVER LN	0	524G	NEF	77494
JADE COVE CT	0	609Q	MC	77459
JADE COVE DR	14100	488N	SWH	77077
JADE COVE LN	0	609P	MC	77459
JADE CREEK CT	6000	297Z	NEH	77345
JADECREST CT	6100	290C	NWC	77389
JADECREST DR	6200	290C	NWC	77389
JADECREST RIDGE	23800	290C	NWC	77389
JADE FALLS CT	7800	407L	NWC	77095
JADE FEATHER LN	26900	324S	NWC	77447
JADE FIELD CT	0	328K	NWC	77377
JADE FOREST LN	0	485J	NEF	77494
JADE GLEN CT	14600	527V	NEF	77498
JADE GREEN CT	4600	578U	SEH	77059
JADE GREEN WAY	0	578T	SEH	77059
JADE HOLLOW	0	572T	SEH	77053
JADE HOLLOW LN	0	488N	SWH	77077
JADE HOLLOW LN	0	488N	SWH	77077
JADE MEADOW CT	14000	618A	SEH	77062
JADEMONT LN	9900	369L	NWC	77070
JADEN MCCADE CT	0	255Q	SEM	77365
JADEN OAKS PLACE	100	249R	NWH	77375
JADEN OAKS PLACE	100	249R	NWH	77375
JADE PARK DR	20300	526S	NEF	77407
JADE PINES	0	297F	SEM	77365
JADE POINTE	0	610J	MC	77459
JADE RIDGE LN	0	407B	NWC	77095
JADE SPRINGS DR	17400	407P	NWC	77095
JADE STAR DR	0	487Z	SWC	77082
JADESTONE LN	20800	291V	NWC	77388
JADESTONE CREEK LN	0	366V	NWC	77433
JADESTONE PARK CT	0	328A	NWC	77429
JADESTONE TERRACE	0	417A	NEC	77044
JADE TREASURE DR	12500	528M	SWH	77072
JADE VIEW CT	20200	335N	NCC	77338
JADE VIEW CT	20200	335N	NCC	77338
JADEWOOD DR	7200	411T	NWH	77088
JADWIN CT	6800	571W	SWH	77489
W. JAGGED RIDGE CIR	0	250N	NWC	77389
E. JAGGED RIDGE CIR	0	250N	NWC	77389
JAGGED RIVER DR	0	250P	NWC	77389
JAG HOLLOW	0	659W	LC	77573
JAGUAR DR	12300	529W	SWH	77477
JAHNKE RD	0	331F	NWC	77379
JAIME KNOLL LN		325S	NWC	77447
JAIMES CT	200	487A	SWC	77094
JAKE SPRINGS CT	0	293L	SEM	77386
JALNA	6900	451S	NWH	77055
JAMAICA	100	535A	SEH	77012
JAMAICA DR	4300	609E	SG	77479
JAMAICA LN	4400	578E	PA	77505
JAMAIL DR	6500	494Y	SEH	77023
JAMARA CIR	12800	488U	SWH	77077
JAMARA LN	2100	488U	SWH	77077
JAMBOREE LN	8500	249P	SWM	77354
JAMEEL RD	8600	410X	NWH	77040
JAMES	0	256Z	SEM	77357
E. JAMES	1	501Y	BT	77520
W. JAMES	100	501Y	BT	77520
JAMES	200	493G	NEH	77009
JAMES	400	537K	PA	77506
JAMES	500	288L	TB	77375
JAMES	800	538L	DP	77536
JAMES	1300	616U	PL	77581
JAMES	1300	292Z	NCC	77373
E. JAMES	1600	542A	BT	77520
JAMES	17200	324E	HK	77447
JAMES	18100	244K	WCO	77447
JAMES CT	0	539Z	LP	77571
JAMES LN	13000	569M	SF	77477
JAMES LN	13100	570J	SF	77477
JAMES RD	2700	569Z	NEF	77477
JAMES RD	18100	325B	NWC	77447
JAMES RD	18300	285X	NWC	77447
JAMES BOWIE DR	1600	502S	BT	77520
JAMES C. LEO DR	0	293U	NCC	77373
JAMES FRANKLIN	7600	412T	NWH	77088
JAMES LANDING	3900	375R	NEC	77396
JAMES LONG CT	0	526W	NEF	77406
JAMES MADISON	0	609C	MC	77459
JAMES MANOR DR	0	253T	SEM	77386
JAMES PLACE	5800	571K	SWH	77085
JAMES RIVER CT	1400	658N	LC	77573
JAMES RIVER LN	14700	408T	NWC	77084
JAMESTOWN	2400	491S	SWH	77057
JAMESTOWN RD	11300	490L	PP	77024
JAMESTOWN COLONY DR	6200	408T	NWC	77084
JAMESTOWN CROSSING LN	0	377E	NEC	77346
JAMIE LN	1700	458V	CV	77530
JAMIE LN	4300	573V	SEH	77048
JAMIE BROOK LN	22900	485U	NEF	77494
JAMIE LEE CT	8800	408A	NWC	77095
JAMIE LEE DR	15800	408A	NWC	77095
JAMISON	100	541S	MP	77571
JAMISON	3200	615R	PL	77581
JAMISON CIR	0	616T	PL	77581
JAMISON LANDING DR	0	616T	PL	77581
JAMISON OAK DR	0	616X	PL	77581
JAMISON PINE DR	0	616T	PL	77581
JAN	0	614F	PL	77581
JAN	3500	611X	FS	77545
JAN CT	3000	444L	KT	77493
JAN LN	0	248N	SWM	77362
JANA LN	2100	538W	PA	77503
JANABROOK DR	11900	570C	SWH	77071
JANACEK RD	17000	380T	NEC	77532
JANAK DR	7400	451X	NWH	77055
JANBAR RD	900	572V	SWH	77047
JANDER DR	1300	252Q	SEM	77386
JANE	1800	297J	SEM	77365
JANE	4300	531H	BL	77401
JANE DR	1600	537N	PA	77502
JANE LN	2000	288Z	NWC	77375
W. JANE LN	11800	288Z	NWC	77375
W. JANE LN	11800	288Z	NWC	77375
E. JANE LN	11800	288Z	NWC	77375
JANE LN	20000	288Z	NWC	77375
JANE RD	23100	287G	NWC	77377
JANE AUSTEN	5600	532A	WU	77005
JANELL DR	0	295C	SEM	77365
JANELL RENE CIR	1700	538M	DP	77536
JANE LYNN LN	16900	329Q	NWC	77070
JANET	7100	451X	NWH	77055
JANET CT	2700	616T	PL	77581
JANET LN	0	610Q	MC	77459
JANET LN	0	656K	FR	77586
JANET LN	2700	616T	PL	77581
JANET PLACE	0	616T	PL	77581
JANEY	12400	496L	NEH	77015
JANEZ LN	0	295M	SEM	77365
JANEZ LN	0	295M	SEM	77365
JAN GLEN LN	9100	329M	NWC	77379
JAN GLEN LN	9900	329M	NWC	77070
JANICE	6700	614D	BK	77581
E. JANISCH RD	100	453E	NWH	77022
JANISCH RD	300	452G	NWH	77018
JAN KELLY LN	400	490L	PP	77024
JANSELLS CROSSING DR	0	369P	NWC	77065
JANUARY	0	614D	BK	77581
JANUARY DR	19800	337U	NEC	77346
JANUS RD	3100	578B	PA	77505
JAPHET	0	539G	SEC	77571
JAPHET	1	494L	NEH	77020
JAPONICA	6600	534H	SEH	77087
JAPONICA	7300	535E	SEH	77012
W. JAQUET	6000	531C	BL	77401
JAQUET DR	800	531C	BL	77401
JAQUINE DR	14200	368T	NWC	77429
JARDEN GLEN CT	0	290K	NWC	77379
JARDIN	3700	532A	SS	77005
JARDIN DES CIR	0	449X	NWH	77043
JARL CT	0	446B	NWC	77449
JARMESE	4800	533V	SEH	77033
JAROD CT	16100	570K	MC	77489
JARRARD	2800	532B	WU	77005
JARRATT SQUARE	20400	335Q	HM	77338
JARRED CT	6800	614T	PL	77584
JARVIS	3000	490X	SWH	77063
JARVIS RD	12600	368E	NWC	77429
JARVIS RD	15100	367H	CY	77429
JARVIS ROW CIR	0	252N	SEM	77380
JASAMINE PATH DR	11900	456C	NEC	77044
JASMINE	100	500E	BT	77520
JASMINE	1300	618W	WB	77598
E. JASMINE	3600	615J	PL	77581
W. JASMINE	4000	615J	PL	77581
JASMINE	600	611Y	FS	77545
JASMINE CIR	0	538V	DP	77536
JASMINE DR	0	460T	NEC	77562
JASMINE DR	1600	537Q	PA	77503
JASMINE ST	100	611Z	NEF	77545
JASMINE ARBOR CT	0	411N	NWH	77088
JASMINE ARBOR LN	0	411N	NWH	77088
JASMINE BLOOM LN	19000	326Y	NWC	77429
JASMINE BROOK LN	12400	616H	SEH	77089
JASMINE CREEK CT	15200	408N	NWC	77095
JASMINE CREST LN	0	406X	NWC	77449
JASMINE FIELD	0	371E	NWC	77066
JASMINE FIELD WAY	0	484Z	NEF	77494
JASMINE FOREST LN	0	405T	NWC	77493
JASMINE HEIGHTS LN	0	406X	NWC	77449
JASMINE HOLLOW LN	0	615F	PL	77581
JASMINE HOLLOW LN	12600	409S	NWC	77041
JASMINE KNOLL WAY	0	326U	NWC	77429
JASMINE LEAF TRAIL	0	334Q	NCC	77373
JASMINE MEADOWS LN	4900	336Z	NEC	77346
JASMINE PARK LN	0	417A	NEC	77044
JASMINE PLACE	6800	330R	NWC	77379
JASMINE RIDGE CT	2400	618A	SEH	77062
JASMINE SPRINGS DR	14500	288E	NWC	77377
JASMINE STONE DR	12800	528H	SWH	77072
JASMINE TERRACE DR	0	332D	NCC	77373
JASMINE TRAIL	7000	408P	NWC	77084
JASMINE TREE LN	15500	457Q	NEC	77049
JASMINE VALLEY CT	0	406X	NWC	77449
JASON	4600	531N	SWH	77096
JASON	5800	530P	SWH	77074
JASON	14500	247N	SWM	77362
JASON CT	0	530Q	SWH	77074
JASON CT	400	252K	SEM	77386
JASON DR	3900	371B	NWC	77014
JASON LN	0	542K	BT	77520
JASON'S CT	0	244C	WCO	77447
JASPER	300	660H	BC	77518
JASPER LN	13000	368Q	NWC	77429
JASPER RD	2000	614Q	PL	77581
JASPER COVE	300	610N	MC	77459
JASPER GROVE CT	5300	297P	NEH	77345
JASPER OAK CT	0	293Z	NCC	77373
JASPER OAKS DR	0	406L	NWC	77433
JASPERSON LN	22500	485U	NEF	77450
JASPERSTONE LN	0	615F	PL	77581
JASPERWOOD	18600	282Z	WCO	77484
JASPERWOOD CIR	19900	446Q	NWC	77449
JASPERWOOD LN	20400	335J	NCC	77338
JASPERWOOD LN	20400	335N	NCC	77338
JAST DR	16000	327Y	CY	77429
JAY	6800	454R	NEH	77028
JAY	7300	455N	NEH	77028
JAY CT	18600	295F	SEM	77365
JAY DR	22000	334E	NCC	77373
JAYALOCH CT	0	329H	NWC	77379
JAYCEE LN	10800	490H	HC	77024
JAYCI CREEK LN	0	375Y	NEC	77396
JAYCIE MEADOW LN	0	412N	NWH	77088
JAYCI HILLS LN	0	366Y	NWC	77433
JAYCI PARK LN	0	375Y	NEC	77396
JAYCREEK CT	13900	369A	NWC	77070
JAYCREEK DR	10500	369B	NWC	77070
JAYCREST DR	13600	413K	NCC	77037
JAYDALE LN	0	575U	SEH	77075
JAYDEN CT	27200	294N	SEM	77386
JAYDEN DR	0	528F	SWC	77083
W. JAYHAWK DR	11300	418N	NEC	77044
E. JAYHAWK DR	11300	418N	NEC	77044
JAYMARS CT	0	295R	SEM	77365
JAYS LN	500	569U	NEF	77477

Street Name	Block	Pg/Sq	Loc	Zips
JAY THRUSH DR	0	526T	NEF	77469
JAY THRUSH DR	0	526T	NEF	77469
JAY WAY	20900	286E	NWC	77447
JAYWOOD DR	9300	410R	NWH	77040
JAZZY COVE	0	406L	NWC	77433
JD NORSWORTHY WAY		609X	NEF	77479
JEAN	1800	534B	SEH	77023
JEAN	2400	536V	PA	77502
JEAN	27700	292L	SP	77373
JEAN LN	0	501M	BT	77521
JEANENE CT	2600	445Q	NWC	77449
JEANETTA	2700	490T	SWH	77063
JEANETTA	3900	530B	SWH	77063
JEANIE DR	17500	326F	NWC	77377
JEANIE LN	1200	501M	BT	77521
JEAN LAFITTE	13200	419R	BR	77532
JEANNA RIDGE CT	16900	527J	NEF	77083
JEANNE LN	100	456L	NEC	77049
JEANNINE DR	1300	452X	NWH	77008
JEBBIA RD	12600	569H	SF	77477
JEB STUART CT	2500	658P	LC	77573
JEB STUART DR	2500	658S	LC	77573
JECKELL ISLES CT	19300	329A	NWC	77375
JECKELL ISLES DR	12200	328D	NWC	77375
JEFF	1000	452B	NWH	77091
JEFFERS CIR	1900	373Q	NCC	77032
JEFFERS CT	1	490G	PP	77024
JEFFERSON	100	580G	LP	77571
JEFFERSON	400	493Q	DT	77002
JEFFERSON	1200	501Z	BT	77520
JEFFERSON	1300	536T	PA	77502
JEFFERSON	1700	493Q	DT	77003
JEFFERSON	3400	614V	PL	77584
JEFFERSON	4200	494W	SEH	77023
JEFFERSON	4400	538Y	DP	77536
JEFFERSON RD	100	537B	PA	77506
JEFFERSON RD	1100	497X	PA	77506
JEFFERSON OAKS	12200	368M	NWC	77429
JEFFERY	1100	538Q	DP	77536
JEFFERY	8000	455P	NEH	77028
JEFFERY	5100	660T	GCO	77539
JEFFERY PINE LN	0	488T	SWH	77077
JEFFERY TRAIL	3800	375R	NEC	77396
JEFF GINN MEMORIAL DR	1100	536R	PA	77506
JELICOE DR	11700	572R	SWH	77047
JELLY PARK STONE DR	16700	327T	NWC	77429
JEN'S WAY	700	612S	FS	77545
JENGO DR	0	528F	SWC	77083
JENIKAY LN	16900	447D	NWC	77084
JENISTA LN	0	326V	NWC	77429
JENKINS	1	494P	SEH	77003
N. JENKINS	100	494P	SEH	77003
JENKINS RD	1300	537J	PA	77506
JENKINS RD	26100	292Q	NEH	77373
JEN MARIE	5800	411Q	NWH	77088
JENNA BETH LN	0	376G	NEC	77396
JENNIFER LN	0	252T	SEM	77386
JENNIFER LN	1300	496K	JC	77029
JENNIFER HEIGHTS CT	25000	250X	NWC	77389
W. JENNIFER WAY DR	0	575R	SEH	77075
E. JENNIFER WAY DR	0	575R	SEH	77075
JENNINGS	8200	535Q	SEH	77017
JENNINGS CT	4000	610K	MC	77459
JENNINGS RD	15800	375R	NEC	77396
JENNS CREEK CT	24500	250X	NWC	77389
JENNY LN	19200	255V	SEM	77365
JENNY ANNE LN	10700	369K	NWC	77070
JENNY CREEK CT	0	286Q	NWC	77377
JENNY GAYE LN	600	459R	HG	77562
JENNY LAKE DR	6900	330C	NWC	77379
JENNYS PARK PLACE	0	572S	SWH	77053
JENNY WOOD CT	13000	368E	NWC	77429
S. JENNY WOOD DR	13000	368E	NWC	77429
JENSEN DR	1	494A	NEH	77020
S. JENSEN DR	100	494J	SEH	77003
JENSEN DR	800	536G	PA	77506
JENSEN DR	1700	494A	NEH	77026
JENSEN DR	3400	454W	NEH	77026
JENSEN DR	6600	454A	NEH	77093
JENSEN DR	10100	414W	NEH	77093
W. JERAD DR	0	452E	NWH	77018
E. JERAD DR	0	452E	NWH	77018
JEREK DR	0	572S	SWH	77053
JEREMY CT	400	252K	SEM	77386
JERICHO CT	5200	452F	NWH	77091
JERNIGAN FORD	2200	659X	DI	77539
JEROME	1000	453T	NWH	77009
JEROME RD	0	658Y	LC	77573
JERRY	500	453J	NWH	77022
JERRY LN	20000	254M	SEM	77365
JERRYCREST DR	5800	614Y	PL	77584
JERSEY	19900	380G	NEC	77532
JERSEY DR	15300	409M	JV	77040
JERSEY HOLLOW DR	16300	409K	JV	77040
JERSEY MEADOW DR	12300	569E	SF	77477
JERSEY SHORE DR	14700	612B	SWC	77047
JERSON RD	0	330C	NWC	77379
JERSON RD	18700	330C	NWC	77379
JERUSALIM CT	0	460Y	MN	77521
JERVIS LN	1800	446X	NWC	77449
JESKE RD	0	613X	NEB	77584
JESSABELLA DR	0	290Q	NWC	77379
JESSALYN LN	0	575Q	SEH	77075
JESSAMINE	100	493C	NEH	77009
JESSAMINE	4700	531K	BL	77401
JESSAMINE	5400	531E	SWH	77081
JESSAMINE WAY	0	659G	LC	77573
JESSE JONES MEM BRDG	0	537D	SEH	77015
JESSE JONES MEM BRDG	0	537D	SEC	77503
JESSICA	0	539Z	LP	77571
JESSICA	0	539Z	LP	77571
JESSICA CT	3000	444M	KT	77493
JESSICA LN	13000	370F	NWC	77069
JESSICA LN	13200	370B	NWC	77069
JESSICA LN	20500	446K	NWC	77449
JESSICA FALLS CIR	14400	377T	NEC	77044
JESSICA HILLS LN	0	293K	SEM	77386
JESSICA ROSE LN	20900	290U	NWC	77379
JESSIE LN	1300	537N	PA	77502
JESSIE ANNE LN	6300	408U	NWC	77041
JESSIE PARKER RD	0	527V	NEF	77498
JESS PIRTLE BLVD	12800	568G	SG	77478
JESTER	7700	533U	SEH	77051
JESTER CT	0	615P	PL	77581
JESTER LN	2500	569V	SF	77477
JESTER, T C BLVD	100	492C	NWH	77007
JESTER, T C BLVD	700	492C	NWH	77008
W. JESTER, T C BLVD	1000	452X	NWH	77008
E. JESTER, T C BLVD	1000	452N	NWH	77008
W. JESTER, T C BLVD	2700	451M	NWH	77018
E. JESTER, T C BLVD	2700	452N	NWH	77018
JESTER, T C BLVD	3700	451D	NWH	77018
JESTER, T C BLVD	5100	411Z	NWH	77091
W. JESTER, T C BLVD	7200	411Z	NWH	77088
JESTER, T C BLVD	13100	371Z	NWC	77038
JESTER, T C BLVD	13700	371R	NWC	77067
JESTER, T C BLVD	13900	371M	NWC	77067
JESTER, T C BLVD	14400	331T	NWC	77014
JESTER, T C BLVD	15000	331T	NWC	77068
JESTER, T C BLVD	16500	330D	NWC	77379
JESTER, T C BLVD	19000	290Y	NWC	77379
JETERO PLAZA DR	0	375F	HM	77396
JETHRO	10100	574A	SEH	77033
JET PILOT	8100	575K	SEH	77075
JETSTREAM CT	800	617B	SEH	77598
JETT	0	258U	NEC	77357
JETTON PARK LN	0	377J	NEC	77346
JETTY CT	17100	379X	NEC	77532
JETTY LN	4600	529E	SWH	77072
JETTY COVE CT	800	485A	NEF	77494
JETTY POINT DR	0	251G	WD	77380
JETTY TERRACE CIR	4100	569Y	MC	77459
JETWAY PLACE CT	0	535Y	SEH	77061
JEWEL	200	536G	PA	77506
JEWEL	2800	494A	NEH	77026
JEWEL CT	10200	252G	SEM	77385
JEWEL ANN DR	3000	488X	SWH	77082
JEWEL ASHFORD RD	5101	526S	NEF	77407
S. JEWEL BEND LN	900	575U	SEH	77075
N. JEWEL BEND LN	900	575U	SEH	77075
W. JEWEL BEND LN	10800	575U	SEH	77075
JEWEL BROOK LN	0	526J	NEF	77407
JEWEL CAVE LN	0	377E	NEC	77346
JEWEL LAKE LN	0	377U	NEC	77044
JEWEL LANDING	400	610N	MC	77459
JEWEL MEADOW DR	14700	572T	SEH	77053
JEWEL PARK LN	200	487A	SWC	77094
JEWEL POINT DR	3701	253X	SEM	77386
JEWEL SPRINGS LN	0	524F	NEF	77494
JEWETT	500	453X	NWH	77009
JEWETT	3900	454T	NEH	77026
JEZEBEL	500	573H	SEH	77033
JEZEBEL	5200	574A	SEH	77033
JIB CT	0	611W	FS	77545
JIB CT	16100	379X	NEC	77532
JIB BOOM CT	1100	379X	NEC	77532
JILL CIR	2400	332A	NWC	77388
JILLANA KAYE DR	10300	371X	NWC	77086
JILLIAN CROSSING WAY	0	372J	NWC	77076
JILLIAN OAKS CT	0	293F	SEM	77386
JILLIAN OAKS LN	0	293F	SEM	77386
JILLIAN WAY CT	24800	250Y	NWC	77389
JILLS WAY LN	18100	326V	NWC	77429
JIM	5700	451K	NWH	77092
JIMBO LN	5500	291E	NWC	77389
JIMMY LN	27000	252E	OR	77385
JIMMY LN	34500	247K	SWM	77362
JIMMY DEAN LN	100	459H	NEC	77562
JIMMY HARNS BLVD	0	578G	SEC	77507
JIM WEST	4300	531M	BL	77401
JIPSIE LN	3000	573F	SEH	77051
JOAN	13100	569M	SF	77477
JOAN	14800	570L	SWH	77085
JOANEL	2600	492T	SWH	77027
JOAN LEIGH CIR	19800	292W	NWC	77388
JOAN LEIGH DR	18900	332A	NWC	77388
JO ANN	2600	569Z	NEF	77477
JO ANN LN	1300	568E	SG	77498
JOANNA CT	28300	246G	SWM	77355
JOAN OF ARC	11800	419Z	BR	77532
JOAN OF ARC DR	11600	490B	HE	77024
JOBAL	500	373W	NCC	77060
JOCELYN	1100	494Y	SEH	77023
JOCELYN PARK CT	24500	445S	NWC	77493
JOCKEY CLUB CT	11400	369W	NWC	77065
JOCKEY CLUB DR	9800	409A	NWC	77065
JOCKEY CLUB DR	10000	369W	NWC	77065
JODI CIR	31900	246S	SWM	77355
JODIE LYNN CIR	0	367N	NWC	77095
JODY CT	10500	528U	SWH	77099
JODYWOOD DR	18700	337Z	NEC	77346
JOE	2200	536V	PA	77502
JOE ANNIE	1100	493N	SWH	77019
JOE CASTILLO	3900	454T	NEH	77026
JOEDELL LN	0	449X	NWH	77043
JO EDNA RD	10900	574R	SEH	77075
JOELLA	3400	374X	NCC	77032
JOE LOUIS LN	6300	412W	NWH	77091
JOEL WHEATON RD	2100	488S	SWH	77077
JOEL WHEATON RD	2500	488S	SWH	77082
JOE PATCH RD	4500	463Z	CCO	77520
JOEY CIR	27800	292L	SP	77373
JOGGERS LN	8500	338W	NEC	77346
JOHANNA DR	1500	451T	NWH	77055
JOHLKE LN	31400	247V	SWM	77355
JOHN	2000	536T	PA	77502
JOHN	2300	616Q	PL	77581
JOHN	2400	616Q	FR	77546
JOHN	7800	535F	SEH	77012
JOHN	16000	458U	CV	77530
JOHN CT	1300	616T	PL	77581
JOHN LN	24700	295L	SEM	77365
JOHN A	100	500P	BT	77520
E. JOHN ALBER RD	100	413S	NEH	77037
JOHN ALBER RD	100	413T	NEH	77076
JOHNATHAN CT	7600	570Z	SWH	77489
JOHNATHAN LANDING CT	0	250K	NWC	77389
JOHN BANK DR	9500	329L	NWC	77379
JOHN CLYDE DR	0	524B	NEF	77494
JOHN COOPER DR	1	250C	WD	77381
JOHN CRUMP LN	2500	445U	NWC	77449
JOHNDALE CT	22700	525F	NEF	77494
JOHN DAVID LN	7800	578C	PA	77505
JOHN DREAPER DR	5400	491U	SWH	77056
JOHN F KENNEDY BLVD	12200	414B	NCC	77039
JOHN F KENNEDY BLVD	16000	374F	NEH	77032
JOHN FREEMAN	6500	532H	SWH	77030
JOHN HANCOCK LN	3600	569Y	MC	77477
JOHN LIZER RD	2800	615T	PL	77581
JOHN LOCKE LN	3000	609D	MC	77459
JOHN MARTIN RD	5400	501A	NEC	77521
JOHN MARTIN RD	6500	461W	NEC	77521
JOHN MARTIN RD	7100	460V	NEC	77521
JOHN RALSTON RD	500	496B	NEH	77013
JOHN RALSTON RD	1900	496F	NEH	77013
JOHN RALSTON RD	6400	456C	NEC	77049
JOHN RALSTON RD	6900	416U	NEC	77044
JOHN ROLFE LN	22500	445U	NWC	77449
JOHNS	0	458B	NEC	77049
JOHNS	3400	615B	PL	77581
JOHNS RD	9000	418X	NEC	77049
JOHNSBURY DR	2500	371M	NWC	77067
JOHNS ENTERPRISE CT	12200	366L	NWC	77433
N. JOHNSON	100	536H	PA	77506
JOHNSON	100	536M	PA	77506
JOHNSON	1000	493F	SWH	77007
JOHNSON	1100	541B	BT	77520
JOHNSON	1700	536R	PA	77502
JOHNSON	4500	500C	NEC	77521
JOHNSON	14500	577T	SEH	77034
JOHNSON DR	0	658T	LC	77573
JOHSON DR	0	614Q	PL	77584
JOHNSON DR	6100	609Z	MC	77459
JOHNSON RD	18700	252A	SEM	77385
JOHNSON RD	23000	256R	SEM	77357
JOHNSON RD	23700	257N	SEM	77357
JOHNSON RD	28000	288Q	TB	77375
JOHNSON, EUNICE LN	0	322A	WCO	77484
JOHNSON LANDING RD	300	495Z	NEH	77029
JOHNSON SPACE CENTER	0	619J	SEH	77058
JOHNS POST RD	0	366K	NWC	77433
JOHNS STAKE CT	12300	366K	NWC	77433
JOHNSTON	1200	453K	NWH	77022
JOHNSTON	2500	614R	PL	77581
JOHNSTON LN	0	420P	NEC	77532
JOHN WARNASCH LN	0	444R	NWC	77493
JOLEN CT	900	531L	BL	77401
JOLIE DR	5000	614V	PL	77584
JOLIET	12800	496D	NEH	77015
JOLIET	12900	497A	NEH	77015
JOLLY BOAT DR	17400	379X	NEC	77532
JOLLY WOOD CT	9400	410D	NWC	77086
JOMAR LN	22900	296D	SEM	77357
JONATHAN	4300	531M	BL	77401
JONATHAN DALTON CT	0	255Q	SEM	77365
JONATHAN WAY BLVD	0	568M	SG	77478
JONATHON CT	0	287A	SWM	77355
JONATHON CT	7600	570Z	SWH	77489
JONES	0	295D	SEM	77365
JONES	0	502X	BT	77520
S. JONES	100	501Y	BT	77520
N. JONES	100	501Y	BT	77520
JONES	2500	494A	NEH	77026
JONES	4600	454G	NEH	77016
JONES	19400	335S	NEH	77338
JONES BLVD	2700	537W	PA	77502
JONES RD	100	459V	HG	77562
JONES RD	800	460V	NEC	77562
E. JONES RD	1800	460U	MN	77521
JONES RD	1800	460V	NEC	77521
JONES RD	8000	409F	JV	77065
JONES RD	11000	369P	NWC	77070
W. JONES RD	11100	369T	NWC	77065
JONES RD	14500	370Y	NWC	77086
JONES RD	15000	329X	NWC	77070
JONES CT	2400	493U	SEH	77004
JONESVILLE	26200	243F	WCO	77484
JONETTE	0	494P	SEH	77003
JONQUIL	100	493C	NEH	77009
JONQUIL PLACE	100	249R	NWH	77375
JONQUIL PLACE	100	249R	NWH	77375
JONSPORT LN	28300	293F	SEM	77386
JOPLIN	7300	535N	SEH	77087
JOPLIN	8000	535P	SEH	77017
JORDAN	0	543X	BC	77520
JORDAN	0	659T	LC	77573
JORDAN	9700	535H	SEH	77017
JORDAN DR	0	614U	PL	77584
JORDAN BRANCH LN	14700	376W	NEC	77396
JORDAN CANYON LN	0	328N	NWC	77429
JORDAN CANYON LN	0	328N	NWC	77429
JORDAN CREEK CT	0	659H	LC	77573
JORDANFALLS DR	0	609U	MC	77479
JORDANFIELD LN	0	484X	NEF	77494
JORDANFIELD LN	0	484X	NEF	77494
JORDANFIELD LN	0	524B	NEF	77494
JORDANFIELD LN	0	524B	NEF	77494
JORDAN OAKS	15100	571U	SWH	77053
JORDANS LANDING LN	19100	526P	NEF	77407
JORDAN TERRACE LN	25600	484Z	NEF	77494
JORDEN RD	1100	448X	NWH	77079
S. JORDEN COVE	1300	451X	NWH	77055
N. JORDEN COVE	1300	451X	NWH	77055
E. JORDEN COVE	7600	451X	NWH	77055
JORDEN FALLS DR	6400	571F	SWH	77085
JORDENS RD	2800	447S	NWC	77084
JORDI DR	0	249V	NWC	77375
JORDONIA	0	615E	PL	77581
JORDY LN	200	660X	LC	77539
JORDYN LAKE DR	16200	328R	NWC	77377
JORDYN RIDGE LN	0	411R	NWH	77088
JORDYN RIDGE LN	0	412N	NWH	77088
JORDYN RIDGE LN	0	573L	SEH	77089
JORENT DR	2600	412J	NWC	77088
JORENT DR	2700	411M	NWH	77088
JORINE DR	7000	530E	SWH	77036
JORNAN HEIGHTS DR	0	415S	NEC	77016
JORNS DR	3100	572K	SWH	77045
JORNS DR	5000	571L	SWH	77045
JOSEPH	900	537K	PA	77506
JOSEPH	1400	535F	SEH	77012
JOSEPH	2200	536V	PA	77502
JOSEPH CIR	0	371G	NWC	77014
JOSEPH CT	0	244M	WCO	77447
JOSEPH CT	1400	288M	TB	77375
JOSEPH DR	23300	296M	SEM	77365
JOSEPH LN	0	463Z	CCO	77520
JOSEPH RD	0	244M	WCO	77447
JOSEPH RD	0	243F	WCO	77447
JOSEPH RD	0	242M	WCO	77484
JOSEPH-LINER RDS	0	242K	WCO	77484
JOSEPHINE	3000	494A	NEH	77026
JOSEPHINE	13100	569M	SF	77477
JOSEPHINE DR	6100	614Q	PL	77584
JOSEPH PARKER DR	1015	486C	SWC	77094
JOSEPH PINE LN	2500	412J	NWH	77088
JOSEY CREEK CT	12800	366H	NWC	77433
E. JOSEY OVERLOOK DR	0	366N	NWC	77433
JOSEY SPRINGS LN	0	484Q	NEF	77494
JOSHNOMI LN	14800	368J	NWC	77429
JOSHUA CIR	4200	331X	NWC	77014
JOSHUA LN	0	656K	FR	77546
JOSHUA LN	1100	490D	SV	77055
JOSHUA LN	9600	329G	NWC	77375
JOSHUA LN	20500	446K	NWC	77449
JOSHUA CREEK CT	0	367W	NWC	77433
JOSHUA KENDALL LN	22000	445V	NWC	77449
JOSHUA LEE LN	500	252P	SEM	77386
JOSHUA MEADOWS DR	0	526N	NEF	77407
JOSHUA TREE LN	1100	332R	NCC	77073
JOSHUA TREE LN	1600	538R	DP	77536
JOSH WAY	300	539Z	LP	77571
JOSIE	8600	495L	NEH	77029
JOURNEY	14000	574X	SEH	77048
JOVE	15700	373W	NCC	77060
JOWETT PLACE	9400	527U	NEF	77498
JOY	7800	455K	NEH	77028
JOY CIR	1	372R	NCC	77060
JOY RD	24900	257T	SEM	77357
JOYCE	200	453U	NEH	77009
JOYCE BLVD	4000	447G	NWC	77084
JOYCEDALE LN	7800	456H	NEC	77044
JOYFUL FOREST DR	0	293X	NCC	77373
JOYFUL RIDGE DR	0	293Y	NCC	77373
JOYFUL WAY	0	293Y	NCC	77373
JOYNER	6200	534U	SEH	77087
JOY OAKS LN	0	373A	NCC	77073
JUANITA	300	536Q	PA	77502
JUANITA	2100	538Q	DP	77536
JUAREZ	6300	500C	NEC	77521
JUAREZ	6500	460Y	MN	77521
JUBILEE CT	8500	528P	SWC	77083
JUBILEE DR	8600	528P	SWC	77083
JUBILEE PARK CT	12800	408D	NWC	77065
JUBILO LN	7000	459K	NEC	77049
JUDALON LN	5300	491X	SWH	77056
JUDALON LN	9500	490W	SWH	77063
JUDD	100	494K	NEH	77020
JUDGE	12400	419V	BR	77532
JUDGE BRY RD	16300	367G	NWC	77429
JUDIA LN	10500	528Z	SWH	77099
JUDIWAY	800	452N	NWH	77018
JUDIWOOD	700	332J	NWC	77090
JUDSON	4100	532A	WU	77005
JUDWIN	8800	575M	SEH	77075
JUDY AVE	2300	616U	FR	77546
JUDY CT	1200	496L	NEH	77015
JUDY LN	1200	501M	BT	77521
JUDY LN	2000	536V	PA	77502
JUDYLEIGH DR	16800	407Y	NWC	77084
JUDY TERRACE	0	570S	MC	77489
JUDYWOOD	19000	337Y	NEC	77346
JUELLA DR	2400	414A	NCC	77039
JUELLA DR	2600	374W	NCC	77039
JUERGEN RD	18000	327A	NWC	77429
JUERGEN RD	18400	326C	NWC	77429
JUI LN	17200	246T	SWM	77355
JULES CT	26500	252P	SEM	77386
JULIA	100	453G	NEH	77022
JULIA CT	0	248U	TB	77375
JULIA LN	21500	248Y	TB	77375
JULIABORA	8000	535U	SEH	77017
JULIABORA CT	700	656B	FR	77546
JULIA MANOR DR		524K	NWF	77406
JULIAN	2400	493B	NWH	77009
JULIAN	3500	453X	NWH	77009
JULIANN ALYES	0	255R	SEM	77365
JULIAN WOODS PLACE	1	250B	WD	77382
JULIA PARK DR	1600	293K	SEM	77386
JULIE	0	287N	NWC	77377
JULIE	2500	615U	PL	77581
JULIE CT	0	577C	PA	77505
JULIE LN	0	538R	DP	77536
JULIE LN	400	460N	HG	77562
JULIE LN	10900	489Q	SWH	77042
JULIE'S CIR	20100	257J	SEM	77357
JULIE ANN DR	2900	614R	PL	77584
JULIEDALE DR	14200	375W	NEC	77396
JULIE MARIE LN	0	446W	NWC	77449
JULIE MEADOWS LN	0	376W	NEC	77396
JULIE POND LN	0	250X	NWC	77389
JULIE RIVERS DR	300	568M	SG	77478
JULIET	2400	536V	PA	77502
JULIET	4000	534L	SEH	77087
JULIETTE SPRINGS LN	6700	609Y	NEF	77459
JULINGTON LN	14000	328T	NWC	77429
JULISSA	0	619Z	LC	77573
JULIUS LN	3800	533H	SEH	77021
JULLIANE CT	11200	529P	SWH	77099
JULY	1800	413R	NCC	77093
JULY SKY CT	0	292D	SEM	77386
JUMADA CIR	5500	451D	NWH	77091
JUMBA	0	489Q	SWH	77042
JUMPING JAY LN	24000	325J	NWC	77447
JUMPING JAY LN	24200	324M	NWC	77447
JUNCO DR	0	411S	NWH	77040
JUNCTION DR	2800	572Q	SWH	77045
JUNCTION BEND LN	3500	484T	NEF	77494
JUNCTION CREEK LN	0	328N	NWC	77429
JUNCTION CREEK LN	0	328N	NWC	77429
JUNCTION PLACE DR	14400	572P	SWH	77045
JUNE	4200	454F	NEH	77016
JUNEAU LN	15700	409M	JV	77040
JUNE FOREST DR	18000	376D	NEC	77346
JUNEGRASS CT	3100	297Q	NEH	77345
JUNE GROVE LN	0	328E	NWC	77377
JUNELL	700	412U	NWH	77088
JUNE OAK ST	18000	327H	NWC	77429
JUNE POINT CT		289G	NWC	77375
JUNE SPRINGS CT	0	446B	NWC	77449
JUNE WOOD WAY	0	620L	SB	77586
JUNIOR	7700	535F	SEH	77012
JUNIORS MAP CT	18500	366K	NWC	77433
JUNIPER	0	375R	NEC	77396
JUNIPER	900	620T	CS	77565
JUNIPER	3800	535N	SEH	77087
JUNIPER CT	400	569V	SF	77477
JUNIPER CT	900	288M	TB	77375
JUNIPER DR	0	461Q	NEC	77521
JUNIPER DR	0	616T	PL	77581
JUNIPER DR	500	580K	LP	77571
JUNIPER LN	0	539W	DP	77571
JUNIPER LN	1400	619C	PA	77586
JUNIPER LN	3900	291G	NWC	77389
JUNIPER BERRY DR	0	526P	NEF	77407
JUNIPER BLUFF CT	5900	338A	NEH	77345
JUNIPER BREEZE LN		329D	NWC	77379
JUNIPER CANYON LN	1100	617H	SEH	77062
JUNIPER CHASE TRAIL	0	526T	NEF	77407
JUNIPER COVE CT	15400	326S	NWC	77433
JUNIPER COVE DR	15200	326S	NWC	77433
JUNIPER COVE LN	0	616E	SEC	77089
JUNIPER CREEK LN	18200	327W	NWC	77429
JUNIPER CROSSING	1250	409S	NWC	77041
JUNIPER DALE CT	0	457G	NEC	77049
JUNIPER FIELDS DR	13200	528L	SWH	77083
JUNIPER FIELD TRAIL	0	325R	NWC	77433
JUNIPER FOREST LN	14500	618B	SEH	77062
JUNIPER FOREST FALL LN	0	484X	NEF	77494
JUNIPER FOREST FALL LN	0	484X	NEF	77494
JUNIPER GLEN DR	10300	450E	NWH	77041
JUNIPER GLEN DR	10400	449H	NWH	77041
JUNIPER GREEN TRAIL	0	376H	NEC	77346
JUNIPER GROVE DR	16000	448A	NWC	77084
JUNIPER HOLLOW WAY	15500	326S	NWC	77433
JUNIPER KNOLL LN	5800	338A	NEH	77345
JUNIPER LANDING BLVD	5200	609S	NEF	77479
JUNIPER MEADOW LN	0	253Q	SEM	77386

Street Name	Block	Pg/Sq	Loc	Zips
JUNIPER MEADOWS DR	0	292N	NWC	77388
JUNIPER MEADOWS LN	3800	572W	SWH	77053
JUNIPER PARK CT	14000	371U	NWC	77066
JUNIPER PLACE CT	9500	576J	SEH	77075
JUNIPER PLACE CT	9500	576J	SEH	77075
JUNIPER POINT DR	13400	528G	SWC	77083
JUNIPER RIDGE LN	21200	289U	NWC	77375
JUNIPER SHORES DR	15800	377P	NEC	77044
JUNIPER SPRINGS DR	0	334K	NCC	77388
JUNIPER SPRINGS DR	0	612E	PL	77545
JUNIPER SPRINGS TRAIL	0	446B	NWC	77449
JUNIPER STONE LN	0	524F	NEF	77494
JUNIPER TERRACE LN	5200	485X	NEF	77494
JUNIPER TREE CT	0	377A	NEC	77346
JUNIPER VALE CIR	19400	446R	NWC	77084
JUNIPER VALLEY LN	0	257F	SEM	77357
JUNIPER WALK LN	0	524C	NEF	77494
JUNIPER WOODS CT	13700	328T	NWC	77429
JUNIUS	0	450E	NWH	77041
JUNIUS	7900	535F	SEH	77012
JUPITER	0	656B	NEB	77546
JUPITER DR	15200	572S	SWC	77053
JUPITER HILLS DR	13800	370B	NWC	77069
JUPITER LANDING CT	27400	294U	SEM	77386
JURA DR	4200	447H	NWC	77084
JURUA DR	0	294D	SEM	77365
JURY RIG CT	16500	419B	NEC	77532
S. JUSTICE	0	578D	LP	77571
JUSTICE	8900	578D	LP	77571
JUSTICE DR	22300	256U	SEM	77357
JUSTICE PARK DR	0	451F	NWH	77092
JUSTIN	4600	414L	NCC	77093
JUSTIN	5700	414M	NEH	77016
JUSTIN CT	200	288M	TB	77375
JUSTIN LN	4200	538U	DP	77536
JUSTINA CT	2500	609A	MC	77478
JUSTIN RIDGE LN	0	376W	NEC	77396
JUSTIN RIDGE RD	0	524B	NEF	77494
JUSTIN TRAIL	12700	369K	NWC	77070
JUSTINWOOD POINT	0	329K	NWC	77375
JUTEWOOD LN	22500	485U	NEF	77450
JUTLAND RD	6400	534N	SEH	77033
JUTLAND RD	7600	533Z	SEH	77033
JUTLAND RD	9400	573D	SEH	77033
JUTLAND RD	10900	573M	SEH	77048
E. K	0	580G	LP	77571
W. K	100	580F	LP	77571

K

Street Name	Block	Pg/Sq	Loc	Zips
K	4100	529A	SWH	77072
K	5900	444T	KT	77493
K ST	0	576Q	SEH	77034
K Z RD	18400	327J	NWC	77429
K Z RD	18500	326M	NWC	77429
K, AVENUE	500	576C	SH	77587
K, AVENUE	1700	496W	GP	77547
K, AVENUE	1800	501S	BT	77520
K, AVENUE	2200	495Z	GP	77547
K, AVENUE	6500	494V	SEH	77011
K, AVENUE	7500	495S	SEH	77012
E. K, AVENUE	9200	535D	SEH	77012
K, J F BLVD	12200	414B	NCC	77039
K, J F BLVD	16000	374F	NEH	77032
K, J H BLVD	0	619C	PA	77586
K, M L BLVD	0	659Y	GCO	77539
KABEE	2300	494B	NEH	77020
KABOOSE DR	0	379J	NEC	77532
KACEE DR	4300	447H	NWC	77084
KACEY LANE CT	19400	337T	NEC	77346
KADABRA DR	0	406U	NWC	77449
KAHLDEN CT	700	488E	SWH	77079
KAHULA	7000	459K	NEC	77049
KAIBAB RD	0	658X	LC	77573
KAILEES CT	28200	293D	SEM	77386
KAILUA DR		325N	NWC	77447
KAINAI CT	0	328N	NWC	77429
KAINER MEADOWS LN	0	573T	SEC	77047
KAINER SPRINGS LN	0	526J	NEF	77407
KAISER	5300	450B	NWH	77040
KAISER	5900	410X	NWH	77040
KAISERSTRASSE	10000	249U	NWC	77375
KAITLYN DR	0	458S	NEC	77530
KAITLYN LN	9800	502G	BT	77521
KAITLYN KERRIA CT	16900	527T	NEF	77407
KAKERGLEN CT	17600	407T	NWC	77084
KALE	0	614X	PL	77584
KALE CT	0	614X	PL	77584
KALE CT	5000	371S	NWC	77066
KALEB PINES CT	24600	250W	NWC	77389
KALE GARDEN CT	0	446C	NWC	77449
KALER RD	14800	413A	NEH	77060
KALE RANCH DR	0	484R	NEF	77494
KALETA PASS LN	0	660K	LC	77573
KALEWOOD DR	8700	529N	SWH	77099
KALEY LN	21600	291R	NWC	77388
KALISTE MEADOW DR	0	332W	NWC	77090
KALISTE MEADOW DR	0	332W	NWC	77090
KALITHEA CT	4900	291N	NWC	77388
KALLIE HILLS LN	0	293K	SEM	77386
KALMER	200	536Z	PA	77502
KALSTON DR	0	326T	NWC	77429
KALTENBRUN RD	13000	371X	NWC	77086
KALWICK DR	3600	538T	DP	77536
KAMA DR	23000	295E	SEM	77365
KAMALA DR	0	458S	NEC	77530
KAMAN LN	0	615P	PL	77581
KAMENA DR	0	408U	NWC	77041
KAMIAH CT	0	410T	NWC	77040
KAMREN DR	1900	458S	NEC	77049
KANAH LN	1000	332J	NWC	77090
KANAWHA DR	19200	254Z	SEM	77365
KANDARIAN	2600	414W	NEH	77093
KANE	500	288G	TB	77375
KANE	1500	493K	SWH	77007
KANE LN	27100	252E	OR	77385
KANGAROO CT	11500	529W	MD	77477
KANSACK LN	10500	370Z	NWC	77086
KANSAS	0	659R	LC	77573
KANSAS	0	659E	LC	77573
KANSAS	0	611Y	FS	77545
KANSAS	100	540Y	LP	77571
KANSAS	400	580C	LP	77571
KANSAS	500	536W	SH	77587
KANSAS	600	537J	PA	77506
KANSAS	1800	541A	BT	77520
KANSAS	5200	492B	NWH	77007
S. KANSAS AVE	100	659J	LC	77573
N. KANSAS AVE	100	658H	LC	77573
KANSAS AVE	2000	660S	GCO	77539
KAPLAN DR	3700	537R	PA	77503
KAPPA	1200	577J	PA	77504

Street Name	Block	Pg/Sq	Loc	Zips
KAPPA DR	9400	573B	SEH	77051
KAPRI LN	9000	532S	SWH	77025
KARA LN	34600	247K	SWM	77362
KARACABEY CT	0	250X	NWC	77389
KARALIS	14000	572Z	SWH	77047
KARANKAWA DR	0	445N	NWC	77493
KARANKAWAS	4000	577F	PA	77504
KARANKAWAS CT	1600	538Q	DP	77536
KARANKAWA TRAIL	0	444S	KT	77493
KARBACH	1900	451U	NWH	77092
KARBO LN	0	373A	NCC	77073
KARCHER	0	339K	HU	77336
KARCHER	5100	453U	NEH	77009
KARDY ST	0	291R	NWC	77388
KARELIAN DR	5500	451D	NWH	77091
KAREN	0	326D	NWC	77377
KAREN	3600	537M	PA	77503
KAREN	7100	413W	NEH	77076
KAREN	7900	413N	NCC	77037
KAREN	13800	369C	NWC	77070
KAREN LN	0	287H	NWC	77377
KAREN LN	0	484P	NWF	77494
KAREN RD	25700	484P	NEF	77494
KARENBETH DR	5100	407Z	NWC	77084
KARENS WAY	5900	614L	PL	77581
KAREY LYNN LN	0	326R	NWC	77429
KARI CT	400	490H	HC	77024
KARI CT	8500	409L	JV	77040
KARI BEND CIR	0	526P	NEF	77407
KARINA DR	0	502H	BT	77520
KARINA LN	0	542L	CCO	77520
KARINA WAY	0	568Z	SG	77478
KARI SPRINGS CT	9400	410J	NWC	77040
KARLANDA LN	0	373A	NCC	77073
KARLOW TRAIL LN	17900	373J	NCC	77060
KARLOW TRAIL LN	17900	373J	NCC	77060
KARLWOOD LN	11600	529T	SWH	77099
KARNAUCH DR	7200	454M	NEH	77028
KARNAUCH PLAZA	7200	454M	NEH	77028
KARNES	200	453Y	NEH	77009
KARNES	7200	495J	NEH	77020
KAROS LN	900	490B	HE	77024
KARPATHOS LN	21500	291N	NWC	77388
KARRYWOOD CT	3900	613Y	NEB	77584
KARSEN DR	1800	458S	NEC	77530
KARSTEN CREEK CT	0	250K	NWC	77389
KARSTEN CREEK WAY	0	250K	NWC	77389
KARTER	0	409F	NWC	77064
KARTER DR	10700	409F	NWC	77064
KARU DR	5100	333H	NCC	77373
KASEY FLOWERS CT	0	376W	NEC	77396
KASEY SPRINGS LN	0	293F	SEM	77386
KASHMERE	2400	494B	NEH	77026
KASHMERE	3500	454T	NEH	77026
KASHMERE SPRING LN	0	611W	FS	77545
KASOS ISLE DR	4900	291N	NWC	77388
KASSARINE PASS	6400	534S	SEH	77033
KASSIKAY DR	16500	447H	NWC	77084
KATE DR	30100	286C	SWM	77355
KATELYN MANOR DR	800	372D	NCC	77073
KATEX BLVD	24000	445S	NWC	77493
KATEX BLVD	24500	444V	KT	77493
KATH LN	0	328X	NWC	77429
KATHARINE LN	700	288L	TB	77375
KATHERINE	100	499R	BT	77520
KATHERINE	100	500N	BT	77520
KATHERINE	2800	569Z	NEF	77477
KATHERINE	16200	498C	CV	77530
KATHERINE CT	10000	616K	SEC	77089
KATHI ANN LN	9700	412F	NWC	77038
KATHIE CT	0	245V	SWM	77355
KATHI LYNN LN	14000	568E	SG	77498
KATHLEEN	3000	463H	MB	77520
KATHLEEN CT	1800	538M	DP	77536
KATHLEEN HANEY DR	10100	371X	NWC	77086
KATHRYN	12400	496L	NEH	77015
KATHRYN CIR	3300	537L	PA	77503
KATHRYN OAKS LN	0	253T	SEM	77386
KATHY	0	286Z	NWC	77377
KATHY	500	335Z	HM	77338
KATHY	1200	577J	PA	77504
KATHY AVE	11700	570L	MC	77071
KATHY LN	0	444P	KT	77493
KATHY LN	2700	444P	KT	77493
KATHY LN	12900	328U	NWC	77429
KATHY LN	27400	247Y	SWM	77355
KATHYWOOD DR	0	328M	NWC	77377
KATIE GRACE CIR	9300	329M	NWC	77379
KATIE HARBOR DR	2600	613W	NEB	77578
KATIE MARIE CT	0	255Q	SEM	77365
KATIE MILL TRAIL	8100	290N	NWC	77379
KATIE RIDGE LN	22000	525D	NEF	77450
KATLYN LN	1800	293E	SEM	77386
KATNER LN	0	253S	SEM	77386
KATNER LN	3100	253S	SEM	77386
KATRINA CT	0	616L	SEC	77089
KATY	3000	569Q	SF	77477
KATY	5800	492B	NWH	77007
KATY	6700	614D	BK	77581
KATY (I.H. 10 W) FRWY	1200	493E	SWH	77007
KATY (I.H. 10 W) FRWY	1200	493E	SWH	77007
KATY (I.H. 10 W) FRWY	4000	492A	SWH	77007
KATY (I.H. 10 W) FRWY	4000	492A	SWH	77007
KATY (I.H. 10 W) FRWY	7200	491B	SWH	77024
KATY (I.H. 10 W) FRWY	7200	491B	SWH	77024
KATY (I.H. 10 W) FRWY	8600	490A	SWH	77024
KATY (I.H. 10 W) FRWY	8600	490A	SWH	77024
KATY (I.H. 10 W) FRWY	10700	489B	SWH	77079
KATY (I.H. 10 W) FRWY	10700	489B	SWH	77079
KATY (I.H. 10 W) FRWY	12200	488C	SWH	77079
KATY (I.H. 10 W) FRWY	12200	488C	SWH	77079
KATY (I.H. 10 W) FRWY	14800	487C	SWH	77094
KATY (I.H. 10 W) FRWY	14800	487C	SWH	77094
KATY (I.H. 10 W) FRWY	19000	486D	SWC	77094
KATY (I.H. 10 W) FRWY	19000	486D	SWC	77094
KATY (I.H. 10 W) FRWY	20000	485B	NWC	77449
KATY (I.H. 10 W) FRWY	20000	485B	NWC	77449
KATY (I.H. 10 W) FRWY	20001	485B	SWC	77450
KATY (I.H. 10 W) FRWY	20001	485B	SWC	77450
KATY (I.H. 10 W) FRWY	24000	484A	KT	77494
KATY (I.H. 10 W) FRWY	24000	484A	KT	77494
KATY (I.H. 10 W) FRWY	24900	444Z	KT	77493
KATY (I.H. 10 W) FRWY	24900	444Z	KT	77493
KATY RD	0	484Y	NEF	77494
KATY RD	6800	492A	NWH	77024
KATY-HOCKLEY	0	324Z	NWC	77447
KATYA GILLIAN DR	10600	576K	SEH	77034
KATY ARBOR LN	0	485W	NEF	77494
KATYBRIAR LN	0	445R	NWC	77449
KATY CITY PARK RD	0	444U	KT	77493
KATY CREEK RANCH DR	0	485N	NWF	77494
KATY FIRST BAPTIST		484C	KT	77494

Street Name	Block	Pg/Sq	Loc	Zips
KATY FLEWELLEN RD	0	484W	NEF	77494
KATY FLEWELLEN RD	0	484W	NEF	77494
KATY FLEWELLEN RD	1000	484K	NEF	77494
KATY FLEWELLEN RD		484G	NEF	77494
KATY FLEWELLEN RD		484N	NEF	77494
KATY FLEWELLEN RD		484S	NEF	77494
KATY FORT BEND RD	0	484D	SWC	77494
KATY FORT BEND RD	0	485E	SWC	77494
KATY FORT BEND RD	600	444Z	KT	77493
KATY FORT BEND RD	2500	444R	NWC	77493
KATY GAP	1000	485F	KT	77494
KATY GASTON RD	0	525P	NEF	77469
KATY GASTON RD	0	525P	NEF	77469
KATYGASTON RD	0	525J	NEF	77406
KATY GASTON RD	0	525E	NEF	77494
KATY GASTON RD	2000	484Y	NEF	77494
KATY GASTON RD	6000	524C	NEF	77494
KATY HOCKLEY RD	0	405A	NWC	77433
KATY HOCKLEY RD	2900	444F	NWC	77493
KATY HOCKLEY RD	5000	404U	NWC	77493
KATY HOCKLEY RD	9000	404D	NWC	77433
KATY HOCKLEY RD	11000	364V	NWC	77433
KATY HOCKLEY RD	14200	324Z	NWC	77447
KATY HOCKLEY CUTOFF	2000	444M	KT	77493
KATY HOCKLEY CUTOFF	5000	404R	NWC	77493
KATY HOLLOW DR	3700	446L	NWC	77449
KATY KNOLL CT	13400	488X	SWC	77082
KATY LAKE ESTATES DR	0	444B	NWC	77493
KATYLAND DR	1000	444Y	KT	77493
KATY MILLS BLVD	2000	484D	SWC	77494
KATY MILLS CIR	5000	484C	KT	77494
KATY MILLS DR	5100	484D	KT	77494
KATY MILLS PKWY	5400	484C	KT	77494
KATY MIST DR	3800	446F	NWC	77449
KATY OAKS BLVD	0	445N	NWC	77493
KATY OAKS RD	0	445N	NWC	77493
KATY POINTE BLVD	0	445E	NWC	77493
KATY PRAIRIE DR	0	444J	KT	77493
KATY PRAIRIE DR	26000	404X	NWC	77493
KATY TOWN LN	0	445N	NWC	77493
KAUFF RANCH CT	0	328N	NWC	77429
KAUFMAN AVE	3500	613S	PL	77584
S. KAUFMAN DR	600	538Q	DP	77536
N. KAUFMAN DR	600	538Q	DP	77536
KAVANAUGH LN	13500	328T	NWC	77429
KAY	1400	537J	PA	77506
KAY	3000	454J	NEH	77093
KAY AVE	2300	616U	PL	77581
KAY CIR	4300	533U	SEH	77051
KAY LN	9300	410B	NWC	77064
KAY LN	11400	612V	PL	77584
KAYAK RIDGE DR	0	250R	NWC	77389
KAYBULL DR	18900	337X	NEC	77346
KAYCEE	600	453J	NWH	77022
KAY JO LN	10800	418S	NEC	77044
KAYLA CT	16200	286C	SWM	77355
KAYLA LN	12300	496Q	GP	77015
KAYLA SPRINGS LN	0	376G	NEC	77396
KAYLYN	500	373W	NCC	77060
KAYLYN ST	0	373X	NCC	77060
KAYVON CT	24900	485N	NEF	77494
KEAGAN FALLS DR	2800	613X	NEB	77578
KEARNEY DR	11500	413X	NEH	77076
KEARNEY HILL LN	7300	250X	NWC	77389
KEARNY BROOK PLACE	1	250D	WD	77381
KEATING	1400	494S	SEH	77003
KEATLEY DR	1800	489P	SWH	77077
KEATON PLACE	0	367P	NWC	77433
KEATS	6600	571S	SWH	77085
KEATS CT	20500	335Q	HM	77338
KEDGE CT	16900	379X	NEC	77532
KEDGWICK LN	0	327Z	NWC	77429
KEE CRESTA CT	0	445E	NWC	77493
KEEFER RD	1300	288F	TB	77375
KEEGAN RD	9600	529S	SWH	77099
KEEGAN HOLLOW LN	2300	293F	SEM	77386
KEEGAN RUN DR	0	447D	NWC	77084
KEEGANS FOREST LN	8700	530X	SWH	77031
KEEGANS GLEN DR	10900	530X	SWH	77031
KEEGANS MEADOW DR	0	527P	NEF	77407
KEEGANS RIDGE RD	11500	569D	SWH	77031
KEEGANS RIDGE WAY DR	16700	527P	NEF	77083
KEEGANS WOOD DR	9000	528P	SWC	77083
KEEHAM	31200	246Y	SWM	77355
KEEL RD	1	453B	NEH	77076
KEELAND	2400	454E	NEH	77093
KEELAND	4700	454G	NEH	77016
KEELBY DR	14800	457Z	NEC	77015
KEELER CT	4100	538N	PA	77503
KEELING TRAIL	18400	378B	NEC	77346
KEELSON CT	300	379U	NEC	77532
KEELY	11700	572A	SWH	77045
KEEN RD	29800	288A	NWC	77377
KEENAN	0	574R	SEH	77048
KEENAN COVE	17900	447B	NWC	77084
KEENBURY LN	0	484Z	NEF	77494
KEENE	100	496S	GP	77547
KEENE	1500	493C	NEH	77009
KEENELAND LN	10500	372W	NWC	77038
KEENE MILL CT	11500	371R	NWC	77067
KEENEN CT	1600	488K	SWH	77077
KEEPERS TRAIL	12400	368J	NWC	77429
KEERAN POINT CT	2200	568A	SG	77498
KEESE DR	10800	576T	SEH	77089
KEESEY CREEK CIR	0	366Z	NWC	77433
KEILER CIR	3000	485V	NEF	77450
KEIRA CT	14200	370A	NWC	77069
KEISER BEND DR	0	328K	NWC	77429
KEISER BEND DR		328k	NWC	77377
KEITH	0	256Y	SEM	77357
KEITH	500	576H	SEH	77504
KEITH	15800	374R	NEH	77032
KEITH	26400	292Q	SP	77373
KEITH RD	5100	577G	PA	77505
KEITH RD	10800	414U	NEC	77093
KEITHHARROW BLVD	16100	448A	NWC	77084
KEITH HARROW BLVD	16400	447C	NWC	77084
KEITH HARROW BLVD	19000	446D	NWC	77084
W. KEITHWOOD CIR	3200	614T	PL	77584
E. KEITHWOOD CIR	3200	614T	PL	77584
S. KEITHWOOD CIR	6700	614T	PL	77584
KEITHWOOD DR	3000	614T	PL	77584
KELBROOK DR	15200	618J	SEH	77062
KELBURN DR	8800	454D	NEH	77016
KELBURN DR	10100	415W	NEH	77016
KELCEY CIR	16200	246Y	SWM	77355
KELFORD	5300	455T	NEH	77028
KELFY ARBOR LN	0	326P	NWC	77433
KELL CIR	9500	410R	NWH	77040
KELL DR	9800	410R	NWH	77040
KELLAN CT	15500	327V	NWC	77429
KELLER	3200	660H	BC	77518

Street Name	Block	Pg/Sq	Loc	Zips
KELLER	6600	534H	SEH	77087
KELLER	7200	535F	SEH	77012
KELLER BAY CT	0	657S	FR	77546
KELLER BROOK LN	0	446A	NWC	77449
KELLER FOREST CT	18000	376D	NEC	77346
KELLERMAN	12200	415R	NEC	77016
KELLERTON CT	14700	368A	NWC	77429
KELLERWOOD DR	15100	370Y	NWC	77086
KELLETT	600	620L	SB	77586
KELLETT	8200	455F	NEH	77028
KELLETT	8800	455G	NEH	77078
KELLEY	100	453Q	NEH	77009
KELLEY	2000	454P	NEH	77026
KELLEY CT	1300	376J	NEC	77396
KELLEY CREEK	18200	487A	SWC	77094
KELLEY GREEN CT	16000	327Y	CY	77429
KELLEY POND	0	293D	SEM	77386
KELLI	16000	458U	CV	77530
KELLICREEK DR	19900	486L	SWC	77450
KELLING DR	3100	572K	SWH	77045
KELLING DR	5100	571L	SWH	77045
KELLINGTON DR	0	295Z	NEH	77365
KELLINGTON DR	0	296W	NEH	77365
KELLINGTON PLACE	0	609K	MC	77459
KELLIWOOD ARBOR LN	21000	486W	NEF	77450
KELLIWOOD COURTS CIR	1	486S	NEF	77450
KELLIWOOD COURTS DR	0	486S	NEF	77450
KELLIWOOD GREENS DR	21200	486W	NEF	77450
KELLIWOOD GROVE CT	4500	486W	NEF	77450
KELLIWOOD GROVE LN	21000	486W	NEF	77450
KELLIWOOD LAKES CT	20400	486P	SWC	77450
KELLIWOOD LAKES DR	2500	486P	SWC	77450
KELLIWOOD MANOR LN	4500	486W	NEF	77450
KELLIWOOD OAKS DR	1300	486L	SWC	77450
KELLIWOOD PARK CT	4500	486W	NEF	77450
KELLIWOOD PARK LN	21000	486W	NEF	77450
KELLIWOOD TRAILS CT	1800	486K	SWC	77450
KELLIWOOD TRAILS DR	1900	486K	SWC	77450
KELLOGG	900	535E	SEH	77012
KELLWAY DR	300	457W	NEC	77015
KELLWOOD DR	7600	410R	NWH	77040
KELLY	0	296P	SEM	77365
KELLY	0	332C	NCC	77373
KELLY	0	502W	BT	77520
KELLY	1	492L	SWH	77007
KELLY	100	292Q	SP	77373
KELLY DR	4000	569S	SG	77478
KELLY DR	5800	614L	PL	77581
KELLY DR	11500	369N	NWC	77065
KELLY LN	100	501Q	BT	77521
KELLY LN	2400	371K	NWC	77066
W. KELLY LN	19700	285Z	NWC	77377
KELLY LN		286W	NWC	77377
KELLY RD	2600	444Q	KT	77493
KELLY RD	24100	296M	SEM	77365
KELLY-JOE SMITH RD	0	296F	SEM	77365
KELLY BROOK TRAIL	2700	371Y	NWC	77038
KELLY COURTS	0	494E	NEH	77020
KELLYDALE CT	2500	291R	NWC	77388
KELLY HILL CT	0	577W	SEH	77034
KELLY KAY CT	19100	332A	NWC	77388
KELLY LAKE TRAIL	10400	616G	SEC	77089
KELLY MEADOWS LN	0	257E	SEM	77357
KELLY MILL LN	5800	337T	NEC	77346
KELLY OAKS CT	19100	337X	NEC	77346
KELLY PINES CT	19200	337T	NEC	77346
KELLY SPRING CIR	5300	331E	NWC	77379
KELLY TIMBERS DR	19400	337T	NEC	77346
KELLYWAY LN	2700	609B	MC	77459
KELLYWOOD LN	14100	489J	SWH	77079
KELLYWOOD LN	14400	488G	SWH	77079
KELLY WOODS CT	0	376W	NEC	77396
KELONA DR	1900	252V	SEM	77386
KELSEY	800	336J	NEH	77339
W. KELSEY CREEK TRAIL	0	325R	NWC	77433
KELSEY CREEK TRAIL	0	326N	NWC	77433
KELSEY GAP CT	0	366V	NWC	77433
KELSEY HILLS LN	0	328M	NWC	77377
KELSEY MEADOWS CT	9500	410J	NWC	77040
KELSEY RAE CT	6900	370A	NWC	77069
KELSEY SPRINGS CT	0	329R	NWC	77379
KELSEY TRACE WAY	16300	326N	NWC	77433
KELSEY TRAIL LN	3900	573V	SEC	77047
KELSO	4900	534N	SEH	77021
KELSO	100	336J	NEH	77339
KELSO CT	600	570S	SF	77477
KELTON	3300	533G	SEH	77021
KELTON HILLS LN	25200	524L	NWF	77406
KELTWOOD LN	0	368A	NWC	77429
KELVIN	4200	538U	DP	77536
KELVIN DR	4500	532C	SWH	77005
KELVIN DR	6700	532G	SWH	77030
KELVING	2300	532L	SWH	77030
KELVING	7400	532L	SWH	77030
S. KEMAH	2300	660F	KE	77565
KEMAH CUT-OFF	0	659C	LC	77573
KEMAH CUT-OFF	0	660A	LC	77573
KEMAH OAKS DR	1700	660B	KE	77565
KEMBERTON DR	1000	618E	SEH	77062
KEMBLE RD	18900	337X	NEC	77346
KEMBLE CREEK CT	0	407U	NWC	77084
KEMBLE CREEK DR	0	407U	NWC	77084
KEMERTON DR	12100	528Z	SWH	77099
KEMP	200	536G	PA	77506
KEMP	5600	494Y	SEH	77023
KEMP CREST CT	5500	251W	NWC	77389
KEMPER DR	2100	659C	LC	77573
KEMPER DR	6800	578K	PA	77505
KEMPER DALE LN	0	446B	NWC	77449
KEMP FOREST DR	9600	450K	NWH	77080
KEMP FOREST DR	10200	449M	NWH	77043
KEMP HOLLOW LN	11900	449L	NWH	77043
KEMPNER	1	568P	SG	77498
KEMPRIDGE	8500	450R	NWH	77080
KEMPSEY LN	0	410M	NWC	77040
KEMPSFORD CT	20200	486F	SWC	77450
KEMPSFORD DR	1000	486F	SWC	77450
KEMPTON PARK DR	16000	330S	NWC	77379
KEMPWOOD DR	7600	451N	NWH	77055
KEMPWOOD DR	8400	450L	NWH	77080
KEMPWOOD DR	10200	449M	NWH	77043
KEMROCK CIR	6100	457S	NEC	77049
KEMROCK CT	6100	457S	NEC	77049
KEMROCK DR	14400	457S	NEC	77049
KEMTON	100	535A	SEH	77012
KEMWOOD DR	10900	490H	HC	77024
KEN	1200	335Z	HM	77338
KENBRIAR DR	15800	570Z	SWH	77489
KENBRIDGE DR	2400	371M	NWC	77067
KENBROOK DR	15800	571W	SWH	77489
KENCHESTER DR	22000	332H	NCC	77073
KENCO	2600	454E	NEH	77093

Street Name	Block	Pg/Sq	Loc	Zips
KENDAHLWOOD LN	0	329F	NWC	77375
KENDALE DR	0	527V	NEF	77083
KENDALIA DR	6900	529M	SWH	77036
KENDALL	1	494N	SEH	77003
N. KENDALL	100	494P	SEH	77003
KENDALL DR	4100	503M	CCO	77520
KENDALL ST	0	612V	PL	77584
KENDALLBROOK DR	14600	408G	NWC	77095
KENDALL CLIFF CT	0	406X	NWC	77449
KENDALL CREEK LN	0	573X	SEC	77047
KENDALL FALLS BLVD	0	578T	SEH	77059
KENDALLHILL CT	0	609U	MC	77479
KENDALL HILL LN	0	609U	NEF	77479
KENDALL LAKE CT	7000	526F	NEF	77407
KENDALL LAKE DR	19700	526F	NEF	77407
KENDALL RIDGE LN	5200	609S	NEF	77479
KENDALL RIDGE LN	17100	407G	NWC	77095
KENDALL ROCK LN	0	446E	NWC	77449
KENDALL SHAY CT	22400	485Z	NEF	77450
KENDALLS PATH CT	0	572S	SWH	77053
KENDAL RIDGE LN	0	253J	SEM	77385
KENDAL RIDGE LN	27100	366Q	NWC	77433
KENDONS WAY LN	16300	326R	NWC	77429
KENDRA LN	20700	486F	SWC	77450
KENDRA FORSET TRAIL		484W	NEF	77494
KENDRICKS PINES BLVD	0	250N	NWC	77389
KENDRICK PLAZA DR	3700	374T	NEH	77032
KENEVA DR	13600	328T	NWC	77429
KENFOREST DR	800	570U	MC	77489
KEN HALL DR	0	568S	SG	77478
KENILWOOD DR	5000	534S	SEH	77033
KENILWORTH	9000	491C	SWH	77024
KENIL WORTH	16200	367G	NWC	77429
KENLAKE DR	22000	485H	SWC	77450
KENLAKE GROVE DR	4900	337C	NEH	77345
KENLEA LN	14900	412D	NEH	77060
KENLY OAKS DR	0	524K	NWF	77406
KENMARK CT	7600	407J	NWC	77433
KENMARK LN	18400	407J	NWC	77433
KENMONT DR	0	377D	NEC	77346
KENMORE	900	535A	SEH	77023
KENNA CT	3800	293C	SEM	77386
KENNA COVE LN	20900	290V	NWC	77379
KENNARD DR	8800	530P	SWH	77074
KENNEBECK PLACE	1500	488K	SWH	77077
KENNEDALE LN	0	330B	NWC	77379
KENNEDY	0	613Y	NEB	77584
KENNEDY	2700	494J	SEH	77003
KENNEDY LN	0	295H	SEM	77365
KENNEDY COMMERCE DR	0	374X	NCC	77032
KENNEDY HEIGHTS BLVD	4700	573M	SEH	77048
KENNEDY OAKS	15100	571U	SWH	77053
KENNEDY RANCH LN	24000	325J	NWC	77447
KENNEDY RANCH LN	24200	324M	NWC	77447
KENNEMER DR	7400	334M	NCC	77338
KENNESAW DR	2900	610U	MC	77459
KENNESAW MOUNTAIN LN	0	377E	NEC	77346
KENNETH ST	0	502W	BT	77520
KENNETH ROYAL DR	0	620L	SB	77586
KENNET VALLEY RD	8600	330S	NWC	77379
KENNEWICK DR	0	370U	NWC	77086
KENNINGHALL DR	0	289R	NWC	77375
KENNINGS AVE	500	419H	CB	77532
KENNINGS RD	100	419R	BR	77532
KENNINGS RD	900	420Q	NEC	77532
KENNINGS RD	4100	421J	NEC	77532
KENNINGTON CT	3600	299S	NEC	77336
KENNINGTON WAY	24700	250Y	NWC	77389
KENNON	3700	453Y	NEH	77009
KENNONS WAY	0	285Q	NWC	77447
KENNONVIEW DR	3300	331N	NWC	77068
KENNOWAY PARK DR	1500	329C	NWC	77379
KENNY	14500	497L	NEC	77015
KENNY	15300	328V	NWC	77377
KENNY LN	1100	538L	DP	77536
KENNY ST	3200	444L	KT	77493
KENO MOON LN	2000	288R	TB	77375
KENOSHA	5200	456N	NEH	77013
KENOVA CANYON CT		526S	NEF	77407
KEN PLACE	1100	568S	SG	77478
KENR	0	331Y	NWC	77014
KENRICK DR	600	373T	NEH	77060
KENRICK DR	800	373P	NCC	77032
KENROSS	2500	449M	NWH	77043
KENS CT	3800	375R	NEC	77396
KENSAL BAY LN	0	329J	NWC	77377
KENSICO RD	7500	530K	SWH	77036
KENSINGTON AVE	0	609G	MC	77459
KENSINGTON BLVD	16100	568X	NEF	77479
KENSINGTON CT	200	490Q	PP	77024
KENSINGTON CT	300	536U	PA	77502
KENSINGTON CT	8700	578D	LP	77571
KENSINGTON DR	1000	613F	NEB	77584
KENSINGTON DR	3200	613K	NEB	77584
S. KENSINGTON DR	9600	569D	SWH	77031
N. KENSINGTON DR	11700	569D	SWH	77031
KENSINGTON BLUFF DR	0	327H	NWC	77429
KENSINGTON BLUFF DR	0	327H	NWC	77429
KENSINGTON BRIAR LN	0	446G	NWC	77449
KENSINGTON CREEK DR	0	293T	NCC	77373
KENSINGTON LAKE DR	0	295Q	SEM	77365
KENSINGTON PARK	2900	615L	PL	77581
KENSINGTON PARK CIR	1800	252R	SEM	77386
KENSINGTON PARK DR	31100	252R	SEM	77386
KENSINGTON PLACE	13700	577W	SEH	77034
KENSINGTON PLACE	14000	617B	SEH	77598
KENSINGTON WAY	1300	336H	NEH	77339
KENSLEY DR	16300	527B	SWC	77082
KENSON LN	14100	368A	NWC	77429
KENS RUN	9200	375R	NEC	77396
KENSTON PLACE	4300	610N	MC	77459
KENSWICK DR	19600	335W	NCC	77338
KENSWICK BLUFF LN	0	290J	NWC	77375
KENSWICK COVE DR	0	329B	NWC	77375
KENSWICK FOREST LN	0	334M	NCC	77338
KENSWICK FOREST LN	8000	334M	NCC	77338
KENSWICK GLEN DR	0	334R	NCC	77338
KENSWICK KEY LN	13900	573Y	SEC	77047
KENSWICK MEADOWS CT	21100	334R	NCC	77338
KENSWICK PARK DR	20700	295R	SEM	77365
KENT	0	256Z	SEM	77357
KENT	0	257H	SEM	77357
KENT	0	615P	PL	77581
KENT	5100	577C	PA	77505
KENT	5300	532D	SWH	77005
KENT CT	0	258F	SEM	77357
KENTBURY	0	488L	SWH	77077
KENTBURY CT	900	486F	SWC	77450
KENT FALLS CT	1700	485L	SWC	77450
KENT FALLS DR	22300	485L	SWC	77450
KENTFIELD DR	9600	453D	NEH	77093
KENTFORD DR	15500	618J	SEH	77062
KENT HOLLOW CT	27400	293F	SEM	77386
KENTINGTON OAK DR	10700	376U	NWC	77396
KENTLAND CT	11700	371M	NWC	77067
KENTLAND DR	1900	371M	NWC	77067
KENTLEY ORCHARD LN	14400	328S	NWC	77429
KENTMERGE RIDGE LN		484N	NEF	77494
KENT OAK DR	1300	489J	SWH	77077
KENTON	7800	455P	NEH	77028
KENTON CROSSING CIR	6600	527E	NEF	77407
KENTON CROSSING LN	17300	527E	NEF	77407
KENTON HILLS CT	0	615H	PL	77089
KENTON HOLLOW LN	0	615H	PL	77089
KENTON PLACE LN		328P	NWC	77429
KENTSHIRE DR	8400	415Y	NEH	77078
KENTSTEAD LN	0	573X	SEC	77047
KENTSTEAD LN	0	573X	SEC	77047
KENT TOWNE LN	9900	528T	NEF	77498
KENTUCKY	200	536W	SH	77587
KENTUCKY	800	538L	DP	77536
KENTUCKY	1200	575D	SH	77587
KENTUCKY	1700	540D	BT	77520
KENTUCKY	2600	659Q	LC	77573
KENTUCKY	2800	494A	NEH	77026
KENTUCKY	3000	659Z	GCO	77539
KENTUCKY RD	2800	611V	FS	77545
KENTUCKY DERBY CIR	18800	337Z	NEC	77346
KENTUCKY TRACE	20200	285M	NWC	77447
KENTWALK DR	4800	449H	NWH	77041
KENTWATER CT	15600	408A	NWC	77095
KENT WAY	1400	656M	FR	77546
KENTWICK DR	6400	408N	NWC	77084
KENTWOOD DR	3200	251N	SWM	77380
KENTWOOD DR	16500	618L	SEH	77058
KENWALL DR	6000	529C	SWH	77072
KENWELL DR	6800	527M	SWC	77083
KENWICH OAKS LN	0	446N	NWC	77449
KENWICK	2700	609R	MC	77459
KENWICK PLACE	1200	577E	PA	77504
KENWOOD	1000	493W	SWH	77006
KENWOOD	0	609Z	MC	77459
KENWOOD LN	500	496B	NEH	77013
KENWOOD HAVEN DR	0	366J	NWC	77433
KENWOOD PARK LN	0	253N	SEM	77386
KENWORTH DR	0	257F	SEM	77357
KENWORTHY DR	2300	610A	MC	77459
KENYA LN	4400	578E	PA	77505
KENYA MANOR DR	0	376N	NEC	77396
KENYON LN	6500	531H	BL	77401
KENZIE CT	11700	529W	MD	77477
KEOUGH RD	9100	410S	NWC	77040
KEOWEE CT	15500	617S	SEC	77546
KEPLER MCVEY CT	9700	329V	NWC	77070
KEPLER WAY	8400	251C	SD	77381
KEPPIE WAY	0	527X	NEF	77407
KERALA ST	0	568J	MC	77498
KERBEY	1300	496J	JC	77029
KERBY PLACE	0	406F	NWC	77433
KERI LEIGH DR	0	292W	NWC	77388
KERMAN DR	11500	368P	NWC	77429
KERMIER RD	17000	323H	HK	77447
KERMIER RD	18200	283V	NWC	77447
KERMIT	4600	453X	NWH	77009
KERN	800	453T	NWH	77009
KERN	1300	541B	BT	77520
KERNEL	6400	534H	SEH	77087
KERNEL	7200	535E	SEH	77012
KERNOHAN	100	419G	CB	77532
KERR	7900	495P	NEH	77029
KERR DR	8500	289H	NWC	77375
KERR LN	0	613S	PL	77584
KERR LN	10200	252F	SEM	77385
KERR COMMONS	0	578T	SEH	77059
KERRIGAN	0	290P	NWC	77379
KERRI LEIGH CT	500	332A	NWC	77388
KERRINGTON GLEN DR	0	406H	NWC	77433
KERRISDALE CT	0	289Q	NWC	77375
KERRWOOD LN	9000	450P	NWH	77080
KERRWOOD LN	10100	450N	NWH	77080
KERRY	100	459R	HG	77562
KERRY CIR	2300	616K	PL	77581
KERRY DR	900	537J	PA	77506
KERRY DR	1900	538P	DP	77536
KERRYBLUE DR	22100	485D	SWC	77450
KERRYBROOK LN	17700	376B	NEC	77396
KERRY GLEN CIR	9200	455D	NEH	77078
KERRY GLEN LN	9600	455D	NEH	77078
KERRY PRAIRIE LN	0	526Q	NEF	77407
KERSHAW	13700	413J	NCC	77037
KERSHOPE FOREST CT	9900	329G	NWC	77379
KERSTEN DR	1800	449Q	NWH	77043
KERVILLE CT	15500	328N	NWC	77429
KERVIN DR	0	571F	SWH	77085
KESNET PARK DR	0	326T	NWC	77433
KESSINGTON LN	1600	486M	SWC	77094
KESSLER	0	493G	SWH	77007
KESSLER'S CROSSING	2600	659S	LC	77573
KESSLER COVE LN	0	524A	NEF	77494
KESSLER PARK CT	1700	572R	SWH	77047
KESSWAY LN	11000	575Y	SEH	77075
KESTREL	33400	324Q	NWC	77447
KESTREL CT	6700	370B	NWC	77069
KESTREL VIEW	0	485E	SWC	77494
KESWICK	0	412Z	NEH	77076
N. KESWICK CT	100	568V	SG	77478
S. KESWICK CT	200	568V	SG	77478
KESWICK CT	1900	615L	PL	77581
KESWICK DR	3000	615L	PL	77581
KESWICK PINES LN	11700	370H	NWC	77066
KETAN LOCH CT	8400	329H	NWC	77379
KETCH CT	1300	619U	LC	77573
KETCH CT	2100	620K	SB	77586
KETCHWOOD DR	8700	529N	SWH	77099
KETTERING CIR	0	258F	SEM	77357
KETTERING DR	2600	491V	SWH	77027
KETTERING DR	2700	501R	BT	77521
KETTERING LN	200	657U	LC	77573
KETTLEBROOK LN	16400	458S	NEC	77049
KETTLE CREEK DR	16800	329R	NWC	77379
KETTLE MAR DR	6900	408P	NWC	77084
KETTLE RUN	2700	609A	SG	77479
KEVA GLEN DR	3000	659D	LC	77573
KEVIN CT	300	539Z	LP	77571
KEVIN LN	2500	450J	NWH	77043
KEVINCREST DR	6700	614T	PL	77584
KEVINDALE CT	16000	409L	JV	77040
KEVINGTON CT	28500	293E	SEM	77386
KEVINKAY DR	4300	447H	NWC	77084
KEWALO BASIN LN	11700	576L	SEH	77034
KEWANEE	4100	533Y	SEH	77051
KEW GARDEN	0	573J	SEH	77047
KEY	0	282U	WL	77484
KEY	600	453X	NWH	77009
KEY CT	4000	609M	MC	77459
KEY BISCAYNE CT	11800	369W	NWC	77065
KEY CREST LN	0	326U	NWC	77429
KEYGATE DR	3200	291U	NWC	77388
KEYHOLE LN	2300	446U	NWC	77084
KEY HOLLOW WAY	3800	291Y	NWC	77388
KEYKO	6200	410W	NWH	77041
KEY LARGO CT	0	610T	MC	77459
KEY MAPS, INC	0	493S	SWH	77006
KEYMILL DR	0	409F	NWC	77064
KEYMIST LN	0	328K	NWC	77377
KEY OAKS LN	0	406K	NWC	77433
KEYPORT LN	900	496G	NEH	77015
KEYRIDGE LN	13500	367C	NWC	77429
KEYSTONE	4500	533M	SEH	77021
KEYSTONE	4600	534K	SEH	77021
KEYSTONE DR	1600	656M	FR	77546
KEYSTONE BEND CT	27300	294N	SEM	77386
KEYSTONE BEND LN	0	327U	NWC	77429
KEYSTONE FAIRWAY CT	16600	367U	NWC	77095
KEYSTONE FAIRWAY DR	10800	367U	NWC	77095
KEYSTONE FALLS CT	0	526P	NEF	77407
KEYSTONE FOREST LN	0	377P	NEC	77044
KEYSTONE GREEN DR	0	326Y	NWC	77433
KEYSTONE GROVE TRAIL	0	328E	NWC	77377
KEYSTONE OAK	0	447N	NWC	77084
KEYSTONE PINE CT	0	446E	NWC	77449
KEYSTONE RIDGE LN	0	329V	NWC	77070
KEYSTONE SPRING WAY	0	616H	SEH	77089
KEYSTONE TRAIL	22300	485L	SWC	77450
KEYSTONE TRAIL	0	615N	PL	77584
KEYTURN LN	18000	337X	NEC	77346
KEY WEST DR	0	445N	NWC	77493
KEYWOOD LN	3200	445M	NWC	77449
KEYWORTH DR	13800	372E	NWC	77014
KIAM	5200	492C	NWH	77007
KIAMESHA CT	14100	330X	NWC	77069
KIAMESHA DR	3400	610J	MC	77459
KIAN CT	5500	531J	SWH	77081
KIAWAH DR	0	326U	NWC	77429
KIBER	10500	530X	SWH	77031
KICKAPOO RD	17000	323G	NWC	77484
KICKAPOO RD	18200	283C	NWC	77484
KICKAPOO RD	23200	243Q	WCO	77447
KICKAPOO RD	29000	243G	WCO	77447
KICKAPOO MEADOWS LN	0	283B	NWC	77484
KICKERILLO CT	400	489J	SWH	77079
KICKERILLO DR	300	488H	SWH	77079
KICKING HORSE PASS	0	366U	NWC	77433
KIDD LN	19500	256L	SEM	77357
KIDD CEMETERY RD	22100	256L	SEM	77357
KIDLINGTON CT	12300	414E	NCC	77039
KIELDER POINTE DR	10100	329C	NWC	77379
KIELDER SHADOW CT		484J	NEF	77494
KIER RD	13300	574T	SEH	77048
KIETH HARROW BLVD	16100	448A	NWC	77084
KIETH HARROW BLVD	16400	447C	NWC	77084
KIETH HARROW BLVD	19000	446D	NWC	77449
KIEV HILLS LN	0	572R	SWH	77047
KILBORNE PARK LN	19600	290Z	NWC	77379
KILBRIDE WAY CT	10400	329C	NWC	77379
KILBURN RD	11500	451P	NWH	77055
KILDARE DR	1100	572R	SWH	77047
KILDARE DR	2100	616K	PL	77581
KILDARE DR	3700	573Q	SEH	77047
KILDARE LN	24300	244R	WCO	77447
KILDEE	0	574B	SEH	77033
KILDEE PARK	7700	375Q	NEC	77396
KILDEER CT	0	658X	LC	77573
KILDEER DR	1300	620G	SB	77586
KILEY DR	500	372H	NCC	77073
KILEY PARK CT	0	616L	SEC	77089
KILGARLIN LN	1400	538N	DP	77536
KILGARNEY KEEP AVE	0	659X	DI	77539
KILGARTH DR	16800	527X	NEF	77407
KILGORE	100	502W	BT	77520
KILGORE	3100	533G	SEH	77021
KILGORE AVE	300	499D	NEC	77520
KILGORE AVE	400	499G	NEC	77520
KILGORE CT	3600	613Y	NEB	77578
KILGORE LN	0	613W	NWB	77578
KILGORE LN	1600	379M	NEC	77532
KILGORE LN	1900	380J	NEC	77532
KILKENNY	2200	538N	DP	77536
KILKENNY DR	1000	572Q	SWH	77047
KILKENNY DR	2100	616J	PL	77581
KILKENNY DR	3500	573Q	SEH	77047
KILKENNY DR	4600	574N	SEH	77048
KILKENNY GLENN DR	12400	408D	NWC	77065
KILLARNEY AVE	1000	656L	FR	77546
KILLARNEY CIR	2400	616J	PL	77581
KILLARNEY CT	1	530R	SWH	77074
KILLARNEY LN	2200	538P	DP	77536
KILLDEER CT	15800	375Q	NEC	77396
KILLDEER LN	2600	375L	HM	77396
KILL DEVIL FALLS DR	0	449T	NWH	77043
KILLEARN DR	6600	578J	PA	77505
KILLENE	8500	455X	NEH	77029
KILLER BEE LN	23000	296D	SEM	77357
KILLIAN CT	4200	609P	MC	77459
KILLINGSWORTH LN	17800	322B	WCO	77484
KILLNEY CT	0	572H	SEH	77051
KILLOUGH	5200	411F	NWC	77038
KILLOUGH	5300	411F	NWC	77086
KILLOUGH ST	5200	411G	NWC	77038
KILMARNOCH WAY	4600	569X	MC	77459
KILMARNOCK DR	0	532E	SWH	77025
KILMER TRAIL	0	295R	SEM	77365
KILMORY CT	0	372A	NWC	77014
KILNAR RD	0	613D	SEH	77048
KILPATRICK DR	700	498A	CV	77530
KILRENNY CT	17000	329M	NWC	77379
KILRENNY DR	8800	329M	NWC	77379
KILRENNY DR	9400	329R	NWC	77379
KILROY	600	496E	NEH	77013
KILROY	1300	496J	JC	77029
KILTS DR	200	490J	BH	77024
KILWINNING DR	16800	407Z	NWC	77084
KIM	3600	611X	FS	77545
KIM DR	1	292Y	NCC	77373
KIMBALL	3500	454Y	NEH	77026
KIMBALL DR	4500	613V	NEB	77584
KIMBALL LN	0	656E	NEB	77511
KIMBALL LN	19700	285T	NWC	77447
KIMBALL PLACE	2700	613V	NEB	77584
KIMBALL PLACE	2700	613R	PL	77584
KIMBALL WAY LN	0	375X	NEC	77396
KIMBERCREEK LN	0	328A	NWC	77429
KIMBERLEE	15700	458E	NEC	77049
KIMBERLEY CT	15000	488G	SWH	77079
KIMBERLEY LN	11900	490E	SWH	77024
KIMBERLEY LN	12900	489E	SWH	77079
KIMBERLEY LN	14600	488D	SWH	77079
KIMBERLEY LN	14900	488G	SWH	77079
KIMBERLING CT		249Q	NWC	77375
KIMBERLY DR	3800	616X	PL	77581
KIMBERLY LN	1900	570S	MC	77489
KIMBERLY CROSSING	4200	485U	NEF	77494
KIMBERLY GLEN LN	23200	334A	NCC	77373
KIMBERLY LOCH LN	9800	616K	SEC	77089
KIMBERWICKE CT	22900	292G	NCC	77373
KIMBLE	7800	535K	SEH	77017
KIMBLE LEDGE LN	0	526R	NEF	77407
KIMBLETON CT	2600	488U	SWH	77082
KIMBRO RD	25400	244L	WCO	77447
KIMBROUGH DR	13100	248U	NWC	77375
KIM CLIFF LN		484W	NEF	77494
KIMSTONE LN	8200	330P	NWC	77379
KIMSWICK CT	200	538U	DP	77536
KIMWOOD DR	8700	450V	NWH	77080
KINA RD	0	288P	NWC	77377
KINBROOK DR	2200	489S	SWH	77077
KINCAID DR	5100	614S	NEB	77584
KINCAID FALLS CT	25600	524K	NWF	77406
KINCHEN TRAILS LN	6000	541F	NWH	77092
KINCROSS CT	1500	485L	SWC	77450
KINDALL TATE LN	6500	609X	NEF	77459
KINDELTREE	0	410R	NWH	77040
KINDER LN	9600	573B	SEH	77051
KINDER BLUFF LN	0	328E	NWC	77429
KINDLEBERGER	0	502Q	BT	77520
KINDLE OAKS DR	20100	486G	SWC	77450
KINDLE TREE CIR	9800	411N	NWH	77040
KINDLETREE DR	9500	411N	NWH	77040
KINDLEWOOD DR	8700	529N	SWH	77099
KINDRED	1900	456L	NEC	77049
KING	0	416D	NEC	77044
KING	100	453Q	NEH	77022
KING	1700	541B	BT	77520
KING	1800	454P	NEH	77026
KING	5000	494G	NEH	77020
KING	7700	455N	NEH	77028
KING CIR	12900	369E	NWC	77429
KING CIR	13600	368H	NWC	77429
KING ST	1100	568T	SG	77478
KING, C E PKWY	7400	456G	NEC	77044
KING, C E PKWY	9100	416V	NEC	77044
KING, M L BLVD	4500	534E	SEH	77021
KING, M L BLVD	6400	534W	SEH	77033
KING, M L BLVD	8500	574J	SEH	77048
KING, M L DR	8800	335T	NEH	77338
KING'S SUMMIT DR	6500	526E	NEF	77450
KING'S WAY	4800	330V	NWC	77069
KING ARTHUR	24700	244R	WCO	77447
KING ARTHUR CT	6700	330Q	NWC	77379
KING ARTHURS CT	1	568M	SG	77478
KING ARTHURS CT	3200	613K	PL	77584
KING BIRD DR	29700	288E	NWC	77377
KINGBIRD DR	29700	248W	NWC	77375
KINGBRIAR CIR	1100	292C	NCC	77373
KINGBRIAR CT	1000	292C	NCC	77373
KINGBRIAR DR	23900	292C	NCC	77373
KING CHARLES CT	0	532L	SWH	77030
KING COTTON LN	4100	609R	MC	77459
KINGCOURT WAY	200	298K	NEC	77336
KING CROSSING BLVD	0	445A	NWC	77493
KINGDOM COME LN	0	574K	SEH	77048
KINGDOM COME PLACE	11800	574J	SEH	77048
KINGDOM EDGE DR	21700	296X	SEM	77339
KINGDOM ISLE LN	0	445A	NWC	77493
KING EDWARDS PLACE	400	461Q	BT	77521
KINGFIELD DR	15300	408S	NWC	77084
KINGFISH DR	4300	620G	SB	77586
KINGFISHER	0	571C	SWH	77035
KINGFISHER CT	0	658X	LC	77573
N. KINGFISHER CT	1200	613M	NEB	77584
S. KINGFISHER CT	1300	613M	NEB	77584
KINGFISHER CT	2100	658T	LC	77573
KINGFISHER DR	200	568T	SG	77478
KINGFISHER DR	2600	375K	HM	77396
KINGFISHER DR	4300	531Z	SWH	77035
KINGFISHER DR	5400	531X	SWH	77096
KINGFORD	0	371J	NWC	77066
KINGFORD TRAIL LN	0	526J	NEF	77407
KING GEORGE LN	0	657G	FR	77546
KING HALLOW LN	0	446D	NWC	77449
KING HARBOUR LN	6300	609K	MC	77459
KINGHAVEN	8600	528P	SWC	77083
KINGHURST	10400	529Y	SWH	77099
KING JAMES CT	2700	657D	SEC	77598
KINGLET	4300	531Z	SWH	77035
KINGLET	5400	531X	SWH	77096
KINGMAN DR	1800	570U	MC	77489
KINGMONT KNOLL CT	23900	292C	NCC	77373
KING PARKWAY M H P	0	456C	NEC	77044
KING POINT VIEW LN	0	332E	NWC	77388
KING POST DR	6300	411T	NWH	77088
KING RANCH LN	10000	528S	NEF	77498
KING RICHARD DR	5300	444U	KT	77493
KING RICHARDS	25600	244M	WCO	77447
KINGS CT	100	569V	SF	77477
KINGS CT	17600	367A	CY	77429
KINGS DR	7100	460Y	MN	77521
KINGS RD	17500	249M	NWC	77375
KINGS RD	18600	250J	NWC	77375
KINGS RD	20400	257P	SEM	77357
W. KINGS ARBOR TRAIL	0	337U	NEC	77346
E. KINGS ARBOR TRAIL	0	337U	NEC	77346
KINGS ARBOR TRAIL	0	337U	NEC	77346
KINGS ARMS WAY	1900	445T	NWC	77493
KINGS BARN CT	0	329N	NWC	77375
KINGS BEND DR	0	296X	SEM	77339
KINGSBRIAR CT	21800	485V	NEF	77450
KINGS BRIAR LN	0	407V	NWC	77084
KINGSBRIAR LN	3200	485V	NEF	77450
KINGSBRIDGE LN	12800	488L	SWH	77077
KINGSBRIDGE RD	900	332M	NCC	77073
KINGSBRIDGE MEADOW DR	8200	527R	NEF	77083
KINGSBRIDGE WAY CT	15100	527R	NEF	77083
KINGSBROOK	500	609D	MC	77459
KINGSBROOK LN	2700	610E	MC	77459
KINGSBROOK RD	8200	491A	SWH	77024
KINGSBURG CT	3700	485V	NEF	77450
KINGSBURY	500	616Y	FR	77546
KINGSBURY	4500	533M	SEH	77021
KINGSBURY	4600	534K	SEH	77021
KINGSBURY LN	0	657U	LC	77573
KINGSBURY PARK LN	0	253N	SEM	77386
KINGS CAMP DR	20200	486F	SWC	77450
KINGS CANYON	0	287A	SWM	77355
KINGS CANYON CT	2700	371L	NWC	77067
KINGS CASTLE DR	1400	486L	SWC	77450
KINGS CHAPEL CT	16800	617X	SEC	77546
KINGS CHAPEL RD	2500	617X	SEC	77546

Street Name	Block	Pg/Sq	Loc	Zips
KINGS CHASE DR	12200	416L	NEC	77044
KINGS CLIFF PLACE	0	295R	SEM	77365
KINGS CLOVER CT	20800	337P	NEC	77346
KINGS CLOVER LN	0	337P	NEC	77346
N. KINGSCOTE DR	0	419B	NEC	77532
W. KINGSCOTE DR	16500	419A	NEC	77532
E. KINGSCOTE DR	16500	419B	NEC	77532
KINGSCOURT DR	300	457X	NEC	77015
KINGS COURT DR	2500	537T	PA	77502
KINGS COVE DR	0	337P	NEC	77346
KINGS COVE LN	0	293F	SEM	77386
KINGS CREEK DR	1	336D	NEH	77339
KINGS CREEK TRAIL	1200	569X	MC	77459
KINGS CRESCENT DR	0	296X	SEM	77339
KINGSCREST LN	0	250Y	NWC	77389
KINGS CROSS DR	0	485F	SWC	77450
KINGS CROSSING DR	2800	337B	NEH	77345
KINGS CROSSS TATION	0	532Z	SWH	77045
KINGS CROWN CT	20700	337R	NEC	77346
KINGS CYPRESS LN	15800	326V	NWC	77429
KINGSDALE	4400	538S	PA	77503
KINGSDALE DR	1700	538T	DP	77536
KINGSDOWN DR	25000	250W	NWC	77389
KINGSFIELD CT	0	657Z	LC	77573
KINGSFLOWER CIR	9200	575Z	SEH	77075
KINGSFORD DR	800	486H	SWC	77094
KINGSFORD DR	12700	372M	NCC	77060
KINGS FOREST DR	2300	336D	NEH	77339
KINGS FOREST DR	23200	285A	SWM	77447
KINGS FOREST DR	23400	245W	SWM	77447
KINGS GARDEN CT	0	416L	NEC	77044
KINGSGATE CIR	0	484F	NEF	77494
KINGS GATE CIR	7200	530Q	SWH	77074
KINGSGATE LN	0	484F	NEF	77494
KINGSGATE LN	800	618Z	WB	77058
KINGS GLEN DR	0	337U	NEC	77346
KINGS GROVE DR	11900	416L	NEC	77044
KINGS GUILD LN	21300	296X	SEM	77339
KINGS HARBOR DR	0	337L	NEC	77345
KINGS HARBOUR CT	0	337L	NEC	77345
KINGS HEAD DR	14400	377X	NEC	77044
KINGSHILL DR	0	296T	SEM	77339
KINGS HILL LN	1	337P	NEC	77346
KINGSHIP CT	0	445A	NWC	77493
KINGS LAKE ESTATES BLVD	1	337P	NEC	77346
KINGSLAKE FOREST DR	11800	416L	NEC	77044
KINGSLAND BLVD	0	484F	KT	77494
KINGSLAND BLVD	0	484H	NEF	77494
KINGSLAND BLVD	18000	487A	SWC	77094
KINGSLAND BLVD	18700	486A	SWC	77094
KINGSLAND BLVD	20000	485C	SWC	77450
KINGSLAND BAY LN	0	377K	NEC	77346
KINGS LANDING LN	4600	485S	NEF	77494
KINGSLEY	7300	535N	SEH	77087
KINGSLEY	8000	535P	SEH	77017
KINGSLEY CT	1	245F	SWM	77355
KINGSLEY DR	0	612L	PL	77584
KINGS LODGE DR	2400	297Z	NEH	77345
KINGS LYNN	18000	618Z	WB	77058
KINGSMAN DR	3600	527C	SWC	77082
N. KINGS MANOR DR	26700	296X	SEM	77339
S. KINGS MANOR DR	26800	296X	SEM	77339
KINGS MARCH CT	27100	296X	SEM	77339
KINGSMARK DR	700	486D	SWC	77094
KINGSMARK SPRINGS LN	1100	338F	NEH	77345
KINGS MEADOW DR	10000	528S	NEF	77083
KINGS MEADOW DR	12200	416L	NEC	77044
KINGSMILL DR	13000	568C	SG	77478
N. KINGS MILL LN	0	296T	SEM	77339
KINGS MILL LN	0	296X	SEM	77339
KINGSMILL RD	5200	617W	FR	77546
KINGS MILL CREST DR	0	296T	SEM	77339
KINGS MILL FOREST DR	0	296T	SEM	77339
KINGS MILL PARK DR	0	296T	SEM	77339
KINGS MOUNTAIN DR	3200	297P	NEH	77345
KINGS MOUNTAIN DR	10000	528S	NEF	77083
KINGSNORTH DR	0	329B	NWC	77375
KINGS OAK LN	0	337U	NEC	77346
KINGS PARK LN	17700	618V	SEH	77058
KINGS PARK HOLLOW	0	296X	SEM	77339
KINGS PARK WAY	0	337Q	NEC	77346
KINGSPASS	9400	576W	SEH	77075
KINGS PATH LN	0	416L	NEC	77044
KINGS PEAK WAY	4000	445H	NWC	77449
KINGSPOINT RD	8600	575Z	SEH	77075
KINGSPOINT RD	9200	576P	SEH	77075
KINGS PORT	300	419C	NEC	77532
KINGS PRESERVE CT	0	337P	NEC	77346
KINGSPUR RIDGE DR	26400	524J	NEF	77494
KINGS RANSOM CT	5400	448C	NWC	77041
KINGS RETREAT CIR	0	337B	NEH	77345
KINGSRIDE LN	12100	490A	SWH	77024
KINGSRIDE LN	13300	489A	SWH	77079
KINGS RIDGE RD	4600	611D	SWH	77053
KINGS RIVER BLVD	0	337Q	NEC	77346
KINGS RIVER CIR	0	337M	NEC	77346
KINGS RIVER CT	21400	337M	NEC	77346
KINGS RIVER DR	7500	337M	NEC	77346
KINGS RIVER POINT	0	337M	NEC	77346
KINGSROSE DR	9200	575Z	SEH	77075
KINGS ROW	0	258E	SEM	77357
KINGS ROW	1	370B	NWC	77069
KINGS ROW	200	257G	RF	77357
KINGS ROW	18000	618Z	WB	77058
KINGS TIMBER TRAIL	0	337P	NEC	77346
KINGSTON	2100	492U	SWH	77019
KINGSTON CT	200	538U	DP	77536
KINGSTON CT	2200	609D	MC	77459
KINGSTON DR	3400	657L	FR	77546
KINGSTON BLUFF LN	0	484N	NEF	77494
KINGSTON COVE	1900	659D	LC	77573
KINGSTON COVE LN	14300	488N	SWH	77077
KINGSTON CREEK LN	0	366U	NWC	77433
KINGSTONE DR	0	618E	SEH	77062
KINGSTON FALLS LN	14200	375Y	NEC	77396
KINGSTON FIELD CROSSING		297K	SEM	77365
KINGSTON GLEN LN	0	524C	NEF	77494
KINGSTON GREEN LN	0	373A	NCC	77073
KINGSTON HARBOR CT	0	619M	TL	77586
KINGSTON HARBOR DR	4700	619M	TL	77586
KINGSTON HILL LN	24500	485S	NEF	77494
KINGSTON HOLLOW CT	0	526R	NEF	77407
KINGSTON LAKE CT	0	297F	SEM	77365
KINGSTON POINT LN	12900	572Q	SWH	77047
KINGSTON RIDGE WAY	0	405P	NWC	77493
KINGSTON RIVER LN	13500	417A	NEC	77044
KINGSTON RIVER BEND	0	417A	NEC	77044
KINGSTON SPRINGS CT	0	617E	SEC	77089
KINGSTON TERRACE LN	0	290Q	NWC	77379
KINGSTON TRACE LN	0	488T	SWH	77077
KINGSTON VALE DR	3500	528B	SWH	77082
KINGSTON VALLEY TRAIL	0	405T	NWC	77493

Street Name	Block	Pg/Sq	Loc	Zips
KINGSTON VILLAGE DR	31400	252R	SEM	77386
KINGSTOWN CT	18400	619W	NB	77058
KINGS TRAIL	2200	337F	NEH	77339
KINGSTREE LN	1400	619W	NB	77058
KINGSVALLEY	9300	576W	SEH	77075
KINGS VIEW DR	2000	337F	NEH	77339
KINGSVILLE	9200	490X	SWH	77063
KINGSVILLE PARK DR	9700	528P	SWH	77099
KINGS WALK LN	16900	329Q	NWC	77070
KINGS WALK ROUND	9900	329Q	NWC	77070
KINGSWAY	3500	502K	BT	77521
KINGSWAY CT	3400	337A	NEH	77339
KINGSWAY DR	100	569V	SF	77477
KINGSWAY DR	1500	658Q	LC	77573
KINGSWAY DR	6800	534V	SEH	77087
KINGSWAY PARK LN	0	253N	SEM	77386
KINGSWICK CT	5500	330Y	NWC	77069
KINGSWOOD	3300	451L	NWH	77092
KINGSWORTHY LN	11100	490Q	PP	77024
KINGUSSIE DR	4500	447D	NWC	77084
KING WILLIAM DR	0	539X	LP	77571
KINGWOOD DR	0	538R	DP	77536
KINGWOOD DR	0	298P	NEC	77336
KINGWOOD DR	100	295Z	NEH	77365
KINGWOOD DR	300	336A	NEH	77339
KINGWOOD DR	4200	337A	NEH	77345
KINGWOOD DR	5000	297Z	NEH	77345
KINGWOOD EXECUTIVE DR	0	335D	NEH	77339
N. KINGWOOD FOREST DR	0	297N	NEH	77339
KINGWOOD GLEN DR	6000	337U	NEC	77346
KINGWOOD GREENS DR	1	337F	NEH	77339
KINGWOOD MEDICAL DR	0	335D	NEH	77339
KINGWOOD PLACE DR	0	295V	NEH	77365
KINGWOOD PLACE DR	23600	335D	NEH	77339
KINGWOOD VILLAS CT	1	337E	NEH	77339
KINKAID	3300	454B	NEH	77093
KINKAID CIR	0	454C	NEH	77093
KINKAID MEADOWS LN	0	377F	NEC	77346
KINKAID SCHOOL RD	200	490Q	PP	77024
KINLEY LN	1100	452K	NWH	77018
KINLEY CREEK LN	0	445W	NWC	77493
KINLOCH DR	4200	447H	NWC	77084
KINMONT CT	16000	330T	NWC	77379
KINNEL LN	9000	289R	NWC	77375
KINNERTON	0	614Y	PL	77584
KINNEY	7000	534R	SEH	77087
KINNEY RD	9600	529U	SWH	77099
KINNEY POINT LN	16800	332Q	NCC	77073
KINO CT	1	251L	WD	77380
KINROSE DR	4400	578F	PA	77505
KINROSS LN	24200	485S	NEF	77494
KINRUSH CT	16200	407D	NWC	77095
KINSALE VALLEY LN	17900	373K	NCC	77060
KINSALE VALLEY LN	17900	373K	NCC	77060
WICKLOW MEADOW LN	17900	373J	NCC	77060
WICKLOW MEADOW LN	17900	373J	NCC	77060
KINSBOURNE LN	14100	332W	NWC	77014
KINSBOURNE LN	14100	372A	NWC	77014
KINSDALE AVE	2400	659X	DI	77539
KINSDALE CT	11600	371M	NWC	77067
KINSDALE CROSSING	0	575V	SEH	77075
KINSFILED CT	0	657Z	LC	77573
KINSLEY DR	4200	578E	PA	77505
KINSLOWE DR	0	409G	NWC	77064
KINSMAN RD	0	457K	NEC	77049
KINSMAN RD	7400	457J	NEC	77049
KINSTON DR	1400	659W	LC	77573
KINTYRE DR	5000	447D	NWC	77084
KINTYRE POINT RD	16100	407H	NWC	77095
KINWICKE CT	3000	485T	NEF	77494
KIOWA	4200	577F	PA	77504
KIOWA	18000	295F	SEM	77365
KIOWA CIR	4700	461S	NEC	77521
KIOWA CT	1200	538Q	DP	77536
KIOWA RIVER LN	17100	367X	NWC	77095
KIOWA TIMBERS DR	5600	337T	NEC	77346
KIP	0	338S	NEC	77346
KIP LN	800	247K	SWM	77362
KIPLANDS CT	0	331U	NWC	77014
KIPLANDS BEND DR	0	331U	NWC	77014
KIPLANDS WAY DR	0	331U	NWC	77014
KIPLING	600	493S	SWH	77006
KIPLING	1700	492V	SWH	77098
KIPLING	3500	492T	SWH	77027
KIPLING DR	2100	502S	BT	77520
KIPLING GLEN CT	0	609T	NEF	77479
KIPLING OAK DR	0	334L	NCC	77373
KIPP AVE	200	620Y	KE	77565
KIPPER CIR	4700	578J	PA	77505
KIPPER LN	21900	256Z	SEM	77357
KIPPERS DR	0	331U	NWC	77014
KIPP WAY	10100	529U	SWH	77099
KIRBY	100	619L	TL	77586
KIRBY DR	0	572Z	PL	77047
KIRBY DR	0	612D	PL	77047
KIRBY DR	0	612M	PL	77584
KIRBY DR	800	492Q	SWH	77019
KIRBY DR	1800	612V	PL	77584
KIRBY DR	2600	492Q	SWH	77098
KIRBY DR	5300	532C	WU	77005
KIRBY DR	6800	532Q	SWH	77030
KIRBY DR	7900	532Q	SWH	77054
KIRBY BEND	0	619D	PA	77586
KIRBY COMMONS DR	0	612R	PL	77584
KIRBY HILL CT	11800	366R	NWC	77433
KIRBY LAKE LN	0	619D	PA	77586
KIRBY OAKS DR	4200	619G	TL	77586
KIRBY PLACE LN	1400	619H	PA	77586
KIRBY RANCH CT	0	366Z	NWC	77433
KIRBYS KNACK DR	0	366X	NWC	77433
KIRBY SPRINGS CT	2000	612H	PL	77584
KIRBYVILLE	6600	534T	SEH	77033
KIRBYWOODS DR	0	619H	TL	77586
KIRK	0	577X	SEH	77034
KIRK	1200	498C	CV	77530
KIRK	2100	494B	NEH	77026
KIRKALDY DR	100	457Y	NEC	77015
KIRKASPEN DR	10000	616A	SEC	77089
KIRKBEND DR	10800	576X	SEC	77089
KIRKBLUFF DR	10000	616A	SEC	77089
KIRKBRIAR DR	11800	576X	SEH	77089
KIRKBROOK DR	8300	615D	SEC	77089
KIRKBRUSH DR	10900	576X	SEC	77089
KIRKBUD DR	10900	576X	SEC	77089
KIRKBY DR	8800	527R	NEF	77083
KIRKCHAPEL CT	9300	329M	NWC	77379
KIRKCHAPEL DR	17000	329M	NWC	77379
KIRKDALE DR	9900	576X	SEC	77089
KIRKFAIR DR	10600	616A	SEC	77089
KIRKFAIR DR	10800	576W	SEC	77089
KIRKFALLS DR	9700	576X	SEC	77089
KIRKFIELD LN	14900	412D	NEH	77060

Street Name	Block	Pg/Sq	Loc	Zips
KIRK FOREST CT	18000	376D	NEC	77346
KIRKGARD DR	12200	572L	SWH	77045
KIRKGLADE CT	7100	407R	NWC	77095
KIRKGLEN DR	9900	576X	SEH	77089
KIRKGREEN DR	10500	576X	SEC	77089
KIRKHALL DR	10400	576T	SEH	77089
KIRKHAM LN	0	657Y	LC	77573
KIRKHAM LN	8100	335N	NCC	77338
KIRKHILL DR	10200	576X	SEH	77089
KIRKHOLLOW DR	11400	576X	SEH	77089
KIRKHOLM DR	11600	576T	SEH	77089
KIRKLAND DR	8700	575Z	SEC	77089
KIRKLAND DR	9000	576W	SEC	77089
KIRKLAND OAKS LN	0	407C	NWC	77095
KIRKLAND WOODS DR	0	368X	NWC	77095
KIRKLANE DR	10400	576T	SEH	77089
KIRKLEIGH LN	9100	329M	NWC	77379
KIRKMEAD DR	10800	576X	SEC	77089
KIRKMEADOW DR	11400	576X	SEH	77089
KIRKMONT DR	8700	575Z	SEC	77089
KIRKMONT DR	9000	576W	SEC	77089
KIRKNOLL DR	11800	576X	SEH	77089
KIRKPARK DR	11100	576X	SEC	77089
KIRKPATRICK BLVD	6800	455N	NEH	77028
KIRKPATRICK WAY	0	609P	MC	77459
KIRKPLUM DR	10000	616A	SEC	77089
KIRKRIDGE DR	10900	576X	SEC	77089
KIRKSAGE CT	10500	616A	SEC	77089
KIRKSHIRE DR	9900	576X	SEC	77089
KIRKSIDE DR	10600	531W	SWH	77096
KIRKSIDE DR	11100	571A	SWH	77035
KIRKSTALL DR	200	372B	NWC	77090
KIRKSTONE DR	9100	329G	NWC	77379
KIRKSTONE MANOR DR	9500	329D	NWC	77379
KIRKSTONE TERRACE		289Y	NWC	77379
KIRKTON DR	9500	368W	NWC	77095
KIRKTON MOOR DR	17100	527W	NEF	77407
KIRKTOWN DR	10800	576X	SEC	77089
KIRKVALE DR	9900	576W	SEC	77089
KIRKVALE DR	10300	616A	SEC	77089
KIRKVALLEY DR	11400	576X	SEH	77089
KIRKVILLE DR	8300	615D	SEC	77089
KIRKVILLE DR	9400	616A	SEC	77089
KIRKVILLE DR	9700	576X	SEH	77089
KIRKWAY DR	11700	576X	SEH	77089
KIRKWELL DR	10800	576X	SEC	77089
KIRKWELL MANOR CT	10500	329B	NWC	77379
KIRKWOOD	500	570S	MC	77489
KIRKWOOD	800	570S	SF	77477
KIRKWOOD	6200	453Q	NEH	77022
KIRKWOOD CT	100	568V	SG	77478
S. KIRKWOOD DR	1100	489S	SWH	77077
S. KIRKWOOD DR	4000	529E	SWH	77072
S. KIRKWOOD DR	8300	529N	SWH	77099
S. KIRKWOOD DR	11500	569F	SF	77477
N. KIRKWOOD RD	100	489E	SWH	77079
N. KIRKWOOD RD	1000	449W	NWH	77043
KIRKWREN CT	10000	616A	SEC	77089
KIRKWREN DR	9900	576W	SEC	77089
KIRKWREN DR	10300	616A	SEC	77089
KIRKWYN DR	11400	576X	SEH	77089
KIRLOCH POINT	0	329G	NWC	77379
KIRSTON DR	6100	290C	NWC	77389
KIRWICK DR	10900	490M	HC	77024
KIRWIN LN	11000	409Y	NWC	77041
KISH LN	9200	573B	SEH	77051
KISKA LN	0	572L	SWH	77045
KISLING ST	0	533F	SWH	77021
KISMET LN	2600	449M	NWH	77043
KISSING CAMEL CT	2700	609H	MC	77459
KIT	9700	531T	SWH	77096
KITA CT	18600	295F	SEM	77365
KITCHENER	11000	413Q	NCC	77093
KITCHEN HILL LN	3800	609A	SG	77479
KITE HILL DR	7200	408Q	NWC	77041
KITMORE DR	8900	529Q	SWH	77099
KITTANSETT CIR	2500	485R	NEF	77450
KITTATINNY PLACE	0	250Q	NWC	77389
KITTEN LN	0	381W	NEC	77532
KITTIWAKE CT	1	251R	WD	77380
KITTIWAKE CT	800	568T	SG	77478
KITTREDGE DR	0	335N	NCC	77338
KITTRELL	9900	576J	SEH	77034
KITTRIDGE	5400	454M	NEH	77028
KITTY	1100	538U	DP	77536
KITTY	1300	570J	SF	77477
KITTY LN	12300	496Q	GP	77015
KITTY BROOK DR	10700	530Y	SWH	77071
KITTY BROOK DR	11200	570C	SWH	77071
KITTYCREST LN	1100	373U	NCC	77032
KITTY DALE DR	14200	375W	NEC	77396
W. KITTY HAWK	1	524J	NWF	77406
E. KITTY HAWK	1	524J	NWF	77406
KITTY HAWK	15000	322T	WCO	77484
KITTY HAWK DR	2000	570W	MC	77489
KITTY HOLLOW DR	4600	610N	MC	77459
KITTY HOLLOW LN	9600	527Q	NEF	77083
KITZMAN CT	0	327F	NWC	77429
KITZMAN RD	16000	327C	NWC	77429
KIWI PLACE	0	334Q	NCC	77388
KLAMATH LN	1000	331H	NWC	77090
KLAMATH FALLS CT	5900	408Y	NWC	77041
KLAMATH FALLS DR	13200	408Z	NWC	77041
KLEB RD	0	330A	NWC	77379
KLEB RD	18000	324D	NWC	77447
KLEBERG	5400	491U	SWH	77056
KLEBERG CT	0	612V	PL	77584
KLEBERG PLACE DR	10800	409B	NWC	77064
KLECKLEY DR	9900	576P	SEH	77075
KLEE CIR	17200	330K	NWC	77379
KLEEWOOD DR	0	409F	NWC	77064
KLEIN	0	288G	TB	77375
S. KLEIN CIR	6900	411J	NWC	77088
N. KLEIN CIR	6900	411J	NWC	77088
KLEIN DR	30100	286C	SWM	77355
KLEINBROOK CT	12200	371J	NWC	77066
KLEINBROOK DR	5000	371J	NWC	77066
KLEIN CEMETERY RD	6300	330C	NWC	77379
KLEIN CHURCH RD	18400	331A	NWC	77379
KLEINDALE CT	5000	371J	NWC	77066
KLEINDALE DR	12100	371J	NWC	77066
KLEINFIELDS CT	4900	371N	NWC	77066
KLEINFIELDS DR	11800	371N	NWC	77066
KLEIN FOREST	16600	330L	NWC	77379
KLEIN FOREST BLVD	0	371E	NWC	77066
KLEIN GARDEN DR	0	371J	NWC	77066
KLEINGATE	12400	371J	NWC	77066
KLEINGREEN LN	7500	330Q	NWC	77379
KLEINMEADOW CT	4800	371J	NWC	77066
KLEINMEADOW DR	11900	371J	NWC	77066
KLEIN OAK DR	0	290G	NWC	77389
KLEIN TERRACE LN	20900	290U	NWC	77379

Street Name	Block	Pg/Sq	Loc	Zips
KLEINWAY DR	4700	371J	NWC	77066
KLEINWOOD DR	16200	330Q	NWC	77379
KLEPPEL RD	9900	249Y	NWC	77375
KLIMER WAY	1600	488K	SWH	77077
KLINGAMANS WAY	0	285L	NWC	77447
KLONDIKE	8800	575M	SEH	77075
KLUGE RD	12000	328Y	NWC	77429
KLUGE RD	12500	368B	NWC	77429
KLUGEBEND CIR	0	368B	NWC	77429
KLUGECORNER LN	0	368B	NWC	77429
KLUGELAKE LN	0	368B	NWC	77429
KNAPP RD	3100	615A	PL	77581
KNEBEL LN	0	282H	NWC	77484
KNEBEL RD	31000	282G	NWC	77484
KNICKERBOCKER	4800	531Y	SWH	77035
KNIGGE CEMETERY RD	12000	368P	NWC	77429
KNIGHT	800	453H	NEH	77022
KNIGHT	2200	453H	NEH	77093
KNIGHT LN	3300	502K	BT	77521
KNIGHT RD	0	610Y	MC	77545
KNIGHT RD	7500	532R	SWH	77054
KNIGHT RD	9400	532V	SWH	77045
KNIGHT HOLLOW CT	23300	485T	NEF	77494
KNIGHT LAKE CT	4500	526X	NEF	77406
KNIGHTON CIR	600	617B	SEH	77034
KNIGHT QUEST DR	0	289P	NWC	77375
KNIGHTRIDER DR	16300	330T	NWC	77379
KNIGHTS CIR	2500	569V	SF	77477
KNIGHTS CT	0	501E	BT	77521
KNIGHTS CT	900	656H	FR	77546
KNIGHTS CT	7000	609U	MC	77459
KNIGHTS DR	9700	408D	NWC	77065
KNIGHTS BLOOM LN	0	332V	NCC	77073
KNIGHTS BRANCH	0	366Y	NWC	77433
KNIGHTS BRIDGE LN	800	618Y	WB	77058
KNIGHTSBROOK LN	21600	445M	NWC	77449
KNIGHTS COVE DR	22000	296X	SEM	77339
KNIGHTS CREST DR	0	528U	SWH	77083
KNIGHTS GLEN LN	0	485T	NEF	77494
KNIGHTS HILL CT	12200	408D	NWC	77065
KNIGHTS HOLLOW CT	0	484U	NEF	77494
KNIGHTSLAND	0	527R	NEF	77083
KNIGHTS MANOR LN	0	615H	PL	77089
KNIGHTSRIDGE LN	19500	486M	SWC	77094
KNIGHTS TOWER CT	0	296X	SEM	77339
KNIGHTS TOWER DR	0	296X	SEM	77339
KNIGHTS WAY DR	13400	528T	SWC	77083
KNIGHTS WAY DR	14700	527R	NEF	77083
KNIGHTWICK DR	1700	452S	NWH	77008
KNIGHTWOOD	5200	414V	NEH	77016
KNIGHTWOOD CT	10600	414V	NEH	77016
KNIGHTWOOD FOREST DR	8000	411L	NWC	77088
KNIPP CT	100	490P	SWH	77024
KNIPP RD	1	490K	BH	77024
KNIPP FOREST	300	490K	BH	77024
KNIPP OAKS	400	490K	BH	77024
KNIPPWOOD LN	11900	490F	BH	77024
KNOBBLEY OAK CT	0	369S	NWC	77070
KNOBBY KNOLL DR	5600	451B	NWH	77092
KNOBBY PINES DR	0	524A	NEF	77494
KNOB CREEK CT	1800	618B	SEH	77062
KNOBCREST CT	12700	372M	NCC	77060
KNOBCREST DR	100	372M	NCC	77060
KNOBCREST DR	11600	369A	NWC	77070
KNOBCREST DR	12000	368D	NWC	77070
KNOB HILL	3300	538U	DP	77536
KNOB HILL AVE	7200	578B	PA	77505
KNOB HILL ST	0	615U	PL	77581
KNOB HILL LAKE LN	0	377A	NEC	77346
KNOB HOLLOW DR	600	498A	CV	77530
KNOBLOCK	2300	534F	SEH	77023
KNOB MOUNTAIN TRAIL	0	415X	NWH	77078
KNOBOAK CIR	1900	450S	NWH	77080
KNOBOAK DR	9800	450S	NWH	77080
KNOBOAK DR	10200	449U	NWH	77043
KNOB PINES CT	0	250V	NWC	77389
KNOCHE DR	16800	376G	NEC	77396
KNOCKOMIE CT	9300	407D	NWC	77095
KNODELL	2900	454W	NEH	77026
KNOLEWOOD LN	0	614S	PL	77584
KNOLL	1700	450V	NWH	77080
KNOLL	2500	450Q	NWH	77080
W. KNOLL	6800	454H	NEH	77028
W. KNOLL	7300	455E	NEH	77028
KNOLL DR	19700	257K	SEM	77357
KNOLL ACRES	27600	258P	SEM	77357
KNOLL ARBOR CT	0	457G	NEC	77049
KNOLL BEND LN	10500	369P	NWC	77070
KNOLLBLOSSOM LN	0	525M	NEF	77407
KNOLLBRIAR LN	7100	525H	NEF	77407
KNOLLBRIDGE LN	6601	290T	NWC	77379
KNOLLBROOK LN	2100	292R	NCC	77373
KNOLLBROOK LN	2400	293N	NCC	77373
KNOLL CLIFF CT	7400	408N	NWC	77095
KNOLL CREEK PLACE	0	446V	NWC	77449
KNOLLCREST	12800	496H	NEH	77015
KNOLLCREST	13000	497E	NEH	77015
KNOLLCREST LN	0	613T	NEB	77584
KNOLL DALE CT	19100	326Y	NWC	77429
KNOLLE LN	25500	339E	NEC	77336
KNOLL FOREST DR	8600	335N	NCC	77338
KNOLL FORREST	300	659H	LC	77573
KNOLL GLEN DR	3900	527D	SWC	77082
KNOLL LAKE DR	15700	408J	NWC	77095
KNOLL LAKE DR	22000	485M	SWC	77450
KNOLL MANOR DR	3000	297X	NEH	77345
KNOLL MILL LN	0	484X	NEF	77494
KNOLL OAKS LN	0	253N	SEM	77386
KNOLL PINES CT	1	251F	WD	77381
KNOLLRIDGE CT	16200	611B	SWH	77053
KNOLL SHADOWS LN	2500	445R	NWC	77449
KNOLLS LANDING	0	407M	NWC	77095
KNOLLS LODGE CT	7700	408J	NWC	77095
KNOLLS LODGE DR	15800	408J	NWC	77095
KNOLLS SPRING DR	0	486K	SWC	77450
KNOLLS SPRING TRAIL	20300	486K	SWC	77450
KNOLL TERRACE DR	4200	297N	NEH	77339
KNOLL TRACE LN	16800	617X	SEC	77546
KNOLLVIEW DR	6100	290C	NWC	77389
KNOLLWEST DR	3200	488Y	SWH	77082
KNOLLWEST DR	6100	528G	SWH	77072
KNOLLWICK CT	4100	572W	SWH	77053
KNOLLWOOD	2000	619V	LC	77565
KNOLLWOOD DR	3600	492N	SWH	77019
KNOLLWOOD TRAIL	6000	334E	NCC	77373
KNOTTED OAK CT	18300	255S	SEM	77365
KNOTTINGHILL DR	13500	568G	SG	77478
KNOTTY CHESTNUT ST	15000	328J	NWC	77429
KNOTTY ELMWOOD TRAIL	800	618J	SEH	77062
KNOTTY GLEN LN	12900	528L	SWH	77072
KNOTTY GREEN DR	18200	447B	NWC	77084
KNOTTYNOLD LN	3900	572S	SWH	77053

Street Name	Block	Pg/Sq	Loc	Zips
KNOTTYNOLD LN	4600	571V	SWH	77053
KNOTTY OAKS TRAIL	2600	572L	SWH	77045
KNOTTY OAKS TRAIL	4600	571M	SWH	77045
KNOTTY OAKS TRAIL	15500	246V	SWM	77355
KNOTTY PINE CIR	1500	616S	PL	77581
KNOTTY PINE TRAIL	11700	415L	NEC	77050
KNOTTY POST LN	6000	334A	NCC	77373
KNOTTY WOOD DR	6000	411W	NWH	77092
KNOTWOOD CT	0	250Q	NWC	77389
KNOTWOOD PLACE	0	249C	SWM	77382
KNOWLTON RD	900	501V	BT	77520
KNOX	1	492L	SWH	77007
KNOX	3100	576D	PA	77504
KNOX	5600	452C	NWH	77091
KNOX	7200	412P	NWH	77088
W. KNOX DR	21100	296N	SEM	77365
E. KNOX DR	21500	296P	SEM	77365
KNOX ESTATE DR	25600	524K	NWF	77406
KNOX PRAIRIE CT	0	366Z	NWC	77433
KNOXVILLE	3900	533Y	SEH	77051
KNOXVILLE DR	2500	658T	LC	77573
KNOXVILLE RUN	0	578D	LP	77571
KNOXVILLE RUN	8900	578D	LP	77571
KNOXWOOD	8800	454F	NEH	77016
KNURLED OAK LN	8200	329H	NWC	77379
KNUTE	6000	455Q	NEH	77028
KOALA DR	8700	575E	SEH	77061
KOBACK CORNERS	22900	333B	NCC	77373
S. KOBAYASHI DR	0	658B	WB	77598
N. KOBAYASHI DR	0	618W	WB	77598
KOBI CT	3000	331P	NWC	77068
KOBI PARK CT	23200	292F	NCC	77373
KOBS RD	21800	287K	NWC	77377
KOBUK VALLEY CIR	0	377J	NEC	77346
KOCH LN	0	448K	NWH	77084
KODES CLAY CT	6500	330R	NWC	77379
KODIAC	5200	291A	NWC	77389
KODIAK CT	2600	371L	NWC	77067
KODY RIDGE CT	0	576R	SEH	77034
KOEHLER	3700	492H	SWH	77007
KOENIG	9900	577N	SEH	77034
KOESTER	8300	409L	JV	77040
KOFA DR	0	658X	LC	77573
KOHLE SPRINGS LN	0	406C	NWC	77433
KOINM	0	375B	HM	77338
KOINM	14000	374X	NCC	77032
KOKOMO	900	497F	NEH	77015
KOLB	4000	492H	NWH	77007
KOLB RD	100	536X	SEH	77017
KOLB RD	200	536X	PA	77502
KOLB RD	300	536X	SH	77587
S. KOLBE CIR	11200	368N	NWC	77429
S. KOLBE DR	11000	368N	NWC	77429
N. KOLBE DR	11700	368N	NWC	77429
W. KOLBE LN	0	450R	NEH	77080
KOLBE BEND LN	0	450R	NEH	77080
KOLBE GROVE LN	0	450R	NEH	77080
KOLBE REACH LN	0	450R	NEH	77080
KOLBE RUN LN	0	450R	NEH	77080
KOLBE SPUR DR	14500	368S	NWC	77429
KOLFAHL	1800	534B	SEH	77023
KOLYMA DR	19300	294D	SEM	77365
KONA CAY DR	11900	456C	NEC	77044
KOPMAN DR	6800	574D	SEH	77061
KORENEK	0	613Z	NEB	77584
KORENEK	13300	414D	NEC	77039
KORFF DR	500	412H	NEH	77037
KORPINK	11400	414N	NCC	77093
KOTAR CT	300	332B	NWC	77388
KOTTAYAM DR	0	570W	MC	77477
E. KOWIS	300	413S	NEH	77037
KOWIS	1400	413V	NCC	77093
KOWIS	2400	414S	NCC	77093
KPRC		611E	NEF	77053
KRACHER SPRINGS DR	0	376S	NEC	77396
KRAHN RD	20100	291T	NWC	77388
KRAMPOTA LN	3800	461A	NEC	77532
KRANSBURG CT	0	407J	NWC	77433
KRANSBURG RANCH DR	7200	407N	NWC	77433
KRANSBURG RIDGE CT	0	295V	SEM	77365
KRANSBURG RIDGE DR	0	296S	SEM	77365
KRANSBURG RIDGE DR	0	295V	SEM	77365
KRANSBURY LN	0	407C	NWC	77095
KRAUSE DR	6600	571W	SWH	77489
KRAYOLA LN	16300	330P	NWC	77379
KREBBS CT	0	612Z	NEB	77578
KREINHOP RD	4000	291T	NWC	77388
KREMMER DR	15000	497D	NEC	77530
KRENEK	0	421E	NEC	77532
KRENEK DR	100	419M	CB	77532
KRENEK DR	1200	420K	NEC	77532
N. KRENEK LN	0	420K	NEC	77532
KRESS	100	494H	NEH	77020
KRESS	3900	454Z	NEH	77026
KREZDORN RD	27000	284A	WCO	77447
KREZDORN RD	28000	283D	WCO	77447
KRISDALE CT	5400	407X	NWC	77084
KRISFORD CT	0	609T	NEF	77479
KRIST DR	1100	451W	SV	77055
KRISTA CT	16000	458S	NEC	77049
KRISTAL LN	0	258F	SEM	77357
KRISTEN	3500	460R	NEC	77562
KRISTEN CT	5200	334E	NCC	77373
KRISTEN FALLS DR	21400	296J	SEM	77365
KRISTEN OAKS CT	19300	337X	NEC	77346
KRISTEN PARK CT	19300	337T	NEC	77346
KRISTEN PARK LN	6000	337T	NEC	77346
KRISTEN PINE DR	19200	337T	NEC	77346
KRISTEN WAY	0	577C	PA	77505
KRISTIN DR	9200	530W	SWH	77031
KRISTINA CT	11900	616F	SEC	77089
KRISTINA WAY	0	539N	DP	77536
KRISTINE DR	34500	247K	SWM	77362
KRISTIN LEE CT	4000	371B	NWC	77014
KRISTIN LEE LN	3800	371B	NWC	77014
KRISWOOD DR	1600	372E	NWC	77014
KROLCZYK	0	286Q	NWC	77377
KRONE CT	9900	376S	NEC	77396
KRUEGER	0	324E	HK	77447
KRUEGER	0	618H	SEH	77062
KRUEGER	17000	324E	NWC	77447
KRUEGER RD	7300	534S	SEH	77033
KRUG RD	16700	287F	NWC	77377
KRUG GLEN CT	0	328M	NWC	77377
KRUG HOLLOW LN	0	328M	NWC	77377
KRYSTAL CT	3900	502J	BT	77521
KRYSTAL'S COVE WAY	0	419D	NEC	77532
KRYSTIN	0	542K	BT	77520
KRYSTINE DR	10200	463G	MB	77520
KUBE CT	16000	409L	JV	77040
KUBIN RD	0	532N	NEC	77532
KUDZU DR	0	293F	SEM	77386

Street Name	Block	Pg/Sq	Loc	Zips
KUEBEN LN	15800	571W	SWH	77489
KUESTER	2500	492V	SWH	77006
KUHLMAN	5600	533H	SEH	77021
KUHLMAN RD	700	491E	HC	77024
KUHN	0	492L	SWH	77007
KULDELL DR	5400	531N	SWH	77096
KULDELL DR	5800	531N	SWH	77074
KULKARNI ST	4400	572E	SWH	77045
KUMQUAT	0	574Q	SEH	77048
KUMQUAT CT	0	417R	NEC	77044
KUNKLE DR	0	448F	NWH	77084
KUNZ LN	11300	574K	SEH	77048
KUNZ RD	0	448K	NWH	77084
KURLAND DR	11900	576V	SEH	77034
KURT LN	15200	375S	NEH	77396
KURTELL LN	12500	368J	NWC	77429
KURTH CANYON CT	0	660J	LC	77573
KURY LN	6200	452X	NWH	77008
KURZPOINT DR	0	526W	NEF	77469
KURZ POINTE CT	6000	406T	NWC	77449
KUYKENDAHL	0	332W	NWC	77090
KUYKENDAHL RD	12400	372B	NWC	77090
KUYKENDAHL RD	13900	331V	NWC	77090
KUYKENDAHL RD	15800	331V	NWC	77068
KUYKENDAHL RD	17200	331A	NWC	77379
KUYKENDAHL RD	19400	291W	NWC	77379
KUYKENDAHL RD	20500	290R	NWC	77379
KUYKENDAHL RD	22400	290A	NWC	77389
KUYKENDAHL RD	23100	290A	NWC	77375
KUYKENDAHL RD	24200	289D	NWC	77375
KUYKENDAHL RD	24500	249Z	NWC	77375
KUYKENDAHL RD	26000	250N	NWC	77375
KUYKENDAHL RD	28000	250B	WD	77381
KWIK KOPY LN	1	367M	NWC	77429
KYACK CT	18500	378A	NEC	77346
KYLA CIR	5300	444L	KT	77493
KYLE	300	568N	SG	77478
KYLE	4300	493W	SWH	77006
KYLE CT	3200	614T	PL	77584
KYLE BEND LN	0	444P	KT	77493
KYLE CANYON DR	0	406C	NWC	77433
KYLE CHAPMAN DR	0	530M	SWH	77074
KYLE CHASE CT	800	292G	NCC	77373
KYLE CREST TRAIL	16200	326P	NWC	77433
KYLER COVE LN	0	524F	NEF	77494
KYLER OAKS PLACE	0	449U	NWH	77043
KYLE TRAIL CT	7300	527J	NEF	77407
KYLEWICK DR	12600	571G	SWH	77085
KYLIE CT	2300	293F	SEM	77386
KYLIE SPRINGS LN	5100	371N	NWC	77066
KYNNDAL SHORE DR	0	253X	SEM	77386
KYREN LN	25800	250S	NWC	77389
W. L	100	580F	LP	77571

L

Street Name	Block	Pg/Sq	Loc	Zips
L	4100	529A	SWH	77072
L ST	0	576Q	SEH	77034
N. L STREET	9700	539V	LP	77571
L, AVENUE	100	501S	BT	77520
L, AVENUE	500	576C	SH	77587
L, AVENUE	5100	494Q	SEH	77011
L, AVENUE	7500	495S	SEH	77012
E. L, AVENUE	9100	535C	SEH	77012
LA ARBRE LN	21000	291U	NWC	77388
LA AVENIDA DR	15800	618N	SEH	77062
LABARRE DR	11400	368P	NWC	77429
LABCO	1200	495J	NEH	77029
LA BELLA MANOR	0	525Z	NEF	77406
LABELLE LN	12700	496D	NEC	77015
LABELLE LN	12900	497A	NEC	77015
LABRADOR DR	13700	572Y	SWC	77047
LA BRANCH	100	493Q	DT	77002
LA BRANCH	800	493Q	DT	77010
LA BRANCH	1200	493Q	DT	77002
LA BRANCH	2300	493U	SWH	77004
LA BREA	8000	527L	NEF	77083
LABURNAME CT	0	289Q	NWC	77375
LA CABANA DR	15600	618N	SEH	77062
LA CASA LN	15600	618N	SEH	77062
LACE BARK PINE DR	0	250V	NWC	77389
LACEBROOK LN	0	612N	PL	77545
LACE FLOWER DR	0	329L	NWC	77379
LACEWING LN	1700	371R	NWC	77067
LACEWING PLACE	1	251X	WD	77380
LACEWOOD CT	2900	613T	NEB	77584
LACEWOOD LN	1	490L	PP	77024
LACEY LN	16500	570E	MC	77489
LACEY RD	10800	329F	NWC	77375
LACEY CREST DR	12500	369L	NWC	77070
LACEYLAND LN	20000	446X	NWC	77449
E. LACEY OAK CIR	2000	251U	WD	77380
W. LACEY OAK CIR	2100	251U	WD	77380
LACEY OAK DR	6100	578J	PA	77505
LACEY OAK MEADOW DR	0	484Z	NEF	77494
LACING CT	16900	379X	NEC	77532
LACK LN	12300	574X	BK	77581
LACOMBE LN	0	289R	NWC	77375
LA CONCHA LN	1300	532Q	SWH	77054
LA CONCHA LN	13500	528L	SWC	77083
LACONIA CT	0	568B	SG	77498
LA COSTA	3200	609H	MC	77459
LA COSTA LN	14900	488G	SWH	77079
LACOSTE LOVE CT	6200	330M	NWC	77379
LA COTE CIR	20700	291Y	NWC	77388
LA COTE LN	20700	291U	NWC	77388
LACREEK LN	5200	331E	NWC	77379
LA CREMA	0	609Z	MC	77459
S. LA CROSSE	10300	496E	JC	77029
N. LA CROSSE	10300	496E	JC	77029
LA CROSSE	10500	496E	JC	77029
LACY	5400	492L	SWH	77007
LACY DR	1300	501V	BT	77520
LACY HILL DR	7000	530J	SWH	77036
LACY WILLOW CT	8800	290J	NWC	77375
LADBROKE LN	12300	414E	NCC	77039
LADBROOK DR	2000	336B	NEH	77339
LADDINGFORD LN	0	657Y	LC	77573
LADEN PINES CT	0	290V	NWC	77379
LADERA DR	6200	527H	SWC	77083
LADERA DR	6300	528E	SWC	77083
LADERA LN	0	609Y	NEF	77459
LADIES TRESSES DR	0	524H	NEF	77494
LADIN DR	2000	413H	NCC	77039
LADINO RD	10500	368S	NWC	77429
LADINO RUN	14700	327Z	CY	77429
LADIU	0	414E	NCC	77039
LADONA CT	0	660G	GCO	77565
LA DUE LN	17800	381N	NEC	77532
LADY	7600	533P	SEH	77021
LADY ANNE DR	12900	377X	NEC	77044
LADY BIRD LAKE CT	0	366N	NWC	77433

Street Name	Block	Pg/Sq	Loc	Zips
LADYBIRD LANDING DR		367N	NWC	77433
LADYBUG CT	24200	295K	SEM	77365
LADYBUG DR	10500	369X	NWC	77064
LADYBUG LN	0	295K	SEM	77365
LADY ELLEN DR	25200	244M	WCO	77447
LADY FERN	8900	369V	NWC	77064
N. LADY FERN LN	1200	332R	NCC	77073
W. LADY FERN LN	16300	332R	NCC	77073
LADY GUINEVERE CIR	24600	245N	WCO	77447
LADY JANE CT	12600	377X	NEC	77044
LADY LESLIE LN	2200	615Q	PL	77581
LADY SHERY LN	0	328N	NWC	77429
LADY SLIPPER DR	0	411D	NWC	77038
LA ENTRADA DR	7000	527L	NEF	77083
LA ESCALONA DR	0	660G	LC	77573
LA ESTANCIA LN	0	452D	NEH	77093
LAFAYETTE	1	501Z	BT	77520
LAFAYETTE	1300	536T	PA	77502
LAFAYETTE	2800	532B	WU	77005
LAFAYETTE	4300	531M	BL	77401
LAFAYETTE CT	2500	620K	SB	77586
LAFAYETTE LN	100	658L	LC	77573
LAFAYETTE HOLLOW LN	17200	377J	NEC	77346
LAFFERTY RD	1100	537N	PA	77502
LAFFERTY RD	1200	536R	PA	77502
LAFFERTY RD	3100	576D	PA	77504
LAFFERTY OAKS DR	10100	495H	NEH	77013
LAFFERTY OAKS DR	10300	496F	NEH	77013
LAFFITE DR	14200	368T	NWC	77429
LAFITTE CT	21800	245V	SWM	77355
LA FLEUR LN	3400	291U	NWC	77388
LA FLEUR PINE LN	1800	537U	PA	77503
LA FONDA DR	200	373W	NEH	77060
LAFONE DR	16000	330M	NWC	77379
LAFONE RD	16600	330M	NWC	77379
LA FONTAINE	2900	371G	NWC	77014
LA FONTE	8600	491D	SWH	77024
LA FOUCHE CT	13300	288Y	NWC	77377
LA FOUCHE DR	25700	288Y	NWC	77377
LAGARTO CT	200	247G	SWM	77362
LAGARTO WAY	300	247G	SWM	77362
LA GLORIA DR	16200	527K	NEF	77083
N. LAGO CT	1600	616K	PL	77581
LAGO BEND LN	12400	409W	NWC	77041
LAGO BLUFF LOOP	0	326T	NWC	77433
LAGO CHASE LOOP	0	326T	NWC	77433
LAGO CREST DR	0	532Y	SWH	77054
LAGO FOREST DR	18000	377A	NEC	77346
LAGO NICOLA	0	659R	LC	77573
LAGOON DR	100	619T	NB	77058
LAGOON LN	23000	338V	NEH	77336
LAGO PARK LOOP	0	326T	NWC	77433
LAGO ROYALE LN	0	409W	NWC	77041
LAGOS AZUL CT	4900	291E	NWC	77389
LAGOS LAGOON WAY	0	291E	NWC	77389
LAGO TERRACE RD	0	526K	NEF	77407
LAGO TRACE DR	400	298P	NEC	77336
LAGO VERDE DR	11400	525J	NEF	77406
LAGO VILLA DR	15400	329T	NWC	77377
LAGO VISTA	100	619V	LC	77565
LAGO VISTA CT	7700	337M	NEC	77346
S. LAGO VISTA DR	1600	616N	PL	77581
N. LAGO VISTA DR	1600	616K	PL	77581
LAGO VISTA LN	1500	485K	NEF	77494
LA GRANADA DR	6600	527L	NEF	77083
LA GROVE LN	12700	496D	NEC	77015
LAGUNA	3100	497E	NEH	77015
LAGUNA CIR	4100	609B	MC	77459
LAGUNA CIR	8000	408L	NWC	77095
LAGUNA BAY CT	0	409W	NWC	77041
LAGUNA BEECH LN	5900	530D	SWH	77036
LAGUNA CORAL CT	400	619Z	LC	77573
LAGUNA DEL REY DR	6100	409W	NWC	77041
LAGUNA EDGE	24800	484M	NEF	77494
LAGUNA FALLS CT	5900	409W	NWC	77041
LAGUNA HEIGHTS LN	0	524M	NEF	77406
LAGUNA LAKE DR	0	290S	NWC	77379
LAGUNA MEADOWS CT	19700	486L	SWC	77094
LAGUNA MEADOWS LN	1600	486L	SWC	77094
LAGUNA POINT CIR	2700	485Q	NEF	77450
LAGUNA POINT DR	22900	485Q	NEF	77450
LAGUNA POINT LN	4000	609Q	MC	77459
LAGUNA POINT LN	12100	449A	NWC	77041
LAGUNA POINTE DR	100	660A	LC	77573
LAGUNA POINTE DR	2700	613E	NEB	77584
LAGUNA RIDGE LN	0	615M	PL	77089
LAGUNA SHORES DR	0	612F	PL	77545
LAGUNA SHORES LN	1100	659M	LC	77573
LAGUNA SPRINGS	0	612L	PL	77584
LAGUNA SPRINGS CT	8000	407G	NWC	77095
LAGUNA SPRINGS DR	17000	407G	NWC	77095
LAGUNA TERRACE DR	12000	409W	NWC	77041
LAGUNA TERRACE WAY	0	409W	NWH	77041
LAGUNA TRACE	6600	525L	NEF	77407
LAGUNA TRACE CT	22300	525L	NEF	77407
LAGUNA TRAIL DR	17200	367U	NWC	77095
LAGUNA TRAIL DR	17300	367T	NWC	77095
LAGUNA VILLAS	7100	530D	SWH	77036
LAGUNA VISTA LN	0	377L	NEC	77346
LAGUNA WOODS CT	19300	329A	NWC	77375
LAGUNA WOODS DR	11800	329A	NWC	77375
LAGUNA WOODS DR	19300	329A	NWC	77375
LAIN RD	22800	290K	NWC	77375
LAINDON SPRINGS LN	0	292U	NCC	77373
LAIRD	900	536M	PA	77506
LAIRD	1300	452Y	NWH	77008
LAIRD FOREST CT	0	444C	NWC	77493
LAIRD KNOLL ST	0	404Z	NWC	77493
LA JOLLA CIR	300	373W	NEH	77060
LA JOLLA DR	15100	373W	NEH	77060
LA JUANA CT	0	332A	NWC	77388
LA JUANA LN	19400	332A	NWC	77388
LA JUANA LN	19600	292W	NWC	77388
LAKE	1800	297J	SEM	77365
LAKE	2500	492U	SWH	77098
LAKE	5800	532C	WU	77005
LAKE CIR	600	248H	SWM	77354
LAKE E. CT	0	338C	NEH	77336
LAKE CT	4100	609B	MC	77459
LAKE CT	16500	498M	CV	77530
W. LAKE DR	0	528Y	SG	77478
N. LAKE DR	0	526X	NEF	77406
E. LAKE DR	0	656V	FR	77546
LAKE W. DR	800	338C	NEH	77336
LAKE DR	800	338C	NEH	77336
LAKE DR	1100	295Y	SEM	77365
W. LAKE DR	1200	338C	NEH	77336
LAKE DR	1600	569Y	MC	77459
S. LAKE DR	2300	659B	LC	77573
LAKE DR	3000	484R	NEF	77494
LAKE DR	3800	616X	PL	77581
LAKE E. LN	0	338C	NEH	77336

Street Name	Block	Pg/Sq	Loc	Zips
LAKE LN	7300	410P	NWC	77040
LAKE RD	2200	459E	NEC	77562
LAKE RD	10200	329T	NWC	77070
LAKE AMISTAD PLACE	0	366S	NWC	77433
LAKE AQUILLA LN	16600	377L	NEH	77044
LAKE ARBOR DR	1600	620E	EL	77586
LAKEARIES LN	3500	446J	NWC	77449
LAKE ARLINGTON LN	0	377G	NEH	77346
LAKE ARLINGTON RD	0	377G	NEH	77346
LAKE BANK CT	1500	620J	EL	77586
LAKE BARDWELL CT	4500	526X	NEF	77406
LAKE BARKLEY LN	0	377G	NEH	77346
LAKE BENBROOK DR	0	377M	NEH	77346
LAKEBEND DR	1700	568V	SG	77478
LAKE BEND DR	18100	407X	NWC	77084
LAKE BEND DR	18200	447B	NWC	77084
LAKE BEND SHORE DR	0	253X	SEM	77386
S. LAKEBLUFF CIR	0	485X	NEF	77494
N. LAKEBLUFF CIR	0	485X	NEF	77494
LAKEBLUFF CT	0	525D	NEF	77450
LAKE BLUFF DR	1500	620E	EL	77586
LAKE BLUFF LN	0	619D	PA	77586
N. LAKE BRANCH LN	0	377H	NEH	77346
LAKE BREEZE LN	2700	378N	NEC	77532
LAKE BRIAN LN	0	377L	NEH	77044
LAKEBRIAR DR	24700	484G	NEF	77494
LAKE BRIDGE	0	658K	LC	77573
W. LAKEBRIDGE LN	0	526J	NEF	77407
E. LAKEBRIDGE LN	0	526J	NEF	77407
LAKEBROOK CT	10300	372W	NWC	77038
LAKEBROOK DR	10500	372W	NWC	77038
LAKE CATHERINE CT	4800	526X	NEF	77407
LAKE CENTER RUN	12300	449A	NWC	77041
LAKE CENTER RUN CT	12700	448D	NWC	77041
LAKE CHAMPLAIN DR	0	377H	NEH	77346
LAKE CHASE CT	0	444P	KT	77493
LAKE CHASE CT	0	444P	KT	77493
LAKE CHASE DR	0	444P	KT	77493
LAKE CHELAN LN	17300	376H	NEC	77346
LAKE CHESDIN RD	0	377L	NEH	77346
LAKE CLARK LN	0	377E	NEC	77346
LAKECLIFF DR	1400	489N	SWH	77077
LAKECLIFFE DR	15800	408E	NWC	77095
LAKE COLONY DR	2800	609F	MC	77459
LAKE COMMONS CT	200	298K	NEC	77336
LAKE COMMONS WAY	29200	298Q	NEC	77336
LAKE COMO CT	0	445J	NWC	77493
LAKE COUNTRY DR	900	619H	TL	77586
LAKECOVE DR	23000	338V	NEH	77336
LAKE COVE POINT LN	0	290T	NWC	77379
LAKE COVE POINT LN	6900	290X	NWC	77379
LAKE COVE WAY	0	620K	SB	77586
LAKE CREEK CIR	4800	609K	MC	77459
LAKE CREEK DR	1900	296U	NEH	77339
W. LAKE CRESCENT DR	3000	336D	NEH	77339
E. LAKE CRESCENT DR	3000	336D	NEH	77339
LAKECREST CIR	12500	368L	NWC	77429
LAKECREST CT	0	445N	NWC	77493
LAKE CREST CT	2500	613V	NEB	77584
LAKE CREST DR	0	287J	NWC	77377
LAKE CREST DR	0	656G	FR	77546
LAKECREST DR	2600	613U	NEB	77584
LAKECREST DR	4200	609B	MC	77459
LAKECREST DR	12700	368G	NWC	77429
LAKECREST DR	12700	368L	NWC	77429
LAKECREST DR	23000	338V	NEH	77336
LAKECREST LN	4300	613V	PL	77584
LAKECREST BEND DR	0	444R	NWC	77493
LAKECREST BEND DR	0	445N	NWC	77493
LAKECREST CREEK DR	0	444R	NWC	77493
LAKECREST FOREST DR	0	444R	NWC	77493
LAKECREST GROVE DR	0	445N	NWC	77493
LAKECREST GROVE DR	0	445N	NWC	77493
LAKECREST HARBOR DR	2400	445N	NWC	77493
LAKECREST HAVEN DR	1800	445S	NWC	77493
LAKECREST MANOR DR	24900	445V	NWC	77493
LAKECREST PASS CT	0	444R	NWC	77493
LAKECREST RIDGE DR	0	445N	NWC	77493
LAKECREST RIVER DR	0	444R	NWC	77493
LAKECREST RUN DR	0	444R	NWC	77493
LAKECREST TERRACE CT	2400	445N	NWC	77493
LAKECREST TOWN DR	2400	445N	NWC	77493
LAKECREST VIEW DR	0	367W	NWC	77433
LAKECREST VILLAGE DR	24400	445N	NWC	77493
LAKECREST WAY DR	0	444R	NWC	77493
LAKE CROSSING LN	0	485W	NEF	77494
LAKE CRYSTAL DR	8300	408E	NWC	77095
LAKE CYPRESS CIR	4300	331W	NWC	77068
LAKE CYPRESS HILL DR	17500	327E	NWC	77429
LAKEDALE DR	15700	408E	NWC	77095
LAKE DANIEL CT	4800	526X	NEF	77407
LAKE EDGE CT	8100	570B	SWH	77071
LAKE EDGE DR	2000	615Z	PL	77581
LAKE ELLA DR	0	375Y	NEC	77396
LAKE ESTATES CT	1200	568J	SG	77498
LAKE ESTATES CT	3000	609F	MC	77459
LAKE ESTATES DR	1100	568J	SG	77498
LAKE EXCURSION CT	13300	377L	NEC	77044
N. LAKEFAIR CT	0	524K	NWF	77406
S. LAKEFAIR CT	0	524K	NWF	77406
N. LAKEFAIR DR	0	524K	NWF	77406
LAKEFAIR DR	0	524K	NWF	77406
E. LAKE FALLS CIR	2900	253W	SEM	77386
S. LAKE FALLS CIR	30000	253W	SEM	77386
N. LAKE FALLS CIR	30000	253W	SEM	77386
LAKE FALLS CT	4100	578Z	PA	77059
S. LAKE FALLS LN	30100	253W	SEM	77386
N. LAKE FALLS LN	30100	253W	SEM	77386
LAKE FERN	0	370S	NWC	77064
LAKEFIELD BLVD	0	245D	SWM	77355
LAKEFIELD BLVD	2400	609J	SG	77479
LAKEFIELD DR	5500	574E	SEH	77033
LAKEFIELD WAY	2400	609E	SG	77479
LAKE FOREST	0	620A	SB	77586
LAKE FOREST BLVD	8800	455H	NEH	77078
LAKE FOREST CIR	1	455H	NEH	77078
LAKE FOREST DR	600	656L	FR	77546
LAKE FOREST DR	12600	368L	NWC	77429
LAKE FORK CT	0	366Z	NWC	77433
LAKE FOUNTAIN DR	0	484K	NEF	77494
LAKEFRONT	0	244B	WCO	77447
LAKE FRONT CIR	0	251G	WD	77380
LAKE FRONT CIR	0	251L	SWM	77380
LAKEFRONT CIR	100	252E	WD	77380
LAKE FRONT CIR	900	251D	WD	77380
LAKEFRONT CIR	900	251G	WD	77380
LAKEFRONT CT	300	568V	SG	77478
LAKEFRONT CT	2400	619X	LC	77573
LAKEFRONT CT	4300	609B	MC	77459
LAKEFRONT DR	1700	569X	MC	77459
LAKEFRONT DR	1800	609B	MC	77459
N. LAKE FRONT DR	2300	619X	LC	77573

Street Name	Block	Pg/Sq	Loc	Zips
LAKE FRONT RD	18900	286L	NWC	77377
LAKEFRONT TERRACE CT	0	615W	PL	77584
LAKEFRONT TERRACE DR	4700	614Z	PL	77584
E. LAKE GABLES DR	0	524K	NWF	77406
E. LAKE GABLES DR	11100	524K	NWF	77406
LAKE GARDENS CT	2500	336C	NEH	77339
LAKE GARDENS DR	2000	336C	NEH	77339
LAKE GENEVA CT	1700	447W	NWH	77084
LAKE GEORGETOWN CT	0	526W	NEF	77407
LAKE GLADEWATER CT	0	526W	NEF	77407
LAKEGLEN CT	300	568U	SG	77478
LAKE GLEN DR	1000	339A	NEH	77336
LAKE GLEN TRAIL	0	378T	NEC	77532
LAKE GRAHAM LN	0	526W	NEF	77406
LAKE GRAYSON DR	800	484K	NEF	77494
LAKE GRAYSON DR	800	484L	NEF	77494
LAKEGREEN CT	0	525H	NEF	77450
LAKEGROVE CT	11800	328R	NWC	77377
LAKE GROVE DR	4100	619G	TL	77586
LAKEGROVE BEND	11800	328V	NWC	77377
LAKEGROVE FOREST	16000	328R	NWC	77377
LAKE HALBERT LN	4500	526W	NEF	77406
LAKE HARBOR LN	0	658X	LC	77573
LAKE HARBOR LN	100	338V	NEH	77336
LAKE HARBOR WAY	1700	447W	NWH	77084
LAKE HARBOR WAY CIR	1700	447W	NWH	77084
LAKE HAVEN CT	7000	609P	MC	77459
LAKEHAVEN DR	3200	296Y	NEH	77339
LAKE HAWKINS CT	0	367S	NWC	77433
LAKEHEAD LN	0	526J	NEF	77407
LAKEHEAD LN	0	526K	NEF	77407
LAKEHEAD LN	0	526P	NEF	77407
LAKEHILL DR	3000	613T	NEB	77584
LAKE HILLS DR	1900	296Y	NEH	77339
LAKE HILL VIEW CIR	0	328S	NWC	77429
LAKE HOLLOW DR	0	612N	PL	77545
LAKE HOLLOW LN	19300	446Z	NWC	77084
LAKE HOUSTON LN	28900	298N	NEC	77336
E. LAKE HOUSTON PKWY	0	338Z	NEC	77532
E. LAKE HOUSTON PKWY	0	338Z	NEC	77532
W. LAKE HOUSTON PKWY	0	377X	NEC	77044
LAKE HOUSTON PKWY	0	337B	NEH	77339
W. LAKE HOUSTON PKWY	2000	337B	NEH	77345
W. LAKE HOUSTON PKWY	3200	297T	NEH	77339
S. LAKE HOUSTON PKWY	5000	456U	NEH	77013
S. LAKE HOUSTON PKWY	7400	417J	NEC	77044
N. LAKE HOUSTON PKWY	9600	416L	NEC	77044
N. LAKE HOUSTON PKWY	13000	417K	NEC	77044
S. LAKE HOUSTON PKWY	13300	417J	NEC	77044
W. LAKE HOUSTON PKWY	18000	337U	NEC	77346
E. LAKE HOUSTON PKWY	24000	338M	NEH	77336
S. LAKE HOUSTON PKWY	5800	456U	NEH	77049
LAKE HURST DR	500	613A	NEB	77584
LAKEHURST DR	7300	534V	SEH	77087
LAKEHURST DR	7400	535S	SEH	77087
LAKE IRIS DR	15600	329U	NWC	77070
LAKE JACKSONVILLE LN	4900	526X	NEF	77407
LAKE KEMP CT	4300	526W	NEF	77406
LAKE KENT LN	24800	250Y	NWC	77389
LAKE KINGWOOD TRAIL	1700	337E	NEH	77339
LAKE KNOLL CT	4600	609P	NEF	77479
LAKE KNOLL DR	0	376C	NEC	77396
LAKE KOLBE LN	0	450R	NEH	77080
S. LAKELAND	0	619X	LC	77573
S. LAKE LAND DR	300	659B	LC	77573
LAKELAND DR	500	335Z	HM	77338
LAKELAND DR	9100	532N	SWH	77025
LAKELAND FALLS DR	20300	326P	NWC	77433
LAKELAND GARDENS CT	22100	445M	NWC	77449
LAKELAND GARDENS DR	3300	445M	NWC	77449
LAKELAND HAVEN DR	0	366K	NWC	77433
LAKE LANDING DR	1800	660L	LC	77573
LAKELANE DR	3200	336Q	NEH	77338
W. LAKELANE DR	19800	336P	NEH	77338
LAKE LAVON CT	4300	526X	NEF	77406
LAKE LAWN DR	25700	251V	SWM	77380
LAKE LEON CT	17900	367S	NWC	77433
LAKE LEWISVILLE CT	0	407A	NWC	77433
LAKE LIMESTONE LN	0	377L	NEH	77346
LAKE LIVINGSTON DR	0	377L	NEH	77346
LAKE LODGE DR	15500	618G	SEH	77062
LAKE LOOP DR	15700	326P	NWC	77433
LAKE LOUISE CT	0	366R	NWC	77433
LAKE LOUISE CT	0	366R	NWC	77433
LAKE MAGNOLIA BLVD	0	377F	NEC	77346
LAKE MALONE CT	0	377F	NEC	77346
LAKE MANOR DR	5300	447C	NWC	77084
LAKE MEAD LN	11900	377E	NEC	77346
LAKE MEADOWS CT	1800	488N	SWH	77077
LAKE MEDINA WAY	0	377M	NEH	77346
LAKEMERE	200	489L	SWH	77079
LAKEMERE PARK CT	31900	252M	SEM	77385
LAKE MICHIGAN AVE	0	377M	NEH	77346
LAKE MIJA CT	0	620F	SB	77586
LAKE MIST CT	7800	337M	NEH	77346
LAKE MIST DR	12900	328Y	NWC	77429
LAKE MIST HARBOUR DR	0	251F	WD	77381
S. LAKEMIST HARBOUR PLACE	1	251F	WD	77381
N. LAKEMIST HARBOUR PLACE	1	251F	WD	77381
LAKEMONT DR	2400	414A	NCC	77039
LAKEMONT DR	6100	415E	NEH	77050
LAKEMONT BEND LN	0	525M	NEF	77407
LAKEMONT BEND LN	20400	526E	NEF	77407
LAKEMONT BEND LN	21000	525M	NEF	77407
LAKEMONT GROVE LN	0	525M	NEF	77407
LAKEMONT HEIGHTS DR	0	526F	NEF	77450
LAKEMONT POINT DR	0	525R	NEF	77407
LAKEN DR	14500	328X	NWC	77429
LAKE NOCONA CT	0	367S	NWC	77433
LAKENSHIRE FALLS LN	0	524E	NEF	77494
LAKE OAK DR	3200	297Z	NEH	77345
LAKE OAKS DR	18300	331H	NWC	77388
LAKE OLYMPIA PKWY	2500	610N	MC	77459
LAKE OLYMPIA PKWY	2700	609Q	MC	77459
LAKE ORANGE CT	0	377H	NEH	77346
LAKE OVERLOOK TRAIL	0	528Y	SWH	77099
LAKE PALOMA TRAIL	0	250L	NWC	77389
LAKE PALOMA TRAIL	0	250L	NWC	77389
LAKEP ARC BEND DR	0	368G	NWC	77429
LAKE PARK	0	658K	LC	77573
LAKE PARK CT	25000	245P	SWM	77355
LAKE PARK DR	0	568D	SG	77478
LAKE PARK DR	9100	455H	NEH	77078
LAKE PARK TRAIL	20700	337P	NEC	77346
LAKE PASSAGE LN	13300	377Q	NEC	77044
LAKE PATH CIR	24400	445S	NWC	77493
LAKE PAULINE CT	1400	526X	NEF	77406
LAKE PINES DR	0	297S	NEH	77339
LAKE PINKSTON DR	4500	526X	NEF	77406
LAKE PLACE DR	5400	448D	NWC	77041
LAKE PLAZA DR	0	292E	NWC	77389
LAKE POINT CT	100	620W	LC	77573
LAKE POINT DR	100	620W	LC	77573
LAKE POINT DR	21500	336L	NEH	77339
LAKE POINTE CT	2500	613U	NEB	77584
LAKE POINTE ESTATES	0	484M	NEF	77494
LAKE POINTE PARKWAY	0	568T	SG	77478
LAKE POINT FOREST	0	620A	SB	77586
LAKEPORT CROSSING DR	15400	367H	CY	77429
LAKEPOST	0	368F	NWC	77429
LAKE PRINCE LN	16600	377L	NEH	77044
LAKE PROMENADE	0	406U	NWC	77449
LAKE RANCH DR	13100	377U	NEH	77044
LAKE RAVEN CT	0	366V	NWC	77433
LAKE RIATA LN	10600	367T	NWC	77433
N. LAKERIDGE CIR	1	251A	WD	77381
LAKERIDGE CT	1	251A	WD	77381
LAKE RIDGE CT	12000	570C	SWH	77071
S. LAKERIDGE DR	0	251A	WD	77381
E. LAKERIDGE DR	1	251A	WD	77381
LAKERIDGE DR	1	251A	WD	77381
LAKERIDGE LN	0	338V	NEH	77336
LAKE RIDGE BEND	3300	251S	SWM	77380
LAKERIDGE PARK LN	0	366R	NWC	77433
LAKE RIDGE PLACE DR	2900	446R	NWC	77084
LAKE RIVERSTONE DR	0	609P	NEF	77479
LAKE ROBBINS DR	2000	251H	SWM	77380
E. LAKE ROSE CT	17300	327P	NWC	77429
W. LAKE ROSE CT	17400	327P	NWC	77429
LAKE ROYAL LN	0	485R	SWC	77450
LAKE RUN DR	4300	609K	MC	77459
LAKE RUN LN	7400	526J	NEF	77407
LAKESAGE LN	0	526J	NEF	77407
LAKE SANDY DR	17200	459X	CV	77530
LAKES AT 610 DR	8800	532U	SWH	77054
LAKE SCENE TRAIL	14100	578X	SEH	77059
LAKES END RD	21800	336L	NEH	77339
LAKE SHADE CT	3700	297U	NEH	77345
LAKE SHADOW DR	0	253J	SEM	77385
LAKESHADOW LN	0	485X	NEF	77494
LAKE SHADOWS DR	3200	378T	NEC	77532
LAKE SHADOWS LN	0	657T	FR	77546
LAKE SHANNON LN	0	366Z	NWC	77433
LAKE SHERWOOD DR	20200	486F	SWC	77450
LAKESHIRE	18700	336V	NEC	77346
LAKESHIRE DR	18500	256H	SEM	77357
LAKESHIRE DR	18700	336Z	NEC	77346
LAKE SHOALS DR	0	612M	PL	77584
LAKESHORE	300	620J	EL	77586
LAKESHORE	17600	499B	CV	77530
LAKESHORE CIR	200	619M	TL	77586
LAKE SHORE DR	0	659B	LC	77573
LAKESHORE DR	0	257A	SEM	77357
LAKESHORE DR	100	619M	TL	77586
LAKESHORE DR	600	568T	SG	77478
LAKE SHORE DR	1000	616X	PL	77581
LAKESHORE DR	1500	336K	NEH	77339
LAKESHORE DR	2300	610P	MC	77459
LAKESHORE BEND DR	0	450Q	NWH	77080
LAKESHORE EDGE DR	0	450Q	NWH	77080
LAKESHORE FOREST CT	2100	610P	MC	77459
LAKESHORE FOREST DR	4100	610P	MC	77459
LAKE SHORE HARBOUR BLVD	0	610T	MC	77459
LAKE SHORE HARBOUR DR	0	610T	MC	77459
LAKESHORE LANDING DR	0	377L	NEC	77044
LAKE SHORE RIDGE	0	448D	NWC	77041
LAKE SHORE RIDGE	12000	449A	NWC	77041
LAKE SHORE RIDGE CT	5300	449A	NWC	77041
LAKESHORES LAGOON LN	0	406D	NWC	77433
LAKESHORE TERRACE DR	0	450R	NWH	77080
LAKESHORE TRAIL DR	0	377L	NEC	77346
LAKESHORE VILLA DR	0	337R	NEC	77346
LAKESHORE WAY	1600	488P	SWH	77077
LAKESHORE WAY CT	13600	488P	SWH	77077
LAKESHORE WAY COVE	13700	488P	SWH	77077
LAKESIDE	0	620B	SB	77586
LAKESIDE	100	619V	LC	77565
LAKESIDE	2100	380C	NEC	77532
LAKESIDE BLVD	0	251C	WD	77381
LAKESIDE BLVD	100	568R	SG	77478
LAKESIDE CT	100	335H	NEH	77339
LAKESIDE CT	5000	577K	PA	77504
LAKESIDE DR	0	613Q	PL	77584
LAKESIDE DR	1	415K	NEC	77050
LAKESIDE DR	100	498M	CV	77530
LAKE SIDE DR	100	254L	SEM	77365
LAKESIDE DR	900	459Z	HG	77562
LAKESIDE DR	1800	620K	SB	77586
E. LAKE SIDE DR	9100	248D	SWM	77354
LAKESIDE DR	23100	296M	SEM	77365
LAKESIDE DR	25000	244R	WCO	77447
LAKESIDE LN	100	335H	NEH	77339
LAKESIDE LN	500	657J	FR	77546
LAKESIDE LN	18000	619T	NB	77058
LAKESIDE BEND CT	2100	488P	SWH	77077
LAKESIDE BEND DR	13600	488P	SWH	77077
LAKESIDE COVE	19000	486H	SWC	77094
LAKESIDE CREEK CT	3400	251S	SWM	77380
LAKESIDE CROSSING	0	484L	NEF	77494
LAKESIDE ENCLAVE DR	1500	488P	SWH	77077
LAKESIDE ESTATES DR	400	489U	SWH	77042
LAKESIDE FOREST DR	8600	411L	NWC	77088
LAKESIDE FOREST LN	10800	489K	SWH	77042
LAKESIDE GABLES DR	10000	369W	NWC	77065
LAKESIDE GREEN	28600	246B	SWM	77355
LAKESIDE HAVEN DR	0	325H	NWC	77377
LAKESIDE HOLLOW CROSSING	0	297K	SEM	77365
LAKESIDE LANDING DR	2000	620J	SB	77586
LAKESIDE MANOR LN	7500	614J	NEB	77581
LAKESIDE MEADOW CT	4700	569X	MC	77459
LAKESIDE MEADOW DR	4300	569X	MC	77459
LAKESIDE OAKS DR	100	489K	SWH	77042
LAKESIDE PARK DR	11600	489T	SWH	77077
LAKESIDE PLACE DR	11300	489P	SWH	77077
LAKESIDE PLAZA DR	1900	568X	NEF	77479
LAKESIDE TERRACE	2600	620N	SB	77586
LAKESIDE TERRACE DR	12600	417D	NEH	77044
LAKESIDE TERRACE DR	13400	377Y	NEH	77346
LAKESIDE TRAIL	3200	488Q	SWH	77077
LAKESIDE VALLEY DR	100	489L	SWH	77042
LAKESIDE VIEW DR	19400	331B	NWC	77388
LAKESIDE VIEW LN	0	376S	NEC	77396
LAKESIDE VIEW WAY	14400	326Y	NWC	77429
LAKESIDE VILLAGE DR	2600	610N	MC	77459
LAKES OF BRIDGEWATER DR	3500	445R	NWC	77449
LAKES OF BRIDGEWATER DR	3600	446J	NWC	77449
LAKES OF CYPRESS FOREST DR	0	332A	NWC	77388
LAKES OF FAIRHAVEN DR	0	326E	NWC	77433
LAKES OF KATY LN	0	444J	KT	77493
LAKES OF MISSION GRV BLVD	0	525X	NEF	77406
LAKES OF PARKWAY	0	488K	SWH	77077
LAKES OF PARKWAY	0	488P	SWH	77077
LAKES OF PINE FOREST CT	17700	447G	NWC	77084
LAKES OF PINE FOREST DR	17600	447G	NWC	77084
LAKES OF ROSEHILL DR	0	327T	NWC	77429
LAKES ON ELDRIDGE DR	12900	448D	NWC	77041
LAKE SOPHIE CT	0	377H	NEH	77346
LAKE SPIRE CT	0	406Q	NWC	77449
LAKESPIRE DR	20000	406Q	NWC	77449
LAKE SPRING CT	20300	326P	NWC	77433
LAKE SPRINGS WAY	25700	292U	NCC	77373
LAKE STERLING GATE DR	1	330N	NWC	77379
LAKESTONE BLVD	0	609K	MC	77459
LAKE STONE CT	19700	286T	NWC	77377
LAKESTONE DR	16000	328R	NWC	77377
LAKE STREAM DR	3100	297S	NEH	77339
LAKE SUPERIOR LN	0	377M	NEH	77346
LAKE SYDNEY DR	0	484L	NEF	77494
LAKE TAHOE CT	0	377M	NEH	77346
LAKE TERRACE CT	1800	251R	WD	77380
LAKE TERRACE CT	4200	609B	MC	77459
LAKE TERRACE DR	12800	448D	NWC	77041
LAKE TIMBER CT	13300	328Q	NWC	77429
LAKE TRAIL BLVD	0	568J	SG	77498
LAKE TRAIL DR	14000	568J	SG	77498
LAKETREE LN	22900	334A	NCC	77373
LAKE TYLOR ST	0	576V	SEH	77034
LAKEVIEW	0	297L	NEH	77365
LAKEVIEW	0	619H	TL	77586
LAKEVIEW	100	619L	PA	77586
LAKEVIEW	1800	499H	NEC	77520
LAKEVIEW	18000	378R	NEC	77532
LAKEVIEW CIR	0	447W	NWH	77084
LAKEVIEW CIR	0	570V	SWH	77489
LAKEVIEW CIR	0	620E	EL	77586
LAKEVIEW CIR	100	657J	FR	77546
LAKEVIEW CIR	700	336K	NEH	77339
W. LAKE VIEW CT	0	244C	WCO	77447
E. LAKE VIEW CT	0	244C	WCO	77447
LAKEVIEW CT	3700	609M	MC	77459
LAKEVIEW CT	17900	255N	SEM	77365
LAKEVIEW DR	100	568K	SG	77498
LAKEVIEW DR	2800	609M	MC	77459
LAKE VIEW DR	3800	616X	PL	77581
LAKEVIEW DR	13500	369E	NWC	77429
LAKEVIEW DR	14900	409Q	JV	77040
LAKEVIEW DR	17600	255N	SEM	77365
LAKEVIEW DR	20100	334T	NEH	77338
LAKEVIEW LN	1900	484K	NEF	77494
LAKEVIEW RD	2000	484L	NEF	77494
LAKEVIEW RD	25100	244L	WCO	77447
LAKEVIEW BEND LN	0	660B	KE	77565
LAKEVIEW BEND LN	31100	252R	SEM	77386
LAKEVIEW HAVEN DR	6500	408N	NWC	77095
LAKEVIEW HAVEN DR	7000	407R	NWC	77095
LAKEVIEW PLACE	11500	329W	NWC	77070
LAKE VILLA DR	0	610T	MC	77459
LAKE VILLA DR	700	619L	TL	77586
LAKE VILLAGE DR	1900	336C	NEH	77339
S. LAKE VILLAGE DR	3100	485U	NEF	77450
N. LAKE VILLAGE DR	22100	485R	NEF	77450
LAKEVILLE CT	2700	336C	NEH	77339
LAKEVILLE DR	600	336B	NEH	77339
LAKEVILLE DR	1900	336C	NEH	77339
LAKE VISTA CIR	4100	609Q	MC	77459
LAKE VISTA DR	12400	328L	NWC	77377
LAKE WALK CT	4300	609K	MC	77459
LAKEWATER DR	0	612N	PL	77545
LAKEWATER DR	25700	338G	NEC	77336
LAKEWAY CT	8200	613V	PL	77584
LAKEWAY CT	12000	570B	SWH	77071
LAKEWAY DR	0	620E	SB	77586
LAKEWAY DR	0	656V	FR	77546
LAKEWAY DR	0	659C	LC	77573
LAKEWAY DR	1	568E	SG	77498
LAKEWAY DR	1300	619D	TL	77586
LAKEWAY DR	22300	333H	NCC	77373
LAKEWAY LN	3200	613V	PL	77584
LAKEWAY PARK	17100	329K	NWC	77375
LAKEWAY VIEW LN	9200	375V	NEC	77396
LAKE WAY VILLAGE DR	0	338M	NEH	77336
LAKE WHITE ROCK DR	0	377M	NEH	77346
LAKE WHITNEY DR	0	407A	NWC	77433
LAKE WICHITA LN	4800	526X	NEF	77407
LAKE WILDERNESS LN	1600	338A	NEH	77345
LAKE WILLOUGHBY LN	13500	377L	NEH	77044
LAKE WILLOW RD	0	570V	SWH	77489
LAKE WILLOWBY LN	0	377G	NEH	77346
LAKEWIND	7700	535T	SEH	77061
LAKEWIND CT	2100	658T	LC	77573
LAKE WIND DR	2200	613J	PL	77584
LAKEWIND LN	2100	658T	LC	77573
LAKEWIND PARK CT	23100	525L	NEF	77407
LAKEWIND PARK LN	22900	525L	NEF	77407
LAKE WINDS DR	1700	569Y	MC	77459
LAKEWOOD	3000	414X	NEH	77093
LAKEWOOD	7200	415W	NEH	77016
LAKEWOOD	8700	415Y	NEH	77078
LAKEWOOD CT	4200	609B	MC	77459
LAKEWOOD DR	100	500J	BT	77520
LAKEWOOD DR	1100	247K	SWM	77362
LAKEWOOD DR	4200	577K	PA	77504
LAKEWOOD DR	4200	610X	MC	77459
LAKEWOOD DR	10200	252G	SEM	77385
LAKEWOOD LN	1	620P	SB	77586
LAKEWOOD BEND	1	369A	NWC	77429
LAKE WOODBRIDGE CT	14900	568A	NEF	77498
LAKE WOODBRIDGE DR	11300	568A	NEF	77498
LAKE WOODBRIDGE DR	11400	528W	NEF	77498
LAKEWOOD COVE	11400	369A	NWC	77070
LAKEWOOD CRSSING BLVD	13800	369A	NWC	77070
LAKEWOOD CRSSING BLVD	14000	329X	NWC	77070
LAKEWOOD CROSSINS	11600	329N	NWC	77377
LAKEWOOD ESTATES	11400	369A	NWC	77070
LAKEWOOD FIELD CT	11300	329N	NWC	77377
LAKEWOOD FIELD DR	13000	368D	NWC	77429
LAKEWOOD FIELD DR	16200	329N	NWC	77377
LAKEWOOD FOREST DR	13700	369A	NWC	77070
LAKEWOOD FOREST DR	14200	329W	NWC	77070
E. LAKEWD FRST NORTH CT	11400	329S	NWC	77377
W. LAKEWD FRST NORTH CT	11500	329S	NWC	77377
LAKEWOOD GLADE CT	12200	368C	NWC	77429
LAKEWOOD GLEN CT	0	329K	NWC	77375
LAKEWOOD GROVE DR	16200	329N	NWC	77377
LAKEWOOD HILLS DR	11800	328R	NWC	77377
LAKE WOODLANDS DR	0	250D	WD	77381
LAKE WOODLANDS DR	0	252E	WD	77381
LAKE WOODLANDS DR	1100	252E	WD	77380
LAKE WOODLANDS DR	10100	251G	WD	77381
LAKEWOOD MANOR DR	0	328V	NWC	77377
LAKEWOOD MEADOW DR	13000	368C	NWC	77429
LAKEWOOD OAKS DR	10700	528W	NEF	77498
LAKEWOOD PINES BLVD	0	377P	NEC	77044
LAKEWOOD PLACE	11500	369A	NWC	77070
LAKEWOODS DR	1500	378R	NEC	77532
LAKEWOOD SPRINGS	0	329N	NWC	77375
LAKEWOOD TRACE DR	12200	368C	NWC	77429
LAKEWOOD TRAIL	11800	329N	NWC	77377
LAKEWOOD VALLEY CT	12200	368C	NWC	77429
LAKEWOOD VIEW CT	19800	486Q	SWC	77450
LAKEWOOD VILLA DR	12300	328V	NWC	77377
LAKEWOOD WEST DR	11900	368D	NWC	77429
LAKEWORTH DR	8900	411R	NWH	77088
LAKIN	400	493J	SWH	77007
LAKIN AVE	900	536F	PA	77506
LAKOTA DR	19100	406Z	NWC	77449
LAKOTA TRAIL	0	291N	NWC	77388
LALEU LN	12500	570G	MC	77071
LA LOMA	15400	527M	NEF	77083
LA LUNA DR	16200	527F	SWC	77083
LALURA BETH DR	0	325S	HK	77447
LA MANCHA DR	15200	527H	SWC	77083
LAMAR	0	499K	NEC	77520
LAMAR	0	619V	LC	77565
LAMAR	100	493Q	DT	77002
LAMAR	1200	493Q	DT	77002
LAMAR	1201	493Q	DT	77010
LAMAR	1300	493Q	DT	77010
W. LAMAR	1900	493J	SWH	77019
LAMAR	2000	493R	SEH	77003
LAMAR	2000	536U	PA	77502
W. LAMAR	3300	492M	SWH	77019
LAMAR	3800	494S	SEH	77023
LAMAR	7300	494Z	SEH	77011
LAMAR CT	3000	609D	MC	77459
LAMAR LN	25100	295Q	SEM	77365
W. LAMAR ST	0	493J	SWH	77019
LAMAR CANYON LN	0	657P	FR	77546
LAMAR FLEMING	6400	533E	SWH	77030
LAMAR PARK LN	0	457P	NEC	77049
LAMB	0	299T	NEC	77336
LAMB	900	493K	SWH	77019
LAMB BROOK LN	0	613P	PL	77584
LAMB CREEK	0	609Z	NEF	77459
LAMBERT	12200	456C	NEC	77044
LAMBETH DR	2700	613K	NEB	77584
LAMBETH PALACE DR	12200	371K	NWC	77066
LAMBORGHINI DR	3100	375M	NEC	77396
LAMBOURNE CIR	1300	329G	NWC	77379
LAMBRIGHT RD	8600	575Q	SEH	77075
E. LAMBUTH LN	300	538Y	DP	77536
W. LAMBUTH LN	7400	538X	DP	77536
LAMELIA LN	0	492B	NWH	77008
LA MER LN	3300	291U	NWC	77388
LAMESA AVE	1300	536K	PA	77506
LA MESA DR	7300	527M	SWC	77083
LAMINA LN	2100	536S	SEH	77017
LA MIRADA DR	6900	527H	SWC	77083
LAMKIN RD	8800	458B	NEC	77049
LAMKIN RD	9100	418X	NEC	77049
LAMOND LN	0	408G	NWC	77095
LAMONT CIR	4300	531D	BL	77401
LAMONTE LN	800	452L	NWH	77018
LAMONTE LN	4800	451M	NWH	77092
LA MORA DR	6500	527G	SWC	77083
LAMPASAS	5300	491Y	SWH	77056
LAMPINO LN	7000	459L	NEC	77049
LAMPLIGHTER	16400	419B	NEC	77532
LAMPLIGHTER CIR	3800	610J	MC	77459
LAMPLIGHTER LN	0	571V	SWH	77053
LAMPLIGHT TRAIL DR	1200	485G	SWC	77450
LAMPPOST CT	7800	410G	NWC	77064
LAMPPOST LN	8300	410G	NWC	77064
LAMPPOST HILL CT	5000	446B	NWC	77449
LAMPPOST PLACE	0	614Y	PL	77584
LAMPREY	11700	529W	SWH	77099
LAMPSON MANOR CT	15400	377X	NEC	77044
LAMPTON CIR	4300	531D	BL	77401
LAMPWICK CIR	20800	291S	NWC	77388
LAN'L	500	459H	NEC	77562
LANA LN	1	491V	SWH	77027
LANA LN	20200	295Z	SEM	77365
LANA LN	26900	252J	OR	77385
LANALEE CT	17000	407Q	NWC	77084
LANARK LN	4000	532E	SWH	77025
LANCASHIRE	0	491Z	SWH	77027
LANCASTER	800	656M	FR	77546
LANCASTER	5200	534R	SEH	77087
LANCASTER LN	300	657U	LC	77573
LANCASTER LN	2500	537K	PA	77506
LANCASTER HILL LN	0	332R	NCC	77073
LANCASTER LAKE DR	0	332Q	NCC	77073
LANCASTER PARK CT	0	611W	FS	77545
LANCASTER PINE DR	0	250V	WD	77389
LANCASTER PINE DR	0	250V	WD	77389
LANCASTER PLACE DR	16400	527P	NEF	77083
LANCASTER WALK DR	3600	371K	NWC	77066
LANCE	3800	460M	NEC	77562
LANCE AVE	7000	578B	PA	77505
LANCE CIR	0	572S	SWH	77053
LANCE LN	2400	569V	SF	77477
LANCEFIELD CT	3100	485S	NEF	77494
W. LANCE LEAF RD	1	250M	WD	77381
E. LANCE LEAF RD	1	251J	WD	77381
LANCELOT	0	502K	BT	77521
LANCELOT DR	12200	570E	SWH	77031
LANCELOT OAKS DR	22100	296X	NEC	77339
LANCEOAK CT	13900	414B	NCC	77039
LANCER PARK	2400	252M	SEM	77385
LANCEWOOD DR	25300	293N	NCC	77373
LAND	2300	613K	PL	77584
LAND RD	13200	573P	SEH	77047
LANDA LN	3700	534G	SEH	77023
LANDAU PARK CT	16200	330T	NWC	77379
LANDAU PARK DR	0	330T	NWC	77379
LANDBREEZE DR	2100	503F	CCO	77520
LANDCIRCLE CT	2100	568C	SG	77478
LANDCROSS DR	12200	528Z	SWH	77099
LANDCROSS TERRACE	0	325H	NWC	77377
LANDEAU CIR	0	371T	NWC	77086
LANDER LN	2000	491N	SWH	77057
LANDERA CT	2600	613S	NEB	77584
LANDFAIR	14000	413E	NCC	77060
LANDFAIR	14800	413A	NCC	77060
LANDFALL LN	6000	534V	SEH	77087
LANDFILL 2 RD	0	334P	NCC	77338
LANDGROVE DR	0	249B	SWM	77382
LANDING BLVD	100	658T	LC	77573
LANDING BROOK DR	4500	376D	NEC	77346
LANDING CREEK DR	0	328F	NWC	77377
LANDING PINES TRAIL	0	447G	NWC	77084
LANDING POINT	0	658K	LC	77573
LANDING POINT DR	0	612N	PL	77545
LANDING WAY CT	2100	293W	NCC	77373
LANDING WAY DR	0	658K	LC	77573
LANDING WAY DR	24000	293W	NCC	77373
LANDMARK	13000	572J	SWH	77045
LANDMARK DR	2700	462X	NEC	77521

Street Name	Block	Pg/Sq	Loc	Zips
LANDMARK DR	3800	569Y	MC	77459
LANDMORE CT	1600	486L	SWC	77450
LANDOLT	200	658D	WB	77598
LANDON LN	11000	490H	HC	77024
LANDON BROOK CT	19800	486Q	SWC	77450
LANDON CREEK LN	0	406Y	NWC	77449
LANDON LAKE DR	9600	613P	PL	77584
LANDON OAKS DR	17400	407K	NWC	77095
LANDON PARK DR	3600	446K	NWC	77449
LANDON POINT CIR	1900	485L	SWC	77450
LANDOR	5600	454M	NEH	77028
LANDOVER LN	2500	445P	NWC	77493
LANDOVER LN	10700	529X	SWH	77099
LANDOVER HILLS LN	0	484T	NEF	77494
LANDRUM AVE	500	659E	LC	77573
LANDRUM LN	4400	610D	SWH	77489
LANDRUM POINT LN	0	332E	NWC	77388
LANDRY BLVD	9000	329M	NWC	77379
LANDRY BLVD	9900	329M	NWC	77070
LANDSBURY CIR	11000	529X	SWH	77099
LANDSBURY CT	11000	529X	SWH	77099
LANDSBURY DR	10200	529X	SWH	77099
LANDSDOWN CT	3500	613Q	NEB	77584
LANDSDOWNE DR	9000	531N	SWH	77096
LANDSDOWNE DR	11400	571A	SWH	77035
LANDSDOWNE POINTE CT	1300	329B	NWC	77379
LANDSDOWNE POINTE DR	10500	329B	NWC	77379
LANDSDOWN RIDGE WAY	0	377A	NEC	77346
LANDS END	0	368G	NWC	77429
LANDS END CIR	11300	529X	SWH	77099
LANDS END DR	10200	529X	SWH	77099
LANDSHIRE DR	20200	335Q	HM	77338
LANDSHIRE DR	23300	256D	SEM	77357
LANDSWALK DR	11000	529X	SWH	77099
LAND VIEW DR	15900	332V	NCC	77073
LANDWARD LN	4900	371N	NWC	77066
LANDWOOD DR	8700	411S	NWH	77040
LANE	7900	495J	NEH	77029
LANE	10300	496J	JC	77029
LANE LN	100	252J	OR	77386
LANECREST LN	500	490G	PP	77024
LANELL	2500	449R	NWH	77043
LANELL DR	700	538Q	DP	77536
LANELL LN	8600	450Z	SV	77055
LANESBOROUGH	0	447D	NWC	77084
LANESBOROUGH DR	3500	569U	MC	77477
LANES END	1	541C	BT	77520
LANESIDE DR	9200	330N	NWC	77379
LANE VIEW	0	328Z	NWC	77070
LANE VIEW	0	329W	NWC	77070
LANEVIEW DR	10500	369B	NWC	77070
LANEVIEW DR	12000	328Z	NWC	77070
LANE WELL	9700	495M	NEH	77029
LANEWOOD DR	8300	454D	NEH	77016
LANEY WAY	0	527T	NEF	77498
LANG RD	1	459F	NEC	77562
LANG RD	2700	458H	NEC	77562
LANG RD	3300	451J	NWH	77092
LANGBOURNE DR	14000	488E	SWH	77077
LANGBROOK CT	16000	407Z	NWC	77084
LANGCART	15700	498F	CV	77530
LANGDALE RD	9600	453C	NEH	77076
LANGDON CT	0	484T	NEF	77494
LANGDON LN	6600	530M	SWH	77074
LANGDON LN	7900	530J	SWH	77036
LANGDON LN	10700	529L	SWH	77072
LANGFIELD CT	8800	410V	NWH	77040
LANGFIELD RD	4400	450H	NWH	77040
LANGFIELD RD	5800	410Z	NWH	77092
LANGFIELD RD	8800	410V	NWH	77040
LANGHAM DR	5700	408S	NWC	77084
LANGHAM CREEK	0	487C	SWH	77094
LANGHAM CREEK DR	1200	447Y	NWH	77084
LANGHAM CROSSING LN	16900	407Z	NWC	77084
LANGHAM DAWN LN	5701	407Y	NWC	77084
LANGHAM HEIGHTS LN	16900	407Z	NWC	77084
LANGHAM MIST LN	0	407V	NWC	77084
LANGHAM ROSE DR	0	524E	NEF	77494
LANGHAM VIEW DR	0	406H	NWC	77433
LANGHAM WAY DR	6300	407T	NWC	77084
LANGHAMWOOD LN	0	407V	NWC	77084
LANGHORNE CT	5500	526A	NEF	77450
LANGKAWI LN	0	378A	NEC	77346
LANG LAKE DR	0	612J	PL	77545
LANGLEY CT	0	658V	LC	77573
LANGLEY RD	2300	413Z	NEH	77093
LANGLEY RD	2400	414W	NEH	77093
LANGLEY RD	5000	415W	NEH	77016
LANGLEY RD	7800	250X	NWC	77389
LANGLEY POND LN	0	257E	SEM	77357
LANGLEY SPRINGS CT	0	407C	NWC	77095
LANGLEY SPRINGS DR	0	407C	NWC	77095
LANGMONT LN	21500	406X	NWC	77449
LANGSBURY CT	3900	447K	NWC	77084
LANGSBURY DR	18100	447K	NWC	77084
LANGSTON	2200	492B	NWH	77007
LANGSTON DR	10500	463N	MB	77580
LANGSTONE PLACE	0	250L	WD	77389
LANGTON CT	700	486B	SWC	77450
LANGTRY	7200	450H	NWH	77040
LANGTRY LN	4300	450G	NWH	77041
LANGWICK DR	800	373N	NEH	77060
LANGWOOD DR	600	488G	SWH	77079
LANHAM	8000	575P	SEH	77075
LANHAM DR	23000	485B	SWC	77450
LANIBETH	5300	374Z	NCC	77032
LANIER DR	1500	658S	LC	77573
LANIER DR	6500	532H	SWH	77030
LANIER SHORE LN	13900	573U	SEC	77047
LANIS DR	5200	660T	GCO	77539
LANKFORD LN	0	286E	SWM	77447
LANNING DR	24300	445S	NWC	77493
LANNY LN	12300	488M	SWH	77077
LA NOCHE DR	7100	527L	SWC	77083
LANSBURY DR	11500	569B	SWH	77099
LANSDALE DR	10000	529V	SWH	77036
LANSDOWN DR	5600	457S	NEC	77049
W. LANSDOWNE CIR	1	249D	WD	77381
N. LANSDOWNE CIR	1	250A	WD	77382
E. LANSDOWNE CIR	1	250A	WD	77382
LANSFIELD	0	569A	SWH	77477
LANSING	1200	494Y	SEH	77023
LANSING CIR	2400	613N	NEB	77584
LANSING CT	2700	613S	NEB	77584
LANSING LN	0	659P	LC	77573
LANSING COVE DR	0	611S	FS	77545
LANSING CREST CIR	200	457Y	NEC	77015
LANSING CREST DR	14500	457Y	NEC	77015
LANSING FIELD LN	0	373A	NCC	77073
LANSING HOLLOW LN	0	371D	NWC	77014
LANSING MEADOWS DR	0	376S	NEC	77396
LANSING RIDGE LN	0	446J	NWC	77449
LANSWICK DR	15400	618J	SEH	77062
LANTANA	5000	535V	SEH	77017
LANTANA CT	0	245R	SWM	77355
LANTANA DR	8000	463S	CCO	77520
LANTANA DR	22000	245Q	SWM	77355
LANTANA DR	22200	245R	SWM	77355
LANTANA BRANCH LN	0	375X	NEC	77396
LANTANA CREEK CT	5300	485X	NEF	77494
LANTANA ESTATES CT	1200	611X	NEF	77545
LANTANA OAKS LN	0	410A	NWC	77064
LANTANA RIDGE CT	20600	326J	NWC	77433
LANTANA SPRING	0	615G	PL	77581
LANTANA WOODS LN	0	407J	NWC	77433
LANTERN	13800	457Y	NEC	77015
LANTERN LN	1900	610J	MC	77459
LANTERN LN	3400	500H	BT	77521
LANTERN LN	12100	247R	SWM	77362
LANTERN LN	25600	257M	SEM	77357
LANTERN LN	26500	258J	SEM	77357
LANTERN BAY LN	3100	446J	NWC	77449
LANTERN BAY LN	3300	445M	NWC	77449
LANTERN BEND DR	100	332K	NWC	77090
LANTERN COVE LN	0	329F	NWC	77375
LANTERN CREEK LN	15000	331T	NWC	77068
LANTERN ELM ST	0	326Y	NWC	77433
LANTERN FALLS LN	0	446B	NWC	77449
LANTERN HILLS DR	0	296X	SEM	77339
LANTERN HOLLOW PLACE	1	250C	WD	77381
LANTERN LAKE CT	500	613F	NEB	77584
LANTERN POINT DR	8200	532Q	SWH	77054
LANTERN RIDGE LN	0	366V	NWC	77433
LANTERN SPRINGS LN	0	406K	NWC	77433
LANTERN VILLAGE LN	19800	486Q	SWH	77450
LANTRY WAY	10400	372W	NWC	77038
LANVILLE LN	3100	446Q	NWC	77449
LANYARD PLACE	16900	379X	NEC	77532
LANYARD POINTE CIR	2000	619Y	LC	77573
LA PALMA LN	0	447J	NWC	77084
LA PALOMA BLVD	0	616N	PL	77581
LA PALOMA DR	15200	527H	SWC	77083
LA PALOMA ESTATES DR	18500	326C	NWC	77429
LAPAS DR	3700	534L	SEH	77023
LA PASEO	6600	534V	SEH	77087
LA PASEO	7300	535S	SEH	77087
LA PAZ	4600	577B	PA	77504
LAPAZ CT	0	658U	LC	77573
LAPEER CT	0	330K	NWC	77379
LA PIEDRA LN	0	660G	GCO	77565
LAPIS CREEK LN	22000	525D	NEF	77450
LAPIS MEADOW DR	0	406R	NWC	77433
LAPIS PARK LN	32500	252R	SEM	77385
LAPIS SPRING DR	0	612L	PL	77584
LA PLACE CT	16400	527K	NEF	77083
LA PLACE DR	7400	527K	NEF	77083
LA PORTADA DR	0	406D	NWC	77433
LA PORTE (S.H. 225) FRWY	1200	537E	LP	77506
LA PORTE (S.H. 225) FRWY	1200	537E	LP	77506
LA PORTE (S.H. 225) FRWY	4600	538H	DP	77536
LA PORTE (S.H. 225) FRWY	4600	538H	DP	77536
LA PORTE (S.H. 225) FRWY	7100	539K	LP	77571
LA PORTE (S.H. 225) FRWY	7100	539K	LP	77571
LA PORTE (S.H. 225) FRWY	7900	535H	SEH	77012
LA PORTE (S.H. 225) FRWY	7900	535H	SEH	77012
LA PORTE (S.H. 225) FRWY	8500	535H	SEH	77017
LA PORTE (S.H. 225) FRWY	8500	535H	SEH	77017
LA PORTE (S.H. 225) FRWY	10000	536E	SEH	77017
LA PORTE (S.H. 225) FRWY	10000	536E	SEH	77017
LA PORTE (S.H. 225) FRWY	12000	540N	LP	77571
LA PORTE (S.H. 225) FRWY	12000	540N	LP	77571
LA PORTE RD	8100	535F	SEH	77012
LAPSTONE DR	3400	488Y	SWH	77082
LA PUENTE DR	6600	527G	SWC	77083
LAPWICK	0	329M	NWC	77379
LAPWING DR	0	610F	MC	77489
LA QUINTA DR	2300	609H	MC	77459
LA QUINTA DR	2800	610E	MC	77459
LA QUINTA LN	14800	488C	SWH	77079
LAR-REEE OAKS CIR	0	455G	NEH	77028
LARABEE	1800	620N	SB	77586
LARA BROOK CT	2900	485P	NEF	77494
W. LARAH LN	200	486D	SWC	77094
E. LARAH LN	19100	486D	SWC	77094
LARAMIE	6100	375W	NEC	77396
LARAMIE RIVER TRAIL	0	406X	NWC	77449
LARAMIR RIVER CT	0	406Y	NWC	77449
LA RANA DR	14700	527M	SWC	77083
LARA NIGHT CT	0	249Q	NWC	77375
LARBOARD CT	17000	379X	NEC	77532
LARCH CIR	4500	500M	BT	77521
LARCH DR	3700	500M	BT	77521
LARCH LN	4500	531D	BL	77401
LARCHBROOK DR	5600	457T	NEC	77049
LARCHFIELD CT	0	250J	NWC	77389
LARCH GROVE CT	0	289R	NWC	77375
LARCHMERE CT	0	372C	NCC	77073
LARCHMONT RD	1700	492T	SWH	77019
LARCHWOOD DR	16500	375J	NEH	77396
LAREDO	100	501W	BT	77520
LAREDO	6300	494D	NEH	77020
LAREDO	8100	495B	NEH	77029
LAREDO	13700	497G	NEC	77015
LA REFORMA BLVD	3300	502F	BT	77521
LAREINA LN	0	531B	SWH	77081
LARENDON	3900	494P	SEH	77003
LA RETAMA DR	3500	455Z	NEH	77013
LARGO	800	501V	BT	77520
LARGO WOODS PLACE	1	250A	WD	77382
LARGS CIR	17400	329L	NWC	77379
LARGS DR	9600	329L	NWC	77379
LARIAT DR	4200	502J	BT	77521
LARIAT DR	9000	490C	SV	77055
LARIAT CANYON DR	20600	486T	SWC	77450
LARIMAR SEA DR	0	296Y	SEM	77339
LARIMER	5800	494M	NEH	77020
LARISSA CIR	6500	406R	NWC	77449
LARISSA DR	19300	406R	NWC	77449
LA RIVIERA DR	300	497A	NEC	77015
LA RIVIERA DR	500	496D	NEC	77015
LARK	32300	322T	WCO	77484
LARK DR	800	537M	PA	77503
LARK LN	2600	375K	HM	77396
LARK LN	4100	532W	SWH	77025
LARK LN	20900	286J	NWC	77447
LARK BROOK LN	10900	368U	NWC	77065
LARK CREEK LN	21400	446J	NWC	77449
LARKDALE DR	2800	613P	NEB	77584
LARKDALE DR	11300	529T	SWH	77099
LARKEN PARK	16500	367C	NWC	77429
LARK FAIR LN	12400	616H	SEH	77089
LARKFIELD CT	3900	618C	SEH	77059
LARKFIELD DR	15700	618C	SEH	77059
LARK GLEN DR	0	297P	NEH	77345
LARKHALL LN	14300	331Y	NWC	77014
LARK HAVEN LN	0	571K	SWH	77085
LARK HILL	0	334Q	NCC	77373
LARKHILL LN	21300	406Y	NWC	77449
LARK HOLLOW LN	200	658N	LC	77573
LARKIN	4800	492C	NWH	77007
LARKIN FALLS CT	14000	377W	NEC	77044
LARKIN HARK LN	0	376J	NEC	77396
LARK MEADOW DR	9500	411N	NWH	77040
LARKMOUNT DR	6100	290C	NWC	77389
LARK MOUNTAIN DR	0	370U	NWC	77086
LARKNOLLS LN	3000	451R	NWH	77092
LARK ORCHARD WAY	0	526T	NEF	77469
LARK ORCHARD WAY	0	526T	NEF	77469
LARK POINT CT	13000	417W	NEC	77044
LARK RIDGE	10300	369L	NWC	77070
LARKRIDGE LN	6400	290Y	NWC	77379
LARKRUN LN	0	326R	NWC	77429
LARK SKY WAY	0	328N	NWC	77429
LARKSONG LN	4700	291S	NWC	77388
LARKSPUR	4000	533Y	SEH	77051
LARKSPUR	4700	533Z	SEH	77033
W. LARKSPUR CIR	600	613F	NEB	77584
E. LARKSPUR CIR	600	613F	NEB	77584
N. LARKSPUR CIR	2700	613F	NEB	77584
LARKSPUR DR	0	460T	NEC	77562
LARKSPUR DR	700	656H	FR	77546
LARKSPUR LN	1100	619H	TL	77586
LARKSPUR HILLS DR	0	406R	NWC	77433
LARKSPUR HILLS DR	0	407N	NWC	77433
LARKSPUR LANDING	0	526P	NEF	77407
LARKSPUR RIDGE DR	0	524E	NEF	77494
LARKSPUR TRAIL	1	250A	WD	77382
LARKSTONE	6700	454M	NEH	77028
LARKS TRACE LN	0	332N	NWC	77090
LARK VALLEY CT	6100	338A	NEH	77345
LARKWAY DR	13700	568F	SG	77498
LARKWOOD DR	6700	530H	SWH	77074
LARKWOOD DR	9800	570C	SWH	77096
LA ROCHE LN	7700	530N	SWH	77036
LA ROCHELLE	0	620K	SB	77586
LA ROCHELLE CIR	7800	570G	MC	77071
LA ROCHELLE DR	12500	496D	NEC	77015
LARRISON CREEK CIR	0	366N	NWC	77433
LARRY	10100	370W	NWC	77064
LARRY	10100	414X	NEH	77093
LARRYCREST DR	5800	614Y	PL	77584
LARRY WAYNE ST	19200	255R	SEM	77365
LARSON	0	450Z	SV	77055
LARSON	8400	575G	SEH	77061
LARSTON	8800	450W	NWH	77055
LARSTON	10200	449Z	NWH	77043
LA RUE	1000	493N	SWH	77019
LARWOOD CT	2600	371V	NWC	77038
LARWOOD LN	13600	371V	NWC	77038
LASABER CT	10000	412B	NWC	77038
LAS ALAMEDAS	0	575R	SEH	77075
LA SALETTE	6000	533L	SEH	77021
LASALETTE	6100	533L	SEH	77021
LA SALLE	1800	656Q	FR	77546
LA SALLE	1900	658K	LC	77573
LA SALLE	3300	492S	SWH	77027
LASALLE LN	0	528Y	SG	77478
LAS BRISAS	100	619V	LC	77565
LAS BRISAS DR	6400	527H	SWC	77083
LAS BRISAS DR	7100	527M	SWC	77083
LASBURY DR	9400	527Q	NEF	77083
LAS CRUCES	7600	455H	NEH	77078
LAS CRUCES CIR	0	539N	DP	77536
LAS CRUCES CIR	8900	455D	NEH	77078
LA SEINE LN	3300	291U	NWC	77388
LAS FLORES DR	7500	527M	SWC	77083
LASHBROOK DR	1100	489J	SWH	77077
LASHLEY CT	2200	485R	SWC	77450
LASKER BROOK CT	0	484V	NWF	77494
LASKEY	1100	576A	SEH	77034
LASKEY MANOR CT	14000	367D	NWC	77429
LASLINA LN	0	659Q	LC	77573
LAS OLAS PASS	0	660F	LC	77573
LA SOMBRA DR	6700	527G	SWC	77083
LAS PALMAS	3000	492W	SWH	77027
LAS PALMAS DR	0	660G	LC	77573
LA SPEZIA LN	0	659Q	LC	77573
LASSEN FOREST LN	0	377E	NEC	77346
LASSEN VILLA CT	400	298X	NEH	77336
LASSITER HOLLOW LN	7400	527J	NEF	77407
LASSO LN	10800	489C	SWH	77079
LAST ARROW DR	700	488B	SWH	77079
LAS TERRAZAS DR	0	574K	SEH	77075
LASTING LIGHT CT	8700	407D	NWC	77095
LASTING LIGHT LN	16200	407D	NWC	77095
LASTING ROSE DR	17600	327N	NWC	77429
LASTING SHADOW CIR	16600	407C	NWC	77095
W. LASTING SPRING CIR	0	250Q	NWC	77389
E. LASTING SPRING CIR	1900	250Q	NWC	77389
LATANA REACH DR		524L	NWF	77406
LATCH LN	2900	411G	NWH	77038
LATCHMORE LN	6700	457Q	NEC	77049
LA TECHE LN	2600	620J	SB	77586
LATEEN CIR	12700	496D	NEC	77015
LATERNA LN	14000	528N	SWC	77083
LA TERRA DR	16200	527K	NEF	77083
LA TERRE DE VIN CT	0	446E	NWC	77449
LATEXO DR	1500	452E	NWH	77018
LATEXO DR	2100	451H	NWH	77018
LATHAM	1	494U	SEH	77011
LATHROP	100	494M	NEH	77020
LATHY	17400	418R	NEC	77044
LATIGO LN		484S	NEF	77494
LATMA CT	9000	532N	SWH	77025
LATMA DR	3500	532N	SWH	77025
LATROBE LN	3100	486S	NEF	77450
LATSON	15000	330U	NWC	77069
LATTA CREEK DR	0	524A	NEF	77494
LATTICEVINE DR	0	367C	NWC	77429
LATTIMER DR	5900	571A	SWH	77035
LATTIMORE CREEK DR	0	447D	NWC	77084
LATVIA CT	5900	330D	NWC	77379
LAUDER RD	900	413C	NCC	77039
LAUDER RD	2400	414H	NEC	77039
LAUDER RD	6000	415E	NEC	77039
LAUDERDALE	1900	533E	SWH	77030
LAUDERWICK CT	6800	525H	NEF	77450
LAUDERWOOD LN	3600	446K	NWC	77449
LAUGHING BROOK CT	1	251Z	WD	77380
LAUGHING GULL LN	2100	658T	LC	77573
LAUGHING WOOD CT	9400	410D	NWC	77086
LAUGHLIN DR	6600	571W	SWH	77489
LAUGHRIDGE	0	247U	SWM	77355
LAUGHTON LN	6400	407U	NWC	77084
LAUMAR CT	14400	328X	NWC	77429
LAUNCH CT	16000	419A	NEC	77532
LAUNCH RD	0	498H	CV	77530
LAURA	0	256Z	SEM	77357
W. LAURA CIR	6500	462X	NEC	77521
E. LAURA CIR	6500	462X	NEC	77521
S. LAURA CIR	8100	462X	NEC	77521
N. LAURA CIR	8100	462X	NEC	77521
LAURA CIR	14600	368S	NWC	77429
LAURA LN	100	252E	OR	77385
LAURA LN	600	659B	LC	77573
LAURA LN	1400	375D	HM	77338
LAURA LN	1900	539V	LP	77571
LAURA LN	2400	615U	PL	77581
LAURA LN	18200	325B	NWC	77447
LAURA ANNE DR	1800	458S	NEC	77049
LAURA HILLS LN	0	293K	SEM	77386
LAURA JEAN	16900	447D	NWC	77084
LAURA KOPPE RD	2800	454E	NEH	77093
LAURA KOPPE RD	4200	454E	NEH	77016
LAURA KOPPE RD	7100	455E	NEH	77028
LAURA KOPPE RD	8800	456E	NEH	77078
LAURAL BREEZE LN	0	417A	NEC	77044
LAURA LEE LN	0	295R	SEM	77365
LAURA LEE LN	5000	577J	PA	77504
LAURA LEIGH LN	3700	657B	FR	77546
LAURA LYNN DR	0	325V	NWC	77433
LAURA MORISON DR	0	568L	SG	77478
LAURAS GLEN CT	22400	485Y	NEF	77450
LAURA SHORE CIR	0	366K	NWC	77433
E. LAURA SHORE CT	12200	366K	NWC	77433
E. LAURA SHORE DR	18300	366K	NWC	77433
W. LAURA SHORE DR	18400	366K	NWC	77433
LAURA SPRINGS	0	336A	SEM	77339
LAURA WAY DR	20000	486P	SWC	77450
LAUREL	3000	612S	FS	77545
LAUREL	4600	531G	BL	77401
LAUREL CT	0	245U	SWM	77355
LAUREL CT	0	329S	NWC	77377
LAUREL CT	500	659G	LC	77573
LAUREL CT	12100	569E	SF	77477
LAUREL DR	0	500E	BT	77520
LAUREL DR	200	656D	FR	77546
LAUREL DR	4300	533H	SEH	77021
LAUREL DR	4400	534E	SEH	77021
LAUREL LN	8100	463S	CCO	77520
LAUREL ARBOR DR	2100	371H	NWC	77014
LAUREL BANK WAY	12700	372E	NWC	77014
LAUREL BAY CT	0	484N	NEF	77494
LAUREL BAY DR	1800	372E	NWC	77014
LAUREL BEND LN	2100	371H	NWC	77014
LAUREL BIRCH DR	2200	371H	NWC	77014
LAUREL BOUGH LN	1800	372E	NWC	77014
N. LAUREL BRANCH DR	10200	369Y	NWC	77064
S. LAUREL BRANCH DR	10300	369Y	NWC	77064
LAUREL BRANCH WAY	2100	371H	NWC	77014
LAUREL BRIAR LN	0	457A	NEC	77044
LAUREL BRIDGE	0	410E	NWC	77040
LAUREL BROOK LN	0	612Q	PL	77584
LAUREL BROOK LN	1900	372E	NWC	77014
LAUREL CANYON DR	0	324J	HK	77447
LAUREL CAVERNS DR	5800	297Z	NEH	77345
LAUREL CHASE LN	24700	485S	NEF	77494
LAUREL CHASE TRAIL	0	332V	NCC	77073
LAUREL CHERRY WAY	2900	251K	WD	77380
LAUREL COVE	15800	329S	NWC	77377
LAUREL CREEK	0	371H	NWC	77014
LAUREL CREEK	0	536S	SEH	77017
LAUREL CREEK CT	4300	609F	MC	77459
LAUREL CREEK CT	9500	410J	NWC	77040
LAUREL CREEK WAY	2700	616N	PL	77581
LAUREL CREEK WAY	5000	535V	SEH	77017
LAUREL CREEK WAY	5200	536T	SEH	77017
LAUREL CREST CT	3400	296Y	NEH	77339
LAUREL CREST DR	3300	296Y	NEH	77339
LAURELDALE CT	10800	449H	NWH	77041
E. LAURELDALE DR	4800	449H	NWH	77041
N. LAURELDALE DR	10400	449H	NWH	77041
LAURELDALE RD	4500	449H	NWH	77041
LAURELDALE PARK LN	0	253N	SEM	77386
LAURELDALE VIEW	0	449H	NWH	77041
LAUREL FALLS CT	12600	371H	NWC	77014
LAUREL FALLS LN	12700	371H	NWC	77014
LAUREL FIELD DR	0	657A	FR	77546
LAURELFIELD DR	15700	618D	SEH	77059
LAUREL FOREST WAY	2100	371H	NWC	77014
LAUREL FORK CT	4100	297S	NEH	77339
LAUREL FORK DR	2900	297S	NEH	77339
LAUREL GARDEN DR	2700	337A	NEH	77339
LAUREL GLEN CT	0	658S	LC	77573
LAUREL GLEN DR	6600	407S	NWC	77449
LAUREL GREEN	25300	293P	NCC	77373
LAUREL GREEN CT	4400	569T	MC	77459
LAUREL GREEN RD	0	569T	MC	77459
LAUREL GROVE DR	4000	619L	TL	77586
LAUREL GROVE LN	700	613F	NEB	77584
LAUREL HAVEN WAY	12500	371H	NWC	77014
LAUREL HEIGHTS CT	4600	448B	NWC	77084
LAUREL HEIGHTS DR	15500	448B	NWC	77084
LAUREL HILL CT	4900	569W	SG	77478
LAUREL HILL DR	1900	336C	NEH	77339
LAUREL HILLS DR	0	257F	SEM	77357
LAUREL HILLS DR	0	371H	NWC	77014
LAUREL HOLLOW DR	3600	331C	NWC	77388
LAUREL KNOLL CIR	15300	326T	NWC	77433
LAUREL LAKE DR	2900	337A	NEH	77339
LAUREL LAND LN	2000	371H	NWC	77014
LAUREL LEAF LN	0	615C	PL	77581
LAUREL LEAF LN	8300	338N	NEC	77346
LAUREL LOCH CT	0	612J	PL	77545
LAUREL LOCH LN	0	612J	PL	77545
LAUREL LOCK DR	20200	486F	SWC	77450
LAUREL MAPLE CT	0	290P	NWC	77379
LAUREL MEADOW DR	11800	329S	NWC	77377
LAUREL MEADOW LN	0	568A	SG	77498
LAUREL MEADOW WAY	12400	371H	NWC	77014
LAUREL MIST CT	2900	297Q	NEH	77345
LAUREL MIST WAY	12700	371H	NWC	77014
LAUREL NOOK WAY	12600	371H	NWC	77014
LAUREL OAK DR	2100	570Y	MC	77489
LAUREL OAK PLACE	1	251U	WD	77380
LAUREL OAKS CT	0	489W	SWH	77082
LAUREL OAKS DR	1800	372E	NWC	77014
LAUREL OAKS DR	2200	371H	NWC	77014
LAUREL PARK LN	19500	486H	SWC	77094
LAUREL PINE DR	400	336E	NEH	77339
LAUREL PLACE LN	0	371H	NWC	77014
LAUREL POINT CT	3200	337E	NEH	77339
LAUREL RAIN CT	0	446K	NWC	77449
LAUREL REACH DR	0	290S	NWC	77379
LAUREL RIDGE DR	0	337C	NEH	77345
LAUREL RIDGE DR	2500	297Y	NEH	77345
LAUREL RIDGE DR	2900	659H	LC	77573
LAUREL RIVER DR	13400	528F	SWC	77083

Street Name	Block	Pg/Sq	Loc	Zips
LAUREL RIVER BEND	2200	371H	NWC	77014
LAUREL ROCK DR	3900	297T	NEH	77345
LAUREL ROSE LN	1800	372E	NWC	77014
LAUREL RUN	6300	408T	NWC	77084
LAUREL RUSTIC OAKS	2300	371H	NWC	77014
LAUREL SAGE DR	400	336E	NEH	77339
LAUREL SHADOWS CT	14600	617H	SEH	77062
LAUREL SPRINGS CT	200	568V	SG	77478
LAUREL SPRINGS LN	1600	336A	NEH	77339
LAURELSTONE CT	14100	568A	SG	77498
LAUREL STONE LN	0	410E	NWC	77064
LAUREL TERRACE CT	22100	525C	NEF	77450
LAUREL TERRACE WAY	2200	371H	NWC	77014
LAUREL TIMBERS DR	400	336E	NEH	77339
LAURELTON CT	0	376C	NEC	77396
LAURELTON DR	0	376C	NEC	77396
LAUREL TRACE	8400	410E	NWC	77040
LAUREL TRAIL DR	19800	406L	NWC	77433
LAUREL TRAILS DR	3600	337E	NEH	77339
LAUREL TRAILS DR	8400	407H	NWC	77095
LAUREL VALE WAY	12700	371H	NWC	77014
LAUREL VALLEY DR	1000	618J	SEH	77062
LAUREL VALLEY DR	1800	372E	NWC	77014
LAURELWALK LN	0	485P	NEF	77494
LAUREL WIND CT	9400	410J	NWC	77040
LAUREL WOOD	0	610K	MC	77459
LAURELWOOD DR	5100	297Y	NEH	77345
LAURELWOOD DR	16100	458Z	CV	77530
LAURELWOOD DR	17100	459W	CV	77530
LAURELWOOD LN	3400	613C	NEB	77584
LAURELWOOD LN	22700	289L	NWC	77375
LAUREN CT	0	538V	DP	77536
LAUREN LN	0	501H	NEC	77521
LAUREN LN	3100	488X	SWC	77082
LAUREN LN	6400	614T	PL	77584
LAUREN BRIAR LN	0	376W	NEC	77396
LAUREN COVE LN	28300	293F	SEM	77386
LAUREN CREEK DR	0	502H	BT	77520
LAUREN CREEK LN	1500	293J	SEM	77386
LAURENHURST CT	1	449Z	NWH	77043
LAUREN LAKE DR	1900	619Z	LC	77573
LAUREN MEADOW LN	22600	525B	NEF	77494
LAUREN OAKS LN	0	376G	NEC	77396
LAUREN PLACE	0	570S	MC	77489
LAUREN ROSE LN	0	616N	PL	77581
LAURENS LANDING	28600	253Y	SEM	77386
LAURENTIDE	1100	495L	NEH	77029
LAUREN TRAIL	0	615Y	PL	77581
LAUREN VERONICA DR	10600	576K	SEH	77034
LAURENWOOD CT	0	375Z	NEC	77396
LAURETTE DR	19600	295G	SEM	77365
LAUREUMONT CT	24100	485T	NEF	77494
LAUREUMONT LN	0	485T	NEF	77494
LAURI LN	10100	460F	NEC	77532
LAURIE LN	6000	614L	PL	77581
LAURIE LN	11900	490K	BH	77024
LAURI LYNN DR	30000	252Y	SEM	77386
LAURUS ESTATES LN	14200	366D	NWC	77429
LAURYNNBROOK DR	5000	578C	PA	77505
LAUSANNE DR	0	329U	NWC	77070
LAUSANNE DR	3000	537Y	PA	77505
LAUSANNE DR	3100	577C	PA	77505
LAUTREC DR	6300	411S	NWH	77088
LAVA LN	0	526S	NEF	77407
LAVACA	700	535B	SEH	77012
LAVACA	1800	656U	FR	77546
LAVACA DR	5400	614Z	PL	77584
LAVACA DR	21000	256N	SEM	77357
LAVACA RANCH LN	0	445M	NWC	77449
LAVACA RANCH LN	0	445R	NWC	77449
LAVAERTON WOOD LN	7400	526J	NEF	77407
LAVAGE LN	8000	461T	NEC	77521
LAVANDER QUARTZ CT	0	524F	NEF	77494
LAVAUN	0	576B	SEH	77034
LAVELL DR	4400	452E	NWH	77018
LAVENDER	2900	494C	NEH	77026
LAVENDER	3700	454U	NEH	77026
LAVENDER	6500	454U	NEH	77028
LAVENDER	7000	454G	NEH	77016
LAVENDER LN	5200	461T	NEC	77521
LAVENDER BAY LN	0	327S	NWC	77429
LAVENDER BEND LN	0	524K	NEF	77406
LAVENDER CANDLE DR	3100	331D	NWC	77388
LAVENDER CREEK CT	16200	326N	NWC	77433
LAVENDER HILLS CT	0	615K	PL	77581
LAVENDER JADE CT	0	296T	SEM	77338
LAVENDER MIST LN	0	524F	NEF	77494
LAVENDER RUN DR	15800	367D	NWC	77429
LAVENDER SHADE CT	0	372D	NCC	77073
LAVENDER TRACE DR	0	253T	SEM	77386
LAVENDERWOOD DR	20800	446N	NWC	77449
LAVER LOVE DR	6200	330M	NWC	77379
LAVERN	3600	611X	FS	77545
LAVERNE	700	536V	PA	77502
LAVERNE	1700	450Q	NWH	77080
LAVERNE CRESCENT	0	450U	NWH	77080
LAVERNE PARK LN	0	450U	NWH	77080
LAVERN ESTATES CT	0	450U	NWH	77080
LAVEROCK RD	3900	331G	NWC	77388
LAVERTON CT	400	486B	SWC	77450
LAVERTON DR	20200	486B	SWC	77450
LA VIOLETTA DR	6500	527F	NEF	77083
LA VISTA DR	9700	450F	NWH	77041
LAVON DR	12200	328D	NWC	77375
LAVONE CT	0	296J	SEM	77365
LAVONE DR	0	295M	SEM	77365
LAVONIA LN	1300	537P	PA	77502
LAVON LAKE LN	0	377G	NEH	77346
LAW	3800	532A	SWH	77005
LAW	3900	492W	SWH	77005
LAWFORD LN	6100	410X	NWH	77040
LAWICK CIR	1600	568Y	SG	77478
LAWLER	7800	533T	SEH	77051
LAWLER RIDGE	6900	451Y	NWH	77055
LAWN	7500	412Q	NWH	77088
LAWN LN	5700	411T	NWH	77088
LAWN ARBOR DR	5100	370D	NWC	77066
LAWNCLIFF LN	8600	410K	NWC	77040
LAWN CREST	0	570Y	MC	77489
LAWNDALE	5100	494Y	SEH	77023
LAWNDALE	6400	534D	SEH	77023
LAWNDALE	7200	535A	SEH	77012
LAWNDALE	9500	536F	SEH	77017
LAWNDALE PLAZA	1500	534D	SEH	77023
LAWNGATE DR	9600	450K	NWH	77080
LAWNHAVEN DR	13300	571M	SWH	77045
LAWNRIDGE	8600	454G	NEH	77016
LAWN WOOD LN	7700	410D	NWC	77086
LAWN WOOD LN	7800	370Z	NWC	77086
LAWRANCE TRACE CT	13700	367C	NWC	77429
LAWRENCE	0	379Q	NEC	77532
LAWRENCE	100	288L	TB	77375
LAWRENCE	700	492D	NWH	77007
LAWRENCE	900	452Z	NWH	77008
LAWRENCE	1200	537J	PA	77506
LAWRENCE	2100	538Q	DP	77536
LAWRENCE	3000	452R	NWH	77018
LAWRENCE CT	0	614Y	PL	77584
LAWRENCE LN	13000	570J	SF	77477
LAWRENCE RD	900	620W	GCO	77565
LAWRENCE RD	1500	660B	KE	77565
LAWRENCE RD	4300	503M	CCO	77520
LAWRENCE RD	27900	288L	TB	77375
LAWRENCE PLACE	0	614Y	PL	77584
LAWSON	1100	494X	SEH	77023
LAWSON	5300	534C	SEH	77023
LAWSON CT	3000	613U	NEB	77584
LAWSON DR	3400	613U	NEB	77584
LAWSON CYPRESS DR	0	329J	NWC	77377
LAWSON LAKE LN	4800	526X	NEF	77407
LAWSON OAKS DR	0	406H	NWC	77433
LAWSON PEAK LN	0	366V	NWC	77433
LAWSONS CREEK LN	0	528L	SWH	77072
LAWSUIT LN	22400	256L	SEM	77357
LAWTHER DR	14900	497H	NEC	77530
W. LAWTHER LN	2200	538Q	DP	77536
E. LAWTHER LN	2200	538Q	DP	77536
LAWTON DR	2500	613U	NEB	77584
LAWTON BEND LN	4700	484Z	NEF	77494
LAWTON LANDING LN	0	484U	NEF	77494
LAWTON RIDGE DR	14400	327X	NWC	77429
LAWTON VALLEY DR	0	377F	NEC	77346
LAXEY GLEN DR	1	329D	NWC	77379
LAXTON CT	200	486B	SWC	77450
LAYFAIR PLACE	900	657J	FR	77546
LAYHILL CT	13600	488P	SWH	77077
LAYNE	3000	580Q	LP	77571
LAYNES RUN DR	0	407E	NWC	77433
LAYTHAM LN	14900	527V	NEF	77498
LAYTON	100	535A	SEH	77012
LAYTON DR	1100	541C	BT	77520
LAYTON CASTLE LN	13400	367G	NWC	77429
LAYTON HILLS DR	13600	367C	NWC	77429
LAYTON MEADOWS LN	0	330H	NWC	77379
LAYTON RIDGE DR	0	376N	NEC	77396
LAZARAS	6300	453Q	NEH	77022
LAZDINS CIR	13000	368L	NWC	77429
LAZEE OAKS	32800	246V	SWM	77355
LAZEE TRAIL	1	490E	BH	77024
LAZY CT	29600	298M	NEC	77336
LAZY LN	0	659S	LC	77573
LAZY LN	1	251Q	WD	77380
LAZY LN	1	620T	KE	77565
LAZY LN	100	500E	BT	77520
LAZY LN	1900	570W	MC	77489
LAZY LN	7600	250W	NWC	77389
LAZY LN	19000	255X	SEM	77365
LAZY LN	29500	252Y	SEM	77386
LAZY BEND	2500	614Q	PL	77581
LAZYBROOK DR	2000	452S	NWH	77008
LAZY BROOK LN	8400	578D	LP	77571
LAZY CREEK DR	20400	258T	SEM	77357
LAZY CREEK LN	1800	616S	PL	77581
LAZY CREEK LN	2000	536T	SEH	77017
S. LAZY DAISY CIR	0	326J	NWC	77433
E. LAZY DAISY CIR	16500	326J	NWC	77433
LAZYDALE LN	9100	455H	NEH	77078
LAZY ELM CT	17000	407L	NWC	77095
LAZY FALLS	0	447N	NWC	77084
LAZY FALLS CT	14500	528S	NEF	77083
LAZYGATE DR	0	334E	NCC	77373
LAZY GREEN DR	0	292N	NWC	77388
LAZY GROVE	14500	248S	SWM	77362
LAZY GROVE DR	1900	336C	NEH	77339
LAZY HILL LN	17000	330J	NWC	77379
LAZY HOLLOW CT	0	615K	PL	77581
LAZY HOLLOW DR	100	657R	LC	77573
LAZY HOLLOW DR	2300	490U	SWH	77063
LAZY HOLLOW LN	0	615K	PL	77581
LAZY HOLLOW LN	23200	285B	SWM	77447
LAZY KAY LN	24000	325E	NWC	77447
LAZY KAY LN	24200	324H	NWC	77447
LAZY KNOLL DR	5300	371N	NWC	77086
LAZY LAGOON	10100	369W	NWC	77065
LAZY LAKE DR	2500	619T	NB	77058
LAZY LANE	0	541C	BT	77520
LAZY LANE	2900	492Q	SWH	77019
LAZY MEADOWS DR	10000	369Y	NWC	77064
LAZY MEADOWS DR	10700	369T	NWC	77064
S. LAZY MEADOW WAY	0	294U	SEM	77386
S. LAZY MEADOW WAY	0	294U	SEM	77386
N. LAZY MEADOW WAY	0	294Q	SEM	77386
N. LAZY MEADOW WAY	0	294Q	SEM	77386
LAZY MIST CT	5300	660X	DI	77539
LAZY MORNING PLACE	1	250D	WD	77381
LAZY MOSS LN	18300	330E	NWC	77379
LAZY NOOK	10500	413X	NEH	77076
LAZY OAK LN	24200	339J	HU	77336
LAZY OAKS	10000	450S	NWH	77080
LAZY OAKS RANCH RD	14400	327Y	CY	77429
LAZY PINE	3000	580P	LP	77571
LAZY PINE DR	29000	298R	NEC	77336
LAZY PINES	1500	453H	NEH	77093
LAZY RAVINE LN	21100	333E	NCC	77073
S. LAZY RIDGE RD	4900	611C	SWH	77053
LAZY RIDGE RD	16100	611C	SWH	77053
LAZY RIVER LN	8900	412L	NWH	77088
LAZY ROCK DR	0	298V	NEC	77336
LAZY ROLL LN	0	367P	NWC	77433
LAZY SHADOWS CT	0	377F	NEC	77346
LAZY SPRING CT	2600	610B	MC	77489
LAZY SPRING DR	0	450Q	NWH	77080
LAZY SPRING DR	1400	610B	MC	77489
LAZY SPRING DR	2400	450L	NWH	77080
LAZY SPRINGS LN	0	615B	PL	77581
LAZY SPRINGS LN	800	292U	NCC	77373
LAZY TEE	0	249Z	NWC	77375
LAZY TIMBERS DR	0	376D	NEC	77346
LAZY TRAIL PATH CT	24700	293S	NCC	77373
LAZY VALLEY DR	19200	446R	NWC	77449
LAZY WILLOW CT	14400	570V	SWH	77489
LAZY WILLOW LN	14500	570V	SWH	77489
LAZY WOOD	100	619H	TL	77586
LAZYWOOD	12500	247M	SWM	77362
LAZY WOOD LN	1	490L	PP	77024
LAZYWOOD LN	3500	534L	SEH	77023
L DES CHAMPS ELYEES WAY	0	491M	SWH	77056
LEA	13000	574N	SEH	77048
LEACASTLE LN	0	573T	SEC	77047
LEACHWOOD DR	24300	445N	NWC	77493
LEACREST CIR	6000	457S	NEC	77049
LEACREST DR	0	457S	NEC	77049
LEACREST DR	14400	457S	NEC	77049
LEADENHALL CIR	900	498A	NEC	77530
LEADENHALL CIR	1000	458W	NEC	77530
LEADER	6300	531E	SWH	77074
LEADER	7700	530F	SWH	77036
LEADER	11500	529F	SWH	77072
LEADER	12700	528H	SWH	77072
LEADER	13100	528G	SWH	77083
LEADERS CROSSING DR	6900	528L	SWH	77072
LEADER TRAIL	13100	528G	SWH	77072
LEADING CIR	13100	528L	SWH	77072
LEADING EDGE DR	2100	617T	SEC	77546
LEADING POINT DR	0	452F	NWH	77091
LEADORE DR	0	410T	NWC	77040
LEADPOINT DR	0	610Q	MC	77459
LEADVILLE CT	0	611N	FS	77545
LEAF	0	616G	SEC	77089
LEAF LN	20500	295M	SEM	77365
LEAF ARBOR DR	6200	451F	NWH	77092
LEAFBROOK CT	100	330E	NWC	77379
LEAFBROOK LN	7700	330E	NWC	77379
LEAF CHASE CT	15800	367D	NWC	77429
LEAF CREEK	1700	485L	NEF	77494
LEAFDALE CT	20600	335J	NCC	77338
LEAFDALE DR	0	372B	NWC	77014
LEAFDALE DR	8400	335J	NCC	77338
LEAF FOREST DR	4200	297Y	NEH	77345
LEAF GLEN LN	12900	528L	SWH	77072
LEAF GROVE	0	326S	NWC	77433
LEAFGROVE LN	0	253N	SEM	77386
LEAFLET LN	200	332A	NWC	77388
LEAFLOCK CIR	4100	485Y	NEF	77450
LEAFLOCK LN	4200	485Y	NEF	77450
LEAF LYNN WAY	0	293K	SEM	77386
LEAF MEADOWS CT	2100	293E	SEM	77386
LEAFMORE CT	8600	527R	NEF	77083
LEAF OAK DR	11800	369S	NWC	77065
LEAFPARK LN	0	335P	NCC	77338
LEAF POINT CT	7800	407G	NWC	77095
LEAF RIDGE DR	23300	485K	NEF	77494
LEAFSAGE CT	300	250C	WD	77381
LEAF SKY LN	0	326L	NWC	77429
LEAFSTONE LN	0	612U	PL	77584
LEAFSTONE LN	23300	292G	NCC	77373
LEAFTEX DR	7400	375T	NEH	77396
LEAFTON LN	0	492D	NWH	77007
LEAFTON LN	26400	248J	SWM	77354
LEAF TRACE CT	1	250H	WD	77381
LEAF VINES DR	0	253T	SEM	77386
LEAF VINES LN	0	253W	SEM	77386
LEAFWIND DR	0	406Q	NWC	77433
LEAFWOOD CIR	100	657Q	LC	77573
LEAFWOOD LN	0	612N	PL	77545
LEAFWOOD LN	19300	446V	NWC	77084
LEAFY LN	8300	451W	SV	77055
LEAFY ARBOR DR	11900	369Q	NWC	77070
LEAFY ARCH WAY	0	377A	NEC	77346
LEAFY ASPEN CT	5900	298W	NEH	77345
LEAFY BROOK CT	0	446D	NWC	77084
LEAFY ELM CT	14200	618E	SEH	77062
LEAFYGATE DR	22500	334C	NCC	77373
LEAFY GLEN DR	2300	618A	SEH	77059
LEAFY GLEN DR	2900	578W	SEH	77059
LEAFY HOLLOW CT	5000	452F	NWH	77018
LEAFY PINE CT	3200	297P	NEH	77345
LEAFY SHORES DR	0	377K	NEC	77044
LEAFY TREE DR	0	332W	NWC	77090
LEAFY TREE DR	0	332W	NWC	77090
LEAFYWOOD DR	25800	252P	SEM	77386
LEAGO	200	452H	NWH	77022
LEAGO	600	452D	NWH	77091
LEAGUE	100	658M	LC	77573
LEAGUE	9900	416W	NEC	77078
LEAGUE CITY PKWY	0	657U	LC	77573
LEAGUE CITY PKWY	0	658T	LC	77573
LEAGUE LINE	26500	284X	NWC	77447
LEAHBELLE	5100	411G	NWC	77088
LEAH MANOR LN	2700	293K	SEM	77386
LEAHOLM LN	800	332N	NWC	77090
LEAL DR	13700	370B	NWC	77069
LEAMAN	16000	246U	SWM	77355
LEAMINGTON DR	9900	329Q	NWC	77070
LEAMINGTON LN	16300	407H	NWC	77095
LEAMINGTON ST	0	568W	SG	77479
LEAMONT DR	7900	529P	SWH	77072
LEAMONT DR	8600	529P	SWH	77099
LEANDER	7900	535G	SEH	77012
LEANDER TRACT LN	0	367S	NWC	77433
LEANDRA DR	6600	527G	SWC	77083
LEANETT WAY	2400	613U	NEB	77584
LEANETT WAY CT	3900	613U	NEB	77584
LEANING ASH LN	10900	489C	SWH	77079
LEANING MAGNOLIA CT	7000	457L	NEC	77049
LEANING OAKS DR	7200	411T	NWH	77088
LEANING OAK TRAIL	0	524W	NWF	77406
LEANING PINE DR	11500	329W	NWC	77070
LEANING TIMBERS DR	19500	337S	NEC	77346
LEANING TREE LN	9500	409D	NWC	77064
LEANNE TRAIL LN	0	293J	SEM	77386
LEA OAK CT	1	251N	WD	77381
LEAR	900	497E	NEH	77015
LEAR	1200	496M	NEH	77015
LEARNING LN	0	609Z	MC	77459
LEARNING LN	0	609Z	MC	77459
LEATH	9600	454B	NEH	77093
LEATHERGATE DR	23800	293Z	NCC	77373
LEATHER MARKET	7600	410H	NWC	77064
LEATHER SADDLE CT	14500	377S	NEC	77044
LEATHERSTEM LN	1800	297V	NEH	77345
LEATHERWOOD DR	1500	486L	SWC	77450
LEATON PARK CT	0	488T	SWH	77077
LEA VALLEY DR	14600	457S	NEC	77049
LEAVINS	900	501Y	BT	77520
LEAWOOD BLVD	7300	529K	SWH	77072
LEAWOOD BLVD	8600	529T	SWH	77099
LE BADIE	2700	454S	NEH	77026
LEBATE	7900	455K	NEH	77028
LE BEAU LN	2200	620J	SB	77586
LEBEN LN	8100	455E	NEH	77028
LE BERGE DR	26000	288Y	NWC	77377
LE BLANC LN	100	419R	BR	77562
LEBON LN	11800	569E	SF	77477
LEBRA	10100	415W	NEH	77016
LE CARPE PLANTATION CT	0	406Z	NWC	77449
LE CHATEAU DR	12700	497A	NEC	77015
LECHUGUILLA DR	2500	293F	SEM	77386
LECLAIRE MEADOW DR	0	335J	NCC	77338
LECLERC LN	11700	489J	SWH	77077
LECONTE LN	21800	333H	NCC	77338
LEDBETTER	5600	534Y	SEH	77087
LEDBURY PARK LN	19000	329H	NWC	77379
LEDBURY WAY LN	0	609S	NEF	77479
LEDFORD LN	11000	415T	NEH	77016
LEDGE	8800	575M	SEH	77075
LEDGE	9700	576J	SEH	77075
LEDGEBROOK LN	2600	617Y	SEC	77546
LEDGECREEK LN	4900	446D	NWC	77449
LEDGECREST DR	2100	411D	NWC	77038
LEDGEFIELD	0	326J	NWC	77433
LEDGER LN	0	609Y	MC	77459
LEDGER LN	1800	496M	GP	77015
LEDGESIDE CT	2900	485S	NEF	77494
LEDGESTONE DR	3400	618D	SEH	77059
LEDGEWAY CT	0	486N	SWC	77450
LEDGEWOOD DR	7900	457E	NEC	77049
LEDGEWOOD PARK DR	15200	367H	NWC	77429
LEDLA DR	15600	373T	NCC	77032
LE DOUX OAKS	200	657R	LC	77573
LEDWICKE	1400	495L	NEH	77029
LEE	0	536R	PA	77506
LEE	100	538L	DP	77536
LEE	500	580C	LP	77571
LEE	1000	537N	PA	77506
LEE	1200	493D	NEH	77009
LEE	1700	494A	NEH	77026
LEE	4400	494C	NEH	77020
LEE AVE	0	257A	SEM	77357
LEE CIR	0	615L	PL	77581
LEE DR	100	501X	BT	77520
LEE DR	500	541F	BT	77520
LEE LN	16100	614Z	PL	77584
LEE RD	0	290U	NWC	77379
LEE RD	0	659V	GCO	77539
LEE RD	100	580V	PA	77586
LEE RD	100	613H	PL	77581
LEE RD	14200	374M	NEH	77396
LEE RD	14201	374H	NEH	77032
LEE RD	18000	375A	NEH	77396
LEE RD	18400	334R	NCC	77338
LEE, ROBERT E RD	11800	456H	NEC	77044
LEE'S CT	2300	658P	LC	77573
LEE ANN LN	800	288C	TB	77375
LEECAST CT	7500	525F	NEF	77407
LEECH RD	0	286F	NWC	77377
LEE CIRCLE CT	3100	615Q	PL	77581
LEEDALE RD	5800	414V	NEH	77016
LEEDALE RD	6000	415S	NEH	77016
LEEDS LN	0	527U	NEF	77083
LEEDS LN	15300	409M	JV	77040
LEEDSCASTLE MANOR	1500	329C	NWC	77379
LEEDS LANDING LN	0	293H	SEM	77386
LEEDSTOWN LN	22500	445U	NWC	77449
LEEDSWELL LN	16300	407V	NWC	77084
LEEDWICK DR	13300	408Y	NWC	77041
LEEK	2500	494W	SEH	77004
LEELAND	700	493Q	DT	77002
LEELAND	1600	493V	SEH	77003
LEELAND	4000	494Y	SEH	77023
LEEMONT CT	12700	369K	NWC	77070
LEEMYERS LN	19700	332A	NWC	77388
LEEN'S LODGE LN	7000	377C	NEC	77346
LEENE'S LODGE LN	18400	377C	NEC	77346
LEE OAKS CT	0	334R	NCC	77338
LEE OTIS	8500	533Z	SEH	77051
LEESA LN	8000	578M	SEH	77507
LEESHIRE DR	4000	532N	SWH	77025
LEE SHORE LN	500	488B	SWH	77079
LEESIDE CT	12500	328L	NWC	77377
LEESIDE DR	17200	328L	NWC	77377
LEE SPRINGS LN	0	334R	NCC	77338
LEESTEAD CT	0	291Z	NWC	77388
LEESVILLE DR	0	257E	SEM	77357
LEESWAY RD	1600	524Y	NEF	77406
LEEWARD CIR	1400	620Y	KE	77565
LEEWARD LN	1	619W	NB	77058
LEEWARD BEND CT	0	366N	NWC	77433
LEEWARD COVE DR	1	251F	WD	77381
LEE WAY DR	16200	367L	CY	77429
LEEWOOD CT	19300	337S	NEC	77346
LE FEVRE, J B RD	0	501W	BT	77520
LEFFINGWELL	2200	494B	NEH	77026
LEFFINGWELL	3800	454T	NEH	77026
LEFTFIELD	0	242R	WCO	77484
LEGACY CT	29000	246A	SWM	77355
LEGACY DR	0	411D	NWC	77038
LEGACY CREEK DR	0	290J	NWC	77375
LEGACY OAK ST	0	445J	NWC	77493
LEGACY PARK DR	10700	409D	NWC	77064
LEGACY PARK DR	10800	369Z	NWC	77064
LEGACY PINES DR	0	253T	SEM	77386
LEGACY PINES DR	0	407N	NWC	77433
W. LEGACY POINT CIR	1	250A	WD	77382
E. LEGACY POINT CIR	1	250A	WD	77382
LEGACY WOODS DR	0	327H	NWC	77429
LEGANO DR	0	445E	NWC	77493
LEGARE CT	5500	408X	NWC	77084
LEGEND LN	1	489M	SWH	77024
LEGENDARY LN	23700	525A	NEF	77494
LEGEND BROOK CT		329K	NWC	77375
LEGEND COVE CT	7800	407K	NWC	77095
LEGEND CREEK CT		329K	NWC	77375
LEGEND FALLS CT	14400	528N	NEF	77083
LEGEND GROVE CT	2000	618A	SEC	77062
LEGEND MANOR DR	11400	489W	SWH	77082
LEGEND MANOR DR	11400	529B	SWH	77082
LEGEND MANOR DR	11900	489W	SWH	77042
LEGEND OAK DR	20000	338S	NEC	77346
LEGEND POINT	1300	620S	CS	77565
LEGEND RUN CT	0	329K	NWC	77375
LEGENDS BEAM DR	0	293B	SEM	77386
LEGENDS BEND DR	3000	253W	SEM	77386
LEGENDS BLUFF DR	0	253W	SEM	77386
LEGENDS BLUFF DR	0	293B	SEM	77386
LEGENDS BRANCH LN	0	253W	SEM	77386
LEGENDS BRIAR DR	0	253X	SEM	77386
S. LEGENDS CHASE CIR	0	253W	SEM	77386
N. LEGENDS CHASE CIR	29800	253W	SEM	77386
S. LEGENDS CHASE CT	0	253W	SEM	77386
N. LEGENDS CHASE CT	0	253W	SEM	77386
S. LEGENDS CREEK CT	0	253W	SEM	77386
N. LEGENDS CREEK CT	0	253W	SEM	77386
LEGENDS CREEK DR	3200	253X	SEM	77386
LEGENDS CREST DR	0	253X	SEM	77386
LEGENDS CROSSING DR	29500	253W	SEM	77386
LEGENDS ESTATES DR	2500	253S	SEM	77386
LEGENDS GARDEN DR	3300	253X	SEM	77386
LEGENDS GATE DR	30300	253S	SEM	77386
LEGENDS GLEN DR	29300	253X	SEM	77386
LEGENDS GREEN DR	3200	253X	SEM	77386
LEGENDS HILL CT	3200	253X	SEM	77386
LEGENDS HILL DR	0	253X	SEM	77386
LEGENDS HOLLOW DR	2200	253S	SWM	77386
LEGENDS KNOLL DR	0	253W	SEM	77386
LEGENDS LANDING DR	3300	253X	SEM	77386
LEGENDS LINE DR	29300	253X	SEM	77386
LEGENDS LINK DR	0	293B	SEM	77386

Street Name	Block	Pg/Sq	Loc	Zips
LEGENDS MEADE DR	0	293B	SEM	77386
LEGENDS MILL DR	3300	253X	SEM	77386
LEGENDS MIST DR	3100	253S	SEM	77386
LEGENDS PASS CT	29700	253W	SEM	77386
LEGENDS PASS LN	29800	253W	SEM	77386
LEGENDS PEAK DR	2300	253V	SEM	77386
LEGENDS PINE CT	29500	253W	SEM	77386
LEGENDS PINE LN	29600	253W	SEM	77386
LEGENDS PLACE DR	29600	253X	SEM	77386
LEGEND SPRINGS DR	800	485F	SWC	77494
LEGENDS RANCH CT	0	253W	SEM	77386
LEGENDS RANCH DR	2700	253X	SEM	77386
LEGENDS REACH DR	0	293A	SEM	77386
LEGENDS RIDGE DR	0	253S	SEM	77386
LEGENDS RIDGE DR	0	253T	SEM	77386
LEGENDS ROCK DR	29500	253W	SEM	77386
LEGENDS RUN DR	2900	253W	SEM	77386
LEGENDS SHADOW DR	3300	253X	SEM	77386
LEGENDS SHORE DR	2300	253S	SEM	77386
LEGENDS SMITH LN	0	293B	SEM	77386
LEGENDS STONE DR	0	253X	SEM	77386
LEGENDS TRACE DR	0	253S	SEM	77386
W. LEGENDS TRAIL DR	29900	253S	SEM	77386
E. LEGENDS TRAIL DR	30100	253W	SEM	77386
LEGENDS TRAIL DR	30100	253S	SWM	77386
LEGENDS TREE DR	0	293B	SEM	77386
LEGENDS VALLEY DR	0	293B	SEM	77386
LEGENDS VALLEY LN	0	293B	SEM	77386
LEGENDS VIEWS DR	30000	253S	SEM	77386
S. LEGENDS VILLAGE CIR	29800	253W	SEM	77386
N. LEGENDS VILLAGE CIR	29800	253W	SEM	77386
S. LEGENDS VILLAGE CT	29700	253W	SEM	77386
N. LEGENDS VILLAGE LN	29700	253W	SEM	77386
LEGENDS WAY	0	444S	KT	77493
LEGENDS WICK DR	0	293B	SEM	77386
LEGENDS WILD DR	3300	293B	SEM	77386
LEGENDS WILLOW DR	29600	253W	SEM	77386
LEGENDS WORTH DR	0	293A	SEM	77386
LEGENDS YORK DR	0	253W	SEM	77386
LEGGETT	5300	614R	PL	77584
LEGGETT DR	1200	495V	GP	77547
LEGHORN	8000	450C	NWH	77040
LEGHRAND CT	200	659D	LC	77573
LEGION	3000	454X	NEH	77026
LEGION LN	22800	256U	SEM	77357
LEGION RD	22800	256U	SEM	77357
LE GREEN	700	453W	NWH	77008
LE GREEN	1000	453W	NWH	77009
LEHALL	1000	532M	SWH	77030
LEHALL	3600	533Q	SEH	77021
LE HARV CT	12300	371G	NWC	77014
LE HAVRE RD	7300	534S	SEH	77033
LEHIGH	4100	532A	WU	77005
LEHIGH	4700	531C	BL	77401
LEHIGH SPRINGS DR	1	251E	WD	77381
LEHMAN	700	452E	NWH	77018
LEICESTER	0	257G	SEM	77357
LEICESTER LN	400	617A	SEH	77034
LEICESTER WAY	4600	569X	MC	77459
LEICHESTER DR	2400	293A	SEM	77386
LEIGHANN LANE DR	4000	573Z	SEC	77047
LEIGH CANYON DR	16000	617X	SEC	77546
LEIGH CREEK DR	21800	290R	NWC	77388
LEIGHTON	6700	454H	NEH	77016
LEIGHTONFIELD CT	7400	406M	NWC	77433
LEIGHTON GARDENS DR	0	488P	SWH	77077
LEIGHWOOD CT	8100	375Y	NEC	77396
LEIGHWOOD LN	14700	375Y	NEC	77396
LEIGH WOODS DR	11000	366U	NWC	77433
LEILA BEND DR	2900	487Z	SWC	77082
LEILA BEND DR	15100	487Z	SWC	77082
LEILA OAKS CIR	14900	487Z	SWC	77082
LEILA OAKS CT	3400	487Z	SWC	77082
LEILA OAKS DR	3200	487Z	SWC	77082
LEILA OAKS LN	15000	487Z	SWC	77082
LEILA PARK CT		366Q	NWC	77433
LEINAD DR	18300	332E	NWC	77090
LEIROP DR	22100	525Q	NEF	77407
LEISURE	1800	659N	LC	77573
LEISURE DR	300	569T	SF	77477
LEISURE LN	0	615N	PL	77584
LEISURE LN	1	251Q	WD	77380
LEISURE LN	1	490F	BH	77024
LEISURE LN	300	657J	FR	77546
LEISURE LAKES BLVD	0	659S	LC	77573
LEISURE PLACE DR	18700	337Z	NEC	77346
LEISURE WOODS	14500	248S	SWM	77362
LEITRIM WAY	10500	573G	SEH	77047
LEITZ RD	10600	575W	SEH	77075
LELAND DR	5300	500G	BT	77521
LELAY CIR	4500	452M	NWH	77022
LELDA LN	0	610Q	MC	77459
LELDA LN	11800	570B	SWH	77071
LELIA	3000	494B	NEH	77026
LELIA LN	2700	569Z	NEF	77477
LEMAC DR	4000	532S	SWH	77025
LEMAC DR	4300	531V	SWH	77096
LEMAY	14500	497L	NEC	77015
LEMING CT	14700	497D	NEC	77015
LEMKE	3600	494P	SEH	77003
LEMM CT	800	332C	NCC	77373
LEMMA DR	7500	408M	NWC	77041
LEMMINGHAM DR	0	291Z	NWC	77388
LEMM ROAD 1	900	292Z	NCC	77373
LEMM ROAD 2	1200	332D	NCC	77373
LEMOINE LN	6300	458N	NEC	77049
LEMON LN	1400	539R	LP	77571
LEMOND DR	11200	415N	NEH	77016
LEMONGRASS AVE	0	461N	NEC	77521
LEMONGRASS DR	0	406D	NWC	77433
LEMON GROVE DR	22700	333E	NCC	77373
LEMONMINT MEADOW DR	8200	525A	NEF	77494
LEMON RIDGE LN	12100	570H	SWH	77035
LEMON TREE CIR	0	570J	MC	77489
LEMON TREE CIR	7500	411U	NWH	77088
LEMON TREE LN	3400	411U	NWH	77088
LEMONWOOD LN	2300	371Z	NWC	77038
LE MOYNE PASS LN	0	609Y	NEF	77459
LEMPIRA CT	6700	370A	NWC	77069
LEMUR LN	12900	328Y	NWC	77429
LENA DR	200	452M	NWH	77022
LENARD	400	453T	NWH	77009
LENA TRAIL DR	18600	331D	NWC	77388
LENCLAIRE DR	15800	571X	SWH	77053
LENEHAN	2700	494J	SEH	77003
LENEN DR	0	285Q	NWC	77447
LENETTE CT	900	531L	BL	77401
LENEVA LN	1300	537P	PA	77502
LENNIE LN	8700	503V	BC	77520
LENNINGTON DR	1500	369V	NWC	77064
LENNON LN	0	293F	SEM	77386
LENNON PARK CT	0	524A	NEF	77494
LENNOX GARDENS DR	12200	371K	NWC	77066
LENNOX RIDGE DR	0	406H	NWC	77433
LENNOX WOODS	0	609Y	MC	77459
LENNY LN	2000	536V	PA	77502
LENORE	8000	535U	SEH	77017
LENOX	1	494U	SEH	77011
N. LENOX	100	494U	SEH	77011
LENOX	600	494U	SEH	77023
LENOX HILL CT	1	250B	WD	77382
LENOX HILL DR	1	250B	WD	77382
LENTANDO LN	12900	328Y	NWC	77429
LENTE CIR	22000	338Y	NEH	77532
LENZE RD	23600	290B	NWC	77389
LEO LN	0	619X	LC	77573
LEO CREEK LN	0	375X	NEC	77396
LEOLYN WOODS LN	0	377K	NEC	77346
LEON	4300	577F	PA	77504
LEON	5900	453U	NEH	77009
LEONA	1700	494E	NEH	77026
LEONA CT	3000	613Y	NEB	77584
LEONARD	900	536M	PA	77506
LEONARD	5600	534B	SEH	77023
LEONARD	21400	256T	SEM	77357
LEONARD RD	16400	458C	NEC	77049
LEONESSA DR	0	525J	NEF	77406
LEONESSA DR	0	525J	NEF	77406
LEONIDAS	3100	492M	SWH	77019
LEONORA	7700	535S	SEH	77061
LEON RIVER CT	0	253U	NWC	77389
LEON SPRINGS LN	13600	328S	NWC	77429
LEON VALLEY LN	0	445M	NWC	77449
LEON VALLEY LN	0	445M	NWC	77449
LEOPOLD CT	5400	533H	SEH	77021
LEORA AVE	100	536L	PA	77506
LEPRECHAUN DR	1000	656M	FR	77546
LEPRECHAUN LN	2500	536X	SEH	77017
LERA	10000	415W	NEH	77016
LERA	10900	415N	NEH	77016
LERIN LN	9400	527U	NEF	77498
LE RIVIERA CIR	600	497A	NEC	77015
LERMA CREEK CT	4200	609Y	NEF	77459
LERNA CT	0	255X	SEM	77365
LERNER DR	14700	497D	NEC	77015
LEROY	2500	616T	PL	77581
LEROY	2900	660H	BC	77518
LEROY DR	1900	536V	PA	77502
LERWICK DR	5100	407Z	NWC	77084
LESA LN	400	292L	SP	77373
LESIKAR	6500	614D	BK	77581
LESINA ST	0	445E	NWC	77493
LESLIE	900	656H	FR	77546
LESLIE	2400	537P	PA	77502
LESLIE	5900	494M	NEH	77020
LESLIE LN	0	539N	DP	77536
LESLIE LN	16100	570J	MC	77489
LESLIE ANN AVE	0	413Y	NEH	77076
LESLIES CT	0	656V	FR	77546
LESOTA CT	13600	328T	NWC	77429
LES TALLEY DR	1600	620E	EL	77586
LESTER	500	492L	SWH	77007
LESTER LN	0	285D	SWM	77355
LESTERGATE DR	23100	333C	NCC	77373
LESTERGATE DR	23900	293Y	NCC	77373
LETCHER	6300	455P	NEH	77028
LETCHFIELD HOLLOW DR	19800	289Z	NWC	77379
LETHAN WAY	0	329C	NWC	77379
LETHBRIDGE	3400	615B	PL	77581
LETHBRIDGE DR	0	371W	NWC	77086
LETICA DR	8100	410K	NWC	77040
LETIEN	6600	492B	NWH	77008
LETO RD	9300	450U	NWH	77080
LETRIM	2500	616J	PL	77581
LETTIE AVE	7700	575W	SEH	77075
LETTIE CT	11000	575Z	SEH	77075
LETZ DR	14200	288B	TB	77375
LEVEL OAK PLACE	2100	251V	WD	77380
LEVEL POND LN	0	334L	NCC	77388
LEVEL RUN	0	568D	SG	77478
LEVEL RUN	12200	569A	MD	77477
LEVERING LN	9200	455E	NEH	77028
LEVERKUHN	500	492M	SWH	77007
LEVERWOOD CT	1	251E	WD	77381
LEVI RD	5800	290H	NWC	77389
LEVIN	0	489F	SWH	77079
LEVONSHIRE DR	4000	532N	SWH	77025
LEW BRIGGS RD	12900	573S	SWH	77047
LEWIS	100	659E	LC	77573
LEWIS	400	536V	PA	77502
LEWIS	1800	493G	NEH	77009
LEWIS	16200	409L	JV	77040
LEWIS DR	1000	660B	KE	77565
LEWIS DR	10900	529T	SWH	77099
LEWIS DR	17000	367K	CY	77433
LEWIS, B J DR	0	412T	NWH	77088
LEWISHAM LN	0	330B	NWC	77379
LEWISTON	6600	456R	NEH	77049
LEWISTON	7200	456M	NEC	77049
LEWISTON CT	6500	456R	NEH	77049
LEWISVILLE DR	0	526W	NEF	77406
LEXA MANOR	0	528C	SWC	77082
LEXANNE CT	0	291Z	NWC	77388
LEXFORD LN	2100	450P	NWH	77080
LEXHAM DR	9400	528S	NEF	77083
LEXI LN	6900	407Q	NWC	77084
LEXINGTON	0	292Q	SP	77373
LEXINGTON	800	656H	FR	77546
LEXINGTON	1700	492Z	SWH	77098
LEXINGTON	1700	538N	DP	77536
LEXINGTON BLVD	0	570W	SF	77477
LEXINGTON BLVD	1100	570Y	MC	77489
LEXINGTON BLVD	1500	568Y	SG	77478
LEXINGTON BLVD	2100	292R	NCC	77373
LEXINGTON BLVD	4600	569X	MC	77459
LEXINGTON CT	0	658R	LC	77573
LEXINGTON CT	700	570Y	MC	77489
LEXINGTON COMMON	3600	569Y	MC	77477
LEXINGTON GREEN DR	1000	569X	MC	77459
LEXINGTON GROVE CT	3800	569U	MC	77459
LEXINGTON GROVE DR	1100	569Y	MC	77459
LEXINGTON LAKE DR	3000	609C	MC	77459
LEXINGTON MANOR CT	3900	569Y	MC	77459
LEXINGTON PARK DR	2200	293N	NCC	77373
LEXINGTON SQUARE	600	336W	HM	77338
LEXINGTON WOODS DR	2000	292R	NCC	77373
LEXINGTON WOODS DR	2300	293N	NCC	77373
LEXOR CT	21500	296A	SEM	77365
LEXOR DR	0	296A	SEM	77365
LEXUS DR	800	375M	NEC	77396
LEXXE CREEK CT	0	325M	NWC	77433
LEY	0	456J	NEH	77078
LEY RD	7100	454M	NEH	77078
LEY RD	7300	455K	NEH	77028
LEY RD	9500	455K	NEH	77078
LEYCREST RD	8700	455M	NEH	77028
LEYCREST RD	8800	455M	NEH	77078
LEYDEN CT	200	486B	SWC	77450
LEYDENWOOD LN	0	526E	NEF	77407
LEYLAND CT	4300	613V	NEB	77584
LEYLAND DR	4400	613V	NEB	77584
LEYTON CT	12500	328Q	NWC	77377
LEYTONSTONE	12500	328Q	NWC	77377
LEYWOOD CIR	9000	528R	SWH	77099
LEZA	19200	379M	NEC	77532
LIAN FALLS LN	0	525M	NEF	77407
LIBBEY DR	1600	452J	NWH	77018
LIBBEY DR	4400	451M	NWH	77092
LIBBY BROOK CT	0	377M	NEH	77346
LIBERTY	1900	659F	LC	77573
LIBERTY CIR	500	616Z	FR	77546
LIBERTY DR	3500	615V	PL	77584
LIBERTY LN	1	288F	TB	77375
LIBERTY RD	2800	494B	NEH	77026
LIBERTY RD	6500	454Z	NEH	77028
LIBERTY RD	6800	455U	NEH	77028
LIBERTY ST	0	256Y	SEM	77357
LIBERTY ST	0	256N	SEM	77357
LIBERTY BELL CIR	1	490K	BH	77024
LIBERTY BLUFF DR	0	457L	NEC	77049
LIBERTY BRANCH BLVD	0	250P	NWC	77389
LIBERTY CREEK TRAIL	0	457L	NEC	77049
LIBERTY CREST	8700	455U	NEH	77028
LIBERTY ELM CT	8000	330E	NWC	77379
LIBERTY FALLS CT	0	457L	NEC	77049
LIBERTY GROVE DR	0	366Y	NWC	77433
LIBERTY HALL DR	0	457L	NEC	77049
LIBERTY KNOLL LN	0	253T	SEM	77386
LIBERTY LAKES DR	15000	457Q	NEC	77049
LIBERTY LANDING DR	0	366P	NWC	77433
LIBERTY MAPLE DR	0	457L	NEC	77049
LIBERTY MESA LN	0	457L	NEC	77049
LIBERTY OAK CT	7100	457L	NEC	77049
LIBERTY PARK DR	0	457L	NEC	77049
LIBERTY PINE LN	15500	457L	NEC	77049
LIBERTY POINT LN	1900	568Y	SG	77478
LIBERTY POINT LN	8100	334R	NCC	77338
LIBERTYPOINT LN	8100	334R	NCC	77338
LIBERTYPOINT LN	8100	334R	NCC	77338
LIBERTY PRAIRIE CT	0	457L	NEC	77049
LIBERTY RIDGE LN	0	457L	NEC	77049
LIBERTY RIVER DR	0	457L	NEC	77049
LIBERTY RUN DR	0	326K	NWC	77433
LIBERTY SKY LN	0	377F	NEC	77346
LIBERTY SPRINGS WAY	0	292U	NCC	77373
LIBERTY SQUARE PLACE	0	250P	NWC	77389
LIBERTY SQUARE TRAIL	0	611W	MC	77545
LIBERTY STONE LN	0	326U	NWC	77429
LIBERTY TRAIL LN	0	610X	MC	77459
LIBERTY TREE LN	0	457L	NEC	77049
LIBERTY VALLEY DR	6400	406T	NWC	77449
LIBERTY VISTA TRAIL	0	457Q	NEC	77049
LIBERTY WAY CT	17300	379X	NEC	77532
LIBERTY WAY DR	800	379X	NEC	77532
LIBERTY WOODS LN	4400	609T	NEF	77479
LIBSON FALLS DR	0	407C	NWC	77095
LICHEN LN	7900	330P	NWC	77379
LIDIA WAY	0	447A	NWC	77449
LIDO LN	4300	451H	NWH	77092
LIDO & PARK CT	14700	375Y	NEC	77396
LIDO BAY LN	0	409W	NWC	77041
LIDO BAY LN	0	409W	NWC	77041
LIDSTONE	1300	620P	SB	77586
LIDSTONE	2300	534F	SEH	77023
LIDSTONE POINT CT	23200	485F	SWC	77494
LIEDER DR	12100	368R	NWC	77065
LIERE LN	0	448K	NWH	77084
LIETNER LN	0	290N	NWC	77379
LIFEWAY VISTA DR		366V	NWC	77433
LIGHT BLUFF CT	0	293Z	NCC	77373
LIGHTBRANCH CT	0	484Y	NEF	77494
LIGHTCLIFFE DR	12400	570A	SWH	77031
LIGHT COMPANY RD	100	536B	PA	77506
LIGHTED HILL CT	19500	366V	NWC	77433
LIGHT FALL CIR	8700	407D	NWC	77095
LIGHT FALL DR	8600	407D	NWC	77095
LIGHT FALLS CT	14400	327Z	NWC	77429
LIGHTFIELD LN	0	485W	NEF	77494
LIGHT FOOT	0	501S	BT	77520
LIGHTGLEN LN	0	525H	NEF	77450
LIGHTHOUSE BLVD	0	619T	LC	77573
LIGHTHOUSE DR	2700	619T	NB	77058
S. LIGHTHOUSE DR	16800	379X	NEC	77532
N. LIGHTHOUSE DR	16800	379X	NEC	77532
LIGHTHOUSE BAY LN	0	658Z	LC	77573
LIGHTHOUSE LAKE LN	0	338W	NEC	77346
LIGHTHOUSE VIEW DR	16600	657C	SEC	77546
LIGHTHOUSE WAY	0	657N	FR	77546
LIGHTNING BAR CT	0	288S	NWC	77377
LIGHTSPUN DR	0	612N	PL	77545
LIGHTSTAR DR	3000	572F	SWH	77045
LIGHTSTONE CT	4800	446D	NWC	77449
LIGHTSTONE LN	0	657V	LC	77573
LIGHTWOODS DR	24200	338L	NEH	77336
LIGONBERRY	4800	533V	SEH	77033
LIGUSTRUM FLOWER	2300	291R	NWC	77388
LIGUSTRUM TRAIL	17100	328Q	NWC	77377
LIGUSTRUM TRAIL CT	12600	328Q	NWC	77377
LILA	0	367M	CY	77429
LILA	0	497J	NEH	77015
LILA	3700	494B	NEH	77026
LILA	6700	614D	BK	77581
LILA LN	12800	496R	NEH	77015
LILAC	100	493C	NEH	77009
LILAC	2400	537Z	PA	77503
LILAC	3200	577D	PA	77505
LILAC	5600	444P	KT	77493
LILAC CIR	100	379P	NEC	77532
LILAC CT	0	569T	NEF	77477
LILAC DR	0	658R	LC	77573
LILAC LN	100	500A	BT	77520
LILAC BLOSSOM WAY	0	616L	SEC	77089
LILAC BREEZE CT		328P	NWC	77429
LILAC BREEZE LN	0	612J	PL	77545
LILACBROOK CT	6700	290Q	NWC	77379
LILAC FALLS BLVD	0	366Z	NWC	77433
LILAC GLEN CT	7600	407L	NWC	77095
LILAC HOLLOW LN	0	406X	NWC	77449
LILAC MANOR CT	0	368U	NWC	77065
LILAC MEADOWS LN	0	525H	NEF	77450
LILAC MEADOWS LN	6600	290T	NWC	77379
LILAC MIST LN	1500	412F	NWC	77038
LILAC RANCH DR	0	484R	NWF	77494
LILAC RANCH DR	0	484R	NWF	77494
LILAC SPRINGS LN	0	407B	NWC	77095
LILAC VALE CT	17200	407Q	NWC	77084
LILAC VALLEY LN	0	367P	NWC	77433
LILAC VIEW CT	0	612J	PL	77545
LILAC WAY	24100	295F	SEM	77365
LILES CT	16800	376L	NEC	77396
LILES LN	3600	376L	NEC	77396
LILIAN FARMS DR	0	366J	NWC	77433
LILIUM CT	1	251L	WD	77380
LILLA LN	16700	458Z	CV	77530
LILLEUX RD	10800	372N	NWC	77067
LILLIAN	900	460S	HG	77562
LILLIAN	1700	536Q	PA	77502
LILLIAN	4000	492G	SWH	77007
LILLIAN	5300	500G	BT	77521
LILLIAN	17100	328R	NWC	77377
LILLIAN SPRINGS	0	292Q	NCC	77373
LILLIE	1100	538U	DP	77536
LILLINGTON MANOR CT	1	329D	NWC	77379
LILLJA RD	11500	413J	NCC	77037
LILLJA RD	13800	413E	NCC	77037
LILLJA RD	14000	373W	NCC	77060
LILLY LN	0	542S	NEC	77520
LILLY FARMS RD	23800	257A	SEM	77357
LILLY HOLLOW DR	0	368E	NWC	77429
LILLY MIST LN	9900	412F	NWC	77038
LILLY RANCH DR	0	484V	NEF	77494
LILY	2400	537Y	PA	77503
LILY	3100	577C	PA	77505
LILY CT	500	659G	LC	77573
LILY CT	27400	248A	SWM	77354
LILY LN	2400	460U	NEC	77562
LILYBLOOM LN	0	525M	NEF	77407
LILY CREEK DR	0	290E	NWC	77375
LILYGATE CT	14400	573X	SEC	77047
LILY GLEN CT	0	524C	NEF	77494
LILYGLEN CT		658T	LC	77573
LILY GLEN LN	0	524G	NEF	77494
LILY HOLLOW CT	6400	290U	NWC	77379
LILY PAD LN	0	526T	NEF	77407
LILY PARK LN	0	571K	SWH	77085
LILY POND CT	3300	609K	MC	77459
LILY RIDGE LN	0	406F	NWC	77433
LILY SPRINGS DR	21200	296J	SEM	77365
LILY TRACE CT	0	253S	SEM	77386
LILYWOOD LN	0	446A	NWC	77449
LILYWOOD SPRINGS DR	0	446M	NWC	77449
LIMA DR	11600	529N	SWH	77099
LIMA DR	12300	528R	SWH	77099
LIMBER BOUGH RD	7600	377D	NEC	77346
LIMBER OAK	14900	487Z	SWC	77082
LIMBER PINE PLACE	12500	369J	NWC	77429
W. LIME BLOSSOM CT	14800	325Q	NWC	77433
E. LIME BLOSSOM CT	14800	325R	NWC	77433
LIME CREEK DR	4000	485Z	NEF	77450
LIME GREEN TRAIL	0	325Q	NWC	77433
LIMERICK	14100	288B	TB	77375
LIMERICK CT	2200	538P	DP	77536
LIMERICK LN	0	245V	SWM	77355
LIMERICK LN	8900	491C	SWH	77024
LIME SPRINGS DR	8300	407H	NWC	77095
LIMESTONE	6300	451J	NWH	77092
LIMESTONE CREST LN	0	445M	NWC	77449
LIMESTONE LAKE DR	16000	328V	NWC	77377
LIMESTONE POINTE LN	0	330B	NWC	77379
LIMESTONE RANCH LN	9300	527N	NEF	77407
LIMESTONE SKY CT	0	578T	SEH	77059
LIMESTON RIDGE TRAIL	20600	326J	NWC	77433
LIMEWOOD LN	10000	528S	NEF	77498
LIMRICK DR	2100	616K	PL	77581
LINA	7100	535J	SEH	77087
LINA RD	15600	323X	NWC	77447
LINARES DR	9700	456A	NEH	77078
LINBROOK DR	10300	615H	SEC	77089
LINCOLN	0	257G	SEM	77357
LINCOLN	0	411V	NWH	77088
LINCOLN	200	538Y	DP	77536
LINCOLN	600	541B	BT	77520
LINCOLN	2700	493S	SWH	77006
LINCOLN	2800	411H	NWC	77038
LINCOLN	3000	411H	NWC	77086
LINCOLN CEDAR DR	100	502G	BT	77520
LINCOLN CREST WAY	0	568B	SG	77498
LINCOLN GREEN DR	5300	444Y	KT	77493
LINCOLN HEIGHTS CT	0	526L	NEF	77407
LINCOLN HEIGHTS LN	0	526F	NEF	77407
LINCOLN PARK DR	0	327U	NWC	77429
LINCOLN RIDGE LN	0	571F	SWH	77085
LINCOLN ROUND DR	1600	444U	KT	77493
W. LINCOLNSHIRE	0	488L	SWH	77077
E. LINCOLNSHIRE	0	488L	SWH	77077
LINCOLNSHIRE RD	4500	574N	SEH	77048
LINCOLNSHIRE FIELD LN	0	485L	NEF	77450
LINCOLNS MEADOW DR	3000	293Y	NCC	77373
LINCOLN TOWN DR	5300	444Y	KT	77493
LINCREST LN	5400	491X	SWH	77056
LINDA	100	538F	DP	77536
LINDA	7600	535N	SEH	77087
LINDA DR	2900	614R	PL	77584
LINDA LN	0	333X	NCC	77073
LINDA LN	400	617U	FR	77546
LINDA LN	400	618X	WB	77598
LINDA LN	1100	613L	NEB	77584
LINDA LN	1600	659A	LC	77573
LINDA LN	1800	537N	PA	77502
LINDA LN	5300	444U	KT	77493
LINDA LN	5300	500H	BT	77521
LINDA LN	12800	570J	SF	77477
LINDA LN	24100	296L	SEM	77365
LINDA LN	28100	248W	TB	77375
LINDA RD	0	323X	NWC	77447
LINDABURY HOLLOW DR	0	524B	NEF	77494
LINDALE	100	453Q	NEH	77022
LINDA LEIGH LN	10300	289L	NWC	77375
LINDALE MANOR CT	0	290Q	NWC	77379
LINDALE ROSE LN	0	375Y	NEC	77396
LINDALL CT	14700	328N	NWC	77429
LINDA MESA DR	6400	527G	SWC	77083
LINDA VISTA RD	7800	455F	NEH	77028
LINDA VISTA RD	8800	455H	NEH	77078
W. LINDBERCH CT	0	501L	BT	77521
N. LINDBERCH CT	0	501L	BT	77521
E. LINDBERCH CT	0	501L	BT	77521
LINDBERG	1000	541A	BT	77520
LINDBERGH	6400	534U	SEH	77087
LINDELL RD	400	292L	SP	77373
LINDELL RUN DR	0	296E	SEM	77365
LINDEN	0	611U	FS	77545
LINDEN	4700	531G	BL	77401
LINDEN	6400	534H	SEH	77087
LINDEN	6900	535E	SEH	77012
LINDEN	13400	568C	SG	77478
LINDEN CT	5300	331E	NWC	77379
LINDEN LN	22800	245Q	SWM	77355

Street Name	Block	Pg/Sq	Loc	Zips
LINDEN BELLE DR		484W	NEF	77494
LINDEN BROOK DR	0	484P	NEF	77494
LINDENBROOK LN	14900	408F	NWC	77095
LINDEN CHASE LN	5300	371J	NWC	77066
LINDEN COVE CT	0	484Q	NEF	77494
LINDEN CREEK LN	0	698M	LC	77539
LINDEN CREEK LN	2100	536S	SEH	77017
LINDENCREST	7300	575A	SEH	77061
LINDENCROFT CT	14100	369D	NWC	77070
LINDENCROFT LN	9500	416Z	NEC	77044
LINDENFIELD CT	19700	446L	NWC	77449
LINDENFIELD DR	3200	446L	NWC	77449
LINDENFIELD PLACE	19800	446L	NWC	77449
LINDEN FOREST LN	0	407S	NWC	77084
LINDEN GATE DR	9700	575Z	SEH	77075
LINDEN GLEN LN	4000	414B	NCC	77039
LINDEN HILL LN	0	658Z	LC	77573
LINDEN HILLS LN	21100	334M	NCC	77338
LINDEN HOLLOW DR	0	376N	NEC	77396
LINDEN HOUSE CT	21200	334M	NCC	77338
LINDEN KNOLL LN	6400	571K	SWH	77085
LINDENLOCH LN	0	571K	SWH	77085
LINDEN MANOR CT	600	292G	NCC	77373
LINDEN MEADOW LN	0	526F	NEF	77407
LINDEN MILL CT	0	484X	NEF	77494
LINDEN OAKS LN	7900	527J	NEF	77407
LINDEN PLACE	4500	614S	NEB	77584
LINDEN PLACE	4800	613V	NEB	77584
LINDEN ROCK DR	0	484K	NEF	77494
LINDEN ROSE CT	0	612U	PL	77584
LINDEN ROSE LN	0	609T	NEF	77479
LINDEN SPRINGS CT	0	253P	SEM	77386
LINDEN SPRINGS CT	16300	367Z	NWC	77095
LINDEN SPRINGS DR	10300	367Z	NWC	77095
LINDEN TREE DR	20200	446T	NWC	77449
LINDENWALK LN	0	367T	NWC	77433
LINDEN WAY LN	0	524F	NEF	77494
LINDENWICK CT	19800	406M	NWC	77433
LINDEN WICK LN	0	446E	NWC	77449
LINDENWOOD	700	501T	BT	77520
LINDENWOOD DR	300	491E	HC	77520
LINDENWOOD CLIFF	0	615B	PL	77581
LINDER	1400	454P	NEH	77026
LINDER GREEN DR	3200	253S	SEM	77386
LINDER PARK LN	2700	253N	SEM	77385
LINDFIELD LN	900	332G	NCC	77073
LINDHAVEN DR	3400	614V	PL	77584
LINDHEIMER RD	21800	285H	SWM	77447
LINDITA DR	14600	527M	SWC	77083
LINDITA DR	14900	527M	NEF	77083
LINDSAY	5000	494X	SEH	77023
LINDSAY LN	1100	444W	KT	77493
LINDSAY RD	13400	368G	NWC	77429
LINDSEY CT	0	570J	SF	77477
LINDSEY LN	0	285X	NWC	77447
LINDSEY LN	0	325B	NWC	77447
LINDSEY RD	19000	287X	NWC	77377
LINDSEY CREEK LN	0	375X	NEC	77396
LINDSEY HILL LN	0	328S	NWC	77429
LINDSEY TERRACE LN	1500	293J	SEM	77386
LINDSTROM RD	14000	420E	NEC	77532
LINDSTROM RD	16700	380W	NEC	77532
LINDY LN	6600	534C	SEH	77023
LINDYANN LN	6200	452X	NWH	77008
LINE	1700	493D	NEH	77009
LINE RD	0	578B	PA	77504
LINEA DEL PINO	2100	488U	SWH	77077
LINEAGE DR	0	444D	NWC	77493
LINECAMP CT	9500	409B	NWC	77064
LINECAMP DR	10300	409B	NWC	77064
LINENHALL DR	10000	528S	NEF	77498
LINEN MILLS LN		366R	NWC	77433
LINER LN	17500	407K	NWC	77095
LINER RD	0	242M	WCO	77484
LINFIELD BLUFF LN	0	524E	NEF	77494
LINFIELD WAY	1700	618R	SEH	77058
LINGARD PARK CT	1800	572R	SWH	77047
LINK CT	8800	532N	SWH	77025
LINK RD	100	658R	LC	77573
LINK RD	100	453T	NWH	77009
LINK RD	800	659N	LC	77573
LINK RD	3200	453N	NWH	77022
W. LINKAGE RD	0	618M	SEH	77058
E. LINKAGE RD	0	619N	SEH	77058
LINKERMUCK	22100	339X	NEC	77532
LINKFAIR LN	8700	532N	SWH	77025
LINKLEA DR	3800	532N	SWH	77025
LINKMEADOW LN	8600	532N	SWH	77025
LINKPASS LN	8600	532N	SWH	77025
LINKS CT	2200	337F	NEH	77345
LINKS CROSSING LN	7800	250S	NWC	77389
LINKSHIRE DR	15400	618J	SEH	77062
LINKSMAN LN	5800	406Y	NWC	77449
LINKS SIDE CT	1	337G	NEH	77339
LINK TERRACE	8700	532N	SWH	77025
LINK VALLEY DR	3500	532T	SWH	77025
LINKVIEW DR	3700	532N	SWH	77025
LINKWOOD	600	656H	FR	77546
LINKWOOD DR	1000	616X	PL	77581
LINKWOOD DR	2800	532P	SWH	77025
LINKWOOD LN	20800	255N	SEM	77365
LINMONT FALLS LN	5400	609T	NEF	77479
LINN	3300	454S	NEH	77026
LINNET LN	10500	574F	SEH	77048
LINNFIELD DR	12700	369M	NWC	77070
LINNHAVEN DR	6100	529C	SWH	77072
LINNMONT LN	0	369M	NWC	77070
S. LINNWOOD	0	257A	SEM	77357
W. LINPAR CT	6400	410Z	NWH	77040
E. LINPAR CT	6400	410Z	NWH	77040
S. LINPAR CT	7500	410Z	NWH	77040
N. LINPAR CT	7500	410Z	NWH	77040
LINSEED DR	0	291Z	NWC	77388
LINSHIRE DR	0	291Z	NWC	77388
LINSLEY LN	0	576V	SEH	77034
LINSON LN	500	656G	FR	77546
LINSTROM GREEN DR	0	295L	SEM	77365
LINTON	6200	492B	NWH	77008
LINVALE DR	11000	415S	NEH	77016
LINWOD TERRACE DR	6601	525Q	NEF	77407
LINWOOD	0	499V	BT	77520
LINWOOD	1	494U	SEH	77011
LINWOOD	3500	615K	PL	77581
LINWOOD CIR	1100	536Q	PA	77502
LINWOOD CT	10900	579C	LP	77571
LINWOOD DR	2400	609B	MC	77459
E. LINWOOD DR	10800	579C	LP	77571
W. LINWOOD DR	18000	257A	WV	77357
N. LINWOOD DR	24300	257A	WV	77357
LINWOOD MANOR CT	15800	367D	NWC	77429
W. LINWOOD OAKS	2100	615K	PL	77581
E. LINWOOD OAKS	2100	615K	PL	77581
LION RIDGE CT	18200	526M	NEF	77407
LIONS GATE CT	19700	335S	NCC	77338
LIONS GATE DR	19900	335N	NCC	77338
LIPAN RD	8600	490Y	SWH	77063
LIPIZZAN LN	0	377S	NEC	77044
LIPPIZANER DR	18500	407N	NWC	77433
LIPPS LN	6300	408U	NWC	77041
LIPSCOMB	2900	534G	SEH	77023
LISA	0	490H	HC	77024
LISA	4000	534J	PA	77503
LISA CT	300	616Y	FR	77546
LISA LN	0	539N	DP	77536
LISA LN	900	336K	NEH	77339
LISA LN	6000	534J	SEH	77021
LISA LN	26500	295Y	SEM	77365
LISA DAWN LN	15400	458N	NEC	77049
LISBOA CIR	0	445E	NWC	77493
LISBOA LN	0	660G	GCO	77565
LISBURN DR	0	484V	NEF	77494
LISCOMB DR	14500	408T	NWC	77084
LISHA LN	2300	570X	MC	77489
LISMAN LN	0	332Q	NCC	77073
LISMORE CIR	11700	368H	NWC	77429
LISMORE CIR	13200	368G	NWC	77429
LISMORE ESTATES LN	11200	252M	SEM	77385
LISMORE LAKE DR	11700	368H	NWC	77429
LISMORE POINT	13200	368G	NWC	77429
LISSIE	3500	611X	FS	77545
LISTI LN	100	459V	HG	77562
LITCHFIELD LN	1	489M	SWH	77024
LITCHFIELD LN	7600	330P	NWC	77379
LITCHFIELD BEND LN	23600	485X	NEF	77494
S. LITE	31900	246T	SWM	77355
N. LITE	31900	246T	SWM	77355
LITTELL	0	373W	NCC	77039
LITTLE	7900	455P	NEH	77028
LITTLE	14500	571Q	SWH	77045
LITTLE CT	13900	488J	SWH	77077
LITTLE RD	5300	500G	NEC	77521
LITTLE ASHLEE CT	4000	371B	NWC	77014
LITTLE BARLEY CT	11000	371S	NWC	77086
LITTLE BEAR DR	2600	336D	NEH	77339
LITTLEBERRY RD	4100	411U	NWH	77088
LITTLE BIG HORN DR	20000	446T	NWC	77449
LITTLE BLUE STEM DR	0	289R	NWC	77375
LITTLEBORNE BIRDWELL LN	13900	573U	SEC	77047
LITTLE BRANCH CT	2900	487Z	SWC	77082
LITTLE BRANCH DR	9400	409D	NWC	77064
LITTLEBROOK RD	11200	539V	LP	77571
LITTLE BUCK DR	100	379A	NEC	77532
LITTLECAPE TRAIL	0	337X	NEC	77346
LITTLE CAPRESE LN	0	451Y	NWH	77055
LITTLE CEDAR DR	2000	296Y	NEH	77339
LITTLE CEDAR BAYOU DR	0	580F	LP	77571
LITTLE COSTILLA WAY	0	290Y	NWC	77379
LITTLE CREEK CT	7100	406Q	NWC	77433
LITTLECREST RD	3900	414T	NEC	77093
LITTLECROFT DR	30100	252V	SEM	77386
LITTLE CROWN WAY	0	568E	NEF	77498
LITTLE CYPRESS LN	16100	367C	CY	77429
LITTLE CYPRESS LN	17100	327P	CY	77429
LITTLE DEER LN	20800	378C	NEC	77532
LITTLE DELL DR	0	446F	NWC	77449
LITTLE DOE DR	400	379A	NEC	77532
LITTLE DOE DR	800	378D	NEC	77532
LITTLE FANS DR	9600	376S	NEC	77396
LITTLE FAWN DR	18300	447P	NWC	77084
LITTLEFIELD CT	11700	328M	NWC	77377
LITTLEFORD	14400	572P	SWH	77045
LITTLE FOREST CT	2400	293S	NCC	77373
LITTLE FORK DR	0	366N	NWC	77433
LITTLE FOX LN	500	373N	NEH	77060
LITTLE FOX CREST	0	294K	SEM	77386
LITTLE GARDEN CT	0	325F	NWC	77447
LITTLEGLEN LN	17000	447C	NWC	77084
LITTLE GREEN CT	0	289R	NWC	77375
LITTLE GROVE DR	0	614L	PL	77581
LITTLE HARBOR WAY	0	525A	NEF	77494
LITTLEHIP HAWTHORN LN	0	463S	CCO	77520
LITTLE JASMINE WAY	0	406W	NWC	77449
LITTLE JOHN	300	491F	SWH	77024
LITTLE JOHN CIR	0	245N	WCO	77447
S. LITTLE JOHN CIR	11700	570L	MC	77071
N. LITTLE JOHN CIR	11700	570L	MC	77071
LITTLE JOHN CIR	25000	244R	WCO	77447
LITTLE JOHN CT	0	381G	LCO	77535
LITTLE JOHN CT	800	536R	PA	77502
LITTLE JOHN LN	5300	444Y	KT	77493
LITTLE JOHN WAY	0	449T	NWH	77043
LITTLE LAKE	5500	531K	BL	77401
LITTLE LEAF CT	14900	487Z	SWC	77082
LITTLE LINK LN	0	376H	NEC	77346
LITTLE LISA LN	10900	490H	HC	77024
LITTLE MCSHAN	0	296G	SEM	77365
LITTLE MISS CREEK DR	0	327R	NWC	77429
LITTLENEVISS DR	0	447C	NWC	77084
W. LITTLE OAK CT	300	252K	SEM	77386
E. LITTLE OAK CT	400	252K	SEM	77386
LITTLE OAK DR	500	254H	SEM	77365
LITTLE OAK DR	10300	462V	CCO	77520
LITTLE OAKS CT	14500	528S	NEF	77083
LITTLE OPEN LN	0	611N	NEF	77545
LITTLE ORCHARD CT	11400	329N	NWC	77377
LITTLE PATH DR	0	328P	NWC	77429
LITTLE PINE LN	19300	406V	NWC	77449
LITTLE PINTO CT	17200	367Q	NWC	77095
LITTLEPORT LN	900	497D	NEC	77530
LITTLEPORT LN	1000	457Z	NEC	77530
LITTLER CT	1800	419A	NEC	77532
LITTLE RANCH RD	13300	368D	NWC	77429
LITTLE REDWOOD DR	6800	578F	PA	77505
LITTLE RIATA DR	17300	367T	NWC	77095
LITTLE RIVER	8200	410G	NWC	77064
LITTLE RIVER CT	0	253V	SEM	77386
LITTLE ROCK CT	0	328P	NWC	77429
LITTLE SAIGON BLVD	0	529Q	SWH	77072
LITTLE SHOE LN	17400	376G	NEC	77396
LITTLE SKIFF WAY	0	378T	NEC	77532
LITTLE SORRELL CT	0	288S	NWC	77377
LITTLE SPRING CIR	2800	293T	NCC	77373
LITTLE SPRINGS LN	0	253P	SEM	77386
LITTLE STAR	12600	617C	SEH	77598
LITTLE THICKET CT	7600	406M	NWC	77433
LITTLETON	400	453L	NEH	77022
LITTLE TRAIL	0	376M	NEC	77346
LITTLE WALNUT LN	0	289C	NWC	77375
LITTLEWICK DR	0	295R	SEM	77365
LITTLE WILLOW DR	7000	578F	PA	77505
LITTLE WILLOW WALK	14300	618E	SEH	77062
LITTLE WIND LN	23400	294W	NCC	77373
LITTLE WING DR	0	291Z	NWC	77388
LITTLE WOLF DR	1500	378C	NEH	77532
LITTLEWOOD DR	500	501R	BT	77521
W. LITTLE YORK RD	100	412U	NWH	77076
E. LITTLE YORK RD	100	412V	NEH	77076
E. LITTLE YORK RD	100	413T	NEH	77076
LITTLE YORK RD	100	413V	NEH	77093
W. LITTLE YORK RD	500	412U	NWH	77091
LITTLE YORK RD	1400	414U	NEC	77093
W. LITTLE YORK RD	2600	411Z	NWH	77091
LITTLE YORK RD	5300	415T	NEH	77016
W. LITTLE YORK RD	6500	410T	NWC	77040
W. LITTLE YORK RD	10300	409T	NWC	77041
LITTLE YORK RD	13500	417T	NEC	77044
W. LITTLE YORK RD	14900	408Z	NWC	77084
W. LITTLE YORK RD	16200	407U	NWC	77084
W. LITTLE YORK RD	18000	406Y	NWC	77449
LITTONWOOD CT	19100	486D	SWC	77094
LIVE CREEK LN	0	613L	PL	77584
LIVELY LN	3200	450K	NWH	77080
LIVELY FICUS LN	0	611T	FS	77545
LIVE MEADOW LN	4700	446H	NWC	77449
LIVE OAK	0	618T	WB	77598
LIVE OAK	1	419G	CB	77532
S. LIVE OAK	100	288H	TB	77375
N. LIVE OAK	100	288H	TB	77375
N. LIVE OAK	100	494J	SEH	77003
LIVE OAK	100	501U	BT	77520
LIVE OAK	100	618X	WB	77598
LIVE OAK	300	536M	PA	77506
LIVE OAK	400	568J	SG	77498
LIVE OAK	500	493V	SEH	77003
LIVE OAK	2300	533B	SEH	77004
LIVE OAK	2400	282Y	WL	77484
LIVE OAK	4500	531H	BL	77401
N. LIVE OAK	19600	257M	SEM	77357
S. LIVE OAK	19800	257M	SEM	77357
LIVE OAK	28100	298Y	NEH	77336
LIVE OAK CIR	17000	254M	SEM	77365
LIVE OAK CT	1400	570T	MC	77489
LIVE OAK DR	300	569V	SF	77477
LIVE OAK DR	7500	375C	HM	77396
LIVE OAK DR	20100	334T	NEH	77338
LIVE OAK DR	20100	381J	NEC	77532
LIVE OAK DR	20300	380H	NEC	77532
LIVE OAK LN	0	616Y	FR	77546
LIVE OAK LN	800	619H	TL	77586
LIVE OAK LN	4200	291K	NWC	77389
LIVE OAK LN	11700	249S	NWC	77375
LIVE OAK RD	20900	256V	SEM	77357
LIVE OAK ST	800	620F	SB	77586
LIVE OAK ALLEY	1	494N	SEH	77003
LIVE OAK BEND WAY	15000	326Z	NWC	77429
LIVE OAK BRANCH DR	16700	254L	SEM	77365
LIVE OAK BURR DR	19900	254L	SEM	77365
LIVE OAK ESTATES DR	19800	254H	SEM	77365
LIVEOAK FOREST	0	456R	NEH	77049
LIVE OAK GLEN LN	13400	328U	NWC	77429
LIVE OAK GREEN CT	0	457G	NEC	77049
LIVE OAK GROVE LN	0	450V	NWH	77080
LIVE OAK HILL	1800	371V	NWC	77067
LIVE OAK HOLLOW	1600	616P	PL	77581
LIVE OAK PLACE	6000	330H	NWC	77379
LIVE OAK SQUARE DR	16200	254G	SEM	77365
LIVE OAKS SPRING DR	21600	486J	SWC	77450
LIVE OAK TRAIL	1	368N	NWC	77429
LIVE OAK TRAIL	2500	539S	DP	77536
LIVE OAK TRAIL	18900	286L	NWC	77377
LIVE OAK VIEW CT	0	299T	NEC	77336
LIVERNOIS RD	9300	450U	NWH	77080
LIVERPOOL	6300	533R	SEH	77021
LIVERPOOL DR	1300	569X	MC	77459
LIVERY LN	7000	407N	NWC	77433
LIVESTOCK LN	0	486J	SWC	77450
LIVESTONE LODGE DR	0	366P	NWC	77433
LIVINGS	9000	455G	NEH	77028
LIVINGSTON	2700	614V	PL	77584
LIVINGSTON	7800	533T	SEH	77051
LIVINGSTONE LN	0	657U	LC	77573
LIVINGSTON LAKE CT	0	615Y	PL	77581
LIVINGSTON RIDGE CT	0	445L	NWC	77449
LIVINGSTON RIDGE CT	0	445L	NWC	77449
LIVING WATER LN	0	366V	NWC	77433
LIVORNO DR	0	657L	FR	77546
LIVORNO WAY	0	533F	SWH	77021
LIVOTTO CT	0	407W	NWC	77449
LIZA CT	2500	291R	NWC	77388
LIZARDS LN	0	449T	NWH	77043
LIZBETH DR	0	571F	SWH	77085
LIZETTE CT	100	576N	SEH	77075
LIZZIE LN	300	289E	TB	77375
LIZZIE RIDGE LN	0	366V	NWC	77433
LJ PARKWAY	0	609N	NEF	77479
LLAMA DR	11100	529W	SWH	77477
LLANO	100	576D	PA	77504
LLANO	1300	577A	PA	77504
LLANO CREEK DR	0	406X	NWC	77449
LLANO LAKE CT	0	578X	SEH	77059
LLANO RIVER LN	0	253U	SEM	77386
LLANO RIVER LN	0	367W	NWC	77095
LLANO RIVER LOOP	0	253T	SEM	77386
LLERENA LN	0	660G	GCO	77565
LLOYD	6300	453Q	NEH	77022
LLOYD	11700	419Y	BR	77532
LLOYD DR	500	501P	BT	77521
LLOYD'S LN	0	245W	SWM	77447
LLOYDMORE	7900	454K	NEH	77093
LO-YANG DR	900	570P	MC	77489
LOBELIA MANOR CT	20000	289Z	NWC	77379
LOBELIA MANOR DR	9200	289Z	NWC	77379
LOBERA DR	7400	527K	NEF	77083
E. LOBIT	100	501Y	BT	77520
W. LOBIT	100	501X	BT	77520
S. LOBIT	100	540Z	LP	77571
N. LOBIT	100	540Z	LP	77571
S. LOBIT	700	580D	LP	77571
LOBLOLLY LN	3400	251S	SWM	77380
LOBLOLLY RD	0	286L	NWC	77377
LOBLOLLY BAY CT	17100	578Y	SEH	77059
LOBLOLLY PINE DR	23500	256Z	SEM	77357
LOBLOLLY PINES WAY	3200	489X	SWH	77082
LOBLOLLY SHADE LN	0	326L	NWC	77429
LOBLOLLY VISTA DR	0	250V	NWC	77389
LOBLOLLY WOOD TRAIL		249T	NWC	77375
LOBO LN	16300	330P	NWC	77379
LOBO TRAIL	17300	407U	NWC	77084
LOCH LN	6100	290C	NWC	77389
LOCH-LOMOND CT	0	531P	SWH	77096
LOCHAMPTON DR	0	289V	NWC	77375
LOCH BEND CT	10900	371S	NWC	77086
LOCHBERRY CT	11700	329N	NWC	77377
LOCH BRIAR CT	1100	485G	SWC	77494
LOCH BRUCERAY DR	6400	407P	NWC	77084
LOCHBURY CT	1	329G	NWC	77379
LOCHBURY DR	18900	329G	NWC	77379
LOCH COURTNEY LN	0	616L	SEC	77089
LOCH CREEK CT	14000	617D	SEH	77062
LOCH DANE DR	9700	329L	NWC	77379
LOCH DANE DR	9900	329L	NWC	77070
LOCHFLORA DR	9300	329G	NWC	77379
LOCHFOREST VIEW LN	0	447C	NWC	77084
LOCH GLEN CT	3800	578X	SEH	77059
LOCH KATRINE	0	448A	NWC	77084
LOCH KATRINE	2200	460F	NEC	77532
LOCH KATRINE CT	4700	447D	NWC	77084
LOCH KATRINE LN	16200	447D	NWC	77084
LOCH LAKE DR	1500	620E	EL	77586
LOCHLAND LN	2200	412J	NWC	77088
LOCH LANGHAM CT	17300	407Q	NWC	77084
LOCH LANGHAM DR	6500	407U	NWC	77084
LOCHLEA RIDGE DR	9200	329H	NWC	77379
LOCHLEVAN CT	28500	299S	NEC	77336
LOCH LOMOND	100	658L	LC	77573
LOCHLOMOND	2200	460F	NEC	77532
LOCHLOMOND CT	8900	531P	SWH	77096
LOCH LOMOND DR	4900	531P	SWH	77096
LOCHMAN CT	3000	614S	NEB	77584
LOCHMAN LN	4800	614S	NEB	77584
LOCH MAREE LN	16500	447H	NWC	77084
LOCHMERE LN	21200	486W	NEF	77450
LOCHMERE LN	21400	485Z	NEF	77450
LOCHMERE WAY	2200	297V	NEH	77345
LOCHMIRE LN	3600	414B	NCC	77039
LOCHMOOR LN	800	616X	FR	77546
LOCHMOOR LN	1100	616X	PL	77581
LOCHNELL DR	200	618J	SEH	77062
LOCHNESS DR	100	459H	NEC	77562
LOCHPOINT CT	0	526E	NEF	77450
LOCHPOINT LN	0	526E	NEF	77450
LOCH RAVEN LN	17000	373N	NEH	77060
LOCHSHIN CIR	16600	447D	NWC	77084
LOCHSHIN DR	4600	447D	NWC	77084
LOCHSHIRE DR	13900	488K	SWH	77077
LOCHSTONE DR	0	373F	NCC	77073
LOCHSTONE DR	0	373F	NCC	77073
LOCHTYNE CIR	1	490G	HE	77024
LOCHTYNE WAY	800	490G	HE	77024
LOCHWOOD WAY N	0	250E	NWC	77375
LOCHWOOD WAY S	0	250E	NWC	77375
LOCKBOURNE DR	12600	412A	NWC	77038
LOCKCREST	2900	573P	SEH	77047
LOCKDALE LN	16000	367D	NWC	77429
LOCKE LN	1500	568U	SG	77478
LOCKE LN	2300	492U	SWH	77019
LOCKE LN	3400	492S	SWH	77027
LOCKE LN	5600	491T	SWH	77056
LOCKE LN	6200	491S	SWH	77057
LOCKE LN	7800	490V	SWH	77063
LOCKE LN	10000	489V	SWH	77042
LOCKE LN	12600	488T	SWH	77077
LOCKE HAVEN DR	16300	618C	SEH	77059
LOCKERIDGE BEND DR	0	293B	SEM	77386
LOCKERIDGE COVE DR	0	293B	SEM	77386
LOCKERIDGE CREEK DR	0	293B	SEM	77386
LOCKERIDGE FARMS DR	0	293B	SEM	77386
LOCKERIDGE OAKS DR	0	293B	SEM	77386
LOCKERIDGE PINES DR	0	293B	SEM	77386
LOCKERIDGE PLACE DR	0	293B	SEM	77386
LOCKERIDGE SPRINGS DR	0	293B	SEM	77386
LOCKERIDGE VIEW DR	0	293B	SEM	77386
LOCKERIDGE VILLAGE DR	0	293B	SEM	77386
LOCKERN	7100	414Z	NEH	77016
LOCKETT	2800	533J	SWH	77021
LOCKETT HILLS LN	0	609X	NEF	77479
LOCKFIELD	4100	451J	NWH	77092
LOCKFORD LN	16900	332Q	NCC	77073
LOCKGATE DR	3200	291Q	NWC	77388
LOCKGATE LN	0	573M	SEH	77048
LOCKGATE LN	10900	573H	SEH	77048
LOCKHART	3900	533U	SEH	77051
LOCKHART DR	5000	614Z	PL	77584
LOCKHARTON CT	0	527W	NEF	77478
LOCKHART REACH LN	0	376N	NEC	77396
LOCKHAVEN DR	100	332Y	NCC	77073
LOCKHEED	3400	615P	PL	77581
LOCKHEED AVE	8100	575E	SEH	77061
LOCKLAINE DR	1300	536Q	PA	77502
LOCKLAND LN	500	658S	LC	77573
LOCKLEE	0	490V	SWH	77063
LOCKRIDGE DR	19000	332C	NCC	77373
LOCKRIDGE DR	19500	292Y	NCC	77373
LOCKRIDGE HARBOR LN	0	297K	NEH	77365
LOCKSFORD	1700	452W	NWH	77008
LOCKSHIRE RIDGE CT	3300	253N	SEM	77386
LOCKSHIRE VALLEY LN	0	253Q	SEM	77386
LOCKSLEY RD	7800	455B	NEH	77078
LOCKSLEY TRACE CT	100	487A	SWC	77094
LOCKSPUR CT	25900	524K	NWF	77406
LOCKSPUR DR	0	524K	NWF	77406
LOCKWAY DR	13800	571Q	SWH	77045
LOCKWOOD DR	0	376X	NEC	77396
S. LOCKWOOD DR	0	494T	SEH	77011
LOCKWOOD DR	100	494L	NEH	77011
S. LOCKWOOD DR	600	494W	SEH	77023
LOCKWOOD DR	700	494G	NEH	77020
E. LOCKWOOD DR	3300	494C	NEH	77026
LOCKWOOD DR	3300	454Y	NEH	77026
LOCKWOOD DR	6300	454Y	NEH	77028
LOCKWOOD DR	7000	454C	NEH	77016
LOCKWOOD RD	11200	416H	NEC	77044
LOCKWOOD RD	13900	376Z	NEC	77396
LOC LOMA LN	2100	539S	LP	77571
LOCUST	1200	282U	WL	77484
LOCUST	1600	536P	PA	77502
LOCUST	4500	531G	BL	77401
LOCUST	11700	419Y	BR	77532
LOCUST GROVE DR	15800	408E	NWC	77095
LOCUST SPRINGS DR	0	407C	NWC	77095
LODDINGTON	28700	293A	SEM	77386
LODENBERRY CT	5000	485W	NEF	77494
LODENBRIAR DR	12800	528H	SWH	77072
LODENSTONE CT	24900	485N	NEF	77494
LODENSTONE LN	15800	407Z	NWC	77084
LODESTAR RD	2800	374A	NEH	77032
LODESTONE CT	16800	367U	NWC	77095
LODGE	6300	451J	NWH	77092
LODGE CT	1300	570T	MC	77489
LODGE RD	700	256R	SEM	77357
LODGE CREEK DR	5000	370D	NWC	77066
LODGE CREEK DR	5100	371A	NWC	77066
LODGE CREST CT	2000	660A	LC	77573
LODGE FALLS CT	1600	338A	NEH	77345
LODGEGATE CT	0	525M	NEF	77407
LODGEGLEN CT	5200	485W	NEF	77494
LODGEGLEN CT	5200	484F	NEF	77494
LODGEGLEN LN	5200	484F	NEF	77494

Street Name	Block	Pg/Sq	Loc	Zips
LODGEHILL LN	700	332E	NWC	77090
LODGEHILL LN	1000	331M	NWC	77090
LODGE HOLLOW CT	300	491G	SWH	77024
LODGE MEADOWS DR	22900	485L	NEF	77494
LODGEPOINT DR	23000	485Q	NEF	77494
LODGEPOLE RD	6400	456R	NEH	77049
LODGEPOLE PINE	0	326Z	NWC	77429
LODGEPOLE PINE	18200	327W	NWC	77429
LODGEPOLE PLACE	8500	290N	NWC	77375
LODGEPOLE VALE TRAIL		249P	NWC	77375
LODGE RUN LN	11300	369N	NWC	77065
LODGESTONE CT	22000	485Z	NEF	77450
LODGE VINE CT	4400	609X	NEF	77479
LODGE WOOD CT	9800	370Z	NWC	77086
LODI DR	1100	459M	HG	77562
LOESER DR	1000	490C	SV	77055
LOETSCH RIDGE WAY	8100	290N	NWC	77379
LOFLAND DR	8400	451W	SV	77055
LOFLAND DR	8500	450Z	SV	77055
LOFT FOREST CT	3800	297W	NEH	77339
LOFTING WEDGE DR	2000	616K	SEC	77089
LOFTON DR	14900	497H	NEC	77530
LOFT SQUARE PLACE	0	376H	NEC	77346
LOFTY EDGE ST	0	327H	NWC	77429
LOFTY ELM ST	2700	371Y	NWC	77038
LOFTY FALLS CT	0	292D	SEM	77386
LOFTY MAGNOLIA CT	5600	297Z	NEH	77345
LOFTY MAPLE TRAIL	1400	338A	NEH	77345
LOFTY MILLS DR	1400	336B	NEH	77339
LOFTY MOUNTAIN TRAIL	14100	618A	SEH	77062
LOFTY OAK CT	2400	578W	SEH	77059
LOFTY PEAK LN	15800	618F	SEH	77062
LOFTY PINES DR	10500	368Z	NWC	77065
LOFTY RIDGE CT	4100	578Z	PA	77059
LOGAN LN	5600	492L	SWH	77007
LOGAN LN	23800	338Q	NEH	77336
LOGAN ST	15600	568T	SG	77478
LOGAN BAY LN	0	572W	SWC	77053
LOGANBERRY CIR	2200	620A	SB	77586
LOGANBERRY PARK LN	2800	331U	NWC	77014
LOGAN BRIAR DR	19700	289W	NWC	77375
LOGAN BRIDGE LN	10300	527Z	NEF	77498
LOGAN CREST CT	3200	485T	NEF	77494
LOGANCREST LN	5800	411B	NWC	77086
LOGANDALE LN	700	373P	NCC	77032
LOGAN FALLS LN	0	375Z	NEC	77396
LOGAN FALLS LN	0	375Z	NEC	77396
LOGAN MILL DR	12400	369K	NWC	77070
LOGAN PARK DR	5700	331E	NWC	77379
LOGAN PASS	0	377B	NEC	77346
LOGAN RIDGE DR	11700	529A	SWH	77072
LOGAN ROCK RD	15700	571W	SWH	77489
LOGANS LANDING LN	0	484Z	NEF	77494
LOGANS RUN LN	0	575V	SEH	77075
LOGAN STAR CT	0	526L	NEF	77407
LOGANS WAY CT	0	616L	SEC	77089
LOGAN TIMBERS LN	19100	328D	NWC	77375
LOG CABIN LN	0	329B	NWC	77375
LOG CRADLE DR	7200	408Q	NWC	77041
LOGGA LN	0	376S	NEC	77396
LOGGER PINE TRAILS	10500	412J	NWC	77088
LOGGERS CHASE CT	600	252T	SEM	77386
LOGGERS DEPOT DR	2600	568Y	SG	77478
LOGGERS LUCK PLACE	10900	251Q	WD	77380
LOGGERS TRAIL CT	9900	410R	NWH	77040
LOGGING TRAIL DR	7200	337Y	NEC	77346
LOGGINS LN	25100	339E	HU	77336
LOG HOLLOW	0	410M	NWH	77040
LOG HOLLOW DR	6500	411J	NWH	77088
LOG HOLLOW DR	7000	410L	NWC	77040
LOG HOUSE CT	100	249R	NWH	77375
LOG HOUSE CT	100	249R	NWH	77375
S. LOGRUN CIR	2700	251Q	WD	77380
N. LOGRUN CIR	2700	251Q	WD	77380
LOGSTON LN	5300	291J	NWC	77389
LOGSTONE DR	6000	525R	NEF	77407
LOGTOWNE DR	0	248N	SWM	77354
LOG TRAIL	0	447J	NWC	77084
LOG VIEW	0	411J	NWH	77088
LOG VIEW DR	7100	410M	NWH	77040
LOGWOOD DR	6200	411T	NWH	77088
LOIRE LN	700	332J	NWC	77090
LOIRE LN	1100	331M	NWC	77090
LOIS LN	7700	575N	SEH	77075
LOIS LN	11800	248N	SWM	77362
LOLA	3500	611X	FS	77545
LOLITA LN	13500	414D	NEC	77039
LOLLIPOP LN	0	375D	HM	77338
LOLLY LN	17000	407Q	NWC	77084
LOMA CT	3700	293G	SEM	77386
LOMA LN	3800	293G	SEM	77386
LOMA ALTA DR	7300	527M	SWC	77083
LOMA LINDA	5500	571T	SWH	77085
LOMA PASEO DR	15100	527R	NEF	77083
LOMA VERDE DR	15600	527L	SWC	77083
LOMA VISTA	6300	571T	SWH	77085
LOMAX	8600	454E	NEH	77093
W. LOMAX DR	1900	539V	LP	77571
E. LOMAX DR	1900	539V	LP	77571
LOMAX SCHOOL RD	1200	539T	LP	77571
LOMBARDIA CT	10900	524R	NEF	77406
LOMBARDY	1300	534B	SEH	77023
LOMBARDY DR	100	568Q	SG	77478
LOMCREST	12000	570M	SWH	77085
LOMELINA LN	0	659R	LC	77573
LOMITAS	4500	492Y	SWH	77098
LOMMEL DR	0	406Z	NWC	77449
LONALLEN	9900	411R	NWH	77088
LONDENBERRY	32900	322J	WCO	77484
LONDON	1100	537P	PA	77506
LONDON	1300	537P	PA	77502
LONDON	6300	533R	SEH	77021
LONDON CT	0	615L	PL	77581
LONDON LN	0	258F	SEM	77357
LONDON LN	0	528K	SWC	77083
LONDONBELLE	0	538Y	PA	77505
LONDONBETTE RD	0	578C	PA	77505
LONDON BRIDSGE STATION	0	532Z	SWH	77045
LONDONDERRY AVE	1000	656M	FR	77546
LONDONDERRY DR	2400	616J	PL	77581
LONDONDERRY DR	10200	449V	NWH	77043
LONDONDERRY DR	33000	322J	WCO	77484
LONDON GREEN DR	1400	458S	NEC	77530
LONDON TOWN DR	8300	250W	NWC	77389
LONDON TOWN DR	25000	250S	NWC	77389
LONDON WAY DR	0	250W	NWC	77389
LONDON WAY DR	8500	249Z	NWC	77375
LONDRES DR	7200	527F	NEF	77083
LONE BRIDGE LN	0	334R	NCC	77338
LONE BRIDGE LN	8200	335N	NEC	77338
LONE BRIDGE LN	8300	335N	NEC	77338
LONE BROOK DR	10300	450E	NWH	77041

Street Name	Block	Pg/Sq	Loc	Zips
LONE BROOK DR	10600	449H	NWH	77041
LONE CEDAR DR	0	658P	LC	77573
LONE CEDAR DR	5500	297Z	NEH	77345
LONE CREEK CT	20700	406T	NWC	77449
LONE CREEK LN	0	612P	PL	77545
LONE CYPRESS LN	0	326Z	NWC	77429
LONE DOVE CT	4000	527G	SWC	77082
LONE EAGLE CIR	1700	378D	NEC	77532
LONE ELM DR	24000	293W	NCC	77373
LONE FIR DR	17000	329R	NWC	77379
LONE HICKORY CT	11800	578Z	PA	77059
LONELY PINE DR	4100	502G	BT	77521
LONELY STAR LN	0	525Z	NEF	77406
LONE MAPLE DR	8300	527Q	NEF	77083
LONE MEADOW CT	7600	407K	NWC	77095
LONE OAK	100	459V	HG	77562
LONE OAK	14800	420J	NEC	77532
LONE OAK CT	4900	501F	BT	77521
LONE OAK DR	1300	659N	LC	77573
LONE OAK DR	1400	413V	NCC	77093
LONE OAK DR	2400	414S	NCC	77093
LONE OAK DR	7300	462Z	BT	77521
LONE OAK RD	4100	414U	NEC	77093
LONE OAK PARK DR	17800	407E	NWC	77095
LONE PINE DR	1	298C	NEC	77336
LONE PINE DR	100	459V	HG	77562
LONE PRAIRIE WAY	0	406T	NWC	77449
LONE QUAIL CT	16700	610C	SWH	77489
LONE QUAIL DR	8200	610C	SWH	77489
LONE RIDGE LN	21500	446N	NWC	77449
LONE RIVER CT	17900	407K	NWC	77095
LONE ROCK DR	2000	296Y	NEH	77339
LONE ROCK LN	0	609U	NEF	77479
LONE SHADOW	15900	246M	SC	77355
LONE SHADOW TRAIL	11700	415L	NEC	77050
LONESOME BAYOU LN	6200	411T	NWH	77088
W. LONESOME DOVE	0	538R	DP	77536
E. LONESOME DOVE	0	538R	DP	77536
LONESOME DOVE CT	10600	367U	NWC	77095
LONESOME DOVE TRL	17300	367T	NWC	77095
LONESOME PINE	16100	286C	SWM	77355
LONESOME PINE RD	3800	291K	NWC	77389
LONESOME QUAIL DR	16400	610B	SWH	77489
LONESOME WOODS TRAIL	6900	337Y	NEC	77346
LONE STAR CT	5600	657V	LC	77573
LONE STAR DR	1000	490C	SV	77055
LONE STAR DR	2100	568X	SG	77479
LONE STAR LN	100	247B	SWM	77362
LONE STAR COLLEGE	0	329X	NWC	77070
LONE STAR JUNCTION	0	525V	NEF	77406
LONESTAR OAK	20300	326T	NWC	77433
LONESTAR OAK CT	20300	326T	NWC	77433
LONESTONE BEND LN	0	446c	NWC	77449
LONE TREE DR	15600	448B	NWC	77084
LONE TUPELO LN	0	326Q	NWC	77429
LONE WILLOW CT	14400	570V	SWH	77489
LONE WILLOW LN	14400	570V	SWH	77489
LONE WILLOW M H	0	413K	NCC	77037
LONE WOLF PASS	17500	367T	NWC	77095
LONE WOLF TRAIL	23100	333B	NCC	77373
LONG	0	492G	SWH	77007
LONG DR	100	501Q	BT	77521
LONG DR	5800	534K	SEH	77087
LONG RD	100	259T	NEC	77336
LONG RD	15100	418T	NEC	77044
LONGACRE DR	1500	450V	NWH	77055
LONG BARREL LN	1900	570Y	MC	77489
LONG BARREL LN	9100	410M	NWC	77040
LONG BAY CT	3100	578X	SEH	77059
LONG BAY LN	0	609Y	NEF	77459
LONG BAY LN	0	609Y	NEF	77459
LONG BOAT CT	16100	419A	NEC	77532
LONGBOAT LN	0	619U	LC	77573
LONG BOUGH CT	3100	578W	SEH	77059
LONGBOW CIR	9400	248M	SWM	77354
LONGBOW LN	1	491G	SWH	77024
LONGBOW LN	27300	248M	SWM	77354
LONG BOW RD	22000	285A	SWM	77447
LONG BRANCH LN	9600	450X	NWH	77055
LONGBROOK DR	11000	529X	SWH	77099
LONGBROOK DR	12400	528V	SWH	77099
LONG CASTLE DR	21400	291R	NWC	77388
LONGCLIFFE DR	18000	447B	NWC	77084
LONGCOMMON DR	9600	569B	SWH	77099
LONG COVE CIR	2200	485Q	NEF	77450
LONG COVE CT	2200	612M	PL	77584
LONG CREEK CT	7600	411U	NWH	77088
LONG CREEK LN	5200	411Q	NWH	77088
LONGCROFT DR	9100	330N	NWC	77379
LONG CYPRESS DR	20400	291Y	NWC	77388
LONGDALE CT	19700	406R	NWC	77433
LONGDRAW DR	1000	484K	NEF	77494
LONGDRAW COVE	2100	484K	NEF	77494
LONGENBAUGH RD	0	406G	NWC	77433
LONGENBAUGH RD	15600	408J	NWC	77095
LONGENBAUGH RD	16000	407G	NWC	77095
LONGENBAUGH RD	22000	405K	NWC	77433
LONGENBAUGH RD	24000	404J	NWC	77493
LONGFELLOW	1	533A	SWH	77005
LONGFIELD CIR	3300	490Z	SWH	77063
LONGFLOWER CT	2000	297V	NEH	77345
LONGFLOWER LN	6100	297V	NEH	77345
LONGFORD DR	12600	456M	NEC	77049
LONGFOREST DR	5400	411K	NWC	77088
LONG GATE DR	10800	573G	SEH	77047
LONG GLEN DR	3700	296V	NEH	77339
LONG GLEN DR	13200	414B	NCC	77039
LONG GROVE DR	4000	619L	TL	77586
LONG HAVEN DR	0	366J	NWC	77433
LONGHERRIDGE	0	615Z	PL	77581
LONGHERRIDGE DR	2000	615V	PL	77581
LONG HILL LN	25300	293N	NCC	77373
LONG HILL LN	25900	292R	NCC	77373
LONGHORN	4100	501M	BT	77521
LONGHORN CIR	0	613W	NEB	77578
LONGHORN CIR	11000	409Y	NWC	77041
LONGHORN DR	0	539N	DP	77536
LONGHORN DR	1400	450N	NWH	77080
LONGHORN DR	3300	447L	NWC	77084
LONGHORN LN	0	409Y	NWC	77041
LONG HUNTER CT	12900	377F	NEC	77346
LONGHURST HILLS LN	0	326U	NWC	77429
LONG IRON CT	25500	250T	NWC	77389
LONG KEY DR	0	366P	NWC	77433
LONG LAKE DR	19300	446Z	NWC	77084
LONG LEAF	0	580P	LP	77571
LONG LEAF	1	299E	NEC	77336
LONGLEAF	4900	614E	PL	77581
LONG LEAF DR	2600	528Y	SG	77478
LONG LEAF DR	6000	411P	NWH	77088
LONG LEAF DR	10200	252H	SEM	77385
LONG LEAF LN	3700	297U	NEH	77345

Street Name	Block	Pg/Sq	Loc	Zips
LONG LEAF LN	7300	462Y	BT	77521
LONGLEAF LN	11700	490K	SWH	77024
LONGLEAF PINES LN	2200	296V	NEH	77339
LONGLEAF PINES LN	2600	297S	NEH	77339
LONGLEAF RIDGE WAY		249T	NWC	77375
LONGLEAF TRAIL	0	326P	NWC	77433
LONGLEAF VALLEY DR	0	524E	NEF	77494
LONGLEAF WOODS TRAIL	0	293D	SEM	77386
LONGLEDGE DR	1200	619G	TL	77586
LONGLEY	700	536Y	SH	77587
LONG LIMB CANYON	0	376S	NEC	77396
LONG LOOK DR	15200	571U	SWH	77053
LONGMARK POINTE DR	0	487E	SWC	77494
LONG MEADOW	5000	534S	SEH	77033
LONG MEADOW CT	3300	613V	PL	77584
LONGMEADOW DR	0	573Y	SEC	77047
LONGMEADOW DR	0	573Y	SEC	77047
LONG MEADOW DR	2900	501R	BT	77521
LONG MEADOW FARMS PKWY	0	525Z	NEF	77406
LONG MEADOW FARMS PKWY	0	526W	NEF	77406
LONGMONT CIR	1900	610B	MC	77489
LONGMONT DR	5000	491Q	SWH	77056
LONGMONT DR	6100	491N	SWH	77057
LONGMONT DR	9400	490N	SWH	77063
LONGMONT DR	10000	489Q	SWH	77042
LONGMONT LN	0	491Q	SWH	77057
LONGMONT PARK CT	0	484Y	NEF	77494
LONGMONT PARK LN	0	484Y	NEF	77494
LONGMONT PLACE CT	0	491L	SWH	77056
LONGMOOR DR	18000	447B	NWC	77084
LONGNECK DR	15500	246T	SWM	77355
LONG OAK CT	12100	328Z	NWC	77070
LONG OAK DR	0	615Z	PL	77581
LONG OAK DR	0	420N	NEC	77532
LONG OAK DR	13900	328Z	NWC	77070
LONG OAKS DR	0	414B	NCC	77039
LONG PEAK LN	0	377E	NEC	77346
LONG PINE DR	11400	489P	SWH	77077
LONG PINE DR	25800	250S	NWC	77389
LONG PLAY LN	11600	417P	NEC	77044
LONG POINT RD	6400	451U	NWH	77055
LONG POINT RD	8600	450X	NWH	77055
LONG POINT RD	10100	450X	NWH	77043
LONGPOINT HILLS LN	0	484X	NEF	77494
LONG PRAIRIE DR	600	485G	SWC	77450
LONG PRAIRIE TRACE	5500	525V	NEF	77407
LONG REACH DR	2300	568Y	SG	77478
LONGREN	10800	576T	SEH	77089
LONGRIDGE DR	7800	451S	NWH	77055
LONG RIVER CIR	14200	528W	NEF	77498
LONG RIVER CT	14100	528W	NEF	77498
LONG RIVER DR	10300	528W	NEF	77498
LONG ROCK DR	2100	610A	MC	77489
LONG SHADOW DR	14000	457U	NEC	77015
LONG SHADOW LN	1900	292X	NWC	77388
LONG SHADOWS CIR	500	332A	NWC	77388
LONG SHADOWS DR	0	251F	SWM	77381
LONG SHADOWS LN	3200	251N	SWM	77380
LONG SHADOWS LN	10800	490H	HC	77024
LONG SHIP CT	19200	330D	NWC	77379
LONGSHIRE LN	7900	410L	NWC	77040
LONGS PEEK CT	17300	328M	NWC	77377
LONGSPRING DR	20300	486K	SWC	77450
S. LONGSPUR DR	1	251X	WD	77380
N. LONGSPUR DR	1	251X	WD	77380
E. LONGSPUR DR	1	251Y	WD	77380
LONGSPUR LN	0	658X	LC	77573
LONGSPUR LN	2100	658X	LC	77573
LONGSTAFF DR	9100	570A	SWH	77031
LONGSTONE RD	25800	250T	NWC	77389
LONGSTRAW PLACE	2000	251R	WD	77380
LONG TIMBER DR	19100	337Y	NEC	77346
LONG TIMBERS LN	1	490H	HC	77024
LONG TIMBERS TRAIL	1	490H	HC	77024
LONGTOM CT	11000	371S	NWC	77086
LONG TRACE DR	18600	377C	NEC	77346
LONG TRACE DR	18700	337Y	NEC	77346
LONG TRAIL LN	24600	338M	NEH	77336
LONG TRAIL PATH CT	2100	293S	NCC	77373
LONGVALE DR	15700	618C	SEH	77059
LONG VALLEY DR	2200	337C	NEH	77345
LONGVIEW	6200	494D	NEH	77020
LONGVIEW	7100	495A	NEH	77020
LONGVIEW	13700	497C	NEC	77015
LONG VIEW DR	0	616T	PL	77581
LONGVIEW DR	300	569N	SG	77478
LONGVIEW CREEK	26300	524F	NEF	77494
LONGVIEW CREEK DR	26300	524F	NEF	77494
LONGVINE CT	12800	528M	SWH	77072
LONGVINE DR	7000	528M	SWH	77072
LONGWOOD	0	459H	NEC	77562
LONGWOOD	2300	616T	PL	77581
W. LONGWOOD	16500	327M	NWC	77429
E. LONGWOOD	16700	327M	NWC	77429
LONGWOOD	0	538V	DP	77536
LONGWOOD CT	0	658S	LC	77573
LONGWOOD DR	3000	537Q	PA	77503
LONGWOOD BEND	14000	328T	NWC	77429
LONGWOOD FOREST DR	0	293T	NCC	77373
LONGWOOD GARDEN WAY	11700	573N	SEH	77047
LONGWOOD GLEN LN	0	657S	FR	77546
LONGWOOD MEADOWS	17200	327M	NWC	77429
LONGWOOD PARK LN	0	253K	SEM	77386
LONGWOODS CT	10100	491E	SWH	77024
LONGWOODS LN	300	491E	SWH	77024
LONGWOOD SPUR	16200	327M	NWC	77429
LONGWOOD TRACE DR	12300	328X	NWC	77429
LONGWOOD TRACE DR	12800	368A	NWC	77429
LONGWOOD TRACE DR	13300	328W	NWC	77429
LONGWORTH LN	12300	490J	BH	77024
LONNIE LN	800	452C	NWH	77091
LONNIEWOOD DR	3600	618D	SEH	77059
LONSFORD DR	9800	371W	NWC	77086
LONZO	3100	490X	SWH	77063
LOOFF	0	368F	NWC	77429
LOOK COVE CT	0	411D	NWC	77038
LOOKMOOR	0	490N	SWH	77024
LOOKOUT CT	1	532K	SWH	77025
LOOKOUT LN	0	378A	NEC	77346
LOOKOUT BEND DR	0	335P	NCC	77338
LOOKOUT MOUNTAIN CT	13100	370C	NWC	77069
LOOKOUT MOUNTAIN DR	5200	370C	NWC	77069
LOOKOUT MOUNTAIN LN	19100	406V	NWC	77449
LOOKOUT RIDGE DR	0	366N	NWC	77433
LOOKOUT SPRINGS		284R	HK	77447
LOOM	1100	379T	NEC	77532
LOOM CT	1000	379T	NEC	77532
LOON DR	0	658X	LC	77573
LOONE CT	700	252T	SEM	77386
LOONRIVER DR	200	338L	NEH	77336
LOOP 207	0	463E	MB	77580
LOOP 207	0	463E	MB	77580

Street Name	Block	Pg/Sq	Loc	Zips
LOOP 410	0	540X	LP	77571
LOOP 410	0	540X	LP	77571
LOOP 410	0	580L	LP	77571
LOOP 410	0	580L	LP	77571
LOOP 494	19300	256U	SEM	77357
LOOP 494	19300	256U	SEM	77357
LOOP 494	22000	335H	NEH	77339
LOOP 494	22000	335H	NEH	77339
LOOP 494	22400	335H	SEM	77339
LOOP 494	22400	335H	SEM	77339
LOOP 494	22600	296S	SEM	77365
LOOP 494	22600	296S	SEM	77365
E. LOOP (I.H. 610) N.	0	495Q	NEH	77029
E. LOOP (I.H. 610) S.	0	535C	SEH	77012
W. LOOP (I.H. 610) N.	1	491M	SWH	77024
W. LOOP (I.H. 610) S.	1	491V	SWH	77027
N. LOOP (I.H. 610)	100	453N	NWH	77008
N. LOOP (I.H. 610) E.	100	454U	NEH	77009
N. LOOP (I.H. 610) W.	100	452Q	NWH	77018
N. LOOP (I.H. 610)	101	453N	NWH	77018
N. LOOP (I.H. 610) E.	101	454U	NEH	77022
N. LOOP (I.H. 610) W.	101	452Q	NWH	77008
S. LOOP (I.H. 610) W.	400	533S	SWH	77054
N. LOOP (I.H. 610)	600	453N	NWH	77009
N. LOOP (I.H. 610)	601	453N	NWH	77022
W. LOOP (I.H. 610) N.	1100	451Z	NWH	77055
S. LOOP (I.H. 610) W.	1400	532U	SWH	77054
W. LOOP (I.H. 610) N.	1500	451Z	NWH	77008
N. LOOP (I.H. 610) E.	2000	454U	NEH	77026
S. LOOP (I.H. 610) E.	2200	533T	SEH	77021
N. LOOP (I.H. 610) W.	2400	452Q	NWH	77092
N. LOOP (I.H. 610) W.	2401	452Q	NWH	77008
S. LOOP (I.H. 610) W.	3200	532U	SWH	77025
S. LOOP (I.H. 610) E.	3900	533T	SEH	77051
S. LOOP (I.H. 610) W.	4300	531V	SWH	77096
S. LOOP (I.H. 610) E.	4400	534N	SEH	77033
W. LOOP (I.H. 610) S.	5200	531M	SWH	77401
W. LOOP (I.H. 610) S.	5201	531M	SWH	77081
W. LOOP (I.H. 610) S.	5500	531M	SWH	77401
S. LOOP (I.H. 610) E.	6051	534N	SEH	77087
S. LOOP (I.H. 610) E.	6052	534N	SEH	77087
S. LOOP (I.H. 610) E.	6100	534N	SEH	77087
N. LOOP (I.H. 610) E.	6600	455X	NEH	77028
S. LOOP (I.H. 610) E.	7700	535F	SEH	77017
S. LOOP (I.H. 610) E.	7701	535F	SEH	77012
N. LOOP (I.H. 610) E.	8100	455X	NEH	77029
W. LOOP (I.H. 610) S.	8500	531M	SWH	77096
S. LOOP (I.H. 610) E.	8500	535F	SEH	77017
N. LOOP (I.H. 610) E.	9400	495C	NEH	77029
LOOP CENTRAL DR	4800	491Z	SWH	77081
LOOSCAN LN	2100	492Q	SWH	77019
LOPER	200	536J	SEH	77017
LOPER	800	535M	SEH	77017
LORALIE LN	6500	609Y	NEF	77459
LORA MEADOWS CT	0	293F	SEM	77386
LORA MEADOWS CT	0	293F	SEM	77386
LORAMIE CREEK CT	0	377M	NEH	77346
LORCA LN	0	660G	GCO	77565
LORD	11500	496K	JC	77029
LORD RD	2900	380L	NEC	77532
LORD NELSON DR	2100	620K	SB	77586
LORDS	200	258F	SEM	77357
LOREN LN	9000	410V	NWC	77040
LORENA SPRINGS LN	0	332V	NCC	77073
LORENE	900	536U	PA	77502
LORENE	4700	452H	NWH	77018
LORENZO	15800	498G	CV	77530
LORETTO DR	4000	492V	SWH	77006
LORI	24400	247X	SWM	77355
LORI CT	0	620K	SB	77586
LORI DR	22400	333H	NCC	77373
LORI LN	1700	458V	CV	77530
LORI LN	9200	410K	NWC	77040
LORI LN	26300	295Y	SEM	77365
LORI BROOK LN	11100	368U	NWC	77065
LORIE LN	500	619L	PA	77586
LORI FALLS CT	11100	368U	NWC	77065
LORI HALL LN	0	488F	SWH	77077
LORIKEET CT	3100	293X	NCC	77373
LORINDA DR	4400	452E	NWH	77018
LORING LN	0	245U	SWM	77355
LORING LN	17200	331G	NWC	77388
W. LORINO	100	412H	NCC	77037
E. LORINO	100	413E	NCC	77037
LORINOWOODS DR	5700	370H	NWC	77066
LORNA CT	8500	413N	NCC	77037
LORNE DR	14000	456V	NEC	77049
LORNE DR	14300	457S	NEC	77049
LORNMEAD DR	600	489H	SWH	77024
LOROCCO WAY	0	656W	AV	77511
LORO LINDA DR	7600	527J	NEF	77083
LORRAINE	1200	493H	NEH	77009
LORRAINE	1700	494E	NEH	77026
LORRAINE	8900	460R	NEC	77562
LORRAINE CT	800	537J	PA	77506
LORRAINE DR	5300	500H	BT	77521
LORREINS LN	13400	367G	NWC	77429
LORRIE DR	8000	532L	SWH	77025
LORRIE LAKE LN	1	490P	SWH	77024
LORTON DR	11200	329X	NWC	77070
LOSA DR	15600	373T	NCC	77032
LOS ALAMOS CIR	0	539N	DP	77536
LOS ALTOS DR	15800	527L	NEF	77083
LOS ANGELES	3400	454K	NEH	77026
LOS ANGELES	6700	454K	NEH	77016
LOS COYOTES DR	6300	578J	PA	77505
LOS ENCINOS CT	1	248G	SWM	77354
LOS ENCINOS DR	1	248C	SWM	77354
LOS FRAILES DR	0	656C	FR	77546
LOSOYA CT	0	291N	NWC	77388
LOST ANCHOR WAY LN	15800	377P	NEC	77044
LOST BRIDGE LN	0	612J	PL	77545
LOST BROOK LN	23100	333B	NCC	77373
LOST CANYON DR	22700	485G	SWC	77450
LOST COVE LN	0	293Z	NCC	77373
LOST CREEK BLVD	3400	569W	SG	77478
LOST CREEK CIR	800	485G	SWC	77450
LOST CREEK CT	31100	248Y	TB	77375
LOST CREEK DR	0	612J	PL	77545
LOST CREEK LN	4900	658W	LC	77573
LOST CREEK RD	13300	248Y	TB	77375
LOST CREEK RD	22400	485G	SWC	77450
LOST CYPRESS DR	17000	327T	CY	77429
LOST EAGLE DR	9500	409C	NWC	77064
LOST ELM CIR	0	366N	NWC	77433
LOST FABLE LN	7200	407L	NWC	77095
LOST FALL CT	0	407S	NWC	77449
LOST FALLS CT	5900	609T	NEF	77479
LOST FOREST DR	5300	451F	NWH	77092
LOST FOREST DR	5600	451B	NWH	77092
LOST HILL CT	2200	293F	SEM	77386
LOST HOLLOW DR	3200	296Y	NEH	77339

Street Name	Block	Pg/Sq	Loc	Zips
LOS TIOS DR	6600	527G	SWC	77083
LOST LAKE DR	3500	297W	NEH	77339
LOST LAKE LN	4200	291T	NWC	77388
LOST LAKE PLACE	0	615L	PL	77581
LOST LEGENDS DR	29500	253W	SEM	77386
LOST MAPLE FOREST CT	3300	297P	NEH	77345
LOST MAPLES CT	18500	337X	NEC	77346
LOST MAPLES DR	0	366S	NWC	77433
LOST MAPLES DR	2700	615N	PL	77581
LOST MAPLES TRAIL	0	377B	NEC	77346
LOST MAPLES TRAIL	12700	337X	NEC	77346
LOST MAPLES TRAIL	2100	297V	NEH	77345
LOST MEADOW LN	14100	489A	SWH	77079
LOST MIDDEN CT	0	366S	NWC	77433
LOST MILL LN	0	367Y	NWC	77095
LOST MINE TRAIL		332E	NWC	77388
LOST OAK DR	3400	331C	NWC	77388
LOST ORCHARD DR	13400	414C	NCC	77039
LOST PATH LN	10200	248G	SWM	77354
LOST PINE LN	10000	462Z	BT	77521
LOST PINES DR	0	524B	NEF	77494
LOST PINES BEND	0	456R	NEH	77049
LOST PINE TRAIL	20900	378C	NEC	77532
LOST PLUM CREEK CIR	0	366N	NWC	77433
LOST QUAIL DR	16400	610C	SWH	77489
LOS TRES RANCHOS	0	371G	NWC	77014
LOST RIDGE CIR	1400	619H	TL	77586
LOST RIVER DR	800	656L	FR	77546
LOST ROCK CT	16000	618S	SEH	77598
LOST ROCK DR	300	618S	SEH	77598
LOST SPRING DR	4400	448E	NWC	77084
LOST STONE DR		329K	NWC	77375
LOST THICKET DR	6700	571J	SWH	77085
LOST TIMBER LN	6300	370L	NWC	77066
LOST TRAIL	10000	411P	NWH	77088
LOST VALLEY TRAIL	21000	378C	NEC	77532
LOST WOODS DR	0	524S	NWF	77406
LOS VERDES DR	4200	577B	PA	77504
LOTEBUSH LN	0	463S	CCO	77520
LOTHBURY DR	0	328N	NWC	77429
LOTTIE LN	100	616Y	FR	77546
LOTTMAN	200	494J	SEH	77003
LOTUS	0	570X	MC	77489
LOTUS	4700	571M	SWH	77045
LOTUS	5400	571L	SWH	77085
LOTUS CIR	0	248H	SWM	77354
LOTUS DR	4000	613V	NEB	77584
LOTUS LN	2900	613V	NEB	77584
LOTUSBRIAR LN	0	488N	SWH	77077
LOTUS CANYON CT		526S	NEF	77407
LOTUS CREEK CT	6900	290T	NWC	77379
LOU LN	100	332B	NWH	77388
S. LOU-AL DR	11500	490F	HE	77024
N. LOU-AL DR	11500	490B	HE	77024
LOU'S LN	21100	256S	SEM	77357
LOUAN CT	14100	568A	SG	77498
LOU ANNA DR	7000	410T	NWC	77040
LOU ANNE LN	4100	451K	NWH	77092
LOUDEN DR	0	289Q	NWC	77375
LOU EDD RD	9700	369P	NWC	77070
LOUEDD RD	9700	369K	NWC	77070
LOU ELLEN LN	1900	452N	NWH	77018
LOUETTA RD	0	326Y	NWC	77429
E. LOUETTA RD	100	292T	NCC	77373
LOUETTA RD	1700	292W	NWC	77388
LOUETTA RD	3400	331B	NWC	77388
LOUETTA RD	4900	330N	NWC	77379
LOUETTA RD	11000	329T	NWC	77070
LOUETTA RD	12400	326V	NWC	77429
LOUETTA RD	12400	328U	NWC	77429
LOUETTAASH DR	0	292W	NWC	77388
LOUETTABOUGH LN	0	292W	NWC	77388
LOUETTA BROOK CT	0	292S	NWC	77388
LOUETTA BROOK LN	0	292S	NWC	77388
LOUETTA CREEK DR	18600	331B	NWC	77388
LOUETTA CROSSING	100	292T	NEH	77373
LOUETTA CROSSING DR	0	292W	NWC	77388
LOUETTA FALLS LN	2200	292S	NWC	77388
LOUETTA GLEN DR	0	292S	NWC	77388
LOUETTA GREEN DR	0	330N	NWC	77379
LOUETTAGUM DR	0	292W	NWC	77388
LOUETTA LAKES DR	19800	291Z	NWC	77388
LOUETTA LEE DR	0	292W	NWC	77388
LOUETTAMAPLE DR	0	292W	NWC	77388
LOUETTAMIST DR	0	292W	NWC	77388
LOUETTA OAK CT	2000	292S	NWC	77388
LOUETTA OAK DR	20600	292S	NWC	77388
LOUETTA OAK TRAIL	0	292S	NWC	77388
LOUETTA PARK CIR	0	292W	NWC	77388
LOUETTA PINE DR	0	292W	NWC	77388
LOUETTA POINT CIR	0	292W	NWC	77388
LOUETTAREACH DR	0	292W	NWC	77388
LOUETTARESERVE	0	292W	NWC	77388
LOUETTASHADOWS LN	0	292W	NWC	77388
LOUETTA SPRING DR	2000	292S	NWC	77388
LOUETTASTREAMWAY	0	292W	NWC	77388
LOUETTA WOODS DR	20600	292S	NWC	77388
LOUIE LN	0	406Z	NWC	77449
LOUIE WELCH DR	19200	335X	NEH	77338
LOUIS	2800	380A	NEC	77532
LOUIS LN	16700	254L	SEM	77365
LOUIS LN	31800	248T	SWM	77362
LOUISA CT	4800	609A	SG	77478
LOUISE	300	453T	NWH	77009
LOUISE	3500	611X	FS	77545
LOUISE	4700	621A	PA	77586
LOUISE	5300	500G	BT	77521
LOUISE	13100	570J	SF	77477
LOUISE LN	0	614W	NEB	77584
W. LOUISE RD	100	412R	NCC	77037
LOUISE OAK CT	8000	290J	NWC	77379
LOUISIANA	0	535Z	SH	77587
LOUISIANA	100	570N	MC	77489
LOUISIANA	100	493Q	DT	77002
LOUISIANA	500	536W	SH	77587
LOUISIANA	1300	538N	DP	77536
LOUISIANA	1400	540D	BT	77520
LOUISIANA	2300	493Q	SWH	77006
LOUISIANA	3400	493Q	SWH	77006
LOUISIANA	4900	493W	SWH	77006
LOUISIANA	600	659C	LC	77573
LOUISVILLE	12800	497A	NEH	77015
LOUPE CT	3500	609Q	MC	77459
LOUPE LN	6800	609Q	MC	77459
LOURDES DR	14000	456V	NEC	77049
LOURDES DR	14400	457S	NEC	77049
LOURES LN	0	660G	GCO	77565
LOUTRE PASS	0	609Y	MC	77459
LOUVRE CT	0	529A	SWH	77042
LOUVRE LN	0	529A	SWH	77042
LOUVRE LN	3300	489W	SWH	77082
LOVAGE AVE	0	419C	NEC	77532

Street Name	Block	Pg/Sq	Loc	Zips
LOVE	3400	454X	NEH	77026
LOVE CT	2800	656X	FR	77546
LOVE LN	2800	656X	FR	77546
LOVEBIRD LN	11300	371R	NWC	77067
LOVE CREEK	0	609Y	MC	77459
W. LOVEGRASS LN	0	293G	SEM	77386
LOVEJOY	3800	494P	SEH	77003
LOVELAND PASS DR	11700	371L	NWC	77067
LOVELY LN	1100	538L	DP	77536
LOVENIA LN	0	375V	NEC	77396
LOVERS LN	700	412Y	NWH	77091
LOVERS WOOD LN	3700	331X	NWC	77014
LOVETT	1000	288D	TB	77375
LOVETT BLVD	400	493S	SWH	77006
LOVETT CT	800	288H	TB	77375
LOVETT LN	18000	330F	NWC	77379
LOVING	0	256Z	SEM	77357
LOVING	2100	576B	SEH	77034
LOVINGTON CT	0	411M	NWH	77088
LOVINNIE	0	539V	LP	77571
LOVIS WAY	0	333G	NCC	77338
LOW BRIDGE LN	10300	527Z	NEF	77498
LOW COUNTRY LN	1	251K	WD	77380
LOWDEN	3800	533Y	SEH	77051
LOWDEN CREST LN	0	369G	NWC	77077
LOWE RD	19600	295G	SEM	77365
LOWELL CT	1800	484H	NEF	77494
LOWELL LN	13700	288X	NWC	77377
LOWELLBERG LN	5600	407Z	NWC	77084
LOWELL LAKE LN	0	377J	NEC	77346
LOWER ARROW DR	6600	371W	NWC	77086
LOWER BIDS AVE	1700	420A	NEC	77532
LOWER CANYON LN	0	485P	NEF	77493
LOWERCOVE CIR	9000	409H	NWC	77064
LOWER LAKE DR	15800	326N	NWC	77433
LOWER LEVEL RD	0	495Y	NEH	77029
LOWER PECOS ST	0	366S	NWC	77433
LOWER RIDGEWAY	9500	576J	SEH	77075
LOWER VALLEY DR	2500	371M	NWC	77067
LOWICK	17300	329M	NWC	77379
LOW OAKS CIR	0	255S	SEM	77365
LOW RIDGE RD	23200	334A	NCC	77373
LOWRIE	10400	414X	NEH	77093
LOXANHACHEE PLACE	0	250U	NWC	77389
LOXLEY DR	1400	372A	NWC	77014
LOXLEY MEADOWS DR	14700	487Z	SWC	77082
LOYAL LN	0	415X	NWH	77078
LOYANNE DR	2300	293W	NCC	77373
LOYEL POINTE DR	7600	370S	NWC	77064
LOYOLA DR	11200	368T	NWC	77429
LOYOLA LN	0	285C	SWM	77447
LOYS COVES CT	0	376U	NEC	77396
LOZAR DR	0	290P	NWC	77379
LOZIER	6600	533L	SEH	77021
LUBBOCK	1400	493K	SWH	77002
LUBBOCK	1500	493K	SWH	77007
LUBY CREEK DR	0	366P	NWC	77433
LUCA	3400	533K	SEH	77021
LUCARIO DR	13100	413J	NCC	77037
LUCAS	2200	494B	NEH	77026
LUCAS ST	0	616T	PL	77581
LUCAS CANYON LN	26500	484Y	NEF	77494
LUCAS TRACE CT	4300	371K	NWC	77066
LUCAYAN DR	0	419E	NEC	77532
LUCCA CT	2800	659M	LC	77573
LUCE	5600	534Q	SEH	77087
LUCERNE	5600	531D	BL	77401
LUCERNE	10800	415S	NEH	77016
LUCIA LN	20000	338S	NEC	77346
LUCIAN LN	4000	657B	FR	77546
LUCIDA LN	3100	293X	NCC	77373
LUCIDOL-PENNWALT	0	380Q	NEC	77532
LUCIEN LN	13400	288Y	NWC	77377
LUCILLE	3600	494B	NEH	77026
LUCILLE DR	0	257A	SEM	77357
LUCINDA	2300	493Z	SEH	77004
LUCINDA MEADOWS DR	0	406U	NWC	77449
LUCKEL DR	5200	444Z	KT	77493
LUCKY	700	412T	NWH	77088
LUCKY	800	539Q	LP	77571
LUCKY	2400	411V	NWH	77088
LUCKY GARDEN WAY	0	527H	SWC	77083
LUCKY HILL WAY	0	527G	SWC	77083
LUCKY LEAF CT	1	251B	WD	77381
LUCKY MEADOW DR	11900	329A	NWC	77375
LUCKY RIVER LN	0	527G	SWC	77083
LUCKY STAR DR	0	487Y	SWC	77082
LUCKY STAR LN	0	525B	NEF	77494
LUCKY STAR LN	0	527H	SWC	77083
LUCORE	9700	535M	SEH	77017
LUCORE	9900	536J	SEH	77017
LUCRETIA	2000	247N	SWM	77362
LUCY LN	300	247F	SWM	77362
LUCY LN	1900	610A	MC	77489
LUCY LN	5800	537Z	PA	77505
LUCYBERRY ST	0	450Q	NWH	77080
LUDGATE DR	23000	333D	NCC	77373
LUDGATE PASS	13700	617B	SEH	77034
LUDINGTON DR	5500	571A	SWH	77035
LUDINGTON DR	7500	570D	SWH	77071
LUDWIG LN	4300	569P	NEF	77477
LUELL	2800	454E	NEH	77093
LUELLA	5100	578C	LP	77571
LUELLA AVE	600	538Y	DP	77536
LUETTA	1	453B	NEH	77076
LUFBERRY PLACE	100	249R	NWC	77375
LUFBERRY PLACE	100	249R	NWH	77375
LUFBOROUGH DR	4000	371E	NWC	77066
LUFKIN	5600	454U	NEH	77026
LUFKIN LN	2400	538P	DP	77536
S. LUGANO DR	0	525J	NEF	77406
S. LUGANO VERDE DR	0	524M	NEF	77406
LUGARY DR	5800	530F	SWH	77036
LUGARY DR	8100	530Q	SWH	77074
LUISTANO LN	0	527W	NEF	77469
LUKE	600	412Y	NWH	77091
LUKE DAVIS BLVD	22300	256L	SEM	77357
LUKE RIDGE LN	5100	484Z	NEF	77494
LULA	1800	453T	NWH	77009
LULA	4300	531M	BL	77401
LULL	3900	534L	SEH	77087
LULLABY LN	1	251Q	WD	77380
LULLABY LN	300	419R	BR	77532
LULLWATER PLACE	1	250D	WD	77381
LUM LN	9800	455D	NEH	77078
LUMA COVE LN	0	328J	NWC	77429
LUMA COVE LN	0	328J	NWC	77377
LUMA LAGO LN	0	526Q	NEF	77407
LUMBER LN	3900	454P	NEH	77016
LUMBERDALE RD	3500	451K	NWH	77092
LUMBERDALE RD	6200	411X	NWH	77092
LUMBER JACK DR	7100	411J	NWH	77040

Street Name	Block	Pg/Sq	Loc	Zips
LUMBER JACK DR	7500	410R	NWC	77040
LUMBER RIDGE TRAIL	0	577S	SEH	77034
LUMBER SPRINGS LN	0	445F	NWC	77493
LUMBERTON DR	0	366P	NWC	77433
LUMPKIN RD	1000	489D	NWH	77043
LUMPKIN RD	1100	449Z	NWH	77043
LUNA	5500	453A	NEH	77076
LUNA	6800	413W	NEH	77076
LUNA BUTTE DR	0	328C	NWC	77377
LUNA FALLS CT	19300	328C	NWC	77377
LUNA FALLS DR	12000	328C	NWC	77377
LUNA LAKES DR	30000	253X	SEM	77386
LUNAR LAKE DR		526S	NEF	77407
LUNA ROSSA DR	0	525E	NEF	77406
LUNA SPRINGS LN	0	366Y	NWC	77433
LUNDAR LN	18100	328H	NWC	77377
LUNDWOOD LN	0	407Z	NWC	77084
LUNDY	9200	454B	NEH	77093
LUNDY LN	1400	656Y	FR	77546
LUNIA LN	0	533F	SWH	77021
LUNS LN	0	373A	NCC	77073
LUNSFORD HOLLOW LN	4700	617X	SEC	77546
LUNSFORD MEWS LN	0	486L	SWC	77094
LUONG FIELD CT	4100	485U	NEF	77494
LUPIN	500	531L	BL	77401
LUPTON CT	9000	450Y	SV	77055
LUPTON LN	8600	450Z	SV	77055
LUQUET LN	0	292J	NWC	77389
LURE CT	9400	408D	NWC	77065
LURE DR	9400	408D	NWC	77065
LURLENE	4200	535Q	SEH	77017
LUSTERLEAF DR	12300	369J	NWC	77429
LUTHE LN	16200	373M	NEH	77032
LUTHE RD	13000	413C	NCC	77039
LUTHE RD	14200	373Y	NCC	77039
LUTHER	1	453C	NEH	77076
LUTHERAN CEMETERY RD	19500	326R	NWC	77429
LUTHERAN CEMETERY RD	23000	287H	NWC	77377
LUTHERAN CHURCH RD	21800	287L	NWC	77377
LUTHERAN SCHOOL RD	16000	287G	NWC	77377
LUTON PARK DR	3400	528C	SWH	77082
LUXEMBOURG DR	15900	329U	NWC	77070
LUZERNE DR	16300	329P	NWC	77070
LUZON	1100	493D	NEH	77009
LYBERT RD	10000	450E	NWH	77041
LYBERT RD	10400	449H	NWH	77041
LYCOMB DR	5600	611B	SWH	77053
LYDEN RIDGE DR	5500	611C	SWH	77053
LYDIA	3400	533N	SWH	77021
LYDIA PLACE	2100	537U	PA	77503
LYERLY	1	453F	NEH	77022
S. LYFORD DR	18500	407W	NWC	77449
N. LYFORD DR	18500	407S	NWC	77449
LYLEWOOD CT	8400	410K	NWC	77040
LYMAN	600	620L	SB	77586
LYMBAR DR	4100	532S	SWH	77025
LYMBAR DR	4400	531X	SWH	77096
LYMBAR DR	6000	530Z	SWH	77096
LYNBRIAR LN	25100	292R	NCC	77373
LYNBRIAR LN	25400	293N	NCC	77373
LYNBROOK CT	3100	569N	SG	77478
LYNBROOK DR	5200	491P	SWH	77056
LYNBROOK DR	5800	491N	SWH	77057
LYNBROOK DR	10000	489Q	SWH	77042
LYNBROOK HOLLOW	10100	489R	SWH	77042
LYNCHBURG RD	0	502F	NEC	77521
LYNCHBURG RD	0	501W	BT	77520
S. LYNCHBURG RD	100	499K	NEC	77520
LYNCHESTER DR	9200	528P	SWC	77083
LYNDA DR	11500	411H	NWC	77038
LYNDALE DR	400	460N	HG	77562
LYNDA LEIGH	19300	332B	NWC	77388
LYNDALL LN	21000	255P	SEM	77365
LYNDBROOK LN	10900	367T	NWC	77433
LYNDEN	0	572J	SWH	77045
LYNDHURST	0	488L	SWH	77077
LYNDHURST DR	5100	534W	SEH	77033
LYNDHURST DR	6200	534Y	SEH	77087
LYNDHURST VILLAGE LN	0	330B	NWC	77379
LYNDON	1000	532M	SWH	77030
LYNDON MEADOWS DR	10300	367U	NWC	77095
LYNDONNVILLE FALLS LN	0	455D	NEH	77078
LYNDONVILLE DR	13300	408Y	NWC	77041
LYNEE LN		611Q	FS	77545
LYNELL DR	13200	420S	BR	77532
LYNETTE	7800	455F	NEH	77028
LYNETTE FALLS DR	9800	368W	NWC	77095
LYNFORD CREST DR	15400	527R	NEF	77083
LYNGROVE DR	800	412G	NWH	77038
LYNKAT LN	6300	528F	SWC	77083
LYNN	400	536X	SH	77587
LYNN	8100	535P	SEH	77017
LYNN CIR	700	536U	PA	77502
LYNN CIR	1000	656H	FR	77546
LYNN DR	0	369F	NWC	77070
LYNN DR	2300	614M	PL	77581
LYNN DR	19200	286Z	NWC	77377
LYNN LN	1100	375D	HM	77338
LYNN LN	5000	491V	SWH	77056
LYNN LN	24800	296R	SEM	77365
LYNNBROOK FALLS LN	0	375X	NEC	77396
LYNN CREST CT	16300	527P	NEF	77083
LYNNFIELD	1900	454N	NEH	77093
LYNNFIELD	3600	454P	NEH	77016
LYNNFIELD	5300	454Q	NEH	77028
LYNNGATE DR	5200	334F	NCC	77373
LYNN HAVEN	12900	368H	NWC	77429
LYNN HAVEN	13000	369E	NWC	77429
LYNN MANOR CT		366T	NWC	77433
LYNNROSE SPRINGS DR	0	329F	NWC	77375
LYNNVIEW DR	1400	451W	NWH	77055
LYNNVILLE DR	13300	368U	NWC	77065
LYNN WAY RD	0	249V	NWC	77375
LYNNWOOD DR	0	462Z	BT	77521
LYNNWOOD DR	0	462Z	BT	77521
LYNNWOOD DR	500	570Y	MC	77489
LYNNWOOD LN	13500	568F	SG	77498
LYNWOOD RD	800	332D	NCC	77373
LYNWOOD BANKS LN	6000	541F	NWH	77092
LYNWOOD HOLLOW LN	0	452Y	NWH	77008
LYNX CT	13600	371C	NWC	77014
LYNX LN	1	251V	WD	77380
LYNX LN	12500	568D	SG	77478
LYONESSE LN	0	410L	NWC	77040
LYONS AVE	1600	493H	NEH	77020
LYONS AVE	2400	494F	NEH	77020
LYONS AVE	7800	495F	NEH	77029
LYONS ALLEY	3400	494F	NEH	77020
LYONS PASS	0	485K	NEF	77494
LYON SPRINGS CT	25500	292U	NCC	77373
LYONS SCHOOL RD	16300	330Q	NWC	77379
LYREBIRD DR	1	251V	WD	77380

Street Name	Block	Pg/Sq	Loc	Zips
LYRIC LN	1100	537R	PA	77503
LYRICAL DR	9700	569H	SF	77477
LYRIC WAY DR	17300	328Q	NWC	77377
LYTHAM LN	1900	485R	NEF	77450
LYTTON SPRINGS	700	292U	NCC	77373

M

Street Name	Block	Pg/Sq	Loc	Zips
M A S	3000	533F	SEH	77021
M D ANDERSON	1100	532H	SWH	77030
M L KING DR	8800	335T	NEH	77338
M L K BLVD	0	659Y	GCO	77539
E. M, AVENUE	100	580G	LP	77571
M, AVENUE	600	576C	SH	77587
MAACK LN	100	413S	NEH	77037
MABEL LN	0	248S	SWM	77355
MABEL'S ISLAND CT	18400	377C	NEC	77346
MABLE	100	499D	NEC	77520
MABLE	200	453L	NEH	77022
MABLE	1500	494X	SEH	77023
MABLE	8900	460R	NEC	77562
W. MABLE	3600	660M	BC	77518
E. MABLE	3600	660M	BC	77518
MABLEHURST DR	0	368E	NWC	77429
MABLE POND LN	0	526R	NEF	77407
MABLE POND LN	18000	526R	NEF	77407
MABRY	0	501R	BT	77521
MABRY	700	502N	BT	77520
MABRY MILL RD	1000	618A	SEH	77062
MABRY STREAM CT	5000	446C	NWC	77449
MACALLAN LN	0	406Z	NWC	77449
MACARTHUR	100	499R	BT	77520
MACARTHUR	100	500N	BT	77520
MACARTHUR	2000	532H	SWH	77030
MACAW	1	251R	WD	77380
MACBETH	10200	460F	NEC	77532
MACBETH DR	4600	333D	NCC	77373
MACCLESBY LN	0	457V	NEC	77049
MACCLESBY LN	900	497D	NEC	77530
MACCLESBY LN	1000	457Z	NEC	77530
MACDUFF	10200	460F	NEC	77532
MACE	0	576Q	SEH	77034
MACE DR	23200	296M	SEM	77365
MACEDONIA SCHOOL RD	23100	244U	WCO	77447
N. MACGREGOR DR	1000	533E	SWH	77030
N. MACGREGOR DR	2200	533B	SWH	77004
MACGREGOR LOOP	4500	534E	SEH	77021
N. MACGREGOR WAY	1200	534D	SEH	77023
S. MACGREGOR WAY	2200	533G	SEH	77021
N. MACGREGOR WAY	2200	533G	SEH	77004
MACGREGOR WAY	2200	533B	SEH	77004
S. MACGREGOR WAY	4300	534E	SEH	77021
MACHA	9800	454B	NEH	77093
MACHAELA'S WAY	8100	375Y	NEC	77396
MACHALA LN	7800	410V	NWC	77040
MACHALL MANOR CT	0	525V	NEF	77406
MACINAC CT	20000	486P	SWC	77450
MACK	0	502W	BT	77520
MACK	900	494V	SEH	77011
MACKAY CT	600	487A	SWC	77094
MACKENZIE DR	10400	371W	NWC	77086
MACKENZIE WAY	1900	570S	MC	77489
MACKEY DR	1500	660T	DI	77539
MACKEY RD	0	610C	SWH	77489
MACKIES RUN LN		366U	NWC	77433
MACKILSEE LN	14400	488H	SWH	77079
MACKINAC LN	3700	577C	PA	77505
MACKINAW	5100	571Y	SWH	77053
MACKINAW ISLE CT	0	326Y	NWC	77433
MACKINSON	5900	534G	SEH	77023
MACKLIN CT	28500	299S	NEC	77336
MACKLIND RIDGE LN	0	484Y	NEF	77494
MACKLIND RIDGE LN	0	484Y	NEF	77494
MACKMILLER DR	5700	457S	NEC	77049
MACKRELL	100	543U	BC	77520
MACKWORTH DR	9700	569M	SF	77477
MACLEISH DR	16800	407Z	NWC	77084
MACMILLAN LN	9200	527Q	NEF	77083
MACNAUGHTON DR	12000	414G	NCC	77039
MACON	23600	291A	NWC	77389
MACON CT	3600	527C	SWC	77082
MACON DR	3600	527C	SWC	77082
MACONDA LN	2000	492S	SWH	77027
MACONDRAY DR	0	376E	HM	77396
MACON PLACE CT	3600	527C	SWC	77082
MACQUAIRE DR	6300	406U	NWC	77449
MACRANTHA CT	5500	331J	NWC	77379
MACRANTHA DR	17600	331J	NWC	77379
MACRIDGE BLVD	4800	571Z	SWH	77053
MACY DR	0	326U	NWC	77429
MACY HILLS CT	0	293K	SEM	77386
MACY HILLS CT	0	293L	SEM	77386
MACZALI CT	15900	570Z	SWH	77489
MACZALI DR	6600	571W	SWH	77489
MACZALI DR	7300	570Z	SWH	77489
MADALYN LN	5000	534E	SEH	77021
MADANAS	0	335C	SEM	77365
MADDEN LN	3900	573L	SEH	77047
MADDEN LN	5100	574J	SEH	77048
MADDEN RD	16900	527S	NEF	77407
MADDEN RD	17900	526Y	NEF	77407
MADDEN OAKS PLACE	0	449U	NWH	77043
MADDIE LN	19200	255V	SEM	77357
MADDINGLY LN	0	657X	LC	77573
W. MADDISON	100	540X	LP	77571
E. MADDISON	100	540Y	LP	77571
MADDOX	9500	455B	NEH	77078
MADDUX DR	21500	296A	SEM	77365
MADELEINE CT	3400	569S	SG	77478
MADELEY	3000	454J	NEH	77093
MADELINE	1700	459H	NEC	77562
MADELINE CIR	6700	407Q	NWC	77084
MADELINE RD	0	571F	SWH	77085
MADELINE ALYSSA CT	9800	532S	SWH	77025
MADELIN MANOR LN	0	293E	SEM	77386
MADERA RD	8200	415X	NEH	77078
MADERA RD	8800	415Z	NEC	77078
MADERA CANYON LN	0	328F	NWC	77377
MADERA RUN PKWY	0	377G	NEC	77346
MADEWOOD	16200	367G	NWC	77429
MADEWOOD DR	2100	609B	MC	77459
MADEWOOD PLACE	5400	614Z	PL	77584
MADGE	1500	373Z	NCC	77039
MADIE DR	8400	453F	NEH	77022
MADIERA CT	0	294H	SEM	77365
MADIERA DR	0	294H	SEM	77365
MADING LN	200	412H	NCC	77037
MADISON	0	537N	PA	77502
MADISON	1100	536R	PA	77502
MADISON	1200	501Z	BT	77520
MADISON	1500	538V	DP	77536
MADISON AVE	0	659W	LC	77573

Street Name	Block	Pg/Sq	Loc	Zips
MADISON AVE	3800	503R	CCO	77520
MADISON CT	0	612V	PL	77584
MADISON DR	0	612V	PL	77584
MADISON DR	0	484D	SWC	77494
MADISON LN	20500	446K	NWC	77449
MADISON BEND DR	0	293L	SEM	77386
MADISON BOULDER LN	0	377K	NEC	77346
MADISON CLAIRE CT	0	407E	NWC	77433
MADISON COVE DR	0	295M	SEM	77365
MADISON CROSSING LN	0	329G	NWC	77375
MADISON ELM ST	0	445K	NWC	77493
MADISON FALLS LN	0	524C	NEF	77494
MADISON HEIGHTS CT	0	407S	NWC	77449
MADISON KAYE CT	0	255Q	SEM	77365
MADISON KENDALL LN	11800	371N	NWC	77066
MADISON LEE LN	5100	577J	PA	77504
MADISON MIDWAY DR	0	366N	NWC	77433
MADISON OAK ST	11701	411G	NWC	77038
MADISON TRAIL	7000	408P	NWC	77084
MADISON VALLEY CT	0	256W	SEM	77365
MADONNA DR	0	371V	NWC	77067
MADRID	6300	533R	SEH	77021
MADRID LN	0	660G	LC	77539
MADRIGAL LN	0	333X	NCC	77073
MADRONA CREEK DR	0	291J	NWC	77389
MADRONE CT	16800	367U	NWC	77095
MADRONE MEADOW CT	0	525A	NEF	77494
MADRONE MEADOW DR	0	524D	NEF	77494
MADRONE TERRACE PLACE	0	249U	NWC	77375
MADUROS	0	415R	NEC	77016
MAE	0	444P	KT	77493
MAE DR	1000	496L	NEH	77015
MAE ST	0	657L	FR	77546
MAELINE	14400	373Z	NCC	77039
MAETE LN	13000	414F	NCC	77039
MAFFITT	1400	493H	NEH	77026
S. MAGAZINE CIR	5600	408X	NWC	77084
N. MAGAZINE CIR	5600	408X	NWC	77084
MAGDALENE DR	700	490B	HE	77024
MAGEE RD	15500	373Q	NCC	77032
MAGELLAN	0	419C	NEC	77532
MAGELLAN MANOR DR	0	525Q	NEF	77407
MAGELLAN POINT LANDING	0	449A	NWC	77084
MAGENTA OAKS DR	12800	528G	SWH	77072
MAGENTA SPRINGS DR	17800	377B	NEC	77346
MAGGIE	3000	533Y	SEH	77051
MAGGIE	4700	533Z	SEH	77033
MAGGIE LN	1	490T	PP	77063
MAGGIE MIST DR	21500	525U	NEF	77406
MAGGIE RIDGE CT	0	293L	SEM	77386
MAGIC DR	12800	414G	NCC	77039
MAGICAL MERLIN WAY		289Q	NWC	77375
MAGIC CREEK DR	0	326E	NWC	77377
MAGIC FALLS DR	12800	328L	NWC	77377
MAGIC LILY DR	0	293W	NCC	77373
MAGIC MOON RD	0	414K	NCC	77039
MAGIC OAKS CT	300	332B	NWC	77388
MAGIC OAKS DR	100	332A	NWC	77388
MAGIC RIVER DR	14400	368E	NWC	77429
MAGIC SPELL DR	0	289P	NWC	77375
MAGLI CT	0	457A	NEC	77044
N. MAGLITTO	17000	328R	NWC	77377
W. MAGLITTO CIR	16800	328R	NWC	77377
E. MAGLITTO CIR	16800	328R	NWC	77377
MAGNA	7600	454K	NEH	77093
MAGNET	2500	533S	SWH	77054
MAGNOLIA	1	297P	NEH	77365
S. MAGNOLIA	100	288M	TB	77375
S. MAGNOLIA	100	459V	HG	77562
N. MAGNOLIA	100	288G	TB	77375
E. MAGNOLIA	100	616Z	FR	77546
MAGNOLIA	100	292Q	SP	77373
MAGNOLIA	100	419Y	BR	77532
MAGNOLIA	100	496W	GP	77547
MAGNOLIA	100	659J	LC	77573
W. MAGNOLIA	300	656D	FR	77546
MAGNOLIA	300	459R	HG	77562
MAGNOLIA	400	570N	MC	77489
MAGNOLIA	1100	500Z	BT	77520
MAGNOLIA	1600	537U	PA	77503
MAGNOLIA	3500	615S	PL	77584
MAGNOLIA	4500	531H	BL	77401
MAGNOLIA	5000	614V	PL	77584
MAGNOLIA	5700	414M	NEC	77050
E. MAGNOLIA	7300	535B	SEH	77012
MAGNOLIA	7400	535A	SEH	77023
MAGNOLIA AVE	0	615Q	PL	77581
MAGNOLIA AVE	100	499A	CV	77530
MAGNOLIA AVE	200	459W	CV	77530
MAGNOLIA AVE	500	658B	WB	77598
MAGNOLIA BLVD	0	259T	NEC	77357
MAGNOLIA CIR	500	490G	PP	77024
MAGNOLIA CIR	500	657V	LC	77573
MAGNOLIA CIR	6800	375X	NEC	77396
MAGNOLIA CIR	17600	527E	NEF	77407
MAGNOLIA CT	2700	569U	NEF	77477
MAGNOLIA DR	0	614U	PL	77584
MAGNOLIA DR	200	298X	NEH	77336
MAGNOLIA DR	12900	419T	NEC	77532
MAGNOLIA DR	21400	257T	SEM	77357
MAGNOLIA LN	0	539N	DP	77536
MAGNOLIA LN	1	298D	NEC	77336
MAGNOLIA LN	200	299A	NEC	77336
MAGNOLIA LN	900	336F	NEH	77339
MAGNOLIA LN	4100	609A	SG	77478
MAGNOLIA LN	6100	444P	KT	77493
MAGNOLIA RD	0	257B	WV	77357
MAGNOLIA RD	0	245X	SWM	77447
MAGNOLIA RD	24500	244Z	WCO	77447
MAGNOLIA RD	25800	284B	WCO	77447
MAGNOLIA ARBOR CT	12800	328G	NWC	77377
MAGNOLIA ARBOR LN	18800	328G	NWC	77377
MAGNOLIA BAY CT	0	526Q	NEF	77407
MAGNOLIA BEND	500	657V	LC	77573
MAGNOLIA BEND	4600	609K	MC	77459
MAGNOLIA BEND	25900	257H	RF	77357
MAGNOLIA BEND DR	1	490M	HC	77024
MAGNOLIA BEND DR	20000	338S	NEC	77346
MAGNOLIA BLOOMTRAIL	0	332V	NCC	77073
MAGNOLIA BLOSSOM	0	658J	LC	77573
MAGNOLIABOUGH PLACE	15000	327W	NWC	77429
MAGNOLIA BROOK CT	8100	610S	MC	77459
MAGNOLIA BROOK LN	20800	326S	NWC	77433
MAGNOLIA CANYON	0	528R	SWH	77099
MAGNOLIA COVE	4900	501F	BT	77521
MAGNOLIA COVE CT	7800	337M	NEC	77346
MAGNOLIA COVE DR	4500	337G	NEH	77345
MAGNOLIA CREEK RD	4600	446H	NWC	77084
MAGNOLIA CREST CT	10100	369G	NWC	77070
MAGNOLIA CREST LN	0	568D	SG	77478
MAGNOLIA CREST LN	0	253P	SEM	77386
MAGNOLIA CREST LN	1900	568D	SG	77478
MAGNOLIA CREST LN	13400	369G	NWC	77070
MAGNOLIA CROSSING	0	658J	LC	77573
N. MAGNOLIA DALE DR	1000	611X	NEF	77545
MAGNOLIA DALE DR	1200	611X	NEF	77545
W. MAGNOLIA DALE DR	3800	611X	NEF	77545
E. MAGNOLIA DALE DR	3800	611X	NEF	77545
MAGNOLIA DELL DR	0	407A	NWC	77433
W. MAGNOLIA ELMS DR	3400	615S	PL	77584
S. MAGNOLIA ELMS DR	3400	615S	PL	77584
E. MAGNOLIA ELMS DR	3400	615S	PL	77584
MAGNOLIA ELMS DR	4300	615S	PL	77584
MAGNOLIA ESTATES DR	100	658J	LC	77573
MAGNOLIA ESTATES DR	1800	252V	SEM	77386
MAGNOLIA FAIR WAY	0	292H	SEM	77386
MAGNOLIA FALLS CT	5400	297P	NEH	77345
MAGNOLIA GLEN DR	8200	338N	NEC	77346
MAGNOLIA GREEN LN	5300	657Z	LC	77573
MAGNOLIA GROVE LN	200	457U	NEC	77049
MAGNOLIA HILL TRAIL	0	371Z	NWC	77038
MAGNOLIA HOLLOW LN	0	525M	NEF	77407
MAGNOLIA LAKE LN	0	526W	NEF	77406
MAGNOLIA LEAF	12700	368V	NWC	77065
MAGNOLIA MANOR DR	13700	367C	CY	77429
MAGNOLIA MEADOW LN	0	658S	LC	77573
MAGNOLIA MEADOW LN		658W	LC	77573
MAGNOLIA OAKS DR	4300	615S	PL	77584
MAGNOLIA PARK	0	327T	CY	77429
MAGNOLIA PINES DR	4300	615S	PL	77584
MAGNOLIA POINT DR	100	298X	NEH	77336
S. MAGNOLIA POND PLACE	0	251E	WD	77381
N. MAGNOLIA POND PLACE	1	251E	WD	77381
MAGNOLIA RIDGE	0	658J	LC	77573
MAGNOLIA RIDGE DR	9300	329Q	NWC	77070
MAGNOLIA RIDGE LN	0	569Q	SF	77477
MAGNOLIA RUN DR	4900	569W	SG	77478
MAGNOLIA SHADOWS LN	7400	407M	NWC	77095
MAGNOLIA SHORES LN	0	377L	NEC	77044
MAGNOLIA SKY DR	0	526T	NEF	77407
MAGNOLIA SPRINGS DR	14100	371U	NWC	77066
MAGNOLIA SUMMIT LN		484Y	NEF	77494
MAGNOLIA TRACE DR	0	658S	LC	77573
MAGNOLIA TRACE DR	12400	371J	NWC	77066
MAGNOLIA TRAIL	0	447N	NWC	77084
MAGNOLIA TRAIL	800	257L	SEM	77357
MAGNOLIA VIEW	0	528R	SWH	77099
MAGNOLIA WALK	2700	332A	NWC	77388
MAGNOLIA WARBLER CREST LN	0	291H	NWC	77389
MAGNOLIA WAY	10000	329T	NWC	77388
MAGNOLIA WAY	200	658J	LC	77573
MAGNOLIA WOODS DR	1800	336L	NEH	77339
MAGNUS LN	13900	528E	SWC	77083
MAGPIE CT	0	328A	NWC	77429
MAGPIE CT	0	328A	NWC	77377
MAHAFFEY RD	10500	289K	NWC	77375
MAHAFFEY RD		289G	NWC	77375
MAHALIA	8300	412U	NWH	77088
MAHAN	16200	331Q	NWC	77068
MAHAN	25100	339E	HU	77336
MAHAN DR	9200	579A	LP	77571
MAHAN WOOD DR	6600	377C	NEC	77346
MAHEJAN CT	4900	614Z	PL	77584
MAHEJAN DR	3500	614Z	PL	77584
MAHOGANY DR	16400	570J	MC	77489
MAHOGANY CREEK CT	5300	331A	NWC	77379
MAHOGANY CREST DR	13900	367C	NWC	77429
MAHOGANY FOREST DR	17800	330J	NWC	77379
MAHOGANY FOREST DR	18300	329H	NWC	77379
MAHOGANY GLEN WAY	0	331A	NWC	77379
MAHOGANY RIDGE CT	0	366R	NWC	77433
MAHOGANY RUN DR	800	485E	SWC	77494
MAHOGANY RUN DR	900	484H	NEF	77494
MAHOGANY TRACE LN	0	527S	NEF	77469
MAHOGANY TRAIL	0	614X	PL	77584
MAHOGANY WIND LN	0	294A	SEM	77386
MAHON RD	28600	323X	NWC	77447
MAHONING DR	7000	530L	SWH	77074
MAHONING DR	8800	530P	SWH	77074
MAHRIAN CT	3300	617Y	SEC	77546
MAIDEN LN	15700	571Y	SWH	77053
MAIDENCANE CT	11000	371S	NWC	77086
MADENCROFT LN	0	458S	NEC	77494
MAIDEN CROSSING DR	21800	296X	SEM	77339
MAIDENFAIR DR	0	289P	NWC	77375
MAIDENGLEN LN	0	571K	SWH	77085
MAIDENGLEN LN	0	571K	SWH	77085
MAIDENHAIR LN	1800	568W	SG	77479
MAIDENHEAD DR	4300	577E	PA	77504
MAIDEN WAY DR	1200	329B	NWC	77379
MAID MARIAN CT	23300	285B	SWM	77447
MAID MARIAN DR	23000	285B	SWM	77447
MAID MARIAN LN	23000	285E	SWM	77447
MAIDSTONE DR	6900	578K	PA	77505
MAIDSTONE LN	7300	408P	NWC	77095
MAIDSTONE MANOR CT	10600	329B	NWC	77379
MAIFEST DR	0	366N	NWC	77433
MAILE PARK DR	0	576R	SEH	77034
MAILLART WAY	0	377D	NEH	77346
MAIL MEADOW LN	12300	568D	SG	77478
MAILY MEADOW LN	0	613V	PL	77584
MAILY MEADOW LN	4100	485Y	NEF	77450
W. MAIN	0	611Z	FS	77545
N. MAIN	0	337B	NEH	77339
MAIN	0	252F	SEM	77385
MAIN	0	297L	NEH	77365
MAIN	0	536H	PA	77506
W. MAIN	0	658N	LC	77573
E. MAIN	0	659E	LC	77573
MAIN	0	611Z	FS	77545
W. MAIN	0	657R	LC	77573
E. MAIN	0	282U	WL	77484
MAIN	0	612W	FS	77545
N. MAIN	1	493H	NEH	77002
MAIN	1	493Q	DT	77002
S. MAIN	100	459Z	HG	77562
E. MAIN	100	335Z	HM	77338
S. MAIN	100	501Y	BT	77520
W. MAIN	100	288G	TB	77375
S. MAIN	100	496W	GP	77547
E. MAIN	100	540Y	LP	77571
W. MAIN	100	540X	LP	77571
E. MAIN	100	288H	TB	77375
MAIN	100	292Q	SP	77373
W. MAIN	100	541B	BT	77520
N. MAIN	100	496S	GP	77547
MAIN	100	298E	NEC	77336
N. MAIN	100	536G	PA	77506
MAIN	100	335Z	HM	77338
W. MAIN	100	493S	SWH	77006
MAIN	100	568J	SG	77498
N. MAIN	100	501L	BT	77520
MAIN	100	535Z	SH	77587
MAIN	100	536L	PA	77506
S. MAIN	300	459R	HG	77562
MAIN	300	463E	MB	77580
S. MAIN	500	570P	MC	77489
S. MAIN	700	541C	BT	77520
MAIN	700	536W	SH	77587
S. MAIN	800	536A	NEH	77029
N. MAIN	1000	615A	PL	77581
MAIN	1200	576A	SH	77587
MAIN	1300	536L	PA	77502
N. MAIN	1500	493H	NEH	77009
W. MAIN	1700	492U	SWH	77098
S. MAIN	2000	569K	SF	77477
N. MAIN	2000	569Q	SF	77477
MAIN	2100	282U	WL	77484
S. MAIN	2400	615N	PL	77581
W. MAIN	2500	539Y	LP	77571
W. MAIN	2600	540D	BT	77520
N. MAIN	2700	461Y	NEC	77521
N. MAIN	3500	453S	NWH	77009
W. MAIN	3900	492S	SWH	77027
S. MAIN	5200	419G	CB	77532
MAIN	5300	493Q	SWH	77004
S. MAIN	5600	533A	SWH	77005
N. MAIN	5700	419C	CB	77532
S. MAIN	6200	532H	SWH	77030
N. MAIN	7000	453J	NWH	77022
S. MAIN	7900	532W	SWH	77025
S. MAIN	11600	571D	SWH	77025
S. MAIN	11700	571D	SWH	77035
MAIN BLVD	22000	286K	NWC	77377
MAIN ST	0	484B	KT	77494
MAIN BENDER TRAM	0	253U	SWM	77386
MAINBLUFF LN	8400	410K	NWC	77040
MAINER	3400	533P	SEH	77021
MAINER LN	900	288D	TB	77375
MAINFORD	3200	493C	NEH	77009
MAIN PLAZA	0	501L	BT	77521
MAIN PLAZA DR	0	532W	SWH	77025
MAINSAIL CIR	4100	569Y	MC	77459
MAINSTAY PLACE LN	12800	377P	NEC	77044
MAINSTREAM PLACE	0	250P	NWC	77389
MAIRCOPA RIDGE DR	0	406G	NWC	77433
MAISEMORE RD	13800	457Y	NEC	77015
MAITLAND CT	0	249A	SWM	77354
MAIZE LN	11000	409U	NWC	77041
MAIZE CLEARING TRAIL	0	334L	NCC	77388
MAIZE FIELD WAY	0	457Q	NEC	77049
MAIZE FLOWER PLACE	0	249Q	NWC	77375
MAIZE MEADOW PLACE	1	250C	WD	77381
MAJESTIC	500	494M	NEH	77020
MAJESTIC	3800	454Z	NEH	77026
MAJESTIC DR	4100	503H	CCO	77520
MAJESTIC LN	1000	616R	FR	77546
MAJESTIC LN	1900	501E	BT	77521
MAJESTICBROOK DR	8500	408G	NWC	77095
MAJESTIC CANYON LN	9500	329U	NWC	77070
MAJESTIC CLIFF WAY	0	290W	NWC	77379
MAJESTIC COVE CT	1000	485F	SWC	77494
MAJESTIC CROWN CT	0	445A	NWC	77493
MAJESTIC FALLS DR	1	336L	NEH	77339
MAJESTIC FOREST DR	17300	330C	NWC	77379
MAJESTIC GLEN LN	16100	332R	NCC	77073
MAJESTIC HARBOR LN	0	297K	NEH	77365
MAJESTIC HILL CT	0	338F	NEH	77345
MAJESTIC LANDING LN	19500	406M	NWC	77433
MAJESTIC MANNER CT		289T	NWC	77375
MAJESTIC MOON	0	369T	NWC	77064
MAJESTIC OAK CT	0	615Z	PL	77581
MAJESTIC OAK DR	0	615Z	PL	77581
MAJESTIC OAK DR	7100	411N	NWH	77040
MAJESTIC PARK LN	0	253N	SEM	77386
MAJESTIC PINES CT	0	338F	NEH	77345
MAJESTIC PINES DR	0	338F	NEH	77345
MAJESTIC PLACE CT	13100	572V	SWH	77047
MAJESTIC POINT DR	0	609T	NEF	77479
MAJESTIC PRINCE DR	9300	409F	NWC	77065
MAJESTIC RIDGE DR	500	457Q	NEC	77049
MAJESTIC SAGE DR	0	328K	NWC	77429
MAJESTIC SAGE DR		328k	NWC	77377
MAJESTIC SPRING LN	0	375Y	NEC	77396
MAJESTIC SPRING LN	0	415C	NEC	77396
MAJESTIC TRAIL	3900	578X	SEH	77059
MAJESTIC VIEW CT	4200	609T	NEF	77479
MAJESTY LN	6100	571K	SWH	77085
MAJESTY ROW	0	251G	WD	77380
MAJOLICA PLACE	0	249B	SWM	77382
MAJOR	7300	575E	SEH	77061
MAJOR BLIZZARD DR	8300	615D	SEC	77089
MAJORCA DR	700	413Y	NEH	77076
MAJOR ELM ST	7300	406R	NWC	77433
MAJOR GLEN CIR	18200	377A	NEC	77346
MAJOR OAK	1	491G	SWH	77024
MAKAH CIR	4700	461S	NEC	77521
MAKAHA CIR	8000	408L	NWC	77095
MAKALU	8400	533T	SEH	77051
MAKANDA DR	16900	366P	NWC	77433
MAKAYLA DR	0	458S	NEC	77049
MAKEIG	5400	454Y	NEH	77026
MAKENNA CT	0	458S	NEC	77530
MAKENNA LN	0	458S	NEC	77530
MAKING DUE WAY	0	328N	NWC	77429
MAKO CT	300	379X	NEC	77532
MALAC RD	7700	250T	NWC	77389
MALADI DR	16000	611D	SWH	77053
MALAGO POINT DR	0	407E	NWC	77433
MALARDCREST DR	8000	377D	NEC	77346
MALARDCREST DR	8300	378A	NEC	77346
MALA WAY	0	333K	NCC	77338
MALBEC LN	0	451S	NWH	77055
MALCA MANOR DR	24700	445W	NWC	77493
MALCOLM DR	10100	453C	NEH	77076
MALCOMBORO DR	5700	408Z	NWC	77041
MALCOMSON RD	11000	329T	NWC	77070
MALCOMSON RD	12200	328Z	NWC	77070
MALCOMS WAY	800	338M	NEH	77336
MALDEN DR	10800	575Z	SEH	77075
MALDEN MOTTE DR	0	484V	NEF	77494
MALDON CT	4300	454K	NEH	77016
MALEDO	0	458F	NEC	77049
MALEEWAN LN	0	528T	NEF	77083
MALEK, R F LN	0	371Q	NWC	77067
MALESA	6600	454R	NEH	77028
MALET	1800	453D	NEH	77093
MALFREY LN	0	407Z	NWC	77084
MALHEAUR DR	0	377G	NEC	77346
MALIBU DR	6600	451E	NWH	77092
MALIBU CREEK LN	0	377F	NEC	77346
MALIN CT	8200	527R	NEF	77083
MALIN MANOR LN	0	446G	NWC	77449
MALL DR	4100	451H	NWH	77092
MALLARD	6000	444K	KT	77493
MALLARD DR	1800	449V	NWH	77043
MALLARD DR	4400	503D	CCO	77520
MALLARD BAY LN	0	524G	NEF	77494
MALLARD BAYOU	100	542J	BT	77520
MALLARD BLUE LN	0	366Y	NWC	77433
MALLARD COVE CT	0	526J	NEF	77407
MALLARD CROSSING DR	26900	324S	NWC	77447
MALLARD ESTATES CT	18100	366D	NWC	77429
MALLARD FIELDS CT	0	609X	NEF	77479
MALLARD LAKE LN	19500	446U	NWC	77084
MALLARD LANDING CT	4700	371K	NWC	77066
MALLARD PASS LN	0	484S	NEF	77494
MALLARD POINT CT	0	406M	NWC	77433
MALLARD RUN CT	0	484S	NEF	77494
MALLARDS POND CT	0	253P	SEM	77386
MALLARD SPRINGS DR	0	296W	SEM	77339
MALLARD STREAM CT	12000	411H	NWC	77038
MALLARDS WAY	8700	461M	NEC	77521
MALLARD WAY	12900	377W	NEC	77044
MALLARD WAY	21500	486A	SWC	77450
MALLET	17400	379W	NEC	77532
MALLETIA DR	19900	335N	NCC	77338
MALLETS BAY CT	19700	526K	NEF	77407
MALLIE CT	8200	491A	HI	77055
MALLORCA CIR	2500	412E	NWC	77038
MALLORCA PASS	0	660G	LC	77539
MALLORY	9200	573C	SEH	77051
MALLORY BRIDGE DR	16700	367Y	NWC	77095
MALLORY CREEK DR	0	376N	NEC	77396
MALLORY PARK LN		484W	NEF	77494
MALLOW	0	574A	SEH	77033
MALLOW	4100	573C	SEH	77051
MALLOW	4700	573C	SEH	77033
MALMAISON RIDGE DR	1200	329B	NWC	77379
MALMEDY RD	4800	534P	SEH	77033
MALON	2400	615P	PL	77581
MALONE	100	492L	SWH	77007
MALONE	500	288G	TB	77375
MALONE DR	0	579F	SEC	77507
MALONE DR	3600	537R	PA	77503
MALOPE RANCH DR	3000	485N	NEF	77494
MAL PASO CT	3600	527C	SWC	77082
MAL PASO DR	15900	527C	SWC	77082
MALPASS	15000	457C	NEC	77049
MALTBY	700	494V	SEH	77011
MALVERN	400	537L	PA	77503
MALVERN	1100	453Z	NEH	77009
MAMMOTH FALLS DR	20000	289W	NWC	77375
MAMMOTH SPRINGS CT	0	407C	NWC	77095
MAMMOTH SPRINGS DR	0	407C	NWC	77095
MANACOR CIR	2500	412E	NWC	77038
MANASOTA	0	660D	KE	77518
MANASSAS LN	8400	527P	NEF	77083
MANASSES SPRINGS LN	11800	376H	NEC	77346
MANATEE	0	338C	NEH	77336
MANATEE LN	1000	332J	NWC	77090
MANBORO CT	12000	371M	NWC	77067
MANCE CT	18200	487A	SWC	77094
MANCHESTER	7400	535A	SEH	77012
MANCHESTER CIR	1200	569X	MC	77459
MANCHESTER LN	2100	615L	PL	77581
MANCHESTER CROSSING DR	0	611S	FS	77545
MANCHESTER POINT LN	0	527J	NEF	77407
MANCHESTER TRAIL DR	700	292G	NCC	77373
MANCOS PARK DR	0	372D	NCC	77073
MANDALAY CT	2600	613S	NEB	77584
MANDALAY WAY	12200	572L	SWH	77045
MANDALE RD	2900	656X	FR	77546
MANDARIN GLEN CIR	0	291N	NWC	77388
MANDATE DR	0	458S	NEC	77049
MANDAVILLA DR	10700	367U	NWC	77095
MANDELL	2400	492V	SWH	77006
MANDELL	5300	532D	SWH	77005
MANDERLY DR	14100	488J	SWH	77077
MANDEVILLE CT	16700	330L	NWC	77379
MANDOLIN CT	10100	369C	NWC	77070
MANDOLIN DR	13800	369C	NWC	77070
MANDOVER LN	4500	297U	NEH	77345
MANDRAKE CT	0	571G	SWH	77085
MANDRILL LN	1700	371R	NWC	77067
MANDY	0	415K	NEH	77050
MANDY LN	0	660Q	LC	77573
MANET CT	3200	489X	SWH	77082
MANETTE DR	20500	486B	SWC	77450
MANFIELD DR	15700	527C	SWC	77082
MANGO	0	576S	SEH	77089
MANGO	9600	576S	SEH	77075
MANGO	10500	576S	SEH	77089
MANGO CT	0	658T	LC	77573
MANGO RIDGE CT	16300	376M	NEC	77396
MANGROVE BEND DR	0	658X	LC	77573
MANGUM RD	1700	451V	NWH	77092
MANGUM RD	5100	451G	NWH	77091
MANHATTAN DR	8500	531P	SWH	77096
MANILA LN	1900	449R	NWH	77043
MANION DR	2800	610U	MC	77459
MANION OAKS CT	0	256M	SEM	77357
MANIRE DR	8600	450Z	NWH	77055
MANIS CT	0	493F	SWH	77007
MANISON PKWY	0	657N	FR	77546
MANITO CIR	2800	485R	NEF	77450
MANITOU DR	3400	455Y	NEH	77013
MANITOU FALLS LN	3000	445R	NWC	77449
MANKAY LN	9500	369M	NWC	77070
MANLEIGH CT	18800	328G	NWC	77377
MANN	2400	454J	NEH	77093
MANNING DR	15600	367R	CY	77429
MANNING LN	7400	575S	SEH	77075
MANNING RD	900	335R	HM	77338
MANNINGTON LN	0	658S	LC	77573
MANNINGTREE LN	16500	330P	NWC	77379
MANO	6700	413X	NEH	77076
MANON LN	20900	291U	NWC	77388
MANOR	0	284C	WCO	77447
MANOR	12300	614D	BK	77581
W. MANOR CIR	25000	250Y	NWC	77389
E. MANOR CIR	25000	250Y	NWC	77389
MANOR CT	12500	528M	SWH	77072
MANOR DR	0	501J	BT	77521
MANOR DR	3400	609S	NEF	77479
MANOR ST	400	497G	NEC	77015
MANOR BAY CT	3000	659M	LC	77573
MANOR BEND	16200	327S	CY	77429
MANOR BRANCH BLVD	0	294J	NWC	77386
MANOR BRIDGE CT	7400	408J	NWC	77095
MANOR BROOK LN	21200	290U	NWC	77379
MANORCLIFF LN	18300	407S	NWC	77449
MANOR COURT DR	5100	446B	NWC	77449
MANOR CREEK LN	5300	451L	NWH	77092
MANOR CREST CT	0	296X	SEM	77339
MANORDALE	4100	578F	PA	77505
MANORDALE DR	3800	527D	SWC	77082
MANOR ESTATES DR	22000	445M	NWC	77449

Street Name	Block	Pg/Sq	Loc	Zips
MANOR FALLS DR	26800	296X	SEM	77339
MANORFIELD DR	4000	619G	TL	77586
MANORFIELD DR	5100	446B	NWC	77449
MANORFORD CT	15600	408A	NWC	77095
MANOR FOREST DR	5500	297N	NEH	77339
MANORGATE DR	11800	570A	SWH	77031
MANORGLEN DR	900	610C	MC	77489
MANOR GLEN DR	5200	297Y	NEH	77345
MANOR GREEN DR	2100	489P	SWH	77077
MANOR GROVE DR	3000	297Y	NEH	77345
MANORHAVEN LN	5100	447B	NWC	77084
MANORHILL DR	15000	618J	SEH	77062
MANOR HOLLOW LN	6800	525H	NEF	77450
MANORHOUSE LN	11500	489X	SWH	77082
MANOR LAKE LN	0	253P	SEM	77386
MANOR LAKE LN	0	612U	PL	77584
MANOR LAKE ESTATES CIR	0	329C	NWC	77379
MANOR LAKE ESTATES DR	18600	329G	NWC	77379
MANOR OAKS DR	5300	296R	NEH	77339
MANOR PARK DR	11600	489P	SWH	77077
MANOR POINT DR	16100	407D	NWC	77095
MANOR RIDGE CT	2800	485N	NEF	77494
MANOR RIDGE LN	600	660E	LC	77573
MANOR SPRING CT	0	328G	NWC	77377
MANOR SQUARE DR	15800	618G	SEH	77062
MANORSTONE LN	0	416Z	NEC	77044
MANOR TREE CT	14900	331T	NWC	77068
MANOR TREE LN	3200	331T	NWC	77068
MANOR WAY	6800	375T	NEH	77396
MANORWOOD	2300	568C	SG	77478
MANORWOOD	2400	528Y	SG	77478
MANORWOOD CIR	0	444K	KT	77493
MANORWOOD CT	0	444K	KT	77493
MANORWOOD DR	3500	444K	KT	77493
MANORWOOD LN	12600	368L	NWC	77429
MANOWAR	16700	617U	SEC	77546
MANRY AVE	6000	614C	BK	77581
MANSARD	2000	532V	SWH	77054
MANSARD	2300	533S	SWH	77054
MANSAS PARK DR	11800	369S	NWC	77065
MANSFIELD	700	452A	NWH	77091
MANSFIELD	3000	451D	NWH	77091
MANSFIELD BAY LN	0	526J	NEF	77407
MANSFIELD BLUFF LN	0	290Q	NWC	77379
MANSFIELD GLEN CT	0	371D	NWC	77014
MANSFIELD PARK CT	500	658N	LC	77573
MANSFIELD PARK LN	20100	291W	NWC	77379
MANSFIELD POINT LN	13600	369C	NWC	77070
MANSION CT	13100	368F	NWC	77429
MANSION RD	0	257Q	SEM	77357
MANSOR DR	13600	408U	NWC	77041
MANTANA CT	17600	331G	NWC	77388
MANTANA DR	17700	331C	NWC	77388
MANTLE CT	10300	369W	NWC	77065
MANTON	5400	455U	NEH	77028
MANTOVA DR	300	372G	NCC	77073
MANTOVA RIVER DR	0	445B	NWC	77493
MANUS	8600	454E	NEH	77093
MANVEL RD	2100	614X	PL	77584
MANVEL RD	2300	611P	FS	77545
MANVILLE	1200	452X	NWH	77008
MANX	6300	528F	SWC	77083
MANY OAK DR	25500	251V	SWM	77380
MANY PINES	1200	251M	WD	77380
MANY PINES RD	1200	252J	WD	77380
MANZANILLA VIEW LN		609S	NEF	77479
MANZANO DR	7800	527L	NEF	77083
MAPLE	0	501E	NEC	77521
MAPLE	100	459Q	HG	77562
MAPLE	100	541S	MP	77571
MAPLE	200	620S	CS	77565
MAPLE	300	536M	PA	77506
MAPLE	1600	493M	DT	77002
MAPLE	4500	531K	BL	77401
MAPLE	5200	419H	CB	77532
MAPLE	5300	531K	BL	77401
MAPLE	5301	531K	SWH	77096
MAPLE	5700	530M	SWH	77074
MAPLE	33000	247R	SWM	77355
MAPLE CIR	0	297E	SEM	77365
MAPLE CT	8300	531Q	SWH	77401
W. MAPLE DR	0	657L	LC	77598
MAPLE DR	6300	334Q	NCC	77338
MAPLE DR	12900	419T	NEC	77532
MAPLE DR	25400	257Y	SEM	77357
MAPLE LN	2700	614Q	PL	77584
MAPLE LN	7200	462Z	BT	77521
MAPLE LN	12200	247M	SWM	77362
MAPLE LN	14100	375X	NEC	77396
MAPLE LN	19500	258J	SEM	77357
MAPLE LN	24400	257B	WV	77357
MAPLE ACE DR	0	444Z	KT	77493
MAPLE ACE DR	0	444Z	KT	77493
MAPLE ACRES CT	16000	408E	NWC	77095
MAPLE ACRES DR	8300	408E	NWC	77095
MAPLE ALLEE DR	26000	250U	NWC	77389
MAPLE ARBOR CT	18200	327W	NWC	77429
MAPLE ASH DR	0	329L	NWC	77379
MAPLE BEND CT	2900	446Q	NWC	77084
MAPLE BEND DR	2800	297Q	NEH	77345
MAPLE BLUFF DR	21700	446B	NWC	77449
MAPLE BOUGH LN	10900	371V	NWC	77067
MAPLE BRANCH	1	251V	WD	77380
MAPLE BRANCH LN	700	613F	NEB	77584
MAPLE BROOK LN	4900	297T	NEH	77345
MAPLE BROOK LN	7800	407H	NWC	77095
MAPLE CHASE LN	19700	486G	SWC	77094
MAPLE CLIFF LN	13900	328S	NWC	77429
MAPLE CREEK DR	1000	539W	LP	77571
MAPLECREEK DR	17600	447W	NWH	77084
MAPLE CREST DR	2300	609D	MC	77459
MAPLECREST DR	8100	529L	SWH	77072
MAPLECREST DR	8500	529U	SWH	77099
MAPLE CROSS DR	4200	578E	PA	77505
MAPLE FALLS CT	15800	329T	NWC	77377
MAPLE FALLS DR	11400	329T	NWC	77377
MAPLE FOX DR	6800	334Q	NCC	77338
MAPLE GABLES LN	0	376N	NEC	77396
MAPLEGATE DR	2100	610A	MC	77489
MAPLEGATE DR	5500	334A	NCC	77373
MAPLE GATE WAY	17300	407Q	NWC	77095
MAPLE GLADE DR	2700	336C	NEH	77339
MAPLE GLEN DR	1	329F	NWC	77375
MAPLE GLEN DR	3600	297X	NEH	77345
MAPLE GREEN LN	0	417W	NEC	77044
MAPLE GROVE LN	3000	451R	NWH	77092
MAPLE HARVEST LN	21300	334M	NCC	77338
MAPLE HEIGHTS DR	3900	297S	NEH	77339
MAPLE HILL DR	3100	657G	FR	77546
MAPLE HILL DR	5700	411U	NWH	77088
MAPLE HILL DR	6300	411T	NWH	77088
MAPLE HILLS CT	0	257E	SEM	77357
MAPLE HILL TRAIL	5100	297L	NEH	77345
MAPLEHURST DR	15800	330T	NWC	77379
MAPLE KNOB CT	5900	298W	NEH	77345
MAPLE KNOLL DR	2900	297N	NEH	77339
MAPLE LAKES DR	1900	336G	NEH	77339
MAPLE LEAF	0	299E	NEC	77336
MAPLE LEAF	9500	410A	NWC	77064
MAPLE LEAF	10700	414V	NEH	77016
MAPLE LEAF	11300	414R	NEH	77016
MAPLE LEAF CIR	3800	579D	LP	77571
MAPLE LEAF CT	1500	616T	PL	77581
MAPLE LEAF DR	100	657Q	LC	77573
MAPLE LEAF LN	12100	569A	SF	77477
MAPLE MANOR DR	15700	408E	NWC	77095
MAPLE MEADOWS CT	20400	326T	NWC	77433
MAPLE MEADOWS DR	15200	326T	NWC	77433
MAPLE MILL DR	18200	327W	NWC	77429
MAPLE MILL DR	18400	326Z	NWC	77429
MAPLE MIST DR	18500	407N	NWC	77449
MAPLEMONT DR	16300	407L	NWC	77095
MAPLE MOSS CT	1400	485L	SWC	77450
MAPLE PARK CT	3700	297W	NEH	77339
MAPLE PARK DR	3300	337B	NEH	77339
MAPLE PARK DR	3400	297W	NEH	77339
MAPLE PARK LN	0	253P	SEM	77386
MAPLE PARK WAY	0	297U	NEH	77345
MAPLE PASS CT	3600	446L	NWC	77449
MAPLE PLACE CT	0	611W	MC	77545
MAPLE POINT CT	19900	406M	NWC	77433
MAPLE POINT DR	19800	406M	NWC	77433
MAPLE RAIN CT	20600	446K	NWC	77449
MAPLE RAPIDS CT	0	294N	SEM	77386
MAPLE RAPIDS CT	20200	335N	NCC	77338
MAPLE RAPIDS CT	20200	335N	NCC	77338
MAPLE RAPIDS LN	0	293R	SEM	77386
MAPLE RAPIDS LN	0	335N	NCC	77338
MAPLE RAPIDS LN	8700	335N	NCC	77338
MAPLE RAPIDS LN	8700	335N	NCC	77338
MAPLE RED DR		484W	NEF	77494
MAPLERIDGE	6500	531F	SWH	77081
MAPLERIDGE	6800	531F	BL	77401
MAPLERIDGE	7000	531F	SWH	77081
MAPLERIDGE	7001	531F	BL	77401
MAPLE ROCK DR	10800	376U	NEC	77396
MAPLE ROCK DR	12100	489J	SWH	77077
MAPLE RUN DR	1000	292F	NCC	77373
MAPLESHIRE DR	0	452P	NWH	77018
MAPLE SHORES DR	15800	377Q	NEC	77044
MAPLES PERCH CT	12900	337X	NEC	77346
MAPLE SPRING	0	538R	DP	77536
MAPLE SPRING PLACE	6300	337P	NEC	77346
MAPLE SPRINGS DR	11200	449X	NWH	77043
MAPLE SQUARE DR	4200	297N	NEH	77339
MAPLE STREAM DR	0	449X	NWH	77043
MAPLE TERRACE DR	4900	297Y	NEH	77345
MAPLE TIMBER CT	0	337P	NEC	77346
MAPLETON	0	500S	BT	77520
MAPLETON	100	499V	BT	77520
MAPLETON DR	1400	449U	NWH	77043
MAPLE TRACE DR	0	370E	NWC	77069
MAPLETRAIL DR	17400	447T	NWH	77084
MAPLE TREE CT	2500	569V	SF	77477
MAPLE TREE DR	7400	411U	NWH	77088
MAPLETWIST	8600	528P	SWC	77083
MAPLE VALLEY RD	100	491F	SWH	77056
MAPLE VIEW DR	23500	293W	NCC	77373
MAPLE VILLAGE CT	15400	326T	NWC	77433
MAPLE VILLAGE DR	19900	326T	NWC	77433
MAPLE VILLAGE DR	20300	326S	NWC	77433
MAPLE VISTA LN	23500	293W	NCC	77373
MAPLE WALK DR	7100	337Y	NEC	77346
MAPLE WAY	500	496H	NEH	77015
MAPLEWICK DR	16100	329N	NWC	77377
MAPLEWOOD	1	494T	SEH	77011
MAPLEWOOD	3500	579A	LP	77571
MAPLEWOOD	25800	252P	SEM	77380
MAPLEWOOD DR	200	616U	FR	77546
MAPLEWOOD DR	700	501T	BT	77520
MAPLE WOOD DR	4000	615Z	PL	77581
MAPLEWOOD DR	22100	405Y	NWC	77449
MAPLEWOOD LN	1200	536P	PA	77502
MAPLEWOOD CREEK	0	610Z	MC	77545
MAPLEWOOD FALLS CT	800	617H	SEH	77062
MAPLEWOOD MILLS CT	0	366V	NWC	77433
MAPLE WOODY LN	0	296Q	SEM	77365
MARA BLVD	34400	247K	SWM	77362
MARABLE DR	4700	453E	NWH	77022
MARABOU PLACE	1	251R	WD	77380
MARANATHA WAY	0	369C	NWC	77070
MARANON LN	700	332E	NWC	77090
MARANON LN	1000	331M	NWC	77090
MARANTA ESTATES CT	14200	366D	NWC	77429
MARANTHA CT	10600	530Z	SWH	77096
MARANTHA RD	0	369C	NWC	77070
MARATHON	200	452R	NWH	77018
MARATHON PLACE	500	569T	NEF	77477
MARATHON WAY	0	569U	NEF	77477
N. MARATHON WAY	300	569T	NEF	77477
S. MARATHON WAY	700	569U	NEF	77477
MARAVILLAS COVE DR	0	366N	NWC	77433
MARBELLA CIR	2000	485M	SWC	77450
MARBELLA CIR	7600	528J	SWC	77083
MARBELLA DR	0	527M	SWC	77083
MAR BELLA PKWY	0	660F	LC	77573
MARBLE	0	500A	BT	77520
MARBLE DR	12600	369L	NWC	77070
MARBLE ACRES CT	0	578T	SEH	77059
MARBLE ARCH CT	8300	335N	NCC	77338
MARBLE BEND	0	526P	NEF	77407
MARBLE BLUFF LN	0	457V	NEC	77049
MARBLE BROOK LN	0	612Q	PL	77584
MARBLE BROOK LN	0	612Q	PL	77584
MARBLE CANYON WAY	15500	417C	NEC	77044
MARBLE COTTAGE LN	100	330U	NWC	77069
MARBLE COVE CT	0	485X	NEF	77494
MARBLE COVE LN	0	485X	NEF	77494
MARBLE CREEK CT	13900	488N	SWH	77077
MARBLE CREEK DR	2600	615R	PL	77581
MARBLE CREEK FALLS CT	16600	330P	NWC	77379
MARBLE CREST DR	10300	367W	NWC	77095
MARBLECREST LN	2300	293F	SEM	77386
MARBLEDALE CT	13800	618A	SEH	77059
MARBLE FALLS DR	2300	333A	NCC	77373
MARBLE FALLS DR	2400	293W	NCC	77373
MARBLE FALLS DR	2900	613P	NEB	77584
MARBLE FALLS BEND	0	484T	NEF	77494
MARBLE FOREST LN	0	406C	NWC	77433
MARBLE GATE LN	5100	330U	NWC	77069
MARBLE GLEN LN	7400	407M	NWC	77095
MARBLEHEAD CT	20500	335Q	HM	77338
MARBLEHEAD DR	9700	335P	HM	77338
MARBLE HILL DR	400	485B	SWC	77450
MARBLE HOLLOW CT	0	657S	FR	77546
MARBLE HOLLOW LN	0	525D	NEF	77450
MARBLE HOLLOW LN	0	253J	SEM	77385
MARBLE LAKES DR	0	484P	NEF	77494
MARBLE MANOR LN	2500	445R	NWC	77449
MARBLE MEADOW CT	0	366V	NWC	77433
MARBLEMOUNT DR	9200	369R	NWC	77064
MARBLE OAK CT	17300	330D	NWC	77379
MARBLE POINT LN	26500	484T	NEF	77494
MARBLEPOINTE LN	0	328P	NWC	77429
MARBLEPOINTE LN	13500	328P	NWC	77429
MARBLE RAVINE DR	5300	526S	NEF	77407
MARBLE RIDGE	14900	330U	NWC	77069
MARBLE RIDGE CT	19900	406M	NWC	77433
MARBLE SPRINGS DR	0	525B	NEF	77494
MARBLE SPRINGS LN	5400	485S	NEF	77494
MARBLE STAFF CT	100	330U	NWC	77069
MARBLE TERRACE CT	0	526R	NEF	77407
MARBLETHORPE LN	0	332R	NCC	77073
MARBLE VISTA WAY	0	445F	NWC	77493
MARBROOK CT	1100	488F	SWH	77077
MARBROOK MEADOW LN	0	524B	NEF	77494
MARBROOK MEADOW LN	0	524B	NEF	77494
MARBROOK SADDLE LN	0	657Y	LC	77573
MARBURG CT	0	568W	SG	77479
MARBURG CT	4700	371N	NWC	77066
MARBURG DR	11600	371N	NWC	77066
MARBURY CT	13100	371D	NWC	77014
MARC	16000	458U	CV	77530
MARCEAU DR	13400	368U	NWC	77065
MARCELIA DR	0	458S	NEC	77049
MARCELLA	300	452D	NWH	77091
MARCELLO LAKES DR	0	445F	NWC	77493
MARCH	12100	614D	BK	77581
MARCHANT RD	3500	573Q	SEH	77047
MARCH CREEK DR	11600	372J	NWC	77067
MARCHCREST LN	18100	526M	NEF	77407
MARCHELLE LN	0	330E	NWC	77379
MARCHENA DR	0	528H	SWC	77083
MARCHMONT DR	700	490G	PP	77024
MARCHWOOD MANOR DR	0	331R	NWC	77090
MARCIA	2100	373Z	NCC	77039
S. MARCIA CIR	11700	570L	MC	77071
N. MARCIA CIR	11700	570L	MC	77071
MARCIA DR	11800	369N	NWC	77065
MARCIN DR	20900	291S	NWC	77388
MARCISZ	0	244J	WCO	77447
MARCOLIN	800	412Q	NWH	77088
MARCONI	1000	493N	SWH	77019
MARCREST CT	12200	369L	NWC	77070
MARCUS	5400	454Y	NEH	77026
MARCY DR	8100	534W	SEH	77033
MARDALE DR	6300	415S	NEH	77016
MARDALE CRESCENT LN	17000	527W	NEF	77407
MARDEL CT	2000	488R	SWH	77077
MARDELL MANOR CT	0	484Y	NEF	77494
MARDELL MANOR CT	0	484Y	NEF	77494
MARDEN CT	15300	568Y	SG	77478
MARDEN LN	1600	568Y	SG	77478
MARDI LN	1300	450Y	NWH	77055
MARDI GRAS DR	12200	371G	NWC	77014
MAREK DR	9600	412G	NWC	77038
MAREK LN	15700	420C	NEC	77532
S. MAREK LN	26500	246N	SWM	77355
MAREK LN	26600	246N	SWM	77355
MARELLA DR	25600	257Q	SEM	77357
MARESCA LN	0	659C	LC	77573
MARFIELD CT	0	289Q	NWC	77375
MARGARET	0	658V	LC	77573
MARGARET	1500	413Z	NEH	77093
MARGARET	2400	414W	NEH	77093
MARGARET FALLS LN	0	484N	NEF	77494
MARGARITA	5200	494G	NEH	77020
MARGATE	10100	529X	SWH	77099
MARGATE CT	1000	613K	NEB	77584
MARGATE DR	1000	613K	NEB	77584
MARGERSTADT RD	23000	243Z	WCO	77447
MARGERSTADT RD	28000	283C	NWC	77484
MARGESON	15000	408T	NWC	77084
MARGIE CT	9800	289U	NWC	77379
MARGIE LN	100	413N	NCC	77037
MARGO	5000	291A	NWC	77389
MARGUERITE LN	1300	537N	PA	77502
MARIA	900	537K	PA	77506
MARIA	1500	659K	LC	77573
MARIA AMORE	21500	334M	NCC	77338
MARIACHI BLVD	0	339W	NEC	77532
MARIACHI BLVD	300	338Z	NEC	77532
MARIA EDNA	8300	413P	NCC	77037
MARIAH	8100	533T	SEH	77051
MARIA HILLS LN	0	293L	SEM	77386
MARIAH ROSE CT	0	366V	NWC	77433
MARIAN	5300	444Y	KT	77493
MARIAN'S HOLLOW	4000	297S	NEH	77339
S. MARIANNE CIR	11700	570L	MC	77071
N. MARIANNE CIR	11700	570L	MC	77071
MARIBELLE WAY	9600	450X	NWH	77055
MARICELLA CIR	17000	407Q	NWC	77084
MARICOPA CT	0	658Y	LC	77573
MARICOPA LN	12300	496L	NEH	77015
MARIE	100	493G	NEH	77009
MARIE	4700	538X	DP	77536
MARIEL CIR	0	408L	NWC	77095
MARIEL DR	0	408L	NWC	77095
MARIETTA LN	4700	534E	SEH	77021
MARIGNY DR	0	371H	NWC	77014
MARIGOLD	3000	493C	NEH	77009
MARIGOLD RD	0	460W	BT	77521
MARIGOLD BLOOM LN	0	417A	NEC	77044
MARIGOLD CREEK CT	20700	326N	NWC	77433
MARIGOLD GLEN WAY	0	576V	SEH	77034
MARILANE	1	492K	SWH	77007
MARILEE LN	2500	490V	SWH	77057
MARILEE CHRIS CT	4500	609Y	NEF	77459
MARILYN	500	612S	FS	77545
MARILYN LN	2900	414W	NEH	77093
MARILYN LN	7200	415W	NEH	77016
MARILYN LN	20500	292S	NWC	77388
S. MARIMAR LAKE BLVD	0	290N	NWC	77375
MARIMONTE LN	0	327W	CY	77429
MARIN	0	327Y	NWC	77429
MARIN DR	14200	367C	CY	77429
MARINA	4000	492H	SWH	77007
MARINA DR	900	336J	NEH	77339
MARINA BAY DR	0	619Y	LC	77573
MARINA CANYON WAY	6200	526B	NEF	77450
MARINA OAKS CT	300	619V	LC	77565
MARINA OAKS DR	100	619V	LC	77565
MARINA PALMS LN	0	619Y	LC	77573
MARINA SHORES CT	0	445A	NWC	77493
MARINA VIEW WAY	2300	619Y	LC	77573
MARINA VISTA LN	5700	449A	NWC	77041
MARINA WAY	2200	619V	LC	77565
MARINA WAY CT	0	619V	LC	77565
MARIN CREEK PLACE	0	250P	NWC	77389
MARINE RD	14600	375W	NEH	77396
MARINE PARK DR	0	619Z	LC	77573
MARINER	2900	660F	LC	77573
MARINER CT	200	419C	NEC	77532
MARINER COVE	1100	568E	SG	77498
MARINER COVE CT	100	619Y	LC	77573
MARINER FALLS WAY	6800	527E	NEF	77407
MARINER GROVE	6900	408P	NWC	77084
MARINER PLACE	18400	378A	NEC	77346
MARINER POINT LN	1900	484K	NEF	77494
MARINER REEF WAY	4500	376N	NEC	77396
MARINERS DR	400	620S	CS	77565
MARINERS LN	1	620S	LC	77565
MARINERS BAY DR	17000	367Y	NWC	77095
MARINERS HARBOR	5100	449A	NWC	77041
MARINER SQUARE CT	6600	527E	NEF	77407
MARINER VILLAGE DR	1	619Q	PA	77586
MARINER WAY	16100	419C	NEC	77532
MARINETTE DR	6100	530G	SWH	77036
MARINETTE DR	7400	530R	SWH	77074
MARIN HILL CT	16000	367C	CY	77429
MARINO RD	0	484E	KT	77494
MARINWOOD DR	6300	611A	SWH	77053
MARION	100	501Y	BT	77520
MARION	1700	493H	NEH	77009
MARION, FRANCIS	6200	411Y	NWH	77091
MARION MEADOW DR	0	253W	SEM	77386
MARION MEADOW LN	0	253W	SEM	77386
MARIOSA	6700	454R	NEH	77028
MARIPOSA	9600	532T	SWH	77025
MARIPOSA BEND LN	9500	616E	SEC	77089
MARIPOSA BLUE LN	0	366Y	NWC	77433
MARIPOSA CANYON	11900	328G	NWC	77377
MARIPOSA CANYON DR	12000	328C	NWC	77377
MARIPOSA GROVE LN	0	377J	NEC	77346
MARISA LN		524M	NEF	77406
MARISA ALEXIS DR	9900	576N	SEH	77075
MARISCAL PLACE	0	250L	NWC	77389
MARISCAL PLACE	0	250L	NWC	77389
MARISOL DR	6500	527G	SWC	77083
MARIS WAY	3300	333G	NCC	77338
MARITIME DR	11000	417V	NEC	77044
MARJORIE	700	412Q	NWH	77088
MARJORIE	1700	412T	NWH	77088
MARK	0	256Y	SEM	77357
MARK	600	538L	DP	77536
MARK	1300	570J	SF	77477
MARK RD	1500	332R	NCC	77073
MARK RD	13400	414D	NEC	77039
MARK ANTHONY CT	18000	256C	RF	77357
MARK CREST DR	0	325S	HK	77447
MARKER DR	0	499T	SEC	77571
MARKER RIDGE DR	0	335P	NCC	77338
MARKET	100	288H	TB	77375
MARKET	1000	501X	BT	77520
MARKET	2600	540D	BT	77520
MARKET	3000	494F	NEH	77020
MARKET	3600	500Z	BT	77520
MARKET	7800	495G	NEH	77029
MARKET	12200	496K	JC	77029
MARKET	13100	497J	NEH	77015
MARKET	14900	497M	CV	77530
MARKET	15100	498H	CV	77530
MARKET	16900	499A	CV	77530
MARKET	18000	499C	CV	77530
MARKET CIR	0	251H	WD	77380
MARKET ST	0	251H	WD	77380
MARKET CENTER DR	0	335S	NEH	77338
MARKET GARDEN LN	0	407V	NWC	77084
N. MARKET LOOP	1200	500B	NEC	77521
MARKET PLACE	0	568R	SG	77478
MARKET PLACE DR	0	256T	SEM	77357
MARKET PLACE DR	0	334Z	NEH	77032
MARKET PLACE DR	0	484D	SWC	77494
MARKET SQUARE LN	22500	445U	NWC	77449
MARKHAM	4000	492W	SWH	77027
MARKHAM WOODS CT	4700	297Q	NEH	77345
MARKHAM WOODS DR	2800	297Q	NEH	77345
MARKHURST DR	14400	328X	NWC	77429
MARKLENA DR	12700	368J	NWC	77429
MARKLEY	4000	534L	SEH	77087
MARKSMAN POINT	0	250U	NWC	77389
MARKRIDGE DR	16800	329V	NWC	77379
MARKS LN	1	257J	SEM	77357
MARKS RD	3300	447Q	NWC	77084
MARKSCOTT DR	3100	488X	SWC	77082
MARKS EDGE DR	0	487A	SWC	77494
MARKSEY CT	800	252P	SEM	77386
MARKSMAN CT	21700	285M	NWC	77447
MARKSPRING LN	0	291X	NWC	77388
MARKSTONE CT	3200	485U	NEF	77494
MARKSTONE KNOLLS DR	0	338M	NEH	77336
MARKS WAY	14300	368P	NWC	77429
MARKVILLE LN	1	570M	SWH	77085
MARKWOOD CT	0	446B	NWC	77449
MARKWOOD CT	15400	571Y	SWH	77053
MARKWOOD LN	4800	571Y	SWH	77053
MARL CT	17500	379T	NEC	77532
MARLAN FOREST LN	26800	366R	NWC	77433
MARLAN WOODS CT	0	253N	SEM	77386
MARLBERRY LN	1900	447X	NWH	77084
MARLBOROUGH DR	4000	451R	NWH	77092
MARLEBONE CT	15000	330U	NWC	77069
MARLEEN	500	576A	SEH	77034
MARLEN AVE	1900	537P	PA	77502
MARLENE	900	538L	DP	77536
MARLE POINT CT	0	290R	NWC	77388
MARLEY HILLS TRAIL	0	616H	SEC	77089
MARLIN	1500	494X	SEH	77023
MARLIN CT	2900	660J	LC	77573
MARLIN LN	1	542A	BT	77520
MARLIN LN	3800	580V	LP	77571
MARLINK LN	0	532S	SWH	77025
MARLIN SPIKE WAY	16000	379X	NEC	77532
MARLIN WATERS DR	18300	377D	NEC	77346
MARLIVE LN	9000	532N	SWH	77025
MARLO	2200	534H	SEH	77023
MARLOCK LN	1300	537P	PA	77502
MARLOWE	3800	532A	WU	77005
MARLOWE GROVE DR	15200	527U	NEF	77498
MARLSTONE CT	19300	486H	SWC	77094
MARLSTONE DR	1300	486H	SWC	77094
MARL WAY	17400	379T	NEC	77532
MARMITE DR	0	249V	NWC	77375
MARMORA CT	2000	658T	LC	77573
MARNE LN	700	332J	NWC	77090
MARNE LN	1100	331M	NWC	77090
MARNEL RD	2000	451N	NWH	77055
MARNERS CT	13900	332W	NWC	77014

Street Name	Block	Pg/Sq	Loc	Zips
MARNIE LN	11900	413T	NEH	77076
MAROBY	200	536J	SEH	77017
MAROBY	900	535R	SEH	77017
MARONEAL	2100	532G	SWH	77030
MARONEAL	3000	532E	SWH	77025
MAROON LN	1200	488J	SWH	77077
MAROON CREEK CT	0	250E	WD	77381
MAROT DR	2000	445S	NWC	77493
MARQUART	3000	492T	SWH	77027
MARQUESA LN	0	447J	NWC	77084
MARQUETTE	3800	532E	WU	77005
MARQUETTE POINT LN	17200	377J	NEC	77346
MARQUETTE TRAIL	2600	485N	NEF	77494
MARQUIS AVE	4500	501F	BT	77521
MARQUITA LN	3500	414E	NCC	77039
MARRAKECH CT	100	531M	BL	77401
MARRAT CT	16400	328V	NWC	77377
MARRON CT	12800	328U	NWC	77429
MARRON DR	12800	328U	NWC	77429
MARRS DR	11100	368Q	NWC	77065
MARS DR	1400	577J	PA	77504
E. MARSALA CT	1400	616K	PL	77581
W. MARSALA CT	2200	616K	PL	77581
N. MARSALA DR	1400	616K	PL	77581
W. MARSALA DR	2100	616K	PL	77581
E. MARSALA DR	2200	616K	PL	77581
MARSDEN	1	494U	SEH	77011
MARSDEN PARK LN	0	485X	NEF	77494
MARSH	0	500V	BT	77520
MARSH	0	501S	BT	77520
MARSHA	10700	490D	HC	77024
MARSHA LN	5800	614K	PL	77581
MARSHAL	100	658H	LC	77573
MARSHALL	200	493S	SWH	77006
MARSHALL	1000	538P	DP	77536
MARSHALL	1700	492V	SWH	77098
MARSHALL	2100	537F	PA	77506
MARSHALL CT	0	249J	SWM	77354
MARSHALL RD	3700	420H	NEC	77532
MARSHALL BRIDGE LN	0	528S	NEF	77498
MARSHALL FALLS DR	0	330P	NWC	77379
MARSHALL OAKS WAY	0	486C	SWC	77094
E. MARSHAM CIR	11900	371K	NWC	77066
W. MARSHAM CIR	12000	371K	NWC	77066
E. MARSHAM SQUARE	3500	371F	NWC	77066
MARSHAVEN WAY	22100	525L	NEF	77407
MARSHBROOK DR	0	250T	NWC	77389
MARSHBURN DR	24200	245S	SWM	77447
MARSHFIELD DR	10800	368U	NWC	77065
MARSH GRASS LN	0	537H	PA	77530
MARSH HAWK	15800	375R	NEC	77396
MARSH HAY CT	11000	371S	NWC	77086
MARSH MILLET CT	1	252N	WD	77380
MARSH WHEN RD	12500	411D	NWC	77038
MARSH WILLOW WAY	0	526T	NEF	77407
MARSHWOOD RD	2700	371U	NWC	77038
MARSILLES LN	0	489X	SWH	77082
MARSTON	800	492M	SWH	77019
MARSTON PARK	0	407Z	NWC	77084
MARSTON RIVER LN	6300	370L	NWC	77066
MARTA DR	6800	527G	SWC	77083
MARTELEY WAY	29500	298Q	NEC	77336
MARTELL	9200	573C	SEH	77051
MARTENS RD	30600	248Y	TB	77375
MARTESIA DR	0	368X	NWC	77095
MARTHA	800	538L	DP	77536
MARTHA	3000	494A	NEH	77026
E. MARTHA LN	1500	537N	PA	77502
MARTHA LN	5500	374R	NEH	77032
MARTHA LN	5800	375N	NEH	77396
MARTHA SPRINGS CT	15800	329U	NWC	77070
MARTHA SPRINGS DR	15800	329U	NWC	77070
MARTHOMAN DR	0	570W	MC	77477
MARTIN	300	452F	NWH	77018
MARTIN	2600	537X	PA	77502
MARTIN N. CIR	23400	296E	SEM	77365
MARTIN S. CIR	23700	296E	SEM	77365
MARTIN CT	1	490C	SV	77055
E. MARTIN DR	0	296K	SEM	77365
W. MARTIN DR	21200	296J	SEM	77365
MARTIN LN	1	490C	SV	77055
MARTIN LN	500	570N	MC	77489
MARTIN LN	13200	614F	BK	77581
MARTINA	0	656X	FR	77546
MARTIN CREEK LN	12100	328V	NWC	77377
MARTINDALE LN	6900	409U	NWC	77041
MARTINDALE RD	10400	409U	NWC	77041
MARTINDALE RD	10900	574K	SEH	77048
MARTIN DOWN LN	22300	485R	NEF	77450
MARTINEAU	15500	373R	NCC	77032
MARTINEC DR	2600	613P	NEB	77584
MARTINEZ	15300	527Z	NEF	77498
MARTINEZ CT	0	657L	FR	77546
MARTINGALE CT	1200	379S	NEC	77532
MARTIN GROVE CT	0	333F	NCC	77338
MARTIN GROVE CT	0	333F	NCC	77338
MARTIN HEIGHTS DR	8800	570A	SWH	77031
MARTINIQUE DR	18500	619W	NB	77058
MARTINIQUE CALLE	5100	660S	GCO	77539
MARTIN LUTHER KING	500	541B	BT	77520
MARTIN LUTHER KING BLVD	4500	534E	SEH	77021
MARTIN LUTHER KING BLVD	8500	574J	SEH	77048
MARTINSHIRE DR	4000	532N	SWH	77025
MARTINS PLACE	1100	493G	SWH	77007
MARTIN TEA TRAIL	0	286Q	NWC	77377
MARTINVILLE DR	2600	536X	SEH	77017
MARTIN WOOD CT	9500	370Z	NWC	77086
MARTIN WOOD LN	7700	370Z	NWC	77086
MARTWAY	0	458L	NEC	77049
MARTY	0	658K	LC	77573
MARUFO VEGA DR	0	293F	SEM	77386
MARVELL DR	1900	373R	NCC	77032
MARVEL OAK CT	7400	337Q	NEC	77346
MARVICK DR	100	536L	PA	77506
MARVIN CIR	1900	620K	SB	77586
MARVIN LN	0	528T	NEF	77498
MARVIN RD	3200	502P	BT	77520
MAR VISTA DR	7300	527M	SWC	77083
MARWELL LN	11600	328T	NWC	77429
MARWICK CT	15900	408A	NWC	77095
MARWOOD	1300	497M	NEC	77015
MARWOOD DR	5900	374M	NEH	77396
MARWOOD ESTATES DR	10200	369Q	NWC	77070
MARWOOD FALLS CT	10200	369L	NWC	77070
MARY	800	494A	NEH	77020
MARY	1500	494A	NEH	77026
MARY	3000	609D	NEF	77477
MARY	3500	577B	PA	77504
MARY AVE	2500	616T	PL	77581
MARY LN	400	460N	HG	77562
MARY LN	1300	539P	LP	77571
MARY'S VILLAGE DR	0	615U	PL	77581

Street Name	Block	Pg/Sq	Loc	Zips
MARY ANN	100	616Y	FR	77546
MARY ANN	400	656C	FR	77546
MARY ANN LN	16000	327D	NWC	77429
MARY BATES BLVD	6700	530K	SWH	77036
MARYDEL	9700	453B	NEH	77076
MARY ELIZ WILBANKS AVE	1	501X	BT	77520
MARY ETHEL RD	5600	500D	NEC	77521
MARYFIELD BLVD	0	615T	PL	77581
MARYFIELD LN	3200	615T	PL	77581
MARY FRANCIS DR	5400	414H	NEC	77039
MARY JAN RD	10300	449D	NWH	77041
MARY JANE LN	14300	288N	NWC	77377
MARY KAY LN	13700	574W	SEH	77048
MARYKNOLL DR	1400	496L	NEH	77015
MARYLAND	1400	492V	SWH	77006
MARYLAND	1600	540D	BT	77520
MARYLAND	1900	492V	SWH	77019
MARYLAND AVE	1200	659U	LC	77573
MARYLAND RD	3300	611T	FS	77545
MARYLEBONE DR	13700	577W	SEH	77034
MARYLIN	500	612S	FS	77545
MARY LOU DR	5000	451G	NWH	77092
MARY MOUNT WAY	1600	618Q	SEH	77058
MARYON	1500	462Z	CCO	77520
MARY POINT LN		366U	NWC	77433
MARYPORT DR	14900	457Z	NEC	77530
MARYS CT	900	616U	FR	77546
W. MARYS CREEK	2000	615V	PL	77581
E. MARYS CREEK	2000	615V	PL	77581
MARYS CREEK CT	2300	615U	PL	77581
MARYS CREEK W. LN	0	615Z	PL	77581
MARYS CREEK LN	1	616U	FR	77546
MARYS CROSSING	0	616Z	FR	77546
MARY SUE CT	14000	568E	SG	77498
MARYSVILLE LN	14800	417V	NEC	77044
MARY THISTLE DR	0	292Z	NCC	77373
MARYVALE DR	1600	485K	NEF	77494
MARYWOOD DR	3400	331C	NWC	77388
MARYWOOD CHASE	700	488B	SWH	77079
MARZELLE	3100	414W	NEH	77093
MARZIA AVE	3800	611Z	FS	77545
MASCARI	4500	453J	NWH	77022
MASCOT	300	495Z	NEH	77029
MASON	0	485Z	NEF	77450
MASON	0	500V	BT	77520
MASON	0	501S	BT	77520
MASON	500	288G	TB	77375
MASON	1300	493N	SWH	77019
MASON	1900	493N	SWH	77006
MASON DR	0	568F	SG	77498
MASON RD	0	525D	NEF	77450
MASON RD	0	526E	NEF	77450
MASON RD	0	526W	NEF	77406
S. MASON RD	100	485D	SWC	77450
N. MASON RD	1000	445R	NWC	77449
MASON RD	2200	568B	NEF	77498
N. MASON RD	5200	405V	NWC	77449
MASON RD	14000	326W	NWC	77433
MASON, LOUIS LN	5600	452B	NWH	77091
MASON BEE LN	0	296D	SEM	77357
MASON CREEK CT	6800	527E	NEF	77407
MASON CREEK DR	19900	406U	NWC	77449
MASON CREEK PATH DR	0	444V	KT	77493
MASON DALE DR	0	367S	NWC	77433
MASON FOREST DR	0	486L	SWC	77094
MASON GROVE CT	18200	376D	NEC	77346
MASON GROVE LN	0	612Q	PL	77584
MASON KNIGHTS CT	0	445W	NWC	77493
MASON KNIGHTS DR	0	445W	NWC	77493
MASON MANOR DR	0	445R	NWC	77449
MASON MOUNTAIN LN	0	578X	SEH	77059
MASON OAKS	0	571L	SWH	77085
MASON PARK BLVD	500	486A	SWC	77450
MASONRIDGE DR	17300	407K	NWC	77095
MASON SPRINGS	0	485Q	NEF	77450
MASON STONE LN	4000	525B	NEF	77494
MASON TERRACE LN	12800	366H	NWC	77433
MASON TRAIL DR	24700	445S	NWC	77493
MASONVILLE LN	1	258R	NEC	77357
MASONWOOD LN	7900	369D	NWC	77070
MASONWOOD FIELD CT		328P	NWC	77429
MASSACHUSETTS	300	495Z	NEH	77029
MASSA MARBLE LN	0	250X	NWC	77389
MASSANET POINT DR	0	366J	NWC	77433
MASSENGALE LN	1	657M	LC	77598
MASSEY	800	541B	BT	77520
MASSEY HIGHWAY	0	614P	PL	77581
MASSEY TOMPKINS RD	100	501M	BT	77521
MASSEY TOMPKINS RD	4000	502K	BT	77520
MASSIE	2000	494E	NEH	77026
MASSON CT	500	332B	NWC	77388
MASSY DR	0	542K	BT	77520
MAST CT	2300	296V	NEH	77339
MASTERS CIR	37200	246G	SWM	77355
MASTERS DR	0	659C	LC	77573
MASTERS DR	2500	619Y	LC	77573
MASTERS DR	5900	330Y	NWC	77069
MASTERS LN	2000	610J	MC	77459
MASTERS GREEN BLVD	0	250X	NWC	77389
MASTERS MANOR	0	446X	NWC	77449
MASTERSON	7900	495P	NEH	77029
MASTERS POINT DR	0	452F	NWH	77091
MASTERS TRACE LN	25500	250T	NWC	77389
MASTERS WAY	600	336B	NEH	77339
MASTER WAY CT	2100	336B	NEH	77339
MASTERWOOD CT	19100	337Z	NEC	77346
MASTIC DR	0	461Q	NEC	77521
MATAGORDA LN	0	657N	FR	77546
MATAGORDA LAKES DR	0	376N	NEC	77396
MATAMORAS	1800	535A	SEH	77023
MATCH PLAY DR	19000	337Z	NEC	77346
MATCH POINT CIR	18700	337Z	NEC	77346
MATCH POINT LN	2800	656X	FR	77546
MATEO PARK DR	0	572R	SWH	77047
MATHER DR	24700	484G	NEF	77494
MATHEW LN	0	542J	BT	77520
MATHEW'S CREST CT	8200	375Y	NEC	77396
MATHEWS	1100	493P	SWH	77019
MATHEWSON LN	10100	489D	NWH	77043
MATHIS	600	453T	NWH	77009
MATHIS DR	5100	444Z	KT	77493
MATHIS RD	14900	322H	NWC	77484
MATHIS RD	18200	282Z	NWC	77484
MATHIS CHURCH RD	16700	331R	NWC	77090
MATHIS LANDING DR	0	326T	NWC	77429
MATILDA DR	2000	373Z	NCC	77039
MATILDA DR	2600	374W	NCC	77032
MATILDA BEND LN	0	406W	NWC	77449
MATILDA CREEK CT	0	527S	NEF	77407
MATILDE CT	3600	613Y	NEB	77584
MATISSE DR	100	489L	SWH	77079
W. MATISSE MEADOW CT	0	249C	SWM	77382

Street Name	Block	Pg/Sq	Loc	Zips
E. MATISSE MEADOW CT	0	249C	SWM	77382
MATLAGE WAY	200	568N	SG	77478
MATLOCK CT	0	366R	NWC	77433
MATLOCK CT	0	366R	NWC	77433
MATON POINT CIR	0	378A	NEC	77346
MATOON LN	22500	485R	NEF	77450
MATSON	7900	455B	NEH	77078
MATSON MANOR CT	1300	329H	NWC	77379
MATT CIR	19000	337X	NEC	77346
MATT RD	5900	337X	NEC	77346
MATTBY	8200	535U	SEH	77061
MATTHEW	24900	249W	NWC	77375
MATTHEW HILLS LN	0	293L	SEM	77386
MATTHEWS LN	28000	249E	SWM	77354
MATTHEWS RD	0	249X	NWC	77375
MATTHEWS CREST CT	0	375Y	NEC	77396
MATTHEWS PLACE	24400	244V	WCO	77447
MATTHEW WAY	0	332Z	NCC	77073
MATTHIAS TRAIL	0	528F	SWC	77083
MATTINA DR	0	489P	SWH	77042
MATTINGHAM DR	3500	371K	NWC	77066
MATTISON DR	8900	411J	NWC	77088
MATTWOOD DR	0	526X	NEF	77469
MATTYE MAYE DR	3500	537Q	PA	77503
MATY LN	23900	295H	SEM	77365
MATZKE RD	0	367R	CY	77429
MAUD	1500	493F	SWH	77007
MAUDEAS DR	13200	420S	BR	77532
MAUDLIN	5100	534Q	SEH	77087
MAUDLIN CIR	0	660D	KE	77546
MAUDLIN RD	0	660C	KE	77565
MAUFFERD	2400	493C	NWH	77009
MAUNA KAI DR	7600	408L	NWC	77095
MAUNA LOA CT	8200	410J	NWC	77040
MAUNA LOA LN	8900	410J	NWC	77040
MAUNA LOA LN	15300	409M	JV	77040
MAUREEN'S WAY	11800	248N	SWM	77362
MAURICE WAY	4100	569P	SF	77477
MAURIENE RD	35	299N	NEC	77336
MAURINE	2100	373Z	NCC	77039
MAURITA DR	4700	333D	NCC	77373
MAURITA LN	8900	456D	NEC	77044
MAURITZ DR	5000	374Z	NCC	77032
MAURY	900	493H	NEH	77020
MAURY	1400	493H	NEH	77026
MAURY	2600	453V	NEH	77009
MAUVE ORCHID WAY	20500	326N	NWC	77433
MAUVEWOOD DR	7800	410L	NWC	77040
MAUX DR	1400	450W	NWH	77043
MAUX DR	1700	450S	NWH	77043
MAVADO CT	3900	293H	SEM	77386
MAVERICK	200	453Y	NEH	77009
MAVERICK	20200	379E	NEC	77532
MAVERICK BEND LN	0	609V	MC	77459
MAVERICK CREEK LN	0	366Z	NWC	77433
MAVERICK PARK LN	2500	446N	NWC	77449
MAVERICK POINT CT	8500	485W	NEF	77494
MAVERICK POINT LN	5300	485W	NEF	77494
MAVERICK SHADOW LN	0	615F	PL	77581
MAVERICK TRACE CT	0	406M	NWC	77433
MAVERICK TRACE LN	0	406M	NWC	77433
MAVERICK VALLEY LN	14800	327Y	NWC	77429
MAVERLY	0	659C	LC	77573
MAVERLY CREST CT	0	484T	NEF	77494
MAVIS LN	5800	537Z	PA	77505
MAX RD	12300	574W	BK	77581
MAX RD	12500	614E	NEB	77581
MAX CONRAD DR	9300	289V	NWC	77379
MAXEY RD	1	456Y	NEH	77013
MAXEY RD	900	496G	NEH	77015
MAXFIELD DR	12800	488Y	SWH	77082
MAXI CIR	0	657L	FR	77546
MAXIE	200	538F	DP	77536
MAXIE	4500	492G	SWH	77007
MAXIM DR	12100	368U	NWC	77065
MAXIMILIAN	2000	373Z	NCC	77039
MAXIMILIAN	2500	374W	NCC	77032
MAXIMOS DR	0	528K	SWC	77083
MAXINE	800	495U	NEH	77029
MAXINE LN	15900	331Q	NWC	77068
MAXROY	2300	492B	NWH	77007
MAXROY	3000	492B	NWH	77008
MAXROY	5900	452B	NWH	77091
MAXROY	7400	412P	NWH	77088
E. MAXROY	7500	412T	NWH	77088
MAX SKY CT		366T	NWC	77433
MAXTED CT	13400	328X	NWC	77429
MAXWELL	5600	534B	SEH	77023
MAXWELL LN	2000	534C	SEH	77023
MAXWELL LN	2400	538Q	DP	77536
MAXWELL RD	0	410Z	NWH	77040
MAXWELL RD	12200	368F	NWC	77429
MAXWOOD DR	7100	330L	NWC	77379
MAY	5600	453A	NWH	77076
MAY	12300	614D	BK	77581
MAY CT	2300	613K	PL	77584
MAY RD	0	327C	NWC	77429
MAYA	9800	248R	SWM	77354
MAYA LN	23600	295F	SEM	77365
MAY APPLE CT	0	325V	NWC	77433
MAYAPPLE DR	2100	503F	CCO	77520
MAYAPPLE BLOSSOM PLACE	0	249Q	NWC	77375
MAYARD RD	6600	408R	NWC	77041
MAYBANK DR	6500	451U	NWH	77055
MAYBANK SHORES CT	0	572E	SWH	77045
MAYBANK SHORES CT	0	572E	SWH	77045
MAY BASKET LN	0	329B	NWC	77375
MAYBELL	5800	452C	NWH	77091
MAYBELL	6500	412Y	NWH	77091
MAYBERRY	9400	455C	NEH	77028
MAYBERRY	9500	415Y	NEH	77078
MAYBERRY HEIGHTS DR	10200	366Z	NWC	77433
MAYBERRY HEIGHTS DR		366V	NWC	77433
MAYBERRY HEIGHTS DR		366Z	NWC	77433
MAYBLOOM CT	0	299X	NEC	77336
MAYBLOOM DR	0	299X	NEC	77336
MAYBROOK	0	612R	PL	77584
MAYBROOK DR	200	457W	NEC	77015
MAYBROOK HOLLOW LN	0	573X	SEC	77047
MAYBROOK HOLLOW LN	0	573X	SEC	77047
MAYBROOK MANOR LN	21100	525M	NEF	77407
MAYBROOK PARK CIR	22300	525C	NEF	77450
MAYBROOK PARK CT	22000	525C	NEF	77450
MAYBROOK PARK LN	5200	525C	NEF	77450
MAY CREEK	0	331Q	NWC	77068
MAYCREST CT	16000	329N	NWC	77377
MAY DAWN DR	0	446F	NWC	77449
MAYDAY	0	292T	NCC	77373
MAYDAY RUN CT	0	293U	NCC	77373
MAYDE CREEK DR	19000	446Z	NWH	77084
MAYDE CREEK FARMS LN	17700	447S	NWH	77084
MAYDE PARK LN	1600	446Z	NWH	77084

Street Name	Block	Pg/Sq	Loc	Zips
MAYER RD	0	295H	SEM	77365
MAYER RD	1	296E	SEM	77365
MAYER RD	32300	242T	NWC	77484
MAYERLING DR	200	490P	BH	77024
MAYER WALLER RD	2000	282Q	WCO	77484
MAYES BLUFF DR		484W	NEF	77494
MAYFAIR	4500	531C	BL	77401
MAYFAIR	6200	534Q	SEH	77087
MAYFAIR CT	100	568V	SG	77478
MAYFAIR DR	0	613P	NEB	77584
MAYFAIR GROVE CT	1	251E	WD	77381
MAYFAIR PARK CT	4600	609S	NEF	77479
MAYFAIR PARK LN	20000	290Z	NWC	77379
MAYFAIR WAY	0	330V	NWC	77069
MAYFAIR WAY	1200	336H	NEH	77339
MAYFIELD RD	10200	449Z	NWH	77043
MAYFIELD RD	11200	449X	NWH	77043
MAYFIELD, R V	3500	411V	NWH	77088
MAYFIELD MEADOW LN	18100	526M	NEF	77407
MAYFIELD OAKS LN	3500	411V	NWH	77088
MAYFLOWER	4000	533U	SEH	77051
MAYFLOWER	4600	533V	SEH	77033
MAYFLOWER LANDING CT	2700	657D	SEC	77598
MAYFLY CT	3200	446Q	NWC	77449
MAYFLY LN	0	296D	SEM	77357
MAYFLY LN	0	297A	SEM	77357
MAYFORD	300	413Y	NEH	77076
MAYFORD BROOK CT	0	295U	SEM	77365
MAYGLEN LN	7800	330E	NWC	77379
MAYGROVE DR	1400	568F	SG	77498
MAYHAW	100	659Q	LC	77573
MAYHAW CT	0	245R	SWM	77355
MAYHAW DR	200	500K	BT	77520
MAYHAW LN	8000	456H	NEC	77044
MAYHILL RIDGE LN	0	657X	LC	77573
MAYKIRK	11000	528Z	NEF	77478
MAY LAUREL DR	12300	372E	NWC	77014
MAYLE	5000	454C	NEH	77016
MAYMIST DR	3300	446R	NWC	77449
MAYMOUNT LN	11600	413R	NCC	77093
MAYNARD PLACE	11100	370S	NWC	77064
MAYO	600	541A	BT	77520
MAYO AVE	800	536N	SEH	77017
MAYOR DR	13100	413H	NCC	77039
MAYORCA DR	27900	298Z	NEH	77336
MAYO SHELL RD	100	496W	GP	77547
MAYO SHELL RD	1000	536A	NEH	77547
MAYPINE LN	0	571K	SWH	77085
MAYPORT LN	0	488N	SWH	77077
MAYPORT CREST LN	0	526J	NEF	77407
MAYRIDGE CIR	8600	529P	SWH	77099
MAYSEL	3000	450M	NWH	77080
MAY SHOWERS CIR	20700	368X	NWC	77095
MAY SHOWERS CT	0	368X	NWC	77095
MAYSIDE LN	8500	410F	NWC	77040
MAYSTAR CT	1	251M	WD	77380
MAY TERRACE DR	0	295L	SEM	77365
MAY VALLEY CIR	0	249A	SWM	77354
MAY VALLEY DR	0	249B	SWM	77382
MAYVIEW DR	2400	412W	NWH	77091
MAYVIEW DR	2600	411Z	NWH	77091
MAYWATER LN	0	367P	NWC	77433
MAYWATER CREST DR	0	377F	NEC	77346
MAYWIND CT	1	251E	WD	77381
MAYWOOD DR	5100	571Y	SWH	77053
MAYWOOD LN	1600	538N	PA	77503
MAYWOOD FALLS CIR	19400	446R	NWC	77084
MAYWOOD FOREST DR	6000	411K	NWC	77088
MAYWOOD RUN CT	0	611S	FS	77545
MAYWOOD RUN CT	2400	611S	FS	77545
MAZE LN	23300	296M	SEM	77365
MAZEFIELD CT	12100	369P	NWC	77070
MAZEN	0	370V	NWC	77066
MC AFEE	9100	530W	SWH	77031
MC AFEE CT	10500	530W	SWH	77031
MC ALEXANDER DR	15600	367R	CY	77429
MCALLISTER AVE	0	568S	SG	77479
MCALLISTER DR	0	609Y	MC	77459
MC ALLISTER RD	2000	451U	NWH	77092
MC ALPINE	300	494N	SEH	77003
MC ASHAN	3300	494N	SEH	77003
MC AULTY	0	373M	NEH	77032
MC AULTY RD	1900	373L	NCC	77032
MC AVOY DR	8000	530M	SWH	77074
MC BEE DR	0	245R	SWM	77355
MC CABE	700	413X	NEH	77076
MC CABE RD	400	580P	LP	77571
MC CADDEN	14200	572P	SWH	77045
MC CALL	0	494J	NEH	77020
MC CALL	100	494E	NEH	77020
McCALL BEND	0	246Z	SWM	77355
McCALL PARK	0	246Z	SWM	77355
McCALL SOUND BLVD	0	247W	SWM	77355
McCALL TRACE	0	246Z	SWM	77355
MC CAMEY DR	21400	368S	NWC	77429
MC CARDELL DR	700	498B	CV	77530
MC CARRON CT	100	659D	LC	77573
MC CARTY	100	495B	NEH	77029
N. MC CARTY	3300	455Y	NEH	77029
N. MC CARTY	3900	455Y	NEH	77013
MC CARTY LN	100	539P	LP	77571
MC CEARLEY DR	15600	367M	CY	77429
MC CHAREN	6500	411B	NWC	77086
MC CLEAREN DR	10700	531W	SWH	77096
MC CLEAREN DR	11600	571E	SWH	77035
MC CLEESTER DR	4000	333D	NCC	77373
MC CLELLAN CIR	1	335H	NEH	77339
MC CLELLAND CIR	1700	453M	NEH	77093
MC CLENDON	2000	532H	SWH	77030
MC CLESKEY RD	21400	256P	SEM	77357
W. MC CLESKY	0	255R	SEM	77357
MC CLOSKY	12700	413P	NCC	77037
MC CLURD CT	13200	328T	NWC	77429
MCCOLLOUGH ST	0	339K	HU	77336
MC COLLUM PARK RD	9900	503V	BC	77520
MC COMB	3000	453N	NWH	77022
MC CONN	15000	617R	SEH	77598
MC CONN CT	400	617R	SEH	77598
MC CONNELL PLACE LN	0	369H	NWC	77070
MC CONNICO DR	100	496W	GP	77547
MC CORMICK	5200	494X	SEH	77023
MC CORMICK	5400	534C	SEH	77023
MC CORMICK CT	7600	407H	NWC	77095
MCCORMICK CT	7600	407G	NWC	77095
MC CORMICK DR	16300	407H	NWC	77095
MC COWN	2800	252A	SEM	77385
MC COY LN	19500	295L	SEM	77365
MC CRACKEN RD	5400	374V	NCC	77032
MC CRAKKEN CIR	11100	369K	NWC	77429
MC CRAREY DR	2800	411M	NWC	77088
MCCRARY PLANTATION	2000	524P	NWF	77406
MC CUE RD	2200	491U	SWH	77056

Street Name	Block	Pg/Sq	Loc	Zips
MC CULLOCH CIR	2700	491Y	SWH	77056
MC CULLOUGH LN	5700	462X	NEC	77521
MC CULLUM RD	6600	571W	SWH	77489
MC DADE	8500	450Q	NWH	77080
MC DANIEL	600	453M	NEH	77022
MC DANIEL	1300	463A	MB	77520
MC DANIEL	1700	454J	NEH	77093
MC DANIEL	7800	462T	NEC	77521
MCDANNALD PARK LN	0	375Y	NEC	77396
MCDANNALD PARK LN	0	375Y	NEC	77396
MC DERMED DR	4000	532W	SWH	77025
MC DERMED DR	4300	531Y	SWH	77035
MC DERMOTT	100	538T	DP	77536
MC DERMOTT CT	2900	615Q	PL	77581
MC DERMOTT DR	4900	414D	NCC	77032
MC DERMOTT DR	13900	374Z	NCC	77032
MC DONALD	0	530C	SWH	77063
MC DONALD	200	536G	PA	77506
MC DONALD	1300	538N	DP	77536
MC DONALD	1400	492F	SWH	77007
MC DONALD	1400	616P	PL	77581
MC DONALD CT	3000	251P	SWM	77380
MC DONALD RD	0	487B	SWC	77094
MC DONALD RD	25500	251P	SWM	77380
MCDONALD RD	25600	251P	WD	77380
MC DOUGAL LN	0	249N	SWM	77354
MC DOWAL	0	333H	NCC	77373
MC DOYLE RD	13400	574U	SEH	77048
MC DUFFIE	1100	492R	SWH	77019
MC DUFFIE	2800	492V	SWH	77098
MC DUGALD	1000	375D	HM	77338
MC ENROE MATCH DR	0	331N	NWC	77379
MC EWEN	4600	453U	NEH	77009
MC FARLAND	300	494Q	SEH	77011
MC FARLAND	1600	502S	BT	77520
MC FARLAND RD	100	412D	NCC	77060
MC FARLAND RD	200	413A	NCC	77060
MC FERON RD	23700	295H	SEM	77365
MC GALLION	8500	453G	NEH	77022
MC GALLION	9400	413Y	NEH	77076
MC GEE	5400	454U	NEH	77026
MC GEE	18000	325B	NWC	77447
MC GEE LN	8200	570B	SWH	77071
MC GEE RD	100	419Q	BR	77532
MCGEE LAKE CT	1400	526X	NEF	77407
MCGILL RD	0	406P	NWC	77433
MC GINNIS	1600	616P	PL	77581
MC GINNIS-MONDAY DR	0	258P	SEM	77357
MC GINTY DR	5700	409Y	NWC	77041
MC GOWEN	100	493T	SWH	77006
MC GOWEN	1000	493T	SWH	77002
MC GOWEN	1100	493V	SEH	77004
MC GOWEN	3500	494W	SEH	77004
MCGOWEN	500	292L	SP	77373
MC GRAGER DR	20300	258T	SEM	77357
MCGRATH DR	0	656W	AV	77511
MC GRATH RD	13400	573S	SWH	77047
MC GREGOR RD	0	253C	SEM	77302
MC GREGOR RD	0	254A	SEM	77302
MC GREW	6400	534Q	SEH	77087
McGUINNESS DR	0	253S	SEM	77386
MCGUIRE RD	0	659E	LC	77573
MCHARD RD	0	615G	PL	77581
MC HARD RD	2600	613G	NEB	77584
MC HARD RD	4100	610H	NEF	77489
MC HARD RD	5000	611E	NEF	77053
MC HARD RD	8200	612E	NEF	77053
MC HENRY	7000	534R	SEH	77087
MC HENRY	7400	535N	SEH	77087
MC ILHENNY	300	493P	SWH	77006
MC ILHENNY	1000	493P	SWH	77002
MC ILHENNY	1400	493V	SEH	77004
MC ILHENNY	3400	494W	SEH	77004
MC INTOSH	600	493C	NEH	77009
MC INTOSH CIR	0	246T	SWM	77355
MC INTOSH RD	26200	246T	SWM	77355
MC INTOSH BEND DR	0	569U	NEF	77477
MC INTYRE	200	612A	NEF	77053
MC KAMY CT	2500	371R	NWC	77067
MC KAMY DR	10900	371R	NWC	77067
MC KAUGHAN RD	2800	374A	NEH	77032
MC KAY	0	335X	NEH	77338
MC KAY	0	375B	NEH	77338
MC KAY BRIDGE	0	338P	NEC	77346
MC KEAN DR	2100	450G	NWH	77080
MC KEE	100	493M	NEH	77002
MC KEE	1500	493D	NEH	77009
MC KEEVER RD	0	610W	MC	77459
MCKENDREE PARK DR	6400	408V	NWC	77041
MCKENZIE PARK CREEK DR	0	291E	NWC	77389
MCKENZIE RIDGE DR	21200	296J	SEM	77365
MC KIBBEN	100	658M	LC	77573
MC KINLEY	3800	533Y	SEH	77051
MC KINLEY	11500	411M	NWC	77038
MCKINLEY CT	0	614U	PL	77581
MC KINLEY LN	3400	411V	NWH	77088
MCKINLEY RUN DR		325N	NWC	77447
MC KINNEY	0	543L	BC	77520
MC KINNEY	100	493Q	DT	77002
MC KINNEY	1100	493Q	DT	77002
MC KINNEY	1101	493Q	DT	77010
MC KINNEY	1200	493Q	DT	77010
MC KINNEY	1700	502N	BT	77520
W. MC KINNEY	1900	493J	SWH	77019
MC KINNEY	1900	541C	BT	77520
MC KINNEY	2000	493R	SEH	77003
MC KINNEY	3200	502N	BT	77521
MC KINNEY	3600	494T	SEH	77023
MC KINNEY	7400	495W	SEH	77011
MC KINNEY	30600	248Y	NWC	77375
MCKINNEY LN	0	417D	NEC	77044
MC KINNEY LN	7900	460T	HG	77562
MC KINNEY RD	0	543K	CCO	77520
MC KINNEY RD	100	419Q	BR	77532
MC KINNEY RD	300	542M	CCO	77520
MC KINNEY PARK LN	0	494S	SEH	77003
MCKINNEY RIDGE DR	0	578S	SEH	77059
JAMES TERRACE LN	0	578S	SEH	77059
MC KINSTRY BLVD	6100	571P	SWH	77085
MCKINZIE CIR	19100	255U	SEM	77365
MCKINZIE W. CIR	21600	255U	SEM	77365
MC KISSICK	2000	657K	FR	77546
MC KNIGHT	5200	571A	SWH	77035
MC KNIGHT LN	19300	335S	NEH	77338
MC KNIGHT RD	5100	614W	NEB	77584
MC LAIN BLVD	11600	570L	MC	77071
MC LEAN	0	500C	SEC	77521
MC LEAN	7500	533Y	SEH	77051
MC LEAN RD	2600	614V	PL	77584
MC LEARY	900	494F	NEH	77020
MC LEOD	14800	413A	NEH	77060
MC LEODS LN	11900	490K	BH	77024

Street Name	Block	Pg/Sq	Loc	Zips
MC MAHON CIR	16000	287G	NWC	77377
MC MASTERS	100	536H	PA	77506
MCMEANS DR	20300	372D	NCC	77073
MC MILLAN	3200	493J	SWH	77007
MCMULLEN LN	1	258R	NEC	77357
MC NAIR	12600	496H	NEH	77015
MC NAIR	13700	497G	NEC	77015
MC NAIR STATION RD	0	460Y	MN	77521
MC NAY DR	2300	537K	PA	77506
MC NEE RD	0	532Q	SWH	77054
MC NEIL	1200	493D	NEH	77009
MC NULTY	13000	574Q	SEH	77048
MC PHAIL	100	288H	TB	77375
MC PHAIL RD	1200	501R	BT	77521
MC SHAN LN	23700	296G	SEM	77365
MC SPADON	23400	296K	SEM	77365
MC SWAIN RD	12600	368C	NWC	77429
MC TIGHE DR	100	531H	BL	77401
MC VOY DR	100	659D	LC	77573
MCWHORTER ST	0	339K	HU	77336
MC WILLIAMS DR	6500	412W	NWH	77091
MEADE CT	2300	658P	LC	77573
MEADE RD	4500	613Z	NEB	77584
MEADOR DR	7100	500K	BT	77520
MEADOW	0	409Q	JV	77040
MEADOW	100	494E	NEH	77020
MEADOW AVE	0	459M	HG	77562
MEADOW CT	300	616Z	FR	77546
N. MEADOW CT	5900	577D	PA	77505
S. MEADOW DR	5800	577D	PA	77505
MEADOW LN	0	381C	LCO	77535
MEADOW LN	0	529W	SWH	77477
MEADOW LN	0	568D	SG	77478
MEADOW LN	0	660C	KE	77565
MEADOW LN	5300	614X	PL	77584
MEADOW LN	11500	569R	SF	77477
MEADOW LN	18800	286M	NWC	77377
MEADOW LN	22900	287H	NWC	77377
MEADOW LN	24400	296L	SEM	77365
MEADOW LN	26300	484P	NEF	77494
MEADOW RD	5400	609S	NEF	77479
MEADOW ABBEY DR	0	366J	NWC	77433
MEADOW ARBOR CT	20000	486P	SWC	77450
MEADOW ASH	21100	525H	NEF	77407
MEADOWBANK DR	0	568W	SG	77479
MEADOWBANK DR	4100	619G	TL	77586
MEADOW BAY CT	1300	568W	SG	77479
MEADOW BEAUTY CT	1	251J	WD	77381
MEADOW BELLE CT	20800	337Q	NEC	77346
MEADOW BEND	0	409A	NWC	77065
MEADOW BEND CT	12200	569A	MD	77477
MEADOWBEND DR	0	446Z	NWH	77084
MEADOW BEND DR	100	659D	LC	77573
MEADOW BEND DR	400	616V	FR	77546
MEADOW BEND LN	9800	408D	NWC	77065
MEADOW BEND TERRACE LN	0	416Z	NEC	77044
MEADOW BERRY	0	568D	SG	77478
MEADOW BERRY DR	12200	569A	MD	77477
MEADOW BIRCH LN	0	446J	NWC	77449
MEADOW BIRCH LN	0	446J	NWC	77449
S. MEADOW BIRD CIR	8300	610G	SWH	77489
N. MEADOW BIRD CIR	8300	610G	SWH	77489
W. MEADOW BIRD CIR	17200	610G	SWH	77489
E. MEADOW BIRD CIR	17200	610G	SWH	77489
MEADOWBLOOM LN	4700	446H	NWC	77449
MEADOW BLUFF CT	6100	526N	NEF	77407
MEADOW BRANCH CT	9200	408B	NWC	77095
MEADOW BRANCH DR	1300	568W	SG	77479
MEADOW BRIAR	600	657Z	LC	77573
MEADOW BRIAR DR	2200	568A	SG	77498
MEADOW BRIAR DR	12300	569E	SF	77477
MEADOW BRIAR DR	13100	488Y	SWH	77082
MEADOWBRIAR LN	7600	490Z	SWH	77063
MEADOWBROOK	800	501K	BT	77521
MEADOW BROOK	17200	459W	CV	77530
MEADOW BROOK CT	2800	659D	LC	77573
MEADOWBROOK DR	8000	535U	SEH	77017
MEADOWBROOK FARM RD	16300	527B	SWC	77082
MEADOWBROOK FARMS RD	0	525A	NEF	77494
MEADOWBROOK M H	0	375H	HM	77396
MEADOWBROOK M H	0	376E	HM	77396
MEADOWBROOK SQUARE	0	408P	NWC	77084
MEADOW BUTTE DR	17200	331R	NWC	77090
MEADOWCHASE CT	9600	409A	NWC	77065
MEADOWCHASE DR	11300	409A	NWC	77065
MEADOWCHASE LN	4200	371B	NWC	77014
MEADOW COVE LN	17400	407Y	NWC	77084
MEADOW CREEK	2800	659H	LC	77573
MEADOW CREEK CT	2800	659H	LC	77573
MEADOW CREEK CT	36800	246C	SWM	77355
MEADOW CREEK DR	1800	616S	PL	77581
MEADOWCREEK DR	2700	609D	MC	77459
MEADOW CREEK LN	5400	536S	SEH	77017
MEADOW CREEK RD	15700	323W	NWC	77447
MEADOWCREEK TRAIL	17700	527E	NEF	77407
MEADOW CREST	4900	539X	LP	77571
MEADOW CREST	8100	570B	SWH	77071
MEADOW CREST CT	12200	569A	MD	77477
MEADOW CREST DR	11700	569A	MD	77477
MEADOWCREST LN	3500	569W	SG	77478
MEADOWCROFT BLVD	0	568W	NEF	77479
MEADOW CROFT DR	7800	490Z	SWH	77063
MEADOW CROSS LN	23200	485P	NEF	77494
MEADOW CROSSING LN	0	407T	NWC	77449
MEADOW CROSSING LN	17600	407F	NWC	77095
MEADOW DALE	0	568D	SG	77478
MEADOWDALE DR	11800	569A	MD	77477
MEADOWDALE DR	12200	568D	MD	77477
MEADOW DAWN CT	0	484Z	NEF	77494
MEADOW DAWN LN	0	484Z	NEF	77494
MEADOW DEW RD	0	411D	NWC	77038
MEADOW EDGE LN	0	446H	NWC	77084
MEADOW EDGE LN	1600	292X	NWC	77388
MEADOW ESTATES LN	14200	367A	NWC	77429
MEADOWFAIR	11900	413T	NEH	77076
MEADOW FAIR CT	0	568W	SG	77479
MEADOWFAIR CT	1	251F	WD	77381
MEADOW FALLS	0	246F	SWM	77355
MEADOW FALLS	11700	328M	NWC	77377
MEADOW FALLS LN	0	408A	NWC	77095
MEADOWFERN DR	100	372L	NWH	77067
MEADOWFIELD ST	0	445N	NWC	77493
MEADOWFIELD CREEK WY	5300	331A	NWC	77379
MEADOW FORD CT	9300	375V	NEC	77396
MEADOW FOREST	0	246E	SWM	77355
MEADOW FOREST LN	4200	297U	NEH	77345
MEADOWFOX PLACE	4900	291E	NWC	77389
MEADOW FROST LN	12400	416Z	NEC	77044
MEADOWGALE LN	0	446H	NWC	77449
MEADOW GARDENS DR	2200	618G	SEH	77062
MEADOW GATE DR	100	658N	LC	77573
MEADOW GATE DR	12300	569E	SF	77477

Street Name	Block	Pg/Sq	Loc	Zips
MEADOWGATE DR	22100	334A	NCC	77373
MEADOW GLADE CIR	3400	297T	NEH	77345
MEADOW GLADE CT	1400	568W	SG	77479
MEADOWGLEN	4800	614N	NEB	77584
MEADOW GLEN	7900	570G	MC	77071
MEADOWGLEN CT	12200	568D	SF	77477
MEADOW GLEN DR	0	381C	LCO	77535
MEADOW GLEN DR	0	381G	LCO	77535
MEADOW GLEN DR	500	501R	BT	77521
MEADOWGLEN DR	12200	569A	MD	77477
MEADOWGLEN LN	7600	490Z	SWH	77063
MEADOWGLEN LN	9300	490W	SWH	77063
MEADOWGLEN LN	9700	489Z	SWH	77042
MEADOWGLEN LN	11100	489Y	SWH	77082
MEADOW GLEN RD	400	616V	FR	77546
MEADOWGLEN CHASE	0	489X	SWH	77082
MEADOWGLEN COVE	0	489X	SWH	77082
MEADOWGLEN CREST	0	489X	SWH	77082
MEADOWGLEN RIDGE LN	0	484N	NEF	77494
MEADOWGOLD LN	4000	297T	NEH	77345
MEADOWGRASS LN	2700	488T	SWH	77082
MEADOWGREEN	11900	413T	NEH	77076
MEADOW GREEN DR	1600	570X	MC	77489
MEADOW GREEN DR	2300	615K	PL	77581
MEADOW GROVE DR	200	412V	NEH	77037
MEADOW GROVE TRAIL	3900	578U	SEH	77059
MEADOW HAVEN CIR	0	366J	NWC	77433
MEADOW HAWK CT	7000	408Q	NWC	77041
MEADOW HAWK DR	11800	616K	SEC	77089
MEADOW HEIGHTS DR	17100	407L	NWC	77095
MEADOWHIGH LN	0	332H	NCC	77373
MEADOWHILL CT	3400	291Q	NWC	77388
MEADOW HILL DR	1400	568W	SG	77479
MEADOWHILL DR	20800	291Q	NWC	77388
MEADOWHILL DR	22000	291Q	NWC	77389
MEADOW HOLLOW	0	528Z	NEF	77478
MEADOWHOLLOW DR	11800	569A	MD	77477
MEADOWHOLLOW DR	12200	529W	MD	77477
MEADOWHURST CIR	22200	286L	NWC	77377
MEADOWHURST DR	2500	614S	NEB	77584
MEADOWICK DR	11000	490R	PP	77024
MEADOWIVY LN	0	406Y	NWC	77449
MEADOW JOY CT	11700	616D	SEC	77089
MEADOW JOY DR	11300	616D	SEC	77089
MEADOW KNOLL DR	500	569U	NEF	77477
MEADOW LAKE	0	247A	SWM	77355
MEADOW LAKE CT	13600	417W	NEC	77044
MEADOWLAKE DR	0	417X	NEC	77044
MEADOW LAKE LN	100	459M	HG	77562
MEADOW LAKE LN	3400	492N	SWH	77027
MEADOW LAKE LN	5200	491T	SWH	77056
MEADOW LAKE LN	6100	491S	SWH	77057
MEADOW LAKE LN	7800	490V	SWH	77063
MEADOW LAKE LN	10000	489V	SWH	77042
MEADOW LAKE LN	11300	489T	SWH	77077
MEADOW LAKE LN	12300	488V	SWH	77077
MEADOWLAKE RD	3500	537H	PA	77503
MEADOW LAKE HILLS CT	0	291H	NWC	77389
MEADOW LAKES DR	0	366V	NWC	77433
MEADOW LAKES DR	1300	568W	SG	77479
MEADOWLAND DR	9600	490W	SWH	77063
MEADOW LANE CT	12200	568D	MD	77477
MEADOW LARK	900	538L	DP	77536
MEADOWLARK	1000	536N	SEH	77017
MEADOW LARK AVE	800	656B	FR	77546
MEADOW LARK LN	600	501L	BT	77521
MEADOWLARK LN	900	568Q	SG	77478
MEADOW LARK LN	1900	539T	LP	77571
MEADOWLARK LN	2100	659S	LC	77573
MEADOWLARK LN	3500	291Q	NWC	77388
MEADOWLARK LN	5000	444Z	KT	77493
MEADOW LARK LN	14000	288P	NWC	77377
MEADOW LARK LN	18800	286H	NWC	77377
MEADOWLARK CREEK CT	0	445E	NWC	77493
MEADOWLARK WAY	3200	614X	PL	77584
MEADOWLAWN	100	580Q	SA	77571
MEADOWLAWN	6600	534C	SEH	77023
MEADOW LEA DR	1	453F	NEH	77022
MEADOWLEAF LN	12700	414F	NCC	77039
MEADOW LIGHT DR	0	527W	NEF	77469
MEADOW LILLY LN	3900	446M	NWC	77449
MEADOWLINE DR	12900	488Y	SWH	77082
MEADOWLINK	100	413S	NEH	77037
MEADOWLINK	200	412V	NEH	77037
MEADOWLOCKE LN	1800	568Y	SG	77478
W. MEADOW LOOP	3400	577D	PA	77505
E. MEADOW LOOP	3400	577D	PA	77505
MEADOW MANOR CT	1900	618F	SEH	77062
MEADOW MILL FOREST LN	0	416Z	NEC	77044
MEADOWMIST CT	3000	612Q	PL	77584
MEADOWMOOR RD	7800	412V	NCC	77037
MEADOW OAK DR	3100	331T	NWC	77068
MEADOW OAKS DR	24700	484L	NEF	77494
MEADOWOOD CIR	4800	501E	BT	77521
MEADOWOOD DR	4600	501E	BT	77521
MEADOW PALM DR	15500	326T	NWC	77433
MEADOW PARK	0	484H	NEF	77494
MEADOW PARK	1500	539S	LP	77571
MEADOW PARK CIR	2100	610N	MC	77459
MEADOW PARK CT	12200	569A	MD	77477
MEADOW PARK DR	4700	573H	SEH	77048
MEADOW PARKWAY	0	659H	LC	77573
MEADOW PARKWAY DR	100	659D	LC	77573
MEADOWPASS	11900	413T	NEH	77076
MEADOW PINES CT	11500	529W	SWH	77477
MEADOW PINES DR	12100	529W	SWH	77477
MEADOW PLACE	4900	539X	LP	77571
MEADOW PLACE CT	11700	570B	SWH	77071
MEADOW PLACE DR	0	570B	SWH	77071
MEADOW PLACE DR	3700	527B	SWC	77082
MEADOW POINT	400	659H	LC	77573
MEADOW POINT CT	0	408B	NWC	77095
MEADOW POND CIR	23000	485U	NEF	77450
MEADOW POND DR	2900	485U	NEF	77450
MEADOW POND DR	8000	609V	MC	77459
MEADOW PRAIRIE ST	0	445N	NWC	77493
MEADOW RANCH PKWY	0	525V	NEF	77407
MEADOW RANCH PKWY	0	526S	NEF	77407
MEADOW RIDGE DR	0	412V	NEH	77037
MEADOW RIDGE DR	12300	569E	SF	77477
MEADOWROCK DR	22200	291L	NWC	77389
MEADOW ROSE CT	19300	337L	HM	77346
MEADOW ROSE PLACE	1	250A	WD	77382
MEADOW RUE	11000	251P	WD	77380
MEADOW RUE CT	1400	568W	SG	77479
MEADOW RUN	0	616V	FR	77546
MEADOW RUN CT	12900	371F	NWC	77066
MEADOWS	0	419M	CB	77532
MEADOWS BLVD	2100	659G	LC	77573
MEADOWS CT	0	283B	NWC	77484
MEADOW SAGE	0	366U	NWC	77433
MEADOWS CROSSING	0	658N	LC	77573

Street Name	Block	Pg/Sq	Loc	Zips
MEADOWS FOREST DR	0	658N	LC	77573
MEADOWSHIRE	7500	413S	NEH	77037
MEADOWSHIRE	9000	413J	NCC	77037
MEADOWSIDE	5800	657V	LC	77573
MEADOWSIDE DR	1	568V	SG	77478
MEADOWSIDE DR	15900	618G	SEH	77062
MEADOWSIDE PARK DR	0	327U	NWC	77429
MEADOWS POND DR	0	660E	LC	77573
MEADOWS PONDS	0	659H	LC	77573
MEADOW SPRINGS DR	0	612K	PL	77545
MEADOW SPRINGS DR	3700	296V	NEH	77339
MEADOW STAR CT	1	251A	WD	77381
MEADOWSTAR DR	1500	568W	SG	77479
MEADOW STONE CT	23300	485K	NEF	77494
MEADOWSTREAM CT	0	525D	NEF	77450
MEADOWS WAY	18500	447J	NWC	77084
MEADOWSWEET DR	1500	568W	SG	77479
MEADOW SWEET DR	13600	328X	NWC	77429
MEADOWSWEET DR	22200	245Q	SWM	77355
MEADOW TERRACE DR	16200	527C	SWC	77082
MEADOWTHORN CT	4700	617X	SEC	77546
MEADOW TIMBERS DR	0	331Q	NWC	77379
MEADOWTRACE DR	6200	290C	NWC	77389
MEADOW TRAIL CT	300	616Z	FR	77546
MEADOW TRAIL LN	400	616Z	FR	77546
MEADOW TRAIL LN	11700	529W	SWH	77477
MEADOW TRAIL LN	11800	569A	MD	77477
MEADOW TREE CT	20300	291Z	NWC	77388
MEADOW TREE LN	2400	291Z	NWC	77388
MEADOW VALE	0	490Z	SWH	77063
MEADOWVALE DR	7600	490W	SWH	77063
MEADOW VALLEY LN	12000	569A	MD	77477
MEADOW VALLEY LN	14200	568A	SG	77498
MEADOW VIEW	0	412V	NEH	77037
MEADOWVIEW	21100	286S	NWC	77377
MEADOWVIEW	21200	285V	NWC	77377
MEADOW VIEW CT	400	616V	FR	77546
MEADOW VIEW CT	8600	409G	JV	77040
MEADOWVIEW DR	2900	610F	MC	77459
MEADOWVIEW DR	7500	413J	NCC	77037
MEADOWVIEW DR	11800	368D	NWC	77429
MEADOW VIEW LN	0	616V	FR	77546
MEADOW VILLAGE DR	15300	408F	NWC	77095
MEADOWVILLE DR	3400	615B	PL	77581
MEADOW VINE	9300	417X	NEC	77044
MEADOWVINE DR	9300	417S	NEC	77044
MEADOW VISTA BLVD	8700	369R	NWC	77064
MEADOW VISTA CT	500	609V	MC	77459
MEADOW VISTA DR	8000	609V	MC	77459
MEADOW WALK LN	10800	371V	NWC	77067
MEADOW WAY CIR	1	524U	NEF	77406
MEADOW WAY DR	2400	610A	MC	77459
MEADOW WAY DR	11400	616C	SEC	77089
MEADOWWICK DR	500	501R	BT	77521
MEADOW WIDE DR	1100	570T	MC	77489
MEADOW WIND DR	0	616J	PL	77089
MEADOW WOOD CT	300	659H	LC	77573
MEADOW WOOD DR	0	614G	PL	77581
MEADOW WOOD DR	3500	537M	PA	77503
MEADOW WOOD LN	400	616V	FR	77546
MEADOW WOOD GREEN	37600	246F	SWM	77355
MEADOW WOOD PARK DR	0	446D	NWC	77449
MEADOWYORK	7500	412V	NEH	77037
MEADS	1000	458Z	CV	77530
MEADVILLE	7700	575B	SEH	77061
MEADWAY CT	12700	488Z	SWH	77082
MEADWAY DR	3000	488Z	SWH	77082
MEADWAY DR	6100	528C	SWH	77072
MEAGAN HILLS CT	0	485X	NEF	77494
MEAGAN SPRINGS DR	0	329M	NWC	77379
MEANDERING BROOKE LN	0	570Z	SWH	77489
MEANDERING MEADOW LN	18200	447P	NWC	77084
MEANDERING OAK LN	0	406L	NWC	77433
MEANDERING TRAIL	2200	296V	NEH	77339
MEANDERING TRAIL	2600	297S	NEH	77339
MEASE CT	4200	538N	PA	77503
MEATH CIR	0	615R	PL	77581
MEAUX DR	9100	530W	SWH	77031
MECCA LN	15600	571Z	SWH	77053
MECHANIC	300	288H	TB	77375
MECO LN	10900	449Y	NWH	77043
MECOM RD	2800	374A	NEH	77032
MEDALLION POINTE CT	5500	525D	NEF	77450
MEDALLION POINTE DR	20700	525D	NEF	77450
MEDANI CT	0	368W	NWC	77095
MEDELL	0	529A	SWH	77072
MEDELLIN	1000	537K	PA	77506
MEDFIELD DR	12600	528D	SWH	77082
MEDFORD CT	100	568V	SG	77478
MEDFORD DR	8500	574A	SEH	77033
MEDICAL CIR	3900	577A	PA	77504
E. MEDICAL CENTER BLVD	100	618U	SEC	77598
MEDICAL CENTER BLVD	100	618X	WB	77598
MEDICAL CENTER DR	0	613E	PL	77584
MEDICAL CENTER DR	5500	484F	KT	77494
MEDICAL COMPLEX DR	13400	288L	TB	77375
MEDICAL PLAZA DR	900	252A	SD	77380
MEDICI CT	0	610T	MC	77459
MEDICINE BOW CIR	11900	371L	NWC	77067
MEDICINE BOW CT	20000	337U	NEC	77346
MEDICINE BOW DR	19800	337U	NEC	77346
MEDINA	200	535B	SEH	77012
MEDINA CT	0	612V	PL	77584
MEDINA BEND LN	12100	449A	NWC	77041
MEDINA HILLS CT	0	367S	NWC	77433
MEDINAH PLACE	4500	531D	BL	77401
MEDINA LAKE CT	0	328S	NWC	77429
MEDINA LAKE DR	12100	328V	NWC	77377
MEDINA LAKE LN	0	328S	NWC	77429
MEDINA RIVER CT	0	253U	SEM	77386
MEDINA RIVER LN	0	253U	SEM	77386
MEDINA RIVER LOOP	0	253U	SEM	77386
MEDIO DR	8000	527M	NEF	77083
N. MEDIO RIVER CIR	1300	569S	SG	77478
S. MEDIO RIVER CIR	1500	569S	SG	77478
MEDIO VISTA LN	0	406G	NWC	77433
S. MEDITERRANEAN	16300	419C	NEC	77532
N. MEDITERRANEAN	16300	419C	NEC	77532
MEDITERRANEAN CT	300	419C	NEC	77532
MEDITERRA WAY	0	250E	WD	77381
MEDLEY GREEN DR	0	325R	NWC	77433
MEDLOWE CT	14300	327Z	NWC	77429
MEDOLLA CIR	23900	525N	NEF	77469
MEDORA	14100	457F	NEC	77049
MEDWAY DR	1600	252Z	SEM	77386
MEEK	800	493L	SWH	77002
MEEK RD	800	335R	HM	77338
MEEKER CIR	300	379J	NEC	77532
MEEK PASS DR	0	366P	NWC	77433
MEEKS	0	288G	TB	77375
MEEKS BAY CT		484J	NEF	77494
MEER DR	1900	457V	NEC	77015

Street Name	Block	Pg/Sq	Loc	Zips
MEETING LN	14500	408X	NWC	77084
MEETING ST	15600	568T	SG	77478
MEGA ENERGY	0	573Z	SEH	77047
MEGA ENERGY DR	0	573Z	SEH	77047
MEGAN	0	255H	SEM	77357
MEGAN	5600	614R	PL	77581
MEGAN	14900	332D	NCC	77373
MEGAN PLACE DR	8100	408F	NWC	77095
MEGANS FALLS CT	0	375Y	NEC	77396
MEGANS WAY	0	486D	SWC	77094
MEGAN WAY	12700	570K	MC	77489
MEGAN WOODS LOOP	0	616L	SEC	77089
MEGELLAN POINT LN	0	612G	PL	77545
MEGELLAN POINT LAND	5500	449A	NWH	77041
MEGGINSON	13400	574U	SEH	77048
MEIKO DR	2800	572L	SWH	77045
MEINEKE	4100	534M	SEH	77087
MEIRWOODS DR	1600	329C	NWC	77379
MEISTERWOOD DR	13300	368Q	NWC	77065
MELANIE	0	247J	SWM	77362
MELANIE	7700	415W	NEH	77016
MELANIE	28300	244K	WCO	77447
MELANIE LN	5300	381N	NEC	77532
MELANIE LN	13900	614L	PL	77581
MELANIE PARK DR	2100	292N	NWC	77388
MELANIE POINTE	0	249S	NWC	77375
MELANITE AVE	5300	571Y	SWH	77053
MELBA	20200	256J	SEM	77357
MELBA LN	0	252B	SEM	77385
MELBA LN	100	660B	KE	77565
MELBA LN	11000	409Y	NWC	77041
MELBA ROSE CIR	14400	327Y	NWC	77429
MELBOURNE	1	453R	NEH	77022
MELBOURNE	1800	454N	NEH	77026
MELBROOK DR	5700	408Y	NWC	77041
MELCHER DR	13400	572J	SWH	77045
MELCREST ESTATES DR	30700	252V	SEM	77386
MELDA	0	251Y	WD	77380
MELDRUM LN	8700	575M	SEH	77075
MELENDY	0	409P	NWC	77041
MELFORD AVE	1000	613F	NEB	77584
MELFORD DR	1200	488K	SWH	77077
MELHAM LN	22700	334B	NCC	77373
MELIDORO	0	290A	NWC	77387
MELINA LN	24000	289D	NWC	77375
MELINDA	19200	379M	NEC	77532
MELINDA LN	5800	577D	PA	77505
MELINE FIELDS DR	3200	253S	SEM	77386
MELISSA	2100	373Z	NCC	77039
MELISSA DR	1500	252V	SEM	77386
MELISSA LEA LN	8900	410K	NWC	77040
MELISSA SPRINGS DR	17800	329G	NWC	77375
MELITA DR	30800	252U	SEM	77386
MELL LN	6400	458N	NEC	77049
MELLENBROOK LN	0	575Q	SEH	77075
MELLENBROOK LN	26600	366R	NWC	77433
MELLISHAW CT	0	289Z	NWC	77379
MELLON	5000	492Y	SWH	77098
MELLOW BREW	32000	246T	SWM	77355
MELLOW BREW CT	31900	246T	SWM	77355
MELLOW BREW PLACE	16500	246U	SWM	77355
MELLOW BROOK DR	9000	528R	SWH	77099
MELLOWGROVE CT	7600	330B	NWC	77379
MELLOWGROVE LN	18500	330B	NWC	77379
MELLOW LEAF CT	1	251E	WD	77381
MELLOW RIDGE DR	17100	330L	NWC	77379
MELLOW RIDGE DR	17600	330G	NWC	77379
MELLOW WOOD PLACE	1	250C	WD	77381
MELLUS	5300	492L	SWH	77007
MELLVILLE DR	0	616L	SEC	77089
MELMORE DR	0	527W	NEF	77478
MELODY CIR	7600	410P	NWC	77040
MELODY LN	100	616U	FR	77546
MELODY LN	3700	660H	BC	77518
MELODY LN	10900	490H	HC	77024
MELODY CANYON CT	0	524G	NEF	77494
MELODY GARDEN	11600	328X	NWC	77429
MELODY GARDEN LN	0	457U	NEC	77049
MELODY GLEN LN	14300	331U	NWC	77014
MELODY OAKS LN	0	485J	NEF	77494
MELODY PARK	5300	370M	NWC	77066
MELODY PARK	5400	371J	NWC	77066
MELODY PARK LN	8900	456D	NEC	77044
MELODY PEAK LN	0	615K	PL	77581
MELODY VIEW CT	0	327U	NWC	77429
MELODYWOOD CT	400	616U	FR	77546
MELODYWOOD DR	300	616U	FR	77546
MELON	1000	412X	NWH	77091
MELON CREEK LN	0	609Y	MC	77459
MELROSE	7600	453G	NEH	77022
MELROSE PARK	0	413U	NEH	77076
MELTING SHADOWS LN	8700	407D	NWC	77095
MELVA	2600	494J	NEH	77020
MELVERN CT	12700	448D	NWC	77041
MELVILLE	0	420S	BR	77532
MELVILLE DR	100	419V	BR	77532
MELVIN OAKS CT	0	407C	NWC	77095
MELVIN UTLEY	0	660X	DI	77539
W. MELWOOD	600	453W	NWH	77009
MELWOOD	600	453X	NWH	77009
MEMBERS DR	10500	576S	SEH	77089
MEMEL	2900	454S	NEH	77026
MEMORIAL	9800	335Y	HM	77338
N. MEMORIAL BLVD	18800	335Y	HM	77338
MEMORIAL CIR	11400	490Q	PP	77024
S. MEMORIAL CT	1900	537T	PA	77502
N. MEMORIAL CT	1900	537T	PA	77502
MEMORIAL CT	3000	493J	SWH	77007
E. MEMORIAL DR	0	296N	SEM	77365
MEMORIAL DR	600	501T	BT	77520
MEMORIAL DR	1400	493J	SWH	77007
MEMORIAL DR	3000	492J	SWH	77007
MEMORIAL DR	8500	491H	SWH	77024
MEMORIAL DR	10700	490L	PP	77024
MEMORIAL DR	12900	489F	SWH	77079
MEMORIAL DR	14400	488B	SWH	77079
MEMORIAL DR	29500	292D	SEM	77386
MEMORIAL-RIVER OAKS	0	296N	SEM	77365
MEMORIAL BEND	100	489H	SWH	77024
MEMORIAL BLOSSOM DR	0	329M	NWC	77379
MEMORIAL BROOK	1200	487D	NWH	77084
MEMORIAL BROOK	1400	447Z	NWH	77084
MEMORIAL CHASE DR	16900	329L	NWC	77070
MEMORIAL CITY WAY	200	490A	SWH	77024
MEMORIAL COVE	10700	490H	HC	77024
MEMORIAL CREEK DR	8800	329M	NWC	77379
MEMORIAL CREST BLVD	3300	493J	SEH	77007
MEMORIAL CREST DR	17400	329M	NWC	77379
MEMORIAL CROSSING CT	9800	329K	NWC	77375
MEMORIAL ESTATES DR	18000	330E	NWC	77379
MEMORIAL FALLS DR	0	329F	NWC	77375
MEMORIAL FALLS DR	17600	329L	NWC	77375
MEMORIAL GATE DR	0	329M	NWC	77379
MEMORIAL GLEN DR	1000	375D	HM	77338
MEMORIAL GREENS DR	0	489E	SWH	77079
MEMORIAL GROVE DR	9100	329M	NWC	77379
MEMORIAL HERMANN DR	10900	613N	PL	77584
MEMORIAL HIEGHTS DR	700	493J	SWH	77007
MEMORIAL HILLS DR	9000	329M	NWC	77379
E. MEMORIAL LOOP	1000	492F	SWH	77007
W. MEMORIAL LOOP	1500	492E	SWH	77007
MEMORIAL MANOR DR	0	329M	NWC	77379
MEMORIAL MEWS	700	488F	SWH	77079
MEMORIAL MILLS DR	0	329M	NWC	77379
MEMORIAL MIST LN	18400	329F	NWC	77375
MEMORIAL OAKS LN	16800	330P	NWC	77379
MEMORIAL OAKS LN	17800	330J	NWC	77379
MEMORIAL PASS DR	17500	329H	NWC	77379
MEMORIAL PASS DR	20200	526E	NEF	77450
MEMORIAL PINES WAY	9000	329M	NWC	77379
MEMORIAL PK ENTRANCE	0	492F	SWH	77007
MEMORIAL POINT LN	1	490P	PP	77024
MEMORIAL POST LN	0	329M	NWC	77379
MEMORIAL RIDGE DR	17500	329H	NWC	77379
MEMORIAL SAGE DR	0	296N	SEM	77365
MEMORIAL SHOP CITY	0	490A	SWH	77024
MEMORIAL SHORES DR	0	329M	NWC	77379
MEMORIAL SPRINGS CT	0	329F	NWC	77375
MEMORIAL SPRINGS DR	17600	329L	NWC	77375
MEMORIAL SPRINGS PASS	0	329B	NWC	77375
MEMORIAL TRACE DR	17400	329M	NWC	77379
MEMORIAL TRACE LN	3000	493J	SWH	77007
MEMORIAL TRAIL DR	9100	329M	NWC	77379
MEMORIAL TRAIL DR	17800	329K	NWC	77375
MEMORIAL VALLEY DR	9100	329M	NWC	77379
MEMORIAL VIEW DR	0	488C	SWH	77079
MEMORIAL VILLAGE DR	900	490B	SWH	77024
N. MEMORIAL WAY	1900	493K	SWH	77007
MEMORIAL WAY DR	10000	329K	NWC	77375
MEMORIAL WOODS	0	256Q	SEM	77357
MEMORIAL WOODS CIR	900	491D	SWH	77024
MEMORIAL WOODS DR	8600	491D	SWH	77024
MEMORY	4700	502G	BT	77521
MEMORY LN	0	619G	TL	77586
MEMORY LN	1	251Q	WD	77380
MEMORY LN	100	412H	NCC	77037
W. MEMORY LN	25600	247Y	SWM	77355
S. MEMORY LN	25600	247Y	SWM	77355
N. MEMORY LN	25600	247Y	SWM	77355
E. MEMORY LN	25600	247Y	SWM	77355
MEMPHIS	7500	495S	SEH	77011
MEMPHIS	17000	375F	HM	77396
MENAGGIO CT	10900	524R	NEF	77406
MENARD	0	620L	SB	77586
MENARD	1300	620L	SB	77586
MENARD	3800	494N	SEH	77003
MENASCO CT	13800	488F	SWH	77077
MENDECINO GLEN CT	400	298T	NEH	77336
MENDECINO GLEN LN	28400	298X	NEH	77336
MENDEZ	7900	495J	NEH	77029
MENDOCINO DR	15400	527L	SWC	77083
MENDOTA LN	5400	374V	NCC	77032
MENEFEE	0	492D	NWH	77007
MENKING CT	400	490H	HC	77024
MENLO DR	6800	527H	SWC	77083
MENLO CREEK CT	7200	525M	NEF	77407
MENN AVE	0	377D	NEH	77346
MENN COVE AVE	0	378A	NEC	77346
MENORCA COVE DR	0	407J	NWC	77433
MENOR CREST DR	6100	290Q	NWC	77388
MENTMORE DR	8300	330N	NWC	77379
MENWOOD CIR	6400	411P	NWH	77088
MERABROOK DR	22200	485Z	NEF	77450
MERALDO DR	9300	455D	NEH	77078
MERCADO DR	17000	527J	NEF	77083
MERCADO RD	26200	246T	SWM	77355
MERCANT MARK LN	19100	526L	NEF	77407
MERCEDELL DR	19600	295G	SEM	77365
MERCEDES	12400	372G	NWH	77090
MERCEDES LN	4900	453E	NWH	77022
MERCEDES BENZ CT	800	375M	NEC	77396
MERCELIE ST	0	530X	SWH	77031
MERCER	2600	492T	SWH	77027
MERCER	5100	532F	WU	77005
MERCER	13000	248U	NWC	77375
MERCER CT	0	609V	MC	77459
MERCER ESTATES CT	1900	252R	SEM	77385
MERCER FALLS LN	0	657Y	LC	77573
MERCER GAP	8500	410F	NWC	77064
MERCER GROVE DR	0	326K	NWC	77433
MERCHANTILE PKWY	0	445X	NWC	77449
MERCHANT SPRINGS LN	4600	447G	NWC	77084
MERCHANTS WAY	0	445Y	NWC	77449
MERCIER DR	25900	244K	WCO	77447
MERCOAL DR	1600	252Z	SEM	77386
MERCURY DR	300	496N	GP	77029
MERCURY DR	900	496J	JC	77013
MERCURY DR	17200	618U	WB	77058
MERCURY COVE CT	9000	575U	SEH	77075
MERCURY RUN CT	0	293U	NCC	77373
MERCY	0	335C	SEM	77365
MERCY MOSS LN	0	524K	NWF	77406
MERE DR	1100	247K	SWM	77362
MEREDITH	6300	531F	BL	77401
MEREDITH CT	1800	538M	DP	77536
MEREDITH DR	8900	460M	NEC	77562
MEREDITH ALICE DR		366U	NWC	77433
MEREDITH ELISE CT	9800	532S	SWH	77025
MEREDITH GATE CIR	14400	377T	NEC	77044
MEREDITH GATE CT	12900	377X	NEC	77044
MEREWOOD LN	12000	570F	SWH	77071
MERGANSER CT	2500	376F	NEC	77396
MERGANSER DR	0	573Y	SEC	77047
MERGANSER DR	0	573Y	SEC	77047
MERIA COVES DR	17300	367X	NWC	77095
MERIBURR LN	3600	533G	SEH	77021
MERIDA DR	13700	572U	SWH	77047
MERIDIAN	3900	535P	SEH	77017
MERIDIAN BLVD	300	501L	BT	77521
MERIDIAN HILL DR	0	253X	SEM	77386
MERIDIAN LAKES DR	10100	367X	NWC	77095
MERIDIAN PARK DR	0	615N	PL	77581
MERIDIAN PARK LN	0	609T	NEF	77479
MERIDIAN PARK LN	14800	376W	NEC	77396
MERIDIAN SPRINGS LN	0	488T	SWH	77077
MERIGLEN LN	20800	291W	NWC	77388
MERILEE CT	13600	328T	NWC	77429
MERION CIR	4600	578F	PA	77505
MERION DR	2300	659C	LC	77573
MERION LN	5000	500M	BT	77521
MERIS LN	12500	496L	NEH	77015
MERIT WAY CT	12500	408D	NWC	77065
MERKEL	3600	494P	SEH	77003
MERLE	1800	536V	PA	77502
MERLE	8600	574A	SEH	77033
MERLE RD	15800	326P	NWC	77433
MERLET DR	4100	614Z	PL	77584
MERLIN CT	8800	450Z	SV	77055
MERLIN DR	8300	451W	SV	77055
MERLIN DR	8600	450Z	SV	77055
MERLIN LN	0	615P	PL	77581
MERLIN ROOST	0	485E	SWC	77494
MERLIN ROOST CT	0	485E	SWC	77494
MERLINS OAKS CT	1200	329G	NWC	77379
MERLINS OAKS DR	1200	329G	NWC	77379
MERLOT LN	0	451S	NWH	77055
MERLOT RIVER DR	26800	296X	NEC	77339
MERMAID LN	1900	618L	SEH	77062
MERNA DR	9200	410K	NWC	77040
MERONA LN	6300	408U	NWC	77041
MERRIBROOK LN	800	616Y	FR	77546
MERRIBROOK LN	1100	616Y	PL	77581
MERRICK	3200	532J	SWH	77025
MERRICK DR	700	569N	SG	77478
MERRIDEL RD	800	490B	HE	77024
MERRIE LN	100	536X	SH	77587
MERRIE LN	4500	531D	BL	77401
MERRIE WAY LN	200	490Q	PP	77024
MERRIEWOOD DR	900	656H	FR	77546
MERRIEWOOD DR	1200	657E	FR	77546
MERRILANE	100	541D	BT	77520
MERRILL	400	493B	NWH	77009
MERRILL RD	0	420J	NEC	77532
MERRILL HILLS CIR	2200	485R	NEF	77450
MERRILLWOOD DR	19200	337T	NEC	77346
MERRIMAC	4000	414Q	NCC	77093
MERRIMAC DR	1600	658T	LC	77573
MERRIMAC HILLS LN	5200	609S	NEF	77479
MERRIMAC RIDGE LN	600	292L	NCC	77373
MERRIMAC TRACE	25500	485S	NEF	77494
MERRIMAN CT	900	616U	FR	77546
MERRIMONT LN	6200	571K	SWH	77085
MERRITT LN	14800	413A	NEH	77060
MERRITT LN	15100	372Z	NEH	77060
MERRIVALE DR	0	448B	NWC	77084
MERRIWEATHER	400	617M	SEH	77598
MERRIWEATHER	4200	609A	SG	77478
MERRIWOOD LN	6900	413W	NEH	77076
MERRY LN	6600	534C	SEH	77023
MERRYGLEN CT	0	332H	NCC	77373
MERRYMEADOW CT	0	609U	MC	77479
MERRY MEADOW DR	14000	456V	NEC	77049
MERRY MEADOW DR	14300	457S	NEC	77049
MERRYMOUNT CT	400	485C	SWC	77450
MERRYMOUNT DR	22000	485C	SWC	77450
MERRY OAKS DR	24000	293T	NCC	77373
MERRY PINE CT	6100	290Z	NWC	77379
MERSEA DR	5300	446C	NWC	77449
MERSEY CT	22800	255W	SEM	77365
MERSEY DR	14201	332W	NWC	77014
MERSEY DR	19300	255W	SEM	77365
MERSMANN CT	0	371D	NWC	77014
MERT LN	6400	444X	KT	77493
MERTON CT	1900	457V	NEC	77015
MERTON DR	1600	457V	NEC	77015
MERWIN	4400	491Z	SWH	77027
MESA CT	4400	461S	NEC	77521
MESA DR	3400	455Z	NEH	77013
MESA DR	4400	502J	BT	77521
MESA DR	5400	455Q	NEH	77028
MESA DR	9500	415U	NEH	77078
MESA DR	11800	415R	NEC	77016
MESA DR	15000	375U	NEC	77396
MESA RIM CT	0	574V	SEH	77048
MESA BLUFF LN	14700	375U	NEC	77396
MESA BROOK LN	5900	409W	NWC	77041
MESA CANYON CT	6400	526E	NEF	77450
MESA CREEK LN	0	366R	NWC	77433
MESA FOREST LN	0	415Y	NEH	77078
MESA GARDENS DR	15700	408J	NWC	77095
MESA GREEN	0	415Y	NEH	77078
MESA HILLS CT	0	415Y	NEH	77078
MESA HILLS LN	0	415Y	NEH	77078
MESA KNOLL LN	0	415Y	NEH	77078
MESA MOUNTAIN	14100	370A	NWC	77069
MESA PARK DR	2500	371L	NWC	77067
MESA PEAK	0	371L	NWC	77067
MESA POINT CT	9800	367Y	NWC	77095
MESA POINT DR	16400	367Y	NWC	77095
MESA RED CT	15200	325R	NWC	77433
MESA RIDGE RD	3600	449L	NWH	77043
MESA RUN LN	0	415Y	NEH	77078
MESA SPRINGS CT	17200	407L	NWC	77095
MESA TERRACE DR	900	485H	SWC	77450
MESA VALLEY DR	0	253T	SEM	77386
MESA VALLEY LN	0	415Y	NEH	77078
MESA VERDE DR	0	538R	DP	77536
MESA VERDE DR	1000	570P	MC	77489
MESA VERDE DR	1500	659W	LC	77573
MESA VERDE DR	15700	618C	SEH	77059
MESA VERDE DR	27000	249J	SWM	77354
MESA VIEW CT	0	415Y	NEH	77078
MESA VIEW LN	0	415Y	NEH	77078
MESA VILLAGE DR	14800	572T	SEH	77053
MESA VISTA CT	6500	528E	SWC	77083
MESA VISTA DR	14700	528E	SWC	77083
MESA VISTA TERRACE DR	0	367T	NWC	77095
MESA WELLS DR	11600	328D	NWC	77377
MESCALERO	7100	462Z	BT	77521
MESCALERO CANYON CT	17600	367X	NWC	77095
MESCALERO CANYON LN	10000	367X	NWC	77095
MESENBRINK LN	0	457V	NEC	77049
MESIA MEADOW LN	0	405R	NWC	77493
MESITA DR	14700	528E	SWC	77083
MESITA DR	14900	527H	SWC	77083
MESKIL OAKS DR	30600	253S	SEM	77386
MESONES DR	7200	527F	NEF	77083
MESQUITE	1300	413Q	NCC	77093
MESQUITE	4400	414Q	NCC	77093
MESQUITE DR	3400	609J	SG	77479
MESQUITE DR	10800	579C	LP	77571
MESQUITE LN	1100	501M	BT	77521
MESQUITE BEND LN	0	407J	NWC	77433
MESQUITE BRANCH CT	19700	332A	NWC	77388
MESQUITE BRUSH LN	17300	367P	NWC	77095
MESQUITE CANYON DR	17400	367X	NWC	77095
MESQUITE CREEK LN	0	484X	NEF	77494
MESQUITE ESTATES LN	18100	366D	NWC	77429
MESQUITE FALLS LN	0	657K	FR	77546
MESQUITE GROVE LN	0	328S	NWC	77429
MESQUITE HOLLOW LN	12500	568D	SG	77478
MESQUITEMANOR LN	0	526J	NEF	77407
MESQUITE MEADOW LN	0	484X	NEF	77494
MESQUITE MEADOW LN	0	484X	NEF	77494
MESQUITE OAKS TRAIL	0	290D	NWC	77389
MESQUITE RIDGE DR	0	333F	NCC	77073
MESQUITE RIVER		284M	HK	77447
MESQUITE TRAIL LN	0	293Z	NCC	77373
MESSARA	0	255T	SEM	77365
MESSARA DR		289Y	NWC	77379
MESSINA CT	0	616K	PL	77089
MESSINA DR	2300	616K	PL	77581
MESSINA CREST CT	0	524S	NWF	77406
MESSINA HARBOR DR	0	445B	NWC	77493
MESTINA	8200	455G	NEH	77028
MESTINA KNOLL DR	0	296E	SEM	77365
META	8400	453F	NEH	77022
METAIRIE	2200	658K	LC	77573
METCALF	2600	535K	SEH	77012
METCALF	2900	535K	SEH	77017
METCALF	4900	611A	SWH	77053
METERS	300	495A	NEH	77020
METHA RD	26700	292M	SP	77373
METHIL DR	16800	329R	NWC	77379
METHODIST DR	0	446Z	NWC	77084
METHVIN LN	5000	381N	NEC	77532
METRO BLVD	6200	528F	SWC	77083
METRODALE DR	8500	410F	NWC	77040
METRONOME DR	10100	450S	NWH	77080
METRONOME DR	10200	449U	NWH	77043
METROPOLITAN	0	492R	SWH	77006
METYCOVE CT	3300	378S	NEC	77532
METYCOVE DR	18300	378T	NEC	77532
METZ	2400	576G	SEH	77034
METZGER CT	5300	609T	NEF	77479
METZLER CREEK DR	25200	250S	NWC	77389
METZLER HILLS LN	0	328L	NWC	77377
MEWS CIR	12500	488V	SWH	77082
MEXIA SPRINGS CT	0	660P	LC	77573
MEXICAN JOHN RD	21300	256F	SEM	77357
MEYER	900	620P	SB	77586
MEYER	3200	534R	SEH	77087
W. MEYER AVE	500	620L	SB	77586
E. MEYER AVE	500	620L	SB	77586
N. MEYER AVE	1100	620L	SB	77586
MEYER RD	1	258V	NEC	77336
MEYER RD	100	259S	NEC	77336
MEYER RD	1600	332M	NCC	77073
MEYER FOREST DR	9600	531V	SWH	77096
MEYERLAND PLAZA	100	531Q	SWH	77096
W. MEYER PARK	0	330Q	NWC	77379
E. MEYER PARK	0	330Q	NWC	77379
MEYER PARK BLVD	0	531V	SWH	77096
MEYER PARK DR	8500	531R	SWH	77096
MEYERS RD	100	459H	NEC	77562
MEYERSVILLE DR	14000	456V	NEC	77049
MEYERSVILLE DR	14300	457S	NEC	77049
MEYERWOOD DR	4100	532N	SWH	77025
MEYERWOOD DR	4300	531R	SWH	77096
MEYRICK CT	16100	330T	NWC	77379
MEZZOMONTE LN	0	659R	LC	77573
MIAMI	7200	375F	HM	77396
MIAMI CT	2700	656U	FR	77546
MIAMI RD	1300	536Q	PA	77502
MIA RIDGE LN	0	293L	SEM	77386
MIA ROSE CT	0	484Q	NEF	77494
MICA DR	3500	488Y	SWH	77082
MI CASTILLO CT	4600	571R	SWH	77045
MICHAEL	2900	660H	BC	77518
N. MICHAEL CIR	11700	570L	MC	77071
S. MICHAEL CIR	11800	570L	MC	77071
MICHAEL DR	0	376A	HM	77338
MICHAEL DR	900	537J	PA	77506
MICHAEL DR	4800	535R	SEH	77017
MICHAEL DR	21800	285D	SWM	77355
MICHAEL LN	13900	614L	PL	77581
MICHAEL LN	19900	295Q	SEM	77365
MICHAELA WAY	21500	333K	NCC	77338
MICHAELIS	2900	462X	NEC	77521
MICHAELS CREST LN	0	375Y	NEC	77396
MICHAUX	2500	493B	NWH	77009
MICHAUX	3500	453X	NWH	77009
MICHEL	0	287A	SWM	77355
MICHEL RD	13600	288L	TB	77375
MICHELE DR	1800	568A	SG	77498
MICHELINE CIR	7800	570G	MC	77071
MICHELLE CT	9000	411S	NWH	77040
MICHELLE DR	34500	247K	SWM	77362
MICHENER FALLS LN	0	484X	NEF	77494
MICHENER FALLS LN	0	484X	NEF	77494
MICHIGAN	200	659E	LC	77573
MICHIGAN	200	536W	SH	77587
MICHIGAN	1000	535Z	SH	77587
MICHIGAN	1400	492R	SWH	77006
MICHIGAN	3100	540D	BT	77520
MICHNIC LN	9400	369M	NWC	77070
MICHULKA LN	10400	413Z	NEH	77093
MICKE	22000	256Y	SEM	77357
MICKEY WAY	1200	450Y	SV	77055
MICKLE CREEK DR	0	458S	NEC	77049
MICKLEHAM DR	16000	330S	NWC	77379
MICKLER	9700	532S	SWH	77025
MICKLETON DR	8700	412N	NWC	77088
MICKWAYNE CT	6900	370A	NWC	77069
MICLIFF BLVD	2300	331Q	NWC	77068
MICMAC CT	14100	328P	NWC	77429
MICOLLET	6100	415N	NEH	77016
MIDBROOK DR	0	617Z	SEH	77546
MIDCOUNTRY LN	0	373E	NCC	77073
MIDDLE	400	494J	SEH	77003
MIDDLE LN	6000	370G	NWC	77066
MIDDLE RD	0	334Z	NEH	77338
MIDDLE BLUFF TRAIL	0	326Y	NWC	77429
MIDDLEBOROUGH LN	0	568A	NEF	77498
MIDDLEBROOK DR	14200	619E	PA	77058
MIDDLEBROOK DR	15000	618D	PA	77058
MIDDLEBROOK DR	16100	578Z	SEH	77059
MIDDLEBROUGH LN	0	569X	MC	77478
MIDDLEBURG DR	11000	329T	NWC	77377
MIDDLEBURY LN	8100	369D	NWC	77070
MIDDLE CANYON CT	0	525A	NEF	77494
MIDDLECREEK	900	656R	FR	77546
MIDDLE CREEK DR	2000	296Z	NEH	77339
MIDDLECREST LN	11600	289W	NWC	77375
MIDDLECREST HILL CT	0	484Y	NEF	77494
MIDDLE FALLS DR	4800	337C	NEH	77345
MIDDLEFIELD DR	6800	578F	PA	77505
MIDDLE FOREST CT	0	578Z	PA	77059
MIDDLE FOREST DR	16800	578Z	PA	77059
MIDDLEGATE LN	0	526F	NEF	77450
MIDDLEGLEN LN	0	576R	SEH	77034
MIDDLELAKE CT	6400	525H	NEF	77450
MIDDLEOAK GROVE LN	0	484Y	NEF	77494
MIDDLEOAK GROVE LN	0	484Y	NEF	77494
MIDDLEOAK GROVE LN	0	524C	NEF	77494
MIDDLEOAK GROVE LN	0	524C	NEF	77494
MIDDLE OAKS BLVD	15000	487Z	SWH	77082
MIDDLE PARK	1400	577J	PA	77504

Street Name	Block	Pg/Sq	Loc	Zips
MIDDLEROSE LN	10400	369F	NWC	77070
MIDDLESBROUGH LN	1400	569X	MC	77459
MIDDLESBROUGH LN	12700	371F	NWC	77066
MIDDLESPRINGS LN	0	484Y	NEF	77494
MIDDLESPRINGS LN	0	484Y	NEF	77494
MIDDLETON	100	660H	BC	77518
MIDDLETON	300	494N	SEH	77003
MIDDLETON RD	4600	500F	BT	77520
MIDDLETON OAKS CIR	0	455G	NEH	77028
MIDDLEWOOD	7500	490R	SWH	77063
MIDDLEWOOD MANOR LN	0	524C	NEF	77494
MIDDLEWOOD MANOR LN	0	524C	NEF	77494
MIDFIELD DR	6600	451J	NWH	77092
MIDFIELD GLEN CT	13600	578W	SEH	77059
MIDFOREST DR	3800	331W	NWC	77068
MIDGELEY	5900	452B	NWH	77091
MIDHURST DR	11000	529F	SWH	77072
MIDLAKE PARK	31700	252M	SEM	77385
MIDLAND	29600	248C	SWM	77354
MIDLAND CT	700	413B	NCC	77060
MIDLAND DR	400	412D	NEH	77037
MIDLAND DR	3600	613X	NEB	77578
MIDLAND CREEK DR	0	328L	NWC	77377
MIDLAND FIELDS DR	13700	528P	SWC	77083
MIDLAND FOREST DR	7900	411N	NWC	77088
MID LANE	2000	491V	SWH	77027
MIDLANE	12400	614C	BK	77581
MIDLOTHIAN LN	2000	336A	SEM	77339
MIDMONT DR	2400	570Y	MC	77489
MIDNIGHT LN	0	572R	SWH	77047
MIDNIGHT DAWN DR	0	527N	NEF	77083
MIDNIGHT GLEN DR	0	326U	NWC	77429
MIDNIGHT GLEN DR	0	326U	NWC	77429
MIDNIGHT SKY CT	0	527N	NEF	77083
MIDNIGHT STAR CT	2600	657C	SEC	77546
MIDNIGHT SUN LN	0	527P	NEF	77407
MID OAKS CT	17800	330C	NWC	77379
MID PEAK WAY	0	445D	NWC	77449
MID PINES	5700	457S	NEC	77049
MID PINES DR	5900	330X	NWC	77069
MIDPORT LN	600	619V	LC	77565
MIDRIDGE DR	15600	408X	NWC	77084
MIDSHIPWAY	16900	379X	NEC	77532
MIDSTREAM DR	4100	569X	MC	77459
MIDVALE	6000	534Q	SEH	77087
MID WAY	0	297N	NEH	77339
MIDWAY	100	292Q	SP	77373
MIDWAY	6300	455P	NEH	77028
MIDWAY BLVD	600	495U	NEH	77029
MIDWAY CT	0	658V	LC	77573
MIDWAY DR	100	501Q	BT	77521
MIDWAY GARDENS DR	0	253Y	SEM	77386
MIDWAY PASS CT	0	293U	NCC	77373
MIDWAY PLAZA DR	0	333R	NCC	77032
MIDWOOD	11900	371M	NWC	77067
W. MIERIANNE	400	412R	NCC	77037
W. MIERIANNE	900	412Q	NWH	77088
MIERIANNE	2000	413R	NCC	77093
MIERIANNE	2400	414Q	NCC	77093
MIER MANOR CT	0	526W	NEF	77406
MIERWOOD MANOR DR	13500	367H	NWC	77429
MIERWOODS DR	0	329C	NWC	77379
MI ESTADO CT	4600	571R	SWH	77045
MIGHTY BUCCANEER DR	3300	617Y	SEC	77546
MIGHTY ELM CT	6200	297Z	NEH	77345
MIGHTY FALLS CT	7500	407K	NWC	77095
MIGHTY OAKS DR	12000	371E	NWC	77066
MIGHTY OAKS DR	12800	370D	NWC	77066
MIGHTY REDWOOD DR	11500	578Z	PA	77059
MIGNON LN	100	489H	SWH	77024
MIJA LN	1400	620K	SB	77586
MIKADO	100	495W	SEH	77011
MIKULA DR	0	449X	NWH	77043
MILAM	100	493Q	DT	77002
MILAM	2300	493Q	SWH	77006
MILAM	3400	493Q	SWH	77002
MILAM	4900	493W	SWH	77006
MILAM	11700	539R	LP	77571
MILAM LN	0	612V	PL	77584
MILAM LN	0	613S	PL	77584
MILAN DR	13700	572U	SWH	77047
MILAN ESTATES	1	491T	SWH	77056
MILANI RIDGE CT	4500	294N	SEH	77386
MILAN MEADOW CT	0	488T	SWH	77077
MILANO CT	0	524R	NEF	77406
MILANO LN	0	331J	NWC	77379
MILANO LN	0	331J	NWC	77379
MILANO LN	0	659G	LC	77573
MILART	5100	534J	SEH	77021
MILAS WAY	0	527T	NEF	77498
MILAZZO DR	0	525J	NEF	77406
MILAZZO LN	0	659M	LC	77573
MILBRAD	3400	454X	NEH	77026
MILBURN	3200	533F	SEH	77021
MILBURN DR	2600	659C	LC	77573
N. MILBY	1	494N	SEH	77003
MILBY	100	494S	SEH	77003
MILBY	600	620L	SB	77586
MILBY	700	494S	SEH	77023
MILBY	1300	494S	SEH	77003
MILBY	2300	493Z	SEH	77004
MILDA DR	9900	411J	NWH	77088
MILDOGE ST	0	573M	SEH	77048
MILDRED	4300	531M	BL	77401
MILE DR	11400	369N	NWC	77065
MILE DR	12100	368R	NWC	77065
MILEHAM LN	21700	291R	NWC	77388
MILEPOST CT	0	249B	SWM	77354
MILE RUN RD	8500	338W	NEC	77346
MILES	100	660H	BC	77518
MILES	1300	497J	NEH	77015
MILES LOOP RD	0	660H	BC	77518
MILES OAKS PLACE	0	449U	NWH	77043
MILESTONE LN	14400	368A	NWC	77429
MILEY	7100	454R	NEH	77028
MILEY	7300	455P	NEH	77028
MILFOIL LN	6300	528G	SWH	77083
MILFORD	900	493W	SWH	77006
MILFORD	1700	492Z	SWH	77098
MILFORD HAVEN DR	0	332R	NCC	77073
MILFORD PLACE	2300	371H	NWC	77014
MILHOLLAND DR	1700	252V	SEM	77386
MILL	0	568N	SG	77478
MILL CT	12500	369L	NWC	77070
MILL RD	14600	375W	NEH	77396
MILLARD	7700	455T	NEH	77028
MILLAU VIADUCT WAY	0	377D	NEC	77346
MILLBANKS DR	12200	569D	SWH	77031
MILLBANKS DR	12400	570E	SWH	77031
S. MILLBEND DR	700	252N	WD	77380
S. MILLBEND DR	900	251U	WD	77380
N. MILLBEND DR	1200	252N	WD	77380
N. MILLBEND DR	1400	251L	WD	77380
MILLBRAE LN	7300	408L	NWC	77041
MILL BRANCH LN	14900	568A	NEF	77498
MILLBRIDGE DR	3600	618D	SEH	77059
MILLBRIDGE HEIGHTS LN	0	295L	SEM	77365
MILL BRIDGE WAY	3600	297T	NEH	77345
MILLBROOK	200	490Q	PP	77024
MILLBROOK DR	0	257E	SEM	77357
MILLBROOK DR	3100	613X	NEB	77584
MILLBROOK DR	7800	407H	NWC	77095
MILLBROOK LN	3100	609M	MC	77459
MILLBURY DR	1600	570U	MC	77489
MILLBURY DR	9400	531U	SWH	77096
MILL CANYON CT	15900	367C	CY	77429
MILL CREEK CT	34200	247L	SWM	77362
MILLCREEK DR	0	571Z	SWH	77053
MILL CREEK DR	0	609A	SG	77479
MILL CREEK DR	1800	452S	NWH	77008
MILL CREEK DR	2200	609A	SG	77478
MILL CREEK DR	4700	461N	BT	77521
MILL CREEK RD	300	247L	SWM	77362
MILLCREEK MANOR LN	0	366U	NWC	77433
MILL CREEK WAY RD	33800	247L	SWM	77362
MILLCREST LN	9300	527P	NEF	77083
MILLCROSS LN	23300	485K	NEF	77494
MILLDALE	0	369K	NWC	77070
MILLENIUM RD	0	333Y	NCC	77073
MILLER	0	418W	NEC	77049
MILLER	0	458A	NEC	77049
MILLER	0	578C	LP	77505
MILLER	300	620T	KE	77565
MILLER	1400	494S	SEH	77003
MILLER	4100	660M	BC	77518
MILLER	10000	370Y	NWC	77086
MILLER AVE	1300	444Z	KT	77493
MILLER'S LANDING DR	16000	458N	NEC	77049
MILLER CUT-OFF RD	300	539A	SEC	77571
MILLER GLEN LN	7600	528L	SWH	77072
MILLER HOUSE LN	15500	370U	NWC	77086
MILLER MEADOWS LN	0	326T	NWC	77433
MILLER MORE DR	0	366P	NWC	77433
MILLER RANCH RD	1500	613K	PL	77584
MILLER RIDGE LN	4500	609Y	NEF	77459
MILLER ROAD 1	15200	458E	NEC	77049
MILLER ROAD 1	15500	457H	NEC	77049
MILLER ROAD 2	6300	458A	NEC	77049
MILLER ROAD 3	7700	457H	NEC	77049
MILLERS LN	24500	404V	NWC	77493
MILLERS CHESTNUT ST	0	457G	NEC	77049
MILLERS CREEK CT	4300	526X	NEF	77406
MILLER SHADOW LN	6600	609Y	NEF	77459
MILLERS ROCK CT	0	250R	NWC	77389
MILLERS RUN LN	15100	527Z	NEF	77498
MILLERS WATER LN	0	659H	LC	77573
MILLERS WAY	7900	407H	NWC	77095
MILLERTON LN	2200	485R	SWC	77450
MILLER VALLEY DR	5800	370C	NWC	77066
MILLER VIEW DR	6000	452D	NWH	77091
MILLER VIEW DR	6300	412Z	NWH	77091
MILLER WILSON RD	0	379L	NEC	77532
MILLER WILSON RD	5400	419C	NEC	77532
MILLER WILSON RD	17000	379Z	NEC	77532
MILLET	8200	535F	SEH	77012
MILLS FALLS DR	12600	411D	NWC	77038
MILL FERRY LN	19100	406V	NWC	77449
MILLFORD CT	6600	457Q	NEC	77049
MILLFORD SPRINGS DR	0	524K	NWF	77406
MILL FOREST RD	17000	618T	WB	77598
MILL GARDEN CT	13800	578W	SEH	77059
MILLGATE DR	22400	334A	NCC	77373
MILLGLEN CT	14100	568A	SG	77498
MILLGROVE LN	900	490B	HE	77024
MILL HAVEN CIR	0	366J	NWC	77433
MILL HEDGE DR	12500	369K	NWC	77070
MILL HOLLOW DR	15800	448E	NWC	77084
MILLHOUSE CIR	21500	333E	NCC	77073
MILLHOUSE CT	21500	333E	NCC	77073
MILLHOUSE RD	1700	333E	NCC	77073
MILLICAN FALLS DR	0	326U	NWC	77429
MILLICAN FALLS DR	0	326U	NWC	77429
MILLICENT	8200	454E	NEH	77093
MILLIE BUSH DR	0	487Y	SWC	77082
MILLIES CREEK LN	0	366R	NWC	77433
MILLIKEN	7500	454K	NEH	77016
MILLIKEN'S BEND	1400	659W	LC	77573
MILLINGHAM CT	4600	337C	NEH	77345
MILL LAKE DR	2300	337A	NEH	77339
MILL LANE DR	12400	369L	NWC	77070
MILL OAK DR	4200	447E	NWC	77084
MILLOAK DR	19100	337X	NEC	77346
MILLOAK STATION CT	19200	337T	NEC	77346
MILLPARK DR	2100	251V	WD	77380
MILL PASS CT	0	484L	NEF	77494
MILLPASS LN	0	366V	NWC	77433
MILL PASS WAY	0	484L	NEF	77494
MILL PATH CT	18500	447S	NWC	77084
MILL PLACE CT	400	568K	SG	77498
MILL POINT DR	15700	618C	SEH	77059
MILL POINT DR	16400	578Y	SEH	77059
MILL POINT PLACE	1	251T	WD	77380
MILLPOND DR	700	568K	SG	77498
MILL POND LN	25300	293N	NCC	77373
MILLPORT	6600	451A	NWH	77092
MILL RIDGE CT	0	296T	SEM	77339
MILL RIDGE DR	0	295R	SEM	77365
MILL RIDGE DR	12300	369J	NWC	77429
MILLRIDGE LN	16600	407G	NWC	77095
MILLRIDGE BEND DR	10200	369L	NWC	77070
MILLRIDGE FOREST CT	0	369K	NWC	77070
MILLRIDGE NORTH DR	10200	369K	NWC	77070
MILLRIDGE PINES	0	369K	NWC	77070
MILLRIDGE PINES CT	10900	369K	NWC	77070
MILL RIVER CT	4400	578E	PA	77505
MILLROCK CIR	3900	609E	SG	77479
MILL RUN DR	900	568K	SG	77498
MILLRUN DR	7800	407H	NWC	77095
MILLS	1800	494E	NEH	77026
MILLS	2000	282U	WL	77484
MILLS CIR	10500	369F	NWC	77070
MILLS CT	1	494E	NEH	77026
MILLS LN	800	656H	FR	77546
MILLS LN	12100	368R	NWC	77065
MILLS RD	0	295D	SEM	77365
MILLS RD	8000	370J	NWH	77064
MILLS RD	9100	369M	NWC	77070
MILLS RD	11100	369K	NWC	77429
MILLS, J W RD	200	619L	PA	77586
MILLS BEND	12900	369F	NWC	77070
MILLS BRANCH DR	0	295M	SEM	77365
MILLS BRANCH DR	0	296N	SEM	77365
MILLS BRANCH DR	2300	297U	NEH	77345
MILLS BREEZE DR	0	369L	NWC	77070
MILLSCOTT DR	12500	369K	NWC	77070
MILLS COVE	10500	369G	NWC	77070
MILLS CREEK CT	1700	336B	NEH	77339
MILLS CREEK DR	2300	336B	NEH	77339
MILLS CREEK MEADOW DR	0	369L	NWC	77070
MILLS CROSSING LN	0	369L	NWC	77070
MILLS CUT	10600	369F	NWC	77070
MILLS FLAT	10600	369F	NWC	77070
MILLSFORK DR	0	366E	NWC	77433
MILLSGLEN DR	0	366J	NWC	77433
MILLS GROVE DR	0	369L	NWC	77070
MILL SHADOW CT	1000	568J	SG	77498
MILL SHADOW DR	1000	568J	SG	77498
MILL SHADOW DR	9700	369L	NWC	77070
MILLSHAW DR	10300	369L	NWC	77070
MILLSHIRE WAY	7600	407G	NWC	77095
MILLSITE RD	12200	416J	NEC	77050
MILLS LAKE CT	24800	484M	NEF	77494
MILLS LANDING	10600	369F	NWC	77070
MILLS MANOR DR	0	484G	NEF	77494
MILLS MEADOW LN	19500	486M	SWC	77094
MILL SONG CT	1000	568J	SG	77498
MILLS PARK LN	14600	327W	NWC	77429
MILLS PASS DR	0	369G	NWC	77070
MILLS POINT DR	0	369L	NWC	77070
MILLS PRAIRIE	10600	369F	NWC	77070
MILL SPRING DR	3600	450K	NWH	77080
MILL SPRINGS DR	17000	330F	NWC	77379
MILLS RAPIDS	13100	369F	NWC	77070
MILLS RIVER	13100	369F	NWC	77070
MILLS RUN DR	0	369G	NWC	77070
MILLS STATION CT	15000	328W	NWC	77429
MILLSTEAD CT	0	408W	NWC	77084
MILLSTONE	0	407H	NWC	77095
MILLSTONE	2200	333J	NCC	77073
MILLSTONE CT	900	568K	SG	77498
MILLSTONE CANYON LN	0	615M	PL	77089
MILLSTONE CANYON LN	4400	609Y	NEF	77459
MILLSTONE ESTATES LN	14300	366D	NWC	77429
MILLSTONE HOLLOW LN	0	484T	NEF	77494
MILLSTONE PARK LN	0	328A	NWC	77429
MILLSTONE RIDGE LN	19700	446C	NWC	77449
MILLSTONE VALLEY CT	900	292C	NCC	77373
MILLS TRACE CT	1800	486K	SWC	77450
MILLS TRAIL LN	0	369L	NWC	77070
MILL STREAM LN	100	372Z	NEH	77060
MILL STREAM LN	200	373W	NEH	77060
MILLSTREAM BEND LN	12900	328K	NWC	77377
MILLSTREAM WAY	12100	449A	NWC	77041
MILLSVIEW RD	9000	369H	NWC	77070
MILLS VILLAGE DR	0	369L	NWC	77070
MILLS WALK DR	10400	369K	NWC	77070
MILLS WAY	10600	369F	NWC	77070
MILLS WHARF	10600	369F	NWC	77070
S. MILL TRACE DR	1	251A	WD	77380
N. MILL TRACE DR	100	251A	WD	77381
MILL TRAIL CT	200	568J	SG	77498
MILL TRAIL DR	100	568J	SG	77498
MILL TRAIL LN	11700	369Q	NWC	77070
MILLVALE DR	2300	337C	NEH	77345
MILL VALLEY DR	900	568K	SG	77498
MILL VALLEY RD	11700	573M	SEH	77048
MILLVAN DR	12300	369K	NWC	77070
MILL VIEW LN	0	376E	HM	77396
W. MILL VILLAGE CIR	17300	407F	NWC	77095
E. MILL VILLAGE CIR	17300	407F	NWC	77095
MILLVILLE DR	600	412Y	NWH	77091
MILL WAY DR	11400	369J	NWC	77429
MILLWAY DR	12400	369K	NWC	77070
MILL WHEEL DR	12500	369K	NWC	77070
MILLWOOD DR	1800	452S	NWH	77008
MILLWOOD COVE DR	0	376N	NEC	77396
MILLWOOD HILL DR	0	407C	NWC	77095
MILLWOOD LAKE DR	2800	609F	NEC	77459
MILLWOOD PASS CIR	0	526T	NEF	77469
MILLWOOD PASS CIR	0	526T	NEF	77469
MILLY	6700	614D	BK	77581
MILNER	100	499V	BT	77520
MILNER RD	14600	374P	NEH	77032
MILNER PASS LN	0	377E	NEC	77346
MILNERS POINT DR	11300	371P	NWC	77066
MILO DR	13200	419R	BR	77532
MILO PASS LN	0	328L	NWC	77377
MILORED	0	495Q	NEH	77029
MILREDGE	8000	535U	SEH	77017
MILRIG CT	17200	527W	NEF	77407
MILROY LN	2500	371P	NWC	77066
MILTON	3800	532A	WU	77005
MILWAUKEE	200	453U	NEH	77009
MILWAUKEE	2400	454S	NEH	77026
MILWEE	4800	451K	NWH	77092
MIMBROUGH	9700	495V	NEH	77029
MIMOSA	0	531R	SWH	77096
MIMOSA	700	536Q	PA	77506
MIMOSA	4500	531P	BL	77401
MIMOSA CT	2200	658P	LC	77573
MIMOSA DR	2200	492Q	SWH	77019
MIMOSA LN	12000	368D	NWC	77429
MIMOSA RD	1200	570T	MC	77489
MIMOSA GLEN DR	20300	291Y	NWC	77388
MIMOSA SPRING DR	12800	328L	NWC	77377
MIMOSA VIEW LN	0	411A	NWC	77086
MIMOSSA	0	658Z	LC	77573
MINARD DR	6000	406T	NWC	77449
MINA WAY	0	531C	SWH	77081
MINCHEN DR	1300	538L	DP	77536
MINCING LN	15200	458W	NEC	77530
MINDEN	5400	454U	NEH	77026
MINDEN OAKS DR	18600	331C	NWC	77388
MINDY PARK CT	5300	330U	NWC	77069
MINDY PARK LN	14200	330U	NWC	77069
MINDYWOOD CT	15800	331N	NWC	77068
MINERAL BLUFF LN	0	377F	NEC	77346
MINERAL CREEK CT	0	660K	LC	77573
MINERAL CREEK CT	5400	330H	NWC	77379
MINERAL HAVEN DR	4100	573Z	SEH	77048
MINERAL ISLAND LN	0	524R	NEF	77406
MINERAL JUNCTION DR	10200	367X	NWC	77095
MENERAL ROCK LN	9300	527S	NEF	77407
MINERAL RUN LN	3400	253P	SEM	77386
MINERAL SPRINGS CIR	0	375Z	NEC	77396
MINERAL SPRINGS LN	0	375Z	NEC	77396
MINERS BEND DR	16600	367U	NWC	77095
MINETTA	14200	570M	SWH	77035
MINGLEWOOD BLVD	3500	534L	SEH	77023
MINGLEWOOD LN	1200	657A	FR	77546
MINIMAX	2300	452W	NWH	77008
MINK CIR	18900	246E	SWM	77355
MINK LAKE DR	18600	246E	SWM	77355
MINNESOTA	500	576A	SH	77587
MINNESOTA	2100	576E	SEH	77034
MINNESOTA	3200	500Z	BT	77520
MINNESOTA	8000	576J	SEH	77034
MINNESOTA	9300	576N	SEH	77075
MINOLA	6300	492F	SWH	77007
MINOLA OAKS DR	0	409F	NWC	77064
MINOOKA	0	458L	NEC	77049
MINOR	0	571K	SWH	77085
MINSMERE CIR	9200	329H	NWC	77379
MINSTREL RD	0	333X	NCC	77073
MINT ARBOR	0	371E	NWC	77066
MINTER	100	453X	NWH	77009
MINTER FALLS CT	16000	327Y	NWC	77429
MINTER FALLS LN	14300	327Y	NWC	77429
MINTGLADE LN	0	371D	NWC	77014
MINTGLADE LN	2300	371D	NWC	77014
MINTGLADE LN	2300	371D	NWC	77014
MINTGLADE LN	2300	371D	NWC	77014
MINTGLADE LN	2300	371D	NWC	77014
MINTO CT	4000	572S	SWH	77053
MINT TEAL CT	0	371K	NWC	77066
MINT TRACE CT	0	253S	SEM	77386
MINT TRAILS	0	371F	NWC	77066
MINTURN LN	10200	409G	NWC	77064
MINTWOOD LN	0	330K	NWC	77379
MINTZ LN	14900	331U	NWC	77014
MINUTEMAN LN	0	656X	FR	77546
MINUTEMEN CT	12000	371M	NWC	77067
MIRABEAU DR	20400	336Q	NEH	77338
MIRABELLA	0	525J	NEF	77406
MIRABELLA DR	0	406C	NWC	77433
MIRA BLOSSOM	7000	377B	NEC	77346
MIRACLE LN	13400	571K	SWH	77085
MIRADOR LN	22300	339W	NEC	77532
MIRAGE CT	500	656B	FR	77546
MIRAGLEN	6500	494Z	SEH	77023
MIRAGLEN DR	3500	613Y	NEB	77584
MIRAMAN CREST DR	22500	289M	NWC	77375
MIRAMAR	1200	493W	SWH	77006
MIRAMAR	3200	580R	SA	77571
MIRAMAR CT	0	620K	SB	77586
MIRAMAR CT	2400	620K	SB	77586
MIRAMAR DR	0	660G	LC	77539
MIRAMAR DR	0	660G	LC	77539
MIRAMAR BEND DR	0	290J	NWC	77375
MIRAMAR CREST CT	8200	290J	NWC	77375
MIRAMAR CREST DR	22400	290J	NWC	77375
MIRAMAR GREEN	1900	620K	SB	77586
MIRAMAR HEIGHTS CIR	0	609T	NEF	77479
MIRAMAR LAKE DR	22700	289M	NWC	77375
MIRAMAR SHORES DR	11800	409A	NWC	77065
MIRAMICHI CT	4100	572W	SWC	77053
MIRA MONTE CT	15600	527L	SWC	77083
MIRA MONTE DR	15500	527L	SWC	77083
MIRANDA	14400	374W	NCC	77039
MIRANDOLA LN	0	524M	NEF	77406
MIRA VISTA DR	15100	527M	SWC	77083
MIRAWOOD	9200	455H	NEH	77078
MIRIAM	1	541B	BT	77520
MIRIAM LN	12500	570G	MC	77071
MIRKWOOD LN	14300	331Y	NWC	77014
MIRMAR ESTATES CT	22900	252L	SEM	77385
MIRMAR ESTATES LN	11200	252M	SEM	77385
MIRO CT	500	332B	NWC	77388
MIRROR CT	3500	331D	NWC	77388
MIRRORCREEK DR	0	376Q	NEC	77396
MIRROR LAKE DR	1500	620J	EL	77586
MIRROR LAKE RD	18700	331D	NWC	77388
W. MIRROR RIDGE CIR	1	250A	WD	77382
E. MIRROR RIDGE CIR	100	250A	WD	77382
MIRROR RIDGE CT	1	250A	WD	77382
MIRROR RIDGE DR	1	250A	WD	77382
MISCHIRE DR	4000	532N	SWH	77025
MISCINDY PLACE	14500	328T	NWC	77429
MISSARAH LN	13400	368B	NWC	77429
MISS CARMEN LN	0	296G	SEM	77365
MISS DEBRA LN	23600	296G	SEM	77365
MISSION	1100	539R	LP	77571
MISSION	2000	619V	LC	77565
MISSION	21100	292P	SP	77373
MISSION DR	6100	614U	PL	77584
MISSION RD	11300	369N	NWC	77065
MISSIONARY RIDGE LN	16700	527P	NEF	77083
MISSION BAY DR	7100	527M	SWC	77083
MISSION BELL DR	6600	527H	SWC	77083
MISSION BLUFF LN	0	527N	NEF	77407
MISSION BRIDGE CT	15800	527Q	NEF	77083
MISSION CANYON LN	0	256X	SEM	77365
MISSION CHASE DR	1300	488K	SWH	77077
MISSION COURT DR	7100	528J	SWC	77083
MISSION COVE LN	0	526P	NEF	77407
MISSION CREEK CIR	1900	446Y	NWC	77084
MISSION CREEK DR	2200	446U	NWC	77084
MISSION CREST CT	15800	527Q	NEF	77083
MISSION ESTATES CT	15800	527Q	NEF	77083
MISSION ESTATES DR	8200	527Q	NEF	77083
MISSION FALLS DR	0	368W	NWC	77095
MISSION FOREST DR	15400	527R	NEF	77083
MISSION FORT LN	0	526Q	NEF	77407
MISSION GATE CT	15800	527Q	NEF	77083
MISSION GLEN DR	15800	527Q	NEF	77083
MISSION GREEN DR	15000	527R	NEF	77083
MISSION GROVE DR	3100	331P	NWC	77068
MISSION HILLS CT	2800	485R	NEF	77450
MISSION HILLS DR	14600	527M	SWC	77083
MISSION HILLS LN	21900	485R	NEF	77450
MISSION LAKE CT	4800	526W	NEF	77407
MISSION MANOR LN	0	526L	NEF	77407
MISSION MEADOW LN	0	526K	NEF	77407
MISSION MILL CIR	2200	446U	NWC	77084
MISSION MILL LN	19500	446U	NWC	77084
MISSION OAK DR	15400	527R	NEF	77083
MISSION OAKS DR	0	527J	NEF	77083
MISSION PARK DR	19300	526G	NEF	77407
MISSION PINES CT	7500	526K	NEF	77407
MISSION PINES LN	19700	526K	NEF	77407
MISSION RIDGE LN	16800	332Q	NCC	77073
MISSION RIDGE PLACE	0	250A	WD	77382
MISSION SPRINGS DR	1400	486L	SWC	77450
MISSION TEJAS PLACE	0	366S	NWC	77433
MISSION TERRACE CT	15800	527Q	NEF	77083
MISSION TERRACE DR	8600	527Q	NEF	77083
MISSION VALLEY CT	13000	370C	NWC	77069
MISSION VALLEY DR	2900	610F	MC	77459
MISSION VALLEY DR	13000	370C	NWC	77069
MISSION VIEJO	3300	502F	BT	77521
MISSION VIEW CT	15800	527Q	NEF	77083
MISSION VILLAGE DR	15800	527G	SWC	77083
MISSISSIPPI	100	495V	NEH	77029
MISSISSIPPI	500	576A	SH	77587
MISSISSIPPI	1500	541A	BT	77520
MISSISSIPPI	8600	495U	NEH	77029
MISSOURI	500	576A	SH	77587
MISSOURI	1000	493S	SWH	77006

Street Name	Block	Pg/Sq	Loc	Zips
MISSOURI	1200	540D	BT	77520
MISSOURI	1900	492V	SWH	77019
MISSOURI AVE	4100	660W	GCO	77539
MISSOURI CITY DR	0	570T	MC	77489
MISSOURI PACIFIC	26600	247Y	SWM	77355
MISSY FALLS DR	0	368U	NWC	77065
MISSY RIDGE CT		366U	NWC	77433
MIST LN	0	370M	NWC	77066
MIST LN	10000	369L	NWC	77070
MIST CREEK CT	5300	657V	LC	77573
MIST CREEK LN	0	375X	NEC	77396
MISTFLOWER LN	6600	407S	NWC	77449
MIST GREEN LN	3500	293P	NCC	77373
MISTIC HILL	19400	486D	SWC	77094
MISTIC MEA CT	10800	369T	NWC	77064
MISTIC MEADOWS CT	10800	369T	NWC	77064
MISTIC MOON CT	11000	369T	NWC	77064
MISTING FALLS LN	0	612K	PL	77545
MISTISSIN LN	3800	572W	SWC	77053
MIST LAKE CT	24900	484M	NEF	77494
MISTLETOE LN	900	336F	NEH	77339
MISTLETOE RD	4800	577C	PA	77505
MISTOVER DR	0	299X	NEC	77336
MISTRA DR	6700	578A	PA	77505
MISTWOOD CT	2000	612H	PL	77584
MISTWOOD LN	0	488F	SWH	77077
MISTY LN	500	656H	FR	77546
MISTY LN	3600	615V	PL	77581
MISTY LN	5100	577C	PA	77505
MISTY LN	18900	286L	NWC	77377
MISTY ALCOVE CT	3300	297P	NEH	77345
MISTY ARBOR DR	6800	571J	SWH	77085
MISTY ARCH LN	11500	366R	NWC	77433
MISTY BAY LN	0	612K	PL	77545
MISTY BEND DR	1200	484G	NEF	77494
MISTY BLUE LN	18900	328F	NWC	77377
MISTY BLUFF DR	13600	571J	SWH	77085
W. MISTYBREEZE CIR	1	250D	WD	77381
E. MISTYBREEZE CIR	1	250D	WD	77381
MISTY BRIDGE	9400	575V	SEH	77075
MISTY BROOK LN	0	615B	PL	77581
MISTY BROOK LN	100	657R	LC	77573
MISTY BROOK LN	3100	447N	NWC	77084
MISTY BROOK BEND CT	6400	290U	NWC	77379
MISTYBROOKBEND LN	21200	290U	NWC	77379
MISTY CANYON LN	17700	407F	NWC	77095
MISTY CHASE LN	15600	572W	SWC	77053
MISTY CLIFF LN	28500	293A	SEM	77386
MISTY CLOUD LN	0	417C	NEC	77044
MISTY COUNTRY DR	0	573E	SEH	77051
MISTY COVE CT	3700	660X	DI	77539
MISTY COVE DR	7700	337M	NEC	77346
MISTY COVE DR	19100	446L	NWC	77449
MISTY CREEK	4200	609K	MC	77459
MISTY CREEK DR	16900	330H	NWC	77379
MISTY CREEK LN	0	615L	PL	77581
MISTY CROSS CT	17200	407Y	NWC	77084
MISTY CROSSING LN	0	290T	NWC	77379
MISTY CYPRESS CT	14300	328P	NWC	77429
MISTY DAISY DR	10800	573F	SEH	77051
MISTY DALE DR	6600	407S	NWC	77449
MISTY DAWN TRAIL	0	326S	NWC	77433
MISTY DAWN TRAIL	15300	325V	NWC	77433
MISTY DAY LN	300	379E	NEC	77532
MISTY DRIFT LN	0	484T	NEF	77494
MISTY EMBER LN	0	524T	NWF	77406
MISTY FALL LN	21600	445M	NWC	77449
MISTY FALLS	0	617X	SEC	77546
MISTY FERN CT	7700	407K	NWC	77095
MISTY FIELD TRAIL	0	337Q	NEC	77346
MISTY FOREST CT	15400	331N	NWC	77068
MISTY GARDENS CT	3900	296V	NEH	77339
MISTYGATE CT	0	293Y	NCC	77373
MISTY GLADE LN	0	484U	NEF	77494
MISTY GLEN LN	1600	658W	LC	77573
MISTY GLEN LN	11500	569B	SWH	77099
MISTY GREEN CT	10800	573F	SEH	77051
MISTY GROVE CIR	1	251X	WD	77380
MISTY GROVE CT	2000	618B	SEH	77062
MISTY GROVE CT	15500	326T	NWC	77433
MISTY GROVE DR	2600	613X	NEB	77578
MISTY HARBOR DR	0	612F	PL	77545
MISTY HARBOUR CIR	1900	619Z	LC	77573
MISTYHAVEN PLACE	1	251A	WD	77381
MISTY HEATH LN	0	408W	NWC	77084
MISTY HEATH LN	0	485S	NEF	77494
MISTY HEATH LN	0	488W	SWH	77082
MISTY HEATHER CT	4300	579W	PA	77059
MISTY HILL LN	1700	338A	NEH	77345
MISTY HILLS DR	13200	328T	NWC	77429
MISTY HOLLOW DR	4500	610P	MC	77459
MISTY HOLLOW DR	15200	330V	NWC	77068
MISTY ISLAND CT	5700	525C	NEF	77494
MISTY ISLE CT	21000	446J	NWC	77449
MISTY JADE LN	18100	326R	NWC	77429
MISTY KNOLL CT	14200	617H	SEH	77062
MISTY LACE DR	17800	376C	NEC	77396
MISTY LAGOON CIR	0	298U	NEC	77336
MISTY LAKE	500	620J	EL	77586
MISTY LAKE BLVD	1	568J	SG	77498
MISTY LAKE CT	1100	568F	SG	77498
MISTY LAKE DR	1100	568E	SG	77498
MISTY LAKE LN	0	614N	PL	77581
MISTY LANDING CT	8200	375Y	NEC	77396
MISTY LANTERN LN	12900	377K	NEC	77044
MISTY LAUREL DR	12300	372E	NWC	77014
MISTY LEA LN	700	332J	NWC	77090
MISTY LEA LN	1000	331M	NWC	77090
MISTYLEAF CT	0	609P	NEF	77479
MISTY LEAF CT	13900	417B	NEC	77044
MISTY LEAF LN	0	417B	NEC	77044
MISTYLEAF LN	6900	609N	MC	77459
MISTY LOCH LN	15800	408S	NWC	77084
MISTY LODGE CT	0	525M	NEF	77407
MISTY LOFT LN	0	366Q	NWC	77433
MISTY MANOR	400	487A	SWC	77094
MISTY MEADOW	0	488D	SWH	77079
MISTY MEADOW	5800	657V	LC	77573
MISTY MEADOW CT	1000	289A	TB	77375
MISTY MEADOW LN	14100	489A	SWH	77079
MISTY MEADOW CREEK LN	0	335N	NCC	77338
MISTY MILL	4400	609E	SG	77479
MISTY MILL DR	12900	408Z	NWC	77041
MISTYMONT DR	12400	369L	NWC	77070
MISTY MOON DR	5300	337S	NEC	77346
MISTY MOORES DR	17400	328L	NWC	77377
MISTY MORNING	100	660A	LC	77573
MISTY MORNING	11300	613J	PL	77584
MISTY MORNING CT	4600	610P	MC	77459
MISTY MORNING CT	11300	613J	PL	77584
MISTY MORNING DR	7100	337Y	NEC	77346
W. MISTY MORNING TRACE	1	251A	WD	77381
N. MISTY MORNING TRACE	1	251A	WD	77381
MISTY MORNING TRACE	6800	525L	NEF	77407
MISTY MOSS CT	22000	255W	SEM	77365
MISTY MOSS LN	12100	369K	NWC	77070
MISTY MOUNTAIN LN	0	484Q	NEF	77494
MISTY OAKS DR	28900	298U	NEC	77336
MISTY OCEAN CT	0	573E	SEH	77051
MISTY PALOMA DR	16400	458N	NEC	77049
MISTY PARK DR	2900	488Y	SWH	77082
MISTY PEAK LN	11800	376H	NEC	77346
MISTY PINES CT	19700	337S	NEC	77346
MISTY PINES DR	19700	337N	NEC	77346
MISTY POINT	1	251X	WD	77380
MISTY POINT DR	0	486N	SWC	77450
MISTY POND CT	0	328E	NWC	77377
MISTY PRAIRIE LN	0	527N	NEF	77407
MISTY RIDGE DR	3600	376G	NEC	77396
MISTY RIDGE LN	8100	570F	SWH	77071
MISTY RIVER DR	10300	371X	NWC	77086
MISTY RIVER TRAIL	2100	297V	NEH	77345
MISTY RIVER WAY	20100	326P	NWC	77433
MISTY SAGE CT	8600	375Z	NEC	77396
MISTY SAGE CT	10800	573F	SEH	77051
MISTY SANDS LN	13501	577W	SEH	77034
MISTY SHADOW CT	10600	449H	NWH	77041
MISTY SHADOW CT	10800	573E	SEH	77051
MISTY SHADOW LN	0	612F	PL	77545
MISTY SHADOWS DR	4300	449H	NWH	77041
MISTY SHORE DR	0	485U	NEF	77450
MISTY SHORE DR	400	660E	LC	77573
MISTY SHORE LN	0	612P	PL	77545
MISTY SPRINGS DR	2800	613X	NEB	77578
MISTY SPRINGS LN	6500	330G	NWC	77379
MISTY STONE CT	15000	377Y	NEC	77044
MISTY SUMMER LN	0	376V	NEC	77396
MISTY SUMMIT DR	10700	371T	NWC	77086
MISTY TERRACE CT	6200	525G	NEF	77494
MISTY TIMBERS WAY	4200	297X	NEH	77345
MISTY TRAIL	10000	411N	NWH	77088
MISTY TRAIL DR	8300	407H	NWC	77095
MISTY TRAILS LN	0	657Z	LC	77573
MISTY VALE LN	8000	575T	SEH	77075
MISTY VALLEY CT	0	573E	SEH	77051
MISTY VALLEY DR	11400	371E	NWC	77066
MISTY VALLEY DR	12100	370H	NWC	77066
MISTY VIEW BLVD	1	568J	SG	77498
MISTY VIEW LN	3500	617Y	SEC	77546
MISTY VILLAGE CT	0	293Z	NCC	77373
MISTY VINE CT	0	411N	NWH	77088
MISTY WATER CIR	9500	409H	NWC	77064
MISTY WATERS LN	0	408J	NWC	77095
MISTY WATERS LN	0	484W	NEF	77494
MISTY WATERS LN	2000	658U	LC	77573
MISTY WAY RD	700	379Q	NEC	77532
MISTY WILLOW DR	13000	369M	NWC	77070
MISTY WILLOW LN	11200	289K	NWC	77375
MISTY WIND CT	2900	659M	LC	77573
MISTY WOOD	18400	255S	SEM	77365
MISTYWOOD DR	300	332T	NWC	77090
MISTYWOODS LN	0	296T	SEM	77365
MITCHELL	0	412R	NCC	77088
MITCHELL	16000	327D	NWC	77429
MITCHELL CT	0	657U	LC	77573
MITCHELL LN	12500	370M	NWC	77066
MITCHELL LN	22300	256Y	SEM	77357
W. MITCHELL RD	100	413N	NCC	77037
MITCHELL RD	100	413N	NCC	77037
E. MITCHELL RD	200	413N	NCC	77037
MITCHELL COVE DR	0	295L	SEM	77365
MITCHELLDALE	5000	451Q	NWH	77092
MITCHELL PASS LN	17200	377J	NEC	77346
MITTLESTEDT	4500	330Y	NWC	77069
MIXON BLVD	0	533J	SWH	77021
MIZE RD	4300	576H	SEH	77504
MIZELL	100	460S	HG	77562
MOARY FIRTH DR	16300	448E	NWC	77084
MOARY FIRTH DR	16500	447H	NWC	77084
MOBILE	0	536P	PA	77506
MOBILE	7100	375F	HM	77396
MOBILE	7400	495S	SEH	77011
MOBILE	13300	497E	NEH	77015
MOBILE CT	0	371Z	NWC	77038
MOBILE DR	500	536K	PA	77506
MOBUD DR	6300	531J	SWH	77074
MOBUD DR	7900	530F	SWH	77036
MOCCASIN CT	11700	329N	NWC	77377
MOCCASIN BEND DR	6300	330G	NWC	77379
MOCK RD	11100	414U	NEC	77093
MOCKER NUT ST	0	463S	CCO	77520
W. MOCKINGBIRD	0	614X	PL	77584
MOCKINGBIRD	100	619L	PA	77586
MOCKINGBIRD	1900	502S	BT	77520
MOCKINGBIRD	2700	619U	LC	77565
MOCKINGBIRD CIR	1	530P	SWH	77074
MOCKINGBIRD LN	0	616U	FR	77546
MOCKINGBIRD LN	100	536U	PA	77502
MOCKINGBIRD LN	800	570P	MC	77489
MOCKINGBIRD LN	1700	492P	SWH	77019
MOCKINGBIRD LN	1900	539T	LP	77571
MOCKINGBIRD LN	5000	444Z	KT	77493
MOCKINGBIRD LN	5300	614X	PL	77584
MOCKINGBIRD LN	11600	490K	BH	77024
MOCKINGBIRD LN	16500	246U	SWM	77355
MOCKINGBIRD LN	18600	286H	NWC	77377
MOCKINGBIRD LN	26200	257H	RF	77357
MOCKING BIRD HILL LN	0	450J	NWH	77080
MOCKINGBIRD MEADOWS CT	0	291H	NWC	77389
MOCKINGBIRD PLACE	10800	252M	SEM	77385
MOCKINGBIRD VALLEY DR	19100	406V	NWC	77449
MOCKINGBIRD WAY	900	568U	SG	77478
MODBURY	17200	329M	NWC	77379
MODENA CT	0	616P	PL	77581
MODENA DR	1200	616K	PL	77581
MODENA GARDENS DR	0	445E	NWC	77493
MODESTE DR	1400	659S	LC	77573
MODESTO DR	6300	527H	SWC	77083
MODICA DR	0	445E	NWC	77493
MODISTE	1200	450Z	SV	77055
MODLEY CT	8200	412Q	NWH	77088
MOERS	8600	575G	SEH	77075
MOERS RD	0	489K	SWH	77077
MOERS RD	9600	575Q	SEH	77075
MOFFITT LN	3000	610D	SWH	77489
MOGGY CT	500	292W	NWC	77388
MOHAVE CIR	4700	461S	NEC	77521
MOHAVE LN	0	336Z	NEC	77346
MOHAVE HILLS	7100	370A	NWC	77069
MOHAVE WAY CT	0	328P	NWC	77429
MOHAVE WAY DR	14000	328P	NWC	77429
MOHAWK	2800	414N	NCC	77093
MOHAWK	4100	461S	NEC	77521
MOHAWK	5500	415S	NEH	77016
MOHAWK DR	9200	579A	LP	77571
MOHAWK RD	23600	295F	SEM	77365
MOHAWK PATH PLACE	0	250Q	NWC	77389
MOHAWK PATH TRAIL	0	250Q	NWC	77389
MOHAWK TRAIL	26100	248R	SWM	77354
MOHEGAN CT	4500	577F	PA	77504
MOHEGAN CT	4700	461S	NEC	77521
MOHICAN DR	0	328P	NWC	77429
MOHLERBRUK DR	3800	371P	NWC	77066
MOJAVE COVE CT	9200	615H	SEC	77089
MOJAVE TRAIL	0	658U	LC	77573
MOLASSES MEADOW LN	21100	289U	NWC	77375
MOLINE	6200	534R	SEH	77087
MOLINE	7400	535N	SEH	77087
MOLLASIS RD	0	405F	NWC	77433
MOLLY	2100	373Z	NCC	77039
MOLLY HILLS CT	0	293K	SEM	77386
MOLLY WINTERS LN	0	366V	NWC	77433
MOLTERE DR	11400	368Q	NWC	77065
MONA	3600	614W	NEB	77584
MONA	9600	454A	NEH	77093
MONACO LN	4400	577H	PA	77505
MONACO RD	12600	369L	NWC	77070
MONALDO CT	0	616P	PL	77581
MONALDO DR	0	616P	PL	77581
MONALDO PLACE	0	616K	PL	77581
MONA LEE LN	2500	450M	NWH	77080
MONARCH CT	0	568E	NEF	77498
MONARCH RD	12600	572R	SWH	77047
MONARCH BEACH DR	1600	485K	NEF	77494
MONARCH BLUFF CT	0	609S	NEF	77479
MONARCH COVE CIR	0	366J	NWC	77433
MONARCH CREEK LN	0	698D	LC	77573
MONARCH CREEK LN	0	327U	NWC	77429
MONARCH CREEK LN	0	444S	KT	77493
MONARCH FIELD LN	0	406C	NWC	77433
MONARCH GARDENS CT	0	615H	PL	77089
MONARCH GLEN LN	4800	446D	NWC	77449
MONARCH GROVE LN	0	484T	NEF	77494
MONARCH HILL LN	0	375Y	NEC	77396
MONARCH HOLLOW LN	2000	446S	NWC	77449
MONARCH LAKE LN	7000	485X	NEF	77494
MONARCH MANOR LN	26600	296X	SEM	77339
MONARCH MEADOW CT	4900	484F	NEF	77494
MONARCH MEADOW LN	3300	615F	PL	77581
MONARCH MEADOW LN	4900	484Z	NEF	77494
MONARCH MIST LN	0	329V	NWC	77070
MONARCH OAKS	1400	451W	NWH	77055
MONARCH RIDGE DR	0	450V	NWH	77080
MONARCH RIVER LN	0	367S	NWC	77433
MONARCH SPRINGS LN	0	375X	NEC	77396
MONARCH TRAIL	0	568J	NEF	77498
MONARCH VALLEY	0	484S	NEF	77494
MONARCH WOODS DR	0	296X	NEC	77339
MONARDA CT	6700	370A	NWC	77069
MONARDA MANOR CT	0	289Z	NWC	77379
MONA VISTA DR	6500	527H	SWC	77083
MONCREY AVE	2500	659S	LC	77573
MONCUR DR	7800	407H	NWC	77095
MODANO CT	2600	611S	NEF	77545
MONDAVI CIR	0	484J	NEF	77494
MONDAY HARGROVE RD	19900	258P	SEM	77357
MONDIAL DR	0	445B	NWC	77493
MONDRIAN DR	15300	527M	NEF	77083
MONEL	0	492L	SWH	77007
MONET	7800	454K	NEH	77093
MONETTA DR	0	257E	SEM	77357
MONICA	11600	490K	BH	77024
MONIQUE DR	11200	368U	NWC	77065
MONIQUE RIDGE LN	0	293K	SEM	77386
MONITOR	4000	414P	NCC	77093
MONKEYSFIST DR	0	617U	SEC	77546
MONKSWOOD DR	20200	486F	SWC	77450
MONMOUTH	3700	577C	PA	77505
MONMOUTH DR	200	459X	CV	77530
MONONA DR	2200	484K	NEF	77494
MONONA TERRACE CT	0	253X	SEM	77386
MONRAD DR	14600	572S	SWH	77045
MONRAD DR	14700	572S	SWH	77053
MONROE	1200	501Z	BT	77520
MONROE	1400	494X	SEH	77023
MONROE	1500	538V	DP	77536
MONROE DR	1100	536R	PA	77502
MONROE RD	6800	535Y	SEH	77017
MONROE RD	7000	575G	SEH	77061
W. MONROE RD	8300	575G	SEH	77061
MONROE RD	9200	575U	SEH	77075
MONSANTA	5900	535S	SEH	77087
MONSEY DR	9200	490X	SWH	77063
MONSOON CT	17500	379X	NEC	77532
MONSTERA RD	14600	328Z	NWC	77070
MONTABELLO DR	0	525J	NEF	77406
MONTAGUE DR	23300	333D	NCC	77373
MONTAGUE DR	23800	293Z	NCC	77373
MONTAGUE MANOR LN	7900	528L	SWH	77072
MONTAIGNE DR	13300	368T	NWC	77065
MONTAIGNE DR	13900	368T	NWC	77429
MONTANA	0	659Z	GCO	77539
MONTANA	700	535Z	SH	77587
MONTANA	700	580C	LP	77571
MONTANA	1600	492H	SWH	77007
MONTANA	1900	541E	BT	77520
MONTANA BEND LN	0	406F	NWC	77433
MONTANA BLUE DR	2400	293W	NCC	77373
MONTANA RIDGE CT	0	409S	NWC	77041
MONTAUK DR	6600	408N	NWC	77084
MONTAY BAY DR	0	250U	NWC	77389
MONTBROOK DR	11700	569B	MD	77099
MONTBURY LN	5400	486W	NEF	77450
MONTCLAIR BLVD	600	569N	SG	77478
MONTCLAIR CT	0	659S	LC	77573
MONT CLAIR DR	6700	532G	SWH	77030
MONTCLAIR BEND LN	0	416Z	NEC	77044
MONTCLAIR COLONY TRAIL	0	405P	NWC	77493
MONTCLAIR LANDING CT	0	248Z	TB	77375
MONTCLAIR MEADOW LN	19200	446H	NWC	77449
MONTCLAIR OAKS LN	2200	252R	SEM	77386
MONTCLAIR ORCHARD TRACE	0	253T	SEM	77386
MONTCLAIR PARK LN	22900	292L	NCC	77373
MONTCLAIR POINT CT	0	572U	SWH	77047
MONTCLIFF CT	12200	370M	NWC	77066
MONTCLIFF BEND CT	4400	609Y	NEF	77459
MONTCLIFF BEND LN	4400	609Y	NEF	77459
MONTE	0	256U	SEM	77357
MONTE LN	29500	299J	NEC	77336
MONTE BELLO	0	656C	FR	77546
MONTEBELLO	0	659S	LC	77573
MONTEBELLO CT	11200	490L	PP	77024
MONTEBELLO CT	11800	329S	NWC	77377
MONTE BELLO RIDGE LN	0	409S	NWC	77041
MONTE CARLO CT	16600	611B	SWH	77053
MONTE CARLO LN	16400	611B	SWH	77053
MONTE CELLO	800	490C	HE	77024
MONTECOLA PINE DR	0	524E	NEF	77494
MONTECREST PARK CT	7500	290S	NWC	77379
MONTECUCCO CT	0	257E	SEM	77357
MONTEGO DR	3700	501L	BT	77521
MONTEGO LN	7000	459L	NEC	77049
MONTEGO BAY CT	0	610T	MC	77459
MONTEIGNE LN	13500	367C	NWC	77429
MONTEITH DR	3800	333C	NCC	77373
MONTEITH DR	5400	334A	NCC	77373
MONTE LAGO LN	0	445F	NWC	77493
MONTELEON	10200	576P	SEH	77075
MONTE LEONE DR	0	525J	NEF	77469
MONTENERO WAY LN	0	533F	SWH	77021
MONTEREY LN	0	660G	LC	77539
MONTEREY BEND LN		484Y	NEF	77494
MONTEREY CLIFF LN	28500	298T	NEH	77336
MONTERO LN	0	257F	SEM	77357
MONTE ROSA CT	11100	525N	NEF	77469
MONTEROSA DR	0	406G	NWC	77433
MONTERREY	0	569Z	NEF	77477
MONTERREY	100	501W	BT	77520
MONTERREY	2000	619V	LC	77565
MONTERREY	9100	455H	NEH	77078
MONTERREY PINE PLACE	8500	289R	NWC	77375
MONTERREY SPRINGS CT	5700	409W	NWC	77041
MONTERREY SPRINGS DR	5700	409W	NWH	77041
MONTERREY SPRINGS DR	5800	449A	NWC	77041
MONTERRY HILLS	0	370A	NWC	77069
MONTERRY OAK LN	0	289C	NWC	77375
MONTESA CT	8000	527L	NEF	77083
MONTESA DR	15400	527L	NEF	77083
MONTES LANDING DR	0	326T	NWC	77433
MONTEVIDEO CIR	4300	577B	PA	77504
MONTE VISTA DR	15400	527G	SWC	77083
MONTEZUMA	6500	500C	NEC	77521
MONTEZUMA LN	0	658Y	LC	77573
MONTFORD CT	3000	569N	SG	77478
MONTFORD DR	9200	529U	SWH	77099
MONTGLEN	7600	535T	SEH	77061
MONTGLEN CT	1	535T	SEH	77061
MONTGOMERY	0	501W	BT	77520
MONTGOMERY	9100	579A	LP	77571
MONTGOMERY LN	1400	335Z	HM	77338
W. MONTGOMERY RD	5600	452C	NWH	77091
W. MONTGOMERY RD	7700	412T	NWH	77088
W. MONTGOMERY RD	11600	411M	NWC	77086
MONTICELLO CT	2000	658T	LC	77573
MONTICELLO DR	2600	572L	SWH	77045
MONTICELLO PINES LN	0	660J	LC	77573
MONTICELLO TERRACE LN	0	446E	NWC	77449
MONTICETO CT	11800	569A	MD	77477
MONTICETO LN	11800	569A	MD	77477
MONTICETO LN	12200	528Z	MD	77477
MONTIERI ST	0	659P	LC	77573
MONTILLA CT	7800	528J	SWC	77083
MONTMARTE BLVD	11700	529B	SWH	77082
MONTOUR DR	1000	618J	SEH	77062
MONTREAL DR	0	328E	NWC	77377
MONTRIDGE DR	8000	451S	NWH	77055
MONTRIDGE DR	9300	450U	NWH	77080
MONTROSE BLVD	1000	493N	SWH	77019
MONTROSE BLVD	1600	493N	SWH	77006
MONTROSE BLVD	5300	493N	SWH	77005
MONTVALE DR	3700	618D	SEH	77059
MONTVERDE LN	10800	569B	SWH	77099
MONTVIEW CT	20600	486F	SWC	77450
MONTVIEW DR	900	486F	SWC	77450
MONTVIEW DR	2600	613S	NEB	77584
MONTWOOD CT	15500	618F	SEH	77062
MONTWOOD DR	15300	618F	SEH	77062
MONUMENT RD	10800	539Q	LP	77571
MONUMENT VALLEY DR	12000	371G	NWC	77067
MONZA DR	3200	371C	NWC	77014
MOODY	100	453U	NEH	77009
MOODY	100	618Y	WB	77598
MOODY	300	659A	LC	77573
MOODY PINES CT	0	297R	NEH	77345
MOOLIT NIGHT DR	14200	528J	SWC	77083
MOON AVE	0	452E	NWH	77018
MOON CT	1300	577J	PA	77504
MOONBEAM	7900	412S	NWH	77088
MOONBEAM CIR	7300	609R	MC	77459
MOON BEAM CT	1	250D	WD	77381
MOONCREST DR	0	616J	SEC	77581
MOONCREST FIELD LN	0	446G	NWC	77449
MOONDANCE LN	7500	570C	SWH	77071
MOONDANCE LN	7800	570C	SWH	77071
MOON DECK CIR	0	288S	NWC	77377
MOONEY RD	1100	413Q	NEH	77037
MOONEY RD	1300	414N	NCC	77093
MOONFLOWER LN	20000	446T	NWC	77449
MOONGLOW	11500	412E	NWC	77038
MOONGLOW DR	16100	332T	NWC	77090
MOON HARVEST LN	0	366N	NWC	77433
MOONHOLLOW DR	19400	446U	NWC	77084
MOONINDIGO LN	0	524B	NEF	77494
MOONLIGHT DR	9600	531P	SWH	77096
MOON LIGHT COVE CIR	0	366J	NWC	77433
MOONLIGHT CREEK CT	15900	408N	NWC	77095
MOONLIGHT FOREST DR	8000	411L	NWC	77088
MOONLIGHT MIST DR	0	376V	NEC	77346
MOONLIGHT RIDGE DR	0	376U	NEC	77396
MOONLIGHT SHADOW CT	4200	579W	PA	77059
MOONLIGHT SPRINGS DR	0	288S	NWC	77377
MOONLITE DR	3600	578A	PA	77505
MOONLIT FALLS DR	0	365M	NWC	77433
MOONLIT FIELDS CT	10900	369T	NWC	77064
MOONLIT LAKE CIR	3100	660A	LC	77573
MOONLIT LAKE CT	22700	485Q	NEF	77450
MOONLIT LAKE LN	0	612P	PL	77545
MOONLIT MEADOWS CT	10800	369T	NWC	77064
MOONLIT POND CT	18700	447E	NWC	77084
MOONLIT RIDGE CT	0	250J	NWC	77375
MOONLIT RIVER	0	366Q	NWC	77433
MOONMIST DR	5800	531E	SWH	77081
MOONMIST DR	7600	530F	SWH	77036
MOONMIST DR	11500	529E	SWH	77072
MOON MIST LN	0	484Z	NEF	77494
MOON RIDGE CT	0	485E	NEF	77494
MOONRIDGE DR	1	457Y	NEC	77015
MOONRIDGE RD	0	405Q	NWC	77449
MOONRISE LN	0	457P	NEC	77049
MOONRISE RIVER	0	406L	NWC	77433
MOONRIVER DR	19800	334R	NCC	77338
MOON ROCK DR	15900	618G	SEH	77062
MOON ROCK DR	16300	618G	SEH	77058
MOON SCAPE VIEW	0	376S	NEC	77396
MOONSEED PLACE	1	250B	WD	77381
MOONSET LN	0	415X	NWH	77078
MOONSHADOWS DR	5100	337S	NEC	77346
MOONSHINE HILL RD	100	336T	NEH	77338

Street Name	Block	Pg/Sq	Loc	Zips
MOONSHINE HILL LOOP	100	336T	NEH	77338
MOONSTONE CIR	3000	452P	NWH	77018
MOONSTONE MIST LN	0	524F	NEF	77494
MOON TRAIL DR	0	337W	NEC	77346
MOONVINE CT	1	251Q	WD	77380
MOON VISTA LN	0	365M	NWC	77433
MOON WALK DR	0	335N	NCC	77338
MOORBERRY	0	449V	NWH	77043
MOORBERRY LN	9500	450S	NWH	77080
MOORBERRY LN	10200	450S	NWH	77043
MOORCREEK DR	10500	369B	NWC	77070
MOORCREEK DR	11900	329W	NWC	77070
MOORCREEK DR	12100	328Z	NWC	77070
MOORCROFT CT	9500	527V	NEF	77498
MOORE	100	288H	TB	77375
MOORE	2300	616N	PL	77581
MOORE	2800	493D	NEH	77009
MOORE	3400	453Z	NEH	77009
MOORE DR	3900	460M	NEC	77562
MOORE RD	0	656W	NEB	77546
MOORE RD	1000	569Z	NEF	77477
MOORE RD	15000	458N	NEC	77049
MOOREBROOK DR	1300	412B	NWC	77038
MOORE CREEK LN	0	377J	NEC	77346
MOOREDALE LN	12400	489D	SWH	77024
MOOREHEAD RD	0	254A	SEM	77302
MOOREHEAD RD	18900	253H	SEM	77302
MOORE HOUSE	0	411V	NWH	77088
MOOREKNOLL LN	12400	489D	SWH	77024
MOOREMEADOW LN	12400	489D	SWH	77024
MOORESIDE LN	900	497D	NEC	77530
MOOREVIEW LN	14300	331Y	NWC	77014
MOORFIELD CT	9300	528S	NEF	77083
MOORFIELD DR	14200	528S	NEF	77083
MOORGATE LN	24600	338M	NEH	77336
MOORHEAD DR	1300	450X	NWH	77055
MOORING POINT CT	4100	569X	MC	77459
MOORING POINT DR	0	612E	PL	77545
MOORING RIDGE LN	11100	575Y	SWH	77075
MOOR LILY CT	20900	291S	NWC	77388
MOOR PARK LN	8700	410F	NWC	77064
MOORTOWN CIR	21600	485V	NEF	77450
MOORWICK LN	1300	449W	NWH	77043
MOOSE DR	100	379A	NEC	77532
MOOSE DR	600	378D	NEC	77532
MOOSE COVE CT	19700	329B	NWC	77375
MOOSE HEAD LN	11800	369R	NWC	77064
MOOSE JAW LN	200	338L	NEH	77336
MOOSEWOOD CT	5500	337S	NEC	77346
MOPAC	0	292R	SP	77373
MOPAN VALLEY LN	11900	370L	NWC	77066
MORALES RD	14400	374N	NEH	77032
MORA WAY	0	656F	NEB	77511
MORAY DR	0	614W	NEB	77584
MORAY LN	11800	415Q	NEC	77016
MORAY VIEW DR	0	368W	NWC	77095
MOREAU	2300	414W	NEH	77093
MOREFORD LN	0	299T	NEC	77336
MOREHOUSE LN	2400	412S	NWH	77088
W. MORELAND DR	0	568W	SG	77479
MORELAND DR	17400	459X	CV	77530
MORELAND GROVE LN	0	416P	NWC	77433
MORELAND PARK LN	0	408G	NWC	77095
MORELEIGH BRANCH DR	0	609U	NEF	77459
MORELEIGH BRANCH DR	0	609U	NEF	77459
MORELOCK AVE	0	660Z	TC	77539
MORELOS RD	3700	500D	NEC	77521
MORELY LAKE DR	0	407C	NWC	77095
MOREN DR	0	256G	SEM	77365
MORENCI	2700	614P	PL	77584
MORENCI DR	0	541M	BT	77520
MORENO AVE	14400	572P	SWH	77045
MORETON CT	7500	330K	NWC	77379
MORETON LN	17400	330K	NWC	77379
MOREWOOD CT	13300	371Z	NWC	77038
MOREWOOD DR	2300	371Z	NWC	77038
MORFONTAINE LN	2600	485R	NEF	77450
MORGAN	0	613Y	NEB	77584
MORGAN	1900	493N	SWH	77006
MORGAN	16000	246U	SWM	77355
W. MORGAN DR	11800	368R	NWC	77065
E. MORGAN DR	11800	368R	NWC	77065
MORGAN DR	25400	249S	NWC	77375
MORGAN LN	0	612Z	NEB	77578
MORGAN RD	0	379K	NEC	77532
MORGAN RD	0	613U	NEB	77584
MORGAN ST	0	568T	SG	77478
MORGAN BAY CT	0	612J	PL	77545
MORGAN BAY DR	0	612J	PL	77545
MORGAN CANYON CT	6200	526A	NEF	77450
MORGAN CREEK	4200	501K	BT	77521
MORGAN CREEK CT	13600	488P	SWH	77077
MORGAN CREEK LN	0	484K	NEF	77494
MORGANFAIR LN	2600	486P	SWC	77450
MORGAN HILL CT	0	253K	SEM	77386
MORGAN ISLE LN	0	653Z	LC	77573
MORGAN JANE WAY	0	366V	NWC	77433
MORGAN KNOLL LN	0	446S	NWC	77449
MORGAN KNOLL LN	0	446S	NWC	77449
MORGANNA	0	569F	SF	77477
MORGAN PARK LN	0	291P	NWC	77388
MORGAN PINES CT	24600	250W	NWC	77389
MORGAN RANCH TRAIL	0	334R	NCC	77338
MORGAN RIDGE LN	2300	293F	SEM	77386
MORGAN RUN	16100	570K	MC	77489
MORGAN SADDLE LN	0	526R	NEF	77407
MORGANS BEND CIR	0	366K	NWC	77433
W. MORGANS BEND DR	0	366K	NWC	77433
E. MORGANS BEND DR	0	366L	NWC	77433
MORGANS COVE CT	0	484U	NEF	77494
MORGANS GOLD DR	0	366L	NWC	77433
MORGANS LAKE DR	0	366Q	NWC	77433
MORGANS MILL CT	0	366L	NWC	77433
MORGANS POINTE CIR	21500	446E	NWC	77449
MORGANS SPRINGS WAY	0	292U	NCC	77373
MORGANS SECRET DR	0	366L	NWC	77433
MORGANS STABLE CT	0	377T	NEC	77044
MORGANS TURN	16200	407H	NWC	77095
MORGAN WILLOW LN	0	327U	NWC	77429
MORGENSEN DR	0	411M	NWH	77088
MORGOOD	5500	454Y	NEH	77026
MORIAH CT	4100	293M	SEM	77386
MORIN PLACE	1200	493L	SWH	77002
MORINSCOTT CT	5600	457S	NEC	77049
MORINSCOTT DR	14000	456V	NEC	77049
MORINSCOTT DR	14300	457S	NEC	77049
MORITZ CT	8400	451S	NWH	77055
MORITZ DR	1400	451S	NWH	77055
MORITZ GLEN	0	451W	NWH	77055
MORITZ GREEN	0	451W	NWH	77055
MORITZ PARK	0	451W	NWH	77055
MORITZ PLACE	1400	451W	NWC	77055
MORITZ WALK	0	451W	NWH	77055
MORLEY	7500	535W	SEH	77061
MORLEY DR	15600	367R	CY	77429
MORLEY PARK LN	900	292B	NCC	77373
MORLEY POINT CT	4500	658N	LC	77573
MORLEY POINTE CT	19900	486Q	SWC	77450
MORNING DR	2200	502S	BT	77520
MORNING DR	7100	461M	NEC	77521
MORNING BLOSSOM PLACE	0	407U	NWC	77084
MORNING BREEZE	5400	448D	NWC	77041
MORNINGBROOK CT	8100	330T	NWC	77379
MORNING BROOK DR	0	612R	PL	77584
MORNINGBROOK DR	16200	330T	NWC	77379
MORNING BROOK LN	19700	486G	SWC	77094
MORNING BROOK WAY	0	612R	PL	77584
MORNING CLOUD CT	0	612R	PL	77584
MORNING CLOUD DR	0	612R	PL	77584
MORNING CLOUD LN	4500	609X	NEF	77479
MORNING COCK WAY	500	338M	NEH	77336
MORNING COVE LN	3500	445M	NWC	77449
MORNING CREEK DR	20300	486P	SWC	77450
MORNING CREEK LN	0	657Y	LC	77573
MORNING CREEK SPRINGS LN	0	297K	NEH	77365
MORNINGCREST CT	6100	290D	NWC	77389
MORNING CREST LN	0	484W	NEF	77494
MORNING CYPRESS CT	0	253P	SEM	77386
MORNING CYPRESS LN	0	366R	NWC	77433
MORNINGDALE	5800	374M	NEH	77396
MORNING DAWN CT	17600	407F	NWC	77095
MORNING DAWN DR	0	612R	PL	77584
MORNING DAWN DR	8200	407F	NWC	77095
MORNING DEW LN	11800	371M	NWC	77067
MORNING DEW PLACE	1600	610P	MC	77459
MORNING DOVE DR	15200	375U	NEC	77396
MORNING DOVE LN	0	461P	NEC	77521
MORNING DOVE LN	800	616U	FR	77546
MORNING DOVE BEND LN	0	291H	NWC	77389
MORNING DUSK DR	0	527N	NEF	77083
MORNING FOREST CT	1	251J	WD	77381
MORNING GALE LN	0	484U	NEF	77494
MORNINGGATE CT	0	445R	NWC	77449
MORNING GLEN LN	8500	527N	NEF	77083
MORNING GLORY CT	4600	610P	MC	77459
MORNING GLORY DR	2400	537Z	PA	77503
MORNING GLORY LN	1	251R	WD	77380
MORNING GLORY MEADOW LN	0	616L	SEC	77089
MORNING GLORY TERR CT	19700	326X	NWC	77433
MORNING GLORY TRACE	6700	525L	NEF	77407
MORNING HILL CT	0	406D	NWC	77433
MORNING ISLAND CT	0	657S	FR	77546
MORNING LAKE DR	2000	619Z	LC	77573
MORNING LAKE DR	22300	485V	NEF	77450
MORNING LEAF CT	2700	291Z	NWC	77388
MORNINGLIGHT DR	2600	446V	NWC	77084
MORNING LODGE LN	14300	417C	NEH	77044
MORNING MEADOW DR	2300	570Y	MC	77489
MORNING MIST CT	1100	568E	SG	77498
MORNING MIST DR	16200	332T	NWC	77090
MORNINGMOUNT LN	0	446C	NWC	77449
MORNING NEWS LN	19300	526F	NEF	77407
MORNING OAK LN	8500	407E	NWC	77433
MORNING PARK DR	1500	485P	NEF	77494
MORNING PINE LN	15000	331T	NWC	77068
MORNING PINE TRAIL	16200	326P	NWC	77433
MORNING POINT LN	0	256W	SEM	77365
MORNING QUAIL CT	16300	610C	SWH	77489
MORNING RAIN DR	12400	328L	NWC	77377
MORNING RAVEN LN	0	485N	NEF	77494
MORNING RIDGE CT	4600	609N	NEF	77479
MORNING RIDGE LN	0	253K	SEM	77386
MORNING RIDGE LN	0	657T	FR	77546
MORNING ROSE LN	8100	407F	NWC	77095
MORNINGSAGE LN	6500	411N	NWC	77088
MORNINGSHADE DR	16300	332T	NWC	77090
MORNING SHADOW WAY	0	376H	NEC	77346
MORNINGSHIRE LN	0	407V	NWC	77084
MORNINGSIDE	100	297L	NEH	77365
MORNINGSIDE	200	616Z	FR	77546
MORNINGSIDE	200	657V	LC	77573
MORNINGSIDE CT	900	616U	FR	77546
MORNINGSIDE DR	3400	492Y	SWH	77098
MORNINGSIDE DR	4500	532G	SWH	77005
MORNINGSIDE DR	5700	532G	SWH	77030
MORNINGSIDE LN	2400	537K	PA	77506
MORNINGSIDE VIEW DR	0	573Y	SEC	77047
MORNING SKY	7000	525E	NEF	77494
MORNING SONG CT	24800	250Y	NWC	77389
MORNING SONG DR	19500	406V	NWC	77449
MORNING STAR AVE	17000	379X	NEC	77532
MORNING STORY DR	22800	334A	NCC	77373
MORNINGTIDE CT	3200	445M	NWC	77449
MORNINGTIDE DR	3400	445M	NWC	77449
MORNING TIDE LN	1900	619Z	LC	77573
MORNINGTON LN	4900	485A	NEF	77494
MORNINGVIEW DR	0	450Q	NWH	77080
MORNINGVIEW DR	2700	450L	NWH	77080
MORNING VIEW BEND LN	0	524L	NEF	77406
MORNING WILLOW DR	4200	486W	NEF	77450
S. MORNINGWOOD CT	1	251Z	WD	77380
N. MORNINGWOOD CT	1	251Z	WD	77380
MOROCCO RD	10000	450A	NWH	77041
MORRELL	1	501T	BT	77520
MORRIS	0	256J	SEM	77357
MORRIS	0	448Z	NWH	77079
MORRIS	0	613S	PL	77584
MORRIS	100	493C	NEH	77009
MORRIS	1000	488D	NWH	77079
MORRIS	1200	541B	BT	77520
MORRIS	2500	494A	NEH	77026
MORRIS CT	4300	613V	NEB	77584
MORRIS DR	4400	613V	NEB	77584
MORRIS RD	0	613N	PL	77584
MORRIS RD	100	248S	SWM	77354
MORRISFIELD CT	19400	486H	SWC	77094
MORRISGLEN CT	6500	407T	NWC	77084
MORRIS HILL LN	0	367Y	NWC	77095
MORRISON	100	543Q	BC	77520
MORRISON	2600	493B	NWH	77009
MORRISON BLVD	5000	444Z	KT	77493
MORRISON LN	0	445J	NWC	77449
MORRISON, W L	0	415A	NEC	77396
MORRISON GROVE DR	0	406B	NWC	77433
MORRIS PARK CT	25000	250Y	NWC	77389
MORRISVILLE CT	0	455D	NEH	77078
MORRISWAY CT	17800	407T	NWC	77084
MORRO CASTLE	10200	576S	SEH	77075
MORROW	6000	412Y	NWH	77091
MORROW MOUNTAIN LN	0	377J	NEC	77346
MORSE	1500	492V	SWH	77019
MORSELLE DR	0	295A	SEM	77365
MORT HALL DR	7600	290S	NWC	77379
MORTIMER DR	11300	371P	NWC	77066
MORTON	0	577T	SEH	77034
MORTON CT	0	447N	NWC	77084
MORTON LN	100	459M	NEC	77562
MORTON RD	0	526X	NEF	77407
MORTON RD	0	525Z	NEF	77406
MORTON RD	5400	444L	KT	77493
MORTON RD	18100	447N	NWC	77084
MORTON RD	20000	446P	NWC	77449
MORTON RD	23000	445P	NWC	77493
MORTON CHASE LN	0	445R	NWC	77449
MORTON COVE LN	0	445R	NWC	77449
MORTON CREEK RANCH RD	0	445F	NWC	77493
MORTON CREEK RANCH RD	0	445P	NWC	77493
MORTON VIEW DR	0	445R	NWC	77449
MORWOOD	5500	454Y	NEH	77026
MOSA RD	0	372J	NWC	77067
MOSA CREEK CT	1800	536N	SEH	77017
MOSAIC LN	14200	568E	SG	77498
MOSAIC CANYON CT	4700	375V	NEC	77396
MOSAICO LN	0	451Y	NWH	77055
MOSAICO LN	0	491C	NWH	77055
MOSAIC POINT TRAIL	0	250Q	NWC	77389
MOSBY CIR	700	493A	NWH	77007
MOSCONE CT	6000	406Z	NWC	77449
MOSES	3400	494F	NEH	77020
MOSEWOOD	7400	410R	NWH	77040
MOSHER LN	600	412M	NEH	77037
MOSHER LN	800	412K	NWH	77088
MOSIELEE	12100	411C	NWC	77086
MOSKOWITZ AVE	1000	620P	SB	77586
MOSLEY CT	3500	493X	SWH	77004
MOSLEY RD	7600	575D	SEH	77017
MOSLEY RD	7900	575H	SEH	77061
MOSLEY RD	8100	575H	SEH	77075
MOSMAN CT	600	486D	SWC	77094
MOSS	100	453X	NWH	77009
MOSS CT	2700	620J	SB	77586
MOSS LN	2700	539S	DP	77536
MOSS LN	16800	254Q	SEM	77365
MOSS AGATE CT	20700	291S	NWC	77388
MOSS ARBOR CT	0	484V	NEF	77494
MOSSBACK PINE RD	0	524B	NEF	77494
MOSS BARK TRAIL	19700	526T	NEF	77407
MOSS BAY CT	0	326U	NWC	77429
MOSS BAY LN	0	326V	NWC	77429
MOSSBERG CT	0	376F	NEC	77396
MOSS BOULDER CT	15000	408P	NWC	77084
MOSS BOULDER DR	6800	408P	NWC	77084
MOSS BRANCH RD	10800	449L	NWH	77043
MOSSBRIAR CT	8800	407C	NWC	77095
MOSSBRIAR LN	17200	407B	NWC	77095
MOSS BRIDGE LN	14900	568A	NEF	77498
MOSS COVE CT	4200	609Y	NEF	77479
MOSS COVE CT	18000	376D	NEC	77346
MOSS COVE LN	0	571K	SWH	77085
S. MOSS CREEK DR	13000	368F	NWC	77429
N. MOSS CREEK DR	13000	368F	NWC	77429
MOSS CREEK LN	2100	616N	PL	77581
MOSS CREEK LN	14500	368J	NWC	77429
MOSSCREST DR	10900	573H	SEH	77048
MOSSDALE CIR	8300	330J	NWC	77379
MOSSEY CREEK	2100	538V	DP	77536
MOSSEY PINES CT	21600	335J	NCC	77338
MOSSEY TERRACE LN	0	290Q	NWC	77379
MOSS FALLS LN	22100	334E	NCC	77373
MOSS FERN DR	0	484X	NEF	77494
MOSS FERN DR	0	484X	NEF	77494
MOSSFORD DR	4500	534L	SEH	77087
MOSSFOREST DR	17400	332E	NWC	77090
MOSS GARDEN LN	0	524D	NEF	77494
MOSS GLENN LN	5200	411Q	NWH	77088
MOSS GREEN CT	0	327U	NWC	77429
MOSS GREEN CT	4500	578U	SEH	77059
MOSSGREY LN	5200	333D	NCC	77373
MOSSGREY LN	5400	334A	NCC	77373
MOSSHALL CT	0	289R	NWC	77375
MOSSHANG CT	8400	410K	NWC	77040
MOSSHILL DR	2300	450N	NWH	77080
MOSSHILL ESTATES LN	18600	366D	NWC	77429
MOSS HOLLOW CT	5000	452F	NWH	77018
MOSSIDE	7600	533P	SEH	77021
MOSS LAKE CT	4300	526W	NEF	77406
MOSS MEADOW LN	19300	446D	NWC	77449
MOSS OAKS DR	6000	414M	NEH	77050
MOSS OAKS DR	6200	415E	NEH	77050
MOSS PARK CT	18000	376D	NEC	77346
MOSSPINE CT	0	447C	NWC	77084
MOSS POINT	100	657K	FR	77546
MOSS POINT	17600	331J	NWC	77379
MOSS POINT CT	5800	330J	NWC	77379
MOSSRIDGE DR	1100	570Y	MC	77489
MOSSRIDGE DR	3700	370B	NWC	77069
MOSS RIDGE RD	10700	449L	NWH	77043
S. MOSSROCK RD	1	251R	WD	77380
N. MOSSROCK RD	1	251R	WD	77380
MOSS ROSE	6500	534H	SEH	77087
MOSS ROSE	7200	535E	SEH	77012
MOSS RUN DR	4900	609F	MC	77459
MOSS SPRING LN	900	490B	HE	77024
MOSS SPRINGS CT	0	406M	NWC	77433
MOSSTEX DR	13700	375T	NEH	77396
MOSSTEX DR	13700	415B	NEC	77396
MOSS TRAIL DR	3500	609K	MC	77459
MOSS TREE RD	3600	449L	NWH	77043
MOSS VALLEY DR	14500	326Z	CY	77429
MOSS VALLEY DR	14700	326Z	NWC	77429
MOSSVILLE CT	3600	331T	NWC	77068
MOSSWILLOW LN	22300	290J	NWC	77375
MOSSWOOD DR	8100	455B	NEH	77028
MOSSY	800	539Q	LP	77571
MOSSY BARK LN	13000	408Z	NWC	77041
MOSSY BEND LN	0	615F	PL	77581
MOSSY BLUFF CT	0	290T	NWC	77379
MOSSY BRANCH CT	0	253T	SEM	77386
MOSSY BRANCH LN	0	253N	SEM	77386
MOSSY BRANCH ST	1100	332V	NCC	77073
MOSSY BROOK CT	10200	367T	NWC	77433
MOSSY BROOK LN	10200	367T	NWC	77433
MOSSY CANYON LN	0	484S	NEF	77494
MOSSY CREEK LN	0	526R	NEF	77469
MOSSY CREEK LN	18000	527N	NEF	77407
MOSSYCUP DR	12100	490E	SWH	77024
MOSSYCUP DR	12400	489H	SWH	77024
MOSSY ELM CT	3100	578X	SEH	77059
MOSSY FIELD LN	21800	291Q	NWC	77388
MOSSY FOREST BLVD	0	253P	SEM	77386
MOSSY FOREST CT	0	289W	NWC	77375
MOSSYGATE DR	4200	333C	NCC	77373
MOSSYGATE DR	4500	293Y	NCC	77373
MOSSY GATE LN	14201	488W	SWH	77082
MOSSY GROVE	16100	376H	NEC	77346
MOSSY GROVE CT	4000	376H	NEC	77346
MOSSY HEDGE LN	0	446M	NWC	77449
MOSSY HILL LN	0	406P	NWC	77449
MOSSY HOLLOW LN	10900	575U	SEH	77075
MOSSY LAKE CIR	1900	446Y	NWC	77084
MOSSY LEAF LN	26900	366R	NWC	77433
MOSSY LEDGE DR	12600	328L	NWC	77377
MOSSY LOG CT	2700	447P	NWC	77084
MOSSY MEADOW LN	13000	571K	SWH	77085
MOSSY OAK DR	100	500E	BT	77520
MOSSY OAK DR	1200	659N	LC	77573
E. MOSSY OAKS	0	292E	NWC	77389
W. MOSSY OAKS DR	0	291E	NWC	77389
E. MOSSY OAKS RD	3800	291G	NWC	77389
W. MOSSY OAKS RD	4100	291F	NWC	77389
MOSSY OAKS RD	22000	291K	NWC	77389
MOSSY PARK	0	327U	NWC	77429
MOSSY PLACE LN	3900	291P	NWC	77388
MOSSY RIDGE LN	17700	407K	NWC	77095
MOSSY RIDGE COVE	13000	408Z	NWC	77041
MOSSYROCK CT	3700	297T	NEH	77345
MOSSY SHORES CT	0	377L	NEC	77044
MOSSY SPRING LN	0	291P	NWC	77388
MOSSY STONE DR	1600	656R	FR	77546
MOSSY STONE DR	1600	489N	SWH	77077
MOSSY TIMBERS DR	5400	337T	NEC	77346
MOSSY TRAIL CT	0	612Q	PL	77584
MOSSY TRAIL DR	2000	486P	SWC	77450
MOSSY TRAIL LN	0	612Q	PL	77584
MOSSY TRAILS CT	22500	525F	NEF	77494
MOSSY TRAILS DR	6300	525F	NEF	77494
MOSSY TREE LN	9800	409D	NWC	77064
MOSSY WOODS DR	12400	328L	NWC	77377
MOSTON DR	1400	252U	SEM	77386
MOSTON DR	1700	252U	SEM	77385
MOTEBELLO MANOR DR	12400	328G	NWC	77377
MOTT CIR	0	525U	NEF	77406
MOTT LN	1	490Q	PP	77024
MOTTLED DUCK LN	0	324S	NWC	77447
MOULTRIE LN	5500	408X	NWC	77084
MOUND RD	0	366H	NWC	77433
MOUND RD	12000	363G	NWC	77447
MOUND RD	25000	324S	NWC	77447
MOUND RD	27000	323V	NWC	77447
MOUND CREEK RD	0	323W	NWC	77484
MOUND CREEK RD	15300	322V	WCO	77484
MOUNT DR	7000	412T	NWH	77091
MOUNT DR	7100	412T	NWH	77088
MOUNTAIN ARBOR CT	0	367P	NWC	77433
MOUNTAIN ASPEN LN	1800	338A	NEH	77345
MOUNTAIN BLUEBIRD PLACE	0	250L	NWC	77389
MOUNTAIN BLUEBIRD PLACE	0	250L	NWC	77389
MOUNTAIN BLUFF LN	5100	297N	NEH	77345
MOUNTAIN CHESTNUT DR	0	369L	NWC	77070
MOUNTAIN CLIFF LN	0	377Y	NEC	77044
MOUNTAIN CREEK	2000	612H	PL	77584
MOUNTAIN CREEK CT	22800	485L	SWC	77450
MOUNTAIN CREEK LN	0	609Y	NEF	77459
MOUNTAIN CREST DR	17100	330N	NWC	77379
MOUNTAIN CYPRESS TRAIL	0	291A	NWC	77389
MOUNTAIN DAISY DR	0	411D	NWC	77038
MOUNTAIN DALE CT	0	406R	NWC	77433
MOUNTAIN DALE DR	19700	406Q	NWC	77433
MOUNTAIN ELM TRAIL	0	445N	NWC	77493
MOUNTAIN FALLS CT	0	657P	FR	77546
MOUNTAIN FLOWER CT	4300	579W	PA	77059
MOUNTAIN FOREST DR	0	446G	NWC	77449
MOUNTAIN FOREST DR	5200	446C	NWC	77449
MOUNTAIN FOREST DR	5200	446C	NWC	77449
MOUNTAIN FORK	4900	609P	MC	77459
MOUNTAIN GREEN TRAIL	2700	298W	NEH	77345
MOUNTAIN GROVE CT	5300	331A	NWC	77379
MOUNTAINHEAD DR	16400	458S	NEC	77049
MOUNTAIN HEIGHTS DR	15200	457Q	NEC	77049
MOUNTAIN HOME LN	15500	328S	NWC	77429
MOUNTAIN LAKE DR	1200	569Y	MC	77459
MOUNTAIN LAKE DR	2100	297Z	NEH	77345
MOUNTAIN LAUREL DR	2600	446S	NWC	77449
MOUNTAIN MAPLE CT	6100	338A	NEH	77345
MOUNTAIN MEADOWS DR	700	485G	SWC	77450
MOUNTAIN MIST CT	0	527J	NEF	77407
MOUNTAIN MIST TRAIL	0	457V	NEC	77049
MOUNTAIN OAK CT	3100	331T	NWC	77068
MOUNTAIN PARK DR	10300	371X	NWC	77086
MOUNTAIN PEAK WAY	4100	297T	NEH	77345
MOUNTAIN PINE LN	6300	407S	NWC	77449
MOUNTAIN PRAIRIE DR	0	406R	NEF	77433
MOUNTAIN RANCH DR	2100	458S	NEC	77049
MOUNTAIN RIDGE RD	11800	449L	NWH	77043
MOUNTAIN ROSE LN	3600	449K	NWH	77043
MOUNTAIN SAGE CT	0	612J	PL	77545
MOUNTAIN SAGE DR	0	612J	PL	77545
MOUNTAIN SHADE DR	18800	331C	NWC	77388
MOUNTAIN SHADOWS DR	16000	448A	NWC	77084
MOUNTAIN SPRING DR	18600	331A	NWC	77379
MOUNTAIN SPRING DR	18800	330D	NWC	77379
MOUNTAIN TIMBER CT	16200	617X	SEC	77546
MOUNTAIN TIMBER DR	4900	617X	SEC	77546
MOUNTAIN VALLEY DR	7300	408N	NWC	77095
MOUNTAIN VIEW DR	5800	297Z	NEH	77345
MOUNTAIN VIEW CREEK CT	5400	330D	NWC	77379
MOUNTAIN VISTA DR	0	406D	NWC	77433
MOUNTAIN WILLOW WAY	0	326Q	NWC	77429
MOUNTAIN WOOD WAY	0	334Q	NCC	77373
MOUNT AIRY CT	13900	367D	NWC	77429
MOUNT AIRY DR	13500	367H	NWC	77429
MOUNT AUBURN DR	24600	484G	NEF	77494
MOUNT BATTEN RD	7300	534S	SEH	77033
MOUNT BAUER DR	0	285L	NWC	77447
MOUNTBURY CT	500	292L	NCC	77373
MOUNT CARMEL DR	6700	534Z	SEH	77087
MOUNT CARSTENZ WAY	0	445H	NWC	77449
MOUNTCLAIR HOLLOW LN	0	249Z	NWC	77375
MOUNT CREST CT	0	368W	NWC	77095
MOUNT DAVIS WAY	0	446E	NWC	77449
MOUNT ECHO DR	0	285Q	NWC	77447
MOUNT ELBRUS WAY	0	446H	NWC	77449
MOUNT EVEREST WAY	0	446E	NWC	77449
MOUNTFIELD DR	18000	447F	NWC	77084
MOUNTFORD DR	0	615W	PL	77584
MOUNT FOREST DR	1900	337D	NEH	77345
MOUNT GREYLOCK DR	0	377K	NEC	77346
MOUNT HOPE DR	0	366N	NWC	77433
W. MOUNT HOUSTON RD	100	413J	NCC	77037
W. MOUNT HOUSTON RD	700	412J	NWH	77038
MOUNT HOUSTON RD	4200	414K	NCC	77093
W. MOUNT HOUSTON RD	4700	411L	NWC	77088
MOUNT HOUSTON RD	5700	415K	NEC	77050
MOUNT LORETTO CT	0	377J	NEC	77346
MOUNT MCKINLEY WAY	21500	445H	NWC	77449
MOUNT PLEASANT	3400	533Q	SEH	77021
MOUNT RIGA DR	0	377G	NEC	77346
MOUNT ROYAL CIR	5400	330Y	NWC	77069

Street Name	Block	Pg/Sq	Loc	Zips
MOUNTSHIRE DR	1900	570Y	MC	77489
MOUNT VERNON	3200	493S	SWH	77006
MOUNT VINSON WAY	0	445H	NWC	77449
MOUNT WHITNEY WAY	4000	445H	NWC	77449
MOUNTWOOD	4400	451H	NWH	77018
MOUNTWOOD	5500	451D	NWH	77091
MOURING CT	0	250U	NWC	77389
MOURNING DOVE DR	3200	291Q	NWC	77388
MOURSUND	1200	533E	SWH	77030
MOUTON CIR	1	419Q	BR	77532
MOUTON PLACE	0	620K	SB	77586
MOWERY RD	2400	572M	SWH	77045
MOWERY RD	4100	573L	SEH	77047
MOY	1000	492G	SWH	77007
MOY	2500	492C	SWH	77019
MOYNIHAN CT	0	447A	NWC	77449
MRSNY CT	4000	293H	SEM	77386
MRSNY DR	4100	293H	SEM	77386
MRYTLE AVE	2400	282Y	WL	77484
MT ANDREW DR	12500	616L	SEC	77089
MT HUNT DR	21700	290R	NWC	77388
MUCKLEROY	6500	413W	NEH	77076
MUDDOBBER LN	0	406R	NWC	77433
MUDDY SPRING DR	17000	367X	NWC	77095
MUECHKE CEMETERY RD	0	333J	NCC	77073
MUELLER LN	6400	330C	NWC	77379
MUELLER CEMETERY RD	11600	367R	CY	77429
MUESCHKE RD	14000	366C	CY	77429
MUESCHKE RD	14200	326L	NWC	77429
MUESCHKE RD	18000	286T	NWC	77377
MUIRFIELD CIR	7700	408L	NWC	77095
MUIRFIELD LN	14000	408L	NWC	77095
MUIRFIELD PLACE	1200	451Y	NWH	77055
MUIRFIELD VALLEY DR	7300	408P	NWC	77095
MUIRFIELD VILLAGE DR	13800	370B	NWC	77069
MUIRWOOD LN	300	568K	SG	77498
MUIRWOOD LN	7300	408L	NWC	77041
MUIRWOOD PLACE LN	19600	329C	NWC	77379
MUIR WOODS TRAIL	12700	377B	NEC	77346
MULA CIR	10200	569M	SF	77477
MULA CT	13100	569M	SF	77477
MULA LN	12800	569M	SF	77477
MULA RD	9700	569M	SF	77477
MULBERRY	0	288M	TB	77375
MULBERRY	0	616T	PL	77581
MULBERRY	0	659T	LC	77573
MULBERRY	100	531H	BL	77401
MULBERRY	2000	288R	TB	77375
MULBERRY	2300	282Y	WL	77484
MULBERRY	3300	493S	SWH	77006
MULBERRY CIR	4900	609K	MC	77459
MULBERRY CT	10900	579C	LP	77571
MULBERRY CT	19200	245H	SWM	77355
MULBERRY CT	25900	248J	SWM	77354
W. MULBERRY DR	10800	579C	LP	77571
MULBERRY LN	2100	537S	PA	77502
MULBERRY LN	7300	462Y	BT	77521
W. MULBERRY FIELD CIR	0	325R	NWC	77433
S. MULBERRY FIELD CIR	0	325R	NWC	77433
N. MULBERRY FIELD CIR	0	325R	NWC	77433
E. MULBERRY FIELD CIR	0	325R	NWC	77433
MULBERRY GROVE DR	5100	297Y	NEH	77345
MULBERRY HILL LN	3200	447N	NWC	77084
MULBERRY HILLS DR	3600	337E	NEH	77339
MULBERRY MEADOWS DR	15000	408T	NWC	77084
MULBERRY PARK LN	4500	297Q	NEH	77345
MULBERRY PARK LN	9800	289U	NWC	77375
MULBERRY RANCH DR	3100	484R	NEF	77494
MULBERRY RIDGE WAY	900	618E	SEH	77062
MULBERRY TERRACE LN	0	297K	NEH	77365
MULBERRY TREE LN	23000	291E	NWC	77389
MULESHOE CT	11100	367P	NWC	77095
MULE SPRINGS DR	11800	576L	SEH	77034
MULEY CT	0	407J	NWC	77433
MULEY CT	0	407J	NWC	77433
MULEY LN	0	407J	NWC	77433
MULEY LN	0	407J	NWC	77433
MULFORD	5100	494X	SEH	77023
MULHOLLAND DR	11200	529W	SWH	77477
MULHOLLAND DR	11800	569A	MD	77477
MULHOLLAND DR		569E	SF	77477
MULLER SKY CT	0	328L	NWC	77377
MULLINS DR	6300	531J	SWH	77081
MULLINS DR	8400	531S	SWH	77096
MULLINS DR	11300	571A	SWH	77035
MULLINS LN	14800	374V	NCC	77032
MULVEY	5300	494C	NEH	77020
MUM LN	0	577S	SEH	77034
MUNCIE	0	257Q	SEM	77357
MUNDARE LN	7300	371W	NWC	77086
MUNFORD	100	453S	NWH	77008
N. MUNGER	100	536G	PA	77506
MUNGER	100	536L	PA	77506
MUNGER	1100	494X	SEH	77023
MUNGER	2000	534B	SEH	77023
MUNICIPAL	0	490J	BH	77024
MUNN	7900	495J	NEH	77029
MUNN	10300	496J	JC	77029
MUNSEY DR	19500	446L	NWC	77449
MUNSHAW	5700	577N	SEH	77034
MUNSON LN	15700	571X	SWH	77053
MURANO GARDENS CT	0	445F	NWC	77493
MURDOCK	3500	573U	SEH	77047
MURFF LN	0	420L	NEC	77532
MURFIELD DR	2100	659C	LC	77573
MURICIA DR	0	659S	LC	77573
MURLEY	9700	412G	NWC	77038
MURPHY	800	656H	FR	77546
MURPHY	5900	534P	SEH	77033
MURPHY	23500	256Z	SEM	77357
MURPHY LN	700	576D	PA	77504
MURPHY RD	2000	609G	MC	77459
MURPHY RD	12000	569G	SWC	77031
MURPHY RD	12100	569Q	SF	77477
MURPHY WOOD DR	0	657U	LC	77573
MURRAY RD	14000	417X	NEC	77044
MURRAYBAY	1400	450W	NWH	77080
MURRAY BROOK DR	9900	530U	SWH	77071
MURRAYHILL DR	1100	449Z	NWH	77043
MURRELET CT	15800	375Q	NEC	77396
MURRELL RD	17600	284H	WCO	77447
MURRELL RD	19000	244Z	WCO	77447
E. MURRILL	1	501Y	BT	77520
W. MURRILL	200	501X	BT	77520
MURR WAY	10500	573R	SEH	77048
MURWORTH DR	2500	532Q	SWH	77054
MURWORTH DR	3000	532N	SWH	77025
MUSCADINE LN	2300	537X	PA	77502
MUSCATINE	10100	495H	JC	77029
MUSCATINE	10300	496E	JC	77029
MUSCATINE	13700	497F	NEC	77015
MUSCLEWOOD RD	0	460W	BT	77521

Street Name	Block	Pg/Sq	Loc	Zips
MUSCORY DR	2500	376F	NEC	77396
MUSCOVY LN	26900	324S	NWC	77447
MUSETTA CT	11500	368P	NWC	77429
MUSGROVE LN	8000	409J	NWC	77041
MUSICAL CT	9500	410J	NWC	77040
MUSKEGON	15800	374R	NEH	77032
MUSKET	11900	490K	BH	77024
MUSKET GROVES	2100	371M	NWC	77067
MUSKET RUN	21800	285M	NWC	77447
MUSKET TRAIL DR	12300	368M	NWC	77429
MUSKINGUM LN	6000	571X	SWH	77053
MUSKMALLOW CT	1	251R	WD	77380
MUSKOGEE TRAIL	1500	296M	SEM	77365
MUSKOGEE TRAIL	1600	297J	SEM	77365
MUSSELBURGH LN	0	569X	MC	77459
MUSTANG	0	490B	HE	77024
MUSTANG	0	612X	NWB	77583
MUSTANG DR	0	457T	NEC	77049
MUSTANG DR	900	656G	FR	77546
MUSTANG LN	0	612Z	NEB	77578
MUSTANG LN	4900	500M	BT	77521
MUSTANG RD	0	614Z	PL	77584
MUSTANG BEND CIR	15400	327V	NWC	77429
MUSTANG CORRAL DR	7400	334R	NCC	77338
MUSTANG CREEK CIR	15600	327V	NWC	77429
MUSTANG CROSSING	1600	610P	MC	77459
MUSTANG CROSSING CIR	15400	327V	NWC	77429
MUSTANG CROSSING CT	4300	610P	MC	77459
MUSTANG DRAW LN	6400	406V	NWC	77449
MUSTANG FALLS CT	20700	486S	SWC	77450
MUSTANG GLEN LN	0	657P	FR	77546
MUSTANG GLEN LN	16000	327Y	NWC	77429
MUSTANG HILL LN	0	446N	NWC	77449
MUSTANG LAKE CT	1400	526X	NEF	77406
MUSTANG MEADOWS LN	0	613S	NEB	77578
MUSTANG MOUNTAIN CT	0	329V	NWC	77070
MUSTANG PARK CT	9400	375V	NEC	77396
MUSTANG POINT CT	1	250A	WD	77382
MUSTANG POINTE LN	19100	526L	NEF	77407
MUSTANG RIDGE RD	11800	371M	NWC	77067
MUSTANG RIVER DR	0	368C	NWC	77429
MUSTANG SPRINGS DR	1800	610E	MC	77459
MUSTANG TRAIL	900	336F	NEH	77339
MUSTANG TRAIL	4500	451M	NWH	77092
MUSTANG TRAIL DR	16500	246Q	SWM	77355
MUSTANG VALLEY CIR	15300	327V	NWC	77429
MUSWELL LN	0	332Q	NCC	77073
MUTCHLER OAKS LN	0	293Y	NCC	77373
MUTINEER LN	12600	328Q	NWC	77377
MUTINY LN	12600	328U	NWC	77377
MYDAS FLY LN	0	297A	SEM	77357
MYERS	2300	501S	BT	77520
MYERS DR	0	332W	NWC	77090
MYERS DR	14500	332W	NCC	77090
MYERS LN	19700	255C	SEM	77357
MYERS MILL DR	1200	570X	MC	77489
MYKAWA RD	1400	615E	PL	77581
MYKAWA RD	5600	534P	SEH	77033
MYKAWA RD	8300	574Z	SEH	77048
MYKAWA RD	12600	615E	PL	77581
MYLLA	12300	496L	NEH	77015
MYNOR WOOD LN	17000	373N	NEH	77060
MYRA	400	656D	FR	77546
MYRA	2100	373Z	NCC	77039
MYRNA LN	1900	444U	KT	77493
MYRNA LN	13100	457W	NEC	77015
MYRTLE	100	493G	NEH	77009
MYRTLE	2500	282Y	WL	77484
MYRTLE	2800	533N	SWH	77054
MYRTLE	6400	534H	SEH	77087
MYRTLE	6800	535A	SEH	77087
MYRTLE	11700	419Y	BR	77532
MYRTLE DR	200	500A	BT	77520
MYRTLE LN	7900	610S	MC	77459
MYRTLE LN	12800	496M	NEH	77015
MYRTLEA DR	13300	489A	SWH	77079
MYRTLEA LN	800	489C	SWH	77079
MYRTLE CREEK	0	289D	NWC	77375
MYRTLE CREEK DR	300	539X	LP	77571
MYRTLE CREST CT	0	615L	PL	77581
MYRTLE FIELD LN	9900	416Z	NEC	77044
MYRTLE LAKE LN	0	524C	NEF	77494
MYRTLELAND LN	15100	368E	NWC	77429
MYRTLE OAK ST	0	414V	NEH	77016
MYRTLE RAIN CT	0	446K	NWC	77449
MYRTLE RANCH DR	3100	484R	NEF	77494
MYRTLE SPRINGS	25000	292U	NCC	77373
MYRTLEWOOD	900	616Q	FR	77546
MYRTLEWOOD	1300	616Q	PL	77581
MYRTLEWOOD	5100	534W	SEH	77033
MYRTLEWOOD DR	0	657Q	LC	77573
MYSTERY	23300	339P	HU	77336
MYSTIC	1300	494G	NEH	77020
MYSTICAL LEGEND DR		289P	NWC	77375
MYSTIC ARBOR LN	0	612F	PL	77545
MYSTIC ARBOR LN	0	488N	SWH	77077
MYSTIC BEND DR	14500	368E	NWC	77429
MYSTIC BERRY DR	0	524E	NEF	77494
MYSTIC BERRY DR	0	524E	NEF	77494
MYSTIC BERRY DR	0	524E	NEF	77494
MYSTIC BLUE TRAIL	0	325R	NWC	77433
MYSTIC BLUFF LN	0	367P	NWC	77433
MYSTIC BRIDGE DR	6300	533F	SWH	77021
MYSTIC CANYON DR	30500	253S	SEM	77386
MYSTIC CASTLE LN	26800	296X	SEM	77339
MYSTIC COVE LN	0	612K	PL	77545
MYSTIC CREEK LN	19600	366V	NWC	77433
MYSTIC CROSSING CT	9600	408D	NWC	77065
MYSTIC CYPRESS DR	0	446D	NWC	77449
MYSTIC FALLS LN	0	375Z	NEC	77396
MYSTIC FOREST LN	4800	375V	NEC	77396
MYSTIC GLEN LOOP	400	336E	NEH	77339
MYSTIC GROVE LN	8400	528Q	SWC	77083
MYSTIC HARBOR LN	16600	367Q	NWC	77095
MYSTIC MANOR CT	0	328A	NWC	77429
MYSTIC MANOR CT	0	328B	NWC	77377
S. MYSTIC MEADOW	2400	533F	SWH	77021
N. MYSTIC MEADOW	2400	533F	SWH	77021
W. MYSTIC MEADOW	6300	533F	SWH	77021
E. MYSTIC MEADOW	6300	533F	SWH	77021
MYSTIC MEADOWS LN	0	617X	SEC	77546
MYSTIC POINT CT	21800	525G	NEF	77494
MYSTIC PORT CT	0	485X	NEF	77494
MYSTIC PORT LN	3200	660J	LC	77573
MYSTIC RIDGE CT	0	615H	PL	77089
MYSTIC SHADOW LN	0	484S	NEF	77494
MYSTIC SHORES LN	0	574V	SEH	77048
MYSTIC SPRINGS DR	4600	376S	NEC	77396
MYSTIC SPRINGS LN	0	527S	NEF	77469
MYSTIC STONE DR	0	289T	NWC	77375
MYSTIC TERRACE LN	0	328Q	NWC	77433
MYSTIC TERRACE LN	0	328A	NWC	77377

Street Name	Block	Pg/Sq	Loc	Zips
MYSTIC TIMBER LN	0	326L	NWC	77429
MYSTIC TRAIL LOOP	400	336E	NEH	77339
MYSTIC VALLEY CT	1	250C	WD	77381
MYSTIC VILLAGE	0	620G	SB	77586
MYSTIC WOOD DR	13300	371Z	NWC	77038
MY WAY	5600	297N	NEH	77339

N

Street Name	Block	Pg/Sq	Loc	Zips
N AVENUE	600	576C	SH	77587
N, AVENUE	6500	494V	SEH	77011
N, AVENUE	7500	495S	SEH	77012
E. N, AVENUE	9100	535D	SEH	77012
NABURN GATE	10800	527X	NEF	77407
NACHITA DR	6300	457N	NEC	77049
NACOGDOCHES VALLEY DR	0	660P	LC	77573
NADALA DR	11800	368V	NWC	77065
NADIA WAY	0	569T	NEF	77459
NADINE	700	453T	NWH	77009
NADOLNEY	400	497F	NEC	77015
NAFF DR	22600	256Q	SEM	77357
N. NAGLE	1	494J	SEH	77003
NAGLE	100	494N	SEH	77003
NAGLE	2300	493V	SEH	77004
NAGRA DR	0	368Z	NWC	77065
NAGY HILL ST	8100	290N	NWC	77379
NAHAS CT	8300	613R	PL	77584
NAILL RD	0	611U	FS	77545
NAILS CREEK DR	1300	569S	SG	77478
NAIRN	7700	530Q	SWH	77074
NAIRN	8300	530P	SWH	77074
NALLE	3400	493Z	SEH	77004
NAMORA CT	9000	450L	NWH	77080
NAMORA LN	4100	450L	NWH	77080
NAN	3800	451K	NWH	77092
NANAK DR	2300	568B	NEF	77498
W. NANAKSAR	0	409S	NWC	77041
S. NANAKSAR	0	409S	NWC	77041
N. NANAKSAR	0	409S	NWC	77041
E. NANAKSAR	0	409S	NWC	77041
NANAKSAR DR	0	409S	NWC	77041
NANCE	1200	493M	NEH	77002
NANCE	1700	494K	NEH	77020
NANCET DR	6100	408Y	NWC	77041
NANCY	400	536V	PA	77502
NANCY	1000	615B	PL	77581
NANCY	4400	531D	BL	77401
NANCY CT	100	252E	OR	77385
NANCY LN	0	375D	HM	77338
NANCY LN	9200	289H	NWC	77375
NANCY LN	28200	252E	OR	77385
NANCY ANN	5900	453U	NEH	77009
NANCY BELL LN	2900	609H	MC	77459
NANCY ROSE	500	497C	NEC	77015
NANDINA CIR	11800	369N	NWC	77065
NANDINA DR	15400	408N	NWC	77095
NANDINA KNOLL	0	526P	NEF	77407
NANES DR	17000	332N	NWC	77090
NANES DR	17400	331H	NWC	77090
NANES RD	0	332N	NWC	77090
NANETTE DR	11700	415M	NEC	77050
NANNETTE LN	20500	292T	NWC	77388
NANPU LN	0	377D	NEC	77346
NANTON DR	25100	252V	SEM	77386
NANTUCKET	1200	538N	PA	77503
NANTUCKET CT	3100	613V	PL	77584
NANTUCKET DR	1000	491N	SWH	77057
NANTUCKET DR	12700	568C	SG	77478
E. NANTUCKET RD	11200	528Z	SG	77478
NANTUCKETWOOD LN	6000	491N	SWH	77057
NAOMI	1900	532R	SWH	77054
NAOMI	2300	533N	SWH	77054
NAOMI	29800	246D	SWM	77355
NAOMI HOLLOW LN	13700	488X	SWH	77082
NAPA CELLARS LN		484J	NEF	77494
NAPA CROSSING LN	28400	298X	NEH	77336
NAPA LAKES DR	0	257F	SEM	77357
NAPA MEADOW LN	0	611W	MC	77545
NAPA VALLEY TRAIL	0	337X	NEC	77346
NAPA VIEW VALLEY DR	0	286D	SWM	77355
NAPA VINE DR	16300	611B	SWH	77053
NAPAWOOD CT	7900	411P	NWC	77088
NAPFIELD DR	9000	330S	NWC	77379
NAPIER CT	14200	330W	NWC	77069
NAPIER LN	6800	330W	NWC	77069
NAPIER ST	0	657Y	LC	77573
NAPLECHASE CREST DR	0	333A	NCC	77373
NAPLES CIR	13400	570J	SF	77477
NAPLES DR	0	578A	PA	77505
NAPLES DR	23000	333C	NCC	77373
NAPLES LN	12800	570J	SF	77477
NAPLES BRIDGE RD	13400	528Y	NEF	77478
NAPLES CLIFF CT	0	366Z	NWC	77433
NAPLES CUT RD	13000	570J	SF	77477
NAPLES GROVE LN	0	573T	SEC	77047
NAPLES HOLLOW LN	21400	256W	SEM	77365
NAPLES PARK CT	7900	369D	NWC	77070
NAPLES PARK LN	13700	369D	NWC	77070
NAPLES SHORE DR	0	445A	NWC	77493
NAPLES TERRACE LN	20500	446W	NWC	77449
NAPOLEON	1700	494S	SEH	77003
NAPOLEON	2200	493Z	SEH	77004
NAPOLEON	3500	533D	SEH	77004
NAPOLEONIC CT	2900	371G	NWC	77014
NAPOLI DR	13700	369C	NWC	77070
NAPPER DR	11800	328R	NWC	77377
NARA VISTA DR	19500	328C	NWC	77377
NARCILLE	300	542A	BT	77520
NARCILLE	1000	502W	BT	77520
NARCISSUS	100	620S	CS	77565
NARCISSUS	6500	534H	SEH	77087
NARCISSUS	7200	535E	SEH	77012
NARCISSUS BROOK LN	19500	406M	NWC	77433
NARCISSUS VIEW TRAIL	0	616H	SEH	77089
NAREMORE CT	17400	330K	NWC	77379
NAREMORE DR	7400	330F	NWC	77379
NARNIA SPRINGS CT	9500	576J	SEH	77075
NARNIA VALE CT	0	326Y	NWC	77433
NARNIA WAY	1	656Q	FR	77546
NARON LN	0	660G	GCO	77565
NARROW BROOK WAY	0	415X	NWH	77078
NARROW CREEK PLACE	1	250G	WD	77381
NARROW GATE DR	21000	368X	NWC	77095
NARROW GLEN CT	0	337U	NEC	77346
NARROWPEAK DR	0	327D	NWC	77429
NARROW STREAM WAY	0	445K	NWC	77493
W. NASA BLVD	700	658E	FR	77598
E. NASA PKWY	0	619L	PA	77586
W. NASA PKWY	100	618X	WB	77598
E. NASA PKWY	100	618Y	WB	77598
W. NASA PKWY	700	658B	WB	77598
E. NASA PKWY	900	618V	SEC	77058

Street Name	Block	Pg/Sq	Loc	Zips
NASA PKWY	1800	620N	SB	77586
E. NASA PKWY	2000	619S	NB	77058
E. NASA PKWY	3000	619P	PA	77058
E. NASA PKWY	3500	619R	SB	77586
NASA RD 1 BYPASS	0	618Y	WB	77598
NASA RD 1 BYPASS	0	658C	WB	77598
NASAS DR	0	255X	SEM	77365
NASH	900	493K	SWH	77019
NASH CREEK CT	6000	525G	NEF	77494
NASHLAND CT	20900	290V	NWC	77379
NASHUA	800	492C	NWH	77008
NASHUA	1100	452Y	NWH	77008
NASHUA DR	2000	570S	SF	77477
NASHUA FALLS LN		484W	NEF	77494
NASHUA PINES CT	18600	337Z	NEC	77346
NASHVILLE	7800	455K	NEH	77028
NASHWOOD CT	8500	410F	NWC	77040
NASSAU CT	5100	534F	SEH	77021
NASSAU DR	1600	620L	SB	77586
NASSAU DR	4300	609J	SG	77479
NASSAU RD	5000	534F	SEH	77021
NASSAU BAY DR	18000	618V	NB	77058
NASWORTHY DR	19200	328D	NWC	77375
NAT	14200	570R	SWH	77085
NATALIAS CT	3100	488X	SWC	77082
NATALIE	14100	572X	SWC	77053
NATALIE BEND RD	0	524B	NEF	77494
NATASHA LN	13300	457T	NEC	77015
NATASHA RUN LN	5100	371N	NWC	77066
NATCHEZ	300	500J	BT	77520
NATCHEZ	900	536K	PA	77506
NATCHEZ	3200	533K	SEH	77021
NATCHEZ CT	0	659W	LC	77573
NATCHEZ BROOK LN	15800	332V	NCC	77073
NATCHEZ CREEK LN	19100	326Y	NWC	77429
NATCHEZ CROSSING ST	21100	525Z	NEF	77406
NATCHEZ HILL TRAIL	3000	446Q	NWC	77084
NATCHEZ PARK LN	0	377E	NEC	77346
NATCHEZ RIDGE CT	5000	446C	NWC	77449
NATCHEZ TRACE	0	412E	NWC	77038
NATHAN'S COVE	0	616L	SEC	77089
NATHANIEL	9000	576J	SEH	77075
NATHANIEL BROWN	3400	533P	SEH	77021
NATHANIEL SPRINGS DR	3700	613X	NEB	77578
NATHANS PARK PLACE	0	572S	SWH	77053
NATION DR	0	569F	SF	77477
NATIONAL	1000	493E	SWH	77007
NATIONAL	2300	537T	PA	77502
NATIONAL RIDGE WAY	0	411H	NWC	77038
NATIONS DR	4000	577H	PA	77505
S. NATIVE	200	453G	NEC	77022
W. NATIVE	8800	453G	NEC	77022
N. NATIVE LN	200	453G	NEC	77022
NATOMA	3200	451Q	NWH	77092
NAT STEEL	0	409S	NWC	77041
NAT TURNER WAY	0	571K	SWH	77085
NATURAL BRIDGE DR	4400	297T	NEH	77345
NATURAL WAY	0	334L	NCC	77388
NATURE PARK LN	2000	252R	SEM	77386
NATURES HARP CT	1	250C	WD	77381
NATURES WAY	0	248F	SWM	77354
NATURES WAY	0	248G	SWM	77354
NATURES WAY	12300	456Y	NEH	77013
NATURE TRAIL	13000	457A	NEC	77044
NAUGHTON	12000	490N	SWH	77024
NAUTICA CIR	18800	338W	NEC	77346
NAUTICAL MILE LN	24700	484D	NEF	77494
NAUTICAL POINTE LN	17000	367Y	NWC	77095
NAUTILUS	500	419B	NEC	77532
NAUTILUS CT	16100	419B	NEC	77532
NAUTILUS LN	5200	461T	NEC	77521
NAUTIQUE WAY	15000	612B	SWC	77047
NAUTS CT	1800	452S	NWH	77008
W. NAVAHO TRAIL	1900	446X	NWC	77449
E. NAVAHO TRAIL	1900	446X	NWC	77449
S. NAVAHO TRAIL	20000	446X	NWC	77449
N. NAVAHO TRAIL	20000	446X	NWC	77449
NAVAJO	3700	492W	SWH	77027
NAVAJO	4200	577F	PA	77504
W. NAVAJO	17200	503F	CCO	77520
E. NAVAJO	17200	503F	CCO	77520
NAVAJO DR	1900	538R	DP	77536
NAVAJO LN	9300	248M	SWM	77354
NAVAJO LN	23600	295F	SEM	77365
NAVAJO PASS	0	658U	LC	77573
NAVAJO PLACE DR	0	249T	NWC	77375
NAVAJO TRAIL	4500	502J	BT	77521
NAVAJO TRAIL DR	17900	331C	NWC	77388
NAVARE	1700	613R	PL	77584
NAVARRO	5000	491Y	SWH	77056
NAVARRO BRANCH DR	18600	366P	NWC	77433
NAVARRO MILLS	0	288Z	NWC	77375
N. NAVASOTA	0	256N	SEM	77357
NAVASOTA	7400	415W	NEH	77016
S. NAVASOTA	20700	256N	SEM	77357
NAVENBY LN	0	457Z	NEC	77530
NAVIA LN	0	660G	GCO	77565
NAVIDAD DR	6500	527L	NEF	77083
NAVIDAD BEND CT	0	406D	NWC	77433
NAVIGATE POINT LN	0	377L	NEC	77346
E. NAVIGATION BLVD	400	495X	SEH	77012
NAVIGATION BLVD	2100	494P	SEH	77003
NAVIGATION BLVD	4400	494V	SEH	77011
NAVIGATION BLVD	7500	495S	SEH	77012
NAVIGATOR	12500	528M	SWH	77072
NAYLAND ROCK DR	3500	371K	NWC	77066
NAYLOR	1100	493H	NEH	77002
W. NAZRO	1	541B	BT	77520
E. NAZRO	1	541B	BT	77520
NEAL	0	247X	SWM	77355
NEAL	100	541B	BT	77520
NEAL	4100	535R	SEH	77017
NEAL	4600	620A	SB	77586
NEAL DR	800	568L	SG	77478
NEAL RD	1400	288D	TB	77375
NEAL RD	1500	248Z	TB	77375
NEAL RIDGE DR	7400	570Z	SWH	77489
NEAP CT	700	379X	NEC	77532
NEARLY WILD WAY	0	286Q	NWC	77377
NEATH	19000	337X	NEC	77346
NEBRASKA	300	536W	SH	77587
NEBRASKA	1000	535Z	SH	77587
NEBRASKA	3100	540D	BT	77520
NECHES	5000	454S	NEH	77026
NECHES CT	0	253Z	SEM	77386
NECHES DR	0	538R	DP	77536
NECHES RIVER DR	2800	614V	PL	77584
NECHES TRAIL LN	4600	291T	NWC	77388
NECKLACE TREE LN	9000	524C	NEF	77494
NECO RIDGE	0	611B	SWH	77053
NECORIDGE DR	16100	571X	SWH	77053
NECTAR BLOOM CT	0	292D	SEM	77386

Street Name	Block	Pg/Sq	Loc	Zips
NECTAR GROVE CT	0	444T	KT	77493
NECTAR GROVE CT	12000	616G	SEC	77089
NEDITH LN	3600	538U	DP	77536
NEDWALD	9700	495R	NEH	77029
NEECE DR	6300	408U	NWC	77080
NEEDHAM	10100	456W	NEH	77013
NEEDHAM LN	25000	296L	SEM	77365
NEEDHAM RD	1200	296R	SEM	77365
NEEDHAM CROSS DR	9400	329D	NWC	77379
NEEDLE BEND CT	0	610Y	MC	77459
NEEDLEPOINT RD	0	503G	CCO	77520
NEEDLEPOINT RD	7800	462T	NEC	77521
NEEDLEPOINT RD	20100	463U	CCO	77520
NEEDLEROCK CT	0	376Q	NEC	77396
NEEDLES NEST DR	0	411D	NWC	77038
NEEDLES THROW LN	0	411D	NWC	77038
NEEDLE WALK LN	20200	291S	NWC	77379
NEELEY	0	457T	NEC	77049
NEELEY DR	1300	450Z	SV	77055
NEELIE CT	0	334R	NCC	77338
NEENAH DR	2100	484K	NEF	77494
NEESHAW DR	11100	369T	NWC	77065
NEFF	6300	531J	SWH	77074
NEFF	7900	530F	SWH	77036
NEFF	11500	529F	SWH	77072
NEHOC LN	19200	338W	NEC	77346
NEIDIGK RD	0	248P	SWM	77354
NEIDIGK SAWMILL RD	100	248K	SWM	77354
NEILS BRANCH DR	13600	488P	SWH	77077
NEIMAN LN	1100	452B	NWH	77091
W. NELDA RD	400	412M	NEH	77037
NELDA RD	900	412L	NWH	77088
NELKINS CT	2700	494A	NEH	77026
NELL	700	536K	PA	77506
NELL	2100	576B	SEH	77034
NELLA CIR	21500	333F	NCC	77338
NELLIE	8000	453H	NEH	77022
NELLIE GAIL TRAIL LN	20300	486T	SWC	77450
W. NELLIS RD	100	412R	NCC	77037
NELLSFIELD LN	0	575V	SEH	77075
NELMS	6900	574H	SEH	77061
NELMS	8300	575G	SEH	77061
NELSON	0	577X	SEH	77034
NELSON	200	620T	SB	77586
NELSON	600	419H	CB	77532
NELSON	6100	614Q	PL	77584
NELSON	14400	571Q	SWH	77045
NELSON	27200	292L	SP	77373
N. NELSON DR	4900	444Z	KT	77493
NELSON BRIDGE DR	0	250X	NWC	77389
NELSON FALLS LN	0	452X	NWH	77008
NELSON LANDING DR	0	326T	NWC	77429
NELSON WAY	0	484B	KT	77494
NELVA PARK CT	20400	446K	NWC	77449
NELVA PARK DR	3800	446K	NWC	77449
NELWOOD DR	2400	371V	NEC	77038
NELWYN	5900	453U	NEH	77009
NEMARD LN	8500	457D	NEC	77049
NEMES LN	0	616N	PL	77581
NEMY RD	0	340P	LCO	77535
NENANA DR	4000	532S	SWH	77025
NENANA DR	4300	531V	SWH	77035
NENTWICH LN	0	457V	NEC	77049
NEON	13500	573V	SEH	77047
NEOSHO	0	248M	SWM	77354
NEPAU DR	11100	529W	SWH	77477
NEPTUNE LN	900	618K	SEH	77062
NERO LAKE DR	0	446D	NWC	77449
NESBY	0	572S	SWH	77053
NESMITH DR	12300	571E	SWH	77035
NEST LN	600	453E	NWH	77022
NESTING CRANE CT	0	250Q	NWC	77389
NESTING WOOD DR	0	376W	NEC	77396
NESTON DR	13600	408Y	NWC	77041
NESTRA DR	0	445F	NWC	77493
NETHERFIELD	6900	534V	SEH	77087
NETHERWOOD CT	2400	613P	NEB	77584
NETLEAF GARDEN DR	5500	524D	NEF	77494
NETT	4500	492G	SWH	77007
NETTLEBROOK LN	20700	525H	NEF	77450
NETTLETON	2000	493Z	SEH	77004
NETTLETON CT	3500	493Z	SEH	77004
NEUCES CREEK	0	609U	MC	77459
NEUENS RD	9400	450S	NWH	77080
NEUENS RD	10200	450S	NWH	77043
NEUHAUS	100	575E	SEH	77061
NEUHAUS	7300	574H	SEH	77061
NEUMANN DR	16600	618M	SEH	77058
NEURATH	100	494N	SEH	77003
NEUTRAL BAY DR	0	327W	NWC	77429
NEUVILLE RD	0	496D	NEC	77015
NEVA CT	0	334R	NCC	77338
NEVADA	400	576B	SH	77587
NEVADA	1400	492R	SWH	77006
NEVADA	1400	540D	BT	77520
NEVELSON CIR	17200	330K	NWC	77379
NEVERMORE DR	13300	368L	NWC	77429
NEVISWAY	16900	447D	NWC	77084
NEW RD	3000	380Y	NEC	77532
NEW RD	4900	381W	NEC	77532
NEW ANN	16200	367L	CY	77429
NEW BARTONC REEK CIR	0	366N	NWC	77433
NEWBEAR DR	5300	446B	NWC	77449
NEW BEDFORD	16300	419C	NEC	77532
NEW BEDFORD CT	100	419C	NEC	77532
NEWBERRY	4500	533V	SEH	77051
NEWBERRY	12700	528Z	SG	77478
NEWBERRY BEND DR	0	296E	SEM	77365
NEWBERRY FOREST DR	0	257E	SEM	77357
NEW BIRMINGHAM DR	0	366N	NWC	77433
NEWBOROUGH DR	10500	529Q	SWH	77099
NEWBRIDGE	6700	451A	NWH	77092
NEWBRIDGE CT	2400	613N	NEB	77584
NEWBROOK CIR	8500	529P	SWH	77072
NEWBROOK DR	3000	613T	NEB	77584
NEWBROOK DR	10300	615D	SEC	77089
NEWBROOK DR	11200	528R	SWH	77072
NEWBROOK DR	12800	528Q	SWC	77072
NEW BRUNSWICK DR	11900	616D	SEH	77089
NEWBURGE LN	0	486D	SWC	77094
NEWBURGH DR	9000	408A	NWC	77095
NEWBURY CT	2700	613T	NEB	77584
NEWBURY DR	6200	407W	NWC	77449
NEWBURY PARK DR	0	525D	NEF	77450
NEWBURY PARK DR	20800	525D	NEF	77450
NEWCASTLE DR	2800	501R	BT	77521
NEWCASTLE DR	3100	491V	SWH	77027
NEWCASTLE DR	5400	531M	SWH	77081
NEWCASTLE DR	5401	531M	BL	77401
NEWCASTLE DR	5500	531M	BL	77401
NEW CASTLE LN	0	657U	LC	77573
S. NEWCASTLE BAY TRAIL	0	251W	SWM	77389

Street Name	Block	Pg/Sq	Loc	Zips
N. NEWCASTLE BAY TRAIL	0	251W	SWM	77389
NEWCASTLE RIDGE LN	0	406X	NWC	77449
NEW CEDARS DR	1300	618E	SEH	77062
NEW CENTURY DR	9300	579E	SEC	77507
NEWCHESTER LN	0	450V	NWH	77080
NEWCOMB WAY	1600	618R	SEH	77058
NEWCOMEN DR	3800	371K	NWC	77066
NEWCOURT BLVD	0	289Q	NWC	77375
NEWCOURT PLACE	0	289Q	NWC	77375
NEWCREST DR	12700	372M	NCC	77060
NEWCROFT CT	0	289R	NWC	77375
NEW CYPRESS DR	12600	368J	NWC	77429
NEWDALE DR	10100	529X	SWH	77099
NEW DECADE DR	0	579E	SEC	77507
NEWEL ELM ST	11700	411G	NWC	77038
NEW ELLENTON DR	0	257E	SEM	77357
NEW ENDING CT	0	574K	SEH	77048
NEW ENGLAND CT	2800	657C	SEC	77598
NEWFALLS CT	20500	526J	NEF	77407
NEW FIELD DR	16100	527C	SWC	77082
NEWFIELD BRIDGE LN	15100	528W	NEF	77498
NEW FOREST DR	18300	255W	SEM	77365
NEW FOREST RD	9100	330S	NWC	77379
NEW FOREST GLEN	6600	457Q	NEC	77049
NEW FOREST PARK LN	0	253Q	SEM	77386
NEW FOREST PARKWAY	0	457P	NEC	77049
NEWFOUNDLAND CT	0	290Z	NWC	77379
NEWGATE DR	23100	333D	NCC	77373
NEWGLEN LN	16800	407V	NWC	77084
NEW GREEN CT	4100	337F	NEH	77339
NEWHALL	11600	414Q	NEC	77093
NEW HAMPSHIRE	300	495Z	NEH	77029
NEW HAMPTON DR	12300	328V	NWC	77377
W. NEW HARMONY PLACE	0	250P	NWC	77389
S. NEW HARMONY PLACE	0	250P	NWC	77389
N. NEW HARMONY PLACE	0	250P	NWC	77389
E. NEW HARMONY PLACE	0	250P	NWC	77389
NEW HARMONY TRAIL	0	250N	NWC	77389
NEW HARMONY TRAIL	300	250P	NWC	77389
W. NEW HARMONY TRAIL	8200	250N	NWC	77389
W. NEW HARMONY TRAIL	9200	249M	NWH	77375
W. NEW HARMONY TRAIL	9200	249M	NWH	77375
NEW HASTINGS DR	15100	408K	NWC	77095
NEW HAVEN DR	200	453A	NEH	77076
NEWHAVEN TRAIL	1100	613L	NEB	77584
NEWHOFF	2500	494A	NEH	77026
NEW HOPE LN	400	485A	NEF	77494
NEWHOPE TERRACE LN	0	446G	NWC	77449
NEW HOPE VIEW LN	0	572F	SWH	77045
NEWHOUSE	3700	492R	SWH	77019
NEW JERSEY	1700	540D	BT	77520
NEWKAY LN	9100	329M	NWC	77379
NEW KENT CT	14700	528S	NEF	77498
NEW KENT DR	9600	528S	NEF	77498
NEW KENTUCKY RD	12600	368L	NWC	77429
NEW KENTUCKY PARK DR	0	285M	NWC	77447
NEW KENTUCKY VILLAGE DR	20200	285M	NWC	77447
NEW KINGS TRAIL	20000	337P	NEC	77346
NEWKIRK LN	5200	534K	SEH	77021
NEWLAND CREST DR	0	411D	NWC	77038
NEWLANDS CT	11700	329N	NWC	77377
NEWLIGHT BEND DR	0	407C	NWC	77095
NEW LONDON DR	0	659E	LC	77573
NEWLY RD	15200	408S	NWC	77084
NEWMAN	800	541C	BT	77520
NEWMAN	2600	492U	SWH	77098
NEWMAN DR	3300	502B	NEC	77521
NEWMARK DR	1400	372E	NWC	77014
NEW MARKET LN	16600	527T	NEF	77083
NEW MEADOW DR	2900	501R	BT	77521
NEW MEADOW DR	11800	370N	NWC	77064
NEW MEXICO	0	541A	BT	77520
NEW MEXICO	300	495V	NEH	77029
NEW MEXICO	2000	540H	BT	77520
NEWMILL CT	20800	290V	NWC	77379
NEWMINT CT	20100	446T	NWC	77449
NEWMINT DR	20200	446T	NWC	77449
NEWMONT	0	530A	SWH	77042
NEW MOON TRAIL	20200	378G	NEC	77532
NEW OAK CT	6300	337P	NEC	77346
NEW OAK TRAIL	1	337P	NEC	77346
NEW ORLEANS	1300	538N	DP	77536
NEW ORLEANS	2400	494F	NEH	77026
NEW ORLEANS	3000	494F	NEH	77020
NEWPARK DR	4700	449H	NWH	77041
E. NEWPARK DR	5000	449D	NWH	77041
N. NEWPARK DR	10400	449H	NWC	77041
NEWPARK DR	12000	328R	NWC	77377
NEW PINES DR	700	292L	SP	77373
NEW PLYMOUTH CT	2900	657D	SEC	77598
NEWPORT	0	258E	SEM	77357
NEWPORT	5500	534C	SEH	77023
NEWPORT BLVD	0	419C	NEC	77532
NEWPORT BLVD	200	658P	LC	77573
NEWPORT CT	0	294J	SEM	77386
NEWPORT LN	0	294J	SEM	77386
NEWPORT LN	0	614S	NEB	77584
W. NEWPORT BEND	0	485A	SWC	77494
S. NEWPORT BEND	0	485A	SWC	77494
N. NEWPORT BEND	0	485A	SWC	77494
E. NEWPORT BEND	0	485A	SWC	77494
NEWPORT BEND CIR	0	485A	SWC	77494
NEWPORT BRIDGE CIR	15200	527Z	NEF	77498
NEWPORT BRIDGE CT	15100	527Z	NEF	77498
NEWPORT BRIDGE LN	10700	527Z	NEF	77498
NEWPORT MIST DR	0	328F	NWC	77429
NEWPORT SHORE DR	11800	369W	NWC	77065
NEWQUAY	5600	571P	SWH	77085
NEW ROCHELLE CT	12500	616H	SEH	77089
NEW ROCHELLE DR	12100	616H	SEH	77089
NEWSHIRE DR	4000	532N	SWH	77025
NEWSOME GLENN DR	0	332W	NWC	77090
NEW SOUTH WALES CT	2300	485R	NEF	77450
NEW STAFFORD RD	0	570E	SWH	77031
NEWTON	10800	576S	SEH	77075
NEWTON	11200	576W	SEH	77089
NEWTON DR	3500	537R	PA	77503
NEWTON DR	22000	256K	SEM	77357
NEWTON RD	0	458Q	NEC	77049
NEWTON BRANCH LN	0	615M	PL	77089
NEWTON FALLS LN	14800	528W	NEF	77498
NEW TRAILS DR	8200	251B	WD	77381
NEW TREE LN	1100	570X	MC	77489
NEW VILLAGE LN	13700	528X	NEF	77498
NEW VISTA LN	11300	371R	NWC	77067
NEW WEST DR	0	579E	SEC	77507
NEW WORLD DR	6200	406T	NWC	77449
NEW YORK	2100	541E	BT	77520
NEW YORK	6300	533R	SEH	77021
NEXUS RD	0	611D	SWH	77053
NEXUS CROSSING LN	0	485M	SWC	77450
NEY	9900	576E	SEH	77034

Street Name	Block	Pg/Sq	Loc	Zips
NEYLAND	0	543Q	BC	77520
NEYLAND	1	453J	NWH	77022
NHATRANG ST	0	529Q	SWH	77072
NIAGARA	900	533U	SEH	77051
NIAGRA FALLS DR	20100	289W	NWC	77375
NIA PLACE	13500	571K	SWH	77085
NIBLICK LN	0	334F	NCC	77373
NICAR	100	413E	NCC	77037
NICE CT	800	496D	NEC	77015
NICECREST DR	0	525L	NEF	77407
NICHE WAY	20800	525D	NEF	77450
NICHILO DR	0	250U	NWC	77389
NICHOLAS	14800	570L	SWH	77085
NICHOLAS DR	2500	615Q	PL	77581
NICHOLAS LN	0	524E	NEF	77494
NICHOLAS MEADOW CT	7100	408R	NWC	77041
NICHOLAS MEADOW DR	13100	408R	NWC	77041
NICHOLAS PASS CT	0	366R	NWC	77433
NICHOLAS PLACE	0	491Y	BL	77401
NICHOLAS POINT CT	0	366Y	NWC	77433
NICHOLAS TRAIL	6500	609Y	NEF	77459
NICHOLE WOODS CT	0	572R	SWH	77047
NICHOLE WOODS DR	1500	573N	SWC	77047
NICHOLE WOODS DR	1801	572R	SWC	77047
NICHOLFOREST DR	0	250T	NWC	77389
NICHOLI LN	5800	660X	DI	77539
NICHOLS	0	246S	SWM	77355
NICHOLS	0	284R	NWC	77447
NICHOLS	4200	494C	NEH	77020
NICHOLS AVE	2200	659Z	GCO	77539
NICHOLS LN	18700	255D	SEM	77357
NICHOLS ALLEY	0	494F	NEH	77020
NICHOLSON	300	620P	SB	77586
NICHOLSON	700	492D	NWH	77007
NICHOLSON	900	452V	NWH	77008
NICHOLSON	4400	452M	NWH	77018
NICHOLS SAWMILL RD	23000	244Y	WCO	77447
NICHOLS SAWMILL RD	24300	245V	SWM	77355
NICHOLS SAWMILL RD	25000	246J	SWM	77355
NICHOLS TRACE DR	24100	296J	SEM	77365
NICKEL DR	15400	570Z	SWH	77489
NICKEL BAUER DR	0	285P	NWC	77447
NICKEL BAUER DR	0	285L	NWC	77447
NICKEL GROVE DR	0	367X	NWC	77095
NICKEL PLANK RD	0	457G	NEC	77049
NICKELWOOD CT	9300	369M	NWC	77070
NICKERSON LN	14900	412D	NEH	77060
NICKERTON LN	21700	291S	NWC	77388
NICKLEBY CT	3000	485T	NEF	77494
NICKS RUN LN	2800	485N	NEF	77494
NICKWILL WAY DR	3200	291Z	NWC	77388
NICLA ST	0	659P	LC	77573
NICOLE CIR	4600	447D	NWH	77084
NICOLE CT	12700	570J	MC	77489
NICOLE DR	3700	537M	PA	77503
NICOLE LN	16700	447D	NWC	77084
NICOLES PLACE TRAIL	10600	616G	SEC	77089
NICOLI CREEK DR	0	335N	NCC	77338
NICOLLET LAKE LN	0	524B	NEF	77494
NIELAN	5300	455P	NEH	77028
NIGHT BEACON POINT DR	9100	289Z	NWC	77379
NIGHT BIRD TRAIL	20000	378G	NEC	77532
NIGHTBROOK LN	0	609U	MC	77459
NIGHTHAVEN CT	0	407B	NWC	77095
NIGHTHAWK CT	400	568T	SG	77478
NIGHT HAWK PLACE	1	251V	WD	77380
NIGHTINGALE DR	5400	536N	SEH	77017
NIGHTINGALE DR	13500	416E	NEC	77050
NIGHTINGALE FALLS CT	0	327X	CY	77429
W. NIGHTINGALE HILL LN	0	524F	NEF	77494
E. NIGHTINGALE HILL LN	0	524G	NEF	77494
NIGHTMIST CT	0	484V	NEF	77494
NIGHTOWL TRAIL	2500	333A	NCC	77373
NIGHT RAIN CT	1	251A	WD	77381
NIGHTSHADE	5300	660X	DI	77539
NIGHTSHADE CT	5000	291S	NWC	77388
NIGHTSHADE CREST LN	0	571G	SWC	77083
NIGHT SONG CT	1	251Z	WD	77380
NIGHTSONG DR	0	612J	PL	77545
NIGHT STAR LN	0	244H	WCO	77447
NIGHT STAR LN	1900	488R	SWH	77077
NIGHTWIND LN	0	485Y	NEF	77450
NIGHTWIND PLACE	1	250C	WD	77381
NIGHTWOOD LN	0	571F	SWH	77085
NIGH WAY	0	576V	SEH	77034
NIHM LN	0	484R	NEF	77494
NIKKI LN	0	570T	MC	77489
NIKKI HILLS CT	0	293F	SEM	77386
NIKKI HILLS CT	0	293F	SEM	77386
NILELAKE CT	0	656U	FR	77546
NILES	8100	535P	SEH	77017
NIMBLE LN	0	458S	NEC	77049
NIMITZ	12700	496M	NEH	77015
NIMITZ	13700	497F	NEC	77015
NIMROD	500	494K	NEH	77020
NINA DR	16700	617Y	SEC	77546
NINA LN	0	569T	SF	77477
NINA LEE LN	1700	452J	NWH	77018
NINA LEE LN	4400	451L	NWH	77092
NINA RIDGE LN	0	293F	SEM	77386
NINA RIDGE LN	0	293F	SEM	77386
NINE IRON CT	2100	616K	SEH	77089
NINE MILE LN	5900	609Z	MC	77459
NINTE	0	490H	HC	77024
NIPPERSINK	0	339W	NEC	77532
NITA	3000	573F	SEH	77051
NITA AVE	0	330Y	NWC	77069
NITIDA	12900	571G	SWH	77045
NITSHILL LN	17100	527W	NEF	77407
NIX	1	494J	SEH	77003
NIXBURG LN	23300	296N	SEM	77365
NOACK RD	12900	247Q	SWM	77355
NOAH	3400	533P	SEH	77021
NOAH LN	0	330K	NWC	77379
NOAH LN	0	660Q	LC	77573
NOAH ARBOR LN	0	486H	SWC	77094
NOAH BLUFF LN	0	376W	NEC	77396
NOAH LANDING DR	8800	370S	NWC	77064
NOAHPINES CT	0	293J	SEM	77386
NOAH RIDGE CT	28000	293J	SEM	77386
NOAHS LANDING LN	0	573Z	SEH	77047
NOBBE HOLLOW DR	0	524B	NEF	77494
NOBEL LN	0	282H	NWC	77484
NOBILITY DR	10600	529W	SWH	77099
NOBILITY DR	11100	529W	SWH	77477
NOBILITY MEADOWS DR	0	494J	NEH	77020
NOBILITY PARK DR	0	494J	NEH	77020
NOBILITY PINES DR	0	494J	NEH	77020
NOBLE	100	292Q	SP	77373
NOBLE	1100	493D	NEH	77009
NOBLE	1700	494A	NEH	77026
NOBLE	3900	494B	NEH	77020

Street Name	Block	Pg/Sq	Loc	Zips
NOBLE CT	4500	501E	BT	77521
NOBLEBRIAR CT	15700	570Z	SWH	77489
NOBLE BROOK CT	15500	457Q	NEC	77049
NOBLE CANYON LN	0	485Y	NEF	77494
NOBLE CEDAR LN	0	289G	NWC	77375
NOBLE CREEK CT	0	457L	NEC	77049
NOBLECREST DR	13200	408R	NWC	77041
NOBLE CRUSADE CT	0	289T	NWC	77375
NOBLE CYPRESS CT	4100	578U	SEH	77059
NOBLE EARL CT	0	404Z	NWC	77493
NOBLE ENERGY WAY	0	329T	NWC	77070
NOBLE FOREST DR	18000	377A	NEC	77346
NOBLE FOREST LN	0	253K	SEM	77386
NOBLE GROVE LN	0	253J	SEM	77385
NOBLE GROVE LN	2800	485N	NEF	77494
NOBLE LAKES LN	3100	489W	SWH	77082
NOBLEMAN DR	7400	408R	NWC	77041
NOBLE MANOR LN	0	612Q	PL	77584
NOBLE MEADOW LN	16300	332R	NCC	77073
NOBLE OAK CT	17700	407K	NWC	77095
NOBLE OAK TRAIL	4200	578U	SEH	77059
NOBLE OAK WAY	0	578U	SEH	77059
NOBLE PASS LN	0	367Y	NWC	77095
NOBLE PINE DR	4200	578U	SEH	77059
NOBLE POINTE CT	10200	329C	NWC	77379
NOBLE POINTE DR	1500	329C	NWC	77379
NOBLE RUN	7700	337M	NEC	77346
NOBLE SAGE CT	4500	578U	SEH	77059
NOBLES CROSSING DR	22000	334E	NCC	77373
NOBLE SPRINGS DR	800	617H	SEH	77062
NOBLETON DR	0	289V	NWC	77375
NOBLE WAY CT	0	660K	LC	77573
NOBLEWOOD CT	2100	658S	LC	77573
NOBLE WOOD DR	0	293H	SEM	77386
NOBLEWOOD BEND	11300	489X	SWH	77082
NOBLEWOOD CREST LN	11300	489X	SWH	77082
NOBLEWOOD WAY	16200	527B	SWH	77082
NOCHE DR	7000	459L	NEC	77049
NOCO DR	12200	328D	NWC	77375
NOCO PYNG RD	0	502E	BT	77520
NOCTURNAL CT	0	445F	NWC	77493
NOCTURNAL CT	0	445K	NWC	77493
NOCTURNE	0	410J	NWC	77040
NOCTURNE LN	1500	449V	NWH	77043
NOD AVE	100	419U	BR	77532
NODAWAY LN	5200	331J	NWC	77379
NODAWAY CREEK CT	0	571F	SWH	77085
NODDING PINES	3200	251N	SWM	77380
NODDING PINES LN	7000	456L	NEC	77044
NODY'S WAY	3000	612S	FS	77545
NOEL	8900	574A	SEH	77033
NOEL CT	3100	613X	NEB	77584
NOELKE CREEK CIR	0	366P	NWC	77433
NOELLE CT	0	334R	NCC	77338
NOGALAS LN	0	660G	GCO	77565
NOGALUS DR	1500	338Y	NEH	77532
NOISY WATERS DR	0	368X	NWC	77095
NOKONAS	0	295F	SEM	77365
NOLA CT	12200	456Y	NEH	77013
NOLA LN	400	247F	SWM	77362
NOLAN	0	500U	BT	77520
NOLAN	1	494N	SEH	77003
S. NOLAN CT	3200	613Z	NEB	77584
S. NOLAN DR	4100	613Z	NEB	77584
N. NOLAN DR	4100	613Z	NEB	77584
NOLAN RD	1500	501V	BT	77520
NOLAN RIVER WAY	0	367S	NWC	77433
NOLAN RYAN EXPRESSWAY	0	613J	PL	77584
NOLAN RYAN EXPRESSWAY	0	613J	PL	77584
NOLD RD	10300	414Y	NEH	77016
NOLDA	4500	492H	SWH	77007
NOLDALE DR	5000	414Y	NEH	77016
NOLEY CT	0	531H	BL	77401
NOLINA DR	2500	293F	SEM	77386
NOLRIDGE DR	5000	414Y	NEH	77016
NOLTE TOSCANO	0	659M	LC	77573
MONTCREST CIR	20400	290S	NWC	77379
NOOK CT	9100	410V	NWC	77040
NOONDAY CT	400	413A	NCC	77060
NOONDAY LN	400	413A	NCC	77060
NOONTIDE CIR	1	251R	WD	77380
NORA'S LN	100	453J	NWH	77022
NORBORNE LN	5200	330U	NWC	77069
NORBURN	12600	528Z	NEF	77478
NORCHESTER VILLAGE DR	10500	369F	NWC	77070
NORCHESTER WAY	24100	290D	NWC	77389
NORCIA CT	0	445A	NWC	77493
NORCREST DR	1800	451S	NWH	77055
NORDIC DR	14100	457N	NEC	77049
NORDLING RD	5400	453A	NEH	77076
NORDLING RD	7500	413S	NEH	77037
NORDWAY DR	17300	407U	NWC	77084
NORELL DR	700	498B	CV	77530
NORENE CT	17000	407Q	NWC	77084
NORFOLK	1600	492Z	SWH	77006
NORFOLK	1700	492Z	SWH	77098
NORFOLK	3700	492X	SWH	77046
NORFOLK	4000	492W	SWH	77027
NORFOLK CT	0	258E	SEM	77357
NORFOLK DR	0	257H	SEM	77357
NORFOLK DR	800	613G	NEB	77584
NORFOLK BROOK CT	0	484J	NEF	77494
NORFOLK PINE	3900	611W	FS	77545
NORFOLK RIDGE WAY	0	526T	NEF	77407
NORFOLK TRAIL LN	0	484X	NEF	77494
NORFOLK TRAIL LN	0	484X	NEF	77494
NORFORD LN	14000	528P	SWC	77083
NORFORK TRAIL LN	0	484X	NEF	77494
NORFORK TRAIL LN	0	484X	NEF	77494
NORGROVE CT	7900	369D	NWC	77070
NORHAM	1100	453H	NEH	77022
NORHAM CT	8700	528N	NEF	77083
NORHAM DR	8800	528N	NEF	77083
NORHAM MANOR DR	0	289X	NWC	77379
NORHILL BLVD	2500	493A	NWH	77009
NORHILL BLVD	3400	453S	NWH	77009
NORHILL FAIR LN	0	328G	NWC	77377
NORHILL HEIGHTS LN	0	377F	NEC	77346
NORHILL POINTE DR	14000	377X	NEC	77044
NORKEY	12300	411A	NWC	77086
NORLAND	6200	453P	NEH	77022
NORLAND POINT LN	0	332R	NCC	77073
NORLINDA	1700	413R	NCC	77093
W. NORMA	100	493C	NWH	77009
NORMA LN	3400	615S	PL	77584
NORMAN	0	613Y	NEB	77578
NORMAN	2100	537K	PA	77506
NORMANDALE	1700	495K	NEH	77029
NORMAN MEADOWS LN	21100	334R	NCC	77338
NORMANDY CT	0	568B	SG	77498
NORMANDY DR	100	456Z	NEC	77015
NORMANDY DR	400	496H	NEC	77015

Street Name	Block	Pg/Sq	Loc	Zips
NORMANDY CROSSING DR	12500	496H	NEC	77015
NORMANDY FOREST CT	3300	291U	NWC	77388
NORMANDY FOREST DR	20700	291U	NWC	77388
NORMANDY WAY	4500	533M	SEH	77021
NORMAN HILL LN	0	660K	LC	77573
NORMANS WOODS	1200	488L	SWH	77077
NORMEADOW LN	10800	413Y	NEH	77076
NORMENTS	5400	414D	NEC	77039
NORMENTS	5900	415A	NEC	77039
NORMONT DR	10500	369B	NWC	77070
NORMONT DR	11700	329W	NWC	77070
NORMONT DR	12100	328Z	NWC	77070
NORRIS DR	3000	532P	SWH	77025
NORSHIRE	2000	573S	SWH	77047
NORSTAND LN	0	408W	NWC	77084
NORSTRUM FALLS CT	12900	367H	NWC	77429
E. NORTH	0	500P	BT	77520
E. NORTH	0	502N	BT	77520
NORTH	0	614M	PL	77581
NORTH	0	616U	PL	77581
NORTH	100	500P	BT	77520
NORTH	100	493C	NWH	77009
NORTH	1000	335V	HM	77338
NORTH	1800	536A	NEH	77015
NORTH	2400	537K	PA	77506
NORTH	5700	484B	KT	77494
NORTH	21200	256S	SEM	77357
NORTH BLVD	1300	493W	SWH	77006
NORTH BLVD	1700	492Y	SWH	77098
NORTH DR	1200	658Z	LC	77573
NORTH DR	1300	458Z	CV	77530
NORTH (I. H. 45 N) FRWY	1000	493C	NWH	77009
NORTH (I. H. 45 N) FRWY	1000	493C	NWH	77009
NORTH (I. H. 45 N) FRWY	2400	453A	NWH	77009
NORTH (I. H. 45 N) FRWY	2400	453A	NWH	77009
NORTH (I. H. 45 N) FRWY	3800	453A	NWH	77022
NORTH (I. H. 45 N) FRWY	3800	453A	NWH	77022
NORTH (I. H. 45 N) FRWY	5400	453A	NWH	77076
NORTH (I. H. 45 N) FRWY	5400	453A	NWH	77076
NORTH (I. H. 45 N) FRWY	6200	412C	NWH	77076
NORTH (I. H. 45 N) FRWY	6200	412C	NWH	77076
NORTH (I. H. 45 N) FRWY	7500	412M	NEH	77037
NORTH (I. H. 45 N) FRWY	7500	412M	NEH	77037
NORTH (I. H. 45 N) FRWY	10700	372Q	NWH	77037
NORTH (I. H. 45 N) FRWY	10700	372Q	NWH	77037
NORTH (I. H. 45 N) FRWY	11400	372Q	NWC	77060
NORTH (I. H. 45 N) FRWY	11400	372Q	NWC	77060
NORTH (I. H. 45 N) FRWY	13700	372Q	NWC	77090
NORTH (I. H. 45 N) FRWY	13700	372Q	NWC	77090
NORTH (I. H. 45 N) FRWY	15200	332K	NWC	77090
NORTH (I. H. 45 N) FRWY	15200	332K	NWC	77090
NORTH (I. H. 45 N) FRWY	18700	332K	NCC	77373
NORTH (I. H. 45 N) FRWY	18700	332K	NCC	77373
NORTH (I. H. 45 N) FRWY	18701	332K	NWC	77388
NORTH (I. H. 45 N) FRWY	18701	332K	NWC	77388
NORTH (I. H. 45 N) FRWY	19500	292K	NCC	77373
NORTH (I. H. 45 N) FRWY	19500	292K	NCC	77373
NORTH (I. H. 45 N) FRWY	19501	292K	NWC	77388
NORTH (I. H. 45 N) FRWY	19501	292K	NWC	77388
NORTH (I. H. 45 N) FRWY	22100	292K	NCC	77373
NORTH (I. H. 45 N) FRWY	22100	292K	NCC	77373
NORTH (I. H. 45 N) FRWY	22101	292K	NWC	77389
NORTH (I. H. 45 N) FRWY	22101	292K	NWC	77389
NORTH (I. H. 45 N) FRWY	24000	252J	SEM	77386
NORTH (I. H. 45 N) FRWY	24000	252J	SEM	77386
NORTH (I. H. 45 N) FRWY	24001	252J	SWM	77380
NORTH (I. H. 45 N) FRWY	24001	252J	SWM	77380
NORTH (I. H. 45 N) FRWY	27000	252J	SEM	77385
NORTH (I. H. 45 N) FRWY	27000	252J	SEM	77385
NORTH (I. H. 45 N) FRWY	27001	252J	SWM	77380
NORTH (I. H. 45 N) FRWY	27001	252J	SWM	77380
NORTH (I. H. 45 N) FRWY	28601	252J	SWM	77381
NORTH (I. H. 45 N) FRWY	28601	252J	SWM	77381
NORTH LN	900	412T	NWH	77088
NORTH RD	0	334Z	NEH	77338
NORTH RD	100	501B	NEC	77521
NORTHACRE DR	900	332V	NCC	77073
NORTHAIRE DR	500	332U	NCC	77073
NORTH ALIANA RD	0	527W	NEF	77469
NORTHAM DR	10900	329B	NWC	77375
NORTHAMPTON	1700	257H	SEM	77357
NORTHAMPTON CT	0	613G	NEB	77584
NORTHAMPTON DR	0	613L	NEB	77584
NORTHAMPTON FOREST DR	24800	250Y	NWC	77389
NORTHAMPTON PINES DR	22800	290H	NWC	77389
W. NORTHAMPTON PLACE	4100	492Y	SWH	77098
E. NORTHAMPTON PLACE	4100	492Y	SWH	77098
NORTHAMPTON TERRACE DR	25000	250Y	NWC	77389
NORTHAMPTON WAY	6800	491B	NWH	77055
NORTHAN HOLLOW LN	0	573T	SEC	77047
NORTH BAY BLVD	0	251G	WD	77380
NORTH BAYOU DR	8200	535Q	SEH	77017
NORTH BAY PLACE	0	251G	WD	77380
E. NORTH BELT	0	375V	NEC	77396
NORTH BELT	0	371U	NWC	77066
NORTH BEND CT	15800	332V	NCC	77073
NORTH BEND DR	0	332U	NCC	77073
NORTHBEND DR	600	501R	BT	77521
NORTH BEND LANDING	13400	367G	CY	77429
NORTH BERWICK DR	22000	368W	NWC	77095
NORTH BLVD PARK	4100	492Y	SWH	77098
NORTHBOROUGH DR	12400	372L	NWH	77067
NORTHBRACE DR	0	409S	NWC	77041
NORTHBRIAR DR	20300	373A	NCC	77073
NORTHBRIAR DR	20400	333W	NCC	77073
NORTHBRIDGE	7700	330N	NWC	77379
NORTHBRIDGE CIR	8000	330J	NWC	77379
NORTHBRIDGE CT	17200	330J	NWC	77379
NORTHBRIDGE DR	8000	330J	NWC	77379
NORTHBROOK DR	10600	449Z	NWH	77043
NORTH BY NORTHWEST	18500	284X	NWC	77447
NORTHCAIRN DR	6200	407T	NWC	77084
NORTHCANYON DR	19000	328H	NWC	77377
NORTH CAROLINA	100	495V	NEH	77029
NORTHCASTLE LN	800	292F	NCC	77373
NORTHCHAPEL	17200	329M	NWC	77379
NORTHCHASE	12000	372R	NEH	77060
NORTHCHASE RIDGE LN	12700	416Z	NEC	77044
NORTHCHASE RIDGE LN	12700	416Z	NEC	77044
NORTHCLIFFE MANOR DR	12200	371F	NWC	77066
NORTHCLIFF PLACE	1800	568C	SG	77478
NORTHCLIFF RIDGE LN	0	657P	FR	77546
NORTH COUNTRY CIR	0	254K	SEM	77365
NORTH COUNTRY DR	15600	254K	SEM	77365
NORTH COURSE DR	5900	529C	SWH	77072
NORTH COURT DR	19700	254F	SEM	77365
NORTHCOURT RD	7000	410Y	NWH	77040
NORTH COVE LN	0	328K	NWC	77377
NORTHCREEK LN	15500	254F	SEM	77365
NORTHCREEK LN	20700	333P	NCC	77073
NORTHCREST CT	0	250U	NWC	77389
NORTHCREST DR	0	250U	NWC	77389

Street Name	Block	Pg/Sq	Loc	Zips
NORTHCREST DR	0	250U	NWC	77389
NORTHCREST DR	0	290Q	NWC	77388
NORTHCREST DR	22000	290L	NWC	77389
NORTHCREST DR	24300	250Y	NWC	77389
NORTHCREST VILLAGE WAY	5900	290L	NWC	77388
NORTHCROSS DR	0	409N	NWC	77041
NORTH CROSS DR	16200	332U	NCC	77073
NORTH DAKOTA	1200	541E	BT	77520
NORTHDALE	0	616X	PL	77581
NORTHDALE	5600	534U	SEH	77087
NORTHDALE	6800	574C	SEH	77087
NORTHEAST DR	0	409S	NWC	77041
NORTHEAST PINES	18800	335X	HM	77338
NORTHERN	8300	530X	SWH	77071
NORTHERN DR	1800	658T	LC	77573
NORTHERN COLONY CT	21000	406P	NWC	77449
NORTHERN LIGHTS DR	0	332Q	NCC	77073
NORTHERN MOUNTAIN CT	14500	332W	NCC	77090
NORTHERN OAK ST	0	414V	NEH	77016
NORTHERN SPRUCE DR	0	293D	SEM	77386
NORTHERN STAR DR	17300	407U	NWC	77084
NORTHEW	600	452D	NWH	77091
NORTHFACE MANOR CT	14200	367D	NWC	77429
NORTHFALK	0	407U	NWC	77084
NORTHFALK DR	17500	407T	NWC	77084
NORTHFIELD DR	0	616U	FR	77546
NORTHFIELD LN	0	245D	SWM	77355
NORTHFIELD LN	4000	451E	NWH	77092
NORTHFLEET CT	3800	528C	SWH	77082
NORTHFLEET DR	13100	528C	SWH	77082
NORTHFOLK VALLEY LN	22000	256X	SEM	77365
NORTH FOREST BLVD	100	332T	NWC	77090
NORTH FORK CT	700	485H	SWC	77450
NORTHFORK CT	2500	613U	NEB	77584
NORTHFORK DR	0	409N	NWC	77041
NORTHFORK DR	3400	613U	NEB	77584
NORTHFORK DR	4800	614S	NEB	77584
NORTHFORK DR	19800	254K	SEM	77365
NORTH FORK DR	22000	485H	SWC	77450
NORTHFORK BEND CT	0	328G	NWC	77377
NORTHFORK BEND LN	0	328G	NWC	77377
NORTHFORK HOLLOW LN	7500	526M	NEF	77407
NORTHFORTY	18000	327E	NWC	77429
NORTHGATE CT	0	613W	NEB	77578
NORTHGATE DR	1	251X	WD	77380
NORTH GATE LN	20800	255N	SEM	77365
NORTHGATE CROSSING BLVD	26300	292F	NCC	77373
NORTHGATE FAIRWAY	0	331U	NWC	77068
NORTHGATE FOREST CIR	17000	331P	NWC	77068
NORTHGATE FOREST DR	15600	331U	NWC	77068
S. NORTHGATE FOREST PLACE	0	331T	NWC	77068
N. NORTHGATE FOREST PLACE	0	331T	NWC	77068
NORTHGATE RIDGE DR	22700	292K	SP	77373
NORTHGATE SPRINGS DR	900	292K	NCC	77373
NORTHGATE VILLAGE DR	2700	331P	NWC	77068
NORTHGATE VILLAS LN	3200	331X	NWC	77014
NORTH GLADE DR	0	332Q	NCC	77073
NORTHGLEN AVE	1900	538N	DP	77536
NORTHGREEN DR	15200	373V	NCC	77032
NORTHGROVE CT	7400	614E	NEB	77581
NORTHHAGEN DR	17400	407T	NWC	77084
NORTH HAVEN DR	7200	411N	NWH	77040
NORTH HEAD DR	25700	252U	SEM	77386
NORTH HILL CT	0	332B	NWC	77388
NORTH HILL DR	0	332B	NWC	77388
W. NORTH HILL DR	100	332B	NCC	77373
E. NORTH HILL DR	200	332C	NCC	77373
NORTH HOLLOW CIR	7500	375C	HM	77396
NORTH HOLLOW DR	1600	375C	HM	77396
NORTH HOU-ROSSLYN	5800	411X	NWH	77091
NORTH HOU-ROSSLYN	7200	411E	NWH	77088
NORTH HOU-ROSSLYN	11600	411E	NWH	77086
NORTHINGTON	5000	414M	NEC	77039
NORTH LAKE	0	619X	LC	77573
NORTHLAKE DR	13700	456R	NEH	77049
NORTHLAKE FOREST DR	15800	327Z	NWC	77429
NORTHLAKE FOREST DR	16400	367C	NWC	77429
NORTHLAND DR	6300	407U	NWC	77084
NORTHLAND DR	15500	254F	SEM	77365
NORTHLANE CIR	12000	411F	NWC	77086
NORTHLAWN DR	500	332U	NCC	77073
NORTHLEAF CT	10900	371S	NWC	77086
NORTHLEAF DR	6500	371T	NWC	77086
NORTHLEIGH BLVD	0	289Q	NWC	77375
NORTHLIGHT	0	484V	NEF	77494
NORTHLIGHT LN	0	484V	NEF	77494
NORTHLINE DR	6100	413S	NEH	77076
NORTHLINE DR	7500	413S	NEH	77037
NORTHLINE LAKE DR	0	377H	NEH	77346
NORTHLINE MALL	100	453K	NEH	77022
NORTH LOOP (I.H. 610)	100	453N	NWH	77008
NORTH LOOP (I.H. 610) E.	100	454U	NEH	77009
NORTH LOOP (I.H. 610) W.	100	452Q	NWH	77018
NORTH LOOP (I.H. 610)	101	453N	NWH	77018
NORTH LOOP (I.H. 610) E.	101	454U	NEH	77022
NORTH LOOP (I.H. 610) W.	101	452Q	NWH	77008
NORTH LOOP (I.H. 610)	600	453N	NWH	77009
NORTH LOOP (I.H. 610)	601	453N	NWH	77022
NORTH LOOP (I.H. 610) E.	2000	454U	NEH	77026
NORTH LOOP (I.H. 610) W.	2400	452Q	NWH	77092
NORTH LOOP (I.H. 610) W.	2401	452Q	NWH	77008
NORTH LOOP (I.H. 610) E.	6600	455X	NEH	77028
NORTH LOOP (I.H. 610) E.	8100	455X	NEH	77029
NORTH LOOP (I.H. 610) E.	9400	495C	NEH	77029
NORTH MACGREGOR	0	532D	SWH	77030
NORTHMARK DR	0	409N	NWC	77041
NORTHMARK DR	6300	407T	NWC	77084
NORTHMARK DR	16000	332V	NCC	77073
NORTH MEADOW DR	16200	332Q	NCC	77073
NORTH MILES DR	14600	488S	SWH	77077
NORTH MISSION CIR	2500	656U	FR	77546
NORTH MIST CT	400	332U	NCC	77073
NORTH MIST DR	16200	332U	NCC	77073
NORTHMOOR	0	485R	NEF	77450
NORTH OAK DR	700	332U	NCC	77073
NORTHOAK FOREST LN	22900	290H	NWC	77389
NORTHOAKS DR	20300	372D	NCC	77073
NORTHOAKS DR	20400	332Z	NCC	77073
NORTH PARK	0	332Y	NEH	77073
NORTH PARK	100	254F	SEM	77365
NORTH PARK CIR	0	296T	SEM	77339
NORTH PARK DR	0	525L	NEF	77407
NORTH PARK DR	0	295V	NEH	77365
NORTH PARK DR	100	296T	SEM	77339
NORTHPARK DR	2600	297S	NEH	77339
NORTHPARK DR	3100	609D	MC	77459
NORTHPARK DR	23900	295E	SEM	77365
NORTHPARK CENTRAL DR	100	332Y	NCC	77073
NORTHPARK PLAZA DR	100	296W	NEH	77365
NORTHPINE DR	19000	291X	NWC	77388
NORTHPINES DR	100	296S	NEH	77339
NORTH PLACE DR	15900	332V	NCC	77073

Street Name	Block	Pg/Sq	Loc	Zips
NORTH PLACE DR	16500	332Q	NCC	77073
NORTHPLAIN DR	0	409N	NWC	77041
NORTHPOINT	0	503Z	BC	77520
NORTHPOINT BLVD	0	329E	NWC	77375
NORTHPOINT DR	1	372V	NEH	77060
NORTHPOINTE BLVD	0	289Z	NWC	77379
NORTHPOINTE BLVD	10400	329E	NWC	77375
NORTHPOINTE BLVD	12700	328F	NWC	77377
NORTHPOINTE BEND DR	12600	328G	NWC	77377
NORTHPOINTE CANYON DR	0	328K	NWC	77429
NORTHPOINTE LAKES BLVD	14000	328P	NWC	77429
NORTHPOINTE LANDING LN	0	328L	NWC	77377
NORTHPOINTE MANOR	0	328B	NWC	77377
NORTHPOINTE MEADOWS DR	0	328H	NWC	77377
NORTHPOINTE RIDGE LN	0	328K	NWC	77377
NORTHPOINTE RIDGE LN	13500	328Q	NWC	77429
NORTHPOINTE RIDGE LN		328k	NWC	77377
NORTHPOINTE TERRACE DR	18700	328G	NWC	77377
NORTHPOINTE VILLAGE DR	0	328C	NWC	77377
NORTHPORT DR	6200	456V	NEC	77049
NORTHPORT LN	600	619V	LC	77565
NORTHPOST	11600	414K	NCC	77093
NORTHRIDGE DR	1	501G	BT	77521
NORTHRIDGE DR	5000	533V	SEH	77033
NORTHRIDGE DR	5200	534W	SEH	77033
NORTHRIDGE FOREST DR	0	252R	SEM	77385
NORTHRIDGE FOREST DR	0	253N	SEM	77386
NORTHRIDGE GREEN LN	0	328K	NWC	77377
NORTHRIDGE PARK DR	20600	332Z	NCC	77073
NORTHRIDGE TERRACE CT	22800	292L	SP	77373
NORTHRIDGE TERRACE LN	600	292L	SP	77373
NORTHRIDGE TRACE LN	0	290Q	NWC	77379
NORTH RIDING DR	0	289D	NWC	77375
NORTH RIM DR	2400	371K	NWC	77067
NORTH ROCK DR	400	332U	NCC	77073
NORTHRUP DR	4600	451F	NWH	77092
NORTHSAGE DR	0	409N	NWC	77041
NORTH SAM HOUSTN PKWY W.	0	370S	NWC	77064
NORTH SAM HOUSTN PKWY E.	100	372V	NEH	77060
NORTH SAM HOUSTN PKWY W.	100	372S	NWH	77038
NORTH SAM HOUSTN PKWY E.	300	373S	NEH	77060
NORTH SAM HOUSTN PKWY E.	800	373S	NCC	77032
NORTH SAM HOSTN PKWY E.	2400	374U	NEH	77032
NORTH SAM HOSTN PKWY W.	3200	371U	NWC	77086
NORTH SAM HOSTN PKWY E.	5700	375U	NEC	77396
NORTH SAM HOSTN PKWY E.	9700	376S	NEC	77396
NORTHSHIRE CT	3000	485T	NEF	77494
NORTHSHIRE LN	24000	485T	NEF	77494
NORTH SHORE	16200	498H	CV	77530
NORTHSHORE CT	4500	569X	MC	77459
NORTHSHORE DR	1500	569X	MC	77459
NORTHSHORE DR	1800	336L	NEH	77339
NORTH SHORELINE POINT	0	251F	WD	77381
NORTH SHORELINE POINT CT	0	251F	WD	77381
NORTHSIDE DR	900	332V	NCC	77073
NORTH SKY CT	16000	332V	NCC	77073
NORTH SKY DR	600	332V	NCC	77073
NORTH SKYFLOWER CT	1	251K	WD	77381
NORTH SPRING	2000	293W	NCC	77373
NORTHSPRING BEND CT	14000	328Q	NWC	77429
NORTHSPRING BEND LN	13400	328Q	NWC	77429
NORTH STAR	7400	412W	NWH	77088
NORTHSTAR DR	0	409N	NWC	77041
NORTHSTAR DR	19800	254F	SEM	77365
NORTH STAR WAY	0	418D	NEC	77532
NORTHSTONE LN	0	328Q	NWC	77429
NORTHSUN LN	0	328P	NWC	77429
NORTHTON	8500	495P	NEH	77029
NORTHTRACE DR	15800	332V	NCC	77073
NORTHTRACE DR	20900	332Z	NCC	77073
NORTH TRAIL DR	16200	332U	NCC	77073
NORTHUMB RD	12800	572R	SWH	77047
NORTHUMBERLAND DR	16400	407D	NWC	77095
NORTHVALE DR	4100	371B	NWC	77014
NORTHVALLEY DR	500	332U	NCC	77073
NORTHVIEW	0	453E	NWH	77022
NORTHVIEW DR	0	616U	FR	77546
NORTHVIEW DR	10100	371X	NWC	77086
NORTHVIEW PARK DR	0	332Y	NCC	77073
NORTHVILLE	400	412H	NEH	77037
NORTHVILLE	700	412G	NWC	77038
NORTHVILLE GARDEN DR	0	412B	NWC	77038
NORTHVILLE PALM DR	0	412F	NWC	77038
NORTHVILLE VILLAGE DR	0	412B	NWC	77038
NORTH VISTA BLVD	100	332U	NCC	77073
NORTHWAY	0	250Z	NWC	77389
NORTHWAY CT	17800	407T	NWC	77084
NORTHWAY DR	6100	290C	NWC	77389
NORTHWAY DR	6300	407T	NWC	77084
NORTHWEST DR	0	409S	NWC	77041
NORTHWST (U.S. 290) FRWY	9800	451E	NWH	77092
NORTHWST (U.S. 290) FRWY	9800	451E	NWH	77092
NORTHWST (U.S. 290) FRWY	12800	450D	NWH	77040
NORTHWST (U.S. 290) FRWY	12800	450D	NWH	77040
NORTHWST (U.S. 290) FRWY	13600	410X	NWH	77040
NORTHWST (U.S. 290) FRWY	13600	410X	NWH	77040
NORTHWST (U.S. 290) FRWY	15100	409K	JV	77040
NORTHWST (U.S. 290) FRWY	15100	409K	JV	77040
NORTHWST (U.S. 290) FRWY	17500	409K	NWC	77065
NORTHWST (U.S. 290) FRWY	17500	409K	NWC	77065
NORTHWST (U.S. 290) FRWY	20000	368X	NWC	77065
NORTHWST (U.S. 290) FRWY	20000	368X	NWC	77065
NORTHWEST 100 DR	7000	451A	NWH	77092
NORTHWEST CENTRAL DR	5400	451A	NWH	77092
NORTHWEST CREEK CIR	5900	371X	NWC	77086
NORTHWESTERN	3800	532A	WU	77005
NORTHWEST JET	0	289V	NWC	77379
NORTHWEST LAKE DR	0	367V	NWC	77095
NORTHWEST MALL	1	451Z	NWH	77092
NORTHWEST MEADOW	0	411B	NWC	77086
NORTHWEST PARK DR	10000	411B	NWC	77086
NORTHWEST PARK DR	10100	371X	NWC	77086
NORTHWST PARK COLONY LN	0	411A	NWC	77086
NORTHWST PARK PLACE DR	9900	411B	NWC	77086
NORTHWEST PINES BLVD	1	331X	NWC	77014
NORTHWEST STATION	9100	409E	JV	77065
NORTHWEST STATION DR	0	409E	JV	77065
NORTHWICK DR	1000	613G	NEB	77584
NORTH WILLOW DR	400	332U	NCC	77073
NORTHWIND DR	9100	369Z	NWC	77064
NORTHWIND LN	4200	331W	NWC	77014
NORTHWINDS DR	6700	409P	NWC	77041
NORTHWOOD	100	453X	NWH	77009
NORTHWOOD	800	501P	BT	77521
NORTHWOOD	2000	453T	NWH	77009
NORTHWOOD	2700	493B	NWH	77009
NORTHWOOD CT	1900	614E	NEB	77581
NORTHWOOD DR	15500	254K	SEM	77365
NORTHWOOD LN	1400	536P	PA	77502
NORTHWOOD COUNTRY LN	1	258Y	NEC	77336
NORTHWOOD COUNTRY RD	11100	258U	NEC	77336
NORTHWOOD FOREST DR	12200	414G	NCC	77039

Street Name	Block	Pg/Sq	Loc	Zips
NORTHWOOD GLEN LN	12900	328F	NWC	77377
NORTHWOOD MILL DR	0	297K	SEM	77365
NORTHWOODS PARK DR	0	409N	NWC	77041
NORTON	0	613Y	NEB	77578
NORTON DR	8500	450Q	NWH	77080
NORTON DR	10400	449R	NWH	77043
NORTON HOUSE LN	23700	445P	NWC	77493
NORVARA TRAIL	6800	330G	NWC	77379
NORVELL	0	299W	NEH	77336
NORVELL CT	1	490J	BH	77024
NORVIC	7900	495J	NEH	77029
NORVIC	10200	496J	JC	77029
NORVIEW DR	100	452H	NWH	77022
NORWALK DR	0	612X	NWB	77583
NORWALK DR	0	659E	LC	77573
NORWALK DR	1500	486K	SWC	77450
NORWAY	14100	572Y	SWH	77047
NORWAY MAPLE LN		289G	NWC	77375
NORWICH	2900	613K	NEB	77584
NORWICH	6100	455Q	NEH	77028
NORWICH HILL LN	0	332R	NCC	77073
NORWICH WAY	4600	569T	MC	77459
NORWOOD	1	494U	SEH	77011
NORWOOD	800	538L	DP	77536
NORWOOD CREST DR	0	248V	NWC	77375
NORWOOD GLEN LN	0	617X	SEC	77546
NORWOOD HILLS DR	2800	485V	NEF	77450
NORWOOD MEADOWS LN	0	524E	NEF	77494
NORWOOD MILLS CT	0	657Y	LC	77573
NORWOOD OAKS DR	0	331J	NWC	77379
NORWOOD PEAK LN		328k	NWC	77429
NORWOOD POINT CT	0	526J	NEF	77407
NORWOOD POINT LN	0	526J	NEF	77407
NORWOOD TRAILS DR	9300	376A	HM	77396
NOTCHWOOD PLACE	100	249R	NWH	77375
NOTCHWOOD PLACE	100	249R	NWH	77375
NOTHINGHAM BLUFF LN	0	484U	NEF	77494
NOTTAWAY CIR	13400	367G	NWC	77429
NOTTAWAY CT	4900	609A	SG	77478
NOTTINGHAM	0	257G	SEM	77357
NOTTINGHAM	1700	536R	PA	77502
NOTTINGHAM	2400	532B	WU	77005
NOTTINGHAM	3100	615P	PL	77581
NOTTINGHAM CIR	0	245J	WCO	77447
NOTTINGHAM CIR	11700	570L	MC	77071
NOTTINGHAM CIR	24600	244M	WCO	77447
NOTTINGHAM CT	0	609D	MC	77459
W. NOTTINGHAM DR	500	658R	LC	77573
S. NOTTINGHAM DR	1100	658R	LC	77573
N. NOTTINGHAM DR	1100	658R	LC	77573
NOTTINGHAM DR	5300	444U	KT	77493
NOTTINGHAM LN	1200	258K	SEM	77357
NOTTINGHAM LN	2800	609D	MC	77459
NOTTINGHAM OAKS TRAIL	300	488G	SWH	77079
NOTTINGHAM WAY	900	656H	FR	77546
NOTTINGHILL DR	21400	291Q	NWC	77388
NOVA CT	12300	488R	SWH	77077
NOVA DR	12000	489N	SWH	77077
NOVA DR	12400	488R	SWH	77077
NOVATO DR	6200	611B	SWH	77053
NOVOSAD	0	529L	SWH	77072
NOWLIN	0	453F	NEH	77022
NOWLIN DR	6200	462X	NEC	77521
NOYCE RD	18000	378R	NEC	77532
NUBEN	6200	411Z	NWH	77091
NUBIA	11500	414L	NCC	77093
NUECES	500	535B	SEH	77012
NUECES LN	5800	290M	NWC	77389
NUECES CANYON CT	2800	486T	SWC	77450
NUECES HOLLOW DR	0	415A	NWC	77039
NUECES RIVER CT	0	253U	NWC	77389
NUECES RIVER LN	0	253U	NWC	77389
NUECES RIVER LOOP	0	253U	NWC	77389
NUECES SPRINGS LN	13800	328S	NWC	77429
S. NUGENT	100	540Y	LP	77571
N. NUGENT	100	540Y	LP	77571
S. NUGENT	500	580D	LP	77571
NUGGENT	3400	414T	NCC	77093
NULAKE EAST CT	0	377H	NEH	77346
NULAKE WEST CT	0	377H	NEH	77346
NULL CT	8000	330E	NWC	77379
NULLARBOR CT	0	406U	NWC	77449
NUMID LAKE CT	0	377H	NEH	77346
NUNN	5600	534Q	SEH	77087
NURSERY RD	100	252N	SWM	77380
NURSERY RD	600	251R	WD	77380
NUTCRACKER CT	15800	375R	NEC	77396
NUTCRACKER LN	1	252N	WD	77380
NUTLEY CIR	25100	295R	SEM	77365
NUTMEG CT	1	250M	WD	77381
NUTMEG LN	0	461P	NEC	77521
NUTMEG HILL LN	0	446A	NWC	77449
NUT PINE CROSSING	0	406C	NWC	77433
NUTTALL OAK DR	14900	487Z	SWC	77082
NUTTY FARMS RD	0	287J	NWC	77377
NUTWOOD DR	2600	613S	NEB	77584
NUTWOOD LN	3400	291L	NWC	77389
NUWOOD LN	14800	572S	SWH	77053
NYACK DR	12700	616D	SEH	77089
NYAD LN	8300	337Z	NEC	77346
NYOKA	6200	410W	NWH	77041
NYSSA	8300	415Y	NEH	77078
NYSSA	9500	416W	NEC	77078
W. NYSTROM CIR	15000	413B	NCC	77060
NYSTROM CIR	15000	413B	NCC	77060
NYSTROM CIR	15100	373W	NCC	77060
W. O S T DR	4400	455Y	NEH	77013
E. O S T DR	4400	455Y	NEH	77013

O

Street Name	Block	Pg/Sq	Loc	Zips
O, AVENUE	6500	494V	SEH	77011
O, AVENUE	7100	495S	SEH	77011
E. O, AVENUE	9100	535D	SEH	77012
O' BRIEN	8900	527S	NEF	77407
O' DONNELL DR	10000	453B	NEH	77076
O' DONNELL DR	10500	413X	NEH	77076
O' HARA DR	14900	571S	SWH	77085
O' HARA DR	15300	571S	SWH	77489
O' MALLY DR	10800	371V	NWC	77067
O' NEAL	0	659F	LC	77573
O' NEIL	1100	493P	SWH	77019
O' REILLY	3900	492M	SWH	77007
O' RILEY BEND	1900	659X	DI	77539
OAK	0	337B	NEH	77339
OAK	0	540T	LP	77571
W. OAK	100	538P	DP	77536
S. OAK	100	288H	TB	77375
N. OAK	100	288H	TB	77375
OAK	100	541S	MP	77571
OAK	100	569K	SF	77477
E. OAK	100	538Q	DP	77536

Street Name	Block	Pg/Sq	Loc	Zips
W. OAK	400	459R	HG	77562
E. OAK	400	459R	HG	77562
OAK	500	541B	BT	77520
OAK	700	452G	NWH	77018
W. OAK	2600	537X	PA	77502
OAK	2700	619U	LC	77565
OAK	3700	580U	LP	77571
OAK	4700	537Y	PA	77503
OAK	4700	581W	PA	77586
OAK	26700	292L	SP	77373
OAK AVE	600	459R	HG	77562
OAK CIR	1100	619H	TL	77586
OAK CIR	14200	375X	NEC	77396
OAK CT	0	295Y	SEM	77365
OAK CT	1	493P	SWH	77006
W. OAK DR	0	657U	LC	77573
OAK DR	0	255V	SEM	77365
W. OAK DR	1	491L	SWH	77056
OAK DR	100	657K	FR	77546
S. OAK DR	23000	296L	SEM	77365
W. OAK DR	24100	296L	SEM	77365
E. OAK DR	24100	296L	SEM	77365
OAK LN	0	296G	SEM	77365
OAK LN	0	459W	CV	77530
OAK LN	100	419U	BR	77532
OAK LN	400	490G	PP	77024
OAK LN	3900	660M	BC	77518
OAK LN	6100	444P	KT	77493
OAK LN	16300	458Z	CV	77530
OAK LN	17400	246T	SWM	77355
OAK LN	17800	380R	NEC	77532
OAK RD	0	614N	PL	77581
OAK RD	100	620S	CS	77565
OAK RD	2500	614S	NEB	77584
OAKA CT	0	295C	SEM	77365
OAK ACRES DR	10300	368U	NWC	77065
OAK ALLEY	0	500Z	BT	77520
OAK ALLEY LN	13400	367G	NWC	77429
OAK ARBOR DR	7000	411Y	NWH	77088
OAK ARBOR DR	7400	411U	NWH	77088
OAK ARBOR WAY	21500	326N	NWC	77433
OAKBANK DR	2400	336D	NEH	77339
OAK BAY CIR	6900	609Q	MC	77459
OAK BAY DR	6000	411Y	NWH	77091
OAK BAYOU LN	10800	409B	NWC	77064
OAK BEND DR	14400	488L	SWH	77079
OAK BEND FOREST DR	13500	528T	SWC	77083
OAK BENT DR	0	615Z	PL	77581
OAKBERRY	10100	529D	SWH	77042
OAK BERRY DR	600	660B	KE	77565
OAK BLOSSOM CT	4100	578U	SEH	77059
OAK BLUFF CT	14600	328Z	NWC	77070
OAK BLUFF DR	12000	328Z	NWC	77070
OAK BOUGH DR	6900	411T	NWH	77088
OAK BOWER DR	18800	337Y	NEC	77346
OAK BRANCH	0	297T	NEH	77345
OAK BRANCH CT	19700	337T	NEC	77346
OAKBRANCH MANOR LN	6700	526H	NEF	77407
OAK BREEZE	1800	447E	NWC	77084
OAK BREEZE DR	0	447A	NWC	77084
OAK BRIAR DR	500	620X	KE	77565
OAK BRIAR DR	19500	337P	NEC	77346
OAK BRIDGE LN	21400	291T	NWC	77388
OAKBRIDGE PARK LN	21500	485M	SWC	77450
OAKBRIDGE PARK LN	21800	486J	SWC	77450
OAKBROOK	0	616W	PL	77581
OAKBROOK CIR	1800	615V	PL	77581
OAKBROOK DR	1700	616V	FR	77581
OAK BROOK DR	10600	456S	NEH	77013
OAKBURY CT	900	570U	MC	77489
OAKBURY DR	1600	570U	MC	77489
OAK CANYON	18600	252D	SEM	77385
OAK CASTLE DR	7800	250W	NWC	77389
OAK CENTER CT	19500	337T	NEC	77346
OAKCENTER DR	11000	529F	SWH	77072
OAK CHASE	1600	615Z	PL	77581
OAK CHASE CIR	1600	616W	PL	77581
OAK CHASE DR	14200	618A	SEH	77062
OAK CHURN PLACE	25600	292U	NCC	77373
OAKCLIFF	2300	534G	SEH	77023
OAK CLOISTER WAY	1900	618R	SEH	77058
OAK CLUSTER CIR	1800	615V	PL	77581
OAK CLUSTER CT	17800	327S	CY	77429
OAK COTTAGE CT	18000	526H	NEF	77407
OAK COUNTRY LN	31600	246Y	SWM	77355
OAK COVE DR	5300	411Y	NWH	77091
OAK COVE DR	5500	337D	NEH	77345
OAK COVE LN	1	337P	NEC	77346
OAK CREEK	0	616S	PL	77581
OAK CREEK	1100	539X	LP	77571
OAK CREEK	3700	615Z	PL	77581
OAK CREEK	10800	490D	HC	77024
OAK CREEK CIR	0	244V	WCO	77447
OAK CREEK CIR	0	659N	LC	77573
OAK CREEK CT	0	657R	LC	77573
OAKCREEK CT	21600	486J	SWC	77450
OAK CREEK DR	0	486E	SWC	77450
OAK CREEK DR	0	657R	LC	77573
OAK CREEK DR	2100	536S	SEH	77017
OAK CREEK LN	0	657R	LC	77573
OAK CREEK LN	6000	330H	NWC	77379
OAK CREEK RD	25000	244V	WCO	77447
OAKCREEK HOLLOW LN	22000	525D	NEF	77450
OAK CREST CT	0	251E	WD	77381
OAK CREST CT	0	252H	SEM	77385
OAK CREST CT	6100	330H	NWC	77379
OAKCREST DR	0	533H	SEH	77021
OAKCREST MANOR LN	0	366R	NWC	77433
OAKCROFT DR	11800	329W	NWC	77070
OAKCROFT DR	12100	328Z	NWC	77070
OAK CROSSING DR	0	615Z	PL	77581
OAK CROSSING LN	0	329X	NWC	77070
OAKDALE	1	493W	SWH	77006
OAKDALE	100	580U	SA	77571
OAKDALE	200	536L	PA	77506
OAKDALE	1000	533B	SEH	77004
OAKDALE CT	2700	569U	NEF	77477
OAK DALE DR	300	569U	NEF	77477
OAK DALE DR	3700	615Z	PL	77581
OAKDALE DR	4500	531D	BL	77401
OAK DALE DR	17100	330D	NWC	77379
OAKDALE LN	0	571V	SWH	77053
OAKDALE BLUFF CT	0	526R	NEF	77407
OAKDALE CLIFF CT	0	405P	NWC	77493
OAKDALE CREEK CT	5300	331A	NWC	77379
OAKDALE HEIGHTS DR	0	326U	NWC	77433
OAKDALE HILLS CT	0	251W	SWM	77389
OAKDALE LAKES TRAIL	0	526P	NEF	77407
OAKDALE LANDING CT	0	484P	NEF	77494
OAKDALE MEADOWS	0	330H	NWC	77379
OAK DALE PLACE	300	657Q	LC	77573
OAK DALE WAY	0	620F	SB	77586
OAKDEN CT	28500	299S	NEC	77336
OAK EDGE CT	7800	330A	NWC	77379
OAKEDGE DR	1800	615Z	PL	77581
OAKEN LN	3100	579C	LP	77571
OAKENDELL DR	15800	448B	NWC	77084
OAKENGATES DR	1200	457Z	NEC	77015
OAKEN GATE WAY	0	334L	NCC	77388
OAK ESTATES CT	800	659K	LC	77573
OAK FAIR DR	5100	297Y	NEH	77345
OAKFAIRBEND	0	368F	NWC	77429
OAK FALLS DR	5300	371N	NWC	77066
OAK FALLS DR	5500	370R	NWC	77066
OAK FERN	7500	410N	NWC	77040
OAKFIELD DR	12600	368L	NWC	77429
OAKFIELD CROSSING	18100	526H	NEF	77407
OAKFIELD FOREST LN	0	253Q	SEM	77386
OAKFIELD VILLAGE LN	0	446M	NWC	77449
OAKFORD CT	9300	491C	SWH	77024
OAKFORD DR	8600	491H	SWH	77024
OAK FOREST DR	0	657R	LC	77573
OAK FOREST DR	3000	452K	NWH	77018
OAK FOREST DR	4100	610P	MC	77459
OAK FOREST LN	0	252M	SEM	77385
OAK FOREST HOLLOW LN	0	253N	SEM	77386
OAK FORK CIR	1800	615Z	PL	77581
OAK GARDENS DR	3300	296Z	NEH	77339
OAK GARDENS DR	3800	297S	NEH	77339
OAK GATE CIR	1800	615V	PL	77581
OAK GATE DR	12100	328Z	NWC	77070
OAK GLADE DR	2700	297S	NEH	77339
OAK GLEN CT	11600	490G	BH	77024
OAK GLEN DR	0	660B	KE	77565
OAKGLEN DR	700	413U	NEH	77076
OAK GLEN MEADOWS	16600	367Y	NWC	77095
OAK GLENN CT	8700	412J	NWC	77088
OAK GREEN CT	19700	337T	NEC	77346
OAK GROVE DR	900	580D	LP	77571
OAKGROVE DR	900	618U	SEC	77058
OAK GROVE LN	0	615Z	PL	77581
OAK GROVE CHURCH ST	0	455G	NEH	77028
OAKHALL DR	3700	371K	NWC	77066
OAKHALL DR	19700	337S	NEC	77346
OAKHAM	5600	571P	SWH	77085
OAK HAMPTON DR	18000	447F	NWC	77084
OAK HARBOR DR	1	617M	SEH	77062
OAK HARBOR DR	600	618J	SEH	77062
OAKHARBORBEND	0	368F	NWC	77429
OAKHARBORMANOR	0	368B	NWC	77429
OAKHAVEN DR	200	500E	BT	77520
OAK HAVEN LN	5400	451C	NWH	77091
OAK HAVEN RD	7900	578C	LP	77571
OAKHEATH LN	0	526S	NEF	77407
OAKHEATH PINE PLACE	0	405P	NWC	77493
OAKHEATH RIVER CT	0	328K	NWC	77429
OAK HEDGE	13300	417S	NEC	77044
OAK HILL	0	295M	SEM	77365
OAKHILL	0	243E	WCO	77484
W. OAK HILL	1	298F	NEC	77336
S. OAK HILL	1	298G	NEC	77336
N. OAK HILL	1	298G	NEC	77336
E. OAK HILL	400	252K	SEM	77386
OAK HILL CT	0	615Z	PL	77581
OAK HILL DR	0	660B	KE	77565
OAK HILL DR	2500	609H	MC	77459
OAK HILL DR	6100	524Y	NWF	77406
OAK HILL DR	6900	534V	SEH	77087
OAK HILL DR	26500	252K	SEM	77386
OAK HILL LN	600	247F	SWM	77362
OAK HILL LN	18900	255K	SEM	77365
OAK HILL ESTATES RD	0	334M	NCC	77338
OAKHILL GATE DR	22200	334B	NCC	77373
OAK HILLS CIR	0	659D	LC	77573
OAK HILL SIDE TRAIL	0	445K	NWC	77493
OAK HOLLOW	0	368H	NWC	77429
OAK HOLLOW	4800	500M	BT	77521
OAK HOLLOW	10800	490D	HC	77024
OAK HOLLOW	23000	287F	NWC	77377
OAK HOLLOW BLVD	25200	244D	WCO	77447
OAK HOLLOW CIR	1	369E	NWC	77429
OAK HOLLOW CT	1900	610F	MC	77489
OAK HOLLOW DR	0	657R	LC	77573
OAK HOLLOW DR	1200	656L	FR	77546
W. OAK HOLLOW DR	1800	616S	PL	77581
E. OAK HOLLOW DR	1900	616S	PL	77581
S. OAK HOLLOW DR	3600	616S	PL	77581
N. OAK HOLLOW DR	3600	616S	PL	77581
OAK HOLLOW DR	13400	369E	NWC	77429
OAK HOLLOW LN	1	245F	SWM	77355
OAK HOLLOW LN	12200	247R	SWM	77362
OAK HOLLOW WAY	17300	330D	NWC	77379
OAKHURST	100	580L	LP	77571
OAKHURST	600	494S	SEH	77023
OAKHURST DR	24700	252P	SEM	77386
OAKHURST CREEK DR	20500	295R	SEM	77365
OAKHURST FOREST DR	20500	295M	SEM	77365
OAKHURST FOREST DR	20500	295V	NEH	77365
OAKHURST GREEN DR	400	372Q	NWH	77067
OAKHURST MEADOWS DR	20700	295R	SEM	77365
OAKHURST TRAILS CT	25500	295R	SEM	77365
OAKHURST TRAILS DR	0	295R	SEM	77365
OAKINGTON DR	7800	530Y	SWH	77071
OAKINGTON LN	22000	445M	NWC	77449
OAK ISLAND DR	15800	329N	NWC	77377
OAKKFIELD GLEN LN	17800	407E	NWC	77433
OAK KNOLL CT	1000	568F	SG	77498
OAK KNOLL DR	200	298F	NEC	77336
OAK KNOLL DR	1100	568F	SG	77498
OAK KNOLL DR	6800	524U	NEF	77406
OAK KNOLL DR	16300	254G	SEM	77365
OAK KNOLL LN	7800	455F	NEH	77028
OAK KNOLL LN	8800	455H	NEH	77078
OAK KNOT CT	8400	250S	NWC	77389
OAK KNOT DR	25300	250S	NWC	77389
OAK LACE DR	3700	291L	NWC	77389
OAK LACE LN	16200	246Y	SWM	77355
OAK LAKE CIR	1800	616W	PL	77581
OAK LAKE DR	3400	296Z	NEH	77339
OAKLAKEBEND	0	368F	NWC	77429
OAKLAKE POINTE DR	0	410N	NWC	77040
OAKLAKE POINTE LN	7500	410N	NWC	77040
OAKLAND	100	499D	NEC	77520
OAKLAND	4800	494X	SEH	77023
OAKLAND	9200	410E	NWC	77064
OAKLAND AVE	9800	410E	NWC	77064
OAKLAND CIR	1800	615Z	PL	77581
OAKLAND CIR	9800	410E	NWC	77064
OAKLAND CT	900	568K	SG	77498
OAKLAND CT	9800	410E	NWC	77064
OAKLAND DR	1100	616R	FR	77546
OAKLAND LN	9800	410A	NWC	77064
OAKLAND BEND	9800	410A	NWC	77064
OAKLAND BROOK ST	2700	371Y	NWC	77038
OAKLAND CLIFF CT	0	484N	NEF	77494
OAKLAND FALLS DR	4100	569T	MC	77459
OAKLAND HILL	9800	410A	NWC	77064
OAKLAND HILLS DR	6500	370B	NWC	77069
OAK LANDING DR	9800	329L	NWC	77375
OAKLAND MANOR LN	0	526Q	NEF	77407
OAKLAND MILLS DR	17800	526H	NEF	77407
OAKLAND PARK DR	0	253J	SEM	77385
OAKLAND VALLEY DR	19700	406R	NWC	77449
OAKLAND WAY	9900	410E	NWC	77064
OAKLAND WOOD TRAIL	0	337Q	NEC	77346
OAKLANE TRAIL	16200	246Y	SWM	77355
OAK LAUREL LN	4600	451G	NWH	77092
OAKLAWN	1	490G	PP	77024
OAKLAWN	400	658H	LC	77573
OAKLAWN	1800	568B	SG	77498
OAKLAWN PARK DR	15100	330U	NWC	77069
OAKLAWN PLACE DR	0	610Q	MC	77459
OAK LEAF	1	299E	NEC	77336
OAK LEAF	800	580P	LP	77571
OAK LEAF	9800	502G	BT	77521
OAK LEAF BLVD	0	255P	SEM	77365
OAKLEAF CIR	1200	580P	SA	77571
OAK LEAF CIR	1800	615Z	PL	77581
OAKLEAF CT	3100	609M	MC	77459
OAK LEAF LN	13300	497A	NEC	77015
OAKLEAF BEND DR	0	376R	NEC	77346
OAKLEAF FOREST DR	8600	411L	NWC	77088
OAKLEAF TRAIL CT	18100	526H	NEF	77407
OAKLEAF TRAIL LN	6700	526H	NEF	77407
OAK LEDGE DR	13100	368U	NWC	77065
OAK LEDGE MEADOW DR	0	335N	NCC	77338
OAKLEIGH DR	0	406L	NWC	77433
OAKLET ST	0	418T	NEC	77044
OAKLEY	600	493W	SWH	77006
OAKLEY RD	22300	256Y	SEM	77357
OAKLEY DOWNS PLACE	1	250A	WD	77382
OAKLEY HILL CT	0	525V	NEF	77406
OAKLEY TERRACE LN	10800	369P	NWC	77070
OAK LIMB CT	20400	335N	NCC	77338
OAK LIMB DR	10300	368Y	NWC	77065
OAK LIMB LN	20500	335J	NCC	77338
OAKLINE DR	12200	574Y	BK	77581
OAKLINE DR	12400	614C	BK	77581
OAK LINKS AVE	2300	618B	SEH	77059
OAK LINKS AVE	2900	578X	SEH	77059
OAK LINKS CT	2300	578X	SEH	77059
OAKLOCH CT	18000	526H	NEF	77407
OAK LODGE CT	800	659K	LC	77573
OAK LODGE DR	1800	615Z	PL	77581
OAKLYNN DR	5200	334A	NCC	77373
OAK MANOR DR	1700	339N	HU	77336
OAKMANTLE DR	6800	571J	SWH	77085
OAK MASTERS CT	17700	330C	NWC	77379
OAK MASTERS DR	6200	330G	NWC	77379
OAKMEAD DR	13700	568F	SG	77498
OAK MEADOW DR	0	620F	SB	77586
OAK MEADOW DR	0	660B	KE	77565
OAK MEADOW LN	11700	569A	MD	77477
OAK MEADOWS	900	536N	SEH	77017
OAKMERE LAKE CT	1200	329G	NWC	77379
OAK MESA CT	11100	369F	NWC	77070
OAK MILL DR	2500	337C	NEH	77345
OAK MIST LN	22500	485Y	NEF	77494
OAKMIST BEND LN	0	253U	SEM	77386
OAKMONT	0	659D	LC	77573
OAKMONT	800	501X	BT	77520
OAKMONT	3200	533F	SEH	77021
OAKMONT	9700	579A	LP	77571
OAKMONT CIR	4600	578E	PA	77505
OAKMONT CT	0	409F	JV	77064
OAKMONT CT	4700	659D	LC	77573
OAKMONT DR	0	296G	SEM	77365
OAKMONT LN	2700	609H	MC	77459
OAKMONT CLUB CT	15400	618B	SEH	77059
OAKMONT CREEK DR	0	330H	NWC	77379
OAKMONT GLEN CT	0	449X	NWH	77043
OAKMONT VILLAGE CIR	0	250S	NWC	77389
OAKMONT VILLAGE DR	0	250S	NWC	77389
OAKMOOR PKWY	0	572H	SEH	77051
OAKMOSS CT	20300	290Z	NWC	77379
OAK MOSS DR	7900	330K	NWC	77379
OAKMOSS HILL CT	18000	526H	NEF	77407
OAKMOSS TRAIL	5700	290Z	NWC	77379
OAK MOTTE DR	0	524C	NEF	77494
OAK MOUNTAIN DR	15700	408A	NWC	77095
OAKNELLA	10100	410W	NWH	77041
OAKNELLA	10400	409Z	NWH	77041
OAKNER DR	11800	328H	NWC	77377
OAKNUT DR	6300	411S	NWH	77088
OAK ORCHARD CT	0	253Q	SEM	77386
OAK ORCHARD CT	20000	326T	NWC	77433
OAK ORCHARD LN	18000	407E	NWC	77433
OAK PARK	0	657M	LC	77573
OAK PARK	12100	328Z	NWC	77070
OAK PARK	15900	373Q	NCC	77032
OAK PARK BLVD	0	487Z	SWC	77082
OAK PARK CIR	12300	328Z	NWC	77070
OAK PARK CT	0	616R	FR	77546
OAK PARK CT	12300	328Z	NWC	77070
OAK PARK DR	0	325R	NWC	77433
OAK PARK LN	0	253J	SEM	77385
OAK PARK LN	0	616R	FR	77546
OAK PARK BEND LN	17800	407F	NWC	77095
OAK PARK TRAILS	0	486N	SWC	77450
OAK PARK TRAILS CT	2100	485R	SWC	77450
OAK PARK TRAILS DR	21500	485R	SWC	77450
OAK PARKWAY DR	900	488F	SWH	77077
OAK PASS CT	0	253J	SEM	77385
OAK PASS DR	6100	411Y	NWH	77091
OAK PATH LN	0	337P	NEC	77346
OAK PINES DR	14700	410J	NWC	77040
OAK PLACE	0	616W	PL	77581
OAK PLACE	100	493P	SWH	77006
OAK PLAINS DR	8400	250S	NWC	77389
OAK PLANK RD	3900	611W	FS	77545
OAK PLAZA CT	0	369J	NWC	77429
OAK PLAZA DR	12300	369J	NWC	77429
OAK POINT CT	1600	615Z	PL	77581
OAK POINT DR	4000	615Z	PL	77581
OAKPOINT DR	9700	450X	NWH	77055
OAKPOINT DR	10200	449Z	NWH	77043
OAK POINT RD	0	542X	CCO	77520
OAK POINTE BLVD	0	609D	MC	77459
OAK PRAIRIE CT	7000	526H	NEF	77407
OAK PRESERVE DR	0	337P	NEC	77336
OAK RAIN CT	20800	446N	NWC	77449
OAK RAMBLING DR		484W	NEF	77494
OAK RANCH DR	27500	299P	NEC	77336
OAK RIDGE	3500	493A	NWH	77009
OAK RIDGE	3600	453W	NWH	77009
OAK RIDGE AVE	800	659J	LC	77573
OAK RIDGE DR	0	660B	KE	77565
OAK RIDGE DR	25800	252N	SWM	77380
OAKRIDGE CANYON LN	0	527J	NEF	77407
OAKRIDGE FOREST CT	25800	252T	SEM	77386
OAKRIDGE FOREST LN	26100	252T	SEM	77386
OAK RIDGE GROVE CIR	0	252P	SEM	77386
OAK RIDGE GROVE DR	0	252P	SEM	77386
OAK RIDGE PARK DR	2800	446R	NWC	77084
OAK RIDGE PARK DR	27200	252K	OR	77385
OAK RIDGE SCHOOL RD	27300	252A	SEM	77385
OAK RIVER DR	2300	333A	NCC	77373
OAKROC GROVE	0	452Q	NWH	77018
OAK ROCK CIR	3100	333B	NCC	77373
OAK ROYAL DR	1700	486K	SWC	77450
OAK RUN	24100	286B	SWM	77355
OAK RUN DR	3800	376D	NEC	77396
OAK RUN DR	6700	526H	NEF	77407
OAKS CT	0	609L	MC	77459
OAKS DR	400	536U	SH	77587
OAKS DR	1200	536Q	PA	77506
OAKS DR	1300	536Q	PA	77502
OAK SAGE DR	0	406L	NWC	77433
OAK SAND DR	2200	486N	SWC	77450
OAKS CROSSING LN	16900	527L	NEF	77083
OAKSEDGE LN	5000	291S	NWC	77388
OAKS FORKS DR	2400	337A	NEH	77339
OAKSHADE DR	20200	256R	SEM	77357
OAK SHADOW	1500	541D	BT	77520
OAK SHADOW CT	0	657R	LC	77573
OAK SHADOW DR	22700	296C	SEM	77357
OAK SHADOWS	0	451D	NWH	77091
OAK SHADOWS CIR	18600	255A	SEM	77302
OAK SHADOWS DR	3600	451C	NWH	77091
OAK SHADOWS LN	11600	490G	BH	77024
OAK SHADOWS PLACE	0	297A	SEM	77357
OAK SHADOWS PLACE	22500	296D	SEM	77357
OAKSHAM LN	17600	331J	NWC	77379
OAKSHIELD LN	11700	366R	NWC	77433
OAKSHIRE CT	0	658M	LC	77573
OAKSHIRE CT	0	615Z	PL	77581
OAKSHIRE DR	4500	491V	SWH	77027
OAK SHORE	6900	415K	NEC	77050
OAKSHORE LAKE DR	0	524C	NEF	77494
OAK SHORES DR	2000	296U	NEH	77339
OAKSIDE DR	3900	572S	SWH	77053
OAKSIDE DR	4600	571V	SWH	77053
OAKSIDE HOLLOW LN	0	407R	NWC	77084
OAK SIDE TRAIL	0	376H	NEC	77346
OAK SIDE TRAIL	4100	376H	NEC	77396
OAK SPRING DR	11200	449X	NWH	77043
OAK SPRING RD	13900	328P	NWC	77429
OAK SPRING PLACE CT	0	292U	NCC	77373
OAK SPRINGS DR	14400	327Y	NWC	77429
OAK STAND CT	5000	446C	NWC	77449
OAK STAR DR	25200	250S	NWC	77389
OAK STATION DR	19500	337T	NEC	77346
OAKSTONE	900	497E	NEH	77015
OAKSTONE PARK DR	0	524K	NWF	77406
OAKS TRAIL	32700	246V	SWM	77355
OAK STREAM DR	1000	449X	NWH	77043
W. OAKS VILLAGE DR	17200	527E	NEF	77407
OAK TERRACE CT	4000	527H	SWC	77082
OAK TERRACE DR	15200	527H	SWC	77082
OAK THICKET CT	31800	253J	SEM	77385
OAK THICKET DR	9600	411N	NWH	77040
OAKTHISTLE LN	0	619U	LC	77565
OAKTHORN CT	0	485J	NEF	77494
OAK TIMBERS DR	19200	337S	NEC	77346
OAKTON SPRINGS DR	0	524G	NEF	77494
OAK TOP DR	0	615Z	PL	77581
OAK TRACE	1600	616W	PL	77581
OAKTRACE CT	17800	376C	NEC	77396
OAKTRACE DR	3800	376C	NEC	77396
OAK TRACE ISLAND DR	0	367X	NWC	77095
OAK TRAIL LN	5500	451C	NWH	77091
OAKTRAIL PRK LN	0	253J	SEM	77385
OAK TREE	0	289H	NWC	77375
OAKTREE	1	657A	FR	77546
OAK TREE CIR	1800	615Z	PL	77581
OAK TREE DR	1100	450X	NWH	77055
OAK TREE DR	1500	450T	NWH	77080
OAK TRUNNEL CT	0	292D	SEM	77386
OAK VALLEY DR	800	490D	HC	77024
OAK VALLEY DR	1700	660B	KE	77565
OAK VALLEY DR	4400	609B	MC	77459
OAK VALLEY DR	11400	369N	NWC	77065
OAK VALLEY LN	400	247F	SWM	77362
OAKVIEW	400	568L	SG	77478
OAKVIEW	2300	609D	MC	77459
OAK VIEW	22800	290J	NWC	77375
OAK VIEW CIR	300	620E	EL	77586
OAK VIEW LN	0	615Z	PL	77581
OAK VIEW LN	22600	284B	WCO	77447
OAKVIEW CREEK LN	4100	573Z	SEH	77048
OAK VIEW TERRACE	19000	486H	SWC	77094
OAK VILLA CIR	8400	250S	NWC	77389
OAK VILLA DR	25200	250S	NWC	77389
OAK VILLAGE DR	6800	375T	NEH	77396
OAKVILLE	3900	414P	NCC	77093
OAK VISTA	300	616Z	FR	77546
OAK VISTA	7500	535S	SEH	77087
OAK VISTA CT	900	616U	FR	77546
OAK VISTA DR	4200	610X	MC	77459
OAK WALK DR	6800	337Y	NEC	77346
OAKWAY	15900	373P	NCC	77032
OAKWAY DR	18800	331D	NWC	77379
OAKWAY DR	18900	337Y	NEC	77346
OAKWELL LN	1700	446X	NWC	77449
OAKWELL STATION CT	5700	337T	NEC	77346
OAK WEST DR	700	332U	NCC	77073
OAKWICK	0	615Z	PL	77581
OAKWICK LN	14000	417X	NEC	77044
OAKWICK FOREST DR	3600	610Y	MC	77459
OAKWILDE CIR	3800	579G	LP	77571
OAK WILDE CT	1	449Z	NWH	77043
OAKWIND CT	18000	526H	NEF	77407
OAK WIND DR	0	615Z	PL	77581
OAKWOOD	200	658M	LC	77573
OAKWOOD	3000	500Z	BT	77520
OAKWOOD	3000	532K	SWH	77025
OAKWOOD	12200	248J	SWM	77362
OAKWOOD CT	0	579C	LP	77571
W. OAKWOOD CT	8000	410V	NWC	77040
E. OAKWOOD CT	8000	410V	NWC	77040
OAKWOOD CT	20100	336S	NEC	77338
OAKWOOD DR	100	252S	SEM	77386
E. OAKWOOD DR	1800	615Z	PL	77581
OAKWOOD DR	8400	249K	SWM	77354
OAKWOOD DR	26000	252P	SEM	77386
OAKWOOD LN	13500	568B	SG	77498
OAKWOOD BEND DR	8000	410V	NWC	77040
OAKWOOD CANYON DR	0	406L	NWC	77433

Street Name	Block	Pg/Sq	Loc	Zips
OAKWOOD COURT DR	1800	501E	BT	77521
OAKWOOD FALLS TRAIL	19600	446Q	NWC	77084
OAKWOOD FOREST DR	3100	297X	NEH	77345
OAKWOOD FOREST DR	8000	410V	NWC	77040
OAKWOOD GARDEN	8000	410U	NWC	77040
OAKWOOD GLEN BLVD	7100	330L	NWC	77379
OAKWOOD GLEN CIR	6900	330G	NWC	77379
OAKWOOD GROVE	6800	410U	NWC	77040
OAKWOOD HOLLOW	7900	410V	NWC	77040
OAKWOOD HOLLOW CT	6700	410V	NWC	77040
OAKWOOD LAKES DR	7700	408J	NWC	77095
OAKWOOD MANOR DR	12900	368E	NWC	77429
OAKWOOD PARK	6900	410U	NWC	77040
OAKWOOD PARK LN	0	253N	SEM	77386
OAKWOOD PLACE	0	250R	NWC	77389
OAKWOOD PLACE	8100	410U	NWC	77040
E. OAKWOOD PLACE CT	6900	410U	NWC	77040
OAKWOOD ROCK LN	0	484X	NEF	77494
OAKWOOD TRACE	8000	410V	NWC	77040
OAKWOOD TRAIL	6700	410Z	NWC	77040
OAKWORTH DR	18000	447B	NWC	77084
OAR BRIDGE	0	575Z	SEH	77075
OARLOCK CT	16000	419A	NEC	77532
OARMAN CT	300	488B	SWH	77079
OASIS DR	9700	531T	SWH	77096
OASIS PALM	0	534J	SEH	77021
OASIS PARK	0	534J	SEH	77021
OASIS POINT	0	444B	NWC	77493
OASIS VIEW LN	11000	577W	SEH	77034
OATES LN	12300	496L	NEH	77015
OATES RD	1	496A	NEH	77013
OATES RD	300	495D	NEH	77013
OATES RD	1000	495H	JC	77029
OATES RD	3600	456S	NEH	77013
OATES RD	5700	456E	NEH	77078
OAT HARVEST CT	2800	411H	NWC	77038
OAT MEADOW TRAIL	0	457G	NEC	77049
OAT MILL RD	16500	407G	NWC	77095
OATS	3000	494F	NEH	77020
OBAFEMI	0	455J	NEH	77028
OBAN	6300	571P	SWH	77085
OBELISK BAY	0	327S	NWC	77429
OBERLIN	3800	532E	WU	77005
W. OBION RD	100	412Z	NWH	77076
OBION RD	100	413W	NEH	77076
W. OBION RD	300	412Z	NWH	77091
W. OBLONG CIR	0	326Y	NWC	77433
S. OBLONG CIR	0	326Y	NWC	77433
N. OBLONG CIR	0	326Y	NWC	77433
OBOE	2200	659B	LC	77573
OBOE DR	9800	532S	SWH	77025
OBRA LN	14400	572Q	SWH	77045
OBSERVATORY	1700	412N	NWH	77088
OBSIDIAN DR	16500	367U	NWC	77095
OBSIDIAN ARROWHEAD	5100	526S	NEF	77407
OCEAN	0	543Q	BC	77520
OCEAN	0	543X	BC	77520
OCEAN CITY BLVD	10700	369K	NWC	77070
OCEANIA CT	1700	486M	SWC	77094
OCEANIC DR	0	445R	NWC	77449
OCEAN LAUREL LN	12300	371H	NWC	77014
OCEAN MANOR LN	1200	659M	LC	77573
OCEAN MIST CT	3300	620E	SB	77586
OCEAN PARK LN	0	657S	FR	77546
OCEAN PARK LN	21200	446J	NWC	77449
OCEAN POINT CT	0	612G	PL	77545
OCEAN POINT DR	0	612G	PL	77545
OCEAN RIDGE CIR	3400	620F	SB	77586
OCEANSIDE DR	8000	408K	NWC	77095
OCEANSIDE LN	1300	619U	LC	77573
OCEANVIEW	11700	570K	MC	77071
OCEANVIEW DR	2000	620P	SB	77586
OCEAN WAY	2900	660K	LC	77573
OCEE	3300	490X	SWH	77063
OCEE	3900	530B	SWH	77063
OCELOT LN	0	576V	SEH	77034
OCHOA RD	6300	614Q	PL	77584
OCHRE LEAF TRAIL	15300	325R	NWC	77433
OCHRE PARK WAY	0	326F	NWC	77433
OCHRE WILLOW TRAIL	20800	326J	NWC	77433
OCHRE WILLOW TRAIL	20800	326F	NWC	77433
OCONEE CT	0	249Z	NWC	77375
OCONEE DR	0	249Z	NWC	77375
OCOTILLO CT	1700	485K	NEF	77494
OCOTILLO DR	11500	367Q	NWC	77095
OCOTILLO ST	0	659G	LC	77573
OCTAVIA	4500	454Y	NEH	77026
OCTAVIAN CT	18100	257D	RF	77357
OCTAVIA WAY	21800	333F	NCC	77073
OCTOBER SHADOW CT	8400	330J	NWC	77379
ODAY RD	1400	614L	PL	77581
ODDO	100	453K	NEH	77022
ODDOM CT	13300	328T	NWC	77429
ODELL SPRINGS DR	21300	295M	SEM	77365
ODELL WAY	3100	537Y	PA	77505
ODEN TERRACE DR	18700	328F	NWC	77377
ODER LN	700	332J	NWC	77090
ODESSA CT	700	413B	NCC	77060
ODESSA DR	10400	528W	NEF	77498
ODET CT	8200	412Q	NWH	77088
ODIN	2100	494E	NEH	77020
ODIN CT	3700	533G	SEH	77021
ODINGLEN DR	7200	407M	NWC	77095
ODOM BLVD	2300	532U	SWH	77054
ODYSSEY	800	570P	MC	77489
ODYSSEY CT	10600	529W	SWH	77099
ODYSSEY DR	1300	610Q	MC	77459
OEDIPUS CT	1300	610Q	MC	77459
OFALLON MILLS DR	0	293F	SEM	77386
OFFER DR	10400	530W	SWH	77031
OFFICE CITY DR	7000	535J	SEH	77087
OFFICE CITY DR	7500	535J	SEH	77012
OGDEN	8100	535Q	SEH	77017
OGDENBURG FALLS DR	19900	289Y	NWC	77379
OGDEN FOREST DR	6000	411K	NWC	77088
OGDEN TRAIL	0	568S	SG	77479
OGILVIE	200	536J	SEH	77017
OGILVIE	1000	535R	SEH	77017
OGLESBY	11500	496K	JC	77029
OGLETHORPE DR	9200	570E	SWH	77031
OHIO	100	540Y	LP	77571
OHIO	500	580D	LP	77571
OHIO	1400	659P	LC	77573
OHIO	3100	540D	BT	77520
OHIO	13800	572T	SWH	77047
OHIO AVE	3100	659Z	GCO	77539
OHIO RD	3000	611T	FS	77545
OHIO CANAL CT	17500	376H	NEC	77346
OHLSON PLACE	0	494E	NEH	77020
OHSFELDT	2500	452T	NWH	77008
OIL BARON LN	0	613W	NEB	77578
OIL CENTER BLVD	19100	333S	NCC	77073

Street Name	Block	Pg/Sq	Loc	Zips
OIL CENTER CT	2200	333S	NCC	77073
OILER DR	0	615Y	PL	77581
OIL FIELD	0	609P	NEF	77479
OIL FIELD RD	0	463F	MB	77520
OIL RANCH	0	284C	WCO	77447
OIL RANCH	0	244Y	WCO	77447
OIL TOWN CT	0	328M	NWC	77377
OJEMAN RD	1500	450V	NWH	77055
OJEMAN RD	1800	450V	NWH	77080
OKACHOBEE DR	0	377M	NEH	77346
OKANELLA	10100	410W	NWC	77041
OKANELLA	10300	409Z	NWC	77041
OKAY	10500	415W	NEH	77016
OKEHAMPTON DR	24400	249Z	NWC	77375
OKINAWA RD	7300	534S	SEH	77033
OKLAHOMA	0	659Z	GCO	77573
OKLAHOMA	100	660M	BC	77518
OKLAHOMA	1300	540D	BT	77520
OKLAHOMA	1500	538S	DP	77536
OKLAHOMA	3000	454N	NEH	77093
OKLAHOMA AVE	1200	659U	LC	77573
OKRA	5000	331A	NWC	77379
OLA DR	5000	374Y	NCC	77032
OLANA DR	5000	414D	NCC	77032
OLAND WAY	0	373A	NCC	77073
OLATHE	9100	450Y	NWH	77055
OLD RD	2300	657P	FR	77546
OLD ALDINE WESTFIELD RD	23700	293W	NCC	77373
OLD ALVIN	0	615F	PL	77581
OLD ALVIN RD	1100	615P	PL	77581
OLD ARBOR TRAIL	0	376H	NEC	77346
OLD ARBOR WAY	0	376H	NEC	77346
OLD ATASCOCITA RD	0	340N	NEC	77336
OLD BAMMEL RD	100	332K	NWC	77090
OLD BAMMEL-N HOUSTON RD	10100	371W	NWC	77086
OLDBAND LN	8400	410F	NWC	77040
OLD BARNGATE LN	0	373E	NCC	77073
OLD BATTLEGROUND RD	0	498Z	DP	77536
OLD BRICKHOUSE DR	4700	450E	NWH	77041
OLD BRIDGE LN	1	568V	SG	77478
OLD BRIDGE LAKE	100	330Z	NWC	77069
OLD CANYON DR	0	328G	NWC	77377
OLD CARRIAGE LN	25300	293N	NCC	77373
OLD CARRIAGE LN	25700	292R	NCC	77373
OLDCASTLE	500	496E	NEH	77013
OLD CEDAR CREEK CIR	0	366N	NWC	77433
OLD CEMETERY	0	340D	LCO	77535
OLD CEMETERY RD	0	295M	SEM	77365
OLD CHAPEL DR	3200	293P	NCC	77373
OLD CHATHAM LN	6400	570D	SWH	77035
OLD CHESTER WAY	4300	577E	PA	77504
OLD CHOATE RD	0	577X	SEH	77034
OLD CHOCOLATE-PEARLAND	3600	613Z	NEB	77578
OLD CHOCOLATE BAYOU RD	2100	613Z	NEB	77584
OLD CHOCOLATE BAYOU RD	13900	573Z	SEH	77048
OLD CHURCH LN	22500	445Q	NWC	77449
OLD CLARK RD	0	539G	SEC	77571
OLD CLINTON RD	5500	494M	NEH	77020
OLD COACH LN	10700	490D	HC	77024
OLD COACH RD	15800	246M	SC	77355
OLD COURSE DR	300	656Q	FR	77546
OLD COURT DR	17400	328L	NWC	77377
OLD CREEK LN	24500	244U	WCO	77447
OLD CREEK RD	14900	413A	NEH	77060
OLD CREEK RD	15300	373W	NEH	77060
OLDCREST DR	9700	569H	SF	77477
OLD CROW LN	0	446D	NWC	77449
OLD CYPRESS-N HOU RD	0	369K	NWC	77065
OLD CYPRESS TRAIL	0	334K	NCC	77338
OLD DESERT RD	9500	579A	LP	77571
OLD DOCK LN	14200	332W	NWC	77090
OLDE BOURBON LN	0	452Q	NWH	77018
OLDE CANYON LN	0	406D	NWC	77433
OLD EDGEWOOD	0	616V	FR	77546
OLDE FALLS DR	0	296X	SEH	77339
OLDE LANTERN WAY	3200	251X	SWM	77380
OLDE MANOR LN	14800	331T	NWC	77068
OLDEN CT	13500	368A	NWC	77429
OLDENBURG LN	9600	408D	NWC	77065
OLDE OAKS ESTATE CT	0	367W	NWC	77095
OLDE ROSE CT	0	249C	SWM	77382
OLDE TAVERN CT	15000	331T	NWC	77068
OLD FAIRBANKS-N HOUSTON	11000	370Z	NWC	77086
OLD FARM RD	2500	490U	SWH	77063
OLD FARMHOUSE LN	6100	406Z	NWC	77449
W. OLDFIELD	100	298G	NEC	77336
S. OLDFIELD	100	298G	NEC	77336
E. OLDFIELD	100	298G	NEC	77336
OLD FIELD PLACE	1900	251V	WD	77380
OLD FINCH CT	0	372C	NCC	77073
OLD FOLTIN RD	11800	411G	NWC	77086
OLD FOREST LN	0	447B	NWC	77084
OLD FORGE	2300	577Q	SEH	77059
OLD FORT RD	2900	609A	SG	77479
OLD FRONTIER TRAIL	0	291N	NWC	77388
OLD GALLEY WAY	18600	378T	NEC	77532
OLD GALVESTON RD	400	618Y	WB	77598
OLD GALVESTON RD	18000	658D	WB	77598
OLDGATE PASS LN	0	407K	NWC	77433
OLD GENOA RED BLUFF RD	500	577N	SEH	77034
OLD GLORY DR	6300	406V	NWC	77449
OLD GREENHOUSE RD	4800	446D	NWC	77084
OLD GREENHOUSE RD	4900	447A	NWC	77084
OLD GREENHOUSE RD	5300	407W	NWC	77084
OLD GREENS RD	1200	373P	NCC	77032
OLD GRUENE CT	0	328S	NWC	77429
OLD GRUENE CT	0	328S	NWC	77429
OLDHAM	1	494U	SEH	77011
OLDHAM ST	0	657T	GCO	77573
OLDHAM FARM	0	372M	NCC	77060
OLD HANNOVER DR	21500	292N	NWC	77388
OLD HARDIN STORE RD	25700	248N	SWM	77354
OLD HARDY RD	0	252B	SEM	77385
OLD HARGRAVES RD	0	340B	LCO	77535
OLDHAVEN	7700	530U	SWH	77074
OLD HEARTH DR	15000	408P	NWC	77084
OLD HICKORY	3100	579C	LP	77571
OLD HICKORY	6400	406V	NWC	77449
OLD HICKORY DR	13000	368L	NWC	77429
OLD HICKORY LN	0	412J	NWC	77038
OLD HICKORY LN	1400	659N	LC	77573
OLD HIGHWAY	0	572A	SWH	77025
OLD HIGHWAY 146	0	502P	BT	77521
OLD HIGHWAY 146	0	501V	BT	77520
OLD HIGHWAY 146	0	541C	BT	77520
OLD HIGHWAY 146	400	540P	BT	77520
OLD HIGHWAY 146	200	580G	LP	77571
OLD HIGHWAY 146	3000	580X	SEC	77586
OLD HIGHWAY 146	5000	620B	SB	77586
OLD HOLLY DR	3400	615S	PL	77584
OLD HOLZWARTH	1700	292S	NWC	77388
OLD HOUSTON RD	18500	254K	SEM	77365

Street Name	Block	Pg/Sq	Loc	Zips
OLD HUFFMEISTER RD	12000	368K	NWC	77429
OLD HUMBLE RD	13900	375W	NEC	77396
OLD JOSEPH RD	30200	243L	WCO	77447
OLD KATY RD	6800	491D	NWH	77024
OLD KATY RD	9100	490B	NWH	77055
OLD KATY RD	10100	489A	NWH	77043
OLD KATY RD	11800	488B	NWH	77079
OLD KICKAPOO	0	243U	WCO	77447
OLD KIRBY RD	1600	619D	TL	77586
OLD LAKE RD	800	491J	SWH	77057
OLD LA PORTE RD	11400	539R	LP	77571
OLD LEDGE LN	8600	412Q	NWH	77088
OLD LEGEND CT	2000	568Z	SG	77478
OLD LEGEND DR	2100	568Z	SG	77478
OLD LIGHTHOUSE LN	6000	408X	NWC	77084
OLD LODGE DR	5300	370C	NWC	77066
OLD LOGGERS RD	0	334V	NCC	77338
OLD LOUETTA RD	16000	329R	NWC	77379
OLD LOUETTA LOOP	2400	291Z	NWC	77388
OLD MAIN	1000	532H	SWH	77030
OLD MAIN STREET LOOP	9600	532X	SWH	77054
OLD MANSE CT	12700	528Z	NEF	77478
OLD MAPLE LN	8200	335N	NCC	77338
OLD MEADOW LN	8300	410G	NWC	77064
OLD MILL CT	1000	568J	SG	77498
OLD MILL LN	900	332L	NCC	77073
OLD MILL RD	19900	256M	NC	77357
OLD MILL RD	19900	256M	NC	77357
OLD MILLSTONE WAY	0	325K	NWC	77447
OLD MINT HOUSE LN	10900	289T	NWC	77375
OLD MISSION RD	11300	367P	NWC	77095
OLD NASA	0	658E	WB	77598
OLD NEEDLEPOINT RD	0	463S	CCO	77521
OLD NEEDLEPOINT RD	7800	462V	CCO	77521
OLD NORTH BELT DR	6900	375T	NEC	77396
OLD OAK LN	2200	296R	NEH	77339
OLD OAKS	200	657V	LC	77573
OLD OAKS BLVD	6400	614T	PL	77584
OLD OAKS DR	3300	500H	BT	77521
OLD OAKS DR	12100	490E	SWH	77024
OLD OAKS DR	12400	489H	SWH	77024
OLD OAKS LN	0	501E	NEC	77521
OLD OAKS LN	11400	252D	SEM	77385
OLD OAKS LN	11600	253A	SEM	77385
OLD ORCHARD	1600	620G	SB	77586
OLD ORCHARD RD	0	539X	LP	77571
OLD OX RD	2000	292D	SEM	77386
OLD OYSTER TRAIL	0	568T	SG	77478
OLD PANAMINT	0	617K	SEH	77546
OLD PIKE RD	0	334A	NCC	77373
OLD PINE LN	12500	456Z	NEC	77015
OLD PINE LN	12800	457W	NEC	77015
OLD PINE GROVE DR	4000	376H	NEH	77346
OLD POST RD	3700	527B	SWC	77082
OLD RAILROAD ST	0	445N	NWC	77493
OLD RAMSEY RD	0	340S	LCO	77535
OLD RANCH RD	21200	333J	NCC	77073
OLD RICHMOND RD	12900	528U	SWC	77099
OLD RICHMOND RD	13200	528U	SWC	77083
OLD RICHMOND RD	13700	528T	NEF	77498
OLD RICHMOND RD	15000	527V	NEF	77498
OLDRIDGE	9500	335P	HM	77338
OLDRIDGE DR	15600	448B	NWC	77084
OLD RIVER DR	16000	458Y	CV	77530
OLD ROCK LN	0	366N	NWC	77433
OLDS DR	11800	295Y	SEM	77365
OLD SAND PIT RD	19600	256G	SEM	77357
OLD SAYBROOK DR	0	447D	NWC	77084
OLD SETTLEMENT CT	4000	609G	MC	77459
OLD SHAWNEE TRACE	0	366N	NWC	77433
OLD SORTERS RD	19900	295H	SEM	77365
OLD SOUTH WAY	0	658J	LC	77573
OLD SPANISH TRAIL	1000	532M	SWH	77054
OLD SPANISH TRAIL	1800	533J	SWH	77054
OLD SPANISH TRAIL	3200	533J	SEH	77021
OLD SPANISH TRAIL	4500	534E	SEH	77021
OLD SPANISH TRAIL	5400	534F	SEH	77023
OLD SPRING LN	100	456Z	NEC	77015
OLD SPRING CYPRESS RD	0	327Z	NWC	77429
OLD SPRING CYPRESS RD	6100	330D	NWC	77379
OLDSQUAW GLEN CT	0	291N	NWC	77388
OLD STABLE RD	0	531D	SWH	77081
OLD STONE CT	5600	609T	NEF	77479
OLD STONE LN	0	366R	NWC	77433
OLD STONE TRAIL	15400	488F	SWH	77079
OLDSTREAM CT	1	251A	WD	77381
OLD TELEGRAPH RD	11300	371M	NWC	77067
OLD TELEGRAPH RD	11700	371R	NWC	77067
OLD TIMBER LN	9600	329C	NWC	77379
OLDTOWN BRIDGE CT	15100	527Z	NEF	77498
OLD TOWNE LN	9900	528T	NEF	77498
OLD TRAIL DR	8200	410Q	NWC	77040
OLD TYBEE RD	14400	408X	NWC	77084
OLD VALLEY WAY	800	486G	SWC	77094
OLD VILLAGE LN	13900	528W	NEF	77498
OLD VISTA RD	5000	577C	PA	77505
OLD WALTERS RD	12200	371G	NWC	77014
OLD WASHINGTON	26800	324E	HK	77447
OLD WASHINGTON RD	0	323C	NWC	77484
OLD WESTFIELD RD	27600	292G	SP	77373
OLDWICK BROOK DR	19200	328D	NWC	77375
OLD WILLOW DR	0	290J	NWC	77375
OLD WINDMILL TRAIL	20200	284R	HK	77447
OLD WOODS LN	21400	333J	NCC	77073
OLD YALE	4400	452M	NWH	77018
OLD YAUPON LN	7700	406M	NWC	77433
OLE	0	299W	NEH	77336
OLEANDER	0	581W	PA	77586
OLEANDER	0	658Y	LC	77573
OLEANDER	100	541W	MP	77571
OLEANDER	1300	493C	NEH	77009
OLEANDER	2300	537Z	PA	77503
OLEANDER	4300	531M	BL	77401
OLEANDER	4700	621A	PA	77586
OLEANDER CT	8200	535V	SEH	77017
OLEANDER DR	1600	612T	NWB	77584
OLEANDER DR	8000	460T	NEC	77562
OLEANDER LN	1	540J	SEC	77571
OLEANDER LN	1200	658Z	LC	77573
OLEANDER ST	4300	501M	BT	77521
OLEANDER GROVE WAY	6800	457L	NEC	77049
OLEANDER HILL ST	0	411H	NWC	77038
OLEANDER POINT DR	10400	367Y	NWC	77095
OLEANDER RIDGE WAY	19500	406M	NWC	77433
OLENTANGY	10100	576N	SEH	77075
OLENTHORPE PARK	22000	332R	NCC	77073
OLEOKE LN	13600	457X	NEC	77015
OLETA LN	24500	404V	NWC	77493
OLGA LN	10000	409Z	NWH	77041
OLGA LN	10100	410W	NWH	77041
OLIN	6000	614L	PL	77581
OLIN RD	14700	288N	NWC	77377

Street Name	Block	Pg/Sq	Loc	Zips
OLINDA DR	6300	408U	NWC	77041
OLIVARA LN		524M	NEF	77406
W. OLIVE	200	536G	PA	77506
OLIVE	500	492M	SWH	77007
OLIVE	1200	501Z	BT	77520
OLIVE	1800	502W	BT	77520
OLIVE	300	659T	LC	77573
OLIVE	500	659U	LC	77573
OLIVE BRANCH	11400	489T	SWH	77042
OLIVE BRANCH CT	8700	528N	SWC	77083
OLIVE BROOK LN	0	367Y	NWC	77095
OLIVE GARDEN	0	488K	SWH	77077
OLIVE GLEN DR	16100	527C	SWC	77082
OLIVE GREEN CT	4500	578U	SEH	77059
OLIVE GROVE CT	6100	338A	NEH	77345
OLIVE HILL BLVD	5100	609S	NEF	77479
OLIVE HILL BLVD		609S	NEF	77479
OLIVE HILL DR	7100	408N	NWC	77095
OLIVE HILL DR	13300	488K	SWH	77077
OLIVE LANDING LN	0	366Z	NWC	77433
OLIVE LEAF DR	18200	447K	NWC	77084
OLIVE MOUNT	0	613K	PL	77584
OLIVE OAK CT	4000	578U	SEH	77059
OLIVE PARK	0	488K	SWH	77077
OLIVE PINE DR	1800	611T	NEF	77545
OLIVE PLACE	0	488K	SWH	77077
OLIVER	1000	493E	SWH	77007
OLIVER LN	1500	463B	MB	77580
OLIVERBROOK LN	0	572Q	SWH	77047
OLIVERIA WAY	0	377D	NEC	77346
OLIVER RIDGE CT	23200	485F	SWC	77494
OLIVER TREE CT	18200	327W	NWC	77429
OLIVE SPRINGS CT	14200	618A	SEH	77062
OLIVE TRACE	0	488K	SWH	77077
OLIVE TRAIL	0	488K	SWH	77077
OLIVEWOOD CT	11500	616C	SEC	77089
OLIVEWOOD DR	10900	616C	SEC	77089
OLIVIA SPRINGS LN	2100	293F	SEM	77386
OLIVIA VIEW LN	0	366U	NWC	77433
OLIVINE LN	3200	291U	NWC	77388
OLLIA CIR	5900	577D	PA	77505
OLMAS WAY LN	0	528L	SWH	77072
OLMSTEAD PARK DR	0	327U	NWC	77429
OLMSTEAD ROW	0	251L	WD	77380
OLNEY OAK DR	800	488D	SWH	77079
OLSEN CT	0	289D	NWC	77375
OLSON LN	6300	578B	PA	77505
OLSTER DR	2600	446U	NWC	77084
OLYMPIA DR	1900	492N	SWH	77019
OLYMPIA DR	2700	609H	MC	77459
OLYMPIA DR	5600	491T	SWH	77056
OLYMPIA DR	6100	491S	SWH	77057
OLYMPIA DR	6600	578A	PA	77505
OLYMPIA DR	7500	490V	SWH	77063
OLYMPIA DR	10000	489U	SWH	77042
OLYMPIA DR	11300	489T	SWH	77077
OLYMPIA DR	12400	488V	SWH	77077
OLYMPIAD DR	5500	448D	NWC	77041
OLYMPIA FALLS CT	0	326K	NWC	77433
OLYMPIA FIELDS LN	5100	330Z	NWC	77069
OLYMPIA FIELDS LN	5200	370C	NWC	77069
OLYMPIA SPRINGS DR	0	660P	LC	77573
OLYMPIA SPRINGS LN	21800	445M	NWC	77449
OLYMPIC CIR	19100	338W	NEH	77346
OLYMPIC DR	0	487X	SWH	77094
OLYMPIC DR	2100	659C	LC	77573
OLYMPIC FOREST DR	0	296A	SEM	77365
OLYMPIC FOREST DR	0	296A	SEM	77365
OLYMPIC PARK LN	0	377E	NEC	77346
OLYMPUS DR	2500	446V	NWC	77084
OMA DR	34600	247K	SWM	77362
OMAHA CIR	3400	291U	NWC	77388
OMAHA DR	7500	461S	NEC	77521
OMAR	400	493B	NWH	77009
OMAR	1200	493B	NWH	77008
OMEARA DR	3500	532S	SWH	77025
OMEARA DR	4300	531V	SWH	77035
OMEGA	3100	453P	NWH	77022
OMEGA CIR	700	537M	PA	77503
OMOLON LN	0	331H	NWC	77090
ONALEIGH DR	700	498A	NEC	77530
ONEIDA	4200	577F	PA	77504
ONEIDA CT	2000	658T	LC	77573
ONEIDA CT	13900	328P	NWC	77429
ONEIDA LAKE LN	0	573Y	SEC	77047
ONENESS AVE	0	371G	NWC	77014
ONE SUGAR CRK PLC BLVD	0	568R	SG	77478
ONE TOKEN DR	11500	368Q	NWC	77065
ONION GULCH CIR	16000	617W	SEC	77546
ONSLOW	10300	414Z	NEH	77016
ONTARIO	1800	501W	BT	77520
ONTONAGON WAY	0	294J	SEM	77386
ONYX LN	21700	291R	NWC	77388
ONYX ROSE CT	0	372C	NCC	77073
OPAL	5100	452E	NWH	77018
OPAL CT	100	453Y	NEH	77009
OPAL CANYON LN	0	488N	SWH	77077
OPAL COVE CT	0	524C	NEF	77494
OPAL CREEK DR	0	612L	PL	77584
OPAL CREST LN	0	524E	NEF	77494
OPAL CREST LN	0	524E	NEF	77494
OPALETTA DR	13400	295G	SEM	77365
OPAL FALLS LN	5000	485S	NEF	77494
OPAL GLEN LN	11100	575Y	SWH	77075
OPAL HILL CT	7500	375U	NEC	77396
OPAL HOLLOW LN	26300	366H	NWC	77433
OPAL MANOR LN	0	407E	NWC	77433
OPAL MEADOW DR	16500	367Y	NWC	77095
OPAL PASS LN	0	328K	NWC	77377
OPAL RIDGE DR	10600	367Y	NWC	77095
OPAL SHORE CT	0	406C	NWC	77433
OPAL SKY CT	0	659H	LC	77573
OPAL SKY DR	5000	446B	NWC	77449
OPAL SPRINGS	2000	486Q	SWC	77450
OPAL STONE CT	0	297K	NEH	77365
OPAL TRAILS CT	0	526L	NEF	77407
OPAL VALLEY DR	0	328L	NWC	77377
OPAL VILLAGE LN	0	524G	NEF	77494
OPAL WAY	100	298X	NEH	77336
OPALWOOD CT	8200	335N	NCC	77338
OPALWOOD LN	8200	335N	NCC	77338
OPATRNY MEADOWS LN	11100	369U	NWC	77064
OPELIKA	8900	450K	NWH	77080
OPELOUSAS	1700	493H	NEH	77020
OPELOUSAS CT	1	494E	NEH	77020
OPEN BAY DR	1700	419A	NEC	77532
OPEN GLADE TRAIL	0	329B	NWC	77375
OPEN GLEN	0	446F	NWC	77449
OPEN OAK WAY	7300	337Q	NEC	77346
OPEN SANDS CT	0	406C	NWC	77433
OPEN SANDS CT	0	609T	NEF	77479
OPEN SLOPE CT	0	376W	NEC	77396

Street Name	Block	Pg/Sq	Loc	Zips
OPERA HOUSE ROW DR	14800	327W	NWC	77429
OPHRYS RD	0	460W	BT	77521
OPPER	8900	409F	NWC	77064
OPUS CT	8900	410K	NWC	77040
OPUS ONE DR	0	484E	NEF	77494
OPUS ONE DR		484J	NEF	77494
ORA	2200	451U	NWH	77092
ORACH MEADOW LN	0	572E	SWH	77045
ORACLE DR	0	658Y	LC	77573
ORALIA DR	12100	368R	NWC	77065
ORANGE	2400	282X	WL	77484
ORANGE	3000	494F	NEH	77020
E. ORANGE	3200	615J	PL	77581
W. ORANGE	4000	615J	PL	77581
W. ORANGE	4700	614M	PL	77581
ORANGE	5800	414M	NEC	77050
S. ORANGE CIR	4600	615J	PL	77581
N. ORANGE CIR	4600	615J	PL	77581
E. ORANGE CIR	4600	615J	PL	77581
ORANGE BLOSSOM	0	460T	NEC	77562
ORANGE BLOSSOM	15100	448H	NWH	77084
ORANGE BLOSSOM CT	700	325Q	NWC	77433
ORANGE BLOSSOM DR	5100	657V	LC	77573
ORANGE BROOK CT	10300	615D	SEC	77089
ORANGE GROVE DR	3500	414K	NCC	77039
ORANGE GROVES	600	659S	LC	77573
ORANGE HILL LN	10200	289U	NWC	77375
ORANGE JASMINE CT	4300	578U	SEH	77059
ORANGE LEAF CT	4400	578V	SEH	77059
ORANGE MAPLE CT	0	325V	NWC	77433
ORANGE OAK WAY	0	326N	NWC	77433
ORANGE ORCHARD LN	0	445N	NWC	77493
ORANGE POPPY DR	20600	326J	NWC	77433
ORANGE SIREN DR	0	335K	NCC	77338
ORANGE TREE DR	4900	578J	PA	77505
ORANGEVALE CT	16800	329R	NWC	77379
ORANGEVALE DR	9600	329R	NWC	77379
ORATORIO CT	9300	410J	NWC	77040
ORCA CT	3600	331B	NWC	77388
ORCHARD	100	618X	WB	77598
ORCHARD	200	570N	MC	77489
ORCHARD CT	0	615S	PL	77584
ORCHARD CT	12000	569A	SF	77477
ORCHARD DR	3000	532T	SWH	77054
ORCHARD LN	0	568P	SG	77498
ORCHARD LN	0	620G	SB	77586
ORCHARD LN	8700	578D	LP	77571
ORCHARD ARBOR LN	0	609X	NEF	77479
ORCHARD BERRY LN	0	289V	NWC	77375
ORCHARD BLOSSOM WAY	4600	446H	NWC	77084
ORCHARD BRIAR LN	0	612Q	PL	77584
ORCHARD BROOK DR	0	486N	SWC	77450
ORCHARD CANYON CT	6200	298W	NEH	77345
ORCHARD CHASE CT	4300	486W	NEF	77450
ORCHARD COUNTRY LN	1800	618B	SEH	77062
ORCHARD COVE LN	0	252M	SEM	77385
ORCHARD CREEK LN	0	485J	NEF	77494
ORCHARD DALE DR	22000	291M	NWC	77389
ORCHARD FARMS LN	14200	617H	SEH	77062
N. ORCHARD FIELD TRAIL	0	325V	NWC	77433
ORCHARD FROST DR	0	614G	PL	77581
ORCHARD GARDEN WAY	0	371J	NWC	77066
ORCHARD GLEN CT	1900	618L	SEH	77062
ORCHARD GROVE DR	29600	288E	NWC	77377
ORCHARD GROVE LN	7200	527E	NEF	77407
ORCHARD HILL DR	1000	488F	SWH	77077
ORCHARD HILL LN	0	253P	SEM	77386
ORCHARD HILL LN	0	253P	SEM	77386
ORCHARD HILLS LN		609X	NEF	77479
ORCHARD HOLLOW WAY	12700	368V	NWC	77065
ORCHARD KNOLL LN	0	485W	NEF	77494
ORCHARD MILL LN	0	612U	PL	77584
ORCHARD MILL LN	19300	446D	NWC	77449
ORCHARD MOUNTAIN DR	11500	578Z	PA	77059
ORCHARD OAK LN	22800	485L	SWC	77450
ORCHARD PARK DR	1500	488K	SWH	77077
ORCHARD PASS DR	0	293D	SEM	77386
ORCHARD PEAK CT	800	617H	SEH	77062
ORCHARD RIDGE LN	8600	335N	NCC	77338
ORCHARD RUN WAY	0	611W	MC	77545
ORCHARD SKY DR	0	366M	NWC	77407
ORCHARD SPRING CT	5800	614G	PL	77581
ORCHARD SPRING DR	1900	614G	PL	77581
ORCHARD SPRINGS CT	0	609U	NEF	77479
ORCHARD SPRINGS DR	10900	371V	NWC	77067
ORCHARD TRAIL DR	0	614L	PL	77581
ORCHARD VALE DR	3600	446Q	NWC	77084
ORCHARD VALLEY CT	3100	447N	NWC	77084
ORCHARD VALLEY CT	5600	338E	NEH	77345
ORCHARD VALLEY LN	0	253K	SEM	77386
ORCHARD VIEW LN	8500	613V	PL	77584
ORCHARD WIND LN	0	612K	PL	77545
ORCHID	400	536N	SEH	77017
ORCHID	6700	614D	BK	77581
ORCHID	20400	282T	WCO	77484
ORCHID DR	0	570T	MC	77489
ORCHID ST	0	460X	BT	77521
ORCHID BEE LN	0	296D	SEM	77357
ORCHID BLOSSOM WAY	20500	326N	NWC	77433
ORCHID BREEZE LN	0	528T	NEF	77498
ORCHID BUD LN	0	326N	NWC	77433
ORCHID COVE CT	0	366Y	NWC	77433
ORCHID CREEK DR	0	612Q	PL	77584
ORCHID CREEK LN	17600	447G	NWC	77084
ORCHID MEADOW DR	0	408F	NWC	77095
ORCHID MIST DR	16500	326J	NWC	77433
ORCHID RIDGE LN	0	527J	NEF	77469
ORCHID SPRING LN	0	524G	NEF	77494
ORCHID TRACE DR	0	253T	SEM	77386
ORCHID TRACE DR	0	612J	PL	77545
ORCHID TRACE LN	0	573X	SEC	77047
ORCHID TRAILS	12600	409S	NWC	77041
ORCHID TREE LN	2800	446N	NWC	77449
ORCHID VALLEY WAY	0	406D	NWC	77433
OREAN	2100	576B	SEH	77034
OREANA CT	3800	293H	SEM	77386
OREBO	7700	412S	NWH	77088
OREGANO CIR	9500	529M	SWH	77036
OREGANO DR	0	461Q	NEC	77521
OREGOLD DR	13200	448D	NWC	77041
OREGON	500	576B	SH	77587
OREGON	900	580G	LP	77571
OREGON	1800	540D	BT	77520
OREGON AVE	2300	659P	LC	77573
W. OREM DR	0	572M	SWH	77045
W. OREM DR	0	573J	SWH	77045
E. OREM DR	1700	573L	SEH	77047
W. OREM DR	2700	572J	SWH	77045
W. OREM DR	4500	571M	SWH	77045
E. OREM DR	4900	574N	SEH	77048
W. OREM DR	7300	570M	SWH	77085
ORIOLE	0	375L	HM	77396
ORIOLE	100	452M	NWH	77018
ORIOLE	1800	658Q	LC	77573
ORIOLE	4800	535R	SEH	77017
ORIOLE	5100	536N	SEH	77017
ORIOLE LN	600	536U	PA	77502
ORIOLE CREEK LN	0	524K	NWF	77406
ORIOLE LAKE WAY	0	616H	SEH	77089
ORIOLE PLACE	10900	252L	SEM	77385
ORIOLE POINT CT	18800	326Z	NWC	77429
ORIOLE SKY WAY	0	445F	NWC	77493
ORIOLE SKY WAY	0	445K	NWC	77493
ORIOLE TRAIL LN	0	333F	NCC	77338
ORIOLE TRAIL LN	0	333F	NCC	77338
ORIOLE WOOD CT	2800	411H	NWC	77038
ORION	2500	658T	LC	77573
ORION	2800	411R	NWH	77088
ORION DR	14100	248X	TB	77375
ORION STAR CT	0	249D	SWM	77382
ORISKYANY CT	0	375V	NEC	77396
ORISON DR	0	408D	NWC	77065
ORKNEY DR	4600	569T	MC	77459
ORLANDO	1600	656U	FR	77546
ORLANDO	3100	414W	NEH	77093
ORLANDO	7200	415W	NEH	77016
ORLEANS	500	659J	LC	77573
ORLEANS	11900	420W	BR	77532
ORLEANS	12500	496D	NEC	77015
ORLEANS	12800	497A	NEH	77015
ORLEANS	25900	288Y	NWC	77377
ORLEANS DR	2600	620K	SB	77586
ORMANDY	11300	570M	SWH	77035
ORMANDY	12100	570M	SWH	77035
ORMEL	14700	373Y	NCC	77039
ORMEL	15000	373Y	NCC	77032
ORMOND CT	14500	408G	NWC	77095
ORMONDE CROSSING DR	16000	367D	NWC	77429
ORNELLA CIR	21500	333F	NCC	77338
ORO GRANDE LN	8800	576L	SEH	77034
ORONO GLEN TRAIL	0	484N	NEF	77494
ORPHELIA	3800	456X	NEH	77013
ORR	1200	493D	NEH	77009
ORREL DR	900	537L	PA	77503
ORTEGA LN	13500	528K	SWC	77083
ORTH LN	27100	252E	OR	77385
ORVILLE	6700	454M	NEH	77028
ORVILLE	7300	455J	NEH	77028
ORYAN CT	100	457X	NEC	77015
OSAGE	3700	530B	SWH	77063
OSAGE	4100	530B	SWH	77036
OSAGE	8800	530Q	SWH	77074
OSAGE DR	0	461S	NEC	77521
OSAGE DR	0	503F	CCO	77520
W. OSAGE DR	2100	503F	CCO	77520
OSAGE BEND LN	0	446B	NWC	77449
OSAGE PARK DR	11900	368V	NWC	77065
OSBORN	5900	534P	SEH	77033
OSBORNE DR	1200	656H	FR	77546
OSBY DR	4000	532S	SWH	77025
OSBY DR	4300	531V	SWH	77096
OSCAR	7400	538X	DP	77536
OSCODA CT	4400	294N	SEM	77386
OSPREY CT	0	657N	FR	77546
OSPREY DR	5400	574E	SEH	77048
OSPREY LN	0	615P	PL	77581
OSPREY BEND DR	16800	366P	NWC	77433
OSPREY LANDING DR	0	324M	NWC	77447
OSPREY LANDING DR	0	324M	NWC	77447
OSPREY PASS	0	485E	SWC	77494
OSPREY POINT DR	0	324M	NWC	77447
OSPREY POINT DR	0	324M	NWC	77447
OSSINEKE CT	0	294K	SEM	77386
N. OSSINEKE DR	0	294K	SEM	77386
OSSINEKE DR	0	294K	SEM	77386
OSTLER DR	0	333D	NCC	77373
S. OSWEGO	10300	496J	JC	77029
N. OSWEGO	10300	496J	JC	77029
OSWEGO	10500	496J	JC	77029
OTHELLO	8500	495L	NEH	77029
OTIS	0	494E	NEH	77020
OTIS	3400	454Y	NEH	77026
OTTAWA LN	1900	449R	NWH	77043
OTTER CIR	10300	462V	CCO	77520
OTTERBURY DR	1800	413H	NCC	77039
OTTERBURY DR	3300	414G	NCC	77039
OTTER CREEK DR	700	539X	LP	77571
OTTER CREEK TRAIL	18300	377B	NEC	77346
OTTER CREST CT	0	377F	NEC	77346
OTTER LODGE PLACE	0	249B	SWM	77354
OTTER PEAK DR	4900	297T	NEH	77345
OTTER POND PLACE	1	250D	WD	77381
OTTER TRAIL CT	19300	406Z	NWC	77449
OTTO	2300	454A	NEH	77093
OTTO LN	400	531F	BL	77401
OTTO RD	3300	293X	NCC	77373
OURAY DR	7900	410F	NWC	77040
OURLANE CIR	700	490F	BH	77024
OURLANE CT	1	490F	BH	77024
OUR LANE PLACE	1	490F	BH	77024
OUR LANE TRAIL	1	490F	BH	77024
OUT DR	12100	572G	SWH	77045
OUTBACK DR	26700	444F	NWC	77493
OUTBACK LAKES TRAIL	18000	377B	NEC	77346
OUTERVALE PLACE	1	250H	WD	77381
OUTFITTER POINT	0	444F	NWC	77493
OUTLAW RIDGE RD	17300	367P	NWC	77095
OUTLOOK DR	100	576G	SEH	77034
OUTPOST DR	9200	450G	NWH	77041
OUTRIGGER CT	16000	419B	NEC	77532
OUTVIEW CT	8800	410K	NWC	77040
OVERBLUFF CT	14800	497D	NEC	77530
OVERBLUFF DR	200	497D	NEC	77530
OVERBROOK	0	488V	SWH	77077
OVERBROOK CIR	1900	610J	MC	77459
OVERBROOK LN	3400	492S	SWH	77027
OVERBROOK LN	5600	491T	SWH	77056
OVERBROOK LN	6200	491S	SWH	77057
OVERBROOK LN	7800	490V	SWH	77063
OVERBROOK LN	10000	489U	SWH	77042
OVERBROOK LN	11300	489T	SWH	77077
OVERBROOK LN	12300	488T	SWH	77077
OVERBROOK TERRACE CT	9700	524G	NEF	77494
OVERBROOK TERRACE LN	25300	524G	NEF	77494
OVERBY PARK LN	3200	485T	NEF	77494
OVERCREST LN	6500	538W	PA	77505
OVERCROSS DR	3000	572F	SWH	77045
OVERCUP DR	12100	490E	SWH	77024
OVERCUP DR	12500	489H	SWH	77024
OVERCUP DR	23900	290B	NWC	77389
OVERDALE	5600	574A	SEH	77033
OVERDALE	6200	574C	SEH	77087
OVERDALE DR	3300	613Y	NEB	77584
OVERDENE PIERCE	0	376R	NEC	77346
OVERGLEN CT	0	528Q	SWC	77072
OVERHILL	1200	452K	NWH	77018
OVERLAKE DR	25700	252S	SWM	77380
OVERLAND	700	570S	SF	77477
OVERLAND GAP CT	0	484S	NEF	77494
OVERLAND HEATH DR	0	250E	NWC	77375
OVERLAND HILLS LN	0	406C	NWC	77433
OVERLAND PARK DR	200	457U	NEC	77049
OVERLAND PASS DR	1600	568U	SG	77478
OVERLAND TRAIL	100	332P	NWH	77090
OVERLAND TRAIL CIR	2400	660X	DI	77539
OVERLAND TRAIL DR	0	524K	NWF	77406
OVERLEA DR	10800	576T	SEH	77089
OVERLOOK DR	300	657J	FR	77546
OVERLOOK DR	6200	409X	NWC	77041
OVERLOOK LN	34900	247F	SWM	77362
OVERLOOK HILL LN	0	609P	NEF	77479
OVERLOOK PARK CT	18000	376H	NEC	77346
OVERLOOK WAY DR	1900	252R	SEM	77385
OVERLYN CT	1	251D	WD	77381
N. OVERLYN PLACE	1	251D	WD	77381
OVERLYN PLACE	1	251D	WD	77381
OVERMAN	6000	452D	NWH	77091
OVERMEAD DR	9700	409A	NWC	77065
OVERMEYER	6800	452W	NWH	77008
OVERO DR	7000	459L	NEC	77049
OVERTON CT	1	493V	SEH	77004
OVERTON DR	10500	368Y	NWC	77065
OVERTON PARK DR	5600	525D	NEF	77450
OVERTON WOODS DR	0	377G	NEC	77346
OVERTURE DR	3500	488Y	SWH	77082
OVERTURE DR	3800	528C	SWH	77082
OVERVIEW DR	9900	528T	NEF	77498
OVID	1200	493F	SWH	77007
OWEN CANYON LN	0	366Q	NWC	77433
OWENDALE DR	14300	457U	NEC	77015
OWEN LAKE	8500	407F	NWC	77095
OWEN OAK DR	18900	338W	NEC	77346
OWENS	0	660X	DI	77539
OWENS	100	495V	NEH	77029
OWENS LN	22500	296C	SEM	77365
OWENS RD	14100	408L	NWC	77095
OWENS RD	22800	296F	SEM	77365
OWENS CREEK LN	4200	291S	NWC	77388
OWENS CROSS DR	2500	371R	NWC	77067
OWENS FALLS DR	12000	328D	NWC	77375
OWENS HILL LN	22100	338Z	NEC	77532
OWENS PARK DR	200	486D	SWC	77094
OWENS TRACE LN	0	446G	NWC	77449
OWL	15800	375R	NEC	77396
OWL LN	7800	463S	CCO	77520
OWL CANYON DR	21700	290Q	NWC	77388
OWL CROSSING LN	0	333F	NCC	77338
OWL CROSSING LN	0	333F	NCC	77338
OWL ECHO CT	4000	527G	SWC	77082
OWL FOREST CT	18500	447N	NWC	77084
OWL LANDING DR	0	485E	SWB	77494
OWL LANDING LN	0	524G	NEF	77494
OWL ROOST LN	11800	415Q	NEC	77016
OWNBY CT	0	615B	PL	77581
OWOSSO CT	27300	294N	SEM	77386
OX	0	656L	FR	77546
OXALIS CT	19700	289Z	NWC	77379
OXBERG TRAIL	0	373A	NCC	77073
OXBOROUGH DR	900	486F	SWC	77450
OXBOW LAKE LN	0	250X	NWC	77389
OXBOW MANOR LN	0	406F	NWC	77433
OXBOW PARK LN	20500	486S	NEF	77450
OXBOW TRAILS	23100	292G	NCC	77373
OXBRIDGE CT	3100	445M	NWC	77449
OXENBERG MANOR LN	18600	328G	NWC	77377
OXENFORD DR	15400	329S	NWC	77377
OXFORD	0	488L	SWH	77077
OXFORD	100	288G	TB	77375
OXFORD	200	493A	NWH	77007
OXFORD	900	453W	NWH	77008
OXFORD	3400	453J	NWH	77022
OXFORD CT	14900	330V	NWC	77069
OXFORD DR	1000	613K	NEB	77584
OXFORD BEND LN	22100	485Z	NEF	77450
OXFORD BROOK CT	2300	445N	NWC	77493
OXFORD CHASE TRAIL	0	526X	NEF	77407
OXFORD CRESCENT CIR	0	489S	SWH	77077
OXFORD GLEN LN	11500	569B	SWH	77072
OXFORD GREEN CT	1700	611W	FS	77545
OXFORD GROVE DR	0	367X	NWC	77095
OXFORD HAVEN DR	0	366J	NWC	77433
OXFORD KNOLLS WAY	0	489W	SWH	77077
OXFORD MEADOW DR	0	332R	NCC	77073
OXFORD OAK ST	0	488Z	SWH	77082
OXFORD PARK	0	488V	SWH	77077
OXFORD PARK DR	12100	489S	SWH	77082
OXFORD POINT LN	0	371D	NWC	77014
OXFORD ROW	2100	612Y	NWB	77578
OXFORDSHIRE DR	7500	330K	NWC	77379
OXFORD TRAILS DR	12100	329A	CY	77429
OXHAM	11500	496K	JC	77029
OXHAM FALLS CT	13800	377Y	NEC	77044
OXHILL CT	2600	613U	NEB	77584
OXHILL CT	17500	331F	NWC	77388
OXHILL RD	3900	331F	NWC	77388
OXLEY CT	18800	328G	NWC	77377
OXNARD LN	16300	657A	FR	77546
OXTED LN	9200	330S	NWC	77379
OXTED LN	9900	329V	NWC	77379
OXWICK CIR	14600	377T	NEC	77044
OYSTER BANK CIR	0	568Y	SG	77478
OYSTER BAY DR	1000	568U	SG	77478
OYSTER COVE CT	12200	569E	SF	77477
OYSTER COVE DR	3100	609L	MC	77459
OYSTER COVE DR	8101	568T	SG	77478
OYSTER CREEK DR	100	568P	SG	77478
OYSTER CREEK DR	8100	609V	MC	77459
OYSTER CREEK DR	8200	610S	MC	77459
OYSTER CREEK LN	100	568U	SG	77478
OYSTER CREEK PLACE	7900	609V	MC	77459
OYSTER CREEK PLACE	8100	610S	MC	77459
OYSTER CREEK VILLAGE DR	400	609V	MC	77459
OYSTER LOOP CT	4900	609A	SG	77478
OYSTER LOOP DR	2300	609A	SG	77478
OYSTER POINT DR	1300	569S	SG	77478
OYSTER TREE DR	3700	447K	NWC	77084
OZARK	3200	533G	SEH	77021
OZARKA TRAIL	0	614T	PL	77584
OZARK FOREST DR	0	377F	NEC	77346
OZARK PASS LN	0	377E	NEC	77346
OZARK TRAIL	0	614U	PL	77584

P

Street Name	Block	Pg/Sq	Loc	Zips
P	0	576R	SEH	77034
N. P	9700	539P	LP	77571
W. P AVE	100	538P	DP	77536
P AVE	1100	538Q	DP	77536
E. P AVE	2800	538Q	DP	77536
E. P AVE	2800	539N	DP	77536
P, AVENUE	6600	494V	SEH	77011
P, AVENUE	7000	495S	SEH	77011
E. P, AVENUE	9100	535D	SEH	77012
PABLO	9800	462M	MB	77580
PABLO TRAIL	3800	375R	NEC	77396
PABST	1000	535E	SEH	77087
PACE DR	0	609Z	MC	77459
PACEMONT DR	0	485A	NEF	77494
PACER CIR	25500	249V	NWC	77375
PACESETTER RD	0	338W	NEC	77346
PACIFIC	0	257B	SEM	77357
PACIFIC	0	284X	NWC	77447
PACIFIC	100	493N	SWH	77006
PACIFIC DR	0	337W	NEC	77346
PACIFICA SPRINGS DR	0	406H	NWC	77433
PACIFIC CREST CT	6700	337Q	NEC	77346
PACIFIC DUNES LN	24800	250X	NWC	77389
PACIFIC GROVE LN	1500	485K	NEF	77494
PACIFIC OCEAN DR	0	291P	NWC	77388
PACIFIC PEARL	7800	528R	SWH	77072
PACIFIC RIDGE CT	7400	408J	NWC	77095
PACIFIC SHORE LN	0	525M	NEF	77407
PACIFIC SPRING LN	0	525M	NEF	77407
PACKARD	13800	450B	NWH	77040
PACKARD	14000	410X	NWH	77040
PACKARD BEND TRAIL	0	616H	SEH	77089
PACKARD ELM CT	5000	446C	NWC	77449
PACKARD ELM ST	2700	371Y	NWC	77038
PACKARD FALLS CT	14500	326Y	NWC	77429
PACKARD GREEN TRAIL	0	328J	NWC	77429
PACKER CT	500	618X	WB	77598
PACKER LN	1200	569Z	NEF	77477
PACKERTON CT	19100	486D	SWC	77094
PACKSADDLE LN	1300	501M	BT	77521
PACKWOOD DR	19800	406Q	NWC	77449
PADDINGTON	6200	571P	SWH	77085
PADDINGTON PLACE DR	8200	527P	NEF	77083
PADDLEFISH WAY	0	366S	NWC	77433
PADDLEWHEEL	17800	331F	NWC	77379
PADDLE WHEEL DR	6200	406V	NWC	77449
PADDOCK CT	9800	409A	NWC	77065
PADDOCK BEND DR	7000	407N	NWC	77433
PADDOCK BROOK LN	2800	411C	NWC	77038
PADDOCK PARK DR	9800	409A	NWC	77065
PADDOCK PARK DR	9900	369W	NWC	77065
PADDOCK WAY	9700	409A	NWC	77065
PADDOCK WAY	12400	408D	NWC	77065
PADDOCK WAY CT	9700	409A	NWC	77065
PADDOCK WOODS LN	0	327U	NWC	77429
PADFIELD	8700	450V	NWH	77055
PADGETT CT	0	568B	SG	77498
PADGETT DR	0	568B	SG	77498
PADO	8900	450V	NWH	77055
PADOK RD	11600	418N	NEC	77044
PADONS TRACE CT	16100	570K	MC	77489
PADOVA CT	0	659M	LC	77573
PADOVA DR	0	524R	NEF	77406
PADOVA GARDENS DR	0	445B	NWC	77493
PADRE SHORES LN	0	367W	NWC	77433
PADSTOW LN	1300	457Z	NEC	77530
PADULA RD	0	445E	NWC	77493
PAGAN CIR	8700	330S	NWC	77379
PAGANINI PLACE	0	444M	NWC	77493
PAGE	0	256T	SEM	77357
PAGE LN	100	338Q	NEH	77336
PAGE LN	200	538P	DP	77536
PAGEANT	0	575J	SEH	77075
PAGE CREST LN	0	612Q	PL	77584
PAGE FOREST DR	0	377A	NEC	77346
PAGEHURST CT	1	250A	WD	77382
PAGEHURST DR	15600	408X	NWC	77084
PAGEMILL LN	26000	524K	NWF	77406
PAGEMILL POINT LN	0	377G	NEC	77346
PAGE RANCH	23100	284C	WCO	77447
PAGE ROCK DR	0	406G	NWC	77433
PAGETREE LN	0	614T	PL	77584
PAGETT PLACE CT	16100	377L	NEC	77044
PAGEWICK CT	0	449D	NWH	77041
W. PAGEWICK DR	0	449D	NWH	77041
E. PAGEWICK DR	4900	449D	NWH	77041
N. PAGEWICK DR	10400	449D	NWH	77041
PAGEWOOD LN	5300	491X	SWH	77056
PAGEWOOD LN	7500	490Y	SWH	77063
PAGEWOOD LN	9700	490W	SWH	77042
PAGO LN	6300	408U	NWC	77041
PAGODA DR	11400	529W	SWH	77477
PAGOSA DR	0	577M	PA	77505
PAGOSA FALLS CT	4900	485Y	NEF	77494
PAGOSA SPRINGS DR	8000	410F	NWC	77040
N. PAIGE	1	494N	SEH	77003
PAIGE	100	494N	SEH	77003
PAIGE	2900	493Y	SEH	77004
PAIGE	5000	533C	SEH	77004
PAIGE HOLLOW DR	24100	296J	SEM	77365
PAIGE MANNER DR	0	488P	SWH	77077
PAIGE PLACE	11800	616G	SEC	77089
PAIGE POINTE CIR		366U	NWC	77433
PAIGE TERRACE CT	0	407E	NWC	77433
PAIGETREE LN	13300	371F	NWC	77014
PAIGEWOOD DR	3500	613Y	NEB	77584
PAINE	6300	453Q	NEH	77022
PAINT BLUFF CIR	0	367W	NWC	77095
PAINTBRUSH AVE	2100	659G	LC	77573
PAINTBRUSH LN	10000	528S	NEF	77498
PAINTBRUSH DAWN CT	0	445K	NWC	77493
PAINTBRUSH LEDGE LN	9500	616E	SEC	77089
PAINTBRUSH PASS CT	0	367W	NWC	77095
PAINTBRUSH TRAIL	7000	525E	NEF	77494
PAINT DESERT DR	0	407J	NWC	77433
PAINTED BLVD	0	255T	SEM	77365
PAINTED CANYON DR	11900	328H	NWC	77377
PAINTED CANYON PLACE	1	250C	WD	77381
PAINTED CRESCENT CT	0	367S	NWC	77433
PAINTEDCUP CT	1	251M	WD	77380
PAINTED DAISY LN	9000	524C	NEF	77494
PAINTED DESERT RD	15600	250J	NWC	77389
PAINTED DUSK CT	0	611W	MC	77545
PAINTEDFERN PLACE	0	446L	NWC	77449
PAINTED MEADOW CIR	3100	446Q	NWC	77449
PAINTED MESA CIR	12800	411D	NWC	77038
PAINTED ROCK TRAIL	0	526N	NEF	77407
PAINTED SANDS TRAIL	0	457C	NEC	77049
PAINTED STONE CT	0	366Y	NWC	77433
PAINTED SUNSET	1	251Z	WD	77380
PAINTED TRAIL DR	5600	408X	NWC	77084
PAINTON LN	7600	250P	NWC	77389
PAINT ROCK RD	16400	657B	FR	77546
PAISLEY	5100	531T	SWH	77096

Street Name	Block	Pg/Sq	Loc	Zips
PAISLEY	6000	530V	SWH	77096
PAISLEY MEADOW DR	2900	659H	LC	77573
PAITER	16300	611C	SWH	77053
PALACE DR	2500	569V	SF	77477
PALACE GREEN CT	1700	445U	NWC	77449
PALACE OAKS CT	15000	487Z	SWH	77082
PALACE OAKS DR	3000	487Z	SWH	77082
PALACE PINES CT	27100	296W	SEM	77339
PALACE PINES DR	21400	296W	SEM	77339
PALACE POINTE DR	13300	414C	NCC	77039
PALACE WAY CT	0	526K	NEF	77407
PALACIO LN	0	660M	GCO	77539
PALACIOS CT	9700	409G	NWC	77064
PALACIOUS FALLS LN	0	524H	NWC	77449
PALADERA PLACE CT	0	253K	SEM	77386
PALADORA DR	15100	527H	SWC	77083
PALADORA PARK LN	8900	527P	NEF	77083
PALADORA POINT CT	0	409S	NWC	77041
PALAMINO CT	5400	337S	NEC	77346
PALAMINO PASS TRAIL	0	377S	NEC	77044
PALARAMO CT	0	525M	NEF	77407
PALAZZO DR	0	329Y	NWC	77070
PALCIO REAL DR	1500	573N	SWC	77047
PALE BLOSSOM DR	0	406D	NWC	77433
PALE IVY LN	0	528Q	SWC	77072
PALE MEADOW CT	21900	485V	NEF	77450
PALEO CT	0	528Y	SG	77478
PALERMO CT	0	659M	LC	77573
PALERMO DR	1300	616K	PL	77581
PALERMO DR	19300	446V	NWC	77084
PALE SAGE DR	0	457U	NEC	77049
PALE STAR DR	9600	409C	NWC	77064
PALESTINE	0	494M	NEH	77020
PALESTINE	600	536W	SH	77587
PALESTINE	6900	495J	NEH	77020
PALESTINE	10100	496J	JC	77029
PALESTINE COVE LN	4300	375R	NEC	77396
PALETTE BLUE BLVD	0	325R	NWC	77429
PALICO	18200	328F	NWC	77429
PALIN	0	411P	NWH	77088
PALIO PASS LN	0	659R	LC	77573
PALISADE DR	4700	573H	SEH	77048
PALISADE FALL TRAIL	5600	337D	NEH	77345
PALISADE GREEN DR	1500	444Z	KT	77493
PALISADE LAKES CT	17100	367X	NWC	77095
PALISADE LAKES DR	9900	367X	NWC	77095
PALISADE ROCK CT	0	526R	NEF	77407
PALISADES HEIGHTS CT	7400	408N	NWC	77095
PALISADES HEIGHTS DR	16000	408N	NWC	77095
PALISADES POINT DR	16600	578Z	PA	77059
PALISANDER CT	17400	331G	NWC	77388
PALLADIO DR	0	328N	NWC	77429
PALLAVI WOODS DR	1	336L	NEH	77339
PALLET RD	2900	374A	NEH	77032
PALLINS WAY	100	659D	LC	77573
PALLWOOD LN	13400	328X	NWC	77429
W. PALM	0	461U	NEC	77521
S. PALM	0	461U	NEC	77521
E. PALM	100	612W	FS	77545
E. PALM	500	611Z	FS	77545
W. PALM	600	611Y	FS	77545
PALM	1000	493W	SWH	77004
PALM	2000	533C	SEH	77004
PALM	3900	660M	BC	77518
PALM	4800	531L	BL	77401
PALM	4800	581W	PA	77586
N. PALM	5900	461U	NEC	77521
PALM	16100	458Y	CV	77530
PALM	4800	621A	PA	77586
PALM BLVD	1	610N	MC	77459
PALM CIR	2300	620F	SB	77586
S. PALM CT	1900	537X	PA	77502
N. PALM CT	1900	537X	PA	77502
PALM CT	6300	614Q	PL	77584
PALM DR	1000	339B	NEC	77336
PALM-AIR	0	660D	KE	77565
PALM AIRE DR	100	656T	FR	77546
PALMANOVA DR	0	525J	NEF	77406
PALM BAY	11300	613J	PL	77584
PALM BAY CT	11200	613J	PL	77584
PALMBEACH	12000	576Q	SEH	77034
PALM BROOK CT	7800	407L	NWC	77095
PALM CASTLE CT	100	660A	LC	77573
PALM CASTLE DR	2100	660A	LC	77573
PALM COCKATOO DR	0	324M	NWC	77447
PALM COCKATOO DR	0	324M	NWC	77447
PALM COVE LN	0	619Y	LC	77573
PALMCREST	1	571G	SWH	77085
PALMCREST	12000	576Q	SEH	77034
W. PALMCREST CT	900	613G	NEB	77584
PALMCROFT	12000	576L	SEH	77034
PALMDALE	12000	576L	SEH	77034
PALMDALE ESTATE DR	0	524K	NWF	77406
PALMDATE	12000	576L	SEH	77034
PALM DESERT LN	3200	609C	MC	77459
PALM DESERT LN	12700	528V	SWH	77099
PALMER	0	493V	SEH	77003
N. PALMER	1	494N	SEH	77003
PALMER	100	494N	SEH	77003
PALMER	3500	493Y	SEH	77004
PALMER	5200	533C	SEH	77004
PALMER DR	2800	656X	FR	77546
PALMERA CT	1700	610K	MC	77459
PALMER COVE DR	0	250X	NWC	77389
PALMER GLEN LN	0	377Y	NEC	77044
PALMER MANOR DR	0	326U	NWC	77429
PALMER OAKS DR	0	299T	NEC	77336
PALMER PARK CT	6200	411B	NWC	77086
PALMER PLACE LN	7800	337Z	NEC	77346
PALMER PLANTATION DR	4100	609R	MC	77459
PALMER SPRINGS DR	0	369G	NWC	77077
PALMER TERRACE LN	0	577W	SEH	77034
PALMERTON DR	11700	369R	NWC	77064
PALMER WAY	3000	251P	WD	77380
PALMETTA SPRING DR	8200	290J	NWC	77375
PALMETTO	100	611Z	FS	77545
PALMETTO	300	612W	FS	77545
PALMETTO	4500	531G	BL	77401
PALMETTO	5300	531G	SWH	77081
PALMETTO	6800	535E	SEH	77087
PALMETTO DR	800	536L	PA	77506
PALMETTO DR	1400	659W	LC	77573
PALMETTO LN	1300	336K	NEH	77339
PALMETTO LN	7300	462Y	BT	77521
PALMETTO CREEK DR	3700	337A	NEH	77339
PALMETTO HILLS DR	0	257F	SEM	77357
PALMETTO LAKES DR	0	376S	NEC	77396
PALMETTO PARK CT	1900	445S	NWC	77493
PALMETTO PARK DR	1900	445S	NWC	77493
PALMETTO PARK DR	24600	445S	NWC	77493
PALMETTO PARK LN	0	445S	NWC	77493
PALMETTO PINES RD	0	374F	NEC	77032

Street Name	Block	Pg/Sq	Loc	Zips
PALMETTO POINT LN	0	488P	SWH	77077
PALMETTO SHORES DR	12000	369W	NWC	77065
PALMETTO SPRINGS TRAIL	0	444S	KT	77493
PALMETTO TRAIL	0	412J	NWC	77038
PALM FALLS CT	17200	407L	NWC	77095
PALMFIELD	9600	576R	SEH	77034
PALM FOREST CT	0	485J	NEF	77494
PALM FOREST LN	1900	488N	SWH	77077
PALMFREE	12000	576Q	SEH	77034
PALM GRASS CT	15400	618B	SEH	77059
PALM GROVE CIR	700	568K	SG	77498
PALM GROVE DR	3500	609G	MC	77459
PALM HARBOUR DR	0	610T	MC	77459
PALMHILL	9800	576R	SEH	77034
PALM ISLAND CIR	3100	660E	LC	77573
PALMITO RANCH DR	0	525V	NEF	77406
PALM LAGOON DR	2100	620W	LC	77573
PALM LAGOON DR	2200	619Z	LC	77573
PALMLAKE	9800	576R	SEH	77034
W. PALM LAKE DR	0	576R	SEH	77034
S. PALM LAKE DR	0	576R	SEH	77034
N. PALM LAKE DR	0	576R	SEH	77034
E. PALM LAKE DR	0	576R	SEH	77034
PALM LEAF CT	12900	377P	NEC	77044
PALMORAL DR	19300	406R	NWC	77449
PALM RAIN CT	20600	446K	NWC	77449
PALM RIDGE CT	6100	338A	NEH	77345
PALMS CENTER	5200	534J	SEH	77021
PALM SHADOWS	10200	575P	SEH	77075
PALM SHORES CT	9100	329R	NWC	77379
PALM SHORES DR	9200	329R	NWC	77379
PALMSPRINGS DR	11200	576Q	SEH	77034
PALM TERRACE BLVD	100	538K	DP	77536
PALMTON	12000	576L	SEH	77034
PALM TRAIL DR	22900	485F	SWC	77494
PALM VALLEY CT	8700	528N	SWC	77083
PALM VISTA DR	2200	618G	SEH	77062
PALMWAY	12000	576Q	SEH	77034
E. PALMWAY	15400	570K	MC	77071
PALMWOOD DR	1600	536P	PA	77502
PALMYRA	100	453L	NEH	77022
PALO ALTO	2000	534D	SEH	77023
PALO ALTO	7900	455M	NEH	77078
PALO BLANCO RD	9300	456J	NEH	77078
PALO DURO	0	614Z	PL	77584
PALO DURO	1800	656U	FR	77546
PALO DURO DR	24000	325J	NWC	77447
PALO DURO CANYON LN	0	660P	LC	77573
W. PALO DURO LAKE TRAIL	0	406D	NWC	77433
S. PALO DURO LAKE TRAIL	0	406D	NWC	77433
N. PALO DURO LAKE TRAIL	0	366Z	NWC	77433
PALO LAKE LN	0	377H	NEH	77346
PALOMA DR	5800	290M	NWC	77389
E. PALOMA DR	18300	326C	NWC	77429
W. PALOMA DR	19700	326C	NWC	77429
PALOMA BAY CT	0	366Z	NWC	77433
PALOMA CREEK DR		289G	NWC	77375
PALOMA GLEN LN	0	375Y	NEC	77396
W. PALOMA LAGO CIR	18500	326C	NWC	77429
E. PALOMA LAGO CT	19600	326C	NWC	77429
PALOMA PARK	0	409W	NWC	77041
PALOMA PARK CT	0	409W	NWC	77041
PALOMA PARK LN	0	409W	NWC	77041
PALOMA PARK LN	0	409W	NWC	77041
PALOMA PINES PLACE	0	250Q	NWC	77389
PALOMAR	0	660H	GCO	77539
PALOMAR LN	2200	620S	BT	77520
PALOMA RANCH CT	7500	406M	NWC	77433
PALOMAR PARK DR	0	526F	NEF	77407
PALOMAR VALLEY DR	3401	253X	SEM	77386
PALOMA TERRACE	6900	407Q	NWC	77084
PALOMINO LN	300	658J	LC	77573
PALOMINO LN	1400	336F	NEH	77339
PALOMINO CREEK CT	22900	290F	NWC	77375
W. PALOMINO LAKE CIR	0	368C	NWC	77429
S. PALOMINO LAKE CIR	0	368C	NWC	77429
N. PALOMINO LAKE CIR	0	368C	NWC	77429
E. PALOMINO LAKE CIR	0	368C	NWC	77429
PALOMINO RIDGE DR	0	334R	NCC	77338
PALOMINO TRAIL	0	612Z	NEB	77578
PALOMINO TRAILS CT	10500	367X	NWC	77095
S. PALOMINTE DR	0	525J	NEF	77406
PALO PINTO CT	3300	609F	MC	77459
PALO PINTO DR	2500	450P	NWH	77080
PALO PINTO DR	4300	450P	NWH	77041
PALO PINTO CREEK DR		367W	NWC	77095
PALOS PARK DR	14500	327W	CY	77429
PALOS PARK DR	14600	327W	NWC	77429
PALOS VERDES DR	4200	577B	PA	77504
PALO VERDE DR	11400	456F	NEC	77044
PALO VISTA DR	800	456F	NEC	77044
PALSTONE BEND LN	3100	331X	NWC	77014
PALTON SPRINGS DR	15100	487Z	SWC	77082
PALUXY CIR	3500	609K	MC	77459
PALUXY RIVER LN	0	253Y	SEM	77386
PAMA CIR	10900	490H	HC	77024
PAMALA	11800	415Q	NEC	77016
PAMBROOKE LN	1400	486H	SWC	77094
PAMELA	13400	572S	SWH	77053
PAMELA DR	100	501P	BT	77521
PAMELA DR	9800	575N	SEH	77034
PAMELA LN	1700	570S	MC	77489
PAMELAHOLLY TRAIL	11900	616G	SEC	77089
PAMELA SUE CT	12200	569A	MD	77477
PAMELA WAY	18300	330H	NWC	77379
PAMELLIA DR	100	531H	BL	77401
PAMPA	100	576D	PA	77504
PAMPA	1300	577A	PA	77504
PAMPAS DR	22900	290G	NWC	77389
PAMPAS LN	1200	658Z	LC	77573
PAMPASS PASS	11300	367U	NWC	77095
PAMPAS TRAIL DR	1800	656R	FR	77546
PAMPLONA DR	1100	298Z	NEH	77336
PAMPLONA LN	0	660L	GCO	77539
PANAGARD DR	2400	488X	SWH	77077
PANAGARD DR	2500	488X	SWH	77082
PANAIR	8500	575C	SEH	77061
PANAMA	900	493D	NEH	77009
PANAMA	3900	577F	PA	77504
PAN AMERICAN CAMP RD	0	656J	NEB	77511
PANAMINT CT	0	250P	NWC	77389
PANATELLA DR	8500	450Z	NWH	77055
PANAY DR	8100	533Z	SEH	77033
PANAY DR	10900	573H	SEH	77048
PANAY CREEK DR	0	573M	SEH	77048
PANAY PARK DR	5100	573M	SEH	77048
PANAY VILLAGE CIR	11900	573M	SEH	77048
PANCALDO CT	0	257F	SEM	77357
PANDA LN	0	408V	NWC	77041
PANDORA DR	10800	456S	NEH	77013
PANHANDLE DR	13900	528S	NEF	77498
PANICUM CT	11000	371T	NWC	77086

Street Name	Block	Pg/Sq	Loc	Zips
PANKY LN	23500	256Z	SEM	77357
PANNELL	1200	494F	NEH	77020
PANNELL	2100	494B	NEH	77026
PANO LN	14700	328Z	NWC	77070
PANOLA	12900	419T	NEC	77532
PANOLA POINTE	13800	367C	CY	77429
PANOLA WAY	9600	450X	NWH	77055
PANORAMA DR	3700	610J	MC	77459
PANORAMA VIEW LN	0	615H	PL	77089
PANSY	2400	537Y	PA	77503
PANSY	3100	577G	PA	77505
PANTANO DR	11500	368R	NWC	77065
PANTEGO LN	0	445L	NWC	77449
PANTHER CT	0	529T	SWH	77099
PANTHER CAVE CT	0	366S	NWC	77433
S. PANTHER CREEK DR	3300	251J	WD	77381
E. PANTHER CREEK DR	3500	251J	WD	77381
W. PANTHER CREEK DR	4700	251E	WD	77381
N. PANTHER CREEK DR	9500	251B	WD	77381
PANTHER CREEK LN	12200	247R	SWM	77362
PANTHER CREEK PINES	4400	250H	WD	77381
PANTHER DEN	700	452G	NWH	77091
PANTHER PASS		332E	NWC	77388
PANTHER PEAK		332E	NWC	77388
PANTHER PLACE DR	12500	528V	SWH	77099
PANTHER POINT DR	10300	528Z	SWH	77099
PANTHER TRAIL	0	250H	WD	77381
PANTHER VILLA CT	12500	528Z	SWH	77099
PANZANO LN	0	659R	LC	77573
PAPADO	5900	411X	NWH	77091
PAPADOSA	14100	572X	SWC	77053
PAPAGO CT	19400	328C	NWC	77377
PAPAGO DR	19300	328D	NWC	77377
PAPALOTE	10000	410W	NWH	77041
PAPALOTE	10200	409Z	NWH	77041
PAPASAN	9300	575H	SEH	77075
PAPAYA BEND DR	0	524E	NEF	77494
PAPER ROSE LN	0	524B	NEF	77494
PAPER WASP LN	0	297A	SEM	77357
PAPINEAU WOODS DR	0	377K	NEC	77346
PAPOOSE TRAIL	1700	378C	NEC	77532
PAR CIR	0	580K	LP	77571
PARABELLO CT	0	525J	NEF	77406
PARABLE LN	14200	327Z	NWC	77429
PARADISE	23900	296H	SEM	77365
PARADISE LN	4700	573H	SEH	77048
PARADISE RD	0	460W	BT	77521
PARADISE BRIDGE LN	15000	528W	NEF	77498
PARADISE CANYON CT	2700	485R	NEF	77450
PARADISE CANYON DR	0	612M	PL	77584
PARADISE GATE DR	22700	334A	NCC	77373
PARADISE PARK BEND	0	526F	NEF	77407
PARADISE PLACE	0	258F	SEM	77357
PARADISE POINT DR	1	568Q	SG	77478
PARADISE RIVER DR	0	609Q	MC	77459
PARADISE SUMMIT DR	19200	328D	NWC	77377
PARADISE VALLEY	0	370C	NWC	77069
PARADISE VALLEY DR	12000	370H	NWC	77066
PARADISE VALLEY DR	13000	330Y	NWC	77069
PARAGON CT	7100	370E	NWC	77069
PARAGUAY CIR	4000	577B	PA	77504
PARAKEET	2100	576B	SEH	77034
PARALEE DR	1100	484K	NEF	77494
PARAMOUNT LN	11300	371Q	NWC	77067
PARANA	0	450P	NWH	77080
PARANA CT	0	450P	NWH	77080
PARANA DR	1600	450T	NWH	77080
PARANA DR	2500	450P	NWH	77080
PARASOL LN	8300	410G	NWC	77064
PARATI CREEK LN	0	406H	NWC	77433
PARAZETTA PLACE	0	285P	NWC	77447
PARC CREST	0	569G	SF	77477
PARCEL THREE	0	572A	SWH	77045
PARC LAKE EDGE DR	0	368G	NWC	77429
PARC LAKE HAVEN DR	0	368G	NWC	77429
PARC MONCEAU LN	0	573N	SWC	77047
PARCO VERDE CIR	2000	485R	SWC	77450
PARDEE	3700	454U	NEH	77026
PARDEE	7700	455T	NEH	77028
PARDOE DR	14600	374U	NEH	77039
PARDUE CT	8000	411P	NWH	77088
PARELLO CT	0	525N	NEF	77469
PARELLO CT	0	525N	NEF	77469
PARENZO ST	0	530X	SWH	77031
PAREMILL DR	7700	408M	NWC	77041
PARESI CT	0	445J	NWC	77493
PARFIELD LN	18700	447J	NWC	77084
PAR FIVE DR	7600	337Z	NEC	77346
PAR FOUR DR	5800	411T	NWH	77088
PARHAM CIR	0	290R	NWC	77388
PARIL CREEK DR	0	333F	NCC	77373
PARIS	6300	533R	SEH	77021
PARISH RD	14700	420H	NEC	77532
PARISH HALL DR	16100	330S	NWC	77379
PARISH MILL LN	14800	528W	NEF	77498
PARISH POINT DR	24300	445S	NWC	77493
PARISH TIMBERS CT	0	325M	NWC	77429
PARISLEY LN	0	659Z	DI	77539
E. PARK	0	536H	PA	77506
PARK	0	291W	NWC	77379
PARK	0	412S	NWH	77088
PARK	1	501S	BT	77520
N. PARK	100	536F	PA	77506
PARK	100	459X	CV	77530
PARK	100	581S	PA	77586
PARK	100	499D	NEC	77562
W. PARK	500	568J	SG	77498
E. PARK	600	568J	SG	77498
PARK	1300	538L	DP	77536
PARK	1400	459S	CV	77530
PARK	1500	492R	SWH	77019
PARK	1600	459W	CV	77530
PARK	2500	500U	BT	77520
PARK	4300	535Q	SEH	77017
PARK	4300	620G	SB	77586
PARK	4500	494T	SEH	77023
PARK	5000	493W	SWH	77006
PARK	5400	444U	KT	77493
PARK	14000	288K	TB	77377
PARK AVE	2000	660D	KE	77565
PARK AVE	2100	615J	PL	77581
PARK CIR	0	660C	KE	77565
W. PARK CT	0	527C	SWC	77082
E. PARK CT	0	527C	SWC	77082
PARK CT	4500	531H	BL	77401
PARK CT	12300	368C	NWC	77429
PARK DR	0	295Y	SEM	77365
PARK DR	0	659J	LC	77573
PARK DR	200	581W	PA	77586
PARK DR	700	580G	LP	77571
PARK DR	1900	540Z	LP	77571
PARK DR	23500	296D	SEM	77357

Street Name	Block	Pg/Sq	Loc	Zips
E. PARK LN	0	537J	PA	77506
PARK LN	0	323D	NWC	77375
PARK LN	0	616V	FR	77546
W. PARK LN	100	536G	PA	77506
PARK LN	1200	485M	SWC	77450
PARK LN	1400	463A	MB	77580
PARK LN	3400	580U	SA	77571
PARK LN	3600	492Y	SWH	77098
PARK LN	6600	534C	SEH	77023
PARK LN	10100	579B	LP	77571
PARK LN	10600	414S	NEH	77093
PARK LN	23100	288E	NWC	77377
PARK RD	0	287H	NWC	77377
PARK RD	100	659J	LC	77573
PARK RD	200	658M	LC	77573
PARK RD	22600	288J	NWC	77377
W. PARK 290 DR	0	324R	NWC	77447
E. PARK 290 DR	0	324R	NWC	77447
N. PARK 290 DR	0	325N	NWC	77447
N. PARK 290 DR	0	324R	NWC	77447
S. PARK 290 DR	0	325S	NWC	77447
S. PARK 290 DR	0	324V	NWC	77447
PARK 90 DR	100	568M	SG	77478
PARK ALMEDA DR	14700	612B	SWC	77047
PARK ANTIQUE LN	0	367D	NWC	77429
PARK ARBOR CT	14600	327W	NWC	77429
W. PARK AT BEVERLY HILLS	3200	491X	SWH	77057
E. PARK AT BEVERLY HILLS	3200	491X	SWH	77057
E. PARK AT FAIRDALE	0	491W	SWH	77057
W. PARK AT FAIRDALE	3000	491W	SWH	77057
N. PARK AT FAIRDALE	6200	491W	SWH	77057
W. PARK AT KINGS MANOR LP	0	296X	SEM	77339
E. PARK AT KINGS MANOR LP	26800	296X	SEM	77339
N. PARK AT KINGS MANOR LP	20100	296X	SEM	77339
W. PARK AT SHADY VILLA	1300	451X	NWH	77055
E. PARK AT SHADY VILLA	1300	451X	NWH	77055
PARK BANK CT	3600	331S	NWC	77068
PARK BAYOU DR	1200	488K	SWH	77077
PARK BEND DR	2900	657G	FR	77546
PARK BEND DR	4300	502F	BT	77521
PARK BEND DR	20600	486E	SWC	77450
PARK BEND DR	21600	485M	SWC	77450
PARK BEND LN	4900	609A	SG	77478
PARK BEND LN	7500	578G	PA	77505
PARK BIRCH LN	1500	486J	SWC	77450
PARK BISHOP DR	21200	486J	SWC	77450
PARK BLUFF DR	21200	486J	SWC	77450
PARKBOROUGH DR	6100	409T	NWC	77041
PARKBRIAR CIR	1	501M	BT	77521
PARK BRIAR DR	1500	486J	SWC	77450
PARKBRIAR LN	2600	613U	NEB	77584
PARK BRIDGE	0	658K	LC	77573
PARK BRIDGE DR	20800	486E	SWC	77450
PARKBROOK DR	0	327T	NWC	77429
PARK BROOK DR	21100	486J	SWC	77450
PARK BROOK DR	21600	485M	SWC	77450
PARK BRUSH CIR	20800	486E	SWC	77450
PARK BRUSH CT	20800	486E	SWC	77450
PARK BRUSH LN	21000	486E	SWC	77450
PARK BUD LN	700	486E	SWC	77450
PARK CANYON DR	20800	486E	SWC	77450
PARKCANYON LN	5000	484Z	NEF	77494
PARK CEDAR CT	11700	328M	NWC	77377
PARK CENTER CT	3800	578X	SEH	77059
PARK CENTER DR	15900	578Y	SEH	77059
PARK CENTER WAY	15700	578X	SEH	77059
PARK CENTRE CT	13400	370E	NWC	77069
PARKCHASE TIMBER CT	7800	370E	NWC	77070
PARKCHASE TIMBER DR	1340	370E	NWC	77070
PARKCHESTER DR	15900	618G	SEH	77062
PARK CIRCLE DR	6000	491J	SWH	77057
PARK CIRCLE WAY	3900	578Y	SEH	77059
PARK COLONY POINT LN	0	411A	NWC	77086
PARKCRAFT DR	7400	570V	SWH	77459
PARK CREEK CT	15000	329W	NWC	77070
PARK CREEK DR	11600	329W	NWC	77070
PARKCREST DR	4000	576G	SEH	77034
PARKCREST DR	4900	539X	LP	77571
PARKCREST FOREST DR	8600	411L	NWC	77088
PARK CROSSING	0	615Q	PL	77581
PARKCROSS PLACE	7400	407J	NWC	77433
PARK CYPRESS	18100	487B	SWC	77094
PARKDALE DR	2000	296Y	NEH	77339
PARKDALE DR	2300	336D	NEH	77339
PARK DALE DR	3300	538U	DP	77536
PARKDALE LN	0	367D	NWC	77429
PARK DOUGLAS DR	4100	447H	NWC	77084
PARK DOWNE LN	21300	486E	SWC	77450
PARK DRIVE CIR	10400	368Z	NWC	77065
PARKE	0	659F	LC	77573
PARK ELLA DR	0	332S	NWC	77090
PARK ELLA DR	1100	332N	NWC	77090
PARK ENTRY DR	16100	409Q	NWH	77041
PARKER	200	492M	SWH	77007
PARKER	21500	287Q	NWC	77377
PARKER CT	100	658K	LC	77573
PARKER CT	11700	249S	NWC	77375
PARKER RD	1	413X	NEH	77076
W. PARKER RD	100	412Z	NEH	77076
E. PARKER RD	100	413X	NEH	77076
W. PARKER RD	400	412Z	NWH	77091
PARKER RD	1500	414W	NEH	77093
PARKER RD	5000	454D	NEH	77016
PARKER RD	8000	415Y	NEH	77078
PARKER RD	24100	296M	SEM	77365
PARKERHAVEN CT	0	452Y	NWH	77008
PARKER MILL CT	0	406F	NWC	77433
PARKER MILL LN	0	406F	NWC	77433
PARKERSBURG DR	5600	530D	SWH	77036
PARKERS COVE CT	13700	417C	NEC	77044
PARKERS HIDEAWAY DR	12000	616G	SEC	77089
PARKERTON LN	28300	293E	SEM	77386
PARKES	7100	412W	NWH	77091
PARKES	7300	412W	NWH	77088
PARKESGATE DR	14400	528N	NEF	77083
PARK ESTATES LN	15200	618F	SEH	77062
PARKESTON DR	0	291Z	NWC	77388
PARKETTE DR	8500	455C	NEH	77028
PARKETTE DR	8800	455D	NEH	77078
PARKEY LN	1700	496Q	GP	77015
PARKEY LN	12400	496Q	GP	77015
PARKFAIR CT	1800	485M	SWC	77450
PARK FALLS CT	11600	612R	PL	77584
PARK FALLS DR	2700	612R	PL	77584
PARK FALLS DR	7600	407M	NWC	77095
PARK FALLS LN	0	660E	LC	77573
PARKFIELD	13300	417S	NEC	77044
PARKFIELD LN	0	609J	MC	77459
PARKFIELD PLACE	3800	446L	NWC	77449
PARK FIRTH DR	16500	447H	NWC	77084
PARKFORD LN	0	528L	SWC	77072
PARKFORD MEADOWS DR	0	406P	NWC	77433

Street Name	Block	Pg/Sq	Loc	Zips
PARK FOREST DR	1700	485M	SWC	77450
PARK FOREST DR	12500	368L	NWC	77429
PARKFOREST DR	12500	368L	NWC	77429
PARK FOREST TRAIL	12900	368E	NWC	77429
PARKFOUR	2900	297N	NEH	77339
PARKFRONT DR	5700	530A	SWH	77036
PARK GABLE DR	24200	293W	NCC	77373
PARK GARDEN DR	2900	297W	NEH	77339
PARK GATE	0	658K	LC	77573
S. PARKGATE CIR	0	251C	SD	77381
PARK GATE CT	5000	452E	NWH	77018
PARKGATE DR	14400	528N	NEF	77083
PARKGLEN	2800	538U	DP	77536
PARKGLEN DR	7900	457E	NEC	77049
PARK GRAND RD	2000	618G	SEH	77062
PARK GREEN	900	538M	DP	77536
PARK GREEN DR	21300	486E	SWC	77450
PARK GREEN WAY	16600	618R	SEH	77058
PARK GROVE DR	4500	502F	BT	77521
PARK GROVE LN	600	485D	SWC	77450
PARK GWEN	24100	293W	NCC	77373
PARK HARBOR CT	1600	446Z	NWH	77084
PARK HARBOR DR	18800	446Z	NWH	77084
PARK HARBOR ESTATES DR	1500	446Z	NWH	77084
PARK HARBOR OAKS CT	1500	447W	NWH	77084
PARK HAVEN DR	1600	489P	SWH	77077
PARKHAVEN DR	2300	568C	SG	77478
PARK HAVEN LN	0	612N	PL	77545
PARKHAVEN LN	1100	488K	SWH	77077
PARK HAVEN LN	3200	538V	DP	77536
PARKHEATH LN	0	292B	NCC	77373
PARK HEATH LN	9600	411N	NWH	77088
PARKHILL DR	700	497D	NEC	77530
PARKHILL FOREST DR	8400	411K	NWC	77088
PARK HOLLOW CT	7800	407M	NWC	77095
PARKHOLLOW DR	14000	488W	SWH	77082
PARK HOLLY CT	1200	486E	SWC	77450
PARKHURST DR	6600	455E	NEH	77028
PARK ISLAND CT	16700	328R	NWC	77377
PARK IVY CT	0	484Y	NEF	77494
PARK IVY LN	0	484Y	NEF	77494
PARK KEY CIR	18800	446V	NWH	77084
PARK KNOLL LN	600	485H	SWC	77450
PARK KNOLL LN	1000	486E	SWC	77450
PARK KOLBE LN	0	450R	NEH	77080
PARK LAKE DR	0	446Q	NWC	77084
PARK LAKES CANYON TRACE	0	376S	NEC	77396
PARKLAKE VILLAGE	1700	486L	SWC	77450
PARKLAND	4200	577J	PA	77504
PARKLAND CT	1	490C	SV	77055
PARKLAND DR	0	366S	NWC	77433
PARK LANDING CT	3900	446L	NWC	77449
PARKLAND MANOR DR	7300	406L	NWC	77433
PARKLAND WAY	0	410E	NWC	77040
PARKLAND WAY	0	410E	NWC	77064
PARKLAND WOODS DR	10700	528X	NEF	77498
PARKLANE	2900	502F	BT	77521
PARKLANE BLVD	1	568M	SG	77478
PARK LAUREATE DR	100	491B	SWH	77024
PARK LAUREL LN	0	526G	NEF	77407
PARK LEAF DR	0	502F	BT	77521
PARK LEAF LN	600	485H	SWC	77450
PARK LINE DR	0	448W	NWH	77084
PARK LINK DR	4300	538U	DP	77536
PARK LODGE CT	1900	618F	SEH	77062
PARK LODGE DR	17100	330N	NWC	77379
PARK LORNE DR	16500	447H	NWC	77084
PARKMAN GROVE DR	0	524K	NWF	77406
PARK MANOR	15200	571Z	SWH	77053
PARK MANOR	16300	611C	SWH	77053
PARK MAPLE DR	1400	486J	SWC	77450
PARKMEAD DR	4300	619G	TL	77586
PARK MEADOW CT	5000	577K	PA	77504
PARK MEADOW CT	11900	616G	SEC	77089
PARK MEADOW DR	0	616L	SEC	77089
PARK MEADOW DR	700	486E	SWC	77450
PARK MEADOW DR	10000	616G	SEC	77089
PARK MEADOWS AVE	2400	538V	DP	77536
PARK MILL DR	21200	486J	SWC	77450
PARK MIST DR	0	486E	SWC	77450
PARKMONT DR	3400	579B	LP	77571
PARKMORE DR	9200	407D	NWC	77095
PARK MOUNT DR	21100	486E	SWC	77450
PARK OAK CT	21100	326N	NWC	77433
PARK OAKS	1800	660C	KE	77565
PARK OAKS DR	2900	535K	SEH	77017
W. PARK ONE DR	800	568G	SG	77478
PARK ONE DR	12800	568G	SG	77478
PARK ON FUQUA DR	10800	576U	SEH	77089
PARK ORCHARD DR	21300	486J	SWC	77450
PARK OVERLOOK CT	15900	326N	NWC	77433
PARK PEBBLE LN	0	485P	NEF	77494
PARKPEBBLE LN	0	485P	NEF	77494
PARK PINE DR	20500	486E	SWC	77450
PARK PINE LN	31400	253P	SEM	77386
PARK PLACE BLVD	7400	535N	SEH	77087
PARK PLACE BLVD	8100	535Q	SEH	77017
PARK PLACE DR	0	524C	NEF	77494
PARK PLACE DR	0	613Q	PL	77584
PARK PLACE ESTATES	29800	288A	NWC	77377
PARK PLAZA	0	256U	SEM	77357
PARK PLAZA DR	4700	452G	NWH	77018
PARK PLAZA DR	5300	452C	NWH	77091
PARK POINT DR	3400	297W	NEH	77339
PARK POINT DR	22300	485L	SWC	77450
PARK POINT LN	0	484F	KT	77494
PARK POINTE DR	0	327U	NWC	77429
PARK POST LN	21300	486J	SWC	77450
PARK RD 138	0	457D	NEC	77049
PARK RD 1836	3800	499T	SEC	77571
PARKRIDGE CT	16500	611C	SWH	77053
PARK RIDGE CT	20800	486E	SWC	77450
S. PARK RIDGE DR	1400	538U	DP	77536
N. PARK RIDGE DR	1400	538U	DP	77536
PARK RIDGE DR	1700	485M	SWC	77450
PARK RIDGE DR	4500	577K	PA	77504
PARKRIDGE DR	5000	611C	SWH	77053
PARKRIDGE GLEN DR	3400	528C	SWH	77082
PARKRIVER DR	11100	329W	NWC	77070
PARK RIVER DR	11400	329W	NWC	77070
PARK ROCK LN	21100	486E	SWC	77450
PARK ROSE DR	0	489T	SWH	77077
PARK ROW	14200	448W	NWH	77079
PARK ROW	15900	447X	NWH	77084
PARK ROW	19900	446X	NWC	77449
PARK ROW	21500	445Z	NWC	77449
PARK ROW DR	0	446Z	NWC	77084
PARK ROYAL	12800	488L	SWH	77077
PARK ROYAL DR	3400	297W	NEH	77339
PARK ROYALE CIR	1200	486E	SWC	77450
PARK ROYALE CT	1200	486E	SWC	77450
PARK ROYALE DR	21100	486E	SWC	77450

Street Name	Block	Pg/Sq	Loc	Zips
PARK ROYALE LN	1200	486E	SWC	77450
PARK RUN DR	21100	486J	SWC	77450
PARK SAGE CT	0	407J	NWC	77433
PARK SAGE LN	0	407J	NWC	77433
PARK SANDS LN	4200	297Y	NEH	77345
PARKS BRANCH LN	4200	484U	NEF	77494
PARK SCOT DR	16500	447H	NWC	77084
PARKSHADOW DR	4500	502F	BT	77521
PARK SHADOW LN	2400	538V	DP	77536
PARK SHADOWS PLACE	0	619A	PA	77058
PARK SHADOWS TRAIL	11800	578Z	PA	77059
PARK SHADOWS TRAIL	12400	619A	PA	77058
PARKSHIRE CT	23200	256D	SEM	77357
PARKSHIRE DR	3500	613W	NEB	77584
PARK SHORE DR	5300	447B	NWC	77084
PARKSIDE	0	614V	PL	77584
PARKSIDE	3800	609K	MC	77459
PARKSIDE DR	1000	496S	GP	77547
PARKSIDE DR	1100	536Z	PA	77502
PARKSIDE DR	1100	537W	PA	77502
N. PARK SIDE DR	1400	538V	DP	77536
S. PARK SIDE DR	1500	538V	DP	77536
PARKSIDE HAVEN DR	0	366J	NWC	77433
PARKSIDE SPRING DR	0	291Q	NWC	77388
PARKSIDE VALLEY LN	0	615R	PL	77581
PARKSIDE VILLAGE BLVD	0	615R	PL	77581
PARKSIDE VILLAGE CT	0	615Q	PL	77581
PARKSIDE VILLAGE DR	0	615Q	PL	77581
PARKSIDE VILLAGE LN	0	615R	PL	77581
PARKSIDE VILLAGE GARDENS	0	615Q	PL	77581
PARK SIX WEST BLVD	0	528A	SWC	77082
PARKSLEY DR	15700	578Y	SEH	77059
PARK SPRING LN	2600	293T	NCC	77373
PARK SPRINGS CT	0	297U	NEH	77345
PARK SPRINGS DR	0	612K	PL	77545
PARK SQUARE LN	4800	375V	NEC	77396
PARKSTEAD DR	1000	619G	TL	77586
PARKSTONE DR	700	413U	NEH	77076
PARKSTONE BEND CT	0	446C	NWC	77449
PARKSTONE BEND LN	0	446c	NWC	77449
PARKSTONE VIEW DR	13400	528F	SWC	77083
PARKSUN CT	7400	525L	NEF	77407
PARK TALON DR	0	371M	NWC	77067
PARK TEN BLVD	1000	487C	NWH	77084
PARK TEN BLVD	1200	447Y	NWH	77084
PARK TEN PLACE	15800	447Y	NWH	77084
PARK TERRACE	8100	535K	SEH	77017
PARK TERRACE, SW	0	569F	SF	77477
PARK THICKET	0	619A	PA	77058
PARK TIMBERS LN	21200	486J	SWC	77450
W. PARKTOWN DR	500	538T	DP	77536
S. PARKTOWN DR	500	538T	DP	77536
N. PARKTOWN DR	500	538T	DP	77536
E. PARKTOWN DR	500	538T	DP	77536
PARK TRAIL	0	658J	LC	77573
PARK TRAIL	10000	491F	SWH	77024
PARKTRAIL DR	8800	456C	NEC	77044
PARKTRAIL DR	9200	416Y	NEC	77044
PARK TRAIL DR	19000	486H	SWC	77094
PARK TRAIL LN	300	493J	SEH	77007
PARK TRAIL LN	4500	578G	PA	77505
PARK TRAIL RUN	1300	493K	SWH	77019
PARK TRAIL VISTA	600	493K	SWH	77019
PARK TRAIL WAY	700	493K	SWH	77019
PARK TREE LN	20000	486E	SWC	77450
PARK TREE LN	21700	485H	SWC	77450
PARK TWO DR	700	568G	SG	77478
PARKVALE DR	9900	529T	SWH	77099
PARK VALLEY DR	21100	486J	SWC	77450
PARK VALLEY DR	21700	485M	SWC	77450
PARKVIEW	100	493C	NWH	77009
PARKVIEW	15400	570G	MC	77071
PARKVIEW CT	500	568K	SG	77498
PARKVIEW CT	4500	610P	MC	77459
PARKVIEW DR	1800	657J	FR	77546
PARKVIEW DR	1800	577F	PA	77504
PARKVIEW DR	2300	615U	PL	77581
PARK VIEW DR	17500	447W	NWH	77084
PARK VIEW LN	0	659S	LC	77573
PARKVIEW LN	1600	610P	MC	77459
PARKVIEW MANOR LN	0	375Y	NEC	77396
PARKVIEW POINT DR	0	487E	SWC	77494
PARK VILLA DR	0	615Q	PL	77581
PARK VILLA DR	21100	486E	SWC	77450
PARK VILLAGE DR	5100	573M	SEH	77048
PARK VILLAGE DR	5200	574J	SEH	77048
PARK VILLAGE LN	0	615R	PL	77581
PARKVILLE DR	14900	331S	NWC	77068
PARKVINE CT	3600	486W	NEF	77494
PARKVINE LN	0	485U	NEF	77450
PARKVINE LN	0	486W	NEF	77450
PARK VISTA DR	7700	528M	SWH	77072
PARK VISTA LN	3200	538V	DP	77536
PARKWALK LN	22700	485Y	NEF	77494
PARKWATER CIR	19800	486Q	SWC	77450
PARKWATER BRIDGE LN	23700	525K	NEF	77407
PARKWAY	500	541C	BT	77520
PARKWAY	900	580D	LP	77571
PARKWAY	9900	579B	LP	77571
PARKWAY	25700	338D	NEC	77336
PARKWAY BLVD	0	569J	SG	77478
PARKWAY BLVD	1500	568U	SG	77478
PARKWAY BLVD	13300	568R	SG	77478
PARKWAY BLVD	13500	568M	SG	77478
PARKWAY CT	0	569J	SF	77477
PARKWAY CT	1300	488K	SWH	77077
S. PARK WAY DR	1400	538V	DP	77536
N. PARK WAY DR	1500	538V	DP	77536
PARKWAY DR	8500	412Q	NWH	77088
PARKWAY BEND LN	0	615M	PL	77089
PARKWAY CROSSING DR	0	292L	SP	77373
PARKWAY FOREST DR	8700	456D	NEC	77044
PARKWAY GLEN DR	0	488U	SWH	77077
PARKWAY GREEN BLVD	0	537M	PA	77530
PARKWAY GREEN BLVD	0	538E	PA	77530
PARKWAY HILLS DR	0	488U	SWH	77077
PARKWAY LAKES CT	0	525L	NEF	77407
PARKWAY LAKES LN	22700	525L	NEF	77407
PARKWAY MANOR DR	12700	570R	SWH	77085
PARKWAY MEADOWS DR	0	488U	SWH	77077
PARKWAY OAKS	37600	246F	SWM	77355
PARKWAY OAKS LN	0	485N	NEF	77494
PARKWAY PLACE	1	409K	JV	77040
PARKWAY PLAZA DR	1400	488K	SWH	77077
PARKWAY RIDGE WAY	0	326W	NWC	77433
PARKWAY SPRING DR	0	488U	SWH	77077
PARKWAY VISTA DR	600	493K	SWH	77019
W. PARKWEST	1	529A	SWH	77072
E. PARKWEST	1	529A	SWH	77072
PARK WEST DR	1	568G	SG	77478
PARK WEST DR	8900	490T	SWH	77063
PARKWEST CENTRAL	14600	528A	SWH	77082

Street Name	Block	Pg/Sq	Loc	Zips
PARKWEST CENTRAL	14800	527D	SWH	77082
PARK WESTHEIMER BLVD	0	525M	NEF	77407
PARK WESTHEIMER LN	0	525L	NEF	77407
PARK WICK LN	3000	538V	DP	77536
PARK WICK LN	21100	486E	SWC	77450
PARKWILLE LN	18000	407K	NWC	77433
PARK WILLOW DR	21100	486J	SWC	77450
PARK WIND CT	21600	486E	SWC	77450
PARK WIND DR	700	486E	SWC	77450
W. PARKWOOD AVE	100	656R	FR	77546
E. PARKWOOD AVE	100	657E	FR	77546
PARKWOOD DR	300	537M	PA	77503
PARK WOOD DR	2900	502F	BT	77521
PARKWOOD DR	3200	533F	SEH	77021
S. PARKWOOD DR	3400	533G	SEH	77021
N. PARKWOOD DR	3400	533G	SEH	77021
PARKWOOD CIRCLE DR	7700	529M	SWH	77036
PARKWOOD COVE CT	4400	609X	NEF	77479
PARKWOOD MANOR DR	2000	296R	NEH	77339
PARK WOODS DR	0	293G	SEM	77386
PARKWOOD VILLAGE DR	0	657E	FR	77546
PARKWOOD WAY	15300	618B	SEH	77059
PARK YORK DR	21100	486J	SWC	77450
PARK YORK DR	21600	485M	SWC	77450
PARLIAMENT	0	257H	SEM	77357
PARLIAMENT DR	0	528K	SWC	77083
PARLIAMENT DR	100	576G	SEH	77034
PARLIAMENT DR	16600	527P	NEF	77083
PARLIAMENT HILLS DR	0	253X	SEM	77386
PARLIAMENT PLACE	26500	258E	SEM	77357
PARLIN RIDGE DR	0	410T	NWC	77040
PARMER CT	8500	409H	NWC	77064
PARMLEY CREEK CT	15800	327R	NWC	77429
PARNELL	7700	533T	SEH	77021
PARNELL	7900	533T	SEH	77051
PAR POINT CT	25500	250T	NWC	77389
PARQUETRY CT	20700	526A	NEF	77450
PARR CT	0	288K	TB	77377
PARRAL CT	700	379X	NEC	77532
PARRAMATTA LN	100	332L	NCC	77073
PARRIS	0	419R	BR	77532
PARRY CT	0	615W	PL	77584
PARRY DR	0	615W	PL	77584
PARRY FIELDS CT	0	615W	PL	77584
PARRY SOUND	1200	577E	PA	77504
PARRYVILLE DR	5600	408Z	NWC	77041
PARSLEY	5100	500H	BT	77521
PARSLEY LN	3600	659Z	GCO	77539
PARSLEY CREEK LN	0	524F	NEF	77494
PARSLEY HAWTHORNE CT	17100	578Y	SEH	77059
PARSLEY PATH LN	0	410E	NWC	77064
PARSLEY RIDGE CT	0	524K	NEF	77406
PARSONFIELD CT	900	292C	NCC	77373
PARSONS	900	535A	SEH	77012
PARSONS FIELD LN	0	524G	NEF	77494
PARSONSGATE DR	22500	334B	NEC	77373
PARSONS GLEN DR	14100	377W	NEC	77044
PARSONS GREEN CT	19900	486Q	SWC	77450
PARSONS KNOLL DR	0	406H	NWC	77433
PARSONS LANDING DR	0	525A	NEF	77494
PARSONS MILL CT	0	295L	SEM	77365
PARSONS MILL DR	0	295L	SEM	77365
PART DR	15800	419F	NEC	77532
PARTAGE LN	13200	370B	NWC	77069
PARTEX	22100	289J	TB	77375
PARTHA WAY	0	333K	NCC	77338
PARTHENON PLACE	17900	257D	RF	77357
PARTHENON PLACE	18200	258A	SEM	77357
PAR THREE	0	258A	SEM	77357
PARTLOW LN	8300	410J	NWC	77040
PARTNERS CT	0	296E	SEM	77365
PARTNERSHIP WAY	0	445Y	NWC	77449
PARTNERS VOICE DR	18500	366K	NWC	77433
PARTNERS WAY	23400	296E	SEM	77365
PARTRIDGE	300	373W	NEH	77060
PARTRIDGEBERRY CT	15800	578Y	SEH	77059
PARTRIDGE GREEN DR	18000	447F	NWC	77084
PARTRIDGE RUN DR	19800	486G	SWC	77094
PAR TWO CIR	18900	337Z	NEC	77346
PARWILL	5700	531F	SWH	77081
PASADENA	0	494Z	SEH	77011
PASADENA	1700	534D	SEH	77023
W. PASADENA BLVD	100	538T	DP	77536
PASADENA BLVD	100	536H	PA	77506
E. PASADENA BLVD	100	538U	DP	77536
PASADENA BLVD	1300	537S	PA	77502
PASADENA BLVD	2600	539S	DP	77536
PASADENA BLVD	2900	537U	PA	77503
W. PASADENA FRWY	100	536E	PA	77506
E. PASADENA FRWY	100	537G	PA	77506
PASADENA FRWY	3200	537G	PA	77503
PASADENA PLAZA	1000	536Y	SH	77587
PASADERO DR	15800	527L	NEF	77083
PASAGUARDA	0	497U	SEH	77503
PASA ROBLES LN	13500	528K	SWC	77083
PASCHALL	100	493G	NEH	77009
PASCHE LN	0	448K	NWH	77084
PASEO ARBOLES AVE	11900	413T	NEH	77076
PASEO CACERES DR	0	492L	SWH	77007
PASEO DEL REY DR	15200	527H	SWC	77083
PASHA DR	8200	410K	NWC	77040
PASKET LN	1900	451U	NWH	77092
PASO DEL FLORES DR	0	571H	SWH	77045
PASO DEL SOL DR	6400	527F	NEF	77083
PASO DOBBLE DR	16200	527F	NEF	77083
PASO FINO DR	0	334R	NCC	77338
PASO HONDO	16300	527F	NEF	77083
PASO HONDO DR	16200	527F	NEF	77083
PASO REAL DR	15100	527M	SWC	77083
PASO RELLO DR	2100	488U	SWH	77077
PASQUA TRAIL	0	658Y	LC	77573
PASS CREEK LN	0	568A	NEF	77498
PASSELANDE DR	0	289Q	NWC	77375
PASSING PINE CT	7400	337Q	NEC	77346
PASSIONFLOWER WAY	0	405T	NWC	77493
PASTEL LN	0	291M	NWC	77389
PASTEL DAWN TRACE	0	457C	NEC	77049
PASTEL SKY WAY	0	334L	NCC	77388
PASTORAL POND CIR	1	291B	WD	77380
PASTORAL TRAIL	0	296T	SEM	77365
PASTORIA DR	11400	527J	NEF	77083
PAS TRAIL	400	338M	NEH	77336
PASTURE BEND CT	0	407J	NWC	77433
PASTURE BEND LN	0	407J	NWC	77433
PASTURE SPRINGS LN	0	407J	NWC	77433
PASTUREVIEW DR	0	614G	PL	77581
PASTURE VIEW LN	8600	491H	SWH	77024
PATAGONIA ST	0	658Y	LC	77573
PATAL	6400	409U	NWC	77041
PATCH	1300	497L	NEC	77015
PATCHESTER DR	300	489F	SWH	77079
PATE	2100	620N	SB	77586

Street Name	Block	Pg/Sq	Loc	Zips
PATE RD	5200	454C	NEH	77016
PATEL LN	12700	414E	NCC	77039
PATERNO DR	0	409F	NWC	77064
PATEWAY DR	600	252P	SEM	77386
PAT FLAHERTY	0	444R	NWC	77493
PATHFIELD DR	15800	448B	NWC	77084
PATHFINDER DR	24400	246S	SWM	77355
PATHFINDER DR	24500	245V	SWM	77355
N. PATHFINDERS CIR	1	251E	WD	77381
S. PATHFINDERS CIR	100	250D	WD	77381
E. PATHFINDERS CIR	100	250D	WD	77381
PATHFINDERS PASS	0	293Y	NCC	77373
PATH GREEN DR	8900	407D	NWC	77095
PATIENCE AVE	3000	371G	NWC	77014
PATINA WAY	6800	406Q	NWC	77449
PATIO DR	2900	536T	SEH	77017
PATIO GLEN DR	7900	570G	MC	77071
PATNA DR	2000	444Q	KT	77493
PATOU DR	700	498B	CV	77530
PATRAS DR	3700	578A	PA	77505
PATRICIA	900	538Q	DP	77536
PATRICIA	1700	570N	MC	77489
PATRICIA	6500	444W	KT	77493
PATRICIA LN	1700	537N	PA	77502
PATRICIA LN	3100	615V	PL	77581
PATRICIA LN	7100	535E	SEH	77012
PATRICIA LN	21000	256N	SEM	77357
PATRICIA LN	22900	256V	SEM	77357
PATRICIA HAVEN LN	0	376W	NEC	77396
PATRICIA MANOR PLACE	2500	535J	SEH	77012
PATRICIA OAKS CT	3300	253N	SEM	77386
PATRICK	1600	537K	PA	77506
PATRICK	5500	452D	NWH	77076
PATRICK CT	1	490E	BH	77024
PATRICK HENRY	5100	531K	BL	77401
PATRICK PALACE	0	616L	SEC	77089
PATRIDGE	6100	614Y	PL	77584
PATRIDGE CIR	12300	247M	SWM	77362
PATRIDGE DR	11200	329X	NWC	77070
PATRIOT CT	3500	569Y	MC	77477
PATRIOT PARK LN	20800	406T	NWC	77449
PATRIOTS WAY	0	656X	FR	77546
PATSY	900	501V	BT	77520
PATSY LN	700	296M	SEM	77365
PATSY LN	27000	252E	OR	77385
PATTEN OAKS LN	0	293Y	NCC	77373
PATTERSON	100	492M	SWH	77007
PATTERSON DR	0	609Y	MC	77459
PATTERSON RD	13000	448P	NWH	77084
PATTERSON RD	13900	573Z	SEH	77048
PATTIBOB	8700	495L	NEH	77029
PATTIGLEN DR	17500	407T	NWC	77084
PATTI LANE CT	900	332Z	NCC	77073
PATTI LYNN LN	1	490P	SWH	77024
PATTINGTON CYPRESS DR	15400	326T	NWC	77433
PATTON	100	453X	NEH	77009
W. PATTON	500	453X	NWH	77009
PATTON	13000	574Q	SEH	77048
PATTY LN	800	580C	LP	77571
PAUL	0	420P	NEC	77532
PAUL	900	537K	PA	77506
PAUL	1400	616U	PL	77581
PAUL RD	15100	527Y	NEF	77498
PAUL'S TRAIL LN	15500	287V	NWC	77377
PAULA	4800	573D	SEH	77033
PAULA LN	27100	252E	OR	77385
PAULA BLUFF LN		366U	NWC	77433
PAULA PLACE	0	251N	SWM	77380
PAUL B KOONCE	7900	575K	SEH	77061
PAULETTE DR	900	538Q	DP	77536
PAULETTE DR	3900	577E	PA	77504
PAULINE	300	536V	PA	77502
PAULINE	900	460S	HG	77562
PAULINE	1000	531L	BL	77401
PAUL OAKS DR	0	524B	NEF	77494
PAUL QUINN	700	452C	NWH	77091
PAUL QUINN	3000	451D	NWH	77091
PAUL REVERE DR	100	489M	SWH	77024
PAULUS DR	10800	409Y	NWC	77041
PAULWOOD DR	10700	530Y	SWH	77071
PAUMA DR	6500	370B	NWC	77069
PAVONIA CT	16500	367Y	NWC	77095
PAVONIA DR	10500	367Y	NWC	77095
PAVERO PLACE	22400	485R	SWC	77450
PAVILION	0	452E	NWH	77091
PAVILION CT	12500	328Q	NWC	77377
PAVILION DR	0	528E	SWC	77083
PAVILION DR	7500	528J	SWC	77083
W. PAVILION PARK CIR	5200	525C	NEF	77494
E. PAVILION PARK CIR	5200	525C	NEF	77494
S. PAVILION PARK CIR	22500	525C	NEF	77494
N. PAVILION PARK CIR	22500	525C	NEF	77494
PAVILION POINT	14100	528J	SWC	77083
PAVONA RIDGE LN	0	410L	NWC	77040
PAWLEY DR	10700	368T	NWC	77065
PAWNEE	3000	533P	SWH	77054
PAWNEE	4400	461S	NEC	77521
PAWNEE DR	1900	538Q	DP	77536
PAWNEE DR	3400	579A	LP	77571
PAWNEE LN	4600	577F	PA	77504
PAWNEE BEND DR	14100	328P	NWC	77429
PAWNEE PASS	0	609Z	MC	77459
PAWNEE TRAIL	12200	247R	SWM	77362
PAWNEE TRAILS DR	13800	328P	NWC	77429
PAXICO	0	577X	SEH	77034
PAXSTON POINT LN	17000	367Y	NWC	77095
PAXTON	10400	413Z	NEH	77093
PAXTON DR	13600	371C	NWC	77014
PAXTON LANDING LN	0	326U	NWC	77429
PAXTON WOODS	0	376R	NEC	77346
PAYETTE DR	1400	410J	NWC	77040
PAYNE	100	493C	NWH	77009
PAYNE CT	27200	252E	OR	77385
PAYNE RD	23100	256M	SEM	77357
PAYNES CREEK DR	0	366Q	NWC	77433
PAYNES CREEK DR		366Q	NWC	77433
PAYSON	2800	533J	SWH	77021
PAYSON PLACE	1	656Q	FR	77546
PAYTON CHASE CT	25600	485S	NEF	77494
PAYTON CHASE LN	4600	485S	NEF	77494
PAYTON GRACE	0	255Q	SEM	77365
PAYTON HAVEN DR	0	366J	NWC	77433
PAYTON MANOR LN	0	446G	NWC	77449
PAYTON SPRINGS DR	0	613X	NEB	77578
S. PAZAREE CT	17500	379X	NEC	77532
N. PAZAREE CT	17500	379T	NEC	77532
PEABLE PATH	12000	369P	NWC	77070
PEABODY	6900	455K	NEH	77028
PEABODY HILL LN	0	524D	NEF	77494
PEACE CT	5500	448D	NWC	77041
PEACEDALE CT	300	457W	NEC	77015
PEACEFUL LN	11400	415P	NEC	77016

Street Name	Block	Pg/Sq	Loc	Zips
S. PEACEFUL CANYON CIR	1	250G	WD	77381
N. PEACEFUL CANYON CIR	1	250G	WD	77381
PEACEFUL CANYON CT	1	250G	WD	77381
PEACEFUL CANYON DR	0	250G	WD	77381
PEACEFUL LIFE LN	0	415S	NEH	77016
PEACEFUL MEADOW TRAIL	0	325R	NWC	77433
PEACEFUL PASS CT		367S	NWC	77433
PEACEFUL VALLEY DR	2300	333A	NCC	77373
PEACEFUL WAY	0	571L	SWH	77085
PEACE RIVER DR	6800	330G	NWC	77379
PEACE ROSE DR	0	251Z	WD	77380
PEACH	0	540T	LP	77571
S. PEACH	100	288H	TB	77375
PEACH	100	288H	TB	77375
E. PEACH	1200	659U	LC	77573
PEACH	9800	454C	NEH	77093
PEACH	10000	414Y	NEH	77093
PEACH CT	2300	615J	PL	77581
PEACH DR	0	257Q	SEM	77357
PEACH LN	2100	537S	PA	77502
PEACH BLOSSOM	10300	575S	SEH	77075
PEACH BLOSSOM DR	900	613E	NEB	77584
PEACH BLUFF LN	0	327U	NWC	77429
PEACH BOUGH CT	16000	407M	NWC	77095
PEACH BOUGH LN	16200	407M	NWC	77095
PEACH BROOK CT	1800	618B	SEH	77062
PEACH COUNTRY CT	4000	578Z	PA	77059
PEACH CREEK DR	5000	535R	SEH	77017
PEACH CREEK DR	25600	257M	SEM	77357
PEACH CREEK DR	26600	258J	SEM	77357
PEACH CREEK LN	0	609U	NEF	77479
E. PEACHFIELD CIR	4100	371F	NWC	77014
W. PEACHFIELD CIR	4200	371F	NWC	77014
S. PEACHFIELD CIR	13400	371F	NWC	77014
N. PEACHFIELD CIR	13400	371F	NWC	77014
PEACHFORD LN	1100	618E	SEH	77062
PEACH FOREST CT	16800	407L	NWC	77095
PEACH GARDEN LN		609X	NEF	77479
PEACHGLEN LN	22100	334E	NCC	77373
PEACH GROVE DR	10200	529W	SWH	77099
PEACH HOLLOW	13800	488X	SWH	77082
S. PEACH HOLLOW CIR	2700	613F	NEB	77584
N. PEACH HOLLOW CIR	2700	613G	NEB	77584
E. PEACH HOLLOW CIR	3600	613G	NEB	77584
S. PEACH HOLLOW CT	900	613F	NEB	77584
PEACH KNOLL LN	24800	485X	NEF	77494
PEACHLEAF	1500	373Z	NCC	77039
PEACHLEAF WILLOW TRACE	0	328A	NWC	77377
PEACHLIGHT LN	0	370L	NWC	77066
PEACH LIMB DR	11700	529W	SWH	77099
PEACH MEADOW DR	12900	328Y	NWC	77429
PEACHMEADOW LN	14800	457V	NEC	77530
PEACHMEADOW LN	15200	458S	NEC	77530
PEACH MILL LN	0	698H	LC	77539
PEACH MOUNTAIN LN	20300	326T	NWC	77433
PEACH OAK CROSSING	0	524D	NEF	77494
PEACH ORCHARD DR	16300	376M	NEC	77396
PEACH PATH CT	0	366Y	NWC	77433
PEACHRIDGE CT	10100	369L	NWC	77070
PEACHRIDGE DR	9800	369L	NWC	77070
PEACHRIDGE RD	0	376H	NEC	77396
PEACH RUN DR	1700	375G	HM	77396
PEACH SPRING DR	500	412M	NEH	77037
PEACH SPRING DR	800	412L	NWH	77088
PEACH STONE CT	9000	526R	NEF	77407
PEACHSTONE PLACE	3300	291L	NWC	77389
PEACHTEX DR	13700	375T	NEH	77396
PEACHTEX DR	13700	415B	NEC	77396
PEACHTREE	6200	454G	NEH	77028
PEACHTREE	7400	454C	NEH	77016
PEACHTREE CT	0	616T	PL	77581
PEACH TREE CT	1	409F	JV	77064
PEACH TREE CT	6100	406Z	NWC	77449
PEACH TREE LN	3100	609M	MC	77459
PEACHTREE HILL CT	6100	338A	NEH	77345
PEACH TREE WAY	0	250E	NWC	77375
PEACH VALLEY CIR	19300	446Z	NWC	77084
PEACHVINE LN	21200	289T	NWC	77375
PEACH WILLOW RD	0	570V	SWH	77489
PEACHWOOD	1800	536P	PA	77502
PEACHWOOD CT	13600	488F	SWH	77077
PEACHWOOD DR	2100	610A	MC	77489
PEACHWOOD BEND DR	800	488F	SWH	77077
PEACOCK	5400	574E	SEH	77033
PEACOCK GAP LN	23500	485K	NEF	77494
PEACOCK HILLS DR	6300	570H	SWH	77035
PEACOCK PARK	7700	375Q	NEC	77396
PEAKWOOD DR	800	332J	NWC	77090
PEAR	0	413B	NCC	77060
E. PEAR	800	659U	LC	77573
PEAR	2800	454W	NEH	77026
E. PEAR	3700	615N	PL	77581
W. PEAR	4100	615J	PL	77581
PEAR CT	2300	614R	PL	77581
PEARBERRY LN	0	524D	NEF	77494
PEAR BLOSSOM LN	0	484Q	NEF	77494
PEAR BROOK TRAIL	1500	618E	SEH	77062
W. PEARCE	100	501X	BT	77520
E. PEARCE	100	501Y	BT	77520
E. PEARCE	600	541D	BT	77520
PEARCE LAKE CT	4900	526X	NEF	77407
PEAR CREEK CIR	1900	446Y	NWC	77084
PEAR GLEN CT	3800	297T	NEH	77345
PEARHAVEN DR	15000	618F	SEH	77062
PEA RIDGE DR	23900	293T	NCC	77373
PEAR KNOLL CT	14400	617H	SEH	77062
PEARL	400	495K	NEH	77029
PEARL	400	501Z	BT	77520
PEARL	1100	538L	DP	77536
PEARL	1500	659F	LC	77573
PEARL DR	10200	409G	NWC	77064
PEARLAND AVE	2100	615J	PL	77581
PEARLAND HEIGHTS	0	614C	PL	77581
PEARLAND PARKWAY	2900	615U	PL	77581
PEARLAND PKWY	0	575Y	SEH	77075
PEARLAND SCHOOL RD	0	615X	PL	77581
PEARLAND SITES RD	2600	615W	PL	77584
PEARL BAY CT	0	612K	PL	77584
PEARL BLUFF LN	3200	573X	SEC	77047
PEARL CREEK LN	0	524H	NEF	77494
PEARL CREST LN	0	250U	NWC	77389
PEARL DRIFT DR	0	286Q	NWC	77377
PEARL HALL DR	3800	576C	SEH	77587
PEARL HOLLOW LN	0	698M	LC	77539
PEAR LIMB DR	10100	529W	SWH	77099
PEARL LAKE DR	8500	408F	NWC	77095
PEARL LAKE DR	21900	445M	NWC	77449
PEARL LANDING DR	0	527W	NEF	77469
PEARLPASS CT	0	609U	MC	77479
PEARLPASS LN	0	609U	MC	77479
PEARL POINT	8600	456H	NEC	77044
PEAR MEADOW LN	3500	414J	NCC	77039
PEAR OAK DR	10300	368Y	NWC	77065
PEAR PLACE CT	0	366Y	NWC	77433
PEAR RIDGE PLACE	16300	376M	NEC	77396
PEARSALL DR	9300	409H	NWC	77064
PEAR SIDE CT	0	292D	SEM	77386
PEARSON	1100	494X	SEH	77023
PEARSON LN	4500	376D	NEC	77346
PEARTEX	0	375T	NEH	77396
PEAR TREE LN	900	332M	NCC	77073
PEARWOOD DR	2400	371Z	NWC	77038
PEAR WOODS CT	13500	578W	SEH	77059
PEASE	500	493Q	DT	77002
PEASE	1600	493Q	SEH	77003
PEASE	3500	494W	SEH	77023
PEATWOOD RD	13900	371U	NWC	77038
PEAVINE CIR	3300	450M	NWH	77080
PEAVY, J W DR	6900	495S	SEH	77011
PEBBLE	25300	339F	NEC	77336
PEBBLE DR	3000	613X	NEB	77578
PEBBLE LN	1900	657N	FR	77546
PEBBLE LN	6000	535S	SEH	77087
PEBBLEBANK LN	0	660J	LC	77573
PEBBLE BANK LN	5700	408Z	NWC	77041
PEBBLE BANKS LN	1400	619D	PA	77586
PEBBLE BANKS LN	1600	619H	PA	77586
PEBBLE BAY CT	4300	578F	PA	77505
PEBBLE BAY DR	3100	660A	LC	77573
PEBBLE BAY DR	3400	485U	NEF	77450
PEBBLE BAY BRIDGE	0	612F	PL	77545
PEBBLE BEACH	6000	370F	NWC	77069
PEBBLE BEACH DR	0	409F	JV	77064
PEBBLE BEACH DR	0	659D	LC	77573
PEBBLE BEACH DR	2000	619Y	LC	77573
W. PEBBLE BEACH DR	2500	609H	MC	77459
E. PEBBLE BEACH DR	2500	609H	MC	77459
N. PEBBLE BEACH DR	3100	609D	MC	77459
PEBBLE BEACH DR	6000	370C	NWC	77069
PEBBLE BEACH LN	3200	613V	PL	77584
PEBBLE BEACH PLACE		484Y	NEF	77494
PEBBLE BEND DR	14600	331N	NWC	77068
PEBBLE BLUFF LN	0	609T	MC	77459
PEBBLE BLUFF LN	4800	446D	NWC	77449
PEBBLEBRIAR LN	0	485S	NEF	77494
PEBBLE BROOK	0	610K	MC	77459
PEBBLEBROOK	300	620J	EL	77586
PEBBLE BROOK	4800	500M	BT	77521
PEBBLEBROOK CT	100	568V	SG	77478
PEBBLE BROOK DR	0	539S	DP	77536
PEBBLE BROOK DR	3500	615S	PL	77584
PEBBLE BROOK DR	3900	660L	LC	77573
PEBBLEBROOK DR	12100	490E	SWH	77024
PEBBLEBROOK DR	13000	489E	SWH	77079
PEBBLE BROOK LN	2900	613V	NEB	77584
PEBBLE CANYON CT	6200	526B	NEF	77450
PEBBLE CHASE DR	1500	486L	SWC	77450
PEBBLE COVE CT	1	251K	WD	77381
PEBBLE COVE DR	1	251K	WD	77381
PEBBLE CREEK DR	2600	615R	PL	77581
PEBBLECREEK LN	12600	368Q	NWC	77429
PEBBLECREEK CROSSING	0	524B	NEF	77494
PEBBLE CREEK TRAIL	15800	326P	NWC	77433
PEBBLE CREST LN	16300	527T	NEF	77083
PEBBLE DOWNE	0	568C	SG	77478
PEBBLEDOWNE CIR	2300	528Y	SG	77478
PEBBLEDOWNE CIR	2300	568C	SG	77478
PEBBLEDOWNE DR	8300	410H	NWC	77064
PEBBLE FALLS DR	7100	407R	NWC	77095
PEBBLE FALLS LN	22300	289K	NWC	77375
PEBBLE FARMS CT	0	377F	NEC	77346
PEBBLE GARDEN LN	3700	446J	NWC	77449
PEBBLEGATE CT	4200	333C	NCC	77373
PEBBLEGLEN DR	16000	407M	NWC	77095
PEBBLE GROVE CT	0	525H	NEF	77407
PEBBLE HEIGHTS LN	4100	609Y	NEF	77479
PEBBLE HILL	12000	490J	BH	77024
PEBBLE HILL CT	1800	569W	SG	77478
PEBBLE HOLLOW	0	251B	WD	77381
PEBBLE HOLLOW	0	526W	NEF	77406
PEBBLE HOLLOW CT	1	251B	WD	77381
PEBBLE LAKE	0	620J	EL	77586
PEBBLE LAKE DR	15000	408F	NWC	77095
PEBBLE LODGE LN	0	407K	NWC	77433
PEBBLE LODGE LN	0	657K	FR	77546
PEBBLE MEADOW CT	14600	367A	NWC	77429
PEBBLE MEADOWS CT	12200	449A	NWC	77041
PEBBLE MESA CIR	8900	412Q	NWH	77088
PEBBLEMILL LN	7200	371W	NWC	77086
PEBBLE PARK LN	10100	529R	SWH	77036
PEBBLE PATH CT	0	369P	NWC	77070
PEBBLEPATH LN	25800	485W	NEF	77494
PEBBLE PINE CT	21500	325V	NWC	77433
PEBBLE PINE TRAIL	21300	325V	NWC	77433
PEBBLE PLACE CT	7000	526F	NEF	77407
PEBBLE POCKET CT	100	249R	NWH	77375
PEBBLE POCKET CT	100	249R	NWH	77375
PEBBLE POINT	0	486L	SWC	77450
PEBBLE POINTE DR	0	612H	PL	77584
PEBBLE ROCK CT	1400	489N	SWH	77077
PEBBLE ROCK DR	11900	489N	SWH	77077
PEBBLE RUN CT	7700	407L	NWC	77095
PEBBLE SANDS DR	11600	329A	NWC	77375
PEBBLESHIRE DR	0	613T	NEB	77584
PEBBLESHIRE DR	0	613X	NEB	77584
PEBBLESHIRE DR	100	618J	SEH	77062
PEBBLE SHORES LN	0	612K	PL	77545
PEBBLE SPRINGS DR	5100	370D	NWC	77066
PEBBLESTONE	12500	528M	SWH	77072
PEBBLESTONE CT	1700	569X	MC	77459
PEBBLESTONE DR	4500	569X	MC	77459
PEBBLE STONE DR	5700	491P	SWH	77057
PEBBLESTONE RIDGE CT		249U	NWC	77375
PEBBLESTONE WAY	0	615A	PL	77581
PEBBLE STREAM CT	2500	298W	NEH	77345
PEBBLE TERRANE LN	0	484U	NEF	77494
PEBBLETON DR	11500	329W	NWC	77070
PEBBLE TRACE DR	3100	331T	NWC	77068
PEBBLE TRAIL CT	0	376B	NEC	77369
S. PEBBLEWALK CIR	13100	408M	NWC	77041
N. PEBBLEWALK CIR	13100	408M	NWC	77041
PEBBLE WAY CT	12500	449A	NWC	77041
PEBBLE WAY LN	5200	449A	NWC	77041
PEBBLEWICK LN	0	446X	NWC	77449
PEBBLEWOOD LN	12100	247R	SWM	77362
PEBWORTH PLACE	22600	333B	NCC	77373
PEBWORTH PLACE	23500	293X	NCC	77373
PECAN	0	247R	SWM	77362
PECAN	0	502T	BT	77520
PECAN	100	419U	BR	77532
PECAN	100	616Z	FR	77546
N. PECAN	200	288G	TB	77375
PECAN	200	658M	LC	77573
PECAN	1100	458Y	CV	77530
PECAN	1300	536P	PA	77502
PECAN	2700	282X	WL	77484
PECAN	2900	534M	SEH	77087
PECAN	5200	419H	CB	77532
PECAN	16300	498H	CV	77530
PECAN CIR	0	251D	SD	77381
PECAN CIR	0	251D	SD	77381
PECAN CIR	1100	619H	TL	77586
PECAN CIR	3800	579C	LP	77571
PECAN CT	2700	609M	MC	77459
PECAN CT	12400	456Y	NEH	77013
PECAN DR	100	502S	BT	77520
S. PECAN DR	400	288G	TB	77375
PECAN DR	400	576B	SH	77587
E. PECAN DR	600	288G	TB	77375
PECAN DR	10800	579C	LP	77571
PECAN DR	12400	456Y	NEH	77013
PECAN DR	24600	257P	SEM	77357
PECAN LN	0	484G	NEF	77494
PECAN LN	1700	375C	HM	77396
PECAN LN	1700	570S	SF	77477
PECAN LN	2000	484L	NEF	77494
PECAN LN	6100	444P	KT	77493
PECAN LN		484L	NEF	77494
PECAN RD	1300	484L	NEF	77494
PECAN ARBOR LN	0	330Z	NWC	77069
PECAN BAYOU LN	0	367W	NWC	77095
PECAN BROOK CT	20400	290V	NWC	77379
PECAN CANYON CT	11500	329N	NWC	77377
PECAN CORNERS	4200	421W	NEC	77532
PECAN CREEK DR	11200	449X	NWH	77043
PECAN CROSSING LN	3500	579A	LP	77571
PECAN DRAW CT	3200	609E	SG	77479
PECAN FOREST	7800	462T	NEC	77521
PECAN FOREST CT	1800	610P	MC	77459
PECAN GAP DR	11600	368P	NWC	77065
PECANGATE DR	5500	334E	NCC	77373
PECAN GLEN CT	9500	410J	NWC	77040
PECAN GLEN DR	1100	570X	MC	77489
PECAN GREEN WAY	0	332V	NCC	77073
PECAN GROVE	200	456Y	NEH	77013
PECAN GROVE CT	2500	613R	NEB	77584
PECAN GROVE DR	3300	500H	BT	77521
PECAN GROVE DR	3500	501E	BT	77521
PECAN GROVE DR	4600	613V	NEB	77584
PECAN GROVE DR	4800	614S	NEB	77584
PECAN HILL CT	0	574Z	SEH	77048
PECAN HOLLOW	1600	616P	PL	77581
PECAN KNOLL DR	4000	297S	NEH	77339
PECAN LANDING CT	0	658T	LC	77573
PECAN LANDING DR	0	332X	NWC	77090
PECAN LEAF DR	6200	330D	NWC	77379
PECAN MANOR DR	2500	502T	BT	77520
PECAN MEADOW DR	12000	570B	SWH	77071
PECAN OAK DR	13300	368X	NWC	77065
PECAN ORCHARD	1800	659S	LC	77573
PECAN ORCHARD CT	0	659S	LC	77573
PECAN PARK	4000	337C	NEH	77345
PECAN PARK CIR	4500	452M	NWH	77018
PECAN PLACE DR	8800	570A	SWH	77071
PECAN POINT CIR	1700	569W	SG	77478
PECAN POINT DR	2800	568Z	SG	77478
PECAN RIDGE	3600	610X	MC	77459
PECAN RIDGE BLVD	4400	331W	NWC	77014
PECAN SHORES DR	12800	377P	NEC	77044
PECAN SPRINGS DR	8800	410E	NWC	77040
PECANTEX DR	13700	415B	NEC	77396
PECANTEX DR	14900	375T	NEH	77396
PECAN TRAIL LN	1	490C	SV	77055
PECAN VALLEY CIR	25500	252S	SWM	77380
PECAN VALLEY CT	200	656T	FR	77546
PECAN VALLEY CT	2300	610J	MC	77459
PECAN VALLEY DR	3800	610J	MC	77459
PECAN VILLAS DR	7600	535W	SEH	77061
PECANWOOD	800	490C	HE	77024
PECAN WOOD DR	2900	609F	MC	77459
PECAN WOOD DR	6200	411P	NWC	77088
PECH RD	1100	451N	NWH	77055
PECK	0	501S	BT	77520
PECKETT, TED LN	700	659J	LC	77573
PECKHAM	2100	492Q	SWH	77019
PECKHAM	2600	492Q	SWH	77098
PECKS PARK CT	0	328M	NWC	77377
PECORE	100	453X	NWH	77009
PECOS	0	614H	PL	77581
PECOS	5400	660T	DI	77539
PECOS	9100	450Y	NWH	77055
PECOS BLUFF CT	12400	377J	NEC	77346
PECOS PARK LN	17200	377J	NEC	77346
PECOS PASS CT	0	407A	NWC	77433
W. PECOS RIVER CT	0	253U	NWC	77389
E. PECOS RIVER CT	0	253U	NWC	77389
PECOS RIVER DR	0	253U	NWC	77389
PECOS RIVER LN	0	253U	NWC	77389
PECOS RIVER BEND DR	0	366Z	NWC	77433
PECOS ROSE LN	0	526R	NEF	77407
W. PECOS VALLEY TRAIL	2000	446X	NWC	77449
E. PECOS VALLEY TRAIL	2000	446X	NWC	77449
S. PECOS VALLEY TRAIL	20000	446X	NWC	77449
N. PECOS VALLEY TRAIL	20000	446X	NWC	77449
PEDDER WAY DR	12400	328Q	NWC	77377
PEDDIE	600	453W	NWH	77008
PEDDIE	1000	453W	NWH	77009
PEDEN	300	493N	SWH	77006
PEDEN	1700	492R	SWH	77019
PEDEN RD	26300	247V	SWM	77355
PEDEN BAY DR	3100	613R	PL	77584
PEDERNALES FALLS DR	2700	615N	PL	77581
W. PEDERNALES RIVER DR	0	366Z	NWC	77433
N. PEDERNALES RIVER DR	0	366Z	NWC	77433
E. PEDERNALES RIVER DR	0	366Z	NWC	77433
PEDERNALES RIVER LN	0	253U	SEM	77386
PEDERNALES TRAILS LN	3200	486T	NEF	77450
PEDERSON	4700	573D	SEH	77033
PEDERSON	5200	574A	SEH	77033
PEDLARS CT	12700	328L	NWC	77377
PEEBLES DR	5000	447D	NWC	77084
PEEK RD	100	445X	NWC	77449
S. PEEK RD	300	485B	SWC	77450
S. PEEK RD	2700	485U	NEF	77450
PEEK RD	3000	445G	NWC	77449
S. PEEK RD	4800	525L	NEF	77407
PEEK RD	5000	405U	NWC	77449
PEEK RD		525Q	NEF	77406
PEEK RD		525T	NEF	77406
PEEK RD		525X	NEF	77406
PEEKSKILL CT	3000	613U	NEB	77584
PEEKSKILL LN	7400	575S	SEH	77075
PEEL CT	5200	452G	NWH	77091
PEER DR	1600	450S	NWH	77043
PEERLESS	6300	533K	SEH	77021
PEERLESS DR	23200	293U	NCC	77373
PEERLESS FOUNTAIN CT	0	533P	SEH	77021
PEERLESS PASS CT	3000	293T	NCC	77373
PEERMONT	15400	618J	SEH	77062
PEG	5900	451K	NWH	77092
PEGASUS CIR	14000	328T	NWC	77429
PEGASUS LN	0	619X	LC	77573
PEGASUS RD	13500	328P	NWC	77429
PEGGY	400	501Z	BT	77520
PEGGY	800	538L	DP	77536
PEGGY	7100	453L	NEH	77022
PEGGY CT	1500	496M	NEH	77015
PEGGY LN	12800	496M	NEH	77015
PELAGO ST	0	659Q	LC	77573
PELHAM DR	2100	492Q	SWH	77019
PELHAM CHASE DR	6600	250U	NWC	77389
PELICAN	1	245T	SWM	77355
PELICAN DR	0	619Y	LC	77573
PELICAN DR	300	379Y	NEC	77532
PELICAN BEACH LN	0	377M	NEC	77346
PELICAN COVE	0	610U	MC	77459
PELICAN COVE CT	0	377F	NEC	77346
PELICAN HILL CT	1200	484H	NEF	77494
PELICAN HILL DR	24500	485E	NEF	77494
PELICAN ISLE CT	12400	328R	NWC	77377
PELICAN MARSH DR	14300	327X	NWC	77429
PELICAN POINTE BLVD	0	448D	NWC	77041
PELICAN WAY RD	17900	447W	NWH	77084
PELLA DR	6900	530J	SWH	77036
PELLY	1800	541B	BT	77520
PELORUS WAY	17000	379X	NEC	77532
PELSEY	9700	495V	NEH	77029
PELTON	3300	371X	NWC	77086
PEMBERTON	500	498G	CV	77530
PEMBERTON DR	2600	532C	WU	77005
PEMBERTON DR	3200	613Y	NEF	77584
S. PEMBERTON CIRCLE DR	3200	532P	SWH	77025
N. PEMBERTON CIRCLE DR	3200	532P	SWH	77025
PEMBERTON CIRCLE DR	3200	532P	SWH	77025
W. PEMBERTON CIRCLE DR	9200	532P	SWH	77025
E. PEMBERTON CIRCLE DR	9200	532P	SWH	77025
PEMBERTON CRESCENT DR	0	532P	SWH	77025
PEMBERTON RIDGE	0	532P	SWH	77025
PEMBERTON TRACE	0	532P	SWH	77025
PEMBERTON WALK	0	532P	SWH	77025
PEMBERWICK PARK LN	13500	369C	NWC	77070
PEMBRIDGE DR	11000	530Y	SWH	77071
PEMBRIDGE DR	11100	570C	SWH	77071
PEMBRIDGE GREEN DR	0	295Q	SEM	77365
PEMBROKE	12900	573R	SEH	77048
PEMBROKE DR	0	569X	MC	77459
PEMBROKE BAY DR	2000	660A	LC	77573
PEMBROKE RIDGE DR	0	369P	NWC	77065
PEMBROOK	9100	454H	NEH	77016
PEMBROOK	9300	455A	NEH	77016
PEMBROOK CT	1	531L	BL	77401
PEMBROOK CT	3300	613Y	NEB	77584
PEMBROOK SPRINGS	0	293W	NCC	77373
PEMBROUGH LN	6900	525F	NEF	77494
PEMETIC TRAIL	0	526T	NEF	77407
PEMFORD DR	11600	329S	NWC	77377
PENANT PARK CT	9500	416Z	NEC	77044
PENCE RD	400	617R	SEH	77598
PENCE HILLS CT	0	366V	NWC	77433
PENCESTER ST	24300	250Z	NWC	77389
PENDER LN	11100	529W	SWH	77477
PENDER LN	11700	569A	MD	77477
PENDERGRASS TRAIL	0	568W	SG	77479
PENDI WAY	5500	448D	NWC	77041
PENDLETON	800	537J	PA	77506
PENELOPE DR	10800	456S	NEH	77013
PENFIELD DR	2500	537P	PA	77506
PENFIELD LN	5200	534K	SEH	77021
PENGUIN	24400	245Q	SWM	77355
PENGUIN CT	1	251V	WD	77380
PENHALLOW LN	0	609U	NEF	77459
PENHALLOW LN	0	609U	NEF	77459
PENHURST	4400	454B	NEH	77093
PENICK	100	282U	WL	77484
PENICK RD	15000	322X	WCO	77484
PENICK RD	16900	322G	WCO	77484
PENINA CT	15900	419E	NEC	77532
PENINA DR	1700	418H	NEC	77532
PENINSULA BLVD	16100	498V	NEC	77015
PENINSULA DR	0	619X	LC	77573
PENINSULA PARK DR	5600	448D	NWC	77041
PENINSULA PLACE	4300	610N	MC	77459
PENINSULAS DR	2400	610J	MC	77459
PENMARK LN	1600	486L	SWC	77450
PENMERE CT	2700	337C	NEH	77345
PENMONT LN	0	330A	NWC	77379
PENN	3200	454K	NEH	77093
PENN	12200	419Y	BR	77532
PENN CIR	1	657A	FR	77546
PENN DR	700	657A	FR	77546
PENNBRIGHT DR	200	332X	NWC	77090
PENNBURY DR	1100	486H	SWC	77094
PENN CITY RD	1400	497R	NEC	77015
PENNE DR	0	616K	PL	77089
PENNER	1000	492A	NWH	77055
PENNERCREST	1000	492A	NWH	77055
PENN HILLS LN	14600	618F	SEH	77062
PENNINGTON	700	453G	NEH	77022
PENNINGTON	2300	454A	NEH	77093
PENNINSULAS	0	609V	MC	77459
PENNISULA GARDEN WAY	0	376S	NEC	77396
PENNLAND LN	0	368N	NWC	77429
PENN MANOR CT	9100	490C	SV	77055
PENNOCK	0	611J	NEF	77489
PENNRIDGE LN	17400	287F	NWC	77377
PENNSGROVE RD	23100	334A	NCC	77373
PENNSHORE LN	0	525H	NEF	77450
PENNSYLVANIA	100	618Y	WB	77598
PENNSYLVANIA	100	495V	NEH	77029
PENNSYLVANIA	100	536W	SH	77587
PENNSYLVANIA	800	576A	SH	77587
PENNSYLVANIA	1300	575D	SH	77587
PENNSYLVANIA	3000	611T	FS	77545
PENNWELL DR	6600	250U	NWC	77389
PENNWORTH LN	6000	407V	NWC	77084
PENNY	0	373X	NCC	77060
PENNY AVE	21000	256T	SEM	77357
PENNY CT	6900	370A	NWC	77069
PENNY LN	0	538Z	DP	77536
PENNY LN	7300	525A	NEF	77494
PENNY LN	14100	370A	NWC	77069
PENNY LN	24500	296L	SEM	77365
PENNY BLUME DR	0	285Q	NWC	77447
PENNYBROOK CT	12000	371J	NWC	77066
PENNYGENT LN	900	497D	NEC	77530
PENNYGENT LN	1000	457Z	NEC	77530
PENNYMILL DR	0	376T	NEC	77396
PENNYMILL DR	0	376T	NEC	77396

Street Name	Block	Pg/Sq	Loc	Zips
PENNY NAIL	5000	452F	NWH	77091
PENNYOAK DR	0	615Z	PL	77581
PENNY PARK	10600	616G	SEC	77089
PENNYRILE LN	22800	485L	SWC	77450
PENNY ROCK CT	0	446J	NWC	77449
PENNYROYAL CT	1400	332V	NCC	77073
PENNYROYAL POINT LN	0	328P	NWC	77375
PENNY SAGE BLVD	0	366V	NWC	77433
PENNYSTONE CT	15600	617W	FR	77546
PENNYSTONE WAY	5000	617W	FR	77546
PENNY WAYNE LN	0	656B	NEB	77581
PENNYWELL LN	3000	485S	NEF	77494
PENNYWOOD CT	12100	369P	NWC	77070
PENRICE DR	20000	486L	SWC	77450
PENROD	8000	455L	NEH	77028
PENROSE CT	0	568W	SG	77479
PENROSE CT	4200	609K	MC	77459
PENROSE DR	0	418X	NEC	77044
PENROSE DR	9100	458B	NEC	77049
PENROSE DR	9900	418T	NEC	77044
PENROSE POINT DR	7700	408J	NWC	77095
PENSACOLA LN	1700	656U	FR	77546
PENSACOLA OAKS LN	0	609T	NEF	77479
PENSDALE	5100	533Z	SEH	77033
PENSGATE	15500	618J	SEH	77062
PENSHORE PARK LN	0	377Y	NEC	77044
PENSHORE PLACE LN	21300	525D	NEF	77450
PENTACLE DR	0	571K	SWH	77085
PENTER	0	375M	HM	77396
PENTLAND CT	17200	527W	NEF	77407
PENTLAND DOWNS ST	0	615S	PL	77584
PENTLAND DOWNS ST	0	377Q	NEC	77044
PENTON DR	9800	528S	NEF	77498
PENTONSHIRE LN	16500	332P	NWC	77090
PENWAY	1	453F	NEH	77022
PENWOOD CT	500	569U	NEF	77477
PENWOOD WAY	3500	534K	SEH	77023
PENZANCE CT	5400	446B	NWC	77449
PENZANCE DR	21300	446C	NWC	77449
PEONIES CT	0	615K	PL	77581
PEONY SPRINGS CT	1	250A	WD	77382
PEORIA	12800	497E	NEH	77015
PEORIA CT	0	496D	NEH	77015
PEPER GLEN LN	2200	293F	SEM	77386
PEPER HOLLOW LN	28200	293F	SEM	77386
PEPPER LN	10800	489C	SWH	77079
PEPPER BEND LN	0	524F	NEF	77494
PEPPERBERRY TRAIL	21300	291R	NWC	77388
PEPPERBROOK DR	7500	408M	NWC	77041
PEPPERBUSH CT	13500	369G	NWC	77070
PEPPER CREEK LN	0	612Q	PL	77584
PEPPER CREEK LN	26800	366M	NWC	77433
PEPPER CREST LN	7000	330B	NWC	77379
PEPPERDINE LN	11400	570C	SWH	77071
PEPPERGATE LN	0	457A	NEC	77044
PEPPERGLEN DR	2100	570Y	MC	77489
PEPPER HILL WAY	1900	618R	SEH	77058
PEPPER HOLLOW LN	0	524F	NEF	77494
PEPPER KNOLL DR	13600	368P	NWC	77065
PEPPERMILL	5100	500H	BT	77521
PEPPERMILL RD	1900	450Q	NWH	77080
PEPPERMILL CREEK DR	0	295V	SEM	77365
PEPPERMILL CREEK DR	25000	296S	SEM	77365
PEPPERMINT DR	0	461T	NEC	77521
PEPPERRELL PLACE	23900	445S	NWC	77493
PEPPERRELL PLACE CT	1900	445T	NWC	77493
PEPPER RIDGE LN	25200	293N	NCC	77373
PEPPER ROOT DR	0	329L	NWC	77379
PEPPERSAGE LN	0	484R	NEF	77494
PEPPERSTONE CT	4000	572S	SWH	77053
PEPPERSTONE LN	13800	417A	NEC	77044
PEPPER TREE CT	1800	568W	SG	77479
PEPPERTREE LN	1400	496K	NEH	77015
PEPPERWEED DR	2300	446U	NWC	77084
PEPPERWOOD LN	1900	447X	NWH	77084
PEQUIN RD	0	419C	NEC	77532
PERALTA CLIFF TRAIL	0	526P	NEF	77407
PERALTA CREEK CT	0	406B	NWC	77433
PERALTA HILL LN	18600	328G	NWC	77377
PERALTA HILLS LN	0	609U	MC	77459
PERALTA LAKE CIR	0	326U	NWC	77429
PERALTA MILLS WAY	0	406W	NWC	77449
PERALTA SHADOW LN	0	377U	NEC	77044
PERALTA SOUND CIR	0	328E	NWC	77377
PERALTA SPRINGS LN	0	326V	NWC	77429
PERALTA VALLEY CT	0	526L	NEF	77407
PERCH	8100	463S	CCO	77520
PERCH DR	0	485B	SWC	77450
PERCH CREEK DR	6200	456Q	NEH	77049
PERCHERON TRAIL	0	334R	NCC	77338
PERCH LANDING CT	0	328G	NWC	77377
PERCIVAL	500	288G	TB	77375
PERCUSSION PLACE	7800	410K	NWC	77040
PERCY RD	2100	414U	NEC	77093
PERDENALES FALLS CT	11900	289W	NWC	77375
PERDIDO DR	2000	418D	NEC	77532
PERDIDO BAY DR	4100	486W	NEF	77450
PERDIDO BAY LN	0	612P	PL	77545
PERDIDO COVE LN	6200	409W	NWC	77041
PERDIDO KEY LN	0	377K	NEC	77346
PEREGRINE DR	1100	657N	FR	77546
PEREIDA	7800	455A	NEH	77028
S. PEREZ	100	536Y	SH	77587
N. PEREZ	100	536Y	SH	77587
PEREZ	4400	569P	SF	77477
PEREZ RD	2200	536Y	PA	77502
PERFECT LANDING WAY	0	290W	NWC	77379
PERFIDIA DR	100	457X	NEC	77015
PERGOLA	0	659M	LC	77573
PERGOLA PLACE	4600	376N	NEC	77396
PERIDOT LN	4300	657B	FR	77546
PERIDOT COVE	10200	367X	NWC	77095
PERIGRINE DR	10700	368U	NWC	77065
PERIMETER PARK DR	6900	409V	NWH	77041
PERIMETER WEST DR	15500	409V	NWH	77041
PERIWINKLE	1600	412F	NWC	77038
PERIWINKLE LN	1300	412F	NWC	77038
PERIWINKLE PLACE	0	460U	NEC	77562
PERKINS	100	659J	LC	77573
PERKINS	300	658H	LC	77573
PERKINS	700	660M	BC	77518
PERKINS	5300	494G	NEH	77020
PERKINS RD	23700	296G	SEM	77365
PERLA RD	0	528W	NEF	77498
PERLA RD	700	536Z	PA	77502
PERLICAN DR	31100	252Q	SEM	77386
PERMESSO LN	0	659R	LC	77573
PERMIAN DR	10400	528W	NEF	77498
PERNOD OAKS DR	0	484X	NEF	77494
PERNOD OAKS DR	0	484X	NEF	77494
PERONI DR	0	524M	NEF	77406
PERRIE	0	577X	SEH	77034

Street Name	Block	Pg/Sq	Loc	Zips
PERRINGTON CIR	3100	487Y	SWC	77082
PERRINGTON CT	21500	486N	SWC	77450
PERRINGTON HEIGHTS LN	0	491Y	SWH	77401
PERRY	0	543Q	BC	77520
PERRY	2200	460T	MN	77521
PERRY	4000	533M	SEH	77021
PERRY	4800	534N	SEH	77021
N. PERRY	7600	460T	MN	77521
PERRY AVE	11700	570L	MC	77071
PERRY LN	24600	250W	NWC	77389
PERRY RD	10500	369Y	NWC	77064
PERRY RD	12200	369L	NWC	77070
PERRYMAN	17400	418R	NEC	77044
PERRYOAK DR	20400	337R	NEC	77346
PERRYS PASS CT	16200	330M	NWC	77379
PERRYS RD	0	257N	SEM	77357
PERRYTON LN	16800	332Q	NCC	77073
PERSA	2000	492Q	SWH	77019
PERSA	2600	492U	SWH	77098
PERSEA RIDGE LN	0	698M	LC	77539
PERSHING	1300	541A	BT	77520
PERSHING	4500	534S	SEH	77033
PERSIAN DR	12600	371G	NWC	77014
S. PERSIMMON	100	289J	TB	77375
PERSIMMON	2400	454J	NEH	77093
PERSIMMON	2600	537T	PA	77502
PERSIMMON DR	0	500A	BT	77520
PERSIMMON DR	0	500E	BT	77520
PERSIMMON COVE	0	526T	NEF	77407
PERSIMMON POINTE	900	658R	LC	77573
PERSIMMON WOODS DR	0	331W	NWC	77068
PERTH	6100	574U	SEH	77048
PERTH MEADOWS CT	19600	406U	NWC	77449
PERTHSHIRE RD	12100	490E	SWH	77024
PERTHSHIRE RD	13000	489E	SWH	77079
PERTHSHIRE RD	14600	488H	SWH	77079
PERU CIR	3900	577A	PA	77504
PERUGIA ST	0	659P	LC	77573
PESSLING	0	249P	SWM	77354
PETAL CT	11700	411H	NWC	77038
PETAL ROSE CT	15000	325V	NWC	77433
PETALUMA DR	16300	611A	SWH	77053
PETE RD	0	659V	GCO	77539
PETERBOROUGH WAY	0	333K	NCC	77073
PETERS RD	1900	379H	NEC	77532
PETERS RD	2700	380A	NEC	77532
PETERSBURG LN	0	527T	NEF	77083
PETERS FOREST DR	0	296A	SEM	77365
PETERSHAM DR	8800	570A	SWH	77031
S. PETERSHAM DR	9600	569D	SWH	77031
N. PETERSHAM DR	11700	569D	SWH	77031
PETINA CYPRESS CT	16300	326F	NWC	77433
PETITT RD	15500	527U	NEF	77498
PETRA DR	8000	527L	NEF	77083
PETREL CT	400	419B	NEC	77532
PETRICH LN	16400	287G	NWC	77377
PETRIE	6800	413W	NEH	77076
S. PETRO LN	100	532X	SWH	77045
PETROPARK DR	6500	409T	NWC	77041
S. PETROPARK DR	11500	409X	NWC	77041
N. PETROPARK DR	11500	409T	NWC	77041
PETTERSON	0	500F	BT	77520
PETTIBONE	9700	454B	NEH	77093
PETTIT	700	453T	NWH	77009
PETTY	5200	492C	NWH	77007
PETUMA MEADOWS DR	25400	249Z	NWC	77375
PETUMA MEADOWS DR		249Z	NWC	77375
PETWORTH DR	11000	529F	SWH	77072
PETVETO	500	493N	SWH	77019
PEWTER CT	1800	445T	NWC	77493
PEWTER CREEK LN	0	406F	NWC	77433
PEWTER STONE	0	371H	NWC	77014
PEYTON	2100	373R	NEH	77032
PEYTON	6800	454R	NEH	77028
PEYTON OAKS PLACE	0	449U	NWH	77043
PEYTON PLACE	2200	538Q	DP	77536
PEYTON RIDGE CIR	0	458T	NEC	77049
PEYTONS GRACE LN		366U	NWC	77433
PEYTON STONE CIR	0	458T	NEC	77049
PFEIFFER DR	15700	527C	SWC	77082
PHANTOM HILL LN	0	609Y	NEF	77459
PHANTOM MIST DR	8300	525Z	NEF	77406
PHANTOM RANCH DR	0	406G	NWC	77433
PHANTURN LN	100	531D	BL	77401
PHEASANT	200	452M	NWH	77018
PHEASANT LN	3400	615U	PL	77581
PHEASANT LN	18800	286G	NWC	77377
PHEASANT RD	28700	323X	NWC	77447
PHEASANTBEND	0	256X	SEM	77365
PHEASANT FIELD DR	18500	378A	NEC	77346
PHEASANT GLEN DR	8100	330J	NWC	77379
PHEASANT GROVE DR	7100	406R	NWC	77433
PHEASANT HILL DR	14200	371B	NWC	77014
PHEASANT LAKE CT	12800	408Z	NWC	77041
PHEASANT OAK DR	0	527F	NEF	77083
PHEASANT RANCH CT	24500	324H	NWC	77447
PHEASANT RIDGE LN	5700	408Z	NWC	77041
PHEASANT RUN	2700	375K	HM	77396
PHEASANT RUN	4900	577G	PA	77505
PHEASANT RUN CIR	2700	375K	HM	77396
PHEASANT RUN DR	2500	336D	NEH	77339
PHEASANT TRACE CT	9000	409F	NWC	77064
PHELPS	7400	495N	SEH	77011
PHIBES TRAIL	6800	330F	NWC	77379
PHIL	4300	531H	BL	77401
PHIL	7800	535F	SEH	77012
PHILCO DR	4100	450G	NWH	77080
PHILFALL	3000	492T	SWH	77098
PHIL HALSTEAD DR	9700	411B	NWC	77086
PHILIBERT LN	7200	455N	NEH	77028
PHILIPPA CREEK LN	0	407V	NWC	77084
PHILIPPA HILLS TRAIL	0	406D	NWC	77433
PHILIPPINE	9300	410J	NWC	77040
PHILIPPINE	15300	409M	JV	77040
PHILIP SPRINGS LN	0	293L	SEM	77386
PHILLIP	0	255C	SEM	77357
PHILLIPS	0	658V	LC	77573
PHILLIPS	5500	452A	NWH	77018
PHILLIPS	7000	412S	NWH	77088
PHILLIPS LN	19500	335S	NEH	77338
PHILLIPS CO RD	100	537F	PA	77506
PHILMONT DR	9600	450K	NWH	77080
PHILPOT DR	700	495Z	GP	77547
PHLOX	4100	573C	SEH	77051
PHOENICIAN DR	1400	485E	NEF	77494
PHOENIX CT	3400	610U	MC	77459
PHOENIX DR	7600	532M	SWH	77030
PHROLAND	18500	526Z	NEF	77407
PHYLLIS	800	538L	DP	77536
PI CIR	1400	577J	PA	77504
PIARES LN	0	660G	GCO	77539
PIAZZA DR		524M	NEF	77406

Street Name	Block	Pg/Sq	Loc	Zips
PICA	3400	493J	SWH	77007
PICADOR DR	7900	527L	NEF	77083
PICARDY LN	14700	417R	NEC	77044
PICASSO PLACE	5800	531S	SWH	77096
PICAYUNE	900	536L	PA	77506
PICCADILLY DR	6700	535W	SEH	77061
PICCADILLY CIRCUS	2900	615L	PL	77581
PICKENS	6200	492F	SWH	77007
PICKERING	400	412Y	NWH	77091
PICKERING CT	2700	613U	NEB	77584
PICKERING LN	3400	613U	NEB	77584
PICKERTON DR	1700	538S	DP	77536
PICKET	2800	658S	LC	77573
PICKETT LN	2700	569V	NEF	77477
PICKETT PLACE	3100	610U	MC	77459
PICKFAIR	3700	454U	NEH	77026
PICKFORD DR	400	485C	SWC	77450
PICKFORD KNOLLS DR	13800	408L	NWC	77041
PICKFORDRUN DR	0	327D	NWC	77429
PICKLING DR	0	461Q	NEC	77521
PICKNEY AVE	0	568S	SG	77479
PICKWELL CT	9500	527V	NEF	77498
PICKWICK PARK DR	3500	297N	NEH	77339
PICKWICK PINE DR	0	376E	HM	77396
PICKWOOD DR	3000	614S	NEB	77584
PICNIC CIR	0	492K	SWH	77007
S. PICNIC LN	0	492J	SWH	77007
N. PICNIC LN	0	492J	SWH	77007
PICO LANDING ST	22100	525L	NEF	77407
PICOLLLO DR	0	525J	NEF	77406
PICO MEADOW CT	2600	293F	SEM	77386
PICTON DR	14300	374Z	NCC	77032
PICTURE ROCK PLACE	0	250P	NWC	77389
PIDDLER DR	2300	293W	NCC	77373
PIEDMONT	300	568P	SG	77478
PIEDMONT	4400	577F	PA	77504
PIEDMONT	5100	414Y	NEH	77016
PIEDMONT CREEK TRAIL	0	332V	NCC	77073
PIEDMONT FOREST DR	0	445A	NWC	77493
PIEDMONT PATH	0	412E	NWC	77038
PIEDRA NEGRAS CT	6200	526B	NEF	77450
PIENZA LN	0	659P	LC	77573
PIERCE	100	493Q	DT	77002
W. PIERCE	300	493N	SWH	77019
PIERCE	1600	493Q	SEH	77003
PIERCE	2700	493Q	SEH	77004
PIERCE MILL LN	0	376M	NEC	77346
PIERCE OAKS DR	0	524K	NWF	77406
PIERCETON CT	20800	485U	NEF	77494
PIERCE VALLEY DR	0	524K	NWF	77406
PIER HOUSE	0	620N	SB	77586
PIERMAIN DR	10200	531V	SWH	77035
PIERRE CT	9900	576S	SEH	77089
PIERREPONT DR	7300	410Q	NWC	77040
PIERRE SCHLUMBERGER BLVD	0	568L	SG	77478
PIER RIDGE LN	0	377Q	NEC	77346
PIERRMONT CT	0	524B	NEF	77494
PIERSON	19400	252B	SEM	77385
PIERSON RANCH LN	0	377K	NEC	77346
PIERWOOD CT	0	253P	SEM	77386
PIER WOOD CT	12500	449A	NWC	77041
PIFER RD	500	490H	HC	77024
PIFER GREEN CIR	700	490H	HC	77024
PIFER WAY	700	490H	HC	77024
PIGEON CT	0	487X	SWH	77094
PIGEON BERRY DR	0	292Z	NCC	77373
PIGEON BLUFF DR	0	369P	NWC	77065
PIGEON COVE CIR	7200	609Q	MC	77459
PIGEONWOOD DR	10900	616C	SEC	77089
PIGTAIL	0	611T	FS	77545
PIKARD WAY CT	4200	294J	SEM	77386
PIKE RD	13500	569M	SF	77477
PIKE RD	13700	570N	MC	77489
PIKECREST DR	24800	250U	NWC	77389
PIKES PEEK CT	17300	328R	NWC	77377
PILGRIM	0	617W	FR	77546
PILGRIM LN	500	616Z	FR	77546
PILGRIM LN	14100	375W	NEC	77396
PILGRIM'S POINT DR	1800	617Y	SEC	77546
PILGRIM'S POINT DR	2400	657C	SEC	77598
PILGRIM'S POINT LN	3000	615L	PL	77581
PILGRIM HALL DR	15500	617W	SEC	77546
PILGRIM HARBOR DR	4800	617W	SEC	77546
PILGRIM OAKS LN	5200	657Z	LC	77573
PILGRIMS CIR	16500	330P	NWC	77379
PILGRIMS BEND DR	2100	617U	SEC	77546
PILGRIMS GATE LN	23000	292G	NCC	77373
PILIBOS PARK CT	0	524A	NEF	77494
PILLAR COVE LN	0	610Q	MC	77459
PILLAR PARK CIR	5500	448C	NWC	77041
PILLOT	7900	495J	NEH	77029
PILLOT	10200	496J	JC	77029
PILOTBIRD LN	0	407V	NWC	77084
PILOT KNOLLS DR	0	366P	NWC	77433
PILOT POINT DR	900	412A	NWC	77038
PILOT ROCK PLACE	100	249M	NWH	77375
PILOT ROCK PLACE	100	249M	NWH	77375
PIMA CT	0	658U	LC	77573
PIMBERTON LN	5200	290Z	NWC	77379
PIMILICO RANCH BLVD	0	326Z	NWC	77429
PIMLICO CT	10300	372X	NWC	77038
PIMLICO DR	100	613F	NEB	77584
PIMLICO LN	1600	538N	PA	77503
PINACLE POINT	5800	571K	SWH	77085
PINAFORE LN	800	373Y	NCC	77039
PINAFORE LN	2400	374W	NCC	77039
PINASTER POINTE LN	5600	290V	NWC	77379
PINASTER POINTE LN	5600	290V	NWC	77379
PINATA LN	0	338Z	NEH	77532
PINCAY OAKS CT	8200	411P	NWC	77088
PINCAY OAKS DR	5900	411P	NWC	77088
PINCHER LN	0	254P	SEM	77365
PINCHER CREEK DR	1600	252Z	SEM	77386
PIN CHERRY LN	14700	288A	NWC	77377
PINCKNEY	100	493H	NEH	77009
PINDER LN	4800	614S	NEB	77584
PINDERFIELD CT	0	527Q	NEF	77083
PINE	0	282U	WCO	77484
PINE	0	282U	WCO	77484
PINE	0	298E	NEC	77336
PINE	0	538S	PA	77503
PINE	0	540T	LP	77571
PINE	0	540T	MP	77571
E. PINE	1	299E	NEC	77336
S. PINE	100	288G	TB	77375
PINE	100	288G	TB	77375
PINE	100	419M	CB	77532
PINE	100	496W	GP	77547
PINE	200	568J	SG	77498
PINE	900	282U	WL	77484
PINE	1100	500Z	BT	77520
PINE	2000	501V	BT	77520

Street Name	Block	Pg/Sq	Loc	Zips
PINE	3400	538U	DP	77536
PINE	3700	580U	LP	77571
PINE	4500	531M	BL	77401
PINE	4700	537U	PA	77503
PINE	4700	581W	PA	77586
PINE	5500	531K	SWH	77081
PINE	16100	458Y	CV	77530
PINE	25400	257Y	SEM	77357
PINE CIR	0	247F	SWM	77362
S. PINE CIR	300	247F	SWM	77362
N. PINE CIR	300	247F	SWM	77362
PINE CIR	600	621A	PA	77586
PINE CIR	1100	619H	TL	77586
PINE CIR	24200	297E	SEM	77365
W. PINE CIR	35200	247F	SWM	77362
E. PINE CIR	35200	247F	SWM	77362
PINE CT	3600	609L	MC	77459
PINE DR	2000	657K	FR	77546
PINE DR	9300	381J	NEC	77532
PINE DR	12300	368D	NWC	77429
PINE DR	25600	257Q	SEM	77357
PINE LN	100	419Q	BR	77532
PINE LN	100	419U	BR	77532
PINE LN	4200	291K	NWC	77389
PINE LN	14000	375X	NEC	77396
PINE LN	17400	246T	SWM	77355
PINE LN	18000	381S	NEC	77532
PINE LN	23600	290A	NWC	77389
PINE RD	100	620S	CS	77565
PINE RD	21800	336L	NEH	77339
PINE ACRES CIR	25600	252S	SWM	77380
PINE ALCOVE CT	3200	297P	NEH	77345
PINEAL PLACE	0	368H	NWC	77429
PINE ARBOR BLVD	31100	253P	SEM	77386
PINE ARBOR DR	5100	371A	NWC	77066
PINE ARBOR DR	5700	370H	NWC	77066
PINE ARBOR TRAIL	3200	297P	NEH	77345
PINE ARBOR WAY	21500	325V	NWC	77433
PINE ARROW CT	6500	250U	NWC	77389
PINE ARROW CT	7300	337Q	NEC	77346
PINEASH CT	1	251J	WD	77381
PINEASH CT	1400	616X	PL	77581
PINEASTER POINTE LN	5600	290V	NWC	77379
PINE BANK CT	0	407C	NWC	77095
PINE BANK DR	0	407C	NWC	77095
PINE BARK CT	3700	616W	PL	77581
PINE BARK DR	6000	411W	NWH	77092
PINE BAY	31100	252R	SEM	77386
PINE BAYOU	10800	490D	HC	77024
PINE BELT DR	11800	368H	NWC	77429
PINE BEND DR	0	249S	NWC	77375
PINE BEND DR	2200	337E	NEH	77339
PINEBEND DR	2600	613T	NEB	77584
PINE BLOSSOM CT	2300	297U	NEH	77345
PINE BLOSSOM TRAIL	4100	578U	SEH	77059
PINE BLUFF	1	580Q	LP	77571
PINE BLUFF DR	0	580Q	LP	77571
PINE BLUFF DR	500	616U	FR	77546
PINE BLUFF DR	19300	328C	NWC	77377
PINE BOUGH LN	12600	368J	NWC	77429
PINE BOWER CIR	18800	337Y	NEC	77346
PINE BOWER CT	7100	337Y	NEC	77346
PINE BRANCH DR	200	332B	NWC	77388
W. PINE BRANCH DR	1600	616W	PL	77581
PINE BRANCH DR	3700	616W	PL	77581
PINE BREEZE DR	4100	297U	NEH	77345
PINE BREEZE LN	0	616R	FR	77546
PINE BRIAR CIR	1	491G	SWH	77056
PINEBRIDGE LN	4100	291T	NWC	77388
PINEBRIDGE PARK LN	0	292K	SP	77373
PINE BROOK	1300	288B	TB	77375
PINE BROOK CT	0	251C	SD	77381
PINEBROOK CT	2400	620L	SB	77586
PINE BROOK DR	2300	538V	DP	77536
PINE BROOK DR	2300	539S	DP	77536
PINEBROOK DR	2600	613T	NEB	77584
PINE BROOK DR	12000	569E	SF	77477
PINEBROOK DR	21700	256F	SEM	77357
PINEBROOK LN	600	501L	BT	77521
PINEBROOK LN	2500	620L	SB	77586
PINEBROOK LN	4600	571V	SWH	77053
PINEBROOK BRIDGE LN	6800	290U	NWC	77379
PINE BROOK COVE	4200	578Y	SEH	77059
PINEBROOK GROVE LN		249V	NWC	77375
PINEBROOK HOLLOW LN	0	253P	SEM	77386
PINEBROOK HOLLOW LN	0	290Y	NWC	77379
PINE BROOK PARK LN	0	484W	NEF	77494
PINEBROOK THICKET LN	0	291A	NWC	77389
PINE BROOK TRAIL	17500	327S	NWC	77429
E. PINE BROOK WAY	3400	578Y	SEH	77059
W. PINE BROOK WAY	3600	578Y	SEH	77059
N. PINE BROOK WAY	4100	578Y	SEH	77059
PINE BURR	7400	411S	NWH	77040
PINE BURR	12200	247M	SWM	77362
PINEBURY LN	22000	526A	NEF	77450
PINE BUSH DR	12600	369L	NWC	77070
PINECANDLE DR	3300	331D	NWC	77388
PINE CANYON DR	24300	251W	SWM	77380
PINE CANYON DR	26300	251N	SWM	77380
PINE CANYON FALLS	0	249Z	NWC	77375
PINE CASTLE CT	0	367Y	NWC	77095
PINE CASTLE DR	0	407C	NWC	77095
PINE CASTLE DR	0	407K	NWC	77095
PINE CENTER DR	7700	407M	NWC	77095
PINE CHASE DR	1200	451W	NWH	77055
PINE CHASE DR	3500	616W	PL	77581
PINE CHASE GROVE	1300	451W	HI	77055
PINECHESTER DR	3400	371P	NWC	77066
PINE CLIFF DR	4800	448B	NWC	77084
PINE CLIFF DR	5200	408X	NWC	77084
PINE CLUSTER LN	19300	338W	NEC	77346
PINE COLONY LN	1500	616T	PL	77581
PINE CONE	0	616R	FR	77546
PINE CONE DR	1800	444T	KT	77493
PINE CONE DR	2200	296V	NEH	77339
PINE CONE DR	21800	333M	NCC	77338
PINE CONE LN	2700	616N	PL	77581
PINE CONE LN	11000	409U	NWC	77041
PINE CONE RANCH RD	0	250W	NWC	77389
PINE CONE TRAIL	3700	577D	PA	77505
PINE COUNTRY LN	31600	246Y	SWM	77355
PINE COVE DR	1000	336J	NEH	77339
PINE COVE DR	6100	411W	NWH	77092
PINE CREEK	8200	451W	HI	77055
PINE CREEK CT	1	536S	SEH	77017
PINE CREEK DR	300	657E	FR	77546
PINE CREEK DR	1500	616X	PL	77581
PINE CREEK DR	5400	539X	LP	77571
PINE CREEK RD	24500	244V	WCO	77447
PINECREEK BEND	0	406F	NWC	77433
PINECREEK COVE DR	0	250V	NWC	77389
PINECREEK HOLLOW LN	17300	407F	NWC	77095

Street Name	Block	Pg/Sq	Loc	Zips
PINECREEK PASS LN	2000	446W	NWC	77449
PINECREEK POINT	24100	292B	NCC	77373
PINECREEK POINT CT	900	292B	NCC	77373
PINECREEK RIDGE CT	6000	290Z	NWC	77379
PINECREEK RIDGE LN	20200	290Z	NWC	77379
PINE CREEK WAY	15800	246R	SC	77355
PINE CRESCENT CT	1	490D	HC	77024
PINE CREST	0	334M	NCC	77338
PINECREST	0	250S	NWC	77389
PINECREST	0	537M	PA	77503
PINE CREST	1600	494G	NEH	77020
PINECREST DR	1	298F	NEC	77336
PINE CREST DR	1500	616S	PL	77581
PINECREST DR	12700	247R	SWM	77362
PINECREST LN	0	296G	SEM	77365
PINECREST PEAK DR	0	293G	SEM	77386
PINE CREST TRAIL	4100	578X	SEH	77059
PINE CROFT DR	0	376E	HM	77396
PINECROFT DR	1100	568F	SG	77498
PINECROFT DR	9200	251D	WD	77380
PINE CROSSING CT	700	292K	SP	77373
PINE CROSSING DR	27100	292L	SP	77373
PINE CUP DR	7400	337V	NEC	77346
PINE CUT RD	17300	374F	NEC	77032
PINEDA CIR	0	525V	NEF	77406
PINEDALE	1	493W	SWH	77006
PINEDALE CIR	12700	247R	SWM	77362
PINEDALE CT	12900	247R	SWM	77362
PINEDALE LN	0	296C	SEM	77365
PINEDELL	0	327U	CY	77429
PINEDELL DR	15600	327V	CY	77429
PINE DESERT LN	10800	412J	NWC	77088
PINE DUST LN	3100	333B	NCC	77373
PINE ECHO DR	19500	338S	NEC	77346
PINE EDGE DR	400	252S	SWM	77380
PINE FALLS DR	7800	408E	NWC	77095
PINE FALLS BLUFF LN	0	484X	NEF	77494
PINE FALLS BLUFF LN	0	484X	NEF	77494
PINEFERN LN	6900	290X	NWC	77379
PINE FIELD CT	1200	616X	PL	77581
PINEFIELD CT	19800	335N	NCC	77338
PINEFIELD LN	2300	490T	SWH	77063
PINEFIELD LN	20300	335N	NCC	77338
PINE FLATS DR	0	367Y	NWC	77095
PINE FOREST	200	379P	NEC	77532
PINE FOREST	35200	247F	SWM	77362
PINE FOREST CIR	1	491L	SWH	77056
PINE FOREST CT	0	616X	PL	77581
PINE FOREST DR	0	246A	SWM	77355
PINE FOREST DR	1500	616T	PL	77581
PINE FOREST DR	5200	491L	SWH	77056
PINE FOREST DR	5900	491J	SWH	77057
PINE FOREST DR	16100	448E	NWC	77084
PINE FOREST DR	16300	447H	NWC	77084
PINE FOREST DR	23300	256Z	SEM	77357
PINE FOREST RD	10000	489M	SWH	77042
PINE FOREST GREEN BLVD	0	447F	NWC	77084
PINE FOREST HOLLOW TRAIL	0	447L	NWC	77084
PINE FOREST LANDING BLVD	0	447G	NWC	77084
PINE FOREST LANDING BLVD	0	447G	NWC	77084
PINE FOREST RIDGE ST	0	444D	NWC	77493
PINE FORK CT	1200	618E	SEH	77062
PINE GAP DR	1400	331M	NWC	77090
PINE GARDEN DR	4800	337C	NEH	77345
PINEGATE DR	0	292F	NCC	77373
PINEGATE DR	2000	452T	NWH	77008
PINEGATE LN	0	292F	NCC	77373
PINE GLEN	11200	329F	NWC	77375
PINE GLEN	12300	369J	NWC	77429
PINE GLEN CT	3700	616W	PL	77581
PINEGLEN TERRACE DR	0	250V	NWC	77389
PINE GREEN LN	7400	337U	NEC	77346
PINE GREEN TRAIL	3800	578X	SEH	77059
PINE GREEN WAY	0	578X	SEH	77059
PINE GROVE CIR	1	490D	HC	77024
PINE GROVE CT	0	251C	SD	77381
PINE GROVE DR	6900	451A	NWH	77092
PINE GROVE DR	7000	411W	NWH	77092
PINE GROVE DR	7300	410Z	NWH	77040
PINE GROVE LN	1500	616T	PL	77581
PINE GULCH CT	5600	457S	NEC	77049
PINE GULLY BLVD	2800	535L	SEH	77017
PINE GULLY DR	400	621A	SB	77586
PINE GULLY DR	600	620D	SB	77586
PINEHALL LN	12900	456D	NEC	77044
PINE HAVEN	19400	252B	SEM	77385
PINE HAVEN DR	300	491H	SWH	77024
PINEHAVEN LN	20100	291S	NWC	77379
PINEHEARTH CT	6800	290T	NWC	77379
PINE HEATH CT	0	375Y	NEC	77396
PINE HEATHER CT	4500	578U	SEH	77059
S. PINE HILL	600	247F	SWM	77362
N. PINE HILL	600	247F	SWM	77362
PINE HILL	700	247F	SWM	77362
W. PINE HILL	35200	247F	SWM	77362
E. PINE HILL	35200	247F	SWM	77362
W. PINE HILL DR	2000	616N	PL	77581
E. PINE HILL DR	2000	616N	PL	77581
S. PINE HILL DR	2700	616N	PL	77581
PINE HILL LN	0	657G	FR	77546
PINEHILL LN	1	492J	SWH	77019
PINEHILL LN	9000	450G	NWH	77041
PINE HILLS DR	0	524A	NEF	77494
PINE HILLS DR	0	524A	NWF	77494
PINE HOLLOW	200	491L	SWH	77056
PINE HOLLOW DR	700	656C	FR	77546
PINE HOLLOW DR	1700	570X	MC	77489
PINE HOLLOW DR	3500	616T	PL	77581
PINE HOLLOW DR	7500	375G	HM	77396
PINE HOLLOW LANDING CT	0	447G	NWC	77084
PINE HOLLOW LANDING CT	0	447G	NWC	77084
PINE HOLLOW TRACE	0	447G	NWC	77084
PINE HOLLOW TRACE	0	447G	NWC	77084
PINEHOLLY CT	1	250C	WD	77381
PINEHOOK LN	7000	415P	NEH	77016
PINEHURST	0	659C	LC	77573
PINEHURST	4700	578J	PA	77505
PINE HURST CT	0	616R	FR	77546
PINEHURST CT	1	409F	JV	77064
PINEHURST CT	1	609C	MC	77459
PINEHURST DR	3600	616X	PL	77581
PINEHURST DR	6400	494Y	SEH	77023
PINEHURST DR	9600	462Z	BT	77521
PINEHURST BEND DR	20000	338S	NEC	77346
PINEHURST GROVE CT	8500	338S	NEC	77346
PINEHURST LOOP	33100	247Q	SWM	77355
PINEHURST PLACE DR	20000	337R	NEC	77346
PINEHURST PLACE DR	20000	338S	NEC	77346
PINEHURST SHADOWS DR	7500	337Q	NEC	77346
PINEHURST TRAIL CIR	8000	337V	NEC	77346
PINEHURST TRAIL DR	19200	338S	NEC	77346
PINEHURST TRAIL DR	19500	337R	NEC	77346
PINE ISLAND DR	6900	415K	NEC	77050
W. PINE IVY LN		289G	NWC	77375
S. PINE IVY LN		289G	NWC	77375
N. PINE IVY LN		289G	NWC	77375
E. PINE IVY LN		289G	NWC	77375
PINE KNOLL DR	11000	529T	SWH	77099
PINE KNOLL DR	12400	528V	SWH	77099
PINE KNOT CT	1400	616X	PL	77581
PINE KNOT RD	22900	290C	NWC	77389
PINE LAKE	400	338V	NEH	77336
PINE LAKE DR	0	538R	DP	77536
PINE LAKE DR	3700	616X	PL	77581
PINE LAKE DR	9600	450W	NWH	77055
PINE LAKE LN	7800	462J	NEC	77521
PINELAKE CANYON CT	5000	447C	NWC	77084
PINELAKE CROSSING CT	20200	290Z	NWC	77379
PINELAKE CROSSING DR	5700	290Z	NWC	77379
PINELAKES BLVD	5700	290Y	NWC	77379
PINE LAKES DR	6100	444P	KT	77493
PINE LAKE TRAIL	2800	331P	NWC	77068
PINELAND DR	1400	616X	PL	77581
PINELAND DR	10200	491E	HC	77024
PINELAND RD	8500	457B	NEC	77044
PINELAND RD	9200	417T	NEC	77044
PINE LANDING DR	10500	412J	NWC	77088
PINE LANDING MIST CT	0	447G	NWC	77084
PINELANDS PARK LN	12100	377E	NEC	77346
PINE LAUREL CT	13100	488Y	SWH	77082
PINE LAWN	12100	414H	NEC	77039
PINE LAWN DR	3700	616X	PL	77581
PINELEAF DR	3700	331N	NWC	77068
PINE LEDGE RD	0	616J	PL	77089
PINELEIGH CT	0	289Q	NWC	77375
PINE LILLY DR	0	245V	SWM	77355
PINELLAS PARK	5800	290Z	NWC	77379
PINELLAS PARK CT	20300	290Z	NWC	77379
PINELOCH DR	600	617M	SEH	77598
PINELOCH DR	700	618E	SEH	77062
PINE LOCK LN	19100	291X	NWC	77388
PINE LODGE DR	700	372B	NWC	77090
PINE MANOR CT	28100	252E	OR	77385
PINE MANOR DR	100	252E	OR	77385
PINE MANOR DR	2100	339P	HU	77336
PINEMEADE LN	11700	289W	NWC	77375
PINE MEADOW	3500	414J	NCC	77039
PINE MEADOW CT	0	570P	MC	77489
PINE MEADOW CT	1400	616X	PL	77581
PINE MEADOW DR	300	570P	MC	77489
PINE MEADOW DR	12000	570B	SWH	77071
PINE MEADOW LN	14000	288P	NWC	77377
PINE MEADOWS BLVD	0	463S	CCO	77520
PINE MEADOWS DR	5900	444T	KT	77493
PINE MILL CT	4000	615S	PL	77584
PINEMILL RD	8600	335N	NCC	77338
PINEMILL HOLLOW	30600	253S	SEM	77386
PINE MILL LANDING LN	0	484X	NEF	77494
PINE MILL RANCH DR	0	484T	NEF	77494
PINE MILL RANCH DR	0	484W	NEF	77494
PINE MILL RANCH DR	0	484W	NEF	77494
PINE MILLS DR	400	659H	LC	77573
PINE MIST LN	22600	333B	NCC	77373
PINEMONT	2100	502S	BT	77520
S. PINEMONT	4300	450G	NWH	77041
PINEMONT DR	700	452E	NWH	77018
PINEMONT DR	4700	451F	NWH	77092
PINEMONT DR	7000	450H	NWH	77040
PINE MONTE RIDGE LN	0	446E	NWC	77449
PINEMONT PLACE	0	541F	NWH	77092
PINEMOOR WAY	16700	618M	SEH	77058
PINE MOSS CT	1200	616X	PL	77581
PINE MOSS DR	10000	411N	NWC	77040
PINE MOUNTAIN CT	4400	448E	NWC	77084
PINE MOUNTAIN DR	15500	448E	NWC	77084
PINENEEDLE DR	400	490G	PP	77024
PINE NEEDLE DR	600	656G	FR	77546
PINE NEEDLE DR	1800	444T	KT	77493
PINE NEEDLE LN	2700	616N	PL	77581
PINE NEEDLE LN	5800	577D	PA	77505
PINENUT BAY CT	15400	618B	SEH	77059
PINE OAK DR	200	459V	HG	77562
PINE OAK LN	20800	286J	NWC	77447
PINE OAK MANOR CT	0	447G	NWC	77084
PINE OAKS DR	25700	244L	WCO	77447
N. PINE ORCHARD DR	1400	616X	PL	77581
W. PINE ORCHARD DR	3600	616X	PL	77581
PINE ORCHARD DR	6000	370M	NWC	77066
PINE PARK	5600	414H	NEC	77039
N. PINE PARKWAY	0	578U	SEH	77059
PINE PASS CT	12000	369Q	NWC	77070
PINE PASS DR	9700	369Q	NWC	77070
PINE PLACE CT	0	406C	NWC	77433
S. PINEPLANK CT	1	251E	WD	77381
N. PINEPLANK CT	1	251E	WD	77381
PINE POINT CT	100	658N	LC	77573
PINE POINT CT	14900	329W	NWC	77070
PINE POST CT	18300	255S	SEM	77365
PINE POST LN	23200	334A	NCC	77373
PINE PRAIRIE LN	4000	297P	NEH	77345
PINE RAIN CT	20700	446K	NWC	77449
PINE RESERVE DR	6400	250U	NWC	77389
PINE REST DR	0	250V	NWC	77389
PINE RIDGE	300	255Z	SEM	77365
PINERIDGE	3500	493B	NWH	77009
PINERIDGE	3600	453X	NWH	77009
PINE RIDGE CT	0	657F	FR	77546
PINE RIDGE DR	0	244V	WCO	77447
PINE RIDGE LN	1500	616T	PL	77581
PINE RIDGE LN	3400	411R	NWH	77088
PINE RIDGE RD	0	244V	WCO	77447
PINE RIDGE FOREST ST	0	444D	NWC	77493
PINE RIDGE KNOLL CT	0	444C	NWC	77493
PINE RIDGE TERRACE RD	7600	531J	SWH	77081
PINE RIVER DR	1900	336C	NEH	77339
PINEROCK LN	12100	490E	SWH	77024
PINEROCK LN	13300	489A	SWH	77079
PINE ROSE	31100	252R	SEM	77386
PINEROW	5600	457S	NEC	77049
PINE RUN CT	20000	291Y	NWC	77388
PINE RUN DR	3200	291Y	NWC	77388
PINERY DR	12800	569J	SF	77477
PINESAGE DR	12900	572F	SWH	77045
PINE SAP CT	1300	616X	PL	77581
PINESAP DR	100	488M	SWH	77079
PINESAP DR	800	488D	SWH	77079
S. PINESAP DR	6100	528D	SWH	77072
PINESBURY DR	3900	447K	NWC	77084
PINESHADE LN	6000	452X	NWH	77008
PINE SHADOW CT	3700	253P	SEM	77386
PINE SHADOWS	0	244K	WCO	77447
PINE SHADOWS	100	619H	TL	77586
PINESHADOWS	12800	247R	SWM	77362
PINE SHADOWS CIR	18500	255B	SEM	77302
PINE SHADOWS DR	200	491L	SWH	77056
PINE SHADOWS LN	7300	462Y	BT	77521
PINE SHADOWS LN	12200	247R	SWM	77362
PINE SHADOWS LN	23200	296F	SEM	77365
PINE SHORES DR	8400	338S	NEC	77346
PINES PLACE DR	8400	338S	NEC	77346
PINE SPLIT WAY DR	0	250U	NWC	77389
PINE SPRING LN	12600	368L	NWC	77429
PINE SPRINGS DR	0	408E	NWC	77095
PINESTEAD CT	100	249R	NWH	77375
PINESTEAD CT	100	249R	NWC	77375
PINE STONE LN	0	484T	NEF	77494
PINE STRAW CT	10600	412J	NWH	77088
S. PINE STREAM	1300	616X	PL	77581
PINE STREAM CT	9100	527R	NEF	77083
PINE STREAM DR	3600	616X	PL	77581
PINESWEPT DR	2800	537Q	PA	77503
PINE TERRACE DR	2300	296Z	NEH	77339
PINETEX	20900	256V	SEM	77357
PINETEX DR	6900	375U	NEH	77396
PINE THICKET CT	700	292K	SP	77373
PINE THICKET LN	13100	571K	SWH	77085
PINE THISTLE CT	17600	330J	NWC	77379
PINE THISTLE DR	8200	330J	NWC	77379
PINE THORN DR	16200	407D	NWC	77095
PINE TIMBERS	4300	450G	NWH	77041
PINE TOP	28600	246E	SWM	77355
PINE TOP LN	0	609Y	NEF	77459
PINETOP LN	2300	293F	SEM	77386
PINETOP GLEN LN	6700	290U	NWC	77379
PINETOWN BRIDGE LN	10300	528W	NEF	77498
PINE TRACE CT	18800	337Y	NEC	77346
PINE TRAIL	0	444P	KT	77493
PINE TRAIL	0	444P	KT	77493
PINE TRAIL LN	6300	337P	NEC	77346
PINE TRAILS	1	245F	SWM	77355
PINE TRAILS	1300	288B	TB	77375
PINE TREE	0	414S	NEH	77093
PINE TREE	1	490L	PP	77024
PINE TREE CIR	1200	580P	SA	77571
PINE TREE CT	1400	616T	PL	77581
PINE TREE DR	2000	413V	NEH	77093
PINE TREE DR	3500	616T	PL	77581
PINE TREE DR	5100	578K	PA	77505
PINETREE LN	19400	283V	NWC	77484
PINE TREE LN	20700	286J	NWC	77447
PINE TREE FORESTTRAIL	0	456R	NEH	77049
PINE TREE GLEN	0	456R	NEH	77049
PINE TREE SPRINGS	0	456R	NEH	77049
PINE VALE LN	13500	413K	NCC	77037
PINE VALLEY	0	245U	SWM	77355
PINE VALLEY	4700	578J	PA	77505
PINE VALLEY DR	2100	492Q	SWH	77019
PINE VALLEY DR	3500	616X	PL	77581
PINE VALLEY TRAIL	15300	326S	NWC	77433
PINE VALLEY WAY	0	326S	NWC	77433
PINE VIEW	6400	457N	NEC	77049
PINE VIEW	12000	368D	NWC	77429
PINEVIEW CIR	300	620E	EL	77586
PINE VIEW CIR	300	620E	EL	77586
PINE VIEW CT	0	616X	PL	77581
PINEVIEW DR	100	495W	SEH	77012
PINE VIEW RD	100	459H	NEC	77562
PINEVIEW TERRACE	0	444R	KT	77493
PINE VILLAGE CT	0	253P	SEM	77386
PINE VILLAGE CT	0	253Q	SEM	77386
PINE VILLAGE DR	1600	450T	NWH	77080
PINE VILLAGE DR	2500	450N	NWH	77080
PINEVILLE DR	3600	502K	BT	77521
PINEVILLE LN	4200	291T	NWC	77388
PINE VISTA LN	6800	411W	NWH	77092
PINE WALK DR	1400	616X	PL	77581
PINEWALKBROOK LN	0	290Q	NWC	77379
PINE WALK TRAIL	500	332A	NWC	77388
PINE WALK TRAIL	1200	291Z	NWC	77388
PINE WARBLER LN	14700	288A	NWC	77377
PINE WATER LN	20200	289W	NWC	77375
PINEWAY BLVD	6000	534F	SEH	77023
PINEWEST CT	14000	456R	NEC	77049
PINEWEST DR	14000	457N	NEC	77049
PINEWICK LN	9000	450G	NWH	77041
PINEWILDE CT	21800	255S	SEM	77365
PINEWILDE DR	5100	371E	NWC	77066
PINEWILDE DR	5700	370H	NWC	77066
PINEWILLE PARK LN	12400	328G	NWC	77377
PINE WILLOW CT	200	656C	FR	77546
PINE WIND CT	0	462Z	BT	77521
PINE WIND CT	0	462Z	BT	77521
PINE WIND CT	7500	337V	NEC	77346
PINE WIND DR	19800	337U	NEC	77346
PINEWOLD CIR	1	491L	SWH	77056
PINEWOLD CT	1	491L	SWH	77056
PINEWOLD DR	200	491L	SWH	77056
PINEWOOD	0	444Q	KT	77493
PINEWOOD	11900	248N	SWM	77362
PINEWOOD CIR	1	490M	HC	77024
PINEWOOD CT	900	498C	CV	77530
PINEWOOD CT	1400	616X	PL	77581
PINEWOOD CT	1800	568B	SG	77498
PINEWOOD CT	6400	444P	KT	77493
PINEWOOD CT	10900	579C	LP	77571
PINEWOOD DR	200	252F	SEM	77385
PINEWOOD DR	2700	659C	LC	77573
PINEWOOD DR	15900	254K	SEM	77365
PINEWOOD LN	800	619H	TL	77586
PINEWOOD LN	1200	536P	PA	77502
PINEWOOD BEND LN	0	253T	SEM	77386
PINEWOOD BLUFF LN	19300	338W	NEC	77346
PINEWOOD CANYON LN	8200	338W	NEC	77346
PINEWOOD COURT DR	1800	501E	BT	77521
PINEWOOD COVE DR	15700	618G	SEH	77062
PINEWOOD CREST LN	8000	338S	NEC	77346
PINEWOOD ECHO LN	0	338W	NEC	77346
PINEWOOD FOREST	17400	330G	NWC	77379
PINEWOOD FOREST CT	1	251A	WD	77381
PINEWOOD GLEN DR	19000	331C	NWC	77388
PINEWOOD GREEN	0	447G	NWC	77084
PINEWOOD GROVE TRAIL	0	257F	SEM	77357
PINE WOOD HILLS CT	0	294K	SEM	77386
PINE WOOD HILLS LN	0	294K	SEM	77386
PINEWOOD MEADOWS LN	0	294J	SEM	77386
PINEWOOD MIST LN	19200	338W	NEC	77346
PINEWOOD PARK DR	0	338S	NEC	77346
PINEWOOD PARK DR	1800	570W	MC	77489
PINEWOOD PARK DR	4300	297X	NEH	77345
PINEWOOD PLACE	22300	289M	NWC	77375
PINEWOOD POINT LN	18900	328F	NWC	77377
PINEWOOD RIDGE DR	0	252T	SEM	77386
PINE WOODS	0	247F	SWM	77362
PINEWOOD SPRINGS DR	5100	371E	NWC	77066
PINEWOOD SPRINGS DR	5700	370H	NWC	77066
PINEWOODS WAY	1800	252Z	SEM	77386
PINEWOOD TERRACE	2600	444Q	KT	77493
PINEWOOD TRACE LN	0	328K	NWC	77377
PINEWOOD TRACE LN	6400	409S	NWC	77041
PINEWOOD VALLEY DR	23800	244H	WCO	77447
PINEY CT	24600	293S	NCC	77373
PINEY BEND CT	25300	250S	NWC	77389
PINEY BEND DR	0	329A	CY	77429
PINEY BEND DR	12200	328D	NWC	77375
PINEY BIRCH CT	5900	338B	NEH	77345
PINEY BROOK DR	3200	579B	LP	77571
PINEY CORNER DR	0	283V	NWC	77484
PINEY CORNERS LN	28200	283Y	NWC	77484
PINEY CREEK LN	4200	291T	NWC	77388
PINEY FOREST CT	19000	446R	NWC	77084
PINEY FOREST DR	2900	446R	NWC	77084
PINEY GROVE LN	13200	328P	NWC	77429
PINEY HEIGHTS LN	25200	250S	NWC	77389
PINEY HILL LN	17400	331K	NWC	77388
PINEY KNOLL CT	6000	407X	NWC	77449
PINEY LAKE CT	2800	411H	NWC	77038
PINEY LAKE DR	19500	291X	NWC	77388
PINEY LINKS	16000	331P	NWC	77068
PINEY MANOR DR	0	250S	NWC	77389
PINEY MEADOW CT	7000	408R	NWC	77041
PINEY OAKS DR	13200	368Y	NWC	77065
PINEY PLACE CT	19600	486H	SWC	77094
PINEY POINT	0	258Q	SEM	77357
PINEY POINT	0	538V	DP	77536
PINEY POINT CIR	11300	490Q	PP	77024
PINEY POINT DR	0	531J	SWH	77081
PINEY POINT RD	200	490L	PP	77024
S. PINEY POINT RD	2000	490T	PP	77063
PINEY RANCH LN	0	484W	NEF	77494
PINEY RIDGE DR	700	616U	FR	77546
PINEY RUN CT	14000	371U	NWC	77066
PINEY VIEW LN	13400	377L	NEC	77044
PINEY WAY CT	12100	329A	CY	77429
PINEY WAY DR	19100	329A	CY	77429
PINEY WAY LN	0	329A	CY	77429
PINEY WOOD LN	27500	249G	SWM	77354
PINEY WOODS DR	1200	656L	FR	77546
PINEY WOODS DR	2300	616T	PL	77581
PINEY WOODS DR	3700	452J	NWH	77018
PIN HOOK CT	2300	620J	SB	77586
PINION CT	16300	376M	NEC	77346
PINION CREEK CIR	17200	246T	SWM	77355
PINION CREEK DR	26100	246T	SWM	77355
PINK AZALEA TRAIL	0	488G	SWH	77079
PINK BLOSSOM TRAIL	0	326J	NWC	77433
PINK BLOSSOM TRAIL	0	326F	NWC	77433
PINK DOGWOOD DR	0	296A	SEM	77365
PINKGRANITE VALLEY	0	526S	NEF	77407
PINKSTONE CT	0	484J	KT	77494
PINKY WAY	1700	496Q	GP	77015
PINNACLE DR	1600	336B	NEH	77339
PINNACLE DR	2600	659C	LC	77573
PINNACLE COVE CT	300	619T	LC	77573
PINNACLE HEIGHTS LN	0	377J	NEC	77346
PINNACLE PEEK	0	485K	NEF	77494
PINNACLE PLACE	13400	370F	NWC	77069
PINNACLE POINT PLACE	28600	253Y	SEM	77386
PINNACLE RUN DR	1200	332V	NCC	77073
PINO LN	22000	338Y	NEH	77532
PIN OAK	100	459Z	HG	77562
PIN OAK	100	500E	BT	77520
PIN OAK CIR	3600	610X	MC	77459
PIN OAK CT	3300	569S	SG	77478
PIN OAK DR	300	298X	NEH	77336
E. PIN OAK DR	1700	616W	PL	77581
S. PIN OAK DR	3700	616W	PL	77581
N. PIN OAK DR	3700	616W	PL	77581
PIN OAK DR	5000	578J	PA	77505
PIN OAK DR	7500	375C	HM	77396
PIN OAK DR	19500	255U	SEM	77365
PIN OAK DR	23800	290A	NWC	77389
PIN OAK DR	26300	248K	SWM	77354
PIN OAK LN	0	616R	FR	77546
PIN OAK LN	100	248K	SWM	77354
PIN OAK LN	4200	291K	NWC	77389
PIN OAK LN	4500	531D	BL	77401
PIN OAK LN	25400	257U	SEM	77357
PIN OAK RD	0	257J	SEM	77357
PIN OAK RD	0	258T	SEM	77357
PIN OAK RD	400	444Y	KT	77494
PIN OAK RD	500	484G	KT	77494
PIN OAK RD	18700	252D	SEM	77385
PIN OAK BEND DR	0	366P	NWC	77433
PIN OAK CREEK LN	4500	297Q	NEH	77345
PIN OAK ESTATES CT	1	531H	BL	77401
PIN OAK ESTATES DR	1	531H	BL	77401
PIN OAK GLEN LN	13300	328U	NWC	77429
PIN OAK LOOP	13900	419Q	BR	77532
PIN OAK PARK	4500	531D	SWH	77081
PIN OAK PLACE	6000	330H	NWC	77379
PIN OAK RIDGE	16000	332V	NCC	77073
PIN OAK SHADOW LN	0	578T	SEH	77059
S. PIN OAK TRAIL	1	257M	SEM	77357
N. PIN OAK TRAIL	1	257M	SEM	77357
PIN OAK TRAIL	24400	257B	WV	77357
PIN OAK TRAILER PARK		484C	KT	77494
PINOLA CT	2000	658S	LC	77573
PINOLE LN	9400	411A	NWC	77086
PINOLE FOREST DR	6200	411P	NWC	77088
PINOLE LANE CT	11500	370L	NWC	77066
PINON DR	4100	451M	NWH	77092
PINON VISTA DR	16200	367Z	NWC	77095
PINOS ALTOS DR	11700	328C	NWC	77377
PINOS VERDES DR	0	406L	NWC	77433
PINPOINT DR	2400	293W	NCC	77373
PINSON DR	18000	367A	CY	77429
PINSONFORK DR	1000	329H	NWC	77379
PINSON MOUND CT	12900	377F	NEC	77346
PINTAIL	3200	444K	KT	77493
PINTAIL CT	24900	484G	NEF	77494
PINTAIL PARK CT	7900	375Q	NEC	77396
PINTAN LN	3700	317B	NWC	77014
PINTO CIR	17900	331M	NWC	77090
PINTO RD	4800	450F	NWH	77041
PINTO BOND LN	0	368C	NWC	77429
S. PINTO POINT CIR	0	250L	NWC	77389
S. PINTO POINT CIR	0	250L	NWC	77389
N. PINTO POINT CIR	0	250K	NWC	77389
N. PINTO POINT CIR	0	250K	NWC	77389
PINTO POINT DR	0	250K	NWC	77389
PINTO POINT DR	0	250K	NWC	77389
PINTO POINT DR	0	250K	NWC	77389
PINTO POINT DR	0	250K	NWC	77389
PINTOPOINTPLACE	0	250K	NWC	77389
PINTOPOINTPLACE	0	250K	NWC	77389
PINTO PONY TRAIL	0	377S	NEC	77044
PINTO SPRINGS LN	600	372H	NCC	77073
PINTO TRAIL	0	612Z	NEB	77578

Street Name	Block	Pg/Sq	Loc	Zips
PINTUCK PLACE	0	250L	NWC	77389
PINTUCK PLACE	0	250L	NWC	77389
PINWOOD DR	15800	571W	SWH	77489
PINYON CREEK CT	8000	407H	NWC	77095
PINYON CREEK DR	15700	408E	NWC	77095
PINYON CREEK DR	16000	407H	NWC	77095
PINYON HILL TRAIL		249T	NWC	77375
PINYON PINE DR	0	251J	WD	77381
PINYON PINE DR	0	524E	NEF	77494
PINYON PLACE	11600	251V	WD	77380
PINYON TRAIL DR	0	250V	NWC	77389
PIONEER CT	19700	337T	NEC	77346
PIONEER BEND CT	20500	486S	NEF	77450
PIONEER BEND LN	3300	486S	NEF	77450
PIONEER CANYON PLACE	100	249R	NWH	77375
PIONEER CANYON PLACE	100	249R	NWH	77375
PIONEER COVE CIR	0	366J	NWC	77433
PIONEER MILL LN	0	406F	NWC	77433
PIONEER PASS	2900	609E	SG	77479
PIONEER RIDGE DR	0	406Q	NWC	77433
PIONEER TRAIL	0	444S	KT	77493
PIONEER TRAIL	4400	609E	SG	77479
PIPE CREEK LN	7400	526K	NEF	77407
PIPELINE	0	659Y	GCO	77539
PIPER	14700	614P	PL	77584
PIPER GATE LN	0	406F	NWC	77433
PIPER GLEN LN	0	609V	MC	77459
S. PIPER GROVE DR	0	446M	NWC	77449
N. PIPER GROVE DR	0	446M	NWC	77449
E. PIPER GROVE DR	0	446M	NWC	77449
PIPER HILL LN	0	326V	NWC	77429
PIPER PASS LN	4400	609Y	NEF	77459
PIPER POINTE LN	19300	329A	NWC	77375
PIPERS FIELD DR	0	446B	NWC	77449
PIPERS GAP CT	14300	332W	NWC	77090
PIPERS LANDING CT	16100	570K	MC	77489
PIPERS VIEW DR	15600	617R	SEH	77598
PIPERS VIEW DR	15900	618S	SEH	77598
PIPER TERRACE LN	22200	485Y	NEF	77450
S. PIPER TRACE	1	250C	WD	77381
PIPER TRACE	1	250C	WD	77381
PIPER TRAIL	100	250C	WD	77381
PIPESTEM DR	0	378P	NEC	77532
PIPESTEM DR	1	245R	SWM	77355
PIPESTONE DR	9400	530S	SWH	77074
PIPESTONE GLEN LN	0	524B	NEF	77494
PIPESTONE POINT CT	0	376H	NEC	77346
PIPING ROCK	0	488V	SWH	77077
PIPING ROCK DR	400	459M	HG	77562
PIPING ROCK LN	3400	492S	SWH	77027
PIPING ROCK LN	5200	491T	SWH	77056
PIPING ROCK LN	6100	491S	SWH	77057
PIPING ROCK LN	7800	490V	SWH	77063
PIPING ROCK LN	10000	489U	SWH	77042
PIPING ROCK LN	11300	489T	SWH	77077
PIPING ROCK LN	12400	488T	SWH	77077
PIPINGWOOD DR	5500	408Y	NWC	77084
PIPIT RD	19600	284V	NWC	77447
PIPPIN GLEN DR	0	376S	NEC	77396
PIRALTA RIDGE LN	0	446E	NWC	77449
PIRATE DR	12600	328Q	NWC	77377
PIRATES COVE	1400	619W	NB	77058
PIRATES GOLD CIR	2700	657C	SEC	77546
PIROUETT PLACE	0	249B	SWM	77382
PIRTLE, JESS BLVD	12900	568G	SG	77478
PIRTLEWOOD CIR	6400	411P	NWH	77088
PISA CT	0	616K	PL	77089
PISTAKEE	0	618V	SEC	77058
PISTOL WHIPPER	0	416C	NEC	77044
PITCAIRN DR	16600	328Q	NWC	77377
PITCAIRN RD	17800	324H	NWC	77447
PITCATAWAY CIR	10300	329B	NWC	77375
PITCATAWAY DR	10300	329B	NWC	77375
PITCHFIELD DR	0	531J	SWH	77074
S. PITCHFORD LN	700	289J	TB	77375
PITCHING WEDGE CT	2100	616K	SEH	77089
PITCHLAKE DR	0	406D	NWC	77433
PITCH PINE DR	16300	329R	NWC	77070
PITCHSTONE CT	11900	328C	NWC	77377
PITCHSTONE DR	19500	328C	NWC	77377
PITKIN RD	24400	252X	SEM	77386
PITKIN IRON CT	1300	488J	SWH	77077
PITNER RD	8500	450M	NWH	77080
PITON MOUNTAIN DR	0	450K	NWH	77080
PITT RD	0	444S	KT	77493
PITTMAN	600	453X	NWH	77009
W. PITTS AVE	100	536F	PA	77506
PITTS AVE	100	536H	PA	77506
PITTS RD	100	444A	NWC	77493
PITTS RD	5000	404S	NWC	77493
PITTSBURGH	2600	532G	WU	77005
PITTSFORD CT	1100	486G	SWC	77450
PITTSFORD DR	20200	486G	SWC	77450
PITTSWOOD LN	7100	415P	NEH	77016
PITZLIN	2800	534F	SEH	77023
PIXIE SPRINGS LN	27500	293F	SEM	77386
PIZER	600	453X	NWH	77009
PIZETTI PLACE	0	444M	NWC	77493
PIZZALATO LN	0	242G	WCO	77484
PIZZITO LN	11100	368U	NWC	77065
PIZZITO LN	11100	368U	NWC	77065
PIZZITOLA	100	577N	SEH	77034
PLAAG	3600	454K	NEH	77093
PLAAG	4100	454K	NEH	77016
PLACE REBECCA LN	1900	331L	NWC	77090
PLACE VENDOME CT	17900	330F	NWC	77379
PLACE VENDOME LN	7400	330F	NWC	77379
PLACEWOOD CT	0	407R	NWC	77084
PLACID	4100	453K	NWH	77022
PLACID BROOK CT	13800	618A	SEH	77059
PLACID OAK CT	17800	407F	NWC	77095
PLACID OAK TRAIL	0	338B	NEH	77345
PLACID POINT	14700	375U	NEC	77396
PLACID POINT CT	14700	375U	NEC	77396
PLACID STREAM CT	4100	578Z	PA	77059
PLACID TRAILS DR	0	328L	NWC	77377
PLACID WOODS CT	13800	568F	SG	77498
PLADDAWA LN	10400	527W	NEF	77407
PLAGENS LN	15800	571W	SWH	77489
PLAINBROOK	11100	539V	LP	77571
E. PLAINBROOK	11600	539V	LP	77571
PLAINFIELD	9600	530S	SWH	77036
PLAINFIELD	10500	570A	SWH	77031
PLAINS RIVER DR	14600	327W	NWC	77429
PLAIN VIEW	0	537X	PA	77502
PLAINVIEW	3200	577B	PA	77504
PLAINVIEW	5600	534V	SEH	77087
PLAINWOOD DR	600	488B	SWH	77079
PLAISANCE	0	611J	NEF	77489
PLAISANCE		611E	FS	77545
PLAISANCE		611L	FS	77545
PLAISTOW CT	17100	407Y	NWC	77084
PLAMER GLEN LN	0	446N	NWC	77449
PLANEVIEW	15500	322T	WCO	77484
PLANTAIN DR	19100	446R	NWC	77449
PLANTAIN LILY CT	0	615K	PL	77581
PLANTATION	0	568R	SG	77478
PLANTATION	0	619M	TL	77586
PLANTATION	100	619X	LC	77573
PLANTATION CT	2500	613R	NEB	77584
PLANTATION DR	0	333W	NCC	77073
PLANTATION DR	0	656Q	FR	77546
PLANTATION DR	2500	613R	NEB	77584
W. PLANTATION DR	3100	538Z	LP	77571
W. PLANTATION DR	3200	578D	LP	77571
E. PLANTATION DR	3200	578D	LP	77571
PLANTATION LN	0	295L	SEM	77365
PLANTATION LN	2500	569N	SG	77478
PLANTATION LN	9900	569R	SF	77477
PLANTATION RD	1	490J	SWH	77024
PLANTATION BAY DR	6100	406Z	NWC	77449
PLANTATION BEND DR	1900	569W	SG	77478
PLANTATION BEND DR	2400	609A	SG	77478
PLANTATION BEND LN	0	406Y	NWC	77449
PLANTATION COLONY CT	5000	609A	SG	77478
PLANTATION COLONY DR	4500	609A	SG	77459
PLANTATION COLONY DR	4800	609A	SG	77478
PLANTATION COVE LN	0	406Z	NWC	77449
PLANTATION CREEK CT	2500	609B	MC	77459
PLANTATION CREEK DR	4400	609B	MC	77459
PLANTATION CREEK DR	20100	295L	SEM	77365
PLANTATION CREST DR	5800	406Y	NWC	77449
PLANTATION ESTATES AVE	24900	295L	SEM	77365
N. PLANTATION ESTATES DR	19700	295L	SEM	77365
S. PLANTATION ESTATES DR	19800	295Q	SEM	77365
PLANTATION FOREST DR	6000	406Z	NWC	77449
PLANTATION GLEN PARK	15300	457U	NEC	77049
PLANTATION GROVE TRAIL	19600	406Y	NWC	77449
PLANTATION HILL	25000	295Q	SEM	77365
PLANTATION HILLS DR	26600	299W	NEH	77336
PLANTATION HOLLOW CT	2600	609G	MC	77459
PLANTATION LAKES DR	2800	609R	MC	77459
PLANTATION MEADOW LN	20100	295M	SEM	77365
PLANTATION MOUNTAIN	100	295L	SEM	77365
PLANTATION MYRTLES DR	0	406Z	NWC	77449
PLANTATION MYRTLES DR	0	406Z	NWC	77449
PLANTATION OAK DR	14700	331T	NWC	77068
PLANTATION ORCHARD CT	7300	526K	NEF	77407
PLANTATION ORCHARD LN	19400	526K	NEF	77407
PLANTATION PASS DR	4300	376D	NEC	77346
PLANTATION POINT DR	0	406V	NWC	77449
PLANTATION RIDGE DR	0	609G	MC	77459
PLANTATION RUN DR	4900	569W	SG	77478
PLANTATION SETTLEMENT LN	0	609G	MC	77459
PLANTATION TRAIL	2700	609A	SG	77478
PLANTATION TREE CT	19600	406Y	NWC	77449
PLANTATION TREE CT	19600	406Y	NWC	77449
PLANTATION VALLEY	0	295L	SEM	77365
PLANTATION VALLEY DR	13900	528T	SWC	77083
PLANTATION WOOD LN	2700	609M	MC	77459
PLANTERS HEATH	0	524E	NEF	77494
PLANTERS HOUSE CT	22800	445Q	NWC	77449
PLANTERS HOUSE LN	2400	445Q	NWC	77449
PLANTERS MOON LN	0	527N	NEF	77083
PLANTERS PATH LN	0	527N	NEF	77407
PLANTERS ROW	2300	568Y	SG	77478
PLANTERS VIEW LN	2600	610N	MC	77459
PLANTERS VIEW LN	2700	609R	MC	77459
PLANTERS WAY	2400	617Y	SEC	77546
PLASTICS AVE	700	494Q	NEH	77020
PLATEAU CT	2300	336B	NEH	77339
PLATINUM SPRINGS DR	17900	329G	NWC	77375
PLATO RD	0	542Y	CCO	77520
PLATO POINT LN	2100	293E	SEM	77386
PLATTSMOUTH LN	16100	326V	NWC	77429
PLATZER DR	0	572P	SWH	77045
PLAYA CT	11700	577X	SEH	77034
PLAYA DR	0	657T	FR	77546
PLAYA DR	5100	614V	PL	77584
PLAYA LUCIA CT	0	377M	NEC	77346
PLAYA VISTA LN	0	409W	NWC	77041
PLAYER	12900	571M	SWH	77045
PLAYER PARK DR	19100	337Z	NEC	77346
PLAYERS PATH	1800	336A	NEH	77339
PLAZA	0	534D	SEH	77023
PLAZA BLVD	1100	537E	PA	77506
PLAZA DR	0	568X	SG	77479
PLAZA 290 BLVD	20000	286W	NWC	77377
PLAZA A DR	0	492X	SWH	77046
PLAZA B DR	0	492X	SWH	77046
PLAZA CIRCLE DR	20200	381E	NEC	77532
PLAZA CIRCLE DR	20600	380H	NEC	77532
PLAZA DALE DR	12900	572F	SWH	77045
PLAZA DEL SOL DR	7000	527M	SWC	77083
PLAZA DEL SOL PARK	200	494J	NEH	77020
N. PLAZA EAST BLVD	1000	332Z	NCC	77073
N. PLAZA EAST BLVD	1300	333W	NCC	77073
PLAZA EAST BLVD	20100	372D	NCC	77073
PLAZA EAST BLVD	20400	332Z	NCC	77073
PLAZA LIBRE DR	15100	527M	SWC	77083
PLAZA PINES DR	3100	297Y	NEH	77345
PLAZA VERDE DR	100	372U	NWH	77038
PLEASANT	100	459V	HG	77562
PLEASANT	800	501V	BT	77520
PLEASANT	4100	492H	NWH	77007
PLEASANTBROOK DR	8700	408G	NWC	77095
PLEASANT COLONY DR	11000	409F	JV	77065
PLEASANT COVE CT	3100	578S	SEH	77059
PLEASANT CREEK DR	1900	337C	NEH	77345
PLEASANT FOREST	0	246C	SWM	77355
PLEASANT FOREST DR		484W	NEF	77494
PLEASANT FOREST BEND DR	0	296A	SEM	77365
PLEASANTGLEN CT	17900	330F	NWC	77379
PLEASANT GLEN LN	0	330F	NWC	77379
PLEASANT GREEN CIR	0	328V	NWC	77377
PLEASANT GROVE DR	0	406M	NWC	77433
PLEASANT GROVE RD	12500	368J	NWC	77429
PLEASANT GROVES	0	255S	SEM	77365
PLEASANT HILL DR	0	657N	FR	77546
PLEASANT HOLLOW LN	0	297P	NEH	77365
PLEASANT KNOLL CT	26100	366R	NWC	77433
PLEASANT KNOLL LN	0	367N	NWC	77095
PLEASANT KNOLL LN	26100	366R	NEC	77433
PLEASANT LILY CT	0	407U	NWC	77084
PLEASANT MEADOW DR	7700	330A	NWC	77379
PLEASANT MILL LN	0	484X	NEF	77494
PLEASANT OAK CT	0	447E	NWC	77084
PLEASANT OAK CT	7000	527E	NEF	77407
PLEASANTON DR	10100	412A	NWC	77038
PLEASANTON DR	10200	372W	NWC	77038
PLEASANT PALM CIR	2100	619Z	LC	77573
PLEASANT PLAINS DR	4800	617S	SEC	77546
PLEASANT POINT CT	0	250P	NWC	77389
PLEASANT POINT PLACE	0	250Q	NWC	77389
PLEASANT PRAIRIE DR	0	485L	SWC	77450
PLEASANT RIDGE DR	0	293D	SEM	77386
PLEASANT RIDGE DR	7400	408J	NWC	77095
PLEASANT RUN CT	3900	611X	NEF	77545
PLEASANT SHADOWS DR	0	250X	NWC	77389
PLEASANT SHORES CT	0	524M	NEF	77406
PLEASANT SPRINGS LN	0	615M	PL	77089
PLEASANT STREAM DR	6100	406T	NWC	77449
PLEASANT TRACE CT	16900	578Z	PA	77059
PLEASANT TRACE DR	4400	578Z	PA	77059
PLEASANT VALLEY	15000	618F	SEH	77062
PLEASANT VALLEY CT	0	609M	MC	77459
PLEASANT VALLEY DR	2100	659C	LC	77573
PLEASANT VALLEY DR	3800	609M	MC	77459
PLEASANT VIEW LN	11800	419V	BR	77532
PLEASANT VILLAS LN	0	575V	SEH	77075
PLEASANTVILLE DR	900	495K	NEH	77029
PLEASANTWOOD DR	18000	330F	NWC	77379
PLEASURE LN	100	299W	NEH	77336
PLEASURE COVE DR	1	251K	WD	77381
PLOVER CT	15900	375Q	NEC	77396
PLOVER DR	4300	620G	SB	77586
PLOVER LN	1	252N	WD	77380
E. PLUM	3000	615K	PL	77581
W. PLUM	4000	614M	PL	77581
PLUM DR	4900	534R	SEH	77087
PLUMB	2600	532B	WU	77005
PLUMBAGO DR	0	575R	SEH	77075
PLUM BOUGH CT	19100	446R	NWC	77084
PLUMBROOK DR	11000	529X	SWH	77099
PLUMBROOK DR	12400	528V	SWH	77099
PLUM BROOK LN	3300	609L	MC	77459
PLUMBWOOD WAY	1700	618R	SEH	77058
PLUM CREEK	7400	535J	SEH	77012
N. PLUM CREEK DR	1300	292C	SEM	77386
S. PLUM CREEK DR	28900	292C	SEM	77386
PLUM CREEK LN	1900	610B	MC	77489
PLUM CREEK LN	2900	534M	SEH	77087
PLUM CREEK FOREST LN	0	534M	SEH	77087
PLUM CREEK MEADOW CT	0	534M	SEH	77087
PLUM CREEK TERRACE LN	0	534M	SEH	77087
PLUM CREEK TRAIL LN	0	534M	SEH	77087
PLUM DALE WAY	0	577S	SEH	77034
PLUMERIA AVE	0	461N	NEC	77521
PLUMERO MEADOW DR	0	524B	NEF	77494
PLUMERO PLACE	0	251Q	WD	77380
PLUME TREE DR	0	335P	NCC	77338
PLUM FALLS CT	900	617H	SEH	77062
PLUM FALLS LN	1900	614L	PL	77581
PLUMFIELD LN	2500	485Q	NEF	77450
PLUM FOREST RD	4400	447A	NWC	77084
PLUM GATE CT		525R	NEF	77469
PLUM GLEN CT	3600	578X	SEH	77059
PLUM GRASS DR	0	328E	NWC	77377
PLUM GREEN CT	0	328E	NWC	77377
PLUM GROVE CT	1	258V	NEC	77357
PLUM GROVE LN	0	614L	PL	77581
PLUM GROVE LN	7000	411Y	NWH	77088
PLUM GROVE RD	200	259A	PG	77357
PLUM HOLLOW DR	3600	618C	SEH	77059
PLUM KNOLL CT	3100	447N	NWC	77084
PLUM LAKE DR	0	612R	PL	77584
PLUM LAKE DR	8200	408E	NWC	77095
PLUM LAKE DR	8700	407H	NWC	77095
PLUM LAKE DR	10600	368Z	NWC	77065
PLUM MEADOW LN	11800	414F	NCC	77039
PLUMMER	7900	495N	NEH	77029
PLUMMER'S LODGE	18500	377D	NEC	77346
PLUM ORCHARD CIR	15200	457T	NEC	77049
PLUM PARK DR	1300	486J	SWC	77450
PLUM POINT	0	259A	PG	77357
PLUM POINT CT	0	609T	MC	77479
PLUMPOINT DR	11300	529X	SWH	77099
PLUMPOINT DR	12300	528V	SWH	77099
PLUM RIDGE DR	9200	410E	NWC	77064
PLUM SPRINGS DR	14200	367B	NWC	77429
PLUM SQUARE CT	0	611W	FS	77545
PLUMTEX DR	14800	375U	NEH	77396
PLUM TRAILS CT	20200	446P	NWC	77449
PLUM TRAILS LN	2800	446P	NWC	77449
PLUM TRAILS RD	20200	446P	NWC	77449
PLUM TREE LN	4100	619G	TL	77586
PLUMTREE FOREST CIR	7600	407M	NWC	77095
PLUMTREE FOREST CT	7500	407M	NWC	77095
PLUM VALE CT	13200	368U	NWC	77065
PLUM VALLEY DR	3500	296V	NEH	77339
PLUMWOOD DR	1400	372E	NWC	77014
PLUMWOOD DR	12900	328Y	NWC	77429
PLUNKETT	2100	538S	DP	77536
PLYMOUTH	300	453L	NEH	77022
PLYMOUTH	300	659J	LC	77573
PLYMOUTH	1300	537P	PA	77502
PLYMOUTH COLONY CT	17600	657D	SEC	77598
PLYMOUTH COLONY DR	2800	657D	SEC	77598
PLYMOUTH LANDING CIR	3100	615K	PL	77581
PLYMOUTH POINTE LN	3200	609Q	MC	77459
PLYMOUTH RIDGE LN	19600	290Z	NWC	77379
PLYMOUTH ROCK CT	2500	657D	SEC	77598
PLYMOUTH ROCK DR	2600	657D	SEC	77598
PLYMOUTH WAY	4600	569X	MC	77459
PLYMPTON DR	24600	484G	NEF	77494
POCAHONTAS	4800	577C	PA	77505
POCAHONTAS	5100	531K	BL	77401
POCAHONTAS DR	4100	461S	NEC	77521
POCATELLO DR	11900	328C	NWC	77377
POCHYLA BLVD	0	415Z	NEH	77078
POCITO CT	19300	337S	NEC	77346
POCO	9000	450U	NWH	77080
POCO DR	2100	570W	MC	77489
POCO DR	2400	610B	MC	77489
POE RD	3000	573K	SEH	77051
POETA LN		524M	NEF	77406
POHL RD	30800	322V	WCO	77484
POINCIANA DR	2300	451M	NWH	77018
POINCIANA DR	4900	451L	NWH	77092
POINSETTA LN	100	459M	HG	77562
POINSETTIA	4700	571H	SWH	77045
N. POINT DR	9000	502P	BT	77520
S. POINT DR	9200	532Y	SWH	77054
E. POINT DR	9200	532Z	SWH	77054
S. POINT LN	0	576V	SEH	77034
S. POINT LN	0	577S	SEH	77034
POINT LN	0	327V	NWC	77429
POINTARBOR CT	0	328C	NWC	77377
POINT BARROW RD	8800	503Z	BC	77520
POINT BLANK DR	800	372X	NWC	77038
POINT BROAD OAKS DR	0	491F	SWH	77056
POINT CLEAR CT	2000	610J	MC	77459
POINT CLEAR DR	500	656P	FR	77546
POINT CLEAR DR	3100	610J	MC	77459
POINT CLEAR DR	6500	370F	NWC	77069
POINT COMFORT CT	2400	657C	SEC	77598
POINT COMFORT LN	17600	617Z	SEC	77598
POINT COMFORT LN	17700	617Y	SEC	77598
POINT COMMERCE DR	8000	375G	HM	77396
POINT CUERO CT	0	484X	NEF	77494
N. POINTE BLVD	0	290Y	NWC	77379
POINTE LN	0	609D	MC	77459
POINTED EDGE LN		328k	NWC	77429
POINTED OAK LN	0	486N	SWC	77450
POINTED OAK LN	20500	486N	SWC	77450
POINTE LEONE LN	0	659R	LC	77573
N. POINTE PLACE	24900	484M	NEF	77494
POINTER	3000	454K	NEH	77016
POINTER RIDGE LN	0	484Z	NEF	77494
POINTER RIDGE LN	11600	366R	NWC	77433
POINTERSCREEK LN	0	327D	NWC	77429
POINTE SERRA DR	0	659G	LC	77573
POINTE SPRINGS CROSSING	5300	251W	NWC	77389
POINTE WAY	0	377Q	NEC	77044
POINT HAVEN CIR	0	366J	NWC	77433
POINT HOLLOW LN	0	366U	NWC	77433
POINT ISABEL LN	0	657N	FR	77546
POINT LOOKOUT DR	18000	619S	NB	77058
POINT NORTHWEST BLVD	15200	408B	NWC	77095
POINT PARK DR	8700	408B	NWC	77095
POINT PENDLETON DR	8200	289M	NWC	77375
POINT ROYAL DR	0	656P	FR	77546
POINT SIX CIRCLE DR	8900	408C	NWC	77095
POINT SUBLIME DR	0	406G	NWC	77433
POINT VILLAGE LN		328P	NWC	77429
POINT WEST DR	5700	530A	SWH	77036
POITIERS CIR	0	570G	MC	77071
POITIERS DR	7600	570G	MC	77071
POIX	0	530Q	SWH	77074
POLARIS BLVD	31200	288B	TB	77375
POLARIS BLVD	31300	248X	TB	77375
POLARIS POINT LN	0	407E	NWC	77433
POLARSTONE CT	13900	377Y	NEH	77044
POLEBROOK DR	0	295R	SEM	77365
POLISHED STONE CIR	8200	407H	NWC	77095
W. POLK	100	540X	LP	77571
E. POLK	100	540Y	LP	77571
POLK	200	493Q	DT	77002
W. POLK	300	493N	SWH	77019
W. POLK	1500	492R	SWH	77019
POLK	1600	493V	SEH	77003
POLK	3900	494S	SEH	77023
POLK	6500	494Y	SEH	77011
POLK AVE	1400	537J	PA	77506
POLK CT	5700	494Y	SEH	77023
POLK LN	3600	538V	DP	77536
POLLARD	900	494F	NEH	77020
POLLETTS COVE CT	0	377K	NEC	77346
POLLUX CT	14100	248X	TB	77375
POLLY	900	501X	BT	77520
POLLY	5200	454C	NEH	77016
POLLY CREEK WAY	20000	486L	SWC	77450
POLO	14300	571U	SWH	77085
POLO MEADOW DR	18100	377D	NEC	77346
POLO MEADOW DR	18600	337Z	NEC	77346
POLO PONY	500	491H	SWH	77024
POLYTHANE LN	0	292J	NWC	77388
POM CT	1	451W	SV	77055
POMANDER RD	5200	534K	SEH	77021
POMEGRANATE LN	20200	446N	NWC	77449
POMERAN DR	2200	450N	NWH	77080
POMEROY AVE	100	536H	PA	77506
POMEROY GROVE DR	24500	295M	SEM	77365
POMINA ST	0	296T	SEM	77365
POMME BAY PASS	0	609Y	MC	77459
POMMEL LN	0	527W	NEF	77407
POMONA DR	2000	537F	PA	77506
POMPANO	11200	529J	SWH	77072
POMPANO LAKE LN	0	609T	NEF	77479
POMPTON CT	0	615W	PL	77584
POMPTON DR	11900	616D	SEH	77089
PONCA	4200	577F	PA	77504
PONCE DR	11200	415Q	NEC	77016
PONCHO SPRINGS CT	0	410T	NWC	77040
POND	200	335Y	HM	77338
POND	7400	455K	NEH	77028
POND CIR	600	247F	SWM	77362
POND ARBOR PATH	19800	526T	NEF	77407
POND BROOK PLACE	2700	609R	MC	77459
POND CYPRESS CT	20900	326N	NWC	77433
PONDE LN	20000	295H	SEM	77365
PONDER LN	0	253C	SEM	77302
PONDER LN	12600	414F	NCC	77039
PONDERA POINT DR	100	249M	NWH	77375
PONDERA POINT DR	100	249M	NWH	77375
PONDERATE CT	11700	369S	NWC	77065
PONDER CHASE CT	0	525Q	NEF	77407
PONDEROSA	0	256Z	SEM	77357
PONDEROSA	3700	500M	BT	77521
PONDEROSA	33100	247R	SWM	77362
PONDEROSA LN	9200	530S	SWH	77074
PONDEROSA LN	9500	530S	SWH	77036
PONDEROSA BEND DR	0	327D	NWC	77429
PONDEROSA HILLS LN		484W	NEF	77494
PONDEROSA PEAK DR	0	293G	SEM	77386
PONDEROSA PINE ST	0	462V	CCO	77520
PONDEROSA PINE PLACE	8500	289R	NWC	77375
PONDEROSA PINES	17300	331Q	NWC	77090
N. PONDS DR	0	617V	SEH	77546
PONDWOOD DR	11900	368D	NWC	77429
PONEAL CT	14200	408Y	NWC	77084
PONNELL LN	8200	412Q	NWH	77088
PONSOT DR	6700	571X	SWH	77489
PONTCHARTRAIN CT	2200	658K	LC	77573
PONTE DE ARTS AVE	0	377D	NEC	77346
PONTE ROSSI	1200	659M	LC	77573
PONTE VECCHIO WAY	0	378A	NEC	77346
PONTIAC DR	8200	531N	SWH	77096
PONT LASALLE LN	1800	537U	PA	77503
PONT PLACE	0	620K	SB	77586
PONY CREEK	7400	609Z	NEF	77459
PONY EXPRESS RD	10200	369X	NWC	77064
POOL CREEK DR	8500	407H	NWC	77095
POOLE RD	6800	330F	NWC	77379
POOL FORGE CT	14800	528W	NEF	77498
POOLVIEW	15400	570K	MC	77071
POPA	0	577X	SEH	77034
POPATOP	21600	333L	NCC	77338
POPE CREEKS LN	0	417C	NEH	77044
POPLAR	0	295Y	SEM	77365
S. POPLAR	100	288L	TB	77375
POPLAR	3400	535N	SEH	77087
POPLAR CT	1400	619D	PA	77586
POPLAR BAY LN	0	406X	NWC	77449
POPLAR BLUFF LN	9200	408A	NWC	77095
POPLAR CANYON CT	17400	527E	NEF	77407
POPLAR COVE	1500	580F	LP	77571
POPLAR CREEK DR	11800	489S	SWH	77077

Street Name	Block	Pg/Sq	Loc	Zips
POPLAR CREEK LN	0	484K	NEF	77494
POPLAR CREEK LN	2800	613F	NEB	77584
POPLAR FIELD LN	0	615M	PL	77089
POPLAR GLEN LN	13100	488Y	SWH	77082
POPLAR GROVE DR	15300	331S	NWC	77068
POPLAR HILL	16800	407L	NWC	77095
POPLAR HILL PLACE	1	250D	WD	77381
POPLAR LAKE TRAIL	0	327R	NWC	77429
POPLAR PARK DR	2100	296Z	NEH	77339
POPLAR PARK WAY	0	657G	FR	77546
POPLAR RIDGE LN	8300	335N	NCC	77338
POPLAR RUN CT	3300	618B	SEH	77059
POPLAR SPRINGS LN	15200	618F	SEH	77062
POPLAR TERRACE LN	5500	406X	NWC	77449
POPLAR TRACE LN	0	253P	SEM	77386
POPLAR TRAILS LN	19100	329A	NWC	77375
POPLAR VALLEY WAY	2900	297Q	NEH	77345
POPLARWOOD CT	11400	616D	SEC	77089
POPLARWOOD DR	11400	616C	SEC	77089
POPOMAN	6300	444X	KT	77493
POPPETS CT	15800	419F	NEC	77532
POPPETS WAY	700	419E	NEC	77532
POPPY	6600	451E	NWH	77092
POPPY ST	0	659G	LC	77573
POPPY'S POINT CT		367W	NWC	77095
POPPYFIELD CT	100	485C	SWC	77450
POPPYFIELD DR	22500	485C	SWC	77450
POPPY TRAILS LN	17500	407P	NWC	77084
POPPY TRAILS LN	18000	407P	NWC	77449
POPS	0	538N	PA	77503
POPULAR CT	0	463S	CCO	77520
POQUENO	0	499L	NEC	77520
PORCHESTER DR	1700	486K	SWC	77450
PORCHLIGHT CT	0	372M	NCC	77073
PORCH SWING	0	411H	NWC	77038
PORPOISE CT	16400	419B	NEC	77532
PORSCHE DR	800	375M	NEC	77396
PORT	100	495A	NEH	77020
PORT RD	10300	579V	SEC	77507
PORT RD	11600	580W	SEC	77586
PORT ACCESS RD	0	495Y	NEH	77029
PORT AEGEAN DR	0	291N	NWC	77388
PORTAGE LN	500	616Y	FR	77546
PORTAGE ROCK LN	5300	486W	NEF	77450
PORTAL DR	5600	531W	SWH	77096
PORTAL DR	7500	530Y	SWH	77071
PORTAL DR	9200	530W	SWH	77031
PORT ANGELES DR	10000	371X	NWC	77086
PORTA ROSA LN	0	659M	LC	77573
PORT BARROW DR	16000	367D	NWC	77429
PORT BISHOP LN	0	526J	NEF	77407
PORT BRANCH DR	0	525Z	NEF	77406
PORT BRIDGE LN	2000	658U	LC	77573
PORT CARISSA DR	2600	617X	SEC	77546
PORTER	600	620Q	SB	77586
PORTER	2500	454S	NEH	77026
PORTER	3900	533M	SEH	77021
PORTER LN	16000	254L	SEM	77365
PORTER RD	2000	445E	NWC	77493
PORTER RD	5500	405S	NWC	77493
PORTER RD	10000	539N	LP	77571
PORTER RD	10000	539N	LP	77571
PORTER MEADOW LN	0	371H	NWC	77014
PORTER RIDGE DR	4700	611C	SWH	77053
PORT ERROLL DR	0	408A	NWC	77095
PORT ERROLL DR	0	368W	NWC	77095
PORTERWAY DR	6300	407T	NWC	77084
PORTFIELD CT	26100	484Z	NEF	77494
PORTGLEN DR	1800	660L	LC	77573
PORTHCAWL CT	24700	484H	NEF	77494
PORT HOUSTON	900	495K	NEH	77029
PORTICO POINT	0	251F	SWM	77380
PORTLAND	1	493W	SWH	77006
PORTLAND LN	0	255T	SEM	77365
PORTLICK CT	0	406U	NWC	77449
PORTLICK DR	0	406U	NWC	77449
PORTMAN GLEN LN	3900	573Z	SEC	77047
PORTMANSHIRE LN	0	407Z	NWC	77084
PORTMAN TRAIL LN	0	526K	NEF	77407
PORT MIRAMAR DR	0	289M	NWC	77375
PORT NORTHWEST	0	409Q	NWH	77041
PORT O'CALL	16100	419B	NEC	77532
PORT O'CALL	16600	379T	NEC	77532
PORTOBELLO DR	13500	528K	SWC	77083
PORTO BIANCO LN	2700	659L	LC	77573
PORT OF HOUSTON	900	495X	NEH	77029
PORTOFINO BLVD	1	620T	KE	77565
PORTOFINO CT	0	610T	MC	77459
PORTOFINO RD	0	529A	SWH	77042
PORTO RICO RD	9800	450A	NWH	77041
PORTO WAY LN	0	660H	GCO	77539
PORTREE DR	12200	371R	NWC	77067
PORT ROSE CT	0	375X	NEC	77396
PORT ROSE LN	2900	659H	LC	77573
PORT ROYAL DR	1900	619W	NB	77058
PORTRUSH CT	1000	485E	NEF	77494
PORT SIDE CT	0	619U	LC	77573
PORTSIDE DR	3700	291Y	NWC	77388
PORTSMOUTH	1700	492Z	SWH	77098
PORTSMOUTH	3000	537K	PA	77503
PORTSMOUTH	4000	492W	SWH	77027
PORTSMOUTH DR	800	613G	NEB	77584
PORTSMOUTH ST	0	492X	SWH	77098
PORTSTOWN	22200	256Y	SEM	77357
PORTUGAL	6000	577H	PA	77505
PORTUGUESE BEND CT	3800	609Q	MC	77459
PORTUGUESE BEND DR	6400	609Q	MC	77459
PORTWALL	200	495F	NEH	77029
PORTWAY DR	900	492A	NWH	77024
PORTWEST DR	6600	492A	NWH	77024
PORTWEST DR	6900	491D	NWH	77024
PORTWOOD	100	494Q	SEH	77011
POSEY	1200	453T	NWH	77009
POSSUM CREEK RD	2000	536S	SEH	77017
POSSUM HILL CT	0	484S	NEF	77494
POSSUM HOLLOW LN	11600	369N	NWC	77065
POSSUM PARK RD	0	336X	NEC	77338
POSSUM PARK RD	200	376C	NEC	77338
POSSUM RUN	17500	376G	NEC	77396
POSSUM TROT	18300	255A	SEM	77302
POSSUMWOOD DR	15200	408N	NWC	77084
POST	500	453L	NEH	77022
POSTANO BLUFF DR	0	406G	NWC	77433
POST BRIDGE LN	7600	250P	NWC	77389
POST GATE DR	22700	334A	NCC	77373
POSTHORN LN	400	497C	NEC	77015
POST MEADOW DR	0	446D	NWC	77449
S. POST OAK	0	491Q	SWH	77056
POST OAK	100	248J	SWM	77354
POST OAK	100	500E	BT	77520
POST OAK BLVD	500	491R	SWH	77027
POST OAK BLVD	700	491Q	SWH	77056

Street Name	Block	Pg/Sq	Loc	Zips
S. POST OAK BLVD	2400	611U	FS	77545
S. POST OAK BLVD	3400	611Y	FS	77545
POST OAK CIR	0	246H	SWM	77355
POST OAK CIR	0	247A	SWM	77355
POST OAK CIR	1	491H	SWH	77024
POST OAK CT	0	616U	FR	77546
POST OAK CT	6100	330D	NWC	77379
POST OAK DR	10000	252C	SEM	77385
POST OAK DR	26300	257M	SEM	77357
POST OAK LN	0	491H	SWH	77024
N. POST OAK LN	1	491M	SWH	77024
POST OAK LN	1	256Q	SEM	77357
S. POST OAK LN	100	491L	SWH	77056
N. POST OAK RD	100	491D	NWH	77024
N. POST OAK RD	1000	451Z	NWH	77055
S. POST OAK RD	9500	531Y	SWH	77096
S. POST OAK RD	10300	531Y	SWH	77035
S. POST OAK RD	12400	571G	SWH	77045
S. POST OAK RD	14900	611B	SWH	77053
POST OAK CENTRAL	0	491U	SWH	77056
POST OAK ESTATES LN	0	491D	NWH	77055
POST OAK GLEN LN	13400	328U	NWC	77429
POST OAK GREEN LN	0	491C	NWH	77055
POST OAK HILL	0	491M	SWH	77024
POST OAK HILL DR	20200	292W	NWC	77388
POST OAK HOLLOW	17100	330D	NWC	77379
POST OAK PARK DR	1100	491R	SWH	77027
POST OAK PKWY	4200	491R	SWH	77027
POST OAK PLACE DR	4500	491R	SWH	77027
POST OAK RUN	29000	246D	SWM	77355
POST OAK RUN	29800	247A	SWM	77355
POST OAK TIMBER DR	4700	491L	SWH	77056
POST OAK VIEW CT	18300	377C	NEC	77346
POST SHADOW ESTATE CT	0	250X	NWC	77389
POST SHADOW ESTATE DR	0	250X	NWC	77389
POSTVINE CT	1	251E	WD	77381
POSTWICK CT	7200	407M	NWC	77095
POST WOOD	0	331C	NWC	77388
POSTWOOD CT	4500	331B	NWC	77388
POSTWOOD DR	3500	331B	NWC	77388
POSTWOOD LN	900	613F	NEB	77584
POSTWOOD GLEN LN	0	334A	NCC	77373
POSTWOOD GREEN LN	5500	334A	NCC	77373
POSTWOOD MANOR CT	0	484W	NEF	77494
POSTWOOD OAKS CT	0	253K	SEM	77386
POSTWOOD OAKS DR	23100	334A	NCC	77373
POSTWOOD PARK DR	5700	334A	NCC	77373
POSTWOOD POINT DR	23100	334A	NCC	77373
POTENZA CT	0	659L	LC	77573
POT LUCK FARM RD	0	249Y	NWC	77375
POTOMAC	1	491N	SWH	77057
POTOMAC	1300	536T	PA	77502
POTOMAC DR	2500	658S	LC	77573
POTTER HOLLOW DR	23200	296N	SEM	77365
POTTINGER DR	8600	528Q	SWC	77083
POTTS RD	1000	336J	NEC	77338
POTTS RD	1400	336J	NEH	77338
POULSON DR	12000	570A	SWH	77031
POUNDBURY CT	900	572U	SWH	77047
POUND RIDGE	11700	490K	BH	77024
POUTER DR	6200	528G	SWC	77083
POUZZOTTO LN	0	527W	NEF	77469
POWDERHORN	1	490F	BH	77024
POWDERHORN	12100	247R	SWM	77362
POWDERHORN LN	1800	445T	NWC	77493
POWDER KEG	0	528K	SWC	77083
POWDER MILL DR	23300	287H	NWC	77377
POWDER MIST LN	2000	446T	NWC	77449
POWDER POINT	0	609A	SG	77479
POWDER RIVER DR	1000	485G	SWC	77450
POWELL	0	459U	HG	77562
POWELL	300	656N	NEB	77511
POWELL LN	200	292R	SP	77373
POWELL LN	12600	496M	NEH	77015
W. POWELL RD	0	580N	SEC	77507
POWELL, W O RD	0	580J	LP	77571
POWELL HOUSE LN	22600	445Q	NWC	77449
POWELL RIDGE DR	0	406B	NWC	77433
POWELL SPRINGS CT	2800	610U	MC	77459
POWELL TERRACE LN	0	376H	NEC	77346
POWER	500	659K	LC	77573
POWER	8000	535F	SEH	77012
POWER CT	300	569J	SG	77478
POWERLINE PASS DR	0	293U	NCC	77373
POWERSCOURT DR	19500	337U	NEC	77346
POWER SPRINGS LN	0	329V	NWC	77070
POYDRAS CT	13000	367H	NWC	77429
POYDRAS ST	0	568J	SG	77498
POYNES DR	9500	409A	NWC	77065
PRADERA DR	16300	527K	NEF	77083
PRADE RANCH LN	15400	328S	NWC	77429
PRADO LN	13200	369G	NWC	77070
PRADO GREEN CT	0	337U	NEC	77346
PRADO GREEN TRAIL	0	337T	NEC	77346
PRADO WOODS	12000	368D	NWC	77429
PRAGUE	0	407R	NWC	77084
PRAGUE	0	408N	NWC	77084
PRAGUE	6200	492F	SWH	77007
PRAIRIE	0	489P	SWH	77077
PRAIRIE	400	493M	DT	77002
PRAIRIE	2200	493M	SEH	77003
PRAIRIE	2500	537P	PA	77506
PRAIRIE	26300	292Q	SP	77373
PRAIRIE DR	8800	410F	NWC	77064
PRAIRIE LN	26800	484N	NEF	77494
PRAIRIE RD	100	460N	HG	77562
PRAIRIE RD	400	460S	HG	77562
PRAIRIE BEND CT	18200	407N	NWC	77433
PRAIRIE BIRD LN	22800	333B	NCC	77373
PRAIRIE BIRD LN	23200	293X	NCC	77373
PRAIRIE BLUFF DR	0	407J	NWC	77433
PRAIRIE BROOK CT	800	617H	SEH	77062
PRAIRIE CLOVER LN	9700	289Y	NWC	77379
PRAIRIE CREEK DR	1900	616S	PL	77581
PRAIRIE CREEK DR	5100	448B	NWC	77084
PRAIRIE CREEK DR	5300	408X	NWC	77084
PRAIRIE CREST DR	0	525U	NEF	77469
PRAIRIE CREST DR	0	525U	NEF	77469
PRAIRIE DALE CT	9500	576J	SEH	77075
PRAIRIE DOG RUN	0	527U	NEF	77498
PRAIRIE DUNES DR	6500	370B	NWC	77069
PRAIRIE FALCON CT	0	250L	NWC	77389
PRAIRIE FALCON CT	0	250L	NWC	77389
PRAIRIE FALCON PLACE	0	250L	NWC	77389
PRAIRIE FALCON PLACE	0	250L	NWC	77389
PRAIRIE FARM LN	0	327U	NWC	77429
PRAIRIE FIRE LN	7700	406M	NWC	77433
PRAIRIE FLAX CT	17700	367T	NWC	77433
PRAIRIE FOREST TRAIL	0	293X	NCC	77373
PRAIRIE GLEN LN	0	445E	NWC	77493
PRAIRIE GRASS LN	0	444S	KT	77493
PRAIRIE GREEN CT	0	525V	NEF	77406

Street Name	Block	Pg/Sq	Loc	Zips
PRAIRIE GROVE DR	1500	489P	SWH	77077
PRAIRIE HAVEN CT	0	327U	NWC	77429
PRAIRIE HAWK DR	10900	409F	NWC	77064
PRAIRIE HILL CT	2800	578W	SEH	77059
PRAIRIE HOLLOW LN	0	488T	SWH	77077
PRAIRIE KNOLL CT	3000	578W	SEH	77059
PRAIRIE LARKSPUR DR	18500	372H	NCC	77073
PRAIRIE LEA	16100	367L	CY	77429
PRAIRIE LILY LN	0	525B	NEF	77494
PRAIRIE MANOR DR	0	526W	NEF	77406
PRAIRIE MARK LN	1600	489P	SWH	77077
PRAIRIE MEADOW DR	4100	446H	NWC	77449
PRAIRIEMILL LN	0	365H	NWC	77433
PRAIRIE MIST	10000	411K	NWH	77088
PRAIRIE MIST LN	0	657T	FR	77546
PRAIRIE OAK DR	7500	370V	NWC	77086
PRAIRIE OAK DR	7600	371S	NWC	77086
PRAIRIE OAKS DR	15300	527Q	NEF	77083
PRAIRIE OAK TRAIL	7500	337R	NEC	77346
PRAIRIE PEBBLE CT	23100	485T	NEF	77494
PRAIRIE PKWY	1200	484D	KT	77494
PRAIRIE RIDGE RD	4800	611C	SWH	77053
PRAIRIE ROSE DR	15000	329W	NWC	77070
PRAIRIE SAGE DR	0	525Z	NEF	77406
PRAIRIE SCHOOL LN	0	484E	KT	77494
PRAIRIE SPRING LN	21700	290K	NWC	77379
PRAIRIESTONE TRAIL LN	0	486T	SWC	77450
PRAIRIE TRAILS DR	9200	330N	NWC	77379
PRAIRIE VALE CT	0	611N	FS	77545
PRAIRIE VALLEY DR	0	366N	NWC	77433
PRAIRIE VIEW DR	8200	412P	NWH	77088
PRAIRIE VIEW WALLER	33000	282E	WCO	77445
PRAIRIE VILLA DR	0	485H	SWC	77450
PRAIRIE VILLAGE DR	6700	406R	NWC	77449
PRAIRIE VILLAGE DR	7000	406M	NWC	77433
PRAIRIE WILDE	100	616Y	FR	77546
PRAIRIE WILDE	200	656C	FR	77546
PRAIRIE WIND LN	8300	410J	NWC	77040
PRAIRIE WING POINT	4600	444F	NWC	77493
PRAISE CT	5600	574J	SEH	77048
PRANCER DR	0	249V	NWC	77375
PRANCING STREAM DR	0	293X	NCC	77373
PRANZO LN	0	659R	LC	77573
PRARIE LAKE CT	23600	525K	NEF	77407
PRATO GARDENS LN	0	445B	NWC	77493
PRATT PARK LN	0	485U	NEF	77450
PRATTSFORD LN	700	332N	NWC	77090
PRATTWOOD CT	400	658N	LC	77573
PRAYING MANTIS LN	0	297A	SEM	77357
PREAKNESS PALM CIR	18800	337Z	NEC	77346
PREAKNESS WAY	12200	570G	SWH	77071
PRECEPTION LN	12900	419V	NEC	77532
PRECIOUS PLACE	22800	291E	NWC	77389
PRECIOUS STONE LN	0	524F	NEF	77494
PREECE CT	12100	328X	NWC	77429
PRELUDE CT	8600	410P	NWC	77040
PRELUDE SPRINGS LN	3700	253P	SEM	77386
PREMIER	5600	450B	NWH	77040
PREMIUM DR	17000	323G	NWC	77447
PRENTISS DR	6800	534Z	SEH	77061
PRENTISS DR	6900	574D	SEH	77061
PRENTISS DR	7100	575A	SEH	77061
PRESA	9300	455D	NEH	77078
PRESCOTIE DR	0	457A	NEC	77044
PRESCOTT	2800	532K	SWH	77025
PRESCOTT DR	0	658Y	LC	77573
PRESCOTT GLEN LN	0	524B	NEF	77494
PRESCOTT GREEN CIR	0	376C	NEC	77396
PRESCOTT MANOR	0	326E	NWC	77433
PRESCOTT RUN LN	6000	524E	NEF	77494
PRESENT	100	569R	SF	77477
PRESENT	200	570S	MC	77489
PRESERVE LN	0	609Z	MC	77459
PRESERVE BEND CIR	23300	291E	NWC	77389
PRESERVE CREEK CT	4800	291E	NWC	77389
PRESERVE GLEN CIR	23300	291E	NWC	77389
PRESERVE PARK DR	5200	291E	NWC	77389
PRESERVE VIEW CIR	23300	291E	NWC	77389
PRESERVE WAY	0	250S	NWC	77389
PRESIDENTS CT	4000	613C	SEC	77047
S. PRESIDENTS DR	4100	573Z	SEC	77047
W. PRESIDENTS DR	14600	573Y	SEC	77047
PRESIDEO	1800	656U	FR	77546
PRESIDIO DR	6100	611B	SWH	77053
PRESIDIO CANYON DR	6200	526B	NEF	77450
PRESIDIO SQUARE BLVD	14500	528E	SWC	77083
PRESLEY	1900	453M	NEH	77093
PRESLEY GROVE DR	0	295M	SEM	77365
PRESLEY GROVE DR	0	295M	SEM	77365
PRESLEY PARK DR	0	293L	SEM	77386
PRESS	500	494K	NEH	77020
PRESSLER DR	1800	532H	SWH	77030
PRESSLER, HERMANN BLVD	1200	532H	SWH	77030
PRESSLER, HERMANN BLVD	1500	533E	SWH	77030
PRESSWOOD CT	0	256M	SEM	77357
PRESSWOOD DR	400	252P	SEM	77386
PRESTIGE ROW	12700	408D	NWC	77065
PRESTON	1	493M	DT	77002
PRESTON	2200	494N	SEH	77003
PRESTON	26200	292Q	SP	77373
PRESTON DR	8400	613V	PL	77584
PRESTON LN	300	657U	LC	77573
PRESTON RD	0	537G	PA	77503
PRESTON RD	800	537T	PA	77503
PRESTON RD	3100	577B	PA	77505
PRESTON BLOOM CT	0	327U	NWC	77429
PRESTON CLIFF CT	0	488T	SWH	77077
PRESTONCOVE CT	0	484T	NEF	77494
PRESTON FIELD LN	8700	407C	NWC	77095
PRESTON GROVE DR	6800	250U	NWC	77389
PRESTON KNOLL DR	0	376N	NEC	77396
PRESTON OAKS DR	0	524F	NEF	77494
PRESTON PARK DR	14700	408F	NWC	77095
PRESTON POINT DR	0	406K	NWC	77433
PRESTON SPRINGS CT	8100	407G	NWC	77095
PRESTON SPRINGS DR	17000	407G	NWC	77095
PRESTON TRAIL DR	6500	370B	NWC	77069
PRESTON TRAILS DR	4500	577L	PA	77505
PRESTONWOOD DR	0	527X	NEF	77407
PRESTONWOOD FRST DR	13200	369D	NWC	77070
PRESTONWOOD FRST DR	14200	329Z	NWC	77070
PRESTONWOOD PARK DR	0	369D	NWC	77070
PRESTWICK	7200	532J	SWH	77025
PRESTWICK CT	400	491K	SWH	77057
PRESTWICK DR	2300	659C	LC	77573
PRESTWOOD DR	6300	531A	SWH	77081
PRESTWOOD DR	7700	530C	SWH	77036
PREVIN CT	6000	411P	NWH	77088
PRICE	1	501X	BT	77520
PRICE	7200	412X	NWH	77088
PRICE CIR	3000	615R	PL	77581
PRICE LN	35000	247B	SWM	77362

Street Name	Block	Pg/Sq	Loc	Zips
PRICE GROVE LN	0	367Y	NWC	77095
PRICE PLAZA DR	0	446X	NWC	77449
PRICEWOOD MANOR CT	0	326J	NWC	77433
PRICHARD CT	2700	610U	MC	77459
PRICHETT DR	8500	531P	SWH	77096
PRICKLY PEAR CT	0	332W	NWC	77090
PRICKLY PEAR CT	0	332W	NWC	77090
PRIDES CROSSING DR	1	250D	WD	77381
PRIDES CROSSING RD	2400	371M	NWC	77067
PRIEST DR	1500	453D	NEH	77093
PRIEST DR	2200	454A	NEH	77093
PRILLERMAN TRAILS DR	10700	415S	NEH	77016
PRIMA	8600	528P	SWC	77083
S. PRIMAVERA DR	1500	616P	PL	77581
N. PRIMAVERA DR	1500	616P	PL	77581
PRIMA VERA DR	4600	571R	SWH	77045
PRIMA VISTA DR	0	406G	NWC	77433
PRIMEROSE VALLEY TRACE	0	616M	SEC	77089
PRIME WEST PKWY	1500	446S	NWC	77449
PRIMO PLACE CT	0	329C	NWC	77379
PRIM PINE CT	20200	326P	NWC	77433
PRIMROSE	5300	536N	SEH	77017
PRIMROSE DR	1300	252G	SEM	77385
PRIMROSE DR	2000	537X	PA	77502
PRIMROSE LN	0	444S	KT	77493
PRIMROSE LN	0	659G	LC	77573
PRIMROSE LN	0	659G	LC	77573
PRIMROSE LN	500	580K	LP	77571
PRIMROSE LN	1300	619H	TL	77586
PRIMROSE RD	0	460W	BT	77521
PRIMROSE ACRES LN	10800	530X	SWC	77031
PRIMROSE BLUFF DR		524A	NEF	77494
PRIMROSE EDGE CT	18700	366D	NWC	77429
PRIMROSE GLEN LN	0	326U	NWC	77429
PRIMROSE MEADOW LN	17600	407F	NWC	77095
W. PRIMROSE MEADOWS CIR	900	613F	NEB	77584
E. PRIMROSE MEADOWS CIR	900	613F	NEB	77584
S. PRIMROSE MEADOWS CIR	3300	613F	NEB	77584
PRIMROSE PARK CIR	0	367W	NWC	77095
PRIMROSE PARK LN	9800	366Z	NWC	77433
PRIMROSE PATH	3800	539S	DP	77536
PRIMROSE PRAIRIE CT	0	366Z	NWC	77433
PRIMROSE SPRINGS CT	0	524F	NEF	77494
PRIMROSE TRACE LN	3600	291L	NWC	77389
PRIMULA DR	0	368A	NWC	77429
PRIMULA PATH	0	526T	NEF	77407
PRIM WATER CT	2100	297V	NEH	77345
PRIMWOOD CT	2200	613Q	NEB	77584
PRIMWOOD DR	11500	329W	NWC	77070
PRINCE	900	492C	NWH	77008
PRINCE	1100	452Y	NWH	77008
PRINCE RD	10400	419S	NEC	77532
PRINCE ST	4500	501F	BT	77521
PRINCE CREEK CT	1300	486F	SWC	77450
PRINCE CREEK DR	20200	486F	SWC	77450
PRINCE EDWARD CT	20400	335Q	HM	77338
PRINCE GEORGE CT	1700	445U	NWC	77449
PRINCE GEORGE DR	0	657H	FR	77546
PRINCE GEORGE DR	3100	657L	FR	77546
PRINCE GEORGE LN	22200	445U	NWC	77449
PRINCE JEFFRY LN	2300	445T	NWC	77493
PRINCE LAWRENCE CT	23700	445T	NWC	77493
PRINCE PINE CT	16900	578Y	SEH	77059
PRINCE PINE TRAIL	4400	578Y	SEH	77059
PRINCE RANCH DR	0	366P	NWC	77433
PRINCE RANCH DR	18700	366P	NWC	77433
PRINCESS DR	100	576G	SEH	77034
PRINCESS LN	2500	609D	MC	77459
PRINCESS BAY CT	3100	613R	PL	77584
PRINCESS DEANNA LN	2300	445T	NWC	77493
PRINCESS GARDEN WAY	11700	573N	SWH	77047
PRINCESS SNOW CIR	2200	445T	NWC	77493
PRINCETON	0	444U	KT	77493
PRINCETON	1200	532M	SWH	77030
PRINCETON	2200	453S	NWH	77009
PRINCETON	7000	532M	SWH	77030
PRINCETON DR	2500	613U	NEB	77584
PRINCETON LN	0	248D	SWM	77354
PRINCETON LN	700	538Y	DP	77536
E. PRINCETON LN	1100	538Y	DP	77536
PRINCETON PARK CT	3800	618D	PA	77058
PRINCETON PEAK	2100	612Y	NWB	77578
PRINCETON PLACE DR	0	249Z	NWC	77375
PRINCETON POINT CT	0	573Y	SEC	77047
PRINCE WILLIAM LN	18500	619W	NB	77058
PRINE LN	0	538V	DP	77536
PRIOR PARK DR	11900	572R	SWH	77047
PRISCILLA CT	300	457W	NEC	77015
PRISM LN	1700	449V	NWH	77043
PRISM COVE PLACE	1	251E	WD	77381
PRISTINE LAKE LN	13600	328S	NWC	77429
PRISTINE PARK CT	5500	448C	NWC	77041
PRISTINE PARK DR	13400	448C	NWC	77041
PRIVADA SARATOGA AVE	12000	413T	NEH	77076
PRIVET LN	13100	328X	NWC	77429
PRIVET GREEN WAY	0	326N	NWC	77433
PROCTOR	200	612E	NEF	77545
PROCTOR	11800	411G	NWC	77038
PROCTOR RD	15500	458X	CV	77530
PRODUCE ROW	2800	534F	SEH	77023
PROFAX DR	0	615F	PL	77581
PROFESSIONAL DR	0	335D	NEH	77339
PROFESSIONAL PARK DR	1	618T	WB	77598
PROFET	1	456W	NEH	77013
PROGRESS	0	463E	MB	77580
PROGRESSO DR	900	412A	NWC	77038
PROGRESS RIDGE WAY DR	0	326V	NWC	77429
PROKOP CT	400	617R	SEH	77598
PROMENADE	0	485D	SWC	77450
PROMENADE BLVD	0	569Q	SF	77477
N. PROMENADE BLVD	13100	569L	SF	77477
PROMENADE LN	6100	614U	PL	77584
PROMENADE ESTATES LN	0	569Q	SF	77477
PROMENADE PARK LN	0	569Q	SF	77477
PROMISE DR	0	285Q	NWC	77447
PRONGHORN DR	0	250K	NWC	77389
PRONGHORN PLACE	0	250L	NWC	77389
PROSE CT	22000	291R	NWC	77389
PROSEWOOD CT	1	251C	WD	77381
PROSEWOOD DR	1	251C	WD	77381
PROSPECT	1000	493W	SWH	77004
PROSPECT	1300	533B	SEH	77004
PROSPECT CANYON LN	0	406G	NWC	77433
PROSPECT GLEN LN	2000	446T	NWC	77449
PROSPECT HILL DR	10000	409C	NWC	77064
PROSPECT MEADOWS DR	17400	367X	NWC	77095
PROSPECT PLACE	1	531K	BL	77401
PROSPECT POINT DR	14000	367D	NWC	77429
PROSPECT RIDGE LN	19100	486D	SWC	77094
PROSPER	700	412U	NWH	77088
PROSPERITY AVE	0	535Z	SEH	77017
PROSPERITY AVE	0	535Z	SEH	77017

Street Name	Block	Pg/Sq	Loc	Zips
PROSPERITY CIR	0	452F	NWH	77018
PROSPERITY RIDGE DR	13900	573V	SEH	77048
PROSPERITY RIVER CT	12500	528M	SWH	77072
PROSPER RIDGE DR	0	368E	NWC	77429
PROST CT	3900	296V	NEH	77339
PROSWIMMER	3100	411R	NWH	77088
PROVDENT GREEN DR	0	406U	NWC	77449
PROVENCE LN	16500	367V	NWC	77095
PROVENCE SPUR	0	285X	NWC	77447
PROVENCE SQUARE	0	285X	NWC	77447
PROVIDENCE	0	617W	FR	77546
PROVIDENCE	1100	493H	NEH	77002
PROVIDENCE	1600	494G	NEH	77020
PROVIDENCE	3700	577C	PA	77505
PROVIDENCE DR	500	616Z	FR	77546
PROVIDENCE BAY DR	0	578T	SEH	77059
PROVIDENCE BLUFF DR	0	290S	NWC	77379
PROVIDENCE CREEK CT	0	405P	NWC	77493
PROVIDENCE GLEN TRAIL	0	405S	NWC	77493
PROVIDENCE LANDING LN	0	526R	NEF	77407
PROVIDENCE OAK	19600	446Q	NWC	77084
PROVIDENCE PARK	11700	490K	BH	77024
PROVIDENCE PINE TRAIL	14200	618A	SEH	77062
PROVIDENCE POINT DR	0	406U	NWC	77449
PROVIDENCE RIDGE TRAIL	0	405T	NWC	77493
PROVIDENCE RIVER LN	0	405T	NWC	77493
PROVIDENCE VIEW LN	0	457Q	NEC	77049
PROVIDENT OAKS LN	1200	488L	SWH	77077
PROVIDENT OAKS LN	1200	488L	SWH	77077
PROVINCE PLACE DR	400	485C	SWC	77450
PROVINCE POINT DR	12400	496D	NEC	77015
PROVINCE VILLAGE DR	0	615R	PL	77581
PROVINCIAL BLVD	21500	486A	SWC	77450
PROVINCIAL BLVD	21900	485C	SWC	77450
PROVOST LN	5700	408X	NWC	77084
PROW WAY	400	379X	NEC	77532
PRUDENCE DR	3200	572N	SWH	77045
PRUDENCE DR	5200	571Q	SWH	77045
PRUDENTIAL CIR	1	568T	SG	77478
S. PRUETT	100	501K	BT	77520
N. PRUETT	100	501Y	BT	77520
S. PRUETT	700	541B	BT	77520
N. PRUETT	3000	501Y	BT	77521
PRUETT	23900	339K	HU	77336
PRUETT ST	0	339K	HU	77336
PRUITT	100	252W	SWM	77380
PRUITT	1000	292L	SP	77373
PRYOR DR	15800	570Z	SWH	77489
PRYSON	6100	375J	NEH	77396
PSEUDO	0	340R	LCO	77535
PUCCOON TRAILS DR	29100	293F	SEM	77386
PUCKETT RIVER DR		367S	NWC	77433
PUEBLA RD	4600	571R	SWH	77045
PUEBLO	9700	462Y	BT	77521
PUEBLO	29000	323C	NWC	77484
PUEBLO CT	2600	659W	LC	77573
PUEBLO DR	18400	295G	SEM	77365
PUEBLO RUN	13900	328P	NWC	77429
PUEBLO TRAIL	4500	502J	BT	77521
PUERTA VALLAEA DR	7600	528K	SWC	77083
PUERTA VALLARTA DR	7200	528K	SWC	77083
PUERTA VISTA DR	6800	407E	NWC	77433
PUERTA VISTA LN	6800	528F	SWC	77083
PUGET LN	19300	331C	NWC	77388
PUGH DR	1100	496S	GP	77547
PULFORD CT	19300	486H	SWC	77094
PULP MILL CT	10500	528W	NEF	77498
PUMA	18800	378Q	NEC	77532
PUMICE POINT	22100	292J	NWC	77389
PUMPKIN ASH LN		289G	NWC	77375
PUMULIA ASH	16500	418Q	NEC	77044
PUNKIN	20700	256P	SEM	77357
PUPPY LN	4900	381W	NEC	77532
PURCELL POINT LN	0	378A	NEC	77346
PURDUE	1000	537P	PA	77502
PURDUE	3000	492W	SWH	77005
PURDUE LN	700	538Y	DP	77536
PURDUE PARK LN	0	253N	SEM	77386
PURDY CT	18500	447N	NWC	77084
PURELI CT		524M	NEF	77406
PURITAN VALLEY DR	20900	406P	NWC	77449
PURPLE CHERRY LN	1700	611T	NEF	77545
PURPLE CORNFLOWER TRAIL	8200	525A	NEF	77494
PURPLE HORSE DR	0	659G	LC	77573
PURPLEMARTIN	13800	528P	SWC	77083
PURPLE MEADOW LN	3600	297T	NEH	77345
PURPLE PLUM LN	2100	618G	SEH	77062
PURPLERIDGE CT	16100	611D	SWH	77053
PURPLE ROSE CT	1300	486H	SWC	77094
PURPLE SAGE RD	5600	457S	NEC	77049
PURPLE SAGE RD	7200	457J	NEC	77049
PURPLETOP CT	1	251J	WD	77381
PURSLANE DR	3300	446R	NWC	77449
PURSTON CT	0	527U	NEF	77083
PURSWELL RD	6600	451U	NWH	77055
PURUS DR	19200	294H	SEM	77365
PURVIS LN	6800	461M	NEC	77521
PUTNAM CT	24700	484G	NEF	77494
PUTTING GREEN DR	19000	337Z	NEC	77346
PYEATT LN	27000	252E	OR	77385
PYRAMID PEAK DR	0	377F	NEC	77346
PYRAMID PLACE	0	571K	SWH	77085
PYRENEES MOUNTAIN DR	0	450K	NWH	77080
PYRON WAY	7000	530E	SWH	77036

Q

Street Name	Block	Pg/Sq	Loc	Zips
Q	0	576R	SEH	77034
Q, AVENUE	6600	494R	SEH	77011
E. Q, AVENUE	9100	535D	SEH	77012
QOP LN	12000	368N	NWC	77429
QUACHITA	4500	414F	NCC	77039
QUADE LN	0	448K	NWH	77084
S. QUADRANT CT	16500	419A	NEC	77532
N. QUADRANT CT	16500	419A	NEC	77532
QUAIL	1500	536P	SEH	77017
QUAIL LN	18700	286H	NWC	77377
QUAIL'S PATH	14400	408K	NWC	77095
QUAIL'S TERRACE	14600	408P	NWC	77095
QUAIL BEND DR	17000	610G	SWH	77489
QUAIL BRIAR DR	16400	610C	SWH	77489
QUAIL BRIDGE LN	5400	611C	SWH	77053
QUAIL BROCK DR	18500	378A	NEC	77346
QUAIL BURG CT	17000	610G	SWH	77489
QUAIL BURG LN	8300	610G	SWH	77489
QUAIL CALL DR	16400	610C	SWH	77489
QUAIL CHASE DR	20500	486K	SWC	77450
QUAIL COVE LN	5400	611C	SWH	77053
QUAIL CREEK CT	100	490Q	PP	77024
QUAIL CREEK CT	14600	329W	NWC	77070
QUAIL CREEK DR	0	612L	PL	77545
QUAIL CREEK DR	2700	609H	MC	77459
QUAIL CREEK DR	11500	329W	NWC	77070
QUAIL CREEK DR	12100	328Z	NWC	77070
QUAIL CREST	0	570Y	MC	77489
QUAILCREST CT	16800	610C	SWH	77489
QUAILCREST DR	8300	610C	SWH	77489
QUAILCROFT DR	8500	610B	SWH	77489
QUAIL DALE DR	16500	610C	SWH	77489
QUAIL DOVE LN	0	658S	LC	77573
QUAIL ECHO DR	16300	610C	SWH	77489
QUAIL FARMS RD	14600	328K	NWC	77429
QUAIL FEATHER CT	1900	570X	MC	77489
QUAIL FEATHER DR	8600	610B	SWH	77489
QUAIL FIELD DR	7100	408P	NWC	77095
QUAIL FOREST DR	13600	328Y	NWC	77429
QUAIL FOREST PARK LN	12900	328Y	NWC	77429
QUAILGATE DR	4400	293Y	NCC	77373
QUAIL GLEN DR	16900	610G	SWH	77489
QUAIL GREEN CT	1900	570X	MC	77489
QUAIL GROVE LN	1800	610K	MC	77459
QUAIL GROVE LN	14700	488L	SWH	77079
QUAIL GULLY DR	16400	610C	SWH	77489
QUAIL HAVEN	2300	333A	NCC	77373
QUAIL HAVEN RD	2300	333A	NCC	77373
QUAIL HAWK DR	2900	371G	NWC	77014
QUAIL HILLS DR	8200	610B	SWH	77489
QUAIL HOLLOW CIR	3000	501E	BT	77521
QUAIL HOLLOW DR	2800	609H	MC	77459
QUAIL HOLLOW DR	4400	501E	BT	77521
QUAIL HOLLOW LN	11400	490L	PP	77024
QUAIL HOLLOW LN	12100	247R	SWM	77362
QUAIL HUNT LN	16300	610C	SWH	77489
QUAIL MEADOW DR	3400	610J	MC	77459
QUAIL MEADOW DR	6200	570D	SWH	77035
QUAIL MEADOW DR	7500	570C	SWH	77071
QUAIL MEADOW DR	16500	610C	SWH	77489
QUAILMONT DR	8600	610C	SWH	77489
QUAIL NEST CT	16300	610C	SWH	77489
QUAIL NEST RD	0	323X	NWC	77447
QUAIL OAK DR	2800	371G	NWC	77014
QUAIL OAK PARK LN	0	253N	SEM	77386
QUAIL PARK DR	8300	610G	SWH	77489
QUAIL PARK DR	12900	328Y	NWC	77429
QUAIL PARK DR	16300	610C	SWH	77489
QUAIL PLACE CT	1600	570X	MC	77489
QUAIL PLACE DR	1900	570X	MC	77489
QUAIL PLACE DR	16300	610C	SWH	77489
QUAIL POINT LN	21300	256W	SEM	77365
QUAIL PRAIRIE DR	16400	610C	SWH	77489
QUAIL RIDGE DR	0	444T	KT	77493
QUAIL RIDGE LN	10500	528X	NEF	77498
QUAIL ROCK CIR	15100	408P	NWC	77095
QUAIL RUN CIR	0	255A	SEM	77302
QUAIL RUN CT	8400	610C	SWH	77489
QUAIL RUN DR	2600	375L	HM	77396
QUAIL RUN DR	4000	614X	PL	77584
QUAIL RUN DR	16300	610C	SWH	77489
QUAIL SHOT DR	8300	610C	SWH	77489
QUAIL SHUTE	23000	291E	NWC	77389
QUAIL TERRACE LN	0	253J	SEM	77385
QUAIL TERRACE LN	0	253J	SEM	77385
QUAIL THICKET LN	0	610G	SWH	77489
QUAIL TRACE DR	1500	610B	MC	77489
QUAIL TREE LN	5300	337N	NEC	77346
QUAIL VALLEY DR	3000	609H	MC	77459
QUAIL VALLEY EAST DR	1800	610E	MC	77459
QUAIL VALLEY EAST DR	2600	610E	MC	77489
QUAIL VIEW CT	16700	610C	SWH	77489
QUAIL VIEW DR	8300	610C	SWH	77489
QUAIL VILLAGE DR	3500	609C	MC	77459
QUAIL VILLAGE DR	5800	611F	SWH	77053
QUAIL VISTA DR	8600	610C	SWH	77489
QUAILWOOD	2600	371G	NWC	77014
QUAILWOOD DR	1	501E	BT	77521
QUAILYNN CT	16300	610C	SWH	77489
QUAILYNN DR	16400	610C	SWH	77489
QUAKER	1700	495L	NEH	77029
QUAKER DR	200	616Z	FR	77546
QUAKER DR	500	656D	FR	77546
QUAKER DR	900	657A	FR	77546
QUAKER LN	14100	375W	NEC	77396
QUAKER BEND DR	900	657A	FR	77546
QUAKING ASPEN LN	14700	288A	NWC	77377
QUALITY HILL	11300	490L	PP	77024
QUANAH	2700	454W	NEH	77026
QUANDER LN	11900	371M	NWC	77067
QUANTAH	11700	490K	BH	77024
QUARK	0	374P	NEH	77032
QUARRY HILL RD	2600	568Z	SG	77478
QUARRY LAKES LN	0	526Q	NEF	77407
QUARR YPATH WAY	0	445K	NWC	77493
QUARRY PATH WAY	0	445K	NWC	77493
QUARRY PLACE LN	0	445F	NWC	77493
QUARRY PLACE LN	0	445K	NWC	77493
QUARRY RIDGE RD	5400	526S	NEF	77407
QUARRY VALE DR	18000	328E	NWC	77377
QUARTER HORSE TRAIL	0	612Z	NEB	77578
QUARTERS LN	2600	491U	SWH	77056
QUARTER WAY	15800	419E	NEC	77532
QUARTZ COVE CT		526S	NEF	77407
QUARTZ CREEK LN	0	334L	NCC	77388
QUARTZ LAKE DR	0	377E	NEC	77346
QUARTZSITE ST	0	658Y	LC	77573
QUARTZ TRAIL	0	292D	SEM	77386
QUAST DR	0	286E	SWM	77447
QUATRO LN		524M	NEF	77406
QUEBEC	4900	491P	SWH	77057
QUEBEC DR	8300	531S	SWH	77096
QUEEN	7700	455P	NEH	77028
QUEEN RD	100	620T	CS	77565
QUEEN ST	1200	568T	SG	77478
QUEEN ANNES RD	800	491A	SWH	77024
QUEENBURY HILLS DR	0	332R	NCC	77073
QUEENCROSS LN	0	332R	NCC	77073
QUEENLOCH CT	0	531S	SWH	77096
QUEENS	1900	535V	SEH	77017
QUEENS CT	100	500N	BT	77520
QUEENS CT	100	569V	SF	77477
QUEENS LN	1	656D	FR	77546
QUEENS RD	100	536U	PA	77502
QUEENS BAY DR	1400	485E	NEF	77494
QUEENSBRIDGE DR	9700	528S	NEF	77498
QUEENSBURG LN	0	657L	FR	77546
QUEENSBURY LN	11900	490A	SWH	77024
QUEENSBURY LN	12900	489A	SWH	77079
QUEENSCLUB DR	6500	330X	NWC	77069
QUEENSDALE DR	16100	527C	SWC	77082
QUEENSFERRY CT	3500	299S	NEC	77336
QUEENSFIELD CT	24600	485S	NEF	77494
QUEENSFORD LN	0	447C	NWC	77084
QUEENSGATE DR	5800	370C	NWC	77066
QUEENS GLEN DR	0	296X	SEM	77339
QUEENSLAKE DR	17200	367A	CY	77429
QUEENSLAND	5400	455Q	NEH	77028
QUEENSLAND WAY	13400	528P	SWH	77099
QUEENSLOCH DR	5100	531S	SWH	77096
QUEENSLOCH DR	6000	530V	SWH	77096
QUEENSMILL CT	700	488E	SWH	77079
QUEENS OAK CT	20000	289Y	NWC	77379
QUEENS RETREAT DR	4300	371A	NWC	77066
QUEENSRIDE LN	13300	369F	NWC	77070
QUEENS RIVER DR	0	416L	NEC	77044
QUEENSTON BLVD	4100	447C	NWC	77084
QUEENSTON BLVD	5200	407Y	NWC	77084
QUEENSTON BLVD	7700	407G	NWC	77095
QUEENSTON BLVD	8400	407C	NWC	77095
QUEENSTON BLVD	12300	367Q	NWC	77095
QUEENSTOWN LN	300	457X	NEC	77015
QUEENS WAY CIR	0	416L	NEC	77044
QUEENSWOOD	4200	502K	BT	77521
QUEENSWOOD LN	6100	492C	NWH	77008
QUEEN VICTORIA	2900	615L	PL	77581
QUE MANOR DR	2000	331Q	NWC	77379
QUENBY	2000	532B	WU	77005
QUENNELL CIR	15500	373Q	NCC	77032
QUENTIN CANYON CT	6200	526E	NEF	77450
QUENTION DR	13800	572N	SWH	77045
QUERIDA CT	0	571H	SWH	77045
QUERIDA CT	0	571H	SWH	77045
QUESO LN	7000	459L	NEC	77049
QUEST BROOK LN	0	296X	SEM	77339
QUETZAL LN	13500	528G	SWC	77083
QUICKSILVER CT	11700	371L	NWC	77067
QUICK STREAM PLACE	1	250G	WD	77381
QUIET LN	11400	415P	NEC	77016
QUIET ARBOR LN	0	614J	NEB	77581
QUIET BAY	2300	613J	PL	77584
QUIET BAY CT	15700	408N	NWC	77095
QUIET BEND DR	2700	610E	MC	77489
QUIET BLUFF LN	14200	488N	SWH	77077
QUIET BROOK DR	19300	446V	NWC	77084
QUIET CANYON	4900	617X	SEC	77546
QUIET CANYON CT	16200	617X	SEC	77546
QUIET CHASE LN	0	328K	NWC	77377
QUIET COUNTRY CT	1800	338A	NEH	77345
QUIET COVE DR	0	568J	NEF	77498
QUIET COVE LN	0	415S	NEH	77016
QUIET COVEY CT	17200	610G	SWH	77489
QUIET CREEK DR	15300	408E	NWC	77095
QUIET CROSSING LN	0	406F	NWC	77433
QUIET DALE CT	17000	407L	NWC	77095
QUIET DAWN CT	17600	407F	NWC	77095
QUIET DAWN LN	0	609Y	NEF	77459
QUIET FALLS	5000	485Y	NEF	77450
QUIET FALLS DR	0	613X	NEB	77578
QUIET FALLS LN	2100	658S	LC	77573
QUIET FOREST	36000	246L	SWM	77355
QUIET FOREST DR	7500	410Q	NWC	77040
QUIET GLADE CT	4000	297T	NEH	77345
QUIET GLEN DR	3200	297Z	NEH	77345
QUIET GREEN CT	1400	618A	SEH	77062
QUIET GROVE CT	18000	376D	NEC	77346
QUIET GROVE LN	7000	376H	NEC	77346
QUIET HERON CT	0	445K	NWC	77493
QUIET HILL RD	9900	579B	LP	77571
QUIET KNOLL CT	3900	618D	PA	77059
QUIET LAKE CT	0	612K	PL	77545
QUIET LAKE CT	2200	619Z	LC	77573
QUIET LAKE CT	22800	485U	NEF	77450
QUIET LAKE DR	3200	485U	NEF	77450
QUIET LAKE LN	0	612K	PL	77545
QUIET LEDGE DR	0	296U	SEM	77365
QUIET LOCH CT	4500	447G	NWC	77084
QUIET LOCH LN	17600	447G	NWC	77084
QUIET LOCH LN	17600	447G	NWC	77084
QUIET MANOR CT	0	657T	FR	77546
QUIET MANOR LN	4600	609J	NEF	77479
QUIET MEADOW CT	3600	613X	NEB	77578
QUIET MEADOW CT	5900	577D	PA	77505
QUIET MEADOW CT	12200	568D	MD	77477
QUIET MEADOWS DR	2400	371M	NWC	77067
QUIET PARK DR	0	568J	NEF	77498
QUIET PATH DR	0	568J	NEF	77498
QUIET PEACE	0	250D	WD	77381
QUIET PEACE PLACE	1	250D	WD	77381
QUIET PINES CT	0	253U	SEM	77386
QUIET PINES LN	0	612U	PL	77584
QUIET PLACE DR	0	568J	NEF	77498
QUIET PLACE DR	3700	527B	SWC	77082
QUIET POINT LN	5900	609U	NEF	77479
QUIET POINTE DR	6300	250U	NWC	77389
QUIET PRAIRIE TRAIL	0	457C	NEC	77049
QUIET QUAIL DR	16500	610C	SWH	77489
QUIET RIDGE LN	18100	326V	NWC	77429
QUIET RIVER LN	0	614J	PL	77581
QUIET ROSE LN	20700	290U	NWC	77379
QUIET SAGE LN	0	485J	NEF	77494
QUIET SHORES DR	0	527W	NEF	77469
QUIET SKY PLACE	0	294P	SEM	77386
QUIET SKY PLACE DR	0	294E	SEM	77386
QUIET SPRINGS LN	800	617H	SEH	77062
QUIET STREAM CT	18000	407K	NWC	77095
QUIET SUMMER CT	0	417C	NEH	77044
QUIET SUMMER LN	0	417C	NEH	77044
QUIET TIMBERS LN	0	484Z	NEF	77494
QUIET TOWN LN	14300	528W	NEF	77498
QUIET TRACE LN	0	614N	PL	77581
QUIET TRAIL DR	16600	376L	NEC	77396
QUIET VALLEY LN	10200	575P	SEH	77075
QUIET VILLAGE CT	6000	611B	SWH	77053
QUIET VILLAS LN	0	575V	SEH	77075
QUIET VISTA DR	0	568J	NEF	77498
QUIET WATER CT	12000	369W	NWC	77065
QUIET WAY	0	246B	SWM	77355
QUIET WAY LN	0	568J	NEF	77498
QUIET WOOD CT	13300	371Z	NWC	77038
QUILL DR	15800	329U	NWC	77070
QUILL BACK DR	4600	617T	SEC	77546
QUILL MEADOW DR	3000	659D	LC	77573
QUILL RUSH WAY	5000	526X	NEF	77406
QUINCANNON LN	2600	449M	NWH	77043
QUINCE	7000	535E	SEH	77087
QUINCEWOOD DR	11400	616C	SEC	77089
QUINCY CT	20300	335P	HM	77338
QUINN	0	656F	NEB	77581
QUINN	300	493B	NWH	77009
QUINN RD	29500	288F	TB	77375
QUINN RD	30300	288B	TB	77375
QUINN RD	30500	248X	TB	77375
QUINN, PAUL	700	452A	NWH	77091
QUINN RIDGE WAY	11600	411H	NWC	77088
QUINTANA ROO PLACE	600	620H	SB	77586
QUINTERO DR	7600	528K	SWC	77083
QUINTHER CT	0	290P	NWC	77379
QUINTO LN	10600	369X	NWC	77064
QUION CT	700	379X	NEC	77532
QUITMAN	100	493C	NEH	77009
QUITMAN	1700	494B	NEH	77026
QUITMAN CT	4200	494B	NEH	77026
QUITMAN DR	3700	577D	PA	77505
QUIVER LN	2200	371M	NWC	77067
QUIVERA PLACE	0	250P	NWC	77389
QUIVIRA TRACE	2600	659C	LC	77573
QUORUM	3300	374P	NEH	77032
S. R	100	580G	LP	77571

R

Street Name	Block	Pg/Sq	Loc	Zips
R F MALEK LN	0	371Q	NWC	77067
R V MAYFIELD	3500	411V	NWH	77088
R W J	0	503M	BC	77520
R, AVENUE	6600	494R	SEH	77011
E. R, AVENUE	9200	535C	SEH	77012
RABBIT HOLLOW DR	7100	461M	NEC	77521
RABBIT HOLLOW DR	7300	462J	NEC	77521
RABBIT OAK DR	10300	368X	NWC	77065
RABBIT RIDGE	0	609Z	NEF	77459
RABBIT RUN PLACE	0	249C	SWM	77382
RABUN CT	0	407W	NWC	77449
RACCOON DR	3800	502F	NEC	77521
RACCOON LN	1	251V	WD	77380
RACCOON RUN CT	3100	333B	NCC	77373
RACE	1700	493M	SWH	77002
RACHAEL LN	200	616Y	FR	77546
RACHEL	600	452C	NWH	77091
RACHEL CT	1300	616U	PL	77581
N. RACHEL CT	2500	616U	PL	77581
RACHEL LN	3000	444L	KT	77493
RACHEL'S WAY	700	612S	FS	77545
RACHELLE CT	4800	485Z	NEF	77450
RACHELLE RIDGE CT	5000	577G	PA	77505
RACHELS CT	6100	525G	NEF	77494
RACHELS MANOR DR	22800	485U	NEF	77494
RACHELS WAY	12700	570K	MC	77489
RACHELS WAY CT	0	329K	NWC	77375
RACHELYNN	0	371K	NWC	77066
E. RACHLIN CIR	8600	570F	SWH	77071
S. RACHLIN CIR	12400	570F	SWH	77071
N. RACHLIN CIR	12400	570F	SWH	77071
RACINE	9700	495R	NEH	77029
W. RACING CLOUD CT	1	251K	WD	77381
E. RACING CLOUD CT	1	251K	WD	77381
RACK	9800	573B	SEH	77051
RACKINGHAM PLACE	19700	335S	NCC	77338
RACQUET CT	7000	330W	NWC	77069
RACQUET RIDGE RD	18700	337Z	NEC	77346
RACQUET SPORTS WAY	18700	338W	NEC	77346
RADBROOK LN	14300	489J	SWH	77079
RADCLIFF	5700	454G	NEH	77016
RADCLIFFE	1700	492C	NWH	77007
RADCLIFFE	4300	535V	SEH	77017
RADCLIFFE	6400	412Y	NWH	77091
RADCLIFF LAKE DR	0	524A	NEF	77494
RADENZ RD	12600	371E	NWC	77066
RADER	12600	371A	NWC	77066
RADFORD LN	10800	569B	SWH	77099
RADFORD PARK CIR	14100	618A	SEH	77062
W. RADHA LN	0	452P	NWH	77018
RADIAL	4900	533R	SEH	77021
RADIANT DAWN	7700	528J	NEF	77083
RADIANT LN	0	445A	NWC	77493
RADIANT LILAC TRAIL	0	326J	NWC	77433
RADIANT REALM DR		289P	NWC	77375
RADIATA PINE CROSSING	0	328E	NWC	77377
RADIO RD	8700	575M	SEH	77075
RADLEY CT	16300	330M	NWC	77379
RADLEY DR	6500	330M	NWC	77379
RADLEY DR	9800	528S	NEF	77498
RADNEY CIR	1	490Q	PP	77024
RADNEY RD	100	490Q	PP	77024
RADNEY ROAD ESTATES	1	490Q	PP	77024
RADNOR	0	490J	SWH	77024
RADRICK LN	22800	485L	SWC	77450
RADS POINT	0	527U	NEF	77498
RADSTOCK DR	14900	618J	SEH	77062
RADWELL CT	15000	617M	SEH	77062
RADWORTHY DR	18000	447B	NWC	77084
RAES CREEK DR	0	250X	NWC	77389
RAESTONE	28700	293A	SEM	77386
RAESTONE	29200	253W	SEM	77386
RAFAEL	9600	455Z	NEH	77013
RAFAM DR	0	578A	PA	77505
RAFFAELLO DR	0	616K	PL	77089
RAFFIA LEAVES WAY	0	332X	NWC	77090
RAFTERS ROW	0	251K	WD	77380
RAFTER THREE DR	24000	325J	NWC	77447
RAGE RD	0	543D	BC	77520
RAGLAND DR	2100	371V	NWC	77067
RAGSDALE CT	1200	485F	SWC	77494
RAGSDALE LN	1200	485F	SWC	77494
RAGUSA LN	0	659M	LC	77573
RAGUS LAKE DR	14000	568E	SG	77498
RAIA LN	12500	570G	MC	77071
W. RAIDER CIR	1	450P	NWH	77080
S. RAIDER CIR	1	450P	NWH	77080
N. RAIDER CIR	1	450P	NWH	77080
E. RAIDER CIR	1	450P	NWH	77080
RAIDER RD	100	620Y	KE	77565
RAILEY	300	453X	NWH	77009
RAILHEAD LN	7300	411A	NWH	77086
RAILHEAD LN	7500	410D	NWH	77086
RAILROAD	0	540T	LP	77571
W. RAILROAD	4800	538F	DP	77536
RAILROAD AVE	0	659E	LC	77573
RAILROAD DR	5200	502B	NEC	77521
RAILROAD BED CROSSING	0	366S	NWC	77433
RAILSPUR	7000	455M	NEH	77078
RAILTON	8900	450K	NWH	77080
RAILWAY	5000	502B	NEC	77521
RAILWOOD	2900	502B	NEC	77521
RAILWOOD DR	8800	455M	NEH	77078
RAINA LN	11600	490G	BH	77024
RAINARCH ST	0	446J	NWC	77449
RAIN BARREL DR	0	299X	NEC	77336
RAINBIRD PLACE	1	251J	WD	77381
RAINBLUFF LN	0	524C	NEF	77494
RAINBOURNE LN	0	657Y	LC	77573
RAINBOW CT	3100	613X	NEB	77584
RAINBOW DR	2000	534H	SEH	77023
RAINBOW LN	0	242D	WCO	77484
RAINBOW LN	0	257K	SEM	77357
RAINBOW LN	0	257K	SEM	77357
RAINBOW BEND DR	7600	578G	PA	77505
RAINBOW BEND LN	22800	485L	SWC	77450
RAINBOW BRIDGE LN	11700	376H	NEC	77346
RAINBOW CREEK DR	0	406U	NWC	77449
RAINBOW FALLS	13400	528F	SWC	77083

Street Name	Block	Pg/Sq	Loc	Zips
RAINBOW GLEN DR	11000	369Y	NWC	77064
RAINBOW GRANITE DR	20600	526S	NEF	77407
RAINBOW LAKE RD	16000	407M	NWC	77095
W. RAINBOW RIDGE CIR	1	250D	WD	77381
N. RAINBOW RIDGE CIR	100	250D	WD	77381
E. RAINBOW RIDGE CIR	100	250D	WD	77381
RAINBOW RUN	4600	609E	SG	77479
RAINBOW VALLEY CT	4600	610P	MC	77459
RAIN CLOUD DR	0	368X	NWC	77095
RAINCOVE DR	11300	415N	NEH	77016
RAIN CREEK CT	8900	289D	NWC	77375
RAIN CREEK DR	24000	289D	NWC	77375
RAINCREST DR	20500	446K	NWC	77449
RAIN DANCE DR	14900	372B	NWC	77090
RAINDREAM PLACE	1	250D	WD	77381
W. RAINDROP	0	614F	PL	77581
E. RAINDROP	0	614F	PL	77581
RAIN DROP CT	0	526J	NEF	77407
RAINDROP HOLLOW DR	4900	449H	NWH	77041
RAINDROP POPPY DR	0	292Z	NCC	77373
RAINDROPS RD	3600	578A	PA	77505
RAINER DR	0	577J	OY	77504
RAINER CREEK DR	0	377L	NEC	77346
RAINER VALLEY LN	0	377E	NEC	77346
RAINESVILLE LN	8800	575U	SEH	77075
S. RAINFALL	0	614F	PL	77581
N. RAINFALL	0	614F	PL	77581
RAINFALL	0	614F	PL	77581
RAINFALL DR	4200	578G	PA	77505
RAINFALL PARK DR	0	291P	NWC	77388
RAIN FERN CT	1	251R	WD	77380
RAINFERN DR	22200	245Q	SWM	77355
RAINFIELD CT	5200	485W	NEF	77494
S. RAINFLOWER CIR	5100	657V	LC	77573
N. RAINFLOWER CIR	5100	657V	LC	77573
RAINFLOWER MEADOW LN	0	484N	NEF	77494
RAINFLOWER TERRACE LN	0	290D	NWC	77389
S. RAIN FOREST CT	1	251Z	WD	77380
N. RAIN FOREST CT	1	251Z	WD	77380
RAINFOREST DR	15400	375P	NWH	77396
RAIN FOREST DR	23500	339P	HU	77336
RAINFOREST TRAIL DR	7500	578L	PA	77505
RAINGATE LN	20000	446T	NWC	77449
RAINGLEN LN	0	457A	NEC	77044
RAINGOLD DR	0	335P	NCC	77338
RAINGREEN DR	20600	446K	NWC	77449
RAINHILL CT	3200	446P	NWC	77449
RAIN HOLLOW	1	490E	SWH	77024
RAINHOLLOW DR	15200	329W	NWC	77070
RAINIER CT	2300	336B	NEH	77339
RAINIER DR	300	490J	BH	77024
RAINLAKE TRAIL	2000	378G	NEC	77532
RAIN LEAF CT	21600	335J	NCC	77338
RAIN LILY	1	245U	SWM	77355
RAIN LILY CT	2100	615K	PL	77581
RAINLILY DR	1900	447W	NWH	77084
RAIN LILY LN	13200	528C	SWH	77083
RAIN LILY CROSSING	0	525A	NEF	77494
RAINMEAD DR	20700	446K	NWC	77449
RAIN MEADOW LN	7400	407J	NWC	77433
W. RAINMILL DR	3400	446K	NWC	77449
E. RAINMILL DR	3400	446K	NWC	77449
N. RAINMILL DR	20700	446K	NWC	77449
RAINMILL DR	20700	446K	NWC	77449
RAINMONT LN	2900	446P	NWC	77449
RAINPARK LN	3100	446P	NWC	77449
RAINPORT CIR	20500	446K	NWC	77449
RAINPORT DR	3300	446K	NWC	77449
RAINPRINT RD	0	250H	WD	77381
RAINS	1	493M	SWH	77003
RAIN SHADOW CT	14900	328Z	NWC	77070
RAINSHORE DR	3300	446K	NWC	77449
RAINSTONE CT	20500	446P	NWC	77449
RAINS WAY	1	492K	SWH	77007
RAINTERRA DR	0	446K	NWC	77449
RAINTREE	1600	502S	BT	77520
RAINTREE	5600	614F	PL	77581
RAINTREE CIR	1300	568W	SG	77479
RAINTREE CIR	1800	620E	EL	77586
RAINTREE CIR	11500	490Q	PP	77024
RAINTREE CT	4300	578L	PA	77505
RAINTREE DR	2700	568V	SG	77478
RAINTREE DR	6100	614Q	PL	77584
RAINTREE PLACE	0	258Q	NEC	77357
RAINTREE RIDGE LN	0	375Y	NEC	77396
RAINTREE VILLAGE DR	2400	446K	NWC	77449
RAINTREE VILLAGE DR	2400	446S	NWC	77449
RAIN VALLEY CT	8600	456H	NEC	77044
RAIN WALK CT	1	251Z	WD	77380
RAINWATER	0	614F	PL	77581
RAINWATER CT	0	612F	PL	77545
RAINWATER DR	0	612E	PL	77545
RAINWATER DR	4800	577C	PA	77505
RAINWATER CREEK LN	0	367S	NWC	77433
RAIN WILLOW CT	4000	572W	SWH	77053
RAINWOOD	600	489E	SWH	77079
RAINWOOD	2900	291V	NWC	77388
RAINWOOD DR	0	612N	PL	77545
RAINWOOD FALLS LN	0	377U	NEC	77044
RAINWOOD PARK LN	0	253N	SEM	77386
RAINWOOD PARK LN	5200	525C	NEF	77450
RAINY CANYON LN	0	524M	NEF	77406
RAINY DAWN CT	0	376V	NEC	77396
RAINY DUSK CT	0	376V	NEC	77396
RAINY HEATH CT	0	446C	NWC	77449
RAINY MEADOW LN	400	496A	NEH	77013
RAINY MORNING DR	0	376V	NEC	77396
RAINY RIVER	4200	577E	PA	77504
RAINY RIVER DR	500	412M	NCC	77037
RAINY RIVER DR	800	412J	NWC	77088
RAINY SUN CIR	6000	457S	NEC	77049
RALEIGH	3200	533K	SEH	77021
RALEIGH CREEK DR	0	248Z	NWC	77375
RALEIGH GREEN TRAIL	15700	325M	NWC	77433
RALEIGH OAK LN	15700	326P	NWC	77433
RALFALLEN	700	453W	NWH	77008
RALFALLEN DR	0	613T	NEB	77584
RALICK CT	7500	330F	NWC	77379
RALLY RUN CIR	8400	338W	NEC	77346
RALPH	2400	492V	SWH	77006
RALPH CIR	21800	245Z	SWM	77355
RALPHCREST DR	1100	373Y	NCC	77039
RALPH CULVER RD	13000	371Y	NWC	77086
RALSTON	2500	494B	NEH	77026
RALSTON	6700	454P	NEH	77016
RALSTON LN	17800	322B	WCO	77484
RALSTON RD	17700	376B	NEC	77396
RALSTON, JOHN	500	496B	NEH	77013
RALSTON, JOHN	6400	456C	NEC	77049
RALSTON, JOHN	6900	416U	NEC	77044
RALSTON, JOHN	14700	376T	NEC	77396
RALSTON BEND LN	0	524G	NEF	77494

Street Name	Block	Pg/Sq	Loc	Zips
RALSTON EDGE LN	0	578X	SEH	77059
RALSTONS RIDGE DR	8500	528Q	SWC	77083
RAM CT	4400	529E	SWH	77072
RAMADA DR	700	618L	SEH	77062
RAMBLEBROOK CT	8300	375Z	NEC	77396
RAMBLEBROOK LN	0	609T	NEF	77479
RAMBLEBROOK LN	14800	375Z	NEC	77396
RAMBLE CREEK DR	3600	610X	MC	77459
RAMBLER DR	9300	417X	NEC	77044
RAMBLERIDGE DR	6400	611B	SWH	77053
RAMBLEWOOD DR	19500	336S	NEC	77338
RAMBLEWOOD RD	400	489E	SWH	77079
RAMBLEWOOD PARK	400	486D	SWC	77094
RAMBLING BROOK DR	2200	333E	NCC	77373
RAMBLING CREEK DR	3200	297Z	NEH	77345
RAMBLING OAK DR	0	524A	NWF	77494
RAMBLING OAKS DR	29000	299J	NEC	77336
RAMBLING PINES DR	3400	297Y	NEH	77345
RAMBLING RIVER WAY	15500	326S	NWC	77433
RAMBLING ROSE DR	12000	488M	SWH	77077
RAMBLING TRAIL	9700	576S	SEH	77089
RAMBLING TREE LN	7000	526F	NEF	77407
RAMBLING WOOD CT	1	252N	WD	77380
RAMEY	9800	576S	SEH	77075
RAMEY CIR	1	576S	SEH	77075
RAMIE	0	375W	NEC	77396
RAMIN DR	8900	454F	NEH	77093
RAMIREZ	800	569P	NEF	77477
RAMLA PLACE TRAIL	0	616H	SEH	77089
RAMONA	12400	368M	NWC	77429
RAMONES DR	0	293G	SEM	77386
RAMOS DR	0	293B	SEM	77386
RAMPART	1800	658K	LC	77573
RAMPART	5400	531E	SWH	77081
RAMPART	10700	531W	SWH	77096
RAMPART	11100	571E	SWH	77035
RAMPART CT	200	658K	LC	77573
RAMPCHESTER LN	13200	457X	NEC	77015
RAMP CREEK LN	11100	568A	NEF	77498
RAMP RDS	0	495T	NEH	77029
RAMPY GREEN DR	0	328M	NWC	77377
RAM ROCK	0	501J	BT	77521
RAMROCK CIR	21000	296N	SEM	77365
RAMROCK CT	21000	296N	SEM	77365
RAMROCK DR	25000	296N	SEM	77365
RAMROD CT	20300	285M	NWC	77447
RAMSAY LN	0	657U	LC	77573
RAMS BOTTOM CT	500	292W	NWC	77388
RAMSEY	0	533N	SWH	77054
RAMSEY	200	501U	BT	77520
RAMSEY DR	3500	537Q	PA	77503
RAMSEY RD	300	338R	NEH	77336
RAMSEY RD	15800	419D	CB	77532
RAMSEY RD	16900	379Z	NEC	77532
RAMSEY RD	18000	380N	NEC	77532
RAMSEY HEIGHTS WAY	0	295Q	SEM	77365
S. RAMSEY LOOP RD	100	380N	NEC	77532
RAMSEY LOOP RD	2400	380J	NEC	77532
RAMSEY RD EXT	0	339R	NEC	77535
RAMSGATE DR	3400	291Q	NWC	77388
RAMUS	4700	451U	NWH	77092
RANA CT	15500	331S	NWC	77068
RANCH	3700	494B	NEH	77026
RANCH LN	0	573L	SEH	77047
RANCH CANYON DR	0	406Y	NWC	77449
RANCH COUNTRY DR	17000	325E	NWC	77447
RANCH CREEK WAY	0	248C	SWM	77354
RANCH CROSS BLVD	0	406Y	NWC	77449
RANCHER HOLLOW CT	0	613W	NEB	77578
RANCHERIA DR	7100	527M	SWC	77083
RANCHERO DR	7800	459L	NEC	77049
RANCHESTER DR	5700	530E	SWH	77036
RANCH GATE DR	0	407J	NWC	77433
RANCHGLEN LN	0	366Q	NWC	77433
RANCH HAVEN CT	20000	256W	SEM	77365
RANCH HOLLOW CT	0	485P	NEF	77494
RANCH HOUSE LN	0	366L	NWC	77433
RANCH LAKE LN	2600	485N	NEF	77494
RANCHLAND LN	0	327U	NWC	77429
RANCHLAND LN	0	613W	NEB	77578
RANCH MILL LN	20500	406G	NWC	77433
RANCHO	0	528J	SWC	77083
RANCHO DR	0	657Q	FR	77546
RANCH OAK DR	0	373E	NCC	77073
RANCH OAKS DR	0	524A	NEF	77494
RANCHO BAUER	36700	246G	SWM	77355
RANCHO BAUER DR	300	489J	SWH	77079
RANCHO BELLA PKWY	0	524R	NEF	77406
RANCHO BERNARDO LN	10200	528X	NEF	77498
RANCHO BLANCO CT	6400	527F	SWC	77083
RANCHO BLANCO DR	16200	527F	SWC	77083
RANCHO GRANDE DR	1900	458S	NEC	77049
RANCHO MIRAGE DR	7100	370A	NWC	77069
RANCHO MISSION DR	7200	528J	SWC	77083
RANCHO MISSION DR	7300	527M	SWC	77083
RANCHO PALOMA BLVD	16400	458N	NEC	77049
RANCHO VERDE WAY	17200	367U	NWC	77095
RANCHO VISTA	0	527H	SWC	77083
RANCHO VISTA DR	4000	577B	PA	77504
RANCHO VISTA DR	14700	528E	SWC	77083
RANCH POINT DR	0	524A	NWF	77494
RANCH POINT DR		484W	NEF	77494
RANCHPORT LN	20400	406T	NWC	77449
RANCH PRAIRIE TRAIL	0	406Y	NWC	77449
RANCH RIATA CT	0	406X	NWC	77449
RANCH RIATA DR	0	406X	NWC	77449
RANCHSTONE DR	10700	409B	NWC	77064
RANCH VALLEY DR	0	324M	NWC	77447
RANCH VIEW LN	0	527S	NEF	77407
RANCH VIEW TRAIL	0	373E	NCC	77073
RANCHWOOD CT	1600	486L	SWC	77450
RANCHWOOD LN	0	657P	FR	77546
RANCHWOOD SPRINGS LN	0	524H	NEF	77494
RAND	3700	454U	NEH	77026
RAND	7700	455T	NEH	77028
RANDALL	1	615P	PL	77581
N. RANDALL	100	536H	PA	77506
RANDALL	100	536M	PA	77506
RANDALL	2400	569V	SF	77477
RANDALL	3000	452Q	NWH	77018
RANDAL LAKE LN	0	332A	NWC	77388
RANDALL OAK DR	4900	569W	SG	77478
RANDALL RIDGE LN	15900	326V	NWC	77429
RANDALL RUN LN		366T	NWC	77433
RANDALLS	0	368W	NWC	77095
RANDAL POINT CT	0	332A	NWC	77388
RANDAL WAY	400	332F	NWC	77388
RANDOLPH	900	412Q	NWH	77088
RANDOLPH	2400	538W	PA	77503
RANDOLPH	8900	575P	SEH	77061
RANDOLPH	9300	575P	SEH	77075
RANDON LN	25800	288X	NWC	77377

Street Name	Block	Pg/Sq	Loc	Zips
RANDON RD	4200	451G	NWH	77092
RANDON RD	5100	451C	NWH	77091
RANDONS POINT DR	1700	568Z	SG	77478
RANDWICK DR	4400	451R	NWH	77092
RANDY DR	9000	450Y	SV	77055
RANDY LN	3100	446P	NWC	77449
RANDY RILEY WAY	0	328M	NWC	77377
RANDY RILEY WAY	32000	253P	SEM	77386
W. RANGECREST PLACE	3200	609E	SG	77479
E. RANGECREST PLACE	3200	609E	SG	77479
RANGE HAVEN CT	0	372M	NCC	77073
RANGE HAVEN LN	0	256W	SEM	77365
RANGELY DR	9100	450Y	NWH	77055
RANGER	400	495E	NEH	77029
RANGER	4500	455S	NEH	77028
RANGER PATH CT	0	250K	NWC	77389
RANGER POINT CT	20400	486T	NEF	77450
RANGER RIDGE	0	327Q	NWC	77429
RANGER RUN	4400	609E	SG	77479
RANGE VALLEY LN	0	327U	NWC	77429
RANGE VALLEY LN	0	327U	NWC	77429
RANGEVIEW DR	22300	485C	SWC	77450
RANGEWOOD CT	1600	618E	SEH	77062
RANIC DR	7800	370S	NWC	77064
RANIER DR	10500	530X	SWH	77031
N. RANKIN CIR	400	372H	NCC	77073
W. RANKIN CIR	13600	372G	NCC	77073
E. RANKIN CIR	13600	372H	NCC	77073
W. RANKIN RD	100	372F	NWH	77090
RANKIN RD	100	372H	NCC	77073
RANKIN RD	800	373G	NCC	77073
RANKIN RD	2100	374F	NEC	77032
RANKIN RD	2100	374J	NEH	77032
RANKIN RD	5700	374H	NEH	77396
RANKIN RD	6000	375E	HM	77396
RANKIN CREEK DR	0	366P	NWC	77433
RANKIN MEADOWS CT	0	326E	NWC	77433
RANKIN PARK DR	0	372H	NCC	77073
RANNA CT	0	568B	SG	77498
RANNIE RD	8400	451J	NWH	77080
RANNIE RD	8500	450M	NWH	77080
RANNOCK WAY	9500	329R	NWC	77379
RANSOM	5600	534Q	SEH	77087
RANSOM RD	27700	258K	SEM	77357
RANSTEN LN	0	291W	NWC	77379
RAOUL WALLENBERG LN	3900	609G	MC	77459
RAPHO DR	2700	378P	NEC	77532
RAPID BROOK CT	5600	337H	NEH	77345
RAPID CREEK CT	5900	338A	NEH	77345
RAPIDCREEK DR	16100	611D	SWH	77053
RAPID CREEK LN	0	660K	LC	77573
RAPIDO RD	5000	534N	SEH	77033
RAPID RIVER LN	4100	410D	NWC	77086
RAPID RIVER LN	9700	370Z	NWC	77086
RAPIDS CT	0	611W	FS	77545
RAPID SPRINGS LN	0	375Z	NEC	77396
RARITAN DR	10000	450S	NWH	77080
RARITAN DR	10200	449V	NWH	77043
RASHELL WAY	2400	612V	PL	77584
RASMUS DR	9200	490X	SWH	77063
RASPBERRY LN	2100	537S	PA	77502
RASTUS AVE	2600	570W	NEF	77477
RATADA CT	700	298Y	NEH	77336
RATAMA	5000	535V	SEH	77017
RATAMA CREEK LN	0	410E	NWC	77064
RATHBONE DR	9700	569H	SWH	77031
RATHBURN	3400	616T	PL	77581
RATHFORD CT	24500	485S	NEF	77494
RATHLIN CT	15900	330T	NWC	77379
RATON	6900	451T	NWH	77055
RATTAN LN	17700	380V	NEC	77532
RAUCH	3300	495C	NEH	77029
RAUCH CT	8600	409M	JV	77040
RAUDABAUGH DR		484W	NEF	77494
RAUL HECTOR DR	9700	575Q	SEH	77075
RAVELLO DR	0	445Y	NWC	77449
RAVEN	0	454S	NEH	77026
RAVEN	600	335Z	HM	77338
RAVEN CT	16400	614X	NEB	77584
RAVEN'S LANDING CT		484S	NEF	77494
RAVENA CT	12500	616D	SEH	77089
RAVEN BLUFF LN	0	485W	NEF	77494
RAVEN CANYON LN	0	407B	NWC	77095
RAVEN CLIFF FALLS		249Z	NWC	77375
RAVEN CLIFFS LN	0	330B	NWC	77379
RAVEN CREEK DR	0	612R	PL	77584
RAVEN CREEK LN	0	406L	NWC	77433
RAVENCREST CT	4000	614Y	PL	77584
RAVENCREST DR	25100	295Q	SEM	77365
RAVENCROSS DR	0	368K	NWC	77429
RAVEN CROSSING LN	10400	616A	SEC	77089
RAVENDALE RD	14000	375W	NEC	77396
RAVENDWOOD LN	31000	282Z	WCO	77484
RAVEN FALLS LN	2600	617X	SEC	77546
RAVENFIELD DR	18000	447B	NWC	77084
RAVEN FLIGHT DR	13300	368Q	NWC	77429
RAVEN FOREST LN	0	484Z	NEF	77494
RAVENGLEN DR	25100	295Q	SEM	77365
RAVENHEAD DR	100	576G	SEH	77034
RAVEN HILL	13000	368F	NWC	77429
RAVEN HOLLOW LN	14700	375U	NEC	77396
RAVENHURST LN	7600	329Z	NWC	77070
RAVENHURST LN	14100	330W	NWC	77070
RAVENKNOLL CT	100	658N	LC	77573
RAVENLAKE CT	0	612K	PL	77545
RAVEN LAKE CT	0	406D	NWC	77433
RAVENLAKE DR	0	612K	PL	77545
RAVENLEA LN	0	416Z	NEC	77044
RAVENLOCH CT	5400	526A	NEF	77450
RAVEN MILL LN	0	406C	NWC	77433
RAVEN MIST CT	0	406X	NWC	77449
RAVENMOOR DR	12200	489J	SWH	77077
RAVENNA LN	0	659L	LC	77573
RAVENNA LN	22000	485Z	NEF	77450
RAVENNA COUNTRY LN	0	491C	NWH	77055
RAVENNA CREEK CROSSING	0	406D	NWC	77433
RAVENNA LANDING LOOP	0	251W	SWM	77389
RAVENNA OAKS CT	0	445J	NWC	77493
RAVENNA WOODS CT	0	328E	NWC	77377
RAVENNO LN	0	331J	NWC	77379
RAVENNO LN	0	331J	NWC	77379
RAVEN OAK CT	1700	486K	SWC	77450
RAVENPARK DR	19900	295Q	SEM	77365
RAVENPASS LN	0	445R	NWC	77449
RAVEN RIDGE DR	0	612N	PL	77545
RAVEN RIDGE DR	4700	611D	SWH	77053
RAVEN RIDGE LN	1	251R	WD	77380
RAVEN RIVER DR	3900	618D	PA	77059
RAVEN RIVER DR	4100	578Z	PA	77059
RAVEN ROCK LN	0	406M	NWC	77433
RAVEN ROCK LN	18200	526M	NEF	77407
RAVEN ROOK DR	12200	368P	NWC	77429

Street Name	Block	Pg/Sq	Loc	Zips
RAVEN ROOST CT	12200	368Q	CY	77429
RAVENS BLUFF LN	0	253K	SEM	77386
RAVENSBROOK LN	18100	326V	NWC	77429
RAVENS CALL LN	18100	526M	NEF	77407
RAVENS CAW DR	13300	368L	NWC	77429
RAVENS CHASE LN	12300	368L	NWC	77429
RAVENSCOURT DR	1100	568F	SG	77498
RAVENS CREEK CT	0	612Q	PL	77584
RAVENSCREEK CT	5200	657Z	LC	77573
RAVENS CREEK DR	0	612Q	PL	77584
RAVENS CREST DR	2000	568Z	SG	77478
RAVENSCROFT LN	20200	290Y	NWC	77379
RAVENSCROFT WAY	14700	527V	NEF	77083
RAVENS GATE LN	0	526W	NEF	77406
RAVENS GLEN CT	12800	368L	NWC	77429
N. RAVEN SHORE DR	0	366K	NWC	77433
RAVENSIDE DR	0	484Z	NEF	77494
RAVENS LAKE CIR	3100	660E	LC	77573
RAVENS LAKE DR	22600	485U	NEF	77450
RAVENS MANOR CT	1400	289X	NWC	77379
RAVENS MATE DR	12300	368K	NWC	77429
RAVENS MILLS CT	5900	609T	NEF	77479
RAVENS NEST CT	9600	527U	NEF	77083
RAVENS NEST LN	12100	616K	SEC	77089
RAVENSONG DR	12700	368L	NWC	77429
RAVEN SOUTH DR	12000	368L	NWC	77429
RAVENS POINT DR	0	525Z	NEF	77406
RAVENSPORT DR	2900	613T	NEB	77584
RAVEN SPRINGS LN	0	660J	LC	77573
RAVENS RIDGE BLVD	0	406C	NWC	77433
RAVEN ROOST DR	13300	368L	NWC	77429
RAVENS RUN LN		366Y	NWC	77433
RAVENS THORPE LN	0	330D	NWC	77379
RAVENS WAY	10500	463S	CCO	77520
RAVENS WAY	10500	502P	BT	77520
RAVENSWAY CT	4000	614X	PL	77584
RAVENSWAY DR	12500	368K	NWC	77429
RAVENSWOOD	0	609Z	MC	77459
RAVENSWORTH	0	569H	SWH	77099
RAVENSWORTH DR	9500	570E	SWH	77031
RAVEN TRAIL	15500	571W	SWH	77489
RAVEN TREE	12500	368F	NWC	77429
RAVEN TREE CT	21700	255S	SEM	77365
RAVEN VIEW DR	11300	371R	NWC	77067
RAVENWIND RD	2000	371M	NWC	77067
RAVENWING DR	13300	368Q	NWC	77429
RAVENWING DR	20000	295R	SEM	77365
RAVENWOOD CIR	7900	451S	NWH	77055
RAVENWOOD CT	4000	614Y	PL	77584
RAVENWOOD CT	20600	295R	SEM	77365
RAVENWOOD DR	5900	614Y	PL	77584
RAVENWOOD DR	19800	295Q	SEM	77365
RAVENWOOD VIEW LN	0	575U	SEH	77075
RAVINE CIR	16900	657B	FR	77546
RAVINE DR	4000	657B	FR	77546
RAWHIDE TRAIL	16500	367B	CY	77429
RAWLEY	3200	494E	NEH	77026
RAWLEY	3400	494F	NEH	77020
RAWLINGS	13800	415A	NEC	77396
RAWLINGS	14000	375W	NEC	77396
RAWLS	3000	492B	NWH	77008
RAWSON LN	2000	619S	NB	77058
RAY	2500	615N	PL	77581
RAY	4600	615N	PL	77581
RAY	7200	454J	NEH	77093
RAY DR	5900	577D	PA	77505
RAY DR	6200	578A	PA	77505
RAYBLUFF LN	8500	410F	NWC	77040
RAYBROOK	0	616A	SEC	77089
RAYBROOK LN	10300	615D	SEC	77089
S. RAYBURN CT	1900	537T	PA	77502
N. RAYBURN CT	2100	537T	PA	77502
RAYBURN LN	1600	616T	PL	77581
RAYBURN LAKE CT	3900	615Y	PL	77581
RAYBURN RIDGE DR	2600	486N	SWC	77450
RAYDELL DR	10500	530W	SWH	77031
RAYDON LN	1	490J	BH	77024
RAY FALLS DR	20200	289W	NWC	77375
W. RAYFORD	6000	250U	NWC	77389
W. RAYFORD RD	0	290A	NWC	77389
RAYFORD RD	0	294J	SEM	77386
RAYFORD RD	0	293F	SEM	77386
RAYFORD RD	1	252T	SEM	77386
RAYFORD RD	2400	253W	SEM	77386
RAYFORD RD	3700	293H	SEM	77386
W. RAYFORD RD	6200	250U	NWC	77389
W. RAYFORD RD	8800	289D	NWC	77375
RAYFORD RD	19700	333M	NCC	77338
RAYFORD RD	23400	291A	NWC	77389
RAYFORD RD	28800	293A	SEM	77386
RAYFORD CREST DR	25101	252T	SEM	77386
RAYFORD FOREST LN	200	252T	SEM	77386
RAYLEINE DR	8400	613V	PL	77584
RAYLIN DR	8400	451W	SV	77055
RAYMAC	100	412H	NCC	77037
RAYMOND	100	288L	TB	77375
RAYMOND	2100	537F	PA	77506
RAYMOND	7000	533Q	SEH	77021
RAYMONDVILLE RD	9900	414W	NEH	77093
RAYMONT CIR	9700	408D	NWC	77065
RAYNOR CT	15700	571W	SWH	77489
RAYPINE DR	100	252S	SEM	77386
RAY SHELL CT	1800	619H	TL	77586
RAYSON RD	8300	451J	NWH	77080
RAYSON RD	8500	450M	NWH	77080
RAYWOOD BLVD	500	450C	NWH	77040
RAYWOOD CT	900	498C	CV	77530
RAYWOOD DR	16000	498C	CV	77530
RAZA RD	5800	614Y	PL	77584
RAZEE CT	700	379X	NEC	77532
RAZORBACK DR	8200	250S	NWC	77389
READING	0	494W	SEH	77004
READING	3600	493Z	SEH	77004
READS CT	13300	457T	NEC	77015
READSLAND LN	6600	408T	NWC	77084
REAGAN	2600	493B	NWH	77009
REAGAN	3700	453X	NWH	77009
REAGAN CANYON DR	24000	325J	NWC	77447
REAGAN MEADOW CT	9100	369V	NWC	77064
REAL	3000	534L	SEH	77087
REALITY RD	12400	414F	NCC	77039
REAMER	5400	531S	SWH	77096
REAMER	5800	530R	SWH	77074
REAMER	8600	530P	SWH	77074
W. REATA DR	2200	538R	DP	77536
E. REATA DR	2200	538R	DP	77536
REAUX, J L	10500	415W	NEH	77016
REAUX, J L	11500	415W	NEH	77016
REBA	900	460S	HG	77562
REBA DR	2300	492U	SWH	77019
REBA LN	27800	298Y	NEH	77336
REBAWOOD DR	8000	337V	NEC	77346

Street Name	Block	Pg/Sq	Loc	Zips
REBAWOOD DR	8300	338N	NEC	77346
REBE	5900	415A	NEC	77039
REBECCA	100	453K	NEH	77022
REBECCA	3400	533P	SEH	77021
REBECCA DR	900	537N	PA	77506
REBECCA LN	1100	375D	HM	77338
REBECCA LN	20151	256K	SEM	77357
S. REBECCA BURWELL LN	22300	445V	NWC	77449
N. REBECCA BURWELL LN	22300	445V	NWC	77449
REBECCA FIELD LN	0	293K	SEM	77386
REBECCA HILL CT	0	525V	NEF	77406
REBECCA MEADOW FALLS DR	0	524B	NEF	77494
REBECCA PINES CT	600	490F	BH	77024
REBEL RD	9800	455A	NEH	77016
REBEL RD	10000	415W	NEH	77016
REBEL RD	11200	415N	NEH	77016
REBEL CREEK DR	0	406V	NWC	77449
REBEL RIDGE DR	4800	609A	SG	77478
REBEL YELL DR	19100	406V	NWC	77449
RECHELLE	11900	414N	NCC	77093
RECORD	7900	455B	NEH	77028
RED RD	1	580V	PA	77586
RED-N-GOLD DR	0	570W	SF	77477
RED ADLER PLACE	0	249B	SWM	77382
RED ALDER CIR	0	332Q	NCC	77073
REDAN	100	493B	NWH	77009
RED ARGAN CT	0	372C	NCC	77073
RED ASH CT	18100	526M	NEF	77407
RED ASHBERRY TRAIL	0	325R	NWC	77433
RED BANK DR	0	332X	NWC	77090
RED BARN WAY	0	250N	NWC	77389
RED BAY CIR	7400	249C	SWM	77354
RED BAY CT	2000	618F	SEH	77062
REDBAY RD	20700	446P	NWC	77449
W. RED BAYBERRY CT	0	325Q	NWC	77433
E. RED BAYBERRY CT	0	325Q	NWC	77433
REDBAY PLACE	14800	487Z	SWC	77082
REDBERRY CT	1	251J	WD	77381
REDBERRY LN	23100	525B	NEF	77494
REDBERRY GLEN LN	6600	409S	NWC	77041
REDBERRY HILL	800	501H	NEC	77521
REDBERRY JUNIPER TRAIL	25900	524D	NEF	77494
REDBERRY JUNIPER TRAIL	25900	524D	NEF	77494
S. RED BIRCH CIR	2300	371Y	NWC	77038
N. RED BIRCH CIR	2800	371Y	NWC	77038
RED BIRCH LN		289G	NWC	77375
REDBIRD LN	8000	456G	NEC	77044
RED BIRD LN	25100	295R	SEM	77365
RED BIRD LN	31600	248S	SWM	77362
REDBIRD KNOLL	0	573X	SEC	77047
REDBIRD PLACE	0	252M	SEM	77385
RED BIRD RIDGE	15500	375Q	NEC	77396
RED BIRD TREE CT	0	328J	NWC	77429
RED BIRD TREE LN	0	445K	NWC	77493
RED BLUFF CT	0	485P	NEF	77493
RED BLUFF LN	0	620A	PA	77586
RED BLUFF RD	100	536H	PA	77506
RED BLUFF RD	900	620G	SB	77586
RED BLUFF RD	1200	537E	PA	77506
RED BLUFF RD	2700	538W	PA	77503
RED BLUFF RD	5500	578B	PA	77505
RED BLUFF RD	7600	578G	PA	77507
RED BLUFF RD	20400	295D	SEM	77365
RED BLUFF TRAIL	24800	485P	NEF	77494
RED BRIAR TRAIL	3900	538Z	DP	77536
REDBRIDGE CT	2500	578W	SEH	77059
RED BRIDGE DR	0	377B	NEC	77346
REDBRIDGE LN	0	657Y	LC	77573
REDBROOK DR	8400	615D	SEC	77089
REDBRUSH DR	14100	528W	NEF	77498
RED BUD	0	257Q	SEM	77357
REDBUD	100	419Q	BR	77532
REDBUD	900	458Z	CV	77530
REDBUD	2800	444P	KT	77493
REDBUD	3200	533T	SEH	77051
REDBUD	4700	533V	SEH	77033
REDBUD AVE	24200	297J	SEM	77365
REDBUD CIR	200	657Q	LC	77573
REDBUD CIR	1100	536P	PA	77506
RED BUD CT	0	616R	FR	77546
RED BUD CT	1500	616T	PL	77581
W. REDBUD DR	3800	579C	LP	77571
S. REDBUD DR	3800	579C	LP	77571
E. REDBUD DR	3800	579C	LP	77571
RED BUD LN	100	500E	BT	77520
RED BUD LN	300	257B	WV	77357
REDBUD LN	700	336F	NEH	77339
RED BUD LN	1800	568W	SG	77479
REDBUD LN	12000	368D	NWC	77429
REDBUD LN	14700	412D	NCC	77060
REDBUD LN	17900	257D	RF	77357
REDBUD RD	0	251R	WD	77380
REDBUD BERRY	15300	326N	NWC	77433
REDBUD BERRY LN	16300	326N	NWC	77433
REDBUD BERRY WAY	15300	325V	NWC	77433
REDBUD BROOK TRAIL	0	616H	SEH	77089
REDBUD DALE CT	0	326V	NWC	77429
REDBUD HILL CT	2500	292W	NWC	77388
REDBUD LEAF LN	14900	326S	NWC	77433
REDBUD POINT LN	0	457G	NEC	77049
REDBUD RAIN DR	0	446K	NWC	77449
REDBUD RIDGE PLACE	1	251R	WD	77380
REDBUD SHORES LN	12900	377K	NEC	77044
REDBUD TERRACE LN	18000	407K	NWC	77433
REDBUD TRAIL	20700	337Q	NEC	77346
REDBUD VALLEY TRAIL	14500	617H	SEH	77062
REDBUD VILLA LN	0	411A	NWC	77086
RED BURR OAK TRAIL	0	524B	NEF	77494
RED BURR OAK TRAIL	0	524B	NEF	77494
RED CANARY CT	14700	325Q	NWC	77433
RED CANDLE DR	3400	331C	NWC	77388
RED CANNA VISTA	5600	376S	NEC	77396
RED CANYON LN	19300	328C	NWC	77377
RED CANYON CREEK	0	335N	NCC	77338
RED CANYON PARK DR	0	484S	NEF	77494
RED CARRIAGE CT	14200	617H	SEH	77062
RED CASCADE CT	0	286L	NWC	77377
RED CASTLE LN	0	375R	NEC	77396
N. RED CEDAR CIR	900	251Q	WD	77380
E. RED CEDAR CIR	1000	251Q	WD	77380
S. RED CEDAR CIR	11800	251Q	WD	77380
RED CEDAR CT	6300	337P	NEC	77346
RED CEDAR DR	3500	502P	BT	77521
RED CEDAR LN	0	339P	HU	77336
REDCEDAR LN	19500	486C	SWC	77094
RED CEDAR BEND	3500	502K	BT	77521
RED CEDAR BLUFF LN	15000	326X	NWC	77433
RED CEDAR CANYON LN	19800	326X	NWC	77433
RED CEDAR COVE LN	15100	326T	NWC	77433
REDCEDAR GROVE PATH	0	445N	NWC	77493
RED CEDAR HOLLOW DR	0	524B	NEF	77494
RED CEDAR PASS	3300	502P	BT	77521
RED CEDAR TRAIL	3200	502P	BT	77521
REDCHASE DR	0	449D	NWH	77041
REDCHURCH DR	8100	330P	NWC	77379
REDCLIFF	8400	410G	NWC	77064
REDCLIFF DR	2100	610A	MC	77489
RED CLIFF DR	5400	337D	NEH	77345
RED CLIFF RIDGE DR	0	524A	NEF	77494
RED CLOUD RD	8900	409F	NWC	77064
RED CLOUD TRAIL	0	609Y	NEF	77459
REDCOAT DR	2100	570Y	MC	77489
RED COAT LN	11800	490F	BH	77024
RED COPPER LN	0	406D	NWC	77433
RED CORAL CT	13700	578W	SEH	77059
RED CORAL DR	7000	578F	PA	77505
RED CREEK CT	0	375X	NEC	77396
RED CREEK COVE LN	0	375Y	NEC	77396
REDCREST DR	16400	367R	NWC	77095
REDCRESTED GLEN CT	0	291N	NWC	77388
RED CYPRESS	0	325K	NWC	77447
RED DEER DR	24200	338L	NEH	77336
RED DEER LN	1	251V	WD	77380
REDDING RD	5900	530E	SWH	77036
REDDING CREST LN	15100	328S	NWC	77429
REDDINGFORD LN	16300	407V	NWC	77084
REDDING OAK CT	7900	411P	NWC	77088
REDDING PINES LN	0	253T	SEM	77386
REDDING RIDGE LN	0	524D	NEF	77494
REDDING RIDGE LN	26000	524D	NEF	77494
REDDING RIDGE LN	26000	524D	NEF	77494
REDDING SPRINGS LN	6400	371W	NWC	77086
REDDINGTON RD	1900	568C	SG	77478
REDDINGWOOD CT	21900	334F	NCC	77373
REDDLESHIRE LN	1300	449W	NWH	77043
REDDLESTON CT	6600	250Y	NWC	77389
REDDY LN	15700	571Z	SWH	77053
REDDY LN	15800	611D	SWH	77053
RED EAGLE CT	18200	377B	NEC	77346
REDELL RD	3700	500G	NEC	77521
REDEMPTION CIR	0	452G	NWH	77018
RED FALLS CIR	0	407C	NWC	77095
RED FAUNA DR	0	406D	NWC	77433
RED FAWN DR	200	338L	NEH	77336
REDFERN	12100	574N	SEH	77048
RED FERN CT	10200	252G	SEM	77385
RED FERN CT	17000	407L	NWC	77095
REDFERN DR	8100	533Z	SEH	77033
REDFIELD CT	0	289Q	NWC	77375
REDFIELD DR	3100	537Q	PA	77503
REDFIELD LN	0	289Q	NWC	77375
RED FINCH CT	7800	375U	NEC	77396
RED FIR DR	3600	411R	NWH	77088
REDFISH LN	13300	569L	SF	77477
REDFORD	1200	576E	SEH	77034
REDFORD	9300	575H	SEH	77075
REDFORD PATH DR	0	376A	NEC	77338
REDFORD PINES LN	0	376A	NEC	77338
RED FOX	27800	288P	NWC	77377
RED FOX DR	1300	378D	NEH	77532
RED FOX LN	28300	248S	SWM	77362
REDGATE CIR	7800	570G	MC	77071
REDGATE DR	13300	457X	NEC	77015
RED GLADE CT	0	332D	NCC	77373
REDGROVE LN	5600	458S	NEC	77494
REDGROVE FALLS CT	0	366Z	NWC	77433
REDGUM DR	3100	446P	NWC	77449
RED HARPER DR	0	292E	NWC	77389
RED HAVEN DR	100	459M	HG	77562
REDHAVEN PLACE	1	250B	WD	77381
RED HAW	1000	488C	NWH	77079
RED HAW	1100	448Y	NWH	77079
RED HAW	4100	453K	NWH	77022
RED HAW RD	15200	457H	NEC	77049
RED HAW RD	15400	458E	NEC	77049
RED HAWK CIR	9000	409F	NWC	77064
REDHEAD CT	13200	377Y	NEC	77044
REDHEAD LN	6000	444K	KT	77493
REDHEAVEN CT	11000	368V	NWC	77065
REDHILL DR	13600	528T	SWC	77083
RED HILL TRAIL	15800	408A	NWC	77095
RED HOLLY LN	0	330E	NWC	77379
REDHORSE DR	0	257E	SEM	77357
RED HUMMINGBIRD DR	0	572R	SWH	77047
RED LAKE CT	0	526X	NEF	77406
RED LAKE LN	0	526X	NEF	77406
RED LAND CT	3400	609M	MC	77459
REDLAND CT	3400	609M	MC	77459
REDLANDS DR	7800	410L	NWC	77040
REDLAND WOODS DR	0	410L	NWC	77040
RED LANTERN DR	4800	617S	SEC	77546
RED LAUREL CT	12900	367H	NWC	77429
REDLEAF LN	700	332J	NWC	77090
REDLEAF FOREST LN	0	484Z	NEF	77494
REDLEAF HOLLOW CT	8600	407F	NWC	77095
REDLEAF HOLLOW LN	17400	407F	NWC	77095
RED LEO LN	22800	291E	NWC	77389
RED LODGE DR	5000	447B	NWC	77084
RED MAGNOLIA CT	1900	336F	NEH	77339
REDMAN	1200	536Q	PA	77506
RED MAPLE	14800	527D	SWC	77082
RED MAPLE CT	0	657H	FR	77546
RED MAPLE CT	7200	407Q	NWC	77095
RED MAPLE DR	9500	410A	NWC	77064
RED MAPLE LN	0	657G	FR	77546
RED MAPLES DR	2800	336D	NEH	77339
RED MEADOWS DR	0	253X	SEM	77386
RED MESA CT	10002	367Z	NWC	77095
RED MESA DR	10000	367Z	NWC	77095
REDMOND	1300	497L	NEC	77015
REDMOND CT	0	568W	SG	77479
RED MOON PLACE	0	250J	NWC	77375
RED MULBERRY LN	14500	377Y	NEH	77044
RED OAK	12900	419T	NEC	77532
RED OAK	24800	247T	SWM	77355
RED OAK	28000	298Y	NEH	77336
RED OAK AVE	100	419Y	BR	77532
RED OAK CT	1300	568W	SG	77479
RED OAK CT	4500	447E	NWC	77084
RED OAK CT	6200	578J	PA	77505
RED OAK DR	100	245F	SWM	77355
RED OAK DR	7700	249G	SWM	77354
RED OAK DR	16300	570J	MC	77489
RED OAK DR	16900	332J	NWC	77090
RED OAK DR	18000	331H	NWC	77090
RED OAK DR	23800	290B	NWC	77389
RED OAK LN	0	330D	NWC	77379
RED OAK LN	0	616V	FR	77546
RED OAK LN	100	245B	SWM	77355
RED OAK LN	2800	614Q	PL	77584
RED OAK LN	20100	256K	SEM	77357
RED OAK RD	15900	498G	CV	77530
RED OAK BEND DR	0	366P	NWC	77433
RED OAK BRANCH LN	3600	297T	NEH	77345
RED OAK FOREST LN	0	253N	SEM	77386
RED OAK GLEN DR	12900	328U	NWC	77429
RED OAK GROVE CT	0	484Y	NEF	77494
RED OAK GROVE CT	0	484Y	NEF	77494
RED OAK HOLLOW	100	245F	SWM	77355
RED OAK LEAF TRAIL	2900	446R	NWC	77084
REDOAK MANOR LN	0	407E	NWC	77433
REDOAK PASS LN	10000	369X	NWC	77064
REDOAK RIDGE LN	10300	369X	NWC	77064
N. RED OAKS LN	19600	257M	SEM	77357
S. RED OAKS LN	19900	257M	SEM	77357
RED OAK TERRACE	1700	336B	NEH	77339
RED OAK TERRACE CT	0	336B	NEH	77339
RED OAK TRAIL	23200	287F	NWC	77377
RED OAK VALLEY DR	0	524B	NEF	77494
RED OLIVE DR	0	285Q	NWC	77447
REDONDO DR	700	496H	NEH	77015
REDONDO VALLEY CT	0	406G	NWC	77433
REDONDO VALLEY DR	0	406G	NWC	77433
RED PHEASANT CT	8600	409G	JV	77040
RED PINE CT	18100	255S	SEM	77365
RED PINE DR	22500	290E	NWC	77375
RED PINE RIDGE WAY	0	457Q	NEC	77049
RED PINE VALLEY TRAIL	0	524F	NEF	77494
RED RIDGE CT	3100	613T	NEB	77578
RED RIPPLE DR	100	452D	NWH	77076
RED RIPPLE RD	300	452D	NWH	77091
RED RIVER	5800	660X	DI	77539
RED RIVER	0	253V	SEM	77386
RED RIVER CT	0	253V	SEM	77386
RED RIVER CT	700	485H	SWC	77450
RED RIVER DR	22000	485G	SWC	77450
RED RIVER ST	0	659L	LC	77573
RED RIVER CANYON DR	0	377F	NEC	77346
RED RIVER LOOP	0	253V	SEM	77386
RED RIVER TRAIL	17200	367T	NWC	77095
RED ROBIN CT	18800	257H	RF	77357
RED ROBIN LN	7400	575N	SEH	77075
REDROCK	2200	412S	NWH	77088
RED ROCK	36900	246D	SWM	77355
REDROCK RD	0	658X	LC	77573
RED ROCK CANYON CT	22200	485G	SWC	77450
RED ROCK CANYON DR	700	485H	SWC	77450
RED ROCK CROSSING DR	13300	414B	NCC	77039
REDROCK FALLS	24400	249Z	NWC	77375
RED ROOSTER LN	0	525A	NEF	77469
REDROOT DR	19700	446Q	NWC	77084
RED ROVER CT	3100	293U	NCC	77373
RED RUGOSA DR	0	367Y	NWC	77095
RED RUGOSA DR	10300	367X	NWC	77095
RED SABLE CT	1	251X	WD	77380
RED SABLE DR	0	291B	WD	77380
RED SABLE DR	1	251Y	WD	77380
RED SABLE PLACE	1	251X	WD	77380
RED SABLE POINT	1	251X	WD	77380
RED SAILS PASS	18400	378B	NEC	77346
RED SHADY OAKS DR	0	524B	NEF	77494
RED SKY CT	1900	293W	NCC	77373
RED SKY DR	23800	293W	NCC	77373
RED SLATE LN	10400	367Y	NWC	77095
RED SPRINGS DR	15700	487Y	SWC	77082
RED SPRUCE LN	0	410M	NWC	77040
RED SQUIRREL DR	0	257A	SEM	77357
REDSTAFF CT	7000	525U	NEF	77406
RED STAR	800	617C	SEH	77598
REDSTART	4500	531Z	SWH	77035
REDSTART	5300	531X	SWH	77096
REDSTEM CT	3900	660X	DI	77539
REDSTONE DR	700	497D	NEC	77530
REDSTONE DR	5100	526T	NEF	77407
REDSTONE BEND DR	0	375Y	NEC	77396
REDSTONE GLEN CT	0	484E	KT	77494
REDSTONEHILLS DR	0	406F	NWC	77433
REDSTONE MANOR DR	1500	329C	NWC	77379
REDSTONE VIEW DR	0	376W	NEC	77396
RED SUN DR	20500	446P	NWC	77449
RED TAILED HAWK CT	13300	377Y	NEH	77044
RED TAILED HAWK DR	13300	377Y	NEH	77044
RED TAIL WAY	4800	376S	NEC	77396
RED TAMARACK LN		289G	NWC	77375
RED TIMBER CT	2100	658S	LC	77573
RED TIMBERS LN	17200	527E	NEF	77407
RED VALLEY DR	2100	458S	NEC	77049
REDVINE TERRACE CT	21000	525R	NEF	77407
RED WAGON DR	0	250Q	NWC	77389
REDWAY LN	400	618N	SEH	77598
REDWAY LN	700	618K	SEH	77062
REDWICK CT	0	291Z	NWC	77388
REDWICK DR	0	291Z	NWC	77388
REDWICKE LN	16300	407V	NWC	77084
RED WILLOW DR	15800	448E	NWC	77084
REDWIN CIR	4000	573L	SEH	77047
RED WING DR	1100	657N	FR	77546
REDWING DR	9000	458A	NEC	77049
REDWING DR	9100	418W	NEC	77049
REDWING LN	7500	375P	HM	77396
REDWING BLUFF DR	1700	453T	NWH	77009
REDWING BROOK TRAIL	4800	446C	NWC	77449
REDWING COVE DR	1700	453T	NWH	77009
REDWING GROVE WAY	2800	411H	NWC	77038
REDWING HAVEN DR	1700	453T	NWH	77009
REDWING KNOLL DR	0	406M	NWC	77433
REDWING PARK DR	700	453T	NWH	77009
REDWING PINES DR	1700	453T	NWH	77009
REDWING PLACE DR	700	453T	NWH	77009
REDWING RIDGE DR	1700	453T	NWH	77009
RED WING TRAIL	22500	289P	NWC	77375
REDWINN DR	2200	536U	PA	77502
RED WOLF CT	17600	407T	NWC	77084
RED WOLF DR	17700	407T	NWC	77084
RED WOLF LN	9900	409C	NWC	77064
RED WOLF LN	10000	369Y	NWC	77064
REDWOOD	800	535E	SEH	77023
REDWOOD	1300	535E	SEH	77087
REDWOOD	2000	619V	LC	77565
REDWOOD CT	1800	568B	SG	77498
REDWOOD DR	10200	462V	CCO	77520
REDWOOD DR	10400	463S	CCO	77520
REDWOOD LN	1200	536P	PA	77502
REDWOOD LN	18600	257B	WV	77357
REDWOOD BEND LN (106CC)	600	613G	NEB	77584
REDWOOD BEND TRAIL	14500	617M	SEH	77062
REDWOOD BOUGH LN	1200	618A	SEH	77062
REDWOOD BRIDGE TRAIL	6100	298W	NEH	77345
REDWOOD CLIFF LN	0	298X	NEH	77336
REDWOOD COVE CT	14900	618F	SEH	77062
REDWOOD CREEK DR	21500	486J	SWC	77450
REDWOOD FALLS	6700	578F	PA	77505
REDWOOD FALLS DR	3700	527D	SWC	77082
REDWOOD GROVE	3300	615U	PL	77581
REDWOOD GROVE CT	4600	297P	NEH	77345
REDWOOD HILL CT	4000	611X	FS	77545
REDWOOD HOLLOW LN	0	377E	NEC	77346
REDWOOD LAKE DR	3200	297X	NEH	77345
REDWOOD LODGE CT	3400	336D	NEH	77339
REDWOOD LODGE DR	2900	336D	NEH	77339
REDWOOD MANOR CT	0	253Q	SEM	77386
REDWOOD MANOR LN	0	406M	NWC	77433
REDWOOD MEADOW LN	0	611X	NEF	77545
REDWOOD PARK LN	0	376H	NEC	77346
REDWOOD PLACE DR	15900	488E	SWH	77079
REDWOOD RIVER DR	5600	297Z	NEH	77345
REDWOOD RUN CT	15200	618F	SEH	77062
REDWOOD SHADOWS CT	3100	447N	NWC	77084
REDWOOD SHORES DR	13400	377L	NEC	77044
REDWOOD TERRACE	6800	250U	NWC	77389
REDWOOD TREE	0	526T	NEF	77407
REDWOOD VILLAGE CIR	1400	252R	SEM	77386
RED WREN CIR	0	484P	NWF	77494
RED WREN CT	2500	338A	NEH	77345
RED YUCCA DR	0	484Y	NEF	77494
RED YUCCA DR	0	484Y	NEF	77494
REECEWOOD LN	500	570U	MC	77489
REED	0	574C	SEH	77087
REED CT	6900	534Z	SEH	77087
REED RD	0	580Q	LP	77571
REED RD	1800	572D	SWH	77051
REED RD	2300	573B	SEH	77051
REED RD	4700	574A	SEH	77033
REED RD	6200	534Z	SEH	77087
REED RD	12500	568H	SG	77478
REED CREEK LN	21300	291X	NWC	77388
REEDCREST	12000	570M	SWH	77085
REED HOLLOW LN	0	452Y	NWH	77008
REEDPOINT DR	1100	332W	NWC	77090
REEDS FERRY DR	6100	408Y	NWC	77041
REEDWOOD DR	500	570Y	MC	77489
REEDWOOD LN	10100	529R	SWH	77036
REEDWOOD RIDGE RD	12700	368V	NWC	77065
REEDY POND CT	1	250H	WD	77381
REEF DR	2000	620W	LC	77573
REEFTON LN	3800	609L	MC	77459
REEF WAY	0	379U	NEC	77532
REESE	300	419G	CB	77532
REESE	1200	535F	SEH	77012
REESE LAKE DR	0	524K	NWF	77406
REESE LOCKETT LN	0	444R	NWC	77493
REEVES	3200	493Z	SEH	77004
REEVESTON RD	12700	413G	NCC	77039
REEVESTON RD	14200	373Y	NCC	77039
REFLECTION CIR	0	501E	BT	77521
REFLECTION CT	2300	609B	MC	77459
REFLECTION BAY DR	0	612G	PL	77584
REFLECTION COVE LN	0	415S	NEH	77016
REFLECTION MEADOWS DR	0	415S	NEH	77016
REFLECTION POINT	1	251E	WD	77381
REFLECTION POINT DR	9800	366Z	NWC	77433
REFLECTION SKY CT	0	484E	KT	77494
REFLECTIONS PATH WAY	9200	375V	NEC	77396
REFUGE CREEK DR	0	325H	NWC	77377
REFUGE CREEK DR	0	326E	NWC	77377
REFUG EFOREST DR	0	325H	NWC	77377
REFUGE LAKE DR	0	325H	NWC	77377
REFUGIO CT	9700	409G	NWC	77064
REGAL	500	576E	SEH	77034
REGAL LN	0	501E	BT	77521
REGAL BROOK	0	408G	NWC	77095
REGAL CREST CT	19700	373A	NCC	77073
REGAL EXETER DR	0	332R	NCC	77073
REGAL GEM LN	0	405W	NWC	77493
REGAL GREEN CT	0	338F	NEH	77345
REGAL GREEN LN	27100	296X	NEH	77339
REGAL HOLLOW LN	600	332Q	NCC	77073
REGALIA CT	0	451X	NWH	77055
REGAL ISLE CT	23100	485F	SWC	77494
REGAL MANOR LN	10800	575U	SEH	77075
REGAL OAK	0	251T	WD	77380
REGAL OAKS DR	3200	615R	PL	77581
REGAL OAKS BEND LN	0	572U	SWH	77047
REGAL OAKS BEND LN	12800	572Q	SWH	77047
REGAL OAK WAY	1301	568W	NEF	77479
REGAL PARK CT	0	253N	SEM	77385
REGAL PASS LN	700	457Q	NEC	77049
REGAL PINE LN	12700	369K	NWC	77070
REGAL PINE TRAIL	4400	578U	SEH	77059
REGAL PINE WAY	5100	617S	FR	77546
REGAL RANCH RD	100	569P	SF	77477
REGAL RIDGE LN	5400	611G	SWH	77053
REGAL ROW	9900	410S	NWC	77040
REGAL ROW	10300	409R	NWC	77040
REGAL SHADOW LN	0	609S	NEF	77479
REGAL SHADOW LN	0	366Y	NWC	77433
REGALSHIRE CT	12900	572Q	SWH	77047
REGAL SHORES CT	0	338F	NEH	77345
REGAL SPRUCE CT	7900	407K	NWC	77095
REGAL STONE LN	0	609U	NEF	77479
REGAL STONE LN		609T	NEF	77479
REGAL TRACE LN	15700	332V	NCC	77073
REGAL WOOD CT	0	293D	SEM	77386
REGAL WOOD DR	2400	371Z	NWC	77038
S. REGAN MEAD CIR	0	249C	SWM	77382
N. REGAN MEAD CIR	0	249C	SWM	77382
REGAN MEAD CT	0	249C	SWM	77382
REGATA RUN DR	2900	657B	SEC	77546
REGATTA RD	18700	378A	NEC	77346
REGATTA CREST	0	485A	NEF	77494
REGATTA LAKE DR	0	524Q	NEF	77406
REGENA	1300	413L	NCC	77039
REGENCY CT	300	657J	FR	77546
REGENCY DR	200	538U	DP	77536
REGENCY DR	3800	572E	SWH	77045
REGENCY LN	1	411K	NWC	77088
REGENCY ASH CT	11800	369J	NWC	77429
REGENCY FOREST DR	11600	369J	NWC	77429
REGENCY GREEN DR	11000	369F	NWC	77429
REGENCY OAK LN	12900	369E	NWC	77429
REGENCY PINE DR	11800	369J	NWC	77429
REGENCY PINES DR	26800	296X	SEM	77339
REGENCY PLACE	7400	330F	NWC	77379
REGENCY SQUARE BLVD	7000	530D	SWH	77036
REGENCY SQUARE CT	7200	530D	SWH	77036
REGENCY VILLA DR	4300	448E	NWC	77084
REGENCY WOOD DR	12900	369E	NWC	77429
REGENT	5100	414L	NEC	77039
REGENT CT	1	568V	SG	77478
REGENT MANOR DR	0	337G	NEC	77345
REGENTS BAY DR	0	612L	PL	77545
REGENTS BAY DR	0	612L	PL	77584
REGENTS CORNER LN	20200	446X	NWC	77449
REGENTS COVE CT	0	528R	SWH	77099
REGENTS CREST LN	3800	446M	NWC	77449
REGENTS PARK	1	609J	SG	77479
REGENTS PARK DR	1200	618Q	SEH	77058
REGENT SQUARE	1	251F	SWM	77381

Street Name	Block	Pg/Sq	Loc	Zips
REGENTVIEW DR	400	489E	SWH	77079
REGENTVIEW DR	8000	529P	SWH	77072
REGG DR	12800	572E	SWH	77045
REGINA DR	15900	408W	NWC	77084
REGIONAL PARK DR	800	373J	NCC	77060
REGNAL	14700	373X	NCC	77039
REHAB RD	0	376K	NEC	77396
REICHERT FARMS	0	490D	HC	77024
REID	1	453Q	NEH	77022
REID	1900	454N	NEH	77026
REID BLVD	0	614P	PL	77581
REID RD	100	379K	NEC	77532
REIDEL WAY	0	490B	SWH	77024
REIDEN DR	7500	570Z	SWH	77489
REIDFALLS DR	23100	296J	SEM	77365
REID LAKE DR	9200	410B	NWC	77064
REIDLAND RD	100	379K	NEC	77532
REIDLAND RD	5000	419G	CB	77532
REIGATE LN	15300	458W	NEC	77530
REIMS RD	5800	530C	SWH	77036
REIMS RD	8400	530Q	SWH	77074
REIN	900	493C	NEH	77009
REINALD RD	4000	371B	NWC	77014
REINER GLEN CT	0	372C	NCC	77073
REINERMAN	1	492C	NWH	77007
REINICKE	100	492L	SWH	77007
REINKE	0	282P	WCO	77484
REISER CT	1600	616X	PL	77581
REISSEN LN	14200	330X	NWC	77069
RELAXING DR	0	296T	SEM	77365
RELAY RD	18900	338W	NEC	77346
REMBRANDT WAY	0	249C	SWM	77382
REMEGAN RD	7300	534S	SEH	77033
REMICK RD	13100	328Q	NWC	77429
REMINGTON CT	900	657A	FR	77546
REMINGTON LN	1	533A	SWH	77005
REMINGTON BEND CT	300	372G	NCC	77073
REMINGTON BEND DR	18900	372G	NCC	77073
REMINGTON BLUFF LN	0	526P	NEF	77407
REMINGTON BRIAR CT	0	578T	SEH	77059
REMINGTON BRIDGE DR	300	372C	NCC	77073
REMINGTON CHASE CT	0	372C	NCC	77073
REMINGTON COVE CT	25600	295V	NEH	77365
REMINGTON CREEK DR	0	372G	NCC	77073
REMINGTON CREST CT	19600	486H	SWC	77094
REMINGTON CREST DR	1300	486G	SWC	77094
REMINGTON CROSS DR	19400	372G	NCC	77073
REMINGTON FALLS LN	0	372G	NCC	77073
REMINGTON GLEN CT	0	372H	NCC	77073
REMINGTON GREEN CT	0	372C	NCC	77073
REMINGTON GROVE CT	0	406R	NWC	77433
REMINGTON GROVE DR	0	406R	NWC	77433
REMINGTON HARBOR CT	200	372G	NCC	77073
REMINGTON HEIGHTS DR	200	372C	NCC	77073
REMINGTON HOLLOW LN	0	372C	NCC	77073
REMINGTON LODGE CT	500	372C	NCC	77073
REMINGTON MANOR	19400	329D	NWC	77379
REMINGTON MANOR DR	0	406R	NWC	77433
REMINGTON MARTIN DR	19400	372C	NCC	77073
REMINGTON MILL DR	0	372H	NCC	77073
REMINGTON OAKS CT	0	406W	NWC	77449
REMINGTON PARK CT	0	372H	NCC	77073
REMINGTON PARK DR	0	372H	NCC	77073
REMINGTON PARK DR	18700	372H	NCC	77073
REMINGTON POINT CT	0	372C	NCC	77073
REMINGTON PRAIRIE DR	19400	372G	NCC	77073
REMINGTON RANCHES DR	0	248D	SWM	77354
REMINGTON RANCHES DR	28000	248C	SWM	77354
REMINGTON RIDGE DR	0	372G	NCC	77073
REMINGTON RUN LN	11800	371N	NWC	77066
REMINGTON SPRINGS DR	0	372D	NCC	77073
REMINGTON SPRINGS DR	0	372H	NCC	77073
REMINGTON TRAIL	500	298T	NEC	77336
REMINGTON VALLEY DR	0	372G	NCC	77073
REMINGTON WALK CT	700	372H	NCC	77073
REMINGTON WALK DR	700	372H	NCC	77073
REMINGTON WICK CT	19400	372G	NCC	77073
REMLAP	6400	451Y	NWH	77055
REMME RIDGE LN	0	572U	SWH	77047
REMMICK DR	0	609T	NEF	77479
REMSON HOLLOW LN	6000	524E	NEF	77494
REMUS DR	4300	572W	SWC	77053
REMUS DR	5100	571Y	SWH	77053
REMWICK DR	600	372H	NCC	77073
REMY ST	12800	571H	SWH	77045
RENA	0	541F	NWH	77092
RENA	6000	451E	NWH	77092
RENAE	600	459H	NEC	77562
RENAISSANCE LN	12100	570F	SWH	77071
RENA JANE LN	3700	537M	PA	77503
RENATA CIR	6700	407Q	NWC	77084
RENAULT	13700	497G	NEC	77015
RENDALE CT	2300	291R	NWC	77388
RENDEZVOUS CT	0	293U	NCC	77373
REND LAKE LN	0	328E	NWC	77429
REND LAKE LN	0	328E	NWC	77377
RENEE SPRINGS CT	0	329R	NWC	77379
RENE HILLS LN	0	293F	SEM	77386
RENE HILLS LN	0	293F	SEM	77386
RENFROW	1000	492R	SWH	77019
RENMARK LN	7400	370A	NWC	77070
RENMARK LN	8100	369D	NWC	77070
RENN RD	13200	528P	SWC	77083
RENNER CROSSING DR	0	326T	NWC	77429
RENNERS CT	700	493K	SWH	77007
RENNIE DR	200	486F	SWC	77450
RENO	4300	451F	NWH	77092
RENO DR	5000	537Y	PA	77505
RENOIR DR	100	489L	SWH	77079
RENO RANCH LN	20800	291T	NWC	77388
RENSHAW	2700	534F	SEH	77023
RENTAL CAR AVE	17300	374F	NEC	77032
RENTON DR	2800	374S	NCC	77032
RENTUR DR	9100	530W	SWH	77031
RENWICK DR	5200	531J	SWH	77081
RENWICK DR	9000	531X	SWH	77096
RENWICK DR	11300	571B	SWH	77035
RENWOOD DR	9200	450Q	NWH	77080
RENWOOD FOREST	0	447G	NWC	77084
RENZ RANCH	0	366J	NWC	77433
RENZ RANCH DR	0	366J	NWC	77433
REO	13800	450B	NWH	77040
REO	14000	410X	NWH	77040
REPA LN	13600	371C	NWC	77014
REPITON WAY	0	445W	NWC	77493
REPPERT	100	660H	BC	77518
E. REPSDORPH	1800	620K	SB	77586
REPSDORPH RD	1900	620J	SB	77586
E. REPUBLIC	100	541C	BT	77520
W. REPUBLIC	200	501Y	BT	77520
REPUBLIC RD	500	258A	SEM	77357
REPUBLICA AVE	0	501W	BT	77520

Street Name	Block	Pg/Sq	Loc	Zips
REPUBLIC RIDGE DR	0	406D	NWC	77433
RESADA PARK LN	0	527N	NEF	77407
RESEARCH FOREST DR	2300	251C	WD	77381
RESEARCH PARK	0	251C	WD	77381
RESEARCH POINT	14000	488W	SWH	77082
RESEDA CIR	16100	618P	SEH	77062
RESEDA DR	300	618N	SEH	77598
RESEDA DR	700	618N	SEH	77062
RESEDA ST	0	568W	SG	77479
RESERVE	400	493A	NWH	77007
RESERVE CT	0	615H	PL	77089
RESERVE BEND DR	0	298P	NEC	77336
RESERVE PARKWAY	0	298T	NEC	77336
RESERVE POINT LN	0	327Z	NWC	77429
RESERVE RIDGE DR	0	298N	NEC	77336
RESERVOIR	8100	457G	NEC	77049
RESICA FALLS LN	18600	486D	SWC	77094
RESOURCE PKWY	10900	616C	SEC	77089
RESTAURANT ROW	0	446Y	NWC	77084
REST HOME RD	3700	614W	NEB	77584
RESTLESS BAY LN	0	612K	PL	77545
RESTON BRIDGE DR	15900	327Y	NWC	77429
RESTON CLIFF CT	31500	253N	SEM	77386
RESTONE BEND DR	0	375Y	NEC	77396
RESTONE BEND DR	0	415C	NEC	77396
RESTON FALLS LN	0	444T	KT	77493
RESTON GLEN LN	16900	332Q	NCC	77073
RESTON GROVE CT	15600	408A	NWC	77095
RESTON GROVE LN	9300	408A	NWC	77095
RESTON HEIGHTS LN	0	446G	NWC	77449
RESTON HILL LN		484T	NEF	77494
RESTON LANDING LN	0	484S	NEF	77494
RESTON POINT DR	0	524L	NWF	77406
RESTON RANCH CT	0	366Y	NWC	77433
RESTON RIVER LN	0	366Y	NWC	77433
RESTON RUN LN	0	406F	NWC	77433
RESTOVER LN	9100	409G	NWC	77064
RESTRIDGE DR	1900	451S	NWH	77055
RETA DR	300	538L	DP	77536
RETAIL RD	0	617V	SEH	77598
RETAMA BLUFF LN	0	326Z	NWC	77429
RETAMA TERRACE LN	0	334R	NEC	77338
RETHA	0	571S	SWH	77085
RETHERFORD DR	9800	371W	NWC	77086
RETIS	200	569Q	SF	77477
RETLIN CT	6200	408Y	NWC	77041
RETREAT	0	371A	NWC	77066
RETREAT CREEK CT	0	484W	NEF	77494
RETREAT TRAIL	12500	368K	NWC	77429
RETRIEVER LN	1900	570X	MC	77489
RETTA	3000	494A	NEH	77026
RETTENDON CT	25000	250W	NWC	77389
RETTON DR	0	451F	NWH	77092
REUBEN WHITE DR	100	419Z	BR	77532
REUBEN WHITE DR	700	420W	BR	77532
REUTERS TRAIL	0	334R	NCC	77338
REVALEN LN	0	527W	NEF	77469
REVA RIDGE DR	600	570S	SF	77477
REVEILLE	3300	535N	SEH	77087
REVELSTOKE DR	10000	371W	NWC	77086
REVERE	1900	492Q	SWH	77019
REVERE	2600	492U	SWH	77098
REVERE DR	1900	536T	PA	77502
REVERE, PAUL DR	100	489M	SWH	77024
REVEREND B.J. LEWIS DR	900	412T	NWH	77088
REVERSE	1600	451Y	NWH	77055
REVERSE ST	0	451Y	NWH	77055
REVOLUTION WAY	0	569Y	MC	77477
S. REVOLUTION WAY	1100	609C	MC	77459
REX	300	536G	PA	77506
REX RD	4100	617T	SEC	77546
REXINE LN	0	407K	NWC	77433
REXORA LN	5200	444Q	KT	77493
REXTON DR	6200	408T	NWC	77084
REY AVE	3100	460Y	MN	77521
REYNALDO DR	3900	333D	NCC	77073
REYNARD CT	0	372C	NCC	77073
REYNOLDS	100	659F	LC	77573
REYNOLDS	200	580L	LP	77571
REYNOLDS	2200	493D	NEH	77009
REYNOLDS DR	3300	613T	NEB	77584
REYNOLDS CREEK DR	2900	291Z	NWC	77388
REYNOLDS PARK DR	0	407W	NWC	77449
REYNOLDS POND DR	0	257E	SEM	77357
REYNOLDSR ESERVE WAY	0	286Q	NWC	77377
REYNOSA CT	200	247G	SWM	77362
REZANOF RD	21400	334M	NCC	77338
RHAPSODY LN	9000	410P	NWC	77040
RHEA	100	577N	SEH	77034
RHEMA LN	11900	574K	SEH	77048
RHETT DR	12100	490J	BH	77024
RHETTA LN	5500	290M	NWC	77389
RHETT BUTLER CT	25000	249S	NWC	77375
RHINE	18100	325B	NWC	77447
RHINE LN	1000	332J	NWC	77090
RHINEBECK DR	11800	616D	SEH	77089
RHINEFIELD	16400	328V	NWC	77377
RHINEY CT	0	616L	SEC	77089
RHOBELL	0	455A	NEH	77078
RHOBELL	7200	415W	NEH	77016
RHOBELL	8000	415X	NEH	77078
RHODE ISLAND	300	495Z	NEH	77029
N. RHODE ISLAND	9200	495Y	NEH	77029
RHODE ISLAND	26500	247Y	SWM	77355
RHODE PLACE	800	493K	SWH	77019
RHODES CIR	300	379N	NEC	77532
RHODES CT	6800	609Q	MC	77459
RHODES DR	3800	578A	PA	77505
RHODES LN	1800	610B	MC	77489
RHODES LN	6200	252F	SEM	77385
RHODES RD	20000	291N	NWC	77388
RHODESDALE LN	0	332Q	NCC	77073
RHODES LANDING BLVD	0	291N	NWC	77388
RHONDA LN	0	248N	SWM	77362
RHYME COURT RD	2100	371R	NWC	77067
RHYTHM LN	9300	410N	NWC	77040
RIAL CT	6700	370A	NWC	77069
RIANA DR	10800	368T	NWC	77065
RIANE LN	0	458S	NEC	77530
RIATA DR	28400	248G	SWM	77354
RIATA LN	2500	450N	NWH	77043
RIATA CANYON CT	0	367P	NWC	77433
RIATA CANYON DR	0	367P	NWC	77433
RIATA CREEK DR	17200	367P	NWC	77095
RIATA CROSSING DR	0	367P	NWC	77433
RIATA GROVE DR	0	367P	NWC	77433
RIATA HILLS LN	7000	330B	NWC	77379
N. RIATA LAKE DR	0	367T	NWC	77433
RIATA LAKE DR	17600	367T	NWC	77433
RIATA MANOR LN	17600	367T	NWC	77433
RIATA PRAIRIE LN	0	367T	NWC	77433
RIATA RANCH BLVD	10400	367T	NWC	77095

Street Name	Block	Pg/Sq	Loc	Zips
RIATA RIVER LN	0	377F	NEC	77346
RIATA SPRINGS LN	17600	367T	NWC	77433
RIATA TRACE LN	0	367T	NWC	77433
RIBBON CREEK WAY	0	291M	NWC	77389
RIBBON FALLS CT	11800	289W	NWC	77375
RIBBON FALLS DR	11900	289W	NWC	77375
RIBBON MEADOW CT	12700	377B	NEC	77346
RIBBONWOOD	9300	455D	NEH	77078
RIBBONWOOD	9900	415Z	NEH	77078
RIBBONWOOD PARK LN	0	253N	SEM	77386
RIBBONWOOD POINT CT	20200	289W	NWC	77375
RIBSTONE CIR	10800	415S	NEH	77016
RIBSTONE DR	11200	415N	NEH	77016
RICABY DR	9700	409G	NWC	77064
RICE	2100	501T	BT	77520
RICE	6300	444X	KT	77493
S. RICE AVE	2800	491Y	SWH	77056
S. RICE AVE	5200	531C	SWH	77081
S. RICE AVE	5900	531L	BL	77401
S. RICE AVE	8800	531Q	SWH	77096
RICE BLVD	1600	532A	WU	77005
RICE RD	0	244E	WCO	77447
RICE RD	6400	614H	PL	77581
RICE RD	33600	244A	WCO	77447
RICECREST	11200	571B	SWH	77035
RICE DRIER RD	4000	615E	PL	77581
RICE FARM RD	7700	542D	CCO	77520
RICEFIELD DR	1500	446Z	NWC	77084
RICEFLOWER DR	2100	503F	CCO	77520
RICEGRASS PLACE	0	250L	NWC	77389
RICEGRASS PLACE	0	250L	NWC	77389
RICELAKE LN	19500	446U	NWC	77084
RICELAND DR	0	501F	BT	77521
RICE MILL AVE	0	445N	NWC	77493
RICE MILL DR	0	444S	KT	77493
RICEVILLE SCHOOL RD	11300	570A	SWH	77031
RICEWOOD DR	3200	297F	SEM	77365
RICEWOOD VILLAGE TRAIL	20100	446B	NWC	77449
RICEWOOD WAY	19800	446Q	NWC	77449
RICH CT	12800	488Q	SWH	77077
RICHARD	0	252U	SEM	77385
RICHARD	0	537E	PA	77506
RICHARD	1100	536M	PA	77506
RICHARD	1400	616T	PL	77581
RICHARD	2700	569V	NEF	77477
RICHARD	7600	460T	MN	77521
RICHARD LN	0	657G	FR	77546
RICHARD RD	25200	252T	SEM	77386
RICHARD ARMS CIR	8600	529P	SWH	77099
RICHARD KAYE LN	28800	248T	SWM	77362
RICHARDS	7900	495P	NEH	77029
RICHARDS DR	0	657L	FR	77546
RICHARDS DR	3100	659Z	GCO	77539
RICHARDSON	2900	494J	NEH	77020
RICHARDSON LN	1600	502W	BT	77520
RICHARDSON RD	300	292G	SP	77373
RICHARDSON RD	6600	370A	NWC	77069
RICHBOURGH LN	13700	372G	NWC	77090
RICHCREST DR	700	373J	NCC	77060
RICHCROFT	8500	495P	NEH	77029
RICHELIEU LN	1000	452E	NWH	77018
N. RICHEY	100	536G	PA	77506
RICHEY	100	536L	PA	77506
RICHEY	700	493M	NEH	77002
RICHEY	1300	536L	PA	77502
S. RICHEY	2600	536T	SEH	77017
S. RICHEY AVE	3700	536S	SH	77587
E. RICHEY RD	0	333T	NCC	77073
W. RICHEY RD	100	332T	NWC	77090
E. RICHEY RD	100	332Z	NCC	77073
E. RICHEY RD	1000	333R	NEH	77338
W. RICHEY RD	4300	371E	NWC	77066
W. RICHEY RD	5500	370M	NWC	77066
W. RICHEY ACCESS	500	536G	PA	77506
RICHFIELD CT	3000	613T	NEB	77584
RICHFIELD LN	4900	573H	SEH	77048
RICHFORD DR	15500	617S	SEC	77546
RICHLAND	0	456E	NEH	77078
RICHLAND	7800	455F	NEH	77028
RICHLAND	8800	455H	NEH	77078
RICHLAND CT	2000	568Z	SG	77478
RICHLAND DR	3200	568Z	SG	77478
RICHLAND CHAMBERS LN	4300	375R	NEC	77396
RICHLAND FALLS LN	0	330C	NWC	77379
RICHLAND HILLS DR	6300	524E	NEF	77494
RICHLAND HOLLOW LN	0	657S	FR	77546
RICHLAND SPRINGS DR	19300	372D	NCC	77073
RICHLAWN DR	1300	329G	NWC	77379
RICH MEADOW DR	0	573R	SEH	77048
RICH MEADOW DR	0	573R	SEH	77048
RICHMOND AVE	100	493W	SWH	77002
RICHMOND AVE	500	493W	SWH	77006
RICHMOND AVE	1700	492W	SWH	77098
RICHMOND AVE	3400	492W	SWH	77046
RICHMOND AVE	3800	492W	SWH	77027
RICHMOND AVE	5000	491W	SWH	77056
RICHMOND AVE	5600	491W	SWH	77057
RICHMOND AVE	7500	490X	SWH	77063
RICHMOND AVE	9700	489Y	SWH	77042
RICHMOND AVE	11100	489W	SWH	77082
RICHMOND AVE	13700	488W	SWH	77082
S. RICHMOND AVE	14800	487Z	SWH	77082
RICHMOND AVE	14800	487V	SWH	77082
RICHMOND LN	500	617W	FR	77546
RICHMOND-GAINES	8100	527V	NEF	77498
RICHMOND-SUGARLAND RD	0	568L	SG	77478
RICHMOND HILL DR	10300	449M	NWC	77041
RICH MOUNTAIN DR	0	376F	NEC	77338
RICH MOUNTAIN LN	0	376F	NEC	77338
RICH PLAZA DR	0	257E	SEM	77357
RICHTON	2300	492U	SWH	77098
RICHTON RD	2800	569Z	NEF	77477
RICHTON FALLS DR	0	524Q	NWF	77406
RICHTOWN LN	9900	528T	NEF	77498
RICHVALE LN	300	617R	SEH	77598
RICHVALE LN	700	618K	SEH	77062
RICH VALLEY LN	14700	528S	NEF	77498
RICHVIEW CT	500	373J	NCC	77060
RICHVIEW DR	600	373J	NCC	77060
RICHWOOD RD	6500	534Y	SEH	77087
RICHWOOD OAKS DR	0	524F	NEF	77494
RICKENBACKER HOLLOW	0	256K	SEM	77357
RICKER PARK CIR	0	407W	NWC	77449
RICKETT RD	30000	246D	SWM	77355
RICKY	4900	573D	SEH	77033
RICKY	5200	574A	SEH	77033
RIDDLELINK LN	0	532S	SWH	77025
RIDDLEWOOD LN	9100	532S	SWH	77025
RIDERDALE PARK LN	10200	369G	NWC	77070
RIDERWOOD DR	10800	529P	SWH	77099
RIDGE	0	420W	BR	77532
RIDGE	500	493B	NWH	77009

Street Name	Block	Pg/Sq	Loc	Zips
RIDGE DR	100	419Z	BR	77532
RIDGE DR	1200	332Z	NCC	77073
W. RIDGE LN	0	612Z	NEB	77578
RIDGE BANK LN	12800	408Z	NWC	77041
RIDGEBAR CIR	15800	611D	SWH	77053
RIDGEBERRY DR	7100	407M	NWC	77095
RIDGEBLUFF LN	0	406Y	NWC	77449
RIDGEBRIAR DR	1500	372E	NWC	77014
RIDGEBRIAR LN	0	571K	SWH	77085
RIDGEBROOK CIR	25600	252S	SWM	77380
RIDGEBROOK LN	0	612K	PL	77545
RIDGEBURG CT	1100	488F	SWH	77077
RIDGEBURG LN	26200	367E	NWC	77433
RIDGEBURY CIR	0	407G	NWC	77095
RIDGE CANYON RD	0	502P	BT	77520
RIDGECHASE LN	14600	331X	NWC	77014
RIDGE CLEARING TRAIL	0	292D	SEM	77386
RIDGECORAL DR	10000	412B	NWC	77038
RIDGE COVE LN	0	366J	NWC	77433
RIDGE CREEK CIR	4800	611C	SWH	77053
W. RIDGECREEK CIR	5600	571Y	SWH	77053
E. RIDGE CREEK DR	4700	611D	SWH	77053
W. RIDGECREEK DR	5000	611C	SWH	77053
RIDGECREEK DR	5000	611C	SWH	77053
W. RIDGECREEK DR	5600	571Y	SWH	77053
W. RIDGECREEK DR	6300	571Y	SWH	77489
RIDGECREST DR	1800	451S	NWH	77055
RIDGECREST DR	5000	577K	PA	77504
RIDGECREST DR	5200	539X	LP	77571
RIDGECREST DR	25800	250S	NWC	77389
RIDGECROFT RD	15700	571Z	SWH	77053
RIDGECROFT RD	15800	611D	SWH	77053
RIDGECROSSING LN	1100	488F	SWH	77077
RIDGECROSS PLACE	1	250D	WD	77381
RIDGEDALE	5400	414D	NEC	77039
RIDGEDALE	6000	415A	NEC	77039
RIDGEDALE DR	2800	297Y	NEH	77345
RIDGE FALLS CT	19700	406R	NWC	77433
RIDGE FALLS DR	0	613X	NEB	77578
RIDGEFIELD RD	3100	579A	LP	77571
RIDGEFIELD PARK LN	0	366R	NWC	77433
RIDGE FOREST DR	8200	411P	NWC	77088
RIDGEGATE RD	15600	571Z	SWH	77053
RIDGE GLEN CT	20900	332Z	NCC	77073
RIDGEGLEN LN	0	488S	SWH	77082
RIDGE GREEN DR	3200	297Z	NEH	77345
RIDGEGREEN DR	16000	527C	SWC	77082
RIDGE GROVE LN	0	407J	NWC	77433
RIDGE HARBOR DR	4800	611C	SWH	77053
RIDGEHAVEN DR	5000	611C	SWH	77053
RIDGE HILL CT	19000	446R	NWC	77084
RIDGE HILL LN	3400	446M	NWC	77084
RIDGE HOLLOW CT	0	244C	WCO	77447
RIDGE HOLLOW DR	1500	372N	NWC	77067
RIDGE HOLLOW DR	1700	371M	NWC	77067
RIDGE LAKE DR	15000	527D	SWC	77082
RIDGELAND	2400	414A	NCC	77039
RIDGELAND CT	700	413B	NCC	77060
RIDGELEY DR	1000	491A	HI	77055
RIDGELEY DR	1200	451W	HI	77055
RIDGELIGHT LN	0	575Y	SEH	77075
RIDGELIGHT LN	0	575Y	SEH	77075
RIDGELINE CT	1	251A	WD	77381
RIDGELOW LN	12400	369L	NWC	77070
RIDGE MANOR CT	3800	297U	NEH	77345
RIDGE MANOR DR	5000	611C	SWH	77053
RIDGE MAPLE ST	0	371Z	NWC	77038
RIDGEMAR CIR	4700	611D	SWH	77053
RIDGEMEADOW CT	16900	527E	NEF	77083
RIDGEMONT	0	611C	SWH	77053
RIDGEMONT	6000	534Q	SEH	77087
RIDGEMONT DR	2300	610A	MC	77489
RIDGEMONT PLACE DR	5400	611C	SWH	77053
RIDGEMOOR ESTATES CT	22900	252R	SEM	77385
RIDGEMOOR ESTATES LN	2000	252R	SEM	77385
RIDGEMORE DR	1900	451S	NWH	77055
RIDGE OAK	0	415A	NEC	77039
RIDGE OAK DR	7200	411T	NWH	77088
RIDGEPARK DR	1100	539X	LP	77571
RIDGE PARK DR	15600	408J	NWC	77095
RIDGE PASS	0	293U	NCC	77373
RIDGE PATH CT	19100	291X	NWC	77388
RIDGE PATH WAY	0	291X	NWC	77388
RIDGE PINE DR	2600	337C	NEH	77345
RIDGEPOINT CT	3300	613Z	NEB	77584
RIDGEPOINT DR	4000	613Z	NEB	77584
RIDGE POINT DR	8500	451S	NWH	77055
RIDGE ROCK RD	15700	571W	SWH	77489
RIDGEROD LN	4600	611D	SWH	77053
RIDGEROE LN	15800	611D	SWH	77053
RIDGE ROW CT	5800	408Z	NWC	77041
RIDGE RUN DR	11500	369U	NWC	77064
RIDGE SCENE WAY	2900	446R	NWC	77084
RIDGESIDE DR	12300	529J	SWH	77072
RIDGE SPRING DR	0	257E	SEM	77357
RIDGE SPRINGS LN		484S	NEF	77494
RIDGESTONE	4800	611D	SWH	77053
RIDGESTONE PARK LN	26400	366H	NWC	77433
RIDGE STREAM LN	18100	326V	NWC	77429
RIDGETON DR	4600	611C	SWH	77053
RIDGE TOP DR	17000	331L	NWC	77090
RIDGETOP POLE LN	0	484X	NEF	77494
RIDGE TRAIL LN	19000	446R	NWC	77084
RIDGE TURN DR	5200	611C	SWH	77053
RIDGETURN DR	5200	571Y	SWH	77053
RIDGEVALLEY DR	1100	539X	LP	77571
RIDGEVAN	4800	611C	SWH	77053
RIDGEVIEW	0	613Z	NEB	77584
RIDGEVIEW DR	3600	609L	MC	77459
RIDGEVIEW DR	7900	451S	NWH	77055
RIDGEVIEW DR	10900	449U	NWH	77043
RIDGE VIEW DR	25200	244R	WCO	77447
RIDGEVIEW POINT	0	298P	NEC	77336
RIDGE VISTA DR	5600	337D	NEH	77345
S. RIDGEWALK DR	4500	611H	SWH	77053
E. RIDGEWALK DR	16600	611H	SWH	77053
RIDGEWAY	10	499R	BT	77520
RIDGEWAY	200	500N	BT	77520
RIDGEWAY DR	4900	577K	PA	77504
RIDGEWAY DR	5000	533V	SEH	77033
RIDGEWAY DR	6200	534V	SEH	77087
RIDGEWAY PARK CT	1800	336B	NEH	77339
RIDGEWELL DR	15200	618J	SEH	77062
RIDGEWEST DR	4800	611C	SWH	77053
RIDGEWICK CT	11500	329N	NWC	77377
RIDGE WIND LN	5400	611B	SWH	77053
RIDGEWOOD	100	298B	NEC	77336
RIDGEWOOD	1500	492R	SWH	77006
S. RIDGEWOOD CIR	11700	570L	MC	77071
N. RIDGEWOOD CIR	11700	570L	MC	77071
RIDGEWOOD DR	200	244C	WCO	77447
RIDGEWOOD DR	200	252J	OR	77386

Street Name	Block	Pg/Sq	Loc	Zips
RIDGEWOOD DR	21500	291Q	NWC	77388
RIDGEWOOD CANYON DR	12000	618D	PA	77059
RIDGEWOOD KNOLL LN	0	572U	SEH	77047
RIDGEWOOD LAKE CT	14200	618A	SEH	77062
RIDGEWOOD PLACE	1200	451X	NWH	77055
RIDGEWOOD REEF	5200	448D	NWC	77041
RIDGEWORTH LN	0	376W	NEC	77396
RIDING	4100	532W	SWH	77025
N. RIDING DR	24000	289D	NWC	77375
RIDINGWOOD DR	15000	570V	SWH	77489
RIDLON	15800	498C	CV	77530
RIEDEL DR	700	490B	SWH	77024
RIESNER	1	493L	SWH	77002
RIETTA	5000	454C	NEH	77016
RIETTA	6100	454D	NEH	77016
RIFLE GAP LN	2900	568Z	SG	77478
RIFLEMAN CIR	13400	368F	NWC	77429
RIFLEMAN TRAIL	12600	368K	NWC	77429
RIFLEWOOD CIR	1900	610J	MC	77459
RIFORD DR	0	328N	NWC	77429
RIGA CT	5400	297J	SEM	77386
RIGBY CT	8500	338W	NEC	77346
RIGBY POINT LN	0	326U	NWC	77429
RIGDALE	15000	408T	NWC	77084
RIGEL	900	656H	FR	77546
RIGEL CT	31400	248X	NWC	77375
RIGEL RD	2800	411R	NWH	77088
RIGGER LN	16600	618T	SEH	77062
RIGGING CT	16000	419A	NEC	77532
RIGGS	400	541B	BT	77520
RIGGS RD	100	453K	NWH	77022
RIGGS MILL LN	11000	524L	NWF	77406
RIGHT WAY	3000	297N	NEH	77339
RIGID RD	0	333Y	NCC	77073
RIGNESS	0	533E	SWH	77030
RIKA POINT	1600	488K	SWH	77077
RILEY	3800	532E	WU	77005
RILEY LN	100	494N	DT	77003
RILEY RD	1	612C	SWC	77047
W. RILEY RD	3400	612B	SWC	77053
RILEYBROOK CIR	18100	487A	SWC	77094
RILEY ESPEN CT	0	372C	NCC	77073
RILEY FUZZELL RD	200	292M	SP	77373
RILEY FUZZELL RD	1000	293E	SEM	77386
RILEY FUZZELL RD	2800	253Y	SEM	77386
RILEY GLEN DR	0	524K	NWF	77406
RILEY RIDGE LN	0	326U	NWC	77429
RILEY WOODS CIR	31300	253P	SEM	77386
RILL LN	15600	618N	SEH	77062
RIMCREST CT	0	484X	NEF	77494
RIMINI CT	23600	525N	NEF	77469
RIMINI LN	0	659R	LC	77573
RIMINI RIVER WAY	0	406X	NWC	77449
RIMMI RIDGE CT	0	328A	NWC	77377
RIMPLE BEND LN	0	574V	SEH	77048
RIMROCK	2000	619V	LC	77565
RIM ROCK DR	1300	412K	NWH	77088
RIMROCK DR	2800	609F	MC	77459
RIMWICK FOREST DR	26000	248J	SWM	77354
RIMWOOD RD	7100	457J	NEC	77049
RINCON DR	0	658Y	LC	77573
RINCON DR	12300	488U	SWH	77077
RINER	3200	454J	NEH	77093
RING CT	2500	609B	MC	77459
RINGFIELD DR	15000	408T	NWC	77084
RINGFORD CT	5400	408W	NWC	77084
RINGFORD RIDGE LN	0	484X	NEF	77494
RINGNECK GLEN DR	0	291N	NWC	77388
RINGOLD	700	412U	NWH	77088
RINGROSE DR	4400	609B	MC	77459
RINGWALD CT	19700	289Z	NWC	77379
RINGWOOD	600	332C	NCC	77373
RINGWOOD CT	22000	255S	SEM	77365
RINGWOOD WAY LN	0	657S	FR	77546
RINN RD	8300	455C	NEH	77078
RIO DR	0	461P	NEC	77521
RIO BELLA CT	0	659R	LC	77573
RIO BLANCO DR	7000	527M	SWC	77083
RIO BONITO RD	13900	528E	SWC	77083
RIO BRAVO RD	10000	369Y	NWC	77064
RIO CRYSTAL CIR	7800	408K	NWC	77095
RIO CRYSTAL DR	7800	408K	NWC	77095
RIO DELL DR	15700	527G	SWC	77083
RIO DEL SOL DR	15400	527L	NEF	77083
RIO GRANDE	0	255X	SEM	77365
RIO GRANDE	8000	409L	JV	77040
RIO GRANDE	8900	409C	NWC	77064
RIO GRANDE	10000	369Y	NWC	77064
RIO GRANDE DR	22800	295B	SEM	77365
RIO GRANDE ST	0	659L	LC	77573
E. RIO GRANDE RIVER	0	367W	NWC	77433
RIO GRANDE RIVER DR	28900	253U	SEM	77386
RIOJA BLUFF LN	0	446E	NWC	77449
RIO LLANO CT	15500	328N	NWC	77429
RIO MESA DR	0	367Z	NWC	77095
RION HILL CT	0	326V	NWC	77429
RIO OAKS CT	3600	331T	NWC	77068
RIO PINAR DR	14600	408K	NWC	77095
RIO PLAZA DR	15200	527H	SWC	77083
RIO QUATRO DR	0	571G	SWH	77045
RIO RANCHO CT	10800	409F	NWC	77064
RIO RIDGE LN	12200	409W	NWC	77041
RIO VALLEY CT	0	256W	SEM	77365
RIO VERDE LN	11500	456F	NEC	77044
RIO VILLA DR	19000	459N	NEC	77049
RIO VISTA	3600	533G	SEH	77021
RIPFORD CT	0	525V	NEF	77406
RIPLEY HILLS DR	0	524K	NWF	77406
RIPLING MEADOW LN	0	609S	NEF	77479
RIPPING LAKE DR	16700	327X	NWC	77429
RIPPLE	5300	291J	NWC	77389
RIPPLE LN	0	491J	HC	77024
RIPPLE BEND CT	3000	615L	PL	77581
RIPPLE BEND LN	2100	615L	PL	77581
RIPPLEBROOK DR	3200	572J	SWH	77045
RIPPLEBROOK DR	4600	571Q	SWH	77045
N. RIPPLE CREEK	0	491J	SWH	77057
S. RIPPLECREEK	500	491J	SWH	77057
RIPPLE CREEK CIR	0	501E	BT	77521
RIPPLE CREEK CIR	3100	500H	BT	77521
RIPPLE CREEK CT	1700	570W	MC	77489
RIPPLECREEK DR	300	491J	HC	77024
RIPPLE CREEK DR	1700	570W	MC	77489
RIPPLE CREEK DR	4600	500H	BT	77521
RIPPLE GLEN DR	12000	570B	SWH	77071
RIPPLE LAKE DR	9900	369W	NWC	77065
RIPPLE RIDGE	0	331S	NWC	77068
N. RIPPLE RIDGE DR	4500	611D	SWH	77053
W. RIPPLE RIDGE DR	16600	611D	SWH	77053
E. RIPPLE RIDGE DR	16600	611D	SWH	77053
RIPPLE RUSH CT	1	251E	WD	77381
RIPPLESTREAM DR	15300	331S	NWC	77068
RIPPLEWAVE DR	10300	528X	NEF	77498
RIPPLEWIND DR	15100	331T	NWC	77068
RIPPLEWIND LN	15100	331N	NWC	77068
RIPPLEWOOD LN	12500	457W	NEC	77015
RIPPLING BEND DR	2600	613W	NEB	77578
RIPPLING BROOK DR	900	620L	SB	77586
RIPPLING BROOK LN	0	289X	NWC	77375
RIPPLING CREEK LN	0	612F	PL	77545
RIPPLING CREEK WAY	14300	618B	SEH	77062
RIPPLING FIELDS CT	11000	369Z	NWC	77064
RIPPLING FIELDS DR	9000	369Z	NWC	77064
RIPPLING HOLLOW DR	6200	330G	NWC	77379
RIPPLING MEADOWS DR	11000	369U	NWC	77064
RIPPLING ROCK CT	0	612U	PL	77584
RIPPLING SHORE CT	22400	525C	NEF	77494
RIPPLING SPRINGS CT	2800	613X	NEB	77578
RIPPLING SPRINGS DR	15400	328N	NWC	77429
RIPPLING SPRINGS LN	0	659M	LC	77573
RIPPLING STREAM LN		525R	NEF	77469
RIPPLING WATER DR	15800	448A	NWC	77084
RIPPON DR	19500	292Y	NCC	77373
RIPTIDE DR	7300	529J	SWH	77072
RIP VAN WINKLE DR	12100	490E	SWH	77024
RIP VAN WINKLE DR	12500	489M	SWH	77024
RIP VAN WINKLE LN	1	490E	BH	77024
RIP VAN WINKLE LN	2600	616N	PL	77581
RISING BAY CT	0	658X	LC	77573
RISING BAY LN	0	612K	PL	77545
RISING BEND LN	0	524B	NEF	77494
RISING BLUFF LN		328P	NWC	77429
RISING BROOK DR	0	406Q	NWC	77449
RISING HILLS CT	25000	295R	SEM	77365
RISING HILLS LN	6600	609Y	NEF	77459
RISING MEADOW LN	0	524D	NEF	77494
RISING OAK LN	0	524D	NEF	77494
RISING SPRINGS LN	0	373E	NCC	77073
RISING STAR DR	19800	334R	NCC	77338
RISING SUN RD	2900	446P	NWC	77449
RISING TIDE LN	2900	660J	LC	77573
RISING WALK LN	0	609U	MC	77459
RISTINA CIR	0	573R	SEH	77048
RISTINA CIR	0	573R	SEH	77048
RITA	0	616S	PL	77581
RITA	3600	611X	FS	77545
RITA	5300	453E	NWH	77022
RITA LN	12800	496M	NEH	77015
RITA RAMBLE LN	0	378A	NEC	77346
RITOW	10800	576T	SEH	77089
RITTENBERG	0	407Z	NWC	77084
RITTENBERG CT	16000	407Z	NWC	77084
RITTENHOUSE	1	413W	NEH	77076
W. RITTENHOUSE	100	412Y	NWH	77076
E. RITTENHOUSE	100	413W	NEH	77076
W. RITTENHOUSE	400	412Y	NWH	77091
RITTENHOUSE PARK CT	18300	331E	NWC	77379
RITTENHOUSE VILLAGE CT	7100	412V	NWH	77091
RITTENHOUSE VILLAGE RD	7100	412V	NWH	77091
RITTENMORE DR	2100	570Y	MC	77489
W. RITTER CIR	15300	570G	MC	77071
E. RITTER CIR	15300	570G	MC	77071
RITZ	7900	455K	NEH	77028
RIVAGE RIDGE DR	0	445E	NWC	77493
RIVA RIDGE DR	6500	524Y	NEF	77406
RIVA RIDGE LN	12200	570G	SWH	77071
RIVA ROW	0	251G	WD	77380
RIVENDELL DR	7500	330F	NWC	77379
RIVENWOOD DR	0	406L	NWC	77433
RIVER	900	495U	NEH	77029
RIVER CIR	1	490R	HC	77063
RIVER CT	0	658L	LC	77573
RIVER DR	3900	535P	SEH	77017
RIVER DR	8100	535T	SEH	77017
RIVER RD	0	336J	NEC	77338
RIVER RD	1	499A	CV	77530
RIVER RD	200	459W	CV	77530
E. RIVER RD	18600	253C	SEM	77357
RIVER BANK	0	459W	CV	77530
RIVERBANK DR	1	251N	WD	77381
RIVERBANK RIDGE CT	9200	616E	SEC	77089
RIVERBANK RIDGE LN	11100	616E	SEC	77089
RIVER BASIN CT	11000	616A	SEC	77089
RIVERBEND	400	501P	BT	77521
RIVER BEND DR	1000	490R	HC	77063
RIVER BEND DR	2700	336L	NEH	77339
RIVERBEND CANYON LN	8300	615H	SEC	77089
RIVERBEND CROSSING	1400	569S	SG	77478
RIVERBEND POINT LN	26800	366R	NWC	77433
RIVER BEND WAY	0	297V	NEH	77345
RIVER BIRCH DR	3000	613B	NEB	77584
RIVER BIRCH DR	22600	290E	NWC	77375
RIVER BIRCH LN	1	252J	WD	77380
RIVER BIRCH WAY	15700	578T	SEH	77059
RIVER BLOSSOM LN	6200	297V	NEH	77345
RIVER BLUFF DR	6500	571J	SWH	77085
RIVER BOTTOM RD	19500	406V	NWC	77449
RIVER BRANCH DR	5700	337D	NEH	77345
RIVER BREEZE DR	19700	289W	NWC	77375
RIVER BROOK CT	19700	337S	NEC	77346
RIVER BROOK DR	19800	337N	NEC	77346
RIVER CANYON LN	0	377E	NEC	77346
RIVERCHASE LN	4200	371B	NWC	77014
RIVERCHASE FOREST CT	0	297U	NEH	77345
RIVERCHASE GLEN DR	0	297V	NEH	77345
RIVERCHASE TRAIL	5900	297V	NEH	77345
RIVERCHASE VILLAGE DR	5700	297V	NEH	77345
RIVER CLIFF LN	8500	407G	NWC	77095
RIVER CLUB	0	525U	NEF	77406
RIVER COURT DR	21100	446C	NWC	77449
RIVER CREEK DR	800	539X	LP	77571
RIVERCREEK WAY	1	569T	SG	77478
W. RIVERCREST DR	1	490S	SWH	77042
E. RIVERCREST DR	1	490S	SWH	77042
RIVERCREST DR	1700	568Y	SG	77478
RIVERCREST DR	2200	336P	NEH	77338
RIVERCROFT LN	11000	615H	SEC	77089
RIVERCROSS RD	8400	410G	NWC	77064
RIVER CYPRESS LN	0	415E	NEH	77050
RIVERDALE	800	458Z	CV	77530
RIVER DALE CANYON LN	0	335P	NCC	77338
RIVER ENDS	0	376Q	NEC	77396
RIVER FALLS DR	1900	336C	NEH	77339
RIVER FERN DR	7100	410P	NWC	77040
RIVERFIELDS DR	0	527Q	NEF	77083
RIVERFORD DR	2200	296V	NEH	77339
RIVER FOREST CT	400	488L	SWH	77079
RIVER FOREST CT	400	488M	SWH	77079
RIVER FOREST DR	14100	489J	SWH	77079
RIVER FOREST DR	14400	488M	SWH	77079
RIVER GARDEN DR	7000	407R	NWC	77095
RIVER GARDEN DR	7300	408J	NWC	77095
RIVERGATE DR	5300	334E	NCC	77373
RIVERGLADE CT	0	609P	NEF	77479
RIVERGLADE DR	8200	408E	NWC	77095
RIVER GLADE LN	5300	609S	NEF	77479
RIVER GLEN CT	6400	614T	PL	77584
RIVER GLEN DR	14300	528W	NEF	77498
RIVERGLEN FOREST DR	1900	337D	NEH	77345
RIVERGLYN DR	1000	490R	HC	77063
RIVERGREEN PARK CT	25500	485W	NEF	77494
RIVERGREEN PARK LN	4900	485S	NEF	77494
RIVERGREEN TERRACE DR		249V	NWC	77375
RIVERGROVE CT	11700	328M	NWC	77377
RIVERGROVE DR	400	497A	NEC	77015
RIVERGROVE DR	14200	329W	NWC	77070
RIVER GROVE RD	200	568P	SG	77478
RIVERGROVE BEND DR	0	337P	NEC	77346
RIVERGROVE PARK DR	0	337P	NEC	77346
RIVERHAVEN DR	1	499B	CV	77530
RIVERHILL CT	0	371H	NWC	77014
RIVER HILL DR	4800	337C	NEH	77345
RIVERHILL ROW CT		367S	NWC	77433
RIVER HOLLOW LN	1	491R	SWH	77027
RIVERINE CT	0	451X	NWH	77055
RIVERINE CT	1300	451X	NWH	77055
RIVERINE TERRACE DR	7900	525Z	NEF	77406
RIVER KEG DR	13700	528P	SWC	77083
RIVER KNOLL CT	5600	406X	NWC	77449
RIVER KNOLL LN	21200	406X	NWC	77449
RIVERLACE DR	900	488E	SWH	77079
RIVERLAND LN	0	410E	NWC	77064
RIVER LAUREL DR	12600	372E	NWC	77014
RIVERLAWN DR	1900	336C	NEH	77339
RIVERLAWN DR	2300	336D	NEH	77339
RIVERLET CT	0	326Z	NWC	77429
RIVER LILLY DR	0	297V	NEH	77345
RIVER LODGE DR	6600	330G	NWC	77379
RIVER MANOR	0	297V	NEH	77345
RIVER MAPLE LN	15600	618G	SEH	77062
RIVERMEAD CT	3300	445M	NWC	77449
RIVERMEAD DR	22000	445M	NWC	77449
RIVER MEADOW LN	11900	569A	MD	77477
RIVER MEADOWS LN	18700	447E	NWC	77084
RIVER MILL CT	6100	330H	NWC	77379
RIVER MILL DR	6500	330G	NWC	77379
RIVER MIST CT	6100	525G	NEF	77494
RIVERMIST CT	11700	328M	NWC	77377
RIVERMOSS LN	0	376W	NEC	77396
RIVERMOSS LN	3800	525B	NEF	77494
RIVER OAK CT	0	297U	NEH	77345
RIVER OAK LN	0	531J	SWH	77081
RIVER OAKS BLVD	1600	492T	SWH	77019
RIVER OAKS DR	3800	578A	PA	77505
RIVER PARK CT	11900	329W	NWC	77070
RIVER PARK DR	15000	329W	NWC	77070
RIVER PARK LN	4600	578G	PA	77505
RIVER PATH	0	484P	NEF	77494
RIVER PEAK	0	609Z	NEF	77459
RIVER PEBBLE LN	0	415E	NEH	77050
RIVER PINES DR	7200	406L	NWC	77433
RIVER PLACE DR	23600	485J	NEF	77494
RIVERPOINT DR	7600	490R	HC	77063
RIVER POINTE LN	0	406Y	NWC	77449
RIVER RANCH DR	4200	578F	PA	77505
RIVER RAPIDS LN	0	330B	NWC	77379
RIVER RAVEN CT	15800	367C	CY	77429
RIVER RIDGE CT	15600	331S	NWC	77068
RIVER RIDGE DR	11800	295Y	SEM	77365
RIVER RIDGE LOOP	0	250Q	NWC	77389
RIVERRIDGE PARK LN	11200	616E	SEC	77089
RIVER RIDGE VIEW LN	0	335N	NCC	77338
RIVER ROADS DR	15800	488E	SWH	77079
RIVERROCK CT	0	656R	FR	77546
RIVER ROCK CT	6600	406U	NWC	77449
RIVER ROCK DR	1100	570Y	MC	77489
RIVER ROCK DR	19600	406U	NWC	77449
RIVER ROCK TRAIL	2300	297V	NEH	77345
RIVER ROSE	5500	297N	NEH	77339
RIVER RUN	25200	244R	WCO	77447
RIVERS RD	3400	613Z	NEB	77578
RIVER SAGE DR	18000	407Y	NWC	77084
RIVERS EDGE TRAIL	3300	297X	NEH	77345
RIVERSHADOWS LN	20900	291X	NWC	77388
RIVERSHIRE LN	20800	333P	NCC	77073
RIVER SHORE LN	0	290P	NWC	77379
RIVERSIDE	17800	499B	CV	77530
RIVERSIDE CT	900	616U	FR	77546
RIVERSIDE DR	0	258U	SEM	77357
RIVERSIDE DR	0	528Y	SG	77478
RIVERSIDE DR	0	659C	LC	77573
RIVERSIDE DR	100	459M	HG	77562
RIVERSIDE DR	2200	533B	SEH	77004
RIVERSIDE DR	3500	616X	PL	77581
RIVERSIDE DR	17400	418R	NEC	77044
RIVERSIDE CREEK DR	25800	524K	NWF	77406
RIVER SIDE CREST LN	0	298T	NEH	77336
RIVERSIDE GROVE DR	15300	527Q	NEF	77083
RIVERSIDE LODGE DR	9200	528T	SWC	77083
RIVERSIDE OAKS DR	4200	297Y	NEH	77345
RIVERSIDE PINES DR	20500	337R	NEC	77346
RIVERSIDE RIDGE LN	21000	446J	NWC	77449
RIVERSIDE WALK LN	8400	410G	NWC	77064
RIVER SLATE CT	0	297U	NEH	77345
RIVER SPRINGS DR	12300	415J	NEH	77050
RIVERSTONE BLVD	0	609K	MC	77459
RIVER STONE DR	0	571J	SWH	77085
RIVERSTONE CROSSING DR	4700	609J	MC	77459
RIVERSTONE FALLS DR		615H	PL	77089
RIVERSTONE LAKE LN	0	616E	SEC	77089
RIVERSTONE LANDING DR	0	615M	PL	77089
RIVERSTONE RANCH	9200	616E	SEC	77089
RIVERSTONE SPRINGS DR	30500	253S	SEM	77386
RIVER TERRACE	0	298E	NEC	77336
RIVERTON	5900	454N	NEH	77026
RIVERTON ASH CT	0	326M	NWC	77429
RIVERTON CREST CT	0	326M	NWC	77429
RIVERTON CROSS RD	0	326L	NWC	77429
RIVERTON MANOR CT	13800	367C	CY	77429
RIVERTON RANCH DR	0	326M	NWC	77429
RIVER TRAIL	0	418F	NEH	77044
RIVER TRAIL	0	539N	DP	77536
RIVER TRAIL DR	12200	415E	NEH	77050
RIVERTREE LN	4600	291W	NWC	77388
RIVER VALE DR	5600	337D	NEH	77345
RIVER VALLEY DR	2000	293W	NCC	77373
RIVER VALLEY DR	2300	610A	MC	77489
RIVER VALLEY DR	3100	297W	NEH	77339
RIVERVIEW CIR	1300	489K	SWH	77077
RIVERVIEW CT	1300	489K	SWH	77077
RIVERVIEW DR	26500	295Y	SEM	77365
RIVERVIEW WAY	5900	491J	SWH	77057
RIVERVIEW WAY	7500	490M	HC	77063
RIVERVIEW WAY	10600	489L	SWH	77042
RIVERVIEW WAY	11300	489N	SWH	77077
RIVER VILLAGE DR	2000	296Y	NEH	77339
RIVER VINE CT	11700	328M	NWC	77377
RIVERWALK DR	0	294D	SEM	77365
RIVERWALK DR	0	295B	SEM	77365
RIVERWAY	1	491L	SWH	77056
RIVERWAY DR	5000	491L	SWH	77056
RIVERWAY OAK CT	2100	297V	NEH	77345
RIVERWAY OAK DR	2200	297V	NEH	77345
W. RIVERWELL CIR	8800	528P	SWC	77083
E. RIVERWELL CIR	8800	528P	SWC	77083
RIVER WESTERN DR	0	327D	NWC	77429
RIVER WILLOW DR	16800	330N	NWC	77379
RIVERWIND LN	0	615H	SEC	77089
W. RIVERWOOD DR	100	412Z	NEH	77076
E. RIVERWOOD DR	100	413W	NEH	77076
RIVERWOOD COVE	0	419A	NEC	77532
RIVERWOOD PARK DR	3400	297T	NEH	77345
RIVERWOOD TRAIL	1800	252Z	SEM	77386
S. RIVIERA CT	1600	616K	PL	77581
RIVIERA DR	2200	659D	LC	77573
RIVIERA LN	3100	336U	NEH	77338
S. RIVIERA CIRCLE	0	616P	PL	77581
N. RIVIERA CIRCLE	1400	616K	PL	77581
RIVIERE LN	20700	291U	NWC	77388
RIVINGTON CT	6700	330M	NWC	77379
RIVOLI DR	0	525J	NEF	77406
RIZZO	0	246T	SWM	77355
ROACH RD	6700	375B	NEH	77396
ROADRUNNER LN	7300	375K	HM	77396
ROADWAY	0	335Y	HM	77338
ROAMING LN	0	251T	WD	77380
ROAMING WOODS LN	3300	251S	SWM	77380
ROAN DR	12000	409A	NWC	77065
ROANDALE DR	10600	573H	SEH	77048
ROANE	8800	455G	NEH	77028
ROANOAK WOODS DR	0	248Z	NWC	77375
ROANOKE	2600	494J	NEH	77020
ROANOKE	6700	454M	NEH	77028
ROANOKE FALLS DR	0	328P	NWC	77429
ROANOKE WOODS DR	0	248V	NWC	77375
ROANWOOD CT	1700	331M	NWC	77090
ROANWOOD DR	1400	331R	NWC	77090
ROARING BLUFFS	0	367X	NWC	77095
ROARING BROOK LN	10800	490H	HC	77024
ROARING CREEK	3400	251S	SWM	77380
ROARING FORK LN	0	408G	NWC	77095
ROARING FORK LN	0	488E	SWH	77077
ROARING HILL CT	0	446N	NWC	77449
ROARING OAKS LN	0	446N	NWC	77449
ROARING PEAKS LN	0	406X	NWC	77449
ROARING POINT DR	8700	411Q	NWH	77088
ROARING RAPIDS DR	3900	578Z	PA	77059
S. ROARING RIVER CT	18400	377B	NEC	77346
N. ROARING RIVER CT	18500	337X	NEC	77346
ROARING SPRINGS DR	7500	410H	NWC	77064
ROARING SPRINGS LN	1400	619D	PA	77586
ROARING SPRINGS RD	4800	577L	PA	77505
ROARK RD	9200	529Y	SWH	77099
ROARK RD	11300	569C	SWH	77031
ROATAN CALLE	0	660S	GCO	77539
ROB LN	31100	286C	SWM	77355
ROBBIE	800	453T	NWH	77009
ROBBIE RD	0	330B	NWC	77379
ROBBIE CREEK LN	0	375X	NEC	77396
ROBBINS DR	300	490L	PP	77024
ROBBINS RD	13500	368G	NWC	77429
ROBBS CROSSING	0	289Z	NWC	77379
ROBCREST WAY	0	570S	MC	77489
ROBECK	19200	326C	NWC	77377
ROBECK	19300	286Y	NWC	77377
ROBERSON	33600	242W	WCO	77484
ROBERSON RD	6600	571S	SWH	77085
ROBERSON RD	7000	571S	SWH	77085
ROBERT	0	454N	NEH	77026
ROBERT	2200	536V	PA	77502
ROBERT	1200	502N	BT	77521
ROBERT DR	24600	296L	SEM	77365
ROBERTA	0	249W	NWC	77375
ROBERTA LN	5800	374R	NEH	77396
ROBERTA LN	5900	375N	NEH	77396
ROBERTCREST	13000	413H	NCC	77039
ROBERT E LEE RD	11800	456H	NEC	77044
ROBERT E LEE RD	13000	457E	NEC	77044
ROBERT JOHN LN	3300	374X	NCC	77032
ROBERT LEE RD	100	453U	NEH	77009
ROBERTS	0	577T	SEH	77034
ROBERTS	100	494N	SEH	77003
ROBERTS	1000	615B	PL	77581
ROBERTS	2000	493V	SEH	77004
ROBERTS	5400	444X	KT	77494
ROBERTS BLVD	3700	502C	NEC	77521
ROBERTS LN	21800	256C	SEM	77357
ROBERTS RD	17000	324G	NWC	77447
ROBERTS RD	18500	284Z	NWC	77447
ROBERTS RD	23200	256M	SEM	77357
ROBERTS CEMETERY LN	0	285M	NWC	77447
ROBERTS CEMETERY LN	20000	285M	NWC	77447
ROBERTS CEMETERY RD	23500	245Y	SWM	77447
ROBERTS HILL DR	0	366N	NWC	77433
ROBERTSON	2800	493D	NEH	77009
ROBERTSON	3500	453V	NEH	77009
ROBERTSON RD	200	656N	NEB	77511
ROBERTS RUN LN	22800	485Y	NEF	77494
ROBERTS TRAIL	300	413J	NCC	77037
ROBERTSVALE RD	13400	413J	NCC	77037
ROBILLARD SPRINGS LN	0	524C	NEF	77494
ROBILLARD SPRINGS LN	0	524C	NEF	77494
ROBIN	100	538F	DP	77536
ROBIN	700	493P	SWH	77019
ROBIN	9700	539T	LP	77571
ROBIN	22000	286J	NWC	77447
ROBIN	32100	322T	WCO	77484
ROBIN AVE	1300	444Z	KT	77493
ROBIN BLVD	12200	572M	SWH	77045
ROBIN CIR	700	536U	PA	77502
ROBIN LN	16000	246Z	SWM	77355
ROBIN LN	18900	286H	NWC	77377
ROBIN RD	100	500E	BT	77520
ROBIN CAPER CT	0	249B	SWM	77382
ROBINDALE LN	0	609H	MC	77459
ROBINDALE CREEK DR	0	487Z	SWC	77082
ROBINDELL DR	8400	530R	SWH	77074
ROBINGLEN DR	13200	528G	SWH	77083
ROBIN GROVE CT	15400	326S	NWC	77433
ROBIN HILL CT	13500	578W	SEH	77059
ROBINHOOD	1700	536R	PA	77502
ROBINHOOD	2200	532C	SWH	77005
ROBINHOOD CIR	1	381G	LCO	77535
ROBINHOOD CIR	2700	615P	PL	77581
ROBIN HOOD CT	0	449T	NWH	77043
ROBINHOOD CT	0	244M	WCO	77447
ROBINHOOD DR	25100	244M	WCO	77447
ROBINHOODS WELL DR	9000	329H	NWC	77379

Street Name	Block	Pg/Sq	Loc	Zips
ROBINHOOD TRAIL	1	381G	LCO	77535
ROBIN KNOLL CT	0	611S	FS	77545
ROBIN LAKE LN	1	490N	SWH	77024
ROBIN MEADOW	5400	614F	PL	77581
ROBIN MEADOW CIR	12300	568H	SF	77477
ROBIN MEADOW CT	4200	446H	NWC	77449
ROBIN NEST WAY	0	332Z	NCC	77073
ROBIN PARK CT	0	297J	SEM	77365
ROBIN RIDGE CIR	0	657N	FR	77546
ROBIN RIDGE DR	8100	375U	NEC	77396
ROBIN RUN DR	1	250C	WD	77381
S. ROBINS	0	577Y	SEH	77034
N. ROBINS	0	577Y	SEH	77034
ROBINS CREST DR	12700	328L	NWC	77377
ROBINS FOREST DR	1400	329C	NWC	77379
ROBINSHIRE LN	0	573T	SEC	77047
ROBINS NEST LN	22900	291E	NWC	77389
ROBINSON DR	700	536M	PA	77506
ROBINSON DR	3300	615B	PL	77581
ROBINSON LN	23600	257J	SEM	77357
ROBINSON RD	100	252J	OR	77386
ROBINSON RD	101	252J	SEM	77385
ROBINSON RD	800	539Q	LP	77571
ROBINSON RD	2900	609H	MC	77459
ROBINSON RD	3300	610J	MC	77459
ROBINSON RD	27200	252K	SEM	77385
ROBINSON BEND DR	0	293G	SEM	77386
ROBINSON PARK CT	0	293L	SEM	77386
ROBINSON POND DR	0	257E	SEM	77357
ROBINSON ROAD CT	2600	610J	MC	77459
ROBIN SOUND	5400	614F	PL	77581
ROBIN SPUR	1900	614F	PL	77581
ROBINS REST	14000	420R	NEC	77532
ROBINS ROSE LN	0	450K	NWH	77080
ROBINS WAY	800	569T	NEF	77477
ROBIN WALK LN	1	251R	WD	77380
ROBINWICK CT	6700	330R	NWC	77379
ROBINWOOD	1	490C	HE	77024
ROBINWOOD	30500	242C	WCO	77484
ROBINWOOD	0	538V	DP	77536
ROBINWOOD DR	300	252P	SEM	77386
ROBINWOOD DR	800	570S	SF	77477
ROBITA	1	493K	SWH	77019
ROBLE CT	0	571H	SWH	77045
ROBLE DR	0	571H	SWH	77045
ROBLE GREEN TRAIL	20300	337U	NEC	77346
ROBLEY	2400	536V	PA	77502
ROBLYNN LN	0	492B	NWH	77008
ROBMORE	100	453B	NEH	77076
ROBSON DR	14600	328X	NWC	77429
ROBS RUN CT	0	366U	NWC	77433
ROBWOOD CT	0	446J	NWC	77449
ROCCOS TRAIL	0	528C	SWH	77082
ROCHDALE	3200	532P	SWH	77025
ROCHELLE CT	14600	367A	NWC	77429
ROCHELLE DR	14300	374Z	NCC	77032
ROCHEN RD	31100	322Y	WCO	77484
ROCHE ROCK DR	0	376T	NWC	77396
ROCHESTER	13500	497F	NEC	77015
ROCHESTER LAKE LOOP	0	405T	NWC	77493
ROCHESTER TRAIL LN	0	658Z	LC	77573
ROCHOW	500	492R	SWH	77019
ROCKAMPTON DR	12400	570E	SWH	77031
ROCKARBOR DR	2800	490X	SWH	77063
ROCKAWAY DR	10100	414Z	NEH	77016
ROCKAWAY POINT LN	7500	525K	NEF	77407
ROCKBEND	16700	407Q	NWC	77084
ROCKBOURNE DR	6100	375E	NCC	77396
ROCKBRIDGE LN	6600	534C	SEH	77023
ROCKBRIDGE MEADOW LN	0	571F	SWH	77085
ROCKBROOK DR	600	497D	NEC	77015
ROCK BROOK FALLS LN	0	660E	LC	77573
ROCKBY DR	6300	571T	SWH	77085
ROCK CANYON CT	0	328P	NWC	77377
ROCK CANYON DR	1000	485H	SWC	77450
ROCKCHAPEL	27100	247Z	SWM	77355
ROCKCHESTER DR	22000	485M	SWC	77450
ROCKCLIFF DR	8400	412M	NCC	77037
ROCK COVE	500	488A	SWH	77079
ROCK CREEK CT	0	377B	NEC	77346
ROCK CREEK DR	0	295V	NEH	77365
ROCK CREEK DR	0	485E	NEF	77494
ROCKCREEK LN	0	458S	NEC	77049
ROCKCREST DR	9700	450E	NWH	77041
ROCKCREST DR	10400	449H	NWH	77041
ROCK DAISY DR	0	293C	SEM	77386
ROCKDALE DR	3200	297J	SEM	77365
ROCKDALE BRIDGE CT	10200	528W	NEF	77498
ROCKDALE BRIDGE LN	15100	528W	NEF	77498
ROCK DOVE LN	14100	377W	NEC	77044
ROCK EAST DR	16500	332Q	NCC	77073
ROCK ELM LN	14700	288A	NWC	77377
ROCKERGATE DR	6600	611A	SWH	77489
ROCKET CRESS CT	0	329L	NWC	77379
ROCKETS	6100	370G	NWC	77066
ROCK FALL MEADOWS ST	0	577S	SEH	77034
ROCK FALLS CT	7600	407M	NWC	77095
ROCK FALLS DR	2700	296W	SEM	77339
ROCK FALLS WAY	12700	448D	NWC	77041
N. ROCKFERN CT	1	251Z	WD	77380
ROCKFERN RD	1	251Z	WD	77380
ROCKFIELD DR	6300	578E	PA	77505
ROCKFORD DR	8100	534W	SEH	77033
ROCKFORD DR	11100	574J	SEH	77048
ROCKFORD HALL DR	8300	330N	NWC	77379
ROCK FOREST LN	13700	415B	NEC	77396
ROCKGATE DR	22000	334E	NCC	77373
ROCKGLEN	13100	497E	NEH	77015
ROCK GREEN CT	0	485E	NEF	77494
ROCKHARBOR	0	369P	NWC	77070
ROCK HARBOR LN	0	407B	NWC	77095
ROCK HARBOR LN	0	660E	LC	77573
ROCK HARBOUR CT	20700	446S	NWC	77449
ROCKHAVEN DR	2100	618G	SEH	77062
ROCKHILL	7500	535X	SEH	77061
ROCKHILL GROVE DR	0	367D	NWC	77429
ROCKHILL POINT DR	13100	367H	CY	77429
ROCK HOLLOW LN	0	250U	NWC	77389
ROCK HOUSE RD	15600	373W	NEH	77060
ROCKHURST DR	8900	450K	NWH	77080
ROCKHURST MOUNTAIN DR	0	450K	NWH	77080
ROCKIN DR	1500	488R	SWH	77077
ROCKINGHAM	3500	573C	SEH	77051
ROCKINGTON LN	15000	457Z	NEC	77530
ROCKIN SEVEN DR	24000	325J	NWC	77447
ROCKIN SEVEN DR	24200	324M	NWC	77447
ROCK KNOLL DR	15000	527R	NEF	77083
ROCKLAND DR	5000	614Q	PL	77584
ROCKLAND DR	11700	370N	NWC	77064
ROCKLEDGE DR	14900	328W	NWC	77429
ROCKLEIGH PLACE	100	535Q	SEH	77017
ROCKLEY RD	10400	529Y	SWH	77099

Street Name	Block	Pg/Sq	Loc	Zips
ROCK MAPLE LN	0	410M	NWC	77040
ROCKMEAD DR	600	336A	SEM	77339
ROCK MILL LN	14900	568A	NEF	77498
ROCKMONT CT	8500	610F	SWH	77489
ROCKMOOR CT	3100	569P	SG	77478
ROCKMORE DR	8600	370N	NWC	77064
ROCKMORE DR	9200	369R	NWC	77064
ROCK OAK PLACE	12200	251V	WD	77380
ROCK PASS DR	9700	409G	NWC	77064
ROCKPATH	0	407U	NWC	77084
ROCK PIGEON CT	0	366S	NWC	77433
ROCK PINE CT	1	251E	WD	77381
ROCKPOINT CIR	3900	660L	LC	77573
ROCKPOINT DR	500	485D	SWC	77450
ROCKPORT CT	0	568E	SG	77498
ROCKPORT HILLS DR	0	367W	NWC	77433
ROCK RANGE LN	0	574V	SEH	77048
ROCKRIDGE CT	1	250D	WD	77381
ROCK RIDGE DR	0	458S	NEC	77049
ROCKRIDGE DR	1	250D	WD	77381
ROCKRILL DR	3000	572F	SWH	77045
ROCK RIVER LN	10600	367T	NWC	77433
ROCK ROSE	7800	533V	SEH	77051
ROCK SHELF DR	0	328E	NWC	77377
ROCKSHIRE DR	13400	414E	NCC	77039
ROCKSHIRE DR	14100	374W	NCC	77039
ROCK SHOALS WAY	0	612L	PL	77584
ROCKSIDE LN	7800	330E	NWC	77379
ROCKSPRAY PLACE	100	249R	NWH	77375
ROCKSPRAY PLACE	100	249R	NWH	77375
ROCK SPRINGS DR	3500	297X	NEH	77345
ROCK SPRINGS DR	5400	539X	LP	77571
ROCKSPRINGS RIDGE	14400	328N	NWC	77429
ROCKSTONE	0	407R	NWC	77084
ROCKSTONE	16700	407Q	NWC	77084
ROCKTON HILLS LN	4600	609S	NEF	77479
ROCKTREE DR	9600	410R	NWH	77040
ROCKVIEW LEDGE LN		366V	NWC	77433
ROCKVILLE DR	11700	369R	NWC	77064
ROCKWALL TRAIL DR	0	377C	NEC	77346
ROCKWATER DR	0	446J	NWC	77449
ROCKWELL BLVD	14400	571S	SWH	77085
ROCKWELL PARK BLVD	200	250N	NWC	77389
ROCKWELL SQUARE PLACE	0	250N	NWC	77389
ROCK WEST DR	16500	332Q	NCC	77073
W. ROCK WING PLACE	0	251B	WD	77381
E. ROCK WING PLACE	0	251B	WD	77381
ROCKWOOD DR	4400	534A	SEH	77004
ROCKWOOD PARK LN	0	366Q	NWC	77433
ROCKY LN	1	410K	NWC	77040
ROCKY BANK DR	19500	329A	NWC	77375
ROCKY BAY RD	0	378Q	NEC	77532
ROCKY BEND DR	500	489P	SWH	77077
ROCKY BEND LN	0	613R	PL	77584
ROCKY BLUFF DR	13600	571J	SWH	77085
ROCKY BRANCH DR	0	448B	NWC	77084
ROCKY BRIAR CT	19000	328G	NWC	77377
ROCKY BRIAR LN	12700	328F	NWC	77377
ROCKY BRIDGE LN	15300	326T	NWC	77433
ROCKY BROOK DR	5600	297Z	NEH	77345
ROCKY BROOK FALLS	0	289D	NWC	77375
ROCKY CANYON DR	0	613R	PL	77584
ROCKY CLIFF CT	17800	407K	NWC	77095
ROCKY CORAL DR	0	446D	NWC	77449
ROCKY COVE CT	0	612L	PL	77584
ROCKY COVE DR	0	612L	PL	77584
ROCKY CREEK	1	413W	NEH	77076
ROCKY CREEK	100	412Z	NEH	77076
ROCKY CREEK DR	0	609R	MC	77459
ROCKY CREEK LN	2100	616N	PL	77581
ROCKY CREST DR	3000	445R	NWC	77449
ROCKY CREST LN	0	613R	PL	77584
ROCKY EDGE DR	0	406C	NWC	77433
ROCKY FALLS LN	0	298V	NEC	77336
ROCKYGATE DR	24000	293Y	NCC	77373
ROCKYGATE LN	0	657P	FR	77546
ROCKY GLEN CT	0	332H	NCC	77373
ROCKY GLEN LN	0	332H	NCC	77373
ROCKY HILL DR	12600	370D	NWC	77066
ROCKY HOLLOW LN	0	659H	LC	77573
ROCKY HOLLOW LN	2200	486N	SWC	77450
ROCKY HOLLOW RD	9700	579B	LP	77571
ROCKY ISLE DR	0	612J	PL	77545
ROCKY KNOLL	0	501N	BT	77521
ROCKY KNOLL DR	11900	489N	SWH	77077
ROCKY KNOLL DR	12300	488R	SWH	77077
ROCKY LAKE CT	12200	328Z	NWC	77070
ROCKY LAKE DR	11900	328Z	NWC	77070
ROCKY LANDING LN	0	484X	NEF	77494
ROCKY LEDGE LN	3600	484T	NEF	77494
ROCKY MANOR LN	4900	446D	NWC	77449
ROCKY MEADOW DR	12600	489D	SWH	77024
ROCKYMEADOW LN	4900	446D	NWC	77084
ROCKY MEADOW LN	12600	615L	PL	77581
ROCKY MILL DR	11200	369J	NWC	77429
ROCKY MOUNT DR	800	412L	NWH	77088
ROCKY MOUNTAIN DR	500	412M	NCC	77037
ROCKY NOOK DR	6100	375J	NEH	77396
ROCKY OAK CT	15400	618B	SEH	77059
ROCKY PEAK LN	7800	527J	NEF	77407
S. ROCKY POINT CIR	0	250Q	NWC	77389
N. ROCKY POINT CIR	0	250Q	NWC	77389
ROCKY POINT CT	0	250Q	NWC	77389
ROCKY POINT DR	0	613R	PL	77584
ROCKY POINT DR	0	250Q	NWC	77389
ROCKYRIDGE DR	2700	490X	SWH	77063
ROCKY RIDGE LN	0	526K	NEF	77407
ROCKY RIVER RD	600	491Q	SWH	77056
ROCKY SHORES DR	19700	289W	NWC	77375
ROCKY SHORES LN	0	615M	PL	77089
ROCKY SPRINGS CT	0	612Q	PL	77584
ROCKY SPRINGS DR	0	612Q	PL	77584
ROCKY SPRINGS TRAIL	12200	572L	SWH	77045
ROCKY TERRACE CT	0	485W	NEF	77494
ROCKYTOP CIR	11700	371L	NWC	77067
ROCKY TRACE LN	0	406L	NWC	77433
ROCKY TRAIL DR	5500	297N	NEH	77339
ROCKY VALLEY DR	8600	527R	NEF	77083
ROCKYWALK CT	25500	485W	NEF	77494
ROCKY WOODS DR	2700	337A	NEH	77339
ROCKY WOODS DR	3700	297W	NEH	77339
RODALE DR	0	458N	NEC	77530
RODEO BEND CIR	2300	659X	DI	77539
RODEO BEND DR	1400	659X	DI	77539
RODEO SQUARE CT	0	528H	SWH	77072
RODEO SQUARE DR	12700	528H	SWH	77072
RODGERDALE	2500	489Y	SWH	77042
RODGERS RD	9300	329U	NWC	77070
RODNEY	2300	576E	SEH	77034
RODNEY LN	1	502T	BT	77520
RODNEY RAY BLVD	9100	410L	NWC	77040
RODRIGO	6200	492F	SWH	77007

Street Name	Block	Pg/Sq	Loc	Zips
RODRIQUEZ RD	0	614N	PL	77584
ROE DR	3000	534M	SEH	77087
ROEBLING CT	0	377D	NEC	77346
ROEBOURNE LN	7500	370A	NWC	77070
ROEBOURNE LN	8100	369D	NWC	77070
ROEBUCK DR	0	335W	NEH	77338
ROEHAMPTON CT	5700	407Y	NWC	77084
ROESMARY KNOLL LN	0	524K	NEF	77406
ROESNER LN	24400	484L	NEF	77494
ROESNER RD	0	485A	SWC	77450
ROESNER RD	900	484M	NEF	77494
ROESNER RD	900	484T	NEF	77494
ROESNER RD	900	485J	NEF	77494
ROESNER RD		484Q	NEF	77494
ROESNER RD		484S	NEF	77494
ROGAN	0	456X	NEH	77013
ROGERDALE	0	529G	SWH	77072
ROGERDALE	4000	529C	SWH	77072
ROGEROVER	0	489W	SWH	77082
ROGERS	0	613S	NEB	77584
E. ROGERS	200	453E	NEH	77022
ROGERS	3100	453K	NWH	77022
ROGERS LAKE LN	1400	526X	NEF	77407
ROGGE	0	458J	NEC	77049
ROGIANO LN	0	659Q	LC	77573
ROGUE CREEK LN	24400	251W	SWM	77380
ROGUE RIVER DR	7000	371S	NWC	77086
ROHM & HAAS	100	538H	DP	77536
ROIDE CT	0	407W	NWC	77449
ROJO ROCK LN	0	406D	NWC	77433
ROLAND	3000	454W	NEH	77026
ROLAND AVE	23300	296D	SEM	77357
ROLAND RD	4000	444H	NWC	77493
ROLAND CANYON DR	0	406H	NWC	77433
ROLAND ORCHARD CT	29700	253X	SEM	77386
ROLAND RUE	2100	615V	PL	77581
ROLBURY LN	12200	370M	NWC	77066
ROLFE LN	5900	408X	NWC	77084
ROLGOM PLACE CT	0	533P	SEH	77021
ROLIDO DR	2700	490U	SWH	77063
ROLK RD	0	488T	SWH	77077
ROLK RD	2200	488T	SWH	77077
ROLKE RD	9700	529T	SWH	77099
ROLLA	6300	451Y	NWH	77055
ROLLAND	200	501X	BT	77520
ROLLAND	6200	412W	NWH	77091
ROLLER MILL LN	10800	527Z	NEF	77498
ROLLESTON LN	0	576R	SEH	77034
ROLLICK DR	0	249V	NWC	77375
ROLLINFORD LN	23600	485X	NEF	77494
ROLLING ACRES DR	16800	375J	NCC	77396
ROLLING BEND LN	0	527N	NEF	77407
ROLLING BONES	16500	527X	NEF	77498
ROLLINGBROOK DR	300	501P	BT	77521
ROLLINGBROOK DR	6100	530Z	SWH	77096
ROLLINGBROOK DR	7600	530Y	SWH	77071
ROLLING CREEK	0	577L	PA	77505
ROLLING CREEK BLVD	0	526P	NEF	77407
ROLLING CREEK DR	500	339A	NEC	77336
ROLLING CREEK DR	700	338D	NEC	77336
ROLLING CREEK DR	16900	331H	NWC	77090
ROLLING FIELD DR	23600	525E	NEF	77494
ROLLING FIELD LN	4400	609N	NEF	77479
ROLLING FOG DR	0	612F	PL	77545
ROLLING FOG DR	2700	657C	SEC	77546
ROLLING FOREST	0	244B	WCO	77447
ROLLING FOREST DR	3500	331G	NWC	77388
ROLLING FORK LN	7300	410P	NWC	77040
ROLLING GLEN	11200	329F	NWC	77375
ROLLING GLEN DR	2100	292R	NCC	77373
ROLLING GLEN DR	2300	293N	NCC	77373
ROLLING GREEN DR	4000	619L	TL	77586
ROLLING GREEN LN	3300	609L	MC	77459
ROLLING HILLS DR	17600	255J	SEM	77365
ROLLING HILLS DR	24300	244C	WCO	77447
ROLLING HILLS LN	2000	446Q	NWC	77449
ROLLING KNOLL	0	525E	NEF	77494
ROLLING KNOLLS	11600	490K	BH	77024
ROLLING LINKS CT	1	252N	WD	77380
ROLLING MEADOW LN	22300	485Z	NEF	77450
ROLLING MEADOWS	24000	289B	NWC	77375
ROLLING MEADOWS	24500	249X	NWC	77375
ROLLING MEADOWS DR	2100	336C	NEH	77339
ROLLING MILL DR	500	568K	SG	77498
ROLLING MILL DR	6500	411J	NWH	77088
ROLLING MILL LN	1	252J	WD	77380
ROLLING MWEADOW CT	0	614G	PL	77581
ROLLING OAKS	9200	249Q	NWC	77375
ROLLING OAKS DR	6700	524Y	NEF	77406
S. ROLLING OAKS DR	8100	250J	NWC	77389
N. ROLLING OAKS DR	8100	250J	NWC	77389
ROLLING OAKS DR	15000	329W	NWC	77070
ROLLING PINE DR	15600	457L	NEC	77049
ROLLING POINTE CIR	3800	446J	NWC	77449
ROLLING RAPIDS RD	0	378A	NEC	77346
ROLLING RIDGE DR	0	524A	NEF	77494
ROLLING RIDGE DR	7700	528M	SWH	77072
ROLLING RIVER CT	0	417D	NEH	77044
ROLLING RIVER LN	0	417D	NEH	77044
ROLLING ROCK	7600	410P	NWC	77040
ROLLING ROCK CT	8900	410P	NWC	77040
ROLLING RUN CT	800	617M	SEH	77062
ROLLING SAGE DR	19200	446M	NWC	77449
ROLLING SHORES CT	18600	378A	NEC	77346
W. ROLLING SILVER LN	0	484T	NEF	77494
E. ROLLING SILVER LN	0	484T	NEF	77494
ROLLING SPRINGS LN	3600	445M	NWC	77449
ROLLING STONE DR	0	538Z	DP	77536
ROLLING STONE DR	1900	656R	FR	77546
ROLLINGSTONE RD	5000	526S	NEF	77407
ROLLING STREAM DR	11700	329A	NWC	77375
ROLLING TERRACE DR	3400	331G	NWC	77388
ROLLING THICKET DR	0	293D	SEM	77386
ROLLING TIMBERS	24000	286B	SWM	77355
ROLLING TIMBERS CT	5100	448B	NWC	77084
ROLLING TIMBERS DR	15600	448B	NWC	77084
ROLLING VALLEY DR	12600	368J	NWC	77429
ROLLING VIEW CT	4700	297Q	NEH	77345
ROLLING VIEW TRAIL	16200	326P	NWC	77433
ROLLING WATER DR	6100	370C	NWC	77069
ROLLING WOOD	100	500E	BT	77520
ROLLINGWOOD CIR	200	500E	BT	77520
ROLLING WOOD DR	1	450X	NWH	77080
W. ROLLINGWOOD DR	100	247G	SWM	77362
ROLLING WOOD DR	33100	248N	SWM	77362
ROLLINGWOOD LOOP N.	0	524A	NEF	77494
ROLLINGWOOD LOOP S.	0	524A	NEF	77494
ROLLINS	5500	451D	NWH	77091
ROLLINSON PARK DR	0	289Y	NWC	77379
ROLLINSON PARK DR		289Y	NWC	77379
ROLLS ROYCE CT	800	375M	NEC	77396
ROLSTER	0	248Q	SWM	77354

Street Name	Block	Pg/Sq	Loc	Zips
ROMA	3400	450M	NWH	77080
ROMAINE LN	700	332E	NWC	77090
ROMAINE LN	1000	331M	NWC	77090
ROMAN LN	0	258B	SEM	77357
ROMAN FOREST BLVD	25300	257E	SEM	77357
ROMAN FOREST BLVD	28000	258D	SEM	77357
ROMAN HILLS CT	10400	369G	NWC	77070
ROMAN HILLS LN	13300	369G	NWC	77070
ROMANO LN	2800	659M	LC	77573
ROMANO PARK LN	1600	332N	NWC	77090
ROMANO PARK LN	1700	331R	NWC	77090
ROMANS	1900	535F	SEH	77012
ROMANY CT	0	299T	NEC	77336
ROMAYOR CT	2300	614M	PL	77581
ROME DR	0	616K	PL	77089
ROMEA	7700	455S	NEH	77028
ROMEO	800	536V	PA	77502
ROMERO DR	1300	616K	PL	77581
ROMERO LN	21800	245V	SWM	77355
ROMFORD LN	15300	458W	NEC	77530
ROMITI CT	0	445E	NWC	77493
ROMNEY RD	7500	530K	SWH	77036
ROMONA BLVD	5700	411F	NWC	77086
ROMSLEY LN	6600	457P	NEC	77049
ROMULUS CT	0	294P	SEM	77386
RON CIR	200	656D	FR	77546
RONALD	11500	414L	NCC	77093
RONALDSAY MEWS	16100	407H	NWC	77095
RONAN RD	0	373N	NEH	77060
RONAN PARK PLACE	300	373S	NEH	77060
RONDA LN	9200	530S	SWH	77074
RONDA DALE DR	0	325S	HK	77447
RONDEL	0	659E	LC	77573
RONDELET DR	3700	293M	SEM	77386
N. RONDELET DR	4000	293M	SEM	77390
S. RONDELET DR	27400	293M	SEM	77390
RONDO CT	8100	410J	NWC	77040
RONDOUT	12900	571H	SWH	77045
RONICO	0	459K	NEC	77049
RONIER	0	538R	DP	77536
RONNIE DR	3200	463H	MB	77520
RONSON LN	2900	462X	NEC	77521
RONSON RD	1500	450Z	NWH	77055
ROOK BLVD	6800	534Y	SEH	77087
ROOKIN	6000	530D	SWH	77074
ROOKIN	6100	530H	SWH	77074
ROOKWOOD CT	0	372C	NCC	77073
ROOS RD	6300	531J	SWH	77074
ROOS RD	7900	530J	SWH	77036
ROOS RD	11600	529E	SWH	77072
ROOSEVELT	1200	535F	SEH	77012
ROOSEVELT DR	1400	538R	DP	77536
ROOSTER ST	0	571R	SWH	77045
ROOT	0	290D	NWC	77389
ROOT	7200	290F	NWC	77389
ROOT RD	5700	290H	NWC	77389
ROOTS DOWN WAY	0	258Q	NEC	77357
ROPER	500	576E	SEH	77034
ROPERS TRAIL CT	20500	486T	SWC	77450
ROSA ALLEN	5100	535M	SEH	77017
ROSA AURORA WAY	0	250X	NWC	77389
ROSALIA CT	0	525J	NEF	77406
ROSALIE	400	493T	SWH	77006
ROSALIE	1000	494W	SEH	77004
ROSALIE PARK CT	0	253Q	SEM	77386
ROSALIE PLACE	1800	493Y	SEH	77004
ROSALINA RIDGE CT	0	328E	NWC	77377
ROSALIND LN	4000	572W	SWH	77053
ROSALINDA LN	0	373A	NCC	77073
ROSALYN CT	2000	568Z	SG	77478
W. ROSAMOND	100	452D	NWH	77076
ROSAMOND	100	453A	NEH	77076
ROSAMOND	2400	492U	SWH	77098
ROSA RIDGE LN	12400	409W	NWC	77041
ROSA RITA DR	0	658Y	LC	77573
ROSAS	1100	569Z	NEF	77477
ROSASTONE TRAIL	0	489D	NWH	77024
ROSBROOK DR	10000	412B	NWC	77038
ROSCOE	1500	580D	LP	77571
ROSCOE DR	0	537E	PA	77506
ROSE	2700	659Z	GCO	77539
ROSE	2800	537Q	PA	77503
ROSE	3900	492G	SWH	77007
ROSE CIR	21800	285D	SWM	77355
ROSE CT	1	493Y	SEH	77004
ROSE LN	5300	334E	NCC	77373
ROSE LN	5700	452B	NWH	77091
ROSE LN	20800	286J	NWC	77447
ROSE RD	2100	614M	PL	77581
ROSE ANN	12800	570J	SF	77477
ROSE ARBOR LN	400	373W	NEH	77060
ROSEBANK CT	4900	609A	SG	77478
ROSEBANK DR	4000	447F	NWC	77084
ROSEBAY	0	609F	MC	77459
ROSEBAY CT	1900	568W	SG	77479
ROSE BAY DR	0	612J	PL	77545
ROSEBAY DR	4400	452E	NWH	77018
ROSEBAY RD	0	460W	BT	77521
ROSE BAY TRAIL	16600	327N	NWC	77429
ROSEBEND DR	1700	485L	NEF	77494
ROSEBERRY DR	3100	579B	LP	77571
ROSEBERRY MANOR DR	1200	329G	NWC	77379
ROSEBLUFF CT	2500	485N	NEF	77494
ROSEBRANCH CT	13800	578W	SEH	77059
ROSEBRIAR DR	15700	570Z	SWH	77489
ROSEBRIER PARK LN	11900	489W	SWH	77082
ROSEBROOK CIR	7000	330F	NWC	77379
ROSEBROOK DR	0	612R	PL	77584
ROSEBROOK DR	0	612R	PL	77584
ROSEBROOK LN	0	330G	NWC	77379
ROSE BUD	0	257Q	SEM	77357
ROSE BUD	0	619H	TL	77586
ROSEBUD DR	2700	613T	NEB	77584
ROSEBUD DR	3800	572S	SWH	77053
ROSEBUD DR	4600	571V	SWH	77053
ROSEBUD LN	18700	286H	NWC	77377
ROSEBUD BEND DR	7200	377C	NEC	77346
ROSEBUD DALE CT	3000	446Q	NWC	77084
ROSEBUD KNOLL CT	18800	326Z	NWC	77429
ROSEBUD MEDIAN	0	619H	TL	77586
ROSEBURY DR	2500	414A	NCC	77039
ROSE BUSH TRAIL	5900	525A	NEF	77494
ROSE CANYON LN	0	485S	NEF	77494
ROSECASTLE DR	8800	329D	NWC	77379
ROSE CLOVER LN	0	293G	SEM	77386
ROSE COTTAGE DR	15000	330U	NWC	77069
ROSECREST CT	3300	569S	SG	77478
ROSECREST DR	13000	571G	SWH	77045
ROSECROFT DR	10400	574J	SEH	77048
ROSE CROSSING LN	20800	290T	NWC	77379
ROSEDALE	700	493X	SWH	77006
ROSEDALE	900	493X	SWH	77002

Street Name	Block	Pg/Sq	Loc	Zips
ROSEDALE	1000	493X	SWH	77004
ROSEDALE	2100	533C	SEH	77004
ROSEDALE AVE	0	571Z	SWH	77053
ROSEDALE CIR	4900	533D	SEH	77004
ROSEDALE BROOK CT	1	251E	WD	77381
ROSEDALE OAKS DR	0	290D	NWC	77389
ROSE DAWN LN	19800	289Y	NWC	77379
ROSE DAWN LN	19800	289Y	NWC	77379
ROSEDOWN CIR	17500	327E	NWC	77429
ROSEDUST TRAIL	0	326N	NWC	77433
ROSE ELFE LN	100	379P	NEC	77532
ROSE FAIR CT	20100	486G	SWC	77450
ROSE FAIR DR	1200	486G	SWC	77450
ROSEFIELD CT	700	613F	NEB	77584
ROSEFIELD DR	2100	450N	NWH	77080
ROSEFORK LN	0	292B	NCC	77373
ROSE GARDEN DR	8300	527Q	NEF	77083
ROSE GARDEN TRAIL	17300	327N	NWC	77429
ROSEGATE DR	4200	333C	NCC	77373
ROSE GLADE DR	16500	367B	NWC	77429
ROSEGLEN CIR	15000	457V	NEC	77530
ROSEGLEN MEADOW LN	0	571F	SWH	77085
ROSEGOLD WAY	20300	290W	NWC	77379
ROSEGROVE LN	0	525B	NEF	77494
ROSEHALL LN	0	408V	NWC	77041
ROSEHAVEN DR	9200	573F	SEH	77051
ROSEHAVEN BAY CT	4600	609J	NEF	77479
ROSEHEARTH CT	26500	484Y	NEF	77494
ROSEHEARTY DR	0	408A	NWC	77095
ROSEHEATH LN	2700	333P	NCC	77073
ROSEHEDGE CT	0	573Y	SEC	77047
ROSEHILL	0	247V	SWM	77355
ROSEHILL CT	14900	328Z	NWC	77070
ROSE HILL DR	2600	659D	LC	77573
ROSEHILL DR	14600	328Z	NWC	77070
ROSEHILL LN	12300	328Z	NWC	77070
ROSEHILL RD	18700	286M	NWC	77377
ROSEHILL CHURCH RD	20500	286R	NWC	77377
ROSEHILL ESTATES LN	14300	366D	NWC	77429
ROSEHILL PARK LN	0	253N	SEM	77386
ROSE HILL PARK LN	17900	367A	NWC	77429
ROSEHILL RESERVE DR	0	286Q	NWC	77377
ROSEHILL RIDGE CT	0	406X	NWC	77449
ROSE HOLLOW CT	20500	486P	SWC	77450
ROSE HOLLOW DR	2400	486P	SWC	77450
ROSE HOLLOW LN	0	486J	SWC	77450
ROSEHOLLOW TRAIL	22600	286H	NWC	77377
ROSEHURST	22000	286L	NWC	77377
S. ROSELAKE DR	18800	286M	NWC	77377
N. ROSELAKE DR	18800	286M	NWC	77377
E. ROSELAKE DR	22100	286M	NWC	77377
ROSELAND	3200	493S	SWH	77006
ROSELAND DR	100	542A	BT	77520
ROSE LANDING DR	0	369M	NWC	77070
E. ROSELANE	100	413T	NEH	77076
ROSELANE	800	413T	NEH	77037
ROSELING RD	1	251L	WD	77380
ROSELLA LN	0	247R	SWM	77362
ROSEL OAKS LN	0	328M	NWC	77377
ROSE LOCH LN	0	286Q	NWC	77377
ROSE MALLOW DR	0	289Y	NWC	77379
ROSE MANOR DR	8500	408E	NWC	77095
ROSE MARBLE CT	100	330U	NWC	77069
ROSEMARIE LN	4500	333M	NCC	77338
ROSE MARIS LN	0	286Q	NWC	77377
ROSEMARY CIR	0	461Q	NEC	77521
ROSEMARY CT	2600	613S	NEB	77584
ROSEMARY DR	0	461Q	NEC	77521
ROSEMARY LN	0	659Z	DI	77539
ROSEMARY LN	2800	414S	NCC	77093
ROSEMARY LN	6300	415S	NEH	77016
ROSEMARY LN	15600	420F	NEC	77532
ROSE MARY BEND	0	528C	SWH	77082
ROSEMARY BEND LN	12400	416Z	NEC	77044
ROSEMARY HILL LN	0	524F	NEF	77494
ROSEMARY PARK LN	2900	489W	SWH	77082
ROSEMARY TRACE DR	0	253T	SEM	77386
ROSEMEAD DR	2100	537F	PA	77506
ROSE MEADOW BLVD	0	460W	BT	77521
ROSEMEADOW CT	1300	486G	SWC	77094
ROSEMEADOW DR	900	486G	SWC	77094
ROSE M H	0	413K	NCC	77037
ROSE MILL DR	0	296Y	SEM	77339
ROSEMIST LN	1800	660L	LC	77573
ROSE MIST LN	9700	412F	NWC	77038
ROSEMONT	3400	533U	SEH	77051
ROSEMONT	3800	579B	LP	77571
ROSEMONT LN	12200	612Q	PL	77584
ROSEMONT ESTATES LN	18000	367A	NWC	77429
ROSEMONT PARK LN	0	457A	NEC	77044
ROSEMONT PARK LN	6800	525B	NEF	77494
ROSEMOUNT TRACE	0	531W	SWH	77096
ROSENEATH DR	3800	533H	SEH	77021
N. ROSENEATH DR	4300	534E	SEH	77021
ROSENFIELD	8700	530C	SWH	77063
ROSENFIELD REACH DR	0	366N	NWC	77433
ROSENGALE CT	0	611S	FS	77545
ROSENRIDGE DR	16100	571X	SWH	77053
ROSENRIDGE DR	16200	611B	SWH	77053
ROSE PARK CT	3000	297N	NEH	77339
ROSEPATH LN	0	525M	NEF	77407
ROSE PETAL LN	9800	412F	NWC	77038
ROSEPINE CT	1	245D	SWM	77355
ROSE PINE CT	15800	327S	NWC	77429
ROSEPOINT	1000	452P	NWH	77018
ROSE POND DR	0	616G	SEH	77089
ROSE QUARTZ LN	3200	291U	NWC	77388
ROSE RIDGE CT	15500	571W	SWH	77489
ROSERIDGE LN	6200	571X	SWH	77053
ROSEROCK LN	4600	291W	NWC	77388
ROSERUSH CT	1	251L	WD	77380
ROSE SAGE	7100	525E	NEF	77494
ROSE SHADOW LN	1500	412F	NWC	77038
ROSESHIRE LN	7400	461T	NEC	77521
ROSESPRING LN	0	290X	NWC	77379
ROSESTONE LN	0	290T	NWC	77379
ROSE SUMMIT LN	17500	527N	NEF	77407
ROSE TERRACE	8000	456H	NEC	77044
ROSE TERRACE LN	0	450Z	NWH	77055
ROSETHORN CT	15800	327S	NWC	77429
ROSETHORN DR	0	456Q	NEH	77049
ROSE TOWER CT	0	444C	NWC	77493
ROSE TRACE DR	0	253T	SEM	77386
ROSE TRAIL	16600	327P	NWC	77429
ROSETRAIL BEND LN	8200	485W	NEF	77494
ROSETTA DR	13800	368P	NWC	77429
ROSEVALE CT	0	249Z	NWC	77375
ROSEVALE CT	17300	327T	NWC	77429
ROSE VALLEY DR	15000	329W	NWC	77070
ROSE VERVIAN DR	0	293G	SEM	77386
ROSE VIEW CT	16600	327P	NWC	77429
ROSEVIEW LN	15800	327T	NWC	77429
ROSE VILLAGE DR	6600	377B	NEC	77346
ROSEVILLE DR	21300	291Q	NWC	77388
ROSEVILLE DR	22300	291L	NWC	77389
ROSEVILLE PARK CT	31300	252R	SEM	77386
ROSEVINE DR	1200	619G	TL	77586
ROSEWATER CT	0	485X	NEF	77494
ROSE WATER CT	3600	613X	NEB	77578
ROSE WATER DR	3400	613X	NEB	77578
ROSEWATER PLACE	1	250C	WD	77381
ROSEWAY	4100	532W	SWH	77025
ROSEWAY LN	3800	579B	LP	77571
ROSEWAY RD	22000	286K	NWC	77377
ROSEWELL CT	9200	407D	NWC	77095
ROSEWICK	800	496H	NEH	77015
ROSEWICK	900	497E	NEH	77015
ROSE WILLOW LN	6400	290U	NWC	77379
ROSEWIN CIR	4000	573L	SEH	77047
ROSEWIND DR	3900	613Y	NEB	77584
ROSEWOOD	100	620T	CS	77565
ROSEWOOD	900	493X	SWH	77004
ROSEWOOD	2500	533C	SEH	77004
ROSEWOOD CT	1500	657E	FR	77546
ROSEWOOD CT	10900	579C	LP	77571
ROSEWOOD DR	700	501X	BT	77520
ROSEWOOD DR	13600	528K	SWC	77083
ROSEWOOD LN	1800	568W	SG	77479
ROSEWOOD GLEN DR	13100	328T	NWC	77429
ROSEWOOD GROVE LN	0	450V	NWH	77080
ROSEWOOD PARK RD	0	286H	NWC	77377
ROSEWOOD PLACE	2600	251U	WD	77380
ROSEWOOD TERRACE DR	0	257F	SEM	77357
ROSEWOOD TRAIL	18900	286L	NWC	77377
ROSEWOOD VALLEY DR	0	484Y	NEF	77494
ROSEWOOD VALLEY DR	0	484Y	NEF	77494
ROSEWOOD WAY LN	12500	409S	NWC	77041
ROSEWORTH CT	18900	328F	NWC	77377
ROSHOLT DR	0	253X	SEM	77386
ROSIE	700	412Y	NWH	77091
ROSIE LN	9000	249N	SWM	77354
ROSIE LN	9300	248R	SWM	77354
ROSILLE	1900	502S	BT	77520
ROSILLON CT	16600	367U	NWC	77095
ROSILLON DR	16700	367U	NWC	77095
ROSILLOS PEAK DR	0	293F	SEM	77386
ROSINE	500	492M	SWH	77019
ROSITA DR	0	527F	SWC	77083
ROSITA CREEK CIR	0	366K	NWC	77433
ROSLYN CT	5500	531J	SWH	77081
ROSLYN SPRINGS DR	18600	331D	NWC	77388
ROSPRIM	9600	410X	NWH	77040
ROSS	500	336J	NEH	77339
ROSS	1100	536K	PA	77506
ROSS	2300	282U	WL	77484
ROSS	4100	573D	SEH	77051
ROSS	12000	576L	SEH	77034
ROSS LN	0	612Z	NEB	77578
ROSS ANDREW RD	0	337X	NEC	77346
ROSSETTE DR	9000	450G	NWH	77080
ROSSINI DR	0	444M	NWC	77493
ROSSINI OPERA DR	0	445A	NWC	77493
ROSSITER LN	14100	457G	NEC	77049
ROSS LAKE CT	0	376M	NEC	77346
ROSSLARE DR	12500	371E	NWC	77066
ROSSLYN	0	411N	NWH	77040
ROSSLYN RD	0	412J	NWH	77088
ROSSLYN RD	3400	452J	NWH	77018
ROSSLYN RD	5200	452J	NWH	77091
ROSSMORE HILL CT	24500	250Z	NWC	77389
ROSS STERLING	1100	532D	SWH	77030
ROSS STERLING	1200	533E	SWH	77030
ROSSTON CIR	3100	487Z	SWC	77082
ROSSTON CT	13500	368A	NWC	77429
ROSSTOWN CT	13400	568B	SG	77498
ROSSTOWN DR	13000	568B	SG	77498
ROSSTOWN WAY	9300	450U	NWH	77080
ROSSULYN LANDING LN	0	411S	NWH	77040
ROSSULYN LANDING LN	0	411S	NWH	77040
ROSSUM CREEK DR	0	376U	NEC	77396
ROSSWOOD DR	2100	659C	LC	77573
ROSSWOOD LN	20000	291Y	NWC	77388
ROSWELL	6800	453L	NEH	77022
ROSY FINCH PLACE	0	250P	NWC	77389
ROSY HILL CT	17300	327T	NWC	77429
ROTAN DR	5000	374Y	NCC	77032
ROTAN DR	5300	374Z	NCC	77032
ROTARY DR	1700	336W	HM	77338
ROTH DR	4200	609K	MC	77459
ROTH DR	11200	413X	NEH	77076
ROTHBURY	9600	450P	NWH	77080
ROTHBURY	10400	450N	NWH	77043
ROTHBURY DR	2900	613U	NEB	77584
ROTHCHILDE CT	5200	330U	NWC	77069
ROTHCREST LN	1000	332Q	NCC	77073
ROTHERHAM DR	21700	291Q	NWC	77388
ROTHERHAM ST	0	657T	LC	77573
ROTHERMEL RD	2900	414S	NEH	77093
ROTHESAY CHASE RD	7900	407H	NWC	77095
ROTH FOREST LN	0	291E	NWC	77389
ROTHGLEN DR	11400	329W	NWC	77070
ROTHKO LN	17200	330K	NWC	77379
ROTHMOORE LN	12200	370M	NWC	77066
ROTHSHIRE CT	23200	292F	NCC	77373
ROTHWAY	6100	410X	NWH	77040
ROTHWELL	900	493M	NEH	77002
ROTHWELL	1200	609C	MC	77477
ROTHWELL	1700	493M	NEH	77020
ROTHWOOD RD	0	291A	NWC	77389
ROTHWOOD RD	22000	291J	NWC	77389
ROTMAN	3800	494P	SEH	77003
ROUEN	0	611F	NEF	77489
ROUFA RD	2300	494N	DT	77003
ROUGE CIR	9200	490T	SWH	77063
ROUGH CUT CT	0	332X	NWC	77090
ROUGHLOCK	6200	415N	NEH	77016
ROUGH NECK DR	1800	336W	HM	77338
ROUGH RIVER CT	0	377F	NEC	77346
ROUKEN GLEN CT	0	527W	NEF	77407
ROUNDABOUT WAY	0	458S	NEC	77049
ROUND BANK CT	8600	410G	NWC	77064
ROUND BANK DR	7600	410G	NWC	77064
ROUNDBLUFF LN	8800	575U	SEH	77075
ROUNDBLUFF LN	8800	575U	SEH	77075
ROUND CREEK CT	0	525H	NEF	77407
ROUND DALE LN	11000	575Y	SWH	77075
ROUND GROVE LN	7600	407M	NWC	77095
ROUND HILL CT	2700	485N	NEF	77494
ROUND HOLLOW CT	0	485S	NEF	77494
ROUNDHOUSE LN	7300	455M	NEH	77078
ROUND KEY DR	0	285Q	NWC	77447
ROUND LAKE DR	1800	488V	SWH	77077
ROUND LAKE DR	2000	489S	SWH	77077
ROUNDLEAF CT	1400	485L	SWC	77494
ROUND LEAF LN	0	446G	NWC	77449
ROUND MOSS LN	0	484P	NEF	77494
ROUND MOUNTAIN DR	0	332W	NWC	77090
ROUND OAK CT	13800	618A	SEH	77059
ROUND RIDGE BLVD	0	527S	NEF	77407
ROUND ROBIN DR	0	406Y	NWC	77449
ROUND ROCK	1800	656R	FR	77546
ROUNDROCK DR	7900	457G	NEC	77049
ROUNDROCK PARK LN	7100	526M	NEF	77407
ROUND ROSE CT	0	290T	NWC	77379
ROUND SPRING DR	1800	296Y	NEH	77339
ROUNDSTONE LN	13900	497C	NEC	77015
ROUND TABLE DR	0	289P	NWC	77375
ROUNDTOP PLACE	1	250D	WD	77381
ROUNDTREE	800	496G	NEH	77015
ROUNDTREE LN	4200	609P	MC	77459
ROUNDUP	0	369Z	NWC	77064
ROUND UP LN	9400	409C	NWC	77064
ROUND VALLEY DR	22500	485L	SWC	77450
ROUNDWIND TRAIL	1800	378G	NEC	77532
ROUSE	100	494H	NEH	77020
ROUSE RD	0	295H	SEM	77365
ROUSELLE LN	12900	328K	NWC	77377
ROUSH RD	0	488E	SWH	77077
ROUSSEAU DR	11200	368T	NWC	77065
ROUTE 4	0	256R	SEM	77357
ROUTHLAND DR	17800	331J	NWC	77379
ROVING MEADOWS LN	3900	460D	NEC	77532
ROWAN LN	6300	531J	SWH	77074
ROWAN LN	6500	530M	SWH	77074
ROWAN LN	7900	530K	SWH	77036
ROWAN LN	11500	529E	SWH	77072
ROWBOAT WAY	0	377Q	NEC	77044
ROWE LN	7700	575P	SEH	77075
ROWELL CT	6600	571W	SWH	77489
ROWENA LN	6300	408U	NWC	77041
ROWENA DALE DR	8000	290J	NWC	77379
ROWLETT RD	9600	576N	SEH	77075
ROWLOCK LN	500	488A	SWH	77079
ROWLOCK VINE DR	3700	447K	NWC	77084
ROWNITA	15600	419H	CB	77532
ROWOOD DR	11800	369P	NWC	77070
ROXANNE DR	100	288G	TB	77375
ROXBORO	0	368T	NWC	77429
ROXBURGH DR	6600	409V	NWH	77041
ROXBURY RD	6500	534U	SEH	77087
ROXDALE RIDGE DR	12500	416Z	NEC	77044
ROXELLA	700	413Y	NEH	77076
ROXELLA	1500	413Z	NEH	77093
ROXETTE CT	0	334R	NCC	77338
ROXTON DR	13900	488F	SWH	77077
ROXTON RIDGE DR	15700	617R	SEH	77598
ROXTON RIDGE DR	15800	618S	SEH	77598
ROY	100	492G	NWH	77007
ROY CIR	2300	492C	NWH	77007
ROY CT	1400	616Q	PL	77581
ROY RD	12600	614F	PL	77581
ROYAL	100	658L	LC	77573
ROYAL	7800	375G	HM	77396
ROYAL AVE	3100	460Y	MN	77521
ROYAL CT	100	616Z	FR	77546
ROYAL DR	12700	569K	SF	77477
ROYAL ADELAIDE DR	2000	485R	NEF	77450
ROYAL ARBOR LN	4900	447C	NWC	77084
W. ROYAL ARCH DR	1	488L	SWH	77077
E. ROYAL ARCH DR	1	488L	SWH	77077
ROYAL ARMS CT	22700	445U	NWC	77449
ROYAL ASCOT CT	9700	409A	NWC	77065
ROYAL BANNER WAY	0	529C	SWH	77082
ROYAL BEAD LN	17800	527N	NEF	77407
ROYAL BELL CT	13100	572V	SWH	77047
ROYAL BEND LN	4500	609S	NEF	77479
ROYAL BEND LN	13100	328F	NWC	77377
ROYAL BIRKDALE RD	14800	408K	NWC	77095
ROYAL BLUE DR	2600	411M	NWH	77088
ROYALBROOK DR	14800	408F	NWC	77095
ROYAL BROOK MANOR DR	0	297J	NEH	77365
ROYAL BROOK MANOR DR	0	297K	SEM	77365
ROYAL CANYON LN	0	484W	NEF	77494
ROYAL CAPE CT	8600	407F	NWC	77095
ROYAL CHASE DR	1600	572M	SWH	77047
ROYAL CHATEAU LN	11200	489X	SWH	77082
ROYAL CIRCLE DR	2600	336D	NEH	77339
ROYAL CLIFF CT	0	526M	NEF	77407
ROYAL COACH DR	26500	258J	SEM	77357
ROYAL COLONY LN	2700	609F	MC	77459
ROYAL COURTSIDE AVE	0	489X	SWH	77082
ROYAL COVE CIR	0	366J	NWC	77433
ROYAL CREEK CT	0	612Q	PL	77584
ROYAL CREEK CT	5200	657Z	LC	77573
ROYAL CREEK TRAIL	0	338B	NEH	77345
ROYAL CRESCENT DR	3100	336H	NEH	77339
ROYAL CREST CT	8000	330J	NWC	77379
ROYAL CREST DR	16800	618Q	SEH	77058
ROYAL CREST WAY	9700	528P	SWH	77099
ROYAL CREST WAY	9700	528Q	SWH	77099
ROYAL CROSSING DR	0	296W	SEM	77365
ROYAL CYPRESS DR	0	446D	NWC	77449
ROYAL DORNOCH DR	4700	578J	PA	77505
ROYAL DOWNS DR	1900	485R	NEF	77450
ROYAL EMERALD LN	0	296T	SEM	77339
ROYAL FALLS CT	0	297K	NEH	77365
ROYAL FERN	1	251R	WD	77380
ROYAL FERN CT	1800	618F	SEH	77062
ROYALFIELD DR	0	578Y	SEH	77059
ROYAL FIELD DR	0	253J	SEM	77385
ROYAL FIELD LN	0	657T	FR	77546
ROYAL FOREST	2300	336A	SEM	77339
ROYAL FORT LN	16300	332R	NCC	77073
ROYAL GALWAY DR	0	332R	NCC	77073
ROYAL GARDENS DR	16000	407M	NWC	77095
ROYAL GATE BLVD	0	376V	NEC	77346
ROYAL GATE LN	17900	527N	NEF	77407
ROYAL GEORGE LN	800	572Q	SWH	77047
ROYAL GLEN DR	2900	297N	NEH	77339
ROYAL GROVE CT	8300	527Q	NEF	77083
ROYAL HAVEN LN	0	366J	NWC	77433
ROYAL HILL CT	0	338F	NEH	77345
ROYAL HILL DR	14100	528S	NEF	77083
ROYAL HOLLOW LN	0	525D	NEF	77450
ROYAL ISLE CT	11900	329A	NWC	77375
ROYAL ISLE DR	19200	329A	NWC	77375
ROYAL IVORY CROSSING	0	489X	SWH	77082
ROYAL JASMINE PLACE	0	406X	NWC	77449
ROYAL KING RD	0	286S	NWC	77377
ROYAL KNOLL CT	6900	578F	PA	77505
ROYALL	6600	453Q	NEH	77022
ROYAL LAGOON DR	19400	332A	NWC	77090
ROYAL LAKE	6900	415K	NEC	77050
ROYAL LAKE DR	0	528Y	SG	77478
ROYAL LANDING DR	0	338B	NEH	77345
ROYAL MANOR	0	578F	PA	77505
ROYAL MANOR DR	3700	527D	SWC	77082
ROYAL MEADOW DR	3900	446H	NWC	77449
ROYAL MELBOURNE CT	0	296A	SEM	77365
ROYAL MILE CT	0	447D	NWC	77084
ROYAL MILE LN	16200	448A	NWC	77084
ROYAL MILE LN	16300	447D	NWC	77084
ROYAL MIST LN	18500	328K	NWC	77377
ROYAL MONTREAL DR	0	485R	SWC	77450
ROYAL MOUNTAIN DR	0	332W	NWC	77090
ROYAL OAK	13800	528P	SWC	77083
ROYAL OAK DR	4200	501K	BT	77521
ROYAL OAK PLACE	2000	251V	WD	77380
ROYAL OAKS	0	616V	FR	77546
ROYAL OAKS DR	2100	659D	LC	77573
ROYAL OAKS DR	3200	251P	SWM	77380
ROYAL OAKS DR	10100	414Z	NEH	77016
ROYAL OAKS DR	18100	257A	WV	77357
ROYAL OAKS CLUB DR	2900	489W	SWH	77082
ROYAL OAKS CREST	2900	489T	SWH	77082
ROYAL OAKS CROSSING	11600	489X	SWH	77082
ROYAL OAKS GREEN	0	489T	SWH	77082
ROYAL OAKS GROVE	2900	489X	SWH	77082
ROYAL OAKS TRACE	0	489X	SWH	77083
ROYAL OAKS VIEW	0	489X	SWH	77082
ROYAL ORCHARD DR	20100	295M	SEM	77365
ROYAL PALISADES LN	0	489W	SWH	77082
ROYAL PALM CT	2400	619Y	LC	77573
ROYAL PALMS	5600	534K	SEH	77021
ROYAL PARK DR	13400	528P	SWH	77083
ROYAL PARKSIDE PLACE	0	489X	SWH	77082
ROYAL PARKWAY	5000	617W	FR	77546
ROYAL PIKE DR	0	404Z	NWC	77493
ROYAL PINE DR	10200	414S	NCC	77093
ROYAL PLACE CT	2600	411M	NWH	77088
ROYAL PLAIN AVE	0	489X	SWH	77082
ROYAL PLANTATION LN	3900	609G	MC	77459
ROYAL POINT CT	0	338F	NEH	77345
S. ROYAL POINT DR	0	338F	NEH	77345
N. ROYAL POINT DR	0	338F	NEH	77345
ROYAL PORTICO PATH	0	489X	SWH	77082
ROYAL PRESS DR	0	404Z	NWC	77493
ROYAL PURPLE LN	23700	296G	SEM	77365
ROYAL RIDGE DR	0	612E	PL	77545
ROYAL RIDGE TRAIL	0	338F	NEH	77345
ROYAL RIVER DR	3700	489Y	SWH	77042
ROYAL ROCK CT	11200	411M	NWC	77088
ROYAL ROSE	11900	489W	SWH	77082
ROYAL ROYCE DR	3600	489Y	SWH	77042
ROYAL SAGE DR	2600	411M	NWH	77088
ROYAL SANDS CT	11200	411M	NWC	77088
ROYAL SANDS LN	0	338B	NEH	77345
ROYAL SASH LN	0	405W	NWC	77493
ROYAL SHADOWS DR	15000	527D	SWC	77082
ROYAL SHORES CIR	0	338F	NEH	77345
ROYAL SHORES DR	1600	338B	NEH	77345
ROYAL SILVER DR	0	489X	SWH	77082
ROYAL SPRINGS CT	13900	488N	SWH	77077
ROYAL STONE LN	16300	332R	NCC	77073
ROYAL SUNSET CT	0	405W	NWC	77493
ROYAL SUNSET CT	0	445A	NWC	77493
ROYAL TERN DR	13100	377X	NEC	77044
ROYAL TERN LN	1	252N	WD	77380
ROYAL TERNS CT	0	658T	LC	77573
ROYAL THISTLE CT	11400	411M	NWH	77088
ROYAL THISTLE DR	0	411M	NWH	77088
ROYAL TIMBERS DR	0	296X	SEM	77339
ROYALTON	5300	531B	SWH	77081
ROYAL TOWER PLACE	0	489X	SWH	77082
ROYALTRACE CT	0	328A	NWC	77429
ROYAL TRAIL DR	2600	337A	NEH	77339
ROYAL TROON DR	0	296A	SEM	77365
ROYAL VEIL LN	0	489X	SWH	77082
ROYAL VILLA DR	21000	406T	NWC	77449
ROYAL VILLAGE DR	11301	411M	NWH	77088
ROYAL WALK	5100	330U	NWC	77069
ROYAL WAY	9300	527R	NEF	77083
ROYALWICK CT	24200	289D	NWC	77375
ROYALWOOD DR	7700	457E	NEC	77049
ROYAL WOODS CT	0	253N	SEM	77385
ROYAN DR	7700	570G	MC	77071
ROY BEAN DR	9200	450G	NWH	77041
S. ROYCE CIR	0	613S	NEB	77578
ROYCE LN	12800	456Y	NEH	77013
ROYCE HOLLY	0	376R	NEC	77346
ROYCE PALMS DR	11100	489Y	SWH	77042
ROYCROFT LN	0	526P	NEF	77407
ROYDENCREST DR	20800	291S	NWC	77388
ROYDER	200	453Y	NEH	77009
ROYDON DR	10300	576U	SEH	77034
ROYSTON DR	0	295Z	NEH	77365
ROZELLE AVE	500	568K	SG	77498
ROZZANO CT	24500	524R	NEF	77406
RUBBLE LN	20601	526S	NEF	77407
RUBENSTEIN	11700	413U	NEH	77076
RUBILEE AVE	6600	415A	NEC	77396
RUBIN	8500	533Y	SEH	77051
RUBIN	10600	573Q	SEH	77047
RUBLE DR	19100	446V	NWC	77084
RUBY DR	5900	614L	PL	77581
RUBY LN	500	248S	SWM	77354
RUBY LN	20100	256L	SEM	77357
RUBY CANYON LN	11400	367U	NWC	77095
RUBY FALLS CT	0	660E	LC	77573
RUBY MEADOW DR	16500	367U	NWC	77095
RUBY RANCH CT	0	372M	NCC	77073
RUBY RED CT	0	372D	NCC	77073
RUBY RED LN	0	524G	NEF	77494
RUBY ROCK WAY	0	526S	NEF	77407
RUBY ROSE	11900	413R	NCC	77093
RUBY STAR DR	0	487Z	SWC	77082
RUBY SUMMERS RD	0	616M	SEC	77089
RUBY TERRACE LN	19000	245D	SWM	77355
RUBY VALLEY CT	0	326J	NWC	77433
RUDDER DR	16000	419A	NEC	77532
RUDDY DUCK CT	0	461N	NEC	77521
RUDEL DR	1200	288F	TB	77375
RUDGEWICK LN	16000	330S	NWC	77379
RUDOLPH RD	800	288C	TB	77375
RUDY BROOK WAY	8100	290N	NWC	77379
RUDY GLEN CT	0	291N	NWC	77388
RUE	4700	573D	SEH	77033
RUE	5100	574A	SEH	77033
RUE BEAUJON	11800	329S	NWC	77377
RUE CAMBON	9000	530Q	SWH	77074
RUE CANYON CT	22300	485Y	NEF	77450
RUE CARRE	7800	530Q	SWH	77074
RUE CHABLIS	7800	530Q	SWH	77074
RUE CRILLON	9000	530Q	SWH	77074
RUE DELA CROIX DR	0	404Z	NWC	77493
RUE DE LA PAIX WAY	0	491Q	SWH	77056
RUE DE VILLE	1	569S	SG	77478
RUE FONTAINE LN	700	496D	NEC	77015

Street Name	Block	Pg/Sq	Loc	Zips
RUE LA FONTAINE	11800	329S	NWC	77377
RUELL	100	536J	SEH	77017
RUELL	800	535M	SEH	77017
RUELLA LN	1300	537P	PA	77502
RUELLEN CT	0	372W	NWC	77038
RUELLEN LN	1100	372W	NWC	77038
RUE MONTEBELLO	15500	329S	NWC	77377
RUE ORLEANS	200	500J	BT	77520
RUE SAINT CYR	7800	530Q	SWH	77074
RUE ST HONORE	15300	329S	NWC	77377
RUE ST LAZARE	11800	329S	NWC	77377
RUFFIAN	0	409E	JV	77065
RUFFIAN CT	4300	617T	SEC	77546
RUFFIAN DR	16100	617T	SEC	77546
RUFFIAN LN	2000	570S	SF	77477
RUFFIAN STAKES LN	0	245Z	SWM	77355
RUFFIN LN	1	251R	WD	77380
RUFFIN GREEN CT	0	611S	FS	77545
RUFFINO RD	9600	569D	SWH	77031
RUFINA ST	0	659Q	LC	77573
RUFUS	6600	412Y	NWH	77091
RUGBY CT	16700	330L	NWC	77379
RUGGED LARK CIR	0	288S	NWC	77377
RUGLEY	3400	493Z	SEH	77004
RUIDOSA CT	16700	611B	SWH	77053
RUIDOSO CIR	0	539N	DP	77536
RUIZ	1500	493M	SEH	77002
RULAND RD	9000	450Y	NWH	77055
RUMAR LN	10100	495H	JC	77029
RUMBLING CANYON CT	0	446C	NWC	77449
RUMBLING CREEK LN	22400	289J	NWC	77375
RUMBLING ROCK LN	0	484S	NEF	77494
RUMBLING WOOD CT	7900	370Z	NWC	77086
RUMBLING WOOD LN	9500	370Z	NWC	77086
RUMFORD LN	6200	408W	NWC	77084
RUMMEL CREEK RD	13000	489C	SWH	77079
RUM RIVER CT	19300	406Y	NWC	77449
RUMSEY SPRINGS DR	20700	296J	SEM	77365
RUMSON DR		484J	NEF	77494
RUNBELL PLACE	15100	408P	NWC	77095
RUNNEBURG RD	400	419H	CB	77532
RUNNEBURG RD	1500	420F	NEC	77532
RUNNELS	1900	493M	SEH	77003
RUNNELS	2300	494N	SEH	77003
RUNNERS LN	19000	338W	NEC	77346
RUNNEY MEADE DR	13600	568F	SG	77498
RUNNING ARABIAN LN	14500	377T	NEC	77044
RUNNING BEAR TRAIL	1200	378G	NEC	77532
RUNNING BIRD LN	8300	610G	SWH	77489
RUNNING BROOK LN	0	612F	PL	77545
RUNNING BROOK LN	17800	330E	NWC	77379
RUNNING CREEK CT	6000	338E	NEH	77345
RUNNING CYPRESS DR	17000	327T	CY	77429
RUNNING DEER	19300	252D	SEM	77385
RUNNING DEER LN	29700	289K	NWC	77375
RUNNING EAGLE FALLS	9100	249Y	NWC	77375
RUNNING EAGLE FALLS		249Z	NWC	77375
RUNNING FOX LN	0	293G	SEM	77386
RUNNING IRON LN	24000	325J	NWC	77447
RUNNING IRON LN	24200	324M	NWC	77447
RUNNING MOON TRAIL	0	334K	NCC	77338
RUNNING PINE CT	4300	658N	LC	77573
RUNNING PINE DR	4300	658N	LC	77573
RUNNING QUAIL CT	16500	610C	SWH	77489
RUNNING SPRING	0	538R	DP	77536
RUNNING SPRINGS DR	1900	336C	NEH	77339
RUNNING SPRINGS DR	3600	618C	SEH	77059
RUNNING TIDE	3500	657B	SEC	77546
RUNNING VINE LN	18300	329H	NWC	77379
RUNNING WATER DR	25600	338C	NEC	77336
RUNNY MEADE DR	9700	531U	SWH	77096
RUN OAKS CT	0	326L	NWC	77429
RUNSWICK DR	15400	618J	SEH	77062
RUNYAN	1500	373Z	NCC	77039
RUPERT	3300	494C	NEH	77026
RUPERT	3600	454Y	NEH	77026
RUPLEY CIR	6200	534Q	SEH	77087
RUPPEL RUNN	17900	332F	NWC	77090
RUPPSTOCK RD	15800	570Z	SWH	77489
RUPSTOCK CT	7400	570Z	SWH	77489
RURAL	3600	493B	NWH	77009
RURAL OAK ST	0	576V	SEH	77034
RURAL OAK ST	0	577S	SEH	77034
RURAL RIDGE RD	0	328N	NWC	77429
RUSHBROOK DR	1700	489N	SWH	77077
RUSHBROOK DR	2300	610A	MC	77489
RUSHCREEK DR	100	372K	NWH	77067
RUSHCROFT DR	3800	527D	SWC	77082
RUSHFIELD GLEN LN	0	328A	NWC	77429
S. RUSH HAVEN CIR	1	250C	WD	77381
N. RUSH HAVEN CIR	1	250C	WD	77381
RUSH HAVEN DR	1	250H	WD	77381
RUSH HOLLOW CT	0	525M	NEF	77407
RUSHING BROOK DR	3000	297Y	NEH	77345
RUSHING CREEK LN	21100	446J	NWC	77449
RUSHING HOLLOW		328k	NWC	77377
RUSHING MEADOW LN	0	615M	PL	77089
RUSHING RIVER DR	5600	337D	NEH	77345
RUSHING SPRING DR	0	612L	PL	77584
RUSHING SPRINGS CT	18100	329K	NWC	77375
RUSHING SPRINGS DR	9800	329K	NWC	77375
RUSHING STREAM CT	8100	290E	NWC	77375
RUSHIRE SQUARE	20200	335P	HM	77338
RUSH MILL CT	9300	408B	NWC	77095
RUSHMORE LN	12500	377E	NEC	77346
RUSHSTONE LN	5400	334A	NCC	77373
RUSHTON CIR	100	659D	LC	77573
RUSH TRACE CT	17200	407Q	NWC	77095
RUSHVILLE CT	21000	406T	NWC	77449
RUSHWATER LN	3500	617X	SEC	77546
RUSHWIND CT	2900	485N	NEF	77494
RUSHWIND LN	0	446D	NWC	77449
S. RUSHWING CIR	0	250H	WD	77381
RUSHWING PLACE	1	250H	WD	77381
RUSHWOOD CIR	2600	371M	NWC	77067
RUSHWORTH DR	1300	372E	NWC	77014
RUSK	400	493R	DT	77002
RUSK	1300	493R	DT	77010
RUSK	1301	493R	DT	77002
RUSK	1600	493R	DT	77010
RUSK	1601	493R	DT	77003
RUSK	2000	493R	SEH	77003
RUSK	3800	494T	SEH	77023
RUSK	6500	494Y	SEH	77011
RUSK	7300	495W	SEH	77011
RUSKIN	3800	532E	WU	77005
RUSKLANDING CT	0	457P	NEC	77049
RUSK MEADOWS LN	0	377A	NEC	77346
RUSS DR	12300	414A	NCC	77039
RUSSELFERN LN	0	457Q	NEC	77049
RUSSELFIELD LN	0	457Q	NEC	77049
RUSSELL	2100	494B	NEH	77026

Street Name	Block	Pg/Sq	Loc	Zips
RUSSELL	3500	454T	NEH	77026
RUSSELL DR	1000	295Y	SEM	77365
RUSSELL DR	21000	256N	SEM	77357
RUSSELL LN	5800	502B	NEC	77521
RUSSELL LN	5900	462X	NEC	77521
RUSSELL CHASE DR	21300	296J	SEM	77365
RUSSELL CREEK CT	28500	293E	SEM	77386
RUSSELL PALMER RD	600	296X	SEM	77339
RUSSELL POINT DR	30401	253S	SEM	77386
RUSSELLWOOD DR	0	327H	NWC	77429
RUSSELS CAVE LN	0	376H	NEC	77346
RUSSELVILLE RD	5100	573V	SEH	77048
RUSSELVILLE RD	5200	574N	SEH	77048
RUSSELWOOD DR	0	327H	NWC	77429
RUSSET BEND LN	0	326V	NWC	77429
RUSSET FIELD CT	10200	369C	NWC	77070
RUSSET LEAF TRACE	0	446F	NWC	77449
RUSSET OAK LN	0	405P	NWC	77493
RUSSETT DR	5500	491K	SWH	77056
RUSSETT DR	10600	489L	SWH	77042
RUSSETT CANYON LN	0	526K	NEF	77407
RUSSET TERRACE LN	17500	407F	NWC	77095
RUSSETT FIELDS CT	9500	416Z	NEC	77044
RUSSETT GREEN DR	18100	328K	NWC	77377
RUSSETT MEADOW CT	0	526N	NEF	77407
W. RUSSETT PLACE	2800	613V	NEB	77584
S. RUSSETT PLACE	4500	613V	NEB	77584
RUSSETT PLACE	4500	613V	NEB	77584
RUSSET TRAIL CT	4800	446D	NWC	77449
RUSSET WOOD CT	1	251F	WD	77381
RUSSO	4100	615E	PL	77581
RUSSWOOD CIR	0	330E	NWC	77379
RUSTIC	6800	534H	SEH	77087
RUSTIC DR	100	536Q	PA	77502
RUSTIC LN	100	656B	FR	77546
RUSTIC LN	600	616X	NEB	77546
RUSTIC BAY CT	0	406C	NWC	77433
RUSTIC BEND CT	10100	369Y	NWC	77064
NICKEL BAUER AVE	0	285L	NWC	77447
RUSTIC BRIDGE LN	0	612P	PL	77545
RUSTIC BRIDGE LN	22000	336E	NEH	77339
RUSTIC BROOK CT	18000	328E	NWC	77377
RUSTIC CANYON TRAIL	17400	331M	NWC	77090
RUSTIC CAPE DR	0	407E	NWC	77433
RUSTIC CHASE DR	0	526L	NEF	77407
RUSTIC COVE LN	0	484Q	NEF	77494
RUSTIC CREEK LN	5900	338A	NEH	77345
RUSTIC FALLS CT	8200	527R	NEF	77083
RUSTIC FIELD LN	4800	446D	NWC	77449
RUSTIC FIELDS LN	14500	327Y	NWC	77429
RUSTIC GARDEN DR	13200	528L	SWH	77083
RUSTIC GARDENS DR	0	253S	SEM	77386
RUSTIC GATE DR	19000	407J	NWC	77433
RUSTIC GATE RD	9400	579C	LP	77571
RUSTIC GLEN CT	17700	407K	NWC	77095
RUSTIC HARBOR CT	800	617M	SEH	77062
RUSTIC HAVEN CT	3700	297U	NEH	77345
RUSTIC HEARTH CT	20600	526J	NEF	77407
RUSTIC HILLS LN	13900	328S	NWC	77429
RUSTIC HOLLOW LN	0	615B	PL	77581
RUSTIC HOLLOW LN	1600	485M	SWC	77450
RUSTIC KNOLLS CT	20300	486F	SWC	77450
RUSTIC KNOLLS DR	1000	486F	SWC	77450
RUSTIC LAKE RD	0	406L	NWC	77433
RUSTIC MAPLE LN	20900	290U	NWC	77379
RUSTIC MEADOW CT	0	614G	PL	77581
RUSTIC MEADOW CT	22400	525C	NEF	77494
RUSTIC MILL LN	0	484Z	NEF	77494
RUSTIC OAK CT	0	293Z	NCC	77373
RUSTIC OAK LN	1500	619D	PA	77586
RUSTIC OAKS	900	248K	SWM	77354
RUSTIC OAKS DR	100	657R	LC	77573
RUSTIC OAR WAY	18500	378A	NEC	77346
RUSTIC PARK CT	8200	527Q	NEF	77083
RUSTIC PARK DR	1700	336B	NEH	77339
RUSTIC PECAN LN	6800	457L	NEC	77049
RUSTIC PIER LN	2900	660E	LC	77573
RUSTIC PINES CT	28500	293E	SEM	77386
RUSTIC PINE TRAIL	17400	331R	NWC	77090
RUSTIC RAIL CT	0	406G	NWC	77433
RUSTIC RANCH LN	0	484T	NEF	77494
RUSTIC RIDGE LN	8300	407E	NWC	77433
RUSTIC ROCK RD	9700	579B	LP	77571
RUSTIC SANDS DR	16000	448A	NWC	77084
RUSTIC SHORES LN	22000	525C	NEF	77450
RUSTIC SPRINGS DR	18100	329F	NWC	77375
RUSTIC STABLE LN	0	327U	NWC	77429
RUSTIC STONE CT	22200	526L	NEF	77407
RUSTIC TIMBERS DR	0	376A	NEC	77338
RUSTIC TRAIL	0	656B	NEB	77581
RUSTIC VIEW CT	1	251B	WD	77381
RUSTIC VILLA DR	3200	297Y	NEH	77345
RUSTIC WAY	0	329Q	NWC	77070
RUSTIC WOODS DR	2600	297X	NEH	77345
RUSTIC WOODS DR	3900	297X	NEH	77339
RUSTIC WOODS LN	0	484F	KT	77494
RUSTING CREEK DR	0	612L	PL	77545
RUSTINGTON DR	17000	330G	NWC	77379
RUSTING WILLOW LN	6100	407U	NWC	77084
RUST LEAF DR	0	406D	NWC	77433
RUSTLER GATE LN	14900	326T	NWC	77433
RUSTLER RIDGE LN	9300	616E	SEC	77089
RUSTLERS TRAIL LN	16000	327Y	NWC	77429
RUSTLERS WAY CT	10800	409F	NWC	77064
RUSTLEWOOD CT	0	335N	NCC	77338
RUSTLEWOOD DR	19800	335N	NCC	77338
RUSTLING ASPEN LN	17500	407K	NWC	77095
RUSTLING BRANCH LN	0	446D	NWC	77449
RUSTLING BROOK LN	1400	486H	SWC	77094
RUSTLING CHESTNUT ST	2900	291M	NWC	77389
RUSTLING ELMS DR	4400	297N	NEH	77339
RUSTLING GATES LN	0	406X	NWC	77449
RUSTLING GLEN LN	4800	446D	NWC	77449
RUSTLING GLEN LN	15300	327V	NWC	77429
RUSTLING LEAVES DR	8300	528P	SWC	77083
RUSTLING MANOR LN	9200	527N	NEF	77407
RUSTLING MAPLE DR	9500	410A	NWC	77064
RUSTLING MOSS DR	3100	331P	NWC	77068
RUSTLING OAKS	24000	247W	SWM	77355
RUSTLING OAKS CT	9000	411J	NWC	77088
RUSTLING PINES LN	3200	251S	SWM	77380
RUSTLING RIDGE LN	18900	328F	NWC	77377
RUSTLING RIVER DR	0	297U	NEH	77345
RUSTLING RIVER DR	0	297U	NEH	77345
RUSTLING RIVER DR	5800	297U	NEH	77345
RUSTLING SPRINGS DR	22000	291J	NWC	77389
RUSTLING TIMBERS CT	20900	290U	NWC	77379
RUSTLING TIMBERS LN	6500	290U	NWC	77379
RUSTLING TRAILS DR	5200	446C	NWC	77449
RUSTLING TREES WAY	2000	293X	NCC	77373
RUSTLING VILLAS LN	0	575V	SEH	77075
RUSTLING WIND LN	1100	659M	LC	77573

Street Name	Block	Pg/Sq	Loc	Zips
RUSTLING WINDS DR	10800	369Z	NWC	77064
RUSTLING WOODS CT	4000	618D	PA	77059
RUSTON	16400	375J	NEH	77396
RUSTON OAKS DR	8800	411J	NWC	77088
RUSTWOOD CT	8400	335N	NCC	77338
RUSTWOOD LN	20400	335N	NCC	77338
RUSTY	11200	413R	NCC	77093
RUSTY ANCHOR CT	18700	378A	NEC	77346
RUSTY BLACKHAW LN	0	463S	CCO	77520
RUSTY BRIDGE CT	0	253N	SEM	77386
RUSTYGATE DR	6000	334B	NCC	77373
RUSTYLEAF LN	600	332J	NWC	77090
RUSTY PINE LN	11100	329F	NWC	77375
RUSTY RIDGE LN	6600	406U	NWC	77449
RUSTY ROCK LN	0	406G	NWC	77433
RUSTY RUNN	17900	332F	NWC	77090
RUTGERS	5300	532F	WU	77005
RUTGERS LN	700	538Y	DP	77536
RUTGERS PARK CT	12200	619A	PA	77058
RUTGERS PLACE	1	532F	WU	77005
RUTH	400	501Z	BT	77520
RUTH	900	493X	SWH	77004
RUTH	2400	533D	SEH	77004
RUTH	2600	570W	NEF	77477
RUTH DR	21000	256J	SEM	77357
RUTH LN	0	656K	FR	77546
RUTHANN DR	21400	333M	NCC	77338
RUTHBY	8300	535Y	SEH	77061
RUTHBY	8800	575C	SEH	77061
RUTHERFORD LN	8700	412K	NWH	77088
RUTHERFORD WAY	10400	329B	NWC	77375
RUTHERGLEN DR	0	569X	MC	77459
RUTHERGLENN DR	5100	531S	SWH	77096
RUTHERGLENN DR	6000	530V	SWH	77096
RUTHIN CT	6700	406U	NWC	77449
RUTHVEN	300	493P	SWH	77019
RUTLAND	0	257G	SEM	77357
RUTLAND	500	492D	NWH	77007
RUTLAND	900	452V	NWH	77008
RUTLAND	4000	452M	NWH	77018
RUTLAND PLACE	500	492D	NWH	77007
E. RUTLEDGE CT	14500	408T	NWC	77084
W. RUTLEDGE CT	14600	408X	NWC	77084
RUTLEDGE DR	0	446S	NWC	77449
RUTLEY CIR	16200	330S	NWC	77379
RUTSON DR	0	327H	NWC	77429
RUTSON DR	0	327H	NWC	77429
RUTTAND PARK LN	4200	485Y	NEF	77450
RYAN CT	2800	376F	NEC	77396
RYAN ACRES DR	5000	614V	PL	77584
RYAN EAGLES CIR	12900	377X	NEC	77044
RYANEAGLES CT	15400	377X	NEC	77044
RYAN EAGLES DR	12900	377X	NEC	77044
RYAN LANDING DR	13300	368U	NWC	77065
RYAN MANOR DR	0	524K	NWF	77406
RYAN MICHAEL DR	0	255Q	SEM	77365
RYANN CT	3500	577C	PA	77505
RYAN OAKS DR	10800	368U	NWC	77065
RYAN PARK DR	8200	408F	NWC	77095
RYAN RIDGE	0	293E	SEM	77386
RYANS BRANCH LN	4400	485Y	NEF	77450
RYANSBROOK LN	1800	293E	SEM	77386
RYANS CREEK CT	25600	484Z	NEF	77494
RYANS RANCH LN	0	524G	NEF	77494
RYANS RUN CT	2000	568Z	SG	77478
RYAN TRAILS DR	10800	368T	NWC	77065
RYANWOOD DR	13500	368T	NWC	77065
RY CREEK WAY CT		289H	NWC	77375
RYCROFT DR	1900	252V	SEM	77386
RYCRUDE	0	287Q	NWC	77388
RYDER CT	2600	659D	LC	77573
RYDERWOOD	0	568C	SG	77478
RYE	100	288H	TB	77375
RYE	200	252S	SWM	77380
RYE	1300	495K	NEH	77029
RYE CT	0	258E	SEM	77357
RYE CREEK DR	0	406T	NWC	77449
RYEGATE DR	6100	408Y	NWC	77041
RYE HARBOR CT	0	377K	NEC	77346
RYE HOLLOW LN	0	296X	SEM	77339
RYEWATER DR	11800	616D	SEH	77089
RYEWATER DR	12200	617A	SEH	77089
RYEWOOD CT	3900	485Y	NEF	77450
RYLAND DR	11400	371Q	NWC	77066
N. RYLANDER CIR	8700	570F	SWH	77071
E. RYLANDER CIR	8700	570F	SWH	77071
S. RYLANDER CIR	12400	570F	SWH	77071
RYLIS	900	493J	SWH	77019
RYMERS SWITCH LN	0	657S	FR	77546
RYMERS SWITCH LN	0	657S	FR	77546
RYMWICK CT	1	251C	WD	77381
RYOAKS DR	15400	408N	NWC	77095
RYON	1100	493D	NEH	77009
RYSON	2900	450M	NWH	77080
RYTON LN	8700	412K	NWC	77088

S

Street Name	Block	Pg/Sq	Loc	Zips
S, AVENUE	6600	494R	SEH	77011
E. S, AVENUE	9300	535D	SEH	77012
SAATHOFF DR	11000	369K	NWC	77429
SABA RD	0	290R	NWC	77388
SABA RD	4600	571R	SWH	77045
SABAL PALM	400	613B	NEB	77584
SABAL PALMS CT	2700	446T	NWC	77449
SABAL PALMS DR	20200	446T	NWC	77449
SABAL PARK CT	300	619X	LC	77573
SABAL PARK LN	300	619X	LC	77573
SABASTIAN DR	9000	527R	NEF	77083
SABASTIAN DR	9000	528N	NEF	77083
SABATINI CT	0	445F	NWC	77493
SABER CT	2000	658T	LC	77573
SABER CT	10300	372W	NWC	77038
SABERO LN	0	660L	LC	77539
SABER OAKS DR	25200	524L	NWF	77406
SABER TRAILS DR	17000	367Y	NWC	77095
SABERWOOD DR	500	570Y	MC	77489
SABINA DR	0	525J	NEF	77406
S. SABINAL DR	20300	446P	NWC	77449
SABINAL CREEK DR	7300	525L	NEF	77407
SABINAL RIVER CT	0	367W	NWC	77433
SABINE	100	493F	NWH	77007
N. SABINE	2600	493B	NWH	77009
SABINE CT	0	538R	DP	77536
SABINE CT	2700	613T	NEB	77584
SABINE DR	0	538R	DP	77536
N. SABINE DR	20400	256N	SEM	77357
S. SABINE DR	20700	256N	SEM	77357
SABINE LN	1700	526W	NEF	77406
SABINE BROOK WAY	1200	332V	NCC	77073
SABINE LAKE CT	0	526X	NEF	77406
SABINE PASS CT	21600	525D	NEF	77450

Street Name	Block	Pg/Sq	Loc	Zips
SABINE POINT DR	0	376V	NEC	77346
SABINE RIDGE DR	0	524A	NEF	77494
SABINE RIVER CT	0	407A	NWC	77433
SABINE SPRING LN	0	445M	NWC	77449
SABINE SPRING LN	0	445M	NWC	77449
SABINE VALLEY TRAIL	0	293D	SEM	77386
SABLE	18300	257A	WV	77357
SABLE CIR	0	371F	NWC	77014
SABLE CT	2700	613T	NEB	77584
SABLE CT	4200	371B	NWC	77014
SABLE DR	1000	616U	FR	77546
SABLE DR	2800	613T	NEB	77584
SABLE LN	13400	371F	NWC	77014
SABLE ACRE CT	20300	326N	NWC	77433
SABLEBEND LN	13700	371B	NWC	77014
SABLEBROOK LN	10300	367X	NWC	77095
SABLE CANYON DR	0	524S	NWF	77406
SABLECHASE CT	13700	371B	NWC	77014
SABLECHASE DR	3400	371B	NWC	77014
S. SABLECHASE LN	13600	371B	NWC	77014
N. SABLECHASE LN	13700	371B	NWC	77014
SABLE CLIFF LN	0	575U	SEH	77075
SABLECLIFF LN	8600	575Y	SEH	77075
SABLE CREEK CT	24500	295M	SEM	77365
SABLE CREEK DR	20500	295M	SEM	77365
SABLE CREEK LN	0	612P	PL	77545
SABLECREST	13600	371C	NWC	77014
SABLE FIELD LN	4800	446D	NWC	77449
SABLE GARDEN CT	0	615B	PL	77581
SABLEGARDEN LN	13700	371B	NWC	77014
SABLEGLEN	13600	371C	NWC	77014
SABLEGROVE CT	4000	371B	NWC	77014
SABLEGROVE LN	13600	371B	NWC	77014
SABLE HILL CT	3700	253P	SEM	77386
SABLE KEY CT	0	326Z	NWC	77429
SABLELEAF DR	12500	369J	NWC	77429
SABLE MEADOW CT	10000	369Y	NWC	77064
SABLE MEADOW LN	10200	369Y	NWC	77064
SABLE MILLS DR	10300	367Y	NWC	77095
SABLEMIST CT	4100	371B	NWC	77014
SABLE OAKS LN	27000	366Q	NWC	77433
SABLE PINES LN	4200	371B	NWC	77014
SABLEPOINT LN	0	371B	NWC	77014
SABLERIDGE CIR	4000	371B	NWC	77014
SABLERIDGE CT	4000	371B	NWC	77014
SABLERIDGE DR	13500	371F	NWC	77014
S. SABLERIDGE LN	13400	371F	NWC	77014
N. SABLERIDGE LN	13400	371F	NWC	77014
SABLE RIVER CT	6800	609Q	MC	77459
SABLE RIVER DR	6900	609Q	MC	77459
SABLERUN CT	4000	371F	NWC	77014
SABLERUN LN	13600	371F	NWC	77014
SABLESPRINGS LN	13700	371B	NWC	77014
SABLE STONE CIR	19800	486Q	SWC	77450
SABLE TERRACE LN	8900	457A	NEC	77044
SABLETON CREST LN	0	326U	NWC	77429
SABLETON CREST LN	0	326U	NWC	77429
SABLE TRAIL CT	10100	369Y	NWC	77064
SABLE TRAIL LN	10200	369Y	NWC	77064
SABLE TREE DR	18200	447K	NWC	77084
SABLE TREE DR	18200	447K	NWC	77084
SABLEWOOD LN	13300	371F	NWC	77014
SABO RD	10300	576T	SEH	77089
SABRA CT	1	573H	SEH	77048
SABRINA DR	4700	371A	NWC	77066
SABRINA OAKS LN	3800	446F	NWC	77449
SABROOKE LN	2600	333N	NCC	77073
SAC CT	13900	328P	NWC	77429
SACATON DR	11000	371S	NWC	77086
SACHAMO	12100	496G	NEH	77013
SACHAR	11700	414M	NEC	77039
SACHNIK	200	536Z	PA	77502
SACHSE CT	0	445L	NWC	77449
SACKETT	2700	492T	SWH	77098
SACKVILLE CLOSE	5800	337X	NEC	77346
SACO RIVER WAY	0	377M	NEH	77346
SACRAMENTO	13500	497F	NEH	77015
N. SACRAMENTO AVE	2100	615N	PL	77581
S. SACRAMENTO AVE	2500	615N	PL	77581
SACRED HAVEN CIR	0	288S	NWC	77377
SADDLE DR	0	656K	FR	77546
SADDLE DR	100	409E	JV	77065
SADDLE LN	9300	450U	NWH	77080
SADDLEBACK PASS	10500	367X	NWC	77095
SADDLEBEND DR	14100	329W	NWC	77070
SADDLEBOUGH DR	11900	409A	NWC	77065
SADDLEBRANCH CT	300	491G	SWH	77024
SADDLEBRED DR	5500	408X	NWC	77084
SADDLEBRED LN	0	612Z	NEB	77578
SADDLEBRED SPRINGS LN	0	368C	NWC	77429
SADDLE BRIAR LN	14600	327Y	NWC	77429
W. SADDLEBROOK	1	491B	SWH	77024
SADDLEBROOK CIR	24400	485J	NEF	77494
SADDLEBROOK CT	1	249Y	NWC	77375
SADDLEBROOK LN	1	491B	SWH	77024
SADDLEBROOK LN	100	249Y	NWC	77375
SADDLEBROOK LN	2000	485J	NEF	77494
N. SADDLEBROOK LN	2700	485J	NEF	77494
S. SADDLEBROOK LN	2800	485J	NEF	77494
SADDLEBROOK CHAMPN WAY	0	249V	NWC	77375
SADDLEBROOK VILLAGE DR	25500	249V	NWC	77375
SADDLEBROOK WAY	25500	485J	NEF	77494
SADDLE BRUSH TRAIL	17400	367T	NWC	77095
SADDLECLIFF TRAIL	0	249V	NWC	77375
E. SADDLE CREEK	0	331S	NWC	77068
SADDLE CREEK	1	490M	HC	77024
SADDLE CREEK DR	1400	331M	NWC	77090
SADDLECREEK DR	1600	331R	NWC	77090
SADDLE CREEK FARMS DR	800	338Z	NEC	77532
SADDLE CREEK FARMS DR	800	339W	NEC	77532
SADDLE HORN CT	0	612Z	NEB	77578
SADDLE HORN DR	200	373W	NEH	77060
SADDLE HORN LN	0	256X	SEM	77365
SADDLEHORN LN	1	490H	HC	77024
SADDLEHORN TRAIL	2000	484H	NEF	77494
SADDLEHORN TRAIL	2700	485J	NEF	77494
SADDLEHORN TRAIL	10200	409B	NWC	77064
SADDLELEAF PLACE	0	251Q	WD	77380
SADDLE MARBROOK CT	6700	609Y	NEF	77459
SADDLE MOUNTAIN LN	0	377F	NEC	77346
SADDLE MOUNTAIN LN	0	377J	NEC	77346
SADDLE PATH CT	24500	293S	NCC	77373
SADDLE RANCH DR	20100	334R	NCC	77338
SADDLE RIDGE	200	251Y	WD	77380
SADDLE RIDGE RD	13000	420P	NEC	77532
SADDLE RIDGE PASS	16400	326K	NWC	77433
SADDLE ROCK DR	500	412M	NCC	77037
SADDLE ROCK DR	800	412K	NWH	77088
SADDLE ROCK LN	26500	258J	SEM	77357
SADDLERS WOODS DR	0	377G	NEC	77346
SADDLE SPRINGS LN	0	367P	NWC	77433
SADDLE SPUR LN	24600	485J	NEF	77494

Street Name	Block	Pg/Sq	Loc	Zips
SADDLE SPUR LN	24900	484R	NEF	77494
SADDLE TREE	700	491B	SWH	77024
SADDLEVILLE MILLS LN	0	406R	NWC	77433
SADDLEWOOD DR	22100	405Y	NWC	77449
SADDLEWOOD LN	500	490H	HC	77024
SADDLEWOOD ESTATES DR	1	490H	HC	77024
SADLER	1100	453H	NEH	77022
SADLER	1700	454F	NEH	77093
SADLER	4800	454G	NEH	77016
SAFEBUY	7900	455K	NEH	77028
SAFEGUARD	8400	533Y	SEH	77051
SAFEGUARD	10600	573G	SEH	77047
SAFE HARBOR CIR	2700	657C	SEC	77546
SAFE HAVEN DR	0	326E	NWC	77377
SAFFLOWER DR	0	461T	NEC	77521
SAFFOLK PUNCH DR	9500	409A	NWC	77065
SAFFRON CT	500	657Z	LC	77573
SAFFRON LN	0	461Q	NEC	77521
SAFFRON LN	4200	657A	FR	77546
SAFFRON HILLS DR	6300	330M	NWC	77379
SAFRANO ST	0	286Q	NWC	77377
SAGAMORE	10800	531W	SWH	77096
SAGAMORE HILLS DR	14800	527D	SWC	77082
SAGAMORE RIDGE PLACE	0	250P	NWC	77389
SAGA VILLA DR	0	257F	SEM	77357
SAGE	100	493B	NWH	77009
SAGE CIR	5200	461T	NEC	77521
SAGE CT	1	250C	WD	77381
SAGE CT	2500	610B	MC	77489
SAGE CT	6400	614T	PL	77584
SAGE DR	200	495V	GP	77547
SAGE DR	4500	500M	BT	77521
SAGE LN	0	659Z	DI	77539
SAGE RD	100	491Y	SWH	77056
SAGE ST	900	501M	BT	77521
SAGEARBOR DR	11000	576Y	SEH	77089
SAGEASPEN LN	9800	616F	SEC	77089
SAGE AUGUST LN	9900	616A	SEC	77089
SAGEBARK DR	9800	616E	SEC	77089
SAGEBEND LN	9500	576W	SEC	77089
SAGEBERRY DR	10300	576W	SEC	77089
SAGEBERRY DR	10500	616B	SEH	77089
SAGEBLOSSOM DR	11200	616E	SEC	77089
SAGEBLUFF DR	10200	576W	SEC	77089
SAGEBLUFF DR	10300	616A	SEC	77089
SAGEBRANCH CT	0	526E	NEF	77450
SAGEBRIAR DR	10400	576Y	SEH	77089
SAGE BROOK DR	10300	615D	SEC	77089
SAGEBRUSH DR	2900	414S	NEH	77093
SAGE BRUSH LN	0	537H	PA	77530
SAGEBRUSH COVE	0	526T	NEF	77407
SAGEBRUSH HOLLOW DR	0	406H	NWC	77433
SAGEBRUSH TRAIL	1100	501M	BT	77521
SAGE BRUSH VALLEY DR	0	406M	NWC	77433
SAGEBUD LN	9800	616E	SEC	77089
SAGEBURROW DR	10100	576W	SEC	77089
SAGEBURROW DR	10300	616B	SEC	77089
SAGECANYON DR	10000	576W	SEC	77089
SAGECANYON DR	10100	616A	SEC	77089
SAGECASTLE LN	9800	616E	SEC	77089
SAGECHERRY DR	11400	616F	SEC	77089
W. SAGECIRCLE	3300	491Y	SWH	77056
E. SAGECIRCLE	3300	491Y	SWH	77056
S. SAGECIRCLE	5200	491Y	SWH	77056
N. SAGECIRCLE	5200	491Y	SWH	77056
SAGECLIFF DR	11800	576Y	SEH	77089
SAGECOMBE CT	20400	291Y	NWC	77388
SAGECOMBE LN	3500	291Y	NWC	77388
SAGECOUNTRY DR	11100	616E	SEC	77089
SAGECOURT DR	9800	616F	SEC	77089
SAGE COVE LN	8800	527N	NEF	77407
SAGECREEK DR	11200	616C	SEC	77089
W. SAGE CREEK PLACE	1	249B	SWM	77382
E. SAGE CREEK PLACE	1	249B	SWM	77382
SAGECREST LN	10800	616B	SEH	77089
SAGECREST LN	11000	576X	SEH	77089
SAGECROFT DR	17900	447C	NWC	77084
SAGE CYPRESS CT	16300	326F	NWC	77433
SAGEDALE DR	9800	616F	SEC	77089
SAGEDECK LN	0	616E	SEC	77089
SAGE DOCK CT	10400	616G	SEH	77089
SAGEDOWNE LN	9800	616B	SEH	77089
SAGEDOWNE LN	11500	576Z	SEH	77089
SAGEELM LN	10300	616B	SEH	77089
SAGE FLOWER CT	21300	335J	NCC	77338
SAGEFORD CT	24800	485N	NEF	77494
SAGEFOREST DR	10400	576Y	SEH	77089
SAGE GALE DR	11100	616E	SEC	77089
SAGEGATE DR	4700	293Y	NCC	77373
SAGEGATE DR	9900	616F	SEC	77089
SAGEGLEN DR	11200	576Y	SEH	77089
SAGEGLEN DR	11400	616C	SEC	77089
SAGEGLOW DR	9900	616F	SEC	77089
SAGEGREEN CT	11500	616F	SEC	77089
SAGEGREEN DR	9900	616F	SEC	77089
SAGEGROVE LN	11400	576Y	SEH	77089
SAGEGULF LN	10800	616B	SEH	77089
SAGEHAMPTON CT	9400	289Y	NWC	77379
SAGEHAVEN DR	11200	576Y	SEH	77089
SAGEHEATHER DR	11000	616C	SEH	77089
SAGEHILL DR	11000	616C	SEH	77089
SAGE HOLLOW LN	0	293G	SEM	77386
SAGEHOLLOW LN	11400	576Y	SEH	77089
SAGEHOLLY CIR	11300	616E	SEC	77089
SAGEHURST LN	11400	576Y	SEH	77089
SAGEKARON DR	11400	616F	SEC	77089
SAGEKING DR	11100	616F	SEC	77089
SAGEKNIGHT CIR	0	616A	SEC	77089
SAGEKNIGHT DR	11100	616A	SEC	77089
SAGEKNOLL LN	9500	576W	SEC	77089
SAGELAKE LN	9800	616E	SEC	77089
SAGELAND DR	11200	576Y	SEH	77089
SAGE LAUREL LN	20900	526E	NEF	77407
SAGELEA LN	9900	616B	SEH	77089
SAGELEAF LN	10800	616B	SEH	77089
SAGELEAF LN	10900	576X	SEH	77089
SAGE LEE	0	616E	SEC	77089
SAGE LINDA LN	11100	616A	SEC	77089
SAGELINK CIR	10300	616F	SEC	77089
SAGELINK CT	10300	616F	SEC	77089
SAGELINK DR	11500	616F	SEC	77089
SAGE MANOR DR	5600	407Y	NWC	77084
SAGE MARIE LN	9900	616A	SEC	77089
SAGEMARK DR	9800	616F	SEC	77089
SAGEMARK RIDGE DR	0	406K	NWC	77433
SAGEMEADOW CT	10500	616G	SEC	77089
SAGEMEADOW LN	10300	576W	SEC	77089
SAGEMEADOW LN	10600	616B	SEH	77089
SAGEMILL DR	9900	616F	SEC	77089
SAGEMIST CT	9600	576W	SEC	77089
SAGEMIST LN	11300	576W	SEC	77089
SAGEMONT SQUARE CT	17600	527E	NEF	77407

Street Name	Block	Pg/Sq	Loc	Zips
SAGEMORGAN DR	10900	616A	SEC	77089
SAGEMOSS LN	9800	616E	SEC	77089
SAGE MOUNTAIN LN	21900	526A	NEF	77450
SAGEOAK DR	11200	576Y	SEH	77089
SAGEORCHARD CT	11100	616A	SEC	77089
SAGEORCHARD LN	9800	616A	SEC	77089
SAGEORCHARD LN	11100	576X	SEH	77089
SAGEPARK LN	10500	576X	SEC	77089
SAGEPARK LN	10700	616B	SEH	77089
SAGEPERRY DR	11400	616C	SEC	77089
SAGEPIKE CIR	11100	616E	SEC	77089
SAGEPIKE DR	9800	616E	SEC	77089
SAGEPINE LN	10500	576Y	SEH	77089
SAGE PLACE DR	8800	570A	SWH	77071
SAGEPLUM DR	9800	616F	SEH	77089
SAGE POINT LN	0	328K	NWC	77377
SAGE POINTE CT	3600	446M	NWC	77449
SAGEQUEEN DR	9800	616A	SEC	77089
SAGER DR	8800	531Q	SWH	77096
SAGE RAIN CT	20600	446K	NWC	77449
SAGERIDGE CIR	10700	616B	SEC	77089
SAGERIVER CT	11100	576X	SEC	77089
SAGERIVER DR	10700	576X	SEC	77089
SAGERIVER DR	11000	616C	SEH	77089
SAGEROCK DR	9900	616B	SEC	77089
SAGEROYAL LN	9800	616F	SEC	77089
SAGE RUN CT	0	299X	NEC	77336
SAGE RUN DR	0	299X	NEC	77336
S. SAGE SPARROW CIR	0	250Q	NWC	77389
S. SAGE SPARROW CIR	0	250Q	NWC	77389
N. SAGE SPARROW CIR	0	250P	NWC	77389
N. SAGE SPARROW CIR	0	250P	NWC	77389
SAGE SPARROW CT	0	250P	NWC	77389
SAGE SPARROW CT	0	250P	NWC	77389
SAGE SQUARE	5200	491Y	SWH	77056
SAGES RAVINE DR	0	377L	NEC	77346
SAGESTANLEY DR	11400	616F	SEC	77089
SAGESTAR LN	10400	576W	SEC	77089
SAGESTONE CT	8500	407G	NWC	77095
SAGE STONE LN	0	609U	MC	77459
SAGE TERRACE	3200	485V	NEF	77450
SAGE THRASHER LN	14700	288A	NWC	77377
SAGETOWN DR	11400	616F	SEC	77089
SAGE TRACE CT	0	253S	SEM	77386
SAGETRAIL DR	9900	576W	SEC	77089
SAGETRAIL DR	10400	616B	SEH	77089
SAGETREE DR	10400	576Y	SEH	77089
SAGE TREE TRAIL	19700	337Q	NEC	77346
SAGEVALE CT	10400	616F	SEC	77089
SAGEVALE LN	10300	576W	SEC	77089
SAGEVALE LN	10500	616B	SEH	77089
SAGEVALLEY DR	11000	616B	SEH	77089
SAGEVIEW DR	11000	616C	SEH	77089
SAGEVILLE DR	11200	576Z	SEH	77089
SAGEWALK CT	6400	290U	NWC	77379
SAGEWALK LN	0	609P	NEF	77479
SAGEWAY DR	11200	576Z	SEH	77089
SAGEWELL DR	9800	616E	SEC	77089
SAGEWHITE DR	11400	616F	SEC	77089
SAGEWICK DR	10400	576Y	SEH	77089
SAGEWILLOW LN	10300	576W	SEC	77089
SAGEWILLOW LN	10800	616B	SEH	77089
SAGEWIND CIR	10700	616G	SEC	77089
SAGEWIND CT	10700	616G	SEC	77089
SAGEWIND DR	10500	576X	SEC	77089
SAGEWIND DR	10700	616B	SEH	77089
SAGEWOOD CT	3100	614U	PL	77584
SAGEWOOD CT	16400	570E	MC	77489
SAGEWOOD DR	100	252N	SEM	77386
SAGEWOOD DR	11200	576Z	SEH	77089
SAGEWOOD BEND LN	0	253T	SEM	77386
SAGEWOOD BEND LN	12600	409W	NWC	77041
SAGEWOOD FOREST DR	0	524E	NEF	77494
SAGEWOOD HILLS DR	12801	528H	SWH	77072
SAGEYORK DR	10000	616A	SEC	77089
SAGGING OAKS DR	19600	292W	NWC	77388
SAG HARBOR LN	0	377J	NEC	77346
SAGINAW DR	11200	413X	NEH	77076
SAGINAW BAY CT	900	292B	NCC	77373
SAGINAW POINT CT	0	445L	NWC	77449
SAGINAW POINT LN	0	445L	NWC	77449
SAGO LN	2000	447S	NWH	77084
SAGO ISLAND DR	0	333F	NCC	77073
SAGO PARK LN	0	409W	NWC	77041
SAGUARD DR	0	658Y	LC	77573
SAHALLE DR	24700	484H	NEF	77494
SAHARA DR	1400	419E	NEC	77532
SAI BABA DR	0	411D	NWC	77038
SAILAWAY DR	1300	619U	LC	77573
SAIL BOAT	2600	619P	NB	77058
SAILE CT	4200	296V	NEH	77339
SAILFIN	16000	419B	NEC	77532
SAILFIN CT	700	419B	NEC	77532
SAILFISH LN	3800	580V	LP	77571
SAILFISH COVE DR	18400	377D	NEC	77346
SAILFISH POINT CT	0	528Y	SG	77478
SAIL HARBOUR CT	22500	485U	NEF	77450
SAILING DR	8700	378A	NEC	77346
SAILOR'S WAY	4400	609R	MC	77459
SAILOR MOON CT	0	657C	SEC	77546
SAILORS MOON CT	17000	657C	SEC	77546
SAILORS MOON DR	2700	657C	SEC	77546
SAIL PORT	2400	613J	PL	77584
SAILPORT LN	0	660J	LC	77573
SAILWIND DR	0	612F	PL	77545
SAILWIND LN	0	660J	LC	77573
SAILWING CREEK CT	11300	613J	PL	77584
SAINT	2600	492S	SWH	77027
SAINT AGNES	1000	532M	SWH	77030
SAINT ALBAN CT	12700	497A	NEC	77015
SAINT ANDREWS	100	656T	FR	77546
SAINT ANDREWS DR	4600	501J	BT	77521
SAINT ANDREWS DR	6300	578J	PA	77505
SAINT ANDREWS RD	600	336B	NEH	77339
SAINT ANDREWS PLACE	2700	659C	LC	77573
SAINT ANNE FOREST DR	6200	411K	NWC	77088
SAINT ARMANDS	0	619Q	PA	77586
SAINT AUGUSTINE	700	494S	SEH	77023
SAINT AUGUSTINE	5800	533M	SEH	77021
SAINT BENEDICT	3400	533P	SEH	77021
SAINT CECILIA	11800	419V	BR	77532
SAINT CHARLES	0	420S	BR	77532
N. SAINT CHARLES	1	494J	SEH	77003
SAINT CHARLES	100	419V	BR	77532
SAINT CHARLES	100	494N	SEH	77003
SAINT CHARLES	500	659J	LC	77573
SAINT CHARLES	2300	493R	SEH	77004
SAINT CHARLES	4600	533B	SEH	77004
SAINT CHRISTOPHER AVE	2000	659F	LC	77573
SAINT CLAIR	900	412U	NWH	77088
SAINT CLAUDE CT	12500	496D	NEC	77015
SAINT CLOUD DR	100	656T	FR	77546

Street Name	Block	Pg/Sq	Loc	Zips
SAINT CLOUD DR	14600	618E	SEH	77062
SAINT EDMUNDS CROSSING	1900	659X	DI	77539
SAINT EDWARDS	17000	332J	NWC	77090
SAINT EDWARDS GREEN DR	700	496C	NEC	77015
SAINT ELMO	600	494F	NEH	77020
SAINT EMANUEL	1	493R	SEH	77002
SAINT EMANUEL	600	493R	SEH	77003
SAINT EMANUEL	2300	493V	SEH	77004
SAINTE MERE EGLISE LN	0	291U	NWC	77388
SAINT EMILION CT	17900	330F	NWC	77379
SAINTES CIR	7800	570G	MC	77071
SAINT FINANS WAY	100	457X	NEC	77015
SAINT FLORENT CT	13400	288Y	NWC	77377
SAINT FLORENT DR	25900	288Y	NWC	77377
SAINT FRANCIS	11800	419V	BR	77532
SAINT FRANCIS LN	800	489B	SWH	77079
SAINT GEORGE LN	800	489C	SWH	77079
SAINT GEORGE PLACE	3200	491Y	BL	77401
SAINT GEORGE SQUARE LN	5300	491Y	BL	77401
SAINT GERMAIN WAY	0	529B	NEF	77082
SAINT HELEN LN	0	330E	NWC	77379
SAINT HELENA WAY	16300	611B	SWH	77053
SAINT HELENS CT	0	526B	NEF	77450
SAINT HELIER	16100	409L	JV	77040
SAINT HONORE CT	11800	329S	NWC	77377
SAINT IVES CT	700	488A	SWH	77079
SAINT JAMES	2500	536U	PA	77502
SAINT JAMES CT	2200	610A	MC	77459
SAINT JAMES PLACE	1700	491P	SWH	77056
SAINT JAMES PLACE	2100	615L	PL	77581
SAINT JOHN CT	10700	530Y	SWH	77071
SAINT JOHN CT	16000	409L	JV	77040
SAINT JOHN DR	1000	613G	NEB	77584
SAINT JOHN DR	18100	619S	NB	77058
SAINT JOHNS WOOD DR	16600	328Q	NWC	77377
SAINT JOHNS WOODS	1200	488L	SWH	77077
SAINT JOSEPH	700	494S	SEH	77023
SAINT JOSEPH PKWY	300	493Q	DT	77002
SAINT JOSEPH PKWY	1600	493Q	SEH	77003
SAINT JUDE DR	6300	578J	PA	77505
SAINT LAURENT LN	0	457Z	NEC	77044
SAINT LAWRENCE CIR	15800	617T	SEC	77546
SAINT LAWRENCE CT	15800	617T	SEC	77546
SAINT LAWRENCE DR	4700	617S	SEC	77546
SAINT LAWRENCE COVE	15800	617W	SEC	77546
ST. LO RD	7000	534S	SEH	77033
ST. LO RD	8600	574A	SEH	77033
SAINT LOUIS	7100	454R	NEH	77028
SAINT LOUIS	7300	455N	NEH	77028
SAINT LUCIA	24800	324H	NWC	77447
SAINT MARKS DR	100	568P	SG	77478
SAINT MARTIN	11800	419V	BR	77532
SAINT MARYS LN	10800	489A	SWH	77079
SAINT MARYS LN	14700	488D	SWH	77079
SAINT MICHAELS PASS	0	406L	NWC	77433
SAINT MICHEL DR	12400	496D	NEC	77015
SAINT MORITZ	5600	531D	BL	77401
SAINT NICHOLAS	0	283F	NWC	77484
SAINT PATRICK LN	2200	538N	DP	77536
SAINT PAUL	5600	531D	BL	77401
SAINT PAULS CT	28600	299S	NEC	77336
SAINT PIERRE CT	16000	327Y	NWC	77429
SAINT PIERRE LN	14300	327Y	NWC	77429
SAINT THOMAS CT	1	369H	NWC	77070
SAINT TROPEZ WAY	0	529A	SWH	77082
SAINT WILLIAM LN	3500	447J	NWC	77084
SAKOWITZ	0	454Y	NEH	77026
SAKOWITZ	700	494C	NEH	77020
SAKOWITZ	3300	494C	NEH	77026
SALADO DR	2600	613S	NEB	77584
SALADO LN	7000	459L	NEC	77049
SALADOCREEK CT	0	366Z	NWC	77433
SALAMA FALLS	0	616H	SEH	77089
SALAMANCA CT	0	328N	NWC	77429
SALAMANCA WAY	2500	659S	LC	77573
SALEM	1700	538S	DP	77536
SALEM	6600	453Q	NEH	77022
SALEM CT	3100	569N	SG	77478
SALEM BLUE CT	0	326J	NWC	77433
SALEM FIELDS CT	0	253X	SEM	77386
SALEM FIELDS DR	0	253X	SEM	77386
SALEM HILLS DR	1	485E	NEF	77494
SALENTO CT	11100	525N	NEF	77469
SALERNO	600	568P	SG	77478
SALERNO CT	1200	659M	LC	77573
SALERNO LN	1	453B	NEH	77076
SALFORD DR	1300	452W	NWH	77008
SALGE DR	7500	410R	NWH	77040
SALIDA CREEK CIR	0	366Y	NWC	77433
SALIDA DE SOL DR	16100	527K	NEF	77083
SALINA	4500	454X	NEH	77026
SALINA	7600	455W	NEH	77020
SALINA CT	3900	375R	NCC	77396
SALINAS LN	0	660G	LC	77539
SALINAS LN	16300	407H	NWC	77095
SALISBURY	2200	492U	SWH	77019
SALISBURY CT	0	657G	FR	77546
SALISBURY DR	13600	568F	SG	77498
SALLAS PITTS RD	18100	295K	SEM	77365
SALMA CT	500	372H	NCC	77073
SALMON CT	10300	462V	CCO	77520
SALMON LN	16000	330S	NWC	77379
SALMON CREEK	12200	449A	NWC	77041
SALMON CREEK LN	0	657P	FR	77546
SALMON PINK PLACE	0	286Q	NWC	77377
W. SALMON RIVER CIR	0	377K	NEC	77346
S. SALMON RIVER CIR	0	377K	NEC	77346
N. SALMON RIVER CIR	0	377K	NEC	77346
SALOP CT	0	258F	SEM	77357
SALTA DR	6600	527H	SWC	77083
SALTA VERDE POINT	0	525A	NEF	77494
SALT CEDAR LN	32800	322B	WCO	77484
SALT CREEK LN	0	524F	NEF	77494
SALTER DR	800	373P	NCC	77032
SALT GRASS	0	539S	DP	77536
SALTGRASS MEADOW DR	0	366J	NWC	77433
SALTGRASS SHORES DR	0	487E	SWC	77494
SALT GRASS TRAIL	13600	367B	CY	77429
SALT GRASS TRAIL	0	539S	DP	77536
SALT GRASS TRAIL WAY	0	444R	NWC	77493
SALTILLO	9600	455Z	NEH	77013
SALT MARSH CT	2100	658T	LC	77573
SALTON POINT DR	16000	617T	SEC	77546
SALT RIVER CT	2800	610U	MC	77459
SALT RIVER CT	19900	446U	NWC	77449
SALT RIVER VALLEY CIR	17500	377E	NEC	77346
SALT RIVER VALLEY LN	12000	377E	NEC	77346
SALT TRAIL	0	371B	NWC	77014
SALTUS	2500	494N	SEH	77003
SALT VALLEY DR	0	445S	NWC	77493
SALT WIND CT	400	379X	NEC	77532
SALTY DOG	6800	375P	NWH	77396

Street Name	Block	Pg/Sq	Loc	Zips
SALUDA CREEK LN	0	571G	SWH	77085
SALVADOR	3600	577B	PA	77504
SALVATO	3000	659Z	GCO	77539
SALZBE	0	415A	NEC	77039
SALZBURG CT	9700	335Q	HM	77338
SALZBURG LN	20100	335Q	HM	77338
SAM	300	536V	PA	77502
SAM	600	412Z	NWH	77091
SAM	10300	527Z	NEF	77498
SAMANTHA LN	12000	248E	SWM	77354
SAMANTHA COVE CT	2900	485N	NEF	77494
SAMANTHA SUZANNE CT	9800	532S	SWH	77025
SAMARA DR	0	253Y	SEM	77386
SAM BROOKINS RD	16000	527U	NEF	77498
SAMBUCO CT	0	525J	NEF	77406
SAM CREEK CT	22400	525C	NEF	77494
SAME WAY	3100	297N	NEH	77339
SAM HOUSTON	5600	414R	NEH	77016
SAM HOUSTON	6100	415R	NEH	77016
SAM HOUSTON DR	3200	609E	SG	77479
S. SAM HOUSTON W. PKWY	3700	572W	SWC	77053
SAM HOUSTON CENTER DR	0	409D	NWC	77064
SAM HOUSTON PARK DR	0	409D	NWC	77064
N. SAM HOUSTON PKWY W	0	370S	NWC	77086
E. SAM HOUSTON PKWY S	0	577P	SEH	77034
E. SAM HOUSTON PKWY S	1	572Z	SWC	77047
W. SAM HOUSTON PKWY N	100	489M	SWH	77024
W. SAM HOUSTON PKWY S	100	489Z	SWH	77042
N. SAM HOUSTON PKWY E	100	372V	NEH	77060
E. SAM HOUSTON PKWY	100	498W	NEC	77015
N. SAM HOUSTON PKWY W	100	372S	NWH	77038
E. SAM HOUSTON PKWY S	100	537V	PA	77503
N. SAM HOUSTON PKWY E	300	373S	NEH	77060
N. SAM HOUSTON PKWY E	800	373S	NCC	77032
W. SAM HOUSTON PKWY N	1000	449U	NWH	77043
S. SAM HOUSTON PKWY E	1800	573Y	SEH	77047
N. SAM HOUSTON PKWY E	2400	374U	NEH	77032
S. SAM HOUSTON PKWY W	3000	571S	SWH	77053
E. SAM HOUSTON PKWY S	3100	577P	PA	77505
N. SAM HOUSTON PKWY W	3200	371U	NWC	77086
S. SAM HOUSTON PKWY E	4100	574X	SEH	77048
W. SAM HOUSTON PKWY N	4300	449G	NWH	77041
E. SAM HOUSTON PKWY N	4800	457A	NEC	77015
E. SAM HOUSTON PKWY N	5600	457A	NEC	77049
N. SAM HOUSTON PKWY E	5700	375U	NEC	77396
W. SAM HOUSTON PKWY S	5800	529M	SWH	77072
W. SAM HOUSTON PKWY N	6000	409Y	NWC	77041
S. SAM HOUSTON PKWY W	6200	571Y	SWH	77085
W. SAM HOUSTON PKWY N	7000	410N	NWC	77040
S. SAM HOUSTON PKWY E	7200	575Y	SEH	77075
E. SAM HOUSTON PKWY N	8200	457A	NEC	77044
W. SAM HOUSTON PKWY N	8500	409D	NWC	77064
W. SAM HOUSTON PKWY S	8800	529M	SWH	77099
E. SAM HOUSTON PKWY N	9200	416H	NEC	77044
S. SAM HOUSTON PKWY E	9400	576Y	SEH	77089
S. SAM HOUSTON PKWY W	9500	570K	SWH	77085
N. SAM HOUSTON PKWY E	9700	376S	NEC	77396
W. SAM HOUSTON PKWY N	10000	369Z	NWC	77064
W. SAM HOUSTON PKWY N	10700	569D	SWH	77031
S. SAM HOUSTON PKWY W	11300	569D	SWH	77031
SAM HOUSTON TOLLWAY	0	369Z	NWC	77064
SAM HOUSTON TRAIL	0	283D	NWC	77484
SAMMIES CT	2700	494E	NEH	77020
SAMMON RD	0	335Z	HM	77338
SAMOA WAY	15600	571X	SWH	77053
SAMOA WAY	16300	611B	SWH	77053
SAMOTH	0	580Z	PA	77586
SAMPLEY WAY	5800	451A	NWH	77092
SAMPRAS ACE CT	6200	331N	NWC	77379
N. SAMPSON	1	494N	SEH	77003
SAMPSON	100	494S	SEH	77003
SAMPSON	2100	493V	SEH	77004
SAMPSON	3500	533D	SEH	77004
SAMPSON	5100	533G	SEH	77004
SAM RAY BURN CT	0	407A	NWC	77433
SAMROSE DR	5400	452C	NWH	77091
SAMS DR	2500	620A	SB	77586
SAMSARAH CIR	17000	407Q	NWC	77084
SAMS HILL RD	20200	257R	SEM	77357
SAMS PLACE	0	494E	NEH	77020
SAMUEL	1500	453T	NWH	77009
SAMUEL LN	12800	496M	NEH	77015
SAMUEL ADAMS DR	10800	369W	NWC	77065
SAMUEL ADAMS LN	3600	569Y	MC	77477
SAMUELS DR	5200	578J	PA	77505
SAMUEL SPRINGS LN	0	377U	NEC	77044
SAM WILSON	1600	494C	NEH	77020
SAN ALBERTO	8800	535Z	SEH	77017
SAN ANGELO	6900	494H	NEH	77020
SAN ANGELO	7100	495E	NEH	77020
SAN ANTONIO	500	535B	SEH	77012
SAN ANTONIO	2100	615J	PL	77581
SAN ANTONIO	6800	410T	NWC	77040
SAN ANTONIO RIVER DR	4700	253V	SEM	77386
W. SAN AUGUSTINE	100	538Q	DP	77536
E. SAN AUGUSTINE	100	538Q	DP	77536
SAN AUGUSTINE AVE	2800	537Q	PA	77503
SAN AUGUSTINE LN	2300	656U	FR	77546
SAN BARRIA DR	0	445E	NWC	77493
SAN BENEDETTO	0	659M	LC	77573
SAN BENITO DR	7400	527M	SWC	77083
SAN BERNADINO	4600	371A	NWC	77066
SAN BERNARD RIVER LN	4600	253Y	SEM	77386
SAN BERNARD RIVER LOOP	28800	253Y	SEM	77386
SAN BIAGO ST	0	530X	SWH	77031
SAN BLAS	6000	535Z	SEH	77017
SAN BONIFACIO	8900	535Z	SEH	77017
SANBORN DR	4300	451H	NWH	77092
SAN CARLO LN	0	659H	LC	77573
SAN CARLOS	9600	455Z	NEH	77013
SANCHEZ	7800	535F	SEH	77012
S. SAN CIRCLE DR	12200	456C	NEC	77044
N. SAN CIRCLE DR	12200	456C	NEC	77044
SAN CLEMENTE	12700	371A	NWC	77066
SAN CLEMENTE POINT CT	0	525B	NEF	77449
SAN CONERO DR	2300	616P	PL	77581
SAN CRISTOBAL	0	527R	NEF	77083
SANCROFT CT	400	486B	SWC	77450
SANCTUARY COVE	2800	485V	NEF	77450
SAND	7700	412S	NWH	77088
SAND, A F RD	13400	408V	NWC	77041
SANDA	16000	458U	CV	77530
SANDAHL CT		484T	NEF	77494
SANDALFOOT	14000	408K	NWC	77095
SANDAL GROVE	0	526T	NEF	77469
SANDAL GROVE	0	526T	NEF	77469
SANDALIA CT	4900	484Y	NEF	77494
SANDALIN CT	13900	368A	NWC	77429
SANDALIN DR	14500	368A	NWC	77429
SANDALISLE LN	0	527S	NEF	77469
SANDAL SPRINGS DR	0	445S	NWC	77493
SANDAL WALK	0	613K	PL	77584

Street Name	Block	Pg/Sq	Loc	Zips
SANDALWOOD CIR	4700	501E	BT	77521
SANDALWOOD DR	1	490P	SWH	77024
SANDALWOOD DR	21900	255U	SEM	77365
SANDALWOOD LN	0	293D	SEM	77386
SAN DARIO DR	16200	527F	NEF	77083
SAND BAR CT	2500	620B	SB	77586
SANDBERRY DR	2800	297Q	NEH	77345
SANDBOW LN	0	417B	NEC	77044
SANDBRIDGE DR	13300	488K	SWH	77077
SANDBROOK DR	3400	371Q	NWC	77066
SAND BUNKER CIR	21400	486S	NEF	77450
SAND CANYON DR	13900	528P	SWC	77083
SAND CASTLE CT	2500	620F	SB	77586
SANDCASTLE LN	0	491X	SWH	77057
SANDCLIFF LN	7100	525H	NEF	77407
SAND COLONY LN	4800	446D	NWC	77449
SANDCOVE CT	0	659M	LC	77573
SAND COVE CT	1	251K	WD	77381
SANDCRANE DR	1400	620G	SB	77586
SAND CREEK CT	19900	446U	NWC	77449
SANDCREST DR	2700	613X	NEB	77578
SAND DOLLAR CT	3300	609E	SG	77479
SAND DOLLAR CT	4000	620F	SB	77586
SAND DOLLAR DR	9900	369W	NWC	77065
SANDEL	300	580L	LP	77571
SANDELFORD DR	18500	406Z	NWC	77449
SANDELFORD DR	18500	407W	NWC	77449
SANDERFORD CT	4800	484Y	NEF	77494
SANDERFORD LN	13300	528Q	SWC	77083
SANDERLING CT	0	461N	NEC	77521
SANDERLING DR	20300	406L	NWC	77433
SANDERLING LN	200	568P	SG	77478
SANDERMEYER DR	0	524K	NWF	77406
SANDERS	300	460T	HG	77562
SANDERS	3300	493Z	SEH	77004
SANDERS	5100	534B	SEH	77023
SANDERS CT	0	659G	LC	77573
SANDERS LN	8700	249J	SWM	77354
SANDERS RD	8600	249J	SWM	77354
SANDERS RD	19400	286B	SWM	77355
SANDERS CEMETERY RD	22100	286F	NWC	77377
SANDERS CEMETERY RD	23000	286F	SWM	77355
SANDERS FOREST CT	8100	335J	NCC	77338
SANDERSGATE LN	0	484Z	NEF	77494
SANDERS GLEN LN	8200	335J	NCC	77338
SANDERS HILL LN	0	375X	NEC	77396
SANDERS WAY	16400	246S	SWM	77355
SANDESTINE DR	17000	407F	NWC	77095
SANDFIELD DR	14000	488J	SWH	77077
SANDFORD LODGE DR	0	372H	NCC	77073
SANDFORD MEADOW LN	0	328K	NWC	77429
SANDFORD SPRINGS TRAIL	0	328A	NWC	77377
SANDGATE RD	200	575E	SEH	77061
SANDGATE FALLS CT	1900	618A	SEH	77062
SANDHILL CRANE DR	14200	377W	NEC	77044
SANDHILL CRANE RD	0	461N	NEC	77521
SANDHILL CRANE PARK DR	0	291H	NWC	77389
SANDHILL GLEN DR	6900	407P	NWC	77084
SANDHILL PARK LN	0	457A	NEC	77044
SANDHILL PINE CT	0	524A	NEF	77494
SAND HILLS DR	0	409F	JV	77064
SANDHILLS PINE COVE	0	293D	SEM	77386
SANDHILL TRAILS CT	0	324M	NWC	77447
SANDHILL TRAILS CT	0	324M	NWC	77447
SAND HOLLOW LN	1800	486L	SWC	77450
SANDHURST DR	8100	534W	SEH	77033
SANDHURST DR	11300	574J	SEH	77048
SANDI LN	25000	485S	NEF	77494
SANDIA COVE CT	12400	409W	NWC	77041
SANDIA CREST ST	0	290U	NWC	77379
SANDIA LAKE LN	0	409W	NWC	77041
SANDIA PINES DR	18800	337Y	NEC	77346
SANDIA SPRINGS CIR	0	367W	NWC	77433
SAN DIMAS DR	7500	527M	SWC	77083
SANDISFIELD LN	15700	408W	NWC	77084
SAND ISLE DR	0	612J	PL	77545
SAND LAKE LN	1400	526X	NEF	77407
SANDLE	7200	412X	NWH	77088
SANDLE	9200	412S	NWH	77088
SANDLE BROOK CT	0	612M	PL	77584
SANDLE CREST CT	5600	448D	NWC	77041
SANDLEHURST DR	3900	577E	PA	77504
SANDLEIGH DR	0	291Y	NWC	77388
SANDLER CT	14600	328X	NWC	77429
SANDLER BEND	11900	328X	NWC	77429
SANDLEWOOD	3900	577E	PA	77504
SANDLEWOOD TRAIL LN	0	371D	NWC	77014
SANDLIGHT LN	26600	368N	NWC	77433
SANDLILY CT	1	251L	WD	77380
SAND LODGE LN	9900	616K	SEC	77089
SANDMAN	100	492G	SWH	77007
S. SANDMAN	3600	492Y	SWH	77098
SANDMAN LN	300	419R	BR	77532
SAND MIST CIR	2100	619Z	LC	77573
SANDMIST DR	0	485V	NEF	77450
SAND MOUNTAIN LN	0	417C	NEH	77044
SAND MYRTLE DR	3700	578Y	SEH	77059
SANDOVER DR	13800	372E	NWC	77014
SANDOWN PARK DR	19200	329D	NWC	77379
SAND PASS LN	9800	409C	NWC	77064
SANDPEBBLE CT	2800	620E	SB	77586
SANDPEBBLE DR	1	250D	WD	77381
SANDPEBBLE DR	2600	620E	SB	77586
SANDPEBBLE CHASE	13600	488F	SWH	77077
SAND PINES	1200	485E	NEF	77494
SANDPIPER	2800	375L	HM	77396
SANDPIPER CIR	4900	501E	BT	77521
SANDPIPER CIR	7400	375L	HM	77396
N. SANDPIPER CT	1200	613M	NEB	77584
S. SANDPIPER CT	1300	613M	NEB	77584
SANDPIPER DR	700	568Q	SG	77478
SANDPIPER DR	1000	620H	SB	77586
SANDPIPER DR	2900	501E	BT	77521
SANDPIPER DR	3200	500H	BT	77521
SANDPIPER DR	7000	530M	SWH	77074
SANDPIPER DR	10300	530V	SWH	77096
SANDPIPER DR	11800	570H	SWH	77035
SANDPIPER LN	100	619Y	LC	77573
SANDPIPER LN	18900	286H	NWC	77377
SANDPIPER TRAILS	23000	333C	NCC	77373
SANDPIT	0	288U	NWC	77377
SAND PIT ACCESS	11000	524P	NWF	77406
SAND PLUM DR	2300	446T	NWC	77449
SAND PLUM LN	0	463S	CCO	77520
SANDPOINT	0	250M	WD	77381
SAND PRAIRIE DR	7700	408J	NWC	77095
SANDRA	1300	616T	PL	77581
SANDRA	6100	454Q	NEH	77028
SANDRA	7500	454C	NEH	77016
SANDRA LN	1400	375D	HM	77338
SANDRA ANN CT	9800	532T	SWH	77025
SANDRADALE	7600	454L	NEH	77016

Street Name	Block	Pg/Sq	Loc	Zips
SAND REEF CT	2900	660J	LC	77573
SAND REEF LN	3100	660J	LC	77573
SANDRI LN	12700	488U	SWH	77077
SANDRIA CT	0	328S	NWC	77429
SANDRIDGE CT	18900	459K	NEC	77049
SANDRINGHAM DR	800	656M	FR	77546
SANDRINGHAM DR	8800	491G	SWH	77024
SAND RIPPLE LN	3900	446E	NWC	77449
SAND ROCK CT	6300	526F	NEF	77450
SANDROCK DR	11400	574J	SEH	77048
SANDS DR	6300	578J	PA	77505
SAND SAGE LN	4700	617X	SEC	77546
SANDSAGE LN	23100	525B	NEF	77494
SAND SHADOW CT	3200	660A	LC	77573
SAND SHADOW DR	3100	660A	LC	77573
SANDS HILL	0	578J	PA	77505
SANDS KEY LN	0	660E	LC	77573
SANDS POINT DR	6400	531E	SWH	77074
SANDS POINT DR	6700	530H	SWH	77074
SANDS POINT DR	7700	530B	SWH	77036
SANDS POINT DR	11000	529B	SWH	77072
SANDSPOINT DR	22100	405Y	NWC	77449
SAND SPRINGS TRAIL	20900	378C	NEC	77532
SANDS TERRACE LN	7300	250T	NWC	77389
SANDSTINE CT	8400	407G	NWC	77095
SANDSTONE	0	613Y	NEB	77584
SANDSTONE	6600	530M	SWH	77074
SANDSTONE	8800	530J	SWH	77036
SANDSTONE	10700	529K	SWH	77072
SANDSTONE LN	6400	407V	NWC	77084
SANDSTONE BEND DR	0	573T	SEC	77047
SANDSTONE BEND LN	4000	609J	NEF	77479
SANDSTONE CANYON DR	0	376U	NEC	77396
SANDSTONE CAVERN	20301	526S	NEF	77407
SANDSTONE CAVERN CIR	20301	526S	NEF	77407
SANDSTONE CREEK DR	2600	615R	PL	77581
SANDSTONE FALLS		289D	NWC	77375
SANDSTONE RIDGE DR	2700	610U	MC	77459
SANDS TRAIL CT	10100	409C	NWC	77064
SANDSWEPT LN	6500	371S	NWC	77086
SAND TERRACE	4000	486S	NEF	77450
SANDTOWN CIR	9800	409G	NWC	77064
SANDTOWN LN	9100	409G	NWC	77064
SAND TRACKS CT	0	370U	NWC	77086
SAND TRAP CT	19000	337Z	NEC	77346
SANDTRAP DR	15500	322T	WCO	77484
SANDUSKY	0	614W	NEB	77584
SANDUSKY CT	25000	249Z	NWC	77375
SANDUSKY DR	0	249Z	NWC	77375
SANDUSKY DR	24500	249Z	NWC	77375
SANDVALLEY CT	0	658X	LC	77573
SANDVALLEY WAY	0	658X	LC	77573
SANDWEDGE DR	32000	322P	WCO	77484
SANDWEDGE POINT CT	6900	250U	NWC	77389
SANDWELL PLACE DR	0	250L	WD	77389
SANDWITH DR	20100	446X	NWC	77449
SANDWOOD CT	11200	616C	SEC	77089
SANDY	7800	455P	NEH	77028
SANDY CT	900	540Z	MP	77571
S. SANDY CT	3900	610K	MC	77459
N. SANDY CT	3900	610K	MC	77459
SANDY CT	12100	367M	CY	77429
SANDY DR	22100	255Y	SEM	77365
SANDY LN	1	459E	NEC	77562
SANDY LN	900	540Z	MP	77571
SANDY LN	1200	502S	BT	77520
SANDY LN	5800	537Z	PA	77505
SANDY LN	25200	295R	SEM	77365
SANDY ARBOR CT	4700	484Y	NEF	77494
SANDY ARBOR LN	26500	484Y	NEF	77494
SANDY BANK CT	0	615L	PL	77581
SANDY BANK DR	19500	329A	NWC	77375
SANDY BANK LN	0	615L	PL	77581
SANDY BAY CT	6500	406T	NWC	77449
SANDY BAY CT	6500	406T	NWC	77449
SANDY BAY LN	20600	406T	NWC	77449
SANDY BEACH CT	0	367S	NWC	77433
SANDY BEACH CT	0	367S	NWC	77433
SANDY BEND CT	13700	417C	NEC	77044
SANDY BLUFF	300	488A	SWH	77079
SANDY BOTTOM POND LN	0	377H	NEH	77346
SANDY BRANCH LN	12200	247R	SWM	77362
SANDY BRIAR CT	20900	290U	NWC	77379
SANDYBROOK LN	12500	368L	NWC	77429
SANDY CEDAR DR	5000	297Y	NEH	77345
SANDY CLIFFS DR	17300	331Q	NWC	77090
SANDY COAST CIR	2000	619Z	LC	77573
SANDY COVE	100	619T	NB	77058
SANDY CREEK	14500	329W	NWC	77070
SANDY CREEK DR	0	502H	BT	77520
SANDY CREEK DR	100	245A	SWM	77355
SANDYDALE LN	1500	413H	NCC	77039
SANDYDALE LN	2400	414G	NCC	77039
SANDY FALLS CT	0	417B	NEC	77044
SANDY FIELDS CIR	28300	293F	SEM	77386
SANDY FIELDS LN	2300	293F	SEM	77386
SANDYFIELDS LN	5000	485W	NEF	77494
SANDY FORKS DR	3400	297W	NEH	77339
SANDYGATE LN	7600	407M	NWC	77095
SANDY GLEN LN	8100	570F	SWH	77071
SANDY GROVE CT	2400	337D	NEH	77345
SANDY GROVE DR	5100	337D	NEH	77345
SANDYHILL CIR	19800	326Q	NWC	77429
SANDY HILL DR	15600	448F	NWC	77084
SANDY HOLLOW DR	6000	407W	NWC	77449
SANDY HOOK DR	12200	616D	SEH	77089
SANDY ISLE LN	7100	250T	NWC	77389
SANDY KNOLL DR	2000	570W	MC	77489
SANDY KNOLLS DR	6800	330L	NWC	77379
SANDY LAKE DR	1700	656R	FR	77546
SANDY LAKE DR	2700	336D	NEH	77339
SANDY LAKE DR	3000	296Z	NEH	77339
SANDY LODGE CT	2500	297U	NEH	77345
SANDY MEADOW LN	3500	414J	NCC	77039
SANDY MEADOW LN	5100	657Z	LC	77573
SANDY MIST CT	2600	485N	NEF	77494
SANDY OAKS DR	6100	415E	NEH	77050
SANDY PARK LN	1500	336B	NEH	77339
SANDY PATH LN	0	407V	NWC	77084
SANDYPINE CIR	16800	330H	NWC	77379
SANDYPINE CT	5900	330H	NWC	77379
SANDYPINE DR	6100	330H	NWC	77379
SANDYPINE LN	16800	330H	NWC	77379
SANDY PLAINS LN	1200	618E	SEH	77062
SANDY POINT LN	14100	371U	NWC	77066
SANDY PORT	500	488A	SWH	77079
SANDY REEF CT	16900	657B	SEC	77546
SANDY RIDGE DR	400	660E	LC	77573
SANDY RING CT	16000	327Y	NWC	77429
SANDY RIVER DR	10600	528W	NEF	77498
SANDY RUNN	700	332J	NWC	77090
SANDY SAGE CT	6200	525G	NEF	77494

Street Name	Block	Pg/Sq	Loc	Zips
SANDY SHOALS DR	1900	619Z	LC	77573
SANDY SHOALS DR	10700	530Y	SWH	77071
SANDY SHORE	19500	337V	NEC	77346
SANDY SHORE DR	100	620W	LC	77573
SANDY SPRINGS LN	14000	568B	SG	77498
SANDY SPRINGS RD	1400	489K	SWH	77042
SANDYSTONE LN	21600	445M	NWC	77449
SANDY STREAM CT	19500	329A	NWC	77375
SANDY STREAM DR	11700	329A	NWC	77375
SANDY TRACE CT	0	485W	NEF	77494
SANDY TRACE LN	0	485W	NEF	77494
SANDY TRAIL CT	1700	336B	NEH	77339
SANDY VALLEY CT	21000	406T	NWC	77449
SANDY VALLEY DR	5900	406T	NWC	77449
SANDY WALK	500	569U	NEF	77477
SANDY WOODS DR	19500	329A	NWC	77375
SAN EMIGDIO WAY	25000	338H	NEH	77336
SAN FELIPE	2100	492N	SWH	77019
SAN FELIPE	3700	492N	SWH	77027
SAN FELIPE	4700	491P	SWH	77056
SAN FELIPE	5700	491P	SWH	77057
SAN FELIPE	7500	490R	SWH	77063
SAN FELIPE	8300	490R	PP	77024
SAN FELIPE	17100	324J	HK	77447
SAN FERNANDO DR	200	412D	NEH	77060
SAN FERNANDO DR	300	373W	NEH	77060
SANFORD	1600	444T	KT	77493
SANFORD	8100	461P	NEC	77521
SANFORD RD	4300	571D	SWH	77035
SANFORD RD	5400	531W	SWH	77096
SANFORD RD	6100	530W	SWH	77031
SANFORD RD	7500	530Y	SWH	77071
SAN GABRIEL DR	19400	446U	NWC	77084
W. SAN GABRIEL RIVER CIR	0	406D	NWC	77433
S. SAN GABRIEL RIVER CIR	0	406D	NWC	77433
N. SAN GABRIEL RIVER CIR	0	406D	NWC	77433
SANGAMON LN	8900	530S	SWH	77074
SANGERBROOK DR	10300	412A	NWC	77038
SANGERBROOK DR	10400	372W	NWC	77038
SAN GREGORIO LN	0	445A	NWC	77493
SAN GUILLERMO	6000	535Z	SEH	77017
SANGUINE SOUND LN	12000	616G	SEC	77089
SANIBEL FALLS CT	10400	367X	NWC	77095
SAN IGNACIO	10000	576N	SEH	77075
SAN JACINTO	1	493Q	DT	77002
E. SAN JACINTO	100	459R	HG	77562
SAN JACINTO	100	459Q	HG	77562
SAN JACINTO	100	540Y	LP	77571
SAN JACINTO	300	580C	LP	77571
N. SAN JACINTO	600	493M	NEH	77002
SAN JACINTO	900	493Q	DT	77010
SAN JACINTO	1000	493Q	DT	77002
SAN JACINTO	1001	493Q	DT	77010
SAN JACINTO	1100	493Q	DT	77002
SAN JACINTO	1100	500Z	BT	77520
S. SAN JACINTO	1600	536Q	PA	77502
SAN JACINTO	2600	493Q	SEH	77004
SAN JACINTO	5500	533A	SWH	77004
SAN JACINTO	10600	539Q	LP	77571
SAN JACINTO	11900	418R	NEC	77044
E. SAN JACINTO DR	28000	258T	NEC	77357
W. SAN JACINTO BAY CT	0	338H	NEH	77336
SAN JACINTO BAY LOOP	0	338H	NEH	77336
SAN JACINTO MONUMENT	0	499T	SEC	77571
SAN JACINTO RIVER CT	29000	253U	SEM	77386
SAN JACINTO RIVER DR	4600	253U	SEM	77386
SAN JOAQUIN PKWY	1800	656U	FR	77546
SAN JOSE	1700	656U	FR	77546
SAN JOSE	5400	494G	NEH	77020
SAN JUAN	5100	494G	NEH	77020
SAN JUANICO ST	0	378A	NEC	77346
SAN LORENZO	8900	535V	SEH	77017
SAN LORENZO CRUZ	16300	527X	NEF	77469
SAN LUCAS DR	7200	527F	NEF	77083
SAN LUCIA RIVER DR	12100	415E	NEH	77050
SAN LUIS REY DR	14700	528J	SWC	77083
SAN MARCOS	600	535A	SEH	77012
SAN MARCOS DR	0	538R	DP	77536
SAN MARINO	800	568P	SG	77478
SAN MARINO DR	1400	616K	PL	77581
SAN MARINO DR	12500	486S	NEF	77450
SAN MARINO COVE DR	0	525J	NEF	77469
SAN MARINO COVE DR	0	525J	NEF	77469
SAN MARTIN LN	13500	528K	SWC	77083
SAN MARZANO CT	0	445J	NWC	77493
SAN MATEO CT	1500	659S	LC	77573
SAN MATEO DR	16300	611B	SWH	77053
SAN MATEO SHORES DR	0	419A	NEC	77532
SAN MIGUEL	200	413A	NEH	77060
SAN MIGUEL	1900	656U	FR	77546
SAN MILO DR	15500	331S	NWC	77068
SAN MORINO DR	7400	527L	NEF	77083
SAN NICHOLAS PLACE	0	525A	NEF	77494
SAN NICOLO LN	2700	659M	LC	77573
SANOUR DR	0	408P	NWC	77084
SAN PABLO DR	6400	527F	NEF	77083
SAN PABLO GARDENS DR	0	571G	SWH	77045
SAN PATRICO CT	8900	409G	NWC	77064
SAN PEDRO	3600	455Z	NEH	77013
SAN PELLINO DR	24500	524R	NEF	77406
SAN PIETRO DR	0	329Y	NWC	77070
SAN RAFAEL LN	13500	528K	SWC	77083
SAN RAMON DR	7200	528E	SWC	77083
SAN RAMON DR	7300	527M	SWC	77083
SAN REMO DR	6000	527H	SWC	77083
SAN REMO LN	1300	659M	LC	77573
SAN RIO DR	16100	527L	NEF	77083
SAN ROCCO ST	0	530X	SWH	77031
SAN SABA	700	535B	SEH	77012
SAN SABA	2500	492U	SWH	77019
SAN SABA CT	9200	579A	LP	77571
SAN SABA CANYON CIR	15900	328S	NWC	77429
SAN SABA CANYON LN	13700	328S	NWC	77479
E. SAN SABA RIVER LN		367W	NWC	77095
SAN SEBASTIAN CT	0	660L	LC	77539
SAN SEBASTIAN CT	2000	619S	NB	77058
SAN SERVERO DR	0	445F	NWC	77493
SANSFORD CIR	3300	446L	NWC	77449
SAN SIMEON DR	7300	527L	NEF	77083
SAN SOLOMON SPRINGS CT	0	367W	NWC	77433
SANSPEREIL DR	11900	573N	SWC	77047
SANS SOUCI DR	0	327W	NWC	77429
SANTA ANITA LN	4300	538N	PA	77503
SANTA ANNA LN	800	539Q	LP	77571
SANTA BERNADETTA	5900	535Z	SEH	77017
SANTA CATALINA CT	3400	485Z	NEF	77450
SANTA CECILIA LN	6000	535V	SEH	77017
SANTA CHRISTI DR	5500	611B	SWH	77053
SANTA CLARA DR	3400	486S	NEF	77450
SANTA CLARA DR	12500	486S	NEF	77450
SANTA CRUZ	9600	455Z	NEH	77013
SANTA CRUZ LN	0	658U	LC	77573

Street Name	Block	Pg/Sq	Loc	Zips
SANTA ELENA	7800	535T	SEH	77061
SANTA ELENA CANYON CT		332E	NWC	77388
SANTA FE	5900	660X	DI	77539
SANTA FE DR	6600	574C	SEH	77061
SANTA FE DR	7200	534Z	SEH	77061
S. SANTA FE DR	7400	574G	SEH	77061
SANTA FE DR	7400	535W	SEH	77061
SANTA FE DR	26600	247Y	SWM	77355
SANTA FE SPRINGS CT	5700	449A	NWC	77041
SANTA FE SPRINGS DR	5700	449A	NWC	77041
SANTA FE SPRINGS DR	12000	409W	NWC	77041
SANTA FE TRAIL	0	539N	DP	77536
SANTA FE TRAIL	0	539N	DP	77536
SANTA INEZ CT	3400	486S	NEF	77450
SANTA ISABEL CT	3400	486S	NEF	77450
SANTA LUCIA CT	7700	527M	SWC	77083
SANTA LUCIA DR	14800	527M	SWC	77083
SANTA LUZ PATH	0	660L	LC	77573
SANTA MARIA	7000	534D	SEH	77023
SANTA MARIA DR	500	568P	SG	77478
SANTA MONICA	0	576N	SEH	77075
SANTA MONICA BLVD	9700	576W	SEH	77089
SANTANA LN	3200	297E	SEM	77365
SANTANDER DR	1000	298Z	NEH	77336
SANTA RITA DR	6500	527K	NEF	77083
SANTA ROSA	1800	534D	SEH	77023
SANTA ROSA LN	3500	569W	SG	77478
SANTA SIENNA DR	0	445B	NWC	77493
SANTA TERESA RD	13200	571L	SWH	77045
SANTEE	4300	451H	NWH	77018
SANTEE DR	4300	501J	BT	77521
SANTEE PASS DR	14400	328P	NWC	77429
SANTIAGO	4600	577B	PA	77504
SANTIAGO	7000	534D	SEH	77023
SANTIAGO LN	0	660L	LC	77539
SANTIAGO COVE LN	12400	409W	NWC	77041
SANTIAGO MOUNTAIN CT	6200	526A	NEF	77450
SANTO DOMINGO	8800	535Z	SEH	77017
SANTO DOMINICO DR	2600	659S	LC	77573
SANTOLINA LN	18000	407N	NWC	77449
SANTONE LN	9900	453B	NEH	77076
SANTOS	17700	327J	NWC	77429
SANTREY DR	5100	407Z	NWC	77084
SANTUARY COVE	2800	485V	NEF	77450
SAN VALENTINO DR	0	445A	NWC	77493
SAN VICENTE LN	3400	486S	NEF	77450
SAO PAULO	4300	577B	PA	77504
SAPHIRE BAY DR	0	612M	PL	77584
SAPLING CREST CT	1000	611X	NEF	77545
SAPLING OAK CT	15000	487Z	SWC	77082
SAPLING OAK DR	3200	487Z	SWC	77082
SAPLING TRAIL	20300	291Y	NWC	77388
SAPLING TRAIL CT	3700	291Y	NWC	77388
SAPLING WAY	10500	530X	SWH	77031
SAPPHIRE CIR	28000	245L	SWM	77355
SAPPHIRE CT	21500	446J	NWC	77449
SAPPHIRE CT	28000	245L	SWM	77355
SAPPHIRE BAY CT	1300	486G	SWC	77094
SAPPHIRE HILL LN	0	524G	NEF	77494
SAPPHIRE LAKE RD	20600	526S	NEF	77407
SAPPHIRE MIST CT	0	372D	NCC	77073
SAPPHIRE SPRINGS LN	0	524G	NEF	77494
SAPPHIRE STAR DR	0	487Y	SWC	77082
SAPPHIRE VALLEY RD	7800	408K	NWC	77095
SAPPHIRE VISTA LN	5700	409W	NWH	77041
SAPPINGTON LN	3100	331U	NWC	77014
SAPULPA LN	0	407J	NWC	77433
SARA LN	0	659W	LC	77573
SARA'S WALK	14200	368N	NWC	77429
SARA BETH WAY	0	616L	SEC	77089
SARACEN DR	12500	368L	NWC	77429
SARADON DR	2200	568C	SG	77478
SARAGOSA BLUE LN	7900	526L	NEF	77407
SARAGOSA CROSSING LN	6300	370L	NWC	77066
SARAGOSA POND LN	0	290P	NWC	77379
SARAH	3400	494B	NEH	77026
SARAH AVE	2100	532V	SWH	77054
SARAH LN	0	248S	SWM	77354
SARAH LN	0	656K	FR	77546
SARAH LN	4500	463Z	CCO	77520
SARAH LN	8000	462X	NEC	77521
SARAH ANN CT	19200	337T	NEC	77346
SARAH BEND DR		325S	NWC	77447
SARAH BLUFF LN		366T	NWC	77433
SARAH DEANN LN	0	255V	SEM	77357
SARAH DEEL	0	618U	WB	77598
SARAH LAKE DR	0	529S	SWM	77099
SARAH RIDGE DR	0	325S	HK	77447
SARAHS LN	12800	496M	NEH	77015
SARAHS LANDING DR	0	612E	PL	77545
SARAH SPRINGS CT	25800	292U	NCC	77373
SARA JO LN	11900	411F	NWC	77086
SARANAC DR	12700	617E	SEH	77089
SARA RIDGE LN	2400	486P	SWC	77450
SARA ROSE	800	452Q	NWH	77018
SARASAM CREEK CT	0	327R	NWC	77429
SARASOTA DR	0	656U	FR	77546
SARATOGA DR	0	658R	LC	77573
SARATOGA DR	3400	411U	NWH	77088
SARATOGA FOREST DR	8400	411K	NWC	77088
SARATOGA HEIGHTS LN	0	484S	NEF	77494
SARATOGA SPRINGS LN	5900	409W	NWC	77041
SARATOGA WOODS LN	0	377E	NEC	77346
SARDANDO DR	0	406G	NWC	77433
SARDINA SHORE DR	0	407E	NWC	77433
SARDINIA DR	0	525J	NEF	77469
SARDINIA DR	0	525J	NEF	77469
SARDINIA DR	11200	525N	NEF	77469
SARDIS LN	3400	411V	NWH	77088
SARDIS LAKE DR	11600	289W	NWC	77375
SARENTO VILLAGE	13400	528Y	NEF	77478
SARGENT TAYLOR MEMORIAL	0	294P	SEM	77386
SARITA	7800	535K	SEH	77012
SARONG DR	4100	532S	SWH	77025
SARONG DR	4300	531V	SWH	77096
SARONNO DR	0	525N	NEF	77469
SARONNO DR	0	525N	NEF	77469
SARSAPARILLA ST	0	461T	NEC	77521
SARTI	12100	371A	NWC	77066
SASHAY DR	10600	529W	SWH	77099
SASHER LN	14300	327X	CY	77429
SASQUATCH DR	19500	328C	NWC	77377
SASSAFRAS LN	22800	296C	SEM	77365
SASSON BLVD	0	457A	NEC	77044
SATCHEL CT	11700	411H	NWC	77038
SATINBIRD CIR	0	328A	NWC	77429
SATIN CLOVER CT	21600	245V	SWM	77355
SATINLEAF PLACE	0	249M	NWH	77375
SATINLEAF PLACE	0	249M	NWH	77375
SATIN TAIL LN	11200	367V	NWC	77095
SATINWOOD	0	332J	NWC	77090
SATINWOOD HILLS LN	19800	366Z	NWC	77433

Street Name	Block	Pg/Sq	Loc	Zips
SATINWOOD TRAIL	19700	337Q	NEC	77346
SATIVA CIR	7800	461T	NEC	77521
SATSUMA	0	408P	NWC	77084
SATSUMA	900	537K	PA	77506
SATSUMA	900	659E	LC	77573
SATSUMA	6300	574R	SEH	77048
SATSUMA	7000	534D	SEH	77023
SATSUMA	7400	535A	SEH	77023
SATSUMA DR	6600	408R	NWC	77041
SATSUMA POINT CT	0	457L	NEC	77049
SATSUMA STATION-HL&P	0	408C	NWC	77041
SATSUMA VALE ST	7300	406R	NWC	77433
SATTERFIELD LN	5500	407Z	NWC	77084
SATTLER PARK DR	6000	411B	NWC	77086
SATURINIA LN	0	659Q	LC	77573
SATURN LN	16600	618Q	SEH	77062
SATURN LN	16800	618Q	SEH	77058
SAUER	1900	493Y	SEH	77004
SAUER	4700	533C	SEH	77004
SAUKI LN	0	527W	NEF	77469
SAULNIER	100	493P	SWH	77019
W. SAULNIER	300	493N	SWH	77019
SAULSWORTH AVE	11500	529X	SWH	77099
SAUMS RD	18000	447S	NWC	77084
SAUMS RD	19900	446T	NWC	77449
W. SAUNDERS	100	658M	LC	77573
E. SAUNDERS	100	659J	LC	77573
SAUNDERS	1000	282U	WL	77484
SAUNDERS RD	3800	414X	NEH	77093
SAUNDERS RD	7200	415W	NEH	77016
SAUNTER DR	200	569Q	SF	77477
SAUNTON DR	21400	486S	NEF	77450
SAURIS CT	1000	412A	NWC	77038
SAUSALITO CIR	0	295R	SEM	77365
SAUSALITO CT	0	295R	SEM	77365
SAUSALITO LN	0	295R	SEM	77365
SAUVE LN	5500	491F	SWH	77056
SAVANA	28500	288E	NWC	77377
S. SAVANNA CT	1900	658Q	LC	77573
N. SAVANNA CT	1900	658Q	LC	77573
SAVANNAH AVE	900	536L	PA	77506
SAVANNAH DR	28700	252A	SD	77381
SAVANNAH LN	3100	610U	MC	77459
SAVANNAH BAY RD	20300	326N	NWC	77433
SAVANNAH BEND	0	538R	DP	77536
SAVANNAH CREEK LN	19400	406V	NWC	77449
SAVANNAH HOLLY DR	0	575R	SEH	77075
SAVANNAH PARK DR	0	327U	NWC	77429
SAVANNAH PINE DR	6300	406V	NWC	77449
SAVANNAH SPRINGS WAY	400	292T	NCC	77373
SAVANNAH TRAILS	9100	408A	NWC	77095
SAVELL DR	3200	502K	BT	77521
SAVELL RD	21800	335H	NEH	77339
W. SAVILE CIR	9500	409E	NWC	77065
E. SAVILE CIR	9500	409E	NWC	77065
SAVILLE CT	9500	528S	NEF	77083
SAVILLE LN	9500	409A	NWC	77065
SAVORY LN	0	419C	NEC	77532
SAVORY SPRINGS LN	0	524F	NEF	77494
SAVOY	100	568P	SG	77478
SAVOY DR	5600	530D	SWH	77036
SAWDUST CT	0	252W	SWM	77380
SAWDUST RD	0	251Y	WD	77380
SAWDUST RD	100	252W	SWM	77380
SAWDUST RD	700	251T	SWM	77380
SAWFLY LN	0	297A	SEM	77357
SAWGRASS CIR	4500	501J	BT	77521
SAWGRASS CT	2400	619Y	LC	77573
SAWGRASS DR	4400	501J	BT	77521
SAWGRASS LN	0	409F	JV	77064
SAWGRASS MEADOW LN	0	524H	NEF	77494
SAWGRASS RIDGE LN	900	332Z	NCC	77073
SAWGRASS TERRACE LN	7400	250X	NWC	77389
SAWHILL BRIDGE LN	11100	568A	NEF	77498
SAWHILL BRIDGE LN	14800	568A	NEF	77498
SAWLAND DR	0	524H	NEF	77494
SAWLAND DR	0	524H	NEF	77494
SAWLEAF CIR	23200	485L	SWC	77494
SAWMILL DR	0	366Z	NWC	77433
SAWMILL DR	18900	246E	SWM	77355
SAWMILL LN	4600	578K	PA	77505
SAW MILL RD	0	340L	LCO	77535
SAWMILL RD	11900	251V	WD	77380
SAWMILL CREEK	0	366V	NWC	77433
SAWMILL CROSSING	0	292G	NCC	77373
SAWMILL GROVE CT	1	251U	WD	77380
SAWMILL GROVE LN	1	251U	WD	77380
SAWMILL PASS	23800	293U	NCC	77373
SAWMILL RUN LN	0	377Z	NEC	77044
SAWMILL STREAM CIR	11700	371L	NWC	77067
SAWMILL TERRACE DR	5000	291J	NWC	77389
SAWMILL TIMBER DR	4800	291J	NWC	77389
SAWMILL TRAIL	7100	411J	NWH	77040
SAWMILL TRAIL	7400	410M	NWC	77040
SAWSTON DR	0	289Q	NWC	77375
SAWTOOTH DR	0	657T	LC	77573
S. SAWTOOTH CANYON DR	12000	328G	NWC	77377
N. SAWTOOTH CANYON DR	12000	328G	NWC	77377
W. SAWTOOTH CANYON DR	19100	328G	NWC	77377
E. SAWTOOTH CANYON DR	19100	328G	NWC	77377
SAWTOOTH OAK DR	14900	487Z	SWC	77082
SAWYER	600	493F	SWH	77007
SAWYER	2500	620J	SB	77586
SAWYER DR	5900	614L	PL	77581
SAWYER BEND LN	0	253P	SEM	77386
SAWYER BEND LN	0	609U	NEF	77479
SAWYER BEND LN	5800	290V	NWC	77379
SAWYER CROSSING LN	0	615G	PL	77581
SAWYERDALE	1800	493F	SWH	77007
W. SAWYER RIDGE DR	0	250N	NWC	77389
E. SAWYER RIDGE DR	0	250N	NWC	77389
SAWYERS CROSSING LN	10300	527Z	NEF	77498
SAWYERS HILL LN	0	411W	NWH	77040
SAXET	6300	451Y	NWH	77055
SAXON	4700	531C	BL	77401
SAXON CT	23000	285B	SWM	77447
SAXON DR	1600	452J	NWH	77018
SAXON DR	4900	451M	NWH	77092
SAXON DR	17400	407K	NWC	77095
SAXON CREEK DR	0	376C	NEC	77369
SAXON GLEN CT	25500	524G	NEF	77494
SAXON GLEN LN	9800	524G	NEF	77494
SAXON HILL LN	0	526K	NEF	77407
SAXON HOLLOW CT	0	407Z	NWC	77084
SAXON HOLLOW CT	3800	617X	SEC	77546
SAXON MEADOW LN	0	366L	NWC	77433
SAXON PLACE CT	0	366Q	NWC	77433
SAXON WAY	23000	285B	SWM	77447
SAXONY DR	0	568B	SG	77498
SAXONY LN	1200	618V	NB	77058
SAXONY LN	1600	619S	NB	77058
SAXTON CT	2900	615P	PL	77581
SAXTON GREEN RD	0	615S	PL	77584
SAXTON MANOR ST	0	451Y	NWH	77055
SAYAN GLEN LN	13000	369G	NWC	77070
SAYBROOK	16400	374M	NEH	77396
SAYBROOK LN	800	490C	HE	77024
SAYBROOK POINT LN	12100	329A	NWC	77375
SAYERS	3300	454T	NEH	77026
SAYERS	6700	454K	NEH	77016
SAYLYNN LN	7700	575P	SEH	77075
SAYRE LN	1700	412F	NWC	77038
SCALES	16200	458Y	CV	77530
SCAMP DR	13300	368L	NWC	77429
SCAMPER LN	16600	381W	NEC	77532
SCANDICCI LN	0	659R	LC	77573
SCANLIN	2900	569Q	SF	77477
SCANLIN RD	1700	570S	MC	77489
SCANLOCK	7700	535F	SEH	77012
SCARAB DR	13300	408U	NWC	77041
SCARBOROUGH LN	0	657Y	LC	77573
SCARBOROUGH LN	400	536K	PA	77506
SCARBOROUGH LN	1300	536K	PA	77502
SCARBOROUGH FAIR	14100	488J	SWH	77077
SCARCELLA LN	12300	568D	MD	77477
SCARLATTI CANTATA DR	0	444M	NWC	77493
SCARLET CIR	0	460W	BT	77521
SCARLET DR	6000	574F	SEH	77048
SCARLET BAY CT	0	525D	NEF	77450
SCARLET BEGONIAS	9600	535D	SEH	77012
SCARLET COVE DR	19300	289W	NWC	77375
SCARLET FOREST DR	17700	328L	NWC	77377
SCARLET GLEN CT	0	488P	SWH	77077
SCARLET OAK CT	2800	657H	FR	77546
SCARLET OAK DR	0	615Z	PL	77581
SCARLET OAK DR	2900	657H	FR	77546
SCARLET OAK LN	14700	288A	NWC	77377
SCARLET PLUME CT	0	291R	NWC	77388
SCARLET RIVER DR	0	416L	NEC	77044
SCARLET SAGE DR	0	659G	LC	77573
SCARLET SUNSET CT	2700	609A	SG	77478
SCARLETT	300	500P	BT	77520
SCARLET TANAGER DR	7900	375Q	NEC	77396
SCARLETT FALLS LN	0	527J	NEF	77407
SCARLETT MANOR CT	25100	249S	NWC	77375
SCARLETT TRAIL CT	0	484Q	NEF	77494
SCARLETT SADDLE CT		366Y	NWC	77433
SCARLETT SAGE CT	0	484U	NEF	77494
SCARLETT SAGE LN	0	484U	NEF	77494
SCARLETT TRACE LN	0	613L	PL	77584
SCARLETT VIEW LN	0	611T	FS	77545
SCARLET WAY	0	615W	PL	77584
SCARLET WOODS CT	1	251V	WD	77380
SCARPINATO PLACE	10400	569L	SF	77477
SCARSDALE BLVD	2100	616K	PL	77581
SCARSDALE BLVD	9800	616G	SEC	77089
SCARSDALE BLVD	12900	576Z	SEH	77089
SCARSDALE BLVD	13100	577W	SEH	77034
SCATTERWOOD CT	1	251E	WD	77381
SCAUP DR	0	410V	NWH	77040
SCENIC	0	660Y	DI	77539
SCENIC DR	500	501Q	BT	77521
SCENIC DR	4700	573H	SEH	77048
SCENIC BLUFF LN	21200	334M	NCC	77338
SCENIC BROOK DR	19800	406L	NWC	77433
SCENIC CANYON LN	7900	407K	NWC	77095
SCENIC COVE	0	376T	NWC	77396
SCENIC COVE CT	0	376T	NWC	77396
SCENIC ELM	3000	578X	SEH	77059
SCENIC FALLS LN	0	484S	NEF	77494
SCENIC GARDENS DR	16700	329R	NWC	77379
SCENIC GLADE DR	13200	578W	SEH	77059
SCENIC GLEN DR	0	610Y	MC	77459
SCENIC GREEN DR	8400	411R	NWH	77088
SCENIC HAVEN DR	15400	527Q	NEF	77083
SCENIC HILLS DR	0	657P	FR	77546
SCENIC HOLLOW CT	2100	486P	SWC	77450
SCENIC HOLLOW DR	0	486P	SWC	77450
SCENIC LAKE CT	17300	327T	NWC	77429
SCENIC LAKES WAY	16900	407L	NWC	77095
SCENIC MEADOW CT	0	614G	PL	77581
SCENIC MOUNTAIN CT	1600	338B	NEH	77345
SCENIC OAKS DR	17700	527E	NEF	77407
SCENIC OAKS DR	17800	526H	NEF	77407
SCENIC PARK DR	1900	252R	SEM	77386
SCENIC PATH CT	14200	367B	NWC	77429
SCENIC PEAKS CT	16500	578Z	PA	77059
SCENIC POINT CT	15500	326T	NWC	77433
SCENIC RIDGE	23300	296M	SEM	77365
SCENIC RIDGE DR	1400	449X	NWH	77043
SCENIC RIVER DR	11500	456F	NEC	77044
SCENIC RIVER RD	0	609N	NEF	77479
SCENIC SHORE	0	620E	SB	77586
SCENIC SHORE CT	8200	568P	SG	77478
SCENIC SHORE DR	1500	338E	NEH	77345
SCENIC SHORE DR	2200	620F	SB	77586
SCENICSIDE LN	7900	330E	NWC	77379
SCENIC SKY WAY	0	457G	NEC	77049
SCENIC TRAIL	900	288B	TB	77375
SCENIC VALLEY DR	3500	297T	NEH	77345
SCENIC VALLEY LN	4100	609T	NEF	77479
SCENIC VIEW	300	616V	FR	77546
SCENIC VIEW CT	3100	620E	SB	77586
SCENIC VIEW DR	15700	618G	SEH	77062
SCENIC VISTA	0	376T	NWC	77396
SCENIC WATER DR	15800	377P	NEC	77044
SCENIC WAY DR	1900	252R	SEM	77385
SCENIC WOODS DR	20300	326T	NWC	77433
SCENIC WOODS TRAIL	4800	297Q	NEH	77345
SCENTED CANDLE WAY	18700	331D	NWC	77388
SCENTED PATH LN	1	250C	WD	77381
SCENT FERN	8900	369V	NWC	77064
SCEPTRE CIR	7800	528R	SWH	77072
SCHADE LN	100	413S	NEH	77037
SCHAFFER LN	8100	369H	NWC	77070
SCHAFF PLACE	8400	535L	SEH	77017
SCHALKER DR	3600	454W	NEH	77026
SCHAMBRAY	6600	571S	SWH	77085
SCHARPE	1200	494X	SEH	77023
SCHARPE	1500	534B	SEH	77023
SCHASPRY	0	330Z	NWC	77069
SCHAUER LN	0	286V	NWC	77377
SCHAUER-JONES RD	0	288J	NWC	77377
SCHAUMBURG DR	6000	290R	NWC	77388
SCHEFFLER DR	10700	449Q	NWH	77043
SCHEPPS	0	489Y	SWH	77042
SCHERER LN	22000	288E	NWC	77377
SCHERER WOODS CT	0	328M	NWC	77377
SCHERZO LN	7900	410K	NWC	77040
SCHEVERS	5600	574A	SEH	77033
SCHEVERS	6200	574C	SEH	77087
SCHIEL RD	0	326Q	NWC	77429
SCHIEL RD	20000	326P	NWC	77433
SCHIEL RD	21400	325M	NWC	77429
SCHIEL NURSERY RD	0	248Z	NWC	77375
SCHILDER DR	1500	453D	NEH	77093
SCHILDER DR	2300	454A	NEH	77093
SCHILLER	6300	451Y	NWH	77055
SCHILLER RD	13800	528A	SWC	77082
SCHILLER PARK LN	0	371D	NWC	77014
SCHILLING	1	493H	NEH	77002
SCHILLING	1	501T	BT	77520
SCHINDEWOLF LN	0	291X	NWC	77388
SCHIVENER HOUSE	23900	445S	NWC	77493
SCHLEIDER DR	2300	615K	PL	77584
SCHLETTY	6400	375J	NCC	77396
SCHLEY	6900	535E	SEH	77087
SCHLOSSER	8600	490Y	SWH	77063
SCHLUMBERGER	2200	534B	SEH	77023
SCHLUMBERGER DR	100	568L	SG	77478
SCHMIDT	13800	368P	NWC	77429
SCHNAUBERT DR	0	366P	NWC	77433
SCHNEIDER	6900	453M	NEH	77093
SCHNEIDER CIR	23600	245X	SWM	77447
SCHNEIDER RD	26000	242C	WCO	77484
SCHOCHLER	0	578C	LP	77571
SCHOLARSHIP ROW	0	488N	SWH	77077
SCHOLL	0	577T	SEH	77034
SCHOLL RD	0	286L	NWC	77377
W. SCHOOL	0	463A	MB	77580
E. SCHOOL	0	463A	MB	77580
SCHOOL	100	288G	TB	77375
SCHOOL	800	659J	LC	77573
SCHOOL	6000	532G	SWH	77030
SCHOOL RD	0	288L	TB	77375
SCHOOL RD	100	570N	MC	77489
SCHOOLEY DR	8600	570B	SWH	77071
SCHOONER	900	419B	NEC	77532
SCHOONER COVE	0	609Y	NEF	77459
SCHOONER COVE LN	800	660E	LC	77573
SCHOONER COVE LN	800	660E	LC	77573
SCHOONERS WAY	16700	617X	SEC	77546
SCHOONER WAY	0	619Z	LC	77573
SCHOPPA LN	5200	500G	NEC	77521
SCHRAMSBERG TRAIL	0	484J	NEF	77494
E. SCHRECK	100	500K	BT	77520
SCHRECK	100	500N	BT	77520
SCHROEDER LN	0	327A	NWC	77429
SCHROEDER RD	4400	494P	SEH	77011
SCHROEDER RD	5800	534J	SEH	77021
SCHROEDER RD	12900	369D	NWC	77070
SCHROEDER RD	14700	329Z	NWC	77070
SCHROEDER OAK CT	0	369K	NWC	77070
SCHULER	4100	492F	SWH	77007
SCHULLER RD	6700	454E	NEH	77093
SCHULLER PLACE CT	0	454N	NEH	77026
SCHULTE LN	0	656Y	FR	77546
SCHULZ LN	0	448F	NWH	77084
SCHUMACHER RD	5300	491X	SWH	77056
SCHUMACHER RD	5600	491X	SWH	77057
SCHUMACHER RD	8600	490Y	SWH	77063
SCHUMANN CT	8200	527Q	NEF	77083
SCHUMANN LN	15300	527Q	NEF	77083
SCHUMANN OAKS DR	3400	253T	SEM	77386
SCHURMIER RD	600	572U	SWH	77047
SCHURMIER RD	3500	573V	SEC	77047
SCHURMIER RD	4000	574S	SEH	77048
SCHURY LN	0	535V	SEH	77017
SCHUTZ	5600	374R	NEH	77032
SCHWARTZ	400	494E	NEH	77020
SCHWARTZ LN	0	288R	TB	77375
SCHWEIKHARDT	400	494B	NEH	77020
SCHWEIKHARDT	2800	494B	NEH	77026
SCHWEINLE CT	0	494E	NEH	77020
SCHWEINLE RD	1	456P	NEC	77049
SCIAACA RD	2000	292V	NCC	77373
SCIAACA RD	2200	293S	NCC	77373
SCOBEY LN	0	452Y	NWH	77008
SCOFIELD LN	10200	531Y	SWH	77096
SCONE	4100	447H	NWC	77084
SCOREGGA LN	13700	413K	NCC	77037
SCORESBY MANOR DR	0	330A	SP	77379
SCOTCH GROVE CT	0	371G	NWC	77014
SCOTCH HOLLOW LN	16300	527Q	NEF	77083
SCOTCH MOSS LN	3100	578C	LP	77571
SCOTCH PINE DR	6200	457N	NEC	77049
SCOTCH PINE PLACE	800	289R	NWC	77375
SCOTCHWOOD DR	6100	406Z	NWC	77449
SCOTLAND	4100	492M	SWH	77007
SCOTNEY CASTLE	14300	408Q	NWC	77095
SCOTSBROOK DR	10100	412B	NWC	77038
SCOTSMAN DR	0	445E	NWC	77493
SCOTT	400	536M	PA	77506
SCOTT	1300	494S	SEH	77003
SCOTT	2200	493Z	SEH	77004
SCOTT	3500	533D	SEH	77004
SCOTT	5400	533Q	SEH	77021
SCOTT	7700	533Y	SEH	77051
SCOTT	9100	573G	SEH	77051
SCOTT	11800	573U	SEH	77047
SCOTT	11600	249W	NWC	77375
W. SCOTT AVE	100	501U	BT	77520
SCOTT CIR	14600	368S	NWC	77429
SCOTT DR	0	538T	DP	77536
SCOTT LN	0	282N	WCO	77484
SCOTT RD	0	299Z	NEC	77336
SCOTT RD	0	339D	NEC	77336
SCOTT RD	0	614H	PL	77581
SCOTT RD	0	615E	PL	77581
SCOTTCREST DR	5800	533M	SEH	77021
SCOTTER DR	14800	457Z	NEC	77015
SCOTTER DR	14900	457Z	NEC	77530
SCOTT GARDNER RD	19800	257L	SEM	77357
SCOTTIE BOY LN	0	525W	NEF	77406
SCOTTISH WOODS LN	0	297P	NEH	77365
SCOTTLAND TERRACE DR	0	376R	NEC	77346
SCOTTLINE DR	5100	578J	PA	77505
SCOTT RANCH RD	0	444T	KT	77493
SCOTTS BLUFF CT	0	377E	NEC	77346
SCOTTSBURY CT	24500	485S	NEF	77494
SCOTTSDALE	0	568D	SG	77478
SCOTTSDALE CT	2300	619Y	LC	77573
SCOTTSDALE CT	11800	569B	MD	77477
SCOTTSDALE DR	11300	569A	MD	77477
SCOTTSDALE PALMS DR	2700	610U	MC	77459
SCOTTS PINE LN	0	457P	NEC	77049
SCOTTS POINT DR	19000	329A	NWC	77375
SCOTTWOOD DR	5100	501E	BT	77521
SCOUTS LN	12600	368L	NWC	77429
SCRANTON	8400	575G	SEH	77061
SCRANTON	8500	575G	SEH	77075
SCREECH OWL CT	24500	485J	NEF	77494
SCRIBE CT	18000	258A	SEM	77357
SCRIBEWOOD CIR	0	249B	SWM	77382
SCRIBNER RD	6300	531E	SWH	77074
SCRIVENER LN	23900	445N	NWC	77493
SCROGGINS RD	0	242D	WCO	77484
SCRUB JAY LN	14700	288A	NWC	77377
SCRUB OAK CT	17700	527E	NEF	77407
SCRUB OAK DR	17800	526H	NEF	77407
SCULL DR	800	419F	NEC	77532
SCULLERS COVE CT	1	251F	WD	77381
SCULLING WAY DR	0	338W	NEC	77346
SCULPTURED ROCK LN	0	377K	NEC	77346
SCUTTLE WAY	17000	379X	NEC	77532
SCYRUS LN	11700	370H	NWC	77066
S D, A I	19300	335T	NEH	77338
SEA ANCHOR WAY	500	379X	NEC	77532
SEABERG RD	12900	421S	NEC	77532
SEABIRD	0	461T	NEC	77521
SEABIRD DR	4400	620G	SB	77586
SEA BISCUIT LN	12400	570G	SWH	77071
SEABISCUIT BAY LN	0	334R	NCC	77338
SEABLOSSOM LN	20100	446T	NWC	77449
SEABLUFF CT	0	366V	NWC	77433
SEABOARD LOOP	10800	529X	SWH	77099
SEABOLD DR	0	610V	MC	77459
SEABOROUGH LN	400	619Z	LC	77573
SEA BRANCH DR	0	447K	NWC	77084
SEABREEZE	100	660F	LC	77573
SEA BREEZE	900	580D	LP	77571
SEABREEZE CT	300	660K	LC	77573
SEA BREEZE CT	1800	569X	MC	77459
SEA BREEZE DR	0	620E	SB	77586
SEABREEZE LN	0	612K	PL	77545
SEABRIGHT CT	0	659M	LC	77573
SEABROOK	3400	533P	SEH	77021
SEABROOK CIR	2100	620F	SB	77586
SEABROOK LN	5300	461T	NEC	77521
SEABROOK ISLAND DR	0	620E	SB	77586
SEABROOK SHIPYARDS	0	620T	SB	77586
SEABROUGH DR	2500	612M	PL	77584
SEABURY CT	1200	484H	NEF	77494
SEABURY PATH CT	0	406Y	NWC	77449
SEABURY PATH CT	0	406Y	NWC	77449
SEA CHANNEL CT	0	620E	SB	77586
SEA CHANNEL DR	3200	620E	SB	77586
SEACLIFF DR	400	618S	SEH	77598
SEACLIFF DR	700	618P	SEH	77062
SEACO AVE	0	538K	DP	77536
SEACO CT	0	538K	DP	77536
SEA COVE CT	2000	619W	NB	77058
SEACREST AVE	0	543W	BC	77520
SEACREST BLVD	300	660K	LC	77573
SEAFIELD DR	1400	457V	NEC	77530
SEAFOAM RD	400	618S	SEH	77598
SEAFOAM RD	700	618P	SEH	77062
SEAFORD DR	10500	576T	SEH	77089
SEAGATE LN	900	618K	SEH	77062
SEAGLER RD	800	489R	SWH	77042
SEAGLER RD	2300	489Z	SWH	77042
SEAGLER GLEN LN	0	446G	NWC	77449
SEAGLER PARK LN	13200	572R	SWH	77047
SEAGLER POND LN	0	373E	NCC	77073
SEAGLERS POINT LN	0	524K	NWF	77406
SEAGLER SPRINGS LN	0	417D	NEH	77044
SEAGRAM	11500	496K	JC	77029
SEAGROOVE	0	612M	PL	77584
SEAGROVE	100	580Q	SA	77571
SEA GROVE CT	12300	449A	NWC	77041
SEAGULL	1600	536N	SEH	77017
SEAGULL LN	8300	613V	PL	77584
SEA HORSE CT	2500	620B	SB	77586
SEAHORSE DR	15000	618F	SEH	77062
SEAHORSE LN	26600	246N	SWM	77355
SEAHORSE COVE	3200	609E	SG	77479
SEAHURST CT	2300	619X	LC	77573
SEA ISLAND DR	13100	370B	NWC	77069
SEAKALE LN	1900	618L	SEH	77062
SEA KING	2000	452T	NWH	77008
SEA LAND	0	540U	MP	77571
SEALANDER	100	419C	NEC	77532
SEALANDER CT	16100	419C	NEC	77532
SEA LARK RD	15700	618J	SEH	77062
SEA LEDGE CT	2600	620A	SB	77586
SEA LEDGE DR	2600	620A	SB	77586
SEALEY	6500	412W	NWH	77091
SEALEY	7700	412T	NWH	77088
SEA LINER DR	15700	618J	SEH	77062
SEAL VALLEY LN	22300	485Y	NEF	77450
SEAMASTER DR	700	618P	SEH	77062
SEA MEADOW CT	4100	446H	NWC	77449
SEAMIST CIR	2300	620F	SB	77586
SEAMIST CT	1800	452W	NWH	77008
SEA MIST DR	100	620W	LC	77573
SEAMIST DR	1100	452W	NWH	77008
SEAMIST DR	3000	452W	NWH	77008
SEA MYRTLE DR	10700	367V	NWC	77095
SEA MYRTLE LN	13900	568B	NEF	77498
SEAN CT	5900	337X	NEC	77346
SEAN PARK CT	8200	408F	NWC	77095
SEA OAK CT	5000	577M	PA	77505
SEA PALMS CT	2000	418D	NEC	77532
SEA PALMS DR	15900	418D	NEC	77532
SEA PINE DR	20700	486F	SWC	77450
SEA PINES DR	0	485E	NEF	77494
SEAPINES HARBOUR DR	0	328D	NWC	77375
SEA PINES PLACE	3000	659D	LC	77573
SEA QUEEN CT	1800	452T	NWH	77008
SEARGENT RD	2800	620N	SB	77586
SEARIDGE LN	0	620G	SB	77586
SEARLE DR	3800	453Y	NEH	77009
SEARLES DR	1500	568U	SG	77478
SEARS DR	19100	335W	NEH	77338
SEARSTON DR	14600	408T	NWC	77084
SEA SHADOW BEND	11800	612M	PL	77584
SEASHELL CT	4100	620A	SB	77586
SEASHORE CIR	3600	620E	SB	77586
SEASHORE DR	2600	620A	SB	77586
SEA SHORE DR	11200	529J	SWH	77072
SEASHORE BEND DR	0	445R	NWC	77449
SEASIDE LN	15600	618J	SEH	77062
SEASIDE SPARROW LN	0	461N	NEC	77521
SEA SMOKE LN	500	488B	SWH	77079
SEASON CT	7400	337Q	NEC	77346
SEASONAL CREST CIR	0	249Q	NWC	77375
SEASONS TRAIL	3200	297P	NEH	77345
SEASONS WAY	0	326P	NWC	77433
SEASPRAY CT	1300	452W	NWH	77008
SEASPRAY CT	1700	452S	NWH	77008
SEASTONE LN	4000	331S	NWC	77068
SEASWEPT DR	12400	570F	SWH	77071
SEATON DR	18500	407W	NWC	77449
SEATON GLEN	200	486D	SWC	77094
SEATON VALLEY DR	6600	330R	NWC	77379
SEATTLE	15600	409R	JV	77040
SEATTLE SLEW DR	12400	409E	JV	77065
SEA TURTLE CT	17900	246N	SWM	77355

Street Name	Block	Pg/Sq	Loc	Zips
SEA TURTLE LN	25000	246W	SWM	77355
SEA TURTLE LN	26700	246N	SWM	77355
SEAVALE RD	15700	618K	SEH	77062
SEAVIEW CT	4100	620A	SB	77586
SEAWARD	0	620E	SB	77586
SEAWAY	0	242G	WCO	77484
SEAWAY DR	500	620E	EL	77586
SEAWOLF DR	16600	618T	SEH	77062
SEAWOOD DR	11700	616D	SEC	77089
SEBAGO CT	0	615W	PL	77584
SEBAGO DR	0	615W	PL	77584
SEBASTIAN CIR	18900	338W	NEC	77346
SEBASTIAN DR	21500	296A	SEM	77365
SEBASTOPOL DR	4600	615N	PL	77584
SEBER DR	8500	289H	NWC	77375
SEBEY RIDGE LN	0	524B	NEF	77494
SECLUSION DR	5600	456V	NEC	77049
SECO CREEK LN	17800	376C	NEC	77396
SECRETARIAT CT	12300	570G	SWH	77071
SECRETARIAT DR	4200	538S	PA	77503
SECRETARIAT DR	9500	408D	NWC	77065
SECRETARIAT LN	7600	570G	SWH	77071
SECRETARIAT RIDGE DR	7400	334R	NCC	77338
SECRETARIET DR	2000	570S	SF	77477
SECRET BRANCH LN	17900	407E	NWC	77433
SECRET CANYON DR	9500	408B	NWC	77095
SECRET FOREST CT	12700	367H	NWC	77429
SECRET HILL LN	0	366Y	NWC	77433
SECURITY	0	374A	NEH	77032
SECURITY LN	9000	458A	NEC	77049
SECURITY LN	9100	418W	NEC	77049
SECURITY WAY	7100	409R	NWC	77040
SEDALIA	6200	533F	SEH	77021
SEDALIA BROOK LN	0	485X	NEF	77494
SEDALIA POINT LN	0	416Z	NEH	77044
SEDALLIA SPRING CT	0	488P	SWH	77077
SEDBERRY	0	619M	TL	77586
SEDDON RD	7900	614E	PL	77581
SEDERS WALK	1	251A	WD	77381
SEDGEBOROUGH CIR	3100	446Q	NWC	77449
SEDGEBOROUGH DR	3100	446Q	NWC	77449
SEDGECREEK DR	19500	446G	NWC	77449
SEDGEFIELD	28700	293A	SEM	77386
SEDGEFIELD CREEK TRACE	0	328K	NWC	77429
SEDGELAND TRAIL LN	0	524C	NEF	77494
SEDGELAND TRAIL LN	0	524C	NEF	77494
SEDGEMOOR DR	8800	289D	NWC	77375
SEDGE WREN CT	9500	527U	NEF	77083
SEDGIE DR	1900	450T	NWH	77080
SEDGWICK DR	400	413T	NEH	77076
SEDONA CT	0	658Y	LC	77573
SEDONA CT	7100	528K	SWC	77083
SEDONA DR	0	658Y	LC	77573
SEDONA DR	0	658Y	LC	77573
SEDONABEND DR	0	328A	NWC	77429
SEDONA CREEK DR	2700	610U	MC	77459
SEDONA HILLS	7100	370A	NWC	77069
SEDONA OAKS DR	0	406G	NWC	77433
SEDONA RANCH LN	20800	291S	NWC	77388
SEDONA RIDGE DR	0	406G	NWC	77433
SEDONA SPRINGS DR	0	330H	NWC	77379
SEDONA WOODS LN	11700	366M	NWC	77433
SEDONA WOODS LN	16300	527F	SWC	77082
SEDORA DR	300	656C	FR	77546
SEDUM GREEN	0	327T	CY	77429
SEDWICK PARK DR	0	295L	SEM	77365
SEEDLING DR	15500	373P	NCC	77032
SEEGERS TRAIL DR	6300	370Q	NWC	77066
SEEKER	8100	455G	NEH	77028
SEEKER	9500	455C	NEH	77078
SEGAR BEND TRAIL	0	293G	SEM	77386
SEGO LILY CT	0	250K	NWC	77389
SEGO LILY CT	0	250K	NWC	77389
SEGOVIA DR	0	659S	LC	77573
SEGOVIA LN	0	660L	LC	77539
SEGREST DR	10700	573L	SEH	77047
SEGUIN CT	9300	579A	LP	77571
SEGUINE DR	0	539N	DP	77536
SEGUIN VALLEY DR	0	484X	NEF	77494
SEGUIN VALLEY DR	0	484X	NEF	77494
SEIDEL RD	17500	287J	NWC	77377
SEIDELSTONE CT	0	328M	NWC	77377
SEINE CT	2900	371G	NWC	77014
SEINFELD CT	6600	370B	NWC	77069
SEKOLA LN	1900	252V	SEM	77386
SELA LN	10700	529K	SWH	77072
SELBY OAKS	0	376R	NEC	77346
SELDER DR	16700	617Y	SEC	77546
SELENE DR	3100	610Q	MC	77459
W. SELF RD	17400	287X	NWC	77377
SELINSKY RD	4700	573H	SEH	77048
SELINSKY RD	5000	573M	SEH	77048
SELINSKY RD	5200	574G	SEH	77048
SELLERS RD	14000	413B	NCC	77060
SELLERS RD	15100	373X	NCC	77060
SELMA	7000	532M	SWH	77030
SELMA	7100	532M	SWH	77030
W. SELPH RD	0	287X	NWC	77377
SELPH RD	17100	287Y	NWC	77377
SELSDON CT	28400	299S	NEC	77336
SELVA	1300	577J	PA	77504
SELWYN DR	14800	457V	NEC	77015
SELZNICK PARK	25143	249S	NWC	77375
SEMINAR DR	500	373N	NEH	77060
SEMINARY RIDGE LN	16600	527P	NEF	77083
SEMINOLE	200	619V	LC	77565
SEMINOLE	1200	538R	DP	77536
SEMINOLE	4200	577F	PA	77504
SEMINOLE	7100	462Y	BT	77521
SEMINOLE	7200	461S	NEC	77521
SEMINOLE DR	4100	614Z	PL	77584
SEMINOLE RD	9500	248R	SWM	77354
SEMINOLE HILL LN	0	484Z	NEF	77494
SEMINOLE LAKES DR	0	376S	NEC	77396
SEMINOLE LODGE LN	0	290Q	NWC	77379
SEMINOLE PARK LN	23100	292G	NCC	77373
SEMINOLE RIDGE DR	0	366P	NWC	77433
SEMINOLE SPRING LN	11000	616E	SEC	77089
SEMINOLE TRAIL	24100	297J	SEM	77365
SEMMES	800	494E	NEH	77020
SEMMES	1600	494E	NEH	77026
SEMMES	3400	454N	NEH	77093
SEMMONS RD	5200	450G	NWH	77040
SEMPIONE DR	0	525E	NEF	77406
SENATE	2100	537T	PA	77502
SENATE	7200	409L	JV	77040
SENCA PARK DR	13700	488K	SWH	77077
SENCA SPRINGS CT	1800	486K	SWC	77450
SENDA CT	6400	337U	NEC	77346
SENDERA OAKS CT	0	406L	NWC	77433
SENDERA OAKS DR	0	406L	NWC	77433
SENEBE WAY	6900	609Y	MC	77459
SENECA	0	503M	BC	77520
SENECA	4200	577F	PA	77504
SENECA	10600	414V	NEH	77016
SENECA CT	2000	658T	LC	77573
SENECA CT	4500	461S	NEC	77521
SENECA POINT	20200	290V	NWC	77379
SENECA TRAIL	9900	248G	SWM	77354
SENEGAL	6900	454Q	NEH	77016
SENIOR	5000	454C	NEH	77016
SENIOR	6200	454D	NEH	77016
SENIOR RD	0	609R	MC	77459
SENIOR RD	2600	610R	NEF	77545
SENISA CT	0	289M	NWC	77375
SENNA	7200	454M	NEH	77028
SENNA AVE	0	659G	LC	77573
SENNA HILL LN	0	290V	NWC	77379
SENNA LEDGE CT	0	616E	SEC	77089
SENNA PLACE	3800	609E	SG	77479
SENOUR CT	3900	296V	NEH	77339
SENOVA CT	2800	613U	NEB	77584
SENOVA DR	3400	613U	NEB	77584
SENOVA LN	0	609T	NEF	77479
SENOVA RIDGE LN	0	253K	SEM	77386
SENS RD	300	540J	SEC	77571
SENTERRA BEND CIR	19200	330D	NWC	77379
SENTERRA LAKES BLVD	19200	290Z	NWC	77379
SENTINAL OAKS	2200	568Y	SG	77478
SENTINEL DR	16500	611B	SWH	77053
SENTINEL OAKS	100	248W	SWM	77362
SENTINEL OAKS	400	247Z	SWM	77362
SENTINEL POINT CT	100	250A	WD	77382
SENTORE CT	2100	616K	PL	77581
SENTORE DR	1300	616K	PL	77581
SENTOSA CLIFF LN	17800	527S	NEF	77407
SENTRY CT	11000	368V	NWC	77065
SENTRY HILL LN	0	375Y	NEC	77396
SENTRY PARK CT	17400	407U	NWC	77084
SENTRY PARK LN	6100	407U	NWC	77084
SENTRY PARK LN		484T	NEF	77494
SENTRY PINE CT	18200	376D	NEC	77346
SENTRY WOODS LN	4800	614S	NEB	77584
SEPTEMBER DR	3700	502G	BT	77521
SEQUIN DR	0	290R	NWC	77388
SEQUOIA	2000	619V	LC	77565
SEQUOIA	4100	461S	NEC	77521
SEQUOIA DR	9200	450G	NWH	77041
SEQUOIA LN	1200	536P	PA	77502
SEQUOIA BEND BLVD	13900	414C	NCC	77032
SEQUOIA BEND BLVD	14000	374Y	NCC	77032
SEQUOIA HILLS DR	0	328R	NWC	77377
SEQUOIA KINGS DR	0	377L	NEC	77346
SEQUOIA LAKE TRAIL	3300	615U	PL	77581
SEQUOIA MEADOW CT	0	376V	NEC	77396
SEQUOIA PARK LN		484W	NEF	77494
SEQUOIA PASS CT	10400	367X	NWC	77095
SEQUOIA TRACE	20200	290V	NWC	77379
SEQUOIA TRACE CT	5800	290V	NWC	77379
SEQUOIA VALLEY LN	11800	377E	NEC	77346
SEQUOIA VIEW LN	17600	376H	NEC	77346
SEREIN MEADOWS DR	3200	253S	SEM	77386
SERENA LN	0	335P	NCC	77338
SERENADE LN	8700	410K	NWC	77040
SERENADE TERRACE DR	4300	609K	MC	77459
SERENATA CT	0	376E	HM	77396
SERENATA LN	0	376E	HM	77396
SERENA VISTA WAY	0	331T	NWC	77068
SERENDIPITY LN	11700	369J	NWC	77429
SERENE ELM ST	0	616H	SEH	77089
SERENE OAK DR	3100	568Z	SG	77478
SERENE SHORE DR	0	328E	NWC	77377
SERENE SPRINGS LN	0	292U	NCC	77373
SERENE TRAILS	1300	288B	TB	77375
SERENE WAVE BLVD	0	325M	NWC	77429
SERENE WAY LN	0	446D	NWC	77084
SERENE WOOD LN	0	407J	NWC	77433
SERENIAH CIR	17000	407Q	NWC	77084
SERENITY	0	296D	SEM	77357
SERENITY LN	1900	659S	LC	77573
SERENITY LN	4400	531D	BL	77401
SERENITY COVE CIR	16900	657C	SEC	77546
SERENITY FALLS LN	0	578T	SEH	77059
SERENITY LOCH DR	18600	329D	NWC	77379
SERENITY MEADOWS CT	0	415S	NEH	77016
SERENITY OAKS DR	0	524K	NWF	77406
SERENITY PINE CT	18200	376D	NEC	77346
SERPENTEER DR	19200	294D	SEM	77365
SERPENTINE DR	1300	496K	JC	77029
SERRANO DR	0	660L	LC	77539
SERRANO BLUFF LN	0	253K	SEM	77386
SERRANO CREEK LN	14400	375Y	NEC	77396
SERRANO GAP CT	0	326V	NWC	77429
SERRANO HILL LN	0	290Q	NWC	77379
SERRANO LAKE CT	22700	289M	NWC	77375
SERRANO TERRACE LN	6000	409W	NWC	77041
SERRANO TRAIL	2900	486S	SWC	77450
SERRANO VALLEY LN	0	609U	MC	77459
SERRINGDON DR	20500	446K	NWC	77449
SERVICE	400	453T	NWH	77009
SERVICE	1200	497F	NEH	77015
SERVICE RD	900	494L	NEH	77020
SESAME	10800	574F	SEH	77048
SESAME ST	0	461Q	NEC	77521
SETON LAKE DR	7200	371W	NWC	77086
SETON LAKE DR	7500	370Z	NWC	77086
SET POINT LN	18700	337Z	NEC	77346
SETTEGAST RD	0	570U	MC	77489
SETTEGAST RD	12000	415B	NEC	77050
SETTEGAST RD	13600	375X	NEC	77396
SETTEGAST RANCH RD	100	524X	NWF	77406
SETTEGAST RANCH RD	6000	524Y	NWF	77406
SETTEMONT RD	12300	570Q	SWH	77085
SETTEMONT RD	12700	570Q	SWH	77489
SETTER CT	16300	610C	SWH	77489
SETTING SUN	6900	525E	NEF	77494
SETTING SUN DR	0	446Q	NWC	77449
SETTLE DR	12400	570F	SWH	77071
SETTLEMENT LN	14000	375W	NEC	77396
SETTLERS BRIDGE LN	20700	291V	NWC	77388
W. SETTLERS LAKE CIR	6100	406T	NWC	77449
E. SETTLERS LAKE CIR	20800	406T	NWC	77449
W. SETTLERS SHORE CIR	12100	366K	NWC	77433
SETTLERS SHORE CIR	12100	366K	NWC	77433
N. SETTLERS SHORE DR	18300	366K	NWC	77433
S. SETTLERS SHORE DR	18400	366K	NWC	77433
SETTLERS SQUARE LN	6100	406T	NWC	77449
SETTLERS VALLEY DR	21000	406P	NWC	77449
SETTLERS VILLAGE DR	6000	406P	NWC	77449
SETTLERS WAY	0	444S	KT	77493
W. SETTLERS WAY	2100	251Q	WD	77380
E. SETTLERS WAY	2100	251R	WD	77380
SETTLERS WAY BLVD	2200	569W	SG	77478
SEUSS DR	7500	532L	SWH	77025
SEVEN COVES CT	23500	525K	NEF	77407
SEVEN HAMPTON LN	200	497B	NEC	77015
SEVEN HAMPTON LN	400	457Y	NEC	77015
SEVEN LEAF LN	6300	297V	NEH	77345
SEVEN MAPLES DR	1600	337D	NEH	77345
SEVEN MAPLES DR	2100	338A	NEH	77345
SEVEN MEADOWS PARKWAY	23600	525B	NEF	77494
SEVEN MILE LN	10600	414S	NCC	77093
SEVEN MILE LN	11600	413R	NCC	77093
SEVEN OAKS	0	488L	SWH	77077
SEVEN OAKS DR	1900	336G	NEH	77339
SEVEN OAKS LN	13500	367G	NWC	77429
SEVEN PINES DR	16800	330G	NWC	77379
SEVEN PINES LN	8700	527N	NEF	77083
SEVEN SEAS	300	419C	NEC	77532
SEVEN SISTERS DR	11200	329B	NWC	77375
SEVEN SISTERS RD	28000	258P	SEM	77357
SEVEN SPRINGS DR	15800	448A	NWC	77084
SEVENTEENTH GREEN CT	19900	337V	NEC	77346
SEVENTEENTH GREEN DR	7300	337V	NEC	77346
SEVENTH HEAVEN	23800	525E	NEF	77494
SEVEN WAVES CT	16400	419C	NEC	77532
SEVERN	10400	528Y	SWH	77099
SEVERO RD	15100	527Z	NEF	77498
SEVILLA DR	0	660G	LC	77539
SEVILLE LN	7200	415T	NEH	77016
SEVILLE MANOR	1800	611T	NEF	77545
SEWALK	14000	572Y	SWH	77047
SEWANEE	5300	532F	WU	77005
SEWANEE	6800	532K	SWH	77025
SEWARD	23600	290D	NWC	77389
SEXTANT	0	618P	SEH	77062
SEXTON	7900	455T	NEH	77028
SEXTUS	16100	409U	NWH	77041
SEYBORN	2300	492S	SWH	77027
SEYMOUR DR	900	536M	PA	77506
SEYMOUR DR	5000	374Y	NCC	77032
SHA CIR	4200	577B	PA	77504
SHABBONA	100	538F	DP	77536
SHAD	10900	449Y	NWH	77043
SHADBURY CT	2300	296V	NEH	77339
SHADBUSH AVE	0	296A	SEM	77365
SHADDER WAY	1	492L	SWH	77019
SHADDOCK DR	7500	408L	NWC	77041
SHADDON MANOR CT	1500	329G	NWC	77379
SHADE CT	0	614S	NEB	77584
SHADE LN	0	614S	NEB	77584
SHADECREST LN	0	658W	LC	77573
SHADED ARBOR DR	0	250N	NWC	77389
SHADED KNOLL LN	0	326L	NWC	77429
SHADED PINES DR	9200	376E	HM	77396
SHADE GAP LN	14900	528W	NEF	77498
SHADELAND DR	1100	449Z	NWH	77043
SHADETREE DR	0	406G	NWC	77433
SHADEWOOD CT	14600	457Y	NEC	77015
SHADIE PINE LN	800	616R	FR	77546
SHADOW CIR	0	541D	BT	77520
SHADOW CIR	1000	658M	LC	77573
SHADOW LN	1	450S	NWH	77080
SHADOW LN	1	490T	SWH	77063
SHADOW LN	600	536L	PA	77506
SHADOW LN	8600	249E	SWM	77354
SHADOW LN	16300	367L	CY	77429
SHADOW LN	26000	257M	SEM	77357
SHADOWBARK DR	3300	488Z	SWH	77082
SHADOW BAY CIR	2100	620W	LC	77573
SHADOW BAY DR	2700	612R	PL	77584
SHADOW BAYOU CT	3400	489W	SWH	77082
SHADOWBEND	1100	616X	PL	77581
SHADOW BEND	1300	619H	TL	77586
SHADOW BEND AVE	0	616Z	FR	77546
SHADOW BEND AVE	0	656C	FR	77546
W. SHADOWBEND AVE	100	656C	FR	77546
S. SHADOWBEND AVE	100	616Z	FR	77546
E. SHADOWBEND AVE	100	616Z	FR	77546
N. SHADOWBEND AVE	300	616Z	FR	77546
SHADOW BEND DR	1400	449V	NWH	77043
SHADOW BEND PLACE	4500	251A	WD	77381
SHADOW BLUFF CT	3400	489W	SWH	77082
SHADOW BRANCH LN	0	253Q	SEM	77386
SHADOWBRANCH LN	1900	488N	SWH	77077
SHADOW BREEZE LN	0	484Z	NEF	77494
SHADOWBRIAR DR	2000	489N	SWH	77077
SHADOWBRIAR DR	3200	488Z	SWH	77082
SHADOW BRIAR LN	2600	333N	NCC	77073
SHADOW BRIAR LN	4100	609F	MC	77459
SHADOWBROOK DR	700	251V	SWM	77380
SHADOW CANYON CT	0	612L	PL	77545
SHADOW CANYON LN	0	612L	PL	77545
SHADOW CANYON LN	2700	485N	NEF	77494
SHADOWCHASE CT	3200	488Z	SWH	77082
SHADOWCHASE DR	3300	488Z	SWH	77082
SHADOWCLIFF CT	600	660E	LC	77573
SHADOWCLIFF LN	0	485X	NEF	77494
SHADOW COVE CT	3600	528D	SWH	77082
SHADOW COVE DR	0	612L	PL	77545
SHADOW COVE DR	3600	528D	SWH	77082
S. SHADOW COVE DR	12200	528D	SWH	77082
N. SHADOW COVE DR	12200	528D	SWH	77082
SHADOW CREEK	0	538V	DP	77536
SHADOW CREEK BLVD	0	250X	NWC	77389
SHADOW CREEK CT	0	502H	BT	77520
SHADOW CREEK CT	23600	485K	NEF	77494
SHADOW CREEK DR	300	620J	EL	77586
SHADOW CREEK DR	2000	536S	SEH	77017
SHADOW CREEK DR	9700	539W	LP	77571
SHADOW CREEK PARKWAY	11700	612G	PL	77584
SHADOW CREEK RIDGE CT	0	250X	NWC	77389
SHADOW CREEK RIDGE DR	0	250X	NWC	77389
W. SHADOW CREEK VILLAS LOOP	0	250X	NWC	77389
S. SHADOW CREEK VILLAS LOOP	0	250X	NWC	77389
E. SHADOW CREEK VILLAS LOOP	0	250X	NWC	77389
SHADOWCREST LN	3200	251N	SWM	77380
SHADOW CREST LN	5500	531S	SWH	77096
SHADOW CREST LN	6100	530R	SWH	77074
SHADOW CYPRESS CT	17800	407F	NWC	77095
W. SHADOWDALE	0	449H	NWH	77041
N. SHADOWDALE	0	449H	NWH	77041
SHADOWDALE DR	1000	489D	SWH	77043
SHADOWDALE DR	1200	449R	NWH	77043
SHADOWDALE DR	4400	449H	NWC	77041
N. SHADOWDALE DR	10400	449H	NWH	77041
SHADOW DANCE LN	0	525R	NEF	77407
SHADOW DUST CT	12400	528D	SWH	77082
SHADOW EDGE CIR	8700	407D	NWC	77095
SHADOW FALLS CT	13500	578W	SEH	77059
SHADOW FALLS LN	0	612K	PL	77545
SHADOWFERN CT	3200	488Z	SWH	77082
SHADOWFERN DR	3300	488Z	SWH	77082
SHADOWFIELD DR	11000	369Z	NWC	77064
SHADOW FOREST DR	1800	484M	NEF	77494
SHADOW FORK CT	3600	528D	SWH	77082
SHADOW GARDEN LN	0	488N	SWH	77077
SHADOW GATE CT	8400	410J	NWC	77040
SHADOW GATE LN	9400	410J	NWC	77040
SHADOWGLADE CT	9700	409D	NWC	77064
SHADOW BLVD	0	609X	NEF	77479
SHADOWGLEN DR	700	498A	CV	77530
SHADOW GLEN LN	2300	252Z	SEM	77386
SHADOW GRANGE CT	0	406G	NWC	77433
SHADOW GRASS DR	4600	444B	NWC	77493
SHADOWGRASS DR	18700	447E	NWC	77084
SHADOW GREEN DR	12300	528D	SWH	77082
SHADOW GROVE LN	18300	378S	NEC	77532
SHADOW HILL LN	7700	528M	SWH	77072
SHADOWHOLLOW DR	12100	489W	SWH	77082
SHADOW ISLAND DR	12300	528D	SWH	77082
SHADOW ISLE LN	6001	408S	NWC	77084
SHADOW KNOLL CT	3800	528D	SWH	77082
SHADOWKNOLL DR	12200	488Z	SWH	77082
SHADOW LAKE CT	8500	407F	HC	77095
W. SHADOWLAKE DR	12300	368M	NWC	77429
N. SHADOWLAKE DR	12300	368M	NWC	77429
E. SHADOWLAKE DR	12300	368M	NWC	77429
SHADOW LAKES CT	500	613F	NEB	77584
SHADOW LAWN	1	493W	SWH	77005
SHADOW LAWN WAY	17500	367T	NWC	77095
SHADOWLEAF DR	3200	488Z	SWH	77082
SHADOW LEDGE DR	17100	367X	NWC	77095
SHADOW LINE CT	0	407S	NWC	77449
SHADOWMEADOWS DR	3400	488Z	SWH	77082
SHADOWMERE DR	0	612K	PL	77545
SHADOWMERE LN	25200	485W	NEF	77494
SHADOW MILL CT	20500	486K	SWC	77450
SHADOWMIST DR	12400	488Z	SWH	77082
SHADOW MIST LN	4300	609X	NEF	77479
SHADOW MOUNTAIN DR	1000	485M	SWC	77450
SHADOW OAK DR	0	327H	NWC	77429
SHADOW OAK DR	0	327H	NWC	77429
SHADOW OAKS	0	450W	NWH	77043
SHADOW OAKS DR	10200	449Z	NWH	77043
SHADOW PARK DR	2000	485Q	NEF	77494
SHADOW PASS TRAIL	15900	329N	NWC	77377
SHADOW PATH DR	16500	618D	PA	77059
SHADOW PINE DR	9800	369L	NWC	77070
SHADOW PLACE DR	0	489W	SWH	77082
SHADOW POINT DR	3900	660L	LC	77573
SHADOW POINT DR	12100	488Z	SWH	77082
SHADOWPOINT DR	12300	488Z	SWH	77082
SHADOWRIDGE DR	5000	611C	SWH	77053
SHADOW RIVER LN	21200	290U	NWC	77379
SHADOW ROCK DR	1800	296Y	NEH	77339
SHADOW ROYAL DR	3800	528D	SWH	77082
SHADOW RUN DR	13500	488X	SWC	77082
SHADOWSIDE CT	3400	489W	SWH	77082
SHADOWS OF ALPSTRINE DR	24700	257P	SEM	77357
SHADOW SPRING CT	3400	489W	SWH	77082
SHADOW STONE	1	251B	WD	77381
SHADOW TERRACE LN	7400	526K	NEF	77407
SHADOW TRACE CIR	3800	528D	SWH	77082
SHADOW TRAIL	3600	447J	NWC	77084
SHADOW TRAIL DR	2900	488X	SWC	77082
SHADOW TREE DR	6300	570H	SWH	77035
SHADOWVALE DR	12400	488Z	SWH	77082
SHADOW VALLEY CT	8400	330N	NWC	77379
SHADOW VALLEY DR	16800	330N	NWC	77379
SHADOW VALLEY DR	17800	330J	NWC	77379
SHADOW VALLEY DR	18000	329M	NWC	77379
SHADOW VALLEY LN	8500	330N	NWC	77379
SHADOW VIEW LN	2400	488V	SWH	77077
SHADOW VILLA LN	9800	416Z	NEF	77044
SHADOWVISTA CT	3500	488Z	SWH	77082
SHADOWVISTA DR	12400	488Z	SWH	77082
SHADOWWALK DR	3200	488Z	SWH	77082
SHADOW WAY	11400	490G	PP	77024
SHADOW WAY CT	500	490G	PP	77024
SHADOW WICK LN	3700	528D	SWH	77082
SHADOW WIND DR	0	612N	PL	77545
SHADOW WIND DR	1800	570X	MC	77489
SHADOW WIND DR	8300	410J	NWC	77040
SHADOW WOOD	0	490Q	PP	77024
SHADOW WOOD DR	100	568J	SG	77498
SHADOW WOOD DR	9600	450S	NWH	77080
SHADOW WOOD DR	10100	449U	NWH	77043
SHADRACK	3700	456X	NEH	77013
SHADSWORTH DR	0	291V	NWC	77388
SHADWAY DR	6700	408T	NWC	77084
SHADWELL DR	800	618J	SEH	77062
SHADWELL LN	0	657A	FR	77546
SHADY DR	8200	454D	NEH	77016
SHADY DR	32200	246U	SWM	77355
SHADY LN	0	454A	NEH	77093
SHADY LN	0	458H	HG	77562
W. SHADY LN	1	490T	SWH	77063
E. SHADY LN	1	490T	SWH	77063
SHADY LN	1	490T	SWH	77063
SHADY LN	100	299W	NEH	77336
S. SHADY LN	300	580U	LP	77571
N. SHADY LN	300	580U	LP	77571
SHADY LN	300	541C	BT	77520
SHADY LN	2700	658J	LC	77598
SHADY LN	9000	249E	SWM	77354
SHADY LN	9300	248H	SWM	77354
SHADY LN	9700	414S	NCC	77093
SHADY LN	16500	458V	CV	77530
SHADY LN	20000	381E	NEC	77532
SHADY RD	1200	298V	NEC	77336
SHADY ACE LN	8200	337Z	NEC	77346
SHADY ACRES CT	0	452U	NWH	77008
SHADY ACRES LANDING	2600	452T	NWH	77008
SHADY ALCOVE CT	6000	338A	NEH	77345
SHADY ARBOR	0	330M	NWC	77379
SHADY ARBOR CT	8900	411S	NWH	77040
SHADY ARBOR CT	8900	410U	NWC	77040
SHADY ARBOR LN	0	253P	SEM	77386
SHADY ARBOR LN	7000	411S	NWH	77040
SHADY ARBOR LN	7300	410U	NWH	77040
SHADY ARBOR WAY	0	331J	NWC	77379
SHADY ARBOUR CT	7400	578F	PA	77505
SHADY ARBOUR DR	4300	578K	PA	77505
SHADY BANK DR	19500	329A	NWC	77375
SHADY BAY LN	3600	609Q	MC	77459
SHADY BAYOU LN	2100	292R	NCC	77373
SHADY BAYOU LN	2400	293N	NCC	77373
SHADY BEND	0	246B	SWM	77355
SHADY BEND DR	2000	615V	PL	77581
SHADY BEND DR	14900	328Z	NWC	77070
SHADY BEND LN	800	616R	FR	77546
SHADY BIRCH HOLLOW	5900	338A	NEH	77345
SHADY BLISS CT	0	366E	NWC	77433
SHADY BLOSSOM DR	0	366J	NWC	77433
SHADY BOUGH DR	10100	329T	NWC	77070
SHADY BRANCH DR	2000	336G	NEH	77339
SHADY BREEZE CT	0	612R	PL	77584

Street Name	Block	Pg/Sq	Loc	Zips
SHADY BREEZE DR	3800	528D	SWH	77082
SHADYBRIAR DR	2000	488V	SWH	77077
SHADY BRIDGE CT	17900	407K	NWC	77095
SHADY BROOK	0	246A	SWM	77355
SHADY BROOK DR	0	612Q	PL	77584
SHADY BROOK DR	500	569U	NEF	77477
SHADYBROOK DR	1400	486H	SWC	77094
SHADYBROOK DR	1600	486M	SWC	77094
SHADY BROOK DR	2300	446V	NWC	77084
SHADYBROOK LN	29600	246A	SWM	77355
SHADYBROOK MEADOW DR	0	450J	NWH	77080
SHADY CANYON CT	16500	367Q	NWC	77095
SHADY CANYON DR	11500	367Q	NWC	77095
SHADY CANYON LN	17800	328M	NWC	77377
SHADY CORNERS LN	7200	411N	NWH	77040
SHADY COVE CT	0	612M	PL	77584
SHADY COVE LN	19500	338T	NEC	77346
SHADY CREEK CIR	0	657A	FR	77546
SHADY CREEK DR	2700	616N	PL	77581
S. SHADY CREEK DR	5300	536S	SEH	77017
N. SHADY CREEK DR	5300	536S	SEH	77017
SHADYCREST DR	3400	615Y	PL	77581
SHADYCREST DR	12400	488Z	SWH	77082
SHADY CYPRESS LN	18100	326V	NWC	77429
SHADY DALE DR	500	569U	NEF	77477
SHADYDALE LN	9800	454D	NEH	77016
SHADYDALE RD	0	367C	NWC	77429
SHADY DAWN LN	0	484U	NEF	77494
SHADY DOWNS DR	12200	528D	SWH	77082
SHADY EDGE DR	0	366E	NWC	77433
SHADY ELM LN	12100	247M	SWM	77362
SHADY ELMS DR	16200	618C	SEH	77059
SHADY END	0	541C	BT	77520
SHADY FALLS DR	0	408A	NWC	77095
SHADY FALLS LN	0	612K	PL	77545
SHADY FERN CT	12700	368V	NWC	77065
SHADY FOREST	0	488G	SWH	77079
SHADY FORK DR	0	366E	NWC	77433
SHADY FORT LN	0	328F	NWC	77377
SHADY GARDENS CT	3000	297N	NEH	77339
SHADY GARDENS DR	5000	297N	NEH	77339
SHADY GATE CT	15100	327V	NWC	77429
SHADY GATE LN	0	615F	PL	77581
SHADY GLADE DR	300	332T	NWC	77090
SHADY GLEN	16600	328P	NWC	77429
SHADY GLEN DR	3200	609H	MC	77459
SHADY GLEN DR	11300	490L	PP	77024
SHADY GLENN DR	1600	257C	WV	77357
SHADY GREEN DR	3600	297W	NEH	77339
SHADY GREEN MEADOWS	0	528Q	SWC	77083
SHADY GROVE CT	1300	619C	PA	77586
SHADY GROVE CT	7000	410V	NWC	77040
SHADY GROVE DR	3600	613W	NEB	77578
SHADY GROVE LN	7300	410V	NWH	77040
SHADY GROVE LN	11600	490K	BH	77024
SHADY HARBOR DR	3800	528D	SWH	77082
SHADY HAVEN CIR	0	366J	NWC	77433
SHADY HEATH LN	21900	525G	NEF	77494
SHADY HILL DR	2800	501N	BT	77521
SHADY HILL DR	3400	500R	BT	77521
SHADY HILLS DR	2900	296Z	NEH	77339
SHADY HILLS LANDING LN	27300	294T	SEM	77386
SHADY HOLLOW	600	491L	SWH	77056
SHADY ISLE CT	0	526J	NEF	77407
SHADY KNOLL LN	0	657Z	LC	77573
SHADY KNOLL LN	12600	368J	NWC	77429
SHADY LAKE	2700	620A	SB	77586
SHADY LAKE DR	100	338V	NEH	77336
SHADY LAKE DR	18200	257D	RF	77357
SHADY LAKE GROVE	0	526J	NEF	77407
SHADY LANE CIR	9300	490T	SWH	77063
SHADY LAWN	100	580U	SA	77571
SHADY LOCH LN	0	366E	NWC	77433
SHADY LODGE LN	700	292L	SP	77373
SHADY MANOR DR	5900	407W	NWC	77449
SHADY MAPLE DR	4900	297N	NEH	77339
SHADY MEADOW LN	11700	414J	NCC	77039
SHADY MILL DR	7100	410U	NWC	77040
SHADY MILL DR	7300	410Q	NWC	77040
SHADYMIST CT	3400	488Z	SWH	77082
SHADY MOSS LN	7100	411S	NWH	77040
SHADY NOOK CT	5000	452F	NWH	77018
SHADY NOOK LN	200	616Z	FR	77546
SHADY OAK DR	24900	244Q	WCO	77447
SHADY OAK LN	1	296G	SEM	77365
SHADY OAKS CT	1900	610F	MC	77489
SHADY OAKS DR	15100	247N	SC	77355
SHADY OAKS DR	15400	246R	SC	77355
SHADY OAKS DR	24800	293N	NCC	77373
SHADY OAKS LN	5000	617W	FR	77546
SHADY PALMS DR	7700	407M	NWC	77095
SHADY PARK DR	2800	535L	SEH	77017
SHADY PECAN CT	15300	328N	NWC	77429
SHADY PINE DR	4200	331K	NWC	77388
SHADY POINT	800	332C	NCC	77373
SHADY RANCH CT	17500	324M	NWC	77447
SHADY RIVER	4200	609K	MC	77459
SHADY RIVER DR	5200	491G	SWH	77056
SHADY RIVER DR	5700	491F	SWH	77057
SHADY RIVER DR	10100	489L	SWH	77042
SHADY RIVER RD	700	580Q	LP	77571
SHADY ROCK LN	300	457W	NEC	77015
SHADY RUN DR	2400	336D	NEH	77339
SHADY RUN LN	0	612U	PL	77584
SHADY SANDS PLACE	0	612Q	PL	77584
SHADY SHORE	100	499B	CV	77530
SHADYSIDE CIR	7200	609Q	MC	77459
SHADY SPRING MEADOW DR	0	450J	NWH	77080
SHADY SPRINGS CT	0	612L	PL	77545
SHADY SPRINGS DR	0	612L	PL	77545
SHADY SPRINGS DR	4000	619L	TL	77586
SHADY SPRUCE CT	4800	484Z	NEF	77494
SHADY SPRUCE LN	25700	484Z	NEF	77494
SHADY SQUARE CT	16900	407L	NWC	77095
SHADY STREAM DR	600	332E	NWC	77090
SHADY TERRACE DR	3900	297T	NEH	77345
SHADY TIMBER LN	0	326L	NWC	77429
SHADY TIMBERS DR	6000	454D	NEH	77016
SHADY TRACE DR	0	253S	SEM	77386
SHADY TRAIL LN	1000	372W	NWC	77038
SHADY TREE	0	295M	SEM	77365
SHADY TREE LN	8600	578D	LP	77571
SHADY TREE LN	9600	370Z	NWC	77086
SHADY VALE DR	7300	410Q	NWC	77040
SHADY VALE LN	7100	410U	NWC	77040
SHADY VALLEY DR	22000	485M	SWC	77450
SHADYVIEW	6000	494U	SEH	77011
SHADY VILLA	33000	246V	SWM	77355
SHADY VILLA LN	6700	451X	NWH	77055
SHADY VILLA COVE	7800	451X	NWH	77055
SHADY VILLA FERN	0	451X	NWH	77055
SHADY VILLA GARDEN	0	451X	NWH	77055
SHADY VILLAGE CT	4200	569X	MC	77459
SHADY VILLAGE DR	3500	297U	NEH	77345
SHADY VILLA HAVEN	1500	451X	NWH	77055
SHADY VILLA MANNER	1500	451X	NWH	77055
SHADY VILLA MEADOW	7800	451X	NWH	77055
SHADY VILLA M H P	0	452D	NWH	77091
SHADY VILLA PINE	1300	451X	NWH	77055
SHADY VILLA WALK	7500	451X	NWH	77055
SHADY VISTA CIR	0	455G	NEH	77028
SHADY VISTA CT	0	455G	NEH	77028
SHADY VISTA LN	0	455G	NEH	77028
SHADY WALK LN	0	484Y	NEF	77494
SHADY WILLOW	8000	290E	NWC	77375
SHADYWIND DR	3200	488Z	SWH	77082
SHADYWOOD	5500	609W	NEF	77479
SHADYWOOD DR	500	616V	FR	77546
SHADYWOOD RD	300	491J	SWH	77057
SHADY WOODS LN	0	253T	SEM	77386
SHAFT DR	13300	368K	NWC	77429
SHAFTSBURY DR	12300	569H	SWH	77031
SHAG BARK DR	7200	249D	SWM	77354
SHAGBARK DR	8800	455D	NEH	77078
SHAGWOOD DR	8000	457F	NEC	77049
E. SHAKER CT	1	251X	WD	77380
W. SHAKER LN	1	251X	WD	77380
SHAKESPEARE	2200	532C	SWH	77030
SHAKESPEARE	2700	615P	PL	77581
SHALE DR	0	461S	NEC	77521
SHALE DR	21700	255U	SEM	77365
SHALE CREEK DR	19100	328D	NWC	77375
SHALE GROVE CT	5000	526S	NEF	77407
SHALFORD CT	24900	250W	NWC	77389
SHALFORD DR	24900	250W	NWC	77389
SHALLOW DR	300	336W	HM	77338
SHALLOW BEND LN	0	525M	NEF	77407
SHALLOWBRIAR LN	0	408V	NWC	77041
SHALLOWBROOK	10700	490H	HC	77024
SHALLOW COVE CT	13400	328Q	NWC	77429
SHALLOW CREEK CT	20100	406Q	NWC	77449
SHALLOW CREEK DR	2500	615R	PL	77581
SHALLOW CREEK LN	0	657S	FR	77546
SHALLOW CREEK LN	22100	525C	NEF	77450
SHALLOW FALLS CT	0	612P	PL	77545
SHALLOW FALLS LN	0	612P	PL	77545
SHALLOWFORD PLACE	100	249M	NWH	77375
SHALLOWFORD PLACE	100	249M	NWH	77375
SHALLOW GLEN LN	21600	525G	NEF	77450
SHALLOWLAKE CT	8500	407F	NWC	77095
SHALLOW LAKE LN	17200	407F	NWC	77095
SHALLOW LEAF LN	0	407K	NWC	77433
SHALLOW OAK CT	0	328L	NWC	77377
SHALLOW OAKS DR	0	369N	NWC	77065
SHALLOW PARK LN	0	524C	NEF	77494
SHALLOW POND CT	1	250H	WD	77381
SHALLOW POND PLACE	1	250H	WD	77381
SHALLOW RIDGE BLVD	16700	367Q	NWC	77095
SHALLOW RIVER CT	6800	290Q	NWC	77379
SHALLOW SHAFT LN	19800	526K	NEF	77407
SHALLOW SPRING CT	22600	525B	NEF	77494
SHALLOW SPRING LN	0	659H	LC	77573
SHALLOW SPRINGS CT	2800	613X	NEB	77578
SHALOM CREEK LN	4200	291T	NWC	77388
SHALY CT	2600	486P	SWC	77450
SHALY BREEZE LN	2100	658U	LC	77573
SHALY COVE LN	0	612K	PL	77545
SHAMAN DR	0	528K	SWC	77083
SHAMBALA WAY	0	524D	NEF	77494
SHAMROCK	5400	536N	SEH	77017
SHAMROCK DR	2500	532H	SWH	77030
SHAMROCK LN	1300	538N	DP	77536
SHAMROCK PARK LN	14000	568A	SG	77498
SHANE	400	412H	NEH	77037
SHANE	20300	446K	NWC	77449
SHANE CREEK LN	4600	291T	NWC	77388
SHANEMOSS CT	3500	331S	NWC	77068
SHANGHAI	15400	409R	JV	77040
SHANGO LN	9100	408A	NWC	77095
SHANGRILA LN	7400	407M	NWC	77095
SHANK DR	7000	614H	PL	77581
SHANK RD	4700	615E	PL	77581
SHANLEY LANDING	0	527W	NEF	77469
SHANLEY LANDING CT	0	527W	NEF	77469
SHANLEY TRACE LN	0	527W	NEF	77469
SHANNA LN	4200	577B	PA	77504
SHANNON	0	247V	SWM	77355
W. SHANNON	2200	538P	DP	77536
E. SHANNON	2200	538P	DP	77536
SHANNON	2300	492S	SWH	77027
SHANNON CIR	0	490H	HC	77024
SHANNON CT	0	610Q	MC	77459
SHANNON CT	2900	376F	NEC	77396
SHANNON LN	2800	376G	NEC	77396
SHANNON BEND	3700	502J	BT	77521
SHANNONN CROSSING LN	0	253X	SEM	77386
SHANNONDALE LN	200	332B	NWC	77388
SHANNON FALLS CT	22700	525B	NEF	77494
SHANNON FOREST CT	2700	485P	NEF	77494
SHANNON GLEN LN	18700	447J	NWC	77084
SHANNON HILLS DR	10700	529P	SWH	77099
SHANNON HILLS DR	12300	528R	SWH	77099
SHANNON LAKE CT	0	377H	NEH	77346
SHANNON MARIE LN	14000	488K	SWH	77077
SHANNON MILLS LN	0	575V	SEH	77075
SHANNON RIDGE RD	14300	618A	SEH	77062
SHANNON VALLEY DR	1200	488M	SWH	77077
SHANNONWOOD CT	0	484Z	NEF	77494
SHAPIRO CT	0	609K	MC	77459
SHAPIRO SPRINGS LN	15200	408B	NWC	77095
SHARIE	900	538L	DP	77536
SHARK CT	1900	418D	NEC	77532
SHARMAN RD	4500	453U	NEH	77009
SHARMON RD	10600	372T	NWH	77038
SHARNOLL CIR	200	659D	LC	77573
SHARON	2000	536T	PA	77502
SHARON	4200	494F	NEH	77020
SHARON	22500	296C	SEM	77357
SHARON CT	0	289V	NWC	77379
SHARON DR	500	335Z	HM	77338
SHARON DR	5600	614F	PL	77581
SHARON LN	300	461X	BT	77521
SHARONDALE	0	614Y	PL	77584
SHARONDALE DR	7700	534W	SEH	77033
SHARONDALE DR	8600	574A	SEH	77033
SHARONDOAH DR	400	460N	HG	77562
SHARON LOUISE	28400	246G	SWM	77355
SHARON PKWY	20800	289V	NWC	77379
SHARP	0	404B	NWC	77447
SHARP	0	364W	NWC	77447
SHARP	0	363Y	NWC	77447
SHARPBILL DR	13200	528K	SWH	77083
SHARPCREST LN	6700	530M	SWH	77074
SHARPCREST LN	7900	530K	SWH	77036
SHARPCREST LN	11200	529J	SWH	77072
SHARP PLACE	1800	492Q	SWH	77019
SHARPSTONE CREEK LN	0	407V	NWC	77084
SHARPSTOWN DR	0	530M	SWH	77074
SHARPSTOWN GREEN CIR	6600	530F	SWH	77036
SHARPTON DR	10000	412B	NWC	77038
SHARPVALE DR	3000	291Z	NWC	77388
SHARPVIEW	0	529K	SWH	77072
SHARPVIEW DR	6300	531J	SWH	77074
SHARPVIEW DR	7900	530J	SWH	77036
SHARPVIEW DR	10600	529J	SWH	77072
SHARPVIEW DR	12500	528M	SWH	77072
SHARTLE CIR	600	491E	HC	77024
SHASTA	2000	620W	LC	77565
SHASTA CT	3500	614Z	PL	77584
SHASTA DR	100	491E	HC	77024
SHASTA DR	2000	619Z	LC	77565
S. SHASTA BEND CIR	0	250P	NWC	77389
N. SHASTA BEND CIR	0	250P	NWC	77389
SHASTA BEND CIR	0	250P	NWC	77389
SHASTA LEAF CT	13800	377Y	NEC	77044
SHASTA SPRINGS DR	9000	576L	SEH	77034
SHASTA SQUARE	7000	408P	NWC	77084
SHATNER DR	4500	371A	NWC	77066
SHATNERWOOD DR	17400	407K	NWC	77095
SHATTUCK	0	292P	NWC	77388
SHAUN DR	4300	577B	PA	77504
SHAUNA LN	0	293K	SEM	77386
SHAUNTEL	2700	616T	PL	77581
SHAVANO CT	0	407J	NWC	77433
SHAVANO CT	0	407J	NWC	77433
SHAVANO LN	0	407J	NWC	77433
SHAVANO LN	0	407J	NWC	77433
SHAVELSON	6800	491B	NWH	77055
N. SHAVER	100	536G	PA	77506
SHAVER	100	536L	PA	77506
SHAVER	1300	536Q	PA	77502
SHAVER	3400	576D	SH	77587
SHAVER	3401	576D	PA	77504
S. SHAVER	4900	576H	SEH	77034
SHAVON CT	20100	291Z	NWC	77388
SHAVON SPRINGS DR	19900	291Z	NWC	77388
W. SHAW	100	536G	PA	77506
SHAW	1200	493Q	SWH	77002
SHAW RD	17000	328J	NWC	77429
SHAWBURG LN	6600	415A	NEC	77396
SHAWNA DR	4400	447D	NWC	77084
SHAWNA LYN DR	2500	333A	NCC	77373
SHAWNBROOK DR	10700	530Y	SWH	77071
SHAWNEE	500	576E	SEH	77034
SHAWNEE	4200	461S	NEC	77521
W. SHAWNEE	17200	503F	CCO	77520
E. SHAWNEE	17200	503F	CCO	77520
SHAWNEE FOREST DR	0	406F	NWC	77433
SHAWNEE PARK DR	21300	525Z	NEF	77406
S. SHAWNEE RIDGE CIR	1	250A	WD	77382
N. SHAWNEE RIDGE CIR	100	250A	WD	77382
SHAWNEE RIDGE CT	1	250A	WD	77382
SHAWNEE RIDGE DR	1	250A	WD	77382
SHAWNWAY LN	19400	486H	SWC	77094
SHAWOOD LN	0	615H	PL	77089
SHAW PERRY LN	24000	445S	NWC	77493
SHAW SPRINGS DR	0	295R	SEM	77365
SHAWWOOD CT	12400	369M	NWC	77070
SHAY LN	18700	336Z	NEC	77346
SHAYNA CT	2500	291R	NWC	77388
SHEA	1000	493M	NEH	77002
SHEALY	500	617R	SEH	77598
SHEALY CT	15300	617R	SEH	77598
SHEA PLACE	1	493H	NEH	77002
SHEARER LN	100	501M	BT	77521
SHEARLING CT	0	250R	NWC	77389
SHEARN	1100	493G	SWH	77007
SHEARWATER CT	0	658T	LC	77573
S. SHEARWATER LN	0	245R	SWM	77355
N. SHEARWATER LN	0	245R	SWM	77355
SHEARWATER BEND DR	2500	376F	NEC	77396
SHEEPHORN CT	0	249A	SWM	77354
SHEEP MEADOW PLACE	1	250D	WD	77381
SHEER WATER DR	13200	528C	SWH	77082
SHEET BEND WAY	16700	617X	SEC	77546
SHEFFIELD	1100	531C	BL	77401
SHEFFIELD	28100	243C	WCO	77484
SHEFFIELD BLVD	900	496M	NEH	77015
SHEFFIELD CT	0	568W	SG	77479
SHEFFIELD CT	4600	577E	PA	77504
SHEFFIELD DR	1200	569X	MC	77459
SHEFFIELD DR	25100	257L	SEM	77357
SHEFFIELD LN	6100	657U	LC	77573
SHEFFIELD BEND CT	7400	407L	NWC	77095
SHEFFIELD BEND DR	17200	407L	NWC	77095
SHEFFIELD ESTATES DR	17100	407Q	NWC	77095
SHEFFIELD FOREST LN	0	332R	NCC	77073
SHEFFIELD GRAY TRAIL	21800	325R	NWC	77433
SHEFFIELD GRAY TRAIL	22000	325R	NWC	77433
SHEFFIELD KNOLL LN	17100	407L	NWC	77095
SHEFFIELDPARK DR	0	325H	NWC	77377
SHEFFIELD PINES LN	17100	407L	NWC	77095
SHEFFIELD TERRACE	14800	497D	NEC	77530
SHEFFIELD TERRACE	15100	498A	NEC	77530
SHEFIELD OAKS DR	0	407Q	NWC	77095
SHEIFELD RUN	0	447D	NWC	77084
SHEKEL LN	200	457X	NEC	77015
SHELBOURNE BAY DR	0	612K	PL	77545
SHELBOURNE CROSSING	21800	332R	NCC	77073
SHELBOURNE PARK LN	6000	407V	NWC	77084
SHELBURNE CIR	7700	330K	NWC	77379
SHELBURNE LN	17500	330K	NWC	77379
SHELBURNE RD	0	375J	NEH	77396
SHELBURNE RD	5800	374M	NEH	77396
SHELBURNE RD	13100	457J	NEC	77049
SHELBY	1000	453Z	NEH	77009
SHELBY CIR	3000	533T	SEH	77051
SHELBY CT	16400	330S	NWC	77379
SHELBY DR	2400	613U	NEB	77584
SHELBY COVE CT	5900	525R	NEF	77407
SHELBY MEADOW LN	0	525M	NEF	77407
SHELBY MEADOW LN	0	526J	NEF	77407
SHELBY OAKS CIR	17700	527E	NEF	77407
SHELBY OAKS DR	6700	527E	NEF	77407
SHELBY PARK DR	2200	486P	SWC	77450
SHELBY PARK LN	19500	373A	NCC	77073
SHELBY RIDGE LN	0	373A	NCC	77073
SHELBY ROW	4000	609A	SG	77479
SHELBY SPRINGS DR	0	612L	PL	77545
SHELBY VIEW LN	0	373A	NCC	77073
SHELBYVILLE DR	21000	525R	NEF	77407
SHELDON	2000	453S	NWH	77008
SHELDON DR	3400	613L	NEB	77584
S. SHELDON RD	100	498K	CV	77530
SHELDON RD	100	498B	CV	77530
SHELDON RD	6300	458F	NEC	77049
SHELDON RD	10500	418T	NEC	77044
SHELDON BEND DR	11100	524L	NWF	77406
SHELDONHAM DR	4800	334M	NCC	77338
SHELDONHAM DR	4900	334J	NCC	77338
SHELDON MARINA	0	418Q	NEC	77044
SHELDON OAKS LN	0	498A	NEC	77530
SHELDON PINES	0	330M	NWC	77379
SHELDON RANCH LN	0	498A	NEC	77530
SHELDON RIDGE WAY	0	418T	NCC	77044
SHELDON SPRINGS DR	0	366V	NWC	77433
SHELDON VILLAS LN	0	498A	NEC	77530
SHELDON WATER LN	0	498A	NEC	77530
SHELDONWOOD CT	0	524H	NWC	77449
SHELDRAKE CT	400	568T	SG	77478
SHELDRICK DR	0	377K	NEC	77346
SHELFORD CT	21100	406T	NWC	77449
SHELIA	2400	615K	PL	77581
SHELIA LN	800	498C	CV	77530
SHELL	22300	256Y	SEM	77357
SHELLBOURNE MEADOWS DR	0	407C	NWC	77095
SHELLBROOK DR	24200	338M	NEH	77336
SHELL CO RD	0	538A	DP	77503
SHELL CREEK CT	10800	409F	NWC	77064
SHELL DOCK RD	0	502L	BT	77521
SHELLDRAKE	0	501E	BT	77521
SHELLDRAKE WAY	3100	500H	BT	77521
SHELLEY	300	453X	NWH	77009
SHELLHORN CT	13200	371C	NWC	77014
SHELL ISLAND CT	3300	613V	PL	77584
SHELL LAKE DR	16300	618P	SEH	77062
SHELLMARK DR	0	376R	NEC	77346
SHELL OIL	0	538C	DP	77536
SHELL OIL CO	0	498X	DP	77536
SHELL PORT SQUARE	0	251L	WD	77380
SHELL ROCK RD	9700	579B	LP	77571
SHELLVILLE CT	8500	410F	NWC	77040
SHELMER DR	8700	450V	NWH	77080
SHELTERING OAKS LN	1400	338E	NEH	77345
SHELTERWOOD DR	800	492C	NWH	77008
SHELTON CT	11100	529X	SWH	77099
SHELTON LN	900	498A	NEC	77530
SHELTON RD	4300	414U	NEC	77093
SHELTON RD	5200	574X	BK	77581
SHELTON GROVE DR	0	369G	NWC	77077
SHELTONS BEND CT	1500	488K	SWH	77077
SHELTON SHADOWS CT	7800	337R	NEC	77346
SHELWICK DR	12200	570A	SWH	77031
SHENANDOAH	2900	533F	SEH	77021
SHENANDOAH DR	100	251D	SD	77381
SHENANDOAH DR	2400	536X	PA	77502
S. SHEPHERD	1000	541D	BT	77520
N. SHEPHERD	1000	501Z	BT	77520
N. SHEPHERD DR	100	492D	NWH	77007
SHEPHERD DR	100	492H	SWH	77007
S. SHEPHERD DR	600	492U	SWH	77019
N. SHEPHERD DR	800	452M	NWH	77008
S. SHEPHERD DR	2600	492U	SWH	77098
N. SHEPHERD DR	3000	452M	NWH	77018
N. SHEPHERD DR	5200	452M	NWH	77091
S. SHEPHERD DR	5300	532D	SWH	77005
N. SHEPHERD DR	6300	412Y	NWH	77091
N. SHEPHERD DR	7500	412Y	NWH	77088
SHEPHERD FALLS LN	0	575V	SEH	77075
SHEPHERD OAKS DR	0	452Q	NWH	77018
SHEPHERDS RIDGE DR	12000	488M	SWH	77077
SHEPHERDS VALLY LN	0	366V	NWC	77433
SHEPHERDS WAY	0	371J	NWC	77066
SHEPPARD	31800	248S	SWM	77362
SHEPPARD RD	5200	501F	NEC	77521
SHEPPERTON CT	9700	409A	NWC	77065
SHERATON	14600	373Z	NCC	77039
SHERATON CROSSING DR	0	250U	NWC	77389
SHERATON OAKS DR	5400	411Y	NWH	77091
SHERBORNE	3000	613F	NEB	77584
SHERBORNE CASTLE CT	0	248Z	NWC	77375
SHERBOURNE	8900	454H	NEH	77016
SHERBOURNE	9200	455E	NEH	77016
SHERBROOKE CT	300	537H	PA	77503
SHERBROOKE RD	1100	491P	SWH	77056
SHERBROOKE RD	3800	537H	PA	77503
SHERBROOKE CANYON LN	0	573T	SEC	77047
SHERBROOK PARK LN	2000	446S	NWC	77449
SHERBURN DR	13700	367D	NWC	77429
SHERBURNE DR	10600	529C	SWH	77072
SHERBURN MANOR DR	14000	367D	NWC	77429
SHEREE	7900	457F	NEC	77049
SHERFIELD RIDGE DR	1000	486F	SWC	77450
SHERI LN	1600	502J	BT	77521
SHERIDAN	2000	532G	SWH	77030
SHERIDAN DR	1500	502W	BT	77520
SHERIDAN RD	1500	537N	PA	77502
SHERIDAN RD	11200	415L	NEC	77016
SHERIDAN RD	11700	415L	NEC	77050
SHERIDAN RD	13800	415C	NEC	77396
SHERIDAN HEIGHTS LN	0	295R	SEM	77365
SHERI HOLLOW LN	13800	488X	SWH	77082
SHERILYNN DR	5200	334E	NCC	77373
SHERINA OAKS	0	408A	NWC	77095
SHERINA PARK DR	8800	408A	NWC	77095
SHERINGHAM	5700	571P	SWH	77085
SHERIOAKS LN	22800	291E	NWC	77389
SHERL	1500	659K	LC	77573
SHERLOCK ACRES	12800	328L	NWC	77377
SHERMAN	100	537G	PA	77503
SHERMAN	400	576A	SH	77587
SHERMAN	2900	494N	SEH	77003
SHERMAN	4400	494U	SEH	77011
SHERMAN	7500	495W	SEH	77012
SHERMAN	1600	535Z	SH	77587
SHERMAN OAK	0	571K	SWH	77085
SHERMAN RIDGE LN	7100	527J	NEF	77083
SHERMONS POND	13100	448D	NWH	77041
SHEROLOCK RD	0	375P	NWH	77396
SHERRI LN	3900	380L	NEC	77532
SHERRILL DR	11900	616D	SEH	77089
SHERROD LN	22000	291J	NWC	77389
SHERROUSE LN	22200	296K	SEM	77365
SHERRY LN	11000	409Y	NWC	77041
SHERRY'S LANDING BLVD	0	616K	SEC	77089
SHERRYLEE LN	5300	334A	NCC	77373
SHERRY MIST LN	0	446E	NWC	77449
SHERRYWOOD DR	8600	456D	NEC	77044
SHERWAY DR	7600	415P	NEC	77016
SHERWELL	0	336P	NEH	77338
SHERWICK	2800	454E	NEH	77093
SHERWICK RIDGE	9500	329D	NWC	77379
SHERWIN	1900	492B	NWH	77007
SHERWIN	6500	412X	NWH	77091
SHERWOOD	1300	502W	BT	77520
W. SHERWOOD	2700	296V	NEC	77339
E. SHERWOOD	4000	297S	NEH	77339
SHERWOOD CIR	600	381G	LCO	77535

Street Name	Block	Pg/Sq	Loc	Zips
SHERWOOD CT	0	251D	SD	77381
SHERWOOD CT	0	251D	SD	77381
SHERWOOD CT	600	381G	LCO	77535
SHERWOOD DR	0	615P	PL	77581
SHERWOOD DR	700	536V	PA	77502
SHERWOOD DR	5300	444U	KT	77493
SHERWOOD DR	6100	533Q	SEH	77021
SHERWOOD DR	13500	568F	SG	77498
SHERWOOD LN	0	452N	NWH	77092
SHERWOOD LN	3600	451R	NWH	77092
SHERWOOD BEND DR	3100	331P	NWC	77068
SHERWOOD FOREST	1000	449T	NWH	77043
SHERWOOD FOREST	1000	489B	NWH	77043
SHERWOOD FOREST CIR	1800	659F	LC	77573
SHERWOOD FOREST GLEN CT	0	449X	SWH	77079
SHERWOOD FOREST GLEN DR	0	449X	SWH	77079
SHERWOOD GARDEN DR	0	489B	NWH	77043
SHERWOOD GLEN DR	600	381G	LCO	77535
SHERWOOD GREEN CT	4400	569T	MC	77459
SHERWOOD GREENS	24700	244R	WCO	77447
SHERWOOD GROVE	0	489B	SWH	77079
SHERWOOD HOLLOW LN	2200	296V	NEH	77339
SHERWOOD HOLLOW LN	2700	297S	NEH	77339
SHERWOOD MILLS LN	0	449X	NWH	77043
SHERWOOD OAK LN	0	449X	NWH	77043
SHERWOOD OAKS DR	13000	457W	NEC	77015
SHERWOOD PARK CIR	0	449X	NWH	77043
SHERWOOD PARK LN	1400	449X	NWC	77043
SHERWOOD PASS CT	0	449X	NWH	77043
SHERWOOD PASS LN	0	290S	NWC	77379
SHERWOOD POINT LN	0	449X	NWH	77043
SHERWOOD RIDGE DR	0	449X	NWH	77043
SHERWOOD RUN	0	489B	SWH	77079
SHERWOOD SPRINGS LN	0	449X	NWH	77043
SHERWOOD TRAILS	0	489B	SWH	77079
SHERYL	1300	496K	JC	77029
SHERYL CIR	0	376N	NEC	77396
SHERYL CIR	1900	376J	NEC	77396
SHERYL CT	0	376J	NEC	77396
SHERYL CT	9800	289U	NWC	77379
SHETLAND LN	800	444X	KT	77493
SHETLAND LN	4500	491V	SWH	77027
SHETLAND OAKS CT	1800	252R	SEM	77385
SHETLAND OAKS DR	31100	252R	SEM	77385
SHETSTONE CIR	12300	367J	NWC	77433
SHEVCHENKO LN	200	413J	NCC	77037
SHIBE PARK CT	22500	291K	NWC	77389
SHIELD	9800	535H	SEH	77017
SHIELD CREST LN	0	296X	SEM	77339
SHIELDHALL LN	0	289Q	NWC	77375
SHIELDS	700	459W	CV	77530
SHIELDS RD	0	247T	SWM	77355
SHIFTING SAND LN	0	526J	NEF	77407
SHILLINGTON CT	20600	486F	SWC	77450
SHILLINGTON DR	800	486F	SWC	77450
SHILLINGTON DR	19800	486G	SWC	77094
SHILO DR	5000	374Y	NCC	77032
SHILOH	2600	494J	NEH	77020
SHILOH CT	3300	610U	MC	77459
SHILOH DR	2900	610U	MC	77459
SHILOH ARBOR DR	0	288S	NWC	77377
SHILOH BEND CT	0	250P	NWC	77389
SHILOH CHURCH RD	12000	370G	NWC	77066
SHILOH CLIFF LN	0	484S	NEF	77494
SHILOH CREEK CT	19400	406V	NWC	77449
SHILOH CREEK LN	19300	406V	NWC	77449
SHILOH MIST LN	0	406X	NWC	77449
SHILOH PARK CT	3800	617X	SEC	77546
SHILOH VALLEY LN	0	377E	NEC	77346
S. SHIMMERING ASPEN DR	0	250Q	NWC	77389
N. SHIMMERING ASPEN DR	0	250Q	NWC	77389
SHIMMERING ASPEN DR	0	250P	NWC	77389
SHIMMERING GREEN TRAIL	0	325L	NWC	77433
SHIMMERING LAKE DR	0	325M	NWC	77433
SHIMMERING MAPLE DR	9500	410A	NWC	77064
SHIMMERING PINES RD	7800	330A	NWC	77379
SHINDLER CIR	8600	409G	NWC	77064
SHINER LN	7300	529J	SWH	77072
SHINGLE OAK	4300	411U	NWH	77088
SHINGLE OAK LN	14700	288A	NWC	77377
SHINING BROOK CT	0	417B	NEC	77044
SHINING LEAF CT	0	407W	NWC	77449
SHINING ROCK LN	0	484X	NEF	77494
SHINING ROCK LN	16200	407H	NWC	77095
SHINING SUMAC AVE	6700	408P	NWC	77084
SHINNECOCK HILLS DR	6500	370B	NWC	77069
SHINNING CREEK CT	5000	485W	NEF	77494
SHINNING CREEK LN	28300	293E	SEM	77386
SHINNING ROCK LN	0	484X	NEF	77494
SHIN OAK DR	24000	338R	NEH	77336
SHINWOOD DR	19500	337S	NEC	77346
SHIP ANCHOR DR	16800	657B	SEC	77546
SHIPMAN LN	3600	331G	NWC	77388
SHIPPING BLVD	0	579R	SEC	77507
SHIPROCK DR	0	539N	DP	77536
SHIPYARD	0	497X	SEC	77503
SHIPYARD RD	0	537B	PA	77506
SHIRE	18800	258G	SEM	77357
SHIRE HORSE	0	255T	SEM	77365
SHIREBROOK DR	13700	568F	SG	77498
SHIREFIELD CT	800	292G	NCC	77373
SHIREFIELD LN	900	292C	NCC	77373
SHIRE GLEN LN	0	527S	NEF	77469
SHIRE GLEN PLACE	0	249A	SWM	77354
SHIREMEADOW DR	700	570Y	MC	77489
SHIRE MILLS CT	0	368C	NWC	77429
SHIREMIST CT	0	524D	NEF	77494
SHIREOAK DR	18000	447F	NWC	77084
SHIRE RIDGE LN	0	334R	NCC	77338
SHIRE TRAIL CT	0	334R	NCC	77338
SHIREVALLEY DR	3800	569Y	MC	77459
SHIRE WOOD LN	2900	489W	SWH	77082
SHIRKMERE RD	800	492B	NWH	77008
SHIRKMERE RD	1100	452X	NWH	77008
W. SHIRLEEN DR	0	619L	PA	77586
S. SHIRLEEN DR	0	619L	PA	77586
N. SHIRLEEN DR	0	619L	PA	77586
E. SHIRLEEN DR	0	619L	PA	77586
SHIRLEEN DR	0	570T	MC	77489
SHIRLEEN DR	100	619L	PA	77586
SHIRLEY	2100	539V	LP	77571
SHIRLEY	5100	500H	BT	77521
SHIRLEY CT	0	246C	SWM	77355
SHIRLEY LN	1400	496L	NEH	77015
SHIRLEY LN	5500	374R	NEH	77032
SHIRLEY LN	5800	375N	NEH	77396
SHIRLEY MAE LN	5900	452A	NWH	77091
SHIRLEY MEADOW	0	246C	SWM	77355
SHIRO DR	3300	371C	NWC	77014
SHIVE DR	9700	456A	NEH	77078
SHIVELEY CIR	2000	373V	NCC	77032
SHOAL	16100	419B	NEC	77532

Street Name	Block	Pg/Sq	Loc	Zips
SHOAL CIR	0	502K	BT	77521
SHOAL CT	700	419B	NEC	77532
SHOAL CREEK CT	11500	612R	PL	77584
SHOAL CREEK DR	2400	619Y	LC	77573
SHOAL CREEK DR	8500	370N	NWC	77064
SHOAL CREEK DR	9100	369R	NWC	77064
SHOAL CREEK DR	11300	612R	PL	77584
SHOAL HAVEN CT	0	290Z	NWC	77379
SHOAL HOLLOW CT	0	366V	NWC	77433
SHOAL LAKE CT	2100	658T	LC	77573
SHOAL LAKE CT	3300	613V	PL	77584
SHOAL LAKE LN	17400	407F	NWC	77095
SHOAL LANDING	11600	612H	PL	77584
SHOAL PARK DR	16800	327U	NWC	77429
SHOAL POINT LN	0	328K	NWC	77377
SHOAL POINTE CT	800	660E	LC	77573
SHOAL POINTE LN	800	660E	LC	77573
SHOAL RIDGE CT	21600	445H	NWC	77449
SHOAL SPRINGS LN	0	366V	NWC	77433
SHOALWATER LN	0	612P	PL	77545
SHOALWATER LN	0	658T	LC	77573
SHOALWATER LN	15700	329U	NWC	77070
SHOALWOOD FALLS DR	0	367U	NWC	77095
SHOEMAKER RD	0	571F	SWH	77085
SHOEMO HILL	0	571R	SWH	77045
SHOOTING CENTER DR	0	487X	SWH	77094
SHOOTING STAR	0	657P	FR	77546
SHOOTING STAR	1200	657S	FR	77546
SHOPPE RD	8800	576M	SEH	77504
N. SHORE DR	100	620T	CS	77565
E. SHORE DR	100	620X	CS	77565
W. SHORE DR	200	620S	CS	77565
S. SHORE DR	1000	620T	CS	77565
E. SHOREACRES BLVD	0	580P	SA	77571
SHOREACRES BLVD	100	580P	SA	77571
SHOREACRES CIR	1	580R	SA	77571
SHORE BAY CT	1400	619D	PA	77586
SHORE BEND CT	0	290K	NWC	77379
SHORE BREEZE DR	0	612F	PL	77545
SHORE BREEZE LN	0	658T	LC	77573
SHORE BREEZE LN	300	619X	LC	77573
SHORE BRIDGE RD	0	366K	NWC	77433
SHORE BROOK CIR	3100	660A	LC	77573
SHORE BROOK CT	3100	660A	LC	77573
SHOREBROOK DR	0	612K	PL	77545
SHOREBROOK DR	14700	408G	NWC	77095
SHORE CASTLE CT	20600	486P	SWC	77450
SHORE CLIFF LN	7400	250X	NWC	77389
SHORE CREEK CT	2200	612M	PL	77584
SHORE CREEK DR	11900	612M	PL	77584
SHORECREST DR	16600	367Q	NWC	77095
SHOREGROVE DR	8200	337R	NEC	77346
SHOREHAM	9100	454A	NEH	77093
SHOREHAVEN CIR	5000	573M	SEH	77048
SHORE HILLS DR	1	337C	NEH	77345
SHORE JUNIPER DR	0	575R	SEH	77075
SHORELAKE DR	1	336D	NEH	77339
SHORELAND CT	18900	328F	NWC	77377
SHORELANDS RD	0	366F	NWC	77433
SHORE LINE CT	3400	620E	SB	77586
SHORELINE DR	1200	568U	SG	77478
SHORE LINE DR	1600	619D	TL	77586
SHORELINE DR	1700	569X	MC	77459
SHORELINE DR	1800	609B	MC	77459
SHORELINE DR	18300	378S	NEC	77532
SHORELINE DR	25100	244R	WCO	77447
SHORELINE POINT DR	1	251F	WD	77381
SHORELINE TERRACE DR	15800	377P	NEC	77044
SHORE MEADOW DR	3100	660A	LC	77573
SHORE MEADOWS LN	0	526J	NEF	77407
SHORE PARK DR	0	366F	NWC	77433
SHORE POINTE DR	1900	619Z	LC	77573
SHORE POINTE DR	11900	612M	PL	77584
SHORES EDGE DR	19700	289W	NWC	77375
SHORE SHADOWS DR	600	338C	NEH	77336
SHORE SHADOWS DR	3400	378N	NEC	77532
SHORESIDE DR	2900	613T	NEB	77584
SHORESIDE DR	3000	378T	NEC	77532
SHOREVIEW CIR	19500	338T	NEC	77346
SHOREVIEW CT	6300	337P	NEC	77346
SHOREVIEW CT	6800	609Q	MC	77459
SHOREVIEW LN	3500	609Q	MC	77459
SHOREVIEW LN	8900	338T	NEC	77346
SHOREWICK DR	2400	459J	NEC	77562
SHOREWOOD DR	600	619H	TL	77586
SHOREWOOD LAKES DR	0	407D	NWC	77095
W. SHOREWOOD LOOP	22400	338V	NEH	77336
E. SHOREWOOD LOOP	22400	338V	NEH	77336
SHORT	0	459E	NEC	77562
SHORT	0	500N	BT	77520
SHORT	2300	460X	MN	77521
SHORT	4100	533M	SEH	77021
SHORT CT	12200	367M	CY	77429
SHORT BRIDGE	11000	576W	SEH	77075
SHORT BROOK LN	13600	408L	NWC	77041
SHORT COUNTRY	1	257K	SEM	77357
SHORTFIN MAKO CT	0	445R	NWC	77449
SHORTGRASSPATH	0	526N	NEF	77407
SHORTHORN CIR	11000	409Y	NWC	77041
SHORTHORN LN	0	409Y	NWC	77041
SHORT LEAF DR	1	298H	NEC	77336
SHORT LEAF RD	0	297U	NEH	77345
SHORT LEAF PINE CT	34300	247G	SWM	77362
SHORTLEAF PINE DR	0	289C	NWC	77375
SHORTLEAF RIDGE DR	0	524A	NEF	77494
SHORT PATH CT	2100	293S	NCC	77373
SHORT PINES DR	0	292Q	SP	77373
SHORT POINT	2000	451S	NWH	77055
SHORT POLK	200	493L	SWH	77002
SHORT SPRINGS CT	0	612L	PL	77584
SHORT SPRINGS DR	0	612L	PL	77584
SHORT T	0	490K	BH	77024
SHORT TRAIL LN	11700	328C	NWC	77377
SHOSHONE DR	7200	461S	NEC	77521
SHOSHONE RD	11500	451P	NWH	77055
SHOSHONI	7100	462Y	BT	77521
SHOSHONI DR	0	577F	PA	77504
SHOSHONI DR	1800	538L	DP	77536
SHOTTERY DR	14800	457V	NEC	77015
SHOTTY	0	540K	SEC	77571
SHOTWELL	100	494G	NEH	77020
SHOTWELL	6000	454L	NEH	77028
SHOTWELL	7600	454L	NEH	77016
SHOTWELL	11200	414Q	NEC	77093
SHOTWELL CT	2800	610U	MC	77459
SHREVEPORT BLVD	4600	455A	NEH	77028
SHREVEPORT BLVD	4700	454Q	NEH	77028
SHREWSBURY CIR	16200	330R	NWC	77379
SHRINER CT	3100	613R	PL	77584
SHRIVER LN	32600	322B	WCO	77484
SHRUB OAK DR	1300	659N	LC	77573
SHRUB OAK DR	16500	376L	NEC	77396

Street Name	Block	Pg/Sq	Loc	Zips
SHUMARD CT	3400	291Y	NWC	77388
SHUMARD OAK CT	0	369S	NWC	77070
SHUMARD OAK DR	0	249V	NWC	77375
SHUMARING DR	0	335T	NCC	77338
SHURLIN PLACE	13500	368A	NWC	77429
SHURMARD DR	5800	451A	NWH	77092
SIAMESE LN	11200	568D	SG	77478
SIANDRA CREEK CT	4500	294J	SEM	77386
SIANDRA CREEK LN	27300	294N	SEM	77386
SIANO PINES DR	0	376E	HM	77396
SIBELIUS LN	100	489L	SWH	77079
SIBERIA BAY CIR	0	328A	NWC	77377
SIBERIAN ELM LN	0	333F	NCC	77073
SIBLEY	1800	534C	SEH	77023
SICA DEER DR	0	293T	NCC	77373
SICA HOLLOW LN	2600	485N	NEF	77494
SICARD CT	0	576K	SEH	77034
SICILY		524M	NEF	77406
SICKLEPOD DR	2600	446U	NWC	77084
SIDE SADDLE WAY	28000	246J	SWM	77355
SIDNEY	1	494T	SEH	77003
N. SIDNEY	100	494P	SEH	77003
SIDNEY	700	494W	SEH	77023
SIDNEY	5800	533M	SEH	77021
SIDONIE DR	0	611H	SWH	77053
SIDONIE ROSE LN	0	524D	NEF	77494
SIEBER DR	1900	536S	SEH	77017
SIEBINTHALER LN	3401	447K	NWC	77084
SIEDEL CEMETERY RD	17800	287N	NWC	77377
SIEGEL	4100	453Y	NEH	77009
SIEGEN TRAIL	0	285P	NWC	77447
SIENA CT	1400	616K	PL	77581
SIENA DR	2100	616K	PL	77581
SIENA SPRINGS BLVD		610X	MC	77459
SIENA VISTA DR	7100	527L	NEF	77083
SIENNA ARBOR LN	6100	409W	NWC	77041
SIENNA BAY CT	5900	409W	NWC	77041
SIENNA BLUFF DR	0	326K	NWC	77433
SIENNA CHRISTUS	0	610W	MC	77459
W. SIENNA COVE LN	8400	527N	NEF	77083
E. SIENNA COVE LN	8401	527N	NEF	77083
S. SIENNA COVE LN	17400	527N	NEF	77083
N. SIENNA COVE LN	17400	527N	NEF	77083
SIENNA FALLS DR	17200	367P	NWC	77095
SIENNA HEIGHTS CT	4500	577G	PA	77505
SIENNA HEIGHTS LN	4700	577G	PA	77505
SIENNA HILL LN	1100	488K	SWH	77077
SIENNAIVY CROSSING	0	526N	NEF	77407
SIENNA LEAF TRAIL	15300	325R	NWC	77433
SIENNA OAK DR	15300	325R	NWC	77433
SIENNA PARK DR	0	527N	NEF	77083
SIENNA PEAK LN	15300	326U	NWC	77429
SIENNA PINES CT	20300	290V	NWC	77379
SIENNA PKWY	3700	610W	MC	77459
SIENNA RANCH RD	0	609Z	MC	77459
SIENNA RANCH RD	0	609Z	MC	77459
SIENNA ROSA LN	12200	409W	NWC	77041
SIENNA SHADOW LN	0	406F	NWC	77433
SIENNA SKY CT	9000	526Q	NEF	77407
SIENNA SPRINGS BLVD	0	609Z	MC	77459
SIENNA SPRINGS DR	2700	612R	PL	77584
SIENNA SPRINGS WAY	0	610W	NEF	77459
SIENNA TERRACE LN	24900	485N	NEF	77494
SIENNA TRACE	8100	528K	SWC	77083
SIENNA TRAILS DR	12700	328L	NWC	77377
SIERRA	2000	619V	LC	77565
SIERRA DR	1500	502J	BT	77521
SIERRA DR	9300	573B	SEH	77051
SIERRA DR	15700	409M	JV	77040
SIERRA LN	0	336Z	NEC	77346
SIERRA BEND DR	0	525M	NEF	77407
SIERRA BLANCA DR	6200	528E	SWC	77083
SIERRA BREEZE	600	487A	SWC	77094
SIERRA BRIDGE LN	0	657S	FR	77546
SIERRA BROOK LN	800	660E	LC	77573
SIERRA BROOK LN	5800	409W	NWC	77041
SIERRA COVE LN	0	293G	SEM	77386
SIERRA CREEK LN	0	377E	NEC	77346
SIERRA CREST DR	0	450U	NWH	77080
SIERRA DAWN DR	8200	290N	NWC	77375
SIERRA FALLS CT	0	328L	NWC	77377
SIERRA GRACE LN	0	616L	SEC	77089
SIERRA GRANDE CT	7400	527K	NEF	77083
SIERRA GRANDE DR	15800	527K	NEF	77083
SIERRA HILL CT	8300	527N	NEF	77083
SIERRA LAKE CT	22400	525C	NEF	77494
SIERRA LAKE DR	800	485G	SWC	77450
SIERRA LONG DR	21600	525M	NEF	77407
SIERRA MADRE DR	0	657T	FR	77546
SIERRA MADRE LN	22100	339W	NEC	77532
SIERRA MEADOW DR	0	526P	NEF	77407
SIERRA NIGHT CT	0	525H	NEF	77407
SIERRA NIGHT DR	0	525M	NEF	77407
SIERRA PARK DR	0	257E	SEM	77357
SIERRA PINES CT	15300	331S	NWC	77068
SIERRA PINES DR	3500	331S	NWC	77068
SIERRA RANCH DR	0	457A	NEC	77044
SIERRA RIDGE DR	14900	376V	NEC	77396
SIERRA SHADOWS DR	900	485H	SWC	77450
SIERRA SKIES DR	15500	527G	SWC	77083
SIERRA SPRINGS LN	900	292U	NCC	77373
SIERRA SPRINGS LN	25200	524E	NEF	77494
SIERRA SUNSET DR	14900	376U	NEC	77396
SIERRA TRAILS DR	6900	527H	SWC	77083
SIERRA VALLE DR	15400	527L	NEF	77083
SIERRA VISTA DR	15900	527G	SWC	77083
SIERRA WILLOW WAY	0	484N	NEF	77494
SIERRA WOODS LN	0	485J	NEF	77494
SIESTA LN	1100	496K	JC	77029
SIFTON DR	30800	252V	SEM	77386
SIGHTING PARK DR	0	526X	NEF	77469
SIGMA	1200	577J	PA	77504
SIGMOND COURT DR	0	404E	NWC	77447
SIGN	7700	570Z	SWH	77489
SIGNAL CREEK DR	15800	408J	NWC	77095
SIGNAL HILL CT	0	612G	PL	77584
SIGNAL HILL DR	3000	657C	SEC	77546
SIGNAL HILL DR	3100	617X	SEC	77546
SIGNAL POINT LN	0	370U	NWC	77086
SIGNAL RIDGE WAY	0	328J	NWC	77429
SIGNAT DR	6600	408R	NWC	77041
SIGNATURE COVE	0	619X	LC	77573
SIGNATURE POINT DR	1	619X	LC	77573
SIGNET	7900	495N	NEH	77029
SIKES	300	452M	NWH	77018
SILBER RD	900	491C	SWH	77024
SILBER RD	1000	451Y	NWH	77055
SILBURY CT	20300	486B	SWC	77450
SILENT CEDARS DR	8100	408E	NWC	77095
SILENT CIRCLE DR	0	568J	NEF	77498
SILENT CREEK DR	0	612G	PL	77584
SILENT ELM ST	0	416M	NEC	77044

Street Name	Block	Pg/Sq	Loc	Zips
SILENT FLIGHT DR	0	485E	SWC	77494
SILENT HILLS LN	0	527N	NEF	77407
SILENT JASMIN CT	21800	325V	NWC	77433
SILENT LAKE LN	14200	568E	SG	77498
SILENT MANOR DR	0	568J	NEF	77498
SILENT MEADOW CT	0	249Z	NWC	77375
SILENT OAKS DR	5900	337T	NEC	77346
SILENT RIVER CT	0	525Z	NEF	77406
SILENT RIVER DR	0	525Z	NEF	77406
SILENT SHORE	0	448D	NWC	77041
SILENT SHORE CT	0	658Y	LC	77573
SILENT SHORES LN	0	612Q	PL	77584
SILENT SPRING CT	0	658T	LC	77573
SILENT SPRING CREEK CT	22900	485Q	NEF	77450
SILENT SPRING CREEK DR	2600	485Q	NEF	77450
SILENT SPRUCE CT	19000	446H	NWC	77084
SILENT STAR CT	7700	407K	NWC	77095
SILENT TIMBER LN	0	527J	NEF	77407
SILENT TIMBER PATH	27400	294T	SEM	77386
SILENT TIMBER PATH LN	0	294E	SEM	77386
SILENT VALE LN	0	406X	NWC	77449
SILENT WALK CT	0	612K	PL	77545
SILENT WALK DR	0	612K	PL	77545
SILENT WAY DR	0	568J	NEF	77498
SILENT WOOD LN	7100	411A	NWC	77086
SILENT WOOD LN	7500	410C	NWC	77086
SILHOUETTE CT	26700	444E	NWC	77493
SILHOUETTE DR	4600	444A	NWC	77493
SILHOUETTE BAY DR	0	612P	PL	77545
SILHOUETTE RIDGE DR	0	376T	NWC	77396
SILICON ALLEY	0	490C	HE	77024
SILK CT	4100	293M	SEM	77386
SILKBAY MEADOW DR	5700	524D	NEF	77494
SILKLEAF LN	1600	486H	SWC	77094
SILK OAK CT	20800	446N	NWC	77449
SILK TASSEL LN	1	251M	WD	77380
SILK TREE LN	2700	446N	NWC	77449
SILKWOOD DR	10400	530W	SWH	77031
SILKY LEAF DR	200	372G	NCC	77073
SILKY MORNING CT	0	377S	NEC	77396
SILKY MOSS DR	0	370U	NWC	77086
SILLS DR	5200	444Y	KT	77493
SILO LN	12300	570G	SWH	77071
SILOUETTE COVE LN	3500	617X	SEC	77546
SILSBEE	6600	534T	SEH	77033
SILSBEE DR	4800	614R	PL	77584
SILVAN WIND LN	8300	410J	NWC	77040
SILVASTONE	0	291N	NWC	77388
SILVER	0	570Z	SWH	77489
SILVER	500	493F	SWH	77007
SILVER DR	6100	614L	PL	77581
SILVERADO DR	0	484E	NEF	77494
SILVERADO DR	1300	488L	SWH	77077
SILVERADO TRACE DR	10600	367T	NWC	77095
SILVER ARROW CT	0	250N	NWC	77389
SILVER ASH LN	17800	407K	NWC	77095
SILVER ASH WAY	18000	407K	NWC	77095
SILVER ASPEN CT	3800	578Z	PA	77059
SILVER BANK CT	1900	619W	NB	77058
SILVER BAY CT	8300	408E	NWC	77095
SILVER BAY CT	11300	612M	PL	77584
SILVER BAY DR	2300	613J	PL	77584
SILVER BELL	4600	571H	SWH	77045
SILVER BELL DR	1500	412B	NWC	77038
SILVER BEND DR	0	376H	NEC	77346
SILVERBERRY TRAIL	2900	297K	NEH	77345
SILVER BIRCH DR	21400	333E	NCC	77073
SILVERBIT TRAIL LN	2800	486T	SWC	77450
SILVER BLUEBERRY TRAIL	21800	325R	NWC	77433
SILVERBLUFF CT	0	367N	NWC	77095
SILVER BONNET	2200	451T	NWH	77055
SILVER BOUGH CIR	2700	578W	SEH	77059
SILVER BOW CIR	0	618A	SEH	77059
SILVERBOW CT	20800	486S	SWC	77450
SILVER BRANCH TRAIL	0	408F	NWC	77095
SILVERBRIDGE LN	0	446E	NWC	77449
SILVER BROOK LN	0	484P	NEF	77494
SILVERBROOK LN	0	613T	NEB	77584
SILVERBROOK LN	21800	445H	NWC	77449
SILVER BRUSH DR	2300	568B	NEF	77498
SILVER CANYON CT	11900	371L	NWC	77067
SILVER CANYON LN	11900	371L	NWC	77067
SILVER CANYON PLACE	1	250D	WD	77381
SILVER CEDAR TRAIL	2900	446P	NWC	77449
SILVER CHALICE DR	6300	411S	NWH	77088
SILVER CHALICE DR	18500	258E	SEM	77357
SILVER CHARM	0	371G	NWC	77014
SILVER CHASE LN	0	525Z	NEF	77406
SILVER CITY DR	10100	409C	NWC	77064
SILVER CLIFF LN	0	657P	FR	77546
SILVER CLIFF LN	23300	292G	NCC	77373
SILVER CLOUD LN	7500	410D	NWC	77086
SILVERCREEK	0	538V	DP	77536
SILVERCREEK CT	2700	613X	NEB	77578
SILVERCREEK DR	3300	613T	NEB	77578
SILVER CREEK DR	5100	535V	SEH	77017
SILVER CREEK DR	12100	328Z	NWC	77070
SILVER CRESCENT DR	0	370U	NWC	77086
SILVERCREST	10100	453C	NEH	77076
SILVER CROSSING CT	17200	407Y	NWC	77084
SILVER CROWN	0	568J	NEF	77498
SILVER CUP	0	371G	NWC	77017
SILVER CYPRESS CT	20200	446T	NWC	77449
SILVER CYPRESS DR	2500	446T	NWC	77449
SILVERDALE	1100	495K	NEH	77029
SILVER DAPPLE DR	19200	255T	SEM	77365
SILVER DAWN CT	0	660K	LC	77573
SILVER DAWN CT	6200	298W	NEH	77345
SILVER DOLLAR CT	3100	613R	PL	77584
SILVER ELM	0	245V	SWM	77355
SILVER ELM PLACE	1	250D	WD	77381
SILVER ELMS CT	0	246S	SWM	77355
SILVER FALLS DR	2100	296Z	NEH	77339
SILVER FALLS DR	3200	297S	NEH	77339
SILVERFIELD LN	12400	371H	NWC	77014
SILVERFIELD PARK LN	21900	446A	NWC	77449
SILVER FIR DR	8000	408E	NWC	77095
SILVER FIR DR	8500	408F	NWC	77095
SILVER FIR LN	0	339N	HU	77336
SILVER FIR LN	0	463S	CCO	77520
SILVER FOREST DR	5800	451B	NWH	77092
SILVER FOX DR	4600	371J	NWC	77066
SILVER FROST DR	4700	371N	NWC	77066
SILVERGATE DR	800	488F	SWH	77079
SILVER GLADE DR	3100	297Y	NEH	77345
SILVER GLADE LN	14100	568A	SG	77498
SILVER GLEN	0	371G	NWC	77017
SILVERGLEN ESTATES DR	12500	371H	NWC	77014
SILVERGLEN NORTH DR	0	371D	NWC	77014
S. SILVER GREEN DR	14700	457Z	NEC	77015
S. SILVER GREEN DR	14900	458W	NEC	77530
N. SILVER GREEN DR	15000	457Z	NEC	77530

Street Name	Block	Pg/Sq	Loc	Zips
N. SILVER GREEN DR	15200	458W	NEC	77530
SILVER GROVE	4300	609N	NEF	77479
SILVER GROVE CT	6900	578F	PA	77505
SILVERHAWK DR	0	446M	NWC	77449
SILVER HAWK DR		289Q	NWC	77375
SILVER HAWKSTONE CT	0	371D	NWC	77014
SILVER HEARTH LN	0	484U	NEF	77494
SILVER HOLLOW LN	14200	488W	SWH	77082
SILVERHORN DR	2600	486P	SWC	77450
SILVER ISLAND CIR	11900	371L	NWC	77067
SILVER JADE CT	27300	294N	SEM	77386
SILVER JADE DR	4400	294N	SEM	77386
SILVER KNIGHT CT	14800	618E	SEH	77062
SILVER KNOLL LN	6800	406Q	NWC	77449
SILVER LACE LN	14400	328Y	NWC	77070
SILVER LAKE	9300	532P	SWH	77025
SILVERLAKE BLVD	0	613L	PL	77584
SILVER LAKE RD	0	376V	NEC	77396
SILVER LAKE RD	0	377S	NEC	77044
SILVERLAKE VILLAGE DR	3000	613N	NEB	77584
SILVER LANCE DR		289P	NWC	77375
SILVER LEAF	24600	247T	SWM	77355
SILVER LEAF CT	500	613A	NEB	77584
SILVER LEAF CT	11900	252H	SEM	77385
SILVERLEAF DR	400	657E	FR	77546
SILVER LEAF DR	1900	292W	NWC	77388
SILVER LEAF DR	2100	610A	MC	77489
SILVER LEAF DR	6100	657Q	LC	77573
SILVER LEAF LN	7000	411Y	NWH	77088
SILVER LEAF LN	10300	289L	NWC	77375
SILVER LEAF LN	11900	252D	SEM	77385
SILVER LEDGE DR	0	404Z	NWC	77493
SILVER LINDEN CT		289G	NWC	77375
SILVERLINE	3200	336Q	NEH	77338
SILVER LINING LN	1800	568A	SG	77498
SILVER LOCK	0	371C	NWC	77017
SILVER LODE DR	22000	485H	SWC	77450
SILVER LURE DR	7700	377D	NEC	77346
SILVER LURE DR	8200	378A	NEC	77346
SILVERMAN	15100	617M	SEH	77598
SILVER MAPLE	24100	338M	NEH	77336
SILVER MAPLE CT	2900	657G	FR	77546
SILVER MAPLE DR	9500	410A	NWC	77064
SILVER MAPLE LN	1300	616T	PL	77581
SILVER MEADOW CT	7200	408R	NWC	77041
SILVERMEADOW DR	2500	371H	NWC	77014
SILVER MESIA CIR	0	406C	NWC	77433
SILVERMILL LN	14200	568A	SG	77498
SILVERMILL PARK LN	0	371D	NWC	77014
SILVERMILL RIMROCK TRAIL	0	371D	NWC	77014
SILVERMIST LN	22400	525C	NEF	77494
SILVER MOON TRAIL	2000	378G	NEC	77532
SILVER MORNING CIR	22200	485M	SWC	77450
SILVER MORNING CT	22200	485M	SWC	77450
SILVER MORNING DR	1200	485M	SWC	77450
SILVER NOBRIGA TRAIL	0	371D	NWC	77014
SILVER OAK	0	609Z	MC	77459
SILVER OAK CT	18100	255S	SEM	77365
SILVER OAK DR	5400	577M	PA	77505
SILVER OAK LN	10500	372W	NWC	77038
SILVER OAK PLACE DR	0	294E	SEM	77386
SILVER OAKS	2200	257D	RF	77357
SILVER OAK TRAIL	20400	337Q	NEC	77346
SILVER PALM TRAIL	0	257F	SEM	77357
SILVERPARK	5500	448D	NWC	77041
SILVERPARK LN	0	568B	SG	77498
SILVERPEAK CT	21800	525G	NEF	77494
SILVER PINES RD	700	618Q	SEH	77062
SILVERPLUME	0	448H	NWH	77084
SILVER POINTE DR	0	295M	SEM	77365
SILVER POPLAR LN	6500	408S	NWC	77084
SILVER PRESS DR	0	404Z	NWC	77493
SILVER RAWLS LN	0	525V	NEF	77406
SILVER RIDGE DR	15400	331R	NWC	77090
SILVER RINGS CT	0	615B	PL	77581
SILVER ROCK CT	6800	406Q	NWC	77449
SILVER ROCK DR	19900	406Q	NWC	77449
SILVER ROD LN	6500	408V	NWC	77041
SILVER ROD LN	12700	409S	NWC	77041
SILVER ROW LN	0	484T	NEF	77494
SILVER RUN LN	4200	256W	SEM	77365
SILVER RUSH DR	11200	367V	NWC	77095
SILVERS	1	491Y	SWH	77056
SILVER SAGE DR	2200	489S	SWH	77077
SILVER SAGEBRUSH CT	17800	367T	NWC	77433
SILVERSAND CT	0	417C	NEH	77044
SILVER SANDS	14700	408K	NWC	77095
SILVER SANDS CIR	7800	408K	NWC	77095
SILVER SHADE DR	0	370Y	NWC	77064
SILVER SHADOWS LN	8200	330E	NWC	77379
SILVER SHADOWS LN	8300	329H	NWC	77379
SILVER SHIELD WAY		289Q	NWC	77375
SILVER SHIRE LN	3400	529A	SWH	77042
SILVER SHORES LN	6800	406Q	NWC	77449
SILVERSIDE DR	3200	446M	NWC	77449
SILVER SKY	0	407R	NWC	77095
SILVER SKY CT	14200	618E	SEH	77062
SILVER SKY LN	16200	407L	NWC	77095
SILVERSMINE DR	12400	371H	NWC	77014
SILVERSMITH LN	23800	445T	NWC	77493
SILVER SPRING CT	3100	609M	MC	77459
SILVER SPRING LN	9000	532N	SWH	77025
SILVER SPRINGS	3100	580P	LP	77571
SILVER SPRINGS DR	3800	613X	NEB	77578
SILVER SPRINGS DR	25000	244R	WCO	77447
SILVER SPRING TRAIL	3000	446P	NWC	77449
SILVER SPRUCE LN	0	617X	SEC	77546
SILVER SPUR	32900	246R	SC	77355
SILVER SPUR DR	3000	446P	NWC	77449
SILVER SPUR TRAIL	3000	446P	NWC	77449
SILVERSTAG TRAIL LN	0	333P	NCC	77073
SILVER STAR CT	3300	613V	PL	77584
SILVER STAR DR	6800	371W	NWC	77086
SILVER STONE	10600	574E	SEH	77048
SILVERSTONE DR	400	657E	FR	77546
SILVERSTREAM CT	12500	371G	NWC	77014
SILVER TEA AVE	0	285P	NWC	77447
SILVERTHORN LN	0	619V	LC	77565
SILVERTHORNE LN	17100	330K	NWC	77379
SILVER THORNGLEN DR	0	331E	NWC	77379
SILVER TIMBER CT	0	407S	NWC	77449
SILVER TIMBERS LN	0	484U	NEF	77494
SILVER TIP DR	9200	329R	NWC	77379
SILVERTON	500	332C	NCC	77373
SILVERTON CREEK LN	9500	410F	NWC	77040
SILVERTON STAR CT	0	253P	SEM	77386
SILVERTON STAR LN	0	329V	NWC	77070
SILVERTON VALLEY LN	0	524H	NEF	77494
SILVER TRAILS	1	256P	SEM	77357
SILVER TREE	0	371G	NWC	77014
SILVER TRUMPET DR	2500	446S	NWC	77449
SILVER VALLEY DR	16000	448A	NWC	77084

Street Name	Block	Pg/Sq	Loc	Zips
SILVER VILLAGE DR	31100	252Q	SEM	77386
SILVER VINEYARD RD	0	484J	NEF	77494
SILVER WILLOW CIR	0	328K	NWC	77429
SILVER WING LN	16201	324S	NWC	77447
SILVER WINTER TRAIL	0	371D	NWC	77014
SILVERWOOD DR	4000	532S	SWH	77025
SILVERWOOD DR	4300	531V	SWH	77035
SILVERWOOD BEND LN	11800	366M	NWC	77433
SILVERWOOD OAKS CT	0	253N	SEM	77386
SILVERWOOD PARK LN	0	253N	SEM	77386
SILVERWOOD TRAIL	7200	337Q	NEC	77346
SILVERWOOD TRAIL	20200	326P	NWC	77433
SILVERWOOD WAY	10000	329T	NWC	77388
SILVERWYCK DR	12400	371H	NWC	77014
SILVER YACHT DR	8700	378A	NEC	77346
SIMCA	0	337X	NEC	77346
SIMMANS	2100	373M	NEH	77032
SIMMONS	0	611Z	FS	77545
SIMMONS	3000	493Z	SEH	77004
SIMMONS	5700	532A	WU	77005
SIMMONS	9100	454F	NEH	77093
SIMMONS	9100	539G	SEC	77571
SIMMONS BLVD	1100	537E	PA	77506
SIMMONS DR	5300	252B	SEM	77385
SIMMS	0	659J	LC	77573
SIMON CT	0	527S	NEF	77469
SIMON LN	0	527S	NEF	77469
SIMONA LN	3200	371U	NWC	77086
SIMONE CT	0	447A	NWC	77449
SIMPSON	0	577T	SEH	77034
SIMPSON	900	660H	BC	77518
SIMPSON	1600	494G	NEH	77020
SIMPSON CREEK LN	10600	528W	NEF	77498
SIMPSON SPRINGS LN	7400	290B	NWC	77389
SIMS	1300	541C	BT	77520
SIMS	7100	534Z	SEH	77061
SIMS AVE	0	252B	SEM	77385
SIMS RD	0	542S	NEC	77520
SIMSBROOK DR	3700	572N	SWH	77045
SIMSBROOK DR	4500	571Q	SWH	77045
SIMSBURY	1200	453K	NWH	77022
SIMSCREST	8500	535R	SEH	77017
SIMSDALE	5600	574A	SEH	77033
SIMSDALE	6200	574C	SEH	77087
SIMSVIEW DR	12900	572F	SWH	77045
SIMSWOOD CT	4600	571R	SWH	77045
SINALOA DR	16300	527K	NEF	77083
SINATRA TRACE	0	293L	SEM	77386
SINCHA	0	533G	SEH	77021
SINCLAIR	100	496T	GP	77547
SINCLAIR	2400	537Z	PA	77503
SINCLAIR	3100	577D	PA	77505
SINCLAIR RIDGE LN	0	526J	NEF	77407
SINEA DR	0	372D	NCC	77073
SINFONIA DR	7900	410J	NWC	77040
SINGAPORE LN	15600	409Q	JV	77040
SINGER	5100	450B	NWH	77040
SINGING BIRD CIR	0	447A	NWC	77084
SINGING BIRD CT	15300	572W	SWH	77053
SINGING CREEK LN	6300	330H	NWC	77379
SINGING SONNET LN	8000	528L	SWH	77072
SINGING SPURS CT	0	485H	SWC	77450
SINGING SPURS DR	22000	485H	SWC	77450
SINGING TREES LN	11400	415P	NEC	77016
SINGING WOODS DR	18600	377C	NEC	77346
SINGING WOODS DR	18900	337Y	NEC	77346
SINGLELEAF LN	22200	290J	NWC	77375
SINGLE OAK ST	0	293X	NCC	77373
SINGLE PINE CT	700	292L	SP	77373
SINGLE RIDGE WAY	0	445F	NWC	77493
SINGLE RIDGE WAY	0	445K	NWC	77493
SINGLE ROSE CT	17400	327T	NWC	77429
SINGLETON	2000	453S	NWH	77008
SINGLETON	3400	502N	BT	77521
SINGLETON RD	3400	501R	BT	77521
SINGLETREE DR	15000	246R	SC	77355
SINGLETREE LN	27800	246J	SWM	77355
SINKS CANYON LN	0	377F	NEC	77346
SINTON CT	2900	446P	NWC	77449
SINTON CREEK DR	0	296E	SEM	77365
SIOUX	0	295F	SEM	77365
SIOUX	4400	461S	NEC	77521
SIOUX DR	6300	538W	PA	77503
SIOUX DR	9300	579A	LP	77571
SIOUX DR	9800	248M	SWM	77354
SIOUX RUN	14400	328P	NWC	77429
SIPSEY WILDERNESS DR	0	377G	NEC	77346
SIR ALEX DR	0	289T	NWC	77375
SIRIL DR	18900	372H	NCC	77073
SIR LANCELOT CIR	24700	244R	WCO	77447
SIROCCO	0	451U	NWH	77055
SIROS ISLE CT	4900	291N	NWC	77388
SIROS ISLE DR	21500	291N	NWC	77388
SIR PENGUIN DR	0	285Q	NWC	77447
SIR RALIEGH WAY	0	568B	SG	77498
SIR WILLIAM DR	16100	330L	NWC	77379
SISKIN TRAIL	0	658X	LC	77573
SISSY LN	700	297J	SEM	77365
SISTERDALE DR	7600	406M	NWC	77433
SITCA	4900	291A	NWC	77389
SITTING BULL DR	0	446T	NWC	77449
SIVLEY	6500	451Y	NWH	77055
SIWANOY CIR	25100	295R	SEM	77365
SIX-PACK DR	32000	246S	SWM	77355
SIX FLAGS DR	6400	410W	NWH	77040
SIX OAKS LN	11000	369S	NWC	77065
SIXPENCE LN	22100	332H	NCC	77073
SIX PINES DR	10500	251M	WD	77380
SIXTUMGRUM LN	27000	284A	WCO	77447
SJOLANDER CIR	6200	462X	NEC	77521
SJOLANDER RD	4400	502A	NEC	77521
SJOLANDER RD	5800	462N	NEC	77521
SKEET CT	16400	610C	SWH	77489
SKEET AND TRAP	0	487X	SWH	77094
SKEG DR	15800	419F	NEC	77532
SKELTON DR	2600	371Q	NWC	77067
SKENE WAY	11700	490F	HE	77024
SKEWEN	5700	337X	NEC	77346
SKIER'S CROSSING DR	0	444J	KT	77493
SKIFF LN	0	377K	NEC	77044
SKIMMER CT	800	568T	SG	77478
SKIMMER WAY	2700	378T	NEC	77532
SKINNER	15700	327P	NWC	77429
SKINNER CT	16900	367A	CY	77429
SKINNER LN	0	525Q	NEF	77407
SKINNER RD	0	525U	NEF	77469
SKINNER RD	0	525U	NEF	77469
SKINNER RD	200	413V	NEH	77093
SKINNER RD	13000	367F	CY	77429
SKINNER RD	13900	327X	CY	77429
SKIPPERS HELM	18500	378A	NEC	77346
SKIPPING FALLS LN	0	484X	NEF	77494

Street Name	Block	Pg/Sq	Loc	Zips
SKIPPING STONE CT	8900	409H	NWC	77064
SKIPPING STONE LN	5000	609S	NEF	77479
SKIPPING STONE LN	9200	409H	NWC	77064
SKIPPY	0	454A	NEH	77093
SKIP ROCK	1900	656R	FR	77546
SKIPWOOD DR	1800	570S	MC	77489
SKOKIE	0	501J	BT	77521
SKYBIRD DR	10900	369Y	NWC	77064
SKY BLUE LN	16200	407R	NWC	77095
SKY BLUE PLACE	16700	407Q	NWC	77095
SKYBRIGHT LN	7200	407R	NWC	77095
SKY BROOK CT	13500	417C	NEC	77044
SKY BROOK LN	15100	417C	NEC	77044
SKYCOUNTRY LN	19800	486G	SWC	77094
SKYDALE DR	11800	329A	NWC	77375
SKYE	4600	447D	NWC	77084
SKYE SPRINGS LN	23500	485W	NEF	77494
N. SKYFLOWER CT	1	251K	WD	77381
SKYFLOWER DR	1	251K	WD	77381
SKYFLOWER PLACE	1	251K	WD	77381
SKY FOREST	0	246B	SWM	77355
SKYGAZE ST	0	332W	NWC	77090
SKY HARBOR CT	4600	609N	NEF	77479
SKY HARBOR CT	16900	657B	SEC	77546
SKY HAVEN AVE	0	571Z	SWH	77053
SKYHAVEN CT	21000	290U	NWC	77379
SKY HAVEN DR	17200	328L	NWC	77377
SKYHAVEN LN	5900	290U	NWC	77379
SKY HAWK DR	10400	369Y	NWC	77064
SKYHILL DR	0	326T	NWC	77433
SKY HOLLOW LN	19900	486Q	SWC	77450
SKYKNOLL LN	12700	488Y	SWH	77082
SKYLA CIR	21500	333G	NCC	77338
SKY LAKE	32100	322T	WCO	77484
SKY LAND DR	15900	332V	NCC	77073
SKYLAND PLACE	1	250D	WD	77381
SKYLANE	0	503R	BC	77520
SKYLARK	1	245U	SWM	77355
SKYLARK LN	1700	491Q	SWH	77056
SKYLARK RD	100	536T	PA	77502
SKYLARK BLUFF TRAIL	0	484P	NEF	77494
SKYLARK FALLS TRAIL	0	405P	NWC	77493
SKYLARK HILL CROSSING	0	405R	NWC	77493
SKYLARK WAY	3200	614X	PL	77584
SKYLAR MEADOWS CT	0	526N	NEF	77407
SKYLIGHT LN	6400	249H	SWM	77354
SKYLIGHT LN	7200	407R	NWC	77095
SKYLINE	0	490Z	SWH	77063
SKYLINE CT	2900	609H	MC	77459
SKYLINE DR	0	613X	NEB	77578
SKYLINE DR	6000	491W	SWH	77057
SKYLINE DR	7600	490X	SWH	77063
SKYLINE ARBOR TERRACE	0	487A	SWC	77094
SKYLINE PARK DR	6900	406R	NWC	77449
SKYLINE TRAIL	800	493K	SWH	77019
SKYLINE VILLAGE DR	0	491W	SWH	77057
SKYLINE VILLAGE PARK	0	491W	SWH	77057
SKYLINE VILLAGE TRAIL	0	491W	SWH	77057
SKYLINE VISTA	800	493K	SWH	77019
SKYMEADOW DR	12900	488Z	SWH	77082
SKY MIST	0	612M	PL	77584
SKYMIST LN	0	485N	NEF	77494
SKYMONT STREAM TRAIL	0	332X	NWC	77090
SKYOAK CT	3700	293C	SEM	77386
SKYPARK DR	2800	488Y	SWH	77082
SKYRIDGE CT	6900	290P	NWC	77379
SKY RIDGE DR	11200	369J	NWC	77429
SKYRIDGE PARK LN	0	524M	NEF	77406
SKYSPRING LN	800	660E	LC	77573
SKY TIMBERS LN	0	446D	NWC	77449
SKYTRAIN RD	2800	374A	NEH	77032
SKYVIEW	100	656D	FR	77546
SKYVIEW	11200	539V	LP	77571
SKYVIEW DR	1600	449U	NWH	77043
SKYVIEW DR	6200	409Y	NWC	77041
SKYVIEW DR	13700	568B	NEF	77498
SKYVIEW BEND DR	13000	573P	SEH	77047
SKYVIEW CHASE DR	2700	573P	SEH	77047
SKYVIEW COVE CT	0	573P	SEH	77047
SKYVIEW CREEK CT	0	573N	SEH	77047
SKYVIEW CREST CT	0	573P	SEH	77047
SKYVIEW DOWNS DR	0	573N	SEH	77047
SKYVIEW FOREST DR	2700	573T	SEH	77047
SKYVIEW GLEN CT	0	573N	SEH	77047
SKYVIEW GREEN DR	13200	573T	SEH	77047
SKYVIEW GROVE CT	0	573N	SEH	77047
SKYVIEW KNOLL CT	0	573N	SEH	77047
SKYVIEW LANDING DR	12900	573P	SEH	77047
SKYVIEW MANOR DR	0	573P	SEH	77047
SKYVIEW MILL DR	2700	573S	SEH	77047
SKYVIEW PARK DR	0	573T	SEH	77047
SKYVIEW RIDGE CT	2600	573N	SEH	77047
SKYVIEW SHADOWS CT	2600	573N	SEH	77047
SKYVIEW TRACE CT	2600	573N	SEH	77047
SKYWALKER LN	0	367P	CY	77433
SKY WAY	32100	322T	WCO	77484
SKY WAY DR	11400	369J	NWC	77429
SKYWING CT	0	293W	NCC	77373
SKYWOOD DR	300	332T	NWC	77090
SLASH PINE CT	11400	251R	WD	77380
SLASH PINE PLACE	8500	289R	NWC	77375
SLASH PINE PLACE	11400	251R	WD	77380
SLASHWOOD LN	5200	331E	NWC	77379
SLASHWOOD LN	5800	331J	NWC	77379
SLATE BEND DR	0	285L	NWC	77447
SLATE BRIDGE CT	21700	445M	NWC	77449
SLATE CREEK LN	0	488T	SWH	77077
SLATE CROSSING LN	0	446N	NWC	77449
SLATE FIELD DR	9700	409G	NWC	77064
SLATE HILLS LN	0	331A	NWC	77388
SLATE HOLLOW LN	0	526F	NEF	77407
SLATE MOUNTAIN	13700	417D	NEC	77044
SLATE RIDGE LN	0	485P	NEF	77494
SLATE RIVER LN	4900	484Z	NEF	77494
SLATE RIVER LN	11000	615H	SEC	77089
SLATERS LN	12900	413G	NCC	77039
SLATE SKY LN	0	253K	SEM	77386
SLATE SPRINGS	21100	525M	NEF	77407
SLATE SPRINGS LN	0	612Q	PL	77584
SLATE STONE CT	9300	409H	NWC	77064
SLATE STONE LN	6400	407V	NWC	77084
SLATESTONE LN	28200	293F	SEM	77386
SLATE VALLEY CT	0	609U	MC	77459
SLATE VALLEY LN	700	292G	NCC	77373
SLEDGE	800	493B	NWH	77009
SLEDGE	2300	282U	WL	77484
SLEEPING COLT PLACE	0	250R	NWC	77389
SLEEPY LN	13500	288C	TB	77375
SLEEPY CREEK DR	5100	535V	SEH	77017
SLEEPY CREEK DR	5200	536S	SEH	77017
SLEEPY CREEK MEADOWS	0	528Q	SWC	77083
SLEEPY CREEK WAY	1800	616S	PL	77581

Street Name	Block	Pg/Sq	Loc	Zips
SLEEPYGATE DR	22500	334E	NCC	77373
SLEEPY HOLLOW	1500	252Y	SEM	77386
SLEEPY HOLLOW	1600	616T	PL	77581
SLEEPY HOLLOW	20500	292S	NWC	77388
SLEEPY HOLLOW CT	200	619H	TL	77586
SLEEPY HOLLOW CT	3300	492P	SWH	77019
SLEEPY HOLLOW RD	9500	252B	SEM	77385
SLEEPY HOLLOW RD	11800	253A	SEM	77385
SLEEPY HOLLOW TRAIL LN	11400	616E	SEC	77089
SLEEPY KNOLL DR	2700	293W	NCC	77373
SLEEPY MEADOW LN	11800	414J	NCC	77039
SLEEPY OAKS CIR	1	490H	HC	77024
SLEEPY PINES DR	12000	370H	NWC	77066
SLEEPY ROSE CT	0	415C	NEC	77396
SLEEPY TERRACE LN	0	290Q	NWC	77379
SLEEPYTIME LN	13000	419U	BR	77532
SLEEPYVALE LN	700	452L	NWH	77018
SLEET RD	6800	408Q	NWC	77041
SLICE RIGHT CIR	0	616J	SEC	77581
SLICK ROCK DR		524L	NWF	77406
SLIDER CT	2600	658T	LC	77573
SLIDING ROCK CIR	0	330B	NWC	77379
SLIPPERY CREEK LN	21200	291T	NWC	77388
SLIPPERY ELM LN	7300	407L	NWC	77095
SLIPPERY ROCK LN	19500	291X	NWC	77388
SLOAN	6300	534L	SEH	77087
SLOANDALE CT	16900	332Q	NCC	77073
SLOANGATE DR	4200	333C	NCC	77373
SLOAN RIDGE LN	0	326U	NWC	77429
SLOCOM DR	3600	446K	NWC	77449
SLOOP CT	500	419B	NEC	77532
SLOSSEN	100	618X	WB	77598
SLOVER CREEK LN	0	524F	NEF	77494
SLUMBER LN	300	419R	BR	77532
SLUMBER LN	3500	534G	SEH	77023
SLUMBERING FALLS LN	10500	366V	NWC	77433
SLUMBERWOOD DR	500	496B	NEH	77013
SMADA CT	2700	609A	SG	77478
SMALL CEDAR	0	658P	LC	77573
SMALLEY RD	28800	323X	NWC	77447
SMALL LEAF CIR	7800	490Z	SWH	77063
SMALL PEBBLE WAY	10000	376S	NEC	77396
SMALLWOOD LN	1100	535A	SEH	77023
SMALLWOOD LN	1400	534D	SEH	77023
SMART	500	412R	NCC	77037
SMILAX	7000	412X	NWH	77088
SMILING WOOD LN	7100	411A	NWC	77086
SMILING WOOD LN	7500	410D	NWC	77086
SMITH	0	499L	NEC	77520
SMITH	100	493L	DT	77002
SMITH	500	576H	PA	77504
SMITH	1200	282U	WL	77484
SMITH	2300	493P	SWH	77006
SMITH	4100	660M	BC	77518
SMITH	11700	415M	NEC	77050
SMITH	16200	409L	JV	77040
SMITH LN	0	615R	PL	77581
SMITH LN	100	659G	LC	77573
SMITH LN	11600	415K	NEC	77050
SMITH RD	0	338M	NEH	77336
SMITH RD	0	613Q	PL	77584
SMITH RD	0	295D	SEM	77365
SMITH RD	0	296A	SEM	77365
SMITH RD	100	419U	BR	77532
SMITH RD	1300	339J	HU	77336
SMITH RD	13600	415B	NEC	77396
SMITH RD	14000	375X	NEC	77396
SMITH BRIDGE LN	0	528W	NEF	77498
SMITHDALE CT	1	490H	HC	77024
SMITHDALE RD	10800	490G	PP	77024
SMITHDALE ESTATES DR	1	490G	PP	77024
SMITHERMAN RD	13900	417X	NEC	77044
SMITHFIELD CROSSING LN	20100	446X	NWC	77449
SMITH LAKE LN	13500	377L	NEH	77044
SMITHLAND DR	0	408N	NWC	77084
SMITH RANCH RD	2200	613N	NEB	77584
SMITH RANCH #1	0	613J	PL	77584
SMITH RANCH #2	2600	613J	PL	77584
SMITH RAPIDS LN	14800	568A	NEF	77498
SMITH SPRINGS	0	292U	NCC	77373
SMITHSTONE	15800	408N	NWC	77084
SMITHSTONE DR	0	407V	NWC	77084
SMOKE CREEK CT	14200	367C	NWC	77429
SMOKEHOLLOW DR	9000	369Z	NWC	77064
SMOKE HOUSE DR	6400	406V	NWC	77449
SMOKE LAKE	24900	249Z	NWC	77375
SMOKERISE PLACE	1	250D	WD	77381
SMOKE ROCK DR	2000	333A	NCC	77373
SMOKEROCK LN	7300	410V	NWH	77040
SMOKESTONE DR	1	251B	WD	77381
SMOKEY DR	7800	410G	NWC	77064
SMOKEY LN	700	379L	NEC	77532
SMOKEY BEAR	2700	411H	NWC	77038
SMOKEY BROOK LN	0	485X	NEF	77494
SMOKEY FOREST LN	2900	253N	SEM	77386
SMOKEYGATE CT	24000	293Y	NCC	77373
SMOKEY HILL RD	22300	485G	SWC	77450
SMOKEY HOLLOW DR	3000	331T	NWC	77068
SMOKEY MOUNTAIN CT	12700	377B	NEC	77346
SMOKEY OAK RD	1	251N	WD	77381
SMOKEY PASS CIR	12800	411D	NWC	77038
SMOKEY RIDGE LN	8900	575Y	SEH	77075
SMOKEY RIVER DR	5100	446B	NWC	77449
SMOKEY SADDLE LN		328P	NWC	77429
SMOKEY SAGE CT	2900	486T	SWC	77450
SMOKEY SAGE DR	20700	486T	SWC	77450
SMOKEY TRAIL DR	13700	408L	NWC	77041
SMOKEY TREE	0	286J	NWC	77377
SMOKEY VALLEY LN		484T	NEF	77494
SMOKEY WOOD LN	7700	410D	NWC	77086
SMOKEY WOOD LN	7800	370Z	NWC	77086
SMOOTH BROME LN	0	293G	SEM	77386
SMOOTH OAK LN	3900	572S	SWH	77053
SMOOTH OAK LN	4600	571V	SWH	77053
SMOOTH ROCK FALLS DR	17600	330F	NWC	77379
SMOOTH STREAM DR	0	249Q	NWC	77375
SMUGGLERS CT	28900	298P	NEC	77336
SNAG LN	3900	331G	NWC	77388
SNAIL HOLLOW DR	8300	410H	NWC	77064
SNAKE CANYON DR	2900	446U	NWC	77449
SNAKE RIVER RD	1900	446X	NWC	77449
SNAPDRAGON CT	1	250M	WD	77381
SNAPDRAGON MEADOW LN	0	524D	NEF	77494
SNAPPING TURTLE DR	0	335P	NCC	77338
SNAPPY CREEK LN	21300	291X	NWC	77388
SNEAD CT	19000	337Z	NEC	77346
SNEIDER	14500	577T	SEH	77034
SNIPES	10100	575N	SEH	77075
SNODDON RD	5800	577D	PA	77505
SNOKOMO	0	610D	SWH	77489
SNOMAC CT	4100	461W	NEC	77521
SNOOK LN	23200	289E	TB	77375

Street Name	Block	Pg/Sq	Loc	Zips
SNOVER	100	492M	SWH	77007
SNOW	3200	444K	KT	77493
SNOW RD	25300	244L	WCO	77447
SNOWBANK DR	8300	410H	NWC	77064
SNOW BAY DR	11300	371R	NWC	77067
SNOWBELL	14800	487Z	SWC	77082
SNOWBELL PLACE	1	250C	WD	77381
SNOWBERRY DR	11700	369J	NWC	77429
SNOWBIRD CT	0	370G	NWC	77066
SNOWBIRD CT	12000	569E	SF	77477
SNOWBIRD MEADOW DR	3100	293Y	NCC	77373
SNOWBLOSSOM CT	3400	615F	PL	77581
SNOWBLOSSOM LN	21300	289T	NWC	77375
SNOWBRIDGE CT	11700	328R	NWC	77377
SNOWCREST CT	12000	328G	NWC	77377
SNOWCREST DR	0	328G	NWC	77377
SNOWDEN	7800	455B	NEH	77028
SNOWDEN	27000	284W	NWC	77447
SNOWDEN	28000	283Z	NWC	77484
SNOWDEN POINT LN	3700	253P	SEM	77386
SNOWDROP LN	2100	371R	NWC	77067
SNOWFLAKE CT	16700	611B	SWH	77053
SNOWFLOWER MEADOW LN	0	525A	NEF	77494
SNOW GOOSE CT	0	291N	NWC	77388
SNOW HILL CT	15100	527Z	NEF	77498
SNOWMASS DR	11600	369A	NWC	77070
SNOWNY HILLS DR	16000	367D	NWC	77429
SNOW PINE LN	0	616J	PL	77089
SNOW POND PLACE	1	250A	WD	77382
SNOWWOOD DR	18400	331D	NWC	77388
SNOWY EGRET DR	0	484P	NWF	77494
SNOWY MEADOW LN	1800	611T	NEF	77545
SNUG HARBOR CT	3100	445M	NWC	77449
SNYDER'S BLUFF	2700	659W	LC	77573
SOAPSTONE LN	24300	292B	NCC	77373
SOARING EAGLE CT	0	411D	NWC	77038
SOARING EAGLE DR	16100	527U	NEF	77083
SOARING FOREST DR	16500	578Z	PA	77059
SOARING PINE CT	5900	338A	NEH	77345
SOARING SUNSET PATH	0	406R	NEF	77433
SOARING WOODS LN	0	296Q	SEM	77365
SOBODA CT	800	488C	SWH	77079
SOCIETY LN	5500	408X	NWC	77084
SOCKEYE DR	2600	572L	NWC	77045
SOCORRO LN	11500	328D	NWC	77377
SODA SPRINGS TRAIL		367W	NWC	77095
SOFFIANO LN	0	659R	LC	77573
SOFIA WILLOW WAY	0	328E	NWC	77377
SOFTBREEZE CT	11300	613J	PL	77584
SOFT BREEZE DR	8000	407F	NWC	77095
SOFT FERN CT	3100	297Q	NEH	77345
SOFT PINE DR	24200	338M	NEH	77336
SOFT PINES CT	22000	255S	SEM	77365
SOFT PINES DR	12000	370H	NWC	77066
SOFT SHADOWS LN	500	496E	NEH	77013
SOHO DR	3700	613G	NEB	77584
SOL	1100	495U	NEH	77029
SOLANA DR	8100	527R	NEF	77083
SOLANO CT	11700	529W	MD	77477
E. SOLANO BAY	5900	409W	NWC	77041
E. SOLANO BAY LN	5900	409W	NWC	77041
W. SOLANO BAY LN	5901	409W	NWC	77041
SOLANO POINT LN	0	406C	NWC	77433
SOLANO POINTE CT	0	609T	NEF	77479
SOLARA BEND	8100	527N	NEF	77083
SOLARA BEND CT	9000	527P	NEF	77083
SOLARI LN	0	659M	LC	77573
SOLAR LEDGE LN	5900	609X	NEF	77479
SOLAR POINT LN	12000	409W	NWC	77041
SOLDIERS CREEK CIR	0	490H	SWH	77024
SOLDIERS FIELD CT	1100	568S	NEF	77479
SOLDIERS FIELD DR	1100	568S	SG	77479
SOLEBROOK PATH	100	249R	NWH	77375
SOLEBROOK PATH	100	249R	NWH	77375
SOLEDAD DR	6400	527F	NEF	77083
SOLEDAD PINE CIR	0	526S	NEF	77407
SOLEDAD RIDGE DR	2400	293N	NCC	77373
SOLEIL DR	14200	528E	SWC	77083
SOLERA LN	0	410M	NWC	77040
SOLERO POINTE LN	0	366Y	NWC	77433
SOLERO RIDGE LN	0	616E	SEC	77089
SOLISBURY HILL DR	0	334M	NCC	77338
SOLITAIRE CIR	0	369L	NWC	77070
SOLITUDE LN	0	539W	DP	77571
SOLITUDE HILL LN		526P	NEF	77407
SOLO	700	494G	NEH	77020
SOLO	2900	494C	NEH	77026
SOLOMON	1900	282U	WL	77484
SOLOMON	7500	409R	JV	77040
SOLOMON RD	11000	329E	NWC	77375
SOLON RD	8800	369R	NWC	77064
SOLSTICE BLVD	0	293F	SEM	77386
SOLVISTA CREEK LN	0	327U	NWC	77429
SOLVISTA HIGH CT	0	253P	SEM	77386
SOLVISTA HILL CT	16400	377L	NEC	77044
SOLVISTA PASS LN	0	329V	NWC	77070
SOLWAY LN	4100	532N	SWH	77025
SOMA DR	16000	527L	NEF	77083
SOMBRERO ST	0	461P	NEC	77521
SOMERCOTES LN	900	498A	NEC	77530
SOMERCOTES LN	1000	458W	NEC	77530
SOMERFORD DR	11000	529F	SWH	77072
SOMERLAND WAY	11300	490G	PP	77024
SOMERSBY BLVD	0	290S	NWC	77379
SOMERSET	800	257H	SEM	77357
SOMERSET	900	258E	SEM	77357
SOMERSET CT	4500	577B	PA	77504
SOMERSET DR	5000	500M	BT	77521
SOMERSET LN	1400	656X	FR	77546
SOMERSET LN	3200	538V	DP	77536
SOMERSET LN	10600	414N	NCC	77093
SOMERSET COMMONS LN	0	492A	NWH	77055
SOMERSET COVE CT	22100	525G	NEF	77494
SOMERSET GREEN DR	0	492A	NWH	77055
SOMERSET GROVE DR	17500	407Y	NWC	77084
SOMERSET HILL CT	20500	526E	NEF	77407
SOMERSET HILL LN	7200	526E	NEF	77407
SOMERSET HORIZON LN	0	377U	NEC	77044
SOMERSET KNOLLS	18000	487A	SWC	77094
SOMERSET KNOLLS CT	200	487A	SWC	77094
SOMERSET LANDING LN	0	657Y	LC	77573
SOMERSET MEADOWS CT	0	484V	NEF	77494
SOMERSET PARK LN	21000	525H	NEF	77450
SOMERSET POINTE DR	2100	660A	LC	77573
SOMERSET VALLEY DR	0	526N	NEF	77407
SOMERSET YORK LN	0	492A	NWH	77055
SOMERSWORTH DR	13300	408Y	NWC	77041
SOMERTON DR	3100	578H	LP	77571
SOMERVEL CT	0	525Z	NEF	77406
SOMERVILLE LAKE CT	3800	615Y	PL	77581
SOMMERALL DR	7000	407R	NWC	77095
SOMMERALL CREEK LN	0	407V	NWC	77084
SOMMERALL LAKE LN	0	407R	NWC	77084
SOMMERMEYER	14200	410W	NWH	77041
SOMMERMEYER	15000	409Z	NWH	77041
SOMMERSET BRANCH CT	0	526J	NEF	77407
SOMMERVILLE AVE	10300	449M	NWC	77041
SONATA CT	7900	410K	NWC	77040
SONATA CT	16700	611B	SWH	77053
SONATA CANYON LN	12400	409W	NWC	77041
SONATA CREEK LN	0	366L	NWC	77433
SONCY WAY	0	286Q	NWC	77377
SONDICK CT	4200	494F	NEH	77020
SONESTA POINT LN	8200	527P	NEF	77083
SONETO DR	7800	527L	NEF	77083
SONGBIRD	0	614V	PL	77584
SONGBIRD LN	3200	336Q	NEH	77338
SONGBROOK DR	6800	528G	SWH	77083
SONGBURY CIR	4100	485Y	NEF	77494
SONGFUL WOODS PLACE	100	251Z	WD	77380
SONGHOLLOW DR	12700	328L	NWC	77377
SONGLARK CIR	0	406D	NWC	77433
SONGLARK BLUFF	0	406X	NWC	77449
SONGLARK VALLEY PLACE	0	405S	NWC	77493
SONG RIDGE CT	5800	408Z	NWC	77041
SONGWIND LN	7400	330F	NWC	77379
SONGWOOD	3500	534K	SEH	77023
SONGWOOD DR	10200	252F	SEM	77385
SONIA LN	0	537T	PA	77502
SONNET GLEN LN	7100	407Q	NWC	77095
SONNET MEADOW CT	12000	573L	SEH	77047
SONNEVILLE DR	8400	451J	NWH	77080
SONNEVILLE DR	8500	450M	NWH	77080
SONNIER	12300	417H	NEH	77044
SONNY LN	1300	463A	MB	77580
SONNY PATH CT	24800	445S	NWC	77493
SONNY PATH DR	1700	445S	NWC	77493
SONOMA DR	6500	611B	SWH	77053
SONOMA BREEZE DR	0	457V	NEC	77049
SONOMA DEL NORTE DR	16700	367U	NWC	77095
SONOMA MISSION CT	0	446E	NWC	77449
SONOMA OAK DR	7900	408L	NWC	77041
SONOMA PARK DR	0	457V	NEC	77049
SONOMA PASS TRAIL	0	251W	SWM	77389
SONOMA RIDGE	0	609Z	MC	77459
SONOMA TRACE	0	458S	NEC	77049
SONOMA TRAIL DR	0	458S	NEC	77049
SONOMA VALLEY DR	23400	287A	SWM	77355
SONOMA WAY	6100	611B	SWH	77053
SONORA	4800	494G	NEH	77020
SONORA	7100	462Z	BT	77521
SONORA DR	0	255X	SEM	77365
SONORA DR	0	658Y	LC	77573
SONORA CANYON CIR	6100	409W	NWC	77041
SONORA CANYON CT	0	409W	NWC	77041
SONORA CANYON LN	0	409W	NWC	77041
SONORA CANYON LN	0	409W	NWC	77041
SONORA CREEK LN	4600	291T	NWC	77388
SONORA MEADOW LN	0	578X	SEH	77059
SONORAN BLUE WAY	0	572E	SWH	77045
SONORA SPRING DR	11900	329A	NWC	77375
SONORITY	0	410J	NWC	77040
SONORITY BLVD	9500	410F	NWC	77040
SONRISA CT	0	247L	SWM	77362
SOOTY TERN DR	0	484P	NEF	77494
SOPHIA SPRINGS LN	0	486H	SWC	77094
SOPHIE ANN DR	3200	537Q	PA	77503
SOPRIS DR	1100	488E	SWH	77077
SORBETE DR	7500	527K	NEF	77083
SORBUS	0	413K	NCC	77037
SORELLA CT	0	489C	NWH	77024
SOREN LN	1	453B	NEH	77076
SORENSON DR	4100	613Z	NEB	77584
SORIA SPRINGS CIR	0	366Y	NWC	77433
SORNEY CT	20000	486C	SWC	77450
SORREL CIR	0	461T	BT	77521
SORREL DR	8300	410H	NWC	77064
SORREL GROVE CT	13900	573V	SEC	77047
SORREL LEAF LN	0	451S	NWH	77055
SORRELL GLEN CT	0	331B	NWC	77388
SORREL MEADOWS DR	8600	249Z	NWC	77375
SORREL OAKS CIR	0	527J	NEF	77407
SORREL OAKS LN	0	527J	NEF	77407
SORREL RIDGE DR	17400	331G	NWC	77388
SORREL TRACE LN	0	527N	NEF	77407
SORRELWOOD DR	300	659H	LC	77573
SORRENTO	100	568P	SG	77478
SORRENTO DR	600	620J	EL	77586
SORRENTO POINT DR	0	257F	SEM	77357
SORSBY DR	10600	573M	SEH	77047
SORSBY WAY	10600	573G	SEH	77047
SORTERS RD	0	335D	NEH	77339
SORTERS RD	23100	295Q	SEM	77365
SOTHERLOCH LAKE DR	9300	329G	NWC	77379
SOTIRED	0	541E	BT	77520
SOTO CIR	7900	535F	SEH	77012
SOTORIA LN	6700	609Y	NEF	77459
SOULINIER	200	536H	PA	77506
SOURIS VALLEY CT	0	571G	SWH	77085
SOURIS VALLEY LN	0	571G	SWH	77085
SOUTH	0	502N	BT	77520
SOUTH	0	540T	LP	77571
SOUTH	0	576U	SEH	77034
N. SOUTH	100	537G	PA	77503
SOUTH	100	537L	PA	77503
SOUTH	200	501S	BT	77520
SOUTH	400	540U	MP	77571
N. SOUTH	1100	497Y	SEC	77503
SOUTH	1700	493G	NEH	77009
SOUTH	5700	484B	KT	77494
SOUTH	21000	256S	SEM	77357
SOUTH BLVD	1300	493W	SWH	77006
SOUTH BLVD	1700	492Z	SWH	77098
SOUTH BLVD	3000	492X	SWH	77005
SOUTH CT	0	529T	SWH	77099
SOUTH DR	0	658Z	LC	77573
SOUTH DR	3600	612A	NEF	77053
SOUTH DR	10300	529T	SWH	77099
SOUTH DR	12300	528V	SWH	77099
SOUTH DR	15000	498E	CV	77530
SOUTH DR	17100	367K	CY	77433
SOUTH (S.H. 288) FRWY	4300	533W	SWH	77004
SOUTH (S.H. 288) FRWY	4300	533W	SWH	77004
SOUTH (S.H. 288) FRWY	7500	533W	SWH	77021
SOUTH (S.H. 288) FRWY	7500	533W	SWH	77021
SOUTH (S.H. 288) FRWY	8100	533W	SWH	77051
SOUTH FRWY	8100	533W	SWH	77051
SOUTH (S.H. 288) FRWY	11900	573J	SWH	77047
SOUTH (S.H. 288) FRWY	11900	573J	SWH	77047
SOUTH LN	900	412T	NWH	77088
SOUTH RD	0	334Z	NEH	77338
SOUTH RD	400	501F	NEC	77521
SOUTH ACRES DR	3700	573G	SEH	77047
SOUTH ACRES DR	4700	574F	SEH	77048
SOUTHAMPTON	0	258L	SEM	77357
SOUTHAMPTON CT	4600	577E	PA	77504
SOUTHAMPTON DR	16000	330Q	NWC	77379
SOUTHAMPTON LN	0	657Y	LC	77573
SOUTH ARBOR DR	11400	616M	SEC	77089
SOUTH ASPEN DR	12200	616H	SEC	77089
SOUTH AUTUMN DR	12000	616M	SEC	77089
SOUTHAVEN DR	19400	446V	NWC	77084
SOUTHBANK	6600	534X	SEH	77033
SOUTHBANK	8600	574B	SEH	77033
SOUTHBAY DR	2900	612R	PL	77584
E. SOUTH BELT	0	575X	SEH	77075
SOUTHBELT INDUSTRIAL DR	1	612B	SWC	77047
SOUTH BEND CIR	1900	610J	MC	77459
SOUTH BERRY LN	12000	616L	SEC	77089
SOUTH BIRCH LN	12000	616L	SEC	77089
SOUTHBLUFF BLVD	8800	576W	SEC	77089
SOUTHBLUFF BLVD	8900	615D	SEC	77089
SOUTHBLUFF LN	0	327Z	NWC	77429
SOUTH BREEZE	8300	570B	SWH	77071
SOUTHBRIAR LN	25100	485N	NEF	77494
SOUTHBRIDGE RD	12600	573Q	SEH	77047
SOUTHBROOK	3500	580V	SA	77571
SOUTHBROOK CIR	100	372L	NCC	77060
SOUTHBROOK DR	5600	574A	SEH	77033
SOUTHBROOK DR	6200	574C	SEH	77087
SOUTH BRUSH DR	11500	616G	SEC	77089
SOUTH CANYON DR	11500	616G	SEC	77089
SOUTHCHASE LN	4200	371F	NWC	77014
SOUTHCHASE LN	5300	657Z	LC	77573
SOUTHCHASE TRAIL LN	0	525H	NEF	77450
SOUTHCHESTER LN	200	489F	SWH	77079
SOUTH CLIFF DR	12200	616L	SEC	77089
SOUTH COAST DR	12400	573Q	SEH	77047
SOUTHCOTT CT	0	525D	NEF	77450
SOUTH CREEK	1200	487B	NWH	77084
SOUTHCREEK	1400	447X	NWH	77084
SOUTHCREEK LN	0	333S	NCC	77073
SOUTHCREST	5800	534P	SEH	77033
SOUTH CREST LN	12100	616G	SEC	77089
SOUTHCROSS LN	0	525H	NEF	77450
SOUTH DAKOTA	0	541A	BT	77520
SOUTHDALE	0	531H	BL	77401
SOUTH DOWN CT	12000	616G	SEC	77089
SOUTHDOWN DR	2600	613K	NEB	77584
SOUTH DOWN DR	11500	616G	SEC	77089
SOUTHDOWN TRACE TRAIL	0	576V	SEH	77034
SOUTHERLAND RD	4000	451J	NWH	77092
SOUTHERN	7600	535N	SEH	77087
SOUTHERN LN	3000	614V	PL	77584
SOUTHERN BAYBERRY DR	0	289C	NWC	77375
SOUTHERN BREEZE CT	15300	457U	NEH	77049
SOUTHERN BROOK TRAIL	23000	291E	NWC	77389
SOUTHERN CHASE DR	0	612P	PL	77545
SOUTHERN COAST DR	0	251L	WD	77380
SOUTHERN COLONY CT	21000	406P	NWC	77449
SOUTHERN CREEK DR	0	612T	PL	77584
SOUTHERN CRESCENT	0	251K	SWM	77380
SOUTHERN CROSS CT	3100	293U	NCC	77373
SOUTHERN CYPRESS CT	0	328S	NWC	77429
SOUTHERN CYPRESS LN	15000	327V	CY	77429
SOUTHERN CYPRESS LN	15000	327V	CY	77429
SOUTHERN GLEN LN	0	484T	NEF	77494
SOUTHERN GREEN DR	0	612P	PL	77545
SOUTHERN GROVE LN	0	612T	PL	77584
SOUTHERN HILLS DR	2200	659C	LC	77573
SOUTHERN HILLS DR	3100	610F	MC	77459
SOUTHERN HILLS DR	5800	330X	NWC	77069
SOUTHERN HILLS RD	900	336A	NEH	77339
SOUTHERN KNOLL LN	0	612P	PL	77545
SOUTHERN LEAF LN	0	335P	NCC	77338
SOUTHERN MAGNOLIA CIR	14500	377Y	NEH	77044
SOUTHERN MANOR CT	0	612P	PL	77545
SOUTHERN MANOR DR	0	612Q	PL	77584
SOUTHERN MAPLE LN	19600	486G	SWC	77094
SOUTHERN MILL CT	0	612P	PL	77545
S. SOUTHERN OAKS DR	2700	331P	NWC	77068
N. SOUTHERN OAKS DR	2700	331P	NWC	77068
SOUTHERN OAKS DR	16500	331P	NWC	77068
SOUTHERN PASS CT	900	618E	SEH	77062
SOUTHERN PINES CT	1500	336G	NEH	77339
SOUTHERN PINES DR	1900	336G	NEH	77339
SOUTHERN RIDGE DR	0	612P	PL	77584
SOUTHERN SPRING LN	0	417B	NEC	77044
SOUTHERN STAR DR	0	612Q	PL	77584
N. SOUTHERN STONE DR	0	367U	NWC	77095
S. SOUTHERN STONE DR	16200	367V	NWC	77095
SOUTHERN STREAM DR	0	406C	NWC	77433
SOUTHERN TRAIL	0	539N	DP	77536
SOUTHERN TRAILS DR	0	612Q	PL	77584
SOUTHERN VALLEY DR	0	612P	PL	77584
SOUTHERN WAY LN	0	612T	PL	77584
SOUTH FALLS DR	0	616L	SEC	77089
SOUTH FALLS TERRACE	10900	367U	NWC	77095
SOUTHFIELD CT	0	572E	SWH	77045
SOUTHFIELD CT	0	572E	SWH	77045
SOUTHFIELD DR	0	616U	FR	77546
SOUTHFIELD DR	13000	572J	SWH	77045
SOUTHFORD	5800	534T	SEH	77033
SOUTHFORD MANOR LN	3100	485T	NEF	77494
SOUTHFORD WAY	0	332R	NCC	77073
SOUTHFORK BLVD	3100	613W	NWB	77578
SOUTH FORK BLVD	11100	616L	SEC	77089
SOUTHFORK DR	0	613Y	NEB	77584
W. SOUTHFORK PINES CIR	1	251A	WD	77381
SOUTHFORK PINES CT	1	251A	WD	77381
SOUTHFORK PINES DR	0	251A	WD	77381
SOUTHFORK PINES PLACE	1	251A	WD	77381
SOUTH FORTY DR	6500	611A	SWH	77053
SOUTH FOUR LN	1	458F	NEC	77049
SOUTHGATE BLVD	1800	532G	SWH	77030
SOUTHGATE DR	0	612V	PL	77584
SOUTHGATE DR	1	251X	WD	77380
SOUTH GLEN DR	11700	529S	SWH	77099
SOUTHGOOD	5800	534T	SEH	77033
SOUTH GREEN DR	12500	576Q	SEH	77034
SOUTH GREENHOUSE RD	900	486H	SWC	77094
SOUTH GROVE LN	12000	616L	SEC	77089
SOUTH HALL	6800	454H	NEH	77028
SOUTH HALL	7300	455E	NEH	77028
SOUTHHAMPTON ESTATES	5300	492Z	SWH	77005
SOUTH HILL DR	11400	616M	SEC	77089
SOUTHHOLLOW LN	0	253N	SEM	77386
SOUTHHOOK CT	20900	332Z	NCC	77073
SOUTH HOU-PASADENA	1300	536T	PA	77502
SOUTHHOVER CT	0	575R	SEH	77075
SOUTH HURST DR	11900	616G	SEC	77089
SOUTHINGTON	5800	534T	SEH	77033
SOUTHLAKE DR	11600	489S	SWH	77077
SOUTHLAND CT	0	610Y	MC	77459
SOUTHLARK	5900	534P	SEH	77033
SOUTHLAWN	3700	533Q	SEH	77021
SOUTHLEA	5200	534N	SEH	77033
SOUTHLEIGH DR	8900	329M	NWC	77379
SOUTHLINE	0	242H	WCO	77484
SOUTHLINE RD	13700	528X	NEF	77498
SOUTHLINE RD	14300	528W	NEF	77498
SOUTH LOOP (I.H. 610) W.	400	533S	SWH	77054
SOUTH LOOP (I.H. 610) W.	1400	532U	SWH	77054
SOUTH LOOP (I.H. 610) E.	2200	533T	SEH	77021
SOUTH LOOP (I.H. 610) W.	3200	532U	SWH	77025
SOUTH LOOP (I.H. 610) E.	3900	533T	SEH	77051
SOUTH LOOP (I.H. 610) W.	4300	531V	SWH	77096
SOUTH LOOP (I.H. 610) E.	4400	534N	SEH	77033
SOUTH LOOP (I.H. 610) E.	6051	534N	SEH	77087
SOUTH LOOP (I.H. 610) E.	6052	534N	SEH	77087
SOUTH LOOP (I.H. 610) E.	6100	534N	SEH	77087
SOUTH LOOP (I.H. 610) E.	7700	535F	SEH	77017
SOUTH LOOP (I.H. 610) E.	7701	535F	SEH	77012
SOUTH LOOP (I.H. 610) E.	8500	535F	SEH	77017
SOUTH MAIN	6200	532L	SWH	77030
SOUTH MAPLE DR	0	444Z	KT	77493
SOUTH MAPLE DR	0	444Z	KT	77493
SOUTHMAYDE CREEK DR	700	488B	SWH	77079
SOUTH MEADOW DR	0	659D	LC	77573
SOUTHMEADOW DR	7500	570C	SWH	77071
SOUTHMEADOW DR	12000	569E	SF	77477
SOUTHMEADOW DR	12300	568H	SF	77477
SOUTHMERE LN	3200	613L	NEB	77584
SOUTH MILL LN	12000	616L	SEC	77089
SOUTHMINSTER DR	5400	571E	SWH	77035
SOUTH MISSION CIR	2100	656U	FR	77546
SOUTHMONT	5800	534P	SEH	77033
SOUTHMORE	200	288H	TB	77375
SOUTHMORE	1000	493W	SWH	77004
SOUTHMORE	1500	533C	SEH	77004
W. SOUTHMORE AVE	100	536P	PA	77502
E. SOUTHMORE AVE	100	536R	PA	77502
E. SOUTHMORE AVE	2800	537P	PA	77503
SOUTHMORE CIR	3900	533H	SEH	77004
SOUTHMUND	5800	534P	SEH	77033
SOUTH OAK CIR	11600	616H	SEC	77089
SOUTH OAK CT	11600	616H	SEC	77089
SOUTH OAK DR	12100	616H	SEC	77089
SOUTH ORCHARD DR	11400	616M	SEC	77089
SOUTH PACIFIC	13900	457F	NEC	77049
SOUTH PARK	0	256K	SEM	77357
SOUTHPARK	21700	256F	SEM	77357
SOUTH PARK DR	0	251Z	SWM	77380
SOUTH PARK GROVE	400	493J	SWH	77007
SOUTH PARK VIEW DR	17900	447W	NWH	77084
SOUTH PASS LN	9100	409G	NWC	77064
SOUTHPINE CT	7000	250T	NWC	77389
SOUTHPOINT WIND LN	9400	410J	NWC	77040
SOUTH PONDS DR	0	618S	SEH	77598
SOUTHPORT DR	9700	576T	SEH	77089
SOUTHPORT LN	500	619V	LC	77565
SOUTHRIDGE	1500	332S	NWC	77090
SOUTHRIDGE	5800	534P	SEH	77033
SOUTHRIDGE DR	17600	255N	SEM	77365
SOUTHRIDGE CROSSING LN	0	332N	NWC	77090
SOUTH RIM TRAIL	19100	332E	NWC	77388
SOUTH ROYALE DR	11100	616L	SEC	77089
SOUTH ROYAL POINT DR	0	338E	NEH	77345
SOUTH RUN DR	0	616G	SEC	77089
SOUTH SAM HOUSTN PKWY E.	1	572Z	SWC	77047
SOUTH SAM HOUSN PKWY E.	1800	573Y	SEH	77047
SOUTH SAM HOUSN PKWY W.	3000	571S	SWH	77053
SOUTH SAM HOUSN PKWY E.	4100	574X	SEH	77048
SOUTH SAM HOUSN PKWY W.	6200	571Y	SWH	77085
SOUTH SAM HOUSN PKWY E.	7200	575Y	SEH	77075
SOUTH SAM HOUSN PKWY E.	9400	576Y	SEH	77089
SOUTH SAM HOUSN PKWY W.	9500	570K	MC	77071
SOUTH SAM HOUS PKWY W.	10700	569D	SWH	77031
SOUTH SAM HOUS PKWY W.	11300	569D	SWH	77031
SOUTHSAND DR	3900	613V	NEB	77584
SOUTHSEAS	5700	534S	SEH	77033
SOUTHSHIP CT	20900	332Z	NCC	77073
SOUTH SHORE BLVD	0	660E	LC	77573
SOUTH SHORE BLVD	2300	619Y	LC	77573
SOUTH SHORE BLVD	5200	659D	LC	77573
SOUTHSHORE DR	3200	336Q	NEH	77338
SOUTHSIDE PLACE	0	532E	SS	77025
SOUTHSPRING DR	12600	573Q	SEH	77047
SOUTH STADIUM LN	6300	484B	KT	77494
SOUTH STAR LN	0	621A	SB	77586
SOUTH TEMPLE DR	0	367Z	NWC	77095
SOUTHTOWN	5800	534T	SEH	77033
SOUTH TRACE DR	12700	371E	NWC	77066
SOUTH TRESA	0	576D	PA	77504
SOUTHURST	5800	534P	SEH	77033
SOUTH VALE DR	12200	616M	SEC	77089
SOUTH VALLEY LN	12000	616L	SEC	77089
SOUTHVIEW	8200	533Y	SEH	77051
SOUTHVIEW	10700	573L	SEH	77047
SOUTH VILLAGE DR	0	617V	SEH	77598
SOUTHVILLE	5800	534T	SEH	77033
SOUTHVINE CT	20900	332Z	NCC	77073
SOUTHWARK	8700	455C	NEH	77028
SOUTHWAY DR	7300	534R	SEH	77087
SOUTHWELL	5800	534P	SEH	77033
SOUTHWELL LN	0	657U	LC	77573
SOUTHWEST (U.S. 59 S) FRWY	100	493X	SWH	77004
SOUTHWEST (U.S. 59 S) FRWY	100	493X	SWH	77004
SOUTHWEST (U.S. 59 S) FRWY	400	493X	SWH	77002
SOUTHWEST (U.S. 59 S) FRWY	400	493X	SWH	77002
SOUTHWEST (U.S. 59 S) FRWY	600	493X	SWH	77006
SOUTHWEST (U.S. 59 S) FRWY	600	493X	SWH	77006
SOUTHWST (U.S. 59 S) FRWY	1900	492X	SWH	77098
SOUTHWST (U.S. 59 S) FRWY	1900	492X	SWH	77098
SOUTHWST (U.S. 59 S) FRWY	3200	492X	SWH	77027
SOUTHWST (U.S. 59 S) FRWY	3200	492X	SWH	77027
SOUTHWST (U.S. 59 S) FRWY	5000	491X	SWH	77056
SOUTHWST (U.S. 59 S) FRWY	5000	491X	SWH	77056
SOUTHWST (U.S. 59 S) FRWY	5600	491X	SWH	77057
SOUTHWST (U.S. 59 S) FRWY	5600	491X	SWH	77057
SOUTHWST (U.S. 59 S) FRWY	6200	531A	SWH	77074
SOUTHWST (U.S. 59 S) FRWY	6200	531A	SWH	77074
SOUTHWST (U.S. 59 S) FRWY	6500	530H	SWH	77074
SOUTHWST (U.S. 59 S) FRWY	6500	530H	SWH	77074
SOUTHWST (U.S. 59 S) FRWY	9900	529Z	SWH	77074
SOUTHWST (U.S. 59 S) FRWY	9900	529Z	SWH	77074
SOUTHWT (U.S. 59 S) FRWY	11000	569E	SWH	77031
SOUTHWT (U.S. 59 S) FRWY	11000	569E	SWH	77031
SOUTHWT (U.S. 59 S) FRWY	11900	569E	SF	77477
SOUTHWT (U.S. 59 S) FRWY	11900	569E	SF	77477
SOUTHWT (U.S. 59 S) FRWY	13100	568X	SG	77478
SOUTHWT (U.S. 59 S) FRWY	13100	568X	SG	77478
SOUTHWESTERN	0	613X	NEB	77578
SOUTHWESTERN	3800	532E	WU	77005
SOUTHWESTERN BLVD	100	568R	SG	77478
SOUTHWEST PLAZA CT	10600	529Z	SWH	77074
SOUTHWEST PLAZA DR	10400	529Z	SWH	77074
SOUTHWICK	1400	450N	NWH	77080

Street Name	Block	Pg/Sq	Loc	Zips
SOUTHWICK DR	9800	335U	HM	77338
SOUTHWICK DR	19500	255Y	SEM	77365
SOUTHWIND	4800	533V	SEH	77033
SOUTHWIND	5100	534T	SEH	77033
SOUTH WIND DR	11900	616L	SEC	77089
SOUTHWOLD LN	11000	530Z	SWH	77096
SOUTHWOOD CIR	200	541D	BT	77520
S. SOUTHWOOD CT	6300	570D	SWH	77035
N. SOUTHWOOD CT	6300	570D	SWH	77035
SOUTHWOOD DR	100	252A	SD	77380
SOUTHWOOD DR	1400	541D	BT	77520
SOUTH WOOD DR	25400	257C	WV	77357
THORNHILL CREEK CT	25600	295V	NEH	77365
SOUTHWOOD OAKS DR	20600	295M	SEM	77365
SOUTHWOOD TRACE LN	15100	457Q	NEC	77049
SOUTHWOOD TRACE LN	15100	457P	NEC	77049
SOUTHWORTH LN	0	613W	NEB	77578
SOUTHWYCK BLVD	0	613U	NEB	77584
SOUTHWYCK PKWY	2000	613T	NEB	77584
SOUTH YORK LN	12000	616L	SEC	77089
SOUTINE ST	0	533F	SWH	77021
SOVEREIGN DR	5800	529D	SWH	77036
SOWAY	2400	450M	NWH	77080
SOWDEN RD	12000	451J	NWH	77055
SOWDEN RD	12100	450M	NWH	77080
SOWLES PARK DR	1900	445S	NWC	77493
SPA DR	2700	538T	DP	77536
SPACE CENTER BLVD	0	538W	PA	77505
SPACE CENTER BLVD	0	578J	PA	77505
SPACE CENTER BLVD	13000	578N	SEH	77059
SPACE CENTER BLVD	14000	618M	SEH	77062
SPACE CENTER BLVD	16300	619J	SEH	77058
SPACE PARK DR	1200	618V	NB	77058
SPACE PARK DR	1600	619S	NB	77058
SPADY	0	453F	NEH	77022
SPALDING GRAY TRAIL	0	325L	NWC	77433
SPALDING GRAY TRAIL	0	325L	NWC	77433
SPANGLER DR	0	295L	SEM	77365
SPANIEL DR	400	496D	NEH	77013
SPANISH ACORN LN	3500	291L	NWC	77389
SPANISH BAY CT	6800	609Q	MC	77459
SPANISH COVE DR	100	338Z	NEC	77532
SPANISH COVE DR	1100	339W	NEC	77532
SPANISH GRANT DR	10400	528W	NEF	77498
SPANISH MILL DR	9300	369R	NWC	77064
SPANISH MOSS CT	5800	330H	NWC	77379
SPANISH MOSS LN	1000	488M	SWH	77077
SPANISH NEEDLE DR	19100	446U	NWC	77084
SPANISH OAK DR	4800	371E	NWC	77066
SPANISH OAK DR	5700	370H	NWC	77066
SPANISH OAK DR	6100	578J	PA	77505
SPANISH OAK HILL CT	2400	292W	NWC	77388
SPANISH OAKS DR	26200	257M	SEM	77357
SPANISH OAKS DR	26500	258J	SEM	77357
SPANISH OAK WAY	6000	330H	NWC	77379
SPANISH RIVER LN	14300	327Y	NWC	77429
SPANISH TRACE	100	339W	NEC	77532
SPANN	1900	492Q	SWH	77019
SPAR CREST CT	0	368A	NWC	77429
SPARKFORD	0	525R	NEF	77469
SPARKLEBERRY	1	251P	WD	77380
SPARKLE BROOK LN	0	367T	NWC	77433
SPARKLE LAKE LN	0	366Z	NWC	77433
SPARKLING BAY LN	14800	618B	SEH	77062
SPARKLING BROOK CT	0	612L	PL	77584
SPARKLING BROOK DR	0	612L	PL	77584
SPARKLING CREEK DR	29700	253W	SEM	77386
SPARKLING SPRINGS DR	8300	407H	NWC	77095
SPARKLING WATER DR	100	338C	NEC	77336
SPARKS	0	568K	SG	77498
SPARKS	3200	454B	NEH	77093
SPARKS VALLEY CT	6100	408T	NWC	77084
SPARKS VALLEY DR	14700	408T	NWC	77084
SPARROW	3000	573B	SEH	77051
SPARROW	9800	539T	LP	77571
SPARROW CIR	2000	657J	FR	77546
SPARROW DR	3600	613Y	NEB	77584
SPARROW CREEK CT	0	524F	NEF	77494
SPARROW CREST DR	0	484J	KT	77494
SPARROW HAWK CT	1	252N	WD	77380
SPARROW KNOLL CT	1200	485G	SWC	77450
SPARROWS GLEN LN	6300	290U	NWC	77379
SPARROWS POINT DR	0	332X	NWC	77090
SPARROWS RIDGE DR	0	486Q	SWC	77450
SPARROWS SPUR ST	0	526W	NEF	77469
SPARROW WAY CT	17300	407L	NWC	77095
SPARTA	7800	455T	NEH	77028
SPARTA DR	3300	610U	MC	77459
SPARTAN CT	13100	448D	NWC	77041
SPARTAN DR	5200	448D	NWC	77041
SPARTAN BATTLE WAY	0	256T	SEM	77357
SPAR WAY	300	379U	NEC	77532
SPATES DR	700	498B	CV	77530
SPATSWOOD LN	22700	445U	NWC	77449
SPAULDING	8200	454D	NEH	77016
SPAULDING RD	100	258Q	NEC	77357
SPAVINAW WAY	0	609Y	NEF	77459
SPEARMAN DR	9400	410E	NWC	77040
SPEAR POINT COVE	800	488F	SWH	77079
SPEARS DR	2200	375G	HM	77396
SPEARS RD	1200	372E	NWC	77067
SPEARS RD	3500	371F	NWC	77066
SPEARS RD	3600	613Y	NEB	77578
SPEARS RD	21900	296K	SEM	77365
S. SPEARS RD	24200	296K	SEM	77365
SPEARS GEARS RD	11300	372K	NWC	77067
SPEAR VALLEY LN	0	256X	SEM	77365
SPECKLED CT	0	332Z	NCC	77073
SPECTRUM BLVD	0	613A	PL	77047
SPECTRUM DR	27300	252K	OR	77385
SPEER LANDING DR	11000	370S	NWC	77064
SPELL	100	452H	NWH	77022
SPELL	200	453E	NWH	77022
SPELL CIR	0	289N	TB	77375
SPELL RD	0	289N	TB	77375
SPELL RD	10500	289P	NWC	77375
SPELLBROOK CT	2400	619Y	LC	77573
SPELLBROOK DR	18000	447F	NWC	77084
SPELLBROOK BEND LN	22800	525K	NEF	77407
SPELLBROOK POINT LN	0	328G	NWC	77377
SPELLMAN RD	4300	531W	SWH	77035
SPELLMAN RD	4300	571D	SWH	77035
SPELLMAN RD	5200	571B	SWH	77035
SPELLMAN RD	5300	571A	SWH	77096
SPELLMAN RD	6400	570D	SWH	77096
SPELLMAN RD	9100	570A	SWH	77031
SPELLMAN RIDGE DR	0	328J	NWC	77429
SPELMAN ST	5600	532A	WU	77005
SPENCE	0	419Q	BR	77532
SPENCE	1900	454N	NEH	77093
SPENCE RD	16000	373S	NEH	77060
SPENCE PARK CT	0	292K	NCC	77373
SPENCER	3700	492H	SWH	77007
SPENCER BLVD	24000	286A	SWM	77355
SPENCER BLVD	24500	246W	SWM	77355
SPENCER RD	10900	409P	NWC	77041
SPENCER RD	14400	408Q	NWC	77095
SPENCER RD	16100	407Q	NWC	77095
SPENCER GATE	0	292K	SP	77373
SPENCER GLEN LN	1400	373A	NCC	77073
SPENCER HWY	1	536X	SH	77587
SPENCER HWY	2100	537Y	PA	77504
SPENCER HWY	4700	537Y	PA	77505
SPENCER HWY	6100	538W	PA	77505
SPENCER HWY	8000	538Z	PA	77505
SPENCER HWY	8001	538Z	DP	77536
SPENCER HWY	8400	538Z	LP	77571
SPENCER HWY	8401	538Z	PA	77505
SPENCER HWY	8900	539X	LP	77571
W. SPENCER LANDING	100	539Z	LP	77571
S. SPENCER LANDING	100	539Z	LP	77571
E. SPENCER LANDING DR	100	539Z	LP	77571
SPENCER TERRACE	24200	286A	SWM	77355
SPENWICK DR	1800	451S	NWH	77055
SPERBER LN	2300	493R	DT	77003
SPERRY GARDENS DR	16500	367Z	NWC	77095
SPERRY GARDENS DR	16500	407C	NWC	77095
SPEYBURN CT	16000	407D	NWC	77095
SPICA	0	248X	TB	77375
SPICE LN	8300	529Q	SWH	77072
SPICEBUSH CT	1	250M	WD	77381
SPICECANYON CT	0	406D	NWC	77433
SPICED CIDER LN	0	326J	NWC	77433
SPICE LEAF TRAIL	0	525B	NEF	77494
SPICE TRAIL CT	0	484Q	NEF	77494
SPICEWOOD	9800	289U	NWC	77375
SPICEWOOD		289Q	NWC	77375
N. SPICEWOOD LN	11400	456F	NEC	77044
SPICEWOOD LN	11400	456F	NEC	77044
SPICEWOOD SPRINGS LN	17400	330G	NWC	77379
SPIKEWOOD DR	8800	455R	NEH	77078
SPILL CREEK DR	11600	612R	PL	77584
SPILLER DR	16900	331K	NWC	77379
SPILLERS LN	1300	449Z	NWH	77043
SPILLERS LN	2500	449V	NWH	77043
S. SPINCASTER CIR	0	250P	NWC	77389
N. SPINCASTER CIR	0	250N	NWC	77389
S. SPINCASTER CT	0	250P	NWC	77389
N. SPINCASTER CT	0	250P	NWC	77389
SPINDLE DR	5100	411F	NWC	77086
SPINDLE ARBOR RD	0	367D	NWC	77429
SPINDLE RIDGE DR	0	252T	SEM	77386
SPINDLETOP CT	3300	613W	NWB	77578
W. SPINDLE TREE CIR	0	249B	SWM	77354
E. SPINDLE TREE CIR	0	249B	SWM	77354
SPINDLE TREE DR	0	249B	SWM	77354
SPINDLEWOOD DR	9200	528T	NEF	77083
SPINDRIFT PLACE	1	251G	WD	77381
SPINET	7600	415W	NEH	77016
SPINKS CREEK LN	4200	291X	NWC	77388
SPINNAKER CT	800	419B	NEC	77532
SPINNAKER DR	2000	660A	LC	77573
SPINNAKER DR	15900	419F	NEC	77532
SPINNAKER BAY LN	8300	613V	PL	77584
SPINNAKER WAY	1100	568E	SG	77498
SPINNER CT	18400	377D	NEC	77346
SPINNER ALDER DR	0	329L	NWC	77379
SPINNEY LN	18500	407N	NWC	77433
S. SPINNING WHEEL CIR	0	249C	SWM	77382
N. SPINNING WHEEL CIR	0	249B	SWM	77382
SPINWOOD DR	100	457X	NEC	77015
S. SPIRAL VINE CIR	1	250H	WD	77381
N. SPIRAL VINE CIR	1	250H	WD	77381
SPIRALWOOD LN	9400	411A	NWC	77086
SPIRIT FALLS CT	0	377K	NEC	77346
SPIRIT LAKE CT	0	377L	NEC	77346
SPIRIT LAKE LN	0	377H	NEH	77346
SPIRIT MOUND LN	0	377F	NEC	77346
SPIVEY RD	7800	460T	HG	77562
SPLASH TOWN DR	100	292T	NCC	77373
SPLENDID CIR	0	444D	NWC	77493
SPLENDORA DR	20500	446P	NWC	77449
SPLINTERED OAK DR	13300	368Y	NWC	77065
SPLINTWOOD CT	2500	297U	NEH	77345
SPLIT RD	28100	288K	NWC	77377
SPLIT BRANCH CT	2000	488N	SWH	77077
SPLIT CEDAR DR	14300	457U	NEC	77015
SPLIT CREEK DR	17800	329M	NWC	77379
SPLIT CREEK LN	0	612F	PL	77545
SPLIT CYPRESS LN	7900	408L	NWC	77041
SPLIT LAKE LN	0	377H	NEH	77346
SPLIT OAK CT	7500	410Q	NWC	77040
SPLIT OAK DR	7800	410R	NWC	77040
SPLIT PINE DR	8000	410L	NWC	77040
SPLIT RAIL LN	12300	570G	SWH	77071
SPLIT RAIL RIDGE	0	293T	NCC	77373
SPLIT RIDGE LN	0	575V	SEH	77075
SPLIT RIVER LN	0	616E	SEC	77089
SPLITROCK CT	1	251A	WD	77381
SPLIT ROCK RD	1	251B	WD	77381
SPLITROCK RD	1	251E	WD	77381
SPLIT ROCK COVE	100	251B	WD	77381
SPLIT ROCK FALLS	9100	249Z	NWC	77375
SPLITTING WILLOW CT	0	297P	NEH	77365
SPLIT WILLOW CT	0	527P	NEF	77083
SPLIT WILLOW DR	16300	527P	NEF	77083
SPODE	9300	456E	NEH	77078
SPOFFORD	0	459H	NEC	77562
SPOKE HOLLOW CT	0	367W	NWC	77095
SPOKE HOLLOW CREEK LN		367N	NWC	77433
SPOON BILL	6000	444K	KT	77493
SPOONBILL DR	2400	619Y	LC	77573
SPOONBILL DR	4300	620G	SB	77586
SPOON CREEK LN	8900	329M	NWC	77379
N. SPOONER	100	536H	PA	77506
SPOONER	100	536M	PA	77506
SPOONER	1500	536R	PA	77502
SPOONWOOD CT	19200	337S	NEC	77346
SPOONWOOD DR	19500	337S	NEC	77346
SPOONWOOD DR	20300	337R	NEC	77346
SPORAN LN	8800	575U	SEH	77075
SPORTS HAVEN DR	8000	377D	NEC	77346
SPORTS HAVEN DR	8300	378A	NEC	77346
SPORTSPLEX DR	0	658R	LC	77573
SPOTSLYVANIA LN	8400	527P	NEF	77083
SPOTTED DEER DR	1	250H	WD	77381
SPOTTED FAWN CT	1	251A	WD	77381
SPOTTED HORSE DR	10000	409C	NWC	77064
SPOTTED LILLY WAY	0	249A	SWM	77354
SPOTTED PONY CT	26900	246P	SWM	77355
SPOTTSWOOD DR	11000	415N	NEH	77016
SPRADS RD	100	413J	NCC	77037
SPRAGUE	6900	578B	PA	77505
SPRANGLETOP AVE	0	461N	NEC	77521
SPRANGLETOP CT	11000	371S	NWC	77086
SPREADING OAK	0	368H	NWC	77429
W. SPREADING OAK AVE	100	656D	FR	77546
E. SPREADING OAK AVE	100	656D	FR	77546
W. SPREADING OAK DR	100	412Z	NEH	77076
E. SPREADING OAK DR	100	413W	NEH	77076
SPREADING OAK DR	12400	369E	NWC	77429
SPREADING OAK LN	12000	248J	SWM	77362
SPREADING OAKS	0	247M	SWM	77362
SPREADING OAKS LN	25600	251N	SWM	77380
SPREY DR	5100	407Z	NWC	77084
SPRIGGS WAY	11600	490F	HE	77024
SPRILA PARK DR	0	327U	NWC	77429
SPRING	1200	493F	SWH	77007
SPRING CT	13500	288C	TB	77375
SPRING DR	400	576D	PA	77504
SPRING DR	22000	256F	SEM	77357
SPRING DR	23500	245W	SWM	77447
SPRING LN	4700	502G	BT	77521
SPRING LN	27500	249G	SWM	77354
SPRING LN	31800	248S	SWM	77362
SPRING-GREEN RD	6200	524U	NWF	77406
SPRING ACRES DR	29800	253W	SEM	77386
SPRING APPLE CT	1200	332R	NCC	77073
SPRING ARBOR CT	3900	614Z	PL	77584
SPRING ARBOR WAY	3600	297T	NEH	77345
SPRING ASH CT	0	485W	NEF	77494
SPRING ASPEN CT	0	485J	NEF	77494
SPRING ASPEN LN	20500	291V	NWC	77388
SPRINGBANK DR	16100	407H	NWC	77095
SPRING BARKER DR	16500	327X	NWC	77429
SPRING BASKET TRAIL	0	250Q	NWC	77389
SPRING BEND DR	2600	253W	SEM	77386
SPRINGBEND LN	21200	486N	SWC	77450
SPRINGBERRY CT	7800	330E	NWC	77379
SPRING BLOSSOM CT	5400	526A	NEF	77450
SPRING BLUFF LN	20500	291V	NWC	77388
W. SPRING BRANCH DR	4000	614Z	PL	77584
S. SPRING BRANCH DR	5000	614Z	PL	77584
SPRING BRANCH DR	8800	450U	NWH	77080
SPRING BREEZE	500	657V	LC	77573
SPRING BRIAR CT	2300	293X	NCC	77373
SPRING BRIAR LN	23800	293X	NCC	77373
SPRING BRIDBE PATH DR	0	293B	SEM	77386
SPRING BRIDGE CT	0	293B	SEM	77386
SPRINGBRIDGE DR	21600	332M	NCC	77073
SPRING BRIDGE PARK CT	0	293B	SEM	77386
SPRING BRIDGE RANCH DR	0	293B	SEM	77386
SPRING BRIDGE TRACE DR	0	293B	SEM	77386
SPRING BRIDGE TRAIL	0	293B	SEM	77386
SPRING BROOK CT	4000	614Z	PL	77584
SPRING BROOK CT	4300	449H	NWH	77041
SPRINGBROOK CT	5300	657Z	LC	77573
SPRING BROOK DR	9700	450F	NWH	77041
SPRING BROOK DR	10600	449H	NWH	77041
SPRINGBROOK GARDEN LN	6100	290V	NWC	77379
SPRINGBROOK HOLLOW CT	21200	290U	NWC	77379
SPRINGBROOK HOLLOW LN	0	290U	NWC	77379
SPRINGBROOK PLAZA DR	0	290R	NWC	77379
SPRINGBURY LN	0	484U	NEF	77494
SPRING BUSINESS CTR N	0	292K	SP	77373
SPRING CANYON CT	2700	371L	NWC	77067
SPRING CANYON DR	0	657Z	LC	77573
SPRING CEDAR LN	1901	488N	SWH	77077
SPRING CHASE DR	2600	253W	SEM	77386
W. SPRING CIRCLE DR	3900	614Z	PL	77584
E. SPRING CIRCLE DR	3900	614Z	PL	77584
N. SPRING CIRCLE DR	5000	614Z	PL	77584
SPRING CITY CT	1300	332W	NWC	77090
SPRING CLIFF CT	0	293W	NCC	77373
SPRING COLONY DR	2700	293A	SEM	77386
SPRINGCOURT DR	15700	618G	SEH	77062
SPRING COVE DR	3400	337B	NEH	77345
SPRING COVE LN	0	485S	NEF	77494
SPRING CREEK	0	251S	SWM	77380
SPRING CREEK	1500	292C	SEM	77386
SPRING CREEK	6000	330H	NWC	77379
SPRING CREEK	6400	407Q	NWC	77084
SPRING CREEK CIR	0	461T	NEC	77521
E. SPRING CREEK CIR	2100	334M	NCC	77338
W. SPRING CREEK CIR	7700	334M	NCC	77338
SPRING CREEK CIR	34200	247G	SWM	77362
SPRING CREEK CT	200	247G	SWM	77362
SPRING CREEK DR	0	656L	FR	77546
SPRING CREEK DR	2000	292V	NCC	77373
SPRING CREEK DR	2200	293S	NCC	77373
SPRING CREEK DR	24300	251N	SWM	77380
SPRING CREEK LN	2100	536T	SEH	77017
SPRING CREEK LN	2900	616N	PL	77581
SPRING CREEK FOREST	0	330M	NWC	77379
SPRING CREEK FOREST DR	16800	330G	NWC	77379
SPRING CREEK FOREST DR	17800	330C	NWC	77379
SPRING CREEK GROVE LN	6000	330H	NWC	77379
SPRING CREEK OAKS CIR	18500	331E	NWC	77379
SPRING CREEK OAKS CT	16800	330H	NWC	77379
SPRING CREEK OAKS DR	5800	330H	NWC	77379
SPRING CREEK TRAIL	0	366N	NWC	77433
SPRING CREEK TRAILS DR	200	292L	SP	77373
SPRINGCRESS	1200	619H	TL	77586
SPRINGCREST	12300	529J	SWH	77072
SPRING CREST CT	3900	614Z	PL	77584
SPRINGCROFT CT	0	289R	NWC	77375
SPRINGCROSS CT	0	488P	SWH	77077
SPRING CROSSING DR	22500	292K	NCC	77373
SPRING CRYSTAL CT	24000	293W	NCC	77373
SPRING CYPRESS RD	100	292P	NWC	77373
SPRING CYPRESS RD	1500	291X	NWC	77388
SPRING CYPRESS RD	4700	331A	NWC	77379
SPRING CYPRESS RD	5400	330E	NWC	77379
SPRING CYPRESS RD	9800	329L	NWC	77070
SPRING CYPRESS RD	11000	329N	NWC	77377
SPRING CYPRESS RD	12000	328S	NWC	77377
SPRING CYPRESS RD	13000	328S	NWC	77429
SPRING CYPRESS RD	15000	327Z	NWC	77429
SPRING CYPRESS RD	15200	367B	CY	77429
SPRING CYPRESS PLAZA DR	0	329P	NWC	77070
SPRINGDALE	7100	455E	NEH	77028
SPRINGDALE CT	2900	613X	NEB	77584
SPRINGDALE DR	3100	613X	NEB	77584
SPRING DANE DR	23900	293U	NCC	77373
SPRING DAY CT	2500	293T	NCC	77373
SPRING DAY LN	23900	293T	NCC	77373
SPRING DEW DR	0	376V	NEC	77346
SPRING DUSK DR	2200	293T	NCC	77373
SPRING ELMS DR	23800	293X	NCC	77373
SPRINGER	6400	534Q	SEH	77087
SPRINGER CEMETERY RD	25900	244Y	WCO	77447
SPRINGERTON CIR	19200	332C	NCC	77373
SPRINGFAIR CT	3000	291V	NWC	77388
SPRING FALLING WAY	0	292Q	NCC	77373
SPRING FALLS CT	0	613X	NEB	77578
SPRING FALLS DR	0	292S	NWC	77388
SPRING FERN LN	7900	410L	NWC	77040
SPRINGFIELD	0	615W	PL	77584
SPRINGFIELD AVE	0	615W	PL	77584
SPRINGFIELD AVE	5000	614Z	PL	77584
SPRING FIELD RD	2000	618G	SEH	77062
SPRINGFIELD GARDEN LN	6600	290Q	NWC	77379
SPRINGFIELD LAKES	4500	609E	SG	77479
SPRINGFIELD RIDGE DR	0	524A	NEF	77494
SPRINGFLIGHT LN	0	324S	NWC	77447
SPRING FLOWER LN	3200	291V	NWC	77388
SPRING FOREST CT	16000	578Y	SEH	77059
SPRING FOREST DR	3900	614Z	PL	77584
SPRING FOREST DR	5000	451C	NWH	77091
SPRING FOREST DR	15700	578Y	SEH	77059
SPRING FOREST DR	29500	252Z	SEM	77386
SPRING FOREST WAY	1300	288C	TB	77375
SPRING FORGE DR	0	293S	NCC	77373
SPRING FORK DR	23800	293X	NCC	77373
SPRING GARDEN	0	296Z	NEH	77339
SPRING GARDEN DR	3900	614Z	PL	77584
SPRING GARDENS DR	3200	296Z	NEH	77339
SPRING GATE DR	22200	334F	NCC	77373
SPRING GLADE DR	16600	327X	NWC	77429
SPRING GLEN DR	11300	329W	NWC	77070
SPRING GLEN LN	1600	615F	PL	77581
SPRING GREEN BLVD	0	524C	NEF	77494
SPRING GREEN CT	1800	570X	MC	77489
SPRING GREEN DR	8500	408E	NWC	77095
SPRING GROVE	0	528V	SWH	77099
SPRING GROVE CT	4000	614Z	PL	77584
SPRING GROVE DR	11400	529S	SWH	77099
SPRING GROVE LN	5700	334A	NCC	77373
SPRING GUM DR	23800	293X	NCC	77373
SPRING HARBOR DR	0	293W	NCC	77373
SPRING HARVEST DR	10300	369X	NWC	77064
SPRING HAVEN CT	0	657Y	LC	77573
SPRINGHAVEN CT	0	484F	NEF	77494
SPRING HAVEN CT	16800	375J	NEH	77396
SPRING HAVEN DR	6100	375J	NEH	77396
SPRING HAVENS	0	292U	NCC	77373
SPRINGHEATH LN	0	290L	NWC	77379
SPRING HEATHER CT	0	330E	NWC	77379
SPRINGHILL	7100	533P	SEH	77021
SPRINGHILL DR	0	571Z	SWH	77053
SPRING HILL DR	100	252X	SEM	77386
SPRINGHILL DR	3100	609D	MC	77459
SPRING HILL LN	0	255P	SEM	77365
SPRING HILL LN	0	659H	LC	77573
SPRINGHILL BEND	15100	327V	NWC	77429
SPRING HILL PLACE	25700	292U	NCC	77373
SPRING HILLS DR	1100	252Y	SEM	77386
SPRING HOLLOW	1	491F	SWH	77024
SPRING HOLLOW DR	13200	248U	TB	77375
SPRINGHOPE CT	500	457U	NEC	77049
SPRINGHURST CT	0	293T	NCC	77373
SPRING IRIS LN	4500	658N	LC	77573
SPRING IRIS LN	25200	485N	NEF	77494
SPRING IVY LN	5800	291W	NWC	77379
SPRING KNOLL DR	1300	288C	TB	77375
SPRING LAKE	0	450Q	NWH	77080
SPRING LAKE DR	7100	249L	SWM	77354
SPRING LAKE DR	14700	328Z	NWC	77070
SPRING LAKE PARK LN	2200	252R	SEM	77386
SPRING LAKES	2800	609F	MC	77459
SPRING LAKES HAVEN	100	292U	NCC	77373
SPRINGLAND CT	10300	369W	NWC	77065
SPRINGLAND DR	10300	369W	NWC	77065
SPRING LANDING	0	291V	NWC	77388
SPRING LANDING	0	658N	LC	77573
SPRING LANDING DR	0	612K	PL	77545
SPRING LANDING LN	0	613T	NEB	77584
SPRINGLEA	4400	336Z	NEC	77346
SPRING LEAF DR	6500	330L	NWC	77379
SPRING LEIGH DR	0	330E	NWC	77379
SPRINGLIGHT LN	20500	291V	NWC	77388
SPRINGLIGHT LN	20700	290V	NWC	77379
SPRING LILY CT	2400	293W	NCC	77373
SPRING LINE CT	13300	370Z	NWC	77086
SPRING LINK CT	22500	292K	NCC	77373
SPRING LODGE DR	5600	297Z	NEH	77345
SPRING MANOR DR	3200	297Z	NEH	77345
SPRING MAPLE LN	14300	618B	SEH	77062
SPRING MARSH CT	14300	367B	NWC	77429
SPRING MEADOW DR	900	292Y	NCC	77373
SPRING MEADOW DR	3900	614Z	PL	77584
SPRING MEADOW LN	3600	450K	NWH	77080
SPRING MEADOW LN	7200	525B	NEF	77494
SPRING MEADOWS	0	461Q	NEC	77521
SPRING MEADOWS LN	0	526G	NEF	77407
SPRINGMERE CT	0	407C	NWC	77095
SPRING MILL LN	23900	293T	NCC	77373
SPRING MILLER DR	9400	369M	NWC	77070
SPRINGMINT CT	13100	328T	NWC	77429
SPRINGMINT DR	13900	328T	NWC	77429
SPRING MISSION LN	20600	291V	NWC	77388
SPRING MIST DR	0	293B	SEM	77386
SPRINGMONT DR	9300	450K	NWH	77080
SPRING MOSS DR	500	609V	MC	77459
SPRING MOSS DR	2700	659G	LC	77573
SPRING MOSS DR	23800	293W	NCC	77373
SPRING MOUNTAIN CT	13900	417D	NEH	77044
SPRING MOUNTAIN DR	14400	288E	NWC	77377
SPRING MOUNTAIN LN	0	291Z	NWC	77388
SPRING MOUNTAIN LN	0	417D	NEH	77044
SPRING MUSIC DR	12500	368V	NWC	77065
SPRING OAK DR	1900	615Z	PL	77581
SPRING OAK DR	5400	577M	PA	77505
SPRING OAK DR	23900	293T	NCC	77373
SPRING OAK HOLLOW	6000	330H	NWC	77379
SPRING OAKS CIR	1300	450Z	SV	77055
SPRING OAKS DR	22100	291K	NWC	77389
SPRING ORCHARD CT	0	526G	NEF	77407
SPRING ORCHARD LN	0	526G	NEF	77407
SPRING ORCHARD LN	20500	291V	NWC	77388
SPRING PALMS CT	4200	297U	NEH	77345
SPRING PARK	5300	491L	SWH	77056
SPRING PARK DR	5100	461P	NEC	77521
SPRING PARK CENTER BLVD	500	332B	NCC	77373
SPRING PATH CT	11700	328M	NWC	77377
SPRING PINE	0	292E	NWC	77389
SPRING PINE CT	5200	297N	NEH	77345
SPRING PINES DR	100	252P	SEM	77386
SPRING PINES DR	14100	288B	TB	77375
SPRING PLACE CT	2500	610B	MC	77489
SPRING PLACE DR	2500	610B	MC	77489
SPRING PLACE DR	10000	369Q	NWC	77070
SPRING POINT	0	292Y	NCC	77373
SPRING POINTE DR	0	332C	NCC	77373
SPRING POINT VIEW	13600	528F	SWC	77083
SPRINGPORT COVE CT	0	525H	NEF	77407
SPRING RAIN DR	2400	331K	NWC	77379
SPRING RANCH LN	3200	291Z	NWC	77388

Street Name	Block	Pg/Sq	Loc	Zips
SPRING RAPID WAY	0	329F	NWC	77375
SPRING RIDGE DR	2600	613X	NEB	77578
SPRING RIDGE RD	1	611D	SWH	77053
SPRING RIDGE RD	25100	252T	SEM	77386
SPRING RIVER CIR	16800	329R	NWC	77379
SPRING RIVER DR	3900	614Z	PL	77584
SPRINGROCK LN	1100	450X	NWH	77055
SPRINGROCK LN	1900	450P	NWH	77080
SPRING ROSE DR	20400	486K	SWC	77450
SPRING RUN LN	6900	485X	NEF	77494
SPRING RUSSELL DR	0	250X	NWC	77389
SPRINGS LN	0	406D	NWC	77433
SPRING SAGE CT	19600	486C	SWC	77094
SPRING SCHOOL RD	100	292R	SP	77373
SPRING SHADOWS DR	10800	369Y	NWC	77064
SPRING SHADOWS PARK CIR	0	450N	NWH	77080
SPRING SHANNON DR	0	293U	NCC	77373
SPRINGSHIRE DR	11500	371P	NWC	77066
SPRING SHOWERS CT	0	446D	NWC	77084
SPRINGSIDE LN	7300	410V	NWH	77040
SPRING SILVER DR	5900	406Z	NWC	77449
SPRING SILVER DR	5900	406Z	NWC	77449
SPRING SONG DR	1	251Y	WD	77380
SPRINGSONG DR	11000	369Z	NWC	77064
SPRING SOURCE PLACE	800	292U	NCC	77373
SPRINGSTONE CT	0	657Z	LC	77573
SPRINGSTONE DR	2500	293A	SEM	77386
SPRING STUEBNER RD	100	292K	SP	77373
SPRING STUEBNER RD	1500	291K	NWC	77389
SPRING STUEBNER RD	5300	290L	NWC	77389
SPRING SUN CT	0	376V	NEC	77346
SPRING SUN DR	0	376V	NEC	77346
SPRING SUNRISE DR	5700	526T	NEF	77407
SPRING SUNSET DR	23000	293W	NCC	77373
SPRINGTAIL LN	11300	371R	NWC	77067
SPRING TAILS BEND	2000	293E	SEM	77386
SPRING TERRACE DR	29700	253W	SEM	77386
SPRING TIDE CT	6300	525F	NEF	77494
SPRINGTIME LN	8000	575T	SEH	77075
SPRINGTON LN	5200	331J	NWC	77379
SPRING TOWNE DR	20800	292N	NWC	77388
SPRING TOWNE DR	23800	293X	NCC	77373
SPRING TRACE CT	400	486D	SWC	77094
SPRING TRAIL	8700	408A	NWC	77095
SPRING TRAIL PARK DR	2600	293K	SEM	77386
SPRING TRAILS BEND	2000	293E	SEM	77386
SPRING TRAILS RIDGE	28500	293E	SEM	77386
SPRINGTREE DR	17800	376C	NEC	77396
N. SPRING TRELLIS CIR	1	250B	WD	77382
SPRING TRELLIS CIR	1	250B	WD	77382
SPRING VALE DR	0	293S	NCC	77373
SPRING VALLEY RD	3300	450K	NWH	77080
SPRING VALLEY RD	4300	450F	NWH	77041
SPRINGVIEW LN	0	612R	PL	77584
SPRINGVIEW LN	8900	450L	NWH	77080
SPRING VILLA DR	11600	329W	NWC	77070
SPRING VILLAGE DR	7900	290F	NWC	77389
SPRINGVILLE DR	7700	407M	NWC	77095
SPRING VINE LN	21600	525G	NEF	77450
SPRING WALK DR	22500	525C	NEF	77494
SPRING WALK LN	14800	326Z	NWC	77429
SPRING WATER DR	500	338D	NEC	77336
SPRING WAY DR	23900	293T	NCC	77373
SPRINGWELL DR	1700	449V	NWH	77043
SPRINGWEST DR	20900	292S	NWC	77388
SPRING WILLOW DR	22900	290E	NWC	77375
SPRING WIND DR	8300	410J	NWH	77040
SPRINGWOOD	18700	258A	RF	77357
SPRINGWOOD DR	300	252F	SEM	77385
SPRINGWOOD DR	1600	450V	NWH	77055
SPRINGWOOD DR	11000	579C	LP	77571
SPRINGWOOD RD	27000	249L	SWM	77354
SPRINGWOOD FOREST DR	0	249G	SWM	77354
SPRINGWOOD FOREST DR	10000	450N	NWH	77080
SPRINGWOOD GLEN LN	0	524H	NEF	77494
SPRINGWOOD LAKE DR	0	524C	NEF	77494
SPRING WOODS DR	300	252T	SEM	77386
SPRINGWOODS PLAZA DR	0	292E	NCC	77373
SPRINGWOODS VILLAGE PKWY	0	292B	NCC	77373
SPRINGWOODS VLLG PKWY	23400	292E	NWC	77389
SPRINTERS DR	19100	337V	NEC	77346
SPRINTERS DR	19100	338S	NEC	77346
SPRINTWOOD CT	19100	338W	NEC	77346
SPRITE	5600	410X	NWH	77040
SPRITE LN	2100	615Y	PL	77581
SPRITE WOODS PLACE	1	249C	SWM	77382
SPROUSE CIR	21100	334R	NCC	77338
SPRUCE	1	493M	SWH	77003
SPRUCE	4400	531G	BL	77401
SPRUCE	16100	458Y	CV	77530
S. SPRUCE DR	10800	579C	LP	77571
N. SPRUCE DR	10800	579C	LP	77571
SPRUCE LN	0	463S	CCO	77520
SPRUCE LN	17400	246T	SWM	77355
SPRUCE BAY DR	3600	297P	NEH	77345
SPRUCE BEND LN	0	253Q	SEM	77386
SPRUCE BOUGH CT	19300	337U	NEC	77346
SPRUCE BOUGH LN	19300	337T	NEC	77346
SPRUCE COVE CT	7800	408J	NWC	77095
SPRUCE CREEK DR	18200	447B	NWC	77084
SPRUCEDALE CT	11000	369E	NWC	77070
SPRUCE FALLS CT	23200	485F	SWC	77494
SPRUCE FOREST DR	5000	451C	NWH	77091
SPRUCE FOREST DR	5800	451B	NWH	77092
SPRUCE GLEN DR	2400	296V	NEH	77339
SPRUCE GROVE DR	2000	336G	NEH	77339
SPRUCE HAVEN DR	7700	407M	NWC	77095
SPRUCE HILL DR	11800	489N	SWH	77077
SPRUCE HOLLOW CT	13400	578X	SEH	77059
SPRUCE KNOB CT	1800	296Y	NEH	77339
SPRUCE KNOB DR	1800	296Y	NEH	77339
SPRUCE KNOLL CIR	10900	368Z	NWC	77065
SPRUCELAKE RD	400	338V	NEH	77336
SPRUCE LODGE DR	2200	296U	NEH	77339
SPRUCE MANOR LN	6200	571K	SWH	77085
SPRUCE MILL DR	8600	408A	NWC	77095
SPRUCE MOUNTAIN DR	11700	371L	NWC	77067
SPRUCE NEEDLE DR	3500	527D	SWC	77082
SPRUCE PARK	14800	527D	SWC	77082
SPRUCE PARK CIR	3500	297U	NEH	77345
SPRUCE PINE DR	2500	337C	NEH	77345
SPRUCE POINT CIR	5400	408X	NWC	77084
SPRUCE POINT DR	15700	408X	NWC	77084
SPRUCE RIDGE WAY	3300	297W	NEH	77339
SPRUCE RUN DR	16800	329R	NWC	77379
SPRUCE TREE LINE TRAIL	0	447J	NWC	77084
SPRUCE VALLEY DR	4000	297Y	NEH	77345
SPRUCE VIEW CT	7000	526F	NEF	77407
SPRUCEWOOD LN	800	490C	HE	77024
SPUNYARD DR	15800	419E	NEC	77532
SPUR	1700	450Y	NWH	77080
SPUR 5	0	494W	SEC	77004

Street Name	Block	Pg/Sq	Loc	Zips
SPUR 5	0	534A	SEC	77004
SPUR 41	100	568M	SG	77478
SPUR 41	100	568M	SG	77478
SPUR 58	100	568S	SG	77478
SPUR 58	100	568S	SG	77478
SPUR 99	2600	541D	BT	77520
SPUR 99	2600	541D	BT	77520
SPUR 99	2700	542B	CCO	77520
SPUR 99	2700	542B	CCO	77520
SPUR 184	0	334V	NEH	77338
SPUR 184	0	334V	NEH	77338
SPUR 184	0	335V	NEH	77338
SPUR 184	0	335V	NEH	77338
SPUR 261	0	412U	NWH	77088
SPUR 261	0	412U	NWH	77088
SPUR 330	0	500A	BT	77520
SPUR 330	0	500A	BT	77520
SPUR 498	0	580K	LP	77571
SPUR 498	0	580K	LP	77571
SPUR 501	0	580U	SA	77571
SPUR 501	0	580U	SA	77571
SPUR 527	0	493W	SWH	77006
SPUR 527	0	493W	SWH	77006
SPUR BRANCH LN	20500	486S	NEF	77450
SPUR CANYON CT	16100	327Y	NWC	77429
SPUR CIRCLE LN	21700	379A	NEC	77532
SPURGEN CT	0	578Q	PA	77059
SPURLIN MEADOW DR	13200	328K	NWC	77377
SPURLIN TRAIL	0	249V	NWC	77375
SPUR RIDGE	0	412E	NWC	77038
SPUR RIDGE CT	0	525V	NEF	77406
SPUR TRAIL	18600	246J	SWM	77355
SPURWOOD CT	1	251A	WD	77381
SPYGLASS CT	1	409F	JV	77064
SPY GLASS DR	2100	659D	LC	77573
SPYGLASS DR	7700	408L	NWC	77095
SPYGLASS LN	2800	609H	MC	77459
SPYGLASS HILLS DR	4100	485Z	NEF	77450
SPYGLEN CT	13400	368B	NWC	77429
SPYGLEN LN	14100	368B	NWC	77429
SQUALL CT	300	379Y	NEC	77532
SQUARE RIGGER LN	16700	617U	SEC	77546
SQUASH	5000	331A	NWC	77379
SQUAW CREEK DR	0	366V	NWC	77433
SQUAW VALLEY	27700	244A	WCO	77447
SQUAW VALLEY TRAIL	20700	378C	NEC	77532
SQUIRE DR	1500	501F	BT	77521
SQUIRECREST DR	6600	250Y	NWC	77389
SQUIREDALE DR	11400	329W	NWC	77070
SQUIRE DOBBINS DR	2100	568C	SG	77478
SQUIRE DOBBINS DR	2400	528Y	SG	77478
SQUIRE HILL CT	10200	369G	NWC	77070
SQUIRE KNOLL ST	0	444D	NWC	77493
SQUIRE PLACE DR	0	335P	NCC	77338
SQUIRES CT	6200	250Y	NWC	77389
SQUIRES BEND	100	569V	SF	77477
SQUIRES PARK DR	0	296X	SEM	77339
SQUIRES PLACE DR	8200	527P	NEF	77083
SQUIRREL TREE	22900	291E	NWC	77389
SQUYRES DR	16400	330P	NWC	77379
SRALLA RD	0	460B	NEC	77532
SRALLA RD	8500	460P	NEC	77562
SRALLA RD	10100	420T	NEC	77532
SSGT MACARIO GARCIA DR	100	494V	SEH	77011
SSGT MACARIO GARCIA DR	2500	494V	SEH	77011
ST. BERNADETTE DR	0	330C	NWC	77379
ST. DOMNINA DR	0	330C	NWC	77379
ST. ELMO'S FIRE	0	539N	DP	77536
ST. HILDEGARDE CT	0	330C	NWC	77379
ST. JOANNA CT	0	330C	NWC	77379
ST. MARCELLA DR	0	330C	NWC	77379
ST. PLACIDIA DR	0	330C	NWC	77379
ST. ROSALIA DR	0	330C	NWC	77379
ST. SEVERA DR	0	330C	NWC	77379
ST. WINFRED DR	0	330C	NWC	77379
STABLE LN	8800	491G	SWH	77024
STABLE BEND CIR	15400	327V	NWC	77429
STABLE BLUFF	0	327U	NWC	77429
STABLE BROOK CIR	15600	327V	NWC	77429
STABLECREEK	14500	327Y	NWC	77429
STABLE CREEK CIR	15700	327V	NWC	77429
STABLE CREST BLVD	8600	491G	SWH	77024
STABLE CREST CT	8800	491G	SWH	77024
STABLEDON DR	13700	371B	NWC	77014
STABLEFIELD LN	0	327U	NWC	77429
STABLEFORD CT	13900	371B	NWC	77014
STABLE GATE DR	15300	327V	NWC	77429
STABLE LAKE DR	15500	327V	NWC	77429
STABLE OAK DR	15400	327V	NWC	77429
STABLE PARK CT	15500	327V	NWC	77429
STABLE PARK DR	15500	327V	NWC	77429
STABLEPOINT LN	16100	327Y	NWC	77429
STABLER LN	10800	413X	NEH	77076
STABLERIDGE CT	13900	371B	NWC	77014
STABLERIDGE DR	3800	371B	NWC	77014
STABLE RUN DR	15300	327V	NWC	77429
STABLE SIDE CT	0	373E	NCC	77073
STABLE SPRINGS CIR	15400	327V	NWC	77429
STABLE STAR CIR	15400	327V	NWC	77429
STABLE STONE LN	1900	615L	PL	77581
STABLETON LN	0	457P	NEC	77049
STABLE TRAIL DR	15400	327V	NWC	77429
STABLEVIEW CT	2800	486N	NEF	77450
STABLE VIEW CT	15700	327V	NWC	77429
STABLEWAY CIR	12100	409A	NWC	77065
STABLEWAY CT	12100	409A	NWC	77065
STABLEWAY DR	9700	409A	NWC	77065
STABLEWOOD BLVD	300	491H	SWH	77024
STABLEWOOD CT	100	491G	SWH	77024
STABLEWOOD DOWNS	0	327U	NWC	77429
STABLEWOOD FARMS DR	14500	327Y	NWC	77429
STABLEWOOD LAKES LN	0	249Z	NWC	77375
STACEY LN	1	541D	BT	77520
STACKSTONE LN	4400	485Z	NEF	77450
STACKWOOD LN	19800	446C	NWC	77084
STACY	4300	619L	PA	77586
STACY DR	2500	615U	PL	77581
STACY LN	3000	538U	DP	77536
STACY RD	4000	447G	NWC	77084
STACY CREST	1701	452T	NWH	77008
STACY FALLS	1701	452T	NWH	77008
STACY GLEN	2100	452T	NWH	77008
STACY KNOLL	2100	452T	NWH	77008
STACY PARK CIR	3500	446J	NWC	77084
E. STADIUM	0	656C	FR	77546
STADIUM	600	501X	BT	77520
STADIUM CIR	800	616Y	FR	77546
W. STADIUM CT	800	616Y	FR	77546
STADIUM DR	1300	463A	MB	77580
N. STADIUM DR	7600	532M	SWH	77030
N. STADIUM DR	8000	532M	SWH	77054
STADIUM LN	200	656C	FR	77546

Street Name	Block	Pg/Sq	Loc	Zips
STADIUM LN	500	616Y	FR	77546
STAFFORD	100	488A	SWH	77079
STAFFORD DR	10600	414T	NEH	77093
STAFFORD RD	12400	569R	SF	77477
STAFFORD RD	12500	570E	SF	77477
STAFFORDALE CT	11500	366Q	NWC	77433
STAFFORDALE LN	0	572Q	SWH	77047
STAFFORD CENTRE	10100	569Q	SF	77477
STAFFORD COLONY LN	13100	570J	SF	77477
STAFFORD HILL COVE	0	524A	NEF	77494
STAFFORD PKWY	1300	570S	SF	77477
STAFFORD POINT DR	13600	569Q	SF	77477
STAFFORD PRIDE DR	600	570S	SF	77477
STAFFORD RUN RD	500	569U	SF	77477
STAFFORDSHIRE	6800	533E	SWH	77030
STAFFORDSHIRE	6800	533E	SWH	77030
STAFFORDSHIRE RD	100	569V	SF	77477
STAFFORDSHIRE RD	1200	570W	MC	77477
STAFFORDSHIRE CRESCENT	1800	533E	SWH	77030
STAFFORD SPRINGS AVE	0	569U	NEF	77477
STAFFORD SPRINGS DR	12400	488R	SWH	77077
STAG CIR	2100	339P	HU	77336
STAG LN	26600	257M	SEM	77357
STAG BROOK CT	0	335P	NCC	77338
STAGECOACH DR	9100	450G	NWH	77041
STAGECOACH RD	0	248S	SWM	77362
STAGECOACH RD	13400	247N	SC	77355
STAGECOACH RD	15300	246M	SC	77355
STAGECOACH CROSSING DR	26500	246P	SWM	77355
STAGERUNN DR	1	332K	NWC	77090
STAGESTOP CIR	0	490H	HC	77024
STAGEWOOD DR	8200	335N	NCC	77338
STAGHILL DR	10200	369X	NWC	77064
STAGHORN LN	0	657L	FR	77546
STAGHORN CORAL LN	0	572E	SWH	77045
STAG MILLER	100	459V	HG	77562
STAGS LEAP DR	0	378Q	NEC	77532
STAGS LEAP BEND LN	0	484E	NEF	77494
STAGS LEAP BEND	0	484J	NEF	77494
STAHMAN LN	0	448K	NWH	77084
STAITI	100	335Z	HM	77338
STALLINGS DR	2700	411R	NWH	77088
STALLINGS SHORE DR		366V	NWC	77433
STALLION LN	11800	570C	SWH	77071
STALLION BROOK LN	4200	291T	NWC	77388
STALLION CREEK CT	0	368C	NWC	77429
STALLION PEAK CIR	15600	327V	NWC	77429
STALLION POINT CIR	15500	327V	NWC	77429
STALLION RIDGE WAY	0	616H	SEC	77089
STALLION RUN	36900	246L	SWM	77355
STALLION TRAIL DR	7400	334R	NCC	77338
STALLONES DR	13400	288L	TB	77375
STALLY	3000	451R	NWH	77092
STALSBY	0	259N	NEC	77357
STALYNN LN	1	491R	SWH	77027
STAMEN DR	7500	408L	NWC	77041
STAMEY	6800	370L	NWC	77066
STAMFORD DR	19400	328D	NWC	77375
STAMFORD DR	19500	288Z	NWC	77375
STAMFORD BROOK CT	0	445M	NWC	77449
STAMFORD BROOK CT	0	445M	NWC	77449
STAMFORD OAKS DR	0	329J	NWC	77377
STAMP	4100	494B	NEH	77026
STAMPEDE CANYON LN	9300	616E	SEC	77089
STAMPEDE PASS DR	15200	408B	NWC	77095
STAMPER WAY	5200	491U	SWH	77056
STAMPFORD DR	13600	488K	SWH	77077
STANART RD	23800	296G	SEM	77365
STANBRIDGE DR	14600	528N	NEF	77083
STANBROOK	10300	615D	SEC	77089
STANBURY PARK LN	12700	328F	NWC	77377
STANBURY PLACE	3500	485X	NEF	77494
STANCLIFF	12900	571M	SWH	77045
STANCLIFF RD	10400	529X	SWH	77099
STANCLIFF OAKS	12800	568C	SG	77478
STANDARD RD	6900	249J	SWM	77354
STANDIFER	100	334Z	NEH	77338
STANDING CYPRESS DR	19900	289Y	NWC	77379
STANDING FIELD CT	0	406F	NWC	77433
STANDING HORN CT	0	253P	SEM	77386
STANDING OAK DR	24200	290B	NWC	77389
STANDING OAKS	6100	415E	NEH	77050
STANDING PINE LN	11600	289W	NWC	77375
STANDING ROCK CT	8700	616A	SEC	77089
STANFIELD CT	19700	406R	NWC	77433
STANFORD	500	493N	SWH	77019
STANFORD	1600	493S	SWH	77006
STANFORD	2700	537T	PA	77502
STANFORD CT	0	657Y	LC	77573
STANFORD CT	4400	450E	NWC	77041
STANFORD PARK CT	1900	486J	SWC	77450
STANFORD PLACE	24300	242S	NWC	77484
STANHOPE CT	15800	448A	NWC	77084
STANHOPE DR	5000	448A	NWC	77084
STANLEY	5100	450B	NWH	77040
STANLEY CT	200	656D	FR	77546
STANLEY BEND CT	0	492C	NWH	77007
STANLEY BRIDG	0	492C	NWH	77007
STANLEY CREST CIR	0	492C	NWH	77007
STANLEY FOREST CT	0	492C	NWH	77007
STANLEY MANOR CT	0	492B	NWH	77007
STANLEY PARK DR	0	492C	NWH	77007
STANLEY POINT DR	0	492C	NWH	77007
STANLING BROOK LN	0	450J	NWH	77080
STANMORE DR	2100	492Q	SWH	77019
STANOLIND RD	24600	249W	NWC	77375
STANSBERG DR	11500	371N	NWC	77066
STANTON	2800	532K	SWH	77025
STANTON CT	3300	613G	NEB	77584
STANTON LAKE DR	0	406H	NWC	77433
STANTON LODGE DR	0	376A	NEC	77338
STANVILLE DR	0	484X	NEF	77494
STANVILLE DR	0	484X	NEF	77494
STANWICK DR	7300	534V	SEH	77087
STANWICK DR	7400	535S	SEH	77087
STANWICK ST	0	568W	SG	77479
STANWICK CROSSING LN	0	524H	NEF	77494
STANWOOD DR	11800	570A	SWH	77031
STAPLEFORD	28700	293A	SEM	77386
STAPLES	200	620P	SB	77586
STAPLES	1700	494B	NEH	77020
STAPLES	1900	494B	NEH	77026
STAPLES DR	100	502D	BT	77520
STAPLES WAY	1	491U	SWH	77056
STAPLETON DR	2000	656Q	FR	77546
STAPLEY DR	16700	375J	NEH	77396
STAR	0	248X	TB	77375
STAR LN	5100	491Y	SWH	77056
STAR LN	5600	491X	SWH	77057
S. STARBOARD	400	419B	NEC	77532
N. STARBOARD	400	419B	NEC	77532
STARBOARD CT	0	485A	SWC	77494

Street Name	Block	Pg/Sq	Loc	Zips
STARBOARD DR	18000	619T	NB	77058
STARBOARD POINT DR	0	532T	SWH	77054
STARBOARD SHORES CT	1700	569X	MC	77459
STARBOARD SHORES DR	4100	569X	MC	77459
STARBOARD VIEW CIR	2100	617U	SEC	77546
STARBOARD VIEW DR	16700	617U	SEC	77546
STARBOROUGH DR	400	659H	LC	77573
STARBRIDGE DR	7200	407R	NWC	77095
STARBRIDGE LAKE LN	23400	525F	NEF	77407
STARBRIDGE PARK LN	3200	445M	NWC	77449
STARBRIDGE POINTE LN	3700	446J	NWC	77449
STARBROOK CREEK DR	6000	524F	NEF	77494
STARBROOK OAK LN	0	366V	NWC	77433
STARBROOK OAK LN		366Z	NWC	77433
STAR CACTUS LN	0	407J	NWC	77433
STAR CACTUS LN	0	407J	NWC	77433
STAR CANYON CT	0	327U	NWC	77429
STAR CREEK CT	4600	609S	NEF	77479
STARCREEK LN	0	417B	NEC	77044
STARCREST LN	0	525C	NEF	77494
STARCROFT CT	2900	659M	LC	77573
STARCROFT CT	6700	290L	NWC	77379
STARDALE LN	16400	657B	FR	77546
STARDUST LN	13900	408U	NWC	77041
STARDUST RIDGE LN	0	249Q	NWC	77375
STAR FERN PLACE	1	251R	WD	77380
STARFIELD DR	5400	408W	NWC	77084
STARFINDER RD	0	367P	CY	77433
STARFIRE LN	9300	529R	SWH	77036
STARFISH LN	8100	529J	SWH	77072
STARFLOWER	7300	525A	NEF	77494
STARFLOWER LN	0	460W	BT	77521
STARGATE CT	3100	331P	NWC	77068
STARGAZER POINT	0	333A	NCC	77373
STARGAZER POINT	0	293W	NCC	77373
STAR GAZER WAY	27000	294P	SEM	77386
STARGRASS CT	3000	659H	LC	77573
STARGRASS DR	21300	291Q	NWC	77388
STAR HAVEN DR	0	366J	NWC	77433
STARHILL CT	13800	488F	SWH	77077
STAR HOLLOW LN	0	377W	NEC	77044
STAR HOLLOW LN	8500	407F	NWC	77095
STARI MOST LN	0	378A	NEC	77346
STAR IRIS PLACE	100	249R	NWH	77375
STAR IRIS PLACE	100	249R	NWH	77375
STARK CT	27100	252J	OR	77385
STARK LN	27200	252J	OR	77385
STARKEY	1200	537Q	PA	77503
STARKEY	3200	493E	SWH	77007
STARK POINT CT	8400	337X	NEC	77346
STARKRIDGE DR	5200	531X	SWH	77035
STARKSBORO CT	500	332Q	NCC	77073
STARK SKY LN	0	377K	NEC	77346
STARKSTONE CT	500	252T	SEM	77386
STAR LAKE CT	17000	375E	NCC	77396
STAR LAKE DR	6100	375E	NCC	77396
STARLAMP LN	8900	407D	NWC	77095
STARLEAF LN	400	613B	NEB	77584
STAR LEDGE CT	0	290C	NWC	77389
STAR LIGHT CT	0	294U	SEM	77386
STAR LIGHT CT	0	294U	SEM	77386
STARLIGHT RD	12800	456M	NEC	77049
STARLIGHT BAY	11300	613J	PL	77584
STARLIGHT BAY	11400	612M	PL	77584
STARLIGHT BAY CT	11500	612M	PL	77584
STARLIGHT CANYON LN	0	484S	NEF	77494
STARLIGHT HARBOUR CT	13600	488P	SWH	77077
STARLIGHT HILL CT	3300	253N	SEM	77386
STARLIGHT PLACE	100	291D	WD	77380
STARLING	5400	536N	SEH	77017
STARLING CT	0	461N	NEC	77521
STARLING CREEK DR	10900	524L	NWF	77406
STARLING GROVE LN	0	405R	NWC	77493
STARLING STREAM CT	0	294J	SEM	77386
STARLING STREAM DR	0	293M	SEM	77386
STARLITE DR	3600	577D	PA	77505
STARLIT MEADOWS CT	10700	369T	NWC	77064
STARLIT RANCH DR	0	484S	NEF	77494
STAR MEADOW LN	24900	338H	NEH	77336
STARMIST LN	0	377Y	NEH	77044
STARMOUNT BLVD	2500	536J	SEH	77017
STAR PEAK DR	2600	411M	NWC	77088
STAR PINE CT	1	251A	WD	77381
S. STARPOINT DR	1900	373L	NCC	77032
N. STARPOINT DR	1900	373L	NCC	77032
STARRUSH CT	1	251Z	WD	77380
STARRY HILLS CT	0	376V	NEC	77396
STARRY MEADOW CT	0	376V	NEC	77396
STARRY NIGHT	7300	525A	NEF	77494
STARRY SPRING CT	0	377S	NEC	77396
STARRY SUMMER LN	0	377S	NEC	77396
STAR SHADOW LN	6300	370L	NWC	77066
STARSHADOW PLACE	1	457U	NEC	77015
STARSHIP CROSSING	0	293G	SEM	77386
STARS HOLLOW DR	19300	372D	NCC	77073
STARS HOLLOW DR	19300	372H	NCC	77073
STAR THISTLE CT	10500	367S	NWC	77433
STARVIOLET	1	251M	WD	77380
STAR WAY	4700	534B	SEH	77023
STAR WISH LN	0	524B	NEF	77494
STARWOOD DR	11600	490F	BH	77024
STARWREATH DR	0	612J	PL	77545
STASSEN	3200	533U	SEH	77051
STATE	0	444Y	KT	77493
STATE	300	536W	SH	77587
STATE	1400	576A	SH	77587
STATE	1500	493K	SWH	77007
STATE	2100	501U	BT	77520
S.H. 3	100	659J	LC	77573
S.H. 3	100	659J	LC	77573
S.H. 3	500	536W	SH	77587
S.H. 3	500	536W	SH	77587
S.H. 3	1300	659T	DI	77539
S.H. 3	1300	659T	DI	77539
S.H. 3	1500	576G	SH	77587
S.H. 3	1500	576G	SH	77587
S.H. 3	7200	576M	SEH	77034
S.H. 3	7200	576M	SEH	77034
S.H. 3	9000	535Z	SEH	77017
S.H. 3	9000	535Z	SEH	77017
S.H. 3	10500	577S	SEH	77034
S.H. 3	10500	577S	SEH	77034
S.H. 3	12000	617G	SEH	77598
S.H. 3	12000	617G	SEH	77598
S.H. 3	15000	618T	WB	77598
S.H. 3	15000	618T	WB	77598
S.H. 3	18200	658C	WB	77598
S.H. 3	18200	658C	WB	77598
S.H. 6	0	282T	WL	77484
S.H. 6	0	282T	WL	77484
S.H. 6	0	323B	NWC	77484
S.H. 6	0	323B	NWC	77484

Street Name	Block	Pg/Sq	Loc	Zips
S.H. 6	0	325U	NWC	77447
S.H. 6	0	325U	NWC	77447
S.H. 6	0	326X	NWC	77433
S.H. 6	0	326X	NWC	77433
S.H. 6	0	366D	NWC	77429
S.H. 6	0	366D	NWC	77429
S.H. 6	0	367K	CY	77433
S.H. 6	0	367K	CY	77433
S.H. 6	0	368X	NWC	77065
S.H. 6	0	368X	NWC	77065
S.H. 6	0	408B	NWC	77095
S.H. 6	0	408B	NWC	77095
S.H. 6	0	610X	MC	77459
S.H. 6	0	610X	MC	77459
S. S.H. 6	100	488E	SWH	77079
S. S.H. 6	100	488E	SWH	77079
S.H. 6	100	568X	SG	77479
S.H. 6	100	568X	SG	77479
S. S.H. 6	1000	488N	SWH	77077
S. S.H. 6	1000	488N	SWH	77077
N. S.H. 6	1000	448W	NWH	77079
N. S.H. 6	1000	448W	NWH	77079
N. S.H. 6	1200	448J	NWH	77084
N. S.H. 6	1200	448J	NWH	77084
S. S.H. 6	2500	488N	SWH	77082
S. S.H. 6	2500	488N	SWH	77082
S. S.H. 6	3500	528A	SWC	77082
S. S.H. 6	3500	528A	SWC	77082
S.H. 6	3900	609G	MC	77479
S.H. 6	3900	609G	MC	77479
N. S.H. 6	5000	408W	NWC	77084
N. S.H. 6	5000	408W	NWC	77084
S. S.H. 6	6200	528A	SWC	77083
S. S.H. 6	6200	528A	SWC	77083
N. S.H. 6	7000	408B	NWC	77095
N. S.H. 6	7000	408B	NWC	77095
S. S.H. 6	9500	528W	NEF	77498
S. S.H. 6	9500	528W	NEF	77498
S.H. 35	1000	615Y	PL	77581
S.H. 35	1000	615Y	PL	77581
S.H. 35	3000	535J	SEH	77087
S.H. 35	3000	535J	SEH	77087
S.H. 35	6400	575W	SEH	77061
S.H. 35	6400	575W	SEH	77061
S.H. 35	9200	575W	SEH	77075
S.H. 35	9200	575W	SEH	77075
S.H. 96	0	659Q	LC	77573
S.H. 96	0	659Q	LC	77573
S.H. 96	0	660F	LC	77573
S.H. 96	0	660F	LC	77573
S.H. 99	0	445T	NWC	77449
S.H. 99	0	445T	NWC	77449
S.H. 99	0	485B	SWC	77450
S.H. 99	0	485B	SWC	77450
S.H. 99	0	525K	NEF	77407
S.H. 99	0	525K	NEF	77407
S.H. 99	0	526X	NEF	77406
S.H. 99	0	526X	NEF	77407
S.H. 134	100	539E	DP	77571
S.H. 134	100	539E	DP	77571
S.H. 134	1900	499N	SEC	77571
S.H. 134	1900	499N	SEC	77571
S.H. 146	0	541A	BT	77520
S.H. 146	0	541A	BT	77520
S.H. 146	0	540H	BT	77520
S.H. 146	0	540H	BT	77520
S.H. 146	0	580F	LP	77571
S.H. 146	0	580F	LP	77571
N. S.H. 146	0	463J	MB	77521
N. S.H. 146	0	463J	MB	77521
S.H. 146	100	501U	BT	77520
S.H. 146	100	501U	BT	77520
S.H. 146	400	620B	SB	77586
S.H. 146	400	620B	SB	77586
S.H. 146	600	620Y	KE	77565
S.H. 146	600	620Y	KE	77565
S.H. 146	2400	502P	BT	77520
S.H. 146	2400	502P	BT	77520
S.H. 146	3000	660C	GCO	77518
S.H. 146	3000	660C	GCO	77518
N. S.H. 146	7000	462V	BT	77520
N. S.H. 146	7000	462V	BT	77520
S.H. 225	100	536E	PA	77506
S.H. 225	100	536E	PA	77506
S.H. 225	1400	537E	PA	77506
S.H. 225	1400	537E	PA	77506
S.H. 225	2900	537E	PA	77503
S.H. 225	2900	537E	PA	77503
S.H. 225	5000	538G	DP	77536
S.H. 225	5000	538G	DP	77536
S.H. 225	7000	535H	SEH	77017
S.H. 225	7000	535H	SEH	77017
S.H. 225	7100	539K	LP	77571
S.H. 225	7100	539K	LP	77571
S.H. 225	10000	536E	SEH	77017
S.H. 225	10000	536E	SEH	77017
S.H. 225	11800	540N	SEC	77571
S.H. 225	11800	540N	SEC	77571
S.H. 249	700	412J	NWC	77038
S.H. 249	700	412J	NWC	77038
S.H. 249	11500	411B	NWC	77086
S.H. 249	11500	411B	NWC	77086
S.H. 249	14000	371W	NWC	77086
S.H. 249	14000	371W	NWC	77086
S.H. 249	14500	370Z	NWC	77086
S.H. 249	14500	370Z	NWC	77086
S.H. 249	16300	370Z	NWC	77064
S.H. 249	16300	370Z	NWC	77064
S.H. 249	17900	369H	NWC	77070
S.H. 249	17900	369H	NWC	77070
S.H. 249	20400	329T	NWC	77070
S.H. 249	20400	329T	NWC	77070
S.H. 249	22600	329T	NWC	77375
S.H. 249	22600	329T	NWC	77375
S.H. 249	24200	328H	NWC	77377
S.H. 249	24200	328H	NWC	77377
S.H. 249	26700	288Z	NWC	77375
S.H. 249	26700	288Z	NWC	77375
S.H. 249	31200	248W	SWM	77362
S.H. 249	31200	248W	SWM	77362
S.H. 249	32000	247M	SWM	77362
S.H. 249	32000	247M	SWM	77362
S.H. 288	0	613W	NEB	77584
S.H. 288	0	613W	NEB	77584
S.H. 288	4000	493T	SWH	77004
S.H. 288	4000	493T	SWH	77004
S.H. 288	7500	533K	SEH	77021
S.H. 288	7500	533K	SEH	77021
S.H. 288	8700	533W	SEH	77051
S.H. 288	8700	533W	SEH	77051
S.H. 288	9100	573J	SEH	77051
S.H. 288	9100	573J	SEH	77051

Street Name	Block	Pg/Sq	Loc	Zips
S.H. 288	11900	573W	SEH	77047
S.H. 288	11900	573W	SEH	77047
S.H. 290	0	410X	NWH	77040
S.H. 290	0	410X	NWH	77040
S.H. 330	0	499D	NEC	77520
S.H. 330	0	499D	NEC	77520
S.H. 330	0	500A	BT	77520
S.H. 330	0	500A	BT	77520
S.H. 330	0	501N	BT	77520
S.H. 330	0	501N	BT	77520
STATE-TEXAS VISTA RD	0	499W	SEC	77571
STATE HWY 6		324L	NWC	77447
STATELY AVE	13800	617B	SEH	77034
STATELY OAK DR	2300	297Z	NEH	77345
STATELY OAK DR	2500	298W	NEH	77345
STATE WALK CIR	9200	409H	NWC	77064
STATFIELD GLEN CT	21600	525D	NEF	77450
N. STATION CT	21100	332U	NCC	77073
STATION DR	7000	574G	SEH	77061
STATLER DR	6200	411Y	NWH	77091
STAUNTON	4500	491Z	SWH	77027
STAYTON CIR	1	490G	PP	77024
STEADMONT DR	5000	450H	NWH	77040
STEAMBOAT LN	15700	488A	SWH	77079
STEAMBOAT INN DR	18400	377C	NEC	77346
STEAMBOAT RUN	2000	568Z	SG	77478
STEAMBOAT SPRINGS CT	11700	371L	NWC	77067
STEAMSIDE BEND DR	100	249R	NWH	77375
STEAMSIDE BEND DR	100	249R	NWH	77375
STEAM SPRINGS DR	9300	329M	NWC	77379
STEARNS	0	620N	SB	77586
STEARNS	6600	533L	SEH	77021
STEBBINS CIR	10600	449Y	NWH	77043
STEBBINS DR	1700	449V	NWH	77043
STEDDUM	200	659E	LC	77573
STEDMAN	8000	495P	NEH	77029
STEEL	2300	492U	SWH	77098
STEEL BLVD	0	579Q	SEC	77507
STEEL, U S RD	0	542V	CCO	77520
STEEL, U S RD	0	543S	CCO	77520
STEELDUST CT	0	287Z	NWC	77377
STEELE	100	460S	HG	77562
STEELE	1300	616Q	FR	77546
STEELE AVE	8400	370Y	NWC	77064
STEELE POINT DR	18200	378P	NEC	77532
STEELE RANCH CT	0	657P	FR	77546
STEELHEAD DR	2600	572L	NWC	77045
STEELMAN	9700	535M	SEH	77017
STEELMAN	9900	536J	SEH	77017
STEEL MEADOWS LN	4900	336Z	NEC	77346
STEEL WOOD DR	0	367D	NWC	77429
STEEP FALLS LN	0	615B	PL	77581
STEEP FOREST CIR	0	524A	NEF	77494
STEEPLE LN	12300	414E	NCC	77039
STEEPLE CANYON RD	0	250T	NWC	77389
STEEPLECHASE RD	14500	570V	SWH	77489
STEEPLE CHASE GLEN DR	7400	377D	NEC	77346
STEEPLECHASE HEIGHTS DR	0	409F	NWC	77064
STEEPLE CHASE HEIGHTS DR	0	409F	NWC	77064
STEEPLECREST DR	11100	409B	NWC	77065
STEEPLEPARK DR	11100	409B	NWC	77065
STEEPLETOP DR	10600	369W	NWC	77065
STEEPLETOP DR	11200	369S	NWC	77065
STEEPLE WAY BLVD	11100	409B	NWC	77065
STEEP PINE TRAIL	0	611W	FS	77545
STEEP ROCK DR	4200	577E	PA	77504
STEEP STEP TRAIL	0	366S	NWC	77433
STEEP WOODS DR	0	253Z	SEM	77386
STEEVE CT	17400	379T	NEC	77532
STEFFANI LN	4300	450E	NWH	77041
STEINBERGS CT	1	494E	NEH	77020
STEINHAGEN RD	16700	327L	NWC	77429
STEINMAN	6600	500N	BT	77520
STELLA	400	541B	BT	77520
STELLA LN	31100	248X	TB	77375
STELLA LANDING LN	0	406C	NWC	77433
STELLA LINK RD	6700	532J	WU	77005
STELLA LINK RD	6800	532J	SWH	77025
STELLAR POINT DR	0	250B	WD	77381
STELLAS POINT CT	14800	375Z	NEC	77396
STEM GREEN CT	15100	325V	NWC	77433
STEMPLY CT	1700	486L	SWC	77094
STEM WAY DR	1200	419B	NEC	77532
STEMWOOD DR	2900	291Z	NWC	77388
STENBURY CT	15800	367D	NWC	77429
STEPENDALE DR	1300	486K	SWC	77450
STEPHANIE DR	500	570U	MC	77489
STEPHANIE LN	7400	538X	DP	77536
W. STEPHANSHIRE	1600	488R	SWH	77077
E. STEPHANSHIRE	1600	488R	SWH	77077
STEPHEN CT	800	656D	FR	77546
STEPHEN LUKE LN	1	657G	FR	77546
STEPHENS LN	10800	418S	NEC	77044
STEPHENS CHARGE CT	12300	366L	NWC	77433
STEPHENS CREEK CT	1700	568V	SG	77478
STEPHENS CREEK LN	3100	568V	SG	77478
STEPHENS FOREST RD	20100	258N	SEM	77357
STEPHENSON RD	15800	374N	NEH	77032
STEPINWOLF LN	23100	333B	NCC	77373
STEPNEY GREEN DR	9900	329Q	NWC	77070
STEPPINGSTONE LN	11900	490J	BH	77024
STEPPINSTONE WAY	1200	289X	NWC	77379
STEPWOOD DR	13800	371V	NWC	77038
E. STERLING	1	501Y	BT	77520
W. STERLING	100	501X	BT	77520
STERLING	1500	462Z	CCO	77520
STERLING	3900	533Y	SEH	77051
STERLING CT	0	484F	KT	77494
STERLING DR	1400	613L	PL	77584
W. STERLING DR	3600	613L	PL	77584
STERLINGAME DR	8700	570A	SWH	77031
STERLING BRIDGE LN	0	568A	NEF	77498
STERLING BROOK	5500	449A	NWC	77041
STERLING BROOK	11600	612H	PL	77584
STERLING CANYON DR	6500	526E	NEF	77450
STERLING CLOUD LN	25200	485J	NEF	77494
STERLING CREEK CIR	0	486A	SWC	77450
STERLING CREEK CT	1700	658W	LC	77573
STERLING CREEK DR	0	656Q	FR	77546
STERLINGCREST RD	13300	456R	NEH	77049
STERLING CROSSING	4900	614S	NEB	77584
STERLING CUP AVE	2300	371H	NWC	77014
STERLING FALLS DR	19900	406Q	NWC	77449
STERLING FIELDS DR	2700	613B	NEB	77584
STERLING GATE CIR	8600	330N	NWC	77379
STERLING GATE CT	16300	330N	NWC	77379
STERLING GREEN BLVD	14700	457Z	NEC	77015
STERLING GREEN CT	1300	457Z	NEC	77015
S. STERLING GREEN DR	900	497D	NEC	77530
S. STERLING GREEN DR	1000	457Z	NEC	77015
STERLING HEIGHTS LN	400	487A	SWC	77094
STERLING HEIGHTS LN	4500	609J	NEF	77479

Street Name	Block	Pg/Sq	Loc	Zips
STERLING HOLLOW DR	6900	406Q	NWC	77449
STERLING LAKE DR	15300	408E	NWC	77095
STERLING MANOR DR	5100	609J	NEF	77479
STERLING MANOR DR	10400	329B	NWC	77375
STERLING MEADOW CT	20000	406Q	NWC	77449
STERLING MEADOW DR	6900	406Q	NWC	77449
STERLING MOON LN	0	366J	NWC	77433
STERLING PARK LN	13400	328X	NWC	77429
STERLING PINES CT	20300	290Z	NWC	77379
STERLING POINT LN	8900	457A	NEC	77044
STERLING POINTE CT	2000	659D	LC	77573
STERLINGSHIRE	7300	455A	NEH	77016
STERLINGSHIRE	8000	455C	NEH	77078
STERLING STONE DR	0	373F	NCC	77073
STERLING STONE DR	0	373F	NCC	77073
STERLINGSTONE DR	12400	371E	NWC	77066
STERLING STONE LN	0	484U	NEF	77494
STERLING VIEW	3800	609K	MC	77459
STERLING VILLAGE DR	1600	252Q	SEM	77386
STERLING VISTA BLVD	0	484T	NEF	77494
STERLING WOOD DR	0	253Z	SEM	77386
STERLING WOOD WAY	4400	578U	SEH	77059
STERN LN	0	377L	NEC	77044
STERN CREEK LN	13600	377L	NEC	77044
STERNWOOD MANOR DR	19700	289Z	NWC	77379
STERRETT	1200	493M	NEH	77002
STETSON CIR	27200	246N	SWM	77355
STETSON LN	2600	450J	NWH	77043
STETSON HEIGHTS LN	0	526K	NEF	77407
STEVEN	0	614L	PL	77581
STEVENAGE LN	900	498A	NEC	77530
STEVENAGE LN	1000	458W	NEC	77530
STEVEN FALLS CT	0	253U	SEM	77386
STEVENS	1500	494E	NEH	77026
STEVENS	20600	256N	SEM	77357
STEVENS	1	255R	SEM	77357
STEVENSON DR	0	609U	MC	77459
STEVENSON RD	0	616W	NEB	77581
STEVENSON RD	0	656A	NEB	77581
STEVEN SPRINGS DR	0	325S	HK	77447
STEVES CROSSING	0	332V	NCC	77073
STEWART	0	484C	KT	77494
STEWART	0	660A	LC	77573
STEWART	1	501U	BT	77520
STEWART	100	496W	GP	77547
STEWART DR	5000	444Z	KT	77493
STEWART LN	21100	256S	SEM	77357
STEWART CREST LN	20700	406K	NWC	77433
STEWARTS GROVE DR	16000	330S	NWC	77379
STIELER DR	0	457V	NEC	77049
STIKINE DR	0	371S	NWC	77086
STILES	1	494T	SEH	77011
N. STILES	100	494P	SEH	77011
STILES LN	12000	568M	SG	77478
STILESBORO CT	14600	618E	SEH	77062
STILL BAY	2400	612M	PL	77584
STILL BAY CT	13600	488P	SWH	77077
STILLBREEZE VALLEY LN	0	328A	NWC	77429
STILLBREEZE VALLEY LN	0	328A	NWC	77377
STILLBRIDGE LN	0	296X	SEM	77339
STILLBROOK CIR	11800	368D	NWC	77429
STILLBROOKE DR	4300	531Z	SWH	77035
STILLBROOKE DR	5300	531X	SWH	77096
STILL CORNER PLACE	1	250H	WD	77381
STILLCOVE LN	9500	616E	SEC	77089
STILLCREEK DR	15100	329W	NWC	77070
STILL CREEK RD	3700	578A	PA	77505
STILLER DR	6700	571W	SWH	77489
STILLER PARK DR	15500	367H	NWC	77429
STILLER RIDGE WAY	0	292D	SEM	77386
W. STILL FOREST	1	490Q	PP	77024
E. STILL FOREST	1	490Q	PP	77024
STILLGATE CT	1000	292B	NCC	77373
STILL GLADE LN	4100	297T	NEH	77345
STILL GLEN CT	1	251J	WD	77381
STILL HARBOUR DR	12500	449A	NWC	77041
STILL HAVEN DR	0	525H	NEF	77407
STILLHAVEN PARK CT	20600	290T	NWC	77389
STILLHAVEN ROAD CT	7100	290T	NWC	77389
STILLHOLLOW LN	19800	486L	SWC	77094
STILLHOUSE DR	19200	288P	NWC	77377
STILLHOUSE DR	19500	288Z	NWC	77375
STILLHOUSE HOLLOW LN	0	657N	FR	77546
STILLHOUSE HOLLOW LN	0	406D	NWC	77433
STILLHOUSE LAKE CT	0	377H	NEH	77346
STILLINGTON DR	12600	456Z	NEC	77015
STILLINGTON DR	12900	457W	NEC	77015
STILLMAN	6100	492F	SWH	77007
STILL MANOR CT	0	446C	NWC	77449
STILL MEADOW	6800	290C	NWC	77389
STILLMEADOW DR	2200	610E	MC	77489
STILLMEADOW DR	14300	488D	SWH	77079
STILLMONT LN	20500	526J	NEF	77407
STILLOAK LN	0	407J	NWC	77433
STILL OAKS LN	0	253N	SEM	77386
STILL POND DR	22900	290F	NWC	77375
STILLRIVER	9200	412L	NWH	77088
STILLROCK DR	0	524T	NWF	77406
STILLSON RD	100	338V	NEH	77336
STILLSON RD	1200	339T	NEC	77532
STILL SPRINGS CT	18000	376D	NEC	77346
STILL SPRINGS DR	4600	376D	NEC	77346
STILLSTONE DR	0	373F	NCC	77073
STILLSTONE DR	0	373F	NCC	77073
STILLVIEW DR	3700	331S	NWC	77068
STILLWATER	0	656V	FR	77546
STILL WATER	7900	461S	NEC	77521
STILLWATER DR	4100	569X	MC	77459
STILLWATER DR	6400	614T	PL	77584
STILLWATER DR	11600	329W	NWC	77070
STILLWATER BAY CT	2100	658V	LC	77573
STILLWATER CANYON LN	0	256W	SEM	77365
STILLWATER COVE BLVD	0	616H	SEC	77089
STILLWATER PLACE DR	18100	376D	NEC	77346
STILLWATER RETREAT LN	0	377U	NEC	77044
STILLWATER VALLEY LN	0	256W	SEM	77365
STILLWELL	6300	534H	SEH	77023
STILLWELL	6600	534H	SEH	77087
STILLWELL DR	2500	610B	MC	77489
STILLWOOD DR	1900	450T	NWH	77080
STILLWOOD DR	2300	450P	NWH	77080
STILLWOOD MEADOW LN	0	484X	NEF	77494
STILLWOOD PARK CT	12600	366H	NWC	77433
STILSON BRANCH LN	6000	541F	NWH	77092
STIMPSON	1	541B	BT	77520
STIMPSON PARK DR	0	376T	NEC	77396
STIMSON	4900	494X	SEH	77023
STING RAY DR	16000	418D	NEC	77532
STINSON DR	8000	609V	MC	77459
STIRRING WINDS LN	5900	411B	NWC	77086
STIRRUP DR	13200	413H	NCC	77039
STIRRUP RANCH	0	289X	NWC	77375

Street Name	Block	Pg/Sq	Loc	Zips
STITCHBIRD LN	0	328A	NWC	77429
ST LAURENT LN	11200	529B	SWH	77082
ST LUCIA CALLE	0	660S	GCO	77539
STOBCROSS DR	17000	527X	NEF	77407
STOCK BRIDGE	0	461S	BT	77521
STOCKBRIDGE DR	3900	609J	SG	77479
STOCKBRIDGE LN	21900	446A	NWC	77449
STOCKDICK	5900	484B	KT	77494
STOCKDICK SCHOOL RD	0	405Z	NWC	77449
STOCKDICK SCHOOL RD	21000	445B	NWC	77449
STOCKDICK SCHOOL RD	23000	444B	NWC	77493
STOCKFIELD LN	6500	406T	NWC	77449
STOCKHOLM CT	5900	406Z	NWC	77449
STOCKLIN CT	14800	527V	NEF	77498
STOCKMAN LN	10400	528X	NEF	77498
STOCKPORT DR	0	657T	LC	77573
STOCKPORT DR	9300	330S	NWC	77379
STOCKTON	6200	532D	SWH	77030
STOCKTON FALLS DR	0	406T	NWC	77449
STOCKTON FALLS DR	0	406U	NWC	77449
STOCKTON SPRINGS DR	0	331E	NWC	77379
STOCKWELL DR	9200	528T	SWC	77083
STOCKWOOD DR	11000	369Y	NWC	77064
STOERNER DR	3300	374X	NCC	77032
STOKES	0	453P	NWH	77022
STOKES RD	19000	282R	NWC	77484
STOKESDALE DR	0	410E	NWC	77064
STOKESMOUNT DR	14000	488E	SWH	77077
STOKSAY DR	0	406U	NWC	77449
STOLZ TRAIL	0	445A	NWC	77493
STONE	8100	535U	SEH	77061
STONE CT	4500	447E	NWC	77084
S. STONE LN	19400	446D	NWC	77449
W. STONE RD	4300	613E	NEB	77584
STONE RD	12500	614E	PL	77581
STONEAGE DR	0	526T	NEF	77407
STONE ANGEL DR	0	377C	NEC	77346
STONE ARBOR LN	7400	614J	NEB	77581
STONE BANK CT	13400	328Q	NWC	77429
STONEBANK DR	0	609P	NEF	77479
STONEBELT DR	0	373F	NCC	77073
STONEBELT DR	0	373F	NCC	77073
STONE BLUFF DR	0	373F	NCC	77073
STONE BLUFF DR	0	373F	NCC	77073
STONEBRANCH LN	0	485V	NEF	77450
STONE BRIAR DR	6300	578J	PA	77505
STONEBRIAR CREEK CROSSING		249V	NWC	77375
STONEBRIDGE	0	244J	WCO	77447
STONE BRIDGE	300	658P	LC	77573
STONE BRIDGE	4700	461N	NEC	77521
STONEBRIDGE DR	4200	609K	MC	77459
STONEBRIDGE DR	4500	615S	PL	77584
STONE BRIDGE DR	11500	369U	NWC	77064
STONEBRIDGE CREEK LN	0	375X	NEC	77396
STONEBRIDGE CROSSING LN	22200	289K	NWC	77375
STONEBRIDGE LAKE DR	9300	249U	NWC	77375
STONEBRIDGE PLACE	9500	249U	NWC	77375
STONEBRIDGE TERRACE CT	20300	526S	NEF	77407
STONEBRIDGE TERRACE DR	20300	526S	NEF	77407
STONEBRIDGE TRAIL DR	17200	367U	NWC	77095
STONEBROOK DR	0	612L	PL	77584
STONEBROOK DR	16600	407G	NWC	77095
STONEBROOK LN	4200	609K	MC	77459
STONE BROOK LN	8800	411S	NWH	77040
STONEBROOK ESTATES DR		329L	NWC	77375
STONEBROOK MANOR LN	0	484N	NEF	77494
STONEBROOK RUN CT		329L	NWC	77375
STONEBROOK TERRACE DR		329L	NWC	77375
STONEBROOK VIEW DR		329k	NWC	77375
STONEBURG DR	4100	485Z	NEF	77450
STONEBURY FALLS CT	0	484J	NEF	77494
STONEBURY TRAIL LN	14400	417C	NEH	77044
STONECACTUS DR	10200	367X	NWC	77095
W. STONE CALDWELL DR		366V	NWC	77433
STONE CANYON CT	20200	286X	NWC	77377
STONE CASTLE DR	9400	409H	NWC	77064
STONE CASTLE TOWER ST	0	444C	NWC	77493
STONECHASE	6500	407U	NWC	77084
STONECLOUD	5600	485S	NEF	77494
STONE COTTAGE LN	0	573Y	SEC	77047
STONECREEK CIR	700	657J	FR	77546
STONE CREEK CT	0	657K	FR	77546
STONE CREEK CT	19900	286X	NWC	77377
STONE CREEK DR	5400	539X	LP	77571
STONECREEK LN	9200	529R	SWH	77036
STONECREEK BEND LN	0	366R	NWC	77433
STONE CREEK MODEL CT	16800	407Q	NWC	77084
STONE CREEK RANCH BLVD	0	325S	HK	77447
STONE CREEK TERRACE	0	657P	FR	77546
STONECREST CT	3400	616S	PL	77581
STONECREST DR	900	452N	NWH	77018
STONECREST DR	2000	616S	PL	77581
STONECROFT LN	4100	485Y	NEF	77450
STONECROP CT	4800	297Q	NEH	77345
STONE CROSS CT	22000	485V	NEF	77450
STONE CROSS BEND DR	0	329U	NWC	77070
STONECROSS CREEK LN	6600	406P	NWC	77449
STONECROSS CREEK LN	6600	406P	NWC	77449
STONECROSS GLEN LN	0	406M	NWC	77433
STONE CROSSING LN	0	446C	NWC	77449
STONECROSS TERRACE LN	21500	446N	NWC	77449
STONEDALE VIEW DR	0	524T	NWF	77406
STONE EAST DR	12100	571F	SWH	77035
STONEFAIR LN	8800	575Y	SWH	77075
STONE FALCON LN	0	485P	NEF	77493
STONE FALLS CT	20200	326N	NWC	77433
STONEFIELD DR	13100	372B	NWC	77014
STONE FIELD CANYON LN	12900	366H	NWC	77433
STONEFIELD MANOR CT	9400	416Z	NEC	77044
STONEFIELD MANOR DR	12000	416Z	NEC	77044
STONEFIELD MANOR DR	12600	417W	NEC	77044
STONEFIR CT	7000	411S	NWH	77040
STONEFORD DR	0	489T	SWH	77077
STONE FOREST DR	19100	331A	NWC	77379
STONEFORT CT	6600	406T	NWC	77449
STONE FOX DR	28700	293A	SEM	77386
STONE GABLES	0	417B	NEC	77044
STONEGATE	1	490F	HE	77024
STONEGATE CIR	3500	615P	PL	77584
STONEGATE CIR	5300	526S	NEF	77407
STONEGATE CT	100	330T	NWC	77379
STONE GATE CT	20100	286Y	NWC	77377
STONEGATE DR	5301	526S	NEF	77407
STONEGATE DR	7200	411S	NWH	77040
STONE GATE DR	10200	252G	SEM	77385
STONEGATE GROVE	5400	526S	NEF	77407
STONEGATE GROVE CT	5400	526S	NEF	77407
STONEGATE PARK CT	1	330T	NWC	77379
STONEGROVE CT	1900	614E	NEB	77581
STONEGROVE CT	20200	289W	NWC	77375
STONEHAM CT	0	484H	NEF	77494
STONE HARBOR DR	4800	617W	SEC	77546

Street Name	Block	Pg/Sq	Loc	Zips
STONE HARBOUR LN	0	484S	NEF	77494
STONEHAVEN DR	7800	250W	NWC	77389
STONEHAVEN DR	15700	578Y	SEH	77059
STONEHAVEN VILLAGE CIR	1600	252Q	SEM	77386
STONE HAVEN WAY	6700	571S	SWH	77085
STONEHEARTH LN	8900	410V	NWH	77040
STONEHEDGE DR	0	373F	NCC	77073
STONEHEDGE DR	0	373F	NCC	77073
STONEHEDGE DR	2700	501E	BT	77521
STONEHEDGE BEND DR	0	373F	NCC	77073
STONEHEDGE BEND DR	0	373F	NCC	77073
STONEHENGE	200	616Y	FR	77546
STONEHENGE DR	13600	568F	SG	77498
STONEHENGE LN	300	457X	NEC	77015
STONEHENGE TRAIL	4100	371E	NWC	77066
STONEHILL DR	15400	618J	SEH	77062
STONE HILL RD	0	250V	NWC	77389
STONEHOLLOW CT	0	615K	PL	77581
STONEHOLLOW DR	1000	336B	NEH	77339
STONE HOUSE LN	1	486M	SWC	77094
STONEHOUSE LN	9400	532S	SWH	77025
STONEHURST CT	3300	613Z	NEB	77584
STONEHURST DR	4000	613Z	NEB	77584
STONEHURST LN	0	524B	NEF	77494
STONE ISLAND CT		526S	NEF	77407
STONE ISLE CT	10700	527W	NEF	77407
STONE IVORY CT	3400	291Y	NWC	77388
STONE IVY LN	0	446C	NWC	77449
STONE LAKE CIR	19900	286X	NWC	77377
STONE LAKE DR	1600	570T	MC	77489
STONE LAKE DR	19600	286T	NWC	77377
STONE LANDING	0	407Z	NWC	77084
STONELEAF DR	0	373F	NCC	77073
STONELEAF DR	0	373F	NCC	77073
STONE LEAF DR	19100	526L	NEF	77407
STONELEDGE DR	400	616X	FR	77546
STONE LEGEND DR		329L	NWC	77375
STONELEIGH CT	1000	289A	TB	77375
STONELEIGH DR	500	489E	SWH	77079
STONELEIGH LAKE DR	0	332S	NWC	77090
STONELEIGH TERRACE DR	0	488U	SWH	77077
STONELICK CT	0	614S	NEB	77584
STONELICK BRIDGE LN	14900	528W	NEF	77498
STONE LOCH CT	0	328P	NWC	77377
STONELODGE	19900	486L	SWC	77450
STONE MALLOW DR	11400	367Q	NWC	77095
STONE MANOR DR	0	329C	NWC	77379
STONEMEADE PLACE	14900	328W	NWC	77429
STONE MEADOWS LN	1600	486M	SWC	77094
STONEMEDE DR	4600	617X	SEC	77546
STONE MESA DR	0	373F	NCC	77073
STONE MESA DR	0	373F	NCC	77073
STONE MILL LN	0	568A	NEF	77498
STONE MILL LN	25300	292R	NCC	77373
STONE MISSION LN	0	526Q	NEF	77407
STONEMIST LN	4500	291T	NWC	77388
STONEMONT LN	0	326R	NWC	77429
STONEMONT RD	9700	579A	LP	77571
STONEMONT GLEN LN	0	525M	NEF	77407
STONE MOSS	20300	290V	NWC	77379
STONEMOUNT CT	8100	335J	NCC	77338
STONE MOUNTAIN LN	20700	333P	NCC	77073
STONE MOUNTAIN FALLS		249Z	NWC	77375
STONE MOUNTAIN FALLS		289D	NWC	77375
STONE OAK CT	4200	609F	MC	77459
STONE OAK CT	7800	370E	NWC	77070
STONE OAK CT	15800	326V	NWC	77429
STONE PARK RD	14400	570V	SWH	77489
STONEPASS CT	4700	609P	NEF	77479
STONEPATH	0	407R	NWC	77084
STONE PEAKS DR	17300	367X	NWC	77095
STONE PINE LN	7300	408Q	NWC	77041
STONEPINE CREEK DR	20000	289W	NWC	77375
STONEPINE MEADOW CT	11500	289W	NWC	77375
STONEPINE MEADOW CT	20200	289W	NWC	77375
STONE POINT	19100	291X	NWC	77388
STONE PORCH LN	9100	409H	NWC	77064
STONEPORT LN	19700	446C	NWC	77449
STONE POST CIR	9200	409H	NWC	77064
STONE PRAIRIE DR	16400	367Q	NWC	77095
STONER CT	6900	411N	NWH	77088
STONER FALLS DR	0	488K	SWH	77077
STONE RIDGE	6400	407U	NWC	77084
STONERIDGE DR	21900	255Y	SEM	77365
STONERIDGE CANYON CT	11000	615H	SEC	77089
STONERIDGE CANYON LN	9200	615H	SEC	77089
STONE RIDGE CROSSING LN	0	366H	NWC	77433
STONERIDGE PARK CT	15100	327V	NWC	77429
STONERIDGE PARK LN	15300	327V	NWC	77429
STONERIDGE TERRACE LN	500	657Y	LC	77573
STONERIVER	0	407R	NWC	77084
STONERIVER CT	0	615K	PL	77581
STONE ROSE DR	0	293L	SEM	77386
STONEROSES TRAIL	0	526S	NEF	77407
STONE RUN	0	407R	NWC	77084
STONERUN	0	407R	NWC	77084
STONERUN	16600	407V	NWC	77084
STONERUN DR	6800	407R	NWC	77084
STONESDALE DR	7700	408J	NWC	77095
STONESFIELD PLACE	7400	250P	NWC	77389
S. STONESHIRE	13800	413E	NCC	77037
STONESHIRE	14000	413E	NCC	77060
STONESHIRE DR	18700	256D	SEM	77357
STONESIDE DR	16600	407G	NWC	77095
STONE SPRINGS DR	0	484S	NEF	77494
STONES RIVER LN	17000	377J	NEC	77346
STONE STABLE LN	16100	327Y	NWC	77429
STONES THROW	100	656D	FR	77546
STONESTHROW LN	0	615K	PL	77581
STONES THROW RD	5900	491J	SWH	77057
STONE STILE DR	17000	617Y	SEC	77546
STONE STREAM DR		329k	NWC	77375
STONE TERRACE CT	9500	616E	SEC	77089
STONE TOWER CT	0	444D	NWC	77493
STONE TRAIL LN	6000	290Z	NWC	77379
STONETRAIL RD	20600	526S	NEF	77407
STONE TRAIL MANOR DR	0	377C	NEC	77346
STONE VALLEY DR	7300	408N	NWC	77095
STONE VIEW DR	0	286U	NWC	77377
STONEVIEW DR	20100	526S	NEF	77407
STONE VILLA	0	409H	NWC	77064
STONE VILLAGE LN	8400	411S	NWH	77040
STONEWALK DR	2000	491U	SWH	77056
STONEWALL	3000	494F	NEH	77020
STONEWALL	5000	494U	SEH	77023
STONEWALL CT	0	407E	NWC	77433
STONEWALL CT	2900	610U	MC	77459
STONEWALL DR	200	658P	LC	77573
STONEWALL PASS	0	656K	FR	77546
STONEWATER	6700	407Q	NWC	77084
STONE WAY DR	2800	488Y	SWH	77082
STONE WEST DR	12100	571F	SWH	77035
STONEWICK DR	15000	331S	NWC	77068
STONEWOOD	10100	415X	NEH	77078
STONEWOOD LN	2200	570Y	MC	77489
STONEWOOD HEIGHTS CT	0	615K	PL	77581
STONEWOOD POINTE LN	6300	370L	NWC	77066
STONEY CT	2000	293W	NCC	77373
STONEY BAY CT	0	405P	NWC	77493
STONEY BEND DR	8800	330J	NWC	77379
STONEY BLUFF LN	21700	445R	NWC	77449
STONEY BROOK	3700	501L	BT	77521
STONEY BROOK	0	538V	DP	77536
STONEY BROOK DR	1800	490Z	SWH	77063
STONEY BROOK DR	6000	530C	SWH	77036
STONEY BROOK LN	3100	609M	MC	77459
STONEY CLOUD DR	0	484X	NEF	77494
STONEY CLOUD DR	0	484X	NEF	77494
STONEY CREEK DR	0	612L	PL	77584
STONEY CREEK DR	100	490J	SWH	77024
STONEY CREEK DR	6200	538W	PA	77503
STONEYCREEK PARK	2100	252M	SEM	77385
STONEYCREEK PARK CT	2200	252M	SEM	77385
STONEYDALE LN	3200	291U	NWC	77388
STONEY ELMS CT	0	407R	NWC	77084
STONEY FALLS DR	11300	367U	NWC	77095
STONEY FORK DR	15500	448B	NWC	77084
STONEY GLADE CT	17800	407K	NWC	77095
STONEY GLEN DR	2200	296V	NEH	77339
E. STONEYGROVE LOOP	5900	408X	NWC	77084
S. STONEYGROVE LOOP	14300	408U	NWC	77084
STONEY HAVEN	0	406T	NWC	77449
STONEY HAVEN DR	19800	406L	NWC	77433
STONEY HEIGHTS	0	291X	NWC	77388
STONEY HILL DR	1000	488E	SWH	77077
STONEY HILLS CT	0	326T	NWC	77433
STONEY KNOLL LN	4200	484U	NEF	77494
STONEY LAKE DR	1600	656R	FR	77546
STONEY LAKE DR	9000	409G	NWC	77064
STONEY MEADOW DR	11200	367V	NWC	77095
STONEY MILL DR	12500	369J	NWC	77429
STONEY OAK DR	3400	331N	NWC	77068
STONEY OAKS CT	0	526P	NEF	77407
STONEY PARK CT	2200	336B	NEH	77339
STONEY PARK DR	1500	336B	NEH	77339
STONEY PASS DR	0	524S	NWF	77406
STONEY PLAIN DR	30100	252V	SEM	77386
STONEY POINT	2200	491U	SWH	77056
STONEY RIDGE CT	4600	609S	NEF	77479
STONEY RIDGE LN	11900	490K	BH	77024
STONEY RISE LN	0	377G	NEC	77346
STONEY RIVER CT	17400	330G	NWC	77379
STONEY RIVER DR	6600	330G	NWC	77379
STONEY RUN PLACE	1	250D	WD	77381
STONEY SHORES LN	0	484P	NEF	77494
STONEYVALE DR	0	527F	NEF	77083
STONEY VIEW DR	4200	578E	PA	77505
STONEYVIEW DR	15000	527R	NEF	77083
STONEYWAY DR	7800	410F	NWC	77040
STONEY WOOD DR	2800	488Y	SWH	77082
STONHAM	3500	573U	SEH	77047
STONHAM	5900	574U	SEH	77048
STONINGTON	5400	410X	NWH	77040
W. STONY BRIDGE CIR	1	250C	WD	77381
S. STONY BRIDGE CIR	1	250C	WD	77381
E. STONY BRIDGE CIR	1	250C	WD	77381
W. STONY BRIDGE CT	1	250C	WD	77381
E. STONY BRIDGE CT	1	250C	WD	77381
STONYDELL CT	8100	535T	SEH	77061
STONY GREEN DR	0	325U	NWC	77433
STONYRIDGE DR	700	498A	NEC	77530
STONY RUN PLACE	1	250D	WD	77381
STOREY DR	6100	375S	NEH	77396
STORMCOVEWAY	0	375V	NEC	77396
STORM CREEK CT	8400	411R	NWH	77088
STORM CREEK DR	3600	411R	NWH	77088
STORMCROFT CIR	1900	485M	SWC	77450
STORMCROFT LN	0	612K	PL	77584
STORMCROFT LN	22300	485M	SWC	77450
STORM MEADOW DR	9900	409C	NWC	77064
STORM MEADOW DR	10100	369Y	NWC	77064
STORM WOOD	8700	410P	NWC	77040
STORMY PINE LN	20100	290Y	NWC	77379
STORMY SKY DR	10500	369Y	NWC	77064
STORNOWAY DR	15800	330T	NWC	77379
STORY	1300	451Y	NWH	77055
STORYBOOK	16900	328Q	NWC	77377
STORY BOOK TRAIL	0	609Z	MC	77459
STORYBROOK FOREST DR	16900	328Q	NWC	77377
STORY CREEK LN	23200	296N	SEM	77365
STORY GLEN DR	0	368E	NWC	77429
STORYWOOD DR	700	490H	HC	77024
STOUGHTON CIR	11400	371Q	NWC	77066
STOUGHTON CT	24600	484H	NEF	77494
STOUT DR	0	285Q	NWC	77447
STOVALL	1900	331L	NWC	77090
STOVEPIPE LN	3800	609A	SG	77479
STOVER	10300	576S	SEH	77075
STOWBRIDGE DR	0	295V	NEH	77365
STOWE	1100	541B	BT	77520
STRACK	0	330V	NWC	77069
S. STRACK DR	0	331K	NWC	77379
W. STRACK DR	17000	331K	NWC	77379
E. STRACK DR	17000	331K	NWC	77379
STRACK RD	4500	330X	NWC	77069
STRACK RD	18000	331E	NWC	77379
STRACKFARM RD	0	331J	NWC	77379
STRACKFIELD LN	0	328M	NWC	77377
STRADBROOK DR	15200	618J	SEH	77062
STRAIGHT ARROW DR	5200	337S	NEC	77346
STRAIGHT CREEK DR	2100	535V	SEH	77017
STRAIGHT ELM	0	611S	FS	77545
STRAIGHTFORK DR	3700	527C	SWC	77082
STRAIGHT WAY	5600	297J	NEH	77339
STRAIT LN	2300	446U	NWC	77084
STRAND CT	300	577W	SEH	77034
STRANG RD	1	540J	SEC	77571
STRANG RD	8200	539L	SEC	77571
STRATA WAY	0	329Y	NWC	77070
STRATBURG LN	0	369G	NWC	77070
STRATFIELD LN	0	575U	SEH	77075
STRATFORD	100	493S	SWH	77006
STRATFORD	400	459Q	HG	77562
STRATFORD	800	537J	PA	77506
STRATFORD	2700	615Q	PL	77581
STRATFORD CANYON DR	0	406H	NWC	77433
STRATFORD HOUSE LN	22700	445Q	NWC	77449
STRATFORD PARK DR	6800	408P	NWC	77084
STRATFORD PLACE	9200	289M	NWC	77375
STRATFORD SKIES LN	13000	528L	SWH	77072
STRATFORD WAY	1300	336H	NEH	77339
STRATFORD WAY LN	1	369D	NWC	77070
STRATHCLYDE SOUND RD	7800	407H	NWC	77095
S. STRATHFORD LN	2500	337B	NEH	77345
N. STRATHFORD LN	2600	337B	NEH	77345
STRATHMERE CT	22900	485B	SWC	77450
STRATHMILL CT	9200	407D	NWC	77095
STRATHMORE DR	8400	455H	NEH	77078
STRATHMORE MANOR LN	16500	332N	NWC	77090
STRATHMORE PLACE LN	0	406R	NWC	77449
STRATMOR CT	6200	250Y	NWC	77389
STRATMORE DR	100	616Y	FR	77546
STRATSBOROUGH DR	23400	525F	NEF	77494
STRATTON	6300	534H	SEH	77023
STRATTON CREEK DR	24500	293T	NCC	77373
STRATTON MEADOWS DR	0	295L	SEM	77365
STRATTON PARK DR	15900	330S	NWC	77379
STRATTON RIDGE DR	0	524S	NWF	77406
STRATTON WOODS DR	0	290D	NWC	77389
STRATUS CT	4100	293H	SEM	77386
STRAT WOOD CT	19900	406M	NWC	77433
STRATWOOD GLEN CT		328P	NWC	77429
STRAUS CT	1	569M	SF	77477
STRAUSS LN	0	377D	NEH	77346
E. STRAWBERRY	200	659Q	LC	77573
STRAWBERRY RD	900	537J	PA	77506
STRAWBERRY RD	1300	537W	PA	77502
STRAWBERRY RD	3900	577E	PA	77504
STRAWBERRY CACTUS LOOP	0	410A	NWC	77064
STRAWBERRY FIELDS DR	0	381L	LCO	77535
STRAWBERRY PARK LN	1200	485H	SWC	77450
STRAWBRIDGE LN	7300	410V	NWH	77040
STRAWFIELD DR	1900	568Y	SG	77478
STRAWGRASS DR	9500	369Y	NWC	77064
STRAWN	1300	541B	BT	77520
STRAWN	1500	413D	NCC	77039
STREAMED TRAIL	4100	331S	NWC	77068
W. STREAMERTRAIL CIR	0	367P	NWC	77433
E. STREAMERTRAIL CIR	0	367P	NWC	77433
STREAM MILL LN	400	485A	NEF	77494
STREAMSIDE DR	1800	657J	FR	77546
STREAMSIDE DR	7600	411Q	NWH	77088
STREAMWOOD DR	6800	527M	SWC	77083
STREATHAM CIR	15300	458W	NEC	77530
STREET CIR	0	298S	NEC	77336
STREET B	0	298S	NEH	77336
STREETCAR CT	15300	326Z	NWC	77429
STREETER LN	0	332A	NWC	77388
STREETER PLACE CT	0	332A	NWC	77388
STRETCH DR	9300	410N	NWC	77040
STREY	400	490E	BH	77024
STREY CT	400	538Y	DP	77536
STRICK LN	12400	496L	NEH	77015
STRICKLAND	900	501Z	BT	77520
STRICKLAND	10500	414T	NEH	77093
STRICKLAND DR	22300	256Q	SEM	77357
STRINGTON DR	13700	408L	NWC	77041
STRIPED ALDER LN	0	329L	NWC	77379
STRIPED MAPLE CT		289G	NWC	77375
STROH CIR	31900	246W	SWM	77355
STROKER RD	100	379G	NEC	77532
STROKER RD	1200	378H	NEC	77532
STROKER RD	2700	380E	NEC	77532
STROLLING STREAM LN	0	527N	NEF	77407
STROLLING WAY	400	569Q	SF	77477
ST ROMAN DR	0	524A	NEF	77494
STROMAN DR	14500	328X	NWC	77429
STRONG BANK	0	609Z	NEF	77459
STRONG CREEK DR	5700	407Z	NWC	77084
STRONG PINE DR	24000	338M	NEH	77336
STRONGS CT	1800	446X	NWC	77449
STRONG WINDS DR	3300	371C	NWC	77014
STROUD DR	6400	530M	SWH	77074
STROUD DR	7900	530J	SWH	77036
STROUD DR	10900	529K	SWH	77072
STROUDWATER LN	0	408W	NWC	77084
STRUTTON DR	14200	528T	NEF	77498
STRYKER LN	21400	406N	NWC	77433
ST SIMON MANOR DR	3800	573U	SEC	77047
STUALISHIOUS DR	0	609T	NEF	77479
STUART	500	493T	SWH	77006
STUART	900	493T	SWH	77002
STUART	1000	493Y	SWH	77004
STUART	28700	288J	NWC	77377
STUART DR	3700	579A	LP	77571
STUART BEND	0	489W	SWH	77082
STUART CREST	0	489S	SWH	77082
STUART MANOR	2600	489X	SWH	77082
STUBBS DR	8600	528Q	SWC	77083
STUCKEY LN	11800	490F	BH	77024
STUDE	1000	493A	NWH	77007
STUDEBAKER LN	3500	375M	NEC	77396
STUDEMONT	400	493E	SWH	77007
STUDER	1100	492G	SWH	77007
STUDEWOOD	400	493A	NWH	77007
STUDEWOOD	900	453W	NWH	77008
STUDEWOOD	2000	453S	NWH	77009
STUEBNER	8100	495P	NEH	77029
STUEBNER DR	23500	289F	NWC	77375
STUEBNER AIRLINE RD	5600	452D	NWH	77091
STUEBNER AIRLINE RD	6300	412Z	NWH	77091
STUEBNER AIRLINE RD	7500	412Z	NWH	77088
STUEBNER AIRLINE RD	14000	331W	NWC	77069
STUEBNER AIRLINE RD	15700	330R	NWC	77379
STUEBNER AIRLINE RD	19200	290S	NWC	77379
STUEBNER AIRLINE RD	23000	289C	NWC	77375
STUEBNER AIRLINE RD	24200	249X	NWC	77375
STUEBNER PARK	2000	412A	NWC	77038
STURBRIDGE DR	5400	491K	SWH	77056
STURDIVANT	12000	569A	MD	77477
STUTTS LN	10800	449U	NWH	77043
STUYVESANT LN	5100	534K	SEH	77021
STYERS	200	453Q	NEH	77022
STYLING CT	1	414Z	NEH	77016
STYLING DR	5300	414Z	NEH	77016
SUBURBAN	4500	494P	SEH	77011
SUBURBAN RD	11300	415J	NEC	77016
SUBURBAN RD	11700	415J	NEC	77050
SUBURBAN GARDEN RD	12200	574X	SEH	77048
SUBURBAN GARDEN RD	12400	614K	PL	77581
SUBURBAN OAKS RD	0	453H	NEH	77093
SUCCESS CT	0	569U	NEF	77477
SUCCESS LN	500	339E	HU	77336
SUCCESS RD	2600	331Q	NWC	77068
SUDAN	4600	494C	NEH	77020
SUDBURY DR	1200	577E	PA	77504
SUDDEN VALLEY LN	0	568A	NEF	77498
W. SUDDLEY CASTLE	7400	408L	NWC	77095
E. SUDDLEY CASTLE	7400	408L	NWC	77095
S. SUDDLEY CASTLE	14000	408L	NWC	77095
N. SUDDLEY CASTLE	14100	408L	NWC	77095
SUDELEY LN	12300	414E	NCC	77039
SUE	200	453U	NEH	77009
SUE DR	1000	660B	KE	77565
SUE LN	0	409M	JV	77040
SUE LN	1	459V	HG	77562
SUE LN	10500	528Z	SWH	77099
SUE LN	32000	248N	SWM	77355
SUE ANN	0	292Z	NCC	77373
SUE ANN LN	1300	332D	NCC	77373
SUE ANN LN	1400	332D	NCC	77373
SUE BARNETT DR	700	452L	NWH	77018
SUE ELLEN	4000	534M	SEH	77087
SUE MARIE LN	5200	452C	NWH	77091
SUEZ	5300	494C	NEH	77020
SUFFIELD CT	1400	332V	NCC	77073
SUFFIELD GLEN CT	4900	484Z	NEF	77494
SUFFIELD GLEN DR	26300	484Z	NEF	77494
SUFFIELD GLEN LN	0	334R	NCC	77338
SUFFIELD GLEN LN	7800	334M	NCC	77338
SUFFIELD PARK LN	0	371H	NWC	77014
SUFFOLK	0	257H	SEM	77357
SUFFOLK DR	2000	491Z	SWH	77027
SUFFOLK BRIDGE LN	16900	332Q	NCC	77073
SUFFOLK CHASE LN	12800	488Q	SWH	77077
SUFFOLK HOLLOW LN	0	526L	NEF	77407
SUFFOLK SKY CT	0	446E	NWC	77449
SUGAR BARS DR	4300	617T	SEC	77546
SUGAR BEAR LN	22800	291E	NWC	77389
SUGARBERRY CIR	1	490P	SWH	77024
SUGARBERRY WAY	20900	289U	NWC	77375
SUGARBLOOM LN	21300	289Q	NWC	77375
SUGARBLOSSOM LN	0	528T	NEF	77083
SUGARBLUFF LN	0	528T	NEF	77083
SUGAR BOW DR	15000	527Z	NEF	77498
SUGAR BOWL LN	0	329B	NWC	77375
SUGAR BRANCH DR	9900	529V	SWH	77036
SUGARBRIDGE LN	20900	289U	NWC	77375
SUGARBRIDGE TRAIL	10100	527V	NEF	77498
SUGAR BUSH	1400	541H	BT	77520
SUGAR BUSH DR	4500	573V	SEH	77048
SUGAR BUSH DR	5300	574N	SEH	77048
SUGARBUSH RIDGE LN	9200	616E	SEC	77089
SUGAR CANE DR	8000	463S	CCO	77520
SUGAR CREEK BLVD	100	568R	SG	77478
SUGAR CREEK DR	5400	539X	LP	77571
SUGAR CREEK LN	1	568R	SG	77478
SUGAR CREEK CENTER BLVD	1	568R	SG	77478
SUGAR CROSSING CT	4100	569W	SG	77478
SUGAR CROSSING DR	1300	569W	SG	77478
SUGAR CRYSTAL CT	14900	527V	NEF	77498
SUGAR CUP CT	14900	527Z	NEF	77498
SUGARDALE CT	900	568K	SG	77498
SUGARDALE DR	12400	569E	SF	77477
SUGAR FALLS CT	14900	527V	NEF	77498
SUGARFIELD CT	900	568K	SG	77498
SUGAR FIELD LN	0	406Z	NWC	77449
SUGAR GLEN LN	9800	289U	NWC	77375
SUGAR GROVE BLVD	4700	569E	SF	77477
SUGAR GROVE CT	11400	370M	NWC	77066
SUGAR HARBOR LN	0	445N	NWC	77493
SUGARHILL	700	539X	LP	77571
SUGAR HILL	0	538R	DP	77536
SUGAR HILL DR	5300	491K	SWH	77056
SUGAR HILL DR	5700	491K	SWH	77057
SUGAR HILL DR	10000	489R	SWH	77042
SUGARHILL RD	0	243F	WCO	77447
SUGAR HILL PRIVATE	0	491P	SWH	77057
SUGAR HOLLOW CT	0	328K	NWC	77377
SUGARHOLLOW CT	10300	527Z	NEF	77498
SUGARHOLLOW DR	14900	527Z	NEF	77498
SUGAR LAKES BLVD	900	568U	SG	77478
SUGARLAND RD	2300	611N	FS	77545
SUGARLAND HOWELL RD	8100	528J	SWC	77083
SUGAR LEAF TRAIL	25900	250S	NWC	77389
SUGARLOAF DR	1100	329H	NWC	77379
SUGAR MAPLE CT	3000	657H	FR	77546
SUGAR MAPLE DR	9500	410A	NWC	77064
SUGARMEADE LN	9900	289P	NWC	77375
SUGARMEADE LN		289Q	NWC	77375
W. SUGAR MEADOW DR	17200	331R	NWC	77090
E. SUGAR MEADOW DR	17200	331R	NWC	77090
SUGAR MILL CIR	14300	408L	NWC	77095
SUGAR MIST LN	14900	527Z	NEF	77498
SUGAR MOTT DR	0	527Z	NEF	77498
SUGAR MOUNTAIN CT	900	568K	SG	77498
SUGAR OAKS CT	7000	527E	NEF	77407
SUGAR ORCHARD LN	10200	289U	NWC	77375
SUGAR PARK LN	0	568N	SG	77478
SUGAR PINE CIR	1900	331V	NWC	77090
SUGAR PINE DR	16600	331R	NWH	77090
SUGAR PINE LN	16600	331V	NWC	77090
SUGAR PINE PLACE	8500	289R	NWC	77375
SUGAR PLACE CT	0	527Z	NEF	77498
SUGAR PLACE DR	0	527Z	NEF	77498
SUGAR PLUM CIR	700	568K	SG	77498
SUGARPLUM LN	14700	618E	SEH	77062
SUGAR RIDGE BLVD	12500	569G	SF	77477
SUGAR RIDGE DR	15600	408N	NWC	77095
SUGAR RIDGE DR	15900	407R	NWC	77095
SUGAR SANDS CT	10400	527Z	NEF	77498
SUGAR SANDS LN	14900	527Z	NEF	77498
SUGARSIDE GLEN DR	0	524A	NEF	77494
SUGARSIDE GLEN DR	0	524B	NEF	77494
SUGAR SPICE DR	0	527Z	NEF	77498
SUGAR SPRINGS DR	12000	489N	SWH	77077
SUGAR STONE DR	14900	527Z	NEF	77498
SUGAR SWEET DR	0	527Z	NEF	77498
SUGAR TRACE DR	0	527Z	NEF	77498
SUGAR TREE CT	9700	329Q	NWC	77070
SUGAR TREE DR	16000	329Q	NWC	77070
SUGAR VALLEY LN	25300	293N	NCC	77373
SUGARVINE CT	4300	658N	LC	77573
SUGARVINE LN	10000	289U	NWC	77375
SUGAR WOOD CT	8500	335N	NCC	77338
SUGARWOOD DR	2700	568U	SG	77478
SUGARWOOD DR	2800	660E	LC	77573
SUITER WAY	3200	537Q	PA	77503
SULGRAVE DR	0	327H	NWC	77429
SULGRAVE DR	0	327H	NWC	77429
SULKY TRAIL	200	373W	NEH	77060
SULKY TRAIL CT	15800	373W	NEH	77060
SULKY TREE	200	372Z	NEH	77060
SULLINS WAY	0	448L	NWH	77084
SULLINS WAY	1700	618R	SEH	77058
SULLIVAN	10600	539U	LP	77571
SULLIVAN	20300	257N	SEM	77357
SULLIVAN AVE	1800	537K	PA	77506
SULLIVAN LN	2400	659X	DI	77539
SULLIVAN FOREST DR	0	296A	SEM	77365
SULLIVAN FOREST DR	0	296A	SEM	77365
SULLIVAN OAKS DR	0	253X	SEM	77386
SULLIVAN SPRINGS DR	1400	485E	NEF	77494
SULLY LN	1300	457Z	NEC	77530
SULPHUR	500	576E	SEH	77034
SULPHUR BRANCH BEND DR	36900	246C	SWM	77355
SULPHUR RIVER CT	0	253Y	SEM	77386
SULPHUR SPRINGS DR	11900	371L	NWC	77067

Street Name	Block	Pg/Sq	Loc	Zips
SULPHUR STREAM CT	10200	367X	NWC	77095
SULPHUR STREAM DR	10200	367X	NWC	77095
SUL ROSS	100	493S	SWH	77002
SUL ROSS	200	493S	SWH	77006
SUL ROSS	1700	492U	SWH	77098
SUL ROSS	4000	492S	SWH	77027
SUL ROSS CT	1700	492V	SWH	77098
SULTAN DR	8300	455H	NEH	77078
SULTANA DR	15600	527L	NEF	77083
SUMAC DR	3000	614U	PL	77584
S. SUMAC DR	6100	614U	PL	77584
SUMAC LN	22200	291L	NWC	77389
SUMAC PARK DR	0	657H	FR	77546
SUMERLIN	9600	576S	SEH	77075
SUMMER	1100	493E	SWH	77007
SUMMER CIR	18700	295F	SEM	77365
SUMMER CT	18400	295A	SEM	77365
SUMMER LN	0	610B	MC	77489
SUMMER LN	0	615N	PL	77584
SUMMER LN	3700	502G	BT	77521
SUMMER LN	19300	256F	SEM	77357
SUMMER LN	28200	248S	SWM	77362
SUMMER AMBLE CT	0	569Q	SF	77477
SUMMER ANNE DR	18600	337Y	NEC	77346
SUMMER ASH LN	14000	417B	NEC	77044
SUMMER BAY CIR	2200	568Z	SG	77478
SUMMER BAY CT	2200	568Z	SG	77478
SUMMER BAY DR	3100	568Z	SG	77478
SUMMERBELL LN	9200	530S	SWH	77074
SUMMERBEND HOLLOW LN	26600	524C	NEF	77494
SUMMERBERRY LN	10000	289U	NWC	77375
SUMMERBLOOM LN	0	612R	PL	77584
SUMMERBLOSSOM LN	2200	488T	SWH	77077
SUMMER BOUNTY TRAIL	0	328A	NWC	77429
SUMMER BREEZE DR	100	579A	LP	77571
SUMMER BREEZE DR	9600	613P	PL	77584
SUMMER BREEZE LN	22200	289J	NWC	77375
SUMMER BREEZES LN	2300	371M	NWC	77067
SUMMER BRIAR CT	15500	571X	SWH	77489
SUMMER BRIDGE LN	0	290T	NWC	77379
SUMMERBROOK CT	10300	372W	NWC	77038
SUMMER BROOK CT	11700	612M	PL	77584
SUMMERBROOK CT	12200	371J	NWC	77066
SUMMERBROOK DR	10500	372W	NWC	77038
SUMMER BROOK DR	14500	377U	NEH	77044
SUMMER CAPE CIR	1000	659H	LC	77573
SUMMERCLIFF CT	12300	328G	NWC	77377
SUMMERCLIFF LN	18600	328G	NWC	77377
SUMMER CLOUD CT	0	251Y	WD	77380
SUMMER CLOUD LN	0	612F	PL	77545
SUMMER COVE CT	3700	617X	SEC	77546
SUMMER CREEK DR	2500	612M	PL	77584
SUMMER CREEK DR	8800	330J	NWC	77379
SUMMER CREST CIR	1	251J	WD	77381
SUMMERCREST DR	3000	613X	NEB	77584
SUMMER CROSSING LN	16901	407Y	NWC	77084
SUMMER CYPRESS CT	16700	327X	CY	77429
SUMMER CYPRESS DR	0	327X	NWC	77429
SUMMER CYPRESS DR	0	327X	CY	77429
SUMMER CYPRESS LN	4600	609J	NEF	77479
SUMMERDALE DR	11900	489N	SWH	77077
SUMMER DAWN LN	16200	407R	NWC	77095
SUMMER DAWN PLACE	16700	407Q	NWC	77095
SUMMER DEW LN	16100	407Q	NWC	77095
SUMMER ELM CT	0	578X	SEH	77059
SUMMERFAIR CT	0	377Y	NEC	77044
SUMMER FALLS	5400	449A	NWC	77041
SUMMER FARM TRAIL	0	526U	NEF	77407
SUMMERFERN CT	0	406L	NWC	77433
SUMMERFERN LN	0	366Q	NWC	77433
SUMMERFIELD CT	3100	613Y	NEB	77584
SUMMERFIELD DR	3800	613Y	NEB	77584
SUMMER FIELD LN	0	657T	FR	77546
SUMMERFIELD LN	5200	331E	NWC	77379
SUMMERFIELD GLADE LN	0	524H	NEF	77494
SUMMERFIELD PLACE	1800	568C	SG	77478
SUMMER FOREST DR	5000	451G	NWH	77091
SUMMER GARDEN DR	14300	528E	SWC	77083
SUMMER GARDENS LN	0	444T	KT	77493
SUMMERGATE DR	23100	333D	NCC	77373
SUMMER GLADE LN	0	367S	NWC	77433
SUMMER GLAZED LN	0	376U	NEC	77396
SUMMER GLEN	0	407Q	NWH	77095
SUMMER GLEN LN	7500	528L	SWH	77072
SUMMER GLOW DR	0	528J	SWC	77083
SUMMER GREEN LN	22900	333B	NCC	77373
SUMMER GROVE CIR	8000	330J	NWC	77379
SUMMER HARVEST	0	369Y	NWC	77064
SUMMER HARVEST	10900	369T	NWC	77064
SUMMER HAVEN CIR	300	660A	LC	77573
SUMMER HAVEN CT	300	660A	LC	77573
SUMMER HAVEN DR	300	660E	LC	77573
SUMMER HEATH CT	0	417B	NEC	77044
SUMMERHILL	11500	490G	PP	77024
SUMMERHILL DR	10300	369Q	NWC	77070
SUMMER HILL CREEK DR	0	377B	NEC	77346
SUMMERHILL MANOR LN	5200	485W	NEF	77494
SUMMER HILLS BLVD	18400	295F	SEM	77365
SUMMER HOLLY LN	0	526N	NEF	77407
SUMMER IRIS TRAIL	0	406H	NWC	77433
SUMMER ISLAND WAY	19200	526Q	NEF	77407
SUMMER ISLE	6600	330M	NWC	77379
SUMMER JASMINE WAY	0	406X	NWC	77449
SUMMER KNOLL LN	14800	377Y	NEH	77044
SUMMER LAKE DR	14500	377U	NEH	77044
SUMMER LAKE CANYON DR	13100	377U	NEH	77044
SUMMER LAKE HOME DR	14600	377U	NEH	77044
SUMMER LAKE RANCH DR	14200	377T	NEC	77044
SUMMER LAKES	4500	609E	SG	77479
SUMMER LAKES	4700	609E	NEF	77459
SUMMER LAKE TRACE DR	14500	377U	NEH	77044
SUMMERLAND CIR	14900	368A	NWC	77429
SUMMERLAND DR	3200	613X	NEB	77578
SUMMERLAND RIDGE CT	5300	449A	NWC	77041
SUMMERLAND RIDGE LN	12200	449A	NWC	77041
SUMMER LAUREL LN	9500	411N	NWH	77088
SUMMERLEAF LN	0	488N	SWH	77077
SUMMERLEE CT	4300	609K	MC	77459
SUMMERLIN LN	19600	406Y	NWC	77449
SUMMER LYNN PLACE LN	0	411P	NWH	77088
SUMMERLYN POINT LN	15200	572S	SWH	77053
SUMMER MANOR DR	3800	660K	LC	77573
SUMMER MANOR LN	5000	609S	NEF	77479
SUMMERMEADE LN	0	525G	NEF	77494
SUMMER MEADOW CT	10800	369T	NWC	77064
SUMMER MILL DR	12600	369L	NWC	77070
SUMMER MIST LN	7100	407R	NWC	77095
SUMMER MOON DR	11600	612M	PL	77584
SUMMER MORNING CT	1	250H	WD	77381
SUMMER MOUNTAIN TRAIL	0	291X	NWC	77388
SUMMER OAK CT	5800	330D	NWC	77379
SUMMER OAK DR	5000	578J	PA	77505
SUMMER OAKS DR	5900	337T	NEC	77346
SUMMER ORCHID CT	0	415X	NWH	77078
SUMMER PALMETTO DR	0	376Z	NEC	77044
SUMMER PARK DR	0	569T	NEF	77477
SUMMER PARK DR	500	569U	NEF	77477
SUMMER PARK LN	1200	485H	SWC	77450
SUMMER PARK LN	32300	252R	SEM	77385
SUMMER PINE LN	22900	333B	NCC	77373
SUMMER PINE LN	23400	293X	NCC	77373
SUMMER PLACE	5300	657V	LC	77573
SUMMER PLACE CT	400	657V	LC	77573
SUMMER PLACE DR	1900	570W	MC	77489
SUMMER PLACE DR	7800	334R	NCC	77338
SUMMER PLAIN LN	0	290T	NWC	77379
SUMMER POINT LN	0	290T	NWC	77379
SUMMER PORCH DR	13100	377U	NEH	77044
SUMMER PORT	1	251F	WD	77381
SUMMER QUAIL DR	8200	610C	SWH	77489
W. SUMMER RAIN CT	1900	336B	NEH	77339
E. SUMMER RAIN CT	1900	336B	NEH	77339
SUMMER RAIN DR	0	614F	PL	77581
SUMMER RAIN DR	1400	336B	NEH	77339
SUMMER RAIN DR	2600	613W	NEB	77578
SUMMER RANCH DR	0	484W	NEF	77494
SUMMER RANGE DR	0	376V	NEC	77346
SUMMER REEF DR	1900	620W	LC	77573
SUMMER REEF DR	8200	407F	NWC	77095
SUMMER RETREAT LN	0	406G	NWC	77433
SUMMER RIDGE CT	15400	571W	SWH	77489
SUMMER RIDGE DR	6400	571W	SWH	77489
E. SUMMER ROSE CT	17300	327P	NWC	77429
W. SUMMER ROSE CT	17400	327P	NWC	77429
SUMMER ROSE LN	0	290U	NWC	77379
SUMMER ROSE LN	14200	488N	SWH	77077
SUMMER RUN DR	9500	409D	NWC	77064
SUMMERS DR	900	570Y	MC	77489
SUMMER SAVORY LN	0	524F	NEF	77494
SUMMERSET DR	0	246T	SWM	77355
SUMMERSET PRAIRIE DR	0	525R	NEF	77407
SUMMERSET RIDGE LN	0	524H	NEF	77494
SUMMERSET WAY	19800	486G	SWC	77094
SUMMERS GLEN CT	0	446S	NWC	77449
SUMMERS GLEN CT	0	446S	NWC	77449
SUMMER SHORE DR	2100	619Z	LC	77573
SUMMER SHOWER DR	22000	325R	NWC	77433
SUMMER SIDE DR	0	525D	NEF	77450
SUMMERSIDE DR	5200	525D	NEF	77450
SUMMER SKY	0	417C	NEC	77044
SUMMER SNOW CIR	13200	448D	NWH	77041
SUMMER SNOW DR	5200	448D	NWC	77041
SUMMER SPRIG RD	1	252J	WD	77380
SUMMER SPRING DR	2300	293T	NCC	77373
SUMMER SPRING DR	11700	612M	PL	77584
SUMMERS SONG DR	0	329E	NWC	77375
S. SUMMER STAR CT	1	251Z	WD	77380
N. SUMMER STAR CT	1	251Z	WD	77380
SUMMERSTONE CT	11600	329N	NWC	77377
SUMMERSTONE LN	0	377Y	NCC	77044
SUMMERSTORM LN	0	660E	LC	77573
SUMMER STREAM DR	14600	377U	NEH	77044
SUMMER SUN DR	0	332X	NWC	77090
SUMMER SUN LN	9400	613L	PL	77584
SUMMER SUNSET DR	14900	376V	NEC	77396
SUMMER SWEET PLACE	2900	251P	WD	77380
SUMMERTIME DR	2700	572G	SWH	77045
SUMMERTON DR	0	294K	SEM	77386
SUMMER TRACE CT	6800	290T	NWC	77379
SUMMER TRACE LN	20900	290U	NWC	77379
SUMMER TRAIL CT	0	253P	SEM	77386
SUMMER TRAIL DR	8000	410L	NWC	77040
SUMMERTREE DR	8200	410L	NWC	77040
SUMMER VALLEY LN	8901	526Q	NEF	77407
SUMMER VILLA CT	15000	417C	NEC	77044
SUMMER VILLA LN	13400	417C	NEC	77044
SUMMERVILLE LN	6100	408Y	NWC	77041
SUMMERVILLE LN	14200	408Y	NWC	77084
SUMMERVILLE LAKE DR	16000	328V	NWC	77377
SUMMERWALK LN	0	485N	NEF	77494
SUMMERWAY LN	14600	331X	NWC	77014
SUMMERWIND CT	3100	613P	NEB	77584
SUMMER WIND DR	16200	332S	NWC	77090
SUMMER WINDS DR	100	579A	LP	77571
SUMMERWOOD LN	400	613B	NEB	77584
SUMMERWOOD LN	11600	496F	NEH	77013
SUMMERWOOD GLEN	12600	409S	NWC	77041
SUMMERWOOD LAKES CT	12800	377X	NEC	77044
SUMMERWOOD LAKES DR	0	417C	NEH	77044
SUMMERWOOD LAKES DR	14200	377X	NEC	77044
SUMMIT	4700	452G	NWH	77018
SUMMIT	5300	444Q	KT	77493
SUMMIT	0	614U	PL	77584
SUMMIT DR	0	614U	PL	77584
SUMMIT DR	1000	288G	TB	77375
SUMMIT LN	3300	609L	MC	77459
SUMMIT BEND LN	9700	524G	NEF	77494
SUMMIT BRIDGE LN	10300	369G	NWC	77070
S. SUMMIT CANYON CT	10200	367W	NWC	77095
E. SUMMIT CANYON DR	10200	367W	NWC	77095
S. SUMMIT CANYON DR	17300	367W	NWC	77095
SUMMIT CLIFF CT	0	526K	NEF	77407
SUMMIT CREST CT	0	366Z	NWC	77433
SUMMIT FALLS CT	3000	297Q	NEH	77345
SUMMIT GROVE LN	0	253P	SEM	77386
SUMMIT HILL DR	0	293L	SEM	77386
SUMMITHILL PLACE	1	250C	WD	77381
SUMMIT HOLLOW DR	0	407Y	NWC	77084
SUMMIT HOLLOW DR	0	407Y	NWC	77084
SUMMIT LAKE DR	1	336D	NEH	77339
SUMMIT LODGE DR	5000	446B	NWC	77449
SUMMIT MEADOW	0	570Y	MC	77489
SUMMIT MIST CT	0	417B	NEC	77044
SUMMIT OAKS LN	16900	330P	NWC	77379
SUMMIT PARK DR	0	488P	SWH	77077
SUMMIT PASS LN	0	375Z	NEC	77396
SUMMIT PASS LN		658T	LC	77573
SUMMIT PINES DR	8600	338S	NEC	77346
SUMMIT PLACE	8200	570B	SWH	77071
SUMMIT RESERVE CT	0	578T	SEH	77059
SUMMIT RIDGE CT	6500	571J	SWH	77085
SUMMIT RIDGE DR	12700	571J	SWH	77085
W. SUMMITRY CIR	0	445Z	NWC	77449
N. SUMMITRY CIR	0	446W	NWC	77449
N. SUMMITRY CIR	0	445Z	NWC	77449
E. SUMMITRY CIR	1400	446W	NWC	77449
SUMMITS EDGE LN	4400	485X	NEF	77494
SUMMIT SPRINGS LN	0	253K	SEM	77386
SUMMIT SPRINGS LN	0	377L	NEC	77346
SUMMIT SPRINGS LN	0	609U	NEF	77479
SUMMIT SPRINGS LN	0	615G	PL	77581
SUMMIT TRAIL RD	18600	378Q	NEC	77532
SUMMIT VALLEY DR	3000	487Z	SWH	77082
SUMMIT VALLEY DR	3600	527D	SWH	77082
SUMMIT WAY CT	2300	336B	NEH	77339
SUMNER DR	4400	452E	NWH	77018
SUMNER CREEK DR	0	293T	NCC	77373
SUMNER ISLE CT	6600	330M	NWC	77379
SUMNERS CREEK CT	23200	485T	NEF	77494
SUMPTER	1800	493H	NEH	77026
SUMPTER	3600	494F	NEH	77020
SUMPTER CT	2000	658T	LC	77573
SUN CT	1	494J	SEH	77003
SUN CT	600	656Q	FR	77546
SUN RD	14600	375W	NEH	77396
SUNBEAM	2900	573C	SEH	77051
SUNBEAM	4700	574A	SEH	77033
SUN BEAM CT	2700	613Q	PL	77584
SUNBEAM PLACE	1	251A	WD	77381
SUNBEAM RIVER DR	16000	448A	NWC	77084
SUNBIRD CT	1	251V	WD	77380
SUNBIRD CT	2600	613Q	PL	77584
SUNBIRD DR	2600	446Q	NWC	77084
SUNBLUFF CT	14400	327Y	NWC	77429
SUNBONNET DR	9100	613L	PL	77584
SUNBONNET LN	7500	410G	NWC	77064
SUNBRIAR LN	0	407B	NWC	77095
SUNBRIDGE LN	19800	486G	SWC	77094
SUNBRIGHT CT	5300	448D	NWC	77041
SUNBRIGHT DR	13200	448D	NWC	77041
SUNBROOK DR	12400	614A	BK	77581
SUNBURST	4500	531D	BL	77401
SUNBURST CT	0	531C	BL	77401
SUNBURST DR	3600	613X	NEB	77578
SUNBURST LN	2400	613M	PL	77584
SUNBURST FALLS DR	0	376U	NEC	77396
SUNBURST MEADOW DR	0	528J	SWC	77083
SUNBURST TRAIL DR	7500	407J	NWC	77433
SUNBURST VIEW DR	19000	407J	NWC	77433
SUNBURST WAY	0	377A	NEC	77346
SUNBURY	7700	455Q	NEH	77028
SUNBURY LN	8100	408F	NWC	77095
SUNBURY SPRINGS DR	0	330H	NWC	77379
SUN CANYON CT	12000	328H	NWC	77377
SUNCHASE CT	3000	446Q	NWC	77449
SUNCHASE WAY	20100	446P	NWC	77449
SUN CITY CT	3000	609H	MC	77459
SUN CITY CT	10300	528V	SWH	77099
SUNCLIFF LN	0	256W	SEM	77365
SUNCOAST DR	20200	446P	NWC	77449
SUNCOVE LN	0	613Q	NEB	77584
SUNCOVE LN	19500	338S	NEC	77346
SUN CREEK DR	0	486A	SWC	77450
SUNCREEK LN	0	698D	LC	77573
SUNCREEK LN	2400	613L	PL	77584
SUNCREST CT	6200	525G	NEF	77494
SUNCREST ESTATES CT	31700	252R	SEM	77385
SUNDALE RD	13000	371Y	NWC	77038
SUNDANCE CT	7900	461S	NEC	77521
SUNDANCE CT	12000	569E	SF	77477
SUNDANCE DR	0	538V	DP	77536
SUNDANCE DR	9400	613L	PL	77584
SUNDANCE DR	19800	337U	NEC	77346
SUNDANCE CREEK LN	22300	289K	NWC	77375
SUNDANCE EDGE CT		526P	NEF	77407
SUNDANCE HILL LN	4000	609T	NEF	77479
SUNDANCE HOLLOW CT	25600	484V	NEF	77494
SUNDANCE HOLLOW LN	4900	484V	NEF	77494
SUNDANCE LAKE LN	0	253P	SEM	77386
SUNDANCE MEADOWS LN	7000	526E	NEF	77407
SUNDANCE SPRINGS DR	0	295L	SEM	77365
SUNDANCE SPRINGS LN	0	290X	NWC	77379
SUNDANCE SUMMIT LN		484S	NEF	77494
SUNDANCE VALLEY DR	800	485G	SWC	77450
SUNDANCE VIEW LN	19500	406H	NWC	77433
SUNDANCE WOODS CT	30901	253N	SEM	77386
SUNDAY HOUSE DR	2600	613Q	PL	77584
SUNDERLAND RD	8500	455G	NEH	77028
SUNDEW CIR	9900	329U	NWC	77070
SUNDEW CT	1	245T	SWM	77355
SUNDEW DR	9700	329U	NWC	77070
SUNDEW COVE CT	12500	409S	NWC	77041
SUNDIAL	0	498K	CV	77530
SUNDIAL STONE LN	0	326Z	NWC	77429
SUNDOWN CT	4600	610P	MC	77459
SUNDOWN DR	7300	455E	NEH	77028
SUNDOWN DR	9000	454D	NEH	77016
SUNDOWN DR	9400	613L	PL	77584
SUNDOWN CANYON CT	0	485W	NEF	77494
SUNDOWN CANYON LN	0	485W	NEF	77494
SUNDOWN COVE LN	0	484Z	NEF	77494
SUNDOWNER	0	503M	BC	77520
SUNDOWNER CT	5400	448C	NWC	77041
SUNDOWNER DR	13400	448C	NWC	77041
SUNDOWN MEADOW	100	379Q	NEC	77532
SUNDOWN M H	0	413M	NCC	77093
SUNDOWN PEAK CT	0	377F	NEC	77346
SUNDOWN WAY DR	3900	446F	NWC	77449
SUNDROP LN	17400	447T	NWH	77084
SUNDROP MEADOW LN	0	484Z	NEF	77494
SUNDROP PARK LN	0	574Z	SEH	77048
SUNFALL BEND LN	0	406X	NWC	77449
SUNFALL CREEK LN	0	415C	NEC	77396
SUNFALL TRAIL LN	31000	253P	SEM	77386
SUNFIELD DR	16700	375J	NEH	77396
SUNFIRE LN	2400	613L	PL	77584
SUNFISH DR	2500	613L	PL	77584
SUNFISH LN	11300	371Q	NWC	77067
SUN FLARE LN	2600	613Q	NEB	77584
SUNFLOWER	4000	533U	SEH	77051
SUNFLOWER	4800	533U	SEH	77033
SUNFLOWER	8500	460P	NEC	77562
SUNFLOWER CT	2700	613P	PL	77584
SUNFLOWER DR	0	570T	MC	77489
SUNFLOWER BLUFF LN	0	410E	NWC	77064
SUNFLOWER CHASE	0	446Q	NWC	77449
SUNFLOWER GROVE CT	0	377C	NEC	77346
SUNFLOWER GROVE DR	0	377C	NEC	77346
SUNFLOWER HILL	0	458A	NEC	77049
SUNFLOWER HILL	15200	457H	NEC	77049
SUNFLOWER PRAIRIE CT	0	457V	NEC	77049
SUNFLOWER RIDGE LN	0	410E	NWC	77064
SUNFLOWER SPRINGS CT	25500	292U	NCC	77373
W. SUNFOREST DR	5800	451B	NWH	77092
SUNFOREST LN	8800	613L	NEB	77584
SUNGAIL DR	1500	252V	SEM	77386
SUNGATE DR	8900	613L	PL	77584
SUNGATE LN	12400	570F	SWH	77071
SUN GLAZE CT	0	376V	NEC	77346
SUN GLAZE DR	0	376V	NEC	77346
SUN GLEN BLVD	0	446P	NWC	77449
SUN GLEN CT	9000	613L	PL	77584
SUN GLEN DR	2500	613L	PL	77584
SUN GLEN CT	3000	446P	NWC	77449
SUNGOLD CT	15500	408E	NWC	77095
SUN HARBOR DR	14200	618E	SEH	77062
SUN HAVEN DR	21000	406T	NWC	77449
SUN HAVEN LN	8800	613Q	NEB	77584
SUNHILL CT	2700	613P	PL	77584
SUN HILL DR	14200	528J	SWC	77083
SUN KING DR	8800	613M	PL	77584
SUN KISS LN	14900	487Z	SWC	77082
SUNLAKE DR	9200	613Q	PL	77584
SUNLAMP CT	16400	407D	NWC	77095
SUNLAND LN	0	250T	NWC	77389
SUN LANDING DR	7000	528E	SWC	77083
SUNLIGHT CT	9000	613L	PL	77584
SUNLIGHT LN	2400	613L	PL	77584
SUNLIGHT LN	7200	407R	NWC	77095
SUNLIGHT HILL LN	0	253P	SEM	77386
SUNLIGHT OAK LN	0	329V	NWC	77070
SUNLIGHT PEAK CIR	0	377J	NEC	77346
SUNLIGHT PEAK LN	0	377J	NEC	77346
SUNLIGHT WAY	16600	618R	SEH	77058
SUNLIGHT WAY DR	0	574P	SEH	77048
SUNLIT BAY DR	11200	613J	PL	77584
SUNLIT FOREST DR	1	251K	WD	77381
SUNLIT LEAF CT	11600	411H	NWC	77088
SUNLIT ORCHARD DR	6300	528H	SWH	77072
SUNLIT PARK DR	9100	375V	NEC	77396
SUNLIT PASS LOOP	4300	375V	NEC	77396
SUNLIT WOOD WAY	0	488Z	SWH	77082
SUN LODGE CT	0	372H	NCC	77073
SUN LODGE DR	0	372H	NCC	77073
SUN MEADOW BLVD	1	656T	FR	77546
SUN MEADOW DR	4100	529B	SWH	77072
SUNMILL CT	15800	367C	CY	77429
SUNMORE CT	8600	412P	NWH	77088
SUNMOUNT PINES DR	13701	528P	SWC	77083
SUNNY DR	1000	413Q	NEH	77037
SUNNY DR	1700	413R	NCC	77093
SUNNY LN	5400	500B	NEC	77521
SUNNYBANK CT	0	330R	NWC	77068
SUNNY BAY CT	2000	619Z	LC	77573
SUNNY BROOK LN	0	613L	PL	77584
SUNNYBROOK LN	800	501K	BT	77521
SUNNYCOAST LN	9700	613P	PL	77584
SUNNYCOVE DR	4600	448E	NWC	77084
SUNNYCREEK CT	2700	613P	PL	77584
SUNNY CREEK DR	11300	370R	NWC	77066
SUNNYCREST	6000	534Q	SEH	77087
SUNNYDALE DR	3000	573F	SEH	77051
SUNNY DAY DR	14300	528J	NEF	77083
SUNNY FIELD DR	8700	528R	SWH	77099
SUNNY GALLOP DR	0	249V	NWC	77375
SUNNYGATE DR	5700	334F	NCC	77373
SUNNYGLEN DR	24000	338L	NEH	77336
SUNNY GROVE DR	14600	329W	NWC	77070
SUNNYHAVEN DR	0	330R	NWC	77068
SUNNYHILL	7000	411V	NWH	77088
SUNNY ISLE LN	1200	660J	LC	77573
SUNNY KNOLL CT	3100	337E	NEH	77339
SUNNYLAND	1500	534C	SEH	77023
SUNNY LEAF LN	0	446D	NWC	77449
SUNNY LEAF LN	0	446D	NWC	77449
SUNNY MEADOWS LN	3200	446Q	NWC	77449
SUNNYNOOK	1	412Z	NEH	77076
SUNNY OAK DR	100	298F	NEC	77336
SUNNY OAKS CT	3700	297U	NEH	77345
SUNNY OAKS WAY	7500	407M	NWC	77095
SUNNY POINT DR	8800	329R	NWC	77379
SUNNY POINT DR	8800	330J	NWC	77379
SUNNY RIDGE DR	7800	407H	NWC	77095
SUNNY RIDGE DR	8500	408A	NWC	77095
SUNNY SHORES DR	2500	613L	PL	77584
SUNNY SHORES DR	20000	337R	NEC	77346
E. SUNNYSIDE	1	413X	NEH	77076
W. SUNNYSIDE	100	412Z	NWH	77076
SUNNYSIDE	200	413W	NEH	77076
W. SUNNYSIDE	300	412Z	NWH	77091
SUNNYSIDE LN	2700	613P	PL	77584
SUNNY SKY PLACE	0	294P	SEM	77386
SUNNYSLOPE LN	0	490Q	PP	77024
SUNNY SPRINGS LN	26300	366R	NWC	77433
SUNNY SQUARE CT	6700	527E	NEF	77407
SUNNY STONE DR	0	408N	NWC	77084
SUNNY STREAM DR	11700	329A	NWC	77375
SUNNY TERRACE LN	0	575Y	SEH	77075
SUNNY VALE DR	3200	297Y	NEH	77345
SUNNYVALE FOREST DR	7900	411P	NWC	77088
SUNNY VALLEY LN	0	528S	NEF	77498
SUNNYVIEW AVE	100	656D	FR	77546
SUNNYVIEW CT	9400	613L	PL	77584
SUNNY VIEW LN	0	294Q	SEM	77386
SUNNY VIEW LN	0	294Q	SEM	77386
SUNNY VIEW LN	0	447E	NWC	77084
SUNNYWOOD DR	8700	412L	NWH	77088
SUNNYWOOD DR	9400	412G	NWC	77038
SUNOCO RD	100	379A	NEC	77532
SUNOCO RD	600	378D	NEC	77532
SUNOCO RD	1800	378D	NEH	77532
SUN OIL CO RD	0	463J	MB	77580
SUNOL	0	528Q	SWC	77099
SUN PARK DR	500	657E	FR	77546
SUN PASS DR	18900	328H	NWC	77377
SUNPERCH CT	9400	613L	PL	77584
SUN POINT CT	0	376B	NEC	77338
SUN POINT CT	0	376B	NEC	77338
SUN PRAIRIE DR	800	332X	NWC	77090
SUNRAY CT	2500	613L	PL	77584
SUNRAY LN	3700	537M	PA	77503
SUNRIDGE CT	9200	613L	PL	77584
SUNRIDGE WAY	6000	534V	SEH	77087
SUNRISE	0	616X	PL	77581
SUNRISE	3700	580V	LP	77571
SUNRISE BLVD	2700	613Q	PL	77584
SUNRISE DR	3300	580Q	SA	77571
SUNRISE DR	4600	610P	MC	77459
SUN RISE LN	7800	528M	SWH	77072
SUNRISE RD	5300	534K	SEH	77021
SUNRISE ARBOR LN	0	328K	NWC	77429
SUNRISE BROOK CT	21400	290P	NWC	77379
SUNRISE CANTER DR	0	249V	NWC	77375
SUNRISE CHASE WAY	0	446Q	NWC	77449
SUNRISE GLEN CT	20200	290Y	NWC	77379
SUNRISE GLEN LN	6300	290Y	NWC	77379
SUNRISE HARBOR LN	2500	613L	PL	77584
SUNRISE KEY	0	619V	LC	77565
SUNRISE KNOLL	0	618E	SEH	77062
SUNRISE KNOLL WAY	800	617M	SEH	77062
SUNRISE LAKE	0	578T	SEH	77059
SUNRISE LIGHT LN	0	574P	SEH	77048
SUNRISE MANOR CT	3200	489X	SWH	77082
SUNRISE MEADOW LN	8500	407F	NWC	77095
SUNRISE MEADOWS DR	0	537Q	PA	77503
SUNRISE PINE VIEW CIR	0	486E	SWC	77450
SUNRISE PINE VIEW LN	0	486A	SWC	77450
SUNRISE PLACE DR	0	570A	SWH	77071

Street Name	Block	Pg/Sq	Loc	Zips
SUNRISE POINT CT	20700	290U	NWC	77379
SUNRISE RANCH CT	0	372M	NCC	77073
SUNRISE RANCH LN	0	484S	NEF	77494
SUNRISE SHORES LN	10400	366V	NWC	77433
S. SUNRISE SHORES LN		366V	NWC	77433
N. SUNRISE SHORES LN		366V	NWC	77433
SUNRISE TERRACE LN	8700	527N	NEF	77407
SUNRISE TRAIL	1500	336K	NEH	77339
SUNRISE VALLEY LN	6600	528F	SWC	77083
SUNRISE WAY	12000	369W	NWC	77065
SUN RIVER CT	11600	328C	NWC	77377
SUN RIVER LN	19300	328C	NWC	77377
SUN RIVER FALLS DR	0	376T	NEC	77396
SUNROSE LN	13000	571Q	SWH	77045
SUNSET	0	580V	LP	77571
SUNSET	0	659Y	DI	77539
SUNSET	900	338C	NEH	77336
SUNSET AVE	0	248G	SWM	77354
SUNSET BLVD	1	533A	SWH	77005
SUNSET BLVD	1500	532A	WU	77005
SUNSET CIR	1000	658M	LC	77573
S. SUNSET CT	1900	658Q	LC	77573
N. SUNSET CT	1900	658Q	LC	77573
SUNSET DR	0	613W	NEB	77578
SUNSET DR	0	614U	PL	77584
N. SUNSET DR	100	656C	FR	77546
SUNSET DR	100	656C	FR	77546
SUNSET DR	800	541C	BT	77520
SUNSET DR	900	536L	PA	77506
N. SUNSET DR	1000	616X	PL	77581
SUNSET DR	1500	657J	FR	77546
SUNSET DR	26600	246N	SWM	77355
SUNSET DR	27600	244A	WCO	77447
SUNSET LN	0	613L	PL	77584
SUNSET LN	10200	252F	SEM	77385
SUNSET ALPS DR	20600	257P	SEM	77357
SUNSET ARBOR DR	17300	328L	NWC	77377
SUNSET BAY CT	0	376U	NEC	77396
SUNSET BAY CT	1400	619D	PA	77586
SUNSET BAY LN	0	612F	PL	77545
SUNSET BEND LN	0	526J	NEF	77407
SUNSET BEND LN	20600	290U	NWC	77379
SUNSET BLUFF DR	17300	367T	NWC	77095
SUNSET BREEZE DR	0	376V	NEC	77396
SUNSET CANYON DR	19000	328F	NWC	77377
SUNSET CLIFF CT	13100	528Y	SG	77478
SUNSET COVE LN	6300	525F	NEF	77494
SUNSET CREEK DR	0	376U	NEC	77396
SUNSET CREST DR	0	377C	NEC	77346
SUNSET DUNE DR	12700	488Y	SWH	77082
SUNSET FALL DR	7000	330P	NWC	77379
SUNSET FALLS DR	0	253T	SEM	77386
SUNSET FIELD DR	0	376V	NEC	77346
SUNSET GARDEN DR	6400	528E	SWC	77083
SUNSET GLEN LN	0	332H	NCC	77373
SUNSET HARBOR LN	0	612F	PL	77545
SUNSET HAVEN DR	0	366J	NWC	77433
SUNSET KNOLL LN	5900	406Z	NWC	77449
SUNSET KNOLLS LN	5900	406Z	NWC	77449
SUNSET LAKE CT	11800	369W	NWC	77065
SUNSET LAKE DR	2600	528Y	SG	77478
SUNSET LAKES DR	1000	616X	PL	77581
SUNSET LANDING	0	446P	NWC	77449
SUNSET LIGHT LN	0	574P	SEH	77048
SUNSET LOCH DR	8400	329H	NWC	77379
SUNSET MANOR LN	3700	485V	NEF	77450
SUNSET MAPLE CT	5100	297L	NEH	77345
SUNSET MEADOW DR	12100	570H	SWH	77035
SUNSET MEADOWS DR	1200	616X	PL	77581
SUNSET OAK	5700	330H	NWC	77379
SUNSET OAKS LN	31300	253P	SEM	77386
SUNSET PARK DR	0	376U	NEC	77396
SUNSET PARK DR	0	446P	NWC	77449
SUNSET PARK LN	0	609T	NEF	77479
SUNSET PASS	2900	446P	NWC	77449
SUNSET PATH WAY	0	611S	FS	77545
SUNSET PINE CIR	0	486A	SWC	77450
SUNSET PINES DR	27100	292P	SP	77373
SUNSET PLACE	11700	570A	SWH	77071
SUNSET PLACE DR	11700	570A	SWH	77071
SUNSET PLACE DR	11800	570B	SWH	77071
SUNSET POND DR	0	249V	NWC	77375
SUNSET PRAIRIE DR	0	376V	NEC	77346
SUNSET RANCH DR	0	406X	NWC	77449
SUNSET RANGE DR	0	376V	NEC	77346
SUNSET RIDGE	11100	539V	LP	77571
SUNSET RIDGE CT	200	620W	LC	77573
SUNSET RIDGE DR	200	620W	LC	77573
SUNSET RIDGE LN	0	574P	SEH	77048
SUNSET RIVER LN	17600	447C	NWC	77084
SUNSET ROCK DR	15600	448B	NWC	77084
SUNSET SHORES LN	0	367W	NWC	77095
SUNSET SKY	23800	525E	NEF	77494
SUNSET SPRINGS CT	0	612E	PL	77545
SUNSET TERRACE DR	3900	660Q	LC	77573
SUNSET TERRACE LN	0	615M	PL	77089
SUNSET TRAIL	2200	568Y	SG	77478
SUNSET TRAIL	18900	379Q	NEC	77532
SUNSET TRAIL LN	22400	289J	NWC	77375
SUNSET VALLEY RD	14500	368E	NWC	77429
SUNSET VIEW DR	13800	528E	SWC	77083
SUNSET VIEW DR	21700	378C	NEC	77532
SUNSET VILLA CT	0	376T	NWC	77396
SUNSET WAY	0	369W	NWC	77065
SUNSET WILLOW DR	0	376V	NEC	77346
SUNSHADOW DR	12200	572K	SWH	77045
SUN SHADOW LN	2300	293F	SEM	77386
SUNSHINE	3600	578A	PA	77505
SUNSHINE	16300	458B	NEC	77049
SUNSHINE CIR	2800	609A	SG	77479
SUNSHINE CT	1600	610P	MC	77459
SUNSHINE DR	4600	609A	SG	77479
SUNSHINE LN	4500	610P	MC	77459
SUNSHINE LN	20000	292S	NWC	77388
SUNSHINE BAY CT	700	373N	NCC	77060
SUNSHINE BAY DR	17000	373N	NEH	77060
SUNSHINE PARK DR	11200	369J	NWC	77429
SUNSHINE POINT DR	2000	337C	NEH	77345
SUNSHINE RIDGE LN	20000	326T	NWC	77433
SUNSHINE TERRACE ST	14300	528J	NEF	77083
SUNSHINE TRACE LN	0	527N	NEF	77407
SUN SHOWER CT	1	250G	WD	77381
SUN SPOT LN	2400	613L	PL	77584
SUN SPRING CT	2300	293X	NCC	77373
SUNSTONE DR	3700	331N	NWC	77068
SUNSTONE LN	2500	613Q	PL	77584
SUNSTONE FALLS LN	0	444T	KT	77493
SUNSTONE TERRACE LN	17800	376C	NEC	77396
SUNSTREAM CT	3100	613T	NEB	77578
SUNSTREAM CT	13600	488T	SWH	77082
SUNSWEPT CT	2200	568Y	SG	77478
SUNSWEPT FIELD LN	10600	369X	NWC	77064
SUNSWEPT WAY	13500	488T	SWH	77082
SUN TERRACE LN	8100	407F	NWC	77095
SUN TOWER LN	0	417D	NEC	77044
SUN TRAIL CT	19400	337S	NEC	77346
SUNTREE CIR	21900	485R	NEF	77450
SUNTREE LN	2600	485R	NEF	77450
SUNTURF LN	9300	417X	NEC	77044
SUNTURF LN	11000	417S	NEC	77044
SUN VALLEY CT	2700	613Q	PL	77584
SUN VALLEY DR	3500	532N	SWH	77025
SUNVIEW CT	17000	407L	NWC	77095
SUNVIEW DR	5400	408X	NWC	77084
SUN VILLAGE DR	7100	528E	SWC	77083
SUNVOLT CT	0	525L	NEF	77407
SUNWICK	14000	413A	NCC	77060
SUNWILLOW CREEK DR	29800	253W	SEM	77386
SUNWOOD DR	2800	371V	NWC	77038
SUNWOOD DR	10200	450J	NWC	77041
SUPER	0	463F	MB	77521
SUPER	1	494T	SEH	77011
N. SUPER	100	494P	SEH	77011
SUPERIOR	1800	501W	BT	77520
SUPERIOR DR	7400	461T	NEC	77521
SUPERIOR WAY	1500	413D	NCC	77039
SUPPLY ROW	6500	494Y	SEH	77011
SUPREMES TRAIL	0	293G	SEM	77386
SUR CT	7000	534S	SEH	77033
SURECROP LN	0	577J	PA	77504
SURF CT	100	619T	NB	77058
SURF OAKS DR	400	620D	SB	77586
S. SURF OAKS DR	4900	621A	SB	77586
SURFRIDER	12300	528M	SWH	77072
SURFSIDE CIR	4200	609K	MC	77459
SURFSIDE LN	6300	609K	MC	77459
SURLES DR	13900	414D	NCC	77032
SURLES DR	14100	374Z	NCC	77032
SURPRISE LN	0	331W	NWH	77069
SURRATT DR	300	452D	NWH	77091
SURREY	0	257H	SEM	77357
SURREY CIR	0	612Z	NEB	77578
SURREY CT	1000	289A	TB	77375
SURREY DR	16200	246M	SC	77355
SURREY LN	0	656X	FR	77546
SURREY LN	3200	538V	DP	77536
SURREY LN	3400	500H	BT	77521
SURREY LN	11900	490J	BH	77024
SURREY CREEK CT	20800	486S	SWC	77450
SURREYDON DR	4100	371B	NWC	77014
SURREYGATE DR	24000	293Z	NCC	77373
SURREY GLEN CT	21400	256W	SEM	77365
SURREY LAKE LN	18000	526R	NEF	77407
SURREY MEADOW CT	6600	457Q	NEC	77049
SURREY OAKS LN	11300	490L	PP	77024
SURREY PARK CIR	4900	484Z	NEF	77494
SURREY PARK LN	26600	484Z	NEF	77494
SURREY SQUARE	5600	535V	SEH	77017
SURREY STONE CT	20700	486S	SWC	77450
SURREY TRAIL LN	2900	486T	SWC	77450
SURREYWEST LN	17600	331J	NWC	77379
SURREY WOODS DR	15900	617X	SEC	77546
SURRY	8700	455G	NEH	77028
SURRY OAKS DR	1700	257C	WV	77357
SURVEY CIR DR	0	299X	NEC	77336
SUSAN	1300	536K	PA	77506
SUSAN	2200	576E	SEH	77034
SUSAN CT	100	252E	OR	77385
SUSAN CT	14000	568E	SG	77498
SUSAN LN	22700	296G	SEM	77365
SUSAN LN	28200	252E	OR	77385
SUSAN ANN CT	1	533D	SEH	77004
SUSAN FOREST LN	11000	616F	SEC	77089
SUSANNA LN	12800	528L	SWH	77072
SUSIE CT	11900	248N	SWM	77355
SUSIE LN	27800	258K	SEM	77357
SUSPIRO DR	8000	527L	NEF	77083
SUSQUEHANNAH DR	11900	368R	NWC	77065
SUSSEX	0	258E	SEM	77357
SUSSEX	0	257H	SEM	77357
SUSSEX CT	0	250Y	NWC	77389
SUSSEX DR	16600	527P	NEF	77083
SUSSEX LN	10000	450A	NWH	77041
SUSSEX MANOR ST	0	451Y	NWH	77055
SUSSEX TRAIL	1000	613K	NEB	77584
SUSSEX WAY LN	0	657G	FR	77546
SUTHERLAND	2500	534G	SEH	77023
SUTHERLAND LN	200	657Q	LC	77573
SUTHERLAND SPRINGS LN	0	485S	NEF	77494
SUTHERLAND SQUARE	6200	531C	SWH	77081
SUTTER	0	614F	PL	77581
SUTTER CREEK LN	14500	375Z	NEC	77396
SUTTER GLEN LN	10400	575V	SEH	77075
SUTTER PARK LN	6300	370Q	NWC	77066
SUTTER PARK LN	9400	411A	NWC	77086
SUTTER PARK LN	9500	371W	NWC	77086
SUTTER RANCH CIR	10800	409B	NWC	77064
SUTTER RANCH DR	9000	409B	NWC	77064
SUTTERS CREEK TRAIL	6600	609K	MC	77459
SUTTERS FIELD DR	7600	528M	SWH	77072
SUTTER SPRINGS LN	31600	253N	SEM	77386
SUTTLE DR	0	370L	NWC	77066
SUTTON	1400	493P	SWH	77006
SUTTON CT	2600	492S	SWH	77027
SUTTON LN	0	620L	SB	77586
SUTTON RD	0	289J	NWC	77375
SUTTON CREST DR	0	290J	NWC	77375
SUTTON FALLS DR	19900	406L	NWC	77433
SUTTONFORD DR	3600	371K	NWC	77066
SUTTON GLEN LN	0	573T	SEC	77047
SUTTON ISLAND CT	0	251G	WD	77380
SUTTON LAKE LN	900	289J	TB	77375
SUTTON MEADOWS CT	9700	411B	NWC	77086
SUTTON MEADOWS DR	6200	411B	NWC	77086
SUTTON PINE LN	0	578T	SEH	77059
SUTTON PLACE	0	488L	SWH	77077
W. SUTTON SQUARE	100	569J	SF	77477
E. SUTTON SQUARE	100	569J	SF	77477
S. SUTTON SQUARE	3300	569J	SF	77477
N. SUTTON SQUARE	3300	569J	SF	77477
SUWANEE LN	800	332J	NWC	77090
SUWANNE	0	331M	NWC	77090
SUZANNA LN	5400	291J	NWC	77389
SUZANNE	13100	569M	SF	77477
SUZANNE CT	7900	330A	NWC	77379
SUZANNE ST	0	659G	LC	77573
SUZANNE WAY	700	332E	NWC	77090
SVENSSON SLADE LN	0	378A	NEC	77346
SWAFFHAM CT	0	299T	NEC	77336
SWAFFHAM LN	0	299T	NEC	77336
SWALLOW	6000	534Z	SEH	77087
SWALLOW CIR	1100	568Q	SG	77478
SWALLOWFIELD DR	14100	488J	SWH	77077
SWALLOW PARK DR	7800	375Q	NEC	77396
SWALLOWS COVE LN	0	485P	NEF	77494
SWALLOW SPRINGS WAY	0	330C	NWC	77379
SWALLOW TAIL CT	1	251B	WD	77381
SWALLOWTAIL LN	0	297A	SEM	77357
SWAN CT	2500	619T	NB	77058
SWAN LN	7900	463S	CCO	77520
SWAN RD	2800	374S	NEH	77032
SWAN CREEK DR	11900	368V	NWC	77065
SWAN CREEK DR	15300	408F	NWC	77095
SWANDALE LN	15700	408A	NWC	77095
SWANFIELD CT	9500	528S	NEF	77083
SWANFIELD DR	14100	528S	NEF	77083
SWAN GLEN DR	10500	529W	SWH	77099
SWAN GREEN LN	14300	408Q	NWC	77095
SWAN HOLLOW CT	7900	408L	NWC	77041
SWAN HOLLOW LN	13800	408L	NWC	77041
SWAN ISLAND DR	4400	610N	MC	77459
SWAN ISLE BLVD	1	610N	MC	77459
SWANK	5600	533G	SEH	77021
SWANLEY CT	15000	617M	SEH	77062
SWAN MEADOW CT	2800	659D	LC	77573
SWAN MEADOW LN	8100	335N	NCC	77338
SWANMORE DR	16800	375J	NEC	77396
SWAN PARK CT	0	406C	NWC	77433
SWANPOND CT	9500	576J	SEH	77075
SWAN RANCH LN	0	526J	NEF	77407
SWAN RIVER DR	12100	415E	NEH	77050
SWANSBURY DR	17200	367A	CY	77429
SWANSEA	6200	574U	SEH	77048
SWANSEA BAY DR	9300	329G	NWC	77379
SWANSEA CREEK DR	0	257E	SEM	77357
SWANSFIELD LN	1400	333S	NCC	77073
SWANSON	1000	532M	SWH	77030
SWANSON	4500	533R	SEH	77021
SWAN SONG PLACE	1	250D	WD	77381
SWAN SPRINGS LN	0	524G	NEF	77494
SWAN VALLEY DR	19700	406M	NWC	77433
S. SWANWICK PLACE	0	250J	NWC	77389
N. SWANWICK PLACE	0	250J	NWC	77389
SWANWOOD LN	0	573X	SEC	77047
SWANWOOD LN	0	573X	SEC	77047
SWARTHMORE	3800	532A	WU	77005
SWAY	6700	571S	SWH	77085
SWAYER KNOLL LN	16400	377L	NEC	77044
SWAYING TREE LN	0	446F	NWC	77449
SWAYZE CT	0	452Q	NWH	77018
SWEDEN CT	19000	330D	NWC	77379
SWEENEY RD	14000	413F	NCC	77060
SWEENEY RD	14200	373X	NCC	77060
SWEENEY PARK CT	5100	408W	NWC	77084
SWEENEY PARK LN	15700	408W	NWC	77084
SWEET ALYSSUM WAY	0	289Y	NWC	77379
SWEET AUBURN LN	0	296E	SEM	77365
SWEET BAY CIR	0	249D	SWM	77354
SWEETBAY DR	2100	503F	CCO	77520
SWEET BAY LN	5400	450A	NWH	77041
SWEET BAY RD	21700	336L	NEH	77339
SWEETBAY MAGNOLIA DR	0	296A	SEM	77365
SWEET BELLS CT	0	406H	NWC	77433
SWEETBERRY LN	9800	289U	NWC	77375
SWEETBETH CT	1	251L	WD	77380
SWEET BIRCH LN	12600	409S	NWC	77041
SWEETBLOOM LN	9800	289U	NWC	77375
SWEET BLOSSOM LN	20900	289U	NWC	77375
SWEET BLUE JASMINE LN	0	335P	NCC	77338
SWEETBRIAR	3600	577D	PA	77505
SWEETBRIAR	5300	536N	SEH	77017
SWEETBROOK DR	10300	372X	NWC	77038
SWEETBRUSH DR	8600	370N	NWC	77064
SWEETBRUSH DR	9100	369R	NWC	77064
SWEETCHERRY DR	13700	415B	NEC	77396
SWEET CICELY CT	4300	578Y	SEH	77059
SWEET FERN	16000	329U	NWC	77070
SWEET FLAG DR	0	250H	WD	77381
SWEET FLOWER DR	600	372H	NCC	77073
SWEET FOREST LN	19600	337V	NEC	77346
SWEET GARDENS CT	0	406F	NWC	77433
SWEETGLEN CT	0	332H	NCC	77373
SWEETGLEN CT	0	609U	MC	77459
SWEETGLEN DR	20600	295R	SEM	77365
SWEET GRASS LN	21300	289U	NWC	77375
SWEET GRASS TRAIL	1400	331M	NWC	77090
SWEET GROVE	21000	289U	NWC	77375
SWEETGROVE BEND LN		328k	NWC	77429
SWEET GROVE RIDGE LN	4900	609S	NEF	77479
SWEET GUM	100	657Q	LC	77573
SWEETGUM	1300	252G	SEM	77385
SWEETGUM	2600	537T	PA	77502
W. SWEET GUM	3600	291Y	NWC	77388
SWEETGUM	6200	444P	KT	77493
SWEETGUM	10000	462Z	BT	77521
SWEETGUM	23400	256V	SEM	77357
SWEETGUM CT	1500	616P	PL	77581
SWEETGUM DR	13700	415B	NEC	77396
SWEETGUM DR	14700	375T	NEH	77396
SWEETGUM DR	24000	257A	WV	77357
SWEET GUM LN	900	336F	NEH	77339
SWEETGUM RD	28000	249C	SWM	77354
SWEETGUM FOREST CT	19700	337V	NEC	77346
SWEETGUM FOREST DR	19500	337V	NEC	77346
SWEETGUM HILL CT	2400	292W	NWC	77388
SWEETGUM HILL LN	3500	297T	NEH	77345
SWEETGUM PARK	0	292N	NWC	77388
SWEETGUM SHORES DR	13000	377P	NEC	77044
SWEET GUM TRACE DR	8000	410Q	NWC	77040
SWEET GUM TRAILS	3900	297S	NEH	77339
SWEET GUM TRAILS	4000	296R	NEH	77339
SWEET GUM WALK	0	331D	NWC	77388
SWEETGUM WALK	0	331D	NWC	77388
SWEETGUM WAY	20200	326P	NWC	77433
SWEET HALL LN	12000	371M	NWC	77067
SWEET HILLS LN		609X	NEF	77479
SWEET JASMINE LN	18500	330E	NWC	77379
SWEET JUNIPER LN	18100	407S	NWC	77449
SWEETLEAF CT	1	251K	WD	77381
SWEETLOUETTA LN	0	292W	NWC	77388
SWEET MAGNOLIA PLACE	19800	335S	NCC	77338
SWEET MAPLE CT	15600	457L	NEC	77049
SWEETMEADOW DR	18500	330B	NWC	77379
SWEET MELISSA DR	8500	525A	NEF	77494
SWEETMELODY LN	0	290Q	NWC	77379
SWEET MINT CT	0	249V	NWC	77375
SWEETNECTAR LN	10000	289U	NWC	77375
SWEET OLIVE WAY	9900	289U	NWC	77375
SWEET ORCHARD CT	5200	297P	NEH	77345
SWEET ORCHID LN	0	524E	NEF	77494
SWEET PASTURE DR	0	249V	NWC	77375
SWEET PEA	7300	412T	NWH	77088
SWEET PEA DR	0	460T	NEC	77562
SWEET PINE DR	0	486A	SWC	77450
SWEET RAIN DR	17600	328L	NWC	77377
SWEET RIVER LN	21100	289U	NWC	77375
SWEETROCK LN	21200	289U	NWC	77375
SWEET ROOT LN	0	377J	NEC	77346
SWEET ROSE CT	0	609X	NEF	77479
SWEETROSE PLACE	15700	408A	NWC	77095
SWEET SAGE DR	0	411N	NWH	77088
SWEET SONG DR	0	328L	NWC	77377
SWEET SONG DR	17400	328L	NWC	77377
SWEET SPICEBERRY TRAIL	0	325Q	NWC	77433
SWEETSPIRE RD	3500	446L	NWC	77449
SWEETSPIRE PLACE	10900	251P	WD	77380
SWEETSPIRE RIDGE	0	526P	NEF	77407
SWEETSTEM CT	6200	297V	NEH	77345
SWEETSTEM DR	1800	297V	NEH	77345
SWEET STONE CT	1400	619H	PA	77586
SWEET STONE BLUFF LN	0	406M	NWC	77433
SWEETSTONE ESTATES CT	14300	366D	NWC	77429
SWEETSTONE FIELD CT	0	406F	NWC	77433
SWEETSTONE GROVE CT	0	406G	NWC	77433
SWEETSTONE GROVE LN	0	406F	NWC	77433
SWEETSTONE SPRINGS CT	0	366V	NWC	77433
SWEETSTONE TRAIL LN	31600	253N	SEM	77386
SWEET SURRENDER CT	13400	448C	NWC	77041
SWEETVINE LN	21300	289U	NWC	77375
SWEET VIOLET CT	20800	337Q	NEC	77346
SWEET VIOLET TRAIL	7000	337L	NEC	77346
SWEET WALNUT CT	0	250M	WD	77381
SWEETWATER	7900	412R	NCC	77037
SWEETWATER	29500	248C	SWM	77354
SWEETWATER CT	12200	568H	SF	77477
SWEETWATER CREEK DR	15700	408E	NWC	77095
SWEETWATER CREEK DR	15900	407H	NWC	77095
SWEETWATER FIELDS LN	16000	328V	NWC	77377
SWEETWATER LAKE CT	0	367W	NWC	77095
SWEETWATER LAKE CT	0	367W	NWC	77433
SWEET WATER POINTE LN	0	657K	FR	77546
SWEETWATER VIEW DR	0	573Y	SEC	77047
SWEET WILLIAM CT	20100	289Y	NWC	77379
SWEET WILLOW CT	11700	570A	SWH	77031
SWEET WIND	0	334A	NCC	77373
SWEET WIND CT	0	612K	PL	77545
SWEET WIND DR	0	612K	PL	77545
SWEETWIND LN	5200	333D	NCC	77373
SWEETWOOD	0	492R	SWH	77019
SWEETWOOD CIR	20900	295R	SEM	77365
SWEETWOOD DR	10300	369Q	NWC	77070
SWELL CT	0	336G	NEH	77339
SWELL DR	0	336G	NEH	77339
SWENO CT	16800	407Z	NWC	77084
SWENSEN DR	3500	615P	PL	77581
SWIFT BLVD	1900	532G	SWH	77030
SWIFTBROOK DR	19600	337S	NEC	77346
SWIFT BROOK GLEN WAY	2900	291M	NWC	77389
SWIFT CREEK DR	0	612F	PL	77545
SWIFT CREEK DR	2600	659W	LC	77573
SWIFT CREEK DR	3600	297W	NEH	77339
SWIFT CURRENT DR	200	338L	NEH	77336
SWIFT FALLS CT	19200	486H	SWC	77094
SWIFT FOX CT	0	366S	NWC	77433
SWIFT RIVER LN	14800	568A	NEF	77498
SWIFTSTREAM PLACE	1	251A	WD	77381
SWIFTWATER LN	7700	575P	SEH	77075
SWIFT WATER BEND	11400	289J	NWC	77375
SWIFTWATER BRIDGE LN	11500	568A	NEF	77498
SWINBROOK LN	12300	414E	NCC	77039
SWINDEN DR	4000	371E	NWC	77066
SWINEY	3200	494J	NEH	77020
SWINGLE RD	2900	573Q	SEH	77047
SWINGLE RD	4400	574N	SEH	77048
SWINTON CT	3500	610U	MC	77459
S. SWIRLING CLOUD CT	0	325M	NWC	77429
N. SWIRLING CLOUD CT	0	325M	NWC	77429
SWIRLING WINDS DR	10100	371X	NWC	77086
SWISS LN	8000	575P	SEH	77075
SWISS HILL DR	13800	488E	SWH	77077
SWISS VILLAGE	9600	454D	NEH	77016
SWITCHBACK DR	0	367X	NWC	77095
SWITCHBUD PLACE	1	251Q	WD	77380
SWITCHGRASS LN	11200	367U	NWC	77095
SWITZER	600	495H	NEH	77013
SWITZER	1300	495M	JC	77029
SWIVEL KNOT CT	0	249V	NWC	77375
SWONKE LN	7000	411N	NWH	77040
SWOPE	1200	495X	SEH	77012
SWORDFERN PLACE	3500	446M	NWC	77449
SWORDS BEND	100	569V	SF	77477
SWORDS CREEK RD	11900	371M	NWC	77067
SYCAMORE	100	288H	TB	77375
SYCAMORE	200	459Q	HG	77562
SYCAMORE	2300	537Y	PA	77503
SYCAMORE	6400	444P	KT	77493
SYCAMORE	7800	535B	SEH	77012
SYCAMORE CIR	14200	375X	NEC	77396
SYCAMORE CIR	26600	248L	SWM	77354
SYCAMORE CT	0	570U	MC	77489
SYCAMORE CT	28100	245K	SWM	77355
SYCAMORE DR	0	616T	PL	77581
S. SYCAMORE DR	10800	579C	LP	77571
N. SYCAMORE DR	10800	539Y	LP	77571
SYCAMORE DR	23900	257A	WV	77357
SYCAMORE LN	0	463S	CCO	77520
SYCAMORE LN	900	336F	NEH	77339
SYCAMORE BEND DR	16600	366P	NWC	77433
SYCAMORE BLUFF DR		484W	NEF	77494
SYCAMORE CREEK DR	5100	297Y	NEH	77345
SYCAMORE CREST LN	0	406T	NWC	77449
SYCAMORE GROVE DR	2300	618G	SEH	77062
SYCAMORE HEIGHTS	13100	368U	NWC	77065
SYCAMORE HILL	15500	246V	SWM	77355
SYCAMORE HILLS	0	282Z	WL	77484
SYCAMORE LAKE RD	14300	618E	SEH	77062
SYCAMORE LEAF LN	15000	328J	NWC	77429
SYCAMORE PARK	0	658M	LC	77573
SYCAMORE PARK CT	19100	486D	SWC	77094
SYCAMORE RIDGE LN	800	332Z	NCC	77073
SYCAMORE SHADOWS DR	3400	297W	NEH	77339
SYCAMORE SHOALS LN	0	377F	NEC	77346
SYCAMORE SIDE WAY	0	328N	NWC	77429
SYCAMORE SPRINGS CT	2900	297S	NEH	77339
SYCAMORE SPRINGS DR	2900	297S	NEH	77339
SYCAMORE TRACE CT	900	332Z	NCC	77073
SYCAMORE TRAIL	16900	254D	SEM	77302
SYCAMORE TREE CT	2900	297Q	NEH	77345
SYCAMORE VALLEY DR	19900	406L	NWC	77433
SYCAMORE VILLAS DR	5100	297Y	NEH	77345
SYCAMORE WIND CT	20700	332Z	NCC	77073
SYCAMORE WOOD DR	20700	332Z	NCC	77073
SYDNEE LOCH CT	0	329H	NWC	77379
SYDNEYANN DR		325S	NWC	77447
SYDNEY BAY CT	0	526J	NEF	77407
SYDNEY CREEK DR	0	325S	HK	77447
SYDNEYPARK LN	0	609U	MC	77479
SYDNEY PARK LN	13100	328F	NWC	77377

Street Name	Block	Pg/Sq	Loc	Zips
SYDNOR	100	494E	NEH	77020
SYDNOR AVE	1900	620P	SB	77586
SYLMAR RD	5500	531J	SWH	77081
SYLMAR RD	6700	530M	SWH	77074
SYLVAN	100	459W	CV	77530
SYLVAN	100	580G	LP	77571
S. SYLVAN LN	0	245R	SWM	77355
N. SYLVAN LN	0	245R	SWM	77355
SYLVAN LN	2200	502A	NEC	77521
SYLVAN RD	6600	534C	SEH	77023
SYLVAN BEACH PARK	0	580D	LP	77571
SYLVAN DALE DR	16400	376H	NEH	77346
SYLVANFIELD DR	4300	331W	NWC	77014
W. SYLVANFIELD DR	14200	371A	NWC	77014
W. SYLVANFIELD DR	14500	331W	NWC	77014
E. SYLVANFIELD DR	14500	331W	NWC	77014
SYLVAN FOREST DR	1	250D	WD	77381
SYLVAN GLEN DR	4500	448F	NWC	77084
SYLVAN GROVE DR	5600	337D	NEH	77345
SYLVAN GROVE LN	0	539Z	LP	77571
SYLVANIA	3800	534G	SEH	77023
SYLVAN LAKE DR	15700	618G	SEH	77062
SYLVANUS DR	0	285P	NWC	77447
SYLVESTER RD	100	453U	NEH	77009
SYLVIA	100	538K	DP	77536
SYLVIA DR	13800	368P	NWC	77429
SYLVIAN HILLS DR	0	573N	SWC	77047
SYLVIA SPRINGS DR	0	293F	SEM	77386
SYLVIA SPRINGS LN	0	293F	SEM	77386
SYMBOL	11100	414P	NCC	77093
SYMPHONIC LN	9100	410K	NWC	77040
SYNOTT RD	2400	488U	SWH	77082
SYNOTT RD	6100	528G	SWH	77083
SYNOTT RD	10100	528Y	SWH	77478
SYRACUSE	3700	532A	SWH	77005
SYRIAN ST	0	570W	MC	77477

T

Street Name	Block	Pg/Sq	Loc	Zips
T	5900	444T	KT	77493
T RICHMOND RD	0	327M	NWC	77429
T BAR M BLVD	6500	330X	NWC	77069
T C JESTER BLVD	100	492C	NWH	77007
T C JESTER BLVD	700	492C	NWH	77008
W. T C JESTER BLVD	1000	452X	NWH	77008
E. T C JESTER BLVD	1000	452N	NWH	77008
W. T C JESTER BLVD	2700	451M	NWH	77018
E. T C JESTER BLVD	2700	452N	NWH	77018
T C JESTER BLVD	3700	451D	NWH	77018
T C JESTER BLVD	5100	411Z	NWH	77091
W. T C JESTER BLVD	7200	411Z	NWH	77088
T C JESTER BLVD	13100	371Z	NWC	77038
T C JESTER BLVD	13700	371R	NWC	77067
T C JESTER BLVD	13900	371M	NWC	77067
T C JESTER BLVD	14400	331T	NWC	77014
T C JESTER BLVD	15000	331T	NWC	77068
T C JESTER BLVD	16500	330D	NWC	77379
T C JESTER BLVD	19000	290Y	NWC	77379
T K C RD	25100	249T	NWC	77375
T K ELLIOTT	0	525V	NEF	77406
T, AVENUE	6600	494R	SEH	77011
W. T, O S DR	4400	455Y	NEH	77013
E. T, O S DR	4400	455Y	NEH	77013
TAB LN	14600	328Z	NWC	77070
TABANA DR	6400	406U	NWC	77449
TABATHA LOOP	0	542J	BT	77520
TABBERTS WAY	0	285K	NWC	77447
TABERNASH DR	0	410L	NWC	77040
TABITHA CT	0	332W	NWC	77090
TABLEROCK DR	10000	369Y	NWC	77064
TABLEROCK DR	10200	409B	NWC	77064
TABOR	1	453T	NWH	77009
TABOR	100	536G	PA	77506
TABOR BROOK DR	0	377C	NEC	77346
TABOR MILLS DR	0	611N	FS	77545
TACCOA DR	0	326K	NWC	77433
TACKABERRY	2200	493D	NEH	77009
TACO CT	14000	568E	SG	77498
TACOMA CT	0	660G	GCO	77539
TACOMA DR	5100	449C	NWC	77041
TACOMA BLUFF DR	0	406H	NWC	77433
TACOMA RIDGE DR	18200	328L	NWC	77377
TACOMA SPRINGS DR	0	326U	NWC	77429
TADLOCK LN	6300	571T	SWH	77085
TADPOLE CT	100	250J	NWC	77375
TADSHIRE LN	0	573T	SEC	77047
TADWORTH CT	15500	618J	SEH	77062
TAFFRAIL WAY	16200	419B	NEC	77532
TAFT	500	493J	SWH	77019
TAFT	1200	537N	PA	77502
TAFT	1700	493N	SWH	77006
TAFT	2100	502W	BT	77520
TAFT CIR	0	502W	BT	77520
TAFT CIR	2300	502W	BT	77520
TAFT DR	0	502W	BT	77520
TAFT DR	1400	538R	DP	77536
TAFTSBERRY DR	9200	407C	NWC	77095
TAGGART	6100	492F	SWH	77007
TAHOE CT	1500	659S	LC	77573
N. TAHOE DR	8200	409M	JV	77040
TAHOE DR	15800	409L	JV	77040
TAHOE CANYON LN	4700	447G	NWC	77084
TAHOE CROSSING LN	6300	370L	NWC	77066
TAHOE LAKE LN	16100	332V	NCC	77073
TAHOE PINES LN	17600	377E	NEC	77346
TAHOE SHORES CT	1	337P	NEC	77346
TAHOKA LN	10000	528S	NEF	77498
TAHOKA SPRINGS DR	19400	406V	NWC	77449
TAHOKA SPRINGS DR	19500	406U	NWC	77449
TAIDSWOOD DR	9100	330S	NWC	77379
TAILPINE LN	0	290P	NWC	77379
TAIN DR	4700	447D	NWC	77084
TAINO DR	4500	461S	NEC	77521
TAIN ROUND CT	16600	447D	NWC	77084
TAINSON DR	6100	408Y	NWC	77041
TAINTOR	12500	572E	SWH	77045
TAL CT	1	451W	SV	77055
TALA	9600	454A	NEH	77093
TALBOTT	2600	532G	WU	77005
TALBROOK DR	1600	372W	NWC	77038
TALCO GARDEN CT	0	660K	LC	77573
TALCOTT	14800	497M	NEC	77015
TALCOTT LN	8800	458A	NEC	77049
TALCOTT LN	9100	418W	NEC	77049
TALCOTT WAY DR	19201	329A	NWC	77375
TALGARTH	0	501C	NEC	77521
TALI DR	5000	414C	NCC	77032
TALIA DR	0	488G	SWH	77079
TALIESIN CT	0	253X	SEM	77386
TALINA WAY	2500	450N	NWH	77080
TALINA WAY	4300	450E	NWH	77041
TALISKER DR	16800	527X	NEF	77407

Street Name	Block	Pg/Sq	Loc	Zips
TALISMAN CT	1	453A	NWH	77076
TALL DR	0	408A	NWC	77095
TALLADEGA SPRINGS LN	0	526R	NEF	77407
TALLANT	100	453B	NEH	77076
TALL CANYON CT	6300	526F	NEF	77450
TALL CEDARS DR	100	379P	NEC	77532
TALL CHASE LN	0	370E	NWH	77070
TALLCREST LN		289G	NWC	77375
TALL CYPRESS DR	17300	331L	NWC	77388
TALL CYPRESS DR	17700	331F	NWC	77388
TALL ELM CT	2800	578W	SEH	77059
TALLEY LN	10000	410W	NWH	77041
TALLEYRAND DR	0	448B	NWC	77084
TALL FIRS LN	8100	408J	NWC	77095
TALL FOREST DR	12000	368L	NWC	77429
TALLGRASS CT	0	250P	NWC	77389
TALLGRASS PRAIRIE LN	0	377J	NEC	77346
TALLGRASS WAY	0	250P	NWC	77389
TALL GROVE LN	0	297U	NEH	77345
TALL HAVEN LN	0	366J	NWC	77433
TALLHEATH CT	13900	377Y	NEH	77044
TALL HILL CIR	0	418T	NCC	77044
TALL JUNIPER HILL	0	524A	NEF	77494
TALL MAPLE CT	17500	407K	NWC	77095
TALL MEADOW CT	9600	411P	NWC	77088
TALL MEADOW LN	9600	411N	NWC	77088
TALLOAK DR	0	615Z	PL	77581
TALL OAKS	12000	490E	BH	77024
TALL OAKS DR	1	298C	NEC	77336
TALLOW	500	409J	NWC	77041
TALLOW CT	1400	619D	PA	77586
TALLOW DR	300	252F	SEM	77385
TALLOW LN	5100	534J	SEH	77021
TALLOWBEND CT	10200	409D	NWC	77064
W. TALLOWBERRY DR	1	250M	WD	77381
S. TALLOWBERRY DR	1	250M	WD	77381
TALLOW BLUFF CT	0	328P	NWC	77377
TALLOW BRIAR LN	10800	575U	SEH	77075
TALLOW BROOK CT	700	485F	SWC	77494
TALLOW CHASE CT	0	657S	FR	77546
TALLOW CHASE LN	0	290Y	NWC	77379
TALLOW COVE DR	4900	501E	BT	77521
TALLOW FOREST CT	14900	618F	SEH	77062
TALLOW GLEN DR	13400	328U	NWC	77429
TALLOW GROVE LN	21500	486N	SWC	77450
TALLOW KNOLL LN	7000	526E	NEF	77407
TALLOWOOD DR	300	620J	EL	77586
TALLOWOOD DR	2700	659C	LC	77573
TALLOWOOD RD	400	489H	SWH	77024
TALLOWPARK LN	0	485X	NEF	77494
TALLOWPINE TERRACE	5200	444Q	KT	77493
TALLOW POINT CT	14100	618A	SEH	77062
TALLOW ROCK LN	0	298U	NEH	77336
TALLOW TREE CIR	9900	329U	NWC	77070
TALLOW TREE DR	9400	329U	NWC	77070
TALLOW VIEW LN	0	406F	NWC	77433
TALLOWWOOD	0	538V	DP	77536
TALLOWWOOD TERRACE	2600	444Q	KT	77493
TALL PINE DR	16000	618D	PA	77059
TALL PINES CT	1	245B	SWM	77355
TALL PINES DR	100	248K	SWM	77354
TALL PINES DR	700	656C	FR	77546
TALL PINES DR	7200	411T	NWH	77088
TALL PINE VALLEY DR	0	412C	NWC	77038
TALL PINE VISTA LN	20000	289W	NWC	77375
TALL RIDGE CT	4500	297U	NEH	77345
TALLSHADOWS DR	15000	373U	NCC	77032
TALL SHIPS LN	2100	617T	SEC	77546
TALL SKY PLACE	1	250H	WD	77381
TALL SPRUCE DR	12900	367H	NWC	77429
TALL SYCAMORE TRAIL	0	445K	NWC	77493
TALL TIMBER DR	10900	369N	NWC	77065
TALL TIMBER RD	24500	257B	WV	77357
TALL TIMBERS CT	300	616V	FR	77546
TALL TIMBERS LN	600	616V	FR	77546
TALL TIMBERS LN	2000	615L	PL	77581
TALL TIMBERS WAY	300	616V	FR	77546
TALL TOWER ST	0	444D	NWC	77493
TALL TREE RIDGE WAY	2900	291M	NWC	77389
TALL TREE TRAIL	19200	331A	NWC	77379
TALLULAH CT	1500	488R	SWH	77077
TALLULAH LN	1900	488R	SWH	77077
TALL WILLOW DR	6300	411T	NWH	77088
TALLWOOD	0	578V	SEH	77059
TALLWOOD DR	6500	337Q	NEC	77346
TALLWOOD CROSSING LN	12600	409S	NWC	77041
TALLYHO RD	8700	575C	SEH	77061
TALLYHO RD	9200	575D	SEH	77017
TALMADGE HILL	0	490J	SWH	77024
TALMADGE REACH	0	376R	NEC	77346
TALMAN RUN DR	0	376V	NEC	77346
TALON DR	1800	657J	FR	77546
TALON COVE LN	0	376S	NEC	77396
TALONCREST CT	9400	527Q	NEF	77083
TALONCREST DR	16100	527Q	NEF	77083
TALTON	7900	455F	NEH	77028
TALTON	8800	455G	NEH	77078
TALTON OAKS DR	0	409F	NWC	77064
TALVERA WAY	0	375Z	NEC	77396
TAM CT	1	451W	SV	77055
TAM-O-SHANTER DR	6300	330X	NWC	77069
TAM-O-SHANTER DR	6900	370A	NWC	77069
TAMAR DR	6300	538W	PA	77503
TAMARA LN	9600	412G	NWC	77038
TAMARACH DR	5000	500M	BT	77521
TAMARACK DR	11800	295Y	SEM	77365
TAMARACK BEND LN	0	377F	NEC	77346
TAMARACK PLACE	4000	527C	SWC	77082
TAMARACK WAY	19500	486C	SWC	77094
TAMARA HEIGHTS LN	0	609S	NEF	77479
TAMARIND DR	0	613T	NEB	77584
TAMARIND PLACE	1	250G	WD	77381
TAMARIND TRAIL	3200	297P	NEH	77345
TAMARING CT	0	570H	SWH	77035
TAMARINO PARK LN	6100	609X	NEF	77479
TAMARISK LN	3500	609G	MC	77459
TAMARISK LN	4700	531C	BL	77401
TAMARRON CT	7800	337R	NEC	77346
TAMARRON DR	20400	337R	NEC	77346
TAMAYO DR	7900	527Q	NEF	77083
TAMBOURINE DR	11900	529W	SWH	77477
TAMERISK CENTRE CT	13800	370A	NWC	77069
TAMERLAINE DR	200	490J	BH	77024
TAMERTON DR	0	291Z	NWC	77388
TAMER VIEW CT	18600	328G	NWC	77377
TAMESI DR	0	255X	SEM	77365
TAMFIELD DR	3600	371K	NWC	77066
TAMINA RD	100	252A	SEM	77385
TAMINA PASS LN	0	657S	FR	77546
TAMI RENEE LN	8700	410K	NWC	77040
TAMMANY LN	15700	527C	SWC	77082
TAMMARACK DR	12400	456Z	NEH	77013

Street Name	Block	Pg/Sq	Loc	Zips
TAMMONY PARK CT	3800	617X	SEC	77546
TAMMONY PARK LN	3800	617X	SEC	77546
TAMMY CT	1	493D	NEH	77026
TAMORA LN	7800	578C	PA	77505
TAM O SHANTER LN	3000	609H	MC	77459
TAM O SHANTER LN	5800	530F	SWH	77036
TAMPA	2600	656T	FR	77546
TAMPA	3200	533G	SEH	77021
TAMPICO	4200	454K	NEH	77016
TAMPINI CT	0	657A	FR	77546
TAMTAM	7700	455L	NEH	77028
TAMWORTH DR	1200	457Z	NEC	77015
TAMWORTH DR	1900	444U	KT	77493
TAMWORTH DR	10900	415S	NEH	77016
TAMWORTH DR	11000	415N	NEH	77016
TAMWORTH ST	0	415S	NEH	77016
TAMY LN	1200	450Y	SV	77055
TAMY LN	9000	450Y	SV	77055
TANAGER	0	529R	SWH	77036
TANAGER	6200	530Q	SWH	77074
TANAGER	8800	530N	SWH	77036
TANAGER	11900	529N	SWH	77072
TANAGER LN	18600	286H	NWC	77377
TANBERRY LN	0	457A	NEC	77044
TANCAH LN	21100	333P	NCC	77073
TANCY RANCH CT	0	484R	NEF	77494
TANDY PARKWAY	0	572R	SWH	77047
TANGA	0	539Z	LP	77571
TANGALA DR	0	326K	NWC	77433
TANG CITY DR	100	570P	MC	77489
TANGERINE	2900	573B	SEH	77051
TANGIERS RD	9900	450A	NWH	77041
TANGLE CIR	5700	491K	SWH	77057
TANGLE LN	5000	491L	SWH	77056
TANGLE BRANCH DR	0	328F	NWC	77429
TANGLEBRIAR	900	619H	TL	77586
TANGLEBRIAR DR	3000	537L	PA	77503
TANGLE BRUSH DR	1	251J	WD	77381
TANGLE BRUSH DR	3500	250M	WD	77381
TANGLE CIRCLE LN	5700	491K	SWH	77057
TANGLE CREEK LN	4200	291X	NWC	77388
N. TANGLE CREEK LN	21100	291T	NWC	77388
TANGLEHEAD CT	11000	371S	NWC	77086
TANGLE LAKE DR	1900	336G	NEH	77339
TANGLE PINES CT	1900	618A	SEH	77062
TANGLE RIVER DR	3700	297W	NEH	77339
TANGLEROSE CT	18600	447E	NWC	77084
TANGLE TREE LN	18200	447P	NWC	77084
TANGLEWILDE	0	502C	BT	77521
TANGLEWILDE	1600	490S	SWH	77063
TANGLEWILDE	3800	530A	SWH	77063
TANGLEWILDE	7700	530F	SWH	77036
TANGLEWOOD CT	12000	569E	SF	77477
TANGLEWOOD DR	100	500E	BT	77520
TANGLEWOOD DR	200	616U	FR	77546
TANGLEWOOD RD	700	491Q	SWH	77056
TANGLEWOOD COVE	0	491K	SWH	77057
TANGLEWOOD PARK	5800	491K	SWH	77057
TANGLEWOOD TRAILS DR	0	366Z	NWC	77433
TANGLEY	2100	532C	SWH	77005
TANGUEY CT	500	332F	NWC	77388
TAN HILL DR	0	377X	NEC	77044
TANNEHILL DR	1500	452W	NWH	77008
TANNER RD	9700	450A	NWH	77041
TANNER RD	10300	449B	NWH	77041
TANNER RD	12700	448D	NWC	77041
TANNER CROSSING LN	0	524A	NEF	77494
TANNER MEADOW LN	0	411R	NWH	77088
TANNER MEADOW LN	0	573L	SEH	77089
TANNER PARK CT	10900	576P	SEH	77075
TANNER TRAIL	0	255Q	SEM	77365
TANNER TRAIL	21600	255U	SEM	77365
TANNER WOODS LN	0	657S	FR	77546
TANNER WOODS LN	4200	609N	NEF	77479
TANNER WOODS LN	21100	334M	NCC	77338
TANNERY HILL RD	100	249M	NWH	77375
TANNERY HILL RD	100	249M	NWH	77375
TAN OAK CIR	8800	290J	NWC	77375
TAN OAK CT	21600	255S	SEM	77365
TANVERN CT	13700	371C	NWC	77014
TANVERN LN	13600	371C	NWC	77014
TANWOOD DR	10900	368V	NWC	77065
TANYA	0	539Z	LP	77571
TANYA CIR	15700	488E	SWH	77079
TAOS LN	11400	369A	NWC	77070
TAOSBLUFF DR	0	328A	NWC	77429
TAOS CREEK CT	0	328J	NWC	77429
TAOS TRAIL	0	539N	DP	77536
TAPALCOMES DR	0	366N	NWC	77433
TAPER GLOW PLACE	1	250G	WD	77381
TAPER REACH DR	0	328K	NWC	77377
TAPESTRY DR	5000	525C	NEF	77494
TAPPENBECK DR	9700	450X	NWH	77055
TAPPENGATE LN	16800	332Q	NCC	77073
TAPPER HILL DR	1200	488F	SWH	77077
TAPPER RIDGE LN	0	377F	NEC	77346
TARA CT	11700	249S	NWC	77375
TARA DR	12100	490J	BH	77024
TARA ASHLEY CT	0	407E	NWC	77433
TARA BEND CT	25200	249S	NWC	77375
TARA GABLES CT	2900	487Z	SWC	77082
TARAGLEN CT	8400	527P	NEF	77407
TARA HILLS CT	11700	576L	SEH	77034
TARANTO LN	200	457Y	NEC	77015
TARANTO LN	400	497C	NEC	77015
TARANTO CREEK CT	0	445J	NWC	77493
TARA OAK DR	13300	368Y	NWC	77065
TARA PLACE	2400	612V	PL	77584
TARA PLACE	3200	578D	LP	77571
TARA PLANTATION DR	11700	249S	NWC	77375
S. TARA PLANTATION DR	12000	249S	NWC	77375
W. TARA PLANTATION DR	25100	249S	NWC	77375
E. TARA PLANTATION DR	25100	249S	NWC	77375
TARA RIDGE OAK BLVD	0	487Z	SWC	77082
TARA RIDGE OAK CT	15000	487Z	SWC	77082
TARARIN LN	0	527N	NEF	77407
TARA SPRINGS LN	0	293F	SEM	77386
TARA TRAIL	0	412E	NWC	77038
TARAWA RD	5100	534S	SEH	77033
TARA WAY DR	22700	445Q	NWC	77449
TARAWOOD CT	3700	291Y	NWC	77388
TARBELL RD	8000	576F	SEH	77034
TARBERRY RD	1300	412Q	NWH	77088
TARBET PLACE CT	13100	367H	CY	77429
TAREN CT	0	289R	NWC	77375
TAREYTON LN	4100	573L	SEH	77047
TAREYTON LN	8000	575K	SEH	77075
TARGET CT	1700	449X	NWH	77043
TARGET DR	1500	449X	NWH	77043
TARIK DR	7800	527L	NEF	77083
TARKINE CT	0	377K	NEC	77346
TARLETON DR	10600	491A	HC	77024

Street Name	Block	Pg/Sq	Loc	Zips
TARLEY	1100	453V	NEH	77009
TARLTON CT	25000	249S	NWC	77375
TARLTON WAY	4300	609A	SG	77478
TARNA LN	6300	531E	SWH	77074
TARNBROOK DR	4600	447B	NWC	77084
TARNEF DR	6000	530D	SWH	77074
TARO LN	8400	461P	NEC	77521
TARO ST	0	419C	NEC	77532
TAR OAKS CT	14900	487Z	SWC	77082
TARONGA LN	0	526P	NEF	77407
TARPANRIDGE	0	334R	NCC	77338
TARPAULIN WAY	600	379X	NEC	77532
TARPLEY CT	1900	445T	NWC	77493
TARPLEY SPRINGS DR	0	526N	NEF	77407
TARPLEY SPRINGS DR	20000	525R	NEF	77407
TARPON	16100	458A	NEC	77049
TARPON CT	0	408A	NWC	77095
TARPON DR	2900	660J	LC	77573
TARPON LN	3800	580V	LP	77571
TARPON BAY CT	0	609T	NEF	77479
TARPON BAY LN	0	366Y	NWC	77433
TARPON SPRINGS LN	8900	408A	NWC	77095
TARRA FIRMA DR	6000	330D	NWC	77379
TARRAGON LN	8300	461P	NEC	77521
TARRAGON LN	9500	529M	SWH	77036
TARRAGONA LN	0	660G	GCO	77539
TARRANT CT	8400	409H	NWC	77064
TARRINGTON CT	900	491A	HC	77024
TARRINGTON DR	10600	491A	HC	77024
TARRYTOWN LN	2600	616N	PL	77581
TARRYTOWN MALL	2400	491S	SWH	77057
TARTAN LN	3500	532J	SWH	77025
TARTAN WALK LN	8600	575U	SEH	77075
TARTAN WALK LN	8600	575U	SEH	77075
TARTON WAY CT	9400	408D	NWC	77065
TARVER	200	453T	NWH	77009
TASCOSA LN	0	660G	GCO	77539
TASCOSA LN	9300	409H	NWC	77064
TASCOTT	100	536G	PA	77506
TASHKENT DR	5100	617W	FR	77546
TASIA DR	12300	570L	SWH	77085
TASK	0	414N	NCC	77093
TASMANIA PLACE	19400	406U	NWC	77449
TASSEL BROOK DR	9800	329U	NWC	77070
TASSEL CREEK DR	11500	329S	NWC	77377
TASSEL FIELD LN	8100	335J	NCC	77338
TASSELL	700	453B	NEH	77076
TASSELWOOD LN	4100	371B	NWC	77014
TASWELL DR	0	485K	SWC	77494
TATE	7900	455T	NEH	77028
TATE CT	10200	252G	SEM	77385
TATEFIELD	8200	455T	NEH	77028
TATOM	9700	454A	NEH	77093
TATOR TOT	0	408Q	NWC	77041
TATTENHALL DR	1800	452S	NWH	77008
TATTERIDGE DR	5600	330Y	NWC	77069
TATTERSHALL CIR	8100	335N	NCC	77338
TATTINGER	0	484E	NEF	77494
TATTON CREST CT	0	290R	NWC	77388
TATUM LN	5300	291J	NWC	77389
TATUM BEND LN	0	293F	SEM	77386
TATUM BEND LN	0	293F	SEM	77386
TAUB RD	8600	410B	NWC	77064
TAUB LOOP	1500	533E	SWH	77030
TAUT CT	15800	419F	NEC	77532
TAUTENHAHN RD	5200	414V	NEH	77016
TAUTENHAHN RD	6000	415S	NEH	77016
TAVENOR CT	0	573M	SEH	77048
TAVENOR LN	3900	573L	SEH	77047
TAVENOR LN	4700	574J	SEH	77048
TAVENOR LN	8000	575K	SEH	77075
TAVENOR LN	9600	576J	SEH	77075
TAVERN	7800	450D	NWH	77040
TAVERNS CORNER CT	0	446H	NWC	77449
TAVERNS CORNER LN	0	446H	NWC	77449
TAVERNS CROSSING LN	0	446H	NWC	77449
TAVERN SPRINGS LN	0	446M	NWC	77449
TAVERTON DR	1400	457Z	NEC	77530
TAVIRA LN	0	660G	GCO	77565
TAVISTOCK DR	8700	570A	SWH	77031
TAVITA TRAIL	0	528K	NWC	77083
TAVOLA DR	0	257E	SEM	77357
TAVOLA ROSE DR	0	257E	SEM	77357
TAWAKOM DR	12200	288Z	NWC	77375
TAWAKON DR	4100	614Z	PL	77584
TAWAKONI CANYON LN	0	660K	LC	77573
TAWINEE	11300	369J	NWC	77065
TAWNAS WAY LN	0	326V	NWC	77429
TAWNEY CT	0	616H	SEC	77089
TAWNY BLUFF CT	0	406L	NWC	77433
TAWNY OAKS DR	1900	338A	NEH	77345
TAWNY TRACE CT	9800	416Z	NEC	77044
TAWNY WOOD CT	20700	335J	NCC	77338
TAWNY WOOD DR	0	335J	NCC	77338
TAXI WAY RD	0	447P	NWC	77449
TAY CT	200	299W	NEH	77336
TAY GROVE PLACE	10900	527W	NEF	77407
TAYLAN HILLS DR	0	293K	SEM	77386
TAYLOE HOUSE LN	23800	445T	NWC	77493
TAYLOR	300	493F	SWH	77007
TAYLOR	300	497N	NEC	77015
TAYLOR	2000	282U	WL	77484
TAYLOR	2400	538Q	DP	77536
TAYLOR AVE	1300	537E	PA	77506
TAYLOR CT	1	494E	NEH	77020
TAYLOR LN	0	570J	SF	77477
TAYLOR LN	1800	616P	PL	77581
TAYLOR LN	19000	380K	NEC	77532
TAYLOR RD	0	408M	NWC	77041
TAYLOR RD	0	576L	SEH	77034
TAYLOR RD	1300	292F	NWC	77389
TAYLOR RD	12000	409J	NWC	77041
TAYLOR BEND DR	0	526E	NEF	77407
TAYLOR BROOK CT	600	486D	SWC	77094
TAYLOR CLIFF LN	0	406C	NWC	77433
TAYLOR COVE CT	0	366Z	NWC	77433
TAYLORCREST	0	257C	WV	77357
TAYLORCREST	12000	490E	BH	77024
TAYLORCREST DR	2900	613T	NEB	77584
TAYLORCREST RD	11400	490G	PP	77024
TAYLORCREST RD	12900	489E	SWH	77079
TAYLOR LAKE CT	4800	526X	NEF	77407
TAYLOR LEIGH LN	0	371N	NWC	77066
TAYLOR MEADOW LN	0	373E	NCC	77073
TAYLOR MEDFORD LN	0	609P	NEF	77479
TAYLOR MILLS CT	0	484L	NEF	77494
TAYLOR PARK CT	0	658X	LC	77573
TAYLOR PARK LN	0	485W	NEF	77494
TAYLOR RIDGE DR	900	292K	SP	77373
TAYLORS CROSSING DR	12200	328D	NWC	77375
TAYLORS GLEN CT	2900	485S	NEF	77494
TAYLOR SKY LN	0	657K	FR	77546

Street Name	Block	Pg/Sq	Loc	Zips
TAYLOR SPRINGS LN	0	329F	NWC	77375
TAYLOR WAY	6600	250Y	NWC	77389
TAYLORWOOD LN	12400	369M	NWC	77070
TAYMAN OAKS DR	0	406K	NWC	77433
TAYMAN PARK LN	23500	485K	NEF	77494
TAYMOUTH DR	1300	252Q	SEM	77386
TAYMOUTH DR	14600	408T	NWC	77084
TAYPORT LN	15000	457Z	NEC	77530
TAYPORT LN	15200	458W	NEC	77530
TAZEWELL POINTE DR	0	524F	NEF	77494
T C JESTER BLVD	0	411D	NWC	77038
T C JESTER BLVD	0	411M	NWH	77088
TEABERRY	3700	291L	NWC	77389
TEABERRY HILL	0	417A	NEC	77044
TEABURY AVE	700	537L	PA	77503
TEAGARDEN CT	22400	485U	NEF	77450
TEAGUE CIR	900	569S	SG	77478
TEAGUE RD	1800	450N	NWH	77080
TEAGUE RD	5400	410W	NWH	77041
TEAK DR	16400	570E	MC	77489
TEAK CANYON TRAIL	0	446B	NWC	77449
TEAK FOREST TRAIL	0	447R	NWC	77084
TEAK FOREST TRAIL	0	447R	NWC	77084
TEAKWOOD	1300	536P	PA	77502
TEAKWOOD CIR	3200	659Z	GCO	77539
TEAKWOOD CT	0	569N	SG	77478
TEAKWOOD DR	300	490M	HC	77024
W. TEAKWOOD DR	3800	579C	LP	77571
E. TEAKWOOD DR	3800	579C	LP	77571
TEAKWOOD FOREST DR	8100	330J	NWC	77379
TEAKWOOD LN (CR 106AA)	3500	613G	NEB	77584
TEAKWOOD PLACE	2000	568Z	SG	77478
TEAKWOOD SPRINGS DR	0	376Q	NEC	77396
TEAL	900	495U	NEH	77029
N. TEAL CT	1200	613M	NEB	77584
S. TEAL CT	1300	613M	NEB	77584
TEAL CT	28400	245H	SWM	77355
TEAL DR	0	444S	KT	77493
TEAL DR	2000	252Z	SEM	77386
TEAL DR	3200	444K	KT	77493
TEAL LN	0	573Y	SEC	77047
TEAL LN	200	568T	SG	77478
TEAL RD	29000	323X	NWC	77447
TEAL ARBOR LN	1800	338B	NEH	77345
TEAL BAY LN	15600	329U	NWC	77070
TEAL BAY BEND	2100	658V	LC	77573
TEAL BAYOU LN	26901	324S	NWC	77447
TEAL BEND BLVD	0	611W	FS	77545
TEAL BLUFF LN	0	488T	SWH	77077
TEAL BREEZE DR	0	526Q	NEF	77407
TEALBRIAR CIR	1	250G	WD	77381
TEALBROOK DR	20600	406Q	NWC	77433
TEAL COVE LN	0	488N	SWH	77077
TEAL CREEK DR	18400	377D	NEC	77346
TEALCREST LN	0	573U	SEC	77047
TEALCREST ESTATES DR	30600	252V	SEM	77386
TEA LEAF DR	0	329B	NWC	77375
N. TEAL ESTATES CIR	1000	611X	NEF	77545
W. TEAL ESTATES CIR	3900	611X	NEF	77545
E. TEAL ESTATES CIR	3900	611X	NEF	77545
TEAL FERN CT	3900	578Z	PA	77059
TEAL FOREST LN	17500	330G	NWC	77379
TEALGATE DR	4400	293Z	NCC	77373
TEAL GLEN	3500	615S	PL	77584
TEAL GLEN CT	1300	618A	SEH	77062
TEAL GROVE LN	0	609U	MC	77459
TEAL HAVEN LN	0	366N	NWC	77433
TEAL HOLLOW DR	12900	367H	NWC	77429
TEAL HOLLOW LN	11600	329N	NWC	77377
TEALIGHT PLACE	0	250E	NWC	77389
TEAL LAKE CT	24900	484M	NEF	77494
TEAL MANOR DR	0	617X	SEC	77546
TEAL MAPLE CT	0	611X	NEF	77545
TEALMEADOW CT	400	490J	BH	77024
TEAL MESA DR	0	573Z	SEH	77048
TEAL OAK DR	900	611Y	NEF	77545
TEAL OAKS LN	6500	408V	NWC	77041
TEAL OAKS LN	12800	408V	NWC	77041
TEAL PARK CT	8100	375U	NEC	77396
TEAL PARK DR	15200	375U	NEC	77396
TEAL POINT DR	20700	486N	SWC	77450
TEAL RUN DR	6300	570D	SWH	77035
TEAL RUN DR	7500	570C	SWH	77071
TEAL RUN PLACE CT	3900	611X	FS	77545
TEAL RUN PLACE DR	1800	611X	FS	77545
TEAL SHADOW CT	0	326T	NWC	77433
TEAL SHORE CT	2400	619Y	LC	77573
TEAL SHORE CT	13700	488P	SWH	77077
TEALSTONE FALLS CT	14000	377X	NEC	77044
TEAL TRAIL	7800	250W	NWC	77389
TEALVIEW LN	2600	485N	NEF	77494
TEAL VISTA CT	3900	611X	FS	77545
TEALWATER CT	3500	446J	NWC	77449
TEAL WAY CT	3900	611X	NEF	77545
TEALWAY DR	1000	577E	PA	77504
TEALWICK LN	0	484Z	NEF	77494
TEALWIND DR	7200	406L	NWC	77433
TEALWOOD	20200	283Q	NWC	77484
TEALWOOD DR	300	489M	SWH	77024
TEALWOOD GLEN LN	3800	611X	NEF	77545
TEALWOOD NORTH CIR	12300	490J	BH	77024
TEALWOOD NORTH DR	12300	490J	BH	77024
TEAMEADOW CT	5200	660X	DI	77539
TEANAWAY LN	1400	495K	NEH	77029
TEANECK DR	11700	616D	SEH	77089
TEA OLIVE CT	0	250U	NWC	77389
TEA ROSE CT	22300	525L	NEF	77407
TEAS	4500	531H	BL	77401
TEASEL CT	20700	526A	NEF	77450
TEASIDE DR	11500	371P	NWC	77066
TEASLY LN	0	249Z	NWC	77375
TEA TREE DR	0	524E	NEF	77494
TEA TREE OLIVE PLACE	0	296A	SEM	77365
TEAWICK CT	3300	331N	NWC	77068
TEBO	9900	453B	NEH	77076
TEBROC CT	19000	486H	SWC	77094
TECHE LN	25100	339E	HU	77336
TECHNIPLEX DR	100	569J	SF	77478
TECHNOLOGY DR	0	529C	SWH	77072
TECHNOLOGY DR	0	568C	SG	77478
TECHNOLOGY FOREST BLVD	0	251B	WD	77381
TECHNOLOGY FOREST BLVD	0	251B	WD	77381
TECK CT	14600	573Z	SEC	77047
TECUMSA	10500	569L	SF	77477
TECUMSEH CIR	5700	491F	SWH	77057
TECUMSEH CT	3000	610U	MC	77459
TECUMSEH LN	200	491F	SWH	77057
TED	5200	450H	NWH	77040
TEDDY LN	22600	290H	NWC	77389
TEDDY BEAR ALLEY	900	335R	HM	77338
TED PICKETT LN	700	659J	LC	77573
TEEPEE TRAIL	0	244A	WCO	77447

Street Name	Block	Pg/Sq	Loc	Zips
TEESDALE DR	7600	455A	NEH	77028
TEE TREE CT	4100	293M	SEM	77386
TEETSHORN	200	493B	NWH	77009
TEJAS	7000	462Y	BT	77521
TEJAS	7800	461S	NEC	77521
TEJAS CT	9200	579E	LP	77571
TEJAS DR	6300	538W	PA	77503
TEJAS DR	23600	295F	SEM	77365
TEJAS TRAIL	16500	367B	CY	77429
TELEAN	6700	574R	SEH	77075
TELEAN	7700	575N	SEH	77075
TELEGRAPH CREEK DR	17100	330G	NWC	77379
TELEGRAPH SQUARE CT	1900	446X	NWC	77449
TELEGRAPH SQUARE LN	20000	446X	NWC	77449
TELEPHONE RD	100	494T	SEH	77023
TELEPHONE RD	1900	534G	SEH	77023
TELEPHONE RD	4000	534R	SEH	77087
TELEPHONE RD	6400	535W	SEH	77061
TELEPHONE RD	6800	575W	SEH	77061
TELEVISTA DR	12900	413P	NEH	77037
TELFAIR CT	14500	408X	NWC	77084
TELFORD WAY	0	329F	NWC	77375
TELGE	3100	533K	SWH	77054
TELGE RD	8500	408A	NWC	77095
TELGE RD	9300	368W	NWC	77095
TELGE RD	11000	368N	NWC	77429
TELGE RD	15000	367D	NWC	77429
TELGE RD	15300	327R	NWC	77429
TELGE RD	18700	287V	NWC	77377
TELGE LAKE TRAIL	0	328E	NWC	77377
TELGE MANOR DR	15700	327R	NWC	77429
TELGE TERRACE	15500	287V	NWC	77377
TELICO JUNCTION LN	7400	377C	NEC	77346
TELKWA DR	1500	252V	SEM	77386
TELLEPSEN	1800	534B	SEH	77023
TELLER BLVD	19500	332A	NWC	77388
TELLER BLVD	19600	292W	NWC	77388
TELLURIDE DR	9500	410F	NWC	77040
TELUCO	6400	451U	NWH	77055
TEMBROOK COVE	2100	484K	NEF	77494
TEMECULA CT	0	484K	NEF	77494
TEMECULA COVE	2200	484K	NEF	77494
TEMPE CIR	17500	367X	NWC	77095
TEMPE CT	17400	367X	NWC	77095
TEMPE ST	0	658U	LC	77573
TEMPELGATE DR	5300	370C	NWC	77066
TEMPERA CT	11700	411H	NWC	77038
E. TEMPERANCE LN	100	538X	DP	77536
W. TEMPERANCE LN	7400	538X	DP	77536
TEMPEST	0	419B	NEC	77532
TEMPLAR LN	13700	528W	NEF	77498
W. TEMPLE	600	453X	NWH	77009
E. TEMPLE	700	453X	NWH	77009
TEMPLE	29500	248B	SWM	77354
TEMPLE AVE	0	453Y	NEH	77009
TEMPLE CT	10000	367Z	NWC	77095
TEMPLE DR	1900	493J	SWH	77019
TEMPLE DR	3600	613X	NEB	77578
TEMPLE BELL DR	4600	291S	NWC	77388
TEMPLE HILL LN	0	326R	NWC	77429
TEMPLE PARK LN	26700	366R	NWC	77433
TEMPLERIDGE LN	10400	575V	SEH	77075
TEMPLE WOODS	0	491G	SWH	77024
TENAHA DR	3300	371C	NWC	77014
TENASSERIM PINE TERRACE	17900	527S	NEF	77407
TENAYA FALLS DR	0	328Y	NWC	77429
TENBURY	15700	409M	JV	77040
TENBURY CT	0	258E	SEM	77357
TENBURY GLEN DR	3600	371K	NWC	77066
TENBY DR	20000	486L	SWC	77450
TEN CURVES CIR	17600	330G	NWC	77379
TEN CURVES CT	17600	330G	NWC	77379
TEN CURVES RD	6800	330G	NWC	77379
TENDERDEN DR	1300	457Z	NEC	77530
TENDERWOOD DR	4700	449H	NWH	77041
TENEHA DR	10100	574A	SEH	77033
TENEYA CANYON	23600	287A	SWM	77355
TENISON CT	16700	330M	NWC	77379
TENKARA PATH	0	249R	NWC	77375
TENLEYTON LN	10400	575V	SEH	77075
TEN MILE LAKE	0	609Y	MC	77459
TENNECO DR	10400	528U	SWH	77099
TENNECO RD	0	537H	PA	77503
TENNESSEE	300	495V	NEH	77029
TENNESSEE	1900	541A	BT	77520
TENNETA DR	10400	528Z	SWH	77099
TEN NINETY TWO DR	13300	569L	SF	77477
TENNIS CT	10700	528U	SWH	77099
TENNIS DR	12700	528V	SWH	77099
TENN OAKS RD	24700	244Q	WCO	77447
TENNYSON	3800	532A	WU	77005
TENNYSON DR	800	613G	NEB	77584
TEN OAKS CT	18300	255S	SEM	77365
TEN OAKS DR	15600	328V	NWC	77377
TEN SLEEP LN	4600	617X	SEC	77546
TENTON PARK LN	6000	541F	NWH	77092
TENUTA LN	0	659P	LC	77573
TEPAJAE	0	573V	SEH	77048
TEPEE	27000	244A	WCO	77447
TEPEE TRAIL	9100	409G	NWC	77064
TERANIA CIR	0	405R	NWC	77493
TERANO LN	0	405R	NWC	77493
TERCELL TRAIL	0	577W	SEH	77034
TERESA DR	500	460N	HG	77562
TERESA DR	1000	490D	SV	77055
TERI CT	19000	252B	SEM	77385
TERI CT	26500	252P	SEM	77386
TERI LN	27700	298Z	NEH	77336
TERIWOOD DR	4200	330V	NWC	77068
TERLIN	13400	415A	NEC	77039
TERLINGUA	4200	577F	PA	77504
S. TERMINAL	0	374B	NEH	77032
TERMINAL	300	495E	NEH	77020
TERMINAL	900	494R	SEH	77011
TERMINAL	3300	455W	NEH	77020
TERMINAL	4900	491Y	BL	77401
N. TERMINAL	2700	334W	NEH	77032
TERN	0	532W	SWH	77025
TERN LAKE DR	3400	297W	NEH	77339
TERRA CANYON LN	7900	406M	NWC	77433
TERRACE	400	620J	EL	77586
TERRACE	2000	501V	BT	77520
E. TERRACE DR	1	492K	SWH	77007
TERRACE DR	200	492K	SWH	77007
TERRACE DR	2300	502A	NEC	77521
S. TERRACE DR	20700	295M	SEM	77365
W. TERRACE DR	23900	295M	SEM	77365
N. TERRACE DR	23900	295H	SEM	77365
E. TERRACE DR	24000	295M	SEM	77365
TERRACE ARBOR LN	25300	485W	NEF	77494
TERRACE BEND	14400	328T	NWC	77429
TERRACE BROOK	0	410L	NWC	77040

Street Name	Block	Pg/Sq	Loc	Zips
TERRACE CLIFF CT	0	526K	NEF	77407
TERRACE COVE LN	0	366J	NWC	77433
W. TERRACE CREEK CIR	4200	371B	NWC	77014
E. TERRACE CREEK CIR	4200	371B	NWC	77014
N. TERRACE CREEK CIR	13600	371B	NWC	77014
TERRACE FALLS DR	0	524A	NEF	77494
W. TERRACE GABLE CIR	0	525A	NEF	77494
E. TERRACE GABLE CIR	0	525A	NEF	77494
TERRACE GATE LN	0	615M	PL	77089
TERRACE GATE LN	22100	485Y	NEF	77450
TERRACE GLADE CT	7900	370E	NWC	77070
TERRACEGLEN CT	21600	290P	NWC	77379
TERRACE HILLS LN	3000	493J	SWH	77007
TERRACE MANOR DR	4400	449M	NWH	77041
TERRACE MEADOW	0	410J	NWC	77040
TERRACE OAKS DR	14900	331T	NWC	77068
TERRACE PARK BLVD	0	447P	NWC	77084
TERRACE PARK CT	0	410L	NWC	77040
TERRACE PARK DR	0	410L	NWC	77040
TERRACE PARK DR	17100	407Q	NWC	77095
TERRACE PASS DR	0	450V	NWH	77080
TERRACE PINES DR	4000	297Y	NEH	77345
TERRACE POINT LN	0	376C	NEC	77338
TERRACE RIDGE	6900	525F	NEF	77494
TERRACE RUN LN	13000	457A	NEC	77044
TERRACE SAGE LN	0	524F	NEF	77494
TERRACES ON MEMORIAL	0	488E	SWH	77077
TERRACE VALLEY CIR	0	526P	NEF	77407
TERRACE VIEW DR	21000	406T	NWC	77449
TERRACE VINE LN	0	290P	NWC	77379
TERRACE WIND LN	8300	410J	NWC	77040
TERRACE WOOD CT	13400	370E	NWC	77070
TERRA CINA CT	0	610P	NEF	77459
TERRACINA DR	0	445J	NWC	77493
TERRA COTTA DR	7800	410L	NWC	77040
TERRA CROSSING LN	6000	409W	NWC	77041
TERRA FOREST CT	0	446D	NWC	77449
TERRA HOLLOW LN	0	526F	NEF	77450
TERRAIN PARK DR	0	293U	NCC	77373
TERRA LAKE CT	0	409W	NWC	77041
TERRA LAKE CT	0	409W	NWC	77041
TERRALYN WAY	13200	528Y	SG	77478
TERRAMARE	0	379K	NEC	77532
TERRANCE	12500	570R	SWH	77085
TERRANCE FALL DR		524A	NEF	77494
TERRANCE SPRINGS LN	0	524C	NEF	77494
TERRA NOVA CT	0	656C	FR	77546
TERRANOVA LN	0	659L	LC	77573
TERRANOVA LN	1000	331H	NWC	77090
TERRANOVA WEST DR	17700	331E	NWC	77379
TERRAPIN DR	0	366K	NWC	77433
TERRAPOINT DR	14900	327X	CY	77429
TERRA RUN CT	27200	294N	SEM	77386
TERRA SPRINGS DR	20500	446F	NWC	77449
TERRASSA LN	0	660G	GCO	77539
TERRA STONE	19100	406M	NWC	77433
TERRAVALE CT	1	251A	WD	77381
TERRA VALLEY LN	8200	290N	NWC	77375
TERRA VERDE DR	26700	284B	WCO	77447
TERRA VERDE LN	2000	299X	NEC	77336
TERRAVISTA MANOR	0	330H	NWC	77379
TERRAVITA DR	0	331J	NWC	77379
TERRAVITA DR	0	331J	NWC	77379
TERRAVITA HILLS	7100	370A	NWC	77069
TERRAWREN LN	17600	331J	NWC	77379
TERRAZA COVE LN	0	409S	NWC	77041
TERRAZZA VERDE DR	0	445A	NWC	77493
TERREBONE DR	11300	368P	NWC	77429
TERREL DR	6000	614Y	PL	77584
TERRELL	4300	414Y	NEH	77093
TERRELL HILLS LN	0	578X	SEH	77059
TERRENCE CT	900	570S	SF	77477
TERRENCE DR	1800	570S	SF	77477
TERRERO DR	19600	328C	NWC	77377
TERRETON DR	0	296N	SEM	77365
TERRI LN	500	247J	SWM	77362
TERRI LN	31000	246Y	SWM	77355
TERRIE LN	3200	615Q	PL	77581
TERRITA LN	21500	256K	SEM	77357
TERRITORY LN	9500	409C	NWC	77064
TERRTON SPRINGS DR	0	296N	SEM	77365
TERRY	100	568N	SG	77478
TERRY	1500	493D	NEH	77009
TERRY	3000	502A	NEC	77521
TERRY	3500	453V	NEH	77009
TERRY LN	3300	446K	NWC	77449
TERRY COURT PLACE	1200	332Z	NCC	77073
TERRYDALE CT	9300	412M	NCC	77037
TERRYDALE DR	9100	412M	NCC	77037
TERRY HOLLOW DR	700	498A	NEC	77530
TERRY SPRINGS CT	20000	526F	NEF	77407
TERUZZI WAY	0	329Y	NWC	77070
TERWILLIGER DR	5600	491P	SWH	77056
TERWILLIGER DR	6200	491N	SWH	77057
TESORO CIR	22200	338Z	NEH	77532
TESSA CT	8300	410K	NWC	77040
TESSIE COVE LN	0	293F	SEM	77386
TESSIE HILLS LN	27900	293K	SEM	77386
TETELA DR	7300	527K	NEF	77083
TETON	4500	533V	SEH	77051
TETON	4700	533V	SEH	77033
TETON LN	18200	295F	SEM	77365
TETON MIL DR	0	334R	NCC	77338
TETON PASS LN	0	377E	NEC	77346
TETON PEAK WAY	0	616H	SEH	77089
TETON RIDGE BLVD		484Y	NEF	77494
TETTER CEMETERY RD	20500	334K	NCC	77338
TEWANTIN DR	8200	575E	SEH	77061
TEXACO	5200	371S	NWC	77086
TEXACO RD	12400	456Y	NEH	77013
TEXANA DR	4000	503H	CCO	77520
TEXAN FOREST TRAIL	0	376H	NEC	77346
TEXARKANA	6200	494D	NEH	77020
TEXARKANA	7100	495A	NEH	77020
TEXARKANA	13700	497B	NEC	77015
W. TEXAS	100	536L	PA	77506
TEXAS	100	288H	TB	77375
TEXAS	100	536M	PA	77506
TEXAS	100	576B	SH	77587
TEXAS	100	659F	LC	77573
TEXAS	400	493M	DT	77002
TEXAS	800	580C	LP	77571
TEXAS	1200	570N	MC	77489
TEXAS	1600	494S	SEH	77003
TEXAS	1700	463B	MB	77580
TEXAS	2200	615N	PL	77581
TEXAS	4700	494U	SEH	77011
TEXAS	7300	495W	SEH	77011
S. TEXAS AVE	0	618X	WB	77598
TEXAS AVE	0	660S	GCO	77539
W. TEXAS AVE	100	501X	BT	77520
E. TEXAS AVE	100	501Y	BT	77520

Street Name	Block	Pg/Sq	Loc	Zips
S. TEXAS AVE	200	658B	WB	77598
TEXAS AVE	400	620T	KE	77565
E. TEXAS AVE	900	541D	BT	77520
E. TEXAS AVE	1800	542A	BT	77520
TEXAS AVE	3100	538P	DP	77536
N. TEXAS AVE	16800	618S	WB	77598
N. TEXAS CT	0	252F	SEM	77385
E. TEXAS CT	0	252F	SEM	77385
W. TEXAS DR	0	252F	SEM	77385
N. TEXAS DR	0	252F	SEM	77385
E. TEXAS DR	0	252F	SEM	77385
TEXAS DR	0	568X	SG	77479
TEXAS ACORN AVE	0	455C	NEH	77078
TEXAS ARMY TRAIL	12400	368F	NWC	77429
N. TEXAS AVE	100	618S	WB	77598
TEXAS BAPTIST HAVEN	0	489M	SWH	77024
TEXAS CHILDREN CIR	0	617D	SEH	77062
TEXAS DANDY DR	0	287V	NWC	77377
TEXAS DANDY DR	0	288S	NWC	77377
TEXAS ELM CT	2600	611S	NEF	77545
TEXAS GARDENS	8500	491M	SWH	77024
TEXAS LANCER DR	0	366J	NWC	77433
TEXAS LANTANA CT	0	406D	NWC	77433
TEXAS LAUREL LOOP	7200	337Q	NEC	77346
TEXAS LAUREL TRAIL	19400	337Q	NEC	77346
TEXAS MEDICAL CENTER	0	533E	SWH	77030
TEXAS OAK DR	3000	446N	NWC	77449
TEXAS PKWY	200	570X	MC	77489
TEXAS PKWY	2500	610G	MC	77489
TEXAS REDBUD CT	10500	376S	NWC	77433
TEXAS SAGE DR	0	575R	SEH	77075
TEXAS SAGE WAY	0	366Z	NWC	77433
TEXAS SOUTHERN DR	100	419Q	BR	77532
TEXAS STAR SPRINGS CT	19600	366V	NWC	77433
TEXAS TRAIL	4400	609E	SG	77479
TEXAS TRAIL LN	3100	613W	NWB	77578
TEXEZ	5500	290M	NWC	77389
TEXIAN CT	0	290R	NWC	77388
TEXICAN TRAIL	6600	461X	BT	77521
TEXMATTI DR	0	484D	SWC	77494
TEXOMA	1800	501W	BT	77520
TEXOMA BEND LN	0	657N	FR	77546
TEXZASH	21100	291V	NWC	77388
THACKERY LN	11000	415P	NEH	77016
THADDS TRAIL	22700	334A	NCC	77373
THALERFIELD DR	0	613V	NEB	77584
THAMER CIR	400	491E	HC	77024
THAMER LN	400	491E	HC	77024
THAMES LN	8300	527P	NEF	77083
THARP	3100	493V	SEH	77003
THARP	3400	494W	SEH	77003
THARP DR	4500	620H	SB	77586
THATCHAM	0	258F	SEM	77357
THATCHER DR	13000	488U	SWH	77077
S. THATCHER BEND CIR	100	250P	NWC	77389
N. THATCHER BEND CIR	100	250P	NWC	77389
THAT WAY	0	297N	NEH	77339
THAYER CT	24700	484G	NEF	77494
THEALL RD	0	370G	NWC	77066
THEALL RD	4700	371A	NWC	77066
THEALL RD	5300	370D	NWC	77066
THE ALLEY	0	335R	HM	77338
THEBES CT	3200	610U	MC	77459
THE HIGHLANDS DR	2500	568Z	SG	77478
THEISS LN	13100	288Q	TB	77375
THEISS RD	3400	333L	NCC	77338
THEISS-HILL DR	7900	330E	NWC	77379
THEISSETTA DR	7700	330K	NWC	77379
THEISS MAIL	0	330K	NWC	77379
THEISS MAIL ROUTE RD	16800	330J	NWC	77379
THEISS PARK LN	17900	330E	NWC	77379
THEISS PARK LN	17900	330J	NWC	77379
THEISSWOOD CIR	17900	330F	NWC	77379
THEISSWOOD CT	17700	330J	NWC	77379
THEISSWOOD LN	17800	330J	NWC	77379
THEISSWOOD RD	7400	330J	NWC	77379
THELF CT	0	290P	NWC	77375
THE LITTLE DIRT RD	22000	256K	SEM	77357
THELMA	14600	614Q	PL	77581
THELMA DR	2200	336N	NEH	77338
THELMA DR	2600	493B	NWH	77009
THELMA LN	100	256V	SEM	77357
THELMA LN	1700	537N	PA	77502
THELMA ANN LN	12800	574P	SEH	77048
THE OAKS	0	328C	NWC	77377
THERESA	1000	533U	SEH	77051
THERESA	2000	537K	PA	77506
THERESA	21100	256S	SEM	77357
THERESA COVE LN	3800	446F	NWC	77449
THE RESERVE DR	25300	250S	NWC	77389
THERIOT TRACE	0	620J	SB	77586
THERMON	10100	576P	SEH	77075
THERON	100	453K	NEH	77022
THERRELL DR	9500	409G	NWC	77064
THETA	2100	576F	SEH	77034
THETFORD LN	8200	369D	NWC	77070
THE WHARF	0	619X	LC	77573
THEYSEN CIR	3300	450L	NWH	77080
THEYSEN DR	8800	450L	NWH	77080
THIBODEAUX	1700	541B	BT	77520
THICKET LN	300	488D	SWH	77079
THICKET EDGE LN	0	484E	KT	77494
THICKET GREEN DR	12100	570H	SWH	77035
THICKET GROVE RD	18200	447P	NWC	77084
THICKET HILL CT	0	373E	NCC	77073
THICKET HOLLOW LN	17300	367A	NWC	77429
THICKETLEAF LN	0	484Z	NEF	77494
THICKET MEADOWS	0	528Q	SWC	77083
THICKET PARK LN	0	376W	NEC	77396
THICKET PATH WAY	0	445K	NWC	77493
THICKET RIDGE LN	0	488P	SWH	77077
THICKET RUN DR	3300	331C	NWC	77388
THICKET TRACE CT	7600	406M	NWC	77433
THICKET TRACE LN	0	406G	NWC	77433
THICKET TRAIL DR	7200	337Y	NEC	77346
THICKEY PINES CT	4200	484U	NEF	77494
THIMBLEBERRY CT	1	251R	WD	77380
THIMBLEWEED DR	0	329L	NWC	77379
THIN LIZZY LN	0	407S	NWC	77449
THIRSTY FISH RD	0	332N	NWC	77090
THISTLE	800	572U	SWH	77047
THISTLE	3500	573U	SEC	77047
THISTLE	4500	574S	SEH	77048
THISTLEBERRY LN	9800	289U	NWC	77375
THISTLEBERRY LN	20900	290U	NWC	77379
THISTLEBRIDGE CT	0	327Z	NWC	77429
THISTLEBURY LN	22900	292L	NCC	77373
THISTLE CREEK CT	12500	416Z	NEC	77044
THISTLECROFT DR	4500	448F	NWC	77084
THISTLEDEW DR	15700	487Y	SWC	77082
THISTLEDOWN DR	0	299X	NEC	77336
THISTLEDOWN DR	2900	659H	LC	77573

Street Name	Block	Pg/Sq	Loc	Zips
THISTLEDOWN LN	3900	577E	PA	77504
THISTLE DOWN LN	5000	330U	NWC	77069
THISTLEGATE CT	24000	293Y	NCC	77373
THISTLE GATE LN	7400	526M	NEF	77407
THISTLEGLEN CIR	7300	407M	NWC	77095
THISTLEGLEN DR	16300	407M	NWC	77095
THISTLEMEADE DR	1100	486H	SWC	77094
THISTLE MEADOW LN	16400	326N	NWC	77433
THISTLEMONT DR	3700	530A	SWH	77042
THISTLEMOOR LN	0	457A	NEC	77044
THISTLE ROCK LN	0	327U	NWC	77429
THISTLE TRAIL DR	9400	329Q	NWC	77070
THISTLE VALLEY CT	25600	295V	NEH	77365
THISTLEWAITE LN	25300	293N	NCC	77373
THISTLE WIND CT	1	250G	WD	77381
THISTLEWOOD	0	609A	SG	77479
THISTLEWOOD	3900	577E	PA	77504
THISTLEWOOD CT	300	659H	LC	77573
THISTLEWOOD DR	600	488G	SWH	77079
THISTLEWOOD PARK CT	0	525B	NEF	77494
THIS WAY	0	297N	NEH	77339
THOM RD	5100	337X	NEC	77346
THOMAS	2000	493C	NEH	77009
W. THOMAS AVE	100	536L	PA	77506
THOMAS AVE	100	536M	PA	77506
THOMAS AVE	700	484C	KT	77494
THOMAS AVE	1300	537E	PA	77506
THOMAS DR	0	252P	SEM	77386
THOMAS DR	1100	375D	HM	77338
THOMAS DR	1200	616U	FR	77546
THOMAS LN	0	246U	SWM	77355
THOMAS LN	0	258Y	NEC	77336
THOMAS LN	20800	256S	SEM	77357
THOMAS RD	1600	501A	SEC	77521
THOMAS RD	5700	449B	NWC	77041
THOMAS RD	5900	409X	NWC	77041
THOMAS RD	27600	298X	NEH	77336
THOMAS JEFFERSON WAY	1300	569Y	MC	77477
THOMAS LINCOLN RIDGE LN	0	325M	NWC	77433
THOMAS MILL LN	14700	528S	NEF	77498
THOMAS PAINE DR	3100	609C	MC	77459
N. THOMAS SHORE CT	0	366F	NWC	77433
N. THOMAS SHORE DR	0	366F	NWC	77433
THOMAS SURVEY DR	0	366F	NWC	77433
THOMASTONE LN	0	377J	NEC	77346
THOMASVILLE DR	9100	369R	NWC	77064
THOMPSON	900	492H	SWH	77007
THOMPSON	1400	541B	BT	77520
THOMPSON CIR	200	569V	SF	77477
THOMPSON LN	0	542S	NEC	77520
THOMPSON RD	6000	500B	NEC	77521
THOMPSON RD	7700	460X	NEC	77562
THOMPSON BEND DR	0	376Q	NEC	77396
THOMPSON CREEK DR	0	371L	NWC	77062
THOMPSON FERRY RD	5600	609X	NEF	77479
THOMPSON POINT DR	17000	366P	NWC	77433
THOMPSONRIDGE DR	0	328A	NWC	77429
THOMPSONS RD	2300	611N	FS	77545
THOMSON ST	0	614A	PL	77581
THONIG RD	1800	451T	NWH	77055
THONIG RD	3800	451K	NWH	77092
THOR LN	2000	618L	SEH	77058
THORA LN	8300	290W	NWC	77379
THORHILL	17200	329M	NWC	77379
THORHURN CT	10400	368Y	NWC	77065
THORN	100	459M	HG	77562
THORN	9800	415Z	NEH	77078
THORN	10000	455D	NEH	77078
THORN BERRY CREEK CT	0	446S	NWC	77449
THORN BERRY CREEK LN	0	446W	NWC	77449
THORNBERRY GROVE DR	0	524T	NWF	77406
THORN BERRY PLACE	1	250C	WD	77381
THORNBILL LN	0	407V	NWC	77084
THORNBLADE CIR	0	250K	NWC	77389
THORNBLUFF CT	14600	367A	NWC	77429
THORNBRANCH DR	700	488C	SWH	77079
THORNBRIAR CT	0	614C	BK	77581
THORNBRIAR DR	0	574Y	BK	77581
THORNBRIAR DR	12200	614C	BK	77581
THORNBROOK DR	1600	570U	MC	77489
THORNBROOK DR	15600	408X	NWC	77084
THORNBROUGH LN	0	575V	SEH	77075
THORNBURG LN	12000	371M	NWC	77067
THORNBURY DR	0	372D	NCC	77073
THORNCLIFF DR	10600	376U	NEC	77396
THORNCREEK CT	1	251A	WD	77381
THORNCREEK WAY	7700	407M	NWC	77095
THORNCROFT DR	0	526E	NEF	77450
THORNCROFT MANOR LN	7900	526L	NEF	77407
THORN CYPRESS DR	16700	327X	CY	77429
THORNDON PARK CT	2400	619Y	LC	77573
THORNE, W W BLVD	2000	333S	NCC	77073
THORNE, W W BLVD	2000	333S	NCC	77073
THORNEBERRY FOREST LN	0	525M	NEF	77407
THORNE CREEK LN	2800	333P	NCC	77073
THORNE CREST	0	289W	NWC	77375
THORNE FIELD RD	400	292M	SP	77373
THORNE HAVEN DR	20600	333P	NCC	77073
THORNGATE CT	5300	485X	NEF	77494
THORNGATE LN	22000	291L	NWC	77389
THORNGATE FOREST LN	0	376C	NEC	77338
THORNHAMPTON CT	0	372A	NWC	77014
THORNHEDGE CT	1	251F	WD	77381
THORNHILL CREEK CT	25600	295V	NEH	77365
THORNHILL OAKS CT	1	456Z	NEC	77015
THORNHILL OAKS DR	1	457W	NEC	77015
THORNHOLLOW DR	1500	332W	NWC	77014
THORNLEA DR	10500	576T	SEH	77089
THORNLEAF LN	10200	369G	NWC	77070
THORNMEAD LN	20000	290Z	NWC	77379
THORN MEADOW	0	407P	NWC	77449
THORNMEADOW LN	7200	407P	NWC	77433
THORNMONT LN	10200	369G	NWC	77070
THORNOAK LN	13200	369G	NWC	77070
THORN RIDGE LN	0	328M	NWC	77377
THORNRIDGE LN	0	369C	NWC	77070
THORNRIDGE LN	0	658S	LC	77573
THORNSBY CT	23700	485T	NEF	77494
THORNTON CIR	4700	452K	NWH	77018
THORNTON DR	0	609U	MC	77459
E. THORNTON RD	100	453J	NWH	77022
THORNTON RD	300	452K	NWH	77018
S. THORNTREE DR	13200	457W	NEC	77015
N. THORNTREE DR	13300	457X	NEC	77015
THORNTON VALLEY CT	0	328K	NWC	77377
THORNVILLE LN	13200	369G	NWC	77070
THORNVINE LN	800	488C	SWH	77079
THORNWALL	6300	451J	NWH	77092
W. THORN WAY	200	456Z	NEC	77015
THORNWELL CT	12600	369K	NWC	77070
THORNWICK DR	800	488C	SWH	77079
THORNWILD RD	6800	571W	SWH	77489
THORNWILDE PARK LN	400	332Q	NCC	77073
THORNWOOD CIR	5300	660X	DI	77539
THORNWOOD CT	800	613F	NEB	77584
THORNWOOD DR	0	616V	FR	77546
THORNWOOD DR	3000	537L	PA	77503
THORNWOOD DR	10900	579C	LP	77571
THORNWOOD LN	1400	618A	SEH	77062
THORNWOOD RD	1	245X	SWM	77447
THOROUGHBRED DR	11900	409A	NWC	77065
THOROUGHBRED TRAILS LN	12600	377T	NEC	77044
THOROUGH GOOD LN	14900	408T	NWC	77084
THORPE LN	0	329F	NWC	77375
THORPESHIRE CT	3300	485S	NEF	77494
THORSBY DR	30100	252V	SEM	77386
THORTON	0	453J	NWH	77022
THORTON KNOLLS DR	24700	250Y	NWC	77389
THORTONS PARK LN	0	290D	NWC	77389
THOUSAND OAKS CIR	5700	451B	NWH	77092
THOUSAND OAKS CT	25100	245P	SWM	77355
THOUSAND PINES DR	1900	336C	NEH	77339
THREADALL PARK DR	13700	488F	SWH	77077
THREADLEAF DR	11500	371N	NWC	77066
THREADNEEDLE	800	488C	SWH	77079
THREEAWN CT	11000	371S	NWC	77086
THREE BARS TRAIL	0	288S	NWC	77377
THREE CHUTES LN	0	326K	NWC	77433
THREE CORNERS DR	500	491E	HC	77024
THREEFLOWER CT	1800	297V	NEH	77345
THREEFLOWER LN	6300	297V	NEH	77345
THREEFOLD RIDGE DR	0	285L	NWC	77447
THREE FORKS DR	900	485H	SWC	77450
THREE LAKES BLVD	12200	328D	NWC	77375
THREE LAKES LN	0	243G	WCO	77447
THREE OAKS CIR	5200	330Y	NWC	77069
THREE PINES DR	3200	296Y	NEH	77339
THREE PINES DR	20600	286J	NWC	77447
THREE RIVERS DR	4000	569S	SG	77478
THREE RIVERS WAY	10500	367S	NWC	77433
THREE SISTERS	3400	414T	NCC	77093
THREE SISTERS CIR	3200	615L	PL	77581
THREE STONE LN	0	289Q	NWC	77375
THREE WOOD DR	2100	616K	SEH	77089
THRELKELD	400	493A	NWH	77007
THROCKMORTON DR	8800	409G	NWC	77064
THRUSH	9800	539T	LP	77571
THRUSH DR	5400	574A	SEH	77033
THRUSH DR	6200	534Z	SEH	77087
THRUSH GROVE PLACE	1	250D	WD	77381
THRUSH TRAIL	22500	286J	NWC	77447
THRUSHWOOD LN	25100	293P	NCC	77373
THUNDER LN	0	297J	SEM	77365
THUNDER BASIN LN	0	377F	NEC	77346
THUNDERBAY	0	618T	SEH	77062
THUNDER BAY DR	4200	577E	PA	77504
THUNDERBAY DR	15600	618J	SEH	77062
THUNDERBIRD	3500	609G	MC	77459
THUNDERBIRD CIR	1	501J	BT	77521
THUNDERBIRD RD	4700	450G	NWH	77041
THUNDERCLOUD PLACE		249Q	NWC	77375
THUNDERHAVEN DR	11000	369V	NWC	77064
THUNDERHEAD CT	10600	409B	NWC	77064
THUNDER LAKE LN	1500	568E	SG	77498
THUNDER RIDGE LN	0	406X	NWC	77449
THUNDER RIDGE WAY	0	616J	PL	77089
THUNDER ROCK DR	19400	406R	NWC	77449
THUNDER VALLEY DR	0	249Q	NWC	77375
THURBER RIDGE DR	0	289Y	NWC	77379
THURLEIGH	9900	529Z	SWH	77031
THURLOW DR	0	615T	PL	77581
THURMON	2100	576A	SEH	77034
THUROW	7300	534M	SEH	77087
THUROW	7400	535J	SEH	77087
THURSA LN	3700	657B	FR	77546
THURSTON LN	23200	296N	SEM	77365
THURSTON CROSSING DR	21300	296N	SEM	77365
THYME CIR	4200	501M	BT	77521
THYME GREEN LN	16400	326N	NWC	77433
TIARA LN	10100	450W	NWH	77043
TIBER	800	490C	HE	77024
TIBET RD	16100	617W	FR	77546
TIBET RD	16400	657B	FR	77546
TIBURON CT	0	250R	NWC	77389
TIBURON WAY	16300	611A	SWH	77053
TICKLESEED LN	19900	289Y	NWC	77379
TICKNER	7100	451X	NWH	77055
TICO DR	6500	527H	SWC	77083
TICONDEROGA LN	0	295G	SEM	77365
TICONDEROGA RD	11900	456H	NEC	77044
TICONDEROGA RD	13000	457E	NEC	77044
TIDAL RD	0	499N	SEC	77571
TIDAL RD	100	538G	DP	77536
TIDAL RD	200	498Z	DP	77536
TIDE ROCK LN	0	612E	PL	77545
TIDESWEPT CT	12000	367Q	NWC	77095
TIDEWATER CT	5100	577C	PA	77505
TIDEWATER DR	2600	572J	SWH	77045
TIDEWATER DR	4500	571M	SWH	77045
TIDEWATER DR	5400	571M	SWH	77085
TIDEWATER CYPRESS TRAIL	0	325K	NWC	77447
TIDEWATER FALLS LN	0	328A	NWC	77429
TIDEWATER FALLS LN	0	328A	NWC	77377
TIDEWIND CT	3100	613S	NEB	77578
TIDFORD	3400	454B	NEH	77093
TIDWELL CT	0	452D	NWH	77076
TIDWELL LN	1600	453D	NEH	77093
TIDWELL RD	1	453B	NEH	77022
W. TIDWELL RD	100	452C	NWH	77022
E. TIDWELL RD	100	453B	NEH	77022
W. TIDWELL RD	300	452A	NWH	77091
TIDWELL RD	1500	454A	NEH	77093
TIDWELL RD	4500	454A	NEH	77016
W. TIDWELL RD	5700	451B	NWH	77092
W. TIDWELL RD	7300	450C	NWH	77040
TIDWELL RD	7700	455A	NEH	77028
TIDWELL RD	8800	456C	NEH	77078
TIDWELL RD	11700	456C	NEH	77044
TIDWELL FOUNTAINS LN		455B	NEH	77078
TIDWILLOW PLACE	0	250J	NWC	77375
TIDY TIPS LN	19800	289Y	NWC	77379
TIEGS AVE	300	659E	LC	77573
TIEL WAY	1	492L	SWH	77019
TIERRA ALTA DR	17100	527J	NEF	77083
TIERRA MIST LN	0	526Q	NEF	77407
TIERRA MOUNTAIN CT	0	576Q	SEH	77034
TIERRA PALMS CT	0	576Q	SEH	77034
TIERRA PARK	0	576L	SEH	77034
TIERRA RIDGE CT	0	576L	SEH	77034
TIERRA RIDGE CT	0	576Q	SEH	77034
TIERRA VERDE DR	7400	527K	NEF	77083
TIERWESTER	2100	493Z	SEH	77004
TIERWESTER	3500	533D	SEH	77004
TIERWESTER	6100	533L	SEH	77021
TIERWOOD CT	3500	331S	NWC	77068
TIFCO	10500	368T	NWC	77429
TIFFANY CT	16500	618M	SEH	77058
TIFFANY DR	3600	572N	SWH	77045
TIFFANY DR	5600	571P	SWH	77085
TIFFANY LN	1	569S	SG	77478
TIFFANY GREEN DR	0	251D	WD	77381
TIFFANY LOOP	0	542J	BT	77520
TIFFANY PLACE	0	532S	SWH	77025
TIFFANY SQUARE	1	569N	SG	77478
TIFFIN	4000	454X	NEH	77026
TIFF TRAIL DR	14100	408L	NWC	77095
TIFWAY LN	13700	417X	NEC	77044
TIGER LN	8100	410K	NWC	77040
TIGER'S WAY		484B	KT	77494
TIGER LILLY WAY	5400	571L	SWH	77085
TIGER MAPLE DR	0	250U	NWC	77389
TIGER SHARK CT	0	445R	NWC	77449
TIGER TRACE CT	4300	371K	NWC	77066
TIGER TRACE LN	4600	371J	NWC	77066
TIGER TRAIL	0	444S	KT	77493
TIGER TRAIL	10400	449V	NWH	77043
TIGER TRAIL	0	450S	NWH	77043
TIGRIS DR	22800	295B	SEM	77365
TIGRIS LN	1000	331H	NWC	77090
TIGRIS RIDGE DR	3900	446M	NWC	77449
TIGRIS SPRINGS CIR	19500	446L	NWC	77449
TIGUAS	4000	577F	PA	77504
TILBROOK CT	10300	372W	NWC	77038
TILBROOK DR	10500	372W	NWC	77038
TILBURY DR	4900	491L	SWH	77056
TILDEN	3000	532K	SWH	77025
TILDEN DR	100	537E	PA	77506
TILDON FOREST DR	0	253W	SEM	77386
TILFER	3100	534M	SEH	77087
TILGHAM DR	7200	495J	NEH	77020
TILGHAM DR	7800	495L	NEH	77029
TILIA	11500	496K	JC	77029
TILLAMOOK CT	0	250U	NWC	77389
TILLER	2200	536V	PA	77502
TILLEY	14700	408X	NWC	77084
TILLISON	1000	412P	NWH	77088
TILSON LN	2400	450Q	NWH	77080
TILSON LN	4300	450L	NWH	77041
TILSTOCK DR	20000	486G	SWC	77450
TILTREE	9600	576S	SEH	77075
TILTRUM LN	12000	411F	NWC	77086
TILTWOOD LN	0	289R	NWC	77375
TIM	2400	454A	NEH	77093
TIM ALLEN CT	4000	371B	NWC	77014
TIMARROM DR	0	250J	NWC	77375
TIMBARRA CIR	0	405T	NWC	77493
TIMBER	100	500N	BT	77520
TIMBER CIR	500	488A	SWH	77079
TIMBER CT	4400	578G	PA	77505
TIMBER CT	27400	249L	SWM	77354
TIMBER DR	2200	659Y	DI	77539
TIMBER LN	0	296J	SEM	77365
TIMBER LN	1	657A	FR	77546
TIMBER LN	100	459M	HG	77562
TIMBER LN	100	500F	BT	77520
TIMBER LN	1500	492S	SWH	77027
TIMBER LN	21600	255U	SEM	77365
TIMBER LN	24300	295M	SEM	77365
TIMBER BAY CT	5600	525D	NEF	77450
TIMBER BEND LN	0	253P	SEM	77386
TIMBER BLUFF CT	21200	256W	SEM	77365
TIMBER BLUFF DR	0	612N	PL	77545
TIMBERBLUFF LN	0	447F	NWC	77084
TIMBERBRANCH CT	2300	247P	SWM	77355
TIMBERBREEZE CT	2300	247N	SWM	77355
TIMBER BRIAR CIR	2700	618A	SEH	77059
TIMBERBRIAR CT	2300	247N	SWM	77355
TIMBER BRIAR CT	14000	618A	SEH	77059
TIMBER BRIGHT CT	0	377Z	NEC	77044
TIMBER BROOK	23200	333B	NCC	77373
TIMBERBROOK TRAIL	2300	297V	NEH	77345
TIMBER CHASE DR	15900	527C	SWC	77082
TIMBERCHASE PLACE	14900	368A	NWC	77429
TIMBER CLIFF CT	17200	327X	NWC	77429
TIMBER CLIFF LN	14600	327X	NWC	77429
TIMBER CORNER	4000	527C	SWC	77082
TIMBER COUNTRY WAY	2800	297Z	NEH	77345
TIMBER COURT HOLLOW DR	0	407Y	NWC	77084
TIMBER COURT HOLLOW DR	0	407Y	NWC	77084
TIMBER COVE DR	700	619H	TL	77586
TIMBERCRAFT DR	8600	408E	NWC	77095
TIMBER CREEK CT	800	616R	FR	77546
TIMBER CREEK CT	4400	610P	MC	77459
TIMBER CREEK DR	1400	616R	FR	77546
TIMBER CREEK DR	1500	610P	MC	77459
TIMBER CREEK DR	1900	616S	PL	77581
TIMBER CREEK DR	4700	535U	SEH	77017
TIMBER CREEK DR	5400	536S	SEH	77017
TIMBERCREEK FALLS DR	11100	367Q	NWC	77095
TIMBER CREEK PLACE CT	16000	408W	NWC	77084
TIMBER CREEK PLACE DR	5100	408W	NWC	77084
TIMBER CREEK PLACE LN	15900	408W	NWC	77084
TIMBERCREEK TRAIL	2300	297V	NEH	77345
TIMBER CREST DR	11000	369N	NWC	77065
TIMBERCREST DR	11700	249S	NWC	77375
TIMBERCREST VILLAGE DR	8200	250S	NWC	77389
W. TIMBER CUT CT	4000	615S	PL	77584
E. TIMBER CUT CT	4000	615S	PL	77584
TIMBERDALE LN	600	332J	NWC	77090
TIMBER DUST CIR	22700	333B	NCC	77373
TIMBER EDGE LN	7000	377C	NEC	77346
TIMBER FALLS CT	4000	527C	SWC	77082
TIMBERFIELD CT	19700	446L	NWC	77449
TIMBERFIELD PLACE	19800	446L	NWC	77449
TIMBER FOREST DR	14200	377X	NEC	77044
TIMBER FOREST DR	17100	377A	NEC	77346
TIMBER FOREST DR	19200	337W	NEC	77346
TIMBER GARDENS DR	0	253S	SEM	77386
TIMBERGATE	0	527C	SWC	77082
TIMBER GLADE CT	3700	297T	NEH	77345
TIMBERGLEN CT	2300	247N	SWM	77355
TIMBER GLEN CT	18100	407S	NWC	77084
TIMBERGLEN DR	10800	490H	HC	77024
TIMBERGREEN CIR	1900	247N	SWM	77355
E. TIMBERGREEN CIR	2200	247P	SWM	77355
TIMBER GREEN CIR	19700	486G	SWC	77094
TIMBERGREEN DR	14000	247P	SWM	77355
TIMBER GROVE CT	15900	329N	NWC	77377
TIMBER GROVE LN	0	253T	SEM	77386
TIMBERGROVE LN	1100	452Y	NWH	77008
TIMBER GROVE PLACE	200	616Z	FR	77546
TIMBER GROVE POINT DR	0	492A	NWH	77008
TIMBERGROVE TRAIL	0	297V	NEH	77345
TIMBERHAVEN DR	14000	371Q	NWC	77066
TIMBERHILL DR	700	490F	HE	77024
TIMBER HOLLOW	0	619E	PA	77058
TIMBER HOLLOW	11600	369N	NWC	77065
TIMBERIDGE CT	16500	327X	CY	77429
TIMBERJACK PLACE	2700	251Q	WD	77380
TIMBERKNOB CT	2300	247N	SWM	77355
TIMBER KNOLL	11700	490K	BH	77024
TIMBERLAKE DR	12000	368L	NWC	77429
TIMBERLAKE CREEK RD	22700	286G	NWC	77377
TIMBERLAKE FOREST LN	19100	286G	NWC	77377
TIMBERLAKE GLEN TRAIL		367S	NWC	77433
TIMBERLAKE GROVE LN	19100	286G	NWC	77377
TIMBERLAKE OAKS DR	19000	286G	NWC	77377
TIMBER LAKES DR	25300	251N	SWM	77380
TIMBERLAKE VIEW LN	19000	286G	NWC	77377
TIMBERLAKE VILLAGE RD	22700	286G	NWC	77377
TIMBERLAKE WOODS LN	19100	286G	NWC	77377
TIMBERLAND BLVD	19000	255T	SEM	77365
TIMBERLAND CT	14900	618F	SEH	77062
TIMBERLAND PATH DR	24600	293S	NCC	77373
TIMBERLAND TRACE	12700	368V	NWC	77065
TIMBER LANE DR	25600	252T	SEM	77386
TIMBERLARK DR	3100	297W	NEH	77339
TIMBERLARK DR	14900	329W	NWC	77070
TIMBERLEA DR	14900	571S	SWH	77489
TIMBERLEA DR	15300	570V	SWH	77489
TIMBERLEAF DR	14100	247N	SWM	77355
TIMBERLEDGE DR	0	249A	SWM	77354
TIMBERLINE DR	700	336J	NEH	77339
TIMBERLINE DR	4300	578G	PA	77505
TIMBER LINE DR	24400	251W	SWM	77380
TIMBER LINE LN	19800	257M	SEM	77357
TIMBERLINE RD	11000	449X	NWH	77043
TIMBERLINE RUN LN	7800	407G	NWC	77095
TIMBERLINE TRAIL	16300	246Y	SWM	77355
TIMBERLINE TRAIL	20200	326P	NWC	77433
W. TIMBERLOCH CT	31500	246Y	SWM	77355
E. TIMBERLOCH CT	31500	246Y	SWM	77355
TIMBERLOCH DR	10300	369L	NWC	77070
TIMBERLOCH PLACE	100	251M	WD	77380
E. TIMBERLOCH TRAIL	31100	246Y	SWM	77355
W. TIMBERLOCH TRAIL	31200	246Y	SWM	77355
TIMBER LODGE LN	21300	256W	SEM	77365
TIMBERLY PARK LN	11500	366Q	NWC	77433
TIMBER MANOR DR	12200	369J	NWC	77429
TIMBERMEADOW DR	12600	369K	NWC	77070
TIMBER MEADOW LN	0	328G	NEC	77377
TIMBERMEADOW OAK DR	0	371E	NWC	77066
TIMBERMEADOW PINES	0	371E	NWC	77066
TIMBER MILL	100	251L	WD	77380
TIMBERMIST CT	0	407E	NWC	77433
TIMBERMOSS CT	6100	657Y	LC	77573
TIMBERMOSS CT	8300	407E	NWC	77095
TIMBER NOOK CT	8300	250S	NWC	77389
TIMBER OAK CIR	1400	659N	LC	77573
TIMBER OAK DR	10000	450S	NWH	77080
TIMBER OAK DR	10200	449U	NWH	77043
TIMBER OAKS CT	28100	246B	SWM	77355
TIMBER OAKS LN	22800	296G	SEM	77365
TIMBER OAKS RIDGE	5800	337T	NEC	77346
TIMBER PARK TRAIL	7900	370E	NWC	77070
TIMBERPATH DR	0	247J	SWM	77355
TIMBER PATH DR	4800	377A	NEC	77346
TIMBER PINES	19300	337T	NEC	77346
TIMBER PINES DR	21300	292N	NWC	77388
TIMBER PINE TRAIL	4500	297P	NEH	77345
TIMBER PLACE	4000	527C	SWC	77082
TIMBER PLATEAU DR	0	376Q	NEC	77396
TIMBER POINT CT	7500	330F	NWC	77379
TIMBER POST LN	7000	377C	NEC	77346
TIMBER QUAIL DR	5200	337W	NEC	77346
TIMBER RAIL CT	17200	376H	NEC	77396
TIMBER RAIL DR	3800	376H	NEC	77396
TIMBER RANCH DR	1900	247J	SWM	77355
TIMBER RIDGE	5000	502B	NEC	77521
TIMBER RIDGE CT	20300	245C	SWM	77355
TIMBER RIDGE DR	0	612N	PL	77545
TIMBER RIDGE DR	19200	246E	SWM	77355
TIMBER RIDGE DR	19300	245D	SWM	77355
TIMBER RIDGE DR	21600	245C	SWM	77355
TIMBER ROCK CT	3600	527C	SWC	77082
TIMBER ROCK DR	15700	527D	SWC	77082
TIMBER RUN DR	15800	527C	SWC	77082
TIMBERS CT	0	337W	NEC	77346
TIMBERS DR	18600	337W	NEC	77346
TIMBERS EDGE DR	18600	337W	NEC	77346
TIMBERSHADE CT	2200	247P	SWM	77355
TIMBER SHADE DR	4800	297Y	NEH	77345
TIMBER SHADE DR	5100	337C	NEH	77345
TIMBERSHADE CROSSING	14900	247J	SWM	77355
TIMBER SHADOWS DR	2300	336B	NEH	77339
TIMBERSHIRE CT	15000	247J	SWM	77355
TIMBER SHORES LN	0	378A	NEC	77346
TIMBERSIDE CIR	3600	532P	SWH	77025
TIMBERSIDE DR	8500	532T	SWH	77025
W. TIMBERSPIRE CT	1	251Z	WD	77380
E. TIMBERSPIRE CT	1	251Z	WD	77380
TIMBERSPIRE LN	1	251Z	WD	77380
TIMBER SPRING CT	18900	337W	NEC	77346
TIMBER SPRING DR	18700	337W	NEC	77346
TIMBER SQUARE CT	6600	527E	NEF	77407
TIMBER STAND	0	292G	NCC	77373
TIMBERSTONE CT	0	367N	NWC	77095
TIMBER STONE LN	20100	290Y	NWC	77379
TIMBERS TRACE DR	18700	337W	NEC	77346
TIMBERS TRAIL DR	5400	337T	NEC	77346
TIMBER STRAND DR	18300	447P	NWC	77084
TIMBER TECH AVE	11200	329E	NWC	77375
TIMBER TERRACE RD	300	491F	SWH	77024
S. TIMBER TOP DR	1	251Q	WD	77380
N. TIMBER TOP DR	1	251L	WD	77380
TIMBER TRACE DR	18700	337Y	NEC	77346
TIMBER TRAIL	0	292D	SEM	77386
TIMBER TRAIL	0	616V	FR	77546
TIMBER TRAIL	2800	610Z	MC	77545
TIMBER TRAIL CT	600	616V	FR	77546
TIMBER TRAIL WAY	20400	326N	NWC	77433
TIMBER TREE CT	19300	337T	NEC	77346
TIMBERTREE LN	11100	369E	NWC	77070
TIMBER TWIST DR	18600	337W	NEC	77346
TIMBER VALLEY DR	15900	329Q	NWC	77070
TIMBER VIEW	600	616V	FR	77546
TIMBER VIEW CT	0	370E	NWC	77070
TIMBER VIEW DR	8600	338S	NEC	77346
TIMBER VILLAGE DR	3100	331P	NWC	77068
E. TIMBERWAGON CIR	10700	251P	WD	77380
W. TIMBERWAGON CIR	10800	251P	WD	77380
TIMBERWALK LN	0	527J	NEF	77407
TIMBERWAY CT	2200	247P	SWM	77355
TIMBER WAY DR	18600	377C	NEC	77346
TIMBER WAY DR	18900	337Y	NEC	77346
TIMBERWAY LN	7400	528M	SWH	77072
TIMBERWILD	11400	251R	WD	77380
TIMBERWILD DR	0	248U	TB	77375

Street Name	Block	Pg/Sq	Loc	Zips
TIMBERWILDE	100	491E	HC	77024
TIMBERWILDE LN	8000	250W	NWC	77389
TIMBERWIND LN	19800	486G	SWC	77094
TIMBERWOOD DR	3000	613T	NEB	77584
TIMBER WOOD DR	10000	450S	NWH	77080
TIMBER WOOD DR	10400	449V	NWH	77043
TIMBER WOOD CREST DR	0	444S	KT	77493
TIMBERWOOD RUN DR	0	366J	NWC	77433
TIMBERWORK RD	16900	330K	NWC	77379
TIMBO LN	6300	408U	NWC	77041
TIMBUCKTOO DR	0	336Y	NEC	77338
TIMES BLVD	2400	532C	SWH	77005
TIMKIN RD	300	288H	TB	77375
TIMKIN RD	600	289E	TB	77375
TIMMEN	6000	534U	SEH	77087
TIMMINS	0	577E	PA	77504
TIMMONS LN	2600	492S	SWH	77027
TIMMONS LN	3800	492S	SWH	77046
TIMOR LN	700	332E	NWC	77090
TIMOR LN	1000	331H	NWC	77090
TIMPANI DR	0	657A	FR	77546
TIMPANI DR	5200	657B	FR	77546
TIMPNOGOS DR	11900	328C	NWC	77377
TIMPSON	900	493K	SWH	77019
TIMPSON RESERVOIR DR	0	366V	NWC	77433
TIMSBURY DR	4400	447F	NWC	77084
TIMS HARBOR DR	0	296T	SEM	77339
TIMUR WAY	0	572R	SWH	77047
TINA LN	100	413N	NCC	77037
TINA LN	25000	484Q	NEF	77494
TINA OAKS CT	2900	487Z	SWC	77082
TINAS TERRACE DR	0	411D	NWC	77038
TINDAREY CT	0	405S	NWC	77493
TINDAREY FALLS LN	0	405P	NWC	77493
TINDEL	1	620W	CS	77565
TINECHESTER DR	2300	296V	NEH	77339
TINECHESTER DR	2600	297S	NEH	77339
TIN HALL RD	0	367D	NWC	77429
TIN HALL RD	0	367D	NWC	77429
TIN HALL RD	0	368A	NWC	77429
TIN HALL RD	0	368A	NWC	77429
TINKER	15000	408T	NWC	77084
TINKER ROUND	5300	444Y	KT	77493
TINKER WAY	26600	257M	SEM	77357
TINSLEY CT	13900	372A	NWC	77014
TINSLEY TRAILS	0	291N	NWC	77388
TINSMAN	6200	375W	NEC	77396
TINTON CT	23300	485K	NEF	77494
TINWAY CT	0	372D	NCC	77073
TINY LN	0	409Q	JV	77040
TINY HUR DR	4200	538N	PA	77503
TINY TRAIL	1	490P	PP	77024
TINY TREE DR	1100	570X	MC	77489
TINY TURTLE POINT	0	376S	NEC	77396
TIOGA PLACE	0	250J	NWC	77389
TIOGA PLACE	0	249M	NWH	77375
TIOGA PLACE	0	249M	NWH	77375
TIPPCREST DR	15000	497D	NEC	77530
TIPPER CT	2600	371M	NWC	77067
TIPPERARY AVE	1000	656L	FR	77546
TIPPERARY DR	1900	538P	DP	77536
TIPPERARY DR	2100	616K	PL	77581
TIPPERARY LN	6700	535X	SEH	77061
TIPPETT	6600	412X	NWH	77091
TIPPETT	7200	412X	NWH	77088
TIPPS	7300	534D	SEH	77023
TIPPS	7400	535A	SEH	77023
TIPPS CT	1	537Y	PA	77505
TIPSHIRE LN	0	406B	NWC	77433
TIPTON	7300	454M	NEH	77028
TIPTON OAKS DR	0	524P	NWF	77406
TIRRANNA DR	0	253Y	SEM	77386
TIRRELL	700	492M	SWH	77019
TISH CT	9200	410K	NWC	77040
TISHA LN	14500	328B	NWC	77377
TITAN DR	16800	618U	SEH	77058
TITAN SPRINGS DR	0	250U	NWC	77389
TITAN SPRINGS DR	0	250U	NWC	77389
TITE	300	495V	NEH	77029
TITE	8900	495U	NEH	77029
TITLEIST DR	3000	333B	NCC	77373
TITUS POINT	13400	571K	SWH	77085
TIVERTON CT	27700	293H	SEM	77386
TIVERTON FOREST CT	25600	295V	NEH	77365
TIVOLI DR	14400	488E	SWH	77077
TIZERTON CT	7900	330E	NWC	77379
TOAD HOLLOW	0	609Z	MC	77459
TOAST HOLLOW CT	0	372D	NCC	77073
TOAST HOLLOW LN	0	372D	NCC	77073
TOBACCO RD	19100	406Z	NWC	77449
TOBAGO LN	0	333R	NCC	77338
TOBAR FALLS CIR	10800	370W	NWC	77064
TOBARRA LN	0	660G	GCO	77539
TOBASA CT	11000	371S	NWC	77086
TOBE DR	700	498B	CV	77530
TOBINN MANOR DR	13500	367H	NWC	77429
TOBRUK LN	7200	534S	SEH	77033
TOCANTINS DR	19400	295E	SEM	77365
TOCATTA BLVD	8600	410Q	NWC	77040
TODD	300	288H	TB	77375
TODD	600	252K	SEM	77385
TODD	10000	451P	NWH	77055
TODD CT	400	252K	SEM	77386
TODDINGTON RD	5700	337X	NEC	77346
TODVILLE RD	200	620G	SB	77586
TODVILLE RD	3200	580Z	PA	77586
TODWICK LN	3900	527C	SWC	77082
TOGGLE CT	15800	419F	NEC	77532
TOHO CT	14400	374Y	NCC	77032
TOHO DR	5000	374Y	NCC	77032
TOKATEE CT	24600	485E	NEF	77494
TOKENEKE TRAIL	1	490G	PP	77024
TOLAR	4000	414T	NEC	77093
TOLEDO	6300	492B	NWH	77008
TOLEDO CT	0	659S	LC	77573
TOLEDO BEND CT	1300	526X	NEF	77406
TOLEDO BEND DR	4300	526X	NEF	77406
TOLEDO BEND TRAILS LN	0	406D	NWC	77433
TOLIMA DR	3900	578A	PA	77505
TOLIVER	200	494J	SEH	77003
TOLIVER	3000	454J	NEH	77093
E. TOLIVER	4100	454K	NEH	77016
TOLKEN WAY	9400	527U	NEF	77498
TOLLIS	8700	450Z	NWH	77055
TOLMAN	9900	576E	SEH	77034
TOLNAY	3900	533M	SEH	77021
TOLSTA WAY	10700	527W	NEF	77407
TOLSTIN LAKES LN	6300	524E	NEF	77494
TOLUCA DR	1500	659S	LC	77573
TOLUCA COVE CT		325N	NWC	77447
TOM	0	502W	BT	77520
TOMAHAWK TRAIL	8000	415L	NEC	77050

Street Name	Block	Pg/Sq	Loc	Zips
TOMAHAWK TRAIL	16700	246M	SC	77355
TOMASA	15100	527Z	NEF	77498
TOMATO	18600	331A	NWC	77379
TOMBALL CEMETERY RD	22100	287M	NWC	77377
TOMBALL PKWY	11500	411B	NWC	77086
TOMBALL PKWY	14100	371W	NWC	77086
TOMBALL PKWY	14500	370Z	NWC	77086
TOMBALL PKWY	16300	370Z	NWC	77064
TOMBALL PKWY	17900	369C	NWC	77070
TOMBALL PKWY	20200	329J	NWC	77070
TOMBALL PKWY	22600	329J	NWC	77375
TOMBALL PKWY	25000	328D	NWC	77375
TOMBALL PKWY	25800	288Q	NWC	77375
TOMBALL PKWY	31000	248S	SWM	77362
TOMICA CT	0	333K	NCC	77073
TOMINTOUL PATH	17300	527W	NEF	77407
TOMKIN CT	0	610Y	MC	77459
TOMKINS COVE DR	8500	528P	SWC	77083
TOMLIN RD	100	413S	NEH	77037
TOMLINSON TRAIL DR	1800	371R	NWC	77067
TOMMANY MANOR LN	0	290Q	NWC	77379
TOMMY LN	1900	570S	MC	77489
TOMMYE	5300	455K	NEH	77028
TOMMY SALLAS RD	20000	258H	SEM	77327
TOMMY TRACE	1500	296M	SEM	77365
TOMMY TRACE	1600	297J	SEM	77365
TOMPKINS DR	3200	502L	BT	77521
TOMSBROOK DR	2500	371M	NWC	77067
TOM THUMB LN	9300	375R	NEC	77396
TOMWOOD	700	494T	SEH	77023
TONAWANDA DR	4300	531Z	SWH	77035
TONBRIDGE LN	0	446W	NWC	77449
TONEY RD	12800	420T	NEC	77532
TONI AVE	900	536N	SEH	77017
TONKAWA	4200	577F	PA	77504
TONKAWA	7100	462Z	BT	77521
TONKAWA CT	0	444S	KT	77493
TONKAWA DR	1300	538M	DP	77536
TONKAWA TRAIL	0	444S	KT	77493
TONNOCHY CT	13700	528P	SWC	77083
TONNOCHY DR	13300	528Q	SWC	77083
TONSLEY SPRINGS DR	0	406M	NWC	77433
TONTO DR	0	658X	LC	77573
TONYA DR	15300	373W	NEH	77060
TONYDALE LN	20900	291V	NWC	77388
TOOKE	2800	534G	SEH	77023
TOOLEY DR	9100	530W	SWH	77031
TOP	700	493M	NEH	77002
TOPAZ	8900	490X	SWH	77063
TOPAZ OAKS LN	0	524G	NEF	77494
TOPAZ RIDGE	19500	245D	SWM	77355
TOPEKA	13400	497F	NEH	77015
TOP GALLANT CT	9600	409A	NWC	77065
TOPHAM CIR	3000	452P	NWH	77018
TOPHILL DR	21300	291Q	NWC	77388
TOP MARK CT	24700	484D	NEF	77494
TOPPING	3300	414X	NEH	77093
TOPPING	4000	454B	NEH	77093
TOPROCK LN	0	406G	NWC	77433
TOPSAIL WAY	400	379T	NEC	77532
TOPSFIELD POINT DR	0	377C	NEC	77346
TOPSIDE CT	1900	418D	NEC	77532
TOPSIDE ROW	0	251G	WD	77380
TOPWAY DR	4900	333H	NCC	77373
TORANO CIR	0	659H	LC	77573
TORCELLO	0	530X	SWH	77031
TORCHLIGHT DR	5100	531Y	SWH	77035
TORCH LITE TERRACE POINT	0	485U	NEF	77450
W. TORCH PINE CIR	1	250M	WD	77381
E. TORCH PINE CIR	1	250M	WD	77381
W. TORCH PINE CT	1	250H	WD	77381
E. TORCH PINE CT	1	250M	WD	77381
TORCHWOOD DR	0	657L	LC	77598
TOREY YUCCA LN	0	372D	NCC	77073
TORIAN WAY	0	527T	NEF	77469
W. TORINO REALE DR	11600	525J	NEF	77406
E. TORINO REALE DR	11600	525J	NEF	77406
TORNADO	0	452A	NWC	77091
TORONADO RIDGE LN	22400	256W	SEM	77365
TORQUAY LN	7300	530L	SWH	77074
TORRANCE CT	19400	328D	NWC	77377
TORRANCE DR	0	659S	LC	77573
TORRANCE DR	0	659S	LC	77573
TORRANCE ELMS CT	0	406U	NWC	77449
TORREGON LN	17800	376B	NEC	77396
TORRENCE FALLS CT	20900	406T	NWC	77449
TORRENS CT	9000	289D	NWC	77375
TORREON	6100	454N	NEH	77026
TORREY CT	0	659G	LC	77573
TORREY RD	31000	322D	NWC	77484
TORREY BROOK TRAIL		249T	NWC	77375
TORREY CHASE BLVD	14300	371B	NWC	77014
TORREY CHASE BLVD	14500	331W	NWC	77014
S. TORREY CHASE CT	14200	371B	NWC	77014
N. TORREY CHASE CT	14300	371B	NWC	77014
TORREY CREEK LN	4200	371B	NWC	77014
TORREY FOREST DR	13500	371B	NWC	77014
TORREY GLEN DR	0	371B	NWC	77014
TORREY GROVE	0	371B	NWC	77014
TORREY PINE PLACE	8500	289R	NWC	77375
TORREY VILLAGE DR	14000	371A	NWC	77014
TORREY VISTA DR	14100	371B	NWC	77014
TORRICELLI CT	0	525L	NEF	77407
TORRIDON CT	9300	407D	NWC	77095
TORRINGTON CT	16600	330M	NWC	77379
TORRINGTON LN	10100	576N	SEH	77075
TORRISDALE LN	0	289R	NWC	77375
TORRY PINES RD	15000	618F	SEH	77062
TORRY VIEW CIR	8600	407H	NWC	77095
TORRY VIEW TERRACE	16400	407H	NWC	77095
TORRY YUCCA LN	0	372D	NCC	77073
TORTOISE CREEK PLACE	0	250P	NWC	77389
TORTOISE CREEK WAY	0	250Q	NWC	77389
TORTOISE SWAMP	25000	246W	SWM	77355
TORTOSA LN	0	660G	GCO	77539
TORTUGA	0	259E	SEM	77357
TORTUGA	0	288T	NWC	77377
TORTUGA HIRSH	0	288B	TB	77375
TORY HILL LN	2900	568V	SG	77478
TOSCA LN	12800	489G	SWH	77024
TOSCA LN	13000	489F	SWH	77079
TOTEM TRAIL	9900	409C	NWC	77064
TOTHILL CT	1400	457Z	NEC	77530
TOTIS RD	15000	323X	NWC	77447
TOTO DELL WAY	0	328N	NWC	77429
TOTTENHAM DR	12400	570A	SWH	77031
TOUCAN LN	11300	371R	NWC	77067
TOUCHE	900	496D	NEC	77015
TOUCHSTONE	7100	454H	NEH	77028
TOUCHSTONE	7300	455E	NEH	77028
TOUCHSTONE	8600	455E	NEH	77016
TOUHY LAKE DR	0	524G	NEF	77494

Street Name	Block	Pg/Sq	Loc	Zips
TOULON	12500	496D	NEC	77015
TOULOUSE	12500	496D	NEC	77015
TOULOUSE AVE	9900	502C	BT	77521
TOULOUSE LN	0	568J	SG	77498
TOURMALINE CT	16800	367Q	NWC	77095
TOURNAMENT CT	1500	419E	NEC	77532
TOURNAMENT CT	14400	330W	NWC	77069
TOURNAMENT DR	6600	330W	NWC	77069
TOURNAMENT LN	37600	246F	SWM	77355
TOURNAMENT TRAILS DR	0	337Z	NEC	77346
TOURNEY LN	2200	445T	NWC	77493
TOURS DR	7000	530F	SWH	77036
TOUSINAU	9500	576J	SEH	77075
TOWARD LN	0	256U	SEM	77357
TOWER	0	528X	NEF	77498
TOWER	100	498G	CV	77530
TOWER	7900	412N	NWH	77088
TOWER BELL LN	1900	610B	MC	77489
TOWER BLUFF LN	0	367P	NWC	77433
TOWER BRIDGE	10800	576S	SEH	77075
TOWER BRIDGE CT	2900	615L	PL	77581
TOWER BRIDGE RD	2000	615L	PL	77581
TOWER FALLS CT	12000	377E	NEC	77346
TOWER FALLS LN	12000	377E	NEC	77346
TOWERGATE DR	4200	333C	NCC	77373
TOWERGLEN CT	14200	408Y	NWC	77084
E. TOWERGLEN LOOP	5500	408Y	NWC	77084
N. TOWERGLEN LOOP	14300	408Y	NWC	77084
TOWER GROVE CT	1600	570T	MC	77489
N. TOWERGUARD DR	21401	296X	SEM	77339
S. TOWERGUARD DR	21471	296X	SEM	77339
TOWER HILL LN	3500	371F	NWC	77066
TOWERING CYPRESS DR	0	326T	NWC	77429
TOWERING OAK	3000	487Z	SWC	77082
TOWERING OAK CT	4300	578U	SEH	77059
TOWERING OAKS	1000	247E	SWM	77355
TOWERING OAKS DR	30500	286C	SWM	77355
TOWERING OAKS TRAIL	16300	286C	SWM	77355
TOWERING PINE DR	28500	246E	SWM	77355
TOWERING PINES DR	1	251A	WD	77381
TOWERMONT LN	4700	291S	NWC	77388
TOWER OAKS BLVD	10600	369S	NWC	77070
TOWER OAKS BLVD	11000	369S	NWC	77065
TOWER POINT DR	13900	528X	NEF	77498
TOWER RIDGE	0	657B	SEC	77546
TOWER RIVER CT	1900	618B	SEH	77062
TOWER SIDE LN	25600	524F	NEF	77494
TOWERSTONE CT	9100	329R	NWC	77379
TOWERSTONE DR	9200	329R	NWC	77379
TOWERVIEW LN	7100	571W	SWH	77489
TOWERVIEW LN	7200	570Z	SWH	77489
TOWN CIR	1300	501V	BT	77520
TOWN ST	0	331W	NWC	77068
TOWN & COUNTRY	1500	659K	LC	77573
TOWN & COUNTRY BLVD	700	489D	SWH	77024
TOWN & COUNTRY LN	800	489D	SWH	77024
TOWN & COUNTRY VLLG	1	489H	SWH	77024
TOWN & COUNTRY WAY	10400	489D	SWH	77024
TOWN BLUFF DR	0	366P	NWC	77433
TOWNBORO DR	800	618J	SEH	77062
N. TOWN CENTER BLVD	2500	568X	SG	77479
W. TOWN CENTER CIR	2800	337B	NEH	77339
E. TOWN CENTER CIR	2800	337B	NEH	77339
TOWN CENTER DR	2301	568Y	SG	77478
TOWN CENTER PLACE	4300	337B	NEH	77339
TOWN CREEK DR	8100	408E	NWC	77095
TOWNE BRIDGE DR	17600	328L	NWC	77377
TOWNE BROOK LN	9900	528T	NEF	77498
TOWNE LAKE DR	0	615Y	PL	77581
TOWNE LAKE PKWY		367S	NWC	77433
TOWNE LAKE PARKWAY	0	407A	NWC	77433
TOWNE LAKE PKWY		366R	NWC	77433
TOWN ELM CT	11100	368U	NWC	77065
TOWNEMIST CT	14000	528S	NEF	77498
TOWNEMIST DR	10000	528S	NEF	77498
TOWNE OAK LN	10300	528X	NEF	77498
TOWNES RD	16200	617W	FR	77546
TOWNES RD	16600	657B	FR	77546
TOWNES FOREST RD	3600	657A	FR	77546
TOWNE TERRACE DR	9200	330N	NWC	77379
TOWNE TOWER LN	9900	528T	NEF	77498
TOWNEVIEW DR	10200	528X	NEF	77498
TOWNE VUE CT	20700	335J	NCC	77338
TOWNEWAY DR	13700	528X	NEF	77498
TOWNEWEST BLVD	13700	528X	NEF	77498
TOWN GATE CT	2800	609G	MC	77459
TOWN GLADE DR	16700	367B	CY	77429
TOWN GREEN DR	15300	527Q	NEF	77083
TOWN GROVE CT	2700	298W	NEH	77345
TOWNHALL CT	22500	445Q	NWC	77449
TOWNHALL LN	2100	445U	NWC	77449
TOWNHALL LN	10400	528X	NEF	77498
TOWN HILL DR	2000	618G	SEH	77062
TOWNHOME LN	1600	569Y	MC	77489
TOWNHOUSE CT	1	531C	BL	77401
TOWNHOUSE LN	1300	537P	PA	77502
TOWNHURST DR	1600	449V	NWH	77043
TOWN LAKE CT	16500	578Z	PA	77059
TOWNLEY DR	800	497D	NEC	77530
TOWN MOOR CT	1300	329H	NWC	77379
TOWN OAKS DR	2200	618G	SEH	77062
TOWN OAKS PLACE	1	531H	BL	77401
TOWN PARK BLVD	5200	444Q	KT	77493
TOWN PARK DR	8700	530A	SWH	77036
TOWN PARK DR	9500	529D	SWH	77036
TOWNPLACE	1000	491J	SWH	77057
TOWN PLACE DR	16700	367B	NWC	77429
TOWN PLAZA DR	4300	572E	SWH	77045
TOWN RIDGE LN	0	617V	SEH	77598
TOWN RIDGE LN	0	618S	SEH	77598
W. TOWNSEN BLVD	0	335Q	HM	77338
E. TOWNSEN BLVD	0	335Q	HM	77338
E. TOWNSEN BLVD	0	336N	NEC	77338
TOWNSEN RD	0	294F	SEM	77386
TOWNSEN RD	0	294Q	SEM	77386
TOWNSEN RD	0	294Q	SEM	77386
TOWNSEND CT	14600	368A	NWC	77429
TOWNSEND MILL CT	100	487A	SWC	77094
TOWNSGATE CIR	6200	526A	NEF	77450
TOWNSGATE CT	20800	526A	NEF	77450
TOWNSHIP DR	0	335Y	HM	77338
TOWNSHIP DR	0	659E	LC	77573
TOWNSHIP LN	0	609L	MC	77459
TOWNSHIP DALE CT	11600	411H	NWC	77088
TOWNSHIP ELM ST	0	293X	NCC	77373
TOWNSHIP GLEN CT	20500	326N	NWC	77433
TOWNSHIP GLEN LN	15500	326S	NWC	77433
TOWNSHIP GROVE LN	0	488Z	SWH	77082
TOWNSHIP MEADOWS CT	16700	407M	NWC	77095
TOWNSHIRE DR	14100	488J	SWH	77077
TOWNSON RD	5800	374M	NEH	77396
TOWNSON RD	6000	375J	NEH	77396

Street Name	Block	Pg/Sq	Loc	Zips
TOWN SQUARE RD	10400	528X	NEF	77498
TOWN SQUARE PLACE	2100	568X	SG	77479
TOWNSVILLE CIR	4000	609L	MC	77459
TOWNWOOD DR	12900	572K	SWH	77045
TOYAH AVE	2400	414A	NCC	77039
TRABAJO DR	7400	527K	NEF	77083
TRACE	0	620N	SB	77586
TRACE CT	3600	376G	NEC	77396
TRACE DR	1200	488L	SWH	77077
TRACE LN	17200	527N	NEF	77083
TRACEBROOK CT	0	525M	NEF	77407
W. TRACE CREEK DR	1	250M	WD	77381
S. TRACE CREEK DR	1	250M	WD	77381
E. TRACE CREEK DR	1	250M	WD	77381
N. TRACE CREEK DR	100	250M	WD	77381
TRACE FOREST DR	18100	330E	NWC	77379
TRACE GLEN LN	17200	527N	NEF	77083
TRACELAWN CT	9200	375V	NEC	77396
TRACELYNN LN	12400	371J	NWC	77066
TRACEMEADOW DR	4300	371J	NWC	77066
TRACE MILL CT	4300	371K	NWC	77066
TRACETON CIR	14400	368B	NWC	77429
TRACE VISTA CIR	28800	298N	NEC	77336
TRACEWOOD LN	12600	371E	NWC	77066
S. TRACEWOOD BEND	13500	488K	SWH	77077
N. TRACEWOOD BEND	13500	488K	SWH	77077
TRACEWOOD CANYON LN		249V	NWC	77375
TRACEWOOD COVE	1300	488K	SWH	77077
TRACEWOOD GLEN	1300	488K	SWH	77077
TRACEWOOD HILLS LN	0	377U	NEC	77044
TRACEWOOD PARK DR	900	488K	SWH	77077
TRACI LN	100	498F	CV	77530
TRACY LN	2500	460U	NEC	77562
TRACY RIDGE CT	0	293K	SEM	77386
TRACY RIDGE CT	0	293G	SEM	77386
TRACY WAY	0	538R	DP	77536
TRADE CENTER DR	0	334V	NEH	77338
TRADE MARKET DR	0	335W	NEH	77338
TRADEMARK PLACE	700	488A	SWH	77079
TRADERS VILLAGE DR	0	408L	NWC	77041
TRADEWINDS DR	2000	609B	MC	77459
TRADE WINDS DR	10100	371X	NWC	77086
TRADINGHOUSE CREEK LN	0	660N	LC	77573
TRADING POST DR	10200	409C	NWC	77064
TRADITIONAL DR	0	444D	NWC	77493
W. TRADITIONS BLVD	3800	527C	SWC	77082
E. TRADITIONS BLVD	3900	527C	SWC	77082
W. TRADITIONS CT	3700	527C	SWC	77082
E. TRADITIONS CT	3700	527C	SWC	77082
W. TRADITIONS COMMON	0	527C	SWC	77082
E. TRADITIONS COMMON	0	527C	SWC	77082
S. TRAFALGAR CT	6000	407W	NWC	77449
N. TRAFALGAR CT	6100	407W	NWC	77449
TRAFALGAR DR	4100	572N	SWH	77045
TRAFALGAR DR	5600	571Q	SWH	77085
TRAFALGAR LN	0	528K	SWC	77083
TRAFALGAR SQUARE	0	408S	NWC	77084
TRAIL CIR	4000	376H	NEC	77346
TRAIL BEND LN	200	616Z	FR	77546
TRAIL BEND LN	18500	447J	NWC	77084
TRAIL BLAZER DR	7700	410L	NWC	77040
TRAILBLAZER E. LN	0	612Z	NWB	77578
TRAILBLAZER LN	2700	612Z	NWB	77578
TRAILBLAZER LN	10200	409C	NWC	77064
TRAIL BLUFF LN	0	293F	SEM	77386
TRAIL BROOK CT	0	658S	LC	77573
TRAILBROOK DR	14700	408G	NWC	77095
TRAILCLIFF CT	0	484Z	NEF	77494
TRAIL CREEK DR	5100	536S	SEH	77017
TRAILCREST	13700	414A	NCC	77039
TRAIL CYPRESS BLVD	0	329N	NWC	77377
TRAILER CT	0	660Z	TC	77539
TRAILER PARK	0	459H	NEC	77562
TRAIL FOREST CT	1600	336E	NEH	77339
TRAIL GLEN DR	6400	457N	NEC	77049
TRAIL HAVEN	0	298J	NEC	77336
TRAIL HEAD	400	616Z	FR	77546
TRAIL HOLLOW	0	609Z	MC	77459
TRAIL HOLLOW DR	0	489L	SWH	77042
TRAIL HOLLOW DR	0	612P	PL	77584
TRAIL HOLLOW DR	12600	489C	SWH	77024
TRAIL HOLLOW DR	12900	489C	SWH	77079
TRAILING CLOVER CT	0	446D	NWC	77084
TRAILING MOSS CT	9700	409D	NWC	77064
TRAILING MOSS DR	9500	409D	NWC	77064
TRAILING OAK LN	0	609G	MC	77459
TRAILING OAKS DR	0	290N	NWC	77379
TRAILING VINE RD	2000	333A	NCC	77373
TRAIL LAKE DR	2800	572J	SWH	77045
TRAIL LAKE DR	4500	571M	SWH	77045
TRAIL LODGE DR	2800	337A	NEH	77339
TRAIL MANOR DR	0	612T	PL	77584
TRAILMEADOW CT	13500	328P	NWC	77429
TRAILMOBILE DR	3400	455Z	NEH	77013
TRAILMONT DR	11600	489S	SWH	77077
TRAILMONT DR	13400	369E	NWC	77070
TRAIL MOUNTAIN CT	0	377E	NEC	77346
TRAIL OAKS CT	1600	336E	NEH	77339
TRAIL POINT DR	0	329J	NWC	77377
TRAILRIDGE CT	2700	609G	MC	77459
TRAIL RIDGE CT	10400	369X	NWC	77064
TRAIL RIDGE DR	0	612Q	PL	77584
TRAIL RIDGE DR	10500	369X	NWC	77064
TRAIL RIDGE DR	10800	409B	NWC	77064
TRAILRIDGE FOREST DR	8800	411L	NWC	77088
TRAIL RIVER DR	2300	337D	NEH	77345
TRAILS CT	400	490H	HC	77024
TRAIL SCENIC SHORE	0	337D	NEH	77345
TRAILS END	400	490H	HC	77024
TRAILS END RD	18800	253A	SEM	77385
TRAIL SIDE DR	8000	410L	NWC	77040
TRAILSIDE DR	15100	408N	NWC	77095
TRAILS PARK LN	31600	252M	SEM	77385
TRAIL SPRINGS CT	1600	336E	NEH	77339
TRAILSTONE CT	24800	485N	NEF	77494
TRAILSTONE LN	3800	485X	NEF	77494
TRAILS WEST DR	20100	406T	NWC	77449
TRAIL TIMBERS DR	5400	337W	NEC	77346
TRAIL TREE LN	21900	336E	NEH	77339
TRAIL VALLEY WAY	6500	371W	NWC	77086
TRAIL VIEW	1800	657N	FR	77546
TRAILVIEW DR	5600	457S	NEC	77049
TRAIL VIEW WAY	400	616V	FR	77546
TRAILVILLE DR	13700	488F	SWH	77077
TRAILVILLE DR	15700	488F	SWH	77079
TRAIL WATER CT	2000	336B	NEH	77339
TRAILWAY LN	6300	330G	NWC	77379
TRAIL WEST	2200	568Y	SG	77478
TRAILWIND CT	5600	456V	NEC	77049
TRAILWOOD CT	0	613X	NEB	77578
TRAILWOOD DR	0	613X	NEB	77578
TRAILWOOD DR	3600	502K	BT	77521

Street Name	Block	Pg/Sq	Loc	Zips
TRAILWOOD DR	3600	534K	SEH	77023
TRAILWOOD ESTATES DR	0	248G	SWM	77354
TRAILWOOD ESTATES DR	0	248G	SWM	77354
TRAILWOOD LANE RD	22400	290J	NWC	77375
TRAILWOOD MANOR LN	21800	445M	NWC	77449
TRAILWOOD VILLAGE DR	900	336C	NEH	77339
TRAIN CT	10800	449C	NWC	77041
TRALEE	0	616J	PL	77581
TRALLE	1400	494F	NEH	77020
TRAMMEL DR	0	291N	NWC	77388
TRAMMEL FRESNO RD	300	611W	NEF	77545
TRAMMEL FRESNO RD	4400	610X	MC	77459
TRAMONTE TRAIL LN	0	484Q	NEF	77494
TRAMONTO DR	0	489P	SWH	77042
TRAMORE DR	14900	527R	NEF	77083
TRAMWOOD DR	600	570Y	MC	77489
TRANCAS CT		366U	NWC	77433
TRANQUIL FOREST	0	447G	NWC	77084
TRANQUIL GLADE PLACE	1	250C	WD	77381
TRANQUILITY DR	18400	337Z	NEC	77346
TRANQUILITY LN	1900	659S	LC	77573
TRANQUILITY LAKES BLVD	2700	614N	PL	77584
TRANQUILITY PARK DR	0	327U	NWC	77429
TRANQUILITY RIDGE DR	10700	376T	NEC	77396
TRANQUILITY TRAIL	0	615N	PL	77584
TRANQUIL OAKS CT	2600	297U	NEH	77345
TRANQUIL PARK CT	15900	330W	NWC	77379
TRANQUIL PARK DR	8500	330T	NWC	77379
S. TRANQUIL PATH DR	1	291C	WD	77380
N. TRANQUIL PATH DR	100	251Y	WD	77380
N. TRANQUIL PATH DR	200	291C	WD	77380
TRANQUIL RIVER DR	7400	578F	PA	77505
TRANQUIL SHORES DR	0	525R	NEF	77407
TRANQUIL SPRINGS LN	0	525B	NEF	77494
TRANQUIL VIEW	0	447E	NWC	77084
TRANSCENTRAL CT	1700	373L	NCC	77032
TRAPPER LN	11300	369N	NWC	77065
TRAPPER HILL DR	1000	488F	SWH	77077
TRAPPERS FOREST DR	3700	411V	NWH	77088
TRAVAGO TRAIL	0	445F	NWC	77493
TRAVELAIR	8200	575E	SEH	77061
TRAVELERS REST	0	412E	NWC	77038
TRAVELERS WAY CIR	9700	409A	NWC	77065
W. TRAVELERS WAY CIR	11200	409A	NWC	77065
E. TRAVELERS WAY CIR	11200	409A	NWC	77065
TRAVELERS WAY LN	9700	409A	NWC	77065
TRAVELLERS DR	2800	658S	LC	77573
TRAVERTINE POINT	0	526X	NEF	77469
TRAVERTINE POINT	0	526X	NEF	77469
TRAVIATA DR	12800	489G	SWH	77024
TRAVICK LN	2900	333P	NCC	77073
TRAVIS	0	500U	BT	77520
TRAVIS	0	539R	LP	77571
TRAVIS	1	493Q	DT	77002
TRAVIS	100	499K	NEC	77520
TRAVIS	100	541B	BT	77520
TRAVIS	100	618X	WB	77598
S. TRAVIS	400	538Y	DP	77536
N. TRAVIS	400	538Y	DP	77536
TRAVIS	700	536U	PA	77502
TRAVIS	2300	493Q	SWH	77006
TRAVIS	3400	493W	SWH	77002
TRAVIS	6500	532H	SWH	77030
TRAVIS LN	0	463H	MB	77520
TRAVIS LN	300	247F	SWM	77362
TRAVIS BLUFF CT	0	660K	LC	77573
TRAVIS BROOK DR	0	524K	NWF	77406
TRAVIS COURT PLACE	1200	332Z	NCC	77073
TRAVIS CREEK WAY	3100	611W	FS	77545
TRAVIS CREEK WAY	3100	611S	FS	77545
TRAVISFALLS DR	0	328A	NWC	77429
TRAVIS HEIGHTS LN	0	578T	SEH	77059
TRAVIS HOUSE LN	24300	445S	NWC	77493
TRAVIS LAKE CT	3800	615Y	PL	77581
TRAVIS MILL CT	0	484X	NEF	77494
TRAVIS MILL CT	0	484X	NEF	77494
TRAVIS PARK DR	1	609J	SG	77479
TRAVIS POINT LN	15200	408S	NWC	77084
TRAVIS TRAIL	0	525E	NEF	77494
TRAWEEK	1000	490C	SV	77055
TREADSLOW LN	2200	371M	NWC	77067
TREADWAY	9000	453F	NEH	77022
TREADWELL CT	1	250D	WD	77381
TREAL RUN MEADOWS DR	3900	611X	FS	77545
TREASCHWIG RD	3100	333G	NCC	77338
TREASCHWIG RD	4300	334B	NCC	77373
TREASCHWIG RD	6700	294X	NCC	77373
TREASURE DR	100	413X	NEH	77076
TREASURE LN	100	335H	NEH	77339
TREASURE LN	4500	613Z	NEB	77584
TREASURE COVE DR	1	251K	WD	77381
TREASURE MOUNTAIN DR	0	292W	NWC	77388
TREASURE OAKS CT	20100	486L	SWC	77450
TREASURE OAKS DR	1600	486L	SWC	77450
TREASURES RIDGE DR	0	296X	SEM	77339
TREASURE TRAIL	4400	609E	SG	77479
TREATY OAKS	15100	571U	SWH	77053
TREBEAU CT	12400	569H	SWH	77031
TREBECK LN	6600	330M	NWC	77379
TREBLE DR	300	336W	HM	77338
TREBOR	2700	538W	PA	77503
TREBOR	6300	578A	PA	77505
TREBORWAY DR	14600	331X	NWC	77014
TRECASTLE DR	14900	457Z	NEC	77530
TRECASTLE DR	15300	458W	NEC	77530
TRECCIA CT	0	445F	NWC	77493
TREE	0	255P	SEM	77365
TREE LN	2100	296Y	NEH	77339
TREE LN	3000	297W	NEH	77339
TREE ARBOR LN	0	328S	NWC	77429
TREEBANK LN	13600	369E	NWC	77070
TREE BARK LN	300	659N	LC	77573
TREEBARK LN	5000	452E	NWH	77018
TREE BRANCH DR	9300	369R	NWC	77064
TREE BRIDGE	9400	575Z	SEH	77075
TREE BRIGHT LN	23000	334A	NCC	77373
TREECREEPER LN	0	367P	NWC	77433
TREE CREST CIR	1	250H	WD	77381
TREEFORK LN	18200	487A	SWC	77094
TREE FROG DR	1	530U	SWH	77074
TREE HOLLOW N. CIR	0	579B	LP	77571
TREEHOPPER LN	0	297A	SEM	77357
TREE HOUSE CIR	3100	333B	NCC	77373
TREE HOUSE CT	3000	333B	NCC	77373
TREE HOUSE LN	22300	333B	NCC	77373
TREE HOUSE LN	22500	293X	NCC	77373
TREE LARK LN	18600	407N	NWC	77449
TREE LINE DR	4300	578G	PA	77505
TREELINE DR	6800	377C	NEC	77346
TREE LINE DR	16700	328Q	NWC	77429
TREELOCH LN	17600	331J	NWC	77379
TREE MANOR LN	3700	297U	NEH	77345
TREE MEADOW	34700	247J	SWM	77362
TREE MEADOW LN	34700	247F	SWM	77362
TREEMILL CT	19100	446M	NWC	77449
TREE MIST CT	0	376H	NEC	77346
TREE MONKEY RD	19800	255F	SEM	77365
TREE MONKEY RD	20700	256E	SEM	77357
TREEMONT CT	0	526T	NEF	77407
TREEMONT FAIR CT	0	526T	NEF	77407
TREEMONT FAIR DR	0	526P	NEF	77407
TREEMONT LANDING	0	447F	NWC	77084
TREE MOSS CT	18200	376D	NEC	77346
TREE MOSS PLACE	4000	376H	NEC	77346
TREE OAKS CT	5600	337T	NEC	77346
TREE ORCHARD DR	19400	446M	NWC	77449
TREE PATH LN	5100	456S	NEH	77013
TREE PINE CT	0	337T	NEC	77346
TREERIDGE PLACE	10400	251L	WD	77380
TREESCAPE CIR	1	251A	WD	77381
TREESDALE CT	2700	485R	NEF	77450
TREESDALE LN	22000	485R	NEF	77450
TREESEY WAY	12800	371F	NWC	77066
TREE SHALLOW BLUFF PATH	0	291H	NWC	77389
TREE SPARROW LN	9500	527Q	NEF	77083
TREETOAD DR	19100	446M	NWC	77449
TREE TOP DR	4200	578F	PA	77505
TREETOP LN	20200	291Y	NWC	77388
TREETOP HILLS LN	0	328M	NWC	77377
TREE TRAIL CT	19300	337T	NEC	77346
TREE TRUNK DR	200	332B	NWC	77388
TREEWATER DR	7000	528M	SWH	77072
TREEWOOD DR	5200	337N	NEC	77346
TREGARNON DR	13000	457W	NEC	77015
TREICHEL RD	12600	408R	NWC	77041
TREICHEL RD	14900	288J	NWC	77377
TREICHEL RD	15400	287M	NWC	77377
TRELAWNEY DR	3400	615B	PL	77581
TRELLIS LN	20700	333P	NCC	77073
TRELLIS ESTATES CT	18000	367A	CY	77429
TREMBLING CREEK CIR	3100	333B	NCC	77373
TREMBLING FOREST LN	4600	451G	NWH	77092
TREMENDO DR	7400	527K	NEF	77083
TREMENTINA DR	0	411M	NWH	77088
TREMONT	7300	455K	NEH	77028
TREMONT BROOK WAY	0	611V	FS	77545
TREMONT GLEN LN	4700	484Y	NEF	77494
TREMONT PARK LN	0	253N	SEM	77386
TREMONT RIDGE LN	0	253T	SEM	77386
TREMONT RIVER LN	0	377F	NEC	77346
TREMONT SPRING LN	0	615H	PL	77089
TREMONT TRAIL LN	2200	486N	SWC	77450
TREMONT WOODS CT	1	251E	WD	77381
TREMOUT HOLLOW LN	0	417B	NEC	77044
TREMPER	5100	494G	NEH	77020
TREMPER	7100	495E	NEH	77020
TRENCH LN	4100	293H	SEM	77386
TRENDALE	5600	534R	SEH	77087
TRENDWEST DR	1700	446Y	NWC	77084
TRENT CT	0	657Y	LC	77573
TRENT RD	3100	578B	PA	77505
TRENT RD	3200	298M	NEC	77336
TRENT RD	3400	299J	NEC	77336
TRENT COVE LN	0	615W	PL	77584
TRENTHAM PLACE	1	493G	NEH	77009
TRENTINO DR	0	445B	NWC	77493
TRENTO CT	0	445F	NWC	77493
TRENT OAKS LN	0	415C	NEC	77396
TRENTON LN	1200	502W	BT	77520
TRENTON RD	2100	414S	NCC	77093
TRENTON RD	2400	414U	NEC	77093
TRENTON ARBOR LN	0	297F	SEM	77365
TRENTON CREEK LN	0	327Z	NWC	77429
TRENTON LAKE LN	6500	408V	NWC	77041
TRENTON MANOR DR	0	578S	SEH	77059
TRENTON REACH DR	0	524E	NEF	77494
TRENTON VALLEY LN	0	446J	NWC	77449
TRENT PARK CT	0	406X	NWC	77449
TRENT SHORES LN	0	611S	FS	77545
TRENT STONE LN	0	445M	NWC	77449
TRENTWAY	7800	450D	NWH	77040
TRENTWOOD DR	8600	527R	NEF	77083
TRENWOOD LN	1	453F	NEH	77022
TRESCH CT	400	617R	SEH	77598
TRESCH LN	15100	617R	SEH	77598
TRESCON DR	5900	574U	SEH	77048
TRESCOTT LN	0	568W	SG	77479
TRESHIRE LN	20700	291S	NWC	77388
TRESLAGOS DR	0	291E	NWC	77389
TRES LAGUNAS	6200	528E	SWC	77083
TRES SABORES LN	0	446E	NWC	77449
TRESTLE TREE CT	0	251Z	WD	77380
TRESVANT DR	400	617R	SEH	77598
TRETOWER RD	0	486L	SWC	77450
TREVI	0	407V	NWC	77084
TREVINO CT	2800	656T	FR	77546
TREVINO TRAILS	19100	337Z	NEC	77346
TREVISO GARDENS DR	0	445J	NWC	77493
TREVISO TERRACE LN	0	447A	NWC	77449
TREVLIG TRAIL	0	373A	NCC	77073
TREVOR HILL DR	3800	371K	NWC	77066
TREVORS TRACE LN	0	524D	NEF	77494
TREVOR WAY	0	332L	NCC	77073
TREY LN	4000	447H	NWC	77084
TREYBURN TRAIL	1800	485L	NEF	77450
TREY ROCK WAY	16300	326P	NWC	77433
TRIANA MEADOW	0	616H	SEC	77089
TRIANA RIVER CT	0	484N	NEF	77494
TRIANA VALLEY CT	0	407S	NWC	77449
TRIANGLE RIDGE	0	296Q	SEM	77365
TRIANON	500	491H	SWH	77024
TRIBANO CT	0	445A	NWC	77493
TRIBE DR	13900	328P	NWC	77429
TRIBECA LN	24500	445S	NWC	77493
TRIBUNE ST	0	258E	SEM	77357
TRICA CT	8200	410K	NWC	77040
TRICHELLE	400	536F	PA	77506
TRI CITY-BEACH RD	0	543X	CCO	77520
TRI CITY-BEACH RD	300	541D	BT	77520
TRI CITY-BEACH RD	3300	542P	BT	77520
TRICKEY RD	11300	372J	NWC	77067
TRICKLING SPRINGS CT	800	292U	NCC	77373
TRIDENS CT	11000	371T	NWC	77086
TRIDENT WAY	0	611T	FS	77545
TRIGATE DR	6600	571W	SWH	77489
TRIGG	4400	454B	NEH	77093
TRILBY WAY	21500	333G	NCC	77338
TRIMBLE	200	453Y	NEH	77009
TRIMM AVE	700	536V	PA	77502
TRIMSTONE DR	6500	578E	PA	77505
TRINIDAD	1400	494S	SEH	77003
TRINITY	200	493K	SWH	77007
TRINITY	500	258A	SEM	77357
TRINITY	600	537K	PA	77506
TRINITY	1800	659F	LC	77573
TRINITY	3200	463G	MB	77520
TRINITY DR	2700	614R	PL	77584
TRINITY DR	12700	569K	SF	77477
TRINITY BAY	0	612L	PL	77584
TRINITY BAY DR	0	612F	PL	77545
TRINITY BEND DR	0	450V	NWH	77080
TRINITY BLUFF LN	0	367P	NWC	77433
TRINITY CREEK CT		484V	NEF	77494
TRINITY CREEK CT		484V	NEF	77494
TRINITY GATE LN	0	377K	NEC	77346
TRINITY GLEN LN	2700	573X	SEC	77047
TRINITY HILLS LN	0	375Y	NEC	77396
TRINITY ISLE CT	5900	338A	NEH	77345
TRINITY JOE LN	0	376G	NEC	77396
TRINITY KNOLL WAY	18200	377C	NEC	77346
TRINITY MEADOW DR	0	570U	MC	77489
TRINITY MEADOW LN	17600	526M	NEF	77407
TRINITY MIST LN	0	373A	NCC	77073
TRINITY OAKS	0	609Z	NEF	77459
S. TRINITY OAKS CIR	1	250B	WD	77381
TRINITY OAKS CIR	1	250B	WD	77381
TRINITY OAKS CT	100	250B	WD	77381
TRINITY PARK CT	0	538R	DP	77536
TRINITY PARK LN	0	253N	SEM	77386
TRINITY PASS CT	3000	293U	NCC	77373
TRINITY RIVER CT	4600	253U	SEM	77386
TRINITY RIVER DR	0	366J	NWC	77433
TRINITY RIVER DR	28801	253U	SEM	77386
TRINITY ROSE CT	0	526P	NEF	77407
TRINITY SPRINGS DR	10400	366V	NWC	77433
TRINITY STAR DR	0	366P	NWC	77433
TRINITY STATION	1800	568Y	SG	77478
TRINITY TRAIL	26800	366H	NWC	77433
TRINITY TRAIL CT	0	407A	NWC	77449
N. TRINITY WAY	20400	256N	SEM	77357
S. TRINITY WAY	20700	256N	SEM	77357
TRINITY WAY DR	0	367S	NWC	77433
TRINKET DR	30700	252U	SEM	77386
TRI OAKS LN	1000	489B	NWH	77043
W. TRI OAKS LN	1100	489B	NWH	77043
TRIOLA LN	6700	530M	SWH	77074
TRIOLA LN	8000	530J	SWH	77036
TRIOLA LN	10700	529K	SWH	77072
TRIPLE CREEK LN		367S	NWC	77433
TRIPLE CROWN DR	7900	570F	SWH	77071
TRIPLE MAST CIR	1900	619Z	LC	77573
TRIPLE OAK CT	1900	489N	SWH	77077
TRIPLE SPUR LN	23200	292G	NCC	77373
TRIPLETT	3200	660H	GCO	77518
TRIPOLI DR	3800	578A	PA	77505
TRIPP LN	10500	527W	NEF	77407
TRIPPELL	10400	413Z	NEH	77093
TRIPPODO	2600	659V	GCO	77539
TRISTAN	3700	533L	SEH	77021
TRISTAN BAY CT	0	293F	SEM	77386
TRISTAN BAY CT	0	293F	SEM	77386
TRISTANDALE LN	0	330B	NWC	77379
TRISTAN MILL LN	0	446G	NWC	77449
TRISTAR DR	100	617B	SEH	77598
TRISTON HILL CT	0	406F	NWC	77433
TRITON CT	20300	486B	SWC	77450
TRIWAY LN	1700	449V	NWH	77043
TRIWAY LN	2200	449R	NWH	77043
TRIWAY LN	5400	450A	NWH	77041
TRIXIE LN	1900	489Q	SWH	77042
TRIZZA CT	0	445F	NWC	77493
TROCADERO LN	0	660G	GCO	77539
TROGON LN	7200	528L	SWH	77083
TROMPILLA LN	13200	528G	SWH	77083
TRONEWOOD	4300	454C	NEH	77093
TRONEWOOD	4500	454C	NEH	77016
TROON	2100	492Q	SWH	77019
TROON CIR	4600	578E	PA	77505
TROON DR	2200	659C	LC	77573
TROON OAK ST	18600	326V	NWC	77429
TROOST	5400	454U	NEH	77026
TROPHY LN	0	525A	NEF	77494
TROPHY CLUB RD	14500	408K	NWC	77095
TROPHY DEER CT	17700	447G	NWC	77084
TROPHY PLACE DR	7600	377D	NEC	77346
TROPHY RIDGE DR	0	293G	SEM	77386
TROPICAL WAY	6000	534V	SEH	77087
TROPICANA CT	700	656C	FR	77546
TROPICANA DR	13100	448D	NWC	77041
TROPPER HILL CT	0	293R	SEM	77386
TROPPER HILL LN	0	293R	SEM	77386
TROTTER DR	2200	445P	NWC	77493
TROTWOOD LN	3100	485S	NEF	77494
TROULON DR	7100	530K	SWH	77074
TROULON DR	8700	530N	SWH	77036
TROULON DR	11900	529N	SWH	77072
TROUT	2500	454A	NEH	77093
TROUT CT	0	614G	PL	77581
TROWBRIDGE CT	15000	618J	SEH	77062
TROWBRIDGE DR	1000	618J	SEH	77062
TROY	24700	249W	NWC	77375
TROY DR	2700	610Q	MC	77459
W. TROY RD	100	452D	NWH	77076
TROY RD	100	413W	NEH	77076
W. TROY RD	300	452D	NWH	77091
TROYAN DR	1	569B	MD	77477
TRUCKEE DR	3400	488Y	SWH	77082
TRUDEAU DR	11300	368P	NWC	77065
TRUDEAU LN	0	568J	SG	77498
TRUDY	7300	455A	NEH	77016
TRUE LN	4800	454L	NEH	77016
TRUE BLUE	0	242R	WCO	77484
TRUESDALE DR	3100	610U	MC	77459
TRUESDELL DR	12400	570E	SWH	77071
TRUETT	5500	534C	SEH	77023
TRULL BROOK LN	24600	250X	NWC	77389
TRULLEY	3000	493V	SEH	77004
TRUMAN	300	452M	NWH	77018
TRUMBALL MANOR	0	376R	NEC	77346
TRUMBULL	6300	453R	NEH	77022
TRUMBULL RIDGE DR	0	406G	NWC	77433
THUMBULL RIDGE LN	0	406G	NWC	77433
TRUMMEL CT	1	251A	WD	77381
TRUMPET	9500	455D	NEH	77078
TRUMPET	9900	415Z	NEH	77078
TRUMPETVINE	13800	528P	SWC	77083
TRUMPET VINE LN	15000	326X	NWC	77433
TRUNNIONS WAY	900	379T	NEC	77532
TRURO	6000	492G	SWH	77007
TRUSCON DR	9500	450P	NWH	77080
TRUSLOW POINT LN	15300	568Y	SG	77478
TRUSS CT	15900	419F	NEC	77532
TRUXILLO	900	493X	SWH	77002
TRUXILLO	1000	493Y	SEH	77004
TRUXTON	16400	374M	NEH	77396
TRUXTON DR	3400	537R	PA	77503
TRYON DR	10700	368T	NWC	77065
TUAM	1	493T	SWH	77006
TUAM	900	493T	SWH	77002
TUAM	1100	493Z	SEH	77004
TUAM	3800	494W	SEH	77004
TUBA CITY DR	0	658Y	LC	77573
TUBBLE CT	0	375V	NEC	77396
TUCK	6900	494H	NEH	77020
TUCK	7100	495J	NEH	77020
TUCKAHOE LN	25000	293S	NCC	77373
TUCKAHOE LN	25300	292R	NCC	77373
TUCKER	5200	484C	KT	77494
TUCKER	5600	534R	SEH	77087
TUCKER RD	1500	502N	BT	77521
TUCKER RD	3100	660E	LC	77573
TUCKER CREEK DR	2500	611S	NEF	77545
TUCKER CYPRESS DR	9700	407B	NWC	77095
TUCKER HOUSE LN	24300	445S	NWC	77493
TUCKERTON RD	0	366Z	NWC	77433
TUCKERTON RD	0	367W	NWC	77095
TUCKERTON RD	0	408A	NWC	77095
TUCSON BEND DR	0	327H	NWC	77429
TUCUMCARI DR	1400	331M	NWC	77090
TUDOR CT	200	538U	DP	77536
TUDOR BEND	0	489X	SWH	77082
TUDOR CREST	0	489S	SWH	77082
TUDOR HEIGHTS LN	0	290W	NWC	77379
TUDOR MANOR	0	489W	SWH	77082
TUDOR POINT CT	16400	527F	SWC	77082
TUDOR RANCH LN	0	446E	NWC	77449
TUDOR WAY	29500	246D	SWM	77355
TUELY CT	700	457Q	NEC	77049
TUFA CT	4400	529E	SWH	77072
TUFFLY	7900	495P	NEH	77029
TUFTED DUCK LN	0	324S	NWC	77447
TUG CT	15900	419F	NEC	77532
TUG CT	19100	255T	SEM	77365
TUHATI FOREST LN	0	407J	NWC	77433
TULANE	700	492D	NWH	77007
TULANE	900	452Z	NWH	77008
TULANE	3900	452M	NWH	77018
TULAROSA LN	19600	328D	NWC	77377
TULIP	2800	537X	PA	77502
TULIP	3200	577F	PA	77504
TULIPA	1	251L	WD	77380
TULIP BLOSSOM CT	0	326N	NWC	77433
TULIP DALE	19100	446R	NWC	77084
TULIP DOWN CT	0	368U	NWC	77065
TULIP GARDEN CT	10900	368U	NWC	77065
TULIP GLEN CT	3900	446G	NWC	77449
TULIP GROVE TRAIL LN	0	406M	NWC	77433
TULIP HILL CT	1	251Y	WD	77380
TULIP POND CT	0	611S	FS	77545
TULIP RANCH DR	0	485S	NEF	77494
TULIP RANCH DR	0	485S	NEF	77494
TULIP RIVER CT	2900	297Q	NEH	77345
TULIP TRACE DR	0	253T	SEM	77386
TULIPTREE LN	1000	332N	NWC	77090
TULL DR	1500	446W	NWC	77449
TULLIBEE LN	0	335J	NCC	77338
TULLIS TRAIL CT	22500	525G	NEF	77494
TULLOS LN	24700	295L	SEM	77365
TULLY	700	488D	SWH	77079
TULLY	7600	415W	NEH	77016
TULLY MEADOWS CT	19600	406U	NWC	77449
TULOMA	0	611E	SWH	77489
TULSA	1300	538N	DP	77536
TULSA RD	4300	451P	NWH	77092
TULUM LN	21100	333P	NCC	77073
TULUM CALLE	2100	660W	GCO	77539
TUMBLEWEED LN	3900	502J	BT	77521
TUMBLEWEED PASS LN	0	406M	NWC	77433
TUMBLEWEED TRAIL	17200	367P	NWC	77095
TUMBLING RD	7500	377D	NEC	77346
TUMBLING FALLS CT	14800	618B	SEH	77062
TUMBLING FALLS DR	3600	613W	NEB	77578
TUMBLING RAPIDS DR	15500	448A	NWC	77084
TUMBLING RIVER LN	0	328F	NWC	77429
TUMLINSON DR	0	366N	NWC	77433
TUNA HILL	100	541W	MP	77571
TUNBRIDGE LN	12300	490J	SWH	77024
TUNBURY LN	7300	408P	NWC	77095
TUNELL LN	1000	373Q	NCC	77032
TUNHAM TRAIL	0	373A	NCC	77073
TUNICA PASS CT	0	250Q	NWC	77389
TUNICA PASS DR	0	250P	NWC	77389
TUNIS	5500	494C	NEH	77020
TUNNEY	11000	409Y	NWC	77041
TUNSON	0	369X	NWC	77064
TUPELO	1300	536K	PA	77506
TUPELO DR	0	327U	NWC	77429
TUPELO DR	15300	327T	NWC	77429
TUPELO GARDEN CIR	0	377J	NEC	77346
W. TUPELO GREEN CIR	0	250Q	NWC	77389
W. TUPELO GREEN CIR	0	250Q	NWC	77389
E. TUPELO GREEN CIR	0	250Q	NWC	77389
E. TUPELO GREEN CIR	0	250Q	NWC	77389
TUPPER BEND CT	0	407J	NWC	77433
TUPPER BEND LN	0	407J	NWC	77433
TUPPER CREEK CT	0	328G	NWC	77377
TUPPER GLEN DR	14900	329W	NWC	77070
TUPPER LAKE DR	5400	491K	SWH	77056
TUPPER LAKE DR	10600	489L	SWH	77042
TURCHIN DR	0	371H	NWC	77014
TURF CT	2700	414A	NCC	77039
TURF VALLEY DR	4500	448E	NWC	77084
TURFWOOD LN	5500	411Q	NWH	77088
TURIN	0	536E	SEH	77017
TURK LN	0	570G	MC	77071
TURKEY CIR	21500	378D	NEH	77532
TURKEY DR	3100	333U	NCC	77073
TURKEY CREEK	0	609Z	NEF	77459
TURKEY CREEK DR	15100	488C	SWH	77079
TURKEY CREEK FARMS	0	334N	NCC	77338
TURKEY SHOOT RD	0	247L	SWM	77355
TURKEY TRAIL	1	488G	SWH	77079
TURKEY TRAIL CT	15000	488G	SWH	77079
TURLEY	600	332C	NCC	77373
TURLOCK CT	12700	448D	NWC	77041
TURMERIC DR	0	461U	NEC	77521
TURN	11300	414P	NCC	77093
TURNABOUT CT	1	568V	SG	77478
TURNBERRY CIR	1400	541G	BT	77520
TURNBERRY CIR	3700	532J	SWH	77025
TURNBERRY CT	5100	577C	PA	77505
TURNBERRY DR	2200	659C	LC	77573
TURNBERRY GLEN CT		249V	NWC	77375
TURNBERRY PARK LN	1000	292B	NCC	77373
TURNBOW	9700	495R	NEH	77029
TURNBRIDGE TRAIL	13000	368Y	NWC	77065
TURNBUCKLE WAY	1700	419A	NEC	77532
TURNBURY ELM CT	2300	292D	SEM	77386
TURNBURY OAK	1200	451Y	NWH	77055

Street Name	Block	Pg/Sq	Loc	Zips
TURNBURY OAK LN	1200	451Y	NWH	77055
TURNBURY VILLAGE DR	29601	292D	SEM	77386
TURNCREEK LN	1200	486G	SWC	77450
TURNER	1100	541B	BT	77520
TURNER AVE	1300	658U	LC	77573
TURNER DR	1	453B	NEH	77076
TURNER DR	1500	454A	NEH	77093
TURNER RD	0	246A	SWM	77355
TURNER RD	0	256L	SEM	77357
TURNER OAKS	0	571L	SWH	77085
TURNER PLACE RD	12700	413P	NCC	77037
TURNER POINT CIR	17400	407P	NWC	77095
TURNER SLATE LN	0	293F	SEM	77386
TURNER SLATE LN	0	293F	SEM	77386
TURNER VINE LN	14100	288B	TB	77375
TURNEY DR	400	412H	NCC	77037
TURNEY DR	700	412G	NWC	77038
TURNEY RD	1800	412F	NWC	77038
TURNING BASIN DR	1200	495Q	NEH	77029
TURNING LEAF LAKE CT	20700	326N	NWC	77433
TURNING LIMB CT	15300	325R	NWC	77433
TURNING MANOR LN	4000	609T	NEF	77479
TURNING POINT CT	14500	457Y	NEC	77015
TURNING ROW LN	2600	610N	MC	77459
TURNING ROW LN	2700	609R	MC	77459
TURNING SPRING LN	0	377Y	NEH	77044
TURNING TREE WAY	15300	325R	NWC	77433
TURNIP	18600	331A	NWC	77379
TURNMILL CT	8200	330P	NWC	77379
TURNPIKE RD	1600	492C	NWH	77008
TURN POINT CT	0	377M	NEC	77346
TURNSTONE CT	16200	527U	NEF	77083
TURNSTONE OAKS CT	25600	524K	NWF	77406
TURPHIN WAY	15000	527V	NEF	77498
TURQUIOISE SPRINGS LN	0	524F	NEF	77494
TURQUOISE LN	7600	451N	NWH	77055
TURQUOISE MIST DR	15000	325R	NWC	77433
TURQUOISE SKY CT	0	524S	NWF	77406
TURQUOISE STREAM DR	17400	367X	NWC	77095
TURRET CROWN DR	1500	485K	NEF	77494
TURRET HILL DR	0	251D	WD	77381
TURRETT POINT LN	0	370U	NWC	77086
TURRIFF	8700	450V	NWH	77055
TURTLE BAY DR	15900	618G	SEH	77062
TURTLE BEACH LN	0	610T	MC	77459
TURTLE BEACH LN	5900	530D	SWH	77036
TURTLE BROOK LN	0	526J	NEF	77407
TURTLE COVE CT	6200	337P	NEC	77346
TURTLE COVE DR	3600	578A	PA	77505
TURTLE CREEK DR	700	610B	MC	77489
TURTLE CREEK DR	1800	610E	MC	77459
TURTLE CREEK DR	6300	578A	PA	77505
TURTLE CREEK LN	18600	246X	SWM	77355
TURTLE CREEK RD	5400	536S	SEH	77017
TURTLE CREEK WAY	18600	246X	SWM	77355
TURTLE DOVE LN	19200	246W	SWM	77355
TURTLE GATE DR	11800	369P	NWC	77070
TURTLE LAGOON	7100	530D	SWH	77036
TURTLE LAKE DR	11500	369R	NWC	77064
TURTLE LOG TRAIL	9300	369R	NWC	77064
TURTLE MANOR DR	0	377C	NEC	77346
TURTLE OAK CT	15500	618C	SEH	77059
N. TURTLE ROCK CT	1	251B	WD	77381
TURTLE ROCK CT	1	251B	WD	77381
TURTLES CORNER LN	12100	329A	NWC	77375
TURTLE SPRINGS LN	0	609Q	MC	77459
TURTLE TRAILS LN	0	609T	NEF	77479
TURTLEWOOD	6400	456R	NEH	77049
TURTLEWOOD CT	10500	529G	SWH	77072
TURTLEWOOD DR	200	659N	LC	77573
TURTLEWOOD DR	6800	529G	SWH	77072
TUSCAN LN	2200	502S	BT	77520
TUSCAN VILLAGE DR	0	659P	LC	77573
TUSCANA SHORES DR	0	407E	NWC	77433
TUSCANIA LN	0	657L	FR	77546
TUSCANIA LN	2800	659M	LC	77573
TUSCAN LAKES BLVD	2300	659M	LC	77573
TUSCAN LILY DR	0	445A	NWC	77493
TUSCAN SHORES DR	0	610T	MC	77459
TUSCANY	100	568P	SG	77478
TUSCANY FARMS DR	0	445B	NWC	77493
TUSCANY PLACE	1600	616J	PL	77581
TUSCARORA	4200	577F	PA	77504
TUSCARORA CT	2000	658S	LC	77573
TUSCOLA LN	19500	406V	NWC	77449
TUSCON	5900	454P	NEH	77026
W. TUSHMAN	0	616N	PL	77581
E. TUSHMAN	0	616P	PL	77581
TUSKEGEE	5600	452B	NWH	77091
TUSKEGEE	6200	412X	NWH	77091
TUSKIN OAKS DR	0	406F	NWC	77433
TUSSENDO DR	7500	528K	SWC	77083
TUSTIN DR	8000	408K	NWC	77095
TUSTIN RANCH CT	23600	485K	NEF	77494
TUTBURY CIR	15400	377X	NEC	77044
TUTOR LN	12800	488Q	SWH	77077
TUTSON PLACE	13500	571L	SWH	77085
TUTTLE CT	0	296N	SEM	77365
TUTTLE POINT DR	14801	487Z	SWC	77082
TUWA RD	22200	289M	NWC	77375
TWAIN	600	332C	NCC	77373
TWAIN MARK LN	0	334Q	NCC	77388
TWAIN MARK LN	0	334Q	NCC	77388
TWEED DR	8700	575E	SEH	77061
TWEEDBROOK DR	8800	330N	NWC	77379
TWEED WAY	0	614U	PL	77584
TWEED WAY	0	614U	PL	77584
TWELFTH FAIRWAY DR	7600	337V	NEC	77346
TWELTH TEE CT	27700	299P	NEC	77336
TWELVE OAKS	0	492W	SWH	77027
TWELVE OAKS DR	3300	609H	MC	77459
TWELVE OAKS DR	10600	491A	HC	77024
TWELVE PINES CT	1	251F	WD	77381
E. TWICKENHAM TRAIL	100	413W	NEH	77076
TWICKENHAM TRAIL	100	412Z	NEH	77076
TWIG DR	10800	576T	SEH	77089
TWIG CORNER CT	100	249R	NWH	77375
TWIG CORNER CT	100	249R	NWH	77375
TWIG LEAF LN	0	447P	NWC	77084
TWIGSWORTH LN	18600	337X	NEC	77346
TWILA SPRINGS CT	0	368X	NWC	77095
TWILA SPRINGS DR	0	368X	NWC	77095
TWILIGHT LN	800	338D	NEH	77336
TWILIGHT BAY DR	0	612K	PL	77545
TWILIGHT CANYON RD	20100	446P	NWC	77449
TWILIGHT CREEK LN	0	366V	NWC	77433
TWILIGHT FALLS LN	19600	446Q	NWC	77084
TWILIGHT GABLE CT	0	253U	SEM	77386
TWILIGHT GABLE CT	0	253U	SEM	77386
TWILIGHT GLEN CT	1	251B	WD	77381
TWILIGHT GROVE LN	26700	366R	NWC	77433
TWILIGHT HOLLOW LN	0	524R	NEF	77406
TWILIGHT KNOLL TRAIL	0	328J	NWC	77429
TWILIGHT MANOR CT	0	417B	NEC	77044
TWILIGHT MOON DR	9400	369Y	NWC	77064
TWILIGHT OAKS CT	0	445F	NWC	77493
TWILIGHT SHORES LN	0	367S	NWC	77433
TWILIGHT SKY CT	12000	618D	PA	77059
TWILIGHT SPRINGS CT	0	657T	FR	77546
TWILIGHT SPRINGS LN	0	609N	NEF	77479
TWILIGHT STAR LN	0	527N	NEF	77083
TWILIGHT TRAIL	20500	378H	NEC	77532
TWILLINGATE LN	8500	411S	NWH	77040
TWIN ARROWS DR	0	524S	NWF	77406
TWIN ASPENS LN	21500	333E	NCC	77073
TWINBROOKE DR	500	412M	NCC	77037
TWINBROOKE DR	800	412K	NWH	77088
TWIN BUTTES DR	19200	328D	NWC	77375
TWIN CANDLE DR	4900	452F	NWH	77018
TWIN CANYON CT	19700	526B	NEF	77450
TWIN CANYON LN	0	539Z	LP	77571
TWIN CIRCLE DR	1	489R	SWH	77042
TWIN CREEK	0	609Z	MC	77459
TWIN CREEKS DR	18100	407T	NWC	77449
TWIN DEER RD	11400	252D	SEM	77385
TWIN DEER RD	11600	253A	SEM	77385
TWIN DIAMOND LN	0	376F	HM	77396
TWIN ELM DR	1700	333E	NCC	77073
TWIN FALLS RD	900	412K	NWH	77088
TWIN FALLS CROSSING LN	0	330B	NWC	77379
TWIN FLOWER DR	12600	328L	NWC	77377
TWIN FORKS CT	3700	610X	MC	77459
TWIN FOUNTAINS DR	0	331U	NWC	77068
TWIN GREENS CT	1	337F	NEC	77339
TWIN GROVE DR	2300	337A	NEH	77339
TWIN HILLS CT	10300	530W	SWH	77031
TWIN HILLS DR	7600	530Y	SWH	77071
TWIN HILLS DR	9100	530W	SWH	77031
TWINING OAKS	7900	330N	NWC	77379
TWINING OAKS LN	1200	570T	MC	77489
TWINKLE CT	4400	529E	SWH	77072
TWINKLE SKY CT	22000	325R	NWC	77433
TWIN KNOLLS DR	2800	296R	NEH	77339
TWIN KNOLLS DR	2900	297N	NEH	77339
TWIN KNOLLS LN	0	660K	LC	77573
TWIN LAKES BLVD	13200	448D	NWC	77041
TWIN LAKES DR	14000	528W	NEF	77498
TWIN LAKES TRAIL	0	615N	PL	77584
TWIN LAMPS LN	8300	410H	NWC	77064
TWINLEAF DR	2900	659H	LC	77573
TWIN LEAF DR	6500	330L	NWC	77379
TWIN MAPLE	14800	527D	SWC	77082
TWIN MEADOW LN	0	445L	NWC	77449
TWIN MILLS LN	0	253T	SEM	77386
TWINMONT LN	3200	485S	NWF	77494
TWIN OAK DR	10300	252G	SEM	77385
TWIN OAKS	0	290A	NWC	77389
TWIN OAKS	300	413Y	NEH	77076
TWIN OAKS	1100	656R	FR	77546
TWIN OAKS	1200	619R	LC	77565
TWIN OAKS BLVD	11300	339J	HU	77336
TWIN OAKS DR	25000	257T	SEM	77357
TWIN OAKS WAY	100	619V	LC	77565
TWIN PINES DR	500	616U	FR	77546
TWIN POINT LN	0	253P	SEM	77386
W. TWIN PONDS CT	0	250N	NWC	77375
E. TWIN PONDS CT	0	250N	NWC	77375
TWIN PONDS PLACE	100	250N	NWC	77375
TWINRIDGE LN	11600	529P	SWH	77099
TWIN RIVERS CT	0	609U	MC	77479
TWIN RIVERS DR	19700	289W	NWC	77375
TWIN RIVERS LN	0	609U	NEF	77479
S. TWINSBERRRY FIELD DR	0	325V	NWC	77433
TWIN SISTERS DR	12500	368G	NWC	77429
TWIN SPRINGS DR	1900	336C	NEH	77339
TWIN SPRINGS PLACE	1	250H	WD	77381
TWIN STONE LN	0	484U	NEF	77494
TWIN TIMBERS LN	0	253P	SEM	77386
TWIN TIMBERS LN	0	619V	LC	77565
TWIN TRAILS DR	0	367X	NWC	77095
TWIN TREE LN	8200	570F	SWH	77071
TWIN TWIST CT	14400	570V	SWH	77489
TWIN VILLAS DR	0	538S	PA	77503
TWINWALKER DR	16400	458S	NEC	77049
TWIN WATERS CT	0	377U	NEC	77044
TWIN WOODS LN	0	253N	SEM	77386
TWISTED ASH CT	14600	457Y	NEC	77015
TWISTED BIRCH CT	0	293S	NCC	77373
TWISTED BIRCH PLACE CT	1	250M	WD	77381
TWISTED BROOK DR	3600	572T	SEH	77053
TWISTED CANYON DR	14300	327X	CY	77429
TWISTED CEDAR CT	14600	457U	NEC	77015
TWISTED CREEK DR	19700	289W	NWC	77375
TWISTED ELM CT	1000	412A	NWC	77038
TWISTED LEAF DR	0	326N	NWC	77433
TWISTED LEAF DR	20800	325R	NWC	77433
TWISTED OAK	5600	502G	BT	77521
TWISTED OAK LN	14300	488M	SWH	77079
TWISTED PECAN CT	14600	457Y	NEC	77015
TWISTED PINE CT	5800	414H	NEC	77039
TWISTED RATTAN LN	13600	457T	NEC	77015
TWISTED SPRUCE CT	100	457Y	NEC	77015
TWISTED TRUNK CT	14300	457Y	NEC	77015
TWISTED TRUNK DR	14300	457U	NEC	77015
TWISTED WILLOW CT	2800	486N	SWC	77450
TWISTED WILLOW LN	21200	486N	SWC	77450
TWISTER TRAIL	25200	293U	NCC	77373
TWISTING RD	4600	447E	NWC	77084
TWISTING FALLS DR	23600	293W	NCC	77373
TWISTING MAPLE CT	22900	333H	NCC	77373
TWISTING OAK	14900	487Z	SWC	77082
TWISTING PINE CT	2500	297U	NEH	77345
TWISTING PINE CT	4400	333G	NCC	77373
TWISTING PINE DR	4400	333G	NCC	77373
TWISTING ROSE CIR	22900	333H	NCC	77373
TWISTING ROSE DR	4400	333G	NCC	77373
TWISTING SPRINGS DR	15500	326S	NWC	77433
TWISTING VINE LN	8500	410V	NWH	77040
TWITCH CT	0	255T	SEM	77365
TWO CREEKS RD	7700	334M	NCC	77338
TWO HARBORS GLEN	0	525B	NEF	77449
TWO LAKES DR	0	289R	NWC	77375
TWO OAKS CIR	11000	368V	NWC	77065
TWOPENNY LN	13600	457X	NEC	77015
TWO RIVERS CT	1900	485Q	NEF	77450
TWO RIVERS LN	22700	485Q	NEF	77450
TWO TRAIL DR	2200	293S	NCC	77373
TYBOR DR	8300	530P	SWH	77074
W. TYLER	100	540X	LP	77571
TYLER	100	288H	TB	77375
TYLER	1900	453T	NWH	77009
TYLER	5600	614M	PL	77581
TYLER CT	0	657G	FR	77546
TYLER CT	12800	570J	SF	77477
TYLER DR	400	612B	SWC	77053
TYLER LN	0	612Z	NEB	77578
TYLER LN	2400	538P	DP	77536
TYLER LN	12900	570J	SF	77477
TYLER CREEK LN	7600	375Y	NEC	77396
TYLERGATE DR	4200	333C	NCC	77373
TYLER HILLS LN	28400	293E	SEM	77386
TYLERMONT DR	15600	367H	NWC	77429
TYLER PARK LN	0	524C	NEF	77494
TYLER PARK LN	0	524C	NEF	77494
TYLER POINT LN	0	615H	PL	77089
TYLER REACH DR		325S	NWC	77447
TYLER SPRINGS LN	0	377E	NEC	77346
TYLER TRACE LN	0	290L	NWC	77379
TYLER TRAILS CT	0	407K	NWC	77433
TYNE	6000	492F	SWH	77007
TYNE CT	11200	490L	PP	77024
TYNEBRIDGE LN	300	490L	PP	77024
TYNEBROOK LN	300	490L	PP	77024
TYNECREEK LN	18500	330E	NWC	77379
TYNEGLEN LN	0	416Z	NEC	77044
TYNELAND CT	7900	369D	NWC	77070
TYNEMEADOW CT	3200	446Q	NWC	77449
TYNEMOUTH DR	1700	577E	PA	77504
TYNEWOOD LN	11200	490Q	PP	77024
TYNHAM SPRINGS DR	0	253S	SEM	77386
TYPHOON WAY	17400	379T	NEC	77532
TYRE	4400	494C	NEH	77020
TYRONE	19000	332C	NCC	77373
W. TYSON RD	1700	458U	CV	77530
E. TYSON RD	1700	458U	CV	77530
TYSOR PARK LN	15000	408B	NWC	77095

U

Street Name	Block	Pg/Sq	Loc	Zips
U S GOVERNMENT RD	0	448W	NWH	77084
U S GOVERNMENT RD	0	447Y	NWH	77084
U S STEEL RD	0	542V	CCO	77520
U S STEEL RD	0	543S	CCO	77520
U, AVENUE	6600	494R	SEH	77011
S. U.S. HWY 59	0	531A	SWH	77081
S. U.S. HWY 59	0	531A	SWH	77081
S. U.S. HWY 59	0	568R	SG	77478
S. U.S. HWY 59	0	568R	SG	77478
U.S. HWY 90	0	380M	NEC	77532
U.S. HWY 90	0	380M	NEC	77532
U.S. HWY 90	0	381F	LCO	77535
U.S. HWY 90	0	381F	LCO	77535
U.S. HWY 90	0	418X	NEC	77049
U.S. HWY 90	0	418X	NEC	77049
U.S. HWY 90	0	420A	NEC	77532
U.S. HWY 90	0	420A	NEC	77532
U.S. HWY 90	0	444Z	KT	77493
U.S. HWY 90	0	444Z	KT	77493
U.S. HWY 90	0	445W	NWC	77493
U.S. HWY 90	0	445W	NWC	77493
U.S. HWY 90	0	455X	NEH	77029
U.S. HWY 90	0	455X	NEH	77029
U.S. HWY 90	0	456N	NEH	77013
U.S. HWY 90	0	456N	NEH	77013
U.S. HWY 90	0	457K	NEC	77049
U.S. HWY 90	0	457K	NEC	77049
U.S. HWY 90	0	458B	NEC	77049
U.S. HWY 90	0	458B	NEC	77049
U.S. HWY 90	0	486D	SWC	77094
U.S. HWY 90	0	486D	SWC	77094
U.S. HWY 90	0	487D	SWH	77094
U.S. HWY 90	0	487D	SWH	77094
U.S. HWY 90	0	492A	SWH	77007
U.S. HWY 90	0	492A	SWH	77007
U.S. HWY 90	0	533L	SEH	77021
U.S. HWY 90	0	533L	SEH	77021
U.S. HWY 90 E.	1500	494G	NEH	77020
U.S. HWY 90 E.	1500	494G	NEH	77020
U.S. HWY 90	5200	444Y	KT	77493
U.S. HWY 90	5200	444Y	KT	77493
U.S. HWY 90 E.	7800	495B	NEH	77029
U.S. HWY 90 E.	7800	495B	NEH	77029
U.S. HWY 90 E.	8100	455T	NEH	77028
U.S. HWY 90 E.	8100	455T	NEH	77028
U.S. HWY 90A	0	532T	SWH	77025
U.S. HWY 90A	0	532T	SWH	77025
U.S. HWY 90A	0	570P	MC	77489
U.S. HWY 90A	0	570P	MC	77489
U.S. HWY 90A	0	571F	SWH	77035
U.S. HWY 90A	0	571F	SWH	77035
U.S. HWY 90A S.	2000	569R	SF	77477
U.S. HWY 90A S.	2000	569R	SF	77477
U.S. HWY 90A S.	5000	568L	SG	77478
U.S. HWY 90A S.	5000	568L	SG	77478
U.S. HWY 90A NORTH	100	495E	NEH	77020
U.S. HWY 90A NORTH	100	495E	NEH	77020
U.S. HWY 90A NORTH	3900	455V	NEH	77013
U.S. HWY 90A NORTH	3900	455V	NEH	77013
W. U.S. HWY 290	22600	367K	CY	77429
W. U.S. HWY 290	22600	367K	CY	77429
W. U.S. HWY 290	26100	366D	NWC	77429
W. U.S. HWY 290	26100	366D	NWC	77429
W. U.S. HWY 290	28000	326X	NWC	77433
W. U.S. HWY 290	28000	326X	NWC	77433
W. U.S. HWY 290	30000	325U	NWC	77429
W. U.S. HWY 290	30000	325U	NWC	77429
W. U.S. HWY 290	32100	324L	NWC	77447
W. U.S. HWY 290	32100	324L	NWC	77447
W. U.S. HWY 290	35700	323D	NWC	77447
W. U.S. HWY 290	35700	323D	NWC	77447
W. U.S. HWY 290	37500	283S	NWC	77484
W. U.S. HWY 290	37500	283S	NWC	77484
UBETCHA	900	489R	SWH	77042
UBUNTU CT	5200	452F	NWH	77091
UCAYALI CT	0	295A	SEM	77365
UDEMI	2400	491V	SWH	77027
ULRICH LN	100	419L	CB	77532
ULRICH RD	100	568N	SG	77498
ULRICH RD	700	288C	TB	77375
ULRICH RD	30700	248Y	NWC	77375
ULYSSES	16300	419B	NEC	77532
ULYSSES LN	7400	461T	NEC	77521
UMBER CT	10600	529W	SWH	77099
UMBER COVE CT	14200	573Z	SEH	77048
UMBER OAK CT	20300	337Q	NEC	77346
UMBRELLA PINE DR	0	289C	NWC	77375
UMBRIA LN	0	659H	LC	77573
UMIAK DR	2800	572L	SWH	77045
UNA	9200	453F	NEH	77022
UNA DR	300	538L	DP	77536
UNCLE BENS	0	494L	NEH	77020
UNDERHILL	6200	451J	NWH	77092
UNDERWOOD	2300	532L	SWH	77030
UNDERWOOD	3000	532J	SWH	77025
UNDERWOOD DR	8000	609Z	MC	77459
UNDERWOOD RD	100	539N	DP	77571
UNDERWOOD RD	3400	579E	LP	77571
UNDERWOOD RD	5700	579N	SEC	77507
UNDERWOOD CREEK WAY	14600	618E	SEH	77062
UNICORN	0	528M	SWH	77072
UNICORNS HORN LN	22100	445U	NWC	77449
UNION	1900	493K	SWH	77007
UNION	14600	328B	NWC	77377
N. UNION CT	21100	332V	NCC	77073
UNION MEADOW LN	0	406C	NWC	77433
UNION MILL RD	2100	371M	NWC	77067
UNION OAK	0	368V	NWC	77065
UNION PARK DR	20800	486E	SWC	77450
UNION POINE CT	16000	367D	NWC	77429
UNION VALLEY DR	1000	615B	PL	77581
UNIQUE CIR	0	418T	NCC	77044
UNISYS	0	450D	NWH	77040
UNITED DR	9800	529H	SWH	77036
UNITED RD	10800	414U	NEC	77093
UNITY DR	2900	490V	SWH	77057
UNITY DR	3000	490Z	SWH	77057
UNITY CANDLE TRAIL	18700	331D	NWC	77388
UNITY THOROUGHFARE	0	419V	NEC	77532
UNIVERSAL DR	4300	529E	SWH	77072
UNIVERSITY BLVD	0	568S	SG	77478
UNIVERSITY BLVD	1900	532B	SWH	77030
UNIVERSITY BLVD	2300	532B	WU	77005
UNIVERSITY BLVD	19700	609P	MC	77459
UNIVERSITY DR	0	618H	SEH	77058
UNIVERSITY GREEN BLVD	0	618L	SEH	77058
UNIVERSITY OAKS BLVD	4400	534A	SEH	77004
UNIVERSITY PARK	0	619A	PA	77058
UNIVERSITY PARK DR	12100	618D	PA	77058
UNIVERSITY PARK DR	22200	485Y	NEF	77450
UPAS	2400	493N	SWH	77006
UPFIELD DR	3500	527C	SWC	77082
UPHALL CT	9200	407D	NWC	77095
UPLAND DR	0	449U	NWH	77043
UPLAND DR	1000	489B	NWH	77043
UPLAND DR	1300	449X	NWH	77043
UPLAND ARBOR DR	0	449X	NWH	77043
UPLAND BROOK LN	5400	331A	NWC	77379
UPLAND CREEK DR	19900	406Q	NWC	77449
UPLAND DALE CT	4800	446C	NWC	77449
UPLAND ELM	19800	446Q	NWC	77084
UPLAND FAIR LN	20200	446F	NWC	77449
UPLAND FOREST DR	0	449T	NWH	77043
UPLAND HILLL	2000	293W	NCC	77373
UPLAND LAKES	0	449X	NWH	77043
UPLAND LAKE WAY	0	449X	NWH	77043
UPLAND MILL LN	0	526K	NEF	77407
UPLAND OAK DR	0	449T	NWH	77043
UPLAND OAK TRACE DR	19100	367B	NWC	77429
UPLAND ORCHARD DR	0	449X	NWH	77043
UPLAND PARK	0	449X	NWH	77043
UPLAND PASS DR	0	449X	NWH	77043
UPLAND PINE ST	0	406R	NWC	77433
UPLAND RAPIDS DR	0	616H	SEH	77089
UPLAND RETREAT DR	0	449X	NWH	77043
UPLAND RETREAT BLUE PL	0	449X	NWH	77043
UPLAND RIDGE LN	0	524F	NEF	77494
UPLAND RIVER DR	0	449T	NWH	77043
UPLAND SKY LN	0	449T	NWH	77043
UPLAND SPRING TRACE	0	445K	NWC	77493
UPLAND VIEW DR	0	611S	FS	77545
UPLAND WILLOW AVE	0	411G	NWC	77038
UPPER BAY RD	18000	619S	NB	77058
UPPER BROOK	8400	410G	NWC	77064
UPPERCOVE CIR	9000	409H	NWC	77064
UPPERFALLS CT	23300	334A	NCC	77373
UPPER FALLS LN	5800	334A	NCC	77373
UPPER GREEN ST	0	334Q	NCC	77388
UPPER HOLLOW DR	11900	371M	NWC	77067
UPPER LAKE DR	3100	336Q	NEH	77338
UPPER LAKE DR	5300	337T	NEC	77346
UPPER LEAF WAY	0	325R	NWC	77433
UPPER RIDGE LN	0	377K	NEC	77346
UPPER RUN WAY	0	328N	NWC	77429
UPPERWAY LN	1	491L	SWH	77056
UPPERWING CT	26800	324S	NWC	77447
UPSHAW DR	5500	374V	NCC	77032
UPSHAW DR	5800	375S	NEH	77396
UPSHIRE DR	16000	458Y	CV	77530
UPSHUR LN	8600	409H	NWC	77064
UPTON	1200	494F	NEH	77020
UPTON HILLS DR	0	366P	NWC	77433
UPTOWN DR	4000	572E	SWH	77045
UPTOWN PARK BLVD	1000	491M	SWH	77056
UPWARD CT	0	373E	NCC	77073
UPWOOD DR	9600	335P	HM	77338
URAGUAY DR	3700	577B	PA	77504
URBAN DR	11700	415M	NEC	77050
URBAN ELM ST	0	328J	NWC	77429
URBAN FOREST CT	2300	292D	SEM	77386
URBAN GLEN CT	0	411H	NWC	77038
URBANNA CT	13000	367H	NWC	77429
URBAN TREES WAY	0	377A	NEC	77346
URBAN WOODS TRAIL	0	492A	NWH	77008
URSA	4400	494K	NEH	77020
US 59 SB-MARKET	200	568M	SG	77478
USENER	700	493B	NWH	77009
US GORT RD	0	449K	NWH	77043
USONIA DR	0	253X	SEM	77386
UTAH	100	540Y	LP	77571
UTAH	600	580C	LP	77571
UTAH	700	535Z	SH	77587
UTAH	1000	492F	SWH	77007
UTAH	1500	541A	BT	77520
UTAH	1900	540D	BT	77520
UTAH	6500	412X	NWH	77091
UTAH AVE	3200	660W	GCO	77539
UTAH BEACH CT	3400	291U	NWC	77388
UTAH OAKS CT	0	406F	NWC	77433
UTE	0	295F	SEM	77365
UTE	4200	577F	PA	77504
UTE MOUNTAIN LN	11900	328C	NWC	77377
UTHER CT	0	290P	NWC	77379
UTICA	13300	497F	NEH	77015
UTOPIA DR	14000	568A	SG	77498
UVALDE RD	1	457T	NEC	77015
UVALDE RD	300	497E	NEC	77015
UVALDE RD	5600	457K	NEC	77049
UVALDE SPRINGS LN	0	328S	NWC	77429
UVALDE SPRINGS LN	0	328S	NWC	77429
UWOOD	0	499S	DP	77536

V

Street Name	Block	Pg/Sq	Loc	Zips
V, AVENUE	6600	494R	SEH	77011
VACCARO CIR	13900	569R	SF	77477
VADINI SHORES LN	0	524E	NEF	77494
VAE DR	5300	500G	BT	77521
VAIDEN FALLS CT	8500	528P	SWC	77083

Street Name	Block	Pg/Sq	Loc	Zips
VAIDEN FALLS DR	8500	528P	SWC	77083
VAIL CT	1800	610K	MC	77459
VAIL DR	0	614U	PL	77584
VAIL DR	0	614U	PL	77584
VAILRUN DR	11600	369A	NWC	77070
VAILVIEW DR	11000	415N	NEH	77016
VAL	0	570H	SWH	77035
VALARNO DR	11300	371P	NWC	77066
N. VALE	0	331X	NWC	77014
N. VALE	0	371B	NWC	77014
VALE	100	536X	SH	77587
VALE	2800	501Q	BT	77521
VALE LN	24400	296L	SEM	77365
VALEBLUFF LN	0	326R	NWC	77429
VALE BROOK DR	0	293S	NCC	77373
VALECHASE LN	14000	371B	NWC	77014
VALEDA LN	7400	538X	DP	77536
VALEDICTORIAN DR	0	488N	SWH	77077
VALEDON CT	14000	371B	NWC	77014
VALEDON LN	4100	371B	NWC	77014
VALE HAVEN DR	0	293S	NCC	77373
VALEMIST CT	17200	407Q	NWC	77084
VALENCIA DR	10100	495H	NEH	77013
VALENCIA DR	10300	496E	NEH	77013
VALENCIA DR	11900	569A	MD	77477
VALENCIA COVE	2500	659S	LC	77573
VALENTINE	600	493K	SWH	77019
VALENTINE LN	0	614T	PL	77584
VALENTINE BRIDGE LN	14900	528W	NEF	77498
VALENTINE WAY	700	493K	SWH	77019
VALENTINO DR	0	610H	NEF	77489
VALE PHEASANT HILL	14000	371B	NWC	77014
VALERA LN	7700	528K	SWC	77083
VALERIAN LN	6600	407T	NWC	77449
VALERIE	4300	531M	BL	77401
VALERIE	5500	531K	SWH	77081
VALERIE AVE	500	536V	PA	77502
VALERIE AVE	24100	297J	SEM	77365
VALERIE LN	3200	251N	SWM	77380
VALERO	1700	656U	FR	77546
VALE SCENE CT	1200	332V	NCC	77073
VALETA DR	8100	527R	NEF	77083
VALEVIEW DR	7100	528M	SWH	77072
VALHALLA DR	6000	330D	NWC	77379
VALHALLAH WAY	17200	407L	NWC	77095
VALIANT DR	9500	417X	NEC	77044
VALIANT BROOK CT	18300	377C	NEC	77346
VALIANT ELM	0	611S	FS	77545
VALIANT KNIGHT DR	0	289P	NWC	77375
VALIANT SCENE CT	2900	411G	NWC	77038
VALIANT SIDE TRAIL	0	377E	NEC	77346
VALIANT SQUARE CIR	0	328N	NWC	77429
VALINDA DR	16200	527K	NEF	77083
VALKA	18600	330A	NWC	77379
VALKEITH DR	4900	531S	SWH	77096
VALKEITH DR	6000	530V	SWH	77096
VALKUS	0	485N	NEF	77494
VALKYRIE DR	19400	290Z	NWC	77379
VALLECITO LN	7800	375G	HM	77396
VALLEJO CT	6200	611B	SWH	77053
VALLEJO DR	16300	611B	SWH	77053
VALLEN DR	16000	409U	NWH	77041
VAL LENA DR	600	489H	SWH	77024
VALLERIE	0	537S	PA	77502
VALLETA DR	1300	452X	NWH	77008
N. VALLEY CT	0	332V	NCC	77073
N. VALLEY CT	21100	332V	NCC	77073
W. VALLEY DR	3700	610J	MC	77459
E. VALLEY DR	3700	610J	MC	77459
VALLEY RD	28000	248S	SWM	77362
VALLEY ACRES RD	1000	618E	SEH	77062
VALLEY BEND CT	14200	568A	SG	77498
VALLEY BEND DR	2300	610A	MC	77489
VALLEY BEND DR	15400	331N	NWC	77068
VALLEY BLOSSOM CT	0	484Z	NEF	77494
VALLEY BLOSSOM LN		658T	LC	77573
VALLEY BLUFF LN	5200	485W	NEF	77494
VALLEY BRANCH DR	3700	296V	NEH	77339
VALLEY BREEZE DR	10100	456B	NEH	77078
VALLEYBROOK	2500	539X	LP	77571
VALLEYBROOK	3100	579B	LP	77571
VALLEY BROOK CT	5200	539X	LP	77571
VALLEY CANYON LN	0	256W	SEM	77365
VALLEY CHASE DR	3500	297U	NEH	77345
VALLEY CLUB DR	9900	456A	NEH	77078
VALLEY COMMONS DR	0	339F	NEC	77336
VALLEY COMMONS DR	700	298U	NEC	77336
VALLEY COVE DR	0	366K	NWC	77433
VALLEY COVE LN	0	571F	SWH	77085
VALLEY CREEK DR	15500	408N	NWC	77095
VALLEY CREST LN	8600	575U	SEH	77075
VALLEY CREST LN	8600	575U	SEH	77075
VALLEY DALE CT	2000	618F	SEH	77062
VALLEY ELM LN	0	410M	NWC	77040
VALLEY ESTATES DR	4000	527D	SWC	77082
VALLEY FAIR DR	5800	338A	NEH	77345
VALLEY FAIR LN	0	660K	LC	77573
VALLEY FALLS CT	10000	456A	NEH	77078
VALLEY FIELD DR	2500	450L	NWH	77080
VALLEY FLAG DR	8600	456B	NEH	77078
VALLEY FOREST DR	2500	610E	MC	77489
VALLEY FOREST DR	8500	456B	NEH	77078
VALLEY FORGE	6000	491P	SWH	77057
VALLEY FORGE DR	1	490F	BH	77024
VALLEY FORGE DR	2400	536T	PA	77502
VALLEY FORGE DR	5800	491N	SWH	77057
VALLEY FORGE DR	10000	489Q	SWH	77042
VALLEY GARDENS DR	2700	297X	NEH	77345
VALLEYGATE LN	0	528Q	SWC	77072
VALLEY GLADE DR	4200	297X	NEH	77345
VALLEY GLEN DR	1300	489K	SWH	77077
VALLEY GOLD CT	8600	456A	NEH	77078
VALLEY GREEN CT	3900	578Z	PA	77059
VALLEY GROVE DR	14000	371U	NWC	77066
VALLEY HAVEN DR	3300	296Z	NEH	77339
VALLEY HAVEN DR	3800	297W	NEH	77339
VALLEY HEATHER CT	6100	338A	NEH	77345
VALLEY HILLS DR	10000	530Y	SWH	77071
VALLEY HILLS DR	11800	570C	SWH	77071
VALLEY HO DR	10200	456B	NEH	77078
VALLEY HOLLOW DR	8900	456A	NEH	77078
VALLEY KINGS DR	0	576W	SEH	77089
VALLEY KNOLL DR	17900	447C	NWC	77084
VALLEY LAKE DR	0	367S	NWC	77433
VALLEY LAKE DR	9900	456B	NEH	77078
VALLEY LANDING DR	1300	485M	SWC	77450
VALLEY LARK CT	5500	337H	NEH	77345
VALLEY LAUREL CT	7500	407M	NWC	77095
VALLEY LEDGE DR	8600	456F	NEH	77078
VALLEYLIGHT DR	24700	484G	NEF	77494
VALLEY LODGE PARKWAY	0	377E	NEC	77346
VALLEY LODGE PARKWAY	0	377J	NEC	77346
VALLEY MANOR CT	2400	610A	MC	77489
VALLEY MANOR DR	2000	610A	MC	77489
VALLEY MANOR DR	2500	337A	NEH	77339
VALLEY MEADOW DR	8600	456B	NEH	77078
VALLEY MILL CT	9900	456A	NEH	77078
VALLEY MOON LN	0	366N	NWC	77433
VALLEY OAKS CT	21500	486J	SWC	77450
VALLEY PALMS DR	16800	330N	NWC	77379
VALLEY PALMS DR	17200	330J	NWC	77379
VALLEY PARK DR	9900	456A	NEH	77078
VALLEY PASS	5400	577Q	SEH	77034
VALLEY PIKE CT	11500	568A	NEF	77498
VALLEY PINES DR	5200	297Y	NEH	77345
VALLEY PLUM CT	15500	326T	NWC	77433
VALLEY POINT DR	0	456A	NEH	77078
VALLEY POND CT	8700	456B	NEH	77078
VALLEY RANCH BLVD	0	256T	SEM	77357
VALLEY RANCH DR	800	485G	SWC	77450
VALLEY RANCH PKWY	0	256T	SEM	77357
VALLEY RANCH PKWY	0	256W	SEM	77365
VALLEY RANCH PKWY	0	296A	SEM	77365
VALLEY RANCH BEND DR	0	256X	SEM	77365
VALLEY RANCH CRSSNG DR	21600	256X	SEM	77365
VALLEY RIDGE DR	3300	613Y	NEB	77584
VALLEY RILL RD	0	446G	NWC	77449
VALLEY RIM DR	0	297N	NEH	77345
VALLEY ROCK DR	8600	456B	NEH	77078
VALLEY ROSE DR	2900	297W	NEH	77339
VALLEY SCENE WAY	5500	291W	NWC	77379
VALLEYSIDE DR	0	524A	NEF	77494
VALLEY SIDE DR	8900	456B	NEH	77078
VALLEY SONG DR	8600	456B	NEH	77078
VALLEY SOUTH DR	8600	456A	NEH	77078
VALLEY SPRING DR	11200	449X	NWH	77043
VALLEY SPRINGS PLACE	25600	292U	NCC	77373
VALLEY SPRING TRAIL	3000	446P	NWC	77449
VALLEY STAR DR	12100	490J	BH	77024
VALLEYSTONE CT	0	609F	MC	77459
VALLEY STONE CT	14600	327W	NWC	77429
VALLEY STREAM	9300	412M	NEH	77037
VALLEY STREAM DR	11200	449X	NWH	77043
VALLEY SUN DR	9900	456A	NEH	77078
VALLEY TRACE LN	0	256W	SEM	77365
VALLEY TREE LN	0	576W	SEH	77089
VALLEY VIEW	0	530U	SWH	77074
VALLEY VIEW	4900	539X	LP	77571
VALLEYVIEW DR	0	609D	MC	77459
VALLEY VIEW DR	1500	539V	LP	77571
VALLEY VIEW LN	7700	530N	SWH	77074
VALLEYVIEW CREEK CT	5300	331A	NWC	77379
VALLEY VISTA CT	11900	489N	SWH	77077
VALLEY VISTA DR	1700	489N	SWH	77077
VALLEY WAY	0	371Z	NWC	77038
VALLEY WAY DR	2800	337A	NEH	77339
VALLEY WELLS DR	20500	446P	NWC	77449
VALLEY WEST CT	8600	456A	NEH	77078
VALLEY WIND DR	9900	456A	NEH	77078
VALLEYWOOD DR	10200	450J	NWC	77041
VALLEYWOOD RD	100	252S	SWM	77380
VALLIE RD	28100	248T	SWM	77362
VALLINGBY DR	23000	485B	SWC	77450
VALMAR	1	619V	LC	77565
VALMONT DR	7200	415T	NEH	77016
VALOR	4000	454F	NEH	77093
VALPARAISO CIR	4300	577B	PA	77504
VAL VERDE	4900	491U	SWH	77056
VAL VERDE	5600	491T	SWH	77057
VAL VERDE	9300	490S	SWH	77063
VAL VERDE	15800	527L	NEF	77083
VAL VERDE CT	5600	491T	SWH	77057
VAL VERDE ST	33000	322J	WCO	77484
VAL VERDE PARK	0	491T	SWH	77057
VAL VERDE SPRINGS CT	0	366Z	NWC	77433
VALVET GRASS LN	0	367V	NWC	77095
VAL VISTA DR	15800	527L	NEF	77083
VALWOOD CT	9300	412L	NWH	77088
VAN	0	458C	NEC	77049
VAN	200	536X	SH	77587
VAN LN	0	446P	NWC	77449
VAN RD	17400	418X	NEC	77049
VAN ALLEN DR	0	251C	WD	77381
VAN ARCHER	11100	415N	NEH	77016
VAN BERKEL LN	0	378A	NEC	77346
VAN BROOK LN	0	367Y	NWC	77095
VAN BUREN	1000	493N	SWH	77019
VAN BUREN	1500	538V	DP	77536
VAN BUREN	1600	493N	SWH	77006
VAN BUREN	12200	369R	NWC	77064
VAN BUREN CIR	1900	537N	PA	77502
VANBURY DR	4900	447B	NWC	77084
VANCE	400	659F	LC	77573
VANCE	1900	453M	NEH	77093
VANCE	3800	454K	NEH	77016
VAN CLEVE	2000	573S	SWH	77047
VANCOUVER LN	11800	369R	NWC	77064
VANDALIA WAY	15200	571Y	SWH	77053
VANDEL	100	453F	NEH	77022
VANDEMAN	6900	535E	SEH	77087
VANDEMAR	13100	371X	NWC	77086
VANDERBILT	6300	532F	WU	77005
VANDERBILT PARK DR	3800	618D	PA	77058
VANDERCROFT CT	10600	369K	NWC	77070
VANDER DALE CT	400	485C	SWC	77450
VANDERFORD DR	10800	569B	SWH	77099
VANDERGRIFT DR	16800	375J	NCC	77396
VANDERHEATH DR	12300	569H	SWH	77031
VANDERMERE CT	4400	337B	NEH	77345
VANDERPOOL LN	200	490J	SWH	77024
VANDERWICK DR	20700	486K	SWC	77450
VANDERWILT CT	0	446W	NWC	77449
VANDER WILT LN	1500	446W	NWC	77449
VANDON	10200	412C	NWC	77038
VANDYKE DR	3200	291Q	NWC	77388
VANESSA CIR	14200	330W	NWC	77069
VANESSA HILLS LN	0	293G	SEM	77386
VANESSA SPRINGS LN	0	250X	NWC	77389
VANETA DR	2100	446Y	NWC	77449
VAN ETTEN	6900	533K	SWH	77021
VANE WAY	400	379T	NEC	77532
VAN FLEET	4800	533V	SEH	77033
VAN FLEET	5100	534S	SEH	77033
VANG CT	1100	379X	NEC	77532
VANHORN CT	0	330B	NWC	77379
VAN HUT LN	7900	457E	NEC	77044
VAN HUT LN	8600	416Z	NEC	77044
VANILLA CIR	0	418T	NCC	77044
VANILLA CIRCLE CT	0	418T	NCC	77044
VANILLA RIDGE CT	0	418T	NCC	77044
VANITY DR	3200	613Z	NEB	77584
VANLYNN LN	6500	407P	NWC	77084
VAN METER	800	572U	SWH	77047
VAN METER	3500	573U	SEC	77047
VAN MOLAN	100	453L	NEH	77022
VANN RD	100	459V	HG	77562
VAN NESS	7500	413S	NEH	77037
VANNEVAR WAY CT	0	251C	WD	77381
VANOVER LN	14400	368B	NWC	77429
VAN SANT LN	0	448F	NWH	77084
W. VANTAGE PKWY	15200	373Q	NCC	77032
E. VANTAGE PKWY	15200	373Q	NCC	77032
VANTAGE POINTE CIR	300	660A	LC	77573
VANTAGE VIEW LN	18700	338W	NEC	77346
W. VAN TREASE DR	2200	538R	DP	77536
E. VAN TREASE DR	2200	538R	DP	77536
VAN WALL	13900	450B	NWH	77040
VANWOOD	9200	410R	NWH	77040
VANYA LN	1300	339E	NEC	77336
VANYA LN	25400	339E	NEC	77336
VAN ZANDT	4800	414Q	NEC	77093
VAN ZANDT	5400	415N	NEH	77016
VAQUERO	1800	656U	FR	77546
VAQUERO WAY	10600	367T	NWC	77095
VARDON CT	19400	486D	SWC	77094
VARESE DR	1300	616P	PL	77581
VARICK CT	0	370Y	NWC	77086
VARLA LN	3700	371C	NWC	77014
VARNELL	11700	414M	NEC	77039
VARNER RD	8700	450V	NWH	77080
VARSITY DR	4300	534A	SEH	77004
VARUNA CT	2000	658S	LC	77573
VASHON LN	3600	331B	NWC	77388
VASHTI DR	200	413S	NCC	77037
VASSAR	1300	493W	SWH	77006
VASSAR	1700	492Z	SWH	77098
VASSER	5900	534Y	SEH	77033
VASSER	8800	574A	SEH	77033
VASSER RIDGE DR	3500	331D	NWC	77388
VATANI DR	10600	576K	SEH	77034
VATICAN CT	0	616L	SEC	77089
VAUGHN	1800	453M	NEH	77093
VAUGHN	3900	454K	NEH	77016
VAUGHN	4600	534B	SEH	77023
W. VAUGHN LN	100	538P	DP	77536
E. VAUGHN LN	100	538P	DP	77536
VAUGHNVILLE DR	14600	408T	NWC	77084
VAULTED CHESTNUT LN	20300	326T	NWC	77433
VAULTED OAKS ST	0	492A	NWH	77008
VAULTED PINES DR	8200	338W	NEC	77346
S. VAUXHALL DR	3900	573Y	SEC	77047
VEENSTRA	1	453F	NEH	77022
VEER DR	1000	419F	NEC	77532
VEERA LN	0	528T	NEF	77498
VEGA	2700	411R	NWH	77088
VEGA CT	2300	619X	LC	77573
VEGA LN	0	286F	SWM	77355
VEGAS	7800	375G	HM	77396
VELASCO	100	494N	SEH	77003
VELASCO	2200	493V	SEH	77004
VELASCO	4400	533C	SEH	77004
VELBUN	5900	454N	NEH	77026
VELLER DR	800	373P	NCC	77032
VELMA	1100	538U	DP	77536
VELMA LN	5800	374V	NEH	77396
VELMA LN	5900	375S	NEH	77396
VELMA LN	21000	255P	SEM	77365
VELURE	0	530A	SWH	77036
VELVET	300	658H	LC	77573
VELVET GRASS LN	11200	367V	NWC	77095
VELVET LEAF PLACE	100	251Z	WD	77380
VELVET SHADOW CT	19400	329A	NWC	77375
VELVET SKY CT	0	294Q	SEM	77386
VELVET SKY CT	0	294Q	SEM	77386
VELVET SKY WAY	0	294U	SEM	77386
VELVET SKY WAY	0	294U	SEM	77386
VEMONE	0	496G	NEH	77013
VENA DR	5800	534V	SEH	77087
VENADO DR	0	366K	NWC	77433
VENDI DR	0	571F	SWH	77085
VENDOME CT	0	330F	NWC	77379
VENETIAN DR	24000	525J	NEF	77406
VENETIAN WAY	4100	537R	PA	77503
VENETO CT	0	659M	LC	77573
VENEZIA DR	0	616K	PL	77089
VENEZIA TERRACE CT	0	406F	NWC	77433
VENICE	100	568P	SG	77478
VENICE	5400	492L	SWH	77007
VENICE CIR	13300	570J	SF	77477
N. VENICE DR	1600	616K	PL	77581
S. VENICE DR	2300	616N	PL	77581
VENICE LN	12800	570J	SF	77477
VENICE VILLA LN	13400	528X	NEF	77498
VENIDA	7800	455B	NEH	77028
VENITO DR	0	447A	NWC	77449
VENNARD RD	8000	576F	SEH	77034
N. VENTANA PKWY	0	445B	NWC	77493
VENTANA MEADOWS DR	0	445E	NWC	77493
VENTANA PRAIRIE DR	0	445F	NWC	77493
VENTURA DR	0	659S	LC	77573
VENTURA LN	4800	534E	SEH	77021
VENTURA CANYON CT	24500	485E	NEF	77494
VENTURA CANYON DR	1200	485E	NEF	77494
VENTURE LN	8600	578D	LP	77571
VENTURE PARK CT	0	525V	NEF	77406
VENTURE PARK DR	0	525U	NEF	77406
VENUS	0	411Z	NWH	77088
VENUS	7000	411R	NWH	77088
VENUS DR	25400	257G	RF	77357
W. VENUS LAKE CIR	0	528Y	SWH	77099
S. VENUS LAKE CIR	0	528Y	SWH	77099
N. VENUS LAKE CIR	0	528Y	SWH	77099
E. VENUS LAKE CIR	0	528Y	SWH	77099
VENUS PARK LN	0	488Z	SWH	77082
VERA DR	14800	375S	NEH	77396
VERA CRUZ	1100	338Z	NEC	77532
VERADO WAY	0	609Y	NEF	77459
VERA JEAN CT	9900	411N	NWH	77088
VERA JEAN DR	6500	411N	NWH	77088
VERA LOU	1100	533U	SEH	77051
VERANDA DR	3700	446L	NWC	77449
VERANDA FALLS	0	619U	LC	77573
VERANDA GREEN TRAIL	6300	337U	NEC	77346
VERANDA MIST	0	619U	LC	77573
VERANDA TERRACE	0	619U	LC	77573
VERANDA VALLEY	0	619U	LC	77573
VERANDA WAY	0	619U	LC	77573
VERANO	10800	496F	JC	77029
VERANO VIEW LN	0	445F	NWC	77493
VERBENA LN	13200	528G	SWH	77083
VERBENA VALLEY WAY	0	331A	NWC	77388
VERCORS MOUNTAIN DR	0	450K	NWH	77080
VERDANT BROOK DR	12600	571F	SWH	77085
VERDANT MEADOW CT	4100	446H	NWC	77449
VERDANT SPRING TRAIL	0	445N	NWC	77493
VERDANT WAY	5100	330Z	NWC	77069
VERDANT WILLOW CT	17100	407Q	NWC	77095
VERDANT WILLOW WAY	17200	407Q	NWC	77095
VERDE CIR	0	485M	SWC	77450
VERDE RD	7700	456J	NEH	77078
VERDE CANYON DR	20300	526E	NEF	77450
VERDECOVE LN	21000	291W	NWC	77388
W. VERDECREEK CIR	0	366Z	NWC	77433
VERDE GLEN LN	12400	570F	SWH	77071
VERDE MAR LN	14100	408L	NWC	77095
VERDE MEADOW CT	7100	408R	NWC	77041
VERDE MIST LN	0	372D	NCC	77073
VERDENBRUK DR	5100	371J	NWC	77066
VERDEN MEADOW CT	0	408R	NWC	77041
VERDE PARK LN	0	367P	NWC	77433
VERDE PLACE LN	0	444T	KT	77493
VERDE TRAILS DR	900	372D	NCC	77073
VERDE VALLEY DR	0	658X	LC	77573
VERDE VALLEY DR	6100	375E	NCC	77396
VERDE VISTA DR	0	406G	NWC	77433
VERDI DR	12800	489G	SWH	77024
VERDINELL	7400	460U	MN	77521
VERDIN PLACE	0	250K	NWC	77389
VERDIN PLACE	0	250K	NWC	77389
VERDI PLACE	0	453G	NEH	77022
VERDI WAY CT	16000	377L	NEC	77044
VERDOME LN	4300	451E	NWH	77092
VERDUN DR	12600	456M	NEC	77049
VERDUN DR	13100	457J	NEC	77049
VERDUN LN	1200	657E	FR	77546
VERHALEN AVE	1000	413C	NCC	77039
VERHALEN AVE	2300	414A	NCC	77039
VERIDIAN GROVE DR	6300	528H	SWH	77072
VERISMO DR	0	293K	SEM	77386
VERLAINE DR	11200	368Q	NWC	77065
VER LEE CT	8900	412M	NEH	77037
VERLIE LN	7800	530K	SWH	77036
VERMARION	13500	370A	NWC	77070
VERME'S PARK LN	7100	377C	NEC	77346
VERMILLION CT	19300	406V	NWC	77449
VERMILLION DR	500	536K	PA	77506
VERMILLION DR	2700	610U	MC	77459
VERMILLION RD	2500	620K	SB	77586
VERMILLION OAK ST	2000	611S	FS	77545
VERMILLION VIEW ST	0	611S	FS	77545
VERMILLON	21300	257T	SEM	77357
VERMONT	0	612W	FS	77545
VERMONT	1400	492R	SWH	77006
VERMONT	1800	541A	BT	77520
VERMONT	1900	492R	SWH	77019
VERMONT GREEN TRAIL	9600	576J	SEH	77075
VERNAGE RD	1100	572R	SWH	77047
VERNAZZA DR	0	257E	SEM	77357
VERNEATH DR	0	446B	NWC	77449
VERNGATE CT	4200	333C	NCC	77373
VERNGATE DR	23400	333C	NCC	77373
VERNIER WOODS LN	19600	290Z	NWC	77379
VERNLAKE CIR	1900	446Y	NWC	77084
VERNON	100	288L	TB	77375
VERNON	3400	494F	NEH	77020
VERNON	13000	368Q	NWC	77429
VERNWOOD	7500	410R	NWH	77040
VERONA	0	258C	SEM	77357
VERONA CT	1200	659L	LC	77573
VERONA DR	2100	616J	PL	77581
VERONA FALLS CT	0	526P	NEF	77407
VERONA RIVER DR	0	445B	NWC	77493
VERONE	4300	531M	BL	77401
VERRET LN	800	332J	NWC	77090
VERRON TRAIL	23600	296H	SEM	77365
VERSAILLES CT	800	496D	NEC	77015
VERSAILLES DR	0	613V	NEB	77584
VERSAILLES DR	12400	496D	NEC	77015
VERSAILLES LAKES LN	11600	489X	SWH	77082
S. VERSHIRE CIR	0	249A	SWM	77354
N. VERSHIRE CIR	0	249A	SWM	77354
VERSOL	8000	410G	NWC	77064
VESPER	8800	575H	SEH	77075
S. VESPER BEND CIR	1	249D	SWM	77382
N. VESPER BEND CIR	100	249C	SWM	77382
VESPER LAKE CT	0	376W	NEC	77396
VEST CT	0	373E	NCC	77073
VESTA CT	37000	246G	SWM	77355
VESTAVIA CT	13400	330Y	NWC	77069
VESTAVIA DR	5600	330Y	NWC	77069
VETERANS DR	2600	615N	PL	77584
VETERANS MEMORIAL	0	331W	NWC	77379
VETERANS MEMORIAL DR	7500	412F	NWH	77088
VETERANS MEMORIAL DR	9500	412F	NWC	77038
VETERANS MEMORIAL DR	10300	372W	NWC	77038
VETERANS MEMORIAL DR	10800	371Q	NWC	77067
VETERANS MEMORIAL DR	12300	371Q	NWC	77014
VEVA DR	2900	614R	PL	77584
VEYBLUM	9700	495R	NEH	77029
VIA ASHFORD TERRACE	0	528M	SWH	77082
VIA BARBARINI	3100	371Y	NWC	77038
VIA BAROLO	0	368C	NWC	77429
VIA BELLA DR	8000	527M	NEF	77083
VIA BELTERRA LN	0	659H	LC	77573
VIA CAPRI CT	11000	525N	NEF	77469
VIA CECILIA	0	659R	LC	77573
VIA CHIANTI CT	12100	368D	NWC	77429
VIA CHIANTI LN	13400	368D	NWC	77429
VIA CORTONA	0	659M	LC	77573
VIA DAVINCI LN	12100	368D	NWC	77429
VIA DEL NORTE DR	14600	528E	SWC	77083
VIA DEL NORTE DR	14800	527H	SWC	77083
VIA DEL SOL DR	7000	528E	SWC	77083
VIA DORA	15600	419F	NEC	77532
E. VIA DORA CT	800	419F	NEC	77532
W. VIA DORA CT	900	419F	NEC	77532
VIA ENCLAVE	0	410Z	NWH	77040
VIA ESPANA DR	6300	527H	SWC	77083
VIA FIRENZE	0	659R	LC	77573
VIA FIRENZE LN	12000	368D	NWC	77429
S. VIA FONTANA CT	11400	525J	NEF	77406
VIAGRA DR	10400	569C	SWH	77031
VIA LA STRADA	0	659L	LC	77573
VIALINDA DR	6500	527G	SWC	77083
VIA LUNA	0	368D	NWC	77429
VIA MICHAELANGELO CT	13500	368D	NWC	77429
VIA MODERNA DR	0	525J	NEF	77406
VIAMONTE LN	0	331J	NWC	77379
VIAMONTE LN	0	331J	NWC	77379
VIA MONTESANO	0	659C	LC	77573
VIANA MEADOW CT	0	366X	NWC	77433
VIANO LN	0	491C	NWH	77055
VIA PALAZZO LN	12000	368D	NWC	77429
VIA PINETTA	0	368C	NWC	77429
VIA PONTE VECCHIO LN	13600	368D	NWC	77429
VIA PORTA ROSA	12100	368D	NWC	77429
VIA PRINCIPLE PKWY	0	257E	SEM	77357
VIA PRIVATO DR	0	525J	NEF	77406

Street Name	Block	Pg/Sq	Loc	Zips
VIA REAL DR	7300	527L	NEF	77083
VIA RICA DR	14200	528J	SWC	77083
VIA ROMA	0	659M	LC	77573
VIA SALERNO CT	24500	524M	NEF	77406
VIA SAN ROCCO	0	368D	NWC	77429
VIASANTORI DR	0	525J	NEF	77406
VIA SIENA	0	659M	LC	77573
VIA SIENA CT	13700	368D	NWC	77429
VIA SIENA LN	12000	368D	NWC	77429
VIA SONOMA	0	659M	LC	77573
VIA SOVANA	0	659R	LC	77573
VIA TORRE DE PISA	0	368C	NWC	77429
VIA TOSCANA	0	659M	LC	77573
VIA TOSCANO CT	12000	368D	NWC	77429
VIA TOSCANO LN	13500	368D	NWC	77429
VIA VENEZIA BLVD	0	524R	NEF	77406
VIA VERDE DR	15100	527M	SWC	77083
VIA VERDONE DR	0	524M	NEF	77406
VIA VIALE DR	0	525J	NEF	77406
VIA VISTA DR	7400	527M	SWC	77083
VICDALE DR	11900	570A	SWH	77031
VICENZA AVE	0	445E	NWC	77493
VICEROY DR	100	576G	SEH	77034
VICK	3200	492M	SWH	77019
VICK RD	0	256L	SEM	77357
VICKERS	400	536X	SH	77587
VICKERS RD	0	326C	NWC	77429
VICKERY DR	0	374Y	NCC	77032
VICKERY DR	0	414C	NCC	77032
VICKERY DR	1300	568E	SG	77498
VICKERY DR	11400	414L	NCC	77093
VICKERY DR	11700	414L	NCC	77039
VICKERY DR	15200	374Q	NEH	77032
VICKI LN	12200	368M	NWC	77429
VICKI RD	15600	323X	NWC	77447
VICKIE LN	13000	497J	NEH	77015
VICKIE SPRINGS LN	6400	371X	NWC	77086
VICKIJOHN CIR	10800	530Y	SWH	77071
VICKIJOHN CT	10800	530Y	SWH	77071
VICKIJOHN DR	5900	531W	SWH	77096
VICKIJOHN DR	7600	530Y	SWH	77071
VICKIJOHN DR	9100	530W	SWH	77031
VICKITA DR	5500	374Z	NCC	77032
VICKRIDGE LN	7900	330K	NWC	77379
VICKSBURG	13100	497E	NEH	77015
VICKSBURG BLVD	0	610Y	MC	77459
VICKSBURG BLVD		610Q	MC	77459
VICKSBURG RD	0	660R	TC	77539
E. VICKSBURG ESTATES	0	610X	MC	77459
W. VICKSBURG ESTATES DR	0	610X	MC	77459
VICKSBURG MANOR LN	0	377J	NEC	77346
VICKSTON LN	13600	371B	NWC	77014
VICTOR	1100	493P	SWH	77019
VICTOR LN	12700	488M	SWH	77077
VICTORIA	0	495A	NEH	77020
VICTORIA	0	500V	BT	77520
VICTORIA	0	658Q	LC	77573
VICTORIA	6300	494D	NEH	77020
VICTORIA	13700	497C	NEC	77015
VICTORIA CT	1800	568Y	SG	77478
VICTORIA CT	1900	658Q	LC	77573
VICTORIA CT	2200	610A	MC	77459
VICTORIA DR	100	452H	NWH	77022
VICTORIA DR	200	453E	NWH	77022
VICTORIA CHASE LN	10000	576N	SEH	77075
VICTORIA CREST LN	9900	576N	SEH	77075
VICTORIA ESTATES DR	30600	252V	SEM	77386
VICTORIA FALLS	10000	576N	SEH	77075
VICTORIA FALLS DR	16600	330P	NWC	77379
VICTORIA FOREST DR	8600	411K	NWC	77088
VICTORIA GROVE	9900	576N	SEH	77075
VICTORIA HEIGHTS LN	9900	576N	SEH	77075
VICTORIA LAKES CIR	17400	329L	NWC	77379
VICTORIA LAKES DR	0	329L	NWC	77379
VICTORIA LAKES DR	800	444X	KT	77493
VICTORIA LANDING TRAIL	0	406W	NWC	77449
VICTORIAN CT	1000	620G	SB	77586
VICTORIAN LN	0	459V	HG	77562
S. VICTORIANA CIR	0	250Q	NWC	77389
N. VICTORIANA CIR	0	250Q	NWC	77389
VICTORIAN MANOR LN	0	573Y	SEC	77047
VICTORIAN RUN	0	568E	NEF	77498
VICTORIAN VILLAGE DR	8600	570F	SWH	77071
VICTORIA PARK LN	10000	576N	SEH	77075
VICTORIA PINE DR	0	293H	SEM	77386
VICTORIA POINT LN	9900	576N	SEH	77075
VICTORIA REACH DR	0	376R	NEC	77346
VICTORIA RIDGE LN	10000	576N	SEH	77075
VICTORIA ROSE LN	0	376W	NEC	77396
VICTORIA SPRINGS DR	0	526P	NEF	77407
VICTORIA WAY	100	657E	FR	77546
VICTORIA WOOD WAY	0	616H	SEH	77089
VICTORIOUS DR	20400	285M	NWC	77447
W. VICTORSON	1300	497K	NEC	77015
E. VICTORSON	1300	497K	NEC	77015
VICTORY DR	600	570S	SF	77477
S. VICTORY DR	700	412S	NWH	77088
N. VICTORY DR	700	412U	NWH	77088
VICTORY DR	3700	411V	NWH	77088
VICTORY LN	7800	457E	NEC	77049
VICTORY CANYON LN	0	249U	NWC	77375
VICTORY LAKES DR	0	659W	LC	77573
VICTORY TERRACE LN	3600	485U	NEF	77450
VICTORY TRACE CT	0	326V	NWC	77429
VIDAILIA POINT	14100	367D	NWC	77429
VIDLER WAY	500	338H	NEH	77336
W. VIEJO DR	100	657T	FR	77546
E. VIEJO DR	100	657Q	FR	77546
VIEJO RD	1500	659S	LC	77573
VIENNA CT	11200	368T	NWC	77429
VIENNA PLACE PKWY	0	536Z	PA	77506
VIENNA TRAILS LN	11200	367U	NWC	77095
VIERA LN	0	575U	SEH	77075
VIETA	7900	457F	NEC	77049
VIEUX CARRE DR	100	493C	NWH	77009
VIEW	2200	536V	PA	77502
VIEWFIELD CT	13800	618A	SEH	77059
VIEW GLEN CT	0	577S	SEH	77034
VIEW MEADOW LN	13700	577W	SEH	77034
W. VIEW MEADOW LOOP	0	577S	SEH	77034
N. VIEW MEADOW LOOP	0	577S	SEH	77034
VIEW PARK LN	7700	407M	NWC	77095
VIEWPOINT CT	0	446F	NWC	77449
VIEW POINT LN	0	577W	SEH	77034
VIEWRIDGE DR	24800	484L	NEF	77494
VIEW VALLEY TRAIL	0	445K	NWC	77493
VIGINIA GRACE DR	0	527T	NEF	77479
VIKING DR	1600	452E	NWH	77018
VIKING DR	4300	451F	NWH	77092
VIKING LN	2200	502S	BT	77520
VIKING LANDING CT	3300	291U	NWC	77388
VIKING LANDING CT	3300	291U	NWC	77388

Street Name	Block	Pg/Sq	Loc	Zips
VIKRAM DR	0	411D	NWC	77038
VILLA	0	575E	SEH	77061
E. VILLA	4200	535Q	SEH	77017
VILLA DR	500	620L	SB	77586
VILLA DR	6900	574D	SEH	77061
N. VILLA DR	9800	409C	NWC	77064
W. VILLA DR	9900	409G	NWC	77064
N. VILLA LN	0	328K	NWC	77377
VILLA LN	3000	609M	MC	77459
VILLA ARBOR DR	0	369D	NWC	77070
VILLA BELLA CT	0	659R	LC	77573
VILLA BEND DR	1	330X	NWC	77069
VILLA BERGAMO CT	0	486H	SWC	77094
VILLA BERGAMO LN	0	487E	SWC	77094
VILLA CANYON PLACE	1	250A	WD	77382
VILLA CAPRI LN	1200	338Z	NEH	77532
VILLA COURT DR	1000	619G	TL	77586
VILLA CREEK	0	334M	NCC	77338
VILLA CREEK DR	2200	296Z	NEH	77339
VILLA DEL	2600	528X	NEF	77498
VILLA DEL LAGO DR	1700	610P	MC	77459
VILLA DEL NORTE DR	16200	332U	NCC	77073
VILLA DEL REY	0	618U	SEC	77058
VILLA DEL SOL DR	7000	527G	SWC	77083
VILLA DE MATEL RD	900	494Y	SEH	77023
VILLA DE MATEL RD	1100	534C	SEH	77023
VILLA DE NORTE ST	0	369D	NWC	77070
VILLA FONTANA WAY	16000	331T	NWC	77068
VILLA FOREST	0	330T	NWC	77069
VILLAGE CIR	1800	577F	PA	77504
VILLAGE CIR	2500	444Q	KT	77493
VILLAGE CIR	14600	368S	NWC	77429
VILLAGE CIR	21600	296E	SEM	77365
VILLAGE CT	0	371Z	NWC	77038
W. VILLAGE CT	1000	537J	PA	77506
E. VILLAGE CT	1000	537J	PA	77506
VILLAGE CT	2600	444Q	KT	77493
VILLAGE CT	4600	569X	MC	77459
VILLAGE CT	21600	296E	SEM	77365
VILLAGE DR	0	257T	SEM	77357
VILLAGE DR	0	615Y	PL	77581
VILLAGE DR	200	568L	SG	77498
VILLAGE DR	16500	409K	JV	77040
VILLAGE DR	22300	405Y	NWC	77449
VILLAGE DR	23600	296E	SEM	77365
VILLAGE LN	0	616R	FR	77546
VILLAGE LN	700	576D	PA	77504
VILLAGE LN	3000	538U	DP	77536
VILLAGE LN	4600	500M	BT	77521
VILLAGE LN	21600	296E	SEM	77365
VILLAGE LN	21630	296E	SEM	77365
VILLAGE ARBOUR DR	5600	444Q	KT	77493
VILLAGE BELL DR	9700	412F	NWC	77038
VILLAGE BEND LN	10900	529K	SWH	77072
VILLAGE BIRCH	14100	618A	SEH	77062
VILLAGE BRANCH LN	0	527J	NEF	77407
VILLAGE BREEZE DR	17300	328L	NWC	77377
VILLAGEBRIAR LN	0	407V	NWC	77084
VILLAGE BRIDGE DR	6700	377C	NEC	77346
VILLAGE BROOK DR	0	610P	MC	77459
VILLAGE BROOK LN	0	612P	PL	77545
VILLAGE BROOK RD	1900	618L	SEH	77062
VILLAGE CENTER CT	9200	409G	NWC	77064
VILLAGE CHASE DR	19800	446Y	NWC	77084
VILLAGE COMMONS DR	17300	328Q	NWC	77377
VILLAGE CORNER CT	16800	578Z	PA	77059
VILLAGE CORNER DR	3800	578Z	PA	77059
VILLAGE COVE CT	0	366K	NWC	77433
VILLAGE COVE LN	0	366J	NWC	77433
VILLAGE CREEK DR	300	618S	SEH	77598
VILLAGE CREEK DR	5000	614Z	PL	77584
VILLAGE CREEK LOOP	0	253U	NWC	77389
VILLAGE CREEK TRAIL	17000	328Q	NWC	77377
VILLAGE CREST CT	12500	328Q	NWC	77377
VILLAGE CROSSING LN	21300	256W	SEM	77365
VILLAGE CROSSING TRAIL	2100	293W	NCC	77373
VILLAGE DALE AVE	2100	617D	SEH	77059
VILLAGE DALE AVE	2200	577Z	SEH	77059
VILLAGE DALE AVE	2400	578W	SEH	77059
VILLAGEDALE DR	3200	297W	NEH	77339
VILLAGE DOGWOOD CT	19000	446H	NWC	77084
VILLAGE ELM	14900	618B	SEH	77062
VILLAGE ESTATES DR	2400	336D	NEH	77339
VILLAGE EVERGREEN TRL	14500	617M	SEH	77062
VILLAGE FALLS CT	3200	296Z	NEH	77339
VILLAGE FOREST CT	5800	451B	NWH	77092
VILLAGE FOREST DR	0	609P	NEF	77479
VILLAGE GARDEN DR	1300	569X	MC	77459
VILLAGE GATE DR	0	614G	PL	77581
VILLAGE GATE DR	12800	488Y	SWH	77082
VILLAGE GREEN CT	1500	488R	SWH	77077
VILLAGE GREEN DR	0	568Z	SG	77478
VILLAGE GREEN DR	5500	444Q	KT	77493
VILLAGE GREEN DR	17400	409K	JV	77040
VILLAGE GROVE DR	3600	376G	NEC	77396
VILLAGE GROVE DR	5800	614L	PL	77584
VILLAGE HEIGHTS CT	4400	578F	PA	77505
VILLAGE HILLS DR	8800	330J	NWC	77379
S. VILLAGE KNOLL CIR	1	250C	WD	77381
E. VILLAGE KNOLL CIR	1	250C	WD	77381
W. VILLAGE KNOLL CIR	100	250C	WD	77381
N. VILLAGE KNOLL CIR	100	250C	WD	77381
VILLAGE KNOLL PLACE	1	250C	WD	77381
VILLAGE LAKE DR	7100	406R	NWC	77433
VILLAGE LEAF DR	2300	252Z	SEM	77386
VILLAGE LINKS TRAILS RD	0	326V	NWC	77429
VILLAGE MANOR DR	3700	297T	NEH	77345
VILLAGE MAPLE CT	19000	446R	NWC	77084
VILLAGE MEADOW CT	0	328L	NWC	77377
VILLAGE MILL LN	7600	527J	NEF	77407
VILLAGE MILLS DR	2700	614R	PL	77584
VILLAGE OAK DR	2500	444Q	KT	77493
VILLAGE OAKS DR	3300	296Z	NEH	77339
VILLAGE OAKS LN	1	450Y	SV	77055
VILLAGE OF FONDREN DR	8600	570F	SWH	77071
VILLAGE OF KINGS LAKE BLVD	0	416G	NEC	77044
VILLAGE PARK CIR	11800	490F	SWH	77024
VILLAGE PARK DR	1900	570W	MC	77489
VILLAGE PARK DR	3100	297W	NEH	77339
VILLAGE PARK DR	4500	577F	PA	77504
VILLAGE PARK DR	5600	444Q	KT	77493
VILLAGE PINE DR	3600	297W	NEH	77339
VILLAGE PKWY	6100	532G	SWH	77005
VILLAGE PLACE DR	11500	489T	SWH	77077
VILLAGE POINT LN	13800	528T	NEF	77498
VILLAGE POND LN	0	611S	FS	77545
VILLAGE RIDGE DR	19700	329A	NWC	77375
VILLAGE ROSE LN	0	528Q	SWC	77072
VILLAGE ROSE LN	8000	528Q	SWH	77072
VILLAGE SPRINGS CT	3000	297N	NEH	77339
VILLAGE SPRINGS DR	5000	297N	NEH	77339
VILLAGE SQUARE DR	800	288G	TB	77375

Street Name	Block	Pg/Sq	Loc	Zips
VILLAGE SQUARE DR	2500	610B	MC	77489
VILLAGE SQUARE DR	12700	488R	SWH	77077
VILLAGE TERRACE	8400	410E	NWC	77040
VILLAGE TOWER DR	0	376B	NEC	77369
VILLAGE TRACE DR	16700	611F	SWH	77053
VILLAGE TRAIL DR	10500	368V	NWC	77065
VILLAGE TRAIL DR	10800	369S	NWC	77065
VILLAGE TREE WAY	19800	446Q	NWC	77084
VILLAGE VIEW DR	4400	569X	MC	77459
VILLAGE WALK	0	419H	CB	77532
VILLAGE WALK CT	4000	337C	NEH	77345
VILLAGE WAY	2500	444P	KT	77493
VILLAGE WAY	2900	536Z	PA	77502
VILLAGE WAY	7000	534M	SEH	77087
VILLAGE WAY	16600	254D	SEM	77302
VILLAGE WAY	17700	255A	SEM	77302
VILLAGE WAY DR	12800	408Z	NWC	77041
VILLAGE WELL DR	3900	376H	NEC	77396
VILLAGE WOODS DR	3100	297W	NEH	77339
VILLAGIO LN	0	485U	NEF	77450
VILLA GLEN DR	3600	411R	NWH	77088
VILLAGROVE DR	13300	457E	NEC	77049
VILLA HEIGHTS DR	11500	370R	NWC	77066
VILLA HILL DR	4200	297X	NEH	77345
VILLA HILLS DR	5900	370M	NWC	77066
VILLA LAGO LN	0	369H	NWC	77070
VILLA LAKE DR	7800	408J	NWC	77095
VILLA LANTE DR	0	326U	NWC	77429
VILLA LANTE DR	0	326U	NWC	77429
VILLA LEA DR	10000	530Y	SWH	77071
VILLA LEA DR	11800	570G	SWH	77071
VILLA LISA DR	0	525J	NEF	77406
VILLAMONTE	0	259E	SEM	77357
VILLA MOUNTAIN LN	7000	330B	NWC	77379
VILLANDRY LN	8100	334R	NCC	77338
VILLANOVA	3800	532E	WU	77005
VILLA PALMS DR	7800	408J	NWC	77095
VILLA PARK DR	3200	296Z	NEH	77339
VILLA PINES DR	3700	297W	NEH	77339
VILLA PISA LN	0	659L	LC	77573
VILLARET DR	16200	527F	SWC	77083
VILLA RIDGE DR	3800	331S	NWC	77068
VILLA ROSE DR	2200	618G	SEH	77062
VILLARREAL DR	6600	571W	SWH	77489
VILLA RUFINO	0	528C	SWH	77082
VILLA SONIA	0	528C	SWH	77082
VILLAS ON POTOMAC	0	491S	SWH	77057
VILLAS PALMS DR	0	369D	NWC	77070
VILLA VERDE	9900	369Y	NWC	77064
VILLA WAY DR	17800	331F	NWC	77379
VILLAWOOD LN	12700	528L	SWH	77072
VILLITA	9600	455Z	NEH	77013
VILLMONT LN	1200	489J	SWH	77077
VILVEN LN	9500	450P	NWH	77080
VINCA CT	13200	328Y	NWC	77429
VINCA RANCH DR	0	484R	NEF	77494
VINCE	200	536G	PA	77506
VINCE	2000	536U	PA	77502
VINCENNES	0	530B	SWH	77036
VINCENNES OAK ST	15000	328J	NWC	77429
VINCENT	100	453Y	NWH	77009
VINCENT CROSSING DR	0	253S	SEM	77386
VINCES BRIDGE	1900	568Z	SG	77478
VINDALE DR	14000	417X	NEC	77044
VINDON DR	12500	489H	SWH	77024
VINE	700	502W	BT	77520
VINE	1000	493M	NEH	77002
VINEARBOR	8600	574A	SEH	77033
VINE BRANCH LN	0	524C	NEF	77494
VINEBRIAR DR	0	253S	SEM	77386
VINE BROOK	0	251R	WD	77380
VINECHASE DR	0	295R	SEM	77365
VINE CREEK DR	2300	337D	NEH	77345
VINE CREST DR	0	370V	NWC	77086
VINECREST DR	3800	613Y	NEB	77584
VINEDALE DR	11400	529X	SWH	77099
VINE FOREST DR	18000	377A	NEC	77346
VINE GROVE CT	7400	407J	NWC	77433
VINEGROVE FALLS CT	0	326T	NWC	77433
VINEHILL DR	13800	568F	SG	77498
VINEMEAD CT	2100	486Q	SWC	77450
VINEMEAD CT	2200	486Q	SWC	77450
VINEMOSS LN	15800	326V	NWC	77429
VINE RIVER DR	3000	528X	NEF	77498
VINERY CT	13200	328U	NWC	77429
VINERY LN	13700	328U	NWC	77429
VINETREE LN	9100	410U	NWC	77040
VINETT	5100	536J	SEH	77017
VINE WALK	0	491F	SWH	77024
VINEWOOD CIR	6900	411T	NWH	77088
VINEWOOD DR	6100	411T	NWH	77088
VINEWOOD LN	6100	657Q	LC	77573
VINEWOOD LN	7300	528L	SWH	77072
VINEYARD CT	2200	568A	SG	77498
VINEYARD DR	3400	487Y	SWC	77082
VINEYARD DR	3500	527C	SWC	77082
VINEYARD BEND	0	614G	PL	77581
VINEYARD BEND CT	0	614G	PL	77581
VINEYARD BEND LN	0	485U	NEF	77494
VINEYARD CREEK LN	0	615J	PL	77089
VINEYARD CREEK LN	0	297J	NEH	77365
VINEYARD FALLS DR	13200	528L	SWH	77083
VINEYARD HAVEN CT	0	446E	NWC	77449
VINEYARD HILL DR	5800	614G	PL	77581
VINEYARD HOLLOW CT		249V	NWC	77375
S. VINEYARD MEADOW TRAIL LN	0	446E	NWC	77449
N. VINEYARD MEADOW TRAIL LN	0	446E	NWC	77449
VINEYARD MEADOW TRAIL CT	0	446E	NWC	77449
VINEYARD TRAIL LN	12500	568D	SG	77478
VINEY CREEK DR	15900	408E	NWC	77095
VINING RD	30100	283E	NWC	77484
VINING RD	30900	282H	NWC	77484
VINITA	2100	576B	SEH	77034
VINKINS CT	12400	570F	SWH	77071
VINKINS RD	8600	570F	SWH	77071
VINLAND DR	18200	619S	NB	77058
VINLAND SHORES CT	0	290Z	NWC	77379
VINO	9000	531G	SWH	77096
VINSON	7300	412W	NWH	77088
VINSONIA	100	541S	MP	77571
VINSON RANCH LN		484W	NEF	77494
VINTAGE	2900	454S	NEH	77026
VINTAGE PKWY	0	329Y	NWC	77070
VINTAGE CENTRE DR	13700	370A	NWC	77069
VINTAGE CREEK DR	7900	330N	NWC	77379
VINTAGE FALLS DR	15400	326S	NWC	77433
VINTAGE GROVE CT	4800	446C	NWC	77449
VINTAGE KNOLL LN	0	293X	NCC	77373
VINTAGE LAKES DR	0	329U	NWC	77070
VINTAGE LEAF CIR	12300	369K	NWC	77070
VINTAGE PARK BLVD	0	329U	NWC	77070
VINTAGE PRESERVE PKWY	0	329Y	NWC	77070

Street Name	Block	Pg/Sq	Loc	Zips
VINTAGE SPRINGS LN	9800	329U	NWC	77070
VINTAGE VALLEY DR	3900	528A	SWC	77082
VINTAGE VILLA DR	9800	329U	NWC	77070
VINTAGE WOOD CIR	8300	329H	NWC	77379
VINTAGE WOOD LN	17000	330N	NWC	77379
VINTAGE WOOD LN	17800	330J	NWC	77379
VINTAGEWOOD LN CIR	17800	330J	NWC	77379
VINTON CT	8400	410K	NWC	77040
VINTON LN	21900	245V	SWM	77355
VINVALE	12600	370K	NWH	77066
VINY RIDGE DR	8200	527R	NEF	77083
VIOLA CT	12000	248N	SWM	77362
VIOLA DR	2200	659B	LC	77573
VIOLA LN	0	539V	LP	77571
VIOLA DALE CT	0	334Q	NCC	77388
VIOLA DALE CT	0	334Q	NCC	77388
VIOLET	2300	537U	PA	77503
VIOLET CT	27400	248E	SWM	77354
VIOLET HAZE TRAIL	0	325M	NWC	77429
VIOLET HOLLOW PARK LN	0	328Q	NWC	77433
VIOLET HOLLOW PARK LN	0	328A	NWC	77377
VIOLET MEADOW LN	25700	484V	NEF	77494
VIOLET PATH LN	0	571G	SWC	77083
VIOLET SUNSET CIR	0	249Q	NWC	77375
VIOLET TRACE CT	16800	326J	NWC	77433
VIOLET VIEW DR	0	460U	NEC	77562
VIOLET WILLOW CT	0	328A	NWC	77377
VIRA CT	13600	371C	NWC	77014
VIRA LN	13700	371C	NWC	77014
VIREO	24700	284V	NWC	77447
VIRGIE COMMUNITY RD	100	248N	SWM	77354
VIRGIL	100	536X	SH	77587
VIRGIL	7400	412T	NWH	77088
VIRGINIA	0	525V	NEF	77406
VIRGINIA	100	540Y	LP	77571
VIRGINIA	100	536W	SH	77587
VIRGINIA	300	616Y	FR	77546
VIRGINIA	400	580C	LP	77571
VIRGINIA	800	659Q	LC	77573
VIRGINIA	1100	575D	SH	77587
VIRGINIA	2600	540D	BT	77520
VIRGINIA	2600	492U	SWH	77098
VIRGINIA	2800	533J	SWH	77054
VIRGINIA AVE	0	538T	DP	77536
VIRGINIA CT	6400	532F	WU	77005
VIRGINIA LN	1800	537N	PA	77502
VIRGINIA LN	24900	296Q	SEM	77365
VIRGINIA COLONY DR	2700	657D	SEC	77598
VIRGINIA FALLS LN	0	366V	NWC	77433
VIRGINIA FERN WAY	15700	578T	SEH	77059
VIRGINIA FIELDS DR	0	524E	NEF	77494
VIRGINIA GARDENS	2400	614U	PL	77584
VIRGINIA PLACE	1	245F	SWM	77355
VIRGINIA WATER LN	7600	408L	NWC	77095
VIRGIN ISLAND DR	3200	609J	SG	77479
VIRLINE LN	0	371M	NWC	77067
VIRTUE CT	2000	658T	LC	77573
VISCARO LN	9200	375R	NEC	77396
VISCARO LN	9400	376N	NEC	77396
VISCO	0	618Y	WB	77598
VISCONTI CT	10900	524R	NEF	77406
VISCOUNT RD	900	374A	NEH	77032
VISCOUNT LANDING	0	527W	NEF	77469
VISION LN	5600	574J	SEH	77048
VISTA AVE	500	501V	BT	77520
VISTA DR	6100	614U	PL	77584
VISTA LN	3000	614V	PL	77584
VISTA RD	100	576D	PA	77504
VISTA RD	1200	577A	PA	77504
VISTA RD	4700	577A	PA	77505
VISTA BAY LN	6000	409W	NWC	77041
VISTA BEND DR	800	332V	NCC	77073
VISTA BLUE LN	0	609S	NEF	77479
VISTA BLUFF LN	0	578T	SEH	77059
VISTA BROOK DR	13100	408M	NWC	77041
VISTA CAMINO DR	6200	527H	SWC	77083
VISTA CANYON CT	0	326U	NWC	77433
VISTA CLIFF WAY	0	445F	NWC	77493
VISTA COVE CIR	1	251E	WD	77381
VISTA COVE DR	1	251E	WD	77381
VISTA CREEK CT	0	568U	SG	77478
VISTA CREEK DR	0	568U	SG	77478
VISTADALE CT	8400	335J	NCC	77338
VISTADALE DR	8300	335J	NCC	77338
VISTA DEL LAGO DR	1000	298Q	NEC	77336
VISTA DEL MAR DR	15900	527G	SWC	77083
VISTA DEL RANCHO DR	8100	527R	SWC	77083
VISTA DEL SOL DR	8000	527M	NEF	77083
VISTA DE ORO	0	369D	NWC	77070
VISTA DE TRES LAGOS DR	23200	291E	NWC	77389
VISTA FOREST	6300	411K	NWC	77088
S. VISTAGLEN LOOP	1400	408X	NWC	77084
W. VISTA GLEN LOOP	5600	408Y	NWC	77084
W. VISTAGLEN LOOP	5600	408X	NWC	77084
VISTA GRANDE DR	6300	527H	SWC	77083
VISTA GROVE CIR	800	332V	NCC	77073
VISTA HAVEN LN	0	487A	SWC	77494
VISTA HEIGHTS DR	14900	326S	NWC	77433
VISTA HILLS DR	0	526Q	NEF	77407
VISTA LAKE CT	2000	568Z	SG	77478
VISTA LAKE CT	19700	406R	NWC	77433
VISTA LAKE DR	3200	568Z	SG	77478
W. VISTA LAKE LN	0	253P	SEM	77386
S. VISTA LAKE LN	0	253P	SEM	77386
N. VISTA LAKE LN	0	253P	SEM	77386
E. VISTA LAKE LN	0	253P	SEM	77386
VISTA MANOR DR	2200	296Z	NEH	77339
VISTA MAR CIR	14100	408L	NWC	77095
VISTA MEADOW CT	0	299S	NEC	77336
VISTAMONT DR	15000	527R	NEF	77083
VISTA NORTE CT	10800	413Y	NEH	77076
VISTA OAK DR	16500	332Q	NCC	77073
VISTA OAKS MANOR	0	455F	NEH	77028
VISTA ORO DR	13100	408M	NWC	77041
VISTA PARK DR	0	568Z	SG	77478
VISTA REACH LN	0	330Z	NWC	77069
VISTA RIDGE DR	4300	296V	NEH	77339
VISTA SPRINGS DR	8800	330N	NWC	77379
VISTA TERRACE LN	0	452Q	NWH	77018
VISTA TRACE DR	21000	332V	NCC	77073
VISTA TRAIL CT	21000	332V	NCC	77073
VISTA VALLEY DR	22500	485L	SWC	77450
VISTA VERDE	7500	535S	SEH	77087
VISTA VILLAGE LN	4900	451G	NWH	77092
VISTA WAY DR	0	367D	NWC	77429
W. VISTAWOOD DR	1300	489K	SWH	77077
E. VISTAWOOD DR	1300	489K	SWH	77077
VISTA WOODS DR	0	455F	NEH	77028
N. VITA CIR	9800	369Q	NWC	77070
W. VITA CIR	11900	369Q	NWC	77070
E. VITA CIR	11900	369Q	NWC	77070
VITRY LN	12500	570G	MC	77071

Street Name	Block	Pg/Sq	Loc	Zips
VITTORIO CT	0	525J	NEF	77469
VITTORIO CT	0	525J	NEF	77469
VIVALDI DR	0	444M	NWC	77493
VIVIAN	900	537J	PA	77506
VIVIAN	900	620W	GCO	77565
VIVIAN	4300	531M	BL	77401
VIVIAN CT	19000	330A	NWC	77379
VIVIAN RD	3100	414T	NCC	77093
VIVIAN POINT LN	16700	367Y	NWC	77095
VIVIENNE WESTMORELAND	12900	367H	NWC	77429
VOBE CT	22100	445V	NWC	77449
VOGEL RD	7000	411Y	NWH	77088
VOGT RD	0	249T	NWC	77375
VOGUE LN	8000	451N	NWH	77055
VOGUE LN	9000	450N	NWH	77080
VOIGHT	1000	493A	NWH	77009
VOIL CT	1000	379X	NEC	77532
VOIX, CHARLIE AVE	500	497A	NEC	77015
VOLGA DR	22800	295B	SEM	77365
VOLGA RIVER DR	0	446D	NWC	77449
VOLLEY	4800	452H	NWH	77022
VOLLEY VALE CT	19000	338W	NEC	77346
VOLLMER RD	2600	451R	NWH	77092
VOLNEY	100	536X	SH	77587
VOLTA	8600	335W	NEH	77338
VOLTAIRE DR	11200	368U	NWC	77065
VOLTERA LAKE DR	0	610Q	MC	77459
VOLTERRA CIR	0	657L	FR	77546
VOLUNTEER	12300	528M	SWH	77072
VOLUNTEER LN	300	252S	SWM	77380
VOLUTE CT	0	411H	NWC	77038
VOLVO CT	800	375M	NEC	77396
VONNETT DR	15400	498B	CV	77530
VORGEN CT	0	290P	NWC	77379
VOSGES MOUNTAIN DR	0	450K	NWH	77080
VOSS RD	100	490H	HC	77024
S. VOSS RD	700	490V	SWH	77057
VOSS RD	1000	490H	SV	77055
VOSS RD	14400	568E	NEF	77498
VOSSDALE RD	2600	491Z	SWH	77027
VOSS PARK DR	1	490D	HC	77024
VOSS PKWY	0	490D	HC	77024
VOSS SPRINGS LN	0	577W	SEH	77034
VOTAW LN	7400	411V	NWH	77088
VOYAGER LN	700	618P	SEH	77062
VRANA DR	10400	418Y	NEC	77049
VUSKOU CT	28000	293H	SEM	77386

W

Street Name	Block	Pg/Sq	Loc	Zips
W. A	100	540X	LP	77571
W RD	0	533N	SWH	77030
W E BILL CROWLEY PK RD	0	414C	NCC	77039
W M	0	580F	LP	77571
W O POWELL RD	0	580J	LP	77571
W W THORNE BLVD	2000	333S	NCC	77073
W, AVENUE	6600	494R	SEH	77011
W. BELFORT RD		526Y	NEF	77469
WABASH	11300	571C	SWH	77035
WABASH DR	22800	255X	SEM	77365
WABASH ELM	1100	332V	NCC	77073
WABING RD	0	568H	SG	77478
WACO	200	494F	NEH	77020
WACO	200	659E	LC	77573
WACO	200	535Z	SH	77587
WACO	900	536W	SH	77587
WACO	1100	576A	SH	77587
WACO	2600	460Y	MN	77521
WACO FALLS DR	0	371L	NWC	77067
WACO TRAILS CIR	0	406D	NWC	77433
WADE RD	4800	500C	NEC	77521
WADE RD	6800	460Q	NEC	77521
WADE RD	9100	460Q	NEC	77562
WADE BRIDGE	0	457X	NEC	77015
WADEBRIDGE WAY	13900	497C	NEC	77015
WADE CREEK LN	0	366K	NWC	77433
WADE HAMPTON DR	800	490D	HC	77024
WADE HAVEN DR	0	366J	NWC	77433
W. WADING POND CIR	0	249M	NWH	77375
W. WADING POND CIR	0	249M	NWH	77375
WADING RIVER DR	19200	329A	NWC	77375
WADLINGTON DR	14400	377X	NEC	77044
WADSWORTH	1400	497M	NEC	77015
WAEBACK DR	17400	527W	NEF	77407
N. WAFER	100	536H	PA	77506
WAFER	100	536H	PA	77506
WAFER	1300	536M	PA	77502
WAGES	9900	454A	NEH	77093
WAGGANNER DR	17200	324M	NWC	77447
WAGG WAY RD	0	408G	NWC	77095
WAGLEY	3900	530C	SWH	77036
WAGNER	500	493E	SWH	77007
WAGNER	14700	577U	SEH	77034
WAGNER POINT CT	0	328M	NWC	77377
WAGON RD	15600	372Z	NEH	77060
WAGON BOSS RD	0	458T	NEC	77049
WAGON BRIDGE LN	0	406F	NWC	77433
WAGON GAP TRAIL	1400	331M	NWC	77090
WAGON POINT DR	1	332K	NWC	77090
WAGON TRAIL	18400	254D	SEM	77302
WAGON TRAIL RD	3300	614U	PL	77584
WAGON TRAIL RD	10300	409G	NWC	77064
WAGONWHEEL CIR	6200	411T	NWH	77088
WAGONWHEEL LN	6700	411T	NWH	77088
WAGON WHEEL RD	15900	246L	SC	77355
WAGON WHEEL WAY	27000	246J	SWM	77355
WAHL	100	419G	CB	77532
WAHL MANOR CT	8200	527R	NEF	77083
WAHOO TRAIL	19700	378L	NEC	77532
WAIALAE CIR	4600	578E	PA	77505
WAINFLEET LN	11000	530Z	SWH	77096
WAINSCOT CT	11700	411H	NWC	77038
WAINSFIELD LN	14900	457Z	NEC	77530
WAINWRIGHT	500	453L	NEH	77022
WAISER CIR	0	411B	NWC	77086
WAITING SPRING CIR	16200	407H	NWC	77095
WAITING SPRING LN	8500	407H	NWC	77095
WAKE CT	17700	379T	NEC	77532
WAKEFIELD CT	2800	613T	NEB	77584
WAKEFIELD DR	300	658M	LC	77573
WAKEFIELD DR	800	452J	NWH	77018
WAKEFIELD DR	2100	451R	NWH	77018
WAKEFIELD MEADOW CT	21100	525M	NEF	77407
WAKEFIELD MEADOW LN	7200	525M	NEF	77407
WAKEFIELD VILLAGE DR	0	367X	NWC	77095
WAKEFORD	0	615R	PL	77581
WAKEFOREST	3600	492X	SWH	77098
WAKEFOREST	4800	532B	WU	77005
WAKE FOREST DR	1900	538N	DP	77536
WAKE ROBIN	1	252N	WD	77380
WAKESHIRE BLVD	3600	538T	DP	77536
WAKETON DR	0	366P	NWC	77433

Street Name	Block	Pg/Sq	Loc	Zips
WAKE VILLAGE DR	15500	617S	SEC	77546
WALBROOK	0	527V	NEF	77498
WALBROOK DR	800	618J	SEH	77062
WALBROOK DR	14800	528S	NEF	77498
WALBROOK MEADOWS LN	0	406M	NWC	77433
WALBURY DR	0	447B	NWC	77084
WALCOTT	0	411Z	NWH	77018
WALCOTT LN	2400	412W	NWH	77088
WALCOTT MILLS DR	0	331E	NWC	77379
WALD RD	8700	576L	SEH	77034
WALDEMAR DR	11900	489N	SWH	77077
WALDEMERE DR	12400	488U	SWH	77077
WALDEN CIR	1100	568F	SG	77498
WALDEN DR	3500	613G	NEB	77584
WALDEN LN	0	657V	LC	77573
WALDEN LN	11400	490Q	PP	77024
WALDENBURG PLACE		289P	NWC	77375
WALDEN CREEK CT	1700	615F	PL	77581
WALDEN CREEK LN	3400	615F	PL	77581
WALDEN FOREST DR	18000	337Z	NEC	77346
WALDEN FOREST DR	19400	338W	NEC	77346
WALDEN GATE LN	0	407J	NWC	77433
WALDEN GLEN CIR	0	378A	NEC	77346
WALDEN GROVE LN	21300	486J	SWC	77450
WALDEN HILL CT	1100	488F	SWH	77077
WALDEN PARK CT	15100	457Q	NEC	77049
WALDEN PARK LN	0	609U	MC	77459
WALDEN TERRACE LN	0	376N	NEC	77396
WALDEN WAY	22300	289L	NWC	77375
WALDEN WOODS	3300	297G	NEH	77365
WALDER CT	20900	406T	NWC	77449
WALDERFORD DR	22900	485B	SWC	77450
WALDINE	14500	497L	NEC	77015
WALDO	3700	530B	SWH	77063
WALDRIDGE DR	0	524K	NWF	77406
WALDRIDGE OAK LN	0	295R	SEM	77365
WALDRON CIR	15500	408S	NWC	77084
WALDRON DR	6400	408S	NWC	77084
WALDWICK DR	15300	329S	NWC	77377
WALES CT	16100	330R	NWC	77379
WALESTON CT	21700	336A	SEM	77339
WALFORD CT	13000	368Y	NWC	77065
WALFORD DR	17100	329R	NWC	77379
WALFORD MILL LN	0	407B	NWC	77095
WALHALLA DR	3200	371Q	NWC	77066
WALHAM CT	4400	337B	NEH	77345
WALK DR	11200	413X	NEH	77076
WALKABOUT CIR	4100	609K	MC	77459
WALKABOUT WAY	5600	526A	NEF	77450
WALKABOUT WAY	5700	525D	NEF	77450
W. WALKER	100	659F	LC	77573
E. WALKER	100	659J	LC	77573
WALKER	300	493L	DT	77002
W. WALKER	600	658M	LC	77573
WALKER	1100	493L	DT	77010
WALKER	1101	493L	DT	77002
WALKER	1300	493L	DT	77010
W. WALKER	1900	493J	SWH	77019
WALKER	2000	493R	SEH	77003
WALKER	3600	494T	SEH	77023
WALKER	7400	495W	SEH	77011
WALKER	10000	370Y	NWC	77064
WALKER	27000	324J	HK	77447
WALKER	27700	323H	HK	77447
W. WALKER	2800	659W	LC	77573
WALKER DR	0	614M	PL	77581
WALKER RD	0	253C	SEM	77302
WALKER RD	0	254A	SEM	77302
WALKER RD	1200	501R	BT	77521
WALKER ST	0	658V	LC	77573
WALKER BRANCH LN	13100	377K	NEC	77346
WALKER LEE PARKWAY	0	375B	NEH	77338
WALKER MEADOW WAY	0	616L	SEC	77089
WALKER MIST LN	0	484T	NEF	77494
WALKER RETREAT LN		524C	NEF	77494
WALKERS FOREST DR	7300	411V	NWH	77088
WALKSEW	14000	572Y	SWH	77047
WALKUP WAY	0	418T	NCC	77044
WALKWAY	7100	530F	SWH	77036
WALKWOOD CIR	800	488B	SWH	77079
WALKWOOD CT	800	488E	SWH	77079
WALKWOOD DR	15300	488E	SWH	77079
WALL	800	412T	NWH	77088
WALL	2400	412S	NWH	77088
WALL	16000	409L	JV	77040
WALL	2400	411V	NWH	77088
WALLA LN	13200	413L	NCC	77037
WALLABY CT	11700	529W	SWH	77477
WALLACE	0	462Z	CCO	77520
WALLACE	100	453L	NEH	77022
WALLACE	8900	495U	NEH	77029
WALLACE DR	100	296P	SEM	77365
WALLACE MIST DR		325S	NWC	77447
WALLACH DR	14800	368J	NWC	77429
WALLBOARD CT	9600	412G	NWC	77038
WALLENBERG LN	0	328F	NWC	77377
WALLER	2000	282U	WL	77484
WALLER	9100	535C	SEH	77012
WALLER PARK LN	10100	409G	NWC	77064
WALLER SPRING CREEK RD	27000	284J	NWC	77447
WALLER SPRING CREEK RD	27500	283J	NWC	77484
WALLER SPRING CREEK RD	31000	282M	NWC	77484
WALLER SPRINGS LN	25500	524F	NEF	77494
WALLER TOMBALL RD	14000	288J	NWC	77377
WALLER TOMBALL RD	15100	287Q	NWC	77377
WALLER TOMBALL RD	18100	286M	NWC	77377
WALLER TOMBALL RD	20600	285Q	NWC	77447
WALLER TOMBALL RD	24100	284Q	NWC	77447
WALLER TOMBALL RD	28000	283T	NWC	77484
WALLER TOMBALL RD	30600	282U	WL	77484
WALLGROVE	0	457J	NEC	77049
WALLING	800	453W	NWH	77009
WALLING DR	800	375D	HM	77338
WALLINGFORD DR	2300	609D	MC	77459
WALLINGFORD DR	2700	489Y	SWH	77042
WALLINGHAM CT	9100	329R	NWC	77379
WALLINGHAM DR	9200	329R	NWC	77379
WALLINGTON DR	8900	531P	SWH	77096
WALLINGTON LN	1800	620G	SB	77586
WALLIS AVE	400	536Q	PA	77502
W. WALLIS DR	21100	296J	SEM	77365
E. WALLIS DR	21600	296K	SEM	77365
WALLIS TRAIL CT	5600	456V	NEC	77049
W. WALLISVILLE RD	100	459P	HG	77562
E. WALLISVILLE RD	100	459R	HG	77562
E. WALLISVILLE RD	800	460Q	NEC	77562
E. WALLISVILLE RD	3000	460Q	NEC	77521
E. WALLISVILLE RD	4100	461R	NEC	77521
WALLISVILLE RD	5400	494D	NEH	77020
E. WALLISVILLE RD	7200	462N	NEC	77521
WALLISVILLE RD	7800	495B	NEH	77029
WALLISVILLE RD	9200	455Z	NEH	77013

Street Name	Block	Pg/Sq	Loc	Zips
WALLISVILLE RD	10400	456W	NEH	77013
WALLISVILLE RD	13300	457U	NEC	77049
WALLISVILLE RD	15200	458N	NEC	77049
WALLISVILLE RD	18500	459N	NEC	77049
WALLSTONE CT	20200	291Y	NWC	77388
WALNE	0	492A	NWH	77055
WALNUT	0	541W	MP	77571
S. WALNUT	100	288M	TB	77375
S. WALNUT	100	618X	WB	77598
N. WALNUT	100	618X	WB	77598
WALNUT	100	282Y	WL	77484
WALNUT	100	288H	TB	77375
WALNUT	700	493M	NEH	77002
E. WALNUT	3300	615P	PL	77581
W. WALNUT	4000	615N	PL	77581
WALNUT	26900	292Q	SP	77373
WALNUT CT	2300	538N	DP	77536
WALNUT DR	21000	257T	SEM	77357
WALNUT DR	21900	255Z	SEM	77365
WALNUT DR	22800	295D	SEM	77365
WALNUT LN	900	336F	NEH	77339
WALNUT LN	2100	537S	PA	77502
WALNUT LN	17400	246T	SWM	77355
WALNUT RD	21800	336L	NEH	77339
WALNUT BEND	0	489Y	SWH	77082
WALNUT BEND CT	12700	570J	MC	77489
WALNUT BEND LN	100	489Q	SWH	77042
WALNUT BEND LN	3800	529C	SWH	77042
WALNUT BRIDGE CT	14300	618A	SEH	77062
WALNUT BROOK CT	9300	410E	NWC	77040
WALNUT CANYON DR	20500	526E	NEF	77450
WALNUT COVE	200	613B	NEB	77584
WALNUT COVE CT	3300	657G	FR	77546
WALNUT COVE DR	3100	657G	FR	77546
WALNUT COVE DR	5000	447B	NWC	77084
WALNUT CREEK CT	27900	245L	SWM	77355
WALNUT CREEK DR	2100	536S	SEH	77017
WALNUT CREEK DR	2100	659C	LC	77573
WALNUT CREEK RD	0	246V	SWM	77355
WALNUT CREEK RD	30400	286C	SWM	77355
WALNUT CREEK RD	31200	246Y	SWM	77355
WALNUT CROSSING	0	247S	SWM	77355
WALNUT DALE CT	11600	411H	NWC	77088
WALNUT FAIR LN	0	293X	NCC	77373
WALNUT FOREST CT	3500	291Y	NWC	77388
WALNUT FOREST LN	3600	291Y	NWC	77388
WALNUTGATE DR	5700	334A	NCC	77373
WALNUT GLEN DR	9000	369Y	NWC	77064
WALNUT GREEN DR	1900	618F	SEH	77062
WALNUT GROVE CIR	25600	252S	SWM	77380
WALNUT GROVE CT	2500	614N	NEB	77584
WALNUT GROVE DR	0	247S	SWM	77355
WALNUT HILL	24200	244H	WCO	77447
WALNUT HILLS DR	5000	297Y	NEH	77345
WALNUT HOLLOW	2500	616P	PL	77581
WALNUT HOLLOW LN	13800	488X	SWH	77082
WALNUT KNOB CT	2500	298W	NEH	77345
WALNUT KNOLL WAY	2900	446R	NWC	77084
WALNUT LAKE RD	13000	368U	NWC	77065
WALNUT LEAF LN	0	328J	NWC	77429
WALNUT MEADOW DR	11300	370M	NWC	77066
WALNUT PEAK CT	5200	297P	NEH	77345
WALNUT POINT DR	5600	337D	NEH	77345
WALNUT POINTE	900	658R	LC	77573
WALNUT POND CT	16900	578Z	PA	77059
WALNUT POND DR	3900	578Z	PA	77059
WALNUT RIDGE DR	2300	610A	MC	77489
WALNUT RIDGE DR	8300	335N	NCC	77338
WALNUT SHORES DR	15900	377L	NEC	77044
WALNUT SPRINGS DR	2900	446P	NWC	77449
WALNUT SPRINGS LN	16100	246U	SWM	77355
WALNUT SQUARE	6700	527E	NEF	77407
WALNUT VALLEY DR	22200	291L	NWC	77389
WALNUT VIEW CT	2900	411G	NWC	77088
WALNUT WOOD DR	15900	448A	NWC	77084
WALRAVEN RD	11900	339J	HU	77336
WALSH	3200	660H	BC	77518
WALSTON RD	500	413F	NCC	77060
WALSTON RIDGE CT	4300	609Y	NEF	77459
WALSTON RIDGE CT	10800	289X	NWC	77379
WALSTON RIDGE DR	1200	289X	NWC	77379
WALSTON RIDGE LN	0	657X	LC	77573
WALSTON SPRINGS CT	0	377U	NEC	77044
WALSTON SPRINGS LN	3900	609T	NEF	77479
N. WALTER	100	536G	PA	77506
WALTER	100	536L	PA	77506
WALTER PEAK LN	25200	524G	NEF	77494
WALTERS RD	11000	371Q	NWC	77067
WALTERS RD	12200	371G	NWC	77014
WALTERS RD	14500	331S	NWC	77068
WALTERVILLE RD	9300	450U	NWH	77080
WALTHALL DR	300	453J	NWH	77022
WALTHAM	29000	293A	SEM	77386
WALTON	200	453T	NWH	77009
WALTON RD	13100	418E	NEC	77044
WALTON HEATH DR	6500	370B	NWC	77069
WALTRIP	5600	534V	SEH	77087
WALTS RUN LN		366U	NWC	77433
WALTWAY DR	1000	452X	NWH	77008
WALWICK DR	10900	490M	HC	77024
WALWORTEN CT	500	486C	SWC	77450
WALWORTH CT	8900	411J	NWC	77088
WALWORTH DR	8900	411J	NWC	77088
WANAKAH DR	5700	370C	NWC	77069
WANAMAKER RD	10600	456N	NEH	77013
WANDA	0	368M	NWC	77429
WANDA	0	458U	CV	77530
WANDA LN	6500	530V	SWH	77074
WANDA LN	7800	456H	NEC	77044
WANDA VERDE LN	0	528C	SWH	77082
WANDERING LAKE LN	0	609Y	MC	77459
E. WANDERING OAK DR	1	250M	WD	77381
WANDERING STREAMS DR	12600	328L	NWC	77377
WANDERING TRAIL	15300	617W	FR	77546
WANDERING WAY CT	0	289D	NWC	77375
WANDERING WAY DR	0	249Z	NWC	77375
WANDERING WOOD DR	14300	457Y	NEC	77015
WANDSWORTH DR	9200	329R	NWC	77379
WANITA PLACE	6600	492F	SWH	77007
WANN PARK DR	19300	372D	NCC	77073
WAR ADMIRAL	4100	537R	PA	77503
WAR ADMIRAL DR	2000	570S	SF	77477
WARATH OAK CT	0	369S	NWC	77070
WARBLER LN	2900	375K	HM	77396
WARBLER WAY	20900	286J	NWC	77447
WARD	100	501Z	BT	77520
WARD	1400	502W	BT	77520
WARD	3400	533L	SEH	77021
WARD	3100	572T	SWH	77053
WARD CT	1900	536R	PA	77502
WARD DR	10300	289B	NWC	77375
WARD LN	300	656W	AV	77511

Street Name	Block	Pg/Sq	Loc	Zips
WARDMONT	1100	413Q	NEH	77037
WARDMONT	2100	414N	NCC	77093
WARDVILLE	11200	414P	NCC	77093
WARE DAIRY RD	2600	656X	FR	77546
WAREHOUSE CENTER	0	335S	NEH	77338
WARFIELD CT	0	407U	NWC	77084
WARFIELD LN	6400	407U	NWC	77084
WARIALDA TRAIL	0	405R	NWC	77493
WARING	4500	491Z	SWH	77027
WARKWORTH DR	14300	571P	SWH	77085
WARLANDER	0	255T	SEM	77365
WAR MEMORIAL DR	3500	448L	NWH	77084
WARM SPRINGS RD	4300	571D	SWH	77035
WARM SPRINGS RD	5200	571A	SWH	77035
WARM SPRINGS RD	6000	570D	SWH	77035
S. WARMSTONE CT	1600	485L	SWC	77494
S. WARMSTONE WAY	23000	485L	SWC	77494
N. WARMSTONE WAY	23000	485L	SWC	77494
WARM TERRACE LN	22200	291J	NWC	77389
WARM WINDS DR	17500	328L	NWC	77377
WARNER	600	453G	NEH	77022
WARNER RD	11000	414U	NEC	77093
WARNER HOLLOW CT	10800	568A	NEF	77498
WARNOCK	0	537Q	PA	77503
WARREN	0	462M	MB	77580
WARREN	1100	538Q	DP	77536
WARREN	9500	463J	MB	77580
WARREN	17000	324E	HK	77447
WARREN RD	8000	410Q	NWC	77040
WARRENFORD DR	8700	527R	NEF	77083
WARREN RANCH RD	14000	364A	NWC	77447
WARREN RANCH RD	15000	324S	NWC	77447
WARRENTON DR	1	490J	BH	77024
WARRENWOOD DR	12400	371F	NWC	77066
WARRINGTON DR	20200	486F	SWC	77450
WARRINGTON LN	6100	657U	LC	77573
WARWANA RD	9700	450S	NWH	77080
WARWANA RD	10800	449U	NWH	77043
WARWICK	0	257G	SEM	77357
WARWICK DR	2600	659C	LC	77573
WARWICK DR	9600	335T	HM	77338
WARWICK LN	1	609C	MC	77459
WARWICK RD	1200	413R	NCC	77093
WARWICK RD	2400	414N	NCC	77093
WARWICK GARDEN LN	0	290Z	NWC	77379
W. WARWICK LAKE LN	6800	250Y	NWC	77389
E. WARWICK LAKE LN	6800	250Y	NWC	77389
WARWICKSHIRE CT	11800	489N	SWH	77077
WARWICKSHIRE DR	0	289T	NWC	77375
WARWICKSHIRE DR	1300	489N	SWH	77077
WARWICK WALK DR	1400	458S	NEC	77530
WARWICK WAY	4300	577F	PA	77504
WASABILAN LN	0	461P	NEC	77521
WASATCH DR	19300	328C	NWC	77377
WASECA	1400	450Y	NWH	77055
WASHAM RD	8600	575U	SEH	77075
WASHBURNE LN	0	407E	NWC	77433
WASHBURN TUNNEL	0	496Y	NEH	77015
WASHBURN TUNNEL	0	536C	SEH	77506
WASHFORDE LN	0	457P	NEC	77049
WASHINGTON	0	283W	NWC	77484
WASHINGTON	100	618Y	WB	77598
WASHINGTON	200	659J	LC	77573
WASHINGTON	500	576A	SH	77587
WASHINGTON	1500	538V	DP	77536
WASHINGTON	1900	541A	BT	77520
WASHINGTON	2100	282Z	WL	77484
WASHINGTON	3000	537G	PA	77503
WASHINGTON	7400	460U	MN	77521
WASHINGTON	11400	414Q	NCC	77093
WASHINGTON AVE	300	493K	SWH	77002
WASHINGTON AVE	1500	493K	SWH	77007
N. WASHINGTON AVE	2100	615J	PL	77581
S. WASHINGTON AVE	2400	615N	PL	77581
WASHINGTON AVE	3900	492B	NWH	77007
WASHINGTON DR	2800	411H	NWC	77038
WASHINGTON IRVING DR	1800	616N	PL	77581
WASHINGTON PARK CT	18300	331E	NWC	77379
WASSIL WAY	23900	445T	NWC	77493
WATCHFUL WILLOW DR	0	366N	NWC	77433
WATEKA CIR	8200	530P	SWH	77074
WATEKA DR	8100	530P	SWH	77074
WATERBEND CT	28600	253Y	SEM	77386
WATERBEND COVE	0	253Z	SEM	77386
WATERBEND COVE	3700	293C	SEM	77386
WATERBEND COVE DR	0	293B	SEM	77386
WATERBEND WAY	28500	293C	SEM	77386
WATER BRIDGE DR	0	366J	NWC	77433
S. WATERBRIDGE DR		249Q	NWC	77375
N. WATERBRIDGE DR		249Q	NWC	77375
WATERBRIDGE DR		249Q	NWC	77375
WATERBURY DR	8300	451W	NWH	77055
WATERBURY EDGE LN	0	377F	NEC	77346
WATERBURY ESTATES DR	2700	613T	NEB	77584
WATERBURY WAY	0	450V	NWH	77055
WATER CANYON CT	2100	488P	SWH	77077
WATER CANYON RD	0	502P	BT	77520
WATER CASTLE CT	0	612M	PL	77584
WATERCASTLE CT	1800	488P	SWH	77077
WATERCASTLE CT	3100	660E	LC	77573
WATERCHASE DR	7700	570V	SWH	77489
WATERCLIFF CT	3200	291U	NWC	77388
WATERCOLOR COVE	4200	578L	PA	77505
WATERCRESS CIR	100	409F	JV	77064
WATERCRESS PARK	12600	409S	NWC	77041
WATERCREST DR	600	620L	SB	77586
WATERCREST DR	1800	452S	NWH	77008
WATERCREST HARBOUR LN	300	658U	LC	77573
WATERCYPRESS CT	26300	366M	NWC	77433
WATER DANCE CT	20200	326P	NWC	77433
WATERDANCE LN	11800	367Q	NWC	77095
WATER EDGE LN	22400	525C	NEF	77494
WATER EDGE POINT LN	9200	375V	NEC	77396
WATER ELM CT	4500	578Y	SEH	77059
WATERELM DR	2000	447S	NWH	77084
WATER ELM WAY	4300	578Y	SEH	77059
WATERFALL DR	200	338H	NEC	77336
WATERFALL DR	1700	656R	FR	77546
WATERFALL DR	2000	610A	MC	77489
WATERFALL COVE	4300	578L	PA	77505
WATERFALL COVE CT	0	659H	LC	77573
WATERFALL CREEK WAY	0	328A	NWC	77377
WATER FALLS LN	21500	446J	NWC	77449
WATERFALL SWIFT	0	367P	NWC	77433
WATERFALL WAY	0	250N	NWC	77375
WATERFALL WAY	4400	609E	SG	77479
WATER FERN LN	2100	615L	PL	77581
WATERFLOWER DR	19700	289W	NWC	77375
WATERFORD	0	487E	SWC	77094
WATERFORD	1300	538N	DP	77536
WATERFORD CT	0	609D	MC	77459
WATERFORD DR	5700	574E	SEH	77033

Street Name	Block	Pg/Sq	Loc	Zips
WATERFORD COVE	19000	486H	SWC	77094
WATERFORD ESTATES CT	11900	328M	NWC	77377
WATERFORD GLEN LN	0	484Y	NEF	77494
WATERFORD GLEN LN	0	484Y	NEF	77494
WATERFORD OAKS LN	0	619V	LC	77565
WATERFORD OAKS LN	1	620S	LC	77565
WATERFORD PARK DR	0	331P	NWC	77068
WATERFORD VILLAGE BLVD	1	609C	MC	77459
WATERFORD WAY	1900	620K	SB	77586
WATERFORD WAY	300	619V	LC	77565
WATERFOWL CT	12500	371G	NWC	77014
WATER FRONT	0	620U	SB	77586
WATER FRONT CT	9200	249A	SWM	77354
WATERFRONT DR	100	620U	SB	77586
WATER GAP DR	1900	568U	SG	77478
WATER GARDEN LN	0	609S	NEF	77479
WATERGATE YACHT CLUB	0	620S	CS	77565
WATERGLEN CT	3200	660J	LC	77573
WATER GLEN DR	200	338H	NEC	77336
WATER GROOVE CT	0	375Y	NEC	77396
WATERHAVEN LN	4700	447G	NWC	77084
WATER HAVEN PARK DR	0	366J	NWC	77433
WATERHAVEN SHORES LN	0	338W	NEC	77346
WATER HICKORY DR	0	289C	NWC	77375
WATER HILL CT	0	485E	NEF	77494
WATERING OAKS LN	16900	527J	NEF	77083
S. WATER IRIS CT	3900	578Y	SEH	77059
N. WATER IRIS CT	4000	578Y	SEH	77059
W. WATERLAKE DR	22700	525K	NEF	77406
S. WATERLAKE DR	23000	525K	NEF	77406
N. WATERLAKE DR	23000	525K	NEF	77406
WATERLAND DR	25600	338H	NEC	77336
WATER LEAF LN	5600	411U	NWH	77088
WATERLILLY LN	0	614J	PL	77581
WATERLILY CT	4300	569X	MC	77459
S. WATERLILY DR	23000	525K	NEF	77406
N. WATERLILY DR	23000	525K	NEF	77406
WATERLILY LN	0	612E	PL	77545
WATERLINE LN	24700	484D	NEF	77494
WATERLOO DR	12900	572F	SWH	77045
WATERLOO DR	14700	572T	SWH	77053
WATERLOO RD	2900	615Q	PL	77581
WATERMELON	7100	451U	NWH	77055
WATERMILL CT	1	251V	WD	77380
WATER MILL DR	18100	326Z	NWC	77429
WATERMIST	0	448D	NWC	77041
WATERMIST DR	0	612P	PL	77545
WATERMIST GLEN CT		484S	NEF	77494
WATERMONT DR	300	338H	NEC	77336
WATER OAK CIR	4900	578J	PA	77505
WATER OAK DR	0	615Z	PL	77581
WATER OAK DR	100	659J	LC	77573
WATER OAK DR	300	659N	LC	77573
WATER OAK DR	4800	578J	PA	77505
WATER OAK DR	12700	570J	MC	77489
WATER OAK DR	16600	458Z	CV	77530
WATER OAK DR	17000	459W	CV	77530
WATER OAK LN	11300	369E	NWC	77429
WATER OAK BEND CT	0	366P	NWC	77433
WATER OAK CROSSING	20900	326N	NWC	77433
WATER OAK HILL DR	20400	292W	NWC	77388
WATER OAK PARK CIR	13200	369E	NWC	77429
WATER OAK TRAIL	22600	287F	NWC	77377
WATER PARK	0	485V	NEF	77450
WATER PARK CT	9500	410D	NWC	77086
WATER PARK LN	7300	411A	NWC	77086
WATER PARK LN	7500	370Z	NWC	77086
WATER PARK WAY	28600	293B	SEM	77386
WATERPINE DR	0	335P	NCC	77338
WATER POINT	4500	609K	MC	77459
WATER POINT CT	6300	337P	NEC	77346
WATER POINT TRAIL	19300	337P	NEC	77346
WATERPORT LN	0	446J	NWC	77449
WATER RIDGE DR	25700	338D	NEC	77336
WATER RIDGE LN	0	502K	BT	77520
WATER ROSE	0	485A	NEF	77494
WATER SCENE TRAIL	0	326Z	NWC	77429
WATERS EDGE	0	609L	MC	77459
WATERS EDGE CT	2000	612H	PL	77584
WATERS EDGE DR	0	656Q	FR	77546
WATERS EDGE DR	3200	613S	NEB	77578
WATERSEDGE DR	3400	568Z	SG	77478
WATERS EDGE LN	1900	620G	SB	77586
WATERS EDGE LN	2200	658X	LC	77573
WATERS EDGE PLACE	12900	448D	NWC	77041
WATERSHED LN	0	366N	NWC	77433
WATER SHOAL LN	3800	609Q	MC	77459
WATERSIDE CT	4200	609B	MC	77459
WATERSIDE DR	1400	619U	LC	77573
WATERSIDE DR	1800	609B	MC	77459
WATERSIDE DR	14800	457V	NEC	77015
WATERSIDE ESTATES CIR	1700	526X	NEF	77407
WATERSIDE ESTATES DR	0	526W	NEF	77406
WATERSIDE RETREAT	4300	609N	NEF	77479
WATERSIDE TRAIL	2700	615N	PL	77584
WATERSIDE VILLAGE CT	4800	526X	NEF	77407
WATERSIDE VILLAGE DR	1600	526W	NEF	77407
WATERSIDE WAY	12600	449A	NWC	77041
WATERSLIDE VIEW CT	0	377U	NEC	77044
WATER STONE	0	609C	MC	77459
WATERSTONE	4000	609C	MC	77459
WATERSTONE DR	10100	530A	SWH	77042
WATERSTONE CREST DR	0	445L	NWC	77449
WATERSTONE CREST DR	0	445L	NWC	77449
WATERSTONE FALLS DR	0	445L	NWC	77449
WATERSTONE FALLS DR	0	445L	NWC	77449
WATERSTONE HILLS DR	0	445L	NWC	77449
WATERS VIEW DR	3100	568Z	SG	77478
WATERS WAY DR	3100	568Z	SG	77478
WATERTHRUSH ST	0	461N	NEC	77521
WATERTON DR	12500	411A	NWC	77086
WATERTOWN MALL	2400	491S	SWH	77057
WATERTREE CIR	1	251T	WD	77380
WATERTREE CT	1	251T	WD	77380
S. WATERTREE LN	1	251T	WD	77380
N. WATERTREE LN	1	251T	WD	77380
WATERVIEW CT	3900	609C	MC	77459
WATERVIEW DR	1600	336B	NEC	77339
WATER VIEW BEND	5000	609S	NEF	77479
WATERVIEW ESTATES TRAIL	0	526T	NEF	77407
WATERVILLE WAY	13800	457Y	NEC	77015
WATER VIOLET LN	0	526T	NEF	77407
WATER WAY	2100	620K	SB	77586
WATERWAY AVE	1	251M	WD	77380
WATERWAY CT	0	251H	WD	77380
WATERWAY PLACE	0	251H	WD	77380
WATERWAY PLACE	0	251M	WD	77380
WATERWAY SOUARE E.	0	251H	WD	77380
WATERWAY SOUARE S.	0	251H	WD	77380
WATERWAY SOUARE W.	0	251H	WD	77380
WATER WELL RD	22000	296K	SEM	77365
WATER WELL RD	22010	296K	SEM	77365
WATER WILLOW LN	0	615L	PL	77581
WATER WILLOW TRACE DR	0	253Y	SEM	77386
WATER WILLOW WAY	0	526T	NEF	77407
WATERWIND CT	3400	617Y	SEC	77546
WATERWOOD CT	1500	569Y	MC	77459
WATERWOOD CT	11600	612R	PL	77584
WATERWOOD DR	4100	501K	BT	77521
WATERWOOD RD	100	338C	NEC	77336
WATER WOOD TRAIL	7500	337R	NEC	77346
WATERWORTH WAY	0	615T	PL	77584
WATFORD DR	0	657U	LC	77573
WATKINS DR	3300	538S	DP	77536
WATKINS WAY	5000	617S	FR	77546
WATKIN WAY	1600	496L	NEH	77015
WATONGA BLVD	3600	451M	NWH	77092
WATSON	2300	493B	NWH	77009
WATSON	3600	453X	NWH	77009
WATSON DR	1400	538Q	DP	77536
WATSON LN	19500	335T	SEH	77338
WATSON CROSSING WAY	0	372J	NWC	77076
WATSONS BAY DR	17800	327W	NWC	77429
WATSONWOOD DR	0	658C	WB	77598
WATTERS RD	2800	537X	PA	77502
WATTERS RD	3100	577B	PA	77504
WATTS	2100	532G	SWH	77030
WATTS AVE	1400	444Z	KT	77493
WATUMBA	0	579Q	SEC	77507
WATZEK WAY	0	615B	PL	77581
WAUGH DR	1	492R	SWH	77007
WAUGH DR	500	492R	SWH	77019
WAUGH DR	1600	493N	SWH	77006
WAUGHCREST	2700	493S	SWH	77006
WAUGHFORD	1	492M	SWH	77007
WAUMSLEY WAY	15300	527U	NEF	77498
WAVECREST	3200	660F	LC	77573
WAVECREST LN	800	618K	SEH	77062
WAVELAND DR	7000	528H	SWH	77072
WAVELAND BEND LN	0	377F	NEC	77346
WAVELL	1900	412N	NWH	77088
WAVERDALE CT	19100	486D	SWC	77094
WAVERLEY	5700	454N	NEH	77026
WAVERLY	500	492D	NWH	77007
WAVERLY	900	452Z	NWH	77008
WAVERLY CT	1	493W	SWH	77005
WAVERLY DR	2600	659C	LC	77573
WAVERLY RD	15400	373L	NCC	77032
WAVERLY BEND CT	22700	485Y	NEF	77450
WAVERLY BEND LN	18300	407N	NWC	77433
WAVERLY CANYON	0	327V	NWC	77429
WAVERLYCANYON CT	0	609U	MC	77479
WAVERLY CANYON LN	4400	658S	LC	77573
WAVERLY CREST CT	13600	367C	NWC	77429
WAVERLY GLEND DR	2000	486J	SWC	77450
WAVERLY GROVE DR	17500	407T	NWC	77084
WAVERLY HILL LN	0	326U	NWC	77429
WAVERLY HILLS CT	0	484Y	NEF	77494
WAVERLY HOLLOW LN	0	326V	NWC	77429
WAVERLY OAKS DR	24500	295M	SEM	77365
WAVERLY PARK LN	19600	291W	NWC	77379
WAVERLY SPRINGS LN	0	615B	PL	77581
WAVERTON CT	14800	527V	NEF	77498
WAVERTREE DR	4400	609B	MC	77459
WAVING FIELDS DR	9000	369Y	NWC	77064
W. WAVY OAK CIR	1	250M	WD	77381
S. WAVY OAK CIR	1	251J	WD	77381
N. WAVY OAK CIR	1	251J	WD	77381
E. WAVY OAK CIR	1	251J	WD	77381
WAXAHACHIE	6900	494H	NEH	77020
WAXAHACHIE	7900	495E	NEH	77029
WAXAHACHIE	13700	497G	NEC	77015
S. WAXBERRY RD	1	251J	WD	77381
N. WAXBERRY RD	1	251J	WD	77381
WAX BILL CT	15800	375Q	NEC	77396
WAXCANDLE DR	3300	331D	NWC	77388
WAXCONDA	0	610D	SWH	77489
WAXLEAF DR	7900	334R	NCC	77338
WAX MALLOW CT	10500	367Z	NWC	77095
WAX MALLOW DR	16500	367Y	NWC	77095
WAXMYRTLE LN	700	489G	SWH	77079
WAXWING	11000	531Y	SWH	77035
WAXWING	11200	571C	SWH	77035
WAXWING DR	0	658X	LC	77573
WAXWING PARK DR	15300	375Q	NEC	77396
WAXWOOD DR	11300	616C	SEC	77089
WAY	7800	455F	NEH	77028
WAYBRIDGE	12800	568C	SG	77478
WAYBRIDGE DR	14900	618J	SEH	77062
WAYBRIDGE GLEN LN	15800	408N	NWC	77095
WAYCREEK RD	16000	331Q	NWC	77068
WAYCREST	2300	494R	SEH	77011
WAYCROSS DR	4300	531Y	SWH	77035
WAYFAIR DR	0	577H	PA	77505
WAYFARE CT	13700	328U	NWC	77429
WAYFARER LN	7700	575P	SEH	77075
WAYFARER GRAY TRAIL	0	325R	NWC	77433
WAYFOREST DR	17200	373J	NEH	77060
WAYLAND	5800	534J	SEH	77021
WAYLORD DR	8200	408L	NWC	77041
WAYMAN	5100	536N	SEH	77017
WAY MANOR	0	490Q	PP	77024
WAYMARE LN	21000	291W	NWC	77388
WAYNE	1400	494F	NEH	77020
WAYNE	2000	537T	PA	77502
WAYNE	2300	494B	NEH	77026
WAYNE	2800	494B	NEH	77020
WAYNE	3600	454T	NEH	77026
WAYNE RD	24500	296L	SEM	77365
WAYNEGATE DR	22200	334G	NCC	77373
WAYNEMER WAY	8100	410K	NWC	77040
WAYNESBORO DR	4300	531Z	SWH	77035
WAYNEWOOD DR	14500	327Z	CY	77429
WAYNOKA DR	22300	485G	SWC	77450
WAY OUT WEST DR	4100	450M	NWH	77092
WAYPARK DR	2800	488X	SWH	77082
WAYSIDE	0	540J	SEC	77571
WAYSIDE CT	2200	538N	DP	77536
WAYSIDE DR	0	657M	FR	77546
S. WAYSIDE DR	100	494V	SEH	77011
N. WAYSIDE DR	100	495J	NEH	77020
WAYSIDE DR	100	494V	SEH	77011
S. WAYSIDE DR	700	534C	SEH	77023
S. WAYSIDE DR	4300	534L	SEH	77087
N. WAYSIDE DR	4600	455F	NEH	77028
S. WAYSIDE DR	7700	534Y	SEH	77033
N. WAYSIDE DR	9600	455B	NEH	77078
S. WAYSIDE DR	13000	574Q	SEH	77048
WAYSIDE VIADUCT	0	494R	SEH	77011
WAYSIDE VILLAGE WAY	0	415X	NWH	77078
WAYSON DR	14800	527V	NEF	77498
WAYWARD RD	8200	410F	NWC	77064
WAYWARD WIND CT	9900	409C	NWC	77064
WAYWARD WIND DR	10000	409C	NWC	77064
WAYWARD WIND LN	10000	409B	NWC	77064
W. B	100	580B	LP	77571
W. C	300	580B	LP	77571
W. D	100	580B	LP	77571
W. E	100	580B	LP	77571
WEAKLEY WAY RD	100	247G	SWM	77362
WEALDEN FOREST DR	1200	329B	NWC	77375
WEALDSTONE DR	12300	328V	NWC	77377
WEALD WAY	20300	291Z	NWC	77388
WEALD WAY CT	2700	291Z	NWC	77388
WEATFIELD DR	16500	407G	NWC	77095
WEATHERFIELD CT	0	609T	MC	77459
WEATHERFORD	3000	580Q	LP	77571
WEATHERFORD CT	2900	613P	NEB	77584
WEATHERFORD DR	2300	613P	NEB	77584
WEATHERHILL LN	7300	408Q	NWC	77041
WEATHERING OAKS DR	11400	370V	NWC	77066
WEATHERLY WAY	100	452H	NWH	77022
WEATHERSBY	5900	452B	NWH	77091
WEATHERSFIELD CT	0	658N	LC	77573
WEATHERSFIELD TRACE CIR	2100	371D	NWC	77014
WEATHERVANE TRAIL	0	325F	NWC	77447
WEATHERWOOD DR	9500	450P	NWH	77080
WEAVER	100	500P	BT	77520
WEAVER	1100	494T	SEH	77023
WEAVER RD	3600	454L	NEH	77093
WEAVER RD	4100	454L	NEH	77016
WEAVER RD	6600	454L	NEH	77028
WEAVER KNOLLS DR	0	338M	NEH	77336
WEBB DR	4800	535R	SEH	77017
WEBB LN	13100	528U	SWH	77498
WEBB RD	0	656S	NEB	77511
WEBB RD	21900	325C	NWC	77447
E. WEBB RD	23600	296M	SEM	77365
WEBB RD	24100	296M	SEM	77365
S. WEBBER CT	3100	613V	NEB	77584
E. WEBBER DR	3100	613V	NEB	77584
S. WEBBER DR	4100	613V	NEB	77584
N. WEBBER DR	4100	613V	NEB	77584
WEBELOS	15800	617T	SEC	77546
WEBELOS CT	4400	617T	SEC	77546
WEBER	1500	493F	SWH	77007
WEBERCREST DR	11500	574K	SEH	77048
WEBSTER	200	493U	SWH	77002
W. WEBSTER	1100	493P	SWH	77019
WEBSTER	1400	659G	LC	77573
WEBSTER	1600	493V	SEH	77003
WEBSTER	2700	493V	SEH	77004
WEBSTER GEN PLANT	0	658D	WB	77598
WEBSTER RANCH RD	2300	617Y	SEC	77546
WECKFORD BLVD	0	376Z	NEC	77044
WEDGEFIELD	5900	455P	NEH	77028
WEDGEFORD CT	9800	416Z	NEC	77044
WEDGEHILL LN	12000	489N	SWH	77077
WEDGEHILL LN	12300	488R	SWH	77077
WEDGEHOLLOW CT	7100	250T	NWC	77389
WEDGEHOLLOW LN	25900	250T	NWC	77389
W. WEDGEMERE CIR	1	250D	WD	77381
E. WEDGEMERE CIR	1	250D	WD	77381
WEDGEOAK CT	0	484X	NEF	77494
WEDGEOAK CT	0	484X	NEF	77494
WEDGEOAK DR	0	484Y	NEF	77494
WEDGEOAK DR	0	484Y	NEF	77494
WEDGEROCK DR	300	618S	SEH	77598
WEDGEWATER LN	0	612P	PL	77545
WEDGEWIND	0	486W	NEF	77450
WEDGEWOOD	0	531D	BL	77401
WEDGEWOOD	1100	536P	PA	77502
WEDGEWOOD	1300	413Q	NCC	77093
WEDGEWOOD	4400	414P	NCC	77093
WEDGEWOOD CIR	1	568V	SG	77478
WEDGEWOOD CT	200	252J	OR	77386
WEDGEWOOD CT	1800	570U	MC	77489
WEDGEWOOD DR	1200	568V	SG	77478
WEDGEWOOD DR	4500	531C	BL	77401
WEDGEWOOD LN	7600	451X	NWH	77055
WEDGEWOOD BAY CT	0	253T	SEM	77386
WEDGEWOOD BLUFF CT	18200	330C	NWC	77379
WEDGEWOOD CHASE WAY	0	406W	NWC	77449
WEDGEWOOD COLONY CT	0	527S	NEF	77407
WEDGEWOOD FOREST DR	1	251F	WD	77381
W. WEDGEWOOD GLEN DR	1	251E	WD	77381
E. WEDGEWOOD GLEN DR	1	251F	WD	77381
WEDGEWOOD GROVE LN	0	326T	NWC	77433
WEDGEWOOD HOLLOW LN	0	290D	NWC	77389
WEDGEWOOD PARK	26300	366H	NWC	77433
WEDGEWOOD PARK CT	12800	366H	NWC	77433
WEDGEWOOD PLACE	0	251E	WD	77381
WEDGEWOOD POINT	1	251E	WD	77381
WEDGEWOOD THICKET WAY	0	368F	NWC	77429
WEDNESBURY LN	8000	530P	SWH	77074
WEEDS RD	6200	370L	NWC	77066
WEEDY LN	8900	454F	NEH	77093
WEEKAPAUG WAY	0	449T	NWH	77043
WEE LADDIE LN	4400	448E	NWC	77084
WEE LASSIE LN	4400	448E	NWC	77084
WEEMS	3800	453Y	NEH	77009
WEENS	5200	492G	SWH	77007
WEEPING CEDAR LN	15000	408T	NWC	77084
WEEPING FIG	0	460J	HG	77562
WEEPING OAK CT	19100	332A	NWC	77388
WEEPING OAKS LN	200	332B	NWC	77388
WEEPINGSPRINGS DR	0	327D	NWC	77429
WEEPING WILLOW LN	10200	576P	SEH	77075
WEEPING WILLOW RD	4900	451F	NWH	77092
WEEPING WILLOW PLACE	8000	610S	MC	77459
WEGESIDE PARK	0	327T	CY	77429
WEILAND MANOR LN	1500	332R	NCC	77073
WEIL PLACE	14800	413A	NEH	77060
WEIMAN	13100	408R	NWC	77041
WEIMAN DR	5100	444Z	KT	77493
WEINGARTEN	4500	533M	SEH	77021
WEINGARTEN	4600	534J	SEH	77021
WEIRICH RD	11200	289F	NWC	77375
WEIR WAY	26600	246P	SWM	77355
WEISENBERGER DR	100	453K	NEH	77022
WEISER RD	3500	537L	PA	77503
WEISS	300	453Y	NEH	77009
WEITLING WAY	0	378A	NEC	77346
WELBECK DR	14800	457Z	NEC	77530
WELBORN CT	2700	610U	MC	77459
WELBORN DR	0	610Q	MC	77459
WELCH	100	493N	SWH	77006
WELCH	500	335Z	HM	77338
WELCH	1900	492R	SWH	77019
WELCH HOUSE LN	23700	445P	NWC	77493
WELCOME LN	14800	331U	NWC	77014
WELD CT	24700	484G	NEF	77494
WELD DR	1100	484G	NEF	77494
WELDON	100	536X	SH	77587
WELDON DR	1700	373C	NCC	77073
WELDON DR	15200	373R	NCC	77032
WELDON SPRINGS DR	0	366Q	NWC	77433
WELDRIDGE DR	9500	527V	NEF	77498
WELFORD DR	4700	531L	BL	77401
WELFORD LN	300	459Q	HG	77562
WELHAM HESTER CIR	13700	367C	NWC	77429
WELK	2300	576E	SEH	77034
WELLAND DR	12300	569D	SWH	77031
WELLAND WAY	1200	336H	NEH	77339
WELLBORN	12300	614C	BK	77581
WELLBROOK CT	0	615F	PL	77581
WELLBROOK LN	0	657Y	LC	77573
WELLBROOK LN	4500	485Y	NEF	77450
WELLER OAKS DR	22200	291J	NWC	77389
WELLERS WAY	16300	407H	NWC	77095
W. WELLESFORD	1600	488R	SWH	77077
E. WELLESFORD	1600	488R	SWH	77077
WELLESLEY CT	3800	613Y	NEB	77584
WELLESLEY DR	500	490H	HC	77024
WELLESLEY MEADOW LN	0	371H	NWC	77014
WELLESLY CT	1	245D	SWM	77355
WELLESLY DR	20000	335U	HM	77338
WELLFLEET CROSSING	0	611S	FS	77545
WELLFORD	1	453F	NEH	77022
WELLFORD POINT DR	0	407C	NWC	77095
WELLFORD TRAIL	0	568W	SG	77479
WELLINGTON	1	413Y	NEH	77076
W. WELLINGTON	100	413W	NEH	77076
E. WELLINGTON	300	413W	NEH	77076
WELLINGTON	1500	413Z	NEH	77093
WELLINGTON	1700	451T	NWH	77055
WELLINGTON CT	1	569N	SG	77478
WELLINGTON CT	1	609C	MC	77459
S. WELLINGTON CT	7900	451T	NWH	77055
N. WELLINGTON CT	7900	451T	NWH	77055
WELLINGTON DR	1	569N	SG	77478
WELLINGTON DR	3400	613L	NEB	77584
WELLINGTON LN	1	569N	SG	77478
WELLINGTON ARCH LN	1300	488L	SWH	77077
WELLINGTON BEND LN	0	332Q	NCC	77073
WELLINGTON CHASE LN	0	376N	NEC	77396
WELLINGTON CIRCLE DR	0	528K	SWC	77083
WELLINGTON COURT BLVD	22900	290G	NWC	77389
WELLINGTON GROVE CIR	26400	484Z	NEF	77494
WELLINGTON GROVE LN	4300	484Z	NEF	77494
WELLINGTON MEADOWS DR	6300	406U	NWC	77449
WELLINGTON PARK	1	502W	BT	77520
WELLINGTON PARK DR	12300	528R	SWH	77072
WELLINGTON PASS DR	3000	293Y	NCC	77373
WELLINGTON PKWY	12300	371G	NWC	77014
WELLINGTON POINT	300	486D	SWC	77094
WELLINGTON WAY	4800	330V	NWC	77069
WELLMAN LN	14900	412D	NEH	77060
WELLNESS LANDING LN	0	528H	SWH	77072
WELLOCK LN	0	329E	NWC	77375
WELLS	200	292L	SP	77373
WELLS LN	27100	252E	OR	77385
WELL SCHOOL RD	0	617K	SEH	77546
WELLSEY CT	1900	568A	SG	77498
WELLS FARGO DR	100	332P	NWC	77090
S. WELLSFORD DR	800	613G	NEB	77584
N. WELLSFORD DR	800	613G	NEB	77584
W. WELLSFORD DR	1300	252Q	SEM	77385
WELLSFORD GLEN DR	21400	406X	NWC	77449
WELLS HEATHER	100	488L	SWH	77077
WELLSHIRE DR	1100	485J	NEF	77494
WELLSLEY CT	1900	568A	SG	77498
WELLS MARK DR	3600	376G	NEC	77396
WELLS RIVER DR	13300	408Y	NWC	77041
WELLSWOOD CT	19300	337S	NEC	77346
WELLSWORTH DR	9200	528T	SWC	77083
WELLWOOD CT	6800	528G	SWH	77083
W. WELSFORD DR	1900	252R	SEM	77386
E. WELSFORD DR	2000	252V	SEM	77386
WELSHPOOL GLEN DR	11600	371P	NWC	77066
WELSH STONE LN	0	457K	NEC	77049
WELSTON TERRACE DR	0	249Q	NWC	77375
WELTY	200	288D	TB	77375
WELWICK CT	21000	406T	NWC	77449
WELWYN DR	15300	409M	JV	77040
WEMBLEY DR	12100	570A	SWH	77031
WEMBLEY DR	12200	569H	SWH	77031
WEMYSS BAY RD	16100	407H	NWC	77095
WENBURY DR	0	289R	NWC	77375
WENDA	4700	573D	SEH	77033
WENDA	5200	574A	SEH	77033
WENDEL	600	493B	NWH	77009
WENDEL RD	0	455K	NEH	77028
WENDELL	4300	531M	BL	77401
WENDELYN LN	13600	330Y	NWC	77069
WENDEMERE	7000	412X	NWH	77088
WENDIGO PLACE	0	408G	NWC	77041
WENDOVER LN	11400	490F	BH	77024
WENDOVER CREEK CT	15500	327V	NWC	77429
WENDOVER GLEN LN	0	445M	NWC	77449
WENDTWOODS DR	100	249R	NWH	77375
WENDTWOODS DR	100	249R	NWH	77375
WENDY HILL WAY	1900	618R	SEH	77058
WENLOCK DR	6000	574U	SEH	77048
WENNINGTON DR	10500	529Q	SWH	77099
WENOAH LOOP	0	250Q	NWC	77389
WENOAH PLACE	0	250R	NWC	77389
WENSLEY DR	30000	252U	SEM	77386
WENTWOOD RD	1200	577E	PA	77504
WENTWORTH	900	493X	SWH	77004
WENTWORTH	2300	533C	SEH	77004
WENTWORTH CT	1300	451X	NWH	77055
WENTWORTH DR	1000	613G	NEB	77584
WENTWORTH LN	2500	537K	PA	77506
WENTWORTH OAKS CT	2400	619Y	LC	77573
WENTWORTH PARK DR	200	457Y	NEC	77015
WENWOOD CIR	7200	411N	NWH	77040
WERCHAN	6100	419D	NEC	77532
WERLEIN	2600	532G	WU	77005
WERNER	4500	453J	NWH	77022
WERNER	5400	453A	NEH	77076
WERNER	6300	413S	NEH	77076
WERNER	7500	413N	NCC	77037
W. WERRINGTON WAY	0	333E	NCC	77073
S. WERRINGTON WAY	0	333K	NCC	77073
N. WERRINGTON WAY	0	333K	NCC	77338
WERTZ	14500	577T	SEH	77034
WESCAN	8200	408M	NWC	77041
WESCOTT AVE	0	568S	SG	77479
WESCO WAY	6400	408U	NWC	77041
WESER DR	22800	295A	SEM	77365
WESLAYAN	2600	492S	SWH	77027
WESLAYAN	5100	532E	WU	77005
WESLEY	1500	494X	SEH	77023
WESLEY DR	100	658L	LC	77573
WESLEY LN	1300	538L	DP	77536
WESLEY MANOR CT	0	407X	NWC	77449
WESLEY OAKS	0	571K	SWH	77085

Street Name	Block	Pg/Sq	Loc	Zips
WESLOW	3600	534Q	SEH	77087
WESSEX DR	11900	617A	SEH	77089
WESSEX PARK DR	13900	367D	NWC	77429
WEST	0	419G	CB	77532
WEST	0	500U	BT	77520
WEST	0	569V	SF	77477
WEST	100	536U	PA	77502
WEST	300	570S	SF	77477
WEST	900	493M	SEH	77020
WEST	1500	494A	NEH	77026
WEST	7600	454E	NEH	77093
WEST BLVD	5100	492Z	SWH	77006
WEST CT	3800	538U	DP	77536
WEST DR	0	658Y	LC	77573
WEST DR	200	619U	LC	77565
WEST DR	500	497H	NEC	77530
WEST DR	14900	612A	NEF	77053
WEST LN	1	492N	SWH	77019
WEST LN	500	536K	PA	77506
WEST LN	2300	491V	SWH	77027
E. WEST RD	100	413A	NEH	77060
WEST RD	100	412B	NEH	77037
WEST RD	200	412B	NWC	77038
WEST RD	1600	532R	SWH	77054
WEST RD	5000	501G	NEC	77521
WEST RD	6000	411B	NWC	77086
WEST RD	7200	411A	NWH	77086
WEST RD	7500	410G	NWC	77064
WEST RD	9800	409B	NWC	77064
WEST RD	11000	409B	NWC	77065
WEST RD	12000	367K	CY	77433
WEST RD	12300	408G	NWC	77041
WEST RD	14600	408F	NWC	77095
WEST RD	16200	407G	NWC	77095
WEST RD	21900	446E	SEM	77357
WESTACRE PLACE	9300	528S	NEF	77083
WEST ALABAMA CT	3000	492T	SWH	77027
WESTBANK AVE	7600	410H	NWC	77064
WESTBAY LN	7700	456H	NEC	77044
WEST BEND	6200	571T	SWH	77085
WEST BEND DR	2300	569V	SF	77477
WEST BEND DR	14600	528A	SWC	77082
WEST BEND DR	14800	527D	SWC	77082
WESTBLUFF DR	1700	446Y	NWC	77084
WESTBOROUGH DR	2000	446X	NWC	77449
WEST BOUGH LN	600	489H	SWH	77024
WESTBOURNE DR	0	484V	NEF	77494
WESTBOURNE PARK DR	0	488Q	SWH	77077
WESTBRAE GARDENS CT	8900	530X	SWC	77031
WESTBRAE MANOR DR	8800	530W	SWC	77031
WESTBRAE MEADOWS DR	10900	530X	SWH	77031
WESTBRAE OAKS LN	10900	530X	SWC	77031
WESTBRAE PARK CT	10800	530X	SWH	77031
WESTBRAE PARK LN	8700	530X	SWH	77031
WESTBRAE PKWY	10600	530W	SWH	77031
WESTBRAE VILLAGE DR	10900	530X	SWH	77031
WESTBRANCH CT	12800	528H	SWH	77072
WESTBRANCH DR	1600	488R	SWH	77077
WESTBRANCH DR	6100	528H	SWH	77072
WESTBRANCH DR	6700	528M	SWH	77072
WESTBRANCH MEADOWS CT	10500	449H	NWH	77041
WESTBRIAR CT	1900	538K	DP	77536
WESTBRIAR LN	5000	491Q	SWH	77056
WESTBRIDGE LN	19600	291W	NWC	77379
WESTBROOK	400	248W	SWM	77362
WESTBROOK	500	247Z	SWM	77362
WESTBROOK CIR	100	242D	WCO	77484
WESTBROOK CIR	3300	537L	PA	77503
WESTBROOK DR	100	242D	WCO	77484
WESTBROOK DR	200	412M	NEH	77037
WESTBROOK RD	5200	454C	NEH	77016
WESTBROOK BRIDGE DR	7800	408L	NWC	77041
WESTBROOK CINCO LN	22500	485Y	NEF	77450
WESTBROOK LAKES BLVD	0	408L	NWC	77095
WESTBROOK OAKS WAY	5400	330D	NWC	77379
WESTBURY CT	14400	408U	NWC	77084
WESTBURY SQUARE	100	571B	SWH	77035
WEST BY NORTHWEST BLVD	5900	410X	NWH	77040
WESTCENTER DR	3300	489Z	SWH	77042
WESTCHASE DR	3300	489Z	SWH	77042
WESTCHASE WAY	0	529G	SWH	77072
WESTCHESTER	4700	578J	PA	77505
WESTCHESTER	5200	492X	SWH	77005
WESTCHESTER	5300	532F	WU	77005
WESTCHESTER	6900	532F	SWH	77025
WESTCHESTER CIR	0	614N	PL	77584
WESTCHESTER CT	1	532F	SWH	77005
WESTCLIFF DR	4400	491R	SWH	77027
WESTCLIFFE CT	19900	406L	NWC	77433
WESTCLIFFE FALLS DR	21500	486J	SWC	77450
WEST CLUB LN	12700	528U	SWH	77099
WESTCOTT	1	492L	SWH	77007
WESTCOTT	6200	492F	SWH	77007
WESTCOTT RD	6300	454H	NEH	77016
WESTCOTT RD	9100	455M	NEH	77016
WEST COURT DR	1	535L	SEH	77017
WESTCOVE CIR	8600	409H	NWC	77064
WESTCREEK LN	2000	491V	SWH	77027
WESTCREST DR	1800	450V	NWH	77055
WESTCROSS	600	452M	NEH	77018
WESTDALE	5600	534V	SEH	77087
WESTEDGE DR	10300	528W	NEF	77498
WESTEGATE SPRINGS LN	0	407J	NWC	77433
WESTELLA DR	12300	488Q	SWH	77077
WESTENFIELD LN	22500	485U	NEF	77450
WESTERBROOK LN	0	375Z	NEC	77396
WESTERCREEK LN	0	617X	SEC	77546
WESTERFIELD LN	0	447N	NWC	77084
WESTERHAM PLACE	5100	330Y	NWC	77069
WESTERLAKE CT	0	375Z	NEC	77396
WESTERLAKE DR	0	612M	PL	77584
WESTERLAND DR	2200	490T	SWH	77063
WESTERLEY LN	12500	488M	SWH	77077
WESTERLOCH DR	13500	488K	SWH	77077
WESTERLY PARK	0	448D	NWC	77041
WESTERMAN	3700	492W	SWH	77005
WESTERMILL DR	4000	527G	SWC	77082
WESTERN DR	8200	451S	NWH	77055
WESTERN DR	9100	450U	NWH	77080
WESTERN LN	0	503V	BC	77520
WESTERN BRANCH CT	4600	371K	NWC	77066
WESTERN BRIAR LN	0	376A	NEC	77396
WESTERN BROOK DR	0	331A	NWC	77388
WESTERN HILLS CT	22000	485H	SWC	77450
WESTERN HILLS DR	900	485H	SWC	77450
WESTERN MEADOWS DR	1000	485G	SWC	77450
WESTERN OAK LN	7600	410L	NWC	77040
WESTERN PASS LN	17800	407K	NWC	77095
WESTERN SADDLE CT	14500	377S	NEC	77044
WESTERN SKIES DR	15100	370U	NWC	77086
WESTERN SKYES DR	0	657T	LC	77573
WESTERN SPRINGS DR	1000	485G	SWC	77450

Street Name	Block	Pg/Sq	Loc	Zips
WESTERN TRAIL DR	8000	410Q	NWC	77040
WESTERN VALLEY DR	21000	406P	NWC	77449
WESTERN VILLAGE LN	1900	449T	NWH	77043
WESTERPINE LN	0	446A	NWC	77449
WESTERWOOD	0	489D	NWH	77043
W. WESTFAIR DR	0	408G	NWC	77041
E. WESTFAIR DR	13800	408H	NWC	77041
WESTFALL AVE	900	536M	PA	77506
WEST FALL DR	14200	528J	SWC	77083
WESTFIELD	100	453K	NWH	77022
WESTFIELD	1500	616W	PL	77581
WESTFIELD	6500	571S	SWH	77085
WESTFIELD LN	600	656B	FR	77546
WESTFIELD BRIDGE	0	333B	NCC	77373
WESTFIELD CREEK RD	0	406X	NWC	77449
WESTFIELD ESTATES DR	20400	446K	NWC	77449
WESTFIELD HOLLOW DR	0	446B	NWC	77449
WESTFIELD LAKE	0	333B	NCC	77373
WESTFIELD LOOP RD	1600	333J	NCC	77073
WESTFIELD PKWY	19200	446L	NWC	77449
WESTFIELD PLACE	0	332K	NWC	77090
WESTFIELD RIDGE DR	0	333F	NCC	77073
WESTFIELD SPRINGS DR	0	446B	NWC	77449
WESTFIELD VILLAGE DR	4100	446F	NWC	77449
WESTFORD	500	453M	NEH	77022
WESTFORD	1700	453M	NEH	77093
WESTFORD PARK LN	7000	526E	NEF	77407
WESTFOREST DR	0	485Q	NEF	77494
WEST FOREST DR	500	489E	SWH	77079
WESTFORK CT	20200	446X	NWC	77449
WESTFORK DR	1600	446W	NWC	77449
WEST FREEWAY	0	492E	SWH	77007
WESTGARD BLVD	11900	456L	NEC	77044
WESTGATE	12000	368Q	NWC	77429
WESTGATE DR	1900	614N	PL	77581
WESTGATE DR	2100	492U	SWH	77019
WESTGATE DR	2600	492U	SWH	77098
WESTGATE DR	10400	252F	SEM	77385
WEST GATE RD	0	580X	SEC	77586
WESTGATE PARK DR	0	253N	SEM	77385
WESTGATE PARK DR	0	407K	NWC	77433
WESTGATE PASTURE LN	0	407J	NWC	77433
WESTGATE VILLAGE LN	22900	292F	NCC	77373
WESTGLEN DR	7800	490Z	SWH	77063
WESTGREEN BLVD	0	446E	NWC	77449
N. WESTGREEN BLVD	1000	446N	NWC	77449
WESTGREEN BLVD	1100	486J	SWC	77450
WESTGREEN CT	20800	486E	SWC	77450
WESTGREEN SPUR	4000	324L	NWC	77447
WESTGREEN SQUARE	16700	324L	NWC	77447
WESTGROVE LN	2600	492S	SWH	77027
WESTGROVE LN	20800	255N	SEM	77365
WESTHALL LN	0	407J	NWC	77433
WEST HAMPTON DR	3000	488X	SWC	77082
WESTHAMPTON DR	3200	572N	SWH	77045
WESTHAVEN DR	19400	446V	NWC	77084
WESTHAWK TRAIL	0	334R	NCC	77338
WESTHEIMER	100	493S	SWH	77006
WESTHEIMER	1700	492T	SWH	77098
WESTHEIMER	3400	492T	SWH	77027
WESTHEIMER	4800	491T	SWH	77056
WESTHEIMER	5700	491T	SWH	77057
WESTHEIMER	7500	490U	SWH	77063
WESTHEIMER	9700	489U	SWH	77042
WESTHEIMER	11300	489U	SWH	77077
WESTHEIMER	12400	488U	SWH	77077
WESTHEIMER	14600	487Z	SWH	77082
WESTHEIMER	16100	527B	SWH	77082
WESTHEIMER CT	5400	491T	SWH	77056
WESTHEIMER DR	2900	485N	NEF	77494
WESTHEIMER AIR PARK		525E	NEF	77494
WESTHEIMER AIR PARK		525J	NEF	77494
WESTHEIMER LAKES N.	26400	524J	NEF	77494
WESTHEIMER PKWY	15000	487U	SWH	77082
WESTHEIMER PKWY	17200	486Y	SWH	77082
WESTHEIMER PKWY	20600	485U	NEF	77450
WESTHEIMER PKWY	23500	485U	NEF	77494
WESTHEIMER PLACE DR	3700	527B	SWC	77082
WESTHEIMER WAY	5400	491T	SWH	77056
WESTHILL DR	12900	488Q	SWH	77077
WESTHOLLOW DR	2500	488W	SWH	77082
WESTHOLLOW PARK DR	13700	488T	SWH	77082
WESTHOLLOW PKWY	3900	528B	SWC	77082
WESTHOLME DR	3900	490Y	SWH	77063
WESTHOPE DR	0	253X	SEM	77386
WESTHORPE DR	12600	488Q	SWH	77077
WESTHURST LN	1500	488Q	SWH	77077
WEST INDIES CT	2000	619W	NB	77058
WESTINGTON LN	7900	410L	NWC	77040
WESTIN HILLS CT	0	488T	SWH	77077
WEST ISLE BLVD	0	251F	WD	77381
WEST ISLE PLACE	1	251F	WD	77381
WESTKNOLL LN	0	528Q	SWC	77072
WEST LAKE CIR	0	657J	FR	77546
WEST LAKE DR	0	657J	FR	77546
WESTLAKE DR	1200	618L	SEH	77062
WESTLAKE PARK BLVD	100	488B	SWH	77079
WESTLAKE PLACE DR	19700	446U	NWC	77084
WESTLAKE RUN BLVD	0	328J	NWC	77429
WESTLAKE RUN BLVD	0	328E	NWC	77377
WESTLAKE WAY	1900	446U	NWC	77084
W. WESTLAND BLVD	8400	408H	NWC	77041
E. WESTLAND BLVD	13600	408H	NWC	77041
WESTLAND CREEK DR	21000	445M	NWC	77449
WEST LANE	2300	491V	SWH	77027
WESTLEA LN	5300	614X	PL	77584
WESTLEIGH DR	12600	488Q	SWH	77077
WESTLINE DR	6000	529H	SWH	77036
WESTLOCK	18200	328H	NWC	77377
WESTLOCK CT	18100	328H	NWC	77377
WESTLOCK DR	11600	328H	NWC	77377
WEST LOOP (I.H. 610) N.	1	491M	SWH	77024
WEST LOOP (I.H. 610) S.	1	491V	SWH	77027
WEST LOOP (I.H. 610) N.	1100	451Z	NWH	77055
WEST LOOP (I.H. 610) N.	1500	451Z	NWH	77008
WEST LOOP (I.H. 610) S.	5200	531M	SWH	77401
WEST LOOP (I.H. 610) S.	5201	531M	SWH	77081
WEST LOOP (I.H. 610) S.	5500	531M	SWH	77401
WEST LOOP (I.H. 610) S.	8500	531M	SWH	77096
WESTMART DR	3800	529D	SWH	77042
WESTMEAD DR	1700	488Q	SWH	77077
WEST MEADOW BLVD	0	460W	BT	77521
WESTMEADOW CT	7300	527J	NEF	77407
WESTMEADOW DR	1700	446Y	NWC	77084
WESTMEADOW DR	3700	527C	SWC	77082
WEST MEMORIAL PK, A	0	491E	SV	77055
WEST MEMORIAL PK, B	0	491A	SV	77055
WEST MEMORIAL PK, C	0	491A	SV	77055
WESTMERE CT	1700	489N	SWH	77077
WESTMERE DR	11800	489N	SWH	77077
WESTMERE DR	12400	488R	SWH	77077
WESTMINISTER	2000	615P	PL	77581

Street Name	Block	Pg/Sq	Loc	Zips
WESTMINISTER CT	5200	330Y	NWC	77069
WESTMINSTER	400	658R	LC	77573
WESTMINSTER DR	300	491F	SWH	77024
WESTMINSTER DR	9800	335Q	HM	77338
WESTMINSTER GLEN LN	0	457K	NEC	77049
WESTMINSTER GLEN LN	0	457K	NEC	77049
WESTMINSTER PLAZA DR	2600	489W	SWH	77082
WESTMINSTER TRACE LN	0	337L	NEC	77345
WESTMINSTER VILLAGE CT	17000	407Y	NWC	77084
WESTMINSTER VILLAGE DR	5700	407Y	NWC	77084
WESTMONT DR	400	496H	NEH	77015
WESTMONT DR	900	497E	NEH	77015
WESTMOOR DR	0	527N	NEF	77407
WESTMOOR DR	0	526M	NEF	77407
WESTMOOR DR	0	526Z	NEF	77469
WESTMOOR DR		526V	NEF	77406
WESTMORELAND	200	493T	SWH	77006
WESTNUT LN	8400	410K	NWC	77040
WESTOAK	0	500J	BT	77520
WEST OAK DR	0	657J	FR	77546
S. WEST OAK DR	1	491L	SWH	77056
N. WEST OAK DR	1	491L	SWH	77056
WEST OAK MEWS	5100	491L	SWH	77056
WEST OAKS BLVD	0	614Q	PL	77584
S. WEST OAKS CIR	0	614Q	PL	77584
N. WEST OAKS CIR	0	614Q	PL	77584
E. WEST OAKS CIR	2700	614Q	PL	77584
WEST OAKS PLAZA	14600	488W	SWH	77082
WESTOFFICE DR	10300	529D	SWH	77042
WESTON	6300	534N	SEH	77021
WESTON	6600	534J	SEH	77021
WESTON OAKS LN	0	326U	NWC	77429
WESTON PARK DR	0	407E	NWC	77433
WESTON VILLAGE DR	31400	252R	SEM	77386
WESTOVER	5100	534W	SEH	77033
WESTOVER	6200	534V	SEH	77087
WESTOVER	7400	535S	SEH	77087
WESTOVER DR	12000	368Q	NWC	77429
WESTOVER PARK AVE	0	657Y	LC	77573
WESTOVER PARK AVE	0	657Y	LC	77573
WESTOVER PARK CIR	2000	252R	SEM	77386
WESTOVER RIDGE DR	0	528H	SWH	77072
WESTPARK DR	2600	492X	SWH	77098
WESTPARK DR	3200	492X	SWH	77005
WESTPARK DR	3700	492W	SWH	77027
WESTPARK DR	5000	491Z	SWH	77056
WESTPARK DR	5600	491X	SWH	77057
WESTPARK DR	6700	530B	SWH	77063
WESTPARK DR	10000	530B	SWH	77042
WESTPARK DR	10100	529D	SWH	77042
WESTPARK DR	10400	529B	SWH	77082
WESTPARK DR	11100	489W	SWH	77082
WESTPARK DR	11600	488Z	SWH	77082
WESTPARK DR	13300	528A	SWC	77082
WESTPARK DR	14900	527C	SWC	77082
WESTPARK MEADOWS		525E	NEF	77494
WESTPARK TOLLROAD	5600	491X	SWH	77057
WESTPARK TOLLROAD	5600	491X	SWH	77057
WESTPARK TOLLROAD	6100	531A	SWH	77057
WESTPARK TOLLROAD	6100	531A	SWH	77057
WESTPARK TOLLROAD	9800	530A	SWH	77057
WESTPARK TOLLROAD	9800	530A	SWH	77057
WESTPARK TOLLROAD	10800	529C	SWH	77057
WESTPARK TOLLROAD	10800	529C	SWH	77057
WESTPARK TOLLROAD	12800	528C	SWH	77057
WESTPARK TOLLROAD	12800	528C	SWH	77057
WEST PARK VIEW DR	0	446V	NWH	77084
WESTPLACE DR	8600	570B	SWH	77071
WESTPLAIN	0	408H	NWC	77041
WESTPOINT	5800	532A	WU	77005
WEST POINT CT	0	290R	NWC	77388
WESTPORT LN	13300	489B	SWH	77079
WESTPORT BRIDGE LN	0	528W	NEF	77498
WESTPORT SHORE DR	1000	486H	SWC	77094
WEST RANCH DR	0	657P	FR	77546
WEST RAY	0	449R	NWH	77043
WESTRAY	9800	450N	NWH	77043
WESTRAY CT	1400	569X	MC	77459
WESTRAY DR	4400	569X	MC	77459
WEST RIDGE	0	251Z	WD	77380
WESTRIDGE	2300	532Q	SWH	77054
WESTRIDGE	3200	532P	SWH	77025
WESTRIDGE DR	500	252W	SWM	77380
WESTRIDGE BEND LN	0	407J	NWC	77433
WEST RIDGE PLACE	5200	448D	NWC	77041
WESTROCK DR	0	446J	NWC	77449
WEST SAM HOUSTN PKWY N.	100	489M	SWH	77024
WEST SAM HOUSTN PKWY S.	100	489Z	SWH	77042
WEST SAM HOUSTN PKWY N.	1000	449U	NWH	77043
WEST SAM HOUSTN PKWY N.	4300	449G	NWH	77041
WEST SAM HOUSTN PKWY S.	5800	529M	SWH	77072
WEST SAM HOUSTN PKWY N.	6000	409Y	NWC	77041
WEST SAM HOUSTN PKWY N.	7000	410N	NWC	77040
WEST SAM HOUSTN PKWY N.	8500	409D	NWC	77064
WEST SAM HOUSTN PKWY S.	8800	529M	SWH	77099
WEST SAM HOUS PKWY N.	10000	369Z	NWC	77064
WEST SHADY LN	1	490T	SWH	77063
WESTSHIRE DR	400	496E	NEH	77013
WESTSHORE CT	0	660J	LC	77573
WESTSHORE CT	4300	609B	MC	77459
WESTSHORE DR	1200	486H	SWC	77094
WESTSHORE DR	2000	609B	MC	77459
WESTSIDE CT	500	536Z	PA	77502
WESTSIDE CT	2000	569W	SG	77478
WESTSIDE DR	1900	538N	DP	77536
WESTSIDE DR	2700	536Z	PA	77502
WESTSIDE DR	3100	576D	PA	77504
WEST SIDE FOREST DR	19800	486L	SWC	77094
WESTSIDE PARKWAY	0	445Y	NWC	77449
WESTSIDE WAY	0	445Y	NWC	77449
WESTSTAR LN	6200	528D	SWH	77072
WEST TEMPLE DR	0	367Y	NWC	77095
WEST TERRACE DR	0	492K	SWH	77007
WEST TEX	9000	490C	SV	77055
WEST TIMBERLOCH TRAIL	31200	246Y	SWM	77355
WESTTOWN	12800	488Q	SWH	77077
WEST TRAIL DR	0	657U	LC	77573
WEST TRAIL DR	0	612P	PL	77545
WEST VALLEY PALMS DR	8900	329M	NWC	77379
WESTVIEW	2500	580L	LP	77571
WESTVIEW DR	3300	580Q	SA	77571
WESTVIEW DR	5800	451X	NWH	77055
WESTVIEW DR	8600	450X	NWH	77055
WESTVIEW DR	10100	449Z	NWH	77043
S. WESTVIEW CIRCLE DR	10800	449Y	NWH	77043
WEST VILLAGE DR	12200	414H	NEC	77039
WEST VIRGINIA	400	453A	NEH	77076
WESTWARD	5400	531A	SWH	77081
WESTWARD LN	0	616U	FR	77546
WESTWARD HO	15800	246R	SC	77355
WESTWARD TRAIL	0	571U	SWH	77085
WESTWAY	100	496S	GP	77547

Street Name	Block	Pg/Sq	Loc	Zips
WEST WAY DR	0	657U	LC	77573
WESTWAY LN	11400	414Q	NEC	77093
WESTWAY LN	14300	488J	SWH	77077
WESTWAY PARK BLVD	0	449H	NWH	77041
WESTWEGO TRAIL	16400	367G	NWC	77429
WESTWICK DR	1600	488Q	SWH	77077
WESTWICK DR	3000	488Y	SWH	77082
WESTWICK DR	6200	528C	SWH	77072
WESTWICK FOREST LN	1200	489A	NWH	77043
WESTWICK FOREST LN	1300	449W	NWH	77043
WESTWILLOW DR	8800	409H	NWC	77064
WESTWIND	1900	538N	DP	77536
WESTWIND CT	0	660K	LC	77573
WESTWIND CT	7800	530U	SWH	77071
WESTWIND LN	7600	530U	SWH	77071
WESTWIND GARDEN PASS	0	484Y	NEF	77494
WESTWIND GARDEN PASS	0	484Y	NEF	77494
WESTWOLD DR	11800	328H	NWC	77377
WESTWOOD	0	254C	SEM	77302
WESTWOOD	1	541D	BT	77520
W. WESTWOOD CIR	15300	570G	MC	77071
E. WESTWOOD CIR	15300	570G	MC	77071
WESTWOOD CT	200	252J	OR	77386
WESTWOOD DR	0	657U	LC	77573
WESTWOOD DR	200	616U	FR	77546
WESTWOOD DR	1800	570S	SF	77477
WESTWOOD DR	1900	451W	NWH	77055
N. WESTWOOD DR	18800	254C	SEM	77302
WESTWOOD DR	26500	252J	OR	77386
WESTWOOD GLEN	800	572Q	SWH	77047
WESTWOOD LAKE CT	1900	336F	HM	77339
WESTWOOD LAKE DR	1900	336F	HM	77339
WESTWOOD MANOR LN	0	573T	SEC	77047
WESTWOOD MEADOWS DR	0	487Z	SWC	77082
WESTWOOD PINES DR	0	446B	NWC	77449
WESTWOOD PLACE DR	7900	529M	SWH	77036
WESTWOOD VILLAGE CIR	0	529M	SWH	77036
WESTWOOD VILLAGE DR	9200	529M	SWH	77036
WETHERBURN LN	22100	445V	NWC	77449
WETHERBY LN	8000	575P	SEH	77075
WETHERFIELD LN	13800	368A	NWC	77429
WETHERILL	8600	454E	NEH	77093
WETHERWIND	19500	446C	NWC	77449
WETNERSFIELD RD	0	408K	NWC	77095
WEXFORD	0	616J	PL	77581
WEXFORD CT	0	490G	PP	77024
WEXFORD DR	1300	538N	DP	77536
WEXFORD PARK DR	6400	411K	NWC	77088
WEYBRIDGE DR	9600	569D	SWH	77031
WEYBURN	6900	454H	NEH	77028
WEYBURN	7300	455E	NEH	77028
WEYBURN GROVE	0	411F	NWH	77086
WEYBURN GROVE DR	8900	411K	NWC	77088
WEYER AVE	1200	658V	LC	77573
WEYGAND	900	282Y	WL	77484
WEYMOUTH DR	8800	570A	SWH	77031
W. F	0	580A	LP	77571
W. F	100	580C	LP	77571
W. G	0	580G	LP	77571
W. G	100	580B	LP	77571
W. H	100	580B	LP	77571
WHARF	8100	495X	SEH	77012
WHARTON	0	500Z	BT	77520
WHARTON	6500	451Y	NWH	77055
WHARTON STA H L & P	0	370P	NWC	77064
WHARTON WEEMS BLVD	0	580K	LP	77571
WHATLEY DR	2100	538S	DP	77536
WHEAT	3000	371Y	NWC	77038
WHEAT	3200	371Y	NWC	77086
WHEAT LN	2000	460X	NEC	77521
WHEATBRIDGE DR	13600	408Y	NWC	77041
WHEAT CROSS DR	0	407F	NWC	77095
WHEAT FARM LN	0	325F	NWC	77447
WHEATFIELD BLVD	3100	615T	PL	77581
WHEATFIELD CT	3400	615U	PL	77581
WHEATFIELD DR	16500	407G	NWC	77095
WHEAT GRASS TRAIL	0	325L	NWC	77433
WHEATHALL CAMP LN	2000	446T	NWC	77449
WHEAT HARVEST LN		484W	NEF	77494
WHEATLAND DR	8700	409G	NWC	77064
S. WHEATLEIGH DR	100	249R	NWH	77375
S. WHEATLEIGH DR	100	249R	NWH	77375
N. WHEATLEIGH DR	100	249R	NWH	77375
N. WHEATLEIGH DR	100	249R	NWH	77375
WHEATLEY	800	541B	BT	77520
WHEATLEY	5400	452B	NWH	77091
WHEATLEY	7200	412P	NWH	77088
WHEATMEADOW CT	3200	615T	PL	77581
WHEATMEADOW LN	3400	615T	PL	77581
WHEATMILL CT	0	407G	NWC	77095
WHEAT MILL LN	16600	407G	NWC	77095
S. WHEATON	0	486T	SWH	77450
N. WHEATON	0	486T	SWH	77450
WHEATON DR	10500	576T	SEH	77089
WHEATON CREEK CT	20700	332Z	NCC	77073
WHEATON CREST LN	0	290T	NWC	77379
WHEATON CREST LN	0	366R	NWC	77433
WHEATON EDGE LN	0	407C	NWC	77095
WHEATON HILL LN	7001	526G	NEF	77407
WHEATON PARK DR	5000	609S	NEF	77479
WHEATRIDGE	3200	615B	PL	77581
WHEATRIDGE DR	11000	369V	NWC	77064
WHEAT SNOW CT	2100	446T	NWC	77449
WHEAT SNOW LN	20100	446S	NWC	77449
WHEATSTALK LN	3400	615T	PL	77581
WHEEDEN RD	6700	574R	SEH	77075
WHEELER	0	537J	PA	77506
WHEELER	1000	493Y	SEH	77002
WHEELER	1100	493Y	SEH	77004
WHEELER	2700	533C	SEH	77004
WHEELER	4300	534A	SEH	77004
WHEELER	5900	534G	SEH	77023
WHEELER PEAK WAY	0	446A	NWC	77449
WHEELHOUSE CT	300	569P	SF	77477
WHEELHOUSE DR	600	569P	NEF	77477
WHEELWRIGHT LN	2500	617Y	SEC	77546
WHELTON CIR	700	537L	PA	77503
WHELTON DR	800	537Q	PA	77503
WHERRY DR	16700	379X	NEC	77532
WHETSTONE LN	7500	410H	NWC	77064
WHICH WAY	0	297N	NEH	77339
WHIDBEY CT	3600	331B	NWC	77388
WHIDBEY ISLAND DR	7700	370Z	NWC	77086
WHIGHAMS PLACE	16800	527X	NEF	77407
WHIMBREL DR	100	568T	SG	77478
WHIMSEY CT	6500	407U	NWC	77084
S. WHIMSEY DR	0	406M	NWC	77433
WHIPPLE DR	100	531L	BL	77401
WHIPPLE TREE DR	15800	329T	NWC	77070
WHIPPOORWILL CIR	0	609F	MC	77459
WHIPPOORWILL DR	500	570U	MC	77489
WHIPPOORWILL RD	11400	490G	HE	77024

Street Name	Block	Pg/Sq	Loc	Zips
WHIRLAWAY DR	2000	570S	SF	77477
WHIRLAWAY DR	4100	537R	PA	77503
WHIRLAWAY ELM DR	8100	337Z	NEC	77346
WHIRLWIND	3000	615Q	PL	77581
WHISPER LN	1	251Q	WD	77380
WHISPER BLUFF DR	10300	376B	NEC	77396
WHISPER HOLLOW LN	0	377U	NEC	77044
WHISPERING BREEZE LN	19300	486H	SWC	77094
WHISPERING BROOK DR	3500	297U	NEH	77345
WHISPERING CREEK	0	610Z	MC	77545
WHISPERING CREEK DR	1400	444X	KT	77493
WHISPERING CREEK WAY	5400	536W	SEH	77017
WHISPERING CYPRESS DR	14600	327X	NWC	77429
WHISPERING DAISY CT	21900	325U	NWC	77433
WHISPERING FALLS CT	15900	448B	NWC	77084
WHISPERING FALLS DR	4700	448B	NWC	77084
WHISPERING FERN CT	2700	297Z	NEH	77345
WHISPERING FOREST DR	1700	336B	NEH	77339
WHISPERING FOREST DR	21700	296X	SEM	77339
WHISPERING FOUNTAINS DR	0	444X	KT	77493
WHISPERING GREEN DR	0	327U	CY	77429
W. WHISPERING GROVE	19400	286L	NWC	77377
E. WHISPERING GROVE	19400	286L	NWC	77377
WHISPERING HOLLOW LN	0	446C	NWC	77449
WHISPERING LAKE CT	14200	328N	NWC	77429
WHISPERING LAKES DR	1400	444X	KT	77493
WHISPERING LAKES RANCH DR	0	660Q	LC	77573
WHISPERING MANOR LN	0	615M	PL	77089
WHISPERING MAPLE DR	23500	293W	NCC	77373
WHISPERING MAPLE WAY	27300	294J	SEM	77386
WHISPERING MAPLE WAY	0	294N	SEM	77386
WHISPERING MEADOW	0	246H	SWM	77355
WHISPERING MEADOWS TRL	10700	369T	NWC	77064
WHISPERING OAK DR	13500	369E	NWC	77429
WHISPERING OAKS	2300	615Q	PL	77581
WHISPERING OAKS DR	100	619H	TL	77586
WHISPERING OAKS DR	1400	444X	KT	77493
WHISPERING OAKS DR	11300	252D	SEM	77385
WHISPERING OAKS LN	31300	253P	SEM	77386
WHISPERING PALMS DR	14000	371Q	NWC	77066
WHISPERING PINE CT	1700	570T	MC	77489
WHISPERING PINE DR	800	570T	MC	77489
WHISPERING PINES	100	657A	FR	77546
WHISPERING PINES	18300	257C	RF	77357
WHISPERING PINES	21300	334M	NCC	77373
WHISPERING PINES DR	1300	451X	NWH	77055
WHISPERING PINES DR	1500	444X	KT	77493
WHISPERING PINES DR	2900	537Q	PA	77503
WHISPERING PINES LN	2600	502B	NEC	77521
WHISPERING RIDGE TERRACE	0	487A	SWC	77094
WHISPERING ROCK LN	4600	291W	NWC	77388
WHISPERING SANDS CT	12500	449A	NWC	77041
WHISPERING SPRINGS DR	2000	292R	NCC	77373
WHISPERING SPRINGS DR	2400	293N	NCC	77373
WHISPERING STAR CT	17500	367T	NWC	77095
WHISPERING THICKET PLACE	100	249R	NWH	77375
WHISPERING THICKET PLACE	100	249R	NWH	77375
WHISPERING TIMBERS WAY	0	296U	SEM	77365
WHISPERING TRAILS CIR	2100	296Y	NEH	77339
WHISPERING TRAILS DR	2100	296Y	NEH	77339
WHISPERING VALLEY DR	14000	368F	NWC	77429
WHISPERING WATER WAY	20300	326N	NWC	77433
WHISPERING WILLOW CT	1200	568W	SG	77479
WHISPERING WILLOW DR	22700	333A	NCC	77373
WHISPERING WIND	23600	525E	NEF	77494
WHISPERING WINDS DR	2900	615Q	PL	77581
WHISPERING WINDS LN	2300	296V	NEH	77339
WHISPERING WOOD LN	7700	410D	NWC	77086
WHISPER PASS	200	486D	SWC	77094
WHISPER POINT DR	0	410L	NWC	77040
WHISPER ROCK DR	0	609S	NEF	77479
WHISPER TRACE CT	1200	485L	SWC	77494
WHISPERTRAIL CT	13900	331X	NWC	77014
WHISPERWILLOW PLACE	10600	251K	WD	77380
WHISPER WOODS DR	0	327Q	CY	77429
WHISTLE CREEK LN	0	406D	NWC	77433
WHISTLER CT	1	251R	WD	77380
WHISTLER DR	0	444S	KT	77493
WHISTLER PINE DR		289G	NWC	77375
WHISTLERS COTTAGE CT	10900	411M	NWC	77088
WHISTLERS WALK PLACE	1	250D	WD	77381
WHISTLING DIXIE	7000	455M	NEH	77078
WHISTLING PINES CT	0	250V	NWC	77389
WHISTLING PINES DR	0	250V	NWC	77389
WHISTLING PINES DR	14300	372B	NWC	77090
WHISTLING SPRINGS DR	12700	377B	NEC	77346
WHISTLING STRAITS DR	0	296A	SEM	77365
WHISTLING WAY	7900	410J	NWC	77040
WHISTLING WIND LN	12600	368J	NWC	77429
WHITAKER AVE	900	536H	PA	77506
WHITAKER DR	1600	656M	FR	77546
WHITAKER DR	19700	335T	HM	77338
WHITAKER CREEK DR	0	407C	NWC	77095
WHITBARROW PLACE	100	249R	NWH	77375
WHITBARROW PLACE	100	249R	NWH	77375
WHITBOURNE DR	6400	408T	NWC	77084
WHITBOURNE MEADOW LN	6800	411S	NWH	77040
WHITCHURCH DR	3500	371K	NWC	77066
WHITCHURCH WAY	13600	457X	NEC	77015
WHITCHURCH WAY LN	0	457W	NEC	77015
WHITE	500	493K	SWH	77007
WHITE	1600	282U	WL	77484
WHITE DR	100	531H	BL	77401
WHITE RD	1	572X	SWC	77047
WHITE ARBOR CT	8100	335J	NCC	77338
WHITE ASH LN	0	407J	NWC	77433
WHITEBACK DR	0	486G	SWC	77094
S. WHITEBACK DR	1600	486G	SWC	77094
WHITEBACK DR	1600	446U	NWC	77084
WHITEBARK PINE WAY	0	366X	NWC	77433
WHITE BARNWOOD	0	407J	NWC	77433
WHITE BARNWOOD CT	0	407J	NWC	77433
WHITEBERRY CT	20500	337Q	NEC	77346
WHITE BIRCH LN	7900	407K	NWC	77095
WHITE BLOSSOM LN	3100	336U	NEH	77338
WHITEBRANCH LN	2100	486P	SWC	77450
WHITEBRIAR DR	1700	538N	DP	77536
WHITEBRIDE LN	0	446B	NWC	77449
WHITE BRIDGE LN	10700	528W	NEF	77498
WHITEBROOK DR	10100	412B	NWC	77038
WHITE BRUSH LN	1	251M	WD	77380
WHITEBRUSH TRACE DR	0	253T	SEM	77386
WHITEBUD DR	3200	487Z	SWC	77082
WHITE CAMELLA CT		526S	NEF	77407
WHITE CANDLE DR	18700	331D	NWC	77388
WHITE CANYON LN	0	417B	NEC	77044
WHITE CAP DR	300	620E	EL	77586
WHITE CAP LN	12000	529J	SWH	77072
WHITE CASTLE LN	8200	412Q	NWH	77088
WHITE CEDAR DR	100	457T	NEC	77015
WHITE CEDAR DR	300	497B	NEC	77015
WHITE CEMETERY	0	459C	NEC	77532

Street Name	Block	Pg/Sq	Loc	Zips
WHITE CHAPEL LN	9200	530S	SWH	77074
WHITE CLIFF DR	13200	368Y	NWC	77065
WHITE CLOUD CT	0	612F	PL	77545
WHITE CLOUD LN	4600	577F	PA	77504
WHITE CLOVER DR	10300	576T	SEH	77089
WHITECOURT DR	0	289V	NWC	77375
WHITE CREEK TRAIL	20000	486L	SWC	77450
WHITECROFT LN	0	292G	NCC	77373
WHITECROSS DR	14200	528S	NEF	77083
WHITE CYPRESS LN	0	325K	NWC	77447
WHITE DAWN DR	0	286Q	NWC	77377
WHITE DEER LN	3400	336Q	NEH	77338
WHITE DOGWOOD TRAIL	0	296A	SEM	77365
WHITE DOVE	18600	257H	RF	77357
WHITE DOVE CT	0	658S	LC	77573
WHITE DOVE TRAIL	19800	378L	NEC	77532
WHITE EAGLE LN	2000	485Q	NEF	77450
WHITE ELK	10200	289L	NWC	77375
WHITE ELM TRAIL		249T	NWC	77375
WHITE FALLS DR	0	612K	PL	77545
WHITE FALLS LN	21500	446J	NWC	77449
WHITE FAWN DR	1	250C	WD	77381
WHITE FAWN DR	10400	449H	NWH	77041
WHITE FEATHER TRAIL	1700	378C	NEC	77532
WHITEFIELD LN	24000	445S	NWC	77493
WHITE FIR DR	7600	411Q	NWH	77088
WHITE FLINT LN	0	367P	NWC	77433
WHITE FRIARS DR	6700	534Y	SEH	77087
WHITEGATE LN	11300	371R	NWC	77067
WHITE GLADE LN	0	407V	NWC	77084
WHITE GLEN LN	0	524D	NEF	77494
WHITEHAIL WAY	1300	336H	NEH	77339
WHITEHALL CIR	0	657U	LC	77573
WHITEHALL DR	200	413A	NEH	77060
WHITEHALL LN	0	657U	LC	77573
WHITEHALL LN	200	616Y	FR	77546
WHITEHALL LN	800	618Z	WB	77058
WHITEHALL PLACE	200	569J	SF	77477
WHITE HART RUN	5800	408U	NWC	77084
WHITEHAVEN	5600	531K	BL	77401
WHITEHAVEN BEND LN	0	526L	NEF	77407
WHITEHAVEN BLUFF TRAIL	0	406W	NWC	77449
WHITEHAVEN FALLS CT	0	484T	NEF	77494
WHITEHAVEN HOLLOW TRACE	0	484N	NEF	77494
WHITEHAVEN MEADOW TRAIL	0	326Q	NWC	77429
WHITEHAWK DR	0	330L	NWC	77379
WHITEHEAD	9900	411R	NWC	77088
WHITEHEATH DR	0	446U	NWC	77084
WHITE HEATHER DR	12900	572E	SWH	77045
WHITE HERON CT	0	327T	CY	77429
WHITEHILL LN	0	524Z	NEF	77406
WHITE HORSE DR	18900	328H	NWC	77377
WHITEHURST CT	500	486B	SWC	77450
WHITE HYACINTH CT	0	326J	NWC	77433
WHITE HYACINTH DR	0	326J	NWC	77433
WHITE IBIS CT	0	658T	LC	77573
WHITE IBIS DR	13300	377Y	NEH	77044
WHITE IBIS LN	0	461N	NEC	77521
WHITE JASMINE TRAIL	0	488G	SWH	77079
WHITEKIRK PLACE	0	249B	SWM	77382
WHITELAKE DR	2300	293X	NCC	77373
WHITE LANE	0	614S	NEB	77584
WHITE LANE CT	0	614S	NEB	77584
WHITE LAUREL LN	0	406D	NWC	77433
WHITELAW DR	1900	252V	SEM	77386
WHITE LILAC TRAIL	0	406X	NWC	77449
WHITELOCK DR	0	368W	NWC	77095
WHITE MANOR DR	4900	578J	PA	77505
WHITE MAPLE LN	9600	410A	NWC	77064
WHITE MARSH CT	8000	330E	NWC	77379
WHITE MEADOW CT	0	329D	SP	77379
WHITEMILLS DR	5700	408Z	NWC	77041
WHITE MOUNTAIN DR	0	377F	NEC	77346
WHITE OAK	22700	256Y	SEM	77357
WHITE OAK CIR	7100	410P	NWC	77040
WHITE OAK CT	0	578J	PA	77505
WHITE OAK CT	23800	297E	SEM	77365
WHITE OAK DR	0	256K	SEM	77357
WHITE OAK DR	300	298X	NEH	77336
WHITE OAK DR	1300	493A	NWH	77009
WHITE OAK DR	2700	493A	NWH	77007
N. WHITE OAK DR	19600	257M	SEM	77357
S. WHITE OAK DR	19900	257M	SEM	77357
WHITE OAK DR	21900	255Z	SEM	77365
WHITE OAK DR	22700	296C	SEM	77357
WHITE OAK DR	24200	257B	WV	77357
WHITE OAK DR	24200	296L	SEM	77365
WHITE OAK LN	0	614Q	PL	77584
WHITE OAK LN	9100	410P	NWC	77040
WHITE OAK BEND DR	10700	369X	NWC	77064
WHITEOAK CANYON DR	0	377K	NEC	77346
WHITE OAK CREEK CT	10800	368T	NWC	77429
WHITE OAK CROSSING	11800	253E	SEM	77385
WHITEOAKELAKE	0	368B	NWC	77429
WHITE OAK FALLS CT	10800	368T	NWC	77429
WHITE OAK FOREST DR	23500	297E	SEM	77365
WHITE OAK GARDENS DR	14000	368T	NWC	77429
WHITE OAK GLEN CT	13900	368T	NWC	77429
WHITE OAK HILL	17700	327S	NWC	77429
WHITE OAK LANDING	11900	253E	SEM	77385
WHITE OAK LANDING BLVD	13300	368T	NWC	77065
WHITE OAK PARK CT	10700	368T	NWC	77429
WHITE OAK PASS	11800	253E	SEM	77385
WHITE OAK PATH	11900	253E	SEM	77385
WHITE OAK PLACE	0	253E	SEM	77385
WHITE OAK PLACE	8000	410P	NWC	77040
WHITE OAK POINT CT	10800	368T	NWC	77429
WHITE OAK POINTE	0	658M	LC	77573
WHITE OAK RIDGE DR	0	368X	NWC	77095
WHITE OAK RUN	11900	253E	SEM	77385
WHITE OAKS HILLS LN	2000	336B	NEH	77339
WHITE OAKS PASS	0	253F	SEM	77385
WHITE OAK SPRINGS DR	13800	368T	NWC	77429
WHITE OAK TRACE DR	10800	368T	NWC	77429
WHITE OAK TRAIL	0	252H	SEM	77385
WHITE OAK TRAIL	0	253E	SEM	77385
WHITE OAK TRAIL LN	10100	409B	NWC	77064
WHITE OAK TRAIL LN	10200	369X	NWC	77064
WHITE OWL	2100	450R	NWC	77080
S. WHITE PEBBLE CT	1	251Z	WD	77380
N. WHITE PEBBLE CT	1	251Z	WD	77380
WHITE PILLARS LN	1	490G	PP	77024
WHITE PINE DR	900	616U	FR	77546
WHITE PINE LN	0	462V	CCO	77520
WHITE PINE LN	5300	414V	NEH	77016
WHITE PINE PLACE	8500	289R	NWC	77375
WHITE PINES DR	0	524A	NEF	77494
WHITE PLAINS DR	12400	616D	SEH	77089
WHITE POPLAR DR	20200	446T	NWC	77449
WHITE POST LN	9600	370Z	NWC	77086
WHITE RIVER CT	0	525V	NEF	77406
WHITE RIVER DR	4200	577E	PA	77504

Street Name	Block	Pg/Sq	Loc	Zips
WHITE RIVER DR	12200	328D	NWC	77375
WHITE RIVERR PASS LN	5700	609T	NEF	77479
WHITE ROCK	4500	533U	SEH	77051
WHITE ROCK	4700	533U	SEH	77033
WHITE ROCK LAKE TRAIL	0	366Z	NWC	77433
WHITE ROCK LANDING CT		366V	NWC	77433
WHITE ROSE LN	0	525Z	NEF	77406
WHITE ROWAN WAY	0	406X	NWC	77449
WHITESAGE CT	16200	527B	SWH	77082
WHITE SAGE CT	16800	326J	NWC	77433
WHITE SAGE COVE LN	0	293G	SEM	77386
WHITE SAIL	3100	660F	LC	77573
WHITESAIL DR	0	245V	SWM	77355
WHITE SAIL DR	24200	338L	NEH	77336
WHITE SANDS DR	0	539N	DP	77536
WHITE SANDS DR	100	335C	SEM	77339
WHITE SANDS RD	1000	485G	SWC	77450
WHITE SANDS WAY	3200	660E	LC	77573
WHITE SHORE LN	21000	290Q	NWC	77379
WHITESIDE LN	10000	450W	NWH	77080
WHITESIDE LN	10100	450W	NWH	77043
WHITE SPARROW DR	0	332S	NWC	77090
WHITE SPRING LN	0	612P	PL	77545
WHITE SPRINGS CT	0	292U	NCC	77373
WHITE STAR DR	16100	618N	SEH	77062
WHITESTONE DR	3500	615S	PL	77584
WHITESTONE LN	900	332H	NCC	77073
WHITE SUMMIT CT	0	417B	NEC	77044
WHITE SWAN DR	7900	375Q	NEC	77396
S. WHITE TAIL CT	17700	447L	NWC	77084
N. WHITE TAIL CT	17700	447G	NWC	77084
WHITE TAIL DR	6800	330F	NWC	77379
WHITE TAIL DR	7100	461M	NEC	77521
WHITE TAIL DR	7300	462J	NEC	77521
WHITE TAIL LN	0	447L	NWC	77084
WHITE TAIL TRAIL	0	376P	NEC	77396
WHITETAIL TRAIL	0	376P	NEC	77396
WHITE THORN	10900	414V	NEH	77016
WHITE TRUFFLE TRAIL	0	325L	NWC	77433
WHITE TRUFFLE TRAIL	0	325L	NWC	77433
WHITEVINE WAY	20700	526E	NEF	77450
WHITE WATER CT	4200	578F	PA	77505
WHITEWATER LN	15600	488B	SWH	77079
WHITE WATER BAY DR	0	612Q	PL	77584
WHITE WATER BAY DR	0	612R	PL	77584
WHITEWATER CREEK CIR	22800	485L	NEF	77450
WHITEWATER FALLS CT	16800	578Z	PA	77059
WHITE WATER TRAIL	11600	496B	NEH	77013
WHITE WAVE CT	0	367S	NWC	77433
WHITEWAY LN	16000	330S	NWC	77379
W. WHITE WILLOW CIR	1	250H	WD	77381
E. WHITE WILLOW CIR	1	250H	WD	77381
WHITE WILLOW LN	0	339N	HU	77336
WHITE WILLOW LN	0	463S	CCO	77520
WHITE WILLOW LN	0	615F	PL	77581
WHITEWIND DR	19700	486G	SWC	77094
WHITE WING	32100	322T	WCO	77484
WHITEWING CIR	1200	656R	FR	77546
WHITE WING CT	0	250B	WD	77381
WHITE WING LN	0	609F	MC	77459
WHITEWING LN	400	489J	SWH	77079
WHITEWING LN	32100	322T	WCO	77484
WHITEWING RD	1	381V	LCO	77535
WHITEWOOD DR	0	292T	NEH	77388
WHITEWOOD DR	18700	332C	NCC	77373
WHITEWOOD DR	19400	292Y	NCC	77373
WHITFORD CT	21900	485Z	NEF	77450
WHITHORN DR	9400	368W	NWC	77095
S. WHITING	1	501X	BT	77520
N. WHITING	100	501X	BT	77520
WHITING ROCK DR	7100	460Y	MN	77521
WHITINHAM DR	2600	371M	NWC	77067
WHITLAM CT	0	615W	PL	77584
WHITLAM DR	0	615W	PL	77584
WHITLAND LN	18900	328F	NWC	77377
WHITLEY	5500	532C	SWH	77005
WHITLOCK DR	0	618A	SEH	77062
WHITMAN	4000	492W	SWH	77027
WHITMAN LN	0	568S	SG	77479
WHITMAN MISSION LN	0	377E	NEC	77346
WHITMAN WAY DR	2300	617Y	SEC	77546
WHITMIRE	2000	535F	SEH	77012
WHITMORE LN	8400	528Q	SWC	77083
W. WHITNEY	1	453J	NWH	77018
E. WHITNEY	100	453J	NWH	77022
WHITNEY	1900	493N	SWH	77006
WHITNEY CT	5200	577C	PA	77505
WHITNEY MEADOWS DR	12100	328R	NWC	77377
WHITNEY OAKS LN	0	569Q	SF	77477
WHITNEY WAY	1500	336B	NEH	77339
WHITSON LN	0	573T	SEC	77047
WHITT	3900	615N	PL	77581
WHITTAKER	900	536H	PA	77506
WHITTAKER WAY	22800	333G	NCC	77373
WHITTER FOREST DR	6000	411K	NWC	77088
WHITTER OAKS	5100	617W	FR	77546
WHITTIER DR	1	657A	FR	77546
WHITTIER DR	2100	373V	NCC	77032
WHITTIER BRIDGE LN	11500	568A	NEF	77498
WHITTINGHAM LN	10900	569B	SWH	77099
S. WHITTINGTON CT	0	488P	SWH	77077
N. WHITTINGTON CT	0	488P	SWH	77077
WHITTINGTON DR	12000	489N	SWH	77077
WHITTINGTON DR	12400	488Q	SWH	77077
WHITTINGTON PARK LN	0	407C	NWC	77095
WHITTMORE FIELDS DR	0	524J	NEF	77494
WHITTON DR	6300	571T	SWH	77085
WHITTY	3800	454S	NEH	77026
WHITWELL DR	5800	406X	NWC	77449
WHITE BIRCH RUN	0	294K	SEM	77386
WICHITA	1000	493W	SWH	77004
WICHITA	1300	537T	PA	77502
WICHITA	1700	533B	SEH	77004
WICHITA CIR	4700	461S	NEC	77521
WICHITA DR	9200	579A	LP	77571
WICHITA FALLS	29500	248B	SWM	77354
WICHITA RIVER WAY	0	367S	NWC	77433
WICHMAN	500	493E	SWH	77007
WICKBRIAR DR	15200	571Z	SWH	77053
WICKBURN DR	1800	252V	SEM	77386
WICKCHESTER LN	11500	449W	NWH	77043
WICKCHESTER LN	12000	448Z	NWH	77079
WICKDALE CT	0	249B	SWM	77354
WICKDALE DR	11100	490M	PP	77024
WICKDALE GARDEN LN	0	377Y	NEC	77044
WICKED WICKET	500	491H	SWH	77024
WICKENBURG DR	9500	569H	SWH	77031
WICKERBAY	1	450W	NWH	77080
WICKER BROOK LN	0	408F	NWC	77095
WICKERHILL FALLS CT	0	377F	NEC	77346
WICKERHILL WAY	100	485L	SWC	77494
WICKERSHAM DR	22000	255Y	SEM	77365

Street Name	Block	Pg/Sq	Loc	Zips
WICKERSHAM LN	3400	492S	SWH	77027
WICKERSHAM LN	5600	491T	SWH	77056
WICKERSHAM LN	6200	491S	SWH	77057
WICKERSHAM LN	7500	490V	SWH	77063
WICKERSHAM LN	10000	489U	SWH	77042
WICKERSHAM LN	11300	489T	SWH	77077
WICKERSHAM LN	12500	488T	SWH	77077
WICKER WAY	0	408P	NWC	77084
S. WICKERWOOD	1	450W	NWH	77080
N. WICKERWOOD	1	450W	NWH	77080
WICKFIELD DR	22000	485M	SWC	77450
WICKFORD CT	0	657U	LC	77573
WICKFORD DR	9000	491C	SWH	77024
WICKFORD DR	30000	288B	TB	77375
WICKGATE	15400	571Z	SWH	77053
WICKHAM CT	20100	486C	SWC	77450
WICKHAMFORD WAY	200	457Y	NEC	77015
WICK HAVEN CIR	0	366J	NWC	77433
WICKHOLLOW LN	11500	449W	NWH	77043
WICKHURST PLACE	14400	368A	NWC	77429
WICKLEY DR	12700	571G	SWH	77085
WICKLINE DR	10900	490M	HC	77024
WICKLOW	0	529Z	SWH	77036
WICKLOW DR	500	538P	DP	77536
WICKLOW DR	2000	616K	PL	77581
WICKLOWE	10300	414V	NEH	77016
WICKLOW MEADOW LN	1200	373J	NCC	77060
WICKLOW MEADOW LN	1200	373J	NCC	77060
WICKMAN GLEN LN	22100	485Z	NEF	77450
WICKMERE DR	15200	618J	SEH	77062
WICKOVER LN	6000	411B	NWC	77086
WICKSHIRE CT	3300	613Z	NEB	77584
WICKSHIRE LN	1300	449W	NWH	77043
WICKSTONE LN	4200	371F	NWC	77014
WICKTON LN	21100	334M	NCC	77338
WICKVIEW LN	4800	571Y	SWH	77053
WICKWAY DR	11100	490M	PP	77024
WICKWAY DR	19400	255Y	SEM	77365
WICKWILD	10900	490M	HC	77024
WICKWILDE	24600	250W	NWC	77389
WICKWOOD CT	3100	613T	NEB	77584
WICKWOOD DR	200	252J	OR	77386
WICKWOOD DR	11000	490R	PP	77024
WICKWOOD LN	2900	613T	NEB	77584
WIDCOMBE DR	18000	447F	NWC	77084
WIDDICOMB CT	1800	452S	NWH	77008
WIDE BRIM CT	0	337X	NEC	77346
WIDE CREEK CT	20100	406Q	NWC	77449
WIDE CREEK CT	0	406Q	NWC	77449
WIDEFIELD PLACE	0	249B	SWM	77382
WIDE OAK CIR	31200	246Y	SWM	77355
WIDE RIVER LN	12400	377A	NEC	77346
WIDEROP LN	4700	617X	SEC	77546
WIDGEEN POND DR	0	328Y	NWC	77429
WIDLEY CIR	12700	488M	SWH	77077
WIDMORE CT	7400	330K	NWC	77379
WIDMORE PLACE	17400	330K	NWC	77379
WIED RD	19500	291Y	NWC	77388
WIEDNER DR	1200	484G	NEF	77494
WIER DR	8000	535U	SEH	77017
WIGEON WAY DR	17300	376F	NEC	77396
WIGGINS	7200	495J	NEH	77020
WIGGINS	7900	495K	NEH	77029
WIGGINS	10300	496J	JC	77029
S. WIGGINS	31900	247V	SWM	77355
WIGHTMAN CT	5000	330Y	NWC	77069
WIGMAKER DR	2000	445S	NWC	77493
WIGTON DR	4300	531S	SWH	77096
WIGTON DR	6000	530V	SWH	77096
WIGWAM LN	9900	248M	SWM	77354
WIGWAM LN	19800	378M	NEC	77532
WIGWAM TRAIL	27100	244A	WCO	77447
WILBARGER	0	502J	BT	77521
WILBARGER CIR	8800	409G	NWC	77064
WILBUR LN	0	289Q	NWC	77375
WILBURFORCE	800	412X	NWH	77091
WILBURN	900	659K	LC	77573
W. WILBURN DR	1	501U	BT	77520
N. WILBURN DR	1500	501U	BT	77520
WILBURY HEIGHTS DR	4700	577G	PA	77505
WILBURY PARK	12600	448D	NWC	77041
WILCANT LN	11600	328T	NWC	77429
WILCHESTER BLVD	100	489G	SWH	77079
WILCOX MANOR DR	0	609S	NEF	77479
WILCOX POINT CT	0	290R	NWC	77388
WILCOX POINT DR	6000	290Q	NWC	77388
WILCREST DR	100	489T	SWH	77042
N. WILCREST DR	300	489B	SWH	77079
WILCREST DR	6700	529F	SWH	77072
S. WILCREST DR	8500	529Y	SWH	77099
S. WILCREST DR	11800	569C	SWH	77031
WILCREST GREEN DR	11100	489Y	SWH	77042
WILCREST PLAZA	1800	538N	DP	77536
WILDACRES DR	4100	529F	SWH	77072
WILD BASIN DR	8500	411R	NWH	77088
WILD BASIN TRAIL	18400	377B	NEC	77346
WILD BERRY CT	3600	446K	NWC	77449
WILD BERRY DR	20400	446K	NWC	77449
WILDBERRY CREEK CT	0	325Q	NWC	77433
WILD BIRD DR	200	332C	NCC	77373
WILDBIRD LN	0	335N	NCC	77338
WILD BLACKBERRY DR	5200	297P	NEH	77345
WILD BLUEBONNET WAY	0	447E	NWC	77084
WILDBROOK DR	0	612L	PL	77584
WILDBROOK DR	1600	372W	NWC	77038
WILDBROOK CANYON LN	0	446W	NWC	77449
WILDBROOK CROSSING LN	25500	485S	NEF	77494
WILDCANDLE DR	3200	331D	NWC	77388
WILD CANYON DR	0	526A	NEF	77450
WILDCAT LN	1600	378C	NEH	77532
WILDCAT BRIDGE LN	10900	568A	NEF	77498
WILD COLUMBINE DR	0	411D	NWC	77038
WILDCROFT DR	21100	406Y	NWC	77449
WILDCROFT DR	21600	446B	NWC	77449
WILD CURRANT CT	0	372C	NCC	77073
WILD CURRENT WAY	0	326J	NWC	77433
WILD DEER DR	0	251B	WD	77381
WILD DOVE CT	0	328N	NWC	77429
WILD DUCK LN	26900	324N	NWC	77447
WILD DUNES CIR	2000	485Q	NEF	77450
WILD DUNES CT	1400	541H	BT	77520
WILDE CREEK DR	0	250R	NWC	77389
WILDEFLOWER PLACE	5300	657V	LC	77573
WILDE FOREST CT	13800	568F	SG	77498
WILDE GLEN LN	13000	528L	SWH	77072
WILDE LAUREL LN	12300	371H	NWC	77014
WILDER	700	453S	NWH	77008
WILDERNESS DR	4800	368Y	NWC	77065
WILDERNESS RD	16500	367F	CY	77429
WILDERNESS RD	24600	251W	SWM	77380
WILDERNESS CLIFF CT	14900	618F	SEH	77062
WILDERNESS FALLS TRAIL	0	297T	NEH	77345

Street Name	Block	Pg/Sq	Loc	Zips
WILDERNESS GLEN CT	4800	446C	NWC	77449
WILDERNESS HILL DR	0	368Y	NWC	77065
WILDERNESS PARK CT	1700	336B	NEH	77339
WILDERNESS PINES CT	600	656G	FR	77546
WILDERNESS PINES DR	1200	656L	FR	77546
WILDERNESS POINT DR	1900	296Y	NEH	77339
WILDERNESS TRAIL	1	656M	FR	77546
WILDERNESS TRAIL	200	248G	SWM	77354
WILDE ROCK WAY	1400	452N	NWH	77018
WILDE WOODS WAY	3200	251X	SWM	77380
W. WILDE YAUPON CIR	1	250H	WD	77381
N. WILDE YAUPON CIR	1	250H	WD	77381
E. WILDE YAUPON CIR	1	250H	WD	77381
S. WILDE YAUPON CT	1	250M	WD	77381
N. WILDE YAUPON CT	1	250H	WD	77381
WILDFERN TRAIL	29400	252Z	SEM	77386
WILDFIRE	5800	657V	LC	77573
WILDFLOWER CIR	23600	525E	NEF	77494
WILDFLOWER CT	0	484E	KT	77494
WILD FLOWER DR	23300	339P	HU	77336
WILDFLOWER DR	25300	248E	SWM	77354
WILDFLOWER COVE	23600	525E	NEF	77494
WILD FOREST DR	0	256C	SEM	77357
WILDFOREST DR	8600	411K	NWC	77088
WILD GINGER CT	1	251P	WD	77380
WILD GOOSE DR	0	329B	NWC	77375
WILDGRASS CT	0	527U	NEF	77498
WILD GROVE CT	16100	329N	NWC	77377
WILDGROVE DR	1200	577E	PA	77504
WILDGROVE HOLLOW DR	0	524S	NWF	77406
WILDHAWK DR	3300	446R	NWC	77449
WILD HEATHER DR	0	289R	NWC	77375
WILD HOLLOW LN	10100	411J	NWH	77088
WILD HORSE LN	24100	325J	NWC	77447
WILD HORSES DR	24200	324M	NWC	77447
WILD HORSE VALLEY RD	700	485G	SWC	77450
WILDHURST DR	15200	327U	NWC	77429
WILDIEN DR	0	484V	NWF	77494
WILD INDIGO	4300	491Z	SWH	77027
WILDING LN	11100	490H	PP	77024
WILDING WIMBLEDON CT	6500	331N	NWC	77379
WILD IVY CT	14800	327W	NWC	77429
WILD JASMINE LN	21200	526A	NEF	77450
WILDLANE DR	0	328F	NWC	77429
WILD LILAC CT	0	612K	PL	77545
WILD LILAC DR	0	612K	PL	77545
WILD LILAC TRAIL	0	377B	NEC	77346
WILD MEADOW CT	1	251R	WD	77380
WILD MILBERRY DR	5500	524D	NEF	77494
WILDMOOR	0	449A	NWC	77041
WILDMOOR CT	200	487A	SWC	77094
WILD MOSS	22800	290E	NWC	77375
WILD MUSTANG LN	12900	377T	NEC	77044
WILD OAK	0	450Z	SV	77055
WILD OAK CIR	1	490D	SV	77055
WILD OAK DR	300	298B	NEC	77336
WILD OAK DR	3600	615Z	PL	77581
WILD OAK DR	17400	332J	NWC	77090
WILD OAK FOREST LN	2500	620F	SB	77586
WILDOAK GLEN LN	0	524B	NEF	77494
WILD OAK LAKE DR	0	524G	NEF	77494
WILD OAK LAKE DR	0	524G	NEF	77494
WILD OAK PARK DR	0	253J	SEM	77385
WILD OAK RUN	200	486D	SWC	77094
WILD OAKS	0	246B	SWM	77355
WILDOATS DR	19100	446M	NWC	77449
WILD OLIVE CT	2300	446T	NWC	77449
WILD ORANGE CT	0	329L	NWC	77379
WILD ORCHARD CT	4200	484Y	NEF	77494
WILD ORCHARD LN	26700	484Y	NEF	77494
WILD ORCHID DR	0	447P	NWC	77084
WILD ORCHID DR	18200	447K	NWC	77084
WILD PEACH	0	257L	SEM	77357
WILD PEACH PLACE	400	609R	MC	77459
WILD PECAN DR	0	248V	NWC	77375
WILD PECAN TRAIL	6700	408S	NWC	77084
WILD PEREGRINE CIR	0	484P	NWF	77494
WILD PINE DR	12200	414H	NEC	77039
WILD PLAINS DR	0	406X	NWC	77449
WILD PLUM	200	456Y	NEH	77013
WILD PLUM	400	496C	NEH	77013
WILD PLUM CT	0	338A	NEH	77345
WILD PLUM DR	0	659N	LC	77573
WILD POPPY DR	19800	289Y	NWC	77379
WILDRIDGE DR	2700	336C	NEH	77339
WILD RIDGE DR	10600	251L	WD	77380
WILD RIVER DR	6400	406T	NWC	77449
WILD ROCK WAY	0	296H	SEM	77357
WILD ROSE	8300	528P	SWC	77083
WILDROSE	18900	286L	NWC	77377
WILDROSE DR	100	500F	BT	77520
WILD ROSE DR	29700	292D	SEM	77386
WILD ROSE DR	29700	252Z	SEM	77386
WILD ROSE TRACE	22300	525L	NEF	77407
WILD ROSE TRAIL	17400	327S	NWC	77429
WILDRYE CREEK DR	0	293C	SEM	77386
WILD RYE TRAIL	0	337R	NEC	77346
WILDSAGE CT	0	290V	NWC	77379
WILD SIDE LN	6300	407S	NWC	77449
WILDSPRUCE CT	8800	411J	NWC	77088
WILDSPRUCE DR	8900	411J	NWC	77088
WILD STRAWBERRY DR	0	411D	NWC	77038
WILD STREAM CT	7500	407K	NWC	77095
WILD THORNBERRY DR	0	328F	NWC	77429
WILD TIMBER TRAIL	15400	325V	NWC	77433
WILD TRAIL	7100	609Y	MC	77459
WILD TURKEY DR	1000	253E	SEM	77385
WILD TURKEY DR	17000	327T	CY	77429
WILD TURKEY LN	3100	615T	PL	77581
WILD TURKEY BEND	0	333R	NEH	77338
WILD VALLEY RD	800	491J	SWH	77057
WILD VIEW CT	20400	486T	NEF	77450
WILDVINE CT	11700	328M	NWC	77377
WILD VIOLET DR	7100	337U	NEC	77346
WILD WILLOW LN	17300	407P	NWC	77084
WILD WILLOW LN	18000	407P	NWC	77449
N. WILDWIND CIR	1	251L	WD	77380
S. WILDWIND CIR	2600	251K	WD	77380
E. WILDWIND CIR	2900	251L	WD	77380
WILD WIND LN	500	496E	NEH	77013
WILD WIND PLACE	2400	251L	WD	77380
WILDWOOD	900	531D	BL	77401
WILDWOOD	3000	615Q	PL	77581
WILDWOOD	26300	257H	RF	77357
WILDWOOD	26500	258A	SEM	77357
WILDWOOD CT	0	484E	KT	77494
WILDWOOD DR	0	296G	SEM	77365
WILDWOOD DR	0	616V	FR	77546
WILDWOOD DR	100	500F	BT	77520
E. WILDWOOD DR	300	296G	SEM	77365
WILDWOOD DR	300	257J	SEM	77357
WILDWOOD DR	400	619L	PA	77586
WILDWOOD DR	900	538N	DP	77536
WILDWOOD DR	13300	248Y	TB	77375
WILDWOOD LN	0	484E	KT	77494
WILDWOOD LN	25400	339E	NEC	77336
S. WILDWOOD RD	23800	296G	SEM	77365
WILDWOOD BEND LN	12400	366H	NWC	77433
WILDWOOD BROOK CT	7500	407L	NWC	77095
WILDWOOD CREEK WAY	5300	331A	NWC	77379
WILDWOOD DALE LN	19400	330D	NWC	77379
WILDWOOD FOREST DR	400	252W	SWM	77380
WILDWOOD GLEN DR	15300	527Q	NEF	77083
WILDWOOD GREEN WAY	0	293X	NCC	77373
WILDWOOD GROVE DR	22300	485L	SWC	77450
WILDWOOD LAKE DR	15300	527Q	NEF	77083
WILDWOOD OAKS DR	23700	257J	SEM	77357
WILDWOOD PARK LN	10200	369G	NWC	77070
WILDWOOD PARK LN	31900	253J	SEM	77385
WILDWOOD RIDGE CT	3400	337A	NEH	77339
WILDWOOD RIDGE DR	1900	570W	MC	77489
WILDWOOD RIDGE DR	3400	297W	NEH	77339
WILDWOOD RIDGE DR	3800	337A	NEH	77339
WILDWOOD RUN	15500	326S	NWC	77433
WILDWOOD SPRINGS CT	0	417C	NEH	77044
WILDWOOD SPRINGS LN	0	417C	NEH	77044
WILDWOOD VALLEY CT	3800	297P	NEH	77345
WILDWOOD WAY	6600	534C	SEH	77023
WILD YAUPON DR	19000	407J	NWC	77433
WILEY	3400	414X	NEH	77093
WILEY	5000	414X	NEH	77016
WILEY	7300	415W	NEH	77016
WILEY MARTIN DR	13300	368K	NWC	77429
WILEYVALE RD	6300	454L	NEH	77028
WILEYVALE RD	7200	454L	NEH	77016
WILEYWOOD DR	13500	456R	NEH	77049
WILKE RD	13000	614H	PL	77581
WILKEN	700	453S	NWH	77008
WILKENBERG DR	10900	370V	NWC	77086
WILKENBERG DR	11200	370R	NWC	77066
WILKENSON	0	493J	SWH	77019
WILKENSON	9	493J	SWH	77019
WILKES	700	493C	NEH	77009
WILKES PARK	25200	249S	NWC	77375
WILKIE LN	11900	413T	NEH	77076
WILKINS	0	296U	SEM	77339
WILKINS	100	659J	LC	77573
WILKINS	400	658M	LC	77573
WILKINS	1100	532H	SWH	77030
WILKINS	23500	338Q	NEH	77336
WILKINS OAKS DR	0	455G	NEH	77028
WILKS DR	19000	326G	NWC	77429
WILKSHIRE CT	15300	330U	NWC	77069
WILKSHIRE WAY	4500	609P	MC	77459
WILLABY LN	900	498A	NEC	77530
WILLABY RD	0	258P	SEM	77357
WILLABY RD	19300	258K	SEM	77357
WILLACY CT	8800	409H	NWC	77064
WILLANCY CT	14800	408F	NWC	77095
WILLANCY LN	8000	408K	NWC	77095
WILLANCY LN	8500	408F	NWC	77095
WILLARD	1	493N	SWH	77006
WILLARDVILLE RD	5600	574Q	SEH	77048
WILLBRIAR LN	15800	570Z	SWH	77489
WILL CLAYTON PKWY	2900	374C	NEH	77032
WILL CLAYTON PKWY	5700	375B	NEH	77338
WILL CLAYTON PKWY	8200	376B	NEC	77338
WILL CLAYTON PKWY	11200	377A	NEC	77346
WILLDCAT BRIDGE LN	0	568A	NEF	77498
WILLERSLEY LN	900	498A	NEC	77530
WILLERSLEY LN	1000	458W	NEC	77530
WILLERS WAY	5200	491P	SWH	77056
WILLERS WAY	6100	491N	SWH	77057
WILLET ST	0	461N	NEC	77521
WILLGUS TRAIL LN	6300	370M	NWC	77066
WILLHANNA DR	22500	445Q	NWC	77449
WILLIA	3500	493J	SWH	77007
WILLIAM	700	493M	NEH	77002
WILLIAMCREST LN	8300	530X	SWH	77071
WILLIAM DOWDELL DR	12300	368M	NWC	77429
WILLIAMETTE DR	22500	445Q	NWC	77449
WILLIAMHURST LN	4500	658N	LC	77573
WILLIAMHURST LN	16600	332N	NWC	77090
WILLIAM JEFFERSON	0	368M	NWC	77429
WILLIAM JUERGENS DR	30200	248Y	TB	77375
WILLIAM PASS LN		366U	NWC	77433
W. WILLIAMS	0	463E	MB	77521
S. WILLIAMS	0	463E	MB	77521
WILLIAMS	0	411S	NWH	77040
WILLIAMS	0	499L	NEC	77520
WILLIAMS	0	577T	SEH	77034
WILLIAMS	0	620T	SB	77586
WILLIAMS	700	536M	PA	77506
WILLIAMS	7200	410V	NWH	77040
WILLIAMS AVE	100	501U	BT	77520
WILLIAMS CIR	3100	446Q	NWC	77449
WILLIAMS DR	1000	659K	LC	77573
WILLIAMS LN	1000	660B	KE	77565
WILLIAMS RD	6000	419C	NEH	77532
WILLIAMS BEND CIR	0	366L	NWC	77433
W. WILLIAMS BEND DR	0	366L	NWC	77433
E. WILLIAMS BEND DR	0	366L	NWC	77433
WILLIAMS BRIDGE LN	0	528W	NEF	77498
WILLIAMSBURG	11300	490L	PP	77024
WILLIAMSBURG CIR	500	616Z	FR	77546
S. WILLIAMSBURG CT	1900	658Q	LC	77573
N. WILLIAMSBURG CT	1900	658Q	LC	77573
WILLIAMSBURG DR	2500	536T	PA	77502
WILLIAMSBURG LN	1	490F	BH	77024
WILLIAMSBURG LN	3300	609G	MC	77459
WILLIAMSCHASE DR	2900	445Q	NWC	77449
WILLIAMS COURT LN	4900	531C	BL	77081
WILLIAMS CREEK DR	0	295R	SEM	77365
WILLIAMS CREEK DR	0	295V	SEM	77365
WILLIAMSDELL	8300	412U	NWH	77088
WILLIAMS ELM DR	0	366Q	NWC	77433
WILLIAMS FIELD DR	0	370U	NWC	77086
WILLIAMS FOREST DR	0	377A	NEC	77346
WILLIAMS OAK DR	0	366Q	NWC	77433
WILLIAMSON	0	374Q	NEH	77032
WILLIAMSON	3200	494J	NEH	77020
WILLIAMS PINE DR	0	366L	NWC	77433
WILLIAMSPORT	200	658K	LC	77573
WILLIAMS REACH DR	0	366Q	NWC	77433
WILLIAMS RIDGE CT	0	366Q	NWC	77433
WILLIAMSTOWN	0	447D	NWC	77084
WILLIAMS TRACE BLVD	1500	568U	SG	77478
WILLIAMS WILLOW LN	0	366L	NWC	77433
WILLIAM TELL	1800	413V	NCC	77093
WILLIAM TELL	2400	414S	NCC	77093
WILLIAM TIGNER DR	0	285P	NWC	77447
WILLIARD'S WAY	200	569U	NEF	77477
WILLIE	10300	414X	NEC	77093
WILLIE WAY	3200	251N	SWM	77380
WILLIFORD	7700	535F	SEH	77012
WILLIMETTE	7900	457F	NEC	77049
WILLINGHAM WAY	16300	407H	NWC	77095
WILLINGTON DR	0	252X	SEM	77386
WILLINGTON LN	0	457P	NEC	77049
WILLIS	14700	373X	NCC	77039
WILLIS	15000	373X	NCC	77032
WILLISTON DR	10700	368T	NWC	77065
WILLITS	1600	616P	PL	77581
WILLIWAW DR	15800	527Q	NEF	77083
WILL JORDAN WAY	8300	531Q	SWH	77401
WILLMONT RD	3700	579A	LP	77571
WILLMORE LN	15400	571W	SWH	77489
WILLOMINE WAY	5200	571L	SWH	77045
WILLOW	0	256V	SEM	77357
N. WILLOW	100	288D	TB	77375
WILLOW	100	292L	SP	77373
WILLOW	100	335Z	HM	77338
WILLOW	100	540V	MP	77571
WILLOW	100	611V	FS	77545
WILLOW	300	536M	PA	77506
WILLOW	600	541B	BT	77520
WILLOW	2100	614M	PL	77581
WILLOW	4600	531G	BL	77401
WILLOW	4700	581W	PA	77586
WILLOW	6100	614Y	PL	77584
WILLOW	6800	412P	NWH	77088
WILLOW	24500	244V	WCO	77447
S. WILLOW CIR	11700	570L	MC	77071
N. WILLOW CIR	11700	570L	MC	77071
WILLOW CT	0	330E	NWC	77379
WILLOW DR	2500	569V	SF	77477
S. WILLOW DR	4900	571B	SWH	77035
WILLOW DR	6300	334T	NEH	77338
WILLOW LN	0	244V	WCO	77447
WILLOW LN	400	500E	BT	77520
WILLOW LN	1200	658Z	LC	77573
WILLOW LN	6300	444P	KT	77493
WILLOW LN	11400	369E	NWC	77429
WILLOW LN	12000	368D	NWC	77429
WILLOW LN	26500	484P	NEF	77494
WILLOW ST	0	282Y	WCO	77484
WILLOW ST	100	335Z	HM	77338
WILLOWBANK RD	16400	328V	NWC	77377
WILLOW BARK DR	8900	290J	NWC	77375
WILLOW BEACH DR	4100	529F	SWH	77072
WILLOWBEND BLVD	3600	532W	SWH	77054
WILLOWBEND BLVD	4000	532W	SWH	77025
WILLOWBEND BLVD	4300	531X	SWH	77035
WILLOWBEND BLVD	5200	531X	SWH	77096
WILLOWBEND BLVD	6100	530Z	SWH	77096
WILLOWBEND DR	1800	538N	DP	77536
WILLOW BEND DR	19100	326D	NWC	77377
W. WILLOW BLUFF RD	6200	407S	NWC	77449
E. WILLOW BLUFF RD	6200	407S	NWC	77449
N. WILLOW BLUFF RD	18300	407S	NWC	77449
WILLOW BOUGH	23200	290E	NWC	77375
WILLOW BRANCH CT	12000	328V	NWC	77070
WILLOW BRANCH CT	12000	328Z	NWC	77070
WILLOW BRANCH DR	1200	659N	LC	77573
WILLOW BRANCH DR	15000	328Z	NWC	77070
WILLOW BRANCH LN	22400	290E	NWC	77375
WILLOW BREEZE DR	12500	328L	NWC	77377
WILLOW BRIAR DR	500	332X	NWC	77090
WILLOWBRIAR LN	900	538P	DP	77536
WILLOW BRIDGE CIR	7000	408N	NWC	77095
WILLOWBRIDGE PARK BLVD	9200	409H	NWC	77064
WILLOWBROOK	4500	533M	SEH	77021
WILLOW BROOK CT	0	612Q	PL	77584
WILLOW BROOK CT	1200	568W	SG	77479
WILLOWBROOK DR	0	406L	NWC	77433
WILLOW BROOK LN	0	612Q	PL	77584
WILLOWBROOK ST	31500	322G	WCO	77484
WILLOWBROOK PARK DR	0	370L	NWC	77066
WILLOWBROOK TOWNS DR	0	370E	NWH	77070
WILLOWBROOK VILLA DR	0	369H	NWC	77070
WILLOWBY	1600	452S	NWH	77008
WILLOW CANYON DR	23100	485F	SWC	77494
WILLOW CENTRE DR	12800	370F	NWH	77066
WILLOWCHASE BLVD	7400	370E	NWH	77070
WILLOW CHASE DR	12800	369M	NWC	77070
WILLOW CHASE LN	0	615M	PL	77089
WILLOW CLIFF LN	5100	609J	MC	77459
WILLOW CLIFF LN	18000	407J	NWC	77433
WILLOW COLONY CT	0	484Z	NEF	77494
WILLOW COLONY LN	0	484Z	NEF	77494
WILLOW COVE CT	6500	407N	NWC	77449
WILLOW COVE DR	18500	407N	NWC	77449
WILLOWCRAFT DR	7400	570V	SWH	77459
WILLOWCREEK	3000	484R	NEF	77494
WILLOW CREEK CT	200	659C	LC	77573
WILLOW CREEK DR	700	539X	LP	77571
WILLOW CREEK DR	2700	659C	LC	77573
WILLOW CREEK DR	23400	290E	NWC	77375
WILLOW CREEK DR	23500	289H	NWC	77375
WILLOW CREEK LN	2000	616N	PL	77581
WILLOW CREEK RD	24900	244V	WCO	77447
WILLOW CREEK BRIDGE LN	22200	289J	NWC	77375
WILLOW CREEK CEMETERY RD	0	289Q	NWC	77375
WILLOW CREEK ESTATES LN	0	289J	NWC	77375
WILLOW CREEK PARK	31500	252R	SEM	77385
WILLOW CREEK PARK	32100	252M	SEM	77385
WILLOWCREEK RANCH RD	0	287Z	NWC	77377
WILLOWCREEK RANCH RD	0	288S	NWC	77377
WILLOWCREEK STABLES RD	22900	290G	NWC	77389
WILLOW CREEK WAY	5400	536S	SEH	77017
WILLOWCREST	11200	289K	NWC	77375
WILLOWCREST CT	6100	250Z	NWC	77389
WILLOW CROSSING	0	409D	NWC	77064
WILLOW CROSSING CIR	10300	369Y	NWC	77064
WILLOW CROSSING CT	10700	369Y	NWC	77064
WILLOW CROSSING DR	9400	369Y	NWC	77064
WILLOWDALE	6000	534Q	SEH	77087
WILLOWDALE CIR	11700	570L	MC	77071
E. WILLOWDELL	0	620K	SB	77586
WILLOWDELL	2100	620K	SB	77586
WILLOW DOWNS DR	21700	290J	NWC	77375
WILLOW END	23000	290E	NWC	77375
WILLOWEND DR	1	490M	HC	77024
WILLOW ESTATES	0	290A	NWC	77389
WILLOW FAIRWAY DR	16500	367U	NWC	77095
WILLOW FIELD DR	11200	369J	NWC	77429
WILLOW FORD CT	5700	525C	NEF	77494
WILLOWFORD CT	16200	527B	SWH	77082
WILLOWFORD PARK DR	21200	526A	NEF	77450
WILLOW FOREST DR	7900	290E	NWC	77375
WILLOW FORK CT	21200	486S	NEF	77450
WILLOW FORK DR	2800	486S	NEF	77450
WILLOW FORK LN	0	485V	NEF	77450
WILLOWGATE DR	22200	334F	NCC	77373
WILLOW GLADE DR	21200	486N	NEF	77450
WILLOWGLEN	600	501L	BT	77521
WILLOWGLEN	5000	534W	SEH	77033
WILLOW GLEN	23000	290E	NWC	77375
WILLOW GREEN DR	1800	570W	MC	77489
WILLOWGREN DR	600	490F	BH	77024
WILLOW GROVE DR	8700	290J	NWC	77375
WILLOWGROVE DR	10000	531V	SWH	77035
WILLOW HEARTH DR	6800	408T	NWC	77084
WILLOW HEIGHTS CT	13500	578W	SEH	77059
WILLOWHERB CT	1	251M	WD	77380
WILLOW HILL DR	4000	619G	TL	77586
WILLOWICK	300	288L	TB	77375
WILLOWICK	1	256V	SEM	77357
W. WILLOWICK AVE	100	656D	FR	77546
E. WILLOWICK AVE	100	656D	FR	77546
WILLOWICK CIR	1	490R	PP	77024
WILLOWICK CT	3300	568Z	SG	77478
WILLOWICK DR	7800	250W	NWC	77389
WILLOWICK RD	2100	492S	SWH	77027
WILLOWICK RD	3600	492N	SWH	77019
WILLOWICK RD	8000	250W	NWC	77389
WILLOWILDE DR	10000	531Z	SWH	77035
WILLOWILDE DR	11100	571D	SWH	77035
WILLOWIND DR	3900	577E	PA	77504
WILLOWISP DR	10300	531Y	SWH	77035
WILLOW KNOLL CT	5300	297P	NEH	77345
WILLOW LAKE DR	1900	616S	PL	77581
WILLOWLAKE DR	1900	489S	SWH	77077
WILLOWLAKE DR	9300	409H	NWC	77064
WILLOW LAKES DR	1800	568W	SG	77479
WILLOW LAND	5400	407X	NWC	77084
WILLOW LANDING LN	0	571K	SWH	77085
WILLOW LEAF	1800	331V	NWH	77090
WILLOW LEAF DR	23300	290E	NWC	77375
WILLOWLEAF GRDEN CRSSNG	0	524D	NEF	77494
WILLOW LOCH DR	8400	329D	NWC	77379
WILLOW LODGE CT	9500	409D	NWC	77064
WILLOW LOG	9500	409D	NWC	77064
WILLOW MANOR DR	0	612Y	NWB	77578
WILLOW MEADOW DR	8600	530W	SWH	77031
WILLOW MILL DR	1500	570T	MC	77489
WILLOW MINT LN	7500	370Z	NWC	77086
WILLOWMIST DR	10800	369Y	NWC	77064
WILLOWMOSS CT	1800	452S	NWH	77008
WILLOW MOSS DR	18300	407S	NWC	77449
WILLOW MOUNTAIN LN	0	573X	SEC	77047
WILLOW OAK CIR	4900	578J	PA	77505
WILLOW OAK DR	0	570U	MC	77489
WILLOW OAK DR	5800	451A	NWH	77092
WILLOW OAK DR	7300	462Z	BT	77521
WILLOW OAK BEND CIR	0	366K	NWC	77433
W. WILLOW OAK BEND DR	0	366K	NWC	77433
E. WILLOW OAK BEND DR	0	366K	NWC	77433
WILLOW OAKS CIR	1000	537J	PA	77506
WILLOWOOD DR	200	657R	LC	77573
WILLOWOOD LN	300	534K	SEH	77023
WILLOWORK	0	490M	HC	77024
WILLOWPARK DR	16000	328R	NWC	77377
WILLOW PARK LN	9800	409C	NWC	77064
WILLOW PARK GREEN	0	369F	NWC	77070
WILLOW PARK TERRACE LN	0	297P	NEH	77365
WILLOW PARK VIEW	0	369F	NWC	77070
WILLOW PARK VILLAGE	0	369F	NWC	77070
WILLOW PASS DR	2200	337E	NEH	77339
WILLOW PATH	7900	290E	NWC	77375
WILLOW PEAK LN	25300	485S	NEF	77494
WILLOW PINE DR	6100	330H	NWC	77379
S. WILLOW PLACE DR	8200	369M	NWC	77070
N. WILLOW PLACE DR	8400	369M	NWC	77070
W. WILLOW PLACE DR	13100	369M	NWC	77070
WILLOW POINT DR	1800	296Y	NEH	77339
WILLOW POINT DR	2300	336D	NEH	77339
WILLOW POINTE	0	658M	LC	77573
WILLOW POND DR	23200	485L	SWC	77494
WILLOW QUILL CT	8800	411J	NWC	77088
WILLOW QUILL DR	8900	411J	NWC	77088
WILLOW RANCH DR	17000	367X	NWC	77095
WILLOW RIDGE DR	3400	297W	NEH	77339
WILLOW RIVER DR	15300	408E	NWC	77095
WILLOW ROCK RD	1400	412K	NWH	77088
WILLOWRON DR	1	490M	HC	77024
WILLOW ROSE DR	0	290U	NWC	77379
WILLOW ROSE DR	0	290D	NWC	77389
WILLOW RUN	17700	325F	NWC	77447
WILLOW RUN	23100	290E	NWC	77375
WILLOW SAGE LN	0	525E	NEF	77494
WILLOW SHADE LN	21900	290J	NWC	77375
W. WILLOW SHADOWS DR	21900	290J	NWC	77375
WILLOWSHIRE LN	0	372A	NWC	77014
WILLOW SHORES DR	15300	618F	SEH	77062
WILLOW SIDE CT	22000	485Z	NEF	77450
WILLOWSONG CT	14400	570R	SWH	77489
WILLOWSONG LN	0	612P	PL	77545
WILLOW SPRING LN	3800	450L	NWH	77080
WILLOW SPRINGS CT	0	657Z	LC	77573
WILLOW SPRINGS DR	0	613X	NEB	77578
WILLOW SPRINGS PLACE	400	292U	NCC	77373
WILLOW SPUR CT	21700	290J	NWC	77375
WILLOW SPUR DR	8800	290J	NWC	77375
WILLOW STONE CT	3800	446L	NWC	77449
WILLOW STREAM DR	18100	407X	NWC	77084
WILLOW SWITCH DR	23600	290D	NWC	77389
WILLOW SWITCH RD	23600	290F	NWC	77389
WILLOW TERRACE DR	1200	338A	NEH	77345
WILLOW TERRACE DR	2200	337D	NEH	77345
WILLOW TERRACE DR	2700	297Z	NEH	77345
WILLOWTEX DR	7000	375T	NEH	77396
WILLOW TIMBER DR	500	332X	NWC	77090
WILLOW TOP LN		328K	NWC	77377
WILLOW TRACE CT	3000	486S	NEF	77450
WILLOW TRACE CT	9500	409H	NWC	77064
WILLOW TRACE DR	20300	326T	NWC	77433
WILLOW TRAIL	2200	539S	DP	77536
WILLOW TRAIL	12000	570D	SWH	77035
WILLOW TREE DR	2900	371U	NWC	77066
WILLOWTWIST	13800	528P	SWC	77083
WILLOW VALE DR	1000	619G	TL	77586
WILLOW VIEW	0	369F	NWC	77070
WILLOWVIEW	1500	539T	LP	77571
WILLOWVIEW DR	3900	577E	PA	77504
WILLOWVIEW DR	5100	500H	BT	77521
WILLOWVIEW LN	0	500H	BT	77521
WILLOWVIEW LN	9200	450U	NWH	77080
WILLOW VISTA DR	300	620J	EL	77586
WILLOW WALK	5600	330Y	NWC	77069
WILLOW WAND	0	369F	NWC	77070
WILLOW WAY	0	257D	RF	77357
WILLOW WAY	17400	246T	SWM	77355
WILLOW WAY	23000	290E	NWC	77375
WILLOW WEST DR	400	332Q	NCC	77073
WILLOW WICK	0	568Z	SG	77478
WILLOW WILDE DR	8800	290J	NWC	77375
W. WILLOWWIND CIR	15300	570G	MC	77071

Street Name	Block	Pg/Sq	Loc	Zips
E. WILLOWWIND CIR	15300	570G	MC	77071
WILLOW WIND CT	4100	609J	NEF	77479
WILLOW WIND LN	0	528P	SWC	77083
WILLOW WISP	2000	620P	SB	77586
WILLOW WISP CIR	500	332A	NWC	77388
WILLOW WISP DR	1400	570T	MC	77489
WILLOW WISP LN	1900	292W	NWC	77388
WILLOW WOOD	23300	290E	NWC	77375
WILLOWWOOD CIR	1	251J	WD	77381
W. WILLOWWOOD CT	1	251J	WD	77381
E. WILLOWWOOD CT	1	251J	WD	77381
WILLOWWOOD DR	22100	405Y	NWC	77449
WILLOW WOOD LN	9300	370Z	NWC	77086
WILLOW WOOD LN	9600	410D	NWC	77086
WILLOW WOOD TRAIL	3000	297Q	NEH	77345
WILLOW WOOD WAY	10000	329T	NWC	77388
WILLOWYCK CIR	2600	613U	NEB	77584
WILLVIEW RD	15300	571W	SWH	77489
WILLWOOD DR	11000	529B	SWH	77072
WILLY LN	25300	339H	NEC	77336
WILMA LOIS AVE	1000	536V	PA	77502
WILMER	3800	494T	SEH	77003
WILMERDEAN	7500	535X	SEH	77061
WILMINGTON	3000	573B	SEH	77051
WILMINGTON	4700	574A	SEH	77033
WILMINGTON DR	500	531H	BL	77401
WILMINGTON PARK LN	0	407Z	NWC	77084
WILO DR	14000	374Z	NCC	77032
WILOAK	9200	455B	NEH	77028
WILOAK	9500	415Y	NEH	77078
WILOMILL DR	9100	410F	NWC	77040
WILOWAY	8800	415R	NEC	77016
WILROSE HAVEN DR	6800	406Q	NWC	77449
WILSHIRE	0	502K	BT	77521
WILSHIRE	2300	534G	SEH	77023
WILSHIRE CIR	2700	615P	PL	77581
WILSHIRE CT	1200	256H	SEM	77357
WILSHIRE CT	2200	538N	DP	77536
WILSHIRE DR	1200	256D	SEM	77357
WILSHIRE FALLS	0	410Z	NWC	77040
WILSHIRE LAKES	0	410Z	NWC	77040
WILSHIRE PARK DR	1400	412A	NWC	77038
WILSHIRE PLACE DR	0	658R	LC	77573
WILSHIRE PLACE DR	7400	410Z	NWH	77040
WILSHIRE POND	0	410Z	NWC	77040
WILSHIRE RIDGE	0	410Z	NWC	77040
WILSON	0	257S	SEM	77359
WILSON	0	377T	NEC	77044
S. WILSON	100	540Z	MP	77571
N. WILSON	100	540Z	MP	77571
WILSON	100	493P	SWH	77019
WILSON	1900	493P	SWH	77006
WILSON	24800	249W	NWC	77375
WILSON CT	0	375H	HM	77396
WILSON CT	0	376E	HM	77396
WILSON DR	1400	538R	DP	77536
WILSON LN	1	288C	TB	77375
WILSON RD	0	375Z	NEC	77396
WILSON RD	100	336W	HM	77338
WILSON RD	1500	502J	BT	77521
WILSON RD	1600	376E	HM	77396
WILSON-BAKER	0	377T	NEC	77044
WILSON PARK CT	15000	376T	NEC	77396
WILSON PINES CT	11700	570A	SWH	77031
WILSON REACH LN	7400	290B	NWC	77389
WILSON REID DR	8700	410K	NWC	77040
WILSONS CREEK LN	16600	527P	NEF	77083
WILSTON CT	1200	489J	SWH	77077
WILSTONE DR	18200	447F	NWC	77084
WILTON	5100	492Z	SWH	77098
WILTON	5300	532D	SWH	77005
WILTON	5800	614Y	PL	77584
WILTON CT	4000	614Y	PL	77584
WILTON PARK CT	17400	330K	NWC	77379
WILTON PARK DR	7600	330K	NWC	77379
WILTSHIRE DR	0	330S	NWC	77379
WILTSHIRE LN	0	657Y	LC	77573
WILTSHIRE DOWNS LN	6600	457Q	NEC	77049
WILTSHIRE WAY CT	0	616L	SEC	77089
WIMAN	800	501P	BT	77521
WIMBERLEY HOLLOW LN	3800	572W	SWC	77053
WIMBERLEY OAKS LN	7200	526H	NEF	77407
WIMBERLY	2800	454E	NEH	77093
WIMBERLY DR	0	539N	DP	77536
WIMBERLY CANYON LN	9000	575U	SEH	77075
WIMBERLY HEIGHTS DR	0	367S	NWC	77433
WIMBERLY HILLS LN	0	366N	NWC	77433
WIMBERLY KNOLL CT	6200	407T	NWC	77084
WIMBERLY KNOLL LN	17400	407T	NWC	77084
WIMBERLY PARK DR	15100	457U	NEC	77049
WIMBERLY PLACE LN	0	484S	NEF	77494
WIMBERLY WAY	15500	328N	NWC	77429
WIMBLEDON DR	13500	568F	SG	77498
N. WIMBLEDON DR	18100	407W	NWC	77449
S. WIMBLEDON DR	18400	407W	NWC	77449
WIMBLEDON LN	0	656X	FR	77546
WIMBLEDON LN	8100	369H	NWC	77070
WIMBLEDON CHAMPIONS	16000	330M	NWC	77379
WIMBLEDON CREEK DR	6600	370M	NWC	77379
WIMBLEDON ESTATES DR	6700	330L	NWC	77379
WIMBLEDON FOREST CT	6600	330M	NWC	77379
WIMBLEDON FOREST DR	16100	330M	NWC	77379
WIMBLEDON OAKS DR	13300	368Y	NWC	77065
WIMBLEDON TRAIL RD	6400	330M	NWC	77379
WIMBLEDON VILLAS DR	6300	330M	NWC	77379
WIMBLETON CT	2100	616K	PL	77581
WINBERIE CT	2100	485R	SWC	77450
WINBERN	800	493T	SWH	77002
WINBERN	1000	493Y	SEH	77004
WINBERRY CT	20000	406T	NWC	77449
WINBUSH CT	13900	367D	NWC	77429
WINCHELL	6300	453R	NEH	77022
WINCHELL PLACE RD	33500	247S	SWM	77355
WINCHELSEA LN	24300	250Z	NWC	77389
WINCHESTER	0	255X	SEM	77365
WINCHESTER	3800	494W	SEH	77003
WINCHESTER CT	0	657A	FR	77546
WINCHESTER BEND	400	298U	NEC	77336
WINCHESTER GROVE LN		325N	NWC	77447
WINCHESTER RANCH TRAIL	0	445J	NWC	77493
WINCHESTER ROCK DR	0	296S	SEM	77365
WINCHESTER VILLAGE CT	9800	409C	NWC	77064
WINCHMORE HILL DR	16000	330T	NWC	77379
WINCOPIN DR	0	408F	NWC	77095
WINCREST CT	12900	328U	NWC	77429
WINCREST FALLS DR	1	328Y	NWC	77429
WINCROFT CT	5200	330U	NWC	77069
N. WIND DR	0	619V	LC	77565
WINDBOURNE DR	0	289R	NWC	77375
WINDBREAK LN	3500	609A	SG	77479
WINDBREAK TRAIL	700	488B	SWH	77079
WINDBRIAR CT	3600	331T	NWC	77068

Street Name	Block	Pg/Sq	Loc	Zips
WIND BROOK	7100	410P	NWC	77040
WIND BRUSH DR	2700	291Z	NWC	77388
WINDBURY CT	20100	290Z	NWC	77379
WINDBURY CT	21900	485Z	NEF	77450
WIND CAVE LN	14700	410J	NWC	77040
WINDCHASE BLVD	2600	488T	SWH	77082
WINDCHASE CT	13500	488X	SWC	77082
WINDCHASE LN	0	615F	PL	77581
WINDCHESTER	2300	615Q	PL	77581
WIND CHIMES DR	4800	371A	NWC	77066
WINDCLIFF CT	5800	407X	NWC	77449
WIND COVE PLACE CT	0	377E	NEC	77346
WIND CREEK	1	656Q	FR	77546
WIND CREEK DR	2000	337C	NEH	77345
WINDCRESS CT	0	409F	JV	77064
WINDCREST CT	0	525D	NEF	77450
WINDCREST CT	3300	616S	PL	77581
WINDCREST CT	5200	525D	NEF	77450
WINDCREST PARK CT	0	253N	SEM	77386
WINDCREST PARK LN	0	252R	SEM	77385
WINDCREST PARK LN	0	253N	SEM	77386
WINDCREST SUMMIT LN	0	578T	SEH	77059
WINDCROFT HOLLOW LN	19900	446C	NWC	77449
WINDCROSS CT	4800	446D	NWC	77449
WIND DALE DR	7200	410P	NWC	77040
WINDELL CT	0	410J	NWC	77040
WINDELL LN	8200	410J	NWC	77040
WINDEMERE	5100	534W	SEH	77033
WINDEMERE CT	9800	335Q	HM	77338
WINDEMERE DR	2900	613F	NEB	77584
WINDEMERE FALLS LN	0	609S	NEF	77479
WINDEMERE ISLE	100	292Q	SP	77373
WINDEMERE PARK CT	24600	485S	NEF	77494
WINDEMERE PARK LN	3000	485S	NEF	77494
W. WINDERBURY	0	488L	SWH	77077
E. WINDERBURY	0	488L	SWH	77077
WINDERMERE LN	1	490Q	PP	77063
WINDERMERE LAKES BLVD	0	369W	NWC	77065
WINDERMERE RETREAT BLVD		484J	NEF	77494
WINDERS	2700	494J	NEH	77020
WINDERWICK LN	12200	371J	NWC	77066
WINDFALL CT	8200	410J	NWC	77040
WINDFALL LN	8300	410J	NWC	77040
WINDFALL PATH DR	24600	293S	NCC	77373
WINDFELLOW PLACE	1	250D	WD	77381
WINDFERN CT	10800	370W	NWC	77064
WINDFERN DR	3300	616S	PL	77581
WINDFERN RD	4300	450A	NWH	77041
WINDFERN RD	6000	410W	NWH	77040
WINDFERN RD	8400	410E	NWC	77064
WINDFERN RD	10400	370W	NWC	77064
WINDFERN RD	11500	369V	NWC	77064
WINDFERN FOREST DR	14400	410J	NWC	77040
WINDFERN LAKES	10800	369V	NWC	77064
WINDFERN TRACE DR	8800	370S	NWC	77064
WIND FIELD LN	20900	290U	NWC	77379
WIND FLOWER LN	9600	370Z	NWC	77086
WINDFORD COVE LN		249Z	NWC	77375
WIND FOREST CT	14600	410J	NWC	77040
WIND FOREST DR	8000	410J	NWC	77040
WIND FREE DR	14700	410J	NWC	77040
WINDGAP CT	3200	251T	SWM	77380
WINDGATE CT	2100	658S	LC	77573
WINDGATE CT	7300	407K	NWC	77433
WINDGROVE CT	8200	527Q	NEF	77083
WINDHAM	0	340V	LCO	77535
WINDHAM	1100	493F	SWH	77007
WINDHAM SPRINGS CT	5300	449A	NWC	77041
WINDHAVEN	13500	456R	NEH	77049
WINDHAVEN LAKE	0	407E	NWC	77433
WINDHAVEN TERRACE CT	0	407E	NWC	77433
W. WINDHAVEN TERRACE TRL	0	407E	NWC	77433
E. WINDHAVEN TERRACE TRL	0	407E	NWC	77433
WINDHILL DR	0	290N	NWC	77379
WINDHOLLOW CIR	400	659H	LC	77573
WIND HOLLOW CIR	14600	410J	NWC	77040
WINDHURST RD	0	525F	NEF	77494
WINDING	100	616U	PL	77546
WINDING LN	0	248G	SWM	77354
WINDING LN	12400	368M	NWC	77429
WINDING RD	400	576M	SEH	77504
WINDING ATWOOD LN	0	328F	NWC	77429
WINDING BAYOU TRACE	0	412C	NWC	77038
WINDING BLACK CHERRY LN	14900	326X	NWC	77433
WINDING BRANCH DR	19100	446M	NWC	77449
WINDINGBROOK CT	5200	660X	DI	77539
WINDINGBROOK DR	5200	660X	DI	77539
WINDING BROOK LN	12500	489H	SWH	77024
WINDING CANYON LN	7200	527J	NEF	77083
WINDING CANYON LN	19500	446C	NWC	77449
WINDING COVE	0	525H	NEF	77450
WINDING CREEK	27200	246K	SWM	77355
WINDING CREEK CT	25300	245K	SWM	77355
WINDING CREEK DR	1800	616S	PL	77581
WINDING CREEK LN	0	657J	FR	77546
WINDING CREEK LN	17500	246N	SWM	77355
WINDING CREEK VIEW	7800	528M	SWH	77072
WINDING CREEK WAY	0	252M	SEM	77385
WINDING CREEK WAY	5300	536S	SEH	77017
WINDING CYPRESS BRK DR	16500	368P	NWC	77429
WINDING FOREST DR	0	615Z	PL	77581
WINDING GLEN LN	0	524B	NEF	77494
WINDING GREEN DR	0	376B	NEC	77369
WINDING HILL LN	8200	330N	NWC	77379
WINDING HOLLOW CT	2100	252M	SEM	77385
WINDING HOLLOW DR	1900	486N	SWC	77450
WINDING HOLLOW LN	11400	289J	NWC	77375
WINDING IVY LN	0	326L	NWC	77429
WINDING KNOLL DR	23100	485Q	NEF	77494
WINDING LAKE CT	22200	485V	NEF	77450
WINDING LAKE WAY	3200	485U	NEF	77450
WINDING MANOR DR	12500	377W	NEC	77044
WINDING MEADOW CT	8200	410Q	NWC	77040
WINDING MOSS DR	15400	331P	NWC	77068
S. WINDING OAK	0	657R	LC	77573
N. WINDING OAK	0	657R	LC	77573
WINDING OAK CIR	0	330K	NWC	77379
WINDING OAK CT	17200	327W	NWC	77429
WINDING OAK LN	8100	330K	NWC	77379
WINDING POINT LN		484S	NEF	77494
WINDING POINT LN		484W	NEF	77494
WINDING RIDGE DR	5400	330H	NWC	77379
WINDING RIVER DR	4900	609A	SG	77478
WINDING RIVER DR	8900	412L	NWH	77088
WINDING RIVER TRAIL	26700	299T	NEC	77336
WINDING RUN LN	2700	485N	NEF	77494
WINDING SHORE CT	22900	485U	NEF	77450
WINDING SHORE LN	2800	485U	NEF	77450
WINDING SHORES DR	0	612L	PL	77584
WINDING SPRING DR	7200	330H	NWC	77379
WINDING SPRINGS DR	2000	658V	LC	77573
WINDING SPRINGS DR	14100	328N	NWC	77429

Street Name	Block	Pg/Sq	Loc	Zips
WINDING STAR LN	0	366Q	NWC	77433
WINDING STREAM LN	0	446H	NWC	77449
WINDING SUMMIT DR	0	257E	SEM	77357
WINDING TIMBERS CIR	4900	377A	NEC	77346
WINDING TIMBERS CT	4800	376D	NEC	77346
WINDING TIMBERS LN	18200	376D	NEC	77346
WINDING TRACE DR	6600	371T	NWC	77086
WINDING TRAIL	10000	579B	LP	77571
WINDING TRAIL LN	19100	406V	NWC	77449
WINDING VALLEY DR	15600	408N	NWC	77095
WINDING VIEW LN	4900	376D	NEC	77346
WINDING WACO CT	0	406D	NWC	77433
WINDING WACO WAY	0	406D	NWC	77433
WINDING WALK DR	7000	408P	NWC	77095
WINDING WATERS DR	14800	327X	NWC	77429
WINDING WATERS LN	17800	609S	NEF	77479
WINDING WATERS LN	18200	609S	NEF	77479
E. WINDING WAY	0	657E	FR	77546
WINDING WAY	0	657K	FR	77546
WINDING WAY	25100	244R	WCO	77447
WINDINGWAY DR	100	657A	FR	77546
WINDINGWAY DR	1100	657E	FR	77546
WINDING WAY DR	5200	411Y	NWH	77091
WINDING WILLOW LN	25300	293P	NCC	77373
WINDING WOOD CT	2300	371Z	NWC	77038
WINDING WOOD DR	13100	371Z	NWC	77038
WINDING WOOD LN	10200	289L	NWC	77375
WINDJAMMER	12300	529J	SWH	77072
WINDJAMMER CT	4100	620E	SB	77586
WINDLAKE CT	12000	369Q	NWC	77070
WINDLAKE DR	10800	369Q	NWC	77070
WINDLASS WAY	700	379X	NEC	77532
WIND LAWN DR	14600	410J	NWC	77040
WINDLEA LN	14700	410J	NWC	77040
WINDLEAF DR	1300	580P	SA	77571
WINDLEWOOD DR	3600	446K	NWC	77449
WINDLEY KEY CT	0	377F	NEC	77346
WIND LOCK CIR	14600	410J	NWC	77040
WINDMARK DR	11100	529X	SWH	77099
WINDMARK LN	10500	529X	SWH	77099
WINDMARK PLACE	11100	529X	SWH	77099
WINDMILL	0	452S	NWH	77008
WINDMILL	3800	609A	SG	77479
WINDMILL BLUFF LN	21900	486W	NEF	77450
WINDMILL CANYON LN	0	524M	NEF	77406
WINDMILL COVE LN	14900	328W	NWC	77429
WINDMILL ELM ST	0	492A	NWH	77008
WINDMILL HILL CIR	0	366M	NWC	77407
WINDMILL LAKES BLVD	9800	576N	SEH	77075
WINDMILL PARK LN	9700	410B	NWC	77064
WINDMIST CIR	6400	407U	NWC	77084
WIND MIST LN	17600	367T	NWC	77433
WINDMONT DR	0	484V	NEF	77494
WINDMOOR CT	19700	446L	NWC	77449
WINDMOOR DR	3200	446L	NWC	77449
WINDMOOR PLACE	3300	446L	NWC	77449
WIND OAK	0	410J	NWC	77040
WINDOAK LN	14700	410J	NWC	77040
WINDOM DR	15900	618N	SEH	77598
WINDOVER	1000	450W	NWH	77055
WINDOVER PARK LN		328P	NWC	77429
WINDOW ROCK DR	0	367Y	NWC	77095
WIND PINE LN	11200	329F	NWC	77375
WIND POINT DR	0	329A	NWC	77375
WIND POPPY CT	1	251J	WD	77381
WIND RIDGE	20500	290V	NWC	77379
WINDRIFT DR	4000	371E	NWC	77066
WINDRIVER CIR	11800	369Q	NWC	77070
WINDRIVER DR	9900	369Q	NWC	77070
WIND RIVER TRAIL	0	409F	NWC	77064
WIND ROCK	8700	410P	NWC	77040
WIND ROCK CT	7200	410P	NWC	77040
WINDROSE CT	100	409F	JV	77064
WINDROSE LN	6200	290U	NWC	77379
WINDROSE LN	32100	322X	WCO	77484
WINDROSE BEND	0	290T	NWC	77379
WINDROSE HOLLOW LN	6000	290U	NWC	77379
WINDROSE TRAIL LN	0	290U	NWC	77379
WINDROW DR	16900	330H	NWC	77379
WINDROW LN	7300	528L	SWH	77072
WINDRUSH DR	9300	330S	NWC	77379
WINDSAIL CT	4400	569X	MC	77459
S. WINDSAIL PLACE	1	251F	WD	77381
N. WINDSAIL PLACE	1	251F	WD	77381
WIND SAND DR	0	446D	NWC	77449
WINDSDOWNE LN	15000	327Z	NWC	77429
WINDSHIRE	5000	609K	MC	77459
WINDSHIRE	13600	368A	NWC	77429
WIND SIDE DR	8700	410P	NWC	77040
WINDSINGER CT	0	249M	NWC	77375
WINDSONG LN	0	612N	PL	77545
WINDSONG LN	1	656Q	FR	77546
WINDSONG CREEK LN	4600	609J	NEF	77479
WIND SONG TRACE	38100	246A	SWM	77355
WINDSONG TRAIL	4000	447K	NWC	77084
WINDSONG TRAIL	5100	407X	NWC	77084
WINDSONG TRAIL	20800	378C	NEC	77532
WINDSONG WAY	0	297P	NEH	77345
WINDSOR	2300	537K	PA	77506
WINDSOR	3200	615P	PL	77581
WINDSOR	3600	538U	DP	77536
WINDSOR	10100	569G	SWH	77031
WINDSOR CT	0	450Y	NWH	77055
WINDSOR CT	1	609C	MC	77459
WINDSOR DR	300	657E	FR	77546
WINDSOR DR	500	656M	FR	77546
WINDSOR DR	11500	569G	SF	77477
WINDSOR LN	1900	492R	SWH	77006
WINDSOR LN	2600	493S	SWH	77006
WINDSOR BLUFF DR	0	327H	NWC	77429
WINDSOR BLUFF DR	0	327H	NWC	77429
WINDSOR CASTLE DR	21500	291R	NWC	77388
WINDSOR CHASE DR	0	253Y	SEM	77386
WINDSOR CHASE LN	1000	292F	NCC	77373
WINDSOR CHASE LN	6100	657Y	LC	77573
WINDSOR CREST DR	18900	486H	SWC	77094
WINDSOR FIELD	20300	290S	NWC	77379
WINDSOR FIELD CT	7500	290S	NWC	77379
WINDSOR FOREST DR	5400	411L	NWC	77088
WINDSOR GARDEN LN	0	417C	NEC	77044
WINDSOR GLEN DR	100	486B	SWC	77450
WINDSOR GROVE LN	17600	447C	NWC	77084
WINDSOR HOLLOW CT	20900	446W	NWC	77449
WINDSOR LAKES DR	18800	487E	SWC	77094
WINDSOR LAKES DR	18900	486M	SWC	77094
WINDSOR LAKES CROSSING	19000	486H	SWC	77094
WINDSOR LOCKS DR	9700	409A	NWC	77065
WINDSOR MANOR	14900	330V	NWC	77069
WINDSOR MIST LN	0	293H	SEM	77386
WINDSOR OAKS LN	14300	618A	SEH	77062
WINDSOR PALMS DR	18900	486H	SWC	77094
WINDSOR PARK DR	1600	486M	SWC	77094

Street Name	Block	Pg/Sq	Loc	Zips
WINDSOR PLACE	0	450Y	NWH	77055
WINDSOR PLACE	0	488L	SWH	77077
WINDSOR POINTE DR	19100	328H	NWC	77375
WINDSOR POINTE DR	19100	329A	NWC	77375
WINDSOR SAILS DR	0	487E	SWC	77094
WINDSOR SQUARE DR	0	337G	NEC	77345
WINDSOR TRACE LN	0	526E	NEF	77450
WINDSOR VALLEY LN	0	457K	NEC	77049
WINDSOR VIEW DR	0	290N	NWC	77379
WINDSOR VILLAGE DR	12600	570F	SWH	77071
WINDSOR WOODS LN	0	484F	NEF	77494
WIND SPRINGS DR	0	450V	NWH	77080
WINDSTAR CT	1	251A	WD	77381
WINDSTAR DR	1	251A	WD	77381
WINDSTONE	0	407R	NWC	77084
WIND STONE	6400	407U	NWC	77084
WINDSTONE MANOR BLVD	0	446G	NWC	77449
WIND STREAM DR	8700	410P	NWC	77040
E. WINDSWEPT	1600	660S	GCO	77539
WINDSWEPT	2300	615Q	PL	77581
WINDSWEPT DR	500	335Z	HM	77338
WINDSWEPT DR	1000	375D	HM	77338
WINDSWEPT LN	5300	491X	SWH	77056
WINDSWEPT LN	6100	491W	SWH	77057
WINDSWEPT LN	7600	490W	SWH	77063
WINDSWEPT GROVE DR	9100	527Q	NEF	77083
WIND TRACE CT	1	251E	WD	77381
WINDTRACE DR	0	446C	NWC	77449
WIND TRACE LN	17900	330E	NWC	77379
WIND TRAIL	7200	410P	NWC	77040
WINDTREE LN	17800	331J	NWC	77379
WIND VEIL DR	8300	410J	NWC	77040
WINDVINE CT	7000	528L	SWH	77072
WINDVINE DR	7200	528L	SWH	77072
WIND WALKER TRAIL	10500	367T	NWC	77095
WINDWARD CT	1	251F	WD	77381
WINDWARD CT	200	660J	LC	77573
WINDWARD DR	300	660K	LC	77573
WINDWARD LN	1	619W	NB	77058
WINDWARD BAY DR	0	612P	PL	77584
W. WINDWARD COVE	1	251F	WD	77381
WINDWARD COVE	1	251F	WD	77381
WINDWARD FALLS WAY	0	297K	SEM	77365
WINDWARD MEADOW	0	296Q	SEM	77365
WINDWARD PASSAGE	7600	528M	SWH	77072
WINDWARD THICKET WAY	0	405P	NWC	77493
WINDWARD WAY	0	378S	NEC	77532
WINDWATER DR	9700	576N	SEH	77075
WINDWATER LAGOON DR	7100	530D	SWH	77036
S. WINDWATER PKWY	7100	530D	SWH	77036
N. WINDWATER PKWY	7100	530D	SWH	77036
WINDWATER POINTE	6100	530D	SWC	77036
WIND WHISPER CT	1	251Z	WD	77380
WIND WILLOW DR	8300	410J	NWC	77040
WINDWOOD	1	656P	FR	77546
WINDWOOD	3000	615Q	PL	77581
WINDWOOD DR	10900	531Y	SWH	77035
WINDWOOD FOREST DR	23100	256D	SEM	77357
WINDWOOD PARK LN	0	253P	SEM	77386
WINDWOOD PARK LN	14600	367A	NWC	77429
WINDY LN	1100	501V	BT	77520
WINDY LN	11600	490K	BH	77024
WINDY ACRES DR	7900	410J	NWC	77040
WINDY BANK LN	0	615L	PL	77581
WINDY BANK LN	23400	525L	NEF	77407
WINDY BAY LN	22100	525C	NEF	77450
WINDY BLUFF CT	4800	446D	NWC	77449
WINDY BRIAR LN	2900	660E	LC	77573
WINDY BRIAR LN	20700	290T	NWC	77379
WINDY BROOK LN	1700	658W	LC	77573
WINDY BROOK LN	4800	446D	NWC	77449
WINDY BROOK LN	22200	289J	NWC	77375
WINDY CANYON LN	0	447B	NWC	77084
WINDY CAPE LN	3200	660E	LC	77573
WINDY CAPE RD	0	368U	NWC	77065
WINDY CHASE LN	4200	484Y	NEF	77494
WINDY CLIFF LN	0	290T	NWC	77379
WINDY COVE CT	2300	619X	LC	77573
WINDY COVE CT	8400	408E	NWC	77095
WINDY COVE DR	15200	408F	NWC	77095
WINDY COVE LN	0	612H	PL	77584
WINDY COVE LN	0	613J	PL	77584
WINDY CREEK DR	0	612M	PL	77584
WINDY CREEK DR	7900	410J	NWC	77040
WINDY CROSSING LN	0	375Y	NEC	77396
WINDY CYPRESS CT	0	446H	NWC	77449
WINDY DAWN DR	11300	612M	PL	77584
WINDY DUNES DR	8100	570F	SWH	77071
WINDYGATE DR	0	293Y	NCC	77373
WINDY GLEN DR	15700	408J	NWC	77095
WINDY GORGE CT	2900	297Q	NEH	77345
WINDY GORGE DR	4500	297P	NEH	77345
WINDY GREEN DR	1900	338A	NEH	77345
WINDY GROVE LN	0	366U	NWC	77433
WINDY HAVEN DR	3700	297W	NEH	77339
WINDY HEATH LN	13100	571K	SWH	77085
WINDY HILLS LN	0	444S	KT	77493
WINDY HILLSIDE TRAIL	0	328K	NWC	77429
WINDY HOLLOW DR	4500	297T	NEH	77345
WINDY ISLE CT	25600	250T	NWC	77389
WINDY ISLE WAY	0	613J	PL	77584
WINDY KNOLL DR	1700	446Y	NWC	77084
WINDY LAKE DR	5100	337D	NEH	77345
WINDYLEA LN	0	525M	NEF	77407
WINDY MARK DR	0	446C	NWC	77449
WINDY MEADOW DR	1700	446Y	NWC	77084
WINDY MEADOW DR	2000	568Z	SG	77478
WINDY MEADOW RD	13800	288P	NWC	77377
WINDY MOUNTAIN LN	0	377E	NEC	77346
WINDY MOUNTAIN LN	0	377E	NEC	77346
WINDY NOOK DR	19900	446U	NWC	77084
WINDY OAKS CT	18100	255S	SEM	77365
WINDY OAKS DR	0	543D	BC	77520
WINDY OAKS DR	8300	410J	NWC	77040
WINDY ORCHARD LN	4900	447C	NWC	77084
WINDY PARK DR	1900	336B	NEH	77339
WINDY PATH LN	0	407E	NWC	77433
WINDY PEAKS CT	1900	371M	NWC	77067
WINDY PIKE TRAIL	0	407A	NWC	77433
WINDYPINE DR	16800	330H	NWC	77379
WINDY PINES CIR	17200	330G	NWC	77379
WINDY PINES DR	6900	330G	NWC	77379
WINDY POINT DR	17200	330G	NWC	77379
WINDY POPLAR TRACE	0	446G	NWC	77449
WINDY PORT LN	0	526E	NEF	77407
WINDY RIDGE DR	1800	486Q	SWC	77450
WINDY RIDGE LN	14500	618B	SEH	77062
WINDY RIDGE TRAIL	37800	246B	SWM	77355
WINDY RIVER LN	6600	406U	NWC	77449
WINDY ROYAL DR	3000	572F	SWH	77045
WINDY RUN CT	0	330B	NWC	77379
WINDY SAGE CT	0	609G	MC	77459

Street Name	Block	Pg/Sq	Loc	Zips
WINDY SHORES DR	2100	612H	PL	77584
WINDY SPRING CT	9200	615H	SEC	77089
WINDY SPRING LN	9300	615H	SEC	77089
WINDY STONE DR	0	447A	NWC	77084
WINDYSTONE DR	0	446C	NWC	77449
WINDY STREAM LN	13900	377Y	NEC	77044
WINDY SUMMER LN	12700	416Z	NEC	77044
WINDYS WAY	1500	446W	NWC	77449
WINDY THICKET LN	2700	488W	SWH	77082
WINDY THICKET LN	8400	407E	NWC	77433
WINDY TRACE LN	0	485X	NEF	77494
WINDY TRAIL DR	14300	410J	NWC	77040
WINDY VALE TRAIL	2500	611S	FS	77545
WINDY VALLEY WAY	0	407A	NWC	77433
WINDY VILLAGE LN	0	407S	NWC	77449
WINDY WAY	4800	577L	PA	77505
WINDY WAY LN	6400	614T	PL	77584
WINDY WILLOW CT	14400	570V	SWH	77489
WINDY WILLOW DR	14500	570V	SWH	77489
WINDY WISP LN	12400	570F	SWH	77071
WINDY WOODS CT	4100	297U	NEH	77345
WINEBERRY DR	2000	486P	SWC	77450
WINEBERRY HILL DR	0	376S	NEC	77396
WINEBROOK CT	2100	612G	PL	77584
WINEBROOK CT	13500	328W	NWC	77429
WINEBROOK DR	12300	612G	PL	77584
WINEBROOK CREEK LN	0	484S	NEF	77494
WINE CEDAR LN	1700	486L	SWC	77450
WINECUP	6900	525F	NEF	77494
WINE CUP CT	9900	329C	NWC	77379
WINECUP LN	2200	659G	LC	77573
WINECUP LN	2500	659G	LC	77573
WINECUP LN	14100	573T	SEC	77047
WINEHILL LN	7800	410L	NWC	77040
WINE MEADOWS CT	16700	327X	NWC	77429
WINE PRESS PASS LN	0	446E	NWC	77449
WINE ROCK DR	15900	329U	NWC	77070
WINESAP LN	13100	328X	NWC	77429
WINESAP BEND DR	0	569T	NEF	77477
WINEWOOD DR	8600	456D	NEC	77044
WINFIELD LN	1000	660B	KE	77565
WINFIELD RD	0	414M	NEC	77050
WINFIELD RD	4600	414M	NCC	77039
WINFIELD RD	5900	415J	NEC	77050
WINFIELD RD	9600	416J	NEC	77050
WINFIELD LAKES TRAIL	0	611S	FS	77545
WINFIELD SQUARE	17300	527E	NEF	77407
WINFORD CT	20000	290Z	NWC	77379
WINFORD DR	5400	446B	NWC	77449
WINFORD ESTATES DR	0	524K	NWF	77406
WINFORD SQUARE DR	0	295Z	NEH	77365
WINFREE DR	4700	534J	SEH	77021
WINFREE DR	6300	534R	SEH	77087
W. WINFREE RD	100	463A	MB	77580
E. WINFREE RD	100	463A	MB	77580
W. WINFREE RD	200	462H	MB	77580
WINFREY LN	1200	289A	TB	77375
WINFREY LN	11900	413U	NEH	77076
WINFRO DR	30300	288B	TB	77375
W. WING DR	2700	613T	NEB	77578
WINGATE	7300	495S	SEH	77011
WINGATE PARK DR	3600	527B	SWH	77082
WINGBORNE LN	0	368N	NWC	77429
WINGDALE CT	3400	527D	SWC	77082
WINGDALE DR	15700	527D	SWC	77082
WINGED DOVE DR	0	658X	LC	77573
WINGEDFOOT DR	2000	610E	MC	77459
WINGED FOOT DR	2100	659D	LC	77573
WINGED FOOT DR	5900	330Y	NWC	77069
WINGFIELD LN	25300	293N	NCC	77373
W. WINGFOOT RD	9400	450F	NWH	77041
WINGLEAF DR	1900	447X	NWH	77084
WINGO	8000	451W	NWH	77055
WINGTAIL WAY	3200	614X	PL	77584
WINGTIP DR	9000	575P	SEH	77061
WINGTIP DR	9100	575P	SEH	77075
WINHALL PLACE	0	249A	SWM	77354
WINK RD	11700	490K	SWH	77024
WINKBOW DR	9100	410K	NWC	77040
WINKIN AVE	100	419U	BR	77532
WINKLEMAN RD	6200	527H	SWC	77083
WINKLER	0	535Z	SEH	77017
WINKLER	100	534M	SEH	77087
WINKLER	8300	535U	SEH	77017
WINKLER DR	100	500J	BT	77520
WINKLER DR	800	535Z	SH	77587
WINKLER WILLOW CT	0	328M	NWC	77377
WINKLE WOOD LN	7500	410D	NWC	77086
WINLOCK GLEN CT		366U	NWC	77433
WINLOCK TRACE CT	0	525D	NEF	77450
WINLOCK TRACE CT	5400	525D	NEF	77450
WINLOCK TRACE DR	0	525D	NEF	77450
WINLOCK TRACE DR	20600	525D	NEF	77450
WINLOCK TRAILS DR	0	253S	SEM	77386
WINMONT CT	3700	527C	SWH	77082
WINMOSS CT	15500	331N	NWC	77068
WINN AVE	0	619V	LC	77565
E. WINN AVE	1800	619V	LC	77565
WINNERS CIR	0	490G	HE	77024
WINNERS CIR	4300	617T	SEC	77546
WINNETKA	4700	534E	SEH	77021
WINNIE	300	493C	NEH	77009
WINNIMAC	2100	539V	LP	77571
WINNINGHAM LN	8300	491A	SV	77055
WINNINGHAM LN	8700	490D	SV	77055
WINNSBORO CT	3300	568V	SG	77478
WINNSBORO DR	9000	411J	NWC	77088
WINNWOOD CT	9400	369M	NWC	77070
WINONA DR	300	536G	PA	77506
WINROCK BLVD	1100	490R	SWH	77057
WINSFORD DR	18000	447B	NWC	77084
WINSFORD HORIZON LN		484J	NEF	77494
WINSHIP	7800	455J	NEH	77028
WINSHIRE DR	11700	490K	BH	77024
WINSLOW	500	531H	BL	77401
WINSLOW	3000	532K	SWH	77025
WINSLOW LN	0	658U	LC	77573
WINSLOW FOREST LN	0	573T	SEC	77047
WINSOME DR	19300	255Y	SEM	77365
WINSOME LN	5600	491T	SWH	77057
WINSOME LN	9300	490S	SWH	77063
WINSOME ROSE CT	0	325U	NWC	77433
WINSOME WAY	0	296H	SEM	77357
WINSOR TERRACE CIR	19800	486Q	SWC	77450
WINSPRING CT	15600	329T	NWC	77377
WINSPRING DR	11000	329T	NWC	77377
WINSTEAD LN	6000	374M	NEH	77396
WINSTEAD LN	6100	375J	NEH	77396
WINSTON	900	453T	NWH	77009
WINSTON CT	2600	613T	NEB	77584
WINSTON COVE CT	0	526J	NEF	77407
WINSTON FALLS CT	8700	375Z	NEC	77396
WINSTON FALLS LN	14700	375Z	NEC	77396
WINSTON HILL DR	19500	406M	NWC	77433
WINSTON HOLLOW LN	25500	485W	NEF	77494
WINSTON LAKE DR	0	526W	NEF	77406
WINSTON POINT LN	0	407V	NWC	77084
WINSTON RANCH CT	21000	525Z	NEF	77406
WINSTON RANCH PKWY	0	525V	NEF	77406
WINSTON RANCH PKWY	7100	526W	NEF	77406
WINSTON WOODS DR	1	491G	SWH	77024
WINSTROME CT	3600	446K	NWC	77449
WINTER	1200	493F	SWH	77007
WINTER LN	3300	502F	BT	77521
WINTER LN	31800	248S	SWM	77362
WINTER BAY LN	1500	412N	NWC	77088
WINTER BERRY CT	0	615L	PL	77581
WINTERBERRY LN	0	698L	LC	77539
WINTERBERRY PLACE	11100	251Q	WD	77380
WINTER BLOOM LN	9600	411P	NWC	77088
WINTER BLOSSOM DR	7100	377C	NEC	77346
WINTERBORNE DR	4200	578E	PA	77505
WINTER BREEZE DR	5900	330D	NWC	77379
WINTER BRIAR CT	15500	571X	SWH	77489
WINTER BROOK DR	12100	371J	NWC	77066
WINTER CANYON LN	19300	328C	NWC	77377
WINTERCOVE CT	14800	487Z	SWC	77082
WINTER CREEK CT	3800	609K	MC	77459
WINTER CREEK CT	13500	488F	SWH	77077
WINTER CREEK LN	0	616J	PL	77089
WINTERCRESS LN	13700	415B	NEC	77396
WINTERFAIR DR	14800	487Z	SWC	77082
WINTER FALCON CROSSING	0	407S	NWC	77449
WINTER FALLS CT	2800	613X	NEB	77578
WINTER FOREST DR	20900	290U	NWC	77379
WINTER GARDEN CT	6500	528E	SWC	77083
WINTERGATE DR	23100	333D	NCC	77373
WINTERGATE DR	23600	293Y	NCC	77373
WINTER GLEN LN	7500	528L	SWH	77072
WINTER GRAPE LN	1800	297V	NEH	77345
WINTER GREEN CT	1000	569T	MC	77459
WINTERGREEN DR	3600	376G	NEC	77396
WINTERGREEN DR	24400	245R	SWM	77355
WINTERGREEN DR	28800	283Q	NWC	77484
WINTERGROVE CT	6700	457Q	NEC	77049
WINTER HARVEST CT	13900	578X	SEH	77059
WINTER HAVEN DR	3600	502G	BT	77521
WINTER HAVEN DR	6000	535S	SEH	77087
WINTERHAVEN DR	15300	329S	NWC	77377
WINTERHAVEN LN	0	613X	NEB	77584
WINTER HEDGE CT	0	527S	NEF	77469
WINTER KNOLL WAY	1800	618F	SEH	77062
WINTER LAKES	2800	609E	MC	77459
WINTERMOUNTAIN LN	6500	290U	NWC	77379
WINTER OAK	0	614U	PL	77584
WINTER OAKS DR	400	488H	SWH	77079
WINTER PARK	11800	371L	NWC	77067
WINTER PARK CT	2700	371L	NWC	77067
WINTERPARK FOREST LN	0	328A	NWC	77429
WINTER PINES CT	700	292K	SP	77373
WINTER ROSE CT	16600	327P	NWC	77429
WINTER ROSE WAY	13800	528E	SWC	77083
WINTER RUN DR	9500	409D	NWC	77064
N. WINTERSAGE LN	6300	370L	NWC	77066
S. WINTERSAGE LN	6301	370L	NWC	77066
WINTER SPRINGS DR	0	612L	PL	77545
WINTER STONE	6400	407U	NWC	77084
N. WINTER SUNRISE CIR	0	249Q	NWC	77375
WINTER SUNRISE CIR	0	249Q	NWC	77375
WINTER THICKET PLACE	100	249R	NWH	77375
WINTER THICKET PLACE	100	249R	NWH	77375
WINTERTON CLIFF CT	0	328A	NWC	77377
WINTERTON TRAIL	0	484N	NEF	77494
WINTERVIEW DR	7500	570Z	SWH	77489
E. WINTER VIOLET CT	0	325M	NWC	77429
W. WINTER VIOLET CT	21600	325M	NWC	77429
WINTER WHEAT PLACE	1	250H	WD	77381
WINTER WIND BLVD	0	368V	NWC	77065
WINTERWOOD DR	5100	657V	LC	77573
WINTERWOOD FOREST DR	0	376A	NEC	77338
WINTERWOOD TRAIL	0	326P	NWC	77433
WINTERWOOD WAY	600	496F	NEH	77013
WINTHORNE LN	12200	370M	NWC	77066
WINTHROP	3700	573L	SEH	77047
WINTHROP	8000	575K	SEH	77075
WINTHROP BEND DR	0	447D	NWC	77084
WINTHROP MANOR WAY	0	326U	NWC	77429
WINTHROP MEADOW WAY	0	484S	NEF	77494
WINTON	100	536X	SH	77587
WINTON	6600	454N	NEH	77093
WINTON	6600	533L	SEH	77021
WINTON WOOD WAY	0	292D	SEM	77386
WINWOOD LN	11900	490J	BH	77024
WINWOOD FALLS LN	0	375Y	NEC	77396
WINWOOD FALLS LN	0	415C	NEC	77396
WIPPRECHT	1400	494G	NEH	77020
WIPPRECHT	2900	454Q	NEH	77026
WIREVINE LN	12800	528L	SWH	77072
WIRFIELD	2400	536Z	PA	77504
WIRKSWORTH DR	3600	371K	NWC	77066
WIRT RD	700	491B	NWH	77024
WIRT RD	1000	451T	NWH	77055
WIRTCREST LN	2100	451P	NWH	77055
WISCONSIN	0	500Y	BT	77520
WISCONSIN	200	659E	LC	77573
WISCONSIN	500	576B	SH	77587
WISCONSIN	3100	540D	BT	77520
WISDOM AVE	300	419V	NEC	77532
WISDOM DR	400	538T	DP	77536
WISDOM WOODS CT	400	486D	SWC	77094
WISDOM WOODS WAY	19200	486D	SWC	77094
WISEMAN RD	0	249U	NWC	77375
WISEMAN RD	300	611G	NEF	77053
WISEWOOD CT	21300	525Z	NEF	77406
WISFORD HORIZON LN	0	484J	NEF	77494
WISHBONE BUSH RD	1	251R	WD	77380
WISHING OAK LANDING	0	294P	SEM	77386
WISHING WELL LN	6200	411T	NWH	77088
WISNER CIR	0	371G	NWC	77014
WISP CT	23700	295F	SEM	77365
WISPER BAY DR	0	486H	SWC	77094
WISP WILLOW WAY	18300	295E	SEM	77365
WISPWIND DR	12600	528M	SWH	77072
WISPY GREEN CT	0	325R	NWC	77433
WISPY WAY	23800	525E	NEF	77494
WISTER CT	6000	452X	NWH	77008
WISTERIA	500	531L	BL	77401
W. WISTERIA CIR	3800	609E	SG	77479
E. WISTERIA CIR	3800	609E	SG	77479
WISTERIA CHASE PLACE	7200	377C	NEC	77346
WISTERIA DALE PATH	0	377A	NEC	77346
WISTERIA ESTATES LN	18200	366D	NWC	77429
WISTERIA HILL ST	16000	332V	NWC	77090
WISTERIA HOLLOW LN	14500	618B	SEH	77062
WISTERIA PARK DR	12700	528H	SWH	77072
WISTERIA RIDGE CT	7500	407M	NWC	77095
WISTERIA RUN CT	14800	617M	SEH	77062
WISTERIA SPRINGS CT	15400	326S	NWC	77433
WISTERIA SPRINGS DR	15200	326S	NWC	77433
WISTERIA TRACE DR	0	253T	SEM	77386
WISTERIA WALK	2700	331D	NWC	77388
WISTERIA WAY	2600	460U	NEC	77562
WISTERWOOD DR	1000	449Z	NWH	77043
WISTFUL DR	7300	525E	NEF	77494
WITCHER	3700	494W	SEH	77003
E. WITCHER LN	100	452D	NWH	77076
WITCHER LN	200	453A	NEH	77076
WITHAM CT	8800	408A	NWC	77095
WITHAM PARK LN	0	611W	FS	77545
WITHERING ELM LN	0	293G	SEM	77386
WITHERS DR	0	293G	SEM	77386
WITHERSDALE DR	14100	488J	SWH	77077
WITHERSPOON DR	0	524J	NWF	77406
WITHERS RIDGE DR	0	527P	NEF	77407
W. WITHERS WAY CIR	9600	409A	NWC	77065
E. WITHERS WAY CIR	11500	409A	NWC	77065
WITHINGTON DR	20400	486B	SWC	77450
WITNEY WAY	0	611S	FS	77545
WITT RD	10900	576L	SEH	77034
WITTE RD	1000	490A	NWH	77055
WITTE RD	1400	450W	NWH	77080
N. WITTER	100	536D	PA	77506
WITTER	100	536H	PA	77506
N. WITTER	1100	496Z	SEH	77506
WITTERSHAW DR	300	372B	NWC	77090
WITTMAN CT	2200	485R	SWC	77450
WITTMAN LN	21500	486N	SWC	77450
WITTMAN LN	21600	485R	SWC	77450
WIXFORD LN	0	289Q	NWC	77375
WOBURN DR	12500	328R	NWC	77377
WODDED CANYON DR	0	484S	NEF	77494
WOERNER RD	200	331L	NWC	77090
WOJO	600	612T	NWB	77584
WOLBROOK	10300	414Z	NEH	77016
WOLCEK RD	2600	420Q	NEC	77532
WOLCEK RD	4100	421N	NEC	77532
WOLCOTT LN	0	657Y	LC	77573
WOLCOTT GREEN	0	376R	NEC	77346
WOLCOTT PARK LN	9000	575V	SEH	77075
WOLF CT	400	490J	BH	77024
WOLF CT	3300	613X	NEB	77584
WOLF RD	100	299Y	NEC	77336
WOLFBORO DR	6000	408Z	NWC	77041
WOLF BRANCH CT	0	327U	NWC	77429
W. WOLF CABIN CIR	0	250N	NWC	77389
E. WOLF CABIN CIR	0	250N	NWC	77389
WOLF CREEK CT	0	444T	KT	77493
WOLF CREEK CT	12700	337X	NEC	77346
WOLF CREEK FALLS CT	0	330P	NWC	77379
WOLF CREEK PASS	2500	371L	NWC	77067
WOLF CREEK TRAIL	18400	337X	NEC	77346
WOLF DEN	1400	252H	SEM	77385
WOLFE	100	496S	GP	77547
WOLFE RD	9800	410A	NWC	77064
WOLFE ISLAND RD	0	340P	NEC	77336
WOLF HOLLOW DR	17500	407P	NWC	77084
WOLFHOUND LN	1	251V	WD	77380
WOLFIELD LN	7800	570C	SWH	77071
WOLF PASS DR	0	326K	NWC	77433
WOLF PUP LN	21400	378C	NEH	77532
WOLF RIDGE LN	0	329V	NWC	77070
WOLF ROCK DR	5300	446B	NWC	77449
WOLF ROSE LN	0	253P	SEM	77386
WOLF RUN DR	0	444T	KT	77493
WOLF RUN LN	11500	368Q	NWC	77065
WOLFS CROSSING CT	23200	292G	NCC	77373
WOLFS KNOLL	1100	486H	SWC	77094
WOLFS MEADOW LN	22500	485Y	NEF	77494
WOLF SPRINGS CT	0	609P	MC	77459
WOLHEB WAY	0	616L	SEC	77089
WOLLASTON CT	0	250E	WD	77381
WOLLY BUCKET PLACE	1	251V	WD	77380
WOLSLEY CT	10700	368Y	NWC	77065
WOLVERHAMPTON WAY	4600	569X	MC	77459
WOLVERTON DR	16400	330L	NWC	77379
WOMACK LN	4800	380R	NEC	77532
WONARD DR	0	615T	PL	77581
WONDER CROSSING	0	293G	SEM	77386
WONDERING FOREST LN	12600	328Q	NWC	77377
WONDER LAND WAY	18700	447J	NWC	77084
WONDERMERE	9000	535Z	SEH	77017
WONDERWOOD DR	0	329R	NWC	77379
WOOD	900	493M	NEH	77002
WOOD	3000	612S	FS	77545
WOOD AVE	100	500N	BT	77520
WOOD BLVD	100	568K	SG	77498
N. WOOD DR	1800	458V	CV	77530
WOOD DR	15800	458U	CV	77530
WOOD LN	11700	490F	BH	77024
WOODACRE DR	16900	418X	NEC	77049
WOODALL LN	100	543U	BC	77520
WOOD ARBOR CT	4100	376H	NEC	77396
WOODARD	200	453U	NEH	77009
WOODARD	2400	453V	NEH	77026
WOODBANK CT	4100	619G	TL	77586
WOODBANK DR	1000	619G	TL	77586
WOOD BARK CIR	8000	330K	NWC	77379
WOODBARK RD	17000	330E	NWC	77379
WOOD BAYOU DR	12100	496C	NEH	77013
WOODBEND DR	0	657T	LC	77573
WOODBEND DR	2600	613S	NEB	77584
WOOD BEND DR	5600	457S	NEC	77049
WOODBEND LN	500	489E	SWH	77079
WOODBEND CREEK DR	1800	451S	NWH	77055
WOODBEND LAKE DR	1800	451S	NWH	77055
WOODBEND OAKS DR	16100	329U	NWC	77388
WOODBEND PARK N	0	451Y	NWH	77055
WOODBEND PARK S	0	451Y	NWH	77055
WOODBEND PARK W	0	451Y	NWH	77055
WOODBEND PINES DR	16100	329T	NWC	77388
WOODBEND TRAIL DR	16100	329T	NWC	77388
WOODBEND VILLA DR	1800	451S	NWH	77055
WOODBEND VILLAGE CT	8101	451S	NWH	77055
WOODBERRY MANOR DR	19700	289Y	NWC	77379
WOODBINE	600	536N	SEH	77017
WOODBINE CT	28600	246E	SWM	77355
WOODBINE LN	23000	285X	NWC	77447
WOODBINE MEADOWS	23000	285X	NWC	77447
WOODBINE PLACE	3400	613Q	NEB	77584
WOOD BLUFF BLVD	7000	410U	NWC	77040
WOODBLUFF BLVD	7000	410Q	NWC	77040
WOODBLUFF CT	7400	410Q	NWC	77040
WOODBOROUGH WAY	0	250P	NWC	77389
WOODBOUGH DR	2300	371Z	NWC	77038
WOODBOURNE DR	15700	618G	SEH	77062
WOODBOURNE FOREST DR	0	377J	NEC	77346
WOODBRANCH LN	900	339A	NEC	77336
WOOD BRANCH PARK DR	1000	488D	NWH	77079
WOOD BRANCH PARK DR	1200	448Z	NWH	77079
WOODBREEZE DR	18600	337Y	NEC	77346
WOODBRIAR DR	3300	331N	NWC	77068
WOODBRIDGE AVE	1000	613F	NEB	77584
WOOD BRIDGE CIR	800	568K	SG	77498
WOODBRIDGE DR	3600	297S	NEH	77339
WOODBRIDGE LN	0	536H	PA	77506
WOODBRIDGE VILLAGES DR	0	568A	NEF	77498
WOOD BROOK	0	568Z	SG	77478
WOODBROOK LN	3300	569W	SG	77478
WOODBROOK LN	6000	452X	NWH	77008
WOODBROOK WAY	0	531C	SWH	77081
WOODBUCK TRAIL	11600	496B	NEH	77013
WOODBURN DR	16900	418X	NEC	77049
WOODBURY	1900	533E	SWH	77030
WOODBURY	2400	613U	NEB	77584
WOODBURY	1900	533E	SWH	77030
WOODBURY CT	1	245D	SWM	77355
WOODBURY MILL DR	4800	291J	NWC	77389
WOODBURY SPRINGS LN	6400	330H	NWC	77379
WOODCAMP DR	8500	411R	NWH	77088
WOOD CANYON DR	7100	410U	NWC	77040
WOODCASTLE BEND	500	486H	SWC	77094
WOODCHASE DR	1100	616X	PL	77581
WOODCHASE DR	3300	490W	SWH	77042
WOODCHASE DR	3800	530A	SWH	77042
WOODCHESTER DR	13400	568F	SG	77498
WOODCHUCK LN	1	251V	WD	77380
WOODCHURCH LN	900	332L	NCC	77073
WOOD CIRCLE LN	200	456Z	NEC	77015
WOODCLIFF DR	12100	496C	NEH	77013
WOODCLIFF LAKE DR	9500	329G	NWC	77379
WOODCLUSTER LN	20600	333T	NCC	77073
WOODCOCK	0	660F	LC	77573
WOODCOMBE DR	100	618J	SEH	77062
WOODCOTE CT	15400	618J	SEH	77062
WOODCOURT	11700	413U	NEH	77076
WOOD COVE DR	1	251F	WD	77381
WOODCRAFT	4000	532W	SWH	77025
WOOD CREEK CT	1	536T	SEH	77017
WOOD CREEK DR	2500	616S	PL	77581
WOOD CREEK LN	0	657T	LC	77573
WOODCREEK LN	2800	333P	NCC	77073
WOODCREEK BEND LN	0	484F	NEF	77494
WOODCREEK BEND LN	0	484K	NEF	77494
WOODCREEK BEND LN	0	484K	NEF	77494
WOODCREEK COVE LN	0	484A	KT	77494
WOODCREEK GLEN LN	3100	333P	NCC	77073
WOODCREEK MEADOWS LN	2800	333P	NCC	77073
WOODCREEK NORTH DR	0	333K	NCC	77073
WOOD CREEK WAY	5500	536T	SEH	77017
WOODCREST	0	451R	NWH	77092
WOOD CREST DR	100	659D	LC	77573
WOODCREST DR	800	452G	NWH	77018
WOODCREST DR	800	616V	FR	77546
WOODCREST DR	1200	452J	NWH	77018
WOODCREST DR	1700	538N	DP	77536
WOODCREST DR	3400	501P	BT	77521
WOODCREST LN	4800	291J	NWC	77389
WOODCROFT CT	7600	408J	NWC	77095
WOODCROFT DR	15700	408J	NWC	77095
WOODCROFT DR	20800	252K	SEM	77385
WOODCYPRESS LN	14900	326Z	NWC	77429
WOOD DALE DR	3700	297T	NEH	77345
WOOD DAWN LN	12600	456Z	NEC	77015
WOODDOVE CIR	11200	616C	SEC	77089
WOOD DOWNE LN	8100	410U	NWC	77040
WOOD DRAKE CT	0	250E	NWC	77375
WOOD DRAKE PLACE	0	250E	NWC	77375
WOOD DRIFT LN	8600	578D	LP	77571
WOOD DUCK CT	5000	609K	MC	77459
WOOD DUCK LN	4400	503D	CCO	77520
WOOD DUCK PARK	7900	375Q	NEC	77396
WOODED ACRES DR	1600	376E	HM	77396
WOODED BEND DR	0	293D	SEM	77386
WOODED CREEK LN	0	366R	NWC	77433
WOODED FIELD TRAIL	15200	328J	NWC	77429
WOODEDGE DR	9800	369P	NWC	77070
WOODEDGE DR	11000	369P	NWC	77065
WOODEDGE PARK	0	369Q	NWC	77070
WOODED GLEN CT	14800	327W	NWC	77429
WOODED GLEN LN	0	253Q	SEM	77386
WOODED HOLLOW CT	0	484F	NEF	77494
WOODED HOLLOW LN	0	484F	NEF	77494
WOODED LAKE CT	21300	525H	NEF	77407
WOODED LAKE LN	21100	525H	NEF	77407
WOODED MIST DR	0	293H	SEM	77386
WOODED OAKS DR	2000	376E	HM	77396
WOODED OVERLOOK DR	100	249R	NWH	77375
WOODED OVERLOOK DR	100	249R	NWH	77375
WOODED PINE LN	1600	333N	NCC	77073
WOODED TERRACE LN	8100	335J	NCC	77338
WOODED TRACE CT	0	446D	NWC	77449
WOODED TREE LN		328P	NWC	77429
WOODED VALLEY DR	7300	408N	NWC	77095
WOODED VILLAS DR	5600	337D	NEH	77345
WOODED WALK LN	0	370E	NWH	77070
WOODED WAY DR	7800	250W	NWC	77389
WOODED WAY DR	8000	250S	NWC	77389
WOODELVES PLACE	1	250D	WD	77381
WOODEN OAK CT	15500	618C	SEH	77059
WOODFAIR DR	9200	529V	SWH	77036
WOODFALL CT	0	372A	NWC	77014
WOOD FALL CT	1200	372F	NWC	77014
WOODFALLS LN	0	527S	NEF	77469
WOOD FERN CT	0	252G	SEM	77385
WOODFERN DR	6900	411S	NWH	77040
WOODFERN GLEN LN (106BB)	800	613G	NEB	77584
WOODFIELD LN	900	332H	NCC	77073
WOODFIN	0	612W	FS	77583
WOODFIN	4000	532W	SWH	77025
WOODFORD	0	295Z	NEH	77365
WOODFORD	4700	461N	NEC	77521
WOODFORD DR	14700	497H	NEC	77015
WOODFORD DR	14900	497H	NEC	77530
WOODFORD GREEN DR	2000	336C	NEH	77339
WOODFORD HOLLOW CT	15300	327V	NWC	77429
WOODFORD PLACE DR	0	295Z	NEH	77365
WOODFOREST BLVD	0	288K	TB	77377
WOODFOREST BLVD	9200	495D	NEH	77013
WOODFOREST BLVD	11500	496B	NEH	77013
WOODFOREST BLVD	12600	457W	NEC	77015
WOODFOREST BLVD	13000	497B	NEC	77015
WOODFOREST BLVD	14800	498A	CV	77530
WOODFOREST CT	400	497B	NEC	77015
WOOD FOREST DR	0	657U	LC	77573
N. WOODFOREST DR	1	457S	NEC	77015
WOODFOX	4000	532W	SWH	77025
WOOD GARDENS CT	3800	296V	NEH	77339
WOODGATE	2400	414A	NCC	77039

Street Name	Block	Pg/Sq	Loc	Zips
WOODGATE DR	0	371Z	NWC	77038
WOODGATE LN	0	484E	KT	77494
WOODGLEN CT	1900	614E	NEB	77581
WOODGLEN DR	2200	610E	MC	77489
WOODGLEN DR	19100	446R	NWC	77449
WOODGLEN DR	25800	252P	SEM	77386
WOODGLEN LN	0	484F	KT	77494
WOOD GLEN LN	18500	447J	NWC	77084
WOODGLEN POINT CT	5900	290Z	NWC	77379
WOODGLEN SHADOWS DR	18500	337X	NEC	77346
WOODGREEN	5600	574A	SEH	77033
WOOD GROVE CT	8100	410U	NWC	77040
WOODGUM DR	18000	331F	NWC	77388
WOODHALL CT	2800	659H	LC	77573
WOODHALL CT	19600	335N	NCC	77338
WOODHALL LN	20000	335N	NCC	77338
WOODHAM DR	14800	372C	NCC	77073
WOODHAM DR	15000	332Y	NCC	77073
WOODHAMPTON DR	4100	578E	PA	77505
WOODHAVEN	100	619H	TL	77586
WOODHAVEN	200	459Q	HG	77562
WOODHAVEN	4000	532W	SWH	77025
WOODHAVEN	6400	614T	PL	77584
WOODHAVEN CT	0	484E	KT	77494
WOODHAVEN WOOD CT	1	252J	WD	77380
WOODHAVEN WOOD DR	1	252J	WD	77380
WOODHEAD	1300	492Z	SWH	77019
WOODHEAD	2600	492Z	SWH	77098
WOOD HEATHER LN	7100	410U	NWC	77040
WOODHILL RD	1100	452Y	NWH	77008
WOODHOLLOW	3900	577F	PA	77504
WOOD HOLLOW DR	0	462V	BT	77521
WOOD HOLLOW DR	0	462V	BT	77521
WOOD HOLLOW DR	100	659D	LC	77573
WOOD HOLLOW DR	1200	490R	SWH	77057
WOODHOLLOW DR	17700	255N	SEM	77365
WOOD HOLLOW DR	19000	255X	SEM	77365
WOOD HOLLOW LN	11800	449L	NWH	77043
WOODHOME	1	490R	SWH	77063
WOODHORN CT	700	618J	SEH	77062
WOODHORN DR	1000	618J	SEH	77062
WOODHORN DR	14900	618J	SEH	77062
WOODHOUSE DR	9100	330N	NWC	77379
WOODHUE CIR	30500	252U	SEM	77386
WOODHUE CT	30500	252U	SEM	77386
WOODHUE DR	700	498B	CV	77530
WOODHUE DR	1600	252V	SEM	77386
WOODHURST	500	496C	NEH	77013
WOODICO CT	10000	412B	NWC	77038
WOODING	800	494V	SEH	77011
WOODINGTON DR	13100	371Z	NWC	77038
WOODKERR	3000	572F	SWH	77045
WOODKNOLL LN	11300	570C	SWH	77071
WOODKNOT DR	11100	616C	SEH	77089
WOODLACE DR	3600	376G	NEC	77396
WOODLAKE	12400	247M	SWM	77362
WOODLAKE CIR	600	568K	SG	77498
WOODLAKE DR	400	338V	NEC	77336
WOODLAKE LN	2200	336G	NEH	77339
WOODLAKE LN	4100	610J	MC	77459
WOODLAKE RD	400	338V	NEH	77336
WOODLAKE SQ LN	0	490N	SWH	77063
WOODLAND	0	620J	EL	77586
WOODLAND	100	619M	EL	77586
WOODLAND	300	493B	NWH	77009
WOODLAND CT	0	615K	PL	77581
WOODLAND CT	3100	580P	LP	77571
WOODLAND DR	400	498D	CV	77530
WOODLAND DR	22800	296G	SEM	77365
WOODLAND BEND WAY DR	0	294A	SEM	77386
WOODLAND BROOK DR	5700	337D	NEH	77345
WOODLAND CREEK DR	5600	297Z	NEH	77345
WOODLAND CREEK LN	17200	367T	NWC	77095
WOODLAND CREST DR	24900	338H	NEH	77336
WOODLAND DRAWN TRAIL	0	376X	NEC	77396
WOODLAND FALLS DR	5800	338A	NEH	77345
WOODLAND FOREST DR	6200	411P	NWC	77088
WOODLAND GARDENS DR	2600	297X	NEH	77345
WOODLAND GLADE DR	5500	370R	NWC	77066
WOODLAND GLEN LN	0	253J	SEM	77385
WOODLAND GREEN DR	21100	446C	NWC	77449
WOODLAND GROVE DR	2700	336C	NEH	77339
WOODLAND HAVEN RD	2000	618G	SEH	77062
WOODLAND HEIGHTS LN	21900	334F	NCC	77373
WOODLAND HILLS DR	0	376V	NEC	77396
WOODLAND HILLS DR	900	336G	NEH	77339
WOODLAND HILLS DR	1900	570W	MC	77489
WOODLAND HILLS DR	2800	296R	NEH	77339
WOODLAND HILLS DR	4200	296R	SEM	77365
WOODLAND HILLS DR	16600	376H	NEC	77346
WOODLAND HILLS DR	18500	336Z	NEC	77338
WOODLAND HILLS LN	0	296Y	SEM	77339
WOODLAND KNOLL LN	8400	407E	NWC	77433
WOODLAND LAKES DR	600	338H	NEH	77336
WOODLAND LEAF LN	0	329B	NWC	77375
WOODLAND MEADOW DR	0	293D	SEM	77386
WOODLAND MEADOWS LN	0	336Z	NEC	77346
WOODLAND OAKS CT	7900	410M	NWC	77040
WOODLAND OAKS DR	9100	410V	NWC	77040
WOODLAND OAKS DR	10600	410M	NWC	77040
WOODLAND OAK TRAIL	7200	337Q	NEC	77346
WOODLAND ORCHARD LN	15200	326S	NWC	77433
WOODLAND PARK DR	0	616V	FR	77546
WOODLAND PARK DR	1700	489T	SWH	77077
WOODLAND PARK DR	2900	489T	SWH	77082
WOODLAND PATH DR	0	376M	NEC	77346
WOODLAND PINE DR	7900	410L	NWC	77040
WOODLAND PLAZA DR	4600	447B	NWC	77084
WOODLAND RIDGE DR	2600	297X	NEH	77345
WOODLANDS	0	538V	DP	77536
WOODLAND SHORE DR	11500	329A	NWC	77375
WOODLANDS PKWY	100	252J	WD	77380
WOODLANDS PKWY	900	251K	WD	77380
WOODLANDS PKWY	3000	252J	WD	77381
WOODLANDS PKWY	4700	250H	WD	77381
WOODLAND SPRINGS DR	1700	489T	SWH	77077
WOODLAND TRAIL DR	0	616V	FR	77546
WOODLAND TRAIL DR	6400	411S	NWH	77088
WOODLAND TRAIL DR	7100	411S	NWH	77040
WOODLAND VALLEY DR	2000	336G	NEH	77339
WOODLAND VIEW DR	3000	297Y	NEH	77345
WOODLAND VIOLET LN	0	526N	NEF	77407
WOODLAND VISTA DR	1700	336G	NEH	77339
WOODLAND WAY	0	616U	FR	77546
WOODLAND WEST DR	7000	410U	NWC	77040
WOODLAND WILLOWS DR	8200	527R	NEF	77083
WOODLARK	5300	536N	SEH	77017
WOODLAWN	100	656D	FR	77546
WOODLAWN	900	459W	CV	77530
WOODLAWN	900	501Z	BT	77520
WOODLAWN	1400	502W	BT	77520
WOODLAWN DR	3800	577B	PA	77504

Street Name	Block	Pg/Sq	Loc	Zips
WOODLAWN CEMETERY	0	491B	NWH	77055
WOODLAWN MANOR CT	15300	367H	NWC	77429
WOODLAWN PLACE	5200	531G	SWH	77401
WOOD LEAF CT	0	462V	BT	77521
WOOD LEAF CT	0	462V	BT	77521
WOOD LEAF CT	12100	496C	NEH	77013
WOODLEAF LAKE LOOP	0	405T	NWC	77493
WOODLEAR	0	368Q	NWC	77065
WOODLEAR LN	11400	368U	NWC	77065
WOODLEIGH	3800	494S	SEH	77023
WOODLEIGH	17800	499C	CV	77530
WOODLEIGH DR	8700	528N	NEF	77083
WOODLEIGH SPRINGS LN	0	484X	NEF	77494
WOODLEIGH SPRINGS LN	0	484X	NEF	77494
WOODLETT CT	7700	407M	NWC	77095
WOODLINE DR	300	252X	SEM	77386
WOODLINE DR	14300	457Y	NEC	77015
WOODLINK CT	0	299T	NEC	77336
WOODLITE LN	12800	457W	NEC	77015
WOODLOCH CT	0	251H	WD	77380
WOODLOCH FOREST DR	1400	251H	WD	77380
WOODLOCK DR	1100	537N	PA	77506
WOODLODE LN	17600	331J	NWC	77379
WOOD LODGE DR	1500	489P	SWH	77077
WOOD LONG DR	7200	411T	NWH	77088
WOOD LOOP	200	456Z	NEC	77015
WOODLOT CT	1	252J	WD	77380
WOODLYN RD	7800	455F	NEH	77028
WOODLYN RD	8800	455H	NEH	77078
WOODMANCOTE DR	5400	337X	NEC	77346
WOODMAPLE CT	14600	457Y	NEC	77015
WOODMARK LN	0	446E	NWC	77449
WOODMEADOW	9300	532P	SWH	77025
WOODMERE LN	3400	569W	SG	77478
WOODMILL PLACE	14800	527D	SWC	77082
WOODMILL TERRACE LN	0	253P	SEM	77386
WOODMILL TERRACE LN	0	253Q	SEM	77386
WOOD MIST DR	500	496B	NEH	77013
WOODMONT DR	3100	572K	SWH	77045
WOODMONT DR	4500	571M	SWH	77045
WOODMOOR PLACE	0	249A	SWM	77354
WOODMOSS CT	22000	255S	SEM	77365
WOODMOSS DR	10400	413K	NCC	77037
WOODNETTLE CT	9600	370Z	NWC	77086
WOODNETTLE LN	7400	371W	NWC	77086
WOODNETTLE LN	7700	370Z	NWC	77086
WOODNOOK DR	14000	488J	SWH	77077
WOOD NYMPH DR	24900	338M	NEH	77336
WOODOAK CT	2400	613Q	NEB	77584
WOODOAK CT	21600	486J	SWC	77450
WOODOAK DR	7300	410Q	NWC	77040
WOOD ORCHARD CT	1100	570X	MC	77489
WOOD ORCHARD DR	1800	570X	MC	77489
WOOD ORCHARD DR	7000	410U	NWC	77040
WOOD PARK	600	619L	TL	77586
WOODPATH LN	0	575U	SEH	77075
WOODPECKER	4800	571C	SWH	77035
WOODPECKER BEND	7400	375K	HM	77396
WOODPILE DR	0	257P	SEM	77357
WOODPINE DR	3700	447J	NWC	77084
WOOD PLACE CT	0	290Y	NWC	77379
WOODPOINT DR	0	295Z	NEH	77365
WOODPORT LN	700	332N	NWC	77090
WOODRAIL DR	400	618S	SEH	77598
WOOD RAIN CT	20600	446K	NWC	77449
WOODREN CT	3000	659H	LC	77573
WOODRIDGE	2800	534M	SEH	77087
WOODRIDGE	7200	535J	SEH	77012
WOODRIDGE DR	18700	254C	SEM	77302
WOODRIDGE PKWY	0	296U	NEH	77365
WOODRIDGE COVE DR	0	535J	SEH	77012
WOODRIDGE MANOR DR	0	535J	SEH	77012
WOODRIDGE PLACE	7500	451X	NWH	77055
WOODRIDGE ROW DR	0	535J	SEH	77012
WOODRIDGE SQUARE DR	0	535J	SEH	77012
WOODRING DR	13300	572K	SWH	77045
WOOD RIVER DR	2000	333B	NCC	77373
WOOD RIVER DR	6900	571J	SWH	77085
WOODROSE DR	22100	485D	SWC	77450
WOODROW	600	493W	SWH	77006
WOODROW	16400	498H	CV	77530
WOODRUFF	8100	535G	SEH	77012
WOODRUFF LN	13600	328W	NWC	77429
WOODRUSH DR	4000	251E	WD	77381
WOODS CT	0	616K	PL	77581
S. WOODS LN	0	484B	KT	77494
N. WOODS LN	0	484B	KT	77494
WOODS LN	500	484B	KT	77494
WOODS ACRE DR	0	296T	SEM	77365
WOODSAGE DR	11600	490B	HE	77024
WOODSBORO CT	20200	291Z	NWC	77388
WOODSBORO DR	2400	292W	NWC	77388
WOODSBORO DR	2700	291Z	NWC	77388
WOODSBOROUGH CIR	1	490D	SV	77055
WOODSBOROUGH DR	1	490D	SV	77055
WOODS BRIDGE WAY	6200	492K	SWH	77007
WOODSBURGH LN	17800	407F	NWC	77433
WOODS CANYON CT	3200	610U	MC	77459
WOODSCAPE	0	530T	SWH	77074
WOOD SCENT CT	1	251Z	WD	77380
WOODSDALE BLVD	2300	371Z	NWC	77038
WOODSDALE CT	13100	371Z	NWC	77038
WOODSDALE CT	18100	255S	SEM	77365
WOODS EDGE DR	3300	331C	NWC	77388
WOODS EDGE LN	1	490R	PP	77024
WOODSEEM CT	0	445M	NWC	77449
WOODSEND LN	0	297U	NEH	77345
WOODS ESTATES DR	1800	337A	NEH	77339
WOODSHADOW DR	11000	496F	NEH	77013
WOOD SHADOWS DR	1900	610F	MC	77489
WOODSHAVER DR	11600	496B	NEH	77013
WOODSHIRE	4000	532W	SWH	77025
WOODSIDE	4400	494T	SEH	77023
WOODSIDE	17500	499B	CV	77530
WOODSIDE DR	1	541D	BT	77520
WOODSIDE DR	2100	618G	SEH	77062
WOODSIDE LN	13300	368B	NWC	77429
WOODSIDE CROSSING LN	0	375X	NEC	77396
WOODSIDE ESTATES	2000	252R	SEM	77385
WOODSIDE GREEN DR	0	368B	NWC	77429
WOODSLAND PARK LN	0	484B	KT	77494
WOODSMAN TRAIL	7000	411N	NWH	77040
WOODSMAN TRAIL	7400	410R	NWC	77040
WOODSMITH CT	1800	570Y	MC	77489
WOOD SMOKE DR	500	496B	NEH	77013
WOODSON RD	100	412D	NEH	77060
WOODSON RD	200	413A	NEH	77060
WOODSON RD	4400	252E	OR	77385
WOODSONG CT	20400	337R	NEC	77346
WOODSONG DR	8100	250S	NWC	77389
WOODSONG TRAIL	0	246C	SWM	77355
WOODSON LAKE DR	28300	293C	SEM	77386

Street Name	Block	Pg/Sq	Loc	Zips
WOODSON PARK DR	0	376Z	NEC	77044
WOODSON PARK DR	12500	377W	NEC	77044
WOODSONS DR	0	253Y	SEM	77386
WOODSONS BEND DR	0	253Y	SEM	77386
WOODSONS EDGE WAY	0	253T	SEM	77386
WOODSONS RESERVE PKWY	0	253Y	SEM	77386
WOODSONS RESERVE PKWY	0	294E	SEM	77386
WOODSONS SHORE DR	0	253Y	SEM	77386
WOODSON TERRACE DR	0	406C	NWC	77433
WOODSON TRACE DR	0	253T	SEM	77386
WOODSON VALLEY CT	7400	415S	NEH	77016
WOODSON VALLEY DR	10700	415S	NEH	77016
WOODSORREL DR	2600	446V	NWC	77084
WOOD SORREL DR	3700	660X	DI	77539
WOODSPIRE DR	13600	571J	SWH	77085
WOOD SPRING LN	12100	496C	NEH	77013
WOODSPRING ACRES CT	0	297U	NEH	77345
WOODSPRING ACRES DR	0	297Q	NEH	77345
WOODSPRING FOREST DR	0	297Q	NEH	77345
WOODSPRING GLEN LN	0	297U	NEH	77345
WOODSTEAD CT	1400	251M	WD	77380
WOODSTOCK DR	800	531K	BL	77401
W. WOODSTOCK CIRCLE DR	1	251E	WD	77381
S. WOODSTOCK CIRCLE DR	1	251E	WD	77381
N. WOODSTOCK CIRCLE DR	1	251E	WD	77381
E. WOODSTOCK CIRCLE DR	1	251E	WD	77381
WOODSTONE	1	490N	SWH	77024
WOODSTONE DR	3000	501E	BT	77521
WOODSTONE DR	3100	500M	BT	77521
WOODSTONE WALK	3700	447J	NWC	77084
WOOD STORK LN	12900	377W	NEC	77044
WOODSTREAM CIR	300	657J	FR	77546
WOODSTREAM DR	2000	336G	NEH	77339
WOODSTREAM VILLAGE DR	4800	297Q	NEH	77345
S. WOODSTREAM WAY	3200	297P	NEH	77345
N. WOODSTREAM WAY	3200	297P	NEH	77345
WOOD SWALLOW WAY	0	328A	NWC	77429
WOOD SWALLOW WAY	0	328A	NWC	77377
WOOD TERRACE DR	13400	371V	NWC	77038
WOOD THORN CT	0	375X	NEC	77396
WOODTHORPE LN	12300	490E	SWH	77024
WOODTHORPE LN	13800	489E	SWH	77079
WOODTHORPE LN	14900	488G	SWH	77079
WOODTHRUSH	0	615C	PL	77581
WOODTIDE RD	17100	376H	NEC	77396
W. WOODTIMBER CT	1	251J	WD	77381
E. WOODTIMBER CT	1	251J	WD	77381
WOOD TOWER CT	0	253N	SEM	77386
WOODTOWN DR	2400	371Z	NWC	77038
WOODTRACE BLVD	0	247L	SWM	77362
WOODTRACE CIR	0	247G	SWM	77362
WOOD TRAIL	0	337R	HM	77346
WOOD TRAIL DR	13100	371Z	NWC	77038
WOOD TRAILS CT	1900	610B	MC	77489
WOOD TREK LN	13000	497A	NEC	77015
WOODTREK LN	13000	457W	NEC	77015
WOODVALE	100	495W	SEH	77012
WOODVALE DR	200	657Q	LC	77573
WOODVALE DR	2500	337C	NEH	77345
WOODVALE LN	1700	570S	MC	77489
WOODVALLEY DR	3500	532S	SWH	77025
WOODVALLEY DR	4300	531V	SWH	77096
WOODVIEW DR	600	616V	FR	77546
WOODVIEW DR	5800	374M	NEH	77396
WOODVIEW DR	5800	375J	NEH	77396
WOOD VILLAGE LN	19300	446V	NWC	77084
WOODVILLE LN	5000	614R	PL	77584
WOODVILLE LN	5200	331E	NWC	77379
WOODVILLE GARDENS DR	14100	488J	SWH	77077
WOODVINE	1300	657A	FR	77546
WOODVINE DR	400	620J	EL	77586
WOODVINE DR	1300	451T	NWH	77055
WOODVINE PLACE CT	7500	451X	NWH	77055
WOODVINE PLACE CT	7500	451X	NWH	77055
WOODVINE RIDGE DR	0	524L	NWF	77406
WOODVINE TRAIL	13100	528L	SWH	77072
WOODVIOLET DR	11300	616C	SEC	77089
WOOD VISTA DR	500	496C	NEH	77013
WOOD WALK LN	19600	337U	NEC	77346
WOODWARD	7900	533T	SEH	77051
WOODWARD GARDENS DR	14700	527D	SWC	77082
WOOD WAY	0	251Q	WD	77380
WOODWAY	0	490U	SWH	77063
WOODWAY	3400	501P	BT	77521
WOODWAY	20900	256R	SEM	77357
WOODWAY CT	200	252N	SEM	77386
WOODWAY DR	0	657U	LC	77573
WOODWAY DR	4500	491H	SWH	77024
WOODWAY DR	4800	491H	SWH	77056
WOODWAY DR	5700	491K	SWH	77057
WOODWAY DR	7500	490R	SWH	77063
WOODWAY DR	25300	257C	WV	77357
WOODWAY OAKS LN	1	491L	SWH	77056
WOODWAY PLACE CT	5900	491K	SWH	77057
WOODWICK	7600	455E	NEH	77028
WOODWICK	9800	415W	NEH	77016
WOODWILD DR	2400	371Z	NWC	77038
WOODWIND	2200	659B	LC	77573
WOODWIND BLVD	0	410J	NWC	77040
WOODWIND DR	9700	532S	SWH	77025
S. WOODWIND LN	0	532S	SWH	77025
N. WOODWIND LN	0	532S	SWH	77025
WOODWIND LN	0	532S	SWH	77025
WOOD WIND DOVE DR	0	327H	NWC	77429
WOODWIND LAKES DR	9100	410K	NWC	77040
WOODWIND SHADOWS DR	0	367S	NWC	77433
WOODWOLF CT	14100	457Y	NEC	77015
WOODWORTH DR	11800	367L	CY	77429
WOODY LN	10600	414S	NEH	77093
WOODY RD	1500	614M	PL	77581
WOODY RD	12300	614D	BK	77581
WOODYARD DR	1200	332Z	NCC	77073
WOODYARD RD	8000	334V	NEC	77338
WOODY CREEK LN	0	488E	SWH	77077
WOODY GUTHRIE DR	0	538V	DP	77536
WOODY HOLLOW DR	12200	328D	NWC	77375
WOODY OAKS DR	0	368W	NWC	77095
WOOLF RD	7800	330A	NWC	77379
WOOLF RD	8000	329D	NWC	77379
WOOLFORD DR	11900	368V	NWC	77065
WOOLONGOING DR	19400	406V	NWC	77449
WOOLSEY CT	9400	375R	NEC	77396
WOOLSEY LN	0	375R	NEC	77396
WOOLWICH DR	1100	373U	NCC	77032
WOOLWORTH	100	494H	NEH	77020
WOOLWORTH	3800	454Y	NEH	77026
WOOSTER	100	500P	BT	77520
WOOTEN RD	1500	613P	NEB	77584
WORCESTER DR	6900	330L	NWC	77379
WORDEN LN	16900	657B	FR	77546
WORDSWORTH	2300	532G	SWH	77030
WORELY DR	0	610Q	MC	77459

Street Name	Block	Pg/Sq	Loc	Zips
WORFIELD CT	9400	527V	NEF	77498
WORGAN CT	16700	330M	NWC	77379
WORLD HOUSTON PKWY	3700	374Q	NEH	77032
WORLD WIDE DR	0	333W	NCC	77073
WORLEY DR	2200	375G	HM	77396
WORMS	1100	494F	NEH	77020
WORNINGTON CT	0	488Q	SWH	77077
WORRELL DR	4100	572E	SWH	77045
WORTHAM BLVD	9400	408D	NWC	77065
WORTHAM BLVD	10000	368Y	NWC	77065
WORTHAM CT	0	368U	NWC	77065
WORTHAM BROOK LN	0	368U	NWC	77065
WORTHAM CENTER DR	0	368Y	NWC	77065
WORTHAM FALLS BLVD	12400	368V	NWC	77065
WORTHAM GATE	11100	368V	NWC	77065
WORTHAM GROVE BLVD	13000	368Y	NWC	77065
WORTHAM GROVE DR	13000	368Y	NWC	77065
WORTHAM LANDING DR	11700	369S	NWC	77065
WORTHAM LANDING DR	12100	368V	NWC	77065
WORTHAM OAKS DR	21100	334M	NCC	77338
WORTHAM RIDGE TRAIL	12500	368Z	NWC	77065
WORTHAM STREAM CT	0	376W	NEC	77396
WORTHAM WAY	6000	534T	SEH	77033
WORTHINGTON	2800	454J	NEH	77093
WORTHINGTON	13000	568C	SG	77478
WORTHINGTON DR	3200	613K	NEB	77584
WORTHINGTON DR	8200	527P	NEF	77083
WORTHSHIRE	700	492C	NWH	77008
WORTLEY DR	0	407Z	NWC	77084
WOVENWOOD LN	7300	408L	NWC	77041
WRANGLER RUN CT	16000	327Y	NWC	77429
WRANGLER SKY CT	0	484S	NEF	77494
WRAY CT	8000	411P	NWH	77088
WREN	1800	658Q	LC	77573
WREN	9800	539T	LP	77571
WREN LN	600	489E	SWH	77079
WREN LN	2200	536U	PA	77502
WREN LN	18700	286H	NWC	77377
WREN RD	21900	256K	SEM	77357
N. WREN ARBOR CIR	0	373E	NCC	77073
WREN BROOK CT	4000	446F	NWC	77449
WREN CREEK CT	0	611S	FS	77545
WRENCREST LN	20600	333P	NCC	77073
WREN CROSSING	0	411H	NWC	77038
WREN CROSSING DR	11600	411H	NWC	77088
WREN DALE LN	18200	377C	NEC	77346
WRENFIELD CT	3900	446L	NWC	77449
WREN FOREST LN	19600	446Q	NWC	77084
WREN HOLLOW WAY	0	334Q	NCC	77388
WREN PARK	7900	375Q	NEC	77396
WREN POND	0	368Z	NWC	77065
WREN SONG DR	0	328E	NWC	77429
WRENSTONE DR	15900	331N	NWC	77068
WRENTHORPE DR	12200	570A	SWH	77031
WREN VALLEY TRAIL	0	445K	NWC	77493
WRENWAY DR	1600	610B	MC	77489
WRENWOOD CIR	9000	528R	SWH	77099
WRENWOOD GREEN	0	449X	NWH	77043
WRENWOOD LAKES	0	449X	NWH	77043
WRENWOOD MAROR	0	449X	NWH	77043
WRENWOOD PARK	0	449X	NWH	77043
WRESSELL CIR	12800	377X	NEC	77044
WRESSELL DR	14500	377X	NEC	77044
WREXHAM SPRINGS CT	25600	292U	NCC	77373
E. WRIGHT	1	501Y	BT	77520
W. WRIGHT	100	501Y	BT	77520
E. WRIGHT	1200	541D	BT	77520
WRIGHT DR	5000	444Z	KT	77493
WRIGHT LN	3900	542T	NEC	77520
WRIGHT RD	3500	374D	NEH	77032
WRIGHT RD	4600	569J	SF	77477
WRIGHT RD	7000	409N	NWC	77041
WRIGHT RD	32400	247R	SWM	77355
WRIGHT OAKS DR	12300	372E	NWC	77014
WRIGHTSBORO DR	14500	328X	NWC	77429
WRIGHTS CROSSING	20000	406U	NWC	77449
WRIGHTS LANDING DR	0	253X	SEM	77386
WRIGHTWOOD	1200	493C	NWH	77009
WRIGLEY	13600	572J	SWH	77045
WRONG WAY RD	7000	404E	NWC	77447
WROTHAM LN	1300	458W	NEC	77530
WROXTON	1700	492Y	SWH	77005
WROXTON CT	1700	532D	SWH	77005
WROXTON RD	1800	492Y	SWH	77005
WUNDER LN	5300	452H	NWH	77091
WUNDER HILL DR	17100	330K	NWC	77379
WUNDERLICH DR	14100	330Z	NWC	77069
WUNSCHE LOOP	800	292P	SP	77373
WUTHERING HEIGHTS DR	2600	572L	SWH	77045
WYANDOTT BLVD	5500	450C	NWH	77040
WYANNGATE DR	4100	293Y	NCC	77373
WYATT	0	538N	PA	77503
WYATT	1100	494X	SEH	77023
WYATT	4200	537R	PA	77503
WYATT OAKS DR	100	249R	NWH	77375
WYATT OAKS DR	100	249R	NWH	77375
WYATT SHORES CT	0	376W	NEC	77396
WYBOURN	0	527V	NEF	77498
WYBOURN CT	0	527V	NEF	77498
WYBOURN WAY	14600	527V	NEF	77083
WYCKCHESTER DR	2400	613R	NEB	77584
WYCLIFFE DR	300	489B	SWH	77079
WYCLIFFE DR	1200	449X	NWH	77043
WYCOMB DR	8100	329Z	NWC	77070
WYCOMB LN	7500	330W	NWC	77070
E. WYE DR	200	501Q	BT	77521
WYETH CIR	17000	330K	NWC	77379
WYLIE	3700	494B	NEH	77026
WYLIE VALLEY LN	0	484T	NEF	77494
WYNBELTS	9000	535Z	SEH	77017
WYNBERRY DR	5700	408Y	NWC	77041
WYNBROOK	8300	535Y	SEH	77061
WYNCHASE DR	1800	538M	DP	77536
WYND AVE	700	537L	PA	77503
WYNDALE	1600	533J	SWH	77030
WYNDALE DR	1800	538M	DP	77536
WYNDEHAVEN LAKES DR	0	485J	NEF	77494
WYNDEMERE LN	1	251U	SWM	77380
S. WYNDEN DR	1	491Q	SWH	77056
N. WYNDEN DR	1	491M	SWH	77056
WYNDEN COMMONS DR	0	491M	SWH	77056
WYNDEN CRESCENT	0	491M	SWH	77024
WYNDEN CRESCENT CT	200	491Q	SWH	77056
WYNDEN ESTATES CT	1	491M	SWH	77056
WYNDEN OAKS CT	1	491R	SWH	77056
WYNDEN OAKS DR	1	491R	SWH	77056
WYNDEN OAKS GARDEN DR	1200	491Q	SWH	77056
WYNDEN PLACE LN	1	491Q	SWH	77056
WYNDEN TRACE LN	100	491Q	SWH	77056
WYNDEN VILLA DR	1100	491Q	SWH	77056
WYNDFIELD CT	0	248V	NWC	77375
WYNDHAM CIR	8300	491A	SV	77024

Street Name	Block	Pg/Sq	Loc	Zips
WYNDHAM CT	8500	409G	JV	77040
WYNDHAM FALLS CT	0	297K	NEH	77365
WYNDHAM HEIGHTS LN	0	488T	SWH	77077
WYNDHAM HILL DR	0	376U	NEC	77396
WYNDHAM LAKE BLVD	0	409F	JV	77064
WYNDHAM PARK DR	8300	491A	SV	77024
WYNDHAM PKWY	0	409F	JV	77040
WYNDHAM TRAIL	0	527R	NEF	77083
WYNDHAM VILLAGE DR	8500	409G	JV	77040
WYNDWOOD DR	100	619H	TL	77586
WYNE	4000	535Q	SEH	77017
WYNELL TERRACE	200	453G	NEH	77022
WYNFIELD DR	800	538M	DP	77536
WYNFIELD DR	14400	368A	NWC	77429
WYNFIELD SPRINGS DR	11000	524L	NWF	77406
WYNFOREST DR	1700	538R	DP	77536
WYNGAARD DR	3000	371U	NWC	77038
WYNGATE DR	1600	538M	DP	77536
WYNLEA	7500	575B	SEH	77061
WYNMAR LN	11900	328X	NWC	77429
WYNMEADOW DR	8500	535Y	SEH	77061
WYNMEADOW DR	8800	575C	SEH	77061
WYNNE	100	453U	NEH	77009
WYNNE AVE	8400	251C	SD	77381
WYNNEWOOD	4800	456T	NEH	77013
WYNNPARK DR	7200	452W	NWH	77008
WYNNVIEW DR	4600	617X	SEC	77546
WYNNWOOD LN	6900	452W	NWH	77008
WYNONA	4000	534M	SEH	77087
WYNRIDGE DR	1800	538M	DP	77536
WYNRUN CT	10500	372W	NWC	77038
WYNWOOD DR	1800	538M	DP	77536
WYOMA TRAIL	7000	330F	NWC	77379
WYOMING	0	659U	LC	77539
WYOMING	1900	541E	BT	77520
WYOMING	2800	659V	GCO	77539
WYOMING	3600	533L	SEH	77021
WYRICK	3400	454Y	NEH	77026
WYSALI CLIFF CT	10800	370S	NWC	77064
WYSTERIA	13800	528P	SWC	77083
WYTCHWOOD CIR	16300	367G	NWC	77429
WYTE LN	4400	454B	NEH	77093

X

Street Name	Block	Pg/Sq	Loc	Zips
X	0	539J	DP	77536
X CAN	9300	248M	SWM	77354
W. X STREET	100	538P	DP	77536
E. X STREET	100	538Q	DP	77536
XAVIER	5700	449C	NWC	77041
XENOPHON DR	3700	527C	SWC	77082
XENOS	0	619M	TL	77586
XINGO CT	19300	295A	SEM	77365

Y

Street Name	Block	Pg/Sq	Loc	Zips
Y	5900	444T	KT	77493
S. Y	100	580L	LP	77571
Y2	0	244F	WCO	77447
YACHT CT	900	379T	NEC	77532
YACHT CLUB LN	1	619R	EL	77586
YACHT HARBOR LN	2100	658U	LC	77573
YALE	1	492H	SWH	77007
YALE	900	452Z	NWH	77008
YALE	2700	537T	PA	77502
YALE	3000	452D	NWH	77018
YALE	5200	452D	NWH	77091
YALE	5300	444Q	KT	77493
YALE	5600	412Z	NWH	77076
YALE	7900	412R	NCC	77037
YALE LN	700	538Y	DP	77536
YALE CT	500	492D	NWH	77007
YALE PARK DR	12200	618D	PA	77058
YALE SQUARE CT	4000	446F	NWC	77449
YALE VILLAGE DR	0	452D	NWH	77091
YALE YARD	2100	612Y	NWB	77358
YAMPA LN	15600	409M	JV	77040
YANCY DR	12400	496M	NEH	77015
YANCY RD	22300	296G	SEM	77365
YANKEE CT	3600	610U	MC	77459
YARBERRY	14600	373X	NCC	77039
YARBERRY	15000	373X	NCC	77032
YARBO CREEK DR	2901	488W	SWC	77082
YARD CT	17300	379X	NEC	77532
YARDLEY DR	6800	525F	NEF	77494
YARDMASTER TRAIL	0	577W	SEH	77034
YARMOUTH	0	258K	SEM	77357
YARMOUTH	5200	455U	NEH	77028
YARNARM CT	16300	418D	NEC	77532
YARROW DR	0	406G	NWC	77433
YARROW CREST CT	12900	571G	SWH	77085
YARROWDALE CT	0	249C	SWM	77382
YARWELL DR	4700	531S	SWH	77096
YARWELL DR	6000	530V	SWH	77096
YASMINE RANCH DR	0	484R	NEF	77494
YATES	1200	494G	NEH	77020
YATES	1400	494B	NEH	77020
YAUPON	100	500J	BT	77520
YAUPON	900	536L	PA	77506
S. YAUPON CIR	17500	287N	NWC	77377
N. YAUPON CIR	17500	287N	NWC	77377
W. YAUPON CIR	21700	287N	NWC	77377
E. YAUPON CIR	21700	287N	NWC	77377
YAUPON GROVE LN	0	336Z	NEC	77346
YAUPON HOLLY LN	13100	377U	NEC	77044
YAUPON MIST DR	0	656L	FR	77546
YAUPON MIST DR	19100	406M	NWC	77433
YAUPON PASS DR	19000	407J	NWC	77433
YAUPON POINT CT	0	367W	NWC	77095
YAUPON RANCH CT	7800	406M	NWC	77433
YAUPON RANCH DR	0	407J	NWC	77433
YAUPON RANCH DR	19200	406M	NWC	77433
YAUPON RIDGE CT	19200	406M	NWC	77433
YAUPON SHORE DR	0	253X	SEM	77386
YAUPON SQUARE LN	0	492A	NWH	77008
YAUPON TRAIL	18700	337Z	NEC	77346
YAUPON VIEW DR	7900	407J	NWC	77433
YAW CT	900	419B	NEC	77532
YAWL CT	700	379X	NEC	77532
YAXLEY CT	0	258E	SEM	77357
YAZOO	0	246P	SWM	77355
YEALING COLT CT	0	411G	NWC	77038
YEANEY DR	0	446B	NWC	77449
YEARLING CIR	9500	409A	NWC	77065
YEARLING CT	9600	409A	NWC	77065
YEARLING DR	11600	409A	NWC	77065
YEARLING DR	12300	408D	NWC	77065
YEARLING BRANCH DR	9500	576J	SEH	77075
YEARLING GROVE RD	0	377E	NEC	77346
YEARLING MEADOWS	19000	486D	SWC	77094
YEARLIING RIDGE CT	4800	446C	NWC	77449
YEATMAH LN	11900	371M	NWC	77067
N. YEGUA RIVER CIR	1300	569S	SG	77478
S. YEGUA RIVER CIR	1500	569S	SG	77478
YELLOW BEGONIA DR	14800	325Q	NWC	77433
YELLOW BIRCH TRAIL	0	377E	NEC	77346
YELLOW BIRD RD	15300	323X	NWC	77447
YELLOW BIRD RD	15700	363A	NWC	77447
W. YELLOW BUD CT	16400	325R	NWC	77433
N. YELLOW BUD CT	21100	325R	NWC	77433
YELLOW CANYON FALLS DR	20100	289W	NWC	77375
YELLOW CORNERSTONE DR	0	524B	NEF	77494
YELLOW CREST RD	0	286Q	NWC	77377
YELLOW DAISY CT	0	325M	NWC	77429
YELLOW DAWN LN	0	325F	NWC	77447
YELLOW HIBISCUS LN	0	406D	NWC	77433
YELLOW JACKET	10200	412C	NWC	77038
YELLOW OAK TRAIL	15300	325R	NWC	77433
YELLOW PEAR WAY	2500	611T	NEF	77545
YELLOW PINE DR	7100	411J	NWH	77040
YELLOW PINE DR	7600	410M	NWC	77040
YELLOW PINE LN	25600	252S	SWM	77380
YELLOW POPLAR TRAIL	0	328N	NWC	77429
YELLOW RAIL DR	13000	377W	NEC	77044
YELLOW ROSE LN	27000	248F	SWM	77354
YELLOW ROSE TRAIL	0	326N	NWC	77433
YELLOWSTAR CT		249Q	NWC	77375
YELLOWSTONE BLVD	3000	533L	SWH	77054
YELLOWSTONE BLVD	3200	533L	SEH	77021
YELLOWSTONE BLVD	5000	534N	SEH	77021
YELLOWSTONE CIR	3500	615S	PL	77584
S. YELLOWSTONE DR	1600	538R	DP	77536
N. YELLOWSTONE DR	1600	538R	DP	77536
YELLOWSTONE DR	4100	577F	PA	77504
YELLOWSTONE DR	4800	577F	PA	77505
YELLOWSTONE PARK DR	0	533K	SWH	77054
YELLOWSTONE TRAIL	18000	377B	NEC	77346
YELLOWSTONE WAY DR	6900	533K	SWH	77054
YELLOW THRUSH DR	0	406R	NWC	77433
YELLOW THYME DR	0	293W	NCC	77373
YELLOW TULIP TRAIL	0	488G	SWH	77079
YELLOWWOOD CT	1	251Q	WD	77380
YELVERTON DR	24300	445S	NWC	77493
YELVERTON GLEN DR	23900	445T	NWC	77493
YEOBRIGHT DR	0	299X	NEC	77336
YEOMAN WAY	17100	379X	NEC	77532
YEPEZ RD	800	577K	PA	77504
YESTEREVE CT	2700	446R	NWC	77084
YESTEREVE CT	2700	446R	NWC	77084
YEW LN	0	333J	NCC	77073
YEWENS CT	14700	368A	NWC	77429
YEWENS LN	13500	368A	NWC	77429
YEWLEAF CT	1	251J	WD	77381
YEWLEAF DR	1	250M	WD	77381
YEWLEAF RD	1	251J	WD	77381
YGNACIO	0	376K	NEC	77396
YIDA LN	100	299W	NEH	77336
YMCA		501Q	BT	77521
YMCA		501Q	BT	77521
YMCA DR	2600	615Q	PL	77581
YOAKUM	24000	339K	HU	77336
YOAKUM BLVD	2400	493W	SWH	77006
YOAKUM ST	0	612V	PL	77584
YOE	7200	415W	NEH	77016
YOE	8000	415X	NEH	77078
YOKE DR	600	419F	NEC	77532
YOLANDITA	9900	576N	SEH	77075
YON RD	13000	369E	NWC	77429
YONDER WAY	28700	298U	NEC	77336
YONGE	0	289N	TB	77375
YORE LN	0	418T	NCC	77044
YORK	0	257H	SEM	77357
YORK	0	258E	SEM	77357
N. YORK	1	494P	NEH	77003
YORK	100	536X	SH	77587
YORK	100	494S	SEH	77003
YORK	7800	375G	HM	77396
YORK CT	0	258E	SEM	77357
YORK LN	0	657U	LC	77573
YORK BEND LN	0	416Z	NCC	77044
YORKBROOK DR	19100	617Z	SEH	77546
YORKCHESTER DR	200	489F	SWH	77079
YORK CREEK DR	1400	332W	NWC	77014
YORKDALE DR	5400	451D	NWH	77091
YORKDALE DR	6400	411Z	NWH	77091
YORKGATE DR	5700	334F	NCC	77373
S. YORKGLEN DR	17300	407Q	NWC	77084
N. YORKGLEN DR	17300	407Q	NWC	77084
YORKGLEN MANOR LN	0	407V	NWC	77084
YORKHAMPTON DR	6600	408T	NWC	77084
YORK HARBOR CT	0	619X	LC	77573
YORKHILL CT	0	527W	NEF	77407
YORK HOLLOW LN	8900	457A	NEC	77044
YORKINGHAM DR	3500	371K	NWC	77066
YORKLYN DR	11300	371P	NWC	77066
YORK MEADOWS	6400	408S	NWC	77084
YORK MINSTER DR	16000	330R	NWC	77379
YORKMONT CT	12900	367H	NWC	77429
YORKMONTE DR	19000	329A	NWC	77375
YORKPINE CT	20100	486L	SWC	77450
YORKPOINT DR	15100	408S	NWC	77084
YORK RIDGE LN	0	484U	NEF	77494
YORKSHIRE	0	257L	SEM	77357
YORKSHIRE	500	453L	NEH	77022
YORKSHIRE	3200	454J	NEH	77093
E. YORKSHIRE	4000	454K	NEH	77016
YORKSHIRE AVE	400	537L	PA	77503
YORKSHIRE BLVD	0	613P	NEB	77584
YORKSHIRE CT	200	538U	DP	77536
YORKSHIRE CT	2900	615Q	PL	77581
YORKSHIRE CT	25700	244M	WCO	77447
YORKSHIRE DR	1200	656M	FR	77546
YORKSHIRE CREEK CT	0	615G	PL	77581
YORKSHIRE MANOR CT	0	330A	SP	77379
YORKSHIRE MANOR DR	0	330A	NWC	77379
YORKSHIRE OAKS DR	11300	409A	NWC	77065
YORKSHIRE WOODS	6000	407Z	NWC	77084
YORKSTONE DR	0	489C	NWH	77024
YORK TIMBERS DR	21700	336B	SEM	77339
YORKTOWN	0	491Y	SWH	77056
YORKTOWN	0	620G	SB	77586
YORKTOWN	1600	491Q	SWH	77056
S. YORKTOWN CT	1900	658Q	LC	77573
N. YORKTOWN CT	1900	658Q	LC	77573
YORKTOWN LN	2600	609D	MC	77459
YORKTOWN COLONY DR	15000	408S	NWC	77084
YORKTOWN CRSSNG PKWY	0	408W	NWC	77084
YORKTOWN HEIGHTS DR	0	295M	SEM	77365
YORKTOWN HEIGHTS DR	0	295M	SEM	77365
YORKTOWN MEADOW LN	6000	407V	NWC	77084
YORKTOWN PASS	0	656X	FR	77546
YORKTOWN PLAZA DR	14900	410S	NWH	77040
YORKWAY DR	20000	486C	SWC	77450
YORKWOOD	2900	414S	NEH	77093
YORKWOOD	5200	414V	NEH	77016
YOSEMITE	3600	533L	SEH	77021
YOSEMITE DR	4200	577F	PA	77504
YOSEMITE FALLS DR	20100	289W	NWC	77375
YOSEMITE GLEN TRAIL	0	411H	NWC	77038
YOSEMITE PLACE DR	0	328N	NWC	77429
YOSEMITE RIDGE CT	0	445T	NWC	77493
YOST BLVD	2500	616N	PL	77581
YOST BLVD	2900	615V	PL	77581
YOUNG	4000	577E	PA	77504
YOUNG DR	1100	375D	HM	77338
YOUNGBERRY	8500	456G	NEC	77044
YOUNGCREST DR	9700	569H	SF	77477
W. YOUNG ELM CIR	0	373E	NCC	77073
N. YOUNG ELM CIR	0	373E	NCC	77073
YOUNGFIELD DR	12900	328Y	NWC	77429
YOUNGLAKE BLVD	19500	446Y	NWC	77084
YOUNG MEADOWS WAY	20900	406T	NWC	77449
YOUNG OAK	19300	291W	NWC	77379
YOUNG PINE ST	0	445K	NWC	77493
YOUNGSTOWN PLACE	9200	375R	NEC	77396
YOUNGTREE CIR	19400	446Y	NWC	77084
S. YOUNGWOOD LN	11800	449L	NWH	77043
N. YOUNGWOOD LN	11800	449L	NWH	77043
YOUPON	100	581W	PA	77586
YOUPON	600	621A	PA	77586
YOUPON	17500	418R	NEC	77044
YOUPON	19300	252C	SEM	77385
YOUPON DR	3800	579C	LP	77571
YOUPON DR	4900	411G	NWC	77086
YOUPON LN	23600	290A	NWC	77389
YOUPON GLEN WAY	0	611S	FS	77545
YOUPON HILL CT	19000	446R	NWC	77084
YOUPON LAKE CT	2700	446R	NWC	77084
YOUPON LAKE CT	2700	446R	NWC	77084
YOUPON LAKE LN	23600	293X	NCC	77373
YOUPON LEAF WAY	19700	446Q	NWC	77084
YOUPON VALLEY CT	1100	332V	NCC	77073
YOUPON VALLEY DR	16000	332V	NCC	77073
YOUPON WOOD CT	1000	617H	SEH	77062
YOUTH CAMPUS RD	0	619L	PA	77586
YUBA CT	7000	454R	NEH	77028
YUCCA	19700	292W	NWC	77388
YUCCA CT	0	658Y	LC	77573
YUCCA FIELD DR	7500	407J	NWC	77433
YUCCA MOUNTAIN DR	0	332W	NWC	77090
YUCCA TIP LN	0	333F	NCC	77073
YUCCA VALLEY LN	19500	406M	NWC	77433
YUKON	0	256V	SEM	77357
YUKON DR	20900	256R	SEM	77357
YUKON COVE DR	0	328F	NWC	77429
YUKON PASS DR	17800	377F	NEC	77346
YUKON RIDGE TRAIL	18200	377B	NEC	77346
YUKON RIVER DR	0	295B	SEM	77365
YUKON STRAIGHT DR	0	524S	NWF	77406
YUKON VALLEY LN	0	377E	NEC	77346
YUMA	2000	495V	NEH	77029
YUMA CT	0	658U	LC	77573
YUMA DR	4200	502J	BT	77521
YUMA CREST LN	19400	328C	NWC	77377
YUMA RIDGE LN	0	406G	NWC	77433
YUMA TRAIL	3900	577G	PA	77505
YUPON	500	541B	BT	77520
YUPON	2100	492R	SWH	77006
YUPON	2400	493W	SWH	77006
YUPON	22800	296Q	SEM	77365
YUPON CIR	2100	615K	PL	77581
YUPON LN	100	254L	SEM	77365
YUPONDALE DR	9500	450T	NWH	77080
YUPON FOREST DR	0	328K	NWC	77377
YUPON RIDGE DR	4100	529F	SWH	77072
YVONNE DR	8700	456D	NEC	77044

Z

Street Name	Block	Pg/Sq	Loc	Zips
Z-Z LN	0	538N	DP	77536
ZABACO	0	609Z	MC	77459
ZABALLOS CT	3400	455Z	NEH	77013
ZABOLIO DR	15400	617R	SEH	77598
ZACHARY	100	495U	NEH	77029
ZACHARY BEND LN	2900	485P	NEF	77494
ZACHARY BEND LN	24400	485P	NEF	77494
ZACHARY STUART CIR	0	609P	MC	77459
ZACKERY CT	2600	660W	DI	77539
ZACK SPRINGS LN	0	293F	SEM	77386
ZADA PARK LN	0	411M	NWH	77088
ZAGAR LN	17900	331H	NWC	77090
ZAHN	24000	286A	SWM	77355
ZAKA RD	0	409D	NWC	77064
ZAKA RD	9200	410A	NWC	77064
ZAMBEZI	0	295A	SEM	77365
ZANARDO CT	0	407W	NWC	77449
ZAPALAC	14500	613R	PL	77584
ZAPATA DR	6500	527F	SWC	77083
ZAPP LN	1300	537P	PA	77502
ZARAGOSA	0	532Y	SWH	77045
ZARAGOSA	6500	500C	NEC	77521
ZARATE AVE	2600	537K	PA	77506
ZAREEN LN	5100	444M	KT	77493
ZARROLL DR	11600	529N	SWH	77099
ZARSKY	0	340H	LCO	77535
ZARZANA ALLEY	3200	494E	NEH	77020
ZAVALA	0	500V	BT	77520
ZAVALLA	6500	500C	SEC	77521
ZAVALLA	12000	570R	SWH	77085
ZAVALLA CIR	2100	656U	FR	77546
ZAVALLA DR	0	538R	DP	77536
ZEDAN WAY DR	0	377L	NEC	77346
ZEENAT BLVD	6700	502C	BT	77521
ZELKO DR	3100	613X	NEB	77584
ZELMA DR	5600	453B	NEH	77076
ZENITH	14400	572T	SWH	77045
ZENITH GLEN LN	15000	328J	NWC	77429
ZENITH RIDGE WAY	0	377A	NEC	77346
ZENOBIE	1	569R	SF	77477
ZEPHYR	3400	533M	SEH	77021
ZEPHYR DR	1100	537N	PA	77506
ZEPHYR GLEN WAY	0	447K	NWC	77084
ZEPHYR GLEN WAY	0	447K	NWC	77084
ZEPPELIN CIR	0	538Z	DP	77536
ZERENE MEADOW LN	24900	338M	NEH	77336
ZETAK LN	19100	379J	NEC	77532
ZEUS DR	4300	610Q	MC	77459
ZIEGLER	1100	536Z	PA	77502
ZILONIS CT	7800	409M	JV	77040
ZIMBY	0	486T	SWH	77450
ZIMMERMAN	8000	411P	NWH	77088
ZINDLER	200	494G	NEH	77020
ZINDLER	15500	527U	NEF	77498
ZINN DR	100	419V	BR	77532
ZINNA DR	16200	367V	NWC	77095
ZINNIA LN	0	376A	NEC	77338
ZINNIA RD	1400	570T	MC	77489
ZION	0	249W	NWC	77375
ZION RD	11900	248Z	NWC	77375
ZION LUTHERAN CEM RD	25500	249U	NWC	77375
ZIRCON CT	10600	529W	SWH	77099
ZOCH LN	3600	451L	NWH	77092
ZOE	100	494H	NEH	77020
ZOEMARK LN	0	533F	SWH	77021
ZOERY	13100	574R	SEH	77048
ZOLA RD	700	453B	NEH	77076
ZOLI CT	0	378A	NEC	77346
ZOLTOWSKI	7000	495N	NEH	77029
ZONOLITE RD	0	292N	NWC	77388
ZOO CIRCLE DR	1500	533A	SWH	77030
ZORA	1300	451Y	NWH	77055
ZORN DR	1200	448L	NWH	77084
ZUBE RD	24200	324M	NWC	77447
ZUBER DR	1200	496S	GP	77547
ZUBIN LN	3200	444M	NWC	77493
ZUINN	11600	411F	NWC	77086
ZUME RD	0	411V	NWH	77088
ZUNI TRAIL	3900	577C	PA	77505
ZURICH CT	9300	329U	NWC	77070
ZWOLLE CIR	3800	573L	SEH	77047

INDEX of SUBDIVISIONS

SEE MC 208 MAP

N
W — E
S

33200

32500

31200

26600

362

GIBONEY

A

B

C

ROBINWD

ROBINWD

D

WESTBRK

SCROGGINS

© KEY MAPS 2017

Fields Store

E

Fieldstore Cemetery

WESTBRK CIR

RAINBOW

SCHNIEDER

WESTBRK WOODS

1488

31500

31100

BUNTING

F.M. 1488

30200

E

362

F

G

SOUTHLINE

Fields Store

H

CHAMPOUX

PIZZALATO

SEAWY

FIELD STORE

JOSEPH-LINER

33100

32900

32800

1488

JOSEPH-LINER

J

K

L

M

F.M. 1488

33500

Spring

Creek

WALLER COUNTY

FIELDS STORE

SEE WC 241 MAP

N

24000

362

N

P

HARRIS COUNTY

Q

© KEY MAPS 2017

KEN-ADA RANCH AIRFIELD (PVT)

TRUE BLUE

LEFTFLD

R

24000

STANFORD

24300

S

33800

MAYER

T

32300

32000

U

31000

V

HARRIS COUNTY

WALLER COUNTY

24000

23200

W

X

Y

FIELDS STORE

Z

ROBERSON

362

23300

© KEY MAPS 2017

0   1/4   1/2   3/4   1 Mile

SEE 282 MAP

© **KEY MAPS** 2017

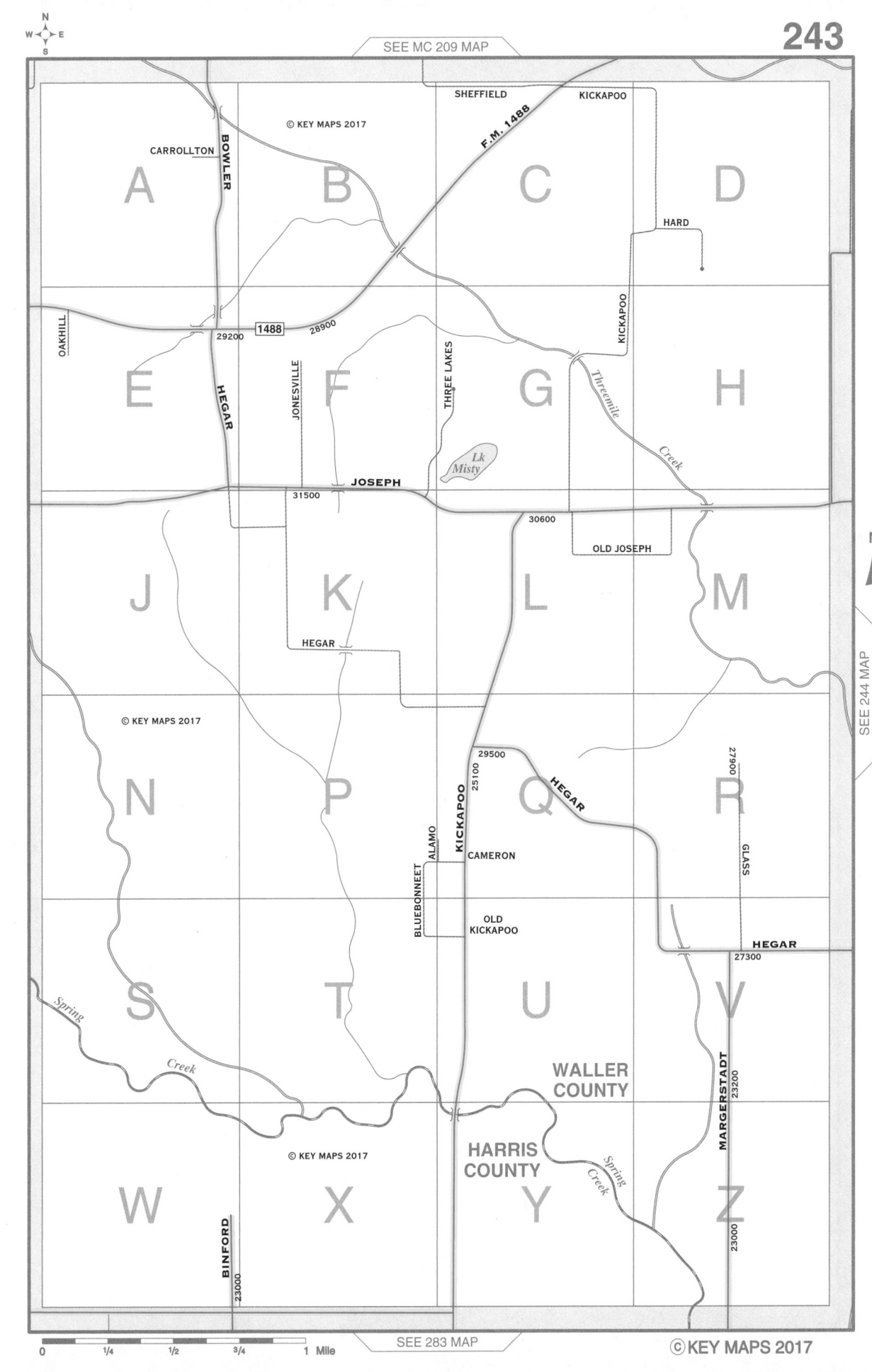

SEE 244 MAP

© KEY MAPS 2017

N
W — E
S

WALLER COUNTY

© KEY MAPS 2017

© KEY MAPS 2017

N

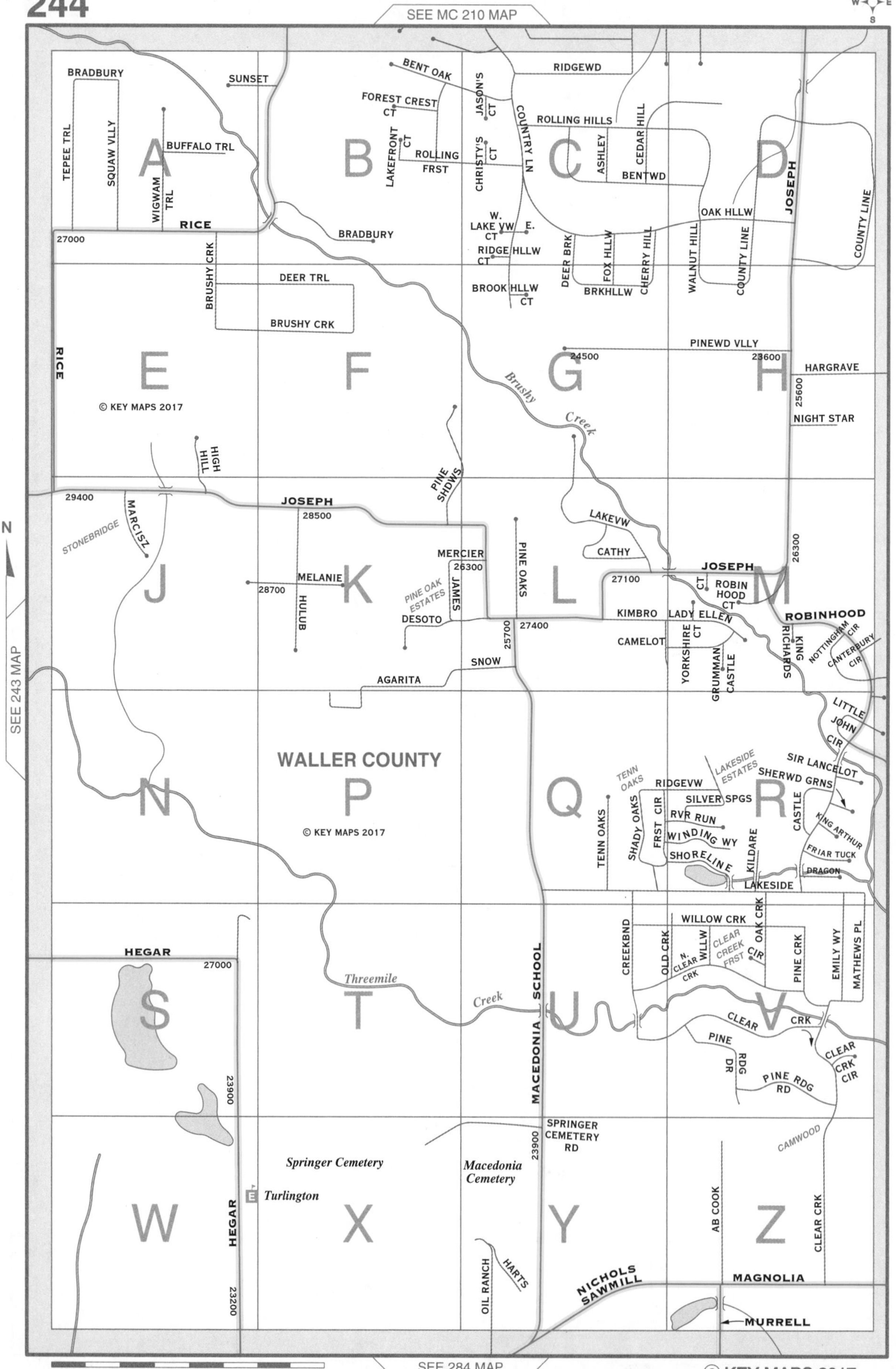

SEE 243 MAP

BRADBURY

TEPEE TRL
SQUAW VLLY
WIGWAM TRL
BUFFALO TRL
SUNSET

A

RICE
27000

RICE

BRUSHY CRK

DEER TRL

BRUSHY CRK

E

HIGH HILL

29400

MARCISZ

STONEBRIDGE

J

28700
MELANIE
HULUB

K

JOSEPH
28500

PINE OAK ESTATES

MERCIER
JAMES
26300
DESOTO
25700

AGARITA
SNOW
27400

BENT OAK

FOREST CREST CT

LAKEFRONT CT

ROLLING FRST

CHRISTY'S CT

JASON'S CT

COUNTRY LN

BRADBURY

W. LAKE VW CT
E. RIDGE HLLW
RIDGE HLLW CT

BROOK HLLW CT

B

RIDGEWD

ROLLING HILLS

ASHLEY
CEDAR HILL
BENTWD

DEER BRK
FOX HLLW
CHERRY HILL
BRKHLLW

C

OAK HLLW
WALNUT HILL
COUNTY LINE

JOSEPH

D

COUNTY LINE

Brushy Creek

24500

PINEWD VLLY
23600

G

LAKEVW
CATHY

PINE SHDWS

PINE OAKS

L

HARGRAVE
25600

NIGHT STAR

26300

H

JOSEPH
27100
ROBIN HOOD CT

KIMBRO
LADY ELLEN

CAMELOT

YORKSHIRE CT
GRUMMAN
CASTLE

RICHARDS KING

ROBINHOOD

NOTTINGHAM CIR
CANTERBURY CIR

LITTLE JOHN CIR

M

SIR LANCELOT

N

TENN OAKS

TENN OAKS
SHADY OAKS
FRST CIR

RIDGEVW
SILVER SPGS
RVR RUN
WINDING WY
SHORELINE

LAKESIDE ESTATES

SHERWD GRNS
CASTLE
KILDARE
FRIAR TUCK
DRAGON
LAKESIDE

KING ARTHUR

R

P

Q

HEGAR
27000

S

23900

Threemile

Creek

MACEDONIA SCHOOL

T

U

CREEKBND
OLD CRK
N. CLEAR CRK
WLLW
WILLOW CRK
CLEAR CREEK FRST
CIR
OAK CRK
PINE CRK
EMILY WY
MATHEWS PL

CLEAR CRK

PINE DR
RDG
PINE RDG RD

CLEAR CRK CIR

V

CAMWOOD

Springer Cemetery

E ▲ *Turlington*

HEGAR

23200

W

Macedonia Cemetery

SPRINGER CEMETERY RD
23900

X

OIL RANCH
HARTS

Y

NICHOLS SAWMILL

AB COOK

CLEAR CRK

MAGNOLIA

Z

MURRELL

0   1/4   1/2   3/4   1 Mile

SEE 284 MAP

© **KEY MAPS** 2017

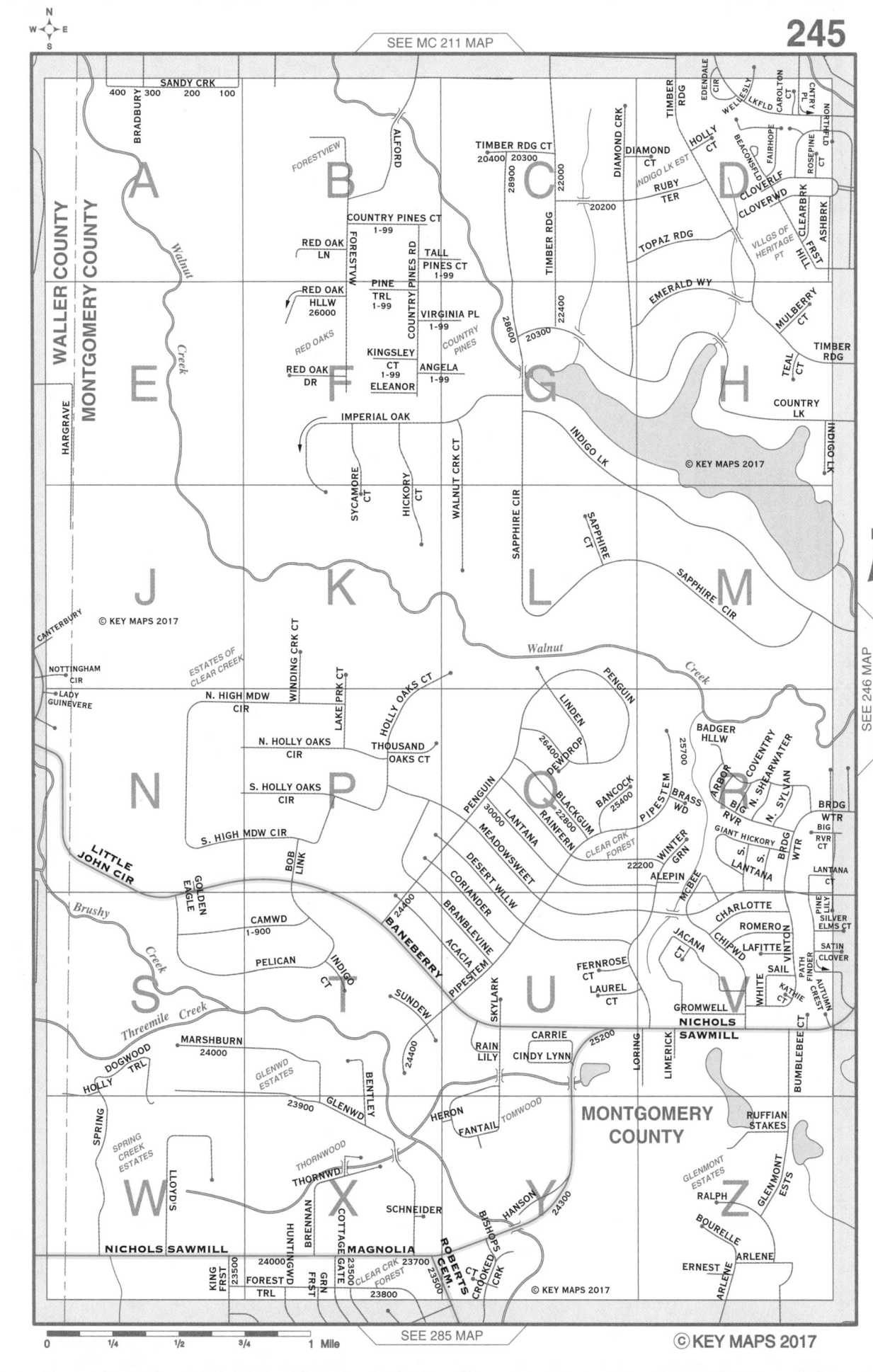

N
W E
S

SANDY CRK
400 300 200 100

BRADBURY

WALLER COUNTY
MONTGOMERY COUNTY

Walnut

Creek

HARGRAVE

A

B

C

D

E

F

G

H

FORESTVIEW
ALFORD

COUNTRY PINES CT
1-99

RED OAK
LN

FORESTVW

PINE
TRL
1-99

COUNTRY PINES RD

TALL
PINES CT
1-99

RED OAK
HLLW
26000

VIRGINIA PL
1-99

RED OAKS

KINGSLEY
CT
1-99

COUNTRY
PINES

RED OAK
DR

ANGELA
1-99

ELEANOR

IMPERIAL OAK

SYCAMORE
CT

HICKORY
CT

WALNUT CRK CT

SAPPHIRE CIR

SAPPHIRE
CT

TIMBER RDG CT
20400 20300

28900

22000

20400

TIMBER RDG

DIAMOND CRK

DIAMOND
CT

INDIGO LK EST

RUBY
TER

TOPAZ RDG

EMERALD WY

20300
22400
28600

20300

INDIGO LK

© KEY MAPS 2017

EDENDALE
CIR

TIMBER
RDG

HOLLY
CT

WE LKFLD
WELLESLY
CAROLTON
CT
CNTRY
PL
NORTHFLD

BEACONSFLD
FAIRHOPE
FAIRHOPE
ROSEPINE
CT

CLOVERLF
CLOVERWD

CLEARBRK
FRST
HILL
ASHBRK

VLLGS OF
HERITAGE
PT

MULBERRY
CT

TIMBER
RDG

TEAL
CT

COUNTRY
LK

INDIGO LK

N

SEE 246 MAP

J

K

L

M

N

P

Q

R

S

T

U

V

W

X

Y

Z

CANTERBURY

NOTTINGHAM
CIR

LADY
GUINEVERE

ESTATES OF
CLEAR CREEK

WINDING CRK CT

N. HIGH MDW
CIR

LAKE PRK CT

N. HOLLY OAKS
CIR

HOLLY OAKS CT

THOUSAND
OAKS CT

S. HOLLY OAKS
CIR

S. HIGH MDW CIR

LITTLE
JOHN CIR

BOB
LINK

Brushy

Creek

Threemile Creek

GOLDEN
EAGLE

CAMWD
1-900

PELICAN

INDIGO
CT

BANEBERRY

24400

SUNDEW

24400

Walnut

Creek

PENGUIN

LINDEN

26400

DEWDROP

PENGUIN

30000

LANTANA

MEADOWSWEET

DESERT WLLW

CORIANDER

BRANBLEVINE

ACACIA

PIPESTEM

SKYLARK

RAIN
LILY

BLACKGUM

RAINFERN

22800

BANCOCK
25400

PIPESTEM

CLEAR CRK
FOREST

22200

ALEPIN

MCBEE

WINTER
GRN

25700

BADGER
HLLW

ARBOR

BIG
RVR

COVENTRY
N. SHEARWATER
N. SYLVAN

BRASS
WD

GIANT HICKORY

S.
LANTANA

S.
BRDG
WTR

BRDG
WTR
BIG
RVR
CT

LANTANA
CT

PINE
LILY

SILVER
ELMS CT

SATIN
CLOVER

CHARLOTTE

ROMERO

LAFITTE

VINTON

JACANA
CT

CHIPWD

SAIL

WHITE

PATH
FINDER

KATHIE
CT

AUTUMN
CREST

FERNROSE
CT

LAUREL
CT

GROMWELL

NICHOLS
SAWMILL

LIMERICK

LORING

25200

BUMBLEBEE CT

CARRIE

CINDY LYNN

MARSHBURN
24000

DOGWOOD
TRL

HOLLY

SPRING

SPRING
CREEK
ESTATES

LLOYD'S

BENTLEY

GLENWD

23900

GLENWD
ESTATES

THORNWOOD

THORNWD

HUNTINGWD

BRENNAN

COTTAGE
GATE

SCHNEIDER

HERON

FANTAIL

TOMWOOD

HANSON

BISHOPS

24300

ROBERTS
CEM.

CLEAR CRK
FOREST

23700
23800

CROOKED
CRK
CT

23500
23600

MAGNOLIA

GRN
FRST

24000

FOREST
TRL

KING
FRST
23500

RUFFIAN
STAKES

MONTGOMERY
COUNTY

GLENMONT
ESTATES

RALPH

BOURELLE

ARLENE

ERNEST

ARLENE

GLENMONT
ESTS

© KEY MAPS 2017

NICHOLS SAWMILL

0 1/4 1/2 3/4 1 Mile

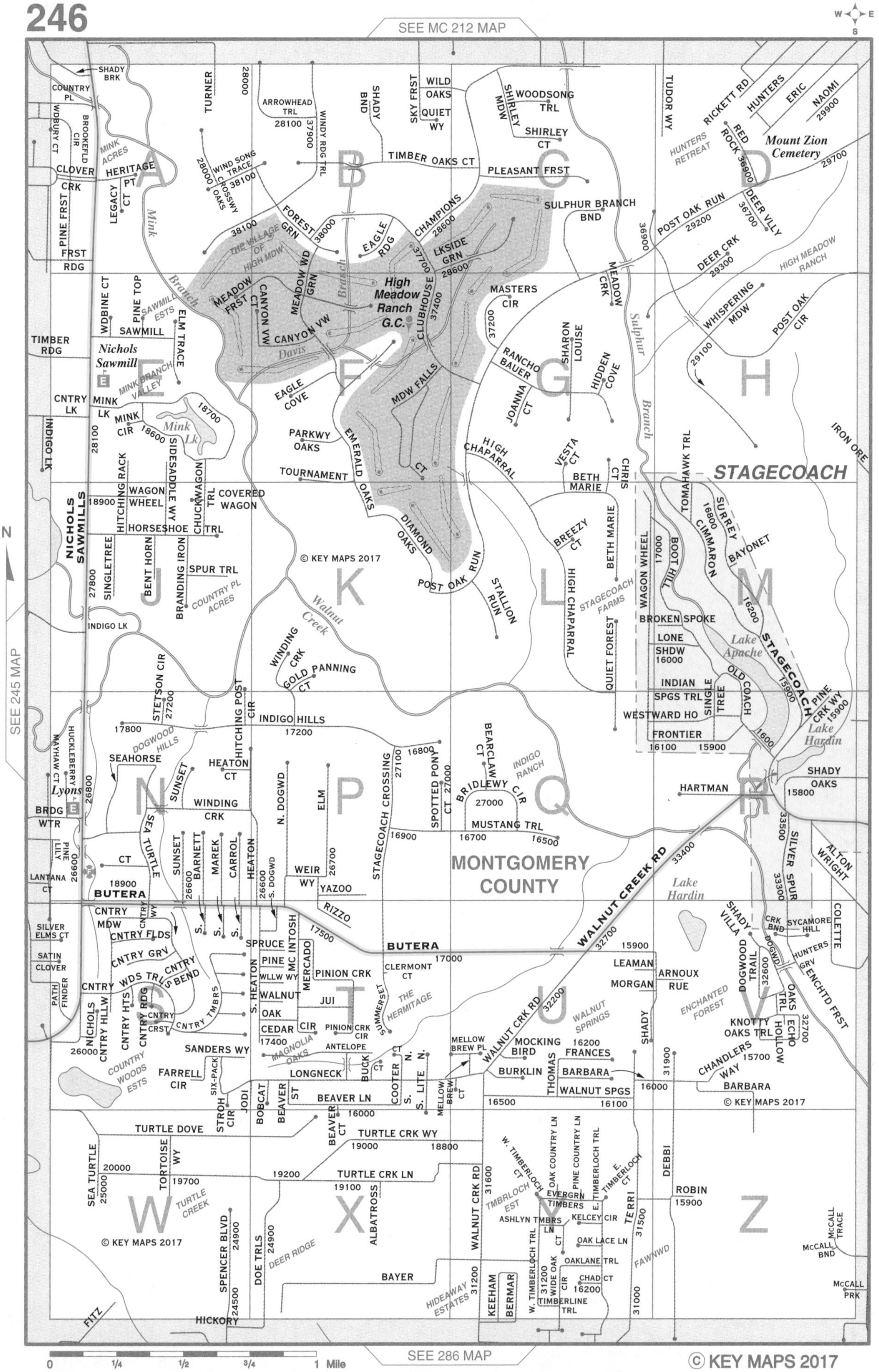

SEE MC 212 MAP

N
W E
S

SHADY BRK

COUNTRY PL
WDBURY CT
BROOKEFLD CIR
MINK ACRES
HERITAGE PT
CLOVER CRK
LEGACY CT
PINE FRST FRST RDG

TURNER
28000
ARROWHEAD TRL
28100 37900
WINDY RDG TRL
WIND SONG TRACE
OAKS CROSSWY
28000
38100 38100
FOREST GRN
38000
MEADOW WD GRN

SHADY BND
SKY FRST
WILD OAKS MDW
QUIET WY
SHIRLEY
WOODSONG TRL
SHIRLEY CT
TIMBER OAKS CT
PLEASANT FRST
CHAMPIONS
28600
LKSIDE GRN
28600
SULPHUR BRANCH BND
MASTERS CIR
37200

TUDOR WY
RICKETT RD
HUNTERS
ERIC
NAOMI
29900
HUNTERS RETREAT
RED ROCK 36900
DEER VLLY
36700
29700
POST OAK RUN
29200
DEER CRK
29300
HIGH MEADOW RANCH
WHISPERING MDW
29100
POST OAK CIR

THE VILLAGE OF HIGH MDW
MEADOW FRST
CANYON VW
MEADOW GRN
CANYON VW
EAGLE RDG
37700
37400
CLUBHOUSE
High Meadow Ranch G.C.
MDW FALLS

TIMBER RDG
WDBINE CT
PINE TOP
SAWMILL ESTS
ELM TRACE
SAWMILL
Nichols Sawmill
MINK BRANCH VALLEY
Davis
EAGLE COVE
PARKWY OAKS
EMERALD OAKS
TOURNAMENT
DIAMOND OAKS
POST OAK RUN

CNTRY LK
MINK LK
MINK CIR
28100 18600
Mink Lk
18700

INDIGO LK

RANCHO BAUER
JOANNA CT
SHARON LOUISE
HIDDEN COVE
VESTA CT
BETH MARIE
CHRIS CT
BREEZY CT
BETH MARIE
HIGH CHAPARRAL
HIGH CHAPARRAL
QUIET FOREST

STAGECOACH
IRON ORE

NICHOLS SAWMILLS
SINGLETREE
27800
18900
HITCHING RACK
WAGON WHEEL
HORSESHOE
SIDESADDLE WY
CHUCKWAGON TRL
COVERED WAGON TRL
BENT HORN
BRANDING IRON
SPUR TRL
COUNTRY PL ACRES
INDIGO LK

Walnut Creek
WINDING CRK CT
GOLD PANNING
HITCHING POST CIR
INDIGO HILLS
17200

STETSON CIR
27200
17800
DOGWOOD HILLS
SEAHORSE
SUNSET
HEATON CT
WINDING CRK
N. DOGWD
ELM
26700
WEIR WY
YAZOO
S. DOGWD
RIZZO

BEARCLAW CT
SPOTTED PONY CT 27000
27100 16800
BRIDLEWY CIR
27000
MUSTANG TRL
16700 16500
INDIGO RANCH

STAGECOACH CROSSING
16900

TOMAHAWK TRL
17000 16800
SURREY
BAYONET
CIMMARON
16200
WAGON WHEEL
BOOT HILL
BROKEN SPOKE
LONE SHDW 16000
INDIAN SPGS TRL
WESTWARD HO
FRONTIER
16100 15900
SINGLE TREE
OLD COACH
STAGECOACH
15900
Lake Apache
PINE CRK WY 15900
Lake Hardin
SHADY OAKS 15800

HARTMAN
16600
STAGECOACH FARMS
STALLION RUN

MONTGOMERY COUNTY

Lake Hardin

33500
33300
SILVER SPUR
33400
WALNUT CREEK RD
32400
CRK BND
16900
DOGWD
SHADY VILLA
HUNTERS GRV
SYCAMORE HILL
COLETTE
ALTON WRIGHT
BENCHTD FRST
32700

SEE 245 MAP

MAYHAW CT
HUCKLEBERRY CT
26800
Lyons
BRDG WTR
PINY LILY
26900
LANTANA CT

SEA TURTLE CT
18900
SUNSET
BARNETT
MAREK
CARROL
HEATON
26600 26600
BUTERA
S. S. S. S.
CNTRY MDW
CNTRY FLDS
CNTRY GRV
CNTRY RDG
WDS TRL
S. HEATON
17500
MC INTOSH
S. DOGWD
SPRUCE
PINE
WLLW WY
WALNUT
OAK
CEDAR
17400
PINION CRK
JUI
ANTELOPE
PINION CRK CIR
MERCADO
CLERMONT CT
17000
THE HERMITAGE
SUMMERSET
BUTERA
MELLOW BREW PL
MELLOW BREW CT
MOCKING BIRD
FRANCES
16200
BURKLIN
THOMAS
BARBARA
WALNUT SPGS
16500 16100

WALNUT CRK RD
32200
WALNUT SPRINGS
SHADY
31900
LEAMAN
MORGAN
ARNOUX RUE
ENCHANTED FOREST
KNOTTY OAKS TRL
32700
ECHO HOLLOW
15700
CHANDLERS WAY
BARBARA
16000
HUNTERS GRV
OAKS TRL

SILVER ELMS CT
SATIN CLOVER
PATH FINDER
NICHOLS CNTRY HLLW
26000
CNTRY HTS
CNTRY CRST
CNTRY TMBRS
CNTRY BEND
COUNTRY WOODS ESTS
SANDERS WY
FARRELL CIR
SIX-PACK
STROH CIR
JODI
BOBCAT
BEAVER
LONGNECK
BUCK CT
COOTER
S. LITE N.
S. LITE N.
BEAVER LN
BEAVER ST
BEAVER CT

TURTLE DOVE
SEA TURTLE
20000
25000
TORTOISE WY
19700
TURTLE CREEK
SPENCER BLVD
24500 24900
DOE TRLS
24900
DEER RIDGE
TURTLE CRK WY
19000 18800
TURTLE CRK LN
19100
ALBATROSS
19200
BAYER
HICKORY
FITZ

WALNUT CRK RD
W. TIMBERLOCH TRL
31600
TMBRLOCH EST
OAK COUNTRY LN
PINE COUNTRY LN
E. TIMBERLOCH TRL
DEBBI
ROBIN
15900
ASHLYN TMBRS
EVERGRN TIMBERS
KELCEY CIR
TERRI
CHAD CT
OAK LACE LN
OAKLANE TRL
W. TIMBERLOCH TRL
TIMBERLINE TRL
31200
WIDE OAK CIR
16200
31000
FAWNWD
KEEHAM
BERMAR
HIDEAWAY ESTATES
W. TIMBERLOCH TRL
31200

McCALL TRACE
McCALL BND
McCALL PRK

Mount Zion Cemetery

MEADOW CRK
SULPHUR
Branch
High Meadow Ranch

© KEY MAPS 2017

SEE 286 MAP

0   1/4   1/2   3/4   1 Mile

© KEY MAPS 2017

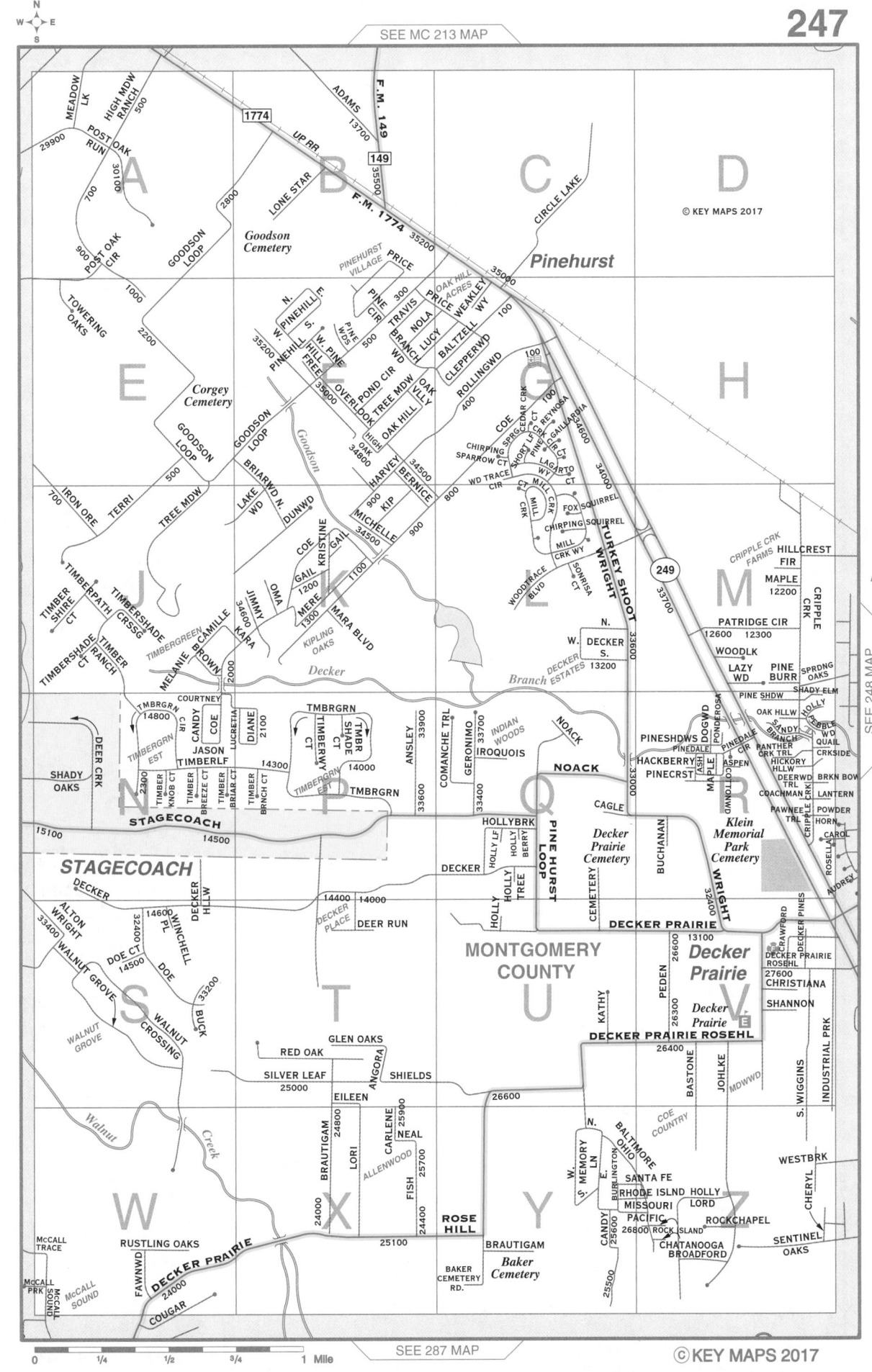

© KEY MAPS 2017

Pinehurst

Goodson Cemetery

Corgey Cemetery

MONTGOMERY COUNTY

Decker Prairie

STAGECOACH

© KEY MAPS 2017

0   1/4   1/2   3/4   1 Mile

SEE MC 214 MAP

N
W E
S

© KEY MAPS 2017

A
B
C
D

Decker Hills
Decker Woods
DALLAS
DENTON
EL PASO
MIDLAND
SWEETWATER
TEMPLE
WICHITA FALLS
DECKER HILLS
LOS ENCINOS
CT
RANCH CRK WY
ASCOT FARMS
CV PRK
HIDDEN CT
E. LAKE SIDE
CHAMPIONS RDG
CHAMPION OAKS
HIDDEN COVE
W. HIDDEN LK
28700
CHAMPION GLEN
Smith
PRINCETON

REMINGTON RANCHES
DOBBIN HUFFSMITH
27200
SHADY
© KEY MAPS 2017

GARDENIA
FLOWER MOUND
VIOLET FLOWER
LILY
IVY
DECKER WDS
CAMELIA
26300
AZALEA
FLOWER MOUND
EAGLES WING
RIATA
HARDIN STORE
27700
WINDING
COUNTRY
SUNSET AVE
GUANG MING WAY
LAKE CIR
LOTUS CIR

Cow
BETH
26900
DUSTIN
WILD FLOWER
YELLOW ROSE
BUTTERCUP
AUTUMNWD
Mill Creek
TRAILWD ESTATES
LOST PATH
WILDERNESS TRL
SENECA TRL
NEOSHO

E
12100
SAMANTHA
F
CARTER
NATURES WY
DECKER FRST
FALLEN LF PL
G
H

RUSTIC OAKS
© KEY MAPS 2017
BAYOU TESCH
LEAFTON
26400
PIN OAK
RUSTIC OAK
ANDERSON
26300
Tall Pines
SYCAMORE
26600
600
AUTUMN LEAF CIR. S.
RANCHERS OF PINEHURST
N. CLINT NEIDIGK
CADDO TRL
10200
9900
SIOUX
N. CREEK
NAVAJO
27200
9800
LONGBOW
27300
9400 CIR
9300
LONGBOW

UP RR
HILL CREST
33700
RIMWICK FOREST
RIMWICK FRST
26000
BIG OAK
J
HOOTEN
K
NEIDIGK SAWMILL
1000
PIN OAK
1300
TALL PINES
400
L
CHEROKEE
APACHE TRL
27200
M

OAKWD
HILLSD
ARROWWD
HEMLOCK
SPREADING OAKS
HOLLY
POST OAK FOREST
GREEN TREE
MULBERRY
25900
ANDY
300
WIGWAM
X CAN

HICKORYWD
PINEWD
12100
Decker
HUGHES
100
25700
S. CREEK
26800
9800
SEMINOLE
26800
9500
SPRING CRK ESTATES

QUAIL HLLW
CRKSIDE
CLEPPER
Branch
NEIDIGK
ROLSTER
26300
MAYA
26100
MOHAWK TRL
ROSIE
9400

BRKN BOW
LANTERN
POWDER
HORN
RHONDA
CAROL
LOIS
DEBBIE
JAN
MAUREEN'S WY
CEDAR
VW
CANYON CRK
HUNTWYCK
LOGTOWNE
HARDIN STORE
100
ELIZABETH CT
Decker Prairie Cemetery
P
Neidigk Lake
Q
MONTGOMERY COUNTY

VIOLA
AUDREY
HELENE
SUSIE
SUE
ANNE
VIRGIE COMMUNITY
500
© KEY MAPS 2017
HARRIS COUNTY

BUNNY
DECKER OAKS
ANNICE
BELLE CT
ASHTON
MORRIS
N
VLLG OF DECKER OAKS
Decker Prairie
RED OAK TER
KIMBROUGH
13100

AUTUMN WOODS
100
ESTELLE
CLARA
SARAH
MABEL
400
RUBY
RICHARD KAYE
28800
HAMILTON PARK
ASHLEY
KENNEDY COVE
GERALDS RUN

SUMMER
AUTUMN
28100
SPRING
LAZY GRV
LEISURE WDS
CATES
SHEPPARD
LOUIS
14500
VALLIE
MERCER
CLEPPER
ISBELL
SPRG HLLW
RHETT BUTLER
UP RR

DECKER IND CIR
31700
WINTER
FALL
VALLEY
RED FOX
FOXWD
28300
DEER
28600
FOXWOOD
Spring Creek
HUNTERWD CT
TIMBER WILD
WILD PECAN
ROANOKE WDS
NORWD CRST
WYNDFLD
SHERBORNE CASTLE

TOMBALL PKWY
BLUE BIRD
FAWN
RED BIRD
BLUE JAY
© KEY MAPS 2017
31000
JULIA
WILDWD
HELEN CRK
LOST CT
ULRICH
30000
SCHIEL NURSERY
ROANOKE WDS
FORT ISABELLA
MONTCLAIR
LNG
BERKSHIRE DOWNS

SENTINAL OAKS
WESTBRK
COCO
31000
DENISE
SENTINEL OAKS
100
W
TOMBALL
TOMBALL HILLS
CRESCENT
12200
NORTH STAR ESTATES
EVERGRN
13300
MOSSY SHORE
12900
SPRING LK
30600
RALEIGH CRK
Z

KINGBIRD
CHRIS
CAMILLE
LINDA
STELLA
ANTONIA
ALICE
ZION
249
CASTOR CT
CAPELLA CIR
STAR
RIGEL
SPICA
CASTOR
BEARING STAR
POLLUX CT
POLARIS
ORION
ALTAIR
COLUMBA
QUINN
CNTRY PINE
CNTRY HILL CT
CNTRY TIME
MARTENS
30800 MDW
CNTRY LN
CNTRY CIR
WM. JUERGENS
30600
McKINNEY
30000
ZION
NEAL
12800
12600

30600
31000
30900
30500
13300
1400

SEE 247 MAP

0   1/4   1/2   3/4   1 Mile

SEE 288 MAP

© KEY MAPS 2017

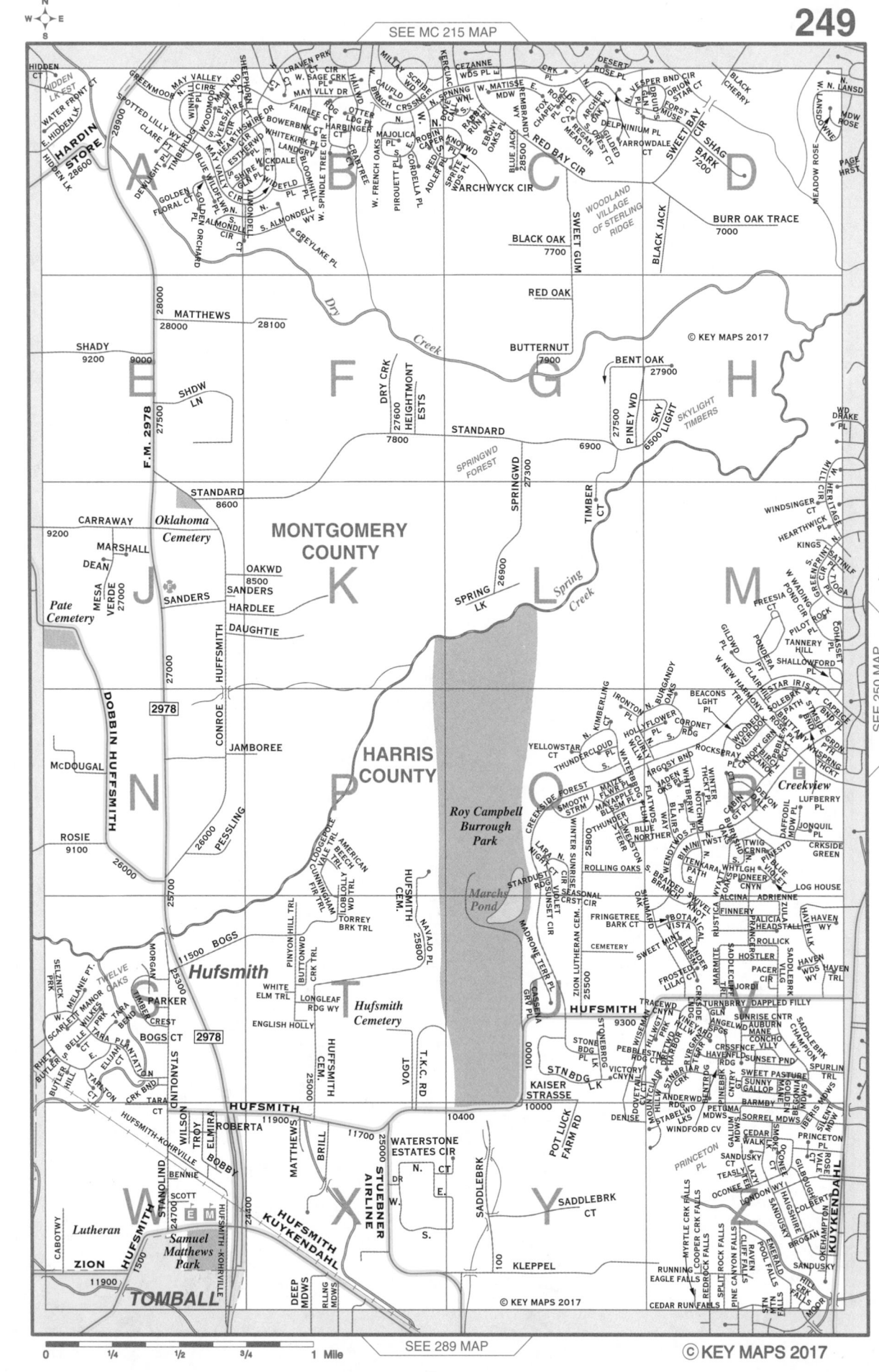

© KEY MAPS 2017

© KEY MAPS 2017

© KEY MAPS 2017

© KEY MAPS 2017

SEE MC 216 MAP

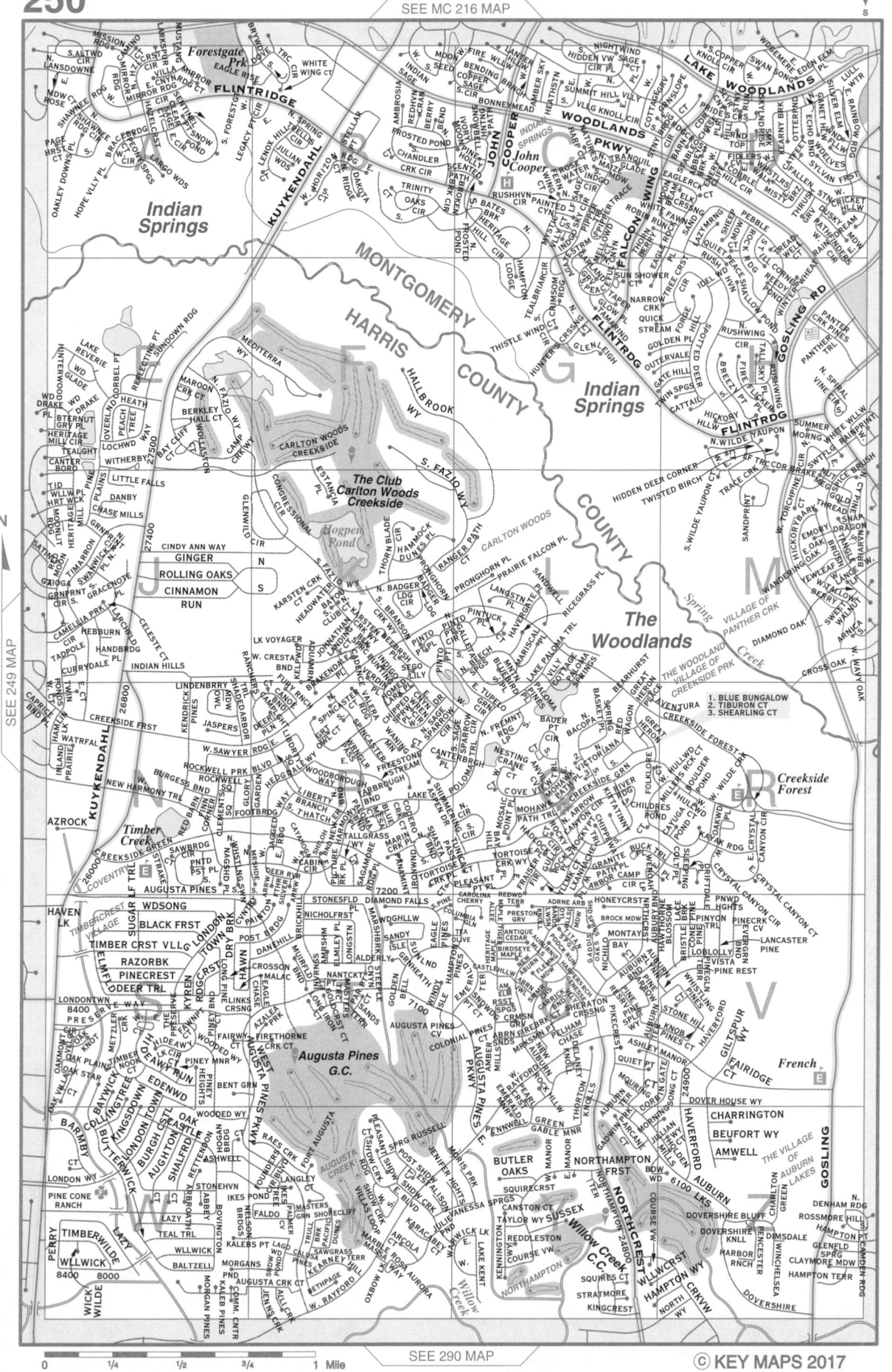

SEE 249 MAP

SEE 290 MAP

© KEY MAPS 2017

0   1/4   1/2   3/4   1 Mile

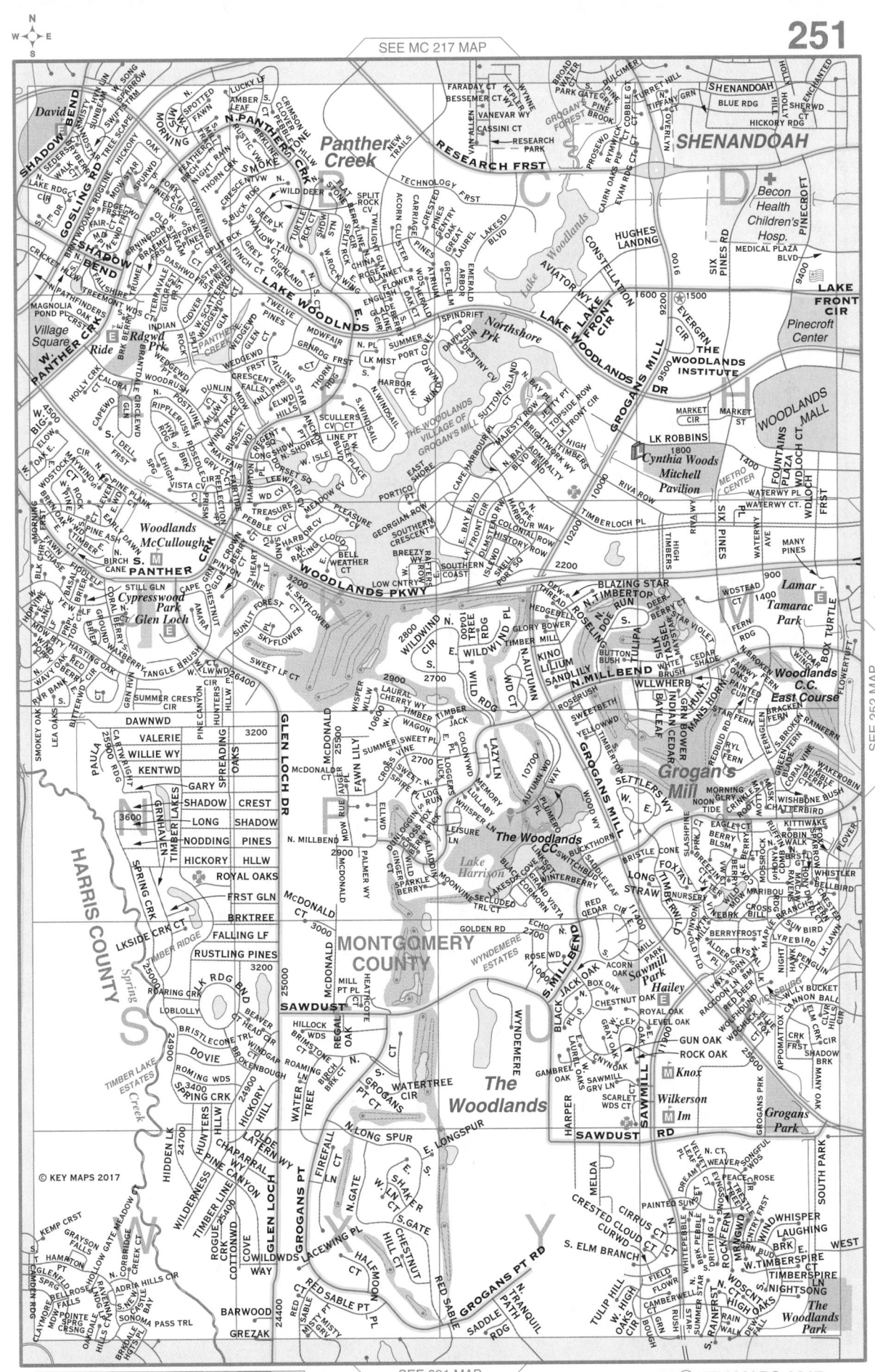

© KEY MAPS 2017

N W E S

SHENANDOAH

OLD OAKS
BIG HOLLY
PIN OAK 18700
WHISPERING OAK
CANYON CROSS
SLEEPY HOLLOW
TWIN DEER
CRK GATE 2100
OAK CANYON 27300

HOLLINS
5300 6200 9400
MELBA
SIMS
BIMMS
SIMMONS 1-99
SIMMONS 300
1400
Tamina Cem
SHADY MEADOW

KENBROOK VALLY
Glen Lake
POST OAK 10500

TAMINA RD 300
Mem. Hermann The Wdlands Hosp.
MEDICAL PLAZA BLVD
I-45
S.WD
DAVID MEMORIAL
DAVID VETTER BLVD
ELMORE
EASLEY
TERI CT
JOHNSON
SCHOOL
MC COWN 300
OLD HARDY 27300
OAK RDG
York
Oak Ridge
9th Grade
Oak Ridge
NANCY
SUSAN CT
P MANOR
LAURA
HEATHER
PATSY
BRENDA
HARLAN 300
PINE
Houser
KERR
MAIN
SUNSET
W GATE
PIERSON
CARMITA
SIMMONS
PINE
RHODES
1400 HAVEN
SONGWD
CACTUS
CHATEAU WDS
TALLOW
SPRINGWD 400
PINEWD
LAKEWD 10200
STONE GATE
JEWEL CT
TATE CT
RED FERN CT
WOODFERN CT
FOREST GLADE CT
BLACK FRST CT
CHATEAU WDS PKWY
FAIRVIEW
TWIN OAK 10900
BEECH
SWEETGUM
PRIMROSE
GLENOAK
FLAMINGO
BRIAR CLIFF
ASHWY 1600
GREAT OAK BLVD
GREAT OAKS
LONGLEAF 10200
BLUE BIRD
ORIDLE PL
HUMMINGBIRD PL
MOCKINGBIRD PL
RED BIRD PL
YOUPON
SILVER CT
SILVER L FLM
BLACK BEAR
WOLF DEN 1-99
HONEY TREE
White Oak Creek
CRK VW LN
E. HARDY EXT
WHITE OAK TRL
OAK CREST CT
CRK VW LN
OAK FRST TRL
11500
18700
Falvey Lake
10000
LAKE FRONT CIR
LAKE
WOODLANDS DR
WDLANDS MALL
Lake Robbins
WOODLANDS PKWY
27000

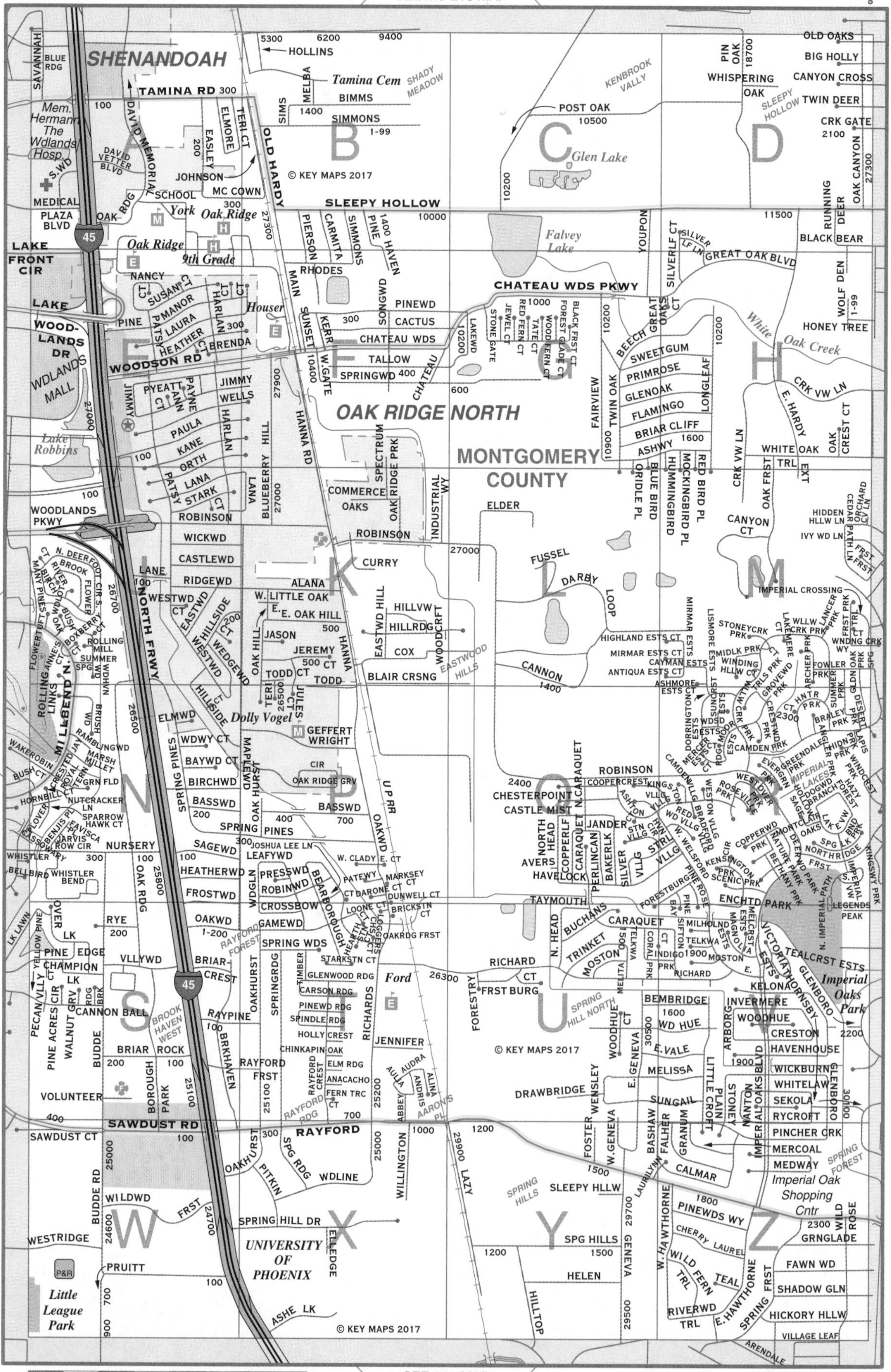

OAK RIDGE NORTH
MONTGOMERY COUNTY
SLEEPY HOLLOW

PYEATT
PAYNE
JIMMY
WELLS
PAULA
KANE
ORTH
LANA
STARK
ROBINSON
JIMMY
ANN
HARLAN
PATSY
LANA CT
LANA
WOODLANDS PKWY 27000

WOODSON RD
27900
10400

SPECTRUM
OAK RIDGE PRK
COMMERCE OAKS
CURRY
ROBINSON
INDUSTRIAL WY
ELDER
27000
FUSSEL
DARBY LOOP
CANNON 1400
HILLVW
HILLRDG
COX
WOODCRFT
EASTWOOD HILLS
BLAIR CRSNG
HIGHLAND ESTS CT
MIRMAR ESTS CT
CAYMAN ESTS CT
ANTIQUA ESTS CT
ASHMORE ESTS CT
MIRMAR ESTS
LISMORE ESTS
IMPERIAL CROSSING

WICKWD
CASTLEWD
RIDGEWD
ALANA
W. LITTLE OAK
E. OAK HILL
JASON
JEREMY
TODD 500 CT
TODD
TERI CT
JULES CT
EASTWD HILL
HANNA
EASTWD HILL
HILLSIDE
BLUEBERRY HILL
HANNA RD 27000
OAK HILL
WEDGEWD
WESTWD
WESTWD CT
EASTWD CT
HILLSIDE CT
500
500

N. DEERFOOT CIR
ROLLING OAKS
MILLBEND DR
NORTH FRWY
MANY PINES
RIVER
BROOK
FLOWER
BUSH
BOXBERG
SUMMER SPG
ANNS CT
WHINN
FLOWERT
ROLLING MILL CT
ROYAL
MARSH MILLET
GRN FLD
RAMBLINGWD
ELMWD
WDWY CT
BAYWD CT
BIRCHWD
BASSWD
SPRING PINES
MAPLEWD
OAK RIDGE GRV
BASSWD 700
CIR
GEFFERT WRIGHT
Dolly Vogel
SPRING PINES 300
JOSHUA LEE LN
LEAFYWD
PRESSWD
ROBINWD
CROSSBOW
GAMEWD
SPRING WDS
STARKSTN CT
HEATHERWD
FROSTWD
OAKWD
WDGLN
BEARBOROUGH
OAKWD
OAKRDG FRST
UP RR
W. CLADY E. CT
PATEWY
MARKSEY
DARONE CT
DUNWELL CT
BRICKSTN
LOONE LN
TIMBER
PINEWD RDG
CHINKAPIN OAK
ELM RDG
ANACACHO
FERN TRC
AULA
AUDRA
ANDRIS
ALINA
AARONS PL
26500
26000
25000

CHESTERPOINT
CASTLE MIST 2400
NORTH HEAD
AVERS
HAVELOCK
COPPERLF
PERLINCAN
BAKERLK
JANDER
SILVER
VLLG
N. CARAQUET
N. CARAQUET
ROBINSON
COOPERCREST
KINGS
CAMDENVILLS
WESTON VLLG
ASHTON
WELSFORD
ROSEVILLER
WESTIER
EVERGRN
COPPERWD
CAMDEN PRK
KENSINGTON
FORESTBURG
SCENIC PRK
TAYMOUTH
BUCHANS
CARAQUET
TRINKET
MOSTON
TELKWA
CORAL PRK
INDIGO
MELITA
RICHARD
FRST BURG
FORESTRY
N. HEAD
RICHARD CT
1900
MOSTON E.
SIFTON
MILHOLND
MAGNO
BRENDALE
DEERWD PARK
NORTHRIDGE
SPG LN
LAK VW
OAKS
BETHANY PRK
LEGENDS PEAK
N. IMPERIAL PATH
Imperial Oaks Park
ENCHTD PARK
VICTORIAL
HORNSBY
GLENBORO
TEALCRST ESTS
KELONAORNSBY
INVERMERE
WOODHUE
ARBORG
IMPERIAL OAKS BLVD
BEMBRIDGE 1600
WD HUE
E. VALE
MELISSA
E. GENEVA 30500
SUNGAIL
GRANUM
DRAWBRIDGE
FOSTER
WENSLEY
W. GENEVA
BASHAW
FALHER
CALMAR
LAURILYNN
NANTON
STONEY
PLAIN
LITTLE CROFT
1900
CRESTON
HAVENHOUSE
WICKBURN
WHITELAW
SEKOLA
RYCROFT
PINCHER CRK
MERCOAL
MEDWAY
Imperial Oak Shopping Cntr
Imperial Oaks Park
2200
2300
SPRING FOREST
GRNGLADE
FAWN WD
SHADOW GLN
HICKORY HLLW
VILLAGE LEAF
WILD ROSE
WILD FERN TRL
TEAL
W. HAWTHORNE
E. HAWTHORNE
CHERRY LAUREL
RIVERWD TRL
SPRING FRST
ARENDALE
PINEWDS WY 1800
SLEEPY HLLW
SPG HILLS 1500
HELEN
HILLTOP
Spring Hills
Spring Hill North

N
SEE 251 MAP

LK LAWN
PLOVER LK
PINE LK
CHAMPION LK
PECAN VLLY CIR
PINE ACRES CIR
CANNON BALL
WALNUT GRV
BRIAR
VOLUNTEER 400
WESTRIDGE
PRUITT
P&R
Little League Park
BELLBIRD
WHISTLER BEND
WHISTLER
NURSERY 300
BUDDE RD 25000
OAK RDG 25800
OAK RDG 24600
WILDWD
FRST 24700
SPRING HILL DR
ELLEDGE
700
900
RYE 200
EDGE
YELLOW PINE
HORNBILL
NUTCRACKER LN
SPARROW
HAWK CT
JAVISCA
BEJUIS PL
ROW CIR
FLOVER
BUSH CT
WAKEROBIN
OAKHURST
SPRINGRDG
RAYPINE
PINEWD RDG
SPINDLE
HOLLY
OAKHURST
PITKIN
SPG RDG
WDLINE
RAYFORD FRST
CARSON RDG
GLENWOOD RDG
CROSS
BRIAR CREST
VLLYWD
BRIAR
ROCK
BUDDE 200
RAYFORD
RAYFORD CREST
RAYFORD RDG
25100
25500
JENNIFER
Ford 26300
E CT
RICHARDS
WILLINGTON 1000
LAZY
SPRING HILLS 1200
GENEVA 26500
29700
29500
RICHARD
N. HEAD

WOODLANDS PKWY

SAWDUST RD
SAWDUST CT 100

I-45

UNIVERSITY OF PHOENIX

SEE 292 MAP

© KEY MAPS 2017

0 1/4 1/2 3/4 1 Mile

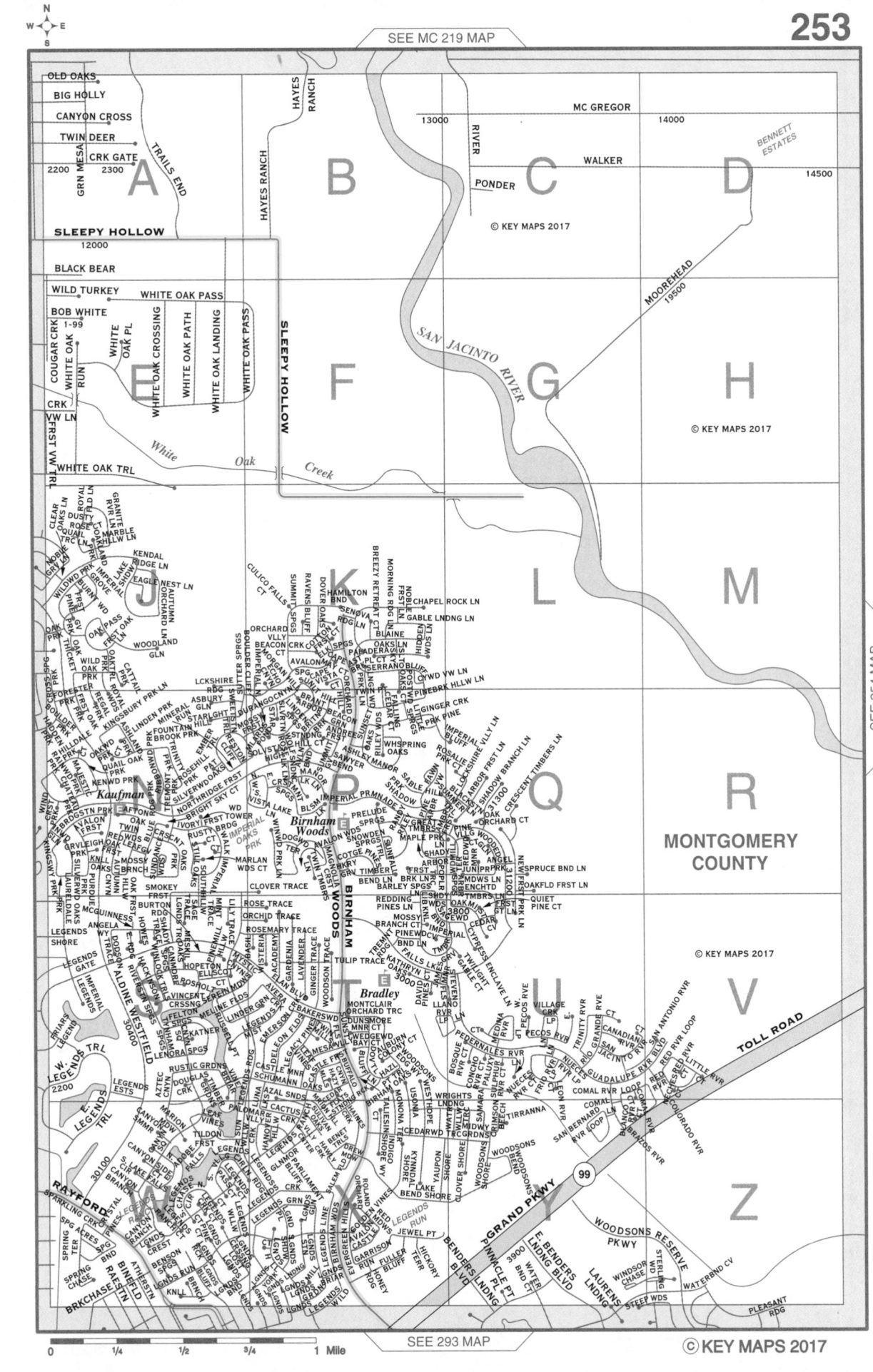

254

N
W E
S

MC GREGOR

WALKER

EAST DR
15000

MOOREHEAD

A

© KEY MAPS 2017

B

Woodridge Estates

N. WESTWD

WESTWD
16300

CLARK

C

WOODRIDGE

OLD HOUSTON RD

19000

VILLAGE WAY

WAGON TRL

CYPRESS CIR
17000

COUNTRY VILLAGE

SYCAMORE TRL
17300

D

© KEY MAPS 2017

MONTGOMERY COUNTY

E

North Country

NORTHSTAR

NORTH CT
100

F

NORTHPARK

NORTHLAND

NORTHCREEK

NORTHWOOD

NORTHFORK

NORTH COUNTRY
CIR 2400   2200

© KEY MAPS 2017

Live Oak Estates

OLD HOUSTON

1314

F.M. 1314

OAK KNOLL
16500

LIVE OAK SQ

G

GOLDEN TRLS

PORTER

CATHY'S

LIVE OAK BURR

17000
LITTLE
OAK

LIVE OAKS
ESTS DR

LIVE OAK
BRNCH

Copeland Ditch

GENE CAMPBELL BLVD

H

LIVE OAK
CIR

J

K

LKSIDE

YOUPON

AIRFIELD LN

L

ALEXANDER

100

DUESTER

LOUIS

BOBBY

200

100

JERRY

INDIAN TRL

M

Williams Lake

PINEWD
300

DOGWD

HOLLY STREET

BAY LN

PINCHER LN

Golden Trails

WILLIAMS AIRFIELD

HECHT

PORTER HEIGHTS

COPELND

N

SAN

JACINTO

P

Q

MOSS

R

© KEY MAPS 2017

SEE 253 MAP

N

RIVER

Black Brnch

TOLL ROAD

GRAND PKWY 99

99

S

T

U

MONTGOMERY COUNTY

V

© KEY MAPS 2017

© KEY MAPS 2017

W

X

Y

KANAWHA

AMAZON

GILA

Z

0   1/4   1/2   3/4   1 Mile

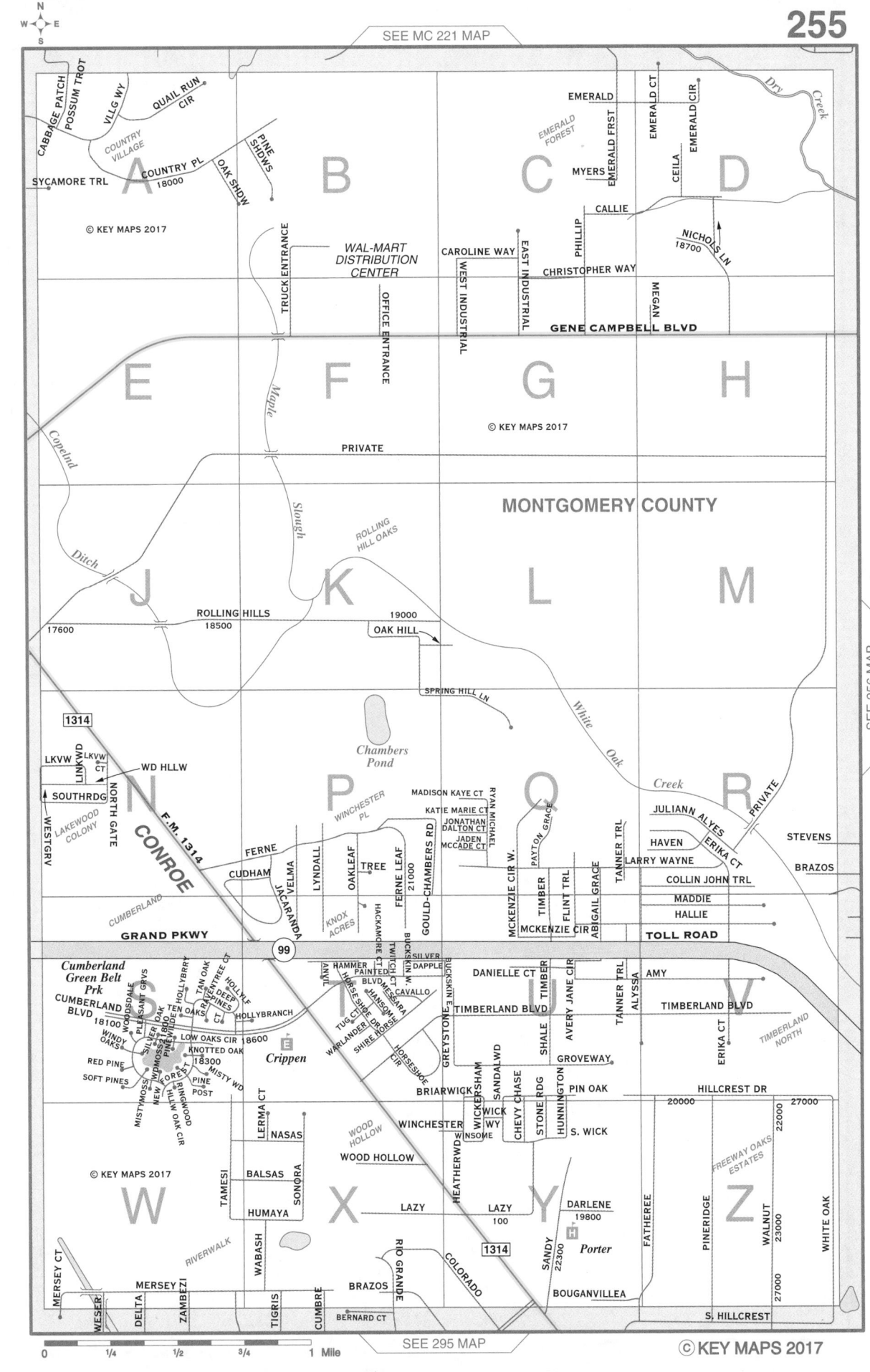

N
W E
S

© KEY MAPS 2017

CABBAGE PATCH
POSSUM TROT
VLLG WY
QUAIL RUN CIR
PINE SHDWS
COUNTRY VILLAGE
COUNTRY PL
18000
OAK SHDW
SYCAMORE TRL

A

B

EMERALD
EMERALD FRST
EMERALD CT
EMERALD CIR
EMERALD FOREST
MYERS
CEILA

C

D

Dry Creek

CAROLINE WAY
WEST INDUSTRIAL
EAST INDUSTRIAL
PHILLIP
CALLIE
CHRISTOPHER WAY
MEGAN
NICHOLS LN
18700

WAL-MART DISTRIBUTION CENTER

TRUCK ENTRANCE
OFFICE ENTRANCE

GENE CAMPBELL BLVD

E

F

G

H

© KEY MAPS 2017

Copeland
Maple
PRIVATE

Slough
Ditch

ROLLING HILL OAKS

MONTGOMERY COUNTY

J

K

L

M

ROLLING HILLS
17600
18500
19000
OAK HILL
SPRING HILL LN

White Oak Creek

SEE 256 MAP

N

1314

LKVWD
LKVW CT
LINKWD
WD HLLW
SOUTHRDG
WESTGRV
LAKEWOOD COLONY
NORTH GATE

N

WINCHESTER PL

P

MADISON KAYE CT
KATIE MARIE CT
JONATHAN DALTON CT
JADEN MCCADE CT
GOULD-CHAMBERS RD
RYAN MICHAEL

Q

PAYTON GRACE
MCKENZIE CIR W.
TIMBER
FLINT TRL
ABIGAIL GRACE
TANNER TRL

JULIANN ALYES
HAVEN
ERIKA CT
LARRY WAYNE
COLLIN JOHN TRL
MADDIE
HALLIE

R

Private
STEVENS
BRAZOS

FERNE
CUDHAM
JACARANDA
VELMA
LYNDALL
OAKLEAF
TREE
FERNE LEAF
21000
KNOX ACRES
HACKAMORE CT
TWITCH CT
BUCKSKIN W.

CONROE F.M. 1314
CUMBERLAND
GRAND PKWY
99
MCKENZIE CIR
TOLL ROAD

Cumberland Green Belt Prk
CUMBERLAND BLVD
18100
WINDY OAKS
RED PINE
SOFT PINES
MISTYMOSS
NEW FOREST
SILVER OAK
NEW WD MOSS
PLEASANT GRVS
TEN OAKS
HOLLYBRRY
TAN OAK
RAVENTREE CT
DEEP PINES
HOLLYF
HOLLYBRANCH
LOW OAKS CIR
18600
KNOTTED OAK
18300
MISTY WD
PINE POST
HLLW OAK CIR
RINGWOOD
SILVER OAK
NEWWILDE
PINEVILLDE

SILVER DAPPLE
PAINTED
HORSE SHOE BLVD
MESSARA
CAVALLO
HANSON
WARLANDER DR
SHIRE HORSE
HORSESHOE CIR
TUG CT
GREYSTONE

HAMMER CT
AMY CT

DANIELLE CT
TIMBERLAND BLVD

S

T

U

AVERY JANE CIR
TANNER TRL
ALYSSA
AMY
TIMBERLAND BLVD
ERIKA CT

V

TIMBERLAND NORTH

Crippen
E

LERMA CT
NASAS
BALSAS
SONORA
HUMAYA
TAMESI
WABASH

WOOD HOLLOW
WINCHESTER
WINSOME
WOOD HOLLOW

BRIARWICK
WICKERSHAM
SANDALWD
WICK WY
CHEVY CHASE
STONE RDG
HUNNINGTON
PIN OAK
S. WICK
GROVEWAY

HEATHERWD
LAZY
LAZY
100

HILLCREST DR
20000
27000
FREEWAY OAKS ESTATES
22000
23000
27000

FATHEREE
PINERIDGE
WALNUT
WHITE OAK

W

X

Y

Z

© KEY MAPS 2017

DARLENE
19800
Porter
SANDY
22300
BOUGANVILLEA

RIVERWALK
MERSEY CT
WESER
MERSEY
DELTA
ZAMBEZI
TIGRIS
CUMBRE
BRAZOS
RIO GRANDE
COLORADO
1314
BERNARD CT

S. HILLCREST

0   1/4   1/2   3/4   1 Mile

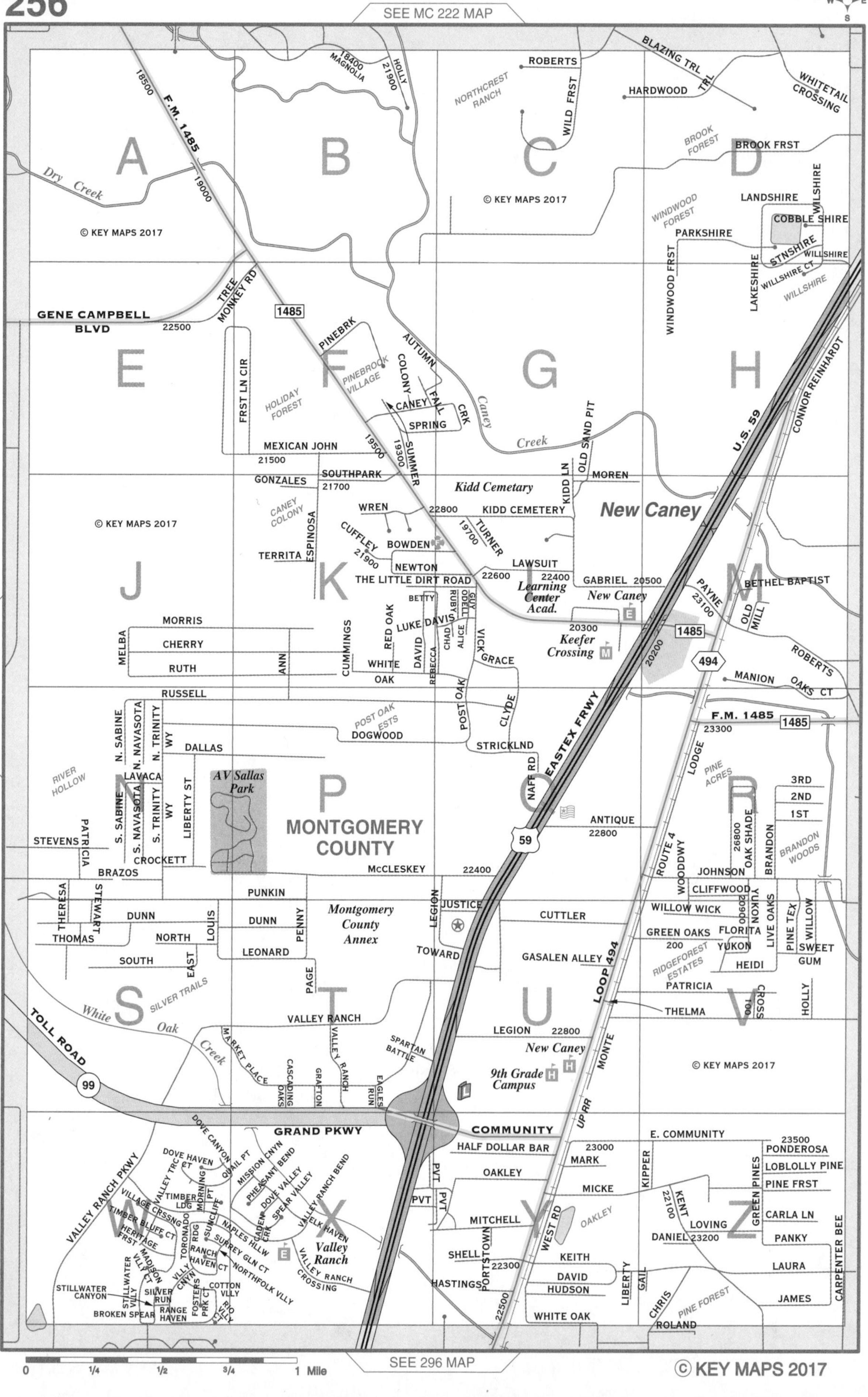

SEE MC 222 MAP

N
W E
S

A

Dry Creek

F.M. 1485

18500

19000

21900 HOLLY

18400 MAGNOLIA

NORTHCREST RANCH

ROBERTS

WILD FRST

HARDWOOD

BLAZING TRL

WHITETAIL CROSSING

© KEY MAPS 2017

B

C

BROOK FOREST

BROOK FRST

WINDWOOD FOREST

D

LANDSHIRE

COBBLE SHIRE

PARKSHIRE

WINDWOOD FRST

LAKESHIRE

STNSHIRE

WILLSHIRE CT

WILLSHIRE

WILLSHIRE

WILLSHIRE

GENE CAMPBELL BLVD

22500

TREE MONKEY RD

1485

E

FRST LN CIR

HOLIDAY FOREST

PINEBRK

PINEBROOK VILLAGE

AUTUMN

FALL

COLONY

CANEY

SPRING

CRK

Caney

Creek

OLD SAND PIT

CONNOR REINHARDT

U.S. 59

F

19500

19300

SUMMER

MEXICAN JOHN 21500

SOUTHPARK 21700

GONZALES

CANEY COLONY

ESPINOSA

WREN

22800

KIDD LN

MOREN

Kidd Cemetary

KIDD CEMETARY

G

New Caney

H

TERRITA

CUFFLEY

BOWDEN

21900

NEWTON

THE LITTLE DIRT ROAD

TURNER 19700

22600

LAWSUIT

22400

GABRIEL 20500

New Caney

BETHEL BAPTIST

OLD MILL

MORRIS

MELBA

CHERRY

RUTH

BETTY

LUKE DAVIS

DAVID

CHAD

REBECCA

ALICE

VICKI

GRACE

Learning Center Acad.

New Caney

23100

PAYNE

1485

23500

20300

Keefer Crossing

20200

494

MANION

ROBERTS

OAKS CT

J

ANN

RED OAK

WHITE OAK

POST OAK

CLYDE

K

CUMMINGS

L

20000

M

RUSSELL

N. SABINE

N. NAVASOTA

N. TRINITY WY

DALLAS

POST OAK ESTS

DOGWOOD

STRICKLND

F.M. 1485

23300

LODGE

PINE ACRES

1485

RIVER HOLLOW

LAVACA

S. SABINE

S. NAVASOTA

S. TRINITY

LIBERTY ST

AV Sallas Park

P

MONTGOMERY COUNTY

NAFF RD

EASTEX FRWY

ANTIQUE 22800

59

26800

OAK SHADE

BRANDON

3RD

2ND

1ST

BRANDON WOODS

STEVENS

PATRICIA

CROCKETT

McCLESKEY

22400

ROUTE 4

WOODDWY

JOHNSON

CLIFFWOOD

YUKON

R

BRAZOS

THERESA

STEWART

THOMAS

DUNN

NORTH

SOUTH

EAST

LOUIS

PUNKIN

PENNY

DUNN

LEONARD

Montgomery County Annex

LEGION

JUSTICE

TOWARD

CUTTLER

GASALEN ALLEY

WILLOW WICK

GREEN OAKS 200

YUKON

HEIDI

RIDGEFOREST ESTATES

PATRICIA

FLORITA

LIVE OAKS

PINE TEX

WILLOW

SWEET GUM

HOLLY

CROSS RD

S

SILVER TRAILS

White Oak Creek

PAGE

VALLEY RANCH

T

MARKET PLACE

CASCADING OAKS

VALLEY RANCH

GRAFTON

SPARTAN BATTLE

EAGLES RUN

U

LEGION 22800

New Caney

9th Grade Campus

MONTE

THELMA

V

© KEY MAPS 2017

TOLL ROAD

99

LOOP 494

UP RR

COMMUNITY

GRAND PKWY

DOVE CANYON

DOVE HAVEN

VALLEY RANCH PKWY

TIMBER TRL

QUAIL PT

VILLAGE CRSSNG

TIMBER LDG

MORNING

SUBCLIFF

MISSION CNYN

PHEASANT BEND

DOVE VALLEY

SPEAR VALLEY

VALLEY RANCH BEND

VALLEY HAVEN

VALLEY RANCH CROSSING

HALF DOLLAR BAR

OAKLEY

MARK 23000

MICKE

MITCHELL

WEST RD

OAKLEY

E. COMMUNITY

KIPPER

22100

KENT

23500 PONDEROSA

LOBLOLLY PINE

PINE FRST

CARLA LN

PANKY

GREEN PINES

LOVING

DANIEL 23200

CARPENTER BEE

W

TIMBER BLUFF CT

HERITAGE

MADISON

FRST

TORONDO

NAPLES HLLW

SURREY GLN CT

NORTHFOLK VLLY

X

Valley Ranch

STILLWATER CANYON

BROKEN SPEAR

SILVER RUN

RANGE HAVEN

FOSTERS

COTTON VLLY

Y

SHELL

HASTINGS

22300

22500

KEITH

DAVID

HUDSON

WHITE OAK

PORTSTOWN

LIBERTY

GAIL

CHRIS

ROLAND

PINE FOREST

LAURA

JAMES

Z

© KEY MAPS 2017

0   1/4   1/2   3/4   1 Mile

SEE 255 MAP

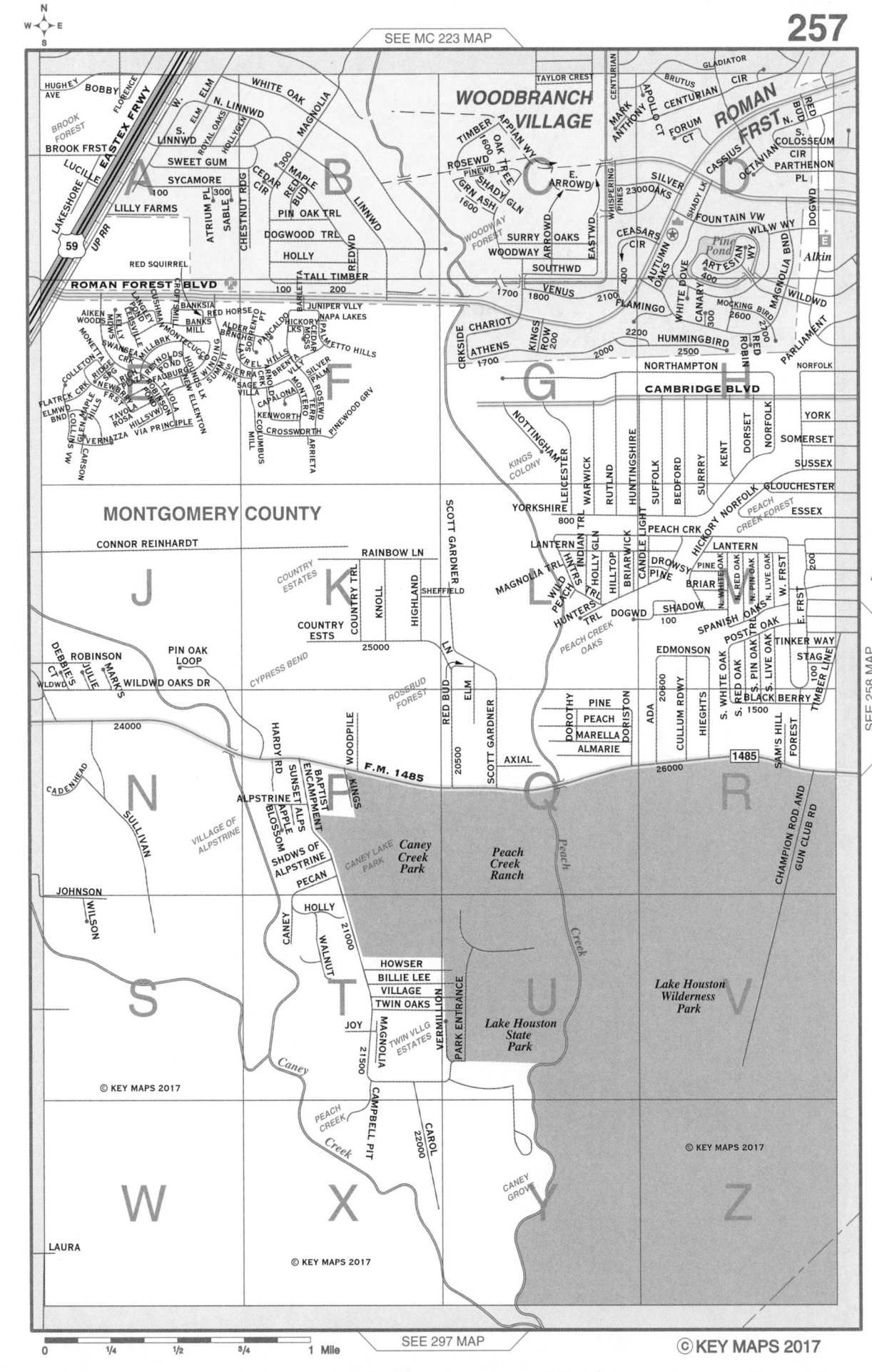

© KEY MAPS 2017

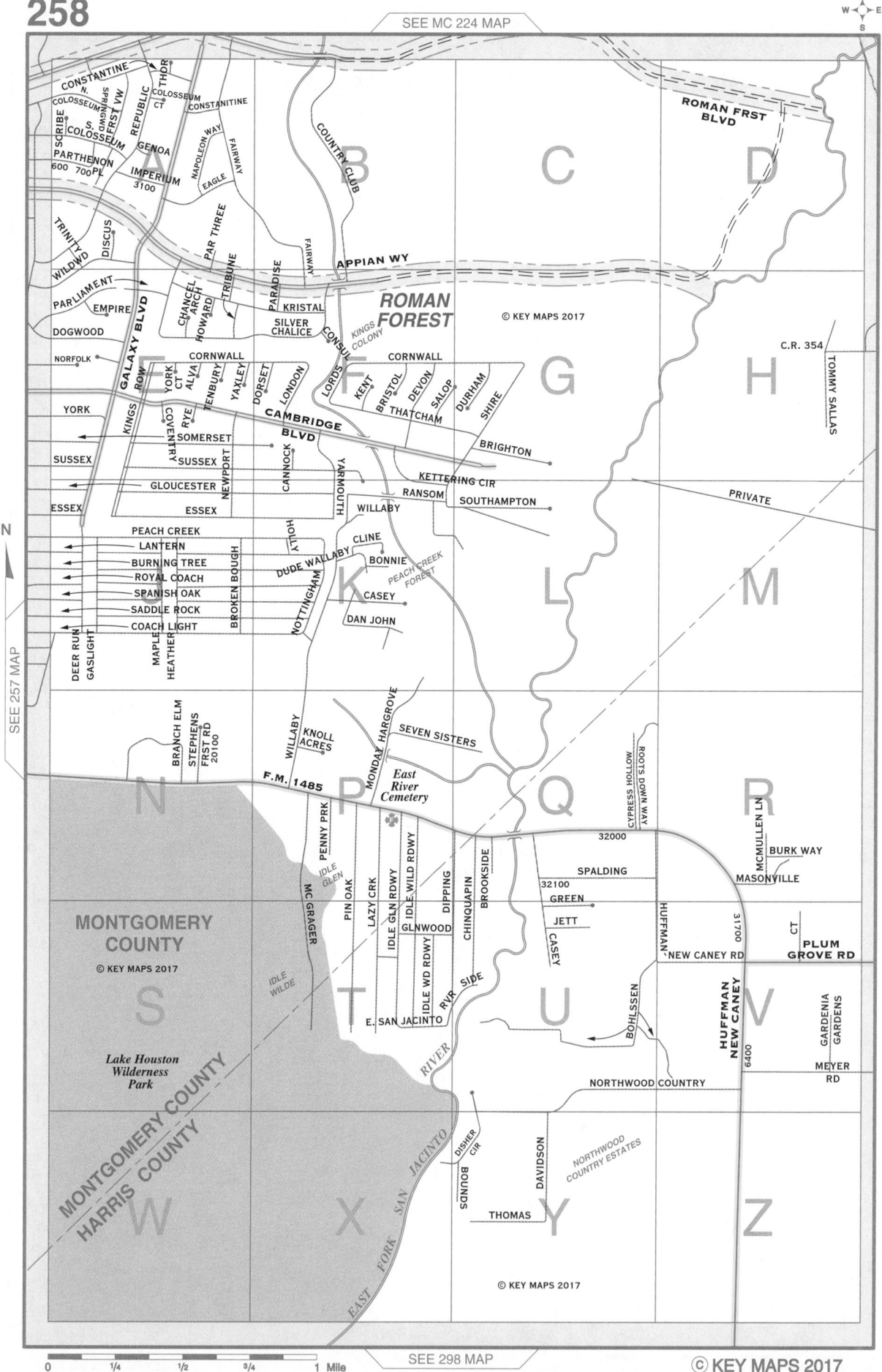

ROMAN FOREST

ROMAN FRST BLVD

MONTGOMERY COUNTY

© KEY MAPS 2017

Lake Houston Wilderness Park

HUFFMAN NEW CANEY

PLUM GROVE RD

© KEY MAPS 2017

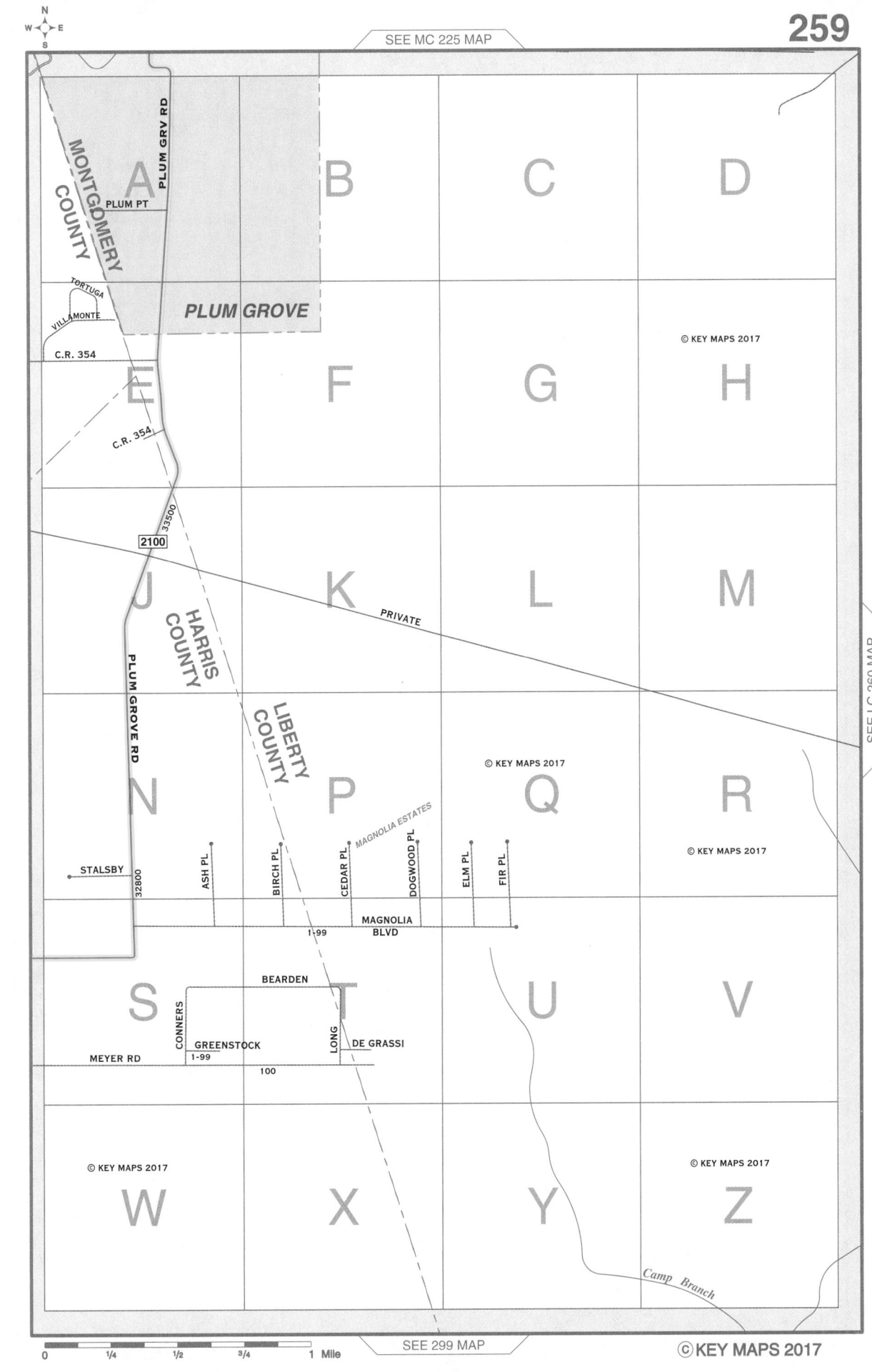

N
W E
S

MONTGOMERY COUNTY

PLUM GRV RD

A

PLUM PT

B

C

D

© KEY MAPS 2017

TORTUGA
VILLAMONTE

C.R. 354

PLUM GROVE

E

F

G

H

C.R. 354

33500

2100

J

HARRIS COUNTY

K

PRIVATE

L

M

PLUM GROVE RD

LIBERTY COUNTY

N

P

Q

R

© KEY MAPS 2017

© KEY MAPS 2017

© KEY MAPS 2017

MAGNOLIA ESTATES

STALSBY

32800

ASH PL

BIRCH PL

CEDAR PL

DOGWOOD PL

ELM PL

FIR PL

MAGNOLIA
BLVD

1-99

BEARDEN

S

CONNERS

T

LONG

DE GRASSI

U

V

GREENSTOCK

1-99

MEYER RD

100

© KEY MAPS 2017

© KEY MAPS 2017

W

X

Y

Z

Camp Branch

N

SEE LC 260 MAP

0   1/4   1/2   3/4   1 Mile

© **KEY MAPS** 2017

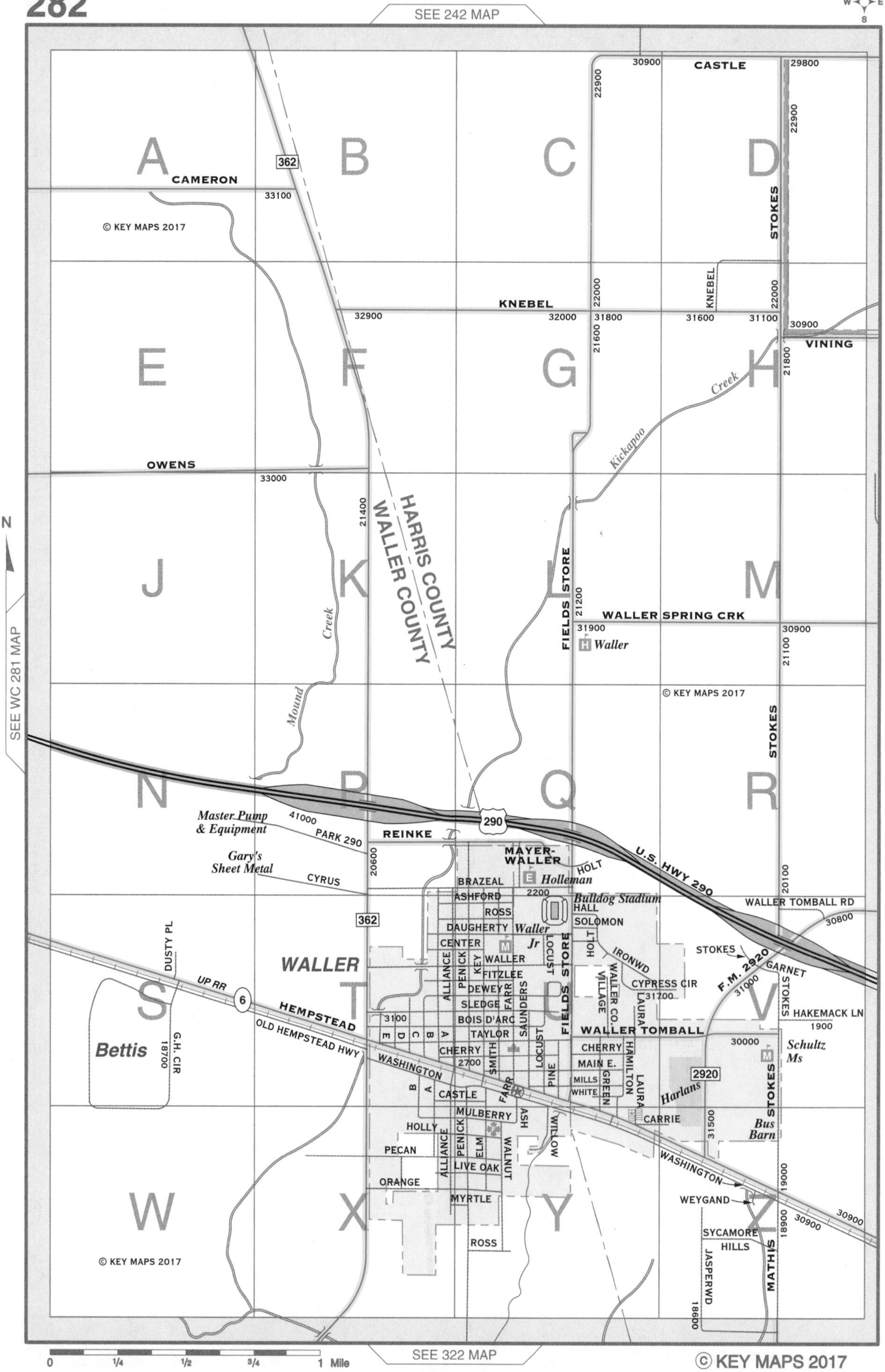

SEE 242 MAP

N
W E
S

A   B   C   D

CAMERON

362
33100

© KEY MAPS 2017

CASTLE
30900   29800
22900   22900
STOKES

KNEBEL
32900   32000   31800   31600   31100   30900

KNEBEL   22000   22000
21600   21800

VINING

E   F   G   H

Kickapoo   Creek

OWENS
33000

21400

HARRIS COUNTY
WALLER COUNTY

N

J   K   L   M

Creek

FIELDS STORE   21200

WALLER SPRING CRK
31900   30900
H Waller   21100

© KEY MAPS 2017

Mound   Creek

STOKES

SEE WC 281 MAP

N   P   Q   R

290

Master Pump
& Equipment   41000   PARK 290
REINKE

Gary's
Sheet Metal   CYRUS   20600

MAYER-
WALLER   HOLT   U.S. HWY 290   20100

Holleman   WALLER TOMBALL RD
30800

362   BRAZEAL   E   Bulldog Stadium
ASHFORD   2200   HALL   SOLOMON
ROSS   Waller   STOKES

DAUGHERTY   Jr   IRONWD   CYPRESS CIR
CENTER   M   WALLER   31700
WALLER   FITZLEE   WALLER CO.
DEWEY   VILLAGE   LAURA

WALLER   S   T   SLEDGE   U   WALLER TOMBALL   V
HEMPSTEAD   BOIS D'ARC   TAYLOR   30000   Schultz
S   3100   E   D   C   B   Ms
Bettis   CHERRY   CHERRY   HAKEMACK LN
2700   MAIN E.   1900

UP RR   6
DUSTY PL   G.H. CIR   18700

MILLS   GREEN   Harlans
WASHINGTON   B   WHITE   CARRIE   31500   Bus
CASTLE   Barn

HOLLY   MULBERRY   2920
PENICK   ELM
PECAN   ALLIANCE   KEY   LIVE OAK   WASHINGTON   WEYGAND
ORANGE   WILLOW   19000   30900
MYRTLE   18900   SYCAMORE
W   X   Y   HILLS   Z
ROSS   JASPERWD
18600

MATHIS

0   1/4   1/2   3/4   1 Mile

SEE 322 MAP

© KEY MAPS 2017

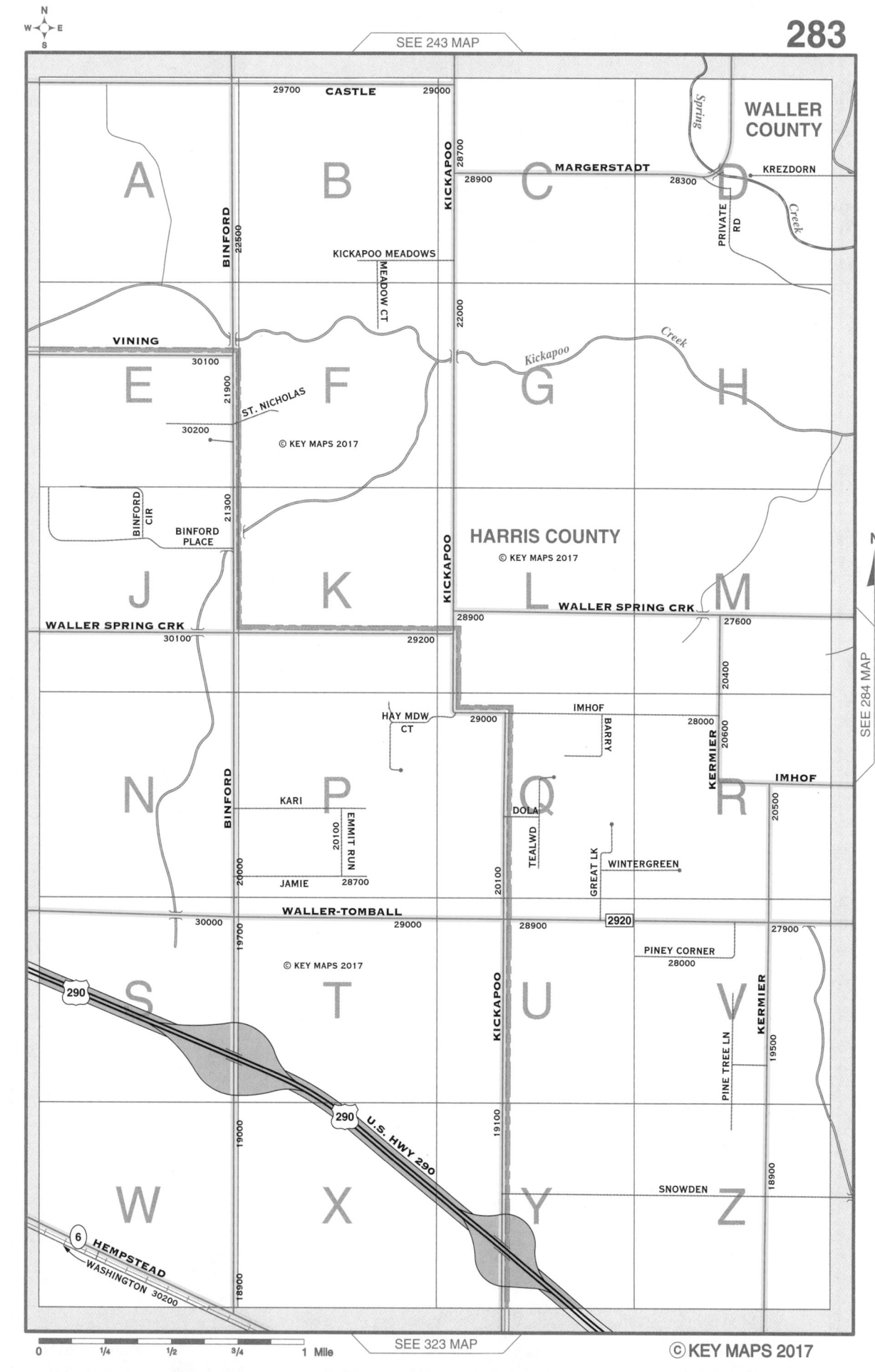

N
W—E
S

CASTLE
29700   29000

WALLER
COUNTY

Spring

A   B   C   MARGERSTADT   D   KREZDORN
28700   28300
KICKAPOO
28900   Creek

BINFORD
22500

KICKAPOO MEADOWS

MEADOW CT

22000

PRIVATE RD

VINING
30100

E   F   Kickapoo   Creek
21900   G   H

ST. NICHOLAS
30200

© KEY MAPS 2017

BINFORD CIR
21300

BINFORD PLACE

HARRIS COUNTY
© KEY MAPS 2017

N

KICKAPOO

J   K   L   WALLER SPRING CRK   M
28900   27600

WALLER SPRING CRK
30100   29200

SEE 284 MAP

20400

IMHOF

29000   BARRY   28000

HAY MDW CT

KERMIER
20600

R   IMHOF

BINFORD

N   P   KARI   Q   DOLA   20500

EMMIT RUN
20000   20100   TEALWD   GREAT LK   WINTERGREEN

JAMIE   28700   20100

WALLER-TOMBALL
30000   29000   28900   2920   27900

PINEY CORNER
28000

© KEY MAPS 2017

19700

290   S   T   U   V
19000   KICKAPOO   KERMIER
19500

290   U.S. HWY 290
19100

PINE TREE LN

W   X   Y   SNOWDEN   18900
Z

6   HEMPSTEAD

WASHINGTON   30200
18900   18900

0   1/4   1/2   3/4   1 Mile

© KEY MAPS 2017

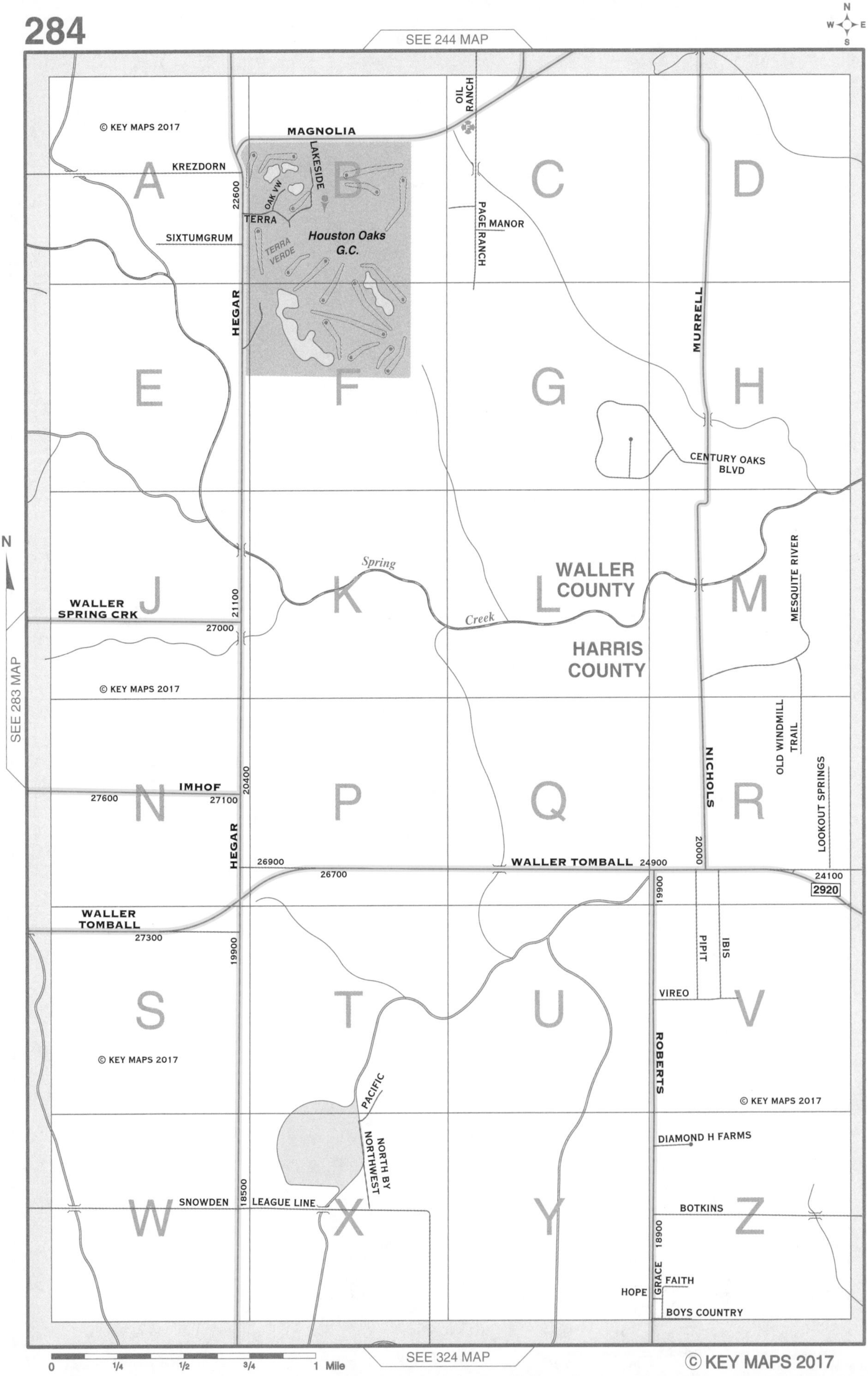

SEE 244 MAP

N
W — E
S

© KEY MAPS 2017

KREZDORN

A

MAGNOLIA

LAKESIDE

OAK VW

TERRA

B

22600

HEGAR

SIXTUMGRUM

TERRA VERDE

Houston Oaks G.C.

OIL RANCH

PAGE RANCH

MANOR

C

D

MURRELL

E

F

G

H

CENTURY OAKS BLVD

SEE 283 MAP

N

Spring

Creek

WALLER COUNTY

HARRIS COUNTY

MESQUITE RIVER

WALLER SPRING CRK

J

21100

27000

K

L

M

© KEY MAPS 2017

IMHOF

27600

N

27100

20400

HEGAR

P

Q

OLD WINDMILL TRAIL

LOOKOUT SPRINGS

NICHOLS

20000

R

26900

26700

WALLER TOMBALL

24900

24100

2920

WALLER TOMBALL

27300

19900

19900

S

T

PIPIT

IBIS

U

VIREO

V

ROBERTS

S

© KEY MAPS 2017

PACIFIC

DIAMOND H FARMS

SNOWDEN

18500

LEAGUE LINE

NORTH BY NORTHWEST

W

X

Y

BOTKINS

Z

18900

GRACE

FAITH

HOPE

BOYS COUNTRY

0   1/4   1/2   3/4   1 Mile

SEE 324 MAP

© KEY MAPS 2017

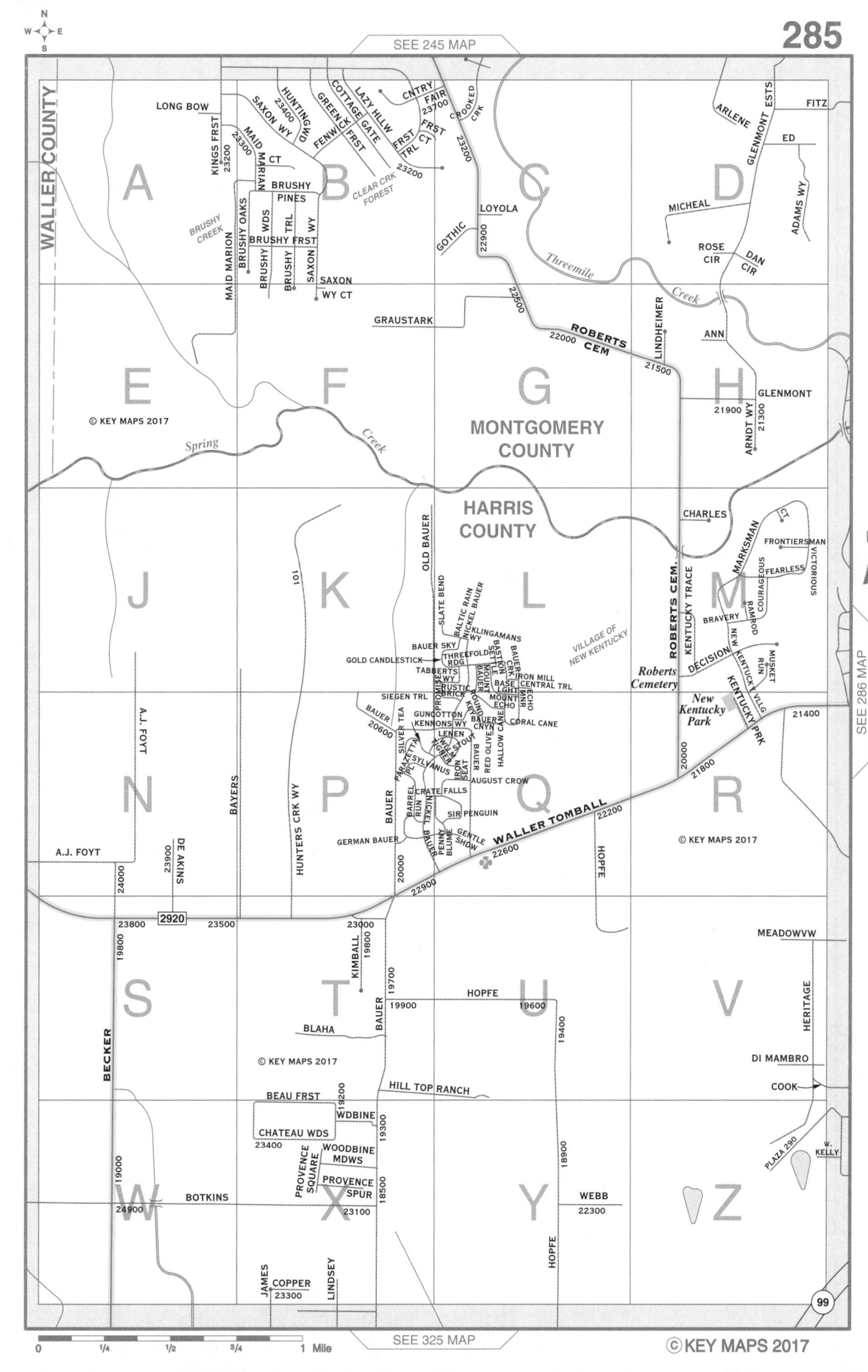

WALLER COUNTY

N
W E
S

LONG BOW

KINGS FRST 23200

MAID MARIAN 23200

HUNTING WD 23400

SAXON WY

GREEN FRST

FENWICK

COTTAGE GATE

LAZY HLLW

FRST CT

FRST TRL

CNTRY FAIR 23700

CROOKED CRK

ARLENE

GLENMONT ESTS

FITZ

ED

ADAMS WY

A

B

C

D

BRUSHY PINES

BRUSHY OAKS

BRUSHY WDS

BRUSHY TRL

BRUSHY FRST

SAXON WY

SAXON WY CT

CLEAR CRK FOREST

LOYOLA

GOTHIC

22900

MICHEAL

ROSE CIR

DAN CIR

Threemile

BRUSHY CREEK

MAID MARION

GRAUSTARK

22500

ROBERTS CEM

22000

LINDHEIMER

21500

Creek

ANN

GLENMONT

21900

ARNDT WY 21300

© KEY MAPS 2017

E

F

G

H

MONTGOMERY COUNTY

Spring

Creek

CHARLES

MARKSMAN

CT

FRONTIERSMAN

VICTORIOUS

FEARLESS

COURAGEOUS

HARRIS COUNTY

VILLAGE OF NEW KENTUCKY

ROBERTS CEM.

KENTUCKY TRACE

BRAVERY

RAMROD

NEW KENTUCKY VLLG

MUSKET

RUN

OLD BAUER

J

101

K

L

M

SLATE BEND

BALTIC RAIN

NICKEL BAUER

KLINGAMANS WY

BAUER SKY

THREEFOLD RDG

GOLD CANDLESTICK

TABBERTS WY

RUSTIC BRICK

SIEGEN TRL

BAUER 20600

SILVER TEA

GUNCOTTON

KENNONS WY

LENEN

BASTION

BATTLE

MOUNT BAUER

MOUNT BAUER

PROMISE

MOUND BAUER CNYN

MOUNT ECHO

BAUER LGHT

BASE

IRON MILL CENTRAL TRL

ECHO MNR

RED OLIVE

BAUER

HALLOW CANE

CORAL CANE

DECISION

KENTUCKY VLLG

New Kentucky Park

KENTUCKY PRK

21400

SEE 286 MAP

N

Roberts Cemetery

20000

21800

N

PLAZETTA

SYLVANUS

TWINER

IRON SEAT

AUGUST CROW

BAUER

BARREL RUN

PARA

NICKEL BAUER

CRATE FALLS

SIR PENGUIN

A.J. FOYT

A.J. FOYT

24000

DE AKINS 23900

BAYERS

HUNTERS CRK WY

GERMAN BAUER

20000

PENNY BLUME

GENTLE SHOW

22600

WALLER TOMBALL

22200

HOPFE

© KEY MAPS 2017

N

P

Q

R

22900

2920

23800

23500

19800

23000

KIMBALL 19800

MEADOWVW

HERITAGE

BECKER

19700

HOPFE

19900

19600

19400

DI MAMBRO

COOK

BAUER

S

BLAHA

T

U

V

© KEY MAPS 2017

19000

HILL TOP RANCH

BEAU FRST

CHATEAU WDS 23400

WDBINE

19200

19300

WOODBINE MDWS

18900

PLAZA 290

W. KELLY

PROVENCE SQUARE

PROVENCE SPUR

18500

BOTKINS

24900

W

X

23100

Y

WEBB 22300

Z

JAMES

COPPER 23300

LINDSEY

HOPFE

0   1/4   1/2   3/4   1 Mile

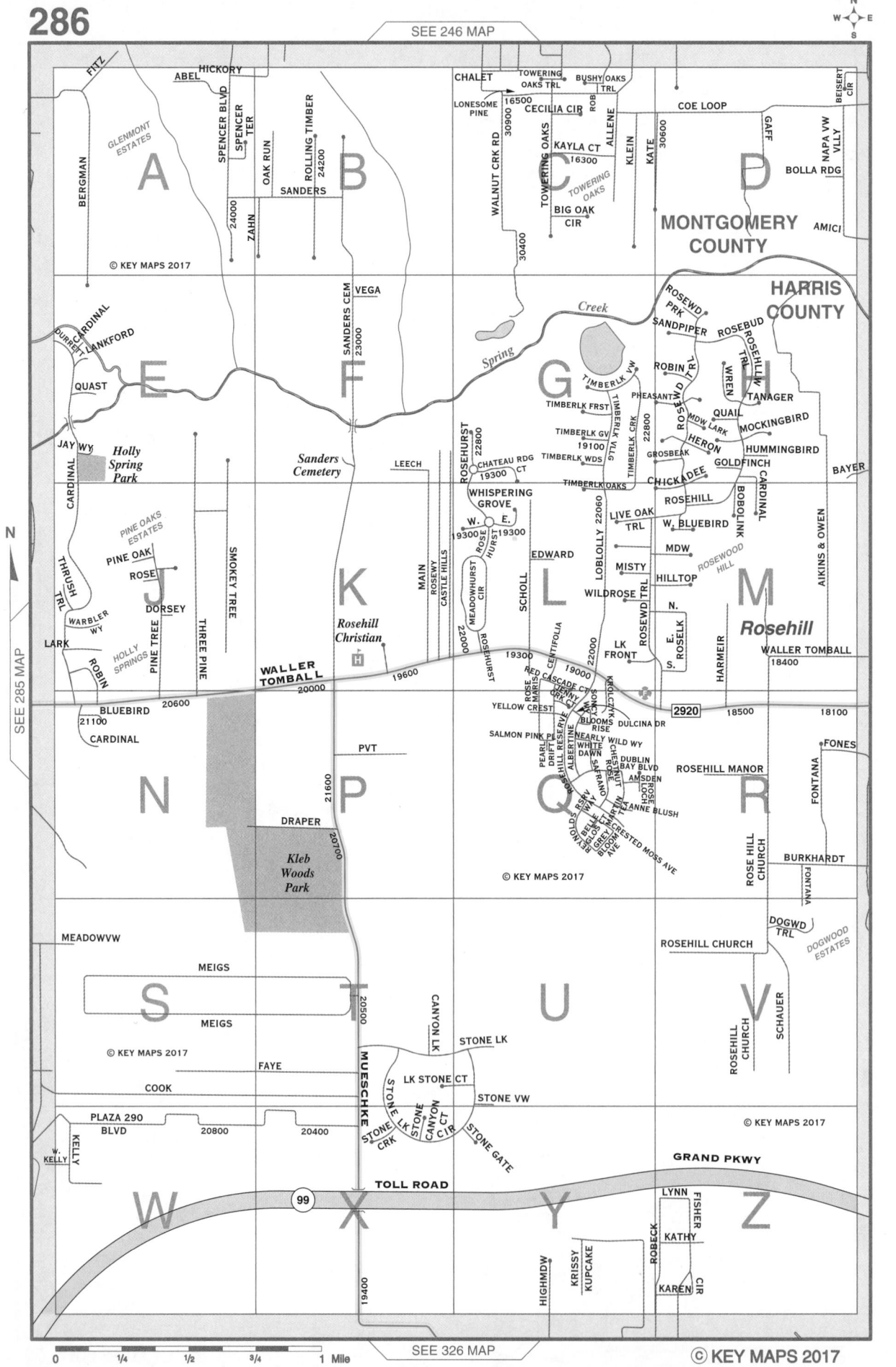

N
W E
S

A

FITZ
ABEL
HICKORY
SPENCER BLVD
SPENCER TER
OAK RUN
ROLLING TIMBER
24200
SANDERS
24000
ZAHN
GLENMONT ESTATES
BERGMAN
© KEY MAPS 2017

B

C

CHALET
TOWERING OAKS TRL
BUSHY OAKS TRL
LONESOME PINE
16500
CECILIA CIR
ROB
ALLENE
COE LOOP
30900
TOWERING OAKS
KAYLA CT
16300
KLEIN
KATE
30600
WALNUT CRK RD
BIG OAK CIR
TOWERING OAKS
30400

D

GAFF
NAPA VW VLLY
BOLLA RDG
AMICI
BEISERT CIR

MONTGOMERY COUNTY

HARRIS COUNTY

Creek
Spring

SANDERS CEM
VEGA
23000

E

DURR
CARDINAL
LANKFORD
QUAST
JAY WY
Holly Spring Park
CARDINAL

F

Sanders Cemetery
LEECH

G

ROSEHURST
22800
CHATEAU RDG CT
19300
TIMBERLK FRST
TIMBERLK GV
19100
TIMBERLK WDS
TIMBERLK OAKS
TIMBERLK VW
TIMBERLK VALG
TIMBERLK CRK
22800

H

ROSEWD PRK
SANDPIPER
ROSEBUD TRL
ROSEHLLW
ROBIN
WREN
TANAGER
PHEASANT
MDW LARK
QUAIL
MOCKINGBIRD
HERON
HUMMINGBIRD
GROSBEAK
GOLDFINCH
CHICKADEE
CARDINAL
BAYER
ROSEWD TRL

J

THRUSH TRL
PINE OAK
ROSE
DORSEY
WARBLER WY
LARK
ROBIN
Pine Oaks Estates
Holly Springs
PINE TREE
Smokey Tree
THREE PINE

K

WHISPERING GROVE
W. 19300
E. 19300
ROSEHURST
MEADOWHURST CIR
22000
Rosehill Christian
MAIN
ROSEWY
CASTLE HILLS
WALLER TOMBALL
20000
19600

L

ROSEHILL
LIVE OAK TRL
W. BLUEBIRD
MDW
MISTY
HILLTOP
WILDROSE
EDWARD
SCHOLL
LOBLOLLY
22060
LK FRONT
19300
19000
CENTIFOLIA
22000

M

BOBOLINK
CARDINAL
AIKINS & OWEN
Rosewood Hill
N. ROSELK
E. ROSELK
S.
HARMEIR
Rosehill
WALLER TOMBALL
18400
ROSEWD TRL

N

BLUEBIRD
20600
21100
CARDINAL
Kleb Woods Park

P

PVT
21600
DRAPER
20700

Q

RED CASCADE CT
ROSE MARLS
CHERRY CRK
YELLOW CREST
BLOOMS RISE
SALMON PINK BLVD
NEARLY WILD WY
WHITE DAWN
PEARL DRIFT
SALMON
DUBLIN BAY BLVD
HILL RESERVE
ALBERTINE
SERRANO
CHESTNUT ROSE
AMSDEN
RSKV WY
BELLE
REYNOLDS
BIGLOW CT
GREG MARTIN
ROSE
JEANNE BLUSH
LOCHE
DULCINA DR
CRESTED MOSS AVE
KNOLOCH
© KEY MAPS 2017

R

FONES
ROSEHILL MANOR
FONTANA
FONTANA
BURKHARDT
ROSE HILL CHURCH

S

MEADOWVW
MEIGS
MEIGS
© KEY MAPS 2017

T

20500
MUESCHKE
FAYE
COOK
PLAZA 290 BLVD
20800
20400
W. KELLY
KELLY

U

CANYON LK
STONE LK
LK STONE CT
STONE VW
CANYON CT
STONE LK STONE CANYON CIR
STONE LK CRK
STONE GATE

V

ROSEHILL CHURCH
SCHAUER
DOGWD TRL
Dogwood Estates
ROSEHILL CHURCH
© KEY MAPS 2017

W

X

19400

Y

HIGHMDW
KRISSY
KUPCAKE
ROBECK

Z

LYNN
FISHER
KATHY
CIR
KAREN

GRAND PKWY

TOLL ROAD
99

2920
18500
18100

0 1/4 1/2 3/4 1 Mile

© **KEY MAPS** 2017

SEE 285 MAP

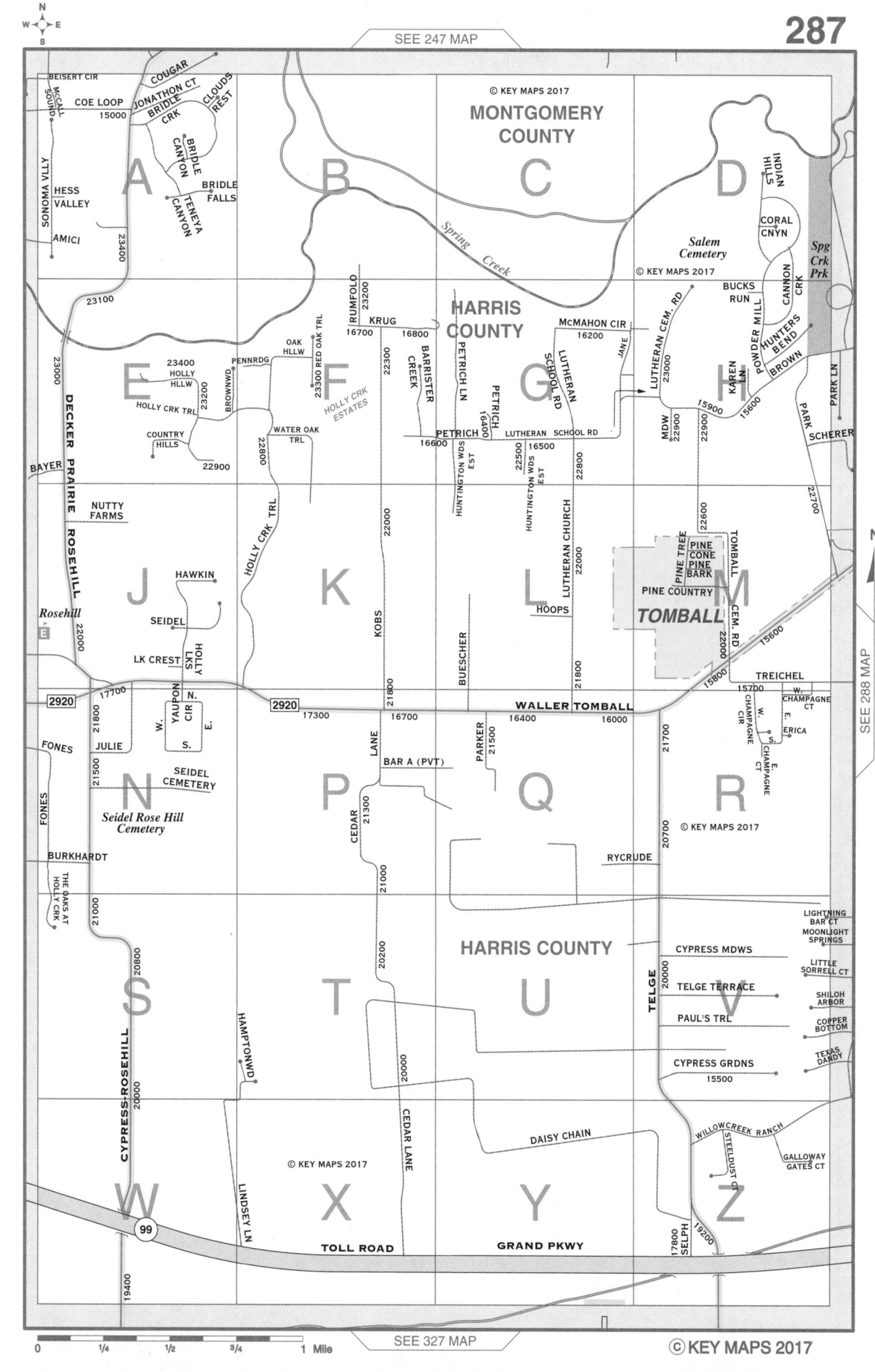

© KEY MAPS 2017

MONTGOMERY
COUNTY

HARRIS
COUNTY

BEISERT CIR
McCALL SOUND
COE LOOP
15000
COUGAR
JONATHON CT
BRIDLE CRK
CLOUDS REST

SONOMA VLLY

HESS VALLEY

AMICI

BRIDLE CANYON
TENEYA CANYON
BRIDLE FALLS

23400

23100

A

B

Spring Creek

C

Salem
Cemetery

© KEY MAPS 2017

INDIAN
HILLS

CORAL CNYN

Spg
Crk
Prk

D

23000

DECKER PRAIRIE ROSEHILL

BAYER

23400
HOLLY HLLW
PENNRDG
BROWNWD
23200
HOLLY CRK TRL

COUNTRY HILLS
22900

OAK HLLW
23300 RED OAK TRL

WATER OAK TRL
22800

HOLLY CRK TRL

22000

E

F

RUMFOLO
23200
KRUG
16700
16800
22300

BARRISTER CREEK

HOLLY CRK ESTATES

PETRICH LN

PETRICH
16400
PETRICH
16600

G

McMAHON CIR
16200

JANE

LUTHERAN CEM. RD.
23000

LUTHERAN SCHOOL RD

LUTHERAN SCHOOL RD
16500

HUNTINGTON WDS EST
22500
HUNTINGTON WDS EST

22800

BUCKS RUN

POWDER MILL
HUNTERS BEND
BROWN

KAREN LN
15900
15600

H

MDW
22900
22900

PARK LN

PARK
SCHERER

22700

NUTTY FARMS

Rosehill

22000

J

HAWKIN

SEIDEL

LK CREST

K

KOBS

22000

21800

L

LUTHERAN CHURCH

HOOPS

22000

21800

BUESCHER

Pine Country

TOMBALL

PINE TREE
PINE CONE
PINE BARK

TOMBALL CEM. RD.

22600

22000

15600

15800

M

N

2920

17700
21800
21500

JULIE

FONES

N

HOLLY LKS
YAUPON CIR
W. N. E. S.

SEIDEL CEMETERY

Seidel Rose Hill
Cemetery

2920
17300

16700

WALLER TOMBALL
16400
16000

P

CEDAR LANE
21300
21000

BAR A (PVT)

Q

PARKER
21500

RYCRUDE

21700

20700

TREICHEL

15700
CHAMPAGNE CIR
CHAMPAGNE CT
ERICA
CHAMPAGNE CT
W. E. S.

R

© KEY MAPS 2017

FONES

BURKHARDT

S

THE OAKS AT HOLLY CRK

21000

CYPRESS-ROSEHILL
20800
20000

HAMPTONWD

T

20200

20000

CEDAR LANE

HARRIS COUNTY

U

TELGE

20000

V

CYPRESS MDWS

TELGE TERRACE

PAUL'S TRL

CYPRESS GRDNS
15500

LIGHTNING BAR CT
MOONLIGHT SPRINGS

LITTLE SORRELL CT

SHILOH ARBOR

COPPER BOTTOM

TEXAS DANDY

W

LINDSEY LN

© KEY MAPS 2017

X

DAISY CHAIN

Y

WILLOWCREEK RANCH
STEELDUST LN
GALLOWAY GATES CT

17800 SELPH
19200

Z

99

TOLL ROAD

GRAND PKWY

19400

SEE 288 MAP

SEE 248 MAP

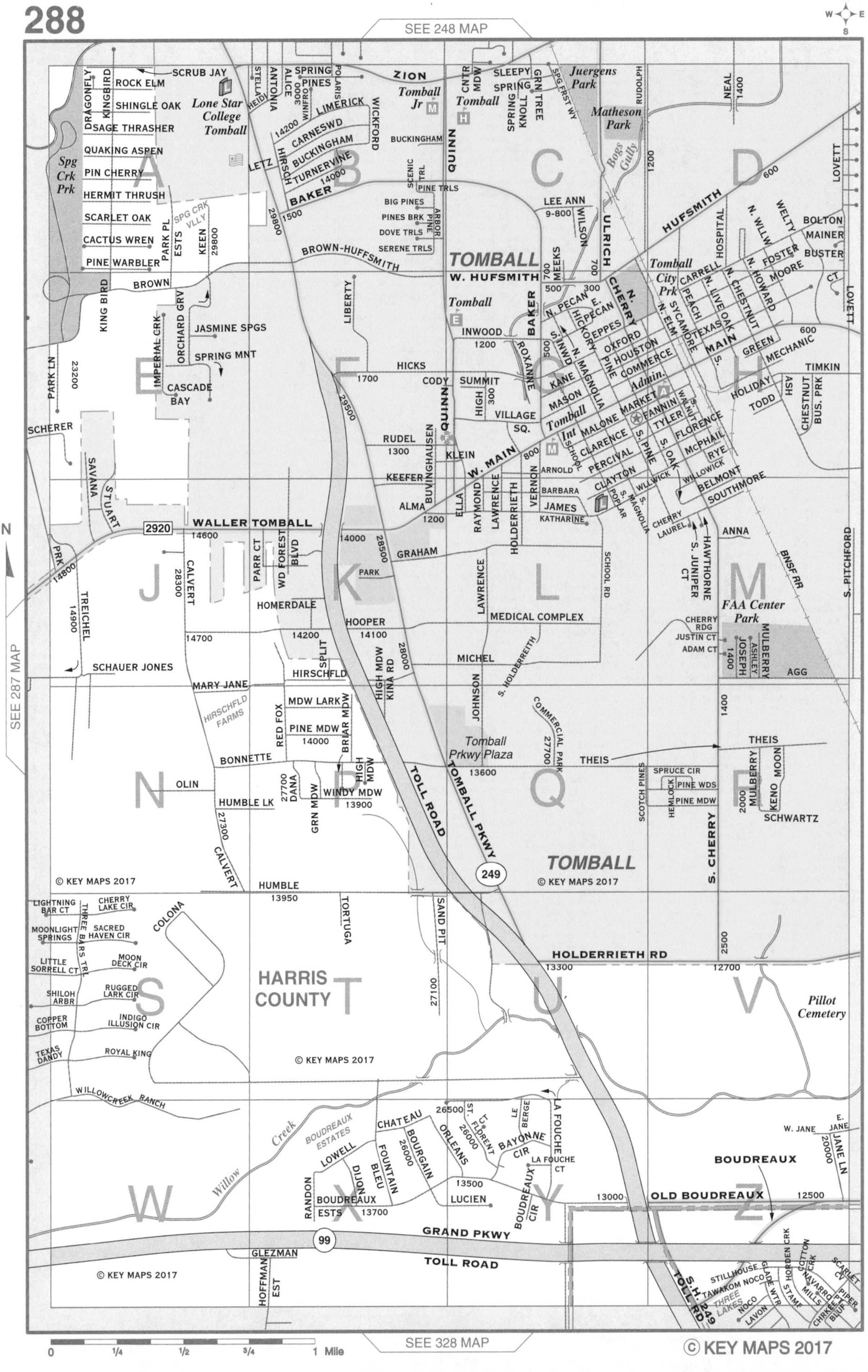

N W E S

DRAGONFLY
KINGBIRD
ROCK ELM
SCRUB JAY
SHINGLE OAK
SAGE THRASHER
QUAKING ASPEN
PIN CHERRY
HERMIT THRUSH
SCARLET OAK
CACTUS WREN
PINE WARBLER

Lone Star College Tomball

STELLA
HEIDIA
ANTONIA
ALICE
SPRING PINES
POLARIS
SPRING
ZION
Tomball Jr

SLEEPY SPRING
SPRING KNOLL
GRN TREE
Juergens Park
Matheson Park

LIMERICK
WICKFORD
CARNESWD
BUCKINGHAM
TURNERVINE
14200
HIRSCH
LETZ
14000
BAKER
1500
29800

Tomball
SCENIC TRL
PINE TRLS
BIG PINES
PINES BRK
DOVE TRLS
SERENE TRLS

QUINN
CNTR MDW
Tomball

Bog's Gully

LEE ANN
9-800
WILSON
ULRICH
MEEKS
700

HUFSMITH

N WLLW
N FOSTER
MOORE
WELTY
BOLTON
MAINER
BUSTER
NEAL
1400
LOVETT
600

Spg Crk Prk

KING BIRD
23200
PARK LN
SCHERER

PARK PL ESTS
KEEN
29800
SPG CRK VLLY

BROWN-HUFFSMITH

W. HUFSMITH
Tomball
INWOOD
1200
500

Tomball City Prk
CARRELL HOSPITAL
PEACH
LINE OAK
N. CHESTNUT
GREEN
HOLIDAY
TODD
MECHANIC
ASH
CHESTNUT BUS. PRK
TIMKIN
600

IMPERIAL CRK
ORCHARD GRV
JASMINE SPGS
SPRING MNT
CASCADE BAY

LIBERTY
HICKS
1700
CODY
SUMMIT
HIGH
VILLAGE SQ.

N. PECAN
E. PECAN
HICKORY
ROXANNE
N. IVWD
N. MAGNOLIA
PINE
OXFORD
HOUSTON
COMMERCE
Admin.
300

BAKER
N. ELM
SYCAMORE
TEXAS
S.

SCHERER
SAVANA
STUART

2920
WALLER TOMBALL
14600
CALVERT
28300
PARR CT
WD FOREST BLVD
14000
28500

RUDEL
1300
KLEIN
KEEFER
ALMA
1200
BUVINGHAUSEN
W. MAIN
800

KANE
MASON
MALONE
CLARENCE
PERCIVAL
CLAYTON
ARNOLD
S. PINE

Int Tomball School
MARKET
FANNIN
TYLER
FLORENCE
McPHAIL
RYE
WILLOWICK
BELMONT
SOUTHMORE

FLORENCE
A
S. MAGNOLIA
POPLAR

HAWTHORNE
S. JUNIPER CT
ANNA

HOMERDALE
14700

PARK
GRAHAM
HOOPER
14100
14200
14000
28000
HIGH MDW KINA RD

ELLA
RAYMOND
LAWRENCE
VERNON
HOLDERRIETH
BARBARA
JAMES
KATHARINE

LAWRENCE
MEDICAL COMPLEX
SCHOOL RD
MICHEL
S. HOLDERRIETH
JOHNSON

CHERRY LAUREL
S. MAGNOLIA
CHERRY RDG
JUSTIN CT
ADAM CT
FAA Center Park
MULBERRY
JOSEPH
ASHLEY
1400
AGG

BNSF RR
S. PITCHFORD

SCHAUER JONES
MARY JANE
HIRSHFLD

HIRSHFLD FARMS
RED FOX
MDW LARK
PINE MDW
14000
SPLIT
BRIAR MDW

Tomball Prkwy Plaza
13600
COMMERCIAL PARK
27700
THEIS
SCOTCH PINES
SPRUCE CIR
HEMLOCK
PINE WDS
PINE MDW
MULBERRY
2000
KENO
MOON
THEIS
SCHWARTZ

BONNETTE
OLIN
HUMBLE LK
27300
CALVERT
DANA
27700
GRN MDW
WINDY MDW
13900
HIGH MDW

TOLL ROAD
TOMBALL PKWY
249

TOMBALL
© KEY MAPS 2017

S. CHERRY
1400
2500

HUMBLE
13950

LIGHTNING BAR CT
CHERRY LAKE CIR
MOONLIGHT SPRINGS
SACRED HAVEN CIR
LITTLE SORRELL CT
MOON DECK CIR
SHILOH ARBR
RUGGED LARK CIR
COPPER BOTTOM
INDIGO ILLUSION CIR
TEXAS DANDY
ROYAL KING

COLONA
TORTUGA
27100
SAND PIT

HOLDERRIETH RD
13300
12700
2500

HARRIS COUNTY
© KEY MAPS 2017

Pillot Cemetery

WILLOWCREEK RANCH

Willow Creek

Boudreaux Estates
LOWELL
CHATEAU
BOURGAIN
26000
FOUNTAIN BLEU
DIJON
RANDON
BOUDREAUX ESTS
13700
ORLEANS
13500
LUCIEN
26500
ST. FLORENT
26000
LE FLORENT
BERGE
BAYONNE CIR
LA FOUCHE
LA FOUCHE CT
BOUDREAUX CIR
13000

BOUDREAUX
OLD BOUDREAUX
12500
W. JANE
E. JANE
JANE LN
20000

99
GRAND PKWY
GLEZMAN
HOFFMAN EST
TOLL ROAD

S.H. 249 TOLL RD
STILLHOUSE
TAWAKOM
NOCO
THREE LAKES
LAVON
HORDEN CRK
COTTON MILLS
NAVARRO
CHRKEE BLUFF
SANDPIPER CT
SCARLET

© KEY MAPS 2017

© KEY MAPS 2017

SEE 287 MAP

SEE 328 MAP

0 1/4 1/2 3/4 1 Mile

© KEY MAPS 2017

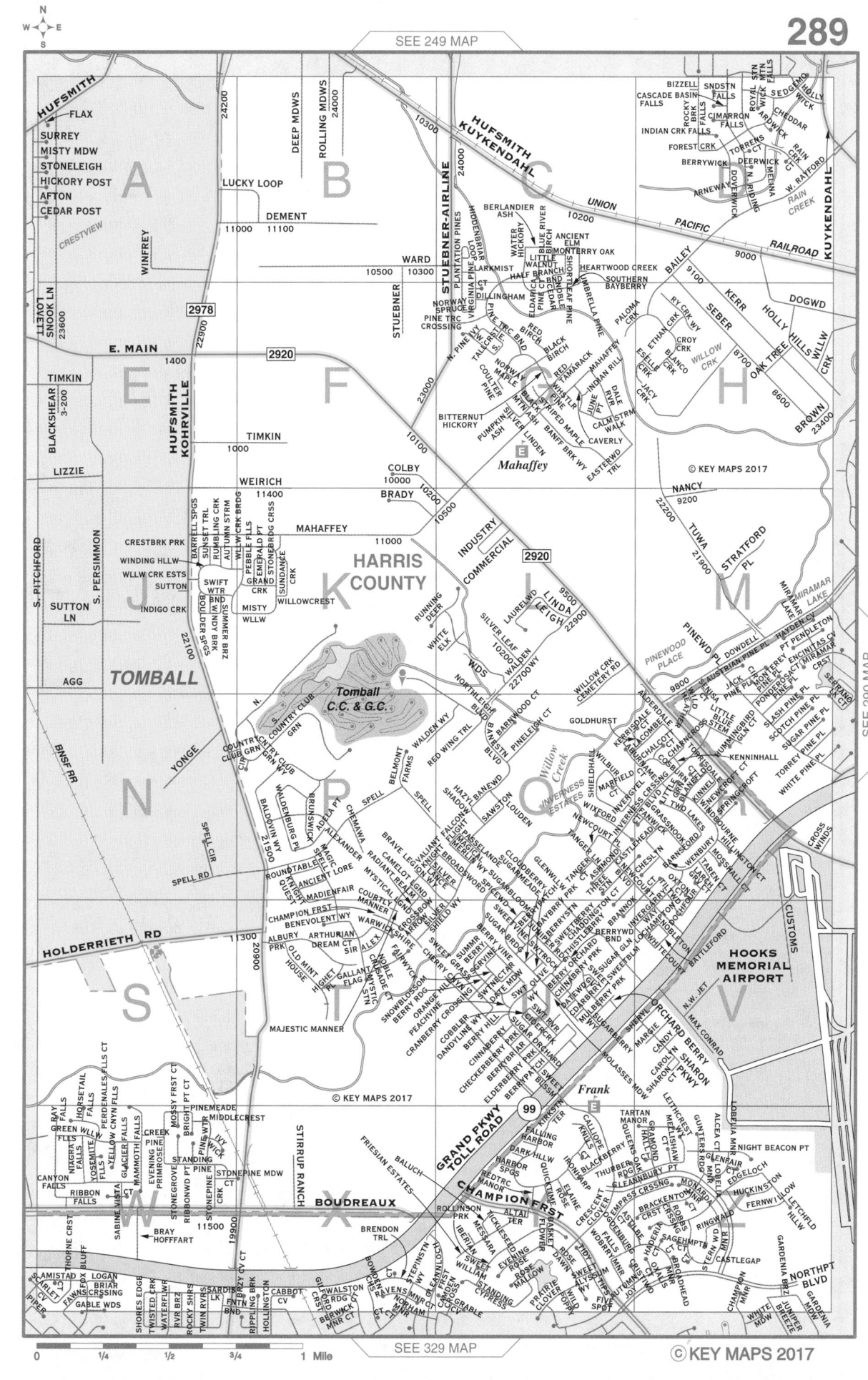

© KEY MAPS 2017

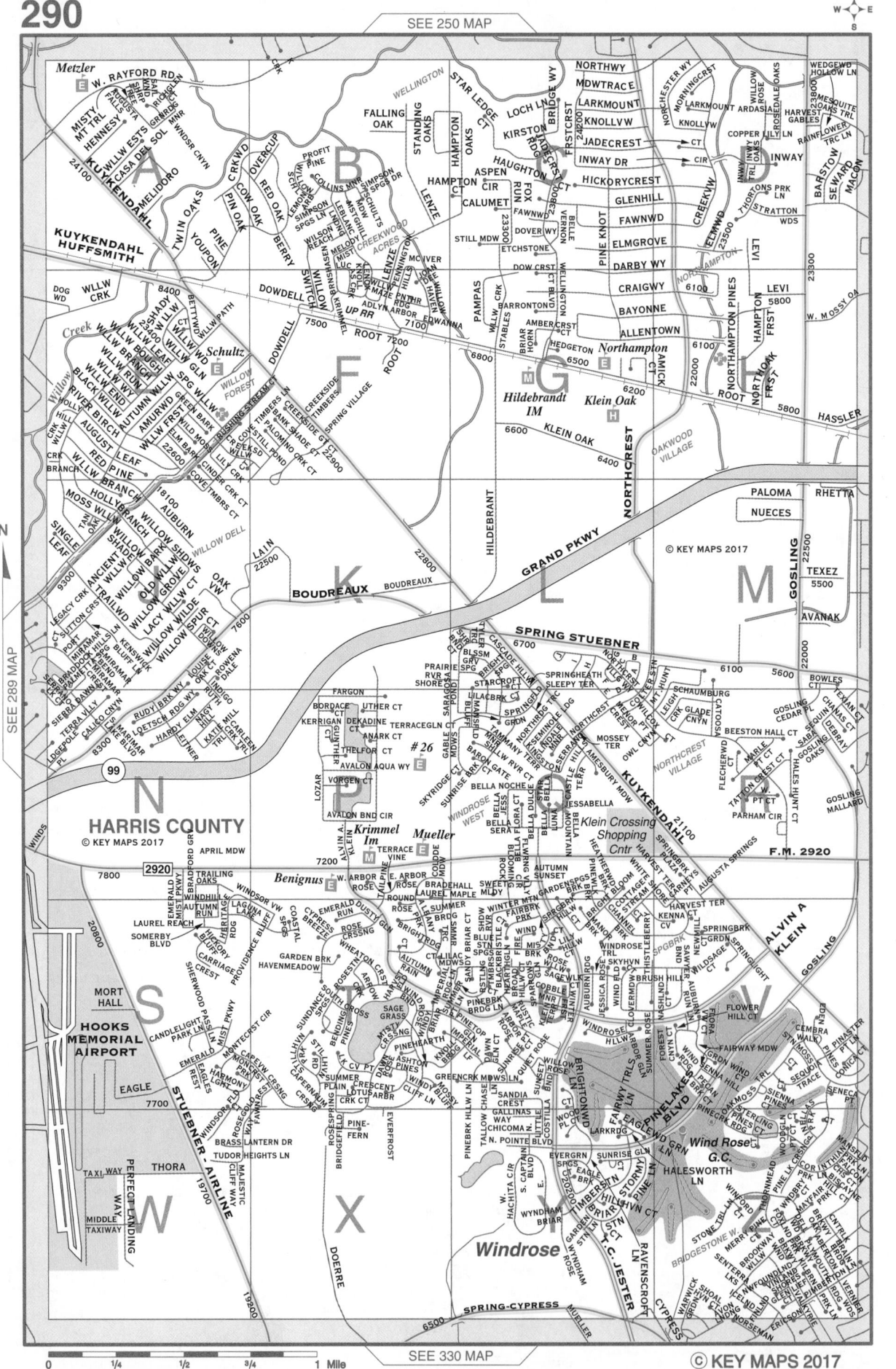

SEE 250 MAP

N
W E
S

Metzler W. RAYFORD RD.

FALLING OAK

MISTY MT TRL

KUYKENDAHL

KUYKENDAHL HUFFSMITH

Creek

Schultz

Willow Forest

STANDING OAKS

HAMPTON OAKS

NORTHWY

MDWTRACE

LARKMOUNT

KNOLLVW

JADECREST

INWAY DR

HICKORYCREST

GLENHILL

FAWNWD

ELMGROVE

DARBY WY

CRAIGWY

BAYONNE

ALLENTOWN

HEDGETON

Northampton

NORTHAMPTON PINES

HAMPTON FRST

LEVI

HASSLER

WEDGEWD HOLLOW LN

BARSTOW

SEWARD

MACON

INWAY

DOWDELL

WILLOW DELL

SPRING VILLAGE

Hildebrandt IM

Klein Oak

KLEIN OAK

NORTHCREST

OAKWOOD VILLAGE

GRAND PKWY

PALOMA

NUECES

RHETTA

© KEY MAPS 2017

GOSLING

TEXEZ

AVANAK

BOUDREAUX

LAIN

OAK VW

SPRING STUEBNER

99

N

HARRIS COUNTY
© KEY MAPS 2017

2920

Krimmel Im

Mueller

Benignus

#26

KUYKENDAHL

Klein Crossing Shopping Cntr

F.M. 2920

ALVIN A KLEIN

GOSLING

MORT HALL

HOOKS MEMORIAL AIRPORT

EAGLE

STUEBNER AIRLINE

THORA

TAXI WAY

MIDDLE TAXIWAY

PERFECT LANDING WAY

W

X

S

T

U

V

DOERRE

PINELAKES BLVD

Wind Rose G.C.

HALESWORTH LN

Y.C. JESTER

RAVENSCROFT

Windrose

SPRING-CYPRESS

MUELLER

CYPRESS

Z

SEE 330 MAP

0   1/4   1/2   3/4   1 Mile

© KEY MAPS 2017

SEE 289 MAP

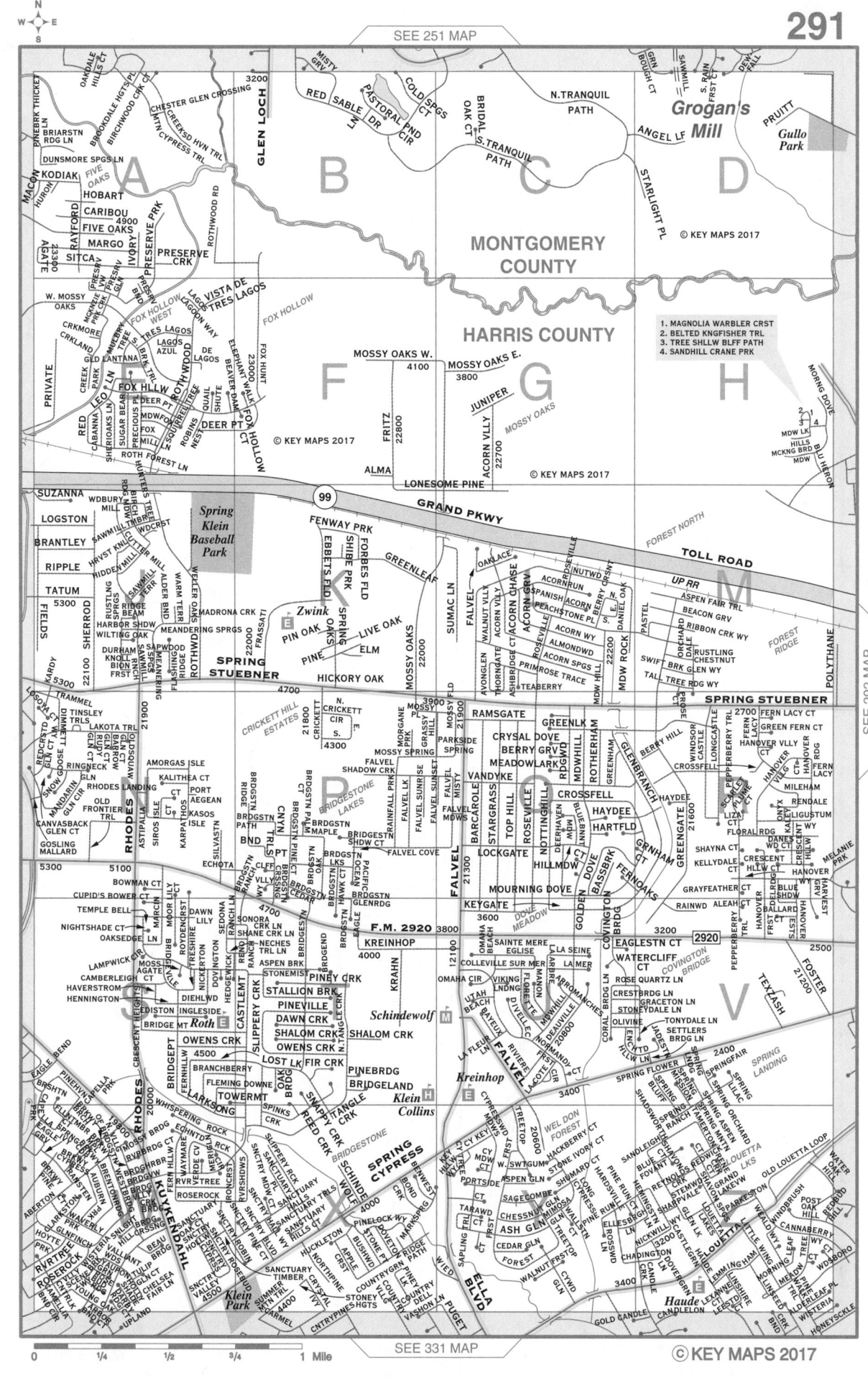

© KEY MAPS 2017

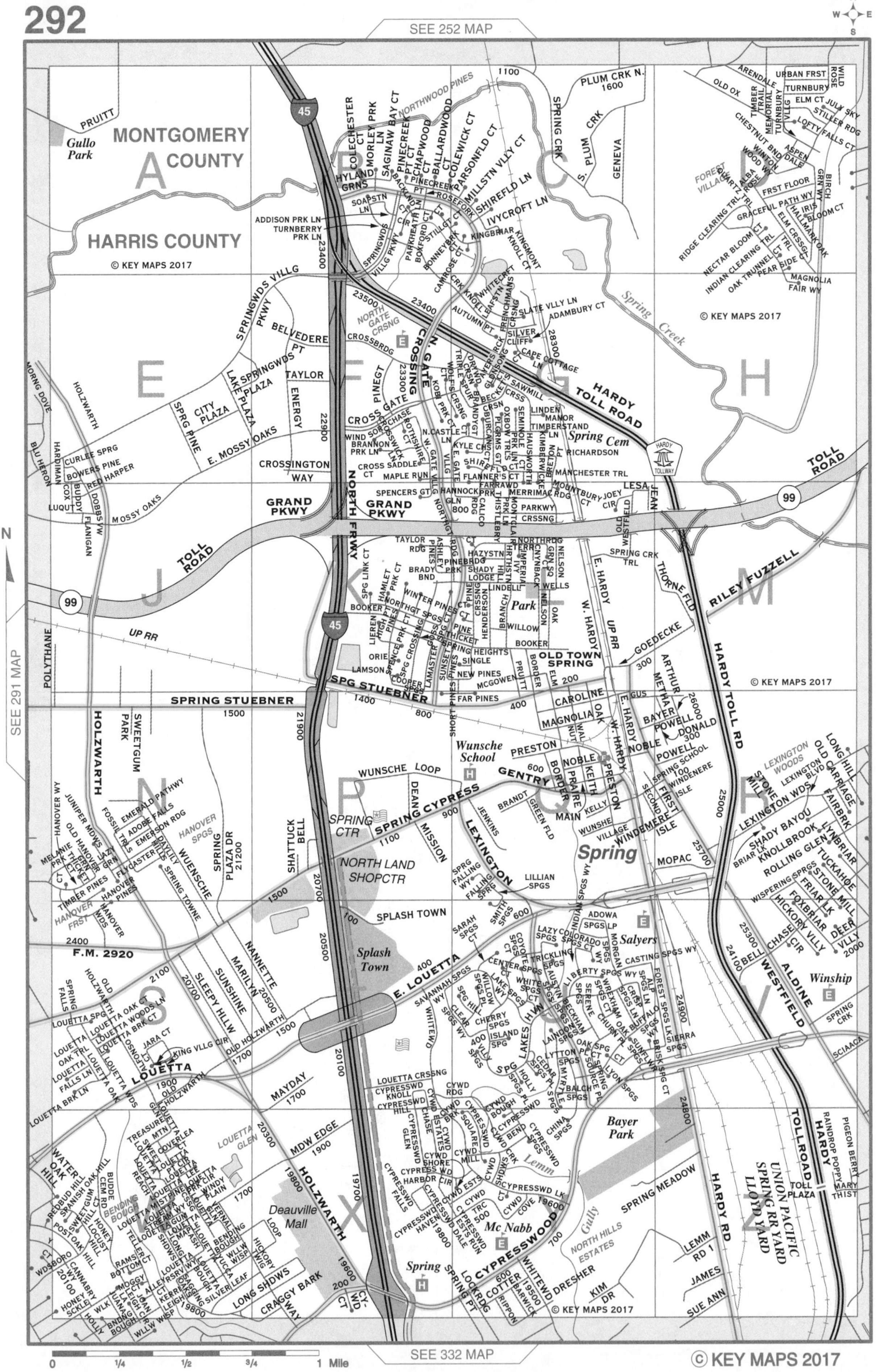

N
W E
S

MONTGOMERY COUNTY

HARRIS COUNTY

© KEY MAPS 2017

Gullo Park

PRUITT

FOREST VILLAGE

© KEY MAPS 2017

HARDY TOLL ROAD

Spring Creek

Spring Cem

HARDY TOLLWAY

TOLL ROAD

99

GRAND PKWY

GRAND PKWY

NORTH FRWY

TOLL ROAD

99

SEE 291 MAP

POLYTHANE

UP RR

SPRING STUEBNER

SPG STUEBNER

Wunsche School

Park

OLD TOWN SPRING

© KEY MAPS 2017

HOLZWARTH

SWEETGUM Park

Hanover Spgs

F.M. 2920

Spring Cypress

SPRING CTR

NORTH LAND SHOPCTR

Spring

SPLASH TOWN

Splash Town

E. LOUETTA

LOUETTA

Salyers

Winship

WESTFIELD

Bayer Park

Spring Meadow

NORTH HILLS ESTATES

McNabb

Deauville Mall

CYPRESSWOOD

Spring

UNION PACIFIC SPRING RR YARD LLOYARD

HARDY TOLLROAD

© KEY MAPS 2017

0   1/4   1/2   3/4   1 Mile

© KEY MAPS 2017

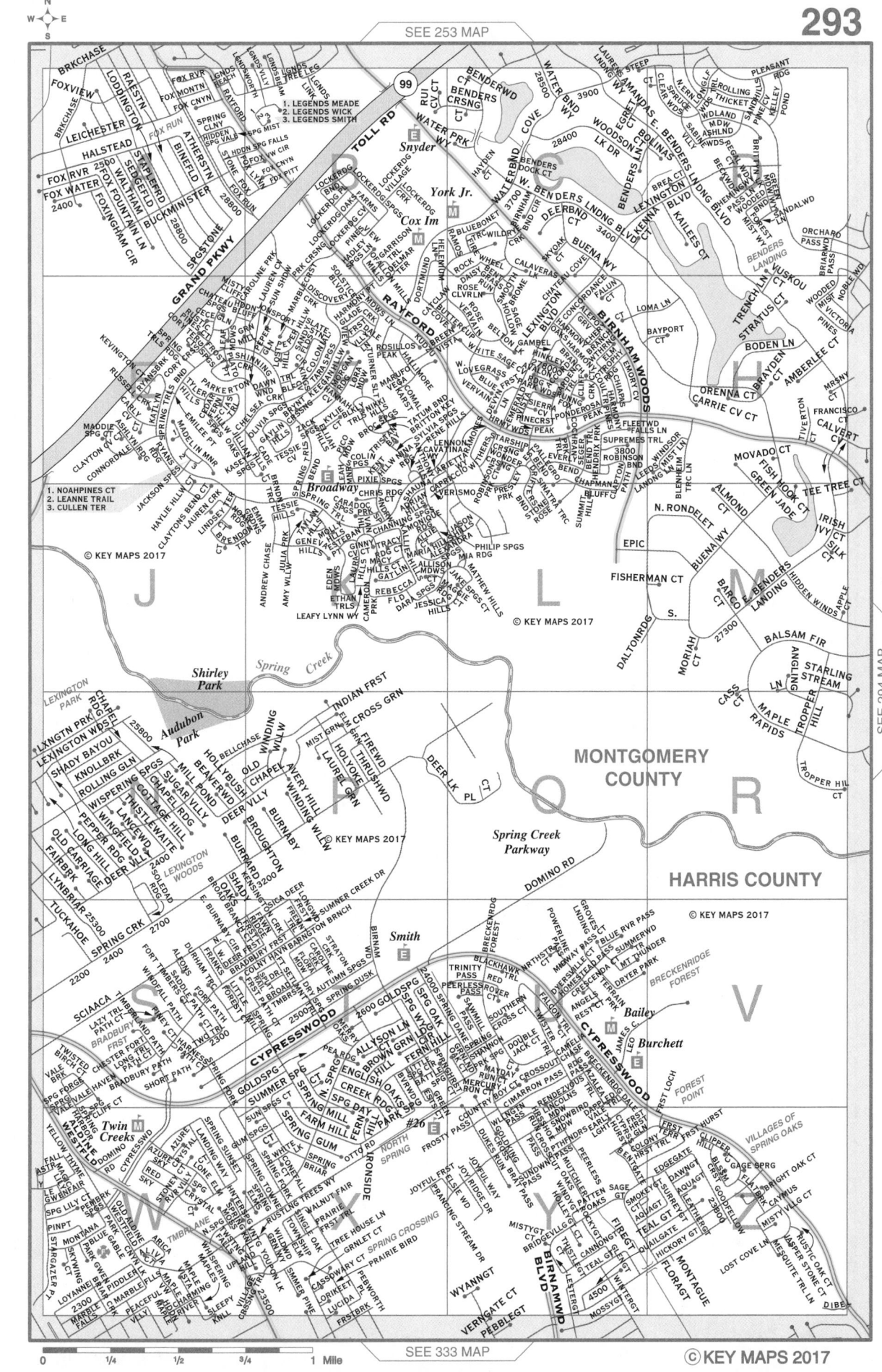

MONTGOMERY
COUNTY

HARRIS COUNTY

Spring Creek
Parkway

Shirley
Park

Spring Creek

Audubon
Park

Twin
Creeks

Smith

Burchett

Bailey

VILLAGES OF
SPRING OAKS

BREckENRIDGE
FOREST

1. LEGENDS MEADE
2. LEGENDS WICK
3. LEGENDS SMITH

Snyder

York Jr.

Cox Im

BIRNHAM
WOODS

BENDERS
LANDING

Broadway

1. NOAHPINES CT
2. LEANNE TRAIL
3. CULLEN TER

© KEY MAPS 2017

© KEY MAPS 2017

© KEY MAPS 2017

© KEY MAPS 2017

© KEY MAPS 2017

© **KEY MAPS** 2017

GRAND PKWY

TOLL RD

RAYFORD

CYPRESSWOOD

CYPRESSWOOD

BIRNAMWD
BLVD

0   1/4   1/2   3/4   1 Mile

SEE 254 MAP

N
W—E
S

A
B
C
D

CHESTNUT PASS WY
Woodson
GANGES CT
RVRWALK
© KEY MAPS 2017
MAHOGANY WIND LN
WOODLAND BND WY
ELBE
BLK WD IRONWD
GRAND OAKS WIND
JURUA
SERPENTER
AMUR
KOLYMA
SILVER OAK PL
CABANGO
DAVIS OAK
ANGARA CT
VICTORIA
PURUS
MADIERA
CT

E
INSPIRE CREST
F
Gully
G
H
BRIGHT TIMBER LANDING
Creek
SAN
CALVERT CV
GREEN JUTE LEDGE
SILENT TIMBER PATH
HANSONS CT
TOWNSEN
JACINTO
ERIC CV CT
HARVEST OAK LANDING
DEWEY MDW
QUIET SKY PL WY
OSSINEKE CT
RIVER

RAYFORD RD
GLDN OAK
HIDDEN
CHASE RUN
IGRV LNDG
N. OSSINEKE
SUMMERTON
© KEY MAPS 2017
WHISPERING MAPLE WY
ONTONAGON WAY
PINE WOOD HILLS CT
N. COLT SHDW LN
EU'S RETREAT
MANOR BRANCH
NEWPORT
CT
OSSINEKE
CHESSFORD
J
BAYLISS RETREAT
K
L
M
PIKARD WAY CT
ATWD PRSRV LN
CANTON ACRES
PINE WOOD MDWS
PINE WD HILLS LN
APPLE CT
HIDDEN WINDS
LITTLE FOX CREST
SIANDRA CRK CT
WHISPERING STREAM MAPLE CT
BLUE CEDAR LN
SIANDRA CRK
WHITE BIRCH RUN
STARLING
OSCODA CT
MILANI RDG CT
N. OSSINEKE
WAY
KEYSTONE BND CT
BLUE CEDAR
SUNNY QUIET SKY PL
E. BALSAM FIR CIR
RAYFORD
MAPLE RAPIDS CT
BLUE CEDAR CT
OWOSSO CT
BALSAM FIR CT
SUNNY SKY PL
N
JAYDEN CT
W. BALSAM FIR CIR
VELVET SKY CT
Q
R
CHATEAU CRK WY
ROMULUS CT
WISHING OAK LANDING
TERRA RUN CT
SILVER JADE
SGT. TAYLOR MEMORIAL
BENTON BRK
N. LAZY MDW WY
SUNNY VW LN
TOWNSEN
BENDERS LANDING
STAR GAZER WAY
HUNTER CRK
HIDDEN GRV LNDG
VELVET SKY WY
HUNTER CRK CT

S
SHADY HILLS LNDG
T
SILENT TIMBER PATH
HAZY LNDG CT
JUNIPER LNDG CT
S. LAZY MDW WY
HALEY LN
STAR LIGHT CT
U
GREEN FRST LN
V

© KEY MAPS 2017
MONTGOMERY COUNTY
© KEY MAPS 2017

HARRIS COUNTY

W
X
Spring Creek
Y
Z
© KEY MAPS 2017

CYPRESSWD
DIBELLO FOREST
LITTLE WIND
POSTWD
CROOKED POST
TREASCHWIG
CARL RD

0   1/4   1/2   3/4   1 Mile

SEE 293 MAP

SEE 334 MAP

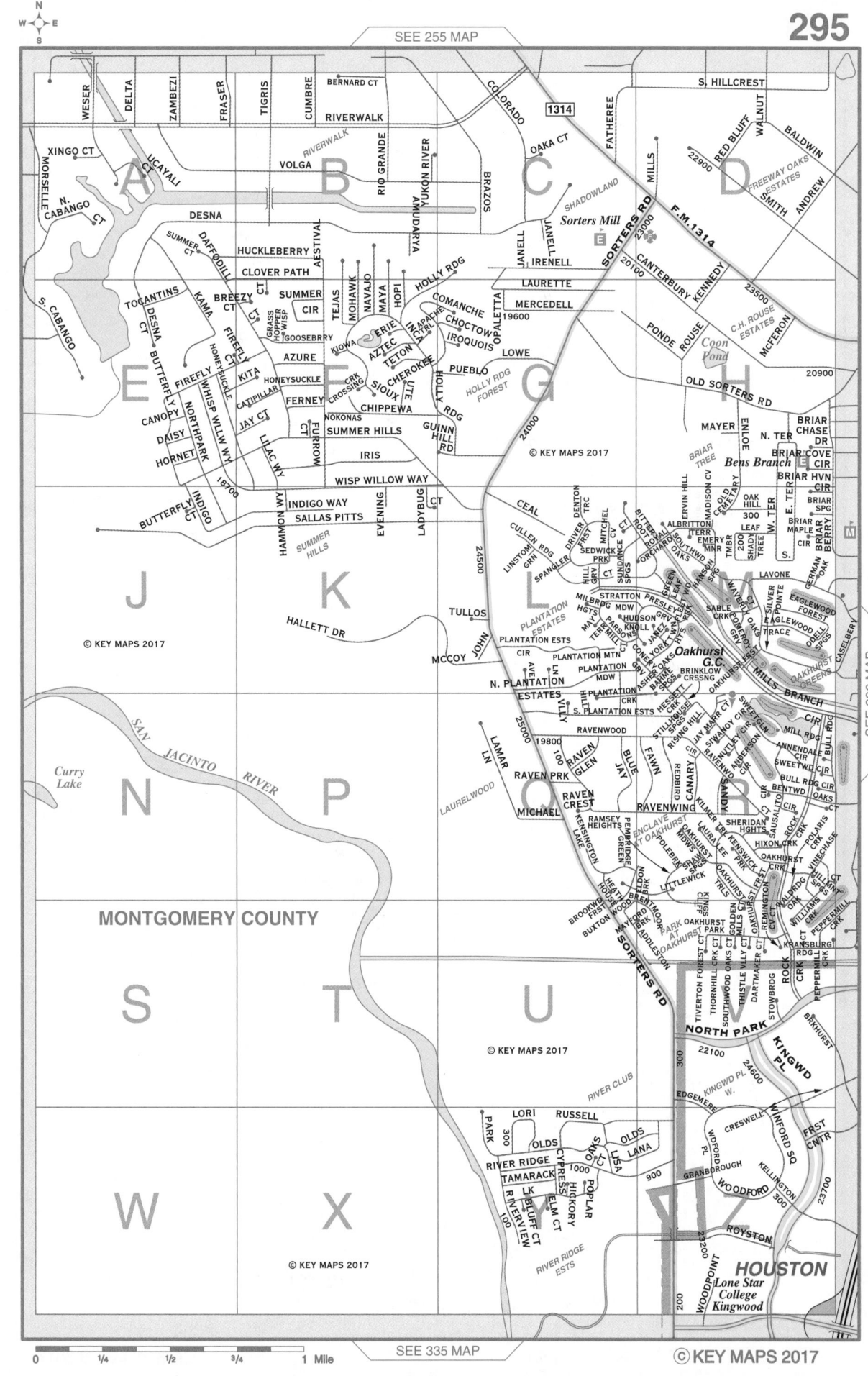

N
W–E
S

WESER
DELTA
ZAMBEZI
FRASER
TIGRIS
CUMBRE
BERNARD CT
RIVERWALK
COLORADO
1314
FATHEREE
S. HILLCREST
RED BLUFF
WALNUT
BALDWIN

XINGO CT
MORSELLE
N. CABANGO CT
UCAYALI
Riverwalk
VOLGA
RIO GRANDE
YUKON RIVER
AMUDARYA
BRAZOS
OAKA CT
SHADOWLAND
MILLS
22900
FREEWAY OAKS ESTATES
SMITH
ANDREW

A
B
C
D

DESNA
Sorters Mill
SORTERS RD
F.M. 1314
KENNEDY
CANTERBURY
23500

SUMMER CT
DAFFODIL
HUCKLEBERRY
CLOVER PATH
AESTIVAL
JANELL
IRENELL
LAURETTE
MERCEDELL
20100
C.H. ROUSE ESTATES
MCFERON

S. CABANGO
TOGANTINS CT
KAMA
BREEZY CT
FIREFLY CT
SUMMER CIR
TEJAS
MOHAWK
NAVAJO
MAYA
HOPI
HOLLY RDG
COMANCHE
OPALETTA
19600
ROUSE
PONDE
Coon Pond
20900

DESNA
BUTTERFLY CT
HONEYSUCKLE
GRASSHOPPER WISP
GOOSEBRRY
KIOWA
ERIE
AZTEC
APACHE
INCA
TETON
CHOCTOWN
IROQUOIS
LOWE
OLD SORTERS RD

E
FIREFLY
KITA
AZURE
TERR
CRK CROSSING
SIOUX
CHEROKEE
UTE
PUEBLO
HOLLY RDG FOREST
MAYER
N. TER
BRIAR CHASE DR

F
CATIPILLAR
HONEYSUCKLE
FERNEY
NOKONAS
CHIPPEWA
HOLLY RDG
ENLOE
BRIAR COVE CIR

CANOPY
JAY CT
FURROW
SUMMER HILLS
GUINN HILL RD
BRIAR TREE
Bens Branch
BRIAR HVN CIR
E

DAISY
WHISP WLLW WY
LILAC WY
IRIS
2400
OAK HILL
BRIAR SPG
GERMAN OAK

HORNET
NORTHPARK
INDIGO CT
WISP WILLOW WAY
24000
OLD CEMETARY
300
LEAF
SHADY TREE
S.
BRIAR MAPLE CIR
BRIAR BERRY

G
H

18700
HAMMON WY
INDIGO WAY
SALLAS PITTS
EVENING
LADYBUG CT
CEAL
ERVIN HILL
MADISON CV
TMBR
200
M

BUTTERFLY CT
SUMMER HILLS
DRIVER
DENTON TRC
MITCHEL
FRST
ALBRITTON
EMERY
LAVONE
SILVER POINTE
EAGLEWOOD FOREST

J
K
CULLEN RDG
LINSTON GRN
SEDWICK PRK
SUNDANCE CV
CT
ORCHARD
SOUTHWD
OAKS
ROYALL
SABLE
WAVERLY OAKS
EAGLEWOOD TRACE
ODELL SPGS
CASELBERRY
N

TULLOS
SPANGLER
HILL GRV
PRESLEY
STRATTON HGTS
MAX
HUDSON KNOLL
GREEN LEAF
WHANSON
LEAF
CRK
POMEROY GRV
SILVER
EAGLEWOOD
OAKHURST GREENS
MILL RDG
BULL RDG

HALLETT DR
MCCOY
Plantation Estates
MILBRG MDW
PARSONS
PERT MILL
J NETT
ASHER OAKS
BRINKLOW
Oakhurst G.C.
MILLS BRANCH
ANNENDALE CIR
SWEETWD CIR

JOHN
CIR
PLANTATION ESTS
PLANTATION MTN
PLANTATION MDW
HESSEY
BRENT OAKS
STILLHOUSE
SPGS
RISNG HILL
JAY MARR CT
SIWANOY CIR
ANDERSON CIR
BENTWD OAKS
BULL RDG CIR

N. PLANTATION
ESTATES
S. PLANTATION ESTS
PLANTATION CRK
REDBIRD
RAVEWND CIR
SAUSALITO CIR
VINECHASE

RAVENWOOD
19800
100
RAVEN GLEN
BLUE JAY
FAWN
CANARY
KILMER DR
SHERIDAN HGTS
POLARIS

LAMAR LN
25000
RAVEN PRK
MICHAEL
RAVEN CREST
RAVENWING
RAMSEY HEIGHTS
PEMBRIDGE GREEN
ENCLAVE AT OAKHURST
OAKHURST MDW
LAUREL LEE
KENSWICK
HIXON CRK
OAKHURST CRK
WILLMNT SPGS
VINECHASE CT

LAURELWOOD
KENSINGTON LAKE
NEATH
OPOLEBRK
BRENTWOOD
LITTLEWICK
Park Oakhurst
SADDLESON
KINGS CLIFF
GOLDEN MILLS CT
REMINGTON
WILDRDG OAK
WILLIAMS CRK
PEPPERMILL CRK

N
P
Q
R
BROOKWALK FRST
BUXTON WOODS
MAYFORD BRK
PARK AT OAKHURST
THISTLE VLLY
STOWBRDG
KRANSBURG RDG
BRKHURST

MONTGOMERY COUNTY
SORTERS RD
TIVERTON FOREST CT
THORNHILL CRK
SOUTHWOOD OAKS CT
DARTMAKER CT
PEPPERMILL CRK

NORTH PARK
KINGWD PL

S
T
U
300
22100
KINGWD PL W.
24600
CRESWELL
WINFORD SQ
23700

River Club
EDGEMERE
WDFORD PL
GRANBOROUGH
WOODFORD
300
KELLINGTON
FRST CNTR

Curry Lake
SAN JACINTO RIVER

LORI
RUSSELL
PARK
300
OLDS
OLDS
LANA
LISA
KINGWD PL

RIVER RIDGE
TAMARACK
OAKS CT
CYPRESS
HICKORY
POPLAR
ELM CT
900
ROYSTON

W
X
LK
BLUFF CT
RIVERVIEW
100
Z

River Ridge Ests
WOODPOINT
200
HOUSTON
Lone Star College Kingwood

© KEY MAPS 2017
© KEY MAPS 2017
© KEY MAPS 2017
© KEY MAPS 2017
© KEY MAPS 2017

0   1/4   1/2   3/4   1 Mile

© KEY MAPS 2017

SEE 296 MAP

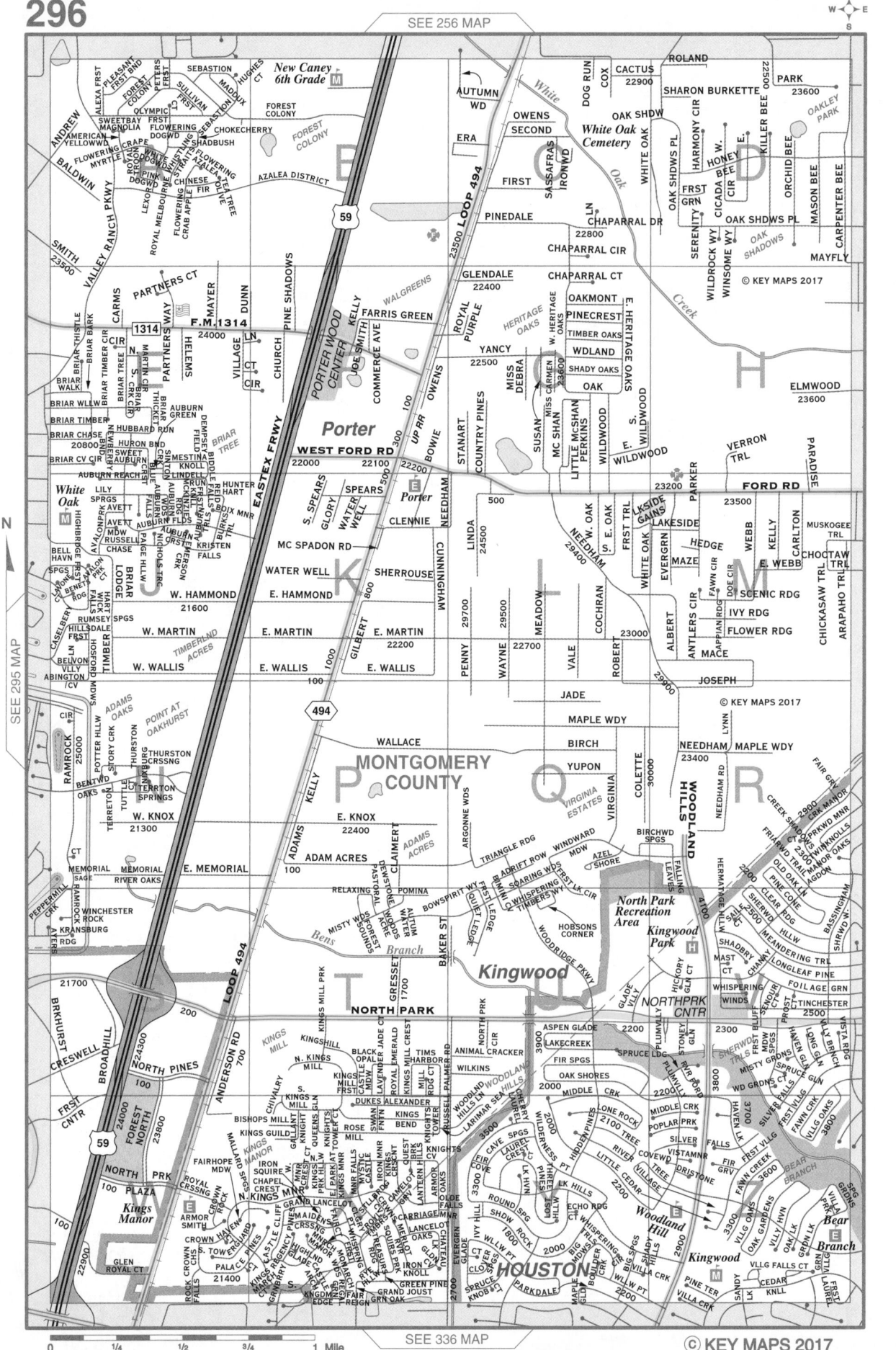

© KEY MAPS 2017

0   1/4   1/2   3/4   1 Mile

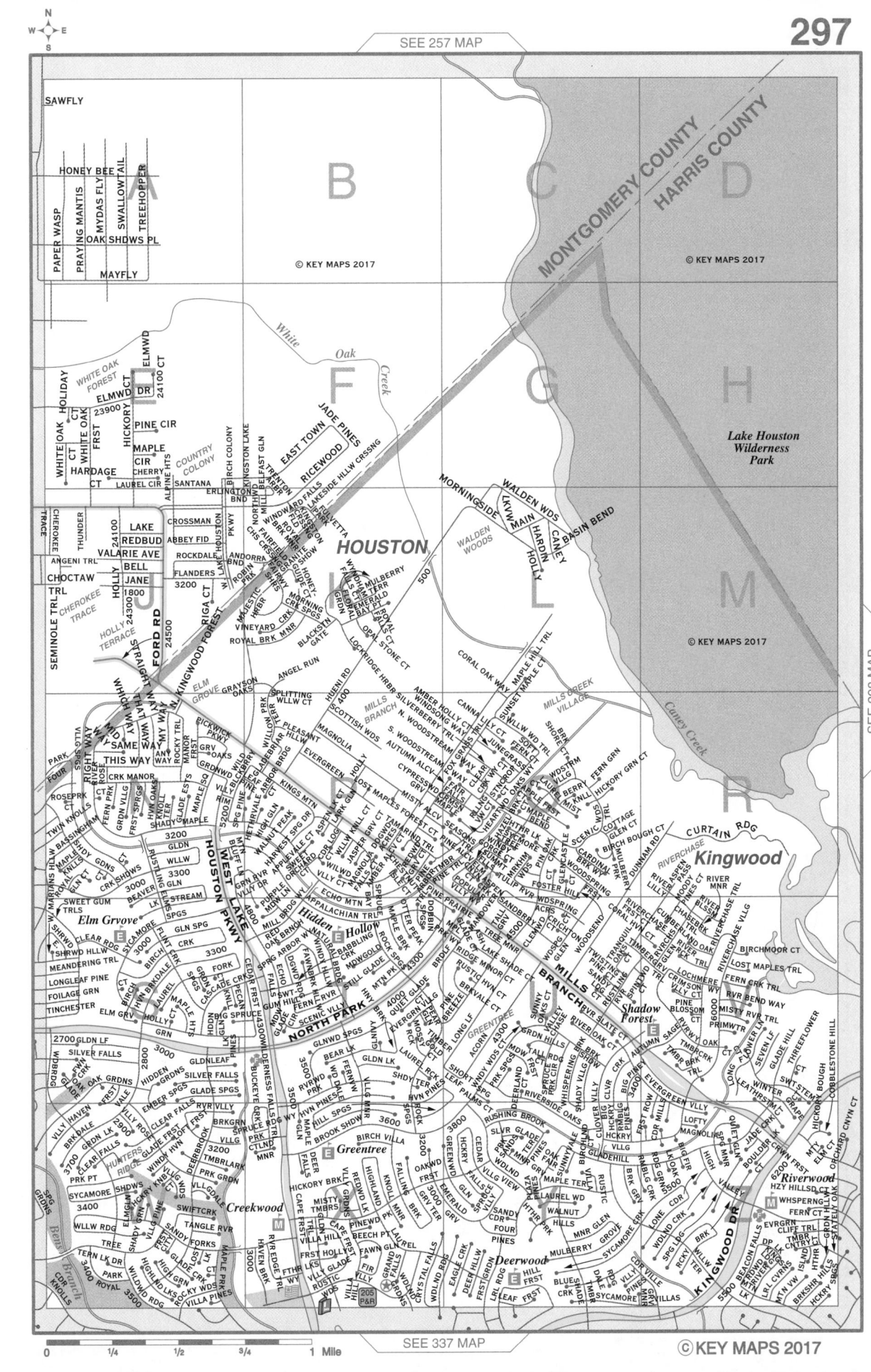

SEE 298 MAP

MONTGOMERY COUNTY

HARRIS COUNTY

Lake Houston Wilderness Park

HOUSTON

Kingwood

Shadow Forest

Riverwood

Deerwood

Creekwood

Greentree

Elm Grvove

Hidden Hollow

Birch Villa

© KEY MAPS 2017

© KEY MAPS 2017

© KEY MAPS 2017

© **KEY MAPS** 2017

0   1/4   1/2   3/4   1 Mile

SEE 258 MAP

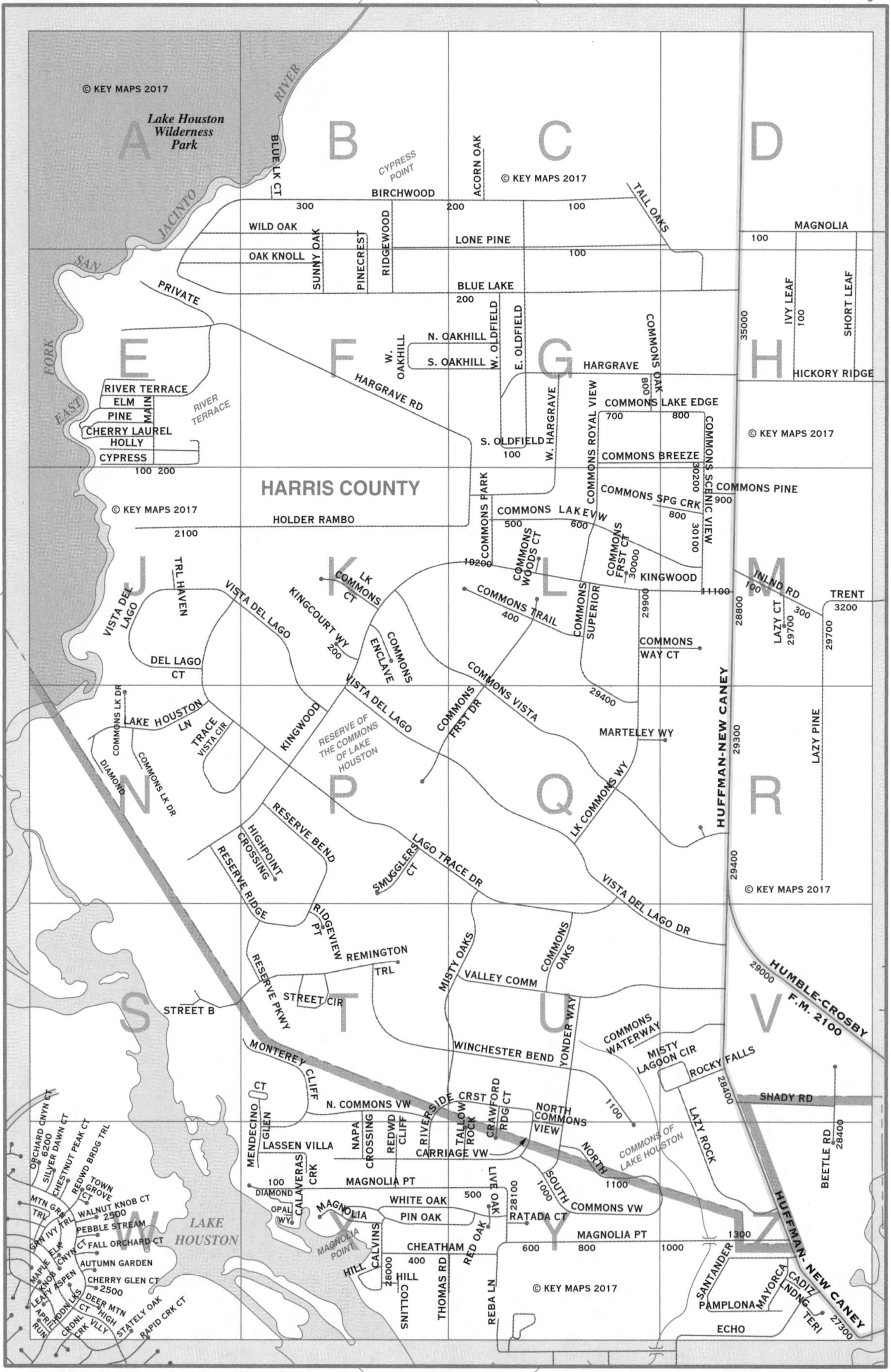

N W E S

© KEY MAPS 2017

A Lake Houston Wilderness Park

SAN JACINTO

EAST FORK

BLUE LK CT

CYPRESS POINT

B BIRCHWOOD 300
WILD OAK
OAK KNOLL
SUNNY OAK
PINECREST
RIDGEWOOD

ACORN OAK 200
LONE PINE
BLUE LAKE 200

C 100
TALL OAKS
© KEY MAPS 2017

D MAGNOLIA 100
IVY LEAF 100
SHORT LEAF
HICKORY RIDGE
35000

H

PRIVATE

E RIVER TERRACE
ELM
PINE
CHERRY LAUREL
HOLLY
CYPRESS
100 200
MAIN
RIVER TERRACE
© KEY MAPS 2017

F HARGRAVE RD
W. OAKHILL
N. OAKHILL
S. OAKHILL
W. OLDFIELD
E. OLDFIELD
S. OLDFIELD 100
W. HARGRAVE

HARRIS COUNTY
HOLDER RAMBO 2100
COMMONS PARK

G HARGRAVE
COMMONS OAK
COMMONS ROYAL VIEW
COMMONS LAKE EDGE 800
700
COMMONS BREEZE
COMMONS SCENIC VIEW
COMMONS SPG CRK 900
800
30200 30100 30000 29900 29700
COMMONS PINE
KINGWOOD 11100
COMMONS LAKEVW 500 600
COMMONS FRST CT
COMMONS SUPERIOR
© KEY MAPS 2017

M INLND RD 100 300
LAZY CT 29700
TRENT 3200
28800 29700
28000

J VISTA DEL LAGO
TRL HAVEN
DEL LAGO CT
LAKE HOUSTON LN
COMMONS LK DR
DIAMOND
TRACE VISTA CIR

K LK COMMONS CT
KINGCOURT WY 200
COMMONS ENCLAVE
VISTA DEL LAGO
10200

L COMMONS WOODS CT
COMMONS TRAIL 400
COMMONS VISTA
COMMONS FRST DR
RESERVE OF THE COMMONS OF LAKE HOUSTON

COMMONS WAY CT
MARTELEY WY
LK COMMONS WY 29400

R HUFFMAN-NEW CANEY
LAZY PINE
29300
© KEY MAPS 2017

N COMMONS LK DR
KINGWOOD

P RESERVE BEND
HIGHPOINT CROSSING
RESERVE RIDGE
RIDGEVIEW PT
REMINGTON TRL
STREET CIR
RESERVE PKWY
SMUGGLERS CT
LAGO TRACE DR

Q VISTA DEL LAGO DR

S STREET B
MONTEREY CLIFF
29400

T MISTY OAKS
VALLEY COMM
WINCHESTER BEND
COMMONS OAKS
YONDER WAY

U COMMONS WATERWAY
MISTY LAGOON CIR
ROCKY FALLS
28000

V HUMBLE-CROSBY F.M. 2100
29000
SHADY RD
BEETLE RD 28400
28400

MENDECINO CT
GLEN
LASSEN VILLA
NAPA CROSSING
N. COMMONS VW
REDWD CLIFF
RIVERSIDE CRST
TALLOW ROCK
CRAWFORD RDG CT
NORTH COMMONS VIEW
NORTH
LAZY ROCK
COMMONS OF LAKE HOUSTON
1100 1100

W LAKE HOUSTON
ORCHARD CNYN CT 6200
SILVER DAWN CT
CHESTNUT PEAK CT
REDWD BRDG TRL
TOWN GROVE 2500
WALNUT KNOB CT
MTN GRN TRL
GRN IVY TRL
PEBBLE STREAM
MAPLE LK KNOB CT
LEAF CT ASPEN
FALL ORCHARD CT
AUTUMN GARDEN
CHERRY GLEN CT 2500
DEER MTN
APRIL HDDN LAS CRK VLLY
CRONL CT HIGH STATELY OAK
RUN RAPID CRK CT
100 DIAMOND
OPAL WY
CALAVERAS CRK
MAGNOLIA POINT
HILL
CALVINS
HILL 400
COLLINS
28000

X MENDECINO
MAGNOLIA PT
WHITE OAK
PIN OAK
CARRIAGE VW
MAGNOLIA
LIVE OAK 500
RED OAK
THOMAS RD
REBA LN

Y RATADA CT
SOUTH COMMONS VW 1000
MAGNOLIA PT
CHEATHAM 600 800 1000
© KEY MAPS 2017

Z HUFFMAN-NEW CANEY 27300
SANTANDER
PAMPLONA
MAYORCA CADIZ
CNDNG TERI
ECHO
1300

SEE 297 MAP
SEE 338 MAP

0 1/4 1/2 3/4 1 Mile

© **KEY MAPS 2017**

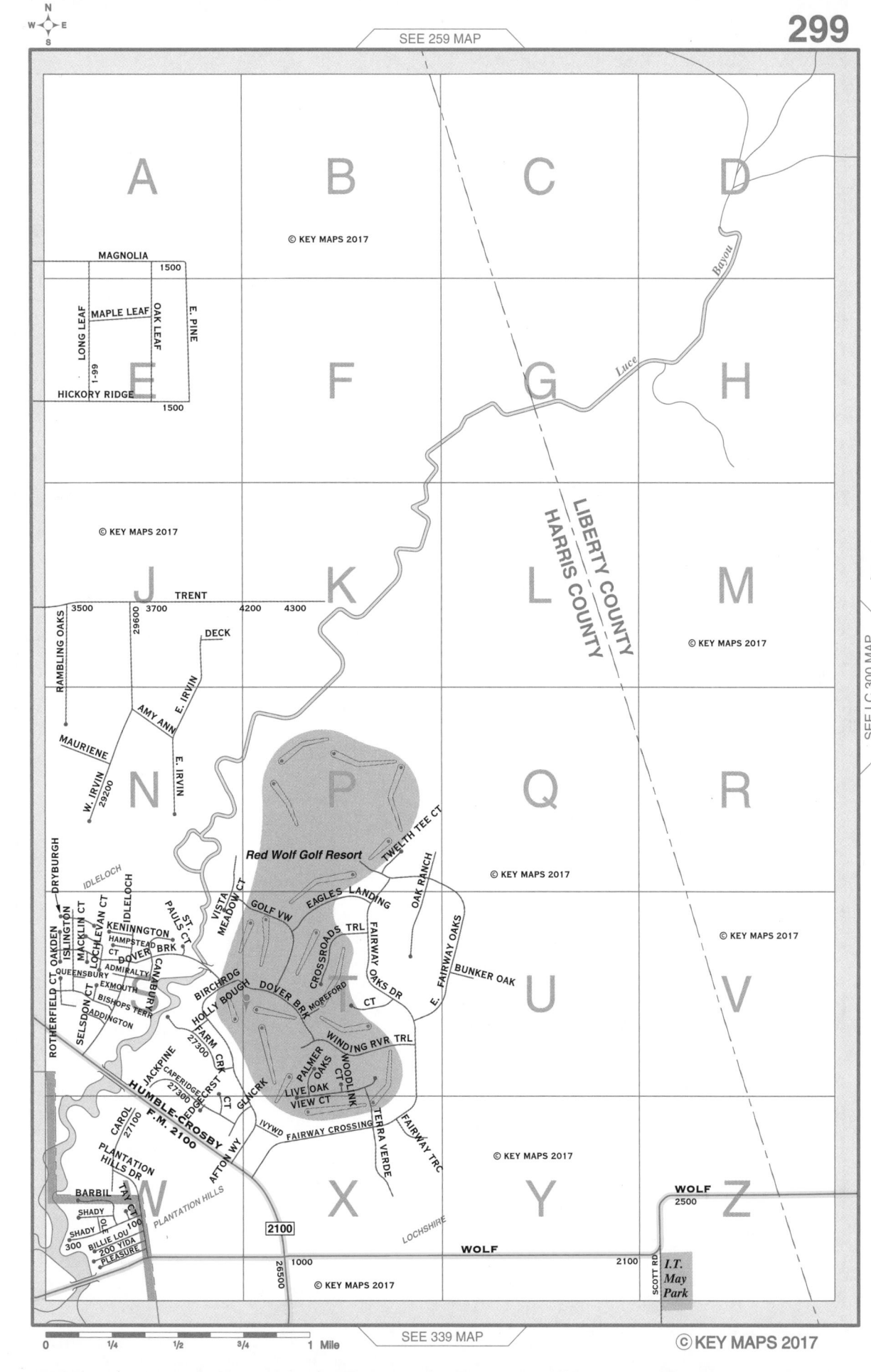

© KEY MAPS 2017

N
W E
S

MAGNOLIA

LONG LEAF | MAPLE LEAF | OAK LEAF | E. PINE
I-99
HICKORY RIDGE
1500

A   B   C   D

E   F   G   H

© KEY MAPS 2017

Luce

Bayou

RAMBLING OAKS

TRENT
3500   29600   3700   4200   4300

DECK

E. IRVIN

AMY ANN

MAURIENE

W. IRVIN
29200

J   K   L   M

© KEY MAPS 2017

LIBERTY COUNTY
HARRIS COUNTY

© KEY MAPS 2017

N   P   Q   R

Red Wolf Golf Resort

TWELTH TEE CT

OAK RANCH

© KEY MAPS 2017

© KEY MAPS 2017

IDLELOCH
DRYBURGH
OAKDEN
ISLINGTON
MACKLIN CT
LOCHLEVAN CT
IDLELOCH
KENINNGTON
HAMPSTEAD CT
ST. PAULS CT
VISTA MEADOW CT
GOLF VW
EAGLE'S LANDING
CROSSROADS TRL
FAIRWAY OAKS DR
E. FAIRWAY OAKS
BUNKER OAK

DOVER BRK
ADMIRALTY
QUEENSBURY
EXMOUTH
BISHOPS TERR
ADDINGTON
ROTHERFIELD CT
SELSDON CT
BIRCHRDG
HOLLY BOUGH
FARM CRK
27300
DOVER BRK
MOREFORD
CT
WINDING RVR TRL

JACKPINE
CAPERIDGE
CEDGECRST
CT
GLNCRK
PALMER OAKS
LIVE OAK
VIEW CT
WOODLNK CT
TERRA VERDE
E. FAIRWAY OAKS
FAIRWAY TRC

CAROL
27100
HUMBLE-CROSBY
F.M. 2100
AFTON WY
IVYWD
FAIRWAY CROSSING

PLANTATION HILLS DR

BARBIL
TAY CT
SHADY
SHADY
100
300
BILLIE LOU
200
YIDA
PLEASURE
PLANTATION HILLS

2100

26500   1000

WOLF

© KEY MAPS 2017

T   U   V

W   X   Y   Z

WOLF
2500

I.T.
May
Park

SCOTT RD

LOCHSHIRE

2100

N

SEE LC 300 MAP

0   1/4   1/2   3/4   1 Mile

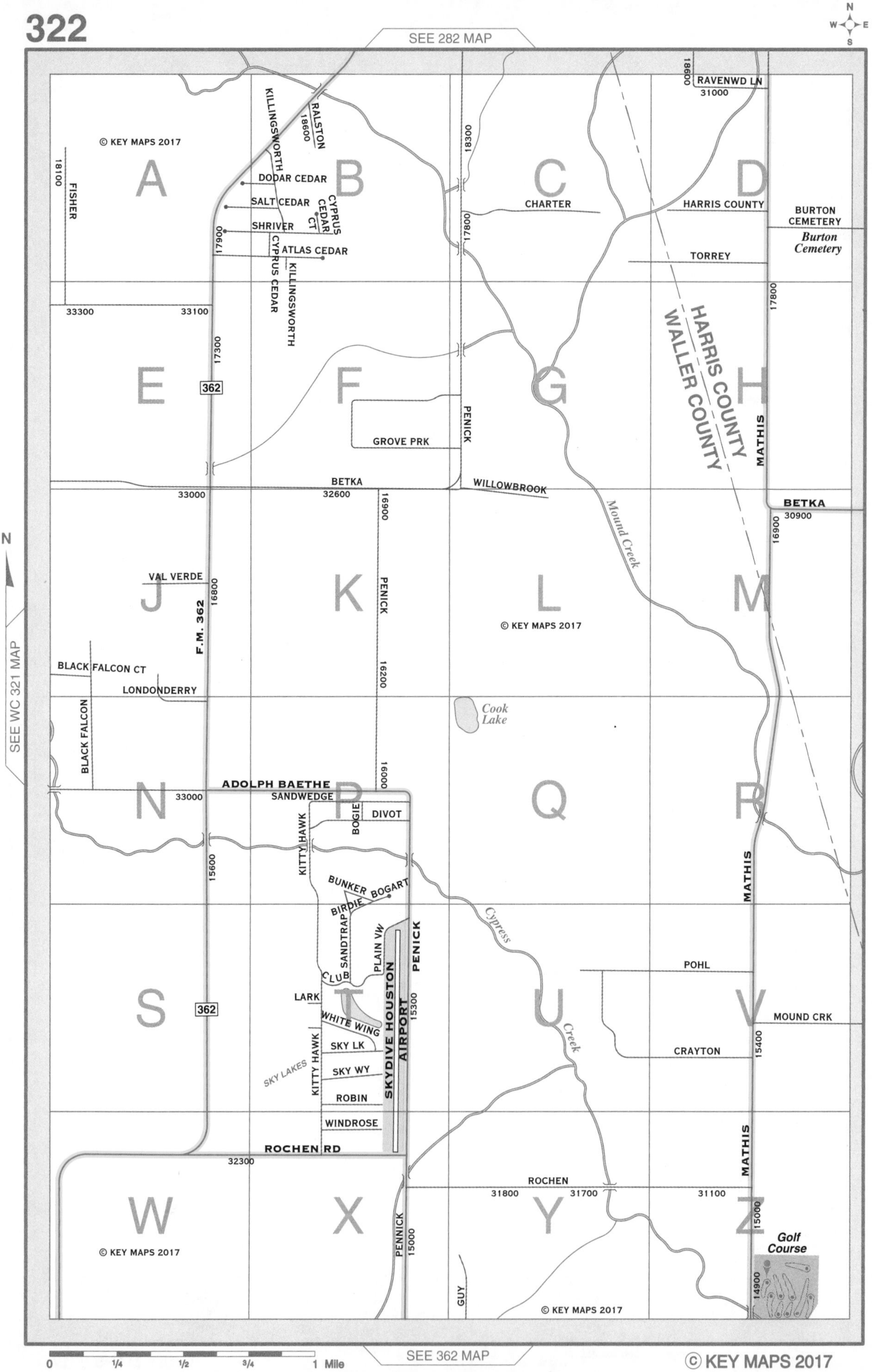

N
W · E
S

SEE 282 MAP

© KEY MAPS 2017

FISHER
18100

KILLINGSWORTH
RALSTON
18600

A
B
C
D

CHARTER

HARRIS COUNTY

BURTON
CEMETERY

*Burton
Cemetery*

DODAR CEDAR

SALT CEDAR

CYPRUS
CEDAR
CT

SHRIVER

TORREY

ATLAS CEDAR

CYPRUS CEDAR

KILLINGSWORTH

33300
33100
17900

HARRIS COUNTY
WALLER COUNTY

MATHIS

17300

362

E
F
G
H

GROVE PRK

PENICK

18300
17800
10800

Mound Creek

BETKA

WILLOWBROOK

BETKA

33000
32600
16900

30900

16900

SEE WC 321 MAP

N

VAL VERDE

F.M. 362
16800

J
K
L
M

PENICK

© KEY MAPS 2017

BLACK FALCON CT

LONDONDERRY

16200

BLACK FALCON

*Cook
Lake*

15600

16000

ADOLPH BAETHE

SANDWEDGE

N
P
Q
R

33000

KITTYHAWK

BOGIE

DIVOT

BUNKER
BOGART

BIRDIE

SANDTRAP

PLAIN VW

Cypress

POHL

CLUB

LARK

PENICK

15300

MATHIS

362
S
T
U
V

WHITE WING

SKYDIVE HOUSTON AIRPORT

SKY LK

KITTY HAWK

Creek

MOUND CRK

Sky Lakes

SKY WY

CRAYTON

15400

ROBIN

WINDROSE

ROCHEN RD

32300

PENNICK
15000

ROCHEN

MATHIS

W
X
Y
Z

31800
31700

31100

© KEY MAPS 2017

GUY

*Golf
Course*

14900

15000

© KEY MAPS 2017

0   1/4   1/2   3/4   1 Mile

SEE 362 MAP

© **KEY MAPS** 2017

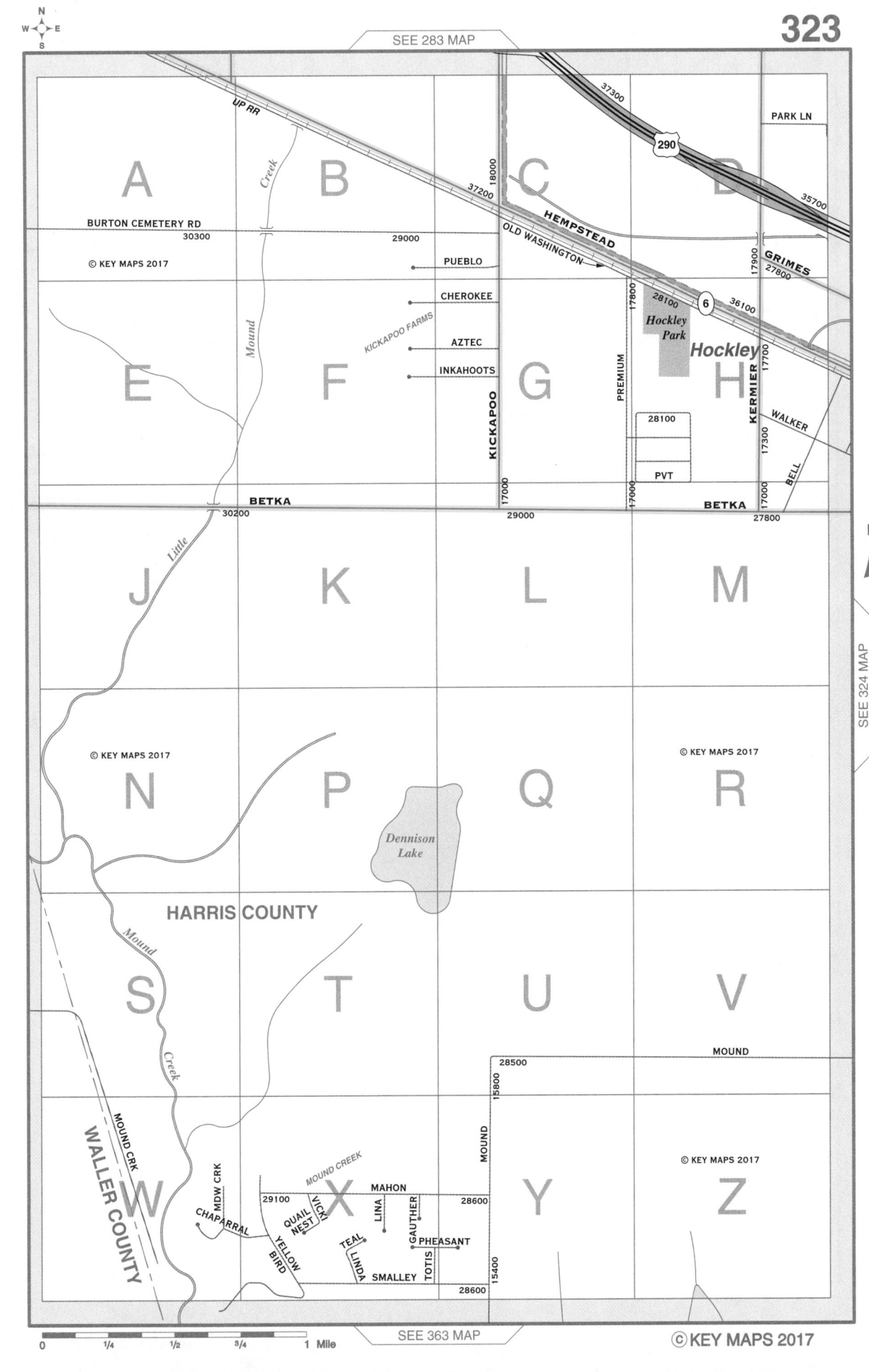

N
W E
S

UP RR

Creek

A   B

BURTON CEMETERY RD
30300   29000

© KEY MAPS 2017

PARK LN

37300

290

C   D

Hempstead

35700

Old Washington

18000
37200

GRIMES
17900   27800

PUEBLO

Mound

Kickapoo Farms

CHEROKEE

28100   6   36100

Hockley Park

Hockley

E   F

AZTEC

INKAHOOTS

KICKAPOO

G   H

PREMIUM

17800

KERMIER

17700

WALKER

28100

17300

BELL

PVT

17000

BETKA
30200

17000   29000   PVT

BETKA
27800   17000

Little

J   K   L   M

SEE 324 MAP

N

© KEY MAPS 2017

© KEY MAPS 2017

N   P   Q   R

Dennison Lake

HARRIS COUNTY

Mound

S   T   U   V

MOUND

28500

15800

MOUND

© KEY MAPS 2017

MOUND CRK

WALLER COUNTY

Creek

MDW CRK

Mound Creek

MAHON

W   X   Y   Z

CHAPARRAL

29100

QUAIL NEST

VICKI

LINA

GAUTHER

28600

YELLOW BIRD

TEAL

LINDA

PHEASANT

SMALLEY

TOTIS

15400

28600

0   1/4   1/2   3/4   1 Mile

© **KEY MAPS** 2017

N
W — E
S

A

B

C

D

© KEY MAPS 2017

HEGAR

18000 KLEB

18000

Little

Cypress

25000

BAUER-HOCKLEY

24700   24200

25700

HOCKLEY

26000

17600

Creek

ST. LUCIA

HOLY SEE

PITCAIRN

GRIMES

27100

HEMPSTEAD

BAUER-
U.S. HWY 290

26600

E

F

G

Zube
Park

H

Hockley

BADTKE

17600

© KEY MAPS 2017

ROBERTS

Ranch
Country

27700

OLD WASHINGTON

KRUGER

17300

HARRIS

17300

Hockley

HICKORY
RANCH

PHEASANT
RANCH

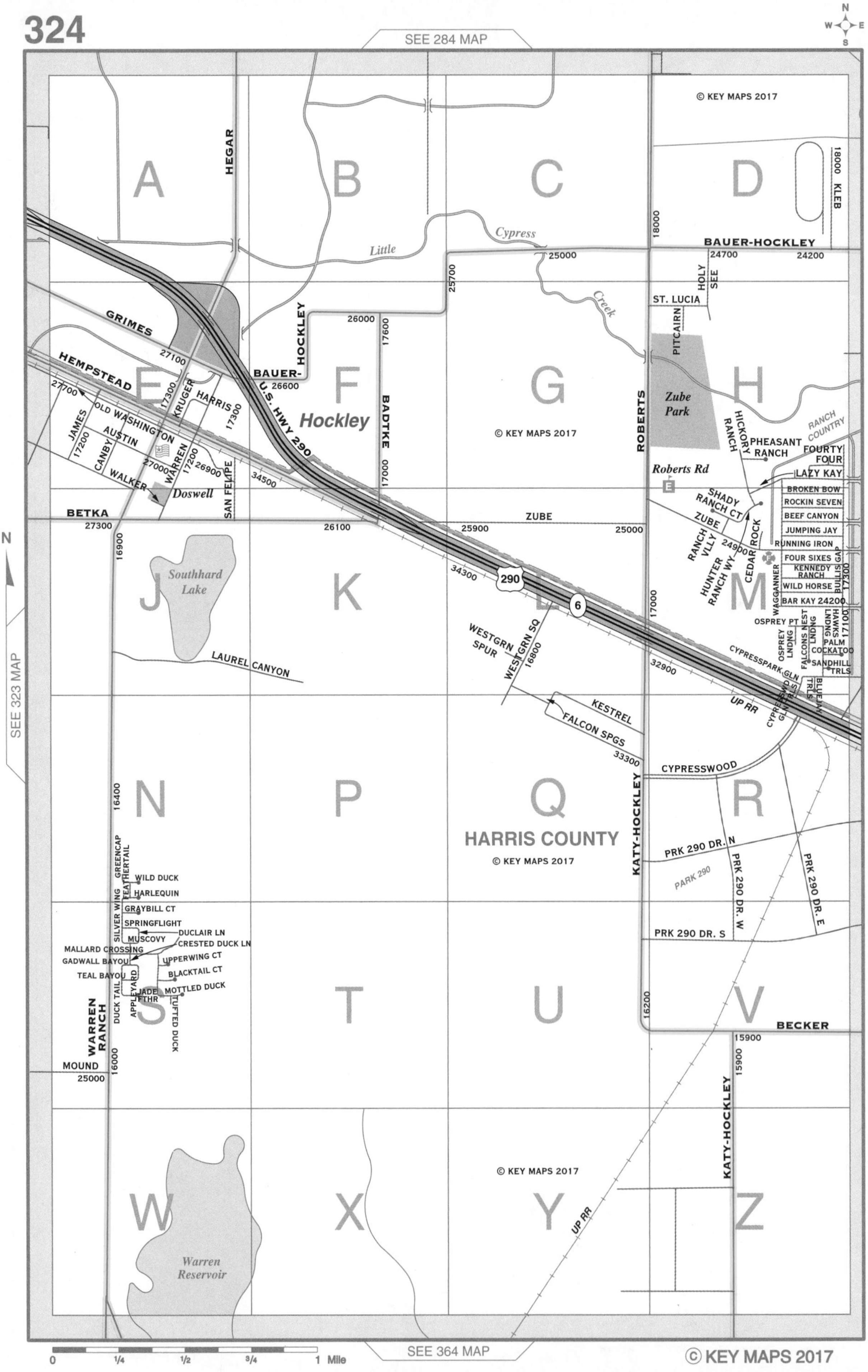

FOURTY
FOUR

JAMES

17200

AUSTIN

CANBY

WARREN

17200

26900

SAN FELIPE

34500

Roberts Rd

Roberts Rd

LAZY KAY

BROKEN BOW

WALKER

27000

Doswell

SHADY
RANCH CT

ROCKIN SEVEN

BEEF CANYON

BETKA

27300

16900

26100

25900

ZUBE

25000

ZUBE
VLLY

JUMPING JAY

RUNNING IRON

FOUR SIXES

CEDAR ROCK

249001

17300

*Southhard
Lake*

J

K

L

290

6

RANCH

HUNTER
RANCH WY

WAGGANNER

KENNEDY
RANCH

WILD HORSE

BAR KAY 24200

OSPREY PT

FALCONS NEST

LNDNG

HAWKS
LNDNG

PALM

COCKATOO

SEE 323 MAP

N

LAUREL CANYON

34300

WESTGRN SQ

WESTGRN
SPUR

16800

17000

32900

CYPRESSPARK GLN

OSPREY

LNDNG

CYPRESOOD GLN TRLS

BLUE JAY

SANDHILL
TRLS

KESTREL

UP RR

FALCON SPGS

33300

CYPRESSWOOD

N

16400

P

Q

PRK 290 DR. N

R

PARK 290

PRK 290 DR. W

PRK 290 DR. E

HARRIS COUNTY

© KEY MAPS 2017

KATY-HOCKLEY

GREENCAP

LEATHERTAIL

WILD DUCK

HARLEQUIN

SILVER WING

GRAYBILL CT

SPRINGFLIGHT

DUCLAIR LN

MUSCOVY

CRESTED DUCK LN

PRK 290 DR. S

MALLARD CROSSING

UPPERWING CT

GADWALL BAYOU

TEAL BAYOU

APPLEYARD

BLACKTAIL CT

16200

DUCK TAIL

JADE
FTHR

MOTTLED DUCK

S

T

U

V

BECKER

WARREN
RANCH

TUFTED DUCK

MOUND

16000

25000

15900

© KEY MAPS 2017

KATY-HOCKLEY

15900

W

X

Y

Z

*Warren
Reservoir*

UP RR

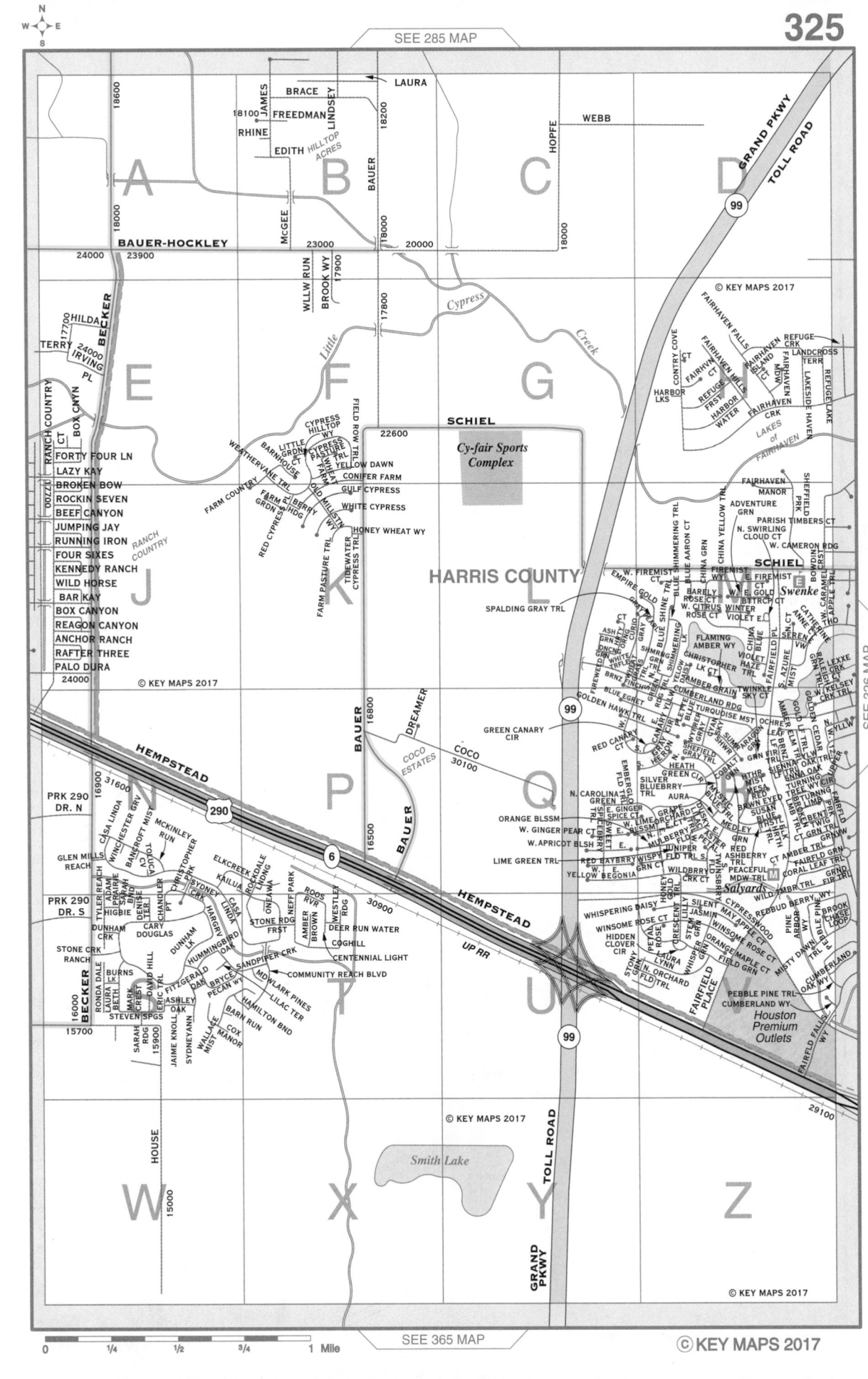

SEE 285 MAP

SEE 326 MAP

SEE 365 MAP

© KEY MAPS 2017

SEE 286 MAP

N
W E
S

A   B   C   D

© KEY MAPS 2017

JUERGEN
19400

HIGHMDW
ROBECK
WLLW BEND
FISHER

W. PALOMA EST
LA PALOMA W.
W. PALOMA W
LAGO CIR
E. PALOMA
VICKERS
PALOMA
E. PALOMA
LAGO CT

BAUER - HOCKLEY

ANGELI
20300
19700
18300

ANGELI
17800
JEANIE

WILKS
HANBERRY

W. CYPRESS HILL
E. CYPRESS HILL
LAKE CYPRESS HILL
DRAGONFLY

CYPRESS HILL

© KEY MAPS 2017

F   G   H

FAIRHAVEN CRK
MAGIC CRK
REFUGE CRK
FAIRHAVEN PARK CT
FAIRHAVEN FOREST CT
FAIRHAVEN SUNSET CT
HAVEN FOREST CT
FAIRHAVEN SUNRISE CT
FAIRHAVEN CROSSING
FAIRHAVEN GATEWAY
SAFE HAVEN
FAIRHAVEN LAKE
MASON

1. SAGE CYPRESS CT
2. PETINA CYPRESS CT
3. DAISY CREEK TRAIL
4. S. AMBER WILLOW TRAIL
5. OCHRE PARK WAY
6. DOGWOOD CREEK CT
7. FIELD HAZE TRAIL
8. GOLDEN SYCAMORE TRL
9. PINK BLOSSOM TRL
10. OCHRE WILLOW TRL
11. CRIMSON FLOWER LN
12. E. AMBER WILLOW TRL

E. FARWD TERR
W. FARWD TERR
LAKES OF FAIRHAVEN
RANKIN MDWS CT
PRESCOTT
RIMANOR

17100

Little Cypress Creek

17700
18900   KZ
SANTOS
CORRAL

RUBY VLLY CT
CALICO PEAK WY
PRICEWD MANOR CT
LEDGEFLD
FLAGSTONE TRL CT
SADDLE RDG PAS

SCHIEL

16900
OLYMPIA FLLS

DRY ARBR CT
RUN OAKS CT
ARBOR OAK
ARBR LF LK
LOBLOLLY SHADE
LEAF SKY
WINDING IVY
RIVERTON RANCH
RIVERTON CREST CT
RIVERTON ASH CT

SIENNA BLFF
MERCER GRV
LANTANA RDG CT
GREEN VELVET TRL
LIMESTONE RDG TRL
ARCHER FLLS
DEEP FALLS
LIBERTY PASS
WOLF PASS
BERDEEN

CORBIN CRK
EVERWOOD GRN
BRIDLE OAK
GLENWOOD
HIDALGO
HARBOR POOL
HAMILTON POOL
TANGALA FALLS
HAVASU
TACCOA
THREE CHUTES

ARBOR VILLAS
MYSTIC TMBR
SHADED KNOLL
SHADY TIMBER
ARBORS EDGE
GREEN IMPERIAL
LONE TUPELO

RIVERTON CROSS
HIDDEN VISTA
BLACKBERRY ARBOR VISTA
LUTHERAN CEM. RD
St. John Cemetery
19500
18400
FENSKE

M
R

WILD CURRENT WY
CACTUS BLOSSOM TRL
RADIANT LILAC TRL
THYME GRN
BASTON CRK
CASCADING FALLS BLVD

MUESCHKE
16500

SCHIEL
20000

SCHIEL
CYPRESS CHURCH

TREY ROCK WY
CHAD ARBOR TRL
EMILY ANN
KYLE CREST TRL
PEBBLE
ROLLING PINE

SANDY HILL
19800

HARRIS COUNTY
Q

CYPRESS HUFFMEISTER
ARROYO
WLLW HTR
MOUNTAIN VALLEY
WHITEHAVEN MDW TRL
BLUE PINE CIR

CYPRESS CHURCH
19100
CY-FAIR FIRE
18900

CHANDLER RDG
VALEBLUFF
LARKRUN
CHATDALE
KENDONS WY
TEMPLE HILL
KAREY LYNN
CORELAND
FENSKE

MORNING PINE TRL
PRIM PINE
SEASONS WY
MISTY RVR WY
CRK TRL
KELFY ARBOR
SWTGUM WY
LONGLF TRL
HEARTWD WY
FAIRFLD LKS CT

MERLE
ESCHER
15800

FAIRFLD PL
EDWORTHY
LONGHURST HILLS
20300

CYPRESS LANDING

JILL'S WY
HAMMONDSPORT
BLAKE VLLY
RIDGE STREAM
QUIET RDG

ELEANOR MEADOW
PERALTA LK CIR
CYPRESS KNOLL
DUNSMORE
CLIFF CRK
LONESTAR CRK CT
ASPENWILDE
EPRIGHTS
WESTON OAKS
OAKDALE HTS
BETHEL
FOLLY FLD
AUBURN TREE
GENEVA FLDS

PROGRESS RDG WY
18500
VINEMOSS
RAVENSBRK
WAVERLY HLLW
KINGS STN
V

TWISTING SPG
20400
WILDWD RUN
MAPLE
PATINGTON
MAPLE MDWS
MAPLE LNDING

FAIRFLD VLLG
FAIRFLD MDWS
1500

Fairfield

290
6
MASON
HEMPSTEAD
28200

UP RR

Cypress Lakes G.C.

CYPRESSWD
18600

W   X   Z

SEE 325 MAP

0   1/4   1/2   3/4   1 Mile

© KEY MAPS 2017

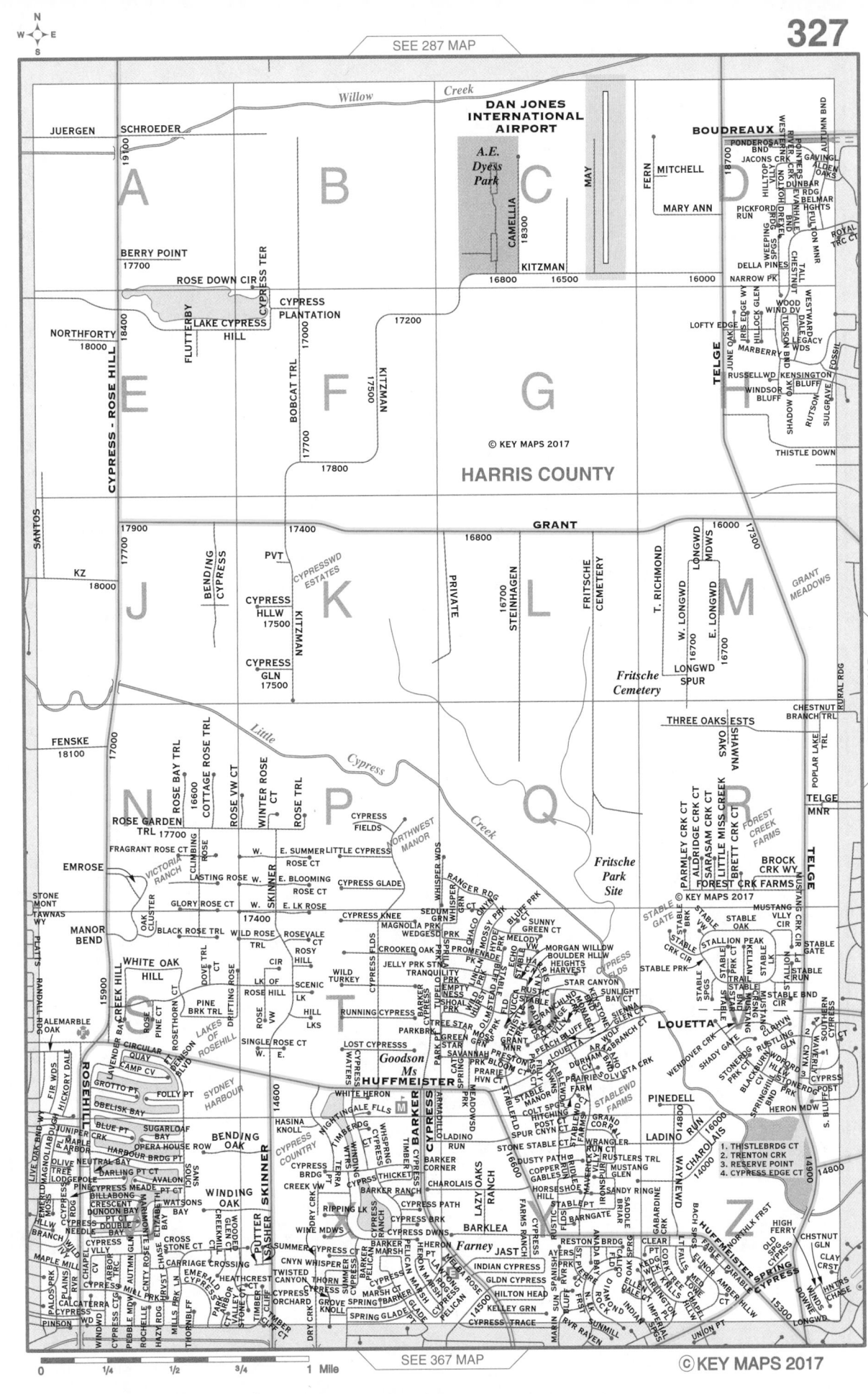

N
W E
S

JUERGEN   SCHROEDER

A

B

DAN JONES
INTERNATIONAL
AIRPORT

A.E.
Dyess
Park

C

BOUDREAUX

MITCHELL

MARY ANN

D

BERRY POINT
17700

ROSE DOWN CIR

CYPRESS
PLANTATION

NORTHFORTY
18000

LAKE CYPRESS
HILL

CYPRESS - ROSE HILL

E

BOBCAT TRL

F

KITZMAN

G

TELGE

H

HARRIS COUNTY

© KEY MAPS 2017

SANTOS

KZ
18000

17900

17400

BENDING
CYPRESS

CYPRESSWD
ESTATES

PVT

CYPRESS
HLLW
17500

KITZMAN

GRANT

16800

PRIVATE

16700
STEINHAGEN

FRITSCHE
CEMETERY

T. RICHMOND

LONGWD
MDWS

GRANT
MEADOWS

J

K

L

M

CYPRESS
GLN
17500

FRITSCHE
CEMETERY

W. LONGWD

E. LONGWD

LONGWD
SPUR

Fritsche
Cemetery

FENSKE
18100

Little

Cypress

Creek

THREE OAKS ESTS

CHESTNUT
BRANCH TRL

POPLAR LAKE
TRL

N

P

Q

Fritsche
Park
Site

© KEY MAPS 2017

R

TELGE
MNR

TELGE

© KEY MAPS 2017

© KEY MAPS 2017

HARRIS COUNTY

DELUCA

BOUDREAUX

SEE 327 MAP

0   1/4   1/2   3/4   1 Mile

© KEY MAPS 2017

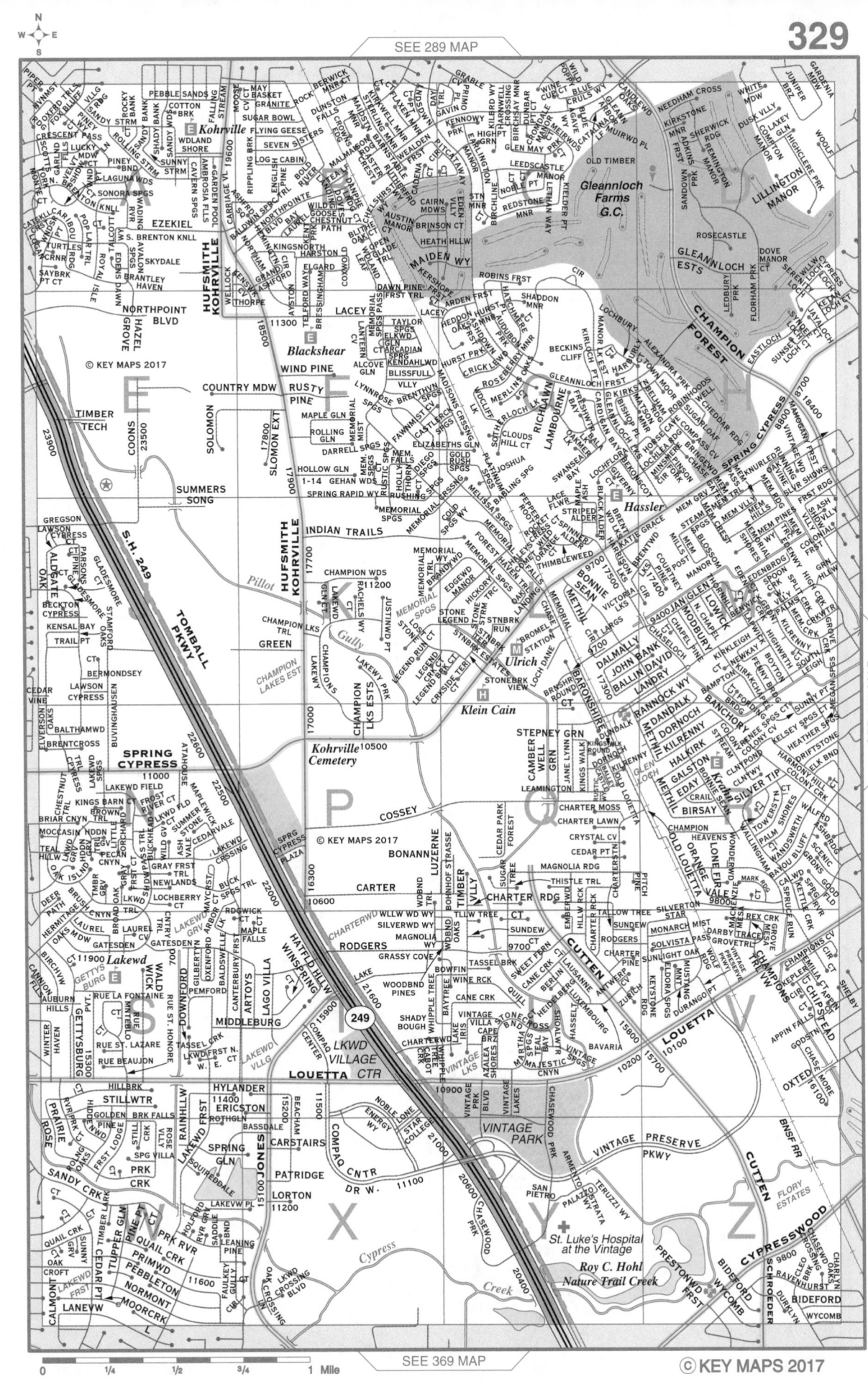

© KEY MAPS 2017

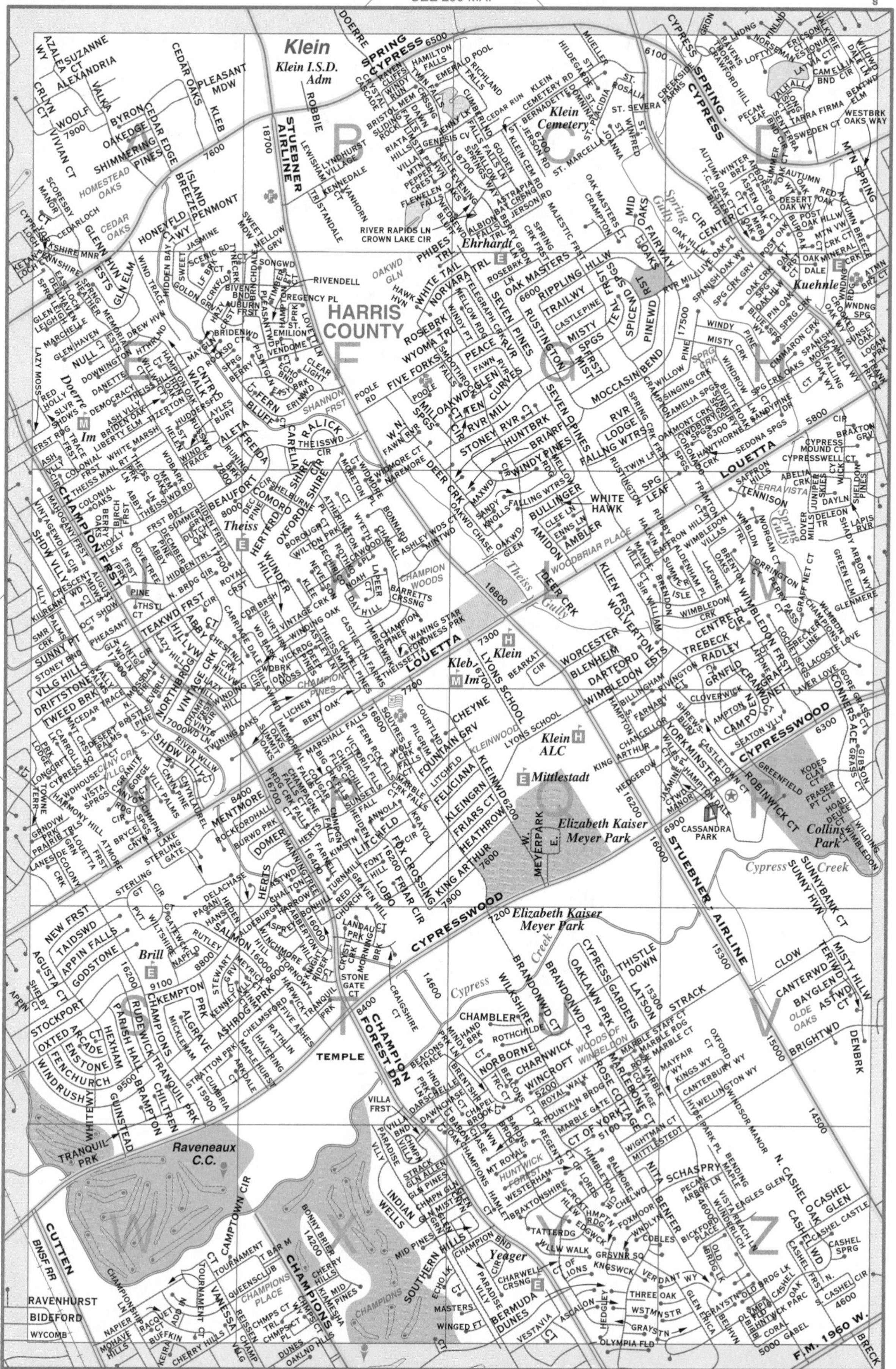

Klein
Klein I.S.D.
Adm

HARRIS
COUNTY

SPRING
CYPRESS

Klein
Cemetery

Kuehnle

Ehrhardt

Theiss

LOUETTA

Louetta

Klein
Kleb
School

Klein
ALC

Mittlestadt

Elizabeth Kaiser
Meyer Park

CYPRESSWOOD

Cassandra
Park

Collins
Park

Cypress Creek

STUEBNER AIRLINE

Elizabeth Kaiser
Meyer Park

Cypress Creek

Brill

TEMPLE

CHAMPION FOREST DR

Raveneaux
C.C.

CUTTEN

RAVENHURST
BIDEFORD
WYCOMB

Yeager

Southern Hills

Bermuda
Dunes

Champions
Place

F.M. 1960 W.

0   1/4   1/2   3/4   1 Mile

© KEY MAPS 2017

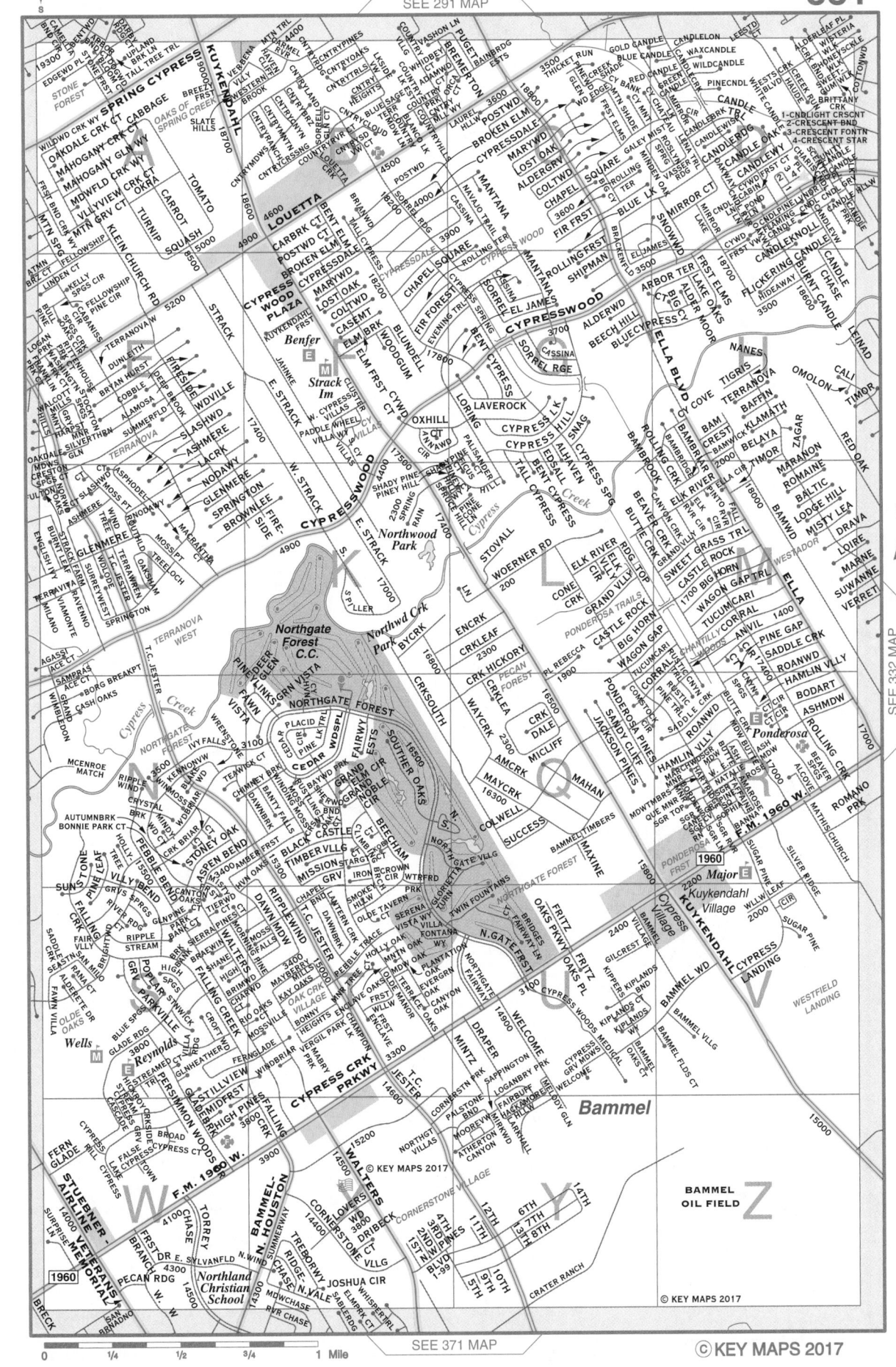

SEE 332 MAP

© KEY MAPS 2017

BAMMEL
OIL FIELD

Bammel

0   1/4   1/2   3/4   1 Mile

SEE 292 MAP

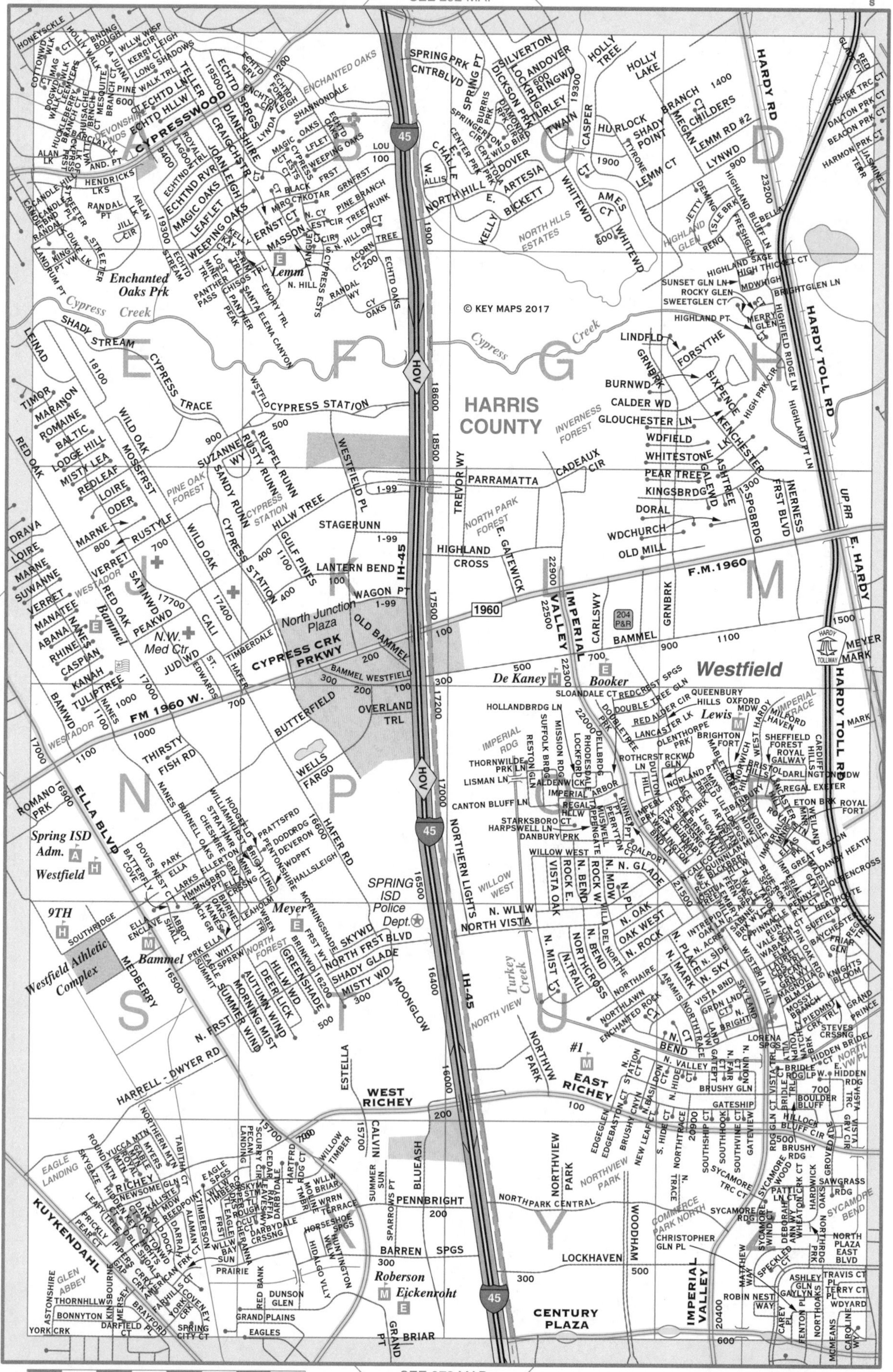

HARRIS COUNTY

CYPRESSWOOD

Enchanted Oaks Prk

Cypress Creek

Cypress Station

North Junction Plaza

CYPRESS CRK PRKWY

FM 1960 W.

F.M. 1960

Westfield

De Kaney

Booker

Spring ISD Adm.

Westfield

9TH

Westfield Athletic Complex

Bammel

Meyer

SPRING ISD Police Dept.

WEST RICHEY

EAST RICHEY

Northview Park

Northpark Central

KUYKENDAHL

Eagle Landing

Roberson

Eickenroht

CENTURY PLAZA

IMPERIAL VALLEY

Turkey Creek

HARDY TOLL RD

HARDY TOLL RD

E. HARDY

HARDY TOLLWAY

MEYER MARK

© KEY MAPS 2017

SEE 331 MAP

SEE 372 MAP

0   1/4   1/2   3/4   1 Mile

© KEY MAPS 2017

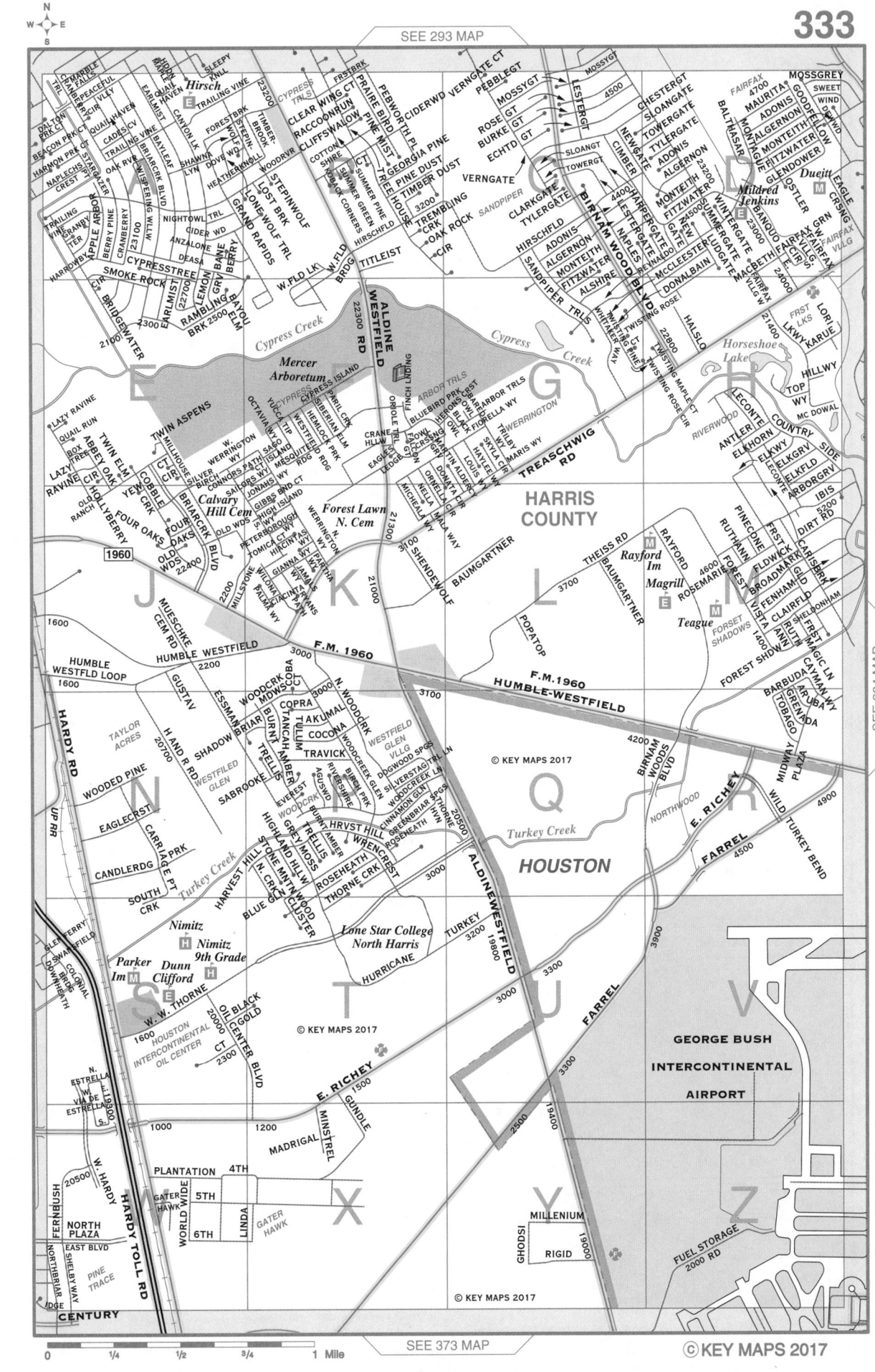

SEE 293 MAP

SEE 373 MAP

SEE 334 MAP

© KEY MAPS 2017

© KEY MAPS 2017

© KEY MAPS 2017

© KEY MAPS 2017

N
W E
S

HARRIS COUNTY

HOUSTON

GEORGE BUSH INTERCONTINENTAL AIRPORT

Mercer Arboretum

Cypress Creek

Cypress Creek

Horseshoe Lake

Turkey Creek

Turkey Creek

Lone Star College North Harris

F.M. 1960

HUMBLE-WESTFIELD

F.M. 1960

HARDY TOLL RD

0   1/4   1/2   3/4   1 Mile

SEE 294 MAP

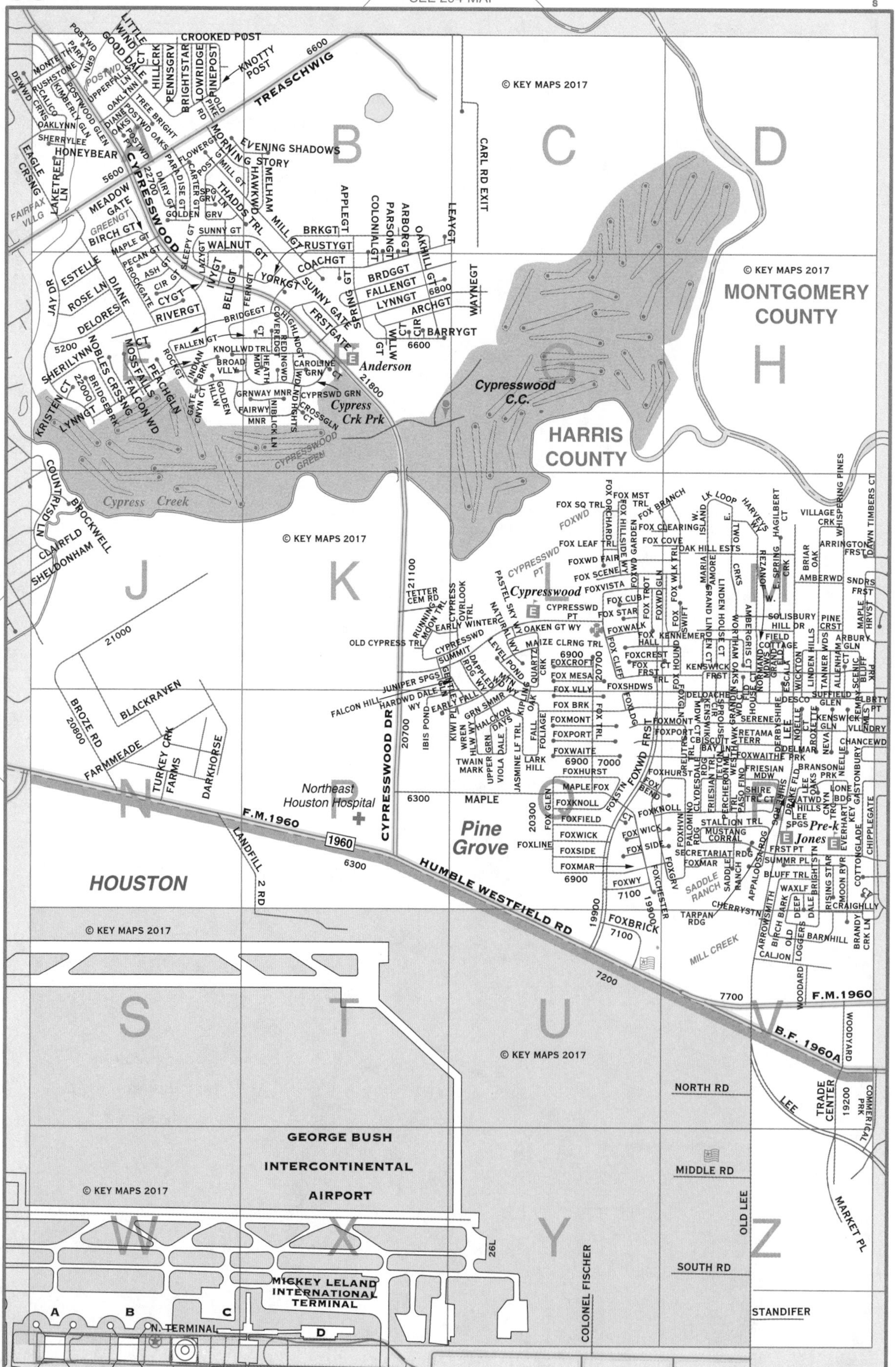

SEE 374 MAP

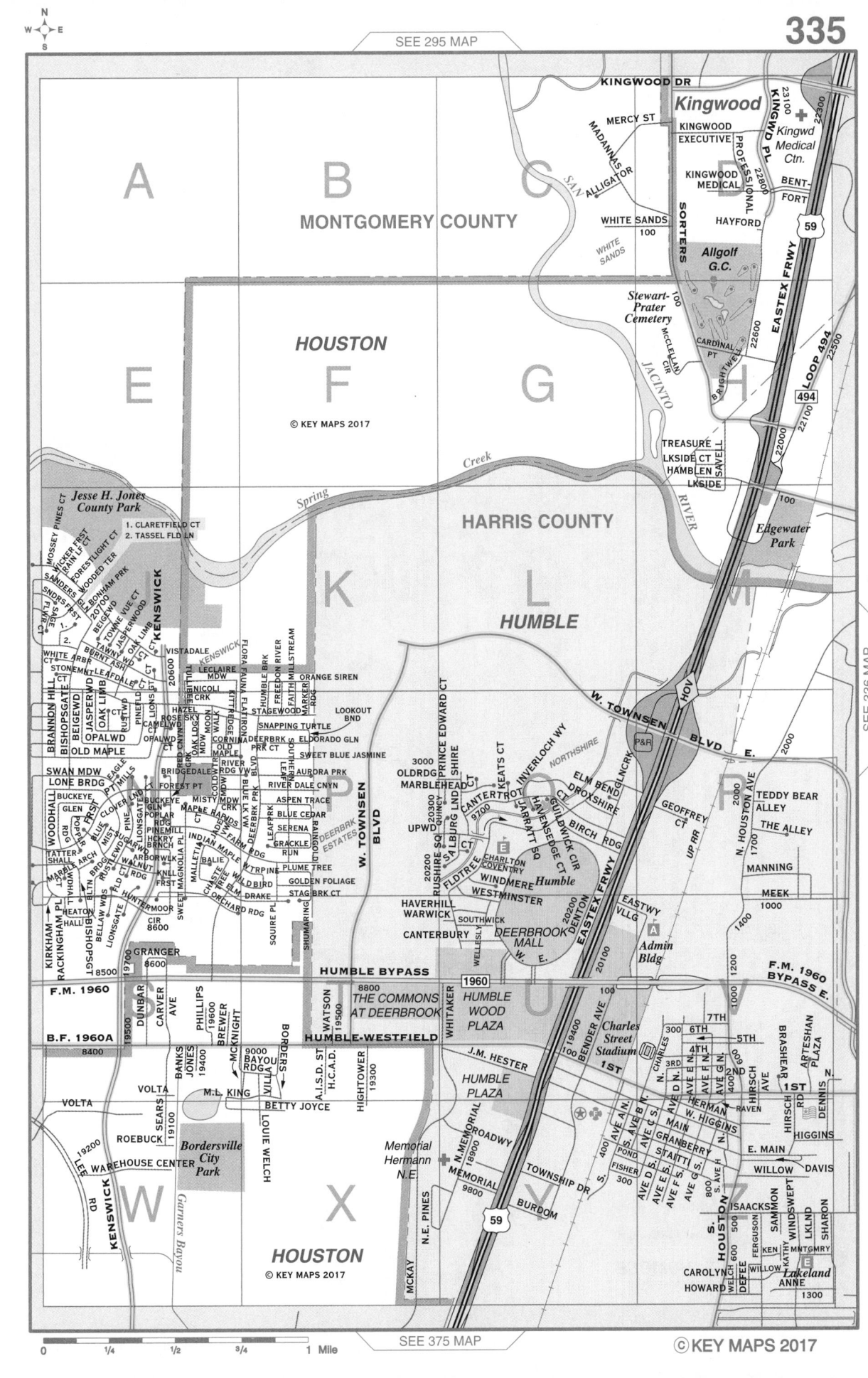

© KEY MAPS 2017

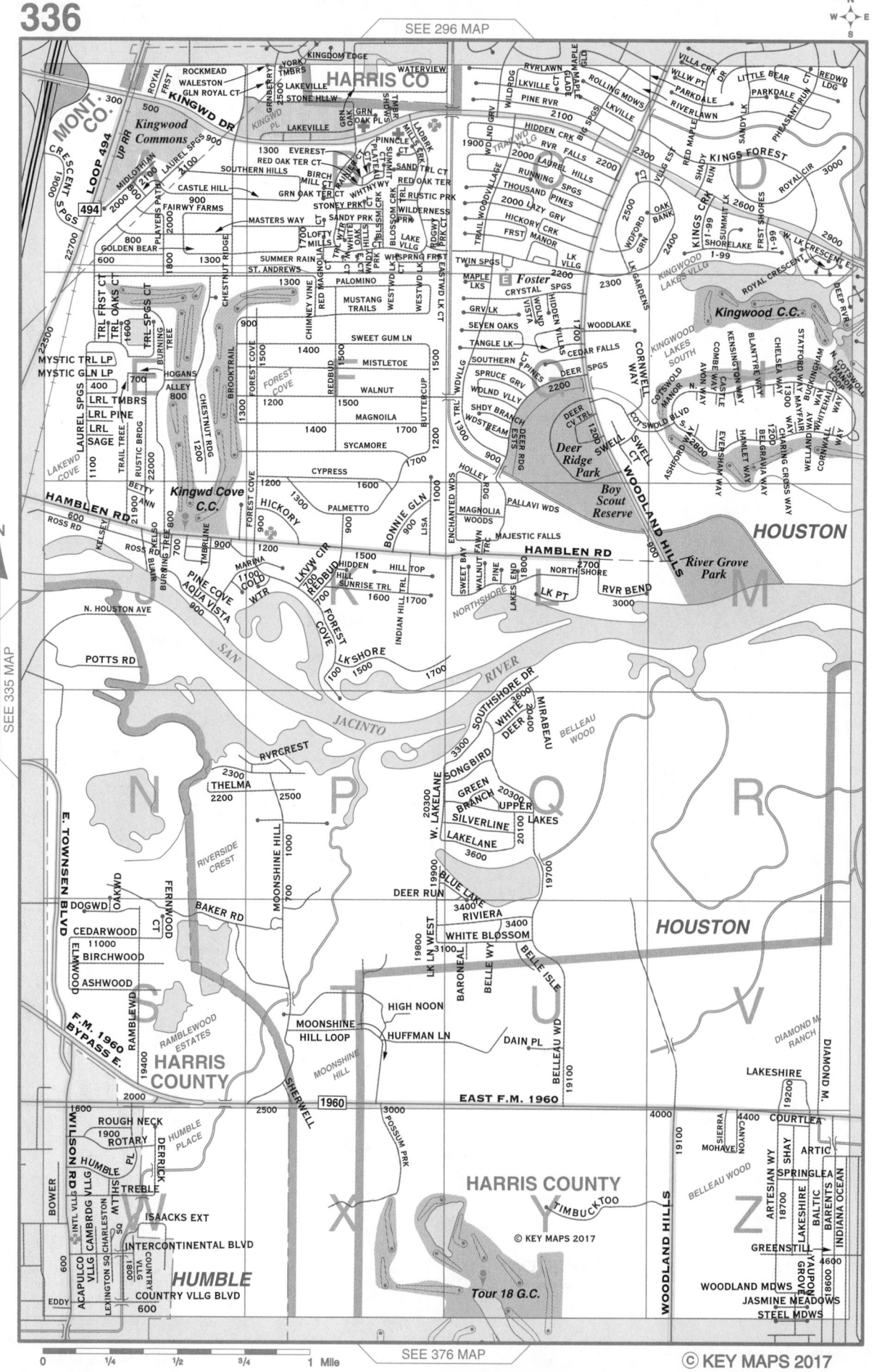

SEE 296 MAP

SEE 335 MAP

SEE 376 MAP

© KEY MAPS 2017

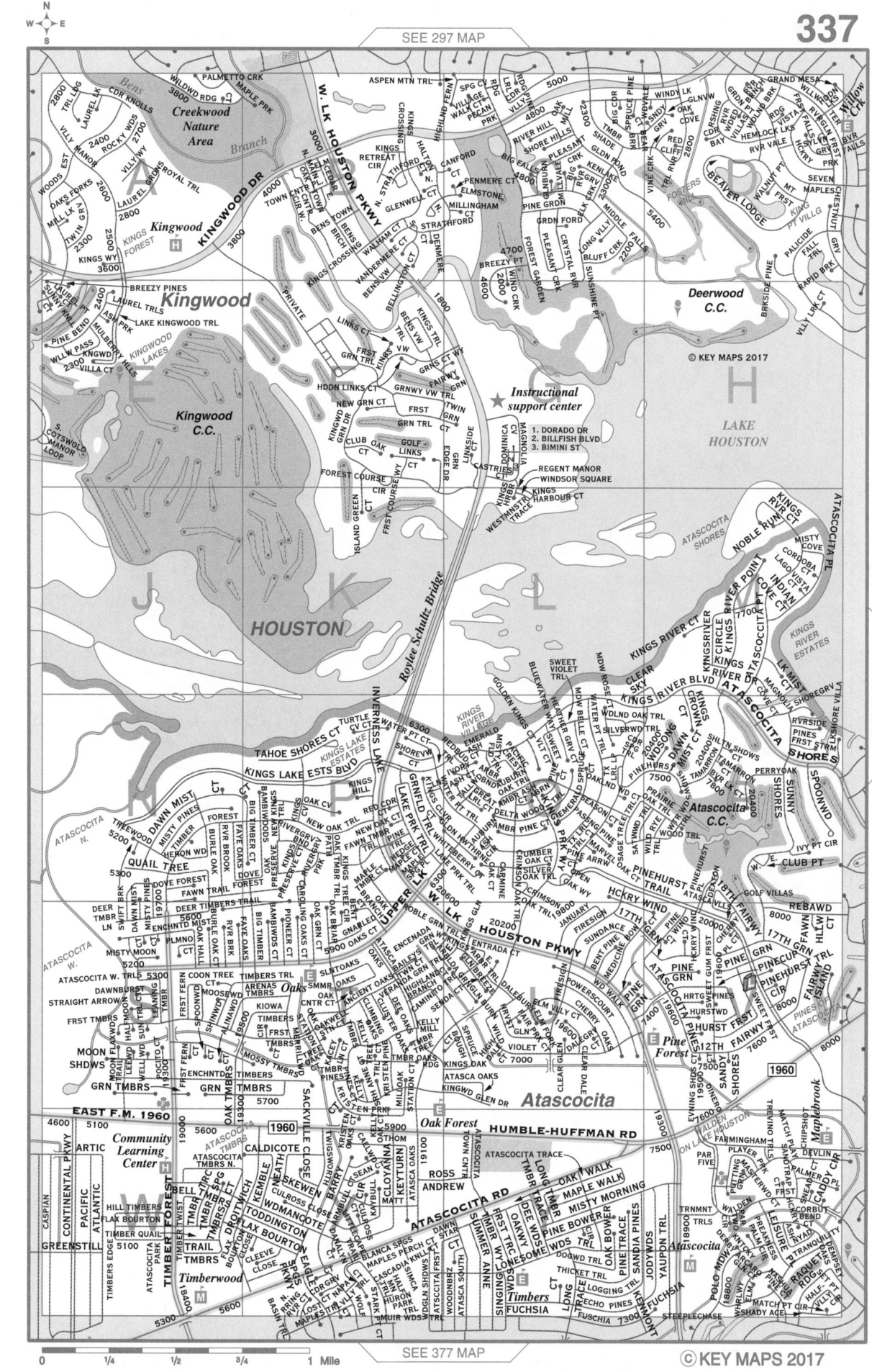

SEE 338 MAP

© KEY MAPS 2017

0   1/4   1/2   3/4   1 Mile

N W E S

HOUSTON

© KEY MAPS 2017

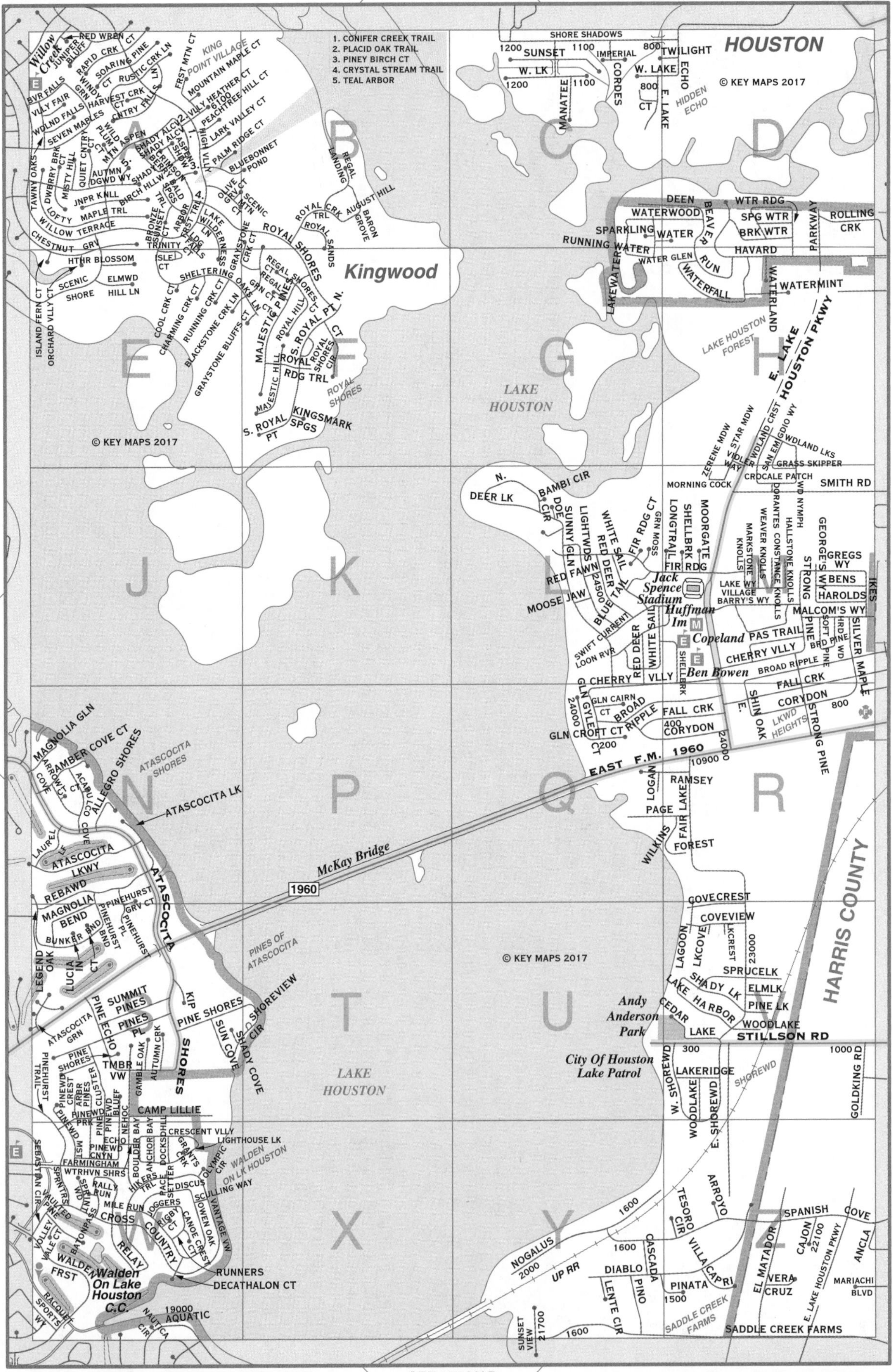

1. CONIFER CREEK TRAIL
2. PLACID OAK TRAIL
3. PINEY BIRCH CT
4. CRYSTAL STREAM TRAIL
5. TEAL ARBOR

Kingwood

© KEY MAPS 2017

LAKE HOUSTON

Lake Houston Forest

WATERWOOD

HOUSTON PKWY

E. LAKE

Jack Spence Stadium

Huffman 1m

Copeland Pas Trail

Ben Bowen

HARRIS COUNTY

ATASCOCITA

McKay Bridge

1960

EAST F.M. 1960

Andy Anderson Park

City Of Houston Lake Patrol

STILLSON RD

PINES OF ATASCOCITA

LAKE HOUSTON

CAMP LILLIE

Walden On Lake Houston C.C.

© KEY MAPS 2017

GOLDKING RD

SADDLE CREEK FARMS

SEE 337 MAP

© KEY MAPS 2017

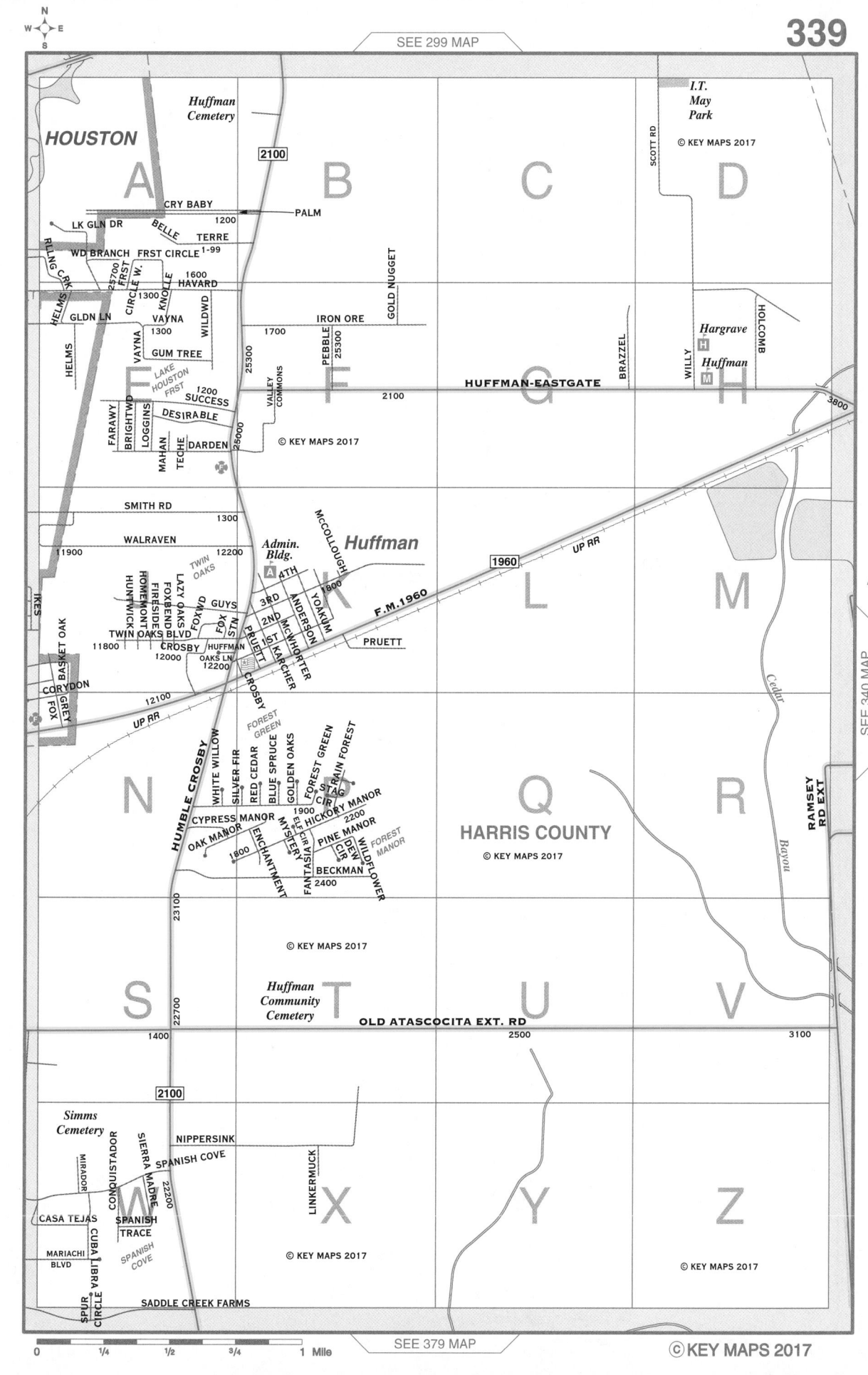

N
W · E
S

*Huffman
Cemetery*

HOUSTON

2100

I.T.
*May
Park*

© KEY MAPS 2017

SCOTT RD

A

B

C

D

CRY BABY
1200
PALM

LK GLN DR
BELLE
TERRE
FRST CIRCLE 1-99

WD BRANCH
FRST
1600
HAVARD

RLLNG CRK
25700
FRST
CIRCLE W.
KNOLLE
WILDWD

HELMS
GLDN LN
VAYNA
1300

HELMS
VAYNA
GUM TREE

LAKE
HOUSTON
FRST
1200
SUCCESS

IRON ORE
1700
PEBBLE
25300

GOLD NUGGET

BRAZZEL

WILLY
Hargrave
H
Huffman
M

HOLCOMB

3800

E

F

G

H

FARAWY
BRIGHTWD
LOGGINS
MAHAN
TECHE
DARDEN
DESIRABLE
25000
25300
VALLEY
COMMONS
2100

HUFFMAN-EASTGATE

© KEY MAPS 2017

SMITH RD
1300

WALRAVEN
11900
12200

IKES

TWIN OAKS

*Admin.
Bldg.*
A
McCOLLOUGH
4TH
3RD
2ND
1800

Huffman

1960
UP RR

LAZY OAKS
FOXBEND
FIRESIDE
HOMEMONT
HUNTWICK
FOXWD
GUYS
FOX
STN

BASKET OAK

TWIN OAKS BLVD
CROSBY
11800
12000
HUFFMAN
OAKS LN
12200
PRUETT
KARCHER
ANDERSON
McWHORTER
YOAKUM
F.M.1960

K

L

M

CORYDON
FOX
GREY
12100

UP RR
23100

HUMBLE CROSBY

PRUETT

PRUETT

N

WHITE WILLOW
SILVER FIR
RED CEDAR
BLUE SPRUCE
GOLDEN OAKS
FOREST GREEN
TRAIN FOREST

*Forest
Green*
STAG
CIR
HICKORY MANOR

CYPRESS MANOR
OAK MANOR
1800
ENCHANTMENT
MYSTERY
ELF
2200
PINE MANOR
DEW
CIR
*Forest
Manor*

FANTASIA
BECKMAN
2400
WILDFLOWER

HARRIS COUNTY

© KEY MAPS 2017

Q

R

Bayou

Cedar

RAMSEY
RD EXT

SEE 340 MAP

N

© KEY MAPS 2017

S

22700

*Huffman
Community
Cemetery*
1400

T

OLD ATASCOCITA EXT. RD
2500

U

3100

V

2100

*Simms
Cemetery*

NIPPERSINK
SPANISH COVE

SIERRA MADRE
22200
SPANISH COVE

LINKERMUCK

MIRADOR
CONQUISTADOR

CASA TEJAS
SPANISH
TRACE
SPANISH
COVE

MARIACHI
BLVD
CUBA LIBRA

SPUR
CIRCLE
SADDLE CREEK FARMS

W

X

Y

Z

© KEY MAPS 2017

© KEY MAPS 2017

0   1/4   1/2   3/4   1 Mile

© **KEY MAPS** 2017

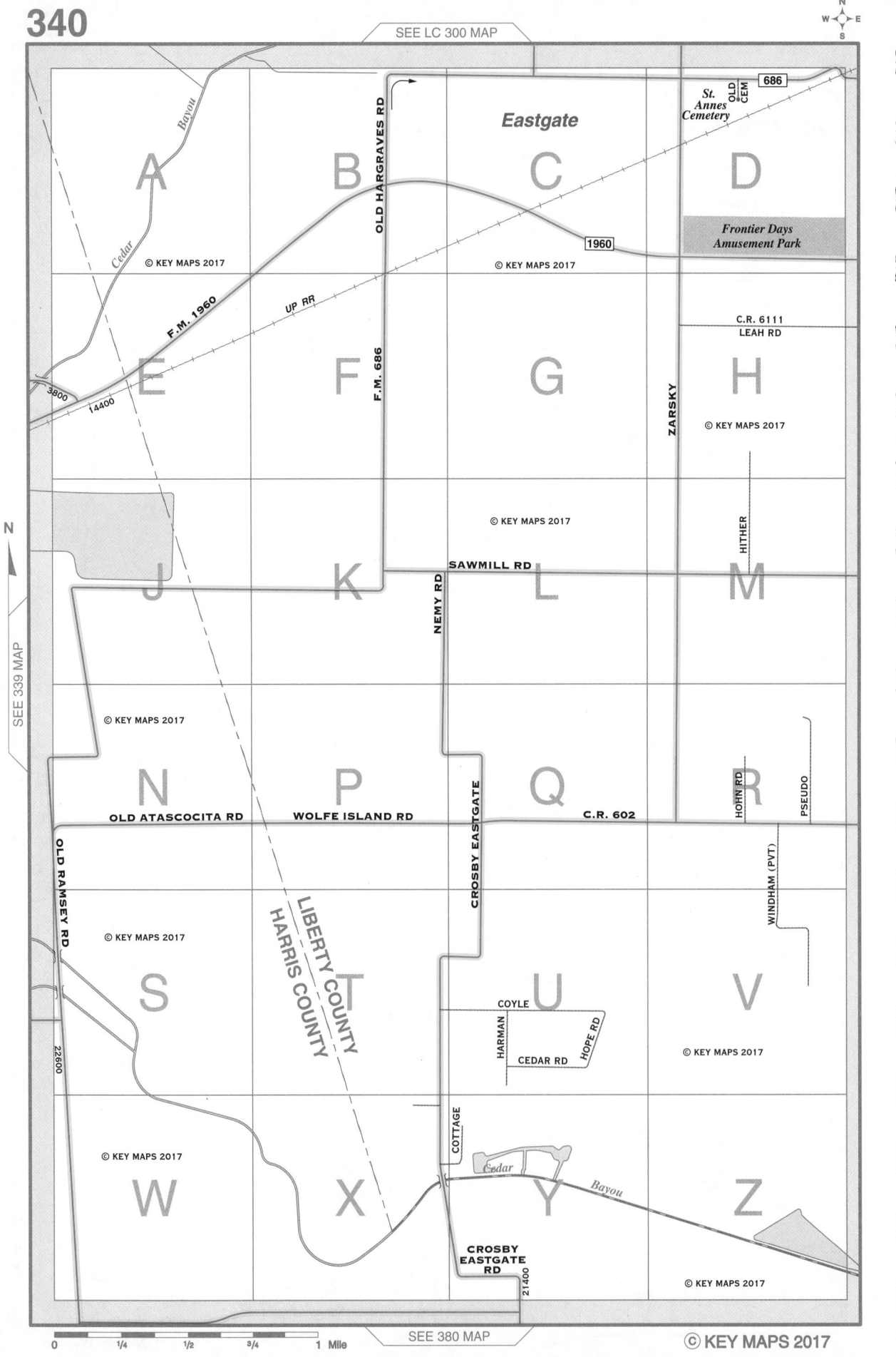

N
W + E
S

Eastgate

686

St.
Annes
Cemetery

OLD CEM

A

B

C

D

Bayou

Cedar

OLD HARGRAVES RD

© KEY MAPS 2017

1960

© KEY MAPS 2017

*Frontier Days
Amusement Park*

F.M. 1960

UP RR

C.R. 6111
LEAH RD

3800

14400

E

F

G

H

F.M. 686

ZARSKY

© KEY MAPS 2017

© KEY MAPS 2017

HITHER

N

SEE 339 MAP

J

K

L

M

SAWMILL RD

NEMY RD

© KEY MAPS 2017

© KEY MAPS 2017

N

P

Q

R

OLD ATASCOCITA RD

WOLFE ISLAND RD

CROSBY EASTGATE

C.R. 602

HOHN RD

PSEUDO

OLD RAMSEY RD

LIBERTY COUNTY
HARRIS COUNTY

WINDHAM (PVT)

© KEY MAPS 2017

22600

S

T

U

V

COYLE

HARMAN

CEDAR RD

HOPE RD

© KEY MAPS 2017

COTTAGE

Cedar

Bayou

© KEY MAPS 2017

W

X

Y

Z

© KEY MAPS 2017

**CROSBY
EASTGATE
RD**

21400

0 1/4 1/2 3/4 1 Mile

© **KEY MAPS** 2017

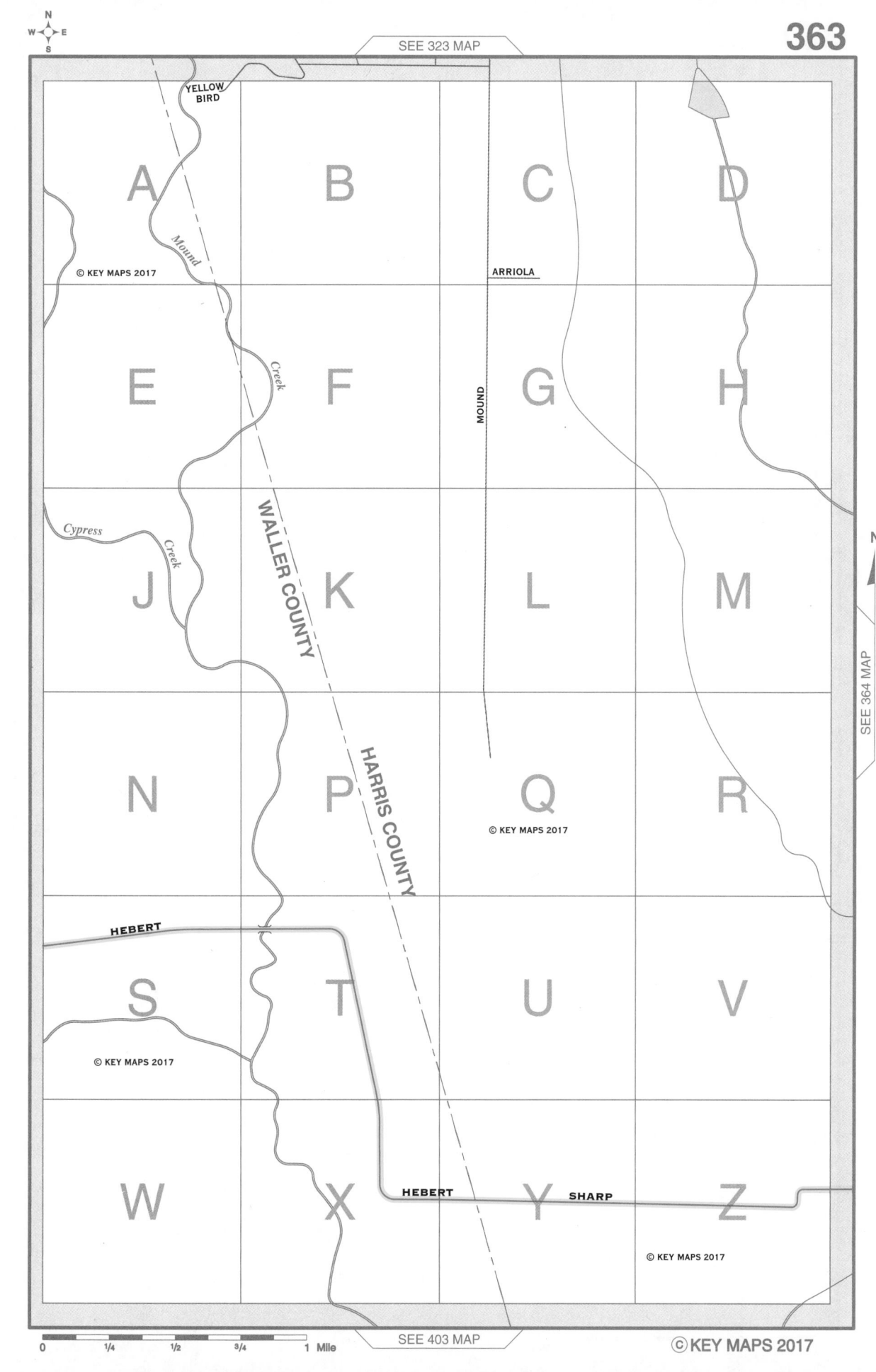

SEE 323 MAP

SEE 364 MAP

SEE 403 MAP

YELLOW BIRD

Mound

Creek

ARRIOLA

MOUND

Cypress

Creek

WALLER COUNTY

HARRIS COUNTY

HEBERT

HEBERT   SHARP

A   B   C   D

E   F   G   H

J   K   L   M

N   P   Q   R

S   T   U   V

W   X   Y   Z

0   1/4   1/2   3/4   1 Mile

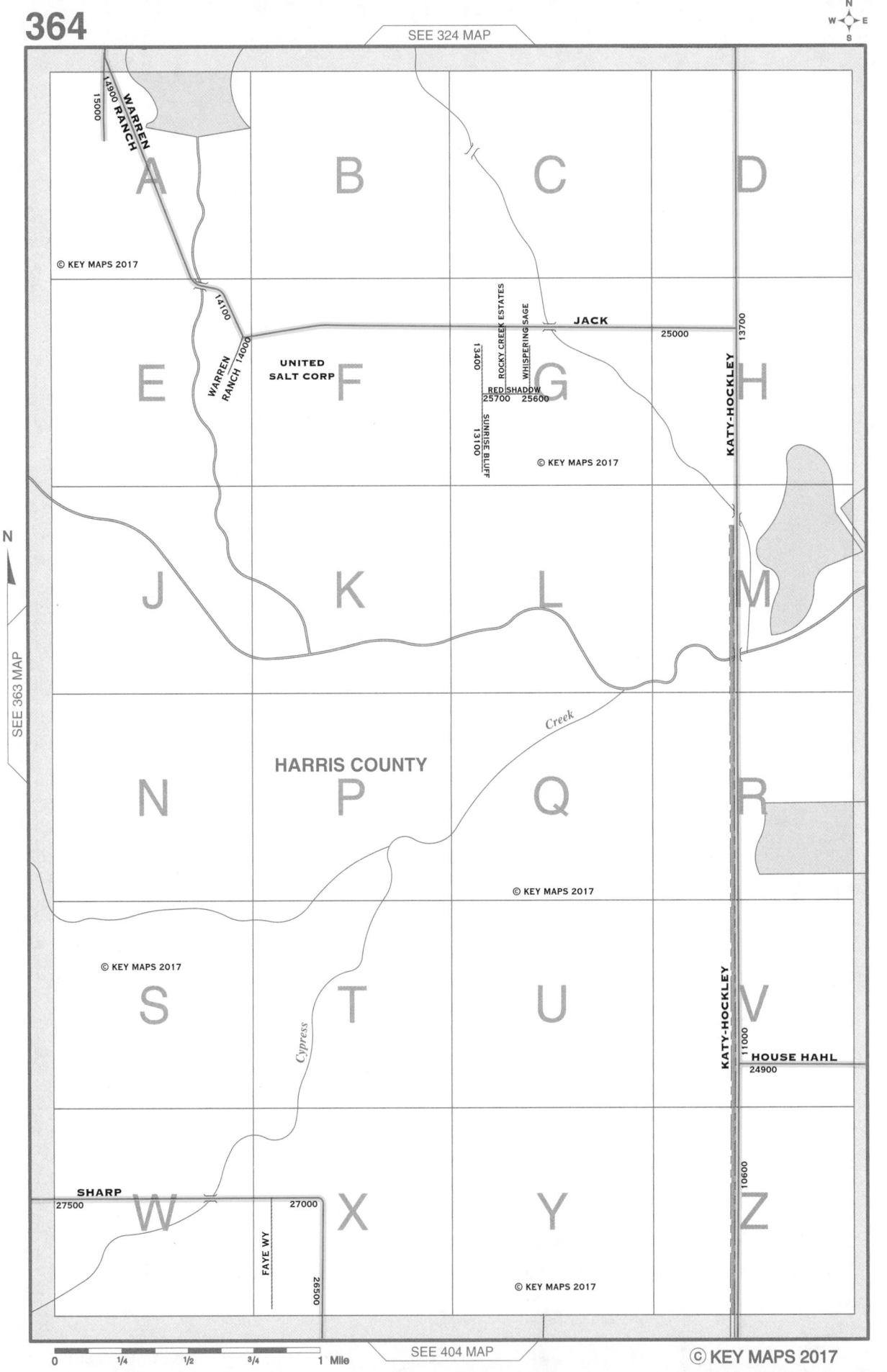

N
W E
S

WARREN RANCH

15000

14900

© KEY MAPS 2017

A

B

C

D

14100

WARREN RANCH 14000

ROCKY CREEK ESTATES

WHISPERING SAGE

JACK

25000

13700

KATY-HOCKLEY

E

UNITED
SALT CORP

F

13400

RED SHADOW

25700   25600

SUNRISE BLUFF

13100

G

© KEY MAPS 2017

H

N

SEE 363 MAP

J

K

L

M

Creek

HARRIS COUNTY

© KEY MAPS 2017

N

P

Q

R

© KEY MAPS 2017

Cypress

KATY-HOCKLEY

S

T

U

V

11000

HOUSE HAHL

24900

10600

SHARP

27500

27000

W

FAYE WY

26500

X

© KEY MAPS 2017

Y

Z

0   1/4   1/2   3/4   1 Mile

© **KEY MAPS** 2017

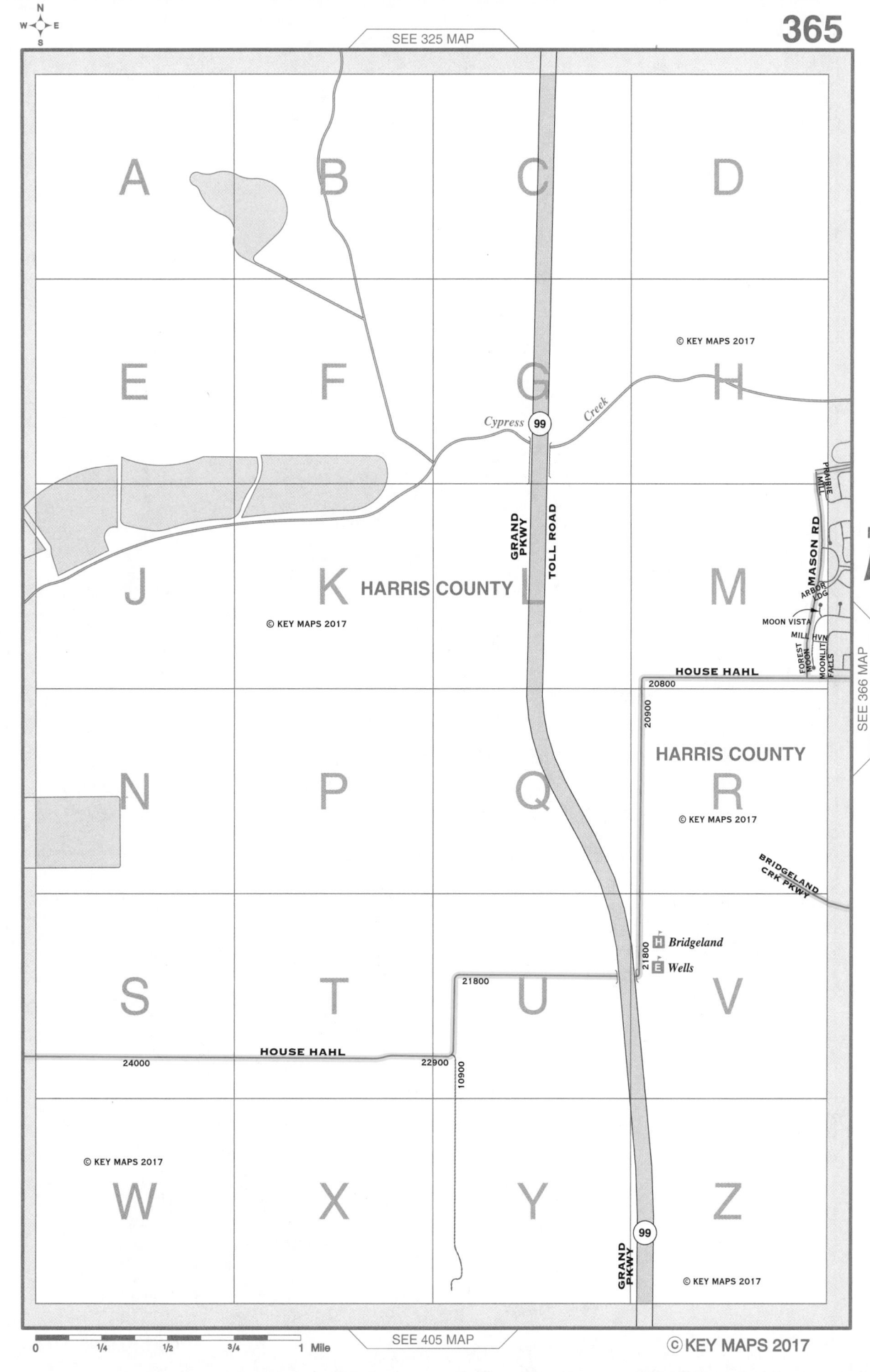

SEE 325 MAP

N
W E
S

A

B

C

D

© KEY MAPS 2017

E

F

G

H

Cypress (99) Creek

GRAND PKWY
TOLL ROAD

J

K

HARRIS COUNTY

L

M

© KEY MAPS 2017

N

SEE 366 MAP

PRAIRIE MIST
MASON RD
ARBOR LDG
MOON VISTA
FOREST MOON
MILL HVN
MOONLIT FALLS

HOUSE HAHL
20800
20900

HARRIS COUNTY

© KEY MAPS 2017

N

P

Q

R

© KEY MAPS 2017

BRIDGELAND CRK PKWY

H Bridgeland
21800
E Wells

S

T

21800

U

V

10900

HOUSE HAHL
24000
22900

© KEY MAPS 2017

W

X

Y

Z

(99)
GRAND PKWY

© KEY MAPS 2017

SEE 405 MAP

0 1/4 1/2 3/4 1 Mile

N
W E
S

MUESCHKE

290 6

UP RR

© KEY MAPS 2017

27100 26200 14000 15600

A   B   C

E   F   G

© KEY MAPS 2017

HOUSE HAHL
CYPRESSCROFT
HOUSE HAHL
FRY RD
STONE RIDGE
GRANITE VLLY
STONE FIELD CANYON
MASON TERRACE
TRINITY TRL
16000 MOUND
WEDGEWD PRK
GATESPRINGS
RIDGESTN
BLACKHORSE TRL
BLACK HORSE
CROSS CANYON
SHETSTONE

Cypress

N. BRIDGELAND LAKE PKWY

Pope

WATER HAVEN PRK
MILLS FORK
LONG HAVEN
SHADY EDGE
BRIDGE COVE
COVE LANDING
CYPRESS PRK
SHOREBRIDGE
SHORELANDS
STEPHENS CHARGE CT
HOLLOW STONE
17400

BlackHorse Golf Club

BLUEBERRY CEDAR

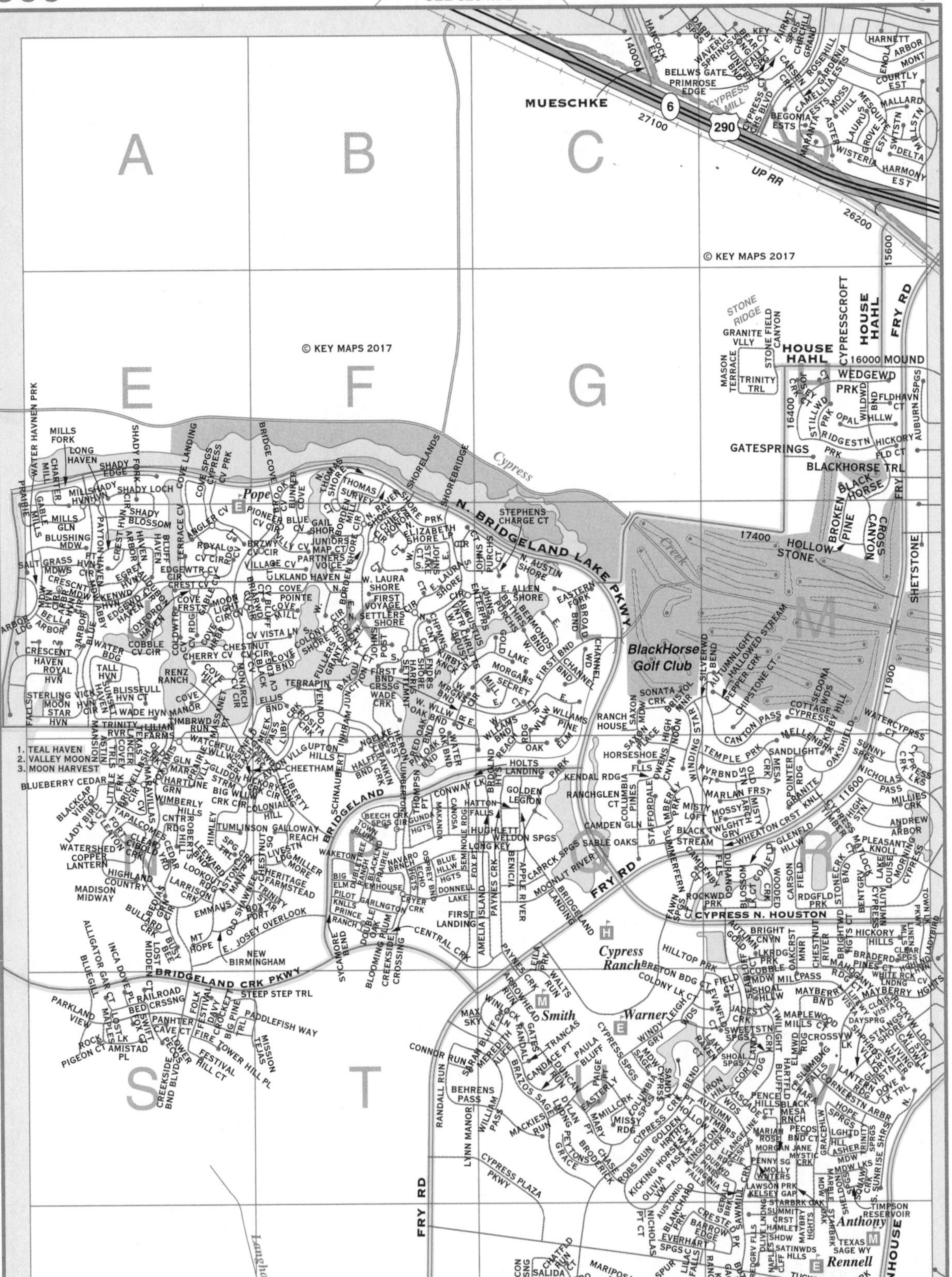

SEE 365 MAP

1. TEAL HAVEN
2. VALLEY MOON
3. MOON HARVEST

BRIDGELAND

FRY RD

CYPRESS N. HOUSTON

Cypress Ranch

BRIDGELAND CRK PKWY
STEEP STEP TRL
PADDLEFISH WAY

Smith
Warner

NEW BIRMINGHAM

FRY RD

CYPRESS PLAZA PKWY

LYNN MANOR

Anthony
Rennell

GREENHOUSE

Langham Creek

W   X

0   1/4   1/2   3/4   1 Mile

© KEY MAPS 2017

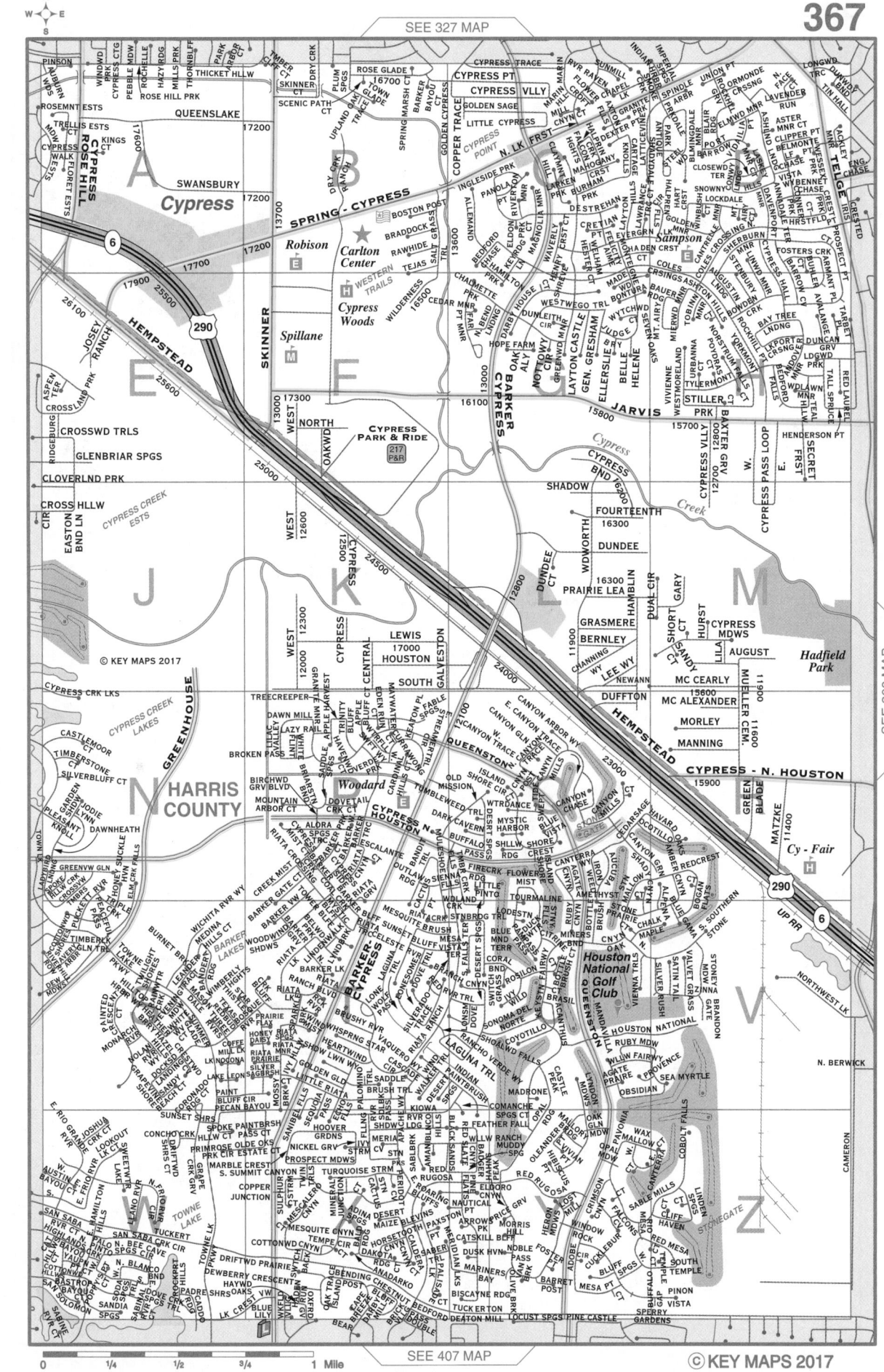

SEE 368 MAP

© KEY MAPS 2017

© KEY MAPS 2017

0   1/4   1/2   3/4   1 Mile

HARRIS COUNTY

CYPRESSWOOD

HUFFMEISTER

JARVIS

TELGE

WHISPERING VLLY

CYPRESS OAKS

ELDRIDGE PKWY N

SHADOWLAKE

Telge Park

Hadfield Park

CYPRESS CRK CEM.

Millsap SHAFT

OLD HUFFMEISTER

Lamkin

CYPRESS CROSSING

N. HOUSTON

CYPRESS

Telge Transportation Cntr

WEISER AIRPARK

Arnold

ELDRIDGE PKWY N.

North Cypress Med Ctr

NORTHWEST FRWY

290

6

HEMPSTEAD

F.M. 1960

1960

Cypress Falls

1. DAWN PT
2. ARBOR VLLY WY
3. ELM BOUGH
4. WORTHAM RDG TRL
5. FERN VALE
6. IRIS BRK WY
7. GRV HLLW

SEE 367 MAP

SEE 408 MAP

0 1/4 1/2 3/4 1 Mile

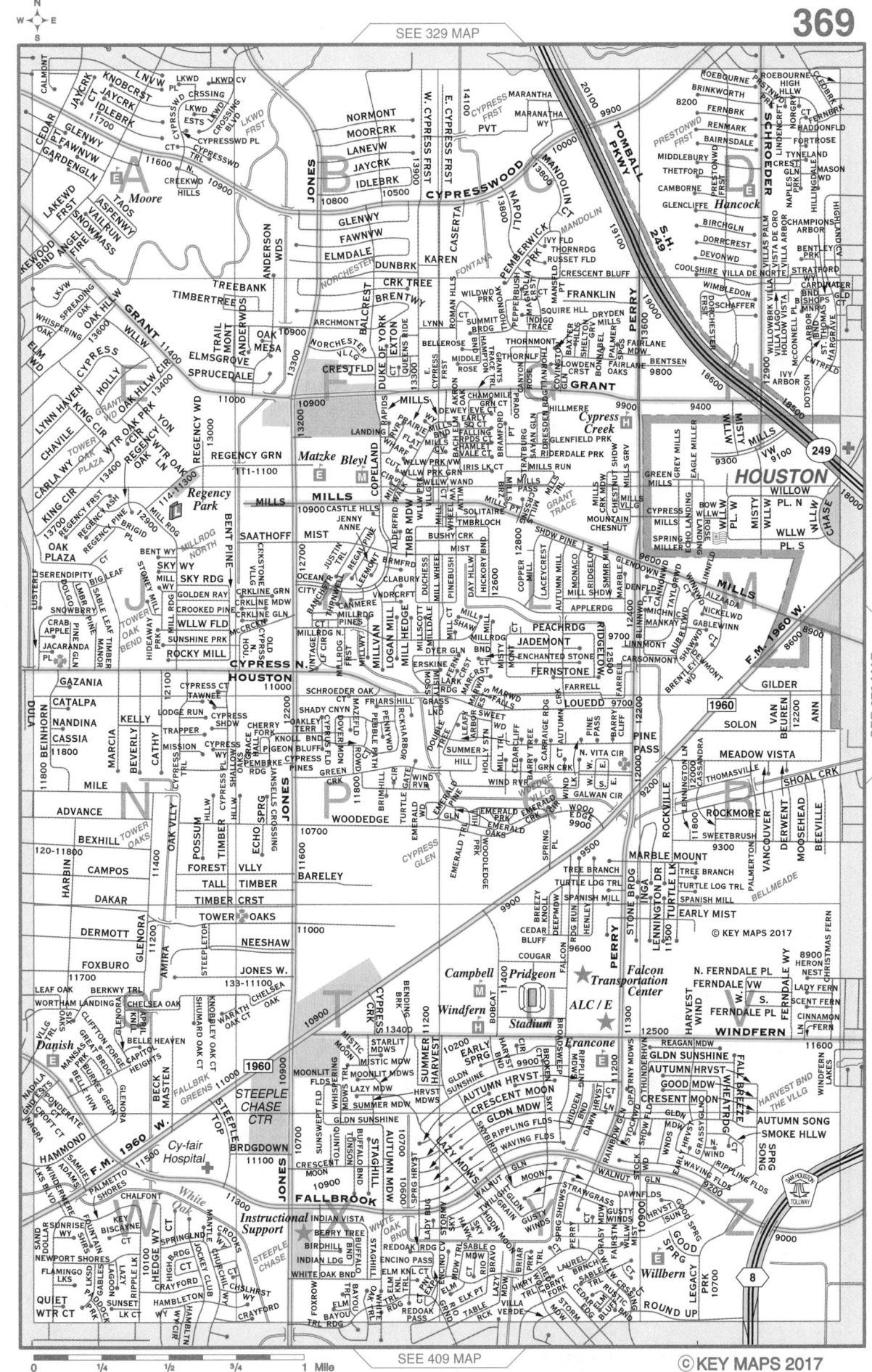

0   1/4   1/2   3/4   1 Mile

© KEY MAPS 2017

SEE 330 MAP

SEE 369 MAP

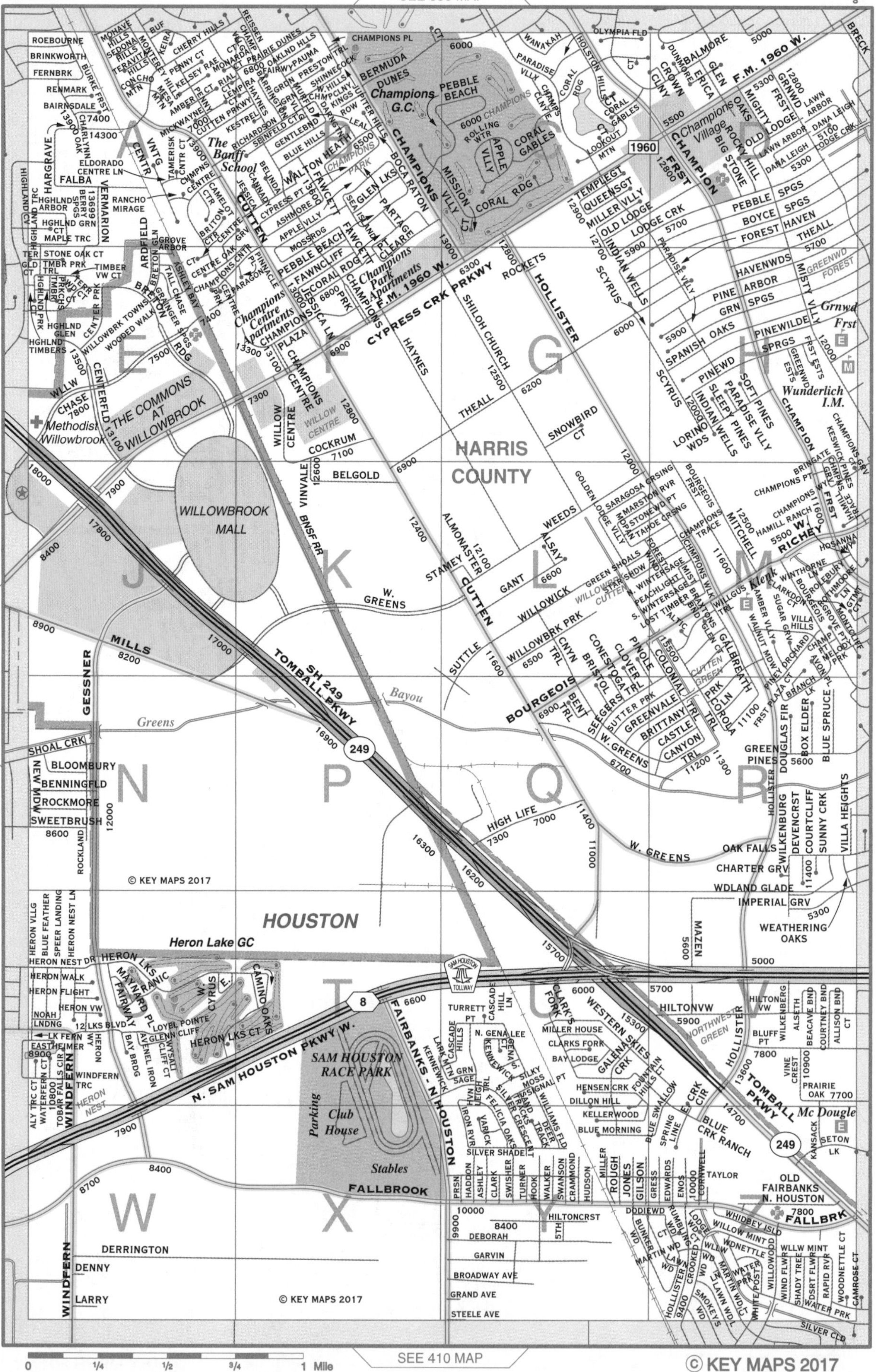

HARRIS COUNTY

HOUSTON

WILLOWBROOK MALL

THE COMMONS AT WILLOWBROOK

Champions G.C.

PEBBLE BEACH

Champions Village

The Banff School

Methodist Willowbrook

Willow Centre

Heron Lake GC

SAM HOUSTON RACE PARK

Club House

Stables

Parking

FM 1960 W.

CYPRESS CRK PRKWY

TOMBALL PKWY

SH 249

N. SAM HOUSTON PKWY W.

SAM HOUSTON TOLLWAY

BNSF RR

GESSNER

WINDFERN

FALLBROOK

FM 1960 W.

W. RICHEY

BOURGEOIS

HOLLISTER

CUTTEN

W. GREENS

Greens Bayou

© KEY MAPS 2017

SEE 410 MAP

0   1/4   1/2   3/4   1 Mile

© KEY MAPS 2017

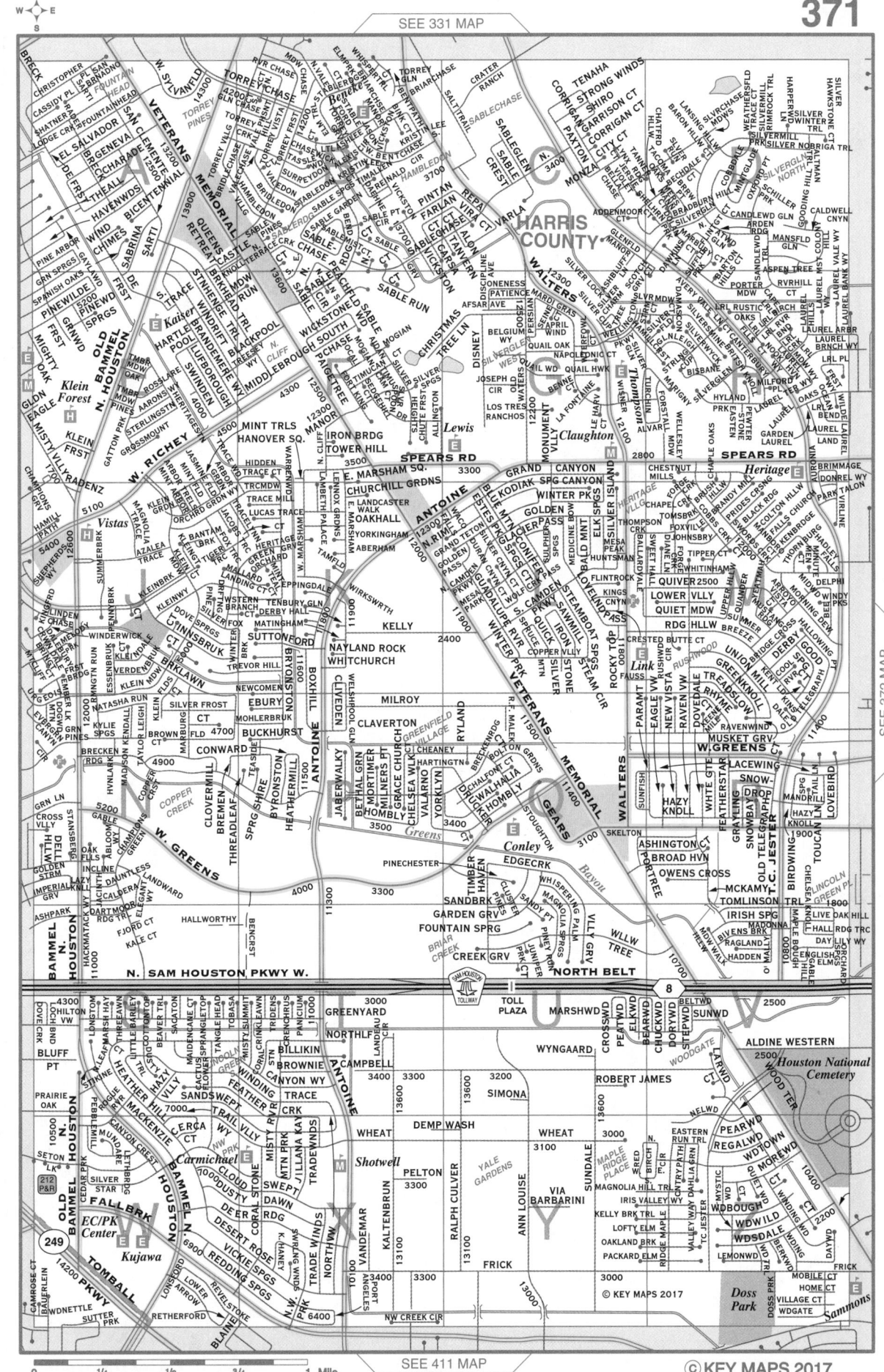

0   1/4   1/2   3/4   1 Mile

© KEY MAPS 2017

SEE 332 MAP

N
W E
S

HARRIS COUNTY

© KEY MAPS 2017

HOUSTON

A B C D E F G H

AIRTEX

IMPERIAL VLLY

AIRTEX

CENTURY PLAZA

Numbered list (Garden area):
1. GARDEN GATE CT
2. REYNARD CT
3. LARCHMERE CT
4. ROOKWOOD CT
5. WILD CURRANT CT
6. RILEY ESPEN CT
7. CASCADE GRN CT
8. CROSSHILL CT
9. OLD FINCH CT
10. FALLS DOCK CT
11. REINER GLN CT
12. RED ARGAN CT
13. GUNTHER SPGS CT
14. FLINT OAK CT
15. ONYX ROSE CT
16. CABELA RDG CT

KUYKENDAHL

ELLA BLVD

Hoyland

Clark

Primary

RUSHWORTH

LAUREL OAKS

SPEARS RD

W. RANKIN

RANKIN RD

RANKIN CIR N.

RANKIN CIR W.

RANKIN CIR E.

RANKIN PARK

Cooper

GILLMAN PARK

REMINGTON

Resthaven Cemetery

IMPERIAL VLLY

OLDHAM FARM

Numbered list (Buckner area):
1. BUCKNER CT
2. BARNESDALE CT
3. FORTON DR
4. BOBCAT PATH CT
5. PORCHLIGHT CT
6. RANGE HAVEN CT
7. BEE LINE CT
8. GOLDMAR CT
9. CORRAL GATE CT
10. SUNRISE RANCH CT
11. RUBY RANCH CT
12. GLEN RYDER CT

N. CRESCENT PARK

MOSA
HODA
DINIA
HUGH
TRICKEY

SPEARS CROSSING

Davis
Davis 9th

FOREST STAR
GREEN PINES
FOREST BARK
FOREST THICKET
FOREST IVY
FOREST HILLSIDE

KUYKENDAHL

RUSH CRK

FRST EDGE

SOUTHBRK

GRUSS
ABNEY

OAKHURST GREEN

GLEN BOROUGH

GREENS RD

Greens Bayou

GREENCHASE

NORTHCHASE

W. GREENS RD

Plummer
Spence

GEARS RD

GEARS RD

NORTH FRWY

GREENSPOINT MALL

GREENSPOINT PARK

BENMAR

CROWN PARK

GREENSMARK

DEPOT NORTH

ELLA BLVD

GREENS PKWY

GREENS CROSSING BLVD

N. SAM HOUSTON PKWY E.

8

N. SAM HOUSTON PKWY

SAM HOUSTON TOLLWAY

BELTWAY 8

ALDINE WESTERN

Houston National Cemetery

© KEY MAPS 2017

NORTHPT

NORTHPOINT

NORTH VILLAGE GREEN

PLAZA VERDE

GREEN PLAZA

ESPLANADE BLVD

ALDINE BENDER

COACH
MILL STREAM
SULKY
TREE
Black Buckboard
COUNTY FAIR
COACH LAMP

VETERANS MEMORIAL

Sammons

FALLBROOK

© KEY MAPS 2017

DEER TRL

GREENS LANDING

Bussey

Thompson

W. DYNA

M Aldine 9th

0   1/4   1/2   3/4   1 Mile

SEE 412 MAP

SEE 371 MAP

© KEY MAPS 2017

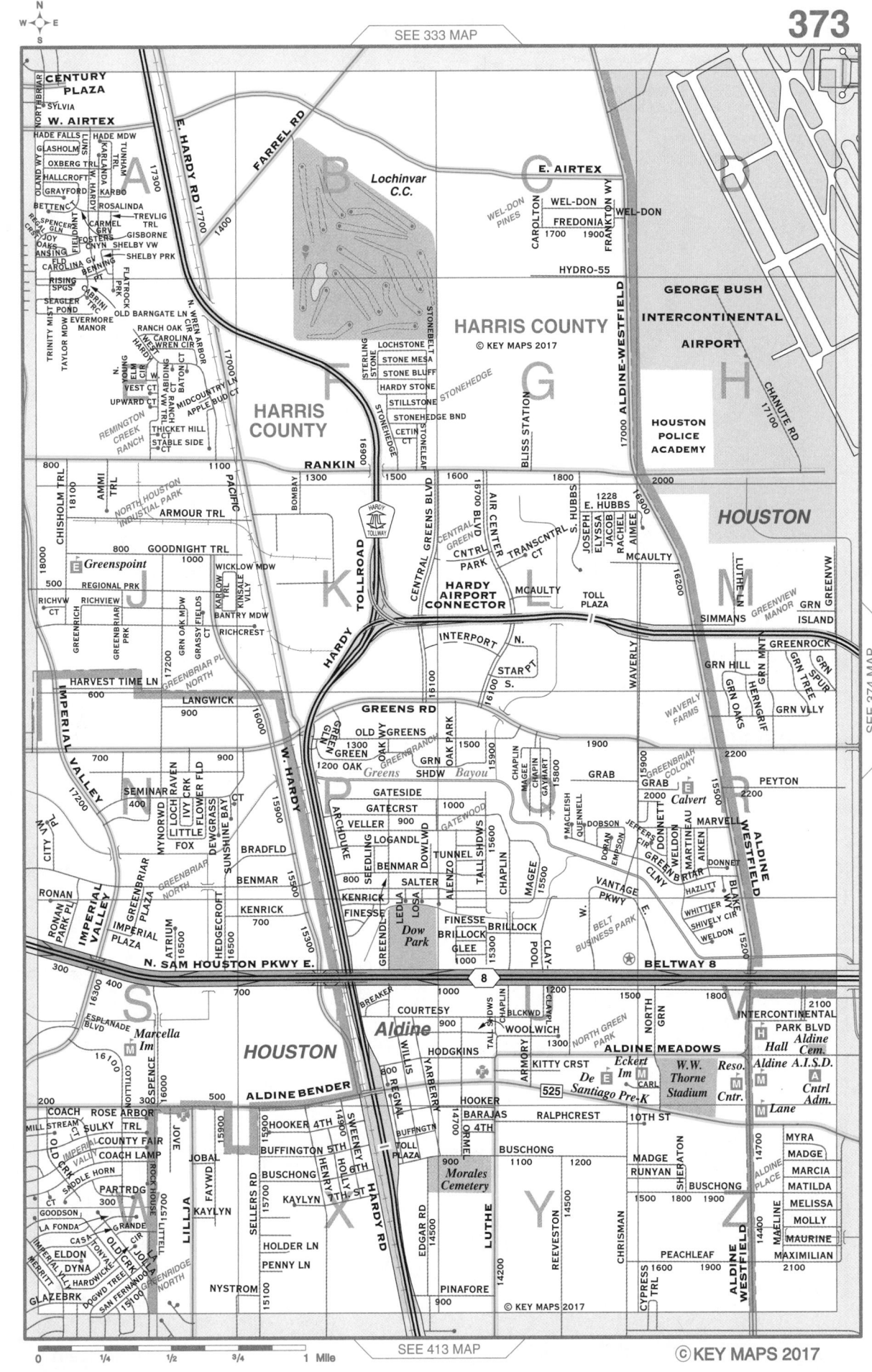

SEE 334 MAP

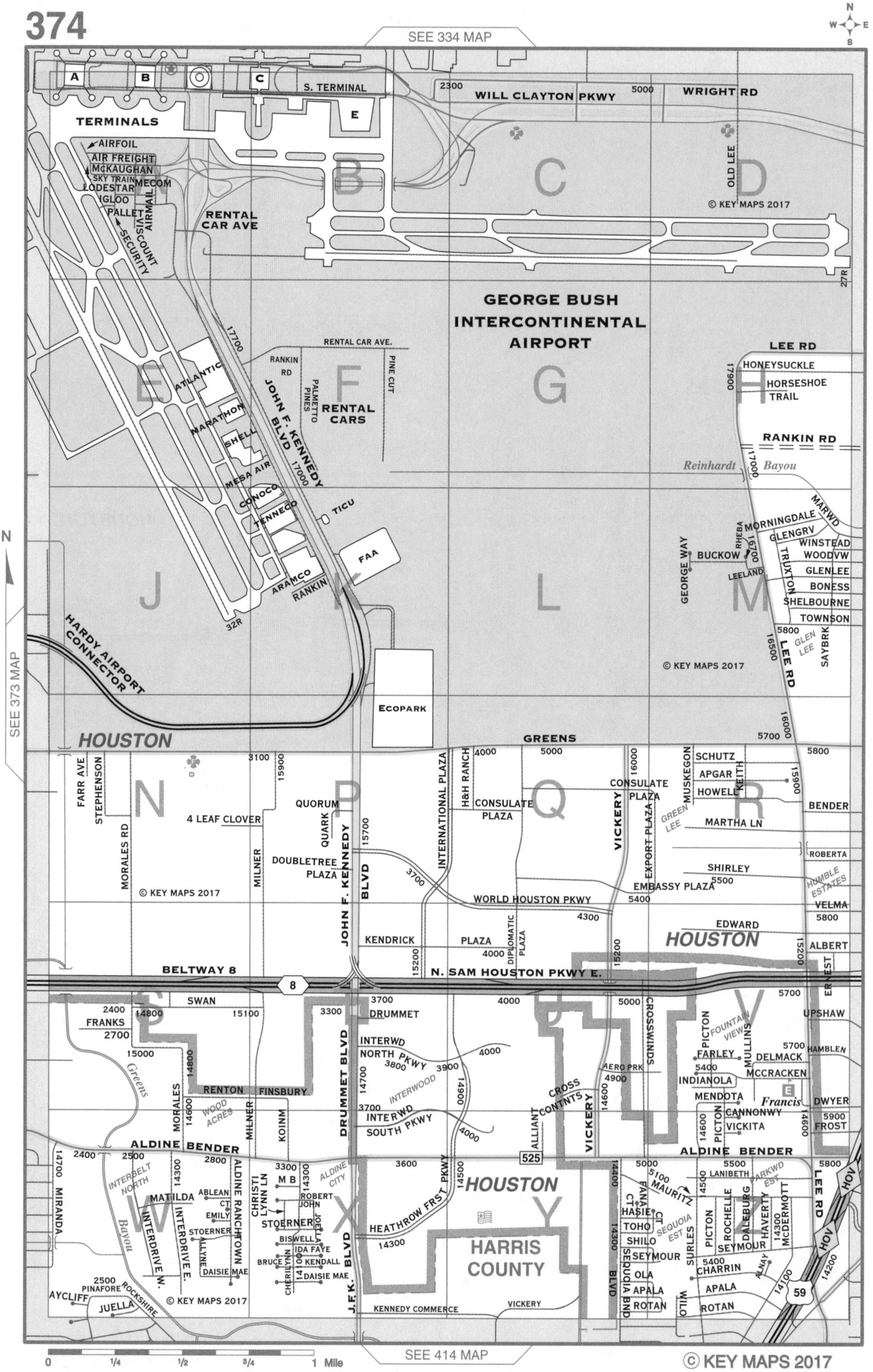

N
W — E
S

TERMINALS

A   B   C

S. TERMINAL

E

WILL CLAYTON PKWY   WRIGHT RD

2300   5000

AIRFOIL
AIR FREIGHT
McKAUGHAN
SKY TRAIN
LODESTAR   MECOM
IGLOO
PALLET   VISCOUNT
AIRMAIL

RENTAL CAR AVE

B

C

D

OLD LEE

© KEY MAPS 2017

27R

**GEORGE BUSH
INTERCONTINENTAL
AIRPORT**

RENTAL CAR AVE.

RANKIN RD

PINE CUT

PALMETTO PINES

ATLANTIC

MARATHON

SHELL

MESA AIR

CONOCO

TENNECO

ARAMCO   RANKIN

32R

E

F

**RENTAL
CARS**

G

LEE RD

HONEYSUCKLE

HORSESHOE TRAIL

H

RANKIN RD

Reinhardt Bayou

MARWD

MORNINGDALE
GLENGRV
WINSTEAD
WOODVW
GLENLEE
BONESS
SHELBOURNE
TOWNSON
SAYBRK

RHEBA
BUCKOW
LEELAND
TRUXTON

GEORGE WAY

GLEN LEE

5800

LEE RD

5700

5800

JOHN F. KENNEDY BLVD

17700

17000

SECURITY

TICU

FAA

J   K

L

© KEY MAPS 2017

16500

16000

HARDY AIRPORT CONNECTOR

Ecopark

SEE 373 MAP

N

HOUSTON

GREENS

5000   5700

FARR AVE
STEPHENSON

MORALES RD

N

3100
15900

4 LEAF CLOVER

© KEY MAPS 2017

QUORUM

QUARK

DOUBLETREE PLAZA

MILNER

P

15700

JOHN F. KENNEDY BLVD

KENDRICK

3700

15200

INTERNATIONAL PLAZA

H&H RANCH   4000

CONSULATE PLAZA

PLAZA
4000

DIPLOMATIC PLAZA

WORLD HOUSTON PKWY

Q

5000

16000

VICKERY

CONSULATE PLAZA

EXPORT PLAZA

Green Lee

SCHUTZ
APGAR
HOWELL

MARTHA LN

SHIRLEY

EMBASSY PLAZA   5500

4300

15200

4300

5400

EDWARD

HOUSTON

5800
KEITH

15900

BENDER

ROBERTA

HMNBLE ESTATES

VELMA

5800

ALBERT

15200

ERNEST

R

BELTWAY 8   N. SAM HOUSTON PKWY E.   8

2400   SWAN   15100
FRANKS
2700   15000

S

14800

Greens

MORALES

RENTON   FINSBURY
WOOD ACRES

MILNER

KOINM

3300   3700   DRUMMET   4000   5000

DRUMMET BLVD

INTERWD
NORTH PKWY
3800   3900   4000

14700

INTERWOOD

14900

3700   INTERWD
SOUTH PKWY   4000

CROSSWINDS

AERO PRK

CROSS CONTNTS

ALLIANT

VICKERY

14600

5000

PICTON
FARLEY

INDIANOLA

MENDOTA
PICTON   CANNONWY
VICKITA

FOUNTAIN VIEWS   UPSHAW

5700   HAMBLEN

DELMACK
McCRACKEN

Francis   DWYER

5900
FROST

5700

14600

ALDINE BENDER

2400   2500   2800
14700

MIRANDA

INTERBELT NORTH
Bayou

INTERDRIVE W.

INTERDRIVE E.

W

14300

MATILDA
EMILY

ABLEAN
CT

STOERNER

ALLYNE

2500   PINAFORE
AYCLIFF
ROCKSHIRE

JUELLA

© KEY MAPS 2017

3300
M B

CHRISTI LYNN LN

BISWELL

CHERILYN

ROBERT JOHN

STOERNER

IDA FAYE   KENDALL
BRUCE LN

DAISIE MAE

JOELLA

J.F.K. BLVD

X

KENNEDY COMMERCE

ALDINE CITY

HEATHROW FRST PKWY

14300

3600

14500

525

HOUSTON

HARRIS COUNTY

Y

VICKERY

ALDINE BENDER

5000   5100
MAURITZ

HASIE
TOHO
SHILO
SEYMOUR
OLA
APALA
ROTAN

5500
LANIBETH

4500

ROCHELLE
SEYMOUR

PICTON
SURLES
CHARRIN

PARKWD
EST

DALEBURG

SHILO

APALA

SEQUOIA BLVD

ALNA

5400

HAVERTY

McDERMOTT

14300

SEQUOIA EST

ALMA

LEE RD

HOV
HOV

5800

14200

ROTAN

59

0   1/4   1/2   3/4   1 Mile

SEE 414 MAP

© **KEY MAPS** 2017

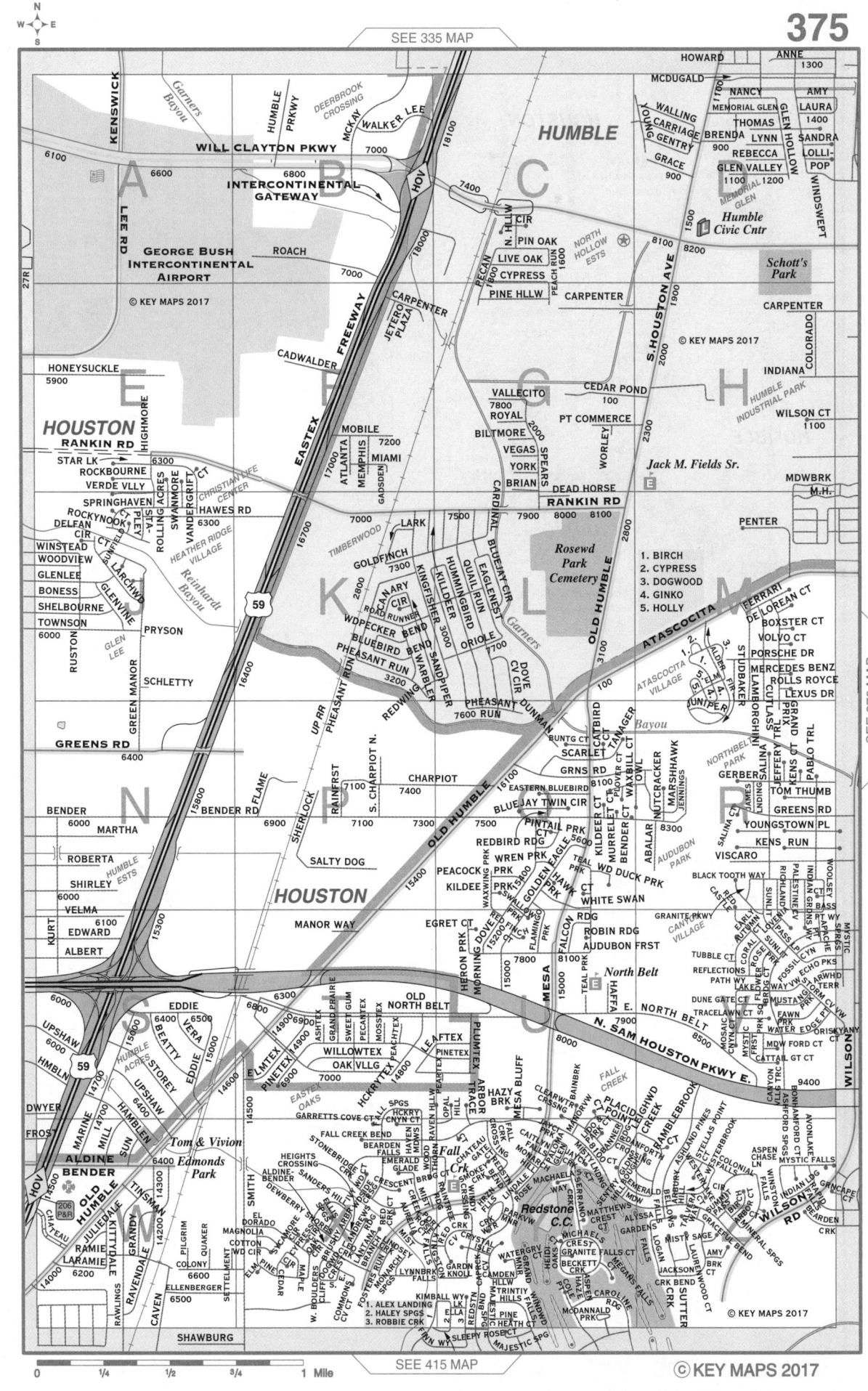

SEE 336 MAP

N W E S 8

EDDY 600 FOOTBALL
1600
1200 Ross Sterling
MICHAEL
1500
Humble High Cate Center
Bus Barn & Warehouse 8900
CARPENTER
ILLINOIS INDIAN
INDIANA 1200
WILSON RD
WILSON CT
HUMBLE
MDWBRK M.H.

STATION LDG
ZINNIA WINTERWD FRST
REDFORD PATH REDFORD PINES
RUSTIC TMBERS
9300
COLD RVR
NORWD TRAILS
ARBURY CASCADE HOUSE
HARMILL HOUSE
WESTERN BRIAR LN SUN PT CT
FLEMING SPGS
SHADED PINES ADOBE STONE WOODED ACRES RICH MTN
ADOBE ROSE MACONDRAY SERENATA
SIANO PINES PICKWICK PINE
CHAMISAL CT COLD RIVER PINES BARR SPG TWIN DIAMOND
DELICADO MILL VW
RICH CROFT
River Pines
Woodland Pines

HOUSTON
DOVER FALLS CT TERRACE PT SAXON CRK
BROKEN TRC CT IVY CLIFF THORNGATE FRST
EAGLE HLLW WINDING GREEN
HAMPTON HILLS HUNTERS TERR
VILLAGE TWR CAMDEN FRST
WHISPERBLUFF CRISWELL FIRE SAGE
SECO CRK RALSTON AVELEIGH SUNSTONE TERR
KERRYBROOK PRESCOTT LAURELEN
TORREGON FIRESAGE CT GREEN CT
3000 ALISA BND
GIANNA SPGS HAYDEN SPGS KAYLA SPGS
EMILY SPGS
JENNA BETH LAUREN DRAWBRDG
HANNAH OAKS HAYLEY SPGS BLACKSTN TRL
BLACKSTN TRLS TRINITY JOE

Tour 18 G.C.
POSSUM PRK

WOODLAND HILLS JASMINE MEADOWS STEEL MDWS
18000 FARMER RD PLANTATION PASS DR WINDING VW
MASON GRV CT TREE MOSS CT
SENTRY PINE CT STILLWTR PL DR
4600 DREW FRST
ATASCOCITA TRL FALCON FRST
LOSS GRV HERON FRST
OVERLOOK STILL SPGS KIRK FRST
TEXAN FRST TRL BLUE SPRUCE
LOFT SQ PL ECHO CLEARING
DUNEBERRY
ADMIRAL LITTLE
WOODSIDE
Whispering Pines

Humble

WILL CLAYTON PKWY
ATASCOCITA RD
ATASCOCITA WY
2300 ATASCOCITA TRACE
2000
1500
1200 2800
LARKIN HARK

OAK TRACE CT MISTY LACE OAK RUN
3700
FAVOR BEND
KNOLL
POSSUM PL
HUNTERS GLN CHESTLINE
GLN HEW CRESTLINE
WINTERFRN WELLSMARK CIR
SHORT FRST WELL
VLLG GRV BECKETT RDG
MISTY RDG PEACH RDG
WDLACE LILES PEA RDG PL
CAPEWD MANGO RDG CT
QUIET OAK CYRIL
SHRUB OAK CYRIL
16700

SHEARWTR BEND
CORMORANT WIGEON WY RYAN CT
2600 BERETTA BND MUSCORY SHANNON
MOSSBERG CT MERGANSER CT SHANNON CT
BENELLI CT DIVING DUCK CT ALLISON
CHAPLIN PL SHANNON 3000
DUSTIN PL KNOCHE
INDIAN RUN
HIGHLAND VILLA
LYGNACIO

Lindsey-Lyons Park Sports Center
Harris County Fire and Sheriff Training Facility
PAM LYNCHER STATE JAIL

APPLE HLLW

ATASCOCITA RECYCLING AND DISPOSAL FACILITY

SEE 375 MAP

SHERYL CT SHERYL CIR
DEER TRAILS
ANTLER
DEER TRL CIR
FAWN MDW WHITE TAIL TRL
DOE PATH CANYON VILLAGE
DEER TRL CIR BLCK RDG

HARRIS COUNTY
Williams Gulley

GREENS RD
Park Lks
VISCARO
BARLOW SPGS
ALABASTER
WOOLSEY MILLW CV
OAKS MATAGORDA
HODGES MAYLAND FALLS
PRESTON KNOLL
CLANTON PINES
MALLORY CRK MAPLE GABLES
KENYA BOUGHTON
LOCKHART REACH ANNE WALDEN TERR PENNYMILL
SEMINOLE LKS LAYTON RDG BRILLIANT
BLANCA TERR DIVERMONT
PALMETTO GROV BONHAM LANSING
CANYON LAKES PRK
ALYSSA HERITAGE
LITTLE FAWN HEAVY ANCHOR
TINY TURTLE TAIL WY
WINEBERRY BLACKMYRTLE
WILSON 4100
ORISKANY

Garners Bayou

HUMBLE GULLY RUN HILLSIDE MILL
HILLSIDE CRK CENTRAL
SUMMER GLAZED TIMBER HILLS
SUN RIVER FALLS DR
SILHOUETTE RDG WYNDHAM HILL
SCENIC CRK THOMPSON BEND EAGLE BRANCH
SCENIC COVE SCENIC VISTA ROSSUM CRK
CEDAR HILLS RDG THORNCLIFF
MAUSER CRK ROCHE VILLA KENTINGTON OAK
AUGUSTA SUNSET JOHN RALSTON AMBERGATE
TRANQUILITY RDG ALMOND GRV
TRANQUILITY HILLS CT DRAKELAND
HARBOR CNYN MAPLE ROCK
STIMPSON PARK CLEAR FORK

ARROWHEAD RDG NEEDLEROCK CT
MIRROR CRK TIMBER PLATEAU FRANKLIN HILLS CT
RIVER ENDS FAIRWOOD CRK CT
TEAKWOOD SPGS GLENDALE RDG CT
CREEKWAY BND
SANDSTONE CNYN CANYON SHORE
HUNTCREST LN
SUNSET BAY AUGUST SUNSET
SIERRA RIDGE ARIZONA SKY
MOONLIGHT RDG SUNBURST
SUNDIA MDW
HARBOUR LK

TALMADGE SHELLMARK DR HOPKINS CEDAR
REACH VICTORIA REACH DR PAXTON WDS
ALLINGTON ROYCE HOLLY BRECKENWD MILLS
DELWDS ALBERT MANOR SELBY OAKS
COTTSEND TRC OAKLEAF
BALMORAL HILLS DR
Ridge Creek
SUNSET RDG GLAZED GOLDEN OASIS LN
DRY RDG CT SPRING SUN CT MOONLIGHT MIST
SUNSET GLAZE SUMMER DAWN RAINY MORNING
CAVE CRK SPRING SUN STARRY MDW MISTY SUMMER
SUNSET FLD SUMMER DUSK BREEZE FRST CT
SUNSET PRAIRIE SILKY MORNING CT
SUNSET RANGE SILVER
CARRIAGE PRK LAKE RD

NORTH SAM HOUSTON PKWY E.
10000 10700 11000 BELTWAY 8 11500
CRYSTAL PRK LOCKWOOD 14500 11700 UP RR

BARTON GRV FOUNTAIN STONE
WORTHAM STREAM PATRICIA HAVEN VESPER LAKE CT
MERIDIAN PRK DIANE MNR ASHLEY CRK AUTUMN LONG TRL
HOGWORTH JULIE MDWS KELLY RDG ASPEN FALLS
VICTORIA ROSE FALL CREEK OPEN SLOPE CT
CARINA ASHTON DEBORAH COLONY
GARNET CT CARINA FRST CT THICKET PRK
FALLS LAUREN BRIAR WOODLAND DRAWN TRL
BEARDEN JUSTIN RDG WYATT SHRS CT
JORDAN BRANCH REDSTN VW
ELLA GATE CT EMMA SPGS CT KASEY FLWRS CT

WOODSON PARK Woodcrk
Summer Creek
WECKFORD BLVD

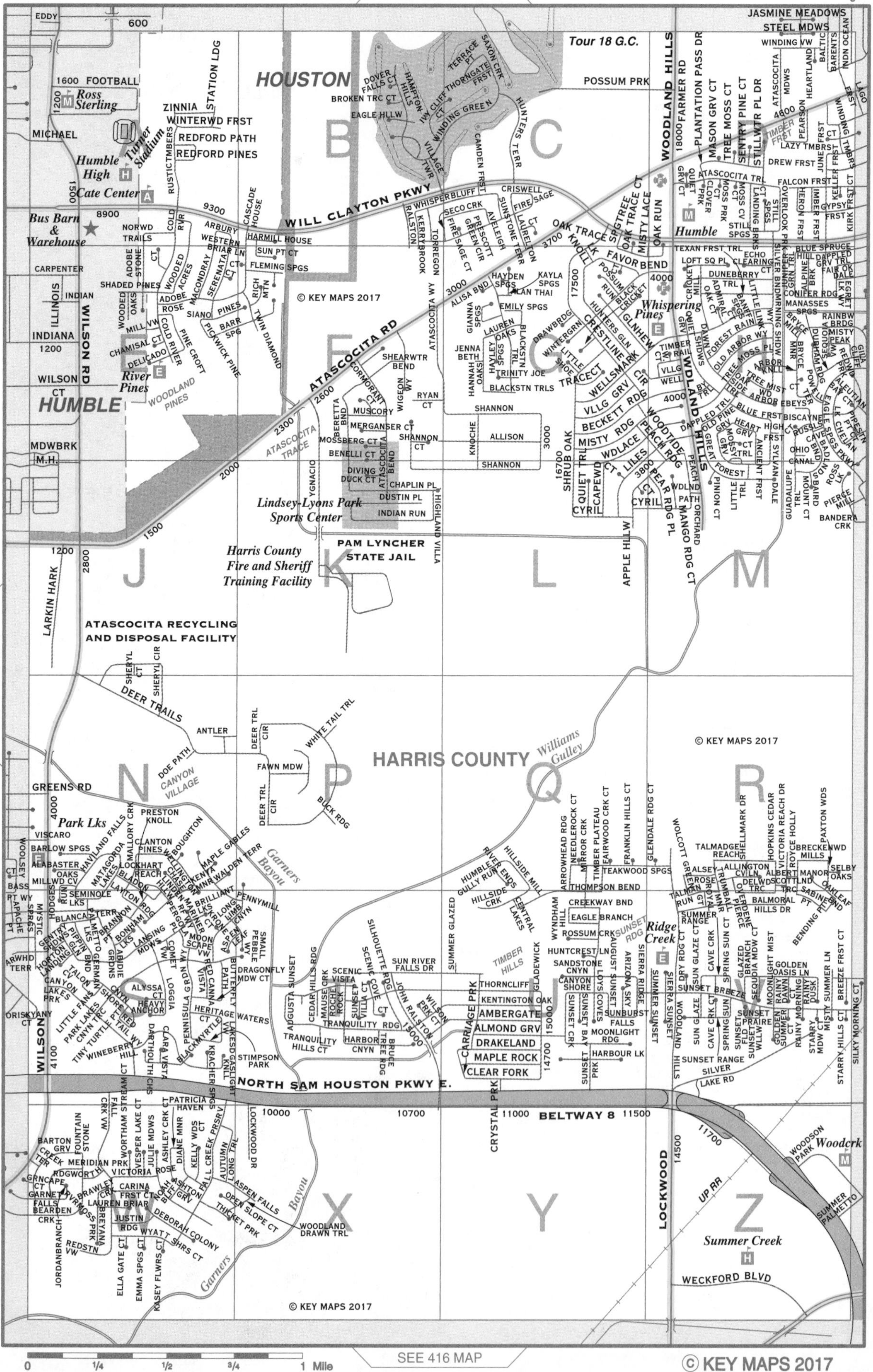

0 1/4 1/2 3/4 1 Mile

SEE 416 MAP

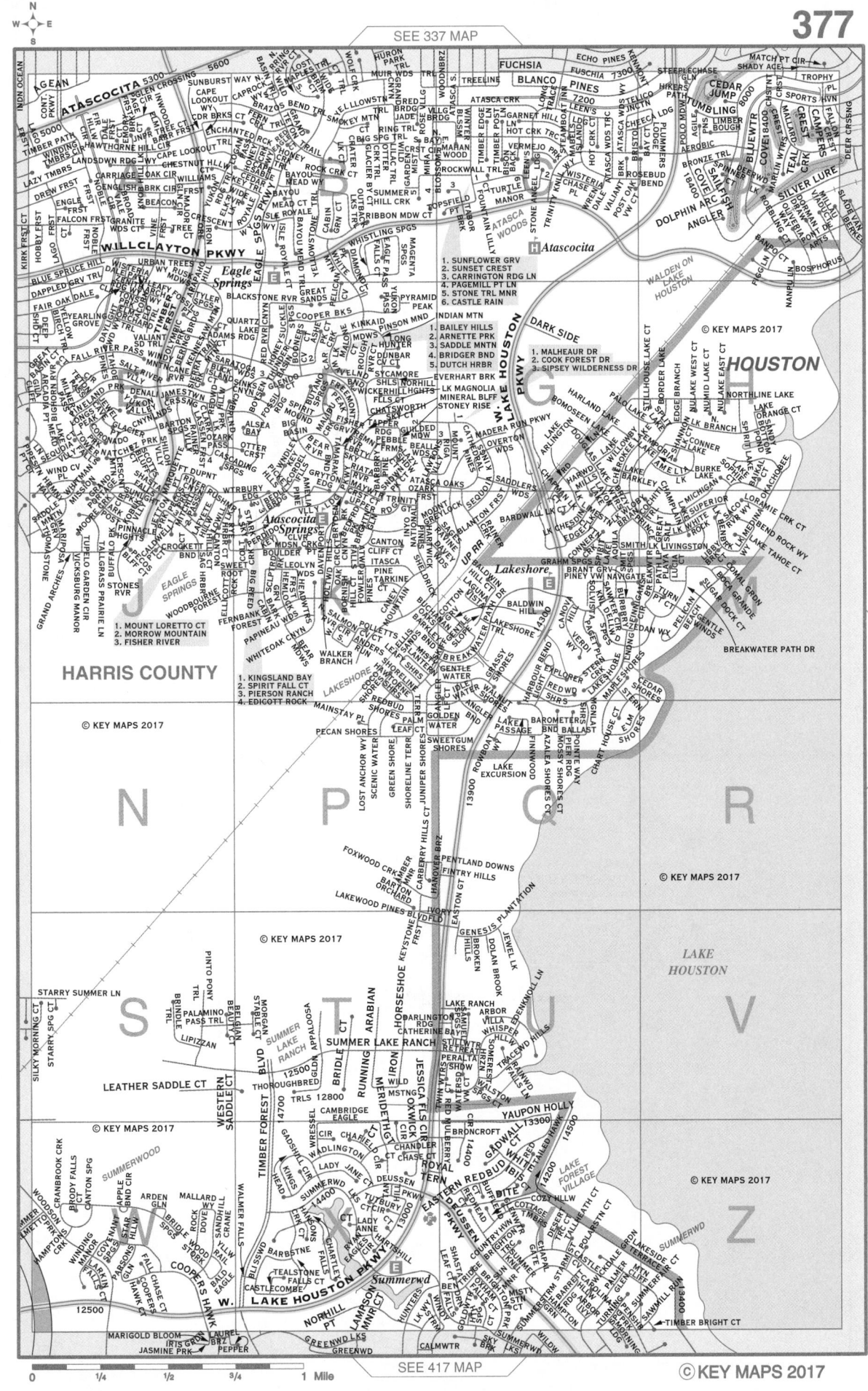

SEE 378 MAP

H Atascocita
1. SUNFLOWER GRV
2. SUNSET CREST
3. CARRINGTON RDG LN
4. PAGEMILL PT LN
5. STONE TRL MNR
6. CASTLE RAIN

INDIAN MTN
1. BAILEY HILLS
2. ARNETTE PRK
3. SADDLE MNTN
4. BRIDGER BND
5. DUTCH HRBR

DARK SIDE
1. MALHEUR DR
2. COOK FOREST DR
3. SIPSEY WILDERNESS DR

1. MOUNT LORETTO CT
2. MORROW MOUNTAIN
3. FISHER RIVER

1. KINGSLAND BAY
2. SPIRIT FALL CT
3. PIERSON RANCH
4. EDICOTT ROCK

HARRIS COUNTY

© KEY MAPS 2017

© KEY MAPS 2017

© KEY MAPS 2017

© KEY MAPS 2017

© KEY MAPS 2017

© KEY MAPS 2017

LAKE
HOUSTON

HOUSTON

N   P   Q   R

S   T   U   V

W   X   Y   Z

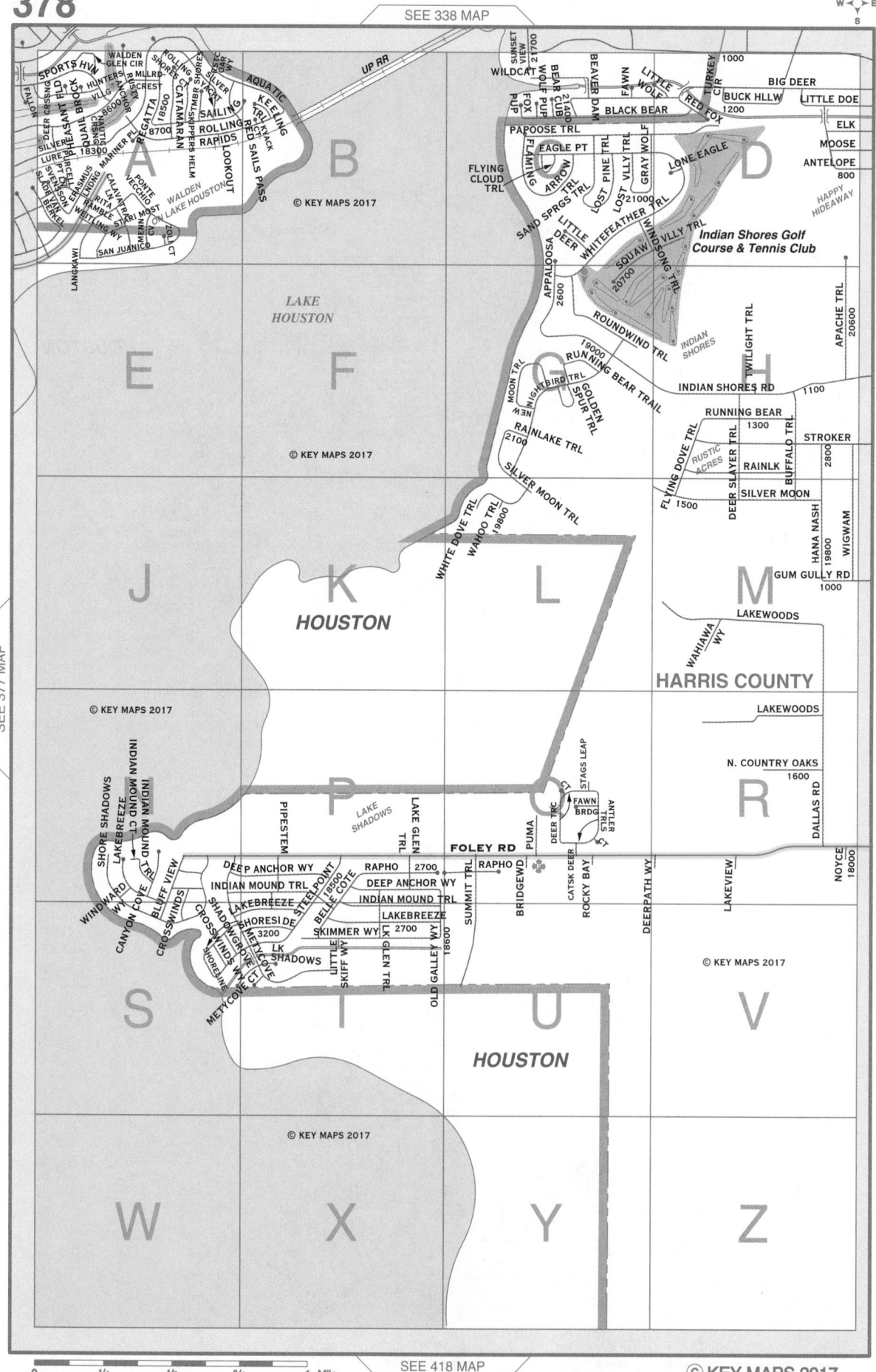

378

N
W E
S

A

SPORTS HVN
WALDEN GLEN CIR
ROLLING CATAMARAN
SHORES ANCHOR
SILVER RMLLRD
HUNTERS RUSTY
VLLG
BROCK
8500
8700
FALLON
SILVER DEER CRSSNG
PLEASANT FLD
QUAIL
REGATTA
LURE
ERASMUS
MARINER
DINGHY
SAILING
ROLLING
RAPIDS
SKIPPERS HELM
RED SAILS PASS
LOOKOUT
18300
18500
PONTO
CALAVTRA
RITA
RAMBLE
SKARI MOST
WHITING WY
CV ON LAKE HOUSTON
WALDEN
SAN JUANICO
LANGKAWI

AQUATIC
KEELING
KYACK
TRL

B

© KEY MAPS 2017

C

SUNSET VIEW 21700
WILDCAT
WOLF PUP
BEAR CUB
BEAVER DAM
FAWN
LITTLE WOLF
TURKEY CIR
1000
BIG DEER
LITTLE DOE
WILDCAT
FOX PUP
BEAR CUB
BLACK BEAR
RED FOX
BUCK HLLW
1200
ELK
PAPOOSE TRL
MOOSE
FLAMING
EAGLE PT
LOST PINE TRL
LOST VLLY TRL
GRAY WOLF
LONE-EAGLE
ANTELOPE
800
FLYING CLOUD TRL
ARROW
HAPPY HIDEAWAY

D

SAND SPRGS TRL
LITTLE DEER
WHITEFEATHER TRL
SQUAW 20700
WINDSONG TRL
Indian Shores Golf Course & Tennis Club
APPALOOSA 2600
ROUNDWIND TRL
INDIAN SHORES
APACHE TRL 20600

E

F

LAKE HOUSTON

© KEY MAPS 2017

G

MOON TRL
NEW
NIGHTBIRD TRL
RUNNING BEAR TRAIL
19000
GOLDEN SPUR TRL
RAINLAKE TRL
2100
SILVER MOON TRL
WAHOO TRL 19800
WHITE DOVE TRL

H

TWILIGHT TRL
INDIAN SHORES RD
1100
FLYING DOVE TRL
RUSTIC ACRES
DEER SLAYER TRL
RUNNING BEAR
1300
RAINLK
BUFFALO TRL
STROKER
2800
SILVER MOON
HANA NASH 19800
WIGWAM
1500
GUM GULLY RD
1000

N

J

© KEY MAPS 2017

K

HOUSTON

L

M

LAKEWOODS
WAHIAWA WY
HARRIS COUNTY

SEE 377 MAP

LAKEWOODS
N. COUNTRY OAKS
1600

P

PIPESTEM
LAKE SHADOWS
LAKE GLEN TRL
STAGS LEAP
DEER TRC
FAWN
ANTLER TRLS CT
BRDG
FOLEY RD
PUMA

R

DALLAS RD

S

SHORE SHADOWS
INDIAN MOUND TRL
LAKEBREEZE
INDIAN MOUND CT
BLUFF VIEW
WINDWARD WY
CANYON COVE
CROSSWINDS
SHADWGROVE
SHORESIDE
METYCOVE
3200
LK SHADOWS
CROSSWINDS CT
SHORELINE
METYCOVE CT
DEEP ANCHOR WY
INDIAN MOUND TRL
LAKEBREEZE
BELLE COTE
STEEL POINT
RAPHO
DEEP ANCHOR WY
INDIAN MOUND TRL
LAKEBREEZE
SKIMMER WY
LITTLE SKIFF WY
LK GLEN TRL 2700
OLD GALLEY WY 18600
SUMMIT TRL
RAPHO 2700
RAPHO
BRIDGEWD
CATSK DEER
ROCKY BAY
DEERPATH WY

I

U

HOUSTON

© KEY MAPS 2017

V

LAKEVIEW
NOYCE 18000

W

© KEY MAPS 2017

X

Y

Z

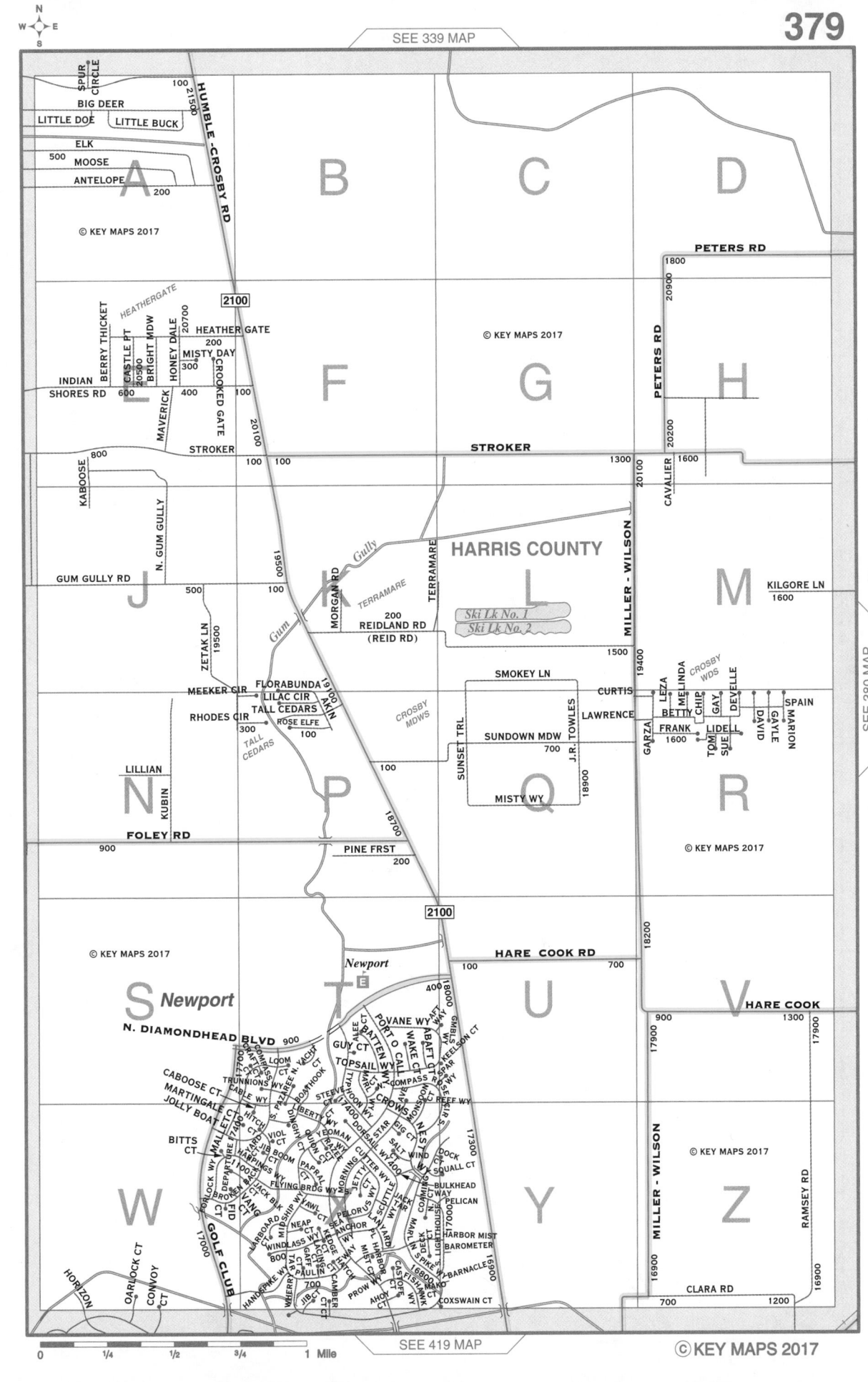

N
W E
S

© KEY MAPS 2017

SPUR CIRCLE
BIG DEER
LITTLE DOE   LITTLE BUCK
ELK
500 MOOSE
ANTELOPE

100
21500

200

A

HUMBLE - CROSBY RD

B

C

D

PETERS RD
1800
20900

2100

HEATHERGATE
BERRY THICKET
CASTLE PT
HEATHER GATE
BRIGHT MDW
20700
HONEY DALE
200
MISTY DAY
300
INDIAN SHORES RD
600 400 100
MAVERICK
CROOKED GATE
20500
20100
STROKER

E

F

© KEY MAPS 2017

G

PETERS RD
20200

H

CAVALIER 1600

STROKER   1300
100 100   20100

KABOOSE 800
N. GUM GULLY
GUM GULLY RD
500 100
19500
ZETAK LN
20500
19100
RAKIN
MEEKER CIR
FLORABUNDA
LILAC CIR
TALL CEDARS
RHODES CIR
ROSE ELFE
300 100
TALL CEDARS
LILLIAN
KUBIN

J

K

MORGAN RD
Gully
TERRAMARE
Terramare
REIDLAND RD
(REID RD)
200
Gum

HARRIS COUNTY

L
Ski Lk No. 1
Ski Lk No. 2
1500

MILLER - WILSON
19400

M
KILGORE LN
1600

GARZA
LEZA
MELINDA
CROSBY WDS
BETTY CHIP GAY DEVELLE
FRANK TOM SUE GAYLE SPAIN
1600 LIDELL DAVID MARION
CURTIS
LAWRENCE

N

P

SMOKEY LN
CROSBY MDWS
SUNDOWN MDW
700
SUNSET TRL
100
MISTY WY
18900
J.R. TOWLES

Q

© KEY MAPS 2017

R

FOLEY RD
900

PINE FRST
200
18700

2100

HARE COOK RD
100 700
18200

Newport
E
S Newport
N. DIAMONDHEAD BLVD 900

T

U

HARE COOK
V 1300
17900

MILLER - WILSON

© KEY MAPS 2017

RAMSEY RD

W

X

Y

Z

CLARA RD
700 1200
16900

© KEY MAPS 2017

0   1/4   1/2   3/4   1 Mile

© KEY MAPS 2017

SEE 380 MAP
N

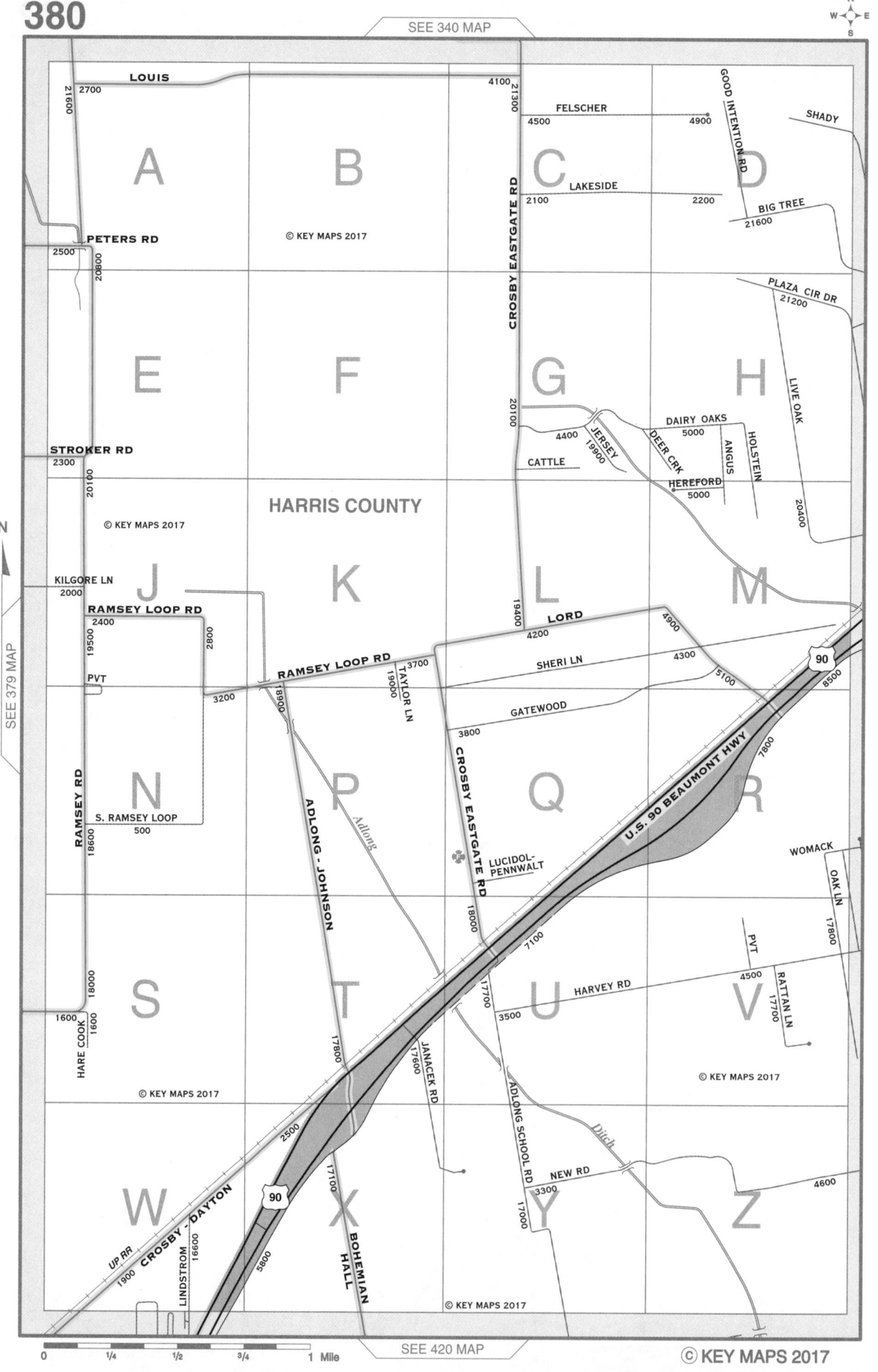

N
W · E
S

LOUIS
21600 2700
4100 21300

FELSCHER
4500 4900

GOOD INTENTION RD

SHADY

A B C D

PETERS RD
2500 20800

LAKESIDE
2100 2200

BIG TREE
21600

CROSBY EASTGATE RD

PLAZA CIR DR
21200

LIVE OAK

E F G H

STROKER RD
2300 20100

20100

20100

DAIRY OAKS
5000

DEER CRK

ANGUS

HOLSTEIN

HARRIS COUNTY

4400

JERSEY
19900

CATTLE

HEREFORD
5000

20400

© KEY MAPS 2017

KILGORE LN
2000

RAMSEY LOOP RD
2400 2800

19500

PVT

J K L M

LORD
4200 4900

SHERI LN
4300 5100

RAMSEY LOOP RD
3200 8900 3700 19000

TAYLOR LN

GATEWOOD
3800

RAMSEY RD
18600

18000

HARE COOK
1600 1600

N P Q R

ADLONG - JOHNSON

Adlong

S. RAMSEY LOOP
500

CROSBY EASTGATE RD
18000

LUCIDOL-PENNWALT

U.S. 90 BEAUMONT HWY
7800

90
8500

WOMACK

OAK LN
17800

S T U V

PVT
4500

RATTAN LN
17700

HARVEY RD
7100 3500

17700

© KEY MAPS 2017

© KEY MAPS 2017

ADLONG SCHOOL RD

Ditch

W X Y Z

UP RR
1900

CROSBY - DAYTON

LINDSTROM
16600

90
5800

BOHEMIAN HALL

JANACEK RD
17600

2500

17100

17000

NEW RD
3300

4600

© KEY MAPS 2017

SEE 379 MAP

N

0   1/4   1/2   3/4   1 Mile

© KEY MAPS 2017

381

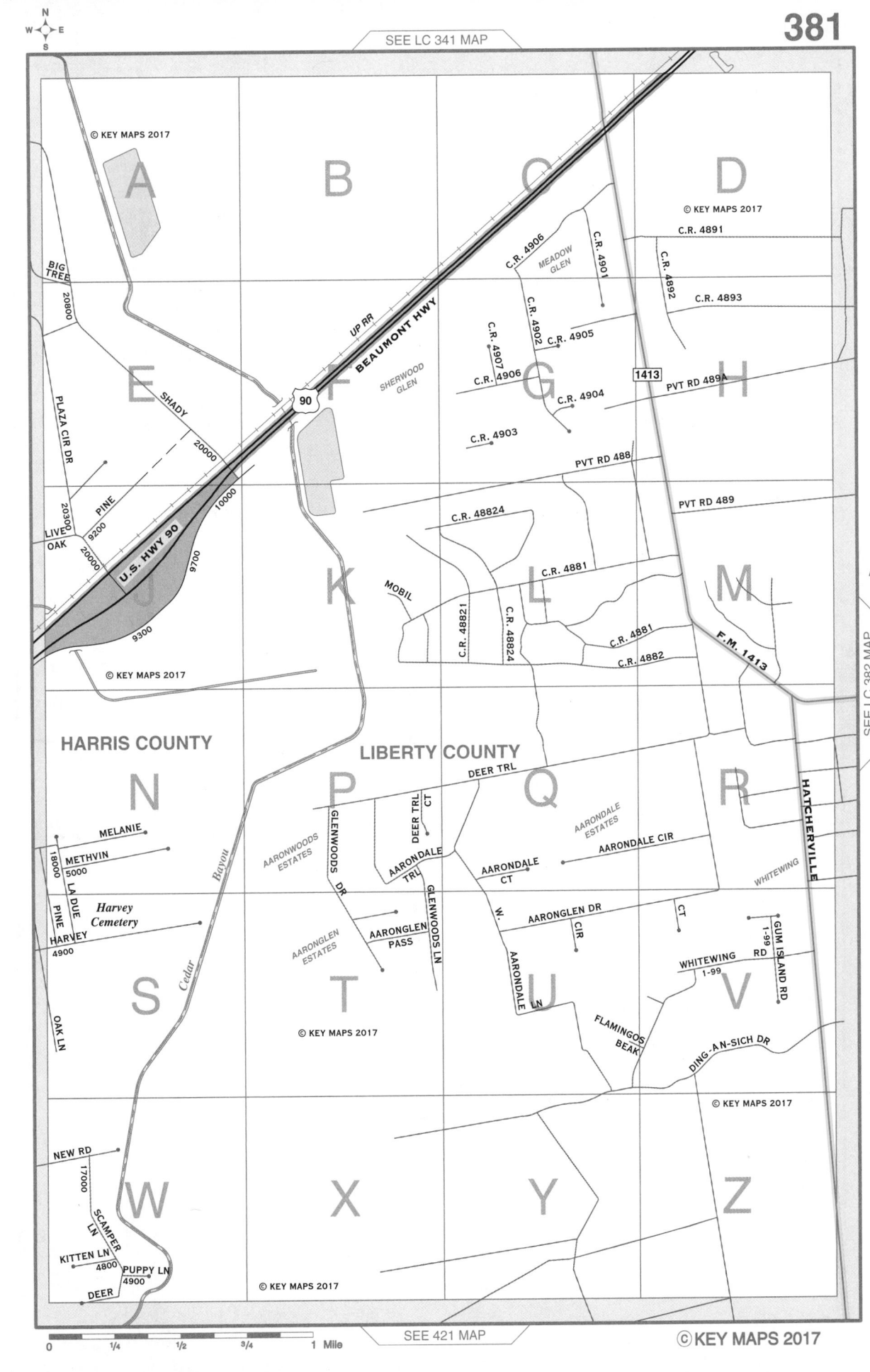

N
W E
S

© KEY MAPS 2017

A   B   C   D

BIG TREE

C.R. 4906
MEADOW GLEN
C.R. 4901
C.R. 4891
C.R. 4892
C.R. 4893

20800

UP RR

BEAUMONT HWY

E   SHADY   F   SHERWOOD GLEN   G   1413   H

C.R. 4902
C.R. 4905
C.R. 4907
C.R. 4906
C.R. 4904
PVT RD 489A

PLAZA CIR DR
20000

90

C.R. 4903

PVT RD 488

20300

PINE
9200

PVT RD 489

C.R. 48824

LIVE OAK
20000

U.S. HWY 90

9700

C.R. 4881

J   K   MOBIL   L   M

9300

C.R. 48821
C.R. 48824
C.R. 4881
F.M. 1413

C.R. 4882

© KEY MAPS 2017

HARRIS COUNTY   **LIBERTY COUNTY**

DEER TRL

N   P   Q   R   HATCHERVILLE

MELANIE
METHVIN
5000
18000
LA DUE

AARONWOODS ESTATES
GLENWOODS DR
DEER TRL CT
AARONDALE TRL
AARONDALE ESTATES
AARONDALE CIR
AARONDALE CT
WHITEWING

PINE
HARVEY
4900

Harvey Cemetery

Cedar   Bayou

AARONGLEN ESTATES
AARONGLEN PASS
GLENWOODS LN
W. AARONGLEN DR
CIR
CT
WHITEWING 1-99
GUM ISLAND RD
1-99

S   T   U   V

OAK LN

© KEY MAPS 2017

AARONDALE LN

FLAMINGOS BEAK

DING-A-N-SICH DR

© KEY MAPS 2017

NEW RD
17000

W   X   Y   Z

SCAMPER LN
KITTEN LN
4800
PUPPY LN
4900
DEER

© KEY MAPS 2017

0   1/4   1/2   3/4   1 Mile

© **KEY MAPS 2017**

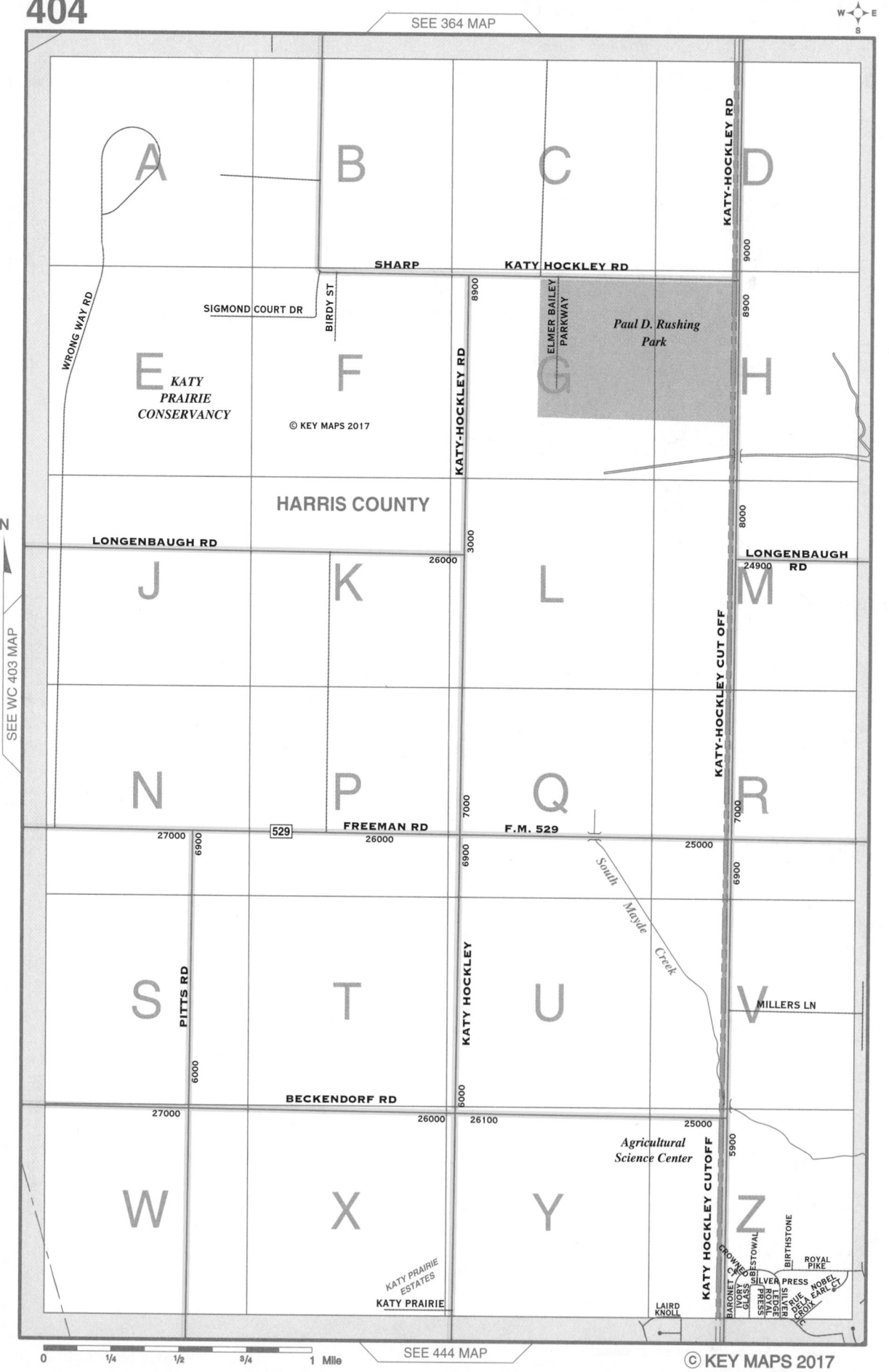

N
W — E
S

A   B   C   D

KATY-HOCKLEY RD

WRONG WAY RD

SHARP   KATY HOCKLEY RD

9000

8900

SIGMOND COURT DR

BIRDY ST

8900

ELMER BAILEY PARKWAY

Paul D. Rushing Park

E   *KATY PRAIRIE CONSERVANCY*   F   G   H

KATY-HOCKLEY RD

© KEY MAPS 2017

HARRIS COUNTY

8000

LONGENBAUGH RD

3000

26000

24900

LONGENBAUGH RD

J   K   L   M

KATY-HOCKLEY CUT OFF

SEE WC 403 MAP

N

N   P   Q   R

7000

7000

27000

6900

529   FREEMAN RD   F.M. 529

26000   25000

6900

6900

South Mayde Creek

S   T   U   V

PITTS RD

KATY HOCKLEY

MILLERS LN

6000

6000

BECKENDORF RD

27000   26000   26100   25000

5900

Agricultural Science Center

W   X   Y   Z

KATY HOCKLEY CUTOFF

KATY PRAIRIE ESTATES

KATY PRAIRIE

LAIRD KNOLL

BIRTHSTONE
ROYAL PIKE
CROWNED CT
BESTOWAL
SILVER PRESS
BARONET CT
IVORY GLASS
LITTLE PRESS
ROYAL LEDGE
SILVER
RUE DELA CROIX
NOBEL EARL CT

0   1/4   1/2   3/4   1 Mile

© **KEY MAPS** 2017

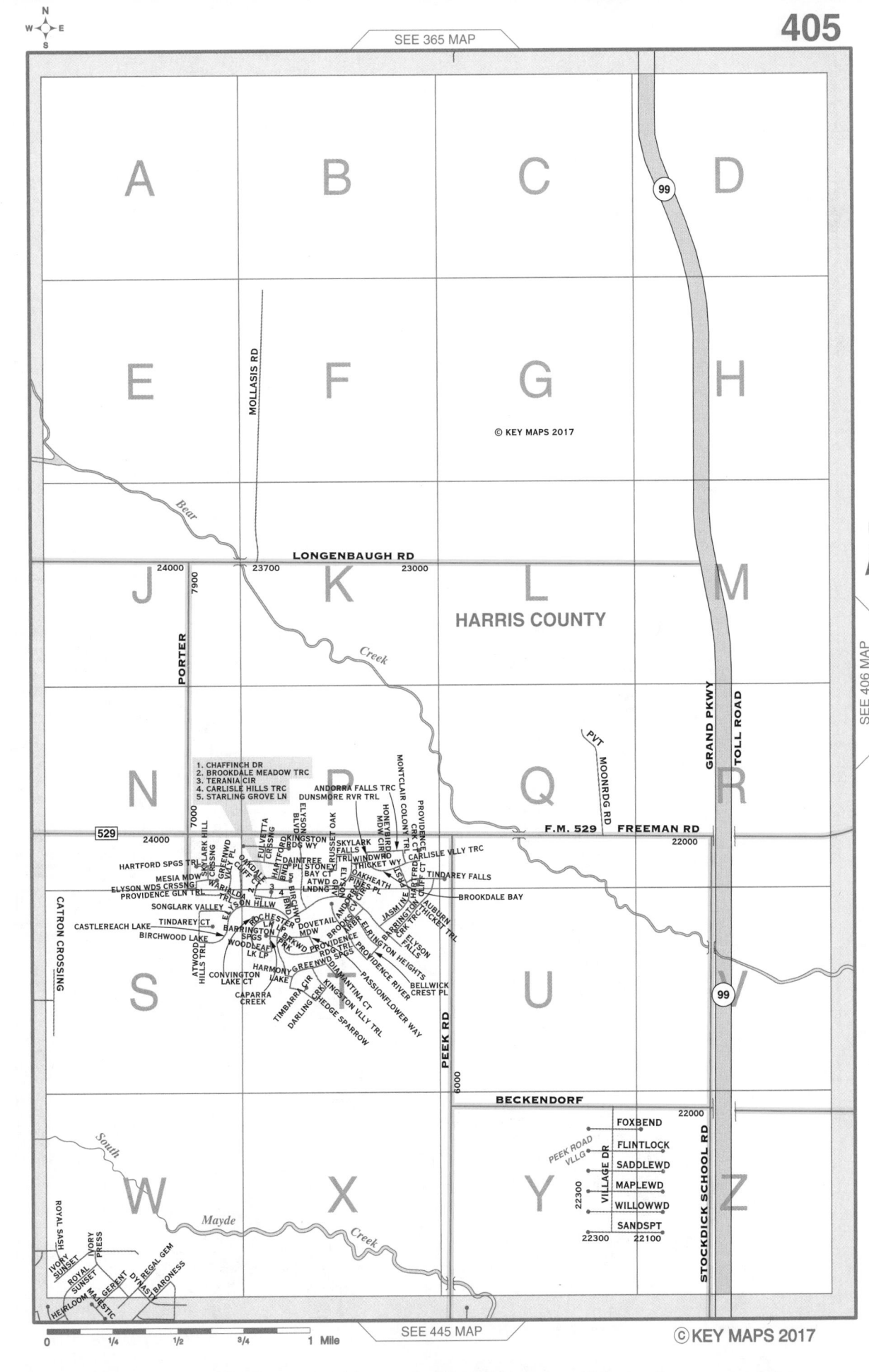

N
W E
S

99

A

B

C

D

MOLLASIS RD

E

F

G

© KEY MAPS 2017

H

Bear

N

LONGENBAUGH RD

24000   23700   23000

J   7900   K   L   HARRIS COUNTY   M

PORTER

Creek

SEE 406 MAP

PVT MOONRDG RD

GRAND PKWY

TOLL ROAD

N   1. CHAFFINCH DR
2. BROOKDALE MEADOW TRC
3. TERANIA CIR
4. CARLISLE HILLS TRC
5. STARLING GROVE LN

ANDORRA FALLS TRC
DUNSMORE RVR TRL

MONTCLAIR COLONY TRL

PROVIDENCE CRK CT

P   Q   R

529   24000   F.M. 529   FREEMAN RD   22000

CATRON CROSSING

HONEYBIRD MDW CIR

ELYSON RDG WY
CARLISLE VLLY TRC

SKYLARK HILL   FULVETTA CRSSNG
KINGSTON FALLS
SKYLARK FALLS

HARTFORD SPGS TRL
DAINTREE BRIDG PL STONEY
WDLF WDLF CLIFF
MESIA MDW CMP LF   HARTFORD BAY CT
ELYSON WDS CRSSNG   WARLDON   OAKHEATH
PROVIDENCE GLN TRL   3 4 LNDNG   ATWD
ELYSON HLLW   PINES
TINDAREY FALLS

SONGLARK VALLEY   THICKET WY

TINDAREY CT   ROCHESTER   AUBURN
CASTLEREACH LAKE   LN LN   DOVETAIL   JASMINE   ELYSON
BARRINGTON   MDW   BARRINGTON   THICKET
BIRCHWOOD LAKE   SPGS BRKWD   PROVIDENCE   HTS   FALLS
WOODLEAF   RDG TRL   ELRINGTON HEIGHTS
ATWOOD   LK LF   PROVIDENCE RIVER
HILLS TRL   HARMONY GREENWD   BROOKDALE BAY
CONVINGTON   LAKE   SKG   BELLWICK
LAKE CT   CIR   PASSIONFLOWER WAY   CREST PL
CAPARRA   TIMBARRA   KINGSTON VLLY TRL
CREEK   DARLING CRK   HEDGE SPARROW

S   T   U

PEEK RD   6000

BECKENDORF   22000

FOXBEND

PEEK ROAD VLLG   FLINTLOCK

VILLAGE DR   SADDLEWD

South   22300   MAPLEWD

W   X   Y   WILLOWWD   Z

Mayde   Creek   SANDSPT

22300   22100

ROYAL SASH
IVORY SUNSET   IVORY PRESS
ROYAL SUNSET   REGAL GEM
GERENT DY   BARONESS
HEIRLOOM   MAJESTIC

STOCKDICK SCHOOL RD

99

0   1/4   1/2   3/4   1 Mile

SEE 445 MAP

© KEY MAPS 2017

HARRIS COUNTY B

1. E. TOWNE LAKE GREENE TRL
2. W. TOWNE LAKE GREENE TRL
3. N. CORAL HONEYSUCKLE LP
4. S. CORAL HONEYSUCKLE LP
5. E. CORAL HONEYSUCKLE LP
6. W. CORAL HONEYSUCKLE LP
7. TEXAS HONYSUCKLE TRL

Langham Creek

WEST

A

HARRIS COUNTY

E

CANYON LAKE WEST

© KEY MAPS 2017

Postma

Longenbaugh

Cypress Springs

FRY RD

Hopper

WESTGREEN BLVD

J

Cypress Park

Andre

SAGEMARK RDG
PRESTON POINT
CYPRESS CRESCENT
DICKINSON MANOR
CYPRESS POST
DESERT SHADOWS
CYPRESS ECHO

FERNWICK VLLG
BENNET RDG
CYPRESS BRZ
STEWART CREST LN

CYPRESS WHITE OAK
CYPRESS NORTHERN OAK
CYPRESS BUR OAK
CYPRESS GOLDEN OAK
CYPRESS VALE

F.M. 529
FREEMAN RD

21300   21100   20900   20200

529

F.M. 529

COMMANDO BRDG BLVD

WINDSONG CT
PHOENIX RDG
JOLLYVILLE
SADLIN TRL
CELADON HILL
HARVESTWOOD TRL
SILVERPIN
SADDLE PASS
ROCK IVY TRL
BELLE BRDG
HUMBLER BRDG
WESTGREEN BLVD

S

Bear Creek

THE LAKE AT SETTLERSWAY

NORTHERN CLNY CT
SOUTHERN CLNY CT
CARMEL VLLY
SETTLERS VLLY
WESTERN VLLY
COVE LK

GARDEN CNYN
NEW WORLD
LIBERTY VALLEY

Walker

BOULDER VLLY

Duryea

Hoover
Towell

CRKSHORE

ALC W

Hemmenway

LITTLE YORK
19900

FLINTOFF
AZALEA ARBOR
WHITEHAVEN BLUFF LN
HARMONT RVR
CAMELLIA CRK
MATILDA BEND LN
REMINGTON OAKS CT
WEDGEWOOD CHS WY
LITTLE JASMINE WAY
VICTORIA LANDING TRL

VILLAGES OF BEAR CREEK

APPLETON MDW TRC

WINFORD

McFee

Gummert RD

Cypress Lakes

Emery

SEE 405 MAP

0   1/4   1/2   3/4   1 Mile

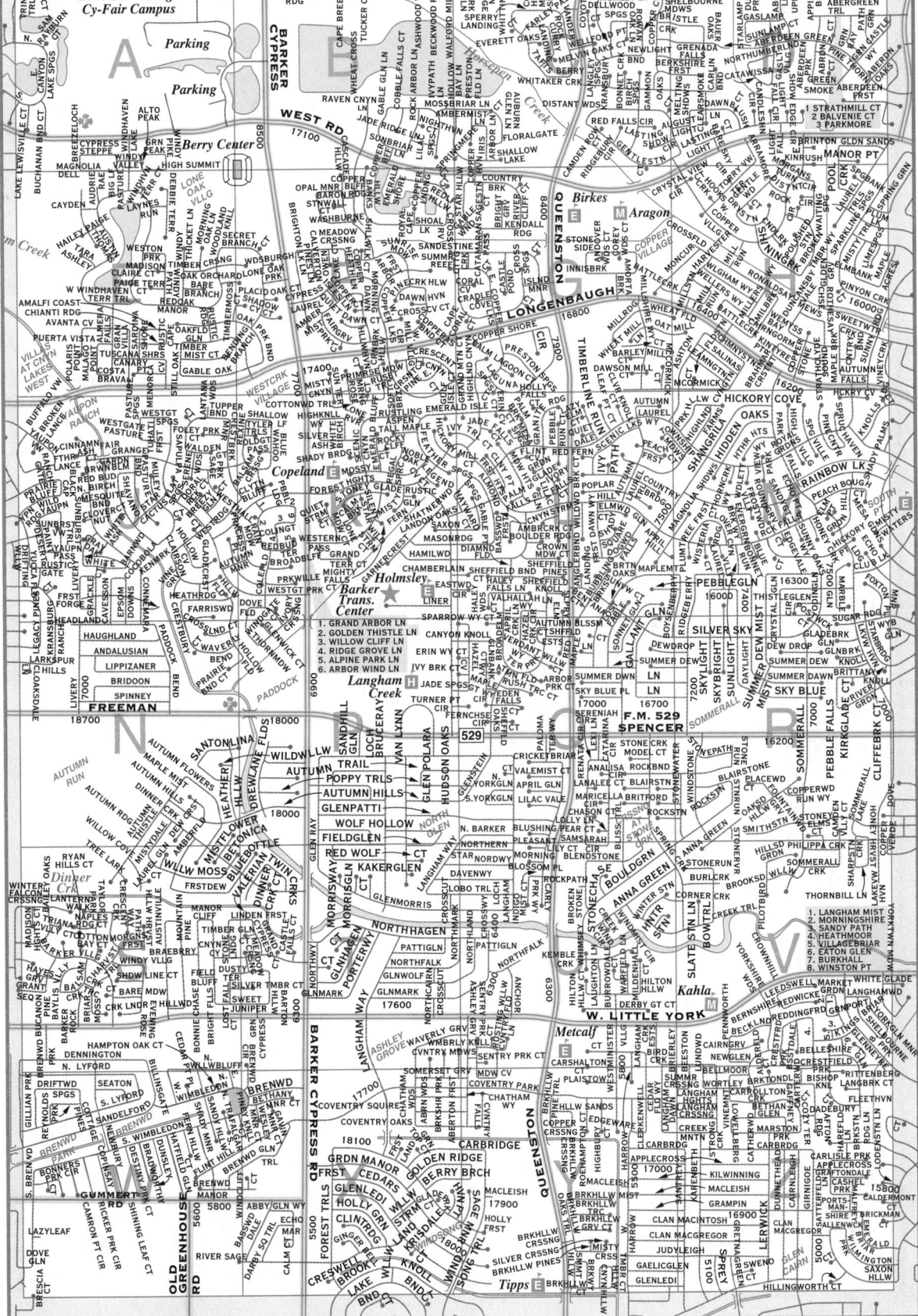

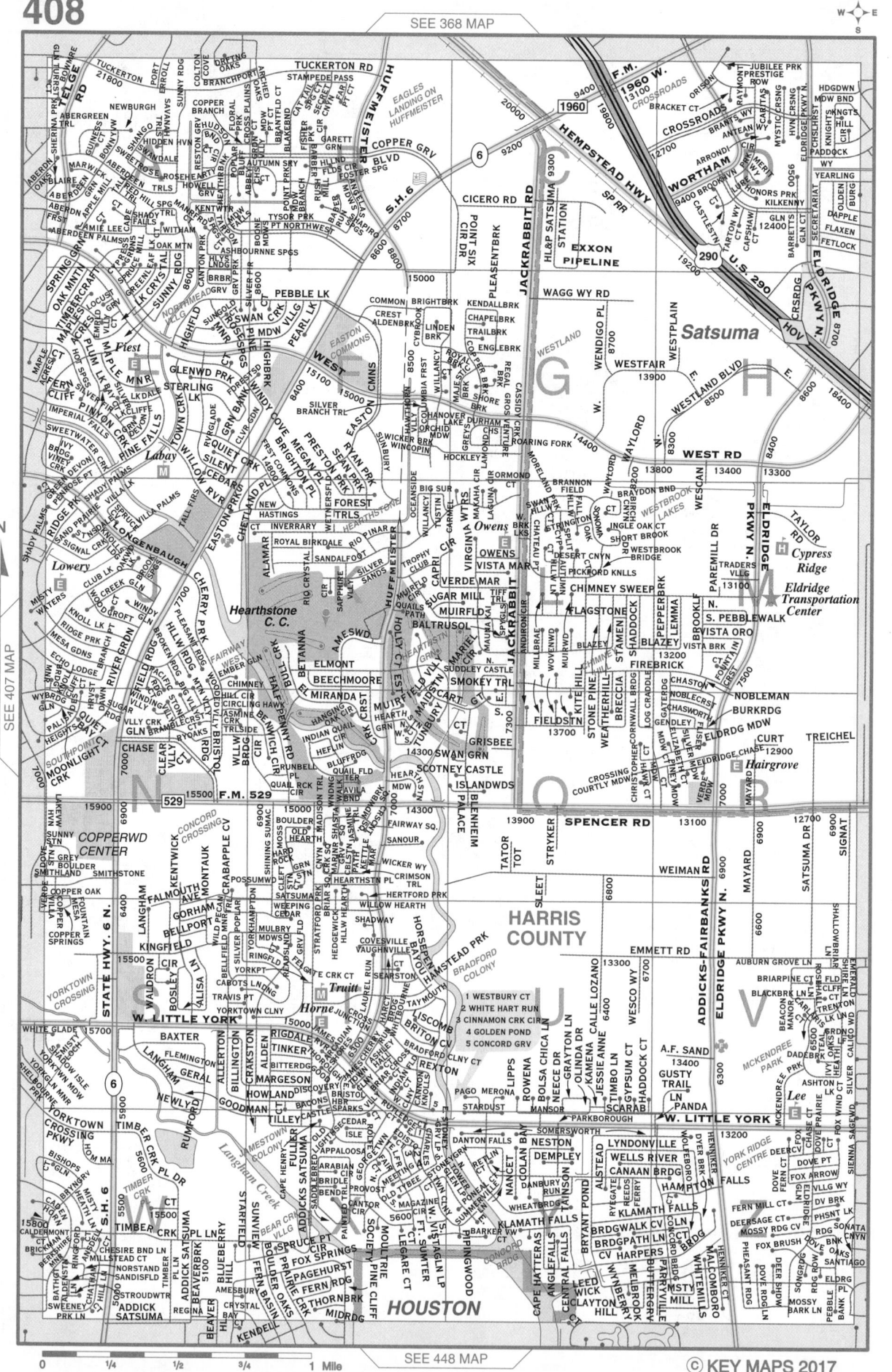

© KEY MAPS 2017

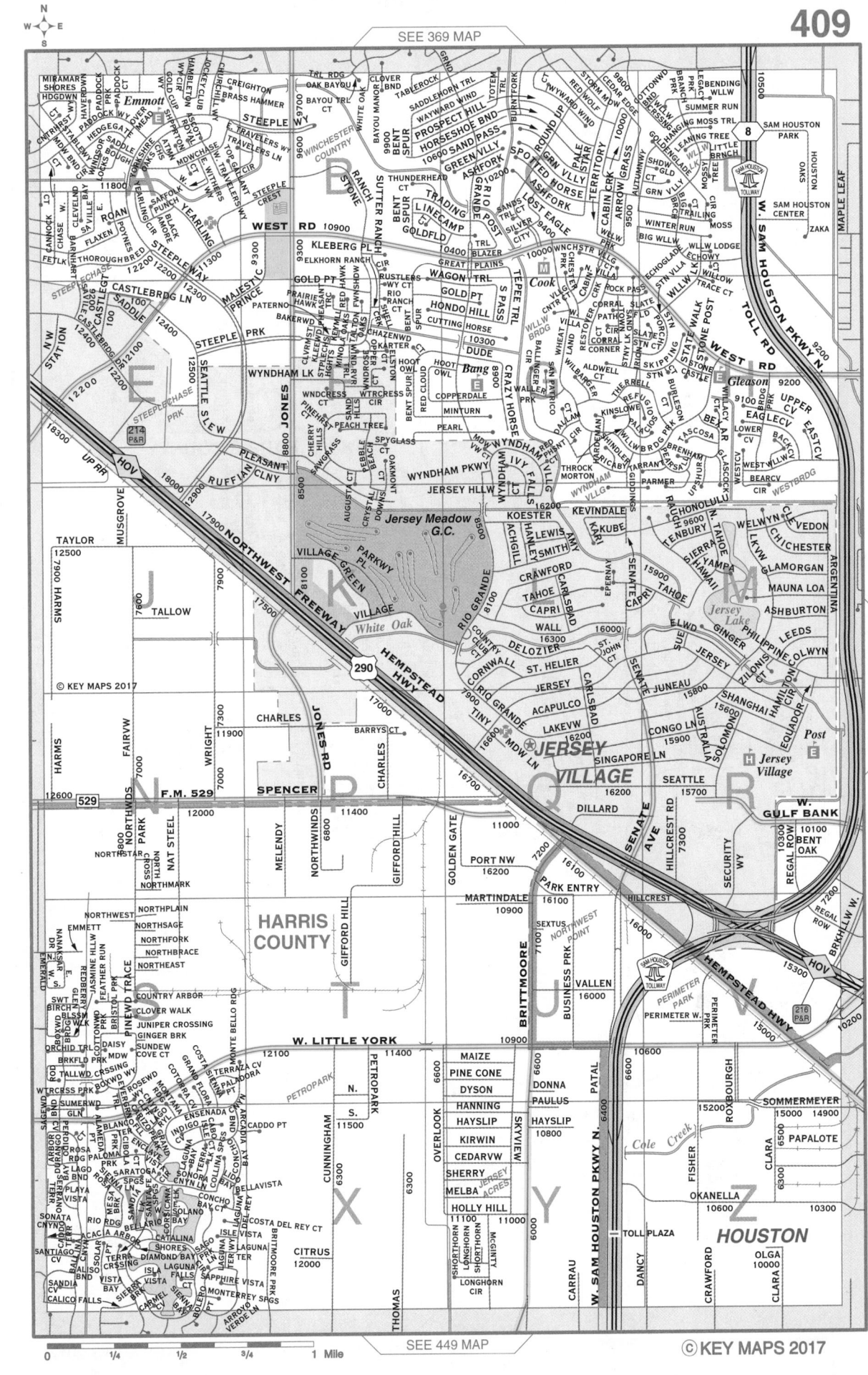

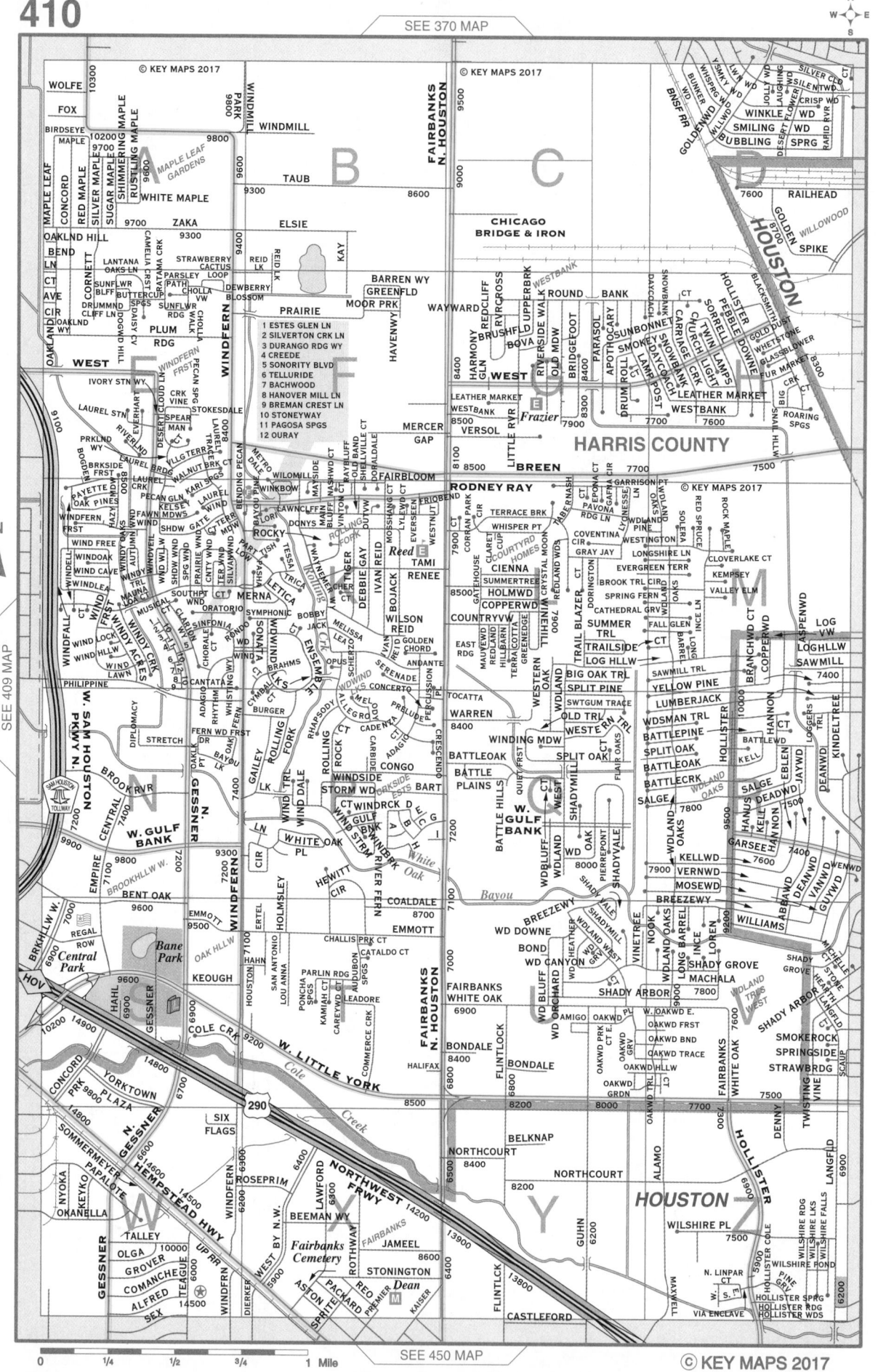

SEE 370 MAP

© KEY MAPS 2017

© KEY MAPS 2017

SEE 450 MAP

© KEY MAPS 2017

0   1/4   1/2   3/4   1 Mile

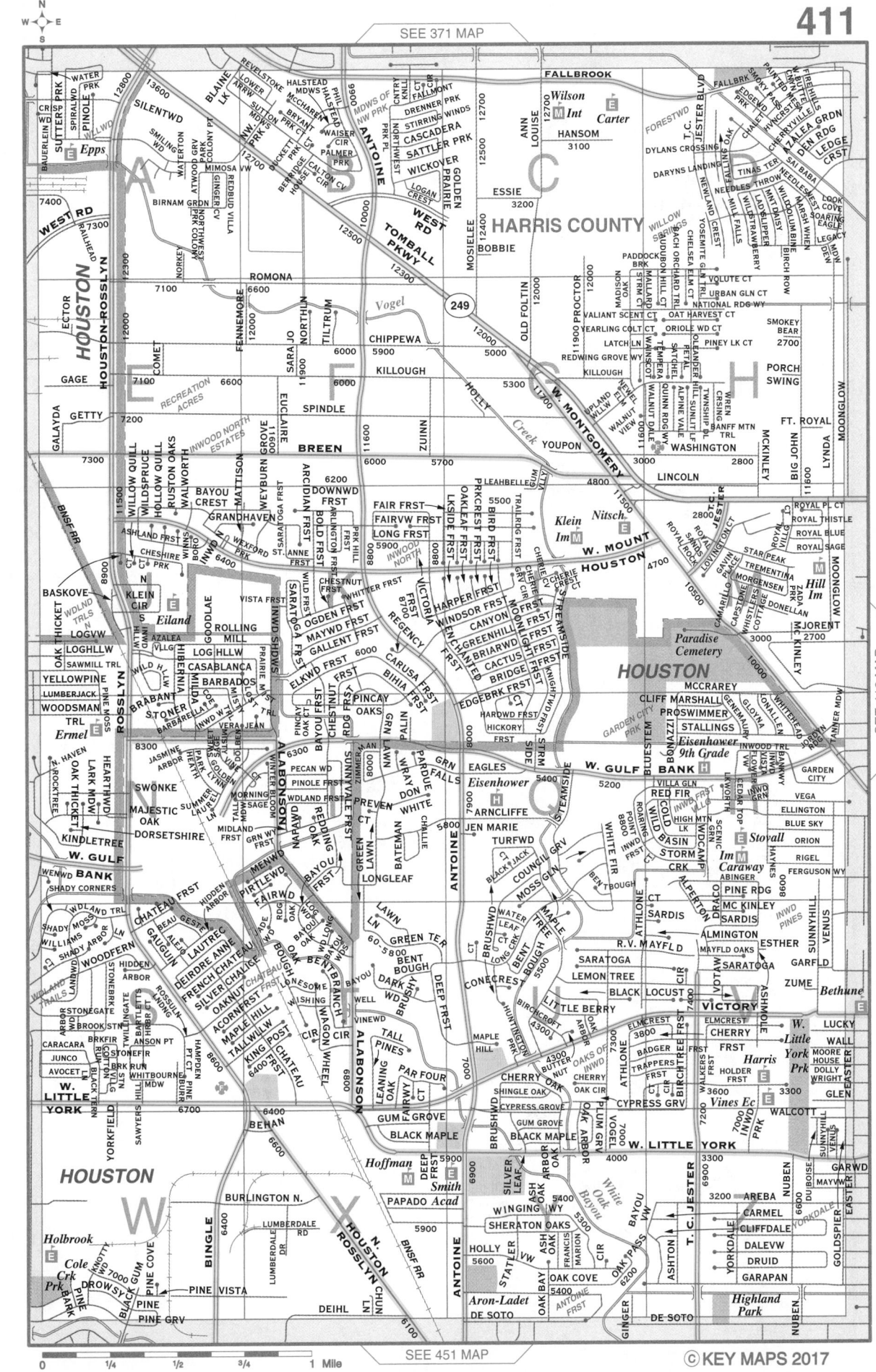

SEE 371 MAP

SEE 412 MAP

SEE 451 MAP

© KEY MAPS 2017

0   1/4   1/2   3/4   1 Mile

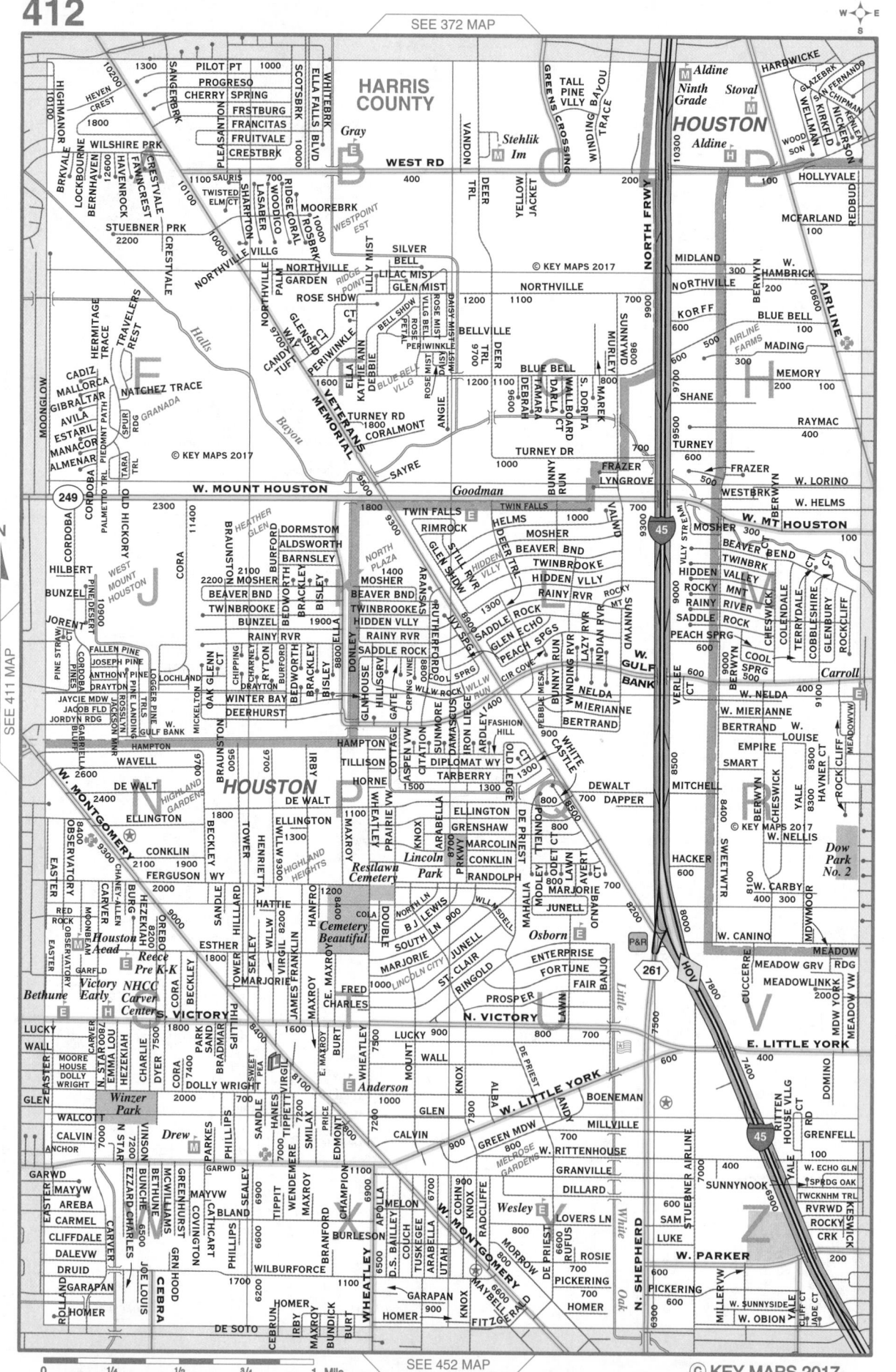

SEE 372 MAP

HARRIS COUNTY

HOUSTON

© KEY MAPS 2017

© KEY MAPS 2017

© KEY MAPS 2017

SEE 411 MAP

0   1/4   1/2   3/4   1 Mile

© KEY MAPS 2017

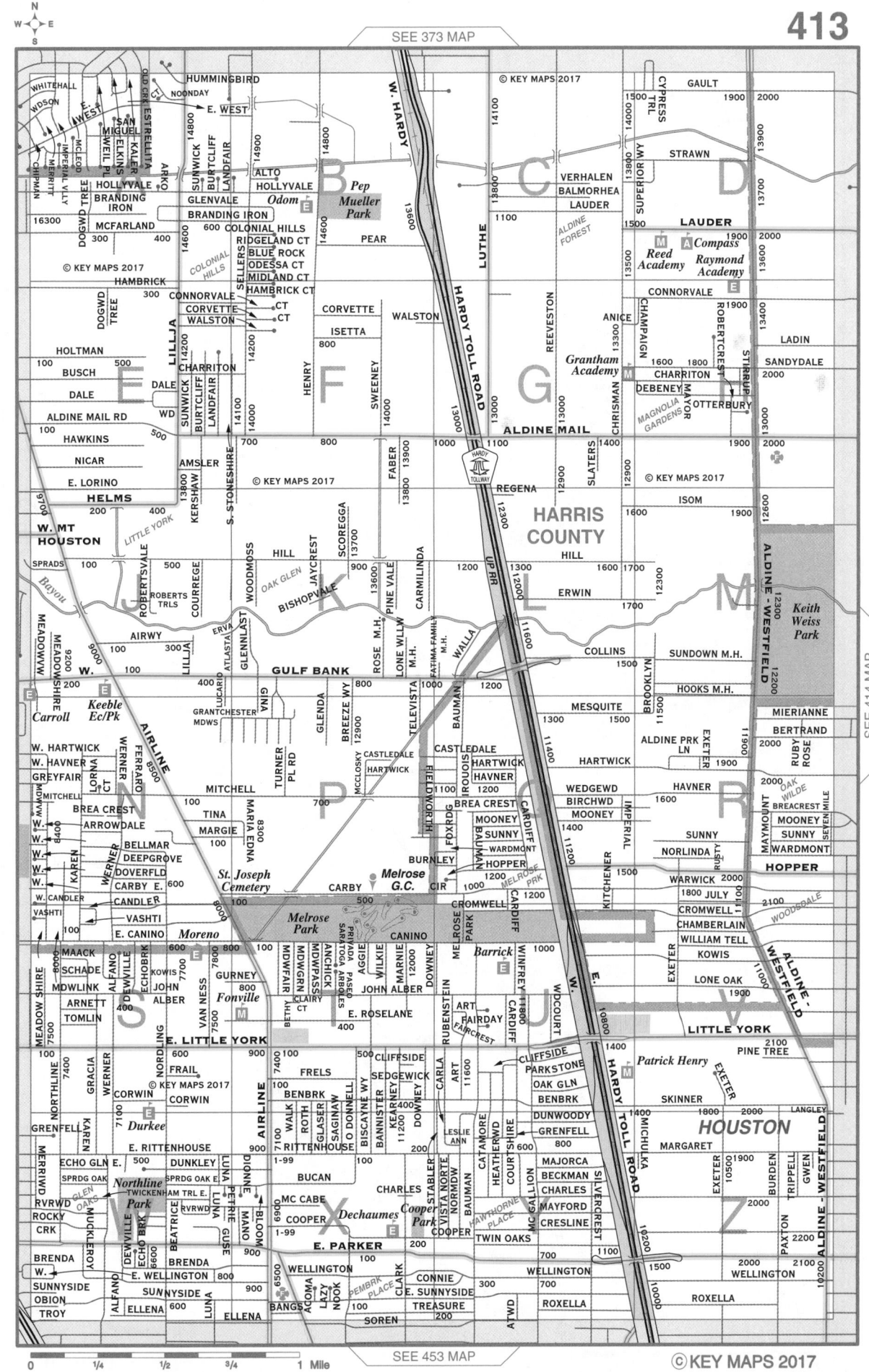

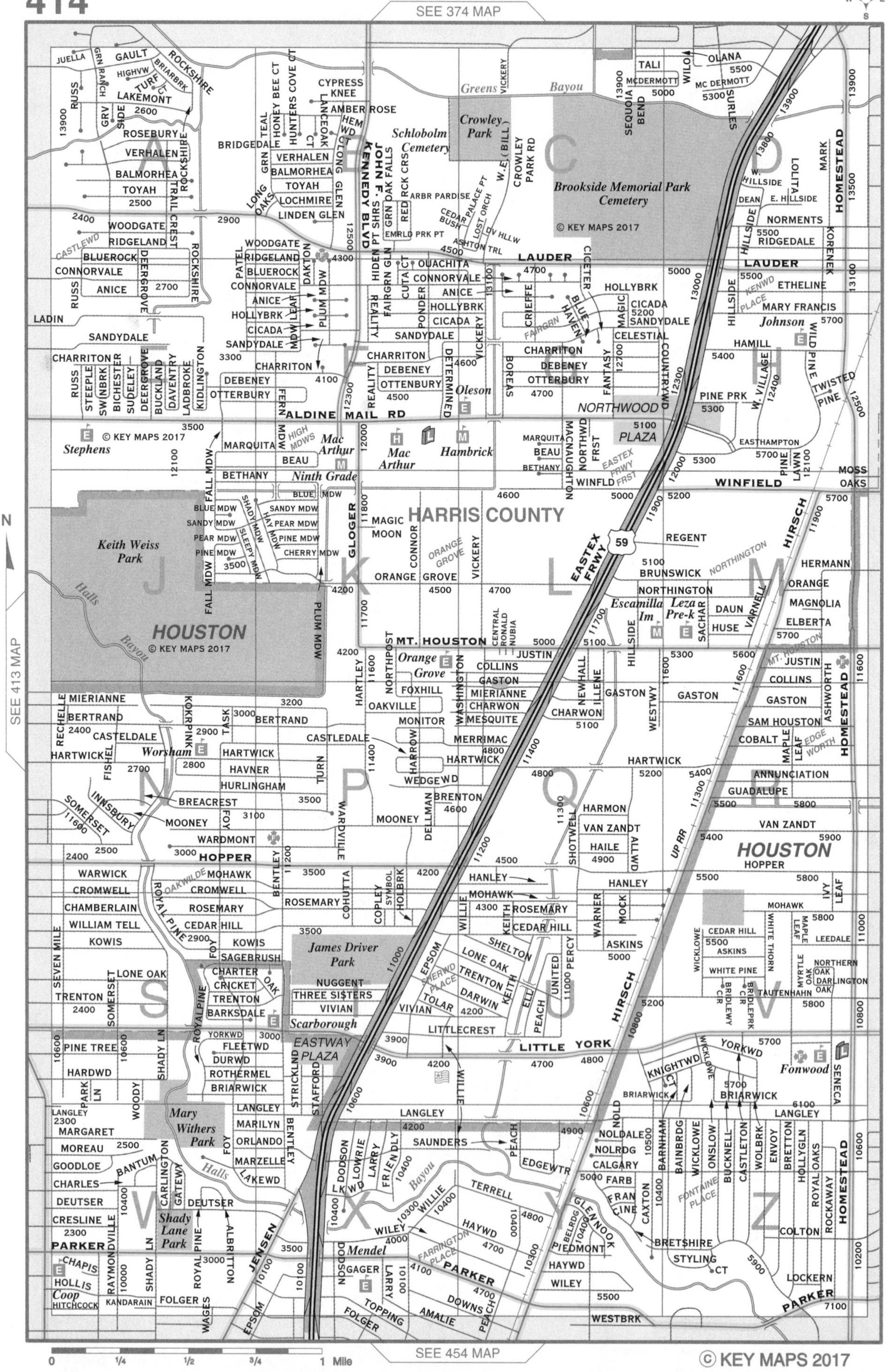

SEE 374 MAP

N W E S

SEE 413 MAP

HARRIS COUNTY

HOUSTON

Keith Weiss Park

James Driver Park

Mary Withers Park

Shady Lane Park

Crowley Park

Schlobolm Cemetery

Brookside Memorial Park Cemetery

© KEY MAPS 2017

NORTHWOOD PLAZA

EASTWAY PLAZA

Fonwood

Scarborough

EASTEX FRWY

59

MT. HOUSTON

LITTLE YORK

LAUDER

WINFIELD

PARKER

Greens Bayou

Halls Bayou

© KEY MAPS 2017

SEE 454 MAP

0   1/4   1/2   3/4   1 Mile

© **KEY MAPS 2017**

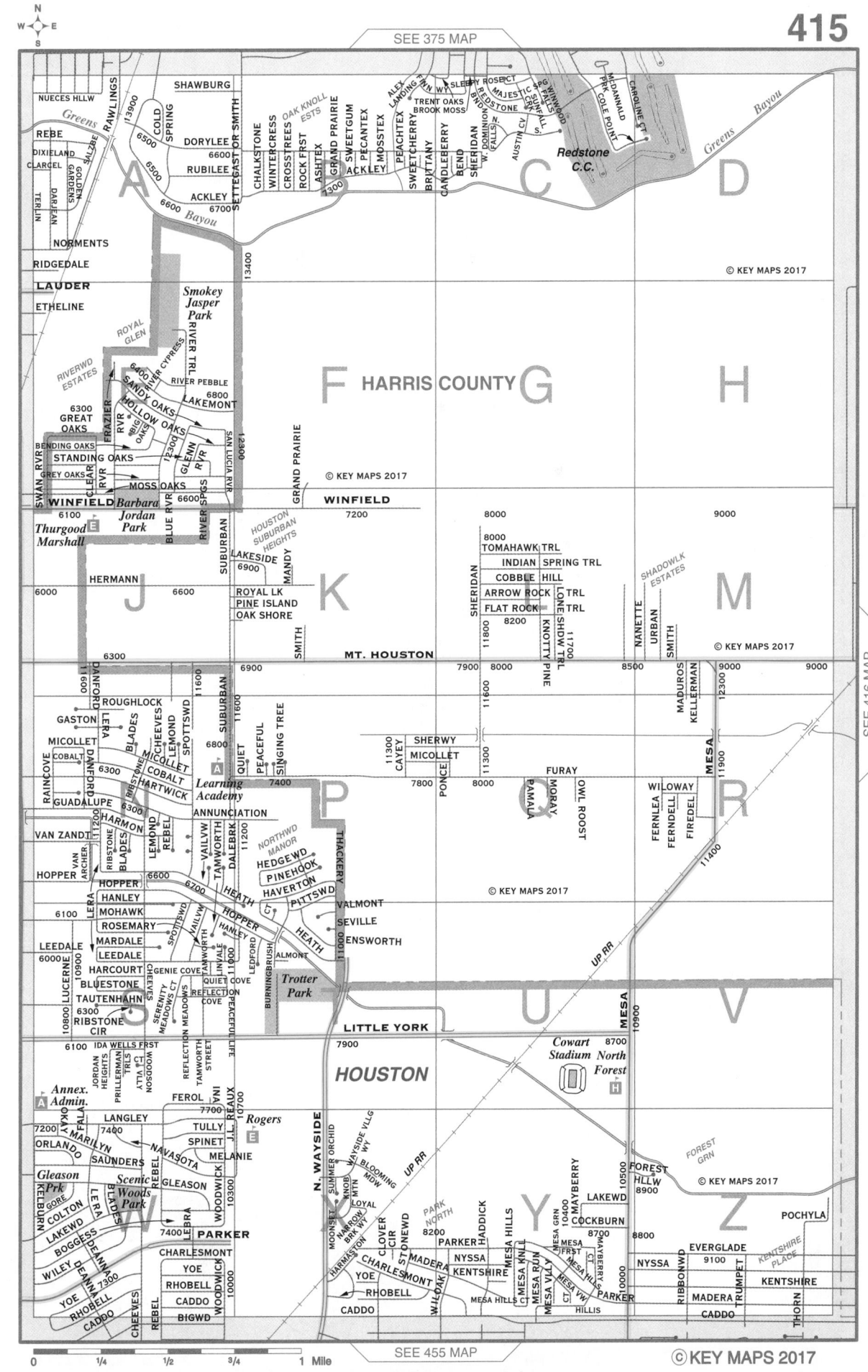

N W E S

HARRIS COUNTY

Greens Bayou

Redstone C.C.

© KEY MAPS 2017

Smokey Jasper Park

Barbara Jordan Park

Thurgood Marshall

WINFIELD

WINFIELD

MT. HOUSTON

Learning Academy

Trotter Park

LITTLE YORK

Cowart Stadium North Forest

HOUSTON

Annex. Admin.

Gleason Prk

Scenic Woods Park

PARKER

SEE 416 MAP

0   1/4   1/2   3/4   1 Mile

© KEY MAPS 2017

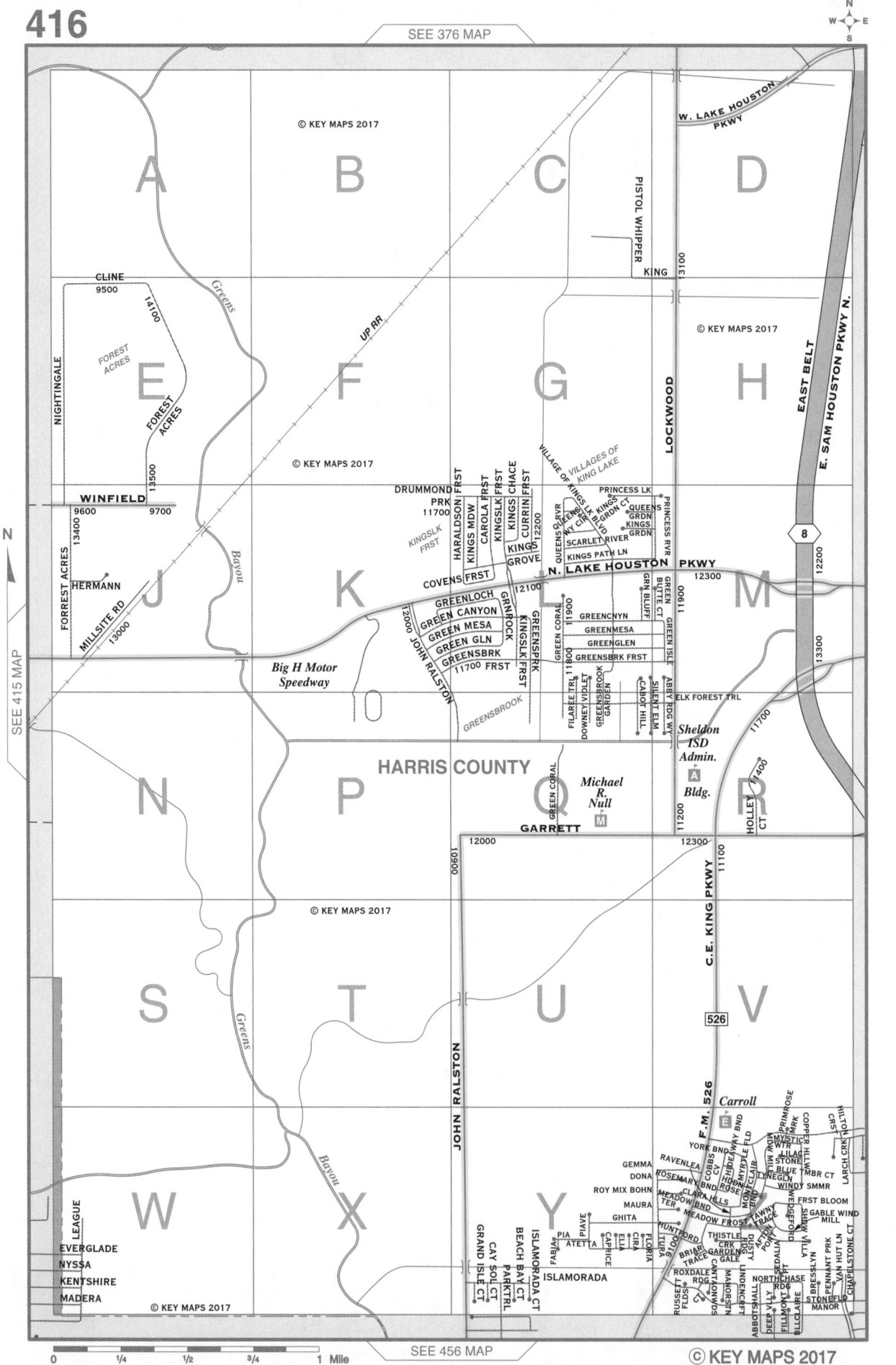

N
W E
S

A   B   C   D

W. LAKE HOUSTON PKWY

PISTOL WHIPPER

KING

3100

© KEY MAPS 2017

CLINE
9500

14100

FOREST
ACRES

E

FOREST
ACRES

13500

Greens

UP RR

F

© KEY MAPS 2017

G

LOCKWOOD

EAST BELT

E. SAM HOUSTON PKWY N.

8

12200

H

NIGHTINGALE

WINFIELD
9600   9700

FORREST ACRES
13400

HERMANN

MILLSITE RD
13000

Bayou

N

SEE 415 MAP

J

VILLAGE OF KINGS LK
VILLAGES OF KING LAKE

DRUMMOND
PRK
11700

HARALDSON FRST

KINGS MDW

CAROLA FRST

KINGSLK FRST

KINGS CHACE

CURRIN FRST

KINGS
GROVE
12200

KINGSLK FRST

QUEVRV

QUEENSLK KINGS

NY CIR KINGS LK BLVD

KINGS GRDN CT

SCARLET RIVER

KINGS PATH LN

PRINCESS LK

QUEENS
GRDN

KINGS
GRDN

PRINCESS RVR

KINGS
GRDN

N. LAKE HOUSTON PKWY
12300

M

12200

COVENS FRST

GREENLOCH

GREEN CANYON

GREEN MESA

GREEN GLN

GREENSBRK

JOHN RALSTON
13000

GRNROCK

KINGSLK FRST

GREENSPRK

KINGSLK FRST

12100

GREENSPRK

GREEN CORAL
11900

GRN BLUFF

GREEN BUTTE CT

GREEN ISLE
11011

GREENCNYN

GREENMESA

GREENGLEN

GREENSBRK FRST

12300

13300

Big H Motor
Speedway

GREENSBROOK

FILAREE TRL
11800

DOWNEY VIOLET

GREENBROOK
GARDEN

SILENT ELM

CABOT HILL

ABBY RDG WY

ELK FOREST TRL

Sheldon
ISD
Admin.

A
Bldg.

11200

11700

HOLLEY
CT
11400

R

HARRIS COUNTY

N

S

GREEN CORAL

Michael
R.
Null
M

GARRETT

Q

12000

10900

12300

11100

C.E. KING PKWY

T

U

526

V

Greens

Bayou

EVERGLADE

NYSSA

KENTSHIRE

MADERA

LEAGUE

W

JOHN RALSTON

X

GEMMA

DONA

ROY MIX BOHN

MAURA

GHITA

PIA

ATETTA

FABIAN

PIAVE

CAY SOL CT

GRAND ISLE CT

PARKTRL

BEACH BAY CT

ISLAMORADA CT

ISLAMORADA

FLORIA

CIRA

ELLA

CAPRICE

HUNTFORD

THISTLE CRK

MEADOW FROST

GARDEN RDG

CANTON

BRIARI TRACE

ROXDALE RDG

RUSSETT FLDS

ABBOTSHALL

DEEP VLY

FILLMONT

BELLCLAIRE

SEDALIA

GALE

AFTON

PORTAL

DUSTY RDG

LINDENCREST

MANORSTN

NORTHCHASE

BRESSLYN

STONEFLD

VAN HUT LN

PENNANT PRK

GABLE WIND MILL

FRST BLOOM

HILTON CRST

LARCH CRK

CHAPELSTONE CT

MANOR

Carroll

F.M. 526

E

YORK BND

RAVENLEA

COBBS

ROSEMARY BND

CLARA HILLS

MEADOW TER

MEADOW BND

MONT CLAIB

MONT ROSE

MAPLE FLD

HICKORY FLD

LYNEGLN

TAWNY TRACE

WEDGEFORD

VILLA

MYSTIC WTR

STONE BLUE

WINDY SMMR

PRIMROSE

COPPER HLLW

LILAC

MBR CT

0   1/4   1/2   3/4   1 Mile

© KEY MAPS 2017

© **KEY MAPS** 2017

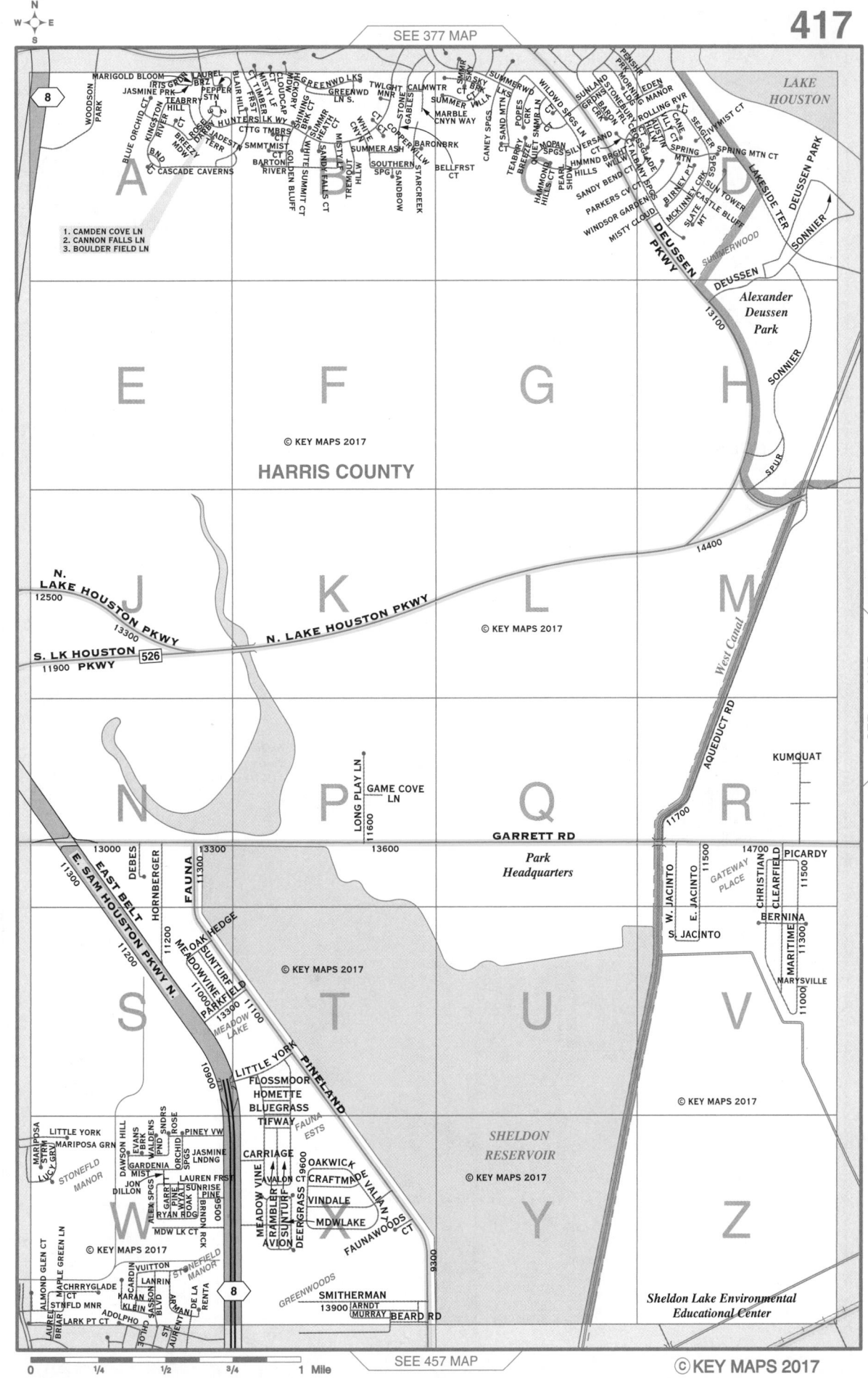

N
W E
S

8

1. CAMDEN COVE LN
2. CANNON FALLS LN
3. BOULDER FIELD LN

LAKE
HOUSTON

© KEY MAPS 2017

HARRIS COUNTY

DEUSSEN PKWY

Alexander
Deussen
Park

N. LAKE HOUSTON PKWY

N. LAKE HOUSTON PKWY

© KEY MAPS 2017

West Canal

S. LK HOUSTON
PKWY 526

SEE 418 MAP

KUMQUAT

LONG PLAY LN

GAME COVE
LN

GARRETT RD

Park
Headquarters

PICARDY

GATEWAY
PLACE

EAST BELT

E. SAM HOUSTON PKWY N.

FAUNA

HORNBERGER

DEBES

OAK HEDGE
SUNTURFIELD
MEADOWVINE
PARKTERR

MEADOW
LAKE

LITTLE YORK

PINELAND

© KEY MAPS 2017

W. JACINTO
E. JACINTO
S. JACINTO

CHRISTIAN
CLEARFIELD

BERNINA
MARITIME

MARYSVILLE

FLOSSMOOR
HOMETTE
BLUEGRASS
TIFWAY

FAUNA
ESTS

SHELDON
RESERVOIR

© KEY MAPS 2017

CARRIAGE

MEADOW VINE
RAMBLER
SUNTURF
AVION

OAKWICK
CRAFTMADE
VINDALE
MDWLAKE

VALIANT
DEERGRASS

FAUNAWOODS
CT

© KEY MAPS 2017

MARIPOSA
STRM
MARIPOSA GRN

LITTLE YORK

STONEFLD
MANOR

DAWSON HILL
EVANS
PARK
GARDENIA
MIST
JON
DILLON
ALEX SPGS
RYAN RDG

VALDENS
PND SNDRS
ORCHID
SPGS
LAUREN FRST
PINE
WYATT
OAK
MDW LK CT

PINEY VW
JASMINE
LNDNG

SUNRISE
PINE
BRNING RCK

8

GREENWOODS

SMITHERMAN
13900

SHELDON
ARNDT
MURRAY
BEARD RD

Sheldon Lake Environmental
Educational Center

ALMOND GLEN CT
LAUREL
BRIAR
MAPLE GREEN LN
CHRRYGLADE
CT
STNFLD MNR
LARK PT CT

CARDIN
KARAN
SASSON
ADOLPHO

VUITTON
LANRIN
BLVD
CHLOE
ST.
AURENT
DE LA
RENTA
ARMANI

© KEY MAPS 2017

0   1/4   1/2   3/4   1 Mile

© KEY MAPS 2017

SEE 378 MAP

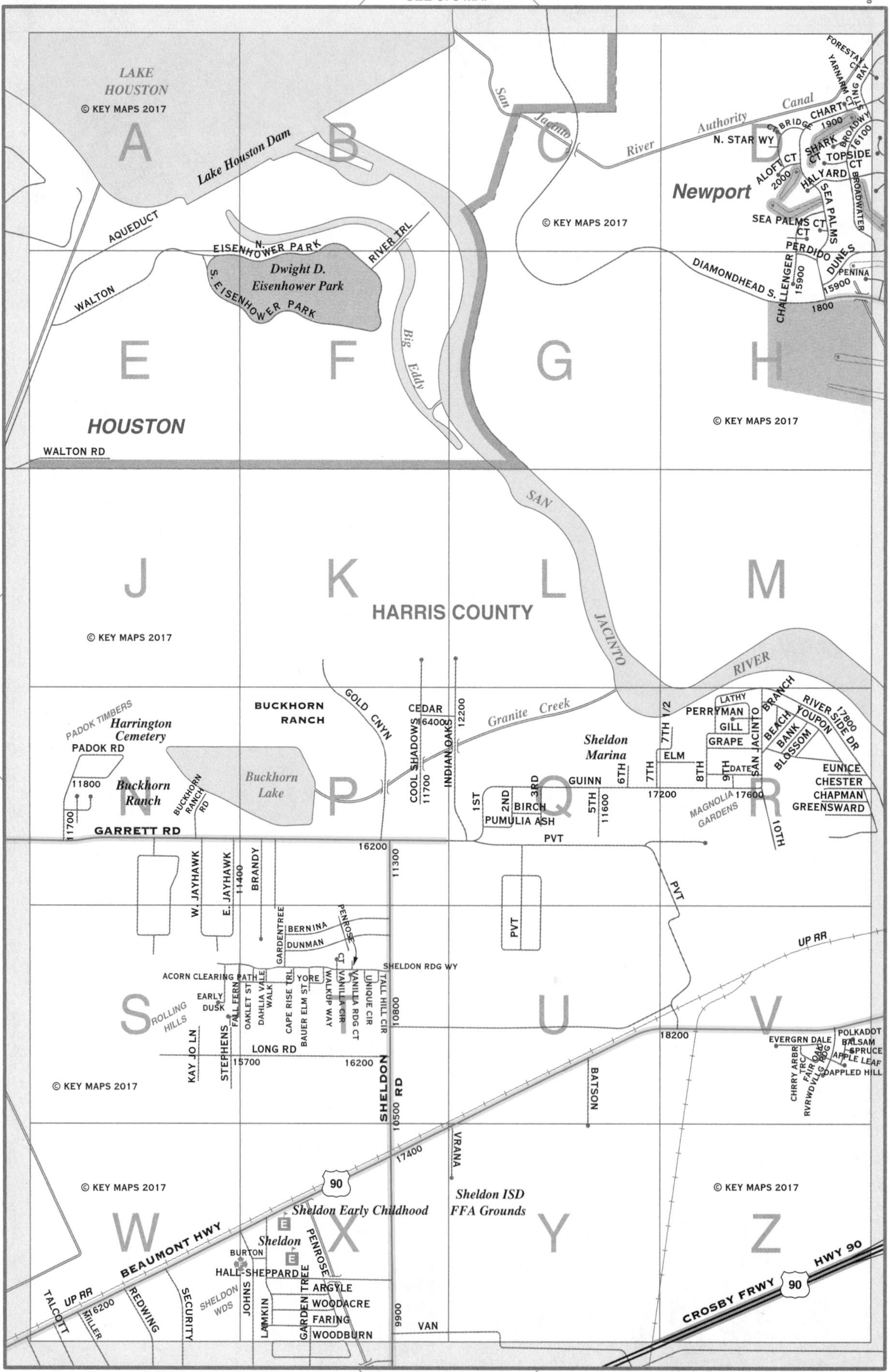

N
W E
S

LAKE HOUSTON
© KEY MAPS 2017

Lake Houston Dam

AQUEDUCT

WALTON

N. EISENHOWER PARK
RIVER TRL
S. EISENHOWER PARK

Dwight D. Eisenhower Park

Big Eddy

A   B   C   D

San Jacinto River

Authority   Canal
N. STAR WY
CAMBRIDGE   CHART
FOREST ST
YARNAM
LONG BAY
Broadway 16100
1900
SHARK   TOPSIDE CT
ALOFT CT   HALYARD CT
2000
SEA PALMS CT
SEA PALMS CT
Newport
PERDIDO   DUNES
15900   PENINA
15900
CHALLENGER
DIAMONDHEAD S.
1800

E   F   G   H

HOUSTON

WALTON RD

© KEY MAPS 2017

© KEY MAPS 2017

SAN JACINTO

J   K   L   M
HARRIS COUNTY

© KEY MAPS 2017

N

SEE 417 MAP

RIVER

17800
RIVER SIDE DR

PADOK TIMBERS
Harrington Cemetery
PADOK RD
GOLD CNYN
BUCKHORN RANCH
CEDAR
64000
COOL SHADOWS
11700
INDIAN OAKS
12200
Granite Creek
7TH 1/2
LATHY
PERRYMAN   BRANCH
GILL
GRAPE   BEACH   YOUPON
BANK   BLOSSOM
DATE
Sheldon Marina
7TH   ELM   8TH   SAN JACINTO
9TH
EUNICE
CHESTER
CHAPMAN
GREENSWARD

11800
11700
Buckhorn Ranch
Buckhorn Lake
BUCKHORN RANCH RD
GUINN
1ST   2ND   3RD   Q   5TH   6TH   7TH
BIRCH
PUMULIA ASH
PVT
17200
11600
MAGNOLIA GARDENS
17600
10TH

GARRETT RD

16200
11300
W. JAYHAWK
E. JAYHAWK
11400
BRANDY
GARDENTREE
BERNINA
DUNMAN
PENROSE
ACORN CLEARING PATH
FALL FERN WALK
EARLY DUSK
OAKLET ST
DAHLIA VALE RD
YORE
CAPE RISE TRL
BAUER ELM ST
WALKUP WAY
VANILLA DG CT
VANILLA CIR
UNIQUE CIR
TALL HILL CIR
SHELDON RDG WY
S
ROLLING HILLS
KAY JO LN
STEPHENS
LONG RD
15700
16200
SHELDON RD
10500
10800

PVT

PVT

UP RR

18200
BATSON

P   Q   R

S   T   U   V

EVERGRN DALE
CHRRY ARBR
RVRWD WS
FAIR OAKS
POLKADOT
BALSAM
SPRUCE
APPLE LEAF
DAPPLED HILL

© KEY MAPS 2017

© KEY MAPS 2017

17400
VRANA
Sheldon ISD FFA Grounds

© KEY MAPS 2017

90

TALCOTT
UP RR
16200
MILLER
REDWING
SECURITY
BEAUMONT HWY

Sheldon Early Childhood

E   *Sheldon*
BURTON
HALL-SHEPPARD
E
SHELDON WDS
JOHNS
LAMKIN
PENROSE
GARDEN TREE
ARGYLE
WOODACRE
FARING
WOODBURN

VAN
9900

W   X   Y   Z

CROSBY FRWY   90   HWY 90

0   1/4   1/2   3/4   1 Mile

SEE 458 MAP

© KEY MAPS 2017

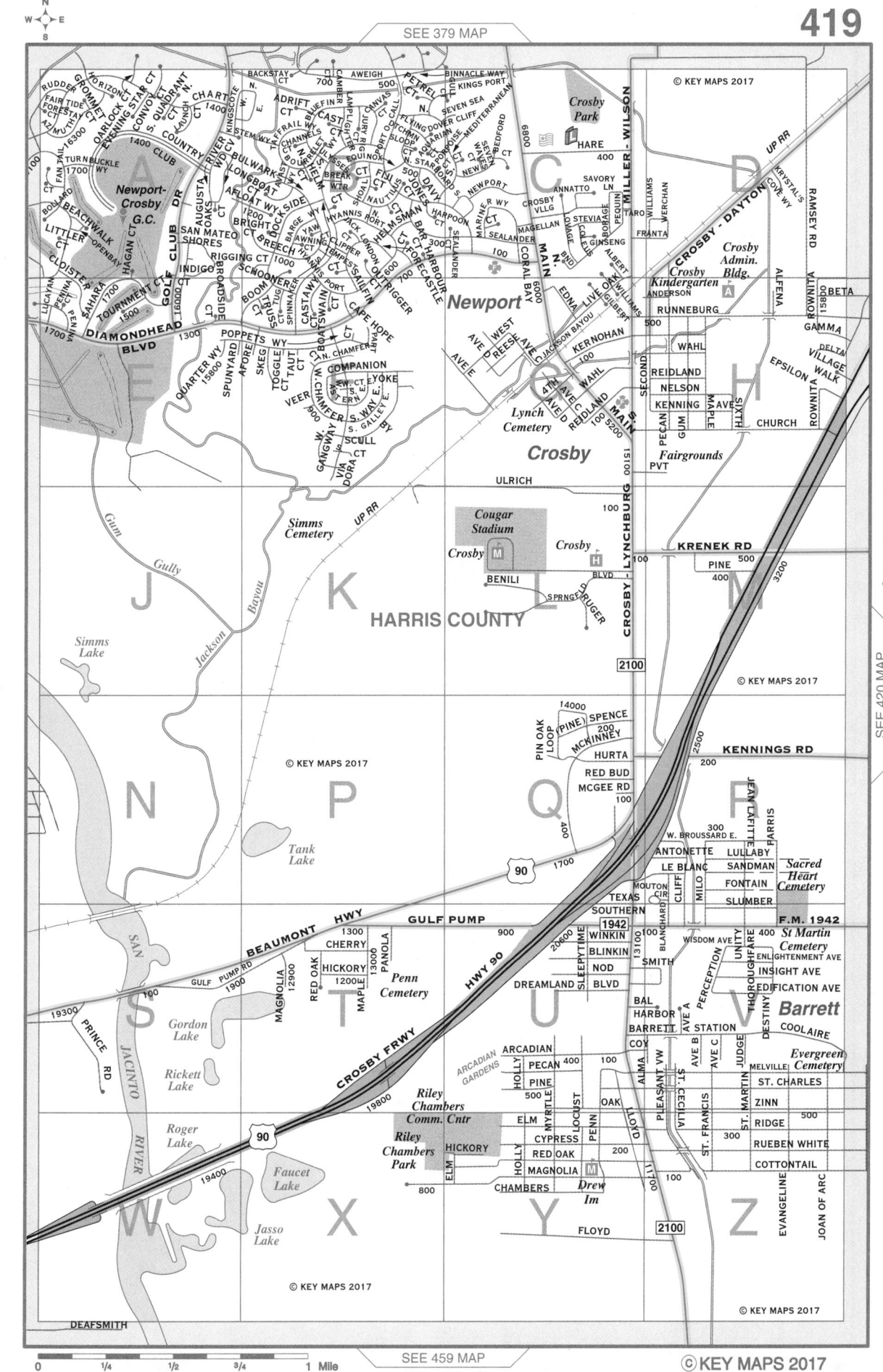

© KEY MAPS 2017

N
W E
S

A

Newport-Crosby G.C.

GOLF CLUB DR

DIAMONDHEAD BLVD

E

C

Crosby Park

HARE

Newport

Crosby Vllg

Crosby

D

CROSBY - DAYTON

Crosby Admin. Bldg.

Crosby Kindergarten

RAMSEY RD

H

VILLAGE WALK

EPSILON WALK

CHURCH

MILLER - WILSON

N. MAIN

G

Lynch Cemetery

West Reese Ave

4TH AVE

Lynch Cemetery

S. MAIN

Fairgrounds

ULRICH

Simms Cemetery

Gun Gully

Jackson Bayou

J

UP RR

K

HARRIS COUNTY

Cougar Stadium

Crosby

BENILI

CROSBY - LYNCHBURG

L

2100

KRENEK RD

PINE

M

3200

Simms Lake

N

Tank Lake

P

Q

PIN OAK LOOP

SPENCE

McKINNEY

HURTA

RED BUD

MCGEE RD

KENNINGS RD

JEAN LAFITTE

FARRIS

R

ANTONETTE

LE BLANC

CLIFF

MILO

LULLABY

SANDMAN

FONTAIN

SLUMBER

Sacred Heart Cemetery

90

BEAUMONT HWY

GULF PUMP

HWY 90

TEXAS SOUTHERN

1942

WINKIN

BLINKIN

NOD

DREAMLAND BLVD

F.M. 1942

St Martin Cemetery

ENLIGHTENMENT AVE

INSIGHT AVE

EDIFICATION AVE

V

Barrett

San Jacinto River

SAN JACINTO RIVER

Gordon Lake

Rickett Lake

Roger Lake

S

CHERRY

HICKORY

MAGNOLIA

RED OAK

PANOLA

MAPLE

GULF PUMP RD

T

Penn Cemetery

CROSBY FRWY

U

HARBOR

BARRETT

STATION

COY

ALMA

Arcadian Gardens

ARCADIAN

PECAN

PINE

HOLLY

Evergreen Cemetery

COOLAIRE

MELVILLE

ST. CHARLES

ZINN

RIDGE

RUEBEN WHITE

COTTONTAIL

Z

Riley Chambers Comm. Cntr

Riley Chambers Park

ELM

CYPRESS

HICKORY

MAGNOLIA

CHAMBERS

Drew Im

Y

ELM

MYRTLE

LOCUST

OAK

PENN

RED OAK

LLOYD

ST. CECILIA

ST. FRANCIS

ST. MARTIN

EVANGELINE

JOAN OF ARC

FLOYD

2100

90

Faucet Lake

Jasso Lake

W

X

DEAFSMITH

0   1/4   1/2   3/4   1 Mile

© KEY MAPS 2017

SEE 420 MAP

N

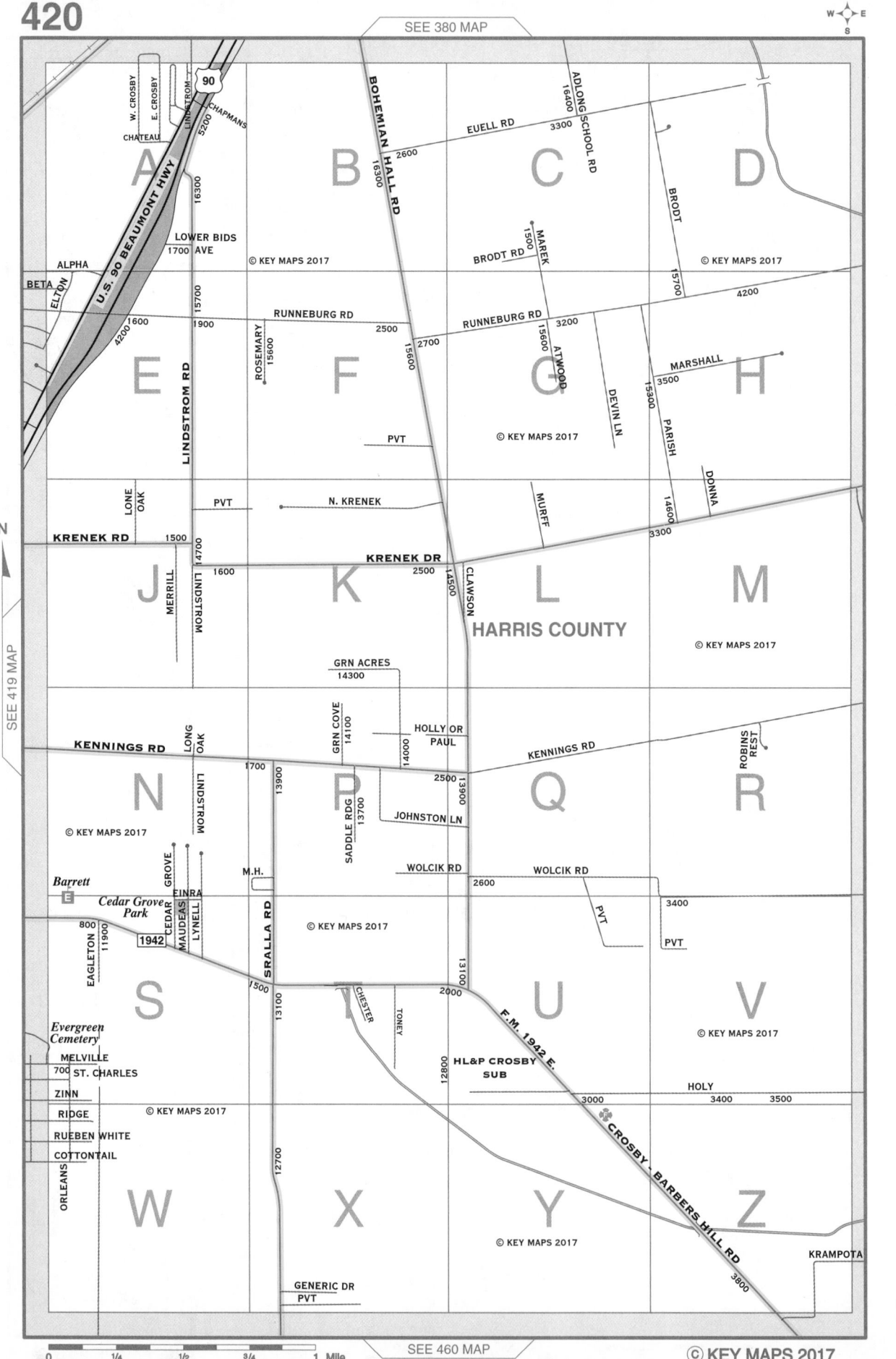

© KEY MAPS 2017

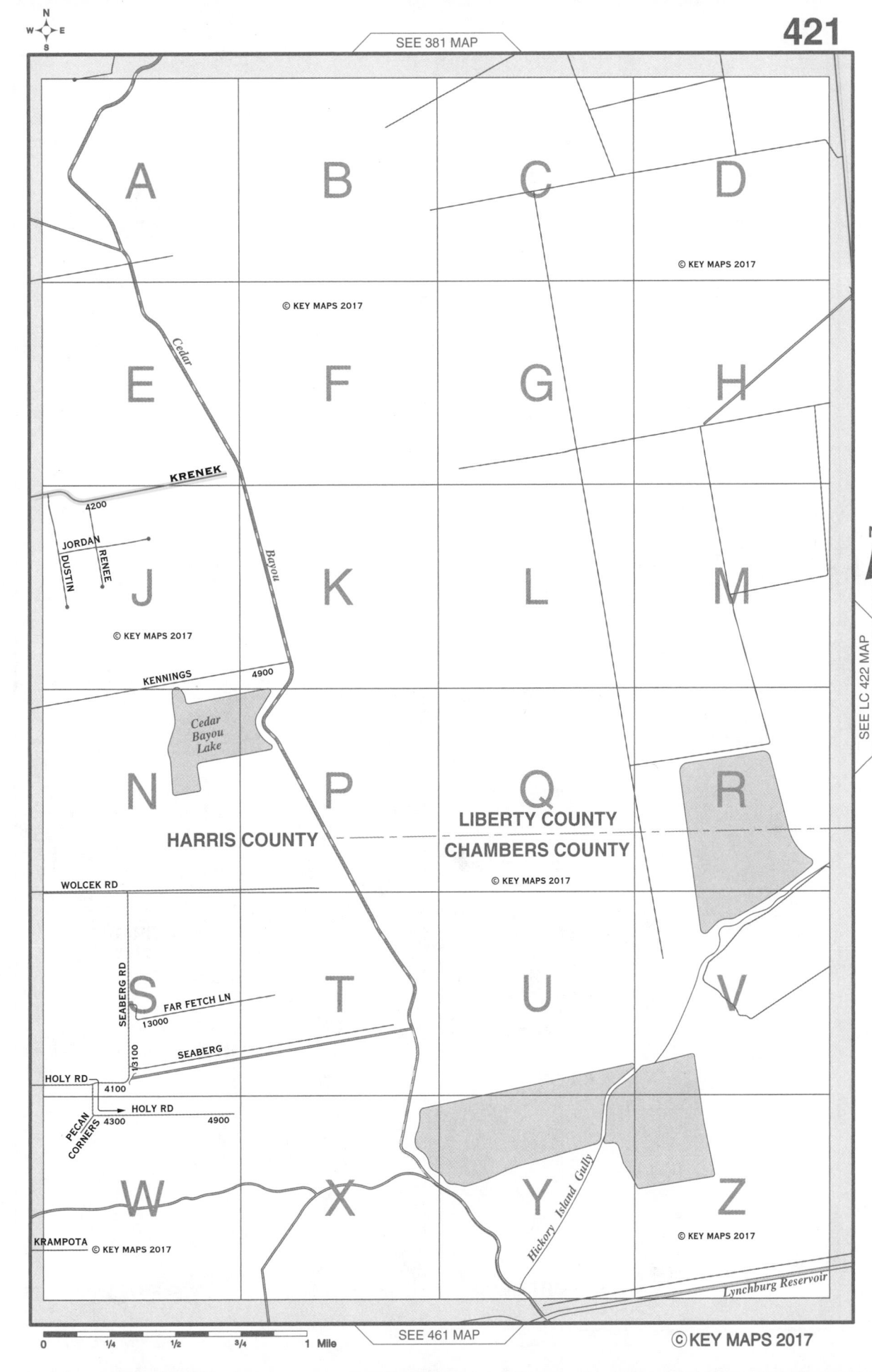

SEE 381 MAP

N
W E
S

A   B   C   D

© KEY MAPS 2017

Cedar

E   F   G   H

KRENEK

4200

JORDAN

DUSTIN   RENEE

J   K   L   M

Bayou

© KEY MAPS 2017

SEE LC 422 MAP

N

KENNINGS   4900

*Cedar
Bayou
Lake*

N   P   Q   R

LIBERTY COUNTY

HARRIS COUNTY   **CHAMBERS COUNTY**

© KEY MAPS 2017

WOLCEK RD

SEABERG RD

S   T   U   V

FAR FETCH LN

13000

13100   SEABERG

HOLY RD

4100

PECAN   HOLY RD

CORNERS   4300   4900

Hickory Island Gully

W   X   Y   Z

KRAMPOTA   © KEY MAPS 2017   © KEY MAPS 2017

Lynchburg Reservoir

0   1/4   1/2   3/4   1 Mile

SEE 461 MAP

© **KEY MAPS** 2017

SEE 404 MAP

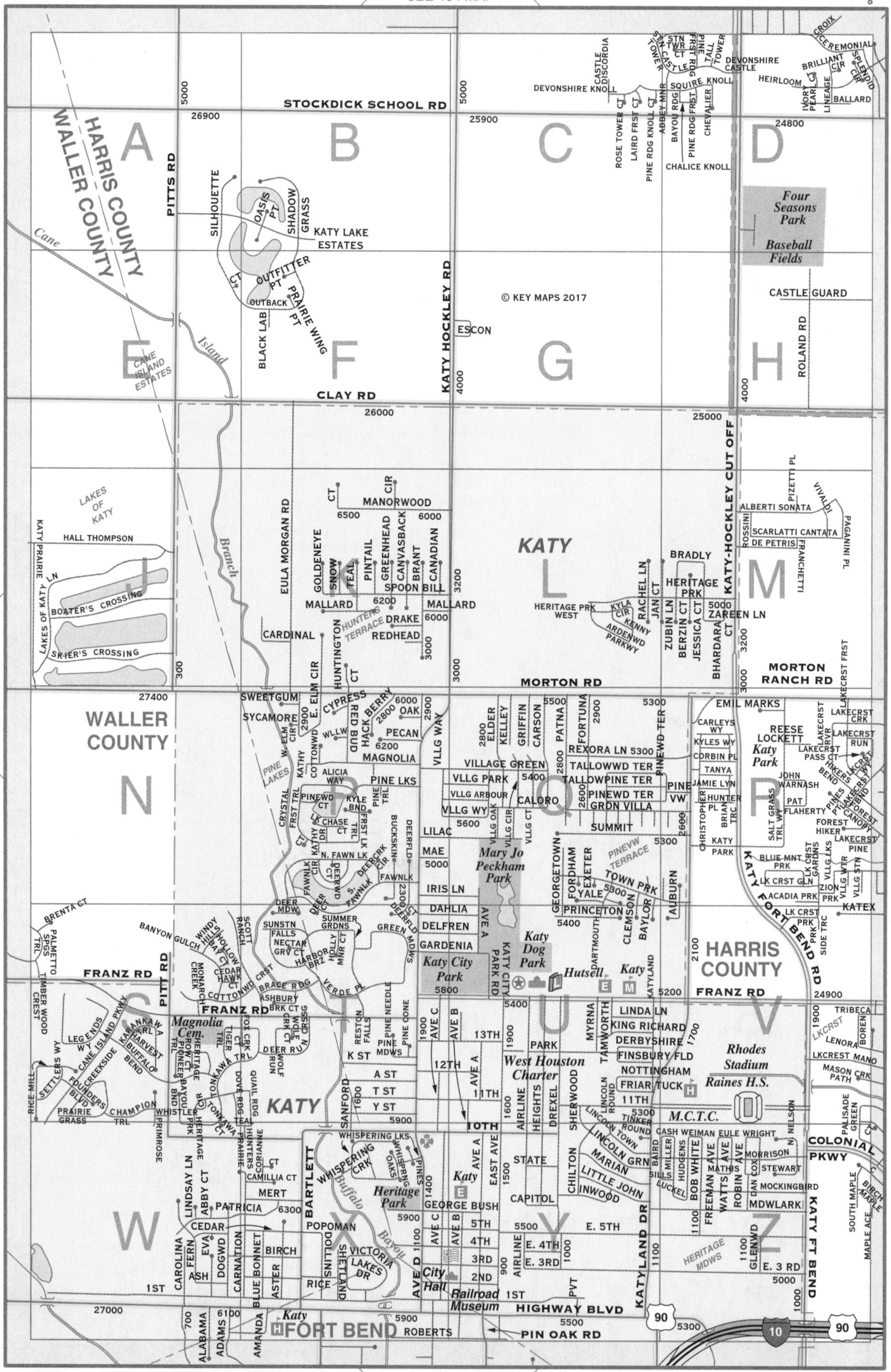

N
W E
S

Grid A–H (top)

A B STOCKDICK SCHOOL RD C D

PITTS RD
5000 26900 5000 25900 24800

SILHOUETTE
OASIS PT
SHADOW GRASS
KATY LAKE ESTATES
OUTFITTER PT
PRAIRIE WING
OUTBACK PT
BLACK LAB

KATY HOCKLEY RD

DEVONSHIRE KNOLL
ROSE TOWER CT
LAIRD FRST CT
PINE RDG KNOLL
CASTLE DISCORDIA
ABBEY MNR
BAYOU RDG
SQUIRE KNOLL
PINE RDG FRST
CHEVALIER
CHALICE KNOLL
STN TWR CT
FERN CASTLE
TALL CASTLE
DEVONSHIRE CASTLE
HEIRLOOM
BRILLIANT CIR
LINEAGE
IVORY PEARL CT
SPLENDID CIR
BALLARD
CROIX
REMONIAL

Four Seasons Park
Baseball Fields

CASTLE GUARD
ROLAND RD

© KEY MAPS 2017

ESCON

CLAY RD

E F G H
Cane
Island
CANE ISLAND ESTATES
26000 4000 25000 4000

Grid J–M

Lakes OF KATY
HALL THOMPSON
KATY PRAIRIE LN
BOATER'S CROSSING
SKIER'S CROSSING
LAKES OF KATY

N

SEE FB 443 MAP

Branch

EULA MORGAN RD
MANORWOOD
CT CIR 6500 6000
GOLDENEYE SNOW TEAL PINTAIL GREENHEAD CANVASBACK BRANT CANADIAN
MALLARD 6200 SPOON BILL MALLARD
HUNTINGTON CARDINAL DRAKE REDHEAD
6000 3000 3200 3000

KATY
L
HERITAGE PRK WEST
KYLA CIR KENNY ARDENWD PARKWY
RACHEL LN
KYLE CIR
BRADLY
HERITAGE PRK
ZUBIN LN JAN CT
BERZIN CT JESSICA CT
ZAREEN LN
BHARDARA CT
KATY-HOCKLEY CUT OFF
PIZETTI PL VIVALDI
ALBERTI SONATA
SCARLATTI CANTATA
ROSSINI DE PETRIS
PAGANINI PL
FRANCHETTI
M
MORTON RANCH RD
LAKECRST FRST

MORTON RD

27400 3200 3000

Grid N–R

WALLER COUNTY
N
SWEETGUM SYCAMORE
W ELM
E. ELM CIR
CYPRESS
HACK BERRY
RED BUD 6000 OAK 2900
PECAN 6200
MAGNOLIA
PINE LKS
PINE TRL
300

CRYSTAL FRST TRL
PINE LAKES
KATHY
PINEWD CT
ALICIA WAY
N. CHASE CT
KYLE BND
COTTONWD
WLLW
VLLG WAY
VILLAGE GREEN
VLLG PARK
VLLG ARBOUR
VLLG WY
CALORO
LILAC
MAE
IRIS LN
DAHLIA
DELFREN
GARDENIA
2800 KELLEY ELDER GRIFFIN CARSON PATNA
REXORA LN 5300
TALLOWWD TER
TALLOWPINE TER
PINEWD TER GRDN VILLA
SUMMIT
FORTUNA 2900 5300
PINEWD TER
PINE VW
5300
PINEVW TERRACE
TOWN PRK
2600

EMIL MARKS
CARLEYS WY
KYLES WY
CORBIN PL
TANYA
JAMIE LYN
HUNTER PL
BRIAN TRC
CHRISTOPHER
SALT GRASS
PAT FLAHERTY
KATY PARK
JOHN WARNASH
REESE LOCKETT
Katy Park
LAKECRST CRK
LAKECRST RVR
LAKECRST RUN
PINERS BEND
BLUE MNT PRK
LK CRST SDE
ACADIA PRK
ZION
LK CRST PRK
VLLG VTR PRK
VLLG STN
FOREST HIKER
FOREST CANOPY
LAKECRST PINE
KATEX
R

P Q
MARY JO PECKHAM PARK
GEORGETOWN FORDHAM EXETER PRINCETON
YALE BAYLOR CLEMSON AUBURN
DARTMOUTH KATYLAND

HARRIS COUNTY

Grid S–Z (bottom)

FRANZ RD
PITT RD
BRENTA CT
PALMETTO SPGS TRL
BANYON GULCH
TIMBER WOOD CREST
SCOTT RANCH
WINDY HOLLOW
MONARCH CREEK
DEER MDW
SUNSTN FALLS
NECTAR
HARBORLY
SUMMER GRDNS
GREEN
HOLLY MIR CT
S. DEER CRK
FAWNLK
DEERFLD
BUCKSKIN
FAWNLK

FRANZ RD
FRANZ RD

MAGNOLIA CEM.
LEGENDS
CANE ISLAND PKWY
KARANKAWA
HARVEST
CREEKSIDE
PIONEER
HERITAGE
TONKAWA TRL
DEER RUN
QUAIL RDG
DOVE RDG
PRAIRIE
WHISTLER
TIGER TRL
CEDAR
BRACE RDG
ASHBURY
BRK CT
RESTON FALLS
PINE NEEDLE
PINE LONE
PINE MDWS
K ST
A ST
T ST
Y ST
5900

S T U V
KATY
SANFORD
13TH
12TH
11TH
AVE C AVE B AVE A

Katy City Park 5800
Katy Dog Park
Hutsell
Katy
5200
FRANZ RD
24900

West Houston Charter
AIRLINE HEIGHTS DREXEL
Park
MYRNA TAMWORTH
SHERWOOD
LINDA LN
KING RICHARD
DERBYSHIRE
FINSBURY FLD
NOTTINGHAM
FRIAR TUCK
Rhodes Stadium
Raines H.S.
TRIBECA
LKCRST
LENORA
MASON CRK PATH
BOREN
LKCREST MANO

M.C.T.C.

SETTLERS WY
FOUNDERS BLVD
PRAIRIE GRASS
CHAMPION TRL
RICE MILL
LINDSAY LN
ABBY CT
CAROLINA
FERN
EVA
ASH
DOGWD
CEDAR
PATRICIA
MERT
CAMILLIA CT
BIRCH
CARNATION
BLUE BONNET
ASTER
VICTORIA
SHETLAND
RICE
POPOMAN
W X
Heritage Park
WHISPERING LKS
WHISPERING CRK
OAKS PINES
6300
Buffalo Bayou
1ST
27000 700 6100

10TH
EAST AVE
STATE
CAPITOL
5500
GEORGE BUSH
5TH 4TH 3RD 2ND
AVE D AVE C AVE B
City Hall
Railroad Museum
Katy FORT BEND
ALABAMA ADAMS AMANDA
HIGHWAY BLVD
PIN OAK RD
ROBERTS 5900 5500

AIRLINE
LINCOLN TOWN
LINCOLN GRN
TINKER ROUND
CASH WEIMAN
BAIRD
SILLS
LUCKEL
CHILTON
MARIAN
LITTLE JOHN
INWOOD
MILLER
HUDGENS
BOB WHITE
FREEMAN
MATHIS
ROBIN
MORRISON
STEWART
DAN COX
MOCKINGBIRD
MDWLARK
EULE
WATTS
WRIGHT
NELSON
COLONIAL PKWY
PALISADE GREEN
SOUTH MAPLE
BIRCH MAPLE
MAPLE ACE
KATY FT BEND
GLENWD
HERITAGE MDWS
5000
Y Z
KATYLAND DR
E. 5TH
E. 4TH
E. 3RD
E. 5TH
1100 1100 1100

90 90
I-10
5300

0 1/4 1/2 3/4 1 Mile

© KEY MAPS 2017

HARRIS COUNTY / WALLER COUNTY
WALLER COUNTY

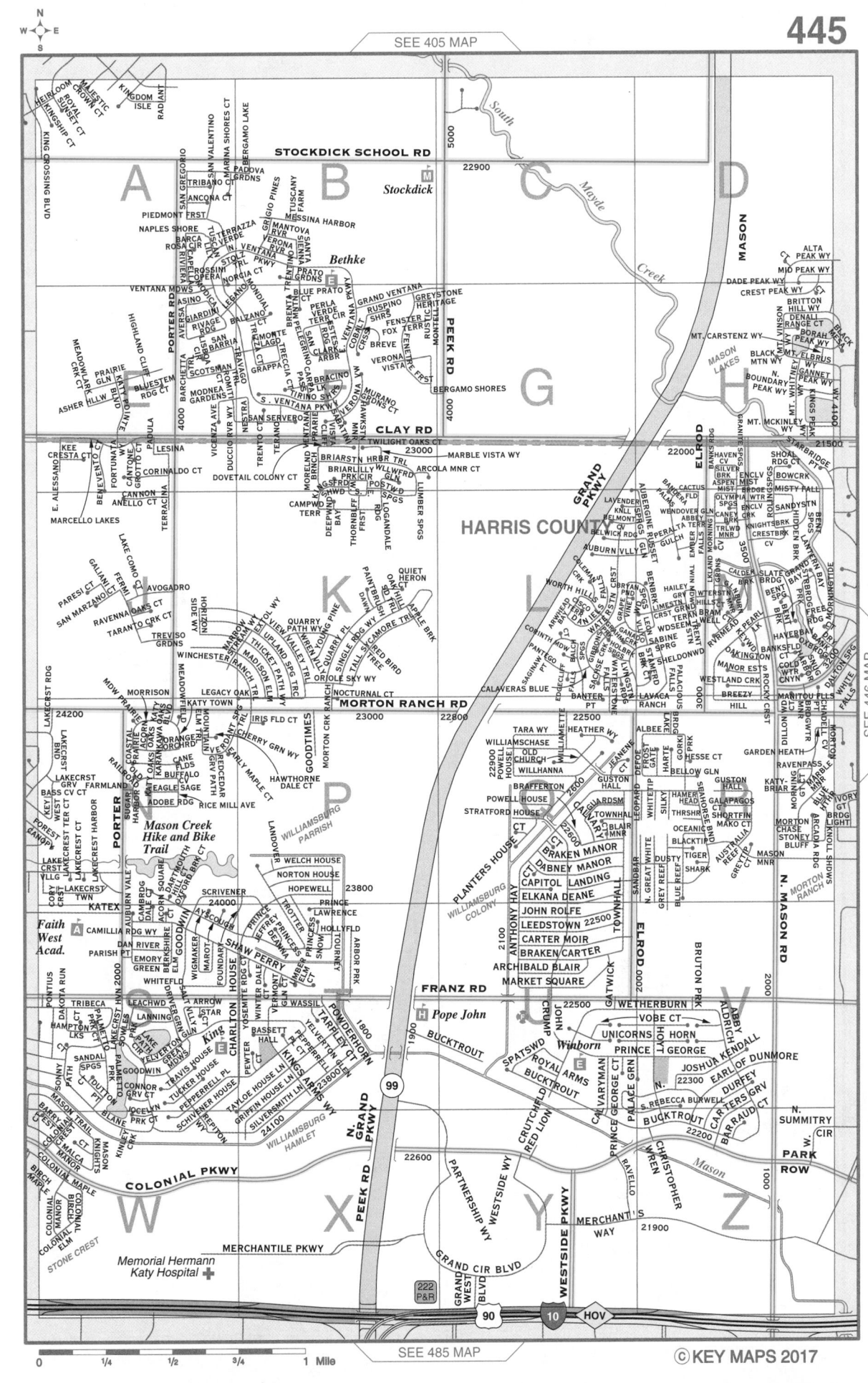

© KEY MAPS 2017

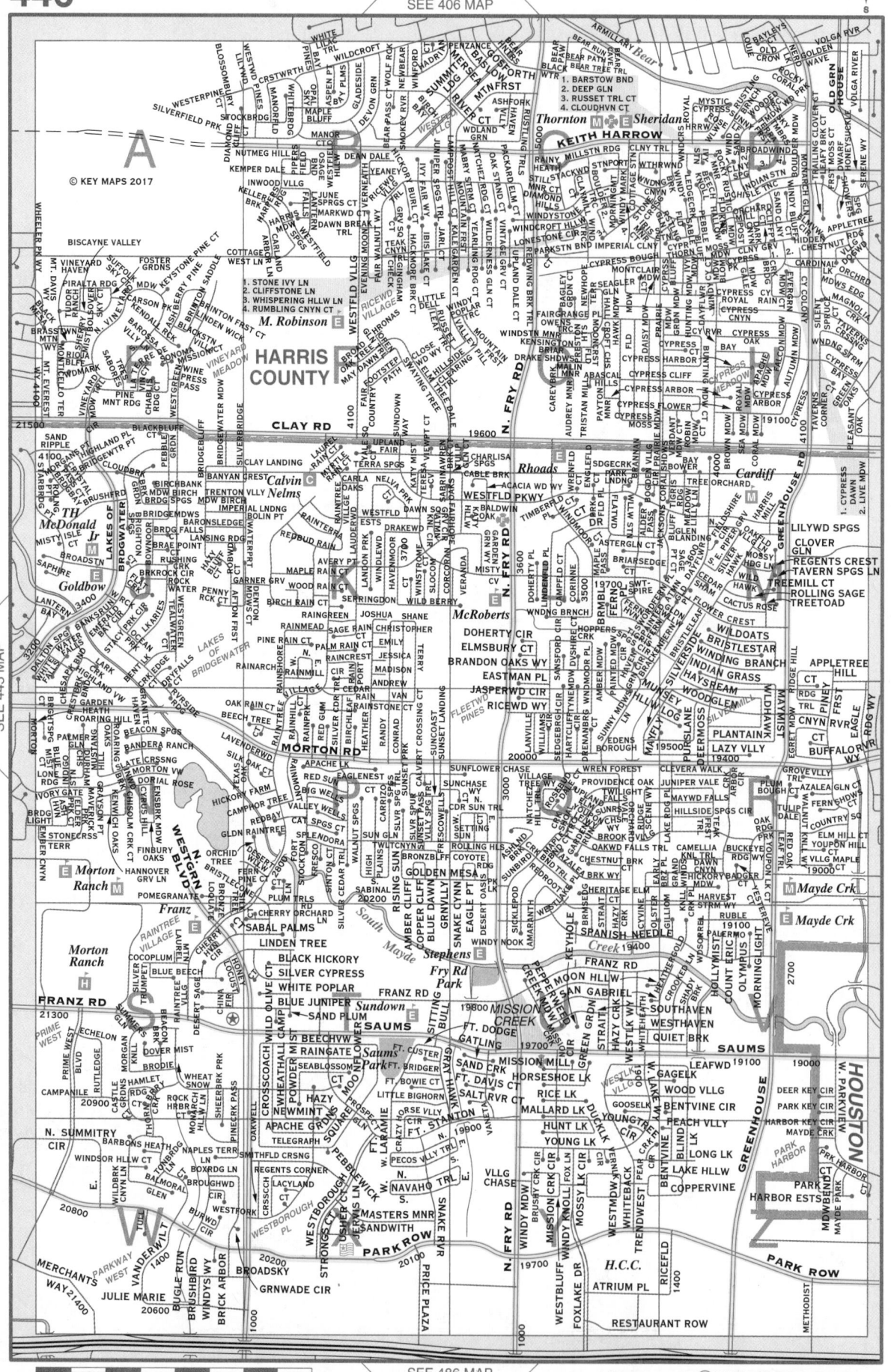

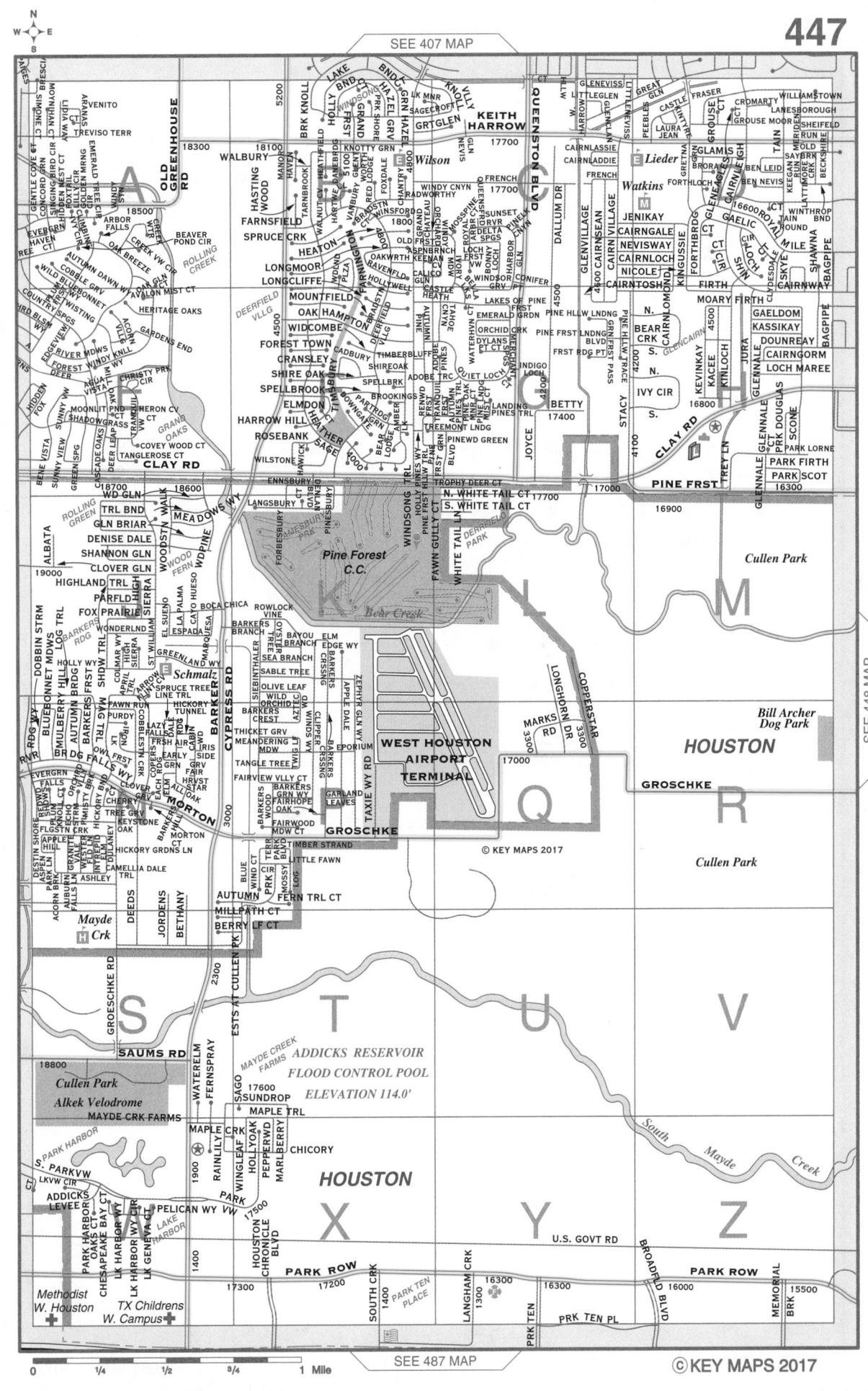

© KEY MAPS 2017

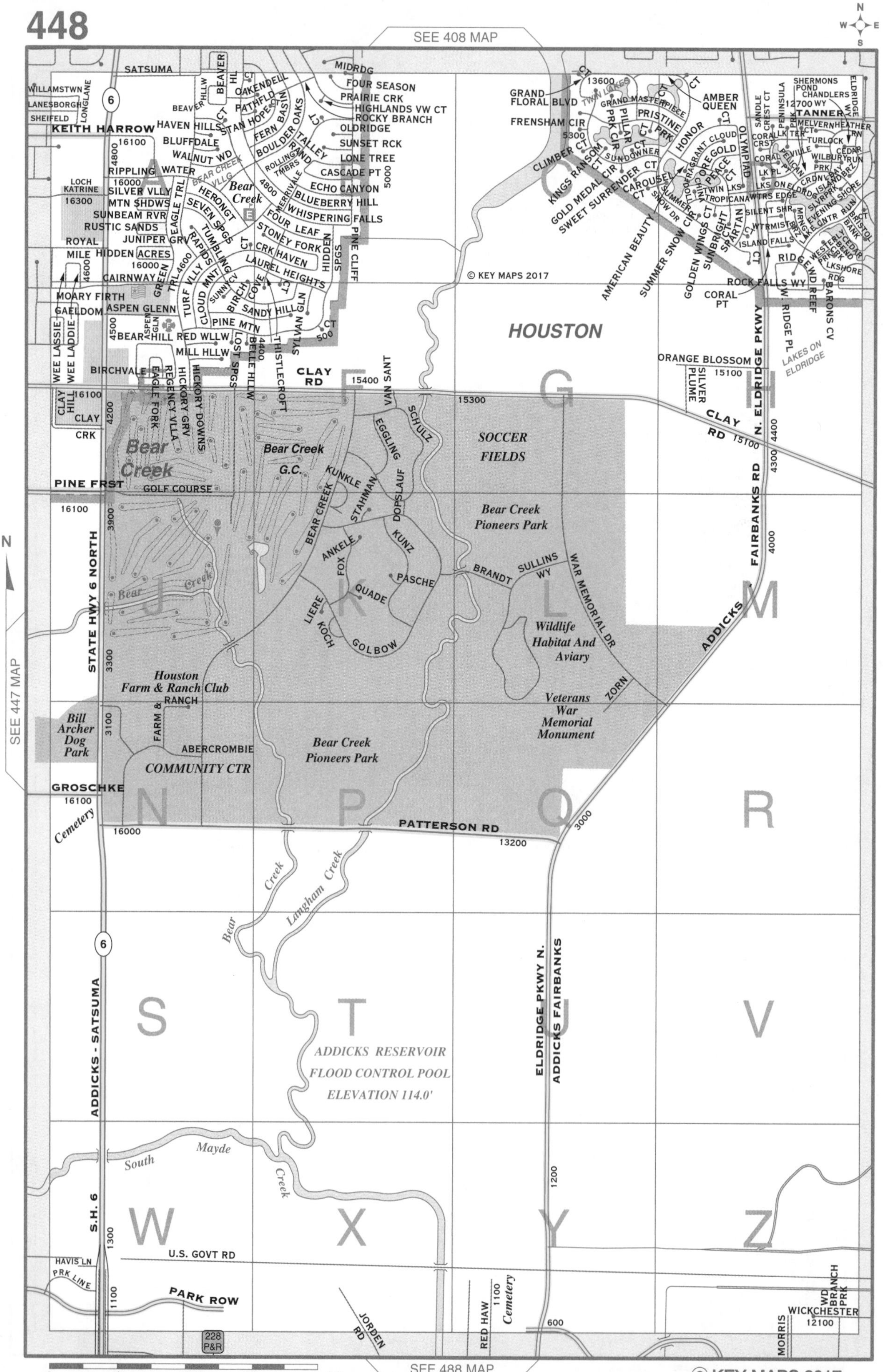

SEE 408 MAP

N
W E
S

SATSUMA

WILLAMSTWN
LANESBORGHN
SHEIFELD

6

KEITH HARROW

MIDRDG
FOUR SEASON
PRAIRIE CRK
HIGHLANDS VW CT
ROCKY BRANCH
OLDRIDGE

BEAVER
PHLLW
BEAVER
HL
OAKENDELL
PATHFLD
STAN HOPE CT

HAVEN HILLS
BLUFFDALE
WALNUT WD
RIPPLING
WATER

16100
14800

LOCH
KATRINE
16300

16000
SILVER VLLY
MTN SHDWS
SUNBEAM RVR
RUSTIC SANDS

ROYAL
MILE HIDDEN
ACRES

16000
14600
JUNIPER GRV
CAIRNWAY

MOARY FIRTH
GAELDOM
ASPEN GLENN

WEE LASSIE
WEE LADDIE

BIRCHVALE

CLAY
HILL
16100
CLAY
CRK

4500
4200
4800

BEAR
CREEK
VLLG

Bear
Creek

E

SEVEN SPGS
HERONGT
TUMBLING
RAPIDS
TURF VLLY
CLOUD MNT

BEAR HILL
RED WLLW

BIRCH
SUNNY

PINE MTN

MILL HLLW
LOST SPGS

REGENCY VLLA
HICKORY GRV
EAGLE FORK

HICKORY DOWNS

FERN BASIN
BOULDER OAKS
ROLLING
TMBRS
4800
KINGVALE
FOUR LEAF
STONEY FORK
CRK HAVEN
LAUREL HEIGHTS
SANDY HILL
SYLVAN GLN
CT
BELLE HLLW
THISTLECROFT

TALLEY
BRAND
ECHO CANYON
BLUEBERRY HILL
WHISPERING FALLS
HIDDEN

SUNSET RCK
LONE TREE
CASCADE PT

5000

PINE CLIFF
PINE SPGS

500

Bear
Creek
G.C.

CLAY RD
15400
15300

VAN SANT
SCHULZ
EGGLING
DORSLAUF
KUNKLE
STAHMAN
KUNZ
KUNZ
BEAR CREEK
ANKELE
FOX
QUADE
PASCHE
LIERE
KOCH
GOLBOW

BRANDT
SULLINS
WY

HOUSTON

ORANGE BLOSSOM
SILVER
PLUME

15100

15000

CLAY
RD
15100
4400
4300
4200

Bear
Creek
GOLF COURSE

PINE FRST
16100
3900

STATE HWY 6 NORTH

Bear Creek

J
K
L

3300

Houston
Farm & Ranch Club
RANCH

FARM &
RANCH

ABERCROMBIE

COMMUNITY CTR

3100

Bill
Archer
Dog
Park

GROSCHKE
16100
16000

Cemetery

N
P
Q
R

SOCCER
FIELDS

Bear Creek
Pioneers Park

WAR MEMORIAL DR

Wildlife
Habitat And
Aviary

ZORN

Veterans
War
Memorial
Monument

Bear Creek
Pioneers Park

PATTERSON RD
13200
3000

ADDICKS

M

FAIRBANKS RD

Lakes On
Eldridge

N. ELDRIDGE PKWY

ROCK FALLS WY
CORAL
PT

SEE 447 MAP

N

Bear Creek
Langham Creek

6

S
T

ADDICKS - SATSUMA

ADDICKS RESERVOIR
FLOOD CONTROL POOL
ELEVATION 114.0'

South
Mayde
Creek

S.H. 6

HAVIS LN
PRK LINE
1100

W
X
Y
Z

U.S. GOVT RD

PARK ROW

ELDRIDGE PKWY N.
ADDICKS FAIRBANKS

1200

V

1300

228
P&R

RED HAW
1100
Cemetery

JORDEN
RD

600

WICKCHESTER
12100
MORRIS
WD
BRANCH
PRK

0   1/4   1/2   3/4   1 Mile

SEE 488 MAP

© KEY MAPS 2017

© KEY MAPS 2017

GRAND
FLORAL BLVD
FRENSHAM CIR

13600
TWIN LKS
CT
GRAND MASTERPIECE
PILLAR
PRK CIR
HONOR
AMBER
QUEEN
PRISTINE
5300

CLIMBER
KINGS RANSON
GOLD MEDAL
SWEET SURRENDER
OLYMPIAD
SUN BRIGHT
SPARTAN

SHERMONS
POND
CHANDLERS
12700 WY
TANNER
MELVERNHEATHER
TURLOCK

AMERICAN BEAUTY
SUMMER SNOW
SNOW DR
CARROUSEL
SILENT SHR
ISLAND FALLS

BARONS CV

RIDGE PL

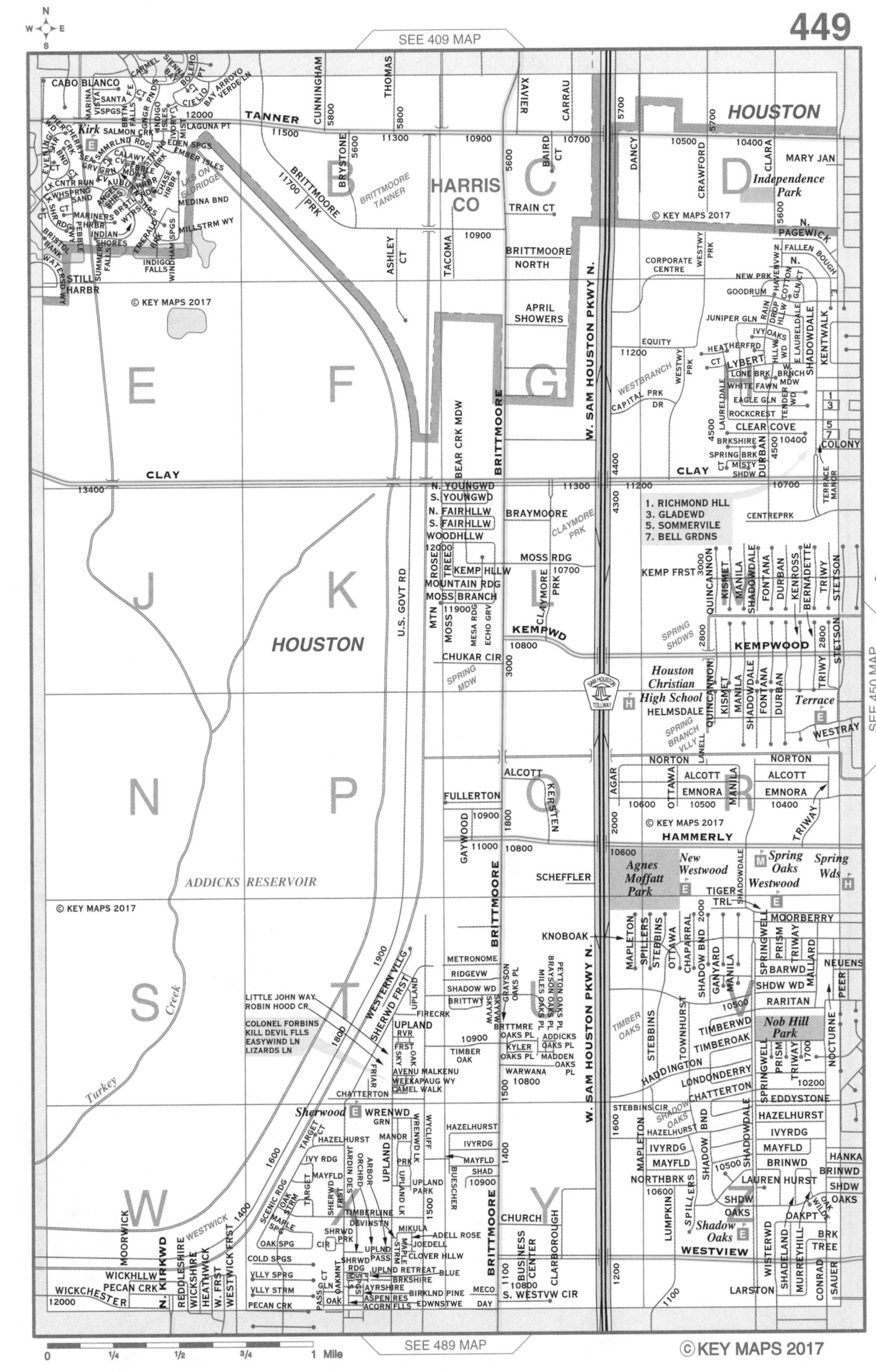

© KEY MAPS 2017

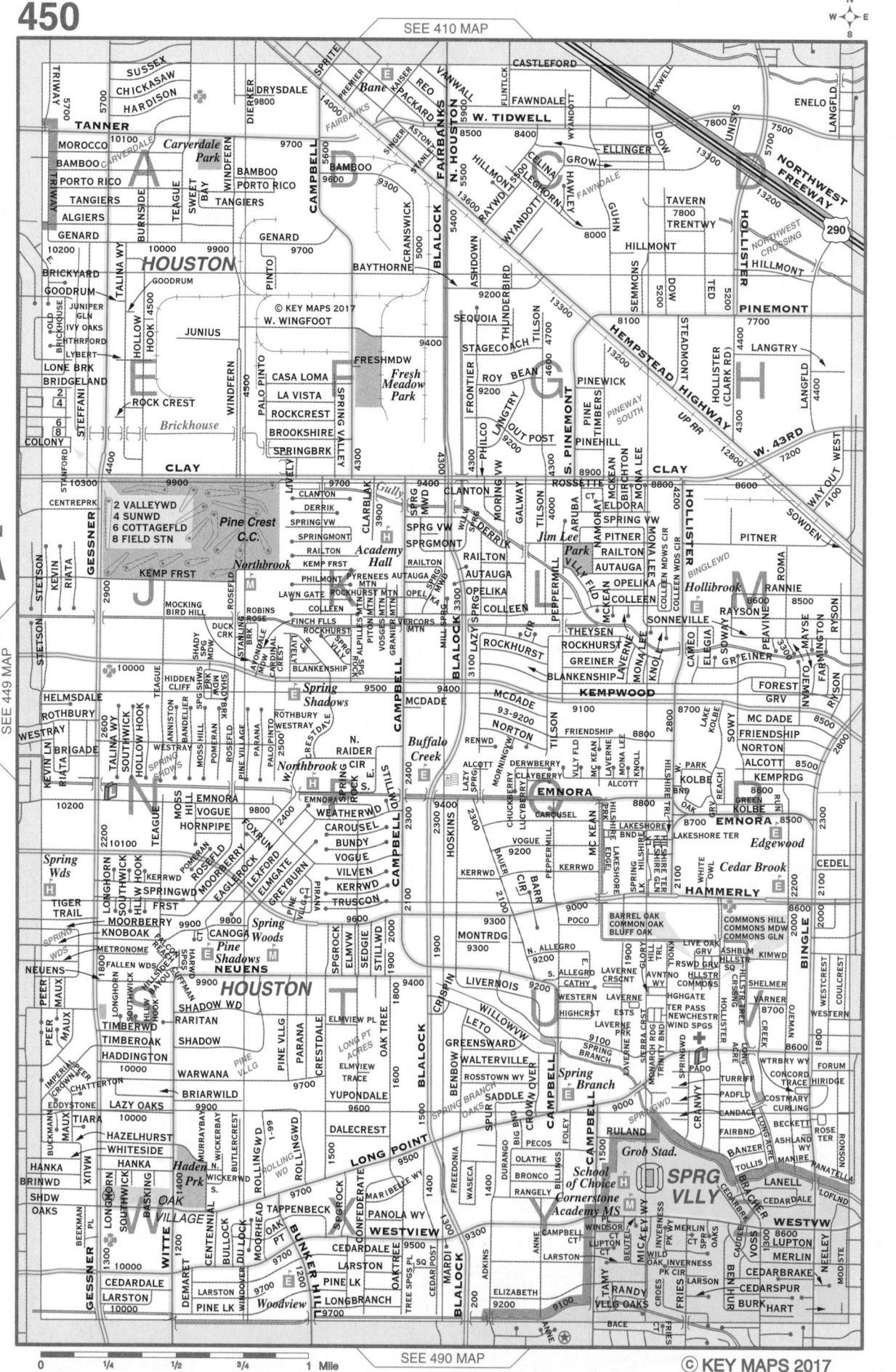

© KEY MAPS 2017

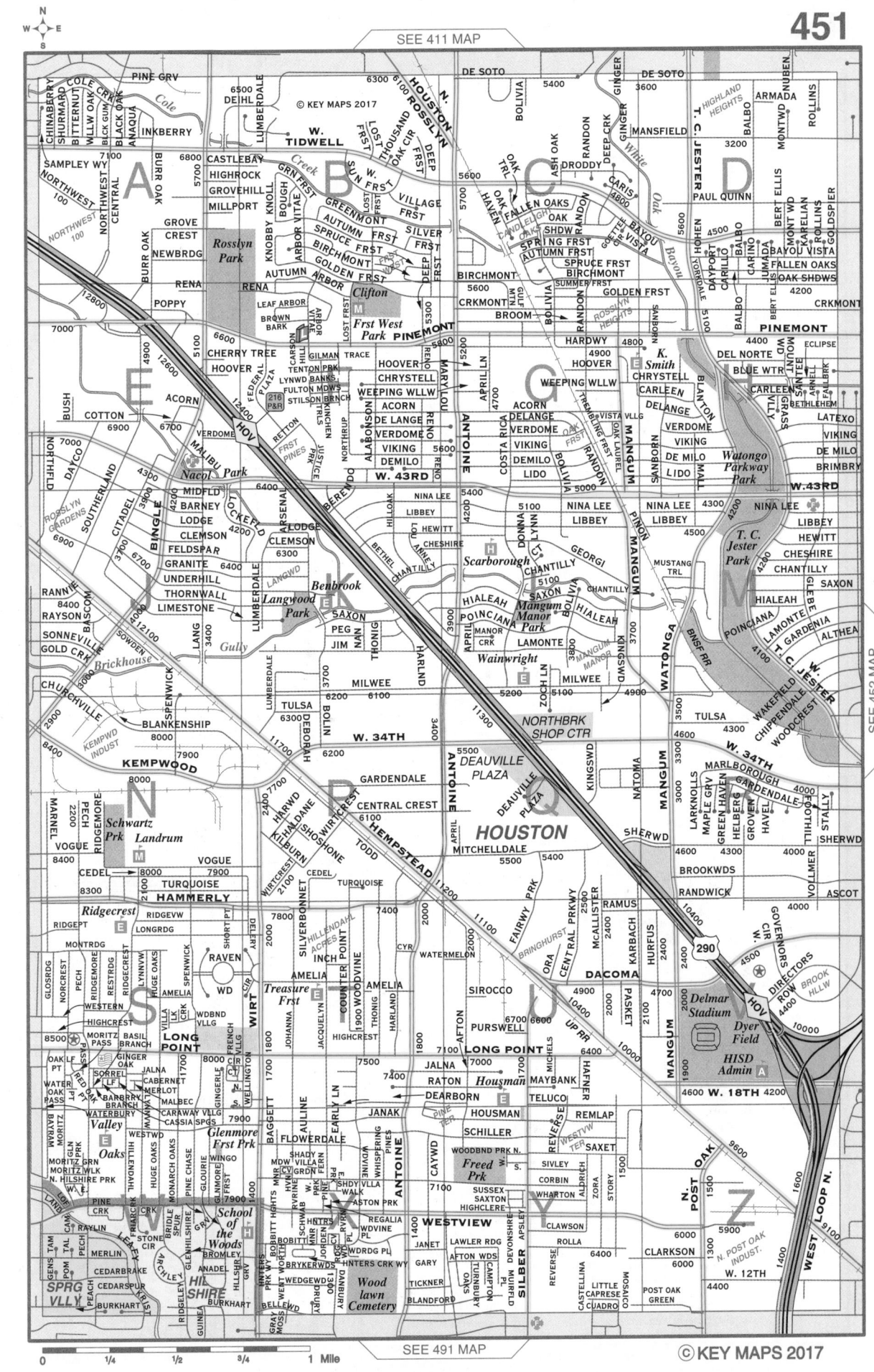

SEE 452 MAP

© KEY MAPS 2017

© KEY MAPS 2017

0   1/4   1/2   3/4   1 Mile

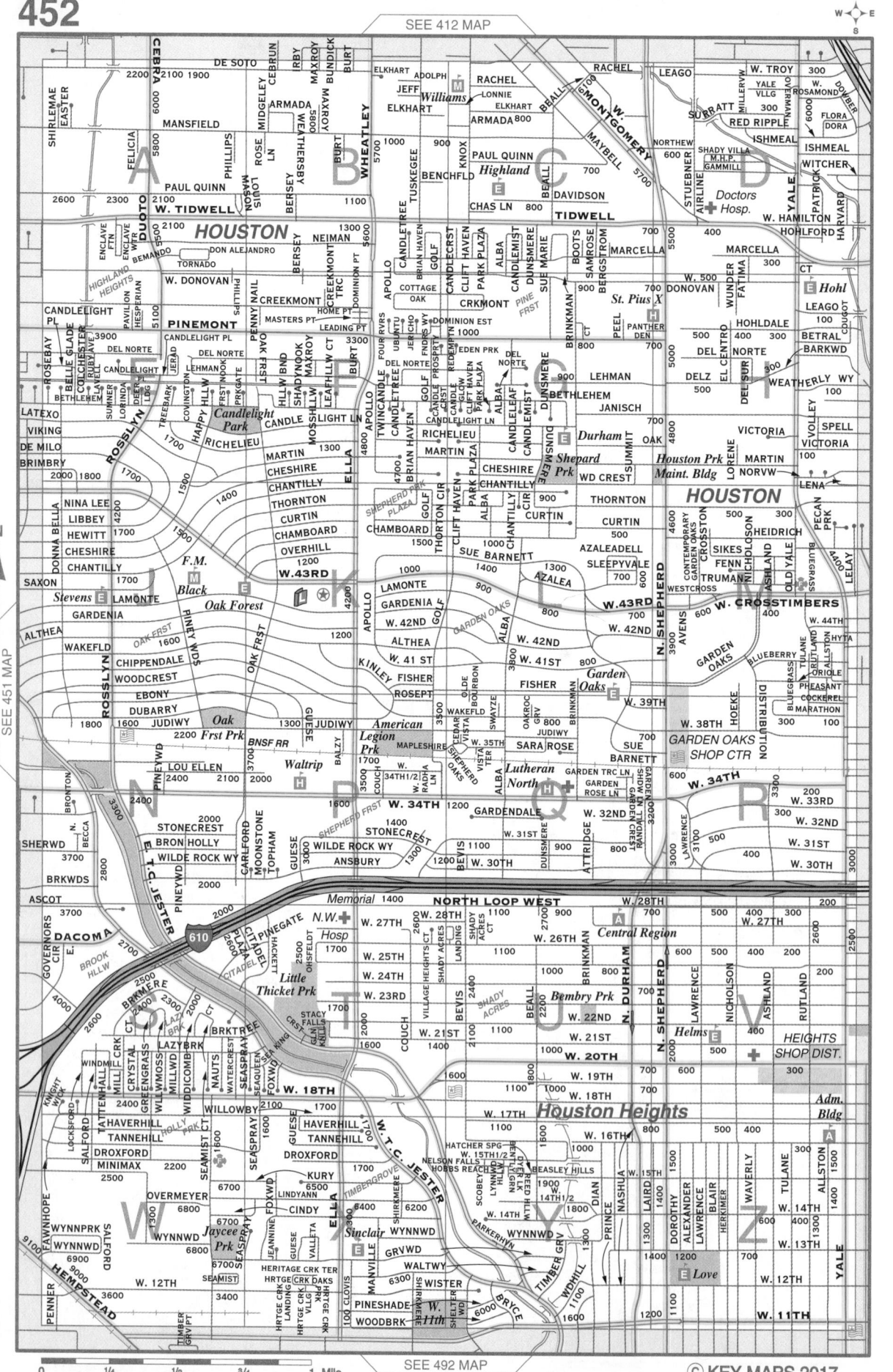

SEE 412 MAP

SEE 451 MAP

SEE 492 MAP

© KEY MAPS 2017

0   1/4   1/2   3/4   1 Mile

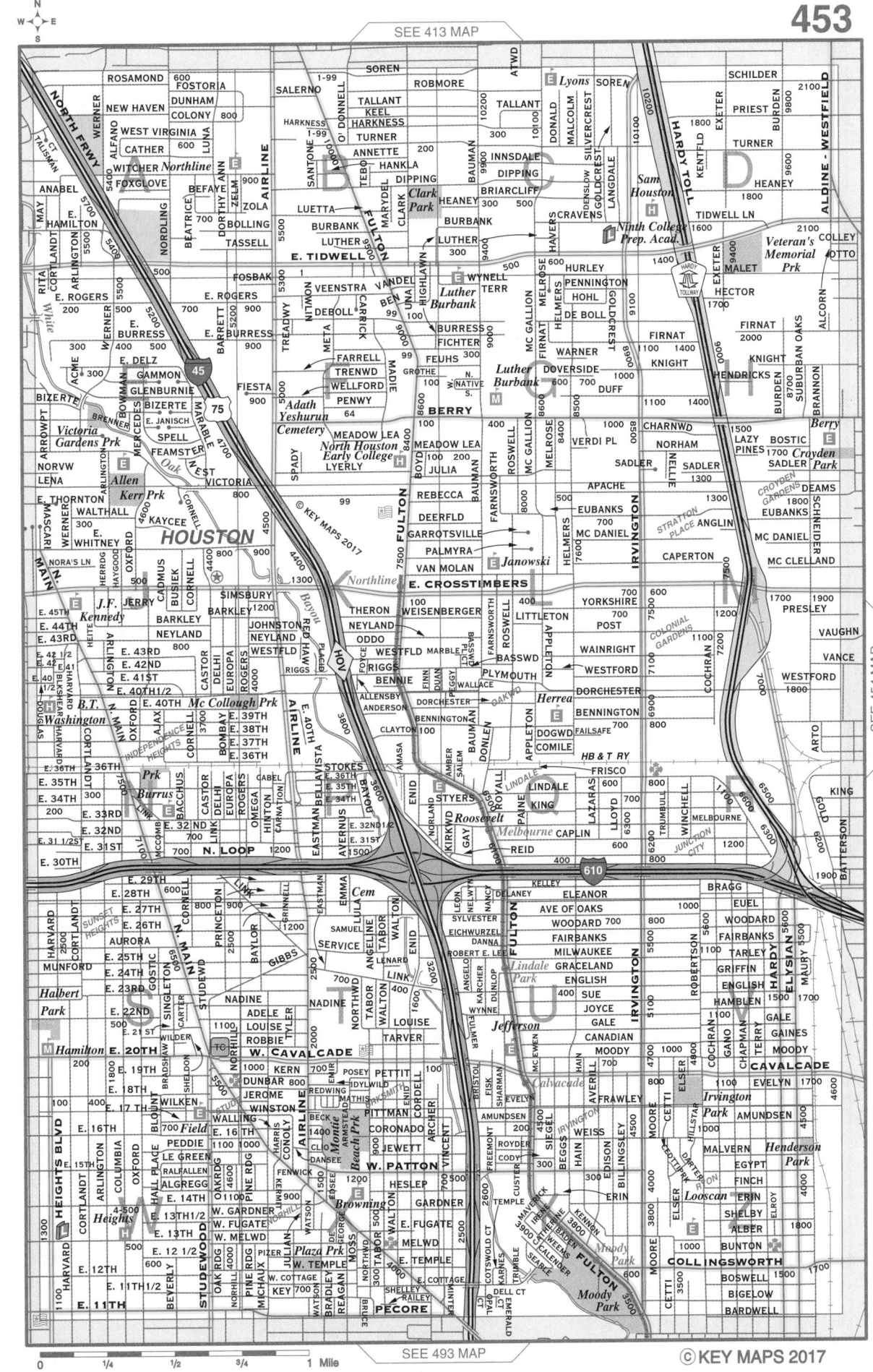

SEE 454 MAP

0   1/4   1/2   3/4   1 Mile

© KEY MAPS 2017

SEE 414 MAP

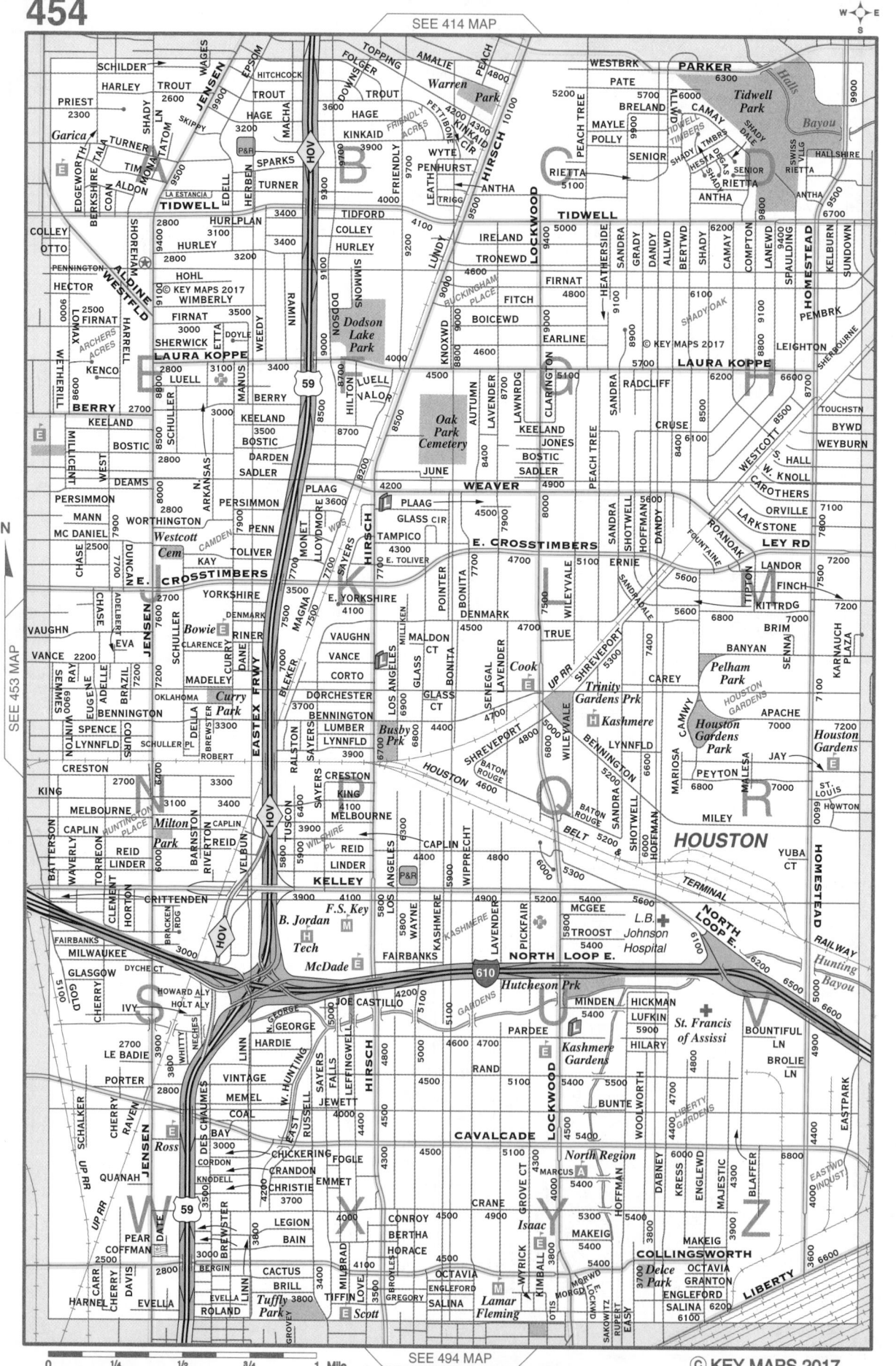

SEE 453 MAP

SEE 494 MAP

0   1/4   1/2   3/4   1 Mile

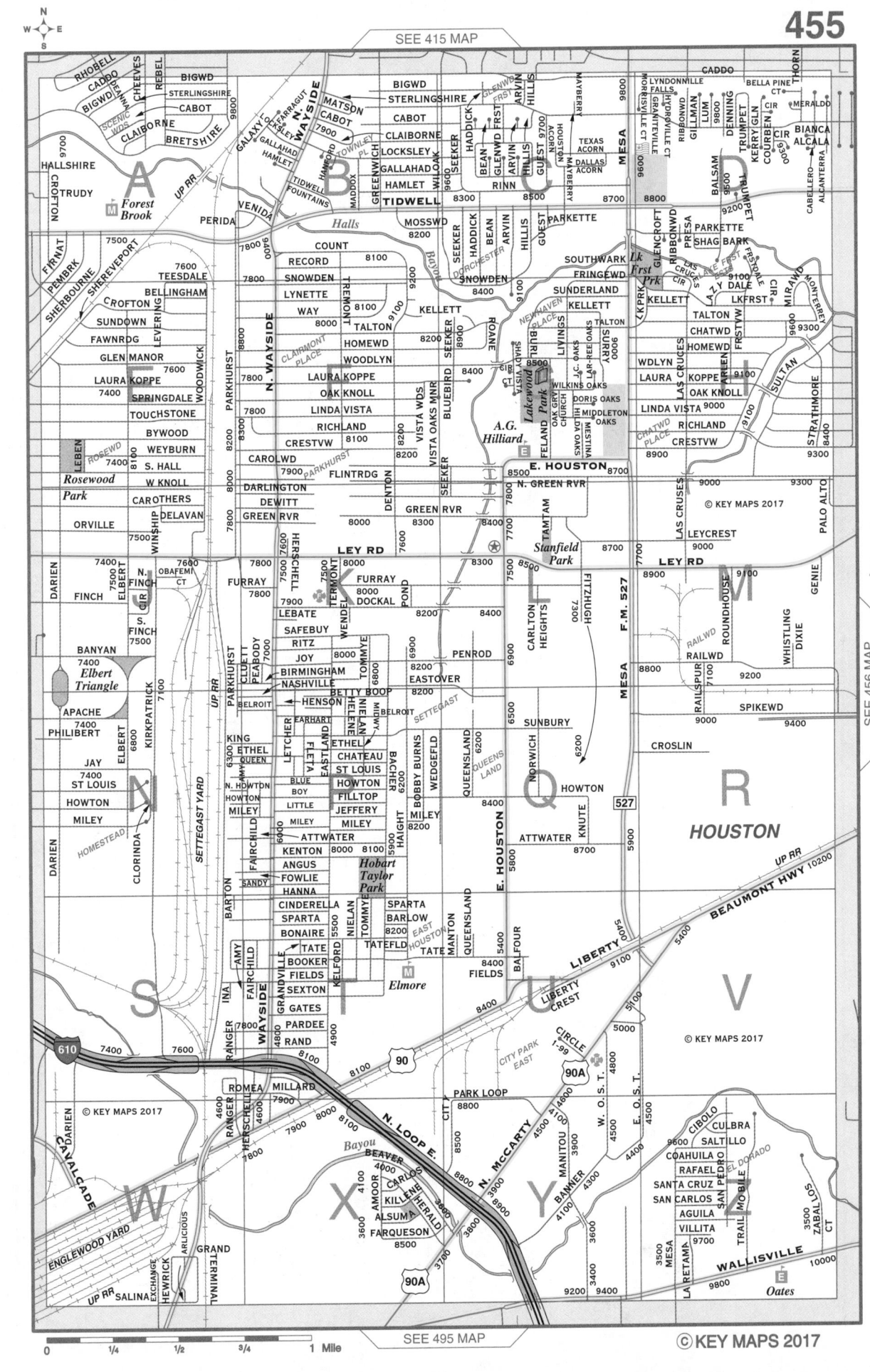

SEE 456 MAP

© KEY MAPS 2017

HOUSTON

0   1/4   1/2   3/4   1 Mile

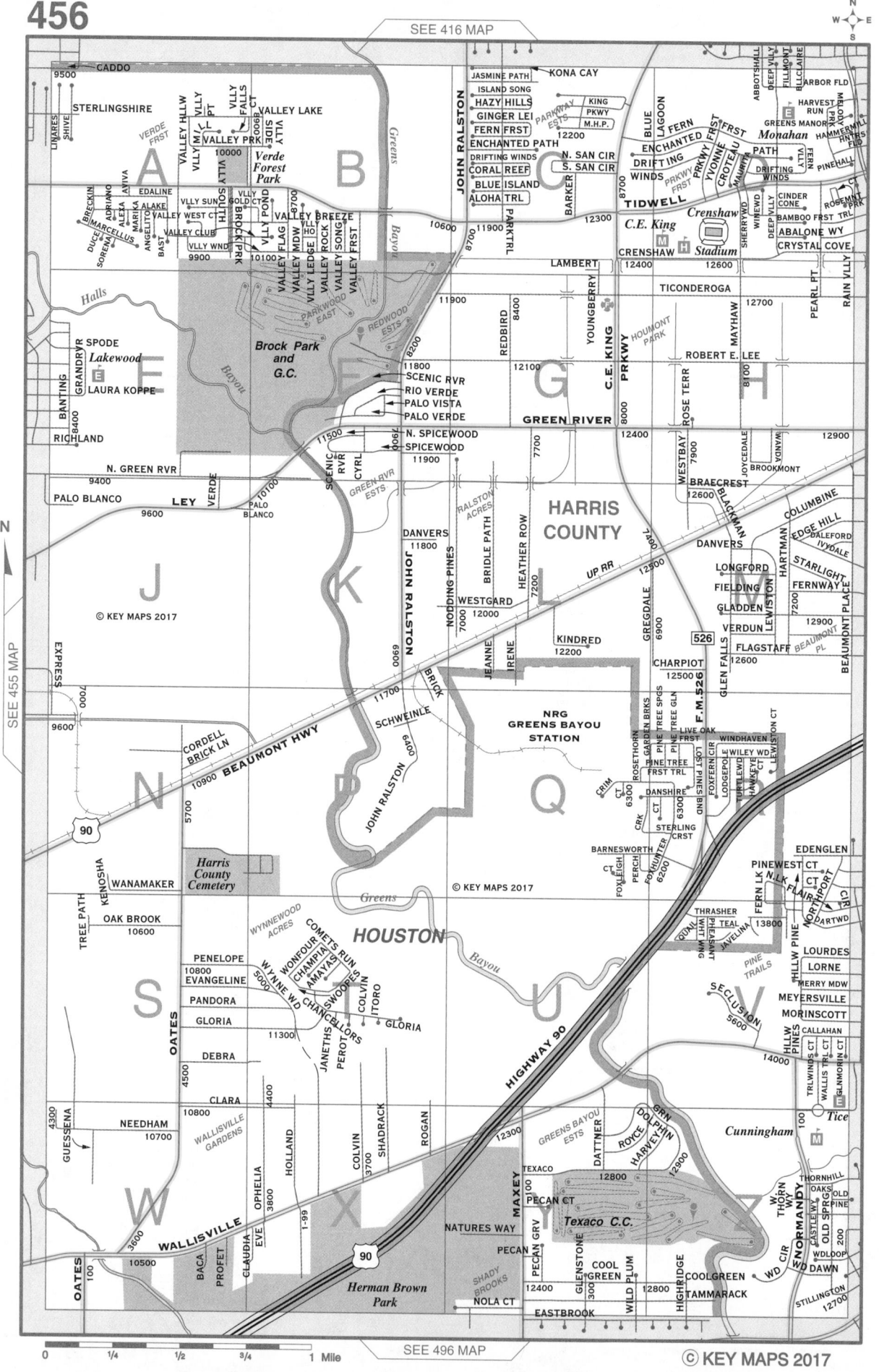

SEE 455 MAP

© KEY MAPS 2017

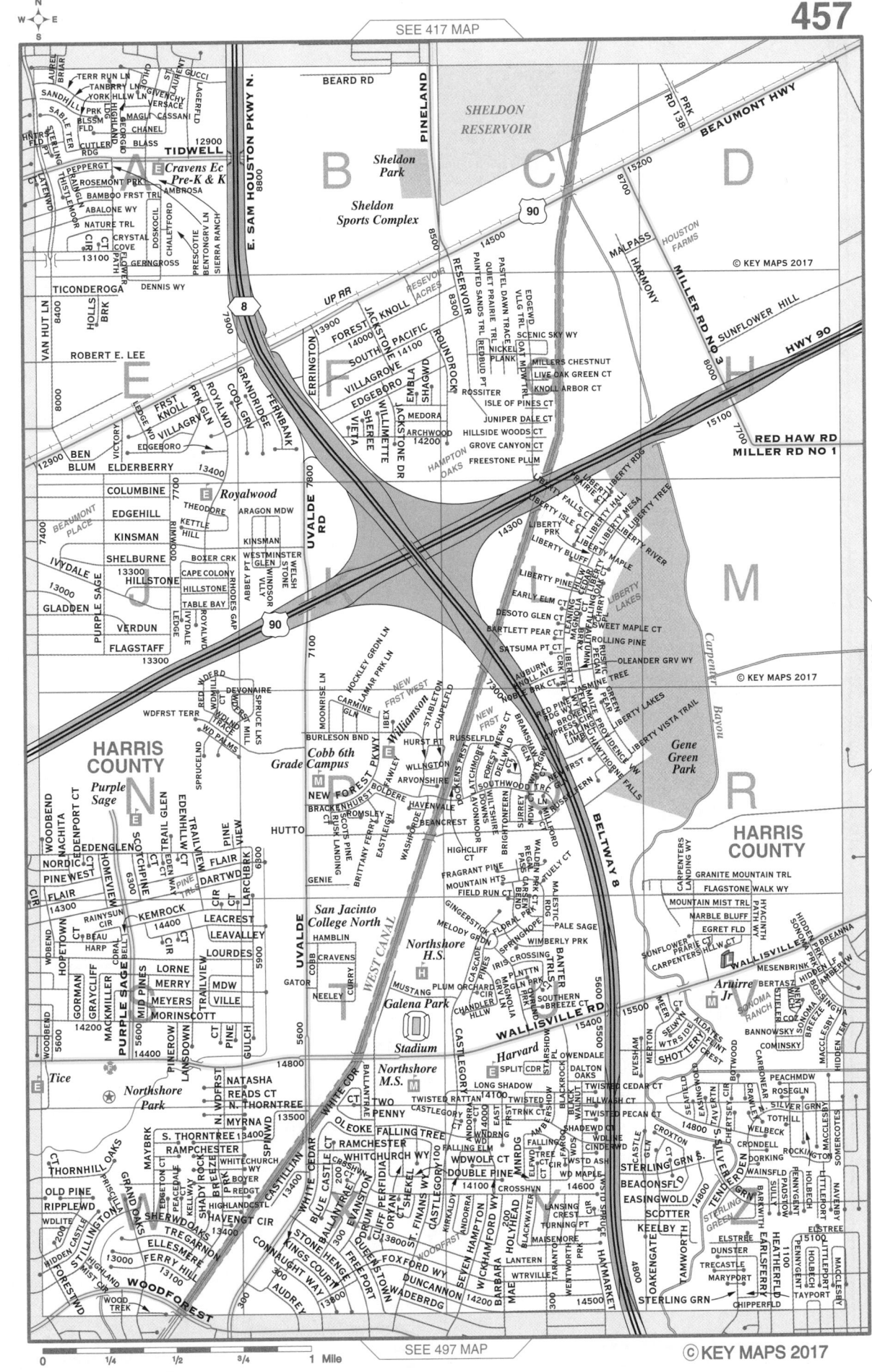

SEE 417 MAP

SEE 458 MAP

SEE 497 MAP

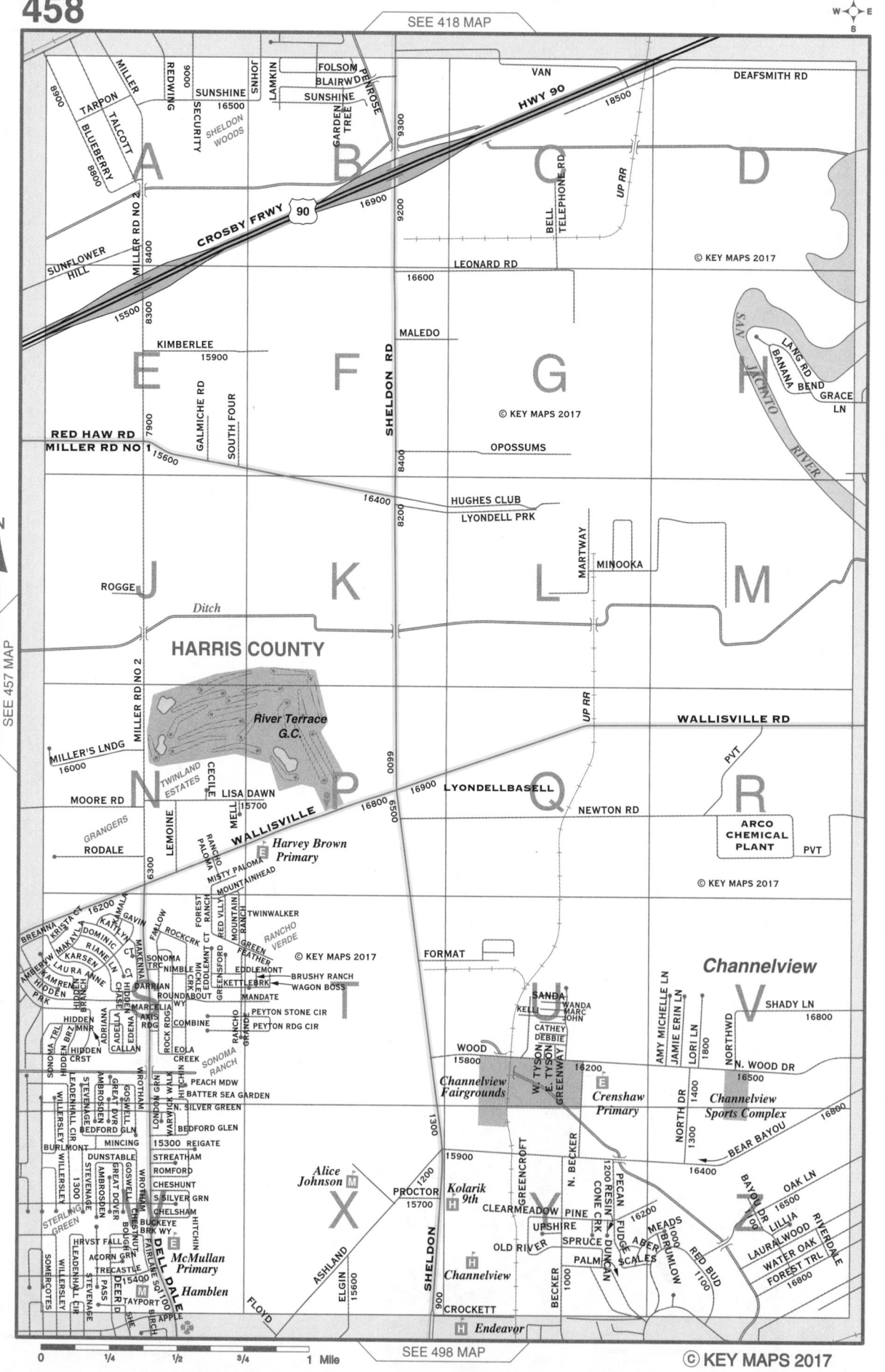

SEE 418 MAP

N
W — E
S

A

8900
TARPON
TALCOTT
BLUEBERRY
8800

MILLER
REDWING
9000
SECURITY
SUNSHINE
16500

JOHNS
LAMKIN
FOLSOM
BLAIRWD
SUNSHINE

GARDEN TREE
PENROSE
BLAIRWD

VAN
DEAFSMITH RD

HWY 90
18500

B

9200
9300

C

BELL TELEPHONE RD

UP RR

D

© KEY MAPS 2017

SUNFLOWER HILL

MILLER RD NO 2
8400
8300
15500

CROSBY FRWY
90
16900

LEONARD RD
16600

MALEDO

SHELDON RD

E

KIMBERLEE
15900

GALMICHE RD
SOUTH FOUR

RED HAW RD
MILLER RD NO 1
9900
15600

F

G

© KEY MAPS 2017

OPOSSUMS
8400

SAN JACINTO RIVER
LANG RD
BANANA
BEND
GRACE LN

H

8200
16400

HUGHES CLUB
LYONDELL PRK

MARTWAY
MINOOKA

J
ROGGE

Ditch

K

L

M

HARRIS COUNTY

MILLER RD NO 2

River Terrace G.C.

TWINLAND ESTATES
CECILE

MILLER'S LNDG
16000

MOORE RD
Grangers
RODALE

N
LEMOINE
6300

LISA DAWN
15700
MELL
RANCHO PALOMA
WALLISVILLE

P
6600
6500
16800
16900

LYONDELLBASELL

UP RR
WALLISVILLE RD

PVT

Q
NEWTON RD

R
ARCO CHEMICAL PLANT
PVT

Harvey Brown Primary

MISTY PALOMA
MOUNTAINHEAD

© KEY MAPS 2017

BREANNA
KRISTA CT
16200
GAVIN
AMBERVW
MAKAY
RIANE LN
DOMINIC
KATHLYN
KARSEN
AMBROSDEN
KAMRENCH
LAURA ANNE
HIDDEN PRK

FARLOW
MAKENNA
SONOMA TRC
NIMBLE
DARRAN
CHASE VW
MARCELIA
AXIS RDG
EDENA
CALLAN

ROCKCRK
FOREST CT RANCH
EDDLEMNT CT
FEATHER
GREEN
CRK
KETTLEBRK
COMBINE
EOLA CREEK
ROCK RDG
SONOMA RANCH

RED VLLY
MOUNTAIN RANCH
GRNSFORD
MANDATE
RANCHO GRAND

TWINWALKER
RANCHO VERDE

EDDLEMONT
BRUSHY RANCH
WAGON BOSS
PEYTON STONE CIR
PEYTON RDG CIR

FORMAT

Channelview

S
T

ADRIANA
BRZ
MNR
HIDDEN CRST
SONOMA TRL
HIDDEN

PEACH MDW
BATTER SEA GARDEN
N. SILVER GREEN
BEDFORD GLEN

SANDA
KELLI
WANDA
MARC
JOHN
CATHEY
DEBBIE
W. TYSON
E. TYSON
GREENWAY

AMY MICHELLE LN
JAMIE ERIN LN
LORI LN
NORTHWD

V
SHADY LN
16800

N. WOOD DR
16500

WROTHAM
HITCHIN
NGN NGON
WARWICK WALK
LEADENHALL WY
STEVENAGE
AMBROSDEN
GOSWELL
GREAT DVR
BEDFORD GLN
MINCING
15300
REIGATE
STREATHAM
ROMFORD
CHESHUNT
CHELSHAM
BURLMONT
DUNSTABLE
WILLERSLEY
1300
WILLERSLEY
STEVENAGE
GOSWELL
GREAT DOVER
S SILVER GRN
CHESTNUT
BOLINGBR
BUCKEYE

WOOD
15800

Channelview Fairgrounds

Crenshaw Primary

N. WOOD DR
NORTH DR
1400
1300
16400

Channelview Sports Complex

BEAR BAYOU
16800

X
Alice Johnson
M
PROCTOR
15700

Kolarik 9th
H
CLEARMEADOW
15900

GREENCROFT
N. BECKER
1200
PECAN
RESIN
CONE CRK
DUNCAN
1200
PINE
UPSHIRE
16200
SPRUCE
AMBER
MEADS
SCALES
PALM
1000
FUDGE
BRUMLOW
GOSLMW

Z
OAK LN
16500
LILLIA
LAURALWOOD
WATER OAK
FOREST TRL
RIVERDALE
16800
BAYOU DR
RED BUD
1100

STERLING GREEN

HRVST FALL
ACORN GRN
TRECASTLE
HLEADENHALL CIR
WILLERSLEY
SOMERCOTES

McMullan Primary
Hamblen

M
DEER LN
TAYPORT
BIRCH
APPLE
PASS

DELL DALE
FAIRLAND
SHE
SOT
15400

Y
ASHLAND
ELGIN
15600

SHELDON
900

15900
Old River
Channelview
H
CROCKETT

BECKER

Endeavor
H

SEE 498 MAP

0   1/4   1/2   3/4   1 Mile

© **KEY MAPS** 2017

SEE 457 MAP

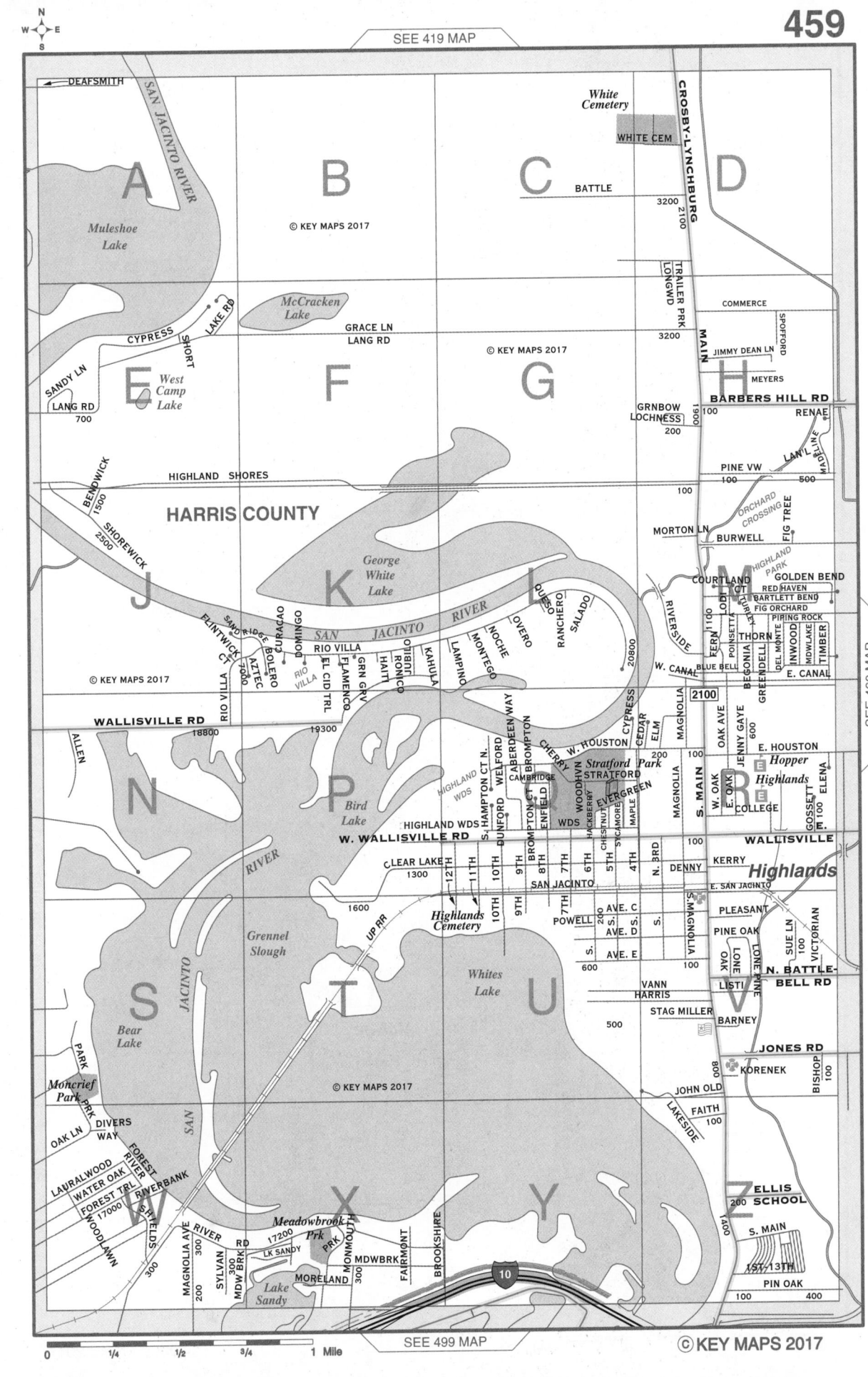

N
W E
S

DEAFSMITH

SAN JACINTO RIVER

A

Muleshoe
Lake

© KEY MAPS 2017

B

C

White
Cemetery

WHITE CEM

BATTLE

3200   2100

D

CROSBY-LYNCHBURG

TRAILER PRK
LONGWD

3200

MAIN

COMMERCE
SPOFFORD

Jimmy Dean Ln
MEYERS

H

BARBERS HILL RD

RENAE

MADLINE

LAN'L

McCracken
Lake

GRACE LN
LANG RD

CYPRESS

SHORT

LAKE RD

SANDY LN

LANG RD
700

E

West
Camp
Lake

F

© KEY MAPS 2017

G

GRNBOW
LOCHNESS
200

1900 100

PINE VW

100   500

100

ORCHARD
CROSSING

FIG TREE

BENDWICK
1500

HIGHLAND SHORES

HARRIS COUNTY

George
White
Lake

MORTON LN
BURWELL

HIGHLAND PARK

COURTLAND

GOLDEN BEND
RED HAVEN
BARTLETT BEND
FIG ORCHARD

SHOREWICK
2500

J

FLINTWICK
CT

SAND RIDGE

CURACAO

DOMINGO

BOLERO

AZTEC

RIO VILLA

K

RIO VILLA

EL CID TRL

FLAMENCO

GRN GRV

HAITI

RONCO

OTIBINI

KAHULA

LAMPINO

SAN   JACINTO   RIVER

MONTEGO

NOCHE

OVERO

RANCHERO

SALADO

QUEO
ROSO

20800

RIVERSIDE

M

FERN

LODI

1100

POINSETTA

BLUE BELL

BEGONIA

GREENDELL

DEL MONTE

THORN

INWOOD

MIDWLAKE

TIMBER

PIPING ROCK

E. CANAL

W. CANAL

2100

© KEY MAPS 2017

WALLISVILLE RD
18800   19300

ALLEN

N

P

Bird
Lake

RIVER

S

JACINTO

Grennel
Slough

T

Bear
Lake

Moncrief
Park

PARK

PRK

OAK LN

DIVERS
WAY

LAURALWOOD

WATER OAK

FOREST TRL

FOREST

RIVER

RIVERBANK

SHIELDS

WOODLAWN

17000

300

MAGNOLIA AVE

SYLVAN

RIVER

MDW BRK

300

LK SANDY

200

300

Lake
Sandy

MORELAND

Meadowbrook
Prk

X

PRK

MONMOUTH

MDWBRK

300

FAIRMONT

BROOKSHIRE

HIGHLAND
WDS

HIGHLAND WDS

W. WALLISVILLE RD

CLEAR LAKE
1300

1600

UP RR

Highlands
Cemetery

SAN JACINTO

HAMPTON CT N.
WELFORD
DUNFORD
CABERDEEN WAY
BROMPTON
CAMBRIDGE
BROMPTON CT
ENFIELD

12TH

11TH

10TH

9TH

8TH

7TH

WDS

CHERRY

WOODVIN

HACKBERRY

CHESTNUT

SYCAMORE

EVERGREEN

MAPLE

W. HOUSTON

CEDAR

ELM

Stratford Park
STRATFORD

MAGNOLIA

200

100

6TH

5TH

4TH

N. 3RD

DENNY

10TH

9TH

7TH

POWELL

AVE. C

AVE. D

AVE. E

200

600

S.

S.

S.

S.

100

MAGNOLIA

S. MAIN

OAK AVE

W. OAK

E. OAK

JENNY GAYE

600

E. HOUSTON

Hopper
Highlands

COLLEGE

GOSSETT

ELENA

E. 100

E.

WALLISVILLE

KERRY

E. SAN JACINTO

PLEASANT

PINE OAK

LONE OAK

LONE PINE

SUE LN

VICTORIAN

100

Highlands

N. BATTLE-
BELL RD

LISTI

VANN
HARRIS

STAG MILLER

500

BARNEY

JONES RD

JOHN OLD

KORENEK

LAKESIDE

FAITH
100

800

BISHOP
100

Z

ELLIS
SCHOOL

200

S. MAIN

1ST-13TH

1400

PIN OAK

100   400

W

V

Whites
Lake

U

Y

10

© KEY MAPS 2017

SEE 499 MAP

SEE 460 MAP

N

WALLISVILLE RD

0   1/4   1/2   3/4   1 Mile

© KEY MAPS 2017

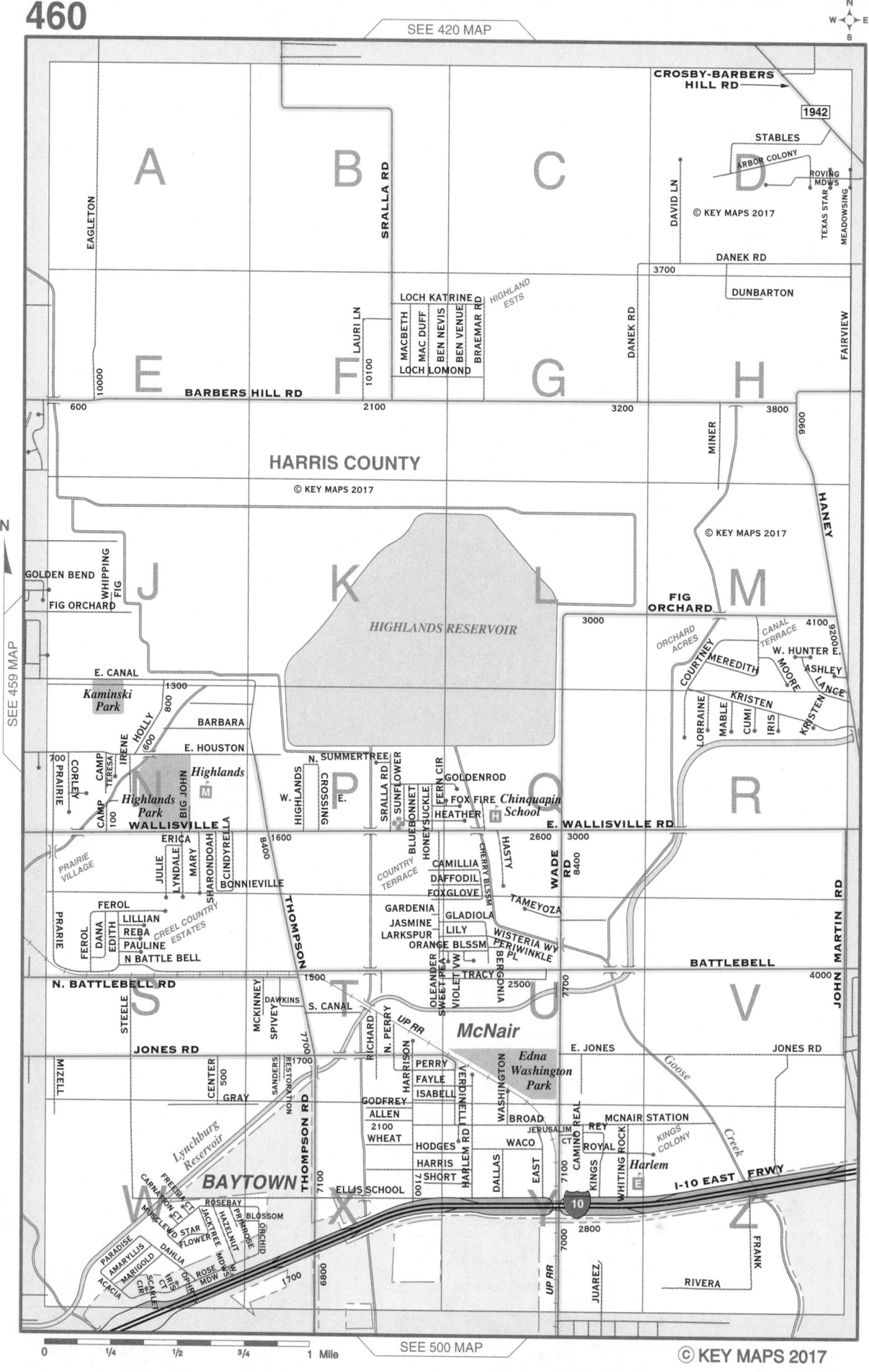

460

SEE 420 MAP

N
W E
S

CROSBY-BARBERS
HILL RD →

1942

A   B   C   D

SRALLA RD

STABLES

ARBOR COLONY

ROVING
MDWS

EAGLETON

DAVID LN

© KEY MAPS 2017

TEXAS STAR

MEADOWSING

DANEK RD

3700

DUNBARTON

LOCH KATRINE

HIGHLAND
ESTS

LAURI LN

MACBETH
MAC DUFF
BEN NEVIS
BEN VENUE
BRAEMAR RD

HIGHLAND RD

DANEK RD

FAIRVIEW

E   F   G   H

10000

10100

BARBERS HILL RD

600   2100   3200   3800

9900

MINER

HANEY

HARRIS COUNTY

© KEY MAPS 2017

© KEY MAPS 2017

N

GOLDEN BEND

WHIPPING
FIG

J   K   L   M

FIG ORCHARD

SEE 459 MAP

HIGHLANDS RESERVOIR

FIG
ORCHARD

3000

4100

92200

ORCHARD
ACRES

CANAL
TERRACE

E. CANAL

COURTNEY

MEREDITH

W. HUNTER E.

MOORE

ASHLEY

LANCE

1300

800

Kaminski
Park

BARBARA

KRISTEN

LORRAINE

MABLE

CUMI

IRIS

KRISTEN

Highlands
Park

E. HOUSTON

N. SUMMERTREE

SUNFLOWER

GOLDENROD

IRENE
HOLLY

600

CORLEY

CAMP
TERESA

BIG JOHN

N

Highlands

M

HIGHLANDS

W.
HIGHLANDS

CROSSING

E.

SRALLA RD

BLUEBONNET

HONEYSUCKLE

FERN CIR

FOX FIRE

HEATHER

Chinquapin
School

H

R

700
PRAIRIE

CAMP

100

WALLISVILLE

CINDYRELLA

GOLDENROD

E. WALLISVILLE RD

2600   3000

ERICA

JULIE

LYNDALE

MARY

SHARONDOAH

BONNIEVILLE

8400

1600

COUNTRY
TERRACE

CAMILLIA

DAFFODIL

FOXGLOVE

CHERRY BLSSM

HASTY

TAMEYOZA

WADE RD

8400

PRAIRIE
VILLAGE

FEROL

FEROL
DANA
EDITH

LILLIAN
REBA
PAULINE

N BATTLE BELL

CREEL COUNTRY
ESTATES

THOMPSON

GARDENIA

JASMINE

LARKSPUR

ORANGE BLSSM

GLADIOLA

LILY

WISTERIA WY

PERIWINKLE
PL

BERGONIA

BATTLEBELL

JOHN MARTIN RD

4000

PRAIRIE

THOMPSON

OLEANDER

SWEET PEA

VIOLET VW

TRACY

2500

2700

N. BATTLEBELL RD

1500

S   T   U   V

STEELE

MCKINNEY

SPIVEY

DAWKINS

S. CANAL

RICHARD

N. PERRY

UP RR

McNair

E. JONES

JONES RD

JONES RD

MIZELL

CENTER

500

SANDERS

PRESTON

1700

HARRISON

PERRY

FAYLE

ISABELLI

VERDINE

Edna
Washington
Park

WASHINGTON

GRAY

GODFREY

ALLEN

2100

WHEAT

BROAD

JERUSALEM

CAMINO REAL

REY

ROYAL

McNAIR STATION

WHITING ROCK

KINGS
COLONY

Lynchburg
Reservoir

HODGES

HARRIS

SHORT

HARLEM RD

WACO

DALLAS

EAST

KINGS

7100

Harlem

E

I-10 EAST FRWY

BAYTOWN

THOMPSON RD

7100

ELLIS SCHOOL

7100

W   X   Y   Z

ROSEBAY

BLOSSOM

ORCHID

HAZELNUT

JACKTREE

MDWS

Goose Creek

FREESIA

CARNATION

MUSELAND

RED STAR

FLOWER

PRIMROSE

10

2800

FRANK

PARADISE

AMARYLLIS

MARIGOLD

DAHLIA

ROSE

MDW

SCARLET
CIR

OPHELIA

ACACIA

1700

JUAREZ

7000

UP RR

RIVERA

0   1/4   1/2   3/4   1 Mile

SEE 500 MAP

© KEY MAPS 2017

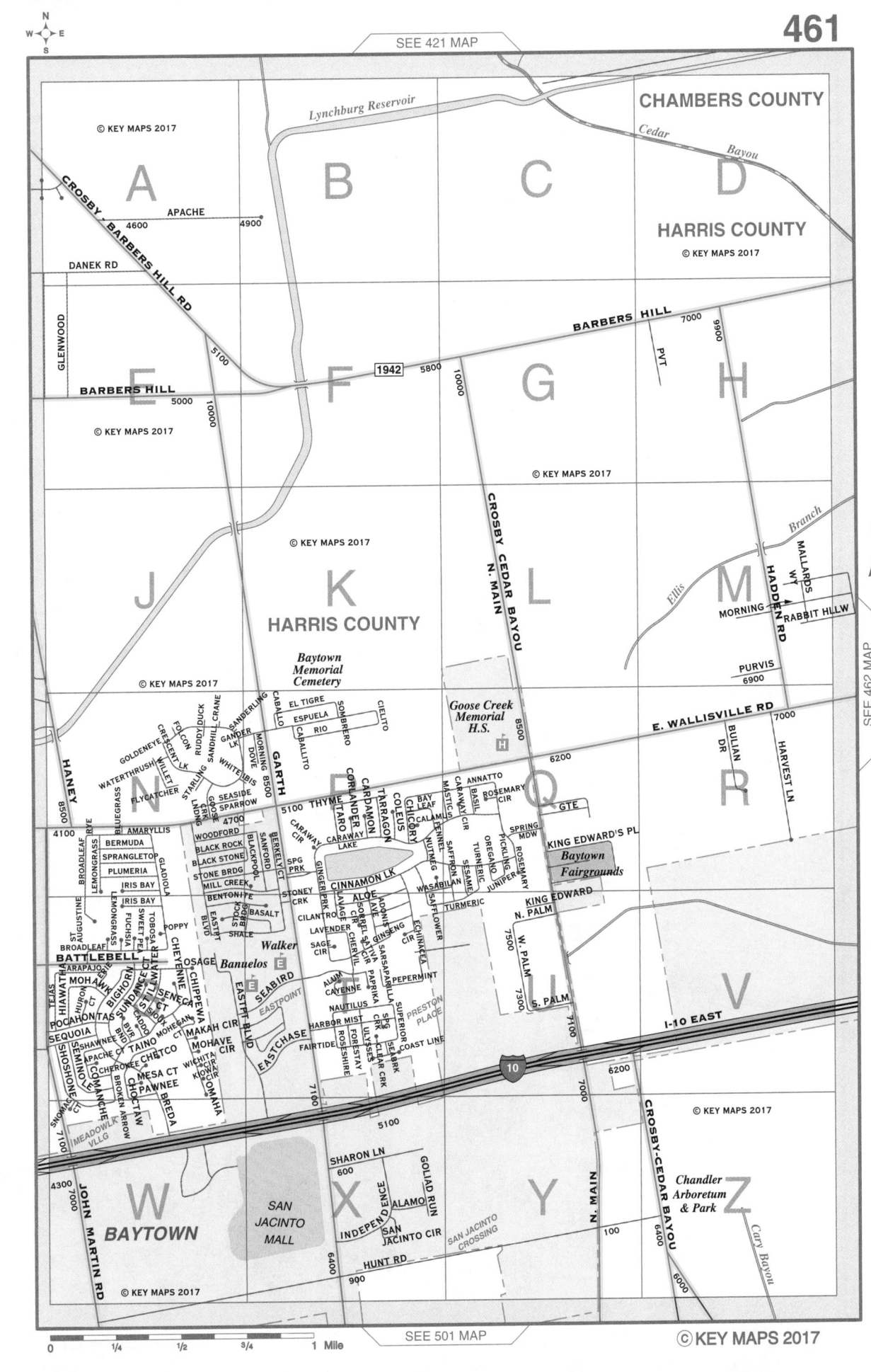

CHAMBERS COUNTY

Lynchburg Reservoir

Cedar Bayou

HARRIS COUNTY

© KEY MAPS 2017

A

APACHE
4600 4900

CROSBY - BARBERS HILL RD

DANEK RD

GLENWOOD

BARBERS HILL
5000
10000

E

5100

1942 5800

F

B

BARBERS HILL 7000
9900
PVT

C

D

© KEY MAPS 2017

G

H

© KEY MAPS 2017

© KEY MAPS 2017

CROSBY CEDAR BAYOU
N. MAIN

Ellis

Branch

MALLARDS WY

MORNING

HADDEN RD

RABBIT HLLW

M

PURVIS
6900

J

HARRIS COUNTY

K

Baytown
Memorial
Cemetery

© KEY MAPS 2017

L

Goose Creek
Memorial H.S.

8500

E. WALLISVILLE RD 7000

6200

R

BULIAN DR

HARVEST LN

© KEY MAPS 2017

HANEY
8500
4100

GARTH

CABALLO
EL TIGRE
ESPUELA
CABALLITO
RIO

SOMBRERO

CIELITO

GOLDENEYE
WATERTHRUSH
BLUEGRASS
FLYCATCHER

CRESCENT LK
FALCON
RUDDY DUCK
SANDHILL CRANE
SANDERLING
WHITE IBIS
DOVE
MORNING 8500
GOOSE LNDG
SEASIDE SPARROW
STARLING
WILLET

GANDER LK

THYME

CORRIANDER
CARDAMON
TARRAGON
COLEUS
CHICORY

ANNATTO
BASIL

CARAWAY CIR

ROSEMARY CIR

GTE

N

AMARYLLIS

WOODFORD
BLACK ROCK
BLACK STONE
STONE BRDG
MILL CREEK
BENTONITE

SANFORD
BLACKPOOL
BERKELY CT

5100

CARAWAY CIR

CARAWAY LAKE

BAY LEAF
MASTICS
FENNEL
NUTMEG
SAFFRON
SESAME

ROSEMARY

SPRING MDW

KING EDWARD'S PL

Q

Baytown
Fairgrounds

BROADLEAF
BERMUDA
SPRANGLETO
PLUMERIA
IRIS BAY

LEMONGRASS
GLADIOLA

IRIS BAY

ST AUGUSTINE
FUCHSIA
SWEET PEA
LEMONGRASS
BROADLEAF

TOBOSA
POPPY

SPG PRK
STONEY CRK

CINNAMON LK

ALOE

BASALT
STOCK
SHALE

CILANTRO
LAVENDER
SAGE CIR

GINGER PRK
SORREL CIR
SILVA
LUVAGE
CHERVIL

GINSENG
ADONIS
SARSAPARILLA
PAPRIKA

TURNERIC
OREGANO
JUNIPER

WASABILAN

TURMERIC

PEPPERMINT

SPRING MDW

KING EDWARD

N. PALM

W. PALM
7500

7300

S. PALM

BATTLEBELL

MOHAWK
HIAWATHA
POCAHONTAS
SEQUOIA
SHOSHONE
SEMINO

TEJAS
HURON
BIGHORN
SUNDANCE CT
OSAGE
CHEYENNE

ARAPAJO
SENECA
CHIPPEWA

MAKAH CIR

Walker

Bannuelos E

EAST PT BLVD

SEABIRD

EASTPOINT

EASTCHASE

ALUM
CAYENNE
NAUTILUS
HARBOR MIST
FAIRTIDE

SAGE CIR
ADONIS

SEA BRK

ULYSSES
ROSSSHIRE
FORESTAY

SUPERIOR
CLEAR CRK
COAST LINE

Preston Place

I-10 EAST

6200

V

10

I

© KEY MAPS 2017

SNOMAC CT
MEADOWLK VLLG
4300 7000

JOHN MARTIN RD

SAN JACINTO MALL

W

BAYTOWN

SHARON LN
600

INDEPENDENCE

GOLIAD RUN
ALAMO
SAN JACINTO CIR

SAN JACINTO CROSSING

HUNT RD
900

X

5100

Y

N. MAIN
7000
100

CROSBY-CEDAR BAYOU

Chandler
Arboretum
& Park

Z

Cary Bayou

6400
6000

© KEY MAPS 2017

0   1/4   1/2   3/4   1 Mile

© **KEY MAPS** 2017

SEE LC 422 MAP

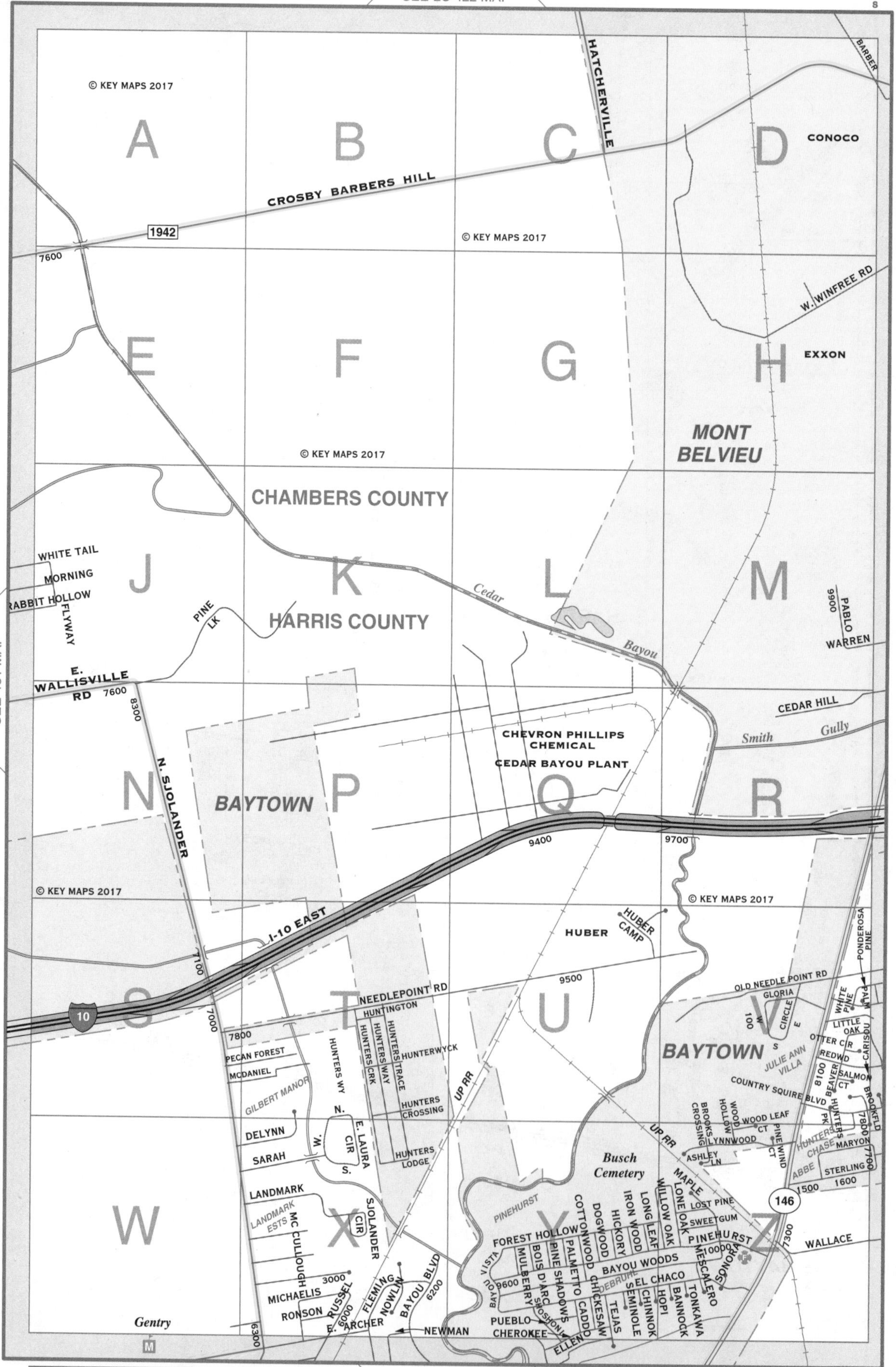

© KEY MAPS 2017

A

B

C

D CONOCO

HATCHERVILLE

BARBER

CROSBY BARBERS HILL

1942

7600

© KEY MAPS 2017

W. WINFREE RD

E

F

G

H EXXON

MONT BELVIEU

CHAMBERS COUNTY

© KEY MAPS 2017

N

SEE 461 MAP

WHITE TAIL

MORNING

RABBIT HOLLOW

FLYWAY

J

PINE LK

HARRIS COUNTY

K

Cedar

L

Bayou

M

9900 PABLO

WARREN

E. WALLISVILLE RD

7600

8300

N. SJOLANDER

N

CHEVRON PHILLIPS CHEMICAL

CEDAR BAYOU PLANT

CEDAR HILL

Smith Gully

BAYTOWN

P

Q

R

© KEY MAPS 2017

9400

9700

© KEY MAPS 2017

PONDEROSA PINE

T7100

I-10 EAST

HUBER CAMP

HUBER

OLD NEEDLE POINT RD

10

S

7000

NEEDLEPOINT RD

7800

HUNTINGTON

PECAN FOREST

MCDANIEL

GILBERT MANOR

HUNTERS WY

HUNTERS CRK

HUNTERS WAY

HUNTERS TRACE

HUNTERWYCK

UP RR

9500

U

BAYTOWN

GLORIA

100 CIRCLE S

WHITE OAK

LITTLE OAK CIR

CARISBU

OTTER CIR

REDWD

SALMON CT

JULIE ANN VILLA

8100 BEAVER

BRONKFLD

7800

DELYNN

N. W. CIR

E. LAURA CIR

S.

HUNTERS CROSSING

HUNTERS LODGE

COUNTRY SQUIRE BLVD

BROOKS CROSSING

WOOD HOLLOW

WOOD LEAF CT

PINEWIND CT

HUNTERS PK

CHASE

MARYON

7700

SARAH

LANDMARK

LYNNWOOD

ASHLEY LN

ABBE

STERLING

W

LANDMARK ESTS

MC CULLOUGH

X

SJOLANDER CIR

Busch Cemetery

PINEHURST

MAPLE

WILLOW OAK

LONE OAK

LONG LEAF

IRON WOOD

SWEET GUM

LOST PINE

PINEWIND

1500

1600

146

7300

WALLACE

Z

MICHAELIS

3000

RUSSEL

FLEMING

NOWLIN

BAYOU BLVD

6200

FOREST HOLLOW

BAYOU VISTA

PINE SHADOWS

PALMETTO

COTTONWOOD

DOGWOOD

HICKORY

PESCADO

MESCALERO

SONORA

RONSON

E. 6000 ARCHER

NEWMAN

9600

BOIS D'ARC

MULBERRY

SHOSHONE

CADDO

CHICKESAW

DEBRUHL

BAYOU WOODS

EL CHACO

SEMINOLE

TEJAS

CHINOOK

HOPI

TONKAWA

BANNOCK

Gentry

6300

PUEBLO

CHEROKEE

ELLEN

0 1/4 1/2 3/4 1 Mile

© KEY MAPS 2017

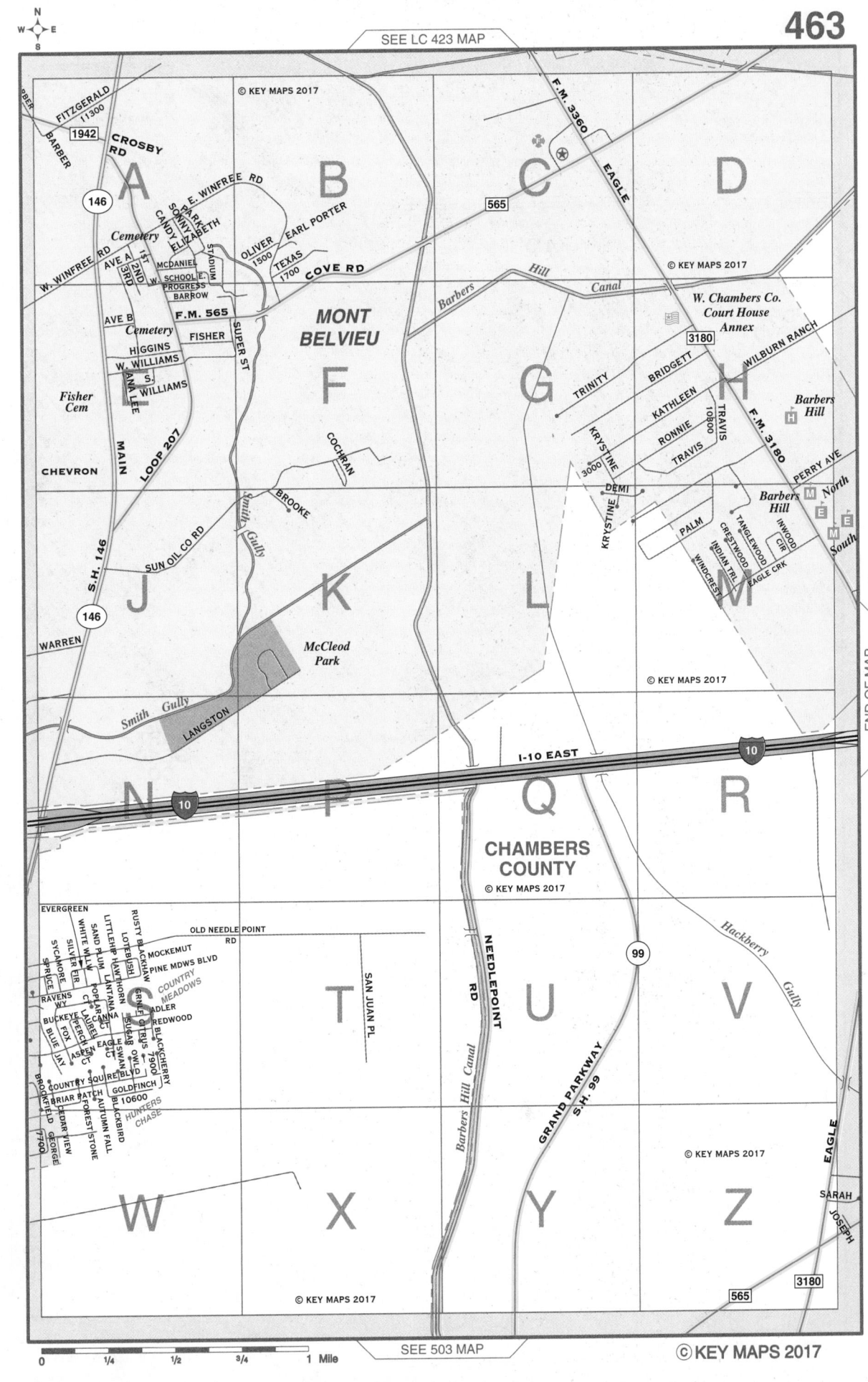

© KEY MAPS 2017

N W E S

FITZGERALD 11300
BARBER
1942
CROSBY RD
(146)

F.M. 3360
EAGLE

A

B

E. WINFREE RD

565
C

D

W. WINFREE RD
Cemetery
AVE A
1ST
SONNY
CANDY
PARK
ELIZABETH
2ND
3RD
W.
McDANIEL
SCHOOL
PROGRESS
BARROW
STADIUM
OLIVER 1500
EARL PORTER
TEXAS 1700
COVE RD

Barbers
Hill
Canal

W. Chambers Co.
Court House
Annex

AVE B
Cemetery
HIGGINS
W. WILLIAMS
ANA LEE
S.
WILLIAMS
FISHER
F.M. 565
SUPER ST

**MONT
BELVIEU**
F

3180
G
TRINITY
BRIDGETT
KATHLEEN
RONNIE
TRAVIS
TRAVIS 10800
WILBURN RANCH

H
Barbers
Hill

Fisher
Cem
MAIN
LOOP 207
CHEVRON

COCHRAN

KRYSTINE
DEMI
KRYSTINE 3000
PALM
CRESTWOOD
WINDCREST
INDIAN TR.
TANGLEWOOD
EAGLE CRK
INWOOD CIR

PERRY AVE
North
South
F.M. 3180

S.H. 146
146
WARREN

J

BROOKE
Smith Gully
SUN OIL CO RD

K
McCleod
Park

L

M

END OF MAP

N

Smith Gully
LANGSTON

I-10 EAST
10

N
10

P

Q

R

**CHAMBERS
COUNTY**
© KEY MAPS 2017

NEEDLEPOINT RD

99

Hackberry
Gully

EVERGREEN
OLD NEEDLE POINT RD

RUSTY BLACKHAW
MOCKEMUT
PINE MDWS BLVD
LITTLEHIP
HAWTHORN
LANTANA
SAND PLUM
LOTEBUSH
WHITE W.L.W.
SILVER FIR
SYCAMORE
SPRUCE
RAVENS WY
BUCKEYE
BEECH
FOX
BLUE JAY
POPLAR
CANNA
LAUREL
ASPEN
SWAN
COUNTRY
MEADOWS
SADLER
GRNFLDS CT
SUGAR TR.
REDWOOD
EAGLE
BLVD
BLACKCHERRY
OWL CT
7900

COUNTRY SQUIRE
BRIAR PATCH
BROOKFIELD
GEORGE
7700
CEDAR VIEW
FOREST STONE
AUTUMN FALL
GOLDFINCH
BLACKBIRD
10600
HUNTERS CHASE
SAN JUAN PL

T

U
GRAND PARKWAY S.H. 99

Barbers Hill Canal

V

Eagle

SARAH
JOSEPH

S

W

X

Y

© KEY MAPS 2017

Z

3180
565

© **KEY MAPS 2017**

0   1/4   1/2   3/4   1 Mile

SEE 444 MAP

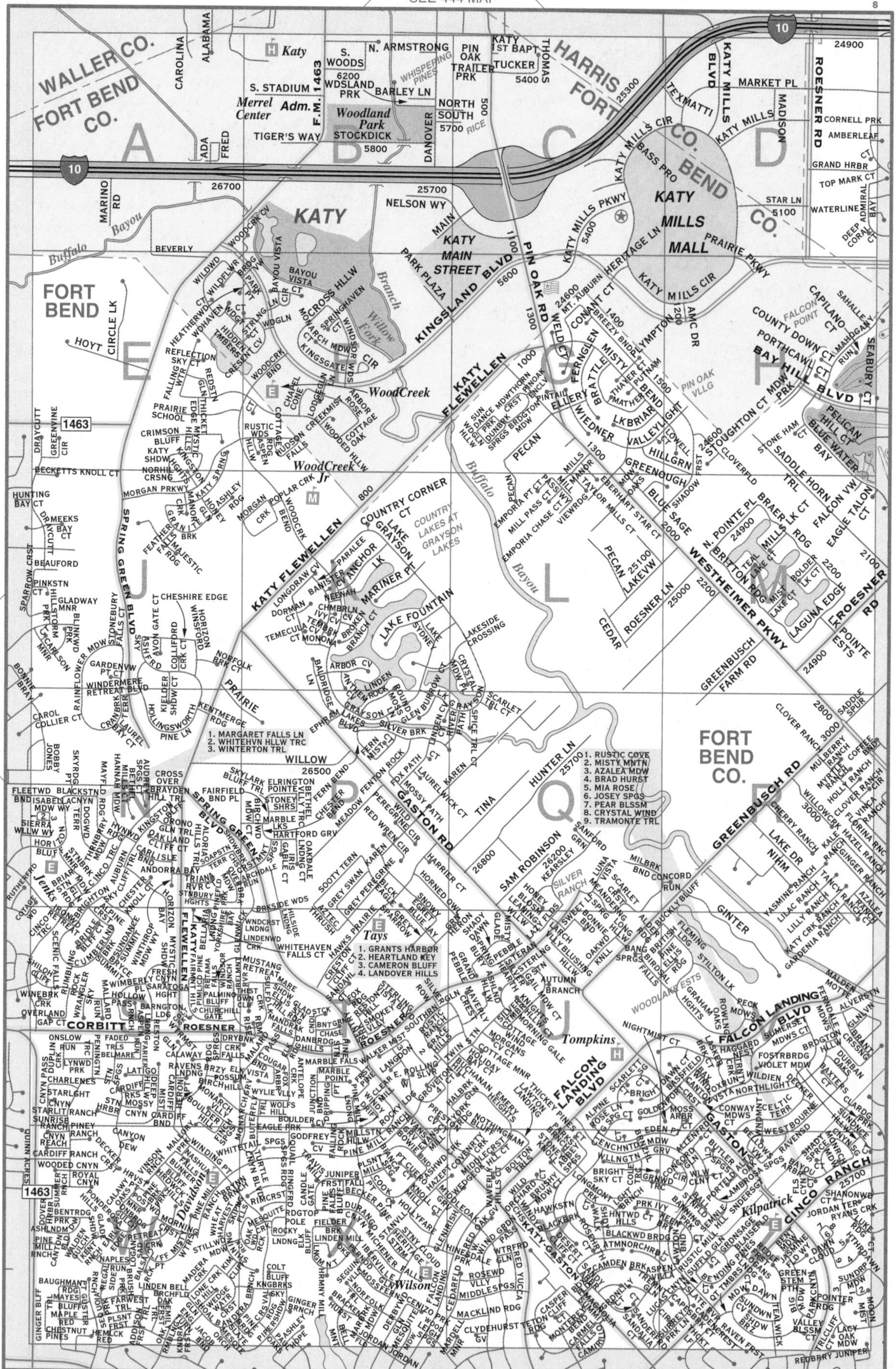

WALLER CO.
FORT BEND CO.

KATY

FORT BEND

CIRCLE LK

Buffalo Bayou
Willow Fork

KINGSLAND BLVD

PIN OAK RD

WELDCTR

KATY MILLS MALL

KATY MILLS PKWY

HARRIS CO.
FORT BEND CO.

ROESNER RD

BAY HILL BLVD

KATY FLEWELLEN

WoodCreek

WoodCreek Jr

COUNTRY CORNER

WESTHEIMER PKWY

ROESNER RD

LAKE GRAYSON

MARINER PT

LAKE FOUNTAIN

FORT BEND CO.

GREENBUSCH FARM RD

GREENBUSCH RD

SPRING GREEN BLVD

WILLOW

1. Margaret Falls Ln
2. Whitehvn Hllw Trc
3. Winterton Trl

GASTON RD

HUNTER LN

1. Rustic Cove
2. Misty Mmtn
3. Azalea Mdw
4. Brad Hurst
5. Mia Rose
6. Josey Spgs
7. Pear Blssm
8. Crystal Wind
9. Tramonte Trl

SAM ROBINSON

SILVER RANCH

CINCO RANCH

CORBITT

ROESNER

KATY FLEWELLEN

Tays
1. Grants Harbor
2. Heartland Key
3. Cameron Bluff
4. Landover Hills

Tompkins

FALCON LANDING BLVD

Kilpatrick

Davidson

Wilson

KATY-GASTON

1463

SEE 524 MAP

0   1/4   1/2   3/4   1 Mile

© KEY MAPS 2017

SEE FB 483 MAP

I-10

SEE 445 MAP

SEE 486 MAP

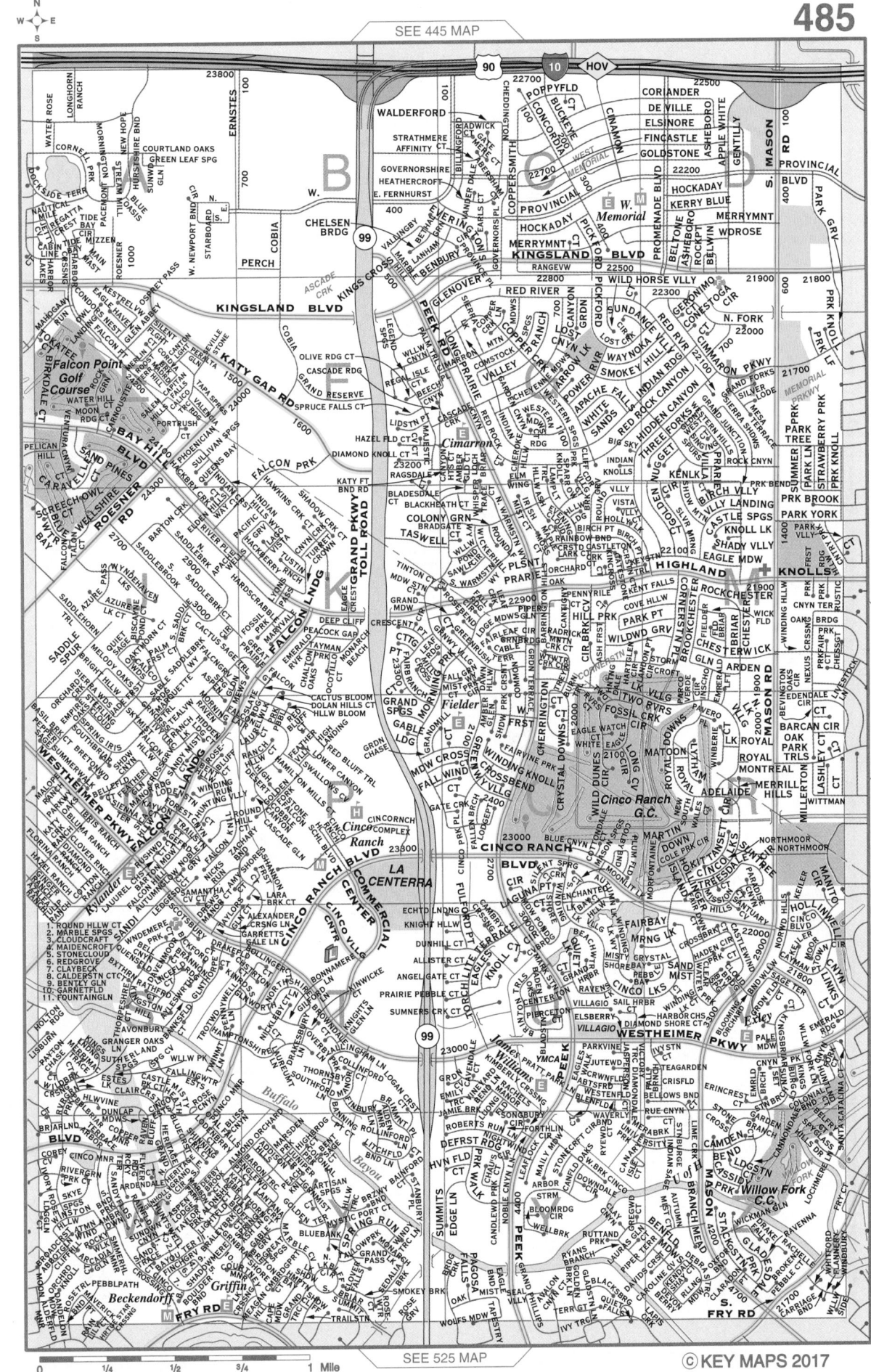

SEE 525 MAP

0   1/4   1/2   3/4   1 Mile

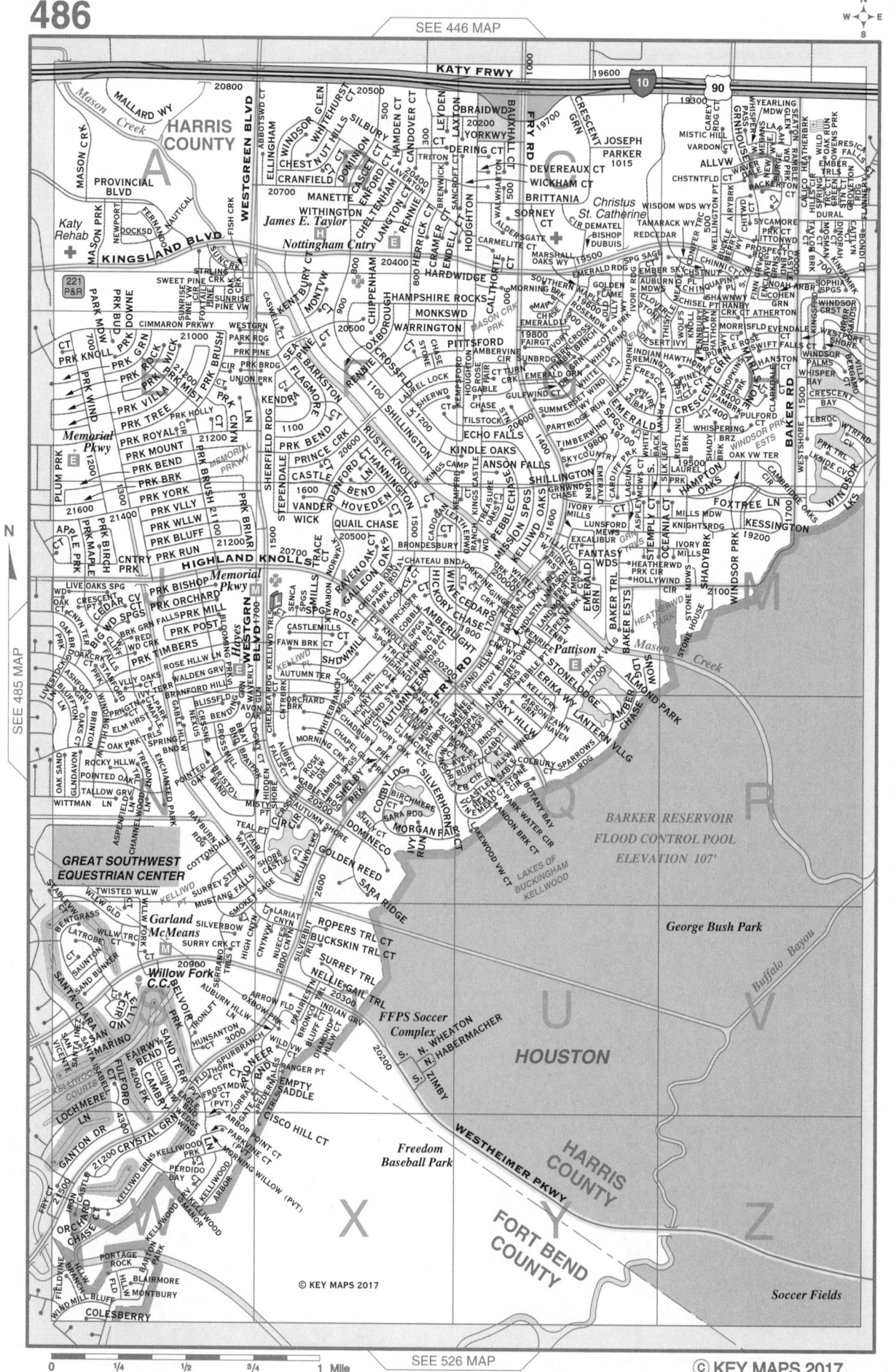

486

KATY FRWY

10

90

HARRIS COUNTY

MASON CREEK

MALLARD WY

PROVINCIAL BLVD

Katy Rehab

MASON PRK

KINGSLAND BLVD

WESTGREEN BLVD

221 P&R

Memorial Pkwy

HIGHLAND KNOLLS

Memorial Pkwy

WESTGRN BLVD

GREAT SOUTHWEST EQUESTRIAN CENTER

Garland McMeans

Willow Fork C.C.

FFPS Soccer Complex

Freedom Baseball Park

WESTHEIMER PKWY

HARRIS COUNTY

FORT BEND COUNTY

HOUSTON

BARKER RESERVOIR FLOOD CONTROL POOL ELEVATION 107'

George Bush Park

Buffalo Bayou

Mason Creek

Pattison

Stonelodge

Snow Park

James E. Taylor

Nottingham Cntry

JOSEPH PARKER

Christus St. Catherine

BAKER RD

KESSINGTON

Soccer Fields

© KEY MAPS 2017

0   1/4   1/2   3/4   1 Mile

© KEY MAPS 2017

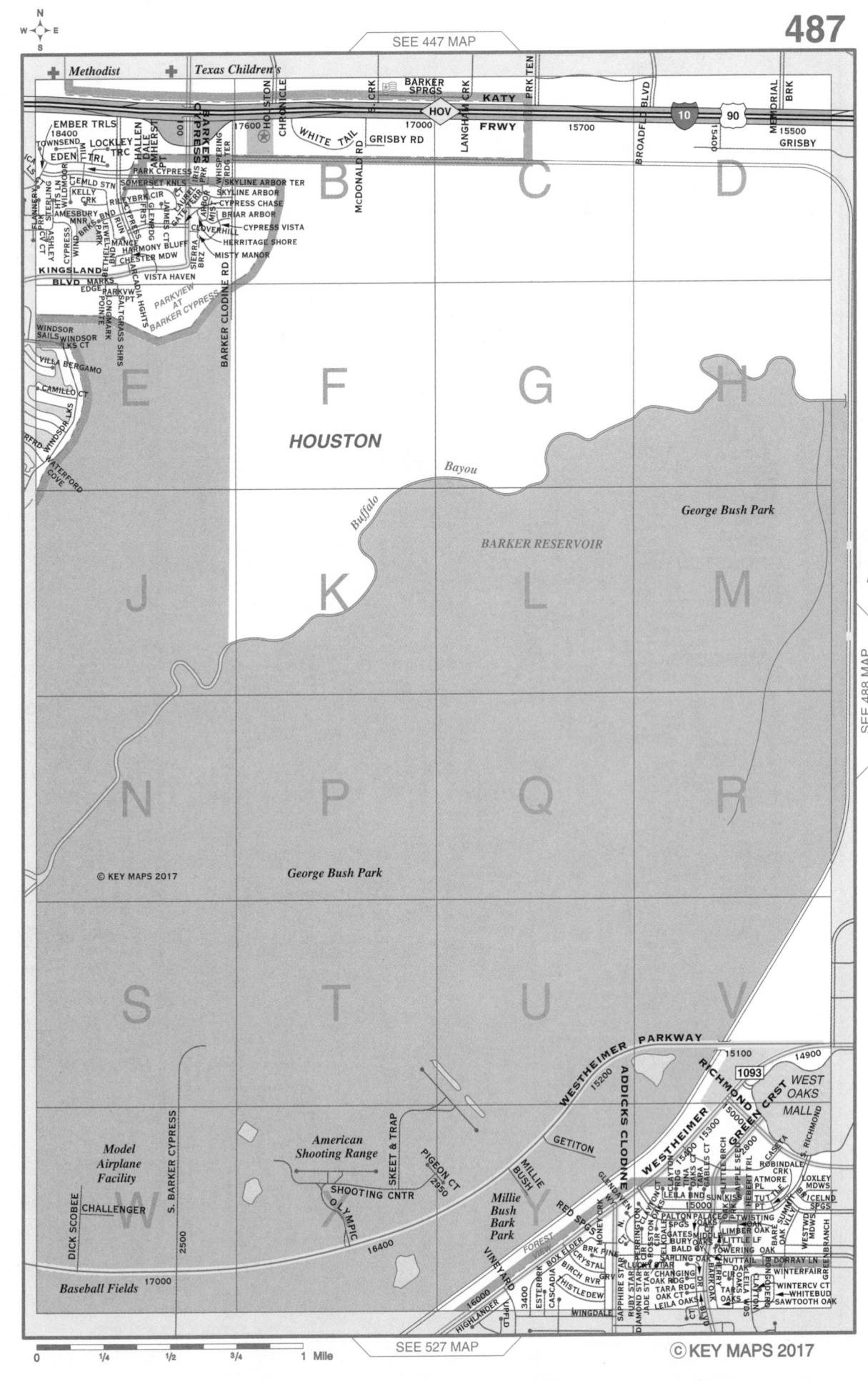

SEE 447 MAP

SEE 488 MAP

SEE 527 MAP

HOUSTON

BARKER RESERVOIR

George Bush Park

George Bush Park

© KEY MAPS 2017

© KEY MAPS 2017

0   1/4   1/2   3/4   1 Mile

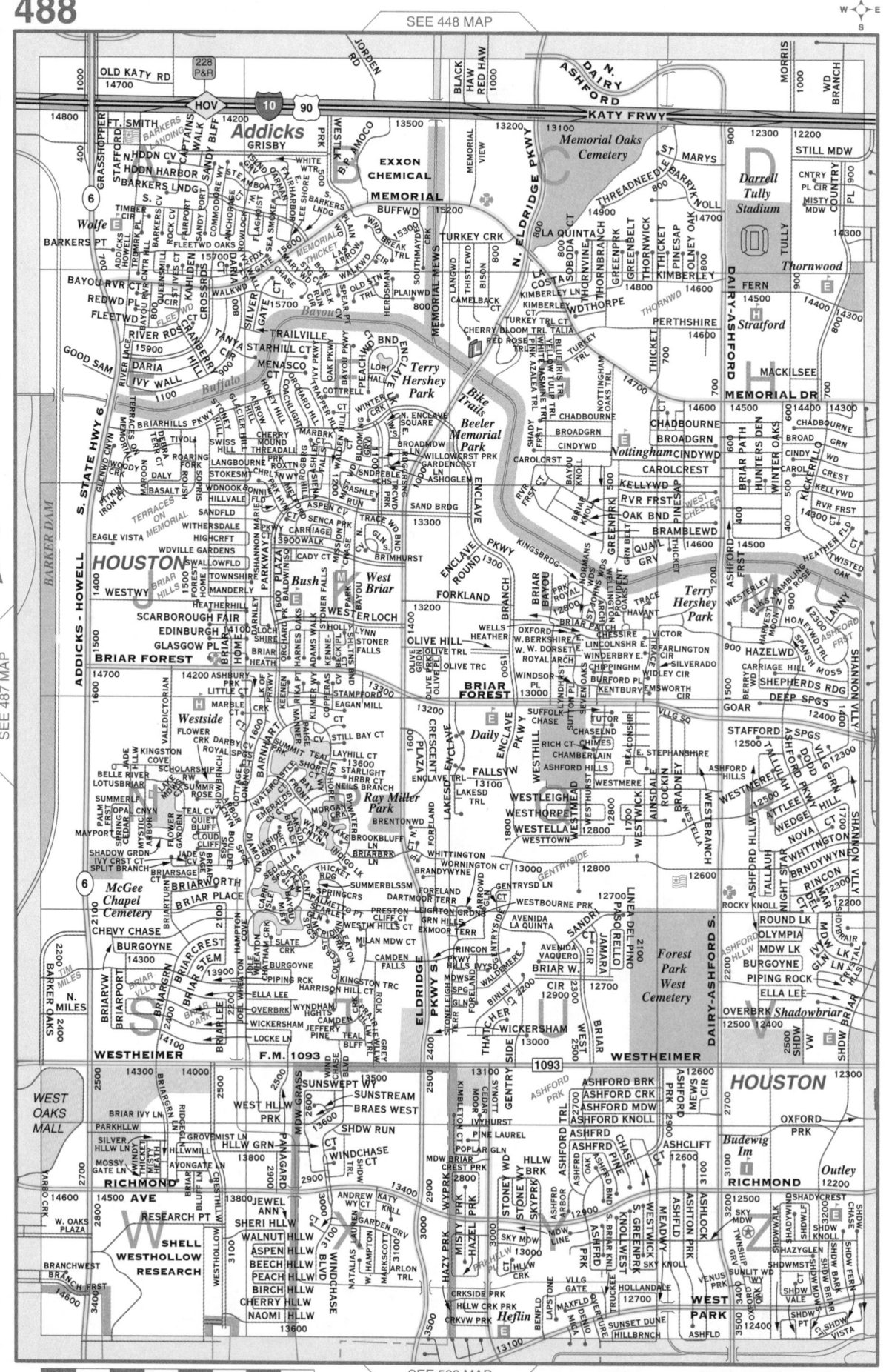

SEE 448 MAP

SEE 487 MAP

SEE 528 MAP

© KEY MAPS 2017

0   1/4   1/2   3/4   1 Mile

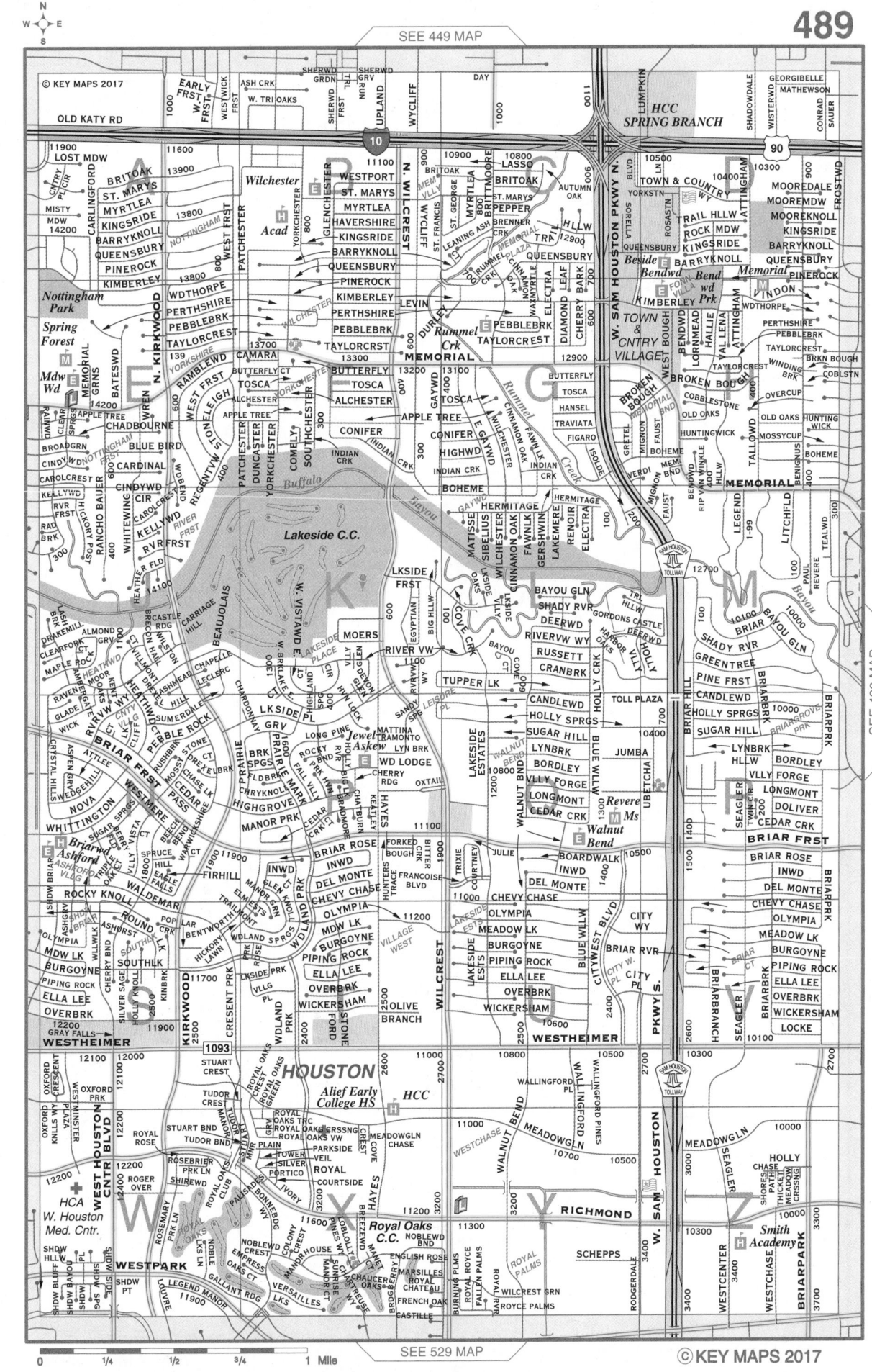

© KEY MAPS 2017

© KEY MAPS 2017

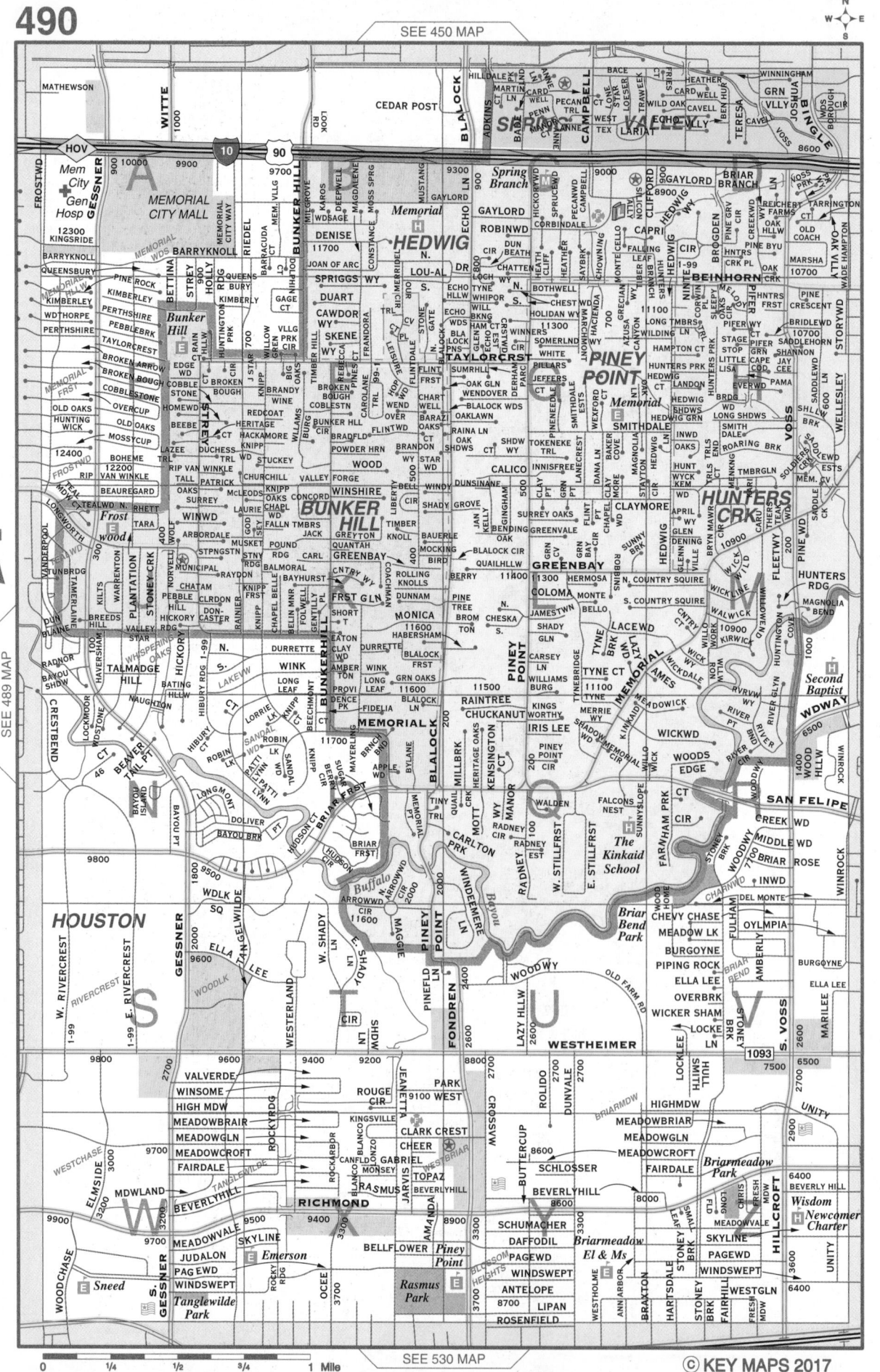

SEE 450 MAP

© KEY MAPS 2017

SEE 530 MAP

491

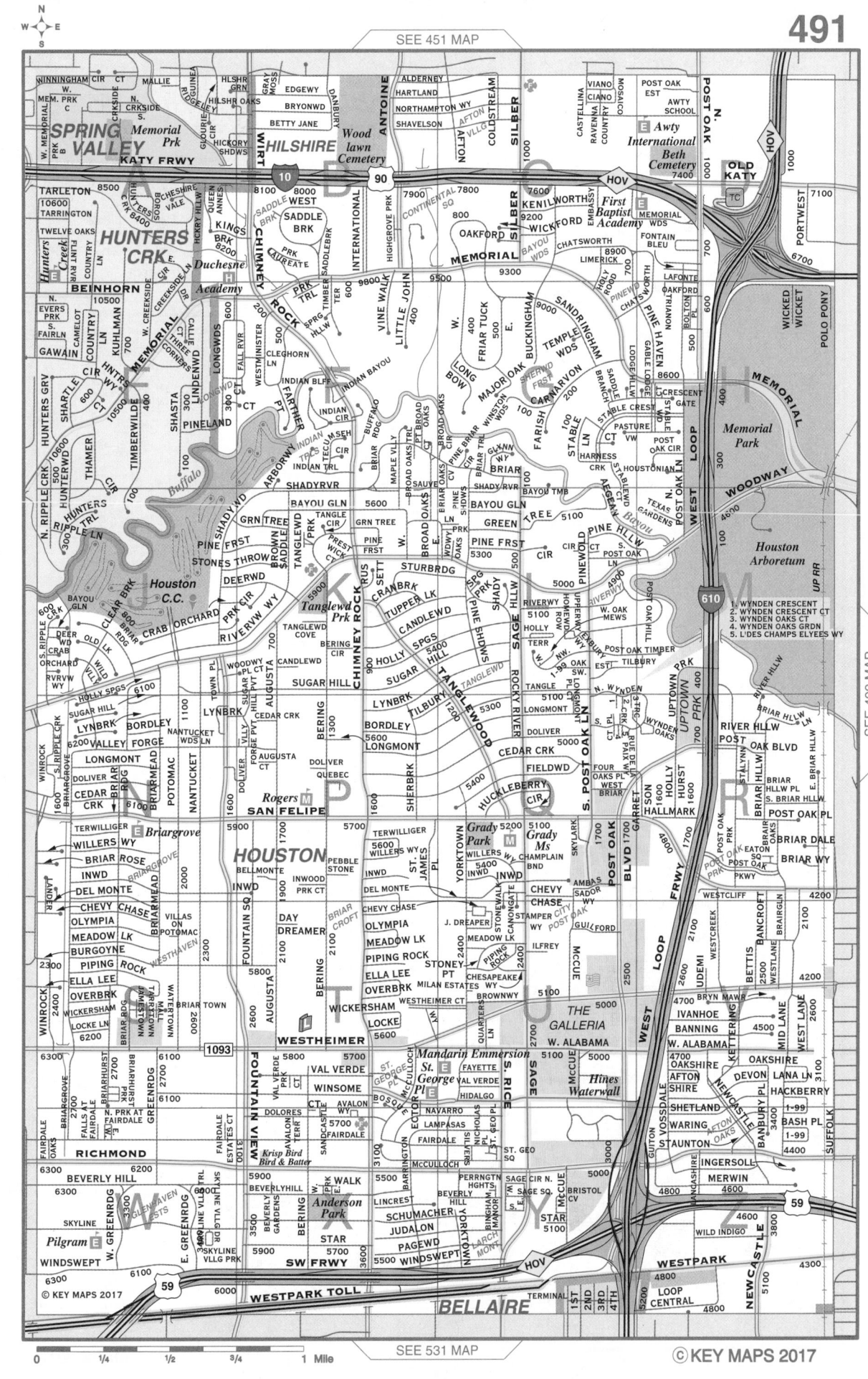

© KEY MAPS 2017

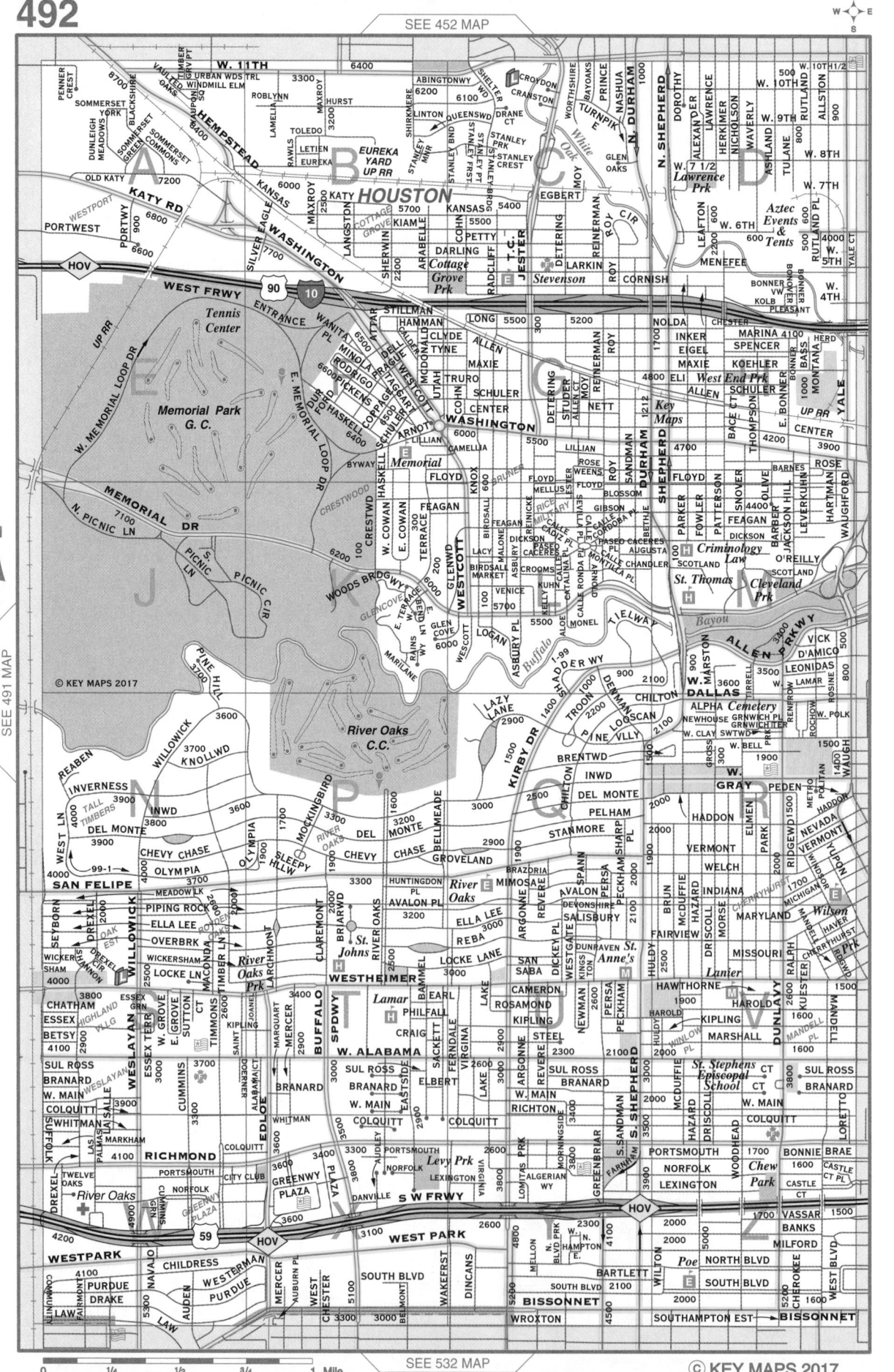

© KEY MAPS 2017

0   1/4   1/2   3/4   1 Mile

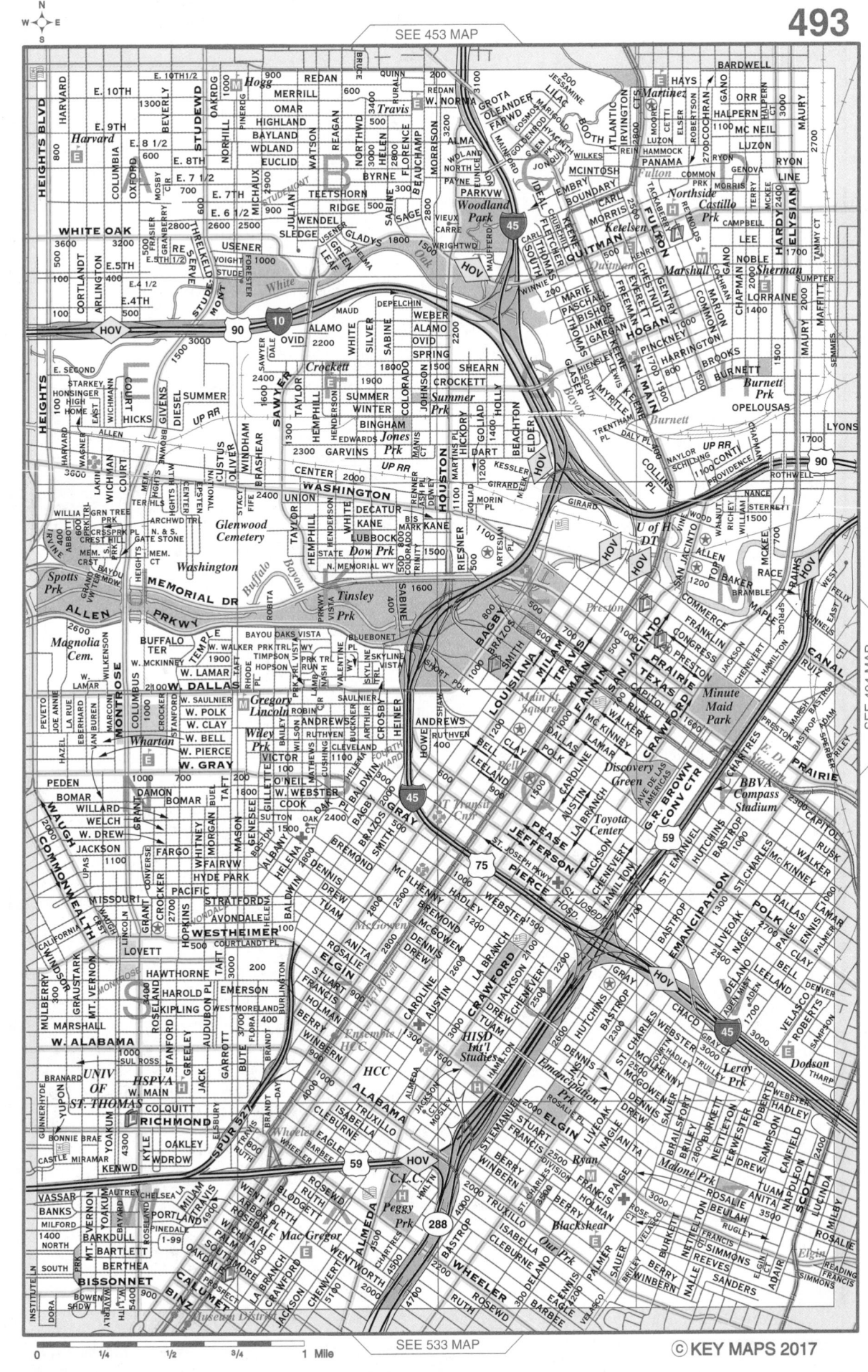

0   1/4   1/2   3/4   1 Mile

SEE 494 MAP

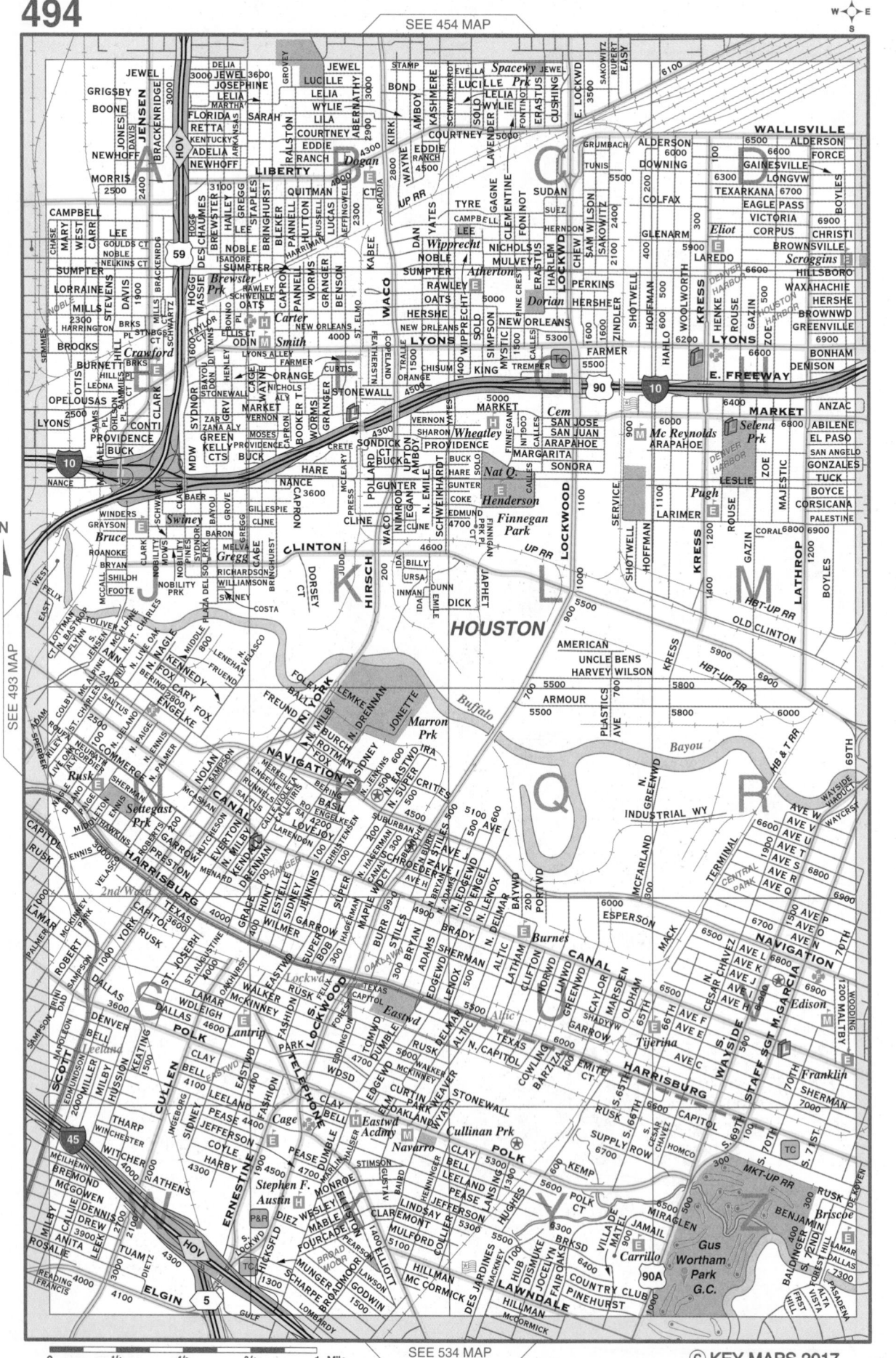

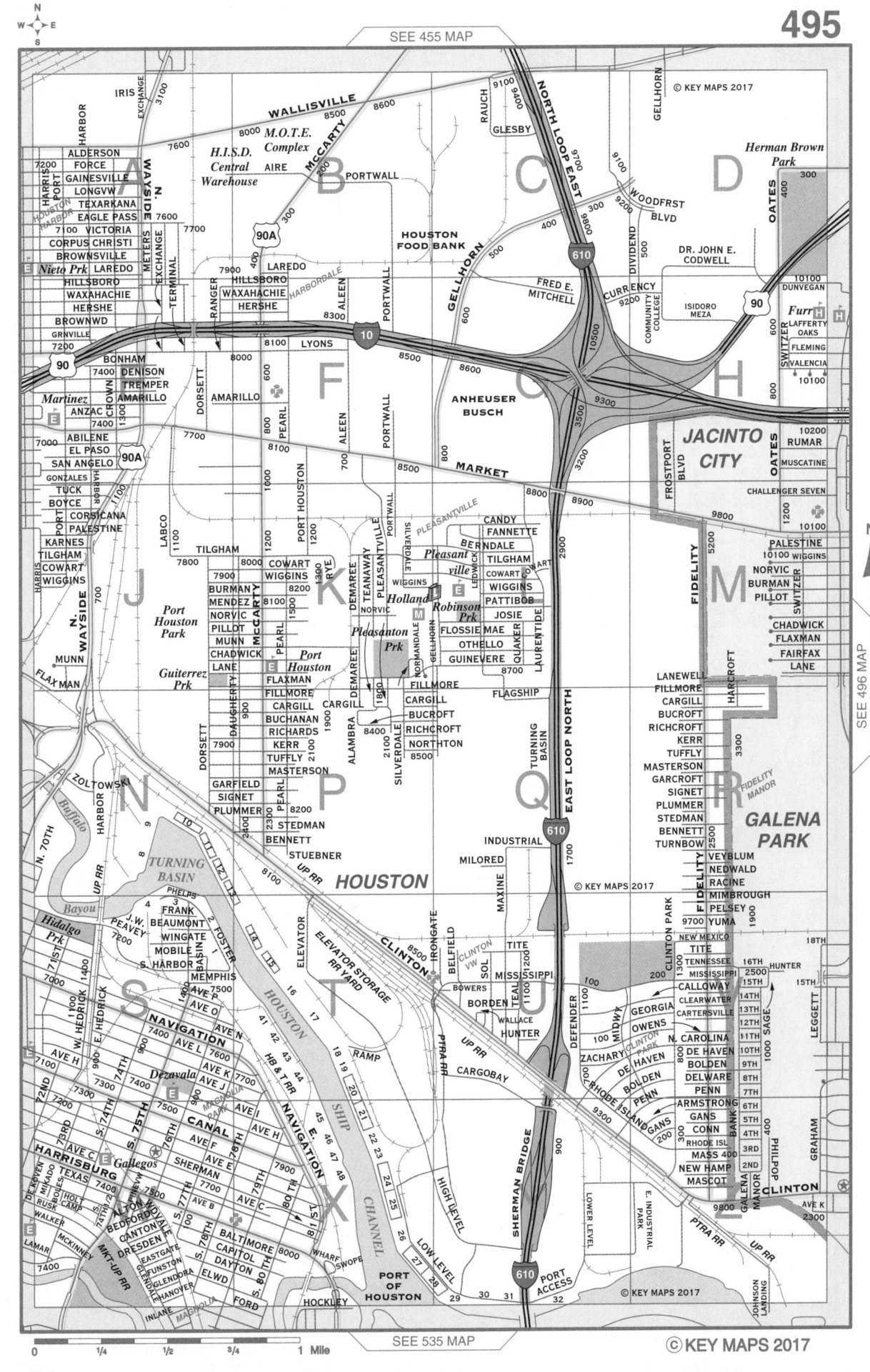

© KEY MAPS 2017

© KEY MAPS 2017

0   1/4   1/2   3/4   1 Mile

496

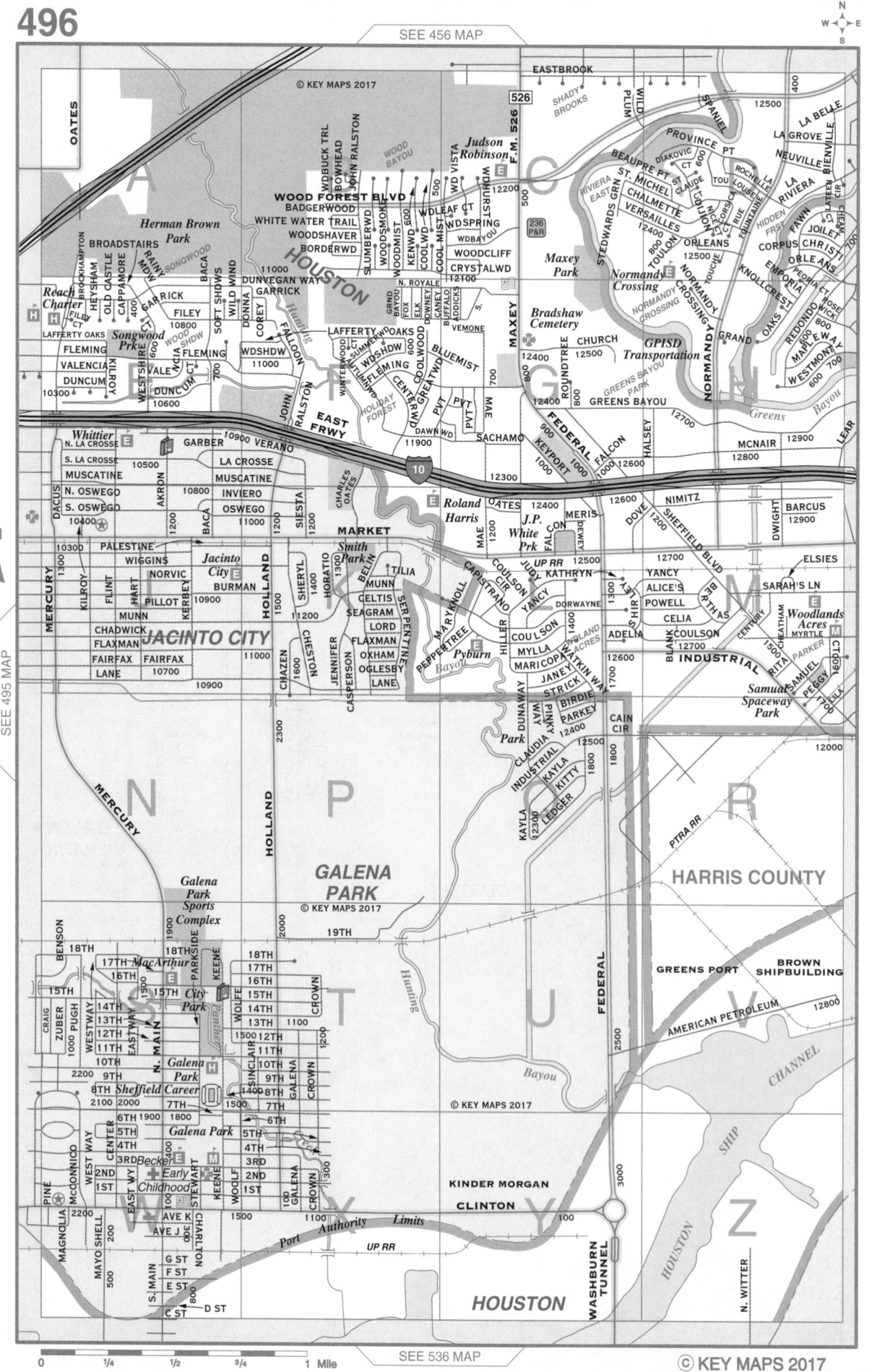

© KEY MAPS 2017

OATES

Herman Brown Park

WDBUCK TRL
BOWHEAD
JOHN RALSTON
WOOD FOREST BLVD
BADGERWOOD
WHITE WATER TRAIL
WOODSHAVER
BORDERWD
SLUMBERWD
WOODSMOKE
WOODMIST
KENWD
COOLWD
COOL MIST
WD VISTA
WDLEAF CT
WDHURST
WDSPRING
WDBAYOU
WOODCLIFF
CRYSTALWD

Judson Robinson

F.M. 526

526

EASTBROOK
SHADY BROOKS
SPANIEL
WILD
PLUM
LA BELLE
LA GROVE
NEUVILLE
PROVINCE PT
BEAUPRE PT ST
DIAKOVIC
ST. MICHEL
CHALMETTE
VERSAILLES
RIVIERA EAST
STEDWARDS GRN
RUE
CORSU
TOULON
ORLEANS
ROCHELLE
LA RIVIERA
FAWN
JOILET
CORPUS CHRISTI
ORLEANS
EMPORIA
KNOLLCREST
REDONDIDO
WICK
MAPLEWAY
WESTMONT

Maxey Park

Normandy Crossing

NORMANDY
GREENS BAYOU PARK
GPISD Transportation
GREENS BAYOU

Bradshaw Cemetery
CHURCH
ROUNDTREE

Greens Bayou

LEAR

McNAIR

BROADSTAIRS
BROCKHAMPTON
HEYSHAM
OLD CASTLE
CAPPAMORE
RAINY MDN
SONGWOOD
BACA
GARRICK
FILEY
DUNVEGAN WAY
GARRICK
Songwood Prke
FLEMING
VALENCIA
DUNCUM
WDSHDW
FLEMING
DUNCUM
FALCON
Hunting
JOHN RALSTON
EAST FRWY
LAFFERTY
SUMMERWOOD
WDSHDW
WINTERWOOD
FLEMING
HOLIDAY FOREST
CENTRWD
GREATWD
COOLWD
BLUEMIST
VEMONE
Reach Charter
FLEMING
SOFT SHWS
WILD WIND
DONNA
COREY
WDSHDW
WOODOAKS
GRND
FOX
DOWNEY
CANEY
ELK
BUFFALO
ADDICKS
N. ROYALE
MAXEY
FEDERAL
FALCON
HALSEY
KEYPORT
SACHAMO
DAWN WD

GARBER
VERANO
LA CROSSE
MUSCATINE
INVIERO
OSWEGO
SIESTA
Whittier
N. LA CROSSE
S. LA CROSSE
MUSCATINE
N. OSWEGO
S. OSWEGO
AKRON
BACA
DACUS
CHARLES OATES
Roland Harris
J.P. White Prk
OATES
MAE
FALCON
MERIS
DOVE
NIMITZ
SHEFFIELD BLVD
DWIGHT
BARCUS
Smith Park

10

MARKET

MERCURY
KILROY
FLINT
HART
PILLOT
MUNN
CHADWICK
FLAXMAN
FAIRFAX
LANE
PALESTINE
WIGGINS
NORVIC
KERBEY
Jacinto City
BURMAN
JACINTO CITY
FAIRFAX
HOLLAND
CHAZEN
CHESTON
JENNIFER
CASPERSON
SHERYL
HORATIO
BELIN
MUNN
CELTIS
SEAGRAM
LORD
FLAXMAN
OKHAM
OGLESBY
LANE
TILIA
PEPPERTREE
MARYKNOLL
PYBURN
Pyburn Park
Bayou
SER PENTINE
CAPISTRANO
COULSON CIR
JUDY
YANCY
HILLER
COULSON
MYLLA
MARICOPA
JANEY
STRICK
BIRDIE
PARKEY
PINKY WAY
DUNAWAY
CLAUDIA
INDUSTRIAL
KAYLA
LEDGER
KITTY
CAIN CIR
KATHRYN
DORWAYNE
WATKIN WAY
WOLAND ACRES
ADELIA
CELIA
POWELL
ALICE'S
YANCY
SARAH'S LN
ELSIES
Woodlands Acres
MYRTLE
INDUSTRIAL
BLANK
COULSON
CENTURY
CHEATHAM
RITA
PARKER
SAMUEL
PEGGY
Samual Spaceway Park

MERCURY

GALENA PARK

HOLLAND

19TH

© KEY MAPS 2017

Galena Park Sports Complex

BENSON
18TH
17TH MacArthur
16TH
15TH
14TH
13TH
12TH
11TH
10TH
9TH
8TH Sheffield Career
7TH
6TH
5TH
4TH
3RD Becker
2ND Early
1ST Childhood
PARKSIDE
KEENE
City Park
WOLFE
SINCLAIR
GALENA
CROWN
18TH
17TH
16TH
15TH
14TH
12TH
11TH
10TH
8TH
7TH
6TH
5TH
4TH
3RD
2ND
1ST
Galena Park Career
Galena Park
CRAIG
ZUBER
PUGH
WESTWAY
EASTWAY
N. MAIN
CENTER
WEST WAY
McCONNICO
PINE
MAGNOLIA
MAYO SHELL
S. MAIN
CHARLTON
STEWART
KEENE
WOOLF
EAST WY
AVE K
AVE J
G ST
F ST
E ST
D ST
C ST

HARRIS COUNTY

GREENS PORT
BROWN SHIPBUILDING
AMERICAN PETROLEUM

Hunting Bayou

FEDERAL

KINDER MORGAN
CLINTON

© KEY MAPS 2017

WASHBURN TUNNEL

N. WITTER

HOUSTON

Port Authority Limits
UP RR

SHIP CHANNEL

HOUSTON

0   1/4   1/2   3/4   1 Mile

© KEY MAPS 2017

SEE 495 MAP

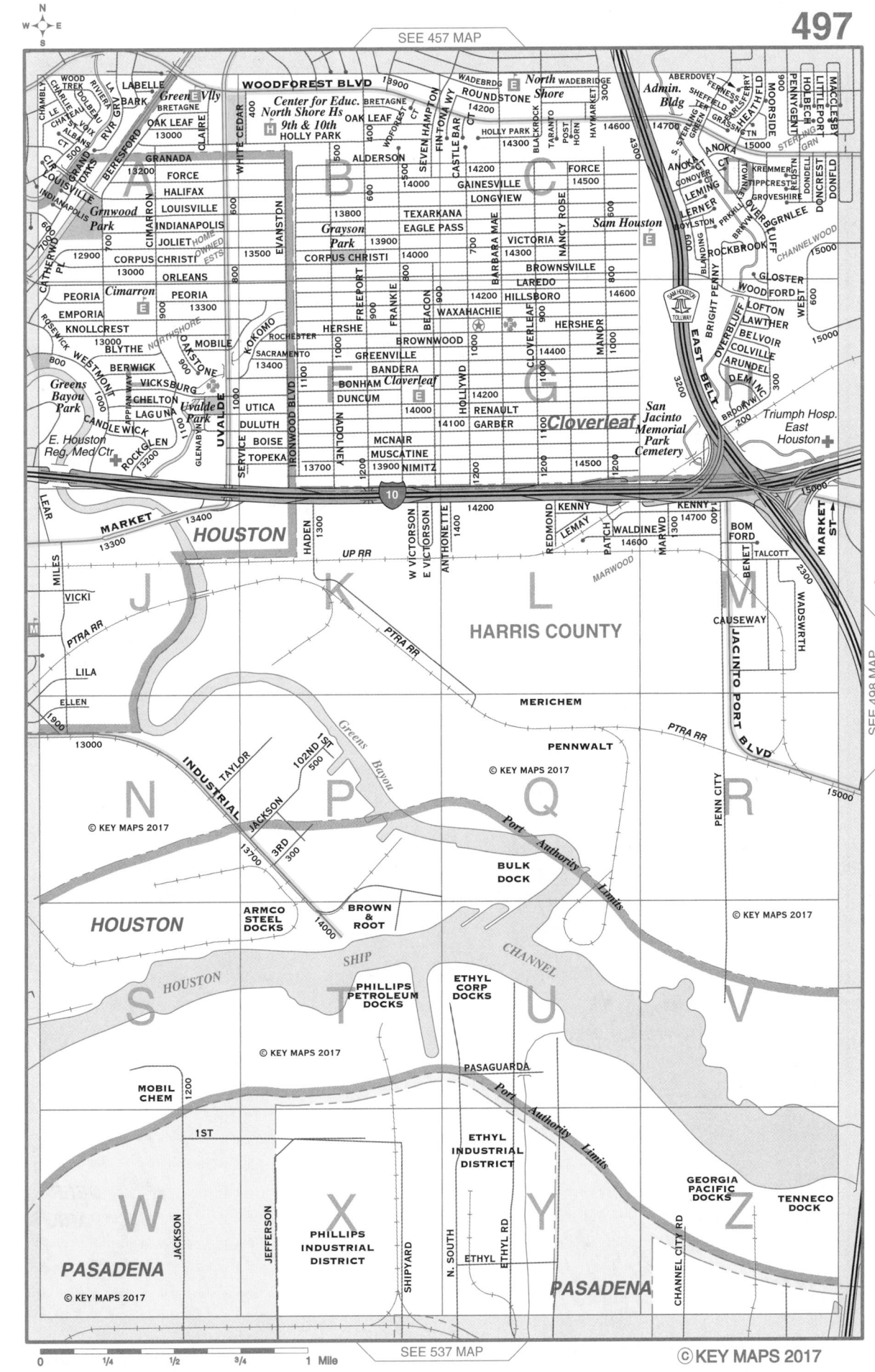

SEE 498 MAP

SEE 537 MAP

0   1/4   1/2   3/4   1 Mile

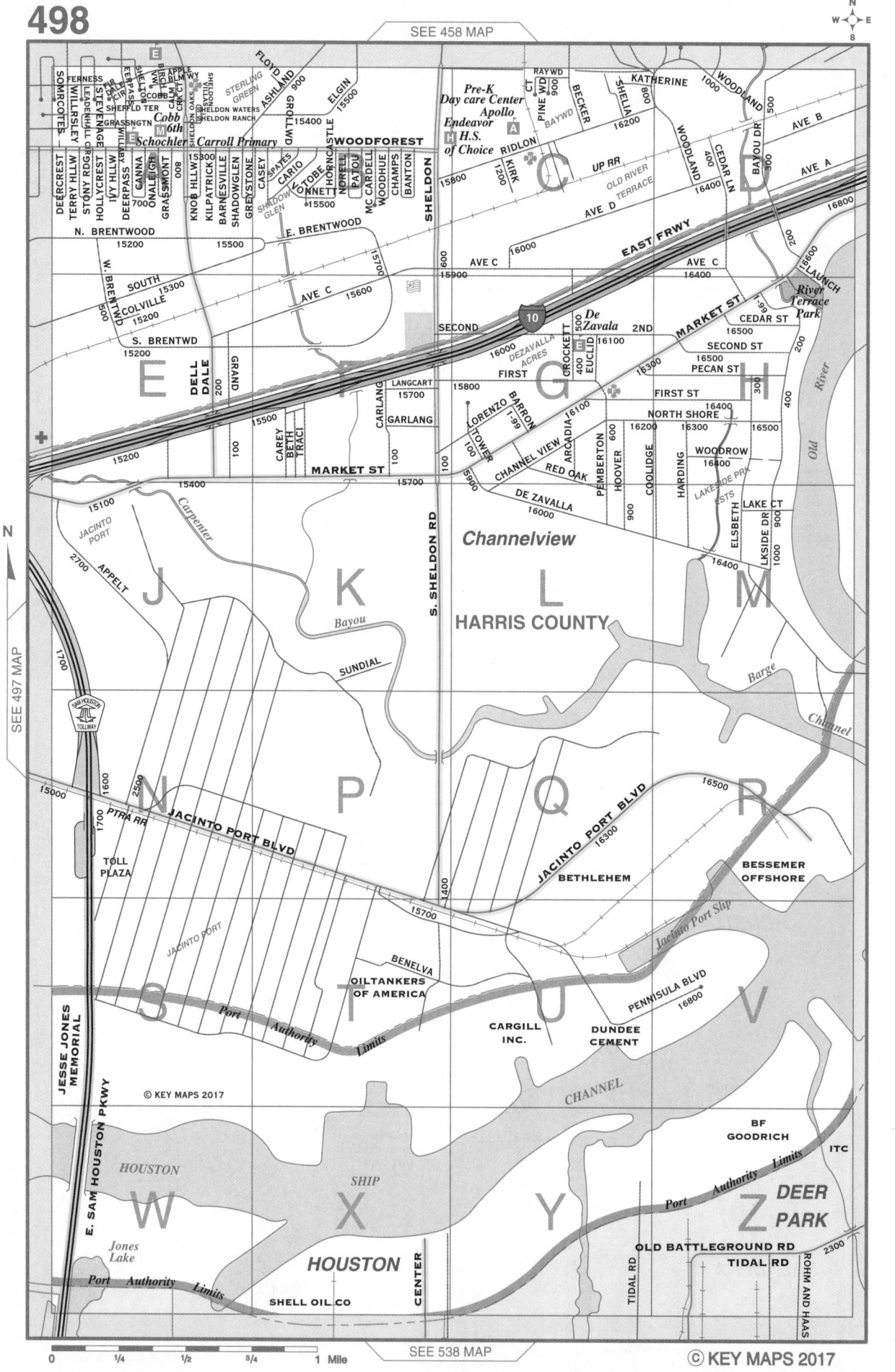

SEE 458 MAP

SEE 497 MAP

SEE 538 MAP

© KEY MAPS 2017

© KEY MAPS 2017

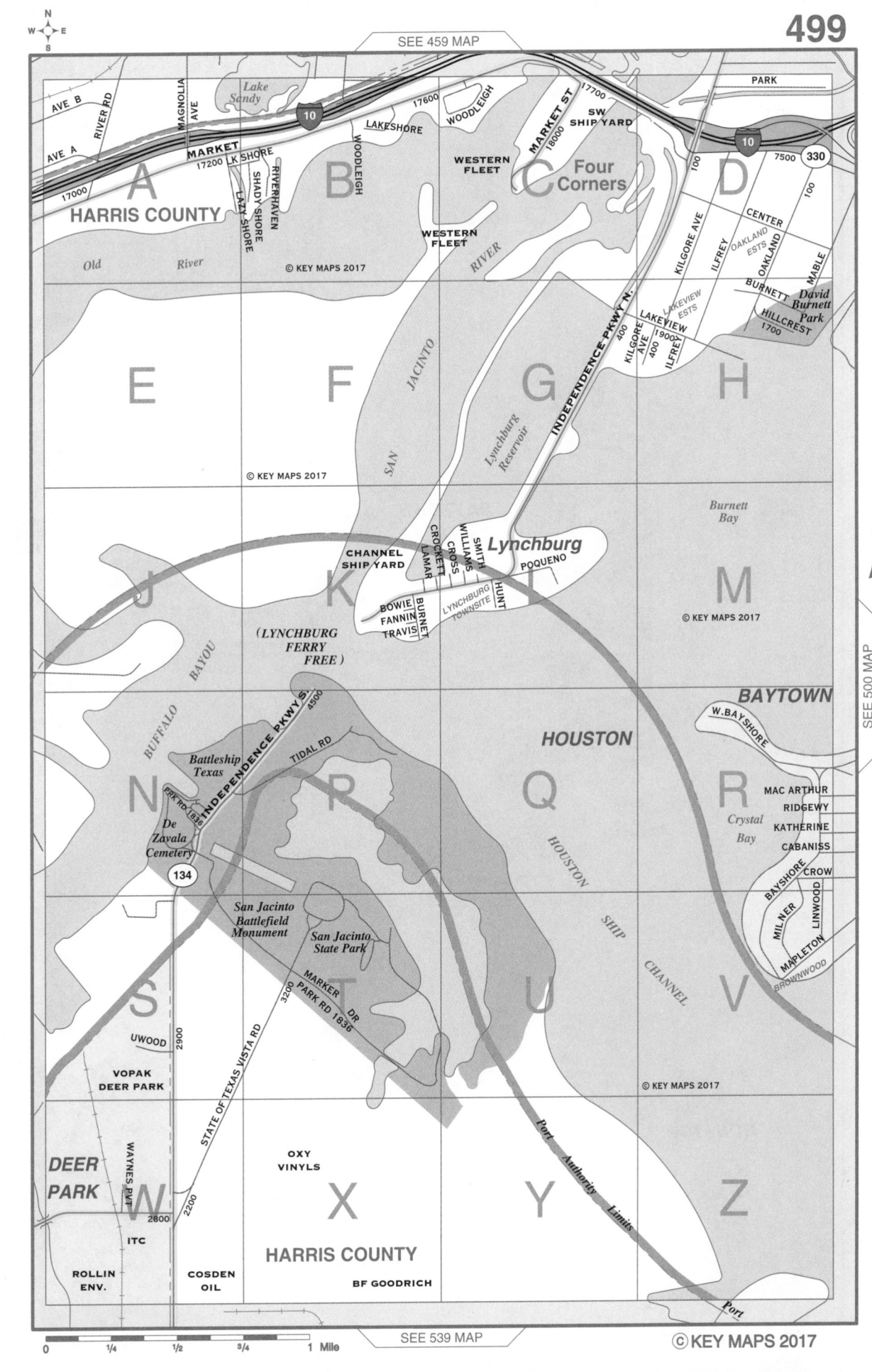

SEE 459 MAP

N
W + E
S

PARK

I-10

AVE B
RIVER RD
MAGNOLIA AVE
Lake Sandy
LAKESHORE
WOODLEIGH
MARKET ST
18000
SW SHIP YARD
17700
I-10
7500
330
100
100

AVE A
MARKET
17200 LK SHORE
WOODLEIGH
17600
WESTERN FLEET
C Four Corners
D
KILGORE AVE
CENTER
OAKLAND ESTS
MABLE

17000
A
SHADY SHORE
RIVERHAVEN
B
WESTERN FLEET
ILFREY
OAKLAND
BURNETT

HARRIS COUNTY
LAZY SHORE
RIVER
INDEPENDENCE PKWY N.
LAKEVIEW ESTS
David Burnett Park

Old River
© KEY MAPS 2017
SAN JACINTO RIVER
400
LAKEVIEW
HILLCREST 1700

E
F
G
KILGORE AVE
1900
ILFREY
H

© KEY MAPS 2017
Lynchburg Reservoir
400
400

Burnett Bay

SMITH
WILLIAMS
Lynchburg
M

CHANNEL SHIP YARD
CROCKETT
CROSS
POQUENO

J
K
LAMAR
HUNT
© KEY MAPS 2017

BOWIE
FANNIN
BURNETT
LYNCHBURG TOWNSITE
TRAVIS

(LYNCHBURG FERRY FREE)

BAYTOWN

W. BAYSHORE

BUFFALO BAYOU
INDEPENDENCE PKWY S.
4500
TIDAL RD
HOUSTON
R
MAC ARTHUR
RIDGEWY

Battleship Texas
N
PRK RD 1836
R
Crystal Bay
KATHERINE
CABANISS

De Zayala Cemetery
134
HOUSTON SHIP CHANNEL
BAYSHORE
CROW
LINWOOD

San Jacinto Battlefield Monument
San Jacinto State Park
MILNER
MAPLETON
BROWNWOOD

S
UWOOD
2900
MARKER DR
PARK RD 1836
320
T
U
V

VOPAK DEER PARK
STATE OF TEXAS VISTA RD

DEER PARK
WAYNES PVT
OXY VINYLS
Port Authority Limits
Z

W
2200
X
Y

2800
ITC
HARRIS COUNTY

ROLLIN ENV.
COSDEN OIL
BF GOODRICH
© KEY MAPS 2017

Port

N
SEE 500 MAP

0   1/4   1/2   3/4   1 Mile

SEE 539 MAP

© **KEY MAPS** 2017

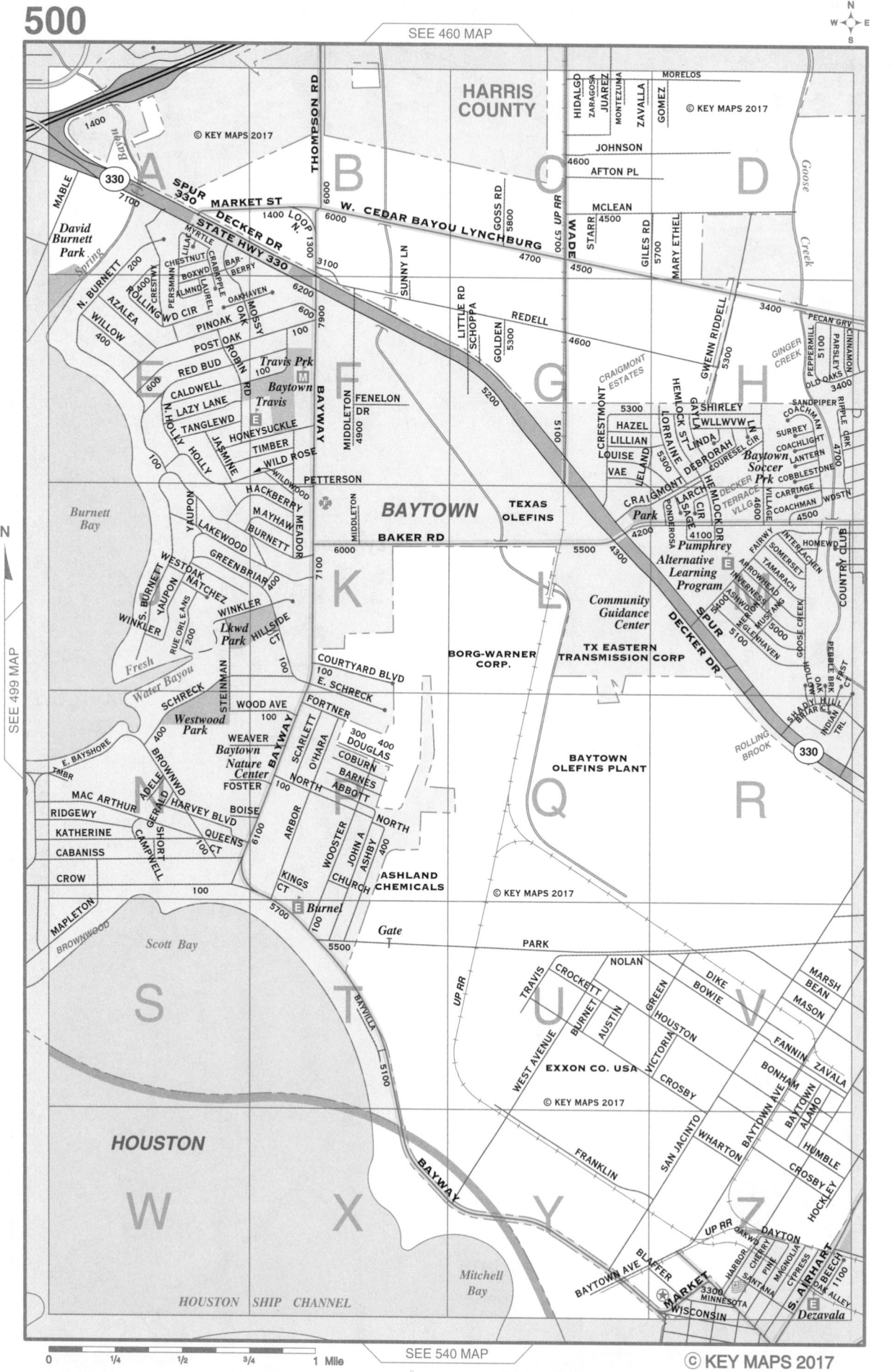

SEE 460 MAP

HARRIS
COUNTY

© KEY MAPS 2017

MORELOS

HIDALGD
ZARAGOSA
JUAREZ
MONTEZUMA
ZAVALLA
GOMEZ

JOHNSON
4600
AFTON PL

MCLEAN
4500
STARR

Goose
Creek

MABLE

David
Burnett
Park

SPUR
330
MARKET ST
DECKER DR
STATE HWY 330

THOMPSON RD

W. CEDAR BAYOU LYNCHBURG

WADE

GILES RD
5700

MARY ETHEL

3400

PECAN GRV
PEPPERMILL 5010
PARSLEY
CINNAMON
OLD OAKS
3400

N. BURNETT
200
AZALEA
ROLLING
WD CIR
WILLOW
400

MYRTLE
CHESTNUT
CRESTVL
PERSMMN
BOXWD
LAUREL
ALMND
CRABAPPLE
BARBERRY

OAKHAVEN
MOSSY
600

SUNNY LN

LITTLE RD
SCHOPPA
GOLDEN
5300

REDELL
4600

GWENN RIDDELL
5300

GINGER
Creek

RIPPLE
CRK
4700

Spring

RED BUD
CALDWELL
N. HOLLY
LAZY LANE
TANGLEWD

PINOAK
POST OAK
ROBIN RD
OAK
100

7900

6200

6000

CRAIGMONT
ESTATES

CRESTMONT
5300
HAZEL
LILLIAN
LOUISE
VAE

HEMLOCK ST
LORRAINE
5300
LIELAND
5300

GALA
LINDA
DEBRORAH
LOUREEL CIR
LARCH
HEMLOCK DR

SHIRLEY
WLLLWVW

SURREY
COACHLIGHT
LANTERN
COBBLESTONE
CARRIAGE
COACHMAN
4500

Baytown
Soccer
Prk

SANDPIPER
COACHMAN

Travis Prk
Baytown
Travis

FENELON
DR
4900

Burnett
Bay

YAUPON
LAKEWOOD
Burnett

HONEYSUCKLE
WILD ROSE
WILDWOOD
PETTERSON

HACKBERRY MEADOR
MAYHAW
BURNETT
400

MIDDLETON

BAYWAY

6000
BAKER RD

BAYTOWN

TEXAS
OLEFINS

Craigmont
Park
4200
PONDEROSA
4100

DECKER
TERRACE
VLLG

FAIRW
SOMERSET
INVERNESS
AIRWD
IMGLENHAVEN
5100

INTERLACHEN
TAMARACH
ARROWHEAD

HOMEWD

Country Club

GOOSE CREEK

PEBBLE BRK

N

SEE 499 MAP

S. BURNETT
WESTOAK
YAUPON
WINKLER
RUE ORLEANS
200
Lkwd
Park

GREENBRIAR
NATCHEZ
WINKLER
CT
HILLSIDE
CT
100

5500

4300

Pumphrey
Alternative
Learning
Program

SHADY HILL
BRIAR
OAK
INDIAN
TRL

Fresh
Water Bayou

SCHRECK
Westwood
Park

STEINMAN

COURTYARD BLVD
100
E. SCHRECK
FORTNER
100
WOOD AVE

Community
Guidance
Center

BORG-WARNER
CORP.

TX EASTERN
TRANSMISSION CORP.

ROLLING
BROOK

330

E. BAYSHORE
TMBR

BROWNWD
ADELE
GERALD
HARVEY BLVD
SHORT
CAMPBELL

WEAVER
Baytown
Nature
Center
FOSTER

SCARLETT
O'HARA
NORTH
100

300
DOUGLAS
COBURN
BARNES
ABBOTT

400

BAYTOWN
OLEFINS PLANT

MAC ARTHUR
RIDGEWY
KATHERINE
CABANISS
CROW

BAYWAY

ARBOR
6100
WOOSTER
JOHN A
CHURCH
NORTH
ASHBY

BOISE
QUEENS
CT
100

ASHLAND
CHEMICALS

© KEY MAPS 2017

MAPLETON
BROWNWOOD

Scott Bay

KINGS
CT
5700
Burnel

5500
Gate

PARK

UP RR

TRAVIS
CROCKETT
WEST AVENUE
BURNETT
AUSTIN

NOLAN

GREEN
HOUSTON
VICTORIAN
CROSBY

DIKE
BOWIE

MARSH
BEAN
MASON

FANNIN
BONHAM

ZAVALA

S

T

EXXON CO. USA

© KEY MAPS 2017

BAYVILLA
5100

HOUSTON

W

X

Mitchell
Bay

BAYWAY

FRANKLIN

SAN JACINTO
WHARTON

BAYTOWN AVE
BAYTOWN
ALAMO
HUMBLE
CROSBY
HOCKLEY

UP RR
BLAFFER
BAYTOWN AVE
HARBOR
PINE
SANTANA

OAKWD
CHERRY
MAGNOLIA
CYPRESS

DAYTON

S. AIRHART
BEECH
100
OAK ALLEY

MARKET
3300
MINNESOTA
WISCONSIN

Dezavala

HOUSTON SHIP CHANNEL

SEE 540 MAP

0   1/4   1/2   3/4   1 Mile

© KEY MAPS 2017

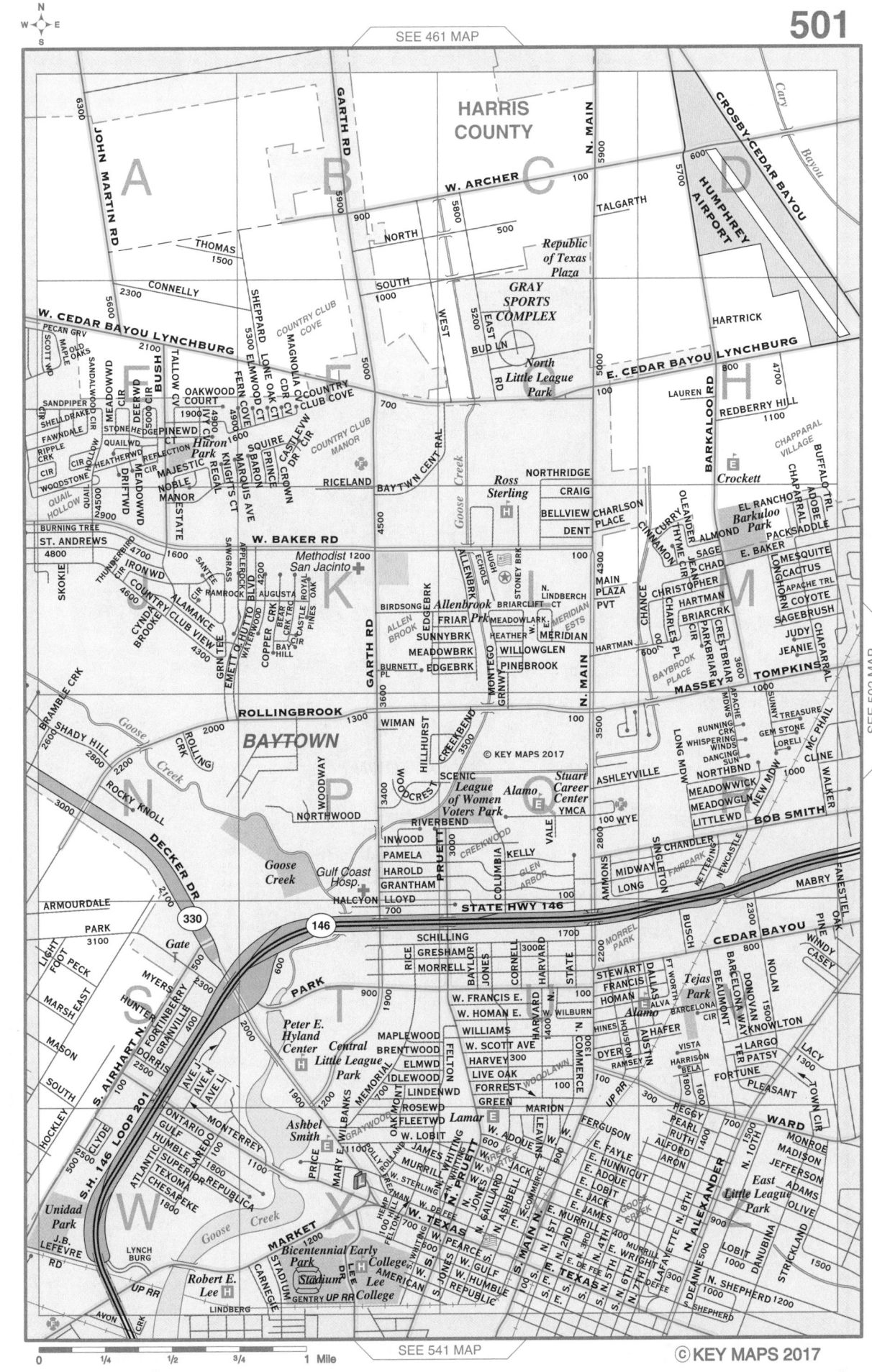

HARRIS COUNTY

BAYTOWN

0   1/4   1/2   3/4   1 Mile

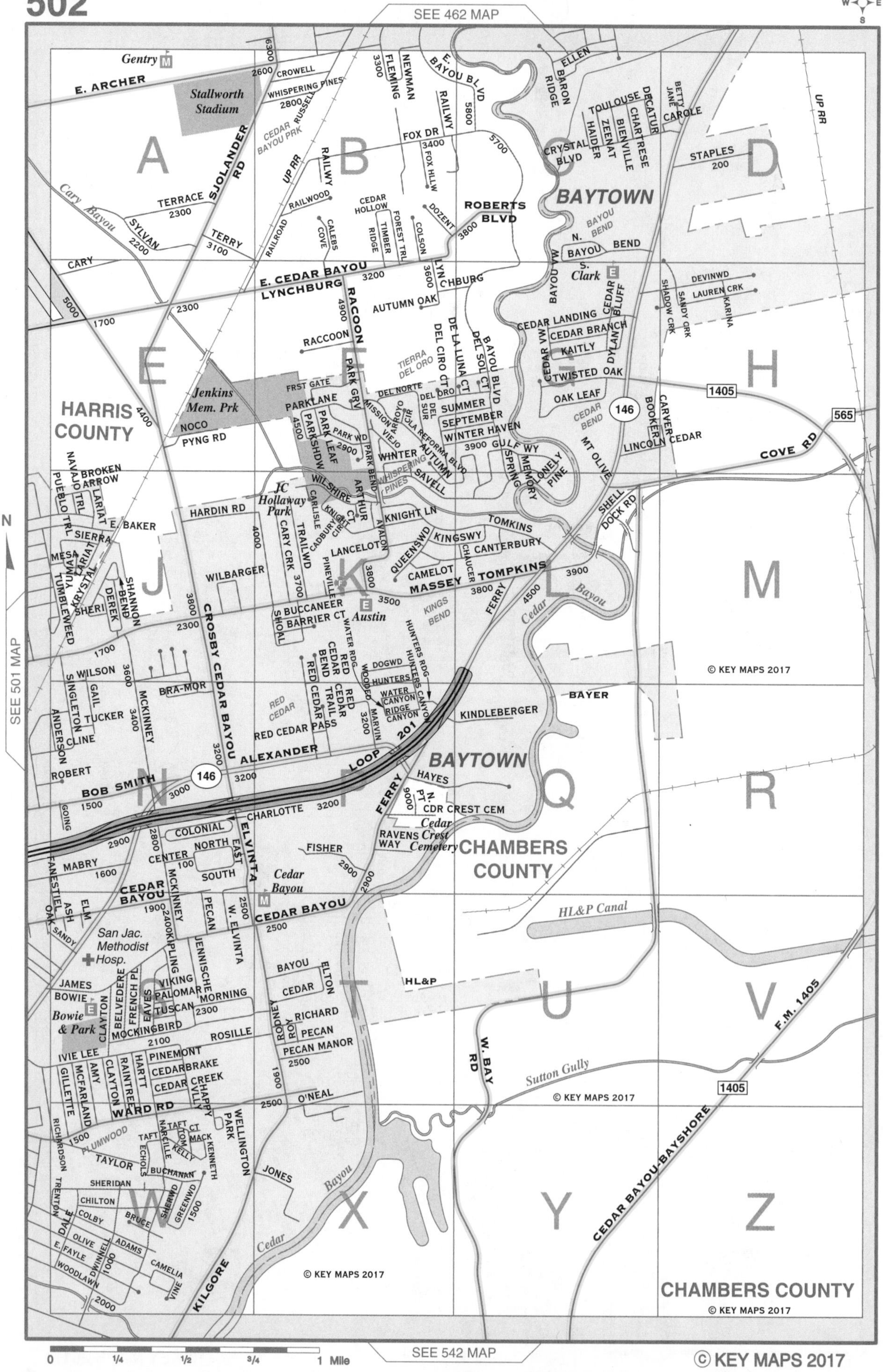

502

N
W E
S

Harris County / **Chambers County**

Grid references: A, B, C, D, E, F, G, H, J, K, L, M, N, P, Q, R, S, T, U, V, W, X, Y, Z

Gentry

E. ARCHER

Stallworth Stadium

CROWELL
WHISPERING PINES
CEDAR BAYOU PRK
FLEMING
NEWMAN
E. BAYOU BLVD
ELLEN
BARON RIDGE
TOULOUSE
DECATUR
BETTY JANE
CAROLE
CHARTRESE
ZEENAT
BIENVILLE
HAIDER
CRYSTAL BLVD

BAYTOWN

STAPLES

FOX DR
FOX HLLW
RAILWY
UP RR
SOLANDER RD
TERRACE
SYLVAN
CARY BAYOU
CARY
TERRY
RAILROAD
RAILWOOD
CALEBS COVE
CEDAR HOLLOW
FOREST TRL
TIMBER RIDGE
DOZENT
COLSON
LYN CHBURG
ROBERTS BLVD

N. BAYOU BEND
S. BAYOU VW
BAYOU BEND
Clark
CEDAR BLUFF
DEVINWD
LAUREN CRK
SHADOW CRK
SANDY CRK
KARINA

E. CEDAR BAYOU LYNCHBURG
AUTUMN OAK
RACCOON
PARK GRV
DE LA LUNA CT
DEL CIRO CT
DEL SOL CT
TIERRA DEL ORO
DEL NORTE
DEL ORO
DEL SUR
SUMMER
SEPTEMBER
WINTER HAVEN
CEDAR LANDING
CEDAR BRANCH
KAITLY
TWISTED OAK
OAK LEAF
BAYOU BLVD
146
1405
565
COVE RD
LINCOLN
CEDAR
BOOKER
CARVER

HARRIS COUNTY

Jenkins Mem. Prk
FRST GATE
PARKLANE
PARKLEAF
PARKSHOW
NOCO
PYNG RD
PARK WD
MISSION
RIOLA REFORMA BLVD
VIEJO
WINTER
AUTUMN
WHISPERING PINES
SAVELL
SPRING
GULF WY
MEMORY
LONELY PINE
MT OLIVE
SHELL DOCK RD

JC Hollaway Park
HARDIN RD
WILBARGER
CARY CRK
TRAILWD
WILSHIRE
ART HUR
KNIGHT CT
CARLISLE
CADBURY
PINEVILLE
LANCELOT
AVALON
KNIGHT LN
QUEENSWD
KINGSWY
CAMELOT
CHAUCER
TOMKINS
CANTERBURY
MASSEY TOMPKINS
CEDAR
Bayou

BROKEN ARROW
NAVAJO TRL
PUEBLO TRL
LARIAT
E. BAKER
SIERRA
MESA
SAVANNA
STA. MARIA
TUMBLEWEED
SHERI
DEREK
SHANNON

BUCCANEER
BARRIER CT
SHOAL
Austin
WATER RDG
RED RDG
WOODED
DOGWD
HUNTERS RDG
HUNTERS CANYON
WATER CANYON
RIDGE CANYON
KINDLEBERGER
BAYER

CROSBY CEDAR BAYOU
S. WILSON
INGLETON
GAIL
TUCKER
MCKINNEY
BRA-MOR
ANDERSON
CLINE
ROBERT
BOB SMITH
RED CEDAR
RED CEDAR BEND
RED CEDAR TRAIL
RED CEDAR PASS
MARVIN
201
LOOP
BAYTOWN

146
ALEXANDER
CHARLOTTE
HAYES
N. PT.
CDR CREST CEM
Cedar Ravens Crest Way
Cedar Cemetery
CHAMBERS COUNTY
FERRY

COLONIAL
NORTH
CENTER
SOUTH
ELVINTA
EAST
FISHER
MABRY
Cedar Bayou
HL&P Canal
HL&P

CEDAR BAYOU
MCKINNEY
OAKPLING
KIPLING
PECAN
W. ELVINTA
CEDAR BAYOU
BAYOU
CEDAR
ELTON
W. BAY RD
Sutton Gully
FM 1405

San Jac. Methodist Hosp.
JAMES
BOWIE
Bowie & Park
JENNISCHE
BELVEDERE
FRENCH PL
EAVES
VIKING
PALOMAR
TUSCAN
MORNING
CLAYTON
IVIE LEE
PINEMONT
CEDARBRAKE
CEDAR CREEK
RICHARD
PECAN
PECAN MANOR
O'NEAL

GILLETTE
MCFARLAND
AMY
RAINTREE
HARTT
CLAYTON
WARD RD
PLUMWOOD
TAFT
NARCILLE
ECHOLS
BUCHANAN
TAYLOR
MACK
KENNETH
Wellington Park
JONES
Cedar Bayou
RICHARDSON
TRENTON
DALE
CHILTON
COLBY
SHERIDAN
BRUCE
ADAMS
CAMELIA
VINE
E. FAYLE
OLIVE
DINNAR
WOODLAWN
KILGORE

CHAMBERS COUNTY

© KEY MAPS 2017

0   1/4   1/2   3/4   1 Mile

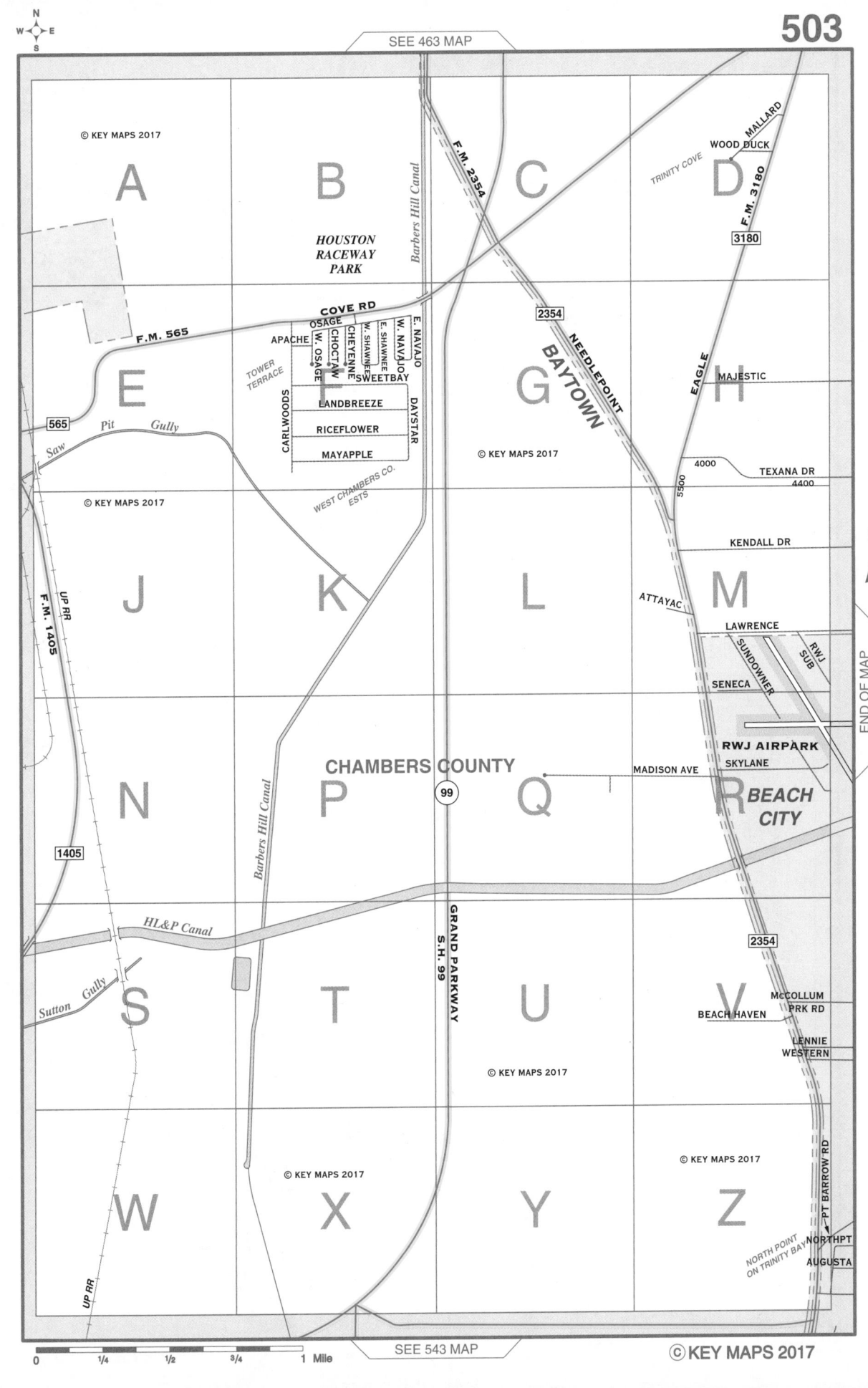

N
W-E
S

© KEY MAPS 2017

A

B

HOUSTON
RACEWAY
PARK

Barbers Hill Canal

F.M. 2354

C

TRINITY COVE

MALLARD
WOOD DUCK

D

F.M. 3180

3180

COVE RD

2354

NEEDLEPOINT

BAYTOWN

EAGLE

F.M. 565

OSAGE
APACHE   W. OSAGE
CHOCTAW
CHEYENNE
W. SHAWNEE
E. SHAWNEE
SWEETBAY

E. NAVAJO
W. NAVAJO

MAJESTIC

H

565

TOWER
TERRACE

E

Saw   Pit   Gully

CARLWOODS

F

LANDBREEZE

RICEFLOWER

MAYAPPLE

DAYSTAR

WEST CHAMBERS CO.
ESTS

G

© KEY MAPS 2017

4000

5500

TEXANA DR
4400

© KEY MAPS 2017

KENDALL DR

UP RR

F.M. 1405

J

K

ATTAYAC

L

LAWRENCE

M

N

RWJ
SUB

SUNDOWNER

© KEY MAPS 2017

Barbers Hill Canal

SENECA

RWJ AIRPARK

SKYLANE

END OF MAP

1405

N

CHAMBERS COUNTY

99

MADISON AVE

BEACH
CITY

N

P

Q

R

HL&P Canal

Sutton   Gully

S

T

GRAND PARKWAY

S.H. 99

U

2354

McCOLLUM
PRK RD

BEACH HAVEN

V

LENNIE
WESTERN

© KEY MAPS 2017

© KEY MAPS 2017

© KEY MAPS 2017

PT BARROW RD

W

UP RR

X

Y

Z

NORTH POINT
ON TRINITY BAY

NORTHPT

AUGUSTA

SEE 484 MAP

N W E S

Stanley

1463

PINE HILLS

ARISTATA

HARMONY SHORES

LADIES TRESSES

COQUINA

TEA TREE

F.M. 1093

CINCO RANCH BLVD

Stanley

CINCO RANCH SW

FRY RD

SPRING GREEN BLVD

FRY RD

Seven Lakes
1. Jacobs Landing
2. Rising Bend Ln
3. Moon Indigo Ln
4. Star Wish Ln
5. Paper Rose Ln
6. Plumero Mdw

SUMMERFLD GLADE

KATY-GASTON RD

INDIANGRASS

1093

25000

Flewellen

WESTHEIMER AIR PARK

1. Dogwood Knoll Ln
2. Skyridge Park Ln
3. Laguna Heights Ln

Hubenak

723

Covey Trails

Covey Trails Airport

W. KITTYHAWK E. KITTYHAWK

359

VILLAS AT WESTHEIMER
1. Anlu
2. Witherspoon

SEE FB 523 MAP

N

SERENITY OAKS

CANYON VLLG AT WESTHEIMER LKS

CRYSTAL CV

CANYON GATE AT WESTHEIMER LKS

CANYON FLDS

FULSHEAR GASTON RD

BELLAIRE BLVD

HINES NURSERIES

N

SAND PIT ACCESS

P

W. HIDDEN LK LN

E. HIDDEN LK LN

Q

R

723

10100

7500

Flewellen Creek

Bentley

S

T

U

V

FORT BEND COUNTY

MEADOW WY CIR

BRANCH

COUNTRYSHIRE

Jones Creek

ROLLING OAKS

2000

1900

7000

Spring Green

ANDRUS

W

F.M. 359

SETTEGAST RANCH RD

X

SETTEGAST RANCH

ANTHONIA LN

OAKHILL ESTATES

LEESWAY

Y

723

HUNTINGTON

CHERIDAN OAKS

CARLTON OAKS

Z

8300

6500

6400

6060

2000

6060

LEANING OAK TRL DEN OAK

COWBOY WY

SEE FB 564 MAP

0 1/4 1/2 3/4 1 Mile

© KEY MAPS 2017

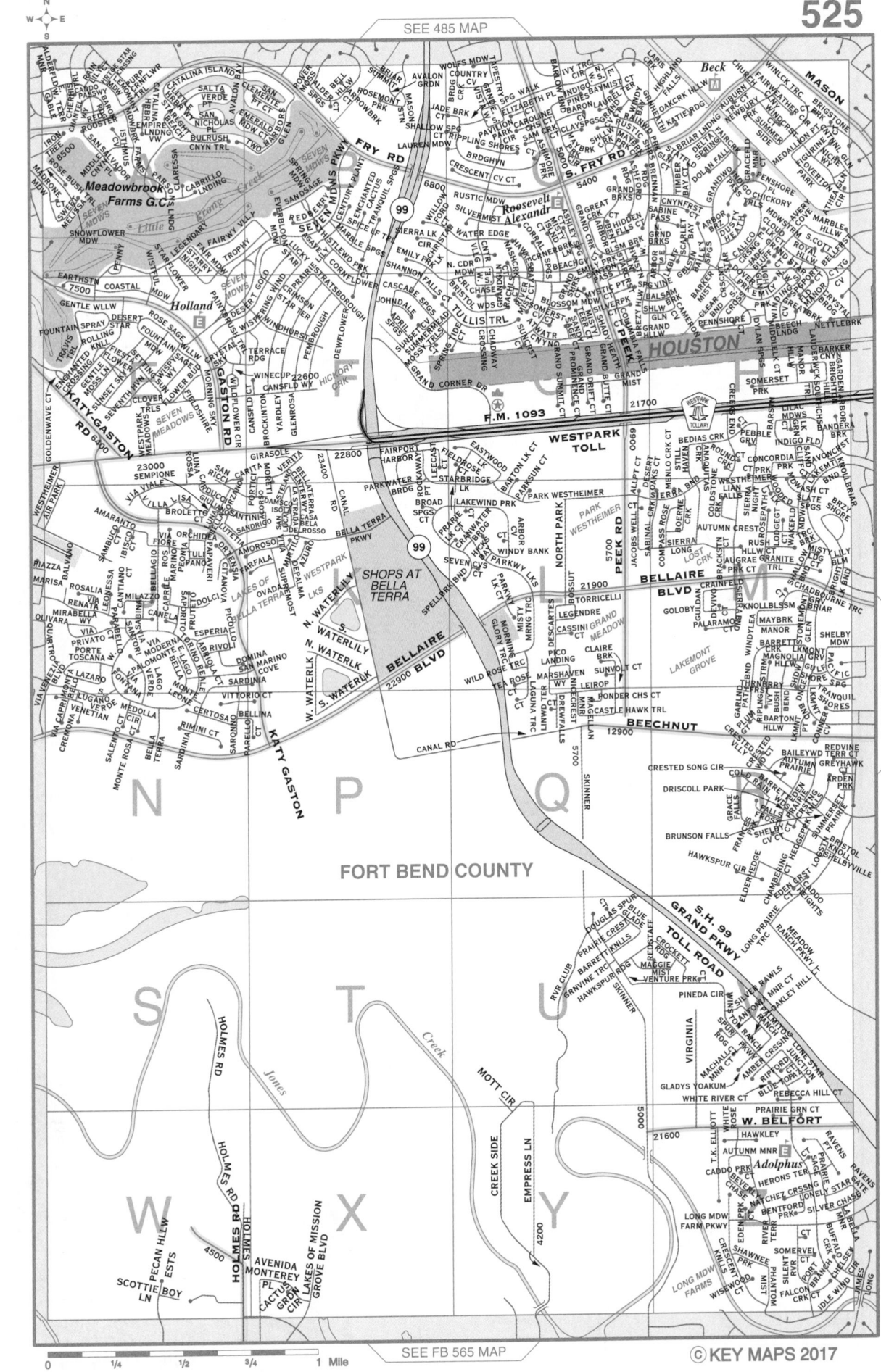

SEE 526 MAP

© KEY MAPS 2017

0   1/4   1/2   3/4   1 Mile

N
W E
S

HARRIS COUNTY
FORT BEND COUNTY

C
HOUSTON

Ft. Bend County Park

Buffalo Bayou

YMCA Camp Park

B

D

BARKER RESERVOIR

BARKER DAM

17900

OAK MOSS HILL CT

F.M. 1093

WESTPARK TOLLWAY

18500

19300

BELLAIRE BLVD

TWIN OAKS VILLAGE

MISSION MANOR

1. AARROYO HILL CT
2. CANYON SHDW
3. WALNUT CANYON
4. BRYCE CANYON

1. HIGHCLIFF LN
2. CLAYHORN CT
3. LINCOLN HEIGHTS CT
4. SUFFOLK HLLW LN

1. DUSTY CANYON LN
2. GARRETT KNOLLS LN
3. HAVEN BEND LN

McNeill

BELLAIRE BLVD

Seguin

Harlem

BEECHNUT

Crockett

HARLEM RD

S. MASON

Fieldstone

W. BELFORT

W. BELFORT

GRAND PKWY

Oakland FARMER

1400

99

TOLL ROAD

W. BELLFORT

18900

W. BELLFORT

WESTMOOR

17900

1. SIGHTING PARK
2. MATTWOOD
3. AUTUMN STONE

Travis

H

W. ALIANA TRC

CARRINGTON WDS

WESTMOOR COMEAUX

LUSITANIA

HAYWARD HILL

NETHERBY

0   1/4   1/2   3/4   1 Mile

SEE 525 MAP

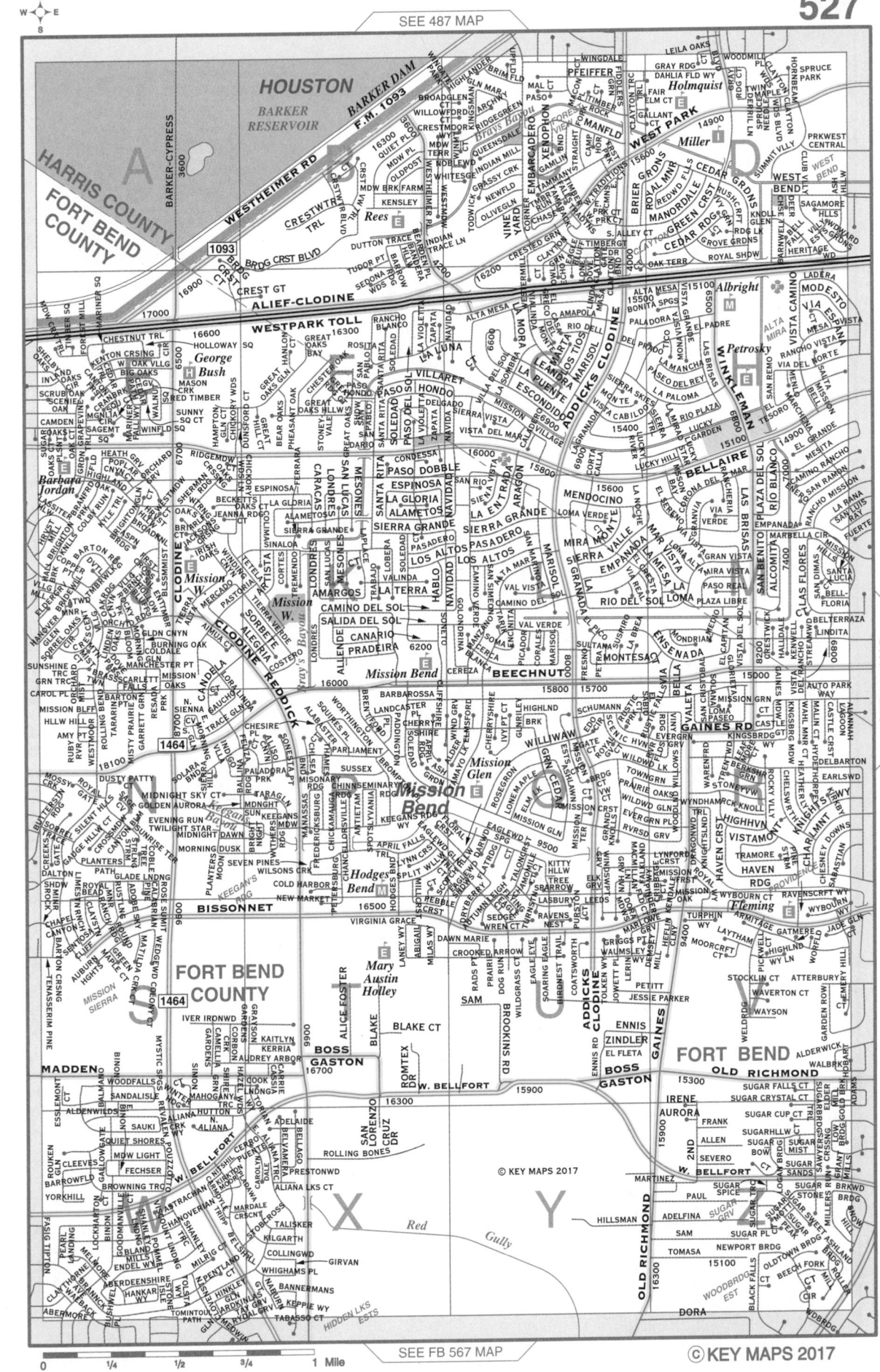

© KEY MAPS 2017

SEE 488 MAP

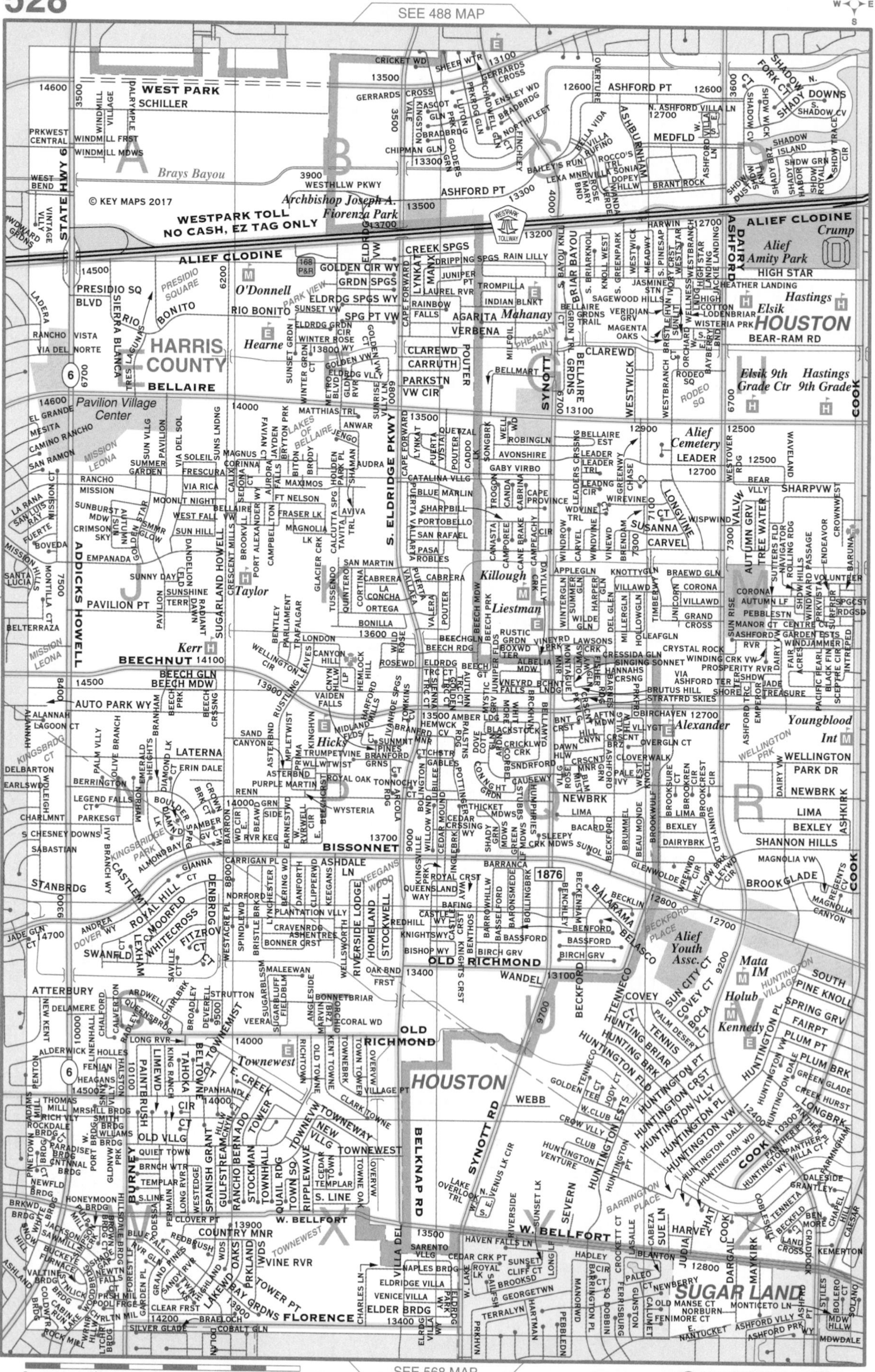

© KEY MAPS 2017

WEST PARK
SCHILLER

Brays Bayou

WESTPARK TOLL
NO CASH, EZ TAG ONLY

Archbishop Joseph A.
Fiorenza Park

ALIEF CLODINE

HARRIS
COUNTY

BELLAIRE

Pavilion Village
Center

PRESIDIO SQ
BLVD

O'Donnell

Hearne

Taylor

Kerr

BEECHNUT

Hicks

Bissonnet

Laterna

ALIEF CLODINE
DAIRY ASHFORD

Alief
Amity Park

Crump

HIGH STAR

HOUSTON

Elsik
BEAR-RAM RD

Hastings

Elsik 9th
Grade Ctr

Hastings
9th Grade

Alief
Cemetery

LEADER

Mahanay

Killough

Liestman

Alexander

Youngblood
Int

Wellington
Park Dr

NEWBRK

LIMA

BEXLEY

SHANNON HILLS

BROOKGLADE

Alief
Youth Assc.

OLD RICHMOND

OLD
RICHMOND

HOUSTON

Townewest

TOWNEWEST

W. BELLFORT

FLORENCE

W. BELLFORT

Mata
IM

Holub

Kennedy

SUGAR LAND

S. ELDRIDGE PKWY

ADDICKS HOWELL

SUGARLAND HOWELL

BELKNAP RD

SYNOTT RD

COOK

SEE 527 MAP

SEE 568 MAP

0   1/4   1/2   3/4   1 Mile

© KEY MAPS 2017

1876

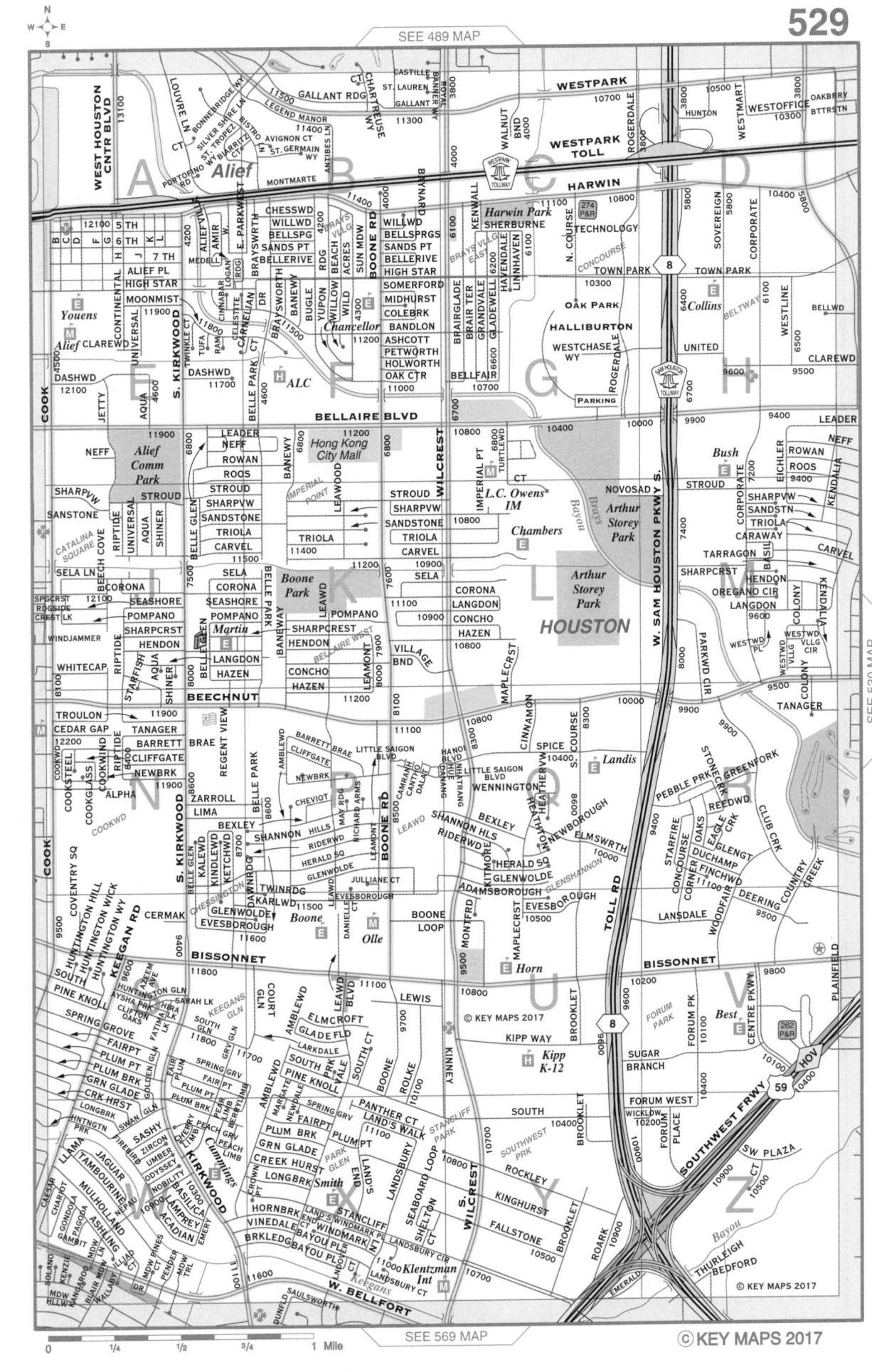

SEE 530 MAP

© KEY MAPS 2017

© KEY MAPS 2017

© KEY MAPS 2017

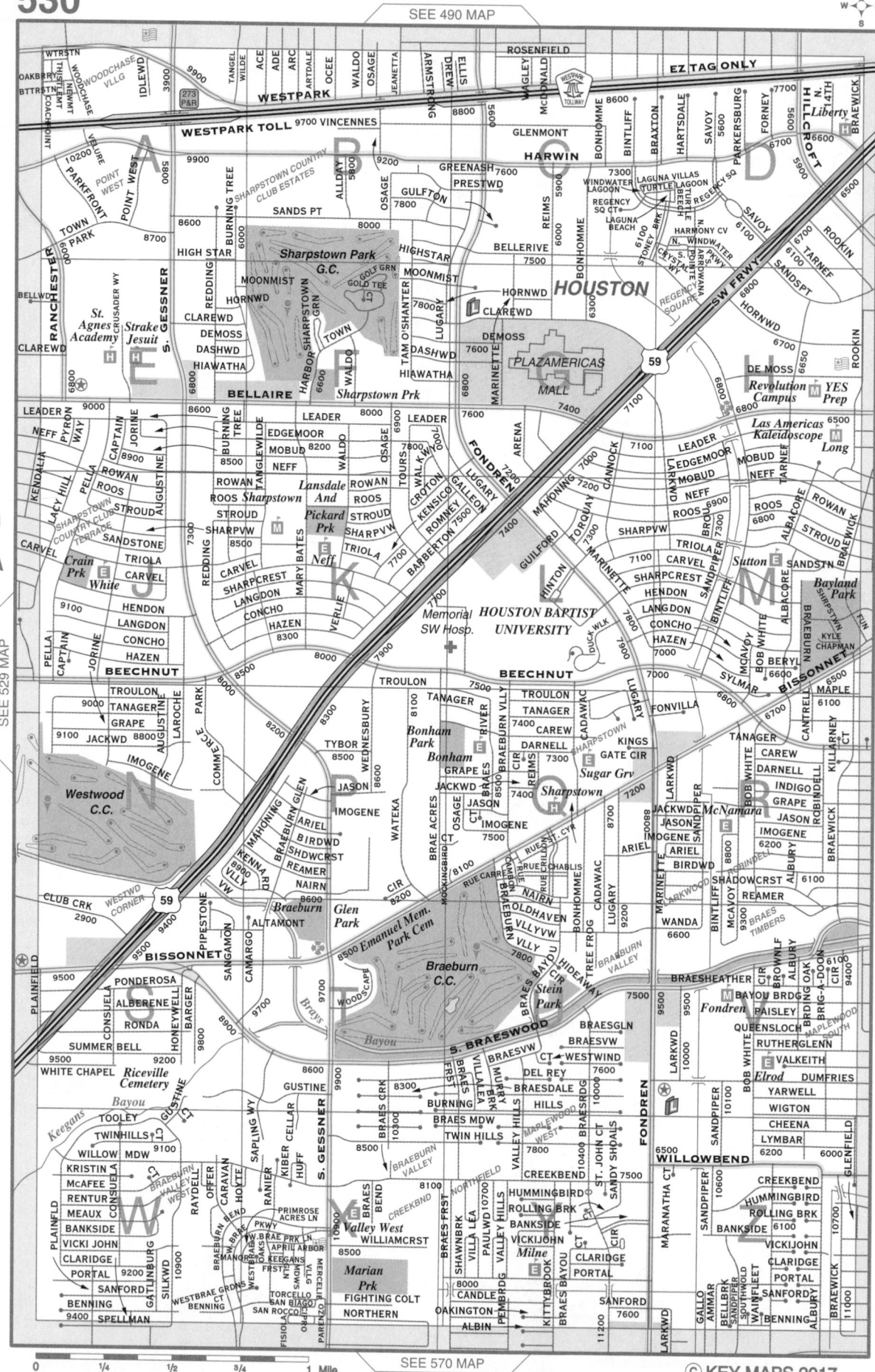

SEE 490 MAP

SEE 529 MAP

© KEY MAPS 2017

0   1/4   1/2   3/4   1 Mile

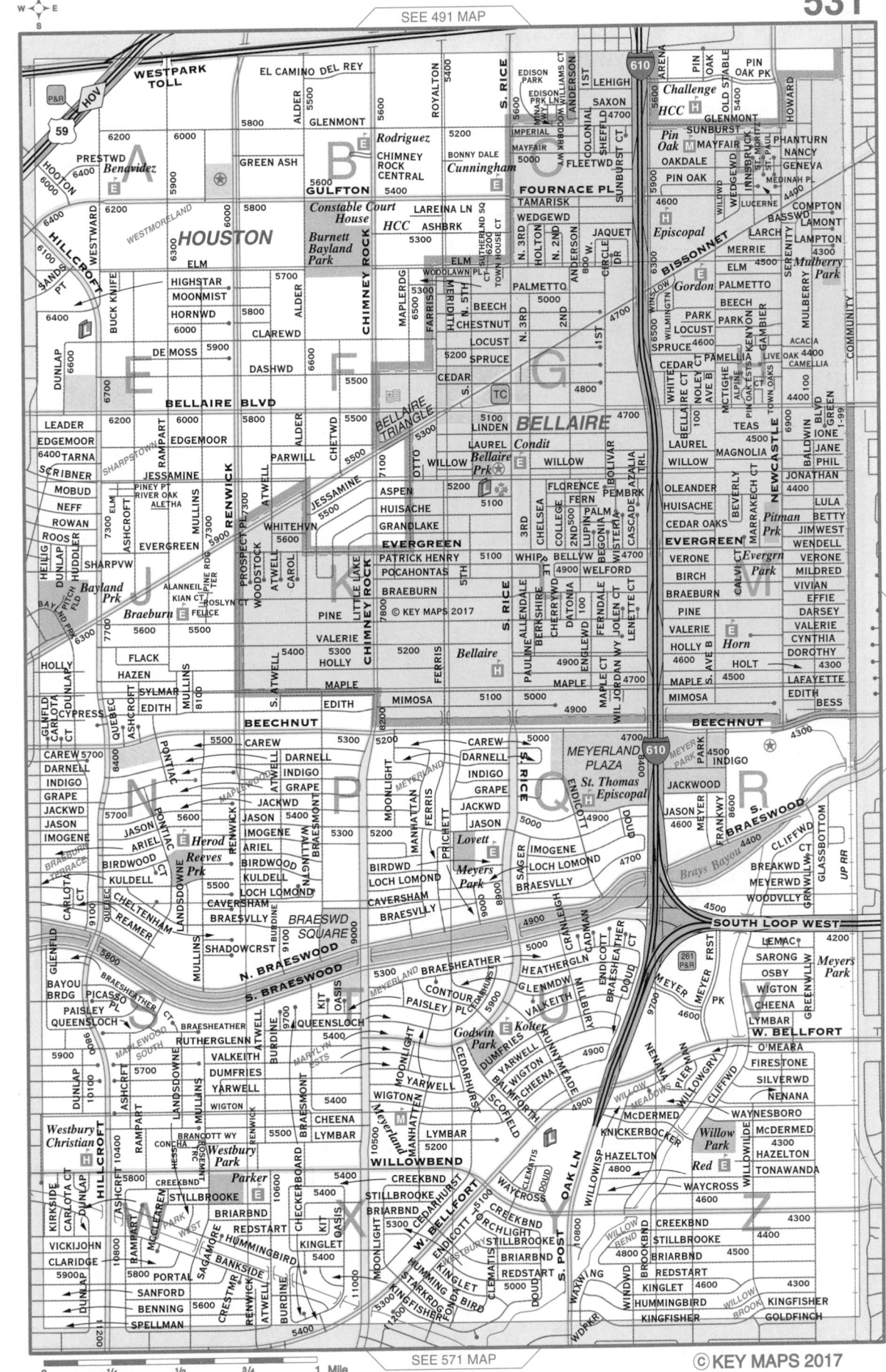

© KEY MAPS 2017

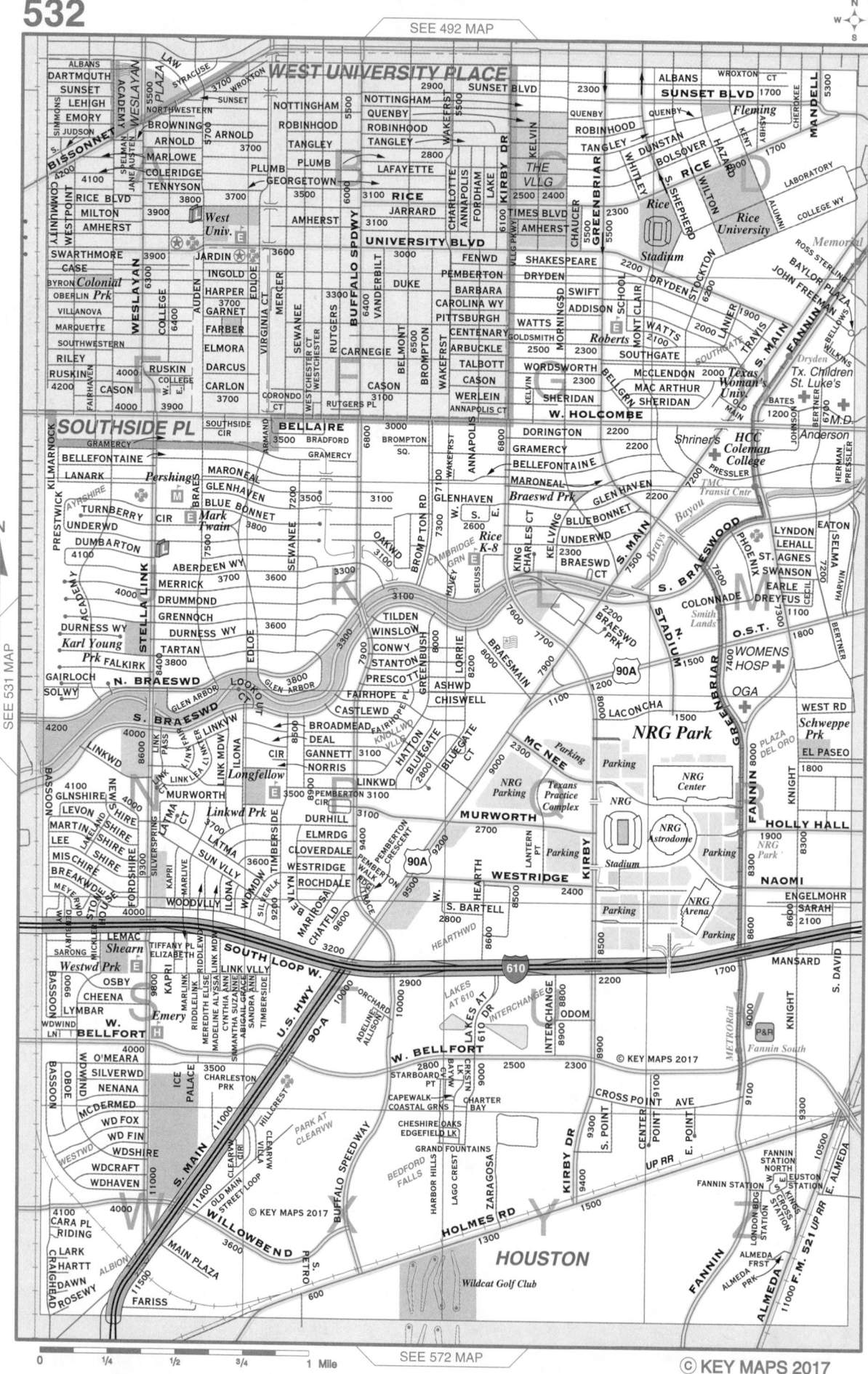

WEST UNIVERSITY PLACE

SOUTHSIDE PL

NRG Park

HOUSTON

Wildcat Golf Club

© KEY MAPS 2017

0   1/4   1/2   3/4   1 Mile

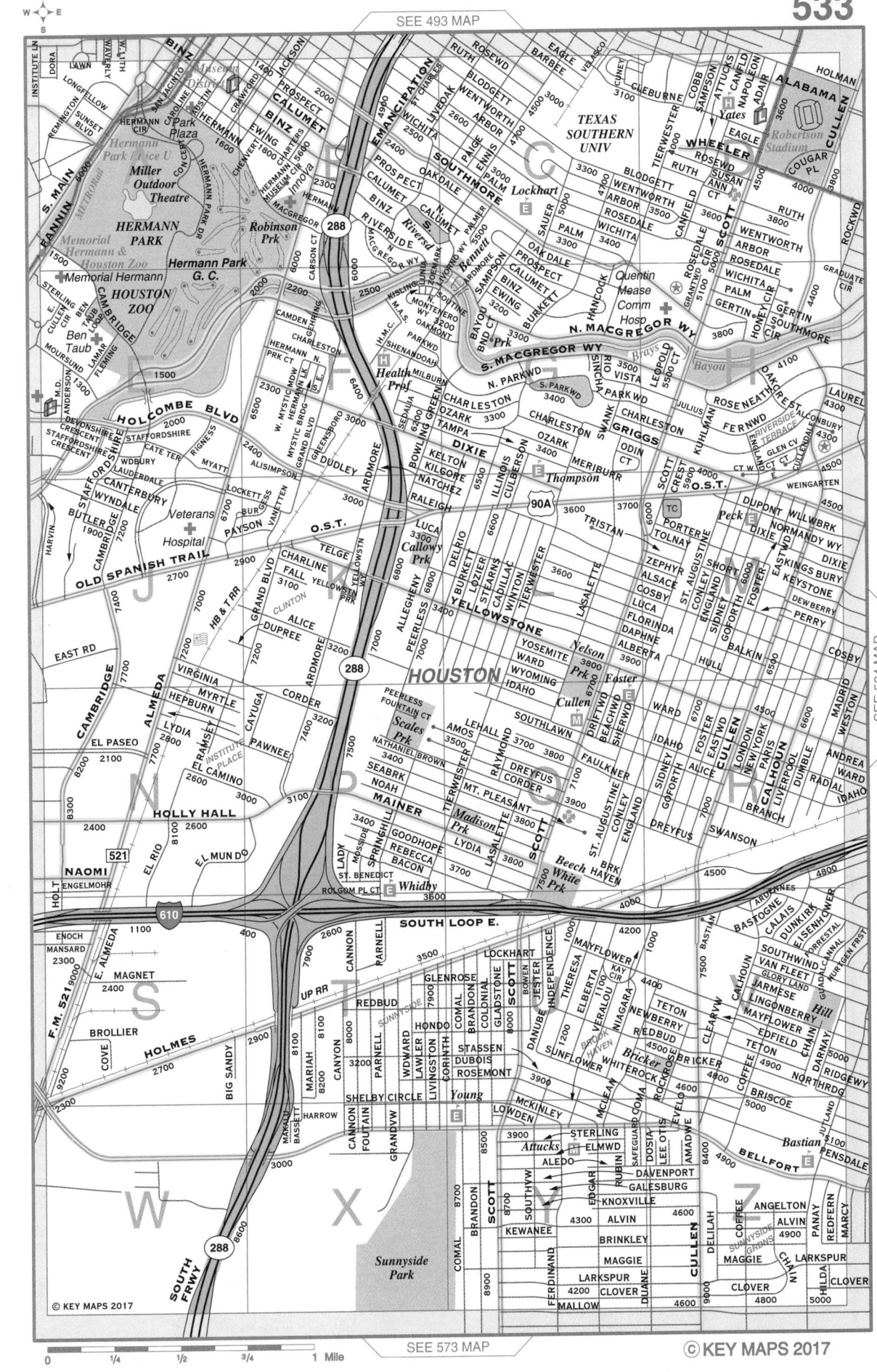

SEE 534 MAP

0   1/4   1/2   3/4   1 Mile

N
W — E
S

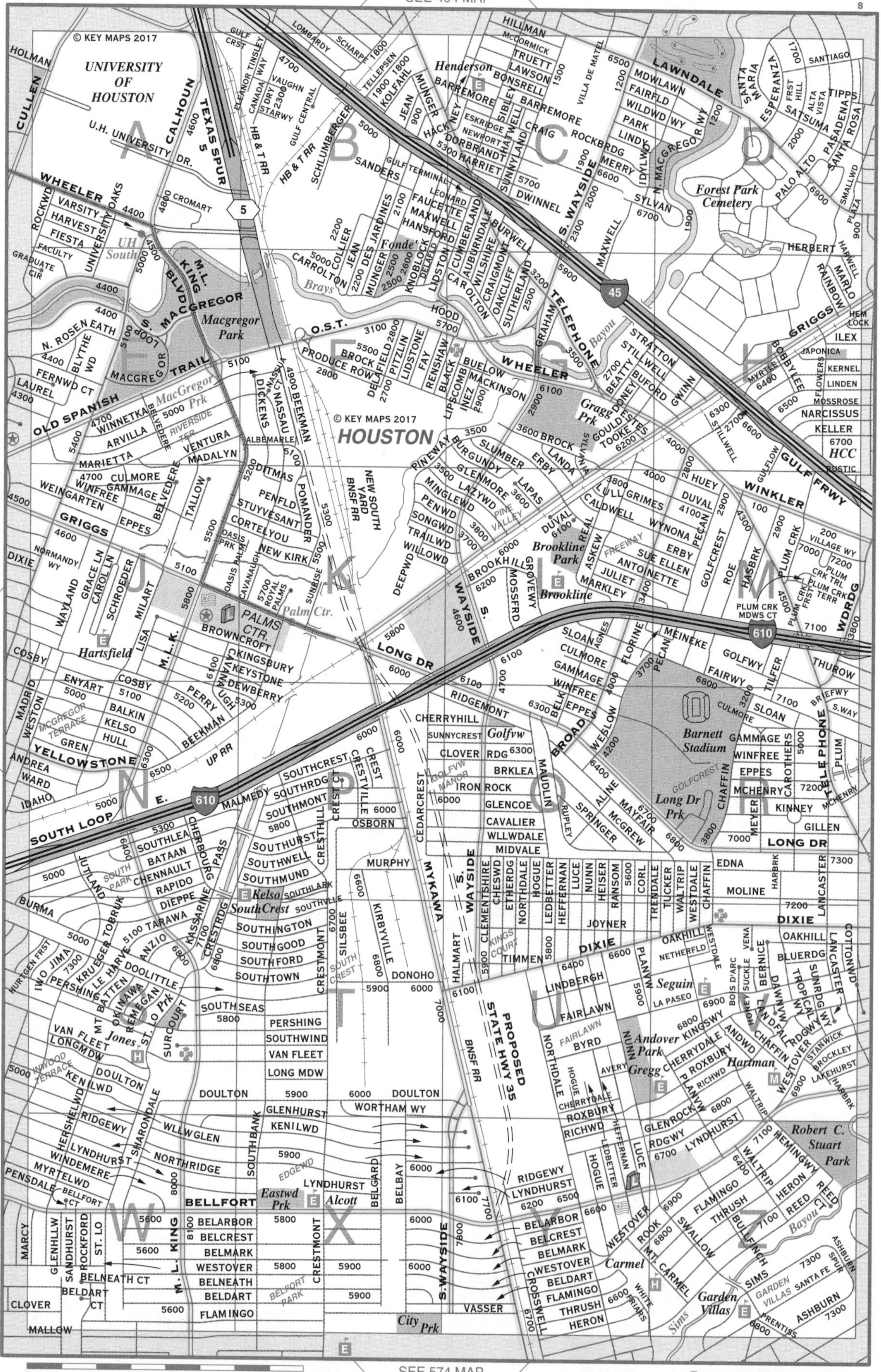

© KEY MAPS 2017

UNIVERSITY OF HOUSTON

U.H. UNIVERSITY DR.

HOLMAN
CULLEN
CALHOUN
TEXAS SPUR 5
HB & T RR

HILLMAN
McCORMICK
TRUETT
LAWSON
SIBLEY
BARREMORE
BARREMORE
HENDERSON
BONSRELL
VILLA DE MATEL

LAWNDALE
MDWLAWN
FAIRFLD
WILDWD WY
PARK
ROCKBRDG
LINDY
IDYLWD
MERRY
N. MACGREGOR WY

SANTA MARIA
ESPERANZA
FIRST HILL
ALTA VISTA
SATSUMA
SANTIAGO
PASADENA
SANTA ROSA
PALO ALTO
SMALLWD
PLAZA
HARWELL
MARLO
RAINBOW

WHEELER
ROCKWD
VARSITY
HARVEST
FIESTA
GRADUATE CIR
UNIVERSITY OAKS
CROMART
UH South
M.L. KING BLVD
S. MACGREGOR

N. ROSEN
EATH
BLYTHE
WD
FERNWD CT
LAUREL
OLD SPANISH
WINNETKA
ARVILLA
MARIETTA

MACGREGOR TRAIL
Macgregor Park
MacGregor Prk
Brays Bayou

O.S.T.
PRODUCE ROW
BROCK
PITZLIN
DELFIELD
LIDSTONE
FAY
RENSHAW
BLACK
BUELOW
MACKINSON
INEZ

WHEELER
STRATTON
STILWELL
BEATTY
BUFORD
GWINN
DONEY

Gragg Prk

HERBERT
GRIGGS
MYRTLE
BOBBYLEE
JAPONICA
KERNEL
LINDEN
MOSSROSE
NARCISSUS
KELLER
HCC
RUSTIC

© KEY MAPS 2017
HOUSTON

NEW SOUTH YARD BNSF RR

PINEWAY
BURGUNDY
SLUMBER
ERBY
LANDA
BROCK
TOOKE
GOULD
DESTES

HUEY
DUVAL
GRIMES
PECAN
WINONA
ERBY
GOLFCREST
ROE
PLUM CRK
VILLAGE WY
WINKLER
GULF FRWY

GRIGGS
DIXIE
NORMANDY WY
GRACE LN
CAROL LN
MILART
WAYLAND
SCHROEDER
LISA

Hartsfield
M.L.K.
PALMS CTR.
BROWNCROFT
KINGSBURY
KEYSTONE
DEWBERRY
PERRY
BEEKMAN

LONG DR

COSBY
ENYART
COSBY
BALKIN
KELSO
HULL
YELLOWSTONE
MADRID
WESTON
GREN

Brookline Park
Brookline
ASKEW
ANTOINETTE
JULIET
MARKLEY

FREEWAY
SUE ELLEN

MEINEKE
GOLFWY
FAIRWY
THUROW
SLOAN
BRIEFWY
S.WAY

CULMORE
GAMMAGE
WINFREE
BELK
EPPES

Barnett Stadium
GOLFCREST
CHAFFIN
Long Dr Prk

GAMMAGE
WINFREE
EPPES
McHENRY
KINNEY
GILLEN
LONG DR

SOUTH LOOP
E. 610
MALMEDY
SOUTHRDG
SOUTHMONT
CRESTVILLE
OSBORN

CHERRYHILL
SUNNYCREST
CLOVER
Golfvw
RDG
BRKLEA
IRON ROCK
GLENCOE
CAVALIER
WLLWDALE
MIDVALE

BROAD
WESLOW
ALINE
MAYFAIR
McGREW
RUPLEY
SPRINGER

SOUTHLEA
BATAAN
CHENNAULT
RAPIDO
DIEPPE
Kelso
SouthCrest
SOUTHINGTON
SOUTH GOOD
SOUTH FORD
SOUTH TOWN

MURPHY
MYKAWA
S. WAYSIDE
CLEMENTSHIRE
CHESWD
ETHERDG
NORTHDALE
HOGUE
LUCE
NUNN
HEISER
RANSOM
TUCKER
WALTRIP
WESTDALE
CHAFFIN
EDNA
MOLINE
DIXIE
LANCASTER
COTTONWD
OAKHILL
BLUERDG

DIXIE
HALMART
KINGS COURT
TIMMEN
SILSBEE
KIRBYVILLE
DONOHO

LINDBERGH
FAIRLAWN
BYRD
SEGUIN
LA PASEO
BERNICE
SUNRDG WY
TROPICAL

IWO JIMA
PERSHING
BATTEN
DOOLITTLE
OKINAWA
REMEGAN
VAN FLEET
LONGMDW
DOULTON
KENILWD
RIDGEWY
LYNDHURST
WINDEMERE
MYRTELWD
PENSDALE

Andover Park
Gregg
CHERRYDALE
ROXBURY
HARTMAN
CHERRYDALE
ROXBURY
RICHWD

Robert C. Stuart Park
HEMINGWY
WALTRIP
FLAMINGO
THRUSH
HERON
REED
BULFINCH

BELLFORT
M.L. KING
BELARBOR
BELCREST
BELMARK
WESTOVER
BELNEATH
BELDART
FLAMINGO
Eastwd Prk
Alcott
LYNDHURST

S. WAYSIDE
BELARBOR
BELCREST
BELMARK
WESTOVER
CROSSWELL
FLAMINGO
THRUSH
HERON
VASSER

Carmel
MT. CARMEL
Garden Villas
GARDEN VILLAS
SIMS
SANTA FE
ASHBURN
PRENTISS

City Prk

0 — 1/4 — 1/2 — 3/4 — 1 Mile

© **KEY MAPS** 2017

SEE 533 MAP

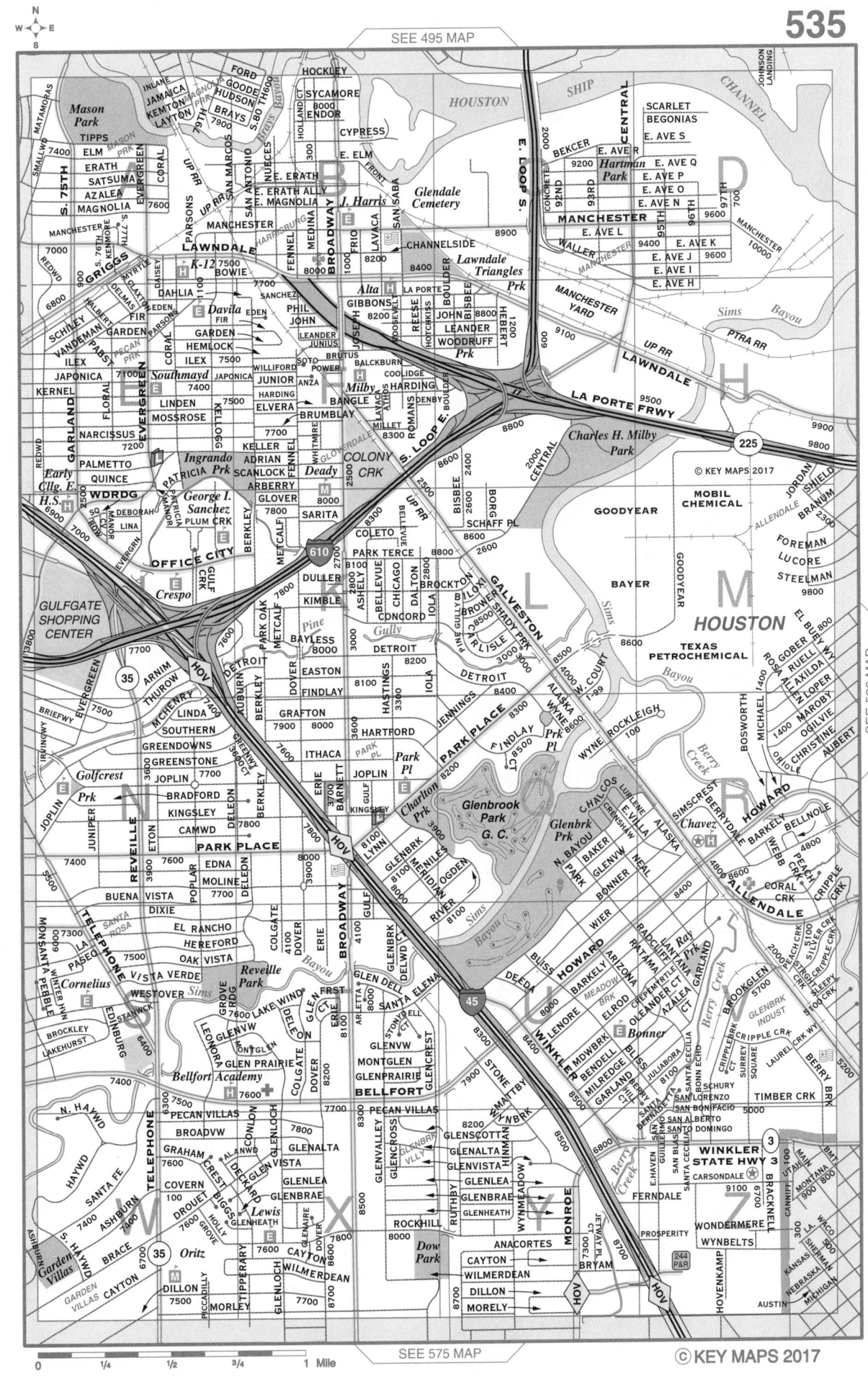

© KEY MAPS 2017

0   1/4   1/2   3/4   1 Mile

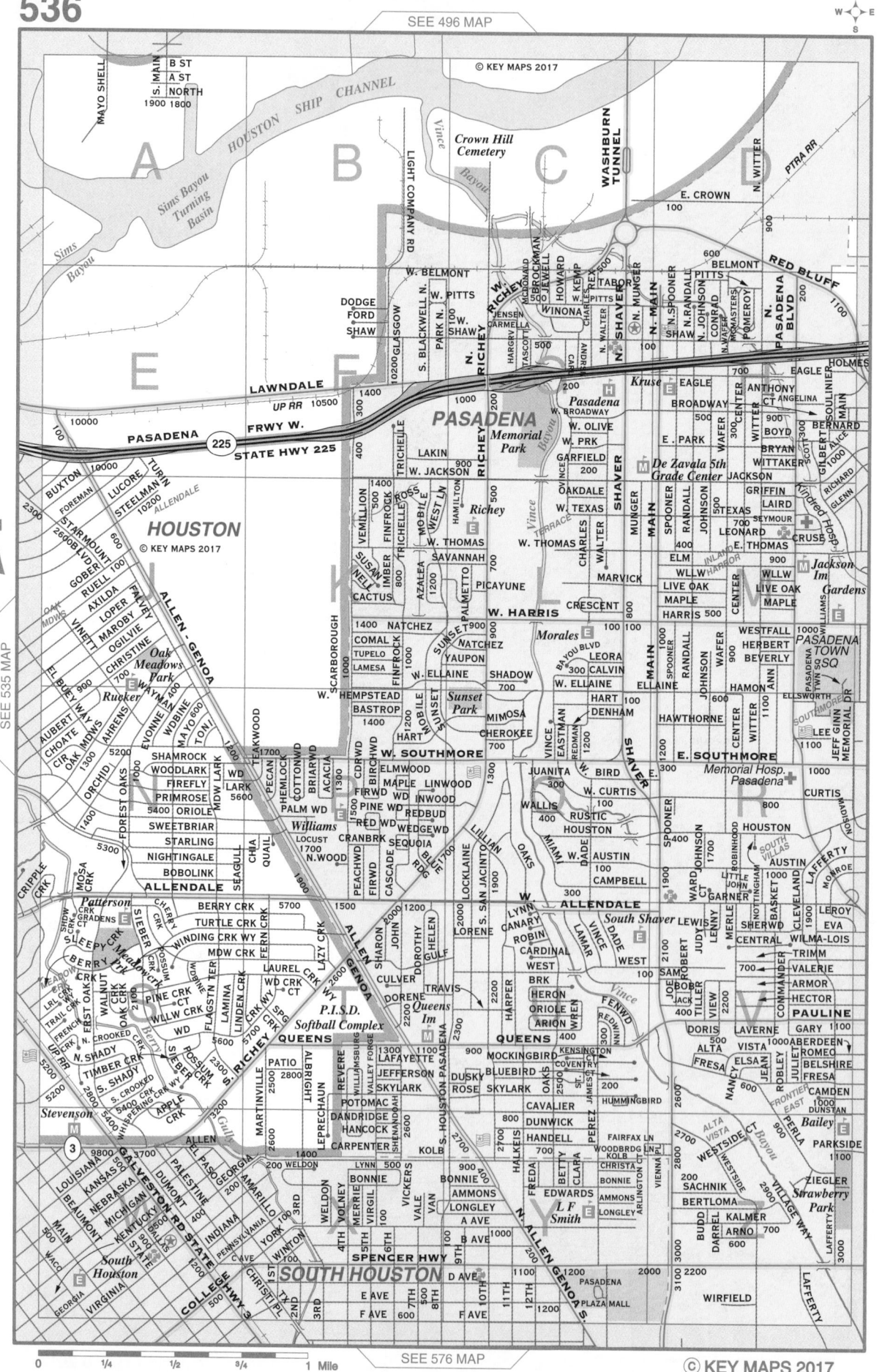

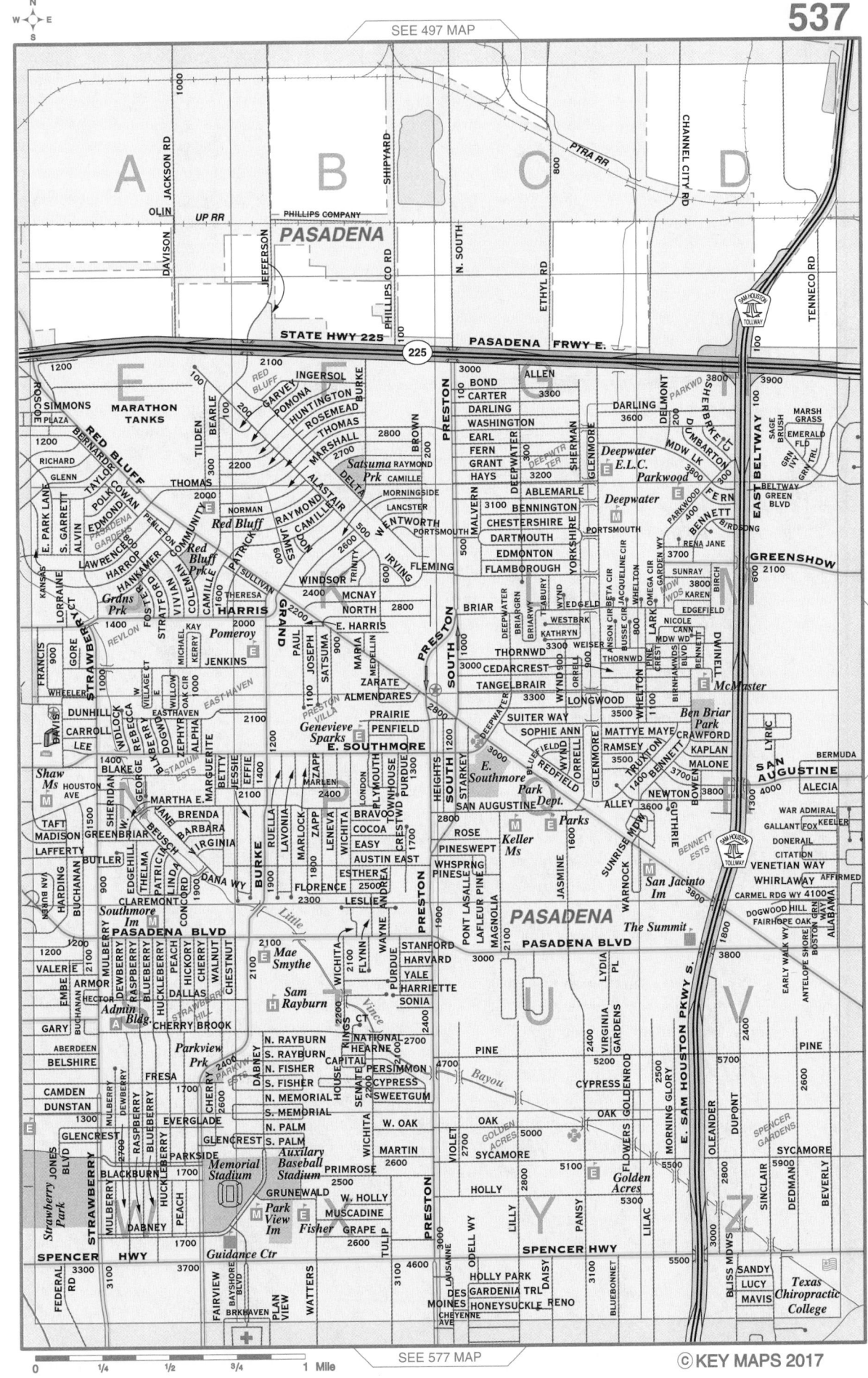

SEE 538 MAP

© KEY MAPS 2017

0   1/4   1/2   3/4   1 Mile

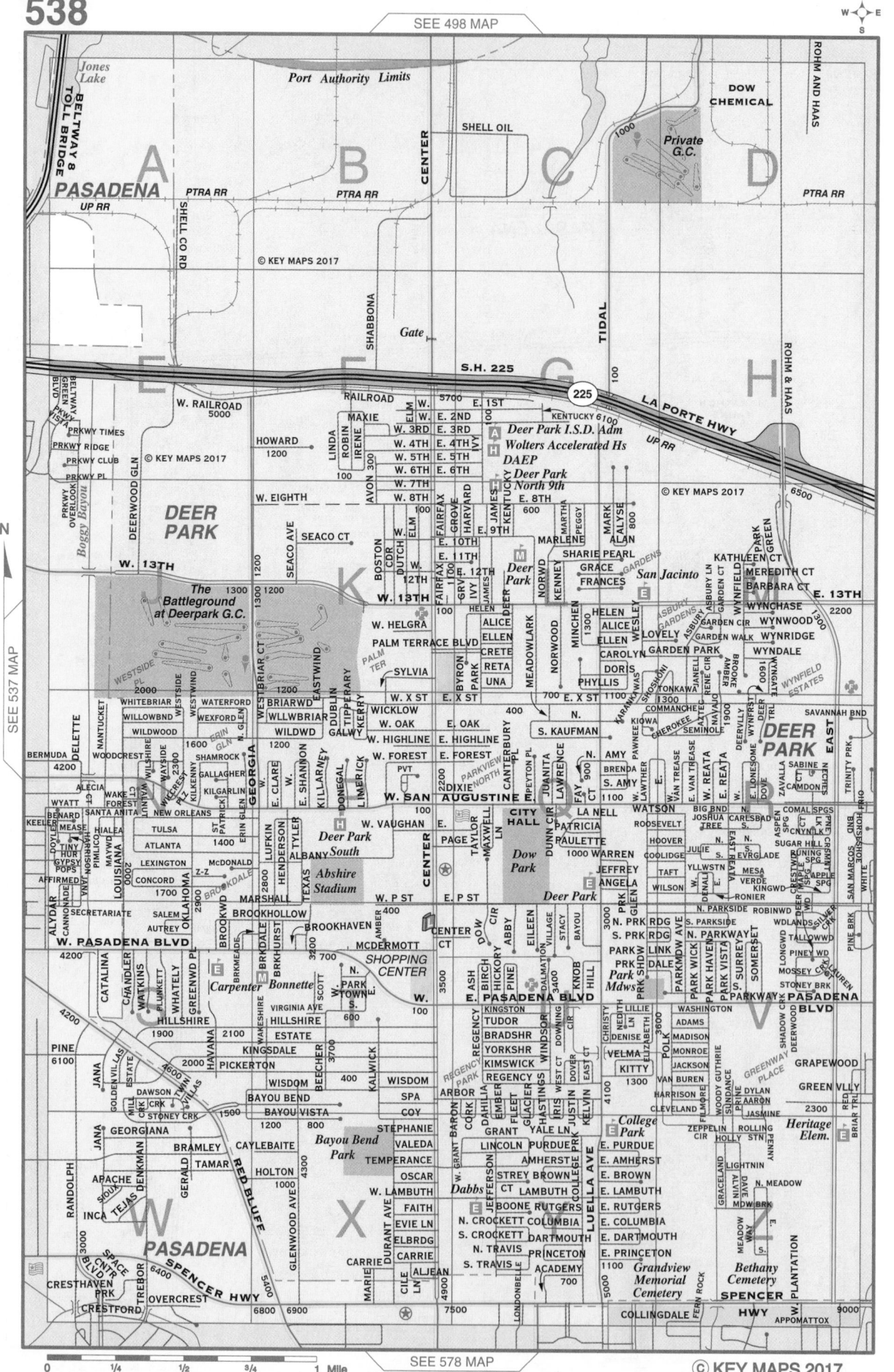

SEE 498 MAP
SEE 537 MAP
SEE 578 MAP

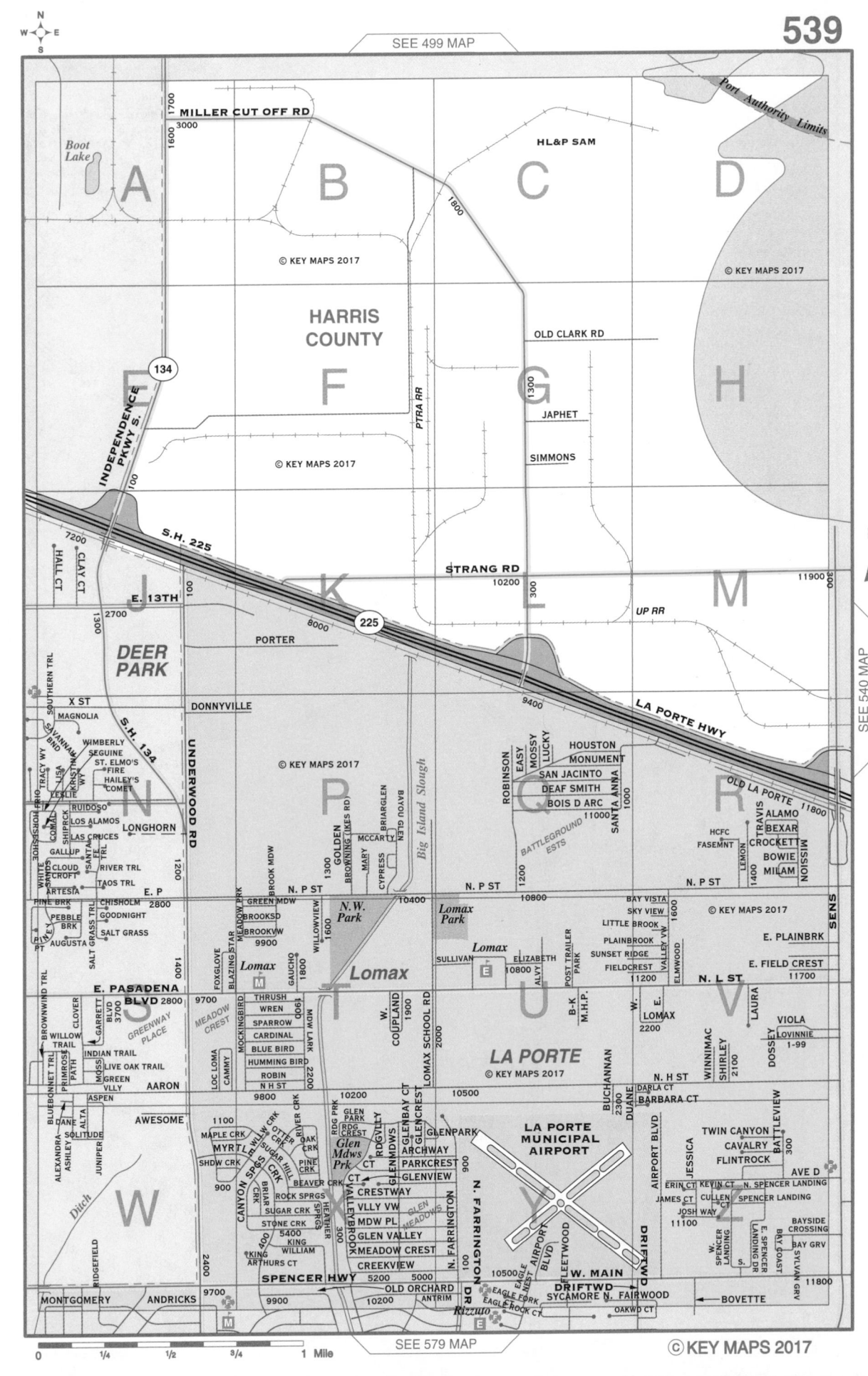

© KEY MAPS 2017

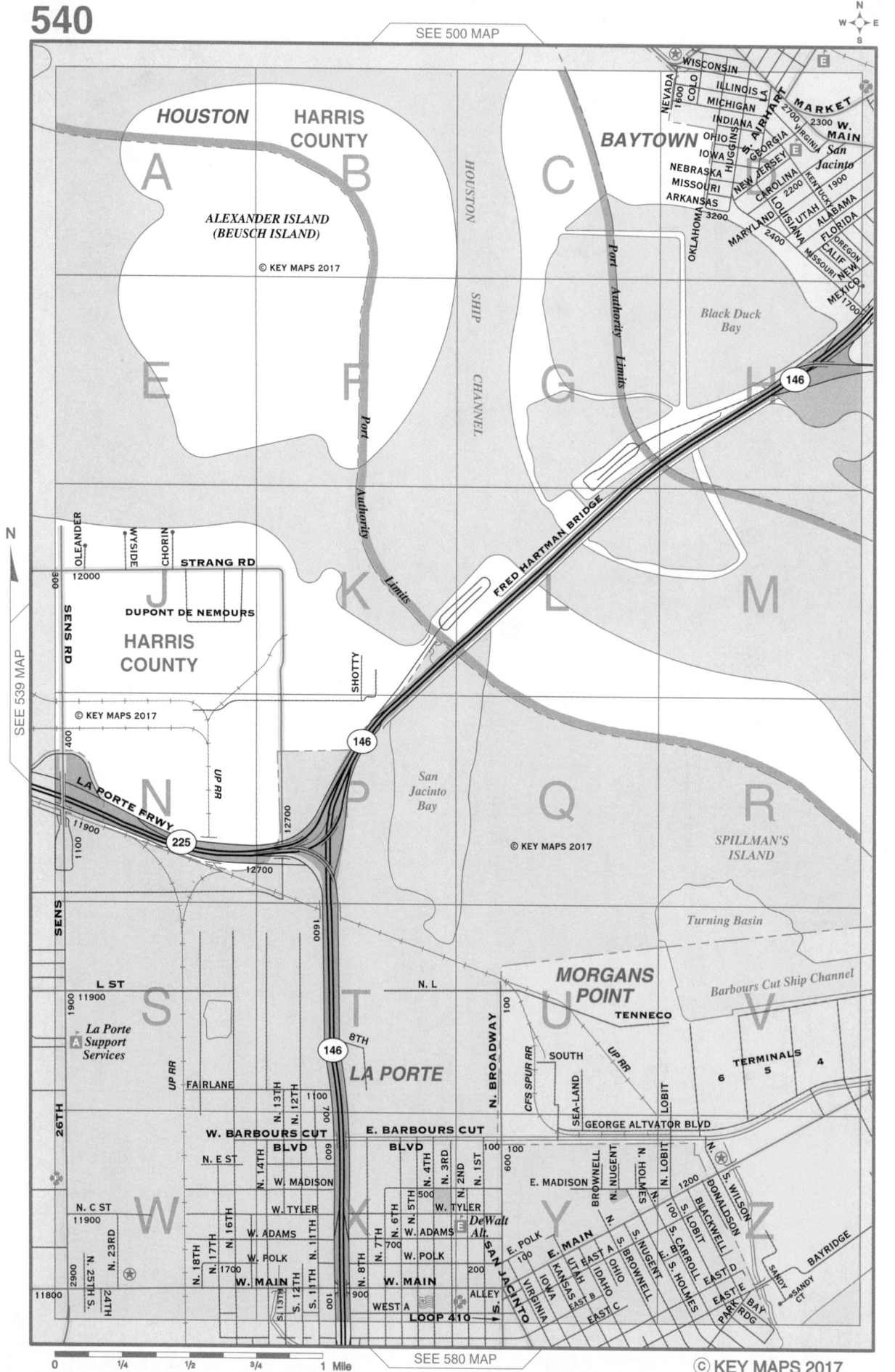

540

HOUSTON   HARRIS
           COUNTY

A   B   C   BAYTOWN

ALEXANDER ISLAND
(BEUSCH ISLAND)
© KEY MAPS 2017

WISCONSIN
NEVADA   COLO
1600   ILLINOIS   LA
         MICHIGAN
         INDIANA
         IOWA   OHIO
NEBRASKA
MISSOURI
ARKANSAS
3200

W. MAIN
San
Jacinto

E   F   G   H   146

Black Duck
Bay

Port Authority Limits

Port Ship Channel

SEE 539 MAP

N

OLEANDER
WYSIDE
CHORIN
STRANG RD
12000

SENS RD
300

DUPONT DE NEMOURS

HARRIS
COUNTY
© KEY MAPS 2017

400

J   K   FRED HARTMAN BRIDGE   L   M

SHOTTY

Port Authority Limits

146

LA PORTE FRWY
11900
1100
225

N   12700   P   San
                               Jacinto
                               Bay
                          © KEY MAPS 2017

Q   R   SPILLMAN'S
                ISLAND

UP RR

12700

1600

Turning Basin

SENS

L ST
1900   11900

La Porte
Support
Services

N. L   100

MORGANS
POINT

Barbours Cut Ship Channel

TENNECO

S   T   U   V

8TH

146   LA PORTE

26TH

UP RR   FAIRLANE

W. BARBOURS CUT
BLVD

N. E ST

N. C ST
11900

N. 23RD
2900

N. 25TH S.
11800   24TH

N. 14TH
N. 13TH
N. 12TH

N. 18TH
N. 17TH
N. 16TH
N. 11TH

1700

S. 13TH
S. 12TH

W. MADISON
W. TYLER
W. ADAMS
W. POLK
W. MAIN

600
700
900

E. BARBOURS CUT
BLVD

100   100
600

1100

N. 6TH
N. 7TH
N. 8TH
100

N. 5TH
N. 4TH
500
N. 3RD
N. 2ND
N. 1ST
W. TYLER
W. ADAMS
W. POLK

WEST A
LOOP 410

N. BROADWAY
CFS SPUR RR
SOUTH
SEA-LAND
UP RR
100
600

GEORGE ALTVATOR BLVD

E. MADISON

BROWNELL
N. NUGENT
N. HOLMES
N. LOBIT
1200

6   5   4
TERMINALS

S. WILSON
DONALDSON
BLACKWELL

E. POLK
E. MAIN
100
EAST A
EAST B
EAST C
EAST D

E. MAIN
UTAH
KANSAS
IOWA
VIRGINIA
IDAHO
OHIO
200
S. NUGENT
S. BROWNELL
S. LOBIT
S. HOLMES
100
S. CARROLL
S. BLACKWELL
EAST E
PARK RDG

1200
BAYRIDGE
SANDY BAY
SANDY CT

S   T   U   V
W   X   Y   Z

SENS
LOBIT

DeWalt
Alt.

SAN JACINTO S.

ALLEY

© KEY MAPS 2017

0   1/4   1/2   3/4   1 Mile

© KEY MAPS 2017

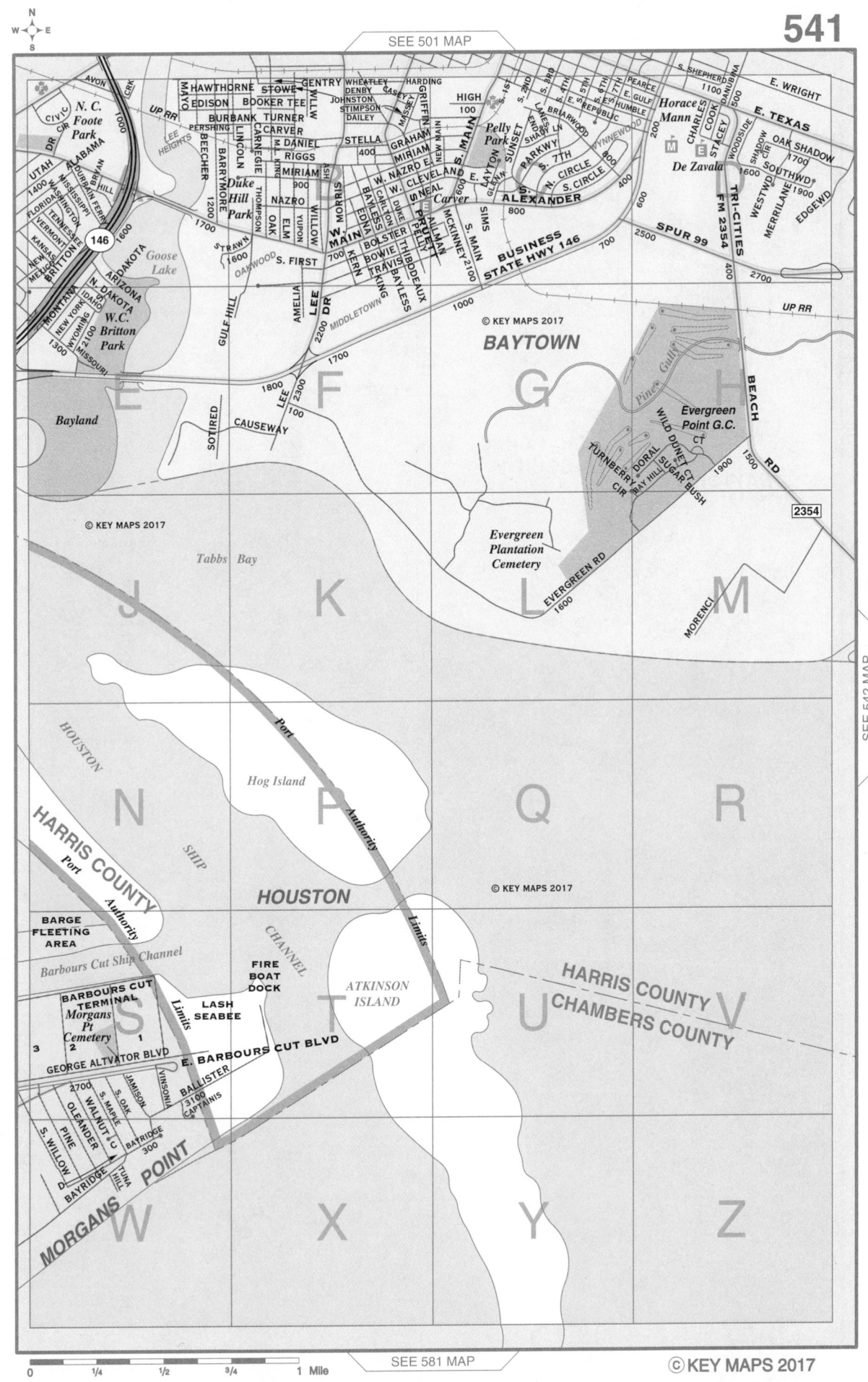

N
W · E
S

N.C. Foote Park
CIVIC CIR
AVON
CRK
1000
UP RR
MAYO
HAWTHORNE STOWE
GENTRY WILLW
WHEATLEY
DENBY
HARDING
CASEY
HIGH 100
S. 1ST
S. 2ND
S. 3RD
S. 4TH
S. 5TH
S. 7TH
PEARCE
S. HUMBLE
E. GULF
S. REPUBLIC
S. SHEPHERD 1100
DANUBMA
E. WRIGHT

EDISON
BOOKER TEE
JOHNSTON
STIMPSON
DAILEY
GRIFFIN
S. MAIN
Pelly Park
LAYTON
SUNSET
S. 7TH
N. CIRCLE
S. CIRCLE
800
WYNNEWOOD
Horace Mann
CHARLES
COOK
STACEY
WOODSIDE
SHADOW CIR
OAK SHADOW 1700
SOUTHWD
E. TEXAS
FM 2354

BURBANK TURNER
CARVER
M. DANIEL
STELLA 400
GRAHAM
W. NAZRO E.
W. CLEVELAND E.
S. ALEXANDER 800
De Zavala
MERRILANE 1900
WESTWD
EDGEWD

PERSHING
BEECHER
BARRYMORE
CARNEGIE
LINCOLN
M. KING
MIRIAM 900
SH
DUKE
W. CARLTON
S. NEAL
Carver
S. MAIN
N. CIRCLE
600
400
SPUR 99
2500
2700

UTAH 1400
ALABAMA
AUBURN
BRYAN
HILL
Duke Hill Park
THOMPSON
NAZRO
OAK
ELM
WILLOW
EDNA
BAYLESS
BOLSTER
BOWIE
McKINNEY 2100
S. MAIN
SIMS
BUSINESS
STATE HWY 146
1000

146

FLORIDA
MISSISSIPPI
WASHINGTON
VERMONT
1700
1200
S. STRAWN 1600
OAKWOOD
S. FIRST
KERN
700
TRAVIS
BAYLESS
THIBODEAUX
PRUETT
ALMAN

KANSAS
NEW YORK
MELICHSON
BRITTON 1600
Goose Lake
AMELIA
LEE DR
2200
KING

N. DAKOTA
ARIZONA
ARIDAKOTA
W.C. Britton Park
MIDDLETOWN

MONTANA
NEW YORK
IDAHO
2100
MISSOURI
1300
WYOMING
1800
LEE 100
BAYTOWN
© KEY MAPS 2017
UP RR

E
Bayland
SOTIRED
CAUSEWAY
F
G
H
BEACH RD
1500
1900
2354

Pines Gulf
Evergreen Point G.C.
CT
WILD DUNE
DORAL
CT
SUGAR BUSH
TURNBERRY
CIR
BAY HILL

J
Tabbs Bay
K
L
Evergreen Plantation Cemetery
EVERGREEN RD
1600
M
MORENCI

HOUSTON
N
SHIP
Hog Island
P
Port Authority
Q
R

HARRIS COUNTY
Port Authority
HOUSTON
© KEY MAPS 2017

BARGE FLEETING AREA
Barbours Cut Ship Channel
CHANNEL
FIRE BOAT DOCK
Limits
ATKINSON ISLAND
Limits

HARRIS COUNTY
U
CHAMBERS COUNTY
V

S
BARBOURS CUT TERMINAL
Morgans Pt Cemetery
3   2   1
GEORGE ALTVATOR BLVD
LASH SEABEE
E. BARBOURS CUT BLVD
T

2700
JAMISON
VINSONIA
BALLISTER
3100
CAPTAINS
WALNUT
S. OAK
S. MAPLE
OLEANDER
BAYRIDGE 300
BATRIDGE
S. PINE
S. WILLOW
D
BAYRIDGE
TUNA
HILL
MORGANS POINT

W
X
Y
Z

0   1/4   1/2   3/4   1 Mile

© KEY MAPS 2017

SEE 542 MAP

N

SEE 502 MAP

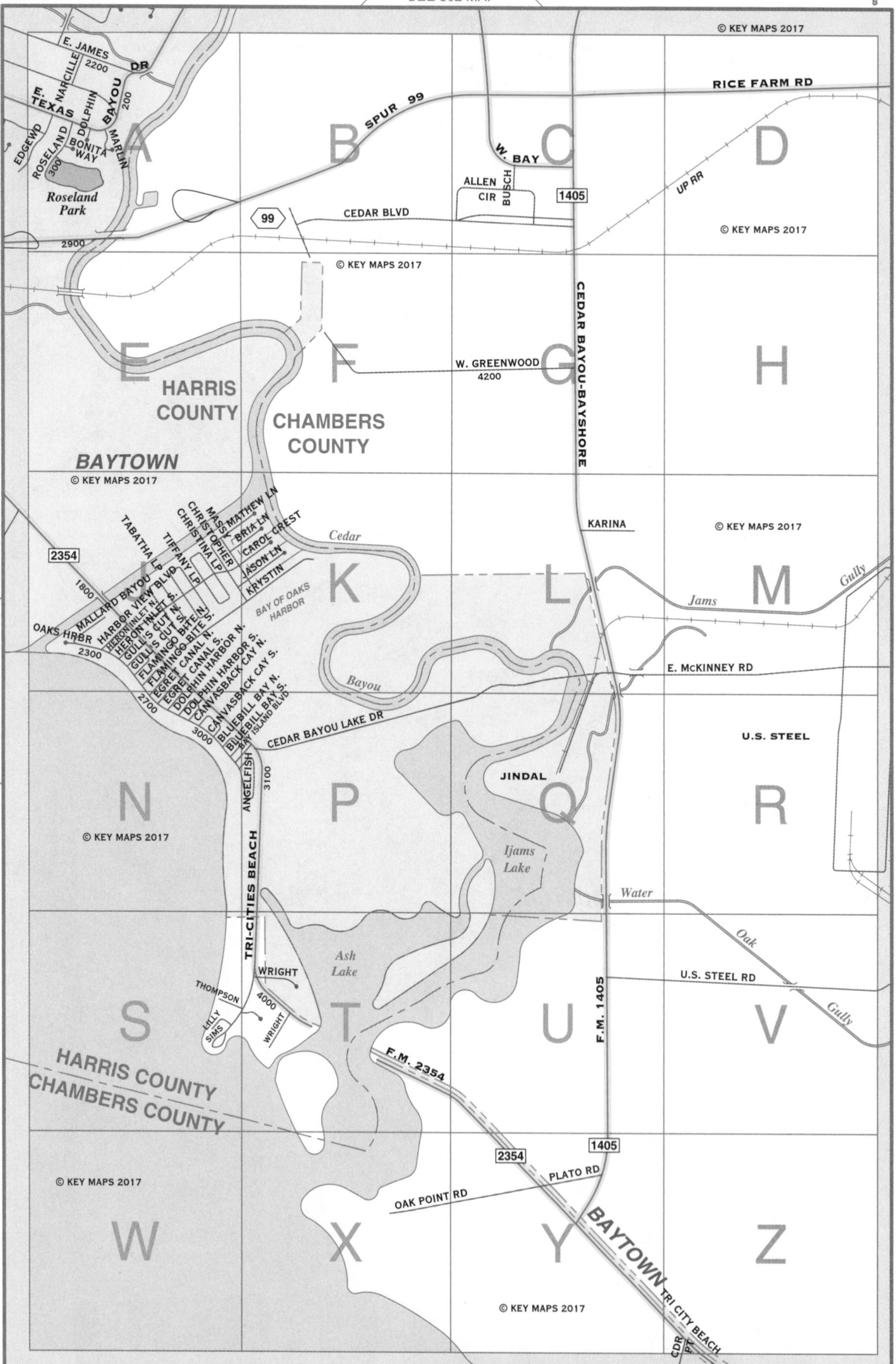

© KEY MAPS 2017

RICE FARM RD

SPUR 99

W. BAY

ALLEN CIR

BUSCH

1405

CEDAR BLVD

99

UP RR

© KEY MAPS 2017

2900

© KEY MAPS 2017

A B C D

E F G H

HARRIS COUNTY

CHAMBERS COUNTY

BAYTOWN

© KEY MAPS 2017

W. GREENWOOD
4200

CEDAR BAYOU-BAYSHORE

KARINA

© KEY MAPS 2017

N

SEE 541 MAP

2354

1800

TABATHA LP

HARBOR VIEW BLVD
HERONINLET N.
HERON INLET S.
GULL'S CUT N.
GULL'S CUT S.
FLAMINGO BITE N.
FLAMINGO BITE S.
EGRET CANAL N.
EGRET CANAL S.
DOLPHIN HARBOR N.
DOLPHIN HARBOR S.
CANVASBACK CAY N.
CANVASBACK CAY S.
BLUEBILL BAY N.
BLUEBILL BAY S.
BAY ISLAND BLVD.

CHRISTOPHER
CHRISTINA LP
TIFFANY LP
JASON LN.
KRYSTIN

MASS N.
MATHEW LN
BRIA LN.
CAROL CREST

MALLARD BAYOU

OAKS HRBR

2300

2700

3000

ANGELFISH BEACH

3100

Cedar

BAY OF OAKS HARBOR

Bayou

CEDAR BAYOU LAKE DR

K L M

Jams

Gully

E. McKINNEY RD

U.S. STEEL

N P Q R

JINDAL

© KEY MAPS 2017

Ijams Lake

Water

Oak

U.S. STEEL RD

Gully

TRI-CITIES BEACH

WRIGHT

THOMPSON

LILY

SIMS

4000

WRIGHT

Ash Lake

S T U V

F.M. 1405

F.M. 2354

HARRIS COUNTY
CHAMBERS COUNTY

© KEY MAPS 2017

2354

1405

PLATO RD

OAK POINT RD

BAYTOWN

TRI CITY BEACH

CDR PT

W X Y Z

© KEY MAPS 2017

0   1/4   1/2   3/4   1 Mile

END OF MAP

© KEY MAPS 2017

E. JAMES DR
2200
E. NARCILLE
BAYOU
200
E. TEXAS
DOLPHIN
MARLIN
EDGEWD
ROSELAND
300
BONITA WAY
Roseland Park

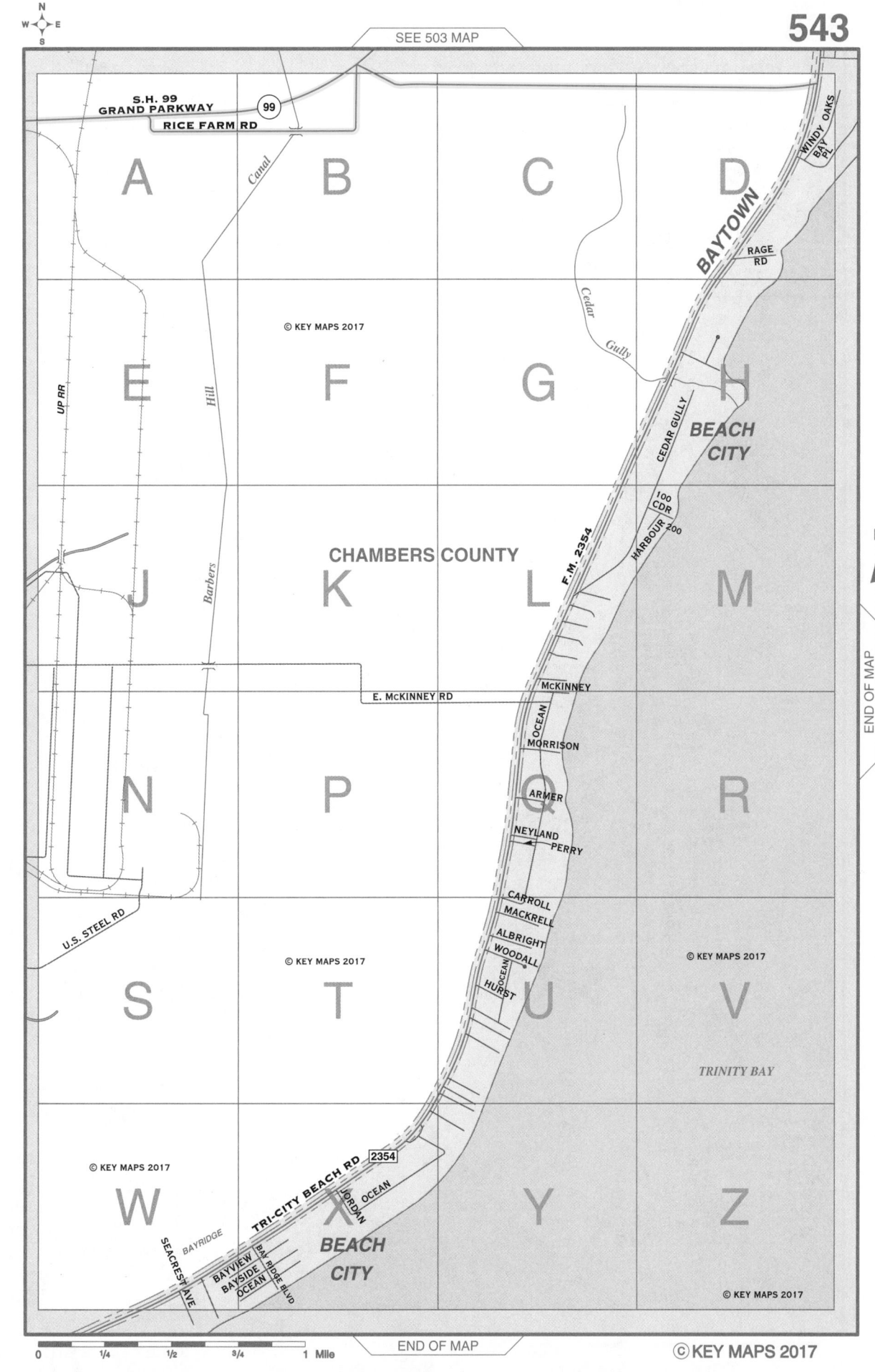

N
W E
S

S.H. 99
GRAND PARKWAY
RICE FARM RD
99

A | **B** | **C** | **D**

BAYTOWN

Canal

WINDY OAKS
BAY PL.

RAGE
RD

Hill

Cedar

Gully

© KEY MAPS 2017

E | **F** | **G** | **H**

UP RR

Barbers

BEACH
CITY

CEDAR GULLY

100
CDR
200

HARBOUR

N
END OF MAP

CHAMBERS COUNTY

F.M. 2354

J | **K** | **L** | **M**

E. McKINNEY RD
McKINNEY

OCEAN

MORRISON

ARMER

N | **P** | **Q** | **R**

NEYLAND
PERRY

U.S. STEEL RD

CARROLL
MACKRELL
ALBRIGHT
WOODALL
OCEAN
HURST

© KEY MAPS 2017

© KEY MAPS 2017

S | **T** | **U** | **V**

TRINITY BAY

© KEY MAPS 2017

TRI-CITY BEACH RD
2354
JORDAN
OCEAN

BAYRIDGE

W | **X** | **Y** | **Z**

SEACREST AVE
BAYVIEW
BAYSIDE
OCEAN
BAY RIDGE BLVD

**BEACH
CITY**

© KEY MAPS 2017

0   1/4   1/2   3/4   1 Mile

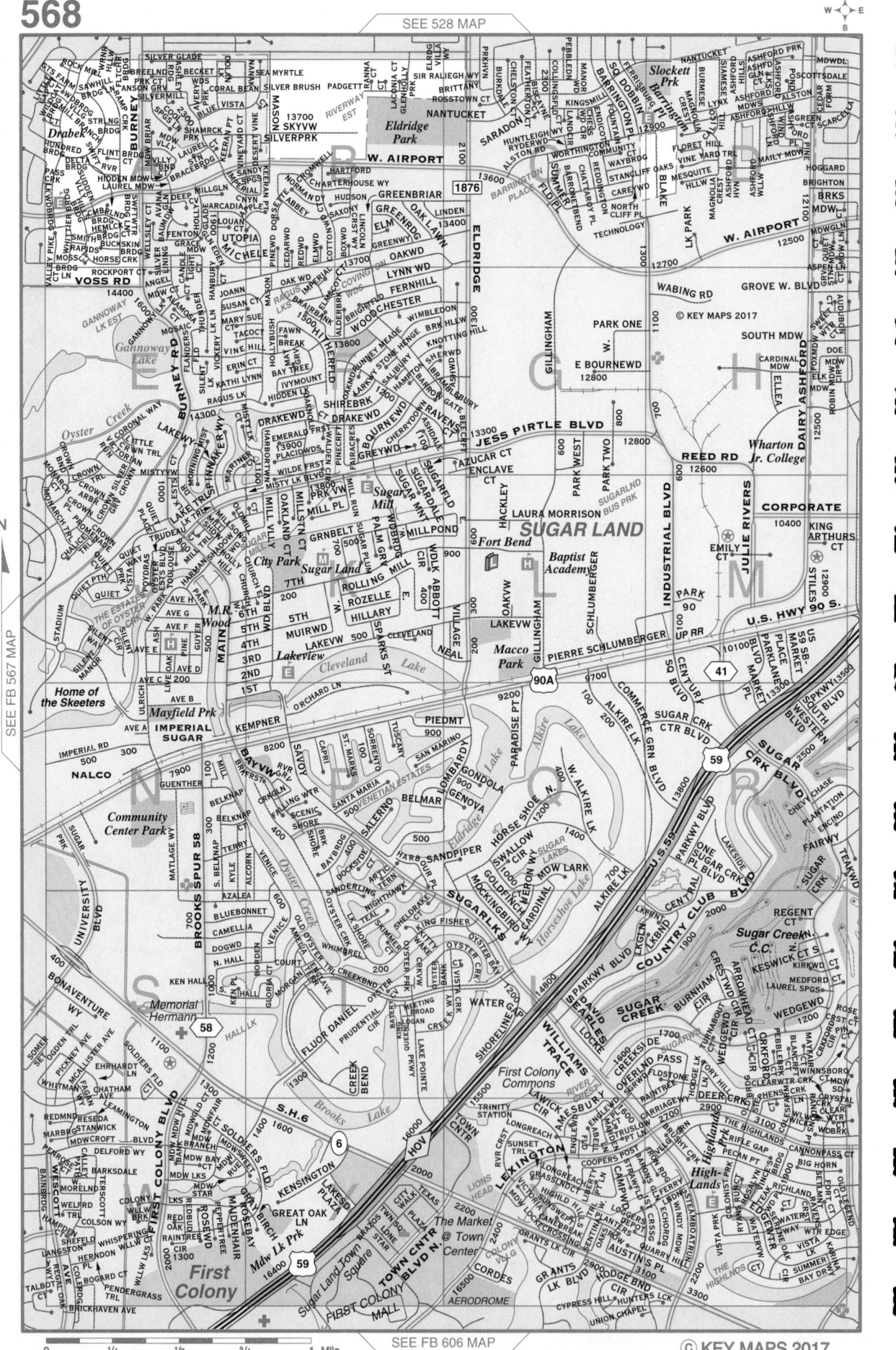

SEE 528 MAP

SEE FB 567 MAP

SEE FB 606 MAP

© KEY MAPS 2017

© KEY MAPS 2017

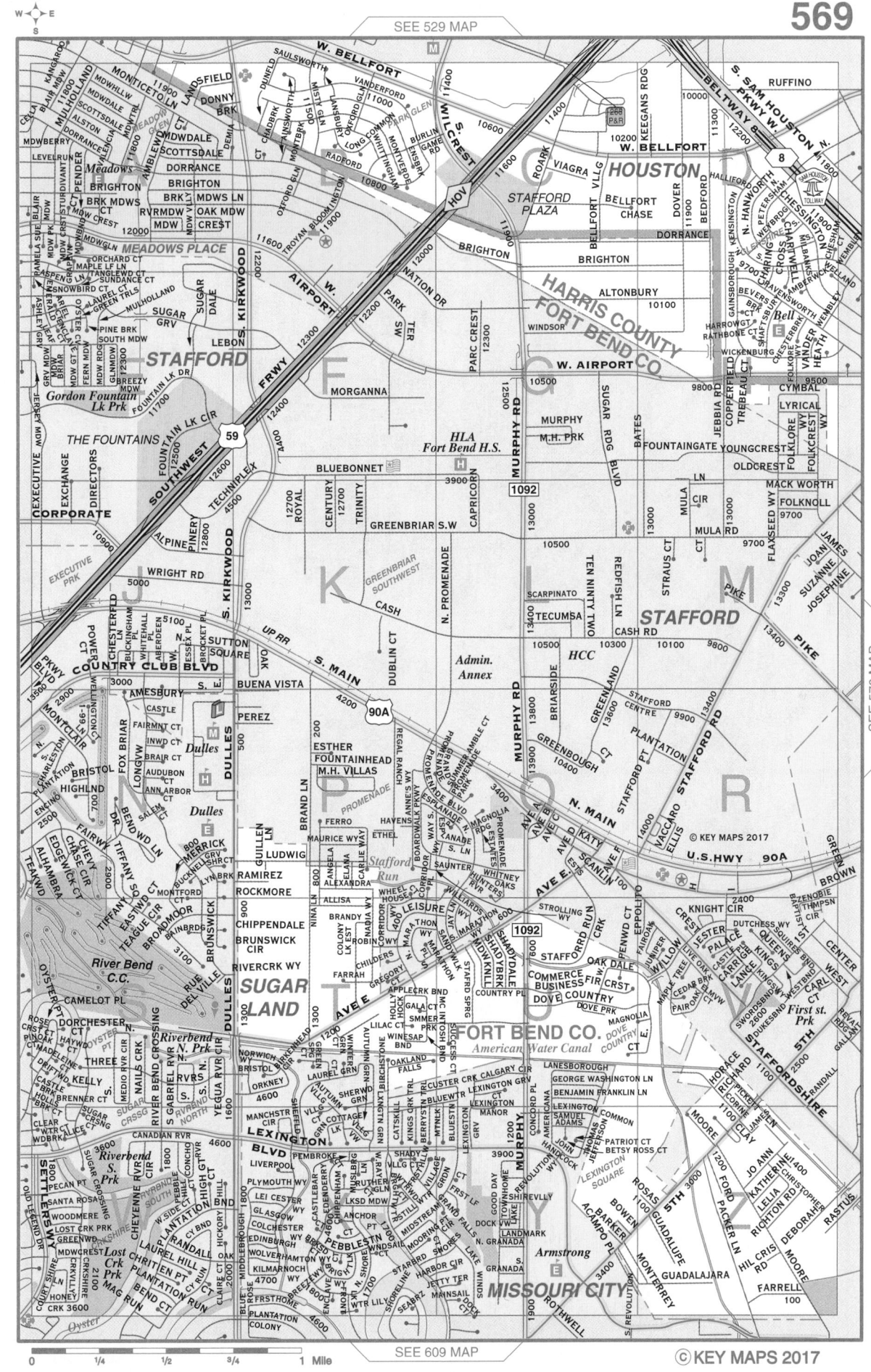

SEE 570 MAP

© KEY MAPS 2017

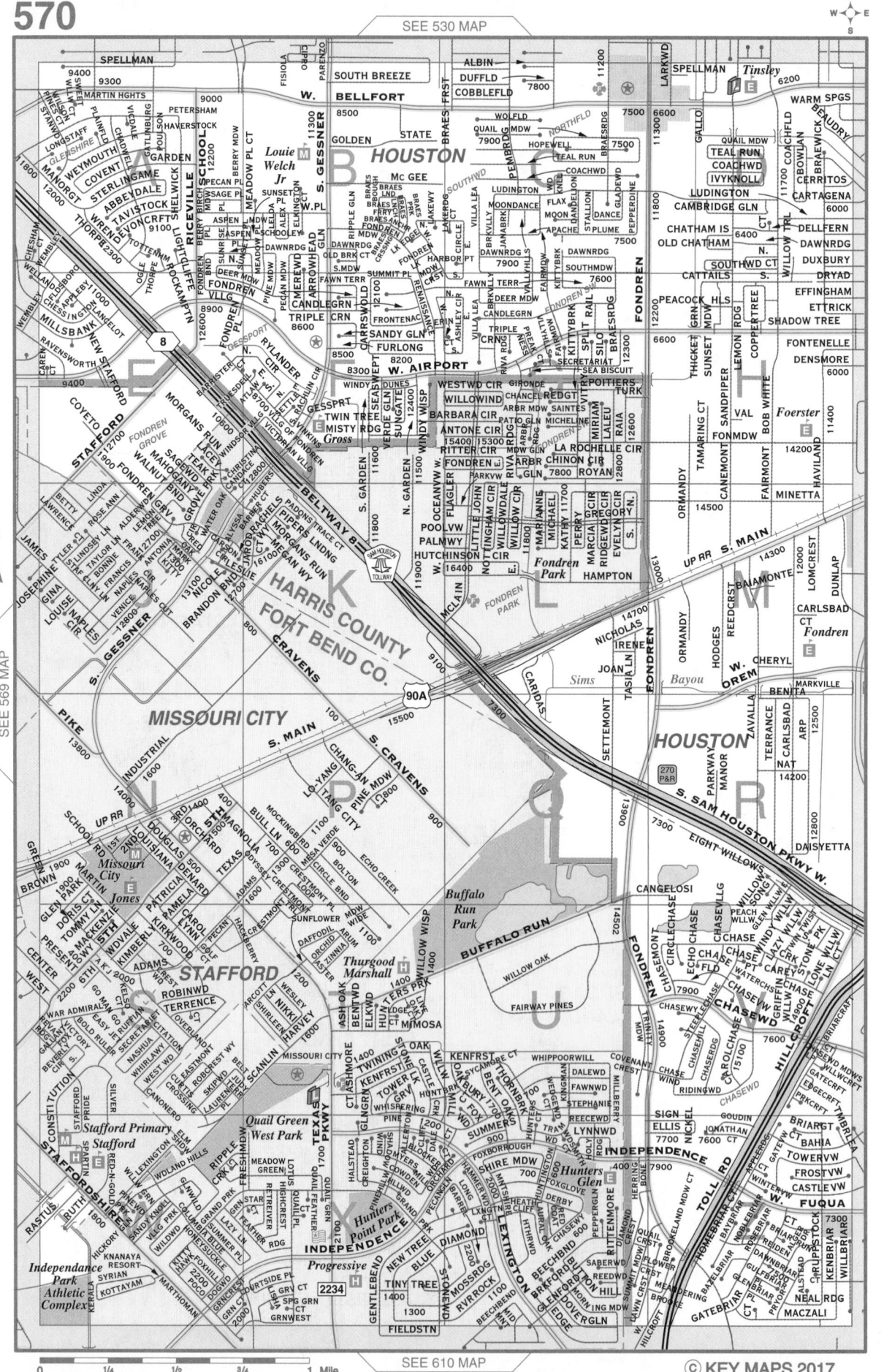

570

SEE 569 MAP

© KEY MAPS 2017

0   1/4   1/2   3/4   1 Mile

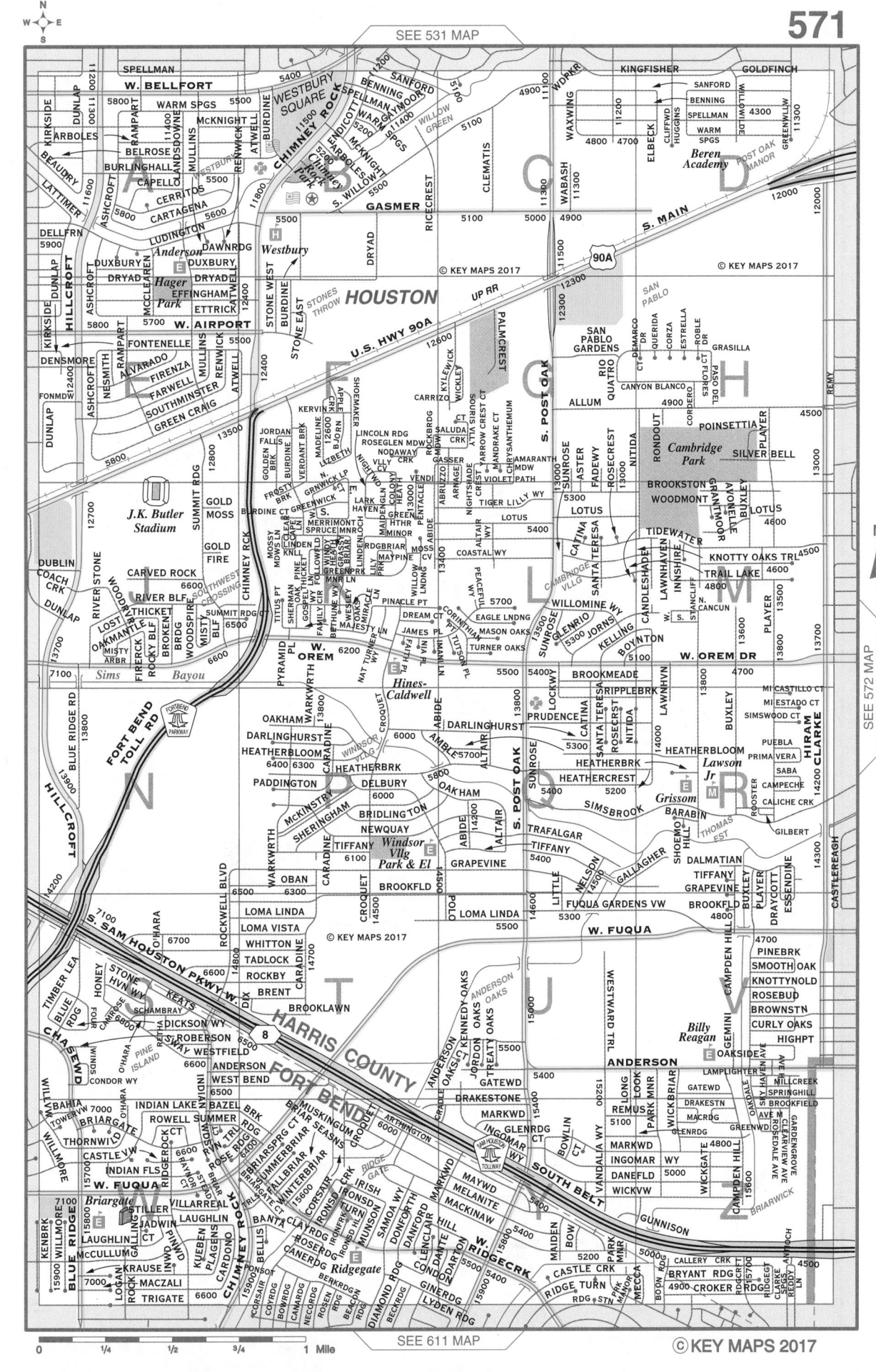

SEE 572 MAP

© KEY MAPS 2017

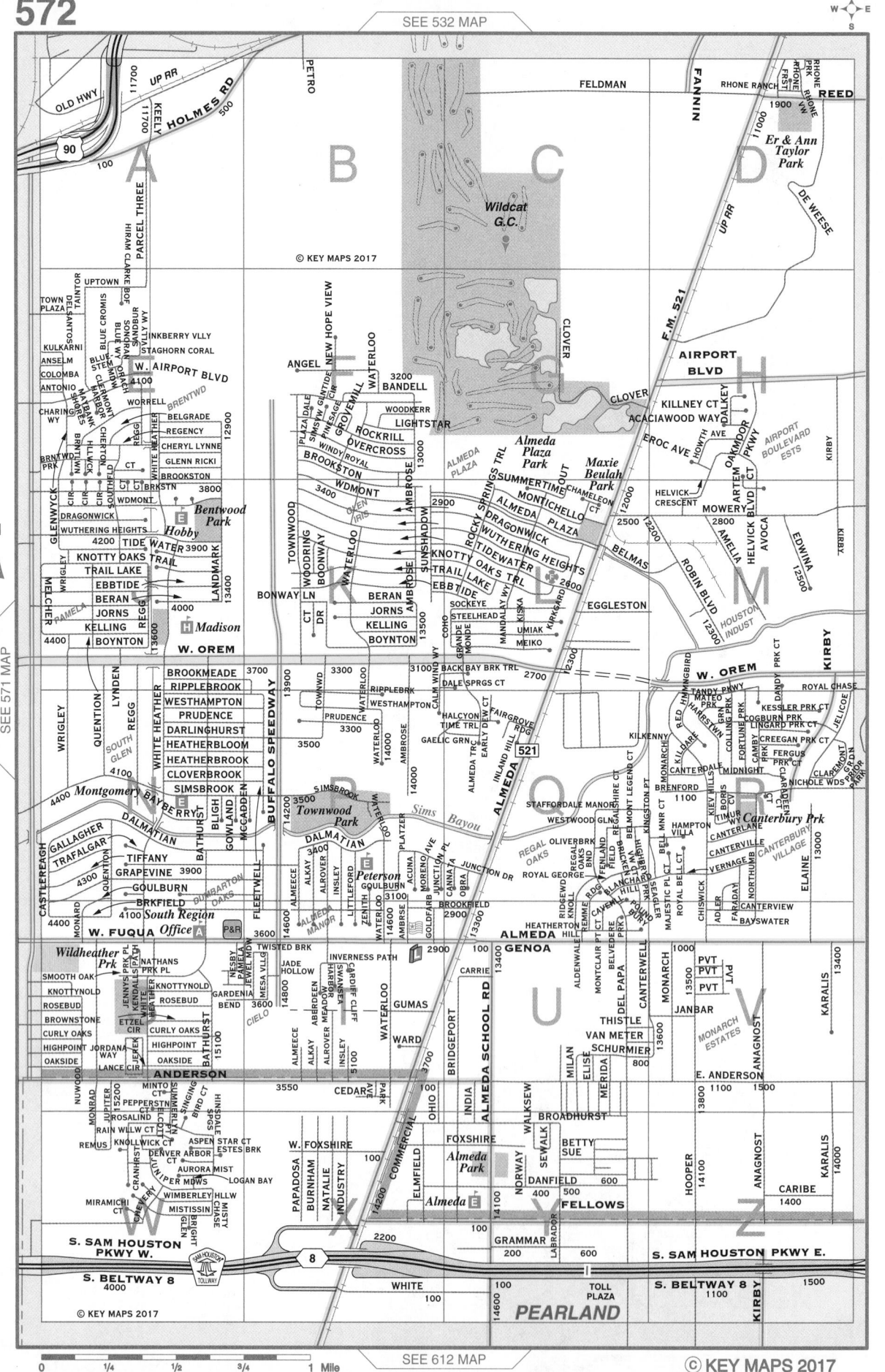

SEE 532 MAP

SEE 612 MAP

© KEY MAPS 2017

© KEY MAPS 2017

© KEY MAPS 2017

PEARLAND

SEE 571 MAP

0   1/4   1/2   3/4   1 Mile

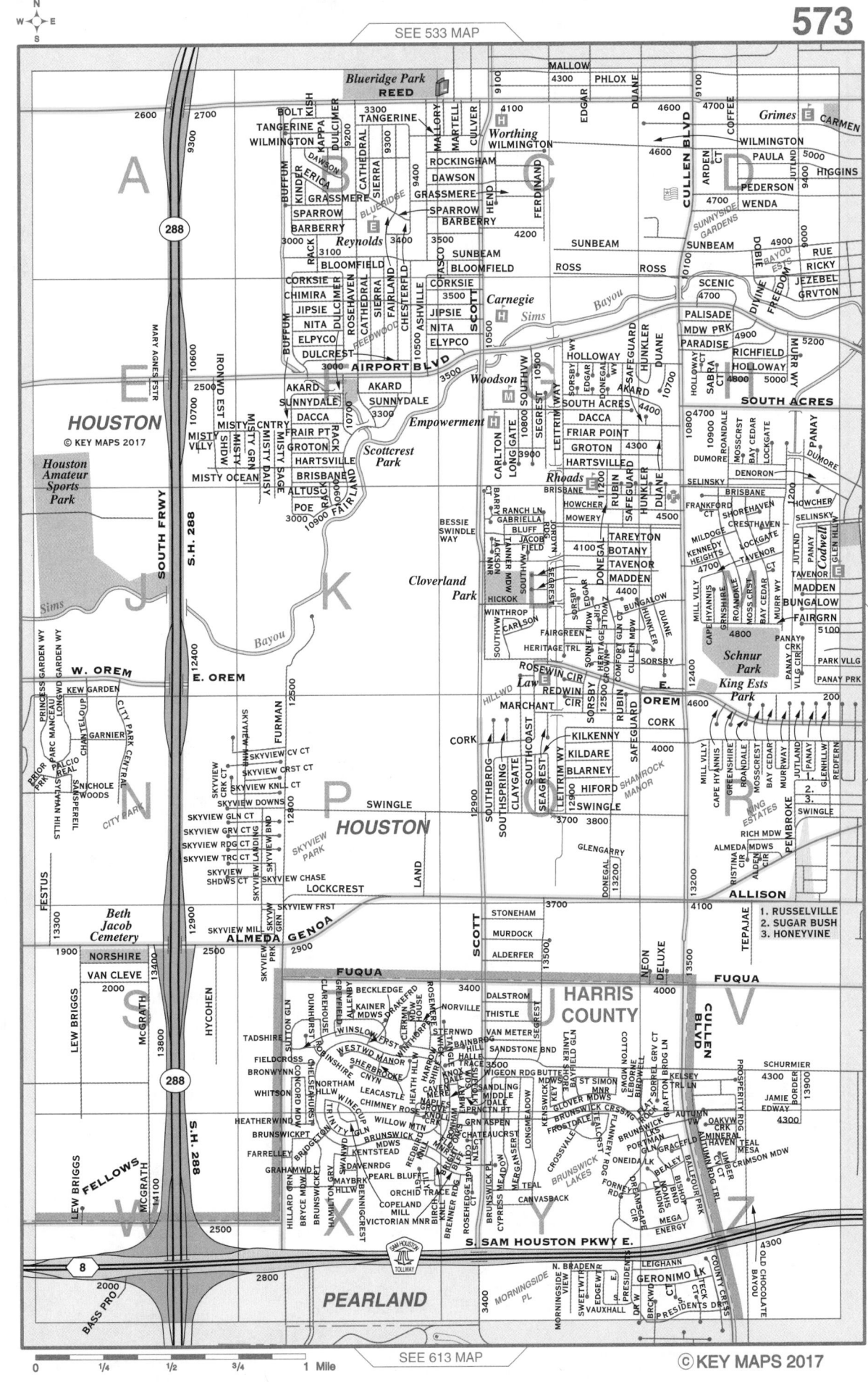

© KEY MAPS 2017

574

N W E S

MALLOW
THRUSH
HERON
REED
Grimes Park
CARMEN
ROCKFORD
ST. LO
GLENSIDE
SHARONDALE
MEDFORD
8500
5700
HERON
REED
HIRONDEL
OVERDALE
KILDEE
CRESTMONT
Mading
WILMINGTON
SCHEVERS
SIMSDALE
SOUTHBRK
6000
HIGGINS
NOEL
PEDERSON
ASHBURN
WDGREEN
5200
WENDA
BAYFLD
5300
9000
VINE ARBOR
MERLE
VASSER
5600

Law Park

REED
CROSWELL
HIRONDEL
OVERDALE
SCHEVERS
SIMSDALE
6200
NORTHDALE
W. ALPINE
E. ALPINE
SOUTHBROOK
ASHBURN
BRACE
PRENTISS
6900
VILLA
6900

A B G D

SANTA FE
CAYTON
KOPMAN
EVANS
7000
DILLON
7100
GARDEN VILLAS
7200

SUNBEAM
JETHRO
RUE
RICKY
JEZEBEL
GRVTON
TENEHA
ELMLAWN
RICKEY
9200
LOT
VINE ARBOR
CRESTMONT
FAIR CROFT
CLEARWAY
RUE
9200
5600

AIRPORT BLVD
7100
FAUNA
CONY

PEACOCK
LAKE
FIELD
PEACOCK
SIMS
WATERFORD

SCARLET
GROSBEAK
CHICKADEE
GALLINULE
6500
10400
0016
BLUE HERON
10700
EVANS
S. SANTA FE
6800
7000
7300
7500
KOPMAN
6900
NEUHAUS
6900
NELMS
BRISBANE
400
800

Sims Bayou Park
AIRPORT BLVD
10500
5300
OSPREY
4TH
3RD
5200
ROCKFORD
5TH
SILVERSTONE
5400
ANNA
HELD
10600
9TH
SOUTH ACRES
LINNET
6100
OSPREY
SESAME
10800
5900

EMSCO
7500
STATION
MYKAWA
6600

Bayou
Sims
GOLDEN GLADE ESTS

VAZCA DEGAMA
PUREZA
ABIERTA
PIEDRAS BLANCAS
CABEZA DE VACA
CORTEZ
COLON
6700
LA PLATA

CANTERWAY
DUMORE
DENORON
Thomas
Frost
11400
SELINSKY
SELINSKY
SESAME
11200
6100
EL GRANATE
EL ORO
EL TOPACIO
EL RUBI
6000
STARLIGHT
RAY
RALSTON FERGE
HANK
KUNZ
ILA SUE
DIAMANTE
MARTINDALE
Ross Sterling
EL TESORO
EL TURQUESA
EL AMBAR
NUEVO PUERTU
MONTE ALTA
LA VACA
MORENA
MI PAIS
MADDEN
6200

ELM SPRG
ELM TREE
GREYLOG
GRACE POINT LN
CEDARBURG
ROSECROFT
M.L. KING
11500
BOTANY
TAVENOR
5600
CRESTMONT PARK
SANDHURST
CANTERWAY
DUMORE
5300
FAWNWAY
ROCKFORD
FAWNGRV
MADDEN
BUNGALOW
FAIRGREEN
5400
SANDROCK
MADDEN
ABUNDANT LIFE
KINGDOM COME LN
RHEMA
PROSPERITY
ROSECROFT
VISION LN
PRAISE CT
WEBERCREST
DAYBREAK

E F H

E K L M

J P

CARSON
6500
MYKAWA
10300

E. OREM
E. OREM
12500
12500

PARK VLLG
PANAY PRK
5300
REDFERN
KILKENNY
SANDROCK
FAWNWAY
ROCKFORD
5300
RUSSELLVILLE
SUGAR BUSH
HONEYVINE
SWINGLE
4800
LINCOLNSHIRE
Frost Replacement
E. OREM
5400
DAWNS EDGE
CLOTELL CIR
DAWN LIGHT CIRCLE
DAWN TERRACE CT
NEW ENDINGS CT
SUNSET RIDGE
DAWN MISTY
DAWN VIEW
DAWN LIGHT
SUNRISE LIGHT
SUNLIGHT
DAWN WY
EARLY HORIZON
WEBERCREST
12800
THELMA ANN
12900
MARTINDALE
5600
WILLARDVILLE
HOUSTON
FOXTON
BEELA
10500
BNSF RR

© KEY MAPS 2017

LEA
GLENGARRY
4600
HENDRICKSEN
ALMEDA GENOA
PENWELL MDW
INGRAM GAP
KATIE RDG
BELTON SPGS
ALLISON
5000
ALMEDA-GENOA
5500
S. WAYSIDE
HOWE RD
6100
13000
PATTON
BLUE JAY
JO EDNA
BURK
WHEEDEN
TELEAN
BURKS CT

Q R

PVT
PVT
PVT
4600
5800
STONEHAM
DUNWICK
WENLOCK
TRESCON
HERTFORD
PERTH
SWANSEA
MCDOYLE
13400
13500
6600
FUQUA
4700
4800
FUQUA
LANGSTON
SOUTH WAYSIDE
MEGGINSON
FOXTON
6600
MYKAWA
14700

S T U V

THISTLE
MARY KAY
COTTINGHAM
SCHURMIER
5200
13900
14100
MARY KAY
5800
SCHURMIER
ATLASRIDGE
BRIMRIDGE
CAPRIDGE
DAYRIDGE
ENRIDGE
FAYRIDGE
GOODRIDGE
CORTENRDG
ALUM ROCK
PECAN HILL CT
BAYRDG CT
MESA RIM CT
ROCK RANGE
MYSTIC SHORES
6900
GRIMPLE BND
SUNDROP PRK
MYKAWA
12000

W X Y Z

© KEY MAPS 2017

TOLL PLAZA
SAM HOUSTON TOLLWAY
S. SAM HOUSTON PKWY E.
8
5200
5500
5800
6100
12200
Clear
Creek
HARRIS COUNTY
C.R. 108
MAX
12400
SHELTON
5200
12300
SLACK
Catherine Keegan Wilderness Prk
BROOKSIDE VLLG
GARDEN
C.R. 109
OAK LINE
THORNBRIAR
ALMA

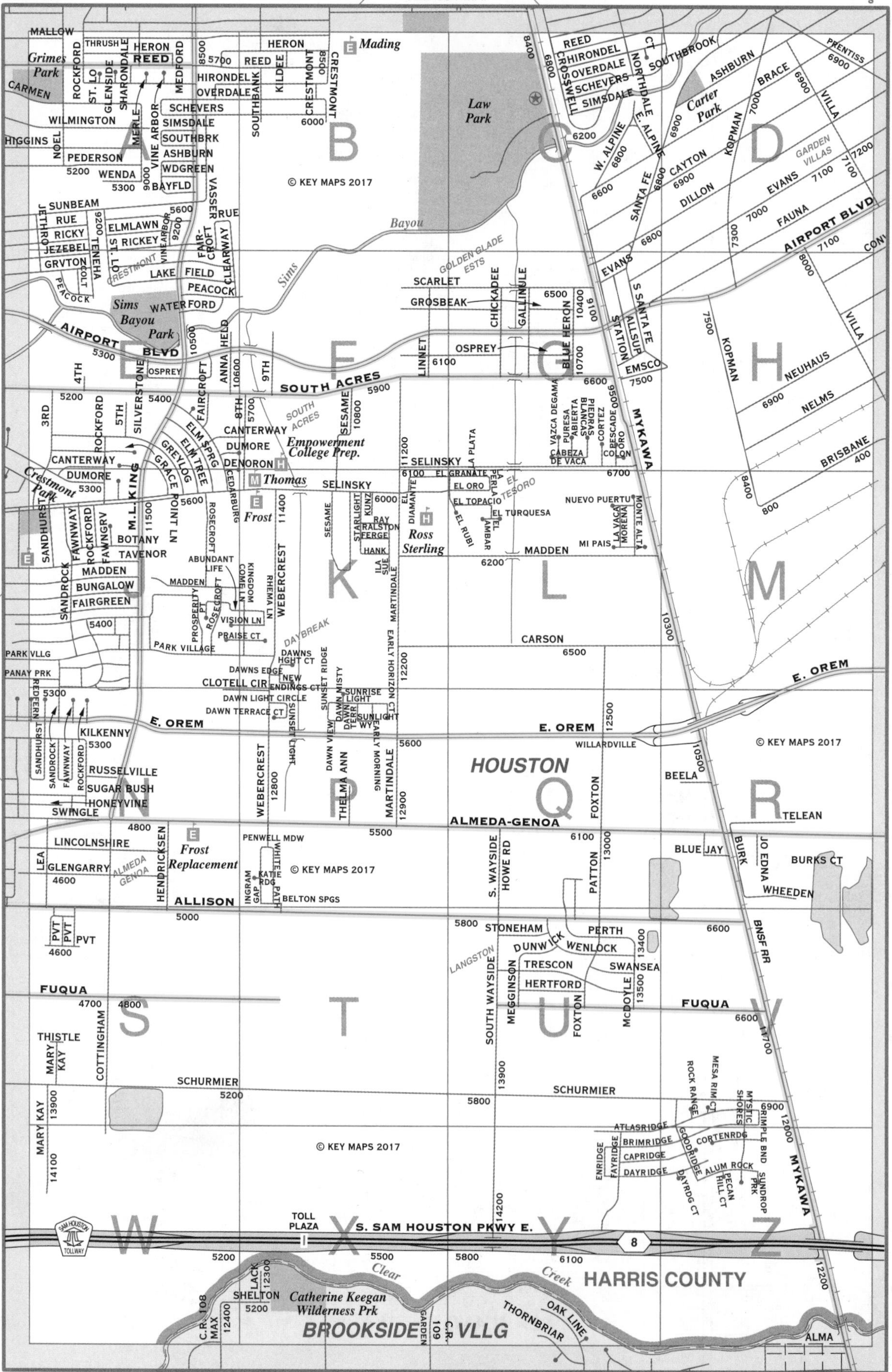

SEE 573 MAP

0 1/4 1/2 3/4 1 Mile

© KEY MAPS 2017

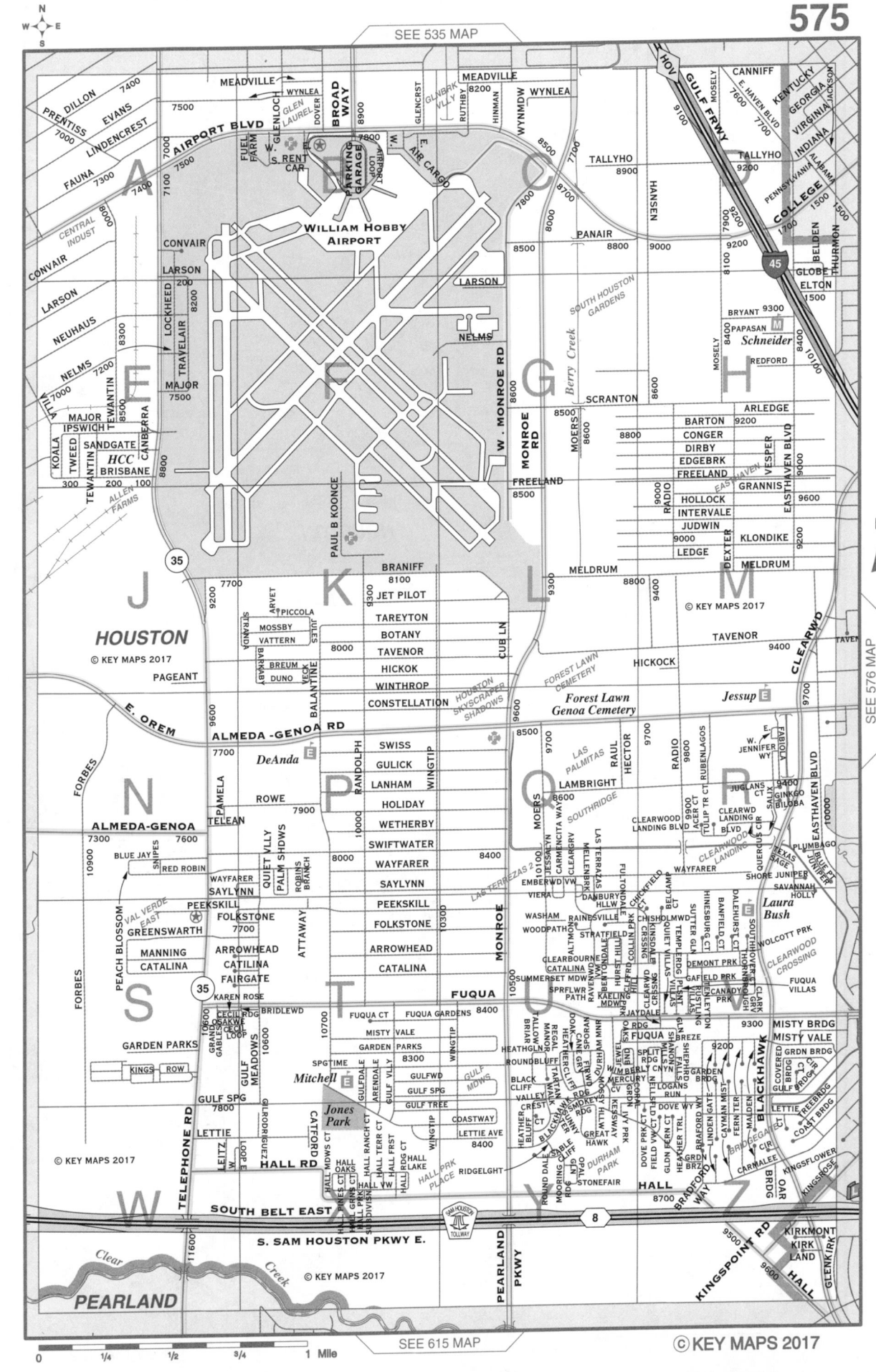

SEE 576 MAP

© KEY MAPS 2017

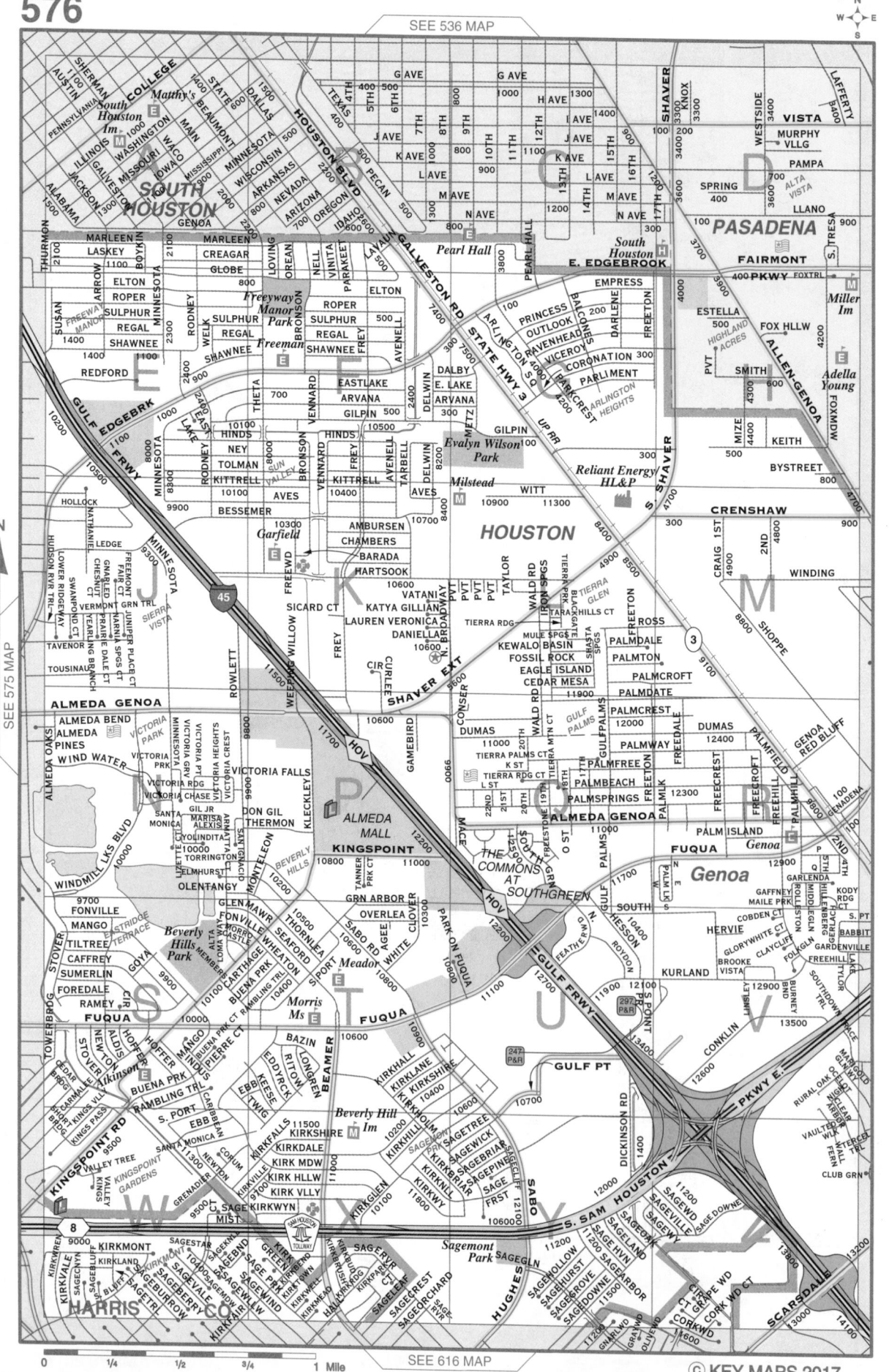

SEE 536 MAP

SEE 575 MAP

SEE 616 MAP

© KEY MAPS 2017

0   1/4   1/2   3/4   1 Mile

PASADENA

SOUTH HOUSTON

HOUSTON

HARRIS CO.

Almeda Mall

Genoa

THE COMMONS AT SOUTHGREEN

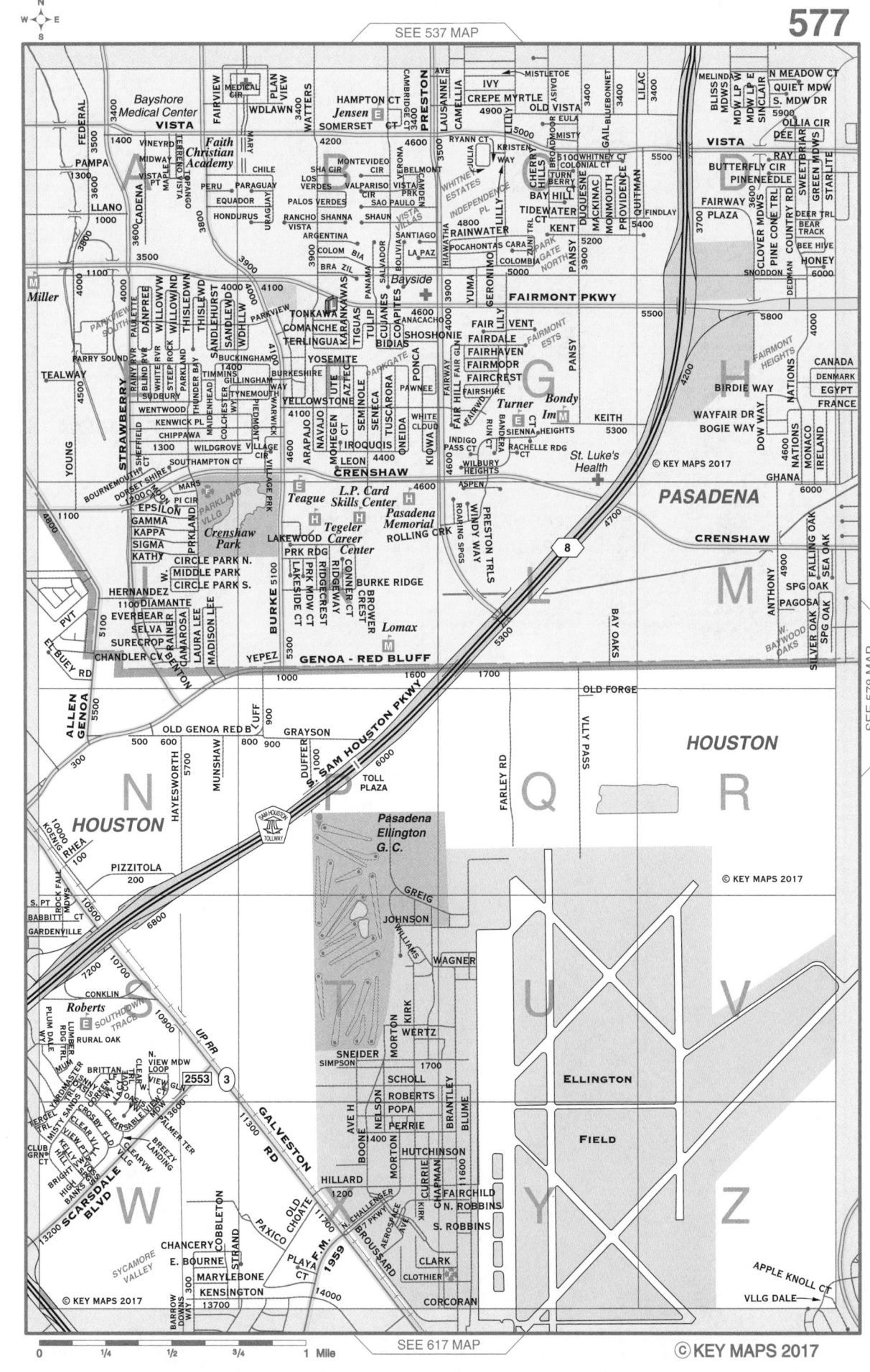

© KEY MAPS 2017

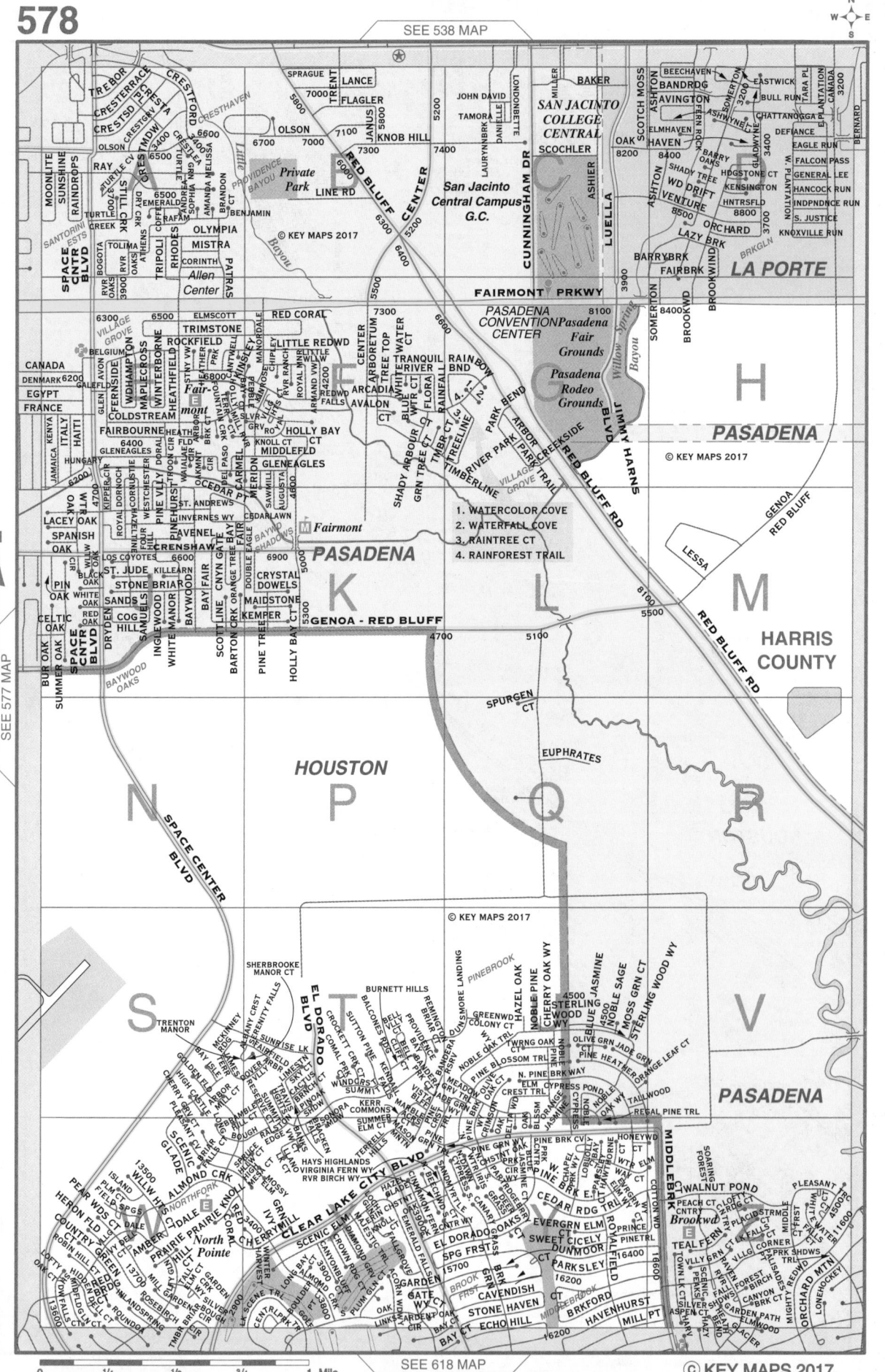

SEE 538 MAP

SEE 577 MAP

SEE 618 MAP

© KEY MAPS 2017

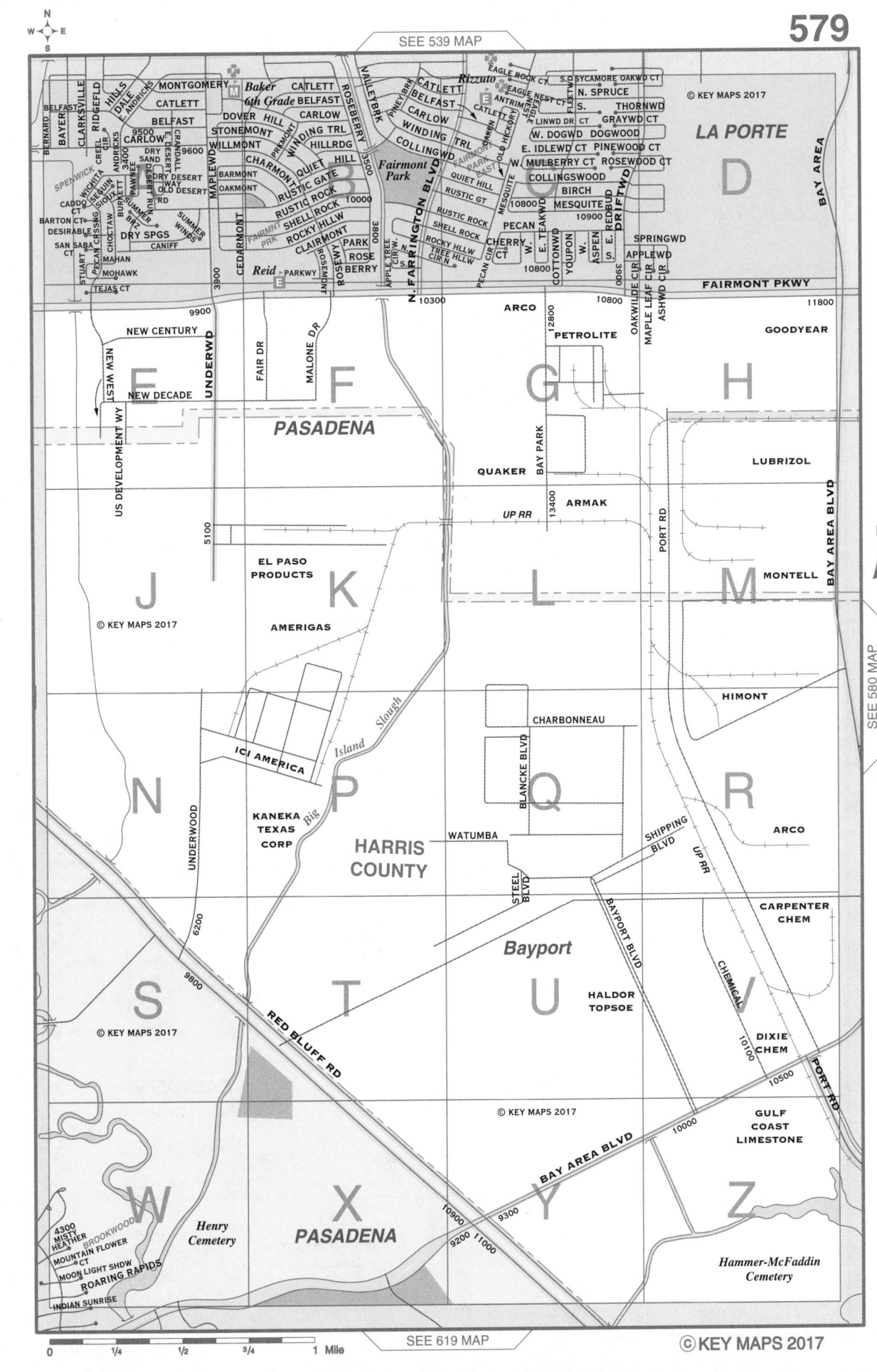

SEE 539 MAP

SEE 580 MAP

SEE 619 MAP

LA PORTE

PASADENA

HARRIS COUNTY

Bayport

PASADENA

© KEY MAPS 2017

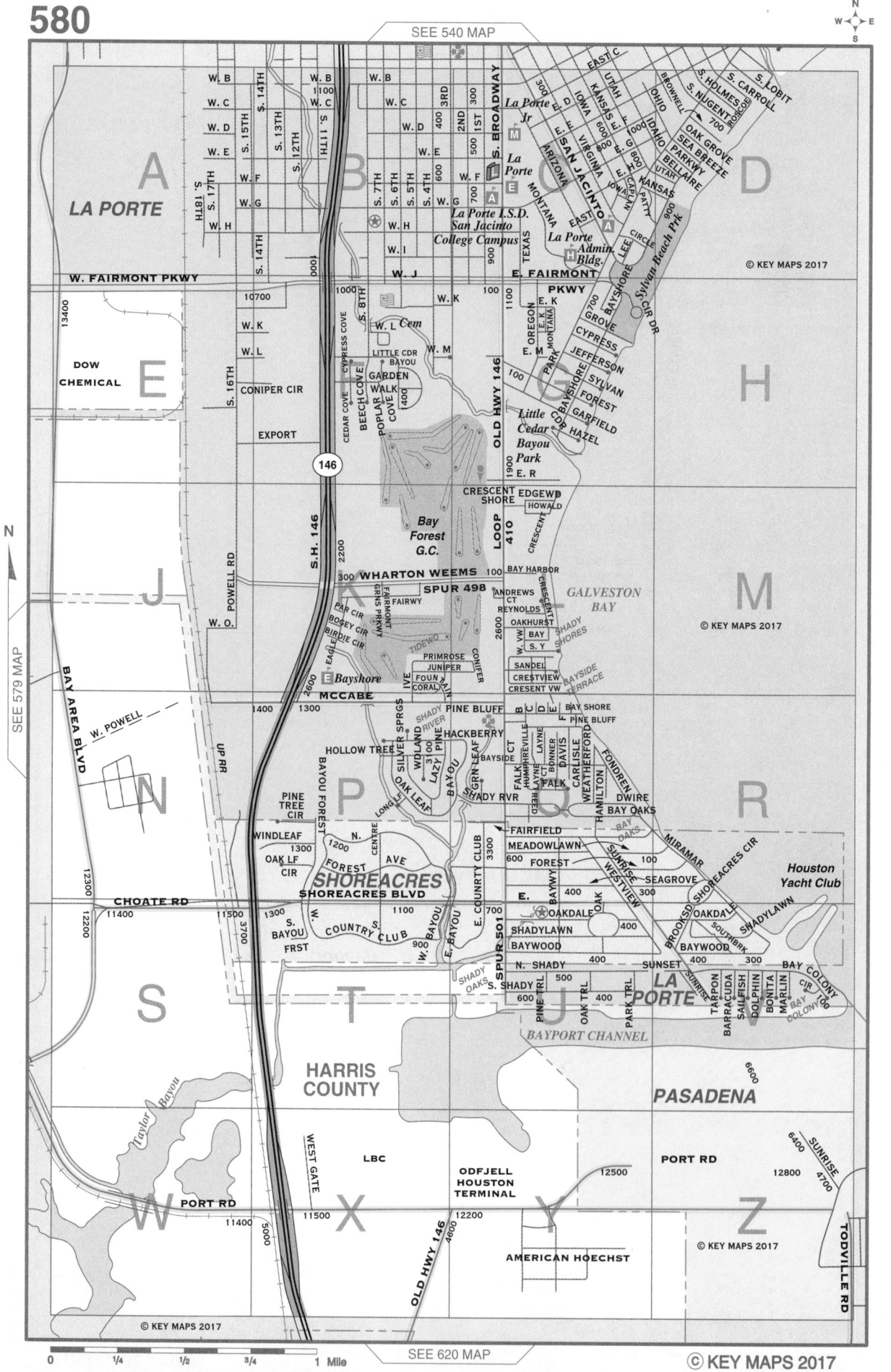

580

LA PORTE

W. B 1100
W. C
W. D
W. E
W. F
W. G
W. H
W. I
W. J

W. FAIRMONT PKWY

10700

W. K
W. L
EXPORT
CONIPER CIR

DOW CHEMICAL

146

S.H. 146

Bay Forest G.C.

WHARTON WEEMS
SPUR 498
FAIRWY
PAR CIR
BOGEY CIR
BIRDIE CIR

Bayshore
McCABE

1400   1300

HOLLOW TREE
SILVER SPRGS
Bayou Forest
PINE TREE CIR
WINDLEAF
OAK LF CIR
FOREST
AVE

SHOREACRES
SHOREACRES BLVD

COUNTRY CLUB

CHOATE RD
11400   1500
12200   3700
12300

SEE 579 MAP

BAY AREA BLVD

W. POWELL

N

UP RR

POWELL RD

PINE TREE CIR

S

HARRIS COUNTY

LBC

WEST GATE

PORT RD
11400   11500
5000

OLD HWY 146

AMERICAN HOECHST

ODFJELL HOUSTON TERMINAL
12200

Taylor Bayou

La Porte Jr

La Porte
S. BROADWAY
3RD   2ND   1ST
400   500   600   700

La Porte I.S.D.
San Jacinto College Campus

S. 8TH

W. K
W. L Cem
W. M

GARDEN WALK
LITTLE CDR BAYOU
POPLAR COVE
BEECH COVE
CYPRESS COVE
CEDAR COVE
S. 16TH

OLD HWY 146
LOOP 410

CRESCENT SHORE
EDGEWD
HOWALD

Little Cedar Bayou Park
E. R

BAY HARBOR
ANDREWS CT
REYNOLDS
OAKHURST
BAY S. Y
SANDEL
CRESTVIEW
CRESENT VW

PINE BLUFF
HACKBERRY
BAYSIDE
SHADY RIVER
LAZY PINE
GRN LEAF
OAK LEAF

FALK
HUMPHREVILLE
LAYNE
BONNER
DAVIS
REED
FALK

Fairfield
MEADOWLAWN
FOREST
BAYWY
E.

SHADYLAWN
BAYWOOD
N. SHADY
S. SHADY

PINE TRL
OAK TRL
PARK TRL

BAYPORT CHANNEL

PASADENA

PORT RD
12500   12800

E. C
UTAH
IOWA
KANSAS
VIRGINIA
OHIO
SAN JACINTO
ARIZONA
MONTANA
TEXAS
EAST

La Porte
Admin. Bldg.

E. FAIRMONT PKWY

OREGON
E. K
E. M
E. R

BAYSHORE
BROWNELL
S. HOLMES
S. NUGENT
OAK GROVE
SEA BREEZE
BELLAIRE
UTAH
KANSAS

S. CARROLL
S. LOBIT
ROSCOE
PARKWY

Sylvan Beach Prk
CIR DR

GROVE
CYPRESS
JEFFERSON
SYLVAN
FOREST
GARFIELD
HAZEL
Little Cdr

GALVESTON BAY

SHADY SHORES
BAYSIDE TERRACE

BAY SHORE
PINE BLUFF

CARLISLE
WEATHERFORD
HAMILTON
FONDREN
DWIRE
BAY OAKS

MIRAMAR
SHOREACRES CIR

Houston Yacht Club

SUNRISE
WESTVIEW
SEAGROVE

OAKDALE
BROOKSD
OAKDAL
SOUTHBRK
SHADYLAWN
BAYWOOD

SUNSET
SUNRISE
LA PORTE

TARPON
BARRACUDA
SAILFISH
DOLPHIN
BONITA
MARLIN
BAY CIR
BAY COLONY

SUNRISE
6400   4700
6600

TODVILLE RD

© KEY MAPS 2017

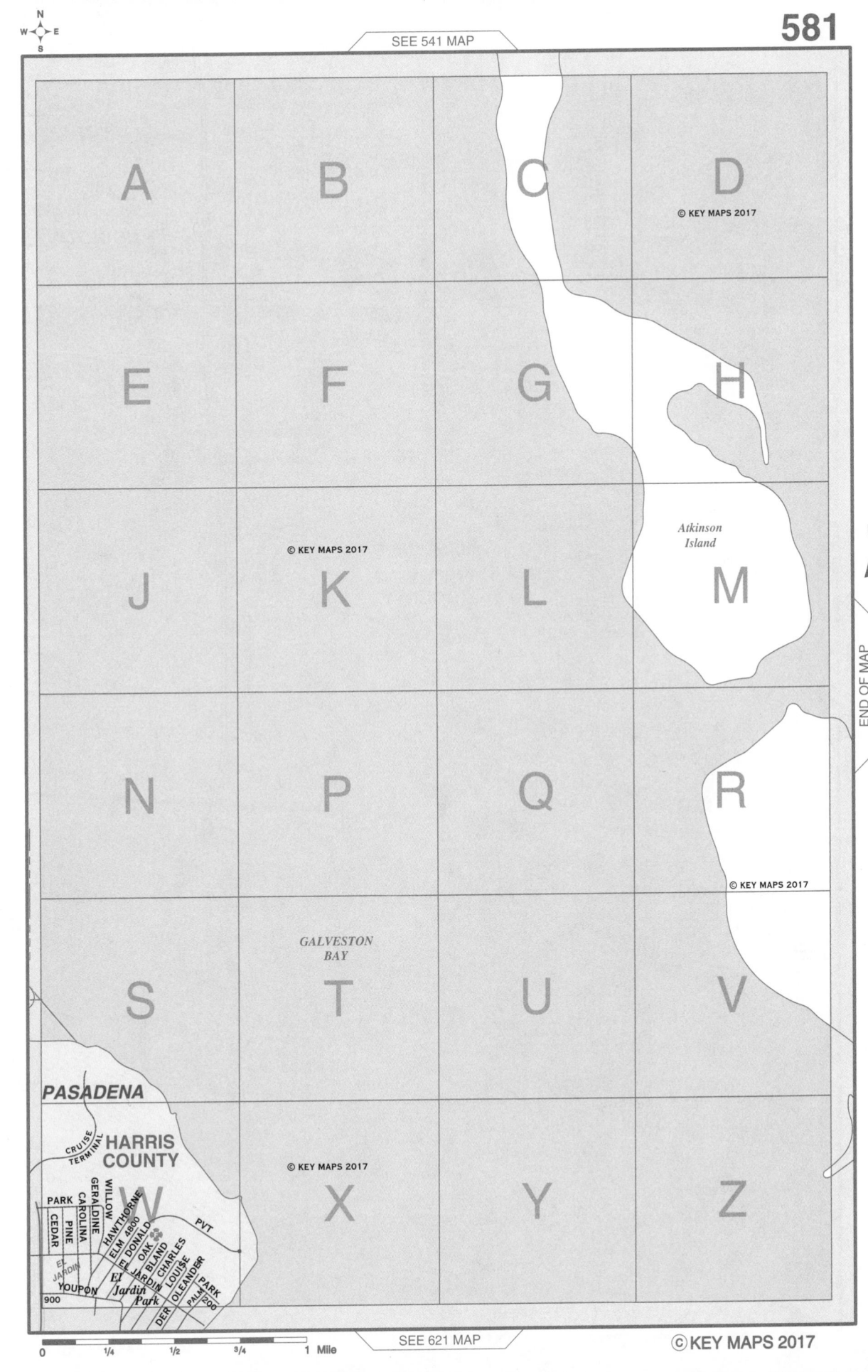

A

B

C

D

© KEY MAPS 2017

E

F

G

H

Atkinson Island

J

K

L

M

© KEY MAPS 2017

N

P

Q

R

© KEY MAPS 2017

GALVESTON BAY

S

T

U

V

PASADENA

HARRIS COUNTY

CRUISE TERMINAL

W

X

Y

Z

© KEY MAPS 2017

PARK
CEDAR
CAROLINA
PINE
GERALDINE
WILLOW
HAWTHORNE
ELM 4800
EL DONALD
OAK
JARDIN
BLAND
CHARLES
LOUISE
PARK
PALM 200
PVT
EL JARDIN
YOUPON
900
El Jardin Park
DER OLEANDER

END OF MAP

N

N
W E
S

© **KEY MAPS 2017**

0   1/4   1/2   3/4   1 Mile

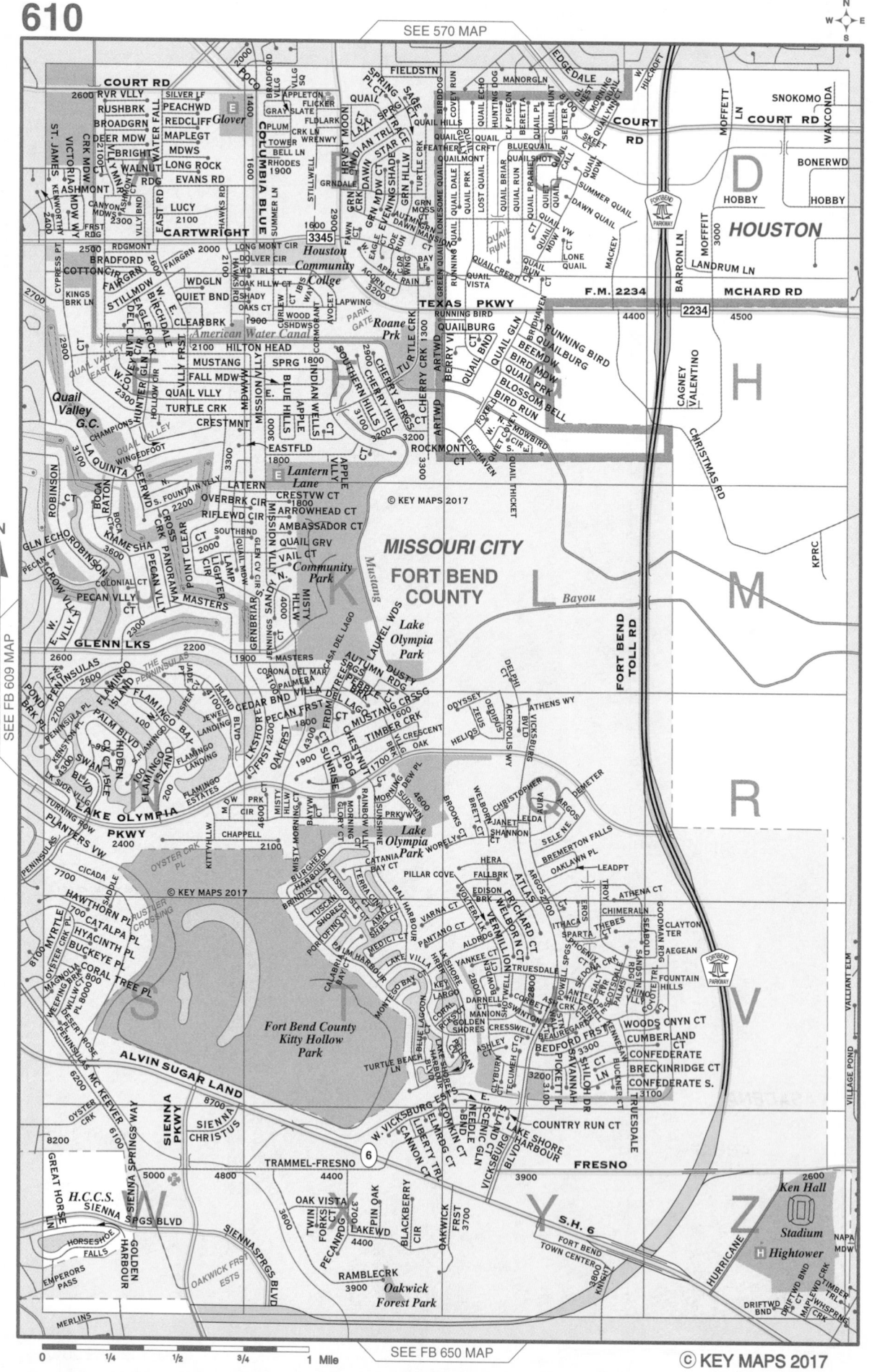

© KEY MAPS 2017

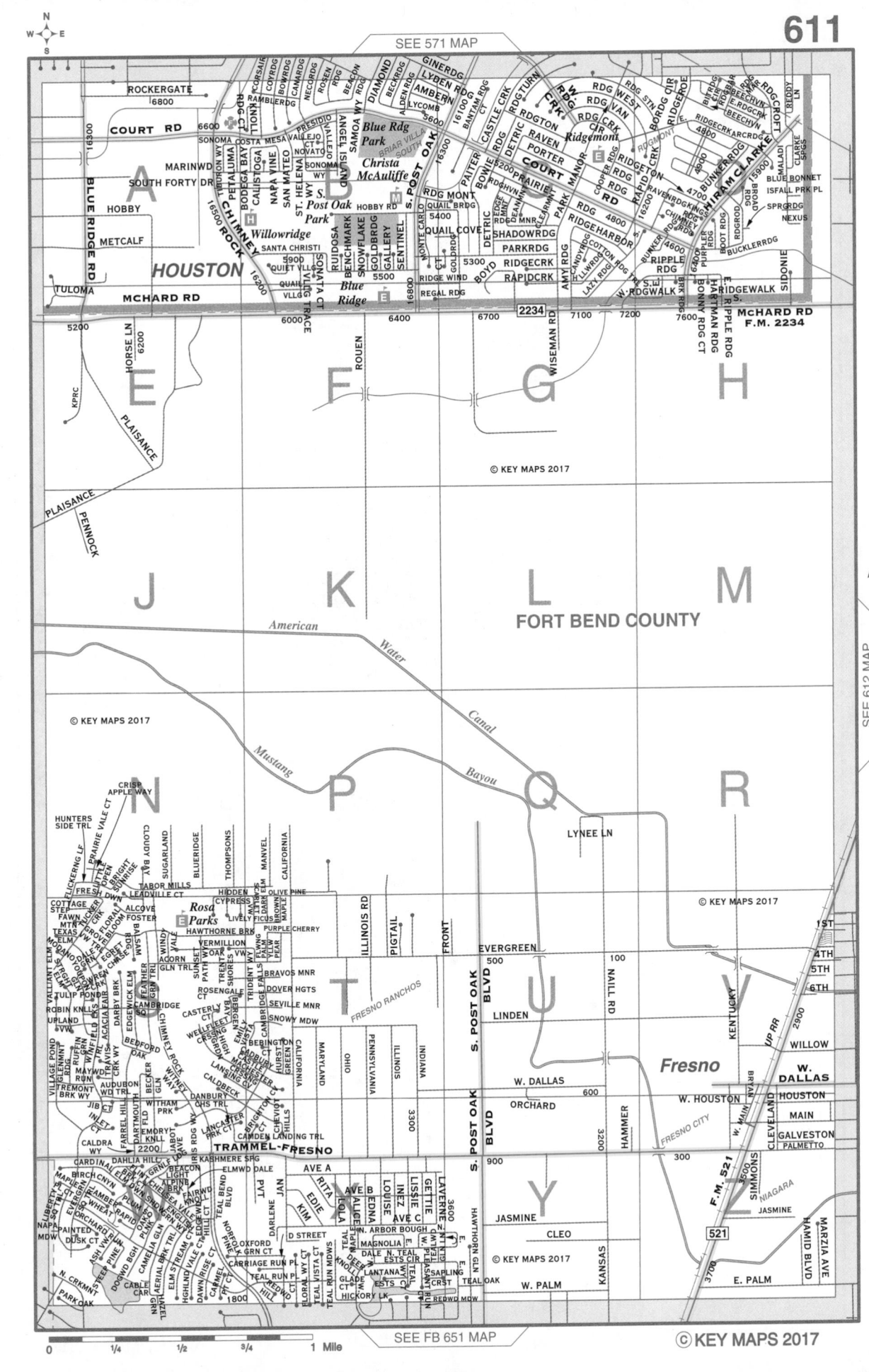

N
W E
S

ROCKERGATE
6800

COURT RD 6600

A

MARINWD

SOUTH FORTY DR

HOBBY

METCALF

HOUSTON

TULOMA

MCHARD RD

5200

BLUE RIDGE RD

CHIMNEY ROCK

HORSE LN
6200

6000

B

Blue Rdg Park

Christa McAuliffe

S. Post Oak Park

Willowridge

SANTA CHRISTI

Blue Ridge

E

KPRC

PLAISANCE

PLAISANCE

PENNOCK

J

F

ROUEN

K

American

Water

L

FORT BEND COUNTY

SEE 612 MAP

N

G

WISEMAN RD

2234

MCHARD RD
F.M. 2234

H

© KEY MAPS 2017

M

© KEY MAPS 2017

Mustang

Canal

Bayou

N

P

Q

LYNEE LN

R

© KEY MAPS 2017

© KEY MAPS 2017

Rosa Parks

ILLINOIS RD

EVERGREEN

500

FRONT

100

1ST
4TH
5TH
6TH

T

Fresno Ranchos

S. POST OAK BLVD

LINDEN

U

NAILL RD

KENTUCKY

UP RR

2900

WILLOW

Fresno

V

W. DALLAS

W. DALLAS

600

W. HOUSTON

ORCHARD

W. HOUSTON
HOUSTON

MAIN

GALVESTON

PALMETTO

Fresno City

TRAMMEL-FRESNO

AVE A

AVE B

3600

900

300

F.M. 521

521

Z

SIMMONS

NIAGARA

JASMINE

MARZIA AVE

HAMID BLVD

Y

JASMINE

CLEO

KANSAS

© KEY MAPS 2017

W. PALM

E. PALM

0   1/4   1/2   3/4   1 Mile

© **KEY MAPS** 2017

SEE 572 MAP

N
W · E
S

HARRIS COUNTY

BLUEBONNET ACRES
BLUEBONNET

SOUTHBELT INDUSTRIAL PARK

Ski School

American Ski Center

Clear Creek

HARRIS COUNTY

PEARLAND

Shadow Creek Ranch Nature Prk

6. SILENT CRK
7. CALYPSO BAY
8. CALYPSO BAY CT

Nolan Ryan

SHADOW CRK PKWY

Marek

1. AUBURN CREEK
2. AMBER CREEK
3. AUBURN SHORES
4. AUBURN FALLS
5. AUBURN FALLS

MCHARD   F.M. 2234

WORTH

ROYAL RIDGE
JUNIPER SPRINGS

F.M. 521

SEE 611 MAP

UP RR

SHADOW CREEK RANCH

FORT BEND COUNTY
BRAZORIA COUNTY

BROADWAY

Wilder

York

Shadow Creek

FIRST
SECOND
3RD
FOURTH
FIFTH
6TH

PEARLAND

RACHEL'S WAY
CUTTER RAYS
JEN'S WAY
SEVENTH

MARILYN

W. DALLAS RD

C.R. 59

C.R. 59

HOUSTON
MAIN
GALVESTON
PALMETTO

FLYIN'B AIRPORT

Stevens & Pruett Ranch

Mustang

American Canal

HARVARD ESTATES

HARVARD CRESCENT
OXFORD ROW
PRINCETON PEAK
YALE YARD
CAMBRIDGE CT
COLUMBIA LANE
HARVARD HOLLOW

JASMINE
VERMONT
E. PALM   C.R. 564A

C.R. 895 MUSTANG
CHESTNUT PARK
NORWALK
COLBROOK

Bayou

© KEY MAPS 2017

0   1/4   1/2   3/4   1 Mile

SEE FB 652 MAP

© KEY MAPS 2017

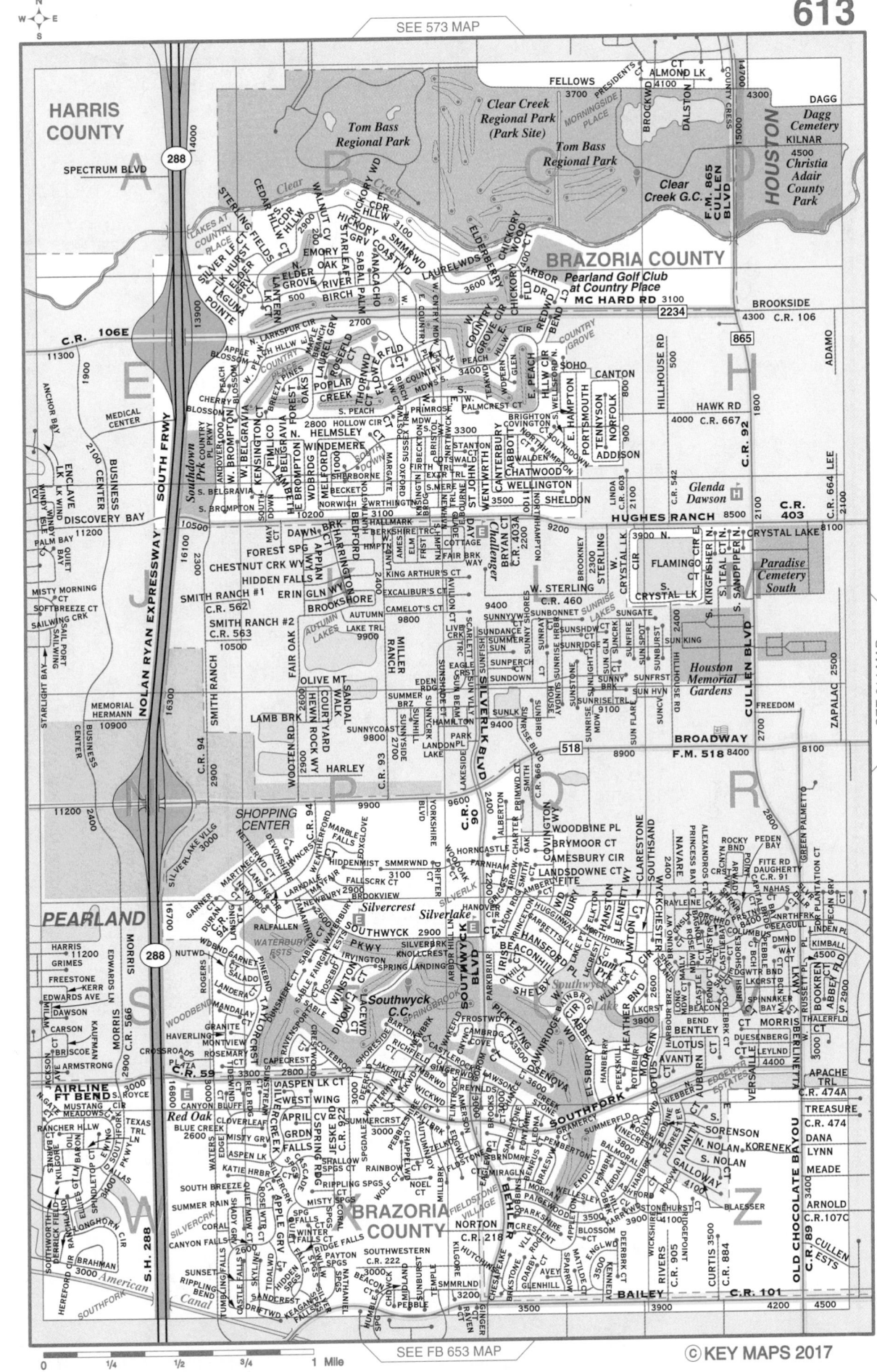

BROOKSIDE VILLAGE

Dagg Cemetery
DAGG
4700

Clear Creek

PEARLAND

BRAZORIA COUNTY

PEARLAND

SEE 613 MAP

© KEY MAPS 2017

© KEY MAPS 2017

0 1/4 1/2 3/4 1 Mile

© **KEY MAPS 2017**

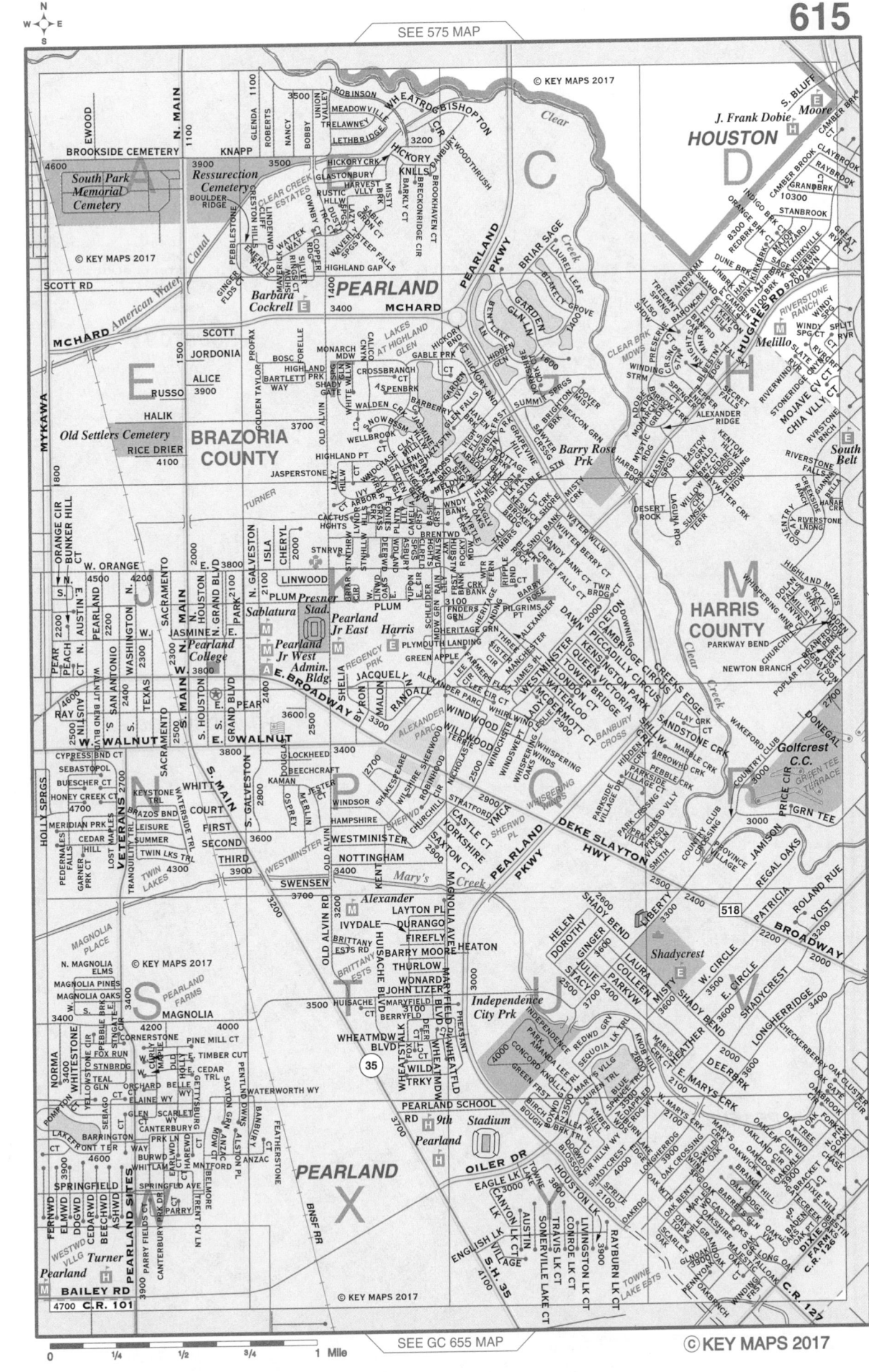

SEE 616 MAP

© KEY MAPS 2017

0   1/4   1/2   3/4   1 Mile

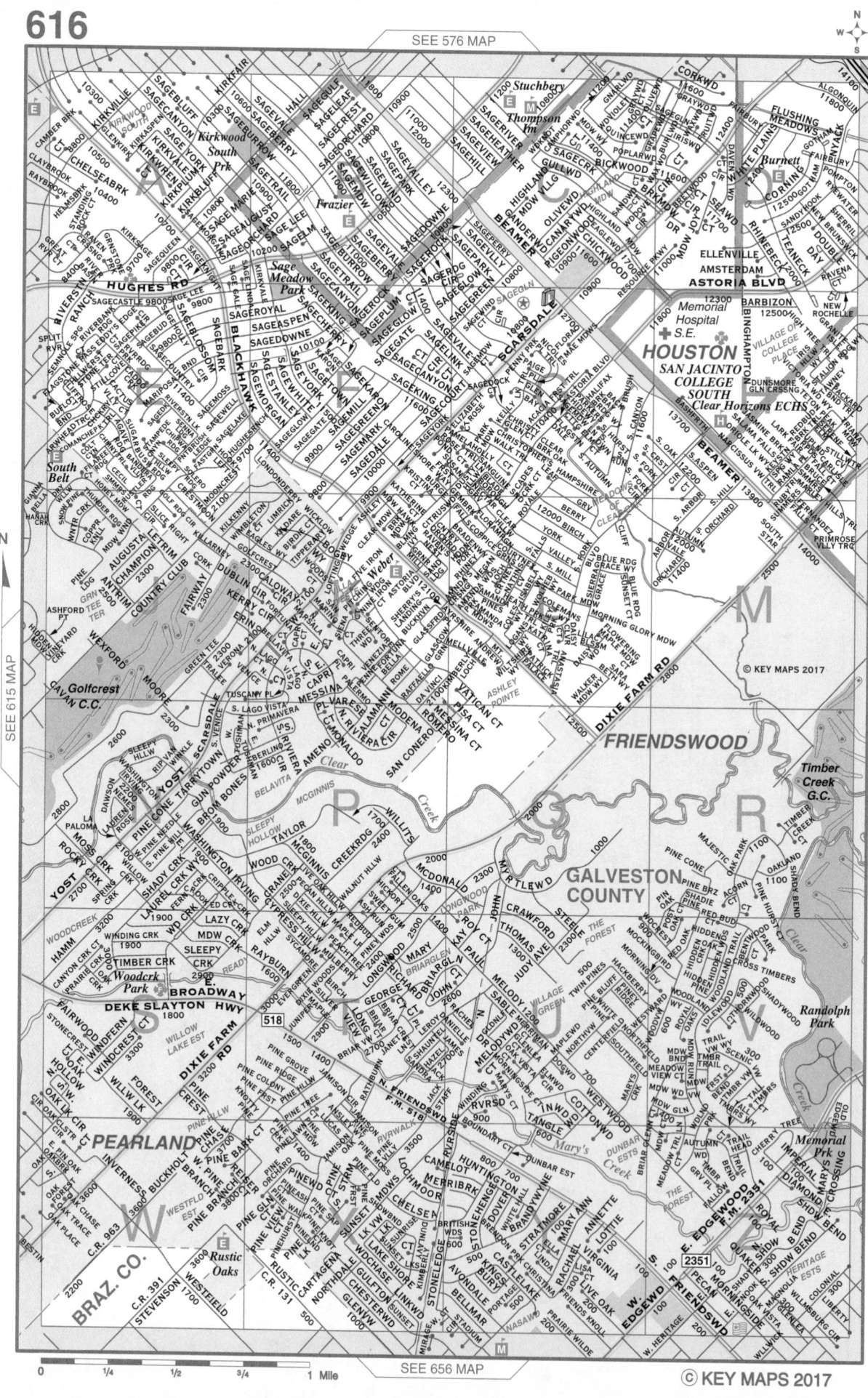

0   1/4   1/2   3/4   1 Mile

© KEY MAPS 2017

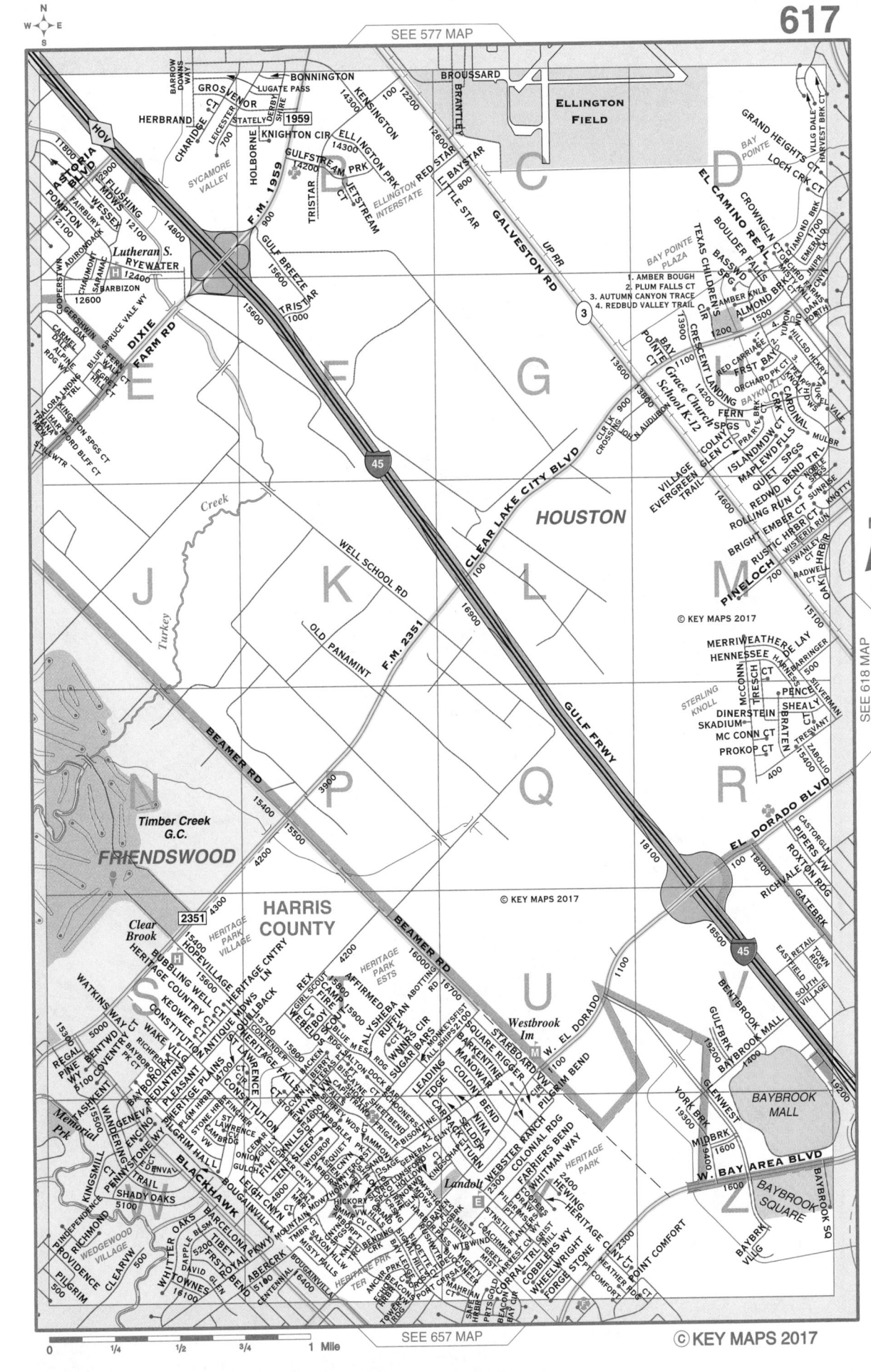

SEE 618 MAP

© KEY MAPS 2017

© KEY MAPS 2017

© KEY MAPS 2017

0   1/4   1/2   3/4   1 Mile

HOUSTON

WEBSTER

UNIVERSITY OF HOUSTON CLEAR LAKE CAMPUS

Clear Lake

Bay Oaks C.C.

Armand Bayou

Clear Lake City

Clear Lake G.C.

Clear Lake Im

NASA

Space Center Im

BAY AREA SQUARE

MEDICAL CENTER BLVD

BAYBROOK SQUARE

Green Acres Park

John F. Ward

G.H. Whitecomb

Walnut Prk

Texas Prk

SEE 617 MAP

SILVERMAN

SPACE CENTER BLVD

E. NASA PKWY

W. NASA PKWY

GALVESTON RD

N. TEXAS RD

W. BAY AREA BLVD

BAY AREA BLVD

EL CAMINO REAL

E. MEDICAL CENTER BLVD

GULF FRWY

45

3

246 P&R

270

F.M. 270 EGRET BAY BLVD

NASA RD BYPASS

OLD GALVESTON RD

CLEAR LAKE CITY BLVD

EL DORADO BLVD

MIDDLEBROOK

© KEY MAPS 2017

1. HOLLINS WY
2. BENTSHIRE WY
3. SUNLIGHT WY
4. PARK GREEN WY
5. BENTFIELD WY
6. BENTFIELD CT
7. BURWOOD CT
8. ASHMOOR CT
9. LINFIELD WY
10. SULLINS WY
11. BARLETON WY
12. PLUMBWOOD
13. PEPPER HILL WY
14. WENDY HILL WY
15. NEWCOMB WY
16. BERNARD WY
17. OAK CLOISTER WY
18. BRAMBLE WY
19. IVY GROVE

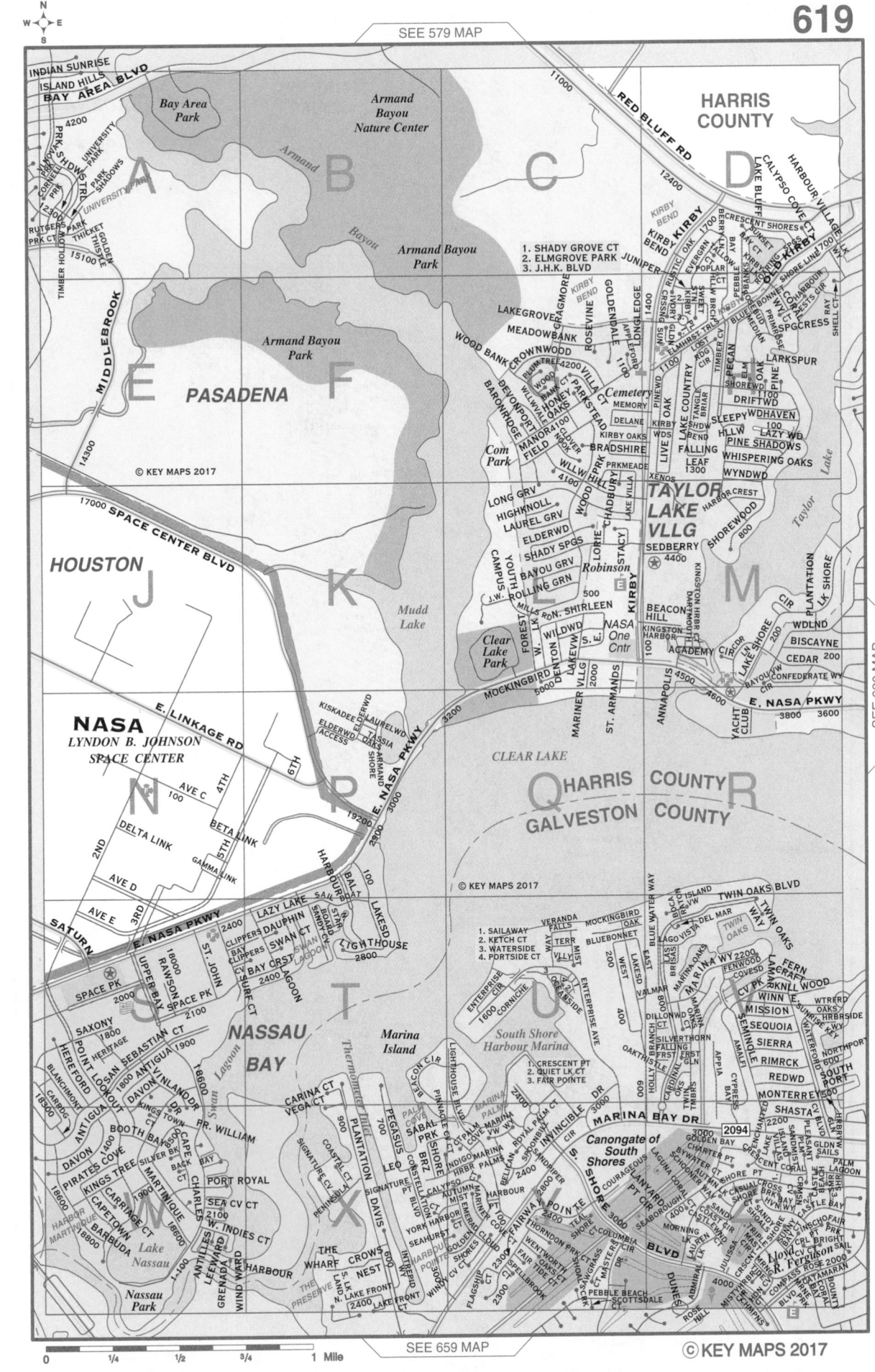

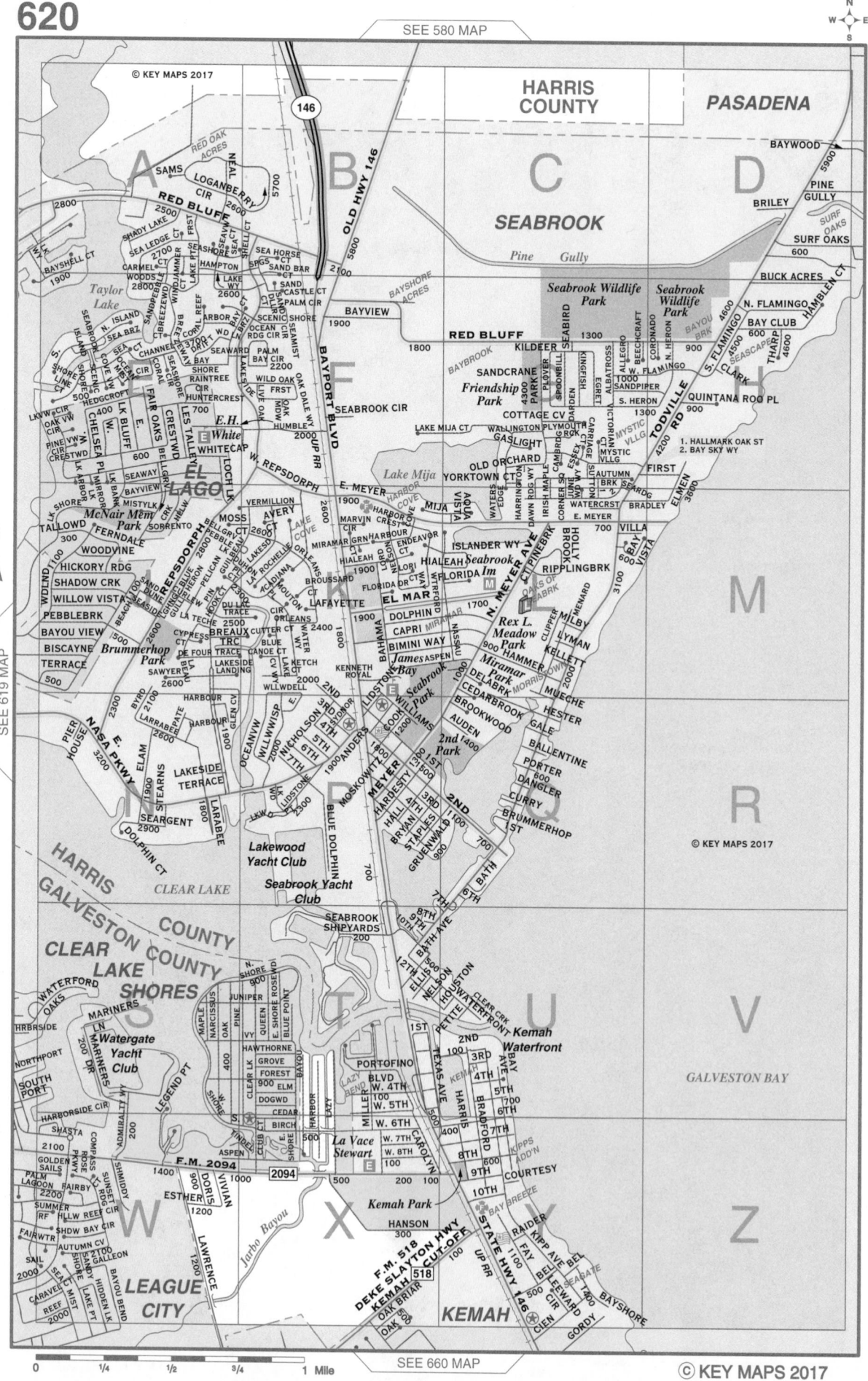

SEE 580 MAP

HARRIS COUNTY

PASADENA

SEE 660 MAP

© KEY MAPS 2017

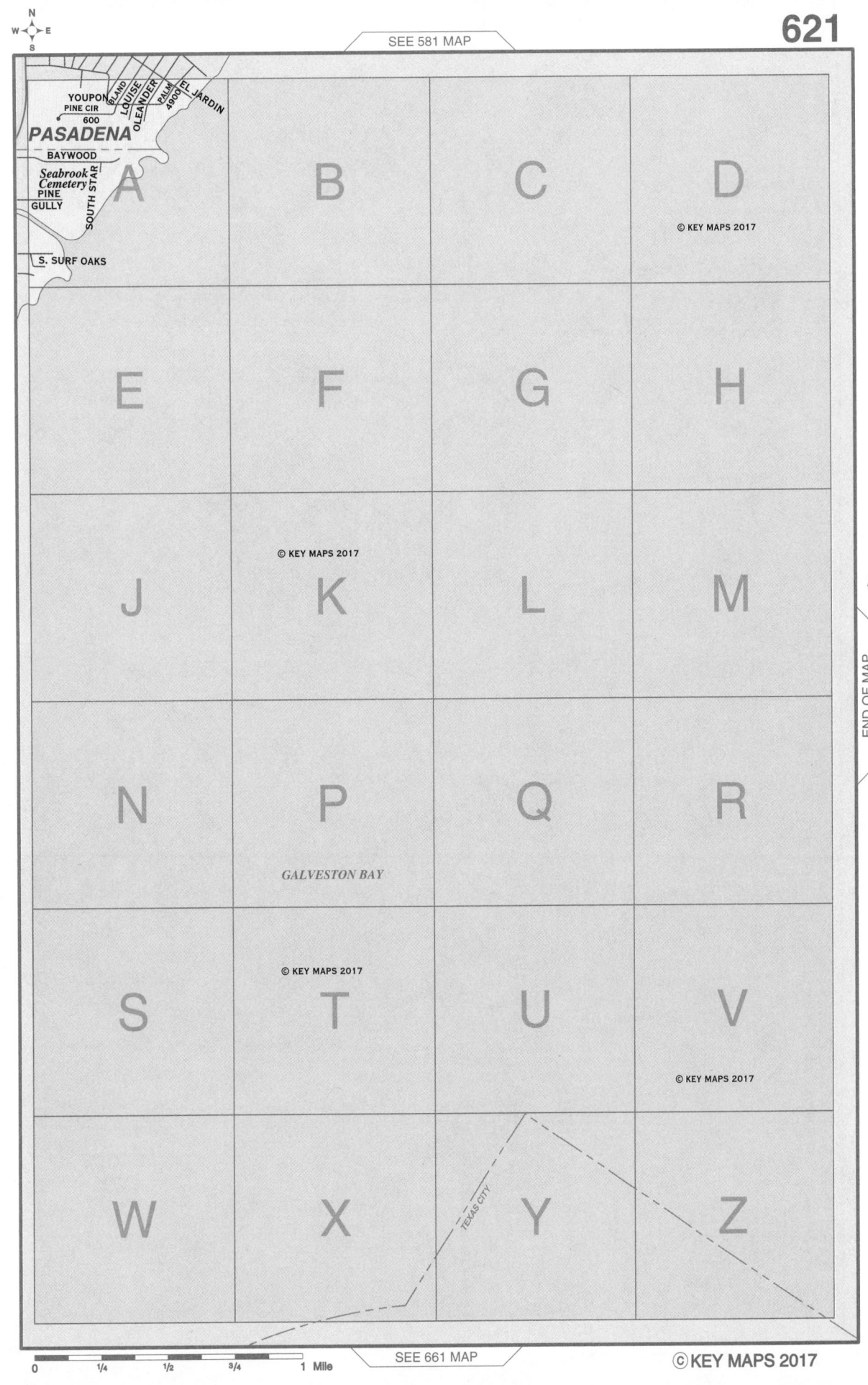

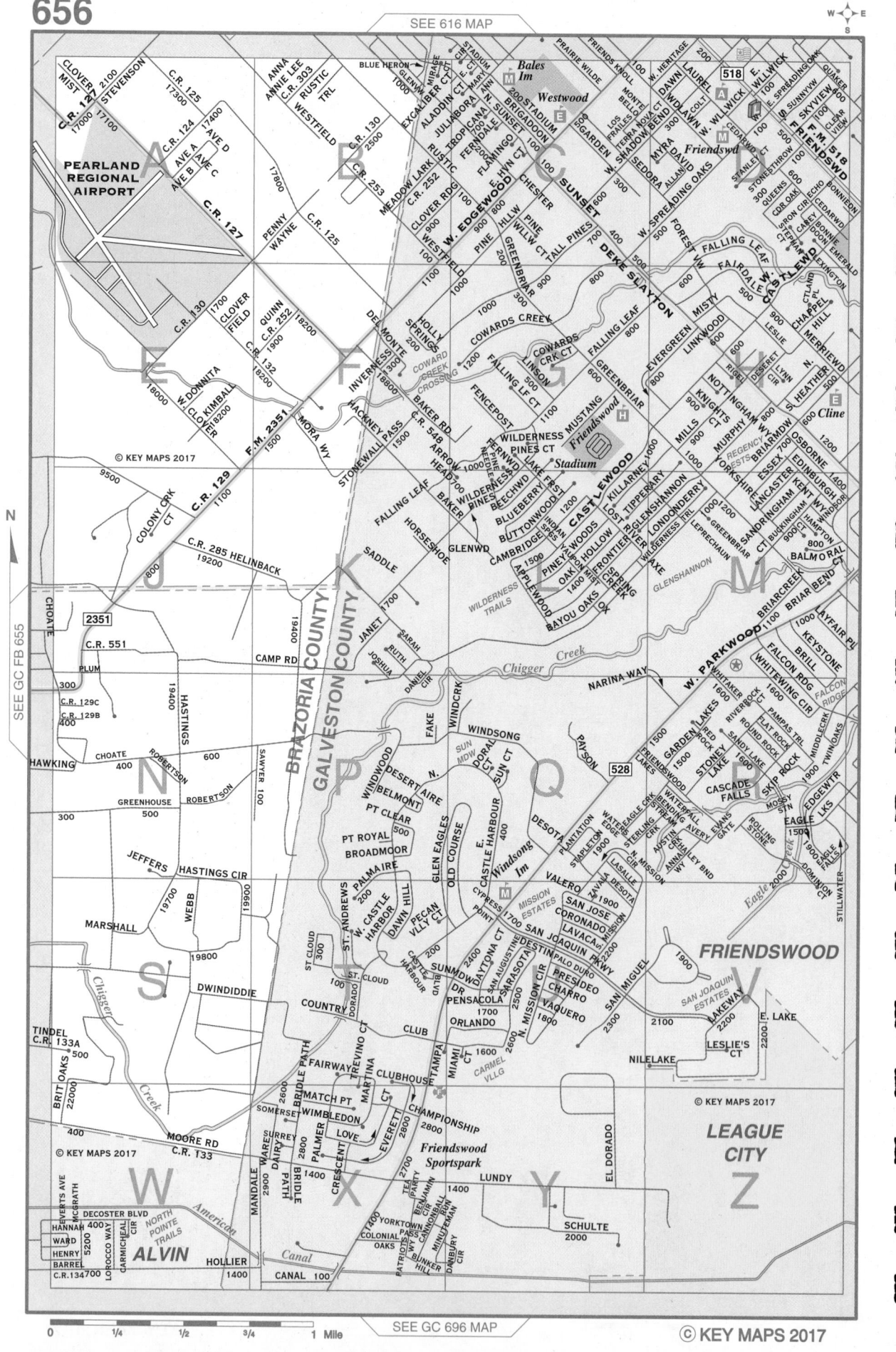

PEARLAND
REGIONAL
AIRPORT

© KEY MAPS 2017

Westwood

Friendswd

Friendswood

FRIENDSWOOD

LEAGUE
CITY

ALVIN

BRAZORIA COUNTY
GALVESTON COUNTY

Chigger Creek

Friendswood
Sportspark

© KEY MAPS 2017

© KEY MAPS 2017

© KEY MAPS 2017

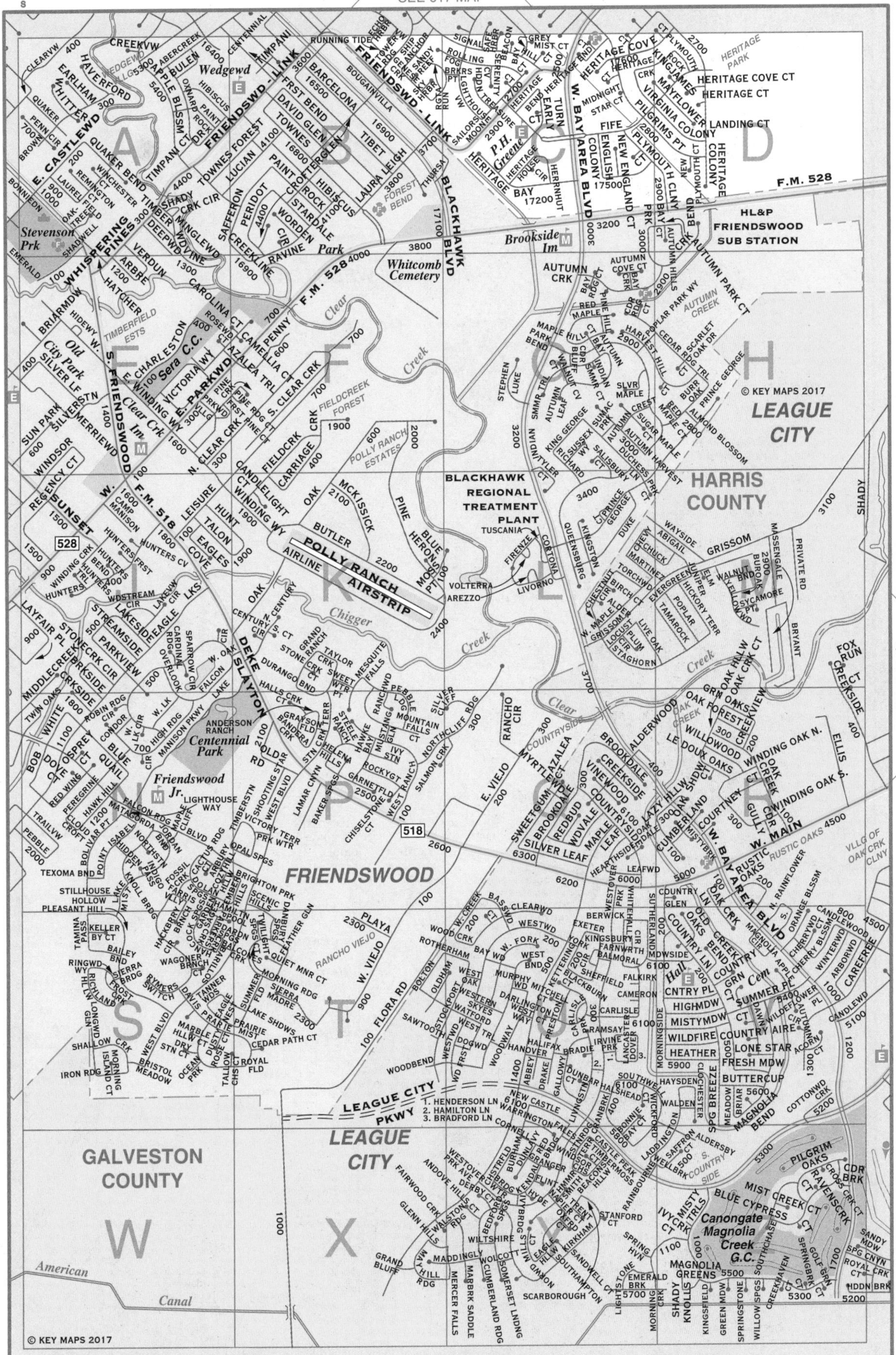

0   1/4   1/2   3/4   1 Mile

SEE 657 MAP

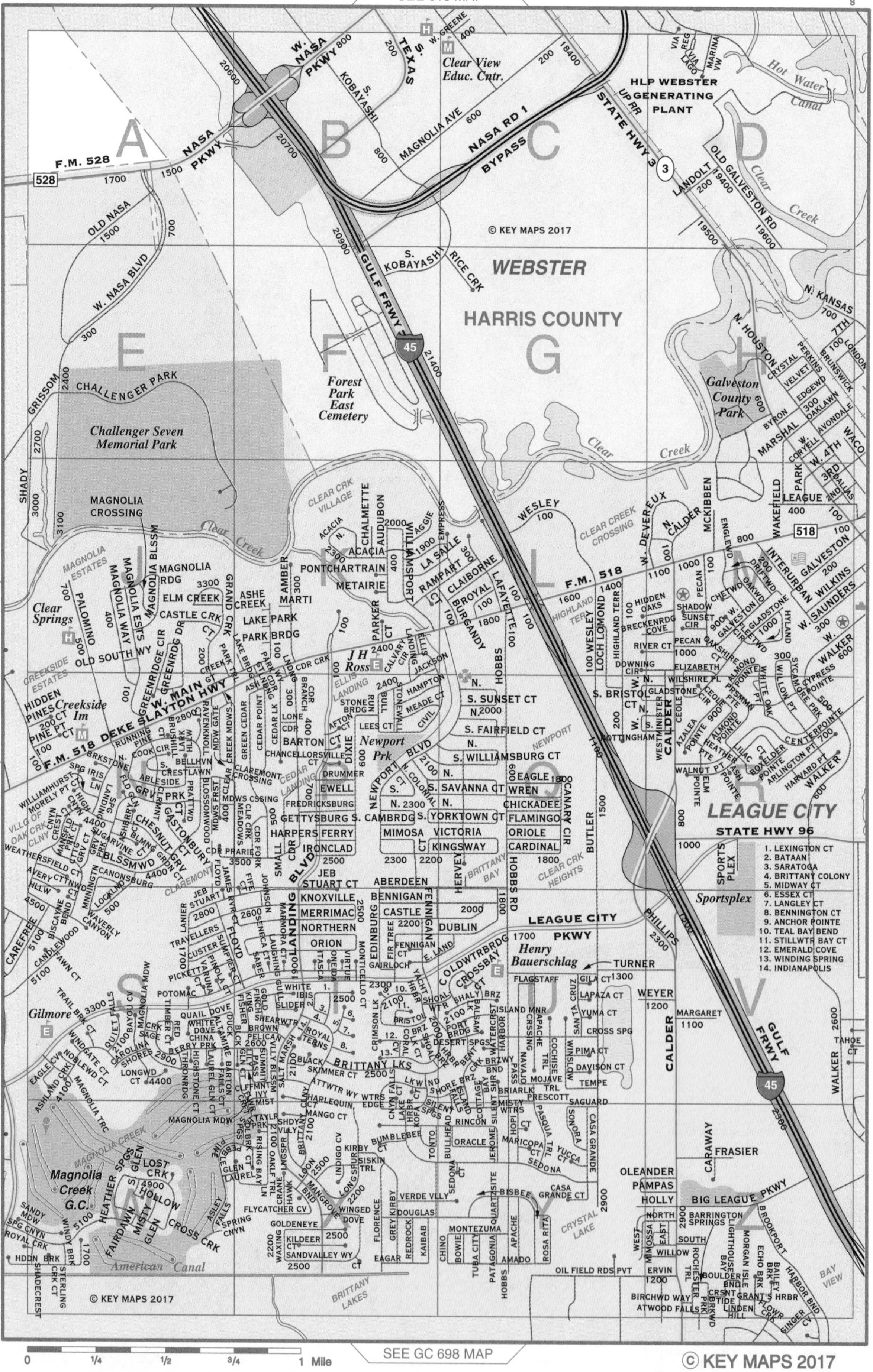

WEBSTER
HARRIS COUNTY

LEAGUE CITY
STATE HWY 96

Clear View Educ. Cntr.

HLP WEBSTER GENERATING PLANT

Galveston County Park

Challenger Park

Challenger Seven Memorial Park

Magnolia Crossing

Forest Park East Cemetery

Clear Creek

Magnolia Estates

Clear Springs

Hidden Pines

Creekside Estates

Creekside Im

J H Ross

Newport Prk

Clear Crk Village

Clear Creek Crossing

Sportsplex

SPORTS PLEX

Magnolia Creek G.C.

Gilmore

Henry Bauerschlag

League City Pkwy

1. LEXINGTON CT
2. BATAAN
3. SARATOGA
4. BRITTANY COLONY
5. MIDWAY CT
6. ESSEX CT
7. LANGLEY CT
8. BENNINGTON CT
9. ANCHOR POINTE
10. TEAL BAY BEND
11. STILLWTR BAY CT
12. EMERALD COVE
13. WINDING SPRING
14. INDIANAPOLIS

NASA PKWY
W. NASA PKWY
NASA RD 1 BYPASS
STATE HWY 3
GULF FRWY 45
F.M. 528
F.M. 518
LEAGUE CITY PKWY
STATE HWY 96
GULF FRWY 45

© KEY MAPS 2017

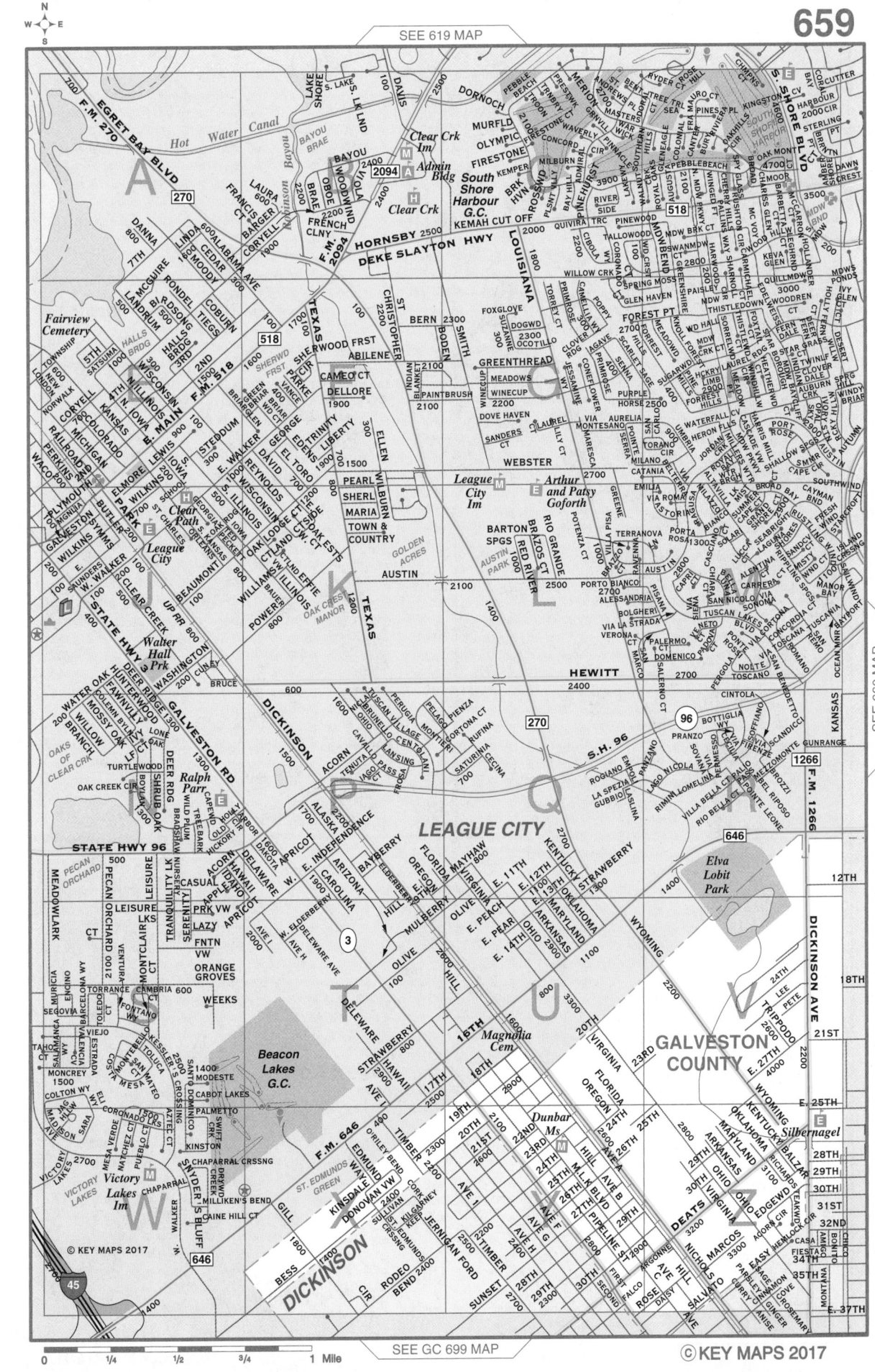

SEE 660 MAP

LEAGUE CITY

GALVESTON COUNTY

© KEY MAPS 2017

0   1/4   1/2   3/4   1 Mile

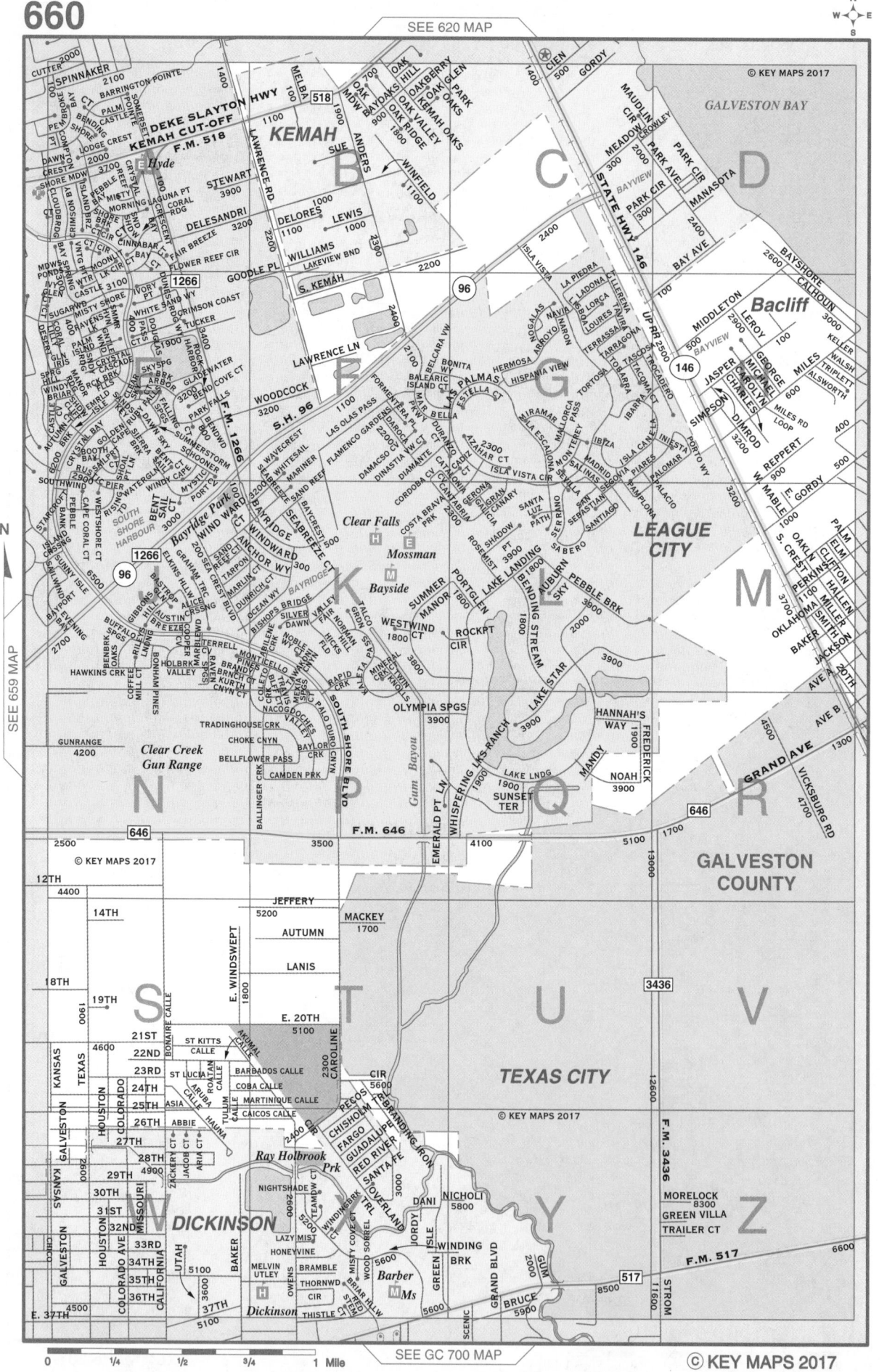

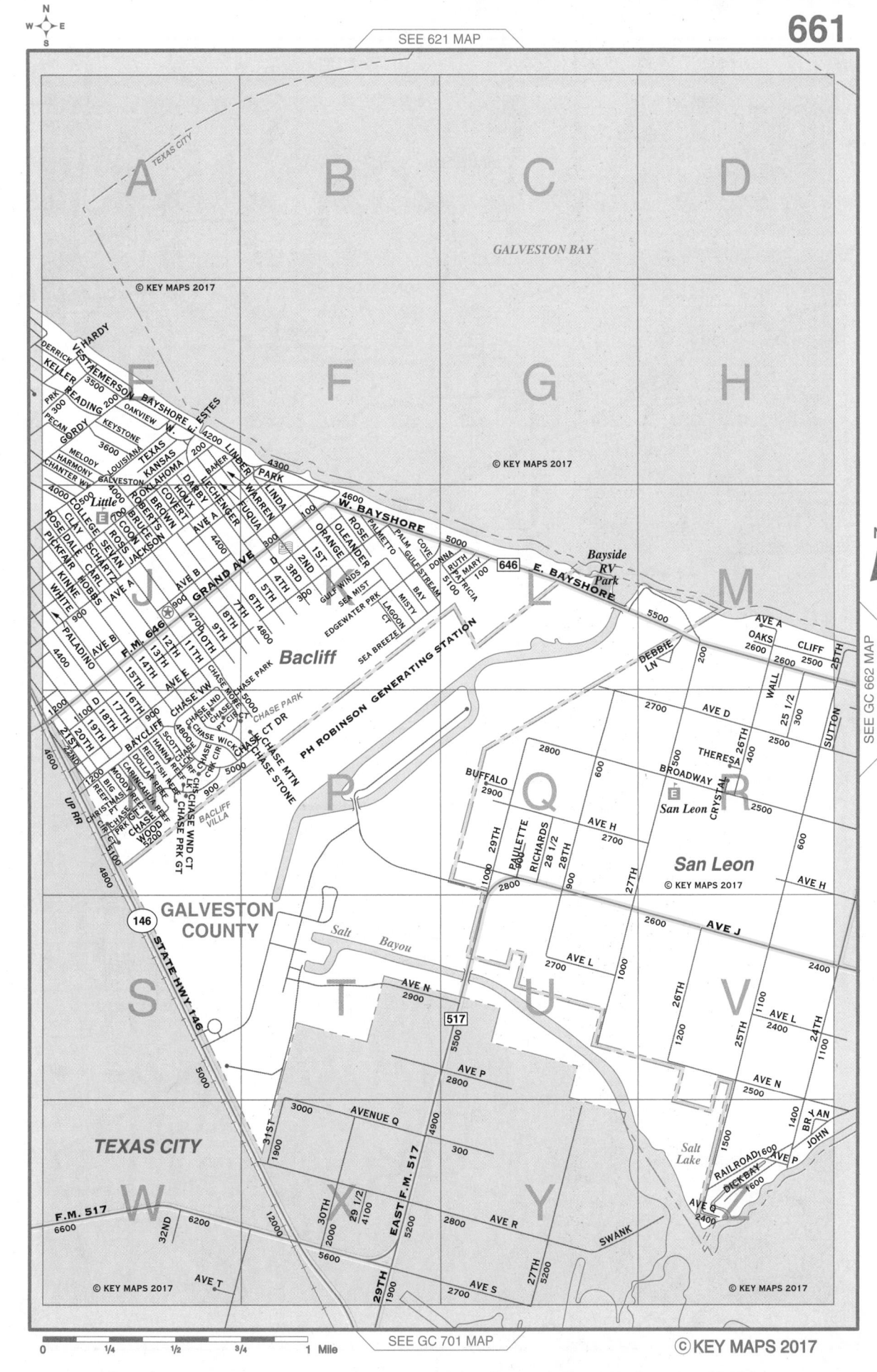

N
W E
S

A B C D

GALVESTON BAY

© KEY MAPS 2017

E F G H

© KEY MAPS 2017

V HARDY
VESTA EMERSON
DERRICK
KELLER 3500
BAYSHORE W. 4200
PRK
READING 200 OAKVIEW ESTES
300 W.
PECAN GORDY KEYSTONE LINDER
MELODY 3600 TEXAS
LOUISIANA KANSAS 200
HARMONY GALVESTON OKLAHOMA BAKER PARK 4300
CHANTER WY 4000 DARBY LECHENGER
COLLEGE 700 RION BROWN WARREN
Little COON ROBERTS COVERT A LINDA 4600 W. BAYSHORE
CLAY SCHARTZ BRUCE SON AVE A ORANGE ROSE PALMETTO COVE 5000
ROSEDALE CARL JACKSON 2ND 1ST GULFSTREAM 5100 646
PICKFAIR HOBBS AVE B GRAND AVE D 3RD OLEANDER BAY E. BAYSHORE
KINNE 900 AVE B 5TH 4TH 300 SEA MIST MISTY
WHITE 646 7TH 4800 LAGOON
4400 PALADINO AVE C 8TH Edgewater PRK CT
4400 12TH 10TH 9TH SEA BREEZE
11TH
14TH *Bacliff*
1200 16TH 13TH CHASE VW CHASE LND
D 18TH 15TH CHASE PRK DR CHASE PARK
19TH CHASE CIR CHASE CT DR
4600 20TH CHASE WICK PH ROBINSON GENERATING STATION
21ST SCOTT HANNA REEF CHASE MTN
22ND DOLLAR REEF CHASE STONE
BAYCLIFF BIG CHASE
CARRINGTON REEF PT *Bacliff*
MOOD WOODY CHRISTMAS CHASE WND CT *Villa*
CHASE PRK GT
CHASE CIR 5100 CHASE WOOD 5200

Bayside RV Park

M
AVE A
OAKS CLIFF 25TH
2600 2600 2500
DEBBIE LN WALL
200 25 1/2 SUTTON
5500 2700 AVE D 300
2500
26TH 400
THERESA CRYSTAL 2500
BUFFALO 2800 500 BROADWAY R
2900 San Leon 600
PAULETTE © KEY MAPS 2017
29TH RICHARDS 28 1/2 AVE H *San Leon*
1000 28TH 2700 AVE H
2800 900 27TH

146 GALVESTON COUNTY

J
F.M. 646

P

Q

2600 AVE J

2700 AVE L 1000

STATE HWY 146

Salt Bayou

AVE N
2900

517
5500

AVE P
2800

S T U V
26TH AVE L 24TH
5000 1200 25TH 2400 1100
31ST 3000 4900 AVE N
1900 AVENUE Q 300 2500
Salt
Lake BR AN
1400
JOHN
1500
RAILROAD 1600 AVE P
DICKBAY 1600
AVE Q Z
2400

TEXAS CITY

W X Y
F.M. 517 30TH 29 1/2 EAST F.M. 517 AVE R
6600 2000 4100 5200 2800 SWANK
32ND 6200 1200 5600 27TH
29TH AVE S 5200
AVE T 1900 2700

© KEY MAPS 2017 © KEY MAPS 2017

0 1/4 1/2 3/4 1 Mile

© KEY MAPS 2017

N

SEE GC 662 MAP

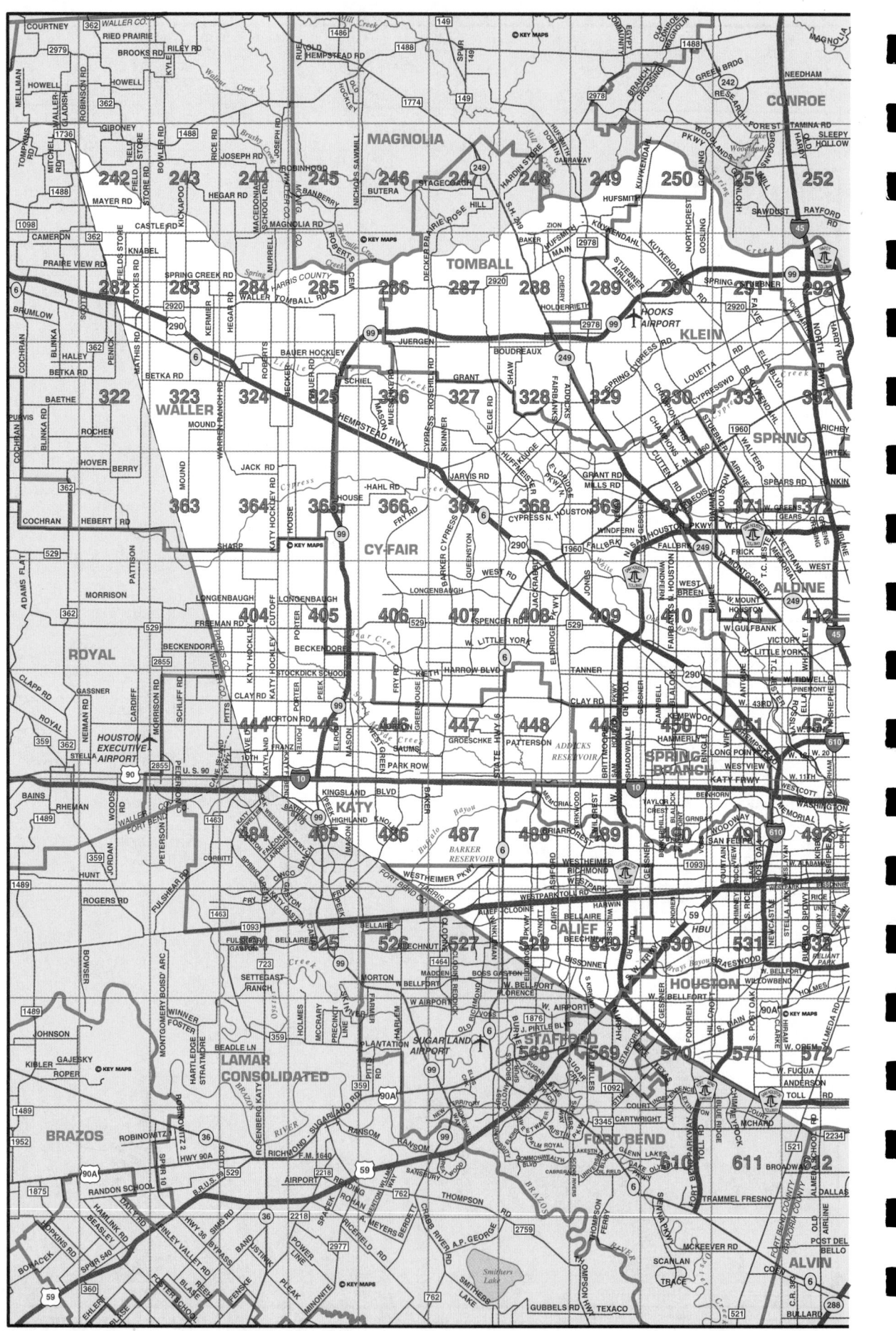

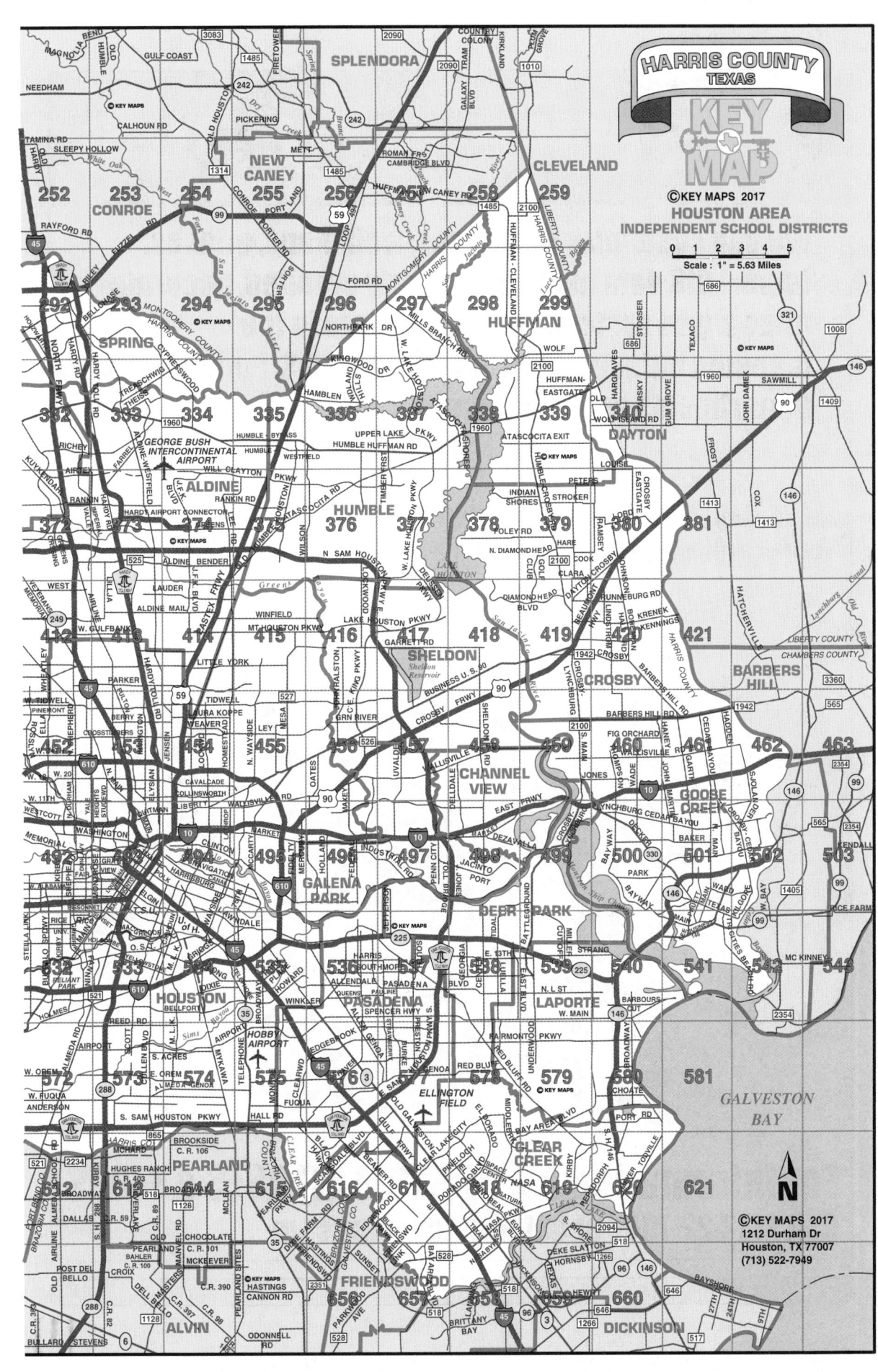